Film
Review
Index

Volume 2: 1950-1985

Film Review Index

Volume 2: 1950-1985

Edited by
Patricia King Hanson
Stephen L. Hanson

Julia Johnson, Assistant Editor

ORYX PRESS
1987

The rare Arabian Oryx is believed to have inspired the myth of the unicorn. This desert antelope became virtually extinct in the early 1960s. At that time several groups of international conservationists arranged to have 9 animals sent to the Phoenix Zoo to be the nucleus of a captive breeding herd. Today the Oryx population is over 400, and herds have been returned to reserves in Israel, Jordan, and Oman.

Copyright © 1987 by
The Oryx Press
2214 North Central at Encanto
Phoenix, Arizona 85004-1483

Published simultaneously in Canada

Printed and Bound in the United States of America

∞ The paper used in this publication meets the minimum requirements of American National Standard for Information Science—Permanence of Paper for Printed Library Materials, ANSI Z39.48, 1984.

Library of Congress Cataloging-in-Publication Data
(Revised for vol. 2)

Film review index.

  Bibliography: v. 1, p.
  Contents: v. 1. 1882–1949 — v. 2. 1950–1985.
  1. Moving-pictures—Reviews—Indexes. I. Hanson, Patricia King. II. Hanson, Stephen L.
Z5784.M9F513   016.79143′75   85-43369
ISBN 0-89774-153-6 (v. 1)
ISBN 0-89774-331-8 (v. 2)

We dedicate this book to our son,
David Grant Hanson,
who went from Blessed Event to
Forty Pounds of Trouble
during its preparation.

Table of Contents

Contributors to Volume 2

Val Armendirez, Academy of Motion Picture Arts and Sciences Library.

Virginia Clark, Frostburg State University.

Donna Darnell, University of Southern California Library.

Marva Felchlin, Alhambra Public Library.

Jeffrey Jensen, Salem Press.

Julia Johnson, University of Southern California Library.

Anne Kail, Beverly Hills Public Library.

Lisa Mosher, Academy of Motion Picture Arts and Sciences Library.

Ellen Snyder, Racine, WI Public Library.

Dennis Thomison, University of Southern California Library.

Don K Thompson, University of Southern California Library.

Lindy Narver, University of Southern California Library.

Elias Savada, American Film Institute.

LaVonne Wuertz, University of Southern California Library.

Introduction

The evolution of the motion picture from scientific experiment to simple entertainment and its ultimate development into a complex art form worthy of serious scholarship in less than a century has created a body of critical writing that is inordinately diverse for a recognized discipline. Its literature has quickly grown to encompass not only the primary source material of the films themselves but also, at one remove, the reminiscences of its practitioners, the opinions of its critics, and finally, the analyses of modern historians and scholars. However, even as the motion picture has gained recognition as a subject worthy of serious scholarship, it has continually outrun even the most ambitious efforts to achieve a measure of bibliographical control over the body of knowledge it represents.

Although the origin of what we now recognize as the "movie review" is shrouded in obscurity, at least one film historian, George C. Pratt, author of *Spellbound in Darkness,* attributes it to Nathaniel Hawthorne, already famous as the "father of American Literature," who was apparently the first writer to critique an instance of projected moving images. Describing a "faux-pas" ridden Diorama presentation in his 1838 *American Notebooks*, Hawthorne wrote:

> There were views of cities and edifices in Europe, of Napoleon's battles and Nelson's sea-fights, in the midst of which would be seen a gigantic, brown, hairy hand (the Hand of Destiny) pointing at the principle points of conflict, while the old Dutchman explained. He gave a good deal of dramatic effect to his descriptions, but his accent and intonation cannot be written. He seemed to take interest and pride in his exhibition, yet when the utter and ludicrous miserability thereof made us laugh, he joined in the joke very readily. When the last picture had been shown, he caused a country boor, who stood gaping beside the machine, to put his head within it, and thrust out his tongue. The head becoming gigantic, a singular effect was produced.

A rudimentery prototype for the film review was thus established—it only remained for the motion picture to be invented.

In 1872, when an English photographer, Eadweard Muybridge, performed his famous "Animals in Motion" experiment utilizing 12 single-frame cameras to record a galloping horse, and then re-created its motion by projecting the resultant images with a Zoopraxiscope and magic lantern, the achievement was purely scientific and the writers of the period treated it accordingly. The invention of "series photography" was properly thought to be of primary interest to journals like the *Scientific American* or the news section of *The New York Times*, both of which debated the merits of Muybridge's 12 camera method vs. Etiene-Jules Morey's technique of taking all of the photographs, sequentially, with one camera. Any artistic considerations centered simply on whether or not all of the horse's feet were ever off of the ground at the same time—the issue that had prompted Muybridge's original experiment. Although the single camera achievement ultimately earned Muybridge's French competitor the accolade as "the father of the motion picture," the greater press coverage gained by the English photographer's demonstrations in the 1880s should certainly allow Muybridge at least a certain "midwife" recognition in the birth of what would finally become the motion picture review.

By the turn of the century, as interest in Muybridge's Zoopraxiscope was supplanted by the newer Kinetoscope and the Cinematographe, with their numerous entertainment possibilities, the subject matter to be photographed and projected became every bit as important as the process itself. The rise of Nickelodeons indicated that the motion picture was arriving as a powerful new mass medium for the working class and so *The New York Times* shifted its coverage of the phenomena to its entertainment pages and began to print reviews regularly as early as 1913. Even the staid *New York Dramatic Mirror* began to intersperse film reviews with its theatrical criticism around the same period.

Yet, prior to 1910, "one-reelers" were usually exhibited in clusters under the headings of their producer and called by such titles as "Edison Program Number One" or "Lumiere Program Number 2." Consequently, local newspaper film reviews more closely resembled the collective type employed for variety shows and vaudeville entertainments than they did more traditional modes of literary and dramatic criticism. Early reviewers rarely singled out individual directors or performers. Florence Lawrence, for example, was routinely called "the Vitagraph Girl" before her immense popularity caused audiences to demand her real name and establish her as the first real "movie star."

During the teens, when motion pictures became big business, a number of trade journals including *Variety* and *Moving Picture World* began to publish a different kind of review. Their critiques were aimed at exhibitors and consequently predated more popular treatments and placed major emphasis on credits and production information. (A tradition continued at present by *The Hollywood Reporter, Motion Picture Herald Product Digest,* and *Variety.*) Today, when many of the films they discussed no longer exist, these appraisals are often the scholar's only indication of what a particular film was about or who was in it. Unfortunately, however, the majority of these reviews were never comprehensively indexed beyond the brief listings done at irregular intervals by some of the publications, while others were not indexed at all.

Historically, the few attempts that have been made to provide a systematic approach to indexing film reviews have usually adopted the arbitrary stance of selecting a fixed universe of anywhere from five to fifteen film journals and then listing citations for every film reviewed by them. Such approaches have, of necessity, ignored a wide range of deserving films and valuable critical perspectives.

Today, as film scholarship approaches the century mark, most researchers still consider the *Readers' Guide to Periodical Literature* as the most comprehensive single index of film reviews. For more scholarly approaches to individual films, there are, of course, *The International Index to Film Periodicals* and *The Film Literature Index,* but they are both highly selective as well as relative newcomers to the field. The *Film Review Index* is an attempt to fill the gap left by traditional indexes and to provide a retrospective bibliography of articles about specific films which have, over the years, established themselves as being of the highest interest to researchers and students. It is thus designed to be a latchkey for scholars, critics, film buffs, librarians, film critics, students and anyone else who is primarily interested in obtaining information on specific films. Accordingly, we have avoided what we consider to be nonessential references to biographical, technical, and other types of material having but a peripheral relationship to the films we have selected for inclusion. All articles, chapters and book citations listed under each film in the *Film Review Index* deal primarily with that film either as a review, as history, or as critical commentary.

Coverage begins in 1882 with some citations to Muybridge's pre-cinema experiments with "Animals in Motion" and a number of other notable nineteenth century landmarks, such as Thomas A. Edison's "The Kiss" (1896), which are regarded as still being of significant importance to scholars. However, the primary focus of the volumes concentrates on the period 1903 (the date of "The Great Train Robbery") to 1986. This affords coverage of more than 7000 feature films, or an average of 75 films a year for each of the high production years between 1914 and 1986. We have obviously not attempted to include every film produced within those years, but primarily those pictures that have established themselves as being of continuing importance to film researchers. At the same time, we have not ignored "programmers" or minor films that could, at some point, become the object of certain highly specialized types of research due to their reflection of certain sociological trends or simply because they were extremely popular for a variety of reasons.

The overriding consideration in the selection of titles was: "Would anybody, at some point in time, ever conceivably want citations to this film?" If the answer was affirmative, we then had to determine "What, if anything can be found?" Often, the options were limited. But in most cases, the basic sources such as *The New York Times, Variety, Film Daily, Hollywood Reporter* and *Moving Picture World* or *Motion Picture Herald* could be counted on to provide a respectable number of citations.

This film-centered approach admittedly places us well out on the proverbial limb, as it is the antithesis of the traditional procedures employed by existing indices which attempt to index journals rather than films. However, it is of more importance to the objectives of the *Film Review Index* to provide a variety of unique, "hard to find" materials for each individual film than it is to provide "in-depth" documentation of various critics, anthologies, histories, and journals which appeal to a small number of film scholars and which are readily available only in a limited number of libraries. In some cases, though, we simply had to settle for what we could find. While this approach may anger some specialists who may find their favorite treatise excluded in favor of a "trade" review or a chapter from a film history, it does provide other advantages. Paramount among these is the fact that the wide variety of entries provided for the most significant films should include some citations that are in reach of users of even the smallest libraries. Individual libraries might not have *Variety* or *The History of Narrative Film* but they certainly will have access to *Saturday Review, Newsweek,* or in the case of the early silents, one of the reprint series or histories cited. Small public or special libraries which cannot afford the major film literature indices will find the *Film Review Index* invaluable as its broad coverage allows it to supplant a variety of more expensive reference works. We hope we have provided something practical and accessible to the scholar and the interested non-professional alike.

Each of the film entries includes several references to the film, with four primary reasons for exclusion: redundancy, foreign language sources, lack of common accessibility, and lack of substance. Thus, an article by French director François Truffaut on one of Alfred Hitchcock's films is included if it is written in English, but omitted if it is in French. At the same time, a minor film review in a popular magazine like *Glamour* or *Family Circle* will not be found here while those in *Time* and *Newweek* will be. One determining factor is often whether or not the popular review includes background or production information that is not commonly available in more critical sources. This is particularly important in reviews of foreign language films where contemporary treatments may contain production details omitted by later historical studies and philosophical critiques.

Great emphasis has also been placed on including references to trade publications—long the most important source of film reviews. Such publications as *The Hollywood Reporter, Variety, The Motion Picture Herald Product Digest* and their antecedents have heretofore never been included in any index. These sources, as mentioned earlier, normally provide the earliest reviews of a film, the most extensive production information and the most complete credits. Yet, they are, historically, the most inaccessible and least indexed avenue of film research. In most cases, the inclusion of citations to these reviews in the *Film Review Index* mandated a page-by-page examination of the complete runs of each journal. In addition to journal, newspaper, and trade reviews, the *Film Review Index* also lists articles in important, freely available books which deal with specific films, such as the *Films of...* books and *Magill's Survey of Cinema.*

Each film in *The Film Review Index* is listed in alphabetical order with cross references for title changes. The bibliographic format was designed for librarians and laypeople alike and thus avoids illogical or complicated abbreviations. The information for each selection includes the film's title, any alternate or foreign titles, the country of origin, director, and year produced. Books are listed by title and page number with full bibliographical information provided separately in an extensive "Books Consulted" section. Periodical titles are cited in full under each film and list the date, volume and page on which the review can be found. [We caution the user to note that in the case of *The New York Times*, a number of reviews may have "np" instead of a section and page number. These dates refer to those used in the bound volumes of *The New York Times Film Reviews* which include reviews not printed in the newspaper during their periods of strikes. We further caution the reader to note that several periodicals in the 1960s and 1970s issued different editions. We have used the National editions unless otherwise noted.]

One interesting and unforeseen result of the *Film Review Index's* alphabetical arrangement was the discovery of a surprising number of films that have been made and remade a number of times during the relatively short history of cinema. For example, the famous version of "Oliver Twist" is the 1949 David Lean version, but that was at least the fifth film adaptation of the Dickens novel, and was followed in the 1970s by Sir Carol Reed's Oscar-winning musical, "Oliver!". Similarly, Walt Disney's "Snow White" was predated by a 1916 version. We hope that such discoveries will be an equally pleasant surprise to users of this book.

Because of the confines of time and space, we were unable to cite every source of value on each film, try as we might. To researchers, then, we would strongly urge a careful perusal of the bibliography at the end of the book. Many of the more theoretical studies provide general background information on a variety of topics beyond those sections cited under particular films elsewhere in the *Film Review Index.* Similarly, if certain books on Howark Hawks or John Ford do not discuss a specific film in depth, they might still offer invaluable insights into the directors' works as a whole.

The user will be happy to know that the indexes of Volume 2 are cumulative for both volumes of the *Film Review Index.* Film titles which are followed by an asterisk as in the case of the 1948 John Ford film "Fort Apache*", are included in *Volume 1: 1882–1949.*

During the course of production of this book, many people offered their help and assistance. We would particularly like to thank Dan Sallitt, Alan Gevinson, and Amy Dunkleberger. We would also like to express our appreciation to the staffs of the following libraries: The Louis B. Mayer Library of the American Film Institute, The Margaret Herrick Library of the Academy of Motion Picture Arts and Sciences, The Reference and Special Collections Departments of the University of Southern California Library, the Theater Arts Library at the University of California at Los Angeles, and the Beverly Hills Public Library.

Among our contributors, we would particularly like to thank Julia Johnson who never stopped giving us citations to "Dr. Strangelove" and "Gone with the Wind," to Dennis Thomison who waded his way through years of the *Hollywood Reporter,* and also to Don K Thompson. At Oryx Press, we would like to thank Jim Thomas for his encouragement and support in the early stages of the project, Anne Thompson who was very patient and supportive in the development of the specifics of the text's format and computerization, and to Sue Johnson and Gene Price who had the rather thankless task of reading through the material citation-by-citation.

Stephen L. Hanson
Patricia King Hanson

Film Listings

A Bout de Souffle *See* Breathless

A Nos Amours (FR; Pialat, Maurice; 1984)
BFI/Monthly Film Bulletin. Jun 1984, v51, p172-73.
Film Comment. Dec 1984, v20, p64.
Film Journal. Nov 1984, v87, p55.
Films and Filming. Jun 1984, n357, p38.
The Los Angeles Times. Nov 9, 1984, SecVI, p16.
The New Leader. Oct 15, 1984, v67, p18-19.
The New Republic. Nov 19, 1984, v191, p26-27.
New Statesman. Jun 15, 1984, v107, p29-30.
New York. Oct 22, 1984, v17, p135-36.
The New York Times. Oct 12, 1984, SecIII, p10.
Newsweek. Nov 5, 1984, v104, p74.
Sight and Sound. Fall 1984, v53, p222-23.
Stills. Jun-Jul 1984, n12, p100-01.
Time. Dec 3, 1984, v124, p79.
The Village Voice. Oct 23, 1984, p64.
Vogue. Jul 1984, v174, p49.

A Tout Prendre (Also titled: Take It All; The Way It Goes) (CAN; Jutra, Claude; 1963)
Film Daily. May 5, 1966, p5.
Film Quarterly. Wint 1963-64, v17, p39-42.
Filmfacts. Jun 15, 1966, v9, p101-02.
Hollywood Reporter. Aug 31, 1966, p3.
Motion Picture Herald Product Digest. May 11, 1966, p519-20.
The New York Times. Apr 26, 1966, p55.
The New Yorker. May 7, 1966, v42, p182.
Newsweek. May 16, 1966, v67, p106.
Private Screenings. p256-58.
Variety. Aug 28, 1963, p18.
The Village Voice. Sep 2, 1965, p15, 17.
The Village Voice. May 19, 1966, p31, 33.

Aan (Also titled: Savage Princess) (INDIA; Khan, Mehboob; 1952)
BFI/Monthly Film Bulletin. Sep 1952, v19, p121.
Dictionary of Films. p1.
Film Criticism and Caricatures, 1943-1953. p145-46.
The London Times. Jul 17, 1952, p9.
The New Statesman and Nation. Jul 19, 1952, v44, p70.
The Spectator. Jul 18, 1952, v189, p96-97.
The Tatler. Jul 30, 1952, v205, p202.

Aaron Slick From Punkin Crick (US; Binyon, Claude; 1952)
Commonweal. May 9, 1952, v56, p117.
Film Daily. Feb 28, 1951, p10.
Hollywood Reporter. Feb 19, 1952, p3.
Motion Picture Herald Product Digest. Feb 23, 1952, p1245-46.
The New York Times. Apr 19, 1952, p18.
Time. Apr 28, 1952, v59, p100.
Variety. Feb 20, 1952, p6.

Abandon Ship (Also titled: Seven Waves Away) (GB; Sale, Richard; 1957)
America. May 4, 1957, v97, p179.
BFI/Monthly Film Bulletin. Apr 1957, v24, p43-44.
Commonweal. May 3, 1957, v66, p127.
Film Daily. Mar 27, 1957, v111, p6.
Films and Filming. May 1957, v3, p24-25.
The Films of Tyrone Power. p196-98.
Hollywood Reporter. May 10, 1957, p4.
Motion Picture Herald Product Digest. Mar 23, 1957, v206, p313.
The New York Times. Apr 18, 1957, p35.
The New York Times. Apr 21, 1957, SecII, p1.
The New Yorker. Apr 27, 1957, v33, p68.
Newsweek. Apr 22, 1957, v49, p124.
Variety. Mar 13, 1957, p6.

Abbott and Costello Lost in Alaska *See* Lost in Alaska

The Abdication (US; Harvey, Anthony; 1974)
BFI/Monthly Film Bulletin. Jan 1975, v42, p3.
Film. Oct 1974, n19, p19.
Films Illustrated. Dec 1974, v4, p130-31.
Films in Review. Oct 1974, v25, p501-02.
Films in Review. Dec 1974, v25, p611-13.
Hollywood Reporter. Sep 18, 1974, p4.
Humanist. Jan-Feb 1975, v35, p64.
Independent Film Journal. Sep 18, 1974, v74, p7.
The Los Angeles Times. Oct 3, 1974, SecIV, p1.
Motion Picture Herald Product Digest. Oct 2, 1974, p35.
Movietone News. Sep 1974, n35, p30-31.
New York. Oct 7, 1974, v7, p93-96.
The New York Times. Oct 25, 1975, p75.
The New Yorker. Oct 7, 1974, v50, p152-54.
Newsweek. Oct 7, 1974, v84, p96.
Senior Scholastic. Oct 24, 1974, v105, p19.
Sight and Sound. Wint 1973, v43, p24-25.
Time. Oct 28, 1974, v104, p5.
Variety. Sep 18, 1974, p19.

About Face (US; Del Ruth, Roy; 1952)
BFI/Monthly Film Bulletin. Nov 1952, v19, p156.
Catholic World. May 1952, v175, p144.
Christian Century. Jul 30, 1952, v69, p887.
Film Daily. Apr 17, 1952, p6.
Hollywood Reporter. Apr 10, 1952, p3.
Motion Picture Herald Product Digest. Apr 12, 1952, p1313.
The New York Times. May 24, 1952, p15.
The New Yorker. May 31, 1952, v28, p81.
Newsweek. Jun 2, 1952, v39, p84.
Time. Jun 2, 1952, v59, p94.
Variety. Apr 16, 1952, p6.

About Mrs. Leslie (US; Mann, Daniel; 1954)
America. Jul 24, 1954, v91, p426.

BFI/Monthly Film Bulletin. Jul 1954, v21, p98.
Catholic World. Jun 1954, v179, p233.
Commonweal. Jul 23, 1954, v60, p388.
Film Daily. Apr 30, 1954, p5.
Films in Review. Jun-Jul 1954, v5, p309.
Hollywood Reporter. Apr 30, 1954, p3.
Library Journal. Jun 15, 1954, v79, p1168.
The London Times. Jul 5, 1954, p11.
Motion Picture Herald Product Digest. May 1, 1954, p2278.
National Parent-Teacher. May 1954, v48, p38.
The New Statesman and Nation. Jul 3, 1954, v48, p14.
The New York Times. Jun 28, 1954, p16.
The New Yorker. Jul 10, 1954, v30, p60.
Newsweek. Jun 21, 1954, v43, p86.
Saturday Review. Jul 3, 1954, v37, p33.
Sight and Sound. Jul-Sep 1954, v24, p36.
The Spectator. Jul 2, 1954, v193, p11.
The Tatler. Jul 14, 1954, v213, p74.
Time. Jul 5, 1954, v64, p76.
Variety. May 5, 1954, p6.

Above and Beyond (US; Frank, Melvin; Panama, Norman; 1952)
BFI/Monthly Film Bulletin. Jan 1953, v20, p3.
Christian Century. Feb 11, 1953, v70, p175.
Commonweal. Feb 20, 1953, v57, p499.
Film Daily. Nov 21, 1952, p13.
Films in Review. Jan 1953, v4, p34-35.
The Films of Robert Taylor. p126-28.
Good Housekeeping. Mar 1953, v136, p16-17.
Hollywood Reporter. Nov 18, 1952, p3.
The London Times. Feb 20, 1953, p2.
Magill's Survey of Cinema. Series II. v1, p1-3.
Motion Picture Herald Product Digest. Nov 22, 1952, p1613.
The Nation. Dec 20, 1952, v175, p585.
The New Statesman and Nation. Feb 28, 1953, v45, p231-32.
The New York Times. Jan 31, 1953, p10.
The New Yorker. Feb 7, 1953, v28, p56.
Newsweek. Feb 2, 1953, v41, p77.
Saturday Review. Jan 24, 1953, v36, p27.
Senior Scholastic. Jan 14, 1953, v61, p30.
The Spectator. Feb 27, 1953, v190, p244.
The Tatler. Mar 4, 1953, v207, p382.
Time. Jan 5, 1953, v61, p70.
Variety. Nov 17, 1952, p6.

Abscheid von Gestern *See* Yesterday Girl

Absence of Malice (US; Pollack, Sydney; 1981)
BFI/Monthly Film Bulletin. Feb 1982, v49, p23.
Christian Century. Mar 3, 1982, v99, p251.
Esquire. Jul 1981, v96, p68-69.
Hollywood Reporter. Nov 17, 1981, p3.
Humanist. Mar-Apr 1982, v42, p60-61.
The Los Angeles Times. Nov 21, 1981, SecVI, p1.
Maclean's. Jan 4, 1982, v95, p50.

Magill's Cinema Annual, 1981. p57-61.
Ms. Jan 1982, v10, p15-16.
The Nation. Jan 2, 1982, v234, p27.
The New Leader. Jan 25, 1982, v65, p21.
The New Republic. Dec 23, 1981, v185, p24-25.
New York. Nov 27, 1981, v14, p70-71.
The New York Times. Nov 19, 1981, SecIII, p21.
The New Yorker. Jan 4, 1982, v57, p83-85.
Newsweek. Nov 23, 1981, v98, p125.
Saturday Review. Nov 1981, v8, p57.
Senior Scholastic. Feb 5, 1982, v114, p28.
Time. Nov 23, 1981, v118, p98.

The Absent Minded Professor (US; Stevenson, Robert; 1961)
America. Apr 1, 1961, v105, p25-26.
The Disney Films. p185-87.
Film Daily. Feb 23, 1961, p6.
Filmfacts. Apr 7, 1961, v4, p62-63.
The New York Times. Mar 17, 1961, p25.
The New Yorker. Apr 1, 1961, v37, p125.
Time. Mar 10, 1961, v77, p66.
Variety. Feb 22, 1961, p3.
Walt Disney: A Guide to References and Resources. p75-76.

Accatone (IT; Pasolini, Pier Paolo; 1961)
BFI/Monthly Film Bulletin. Dec 1964, v29, p134.
Commonweal. Apr 26, 1968, v88, p185.
Film Quarterly. Wint 1966-67, v20, p28-33.
Filmfacts. Jul 1, 1968, v11, p164-66.
Films and Filming. Apr 1967, v13, p4-5.
International Film Guide. 1968, v5, p89-90.
Magill's Survey of Cinema. Foreign Language Films. v1, p5-8.
The New York Times. Sep 17, 1961, p20.
The New York Times. Apr 5, 1968, p56.
Pier Paolo Pasolini (Snyder). p33-47.
Sight and Sound. Aut 1962, v31, p193-94.
Variety. Sep 6, 1961, p18.

Accident (GB; Losey, Joseph; 1967)
America. Jun 3, 1967, v116, p821-22.
BFI/Monthly Film Bulletin. Mar 1967, v34, p39-40.
Christian Century. Jun 7, 1967, v84, p754-55.
Cinema. Spr 1968, v4, p22-23, 38.
Commonweal. Apr 28, 1967, v86, p117-78.
Esquire. Jul 1967, v68, p20.
Film Daily. Apr 11, 1967, p11.
Film Quarterly. Sum 1967, v20, p60-63.
Filmfacts. Jun 1, 1967, v10, p95.
Films and Filming. Apr 1967, p54.
The Films of Dirk Bogarde. p164-67.
Harper's. Jun 1967, v234, p110-11.
Hollywood Reporter. Apr 17, 1967, p3.
International Film Guide. 1968, v5, p89-90.
Joseph Losey (Hirsch). p113-26.
Life. Apr 21, 1967, v62, p12.
Magill's Survey of Cinema Series II. v1, p4-7.
Making Pictures: The Pinter Screenplays. p50-76.
Motion Picture Herald Product Digest. Apr 12, 1967, p675.
The Nation. May 15, 1967, v204, p638.
The New Republic. Jun 3, 1967, v156, p38-41.
The New York Times. Apr 18, 1967, p33.
The New Yorker. Apr 22, 1967, v43, p150-51.
Newsweek. Apr 24, 1967, v69, p96.
Saturday Review. Apr 29, 1967, v50, p47.
Sight and Sound. Aut 1966, v35, p179-84.
Sight and Sound. Spr 1967, v36, p57-59.
Take One. Jun 1967, v1, p28.
Time. Apr 21, 1967, v89, p101.
Variety. Feb 15, 1967, p17.
The Village Voice. Apr 20, 1967, p25.
The Village Voice. May 18, 1967, p26, 29.

The Village Voice. Jun 8, 1967, p23.
Vogue. Jun 1967, v149, p77.

The Ace *See* The Great Santini

Ace in the Hole (Also titled: The Big Carnival) (US; Wilder, Billy; 1951)
BFI/Monthly Film Bulletin. Apr 1951, v18, p242.
Billy Wilder (Dick). p57-61.
Billy Wilder in Hollywood. p175-76.
Billy Wilder (Madsen). p91-94.
Christian Century. Oct 17, 1951, v68, p1207.
Cinema, the Magic Vehicle. v2, p98-99.
Commonweal. Jul 13, 1951, v54, p334.
Dark City: The Film Noir. p105-09.
Dictionary of Films. p2.
The Film Career of Billy Wilder. p80-82.
Film Daily. May 8, 1951, p6.
Film Quarterly. Sum 1970, v23, p2-9.
Films in Review. Aug-Sep 1951, v2, p38-39.
The Films of Kirk Douglas. p71-75.
Halliwell's Hundred. p342-45.
Hollywood Reporter. May 7, 1951, p3.
Metro. Nov 1980, n53, p14-17.
Motion Picture Herald Product Digest. May 12, 1951, p845.
Movietone News. May 1975, n41, p21-24.
The Nation. Jul 14, 1951, v173, p37.
The New Republic. Jul 16, 1951, v125, p22.
The New Statesman and Nation. Jun 23, 1951, v41, p708.
The New York Times. Jun 30, 1951, p8.
The New Yorker. Jul 7, 1951, v27, p35.
Newsweek. Jul 2, 1951, v38, p78.
Quarterly Review of Film Studies. 1984, v9, n2, p101-12.
Rotha on Film. p178-80.
Saturday Review. Jul 7, 1951, v34, p24.
Sight and Sound. Jun 1951, v20, p45.
The Spectator. Jun 15, 1951, v186, p781.
Time. Jul 9, 1951, v58, p84.
Variety. May 9, 1951, p6.

Across the Bridge (GB; Annakin, Ken; 1957)
America. Nov 16, 1957, v98, p228.
BFI/Monthly Film Bulletin. Sep 1957, v24, p110.
Commonweal. Nov 1, 1957, v67, p131.
Film Daily. Nov 8, 1957, v112, p8.
Films and Filming. Sep 1957, v3, p23.
Films in Review. Dec 1957, v8, p523-24.
The Nation. Nov 23, 1957, v185, p396.
The New York Times. Oct 30, 1957, p24.
The New Yorker. Nov 9, 1957, v33, p109.
Newsweek. Nov 4, 1957, v50, p112.
Sight and Sound. Aut 1957, v27, p94.
Variety. Aug 28, 1957, p6.

Across the Wide Missouri (US; Wellman, William A.; 1951)
American Cinematographer. May 1951, v32, p178-79.
BFI/Monthly Film Bulletin. Nov 1951, v18, p359.
Catholic World. Nov 1951, v174, p145.
Christian Century. Nov 21, 1951, v68, p1359.
Film Daily. Sep 24, 1951, p20.
The Films of Clark Gable. p222-24.
Hollywood Reporter. Sep 18, 1951, p3.
Library Journal. Nov 1, 1951, v76, p1818.
Motion Picture Herald Product Digest. Sep 29, 1951, p1041-42.
The New York Times. Nov 7, 1951, p35.
Newsweek. Nov 19, 1951, v38, p102.
Saturday Review. Oct 27, 1951, v34, p30.
Time. Nov 19, 1951, v58, p110.
Variety. Sep 19, 1951, p6.
William A. Wellman (Thompson). p231-35.

Act One (US; Schary, Dore; 1963)
America. Jan 11, 1964, v110, p54-55.
Film Daily. Dec 17, 1963, p6.
Filmfacts. Jan 23, 1964, v6, p321-23.
Films in Review. Feb 1964, v15, p117.
The New Republic. Jan 18, 1964, v150, p26.
The New York Times. Dec 27, 1963, p17.
Photoplay. v65, p19.
Time. Dec 27, 1963, v82, p57.
Variety. Dec 18, 1963, p7.

Actors and Sin (US; Hecht, Ben; 1952)
Ben Hecht: Hollywood Screenwriter. p169-73.
BFI/Monthly Film Bulletin. May 1953, v20, p63.
The Cinema of Edward G. Robinson. p181-83.
Commonweal. Jun 13, 1952, v56, p245.
Film Daily. May 29, 1952, p6.
Films in Review. Aug-Sep 1952, v3, p358.
The Five Lives of Ben Hecht (Fetherling). p153-55.
Hollywood Reporter. May 23, 1952, p4.
Library Journal. Jul 1952, v77, p1185.
Life. Jun 23, 1952, v32, p121-22.
Motion Picture Herald Product Digest. May 31, 1952, p1382.
The New York Times. May 30, 1952, p11.
The New Yorker. Jun 7, 1952, v28, p124.
Newsweek. Jun 9, 1952, v39, p89.
Saturday Review. Jun 7, 1952, v35, p28.
Theatre Arts. Apr 1952, v36, p42.
Time. Jun 23, 1952, v59, p96.
Variety. May 28, 1952, p22.

The Actress (US; Cukor, George; 1953)
America. Nov 7, 1953, v90, p159.
BFI/Monthly Film Bulletin. Jan 1954, v21, p2.
Catholic World. Sep 1955, v177, p463.
Commonweal. Oct 30, 1953, v59, p92.
Farm Journal. Nov 1953, v77, p161.
Film Daily. Aug 10, 1953, p6.
The Films in My Life. p85-88.
Films in Review. Oct 1953, v4, p433.
The Films of Spencer Tracy. p215-16.
George Cukor (Phillips). p85-88.
Hollywood Reporter. Aug 4, 1953, p3.
Library Journal. Oct 15, 1953, v78, p1840.
Life. Nov 9, 1953, v35, p107.
Magill's Survey of Cinema. Series II. v1, p18-20.
The Nation. Nov 21, 1953, v177, p434.
National Parent Teacher. Oct 1953, v48, p38.
The New York Times. Oct 13, 1953, p34.
The New York Times. Oct 25, 1953, SecII, p1.
The New Yorker. Oct 24, 1953, v29, p129.
Newsweek. Sep 28, 1953, v42, p101.
Saturday Review. Oct 3, 1953, v36, p43.
Senior Scholastic. Nov 4, 1953, v63, p35.
Time. Oct 19, 1953, v62, p112.
Variety. Aug 5, 1953, p6.

Adam and Eve (Also titled: Adan y Eva) (SP; Gout, Albert; 1957)
BFI/Monthly Film Bulletin. Nov 1958, v25, p141.
Film Daily. Nov 26, 1957, v112, p11.
Filmfacts. 1958, v1, p210.
Hollywood Reporter. Nov 18, 1957, p3.
The New York Times. Oct 18, 1958, p17.
Variety. Nov 28, 1956, p6.

Adele Hasn't Had Her Supper Yet *See* Dinner for Adele

Admirable Crichton (Also titled: Paradise Lagoon) (GB; Gilbert, Lewis; 1957)
America. Feb 1, 1958, v98, p522.
BFI/Monthly Film Bulletin. Jul 1957, v24, p82.
Commonweal. Jan 31, 1958, v67, p458.
Film Daily. Dec 20, 1957, v92, p6.
Films and Filming. Jul 1957, v3, p23.

Hollywood Reporter. Dec 18, 1957, p3.
Motion Picture Herald Product Digest. Dec 21, 1957, p649.
The New York Times. Dec 17, p45.
Newsweek. Dec 16, 1957, v50, p119.
Saturday Review. Jan 18, 1958, v41, p24.
Time. Jan 6, 1958, v71, p74.
Variety. Jun 19, 1957, p6.

Adolescente, L' (FR; Moreau, Jeanne; 1979)
Hollywood Reporter. Oct 18, 1982, p10.
The Los Angeles Times. Sep 29, 1982, SecVI, p1.
Magill's Cinema Annual, 1983. p53.
The Nation. Oct 9, 1982, v235, p346.
The New Republic. Oct 11, 1982, v187, p25.
The New York Times. Sep 12, 1982, p84.
Newsweek. Sep 27, 1982, v100, p76.
Variety. Jan 31, 1979, p24.

Adua and Her Colleagues *See* Love a La Carte

Adua e le Compagne *See* Love a La Carte

Adventures of a Young Man *See* Hemingway's Adventures of a Young Man

The Adventures of Buckaroo Banzai Across the Eighth Dimension (Also titled: Buckaroo Banzai) (US; Richter, W.D.; 1984)
Cinefex. Nov 1984, n19, p44-59.
Film Journal. Sep 1984, v87, p25-26.
Hollywood Reporter. Aug 4, 1984, p4.
The Los Angeles Times. Aug 10, 1984, SecIV, p1.
Maclean's. Aug 27, 1984, v97, p54.
Magill's Cinema Annual, 1985. p47-51.
New York. Oct 22, 1984, v17, p136.
The New York Times. Oct 5, 1984, SecIII, p8.
The New Yorker. Aug 20, 1984, v60, p87-89.
Newsweek. Aug 20, 1984, v104, p75.
School Update. May 11, 1984, v116, p18.
Time. Aug 13, 1984, v124, p93.
Variety. Aug 8, 1984, p14.
The Village Voice. Oct 16, 1984, p59.

The Adventures of Captain Fabian (US; Marshall, William; 1951)
BFI/Monthly Film Bulletin. Oct 1951, v18, p345.
Film Daily. Oct 1, 1951, p6.
The Films of Errol Flynn. p174-75.
Hollywood Reporter. Sep 21, 1951, p4.
Motion Picture Herald Product Digest. Sep 29, 1951, p1042.
The New York Times. Dec 14, 1951, p36.
Variety. Sep 26, 1951, p6.

The Adventures of Hajji Baba (US; Weis, Don; 1954)
America. Oct 16, 1954, v92, p83.
BFI/Monthly Film Bulletin. Mar 1955, v22, p31.
Film Daily. Oct 8, 1954, p6.
Hollywood Reporter. Oct 7, 1954, p3.
Library Journal. Nov 1, 1954, v79, p2095.
Life. Sep 27, 1954, v37, p51.
Motion Picture Herald Product Digest. Oct 16, 1954, p177.
National Parent-Teacher. Dec 1954, v49, p39.
The New York Times. Oct 9, 1954, p8.
Newsweek. Nov 8, 1954, v44, p101.
Time. Nov 1, 1954, v64, p98.
Variety. Oct 13, 1954, p6.

The Adventures of Robinson Crusoe (Spanish title: Aventuras de Robinson Crusoe, Las; Also titled: Robinson Crusoe) (MEX, US; Buñuel, Luis; 1954)
BFI/Monthly Film Bulletin. Sep 1954, v21, p126.
Catholic World. Jun 1954, v179, p220.
Cinema Eye, Cinema Ear. p98-99.
The Cinema of Luis Buñuel. p71-73.
Commonweal. Jul 30, 1954, v60, p413.
Farm Journal. Jul 1954, v78, p92.
Film Daily. Jun 16, 1954, p6.
Films and Filming. Oct 1954, v1, p20.
Films and Filming. Aug 1969, v15, p78-79.
Films in Review. Aug-Sep 1954, v5, p364-65.
The Great Adventure Films. p180-83.
Hollywood Reporter. Jun 11, 1954, p3.
Illustrated London News. Aug 21, 1954, v225, p306.
Kiss Kiss Bang Bang. p281.
Library Journal. Jun 1, 1954, v79, p1048.
Life. Aug 23, 1954, v37, p59-60.
The London Times. Aug 9, 1954, p9.
Luis Buñuel (Aranda). p156-59.
Luis Buñuel (Durgnat). p78-82.
Luis Buñuel (Higginbotham). p73-74.
Luis Buñuel (Kyrou). p61-63.
Motion Picture Herald Product Digest. Jun 12, 1954, p26.
National Parent-Teacher. Jun 1954, v48, p38.
Natural History. Nov 1954, v63, p426.
The New Statesman and Nation. Aug 14, 1954, v48, p183-84.
The New York Times. Aug 6, 1954, p10.
The New York Times Magazine. May 30, 1954, p30.
The New Yorker. Aug 14, 1954, v30, p58.
Newsweek. Apr 19, 1954, v43, p106.
Reporter. Sep 23, 1954, v11, p46.
Saturday Review. Jul 17, 1954, v37, p27.
Senior Scholastic. May 5, 1954, v64, p37.
Sight and Sound. Oct-Dec 1954, v24, p86-87.
Time. May 24, 1954, v63, p102.
Variety. Jun 2, 1954, p6.

The Adventures of Sherlock Holmes' Smarter Brother (Also titled: Sherlock Holmes' Smarter Brother) (US; Wilder, Gene; 1975)
BFI/Monthly Film Bulletin. Feb 1976, v43, p23.
Films in Review. Jan 1976, v27, p55.
The Films of Sherlock Holmes. p226-33.
Hollywood Reporter. Dec 1, 1975, p3.
The Los Angeles Times. Dec 14, 1975, Calendar, p54.
Motion Picture Herald Product Digest. Dec 24, 1975, p54.
The New Republic. Jan 31, 1976, v174, p25.
The New York Times. Dec 15, 1975, p42.
The New Yorker. Dec 22, 1975, v51, p70-71.
Newsweek. Dec 22, 1975, v86, p50.
Saturday Review. Jan 24, 1976, v3, p49.
Sherlock Holmes on the Screen. p229-38.
Time. Dec 22, 1975, v106, p72.
Variety. Dec 3, 1975, p22.
Vogue. Feb 1976, v166, p80.

Advise and Consent (US; Preminger, Otto; 1962)
America. Jun 30, 1962, v107, p449.
BFI/Monthly Film Bulletin. Sep 1962, v29, p122.
The Cinema of Otto Preminger. p136-40.
Commonweal. Jun 8, 1962, v76, p280.
Film. Aut 1962, v33, p21-22.
Film Culture. Fall 1964, n34, p28-34.
Film Daily. Jun 7, 1962, v7, p9.

Filmfacts. Jun 15, 1962, v5, p113-15.
Films and Filming. Oct 1962, v9, p29.
Films in Review. Aug-Sep 1962, v13, p430-32.
The Films of Henry Fonda. p166-67.
The Fondas (Springer). p180-82.
Hollywood Reporter. May 16, 1962, v16, p3.
Life. Jul 6, 1962, v53, p73-75.
Magill's Survey of Cinema. Series I. v1, p18-21.
Motion Picture Herald Product Digest. May 30, 1962, p572.
Movie. Sep 1962, n2, p26-30.
Movie. Nov 1962, n4, p14-17.
The New Republic. Jul 4, 1962, v142, p28.
The New York Times. May 13, 1962, p70.
The New York Times. Jul 7, 1962, p31.
The New Yorker. Jul 9, 1962, v38, p116.
Newsweek. Jul 11, 1962, v59, p99-100.
Saturday Review. Jul 2, 1962, v45, p23.
Sight and Sound. Aut 1962, v31, p144-45.
Time. Mar 30, 1962, v79, p13.
Time. Jul 8, 1962, v79, p66.
Variety. May 26, 1962, p6.
The Village Voice. Jun 14, 1962, p11.
The Village Voice. Sep 6, 1962, p9, 12.
The Village Voice. Sep 6, 1962, p47.

Affair in Monte Carlo *See* Twenty Four Hours of a Woman's Life

Affair in Trinidad (US; Sherman, Vincent; 1952)
BFI/Monthly Film Bulletin. Sep 1952, v19, p121.
Commonweal. Aug 15, 1952, v56, p462.
Film Daily. Jul 31, 1952, p6.
Films in Review. Aug-Sep 1952, v3, p359.
The Films of Rita Hayworth. p180-86.
Hollywood Reporter. Jul 30, 1952, p3.
The London Times. Sep 1, 1952, p8.
Motion Picture Herald Prooduct Digest. Aug 2, 1952, p1470.
National Parent-Teacher. Sep 1952, v47, p38.
The New Statesman and Nation. Sep 6, 1952, v44, p263.
The New York Times. Jul 31, 1952, p14.
Newsweek. Aug 11, 1952, v40, p86.
The Tatler. Sep 10, 1952, v205, p464.
Time. Aug 4, 1952, v60, p76.
Variety. Jul 30, 1952, p6.

An Affair of the Heart *See* Love Affair, or The Case of the Missing Switchboard Operator

An Affair to Remember (US; McCarey, Leo; 1957)
America. Jul 27, 1957, v97, p451.
BFI/Monthly Film Bulletin. Oct 1957, v24, p122.
Commonweal. Aug 9, 1957, v66, p472.
Film Comment. Fall 1971, v7, p58-59.
Film Daily. Jul 12, 1957, v112, p9.
Films and Filming. Oct 1957, v4, p24-25.
The Films of Cary Grant. p227-29.
Hollywood Reporter. Jul 12, 1957, p3.
Magill's Survey of Cinema. Series II. v1, p24-26.
The New York Times. Jul 20, 1957, p8.
The New York Times. Jul 28, 1957, SecII, p1.
The New Yorker. Aug 3, 1957, v33, p48.
Newsweek. Jul 15, 1957, v40, p100.
Saturday Review. Jul 20, 1957, v40, p27.
Saturday Review. Aug 10, 1957, v40, p24.
Talking Pictures. p307-13.
Time. Aug 5, 1957, v70, p76.
Variety. Jul 17, 1957, p6.

Africa, Addio (IT; Jacopetti, Gualtiero; Prosperi, Franco; 1966)
America. Apr 22, 1967, v116, p601-02.

Christian Science Monitor (Western edition).
Jun 12, 1967, p6.
Film 67/68. p240-41.
Film Daily. Jan 13, 1967, p6.
Filmfacts. Jun 1, 1967, v10, p98-100.
Films and Filming. Sep 1967, v13, p22.
Films in Review. Apr 1967, v18, p243-44.
Motion Picture Herald Product Digest. Feb 1,
1967, p654.
The New York Times. Mar 13, 1967, p43.
Newsweek. Mar 20, 1967, v69, p101.
Variety. Mar 9, 1966, p6.

African Fury *See* Cry, the Beloved Country

The African Queen (US, GB; Huston, John;
1951)
America's Favorite Movies. p234-52.
Audience. Jun 1973, v5, p1-2.
BFI/Monthly Film Bulletin. Feb 1952, v19,
p15.
Catholic World. Mar 1952, v174, p457-58.
Christian Century. Mar 19, 1952, v69, p351.
The Cinema of John Huston. p88-93.
Cinema, the Magic Vehicle. v2, 79-80.
Classic Images. Mar 1985, n117, p56.
Commonweal. Mar 14, 1952, v55, p566.
The Complete Films of Humphrey Bogart.
p161-62.
Dictionary of Films. p3.
Film Comment. May-Jun 1980, v16, p25-26.
Film Criticism and Caricatures, 1943-1953.
p135-36.
Film Culture. 1959, n19, p66-101.
Film Daily. Dec 26, 1951, p11.
Films and Filming. Oct 1959, v6, p10, 25.
Films in Review. Feb 1952, v3, p81-84.
The Films of Katharine Hepburn. p147-50.
The Films of the Fifties. p59-60.
The Great Adventure Films. p162-65.
Hollywood Reporter. Dec 26, 1951, p3.
Humphrey Bogart: The Man and His Films.
p159.
*The International Dictionary of Films and
Filmmakers.* v1, p13-15.
John Huston: Maker of Magic. p83-90.
Kiss Kiss Bang Bang. p281-82.
Library Journal. Mar 1, 1952, v77, p426.
Literature/Film Quarterly. 1982, v10, n1, p13-
24.
Magill's Survey of Cinema. Series I. v1, p22-25.
Motion Picture Herald Product Digest. Dec 29,
1951, p1169.
The New Republic. Mar 10, 1952, v126, p21.
The New Statesman and Nation. Jan 12, 1952,
v43, p37.
The New York Times. Feb 21, 1952, p24.
The New York Times Magazine. Feb 10, 1952,
p20-21.
The New Yorker. Feb 23, 1952, v28, p77.
Newsweek. Mar 3, 1952, v39, p88.
· *An Open Book.* p187-204.
Reruns. p82-86.
Saturday Review. Feb 23, 1952, v35, p29.
Selected Film Criticism, 1951-1960. p4-5.
Senior Scholastic. Mar 12, 1952, v60, p24.
Sight and Sound. Apr-Jun 1952, v21, p172.
The Spectator. Jan 11, 1952, v188, p44.
Theatre Arts. Mar 1952, v36, p45, 73.
Theatre Arts. Feb 1952, v36, p48-49, 92.
Time. Feb 25, 1952, v59, p68.
Variety. Dec 26, 1951, p6.

After Hours (US; Scorsese, Martin; 1985)
BFI/Monthly Film Bulletin. Jun 1986, v53,
p165-66.
Hollywood Reporter. Sep 9, 1985, p3.
Humanist. Jan-Feb 1986, v46, p39-40.
The Los Angeles Times. Sep 29, 1985,
Calendar, p22.

Maclean's. Oct 14, 1985, v98, p93.
Magill's Cinema Annual, 1986. p51-55.
The Nation. Dec 7, 1985, v241, p623-24.
The New Republic. Oct 14, 1985, v193, p26-27.
New York. Sep 23, 1985, v18, p93-95.
The New York Times. Sep 13, 1985, SecIII, p6.
The New Yorker. Sep 23, 1985, v61, p101-03.
Newsweek. Sep 16, 1985, v106, p68.
Rolling Stone. Nov 7, 1985, p45-46.
Time. Sep 23, 1985, v126, p91.
Variety. Sep 11, 1985, p4.
Vogue. Sep 1985, v175, p102.
The Wall Street Journal. Sep 5, 1985, p24.

After the Fox (Italian title: Caccia Alla
Volpe) (IT, US, GB; De Sica, Vittorio;
1966)
BFI/Monthly Film Bulletin. Nov 1966, v33,
p168.
Film Daily. Dec 8, 1966, p7.
Film Quarterly. Sep 1967, v20, p60-61.
Filmfacts. Jan 15, 1967, v9, p366-68.
Films in Review. Jan 1967, v18, p55.
Hollywood Reporter. Dec 7, 1966, p3.
The London Times. Sep 29, 1966, p7.
Motion Picture Herald Product Digest. Dec 14,
1966, p639-40.
New Statesman. Sep 30, 1966, v72, p488.
The New York Times. Dec 24, 1966, p11.
The New Yorker. Jan 7, 1967, v42, p89.
Newsweek. Jan 2, 1967, v69, p64.
Saturday Review. Dec 31, 1966, v49, p36.
Variety. Oct 12, 1966, p6.
*Vittorio De Sica: A Guide to References and
Resources.* p128-33.

After the Rehearsal (Swedish title: Efter
Reptitionen) (SWED; Bergman,
Ingmar; 1984)
Christian Century. Sep 5, 1984, v101, p812.
Film Journal. Jul 1984, v87, p22-23.
Films in Review. Aug-Sep 1984, v35, p431.
Hollywood Reporter. Jun 21, 1984, p4.
Informer. Jul 1984, p5-6.
The Los Angeles Times. Jun 20, 1984, SecIV,
p1.
Maclean's. Jul 16, 1984, v97, p53.
Magill's Cinema Annual, 1985. p52-56.
National Review. Aug 24, 1984, v36, p56-59.
The New Leader. Sep 3, 1984, v67, p22.
The New Republic. Jun 25, 1984, v190, p24-26.
New York. Jul 16, 1984, v17, p46-47.
The New York Times. Jun 21, 1984, SecIII,
p14.
Penthouse. Sep 1984, v16, p54.
Time. Jul 9, 1984, v124, p82.
Variety. Apr 25, 1984, p54.
Vogue. Sep 1984, v174, p86.

Against All Flags (US; Sherman, George;
1952)
BFI/Monthly Film Bulletin. Dec 1952, v19,
p169.
Christian Century. Feb 18, 1953, v70, p207.
Film Daily. Dec 3, 1952, p6.
The Films of Anthony Quinn. p128-29.
The Films of Errol Flynn. p178-80.
Hollywood Reporter. Nov 26, 1952, p3.
Look. Jan 13, 1953, v17, p66-67.
Motion Picture Herald Product Digest. Nov 29,
1952, p1621-22.
National Parent-Teacher. Dec 1952, v47, p36.
The New York Times. Dec 25, 1952, p34.
Newsweek. Jan 12, 1953, v41, p76.
Time. Dec 22, 1952, v60, p67.
Variety. Nov 26, 1952, p6.

Against All Odds (US; Hackford, Taylor;
1984)
Armchair Detective. Fall 1984, v17, p325-6.

BFI/Monthly Film Bulletin. Jun 1984, v51,
p171.
Film Journal. Apr 1984, v87, p35-36.
Films and Filming. Jun 1984, n357, p11.
Films in Review. Apr 1984, v35, p237-38.
Hollywood Reporter. Feb 15, 1984, p3.
The Los Angeles Times. Mar 2, 1984, SecVI,
p1.
Maclean's. Mar 5, 1984, v97, p61.
Millimeter. Apr 1984, v12, p167.
New Statesman. May 18, 1984, v107, p28-29.
New York. Mar 5, 1984, v17, p112.
The New York Times. Mar 11, 1984, SecII, p17.
The New York Times. Mar 2, 1984, SecIII, p14.
The New Yorker. Mar 19, 1984, v60, p127-30.
Newsweek. Mar 5, 1984, v103, p82.
Photoplay. Jul 1984, v35, p19.
Soundtrack. Jun 1984, v3, p10-11.
Time. Mar 19, 1984, v123, p91.
Variety. Feb 15, 1984, p24.
The Village Voice. Mar 13, 1984, p41.

Agatha (US; Apted, Michael; 1979)
BFI/Monthly Film Bulletin. Jun 1979, v46,
p115.
Commonweal. May 11, 1979, v106, p273-74.
Films in Review. Apr 1979, v30, p243.
The Films of Dustin Hoffman. p195-202.
Hollywood Reporter. Feb 9, 1979, p10.
The Los Angeles Times. Feb 8, 1979, SecIV, p1.
Magill's Cinema Annual, 1983. p435-38.
Motion Picture Herald Product Digest. Feb 21,
1979, p74.
The Nation. Mar 10, 1979, v228, p285.
The New Republic. Mar 3, 1979, v180, p25.
New York. Jun 4, 1979, v12, p71.
The New York Times. Feb 9, 1979, v3, p10.
The New Yorker. Feb 26, 1976, v55, p101-03.
Newsweek. Feb 19, 1979, v93, p57.
Saturday Review. Apr 14, 1979, v6, p41.
Time. Feb 26, 1979, v113, p76.
Variety. Feb 14, 1979, p23.

Agnes of God (US; Jewison, Norman;
1985)
America. Oct 19, 1985, v153, p242.
BFI/Monthly Film Bulletin. Mar 1986, v53,
p73.
Christian Century. Aug 28, 1985, v102, p774.
Christianity Today. Dec 13, 1985, v29, p4.
Commonweal. Oct 4, 1985, v112, p530-32.
Film Comment. Sep-Oct 1985, v21, p13-17.
Films in Review. Dec 1985, v36, p619.
Hollywood Reporter. Aug 15, 1985, p3.
The Los Angeles Times. Sep 13, 1985, SecVI,
p1.
Maclean's. Sep 16, 1985, v98, p62.
Magill's Cinema Annual, 1986. p56-59.
Ms. Dec 1985, v14, p29.
New York. Sep 23, 1985, v18, p95.
The New York Times. Sep 13, 1985, SecIII, p12.
Newsweek. Sep 9, 1985, v106, p89.
Time. Aug 26, 1985, v126, p64.
Variety. Aug 21, 1985, p16.
Vogue. Oct 1985, v175, p92.

The Agony and the Ecstasy (US, IT; Reed,
Carol; 1965)
America. Oct 16, 1965, v113, p448.
BFI/Monthly Film Bulletin. Nov 1965, v32,
p159-60.
Cahiers du Cinema in English. Dec 1966, n6,
p54-55.
Catholic World. Nov 1965, v202, p127-28.
Christian Century. Dec 15, 1965, v82, p1548.
Christian Science Monitor (Western edition).
Nov 11, 1965, p4.
Commonweal. Oct 15, 1965, v83, p61.
Film Daily. Sep 14, 1965, p5, 7.
Films and Filming. Sep 1966, v12, p53.

Films and Filming. Oct 1965, v12, p39-40.
Films and Filming. Dec 1965, v12, p24.
Films in Review. Oct 1965, v16, p511-12.
The Films of Charlton Heston. p144-49.
Hollywood Reporter. Sep 14, 1965, p3.
Life. Nov 12, 1965, v59, p75-76.
The London Times. Oct 27, 1965, p15.
Look. Mar 9, 1965, v29, p41-48.
Motion Picture Herald Product Digest. Sep 15, 1965, p361.
The New Republic. Nov 6, 1965, v153, p31.
New Statesman. Nov 5, 1965, v70, p667.
The New York Times. Oct 9, 1965, p5.
The New Yorker. Oct 16, 1965, v41, p228-29.
Playboy. Dec 1965, v12, p40, 42.
Saturday Review. Sep 25, 1965, v48, p50.
Senior Scholastic. Nov 11, 1965, v87, p44.
The Spectator. Nov 5, 1965, v215, p586.
Time. Oct 15, 1965, v86, p117.
Variety. Sep 15, 1965, p6.

Aguirre, the Wrath of God (German title: Aguirre, der Zorn Göttes) (WGER; Herzog, Werner; 1973)
BFI/Monthly Film Bulletin. Jan 1975, v22, p3-4.
Films in Review. Jun-Jul 1977, v28, p376.
The Great German Films. p260-68.
Hollywood Reporter. Apr 6, 1977, p11.
The International Dictionary of Films and Filmmakers. v1, p15-16.
The Los Angeles Times. Jun 8, 1977, SecIV, p1.
Magill's Survey of Cinema. Foreign Language Films. v1, p45-49.
The Nation. Apr 23, 1977, v224, p508.
The New Republic. Apr 16, 1977, v176, p23-24.
New York. Apr 18, 1977, v10, p94-96.
The New York Times. Apr 4, 1977, p43.
The New York Times. Dec 11, 1977, SecII, p15.
The New Yorker. Apr 11, 1977, v53, p127-28.
Time. May 16, 1977, v109, p92-93.
Variety. May 30, 1973, p26.

Ai No Corrida *See* In the Realm of the Senses

Aida (IT; Fracassi, Clemente; 1954)
America. Dec 11, 1954, v92, p306.
BFI/Monthly Film Bulletin. Sep 1956, v23, p115.
Catholic World. Oct 1954, v180, p66.
Commonweal. Dec 10, 1954, v61, p290.
Film Daily. Oct 14, 1954, p6.
Films in Review. Oct 1954, v5, p434.
Harper's Magazine. Jan 1955, v210, p87.
Hollywood Reporter. Mar 26, 1954, p3.
Motion Picture Herald Product Digest. Nov 6, 1954, p202.
National Parent-Teacher. Sep 1954, v49, p37.
The New York Times. Nov 12, 1954, p17.
The New York Times Magazine. Sep 26, 1954, p26.
Newsweek. Nov 15, 1954, v44, p112.
Saturday Review. Nov 6, 1954, v37, p39-40.
Time. Nov 29, 1954, v64, p75.
Variety. Oct 13, 1954, p6.

Airplane (US; Abrahams, Jim; Zucker, David; Zucker, Jerry; 1980)
BFI/Monthly Film Bulletin. Aug 1980, v47, p151.
Commonweal. Sep 12, 1980, v107, p503.
Commonweal. Sep 26, 1980, v107, p529-30.
Hollywood Reporter. Jun 27, 1980, p2.
Humanist. Nov-Dec 1980, v41, p45-46.
The Los Angeles Times. Jul 2, 1980, SecIV, p1.
Maclean's. Aug 11, 1980, v93, p55.
Motion Picture Herald Product Digest. Jul 9, 1980, p9.
The Nation. Jul 19, 1980, v231, p93.

The New Republic. Aug 2, 1980, v183, p26.
The New York Times. Aug 24, 1980, p69.
Newsday. Jul 4, 1980, SecII, p7.
Rolling Stone. Oct 2, 1980, p31.
Time. Jul 14, 1980, v116, p71.
Variety. Jul 2, 1980, p18.
The Village Voice. Jul 2, 1980, p36.

Airport (US; Seaton, George; 1970)
America. Mar 21, 1970, v122, p312.
BFI/Monthly Film Bulletin. Jun 1970, v37, p126-27.
Burt Lancaster: A Pictorial Treasury of His Films. p143-46.
Burt Lancaster: The Man and His Movies. p114-16.
Deeper into Movies. p136-37.
Film Daily. Feb 17, 1970, p3.
Films and Filming. Jun 1970, v16, n9, p84-85.
Films in Review. Apr 1970, v21, p243-44.
Hollywood Reporter. Feb 16, 1970, p3.
Magill's Survey of Cinema. Series II. v1, p27.
The New York Times. Mar 6, 1970, p34.
The New York Times. Mar 8, 1970, SecII, p1.
The New Yorker. Mar 21, 1970, v46, p165.
Newsweek. Mar 16, 1970, v75, p103-04.
Senior Scholastic. Apr 13, 1970, v96, p20-21.
Sight and Sound. Wint 1969-70, v39, n1, p49-50.
Variety. Feb 18, 1970, p17.

Airport 1975 (US; Smight, Jack; 1974)
America. Nov 9, 1974, v131, p288.
BFI/Monthly Film Bulletin. Feb 1975, v42, p27.
The Fifty Worst Films of All Time. p17-20.
Films in Review. Dec 1974, v25, p627.
The Films of Charlton Heston. p216-17.
The Films of Gloria Swanson. p 249-52.
The Films of Myrna Loy. p248-50.
Hollywood Reporter. Oct 11, 1974, p3.
The Los Angeles Times. Oct 18, 1974, SecIV, p1.
Magill's Survey of Cinema. Series II. v1, p27-29.
Motion Picture Herald Product Digest. Oct 30, 1974, p42.
The New York Times. Oct 19, 1974, p63.
The New Yorker. Oct 28, 1974, v50. p71-72.
Reeling. p484-86.
Time. Nov 4, 1975, v104, p8.
Variety. Oct 16, 1974, p14.

Akahige *See* Red Beard

The Alamo (US; Wayne, John; 1960)
The Alamo. 1960.
America. Nov 12, 1960, v104, p230.
BFI/Monthly Film Bulletin. Dec 1960, v27, p163.
Commonweal. Oct 28, 1960, v70, p124.
The Complete Films of John Wayne. p227-29.
Film Daily. Oct 24, 1960, p5.
Film Quarterly. Wint 1960, v14, p61.
Filmfacts. Nov 18, 1960, v3, p255.
Films and Filming. Dec 1960, v7, p32-33.
Films in Review. Nov 1960, v11, p549-551.
Hollywood Reporter. Oct 24, 1960, p3.
Life. Sep 19, 1960, v49, p120-23.
McCall's. Jan 1961, v88, p8.
Motion Picture Product Herald Digest. Nov 5, 1960, p907.
The New York Times. Oct 27, 1960, p45.
The New Yorker. Nov 5, 1960, v36, p187.
Redbook. Jan 1961, v116, p11.
Senior Scholastic. Nov 30, 1960, v71, p38.
Time. Nov 7, 1960, v76, p76.
Variety. Oct 26, 1960, p6.

Alamo Bay (US; Malle, Louis; 1985)
BFI/Monthly Film Bulletin. Jan 1986, v53, p5.
California. May 1985, v10, p55.
Chatelaine. Jul 1985, v58, p6.
Hollywood Reporter. Apr 1, 1985, p3.
The Los Angeles Times. Apr 3, 1985, SecVI, p1.
Maclean's. Apr 22, 1985, v98, p74.
Ms. Apr 1985, v13, p119.
New Statesman. Jan 31, 1986, v111, p34.
New York. Apr 15, 1985, v18, p97.
The New York Times Magazine. Apr 7, 1985, p28-31.
Newsweek. Apr 8, 1985, v105, p85.
Playboy. May 1985, v32, p37.
Texas Monthly. May 1985, v13, p176.
Time. Apr 8, 1985, v125, p83.
Variety. Apr 3, 1985, p15.
Vogue. Mar 1985, v175, p128.
Washingtonian. May 1985, v20, p72.
World Press Review. Nov 1985, v32, p59.

Albero degli Zoccoli, L' *See* The Tree of Wooden Clogs

Alex and the Gypsy (US; Korty, John; 1976)
America. Oct 30, 1976, v135, p286-88.
BFI/Monthly Film Bulletin. Apr 1977, v44, p63.
Films in Review. Nov 1976, v27, p567-68.
Independent Film Journal. Oct 11, 1976, v78, p32.
New York. Oct 18, 1976, v9, p79-81.
The New York Times. Oct 4, 1976, p16.
The New Yorker. Oct 18, 1976, v52, p75-78.
Time. Nov 1, 1976, v108, p84.
Variety. Sep 29, 1976, p30.
The Village Voice. Dec 20, 1976, p57.
When the Lights Go Down. p183-84.

Alexander the Great (US; Rossen, Robert; 1956)
America. Apr 14, 1956, v95, p72.
BFI/Monthly Film Bulletin. Mar 1956, v23, p55.
Commonweal. Apr 27, 1956, v64, p96.
Film Culture. 1956, v2, p29-30.
Film Daily. Mar 29, 1956, p9.
Films and Filming. Apr 1956, v2, p14-15.
Films in Review. May 1956, v7, p218-220.
The Films of Fredric March. p216-18.
Hollywood Reporter. Mar 29, 1956, p3.
Magill's Survey of Cinema. Series II. v1, p30-33.
The Nation. Apr 21, 1956, v182, p350.
The New York Times. Mar 29, 1956, p23.
The New York Times. Apr 1, 1956, SecII, p1.
The New Yorker. Apr 7, 1956, v32, p110.
Saturday Review. Mar 31, 1956, v39 p28.
Time. Apr 16, 1956, v67, p104.
Variety. Apr 4, 1956, p6.

Alfie (GB; Gilbert, Lewis; 1966)
America. Sep 3, 1966, v115, p232-33.
BFI/Monthly Film Bulletin. May 1966, v33, p70.
Christian Century. Feb 8, 1967, v84, p178-79.
Christian Science Monitor (Western edition). Nov 11, 1966, p4.
Commonweal. Sep 16, 1966, v84, p585.
Film Daily. Aug 23, 1966, p4.
Film Quarterly. Spr 1967, v20, p42-46.
Filmfacts. Sep 15, 1966, v9, p181-83.
Films and Filming. Dec 1965, v12, p10.
Films and Filming. Jun 1966, v12, p10.
Films in Review. Oct 1966, v17, p520-21.
The Films of the Sixties. p169-70.
Hollywood Reporter. Aug 23, 1966, p3.
Life. Sep 2, 1966, v61, p6.
The London Times. Mar 24, 1966, p16.

Magill's Survey of Cinema. Series I. v1, p31-32.
Motion Picture Herald Product Digest. Aug 31, 1966, p587.
Movie Comedy (Byron). p146-48.
The Nation. Sep 12, 1966, v203, p229.
New Statesman. Mar 25, 1966, v71, p437.
The New York Times. Aug 25, 1966, p42.
The New Yorker. Aug 27, 1966, v42, p90.
Newsweek. Aug 29, 1966, v68, p68.
Playboy. Nov 1966, v13, p38.
Private Screenings. p275-80.
Saturday Review. Aug 27, 1966, v49, p40.
Second Sight. p81-83.
See No Evil. p323-28.
The Spectator. Apr 1, 1966, v216, p405-06.
Take One. Nov-Dec 1966, v1, p28.
Time. Sep 2, 1966, v88, p66.
Variety. Mar 30, 1966, p6.
The Village Voice. Aug 25, 1966, p21.
Vogue. Sep 1, 1966, v148, p207.

Alfred the Great (GB; Donner, Clive; 1969)
America. Dec 13, 1969, v121, p600.
Deeper Into Movies. p84-85.
Film Daily. Oct 27, 1969, p4.
Films and Filming. Sep 1969, v15, p59-60.
Films in Review. Oct 1969, v20, p513-14.
The New York Times. Dec 4, 1969, p70.
The New Yorker. Dec 13, 1969, v45, p175.
Variety. Jul 23, 1969, p6.

Alfredo Alfredo (IT; Germi, Pietro; 1973)
The Films of Dustin Hoffman. p147-56.
Hollywood Reporter. Dec 13, 1973, p3.
The New York Times. Dec 18, 1973, v54, p1.
Newsweek. Jan 14, 1974, v83, p74.
Reeling. p349-51.
Time. Jan 7, 1974, v103, p61.
Variety. Dec 19, 1973, p12.

Ali (German title: Angst Essen Seele Auf; Also titled: Fear Consumes the Soul) (WGER; Fassbinder, Rainer Werner; 1974)
BFI/Monthly Film Bulletin. Nov 1974, v41, p243-44.
Christian Century. Sep 4, 1974, v91, p824-25.
Fassbinder: Filmmaker. p66-67.
Fassbinder (Tanem). p49, 110.
Film. Nov 1974, n20, p18.
The Great German Films. p272-73.
Hollywood Reporter. Oct 16, 1974, p8.
Magill's Survey of Cinema. Foreign Language Films. v1, p64-68.
The Nation. Oct 26, 1974, v219, p413.
New Statesman. Sep 27, 1974, v88, p440.
The New York Times. Sep 18, 1975, p50.
Newsweek. Oct 14, 1974, v84, p133.
Sight and Sound. Fall 1974, v43, p245.
Variety. May 22, 1974, p26.
The Village Voice. Oct 3, 1974, p88-89.

Alice Doesn't Live Here Anymore (US; Scorsese, Martin; 1974)
Audience. Feb 1975, v7, p11-12.
BFI/Monthly Film Bulletin. Jun 1975, v42, p127-28.
Cineaste. 1975, v7, p32-34.
Cinema Papers. Jul-Aug 1975, v2, p149-50.
Commentary. May 1975, v59, p67-70.
Esquire. May 1975, v83, p38.
Film. Jul 1975, n28, p19-20.
Film Comment. Mar-Apr 1975, v11, p42-46.
Film Quarterly. Spr 1975, v28, p55-59.
Filmmakers Newsletter. Mar 1975, v8, p21-26.
Films and Filming. Aug 1975, v21, p39-40.
Films Illustrated. Jun 1975, v4, p364.
Films Illustrated. Dec 1975, v5, p152.
Films in Review. Feb 1975, v26, 121-22.
Films in Review. Feb 1975, v26, p121.

Hollywood Reporter. Dec 9, 1974, p3.
Hudson Review. Sum 1975, v28, p413-20.
Independent Film Journal. Jan 22, 1975, v75, p13.
Jump Cut. May-Jun 1975, n7, p4-5.
The Los Angeles Times. Dec 9, 1974, SecIV, p16.
Martin Scorsese and Michael Cimino. p64-84.
Motion Picture Herald Product Digest. Jan 15, 1974, p62.
Movietone News. Sep 29, 1975, n44, p9-10.
Ms. Jan 1975, v3, p34.
The Nation. Feb 15, 1975, v220, p190.
The New Republic. Feb 15, 1975, v172, p22.
New York. Jun 27, 1975, v8, p64-65.
The New York Times. Mar 30, 1975, SecII, p1.
The New York Times. Feb 2, 1975, SecII, p13.
The New Yorker. Jan 13, 1975, v50, p74-78.
Newsweek. Jun 27, 1975, v85, p64.
Penthouse. May 1975, v6, p40-41.
Ramparts. May-Jun 1975, v13, p56-60.
Saturday Review. Jan 25, 1975, v2, p49.
Senior Scholastic. Apr 10, 1975, v106, p18.
Sight and Sound. Sum 1975, v44, p188-89.
Take One. 1975, v4, n8, p25-27.
Time. Feb 3, 1975, v6, p40-41.
Time. Feb 3, 1975, v104, p4.
Variety. Dec 11, 1974, p16.
The Village Voice. Jun 13, 1975, p71-72.
The Village Voice. Feb 17, 1975, p67-68.
Vogue. Apr 1975, v165, p90.

Alice in Wonderland (US; Geronimi, Clyde; Luske, Hamilton; Jaxon, Wilfrid; 1951)
The Art of Walt Disney. p286, 291, 300.
BFI/Monthly Film Bulletin. Aug 1951, v18, p306.
Christian Century. Oct 3, 1951, v68, p1143.
Cinema, the Magic Vehicle. v2, p91-92.
Commonweal. Aug 10, 1951, v54, p430.
Cue. Aug 4, 1951, p19.
The Disney Films. p101-03.
Film Daily. Jul 2, 1951, p6.
Films in Review. May 1951, v2, p7-11.
Hollywood Reporter. Jul 2, 1951, p4.
The London Times. Jul 25, 1951, p6.
Motion Picture Herald Product Digest. Jul 7, 1951, p921.
The New Republic. Aug 13, 1951, v125, p21.
The New Statesman and Nation. Aug 4, 1951, v42, p126.
The New York Times. Jul 30, 1951, p12.
The New York Times. Apr 21, 1974, p1.
The New Yorker. Aug 4, 1951, v27, p53.
Saturday Review. Aug 11, 1951, v34, p30-32.
Selected Film Criticism, 1951-1960. p5-6.
Sight and Sound. 1985, v54, p136-38.
The Spectator. Jul 27, 1951, v186, p124.
Time. Jul 16, 1951, v58, p90.
Time. Jul 23, 1951, v58, p82.
Time. Aug 6, 1951, v58, p69.
Variety. Jul 4, 1951, p8.
Walt Disney: A Guide to References and Resources. p41-42.

Alice's Restaurant (US; Penn, Arthur; 1969)
Alice's Restaurant. 1970.
Arthur Penn (Wood). p92-117.
Atlantic. Nov 1969, v224, p170-72.
Christian Century. Dec 3, 1969, v86, p1555-56.
Cinema. v5, p47-48.
Confessions of a Cultist. p457-59.
Esquire. Nov 1969, v72, p82.
Figures of Light. p198-200.
Film 69/70. p62-66.
Film Daily. Aug 18, 1969, p7.
Film Society Review. Nov 1969, v5, p38-42.

Filmfacts. 1969, v12, n13, p289.
Films and Filming. Apr 1970, v16, p39-41.
Films in Review. Aug-Sep 1969, v20, p442-43.
The Films of the Sixties. p277-78.
Focus. Spr 1970, n6, p27-31.
Godard and Others: Essays on Film Form. p162-80.
Hollywood Reporter. Aug 13, 1969, p3.
Journal of Popular Culture. Sum 1970, v4, p273-85.
Life. Aug 29, 1969, v67, p8.
Mademoiselle. Oct 1969, v64, p54.
Magill's Survey of Cinema. Series II. v1, p47-49.
Movies Into Film. p118-19.
The Nation. Sep 22, 1969, v209, p294.
National Review. Sep 23, 1969, v21, p971.
The New Republic. Sep 27, 1969, v161, p22.
The New York Times. Aug 25, 1969, p38.
The New York Times. Aug 31, 1969, SecII, p1.
The New Yorker. Sep 6, 1969, v155, p96.
Newsweek. Sep 1, 1969, p68-69.
Newsweek. Sep 29, 1969, v74, p101-04.
Saturday Review. Aug 30, 1969, v52, p35.
Sight and Sound. Wint 1969-70, v39, p44-45.
Take One: The Canadian Film Magazine. 1969, v2, p24-25.
Time. Aug 29, 1969, v94, p64.
Unholy Fools, Wits, Comics, Disturbers of the Peace. p199-201.
Variety. Aug 13, 1969, p18.

Alien (US; Scott, Ridley; 1979)
Alien. 1979.
BFI/Monthly Film Bulletin. Sep 1979, v46, p191.
Film Comment. Sep 1979, v15, p52-53.
Films in Review. Aug-Sep 1979, v30, p436.
The Films of the Seventies. p251-53.
Hollywood Reporter. May 18, 1979, p3.
The Los Angeles Times. May 20, 1979, Calendar, p1.
Magill's Survey of Cinema. Series I. v6, p37-39.
Motion Picture Herald Product Digest. Jun 6, 1979, p1.
The New Republic. Jun 16, 1979, v180, p20.
New York. Jun 4, 1979, v12, p71.
The New York Times. May 25, 1979, SecIII, p16.
The New York Times. Jun 24, 1979, p19.
Newsweek. May 28, 1979, v93, p101.
Saturday Review. Aug 4, 1979, v6, p51.
Time. Jun 4, 1979, v113, p60.
Variety. May 23, 1979, p22.
The World of Fantastic Films. p104-06.

Aliza the Policeman *See* The Policeman

All About Eve (US; Mankiewicz, Joseph L.; 1950)
American Cinematographer. Jan 1951, v32, p10-11.
American Film. Jul-Aug 1983, v8, p66-67.
America's Favorite Movies. p200-14.
Bette Davis: Her Films and Career. p148-50.
BFI/Monthly Film Bulletin. Jan 1951, v18, p199.
Christian Century. Nov 29, 1950, v67, p1439.
Cinema, the Magic Vehicle. v2, p54-55.
Classic Movies. p38-39.
Commonweal. Oct 27, 1950, v53, p62-63.
Cult Movies. p4-7.
Dictionary of Films. p7.
Esquire. Dec 1950, v34, p74.
Fifty From the Fifties. p1-8.
Film Criticism and Caricatures, 1943-1953. p118.
Film Daily. Sep 13, 1950, p6.
Film Quarterly. n4 1983, v36, p4-17.
Films in Review. Dec 1950, v1, p37-38.

The Films of Marilyn Monroe. p42-45.
The Films of the Fifties. p25-26.
The Great Movies. p170-71.
Halliwell's Hundred. p5-8.
Harper's Magazine. Jan 1951, v202, p103-04.
Hollywood Reporter. Sep 13, 1950, p3.
Hollywood Reporter. Jan 12, 1962, p3.
The International Dictionary of Films and Filmmakers. v1, p20-21.
Joseph L. Mankiewicz (Dick). p151-57.
Kiss Kiss Bang Bang. p283.
Life. Oct 30, 1950, v29, p79-80.
Magill's Survey of Cinema. Series I. v1, p40-42.
More About All About Eve.
Mother Goddam. p242, 248-53.
Motion Picture Herald Product Digest. Sep 16, 1950, p485.
Motion Picture Herald Product Digest. Jul 22, 1961, p213.
The Nation. Oct 28, 1950, v171, p397.
New American Mercury. Jan 1951, v72, p95-96.
The New Republic. Nov 6, 1950, v123, p21.
The New Statesman and Nation. Dec 16, 1950, v40, p624.
The New York Times. Oct 14, 1950, p13.
The New Yorker. Oct 21, 1950, v26, p101.
Newsweek. Oct 16, 1950, v36, p94.
Pictures Will Talk. p158-72.
Running Time: Films of the Cold War. p141, 145.
Saturday Review. Oct 21, 1950, v33, p31.
Selected Film Criticism, 1941-1950. p4.
Senior Scholastic. Nov 29, 1950, v57, p19.
Shots in the Dark. p258-60.
Sight and Sound. Jan 1951, v19, p373-74, 376.
The Spectator. Dec 8, 1950, v185, p648.
Star Acting. p293-14.
Talking Pictures. p241-43.
Theatre Arts. Dec 1950, v34, p8-9.
Time. Oct 16, 1950, v56, p96.
Vintage Films. p114-18.

All Fall Down (US; Frankenheimer, John; 1962)
America. May 5, 1962, v107, p210.
BFI/Monthly Film Bulletin. Jun 1962, v29, p74.
The Cinema of John Frankenheimer. p69-80.
Commonweal. Apr 27, 1962, v76, p112.
Film Daily. Mar 27, 1962, v27, p7.
Filmfacts. Apr 27, 1962, v5, p71-73.
Films and Filming. Jun 1962, v8, p38.
Films in Review. May 1962, v13, p297-98.
The Films of Warren Beatty. p79-87.
Hollywood Reporter. Mar 26, 1962, v169, p3.
Motion Picture Herald Product Digest. Mar 28, 1962, p491, 493.
Movie. Dec 1962, n5, p35.
The New Republic. Apr 23, 1962, v146, p37-38.
The New York Times. Apr 12, 1962, p41.
The New Yorker. Apr 21, 1962, v38, p170.
Newsweek. Apr 23, 1962, v59, p96-97.
Saturday Review. May 5, 1962, v45, p28.
Screen. Jul-Oct 1969, v10, p160-73.
Sight and Sound. Aut 1962, v31, p144.
Time. Apr 13, 1962, v79, p100.
Variety. Mar 28, 1962, p6.

All My Good Countrymen (Czech title: Vsichni Dobri Rodaci) (CZECH; Vojteck, Jasny; 1968)
Filmfacts. Jun 1, 1968, v11, p133-34.
Magill's Survey of Cinema. Foreign Language Films. v1, p69-73.
The New Republic. May 6, 1985, v192, p26.
The New York Times. Apr 4, 1985, p13.
Variety. May 28, 1969, p34.
The Village Voice. Apr 9, 1985, p54.

All Night Long (US; Ralph, Michael; 1981)
BFI/Monthly Film Bulletin. Jun 1982, v48, p107.
Films Illustrated. Jun 1981, v10, p325.
Films In Review. Apr 1981, v32, p246-47.
The Los Angeles Times. Mar 6, 1981, SecVI, p1.
Maclean's. Mar 30, 1981, v94, p57.
The New Republic. Mar 21, 1981, v184, p25.
New Statesman. Jun 26, 1981, v101, p23.
New York. Mar 23, 1981, v14, p53-54.
The New York Times. Mar 6, 1981, SecIII, p5.
The New Yorker. Mar 9, 1981, v57, p104.
Newsweek. Mar 16, 1981, v97, p97.
Rolling Stone. Apr 2, 1981, p46.
Time. Mar 9, 1981, v117, p69.
Variety. Mar 11, 1981, p16.
The Village Voice. Mar 11, 1981, p47.

All of Me (US; Reiner, Carl; 1984)
BFI/Monthly Film Bulletin. Jan 1985, v52, p13.
Commonweal. Nov 30, 1984, v111, p660.
Film Comment. Sep-Oct 1984, v20, p24-27.
Film Journal. Aug 1984, v87, p9.
Film Journal. Oct 1984, v87, p17-18.
The Los Angeles Times. Sep 10, 1984, SecVI, p1.
Maclean's. Oct 1, 1984, v97, p82.
Magill's Cinema Annual, 1985. p58-62.
Ms. Sep 1984, v13, p34.
The Nation. Nov 10, 1984, v239, p491-93.
The New York Times. Sep 21, 1984, SecIII, p6.
The New Yorker. Sep 17, 1984, v60, p124.
Newsweek. Sep 17, 1984, v104, p89.
Penthouse. Oct 1984, v16, p56.
Rolling Stone. Nov 8, 1984, p16-18.
Time. Sep 17, 1984, v124, p92.
Variety. Jul 11, 1984, p17.
The Village Voice. Sep 25, 1984, p59.
Vogue. Sep 1984, v174, p90.

All Screwed Up (Italian title: Tutto a Posto e Niente In Ordine) (IT; Wertmuller, Lina; 1974)
America. Feb 7, 1976, v134, p99-100.
Before My Eyes. p28.
Film Bulletin. Feb 1976, v45, p37.
Independent Film Journal. Feb 4, 1976, v77, p9.
The Los Angeles Times. Apr 23, 1976, SecIV, p1.
The Nation. Jan 31, 1976, v222, p123-24.
The New Republic. Feb 14, 1976, v174, p22-23.
New York. Feb 16, 1976, v9, p79-80.
New York Review of Books. Mar 18, 1976, v23, p5.
The New York Times. Jan 15, 1976, p28.
The New York Times. Jan 25, 1976, SecII, p1.
Saturday Review. Feb 21, 1976, v3, p49-50.
Variety. Aug 14, 1974, p16.
Vogue. Mar 1976, v166, p68.

All That Heaven Allows (US; Sirk, Douglas; 1955)
America. Mar 10, 1956, v94, p647.
BFI/Monthly Film Bulletin. Oct 1955, v22, p151.
Catholic World. Jan 1956, v182, p306.
Commonweal. Feb 3, 1956, v63, p459.
Douglas Sirk (Stern). p111-32.
Film Daily. Oct 25, 1955, p5.
The Great Romantic Films. p168-71.
Hollywood Reporter. Oct 25, 1955, v136, n47, p3.
Library Journal. Jan 1, 1956, v81, p74.
Magill's Survey of Cinema. Series II. v1, p53-56.
The New York Times. Feb 29, 1956, p35.
The New York Times. Mar 4, 1956, SecII.
Saturday Review. Dec 3, 1955, v38, p39.

Time. Mar 26, 1956, v67, p104.
Variety. Oct 26, 1955, p6.

All That Jazz (US; Fosse, Bob; 1979)
America. Jan 19, 1980, v142, p43.
BFI/Monthly Film Bulletin. Aug 1980, v47, p151-52.
Dance Magazine. Feb 1980, v54, p56-57.
The Hollywood Musical. p412-14.
Hollywood Musicals. p362-67.
Hollywood Reporter. Dec 12, 1979, p3.
The Los Angeles Times. Dec 16, 1979, Calendar, p1.
Magill's Survey of Cinema. Series 1, v1, p46-50.
Motion Picture Herald Product Digest. Dec 26, 1979, p58.
The New Republic. Jan 26, 1980, v182, p24-25.
New York. Dec 31, 1979, v13, p61-62.
The New York Times. Dec 20, 1979, SecIII, p13.
Newsweek. Dec 24, 1979, v94, p78-79.
Saturday Review. Feb 2, 1980, v7, p28.
Variety. Dec 12, 1979, p22.

All the Brothers Were Valiant (US; Thorpe, Richard; 1953)
America. Dec 19, 1953, v90, p327.
BFI/Monthly Film Bulletin. Jan 1954, v21, p7.
Commonweal. Nov 20, 1953, v59, p165.
Film Daily. Oct 19, 1953, p6.
The Films of Robert Taylor. p132-34.
Hollywood Reporter. Oct 16, 1953, p3.
Library Journal. Dec 1, 1953, v78, p2098.
The New York Times. Dec 29, 1953, p19.
Newsweek. Jan 18, 1954, v43, p88.
Saturday Review. Nov 7, 1953, v36, p37.
Time. Jan 18, 1954, v63, p103.
Variety. Oct 21, 1953, p6.

All the Fine Young Cannibals (US; Anderson, Michael; 1960)
America. Sep 10, 1960, v103, p623.
BFI/Monthly Film Bulletin. May 1960, v27, p62.
Commonweal. Sep 9, 1960, v72, p470.
Film Daily. Jul 15, 1960, p6.
Filmfacts. Oct 21, 1960, v3, p233.
Films and Filming. Jun 1960, v6, p23.
McCall's. Oct 1960, v88, p162.
Motion Picture Product Herald Digest. Jul 16, 1960, p771.
The New York Times. Sep 23, 1960, p33.
Time. Sep 12, 1960, v76, p80.
Variety. Jul 20, 1960, p6.

All the President's Men (US; Pakula, Alan J.; 1976)
Action. Mar-Apr 1976, v11, p12-19.
America. Apr 17, 1976, v134, p346-47.
American Cinematographer. Jul 1976, v57, p774-75.
American Film. Jul-Aug 1976, v1, p6-7.
Audience. Oct 1976, v9, p8.
Before My Eyes. p205.
BFI/Monthly Film Bulletin. May 1976, v43, p95.
Christian Century. Jan 9, 1976, v93, p571-72.
Cinema Papers. Sep-Oct 1976, n10, p171-72.
Columbia Journalism Review. May-Jun 1976, v15, p46-47.
Commentary. Jul 1976, v62, p59-61.
Commonweal. Apr 23, 1976, v103, p276-78.
Film Bulletin. Apr 1976, v45, pA.
Film Comment. Sep-Oct 1976, v12, p8-19.
Films and Filming. Jun 1976, v22, p30-31.
Films and Filming. May 1976, v22, p25-27.
Films Illustrated. Jun 1976, v5, p374-75.
Films Illustrated. May 1976, v5, p326-28, 340-43.
The Films of Dustin Hoffman. p167-76.
The Films of Robert Redford. p225-38.

Motion Picture Herald Product Digest. Oct 5, 1966, p611.
The New York Times. Nov 17, 1966, p55.
Newsweek. Dec 5, 1966, v68, p109-09A.
Playboy. Dec 1966, v13, p56, 62.
The Private Eye, the Cowboy and the Very Naked Girl. p215-17.
Time. Oct 14, 1966, v88, p117.
Variety. Oct 5, 1966, p6.

Always (US; Jaglom, Henry; 1985)
Chicago. Oct 1985, v 34, p105.
The Los Angeles Times. Oct 3, 1985, SecVI, p3.
Magill's Cinema Annual, 1986. p60-64.
The New York Times. Jan 24, 1986, SecIII, p8.
Variety. Mar 27, 1985, p17.

Amadeus (US; Forman, Milos; 1984)
America. Oct 13, 1984, v151, p210.
BFI/Monthly Film Bulletin. Jan 1985, v52, p14.
Christian Century. Oct 24, 1984, v101, p995-96.
Christianity Today. Apr 19, 1985, v29, p32.
Commonweal. Oct 19, 1984, v111, p557-58.
Film Comment. Sep-Oct 1984, v20, p50-57.
Film Comment. Jan-Feb 1985, v21, p70-75.
Film Journal. Oct 1984, v87, p26.
Films in Review. Apr 1985, v36, p246.
Hollywood Reporter. Sep 7, 1984, p3.
Horizon. Sep 1984, v27, p49-52.
Informer. Sep-Oct 1984, p8.
Life. Sep 1984, v7, p66-68.
The Los Angeles Times. Sep 19, 1984, SecIV, p1.
Maclean's. Oct 1, 1984, v97, p83.
Magill's Cinema Annual, 1985. p58-62.
The Nation. Dec 22, 1984, v239, p692-93.
National Review. Oct 19, 1984, v36, p56-57.
The New Republic. Oct 22, 1984, v191, p30-32.
New York. Sep 24, 1984, v17, p93-95.
New York Review of Books. Apr 11, 1985, v32, p11-12.
The New York Times. Sep 19, 1984, SecIII, p23.
The New York Times. Sep 20, 1984, SecIII, p18.
The New Yorker. Oct 29, 1984, v60, p122-23.
Newsweek. Sep 24, 1984, v104, p85.
Penthouse. Dec 1984, v16, p60.
Rolling Stone. Sep 27, 1984, p19-20.
Sight and Sound. Spr 1985, v54, p142.
Time. Sep 10, 1984, v124, p74-75.
Time. Apr 8, 1985, v125, p74.
Variety. Sep 5, 1984, p12.
The Village Voice. Sep 5, 1984, p63.
Vogue. Oct 1984, v174, p636.

Amants, Les (Also titled: The Lovers) (FR; Malle, Louis; 1958)
BFI/Monthly Film Bulletin. 1959, v26, p136.
Cinema, the Magic Vehicle. v2, p429-30.
Commonweal. Nov 27, 1959, v71, p265.
Double Takes. p214-16.
Film Daily. Nov 2, 1959, v116, p6.
Filmfacts. Dec 2, 1959, v2, p261-62.
The Films in My Life. p314-15.
Films in Review. Nov 1959, v10, p561-62.
Hollywood Reporter. Nov 2, 1959, p3.
The International Dictionary of Films and Filmmakers. v1, p24-25.
Magill's Survey of Cinema. Foreign Language Films. 4, p1844-47.
The Nation. Nov 28, 1959, v189, p407.
The New Republic. Dec 7, 1959, v141, p407.
The New York Times. Oct 27, 1959, p40.
The New Yorker. Nov 7, 1959, v35, p204.
Newsweek. Sep 21, 1959, v54, p125.
Saturday Review. Aug 8, 1959, v40, p24.
Time. Jan 25, 1960, v75, p93.
Variety. Sep 17, 1958, p7.

Amarcord (IT, FR; Fellini, Federico; 1974)
BFI/Monthly Film Bulletin. 1974, v41, p195.
Esquire. Dec 1974, v82, p20.

Federico Fellini: A Guide to References and Resources. p126-33.
Film Quarterly. Fall 1975, v29, p50-52.
Films in Review. Nov 1974, v25, p566.
Hollywood Reporter. Apr 4, 1975, p14.
The Los Angeles Times. Apr 9, 1975, SecIV, p27.
Magill's Survey of Cinema. Foreign Language Films. v1, p91-94.
Motion Picture Herald Product Digest. Oct 2, 1974, p34.
The Nation. Oct 12, 1974, v219, p350.
The New Republic. Sep 28, 1974, v171, p22.
The New York Times. May 26, 1975, SecII, p1.
The New York Times. Sep 20, 1975, p32.
The New York Times. Sep 29, 1975, SecII, p1.
The New York Times. Dec 8, 1975, SecII, p15.
The New Yorker. Sep 23, 1974, v50, p95-96.
Newsweek. Sep 30, 1974, v84, p106-07.
Saturday Review (World). Oct 19, 1974, v2, p41-42.
Time. Oct 7, 1974, v104, p7.
Variety. Jan 16, 1974, p18.

Amator (Also titled: Camera Buff) (POL; Kreslowski, Kryzysztof; 1979)
BFI/Monthly Film Bulletin. Feb 1982, v49, p23.
Cineaste. Wint 1980-81, p37.
Hollywood Reporter. Mar 17, 1980, p24.
New Statesman. Jan 1, 1982, v61, p24.
The New York Times. Oct 3, 1980, SecIII, p18.
Variety. Sep 5, 1979, p22.

The Amazing Monsieur Fabre (FR; Diamant-Berger, Henri; 1951)
BFI/Monthly Film Bulletin. May 1954, v21, p67.
Christian Century. Apr 8, 1953, v70, p431.
Commonweal. Oct 17, 1952, v57, p38.
Film Daily. Sep 3, 1952, p6.
Library Journal. Oct 1, 1952, v77, p1605.
Motion Picture Herald Product Digest. Aug 30, 1952, p1511.
National Parent-Teacher. Nov 1952, v47, p36.
Natural History. Nov 1952, v61, p424.
The New York Times. Sep 9, 1952, p21.
Newsweek. Sep 22, 1952, v40, p112.
Saturday Review. Aug 30, 1952, v35, p24.
Theatre Arts. Oct 1952, v36, p96.
Variety. Sep 3, 1952, p12.

Amère Victoire *See* Bitter Victory

America, America (Also titled: The Anatolian Smile) (US; Kazan, Elia; 1963)
America. Feb 1, 1964, v110, p173.
America, America. 1962.
An American Odyssey. p239-41.
BFI/Monthly Film Bulletin. May 1964, v31, p66.
Cinema. Feb 1964, v2, p46.
Commonweal. Jan 24, 1964, v79, p484.
Confessions of a Cultist. p115-16.
Elia Kazan: A Guide to References and Resources. p81-84.
Esquire. Mar 1964, v61, p22.
Film Daily. Dec 16, 1963, v123, p15.
Film Quarterly. Sum 1964, v17, p55-56.
Filmfacts. Jan 30, 1964, v6, p329-31.
Films and Filming. May 1964, v10, p20.
Films in Review. Jan 1964, v15, p44-45.
The Films of the Sixties. p95.
Hollywood Reporter. Dec 16, 1963, v178, p3.
Kazan on Kazan. p145-55.
Life. Mar 6, 1964, v56, p113-14.
Magill's Survey of Cinema. Series II. v1, p68-70.

Motion Picture Herald Product Digest. Jan 8, 1964, v231, p961.
National Review. May 19, 1964, v16, p413-15.
The New Republic. Jan 4, 1964, v150, p20-22.
The New York Times. Dec 16, 1963, p44.
The New York Times. Dec 22, 1963, p3.
Newsweek. Dec 23, 1963, v62, p74.
Photoplay. Mar 1964, v65, p18.
Saturday Review. Dec 28, 1963, v46, p29.
Time. Jan 3, 1964, v83, p78.
Variety. Dec 18, 1963, p6.
Vogue. Feb 1964, v143, p64.
A World on Film. p155-56.

America at the Movies (US; Stevens, George Jr.; 1976)
Commonweal. Oct 22, 1976, v103, p695-96.
Hollywood Reporter. Aug 2, 1976, p12.
Independent Film Journal. Oct 11, 1976, v78, p33.
The Los Angeles Times. Aug 2, 1976, SecIV, p1.
New York. Oct 4, 1976, v9, p86-88.
The New York Times. Oct 3, 1976, SecII, p15.
The New Yorker. Oct 11, 1976, v52, p138-44.
Variety. Jul 14, 1976, p21.
The Village Voice. Oct 4, 1976, p123.
When the Lights Go Down. p178-79.

An American Dream (Also titled: See You in Hell, Darling) (US; Gist, Robert; 1966)
BFI/Monthly Film Bulletin. Nov 1966, v33, p171-72.
Christian Science Monitor (Western edition). Oct 19, 1966, p10.
Film Daily. Sep 9, 1966, p6.
Film Quarterly. Wint 1966-67, v20, p59-60.
Filmfacts. Nov 1, 1966, v9, p234-35.
Films and Filming. Jan 1967, v13, p37-38.
Hollywood Reporter. Aug 25, 1966, p3.
Motion Picture Herald Product Digest. Sep 14, 1966, p596.
The New York Times. Sep 1, 1966, p28.
The New Yorker. Sep 10, 1966, v42, p103.
Newsweek. Sep 5, 1966, v68, p88.
Playboy. Nov 1966, v13, p34, 38.
Saturday Review. Sep 17, 1966, v49, p30.
Variety. Aug 31, 1966, p6.
The Village Voice. Sep 22, 1966, v11, p27.

American Flyers (US; Badham, John; 1985)
California Magazine. Sep 1985, v10, p46.
Films in Review. Oct 1985, v36, p486-87.
Hollywood Reporter. Aug 12, 1986, p3.
Los Angeles. Aug 1985, v30, p38.
The Los Angeles Times. Aug 15, 1985, SecVI, p1.
Maclean's. Oct 28, 1985, v98, p70.
The New York Times. Aug 16, 1985, SecIII, p6.
Newsweek. Sep 9, 1985, v106, p90.
Sports Illustrated. Sep 9, 1985, v63, p6.
Variety. Aug 14, 1985, p16.
The Village Voice. Aug 20, 1985, p56.

The American Friend (German title: Amerikanishe Freund, Der) (FR, WGER, US; Wenders, Wim; 1977)
BFI/Monthly Film Bulletin. Jan 1978, v45, p3.
Commonweal. Nov 11, 1977, v104, p725-26.
Films in Review. Dec 1977, v28, p632.
The Great German Films. p277-78.
Hollywood Reporter. Sep 30, 1977, p3.
The International Dictionary of Films and Filmmakers. v1, p27-28.
The Los Angeles Times. Nov 30, 1977, SecIV, p1.
Motion Picture Herald Product Digest. Sep 21, 1977, p29-32.
The Nation. Oct 15, 1977, v225, p380.
The New German Cinema. p148-55.

The New Republic. Oct 1, 1977, v177, p27-28.
The New York Times. Sep 24, 1977, p15.
The New Yorker. Oct 17, 1977, v53, p174-79.
Newsweek. Oct 3, 1977, v90, p71-73.
Variety. Jun 8, 1977, p26.

American Gigolo (US; Schrader, Paul; 1980)
BFI/Monthly Film Bulletin. May 1980, v47, p87.
The Christian Science Monitor. Feb 22, 1980, p19.
Film Comment. Mar-Apr 1980, v16, p49-52.
Films in Review. Mar 1980, v31, p177.
Hollywood Reporter. Feb 1, 1980, p3.
Hollywood Reporter. Nov 7, 1979, p3.
The Los Angeles Times. Feb 1, 1980, SecV, p1.
Maclean's. Feb 4, 1980, v93, p49.
Motion Picture Herald Product Digest. Feb 6, 1980, p71.
The Nation. Feb 23, 1980, v230, p219.
National Review. Apr 4, 1980, v32, p425-26.
The New Leader. Feb 25, 1980, v63, p21.
The New Republic. Mar 1, 1980, v182, p25.
New York. Feb 4, 1980, v13, p62-63.
The New York Times. Feb 3, 1980, SecII, p15.
The New York Times. Feb 1, 1980, SecIII, p14.
The New Yorker. Feb 4, 1980, v55, p107-08.
Newsday. Feb 1, 1980, SecII, p7.
Newsweek. Feb 11, 1980, v95, p82.
Time. Feb 11, 1980, v115, p95.
Variety. Jan 30, 1980, p28.
The Village Voice. Mar 10, 1980, p56.
The Washington Post. Feb 1, 1980, SecIII, p1.

American Graffiti (US; Lucas, George; 1973)
American Scholar. Wint 1973, v43, p147-51.
Atlantic. Oct 1973, v232, p125-27.
Atlantic. Dec 1973, v232, p132-34.
Commentary. Nov 1973, v56, p74-75.
Commonweal. Oct 5, 1973, v99, p12-13.
Esquire. Oct 1973, v80, p46.
Film Heritage. Wint 1973-74, n9, n2, p32.
Film Quarterly. Fall 1973, v27, p58-60.
Hollywood Reporter. Jun 19, 1973, p3.
Hot Rod. Aug 1973, v26, p18.
Magill's Survey of the Cinema. English Language Films. Series I, v1, p56.
The Nation. Sep 24, 1973, v217, p283.
National Review. Nov 9, 1973, v25, p1251.
The New Republic. Sep 15, 1973, v169, p22.
The New York Times. Aug 5, 1973, SecII, p4.
The New York Times. Aug 13, 1973, p21.
The New York Times. Sep 16, 1973, SecII, p1.
The New York Times. Dec 2, 1973, SecII, p13.
The New York Times. Jan 6, 1974, SecII, p1.
The New York Times. Jan 7, 1974, p38.
The New York Times. Sep 29, 1974, SecII, p15.
The New Yorker. Aug 13, 1973, v49, p66-67.
The New Yorker. Oct 29, 1973, v49, p154-56.
PTA Magazine. Dec 1973, v68, p4.
Senior Scholastic. Oct 1973, v103, p24.
Time. Aug 20, 1973, v102, p58.
Variety. Jun 20, 1973, p20.

American Guerilla in the Philippines (Also titled: I Shall Return) (US; Lang, Fritz; 1950)
BFI/Monthly Film Bulletin. Jan 1951, v18, p200.
Christian Century. Dec 6, 1950, v67, p1471.
The Cinema of Fritz Lang. p171-74.
Commonweal. Nov 24, 1950, v53, p173.
Film Daily. Nov 8, 1950, p6.
The Films of Fritz Lang. p231-33.
The Films of Tyrone Power. p164-66.
Fritz Lang: A Guide to References and Resources. p102-04.
Fritz Lang (Armour). p143-45.

Fritz Lang (Eisner). p295-300.
Hollywood Reporter. Nov 6, 1950, p3.
Library Journal. Dec 15, 1950, v75, p2163.
Motion Picture Herald Product Digest. Nov 18, 1950, p571.
The New Republic. Dec 11, 1950, v123, p29.
The New York Times. Nov 8, 1950, p37.
The New Yorker. Nov 18, 1950, v26, p157.
Newsweek. Nov 20, 1950, v36, p103.
The Spectator. Dec 15, 1950, v185, p693.
Time. Nov 27, 1950, v56, p98.
Variety. Nov 8, 1950, p6.

American Hot Wax (US; Mutrux, Floyd; 1978)
BFI/Monthly Film Bulletin. Jul 1978, v45, p152.
Encore. Apr 17, 1978, v7, p30.
Films in Review. May 1978, v29, p312.
The Hollywood Musical. p409.
Hollywood Reporter. Mar 10, 1978, p3.
The Los Angeles Times. Mar 17, 1978, SecIV, p30.
New York. Apr 3, 1978, v11, p67-68.
The New York Times. Mar 17, 1978, SecIII, p13.
The New York Times. Apr 30, 1978, SecII, p14.
The New Yorker. Mar 20, 1978, v54, p124-26.
Newsweek. Mar 27, 1978, v91, p96.
Rolling Stone. Apr 20, 1978, p46-47.
Time. Mar 27, 1978, v111, p77.
Variety. Mar 15, 1978, p21.

An American in Paris (US; Minnelli, Vincente; 1951)
American Cinematographer. Jan 1952, v33, p18-19.
BFI/Monthly Film Bulletin. Sep 1951, v18, p323.
Christian Century. Dec 5, 1951, v68, p1423.
Cinema, the Magic Vehicle. v2, p97-98.
Classic Film Collector. Fall 1976, n52, p22-23.
Commonweal. Oct 19, 1951, v55, p39.
Cue. Oct 6, 1951, p18.
Dictionary of Films. p9.
Film Daily. Aug 28, 1951, p7.
Films and Filming. Sep 1964, v10, p34-35.
Films in Review. Oct 1951, v2, p48-49.
The Films of Gene Kelly. p120-30.
Hollywood Reporter. Aug 28, 1951, p3.
I Remember It Well. p222-53.
The International Dictionary of Films and Filmmakers. v1, p26-27.
Journal of Popular Film and Television. n4, 1982, v9, p181-93.
Life. Apr 23, 1951, v55, p39.
The London Times. Aug 23, 1951, p2.
The Magic Factory: How MGM Made An American in Paris.
Magill's Survey of Cinema. Series I. v1, p60-63.
Motion Picture Herald Product Digest. Sep 1, 1951, p997.
The New Republic. Oct 22, 1951, v125, p21.
The New Statesman and Nation. Aug 18, 1951, v42, p180.
The New York Times. Oct 5, 1951, p24.
The New Yorker. Oct 6, 1951, v27, p69.
Newsweek. Oct 8, 1951, v38, p100.
Saturday Review. Nov 3, 1951, v34, p28.
Selected Film Criticism 1951-1960. p6-7.
Senior Scholastic. Nov 14, 1951, v59, p26.
Sequence. New Year 1952, n14, p36-38.
Sight and Sound. Oct-Dec 1951, v21, p77-78.
The Spectator. Aug 17, 1951, v187, p212.
Time. Oct 8, 1951, v58, p108.
Variety. Aug 29, 1951, p6.
Vincente Minnelli and the Film Musical. p50-53, 91-96.
The World of Entertainment. p306-32.

American Pop (US; Bakshi, Ralph; 1981)
Christian Century. Apr 22, 1981, v98, p40.
Commonweal. Apr 10, 1981, v108, p209.
Film Comment. Jan-Feb 1981, v17, p18-20.
Hollywood Reporter. Feb 9, 1981, p3.
The Los Angeles Times. Feb 13, 1981, SecVI, p1.
Maclean's. Mar 16, 1981, v94, p61-62.
Magill's Cinema Annual, 1982. p62-65.
The Nation. Mar 14, 1981, v232, p317.
The New York Times. Feb 13, 1981, SecIII, p5.
Newsweek. Mar 16, 1981, v97, p94.
Time. Apr 6, 1981, v117, p71.

An American Werewolf in London (US; Landis, John; 1981)
BFI/Monthly Film Bulletin. Nov 1981, v48, p215.
Film Journal. Aug 24, 1981, v84, p15-16.
Films Illustrated. Aug 1981, v10, p422-23.
Hollywood Reporter. Aug 17, 1981, p3.
Magill's Cinema Annual, 1982. p66-70.
New Statesman. Nov 13, 1981, v102, p30.
New York. Sep 14, 1981, v14, p62.
The New York Times. Aug 21, 1981, SecIII, p12.
Newsweek. Sep 7, 1981, v98, p82.
Variety. Aug 19, 1981, p21.
The Village Voice. Apr 1, 1981, p26.
The Village Voice. Aug 26, 1981, p42.

The Americanization of Emily (US; Hiller, Arthur; 1964)
America. Nov 14, 1964, v3, p641-43.
BFI/Monthly Film Bulletin. Jun 1965, v32, p86.
Commonweal. Dec 4, 1964, v81, p355.
Film Daily. Oct 28, 1964, v125, p6-7.
Films and Filming. May 1965, v11, p24.
Films in Review. Nov 1964, v15, p575.
The Films of the Sixties. p143-44.
Hollywood Reporter. Oct 28, 1964, v182, p3.
Magill's Survey of Cinema. Series I. v1, p64-67.
Motion Picture Herald Product Digest. Nov 11, 1964, v232, p161.
The New Republic. Dec 5, 1964, v151, p22.
The New York Times. Oct 28, 1964, p51.
Newsweek. Feb 10, 1964, v63, p83.
Newsweek. Nov 1964, v64, p96-97.
Saturday Review. Oct 24, 1964, v47, p29.
Time. Nov 13, 1964, v84, p128.
Variety. Oct 28, 1964, p6.
Vogue. Jan 1, 1965, v145, p66.

The Americano (US; Castle, William; 1954)
BFI/Monthly Film Bulletin. Mar 1955, v22, p37.
Film Daily. Jan 5, 1955, p12.
Films and Filming. Mar 1955, v1, p20.
Hollywood Reporter. Dec 29, 1954, p3.
National Parent-Teacher. Mar 1955, v49, p38.
The New York Times. Jan 20, 1955, p35.
Variety. Dec 29, 1954, p6.

Amerikanishe Freund, Der *See* The American Friend

The Amityville Horror (US; Rosenberg, Stuart; 1979)
BFI/Monthly Film Bulletin. Jan 1980, v47, p3.
Film Comment. Sep 1979, v15, p51-52.
Hollywood Reporter. Jul 27, 1979, p3.
The Los Angeles Times. Jul 27, 1979, SecIV, p1.
Motion Picture Herald Product Digest. Aug 15, 1979, p21.
The New York Times. Jul 27, 1979, SecIII, p9.
The New Yorker. Aug 13, 1979, v55, p97-98.
Newsweek. Aug 13, 1979, v94, p75.
Time. Sep 17, 1979, v114, p102.
Variety. Aug 1, 1979, p20.

The Amorous Adventures of Moll Flanders
(GB; Young, Terence; 1965)
America. Jun 19, 1965, v112, p887.
Christian Science Monitor (Western edition).
Jun 2, 1965, p12.
Film Daily. Jun 2, 1965, p6.
Films and Filming. Sep 1965, v11, p30.
Films in Review. Aug-Sep 1965, v16, p447.
Hollywood Reporter. May 26, 1965, p3.
Life. Jun 11, 1965, v58, p17.
The London Times. Jul 22, 1965, p15.
Motion Picture Herald Product Digest. Jun 9,
1965, p306.
The New Republic. Jun 5, 1965, v152, p26.
New Statesman. Jul 30, 1965, v70, p163.
The New York Times. May 27, 1965, p28.
The New Yorker. May 29, 1965, v41, p68.
Newsweek. May 31, 1965, v65, p85.
Playboy. Aug 1965, v12, p24.
Time. Jun 4, 1965, v85, p67.
Variety. May 26, 1965, p6.

Amour de Swann, Un *See* Swann in Love

Amour L'après-Midi, L' *See* Chloe in the
Afternoon

Anastasia (US; Litvak, Anatole; 1956)
America. Dec 29, 1956, v96, p378-79.
BFI/Monthly Film Bulletin. Jan 1957, v24, p14.
Commonweal. Jan 11, 1957, v65, p383.
Film Daily. Dec 14, 1956, p6.
Films and Filming. Mar 1957, v3, p25.
The Films in My Life. p123-24.
Films in Review. Jan 1957, v8, p28-30.
The Films of Ingrid Bergman. p147-51.
Hollywood Reporter. Dec 14, 1956, p3.
Magill's Survey of Cinema. Series II. v1, p71-
75.
The New Republic. Feb 4, 1957, v136, p22.
The New York Times. Dec 14, 1956, p35.
The New Yorker. Dec 22, 1956, v32, p65.
Newsweek. Dec 10, 1956, v48, p118.
Saturday Review. Dec 8, 1956, v39, p30.
Sight and Sound. Spr 1957, v26, p210-11.
Time. Dec 17, 1956, v68, p100.
Variety. Dec 19, 1956, p6.

Ana-ta-han (Also titled: The Saga of
Anatahan; Devil's Pitchfork) (JAPAN;
Sternberg, Josef von; 1953)
BFI/Monthly Film Bulletin. May 1954, v21,
p67-68.
BFI/Monthly Film Bulletin. May 1979, v46,
p107.
Commonweal. May 28, 1954, v60, p198.
Film Heritage. Wint 1965-66, v1, p13-17.
Film News. Nov-Dec 1975, v32, p25-26.
Films in Review. Feb 1954, v5, p93-95.
The Films of Josef von Sternberg. p53-54.
Hollywood Reporter. Sep 24, 1954, p6.
The London Times. Mar 15, 1954, p4.
Motion Picture Herald Product Digest. May 22,
1954, p2-3.
Movie Man (Thomson). p47-48.
The New Statesman and Nation. Mar 20, 1954,
v47, p356.
The New York Times. May 18, 1954, p38.
The New Yorker. May 29, 1954, v30, p53.
Newsweek. Mar 1, 1954, v43, p80.
Saint Cinema: Selected Writings, 1929-1970.
p112-15.
Saturday Review. May 22, 1954, v37, p29.
Sight and Sound. Apr-Jun 1953, v22, p152-53.
Sight and Sound. Jul-Sep 1954, v24, p34-35.
The Spectator. Mar 19, 1954, v192, p322.
Sternberg (Baxter). p119-29.
Variety. Jul 15, 1953, p6.
Variety. May 26, 1954, p6.

The Anatolian Smile *See* America, America

Anatomy of a Murder (US; Preminger,
Otto; 1959)
America. Jul 18, 1959, v101, p539.
Anatomy of a Motion Picture. 1959.
BFI/Monthly Film Bulletin. Oct 1959, v26,
p131.
The Cinema of Otto Preminger. p127-31.
Fifty from the Fifties. p9-16.
Film Daily. Jul 1, 1959, v114, p8,.
Filmfacts. Aug 19, 1959, v2, p163-65.
Films in Review. Aug-Sep 1959, v10, p415-16.
The Films of James Stewart. p127-31.
Hollywood Reporter. Jul 1, 1959, p3.
Life. Jul 27, 1959, v47, p66-68.
Look. Jun 23, 1959, v23, p48.
Magill's Survey of Cinema. Series II. v1, p75-
78.
The Nation. Jul 18, 1959, v189, p39-40.
The New Republic. Jul 13, 1959, v141, p22.
The New York Times. Jul 3, 1959, p10.
The New Yorker. Jul 11, 1959, v35, p55.
Newsweek. Jul 13, 1959, v54, p88.
Saturday Review. Jul 11, 1959, v42, p24-25.
Time. Jul 13, 1959, v70, p68.
Variety. Jul 1, 1959, p6.

And God Created Woman (French title: Et
Dieu...Créa la Femme; Also titled:
And Woman...Was Created) (FR;
Vadim, Roger; 1957)
BFI/Monthly Film Bulletin. May 1957, v24,
p54.
Film Daily. Oct 28, 1957, p6.
Films and Filming. May 1957, v3, p26.
The Films in My Life. p311-12.
Films in Review. Jan 1958, v9, p28.
The Films of the Fifties. p235-36.
The Great French Films. p258.
*Magill's Survey of Cinema. Foreign Language
Films.* v1, p105-09.
The New York Times. Oct 22, 1957, p41.
Time. Nov 11, 1957, v70, p120.
Variety. Jan 23, 1957, p6.

. . . And Justice for All (US; Jewison,
Norman; 1979)
BFI/Monthly Film Bulletin. Apr 1980, v47,
p63.
Films in Review. Dec 1979, v30, p630.
Hollywood Reporter. Sep 17, 1979, p2.
Motion Picture Herald Product Digest. Oct 31,
1979, p42.
The Nation. Oct 27, 1979, v229, p412.
New York. Oct 29, 1979, v12, p155-56.
The New York Times. Oct 19, 1979, SecIII, p18.
The New Yorker. Oct 22, 1979, v55, p179-81.
Newsweek. Oct 22, 1979, v94, p102.
Saturday Review. Dec 1979, v6, p48.
Time. Oct 22, 1979, v114, p84-85.
Variety. Sep 19, 1979, p18.

And Now Miguel (US; Clark, James B.;
1966)
BFI/Monthly Film Bulletin. Jan 1967, v34, p7.
Christian Science Monitor (Western edition).
Mar 17, 1966, p6.
Christian Science Monitor (Western edition).
Aug 6, 1966, p6.
Film Daily. May 12, 1966, p5.
Filmfacts. Nov 15, 1966, v9, p257-58.
Hollywood Reporter. May 10, 1966, p3.
Life. Jul 29, 1966, v61, p12.
Motion Picture Herald Product Digest. May 25,
1966, p527.
The New York Times. Sep 8, 1966, p43.
Newsweek. Jun 27, 1966, v67, p94.
Saturday Review. May 14, 1966, v49, p50.
Time. Jun 10, 1966, v87, p115.
Variety. May 18, 1966, p18.

And Now My Love (French title: Toute une
vie) (FR, IT; Lelouch, Claude; 1974)
BFI/Monthly Film Bulletin. Jun 1975, v42,
p145.
Hollywood Reporter. Mar 25, 1975, p19.
The Los Angeles Times. Mar 26, 1975, SecIV,
p1.
*Magill's Survey of Cinema. Foreign Language
Films.* v1, p110-15.
Motion Picture Herald Product Digest. Apr 9,
1975, p88.
The Nation. Apr 12, 1975, v220, p33.
The New Republic. May 17, 1975, v172, p33.
The New York Times. Mar 22, 1975, p36.
The New Yorker. Apr 7, 1975, v51, p126-28.
Variety. May 29, 1974, p16.

And There Came a Man (Italian title: E
Venne un Uomo; Also titled: A Man
Named John) (IT, FR; Olmi,
Ermanno; 1965)
BFI/Monthly Film Bulletin. Nov 1968, v35,
p169.
Commonweal. Apr 26, 1968, v88, p184-85.
Film Daily. Apr 9, 1968, p4.
Filmfacts. May 15, 1968, v11, p133-34.
Films and Filming. Dec 1968, v15, p49-50.
The London Times. Oct 3, 1968, p8.
Motion Picture Herald Product Digest. Apr 10,
1968, p794.
The New Republic. Apr 13, 1968, v158, p24.
The New York Times. Apr 5, 1968, p56.
Saturday Review. Apr 13, 1968, v51, p50.
The Spectator. Oct 11, 1968, v221, p519.
Variety. Sep 8, 1965, p6.

And Woman...Was Created *See* And God
Created Woman

The Anderson Tapes (US; Lumet, Sidney;
1971)
BFI/Monthly Film Bulletin. Dec 1973, v38,
p235.
Commonweal. Apr 6, 1971, v94, p408.
Deeper into Movies. p277.
Filmfacts. 1971, v14, p152-56.
Films and Filming. Mar 1972, v18, n6, p57-58.
Focus on Film. Sum 1971, n7, p7.
Hollywood Reporter. May 12, 1971, v217, n11,
p3.
The New York Times. Jun 18, 1971, p23.
Newsweek. Jul 12, 1971, v78.
Saturday Review. Jul 10, 1971, v54, p12.
*Sidney Lumet: A Guide to References and
Resources.* p90-92.
Time. Jul 19, 1971, v98, p69-70.
Variety. May 12, 1971, p19.
The Village Voice. Jul 22, 1971, v16, p55.

Andrei Rublev (Also titled: Andrei
Roublov) (USSR; Tarkovsky, Andrei;
1966)
Cinema Papers. Mar-Apr 1975, v2, p63.
Classic Movies. p115.
Films and Filming. Nov 1973, v20, p47-48.
Independent Film Journal. Feb 4, 1974, v73,
p12.
Living Images. p233.
*Magill's Survey of Cinema. Foreign Language
Films.* v1, p122-25.
The New Republic. Nov 3, 1973, v169, p20.
New Statesman. Aug 17, 1973, v86, p230-31.
The New Yorker. Dec 13, 1969, v45, p179-81.
Sight and Sound. n2, 1973, v42, p89-94.
Variety. Jun 4, 1969, p36.
The Village Voice. Nov 1, 1973, v18, p75.
Young Cinema and Theatre. 1973, n3, p26-34.

Androcles and the Lion (US; Erskine,
Chester; 1952)
BFI/Monthly Film Bulletin. Jul 1953, v20, p99.

Catholic World. Jan 1953, v176, p303.
Christian Century. Apr 1, 1953, v70, p399.
Commonweal. Jan 30, 1953, v57, p425.
Film Daily. Oct 29, 1952, p6.
Films in Review. Jan 1953, v4, p39.
Hollywood Reporter. Oct 29, 1952, p3.
Illustrated London News. Oct 24, 1953, v223, p665.
Library Journal. Dec 15, 1952, v77, p2170.
The London Times. Jan 16, 1953, p9.
Motion Picture Herald Product Digest. Nov 22, 1952, p1614.
National Parent-Teacher. Jan 1953, v47, p37.
The New Republic. Jun 15, 1953, v128, p22-23.
The New Statesman and Nation. Oct 24, 1953, v46, p487.
The New York Times. Jan 15, 1953, p23.
The New Yorker. Jan 31, 1953, v28, p54.
Newsweek. Jan 19, 1953, v41, p89-90.
Saturday Review. Dec 20, 1952, v35, p27.
Sight and Sound. Apr-Jun 1953, v22, p199.
The Spectator. Oct 16, 1953, v190, p422.
The Tatler. Oct 28, 1953, v210, p208.
Theatre Arts. Dec 1952, v36, p66-69.
Time. Jan 12, 1953, v61, p94.
Variety. Oct 29, 1952, p6.

The Andromeda Strain (US; Wise, Robert; 1971)
America. Apr 3, 1971, v124, p354.
American Cinematographer. May 1971, v52, n5, p436-53.
Atlantic. May 29, 1971, v27, p97-98.
BFI/Monthly Film Bulletin. Jul 1971, v38, p135.
Commonweal. Apr 30, 1971, v94, p190-91.
Deeper into Movies. p270.
Filmfacts. 1971, v14, n5, p102.
Films and Filming. Aug 1971, v17, n11, p49-50.
Films in Review. Apr 1971, v22, n4, p232-33.
Holiday. May 1971, v49, p10.
Hollywood Reporter. Mar 10, 1971, v215, n16, p3.
The New York Times. Mar 22, 1971, p40.
Newsweek. Mar 29, 1971, v77, p98.
Saturday Review. Aug 8, 1970, v53, p22-25.
Saturday Review. Apr 3, 1971, v54, p52.
Science Fiction Films of the Seventies. p28-34.
Variety. Mar 10, 1971, p16.
The Village Voice. 1971, p69.

Andy Warhol's Dracula (Also titled: Blood For Dracula) (US; Warhol, Andy; 1974)
Hollywood Reporter. Nov 5, 1974, p3.
The New York Times. Jul 14, 1974, SecII, p1.
Newsweek. Feb 24, 1975, v85, p84.
Variety. Feb 20, 1974, p16.

Andy Warhol's Frankenstein (US; Warhol, Andy; 1974)
The New York Times. May 16, 1974, p52.
The New York Times. Jun 30, 1974, SecII, p1.
The New York Times. Jul 7, 1974, SecII, p11.
Newsweek. May 20, 1974, v83, p105.
Rolling Stone. Jul 18, 1974, p70.

Ange Exterminateur, L' *See* The Exterminating Angel

Angel Exterminador, El *See* The Exterminating Angel

Angel Face (US; Preminger, Otto; 1952)
America. Apr 25, 1953, v89, p118.
BFI/Monthly Film Bulletin. Feb 1953, v20, p21-22.
The Cinema of Otto Preminger. p95-96.
Commonweal. May 1, 1953, v58, p99.
Film Daily. Dec 11, 1952, p6.
Hollywood Reporter. Dec 1, 1952, p3.

Library Journal. Jan 1, 1953, v78, p50.
McCall's. Apr 1953, v80, p8.
Motion Picture Herald Product Digest. Dec 6, 1952, p1629.
Movie. Sep 1962, n2, p14-16.
The Nation. Apr 11, 1953, v176, p314.
National Parent-Teacher. Feb 1953, v47, p37.
The New York Times. Apr 25, 1953, p11.
Newsweek. May 4, 1953, v41, p95.
A Reference Guide to the American Film Noir. p11-12.
Robert Mitchum on the Screen. p126-27.
Time. Feb 23, 1953, v61, p104.
Variety. Dec 3, 1952, p6.

The Angel Who Pawned Her Harp (GB; Bromly, Alan; 1954)
BFI/Monthly Film Bulletin. Oct 1954, v21, p146.
Films and Filming. Oct 1954, v1, p29.
The London Times. Sep 6, 1954, p5.
Motion Picture Herald Product Digest. Feb 4, 1956, p770.
National Parent-Teacher. May 1956, v50, p38.
The New Statesman and Nation. Sep 11, 1954, v48, p294.
The New York Times. Feb 29, 1956, p35.
Newsweek. Mar 5, 1956, v47, p91.
The Tatler. Sep 15, 1954, v213 p492.
Variety. Sep 15, 1954, p6.

Angelo My Love (US; Duvall, Robert; 1983)
Commonweal. Jun 3, 1983, v110, p339-41.
Hollywood Reporter. May 6, 1983, p19.
The Los Angeles Times. May 7, 1983, SecVI, p1.
Magill's Cinema Annual, 1984. p47-51.
The Nation. Jun 4, 1983, v236, p714.
The New Republic. May 30, 1983, v188, p25.
New York. Jun 4, 1983, v16, p20-21.
The New York Times. Apr 27, 1983, SecIII, p17.
Newsweek. May 9, 1983, v101, p87.
Time. May 30, 1983, v121, p76.
Variety. Apr 27, 1983, p30.

Angels in the Outfield (US; Brown, Clarence; 1951)
Catholic World. Oct 1951, v174, p65.
Christian Century. Oct 17, 1951, v68, p1207.
Commonweal. Oct 26, 1951, v55, p64.
Film Daily. Aug 27, 1951, p5.
Hollywood Reporter. Aug 27, 1951, p3.
Motion Picture Herald Product Digest. Sep 1, 1951, p997.
The New York Times. Oct 18, 1951, p32.
Newsweek. Sep 17, 1951, v38, p91.
Saturday Review. Sep 22, 1951, v34, p30.
Time. Oct 1, 1951, v58, p102.
Variety. Aug 29, 1951, p6.

Angels One Five (GB; O'Ferrall, George More; 1952)
BFI/Monthly Film Bulletin. May 1952, v19, p63.
Film Daily. Jun 14, 1954, p6.
The London Times. Mar 21, 1952, p2.
Motion Picture Herald Product Digest. May 8, 1954, p2285-86.
The New Statesman and Nation. Mar 29, 1952, v43, p373.
The New York Times. Apr 30, 1954, p28.
The Spectator. Mar 21, 1952, v188, p365-66.
The Tatler. Apr 2, 1952, v204, p30.
Variety. Apr 2, 1952, p22.

Angi Vera (HUNG; Gabor, Pal; 1980)
BFI/Monthly Film Bulletin. Jul 1980, v47, p123.
Film Quarterly. Fall 1980, v34, p45.

Films in Review. Mar 1980, v31, p183.
Hollywood Reporter. Nov 7, 1979, p3.
The Los Angeles Times. Jan 7, 1980, SecVI, p7.
Maclean's. Feb 4, 1980, v93, p50.
The Nation. Feb 9, 1980, v230, p154-55.
The New Republic. Jan 19, 1980, v183, p26.
The New York Times. Jan 9, 1980, SecIII, p24.
The New Yorker. Jan 14, 1980, v56, p79.
Newsday. Jan 11, 1980, SecII, p5.
Time. Mar 24, 1980, v115, p83.
The Village Voice. Jan 21, 1980, p53.

The Angry Silence (GB; Green, Guy; 1960)
America. Jan 21, 1961, v104, p549-50.
BFI/Monthly Film Bulletin. Apr 1960, v27, p47.
Commonweal. Dec 30, 1960, v70, p365.
Film Daily. Dec 13, 1960, p6.
Film Quarterly. Fall 1961, v15, p41-43.
Filmfacts. 1960, v3, p309.
Films and Filming. Apr 1960, v6, p23.
Films in Review. Jan 1961, v12, p36.
Hollywood Reporter. Dec 8, 1960, p3.
Hollywood UK. p97-101.
Magill's Survey of Cinema. Series II. v1, p89-91.
McCall's. Feb 1961, v80, p167.
Motion Picture Product Herald Digest. Dec 17, 1960, p956.
The Nation. Jan 7, 1961, v192, p19-20.
The New Republic. Dec 26, 1960, v143, 21-22.
The New York Times. Dec 13, 1960, p25.
The New Yorker. Dec 24, 1960, v34, p51.
Saturday Review. Dec 17, 1960, v43, p30.
Sight and Sound. Spr 1960, v29, p89.
Time. Jan 2, 1961, v70, p50.
Variety. Mar 23, 1960, p6.
A World on Film. p192-94.

Angst des Tormanns beim Elfmeter, Die
See The Anxiety of the Goalie at the Penalty Kick

Angst Essen Seele Auf *See* Ali

Animal House *See* National Lampoon's Animal House

Anna (IT; Lattuada, Alberto; 1952)
BFI/Monthly Film Bulletin. Nov 1952, v19, p153.
Commonweal. Mar 6, 1953, v57, p551.
Films in Review. Aug-Sep 1952, v3, p359.
Motion Picture Herald Product Digest. Aug 9, 1952, p1477-78.
The New York Times. Feb 19, 1953, p20.
Newsweek. Mar 2, 1953, v41, p90.
Theatre Arts. Mar 1953, v37, p86.
Time. Mar 2, 1953, v61, p90.
Variety. Mar 5, 1952, p22.

Anne of the Indies (US; Tourneur, Jacques; 1951)
BFI/Monthly Film Bulletin. Nov 1951, v18, p360.
Christian Century. Dec 26, 1951, v68, p1521.
Film Daily. Oct 18, 1951, p10.
Hollywood Reporter. Oct 15, 1951, p3.
Motion Picture Herald Product Digest. Oct 20, 1951, p1065.
The New York Times. Oct 25, 1951, p36.
Variety. Oct 17, 1951, p6.

Annee Derniere a Marienbad, L' *See* Last Year at Marienbad

Anni Difficili (Also titled: The Little Man; The Difficult Years) (IT; Zampa, Luigi; 1948)
BFI/Monthly Film Bulletin. Oct 1952, v19, p137.
Commonweal. Sep 15, 1950, v52, p559.
Library Journal. Oct 1, 1950, v75, p1677.

The London Times. Aug 15, 1952, p7.
The London Times. Aug 18, 1952, p8.
The New Republic. Sep 11, 1950, v123, p21.
The New Statesman and Nation. Aug 23, 1952, v44, p210.
The New York Times. Aug 22, 1950, p31.
The New Yorker. Sep 2, 1950, v26, p66.
Newsweek. Sep 4, 1950, v36, p70.
Saturday Review. Sep 16, 1950, v33, p32-33.
Sight and Sound. Oct-Dec 1952, v22, p80.
The Spectator. Aug 15, 1952, v189, p215.
The Tatler. Sep 3, 1952, v205, p418.
Theatre Arts. Oct 1950, v34, p8-9.
Time. Aug 28, 1950, v56, p72.
Variety. Aug 23, 1950, p20.

Annie (US; Huston, John; 1982)
BFI/Monthly Film Bulletin. Aug 1982, v44, p164-65.
Christian Century. Jun 9, 1982, v99, p708.
Christianity Today. Aug 6, 1982, v26, p61.
Commonweal. Jun 4, 1982, v109, p338-39.
Commonweal. Jun 18, 1982, v109, p371-72.
Dance Magazine. Jun 1982, v56, p56.
Film Comment. Jul-Aug 1982, v18, p47-48.
Fortune. Jun 28, 1982, v105, p31.
Hollywood Reporter. May 12, 1982, p3.
Horizon. Apr 1982, v25, p37.
The Los Angeles Times. May 21, 1982, SecVI, p1.
Maclean's. May 31, 1982, v95, p57.
Magill's Cinema Annual, 1983. p56-59.
The New Republic. Jun 9, 1982, v186, p22-23.
New York. May 31, 1982, v15, p79-80.
The New York Times. May 21, 1982, SecIII, p4.
The New York Times Magazine. May 2, 1982, p40-43.
The New Yorker. May 31, 1982, v58, p82-84.
Newsweek. May 24, 1982, v99, p82.
Saturday Review. Jun 1982, v9, p64-65.
Time. May 24, 1982, v119, p75.
Variety. May 12, 1982, p3.

Annie Get Your Gun (US; Sidney, George; 1950)
BFI/Monthly Film Bulletin. Jul 1950, v17, p98.
Christian Century. Jul 19, 1950, v67, p879.
Commonweal. Jun 2, 1950, v52, p198.
Film Daily. Apr 12, 1950, p4.
The Great Western Pictures. p9-11.
Hollywood Reporter. Apr 12, 1950, p3.
Journal of Popular Culture. n3, 1978-79, v12, p531-39.
Library Journal. May 1, 1950, v75, p786.
Life. Apr 17, 1950, v28, p174-75.
The London Times. Jul 3, 1950, p8.
Motion Picture Herald Product Digest. Apr 15, 1950, p261.
The Musical: From Broadway to Hollywood. p33-37.
The New Republic. May 29, 1950, v132, p22.
The New York Times. May 18, 1950, p37.
The New Yorker. May 20, 1950, v26, p99.
Newsweek. Jun 5, 1950, v35, p86.
The Spectator. Jun 30, 1950, v184, p886.
Time. Apr 24, 1950, v55, p66.
Variety. Apr 12, 1950, p6.
The Velvet Light Trap. 1973, n8, p11-13.
The World of Entertainment. p271-83.

Annie Hall (US; Allen, Woody; 1977)
America. May 7, 1977, v136, p431.
American Film. Jul-Aug 1977, v2, p8-9.
BFI/Monthly Film Bulletin. Oct 1977, v44, p207.
Christian Century. Jun 22, 1977, v94, p593-94.
Commonweal. May 13, 1977, v104, p306-07.
Fifty Grand Movies from the 1960s and 1970s. p3-8.
Films and Filming. Oct 1977, v24, p37.

Films in Review. Jun-Jul 1977, v28, p373.
The Films of the Seventies. p184-85.
Hollywood Reporter. Apr 6, 1977, p3.
The International Dictionary of Films and Filmmakers. v1, p32-33.
The Los Angeles Times. Apr 17, 1977, Calendar, p1.
Magill's Survey of Cinema. Series I. v1, p86-89.
Motion Picture Herald Product Digest. May 11, 1977, p93.
The Nation. Apr 30, 1977, v224, p540.
The New Republic. May 14, 1977, v176, p22.
New York. May 2, 1977, v10, p74-76.
The New York Times. Apr 21, 1977, SecIII, p22.
The New York Times. Apr 24, 1977, SecII, p19.
The New York Times. Sep 18, 1977, SecII, p17.
The New Yorker. Apr 25, 1977, v53, p136.
Newsweek. May 2, 1977, v89, p78.
Saturday Review. Sep 26, 1977, v4, p38-39.
Time. Apr 25, 1977, v109, p70.
Time. Sep 26, 1977, v110, p69-71.
Variety. Mar 30, 1977, p18.
The Village Voice. Apr 25, 1977, p45.
Vogue. Jun 1977, v167, p22.
Woody Allen: His Films and Career. p167-78.
Woody Allen (Palmer). p83-96.

Another Country (GB; Kanievska, Marek; 1984)
BFI/Monthly Film Bulletin. Jun 1984, v51, p173-74.
Commentary. Sep 1984, v78, p61-64.
Contemporary Review. Nov 1984, v245, p267-70.
Film Comment. Jul-Aug 1984, v20, p9-14.
Film Journal. Aug 1984, v87, p6, 20.
Films and Filming. Apr 1984, n355, p32.
Films in Review. Oct 1984, v35, p499.
Hudson Review. Wint 1984, v37, p585-87.
The Los Angeles Times. Jul 19, 1984, SecVI, p1.
Ms. Sep 1984, v13, p34.
The Nation. Jul 7, 1984, v239, p25-26.
The New Republic. Jul 9, 1984, v191, p24-25.
New Statesman. Jun 8, 1984, v107, p28-29.
New York. Jul 16, 1984, v17, p47-48.
The New York Times. Jun 29, 1984, SecIII, p8.
Newsweek. Jun 25, 1984, v103, p69.
Photoplay. Aug 1984, v35, p20.
Sight and Sound. Sum 1984, v53, p148-49.
Time. Jul 23, 1984, v124, p102.
Variety. May 23, 1984, p14.
The Village Voice. Jul 3, 1984, p59, 65.
Vogue. Aug 1984, v174, p66.

Another Man's Poison (GB; Rapper, Irving; 1951)
Bette Davis: Her Films and Career. p154-55.
BFI/Monthly Film Bulletin. Dec 1951, v18, p370.
Christian Century. Feb 20, 1952, v69, p231.
Film Daily. Jan 7, 1952, p 6.
Hollywood Reporter. Jan 2, 1952, p4.
Mother Goddam. p254-56.
Motion Picture Herald Product Digest. Jan 5, 1952, p1178.
The New Statesman and Nation. Dec 1, 1951, v42, p623.
The New York Times. Jan 7, 1952, p14.
Newsweek. Jan 21, 1952, v39, p91.
The Spectator. Nov 23, 1951, v187, p704.
Variety. Nov 28, 1951, p6.

Ansikte mot Ansikte *See* Face to Face

Ansiktet *See* The Magician

The Anxiety of the Goalie at the Penalty Kick (German title: Angst des Tormanns beim Elfmeter, Die; Also

titled: The Goalie's Anxiety at the Penalty Kick) (WGER; Wenders, Wim; 1972)
The Los Angeles Times. Nov 18, 1977, SecIV, p26.
Magill's Survey of Cinema. Foreign Language Films. v1, p140-45.
Modern European Filmmakers and the Art of Adaptation. p188-202.
The New York Times. Mar 11, 1972, p16.
Sight and Sound. Wint 1972-73, v42, p6-7.
Variety. Mar 29, 1972, p30.

Any Number Can Win (French title: Mélodie en Sous-Sol; Also titled: The Big Snatch) (FR; Verneuil, Henri; 1963)
Commonweal. Nov 8, 1963, v79, p195.
Film Daily. Oct 8, 1963, p3.
Film Facts. Nov 14, 1963, v6, p247-48.
Films and Filming. May 1976, v13, p29-30.
Films in Review. Dec 1963, v14, p627-28.
The New York Times. Oct 9, 1963, v47, p2.
The New Yorker. Oct 19, 1963, v39, p140.
Newsweek. Oct 7, 1963, v62, p110.
Photoplay. Dec 1963, v64, p12.
Variety. Apr 17, 1963, p7.

Any Wednesday (Also titled: Bachelor Girl Apartment) (US; Miller, Robert Ellis; 1966)
America. Nov 5, 1966, v115, p560.
BFI/Monthly Film Bulletin. Apr 1967, v34, p59.
Big Screen, Little Screen. p335.
Christian Science Monitor (Western edition). Nov 21, 1966, p12.
Commonweal. Oct 28, 1966, v85, p104.
Film Daily. Oct 17, 1966, p5.
Filmfacts. Dec 1, 1966, v9, p268-70.
Films and Filming. May 1967, v13, p29-30.
Films in Review. Nov 1966, v17, p588-89.
The Films of Jane Fonda. p122-26.
The Fondas (Springer). p268-69.
Hollywood Reporter. Oct 13, 1966, p3.
The London Times. Apr 6, 1967, p12.
Motion Picture Herald Product Digest. Oct 26, 1966, p622.
The New Republic. Oct 22, 1966, v155, p34.
The New York Times. Oct 14, 1966, p50.
The New Yorker. Oct 22, 1966, v42, p164.
Playboy. Jan 1967, v14, p22.
Variety. Oct 19, 1966, p6.
The Village Voice. Nov 10, 1966, v12, p27.

Any Which Way You Can (US; Van Horn, Buddy; 1980)
BFI/Monthly Film Bulletin. Feb 1981, v48, p23.
Clint Eastwood (Guérif). p139-46.
The Films of Clint Eastwood. p221-25.
Hollywood Reporter. Dec 15, 1980, p3.
Motion Picture Herald Product Digest. Dec 31, 1980, p57.
The New Leader. Jan 12, 1981, v64, p20.
The New York Times. Dec 17, 1980, SecIII, p26.
Time. Jan 12, 1981, v64, p20.
Variety. Dec 17, 1980, p16.
The Village Voice. Dec 17, 1980, p66.

Anything Can Happen (US; Seaton, George; 1952)
BFI/Monthly Film Bulletin. Sep 1953, v20, p130.
Catholic World. Apr 1952, v175, p63.
Christian Century. Jan 25, 1952, v69, p761.
Commonweal. Apr 25, 1952, v56, p69.
Film Daily. Feb 28, 1952, p10.
Hollywood Reporter. Feb 27, 1952, p4.

Library Journal. Apr 1, 1952, v77, p586.
Motion Picture Herald Product Digest. Mar 1, 1952, p1253.
The New York Times. Apr 4, 1952, p21.
The New Yorker. Apr 12, 1952, v28, p119.
Newsweek. Apr 14, 1952, v39, p95.
Senior Scholastic. Apr 23, 1952, v60, p23.
The Spectator. Jul 31, 1953, v191, p125.
Theatre Arts. May 1952, v36, p104.
Time. Apr 14, 1952, v59, p106.
Variety. Feb 27, 1952, p6.

Apache (US; Aldrich, Robert; 1954)
BFI/Monthly Film Bulletin. Sep 1954, v21, p126.
Burt Lancaster: A Pictorial Treasury of His Films. p78.
Burt Lancaster: The Man and His Movies. p62-63.
Commonweal. Jul 30, 1954, v60, p413.
Dictionary of Films. p13.
Farm Journal. Jul 1954, v78, p92.
Film Daily. Jul 7, 1954, p10.
The Films and Career of Robert Aldrich. p23-30.
Hollywood Reporter. Jun 30, 1954, p3.
The London Times. Aug 30, 1954, p5.
Magill's Cinema Annual, 1982. p395-98.
Motion Picture Herald Product Digest. Jul 3, 1954, p49.
National Parent-Teacher. Jun 1954, v48, p38.
The New Statesman and Nation. Sep 4, 1954, v48, p264.
The New York Times. Jul 10, 1954, p7.
Robert Aldrich: A Guide to References and Resources. p19-20.
Seeing is Believing (Biskind). p244-45.
Time. Aug 9, 1954, v64, p84.
Variety. Jun 30, 1954, p6.

The Apartment (US; Wilder, Billy; 1960)
America. Jun 25, 1960, v103, p403.
BFI/Monthly Film Bulletin. Aug 1960, v27, p107.
Billy Wilder (Dick). p91-94.
Billy Wilder (Madsen). p121-23.
The Bright Side of Billy Wilder, Primarily. p45-46, 185-89.
Commonweal. Jul 8, 1960, v70, p351.
Film Daily. May 19, 1960, p6.
Film Quarterly. Sum 1960, v13, p60.
Filmfacts. 1960, v3, p135.
Films and Filming. Sep 1960, v6, p21-22.
Films in Review. Aug-Sep 1960, v11, p428.
The Films of Jack Lemmon. p106-12.
The Films of Shirley MacLaine. 1980, p94-98.
Hollywood Reporter. May 18, 1960, p3.
Journey Down Sunset Boulevard. p147-71.
Magill's Survey of Cinema. Series I. v1, p90-93.
Motion Picture Product Herald Digest. May 21, 1960, p700.
The New Republic. Jun 27, 1960, v140, p20.
The New York Times. Jun 16, 1960, p37.
The New York Times. Jun 26, 1960, SecII, p1.
The New Yorker. Jun 25, 1960, v36, p70.
Newsweek. Jun 20, 1960, v55, p110.
Reruns. p111-15.
Saturday Review. Jun 11, 1960, v43, p24.
Sight and Sound. Aut 1960, v29, p195-96.
Time. Jun 6, 1960, v15, p47.
Variety. May 18, 1960, p6.
A World on Film. p149.

Ape regina, L' *See* The Conjugal Bed

Apocalypse Now (US; Coppola, Francis Ford; 1979)
America. Sep 1, 1979, v141, p96.
BFI/Monthly Film Bulletin. Dec 1979, v46, p247-49.
Commonweal. Sep 28, 1979, v106, p532.

Commonweal. Oct 12, 1979, v106, p560-61.
Double Exposure. p110-17.
The English Novel and the Movies. p211-17.
Fifty Grand Movies from the 1960s and 1970s. p181-84.
Film Comment. Sep 1979, v15, p27.
Films in Review. Oct 1979, v30, p495.
The Films of the Seventies. p257-60.
Francis Ford Coppola: A Guide to References and Resources. p638-44, 63-69.
Hollywood Reporter. Aug 13, 1979, p3.
The International Dictionary of Films and Filmmakers. v1, p34-36.
The Los Angeles Times. Aug 12, 1979, Calendar p1.
Magill's Survey of Cinema. Series I. v1, p94-97.
Motion Picture Herald Product Digest. Aug 29, 1979, p25.
The Nation. Aug 25, 1979, v229, p153-54.
The New Republic. Sep 15, 1979, v181, p74-75.
New York. May 28, 1979, v12, p101-02.
New York. Aug 27, 1979, v12, p87-89.
The New York Times. Aug 15, 1979, SecIII, p15.
The New York Times. Dec 9, 1979, SecII, p21.
The New Yorker. Sep 3, 1979, v55, p70-72.
Newsweek. May 21, 1979, v93, p97.
Newsweek. May 28, 1979, v93, p100-01.
Newsweek. Aug 20, 1979, v94, p56-57.
Newsweek. Jun 13, 1977, v89, p57-58.
Rolling Stone. Nov 1, 1979, p46-50, 51-57.
Saturday Review. Jan 5, 1980, v7, p44.
Time. Aug 27, 1979, v114, p55.
Variety. May 16, 1979, v21.
Variety. Aug 15, 1979, p30.
Variety. May 30, 1979, p17.

The Appaloosa (Also titled: Southwest to Sonora) (US; Furie, Sidney J.; 1966)
BFI/Monthly Film Bulletin. Dec 1966, v33, p182.
Christian Science Monitor (Western edition). Nov 25, 1966, p10.
Commonweal. Sep 3, 1966, v84, p638.
Film Daily. Sep 14, 1966, p6.
Film Quarterly. Wint 1966-67, v20, p60.
Filmfacts. Oct 1, 1966, v9, p202-04.
Films and Filming. Dec 1966, v13, p9, 12.
Films in Review. Oct 1966, v17, p523.
The Films of Marlon Brando. p172-79.
Hollywood Reporter. Sep 12, 1966, p3.
The London Times. Oct 27, 1966, p6.
Motion Picture Herald Product Digest. Sep 28, 1966, p604-05.
New Statesman. Oct 21, 1966, v72, p642.
The New York Times. Sep 15, 1966, p51.
The New Yorker. Sep 24, 1966, v42, p111.
Newsweek. Sep 26, 1966, v68, p113.
Playboy. Dec 1966, v13, p62.
Saturday Review. Sep 17, 1966, v49, p30.
Senior Scholastic. Oct 21, 1966, v89, p29.
Time. Sep 30, 1966, v88, p123.
Variety. Sep 14, 1966, p6.
Vogue. Nov 1, 1966, v148, p151.

The Apprenticeship of Duddy Kravitz (CAN; Kotcheff, Ted; 1974)
Audience. Aug 1974, v7, p11-13.
BFI/Monthly Film Bulletin. Dec 1974, v41, p267-68.
Cinema Canada. Jun-Jul 1974, v14, p72.
Commonweal. Sep 20, 1974, v100, p503-04.
Esquire. Sep 1974, v82, p42.
Films in Review. Oct 1974, v25, p502.
Hollywood Reporter. Jul 29, 1974, p3.
Independent Film Journal. Jul 10, 1974, v74, p13.
The Los Angeles Times. Aug 7, 1974, SecIV, p1.

Magill's Survey of Cinema. Series I. v1, p98-100.
Motion. May-Jun 1974, p27.
Motion. Jul-Aug 1974, p52.
Motion Picture Herald Product Digest. Jun 19, 1974, p5.
Movietone News. May-Jun 1974, n32, p32-33.
The Nation. Aug 17, 1974, v219, p123-24.
New Canadian Film. 1974, v6, p21.
The New Republic. Aug 24, 1974, v171, p22.
New York. Jul 29, 1974, v7, p54-55.
The New York Times. Jul 3, 1974, p18.
The New York Times. Oct 27, 1974, SecII, p17.
The New York Times. Sep 8, 1974, SecII, p13-14.
The New York Times. May 30, 1974, SecII, p32.
The New Yorker. Jul 22, 1974, v50, p65-67.
Newsweek. Jul 29, 1974, v84, p68.
Take One. Jan-Feb 1973, v4, p32-33.
Time. Sep 2, 1974, v104, p5-6.
Variety. Apr 10, 1974, p17.
Variety. Apr 10, 1974, p17.
The Village Voice. Aug 1, 1974, p20.

The April Fools (US; Rosenberg, Stuart; 1969)
Commonweal. Jun 27, 1969, v90, p417.
Film Daily. May 27, 1969, p8.
Filmfacts. 1969, v12, p296.
Films and Filming. May 1970, v16, p40-41.
Films in Review. Aug-Sep 1969, v20, p448.
The Films of Jack Lemmon. p180-85.
The Films of Myrna Loy. p248-50.
Hollywood Reporter. May 29, 1969, p3.
The New York Times. May 29, 1969, p43.
The New Yorker. Jun 14, 1969, v45, p83.
Newsweek. Jun 9, 1969, v73, p111.
Saturday Review. Jun 14, 1969, v52, p26.
Time. Jun 6, 1969, v93, p108.
Variety. May 28, 1969, p6.

April in Paris (US; Butler, David; 1952)
BFI/Monthly Film Bulletin. Apr 1953, v20, p52.
Catholic World. Jan 1953, v176, p301.
Christian Century. Jan 28, 1953, v70, p119.
Commonweal. Jan 2, 1953, v57, p334.
Film Daily. Nov 21, 1952, p4.
The Films of Doris Day. p125-28.
Hollywood Reporter. Nov 13, 1952, p3.
The London Times. Mar 3, 1953, p2.
Motion Picture Herald Product Digest. Nov 15, 1952, p1605.
National Parent-Teacher. Feb 1953, v47, p37.
The New York Times. Dec 25, 1952, p34.
Newsweek. Jan 5, 1953, v41, p61.
The Spectator. Feb 27, 1952, v190, p244.
Variety. Nov 19, 1952, p6.

April Love (US; Levin, Henry; 1957)
America. Nov 30, 1957, v98, p300.
BFI/Monthly Film Bulletin. Feb 1958, p18.
Film Daily. Nov 15, 1957, v112, p6.
Hollywood Reporter. Nov 15, 1957, p3.
Magill's Survey of Cinema. Series II. v1, p104-06.
Motion Picture Herald Product Digest. Nov 23, 1957, p617.
The New York Times. Nov 28, 1957, p57.
Newsweek. Dec 2, 1957, v50, p97.
Variety. Nov 20, 1957, p6.

Apur Sanshar *See* The World of Apu

Arabesque (GB; Donen, Stanley; 1966)
America. May 21, 1966, v114, p754-55.
BFI/Monthly Film Bulletin. Aug 1966, v33, p118-19.
Christian Century. Jun 22, 1966, v83, p810.

Christian Science Monitor (Western edition).
Jun 17, 1966, p6.
Commonweal. May 20, 1966, v84, p257.
Film Daily. May 4, 1966, p5.
Film Quarterly. Fall 1966, v20, p57-58.
Filmfacts. Jul 1, 1966, v9, p109-10.
Films and Filming. Sep 1966, v12, p12.
Films in Review. May 1966, v17, p315-16.
The Films of Gregory Peck. p197-99.
The Films of Sophia Loren. p183-86.
The Great Spy Pictures. p59-60.
Hollywood Reporter. May 4, 1966, p3.
Life. May 13, 1966, v60, p12.
The London Times. Jul 28, 1966, p7.
Motion Picture Herald Product Digest. May 11,
1966, p517.
New Statesman. Jul 29, 1966, v72, p176-77.
The New York Times. May 6, 1966, p54.
The New Yorker. May 14, 1966, v42, p120.
Newsweek. May 16, 1966, v67, p106.
Playboy. Jul 1966, v13, p26.
Saturday Review. May 21, 1966, v49, p48.
Senior Scholastic. May 13, 1966, v88, p27-28.
The Spectator. Aug 26, 1966, v217, p261.
Stanley Donen (Casper). p174-79.
Variety. May 4, 1966, p6.
The Village Voice. Oct 13, 1966, v11, p27.

Are We All Murderers? *See* We Are All
Murderers

Argent de Poche *See* Small Change

Argent, L' (US; Bresson, Robert; 1983)
America. Mar 3, 1984, v150, p150-51.
American Film. Oct 1983, v9, p70.
Commonweal. Jun 1, 1984, v111, p337-38.
Film Quarterly. Sum 1984, v37, p18.
Films and Filming. Aug 1983, n347, p27-28.
Hollywood Reporter. Sep 26, 1983, p16.
The Los Angeles Times. May 2, 1984, SecVI,
p1.
Magill's Cinema Annual, 1985. p74-79.
The New Republic. Apr 16, 1984, v190, p24-25.
New York. Apr 23, 1984, v17, p102.
The New York Times. Sep 24, 1984, p11.
The New York Times. Mar 23, 1984, SecIII,
p10.
Newsweek. Apr 16, 1984, v103, p93.
Sight and Sound. Oct 1983, v52, p273.
Time. Apr 16, 1984, v123, p81.
Variety. Mar 28, 1984, p26.
The Village Voice. Apr 10, 1984, p41.

Around the World in Eighty Days (Also
titled: Around the World in 80 Days)
(US; Anderson, Michael; 1956)
America. Nov 3, 1956, v96, p140.
BFI/Monthly Film Bulletin. Jul 1957, v24, p94-
95.
Classic Film Collector. Sep 1979, v65, p20-21.
Commonweal. Nov 9, 1956, v65, p151-52.
Film Daily. Oct 18, 1956, p6.
Film News. Nov-Dec 1979, v36, p38.
Films and Filming. Aug 1957, v3, p23-24.
Films in Review. Nov 1956, v7, p457-59.
The Films of David Niven. p127-33.
The Films of Frank Sinatra. p120-22.
The Films of Marlene Dietrich. p196-98.
The Films of Ronald Colman. p245-48.
The Films of Shirley MacLaine. p53-58.
The Films of the Fifties. p187-88.
The Great Adventure Films. p196-203.
Hollywood Reporter. Oct 18, 1956, p3.
Magill's Survey of Cinema. Series I. v1, p101-
05.
The Nation. Nov 10, 1956, v183, p417.
The Nation. Dec 1, 1956, v183, p470.
The New York Times. Oct 18, 1956, p37.
The New York Times. Oct 28, 1956, Sec 2, p1.
The New York Times. Jan 20, 1984, SecIII, p1.

The New Yorker. Oct 27, 1956, v32, p158.
Newsweek. Oct 29, 1956, v48, p98.
Newsweek. Nov 5, 1956, v48, p114-15.
Saturday Review. Nov 3, 1956, v39, p28.
Time. Oct 29, 1956, v68, p72.
Variety. Oct 24, 1956, p6.
Vintage Films. p155-63.

Around the World Under the Sea (US;
Marton, Andrew; 1966)
BFI/Monthly Film Bulletin. Jul 1966, v33,
p107.
Film Daily. Apr 6, 1966, p6.
Filmfacts. Oct 1, 1966, v9, p210-11.
Films and Filming. Aug 1966, v12, p12.
Hollywood Reporter. Apr 6, 1966, p3.
Kiss Kiss Bang Bang. p222-23.
The London Times. Jun 9, 1966, p8.
Motion Picture Herald Product Digest. Apr 13,
1966, p500.
The New York Times. Jul 21, 1966, p20.
Variety. Apr 6, 1966, p24.

The Arrangement (US; Kazan, Elia; 1969)
An American Odyssey. p242-44.
Deeper Into Movies. p60-66.
*Elia Kazan: A Guide to References and
Resources.* p84-87.
Film Daily. Nov 18, 1969, p3.
Film Quarterly. Sum 1970, v23, p52-54.
Films and Filming. Apr 1970, v16, p38-39.
Films in Review. Dec 1969, v20, p639.
The Films of Kirk Douglas. p233-36.
Hollywood Reporter. Nov 19, 1969, p3.
Kazan on Kazan. p155-62.
Movie. Wint 1970-71, n18, p14-17.
Movies Into Film. p324-26.
The New York Times. Nov 19, 1969, p48.
The New York Times. Nov 30, 1969, SecII, p13.
The New Yorker. Nov 22, 1969, v45, p211-12.
Newsweek. Nov 24, 1969, v74, p118.
Saturday Review. Nov 22, 1969, v52, p68.
Time. Nov 21, 1969, v94, p92.
Variety. Nov 19, 1969, p22.
Vogue. Jan 1, 1960, v155, p74.

Arriverderci, Baby (Also titled: Drop Dead,
Darling) (GB; Hughes, Ken; 1966)
BFI/Monthly Film Bulletin. Mar 1967, v34,
p45.
Christian Science Monitor (Western edition).
Jan 30, 1967, p4.
Film Daily. Jan 3, 1967, p6.
Filmfacts. Jan 15, 1967, v9, p377-79.
Films and Filming. Apr 1967, v13, p10.
Hollywood Reporter. Dec 20, 1966, p3.
Motion Picture Herald Product Digest. Jan 4,
1967, p646.
The New York Times. Dec 29, 1966, p22.
Newsweek. Jan 16, 1967, v69, p88.
Playboy. Jan 1967, v14, p22.
Time. Jan 20, 1967, v89, p83.
Tony Curtis: The Man and His Movies. p110-
13.
Variety. Dec 21, 1966, p7.

The Art of Love (US; Jewison, Norman;
1965)
BFI/Monthly Film Bulletin. Jul 1965, v32,
p107-08.
Christian Science Monitor (Western edition).
Jul 15, 1965, p4.
Film Daily. May 6, 1965, p6.
Films and Filming. Aug 1965, v11, p32.
Hollywood Reporter. May 5, 1965, p3.
The London Times. May 27, 1965, p16.
Motion Picture Herald Product Digest. May 12,
1965, p282.
The New York Times. Jul 1, 1965, p34.
Time. Jul 16, 1965, v86, p94.
Variety. May 12, 1965, p6.

Arthur (US; Gordon, Steve; 1981)
BFI/Monthly Film Bulletin. Nov 1981, v48,
p215-16.
Films In Review. v32, p491.
Hollywood Reporter. Jul 13, 1981, p3.
The Los Angeles Times. Jul 17, 1981, SecVI,
p1.
Magill's Cinema Annual, 1982. p71-73.
National Review. Oct 2, 1981, v33, p1151-52.
New Statesman. Dec 18, 1981, v102, p50-51.
New York. Jul 27, 1981, v14, p50-51.
New York. Aug 24, 1981, v14, p27-29.
The New York Times. Jul 17, 1981, SecIII, p10.
The New Yorker. Jul 27, 1981, v57, p78-79.
Newsweek. Jul 27, 1981, v98, p75.
Theater Crafts. Jun-Jul 1981, v15, p60-62.
Time. Aug 3, 1981, v118, p67.
Variety. Jul 15, 1981, p24.

Artists and Models (US; Tashlin, Frank;
1955)
Film Daily. Nov 11, 1955, p5.
The Films of Shirley MacLaine. p49-52.
The Films of the Fifties. p141-42.
Hollywood Reporter. Nov 9, 1955, p3.
Motion Picture Herald Product Digest. Nov 12,
1955, p665.
The New York Times. Dec 22, 1955, p20.
Time. Jan 9, 1956, v67, p86.
Variety. Nov 9, 1955, p6.

As for All These Women *See* Now About
These Women

As Young As You Feel (US; Jones,
Harmon; 1951)
BFI/Monthly Film Bulletin. Aug 1951, v18,
p310.
Christian Century. Jul 11, 1951, v68, p831.
Film Daily. Jun 13, 1951, p6.
The Films of Marilyn Monroe. p57-59.
Hollywood Reporter. Jun 5, 1951, p3.
Library Journal. Jun 1, 1951, v76, p972.
The London Times. Jul 23, 1951, p2.
Motion Picture Herald Product Digest. Jun 9,
1951, p878.
The New Statesman and Nation. Jul 28, 1951,
v42, p97-98.
The New York Times. Aug 3, 1951, p10.
Newsweek. Jul 23, 1951, v38, p84.
Variety. Jun 6, 1951, p6.

Ashani Sanket *See* Distant Thunder

Ashes and Diamonds (Polish title: Popiol y
Diament) (POL; Wajda, Andrzej;
1958)
BFI/Monthly Film Bulletin. Aug 1959, v26,
p103.
Boxoffice. Sep 4, 1961, p10.
The Cinema of Andrzej Wajda. p37-46.
Commonweal. Oct 9, 1959, v71, p45-46.
Hollywood Reporter. Jan 12, 1962, p3.
*The International Dictionary of Films and
Filmmakers.* v1, p368-70.
*Magill's Survey of Cinema. Foreign Language
Films.* v1, p156-60.
Motion Picture Herald Product Digest. Jul 22,
1961, p213.
The New York Times. May 30, 1961, p8.
Newsweek. Jun 12, 1961, p8, v57, p94-95.
Saturday Review. Jun 10, 1961, v44, p37.
Time. May 19, 1961, v77, p88.
Variety. Sep 16, 1959, p16.

Ask Any Girl (US; Walters, Charles; 1959)
America. Jun 6, 1959, v101, p418.
BFI/Monthly Film Bulletin. Oct 1959, v26,
p131.
Commonweal. Jun 5, 1959, v70, p258.
Film Daily. May 13, 1959, v115, p6.
Filmfacts. Jul 1, 1959, v2, p119-20.

Films in Review. Jun-Jul 1959, v10, p355.
The Films of David Niven. p154-57.
The Films of Shirley MacLaine. p77-81.
Hollywood Reporter. May 13, 1959, p3.
Library Journal. Jun 1, 1959, v84, p1801.
The New York Times. May 22, 1959, p32.
The New Yorker. May 30, 1959, v35, p90.
Newsweek. Jun 1, 1959, v53, p95.
Saturday Review. May 23, 1959, v42, p24.
Time. Jun 1, 1959, v73, p60.
Variety. May 13, 1959, p6.

The Asphalt Jungle (US; Huston, John; 1950)
American Cinematographer. Aug 1950, v31, p271.
BFI/Monthly Film Bulletin. Sep 1950, v17, p134.
Christian Century. Jul 5, 1950, v67, p831.
The Cinema of John Huston. p72-87.
Cinema, the Magic Vehicle. v2, p53.
Classics of the Gangster Film. p188-94.
Commonweal. Jun 16, 1950, v52, p249.
Dictionary of Films. p15.
Fifty From the Fifties. p17-26.
Film Comment. May-Jun 1980, v16, p25-26.
Film Criticism and Caricatures, 1943-1953. p114-15.
Film Culture. 1959, n19, p66-01.
Film Daily. May 5, 1950, p8.
Films and Filming. Oct 1959, v6, p9-10.
Films in Review. Jul-Aug 1950, v1, p15-17.
The Films of Marilyn Monroe. p38-41.
The Films of the Fifties. p39-42.
Fortnight. Jun 23, 1950, v8, p32.
The Great Gangster Pictures. p27-28.
Hollywood Reporter. May 5, 1950, p3, 8.
John Huston (Hammen). p52-53.
John Huston: Maker of Magic. p69-73.
Library Journal. Jul 1950, v75, p1201.
Magill's Survey of Cinema. Series II. v1, p124-26.
Motion Picture Herald Product Digest. May 6, 1950, p285.
The Nation. Jul 15, 1950, v171, p65.
The Nation. Oct 28, 1950, v171, p397.
The New Republic. Jun 26, 1950, v122, p23.
The New Statesman and Nation. Oct 28, 1950, v40, p395.
The New York Times. Jun 9, 1950, p29.
The New Yorker. Jun 17, 1950, v26, p59.
Newsweek. Jun 12, 1950, v35, p88.
Reruns. p72-76.
Saturday Review. Jun 24, 1950, v33, p34.
Selected Film Criticism, 1941-1950. p8-10.
Shots in the Dark. p225-28.
Sight and Sound. Nov 1950, v19, p286-88.
Time. Jun 19, 1950, v55, p92.
Variety. May 10, 1950, p6.

The Assassin *See* Venetian Bird

Assault Force *See* ffolkes

Assault on a Queen (US; Donohue, Jack; 1966)
BFI/Monthly Film Bulletin. Oct 1966, v33, p153-54.
Christian Science Monitor (Western edition). Aug 13, 1966, p4.
Film Daily. Jun 17, 1966, p4.
Filmfacts. Sep 15, 1966, v9, p193-94.
The Films of Frank Sinatra. p219-22.
Hollywood Reporter. Jun 17, 1966, p3.
The London Times. Sep 8, 1966, p17.
Motion Picture Herald Product Digest. Jun 22, 1966, p545-46.
The New York Times. Jul 28, 1966, p23.
Playboy. Oct 1966, v13, p26-27.
Time. Aug 12, 1966, v88, p59.
Variety. Jun 22, 1966, p6.

Assignment—Paris (US; Parrish, Robert; 1952)
BFI/Monthly Film Bulletin. Jan 1953, v20, p3.
Catholic World. Oct 1952, v176, p63.
Film Daily. Sep 4, 1952, p6.
Hollywood Reporter. Sep 3, 1952, p3.
Library Journal. Oct 15, 1952, v77, p1801.
Motion Picture Herald Product Digest. Sep 13, 1952, p1525.
The New York Times. Oct 25, 1952, p12.
Newsweek. Oct 27, 1952, v40, p114.
Theatre Arts. Oct 1952, v36, p73.
Time. Nov 10, 1952, v60, p124.
Variety. Sep 10, 1952, p6.

The Astonished Heart (GB; Fisher, Terence; Darnborough, Anthony; 1949)
BFI/Monthly Film Bulletin. Feb-Mar 1950, v17, p23.
Christian Century. Jul 19, 1950, v67, p879.
Commonweal. Feb 24, 1950, v51, p537.
Hollywood Reporter. Feb 15, 1950, p3.
Library Journal. Mar 15, 1950, v75, p503.
Motion Picture Herald Product Digest. Feb 18, 1950, p197.
The New Republic. Feb 27, 1950, v122, p22.
The New Statesman and Nation. Mar 11, 1950, v39, p272.
The New York Times. Feb 15, 1950, p23.
The New Yorker. Feb 18, 1950, v25, p83-84.
Newsweek. Feb 27, 1950, v35, p80.
The Spectator. Mar 3, 1950, v184, p273.
Time. Feb 27, 1950, v55, p100.
Variety. Feb 15, 1950, p13.

At Long Last Love (US; Bogdanovich, Peter; 1975)
BFI/Monthly Film Bulletin. Apr 1975, v42, p75.
Esquire. Jan 1975, v83, p64.
The Fifty Worst Films of All Time. p37-42.
Films in Review. Apr 1975, v26, p245.
The Films of Burt Reynolds. p175-78.
Hollywood Reporter. Mar 5, 1975, p3.
Motion Picture Herald Product Digest. Mar 26, 1975, p82.
The New Republic. Apr 5, 1975, v172, p20.
The New York Times. Mar 7, 1975, p22.
The New York Times. Mar 16, 1975, SecII, p17.
The New Yorker. Mar 24, 1975, v51, p93-94.
Newsweek. Mar 24, 1975, v85, p54-59.
Reeling. p613-17.
Saturday Review. Apr 19, 1975, v2, p46.
Time. Mar 31, 1975, v105, p6.
Variety. Mar 5, 1975, p20.

At War With the Army (US; Walker, Hal; 1950)
BFI/Monthly Film Bulletin. Apr 1951, v18, p248-49.
Christian Century. Feb 14, 1951, v68, p222.
Commonweal. Mar 9, 1951, v53, p544.
Film Daily. Dec 13, 1950, p14.
Hollywood Reporter. Dec 12, 1950, p4.
The London Times. Mar 19, 1951, p2.
Motion Picture Herald Product Digest. Dec 16, 1950, p614.
The New York Times. Jan 25, 1951, p21.
Newsweek. Feb 5, 1951, v37 p80.
Time. Jan 29, 1951, v57, p104.
Variety. Dec 13, 1950, p8.

Athena (US; Thorpe, Richard; 1954)
America. Dec 25, 1954, v92, p346.
BFI/Monthly Film Bulletin. Jan 1955, v22, p7.
Catholic World. Jan 1955, v180, p303.
Commonweal. Nov 26, 1954, v61, p224.
Film Daily. Nov 4, 1954, p6.
Films and Filming. Feb 1955, v1, p18.

Hollywood Reporter. Oct 29, 1954, p3.
Motion Picture Herald Product Digest. Nov 6, 1954, p201.
National Parent-Teacher. Jan 1955, v49, p38.
The New York Times. Dec 22, 1954, p28.
Newsweek. Nov 22, 1954, v44, p108.
Saturday Review. Nov 27, 1954, v37, p28.
Time. Nov 22, 1954, v64, p102.
Variety. Nov 3, 1954, p6.

Atlantic City (CAN, FR; Malle, Louis; 1980)
America. May 9, 1981, v144, p387.
BFI/Monthly Film Bulletin. Jan 1981, v48, p3-4.
Burt Lancaster: The Man and His Movies. p150-53.
Christian Century. Jul 15, 1981, v98, p723-24.
Commonweal. Jun 19, 1981, v108, p374.
Films in Review. Jun-Jul 1981, v32, p376-77.
Humanist. Jul-Aug 1981, v41, p57-58.
Humanities. Jul-Aug 1981, v41, p57-58.
The Los Angeles Times. Apr 5, 1981, Calendar, p29.
Maclean's. Apr 27, 1981, v94, p50-51.
The Nation. Apr 25, 1981, v232, p508-09.
National Review. Jul 24, 1981, v33, p853-54.
The New Leader. Apr 20, 1981, v64, p21.
The New Republic. Apr 18, 1981, v184, p29.
New Statesman. Jan 23, 1981, v101, p25.
New York. Apr 6, 1981, v14, p56.
New York. Jun 1, 1981, v14, p48-49.
The New York Times. Apr 3, 1981, SecIII, p15.
The New Yorker. Apr 6, 1981, v57, p154.
Newsweek. Apr 6, 1981, v97, p103.
Rolling Stone. Apr 30, 1981, p38-39.
Time. Apr 6, 1981, v117, p68.

The Atomic Cafe (US; Rafferty, Kevin; Loader, Jayne; Rafferty, Pierce; 1982)
American Film. May 1982, v7, p9.
BFI/Monthly Film Bulletin. Dec 1982, v49, p289.
Commonweal. Jul 16, 1982, v109, p405-06.
Hollywood Reporter. Mar 26, 1982, p45.
New York. May 3, 1982, v15, p75-76.
The New York Times. Mar 17, 1982, SecIV, p16.
Newsweek. Jan 28, 1982, v99, p73.
Progressive. Aug 1982, v46, p52.
Rolling Stone. Jun 10, 1982, p54.
Variety. Mar 17, 1982, p26.
The Village Voice. Mar 23, 1982, p50.

The Atomic City (US; Hopper, Jerry; 1952)
BFI/Monthly Film Bulletin. Jun 1952, v19, p78.
Christian Century. Jul 23, 1952, v69, p863.
Film Daily. Apr 11, 1952, p11.
Films in Review. Jun-Jul 1952, v3, p292.
Hollywood Reporter. Apr 8, 1952, p3.
Motion Picture Herald Product Digest. Apr 12, 1952, p1314.
The New York Times. May 2, 1952, p21.
The New Yorker. May 10, 1952, v28, p86.
Newsweek. May 12, 1952, v39, p104.
Theatre Arts. Jul 1952, v36, p88.
Time. May 12, 1952, v59, p103.
Variety. Apr 9, 1952, p6.

The Atomic Kid (US; Martinson, Leslie H.; 1954)
BFI/Monthly Film Bulletin. Apr 1955, v22, p56.
Film Daily. Dec 7, 1954, p12.
Hollywood Reporter. Dec 8, 1954, p3.
Motion Picture Herald Product Digest. Dec 18, 1954, p250-51.
National Parent-Teacher. Feb 1955, v49, p38.
The New York Times. Dec 4, 1954, p14.
Variety. Dec 8, 1954, p6.

Att Alska *See* To Love

Attack! (US; Aldrich, Robert; 1954)
America. Sep 29, 1956, v95, p632.
BFI/Monthly Film Bulletin. Nov 1956, v23, p136.
Commonweal. Oct 5, 1956, v65, p16.
Film Daily. Sep 6, 1956, p6.
The Films and Career of Robert Aldrich. p60-75.
Films and Filming. Dec 1956, v3, p24.
Hollywood Reporter. Sep 5, 1956, p3.
Journal of Popular Film. 1973, v2, p262-76.
Magill's Survey of Cinema. Series II. v1, p130-35.
The Nation. Oct 6, 1956, v183, p294.
The New York Times. Sep 20, 1956, p29.
The New Yorker. Sep 29, 1956, v32, p88.
Newsweek. Sep 17, 1956, v48, p116.
Robert Aldrich: A Guide to References and Resources. p26-28.
Saturday Review. Sep 1, 1956, v39, p25-26.
Time. Sep 10, 1956, v68, p116.
Variety. Sep 12, 1956, p6.
The Velvet Light Trap. Wint 1974, n11, p46-49.

Au Hasard, Balthazar (Also titled: Balthazar) (FR, SWED; Bresson, Robert; 1966)
Babel. p128-32.
BFI/Monthly Film Bulletin. Jan 1967, v34, p2.
Cahiers du Cinema in English. Sep 1967, n11, p54-56.
Cahiers du Cinema in English. Feb 1967, n8, p6-27.
Film Quarterly. Wint 1971-72, v25, p30-32.
Film Quarterly. Spr 1967, v20, p24-28.
Film Quarterly. Fall 1977, v31, p19-31.
Films and Filming. Dec 1966, v13, p18, 51-52.
The Films of Robert Bresson. p106-14.
The Great French Films. p265.
The Great Movies. p191-92.
International Film Guide. 1967, v4, p70.
The London Times. Oct 13, 1966, p18.
The London Times. Sep 7, 1966, p16.
Magill's Survey of Cinema. Foreign Language Films. v1, p174-77.
Movie Journal (Mekas). p374.
New Society. Oct 20, 1966, p619-20.
New Statesman. Oct 21, 1966, v72, p598-99.
The New York Times. Feb 20, 1970, p31.
Newsweek. Mar 16, 1970, v65, p101-02.
The Primal Screen. p157-60.
Quarterly Review of Film Studies. Spr 1985, v10, p122-23.
Renaissance of the Film. p32-40.
Robert Bresson: A Guide to References and Resources. p25, 66-71.
Sight and Sound. Wint 1966-67, v36, p7-9.
Sight and Sound. Sum 1966, v35, p112-16.
The Spectator. Oct 21, 1966, v217, p519.
Take One. Jun 1967, v1, p33.
Variety. May 11, 1966, p28.
The Velvet Light Trap. Sum 1973, n9, p19-22.
The Village Voice. Feb 19, 1970, v15, p55, 60.

Auberge Rouge, L' *See* The Red Inn

Au-Dela des Grilles (Also titled: The Walls of Malapaga; Mura di Malapaga, La; Beyond the Gates) (FR; Clément, René; 1949)
BFI/Monthly Film Bulletin. Mar-Apr 1950, v17, p42-43.
Cinema, the Magic Vehicle. v1, p486.
Commonweal. Apr 7, 1950, v51, p677.
Film Daily. Apr 4, 1950, p6.
Films in Review. May-Jun 1950, v1, p26-28.
The Great French Films. p251.
Hollywood Reporter. Oct 19, 1950, p3.

Magill's Survey of Cinema. Foreign Language Films. v7, p3321-24.
The New Republic. Apr 3, 1950, v122, p22.
The New Statesman and Nation. Mar 25, 1950, v39, p339.
The New York Times. Mar 21, 1950, p34.
The New Yorker. Apr 1, 1950, v26, p90.
Newsweek. Apr 10, 1950, v35, p82.
The Spectator. Mar 10, 1950, v184, p305-06.
Variety. Mar 29, 1950, p11.

Auntie Mame (US; Da Costa, Morton; 1958)
America. Dec 20, 1958, v100, p381.
BFI/Monthly Film Bulletin. 1959, v26, p14.
Commonweal. Dec 26, 1958, v340, p340.
Film Daily. Nov 26, 1958, p7.
Filmfacts. Jan 7, 1959, v1, p241-42.
Films in Review. Jan 1959, v10, p42-43.
Hollywood Reporter. Nov 26, 1958, p3.
Library Journal. Jan 1, 1959, v84, p70.
Magill's Survey of Cinema. Series II. v1, p134-36.
The New Republic. Jan 19, 1959, v140, p20-21.
The New York Times. Dec 5, 1958, p39.
Newsweek. Dec 15, 1958, v52, p112.
Saturday Review. Dec 27, 1958, v41, p21.
Variety. Nov 26, 1958, p6.

Aus dem Leben der Marionetten *See* From the Life of the Marionettes

Author! Author! (US; Hiller, Arthur; 1982)
BFI/Monthly Film Bulletin. Nov 1982, v49, p258-59.
Christian Century. Jul 7, 1982, v99, p768.
Commonweal. Sep 10, 1982, v109, p468-69.
Hollywood Reporter. Jun 14, 1982, p3.
The New Republic. Jul 19, 1982, v187, p31.
New York. Jul 19, 1982, v15, p52-53.
The New York Times. Jun 18, 1982, SecIII, p10.
The New Yorker. Jul 26, 1982, v58, p66-67.
Newsweek. Jul 5, 1982, v100, p72.

An Autumn Afternoon (Japanese title: Samma no Aji; Also titled: The Widower; The Taste of Mackerel; A Taste of the Fish Called Samma) (JAPAN; Ozu, Yasujiro; 1962)
Dictionary of Films. p325.
Film. Wint 1966, n47, p22.
Film 73/74. p36-38.
Film News. Jan-Feb 1975, v32, p27.
Film Quarterly. Wint 1965-66, v19, p48-50.
The London Times. Oct 6, 1966, p18.
The London Times. Oct 21, 1963, p14.
The Nation. May 21, 1973, v216, p670.
New Statesman. Oct 7, 1966, v72, p528, p530.
The New Yorker. May 19, 1973, v49, p83-84.
Newsweek. Jun 11, 1973, v81, p103-04.
Ozu (Richie). p43-44.
Something to Declare. p147-50.
Time. Jun 4, 1973, v101, p96-97.
Transcendental Style in Film. p47-55.
Variety. Sep 18, 1963, p6.

Autumn Sonata (Swedish title: Herbstonate) (SWED; Bergman, Ingmar; 1978)
America. Oct 28, 1978, v139, p288.
Autumn Sonata. 1978.
Encore. Nov 20, 1978, v7, p30.
Films in Review. Nov 1978, v29, p569.
Hollywood Reporter. Sep 19, 1978, p3.
Human Behavior. Jan 1979, v8, p77.
The Los Angeles Times. Oct 15, 1978, Calendar, p35.
Maclean's. Nov 20, 1978, v91, p66-67.
Magill's Survey of Cinema. Foreign Language Films. v1, p184-89.

Motion Picture Herald Product Digest. Oct 4, 1978, p33.
Ms. Dec 1978, v7, p30.
The Nation. Dec 2, 1978, v227, p619-20.
National Review. Nov 24, 1978, v30, p1490-91.
The New Republic. Oct 7, 11978, v179, p24-26.
New York. Oct 9, 1978, v11, p113.
The New York Times. Nov 6, 1978, np.
The New York Times. Dec 3, 1978, SecII, p13.
The New Yorker. Nov 6, 1978, v54, p165-66.
Newsweek. Oct 16, 1978, v92, p76.
Time. Oct 16, 1978, v112, p112.
Variety. Sep 13, 1978, p21.

Aux Postes de Combat *See* The Bedford Incident

Aventuras de Robinson Crusoe, Las *See* The Adventures of Robinson Crusoe

Aveu, L' *See* The Confession

Avventura, L' (IT; Antonioni, Michelangelo; 1960)
America. Jun 3, 1961, v105, p411.
Antonioni (Chatman). p5-30.
Cahiers du Cinema in English. 1966, n2, p77-78.
Christian Century. Apr 30, 1961, v78, p1031-32.
Classic Movies. p182-85.
Commonweal. Apr 14, 1961, v74, p79.
Esquire. Apr 1961, v55, p21-22.
Esquire. May 1962, v57, p65-66.
Favorite Movies. p172-89.
Film and the Critical Eye. p396-429.
Great Film Directors. p14-22.
The International Dictionary of Films and Filmmakers. v1, p41-42.
Italian Cinema (Bondanella). p210-13.
Magill's Survey of Cinema. Foreign Language Films. v1, p190-93.
Michelangelo Antonioni: A Guide to References and Resources. p96-101.
Motion Picture Herald Product Digest. Apr 15, 1961, p93.
The Nation. Apr 15, 1961, v192, p329-30.
The New Republic. Apr 10, 1961, v144, p26.
The New York Times. Apr 5, 1961, p30.
The New Yorker. Apr 22, 1961, v37, p144-45.
Newsweek. Apr 17, 1961, v57, p107.
Renaissance of the Film. p24-31.
Saturday Review. Apr 8, 1961, v44, p41.
Time. Apr 7, 1961, v77, p60.
Variety. May 25, 1960, p7.
Yale Review. Oct 1964, v54, p41-50.

Baby Blue Marine (US; Hancock, John; 1976)
BFI/Monthly Film Bulletin. Sep 1976, v43, p188.
Film Bulletin. Apr 1976, v45, pB.
Hollywood Reporter. Apr 28, 1976, p6.
Independent Film Journal. May 14, 1976, v77, p10-11.
The Los Angeles Times. Apr 27, 1976, SecIV, p1.
Motion Picture Herald Product Digest. May 19, 1976, p100.
New York. May 10, 1976, v9, p64-65.
The New York Times. May 6, 1976, p45.
Time. May 17, 1976, v107, p72.
Variety. Apr 28, 1976, p28.

Baby Doll (US; Kazan, Elia; 1956)
America. Dec 29, 1956, v96, p367.
An American Odyssey. p217-19.
BFI/Monthly Film Bulletin. Jan 1957, v24, p14.
Commonweal. Dec 28, 1956, v65, p335.
Elia Kazan: A Guide to References and Resources. p68-71.
Film Culture. 1957, v3, p19-20.

Film Daily. Dec 5, 1956, p6.
Films and Filming. Feb 1957, v3, p21-22.
The Films in My Life. p110-13.
Films in Review. Jan 1957, p32-33.
The Films of the Fifties. p200-01.
Hollywood Reporter. Dec 5, 1956, p3.
Kazan on Kazan. p66-83.
Magill's Survey of Cinema. Series II. v1, p141-45.
The Nation. Dec 29, 1956, v183, p567.
The New Republic. Jan 21, 1957, v136, p21.
The New Republic. Feb 4, 1957, v136, p3.
The New York Times. Dec 19, 1956, p40.
The New Yorker. Dec 29, 1956, v32, p59.
Newsweek. Dec 17, 1956, v48, p106.
Saturday Review. Dec 29, 1956, v39, p22-24.
Sight and Sound. Wint 1956-57, v26, p150-51.
Time. Dec 24, 1956, v68, p61.
Time. Jan 14, 1956, v69, p100.
Variety. Dec 5, 1956, p6.

Baby Face Nelson (US; Siegel, Don; 1957)
BFI/Monthly Film Bulletin. Feb 1958, v25, p18-19.
Film Daily. Nov 18, 1957, v112, p6.
Film Noir. p15-16.
Films and Filming. Feb 1958, v4, p26.
Hollywood Reporter. Nov 6, 1957, p3.
Motion Picture Herald Product Digest. Nov 9, 1957, p593.
The New York Times. Dec 12, 1957, p35.
Newsweek. Nov 25, 1957, v50, p125.
Variety. Nov 6, 1957, p6.

Baby, It's You (US; Sayles, John; 1983)
BFI/Monthly Film Bulletin. Nov 1984, v51, p330.
Commonweal. May 20, 1983, v110, p304-05.
Films in Review. May 1983, v34, p302-03.
Hollywood Reporter. Mar 4, 1983, p3.
The Los Angeles Times. Apr 22, 1983, SecVI, p1.
Maclean's. May 9, 1983, v96, p66.
The New Leader. Apr 4, 1983, v66, p19-20.
New York. Apr 11, 1983, v16, p72.
The New York Times. Mar 25, 1983, SecIII, p6.
Newsweek. Apr 11, 1983, v101, p78.
Variety. Mar 9, 1983, p18.
Vogue. May 1983, v173, p50.

Baby, the Rain Must Fall (US; Mulligan, Robert; 1965)
America. Feb 13, 1965, v112, p231.
BFI/Monthly Film Bulletin. Jun 1965, v32, p86-87.
Christian Science Monitor (Western edition). Mar 6, 1965, p12.
Commonweal. Jan 22, 1965, v81, p544.
Film Daily. Jan 12, 1965, p4.
Film Quarterly. Spr 1965, v18, p59.
Filmfacts. Feb 5, 1965, v8, p1-3.
Films and Filming. Jul 1965, v11, p28.
Films and Filming. Jun 1965, v11, p18.
Films in Review. Jan 1965, v16, p47-48.
The Films of Steve McQueen. p91-100.
Hollywood Reporter. Jan 12, 1965, p3.
The London Times. May 6, 1965, p10.
Motion Picture Herald Product Digest. Jan 20, 1965, p209.
Movie. Sum 1965, n13, p45.
The New York Times. Jan 14, 1965, p44.
The New Yorker. Jan 23, 1965, v40, p104.
Newsweek. Jan 25, 1965, v65, p90.
Playboy. Feb 1965, v12, p24.
Saturday Review. Jan 30, 1965, v48, p40.
Sight and Sound. Sum 1965, v34, p148.
Time. Feb 5, 1965, v85, p64.

Bachelor Girl Apartment *See* Any Wednesday

Bachelor Party (US; Mann, Delbert; 1957)
America. Apr 27, 1957, v97, p152.
BFI/Monthly Film Bulletin. Aug 1957, v24, p95.
Commonweal. Apr 12, 1957, v66, p35-36.
Film Daily. Mar 4, 1957, v111, p6.
Films and Filming. Aug 1957, v3, p28.
Films in Review. Apr 1957, v8, p175-76.
Hollywood Reporter. Feb 26, 1957, p3.
Motion Picture World. Mar 9, 1957, v206, p289.
The Nation. Apr 27, 1957, v184, p379.
The New Republic. May 27, 1957, v136, p29.
The New York Times. Apr 10, 1957, p37.
The New York Times. Apr 14, 1957, SecII, p1.
The New Yorker. Apr 20, 1957, v33, p135.
Newsweek. Apr 22, 1957, v49, p124-25.
Saturday Review. Apr 27, 1957, v40, p25.
Time. Apr 15, 1957, v69, p116.
Variety. Mar 6, 1957, p6.
The Village Voice. Jun 26, 1957, p6.

Back at the Front (Also titled: Willie and Joe Back at the Front) (US; Sherman, George; 1952)
Film Daily. Oct 2, 1952, p6.
Hollywood Reporter. Sep 26, 1952, p3.
Motion Picture Herald Product Digest. Oct 4, 1952, p1550-51.
National Parent-Teacher. Nov 1952, v47, p37.
Time. Oct 20, 1952, v60, p112.
Variety. Oct 1, 1952, p6.

Back Roads (US; Ritt, Martin; 1981)
BFI/Monthly Film Bulletin. Dec 1981, v48, p240.
Maclean's. Mar 16, 1981, v94, p61.
The New Leader. Apr 20, 1981, v64, p20.
The New Republic. Mar 28, 1981, v184, p23.
New York. Mar 23, 1981, v14, p54-55.
The New York Times. Mar 13, 1981, SecIII, p6.
Newsweek. Mar 16, 1981, v97, p97.
Variety. Mar 11, 1981, p17.
The Village Voice. Mar 11, 1981, v26, p47.

Back to the Future (US; Zemeckis, Robert; 1985)
BFI/Monthly Film Bulletin. Dec 1985, v52, p375-76.
Chatelaine. Sep 1985, v58, p18.
Commonweal. Aug 9, 1985, v112, p439-40.
Hollywood Reporter. Jun 24, 1985, p3.
The Los Angeles Times. Jul 3, 1985, SecVI, p1.
Maclean's. Jul 15, 1985, v98, p54.
Magill's Cinema Annual, 1986. p65-74.
The New Republic. Aug 5, 1985, v193, p24.
New Statesman. Dec 6, 1985, v110, p30.
New York. Jul 15, 1985, v18, p64-66.
The New York Times. Jul 3, 1985, SecIII, p18.
The New Yorker. Jul 29, 1985, v61, p57-58.
Newsweek. Jul 8, 1985, v106, p76.
Philadelphia Magazine. Sep 1985, v76, p89.
Popular Mechanics. Aug 1985, v162, p84-87.
Progressive. Sep 1985, v49, p38.
Time. Jul 1, 1985, v125, p62.
Variety. Jun 26, 1985, p18.
The Village Voice. Jul 9, 1985, p48.
The Wall Street Journal. Jul 3, 1985, p12.
Washingtonian. Aug 1985, v20, p56.

Backfire (US; Sherman, Vincent; 1950)
Film Daily. Jan 19, 1950, p12.
Hollywood Reporter. Jan 17, 1950, p3.
Motion Picture Herald Product Digest. Jan 21, 1950, p161, 163.
The New York Times. Jan 27, 1950, p29.
Variety. Jan 18, 1950, p6.

Backfire (French title: Echappement Libre; Also titled: Free Escape) (FR; Becker, Jean; 1964)

Film Daily. Apr 26, 1965, p4.
Filmfacts. Jun 25, 1965, v8, p117-18.
Films. 1965, v8, p117.
Hollywood Reporter. Jun 10, 1965, p3.
The London Times. Apr 12, 1966, p13.
Motion Picture Herald Product Digest. May 12, 1965, p282.
The New York Times. Apr 27, 1965, p27.
The New Yorker. May 1, 1965, v41, p120.
Newsweek. May 10, 1965, v65, p118.
Saturday Review. May 15, 1965, v48, p34.
Time. May 7, 1965, v85, p107.
Variety. Oct 7, 1964, p6.

The Bad and the Beautiful (US; Minnelli, Vincente; 1952)
BFI/Monthly Film Bulletin. Feb 1953, v20, p18.
Catholic World. Jan 1953, v176, p302.
Christian Century. Mar 11, 1953, v70, p303.
Commonweal. Feb 6, 1953, v57, p450.
Cue. Jan 17, 1953, p12.
Fifty From the Fifties. p28-35.
Film Daily. Nov 21, 1952, p4.
Films in Review. Jan 1953, v4, p35-37.
The Films of Kirk Douglas. p192-97.
The Films of Lana Turner. p178-83.
The Films of the Fifties. p75-78.
The Great Movies. p172-74.
Hollywood Reporter. Nov 19, 1952, p4.
I Remember It Well. p262-66, 268-70.
Kiss Kiss Bang Bang. p286-87.
The London Times. Mar 9, 1953, p4.
Look. Jan 27, 1953, v17, p80-81.
Magill's Survey of Cinema. Series II. v1, p112-15.
Motion Picture Herald Product Digest. Nov 22, 1952, p1613.
Movie. Wint 1977-78, n25, p30-52.
National Parent-Teacher. Jan 1953, v47, p37.
The New Statesman and Nation. Mar 14, 1953, v45, p295.
The New York Times. Jan 16, 1953, p19.
The New Yorker. Jan 17, 1953, v28, p89.
Newsweek. Jan 26, 1953, v41, p100.
Saturday Review. Jan 3, 1953, v36, p54.
Selected Film Criticism, 1951-1960. p12-13.
Sight and Sound. Apr-Jun 1953, v22, p193-94.
The Spectator. Mar 6, 1952, v190, p276.
Theatre Arts. Feb 1953, v37, p80.
Time. Jan 12, 1953, v61, p94.
Variety. Nov 19, 1952, p6.

Bad Birds and Good Birds *See* The Hawks and the Sparrows

Bad Boys (US; Rosenthal, Rick; 1983)
BFI/Monthly Film Bulletin. May 1983, v50, p128.
Commonweal. May 16, 1983, v110, p274.
Esquire. Mar 1983, v99, p217-18.
Hollywood Reporter. Feb 28, 1983, p6.
Humanist. Jul-Aug 1983, v43, p41.
The Los Angeles Times. Mar 25, 1983, SecVI, p26.
New York. Mar 28, 1983, v16, p72.
The New York Times. Mar 25, 1983, SecIII, p8.
The New Yorker. Apr 4, 1983, v59, p128-31.
Newsweek. Mar 28, 1983, v101, p73-74.
Rolling Stone. Apr 14, 1983, p51.
Variety. Mar 2, 1983, p10.

Bad Day at Black Rock (US; Sturges, John; 1954)
America. Feb 12, 1955, v92, p518.
American Film. Nov 1979, v5, p54.
BFI/Monthly Film Bulletin. Apr 1955, v22, p50.
Catholic World. Feb 1955, v180, p382.
Collier's. Mar 18, 1955, v135, p6.
Commonweal. Jan 14, 1955, v61, p407.

Farm Journal. Feb 1955, v79, p149.
Film Culture. May-Jun 1955, v1, p27.
Film Daily. Dec 15, 1954, p6.
Film Society Review. Apr 1966, p19-20.
Films and Filming. May 1955, v1, p20.
Films in Review. Feb 1955, v6, p83-84.
The Films of Spencer Tracy. p221-23.
The Films of the Fifties. p153-55.
Hollywood Reporter. Dec 15, 1954, p3.
Kiss Kiss Bang Bang. p287.
Library Journal. Jan 1, 1955, v80, p63.
The London Times. Mar 14, 1955, p11.
Magill's Survey of Cinema. Series I. v1, p116-18.
The Nation. Feb 19, 1955, v180, p165.
National Parent-Teacher. Mar 1955, v49, p38.
The New Statesman and Nation. Mar 26, 1955, v49, p434.
The New York Times. Feb 2, 1955, p22.
The New Yorker. Feb 12, 1955, v30, p92.
Newsweek. Feb 21, 1955, v45, p94.
Saturday Review. Jan 29, 1955, v38, p26.
The Spectator. Mar 18, 1955, v194, p326.
The Tatler. Mar 23, 1955, v215, p592.
Time. Jan 17, 1955, v65, p74.
Variety. Dec 15, 1954, p6.

The Bad News Bears (US; Ritchie, Michael; 1976)
American Film. Mar 1976, v1, p50-53.
BFI/Monthly Film Bulletin. Nov 1976, v43, p228.
Film Bulletin. Apr 1976, v45, pB.
Films and Filming. Dec 1976, v23, p34.
Films and Filming. Nov 1976, v23, p22-23.
Films in Review. May 1976, v27, p312.
Hollywood Reporter. Apr 6, 1976, p3.
Independent Film Journal. Apr 14, 1976, v77, p7.
Magill's Survey of Cinema. Series II. v1, p157-58.
Motion Picture Herald Product Digest. Apr 7, 1976, p88.
New Statesman. Nov 12, 1976, v92, p689.
New York. Apr 19, 1976, v9, p84-86.
Newsweek. Apr 12, 1976, v87, p97.
Penthouse. Jul 1976, v7, p47-49.
Saturday Review. Apr 17, 1976, v3, p44.
Sight and Sound. Spr 1976, v45, p14-15.
The Thousand Eyes Magazine. May 1976, n10, p11-12.
Time. Apr 26, 1976, v107, p45.
Variety. Apr 7, 1976, p23.
The Village Voice. May 3, 1976, p123-24.

The Bad Seed (US; LeRoy, Mervyn; 1956)
America. Sep 22, 1956, v95, p604.
BFI/Monthly Film Bulletin. Oct 1956, v23, p124.
Commonweal. Sep 28, 1956, v64, p633.
Film Daily. Jul 25, 1956, p6.
Films and Filming. Oct 1956, v3, p26.
The Films in My Life. p121-24.
Films in Review. Oct 1956, v7, p415-16.
Hollywood Reporter. Jul 25, 1956, p3.
Magill's Survey of Cinema. Series II. v1, p159-62.
The Nation. Oct 20, 1956, v183, p333-34.
The New York Times. Sep 13, 1956, p39.
The New Yorker. Sep 22, 1956, v32, p159.
Newsweek. Sep 17, 1956, v48, p118.
Saturday Review. Sep 22, 1956, v39, p31.
Time. Sep 17, 1956, v68, p100.
Variety. Jul 25, 1956, p6.

Bad Timing: A Sensual Obsession (GB; Roeg, Nicolas; 1980)
BFI/Monthly Film Bulletin. Mar 1980, v47, p43.
Christian Century. Nov 12, 1980, v97, p1108.

Film Comment. Nov-Dec 1980, v16, p59-61.
Films in Review. Nov 1980, v31, p568.
Hollywood Reporter. Sep 26, 1980, p11.
The Los Angeles Times. Oct 12, 1980, Calendar, p1.
Maclean's. Sep 22, 1980, v93, p61.
Motion Picture Herald Product Digest. Oct 8, 1980, p36.
The Nation. Oct 25, 1980, v231, p420.
The New Republic. Oct 4, 1980, v183, p26-27.
The New York Times. Sep 21, 1980, p70.
Newsday. Sep 19, 1980, SecII, p7.
Newsweek. Oct 6, 1980, v96, p72.
Rolling Stone. Oct 30, 1980, p37.
Saturday Review. Sep 1980, v7, p90-91.
Time. Nov 3, 1980, v116, p108.
Variety. Sep 1980, v170, p72.
Variety. Feb 20, 1980, p22.
The Village Voice. Sep 24, 1980, p52.

Baie des Anges, La *See* Bay of Angels

The Bailiff *See* Sansho the Bailiff

Baisers Volés *See* Stolen Kisses

The Baker of Valorgue, Le *See* Boulanger de Valorgue, Le

Bal, Le (FR, IT, ALG; Scola, Ettore; 1983)
BFI/Monthly Film Bulletin. Dec 1984, v51, p374.
Christian Century. Jul 18, 1984, v101, p73.
Dance Magazine. Jun 1984, v58, p54-55.
Film Journal. May 1984, v87, p27.
Hollywood Reporter. Mar 27, 1984, p12.
Hudson Review. Fall 1984, v37, p457-60.
The Los Angeles Times. Mar 30, 1984, SecVI, p15.
Magill's Cinema Annual, 1985. p80-87.
New York. Mar 26, 1984, v17, p80-81.
The New York Times. Mar 18, 1984, SecII, p17.
The New York Times. Mar 23, 1984, SecIII, p6.
Newsweek. Apr 2, 1984, v103, p85.
Time. Apr 16, 1984, v123, p81.
Variety. Jan 4, 1984, p20.

Bal Taborin (US; Ford, Philip; 1952)
BFI/Monthly Film Bulletin. Dec 1952, v19, p169.
Film Daily. Jun 23, 1952, p6.
Hollywood Reporter. Jun 18, 1952, p3.
Motion Picture Herald Product Digest. Jun 28, 1952, p1426.
Variety. Jun 18, 1952, p6.

The Balcony (US; Strick, Joseph; 1963)
BFI/Monthly Film Bulletin. Dec 1963, v30, p167-68.
Christian Century. Apr 12, 1963, p430-31.
Christian Science Monitor. Apr 2, 1963, p4.
Commonweal. Apr 12, 1963, v78, p74.
Film Daily. Mar 21, 1963, p5.
Filmfacts. Apr 4, 1963, v6, p43-45.
Films and Filming. Nov 1963, v10, p21.
Films in Review. Apr 1963, v14, p243.
Hollywood Reporter. Apr 23, 1963, p3.
The Nation. May 18, 1963, v196, p430-31.
The New Republic. Mar 23, 1963, v148, p34.
New Statesman. Oct 18, 1963, v66, p538.
The New York Times. Mar 22, 1963, p7.
The New Yorker. Mar 30, 1963, v39, p143-44.
Newsweek. Apr 1, 1963, v61, p81.
Saturday Review. Mar 30, 1963, v46, p34.
Sight and Sound. Wint 1963-64, v33, p40.
Spectator. Oct 25, 1963, v211, p528.
Time. Mar 29, 1963, v81, p92.
Variety. Mar 20, 1963, p6.

Ballad of a Soldier (Russian title: Ballada o Soldatye) (USSR; Chukhari, Grigoi; 1959)
Cinema, the Magic Vehicle. v2, p452-53.

Commonweal. Jan 13, 1961, v73, p414.
Fifty from the Fifties. p37-43.
Film Culture. Spr 1962, n24, p34-39.
Film Culture. Fall 1962, n26, p34-39.
Film Daily. Dec 28, 1960, p6.
Film Quarterly. Wint 1960, v14, p46-47.
Films and Filming. Jul 1961, v7, p25-26.
Films in Review. Jan 1961, v12, p36-37.
The International Dictionary of Films and Filmmakers. v1, p43-44.
Magill's Survey of Cinema. Foreign Language Films. v1, p207-09.
Motion Picture Herald Product Digest. Dec 31, 1960, p972.
The Nation. May 13, 1961, v192, p420.
The New Republic. Jan 9, 1961, v144, p26.
The New York Times. Dec 27, 1960, p22.
The New York Times. Jan 1, 1961, SecII, p1.
The New Yorker. Jan 7, 1961, v36, p63.
Newsweek. Jan 9, 1961, v57, p80.
On Movies. p269-70.
Saturday Review. Dec 24, 1960, v43, p42.
Sight and Sound. Sum 1961, v30, p151-52.
Time. Jan 13, 1961, v77, p47.
Variety. May 18, 1960, p7.

The Ballad of Berlin *See* The Berliner

The Ballad of Cable Hogue (US; Peckinpah, Sam; 1970)
America. May 23, 1970, v122, p570.
Commonweal. Jul 24, 1970, v92, p369.
Esquire. Jun 1970, v73, p68.
The Films of Sam Peckinpah. p41-48.
Holiday. May 1970, v47, p34-35.
Life. Mar 27, 1970, v68, p11.
The New Republic. Jun 6, 1970, v162, p19.
The New York Times. May 14, 1970, p42.
Newsweek. Mar 23, 1970, v75, p102.
Peckinpah (Simmons). p108-20.
Sam Peckinpah (McKinney). p101-10.
Saturday Review. Apr 11, 1970, v53, p42.
Time. Mar 16, 1970, v95, p81.
Variety. Mar 11, 1970, p17.

A Ballad of Love (Russian title: Dvoye; Also titled: Father of a Soldier; Two in Two) (USSR; Bogin, Mikhail; 1965)
Christian Science Monitor (Western edition). Jul 17, 1966, p6.
Commonweal. Apr 8, 1966, v84, p81.
Film Society Review. May 1968, p28.
Filmfacts. Apr 1, 1966, v9, p44.
Motion Picture Herald Product Digest. Mar 2, 1966, p477.
The New York Times. Feb 21, 1966, p51.
Variety. Jul 14, 1965, p7.

Ballada o Soldatye *See* Ballad of a Soldier

Ballon Rouge, Le *See* The Red Balloon

Balthazar *See* Au Hasard, Balthazar

Bambole, Le (Also titled: Four Kinds of Love) (IT, FR; Risi, Dino; Comencini, Luigi; Rosi, Francesco; 1964)
BFI/Monthly Film Bulletin. Dec 1965, v32, p181-82.
Film Daily. Jul 14, 1965, p6.
Films and Filming. Dec 1965, v12, p31.
Films and Filming. Sep 1965, v11, p20-21.
The London Times. Oct 14, 1965, p16.
The New York Times. Jun 29, 1965, p26.
The New Yorker. Jul 17, 1965, v41, p60-61.
The Spectator. Oct 15, 1965, v215, p485.
Time. Jul 9, 1965, v86, p96.
Variety. Feb 3, 1965, p6.

Banana Peel (French title: Peau de Banane) (FR; Ophuls, Marcel; 1963)
Christian Science Monitor (Western edition). Apr 27, 1965, p2.

Filmfacts. Feb 12, 1965, v8, p6-8.
Films in Review. Feb 1965, v16, p114-15.
Life. Feb 12, 1965, v58, p15.
Motion Picture Herald Product Digest. Feb 3, 1965, p218-19.
The New Republic. Feb 6, 1965, v152, p28.
The New York Times. Jan 19, 1965, p29.
The New Yorker. Jan 30, 1965, v40, p114.
Newsweek. Jan 25, 1965, v65, p90.
Playboy. Apr 1965, v12, p24.
Time. Jan 29, 1965, v85, p85.
Variety. Nov 13, 1963, p17.

Bananas (US; Allen, Woody; 1971)
America. Jun 12, 1971, v124, p619.
Atlantic. Aug 1971, v218, p92-94.
BFI/Monthly Film Bulletin. Oct 1971, v38, p191.
Films and Filming. Nov 1971, v18, n2, p51.
Hollywood Reporter. Apr 28, 1971, v216, n1, p3.
Look. Jun 15, 1971, v25, p80.
Magill's Survey of Cinema. Series II. v1, p166.
The New Republic. May 22, 1971, v164, p24.
The New York Times. Apr 29, 1971, p46.
The New Yorker. May 15, 1971, v47, p127-29.
Newsweek. May 17, 1971, v77, p102.
Variety. Apr 28, 1971, p6.
The Village Voice. May 6, 1971, v16, n18, p65.
Woody Allen: His Films and Career. p99-117.
Woody Allen (Palmer). p49-56.

Band of Angels (US; Walsh, Raoul; 1957)
BFI/Monthly Film Bulletin. Oct 1957, v24, p125.
Commonweal. Jul 26, 1957, v66, p425.
Film Daily. Jul 10, 1957, p8.
The Films of Clark Gable. p240-42.
The Films of Sidney Poitier. p64-66.
From Sambo to Superspade. p212.
Hollywood Reporter. Jul 10, 1957, p3.
The New York Times. Jul 11, 1957, p21.
The New Yorker. Jul 20, 1957, v33, p61.
Newsweek. Jul 29, 1957, v50, p86.
Time. Aug 5, 1957, v70, p76.
Variety. Jul 10, 1957, p6.

Band of Outsiders (French title: Bande a Part; Also titled: The Outsiders) (FR; Godard, Jean-Luc; 1964)
BFI/Monthly Film Bulletin. Dec 1964, v31, p170.
Dictionary of Films. p23.
Film Daily. Apr 25, 1966, p5.
Film Heritage. Spr 1968, v3, p11-22, 47.
Film Quarterly. Wint 1964, v18, p54-55.
Filmfacts. Apr 1, 1966, v9, p44-46.
Films and Filming. Jan 1965, v11, p31.
The Films of Jean-Luc Godard. p61-71.
Focus on Godard. p40-45.
Jean-Luc Godard: A Critical Anthology. p170-78.
Jean-Luc Godard: A Guide to References and Resources. p58-61.
Kiss Kiss Bang Bang. p137-41.
The London Times. May 12, 1964, p15.
Magill's Survey of Cinema. Foreign Language Films. v1, p217-23.
Motion Picture Herald Product Digest. Mar 30, 1966, p493.
The Nation. Apr 4, 1966, v202, p406.
The New Republic. Sep 10, 1966, v155, p27-29.
New Statesman. Nov 6, 1964, v68, p708.
The New Wave. p141-45.
The New York Times. Mar 16, 1966, p48.
Newsweek. Mar 28, 1966, v67, p101.
Private Screenings. p312-15.
Sight and Sound. Wint 1964-65, v34, p11-12.
Variety. Apr 29, 1964, p6, 26.

The Village Voice. Oct 8, 1964, v9, p15-16.
The Village Voice. Mar 24, 1966, v11, p29.

The Bandwagon (US; Minnelli, Vincente; 1953)
America. Jul 18, 1953, v89, p405.
American Film Genres. p196-202.
BFI/Monthly Film Bulletin. Nov 1953, v20, n238, p170.
Catholic World. Aug 1953, v177, p384.
Commonweal. Jul 31, 1953, v58, p423.
Dance Magazine. Sep 1953, v27, p68-69.
Farm Journal. Sep 1953, v77, p118.
Film Daily. Jul 7, 1953, p6.
Films in Review. Aug-Sep 1953, v4, p360-61.
Holiday. Jan 1954, v15, p17.
Hollywood Reporter. Jul 6, 1953, p3.
Life. Aug 10, 1953, v35, p79.
Magill's Survey of Cinema. Series I. v1, p123-25.
McCall's. Sep 1953, v86, p6.
National Parent-Teacher. Sep 1953, v48, p38.
The New York Times. Jul 10, 1953, p10.
The New York Times. Jul 19, 1953, SecII, p1.
The New Yorker. Jul 18, 1953, v29, p63.
Newsweek. Jul 6, 1953, v42, p48-50.
Saturday Review. Jul 25, 1953, v36, p28.
Senior Scholastic. Sep 16, 1953, v63, p37.
Sight and Sound. Jan-Mar 1954, v23, p142-43.
Starring Fred Astaire. p381-96.
Time. Jul 13, 1953, v62, p94.
Variety. Jul 8, 1953, p6.
Vincente Minnelli and the Film Musical. p112.

Bang, Bang, You're Dead! (Also titled: Our Man in Marrakesh) (GB; Sharp, Don; 1966)
BFI/Monthly Film Bulletin. Jun 1966, v33, p96.
Film Daily. Sep 29, 1966, p5.
Filmfacts. Feb 15, 1967, v10, p15-16.
Films and Filming. Aug 1966, v12, p10.
The Great Spy Pictures. p74-75.
Motion Picture Herald Product Digest. Aug 31, 1966, p588.
The New York Times. Jan 19, 1967, p41.
Newsweek. Sep 5, 1966, v68, p88A.
Variety. Aug 24, 1966, p6.

Bang the Drum Slowly (US; Hancock, John; 1973)
America. Sep 1, 1973, v129, inside back cover.
Commonweal. Oct 19, 1973, v99, p62.
Esquire. Oct 1973, v80, p48.
Film Quarterly. Wint 1973-74, v17, p49.
Holiday. Nov 1973, v54, p13-14.
Hollywood Reporter. Aug 3, 1973, p3.
Mademoiselle. Sep 1973, v77, p66.
The Nation. Sep 24, 1973, v217, p283.
The New Republic. Sep 1, 1973, v169, p24.
The New York Times. Aug 27, 1973, p35.
The New York Times. Sep 2, 1973, SecII, p1.
The New York Times. Sep 30, SecII, p1.
The New York Times. Jan 6, 1974, SecII, p2.
The New York Times. Jan 20, 1974, SecII, p4.
The New Yorker. Sep 10, 1973, v49, p102.
Newsweek. Sep 10, 1973, v82, p85.
PTA Magazine. Oct 1973, v68, p8.
Time. Sep 3, 1973, v102, p60.
Variety. Aug 15, 1973, p12.
Vogue. Sep 1973, v162, p174.

Bank Shot (US; Champion, Gower; 1974)
Audience. Sep 1974, v7, p14-15.
BFI/Monthly Film Bulletin. Dec 1974, v41, p246.
Films Illustrated. Oct 1974, v4, p46.
Hollywood Reporter. Jul 8, 1974, p3.
Independent Film Journal. Jul 10, 1974, v74, p14.

The Los Angeles Times. Aug 14, 1974, SecIV, p19.
New Statesman. Sep 20, 1974, v88, p390.
New York. Aug 19, 1974, v7, p62-63.
The New York Times. Aug 1, 1974, p18.
The New Yorker. Aug 12, 1974, v50, p76, 79-80.
PTA Magazine. Oct 1974, v69, p6.
Time. Sep 23, 1974, v104, p6.
Variety. Jul 10, 1974, p16.
The Village Voice. Aug 22, 1974, v19, p75.

Barbarella (US, FR; Vadim, Roger; 1968)
Atlantic. Apr 1969, v223, p141.
BFI/Monthly Film Bulletin. Nov 1968, v35, p167-68.
Christian Century. Feb 12, 1969, v86, p238.
Christian Science Monitor (Western edition). Nov 11, 1968, p12.
Film Daily. Oct 16, 1968, p9.
Film Quarterly. Spr 1969, v22, p58.
Filmfacts. Jan 1, 1968, v11, p412-14.
Films and Filming. Dec 1968, v15, p38-39.
The Films of Jane Fonda. p142-46.
The Films of the Sixties. p221-23.
Future Tense: The Cinema of Science Fiction. p170-71.
Hollywood Reporter. Oct 7, 1968, p3.
London Sunday Times Magazine. Sep 13, 1968, p50-53.
The London Times. Oct 17, 1968, p18.
Magill's Survey of Cinema. Series II. v1, p170-73.
Motion Picture Herald Product Digest. Oct 23, 1968, p45.
Movies Into Film. p142-43.
The New Republic. Nov 9, 1968, v159, p22.
New Society. Oct 31, 1968, p629-30.
New Statesman. Oct 25, 1968, v76, p557.
The New York Times. Oct 12, 1968, p43.
The New York Times. Oct 13, 1968, p1.
The New Yorker. Nov 2, 1968, v44, p182.
Newsweek. Oct 21, 1968, v72, p100.
Science Fiction Studies in Film. p185-87.
Sight and Sound. Wint 1968-69, v38, p46-47.
The Spectator. Oct 25, 1968, v221, p599.
Time. Oct 18, 1968, v92, p108.
Variety. Oct 9, 1968, p6.
The Village Voice. Oct 17, 1968, v14, p53.
A Year In the Dark. p267-70.

The Barbarian and the Geisha (US; Huston, John; 1958)
America. Oct 18, 1958, v100, p89.
BFI/Monthly Film Bulletin. Nov 1958, v25, p139.
Catholic World. Dec 1958, v188, p241.
The Cinema of John Huston. p116-18.
Commonweal. Oct 17, 1958, v69, p73.
The Complete Films of John Wayne. p220-22.
Film Daily. Sep 30, 1958, v114, p6.
Filmfacts. Nov 5, 1958, v1, p181-82.
Films in Review. Oct 1958, v9, p462.
Hollywood Reporter. Sep 30, 1958, p3.
John Huston (Hammen). p90-93.
Library Journal. Oct 15, 1958, v83, p2825.
Look. Nov 25, 1958, v22, p108.
The New Republic. Nov 3, 1958, v139, p21-22.
The New York Times. Oct 3, 1958, p23.
The New Yorker. Oct 11, 1958, v34, p94.
Newsweek. Oct 6, 1958, v52, p90-91.
Saturday Review. Oct 11, 1958, v41, p29.
Time. Oct 6, 1958, v72, p90.
Variety. Oct 1, 1958, p6.

Barbarosa (IT; Schepisi, Fred; 1982)
Hollywood Reporter. Jan 18, 1982, p4.
The Los Angeles Times. Oct 23, 1982, SecV, p1.
Magill's Cinema Annual, 1983. p60-64.
National Review. Sep 3, 1982, v34, p1097.

The New Republic. Sep 13, 1982, v187, p26-27.
New York. Aug 9, 1982, v15, p59-60.
The New York Times. Sep 12, 1982, II, p17.
The New Yorker. Aug 9, 1982, v58, p78-79.
Newsweek. Aug 2, 1982, v100, p62.
Progressive. Oct 1982, v46, p55.
Rolling Stone. Mar 18, 1982, p45-46.
Time. Aug 9, 1982, v120, p58.
Variety. Jan 19, 1982, p3.

Bardouzes, Les *See* The Great Spy Chase

The Barefoot Battalion (GREECE; Tallas, Gregg; 1954)
BFI/Monthly Film Bulletin. Sep 1955, v22, p134.
Catholic World. Feb 1954, v178, p382.
Commonweal. Jun 11, 1954, v60, p249.
Film Daily. Jul 9, 1954, p6.
Films and Filming. Oct 1955, v2, p20-21.
Hollywood Reporter. Jun 3, 1954, p3.
Motion Picture Herald Product Digest. Jun 19, 1954, p34.
The New Statesman and Nation. Aug 13, 1955, v50, p186.
The New York Times. May 29, 1954, p13.
Saturday Review. Feb 20, 1954, v37, p33.
Variety. Jun 9, 1954, p20.

The Barefoot Contessa (US, IT; Mankiewicz, Joseph L.; 1954)
America. Oct 30, 1954, v92, p139.
BFI/Monthly Film Bulletin. Dec 1954, v21, p170-71.
Catholic World. Nov 1954, v180, p138.
Commonweal. Oct 8, 1954, v61, p15.
The Complete Films of Humphrey Bogart. p178-80.
Coronet. Nov 1954, v37, p6.
Dictionary of Films. p24.
Farm Journal. Nov 1954, v78, p73.
Film Daily. Sep 27, 1954, p6.
Films and Filming. Dec 1954, v1, p18.
Films and Filming. Jan 1955, v1, p21.
The Films in My Life. p129-32.
Films in Review. Oct 1954, v5, p430-32.
Hollywood Reporter. Sep 27, 1954, p3.
Humphrey Bogart: The Man and His Films. p171.
Illustrated London News. Nov 27, 1954, v225, p962.
Joseph L. Mankiewicz (Dick). p107-13.
Kiss Kiss Bang Bang. p289.
The London Times. Nov 8, 1954, p10.
Magill's Cinema Annual, 1983. p399-402.
Motion Picture Herald Product Digest. Oct 2, 1954, p169.
National Parent-Teacher. Nov 1954, v49, p39.
The New Statesman and Nation. Nov 13, 1954, v48, p612.
The New York Times. Sep 30, 1954, p37.
The New Yorker. Oct 9, 1954, v30, p173.
Newsweek. Oct 4, 1954, v44, p86-87.
Pictures Will Talk. p340-53.
Saturday Review. Oct 23, 1954, v37, p31.
Sight and Sound. Jan-Mar 1955, v24, p146.
Talking Pictures. p243-46.
Time. Oct 18, 1954, v64, p102.
Variety. Sep 29, 1954, p6.

The Barefoot Executive (US; Butler, Robert; 1971)
BFI/Monthly Film Bulletin. May 1971, v38, p92.
Filmfacts. 1971, v14, p315-16.
Films in Review. Apr 1971, v22, n4, p234-35.
Hollywood Reporter. Feb 24, 1971, v215, n6, p3.
The New York Times. May 27, 1967, p33.
Variety. Feb 24, 1971, p18.
The Village Voice. Mar 25, 1971, v16, n12, p59.

Barefoot in the Park (US; Saks, Gene; 1967)
BFI/Monthly Film Bulletin. Aug 1967, v34, p119.
Commonweal. Jun 16, 1967, v86, p369.
Film Daily. May 24, 1967, p5.
Films and Filming. Jul 1967, v13, p21-22.
Films in Review. May 1967, v18, p310-11.
The Films of Jane Fonda. p137-41.
The Films of Robert Redford. p102-09.
The Films of the Sixties. p185-86.
Hollywood Reporter. May 24, 1967, p3.
Life. Jun 9, 1967, v62, p12.
Magill's Survey of Cinema. Series II. v1, p174-76.
Motion Picture Herald Product Digest. May 24, 1967, p687.
The New York Times. May 26, 1967, p51.
The New Yorker. Jun 10, 1967, v43, p72.
Saturday Review. Jun 3, 1967, v50, p43.
Time. Jun 9, 1967, v89, p111.
Variety. May 24, 1967, p6.
The Village Voice. Jun 15, 1967, p31.

The Barefoot Mailman (US; McEvoy, Earl; 1951)
Commonweal. Jan 18, 1952, v55, p374.
Film Daily. Nov 5, 1951, p6.
Hollywood Reporter. Nov 1, 1951, p4.
Library Journal. Nov 15, 1951, v76, p1948.
Motion Picture Herald Product Digest. Nov 10, 1951, p1102.
Time. Dec 17, 1951, v58, p104.
Variety. Nov 7, 1951, p6.

Bariera *See* Barrier

The Baron of Arizona (US; Fuller, Sam; 1950)
BFI/Monthly Film Bulletin. Sep 1950, v17, p139.
Film Daily. Feb 14, 1950, p6.
Hollywood Reporter. Feb 8, 1950, p3.
Motion Picture Herald Product Digest. Feb 18, 1950, p198.
The New York Times. Jun 23, 1950, p29.
Samuel Fuller (Hardy). p128-31.
Variety. Feb 15, 1950, p13.
Vincent Price: Unmasked. p183-84.

Barrier (Polish title: Bariera) (POL; Skolimowski, Jerzy; 1966)
BFI/Monthly Film Bulletin. Dec 1967, v34, p183.
Cahiers du Cinema in English. Dec 1967, n12, p6-16.
The London Times. Oct 26, 1967, p8.
Magill's Survey of Cinema. Foreign Language Films. v1, p224-27.
The New York Times. Sep 27, 1967, p39.
Variety. Dec 21, 1966, p7.

Barry Lyndon (US; Kubrick, Stanley; 1975)
American Cinematographer. Mar 1976, v52, p276-77.
Audience. Aug 1976, v9, p7.
Audience. Apr 1976, v8, p8-10.
Audience. Mar 1976, v8, p10-11.
Before My Eyes. p180.
BFI/Monthly Film Bulletin. Jan 1976, v43, p3-4.
Cinema Papers. Mar-Apr 1976, p363.
Commentary. Mar 1976, v61, p60-62.
Commonweal. Mar 26, 1976, v103, p208-09.
Commonweal. Apr 9, 1976, v103, p243-45.
The English Novel and the Movies. p95-107.
Fifty Classic British Films. p142-44.
Film Comment. Mar-Apr 1976, v12, p26-28.
Film Quarterly. Fall 1976, v30, p13, 49-54.
Filming Literature. p130-35.
Films and Filming. Feb 1976, v22, p33-34 .

Films Illustrated. Mar 1976, v5, p270.
Films Illustrated. Jan 1976, v5, p166.
Films in Review. Feb 1976, v21, p121-22.
Georgia Review. 1976, v30, n4, p827-53.
Kubrick (Ciment). p166-79.
The Los Angeles Times. Dec 19, 1975, SecIV, p1.
Magill's Survey of Cinema. Series I. v1, p132-34.
Media Montage. 1976, v1, n1, p29.
Medium. Oct 1976, v6, p29.
Modern Photography. Aug 1976, v40, p41-42.
Movietone News. Feb 1976, n48, p30-31.
The Nation. Jan 3, 1976, v222, p30.
National Review. Apr 16, 1976, v28, p399-400.
The New Republic. Jan 3, 1976, v174, p22-23.
New York. Dec 29, 1976, v9, p84-87.
The New York Review of Books. Feb 5, 1976, v23, p3-4.
The New York Times. Jan 11, 1976, SecII, p13.
The New York Times. Feb 29, 1976, SecII, p1.
The New Yorker. Dec 29, 1975, v51, p49-51.
Newsweek. Dec 22, 1976, v86, p49-50.
Penthouse. Apr 1976, v7, p54-55.
Quarterly Review of Film Studies. 1976, v1, n2, p141-54.
Saturday Review. Jan 10, 1976, v3, p61.
Sight and Sound. Sum 1976, v45, p77-80.
Society. Jul 1976, v13, p81-82.
Stanley Kubrick: A Film Odyssey. p173-80.
Stanley Kubrick: A Guide to References and Resources. p56-57.
Times Literary Supplement. Jan 9, 1976, n3852, p32.
Variety. Jan 14, 1976, p6.
Variety. Dec 17, 1975, p23.
When the Lights Go Down. p101-06.

Batman (US; Martinson, Leslie H.; 1966)
BFI/Monthly Film Bulletin. Jan 1967, v34, p8.
Film Daily. Jul 20, 1966, p6.
Filmfacts. Oct 15, 1966, v9, p225-26.
Films and Filming. Mar 1967, v13, p31-32.
Films and Filming. Apr 1966, v12, p6, 8.
Hollywood Reporter. Jul 18, 1966, p3.
The London Times. Feb 3, 1966, p18.
The London Times. Dec 8, 1966, p18.
Motion Picture Herald Product Digest. Aug 3, 1966, p570.
New Statesman. Dec 16, 1966, v72, p916.
The New York Times. Aug 25, 1966, p42.
The Spectator. Feb 18, 1966, v216, p199.
Variety. Jul 20, 1966, p6.

Battaglia di Algeri, La *See* The Battle of Algiers

Battle Cry (US; Walsh, Raoul; 1955)
America. Feb 19, 1955, v92, p547.
BFI/Monthly Film Bulletin. Jun 1955, v22, p82.
Catholic World. Mar 1955, v180, p464.
Commonweal. Feb 25, 1955, v61, p551.
Film Daily. Feb 1, 1955, p7.
Guts & Glory. p100-01.
Hollywood Reporter. Feb 1, 1955, v133, n10, p3.
The New York Times. Feb 3, 1955, p18.
The New York Times. Feb 6, 1955, SecII, p1.
The New Yorker. Feb 12, 1955, v30, p93.
Newsweek. Feb 14, 1955, v45, p91.
Saturday Review. Feb 19, 1955, v38, p25.
Time. Feb 14, 1955, v65, p102.
Variety. Feb 5, 1955, p6.

Battle Hell (Also titled: Yangtse Incident; Escape of the Amethyst) (GB; Anderson, Michael; 1957)
America. Sep 21, 1957, v97, p660.
BFI/Monthly Film Bulletin. May 1957, v24, p57.
Film Daily. Jul 10, 1957, p8.

Films and Filming. May 1957, v3, p24.
Films in Review. Oct 1957, v8, p407-08.
Hollywood Reporter. May 10, 1957, p4.
Motion Picture Herald Product Digest. May 25, 1957, p386.
The New York Times. Aug 22, 1957, p23.
Saturday Review. Sep 14, 1957, v40, p30.
Sight and Sound. Spr 1957, v26, p209.
Time. Sep 2, 1957, v70, p60.
Variety. Apr 10, 1957, p6.

Battle Hymn (US; Sirk, Douglas; 1957)
America. Mar 16, 1957, v96, p686.
BFI/Monthly Film Bulletin. Mar 1957, v24, p27-28.
Commonweal. Mar 8, 1957, v65, p591.
Film Daily. Dec 18, 1957, p6.
Films and Filming. Mar 1957, v3, p25.
Hollywood Reporter. Dec 18, 1956, p3.
The New York Times. Feb 16, 1957, p14.
The New York Times. Feb 24, 1957, SecII, p1.
The New Yorker. Feb 23, 1957, v33, p75.
Newsweek. Feb 25, 1957, v49, p119.
Saturday Review. Feb 16, 1957, v40, p28.
Time. Mar 11, 1957, v69, p98.
Variety. Dec 19, 1956, p7.

The Battle of Algiers (Italian title: Battaglia di Algeri, La) (IT, ALG; Pontecorvo, Gillo; 1966)
America. Nov 4, 1967, v117, p521.
BFI/Monthly Film Bulletin. Apr 1971, v38, p68.
Commonweal. Oct 20, 1967, v87, p88.
Esquire. Jan 1968, v69, p32.
Fifty Grand Movies of the 1960s and 1970s. p161-64.
Film Daily. Sep 25, 1967, p14.
Film Quarterly. Wint 1967, v21, p27-29, p37-41.
Film Quarterly. Spr 1969, v22, p26-31.
Harper's. Dec 1967, v235, p133.
Hollywood Reporter. Mar 16, 1967, p3.
The International Dictionary of Films and Filmmakers. v1, p47-48.
Life. Oct 27, 1967, v63, p16.
Magill's Survey of Cinema. Foreign Language Films. v1, p228-33.
Motion Picture Herald Product Digest. Oct 11, 1967, p730.
The Nation. Oct 9, 1967, v205, p348-49.
The New Republic. Dec 16, 1967, v157, p19.
The New York Times. Sep 21, 1967, p56.
The New Yorker. Sep 23, 1967, v43, p93.
Newsweek. Oct 23, 1967, v70, p102.
Reporter. Nov 2, 1967, v37, p52.
Saturday Review. Apr 22, 1967, v50, p75.
Sight and Sound. Sum 1971, v40, p160-61.
Take One. 1968, v1, p25-26.
Time. Sep 29, 1967, v90, p100-01.
Variety. Sep 7, 1966, p6.

The Battle of Britain (GB; Hamilton, Guy; 1969)
America. Nov 1, 1969, v121, p399-400.
The Battle of Britain: The Making of a Film. 1969.
Film Daily. Oct 9, 1969, p4.
Films and Filming. Nov 1969, v16, p41.
Films in Review. Nov 1969, v20, p569-71.
The Films of Laurence Olivier. p156-59.
Holiday. Dec 1969, v46, p30.
Laurence Olivier: Theater & Cinema. p191-96.
The New York Times. Oct 21, 1969, p38.
Saturday Review. Oct 25, 1969, v52, p32.
Senior Scholastic. Oct 27, 1969, v95, p24.
Time. Oct 24, 1969, v94, p102.
Variety. Sep 17, 1969, p13.

Battle of the Bulge (US; Annakin, Ken; 1965)
America. Jan 8, 1966, v114, p52.
BFI/Monthly Film Bulletin. Feb 1966, v33, p14.
Christian Science Monitor (Western edition). Jan 6, 1966, p4.
Cinema. Mar 1966, v3, p46-47.
Commonweal. Jan 28, 1966, v83, p507.
Film Daily. Dec 20, 1965, p3.
Film Library Quarterly. Sum 1968, v1, p50.
Films and Filming. Feb 1966, v12, p7-8.
Films in Review. Jan 1966, v17, p50-51.
The Films of Henry Fonda. p187-89.
Guts & Glory. p243.
Hollywood Reporter. Dec 17, 1965, p3.
The London Times. Dec 9, 1965, p13.
Motion Picture Herald Product Digest. Jan 5, 1966, p434.
New Statesman. Dec 10, 1965, v70, p946.
The New York Times. Dec 18, 1965, p36.
Newsweek. Jan 10, 1966, v67, p62.
Saturday Review. Jan 29, 1966, v49, p43.
Senior Scholastic. Feb 25, 1966, v88, p18.
The Spectator. Dec 10, 1965, v215, p780.
Time. Dec 31, 1965, v86, p77-78.
Variety. Dec 22, 1965, p6.

The Battle of the River Plate *See* Pursuit of the Graf Spee

Battle of the Sexes (GB; Crichton, Charles; 1960)
BFI/Monthly Film Bulletin. Feb 1960, v27, p18.
Commonweal. May 27, 1960, v72, p229.
Film Daily. Apr 25, 1960, p6.
Film Quarterly. Fall 1960, v14, p51-54.
Films and Filming. Feb 1960, p22.
The Nation. Apr 30, 1960, v190, p392.
The New York Times. Apr 19, 1960, p40.
The New York Times. May 1, 1960, SecII, p1.
The New Yorker. Apr 30, 1960, v36, p168-69.
Newsweek. May 2, 1960, v55, p89.
Time. May 2, 1960, v75, p34.

The Battle of the Villa Fiorita (GB; Daves, Delmer; 1965)
BFI/Monthly Film Bulletin. Sep 1964, v32, p130-31.
Christian Science Monitor (Western edition). Jun 17, 1965, p10.
Commonweal. Jun 18, 1965, v82, p414-15.
Film Daily. May 27, 1965, p7.
Films and Filming. Sep 1965, v11, p31-32.
Hollywood Reporter. May 24, 1965, p3.
The London Times. Aug 5, 1965, p5.
Motion Picture Herald Product Digest. Jun 9, 1965, p306.
The New York Times. May 27, 1965, p28.
Time. Jun 4, 1965, v85, p67.
Variety. May 26, 1965, p14.

Battle Stripe *See* The Men

Battle Zone (US; Selander, Lesley; 1952)
BFI/Monthly Film Bulletin. Aug 1953, v20, p120.
Hollywood Reporter. Oct 9, 1952, p4.
Motion Picture Herald Product Digest. Oct 18, 1952, p1565.
The New York Times. Nov 1, 1952, p17.
Variety. Oct 15, 1952, p6.

Bay of Angels (French title: Baie des Anges, La; Also titled: Bay of the Angels) (FR; Demy, Jacques; 1962)
BFI/Monthly Film Bulletin. Jul 1965, v32, p103.
Christian Science Monitor (Western edition). Feb 16, 1965, p10.

Commonweal. Dec 11, 1964, v81, p390.
Confessions of a Cultist. p171-72.
Film. 1964, n41, p21-23.
Film Comment. Wint 1965, v3, p72-73.
Film Daily. Nov 25, 1964, p4.
Film Society Review. Sep 1965, p14-15.
Filmfacts. 1964, v7, p264.
Films and Filming. Aug 1965, v11, p27.
The London Times. May 27, 1965, p16.
Motion Picture Herald Product Digest. Dec 9, 1964, p185-86.
Movie. Aut 1965, n14, p33-35.
The New Republic. Dec 19, 1964, v151, p28.
The New York Times. Nov 24, 1964, p44.
The New Yorker. Dec 5, 1964, v40, p156.
Private Screenings. p159-60.
Saturday Review. Dec 12, 1964, v47, p42.
Sight and Sound. Wint 1964-65, v34, p9-11.
Sight and Sound. Sum 1964, v33, p136-39.
The Spectator. Jun 11, 1965, v214, p758.
Time. Nov 27, 1964, v84, p109.
Variety. Mar 20, 1963, p18.
The Village Voice. Nov 26, 1964, v10, p19, 25.

Beach Blanket Bingo (US; Asher, William; 1965)
Film Daily. Jun 3, 1965, p6.
Hollywood Reporter. Apr 8, 1965, p3.
Motion Picture Herald Product Digest. Jun 23, 1965, p316.
Variety. Apr 7, 1965, p6.

Beach Party (US; Asher, William; 1963)
BFI/Monthly Film Bulletin. Sep 1964, v31, p132.
Film Daily. Jul 17, 1963, p6.
Film Quarterly. Spr 1964, v17, p61.
Filmfacts. Sep 5, 1963, p177-78.
The Films of the Sixties. p99.
Hollywood Reporter. Jul 15, 1963, v176, p3.
The New York Times. Sep 26, 1963, p40.
Time. Aug 16, 1963, v82, p74.
Variety. Jul 17, 1963, p6.

Beachhead (US; Heisler, Stuart; 1954)
BFI/Monthly Film Bulletin. Jun 1954, v21, p86.
Film Daily. Jan 28, 1954, p12.
Hollywood Reporter. Jan 28, 1954, p3.
Library Journal. Feb 15, 1954, v79, p314.
Motion Picture Herald Product Digest. Jan 30, 1954, p2165.
National Parent-Teacher. Apr 1954, v48, p38.
The New York Times. Apr 17, 1954, p8.
Newsweek. Mar 1, 1954, v43, p80.
Time. Apr 19, 1954, v63, p104.
Tony Curtis: The Man and His Movies. p46-47.
Variety. Feb 3, 1954, p6.

Beat the Devil (US; Huston, John; 1954)
American Film. Sep 1980, v5, p45.
BFI/Monthly Film Bulletin. Jan 1954, v21, p2.
Catholic World. Apr 1954, v179, p63-64.
The Cinema of John Huston. p98-102.
Cinema, the Magic Vehicle. v2, p180-81.
Commonweal. Mar 19, 1954, v59, p600.
The Complete Films of Humphrey Bogart. p170-72.
Coronet. Apr 1954, v35, p6.
Farm Journal. May 1954, v78, p137.
Film Comment. May-Jun 1980, v16, p25-56.
Film Daily. Mar 3, 1954, p10.
Film Society Review. Jan 1966, p13.
Films in Review. Mar 1954, v5, p143-44.
The Films of Jennifer Jones. p117-22.
The Films of Peter Lorre. p205-07.
Hollywood Reporter. Mar 2, 1954, p3.
Humphrey Bogart: The Man and His Films. p164-66.
John Huston (Hammen). p71-75.
Kiss Kiss Bang Bang. p290-91.
Library Journal. Mar 1, 1954, v79, p444.

Look. Sep 22, 1953, v17, p128-29.
Magill's Survey of Cinema. Series II. v1, p190-92.
Millimeter. Dec 1975, v3, p56-57.
Motion Picture Herald Product Digest. Mar 6, 1954, p2205-06.
Movie Comedy (Byron). p107-09.
National Parent-Teacher. Apr 1954, v48, p38.
The New Statesman and Nation. Dec 5, 1953, v46, p715.
The New York Times. Mar 13, 1954, p11.
The New York Times Magazine. Sep 27, 1953, p32-33.
The New Yorker. Mar 20, 1954, v30, p118.
Newsweek. Mar 8, 1954, v43, p82.
Saturday Review. Mar 13, 1954, v37, p28.
Senior Scholastic. Mar 10, 1954, v64, p27.
Sight and Sound. Jan-Mar 1954, v23, p147-48.
Time. Mar 8, 1954, v63, p94.
Variety. Dec 2, 1953, p6.

Beau Brummell (GB; Bernhardt, Curtis; 1954)
America. Oct 30, 1954, v92, p138.
BFI/Monthly Film Bulletin. Jan 1955, v22, p2.
Farm Journal. Dec 1954, v78, p141.
Film Daily. Oct 6, 1954, p6.
Films and Filming. Jan 1955, v1, p19.
Films in Review. Nov 1954, v5, p483-84.
The Films of Elizabeth Taylor. p110-14.
Hollywood Reporter. Oct 6, 1954, p3.
Illustrated London News. Nov 27, 1954, v225, p962.
Library Journal. Nov 1, 1954, v79, p2095.
Life. Oct 18, 1954, v37, p115-16.
Motion Picture Herald Product Digest. Oct 16, 1954, p179.
National Parent-Teacher. Dec 1954, v49, p39.
The New Statesman and Nation. Nov 27, 1954, v48, p693.
The New York Times. Oct 21, 1954, p31.
The New Yorker. Oct 30, 1954, v30, p126.
Newsweek. Oct 25, 1954, v44, p102.
Saturday Review. Oct 23, 1954, v37, p33.
The Tatler. Dec 1, 1954, v214, p570.
Time. Oct 18, 1954, v64, p102.
Variety. Oct 6, 1954, p6.

Beau Geste (US; Heyes, Douglas; 1966)
America. Sep 17, 1966, v115, p298.
BFI/Monthly Film Bulletin. Nov 1966, v33, p167.
Christian Science Monitor (Western edition). Sep 19, 1966, p6.
Cinema. Dec 1966, v3, p47.
Film Daily. Jul 20, 1966, p7.
Filmfacts. Nov 1, 1966, v9, p240-41.
Films and Filming. Dec 1966, v13, p16, 18.
Hollywood Reporter. Jul 20, 1966, p3.
Motion Picture Herald Product Digest. Aug 3, 1966, p569.
The New York Times. Sep 8, 1966, p43.
Senior Scholastic. Oct 7, 1966, v89, p26.
Variety. Jul 20, 1966, p6.

Beau James (US; Shavelson, Melville; 1957)
America. Jul 6, 1957, v97, p392.
BFI/Monthly Film Bulletin. Jun 1957, v24, p66.
Commonweal. Jul 12, 1957, v66, p377.
Film Daily. Jun 7, 1957, p8.
Films and Filming. Sep 1957, v3, p26.
Films in Review. Jun-Jul 1957, v8, p282-83.
Hollywood Reporter. Jun 7, 1957, p3.
Motion Picture Herald Product Digest. Jun 15, 1957, p417.
The New York Times. Jun 27, 1957, p21.
The New Yorker. Jul 6, 1957, v33, p58.
Newsweek. Jul 1, 1957, v50, p77.

Time. Jul 1, 1957, v70, p80.
Variety. Jun 12, 1957, p6.

Beau Mariage, Le (FR; Rohmer, Eric; 1982)
BFI/Monthly Film Bulletin. Nov 1982, v49, p254-60.
Hollywood Reporter. Aug 26, 1982, p2.
The Los Angeles Times. Nov 2, 1982, SecVI, p2.
Magill's Cinema Annual, 1983. p65-67.
The Nation. Sep 25, 1982, v235, p284-85.
National Review. Oct 15, 1982, v34, p1293-94.
The New Republic. Oct 4, 1982, v187, p24-25.
New Statesman. Nov 19, 1982, v104, p30-31.
New York. Aug 30, 1982, v15, p62.
The New York Times. Aug 27, 1982, SecIII, p6.
The New Yorker. Oct 4, 1982, v58, p140-41.
Newsweek. Sep 20, 1982, v100, p92.
Time. Aug 30, 1982, v120, p89.
Variety. Jul 28, 1982, p20.
The Village Voice. Aug 31, 1987, p43.

Beau Pere (FR; Blier, Bertrand; 1981)
Hollywood Reporter. Jan 12, 1982, p82.
The Los Angeles Times. Oct 20, 1981, SecVI, p4.
The New Leader. Nov 16, 1981, v64, p18.
New Statesman. Nov 27, 1981, v102, p32-33.
New York. Nov 2, 1981, v14, p58-60.
The New York Times. Oct 9, 1981, p20.
Newsweek. Oct 19, 1981, v98, p93.
Saturday Review. Nov 1981, v8, p57.
Time. Nov 9, 1981, v119, p98.
Variety. May 27, 1981, p18.

Beau Serge, Le (Also titled: Handsome Serge) (FR; Chabrol, Claude; 1958)
Boxoffice. Sep 25, 1961, p10.
Filmfacts. Sep 16, 1959, v2, p194.
The Films in My Life. p313-14.
Films in Review. Oct 1959, v10, p495-96.
Magill's Survey of Cinema. Foreign Language Films. v1, p234-37.
The New York Times. Aug 3, 1959, p21.
Variety. Jun 4, 1958, p6.

Beaute du Diable, La (Also titled: Beauty and the Devil) (FR, IT; Clair, René; 1949)
BFI/Monthly Film Bulletin. Dec 1950, v17, p182.
Cinema, the Magic Vehicle. v1, p501-02.
Dictionary of Films. p27.
Film Daily. Dec 8, 1952, p6.
Film Society Review. Sep 1965, p12-13.
Films in Review. Jan 1951, v2, p19-20.
Films in Review. Oct 1952, v3, p417-18.
Magill's Survey of Cinema. Foreign Language Films. v1, p248-52.
Motion Picture Herald Product Digest. Aug 30, 1952, p1510-11.
The New Statesman and Nation. Nov 11, 1951, v40, p424.
Newsweek. Sep 8, 1952, v40, p96.
René Clair (McGerr). p170-74.
Saturday Review. Sep 13, 1952, v35, p34.
Sequence. New Year 1951, n13, p14-15.
Sight and Sound. Mar 1950, v19, p10-11.
Sight and Sound. Dec 1950, v19, p331, 339.
Theatre Arts. Jul 1951, v35, p34-35.
Theatre Arts. Nov 1952, v36, p93.
Time. Sep 15, 1952, v60, p109.
Variety. Apr 19, 1950, p8.

Beauties of the Night *See* Belles-de-Nuit, Les

Beautiful Stranger *See* Twist of Fate

Beauty and the Devil *See* Beaute du Diable, La

Because of You (US; Pevney, Joseph; 1952)
BFI/Monthly Film Bulletin. Nov 1952, v19, p156.
Commonweal. Dec 19, 1952, v57, p284.
Film Daily. Oct 9, 1952, p6.
Hollywood Reporter. Oct 9, 1952, p3.
McCall's. Nov 1952, v80, p8.
Motion Picture Herald Product Digest. Oct 11, 1952, p1558.
National Parent-Teacher. Dec 1952, v47, p36.
The New York Times. Dec 4, 1952, p47.
Newsweek. Dec 15, 1952, v40, p102.
Variety. Oct 8, 1952, p12.

Because You're Mine (US; Hall, Alexander; 1952)
BFI/Monthly Film Bulletin. Dec 1952, v19, p169-70.
Christian Century. Nov 12, 1952, v69, p1335.
Film Daily. Sep 11, 1952, p6.
Hollywood Reporter. Aug 29, 1952, p3.
Motion Picture Herald Product Digest. Sep 6, 1952, p1517.
National Parent-Teacher. Oct 1952, v47, p36.
The New York Times. Sep 26, 1952, p18.
The New Yorker. Oct 4, 1953, v28, p74.
Newsweek. Oct 13, 1952, v40, p100.
The Spectator. Oct 31, 1952, v189, p565.
Time. Oct 13, 1952, v60, p108.
Variety. Sep 3, 1952, p12.

Beckett (GB; Glenville, Peter; 1964)
America. Mar 21, 1964, v110, p379-80.
BFI/Monthly Film Bulletin. May 31, 1964, v31, p66-67.
Christian Century. Sep 9, 1964, v81, p1112-13.
Commonweal. Mar 13 1964, v79, p722.
Film Daily. Mar 4, 1964, v124, p6-7.
Films and Filming. May 1964, v10, p21.
Films in Review. Apr 1964, v15, p237-39.
The Films of the Sixties. p124-24.
Hollywood Reporter. Mar 4, 1964, v179, p3.
Life. Mar 13, 1964, v58, p81-82.
Magill's Survey of Cinema. Series I. v1, p138-40.
Motion Picture Herald Product Digest. Mar 18, 1964, v231, p28, 36.
The New Republic. Mar 14, 1964, v150, p26-27.
The New York Times. Mar 12, 1964, p40.
The New Yorker. Mar 14, 1964, v40, p155.
Newsweek. Mar 23, 1964, v63, p95.
The Private Eye, The Cowboy and the Very Naked Girl. p67-70.
Saturday Review. Mar 7, 1964, v47, p24-25.
Time. Mar 20, 1964, v83, p94-95.
Variety. Mar 4, 1964, p6.

Bed and Board (French title: Domicile Conjugal) (FR; Truffaut, François; 1971)
The Adventures of Antoine Doinel. p260-325.
America. Feb 6, 1971, v124, p128.
BFI/Monthly Film Bulletin. Aug 1971, v38, p163.
Filmfacts. 1971, v16, n2, p21.
Films and Filming. Sep 1971, v17, n12, p36-37.
Films in Review. Mar 1971, v22, n3, p171-73.
François Truffaut: A Guide to References and Resources. p65-67.
François Truffaut (Insdorf). p77-85.
Hollywood Reporter. Jan 20, 1971, v214, n32, p3.
The Nation. Mar 1, 1971, v212, p284.
National Review. Jun 15, 1971, v23, p662.
The New Republic. Feb 13, 1971, v164, p24.
The New York Times. Jan 22, 1971, p16.
The New York Times. Jan 24, 1971, SecII, p1.

The New Yorker. Feb 6, 1971, v46, p89.
Newsweek. Jan 25, 1971, v77, p79.
Saturday Review. Jan 23, 1971, v54, p84.
Sight and Sound. Aut 1971, v40, n4, p225-26.
Take One. Nov-Dec 1969, v11, n8, p20.
Time. Feb 8, 1971, v97, p82.
Variety. Aug 26, 1970, p16.
The Village Voice. Jan 28, 1971, v16, n4, p61.

The Bed Sitting Room (GB; Lester, Richard; 1969)
Deeper Into Movies. p20-21.
Figures of Light. p204-06.
Films and Filming. May 1970, v16, p42.
The Nation. Oct 27, 1969, v209, p452.
The New Republic. Oct 18, 1969, v161, p22.
The New York Times. Sep 29, 1969, p53.
The New Yorker. Oct 11, 1969, v65, p159.
Newsweek. Nov 3, 1969, v74, p97-97A.
Richard Lester: A Guide to References and Resources. p34-35.
Variety. Jul 16, 1969, p6.

Bedazzled (GB; Donen, Stanley; 1967)
America. Feb 3, 1968, v118, p166-67.
BFI/Monthly Film Bulletin. Jan 1968, v35, p2.
Commonweal. Feb 9, 1968, v87, p564.
Film Daily. Dec 11, 1967, p8.
Films and Filming. Jan 1968, v14, p26-27.
Films in Review. Jan 1968, v19, p55-56.
Hollywood Reporter. Dec 8, 1967, p3.
Life. Jan 26, 1968, v64, p8.
Motion Picture Herald Product Digest. Dec 20, 1967, p752.
The Nation. Jan 1, 1968, v206, p28.
The New Republic. Jan 6, 1968, v158, p30.
The New York Times. Dec 11, 1967, p65.
Reporter. May 16, 1968, v38, p33.
Saturday Review. Jan 6, 1968, v51, p38.
Stanley Donen (Casper). p186-91.
Variety. Dec 13, 1967, p6.
The Village Voice. Dec 21, 1967, p39.

The Bedford Incident (Also titled: Aux Postes de Combat) (GB; Harris, James B.; 1965)
America. Nov 13, 1965, v113, p609-10.
BFI/Monthly Film Bulletin. Nov 1965, v32, p160.
Cahiers du Cinema in English. 1966, n5, p56.
Christian Science Monitor (Western edition). Nov 13, 1965, p6.
Cinema. Dec 1965, v3, p28-31.
Film Daily. Oct 11, 1965, p12.
Film Quarterly. Spr 1966, v19, p51.
Films and Filming. Mar 1966, v12, p57-58.
The Films of Sidney Poitier. p122-24.
Guts & Glory. p205-10.
Hollywood Reporter. Oct 11, 1965, p3.
Life. Nov 5, 1965, v59, p22.
The London Times. Oct 14, 1965, p16.
Motion Picture Herald Product Digest. Oct 27, 1965, p393.
The New York Times. Nov 3, 1965, p43.
The New Yorker. Nov 6, 1965, v41, p122.
Newsweek. Nov 22, 1965, v66, p108.
Nuclear War Films. p76-80.
Playboy. Nov 1965, v12, p56-57.
Redbook. Nov 1965, v126, p48.
Saturday Review. Nov 13, 1965, v48, 73.
Saturday Review. Dec 4, 1965, v48, p75.
Variety. Oct 13, 1965, p6.

Bedknobs and Broomsticks (US; Stevenson, Robert; 1971)
BFI/Monthly Film Bulletin. Nov 1971, v38, p216.
Filmfacts. 1971, v14, n24, p701.
Films and Filming. Dec 1971, v18, n3, p54.
Films in Review. Dec 1971, v22, n10, p640-42.

Hollywood Reporter. Nov 9, 1971, v218, n35, p3.
The New York Times. Nov 12, 1971, p54.
The New Yorker. Dec 11, 1971, v47, p138-39.
Saturday Evening Post. Sum 1971, v243, p86-87.
Variety. Oct 13, 1971, p16.

Bedtime For Bonzo (US; De Cordova, Frederick; 1951)
Cult Movies. p18-20.
Film Daily. Jan 15, 1951, p6.
The Films of Ronald Reagan. p179-81.
Hollywood Reporter. Jan 15, 1951, p3.
Magill's Cinema Annual, 1984. p512-16.
Motion Picture Herald Product Digest. Jan 20, 1951, p669.
The New York Times. Apr 6, 1951, p31.
Newsweek. Mar 12, 1951, v37, p87.
Senior Scholastic. Feb 28, 1951, v58, p19.
Variety. Jan 17, 1951, p11.
The Village Voice. Dec 18, 1984, p82.
The Village Voice. Apr 23, 1985, p51.

Bedtime Story (US; Levy, Ralph; 1964)
BFI/Monthly Film Bulletin. Jul 1964, v31, p102.
Commonweal. Jun 19, 1964, v80, p399.
Film Daily. Jun 2, 1964, v124, p4.
Films and Filming. Sep 1964, v10, p17-18.
Films in Review. Aug-Sep 1964, v15, p444.
The Films of David Niven. p189-93.
The Films of Marlon Brando. p150-55.
Hollywood Reporter. Jun 2, 1964, v180, p3.
Motion Picture Herald Product Digest. Jun 10, 1964, v231, p65.
The New Republic. Jul 4, 1964, v151, p29.
The New York Times. Jun 11, 1964, p27.
Newsweek. Jun 22, 1964, v63, p84.
Saturday Review. Jun 13, 1964, v47, p45.
Time. Jun 26, 1964, v83, p91-92.
Variety. Jun 3, 1964, p6.

Been Down So Long It Looks Like Up to Me (US; Young, Jeff; 1971)
Filmfacts. 1971, v14, p476-78.
Hollywood Reporter. Sep 9, 1971, v217, n44, p3.
The New York Times. Sep 16, 1971, p52.
Variety. Sep 8, 1971, p6.
The Village Voice. Oct 7, 1971, p67.

Before the Revolution (Italian title: Prima della Rivoluzione) (IT; Bertolucci, Bernardo; 1964)
Bernardo Bertolucci (Kolker). p40-68.
Cinema Journal. 1984, v23, n2, p4-28.
Confessions of a Cultist. p201-02.
Film. 1964, n41, p17-19.
Film Comment. May-Jun 1974, v10, p22.
Film Quarterly. Fall 1966, v20, p55-57.
Film Society Review. Sep 1966, p15-17.
Films and Filming. May 1969, v15, p39-40.
Films in Review. Aug-Sep 1965, v16, p452.
International Film Guide. 1967, v4, p109.
Italian Cinema (Bondanella). p189-90.
Kiss Kiss Bang Bang. p151-53.
Life. Aug 13, 1965, v59, p12.
Literature/Film Quarterly. Jul 1976, v4, p215-21.
Magill's Survey of Cinema. Foreign Language Films. v1, p258-61.
Massachusetts Review. 1975, v16, n4, p807-28.
Motion Picture Herald Product Digest. Aug 4, 1965, p339.
The New Italian Cinema. p84-87.
The New York Times. Sep 25, 1964, p32.
The New Yorker. Aug 7, 1965, v41, p66.
Newsweek. Aug 2, 1965, v66, p66-67.
Variety. May 6, 1964, p16.

The Village Voice. Oct 8, 1964, p15-16.
The Village Voice. Jul 22, 1965, p14, 16.

The Beguiled (US; Siegel, Don; 1971)
BFI/Monthly Film Bulletin. Jan 1971, v39, p3.
Clint Eastwood (Guérif). p77-80.
Commonweal. Jun 11, 1971, v94, p310.
Film Heritage. Wint 1971-72, v7, n2, p15-20.
Filmfacts. 1971, v14, p48-50.
The Films of Clint Eastwood. p117-23.
The Films of The Seventies. p40-41.
Hollywood Reporter. Mar 8, 1971, p3.
Magill's Survey of Cinema. Series I. v1, p141-45.
The New York Times. Apr 1, 1971, p48.
Newsweek. Apr 19, 1971, v77, p126.
Time. Apr 12, 1971, v97, p94.
Variety. Mar 10, 1971, p16.
The Village Voice. Apr 8, 1971, p61.

Behold a Pale Horse (US; Zinnemann, Fred; 1964)
America. Sep 5, 1964, v111, p240.
BFI/Monthly Film Bulletin. Nov 1964, v31, p158-59.
Catholic World. Oct 1964, v200, p67-68.
Commonweal. Aug 21, 1964, v80, p579.
Film Daily. Aug 14, 1964, p6.
Films and Filming. Nov 1964, v11, p24.
Films in Review. Oct 1964, v15, p500-01.
The Films of Anthony Quinn. p200-01.
The Films of Gregory Peck. p191-93.
Hollywood Reporter. Aug 14, 1964, v181, p3.
Life. Aug 21, 1964, v57, p12.
Motion Picture Herald Product Digest. Aug 19, 1964, v232, p113.
The New York Times. Aug 14, 1964, p16.
The New Yorker. Aug 29, 1964, v40, p78.
Newsweek. Aug 24, 1964, v64, p79.
Saturday Review. Aug 8, 1964, v47, p24.
Sight and Sound. Aut 1964, v33, p198.
Time. Aug 28, 1964, v84, p70.
Variety. Aug 19, 1964, p6.

Being There (US; Ashby, Hal; 1979)
America. Feb 23, 1980, v142, p149.
BFI/Monthly Film Bulletin. Jul 1980, v47, p124.
Commonweal. Feb 29, 1980, v107, p117-18.
Films in Review. Mar 1980, v31, p176.
The Films of Shirley MacLaine. p179-82.
Hollywood Reporter. Dec 17, 1979, p3.
The Los Angeles Times. Dec 28, 1979, SecIV, p1.
Magill's Survey of Cinema. Series I. v6, p145-48.
Motion Picture Herald Product Digest. Jan 23, 1979, p65.
The Nation. Jan 26, 1980, v230, p91-92.
The Nation. Feb 2, 1980, v230, p122-24.
New York. Jan 14, 1980, v13, p69-70.
The New York Times. Dec 20, 1979, SecIII, p20.
Saturday Review. Mar 1, 1980, v7, p34.
Time. Mar 3, 1980, v115, p64-68.
Variety. Dec 19, 1979, p19.

Bella Mugnaia, La *See* The Miller's Beautiful Wife

Belle de Jour (FR; IT; Buñuel, Luis; 1966)
America. May 25, 1968, v118, p716.
Christian Century. Jul 31, 1968, v85, p969-70.
Cineaste. Wint 1967-68, v1, p23.
Cinema. 1969, v5, n1, p44.
The Cinema of Luis Buñuel. p165-75.
The Classic Cinema. 295-316.
Commonweal. May 10, 1968, v88, p240.
Confessions of a Cultist. p353-59.
The Discreet Art of Luis Buñuel. p195-20.
Esquire. Feb 1968, v69, p20.

Senior Scholastic. Feb 17, 1954, v64, p30.
Time. Dec 28, 1953, v62, p56.
Variety. Dec 16, 1953, p6.

Bengal Brigade (US; Benedek, Laslo; 1954)
America. Nov 20, 1954, v92, p222.
Farm Journal. Dec 1954, v78, p141.
Film Daily. Oct 21, 1954, p6.
Films in Review. Nov 1955, v6, p449-51.
Hollywood Reporter. Oct 19, 1954, p3.
Library Journal. Oct 1, 1954, v79, p1755.
Motion Picture Herald Product Digest. Oct 23, 1954, p185.
National Parent-Teacher. Oct 1954, v49, p39.
The New York Times. Nov 13, 1954, p13.
Time. Dec 6, 1954, v64, p116.
Variety. Oct 20, 1954, p6.

Ben-Hur (US; Wyler, William; 1959)
America. Dec 5, 1959, v102, p333-34.
BFI/Monthly Film Bulletin. Feb 1960, v27, p18.
Christian Century. Jan 13, 1960, v77, p51-52.
Classic Movies. p136-37.
Commonweal. Dec 11, 1959, v77, p320-21.
Cosmopolitan. Dec 1959, v147, p26-29.
Fifty from the Fifties. p45-54.
Film Daily. Nov 18, 1959, p5.
Filmfacts. Dec 16, 1959, v2, p275-78.
Films in Review. Dec 1959, v10, p617-20.
The Films of Charlton Heston. p100-17.
The Films of the Fifties. p262-65.
Hollywood Reporter. Nov 18, 1959, p3.
Magill's Survey of Cinema. Series I. v1, p149-54.
Make It Again, Sam. p32-37.
McCall's. Feb 1960, v87, p6.
The New Republic. Dec 28, 1959, v141, p27.
The New York Times. Nov 19, 1959, p50.
The New Yorker. Dec 5, 1959, v35, p153-54.
Newsweek. Nov 30, 1959, v54, p65.
On Movies. p136-37.
Saturday Review. Dec 5, 1959, v42, p32.
Senior Scholastic. Jan 13, 1960, v75, p33.
Time. Nov 30, 1959, v74, p55.
Variety. Nov 18, 1959, p6.
Vintage Films. p179-83.
William Wyler: A Guide to References and Resources. p144-48.
William Wyler (Madsen). p43-46.

Benjamin, or The Diary of an Innocent Young Boy (French title: Benjamin, ou Les Memoires d'un Puceau; Memoires d'un Puceau, Les; Also titled: Innocent Young Man) (FR; Deville, Michel; 1968)
BFI/Monthly Film Bulletin. Feb 1969, v36, p31.
Commonweal. Apr 12, 1968, v88, p104.
Film Daily. Mar 27, 1968, p6.
Filmfacts. Apr 15, 1968, v11, p100-02.
Films and Filming. May 1968, v14, p54-56.
Films and Filming. Mar 1969, v15, p47.
Films in Review. Apr 1968, v19, p245-46.
Going Steady. p86-88.
Hollywood Reporter. Mar 25, 1968, p3.
The London Times. Jan 16, 1969, p11.
Motion Picture Herald Product Digest. Apr 3, 1968, p791.
The New Republic. Apr 13, 1968, v158, p24.
The New York Times. Mar 26, 1968, p41.
The New Yorker. Feb 3, 1968, v43, p80.
The New Yorker. Mar 30, 1968, v44, p114.
Newsweek. Apr 8, 1968, v7, p120.
Sight and Sound. Spr 1968, v37, p74.
Variety. Jan 24, 1968, p6.
The Village Voice. Mar 28, 1968, p47.
A Year In the Dark. p94-95.

The Berliner (Also titled: The Ballad of Berlin; Berliner Ballade) (WGER; Stemmle, Robert A.; 1948)
Commonweal. Nov 14, 1952, v57, p142.
Film Daily. Dec 3, 1952, p6.
The German Cinema (Manvell and Fraenkel). p108-09.
The Great German Films. p243-45.
Motion Picture Herald Product Digest. Nov 1, 1952, p1590.
The New York Times. Oct 28, 1952, p37.
Newsweek. Nov 10, 1952, v40, p108.
Theatre Arts. Dec 1952, v36, p86.

Bernardine (US; Levin, Henry; 1957)
America. Aug 3, 1957, v97, p472.
BFI/Monthly Film Bulletin. Oct 1957, v24, p125-26.
Film Daily. Jun 25, 1957, p14.
Films and Filming. Sep 1957, v3, p27.
Films in Review. Aug-Sep 1957, v8, p356.
The Films of the Fifties. p239-40.
Hollywood Reporter. Jun 21, 1957, p3.
Motion Picture Herald Product Digest. Jun 29, 1957, v207, p433.
The New York Times. Jul 25, 1957, p28.
Newsweek. Aug 5, 1957, v50, p94.
Variety. Jul 3, 1957, p6.

The Best Little Whorehouse in Texas (US; Higgins, Colin; 1982)
Hollywood Reporter. Jul 21, 1982, p3.
The Los Angeles Times. Jul 24, 1982, SecVI, p1.
Maclean's. Aug 2, 1982, v95, p50-51.
Magill's Cinema Annual, 1983. p72-75.
New York. Aug 2, 1982, v15, p47.
The New Yorker. Aug 9, 1982, v58, p79-81.
Newsweek. Jul 26, 1982, v100, p79.
Rolling Stone. Sep 2, 1982, p33.
Time. Jul 26, 1982, v120, p44-45.
Variety. Jul 20, 1982, p3.

The Best Man (US; Schaffner, Franklin J.; 1964)
BFI/Monthly Film Bulletin. Oct 1964, v31, p144.
Commonweal. Apr 24, 1964, v80, p147.
Esquire. Jun 1964, v61, p18.
Film Daily. Apr 1, 1964, v124, p4.
Films in Review. May 1964, p301-03.
The Films of Henry Fonda. p174-76.
The Fondas (Springer). p199.
Hollywood Reporter. Apr 11, 1964, v179, p3.
Magill's Survey of Cinema. Series II. v1, p199-201.
Motion Picture Herald Product Digest. Apr 15, 1964, p26.
The New Republic. Apr 18, 1964, v150, p24.
The New York Times. Apr 7, 1964, p29.
The New Yorker. Apr 18, 1964, v40, p118.
Saturday Review. Apr 4, 1964, v47, p36.
Sight and Sound. Aut 1964, v33, p198.
Variety. Apr 1, 1964, p6.
Vogue. Apr 15, 1964, v143, p52.

The Best of Enemies (Italian title: Due Nemici, I; Also titled: The Two Enemies) (GB, IT; Hamilton, Guy; 1962)
America. Aug 4, 1962, v107, p572.
BFI/Monthly Film Bulletin. Jan 1962, v29, p4.
Commonweal. Sep 7, 1962, v76, p498.
Film Daily. Aug 3, 1962, p4.
Filmfacts. Sep 14, 1962, v5, p198-200.
Films and Filming. Jan 1962, v8, p31.
The Films of David Niven. p172-73.
Hollywood Reporter. Aug 3, 1962, p3.
Motion Picture Herald Product Digest. Aug 8, 1962, p634.

The New Republic. Sep 10, 1962, v147, p29.
The New York Times. Aug 7, 1962, p35.
The New Yorker. Aug 18, 1962, v38, p69.
Newsweek. Aug 13, 1962, v60, p82.
Saturday Review. Jul 14, 1962, v45, p16.
Time. Aug 10, 1962, v80, p68.
Variety. Dec 20, 1961, p7.

The Best of Everything (US; Negulesco, Jean; 1959)
America. Oct 24, 1959, v102, p111-12.
BFI/Monthly Film Bulletin. Dec 1959, v26, p154.
Commonweal. Nov 6, 1959, v71, p185.
Double Takes. p21.
Film Daily. Oct 8, 1959, p6.
Filmfacts. Nov 18, 1959, v2, p247-49.
Films in Review. Nov 1959, v10, p558.
Hollywood Reporter. Oct 8, 1959, p3.
The New Republic. Nov 2, 1959, v141, p22.
The New York Times. Oct 9, 1959, p24.
Newsweek. Oct 19, 1959, v54, p108.
Saturday Review. Oct 31, 1959, v42, p24.
Time. Oct 26, 1959, v74, p59.
Variety. Oct 14, 1959, p6.

Besuch, Der *See* The Visit

Bete S'eveille, La *See* The Sleeping Tiger

Betrayal (GB; Jones, David; 1983)
America. May 21, 1983, v148, p402.
Christian Century. Apr 13, 1983, v100, p346-40.
Commonweal. Jul 15, 1983, v110, p399-401.
Films in Review. Apr 1983, v34, p239.
Hollywood Reporter. Feb 16, 1983, p3.
The Los Angeles Times. Mar 9, 1983, SecVI, p1.
Maclean's. Feb 28, 1983, v96, p50.
Magill's Cinema Annual, 1984. p67-73.
The Nation. Mar 12, 1983, v236, p315-16.
National Review. Aug 5, 1983, v35, p951-52.
The New Republic. Feb 28, 1983, v188, p22-23.
New York. Feb 21, 1983, v16, p62-63.
New York. Feb 28, 1983, v16, p84.
The New York Times. Feb 20, 1983, SecI, p78.
The New Yorker. Jul 11, 1983, v59, p95.
Newsweek. Feb 28, 1983, v101, p74.
Progressive. May 1983, v47, p51.
Time. Mar 7, 1983, v121, p84.
Vogue. Mar 1983, v173, p100.

Betrayed (US; Reinhardt, Gottfried; 1954)
America. Sep 11, 1954, v91, p574.
BFI/Monthly Film Bulletin. Oct 1954, v21, p146.
Commonweal. Oct 1, 1954, v60, p632.
Farm Journal. Oct 1954, v78, p137.
Film Daily. Jul 27, 1954, p6.
Films and Filming. Oct 1954, v1, p29.
The Films of Clark Gable. p232-34.
The Films of Lana Turner. p191-93.
Hollywood Reporter. Jul 19, 1954, p3.
The London Times. Aug 23, 1954, p10.
Motion Picture Herald Product Digest. Jul 24, 1954, p81.
National Parent-Teacher. Sep 1954, v49, p38.
The New York Times. Sep 9, 1954, p36.
Newsweek. Sep 27, 1954, v44, p98.
The Tatler. Sep 1, 1954, v213, p372.
Time. Sep 20, 1954, v64, p111.
Variety. Jul 21, 1954, p6.

The Betsy (US; Petrie, Daniel; 1978)
BFI/Monthly Film Bulletin. May 1978, v45, p84.
Films in Review. Jun-Jul 1978, v29, p372.
Hollywood Reporter. Feb 8, 1978, p3.
The Los Angeles Times. Feb 10, 1978, SecIV, p30.
Maclean's. Mar 6, 1978, v91, p67.

Motion Picture Herald Product Digest. Feb 22, 1978, p73.
The New York Times. Feb 10, 1978, SecIII, p5.
The New Yorker. Feb 27, 1978, v54, p87.
Newsweek. Feb 20, 1978, v91, p90.
Time. Feb 27, 1978, v111, p62.
Variety. Feb 15, 1978, p19.

Beverly Hills Cop (US; Brest, Martin; 1984)
BFI/Monthly Film Bulletin. Mar 1985, v52, p76.
Chatelaine. Feb 1985, v58, p4.
Commentary. Mar 1985, v79, p63.
Esquire. Jan 1985, v103, p112.
Films in Review. Feb 1985, v36, p108.
Hollywood Reporter. Nov 30, 1984, p3.
Jet. Jan 21, 1985, v67, p56-59.
Los Angeles. Jan 1985, v30, p34.
The Los Angeles Times. Dec 5, 1984, SecVI, p1.
Maclean's. Dec 24, 1984, v60, p78.
Magill's Cinema Annual, 1985. p88-92.
The New Republic. Dec 31, 1984, v191, p24.
New Statesman. Apr 26, 1985, v109, p37.
New Statesman. Mar 22, 1985, v109, p30.
New York. Dec 10, 1984, v17, p94.
The New York Times. Dec 5, 1984, SecIII, p25.
The New Yorker. Dec 24, 1984, v60, p78.
Newsweek. Dec 3, 1984, v104, p81.
Newsweek. Jan 7, 1985, v105, p48-49.
Playboy. Mar 1985, v32, p26.
Saturday Review. Jan-Feb 1985, v11, p81.
Texas Monthly. Feb 1985, v13, p135.
Time. Jan 7, 1985, v125, p103.
Variety. Nov 28, 1984, p19.
Washingtonian. Jan 1985, v20, p66.
Washingtonian. Feb 1985, v20, p53.

Beware, My Lovely (US; Horner, Harry; 1952)
BFI/Monthly Film Bulletin. Jul 1953, v20, p104-05.
Christian Century. Nov 5, 1952, v69, p1303.
Commonweal. Jul 4, 1952, v56, p316.
Film Daily. Aug 7, 1952, p7.
Hollywood Reporter. Jul 29, 1952, p3.
The London Times. Jun 22, 1953, p10.
Motion Picture Herald Product Digest. Aug 2, 1952, p1470.
The New York Times. Sep 13, 1952, p10.
Newsweek. Sep 29, 1952, v40, p94.
Saturday Review. Jun 14, 1952, v35, p36.
The Tatler. Jul 1, 1953, v209, p31.
Theatre Arts. Jul 1952, v36, p88.
Time. Sep 22, 1952, v60, p104.
Variety. Jul 30, 1952, p6.

Beyond a Reasonable Doubt (US; Lang, Fritz; 1956)
BFI/Monthly Film Bulletin. Dec 1956, v23, p148-49.
Film Daily. Oct 1, 1956, p7.
The Films of Fritz Lang. p262-66.
Fritz Lang: A Guide to References and Resources. p124-27.
Fritz Lang (Armour). p111-13.
Fritz Lang (Eisner). p358-46.
Hollywood Reporter. Sep 12, 1956, p3.
Magill's Survey of Cinema. Series II. v1, p202-06.
The New York Times. Sep 14, 1956, p27.
Newsweek. Sep 10, 1956, v48, p104.
Saturday Review. Sep 29, 1956, v39, p22.
Variety. Sep 12, 1956, p6.

Beyond the Gates *See* Au-Dela des Grilles

Bhowani Junction (US; Cukor, George; 1956)
America. Jun 9, 1956, v95, p272.

BFI/Monthly Film Bulletin. Nov 1956, v23, p112.
Commonweal. Jun 8, 1956, v64, p251.
Film Daily. May 7, 1956, p10.
Films and Filming. Sep 1956, v2, p23.
Films in Review. Jun-Jul 1956, v7, p287.
George Cukor (Phillips). p117-21.
Hollywood Reporter. May 4, 1956, p3.
Magill's Survey of Cinema. Series II. v1, p205-09.
The New York Times. May 25, 1956, p26.
The New York Times. Jun 3, 1956, SecII, p1.
The New Yorker. Jun 2, 1956, v32, p130.
Newsweek. Jun 11, 1956,, v47, p118.
Saturday Review. Jun 2, 1956, v39, p25.
Time. Jun 4, 1956, v67, p109.
Variety. May 9, 1956, p6.

The Bible . . . In the Beginning (Italian title: Bibbia, La) (IT, US; Huston, John; 1966)
America. Oct 8, 1966, v115, p433-35.
BFI/Monthly Film Bulletin. Nov 1966, v33, p163.
Big Screen, Little Screen. p367-70.
Cahiers du Cinema in English. 1966, n5, p7-8.
Catholic World. Oct 1966, v204, p64.
Christian Century. Sep 7, 1966, v83, p1083.
Christian Century. Nov 16, 1966, v83, p1410.
Christian Science Monitor (Western edition). Oct 10, 1966, p6.
Cinema. Dec 1966, v3, p47.
The Cinema of John Huston. p146-55.
Commonweal. Oct 21, 1966, v85, p79.
Film Daily. Sep 28, 1966, p38-39.
Film Quarterly. Sum 1967, v20, p11-22.
Filmfacts. Oct 15, 1966, v9, p213-17.
Films and Filming. Nov 1966, v13, p8.
Films in Review. Oct 1966, v17, p517-19.
Harper's Magazine. Oct 1966, v233, p132-34.
Hollywood Reporter. Sep 28, 1966, p3-4.
Illustrated London News. Oct 8, 1966, v249, p11.
John Huston (Hammen). p108-10.
Kiss Kiss Bang Bang. p160-64.
Life. Oct 7, 1966, v61, p22.
The London Times. Oct 16, 1966, p18.
Look. Oct 18, 1966, v30, p104.
Motion Picture Herald Product Digest. Sep 28, 1966, p13, 26.
Motion Picture Herald Product Digest. Oct 12, 1966, p614-15.
National Review. Apr 18, 1967, v19, p428-30.
The New Republic. Oct 22, 1966, v155, p30-32.
The New York Times. Sep 29, 1966, p60.
The New Yorker. Oct 1, 1966, v42, p184-85.
Newsweek. Oct 3, 1966, v68, p105.
Playboy. Nov 1966, v13, p32, 34.
The Private Eye, the Cowboy and the Very Naked Girl. p198-201.
Reporter. Nov 3, 1966, v35, p56.
Saturday Review. Oct 1, 1966, v49, p34.
Senior Scholastic. Nov 11, 1966, v89, p26.
Sight and Sound. Aut 1966, v35, p199-200.
The Spectator. Oct 14, 1966, v217, p487.
Time. Oct 7, 1966, v88, p119.
Variety. Sep 28, 1966, p6.
Vogue. Oct 1, 1966, v148, p162.

Biches, Les (Also titled: The Does; The Girlfriends) (FR, IT; Chabrol, Claude; 1968)
Atlantic. Apr 1969, v223, p140.
BFI/Monthly Film Bulletin. Feb 1969, v36, p23.
Claude Chabrol (Wood and Walker). p103-12.
Directors and Directions: Cinema for the Seventies. p29-31.
Film Heritage. Sum 1969, v44, p16-26.

Film Quarterly. Spr 1969, v22, p58-59.
Filmfacts. Jan 1, 1968, v11, p395-96.
Films and Filming. Mar 1969, v15, p40-42.
Going Steady. p178-79.
Hollywood Reporter. Dec 12, 1968, p3.
The London Times. Jul 2, 1968, p13.
The London Times. Jan 17, 1969, p12.
Magill's Survey of Cinema. Foreign Language Films. v1, p282-86.
Movie. Wint 1969-70, n17, p16-24.
Movies Into Film. p261-64.
New Statesman. Jan 17, 1969, v77, p94.
The New York Times. Sep 27, 1968, p34.
Sight and Sound. Wint 1968-69, v38, p33-34.
The Spectator. Jan 17, 1969, v222, p84.
Variety. Apr 10, 1968, p24.
The Village Voice. Oct 17, 1968, v14, p53.
A Year In the Dark. p250-51.

Bidone, Il (IT; Fellini, Federico; 1955)
BFI/Monthly Film Bulletin. Dec 1956, v23, p149.
Cinema, the Magic Vehicle. v2, p234-35.
Commonweal. Dec 11, 1964, v81, p389.
Federico Fellini: A Guide to References and Resources. p68-72.
Fellini (Budgen). p30-33.
Fellini (Solmi). p50-85.
Fellini the Artist. p84-87.
Film Quarterly. Fall 1964, v18, p55-57.
Films and Filming. Jan 1957, v3, p23.
The Films of Federico Fellini. p85-90.
Magill's Survey of Cinema. Foreign Language Films. v1, p292-97.
The New York Times. Nov 20, 1964, p42.
Newsweek. Nov 23, 1964, v64, p117.
Sight and Sound. Wint 1956-57, v26, p153-54.
Time. Dec 4, 1964, v84, p111.
Variety. Nov 2, 1955, p18.
The Village Voice. Nov 19, 1964, p13.

Bienvenido, Mr. Marshall *See* Welcome, Mr. Marshall

Big Bad Mama (US; Corman, Roger; 1974)
The Films of Roger Corman. p59, 78.
Hollywood Reporter. Jul 2, 1974, p3.
Variety. Sep 4, 1975, p20.

Big Boodle (Also titled: Night in Havana) (US; Wilson, Richard; 1957)
BFI/Monthly Film Bulletin. Jun 1957, v24, p74.
Film Daily. Jan 31, 1957, v111, p10.
The Films of Errol Flynn. p209-11.
Hollywood Reporter. Jan 25, 1957, p3.
Motion Picture Herald Product Digest. Feb 2, 1957, v206, p250.
The New York Times. Mar 12, 1957, p38.
Newsweek. Mar 18, 1957, v49, p118.
Variety. Jan 30, 1957, p6.

The Big Carnival *See* Ace in the Hole

The Big Chill (US; Kasdan, Lawrence; 1983)
Commonweal. Nov 18, 1983, v110, p631-32.
Esquire. Oct 1983, v100, p124.
Film Comment. Sep-Oct 1983, v19, p20-21.
Films in Review. Oct 1983, v34, p501.
Hollywood Reporter. Sep 9, 1983, p3.
The Los Angeles Times. Sep 28, 1983, SecVI, p1.
Maclean's. Oct 10, 1983, v96, p54.
Magill's Cinema Annual, 1984. p78-83.
Ms. Oct 1983, v12, p37-38.
The Nation. Oct 22, 1983, v237, p380-81.
National Review. Oct 28, 1983, v35, p1350-51.
The New Republic. Oct 31, 1983, v189, p22-24.
New York. Sep 26, 1983, v16, p78-80, 92.
The New York Times. Sep 18, 1983, SecII, p1.
The New Yorker. Oct 17, 1983, v59, p189-92.
Newsweek. Sep 26, 1983, v102, p90.

Progressive. Dec 1983, v47, p38.
Saturday Review. Sep 10, 1983, v9, p36-37.
Time. Sep 12, 1983, v122, p66.
Variety. Sep 7, 1983, p16.

The Big Country (US; Wyler, William; 1958)
America. Oct 18, 1958, v100, p87.
BFI/Monthly Film Bulletin. Feb 1959, v26, p14.
Catholic World. Oct 1958, v188, p62.
Commonweal. Oct 10, 1958, v69, p48.
Film Daily. Aug 8, 1958, v114, p1.
Filmfacts. Oct 29, 1958, v1, p173-74.
Films in Review. Oct 1958, v9, p453-54.
The Films of Charlton Heston. p93-97.
The Films of Gregory Peck. p151-56.
Hollywood Reporter. Aug 8, 1958, p3.
Library Journal. Oct 1, 1958, v83, p2667.
Life. Sep 29, 1958, 45, p82-84.
Magill's Survey of Cinema. Series II. v1, p212-15.
The New York Times. Oct 2, 1958, p44.
The New Yorker. Oct 11, 1958, v34, p93.
Newsweek. Sep 8, 1958, v52, p95.
Saturday Review. Aug 23, 1958, v41, p25.
Senior Scholastic. Nov 7, 1958, v73, p29.
Time. Sep 8, 1958, v72, p96.
Variety. Aug 13, 1958, p6.
William Wyler: A Guide to References and Resources. p141-44.
William Wyler (Anderegg). p192-203.
William Wyler (Madsen). p328-34.

The Big Day *See* Jour de Fete

Big Deal At Dodge City *See* A Big Hand For the Little Lady

The Big Fix (US; Kagan, Jeremy Paul; 1978)
BFI/Monthly Film Bulletin. Feb 1979, v46, p20.
Films in Review. Dec 1978, v29, p636.
Hollywood Reporter. Oct 3, 1978, p3.
The Los Angeles Times. Oct 6, 1978, SecIV, p1.
Maclean's. Oct 23, 1978, v91, p63-64.
Motion Picture Herald Product Digest. Oct 18, 1978, p37.
The New Leader. Nov 6, 1978, v61, p18-19.
The New Republic. Nov 4, 1978, v179, p41.
New York. Oct 23, 1978, v11, p131-32.
The New York Times. Nov 6, 1978, np.
The New Yorker. Oct 23, 1978, v54, p154-56.
Newsweek. Oct 9, 1978, v92, p92.
Time. Oct 16, 1978, v112, p111.
Variety. Oct 4, 1978, p18.

A Big Hand For the Little Lady (Also titled: Big Deal At Dodge City) (US; Cook, Fielder; 1966)
BFI/Monthly Film Bulletin. Sep 1966, v33, p135-36.
Big Screen, Little Screen. p331.
Christian Science Monitor (Western edition). Aug 19, 1966, p4.
Film Daily. Apr 25, 1966, p5.
Film Quarterly. Wint 1966-67, v20, p60.
Filmfacts. Aug 1, 1966, v9, p133-34.
Films and Filming. Oct 1966, v13, p54-55.
The Films of Henry Fonda. p192-94.
The Fondas (Springer). p278-79.
Hollywood Reporter. Apr 25, 1966, p3.
Life. Jun 24, 1966, v60, p16.
Motion Picture Herald Product Digest. May 11, 1966, p518.
The New Republic. Oct 22, 1966, v155, p33.
The New York Times. Jun 9, 1966, p54.
The New Yorker. Jun 18, 1966, v42, p110.
Newsweek. Jun 20, 1966, v67, p104.
Playboy. Sep 1966, v13, p60, 62.

Senior Scholastic. May 6, 1966, v88, p37-38.
Time. Jun 24, 1966, v87, p103.
Variety. Apr 27, 1966, p6.

The Big Hangover (US; Krasna, Norman; 1950)
Christian Century. Jun 21, 1950, v67, p775.
The Films of Elizabeth Taylor. p79-80.
Hollywood Reporter. Mar 14, 1950, p3.
Motion Picture Herald Product Digest. Mar 18, 1950, p229.
The New York Times. May 26, 1950, p20.
Newsweek. Jun 12, 1950, v35, p91.
Time. Jun 19, 1950, v55, p93.
Variety. Mar 15, 1950, p12.

The Big Heat (US; Lang, Fritz; 1953)
America. Nov 7, 1953, v90, p159.
BFI/Monthly Film Bulletin. Apr 1954, v21, p51.
Catholic World. Oct 1953, v178, p63.
Farm Journal. Dec 1953, v77, p73.
Film Daily. Oct 6, 1953, p8.
The Films of Fritz Lang. p245-49.
The Films of the Fifties. p88-90.
Fritz Lang: A Guide to References and Resources. p113-16.
Fritz Lang (Armour). p159-62.
Fritz Lang (Eisner). p329-37.
Hollywood Reporter. Sep 23, 1953, p3.
Library Journal. Oct 1, 1953, v78, p1677.
Magill's Survey of Cinema. Series II. v1, p216.
The Nation. Nov 21, 1953, v177, p434.
National Parent-Teacher. Nov 1953, v48, p36.
The New York Times. Oct 15, 1953, p43.
Newsweek. Nov 2, 1953, v42, p90-91.
Sight and Sound. Jul-Sep 1954, v24, n1, p36.
Time. Nov 2, 1953, v62, p112.
Variety. Sep 23, 1953, p6.

Big Jim McLain (US; Ludwig, Edward; 1952)
BFI/Monthly Film Bulletin. Dec 1952, v19, p165.
The Complete Films of John Wayne. p186-87.
Film Daily. Sep 3, 1952, p6.
Hollywood Reporter. Aug 25, 1952, p3.
Motion Picture Herald Product Digest. Aug 30, 1952, p1509.
National Parent-Teacher. Nov 1952, v47, p37.
The New Statesman and Nation. Nov 1, 1952, v44, p509.
The New York Times. Sep 18, 1952, p35.
Newsweek. Nov 3, 1952, v40, p104.
Time. Sep 29, 1952, v60, p93.
Variety. Apr 27, 1952, p6.

The Big Knife (US; Aldrich, Robert; 1955)
America. Nov 19, 1955, v94, p224.
Catholic World. Oct 1955, v181, p58.
Commonweal. Dec 2, 1955, v63, p225.
Film Daily. Sep 23, 1955, p5.
The Films and Career of Robert Aldrich. p46-53.
The Films in My Life. p98-100.
Films in Review. Nov 1955, v6, n9, p466.
Hollywood Reporter. Sep 16, 1955, v136, n20, p3.
Library Journal. Oct 15, 1955, v80, p2230.
Magill's Survey of Cinema. Series I. v1, p159-61.
The Nation. Nov 12, 1955, v181, p427.
The New Republic. Jan 9, 1956, v134, p19-20.
The New York Times. Nov 6, 1955, SecII, p5.
The New York Times. Nov 9, 1955, p41.
The New Yorker. Nov 19, 1955, v31, p194.
Newsweek. Nov 21, 1955, v46, p114.
Robert Aldrich: A Guide to References and Resources. p24-25.
Saturday Review. Nov 19, 1955, v38, p38.

Time. Oct 24, 1955, v66, p106.
Variety. Sep 21, 1955, p6.

Big Land (Also titled: Stampeded) (US; Douglas, Gordon; 1957)
America. Mar 16, 1957, v96, p686.
BFI/Monthly Film Bulletin. May 1957, v24, p61.
Film Daily. Feb 6, 1957, p6.
Films and Filming. Jun 1957, v3, p23-24.
Hollywood Reporter. Jan 30, 1957, p3.
Motion Picture Herald Product Digest. Feb 2, 1957, v206, p251.
The New York Times. Mar 2, 1957, p18.
The New Yorker. Mar 9, 1957, v33, p76.
Time. Apr 1, 1957, v69, p96.
Variety. Jan 30, 1957, p6.

The Big Lift (US; Seaton, George; 1950)
BFI/Monthly Film Bulletin. Apr-May 1950, v17, p58-59.
Christian Century. Jun 14, 1950, v67, p743.
Commonweal. May 5, 1950, v52, p98.
Film Daily. Apr 7, 1950, p7.
Films in Review. May-Jun 1950, v1, p9-11,23-25.
The Films of Montgomery Clift. p119-24.
Hollywood Reporter. Apr 10, 1950, p3.
Motion Picture Herald Product Digest. Apr 15, 1950, p261.
The New Republic. May 15, 1950, v122, p23.
The New Statesman and Nation. May 6, 1950, v39, p513.
The New York Times. Apr 27, 1950, p37.
The New Yorker. Apr 29, 1950, v26, p91.
Newsweek. May 1, 1950, v35, p75.
Senior Scholastic. May 10, 1950, v56, p30.
Time. May 8, 1950, v55, p90.

The Big Night (US; Losey, Joseph; 1951)
BFI/Monthly Film Bulletin. Jun 1952, v19, p73.
Christian Century. Feb 6, 1952, v69, p175.
Commonweal. Mar 21, 1952, v55, p593.
Film Culture. Spr 1966, v40, p35-37.
Film Daily. Nov 13, 1951, p6.
Holiday. Mar 1952, v11, p19.
Hollywood Reporter. Nov 2, 1951, p3.
Joseph Losey (Hirsch). p51-53.
Library Journal. Apr 15, 1952, v77, p713.
Motion Picture Herald Product Digest. Nov 10, 1951, p1101-02.
The New York Times. Mar 20, 1952, p37.
Newsweek. Nov 26, 1951, v38, p100.
Saturday Review. Dec 8, 1951, v34, p31.
Time. Nov 12, 1951, v58, p112.
Variety. Nov 7, 1951, p6.

The Big North *See* The Wild North

The Big Red One (US; Fuller, Sam; 1980)
BFI/Monthly Film Bulletin. Jul 1980, v47, p125.
Christian Century. Nov 12, 1980, v97, p1108.
The Christian Science Monitor. Aug 28, 1980, p18.
Hollywood Reporter. May 14, 1980, p3.
The Los Angeles Times. Jul 18, 1980, SecVI, p1.
Maclean's. Jul 21, 1980, v93, p51.
Magill's Survey of Cinema. Series II. v1, p223-28.
Motion Picture Herald Product Digest. Jul 23, 1980, p13.
The Nation. Jul 19, 1980, v231, p92-93.
National Review. Apr 8, 1980, v32, p976.
The New Leader. Aug 11, 1980, v63, p26-27.
New York. Jul 21, 1980, v13, p52-53.
The New York Times. May 25, 1980, SecII, p1.
The New York Times. Jul 18, 1980, SecIII, p6.
The New York Times Magazine. May 4, 1980, p48-49.

Newsday. Jul 18, 1980, SecII, p7.
Newsweek. Jul 28, 1980, v96, p68.
Time. Jul 21, 1980, v116, p73-74.
Variety. May 14, 1980, p14.
Washington Post. Jul 18, 1980, p25.

The Big Sky (US; Hawks, Howard; 1952)
BFI/Monthly Film Bulletin. Dec 1952, v19, p165.
Catholic World. Sep 1952, v175, p465.
Christian Century. Sep 19, 1952, v69, p1046.
Commonweal. Sep 5, 1952, v56, p535.
Film Daily. Jul 14, 1952, p6.
Films in Review. Aug-Sep 1952, v3, p357.
The Films of Howard Hawks. p68-71.
The Films of Kirk Douglas. p88-91.
Hollywood Reporter. Jul 9, 1952, p3.
Library Journal. Oct 1, 1952, v77, p1605.
Life. Sep 8, 1952, v33, p59.
Magill's Survey of Cinema. Series I. v1, p229-33.
Motion Picture Herald Product Digest. Jul 12, 1952, p1441.
The Nation. Sep 27, 1952, v175, p283.
National Parent-Teacher. Sep 1952, v47, p38.
Natural History. Oct 1952, v61, p381.
The New York Times. Aug 20, 1952, p21.
The New Yorker. Sep 6, 1952, v28, p91.
Newsweek. Aug 25, 1952, v40, p85.
Saturday Review. Aug 16, 1952, v35, p28-29.
Time. Aug 11, 1952, v60, p88.
Variety. Jul 9, 1952, p6.

The Big Sleep (GB; Winner, Michael; 1978)
BFI/Monthly Film Bulletin. Sep 1978, v45, p172.
Films in Review. Jun-Jul 1978, v29, p373.
The Films of Michael Winner. p126-34.
The Los Angeles Times. Mar 29, 1978, SecIV, p1.
Maclean's. Mar 20, 1978, v91, p68.
Motion Picture Herald Product Digest. Mar 22, 1978, p84.
The New York Times. Mar 15, 1978, SecIII, p19.
Raymond Chandler and Film. p179-86.
Raymond Chandler in Hollywood. p143-48.
Robert Mitchum on the Screen. p234-35.
Variety. Mar 15, 1978, p19.

The Big Snatch *See* Any Number Can Win

The Big T.N.T. Show (US; Peerce, Larry; 1966)
Film Daily. Feb 3, 1966, p8.
Filmfacts. Mar 15, 1966, v9, p33.
Hollywood Reporter. Jan 19, 1966, p3.
Motion Picture Herald Product Digest. Jan 26, 1966, p458.
Variety. Jan 19, 1966, p28.

The Big Trees (US; Feist, Felix; 1952)
BFI/Monthly Film Bulletin. May 1952, v19, p63.
Film Daily. Feb 7, 1952, p10.
The Films of Kirk Douglas. p84-87.
Hollywood Reporter. Feb 5, 1952, p4.
Motion Picture Herald Product Digest. Feb 9, 1952, p1229-30.
The New York Times. Feb 6, 1952, p24.
Newsweek. Feb 25, 1952, v39, p100.
Variety. Feb 6, 1952, p6.

Bigger Than Life (US; Ray, Nicholas; 1956)
America. Aug 11, 1956, v95, p452.
BFI/Monthly Film Bulletin. Oct 1956, v23, p124.
Cinema Journal. 1983, v22, p38-57.
Commonweal. Aug 10, 1956, v64, p466.
Film Daily. Aug 3, 1956, p8.

Films and Filming. Nov 1956, v3, p25.
The Films in My Life. p143-47.
Films in Review. Oct 1956, v7, p417-18.
The Films of James Mason. p132-33.
Hollywood Reporter. Aug 3, 1956, p3.
Magill's Survey of Cinema. Series II. v1, p234-40.
The New York Times. Aug 3, 1956, p11.
The New York Times. Aug 5, 1956, SecII, p1.
The New Yorker. Aug 11, 1956, v32, p58.
Nicholas Ray: A Guide to References and Resources. p92-97.
Nicholas Ray (Kreidl). p169-71.
Saturday Review. Jul 28, 1956, v39, p24.
Time. Aug 6, 1956, v68, p53.
Variety. Aug 15, 1956, p6.

Billie (US; Weis, Don; 1965)
BFI/Monthly Film Bulletin. Jan 1966, v33, p5-6.
Film Daily. Sep 7, 1965, p15.
Films and Filming. Mar 1966, v12, p53-54.
Hollywood Reporter. Sep 2, 1965, p3.
The London Times. Dec 9, 1965, p13.
Motion Picture Herald Product Digest. Sep 15, 1965, p361-62.
The New York Times. Sep 16, 1965, p55.
Newsweek. Sep 27, 1965, v66, p99.
Variety. Sep 8, 1965, p6.

Billion Dollar Brain (GB; Russell, Ken; 1967)
America. Jan 13, 1968, v118, p48.
BFI/Monthly Film Bulletin. Jan 1968, v35, p2-3.
Film Daily. Dec 15, 1967, p7.
Films and Filming. Jan 1968, v14, p24.
Hollywood Reporter. Dec 12, 1967, p3.
Ken Russell: A Guide to References and Resources. p20-21.
Ken Russell (Phillips). p77-81.
Ken Russell's Films. p42-50.
Motion Picture Herald Product Digest. Dec 20, 1967, p752.
The New York Times. Dec 23, 1967, p29.
Newsweek. Jan 15, 1968, v71, p76.
Saturday Review. Jan 6, 1968, v51, p38.
Senior Scholastic. Jan 11, 1968, p19.
Time. Jan 5, 1968, v91, p74.
Variety. Nov 22, 1967, p6.
The Village Voice. Jan 18, 1968, p33.

Billy Budd (GB; Ustinov, Peter; 1962)
America. Dec 22, 1962, v107, p1279.
BFI/Monthly Film Bulletin. Dec 1962, v29, p163-64.
Cinema. 1963, v1, n3, p33.
Cinema. 1963, v1, n1, p41.
The Classic American Novel and the Movies. p124-31.
Commonweal. Nov 16, 1962, v77, p202-03.
Film Daily. Aug 27, 1962, p4.
Film Quarterly. Spr 1963, v16, p53-56.
Filmfacts. Nov 23, 1962, v5, p267-69.
Films and Filming. Oct 1962, v9, p29, 31.
Films and Filming. Jan 1962, v9, p16-18, 42.
Films in Review. Nov 1962, v13, p552-53.
Hollywood Reporter. Aug 27, 1962, v27, p3.
I Lost It At the Movies. p211-15.
Life. Dec 7, 1962, v53, p128.
Literature/Film Quarterly. 1976, v4, n3, p271-85.
Magill's Survey of Cinema. Series I. v1, p165-68.
Motion Picture Herald Product Digest. Sep 5, 1962, p649-50.
The Nation. Dec 8, 1962, v195, p412.
The New Republic. Nov 10, 1962, v147, p25.
The New York Times. Oct 31, 1962, p32.
The New Yorker. Nov 3, 1962, v38, p116.

Newsweek. Nov 5, 1962, v60, p112.
Saturday Review. Nov 10, 1962, v45, p27.
Sight and Sound. Aut 1962, v31, p197.
Time. Nov 9, 1962, v80, p99.
A World on Film. p116-17.

Billy Jack (US; Frank, T. C.; 1971)
BFI/Monthly Film Bulletin. Sep 1972, v39, p184.
Deeper into Movies. p341.
Filmfacts. 1971, v14, n17, p430-33.
Films and Filming. Oct 1972, v19, n1, p49.
Hollywood Reporter. Apr 30, 1971, p3.
Magill's Survey of Cinema. Series II. v1, p242-44.
The New York Times. Jul 29, 1971, p42.
The New York Times. Mar 11, 1973, SecII, p1.
The New Yorker. Nov 27, 1971, v47, p148.
Newsweek. Aug 30, 1971, v78, p76.
Newsweek. Mar 26, 1973, v81, p72.
Variety. May 5, 1971, p22.
The Village Voice. Aug 19, 1971, p47.

Billy Liar (GB; Schlesinger, John; 1963)
America. Feb 8, 1963, v110, p202-3.
BFI/Monthly Film Bulletin. Sep 1963, v30, p126-27.
Commonweal. Dec 6, 1963, v79, p314.
Fifty Classic British Films. p112-15.
Film Daily. Dec 17, 1963, p6.
Filmfacts. Nov 28, 1963, p257-58.
Films and Filming. Sep 1963, v9, p21.
Films in Review. Nov 1963, v14, p567.
Illustrated London News. Aug 31, 1963, p322.
John Schlesinger: A Guide to References and Resources. p43-45.
John Schlesinger (Phillips). p52-61.
Magill's Survey of Cinema. Series II. v1, p245-48.
The New Republic. Dec 14, 1963, v149, p27.
New Statesman. Aug 16, 1963, p204.
The New York Times. Dec 17, 1963, p49.
The New Yorker. Dec 21, 1963, v39, p88-89.
Newsweek. Dec 1963, v62, p74.
Sight and Sound. Aut 1963, v32, p193-94.
Spectator. Aug 16, 1963, v211, p204.
Variety. Aug 21, 1963, p6.
The Village Voice. Dec 19, 1963, p17.

Billy Rose's Jumbo *See* Jumbo

Bingo Long Traveling All Stars & Motor Kings (US; Badham, John; 1976)
American Film. Jul-Aug 1976, v1, p8-13.
Before My Eyes. p225.
BFI/Monthly Film Bulletin. Nov 1976, v43, p229.
Ebony. Jul 1976, v31, p66-68.
Film Bulletin. May 1976, v45, p13.
Films and Filming. Dec 1976, v23, p40.
Films in Review. Oct 1976, v27, p505.
Hi Fi. Dec 1976, v26, p131-32.
Independent Film Journal. Jul 9, 1976, v78, p11.
The Los Angeles Times. Jul 16, 1976, SecIV, p1.
Movietone News. Oct 11, 1976, n 52, p42.
The New Republic. Aug 7, 1976, v175, p26.
New York. Jul 26, 1976, v9, p54.
The New York Times. Jul 17, 1976, p10.
Newsweek. Jul 19, 1976, v88, p77.
Penthouse. Nov 1976, v8, p55-57.
Saturday Review. Aug 7, 1976, v3, p45.
Time. Aug 2, 1976, v108, p60.
Variety. May 19, 1976, p19.

Bird Man of Alcatraz *See* Birdman of Alcatraz

Bird of Paradise (US; Daves, Delmer; 1951)
BFI/Monthly Film Bulletin. Jul 1951, v18, p291.
Christian Century. May 9, 1951, v68, p599.
Film Daily. Mar 12, 1951, p6.
Hollywood Reporter. Mar 12, 1951, p3.
Motion Picture Herald Product Digest. Mar 17, 1951, p757-58.
The New York Times. Mar 15, 1951, p37.
The New Yorker. Mar 24, 1951, v27, p93.
Newsweek. Mar 12, 1951, v37, p88.
The Spectator. Jul 6, 1951, v187, p14.
Time. Mar 19, 1951, v57, p106.
Variety. Mar 14, 1951, p6.

The Bird With the Crystal Plumage (Italian title: Uccello dalle piume di Cristallo, L') (IT; Argento, Dario; 1970)
The New York Times. Jul 23, 1970, p25.
The New Yorker. Aug 1, 1970, v46, p70.
Variety. Jul 29, 1970, p15.

Birdman of Alcatraz (Also titled: Bird Man of Alcatraz) (US; Frankenheimer, John; 1962)
America. Jul 28, 1962, v107, p552.
BFI/Monthly Film Bulletin. Sep 1962, v29, p122-23.
Burt Lancaster: A Pictorial Treasury of His Films. p114-17.
Burt Lancaster: The Man and His Movies. p92-93.
Commonweal. Aug 10, 1962, v76, p446.
Film Daily. Jun 18, 1962, p6.
Filmfacts. Aug 3, 1962, v5, p159-60.
Films and Filming. Sep 1962, v8, p31.
Films and Filming. Jul 1962, v8, p28-29.
Films in Review. Jun-Jul 1962, v13, p359-60.
Hollywood Reporter. Jun 18, 1962, p3.
Life. Aug 24, 1962, v53, p39.
The Los Angeles Times. May 1962, SecVI, p7.
Magill's Survey of Cinema. Series I. v1, p169-71.
Motion Picture Herald Product Digest. Jun 20, 1962, p597.
Movie. Sep 1962, n2, p35.
Movie. Dec 1962, n5, p35.
The New Republic. Aug 13, 1962, v147, p28.
The New Republic. Sep 17, 1962, p30.
The New Republic. Sep 24, 1962, p30-31.
The New York Times. Jul 19, 1962, p19.
Newsweek. Jul 9, 1962, v60, p72-73.
Saturday Review. May 19, 1962, v45, p31.
Screen. Jul-Oct 1969, v10, p160-73.
Time. Jul 20, 1962, v80, p79.
Variety. Jun 20, 1962, p6.

The Birds (US; Hitchcock, Alfred; 1963)
America. Apr 20, 1963, v108, p589.
The Art of Alfred Hitchcock. p383-96.
BFI/Monthly Film Bulletin. Sep 1963, v30, p127.
Commonweal. Apr 12, 1963, v78, p73-74.
Esquire. Oct 1963, v60, p23.
Film Daily. Mar 28, 1963, p3.
Film Quarterly. Sum 1963, v16, p44-46.
Filmfacts. Apr 11, 1963, v6, p49-51.
Films and Filming. Sep 1963, v9, p20.
The Films in My Life. p86-89.
Films in Review. May 1963, v14, p309.
The Films of Alfred Hitchcock. p221-25.
The Films of the Sixties. p96-98.
Focus on the Horror Film. p141-48.
Hitchcock (Truffaut). p285-300.
Hitchcock's Films. p115-33.
Hollywood Reporter. Mar 28, 1963, v174, p3.
Illustrated London News. Sep 14, 1963, v243, p396.

Magill's Survey of Cinema. Series II. v1, p249-52.
Movie. Jul-Aug 1963, p22-23.
The New Republic. Apr 13, 1963, v148, p34-35.
New Statesman. Aug 30, 1963, v66, p265.
The New York Times. Mar 29, 1963, SecIII, p5.
The New York Times. Apr 1, 1963, p54.
The New Yorker. Apr 6, 1963, v39, p177.
Newsweek. Apr 8, 1963, v61, p92.
On Movies. p302-05.
Saturday Review. Apr 6, 1963, v46, p39.
Surrealism and the Cinema. p109-12, 114-16.
Time. Apr 5, 1963, v81, p103.
Variety. Mar 27, 1963, p6.
The Village Voice. Apr 4, 1963, p15.

Birds Do It (US; Marton, Andrew; 1966)
Film Daily. Aug 2, 1966, p6.
Filmfacts. Jan 15, 1967, v9, p346.
The Great Spy Pictures. p86.
Hollywood Reporter. Jul 28, 1966, p3.
Variety. Aug 3, 1966, p6.

The Birds, the Bees and the Italians (Italian title: Signore e Signori; Also titled: Ladies and Gentlemen) (FR, IT; Germi, Pietro; 1966)
America. Oct 14, 1967, v117, p424.
Christian Science Monitor (Midwestern Edition). Oct 27, 1967, p4.
Film Daily. Apr 11, 1967, p11.
Filmfacts. Oct 15, 1967, v10, p257-58.
Films and Filming. Nov 1968, v15, p50-51.
Hollywood Reporter. Feb 14, 1967, p3.
The London Times. Sep 23, 1968, p7.
The New York Times. Aug 8, 1967, p33.
The New Yorker. Aug 12, 1967, v43, p74-75.
Playboy. Nov 1967, v14, p42, 47.
Time. Aug 18, 1967, v90, p63.
Variety. Mar 9, 1966, p17.
The Village Voice. Nov 16, 1967, v13, p31.

Birdy (US; Parker, Alan; 1984)
America. Mar 23, 1985, v152, p236.
BFI/Monthly Film Bulletin. Jun 1985, v52, p204.
Christian Century. Jun 5, 1985, v102, p590.
Commonweal. Jan 25, 1985, v112, p50.
Films in Review. Mar 1985, v36, p181.
Hollywood Reporter. Dec 12, 1984, p3.
Horizon. May 1985, v28, p18.
Los Angeles. Jan 1985, v30, p36.
Maclean's. Jan 7, 1985, v98, p70.
Magill's Cinema Annual, 1985. p93-97.
Ms. Apr 1985, v13, p118.
The Nation. Jun 22, 1985, v240, p77.
New Statesman. Jun 14, 1985, v109, p38.
New York. Jan 21, 1985, v18, p53.
The New York Times. Dec 21, 1984, SecIII, p25.
The New Yorker. Feb 11, 1985, v60, p110-11.
Philadelphia Magazine. Jul 1985, v76, p60.
Playboy. Mar 1985, v32, p25.
Rolling Stone. Mar 14, 1985, p39-41.
Time. Jan 7, 1985, v125, p96.
Variety. Dec 12, 1984, p16.
Vogue. Feb 1985, v175, p76.
Washingtonian. Feb 1985, v20, p53.
Washingtonian. Mar 1985, v20, p75.
Washingtonian. Apr 1985, v20, p59.

The Birthday Party (GB; Friedkin, William; 1968)
BFI/Monthly Film Bulletin. Apr 1970, v37, p68-69.
Commonweal. Feb 7, 1969, v89, p591.
Confessions of a Cultist. p409-15.
Figures of Light. p128-29.
Film 68/69. p211-16.
Filmfacts. Jan 15, 1969, v11, p497-99.

Films and Filming. Apr 1970, v16, p41-42.
Films in Review. Jan 1969, v20, p55-56.
Going Steady. p260-61.
Hollywood Reporter. Dec 17, 1968, p3.
The London Times. Jan 9, 1968, p6.
Motion Picture Herald Product Digest. Dec 11, 1968, p75, 78.
The Nation. Jan 6, 1969, v208, p29-30.
The New Republic. Jan 4, 1969, v160, p34.
The New York Times. Dec 10, 1968, p54.
The New Yorker. Dec 21, 1968, v44, p90-91.
Newsweek. Dec 23, 1968, v72, p89-80.
Saturday Review. Dec 7, 1968, v51, p68.
Variety. Dec 18, 1968, p26.
The Village Voice. Dec 19, 1968, v14, p51, 53-54.
Vogue. Jan 1, 1969, v153, p66.

Biruma no Tategoto *See* The Burmese Harp

Bitter Victory (Also titled: Amère Victoire) (FR; Ray, Nicholas; 1957)
BFI/Monthly Film Bulletin. Mar 1958, v25, p30.
Filmfacts. 1958, v4, p25.
Filmfacts. 1958, v1, p270.
Films and Filming. Mar 1958, v4, p25.
Films in Review. Apr 1958, v9, p205.
Hollywood Reporter. Feb 19, 1958, p4.
Magill's Survey of Cinema. Series II. v1, p259-63.
Variety. Sep 4, 1957, p26.

Bizet's Carmen (Also titled: Carmen) (IT, FR; Rosi, Francesco; 1983)
BFI/Monthly Film Bulletin. Mar 1985, v52, p79.
Films and Filming. Jan 1984, n352, p33.
Films in Review. Feb 1984, v35, p111.
Hollywood Reporter. Oct 1, 1984, p3.
Maclean's. Mar 4, 1985, v98, p54.
Magill's Cinema Annual, 1985. p98-104.
The New Republic. Oct 1, 1984, v191, p24.
The New York Times. Sep 20, 1984, SecIII, p21.
The New York Times. Sep 23, 1984, SecII, p19.
The New Yorker. Oct 29, 1984, v60, p123.
Newsweek. Sep 17, 1984, v104, p89.
Opera News. Oct 1984, v49, p10.
Saturday Review. Dec 1983, v9, p43.
Theater Crafts. Jan 1985, v19, p22-23.
Time. Oct 8, 1984, v124, p82.
Variety. Mar 14, 1984, p22.

Black and White in Color (French title: Victoire en Chantant, La) (FR, IVORY COAST; Annaud, Jean-Jacques; 1977)
America. Jun 11, 1977, v136, p527-28.
The Great French Films. p272-73.
Hollywood Reporter. Apr 25, 1977, p3.
The Los Angeles Times. Jul 20, 1977, SecIV, p1.
Magill's Survey of Cinema. Foreign Language Films. v1, p321-25.
The Nation. Jun 4, 1977, v224, p700.
The New Republic. Jun 18, 1977, v176, p23.
The New York Times. May 9, 1977, p27.
The New Yorker. May 23, 1977, v53, p109-10.
Saturday Review. May 28, 1977, v40.
Time. May 16, 1977, v109, p91-92.
Variety. Oct 13, 1976, p23.

The Black Bird (US; Giler, David; 1975)
Hollywood Reporter. Dec 22, 1975, p4.
The Los Angeles Times. Dec 25, 1975, SecIV, p1.
Motion Picture Herald Product Digest. Dec 31, 1975, p60.
The New York Times. Dec 26, 1975, p43.
The New Yorker. Jan 19, 1976, v51, p53-54.
Newsweek. Jan 12, 1976, v87, p69.

Saturday Review. Feb 7, 1976, v3, p45-46.
Variety. Dec 24, 1975, p18.

The Black Castle (US; Juran, Nathan; 1952)
BFI/Monthly Film Bulletin. Mar 1953, v20, p35.
Christian Century. Nov 26, 1952, v69, p1391.
Film Daily. Oct 23, 1952, p6.
The Films of Boris Karloff. p212-14.
Hollywood Reporter. Oct 22, 1952, p3.
Motion Picture Herald Product Digest. Oct 25, 1952, p1582.
National Parent-Teacher. Dec 1952, v47, p37.
The New York Times. Dec 26, 1952, p20.
Time. Dec 8, 1952, v60, p100.
Variety. Oct 22, 1952, p6.

The Black Cauldron (US; Berman, Ted; Rich, Richard; 1985)
BFI/Monthly Film Bulletin. Oct 1985, v52, p305.
California Magazine. Aug 1985, v10, p57.
Fantasy and Science Fiction. Oct 1985, v69, p109.
Hollywood Reporter. Jul 22, 1985, p3.
The Los Angeles Times. Jul 24, 1985, SecVI, p1.
Maclean's. Aug 1985, v98, p48.
Magill's Cinema Annual, 1986. p75-79.
New Statesman. Oct 11, 1985, v110, p38.
The New York Times. Sep 8, 1985, SecVI, p35.
Newsweek. Aug 12, 1985, v106, p71.
Philadelphia Magazine. Oct 1985, v76, p85.
Time. Aug 5, 1985, v126, p68.
Variety. Jul 24, 1985, p16.

The Black Hand (US; Thorpe, Richard; 1950)
BFI/Monthly Film Bulletin. Apr-May 1950, v17, p65.
Christian Century. Apr 5, 1950, v67, p447.
Commonweal. Mar 24, 1950, v51, p630.
Film Daily. Jan 19, 1950, p12.
Films and Filming. Sep 1964, v10, p34.
The Films of Gene Kelly. p112-14.
The Great Gangster Pictures. p40, 42.
Hollywood Reporter. Jan 19, 1950, p3.
Motion Picture Herald Product Digest. Jan 21, 1950, p161.
The New Republic. Mar 20, 1950, v122, p23.
The New York Times. Mar 13, 1950, p15.
The New Yorker. Mar 25, 1950, v26, p100.
Newsweek. Mar 27, 1950, v35, p84.
Time. Mar 20, 1950, v55, p92.
Variety. Jan 25, 1950, p18.

The Black Hole (US; Nelson, Gary; 1979)
BFI/Monthly Film Bulletin. Feb 1980, v47, p19-20.
The Films of the Seventies. p276-78.
Hollywood Reporter. Dec 19, 1979, p3.
Horizon. Sep 1979, v22, p60-62.
The Los Angeles Times. Dec 21, 1979, SecVI, p1.
Motion Picture Herald Product Digest. Jan 9, 1979, p61.
The New York Times. Dec 21, 1979, SecIII, p16.
Newsweek. Dec 24, 1979, v94, p79.
Variety. Dec 19, 1979, p20.

Black Jack *See* Captain Black Jack

The Black Knight (GB; Garnett, Tay; 1954)
America. Nov 27, 1954, v92, p259.
BFI/Monthly Film Bulletin. Oct 1954, v21, p146.
Commonweal. Nov 19, 1954, v61, p188.
Film Daily. Oct 21, 1954, p6.
The Films of Alan Ladd. p198-200.
Hollywood Reporter. Nov 9, 1954, p3.

Motion Picture Herald Product Digest. Oct 23, 1954, p185.
National Parent-Teacher. Jan 1955, v49, p38.
The New York Times. Oct 29, 1954, p27.
Newsweek. Nov 15, 1954, v44, p112.
Time. Nov 8, 1954, v64, p110.
Variety. Sep 8, 1954, p6.

Black Like Me (US; Lerner, Carl; 1964)
Christian Century. Jun 17, 1964, v81, p807.
Commonweal. May 15, 1964, v80, p236.
Ebony. May 1964, v19, p37-38.
Film Daily. May 25, 1964, v124, p11.
Motion Picture Herald Product Digest. Jun 10, 1964, p68.
The New Republic. May 23, 1964, v150, p24.
The New York Times. May 21, 1964, p42.
The New Yorker. May 23, 1964, v40, p151-52.
Newsweek. May 25, 1964, v63, p110B.
Saturday Review. Apr 25, 1964, v47, p25.
Variety. May 20, 1964, p6.

The Black Marble (US; Becker, Harold; 1980)
The Christian Science Monitor. Mar 26, 1980, p22.
Films in Review. Apr 1980, v31, p244.
Hollywood Reporter. Feb 22, 1980, p3.
Humanist. Jul-Aug 1980, v40, p46-47.
The Los Angeles Times. Mar 21, 1980, SecVI, p1.
Motion Picture Herald Product Digest. Mar 26, 1980, p81.
The New Yorker. Mar 10, 1980, v56, p136.
Newsday. Mar 7, 1980, SecII, p7.
Newsweek. Mar 17, 1980, v95, p101.
Time. Mar 31, 1980, v115, p84.
Variety. Feb 27, 1980, p20.
The Village Voice. Mar 17, 1980, p46.

Black Moon (US; Malle, Louis; 1975)
Hollywood Reporter. Nov 5, 1975, p6.
Motion Picture Herald Product Digest. Oct 22, 1975, p38.
The New York Times. Sep 30, 1975, p31.
The New York Times. Oct 3, 1975, p40.
The New York Times. Oct 5, 1975, SecII, p15.
The New Yorker. Nov 24, 1975, v51, p168.
Saturday Review. Nov 29, 1975, v3, p37.
Time. Nov 17, 1975, v106, p78-79.
Variety. Sep 24, 1975, p22.

Black Orpheus (Also titled: Orfeu Negro; Orfeo de Conceicao) (FR; Camus, Marcel; 1959)
America. Jan 30, 1960, v102, p537.
BFI/Monthly Film Bulletin. Jul 1960, v27, p93.
Commonweal. Jan 1, 1960, v71, p396.
Dance Magazine. Dec 1959, v33, p16-17.
Film Daily. Jan 4, 1960, v117, p6.
Filmfacts. Jan 13, 1960, v2, p311-12.
Films in Review. Dec 1959, v10, p621-22.
The International Dictionary of Films and Filmmakers. v1, p345-46.
McCall's. Feb 1960, v87, p8.
The Nation. Jan 16, 1960, v190, p59-60.
The New Republic. Jan 4, 1960, v142, p21.
The New York Times. Dec 22, 1959, p41.
The New Yorker. Jan 2, 1960, v35, p47.
Saturday Review. Dec 19, 1959, v42, p12-13.
Time. Nov 16, 1959, v74, p114.
Variety. May 20, 1959, p6.

Black Peter (Also titled: Cerny Petr) (CZECH; Forman, Milos; 1964)
Filmfacts. 1971, v14, p521-22.
Films and Filming. Dec 1965, v12, n3, p27-28.
The Milos Forman Stories. p39-47, 51-58.
Newsweek. Aug 2, 1971, v78, p75.
Variety. Aug 12, 1964, p6.

The Black Rose (GB; Hathaway, Henry; 1950)
American Cinematographer. Nov 1950, v31, p378-79.
BFI/Monthly Film Bulletin. Sep 1950, v17, p118.
Christian Century. Oct 11, 1950, v67, p1215.
Commonweal. Sep 22, 1950, v52, p581.
Film Daily. Aug 8, 1950, p12.
The Films of Tyrone Power. p161-63.
The Hollywood Professionals. v1, p158-62.
Hollywood Reporter. Aug 7, 1950, p3.
Library Journal. Oct 1, 1950, v75, p1677.
Motion Picture Herald Product Digest. Aug 12, 1950, p433.
The New York Times. Sep 5, 1950, p11.
The New Yorker. Sep 9, 1950, v26, p98.
Newsweek. Sep 11, 1950, v36, p87.
Senior Scholastic. Oct 11, 1950, v57, p37.
Time. Sep 11, 1950, v56, p102.

The Black Shield of Falworth (US; Maté, Rudolph; 1954)
America. Oct 23, 1954, v92, p110.
BFI/Monthly Film Bulletin. Oct 1954, v21, p142-43.
Farm Journal. Sep 1954, v78, p140.
Film Daily. Aug 3, 1954, p3.
Films and Filming. Oct 1954, v1, p24.
Hollywood Reporter. Aug 3, 1954, p3.
Library Journal. Sep 1, 1954, v79, p1485.
Motion Picture Herald Product Digest. Aug 7, 1954, p97.
National Parent-Teacher. Dec 1954, v49, p38.
The New York Times. Oct 7, 1954, p16.
Senior Scholastic. Oct 27, 1954, v65, p29.
Time. Oct 25, 1954, v64, p88.
Tony Curtis: The Man and His Movies. p50-51.
Variety. Aug 4, 1954, p6.

The Black Stallion (US; Ballard, Carroll; 1979)
BFI/Monthly Film Bulletin. Jun 1980, v47, p107.
Hollywood Reporter. Oct 22, 1979, p6.
Motion Picture Herald Product Digest. Oct 31, 1979, p44.
The New York Times. Oct 13, 1979, p12.
The New Yorker. Nov 5, 1979, v55, p180.
Newsweek. Oct 29, 1979, v94, p105.
Time. Dec 10, 1979, v114, p111.
Variety. Oct 17, 1979, p10.

Black Sunday (US; Frankenheimer, John; 1977)
America. Apr 23, 1977, v136, p383.
BFI/Monthly Film Bulletin. Jul 1977, v44, p140.
Films and Filming. May 1977, v23, p17-19.
Films in Review. May 1977, v28, p312.
The Films of the Seventies. p171-72.
Hollywood Reporter. Mar 25, 1977, p3.
The Los Angeles Times. Mar 27, 1977, Calendar, p56.
Motion Picture Herald Product Digest. Apr 4, 1977, p87.
The New Republic. Apr 9, 1977, v176, p22.
The New York Times. Apr 1, 1977, SecIII, p10.
The New York Times. Apr 3, 1977, SecII, p17.
The New York Times. Sep 18, 1977, SecII, p1.
The New Yorker. Apr 4, 1977, v53, p118.
Newsweek. Apr 4, 1977, v89, p73.
Saturday Review. Apr 30, 1977, v4, p34-35.
Sports Illustrated. Apr 11, 1977, v46, p66.
Time. Apr 4, 1977, v109, p68.
Variety. Mar 30, 1977, p19.

Black Thursday (French title: Guichets du Louvre, Les) (FR; Mizrahi, Moshe; 1974)

Esquire. Apr 1975, v83, p54.
Hollywood Reporter. Dec 24, 1974, p3.
Independent Film Journal. Dec 25, 1974, v75, p51-52.
Magill's Survey of Cinema. Foreign Films. v2, p334-36.
Motion Picture Herald Product Digest. Dec 25, 1974, p28.
The Nation. Jan 18, 1975, v220, p62.
The New Republic. Mar 15, 1975, v172, p22.
New York. Dec 23, 1974, v7, p70-71.
The New York Times. Oct 14, 1974, SecII, p2.
Newsweek. Jan 13, 1975, v85, p69.
Time. Jan 27, 1975, v105, p9.
Variety. Jul 3, 1974, p16.

Black Widow (US; Johnson, Nunnally; 1954)
America. Nov 13, 1954, v92, 194.
BFI/Monthly Film Bulletin. Mar 1955, v22, p32.
Catholic World. Dec 1954, v180, p220.
Commonweal. Dec 3, 1954, v61, p255.
Film Daily. Oct 28, 1954, p6.
Films and Filming. Jun 1955, v1, p20.
The Films of Ginger Rogers. p216.
Hollywood Reporter. Oct 27, 1954, p3.
Library Journal. Nov 15, 1954, v79, p2182.
Motion Picture Herald Product Digest. Oct 30, 1954, p193.
National Parent-Teacher. Jan 1955, v49, p39.
The New Statesman and Nation. Apr 23, 1955, v49, p578.
The New York Times. Oct 28, 1954, p46.
The New Yorker. Nov 13, 1954, v30, p211.
Newsweek. Nov 8, 1954, v44, p100.
Saturday Review. Nov 13, 1954, v37, p27.
Time. Nov 8, 1954, v64, p110.
Variety. Oct 27, 1954, p6.

The Black Windmill (US; Siegel, Don; 1974)
BFI/Monthly Film Bulletin. Aug 1974, v41, p168-69.
Film. Aug 1974, n17, p22.
Films Illustrated. Aug 1974, v3, p470.
Films in Review. Jun-Jul 1974, v25, p373.
Hollywood Reporter. May 6, 1974, p3.
Independent Film Journal. May 15, 1974, v73, p19.
The Los Angeles Times. May 19, 1974, Calendar, p28.
Motion Picture Herald Product Digest. May 8, 1974, p97.
Movietone News. Oct 1974, n36, p36.
New Statesman. Jul 29, 1974, v88, p92-93.
The New York Times. May 18, 1974, p18.
The New Yorker. Jun 3, 1974, v50, p97-99.
Newsweek. Jun 17, 1974, v83, p112.
Saturday Review. Jul 13, 1974, v1, p38.
Take One. 1974, v4, n4, p27-28.
Time. Jun 3, 1974, v103, p57-58.
Variety. May 8, 1974, p37.
The Village Voice. May 30, 1974, p81.

Blackbeard, the Pirate (US; Walsh, Raoul; 1952)
BFI/Monthly Film Bulletin. Mar 1953, v20, p34-35.
Film Daily. Dec 12, 1952, p6.
Hollywood Reporter. Nov 26, 1952, p3.
Motion Picture Herald Product Digest. Dec 6, 1952, p1629.
National Parent-Teacher. Feb 1953, v47, p37.
The New York Times. Dec 26, 1952, p20.
Newsweek. Jan 19, 1953, v41, p98.
Theatre Arts. Feb 1953, v37, p84.
Time. Dec 22, 1952, v60, p66.
Variety. Dec 3, 1952, p6.

Blackboard Jungle (US; Brooks, Richard; 1955)
America. Mar 26, 1955, v92, p686-87.
BFI/Monthly Film Bulletin. Oct 1955, v22, p147.
Catholic World. Apr 1955, v181, p63.
Cinema. Wint 1967, v3, n6, p50.
Commonweal. Mar 18, 1955, v61, p630-31.
Fifty from the Fifties. p55-60.
Film Culture. May-Jun 1955, v1, n3, p25-26.
Film Daily. Feb 28, 1955, p6.
Films and Filming. Nov 1955, v2, n2, p18.
Films in Review. Apr 1955, v6, n4, p188-89.
The Films of Sidney Poitier. p58-61.
The Films of the Fifties. p161-62.
Hollywood Reporter. Feb 28, 1955, v133, n29, p3.
Library Journal. Mar 15, 1955, v89, p642.
Life. Mar 28, 1955, v38, p49-50.
Magill's Survey of Cinema. Series II. v1, p26-66.
Movie. Spr 1965, n12, p10-12.
The Nation. Apr 2, 1955, v180, p294-95.
The New Republic. Apr 11, 1955, v132, p29-30.
The New York Times. Mar 21, 1955, p21.
The New York Times. Mar 27, 1955, SecII, p1.
The New Yorker. Mar 26, 1955, v31, p120.
Newsweek. Mar 28, 1955, v45, p94.
Saturday Review. Apr 2, 1955, v38, p31.
Sight and Sound. Wint 1955-56, v25, n3, p150.
Time. Mar 21, 1955, v65, p98.
Variety. Mar 2, 1955, p8.

Blackmailed (GB; Allégret, Marc; 1951)
BFI/Monthly Film Bulletin. Feb 1951, v18, p214.
Films in Review. Mar 1951, v2, p37-38.
The Films of Dirk Bogarde. p56-57.
Hollywood Reporter. Jul 28, 1952, p3.
The London Times. Feb 5, 1951, p3.
Motion Picture Herald Product Digest. Sep 15, 1951, p1015.
The Spectator. Feb 2, 1951, v186, p146.
Variety. Feb 7, 1951, p6.

Blade Runner (US; Scott, Ridley; 1982)
American Cinematographer. Jul 1982, v63, p692-93.
Christianity Today. Sep 3, 1982, v26, p97.
Commentary. Aug 1982, v74, p67-70.
Film Comment. Jul-Aug 1982, v18, p64-65.
Film Journal. May 24, 1982, v85, p24-25.
Films in Review. Aug-Sep 1982, v33, p429.
Hollywood Reporter. Jun 15, 1982, p3.
The International Dictionary of Films and Filmmakers. v1, p59-60.
The Los Angeles Times. Jun 25, 1982, SecVI, p1.
Maclean's. Jun 28, 1982, v95, p58-59.
Magill's Cinema Annual, 1983. p76-81.
The New Republic. Jul 19, 1982, v187, p30.
New Statesman. Sep 10, 1982, v104, p27-28.
The New York Times. Jun 25, 1982, SecIII, p10.
The New Yorker. Jul 12, 1982, v58, p82-85.
Newsweek. Jun 28, 1982, v99, p72.
Rolling Stone. Aug 6, 1982, p33-34.
Time. Jul 12, 1982, v120, p68.
Variety. Jun 14, 1982, p3.
The Village Voice. Jul 6, 1982, p47.

Blame it on Rio (US; Donen, Stanley; 1984)
BFI/Monthly Film Bulletin. Oct 1984, v51, p301.
Film Journal. Mar 1984, v87, p41-42.
Films and Filming. Sep 1984, n364, p36.
Films in Review. Apr 1984, v35, p24.
Hollywood Reporter. Feb 9, 1984, p3.

The Los Angeles Times. Feb 17, 1984, SecVI, p15.
Ms. May 1984, v12, p59.
The New Republic. Mar 19, 1984, v190, p24-25.
New Statesman. Aug 17, 1984, v108, p27-28.
New York. Feb 20, 1984, v17, p77.
The New York Times. Feb 17, 1984, SecIII, p10.
The New Yorker. Feb 20, 1984, v60, p115.
Newsweek. Mar 5, 1984, v103, p82.
Photoplay. Oct 1984, v35, p47-49.
Time. Feb 27, 1984, v123, p98.
Variety. Feb 1, 1984, p18.
The Village Voice. Feb 21, 1984, p57.
Vogue. Feb 1984, v174, p52.

Blazing Saddles (US; Brooks, Mel; 1974)
Audience. Apr 1974, v6, p10-11.
BFI/Monthly Film Bulletin. Jan 1974, v41, p120-21.
Christian Century. Jul 17, 1974, v91, p727.
Cinefantastique. 1975, v4, n1, p33.
Commentary. May 1974, v57, p61-63.
Commonweal. Mar 22, 1974, v100, p61-62.
Esquire. May 1974, v82, p32.
Film Heritage. 1974, v9, n4, p35-36.
Films and Filming. Aug 1974, v20, p43.
Films and Filming. Jul 1974, v20, p49-51.
Films Illustrated. May 1974, v3, p327-28.
Films in Review. Mar 1974, v25, p182-83.
Hollywood Reporter. Feb 6, 1974, p3.
Independent Film Journal. Feb 18, 1974, v73, p9-10.
Jump Cut. Sep-Oct 1974, n3, p3-4.
The Los Angeles Times. Feb 7, 1974, SecIV, p1.
Magill's Survey of Cinema. Series I. v1, p184-87.
Millimeter. May 1974, v2, p42.
Motion Picture Herald Product Digest. Feb 13, 1974, p73.
Movietone News. May-Jun 1974, n32, p40-41.
The New Republic. Mar 16, 1974, v170, p20.
New Statesman. Jun 21, 1974, v87, p895.
New York. Feb 25, 1974, v7, p52-53.
The New York Times. Jun 30, 1974, SecII, p1.
The New York Times. Mar 17, 1974, SecII, p15.
The New Yorker. Feb 18, 1974, v49, p100.
Newsweek. Feb 18, 1974, v83, p101.
Newsweek. Apr 22, 1974, v83, p98.
Penthouse. Jun 1974, v5, p37.
Rolling Stone. Mar 28, 1974, p54.
Sight and Sound. Fall 1974, v43, p180-81.
Time. Mar 4, 1974, v103, p62-63.
Variety. Feb 13, 1974, p18.
The Village Voice. Mar 14, 1974, p71.

Blazing Sun *See* Purple Noon

Blé en Herbe, Le (Also titled: Ripening Seed; The Game of Love; The Flowering Wheat) (FR; Autant-Lara, Claude; 1953)
BFI/Monthly Film Bulletin. Nov 1954, v21, p155.
Film Daily. Dec 16, 1954, p6.
Films and Filming. Nov 1954, v1, p20.
Films in Review. Jan 1955, v6, p38.
The Great French Films. p255.
Hollywood Reporter. Aug 25, 1955, p3.
The London Times. Sep 16, 1954, p9.
The Nation. Dec 25, 1954, v179, p557.
The New Statesman and Nation. Sep 25, 1954, v48, p360.
The New York Times. Dec 15, 1954, p41.
Newsweek. Jan 3, 1955, v45, p45.
Saturday Review. Jan 8, 1955, v38, p26.
The Spectator. Sep 17, 1954, v193, p332.
The Tatler. Feb 17, 1954, v211, p272.
The Tatler. Sep 29, 1954, v213, p618.
Time. Jan 24, 1955, v65, p76.

Variety. Mar 24, 1954, p24.
Variety. Mar 31, 1954, p6.

Blechtrommel, Die *See* The Tin Drum

Bless the Beasts & Children (US; Kramer, Stanley; 1971)
Filmfacts. 1971, v14, p598-600.
Films in Review. Oct 1971, v12, n8, p511-12.
Hollywood Reporter. Jul 8, 1971, v216, n50, p3.
The New York Times. Oct 29, 1971, p29.
Newsweek. Sep 6, 1971, v78, p67.
Saturday Review. Oct 23, 1971, v54, p25.
Stanley Kramer, Film Maker. p303-10.
Variety. Jul 14, 1971, p16.
The Village Voice. Nov 25, 1971, v16, n47, p87.

Blind Date (Also titled: Chance Meeting) (GB; Losey, Joseph; 1959)
BFI/Monthly Film Bulletin. Sep 1959, v26, p119.
Commonweal. Mar 11, 1960, v71, p655.
Joseph Losey (Hirsch). p68-72.
Magill's Survey of Cinema. Series II. v1, p270-72.
The New Republic. Apr 4, 1960, v142, p30.
The New York Times. Oct 27, 1960, p45.
Saturday Review. Feb 27, 1960, v43, p26.
Variety. Aug 26, 1959, p6.

Blind Terror (Fleischer, 1971) *See* See No Evil

Blind Terror (Hough, 1971) *See* Sudden Terror

Blindfold (Also titled: Lax Yeux Bandés) (US; Dunne, Philip; 1966)
BFI/Monthly Film Bulletin. Mar 1966, v33, p35.
Cahiers du Cinema in English. 1966, n4, p61.
Christian Science Monitor (Western edition). Jul 1, 1966, p4.
Film Daily. May 19, 1966, p7.
Film Quarterly. Fall 1966, v20, p58.
Filmfacts. Aug 15, 1966, v9, p153-54.
Films and Filming. Feb 1966, v12, p58-59.
The Great Spy Pictures. p88-89.
Hollywood Reporter. May 18, 1966, p3.
The London Times. Feb 10, 1966, p16.
Motion Picture Herald Product Digest. May 25, 1966, p526.
The New York Times. May 26, 1966, p55.
Newsweek. Jun 20, 1966, v67, p104.
Playboy. May 1966, v13, p30, 32.
Time. Jun 10, 1966, v87, p112.
Variety. May 18, 1966, p6.

A Blonde in Love *See* Loves of a Blonde

A Blonde's Love *See* Loves of a Blonde

Blood and Black Lace (Italian title: Su Donne Per L'Assassino) (IT, FR, WGER; Bava, Mario; 1964)
BFI/Monthly Film Bulletin. Feb 1966, v33, p18.
Hollywood Reporter. Jun 11, 1965, p3.
The London Times. Mar 19, 1966, p15.
The New York Times. Nov 11, 1965, p58.
Variety. Jun 23, 1965, p6.

Blood Feast (US; Lewis, Herschell G.; 1964)
Boxoffice. Nov 18, 1963, v84, p2779.
Motion Picture Herald Product Digest. Sep 4, 1963, v230, p884.
Newsweek. May 18, 1964, v63, p100.
Variety. May 6, 1964, p17.

Blood Feud (Italian title: Fatto di sangue fra due uomini per causa de un vedova; Also titled: Revenge) (IT; Wertmuller, Lina; 1979)

Films in Review. Apr 1980, v31, p249.
Hollywood Reporter. Feb 15, 1980, p3.
Italian Cinema (Bondanella). p365-66.
The Los Angeles Times. Feb 15, 1980, SecVI, p2.
The Nation. Mar 15, 1980, v230, p317.
The New Italian Cinema (Witcombe). p256-58.
The New Republic. Mar 15, 1980, v182, p25.
The New York Times. Feb 22, 1980, SecIII, p7.
The New Yorker. Mar 3, 1980, v56, p112-16.
Newsday. Feb 22, 1980, p7.
Variety. Feb 7, 1979, p20.
The Village Voice. Feb 25, 1980, p39.

Blood for Dracula *See* Andy Warhol's Dracula

Blood Simple (US; Berman, Ted; Coen, Joel; 1985)
BFI/Monthly Film Bulletin. Jan 1985, v52, p17.
Commonweal. Apr 5, 1985, v112, p213.
Film Comment. Mar-Apr 1985, v21, p14-19.
Humanist. Jul-Aug 1985, v45, p43-44.
The Los Angeles Times. May 5, 1985, Calender, p24.
Maclean's. Apr 15, 1985, v98, p58.
National Review. Mar 22, 1985, v37, p55-56.
The New Republic. Feb 25, 1985, v192, p24-25.
New York. Jan 21, 1985, v18, p51-53.
The New York Times. Jan 20, 1985, SecII, p17.
The New Yorker. Feb 25, 1985, v61, p81-83.
Newsweek. Jan 21, 1985, v105, p74.
Time. Jan 28, 1985, v125, p90-91.
Variety. Jul 24, 1985, p16.

Blood Wedding (Spanish title: Bodas de Sangre) (SP; Saura, Carlos; 1981)
Cineaste. 1982, v12, n1, p60.
Dance Magazine. Jan 1982, v56, p112-13.
Film. Nov 1982, n110, p9.
Film. Mar 1982, v104, p3.
The Los Angeles Times. Jan 15, 1982, SecVI, p1.
New Statesman. Feb 12, 1982, v103, p28.
The New York Times. Oct 25, 1981, p63.
The New York Times. Nov 8, 1981, SecII, p14.
Newsweek. Nov 9, 1981, v98, p4.
Quarterly Review of Film Studies. 1983, v8, n2, p49-55.

Bloodbrothers (US; Mulligan, Robert; 1978)
BFI/Monthly Film Bulletin. Apr 1979, v46, p68.
Hollywood Reporter. Sep 15, 1978, p3.
Human Behavior. Dec 1978, v7, p77.
The Los Angeles Times. Oct 6, 1978, SecIV, p23.
New York. Oct 2, 1978, v11, p118.
The New Yorker. Oct 2, 1978, v54, p117-20.
Newsweek. Oct 2, 1978, v92, p85.
Time. Oct 2, 1978, v112, p66.
Variety. Sep 20, 1978, p26.

Bloodhounds of Broadway (US; Jones, Harmon; 1952)
BFI/Monthly Film Bulletin. Jan 1953, v20, p7-8.
Film Daily. Oct 29, 1952, p6.
Hollywood Reporter. Oct 27, 1952, p3.
Library Journal. Dec 1, 1952, v77, p2066.
Motion Picture Herald Product Digest. Nov 1, 1952, p1589.
National Parent-Teacher. Dec 1952, v47, p37.
The New York Times. Nov 15, 1952, p15.
Newsweek. Dec 15, 1952, v40, p102.
Time. Dec 1, 1952, v60, p64.
Variety. Oct 29, 1952, p6.

Bloody Mama (US; Corman, Roger; 1971)
BFI/Monthly Film Bulletin. May 1971, v38, p93.
Big Screen, Little Screen. p284-85.

Film Daily. Mar 24, 1970, p8.
Film Quarterly. Sum 1970, v23, p60.
Films and Filming. Aug 1970, v16, p48-49.
The Films of Roger Corman. p70-71.
Hollywood Reporter. Mar 18, 1970, p3.
The New York Times. May 7, 1970, p62.
The New York Times. May 24, 1970, SecII, p13.
Newsweek. May 25, 1970, v75, p102.
Sight and Sound. Aut 1970, v39, n4, p183-84.
Variety. Mar 18, 1970, p18.

Blow Out (US; De Palma, Brian; 1981)
BFI/Monthly Film Bulletin. Nov 1981, v48, p216-17.
Brian De Palma (Bliss). p98-118.
Commonweal. Sep 25, 1981, v108, p529-31.
The New Republic. Aug 22, 1981, v185, p22-23.
New Statesman. Oct 23, 1981, v102, p27.
New York. Aug 3, 1981, v14, p52-53.
The New York Times. Jul 24, 1981, SecIII, p6.
The New Yorker. Jul 27, 1981, v57, p74.
Newsweek. Jul 27, 1981, v98, p74.
Rolling Stone. Sep 3, 1981, p38.
Time. Jul 27, 1981, v118, p62.
Variety. Jul 29, 1981, p20.

Blow-Up (Also titled: Blow Up) (GB, IT; Antonioni, Michelangelo; 1966)
America. Jan 14, 1967, v116, p60-61.
American Imago. Fall 1975, v32, p240-63.
American Scholar. Wint 1967, v37, p120-31.
Antonioni (Cameron). p125-40.
Antonioni (Chatman). p138-58.
Antonioni's Visual Language. p102-09.
BFI/Monthly Film Bulletin. Jun 1967, v34, p86.
Big Screen, Little Screen. p378-79.
Blow-Up: A Film.
Christian Century. Feb 8, 1967, v84, p178.
Christian Science Monitor (Western edition). May 28, 1966, p6.
Christian Science Monitor (Western edition). Jan 4, 1967, p8.
Cinema Journal. Spr 1971, v10, p43-45.
Close-Up: A Critical Perspective on Film. p255-62.
Commentary. Apr 1967, v43, p86-89.
Commonweal. Jan 13, 1967, v85, p403.
Confessions of a Cultist. p280-84.
Dictionary of Films. p39.
Esquire. Apr 1967, v67, p47-48.
Figures of Light. p5-13.
Film 67/68. p274-81.
Film and Literature: An Introduction. p277-82.
Film As Film. p61-95.
Film Comment. Fall 1970, v6, p64-69.
Film Daily. Dec 19, 1966, p10.
Film Heritage. Spr 1967, v2, p3-15.
Film Heritage. Wint 1968-69, v4, p26-30.
Film Heritage. Spr 1970, v5, p13-21.
Film Quarterly. Spr 1967, v20, p28-31.
Filmfacts. Jan 1, 1967, v9, p301-04.
Films and Filming. May 1967, v13, p24-25.
Films in Review. Jan 1967, v18, p52.
The Films of the Sixties. p174-76.
Focus on Blow-Up. 1971.
The Great Films. p242-46.
The Great Movies. p193-95.
Hollywood Reporter. Dec 19, 1966, p3.
The International Dictionary of Films and Filmmakers. v1, p61-63.
International Film Guide. 1968, v5, p87-89.
Italian Cinema (Bondanella). p221-26.
Journal of Aesthetic Education. 1974, v8, n1, p27-42.
Journal of Aesthetic Education. 1975, v9, n2, p109-22.
Journal of Aesthetic Education. 1982, v16, n1, p57-67.

Variety. May 12, 1971, p19.
The Village Voice. Jun 17, 1971, v16, n24, p79.

The Blues Brothers (US; Landis, John; 1980)
BFI/Monthly Film Bulletin. Oct 1980, v47, p187.
Commonweal. Sep 26, 1980, v107, p529-30.
Hollywood Reporter. Jun 18, 1980, p2.
Jump Cut. Oct 1980, p1.
The Los Angeles Times. Jun 20, 1980, SecVI, p1.
Maclean's. Jun 30, 1980, v93, p53.
Motion Picture Herald Product Digest. Jul 23, 1980, p14.
The Nation. Jul 19, 1980, v231, p93.
New York. Jun 30, 1980, v13, p52-53.
The New York Times. Jun 20, 1980, SecIII, p16.
The New York Times. Jun 29, 1980, SecII, p1.
The New York Times. Jul 13, 1980, SecII, p15.
The New Yorker. Jul 7, 1980, v56, p95-97.
Newsday. Jun 20, 1980, SecII, p7.
Newsweek. Jun 30, 1980, v95, p62.
Rolling Stone. Aug 7, 1980, p28-30.
Time. Jul 7, 1980, v116, p44.
Variety. Jun 18, 1980, p22.
The Village Voice. Jul 2, 1980, p33.

Blume in Love (US; Mazursky, Paul; 1973)
Commentary. Nov 1973, v56, p75-77.
Commonweal. Aug 24, 1973, v98, p456.
Filmfacts. 1973, v16, n7, p165.
Holiday. Sep 1973, v54, p8.
Magill's Survey of Cinema. Series II. v1, p298.
The New Republic. Jul 23, 1973, v168, p24.
The New York Times. Jul 23, 1973, p69-71.
The New York Times. Sep 30, 1973, SecII, p4.
The New York Times. Jan 6, 1974, SecII, p2.
Newsweek. Jul 25, 1973, v81, p54.
PTA Magazine. Oct 1973, v68, p8.
Time. Jul 25, 1973, v101, p76-77.
Variety. May 23, 1973, p19.

The Boat *See* Boot, Das

The Boatniks (US; Tokar, Norman; 1970)
BFI/Monthly Film Bulletin. Aug 1970, v37, p163.
The New York Times. Jul 2, 1970, p25.
Variety. May 27, 1970, p20.

Bob and Carol and Ted and Alice (US; Mazursky, Paul; 1969)
America. Oct 4, 1969, v121, p267-69.
Cinema. v5, p32-33.
Commonweal. Nov 21, 1969, v91, p247-49.
Deeper Into Movies. p9-17.
Esquire. Jan 1970, v53, p38.
Film 69/70. p47-61.
Film Daily. Jul 11, 1969, p6.
Film Quarterly. Wint 1969-70, v23, p62.
Film Society Review. May 1970, v5, p38-41.
Filmfacts. 1969, v12, p409.
Films and Filming. May 1970, v16, p41-42.
Holiday. Oct 1969, v46, p53.
Journal of Popular Culture. Sum 1970, v4, p292-98.
Life. Oct 3, 1969, v67, p17.
Mademoiselle. Oct 1969, v69, p54.
Magill's Survey of Cinema. Series II. v1, p301-04.
Movie Comedy (Byron). p158-61.
The New Republic. Oct 25, 1969, v161, p32.
The New York Times. Sep 17, 1969, p50.
The New York Times. Sep 21, 1969, SecII, p1.
The New Yorker. Oct 4, 1969, v45, p144.
Saturday Review. Oct 11, 1969, v52, p51.
Second Sight. p259-62.
Time. Sep 26, 1969, v94, p94.

Variety. Jul 2, 1969, p6.
Vogue. Nov 1, 1969, v154, p118.

Bob le Flambeur (Also titled: Fever Heat) (FR; Melville, Jean-Pierre; 1955)
Boxoffice. Aug-Sep 1982, v118, p135-36.
Filmfacts. Feb 17, 1961, v4, p16.
Hollywood Reporter. Jun 25, 1982, p11.
The Los Angeles Times. Aug 20, 1982, SecVI, p1.
Magill's Cinema Annual, 1984. p526-29.
The Nation. Jul 3, 1982, v235, p26-28.
The New Republic. Aug 9, 1982, v187, p26-27.
New York. Nov 23, 1981, v14, p70-72.
New York. Jul 19, 1982, v15, p51-53.
The New York Times. Sep 26, 1981, p12.
The New York Times. Jun 23, 1982, p22.
Penthouse. Oct 1982, v13, p52-54.
Time. Aug 16, 1982, v120, p70.
Variety. Nov 7, 1956, p6.
The Village Voice. Jun 29, 1982, v27, p63.

Bobby Deerfield (US; Pollack, Sydney; 1977)
BFI/Monthly Film Bulletin. Nov 1977, v44, p228.
Films in Review. Dec 1977, v28, p630.
Hollywood Reporter. Sep 9, 1977, p3.
The Los Angeles Times. Oct 5, 1977, SecIV, p1.
Motion Picture Herald Product Digest. Oct 5, 1977, p34.
The New Republic. Oct 22, 1977, v177, p20-22.
The New York Times. Sep 30, 1977, SecIII, p8.
The New Yorker. Oct 3, 1977, v53, p130-33.
Newsweek. Oct 3, 1977, v90, p71.
Saturday Review. Nov 26, 1977, v5, p46.
Time. Oct 10, 1977, v110, p83-84.
Variety. Sep 14, 1977, p16.
Vogue. Oct 1977, v167, p50.

The Bobo (GB; Parrish, Robert; 1967)
BFI/Monthly Film Bulletin. Sep 1967, v34, p138.
Film Daily. May 31, 1967, p6.
Filmfacts. 1967, v10, p263.
Hollywood Reporter. May 29, 1967, p3.
Life. Sep 15, 1967, v63, p12.
Motion Picture Herald Product Digest. Jun 7, 1967, p691.
The New York Times. Sep 29, 1967, p53.
Newsweek. Sep 25, 1967, v70, p107.
Time. Oct 13, 1967, v90, p107.
Variety. May 31, 1967, p6.

Boccaccio 70 (IT, FR; Fellini, Federico; Visconti, Luchino; De Sica, Vittorio; 1962)
America. Sep 8, 1962, v107, p697.
BFI/Monthly Film Bulletin. May 1963, v30, p58.
Commonweal. Jul 13, 1962, v76, p401.
Federico Fellini: A Guide to References and Resources. p87-90.
Federico Fellini (Solmi). p160-64.
Film Daily. Jun 28, 1962, v28, p7.
Filmfacts. Jul 20, 1962, v5, p145-47.
Films in Review. Jun-Jul 1962, v13, p363-64.
The Films of Federico Fellini. p106-09.
Hollywood Reporter. Jul 30, 1962, v30, p3.
Motion Picture Herald Product Digest. Jul 11, 1962, p609.
The New Republic. Jul 16, 1962, v147, p28-29.
The New York Times. Jul 27, 1962, p40.
The New Yorker. Jul 7, 1962, v38, p64.
Newsweek. Jul 9, 1962, v60, p73.
Saturday Review. Jul 7, 1962, v45, p16.
Sight and Sound. Spr 1963, v32, p91-92.
Time. Mar 23, 1962, v79, p75.
Time. Jul 29, 1962, v79, p60.
Variety. May 16, 1962, p6.

Bodas de Sangre *See* Blood Wedding

Body Double (US; De Palma, Brian; 1984)
America. Nov 24, 1984, v151, p345.
BFI/Monthly Film Bulletin. Apr 1984, v52, p147.
Film Comment. Sep-Oct 1984, v20, p12-17.
Hollywood Reporter. Oct 3, 1984, p3.
Informer. Nov 1984, p6.
The Los Angeles Times. Oct 26, 1984, SecVI, p20.
Ms. Jan 1985, v13, p30.
The Nation. Nov 24, 1984, v239, p562-63.
New York. Nov 5, 1984, v17, p67-69.
The New York Times. Oct 26, 1984, SecIII, p8.
The New York Times. Dec 30, 1984, SecVI, p17.
The New Yorker. Nov 12, 1984, v60, p184-86.
Newsweek. Oct 29, 1984, v104, p134-35.
Time. Oct 29, 1984, v124, p102.
Variety. Oct 17, 1984, p15.
Vogue. Sep 1984, v174, p727.
Vogue. Nov 1984, v174, p110.

Body Heat (US; Kasdan, Lawrence; 1981)
Commonweal. Dec 18, 1981, v108, p722-23.
Film Comment. Sep-Oct 1981, v17, p49-52.
Hollywood Reporter. Aug 17, 1981, p10.
The International Dictionary of Films and Filmmakers. v1, p63-64.
The Los Angeles Times. Aug 28, 1981, SecVI, p5.
Maclean's. Aug 31, 1981, v94, p58.
Magill's Cinema Annual, 1982. p87-92.
The New Leader. Sep 21, 1981, v64, p22.
The New Republic. Dec 9, 1981, v185, p20-21.
New York. Aug 31, 1981, v14, p52-53.
The New York Times. Oct 25, 1981, SecII, p15.
The New Yorker. Nov 9, 1981, v57, p182-84.
Newsweek. Aug 31, 1981, v98, p36.
Rolling Stone. Oct 4, 1981, p72.
Saturday Review. Sep 1981, v8, p49.
Time. Aug 24, 1981, v118, p62.
Variety. Aug 17, 1981, p3.
The Village Voice. Aug 19, 1981, p46.

Boeing Boeing (US; Rich, John; 1965)
BFI/Monthly Film Bulletin. Jun 1966, v33, p92.
Christian Science Monitor (Western edition). Jan 5, 1966, p8.
Film Daily. Nov 23, 1965, p8.
Films and Filming. Aug 1966, v12, p15.
Hollywood Reporter. Nov 17, 1965, p3.
The London Times. May 26, 1966, p19.
Motion Picture Herald Product Digest. Dec 8, 1965, p418.
New Statesman. May 27, 1966, v71, p788.
The New York Times. Dec 24, 1965, p24.
The New Yorker. Jan 15, 1966, v41, p71.
Newsweek. Jan 10, 1966, v67, p62.
Playboy. Feb 1966, v13, p33-34.
Time. Jan 21, 1966, v87, p80.
Variety. Dec 1, 1965, p6.

Boheme, La (SWITZ; Zeffirelli, Franco; 1965)
BFI/Monthly Film Bulletin. Jul 1966, v33, p102-03.
Christian Science Monitor (Western edition). Oct 23, 1965, p6.
Film Daily. Oct 6, 1965, p7.
Hollywood Reporter. Oct 6, 1965, p3.
Life. Oct 29, 1965, v59, p23.
The London Times. Jun 4, 1966, p7.
Motion Picture Herald Product Digest. Oct 27, 1965, p393.
The New York Times. Oct 20, 1965, p51.
Opera News. Oct 23, 1965, v30, p42.
Private Screenings. p218-19.
Variety. Oct 13, 1965, p18.

Bombers B-52 (Also titled: No Sleep till Dawn) (US; Douglas, Gordon; 1957)
America. Dec 7, 1957, v98, p328.
BFI/Monthly Film Bulletin. Oct 1957, v24, p129.
Film Daily. Nov 8, 1957, v112, p8.
Hollywood Reporter. Oct 30, 1957, p3.
The New York Times. Nov 23, 1957, p11.
The New Yorker. Dec 7, 1957, v33, p100.
Time. Dec 9, 1957, v70, p108.
Variety. Oct 30, 1957, p6.

Bonaventure *See* Thunder on the Hill

Bonheur, Le (Also titled: Happiness) (FR; Varda, Agnés; 1965)
BFI/Monthly Film Bulletin. Aug 1965, v32, p118.
Christian Science Monitor (Western edition). Jul 31, 1965, p4.
Cinema. Dec 1966, v3, p48.
Commonweal. Jun 17, 1966, v84, p369.
Dictionary of Films. p39.
Film and the Critical Eye. p508-12.
Film Comment. Sum 1965, v3, p32-33.
Film Quarterly. Wint 1966-67, v20, p35-37.
Filmfacts. Aug 1, 1966, v9, p138-39.
Films and Filming. Sep 1965, v11, p30-31.
Life. May 20, 1966, v60, p22.
The London Times. Jul 8, 1965, p7.
Magill's Survey of Cinema. Foreign Language Films. v1, p372-75.
Motion Picture Herald Product Digest. Jun 1, 1966, p534.
Movie. Aut 1965, n14, p24-25.
New Statesman. Jul 9, 1965, v70, p59.
The New York Times. May 24, 1966, p55.
The New Yorker. May 28, 1966, v42, p113-14.
Newsweek. Jun 13, 1966, v67, p114-14A.
Playboy. Jul 1966, v13, p30.
Private Screenings. p258-62.
Saturday Review. May 28, 1966, v49, p45.
Sight and Sound. Aut 1965, v34, p200-01.
The Spectator. Jul 16, 1965, v215, p78.
Time. May 27, 1966, v87, p97-98.
Tynan Right and Left. p235-36.
Variety. Mar 3, 1965, p7.
The Village Voice. Jun 23, 1966, v11, p27.
Vogue. May 1966, v147, p147.

Bonjour Élephant! *See* Hello, Elephant!

Bonjour Tristesse (US; Preminger, Otto; 1958)
America. Jan 25, 1958, v98, p496.
BFI/Monthly Film Bulletin. May 1958, v25, p55.
Commonweal. Jan 31, 1958, v60, p457.
Double Takes. p19-21.
Film Daily. Jan 16, 1958, v113, p6.
The Films in My Life. p137-40.
Films in Review. Feb 1958, v9, p87-88.
The Films of David Niven. p146-49.
Hollywood Reporter. Jan 15, 1958, p3.
Library Journal. Feb 1, 1958, v83, p396.
The Nation. Feb 1, 1958, v186, p396.
The New York Times. Jan 16, 1958, p32.
The New Yorker. Jan 25, 1958, p33, p106.
Newsweek. Jan 20, 1958, v59, p89.
Saturday Review. Feb 15, 1958, v41, p30.
Time. Jan 20, 1958, v71, p86.
Variety. Jan 15, 1958, p6.

Bonnes Femmes, Les (FR, IT; Chabrol, Claude; 1960)
Claude Chabrol (Wood and Walker). p39-57.
Commonweal. May 27, 1966, v84, p285.
Confessions of a Cultist. p243-45.
Dictionary of Films. p39-40.
Filmfacts. Jul 15, 1966, v9, p123-24.
Films and Filming. May 1961, v7, p26-27.

Magill's Survey of Cinema. Foreign Language Films. v1, p380-85.
Movie. Jun 1963, n10, p8-9, 16-20.
National Review. Jul 25, 1967, v19, p814.
The New Wave. p263-65.
The New York Times. May 13, 1966, p32.
Newsweek. May 16, 1966, v67, p106.
Time. May 20, 1966, v87, p117.
Variety. May 4, 1960, p6.
The Village Voice. May 5, 1966, v11, p27.

Bonnie and Clyde (US; Penn, Arthur; 1967)
America. Sep 2, 1967, v117, p227.
Arthur Penn (Wood). p72-91.
BFI/Monthly Film Bulletin. Oct 1967, v34, p150.
The Bonnie and Clyde Book. 1972.
Catholic World. May 1968, v207, p76-79.
Christian Century. Oct 18, 1967, v84, p1326.
Cineast. Fall 1967, v1, p14-17.
Cineaste. Fall 1968, v2, p2-6.
Cinema. Sum 1967, p4-7, 7-10, 11-16.
Cinema. Sum 1969, v5, p28-30.
Cinema Journal. Spr 1971, v10, p19-33.
Classic Movies. p126-67.
Classics of the Gangster Film. p220-25.
Commonweal. Nov 10, 1967, v87, p170-71.
Esquire. Nov 1967, v68, p32.
Esquire. Dec 1967, v68, p46.
Fifty Grand Movies of the 1960s and 1970s. p209-13.
Film Comment. Fall 1970, v6, p64-69.
Film Daily. Aug 7, 1967, p3.
Film Heritage. Wint 1967-68, v3, p1-6, 7-21.
Film Quarterly. Wint 1967, v21, p45-48.
Film Quarterly. Sum 1968, v21, p2-13.
Film Society Review. Jan 1968, p42-45, 45-46.
Films and Filming. Oct 1967, v14, p20-21.
Films in Review. Oct 1967, v18, p504-05.
The Films of the Sixties. p202-05.
The Films of Warren Beatty. p131-44.
The Great Movies. p243-45.
Hollywood Reporter. Aug 7, 1967, p3.
The International Dictionary of Films and Filmmakers. v1, p64-66.
Landmark Films. p290-301.
Life. Oct 13, 1967, v63, p16.
Magill's Survey of Cinema. Series I. v1, p205-08.
Motion Picture Herald Product Digest. Aug 16, 1967, p713.
The Nation. Oct 30, 1967, v205, p444-45.
The New Republic. Nov 4, 1967, v157, p27-29.
The New York Times. Aug 14, 1967, p36.
The New York Times Magazine. Feb 18, 1968, p26-29.
The New Yorker. Aug 19, 1967, v43, p77-79.
The New Yorker. Oct 21, 1967, p147-48.
Ramparts Magazine. May 1968, v6, p16.
Reporter. Oct 5, 1967, v37, p46-47.
Reruns. p200-04.
Saturday Review. Aug 5, 1967, v50, p40.
Senior Scholastic. Dec 7, 1967, v91, p25.
Sight and Sound. Wint 1967, v37, p2-8.
Sight and Sound. Aut 1968, v37, p170-76.
Sight and Sound. Aut 1967, v36, p203-04.
Take One. 1967, v1, p20-22.
Ten Film Classics. p149-66.
Time. Aug 25, 1967, v90, p78.
Time. Dec 8, 1967, v90, p67-68.
Trans-Action. May 1968, v5, p15-21.
Variety. Aug 9, 1967, p6.
The Village Voice. Aug 24, 1967, p21.
The Village Voice. Aug 31, 1967, p25.
The Village Voice. Dec 21, 1967, p43.
Vogue. Sep 15, 1967, v150, p68.

Bonnie Prince Charlie (GB; Kimmins, Anthony; 1948)
BFI/Monthly Film Bulletin. Dec 1948, v15, p170.
Christian Century. Feb 27, 1952, v69, p263.
Commonweal. Jan 18, 1952, v55, p375.
Film Criticism and Caricatures, 1943-53. p89.
The Films of David Niven. p86-89.
Hollywood Reporter. Feb 18, 1952, p3.
Motion Picture Herald Product Digest. Jan 19, 1952, p1194.
The New York Times. Jan 7, 1952, p14.
The New Yorker. Jan 12, 1952, v27, p50.
Newsweek. Jan 21, 1952, v39, p90.
Variety. Nov 3, 1948, p11.

Bonzo Goes to College (US; De Cordova, Frederick; 1952)
BFI/Monthly Film Bulletin. Dec 1952, v19, p170.
Film Daily. Sep 2, 1952, p6.
Hollywood Reporter. Aug 29, 1952, p3.
Motion Picture Herald Product Digest. Aug 30, 1952, p1509.
National Parent-Teacher. Oct 1952, v47, p36.
Time. Oct 20, 1952, v60, p114.
Variety. Sep 3, 1952, p12.

Boom (GB; Losey, Joseph; 1968)
America. Jun 8, 1968, v118, p760.
BFI/Monthly Film Bulletin. Feb 1969, v36, p23-244.
Christian Science Monitor (Western edition). Jun 1, 1968, p4.
Commonweal. Jun 14, 1968, v88, p385.
Conversations With Losey. p273-82.
Film Daily. May 27, 1968, p7.
Film Quarterly. Wint 1968, v22, p52-55.
Filmfacts. Aug 15, 1968, v11, p216-18.
Films and Filming. Mar 1969, v15, p43-44.
Films in Review. Aug-Sep 1968, v19, p454.
The Films of Elizabeth Taylor. p198-202.
Hollywood Reporter. May 27, 1968, p3.
Joseph Losey (Hirsch). p157-67.
Life. Jun 21, 1968, v64, p12.
The London Times. Feb 13, 1968, p8.
The London Times. Jan 2, 1969, p6.
Motion Picture Herald Product Digest. Jun 5, 1968, p819.
Movies Into Film. p313-14.
The New Republic. Jun 8, 1968, v158, p26.
The New York Times. May 27, 1968, p56.
Newsweek. Jun 3, 1968, v71, p104.
Saturday Review. Jun 1, 1968, v51, p19.
Sight and Sound. Spr 1969, v38, p77-78.
The Spectator. Jan 10, 1969, v222, p51.
Time. May 31, 1968, v91, p56.
Variety. May 19, 1968, p20.
The Village Voice. Jun 6, 1968, v13, p47.

Boot, Das (Also titled: The Boat) (WGER; Peterson, Wolfgang; 1982)
American Cinematographer. Dec 1982, v63, p1277-81.
BFI/Monthly Film Bulletin. May 1982, v49, p81.
Christian Century. Aug 18, 1982, v99, p868.
Christianity Today. Oct 8, 1982, v26, p103.
Contemporary Review. Aug 1982, v247, p101-04.
Film Journal. Feb 19, 1982, 85, p42.
Films in Review. Apr 1982, v33, p241-42.
The Great German Films. p296-99.
Hollywood Reporter. Mar 17, 1982, p3.
Humanist. Sep-Oct 1982, v42, p57-58.
The Los Angeles Times. Mar 22, 1982, SecVI, p1.
Magill's Cinema Annual, 1983. p86-90.
New Statesman. Apr 9, 1982, v103, p29.
New York. Feb 15, 1982, v15, p70-71.

The New York Times. Feb 10, 1982, p24.
Newsweek. Mar 1, 1982, v99, p70.
Variety. Oct 2, 1981, p3.
The Village Voice. Feb 10, 1962, p60.

Boots Malone (US; Dieterle, William; 1952)
BFI/Monthly Film Bulletin. May 1952, v19, p60.
Film Daily. Jan 11, 1952, p7.
The Films of William Holden. p125-28.
Hollywood Reporter. Dec 19, 1951, p4.
Motion Picture Herald Product Digest. Dec 29, 1951, p1169.
The Nation. Apr 5, 1952, v174, p332-33.
The New York Times. Mar 13, 1952, p26.
The New Yorker. Mar 22, 1952, v28, p115.
Saturday Review. Jan 26, 1952, v35, p24.
The Spectator. Mar 21, 1952, v188, p366.
Theatre Arts. Feb 1952, v36, p90.
Time. Feb 4, 1952, v59, p72.
Variety. Dec 26, 1951, p6.

Bora Bora (IT; Liberatore, Ugo; 1971)
Filmfacts. 1971, v14, p58.
Hollywood Reporter. Feb 17, 1970, v214, p3.
The New York Times. Mar 18, 1971, p48.
Variety. Dec 4, 1968, p26.

The Border (US; Richardson, Tony; 1982)
The New Republic. Feb 24, 1982, v186, p22-24.
New York. Feb 8, 1982, v15, p54-55.
The New York Times. Jan 29, 1982, SecIII, p10.
The New Yorker. Feb 1, 1982, v57, p120-21.
Newsweek. Feb 1, 1982, v99, p72.
Rolling Stone. Mar 18, 1982, p45-46.
Time. Feb 1, 1982, v119, p79.
Variety. Jan 27, 1982, p16.

Borderline (US; Seiter, William A.; 1950)
Christian Century. Feb 22, 1950, v67, p255.
Commonweal. Mar 24, 1950, v51, p630.
Film Daily. Jan 12, 1950, p5.
Hollywood Reporter. Jan 11, 1950, p3.
Motion Picture Herald Product Digest. Jan 14, 1950, p153.
The New York Times. Mar 6, 1950, p17.
Time. Mar 27, 1950, v55, p104.
Variety. Jan 11, 1950, p6.

Born Free (GB; Hill, James; 1966)
America. Jul 9, 1966, v115, p42.
BFI/Monthly Film Bulletin. May 1966, v33, p73.
Big Screen, Little Screen. p348.
A Cast of Lions: the Story of the Filming of Born Free. 1966.
Christian Science Monitor (Western edition). Apr 8, 1966, p4.
Commonweal. May 6, 1966, v84, p201.
Film Daily. Mar 23, 1966, p4.
Film Quarterly. Sum 1966, v19, p67-68.
Filmfacts. Aug 1, 1966, v9, p145-46.
Films in Review. May 1966, v17, p314-15.
Hollywood Reporter. Mar 23, 1966, p3.
Kiss Kiss Bang Bang. p220-22.
Life. Apr 8, 1966, v60, p16.
The London Times. Jul 7, 1965, p12.
Look. Apr 19, 1966, v30, p106.
Mademoiselle. Jun 1966, v63, p52.
Magill's Survey of Cinema. Series II. v1, p312-14.
Motion Picture Herald Product Digest. Jun 1, 1966, p533.
Motion Picture Herald Product Digest. Mar 30, 1966, p491.
New Statesman. Mar 18, 1966, v71, p401.
The New York Times. Jun 23, 1966, p29.
The New Yorker. Jul 9, 1966, v42, p78.
Newsweek. Apr 11, 1966, v67, p110.
Senior Scholastic. Apr 15, 1966, v88, p35.

The Spectator. Mar 18, 1966, v216, p330.
Time. Apr 8, 1966, v87, p105.
Variety. Mar 23, 1966, p6.

Born to be Bad (US; Ray, Nicholas; 1950)
BFI/Monthly Film Bulletin. Jan 1951, v18, p202-03.
Film Daily. Aug 22, 1950, p5.
Hollywood Reporter. Aug 22, 1950, p3.
Library Journal. Oct 15, 1950, v75, p1843.
The London Times. Jan 8, 1951, p2.
Motion Picture Herald Product Digest. Aug 26, 1950, p449-50.
The New York Times. Sep 29, 1950, p31.
The New Yorker. Oct 7, 1950, v26, p63.
Newsweek. Oct 2, 1950, v36, p86.
Nicholas Ray: A Guide to References and Resources. p53-57.
The Spectator. Jan 5, 1951, v186, p13.
Time. Sep 18, 1950, v56, p103.
Variety. Aug 23, 1950, p8.
The Velvet Light Trap. Fall 1973, n10, p46-53.

Born Yesterday (US; Cukor, George; 1950)
BFI/Monthly Film Bulletin. Mar 1951, v18, p227.
Christian Century. Feb 7, 1951, v68, p191.
Commonweal. Dec 29, 1950, v53, p301-02.
Dictionary of Films. p40-41.
Fifty From the Fifties. p61-66.
Film Daily. Nov 20, 1950, p4.
Films in Review. Feb 1951, v2, p36-38.
The Films of William Holden. p115-18.
Fortnight. Dec 25, 1950, v9, p32.
George Cukor (Phillips). p108-10.
Hollywood Reporter. Nov 17, 1950, p3.
Kiss Kiss Bang Bang. p296-97.
Library Journal. Jan 15, 1951, v76, p124.
Magill's Survey of Cinema. Series I. v1, p209-11.
Motion Picture Herald Product Digest. Nov 25, 1950, p590-91.
The Nation. Feb 3, 1951, v172, p114.
The New Republic. Jan 15, 1951, v124, p31.
The New Statesman and Nation. May 5, 1951, v41, p504.
The New York Times. Dec 27, 1950, p30.
The New Yorker. Dec 23, 1950, v26, p59.
Newsweek. Jan 1, 1951, v37, p57.
On Cukor. p214-17.
Rotha on Film. p174-75.
Saturday Review. Jan 6, 1951, v34, p26.
Selected Film Criticism, 1941-1950. p32-33.
Sight and Sound. Mar 1951, v19, p441, 456.
The Spectator. Apr 27, 1951, v186, p553.
Time. Dec 25, 1950, v56, p56-57.
Variety. Nov 22, 1950, p8.

The Boston Strangler (US; Fleischer, Richard; 1968)
America. Oct 26, 1968, v119, p392.
American Cinematographer. Feb 1969, v50, p202-05.
BFI/Monthly Film Bulletin. Jun 1969, v36, p119.
Commonweal. Nov 15, 1968, v89, p254.
Esquire. Mar 1969, v71, p32.
Film 68/69. p182-84.
Film Daily. Oct 15, 1968, p8.
Filmfacts. Jan 15, 1969, v11, p465-67.
Films and Filming. Jul 1969, v15, p40-41.
Films in Review. Nov 1968, v19, p581-82.
Going Steady. p201-03.
Hollywood Reporter. Oct 14, 1968, p3.
The London Times. May 15, 1969, p14.
The London Times. May 17, 1969, p19.
Magill's Survey of Cinema. Series II. v1, p315-17.
Motion Picture Herald Product Digest. Oct 16, 1968, p39.

New Statesman. May 16, 1969, v77, p709-10.
The New York Times. Oct 17, 1968, p52.
The New Yorker. Oct 26, 1968, v44, p209-10.
Newsweek. Oct 28, 1968, v72, p114.
Saturday Review. Oct 26, 1968, v51, p55.
Variety. May 29, 1968, p20.
A Year In the Dark. p271-72.

The Bostonians (GB; Ivory, James; 1984)
BFI/Monthly Film Bulletin. Sep 1984, v51, p271.
Christian Century. Aug 29, 1984, v101, p811.
Commentary. Oct 1984, v78, p60-65.
Film Journal. Sep 1984, v87, p30.
Films and Filming. Sep 1984, n360, p35.
Films in Review. Nov 1984, v35, p498.
Hollywood Reporter. Jul 30, 1984, p4.
Horizon. May 1984, v27, p35-36.
Informer. Nov 1984, p6.
Maclean's. Dec 10, 1984, v97, p69.
Magill's Cinema Annual, 1985. p105-11.
Ms. Oct 1984, v13, p133-34.
The New Republic. Aug 6, 1984, v191, p26-27.
New Statesman. Sep 28, 1984, v108, p36-37.
New York. Aug 13, 1984, v17, p51-52.
The New York Times. Aug 5, 1985, SecII, p15.
The New York Times. Aug 2, 1984, SecIII, p15.
The New Yorker. Aug 6, 1984, v60, p68.
Newsweek. Aug 13, 1984, v104, p67.
On Location. Jun 1984, v8, p76.
Photoplay. Nov 1984, v35, p21.
Sight and Sound. Oct 1984, v53, p295.
Time. Oct 15, 1984, v124, p99.
Variety. May 23, 1984, p15.
The Village Voice. Aug 7, 1984, p52.
Vogue. Oct 1984, v174, p76.

Both Ends of the Candle *See* The Helen Morgan Story

Boucher, Le *See* The Butcher

Boulanger de Valorgue, Le (Also titled: The Baker of Valorgue) (FR, IT; Verneuil, Henri; 1952)
BFI/Monthly Film Bulletin. Mar 1955, v22, p32.
Films and Filming. Apr 1955, v1, p20.
The New Statesman and Nation. Feb 5, 1955, v49, p178.
Variety. Mar 25, 1953, p78.

Bound for Glory (US; Ashby, Hal; 1976)
America. Feb 12, 1977, v136, p135-36.
American Cinematographer. Jul 1976, v57, p788-91.
American Cinematographer. May 1977, v58, p496-98.
Film Bulletin. Nov-Dec 1976, v45, p8, 42.
Film Comment. Nov-Dec 1976, v12, p26-28.
Films and Filming. Jun 1977, v23, p34-36.
Films In Review. Feb 1977, v28, p118.
The Films of the Seventies. p150-51.
Hollywood Reporter. Oct 26, 1976, p8.
Independent Film Journal. Nov 12, 1976, v78, p9.
The Los Angeles Times. Dec 5, 1976, Calendar, p1.
The New Republic. Nov 27, 1976, v175, p18.
New Times. Jan 1, 1977, v8, p87-88.
The New York Times. Dec 5, 1976, SecII, p1.
The New York Times. Dec 4, 1976, p17.
The New York Times. Dec 12, 1977, SecII, p1.
The New Yorker. Dec 13, 1976, v52, p148-52.
Newsweek. Dec 13, 1976, v88, p104.
Saturday Review. Dec 11, 1976, v4, p78.
Sight and Sound. Fall 1976, v45, p140-49.
Time. Dec 20, 1976, v108, p62.
Variety. Oct 27, 1976, p26.
The Village Voice. Dec 13, 1976, p85.
When the Lights Go Down. p224-30.

The Bounty (US; Donaldson, Roger; 1984)
BFI/Monthly Film Bulletin. Aug 1984, v51, p237-38.
Cinema Papers. Aug 1984, n47, p267-68.
Commentary. Aug 1984, v78, p56-62.
Commonweal. Jun 1, 1984, v111, p338-39.
Contemporary Review. Nov 1984, v245, p267-70.
Film Journal. Jun 1984, v87, p23-24.
Films and Filming. Aug 1984, n359, p32-33.
Films in Review. Aug-Sep 1984, v35, p432-33.
Hollywood Reporter. Apr 24, 1984, p4.
Horizon. Apr 1984, v27, p46-49.
Informer. May-Jun 1984, p3-4.
The Los Angeles Times. May 4, 1984, SecVI, p1.
Maclean's. May 14, 1984, v97, p74.
The New Republic. Jun 14, 1984, v190, p24-26.
New Statesman. Sep 28, 1984, v108, p36-37.
New York. May 14, 1984, v17, p72.
The New York Times. May 4, 1984, SecIII, p8.
The New York Times. Apr 29, 1984, SecII, p17.
The New Yorker. Jun 11, 1984, v60, p109-11.
Newsweek. May 14, 1984, v103, p81.
Penthouse. Jul 1984, v15, p48.
Photoplay. Aug 1984, v35, p24-27.
Photoplay. Oct 1984, v35, p22.
Stills. Jun-Jul 1984, n12, p55-60.
Time. May 7, 1984, v123, p121.
Variety. Apr 25, 1984, p18.
The Village Voice. May 15, 1984, p53.
Vogue. Jun 1984, v174, p52.

Boy, Did I Get a Wrong Number (US; Marshall, George; 1966)
BFI/Monthly Film Bulletin. Aug 1966, v33, p122.
Film Daily. Jun 8, 1966, p4.
Filmfacts. Aug 1, 1966, v9, p136-38.
Films and Filming. Aug 1966, v12, p7.
Hollywood Reporter. Jun 1, 1966, p3.
The New York Times. Jun 9, 1966, p54.
Newsweek. Jun 20, 1966, v67, p102.
Time. Jun 24, 1966, v87, p104.
Variety. Jun 8, 1966, p6.

The Boy Friend (GB, US; Russell, Ken; 1971)
BFI/Monthly Film Bulletin. Mar 1972, v39, p48.
Commonweal. Jan 7, 1972, v95, p326.
Deeper into Movies. p378.
Filmfacts. 1971, v14, p469-73.
Films and Filming. Oct 1971, v18, n1, p34-35.
Hollywood Reporter. Dec 16, 1971, v219, n11, p3.
Ken Russell: A Guide to References and Resources. p30-32.
Ken Russell (Phillips). p152-58.
Ken Russell's Films. p118.
Life. Jan 21, 1972, v72, p16.
Magill's Survey of Cinema. Series II. v1, p318-21.
The New York Times. Dec 17, 1971, p29.
The New Yorker. Jan 8, 1971, v47, p74-77.
Newsweek. Dec 27, 1971, v78, p61-62.
Saturday Review. Jan 29, 1972, v75, p23.
Sight and Sound. Spr 1972, v41, n2, p111-12.
Time. Dec 20, 1971, v98, p82-83.
Variety. Dec 22, 1971, p6.
The Village Voice. Dec 23, 1971, p51.

The Boy From Oklahoma (US; Curtiz, Michael; 1954)
BFI/Monthly Film Bulletin. Jun 1954, v21, p86-87.
Commonweal. Mar 19, 1954, v59, p600.
Film Daily. Jan 28, 1954, p14.

Hollywood Reporter. Jan 14, 1954, p3.
Motion Picture Herald Product Digest. Jan 16, 1954, p2141.
National Parent-Teacher. Jan 1954, v48, p38.
Time. Mar 8, 1954, v63, p100.
Variety. Jan 20, 1954, p6.

Boy on a Dolphin (US; Negulesco, Jean; 1957)
America. May 4, 1957, v97, p180.
American Cinematographer. May 1957, v38, p298-99.
BFI/Monthly Film Bulletin. Jun 1957, v24, p68.
Commonweal. May 3, 1957, v66, p127.
Film Daily. Apr 11, 1957, p6.
Films and Filming. Jun 1957, v3, p24.
Films in Review. May 1957, v8, p222-23.
The Films of Alan Ladd. p219-22.
The Films of Sophia Loren. p81-84.
The Films of the Fifties. p233-24.
Hollywood Reporter. Apr 11, 1957, p3.
Motion Picture Herald Product Digest. Apr 13, 1957, p337.
The New York Times. Apr 20, 1957, p21.
The New Yorker. Apr 27, 1957, v33, p68.
Newsweek. Apr 22, 1957, v49, p122.
Saturday Review. May 11, 1957, v40, p27.
Time. Apr 22, 1957, v69, p108.
Variety. Apr 17, 1957, p6.

A Boy Ten Feet Tall (Also titled: Sammy Going South) (GB; Mackendrick, Alexander; 1963)
BFI/Monthly Film Bulletin. May 1963, v30, p61.
Commonweal. Jan 29, 1965, v81, p573.
Film Daily. Jan 6, 1965, p9.
Filmfacts. Apr 16, 1965, v8, p59-61.
Films and Filming. May 1963, v9, p28.
Hollywood Reporter. Jan 6, 1965, p3.
Illustrated London News. Mar 30, 1963, v242, p478.
Life. Mar 12, 1965, v58, p19.
Motion Picture Herald Product Digest. Jan 20, 1965, p210-11.
New Statesman. Mar 22, 1963, v65, p436.
The New York Times. May 13, 1965, p32.
The Private Eye, the Cowboy and the Very Naked Girl. p131-32.
The Spectator. Mar 22, 1963, v210, p360.
Variety. Mar 27, 1963, p6.
The Village Voice. May 27, 1965, v10, p19.

The Boys from Brazil (US; Schaffner, Franklin J.; 1978)
BFI/Monthly Film Bulletin. Apr 1979, v46, p48.
Encore. Oct 16, 1978, v7, p30.
Films in Review. Nov 1978, v29, p569.
The Films of Gregory Peck. p233-36.
The Films of the Seventies. p229-31.
Hollywood Reporter. Sep 25, 1978, p3.
Laurence Olivier: Theater & Cinema. p244-52.
The Los Angeles Times. Oct 5, 1978, SecIV, p1.
Maclean's. Oct 16, 1978, v91, p70.
Magill's Cinema Annual, 1986. p480-83.
New York. Oct 9, 1978, v11, p112.
The New York Times. Dec 3, 1978, SecII, p13.
The New Yorker. Oct 9, 1978, v54, p164.
Newsweek. Oct 9, 1978, v92, p92.
Time. Oct 9, 1978, v112, p100-01.
Variety. Sep 27, 1978, p20.

The Boys in Company C (US; Furie, Sidney J.; 1978)
BFI/Monthly Film Bulletin. Mar 1978, v45, p41.
Films in Review. Mar 1978, v29, p186.
Hollywood Reporter. Jan 25, 1978, p3.
Human Behavior. Apr 1978, v7, p75.

The Los Angeles Times. Apr 28, 1978, SecIV, p1.
Motion Picture Herald Product Digest. Jan 25, 1978, p68.
The New Republic. Mar 4, 1978, v178, p27.
New York. Jan 23, 1978, v11, p65-66.
The New York Times. Feb 2, 1978, SecIII, p15.
Newsweek. Feb 6, 1978, v91, p89.
Variety. Jan 25, 1978, p24.

The Boys in the Band (US; Friedkin, William; 1970)
America. Apr 11, 1970, v122, p398.
BFI/Monthly Film Bulletin. Oct 1970, v37, n441, p199.
Christian Century. Aug 5, 1970, v87, p944.
Deeper into Movies. p137-38.
Film Daily. Mar 18, 1970, p3.
Films and Filming. Oct 1970, v17, n1, p38.
The Films of the Seventies. p26-29.
Hollywood Reporter. Mar 13, 1970, p3.
Life. Apr 10, 1970, v48, p12.
Magill's Survey of Cinema. Series II. v1, p321-33.
The New Republic. Apr 18, 1970, v162, p20.
The New York Times. Mar 18, 1970, p36.
The New York Times. Mar 21, 1970, v46, p166-67.
Newsweek. Mar 30, 1970, v75, p91.
Saturday Review. Apr 4, 1970, v53, p24.
Time. Mar 30, 1970, v95, p97.
Variety. Mar 18, 1970, p18.
Vogue. May 1970, v155, p152.

The Brain (French title: Cerveau, Le) (FR; Oury, Gerard; 1969)
America. Nov 29, 1969, v121, p544.
Film Daily. Sep 25, 1969, p7.
Films and Filming. Feb 1970, v16, p42-43.
Films in Review. Dec 1969, v20, p638-39.
The Films of David Niven. p225-29.
Hollywood Reporter. Sep 17, 1969, p3.
The New York Times. Nov 14, 1969, p40.
Newsweek. Dec 1, 1969, v74, p89.
Time. Dec 5, 1969, v94, p114.

Brainstorm (US; Conrad, William; 1965)
BFI/Monthly Film Bulletin. Mar 1966, v33, p41.
Film Daily. May 14, 1965, p6.
Films and Filming. Mar 1969, v15, p84.
Hollywood Reporter. May 10, 1965, p3.
Motion Picture Herald Product Digest. May 26, 1965, p291.
The New York Times. Jun 10, 1965, p38.
Time. Jun 18, 1965, v85, p102.
Variety. May 12, 1965, p28.

Brainstorm (US; Trumbull, Douglas; 1983)
Christianity Today. Nov 11, 1983, v27, p91.
Film Comment. Sep-Oct 1983, v19, p76-82.
Films in Review. Oct 1983, v34, p502-03.
Hollywood Reporter. Sep 27, 1983, p3.
The Los Angeles Times. Sep 30, 1983, SecVI, p13.
Maclean's. Oct 10, 1983, v96, p56.
The New York Times. Sep 30, 1983, SecIII, p17.
Newsweek. Oct 10, 1983, v102, p94.
Psychology Today. Nov 1983, v17, p79.
Time. Oct 17, 1983, v122, p90.
Variety. Sep 28, 1983, p10.

Branded (US; Maté, Rudolph; 1950)
Christian Century. Feb 21, 1951, v68, p254.
Commonweal. Jan 26, 1951, v53, p399.
Film Daily. Nov 16, 1950, p6.
The Films of Alan Ladd. p149-52.
Hollywood Reporter. Nov 15, 1950, p4.
The London Times. Jan 22, 1951, p2.
Motion Picture Herald Product Digest. Nov 18, 1950, p570.
The Nation. Feb 3, 1951, v172, p114.

The New York Times. Jan 11, 1951, p28.
Saturday Review. Feb 17, 1951, v34, p30.
The Spectator. Jan 19, 1951, v186, p76.
Time. Jan 15, 1951, v57, p78.
Variety. Nov 15, 1950, p6.

Brandy For the Parson (GB; Eldridge, John; 1952)
Motion Picture Herald Product Digest. Aug 30, 1952, p1511.
The New York Times. Apr 18, 1952, p13.
The New Yorker. Aug 30, 1952, v28, p51.
Newsweek. Sep 8, 1952, v40, p95.
Sight and Sound. Apr-Jun 1951, v21, p171.
The Tatler. Jun 4, 1952, v204, p540.
Theatre Arts. Oct 1952, v36, p96.
Variety. Jun 4, 1952, p6.

Bratya Karamazovy *See* The Brothers Karamazov

The Brave Bulls (US; Rossen, Robert; 1951)
BFI/Monthly Film Bulletin. Oct 1951, v18, p338.
Christian Century. Aug 8, 1951, v68, p927.
Commonweal. May 4, 1951, v54, p90.
Fifty From the Fifties. p67-74.
Film Criticism and Caricatures, 1943-1953. p130-31.
Film Daily. Apr 18, 1951, p6.
Films in Review. Jun-Jul 1951, v2, p34-35.
The Films of Anthony Quinn. p118-19.
Hollywood Reporter. Apr 18, 1951, p3.
Library Journal. May 1, 1951, v76, p785.
Motion Picture Herald Product Digest. Apr 21, 1951, p809.
The Nation. May 26, 1951, v172, p497.
The New York Times. Apr 19, 1951, p39.
The New Yorker. Apr 21, 1951, v27, p97.
Newsweek. Apr 23, 1951, v37, p54-55.
Saturday Review. May 5, 1951, v34, p26-27.
Senior Scholastic. May 9, 1951, v58, p29.
Sight and Sound. Oct-Dec 1951, v21, p82.
Time. Apr 23, 1951, v57, p106.

The Brave Italian People *See* Italiano brava Gente

The Brave One (US; Rapper, Irving; 1956)
America. Dec 22, 1956, v96, p360.
Commonweal. Dec 7, 1956, v64, p254.
Film Daily. Sep 19, 1956, p6.
Films and Filming. Nov 1957, v4, p24.
Films in Review. Aug-Sep 1956, v7, p346-47.
Hollywood Reporter. Sep 19, 1956, p3.
Magill's Survey of Cinema. Series II. v1, p328-31.
Newsweek. Oct 15, 1956, v48, p132.
Saturday Review. Oct 20, 1956, v39, p59.
Talking Pictures. p259-60.
Variety. Sep 19, 1956, p6.

Brazil (GB; Gilliam, Terry; 1985)
BFI/Monthly Film Bulletin. Apr 1985, v52, p107.
California Magazine. Dec 1985, v10, p121.
Chicago. Feb 1986, v35, p80.
Commonweal. Feb 28, 1986, v113, p114-15.
Film Quarterly. Spr 1985, v38, p50.
Hollywood Reporter. Dec 18, 1985, p3.
The Los Angeles Times. Dec 25, 1985, SecVI, p1.
Maclean's. Feb 10, 1986, v99, p74.
Magill's Cinema Annual, 1986. p80-83.
The Nation. Feb 15, 1986, v242, p185.
The New Republic. Feb 17, 1986, v194, p26.
New Statesman. Feb 22, 1985, v109, p35.
New York. Jan 27, 1986, v19, p55.
The New York Times. Dec 18, 1985, SecIII, p22.
Newsweek. Dec 16, 1985, v106, p82.

Progressive. Apr 1986, v50, p39.
Saturday Review. Sep-Oct 1985, v11, p76.
Time. Dec 30, 1985, v126, p84.
Variety. Feb 13, 1985, p18.

Bread and Chocolate (Italian title: Pane e cioccolata) (IT; Brusati, Franco; 1973)
BFI/Monthly Film Bulletin. Nov 1979, v46, p230-31.
Hollywood Reporter. Jul 18, 1978, p6.
Human Behavior. Nov 1978, v7, p77.
The Los Angeles Times. Oct 25, 1978, SecIV, p16.
Magill's Survey of Cinema. Foreign Language Films. v1, p402-04.
Motion Picture Herald Product Digest. Jul 26, 1978, p14.
The Nation. Aug 5, 1978, v227, p123-24.
New York. Jul 31, 1978, v11, p62.
The New York Times. Jul 14, 1978, SecIII, p14.
The New York Times. Dec 14, 1978, SecIII, p20.
Newsweek. Aug 14, 1978, v112, p63.
Time. Aug 28, 1978, v112, p57.
Variety. Feb 27, 1974, p26.
Vogue. Jul 24, 1978, v168, p40.

Bread, Love and Dreams (Italian title: Pane, Amore e Fantasia) (IT; Comencini, Luigi; 1953)
BFI/Monthly Film Bulletin. Dec 1954, v21, p174.
Commonweal. Sep 10, 1954, v60, p557.
Film Daily. Oct 4, 1954, p6.
Films and Filming. Jan 1956, v2, p21.
Films in Review. Oct 1954, v5, p433-34.
Hollywood Reporter. Nov 2, 1954, p3.
Life. Sep 20, 1954, v37, p125.
The London Times. Oct 25, 1954, p2.
Motion Picture Herald Product Digest. Sep 25, 1954, p153-54.
National Parent-Teacher. Nov 1954, v49, p39.
The New Statesman and Nation. Oct 30, 1954, v48, p537.
The New York Times. Sep 21, 1954, p24.
The New York Times Magazine. Aug 15, 1954, p54.
The New Yorker. Oct 2, 1954, v30, p131.
Newsweek. Oct 4, 1954, v44, p85-86.
Passion and Defiance. p142.
Reporter. Oct 21, 1954, v11, p42.
Saturday Review. Sep 4, 1954, v37, p26.
Saturday Review. Jan 1, 1955, v38, p63.
The Tatler. Nov 3, 1954, v214, p286-87.
Time. Oct 4, 1954, v64, p100.
Variety. Jan 20, 1954, p18.

Breaker Morant (AUSTRALIA; Beresford, Bruce; 1981)
America. Feb 14, 1981, v144, p124.
BFI/Monthly Film Bulletin. Aug 1980, v47, p153.
Christian Science Monitor. Jan 15, 1981, p19.
Cineaste. Fall 1981, v10, p43.
Cinema Papers. Dec 1980, n30, p420-21.
Cinema Papers. Feb 1982, n36, p48-49.
Commentary. May 1981, v71, p73-81.
Critical Arts. Sum 1983, v2, p51-53.
Critical Arts. Fall 1982, v2, p61-68.
Film Journal. Jan 15, 1981, v84, p33.
Films In Review. Mar 1981, v32, p183-84.
Films in Review. Mar 1982, v32, p183.
Hollywood Reporter. Dec 24, 1980, p3.
Horizon. Feb 1981, v24, p70-71.
Jump Cut. Jul 1982, n27, p13-14.
Magill's Survey of Cinema. Series II. v1, p331-35.
Millimeter. Apr 1981, v9, p184-86.
The Nation. Jan 31, 1981, v232, p124-25.
National Review. Mar 20, 1981, v33, p304-05.

The New Republic. Dec 27, 1980, v183, p24.
New York. Jan 26, 1981, v14, p47-48.
The New York Times. Jan 2, 1981, SecIII, p8.
The New York Times. Dec 22, 1980, SecIII, p22.
Progressive. Mar 1981, v45, p54.
Saturday Review. Jan 1981, v8, p84-85.
Time. Jan 5, 1981, v117, p85.
Variety. Apr 23, 1980, p18.
The Village Voice. Dec 24, 1980, p42.

Breakfast at Tiffany's (US; Edwards, Blake; 1961)
America. Nov 25, 1961, v106, p310-11.
BFI/Monthly Film Bulletin. Nov 1961, v28, p151.
Blake Edwards (Lehman and Luhr). p60-66, 161-62.
Commonweal. Oct 20, 1961, v75, p93.
Esquire. Dec 1961, v56, p64.
Film Daily. Oct 5, 1961, p6.
Filmfacts. Oct 20, 1961, v4, p233-35.
Films in Review. Nov 1961, v7, p553-54.
The Films of the Sixties. p57-59.
Life. Sep 8, 1961, v51, p133-36.
Magill's Survey of Cinema. Series I. v1, p215-17.
The Modern American Novel and the Movies. p236-47.
The New Republic. Sep 18, 1961, v145, p28.
The New York Times. Oct 6, 1961, p28.
The New Yorker. Oct 16, 1961, v37, p198-99.
Newsweek. Oct 16, 1961, v58, p114.
Saturday Review. Sep 30, 1961, v44, p28.
Time. Oct 20, 1961, v78, p94.
Unholy Fools, Wits, Comics, Disturbers of the Peace. p218-19.
Variety. Oct 11, 1961, p7.

The Breakfast Club (US; Hughes, John; 1985)
BFI/Monthly Film Bulletin. May 1985, v52, p148.
Chicago. Mar 1985, v34, p125.
Films in Review. May 1985, v36, p306.
Los Angeles. Mar 1985, v30, p36.
The Los Angeles Times. Feb 15, 1985, SecVI, p1.
Maclean's. Feb 18, 1985, v98, p58.
Magill's Cinema Annual, 1986. p85-89.
Ms. Jun 1985, v13, p90.
New Statesman. Jan 7, 1985, v109, p36.
New York. Feb 18, 1985, v18, p95-96.
The New York Times. Feb 15, 1985, SecIII, p18.
The New Yorker. Apr 8, 1985, v61, p123-25.
Newsweek. Feb 25, 1985, v105, p85.
Playboy. May 1985, v32, p37.
Saturday Review. Apr 1985, v11, p78.
Texas Monthly. Apr 1985, v13, p176.
Time. Feb 18, 1985, v125, p90.
Variety. Feb 13, 1985, v318, p19.
Washingtonian. Mar 1985, v20, p80.

Breakheart Pass (US; Gries, Tom; 1976)
BFI/Monthly Film Bulletin. Feb 1976, v43, p24-25.
Films and Filming. Apr 1976, v22, p40.
Films in Review. Mar 1976, v27, p187.
Hollywood Reporter. Mar 10, 1976, p8.
Independent Film Journal. Feb 18, 1976, v77, p11.
The Los Angeles Times. Mar 10, 1976, SecIV, p9.
Movietone News. Apr 1976, n49, p47-48.
New Statesman. Jan 16, 1976, v91, p110.
The New York Times. May 6, 1976, p46.
Time. Apr 19, 1976, v107, p82.
Variety. Feb 4, 1976, p16.

Breaking Away (US; Yates, Peter; 1979)
BFI/Monthly Film Bulletin. Nov 1979, v46, p224-25.
Commonweal. May 23, 1980, v107, p305-07.
Films in Review. Oct 1979, v30, p501.
Hollywood Reporter. Jul 9, 1979, p5.
The Los Angeles Times. Jul 8, 1979, Calendar, p1.
Magill's Survey of Cinema. Series I. v1, p218-21.
Motion Picture Herald Product Digest. Aug 1, 1979, p18.
The New Republic. Aug 18, 1979, v181, p24.
New York. Jul 30, 1979, v12, p58.
The New York Times. Sep 2, 1979, SecIV, p13.
The New Yorker. Aug 6, 1979, v55, p65.
Newsweek. Jul 23, 1979, v94, p71.
Rolling Stone. Sep 20, 1979, p42.
Rolling Stone. Apr 17, 1980, p31-32.
Saturday Review. Oct 13, 1979, v6, p60.
Sports Illustrated. Aug 6, 1979, v5, p32.
Time. Jul 30, 1979, v114, p83.
Variety. Jul 11, 1979, p19.

The Breaking Point (US; Curtiz, Michael; 1950)
BFI/Monthly Film Bulletin. Jan 1951, v18, p199-200.
Commonweal. Oct 13, 1950, v53, p14.
Film Daily. Sep 12, 1950, p8.
Films in Review. Dec 1950, v1, p41.
The Films of John Garfield. p171-75.
Hemingway on Film. p48-65.
Hollywood Reporter. Sep 11, 1950, p3.
Library Journal. Oct 1, 1950, v75, p1677.
The London Times. Jan 31, 1951, p9.
Motion Picture Herald Product Digest. Sep 16, 1950, p486.
The New York Times. Oct 7, 1950, p10.
The New Yorker. Oct 21, 1950, v26, p101.
Newsweek. Oct 16, 1950, v36, p92.
Sight and Sound. Feb 1951, v19, p413.
The Spectator. Jan 26, 1951, v18, p108.
Time. Sep 25, 1950, v56, p96.
Variety. Sep 13, 1950, p4.
The Velvet Light Trap. Wint 1975, n14, p17-20.

Breaking Through the Sound Barrier (Also titled: The Sound Barrier; Through the Sound Barrier; Breaking the Sound Barrier) (GB; Lean, David; 1952)
American Photography. Mar 1953, v47, p15.
BFI/Monthly Film Bulletin. Sep 1952, v19, p124-25.
Catholic World. Dec 1952, v176, p222-23.
Christian Century. Dec 17, 1952, v69, p1487.
The Cinema of David Lean. p99-108.
Commonweal. Nov 14, 1952, v57, p141.
David Lean: A Guide to References and Resources. p81-82.
David Lean and His Films. p103-14.
David Lean (Anderegg). p73-79.
Film Daily. Oct 30, 1952, p6.
Films in Review. Dec 1952, v3, p527-28.
Illustrated London News. Aug 9, 1952, v221, p232.
Kiss Kiss Bang Bang. p297.
The London Times. Jul 23, 1952, p3.
Magill's Cinema Annual, 1985. p621-25.
Motion Picture Herald Product Digest. Nov 15, 1952, p1605.
National Parent-Teacher. Jan 1953, v47, p37.
The New Statesman and Nation. Aug 2, 1952, v44, p134.
The New York Times. Nov 7, 1952, p19.
The New Yorker. Aug 30, 1952, v28, p68.
The New Yorker. Nov 22, 1952, v28, p107.
Newsweek. Dec 1, 1952, v40, p82.
Saturday Review. Nov 22, 1952, v35, p38.

Senior Scholastic. Dec 10, 1952, v61, p25.
Sight and Sound. Oct-Dec 1952, v22, p80.
The Spectator. Jul 25, 1952, v189, p129.
The Tatler. Aug 6, 1952, v205, p246.
The Tatler. Feb 11, 1953, v207, p238.
Time. Nov 10, 1952, v60, p120.
Variety. Jul 20, 1952, p18.

Breathless (French title: A Bout de Souffle; Also titled: The Last Gasp) (FR; Godard, Jean-Luc; 1960)
Commentary. Sep 1960, v30, p230-32.
Commonweal. Feb 17, 1961, v73, p533.
Dictionary of Films. p1.
Esquire. Jul 1961, v56, p20.
Film. Sum 1961, v29, p10.
Film Quarterly. Spr 1961, v14, p54-56.
Filmfacts. Mar 13, 1961, v4, p35.
Films and Filming. Aug 1961, v7, p25.
The Films in My Life. p316.
Films in Review. Jun-Jul 1960, v11, p367-68.
Films in Review. Mar 1961, v12, p175-77.
The Films of Jean-Luc Godard. p11-16.
Great Film Directors. p361-64.
I Lost It at the Movies. p127-32, 210-12.
Jean-Luc Godard: A Guide to References and Resources. p36-39.
Jean-Luc Godard (Collet). p164-65, 171-75.
Jean-Luc Godard (Kreidl). p39-40, 45-46.
Landmark Films. p248-57.
The Nation. Mar 11, 1961, v192, p223.
The New Republic. Feb 13, 1961, v144, p20.
The New Wave. p108-13.
The New York Times. Feb 8, 1961, p26.
The New York Times. Feb 12, 1961, SecII, p1.
The New Yorker. Feb 11, 1961, v36, p102-4.
Newsweek. Feb 6, 1961, v57, p84.
On Movies. p372-74.
Reruns. p132-35.
Sight and Sound. Spr 1960, v29, p84-85.
Time. Feb 17, 1961, v77, p62.
Variety. Jan 27, 1960, p6.

Breathless (US; McBride, Jim; 1983)
Commonweal. Jun 17, 1983, v110, p371.
Film Comment. May-Jun 1983, v19, p34-38.
Hollywood Reporter. May 12, 1983, p3.
Horizon. Jul-Aug 1983, v26, p61.
The Los Angeles Times. May 13, 1983, SecVI, p1.
Magill's Cinema Annual, 1984. p89-93.
The New Republic. Jun 13, 1983, v188, p24-25.
The New York Times. May 13, 1983, SecIII, p10.
Newsweek. May 23, 1983, v101, p54.
Sight and Sound. Aut 1983, v52, p276.
Time. May 30, 1983, v121, p76.

Breve vacanza, Una *See* Brief Vacation

Brewster's Millions (US; Hill, Walter; 1985)
BFI/Monthly Film Bulletin. Aug 1985, v52, p243.
Hollywood Reporter. May 20, 1985, p3.
Jet. Jun 3, 1985, v68, p58-60.
The Los Angles Times. May 22, 1985, SecVI, p1.
Maclean's. Jun 3, 1985, v98, p51.
New York. Jun 10, 1985, v18, p78.
The New York Times. May 22, 1985, SecIII, p23.
The New York Times. Jun 2, 1985, SecII, p19.
Newsweek. Jun 3, 1985, v105, p65.
Time. Jun 3, 1985, v125, p71.
Variety. May 22, 1985, p14.

The Bride Wore Black (French title: Mariée Était en Noir, La) (FR; Truffaut, François; 1967)

BFI/Monthly Film Bulletin. Sep 1968, v35, p133.
Christian Century. Oct 23, 1968, v85, p1342.
Christian Science Monitor (Western edition). Aug 5, 1968, p6.
Cinema. Spr 1968, v4, p30-33.
The Cinema of François Truffaut. p88-97.
Commonweal. Aug 9, 1968, v88, p534.
Confessions of a Cultist. p380-82.
Film Daily. Jul 19, 1968, p4.
Film Quarterly. Fall 1968, v22, p72.
Filmfacts. Aug 1, 1968, v11, p196-98.
Films and Filming. Oct 1968, v15, p38-39.
Films in Review. Aug-Sep 1968, v19, p454-55.
Finally Truffaut. p123-30.
François Truffaut (Crisp). p92-99.
François Truffaut (Insdorf). p55-67, 105-12, 240.
Hollywood Reporter. May 16, 1968, p3.
Life. Aug 9, 1968, v65, p4.
Literature/Film Quarterly. 1973, v1, n3, p218-25.
The London Times. May 18, 1968, p23.
The London Times. Aug 1, 1968, p7.
Magill's Survey of Cinema. Foreign Language Films. v1, p410-13.
Motion Picture Herald Product Digest. Jul 31, 1968, p836.
Movie. Wint 1968-69, n16, p34-36.
Movies Into Film. p182-84.
The Nation. Jul 22, 1968, v207, p61.
The New Republic. Jul 13, 1968, v159, p22.
The New Republic. Jul 7, 1968, v159, p17.
New Statesman. Aug 2, 1968, v76, p150-51.
The New York Times. Jun 26, 1968, p42.
The New Yorker. Jul 6, 1968, v44, p46-47.
Newsweek. Jul 1, 1968, v72, p94.
Saturday Review. Jun 22, 1968, v51, p55.
Sight and Sound. Aut 1968, v37, p188-89.
Sight and Sound. Spr 1969, v38, p87-88.
The Spectator. Aug 9, 1968, v221, p202.
Take One. May-Jun 1968, v1, p24.
Time. Jul 5, 1968, v92, p54-55.
Variety. Apr 24, 1968, p26.
The Village Voice. Aug 22, 1968, p31.
Vogue. Aug 1, 1968, v152, p60.
A Year In the Dark. p183-85.

The Bridge on the River Kwai (GB; Lean, David; 1957)
America. Jan 4, 1958, v98, p403.
BFI/Monthly Film Bulletin. Nov 1957, v24, p134-35.
The Cinema of David Lean. p129-44.
Cinema, the Magic Vehicle. v2, p369-71.
Combat Films. p143-73.
Commonweal. Dec 20, 1957, v67, p311.
David Lean: A Guide to References and Resources. p86-87.
David Lean and His Films. p149-59.
David Lean (Anderegg). p91-102.
Fifty from the Fifties. p75-82.
Film Culture. Feb 1958, v4, p15-16.
Film Daily. Nov 20, 1957, p10.
Film Quarterly. Fall 1958, v12, p45-50.
Films and Filming. Nov 1957, v4, p26-27.
Films and Filming. Feb 1963, v9, p44.
Films in Review. Jan 1958, v9, p23-24.
The Films of the Fifties. p229-30.
The Films of William Holden. p180-85.
The Great Adventure Films. p212-18.
The Great Movies. p108-10.
Hollywood Reporter. Nov 20, 1957, p3.
Magill's Survey of Cinema. English Language Films. Series I, v1, p225-29.
Motion Picture Herald Product Digest. Nov 23, 1957, p26.
The Nation. Jan 11, 1958, v185, p38.
The New Republic. Jan 27, 1958, v138, p22.

The New York Times. Jan 6, 1957, SecII, p7.
The New York Times. Nov 24, 1957, SecVI, p44-45.
The New York Times. Dec 15, 1957, SecII, p7.
The New York Times. Dec 19, 1957, p39.
The New York Times. Dec 22, 1957, SecII, p3.
The New York Times. Jan 12, 1958, SecII, p1.
The New York Times Magazine. Nov 24, 1957, p44-45.
The New Yorker. Dec 28, 1957, v33, p48.
Newsweek. Dec 23, 1957, v1, p77.
Saturday Review. Dec 14, 1957, v40, p23.
Time. Dec 23, 1957, v70, p70.
Variety. Nov 20, 1957, p6.
Vintage Films. p164-69.

A Bridge Too Far (GB; Attenborough, Richard; 1977)
BFI/Monthly Film Bulletin. Jul 1977, v44, p141-42.
Commonweal. Jul 8, 1977, v104, p432-33.
Films in Review. Oct 1977, v28, p503.
The Films of Laurence Olivier. p188-98.
The Films of Robert Redford. p239-42.
Hollywood Reporter. Jun 8, 1977, p3.
Laurence Olivier: Theater & Cinema. p234-36.
Motion Picture Herald Product Digest. Jun 22, 1977, p5.
The New York Times. Jun 16, 1977, SecIII, p20.
The New Yorker. Jun 20, 1977, v53, p90-91.
Newsweek. Jun 20, 1977, v89, p65.
Saturday Review. Jun 25, 1977, v109, p92.
Sean Connery (Callan). p211-12.
Time. Jun 13, 1977, v109, p92.
Variety. Jun 8, 1977, p23.
William Goldman's Story of A Bridge Too Far. 1977.

The Bridges at Toko-Ri (US; Robson, Mark; 1954)
America. Jan 29, 1955, v92, p463.
BFI/Monthly Film Bulletin. Feb 1955, v22, p18.
Catholic World. Feb 1955, v180, p381.
Commonweal. Feb 4, 1955, v61, p477.
Farm Journal. Feb 1955, v79, p149.
Film Daily. Dec 28, 1954, p6.
Films and Filming. Feb 1955, v1, p19.
Films in Review. Feb 1955, v6, p81-82.
The Films of Fredric March. p211-12.
The Films of the Fifties. p158-60.
The Films of William Holden. p161-63.
Guts & Glory. p114-15.
Hollywood Reporter. Dec 28, 1954, p3.
Library Journal. Jan 15, 1955, v80, p150.
Life. Feb 7, 1955, v38, p91-92.
The London Times. Jan 10, 1955, p10.
Look. Feb 8, 1955, v19, p92.
Magill's Survey of Cinema. Series II. v1, p336-38.
Motion Picture Herald Product Digest. Jan 1, 1955, p265.
National Parent-Teacher. Jan 1955, v49, p39.
The New Republic. Mar 14, 1955, v132, p28-29.
The New Statesman and Nation. Jan 15, 1954, v49, p73.
The New York Times. Jan 21, 1955, p20.
The New Yorker. Jan 29, 1955, v30, p82.
Newsweek. Jan 17, 1955, v45, p86.
Saturday Review. Jan 22, 1955, v38, p43.
The Spectator. Jan 14, 1955, v194, p46.
The Tatler. Jan 19, 1955, v215, p111.
Time. Jan 24, 1955, v65, p75.
Variety. Dec 29, 1954, p6.

Brief Vacation (Italian title: Breve vacanza, Una) (IT, SP; De Sica, Vittorio; 1973)
BFI/Monthly Film Bulletin. May 1975, v42, p101.

Commonweal. Mar 28, 1975, v102, p19-20.
Esquire. May 1975, v83, p43-44.
Hollywood Reporter. Mar 18, 1975, p19.
Italian Cinema (Bondanella). p325-26.
The Los Angeles Times. Mar 25, 1975, SecIV, p1.
Motion Picture Herald Product Digest. Feb 12, 1975, p71.
The Nation. Mar 8, 1975, v220, p284-85.
The New Republic. Mar 8, 1975, v172, p22.
The New York Times. Feb 10, 1975, p20.
The New Yorker. Mar 3, 1975, v51, p83-84.
Newsweek. Feb 24, 1975, v85, p81-82.
Reeling. p598-600.
Saturday Review. Mar 8, 1975, v2, p36.
Time. Mar 10, 1975, v105, p6.
Variety. Aug 22, 1973, p19.
Vittorio De Sica: A Guide to References and Resources. p162-68.

The Brig (US; Mekas, Jonas; 1964)
Film Daily. Jul 13, 1966, p4.
Film Society Review. May 1966, p16-17.
The London Times. Nov 7, 1964, p5.
Movie Journal (Mekas). p190-94.
The New York Times. Sep 21, 1964, p37.
The New Yorker. Apr 23, 1966, v42, p131-32.
Newsweek. Apr 25, 1966, v67, p90C.
Private Screenings. p232.
Variety. Sep 9, 1964, p24.
The Village Voice. Oct 1, 1964, v9, p13, 17.
The Village Voice. Jun 24, 1965, v10, p21.
The Village Voice. Apr 21, 1966, v11, p29.

Brigadoon (US; Minnelli, Vincente; 1954)
America. Sep 18, 1954, v91, p600.
BFI/Monthly Film Bulletin. Jul 1955, v22, p99-100.
Catholic World. Oct 1954, v180, p66.
Commonweal. Oct 15, 1954, v61, p37-38.
Cue. Sep 18, 1954, p16.
Dictionary of Films. p42.
Farm Journal. Oct 1954, v78, p137.
Film Daily. Aug 11, 1954, p4.
Films and Filming. Oct 1954, v1, p26.
Films and Filming. Jul 1955, v1, p15.
Films in Review. Oct 1954, v5, p429-30.
The Films of Gene Kelly. p146-52.
Hollywood Reporter. Aug 11, 1954, p3.
Library Journal. Oct 1, 1954, v79, p1755.
Look. Oct 5, 1954, v18, p74-75.
Magill's Survey of Cinema. Series II. v1, p339-42.
Motion Picture Herald Product Digest. Aug 14, 1954, p105.
National Parent-Teacher. Oct 1954, v49, p38.
The New York Times. Sep 17, 1954, p18.
The New Yorker. Sep 25, 1954, v30, p61.
Newsweek. Sep 13, 1954, v44, p108-09.
Saturday Review. Sep 25, 1954, v37, p26.
Selected Film Criticism, 1951-1960. p19-20.
Senior Scholastic. Sep 29, 1954, v65, p45.
Time. Oct 4, 1954, v64, p103.
Variety. Aug 11, 1954, p6.
Vincente Minnelli and the Film Musical. p55-57, 141-42, 180.
Woman's Home Companion. Aug 1954, v81, p10-11.
The World of Entertainment. p420-29.

Bright Leaf (US; Curtiz, Michael; 1950)
Christian Century. Jul 26, 1950, v67, p903.
Film Daily. May 24, 1950, p7.
The Films of Gary Cooper. p223-24.
Hollywood Reporter. May 23, 1950, p3.
Lauren Bacall: Her Films and Career. p105-09.
Library Journal. May 15, 1950, v75, p885.
The London Times. Sep 25, 1950, p6.
Motion Picture Herald Product Digest. May 27, 1950, p313.

The New York Times. Jun 17, 1950, p7.
The New Yorker. Jun 24, 1950, v26, p65.
Newsweek. Jul 3, 1950, v36, p69.
Time. Jun 26, 1950, v55, p94.
Variety. May 24, 1950, p6.

Bright Victory (Also titled: Lights Out) (US; Robson, Mark; 1951)
BFI/Monthly Film Bulletin. Apr 1951, v18, p246-47.
Christian Century. Oct 31, 1951, v68, p1263.
Commonweal. Aug 17, 1951, v54, p454.
Film Daily. Jul 23, 1951, p6.
From Sambo to Superspade. p166-67.
Hollywood Reporter. Jul 20, 1951, p3.
Life. Sep 3, 1951, v31, p77-78.
Magill's Survey of Cinema. Series I. v1, p234-36.
Motion Picture Herald Product Digest. Jul 28, 1951, p946-47.
The Nation. Aug 11, 1951, v173, p118.
The New Republic. Aug 27, 1951, v125, p21.
The New York Times. Aug 1, 1951, p19.
The New Yorker. Aug 4, 1951, v27, p53.
Newsweek. Jul 23, 1951, v38, p84.
Saturday Review. Jul 21, 1951, v34, p26.
Senior Scholastic. Sep 19, 1951, v59, p35.
Sight and Sound. May 1951, v20, p20.
The Spectator. Mar 30, 1951, v186, p412-13.
Time. Aug 13, 1951, v58, p98.
Variety. Jul 25, 1951, p6.

Brimstone and Treacle (GB; Loncraine, Richard; 1982)
BFI/Monthly Film Bulletin. Sep 1982, v49, p195-96.
Hollywood Reporter. Nov 9, 1982, p3.
The Los Angeles Times. Nov 18, 1982, SecVI, p8.
Maclean's. Nov 29, 1982, v95, p60-61.
Magill's Cinema Annual, 1983. p93-94.
The New Republic. Nov 29, 1982, v187, p22-23.
New Statesman. Sep 10, 1982, v104, p27-28.
The New York Times. Nov 5, 1982, SecIII, p7.
Variety. Sep 3, 1982, p3.
The Village Voice. Nov 9, 1982, p46.

Bring Me the Head of Alfredo Garcia (US, MEX; Peckinpah, Sam; 1974)
Audience. Nov 1974, v7, p9-11.
BFI/Monthly Film Bulletin. Feb 1975, v42, p29.
Commonweal. Oct 4, 1974, v101, p17-18.
The Fifty Worst Films of All Time. p51-56.
Film Heritage. 1974, v10, n1, p47-48.
Film Quarterly. Spr 1975, v28, p2-17.
Films and Filming. Feb 1975, v21, p35.
Films in Review. Nov 1974, v25, p569.
The Films of Sam Peckinpah. p80-86.
Hollywood Reporter. Aug 7, 1974, p3.
Independent Film Journal. Aug 7, 1974, v74, p7-8.
The Los Angeles Times. Aug 7, 1974, SecIV, p12.
Motion Picture Herald Product Digest. Aug 14, 1974, p24.
Movietone News. Jul 1975, n42, p40-41.
The New Republic. Aug 31, 1974, v171, p20.
New York. Aug 12, 1974, v7, p57.
The New York Times. Sep 15, 1974, SecII, p1.
Newsweek. Aug 26, 1974, v84, p82.
Peckinpah (Simmons). p189-208.
Sam Peckinpah (McKinney). p175-90.
Sight and Sound. Spr 1975, v44, p121.
Take One. 1974, v4, n6, p25-26.
Time. Sep 16, 1974, v104, p6.
Variety. Aug 7, 1974, p18.
The Village Voice. Sep 12, 1974, v75.

Britannia Hospital (GB; Anderson, Lindsay; 1982)
Christian Century. Jun 1, 1983, v100, p555.
Cineaste. 1983, v11, n4, p36-37.
Hollywood Reporter. Jan 14, 1983, p6.
The Los Angeles Times. Mar 31, 1983, SecVI, p6.
The Nation. Apr 16, 1983, v236, p489-90.
The New Republic. Apr 25, 1983, v188, p22-23.
The New York Times. Mar 4, 1983, SecIII, p10.
Newsweek. Mar 21, 1983, v101, p70-71.
Progressive. May 1983, v47, p50-51.
Variety. Mar 2, 1983, p323.

Broadway Danny Rose (US; Allen, Woody; 1984)
America. Feb 25, 1984, v150, p135.
BFI/Monthly Film Bulletin. Sep 1984, v51, p272.
Christian Century. Feb 29, 1984, v101, p226.
Christianity Today. Mar 16, 1984, v28, p58.
Cineaste. 1984, v13, n3, p40-42.
Commonweal. Mar 23, 1984, v111, p182-83.
Film Journal. Mar 1984, v87, p43-44.
Films and Filming. Jul 1984, n358, p15.
Hollywood Reporter. Jan 16, 1984, p3.
Informer. Mar 1984, p3-4.
The Los Angeles Times. Jan 27, 1984, SecIV, p1.
Maclean's. Jan 30, 1984, v97, p50.
Magill's Cinema Annual, 1985. p112-17.
The Nation. Mar 17, 1984, v238, p331-32.
The New Leader. Mar 5, 1984, v67, p19-20.
The New Republic. Feb 20, 1984, v190, p24-25.
New Statesman. Aug 17, 1984, v108, p27-28.
New York. Feb 6, 1984, v17, p64.
The New York Times. Mar 5, 1984, SecIII, p13.
The New York Times. Jan 29, 1984, SecII, p13.
The New York Times. Feb 5, 1984, SecII, p1.
The New Yorker. Feb 6, 1984, v59, p118-20.
Newsweek. Jan 30, 1984, v103, p69.
Photoplay. Sep 1984, v35, p20.
Sight and Sound. Wint 1984, v53, p300.
Time. Jan 23, 1984, v123, p68.
Variety. Jan 18, 1984, p22.
Visions. Jun 5, 1984, n20, p7.
Woody Allen: His Films and Career. p232-42.

Broken Arrow (US; Daves, Delmer; 1950)
Christian Century. Sep 13, 1950, v67, p1087.
Commonweal. Aug 4, 1950, v52, p413.
Film Daily. Jun 14, 1950, p12.
The Filming of the West. p533-34.
The Films of James Stewart. p131-33.
The Films of the Fifties. p33-34.
The Great Western Pictures. p37-39.
Hollywood Quarterly. Wint 1950, v5, p178-81.
Hollywood Reporter. Jun 12, 1950, p3.
Kiss Kiss Bang Bang. p298.
Library Journal. Jun 1, 1950, v75, p991.
The London Times. Aug 28, 1950, p6.
Magill's Survey of Cinema. Series I. v1, p248-51.
The Making of the Great Westerns. p185-94.
Motion Picture Herald Product Digest. Jun 17, 1950, p345.
The New Republic. Jul 31, 1950, v123, p23.
The New Statesman and Nation. Sep 2, 1950, v40, p252.
The New York Times. Jul 21, 1950, p15.
The New Yorker. Jul 22, 1950, v26, p45.
Newsweek. Aug 7, 1950, v36, p76.
One Good Film Deserves Another. p59-64.
Saturday Review. Aug 5, 1950, v33, p30-31.
Time. Jul 31, 1950, v56, p62.
Variety. Jun 14, 1950, p8.

Broken Lance (US; Dmytryk, Edward; 1954)
America. Aug 14, 1954, v91, p486.

BFI/Monthly Film Bulletin. Nov 1954, v21, p155-56.
Catholic World. Sep 1954, v179, p464.
Commonweal. Aug 27, 1954, v60, p513.
Film Daily. Jul 23, 1954, p10.
Films and Filming. Oct 1954, v1, p24.
Films and Filming. Dec 1954, v1, p19.
Films in Review. Oct 1954, v5, p434-35.
The Films of Spencer Tracy. p217-20.
The Great Western Pictures. p39.
Hollywood Reporter. Jul 23, 1954, p3.
The London Times. Nov 15, 1954, p11.
Magill's Survey of Cinema. Series II. v1, p343-45.
Motion Picture Herald Product Digest. Jul 31, 1954, p89.
National Parent-Teacher. Oct 1954, v49, p39.
The New York Times. Jul 30, 1954, p9.
Newsweek. Aug 16, 1954, v44, p82.
One Good Film Deserves Another. p75-80.
The Tatler. Nov 24, 1954, v214, p486-87.
Time. Aug 23, 1954, v64, p72.
Variety. Jul 28, 1954, p6.

Bronco Billy (US; Eastwood, Clint; 1980)
America. Jul 5, 1980, v143, p16.
BFI/Monthly Film Bulletin. Jul 1980, v47, p126.
Christian Science Monitor. Jun 27, 1980, p19.
Clint Eastwood (Guérif). p139-46.
Films in Review. Aug 1980, v31, p437.
The Films of Clint Eastwood. p216-20.
Hollywood Reporter. Jun 12, 1980, p3.
Jump Cut. Oct 1980, p3.
The Los Angeles Times. Jun 12, 1980, SecVI, p4.
Magill's Survey of Cinema. Series II. v1, p346-48.
Motion Picture Herald Product Digest. Jun 25, 1980, p6.
The Nation. Jul 5, 1980, v231, p28.
The New York Times. Jun 11, 1980, SecIII, p24.
Newsday. Jun 11, 1980, SecII, p66.
Newsweek. Jun 23, 1980, v95, p77.
Time. Jun 16, 1980, v115, p50.
Variety. Jun 11, 1980, p20.

Brother and Sister Bed *See* My Sister, My Love

The Brothers in Law (GB; Boulting, John; 1957)
BFI/Monthly Film Bulletin. Apr 1957, v24, p42.
Commonweal. Aug 23, 1957, v66, p523.
Films and Filming. Apr 1957, v3, p27.
Motion Picture Herald Product Digest. Oct 12, 1957, v209, p561.
The New York Times. Aug 20, 1957, p22.
Saturday Review. Sep 14, 1957, v40, p30.
Sight and Sound. Spr 1957, v26, p212.
Variety. Mar 13, 1957, p6.

The Brothers Karamazov (US; Brooks, Richard; 1958)
America. Mar 1, 1958, v98, p643.
BFI/Monthly Film Bulletin. Aug 1958, v25, p98.
Catholic World. Apr 1958, v188, p66.
Christian Century. Apr 2, 1958, v75, p410-41.
Commonweal. Feb 28, 1958, v67, p568.
Film Daily. Feb 19, 1958, v113, p6.
Filmfacts. Mar 12, 1958, v1, p21-22.
Films in Review. Feb 1958, v9, p49-52.
Films in Review. Mar 1958, v9, p140-42.
Hollywood Reporter. Feb 19, 1958, p3.
Library Journal. Mar 1, 1958, v83, p748.
Life. Mar 10, 1958, v44, p60-66.
The Nation. Mar 8, 1958, v186, p216.
The New Republic. Apr 21, 1958, v13, p21.

The New York Times Magazine. Nov 3, 1957, p78.
The New York Times Magazine. Feb 21, 1958, p18.
The New Yorker. Mar 1, 1958, v34, p104.
Newsweek. Feb 24, 1958, v51, p102.
Saturday Review. Feb 22, 1958, v27, p27.
Time. Feb 24, 1958, v71, p98.
Variety. Feb 19, 1958, p6.

The Brothers Karamazov (Russian title: Bratya Karamazovy) (USSR; Pyriev, Ivan; 1968)
BFI/Monthly Film Bulletin. May 1972, v39, p92.
The London Times. Jul 23, 1969, p11.
Magill's Survey of Cinema. Foreign Language Films. v1, p418-23.
The New York Times. Jun 13, 1980, SecIII, p12.
Variety. Jul 30, 1969, p36.
The Village Voice. Jun 16, 1980, p42.

The Brothers Rico (US; Karlson, Phil; 1957)
BFI/Monthly Film Bulletin. Sep 1957, v24, p113.
Dreams and Dead Ends. p234-64.
Film Daily. Aug 26, 1957, v112, p6.
Film Noir. p43-44.
Hollywood Reporter. Aug 21, 1957, p3.
Motion Picture Herald Product Digest. Aug 24, 1957, v208, p506.
Newsweek. Sep 16, 1957, v50, p120.
Time. Sep 16, 1957, v70, p115.
Variety. Aug 21, 1957, p18.

The Browning Version (GB; Asquith, Anthony; 1951)
BFI/Monthly Film Bulletin. Apr 1951, v18, p243.
Christian Century. Feb 6, 1952, v69, p175.
Cinema, the Magic Vehicle. v2, p78-79.
Commonweal. Nov 16, 1951, v55, p144.
Film Daily. Nov 12, 1951, p7.
Film News. Sep 1974, v3, p22-23.
Films in Review. Aug-Sep 1951, v2, p36-38.
The Films of Anthony Asquith. p130-32.
Hollywood Reporter. Mar 27, 1952, p3.
Library Journal. Nov 1, 1951, v76, p1818.
The London Times. Mar 19, 1951, p2.
Magill's Survey of Cinema. Series II. v1, p353-55.
Motion Picture Herald Product Digest. Nov 3, 1951, p1093.
The New Republic. Nov 19, 1951, v125, p21.
The New Statesman and Nation. Mar 31, 1951, v41, p366.
The New York Times. Oct 30, 1951, p33.
The New Yorker. Nov 3, 1951, v27, p129.
Newsweek. Nov 12, 1951, v38, p99.
Saturday Review. Nov 10, 1951, v34, p27.
Senior Scholastic. Nov 14, 1951, v59, p26.
Sight and Sound. Apr 1951, v19, p475.
The Spectator. Mar 16, 1951, v186, p341-42.
Time. Nov 12, 1951, v58, p110.
Variety. Mar 21, 1951, p7.

Brubaker (US; Rosenberg, Stuart; 1980)
BFI/Monthly Film Bulletin. Sep 1980, v47, p172.
Christian Science Monitor. Aug 14, 1980, p19.
Films in Review. Aug 1980, v31, p436.
The Films of Robert Redford. p254-58.
Hollywood Reporter. Jun 18, 1980, p3.
The Los Angeles Times. Jun 15, 1980, Calendar, p1.
Maclean's. Jun 30, 1980, v93, p51-52.
Magill's Survey of Cinema. Series II. v1, p356-59.

Motion Picture Herald Product Digest. Jun 25, 1980, p5.
The New Republic. Jul 19, 1980, v183, p22.
New York. Jun 30, 1980, v13, p53-54.
The New York Times. Jun 20, 1980, SecIII, p8.
The New York Times. Jun 22, 1980, SecII, p17.
The New York Times. Jul 6, 1980, SecII, p1.
The New Yorker. Jul 7, 1980, v56, p90.
Newsday. Jun 20, 1980, SecII, p7.
Newsweek. Jun 23, 1980, v95, p75.
Time. Jun 30, 1980, v115, p72.
Variety. Jun 18, 1980, p22.
The Village Voice. Jun 25, 1980, p41.

Buckaroo Banzai *See* The Adventures of Buckaroo Banzai Across the Eighth Dimension

Budapest Tales (Hungarian title: Budapesti Mesek) (HUNG; Szabo, Istvan; 1976)
Film. Aug 1977, n52, p3-4.
Film Quarterly. 1978, v32, n1, p30-31.
Magill's Survey of Cinema. Foreign Language Films. v1, p427-30.
Variety. Mar 2, 1977, p26.

Buddy Buddy (US; Wilder, Billy; 1981)
The Los Angeles Times. Dec 11, 1981, SecVI, p1.
Magill's Cinema Annual, 1982. p92-96.
The New Republic. Jan 1982, v186, p28.
New York. Dec 21, 1981, v14, p56.
The New York Times. Dec 11, 1981, SecIII, p12.
Newsweek. Dec 14, 1981, v98, p124.
Time. Jan 4, 1982, v119, p87.
Variety. Dec 9, 1981, p20.
The Village Voice. Dec 16, 1981, p73.

The Buddy Holly Story (US; Rash, Steve; 1978)
BFI/Monthly Film Bulletin. Jun 1979, v46, p116-17.
Commonweal. Sep 1, 1978, v105, p565.
Films in Review. Nov 1978, v29, p567.
The Films of The Seventies. p224-25.
The Hollywood Musical. p409, 411.
Hollywood Reporter. May 17, 1978, p3.
The Los Angeles Times. Jun 14, 1978, SecIV, p13.
Maclean's. Jul 24, 1978, v91, p59.
Motion Picture Herald Product Digest. Jul 26, 1978, p13.
National Review. Sep 1, 1978, v30, p1097.
The New Leader. Aug 14, 1978, v61, p23-24.
The New York Times. Jul 21, 1978, SecIII, p14.
The New York Times. Jul 30, 1978, SecII, p13.
Newsweek. Jun 26, 1978, v91, p79-80.
Rolling Stone. Jul 27, 1978, p32.
Rolling Stone. Sep 21, 1978, p49-51.
Time. Jul 24, 1978, v112, p56.
Variety. May 17, 1978, p54.

Buffalo Bill and the Indians or Sitting Bull's History Lesson (US; Altman, Robert; 1976)
Atlantic Monthly. Oct 1976, v238, p106-8.
BFI/Monthly Film Bulletin. Sep 1976, v43, p188-89.
Burt Lancaster: The Man and His Movies. p134-35.
Commentary. Oct 1976, v62, p75-77.
Commonweal. Aug 13, 1976, v103, p528-29.
Film Heritage. 1976, v11, n3, p39-40.
Film Quarterly. Fall 1976, v30, p54-56.
Films and Filming. Sep 1976, v22, p33-34.
Films in Review. Oct 1976, v27, p505-06.
The Films of Robert Altman. p75-82.
Hi Fi. Aug 1976, v26, p32-34.
Hollywood Reporter. Jun 24, 1976, p2.

Independent Film Journal. Jun 25, 1976, v78, p13-14.
The Los Angeles Times. Jun 30, 1976, SecIV, p1.
Motion Picture Herald Product Digest. Jun 30, 1976, p9.
The Nation. Jul 31, 1976, v223, p93-94.
The New Republic. Jul 24, 1976, v175, p22.
New Statesman. Jul 23, 1976, v91, p123-24.
New York. Jul 5, 1976, v9, p70.
The New York Review of Books. Jul 15, 1976, v23, p29-30.
The New York Times. Jul 4, 1976, SecII, p1.
The New York Times. Jun 25, 1976, SecIII, p8.
The New Yorker. Jun 28, 1976, v52, p62.
Newsweek. Jun 28, 1976, v87, p77.
Penthouse. Oct 1976, v8, p45-47.
Robert Altman A Guide to Reference and Resources. p59-62.
Robert Altman, American Innovator. p213-30.
Robert Altman (Plecki). p91-98.
Saturday Review. Jul 10, 1976, v3, p62.
Sight and Sound. Wint 1976, v45, p254.
The Thousand Eyes Magazine. Jul-Aug 1976, n12, p12.
Time. Jul 19, 1976, v108, p66.
Times Educational Supplement. Aug 6, 1976, n3192, p42.
Variety. Jun 30, 1976, p20.
Vogue. May 1976, v166, p116-17.

Bugles in the Afternoon (US; Rowland, Roy; 1952)
BFI/Monthly Film Bulletin. Jun 1952, v19, p78.
Film Daily. Jan 31, 1952, p6.
Hollywood Reporter. Jan 31, 1952, p3.
Library Journal. Apr 1, 1952, v77, p586.
Motion Picture Herald Product Digest. Feb 2, 1952, p1221.
The New York Times. Mar 5, 1952, p32.
Newsweek. Mar 10, 1952, v39, p102.
The Spectator. May 2, 1952, v188, p576-77.
Time. Feb 11, 1952, v59, p97.
Variety. Feb 6, 1952, p6.

Bugsy Malone (GB; Parker, Alan; 1976)
BFI/Monthly Film Bulletin. Jul 1976, v43, p145-46.
Film Bulletin. Sep-Oct 1976, v45, p37.
Films and Filming. Sep 1976, v22, p31-32.
Films in Review. Nov 1976, v27, p565-66.
Hollywood Reporter. Sep 15, 1976, p2.
Independent Film Journal. Sep 3, 1976, v78, p7.
Interview. Oct 1976, v6, p10-13.
The Los Angeles Times. Oct 13, 1976, SecIV, p1.
Motion Picture Herald Product Digest. Sep 29, 1976, p34.
The Nation. Oct 9, 1976, v223, p350.
New Statesman. Jul 24, 1976, v91, p123-24.
New York. Sep 27, 1976, v9, p85-87.
The New York Times. Sep 26, 1976, p15.
The New Yorker. Sep 27, 1976, v52, p124-25.
Newsweek. Sep 27, 1976, v88, p89-90.
Saturday Review. Oct 2, 1976, v4, p39.
Sight and Sound. Wint 1976, v45, p255.
Time. Sep 6, 1976, v108, p60-63.
Times Educational Supplement. Jul 30, 1976, n3191, p39.
Variety. Jun 9, 1976, p22.
Vogue. Oct 1976, v166, p142.
When the Lights Go Down. p163-65.

A Bullet Is Waiting (US; Farrow, John; 1954)
America. Nov 20, 1954, v92, p222.
BFI/Monthly Film Bulletin. Dec 1954, v21, p177.
Catholic World. Oct 1954, v180, p65.

Film Daily. Aug 26, 1954, p6.
Hollywood Reporter. Aug 20, 1954, p3.
Motion Picture Herald Product Digest. Aug 21, 1954, p113.
National Parent-Teacher. Oct 1954, v49, p39.
The New Republic. Jun 27, 1955, v132, p22.
The New Statesman and Nation. Aug 21, 1954, v48, p208-09.
The New York Times. Nov 12, 1954, p17.
Time. Dec 6, 1954, v64, p114.
Variety. Sep 1, 1954, p6.

The Bullfighter and the Lady (US; Boetticher, Budd; 1951)
BFI/Monthly Film Bulletin. Jul 1951, v18, p296.
Christian Century. Jun 20, 1951, v68, p751.
Cinema. Fall 1970, v6, p22-29.
Commonweal. May 4, 1951, v54, p91.
Film Criticism and Caricatures, 1943-1953. p131.
Film Daily. May 3, 1951, p18.
Films in Review. Jun-Jul 1951, v2, p34-35.
Hollywood Reporter. Apr 25, 1951, p3.
Kiss Kiss Bang Bang. p299.
The London Times. Sep 24, 1951, p8.
Motion Picture Herald Product Digest. May 5, 1951, p825-26.
The Nation. May 26, 1951, v172, p498.
The New York Times. Apr 27, 1951, p19.
The New Yorker. May 5, 1951, v27, p98.
Newsweek. May 14, 1951, v37, p100.
Saturday Review. May 5, 1951, v34, p26.
Sight and Sound. Oct-Dec 1951, v21, p82.
Time. Apr 23, 1951, v57, p106.
Variety. May 2, 1951, p6.

Bullitt (US; Yates, Peter; 1968)
America. Oct 26, 1968, v119, p392.
BFI/Monthly Film Bulletin. Jan 1969, v36, p4.
Christian Science Monitor (Western edition). Nov 18, 1968, p12.
Commonweal. Nov 15, 1968, v89, p254.
Figures of Light. p118-20.
Film 68/69. p165-66.
Film Daily. Oct 16, 1968, p7.
Film Quarterly. Wint 1968-69, v22, p55.
Filmfacts. Jan 15, 1969, v11, p433-34.
Films and Filming. Mar 1969, v15, p39-40.
Films in Review. Nov 1968, v19, p582-83.
The Films of Steve McQueen. p141-53.
The Films of the Sixties. p255-57.
Going Steady. p201.
Hollywood Reporter. Oct 16, 1968, p3.
Life. Nov 22, 1968, v65, p28.
London Magazine. Mar 1969, v8, p76-79.
The London Times. Dec 28, 1968, p15.
Magill's Survey of Cinema. Series I. v1, p255-58.
Motion Picture Herald Product Digest. Oct 23, 1968, p47.
Movies Into Film. p294-95.
The New Republic. Nov 23, 1968, v159, p26.
New Statesman. Jan 10, 1969, v77, p56.
The New York Times. Oct 18, 1968, p41.
The New York Times. Nov 3, 1968, p1.
Saturday Review. Nov 9, 1968, v51, p55.
Sight and Sound. Wint 1968-69, v38, p45.
The Spectator. Dec 27, 1968, v221, p918-19.
Take One. Jul-Aug 1968, v1, p22-24.
Time. Nov 8, 1968, v92, p111.
Variety. Oct 16, 1968, p6.
The Village Voice. Oct 31, 1968, p49-50.
A Year In the Dark. p270-71.

Bunny Lake Is Missing (GB; Preminger, Otto; 1965)
America. Nov 6, 1965, v113, p542.
BFI/Monthly Film Bulletin. Mar 1966, v33, p35-36.

Christian Science Monitor (Western edition).
Nov 23, 1965, p6.
Christian Science Monitor (Western edition).
Feb 21, 1966, p6.
Cinema. Mar 1966, v3, p4-8, 13-14.
The Cinema of Otto Preminger (Pratley). p150-53.
Commonweal. Oct 22, 1965, v83, p100.
Confessions of a Cultist. p212-14.
Film Daily. Oct 5, 1965, p1.
Film Quarterly. Spr 1966, v19, p51.
Film Quarterly. Fall 1966, v20, p22-27.
Films and Filming. Mar 1966, v12, p18-19.
Films in Review. Nov 1965, v16, p580-81.
The Films of Laurence Olivier. p138-41.
Hollywood Reporter. Oct 5, 1965, p3.
International Film Guide. 1967, v4, p160.
Laurence Olivier (Hirsch). p153-54.
Laurence Olivier: Theater & Cinema. p164-67.
Life. Dec 3, 1965, v59, p20.
The London Times. Feb 10, 1966, p16.
Motion Picture Herald Product Digest. Oct 13, 1965, p385.
Moviegoer. Sum 1966, v3, p57-60.
The New Republic. Nov 6, 1965, v153, p31.
New Statesman. Feb 11, 1965, v71, p201.
The New York Times. Oct 4, 1965, np.
The New Yorker. Oct 16, 1965, v41, p229-30.
Newsweek. Oct 18, 1965, v66, p120.
Saturday Review. Oct 30, 1965, v48, p75.
Sight and Sound. Spr 1966, v35, p95-96.
The Spectator. Feb 18, 1966, v216, p199.
Variety. Oct 6, 1965, p6.
The Village Voice. Oct 21, 1965, v11, p21.

Buongiorno Elefante! *See* Hello, Elephant!

Buono, Il Brutto, Il Cattivo, Il *See* The Good, The Bad and The Ugly

The Burmese Harp (Japanese title: Biruma no Tategoto; Also titled: The Harp of Burma) (JAPAN; Ichikawa, Kon; 1956)
BFI/Monthly Film Bulletin. Mar 1960, v27, p31.
Christian Science Monitor (Western edition). Sep 30, 1966, p6.
Cinema East. p88-100.
Dictionary of Films. p36.
Film Daily. May 4, 1967, p8.
Film Journal. Nov 1959, n14, p27-28.
Filmfacts. Jul 15, 1967, v10, p145-46.
Films and Filming. Apr 1960, v6, p22.
Japan: Film Image. p85-88.
Japanese Film Directors. p226-27.
The London Times. Feb 1960, p13.
Magill's Survey of Cinema. Foreign Language Films. v1, p431-36.
Motion Picture Herald Product Digest. May 10, 1967, p683.
The New York Times. Apr 29, 1967, p25.
Private Screenings. p281-82.
Senior Scholastic. May 19, 1967, v90, p43.
Variety. Sep 19, 1956, p6.

Burn! (Also titled: Quemada!) (IT, FR; Pontecorvo, Gillo; 1970)
America. Nov 14, 1970, v123, p414.
Atlantic. Jan 1971, v227, p100-02.
Commonweal. Nov 27, 1970, v93, p223.
The Films of Marlon Brando. p216-19.
Life. Nov 27, 1970, v69, p20.
The New Republic. Nov 14, 1970, v163, p20.
The New York Times. Oct 22, 1970, p62.
The New Yorker. Nov 7, 1970, v46, p159-62.
Newsweek. Nov 2, 1970, v76, p112.
Reeling. p291-94.
Saturday Review. Nov 21, 1970, v53, p56.

Time. Nov 2, 1970, v96, p94.
Variety. Oct 21, 1970, p14.

Bus Riley's Back in Town (US; Hart, Harvey; 1965)
BFI/Monthly Film Bulletin. Oct 1965, v32, p146-47.
Christian Science Monitor (Western edition). Mar 24, 1965, p6.
Commonweal. Apr 30, 1965, v82, p192.
Film Daily. Mar 18, 1965, p6.
Film Quarterly. Sum 1965, v18, p59.
Filmfacts. Apr 16, 1965, v8, p54-56.
Films and Filming. Nov 1965, v12, p27.
Hollywood Reporter. Mar 17, 1965, p4.
The London Times. Mar 10, 1966, p14.
Motion Picture Herald Product Digest. Mar 31, 1965, p257-58.
The New York Times. Apr 8, 1965, p45.
Newsweek. Apr 12, 1965, v65, p110.
Saturday Review. Apr 24, 1965, v48, p39-40.
Sight and Sound. Wint 1965-66, v35, p43.
Time. Apr 23, 1965, v85, pC9.
Variety. Mar 17, 1965, p7.
The Village Voice. May 13, 1965, v10, p20.

Bus Stop (US; Logan, Joshua; 1956)
America. Sep 15, 1956, v95, p576.
BFI/Monthly Film Bulletin. Nov 1956, v23, p136-37.
Commonweal. Sep 7, 1956, v64, p561.
Film Daily. Aug 15, 1956, p4.
Films and Filming. Nov 1956, v3, p24.
Films in Review. Oct 1956, v7, p413-14.
The Films of Marilyn Monroe. p129-34.
Hollywood Reporter. Aug 14, 1956, p3.
Magill's Survey of Cinema. Series I. v1, p259-64.
The Nation. Oct 6, 1956, v183, p294.
The New York Times. Sep 1, 1956, p19.
The New York Times. Sep 2, 1956, SecII, p1.
The New Yorker. Sep 15, 1956, v32, p76.
Newsweek. Aug 27, 1956, v48, p90.
Saturday Review. Sep 15, 1956, v39, p37.
Time. Sep 3, 1956, v68, p74.
Variety. Aug 15, 1956, p6.

Buster and Billie (US; Petrie, Daniel; 1974)
BFI/Monthly Film Bulletin. Aug 1974, v41, p169-70.
Christian Century. Aug 21, 1974, v91, p805.
Film. Aug 1974, n17, p20.
Films and Filming. Sep 1974, v20, p53-56.
Films Illustrated. Aug 1974, v3, p468.
Films in Review. Dec 1974, v25, p627.
Hollywood Reporter. Jun 11, 1974, p3.
Independent Film Journal. Jun 26, 1974, v74, p7.
The Los Angeles Times. Oct 9, 1974, SecIV, p11.
Motion Picture Herald Product Digest. Jun 19, 1974, p6.
Movietone News. Oct 1974, n36, p31-32.
New York. Sep 9, 1974, v7, p62-63.
The New York Times. Aug 22, 1974, p28.
Newsweek. Jul 15, 1974, v84, p83.
Time. Sep 16, 1974, v104, p7.
Variety. Jun 12, 1974, p18.

The Buster Keaton Story (US; Sheldon, Sidney; 1957)
America. May 4, 1957, v97, p180.
BFI/Monthly Film Bulletin. Jul 1957, v24, p86.
Film Daily. Apr 17, 1957, v111, p8.
Films and Filming. Jul 1957, v3, p23.
Films in Review. May 1957, v7, p220-21.
Hollywood Reporter. Apr 17, 1957, p3.
Motion Picture Herald Product Digest. Apr 20, 1957, v207, p345.
The New York Times. Apr 22, 1957, p31.
The New Yorker. May 4, 1957, v33, p163.

Newsweek. Apr 29, 1957, v49, p110.
Time. May 6, 1957, v69, p104.
Variety. Apr 17, 1957, p6.

Bustin' Loose (US; Scott, Oz; 1981)
Maclean's. Jan 8, 1981, v94, p49.
The New Republic. Jun 6, 1981, v184, p26-27.
New York. Jun 8, 1981, v14, p51-52.
The New York Times. May 22, 1981, SecIII, p13.
Newsweek. Jun 1, 1981, v97, p91.
Time. Jun 1, 1981, v117, p75.
Variety. May 27, 1981, p16.
The Village Voice. Jun 17, 1981, p46.

Busting (US; Hyams, Peter; 1974)
BFI/Monthly Film Bulletin. Feb 1974, v42, p24-25.
Films in Review. Apr 1974, v25, p246-47.
Hollywood Reporter. Jan 25, 1974, p3.
Independent Film Journal. Feb 4, 1974, v73, p10-11.
The Los Angeles Times. Feb 6, 1974, SecIV, p1.
Millimeter. May 1974, v2, p42-43.
Motion Picture Herald Product Digest. Feb 13, 1974, p75.
Movietone News. Apr 1974, n31, p27-28.
New Statesman. May 24, 1974, v87, p747.
New York. Mar 4, 1974, v7, p58-59.
The New York Times. Mar 3, 1974, SecII, p11.
Rolling Stone. Mar 28, 1974, p54-55.
Time. Mar 25, 1974, v103, p72.
Variety. Jan 30, 1974, p13.
The Village Voice. Mar 21, 1974, p69.

Butch Cassidy and the Sundance Kid (US; Hill, George Roy; 1969)
America. Oct 11, 1969, v121, p306-08.
Deeper Into Movies. p5-9.
Fifty Grand Movies of the 1960s and 1970s. p125-26.
Film Daily. Sep 10, 1969, p6.
Film Quarterly. Wint 1969-70, v23, p62-63.
Film Society Review. v5, p33-37.
Films in Review. Oct 1969, v20, p510-11.
The Films of George Roy Hill. p64-80.
The Films of Paul Newman. p179-85.
The Films of Robert Redford. p100-19.
The Films of the Sixties. p272-74.
Focus. Spr 1970, p12-13, 15-16.
George Roy Hill (Shores). p15-17, 19-20, 25-39.
Hollywood Reporter. Sep 10, 1969, p3.
Life. Oct 24, 1969, v67, p16.
Look. Oct 21, 1969, v33, p70.
Magill's Survey of Cinema. Series I. v1, p264-66.
The Making of the Great Westerns. p409-28.
Movies Into Film. p177-78.
The New Republic. Oct 25, 1969, v161, p32.
The New York Times. Sep 25, 1969, p54.
The New York Times. Oct 5, 1969, SecII, p20.
The New Yorker. Sep 27, 1969, v45, p127-29.
Newsweek. Oct 13, 1969, v74, p116.
Saturday Review. Sep 20, 1969, v52, p30.
Saturday Review. Sep 26, 1969, v52, p94.
Second Sight. p253-55.
Sight and Sound. Spr 1970, v39, p101-02.
Time. Sep 26, 1969, v94, p94.
Variety. Sep 10, 1969, p36.

The Butcher (French title: Boucher, Le) (FR; Chabrol, Claude; 1970)
America. Feb 5, 1972, v126, p122-23.
BFI/Monthly Film Bulletin. Jul 1971, v39, n462, p131.
Commonweal. Feb 4, 1972, v95, p421-22.
Deeper into Movies. p399.
Film Quarterly. Fall 1972, v26, p54-58.
Filmfacts. 1971, v14, n23, p601-04.
Films and Filming. Jul 1972, v18, p51-52.
Films in Review. Feb 1972, v23, p112-13.

Life. May 26, 1972, v72, p16.
Movie. Wint 1970-71, n18, p38.
The Nation. Jan 31, 1972, v214, p705.
The New York Times. Sep 14, 1970, p46.
The New York Times. Dec 20, 1971, p47.
The New Yorker. Feb 5, 1972, v47, p79-80.
Sight and Sound. Wint 1970-71, v40, n1, p16-17.
Time. Sep 21, 1970, v96, p100.
Time. Jan 17, 1972, v99, p55-56.
Variety. Mar 11, 1970, p22.

Butley (US; Pinter, Harold; 1974)
Audience. May 1974, v6, p12-13.
Hollywood Reporter. Jan 18, 1974, p3.
Independent Film Journal. Apr 15, 1974, v73, p9-10.
The Los Angeles Times. Jan 18, 1974, SecIV, p1.
Magill's Survey of Cinema. Series II, v1, p367-71.
Motion Picture Herald Product Digest. Apr 10, 1974, p89.
Movietone News. Mar 1974, n30, p32.
New York. Apr 15, 1974, v7, p79-81.
The New York Times. Apr 9, 1974, p34.
Newsweek. May 20, 1974, v83, p106.
Time. Apr 29, 1974, v103, p76-78.
Variety. Jan 23, 1974, p14.
The Village Voice. Feb 28, 1974, v19, p68.

Butterfield 8 (US; Mann, Daniel; 1960)
America. Dec 3, 1960, v104, p350.
BFI/Monthly Film Bulletin. Dec 1960, v27, p163.
Commonweal. Nov 11, 1960, v73, p179.
Film Daily. Oct 25, 1960, p10.
Filmfacts. 1960, v3, p269.
Films and Filming. Jan 1961, v7, p33-34.
Films in Review. Dec 1960, v11, p613-14.
The Films of Elizabeth Taylor. p146-51.
Magill's Survey of Cinema. Series II. v1, p372-74.
Motion Picture Product Herald Digest. Oct 29, 1960, p900.
The New York Times. Nov 17, 1960, p46.
The New York Times. Nov 27, 1960, SecII, p1.
The New Yorker. Nov 19, 1960, v36, p152.
Newsweek. Nov 7, 1960, v56, p121.
Saturday Review. Nov 19, 1960, v43, p39.
Time. Mar 21, 1960, v75, p83.
Variety. Oct 26, 1960, p6.

Butterflies are Free (US; Katselas, Milton; 1972)
America. Aug 5, 1972, v127, p76.
Films in Review. Aug-Sep 1972, v23, p435.
Hollywood Reporter. Jun 21, 1972, p3.
Life. Aug 4, 1972, v73, p19.
National Review. Sep 15, 1972, v24, p1024.
The New York Times. Jul 7, 1972, p19.
Newsweek. Jul 31, 1972, v80, p65.
Saturday Review. Jul 1, 1972, v55, p63.
Time. Jul 24, 1972, v100, p60.
Variety. Jul 5, 1972, p16.

Bye Bye Birdie (US; Sidney, George; 1963)
America. Apr 20, 1963, v108, p590-91.
BFI/Monthly Film Bulletin. Dec 1963, v30, p170-71.
Commonweal. Apr 15, 1963, v61, p103.
Film Daily. Apr 5, 1963, p3.
Filmfacts. May 9, 1963, v6, p73-75.
Films and Filming. Nov 1963, v10, p23.
Films in Review. Apr 1963, v14, p240-41.
Hollywood Reporter. Apr 4, 1963, p3.
Magill's Survey of Cinema. Series II. v1, p375-78.
The Musical: From Broadway to Hollywood. p96-100.
The New York Times. Apr 5, 1963, p27.

Photoplay. Jul 1963, v64, p8.
Saturday Review. Apr 27, 1963, v46, p26.
Variety. Apr 10, 1963, p6.

Bye Bye Braverman (US; Lumet, Sidney; 1968)
America. Mar 9, 1968, v118, p332.
Christian Science Monitor (Western edition). Mar 25, 1968, p12.
Commonweal. Mar 8, 1968, v87, p690.
Commonweal. Apr 5, 1968, v88, p76.
Film Daily. Feb 6, 1968, p7.
Filmfacts. Mar 1, 1968, v11, p42-44.
Films in Review. Apr 1968, v19, p242-43.
Five Thousand One Nights At the Movies. p85.
Going Steady. p62-64.
Harper's Magazine. May 1968, v236, p92-94.
Hollywood Reporter. Feb 2, 1968, p3.
Life. Mar 15, 1968, v64, p10.
Motion Picture Herald Product Digest. Feb 14, 1968, p773-74.
Movies Into Film. p311.
The Nation. Mar 11, 1968, v206, p356.
The New Republic. Mar 9, 1968, v158, p37.
The New York Times. Feb 22, 1968, p36.
The New York Times. Apr 23, 1967, p15.
The New Yorker. Mar 2, 1968, v44, p125.
Newsweek. Mar 11, 1968, v71, p92.
Saturday Review. Mar 2, 1968, v51, p40.
Sidney Lumet: A Guide to References and Resources. p82-84, 135.
Sight and Sound. Aut 1969, v38, p190-95.
Time. Mar 15, 1968, v91, p90.
Variety. Feb 7, 1968, p6.
The Village Voice. Mar 21, 1968, p47.
A Year In the Dark. p53-54.

Bye Bye Brazil (Also titled: Bye-Bye Brasil) (BRAZ; Diegues, Carlos; 1980)
Christian Science Monitor. Oct 30, 1980, p18.
Cineaste. Wint 1980-81, v10, p34.
Hollywood Reporter. Oct 6, 1980, p6.
The Los Angeles Times. Feb 8, 1981, Calendar, p34.
Maclean's. Nov 3, 1980, v93, p64-65.
Magill's Survey of Cinema. Foreign Language Films. v1, p441-45.
The Nation. Nov 22, 1980, v231, p556-57.
The New York Times. Sep 27, 1980, SecIII, p13.
Newsday. Jan 16, 1981, SecII, p7.
Newsweek. Nov 3, 1980, v96, p92.
Time. Nov 24, 1980, v116, p103.
Variety. Dec 19, 1979, p36.
Variety. May 2, 1980, p18.
The Village Voice. Oct 1, 1980, p50.

Cabaret (US; Fosse, Bob; 1972)
America. Mar 11, 1972, v126, p264.
Christian Century. May 3, 1972, v89, p524.
Commonweal. Apr 21, 1972, v96, p167.
Deeper into Movies. p409-12.
Fifty Grand Movies of the 1960s and 1970s. p95-98.
Filmfacts. 1972, v15, n2, p21.
Films in Review. Mar 1972, v23, n3, p187.
The Great Movies. p96.
HiFi. May 1972, v22, p73-75.
Hollywood Reporter. Feb 15, 1972, p3.
The International Dictionary of Films and Filmmakers. v1, p72-73.
Life. Mar 10, 1972, v72, p24.
Magill's Survey of Cinema. Series I. v1, p267.
The Musical: from Broadway to Hollywood. p143-47.
National Review. Apr 28, 1972, v24, p476.
The New Republic. Mar 4, 1972, v166, p22.
The New York Times. Feb 14, 1972, p22.
The New York Times. Feb 20, 1972, SecII, p1.
The New York Times. Feb 27, 1972, SecII, p1.
The New Yorker. Feb 19, 1972, v47, p84.

The Novel and the Cinema. p335-37.
Redbook. May 1972, v139, p16.
Saturday Review. Mar 4, 1972, v55, p66.
Senior Scholastic. Apr 17, 1972, , v100, p23.
Time. Feb 21, 1972, v99, p80.
Variety. Feb 16, 1972, p18.
Vintage Films. p210-14.

Cabiria *See* The Nights of Cabiria

Cabriola *See* Every Day Is a Holiday

Caccia Alla Volpe *See* After the Fox

Cactus Flower (US; Saks, Gene; 1969)
Big Screen, Little Screen. p249-50.
Film Daily. Sep 11, 1969, p7.
Films in Review. Dec 1969, v20, p638.
The Films of Ingrid Bergman. p177-80.
Holiday. Nov 1969, v46, p23.
Hollywood Reporter. Sep 3, 1969, p3.
Magill's Survey of Cinema. Series II. v1, p379-82.
The New York Times. Dec 17, 1969, p62.
Newsweek. Dec 29, 1969, v74, p55.
Saturday Review. Dec 20, 1969, v52, p38.
Time. Dec 19, 1969, v94, p78.
Variety. Sep 3, 1969, p19.
Vogue. Nov 1, 1969, v154, p118.

The Caddy (US; Taurog, Norman; 1953)
BFI/Monthly Film Bulletin. Oct 1953, v20, n237, p147.
Film Daily. Aug 10, 1953, p6.
Hollywood Reporter. Aug 4, 1953, p3.
McCall's. Oct 1953, v81, p10.
The New York Times. Sep 18, 1953, p16.
Newsweek. Oct 5, 1953, v42, p88.
Time. Sep 28, 1953, v62, p84.
Variety. Aug 5, 1953, p6.

Caddyshack (US; Ramis, Harold; 1980)
BFI/Monthly Film Bulletin. Sep 1980, v47, p173.
Christian Science Monitor. Aug 7, 1980, p19.
Hollywood Reporter. Jul 25, 1980, p10.
The Los Angeles Times. Jul 25, 1980, SecVI, p2.
Motion Picture Herald Product Digest. Aug 6, 1980, p18.
New York. Aug 11, 1980, v13, p39.
The New York Times. Jul 25, 1980, SecIII, p8.
Newsday. Jul 25, 1980, SecII, p7.
Newsweek. Aug 11, 1980, v96, p69.
Variety. Jul 23, 1980, p18.
The Village Voice. Aug 6, 1980, p41.

Caduta Degli Dei, La *See* The Damned

Cage Aux Folles, La (FR; Molinaro, Edouard; 1978)
BFI/Monthly Film Bulletin. Jan 1980, v47, p5.
Films in Review. Aug-Sep 1979, v30, p435.
The Great French Films. p274-76.
Hollywood Reporter. Jun 1, 1979, p3.
Magill's Survey of Cinema.Foreign Language Films. v1, p446-51.
Motion Picture Herald Product Digest. May 16, 1979, p97.
The Nation. May 19, 1979, v228, p581.
The New York Times. May 13, 1979, p41.
The New York Times. Dec 14, 1980, SecII, p21.
The New Yorker. May 28, 1979, v55, p122.
Newsweek. Aug 13, 1979, v94, p77.
Time. Aug 20, 1979, v114, p58.
Variety. Nov 1, 1978, p40.

Cage Aux Folles II, La (FR; Molinaro, Edouard; 1981)
The Nation. Mar 21, 1981, v232, p349.
The New Republic. Mar 7, 1981, v184, p26.
New York. Mar 2, 1981, v14, p50-51.
The New Yorker. Mar 23, 1981, v57, p136.
Newsweek. Mar 9, 1981, v97, p77.

Rolling Stone. Apr 16, 1981, p34.
Time. Mar 2, 1981, v117, p93.

Cage of Gold (GB; Dearden, Basil; 1950)
BFI/Monthly Film Bulletin. Oct 1950, v17, p148-49.
The London Times Sep 25, 1950. p6.
Motion Picture Herald Product Digest. Feb 2, 1952, p1222.
The New York Times. Jan 19, 1952, p13.
Newsweek. Jan 28, 1952, v39, p90.
Variety. Oct 4, 1950, p22.

Caged (US; Cromwell, John; 1950)
BFI/Monthly Film Bulletin. Sep 1950, v17, p134-35.
Commonweal. Jun 9, 1950, v52, p221.
Film Daily. May 4, 1950, p6.
The Great Gangster Pictures. p73-75.
Hollywood Reporter. May 2, 1950, p3.
The London Times. Aug 26, 1950, p6.
Magill's Survey of Cinema. Series II. v1, p386-88.
Motion Picture Herald Product Digest. May 6, 1950, p286.
The New Statesman and Nation. Sep 2, 1950, v40, p251-52.
The New York Times. May 20, 1950, p8.
Newsweek. Jun 19, 1950, v35, p90.
The Spectator. Aug 25, 1950, v185, p240.
Time. Jun 19, 1950, v55, p96.
Variety. May 3, 1950, p6.

The Caine Mutiny (US; Dmytryk, Edward; 1954)
America. Jul 3, 1954, v91, p367.
BFI/Monthly Film Bulletin. Sep 1954, v21, p127.
Catholic World. Jun 1954, v179, p221-22.
Cinema, the Magic Vehicle. v2, p228-29.
Collier's. Nov 13, 1953, v132, p50-53.
Commonweal. Jun 25, 1954, v60, p293-94.
The Complete Films of Humphrey Bogart. p173-75.
Cue. Jun 26, 1954, p16.
Farm Journal. Jul 1954, v78, p92.
Fifty From the Fifties. p83-90.
Film Daily. Jun 9, 1951, p6.
Film News. Sum 1980, v37, p36-37.
Films and Filming. Oct 1954, v1, p30.
Films in Review. Jun-Jul 1954, v5, p304-05.
Fortnight. Aug 4, 1954, v17, p29.
Guts & Glory. p129-39.
Hollywood Reporter. Jun 9, 1954, p3.
Humphrey Bogart: The Man and His Films. p167.
Illustrated London News. Sep 4, 1954, v225, p378.
Library Journal. Jul 1954, v79, p1304.
Life. May 3, 1954, v36, p67-70.
The London Times. Aug 16, 1954, p4.
Look. Jun 29, 1954, v18, p84-85.
Magill's Survey of Cinema. Series I. v1, p275-79.
Motion Picture Herald Product Digest. Jun 12, 1954, p25.
National Parent-Teacher. Jun 1954, v48, p39.
The New Statesman and Nation. Aug 21, 1954, v48, p208.
The New York Times. Jun 25, 1954, p17.
The New Yorker. Jul 3, 1954, v30, p48-49.
Newsweek. Jun 28, 1954, v43, p72.
Saturday Review. Jun 26, 1954, v37, p28.
Selected Film Criticism, 1951-1960. p21-23.
Senior Scholastic. May 12, 1954, v64, p29.
Sight and Sound. Oct-Dec 1954, v24, p87-88.
The Spectator. Aug 13, 1954, v193, p194.
Stanley Kramer, Film Maker. p167-76.
The Tatler. Aug 25, 1954, v213, p332.

Time. Jun 28, 1954, v63, p90.
Variety. Jun 9, 1954, p6.

Čajkovskij *See* Tchaikovsky

Cal (GB; O'Connor, Pat; 1984)
American Film. Oct 1984, v10, p94.
BFI/Monthly Film Bulletin. Sep 1984, v51, p273.
Commonweal. Oct 5, 1984, v111, p534-55.
Films and Filming. Aug 1984, n359, p33.
Films in Review. Dec 1984, v35, p622-23.
Hollywood Reporter. Sep 3, 1984, p3.
Maclean's. Oct 15, 1984, v97, p77-78.
Magill's Cinema Annual, 1985. p124-29.
New Statesman. Sep 14, 1984, v108, p34-35.
The New York Times. Aug 24, 1984, p6.
The New York Times. Sep 9, 1984, SecII, p25.
Photoplay. Oct 1984, v35, p19.
Time. Sep 3, 1984, v124, p83.
Variety. May 23, 1984, p26.
The Village Voice. Sep 4, 1984, p55.

Calamity Jane (US; Butler, David; 1953)
America. Dec 12, 1953, v90, p305.
Catholic World. Dec 1953, v178, p224.
Farm Journal. Jan 1954, v78, p83.
Film Daily. Oct 29, 1953, p7.
The Films of Doris Day. p133-36.
Hollywood Reporter. Oct 28, 1953, p3.
Library Journal. Dec 1, 1953, v78, p2098.
Magill's Survey of Cinema. Series II. v1, p389.
National Parent-Teacher. Dec 1953, v48, p38.
The New York Times. Nov 5, 1953, p40.
Newsweek. Nov 23, 1953, v42, p100.
Saturday Review. Nov 14, 1953, v36, p40.
Time. Nov 23, 1953, v62, p120.
Variety. Oct 21, 1953, p6.

California Holiday *See* Spinout

California Split (US; Altman, Robert; 1974)
Audience. Oct 1974, v7, p6-8.
BFI/Monthly Film Bulletin. Dec 1974, v41, p269-70.
Commonweal. Oct 11, 1974, v101, p37.
Esquire. Nov 1974, v82, p44.
Film Quarterly. Spr 1975, v28, p54-55.
Filmmakers Newsletter. Oct 1974, v7, p24-27.
Films in Review. Nov 1974, v25, p570.
The Films of Robert Altman. p29-39.
Hollywood Reporter. Aug 7, 1974, p3.
Independent Film Journal. Aug 21, 1974, v74, p9.
The Los Angeles Times. Aug 14, 1974, SecIV, p1.
Motion Picture Herald Product Digest. Aug 14, 1974, p21.
The New Republic. Aug 31, 1974, v171, p20.
New York. Aug 19, 1974, v7, p62-63.
The New York Times. Sep 29, 1974, SecII, p1.
The New York Times. Sep 1, 1974, SecII, p9.
The New Yorker. Aug 19, 1974, v50, p78-80.
Newsweek. Aug 26, 1974, v84, p84.
Penthouse. Dec 1974, v6, p61-62.
Robert Altman: A Guide to References and Resources. p51-54.
Robert Altman: American Innovator. p177-92.
Robert Altman (Plecki). p69-71.
Saturday Review. Sep 21, 1974, v2, p42-43.
Time. Sep 2, 1974, v104, p6.
Variety. Aug 7, 1974, p18.
The Village Voice. Oct 3, 1974, p81-82.

California Suite (US; Ross, Herbert; 1978)
BFI/Monthly Film Bulletin. Apr 1979, v46, p69.
Films in Review. Feb 1979, v30, p120.
The Films of Jane Fonda. p215-20.
Hollywood Reporter. Dec 16, 1978, p16.
The Los Angeles Times. Dec 22, 1978, SecIV, p1.

Maclean's. Dec 25, 1978, v91, p51.
Motion Picture Herald Product Digest. Mar 3, 1978, p64.
The New York Times. Dec 22, 1978, SecIII, p12.
The New York Times. Dec 24, 1978, SecII, p11.
The New Yorker. Jan 8, 1979, v54, p49-51.
Newsweek. Jan 8, 1979, v93, p59.
Time. Jan 8, 1979, v113, p69.
Variety. Dec 13, 1978, p24.

Caligula (US; Brass, Tinto; 1980)
BFI/Monthly Film Bulletin. Dec 1980, v47, p232.
Christianity Today. Oct 24, 1980, v24, p64-65.
Films in Review. Apr 1980, v31, p244.
Hollywood Reporter. Apr 23, 1980, p2.
National Review. Oct 3, 1980, v32, p1197-98.
The New Republic. Feb 23, 1980, v182, p24.
New York. Feb 25, 1980, v13, p61.
The New York Times. Feb 2, 1980, p9.
Newsweek. Feb 25, 1980, v95, p76.
Variety. Feb 21, 1980, p24.

Call Me Madam (US; Lang, Walter; 1953)
America. Apr 4, 1953, v89, p25.
BFI/Monthly Film Bulletin. Jun 1953, v20, n233, p83.
Catholic World. May 1953, v177, p142.
Commonweal. Apr 3, 1953, v57, p649.
Film Daily. Mar 6, 1953, p7.
Films in Review. Apr 1953, v4, n4, p193-94.
Hollywood Reporter. Mar 4, 1953, p3.
Library Journal. v78, p588.
The New York Times. Mar 15, 1953, SecVI, p40.
The New York Times. Mar 26, 1953, p37.
The New Yorker. Mar 28, 1953, v29, p74.
Newsweek. Mar 30, 1953, v41, p91.
Saturday Review. Apr 4, 1953, v36, p43.
Theatre Arts. May 1953, v37, p82.
Time. Mar 23, 1953, v61, p108.
Variety. Mar 4, 1953, p6.

Call Me Mister (US; Bacon, Lloyd; 1951)
BFI/Monthly Film Bulletin. Jun 1951, v18, p279.
The Busby Berkeley Book. p163-66.
Christian Century. Apr 11, 1951, v68, p479.
Commonweal. Mar 9, 1951, v53, p544.
Film Daily. Jan 25, 1951, p12.
Hollywood Reporter. Jan 24, 1951, p3.
Library Journal. Mar 1, 1951, v76, p418.
Motion Picture Herald Product Digest. Jan 27, 1951, p689-90.
The New York Times. Feb 1, 1951, p21.
The New Yorker. Feb 10, 1951, v26, p90.
Newsweek. Feb 5, 1951, v37, p80.
Saturday Review. Feb 24, 1951, v34, p26.
The Spectator. May 25, 1951, v186, p684.
Time. Feb 5, 1951, v57, p78.
Variety. Jan 24, 1951, p6.

Callaway Went Thataway (US; Panama, Norman; Frank, Melvin; 1951)
Catholic World. Dec 1951, v174, p221.
Christian Century. Jan 16, 1952, v69, p87.
Film Daily. Nov 15, 1951, p6.
The Films of the Fifties. p47-48.
Motion Picture Herald Product Digest. Nov 17, 1951, p1100.
The New York Times. Dec 6, 1951, p42.
The New Yorker. Dec 15, 1951, v27, p148.
Newsweek. Dec 17, 1951, v38, p100.
Theatre Arts. Jan 1952, v36, p29.
Variety. Nov 14, 1951, p6.

Calling Bulldog Drummond (GB; Saville, Victor; 1951)
BFI/Monthly Film Bulletin. Aug 1951, v18, p310.

Film Daily. Oct 18, 1951, p10.
Library Journal. Jan 15, 1952, v77, p140.
The London Times. Jul 23, 1951, p2.
Motion Picture Herald Product Digest. Oct 20, 1951, p1066.
The New Statesman and Nation. Jul 21, 1951, v42, p69.
Variety. Jul 11, 1951, p6.

Camelot (US; Logan, Joshua; 1967)
America. Nov 11, 1967, v117, p582-83.
BFI/Monthly Film Bulletin. Jan 1968, v35, p3.
Christian Century. Jan 10, 1968, v85, p52-53.
Commonweal. Nov 17, 1967, v87, p207.
Film Daily. Oct 26, 1967, p3.
Film Quarterly. Spr 1968, v21, p56.
Films and Filming. Jan 1968, v14, p22.
Films and Filming. Nov 1967, v14, p15-17.
Films in Review. Dec 1967, v18, p649-50.
Harper's. Jan 1968, v236, p81-82.
The Hollywood Musical. p387-91.
Hollywood Reporter. Oct 25, 1967, p3.
Life. Sep 22, 1967, v63, p70-75.
Motion Picture Herald Product Digest. Nov 1, 1967, p737.
National Review. Feb 27, 1968, v20, p199-201.
The New York Times. Oct 26, 1967, p54.
Newsweek. Nov 6, 1967, v70, p90.
Senior Scholastic. Dec 14, 1967, v91, p21.
Time. Nov 3, 1967, v90, p100.
Variety. Oct 25, 1967, p6.

Camera Buff *See* Amator

Cammino della speranza, Il (Also titled: The Path of Hope; The Road to Hope) (IT; Germi, Pietro; 1950)
Cinema, the Magic Vehicle. v2, p56-57.
Dictionary of Films. p51.
Film Daily. Oct 3, 1951, p6.
Hollywood Quarterly. Sum 1951, v5, p389-400.
Hollywood Reporter. Dec 24, 1951, p3.
Italian Cinema (Bondanella). p85-86.
Italian Cinema (Leprohon). p119-20.
The New Statesman and Nation. Jul 19, 1952, v44, p71.
The New York Times. Aug 5, 1952, p15.
Newsweek. Aug 18, 1952, v40, p84.
Saturday Review. Nov 17, 1951, v34, p64.

Campanadas a Medianoche *See* Chimes at Midnight

Can Heironymus Merkin Ever Forgive Mercy Humppe and Find True Happiness? (GB; Newley, Anthony; 1969)
Big Screen, Little Screen. p158-60.
Christian Century. Jan 7, 1970, v87, p24.
Commonweal. Apr 18, 1969, v90, p144-45.
Film Daily. Mar 11, 1969, p6.
Films and Filming. Aug 1969, v15, p41-43.
The New York Times. Mar 20, 1969, p55.
Newsweek. Apr 7, 1969, v73, p82.
Saturday Review. Apr 5, 1969, v52, p50.
Time. Mar 28, 1969, v93, p88.
Variety. Mar 12, 1969, p6.

Can-Can (US; Lang, Walter; 1960)
America. Mar 26, 1960, v102, p773.
BFI/Monthly Film Bulletin. May 1960, v27, p62.
Chevalier: The Films and Career of Maurice Chevalier. p185-88.
Commonweal. Apr 1, 1960, v72, p16-17.
Dance Magazine. Apr 1960, v34, p14.
Film Daily. Mar 10, 1960, p10.
Films and Filming. May 1960, v6, p21-22.
Films in Review. Apr 1960, v11, p235-36.
The Films of Frank Sinatra. p160-62.
The Films of Shirley MacLaine. p88-93.
Hollywood Reporter. Mar 10, 1960, p3.

Life. Mar 14, 1960, v48, p72-54.
Motion Picture Herald Product Digest. Mar 19, 1960, p627.
The New York Times. Mar 10, 1960, p36.
The New York Times. Mar 20, 1960, SecII, p1.
The New Yorker. Mar 19, 1960, v36, p170.
Newsweek. Mar 21, 1960, v55, p120.
Time. Mar 21, 1960, v75, p83.
Variety. Mar 9, 1960, p6.

The Candidate (US; Ritchie, Michael; 1972)
America. Aug 5, 1972, v127, p76.
Commonweal. Aug 25, 1972, v96, p455.
Filmfacts. 1972, v15, n9, p189.
Films in Review. Aug-Sep 1972, v23, n7, p436.
The Films of Robert Redford. p155.
Hollywood Reporter. Jun 20, 1972, p3.
Life. Jul 7, 1972, v73, p22.
Life. Jul 28, 1972, v73, p45-48.
Magill's Survey of Cinema. Series II. v1, p393.
The New Republic. Aug 5, 1972, v167, p24.
The New York Times. Jul 30, 1972, v25, p1.
The New Yorker. Jul 1, 1972, v48, p64-65.
Newsweek. Jul 17, 1972, v80, p78-79.
Saturday Review. Jul 15, 1972, v55, p60.
Senior Scholastic. Oct 9, 1972, v101, p20.
Time. Jul 17, 1972, v100, p49.
Variety. Jun 21, 1972, p18.

Cannery Row (US; Ward, David S.; 1982)
BFI/Monthly Film Bulletin. Sep 1983, v50, p253, 269.
Hollywood Reporter. Feb 3, 1982, p3.
Literature/Film Quarterly. v10, n2, p82-84.
The Los Angeles Times. Feb 12, 1982, SecVI, p1.
Maclean's. Feb 22, 1982, v95, p56.
Magill's Cinema Annual, 1983. p95-99.
The New York Times. Feb 12, 1982, SecIII, p10.
Oceans. May-Jun 1982, v15, p60.
Rolling Stone. Apr 2, 1981, p16-22.
Steinbeck on Film. p172-75.
Time. Feb 15, 1982, v119, p64.
Variety. Feb 1, 1982, p3.
The Village Voice. Mar 16, 1982, p48.

Can't Stop the Music (US; Walker, Nancy; 1980)
BFI/Monthly Film Bulletin. Aug 1980, v47, p153.
Film Comment. Sep-Oct 1980, v16, p51.
Hollywood Reporter. Jun 12, 1980, p3.
The Los Angeles Times. Jun 20, 1980, SecVI, p13.
Motion Picture Herald Product Digest. Jul 9, 1980, p12.
The New York Times. Jun 20, 1980, SecIII, p12.
Newsday. Jun 20, 1980, SecII, p10.
Newsweek. Jul 7, 1980, v96, p68.
Variety. Jun 4, 1980, p20.
The Village Voice. Jul 2, 1980, p33.

Cape Fear (US; Thompson, J. Lee; 1962)
America. Apr 21, 1962, v107, p85.
BFI/Monthly Film Bulletin. Jan 1963, v30, p7.
Commonweal. May 11, 1962, v76, p179.
Film Daily. Mar 7, 1962, p6.
Film Quarterly. Sum 1962, v15, p63.
Filmfacts. May 25, 1962, v5, p99-100.
Films and Filming. Feb 1963, v9, p35-36.
Films in Review. May 1962, v13, p299.
The Films of Gregory Peck. p174-78.
Hollywood Reporter. Mar 7, 1962, v169, p3.
Motion Picture Herald Product Digest. Mar 14, 1962, p476.
Movie. Feb 1963, n7, p36.
The New York Times. Apr 19, 1962, p35.
Newsweek. Apr 30, 1962, v59, p98.

Robert Mitchum on the Screen. p175-76.
Saturday Review. May 5, 1962, v45, p28.
Time. Apr 27, 1962, v79, p87.
Variety. Mar 7, 1962, p6.

Caprice (US; Tashlin, Frank; 1967)
BFI/Monthly Film Bulletin. Jun 1967, v34, p87.
Commonweal. Jun 23, 1967, v86, p392.
Film Daily. May 18, 1967, p4.
Film Quarterly. Fall 1967, v21, p58.
Films and Filming. Jul 1967, v13, p20-21.
The Films of Doris Day. p235-38.
Hollywood Reporter. May 16, 1967, p3.
Motion Picture Herald Product Digest. May 24, 1967, p688.
The New York Times. Jun 8, 1967, p52.
Newsweek. Jun 26, 1967, v69, p73.
Saturday Review. Jun 3, 1967, v50, p43.
Variety. May 17, 1967, p6.

Capricious Summer (Czech title: Rozmarne Neto) (CZECH; Menzel, Jiri; 1968)
BFI/Monthly Film Bulletin. Oct 1969, v36, p209-10.
The Czechoslovak New Wave. p180-85.
Film Quarterly. Spr 1969, v22, p59-60.
Film Society Review. Oct 1969, v4, p29-36.
Filmfacts. Dec 15, 1968, v11, p383-85.
Magill's Survey of Cinema. Foreign Language Films. v1, p460-63.
The New Republic. Oct 5, 1968, v159, p18.
New Statesman. Sep 19, 1969, v78, p389.
The New York Times. Sep 18, 1968, p50.
The New York Times. Sep 25, 1968, p38.
The Spectator. Sep 20, 1969, v223, p382.
Variety. Jun 19, 1968, p6.
Vogue. Sep 15, 1968, v152, p72.

Capricorn One (US; Hyams, Peter; 1978)
Films in Review. Oct 1978, v29, p501.
Hollywood Reporter. Jun 2, 1978, p3.
The Los Angeles Times. Jun 2, 1978, SecIV, p24.
Motion Picture Herald Product Digest. Jun 28, 1978, p8.
The New York Times. Jun 2, 1978, SecIII, p8.
The New York Times. Jun 11, 1978, SecII, p12.
Newsweek. Jun 19, 1978, v91, p75.
Saturday Review. Oct 28, 1978, v5, p36.
Time. Jun 12, 1978, v111, p90.
Variety. Jun 7, 1978, p25.

Captain Black Jack (Also titled: Black Jack) (FR, US; Duvivier, Julien; 1951)
Hollywood Reporter. Jul 17, 1952, p3.
The New York Times. Oct 22, 1952, p31.
Newsweek. Nov 3, 1952, v40, p107.
Variety. Jan 31, 1951, p6.

Captain Carey, U.S.A. (US; Leisen, Mitchell; 1950)
Christian Century. May 10, 1950, v67, p599.
Commonweal. Apr 7, 1950, v51, p677.
Film Daily. Feb 21, 1950, p5.
The Films of Alan Ladd. p146-48.
Hollywood Director. p280-81.
Hollywood Reporter. Feb 20, 1950, p3.
Motion Picture Herald Product Digest. Feb 25, 1950, p205.
The New York Times. Mar 30, 1950, p40.
Newsweek. Apr 10, 1950, v35, p83.
Time. May 1, 1950, v55, p92.
Variety. Feb 22, 1950, p6.

Captain Horatio Hornblower RN (GB; Walsh, Raoul; 1951)
BFI/Monthly Film Bulletin. May 1951, v18, p258.
Catholic World. Oct 1951, v174, p64.
Christian Century. Sep 19, 1951, v68, p1087.
Film Daily. Jun 15, 1951, p6.
Films in Review. Aug-Sep 1951, v2, p43.

The Films of Gregory Peck. p111-13.
The Great Adventure Films. p156-61.
High Fidelity. Oct 1979, v29, p125.
Hollywood Reporter. Apr 13, 1951, p4.
Hollywood Reporter. Jun 14, 1951, p4.
Library Journal. Sep 1, 1951, v76, p1344.
Motion Picture Herald Product Digest. Jun 16, 1951, p886.
The New York Times. Sep 14, 1951, p21.
The New Yorker. Sep 22, 1951, v27, p91.
Newsweek. Sep 24, 1951, v38, p87.
The Spectator. Apr 13, 1951, v186, p490.
Time. Sep 10, 1951, v58, p96.
Variety. Apr 18, 1951, p6.
Variety. Jun 20, 1951, p6.

Captain Newman, M.D. (US; Miller, David; 1964)
America. Feb 29, 1964, v110, p295.
BFI/Monthly Film Bulletin. Apr 1964, v31, p54.
Commonweal. Mar 6, 1964, v79, p694.
Film Daily. Oct 22, 1963, v123, p6.
Films in Review. Feb 1964, v15, p118-19.
The Films of Gregory Peck. p188-90.
Hollywood Reporter. Oct 22, 1963, v177, p3.
Look. Apr 7, 1964, v28, p92-94.
Magill's Survey of Cinema. Series II. v1, p405-07.
Motion Picture Herald Product Digest. Oct 30, 1963, p921-22.
The New York Times. Feb 21, 1964, p36.
The New Yorker. Feb 29, 1964, v40, p122.
Newsweek. Mar 2, 1964, v63, p84.
Saturday Review. Feb 15, 1964, v47, p33.
Time. Feb 28, 1964, v83, p105.
Variety. Oct 23, 1963, p6.
Vogue. Apr 1, 1964, v143, p42.

The Captain's Paradise (GB; Kimmins, Anthony; 1953)
BFI/Monthly Film Bulletin. Jul 1953, v20, p100.
Commonweal. Sep 25, 1953, v58, p610.
Film Daily. Oct 7, 1953, p6.
Films in Review. Nov 1953, v4, n9, p483.
Hollywood Reporter. Nov 23, 1953, p3.
The New York Times. Aug 30, 1953, SecVI, p36.
The New York Times. Sep 29, 1953, p25.
The New York Times. Oct 4, 1953, SecII, p1.
The New Yorker. Oct 10, 1953, v29, p127.
Newsweek. Oct 12, 1953, v42, p100.
Saturday Review. Sep 26, 1953, v36, p34.
Time. Oct 12, 1953, v62, p110.
Variety. Jun 24, 1953, p22.

The Captive City (US; Wise, Robert; 1952)
BFI/Monthly Film Bulletin. Aug 1952, v19, p105.
Christian Century. Sep 3, 1952, v69, p1015.
Commonweal. Apr 11, 1952, v56, p14.
Film Daily. Mar 31, 1952, p6.
Hollywood Reporter. Mar 27, 1952, p3.
Motion Picture Herald Product Digest. Mar 29, 1952, p1297.
The New York Times. Mar 27, 1952, p34.
Newsweek. Apr 7, 1952, v39, p101.
Saturday Review. Apr 12, 1952, v35, p41.
Sight and Sound. Oct-Dec 1952, v22, p80.
The Tatler. Jul 23, 1952, v205, p158.
Variety. Mar 26, 1952, p6.

The Capture (US; Sturges, John; 1950)
BFI/Monthly Film Bulletin. Jun 1950, p84.
Commonweal. Jun 9, 1950, v52, p221.
Film Daily. Apr 12, 1950, p4.
Hollywood Reporter. Mar 29, 1950, p3.
Motion Picture Herald Product Digest. Apr 8, 1950, p254.
The New York Times. May 20, 1950, p8.

The Spectator. May 19, 1950, v184, p681.
Time. Jun 19, 1950, v55, p94.
Variety. Apr 5, 1950, p6.

Car Wash (US; Schultz, Michael; 1976)
Film Bulletin. Sep-Oct 1976, v45, p36-37.
Independent Film Journal. Oct 29, 1976, v78, p10.
The Los Angeles Times. Aug 29, 1976, Calendar, p48.
The New York Times. Oct 16, 1976, p13.
The New York Times. Oct 24, 1976, SecII, p15.
The New Yorker. Oct 25, 1976, v52, p68.
Newsweek. Oct 4, 1976, v88, p89-90.
Time. Nov 22, 1976, v108, p95.
Variety. Sep 1, 1976, p22.
The Village Voice. Nov 8, 1976, p53-54.

Carbine Williams (US; Thorpe, Richard; 1952)
BFI/Monthly Film Bulletin. Jun 1952, v19, p79.
Christian Century. Jun 4, 1952, v69, p687.
Commonweal. May 23, 1952, v56, p174.
Film Daily. Apr 21, 1952, p10.
The Films of James Stewart. p152-54.
Hollywood Reporter. Apr 15, 1952, p3.
Library Journal. Jun 1, 1952, v77, p970.
Motion Picture Herald Product Digest. Apr 19, 1952, p1321.
The New York Times. May 8, 1952, p37.
Newsweek. May 26, 1952, v39, p92.
Saturday Review. May 3, 1952, v35, p31.
Theatre Arts. Jun 1952, v36, p96.
Time. May 12, 1952, v59, p108.
Variety. Apr 16, 1952, p6.

The Card *See* The Promoter

The Cardinal (US; Preminger, Otto; 1963)
America. Jan 4, 1963, v110, p27.
BFI/Monthly Film Bulletin. Feb 1964, v31, p18.
Catholic World. Mar 1964, v198, p365-71.
Catholic World. Feb 1964, v198, p327-28.
The Cinema of Otto Preminger. p146-47.
Commonweal. Dec 20, 1963, v79, p371-72.
Ebony. Dec 1963, v19, p126-28.
Esquire. Mar 1964, v61, p24.
Film Daily. Oct 17, 1963, p4.
Filmfacts. Dec 19, 1963, v6, p281-84.
Films and Filming. Feb 1964, v10, p28-29.
National Review. Jan 28, 1964, v16, p77-79.
The New Republic. Dec 21, 1963, v149, p29.
New Statesman. Dec 20, 1963, v66, p921.
The New York Times. Dec 13, 1963, p41.
The New York Times. Dec 15, 1963, SecII, p3.
The New Yorker. Dec 14, 1963, v39, p198.
Newsweek. Dec 16, 1963, v62, p90.
Reporter. Feb 13, 1964, v30, p44.
Saturday Review. Dec 7, 1963, v46, p32.
Sight and Sound. Wint 1963-1964, v33, p39-40.
Time. Dec 13, 1963, v82, p97-98.
Variety. Oct 16, 1963, p6.
The Village Voice. Dec 12, 1963, p23.

The Care Bears Movie (US; Selznick, Arna; 1985)
BFI/Monthly Film Bulletin. Aug 1985, v52, p244.
The Los Angeles Times. Mar 29, 1985, SecVI, p4.
Maclean's. May 27, 1985, v98, p54.
The New York Times. Mar 29, 1985, SecIII, p16.
Variety. Mar 27, 1985, p17.

Career (US; Jason, Leigh; 1959)
America. Oct 17, 1959, v102, p90-91.
BFI/Monthly Film Bulletin. Jan 1960, v27, p2.
Commonweal. Nov 6, 1959, v71, p185.
Film Daily. Sep 25, 1959, v116, p6.
Filmfacts. Nov 4, 1959, v2, p233-34.

The Films of Shirley MacLaine. p82-84.
Hollywood Reporter. Sep 25, 1959, p3.
The New York Times. Oct 9, 1959, p24.
The New Yorker. Oct 17, 1959, v35, p197.
Newsweek. Oct 19, 1959, v54, p108.
Saturday Review. Oct 10, 1959, v42, p32.
Time. Oct 19, 1959, v74, p108.
Variety. Sep 30, 1959, p12.

Careful He Might Hear You (AUSTRALIA; Schultz, Carl; 1984)
BFI/Monthly Film Bulletin. Jul 1985, v52, p210.
Cinema Papers. Mar-Apr 1984, n44/45, p86-87.
Hollywood Reporter. Jun 18, 1984, p4.
The Los Angeles Times. Jun 30, 1984, SecVI, p3.
The Los Angeles Times. Jul 15, 1984, SecVI, p3.
Maclean's. Jul 23, 1984, v97, p46.
Magill's Cinema Annual, 1985. p130-34.
The New Leader. Jul 9, 1984, v67, p18-19.
The New York Times. Jun 15, 1984, SecIII, p8.
The New York Times. Jul 8, 1984, SecII, p15.
Variety. Jun 15, 1984, p14.
Variety. Jun 13, 1984, p20.
The Village Voice. Jun 26, 1984, p49, 56.

The Caretakers (US; Bartlett, Hall; 1963)
Commonweal. Oct 4, 1963, v79, p46.
Film Daily. Aug 16, 1963, p14.
Filmfacts. Sep 5, 1963, v6, p179-80.
Films and Filming. Jan 1966, v12, p28-29.
Films in Review. May 1963, v14, p307-8.
The Films of Joan Crawford. p212-13.
Hollywood Reporter. Aug 15, 1963, v176, p3.
The New York Times. Aug 22, 1963, p19.
Photoplay. Nov 1963, v64, p12.
Saturday Review. Aug 10, 1963, v46, p34.
Time. Sep 6, 1963, v82, p84.
Variety. Jul 1963, p6.

Cargo to Capetown (US; McEvoy, Earl; 1950)
Film Daily. Apr 11, 1950, p6.
Hollywood Reporter. Apr 7, 1950, p3.
The London Times. Aug 21, 1950, p6.
Motion Picture Herald Product Digest. Apr 1, 1950, p246.
The New York Times. Mar 31, 1950, p36.
The Spectator. Aug 18, 1950, v185, p209.
Variety. Apr 5, 1950, p6.

Caribbean (Also titled: Caribbean Gold) (US; Ludwig, Edward; 1952)
BFI/Monthly Film Bulletin. Feb 1953, v20, p23.
Film Daily. Aug 7, 1952, p7.
Hollywood Reporter. Aug 1, 1952, p3.
Motion Picture Herald Product Digest. Aug 2, 1952, p1469-70.
National Parent-Teacher. Oct 1952, v47, p37.
Newsweek. Nov 3, 1952, v40, p107.
Variety. Aug 6, 1952, p6.

Carmen *See* Bizet's Carmen

Carmen Jones (US; Preminger, Otto; 1954)
America. Nov 6, 1954, v92, p165.
American Cinematographer. Dec 1954, v35, p610-11.
Behind the Scenes of Otto Preminger. p134-37, 262.
BFI/Monthly Film Bulletin. Feb 1955, v22, p18-19.
Black Films and Film-Makers. p88-94.
Catholic World. Dec 1954, v180, p221.
The Cinema of Otto Preminger. 1977, p109-11.
Commentary. Jan 1955, v19, p74-77.
Commonweal. Nov 19, 1954, v61, p188.
Dictionary of Films. p53-54.
Farm Journal. Dec 1954, v78, p141.

Film Daily. Oct 5, 1954, p10.
Films and Filming. Feb 1955, v1, p18.
Films and Filming. Dec 1954, v1, p24.
Films in Review. Dec 1954, v5, p543-44.
From Sambo to Superspade. p203-06.
Harper's Magazine. Jan 1955, v210, p87.
Hollywood Reporter. Sep 28, 1954, p3.
Library Journal. Nov 15, 1954, v79, p2182.
Life. Nov 1, 1954, v37, p87-90.
The London Times. Jan 10, 1955, p10.
Motion Picture Herald Product Digest. Oct 16, 1954, p179.
Movie. Nov 1962, n4, p21-23.
The Nation. Nov 13, 1954, v179, p430.
National Parent-Teacher. Dec 1954, v49, p39.
The New Statesman and Nation. Jan 15, 1954, v48, p73.
The New York Times. Oct 29, 1954, p27.
The New York Times Magazine. Oct 17, 1954, p64-65.
The New Yorker. Nov 6, 1954, v30, p181.
Newsweek. Oct 25, 1954, v44, p102.
Preminger: An Autobiography. p133-36.
Saturday Review. Jan 1, 1955, v38, p63.
Saturday Review. Nov 6, 1954, v37, p39-40.
Sight and Sound. Spr 1955, v24, p198-99.
The Spectator. Jan 7, 1955, v194, p16, 18.
The Tatler. Jan 19, 1955, v215, p111.
Time. Nov 1, 1954, v64, p98.
Variety. Oct 6, 1954, p6.

Carnal Knowledge (US; Nichols, Mike; 1971)
America. Jul 24, 1971, v125, p48.
Atlantic. Nov 1971, v228, p144.
BFI/Monthly Film Bulletin. Oct 1971, v38, p193.
BFI/Monthly Film Bulletin. Nov 1971, v38, n454, p230.
Cineaste. Wint 1971-72, v5, n1, p12-14.
Commonweal. Sep 3, 1971, v94, p453.
Esquire. Oct 1971, v76, p45-46.
Fifty Grand Movies of the 1960s and 1970s. p13-16.
Film Library Quarterly. Wint 1971-72, v5, n1, p14-21.
Film Quarterly. Wint 1971, v25, p56.
Films and Filming. Dec 1971, v18, n3, p50.
Films in Review. Aug-Sep 1971, v22, p441-42.
The Films of The Seventies. p33-34.
Focus on Film. Sum 1971, n7, p8.
Hollywood Reporter. Jun 30, 1971, p3.
Life. Aug 6, 1971, v71, p12.
Magill's Survey of Cinema. Series I. v1, p295-27.
Mike Nichols (Schuth). p65-84.
National Review. Oct 22, 1971, v23, p1192.
The New Republic. Aug 21, 1971, v165, p22.
The New York Times. Jul 1, 1971, p63.
The New York Times. Jul 4, 1971, SecII, p1.
The New York Times. Aug 1, 1971, SecII, p9.
The New Yorker. Jul 3, 1971, v47, p43-44.
Newsweek. Jul 5, 1971, v78, p71.
Newsweek. Aug 2, 1971, v78, p9.
Saturday Review. Jul 3, 1971, v54, p18.
Sight and Sound. Aut 1971, v40, p222-23.
Time. Jul 5, 1971, v98, p66-67.
Variety. Jun 30, 1971, p22.
The Village Voice. Jul 8, 1971, p49.

Carnets du Major Thompson, Les *See* The French They Are a Funny Race

Carnival Story (US; Neumann, Kurt; 1954)
America. May 15, 1954, v91, p203.
BFI/Monthly Film Bulletin. Jun 1954, v21, p86.
Commonweal. May 7, 1954, v60, p118.
Film Daily. Mar 24, 1954, p6.
Hollywood Reporter. Mar 24, 1954, p3.
The London Times. May 17, 1954, p4.

Motion Picture Herald Product Digest. Mar 27, 1954, p2237.
National Parent-Teacher. May 1954, v48, p38.
The New York Times. Apr 17, 1954, p8.
The New Yorker. Apr 24, 1954, v30, p81.
Newsweek. Apr 5, 1954, v43, p81.
Saturday Review. May 8, 1954, v37, p26.
The Spectator. May 14, 1954, v192, p578-79.
The Tatler. May 26, 1954, v212, p462.
Time. Apr 19, 1954, v63, p100.
Variety. Mar 24, 1954, p6.

Carny (US; Kaylor, Robert; 1980)
Films in Review. Aug 1980, v31, p440.
Hollywood Reporter. May 21, 1980, p3.
The Los Angeles Times. Sep 7, 1980, Calendar, p27.
Motion Picture Herald Product Digest. Jun 11, 1980, p2.
National Review. Jul 25, 1980, v32, p915-16.
New York. Jun 23, 1980, v13, p56-57.
Newsday. Jun 13, 1980, SecII, p7.
Newsweek. Jun 23, 1980, v95, p75.
Rolling Stone. Jun 26, 1980, p28-29.
Time. Jun 16, 1980, v115, p50.
Variety. May 21, 1980, p20.
The Village Voice. Jun 25, 1980, p41.
The Village Voice. Sep 10, 1980, p46.

Caroline Cherie (FR; Pottier, Richard; 1951)
BFI/Monthly Film Bulletin. Jul 1952, v19, p93.
Film Daily. Jun 11, 1954, p6.
The New Statesman and Nation. Jun 7, 1952, v43, p572.
The New York Times. May 25, 1954, p23.
Saturday Review. Jun 5, 1954, v37, p27.
Variety. Mar 21, 1951, p7.

Carosse d'Or, Le *See* The Golden Coach

Carousel (US; King, Henry; 1956)
America. Mar 3, 1956, v94, p620.
BFI/Monthly Film Bulletin. May 1956, v23, p56.
Commonweal. Mar 9, 1956, v63, p592.
Film Culture. 1956, v2, p25-26.
Film Daily. Feb 17, 1956, p6.
Films and Filming. May 1956, v2, p20.
Films in Review. Mar 1956, v7, p127-28.
Hollywood Musicals. p352.
Hollywood Reporter. Feb 17, 1956, p3.
Magill's Survey of Cinema. Series I. v1, p298-302.
Motion Picture Herald Product Digest. Mar 3, 1956, p802.
The Musical: From Broadway to Hollywood. p61-65.
The New York Times. Feb 17, 1956, p13.
The New York Times. Feb 19, 1956, SecII, p1.
The New York Times. Mar 3, 1956, v32, p68.
Newsweek. Mar 5, 1956, v47, p90.
Saturday Review. Mar 3, 1956, v39, p23.
Time. Mar 19, 1956, v67, p108.
Variety. Feb 22, 1956, p6.

The Carpetbaggers (US; Dmytryk, Edward; 1964)
BFI/Monthly Film Bulletin. Nov 1964, v31, p159.
Commonweal. Jul 24, 1964, v80, p514.
Esquire. Oct 1965, v64, p34.
Film Daily. Apr 10, 1964, v124, p10.
Films and Filming. Dec 1964, v11, p27-28.
Films in Review. Jun-Jul 1964, v15, p368-69.
The Films of the Sixties. p120-21.
Hollywood Reporter. Apr 10, 1964, v180, p3.
Life. Jun 26, 1964, v56, p12.
Motion Picture Herald Product Digest. Apr 15, 1964, v231, p26.
The New York Times. Jul 2, 1964, p24.

Saturday Review. Jun 20, 1964, v47, p29.
Time. Jul 3, 1964, v84, p86.
Variety. Apr 15, 1964, p6.

Carrie (US; Wyler, William; 1952)
BFI/Monthly Film Bulletin. Jul 1952, v19, p89.
Catholic World. Aug 1952, v175, p383-84.
Christian Century. Oct 8, 1952, v69, p1175.
The Classic American Novel and the Movies. p152-64.
Commonweal. Aug 1, 1952, v56, p412.
Film Comment. Fall 1970, v6, p25-27.
Film Daily. Jun 11, 1952, p7.
Films in Review. Mar 1952, v3, p134-36.
The Films of Jennifer Jones. p117-22.
The Films of Laurence Olivier. p110-11.
Hollywood Reporter. Jun 9, 1952, p3.
Illustrated London News. Jul 26, 1952, v221, p150.
Laurence Olivier (Hirsch). p136-39.
Laurence Olivier: Theater & Cinema. p113-16.
Library Journal. Jul 1952, v77, p1185.
The London Times. Jul 7, 1952, p8.
Magill's Survey of Cinema. Series II. v1, p408-11.
Motion Picture Herald Product Digest. Jun 14, 1952, p1397.
The Nation. May 17, 1952, v174, p485.
The New Statesman and Nation. Jul 12, 1952, v44, p40.
The New York Times. Jul 17, 1952, p20.
The New Yorker. Jul 26, 1952, v28, p50.
Newsweek. Jul 28, 1952, v40, p81.
Saturday Review. Jul 12, 1952, v35, p25.
Sight and Sound. Jul-Sep 1952, v22, p26-27.
The Spectator. Jul 4, 1952, v189, p15.
The Tatler. Jul 16, 1952, v205, p114.
Time. Jun 30, 1952, v59, p59.
Variety. Jun 11, 1952, p6.
William Wyler: A Guide to References and Resources. p127-31.
William Wyler (Anderegg). p165-73.
William Wyler (Madsen). p434.

Carrie (US; De Palma, Brian; 1976)
BFI/Monthly Film Bulletin. Jan 1977, v44, p3-4.
Cinefantastique. 1976, v5, n3, p20.
De Palma (Bliss). p8-29, 50-71.
Film Bulletin. Nov-Dec 1976, v45, p43.
The Films of the Seventies. p159-61.
Hollywood Reporter. Nov 1, 1976, p4.
Independent Film Journal. Nov 26, 1976, v78, p7-8.
The Los Angeles Times. Nov 17, 1976, SecIV, p23.
Magill's Survey of Cinema. Series II. v1, p408-11.
Motion Picture Herald Product Digest. Nov 24, 1976, p50.
The New York Times. Dec 5, 1976, SecII, p13.
The New York Times. Sep 17, 1976, SecII, p6.
The New York Times. Dec 12, 1976, SecII, p13.
The New Yorker. Nov 22, 1976, v52, p177-80.
Newsweek. Nov 22, 1976, v88, p113.
Time. Nov 8, 1976, v108, p110.
Variety. Nov 3, 1976, p27.
The Village Voice. Nov 29, 1976, p53.
The Village Voice. Dec 6, 1976, p59-60.

Carrington V.C. *See* Court-Martial

Carrozza d'Oro, La *See* The Golden Coach

Carry on Nurse (GB; Thomas, Gerald; 1960)
The Carry-On Book. 1978.
Fifty Classic British Films. p97-99.
Film Daily. Mar 22, 1960, p7.
Films and Filming. May 1959, v5, p22.
Hollywood Reporter. Mar 15, 1960, p3.

Magill's Survey of Cinema. Series I. v1, p301-04.
The New York Times. Sep 10, 1960, p11.
The New Yorker. Sep 24, 1960, v36, p168.
Time. Sep 26, 1960, v76, p94.
Variety. Mar 18, 1959, p23.

Cartouche (Also titled: Swords of Blood) (FR; Broca, Philippe de; 1962)
BFI/Monthly Film Bulletin. Sep 1964, v31, p130-31.
Boxoffice. Aug 10, 1964, v85, p10.
Film Daily. Jul 21, 1964, v125, p6.
Films in Review. Aug-Sep 1964, v15, p439.
Motion Picture Herald Product Digest. Aug 5, 1964, v232, p98-99.
The New York Times. Jul 22, 1964, p39.
The New Yorker. Aug 8, 1964, p40, p74.
Time. Jul 31, 1964, v84, p63.
Variety. May 9, 1962, p17.

Casanova *See* Fellini's Casanova

Casanova di Fellini, Il *See* Fellini's Casanova

Casanova '70 (IT, FR; Monicelli, Mario; 1965)
America. Aug 28, 1965, v113, p224-26.
BFI/Monthly Film Bulletin. Jun 1966, v33, p92.
Christian Science Monitor (Western edition). Aug 20, 1965, p2.
Commonweal. Aug 20, 1965, v82, p599.
Esquire. Oct 1965, v64, p34, 36.
Film Daily. Jul 21, 1965, p4.
Films and Filming. Dec 1965, v12, p40-41.
Films and Filming. Jun 1966, v12, p56-57.
Hollywood Reporter. Jul 21, 1965, p3.
Life. Aug 20, 1965, v59, p8.
The London Times. Apr 21, 1966, p9.
Motion Picture Herald Product Digest. Aug 4, 1965, p338.
The New Republic. Aug 7, 1965, v153, p36-38.
The New York Times. Jul 21, 1965, p43.
The New Yorker. Jul 31, 1965, v41, p56.
Newsweek. Aug 9, 1965, v66, p79.
Playboy. Oct 1965, v12, p24, 26.
Saturday Review. Sep 4, 1965, v48, p44.
Time. Aug 6, 1965, v86, p85.
Variety. Jul 21, 1965, p7.

Casanova's Big Night (US; McLeod, Norman Z.; 1954)
America. May 1, 1954, v91, p147.
Basil Rathbone: His Life and His Films. p319-20.
BFI/Monthly Film Bulletin. Apr 1954, v21, p55-56.
Farm Journal. May 1954, v78, p137.
Film Daily. Mar 1, 1954, p6.
Hollywood Reporter. Mar 1, 1954, p3.
The London Times. Apr 12, 1954, p6.
Motion Picture Herald Product Digest. Mar 6, 1954, p2205.
National Parent-Teacher. May 1954, v48, p39.
The New Statesman and Nation. Apr 17, 1954, v47, p501.
The New York Times. Apr 19, 1954, p19.
The New Yorker. May 1, 1954, v30, p110.
Newsweek. Apr 5, 1954, v43, p80.
Saturday Review. Apr 10, 1954, v37, p36.
Senior Scholastic. Apr 21, 1954, v64, p30.
The Spectator. Apr 9, 1954, v192, p430.
Time. Apr 19, 1954, v63, p110.
Variety. Mar 3, 1954, p6.

Case of the Missing Switchboard Operator
See Love Affair, or The Case of the Missing Switchboard Operator

Cash McCall (US; Pevney, Joseph; 1960)
BFI/Monthly Film Bulletin. Apr 1960, v27, p47.
Commonweal. Feb 19, 1960, v71, p573.
Film Daily. Dec 14, 1959, p14.
The New York Times. Jan 28, 1960, p1.
Newsweek. Jan 18, 1960, v55, p91.
Time. Feb 1, 1960, v75, p76.
Variety. Dec 9, 1959, p6.

Casino Royale (GB; Huston, John, et. al.; 1967)
America. May 20, 1967, v116, p764.
BFI/Monthly Film Bulletin. Jun 1967, v34, p87-88.
The Cinema of John Huston. p 156-59.
Commonweal. May 19, 1967, v86, p264.
Esquire. Aug 1967, v68, p30.
Film Daily. May 1, 1967, p8.
Film Quarterly. Sum 1967, v20, p77-78.
Films in Review. Jun-Jul 1967, v18, p367-68.
The Films of David Niven. p206-11.
The Films of William Holden. p226-28.
Hollywood Reporter. May 1, 1967, p3.
James Bond in the Cinema. p283-86.
James Bond's Bedside Companion. p238-39.
John Huston (Madsen). p119-20.
John Huston, Maker of Magic. p171-73.
John Huston (Pratley). p156-59.
Life. Apr 21, 1967, v62, p108-10.
Look. Nov 15, 1966, v30, p50-54.
Motion Picture Herald Product Digest. May 10, 1967, p681.
The New York Times. Apr 29, 1967, p25.
The New Yorker. May 6, 1967, v43, p172.
Newsweek. May 15, 1967, v69, p94.
Saturday Review. May 20, 1967, v50, p65.
Time. May 12, 1967, v89, p100.
U.S. Camera. Aug 1967, v30, p61.
Variety. Apr 19, 1967, p6.
The Village Voice. Jun 15, 1967, p41.
Woody Allen: His Films and Career. p67-76.

Casque D'Or (Also titled: Golden Marie; Golden Helmet) (FR; Becker, Jacques; 1952)
BFI/Monthly Film Bulletin. Oct 1952, v19, p137.
Cinema, the Magic Vehicle. v2, p119-21.
Commonweal. Sep 12, 1952, v56, p559.
Dictionary of Films. p55-56.
Film Criticism and Caricatures, 1943-53. p148-49.
The Great French Films. p139-42.
The International Dictionary of Films and Filmmakers. v1, p79-80.
Kiss Kiss Bang Bang. p303-04.
The London Times. Sep 8, 1952, p8.
Motion Picture Herald Product Digest. Sep 6, 1952, p1517.
The New Statesman and Nation. Sep 13, 1952, v44, p290-91.
The New York Times. Aug 19, 1952, p19.
The New Yorker. Aug 30, 1952, v28, p52.
Newsweek. Sep 1, 1952, v40, p64.
Sight and Sound. Oct-Dec 1952, v22, p75-77.
Sight and Sound. Sum 1969, v38, p142-47.
The Spectator. Sep 5, 1952, v189, p295.
Theatre Arts. Oct 1952, v36, p96.
Variety. May 28, 1952, p24.

Cast a Dark Shadow (GB; Gilbert, Lewis; 1957)
BFI/Monthly Film Bulletin. Oct 1955, v22, p152.
Film Daily. Dec 5, 1957, v2, p9.
Films and Filming. Nov 1955, p22, p18.
The Films of Dirk Bogarde. p87.
The New York Times. Nov 28, 1957, p57.

The New Yorker. Dec 7, 1957, v33, p99.
Variety. Nov 28, 1955, p9.

Cast a Giant Shadow (US; Shavelson, Melville; 1966)
America. Apr 30, 1966, v114, p631.
BFI/Monthly Film Bulletin. Sep 1966, v33, p136.
Christian Science Monitor (Western edition). Apr 23, 1966, p4.
Cinema. Jul 1966, v3, p48.
The Complete Films of John Wayne. p262-63.
Film Daily. Mar 30, 1966, p3.
Filmfacts. May 15, 1966, v9, p78-81.
Films and Filming. Nov 1966, v13, p55-56.
Films in Review. May 1966, v17, p315.
The Films of Frank Sinatra. p212-15.
The Films of Kirk Douglas. p210-13.
Hollywood Reporter. Mar 30, 1966, p3.
The London Times. Aug 11, 1966, p12.
Motion Picture Herald Product Digest. Apr 13, 1966, p499-500.
The New York Times. Mar 31, 1966, p43.
Newsweek. Apr 18, 1966, v67, p110.
Saturday Review. Apr 9, 1966, v49, p54.
Senior Scholastic. May 20, 1966, v88, p35.
The Spectator. Aug 26, 1966, v217, p261.
Time. Apr 15,1966, v87, p103.
Variety. Mar 30, 1966, p6.

Castle in the Air (Also titled: Castles in the Air) (GB; Cass, Henry; 1952)
BFI/Monthly Film Bulletin. Sep 1952, v19, p126.
The London Times. Jul 14, 1952, p3.
National Parent-Teacher. Mar 1953, v47, p26.
The New York Times. Jan 5, 1953, p19.
The New Yorker. Jan 10, 1953, v28, p75.
The Spectator. Jul 11, 1952, v188, p65.
Time. Jan 26, 1953, v61, p96.
Variety. Jul 16, 1952, p20.

The Castle of the Spider's Web *See* Throne of Blood

Castles in the Air *See* Castle in the Air

Cat Ballou (US; Silverstein, Elliot; 1965)
BFI/Monthly Film Bulletin. Sep 1965, v32, p131.
Christian Science Monitor (Western edition). Jul 10, 1965, p4.
Commonweal. Apr 30, 1965, v82, p192.
Esquire. Sep 1965, v64, p40.
Film Daily. May 6, 1965, p6.
Film Quarterly. Fall 1965, v19, p54-55.
The Filming of the West. p559-60.
Films and Filming. Oct 1965, v12, p26-27.
Films in Review. Jun-Jul 1965, v16, p383-84.
The Great Western Pictures. p49-51.
Hollywood Reporter. May 6, 1965, p3.
Kiss Kiss Bang Bang. p36-38.
Life. Jun 11, 1965, v58, p121-22.
The London Times. Aug 12, 1965, p5.
Magill's Survey of Cinema. Series II. v1, p412-14.
Motion Picture Herald Product Digest. May 26, 1965, p289.
Movie. Aut 1965, n14, p45.
Movie Comedy (Byron). p110-11.
The Nation. Aug 2, 1965, v201, p68.
The New Republic. May 22, 1965, v152, p27-28.
New Statesman. Aug 13, 1965, v70, p227-28.
The New York Times. Jun 25, 1965, p36.
The New Yorker. Jun 26, 1965, v41, p78.
Newsweek. May 10, 1965, v65, p118A.
Playboy. Jun 1965, v12, p26, 28.
The Private Eye, the Cowboy and the Very Naked Girl. p140.
Private Screenings. p194.
Saturday Review. May 15, 1965, v48, p34.

Senior Scholastic. May 13, 1965, v86, p36.
Sight and Sound. Aut 1965, v34, p197-98.
Time. May 21, 1965, v85, p107.
Variety. May 12, 1965, p6.
Vogue. Sep 1, 1965, v146, p180.

Cat on a Hot Tin Roof (US; Brooks, Richard; 1958)
America. Sep 27, 1958, v99, p679.
Authorship and Narrative in the Cinema. p197-205.
BFI/Monthly Film Bulletin. Nov 1958, v25, p140.
Catholic World. Nov 1958, v188, p153.
Commonweal. Sep 26, 1958, v68, p637.
Cosmopolitan. Sep 1958, v145, p145.
Film and Literature: An Introduction. p197-205.
Film Daily. Aug 13, 1958, v114, p6.
Filmfacts. Oct 15, 1958, v1, p161-62.
Films in Review. Oct 1958, v9, p454-55.
The Films of Elizabeth Taylor. p131-38.
The Films of Paul Newman. p71-75.
The Films of Tennessee Williams. p133-54.
Hollywood Reporter. Aug 13, 1958, p3.
Library Journal. Oct 1, 1958, v83, p2667.
Magill's Survey of Cinema. Series I. v1, p308-11.
The Nation. Oct 11, 1958, v187, p220.
The New Republic. Sep 9, 1958, v139, p21-22.
The New York Times. Sep 19, 1958, p24.
The New Yorker. Sep 27, 1958, v34, p163-64.
Newsweek. Sep 1, 1958, v52, p56.
Saturday Review. Sep 13, 1958, v41, p58.
Tennessee Williams and Film. p38-48.
Time. Sep 15, 1958, v72, p92.
Variety. Aug 13, 1958, p6.

Cat People (US; Schrader, Paul; 1982)
American Film. Apr 1982, p38-45.
Christian Century. May 5, 1982, v99, p547.
Hollywood Reporter. Mar 26, 1982, p3.
Horizon. Sep 1982, v25, p60-61.
The Los Angeles Times. Apr 2, 1982, SecVI, p1.
Maclean's. Apr 12, 1982, v96, p66.
Magill's Cinema Annual, 1983. p100-03.
The New Leader. May 3, 1982, v65, p20.
New York. Apr 12, 1982, v15, p60-61.
The New York Times. Apr 2, 1982, SecIII, p3.
The New Yorker. May 3, 1982, v58, p130-31.
Newsweek. Apr 5, 1982, v99, p74.
Time. Apr 5, 1982, v119, p70.
Variety. Mar 22, 1982, p3.

Catch-22 (US; Nichols, Mike; 1970)
BFI/Monthly Film Bulletin. Nov 1970, v37, p215-16.
Catholic World. Aug 1970, v211, p199-202.
Christian Century. Sep 23, 1970, v87, p1129-30.
Commonweal. Aug 21, 1970, v92, p416-17.
Commonweal. Oct 16, 1970, v93, p69-70.
Esquire. Sep 1970, v74, p12.
Film Quarterly. Fall 1970, v24, p7-17.
Films in Review. Aug-Sep 1970, v21, p437-38.
Hollywood Reporter. Jun 5, 1970, p3, 8.
Mike Nichols (Schuth). p65-84.
The Modern American Novel and the Movies. p256-65.
The Nation. Jul 20, 1970, v211, p60.
The New Republic. Jul 4, 1970, v163, p22.
The New York Times. Jun 25, 1970, p54.
The New York Times. Jun 28, 1970, SecII, p1.
The New York Times. Jul 19, 1970, SecII, p9.
The New Yorker. Jun 27, 1970, v46, p62-63.
Newsweek. Jun 22, 1970, v75, p81.
The Novel and the Cinema. p304-06.
Saturday Review. Jun 27, 1970, v53, p24.
Sight and Sound. Aut 1970, v39, n4, p218-19.
Time. Jun 15, 1970, v95, p66-68.
Variety. Jun 10, 1970, p18.

Catch Us If You Can *See* Having a Wild Weekend

Cattle Annie and Little Britches (US; Johnson, Lamont; 1980)
Film Bulletin. Jul 1981, v37, p37.
Film Journal. Jun 8, 1981, v84, p17-18.
Hollywood Reporter. Apr 24, 1981, p3.
Magill's Cinema Annual, 1982. p97-100.
The New Republic. Jun 6, 1981, v184, p26.
The New York Times. May 15, 1981, SecIII, p8.
The New Yorker. Jun 15, 1981, v57, p135-36.
Rolling Stone. Jul 23, 1981, p31-32.
Variety. Apr 29, 1981, p18.
The Village Voice. Jun 24, 1981, p49.

Cattle Queen of Montana (US; Dwan, Allan; 1954)
BFI/Monthly Film Bulletin. Jul 1955, v22, p105.
Film Daily. Dec 7, 1954, p12.
The Films of Barbara Stanwyck. p233-35.
The Films of Ronald Reagan. p210-13.
Hollywood Reporter. Nov 17, 1954, p4.
Motion Picture Herald Product Digest. Nov 20, 1954, p218.
National Parent-Teacher. Jan 1955, v49, p39.
The New York Times. Jan 26, 1955, p22.
Starring Miss Barbara Stanwyck. p248, 255.
Variety. Nov 17, 1954, p6.

Cause For Alarm (US; Garnett, Tay; 1951)
BFI/Monthly Film Bulletin. May 1951, v18, p262-63.
Christian Century. Mar 21, 1951, v68, p383.
Commonweal. Feb 16, 1951, v53, p470.
Film Daily. Jan 26, 1951, p6.
Hollywood Reporter. Jan 26, 1951, p3.
Motion Picture Herald Product Digest. Jan 27, 1951, p690.
The New York Times. Mar 30, 1951, p28.
Time. Feb 26, 1951, v57, p100.
Variety. Jan 31, 1951, p6.

Cavaleur, La *See* Practice Makes Perfect

Caza, La *See* The Hunt

Celeste (WGER; Adlon, Percy; 1981)
The Great German Films. p300-02.
Hollywood Reporter. Nov 15, 1982, p8.
The Los Angeles Times. Jan 13, 1983, SecVI, p7.
Magill's Cinema Annual, 1983. p104-07.
The New Republic. Oct 25, 1982, v187, p22.
The New York Times. Oct 6, 1982, SecIII, p21.
Newsweek. Nov 22, 1982, v100, p118.
Variety. Jun 3, 1982, p22.

Celine and Julie Go Boating (French title: Celine et Julie vont bateau) (FR; Rivette, Jacques; 1974)
BFI/Monthly Film Bulletin. Aug 1976, v45, p163.
Film. Oct 1974, n19, p20.
Film. Mar 1975, n25, p21-23.
Film Quarterly. Wint 1974, v28, p32-39.
Hollywood Reporter. Mar 21, 1975, p6.
Magill's Survey of Cinema. Foreign Language Films. v2, p497-500.
Movietone News. Aug 14, 1978, n58/59, p42-43.
The New York Times. Feb 24, 1978, SecIII, p10.
Sight and Sound. Fall 1974, v43, p190-94.
Variety. Aug 21, 1974, p22.
The Village Voice. Oct 23, 1978, p76.

Celui Qui doit Mourir (Also titled: He Who Must Die) (FR, IT; Dassin, Jules; 1957)
America. Jun 15, 1957, v97, p325.
BFI/Monthly Film Bulletin. Dec 1957, v24, p146.

Films and Filming. Dec 1957, v4, p21-22.
Films in Review. Dec 1958, v9, p594-95.
Sight and Sound. Wint 1957-58, v27, p146-47.
Variety. May 15, 1957, p17.

The Centurions *See* The Lost Command

C'era una volta il West *See* Once Upon a Time in the West

The Ceremony (GB; Harvey, Laurence; 1963)
America. May 23, 1964, v110, p749-50.
BFI/Monthly Film Bulletin. May 1964, v31, p67.
Film Daily. Dec 16, 1963, p14.
Films and Filming. May 1964, v10, p23-24.
The New York Times. May 14, 1964, p39.
Newsweek. Feeb 24, 1964, v63, p89.
Photoplay. Mar 1964, v65, p79.
Saturday Review. Jan 18, 1964, v47, p27.
Variety. Dec 18, 1963, p7.

The Ceremony (Japanese title: Gishiki) (JAPAN; Oshima, Nagisa; 1971)
BFI/Monthly Film Bulletin. Jun 1971, v39, p113.
Cineaste. Spr 1974, v6, n2, p20-26.
Films and Filming. Aug 1972, v18, n11, p52.
Movietone News. Jan 1975, n38, p18-20.
New York Magazine. Feb 11, 1974, v7, p75.
The New York Times. Feb 8, 1974, p18.
Variety. Jul 14, 1971, p16.

Cerny Petr *See* Black Peter

A Certain Smile (US; Negulesco, Jean; 1958)
America. Aug 23, 1958, v99, p539.
BFI/Monthly Film Bulletin. Sep 1958, v25, p123.
Commonweal. Aug 15, 1958, v68, p496.
Film Daily. Jul 30, 1958, v114, p6.
Filmfacts. Sep 17, 1958, v1, p137-38.
Films in Review. Oct 1958, v9, p456-57.
Hollywood Reporter. Jul 30, 1958, p3.
Library Journal. Sep 1, 1958, v83, p496.
The New York Times. Aug 1, 1958, p13.
The New Yorker. Aug 9, 1958, v34, p58.
Newsweek. Aug 11, 1958, v52, p87.
Time. Aug 11, 1958, v72, p70.
Variety. Jul 30, 1958, p6.

Cerveau, Le *See* The Brain

Cet Obscur Object du Desir *See* That Obscure Object of Desire

Chagrin et la Pitie, Le *See* The Sorrow and the Pity

Chain Lightning (US; Heisler, Stuart; 1950)
Christian Century. Mar 22, 1950, v67, p383.
Commonweal. Mar 10, 1950, v51, p582.
Film Daily. Feb 2, 1950, p9.
The Films of Humphrey Bogart. p152-53.
Hollywood Reporter. Jan 31, 1950, p3.
Humphrey Bogart: The Man and His Films. p151.
The London Times. Mar 6, 1950, p8.
The New York Times. Feb 20, 1950, p21.
The New Yorker. Mar 4, 1950, v26, p80.
Newsweek. Mar 6, 1950, v35, p84.
Senior Scholastic. Jan 11, 1950, v55, p25.
The Spectator. Mar 3, 1950, v184, p273-74.
Time. Mar 6, 1950, v55, p92.
Variety. Feb 8, 1950, p11.

The Chalk Garden (GB; Neame, Ronald; 1964)
America. Jun 6, 1964, v110, p805.
BFI/Monthly Film Bulletin. Apr 1964, v31, p50.
Boxoffice. Apr 13, 1964, v84, p2818.

Commonweal. May 29, 1964, v80, p298.
Film Daily. Apr 8, 1964, p3.
Films and Filming. May 1964, v10, p28.
Films in Review. May 1964, v15, p303.
Hollywood Reporter. Apr 8, 1964, p3.
Life. Jun 12, 1964, v56, p21.
Magill's Survey of Cinema. Series II. v1, p418-20.
Motion Picture Herald Product Digest. Apr 15, 1964, p25-26.
The New Republic. May 30, 1964, v150, p25-26.
The New York Times. May 22, 1964, p42.
The New Yorker. May 30, 1964, v40, p112.
Newsweek. Jun 1, 1964, v63, p84.
Saturday Review. Jun 27, 1964, v47, p50.
Time. May 29, 1964, v83, p85.
Variety. Apr 8, 1964, p6.

Chamade, La (Also titled: Heartbeat) (FR; Cavalier, Alain; 1968)
Film Daily. Aug 11, 1969, p4.
Films and Filming. Feb 1970, v16, p54.
Hollywood Reporter. Sep 2, 1969, p3.
Movies Into Film. p264-66.
The New York Times. Jul 28, 1969, p25.
Saturday Review. Aug 16, 1969, v52, p37.
Time. Aug 22, 1969, v99, p65.
Variety. Nov 20, 1968, p36.

The Champ (US; Zeffirelli, Franco; 1979)
BFI/Monthly Film Bulletin. Jun 1979, v46, p118.
Films in Review. Jun-Jul 1979, v30, p379.
Hollywood Reporter. Mar 30, 1979, p3.
The Los Angeles Times. Apr 1, 1979, Calendar, p1.
Motion Picture Herald Product Digest. Apr 18, 1979, p89.
New York. Apr 16, 1979, p86-87.
The New York Times. Apr 4, 1979, SecIII, p19.
Newsweek. Apr 9, 1979, v93, p87.
Newsweek. Apr 23, 1979, v93, p69.
Time. Apr 9, 1979, v113, p53.
Variety. Mar 28, 1979, p20.

Champagne for Caesar (US; Whorf, Richard; 1950)
BFI/Monthly Film Bulletin. Jun 1950, v17, p78.
Christian Century. Jun 28, 1950, v67, p800.
Commonweal. May 26, 1950, v52, p172.
Film Daily. Feb 7, 1950, p8.
The Films of Ronald Colman. p241-44.
Hollywood Reporter. Feb 7, 1950, p3.
Life. Apr 10, 1950, v28, p119-22.
Magill's Survey of Cinema. Series I. v1, p320-22.
Motion Picture Herald Product Digest. Feb 11, 1950, p186.
The New Republic. May 29, 1950, v122, p23.
The New York Times. May 12, 1950, p33.
The New Yorker. May 20, 1950, v26, p99.
Newsweek. May 8, 1950, v35, p87-88.
The Spectator. May 5, 1950, v184, p609.
Time. May 8, 1950, v55, p94.
Variety. Feb 8, 1950, p11.
Vincent Price: Unmasked. p182-83.

The Champagne Murders (French title: Scandale, Le) (FR; Chabrol, Claude; 1966)
BFI/Monthly Film Bulletin. Feb 1968, v35, p23-24.
Claude Chabrol (Wood). p98-01.
Filmfacts. Jun 1, 1968, v11, p134-35.
The London Times. Feb 15, 1968, p6.
Motion Picture Herald Product Digest. May 15, 1968, p812.
The New York Times. Apr 25, 1968, p53.
Sight and Sound. Spr 1968, v37, p102-03.

Variety. Mar 15, 1967, p26.
The Village Voice. May 23, 1968, p43.

Chan Is Missing (US; Wang, Wayne; 1982)
The Los Angeles Times. Aug 13, 1982, SecVI, p7.
Maclean's. Sep 6, 1982, v95, p54.
Magill's Cinema Annual, 1983. p113-15.
The Nation. Jul 3, 1982, v235, p26-27.
The New Republic. Jun 16, 1982, v186, p25.
New York. Jun 7, 1982, v15, p72-73.
The New York Times. Apr 24, 1982, p13.
Newsweek. Jun 21, 1982, v99, p65-66.
Progressive. Jul 1982, v46, p50-51.
Variety. Mar 19, 1982, p3.

Chance Meeting (Asquith, 1954) *See* The Young Lovers

Chance Meeting (Losey, 1959) *See* Blind Date

Chance of a Lifetime (GB; Miles, Bernard; 1950)
BFI/Monthly Film Bulletin. Mar-Apr 1950, v17, p43.
Film Daily. Jan 25, 1951, p12.
Films in Review. Mar 1951, v2, p3.
Illustrated London News. May 13, 1950, v216, p750.
Motion Picture Herald Product Digest. Feb 3, 1951, p697.
The New Republic. Mar 26, 1951, v124, p22.
The New York Times. Mar 15, 1951, p37.
The New Yorker. Mar 17, 1951, v27, p107.
Newsweek. Mar 5, 1951, v37, p87.
Rotha on Film. p151-53.
Saturday Review. Mar 10, 1951, v34, p25.
Shots in the Dark. p159-63.
Sight and Sound. May 1950, v19, p123-24.
Sight and Sound. Jan 1951, v19, p349-50.
Time. May 8, 1950, v55, p90.
Variety. May 3, 1950, p20.

A Change of Seasons (US; Lang, Richard; 1980)
BFI/Monthly Film Bulletin. Jun 1981, v48, p109.
Films in Review. Feb 1981, v32, p121.
Hollywood Reporter. Dec 18, 1980, p2.
Motion Picture Herald Product Digest. Jan 21, 1981, p62.
The New Leader. Jan 12, 1981, v64, p19.
The New Republic. Dec 27, 1980, v183, p24.
The New York Times. Dec 19, 1980, SecIII, p8.
Time. Jan 26, 1981, v117, p62.
Variety. Dec 24, 1980, p14.
The Village Voice. Dec 17, 1980, p66.

The Changeling (CAN; Medak, Peter; 1979)
BFI/Monthly Film Bulletin. Sep 1980, v47, p173.
Christian Science Monitor. Mar 21, 1980, p15.
Films in Review. Apr 1980, v31, p248.
Hollywood Reporter. Mar 14, 1980, p3.
The Los Angeles Times. Mar 26, 1980, SecVI, p1.
Maclean's. Apr 14, 1980, v93, p66.
The New York Times. Mar 28, 1980, SecIII, p8.
Newsday. Mar 28, 1980, SecII, p7.
Newsweek. Mar 31, 1980, v95, p82.
Time. Apr 28, 1980, v115, p77.
Variety. Feb 20, 1980, p22.
The Village Voice. Mar 31, 1980, p44.

The Chant of Jimmy Blacksmith (AUSTRALIA; Schepisi, Fred; 1978)
Christian Science Monitor. Sep 4, 1980, p19.
Cineaste. Fall 1980, v10, p37.
Hollywood Reporter. Sep 25, 1978, p27.

The Los Angeles Times. Nov 20, 1980, SecVI, p2.
Maclean's. Oct 13, 1980, v93, p66.
The Nation. Sep 27, 1980, v231, p292-93.
National Review. Oct 17, 1980, v32, p1276-78.
National Review. Oct 31, 1980, v32, p1341-42.
The New Australian Cinema. p87-88.
The New Leader. Oct 6, 1980, v63, p19-20.
The New Republic. Sep 20, 1980, v183, p26-27.
New York. Sep 8, 1980, v13, p69-71.
The New York Times. Sep 3, 1980, SecIII, p15.
The New Yorker. Sep 15, 1980, v56, p148.
Newsday. Sep 5, 1980, SecII, p7.
Progressive. Nov 1980, v44, p51-52.
Sight and Sound. Spr 1979, v48, p126.
Time. Sep 8, 1980, v116, p74.
The Village Voice. Sep 3, 1980, p40.

Chaos *See* Ran

The Chapman Report (US; Cukor, George; 1962)
America. Nov 3, 1962, v107, p1012.
BFI/Monthly Film Bulletin. Dec 1962, v29, p165.
Commonweal. Dec 14, 1962, v77, p315.
Film Daily. Aug 29, 1962, v29, p5.
Film Quarterly. Spr 1963, v61, p58.
Filmfacts. Nov 23, 1962, v5, p272-74.
Films and Filming. Dec 1962, v9, p46.
Films in Review. Oct 1962, v13, p489.
The Films of Jane Fonda. p83-87.
The Fondas (Springer). p183-84.
George Cukor (Phillips). p137-40.
Hollywood Reporter. Aug 29, 1962, p3.
Motion Picture Herald Product Digest. Sep 5, 1962, p651.
Movie. Nov 1962, n4, p35.
Movie. Dec 1962, n5, p38-39.
The New York Times. Oct 18, 1962, p49.
The New Yorker. Oct 27, 1962, v38, p205.
Newsweek. Oct 29, 1962, v60, p88.
Time. Nov 2, 1962, v80, p101.
Variety. Aug 29, 1962, p6.

Chapter Two (US; Moore, Robert; 1979)
BFI/Monthly Film Bulletin. Sep 1980, v47, p174.
Hollywood Reporter. Dec 10, 1979, p21.
The Los Angeles Times. Dec 9, 1979, Calendar, p1.
Motion Picture Herald Product Digest. Dec 26, 1979, p59.
The New Republic. Jan 26, 1980, v182, p24-25.
The New York Times. Dec 14, 1979, SecIII, p14.
The New Yorker. Dec 24, 1979, v55, p82.
Variety. Dec 12, 1979, p22.

Charade (US; Donen, Stanley; 1963)
America. Dec 21, 1963, v109, p810.
BFI/Monthly Film Bulletin. Apr 1964, v31, p50-51.
Commonweal. Dec 13, 1963, v79, p349.
Film Daily. Sep 25, 1963, p4.
Films and Filming. Mar 1964, v10, p26.
Films in Review. Dec 1963, v14, p627.
The Films of Cary Grant. p258-61.
Hollywood Reporter. Sep 24, 1963, p3.
Magill's Survey of Cinema. Series I. v1, p323-25.
Motion Picture Herald Product Digest. Oct 2, 1963, p897.
The New Republic. Dec 21, 1963, v149, p29.
The New York Times. Dec 6, 1963, p40.
The New Yorker. Dec 14, 1963, v39, p196.
Newsweek. Dec 16, 1963, v62, p90.
Saturday Review. Dec 14, 1963, v46, p24.
Sight and Sound. Spr 1964, v33, p98.
Stanley Donen (Casper). p166-73.
Talking Pictures. p97-99.

Time. Dec 20, 1963, v82, p63.
Variety. Sep 25, 1963, p6.
Vogue. Jan 1, 1964, v143, p24.

The Charge at Feather River (US; Douglas, Gordon; 1953)
America. Jul 4, 1953, v89, p366.
BFI/Monthly Film Bulletin. Nov 1953, v20, p158.
Film Daily. Jul 8, 1953, p10.
Hollywood Reporter. Jun 30, 1953, p3.
The New York Times. Jul 16, 1953, p17.
The New Yorker. Jul 25, 1953, v29, p47.
Newsweek. Aug 3, 1953, v42, p76.
Saturday Review. Jul 11, 1953, v36, p36.
Time. Jul 13, 1953, v62, p97.
Variety. Jul 1, 1953, p6.

The Charge Is Murder *See* Twilight of Honor

The Charge of the Light Brigade (GB; Richardson, Tony; 1968)
America. Oct 12, 1968, v119, p335.
Atlantic. Jan 1969, v223, p115-16.
BFI/Monthly Film Bulletin. Jul 1968, v35, p98-99.
Christian Century. May 21, 1969, v86, p715-16.
Christian Science Monitor (Western edition). Oct 11, 1968, p4.
Christian Science Monitor (Western edition). Dec 9, 1969, p17.
Cinema. Sum 1968, v4, p55-56.
Figures of Light. p106-09.
Film 68/69. p89-93.
Film Daily. Sep 26, 1968, p4.
Film Society Review. Mar 1969, v4, p14-34.
Filmfacts. Jan 1, 1969, v11, p399-402.
Films in Review. Oct 1968, v19, p515-16.
Five Thousand One Nights At the Movies. p102-03.
Going Steady. p175-78.
Hollywood Reporter. Jun 20, 1968, p3.
Life. Oct 11, 1968, v65, p14.
The London Times. Mar 2, 1968, p19.
Look. Feb 6, 1968, v32, p58-61.
Motion Picture Herald Product Digest. Sep 25, 1968, p23.
Movies Into Film. p315-16.
The New Republic. Oct 12, 1968, v159, p32.
New Statesman. Apr 19, 1968, v75, p522-23.
The New York Times. Oct 7, 1968, p59.
The New Yorker. Oct 12, 1968, v44, p166.
Newsweek. Oct 14, 1968, v72, p101.
Saturday Review. Oct 12, 1968, v51, p54.
Senior Scholastic. Oct 25, 1968, v93, p20-21.
Sight and Sound. Sum 1969, v38, p130-33.
The Spectator. Apr 19, 1968, v220, p534.
Take One. Sep-Oct 1968, v2, p10-13.
Variety. Apr 17, 1968, p6.
Vogue. Oct 15, 1968, v152, p58.

Chariots of Fire (GB; Hudson, Hugh; 1981)
America. Oct 17, 1981, v145, p223.
BFI/Monthly Film Bulletin. May 1981, v48, p90.
Christian Century. Dec 9, 1981, v98, p1292.
Christianity Today. Jan 22, 1982, v26, p40-41.
Christianity Today. Mar 19, 1982, v26, p34-35.
Commonweal. Dec 4, 1981, v108, p687-88.
Commonweal. Mar 26, 1982, v109, p81.
Commonweal. Apr 23, 1982, v109, p230-31.
Fifty Classic British Films. p145-47.
Hollywood Reporter. Aug 7, 1981, p2.
The Los Angeles Times. Sep 20, 1981, Calendar, p28.
Maclean's. Oct 5, 1981, v94, p59-60.
Magill's Cinema Annual, 1982. p101-05.
The Nation. Oct 10, 1981, v233, p354-55.
National Review. Nov 13, 1981, v33, p1360.
The New Leader. Oct 5, 1981, v64, p21-22.

The New Republic. Oct 7, 1981, v185, p26-27.
The New Republic. Jan 27, 1982, v186, p24.
New York. Oct 5, 1981, v14, p60-61.
The New York Times. Sep 25, 1981, SecIII, p14.
The New York Times. Sep 20, 1981, SecII, p1.
The New Yorker. Oct 26, 1981, v57, p176-78.
Newsweek. Sep 1981, v98, p88.
Progressive. Dec 1981, v45, p54.
Rolling Stone. Oct 1981, p72.
Saturday Evening Post. Jul-Aug 1982, v254, p18.
Saturday Review. Sep 1981, v8, p48-49.
Senior Scholastic. Oct 16, 1981, v114, p27.
Sports Illustrated. Sep 28, 1981, v55, p63.
Time. Sep 21, 1981, v118, p73.
Variety. Apr 8, 1981, p8.

Charley (US; Nelson, Ralph; 1968)
America. Oct 26, 1968, v119, p392.
BFI/Monthly Film Bulletin. Dec 1968, v35, p191-92.
Christian Science Monitor (Western edition). Feb 7, 1969, p8.
Commonweal. Oct 11, 1968, v89, p64.
Film 68/69. p181-82.
Film Daily. Sep 24, 1968, p14.
Film Quarterly. Spr 1969, v22, p60.
Filmfacts. Dec 15, 1968, v11, p378-80.
Films and Filming. Dec 1968, v15, p34-35.
Films and Filming. Nov 1968, v15, p63-64.
Films in Review. Nov 1968, v19, p578-79.
Five Thousand One Nights At the Movies. p104.
Going Steady. p181-84.
Hollywood Reporter. Sep 23, 1968, p3.
Life. Nov 1, 1968, v65, p12.
The London Times. Nov 7, 1968, p17.
The London Times. May 17, 1969, p19.
Magill's Survey of Cinema. Series I. v1, p326-28.
Motion Picture Herald Product Digest. Sep 25, 1968, p23.
New Statesman. Nov 8, 1968, v76, p643.
The New York Times. Sep 24, 1968, p55.
The New Yorker. Oct 12, 1968, v44, p170-72.
Newsweek. Sep 30, 1968, v72, p96.
Saturday Review. Sep 21, 1968, v51, p47.
Science Fiction Studies in Film. p200-01.
Senior Scholastic. Nov 22, 1968, v93, p33.
The Spectator. Nov 15, 1968, v221, p707-08.
Take Twenty Two. p103-07.
Variety. Jul 3, 1968, p6.

Charlie Bubbles (GB; Finney, Albert; 1967)
BFI/Monthly Film Bulletin. Oct 1968, v35, p147-48.
Christian Century. May 8, 1968, v85, p624.
Christian Science Monitor (Western edition). Feb 17, 1968, p8.
Commonweal. Mar 1, 1968, v87, p656.
Confessions of a Cultist. p339-42.
Esquire. Jun 1968, v69, p60.
Film 68/69. p136-41.
Film Daily. Feb 14, 1968, p4.
Film Quarterly. Sum 1968, v21, p57.
Filmfacts. Mar 1, 1968, v11, p31-33.
Films and Filming. Nov 1968, v15, p39-40.
Films in Review. Mar 1968, v19, p182-83.
Going Steady. p57-58.
Harper's Magazine. May 1968, v236, p94.
Hollywood Reporter. Feb 9, 1968, p3.
Life. Mar 8, 1968, v64, p18.
The London Times. May 18, 1968, p23.
The London Times. Sep 9, 1968, p4.
The London Times. Sep 19, 1968, p11.
Magill's Survey of Cinema. Series II. v1, p433-36.
Motion Picture Herald Product Digest. Feb 7, 1968, p772.
Movie. Spr 1968, n15, p40.
Movies Into Film. p309-10.

The Nation. Mar 4, 1968, v206, p318.
National Review. Jul 2, 1968, v20, p664.
The New Republic. Mar 9, 1968, v158, p24.
New Statesman. Sep 20, 1968, v76, p373.
The New York Times. Feb 12, 1968, p47.
The New York Times. Feb 25, 1968, p4.
The New Yorker. Feb 24, 1968, v44, p106-07.
Newsweek. Feb 24, 1968, v71, p92.
Reporter. May 16, 1968, v38, p33.
Saturday Review. Mar 2, 1968, v51, p40.
Sight and Sound. Aut 1968, v37, p207-08.
The Spectator. Sep 27, 1968, v221, p441.
Time. Feb 23, 1968, v91, p95.
Variety. Feb 14, 1968, p6.
The Village Voice. Feb 29, 1968, p41, 44.
Vogue. Mar 15, 1968, v151, p42.
A Year In the Dark. p44-46, 58-59.

Charlotte's Web (US; Nichols, Charles A.; Talcamoto, Iwao; 1973)
Children's Novels and the Movies. p171-81.
Films in Review. Apr 1973, v24, n4, p241.
The New York Times. Feb 23, 1973, p18.
The New York Times. Apr 15, 1973, SecII, p13.
Variety. Feb 21, 1973, p18.
The Village Voice. Mar 15, 1973, p75.

Charme Discret de la Bourgeoisie, Le *See* The Discreet Charm of the Bourgeoisie

Charulata (Also titled: The Lonely Wife) (INDIA; Ray, Satyajit; 1964)
BFI/Monthly Film Bulletin. Dec 1965, v32, p178.
The Cinema of Satyajit Ray. p36-39.
Commonweal. Oct 16, 1970, v93, p71.
Esquire. Dec 1965, v64, p86.
Film Quarterly. Fall 1967, v21, p42-45.
Films and Filming. Dec 1965, v12, p25-26.
The International Dictionary of Films and Filmmakers. v1, p84-85.
The London Times. Oct 14, 1965, p16.
Magill's Survey of Cinema. Foreign Language Films. v2, p517-21.
New Statesman. Oct 22, 1965, v70, p615-16.
The New York Times. Sep 11, 1965, p16.
The New Yorker. Jul 8, 1974, v50, p48-51.
Portrait of a Director: Satyajit Ray. p180-85.
Sight and Sound. Wint 1965-66, v35, p31-33.
The Spectator. Oct 22, 1965, v215, p512-13.
Variety. Jul 7, 1965, p16.

The Chase (US; Penn, Arthur; 1966)
America. Mar 5, 1966, v114, p337.
Arthur Penn (Wood). p52-70.
BFI/Monthly Film Bulletin. Oct 1966, v33, p150.
Big Screen, Little Screen. p355-58.
Christian Science Monitor (Western edition). Feb 23, 1966, p4.
Cinema. Mar 1966, v3, p32.
Commonweal. Apr 1, 1966, v84, p55.
Film Daily. Feb 2, 1966, p4.
Film Quarterly. Fall 1966, v20, p58-59.
Filmfacts. Apr 1, 1966, v9, p41-44.
Films and Filming. Oct 1966, v13, p6, 8, 10-11.
Films in Review. Mar 1966, v17, p183-84.
The Films of Jane Fonda. p117-21.
The Films of Marlon Brando. p164-71.
The Films of Robert Redford. p86-94.
Holiday. Feb 1966, v39, p87-88.
Hollywood Reporter. Feb 2, 1966, p3.
Kiss Kiss Bang Bang. p185-88.
Life. Mar 4, 1966, v60, p12.
London Magazine. Nov 1966, v6, p76-79.
The London Times. Mar 3, 1965, p15.
The London Times. Sep 8, 1966, p17.
Magill's Survey of Cinema. Series II. v1, p442-45.
McCall's. Apr 1966, v93, p192-93.

Motion Picture Herald Product Digest. Feb 2, 1966, p459.
Movie Man (Thomson). p208-10.
The Nation. Mar 7, 1966, v202, p280.
New Statesman. Sep 11, 1966, v72, p406-07.
The New York Times. Feb 19, 1966, p24.
The New York Times. Feb 20, 1966, p3.
Newsweek. Feb 28, 1966, v67, p91.
Playboy. Apr 1966, v13, p41-42.
Saturday Review. Feb 19, 1966, v49, p64.
Screen. Jul-Oct 1969, v10, p88-14.
Senior Scholastic. Mar 18, 1966, v88, p32.
Sight and Sound. Aut 1966, v35, p197-98.
The Spectator. Sep 9, 1966, v217, p321.
Time. Feb 25, 1966, v87, p105.
Variety. Feb 23, 1966, p4.
Variety. Feb 2, 1966, p6.
The Village Voice. Apr 7, 1966, p31.

Chasse a l'Homme, La *See* Male Hunt

Chateau Life *See* Vie de Chateau, La

Che! (US; Fleischer, Richard; 1969)
Christian Century. Aug 6, 1969, v86, p1045.
The Fifty Worst Films of All Time. p57-60.
Film 69/70. p190-95.
Film Daily. Jun 17, 1969, p4.
Film Quarterly. Fall 1969, v23, p49.
Films in Review. Aug-Sep 1969, v20, p444-45.
Focus. Oct 1969, n5, p32-33.
The Nation. Jun 23, 1969, v108, p806.
The New Republic. Jun 21, 1969, v160, p22.
The New York Times. Jun 15, 1969, SecII, p1.
The New Yorker. Jun 14, 1969, v45, p83.
Newsweek. Jun 16, 1969, v73, p101-02.
Politics and Film. p150-51.
Time. Jun 13, 1969, v93, p103.
Variety. Jun 4, 1969, p6.

The Cheap Detective (US; Moore, Robert; 1978)
BFI/Monthly Film Bulletin. Oct 1978, v45, p195.
Films in Review. Oct 1978, v29, p502.
Hollywood Reporter. Jun 5, 1978, p4.
The Los Angeles Times. Jun 1978, Calendar, p1.
Motion Picture Herald Product Digest. Jul 5, 1978, p10.
The Nation. Jul 8, 1978, v227, p61-62.
The New Republic. Jul 22, 1978, v179, p28.
New York. Jul 10, 1978, v11, p75.
The New York Times. Jun 23, 1978, SecIII, p8.
The New York Times. Jul 2, 1978, SecII, p1.
The New Yorker. Jul 3, 1978, v54, p74-75.
Newsweek. Jun 26, 1978, v91, p80.
Time. Jul 10, 1978, v112, p78.
Variety. Jun 7, 1978, p25.
Vogue. Jul 1978, v168, p30.

Cheaper by the Dozen (US; Lang, Walter; 1950)
Christian Century. May 3, 1950, v67, p575.
Commonweal. Apr 14, 1950, v52, p17.
Film Daily. Mar 28, 1950, p10.
The Films of Myrna Loy. p238-49.
Hollywood Reporter. Mar 27, 1950, p3.
Illustrated London News. May 13, 1950, v216, p750.
Library Journal. Apr 15, 1950, v75, p708.
Motion Picture Herald Product Digest. Apr 1, 1950, p245.
The New York Times. Apr 1, 1950, p12.
The New Yorker. Apr 8, 1950, v26, p98.
Newsweek. Apr 10, 1950, v35, p82.
One Good Film Deserves Another. p65-68.
Parents Magazine. May 1950, v25, p34-35.
Senior Scholastic. Apr 26, 1950, v56, p23.
The Spectator. May 5, 1950, v184, p609.

Time. Apr 10, 1950, v55, p90.
Variety. Mar 29, 1950, p11.

The Chelsea Girls (US; Warhol, Andy; 1966)
BFI/Monthly Film Bulletin. Jul 1972, v39, p134-35.
Cahiers du Cinema in English. May 1967, n10, p43-49.
Cineaste. Wint 1967-68, v1, p20-21.
Cineaste. Spr 1968, v1, p12-15, 33.
Confessions of a Cultist. p274-76.
Esquire. Apr 1967, v67, p48.
Film Culture. Fall 1966, n42, p8-9.
Film Culture. Sum 1967, n45, p22, 41-44, 46.
Film Quarterly. Sum 1967, v20, p73-76.
Film Quarterly. Wint 1967-68, v21, p60.
Filmfacts. Jan 15, 1967, v9, p369-70.
Films and Filming. Aug 1969, v15, p21, 24, 36-38.
Hollywood Reporter. Mar 30, 1967, p3.
Movie Journal (Mekas). p254-57.
The New American Cinema (Battcock). p246-52.
The New York Times. Dec 2, 1966, p46.
Newsweek. Nov 14, 1966, v68, p109.
Playboy. Apr 1967, v14, p40-41.
Private Screenings. p294-95.
Sight and Sound. Spr 1968, v37, p102-03.
Take One. Apr 1967, v1, p23-24.
Take One. Sep-Oct 1971, v3, p13.
Time. Dec 30, 1966, v88, p37.
Variety. Jan 18, 1967, p6.
The Village Voice. Dec 15, 1966, p33.
The Village Voice. Sep 29, 1966, p27.
The Village Voice. Nov 24, 1966, p29.

Cher Disparu, Le *See* The Loved One

The Chess Players (Indian title: Shatranj Ke Khilari) (INDIA; Ray, Satyajit; 1977)
Hollywood Reporter. Apr 11, 1978, p2.
Human Behavior. Sep 1978, v7, p77.
The Los Angeles Times. Aug 4, 1978, SecIV, p20.
The Nation. Jun 17, 1978, v226, p741.
The New Republic. Jun 3, 1978, v178, p24.
New York. Jun 5, 1978, v11, p86.
The New York Times. May 1978, SecIII, p17.
The New York Times. Jun 11, 1978, SecII, p21.
The New Yorker. May 22, 1978, v54, p113-15.
Newsweek. Jun 12, 1978, v91, p93.
Variety. Dec 1, 1977, p44.

Cheyenne Autumn (US; Ford, John; 1964)
America. Jan 16, 1965, v112, p85.
BFI/Monthly Film Bulletin. Dec 1964, v31, p171.
Film Daily. Oct 7, 1964, v125, p5.
Films and Filming. Dec 1964, v11, p27.
Films in Review. Jan 1965, v16, p52.
The Great Western Pictures. p53-54.
Hollywood Reporter. Oct 7, 1964, p3.
John Ford (Bogdanovich). p104-06.
Life. Nov 27, 1964, v57, p19.
Magill's Survey of Cinema. Series II. v1, p449-53.
Motion Picture Herald Product Digest. Oct 14, 1964, p22.
The New Republic. Jan 23, 1965, v152, p36-37.
The New York Times. Dec 24, 1964, p8.
The New Yorker. Jan 2, 1965, v40, p65.
Newsweek. Jan 11, 1965, v65, p79.
Saturday Review. Jan 16, 1965, v48, p36.
Sight and Sound. Wint 1964-65, v34, p36-37.
Time. Jan 8, 1965, v85, p54.
Variety. Oct 7, 1964, p6.
Vogue. Dec 1964, v144, p150.
The Western Films of John Ford. p228-35.

Chicago, Chicago *See* Gaily, Gaily

A Child Is Waiting (US; Cassavetes, John; 1963)
America. Feb 23, 1963, v108, p275.
American Dreaming (Carney). p77-81.
Catholic World. Mar 1963, v196, p387-89.
Commonweal. Feb 1, 1963, v77, p494.
Filmfacts. Feb 21, 1963, v6, p9-11.
Films and Filming. Oct 1966, v13, p8.
Films in Review. Mar 1963, v14, p175-76.
Hollywood Reporter. Jan 9, 1963, p3.
Judy: The Films and Career of Judy Garland. p176-79.
The London Times. Jul 14, 1966, p19.
Motion Picture Herald Product Digest. Jan 23, 1963, p737.
The New Republic. Jan 26, 1963, v148, p28.
New Statesman. Jul 22, 1966, v72, p141.
The New York Times. Feb 14, 1963, p5.
The New Yorker. Feb 23, 1963, v39, p126.
Newsweek. Feb 4, 1963, v61, p78.
Saturday Review. Jan 26, 1963, v46, p31.
The Spectator. Jul 22, 1966, v217, p123.
Time. Feb 8, 1963, v81, p66.
Variety. Jan 16, 1963, p6.
The Village Voice. Feb 14, 1963, p25.

The Children of Marx and Coca-Cola *See* Masculin-Féminin

The Children's Hour (US; Wyler, William; 1962)
America. Jul 2, 1962, v107, p360.
Cinema. 1963, n1, v1, p43.
Commonweal. Mar 2, 1962, v75, p598.
Film Daily. Jan 12, 1962, p10.
Film Quarterly. Spr 1963, v16, p58.
Filmfacts. Mar 23, 1962, v5, p41-43.
Films and Filming. Sep 1962, v8, p31-32.
Films in Review. Apr 1962, v13, p236-37.
The Films of Shirley MacLaine. p107-12.
Hollywood Reporter. Dec 8, 1961, v8, p3.
I Lost It at the Movies. p158-59.
Magill's Survey of Cinema. Series I. v1, p329-31.
Motion Picture Herald Product Digest. Dec 20, 1961, p388-89.
The New Republic. Apr 16, 1962, v146, p28.
The New York Times. Mar 15, 1962, p28.
The New Yorker. Mar 17, 1962, v38, p123-24.
Newsweek. Mar 12, 1962, v59, p101.
Saturday Review. Feb 24, 1962, v45, p37.
Time. Feb 9, 1962, v79, p83.
Variety. Dec 13, 1961, p6.
The Village Voice. Mar 1, 1962, p11.
William Wyler: A Guide to References and Resources. p50-56.

The Chimes at Midnight (Spanish title: Campanadas a Medianoche; Also titled: Falstaff) (SP, SWITZ; Welles, Orson; 1965)
BFI/Monthly Film Bulletin. May 1967, v34, p70.
Cahiers du Cinema in English. Sep 1967, n11, p6-23.
Confessions of a Cultist. p292-94.
Dictionary of Films. p51-52.
Film 67/68. p69-75.
Film Criticism. Wint-Spr 1978, v2, p66-71.
Film Daily. Feb 1, 1967, p7.
Film Quarterly. Fall 1969, v23, p11-20.
Filmfacts. Jun 1, 1967, v10, p104-05.
Films and Filming. May 1967, v13, p25.
The Films of Orson Welles. p167-77.
Focus on Orson Welles. p178-86.
Harper's Magazine. Jan 1967, v234, p102.
The International Dictionary of Films and Filmmakers. v1, p89-90.

International Film Guide. 1967, v4, p141.
Kiss Kiss Bang Bang. p245-48.
Literature/Film Quarterly. Jul 1983, v11, p197-202.
The London Times. May 13, 1966, p12.
The London Times. Mar 18, 1967, p7.
The London Times. Mar 23, 1967, p10.
Magill's Cinema Annual, 1983. p443-46.
Motion Picture Herald Product Digest. Feb 1, 1967, p654.
Movies Into Film. p30-31.
National Review. Jul 25, 1967, v19, p816-17.
The New Republic. Jun 24, 1967, v156, p27-32.
New Statesman. Mar 31, 1967, v73, p447-48.
The New York Times. Mar 18, 1967, p19.
The New Yorker. Mar 25, 1967, v43, p152.
The New Yorker. Aug 13, 1966, v42, p116.
Newsweek. Mar 27, 1967, v69, p96.
Orson Welles (McBride). p148-58.
Playboy. Feb 1967, v14, p19-20.
Shakespeare and the Film. p64-71.
Shakespeare on Film. p106-21.
Sight and Sound. Sum 1967, v36, p146-47.
Sight and Sound. Aut 1966, v35, p158-63.
Sight and Sound. Spr 1965, v34, p64-65.
Time. Mar 24, 1967, v89, p89.
Variety. May 18, 1966, p7.
The Village Voice. Mar 30, 1967, p33.
Vogue. Jan 1, 1967, v149, p53.

China Is Near (Italian title: Cina è Vicina, La) (IT; Bellochio, Marco; 1967)
America. Feb 10, 1968, v118, p203.
China Is Near. p1-35.
Christian Science Monitor (Western edition). Jan 17, 1968, p8.
Cineaste. Sum 1970, v4, p24-25.
Confessions of a Cultist. p336-39.
Esquire. Jun 1968, v69, p60.
Figures of Light. p50-51.
Film 68/69. p75-83.
Film Daily. Jan 15, 1968, p12.
Film Quarterly. Fall 1968, v22, p70-72.
Film Society Review. Sep 1968, v4, p26-36.
Filmfacts. Feb 1, 1968, v11, p5-6.
Five Thousand One Nights At the Movies. p106-07.
Going Steady. p5-9.
Hollywood Reporter. Feb 15, 1968, p3.
Motion Picture Herald Product Digest. Jan 17, 1968, p760-61.
Movies Into Film. p286-90.
The Nation. Jan 29, 1968, v206, p156.
The New Italian Cinema. p44-46.
The New Republic. Feb 3, 1968, v158, p26.
The New York Times. Jan 9, 1968, p37.
The New Yorker. Jan 13, 1968, v43, p90.
Newsweek. Jan 22, 1968, v71, p84.
Saturday Review. Feb 17, 1968, v51, p41.
Sight and Sound. Wint 1967-68, v37, p14-16.
Time. Jan 12, 1968, v91, p59.
Variety. Sep 20, 1967, p20.
The Village Voice. Feb 1, 1968, p16.
A Year In the Dark. p8-9.

The China Syndrome (US; Bridges, James; 1979)
BFI/Monthly Film Bulletin. Sep 1979, v46, p194, 262.
Commonweal. Apr 27, 1979, v106, p242-43.
Film Comment. May 1979, v15, p28-31.
Films in Review. Jun-Jul 1979, v30, p372.
The Films of Jane Fonda. p221-29.
The Films of the Seventies. p245-47.
The Los Angeles Times. Mar 11, 1979, Calendar, p1.
Motion Picture Herald Product Digest. Apr 4, 1979, p85.
The Nation. Mar 31, 1979, v228, p347-48.

The New Republic. Apr 7, 1979, v180, p24-25.
New York. Apr 2, 1979, v12, p79.
The New York Times. Mar 16, 1979, SecIII, p16.
The New Yorker. Apr 2, 1979, v55, p109.
Newsweek. Mar 19, 1979, v93, p103.
Newsweek. Apr 2, 1979, v93, p96.
Rolling Stone. Apr 5, 1979, p50-55.
Saturday Review. May 12, 1979, v6, p40.
Time. Mar 26, 1979, v113, p54.
Variety. Mar 7, 1979, p20.

Chinatown (US; Polanski, Roman; 1974)
American Cinematographer. May 1975, v55, p526-29.
Audience. Nov 1974, v7, p8-9.
BFI/Monthly Film Bulletin. Aug 1974, v41, p171-72.
Christian Century. Sep 18, 1974, v91, p860-61.
Cineaste. 1974, v6, n3, p38-39.
Classic Movies. p128-31.
Commentary. Sep 1974, v58, p71-73.
Commonweal. Jul 26, 1974, v100, p405.
Esquire. Oct 1974, v82, p14.
Fifty Grand Movies of the 1960s and 1970s. p155-58.
Film. Sep 1974, n18, p18.
Film. Oct 1974, n19, p20.
Film Comment. Nov-Dec 1974, v10, p30-33.
Film Heritage. 1974, v10, n1, p44-46.
Film Quarterly. Wint 1974, v28, p25-32.
Films and Filming. Oct 1974, v21, p38-39.
Films and Filming. Aug 1974, v20, p25-27.
Films Illustrated. Aug 1974, v3, p472.
Films Illustrated. Sep 1974, v4, p28-29.
Films in Review. Aug-Sep 1974, v25, p442.
Films in Review. Nov 1974, v25, p560-63.
The Films of the Seventies. p107-10.
Hollywood Reporter. Nov 28, 1973, p3.
Independent Film Journal. Jun 26, 1974, v74, p7-8.
The International Dictionary of Films and Filmmakers. v1, p90-91.
Jump Cut. Sep-Oct 1974, n3, p9-10.
The Los Angeles Times. Sep. 20, 1974, SecIV, p8.
Magill's Survey of Cinema. Series I. v1, p332-35.
Movietone News. Aug 1974, n34, p37-38.
Movietone News. Jul 1974, n33, p1-8.
The Nation. Jul 6, 1974, v219, p29-30.
The New Republic. Jul 20, 1974, v171, p16.
New Statesman. Aug 9, 1974, v88, p197-98.
New York. Aug 26, 1974, v7, p64.
New York. Jul 8, 1974, v7, p74-75.
The New York Times. Aug 11, 1974, SecII, p11.
The New York Times. Oct 20, 1974, SecII, p1.
The New York Times. Sep 1, 1974, SecII, p9.
The New Yorker. Jul 1, 1974, v50, p70.
Newsweek. Jul 1, 1974, v84, p74.
Partisan Review. 1974, v41, n4, p581-85.
Penthouse. Sep 1974, v6, p35-36.
Progressive. Sep 1974, v38, p53-54.
Roman Polanski: A Guide to References and Resources. p31-33.
Roman Polanski (Wexman). p91-108.
Saturday Review. Jul 27, 1974, v1, p46.
Sight and Sound. Fall 1974, v43, p243-44.
Social Policy. Nov-Dec 1974, v5, p48-49.
Society. Nov 1974, v12, p73-77.
Take One. 1974, v4, n4, p32.
Time. Jul 1, 1974, v104, p42.
Variety. Jun 19, 1974, p16.
The Velvet Light Trap. Fall 1974, n13, p13-16.
The Village Voice. Nov 7, 1974, p85.
The Village Voice. Aug 1, 1974, p63.

Chitty Chitty Bang Bang (GB; Hughes, Ken; 1968)
BFI/Monthly Film Bulletin. Feb 1969, v36, p24-25.
Children's Novels and the Movies. p197-204.
Christian Science Monitor (Eastern edition). Aug 7, 1968, p12.
Film Daily. Nov 20, 1968, p3.
Filmfacts. Jan 15, 1969, v11, p513-15.
Films and Filming. May 1969, v15, p42.
Films in Review. Jan 1969, v11, p513-15.
Going Steady. p278-81.
Hollywood Reporter. Nov 25, 1968, p3.
The London Times. Dec 14, 1968, p14.
Motion Picture Herald Product Digest. Nov 27, 1968, p67, 69.
The New York Times. Dec 19, 1968, p64.
The New Yorker. Jan 4, 1969, v44, p70-71.
Newsweek. Dec 30, 1968, v72, p61.
Saturday Review. Dec 21, 1968, v51, p16.
The Spectator. Dec 27, 1968, v221, p919.
Time. Dec 27, 1968, v92, p56.
Variety. Nov 20, 1968, p6.
A Year In the Dark. p321-23.

Chloe in the Afternoon (French title: Amour L'après-Midi, L') (FR; Rohmer, Eric; 1972)
Atlantic. Dec 1972, v230, p138-41.
Commonweal. Nov 3, 1972, v97, p109.
Film Quarterly. Sum 1973, v26, p57-60.
Filmfacts. 1972, v15, n15, p33.
Life. Nov 17, 1972, v73, p30.
The Nation. Oct 9, 1972, v215, p316-17.
The New Republic. Oct 14, 1972, v167, p22.
The New York Times. Sep 30, 1972, v19, p2.
The New Yorker. Oct 7, 1972, v48, p135-37.
Reeling. p29-32.
Saturday Review. Nov 4, 1972, v55, p90.
Time. Oct 16, 1972, v100, p76.
Variety. Aug 30, 1972, p18.
Women and their Sexuality in the New Film. p147-78.

The Choirboys (US; Aldrich, Robert; 1977)
Films in Review. Feb 1978, v29, p118.
The Films of Robert Aldrich. p71-74.
Hollywood Reporter. Dec 21, 1977, p3.
The Los Angeles Times. Dec 23, 1977, SecIV, p18.
Motion Picture Herald Product Digest. Jan 4, 1977, p61.
The New York Times. Dec 24, 1977, p8.
The New York Times. Feb 19, 1978, SecII, p1.
Newsweek. Jan 2, 1978, v91, p59.
Time. Jan 16, 1978, v111, p82.
Variety. Dec 21, 1977, p20.

Choose Me (US; Rudolph, Alan; 1984)
BFI/Monthly Film Bulletin. Apr 1985, v52, p99.
California Magazine. Sep 1984, v9, p64.
Christian Century. Jan 30, 1985, v102, p105.
Film Journal. Nov 1984, v87, p51-52.
Films in Review. Jan 1985, v36, p49.
Los Angeles. Sep 1984, v29, p40.
The Los Angeles Times. Aug 29, 1984, SecVI, p1.
Maclean's. Oct 15, 1984, v97, p78.
Magill's Cinema Annual, 1985. p135-40.
New Statesman. Apr 26, 1985, v109, p37.
The New York Times. Nov 28, 1984, SecIII, p19.
The New York Times. Nov 1, 1984, SecIII, p18.
The New Yorker. Dec 24, 1984, v60, p79.
Newsweek. Nov 19, 1984, v104, p135.
Playboy. Oct 1984, v31, p3.
Progressive. Jan 1985, v49, p36.
Time. Feb 4, 1985, v125, p83.
Variety. Aug 22, 1984, p17.

The Village Voice. Nov 13, 1984, p62.
Vogue. Aug 1984, v174, p70.
Washingtonian. Dec 1984, v20, p68.
Whole Earth Review. Jan 1985, p73.

A Chorus Line (US; Attenborough, Richard; 1985)
BFI/Monthly Film Bulletin. Jan 1986, v53, p6.
Dance Magazine. Dec 1985, v59, p46-50.
Films in Review. Jan 1986, v37, p46.
Hollywood Reporter. Dec 3, 1985, p3.
Life. Dec 1985, v8, p160-61.
The Los Angeles Times. Dec 12, 1985, SecVI, p1.
Magill's Cinema Annual, 1986. p91-95.
The Nation. Jan 25, 1986, v242, p90.
The New Republic. Dec 30, 1985, v193, p24-25.
New York. Dec 16, 1985, v18, p76.
The New York Times. Dec 10, 1985, p20.
The New York Times. Dec 29, 1985, SecII, p25.
The New York Times. Dec 10, 1985, SecIII, p17.
Newsweek. Dec 30, 1985, v106, p62.
Saturday Review. Nov-Dec 1985, v11, p22.
Theatre Crafts. Jan 1986, v20, p79-81.
Time. Dec 9, 1985, v126, p111.
Variety. Dec 4, 1985, p24.
Vogue. Dec 1985, v175, p304-05.
The Wall Street Journal. Dec 12, 1985, p32.

The Chosen (US; Kagan, Jeremy Paul; 1981)
Hollywood Reporter. May 13, 1982, p10.
The Los Angeles Times. May 9, 1982, Calendar, p28.
Magill's Cinema Annual, 1983. p116-19.
The Nation. May 8, 1982, v234, p568-70.
New York. May 17, 1982, v15, p54-55.
The New York Times. Apr 30, 1982, SecIII, p5.
Newsweek. May 17, 1982, v99, p100-01.
Progressive. Jul 1982, v46, p51.
Saturday Review. Apr 1982, v9, p52.
Variety. Sep 16, 1981, p3.

Christ in Concrete *See* Give Us this Day

Christiane F. (German title: Wir Kinden Vom Bahnof 200) (WGER; Edel, Ulrich; 1981)
BFI/Monthly Film Bulletin. Jan 1982, v49, p5-6.
Film Journal. Mar 22, 1982, v85, p17.
Maclean's. Apr 12, 1982, v95, p67.
Ms. Jun 1982, v10, p100.
The Nation. Mar 20, 1982, v234, p346-48.
New York. Mar 28, 1982, v15, p64-65.
The New York Times. Apr 16, 1982, SecIII, p8.
Variety. Mar 10, 1982, p10.
The Village Voice. Mar 23, 1982, p48.

A Christmas Carol (Also titled: Scrooge) (GB; Hurst, Brian Desmond; 1951)
BFI/Monthly Film Bulletin. Nov 1951, v18, p359.
Christian Century. Dec 19, 1951, v68, p1495.
Commonweal. Dec 21, 1951, v55, p278.
Dickens and Film. p316-18.
Film Daily. Nov 8, 1951, p6.
Films in Review. Dec 1951, v2, p57-58.
Hollywood Reporter. Oct 30, 1951, p3.
Library Journal. Dec 15, 1951, v76, p2110.
Magill's Survey of Cinema. Series I. v1, p336-38.
Motion Picture Herald Product Digest. Nov 3, 1951, p1094.
The New Republic. Dec 17, 1951, v125, p20.
The New Statesman and Nation. Dec 1, 1951, v42, p623.
The New York Times. Nov 29, 1951, p41.
The New Yorker. Dec 8, 1951, v27, p69.
Newsweek. Dec 10, 1951, v38, p98.

Saturday Review. Dec 1, 1951, v34, p38.
Senior Scholastic. Dec 12, 1951, v59, p26.
The Spectator. Nov 23, 1951, v186, p704.
Time. Dec 3, 1951, v58, p104.
Variety. Nov 14, 1951, p16.

A Christmas Story (US; Clark, Bob; 1983)
BFI/Monthly Film Bulletin. Nov 1984, v51, p332.
Film Journal. Jan 1984, v87, p14-15.
Films and Filming. Nov 1984, v20, p35-36.
Hollywood Reporter. Nov 14, 1983, p4.
The Los Angeles Times. Nov 18, 1983, SecIV, p18.
Magill's Cinema Annual, 1984. p110-15.
The New York Times. Nov 18, 1983, SecIII, p36.
Variety. Nov 1983, p16.

Chronicle of a Summer (French title: Chronique d'un Été) (FR; Rouch, Jean; Morin, Edgar; 1961)
American Anthropologist. 1978, v80, n4, p1020-22.
BFI/Monthly Film Bulletin. Aug 1962, v29, p103-04.
Cineaste. 1978, v8, n4, p16-24.
Cinema Verité (Issari). p72-74.
Dictionary of Films. p62.
Documentary: A History of Non-Fiction Film. p254-55.
The Documentary Tradition. p437-43.
Film. Aut 1963, n33, p17-18.
Film Comment. Fall-Wint 1967, v4, p82-86.
Film Daily. May 17, 1965, p3.
Film Quarterly. Sum 1964, v17, p30-36.
Film Quarterly. Wint 1961-62, v15, p57-59.
Films and Filming. Aug 1962, v8, p33.
The International Dictionary of Films and Filmmakers. v1, p94-95.
Motion Picture Herald Product Digest. Jun 9, 1965, p307.
Movie. Apr 1963, n8, p21-23.
The New Republic. May 15, 1965, v152, p33.
The New York Times. May 7, 1965, p34.
The New Yorker. May 8, 1965, v41, p167.
Sight and Sound. Sum 1962, v31, p144-45.
Studies in Visual Communication. 1985, v11, n1, p4-78.
Variety. May 24, 1961, p6.
A World on Film. p266-67.

Chronicle of Anna Magdalena Bach (Also titled: Chronik der Anna Magdalena Bach) (IT, WGER; Straub, Jean-Marie; 1968)
BFI/Monthly Film Bulletin. May 1970, v37, p96.
Cinema. Jan 1978, n229, p53-57.
Film Quarterly. Wint 1968-69, v22, p55-56.
Filmfacts. 1969, v12, n12, p282-83.
Jean-Marie Straub (Roud). p64-86, 173-75.
New German Cinema (Franklin). p83-88.
The New German Cinema (Sandford). p29.
New Statesman. May 1, 1969, v78, p638.
The New York Times. Sep 20, 1968, p37.
The New York Times. Apr 7, 1969, p49.
The New Yorker. Sep 21, 1968, v44, p145-46.
The Reader. Apr 30, 1982, p22.
Sight and Sound. Sum 1968, v37, p134-35.
Variety. May 15, 1968, p7.

Chronique d'un Été *See* Chronicle of a Summer

Cid, El (US; Mann, Anthony; 1961)
America. Dec 16, 1961, v106, p405.
Anthony Mann (Basinger). p161-76.
Commonweal. Dec 22, 1961, v75, p340.
Film Daily. Dec 6, 1961, p6.
Filmfacts. Dec 29, 1961, v4, p307-09.

Films in Review. Jan 1962, v8, p45-46.
The Films of Charlton Heston. p121-28.
The Films of Sophia Loren. p125-26.
The Great Adventure Films. p240-47.
Magill's Survey of Cinema. Series II. v1, p458-61.
National Review. Feb 13, 1962, v12, p103.
The New Republic. Jan 8, 1962, v146, p22.
The New York Times. Dec 15, 1961, p49.
Newsweek. Dec 18, 1961, v58, p98.
Saturday Review. Dec 23, 1961, v44, p39.
Time. Dec 22, 1961, v78, p45.
Variety. Dec 6, 1961, p6.

Ciel et la Boue, Le *See* The Sky Above, the Mud Below

Cina è Vicina, La *See* China Is Near

The Cincinnati Kid (French title: Kid de Cincinnati, Le) (US; Jewison, Norman; 1965)
America. Nov 6, 1965, v113, p544.
American Cinematographer. Nov 1965, v46, p712-15.
BFI/Monthly Film Bulletin. Dec 1965, v32, p178-79.
Cahiers du Cinema in English. 1966, n4, p58-59.
Cinema. Jul-Aug 1965, v2, p4-6.
Commonweal. Nov 19, 1965, v83, p217.
Film Daily. Oct 14, 1965, p6.
Films and Filming. Jan 1966, v12, p27.
Films and Filming. Dec 1965, v12, p39.
Films in Review. Dec 1965, v16, p642.
The Films of Steve McQueen. p101-12.
Hollywood Reporter. Oct 14, 1965, p3.
Life. Nov 19, 1965, v59, p15.
The London Times. Oct 28, 1965, p8.
Motion Picture Herald Product Digest. Oct 13, 1965, p386.
New Statesman. Nov 5, 1965, v70, p708.
The New York Times. Oct 28, 1965, p48.
The New Yorker. Nov 13, 1965, v41, p235.
Newsweek. Nov 8, 1965, v66, p113.
Playboy. Jan 1966, v13, p48.
The Private Eye, the Cowboy and the Very Naked Girl. p154.
Variety. Oct 20, 1965, p6.
The Village Voice. Nov 4, 1965, p11, 14, 23.
Vogue. Nov 1, 1965, v146, p116.

Cinderella (US; Jackson, Wilfred; Luske, Hamilton; Geronimi, Clyde; 1950)
The Art of Walt Disney. p282-90.
BFI/Monthly Film Bulletin. Feb 1951, v18, p214.
Christian Century. Mar 15, 1950, v67, p351.
Commonweal. Mar 17, 1950, v51, p607.
Commonweal. Jun 26, 1953, v58, p298.
The Disney Films. p93-96.
Film Daily. Dec 13, 1949, p4.
Films and Filming. Mar 1959, v15, p56.
Films in Review. Apr 1950, v1, p27-29.
Illustrated London News. Dec 23, 1950, v217, p1053.
Library Journal. Mar 1, 1950, v75, p410.
The London Times. Jul 15, 1950, p8.
Motion Picture Herald Product Digest. Dec 17, 1949, p121.
The New Statesman and Nation. Dec 30, 1950, v40, p678.
The New York Times. Feb 23, 1950, p33.
Newsweek. Feb 13, 1950, v35, p84.
Saturday Review. Jun 3, 1950, v33, p28-30.
Selected Film Criticism, 1941-1950. p39-40.
Senior Scholastic. Apr 5, 1950, v56, p29.
The Spectator. Dec 22, 1950, v185, p729.
Time. Feb 20, 1950, v55, p88.

Variety. Dec 14, 1949, p8.
Walt Disney: A Guide to References and Resources. p39-40.

Cinderella Liberty (US; Rydell, Mark; 1973)
Guts & Glory. p292-94.
Hollywood Reporter. Dec 6, 1973, p3.
Magill's Survey of Cinema. English Language Films. Series II, v1, p462.
The New York Times. Dec 19, 1973, p2.
Newsweek. Dec 31, 1973, v82, p33.
Reeling. p351-370.
Time. Jan 7, 1974, v103, p61.
Variety. Dec 12, 1973, p20.

Ciociara, La *See* Two Women

Circle of Danger (GB; Tourneur, Jacques; 1951)
BFI/Monthly Film Bulletin. Jun 1951, v18, p279.
Christian Century. May 30, 1951, v68, p671.
Commonweal. Apr 20, 1951, v54, p38.
Film Daily. Apr 17, 1951, p6.
Hollywood Reporter. Mar 27, 1951, p3.
Motion Picture Herald Product Digest. Mar 31, 1951, p785.
The New Republic. Jul 30, 1951, v125, p23.
The New York Times. Jul 12, 1951, p21.
The New Yorker. May 26, 1951, v27, p79.
The New Yorker. Jul 21, 1951, v27, p63.
Newsweek. Jul 30, 1951, v38, p68.
The Spectator. Apr 20, 1951, v186, p520-21.
Time. Jul 30, 1951, v58, p69.
Variety. Mar 28, 1951, p6.

Circle of Deceit (German title: Faelschung, Die) (FR, WGER; Schlöndorff, Volker; 1981)
Commonweal. Mar 26, 1982, v109, p180.
Films in Review. May 1982, v33, p305.
The Nation. Mar 6, 1982, v234, p282.
The New Republic. Feb 17, 1982, v186, p267.
New Statesman. Apr 10, 1982, v103, p22-23.
New York. Mar 8, 1982, v15, p87-88.
The New York Times. Mar 7, 1982, SecII, p15.
Progressive. Mar 1982, v46, p54.
The Village Voice. Mar 2, 1982, p45.

Circle of Love (French title: Ronde, La; Also titled: The Round) (FR; Vadim, Roger; 1964)
BFI/Monthly Film Bulletin. Feb 1965, v32, p21-22.
Commonweal. Apr 23, 1965, v82, p157.
Dictionary of Films. p319.
Film Daily. Mar 25, 1965, p7.
Film Quarterly. Sum 1965, v18, p59.
Filmfacts. May 14, 1965, v8, p84-86.
Films and Filming. Mar 1965, v11, p32.
Films in Review. Apr 1965, v16, p253.
The Films of Jane Fonda. p108-16.
Hollywood Reporter. Jul 15, 1965, p3.
Listener. Jan 21, 1965, v73, p104.
Motion Picture Herald Product Digest. Apr 14, 1965, p267.
New Statesman. Jan 8, 1965, v69, p51-52.
The New York Times. Mar 25, 1965, p42.
The New Yorker. Apr 3, 1965, v41, p104, 106.
Newsweek. Apr 12, 1965, v65, p112.
Playboy. Jul 1965, v12, p28.
Saturday Review. Apr 10, 1965, v48, p30.
The Spectator. Jan 8, 1965, v214, p45.
Time. Apr 9, 1965, v85, p105-06.
Variety. Oct 28, 1964, p7.
The Village Voice. May 20, 1965, p19-20.

Circle of Love (Ophuls, 1950) *See* Ronde, La

Cisaruv pekar a pekaruv cisar *See* The Emperor's Baker

Cisaruv Slavik *See* The Emperor's Nightingale

Cittá delle Donne, La *See* City of Women

City Heat (US; Benjamin, Richard; 1984)
BFI/Monthly Film Bulletin. Mar 1985, v52, p80.
Hollywood Reporter. Dec 4, 1984, p3.
Los Angeles. Jan 1985, v30, p38.
The Los Angeles Times. Dec 7, 1984, SecVI, p10.
New York. Dec 10, 1984, v17, p95.
The New York Times. Dec 7, 1984, SecIII, p4.
Newsweek. Dec 10, 1984, v104, p97.
Playboy. Mar 1985, v32, p26.
Time. Dec 10, 1984, v124, p92.
Variety. Dec 5, 1984, p17.
Vogue. Feb 1985, v175, p66.
Washingtonian. Jan 1985, v20, p66.

The City Jungle *See* The Young Philadelphians

City of Women (Italian title: Cittá delle Donne, La) (IT; Fellini, Federico; 1981)
America. Apr 11, 1981, v144, p301.
BFI/Monthly Film Bulletin. Sep 1981, v48, p172-73.
Hollywood Reporter. Apr 10, 1981, p37.
Horizon. May 1981, v24, p70-71.
The Los Angeles Times. May 1, 1981, SecVI, p12.
Maclean's. Apr 13, 1981, v94, p52.
Magill's Cinema Annual, 1982. p106-10.
The Nation. Apr 11, 1981, v232, p444-45.
National Review. Jun 26, 1981, v33, p734-36.
The New Republic. Apr 4, 1981, v184, p26.
New Statesman. Sep 18, 1981, v102, p24.
New York. Apr 6, 1981, v14, p81-82.
New York. Apr 13, 1981, v14, p50-54.
The New York Times. Apr 8, 1981, SecIII, p1, 21.
The New York Times. Apr 5, 1981, SecII, p1.
Newsweek. Apr 20, 1981, v97, p93.
Rolling Stone. May 28, 1981, p52.
Saturday Review. May 1981, v8, p76-77.
Time. Apr 20, 1981, v117, p84.
Variety. Mar 4, 1981, p22.

Clair de Femme (FR; Costa-Gavras, Constantin; 1980)
Christian Science Monitor. Apr 3, 1980, p18.
Commonweal. Jun 20, 1980, v107, p374-75.
Costa-Gavras: The Political Fiction Film. p215-35.
Films in Review. May 1980, v31, p307.
Hollywood Reporter. Mar 26, 1980, p21.
The Los Angeles Times. Apr 2, 1980, SecVI, p1.
The Nation. Apr 5, 1980, v230, p410.
The New Republic. Apr 12, 1980, v182, p24-25.
New York. Apr 21, 1980, v13, p86-87.
The New York Times. Mar 23, 1980, p54.
The New Yorker. Apr 7, 1980, v56, p138-39.
Newsday. Jun 6, 1980, SecII, p7.
Philadelphia Magazine. Jun 1980, v71, p56.
Variety. Sep 26, 1979, p20.
The Village Voice. Apr 7, 1980, p37.
Washingtonian. Aug 1980, v15, p45.

Claire's Knee (French title: Genou de Claire, Le) (FR; Rohmer, Eric; 1971)
America. Mar 6, 1971, v124, p244.
BFI/Monthly Film Bulletin. Aug 1971, v38, p164.
Cinema. Fall 1971, v7, n1, p16-21.
Commonweal. Apr 9, 1971, v94, p112.
Esquire. Jun 1971, v75, p36.

Film Quarterly. Sum 1971, v24, p4.
Films in Review. Apr 1971, v22, n4, p231-33.
Movies Plus One. p30-31.
The Nation. Mar 8, 1971, v212, p317-18.
National Review. Jul 27, 1971, v23, p20.
The New Republic. Mar 20, 1971, v164, p20.
The New York Times. Jan 11, 1971, p20.
The New York Times. Feb 22, 1971, p23.
The New York Times. Mar 7, 1971, SecII, p1.
The New York Times. Oct 29, 1972, SecII, p1.
The New Yorker. Mar 20, 1971, v47, p136.
Newsweek. Mar 1, 1971, v77, p136.
Saturday Review. Feb 20, 1971, v54, p14.
Sight and Sound. Sum 1971, v40, p122-23.
Take One. May-Jun 1970, v11, n11, p24-27.
Time. Apr 12, 1971, v97, p93.
Variety. Dec 2, 1970, p16.
The Village Voice. Feb 25, 1971, p51.
The Village Voice. Mar 11, 1971, p59.

Clash by Night (US; Lang, Fritz; 1952)
American Film. Jul-Aug 1983, v8, p66-67.
BFI/Monthly Film Bulletin. Sep 1952, v19, p122.
Catholic World. Jul 1952, v175, p307.
The Cinema of Fritz Lang. p179-81.
Film Daily. May 16, 1952, p7.
The Films of Barbara Stanwyck. p210-13.
The Films of Fritz Lang. p237-40.
The Films of Marilyn Monroe. p68-71.
Fritz Lang: A Guide to References and Resources. p108-09.
Fritz Lang (Eisner). p313-20.
Fritz Lang in America. p80-84.
Hollywood Reporter. May 14, 1952, p3.
Library Journal. Jun 15, 1952, v77, p1071.
The London Times. Aug 4, 1952, p9.
Motion Picture Herald Product Digest. May 17, 1952, p1366.
The Nation. Jul 26, 1952, v175, p77.
National Parent-Teacher. Sep 1952, v47, p38.
The New York Times. Jun 19, 1952, p32.
The New Yorker. Jun 28, 1952, v28, p62.
Newsweek. Jun 2, 1952, v39, p84.
A Reference Guide to the American Film Noir. p40-41.
Saturday Review. Jun 14, 1952, v35, p35.
Sight and Sound. Oct-Dec 1952, v22, p80.
Theatre Arts. Jul 1952, v36, p36.
Time. Jun 9, 1952, v59, p104.
Variety. May 14, 1952, p6.

Claudine (US; Berry, John; 1974)
Audience. Jul 1974, v7, p10.
BFI/Monthly Film Bulletin. Oct 1974, v41, p221.
Commonweal. Oct 18, 1974, v101, p65-66.
Films in Review. Jun-Jul 1974, v25, p372-73.
Hollywood Reporter. Apr 5, 1974, p3.
Independent Film Journal. Apr 29, 1974, v73, p7-8.
The Los Angeles Times. May 12, 1974, Calendar, p26.
Motion Picture Herald Product Digest. May 8, 1974, p98.
New York. Apr 22, 1974, v7, p90-91.
The New York Times. May 5, 1974, SecII, p1.
The New York Times. May 26, 1974, SecII, p8.
The New Yorker. Apr 29, 1974, v50, p115-19.
Rolling Stone. May 23, 1974, p82.
Social Policy. Sep-Oct 1974, v5, p59-60.
Time. May 20, 1974, v103, p66-68.
Variety. Apr 10, 1974, p17.
The Village Voice. May 16, 1974, p101.

Cleo from 5 to 7 (French title: Cleo de 5 a' 7) (FR, IT; Varda, Agnés; 1961)
America. Aug 24, 1962, v76, p474.
BFI/Monthly Film Bulletin. Dec 1962, v29, p165-66.

Cinema Texas Program Notes. Aug 13, 1973, v14, p86-89.
Enclitic. 1983, v7, n2, p82-90.
Film. Wint 1962, n34, p24.
Film Daily. Aug 31, 1962, v31, p3.
Filmfacts. Oct 19, 1962, v5, p232-34.
Films and Filming. Dec 1962, v9, p38.
The International Dictionary of Films and Filmmakers. , v1, p100-01.
Magill's Survey of Cinema. Foreign Language Films. v2, p583-87.
Motion Picture Herald Product Digest. Nov 14, 1962, p692.
Movie. Oct 1962, n3, p32.
The Nation. Oct 13, 1962, v195, p228.
The New Republic. Sep 10, 1962, v147, p28-29.
The New York Times. Sep 5, 1962, p43.
The New Yorker. Sep 15, 1962, v38, p95.
Newsweek. Sep 10, 1962, v60, p106.
Saturday Review. Aug 4, 1962, v45, p14.
Saturday Review. Sep 29, 1962, v45, p22.
Sight and Sound. Sum 1962, v31, p145-46.
Time. Sep 14, 1962, v80, p103.
Variety. Dec 20, 1961, p7.
Wide Angle. 1981, n4, p38-49.
A World on Film. p252-54.

Cleopatra (US; Mankiewicz, Joseph L.; 1963)
America. Jun 29, 1963, v108, p910.
BFI/Monthly Film Bulletin. Sep 1963, v30, p127-28.
Business Week. Jun 15, 1963, p24.
The Cleopatra Papers. 1963.
Commonweal. Jul 5, 1963, v78, p398.
Film Daily. Jun 13, 1963, p1.
Filmfacts. Jul 4, 1963, v6, p121-24.
Films and Filming. Sep 1963, v9, p24.
Films in Review. Aug-Sep 1963, v14, p431-33.
The Films of Elizabeth Taylor. p152-61.
The Films of the Sixties. p113-15.
Illustrated London News. Aug 17, 1963, v243, p252.
Joseph L. Mankiewicz (Dick). p138-48.
Life. Jun 21, 1963, v54, p30.
Magill's Survey of Cinema. Series II. v1, p466-71.
My Life with Cleopatra. 1963.
National Review. Aug 13, 1963, v15, p78.
The New Republic. Jun 29, 1963, v148, p27-28.
New Statesman. Aug 2, 1963, v66, p149.
The New York Times. Jun 13, 1963, p29.
The New York Times. Jun 16, 1963, SecII, p1.
The New Yorker. Jun 22, 1963, v39, p61-62.
Newsweek. Jun 24, 1963, v61, p110-12.
Newsweek. Jul 8, 1963, v62, p78.
On Movies. p301-02.
Photoplay. Oct 1963, v64, p6.
Saturday Evening Post. Jun 1, 1963, v236, p26.
Saturday Review. Jun 29, 1963, v46, p20.
Sight and Sound. Aut 1963, v32, p198.
Spectator. Aug 9, 1963, v211, p176.
Time. Jun 21, 1963, v81, p90.
Variety. Jun 19, 1963, p6.
The Village Voice. Jun 20, 1963, p13.

The Climax (Italian title: Immorale, L'; Also titled: The Immoralist) (IT, FR; Germi, Pietro; 1967)
America. Oct 14, 1967, v117, p424.
Film Daily. Sep 15, 1967, p6.
Filmfacts. Nov 15, 1967, v10, p291-93.
Hollywood Reporter. Oct 23, 1966, p3.
Motion Picture Herald Product Digest. Sep 27, 1967, p726-27.
The New York Times. Sep 12, 1967, p55.
The New Yorker. Sep 16, 1967, v43, p187-88.
Playboy. Dec 1967, v14, p46, 48.
Saturday Review. Oct 7, 1967, v50, p52.

Time. Sep 22, 1967, v90, p105.
Variety. May 17, 1967, p18.

The Clockmaker (French title: Horloger de Saint Paul) (FR; Tavernier, Bertrand; 1974)
Film News. Nov-Dec 1976, v33, p29.
Hollywood Reporter. Aug 4, 1976, p2.
Independent Film Journal. Jun 25, 1976, v78, p16.
The Los Angeles Times. Oct 11, 1976, SecIV, p1.
Modern European Filmmakers and the Art of Adaptation. p238-47.
The New Republic. Sep 4, 1976, v175, p32.
New York. Aug 9, 1976, v9, p53-54.
The New York Times. Sep 13, 1976, SecII, p11.
The New York Times. Jun 29, 1976, p19.
The New York Times. Aug 22, 1976, SecII, p11.
The New Yorker. Aug 9, 1976, v52, p49-50.
Newsweek. Aug 30, 1976, v88, p74.
Saturday Review. Sep 18, 1976, v3, p42.
Time. Sep 13, 1976, v108, p80.
Variety. Jan 30, 1974, p16.

A Clockwork Orange (GB; Kubrick, Stanley; 1971)
BFI/Monthly Film Bulletin. Feb 1972, v39, p28.
Classic Movies. p118-21.
Commonweal. Jan 14, 1972, v95, p351-52.
Commonweal. Jul 14, 1972, v96, p383-86.
Deeper into Movies. p470-75.
Double Exposure. p162-68.
Double Takes. p136-39.
Fifty Grand Movies of the 1960s and 1970s. p213-16.
Film and Literature: An Introduction. p293-302.
Film Heritage. Sum 1972, v7, n4, p1-6.
Film Quarterly. Spr 1972, v25, p33-36.
Film Quarterly. Fall 1976, v30, p13-19.
Films and Filming. Feb 1972, v18, n5, p43-49.
Films in Review. Jan 1972, v23, p51.
The Films of The Seventies. p45-46.
Hollywood Reporter. Dec 14, 1971, p3.
Kubrick (Ciment). p148-65.
Magill's Survey of Cinema. Series II. v1, p475-79.
Marshall Delaney at the Movies. p150-51.
The Nation. Jan 3, 1972, v214, p28.
The New Republic. Jan 1, 1972, v166, p22.
The New York Times. Dec 20, 1971, p44.
The New York Times. Jan 9, 1972, SecII, p1.
The New York Times. Feb 6, 1972, SecII, p13.
The New York Times. Feb 13, 1972, SecII, p1.
The New York Times. Aug 26, 1972, p25.
The New Yorker. Jan 1, 1972, v47, p50-53.
Newsweek. Jan 3, 1972, v129, p28-33.
The Novel and the Cinema. p307-13.
Saturday Review. Dec 25, 1971, v54, p40-41.
Science Fiction Films of the Seventies. p41-46.
Science Fiction Studies in Film. p176-81.
Screen. Sum 1972, v13, n2, p17-31.
Sight and Sound. Wint 1971-72, v41, n1, p44-46.
Stanley Kubrick: A Guide to References and Resources. p52-55.
Take One. Apr 1972, v3, n3, p20-21.
Time. Dec 20, 1971, v98, p80-81.
Time. Dec 27, 1971, v98, p59.
Twenty All-Time Great Science Fiction films. p223-36.
Variety. Dec 15, 1971, p14.
The Village Voice. Dec 30, 1971, p49.

Cloportes (French title: Metamorphose des Cloportes, Le; Also titled: The Metamorphosis of Bugs) (FR; Granier-Deferre, Pierre; 1965)

Christian Science Monitor (Western edition). May 6, 1966, p4.
Film Daily. Apr 22, 1966, p6.
Filmfacts. Jun 15, 1966, v9, p104-06.
Hollywood Reporter. May 5, 1966, p4.
Motion Picture Herald Product Digest. Apr 13, 1966, p501.
The New York Times. Apr 19, 1966, p36.
The New Yorker. Apr 30, 1966, v42, p155.
Newsweek. May 2, 1966, v67, p103-04.
Saturday Review. Apr 30, 1966, v49, p53.
Variety. Oct 27, 1965, p26.

Close Encounters of a Third Kind (Rerelease title: Special Edition: Close Encounters of a Third Kind) (US; Spielberg, Steven; 1977; 1980)
An Album of Great Science Fiction Films. p65, 69.
America. Dec 17, 1977, v137, p445.
American Cinematographer. Jan 1978, v59, p26-72.
American Film. Nov 1977, v2, p 24-29.
Atlantic. Jan 1978, v241, p90-91.
BFI/Monthly Film Bulletin. Oct 1980, v47, p189.
BFI/Monthly Film Bulletin. Apr 1978, v45, p63.
Christian Science Monitor. Aug 14, 1980, p19.
Classic Movies. p70-72.
Close Encounters of a Third Kind: A Document of the Film. 1977.
The Close Encounters of a Third Kind Diary. 1978.
Commonweal. Mar 17, 1978, v105, p179-81.
Commonweal. Mar 31, 1978, v105, p213-14.
Film Comment. Jan 1978, v14, p49-55.
Film Review Annual. 1981, p185-91.
Films in Review. Dec 1977, v28, p634.
Films in Review. Oct 1980, v31, p499.
The Films of the Seventies. p191-92.
Hollywood Reporter. Nov 4, 1977, p3.
Hollywood Reporter. Aug 1, 1980, p3.
The Humanist. Mar 1978, v38, p51.
The International Dictionary of Films and Filmmakers. v1, p103-04.
The Los Angeles Times. Nov 18, 1977, SecIV, p1.
The Los Angeles Times. Aug 3, 1980, Calendar, p1.
Maclean's. Sep 1, 1980, v93, p60-61.
Magill's Survey of Cinema. Series I. v1, p362-64.
Motion Picture Herald Product Digest. Nov 23, 1977, p49-50.
The Nation. Dec 17, 1977, v225, p668-69.
National Review. Dec 23, 1977, v29, p1500-02.
The New Republic. Dec 10, 1977, v177, p20-22.
The New Republic. Sep 6, 1980, v183, p24.
New York. Aug 18, 1980, v13, p70.
The New York Review of Books. Jan 26, 1978, v24, p21-22.
The New York Times. Nov 17, 1977, SecIII, p19.
The New York Times. Nov 20, 1977, SecII, p15.
The New York Times. Aug 31, 1980, SecII, p10.
The New Yorker. Nov 28, 1977, v53, p174-78.
The New Yorker. Sep 1, 1980, v56, p80.
Newsday. Aug 8, 1980, SecII, p7.
Newsweek. Nov 21, 1977, v90, p88-89.
Newsweek. Aug 18, 1980, v96, p87.
Philadelphia Magazine. Sep 1980, v71, p69-71.
Rolling Stone. Jan 26, 1978, p33-37.
Saturday Review. Jan 7, 1978, v5, p46.
Saturday Review. Dec 10, 1977, v5, p80.
Science Digest. Feb 1978, v83, p16-18.
Science Digest. Apr 1978, v83, p17-21.
The Steven Spielberg Story. p53-74.

Time. Nov 7, 1977, v110, p102-03.
Time. Aug 18, 1980, v116, p58.
Variety. Nov 9, 1977, p16.
Variety. Aug 6, 1980, p22.
The Village Voice. Nov 28, 1977, 47-58.
Washingtonian. Jan 1978, v13, p27.
The World of Fantastic Films. p107-10.

Close To My Heart (US; Keighley,
William; 1951)
BFI/Monthly Film Bulletin. Feb 1952, v19,
p34.
Christian Century. Mar 19, 1952, v69, p351.
Film Daily. Oct 5, 1951, p6.
The London Times. Jan 21, 1952, p2.
Motion Picture Herald Product Digest. Oct 6,
1951, p1049.
Variety. Oct 10, 1951, p6.

Closely Watched Trains (Czechoslovakian
title: Ostre Sledovane Vlasky; Also
titled: Closely Observed Trains;
Strictly Controlled Trains; On the
Lookout for Trains; Special Priority
Trains) (CZECH; Menzel, Jirí; 1966)
America. Dec 9, 1967, v117, p722.
BFI/Monthly Film Bulletin. Jun 1968, v35, p88.
Christian Science Monitor (Western edition).
Dec 13, 1967, p12.
Closely Watched Trains. p5-12.
Commonweal. Dec 8, 1967, v87, p336-37.
Dictionary of Films. p265.
Esquire. May 1968, v69, p84.
Figures of Light. p29-30.
Film 67/68. p119-21.
Film Criticism. 1984-85, v9, n2, p78-80.
Film Quarterly. 1984, v37, n4, p58-59.
Filmfacts. Dec 1, 1967, v10, p304-06.
Films and Filming. Jul 1968, v14, p27.
Harper's Magazine. Jan 1968, v236, p82-83.
Hollywood Reporter. Nov 17, 1966, p3.
*The International Dictionary of Films and
Filmmakers.* v1, p348-49.
*Jiri Menzel and the History of "The Closely
Watched Trains"* 1982.
Life. Nov 10, 1967, v63, p12.
The London Times. May 9, 1967, p8.
*Magill's Survey of Cinema. Foreign Language
Films.* v2, p588-92.
Motion Picture Herald Product Digest. Nov 22,
1967, p744.
Movie Comedy (Byron). p257-58.
Movies Into Film. p279-80.
The Nation. Nov 13, 1967, v205, p506.
The New Republic. Dec 2, 1967, v157, p20.
New Statesman. May 10, 1968, v75, p623-24.
The New York Times. Jun 19, 1967, p41.
The New York Times. Oct 16, 1967, p59.
Newsweek. Nov 27, 1967, v70, p97.
Playboy. Dec 1967, v14, p50, 52.
Reruns. p196-99.
Saturday Review. Dec 9, 1967, v50, p44.
Second Sight. p152-54.
The Spectator. May 17, 1968, v220, p677-78.
Time. Sep 15, 1967, v90, p101-02.
Variety. Oct 26, 1966, p6.

The Clouded Yellow (GB; Thomas, Ralph;
1950)
BFI/Monthly Film Bulletin. Dec 1950, v17,
p187.
Commonweal. Nov 30, 1951, v55, p200.
Film Daily. Oct 2, 1951, p6.
Hollywood Reporter. Sep 28, 1951, p4.
Motion Picture Herald Product Digest. Oct 6,
1951, p1049-50.
The New Republic. Dec 3, 1951, v125, p22.
The New York Times. Nov 13, 1951, p33.
The New Yorker. Nov 24, 1951, v27, p131-32.
Newsweek. Nov 26, 1951, v38, p100.

Senior Scholastic. Nov 28, 1951, v59, p22.
The Spectator. Nov 24, 1950, v185, p548.
Variety. Nov 29, 1950, p14.

The Clowns (Italian title: Clowns, I) (IT;
Fellini, Federico; 1971)
BFI/Monthly Film Bulletin. Sep 1971, v39,
p184.
Commonweal. Sep 24, 1971, v94, p501-02.
*Federico Fellini: A Guide to References and
Resources.* p118-20.
Fellini the Artist. p190-201.
Film Quarterly. Fall 1971, v25, p53-55.
Films in Review. Jun-Jul 1971, v22, n6, p367-
69.
The Films of Federico Fellini. p139-44.
Hollywood Reporter. Jun 23, 1971, p3.
Life. Jul 9, 1971, v71, p9.
The Nation. Jun 28, 1971, v212, p828-29.
National Review. Oct 22, 1971, v23, p1191.
The New Republic. Jul 3, 1971, v165, p22.
The New York Times. Jun 5, 1971, p50.
The New York Times. Jun 20, 1971, SecII, p1.
The New York Times. Jul 4, 1971, SecII, p11.
The New Yorker. Jun 12, 1971, v47, p96.
Newsweek. Jun 21, 1971, v77, p86.
Sight and Sound. Aut 1972, v41, n4, p229-30.
Time. Jun 21, 1971, v97, p84.
*Unholy Fools, Wits, Comics, Distrubers of the
Peace.* p15-20.
Variety. Sep 16, 1970, p14.
The Village Voice. Jul 1, 1971, p47.

Coal Miner's Daughter (US; Apted,
Michael; 1980)
BFI/Monthly Film Bulletin. Jun 1980, v47,
p108.
Christian Science Monitor. Mar 20, 1980, p17.
Cineaste. Sum 1980, v10, p32.
Films in Review. Apr 1980, v31, p242.
Hollywood Reporter. Feb 20, 1980, p3.
The Los Angeles Times. Mar 2, 1980, Calendar,
p29.
Magill's Survey of Cinema. Series I. v1, p365-
69.
Motion Picture Herald Product Digest. Mar 26,
1980, p82.
The New York Times. Mar 7, 1980, SecIII, p8.
Newsday. Mar 7, 1980, SecII, p7.
Sight and Sound. Sum 1980, v49, p197.
Variety. Feb 20, 1980, p19.
The Village Voice. Mar 10, 1980, p51.

Cobweb Castle *See* Throne of Blood

Cocktails in the Kitchen *See* For Better,
For Worse

Cocoon (US; Howard, Ron; 1985)
BFI/Monthly Film Bulletin. Sep 1985, v52,
p273.
Christian Century. Jul 17, 1985, v102, p684.
Christianity Today. Oct 4, 1985, v29, p85-86.
Commonweal. Aug 9, 1985, v112, p439.
Films in Review. Aug 1985, v36, p427.
Hollywood Reporter. Jun 13, 1985, p3.
Horizon. Jun 1985, v28, p21-24.
Humanist. Nov-Dec 1985, v45, p41.
The Los Angeles Times. Jun 21, 1985, SecVI,
p1.
Maclean's. Jul 1, 1985, v98, p67.
Magill's Cinema Annual, 1986. p96-99.
The New Leader. May 6, 1985, v68, p20-21.
The New Republic. Jul 15, 1985, v193, p32-33.
New York. Jun 24, 1985, v18, p66.
The New York Times. Jun 21, 1985, SecIII, p5.
The New Yorker. Jul 15, 1985, v61, p73-75.
Newsweek. Jun 24, 1985, v105, p70.
Time. Jun 24, 1985, v125, p89.
Variety. Jun 19, 1985, p24.
Vogue. Jun 1985, v175, p56.

Code Name Morituri *See* Morituri

Cold Days *See* Hideg Napok

Cold Turkey (US; Lear, Norman; 1971)
America. Jun 12, 1971, v124, p619.
BFI/Monthly Film Bulletin. Sep 1971, v38,
p180.
Filmfacts. 1971, v14, n3, p44.
Hollywood Reporter. Jan 29, 1971, p3.
The New Republic. Apr 24, 1971, v164, p22.
The New York Times. Mar 18, 1971, p46.
The New York Times. Mar 28, 1971, SecII, p1.
Newsweek. Apr 19, 1971, v77, p136.
Time. May 3, 1971, v97, p89.
Variety. Feb 31, 1971, p17.

Collectionneuse, La (FR; Rohmer, Eric;
1967)
Commonweal. Jun 11, 1971, v94, p310.
Commonweal. Jun 25, 1971, v94, p336-37.
Filmfacts. 1971, v14, n15, p382-84.
Films and Filming. Jul 1969, v15, p42.
Films in Review. Jun-Jul 1971, v22, p373.
Hollywood Reporter. Apr 26, 1971, p2.
The Nation. May 3, 1971, v212, p574.
The New Republic. May 29, 1971, v164, p26.
The New York Times. Apr 26, 1971, p41.
The New Yorker. May 8, 1971, v47, p119.
Newsweek. May 3, 1971, v77, p100-01.
Sight and Sound. Sum 1969, v38, p157-58.
Time. May 17, 1971, v97, p100.
Variety. Mar 8, 1967, p6.
The Village Voice. Apr 29, 1971, p73.
Women and their Sexuality in the New Film.
p147-78.

The Collector (US, GB; Wyler, William;
1965)
America. Jun 26, 1965, v112, p905-06.
BFI/Monthly Film Bulletin. Nov 1965, v32,
p161-62.
Christian Science Monitor (Western edition).
Jul 21, 1965, p4.
Commonweal. Jun 25, 1965, v82, p446.
Confessions of a Cultist. p195-99.
English Journal. Mar 1968, v57, p328-33.
Film Daily. May 21, 1965, p6.
Film Quarterly. Fall 1965, v19, p39-51.
Films and Filming. Oct 1966, v13, p36-37.
Films and Filming. Nov 1965, v12, p30.
Films in Review. Aug-Sep 1965, v16, p445-46.
Hollywood Reporter. May 21, 1965, p3.
International Film Guide. 1966, v3, p143.
Life. May 14, 1965, v58, p153-54.
London Magazine. Dec 1965, v5, p66-69.
The London Times. Oct 13, 1965, p13.
Look. Oct 20, 1964, v28, p90-93.
Magill's Survey of Cinema. Series II. v2, p494-
97.
Marshall Delaney at the Movies. p85-88.
Motion Picture Herald Product Digest. May 26,
1965, p290.
Movie. Aut 1965, n14, p39.
The New Republic. Jun 19, 1965, v152, p26-27.
New Statesman. Oct 15, 1965, v70, p574.
The New York Times. Jun 18, 1965, p28.
Newsweek. Jun 21, 1965, v65, p96.
Playboy. Jul 1965, v12, p28.
*The Private Eye, the Cowboy and the Very
Naked Girl.* p136-38.
Private Screenings. p186-90.
Saturday Review. Jun 12, 1965, v48, p57.
Sight and Sound. Aut 1965, v34, p201.
The Spectator. Oct 22, 1965, v215, p513.
Time. Jun 25, 1965, p103-04.
Variety. May 26, 1965, p6.
The Village Voice. Jun 24, 1965, v10, p22-23.
Vogue. Aug 15, 1965, v146, p52.
*William Wyler: A Guide to References and
Resources.* p152-55.

Comes a Horseman (US; Pakula, Alan J.; 1978)
BFI/Monthly Film Bulletin. Mar 1979, v46, p41.
Films in Review. Dec 1978, v29, p634.
The Films of Jane Fonda. p209-15.
Hollywood Reporter. Oct 10, 1978, p3.
The Los Angeles Times. Oct 22, 1978, Calendar, p35.
Maclean's. Nov 29, 1978, v91, p66-67.
Motion Picture Herald Product Digest. Nov 1, 1978, p43.
The Nation. Nov 11, 1978, v227, p519.
The New Republic. Nov 25, 1978, v179, p24.
New York. Nov 13, 1978, v11, p128.
The New York Times. Dec 3, 1978, SecII, p13.
The New Yorker. Nov 13, 1978, v54, p225-28.
Time. Nov 6, 1978, v112, p78.
Variety. Oct 11, 1978, p31.

Comfort and Joy (US; Forsyth, Bill; 1984)
BFI/Monthly Film Bulletin. Aug 1984, v51, p232.
Film Journal. Nov 1984, v87, p54.
Films and Filming. Aug 1984, n359, p33-34.
Films in Review. Nov 1984, v35, p568.
Hollywood Reporter. Oct 18, 1984, p3.
Informer. Nov 1984, p4.
The Los Angeles Times. Nov 1, 1984, SecVI, p1.
Maclean's. Nov 5, 1984, v97, p61-62.
Magill's Cinema Annual, 1985. p146-49.
The New Republic. Nov 12, 1984, v191, p32-33.
New York. Oct 15, 1984, v17, p83.
The New York Times. Oct 10, 1984, SecIII, p19.
The New Yorker. Nov 26, 1984, v60, p114-17.
Newsweek. Oct 22, 1984, v104, p99.
Photoplay. Oct 1984, v60, p112-19.
Sight and Sound. Sum 1984, v53, p84-85.
Sight and Sound. Wint 1984, v53, p296-97.
Variety. May 23, 1984, p22.
The Village Voice. Oct 16, 1984, p59.

The Comic (US; Reiner, Carl; 1969)
Deeper Into Movies. p74-78.
Film Daily. Nov 12, 1969, p4.
Hollywood Reporter. Nov 5, 1969, p3.
The New York Times. Nov 20, 1969, p58.
The New Yorker. Dec 6, 1969, v45, p190.
Time. Dec 12, 1969, v94, p103.
Variety. Nov 12, 1969, p84.

Comic Strip Hero *See* Jeu de Massacre

Coming Home (US; Ashby, Hal; 1978)
America. Mar 18, 1978, v138, p211.
BFI/Monthly Film Bulletin. May 1978, v45, p86.
Film Comment. Mar 1978, v14, p54-57.
Films in Review. Apr 1978, v29, p239.
The Films of Jane Fonda. p201-08.
The Films of the Seventies. p210-12.
Hollywood Reporter. Feb 15, 1978, p3.
Human Behavior. Jun 1978, v7, p75.
The Los Angeles Times. Feb 12, 1978, Calendar, p1.
Maclean's. May 1, 1978, v91, p82-83.
Magill's Survey of Cinema. Series I. v1, p374-79.
Motion Picture Herald Product Digest. Feb 22, 1978, p25.
Ms. May 1978, v6, p27-28.
The New Republic. Mar 4, 1978, v178, p26-27.
The New York Times. Feb 16, 1978, SecIII, p20.
The New Yorker. Feb 20, 1978, v54, p119-21.
Newsweek. Feb 20, 1978, v91, p89-90.
Saturday Review. Apr 29, 1978, v5, p24.
Time. Feb 20, 1978, v111, p68.
Variety. Feb 15, 1978, p19-21.

The Command (US; Butler, David; 1954)
America. Feb 6, 1954, v90, p491.
BFI/Monthly Film Bulletin. May 1954, v21, p68.
Catholic World. Mar 1954, v178, p460.
Commonweal. Feb 26, 1954, v59, p525.
Farm Journal. Apr 1954, v78, p165.
Film Daily. Jan 18, 1954, p6.
Films in Review. Feb 1954, v5, p93.
Hollywood Reporter. Jan 18, 1954, p3.
The London Times. Apr 5, 1954, p5.
Motion Picture Herald Product Digest. Jan 23, 1954, p2157.
National Parent-Teacher. Mar 1954, v48, p39.
The New York Times. Jan 16, 1954, p10.
Newsweek. Feb 1, 1954, v43, p76.
The Spectator. Apr 9, 1954, v192, p430.
Time. Feb 1, 1954, v63, p74.
Variety. Jun 20, 1954, p6.

Commando (US; Lester, Mark L.; 1985)
BFI/Monthly Film Bulletin. Feb 1986, v53, p41.
Films in Review. Jan 1986, v37, p42.
Hollywood Reporter. Oct 3, 1985, p3.
The Los Angeles Times. Oct 4, 1985, SecVI, p8.
Magill's Cinema Annual, 1986. p111-14.
New York. Nov 4, 1985, v18, p78.
The New York Times. Oct 4, 1985, SecII, p18.
Time. Oct 28, 1985, v126, p111.
Variety. Oct 9, 1985, p23.

Compagni, I *See* The Organizer

Companions of the Night (French title: Compagnes de la Nuit, Les) (FR; Habib, Ralph; 1953)
BFI/Monthly Film Bulletin. May 1954, v21, p69.
Film Daily. Dec 3, 1954, p6.
Hollywood Reporter. Aug 20, 1954, p3.
Illustrated London News. May 1, 1954, v224, p720.
The London Times. Apr 12, 1954, p6.
The New Statesman and Nation. Apr 17, 1954, v47, p501.
The New York Times. Nov 25, 1954, p44.
The Tatler. Apr 21, 1954, v212, p168.

The Company of Wolves (GB; Jordan, Neil; 1985)
BFI/Monthly Film Bulletin. Sep 1984, v51, p264.
Film Comment. Mar-Apr 1985, v21, p51-59.
Film Direction. Spr 1985, p7.
Films and Filming. Sep 1984, p36.
Hollywood Reporter. Apr 19, 1985, p3.
The Los Angeles Times. Apr 19, 1985, SecVI, p4.
Maclean's. May 6, 1985, v98, p63.
Magill's Cinema Annual, 1986. p115-19.
The New York Times. Apr 28, 1985, SecII, p18.
Newsweek. May 6, 1985, v105, p73.
Screen International. Sep 22-29, 1984, No. 464, p18.
Sight and Sound. Aut 1984, v53, p299.
Variety. Jul 18, 1985, p17.

The Company She Keeps (US; Cromwell, John; 1950)
BFI/Monthly Film Bulletin. Jun 1951, v18, p279.
Commonweal. Feb 9, 1951, v53, p448.
Film Daily. Dec 22, 1950, p6.
Hollywood Reporter. Dec 19, 1950, p3.
Motion Picture Herald Product Digest. Dec 23, 1950, p633.
The New York Times. Jan 29, 1951, p14.
Time. Feb 19, 1951, v57, p100.
Variety. Dec 20, 1950, p6.

Compartiment Tuers *See* The Sleeping Car Murders

The Competition (US; Oliansky, Joel; 1980)
BFI/Monthly Film Bulletin. Apr 1981, v48, p63.
Christian Century. Apr 22, 1981, v98, p60.
Films in Review. Mar 1981, v32, p184.
Hollywood Reporter. Dec 2, 1980, p4.
Humanist. May-Jun 1981, v41, p53-54.
Maclean's. Dec 15, 1980, v93, p62.
Motion Picture Herald Product Digest. Dec 17, 1980, p56.
New Statesman. Jun 12, 1981, v101, p22.
New West. Dec 22, 1980, v5, p145.
The New York Times. Dec 3, 1980, SecIII, p27.
The New Yorker. Jan 19, 1981, v56, p104.
Newsweek. Dec 8, 1980, v96, p105.
Senior Scholastic. Feb 20, 1981, v113, p23.
Time. Dec 15, 1980, v116, p68.
Variety. Dec 3, 1980, p24.
Washingtonian. Jan 1981, v16, p45.

Compromising Positions (US; Perry, Frank; 1985)
BFI/Monthly Film Bulletin. Jul 1986, v53, p205.
Commonweal. Sep 20, 1985, v112, p500.
Hollywood Reporter. Aug 16, 1985, p3.
The Los Angeles Times. Aug 30, 1985, SecVI, p1.
Magill's Cinema Annual, 1986. p120-23.
The Nation. Nov 23, 1985, v241, p560-61.
National Review. Oct 18, 1985, v37, p56-59.
The New Leader. Oct 21, 1985, v68, p21.
The New Republic. Oct 7, 1985, v193, p26-28.
New York. Sep 9, 1985, v18, p76.
The New York Times. Aug 30, 1985, SecIII, p5.
The New Yorker. Sep 9, 1985, v61, p74-75.
Newsweek. Sep 9, 1985, v106, p90.
Time. Sep 23, 1985, v126, p91.
Variety. Aug 21, 1985, p18.

Compulsion (US; Fleischer, Richard; 1959)
America. Apr 25, 1959, v101, p257.
BFI/Monthly Film Bulletin. Apr 1959, v26, p42.
Catholic World. May 1959, v189, p154.
Commonweal. May 1, 1959, v70, p130.
Film Daily. Feb 5, 1959, p6.
Filmfacts. May 13, 1959, v2, p75-77.
Films in Review. Apr 1959, v10, p239-40.
Hollywood Reporter. Feb 4, 1959, p3.
Library Journal. Apr 1, 1959, v84, p1119.
Life. Apr 13, 1959, v46, p60.
Magill's Survey of Cinema. Series I. v1, p380-83.
The Nation. Apr 25, 1959, v188, p395.
The New Republic. Apr 20, 1959, v140, p20.
The New York Times. Apr 2, 1959, p26.
The New Yorker. Apr 11, 1959, v35, p163.
Newsweek. Apr 13, 1959, v53, p118.
Saturday Review. Mar 28, 1959, v42, p27.
Time. Apr 13, 1959, v83, p98.
Variety. Feb 4, 1959, p6.

Conan the Barbarian (US; Milius, John; 1982)
BFI/Monthly Film Bulletin. Aug 1982, v49, p167-68.
Christian Century. Aug 18 1982, v99, p868.
Film Comment. May-Jun 1982, v18, p26-28.
The Los Angeles Times. May 14, 1982, SecVI, p1.
Maclean's. May 17, 1982, v95, p65-66.
The New Leader. Jun 14, 1982, v65, p19-20.
New Statesman. Aug 27, 1982, v104, p24.
New York. May 24, 1982, v15, p68.
The New York Times. May 15, 1982, p13.

The New York Times. Mar 16, 1982, SecIII,
p11.
Newsweek. May 17, 1982, v99, p100.
Photoplay. Oct 1982, v33, p24.
Rolling Stone. Jun 10, 1982, p37.
Sight and Sound. Sum 1982, v51, p152-53.
Time. May 24, 1982, v119, p76.
Variety. Mar 17, 1982, p24.
The Village Voice. May 18, 1982, p54.

Conan the Destroyer (US; Fleischer,
Richard; 1984)
BFI/Monthly Film Bulletin. Oct 1984, v51,
p303.
Cinefantastique. 1984, v14, n4/5, p4-7.
Film Journal. Jul 1984, v87, p42.
Film Journal. Aug 1984, v87, p18.
Films and Filming. Sep 1984, n360, p37-38.
Hollywood Reporter. Jun 27, 1984, p4.
The Los Angeles Times. Jun 29, 1984, SecVI,
p1.
The New York Times. Jun 29, 1984, SecIII, p8.
Newsweek. Jul 2, 1984, v104, p45.
Photoplay. Nov 1984, v35, p20, 40-42.
Variety. Jun 27, 1984, p19.
The Village Voice. Jul 10, 1984, p46.

Concrete Jungle (Also titled: The Criminal)
(GB; Losey, Joseph; 1960)
The Cinema of Joseph Losey. p89-97.
Film Quarterly. Spr 1963, v16, p58.
Films and Filming. Nov 1960, v7, p32.
Joseph Losey (Hirsch). p76-78.
Magill's Survey of Cinema. Series II. v2, p503-
06.
Newsweek. Jun 18, 1962, v59, p87.
Sight and Sound. Aut 1960, v29, p196.
Time. Jul 13, 1962, v80, p66.

Condamne a Mort s'est Echappe, Un (Also
titled: A Man Escaped; A Condemned
Man Escaped) (FR; Bresson, Robert;
1956)
America. Jun 15, 1957, v97, p325.
BFI/Monthly Film Bulletin. Jun 1957, v24, p95.
Film. Sep-Oct 1957, v13, p21-22.
Film Culture. Oct 1957, v3, p6.
Film Daily. Aug 29, 1957, p6.
Films and Filming. Jul 1957, v3, p23-24.
Films in Review. Oct 1957, v8, p412-13.
*The International Dictionary of Films and
Filmmakers.* v1, p105-06.
The New York Times. Aug 27, 1957, p33.
Quarterly Review of Film Studies. 1976, v1,
p453-77.
*Robert Bresson: A Guide to References and
Resources.* p56-60.
Sight and Sound. Sum 1957, v27, p30-33.
Variety. Dec 12, 1956, p6.

Conde, Un *See* The Cop

A Condemned Man Escaped *See*
Condamne a Mort s'est Echappe, Un

The Condemned of Altona (Italian title:
Sequestrati di Altona, I) (IT; De Sica,
Vittorio; 1963)
BFI/Monthly Film Bulletin. Oct 1963, v30,
p142-43.
Film Daily. Sep 11, 1963, p4.
Filmfacts. Oct 24, 1963, v6, p219-21.
Films and Filming. Sep 1963, v9, p21-22.
Films in Review. Oct 1963, v14, p493-94.
The Films of Fredric March. p231-34.
The Films of Sophia Loren. p146-49.
The New Republic. Sep 28, 1963, v149, p28.
The New York Times. Oct 31, 1963, p26.
The New Yorker. Nov 9, 1963, v39, p209.
Newsweek. Oct 7, 1963, v62, p110.
Photoplay. Nov 1963, v64, p12.

Saturday Review. Oct 19, 1963, v46, p46.
Time. Sep 27, 1963, v82, p83.
Variety. Sep 11, 1963, p6.

Conduct Unbecoming (GB; Anderson,
Michael; 1975)
BFI/Monthly Film Bulletin. Jan 1976, v43, p5.
Commonweal. Nov 21, 1975, v102, p564-65.
Hollywood Reporter. Oct 6, 1975, p3.
Motion Picture Herald Product Digest. Oct 8,
1975, p34.
The New York Times. Oct 6, 1975, p42.
The New Yorker. Nov 3, 1975, v51, p141-43.
Saturday Review. Nov 1, 1975, v3, p48.
Time. Oct 13, 1975, v106, p79.
Variety. Sep 17, 1975, p18.

The Confession (French title: Aveu, L')
(FR; Costa-Gavras, Constantin; 1970)
America. Feb 13, 1971, v124, p158.
BFI/Monthly Film Bulletin. Dec 1970, v37,
p243.
Commonweal. Mar 5, 1971, v93, p548-49.
Deeper into Movies. p200-05.
Film Quarterly. Sum 1971, v24, p54-56.
Films and Filming. Dec 1970, v17, p47-48.
Films in Review. Jan 1971, v22, p41-43.
Hollywood Reporter. Dec 7, 1970, p3.
The New York Times. Dec 10, 1970, p58.
Sight and Sound. Wint 1970-71, v40, p49-50.
Take One. 1970, v2, n7, p22.
Variety. May 6, 1970, p15.

Confidential File *See* Mr. Arkadin

Confidential Report *See* Mr. Arkadin

Confidentially Yours (French title:
Vivement Dimanche) (FR; Truffaut,
François; 1983)
BFI/Monthly Film Bulletin. Nov 1983, v50,
p312-13.
Film. Nov 1983, n120, p4.
Film Journal. Mar 1984, v87, p46.
Films and Filming. Nov 1983, n350, p37.
Hollywood Reporter. Jan 20, 1984, p3.
The Los Angeles Times. Jan 26, 1984, SecVI,
p7.
Maclean's. Feb 13, 1984, v97, p62.
The New Republic. Feb 20, 1984, v190, p25.
New Statesman. Nov 18, 1983, v106, p28.
New York. Jan 30, 1984, v17, p53.
The New York Times. Jan 20, 1984, SecIII, p6.
Newsweek. Jan 30, 1984, v103, p69.
Penthouse. May 1984, v15, p48.
Photoplay. Dec 1983, v34, p19-20.
Sight and Sound. Spr 1983, v53, p61.
Stills. Nov-Dec 1983, n9, p84.
Time. Jan 30, 1984, v123, p78.
Variety. Jan 18, 1984, p24.
Variety. Aug 17, 1983, p23.
The Village Voice. Jan 31, 1984, p55.

The Conformist (Italian title: Conformista,
Il) (IT; Bertolucci, Bernardo; 1971)
Bernardo Bertolucci (Kolker). p86-106.
BFI/Monthly Film Bulletin. Dec 1971, v38,
n455, p237.
Cineaste. Spr 1971, v4, n4, p19-23.
Commonweal. Oct 30, 1970, v93, p129.
Deeper into Movies. p270-76.
Esquire. Aug 1971, v76, p42.
Film Quarterly. Sum 1971, v24, p2-19.
Filmfacts. 1971, v14, n5, p81-85.
Films and Filming. Jan 1972, v18, n4, p54-55.
Films in Review. Apr 1971, v22, n4, p235.
Hollywood Reporter. Mar 19, 1971, v215, n23,
p3.
Life. Apr 16, 1971, v70, p18.
*Modern European Filmmakers and the Art of
Adaptation.* p222-37.
The Nation. Apr 5, 1971, v212, p446.

National Review. Oct 22, 1971, v23, p1191.
The New Republic. Apr 10, 1971, v164, p24.
The New York Times. Sep 19, 1970, p32.
The New York Times. Mar 23, 1971, p31.
The New York Times. Apr 11, 1971, SecII, p1,
15.
The New Yorker. Mar 13, 1971, v47, p118.
The New Yorker. Mar 27, 1971, v47, p99.
Newsweek. Apr 10, 1971, v54, p40.
Sight and Sound. Spr 1971, v40, p64-66.
Time. Apr 5, 1971, v97, p86.
Variety. Jul 8, 1970, p15.
The Village Voice. Oct 8, 1970, v15, n41, p53-
58.
The Village Voice. Apr 1, 1971, v16, n13, p72.
Women and their Sexuality in the New Film.
p87-96.

Congolaise (FR; Dupont, Jacques; 1950)
Film Daily. May 19, 1950, p6.
Hollywood Reporter. May 8, 1950, p3.
Motion Picture Herald Product Digest. May 13,
1950, p294.
The New York Times. May 22, 1950, p17.
Variety. May 10, 1950, p16.

The Conjugal Bed (Italian title: Storia
moderna, Una; Ape regina, L') (IT;
Ferreri, Marco; 1963)
Commonweal. Oct 11, 1963, v79, p79.
Film Daily. Sep 16, 1963, p4.
Filmfacts. Oct 17, 1963, v6, p213-14.
The New Republic. Oct 12, 1963, v149, p29.
The New York Times. Sep 27, 1963, v30, p1.
The New Yorker. Sep 21, 1963, v46, p, p44.
Photoplay. Dec 1963, p12.
Time. Sep 27, 1963, v82, p84.
Variety. Jan 30, 1963, p6.
The Village Voice. Nov 27, 1963, p15.

Conrack (US; Ritt, Martin; 1974)
America. Apr 20, 1974, v130, p316.
BFI/Monthly Film Bulletin. Sep 1974, v41,
p197.
Christian Century. Apr 3, 1974, v91, p378.
Filmmakers Newsletter. Apr 1974, v7, p27-31.
Films and Filming. Sep 1974, v20, p66-67.
Films Illustrated. Jul 1974, v3, p427.
Films in Review. Apr 1974, v25, p246.
Hollywood Reporter. Feb 15, 1974, p3.
Independent Film Journal. Mar 4, 1974, v73,
p19.
The Los Angeles Times. Mar 10, 1974,
Calendar, p1.
Media and Methods. Apr 1974, v10, p16.
Motion Picture Herald Product Digest. Mar 13,
1974, p32.
The New Republic. Mar 16, 1974, v170, p20.
The New York Times. Apr 21, 1974, SecII, p11.
The New Yorker. Mar 11, 1974, v50, p119-22.
Newsweek. Apr 8, 1974, v83, p90.
PTA Magazine. May 1974, v68, p6.
Rolling Stone. Apr 11, 1974, p70.
Saturday Review. Apr 6, 1974, v1, p50.
Time. Apr 8, 1974, v103, p64.
Variety. Feb 20, 1974, p14.
The Village Voice. Apr 18, 1974, p85-86.

Constans (Also titled: The Constant Factor)
(POL; Zanussi, Krzysztof; 1980)
BFI/Monthly Film Bulletin. Nov 1981, v48,
p217.
Christian Science Monitor. Feb 12, 1981, p18.
New Statesman. Sep 25, 1981, p34.
The New York Times. Oct 9, 1980, SecIII, p24.
Variety. May 21, 1980, p18.

Conteau dans la Plaie, Le *See* Five Miles to
Midnight

Contempt (French title: Mépris, Le) (FR, IT; Godard, Jean-Luc; 1963)
BFI/Monthly Film Bulletin. Jul 1970, v37, p141-42.
Christian Science Monitor (Western edition). Jan 20, 1965, p6.
Close-Up: A Critical Perspective on Film. p262-67.
Commonweal. Feb 5, 1965, v81, p611.
Confessions of a Cultist. p183-89.
Dictionary of Films. p216.
Film Heritage. Spr 1968, v3, p11-22, 47.
Film Quarterly. Sum 1966, v19, p24-29.
Film Quarterly. Spr 1965, v18, p5-9.
Films and Filming. Jul 1970, v16, p40-41.
Films in Review. Jan 1965, v16, p51-52.
The Films of Jean-Luc Godard. p54-60.
Focus on Godard. p37-39.
Godard on Godard. p200-01.
The Great Movies. p175-76.
Jean-Luc Godard: A Critical Anthology. p152-69.
Modern European Filmmakers and the Art of Adaptation. p100-14.
Motion Picture Herald Product Digest. Dec 23, 1964, p196.
The New Republic. Jan 2, 1965, v152, p21-22.
The New Wave (Monaco). p134-39.
The New York Times. Dec 19, 1964, p25.
The New Yorker. Dec 26, 1964, v40, p73.
The Novel and the Cinema. p348-57.
Private Screenings. p166-67.
Saturday Review. Feb 6, 1965, v48, p43.
Sight and Sound. Sum 1970, v39, p163-64.
Take One. Nov-Dec 1968, v2, p12-13.
Time. Jan 8, 1965, v85, p54.
Variety. Jan 1, 1964, p6.
The Village Voice. Jan 28, 1965, v10, p14, 18.
The Village Voice. Jan 7, 1965, v10, p13-14.
The Village Voice. Feb 4, 1965, v10, p15, 18.
A World on Film. p243-44.

Continental Divide (US; Apted, Michael; 1981)
Hollywood Reporter. Sep 8, 1981, p3.
The Los Angeles Times. Sep 18, 1981, SecVI, p1.
Magill's Cinema Annual, 1982. p115-18.
The New York Times. Sep 18, 1981, SecIII, p14.
The New Yorker. Nov 9, 1981, v57, p80.
Newsweek. Oct 5, 1981, v98, p78.
Time. Sep 14, 1981, v118, p90.

The Conversation (US; Coppola, Francis Ford; 1974)
Atlantic. May 1974, v233, p132-34.
Audience. Nov 1974, v7, p6-8.
BFI/Monthly Film Bulletin. Jul 1974, v41, p145-46.
Christian Century. May 22, 1974, v91, p570.
Cineaste. 1974, v6, n3, p32.
Cinefantastique. 1974, v3, n3, p35.
Commentary. Jul 1974, v58, p61-64.
Commonweal. May 2, 1974, v100, p214.
Esquire. Jun 1974, v81, p40.
Film. Aug 1974, n17, p18.
Film Heritage. 1974, v10, n1, p46-47.
Film Quarterly. Fall 1974, v28, p54-60.
Film Quarterly. Spr 1974, v28, p54-60.
Filmmakers Newsletter. May 1974, v7, p30-34.
Films and Filming. Jul 1974, v20, p19-21, 41-42.
Films Illustrated. Jul 1974, v3, p427, 436-37.
Films in Review. May 1974, v25, p307.
Focus on Film. Sum 1974, n18, p15-16.
Francis Ford Coppola: A Guide to References and Resources. p52-54.
Hollywood Reporter. Apr 1, 1974, p3.

Independent Film Journal. Apr 15, 1974, v73, p9.
The Los Angeles Times. Apr 7, 1974, Calendar, p1.
Magill's Survey of Cinema. Series II. v2, p515-19.
Motion Picture Herald Product Digest. Apr 10, 1974, p89.
Movietone News. May-Jun 1974, n32, p34.
The Nation. Apr 27, 1974, v218, p539-40.
The New Republic. Apr 27, 1974, v170, p22.
New Statesman. Jul 12, 1974, v88, p59-60.
New York. Apr 8, 1974, v7, p77-78.
The New York Times. Apr 21, 1974, SecII, p1.
The New York Times. May 12, 1974, SecII, p13.
The New York Times. May 25, 1974, p16.
The New Yorker. Apr 15, 1974, v50, p116.
Newsweek. May 13, 1974, v83, p130-31.
Penthouse. Aug 1974, v5, p35-36.
PTA Magazine. Jun 1974, v68, p4.
Rolling Stone. May 23, 1974, n161, p82.
Saturday Review. May 4, 1974, v1, p60-61.
Sight and Sound. Sum 1974, v43, p131-33.
Take One. Jan-Feb 1973, v4, p36-37.
Time. Apr 15, 1974, v103, p90.
Times Literary Supplement. Jul 26, 1974, p790-91.
Variety. Apr 3, 1974, p14.
The Village Voice. Jun 6, 1974, p89-90.
The Village Voice. Jun 13, 1974, p89-90.
The Village Voice. Jun 20, 1974, p79-80.

Convoy (US; Peckinpah, Sam; 1978)
BFI/Monthly Film Bulletin. Jul 1978, v45, p155.
Hollywood Reporter. Jun 22, 1978, p3.
The Los Angeles Times. Jun 28, 1978, SecIV, p1.
Motion Picture Herald Product Digest. Jul 5, 1978, p9.
The New Leader. Jul 17, 1978, v61, p24.
The New Republic. Jul 22, 1978, v179, p23.
The New York Times. Jun 28, 1978, SecIII, p17.
The New York Times. Jul 2, 1978, SecII, p1.
The New Yorker. Sep 25, 1978, v54, p137-45.
Newsweek. Jul 10, 1978, v54, p137-45.
Sam Peckinpah (McKinney). p217-30.
Time. Jul 4, 1977, v110, p73-74.
Time. Jul 10, 1978, v112, p78.
Variety. Jun 28, 1978, p22.

Coogan's Bluff (US; Siegel, Don; 1968)
American Film Genres (Kaminsky). p231-32.
BFI/Monthly Film Bulletin. Mar 1969, v36, p47-48.
Don Siegel: American Cinema. p58, p73-74.
Don Siegel: Director. p215-24.
Film Daily. Oct 7, 1968, p4.
Film Quarterly. Fall 1969, v23, p48-49.
Filmfacts. Dec 15, 1968, v11, p368-70.
Films and Filming. May 1969, v15, p51-52.
Films and Filming. Jan 1969, v15, p22.
The Films of Clint Eastwood. p80-85.
Hollywood Reporter. Oct 2, 1968, p3.
The London Times. Jan 24, 1969, p7.
Motion Picture Herald Product Digest. Oct 9, 1968, p35.
New Statesman. Jan 31, 1969, v77, p165.
The New York Times. Oct 3, 1968, p56.
The New York Times. Nov 10, 1968, p1.
Sight and Sound. Spr 1969, v38, p96-97.
Time. Nov 15, 1968, v92, pLA19, 21.
Variety. Oct 2, 1968, p6.
The Village Voice. Oct 31, 1968, p49-50.

Cool Hand Luke (US; Rosenberg, Stuart; 1967)
America. Dec 2, 1967, v117, p694.

BFI/Monthly Film Bulletin. Jan 1968, v35, p3-4.
Christian Century. Apr 10, 1968, p457-58.
Cinema. Sum 1967, v3, p50.
Commonweal. Dec 1, 1967, v87, p305-06.
Esquire. Sep 1967, v68, p24.
Fifty Grand Movies of the 1960s and 1970s. p59-64.
Film Daily. Jun 6, 1967, p3.
Films and Filming. Jan 1968, v14, p21.
Films in Review. Dec 1967, v18, p647.
The Films of Paul Newman. p161-65.
The Films of the Sixties. p195-97.
Hollywood Reporter. May 31, 1967, p3.
Life. Nov 3, 1967, v63, p20.
Magill's Survey of Cinema. Series I. v1, p384-86.
Motion Picture Herald Product Digest. Jun 7, 1967, p691.
The New York Times. Nov 2, 1967, p58.
The New Yorker. Nov 11, 1967, v43, p196-97.
Newsweek. Nov 13, 1967, v70, p123.
Saturday Review. Nov 11, 1967, v50, p82.
Senior Scholastic. Nov 9, 1967, v91, p17.
Time. Nov 10, 1967, v90, p102.
Variety. May 31, 1967, p6.
The Village Voice. Nov 16, 1967, p31.
Vintage Films. p207-09.

The Cool World (US; Clarke, Shirley; 1964)
BFI/Monthly Film Bulletin. Mar 1974, v41, p44-45.
Commonweal. May 15, 1964, v80, p236.
Esquire. Jul 1964, v62, p111-13.
Film Comment. 1964, v2, p51-53.
Life. Apr 24, 1964, v56, p15.
Motion Picture Herald Product Digest. Jun 10, 1964, p67-68.
The Nation. Apr 27, 1964, v198, p447-48.
The New Republic. May 23, 1964, v150, p24.
The New York Times. Apr 21, 1964, p42.
The New Yorker. Apr 25, 1964, v40, p171-72.
Newsweek. Apr 20, 1964, v63, p114.
Saturday Review. Apr 25, 1964, v47, p25.
Time. Apr 17, 1964, v83, p123.
Variety. Sep 11, 1963, p6.
A World on Film. p164-66.

Cooley High (US; Schultz, Michael; 1975)
BFI/Monthly Film Bulletin. Feb 1976, v44, p21.
Hollywood Reporter. Jun 25, 1975, p9.
The Los Angeles Times. Jul 13, 1975, Calendar, p36.
The New York Times. Jun 26, 1975, p35.
The New York Times. Jul 6, 1975, SecII, p9.
The New York Times. Aug 10, 1975, SecII, p13.
Newsweek. Jul 21, 1975, v86, p64.
Senior Scholastic. Sep 23, 1975, v107, p40.
Time. Sep 1, 1975, v106, p45.
Variety. Jun 25, 1975, p23.

The Cop (French title: Conde, Un; Also titled: Murder-Go-Round) (FR; Boisset, Yves; 1971)
BFI/Monthly Film Bulletin. Dec 1971, v38, p237.
Filmfacts. 1971, v14, n17, p428-29.
Films and Filming. Jan 1972, v18, n4, p61.
Hollywood Reporter. Jun 1, 1971, p3.
The Nation. Jun 14, 1971, v212, p765.
The New York Times. May 27, 1971, p34.
Variety. Sep 30, 1970, p22.

Copper Canyon (US; Farrow, John; 1950)
Commonweal. Nov 24, 1950, v53, p173.
Film Daily. Jul 24, 1950, p6.
The Films of Hedy Lamarr. p215-17.
Hollywood Reporter. Jul 21, 1950, p3.
The London Times. Jan 30, 1950, p2.

Motion Picture Herald Product Digest. Jul 29, 1950, p405.
The New York Times. Nov 16, 1950, p39.
Newsweek. Nov 27, 1950, v36, p84.
The Spectator. Jan 27, 1950, v184, p106-07.
Time. Dec 4, 1950, v56, p98.
Variety. Aug 26, 1950, p10.

Cops and Robbers (US; Avakian, Aram; 1973)
American Scholar. Wint 1973, v43, p147-51.
Commonweal. Sep 28, 1973, v98, p526-27.
The New Republic. Sep 8, 1973, v169, p35.
The New York Times. Aug 16, 1973, p40.
The New York Times. Sep 23, 1973, SecII, p1.
The New York Times. Jan 20, 1974, SecII, p1.
The New Yorker. Aug 27, 1973, p49.
Newsweek. Aug 27, 1973, v82, p86.
PTA Magazine. Nov 1973, v68, p6.
Time. Oct 1, 1973, v102, p105.
Variety. Aug 15, 1973, p12.

Corniaud, Le *See* The Sucker

Corvette Summer (Also titled: The Hot One) (US; Robins, Matthew; 1978)
BFI/Monthly Film Bulletin. Jun 1979, v46, p124.
Films in Review. Oct 1978, v29, p502.
Hollywood Reporter. May 19, 1978, p3.
The Los Angeles Times. Aug 30, 1978, SecIV, p13.
Maclean's. Aug 21, 1978, v91, p52.
Motion Picture Herald Product Digest. Jun 7, 1978, p1.
The New York Times. Aug 4, 1978, SecIII, p13.
Variety. May 24, 1978, p27.

The Cotton Club (US; Coppola, Francis Ford; 1984)
BFI/Monthly Film Bulletin. May 1985, v52, p149.
Christianity Today. Feb 5, 1985, v29, p53.
Down Beat. Mar 1985, v52, p12.
Film Quarterly. Sum 1985, v38, p16.
Hollywood Reporter. Dec 10, 1984, p3.
Los Angeles. Jan 1985, v30, p34.
The Los Angeles Times. Dec 14, 1984, SecVI, p1.
Maclean's. Dec 17, 1984, v97, p60.
New Statesman. May 3, 1985, v109, p34.
The New York Times. Mar 22, 1984, SecIII, p17.
The New York Times. Dec 14, 1984, SecIII, p4.
The New Yorker. Jan 7, 1985, v60, p67-70.
Newsweek. Dec 24, 1984, v104, p52.
Playboy. Mar 1985, v32, p26.
Saturday Review. Apr 1985, v11, p72.
Texas Monthly. Feb 1985, v13, p134.
Variety. Feb 13, 1985, p145.
Variety. Dec 12, 1984, p16.
Washingtonian. Jan 1985, v20, p66.
Whole Earth Review. May 1985, p80.

Cotton Comes to Harlem (US; Davis, Ossie; 1970)
BFI/Monthly Film Bulletin. Jun 1971, v38, p118-19.
Black Films and Film-Makers. p101-05.
Christian Century. Dec 2, 1970, v87, p1454-1455.
Esquire. Oct 1970, v74, p67.
From Sambo to Superspade. p239-41.
Life. Aug 28, 1970, v69, p58-59.
Magill's Survey of Cinema. Series II. v2, p528.
The New York Times. Jun 11, 1970, p50.
The New York Times. Jul 19, 1970, SecII, p1.
Newsweek. Jun 22, 1970, v75, p82.
Saturday Review. Jul 18, 1970, v53, p22.
Time. Jul 6, 1970, v96, p70.
Variety. Jun 10, 1970, p18.

Countdown (US; Altman, Robert; 1968)
American Skeptic: Robert Altman's Genre-Commentary Films. p1-16.
BFI/Monthly Film Bulletin. Sep 1967, v34, p138.
Film Daily. Feb 20, 1968, p8.
Filmfacts. Jul 1, 1968, v11, p172-73.
The Films of Robert Altman. p109-10.
Hollywood Reporter. Feb 12, 1968, p3.
Motion Picture Herald Product Digest. Feb 28, 1968, p777.
The New York Times. May 2, 1968, p57.
Robert Altman: A Guide to References and Resources. p33-34, 90-91.
Robert Altman, American Innovator. p47-51.
Variety. Feb 14, 1968, p6.

The Counterfeit Traitor (US; Seaton, George; 1962)
America. May 19, 1962, v107, p276.
BFI/Monthly Film Bulletin. Aug 1962, v29, p104.
Commonweal. May 18, 1962, v76, p211.
Film Daily. Apr 4, 1962, p8.
Filmfacts. May 4, 1962, v5, p77-79.
Films in Review. May 1962, v13, p291-92.
The Films of William Holden. p206-09.
Hollywood Reporter. Apr 4, 1962, p3.
Life. Apr 27, 1962, v52, p57.
Magill's Survey of Cinema. Series II. v2, p534-37.
Motion Picture Herald Product Digest. Apr 11, 1962, p516.
The New York Times. Apr 18, 1962, p28.
Newsweek. Apr 23, 1962, v59, p96.
Saturday Review. Apr 28, 1962, v45, p37.
Time. May 4, 1962, v79, p65.

Country (US; Pearce, Richard; 1984)
American Film. Sep 1984, v9, p14.
BFI/Monthly Film Bulletin. Apr 1985, v52, p108.
Commonweal. Nov 30, 1984, v111, p661-62.
Film Journal. Oct 1984, v87, p15-16.
Films in Review. Dec 1984, v35, p620-21.
Hollywood Reporter. Sep 24, 1984, p3.
The Los Angeles Times. Oct 5, 1984, SecVI, p1.
Maclean's. Oct 29, 1984, v97, p69.
Magill's Cinema Annual, 1985. p156-60.
Ms. Nov 1984, v13, p44.
The Nation. Oct 27, 1984, v239, p426.
The New Republic. Oct 29, 1984, v191, p25-26.
The New Republic. Dec 10, 1984, v191, p8.
New York. Oct 15, 1984, v17, p81-82.
The New York Times. Sep 28, 1984, SecIII, p20.
The New York Times. Nov 23, 1984, SecIII, p13.
The New Yorker. Oct 1, 1984, v60, p108.
Newsweek. Oct 1, 1984, v104, p52-53.
Saturday Review. Oct 8, 1984, v10, p66-67.
Time. Oct 8, 1984, v124, p82.
Variety. Sep 26, 1984, p15.
The Village Voice. Oct 2, 1984, p49.

The Country Girl (US; Seaton, George; 1954)
BFI/Monthly Film Bulletin. Mar 1955, v22, p33.
Catholic World. Dec 1954, v180, p222.
Commonweal. Dec 17, 1954, v61, p312.
Farm Journal. Jan 1955, v79, p70.
Film Culture. Mar-Apr 1955, v1, p41-42.
Film Daily. Nov 29, 1954, p6.
Films and Filming. May 1955, v1, p19.
Films in Review. Jan 1955, v6, p30-31.
The Films of Bing Crosby. p211-16.
The Films of William Holden. p157-60.
Fortnight. Jan 19, 1955, v18, p44.
Hollywood Reporter. Nov 29, 1954, p3.
Library Journal. Dec 15, 1954, v79, p2438.

Life. Dec 6, 1954, v37, p106.
The London Times. Mar 10, 1955, p7.
Look. Dec 14, 1954, v18, p163-65.
Magill's Survey of Cinema. Series I. v1, p390-92.
Motion Picture Herald Product Digest. Dec 4, 1954, p233.
The Nation. Dec 11, 1954, v179, p518.
National Parent-Teacher. Jan 1955, v49, p39.
The New Republic. Apr 4, 1955, v132, p21.
The New Statesman and Nation. Mar 19, 1955, v49, p387.
The New York Times. Dec 16, 1954, p51.
The New York Times Magazine. Nov 14, 1954, p39.
The New Yorker. Dec 25, 1954, v30, p60.
Newsweek. Dec 6, 1954, v44, p107.
Reporter. Feb 24, 1955, v12, p47.
Saturday Review. Dec 18, 1954, v37, p27.
Selected Film Criticism, 1951-1960. p27-28.
The Tatler. Mar 23, 1955, v215, p592.
Time. Dec 13, 1954, v64, p96.
Variety. Dec 1, 1954, p6.

Coup de Foudre *See* Entre Nous

Coup de Grace (German title: Fangschuss, Der) (FR, WGER; Schlöndorff, Volker; 1965)
BFI/Monthly Film Bulletin. Apr 1977, v44, p67.
Films in Review. Mar 1978, v29, p185.
Hollywood Reporter. Feb 23, 1978, p3.
Magill's Survey of Cinema. Foreign Language Films. v2, p631-35.
New York. Feb 13, 1977, v11, p71.
Variety. Mar 24, 1965, p6.

Coup de tete (Also titled: Hothead) (FR; Annaud, Jean-Jacques; 1979)
Commonweal. Mar 14, 1980, v107, p149.
Films in Review. Mar 1980, v31, p178.
Forbes. Mar 31, 1980, v125, p22.
Hollywood Reporter. Feb 1, 1980, p48.
The Los Angeles Times. Mar 20, 1980, SecVI, p3.
The Nation. Feb 9, 1980, v230, p155.
The New York Times. Jan 21, 1980, SecIII, p15.
The New Yorker. Jan 28, 1980, v55, p63.
Newsday. Jan 18, 1980, SecII, p5.
Playboy. Jun 1980, v27, p47.
Variety. Oct 31, 1979, p22.
The Village Voice. Jan 28, 1980, p47.

Coup de Torchon (FR; Tavernier, Bertrand; 1981)
America. Feb 26, 1983, v148, p154.
BFI/Monthly Film Bulletin. May 1982, v49, p82.
Commonweal. Feb 11, 1983, v110, p86-87.
Film Journal. Dec 27, 1982, v85, p16.
The Los Angeles Times. Apr 10, 1983, Calendar, p6.
Magill's Cinema Annual, 1983. p124-29.
The Nation. Feb 5, 1983, v236, p154-56.
The New Republic. Jan 24, 1983, v188, p25.
New Statesman. May 7, 1982, v103, p24-25.
New York. Jan 10, 1983, v16, p68-69.
The New York Times. Dec 20, 1982, SecIII, p12.
The New Yorker. Jan 24, 1983, p92.
Newsweek. Jan 3, 1983, v101, p53.
Photoplay. Jul 1982, v33, p27.
Time. Jan 24, 1983, v121, p93.
Variety. Nov 27, 1981, p3.
The Village Voice. Dec 21, 1982, p85.

The Court Jester (US; Panama, Norman; Frank, Melvin; 1956)
America. Feb 11, 1956, v94, p542.

BFI/Monthly Film Bulletin. Mar 1956, v23, p28.
Commonweal. Feb 24, 1956, v63, p544.
Film Daily. Jan 27, 1956, p6.
The Great Adventure Films. p192-95.
Halliwell's Hundred. p57-60.
Magill's Survey of Cinema. Series I. v1, p393-97.
Motion Picture Herald Product Digest. Jan 28, 1956, p761.
The New Republic. Mar 5, 1956, v134, p21.
The New York Times. Feb 2, 1956, p19.
The New York Times. Feb 5, 1956, SecII, p1.
The New Yorker. Feb 11, 1956, v31, p117.
Newsweek. Feb 6, 1956, v47, p86.
Saturday Review. Feb 4, 1956, v39, p21.
Time. Feb 6, 1956, v67, p92.
Variety. Feb 1, 1956, p6.

Court-Martial (Also titled: Carrington V.C.) (GB; Asquith, Anthony; 1954)
America. Aug 13, 1955, v93, p479.
BFI/Monthly Film Bulletin. Jan 1955, v22, p2.
Catholic World. Jun 1955, v181, p222.
Commonweal. May 20, 1955, v62, p183.
Confessions of a Cultist. p20-21.
Film Culture. Wint 1955, n5/6, p37.
Film Daily. Aug 5, 1955, p8.
Films and Filming. Feb 1955, v1, p20.
Films in Review. May 1955, v6, p237-39.
The Films of David Niven. p119-21.
Motion Picture Herald Product Digest. Aug 20, 1955, p561.
National Parent-Teacher. Sep 1955, v50, p39.
The New Statesman and Nation. Dec 18, 1954, v48, p826.
The New York Times. Aug 2, 1955, p17.
The New Yorker. Aug 13, 1955, v31, p49.
Newsweek. Aug 8, 1955, v46, p76.
Quarterly of Film, Radio and Television. Fall 1956, v11, p33-38.
The Spectator. Dec 17, 1954, v193, p787.
Time. Aug 22, 1955, v66, p84.
Variety. Dec 15, 1954, p28.

The Court Martial of Billy Mitchell (Also titled: One Man Mutiny) (US; Preminger, Otto; 1955)
America. Dec 31, 1955, v94, p384.
The Cinema of Otto Preminger (Pratley). p114-16.
Commonweal. Dec 30, 1955, v63, p332.
Film Daily. Dec 9, 1955, p6.
Films in Review. Jan 1956, v7, p33-34.
The Films of Gary Cooper. p 252-54.
Library Journal. Jan 1, 1956, v81, p74.
Motion Picture Herald Product Digest. Dec 10, 1955, p697.
Movie. Sep 1962, n2, p20.
The New York Times. Aug 2, 1955, p17.
The New York Times. Dec 23, 1955, p14.
The New Yorker. Dec 31, 1955, v31, p36.
Newsweek. Jan 9, 1956, v47, p71.
Saturday Review. Jan 14, 1956, v39, p21.
Time. Dec 26, 1955, v66, p59-61.
Variety. Dec 14, 1955, p6.

The Courtship of Eddie's Father (US; Minnelli, Vincente; 1963)
BFI/Monthly Film Bulletin. Apr 1963, v30, p42.
Commonweal. Mar 22, 1963, v77, p665.
Film Daily. Mar 13, 1963, p6.
Filmfacts. Apr 18, 1963, v6, p55-56.
Films and Filming. Apr 1963, v9, p34.
Films in Review. Apr 1963, v14, p238-39.
Hollywood Reporter. Mar 12, 1963, p3.
Movie. Jun 1963, p29-32.
The New York Times. Mar 28, 1963, p8.
Newsweek. Apr 8, 1963, v61, p93.

Photoplay. May 1963, v63, p6.
Time. Apr 15, 1963, v81, p103-4.
Variety. Mar 13, 1963, p6.

Cousin Angelica (Spanish title: Prima Angelica, La) (SP; Saura, Carlos; 1974)
Cinema Papers. Jul-Aug 1975, n2, p131.
Film Quarterly. Spr 1979, v32, p14-25.
Magill's Survey of Cinema. Foreign Language Films. v2, p636-39.
Medium. Sep 1978, v8, p27-29.
The New York Times. May 13, 1977, SecIII, p5.
The New York Times. May 29, 1977, SecII, p11.
Variety. May 8, 1974, p37.

Cousins, Les (Also titled: The Cousins) (FR; Chabrol, Claude; 1958)
BFI/Monthly Film Bulletin. Nov 1959, v26, p146.
Filmfacts. Dec 30, 1959, v2, p296-97.
Films in Review. Oct 1959, v10, p495-96.
I Lost it at the Movies. p132-36.
The New York Times. Nov 24, 1959, p44.
Saturday Review. Sep 19, 1959, v42, p27.
Time. Jan 25, 1960, v75, p93.
Variety. Mar 4, 1959, p6.

The Cowboy (US; Williams, Elmo; 1954)
Catholic World. Jun 1954, v179, p223.
Commonweal. Aug 27, 1954, v60, p513.
Farm Journal. Jun 1954, v78, p141.
Film Daily. Jan 20, 1954, p7.
Films in Review. May 1954, v5, p240-41.
Films in Review. Aug-Sep 1954, v5, p347-49, 373.
Hollywood Reporter. Dec 31, 1953, p3.
The London Times. Mar 8, 1955, p4.
Motion Picture Herald Product Digest. Jan 9, 1954, p2134.
National Parent-Teacher. Jun 1954, v48, p38.
The New York Times. Aug 3, 1954, p14.
Newsweek. Apr 26, 1954, v43, p102.
Saturday Review. Aug 21, 1954, v37, p30.
Senior Scholastic. Sep 15, 1954, v65, p35.
Variety. Jan 20, 1954, p18.

Cowboy (US; Daves, Delmer; 1958)
America. Mar 1, 1958, v98, p643.
BFI/Monthly Film Bulletin. Mar 1958, v25, p31.
Commonweal. Mar 7, 1958, v67, p593.
Film Daily. Feb 13, 1958, p6.
Filmfacts. Mar 19, 1958, v1, p27-28.
Films in Review. Mar 1958, v9, p143.
The Films of Jack Lemmon. p86-90.
Hollywood Reporter. Feb 11, 1958, p3.
Library Journal. Mar 1, 1958, v33, p748.
The Los Angeles Times. Feb 9, 1958, SecV, p1.
Magill's Cinema Annual, 1982. p417-21.
The New York Times. Feb 20, 1958, p29.
The New Yorker. Mar 1, 1958, v34, p107.
Newsweek. Feb 17, 1958, v51, p106.
Saturday Review. Mar 1, 1958, v41, p26.
Time. Feb 17, 1958, v71, p64.
Variety. Feb 12, 1958, p6.

Crack in the Mirror (US; Fleischer, Richard; 1960)
America. Jun 4, 1960, v103, p342.
BFI/Monthly Film Bulletin. Jun 1960, v27, p83.
Commonweal. Jun 10, 1960, v72, p279.
Film Daily. May 11, 1960, p6.
Films and Filming. Jul 1960, v6, p24.
Films in Review. Jun-Jul 1960, v11, p358-59.
Hollywood Reporter. May 11, 1960, p3.
Life. May 23, 1960, v48, p81-82.
The New York Times. May 20, 1960, p26.
Newsweek. May 23, 1960, v55, p116.
Saturday Review. May 14, 1960, v43, p29.

Time. May 30, 1960, v75, p46.
Variety. May 11, 1960, p6.

Crack in the World (US; Marton, Andrew; 1965)
BFI/Monthly Film Bulletin. Apr 1965, v32, p56.
Film Daily. Feb 16, 1965, p4.
Films and Filming. Apr 1965, v11, p28-29.
Hollywood Reporter. Feb 9, 1965, p3.
The London Times. Mar 4, 1965, p17.
Motion Picture Herald Product Digest. Mar 3, 1965, p243.
New Statesman. Mar 12, 1965, v69, p413-14.
The New York Times. May 13, 1965, p32.
Variety. Feb 10, 1965, p7.
Vogue. May 1965, v145, p143.

Crackers (US; Malle, Louis; 1984)
BFI/Monthly Film Bulletin. Jan 1985, v52, p19.
Film Journal. Mar 1984, v87, p42-43.
Film Journal. Feb 1984, v87, p4.
Hollywood Reporter. Jan 25, 1984, p3.
The Los Angeles Times. Feb 17, 1984, SecVI, p15.
The New Republic. Mar 19, 1984, v190, p24-26.
The New York Times. Feb 17, 1984, SecIII, p19.
Saturday Review. Jan-Feb 1984, v10, p40-41.
Time. Feb 13, 1984, v123, p74.
Variety. Jan 25, 1984, p21.
The Village Voice. Feb 28, 1984, p57.

The Crash of Silence *See* Mandy

Craze (GB; Francis, Fred; 1974)
BFI/Monthly Film Bulletin. Jun 1974, v41, p123.
Cinefantastique. 1974, v3, n4, p32.
Hollywood Reporter. Jun 4, 1974, p3.
Independent Film Journal. Jul 24, 1974, v74, p15.
The Los Angeles Times. Jun 5, 1974, SecIV, p17.
Motion Picture Herald Product Digest. Jul 31, 1974, p20.
New Statesman. May 17, 1974, v87, p705-6.
PTA Magazine. Oct 1974, v69, p6.
Variety. Jun 12, 1974, p18.
The Village Voice. Aug 22, 1974, p79.

Crazy Joe (US; Lizzani, Carlo; 1974)
Atlantic. Feb 1974, v233, p92-93.
BFI/Monthly Film Bulletin. Nov 1974, v41, p248-49.
Films in Review. Apr 1974, v25, p249.
Independent Film Journal. Feb 18, 1974, v73, p10-11.
The Los Angeles Times. Mar 6, 1974, SecIV, p14.
Motion Picture Herald Product Digest. Feb 13, 1974, p76.
New York. Feb 18, 1974, v7, p74-75.
The New York Times. Feb 16, 1974, p36.
PTA Magazine. May 1974, v68, p6.
Time. Mar 11, 1974, v103, p80.
Variety. Feb 6, 1974, p18.
The Village Voice. Mar 28, 1974, p77-78.

Crazy Pete *See* Pierrot Le Fou

Crazy Quilt (US; Korty, John; 1966)
Catholic World. Feb 1967, v204, p301-06.
Film Daily. Oct 28, 1966, p7.
Film Quarterly. Spr 1967, v20, p32-33.
Film Quarterly. Spr 1966, v19, p20-25.
Filmfacts. Dec 1, 1966, v9, p270-71.
Motion Picture Herald Product Digest. Nov 9, 1966, p626-27.
The Nation. Oct 24, 1966, v203, p430.
The New York Times. Oct 4, 1966, p50.
The New Yorker. Oct 15, 1966, v42, p203-04.

Newsweek. Oct 10, 1966, v68, p114.
The Private Eye, the Cowboy and the Very Naked Girl. p231-32.
Senior Scholastic. Feb 3, 1967, v90, p18.
Time. Sep 16, 1966, v88, p117.
The Village Voice. Oct 13, 1966, p27.

Creature From the Black Lagoon (US; Arnold, Jack; 1954)
BFI/Monthly Film Bulletin. Jan 1955, v22, p7-8.
Classic Images. Jul 1982, n85, p23.
Commonweal. May 14, 1954, v60, p145.
Cue. May 1, 1954, p15.
Film Daily. Feb 18, 1954, p6.
The Films of the Fifties. p109-10.
Future Tense: The Cinema of Science Fiction. p99-100.
Hollywood Reporter. Feb 9, 1954, p3.
Journal of Popular Film. 1973, v2, n1, p14-28.
Magill's Cinema Annual, 1982. p422-25.
Motion Picture Herald Product Digest. Feb 13, 1954, p2182.
National Parent-Teacher. Apr 1954, v48, p38.
The New York Times. May 1, 1954, p13.
One Good Film Deserves Another. p79-83.
Science Fiction Gold. p123-34.
Selected Film Criticism, 1951-1960. p28-29.
Variety. Feb 10, 1954, p7.

Creepshow (US; Romero, George; 1982)
BFI/Monthly Film Bulletin. Nov 1982, v49, p260-61.
Esquire. Jan 1982, v97, p72-73.
Film Comment. Sep-Oct 1982, v18, p13-17.
Film Journal. Nov 19, 1982, v85, p52.
The New York Times. Nov 10, 1982, SecIII, p23.
The New York Times. Nov 7, 1982, SecII, p15.
Newsweek. Nov 22, 1982, v100, p118.
Time. Nov 22, 1982, v120, p110.
Variety. May 26, 1982, p17.
The Village Voice. Nov 23, 1982, p62.

Crest of the Wave (Also titled: Seagulls Over Sorrento) (GB; Boulting, John; Boulting, Roy; 1954)
America. Nov 20, 1954, v92, p222.
BFI/Monthly Film Bulletin. Aug 1954, v21, p116.
Farm Journal. Jan 1955, v79, p70.
Film Daily. Nov 12, 1954, p22.
The Films of Gene Kelly. p153-55.
Hollywood Reporter. Nov 10, 1954, p3.
Library Journal. Dec 15, 1954, v79, p2438.
The London Times. Jul 19, 1954, p11.
Motion Picture Herald Product Digest. Nov 13, 1954, p209-10.
National Parent-Teacher. Jan 1955, v49, p39.
The New York Times. Nov 11, 1954, p43.
The New Yorker. Nov 20, 1954, v30, p82.
Newsweek. Jan 3, 1955, v45, p45.
Saturday Review. Nov 27, 1954, v37, p28.
The Tatler. Jul 28, 1954, v213, p164.
Time. Nov 15, 1954, v64, p113.
Variety. Jul 21, 1954, p6.

Cries and Whispers (Swedish title: Viskningar och rop) (SWED; Bergman, Ingmar; 1973)
America. Jan 27, 1973, v128, p74-75.
American Scholar. Sum 1973, v42, p500-02.
Christian Century. Feb 21, 1973, v90, p238-39.
Commonweal. Apr 6, 1973, v98, p112-13.
Film Quarterly. Fall 1973, v27, p2-11.
The Films in My Life. p257-60.
Hollywood Reporter. Jan 9, 1973, p4.
Ingmar Bergman: A Critical Biography. p275-82.

Ingmar Bergman and the Rituals of Art. p52-242.
Ingmar Bergman: Essays in Criticism. p297-12.
National Review. Mar 2, 1973, v25, p266.
The New Republic. Feb 3, 1973, v168, p24.
The New York Times. Jan 14, 1973, SecII, p13.
The New York Times. May 27, 1973, SecII, p1.
The New York Times. Feb 17, 1974, SecII, p1.
The New York Times. Apr 3, 1974, p36.
Reeling. p132-39.
Reruns. p233-37.
Saturday Review. Feb 1973, v1, p72.
Variety. Dec 20, 1972, p18.
Women and their Sexuality in the New Film. p106-27.

Crimes of Passion (US; Russell, Ken; 1984)
America. Nov 24, 1984, v151, p345.
American Film. Nov 1984, v10, p24.
BFI/Monthly Film Bulletin. Sep 1985, v52, p274.
Film Journal. Dec 1984, v87, p18-19.
Films in Review. Jan 1985, v36, p50.
Hollywood Reporter. Oct 17, 1984, p3.
The Los Angeles Times. Oct 19, 1984, SecVI, p6.
Magill's Cinema Annual, 1985. p161-65.
New York. Nov 19, 1984, v17, p53-54.
The New York Times. Oct 19, 1984, SecIII, p19.
The New York Times. Nov 8, 1984, SecIII, p23.
Newsweek. Oct 29, 1984, v104, p134-35.
Time. Oct 29, 1984, v124, p102.
Variety. Sep 19, 1984, p23.
The Village Voice. Nov 6, 1984, p64.

The Criminal *See* Concrete Jungle

The Crimson Pirate (US; Siodmak, Robert; 1952)
BFI/Monthly Film Bulletin. Dec 1952, v19, p170.
Burt Lancaster: A Pictorial Treasury of His Films. p65-66.
Burt Lancaster: the Man and His Movies. p52-54.
Catholic World. Oct 1952, v176, p63.
Commonweal. Sep 12, 1952, v56, p559.
Film Criticism and Caricatures, 1943-53. p150-51.
Film Daily. Sep 2, 1952, p6.
The Films of the Fifties. p83-85.
Hollywood Reporter. Aug 27, 1952, p3.
Kiss Kiss Bang Bang. p312-13.
Magill's Survey of Cinema. Series II. v2, p545-47.
Motion Picture Herald Product Digest. Aug 30, 1952, p1509.
The New York Times. Aug 28, 1952, p21.
Newsweek. Sep 8, 1952, v40, p97-98.
Saturday Review. Aug 2, 1952, v35, p29.
The Tatler. Jan 7, 1953, v207, p24.
Time. Sep 15, 1952, v60, p106.
Variety. Aug 27, 1952, p6.

Crisis (US; Brooks, Richard; 1950)
BFI/Monthly Film Bulletin. Dec 1950, v17, p183.
Christian Century. Aug 16, 1950, v67, p983.
Commonweal. Jul 14, 1950, v52, p346.
Film Daily. Jun 19, 1950, p6.
The Films of Cary Grant. p203-05.
Hollywood Reporter. Jun 16, 1950, p3.
Motion Picture Herald Product Digest. Jun 17, 1950, p346.
The New Republic. Jul 24, 1950, v123, p22-23.
The New Statesman and Nation. Dec 2, 1950, v40, p542.
The New York Times. Jul 4, 1950, p10.
The New Yorker. Jul 15, 1950, v26, p57.
Newsweek. Jul 10, 1950, v36, p85.
Sight and Sound. Dec 1950, v19, p334.

The Spectator. Dec 1, 1950, v185, p613.
Time. Jul 17, 1950, v56, p92.
Variety. Jun 21, 1950, p8.
The World of Entertainment. p284-89.

Cristo Proibito, Il *See* Strange Deception

Cristo Si è Fermato a Eboli *See* Eboli

Critic's Choice (US; Weis, Don; 1963)
America. May 11, 1963, v108, p692.
BFI/Monthly Film Bulletin. Mar 1963, v30, p36-37.
Commonweal. Apr 19, 1963, v78, p106.
Film Daily. Mar 29, 1963, p6.
Filmfacts. Apr 18, 1963, v6, p59-60.
Films and Filming. Mar 1963, v9, p40.
Hollywood Reporter. Mar 29, 1963, p3.
Illustrated London News. Feb 16, 1963, v242, p242.
The New York Times. May 2, 1963, p2.
Newsweek. Apr 15, 1963, v61, p104.
Photoplay. May 1963, v63, p6.
Saturday Review. Mar 2, 1963, v46, p31.
Variety. May 3, 1963, p6.

Cronaca di un Amore *See* Story of a Love Affair

Cronaca Familiare *See* Family Diary

The Crook (French title: Voyou, Le (The Hoodlum); Also titled: Simon the Swiss) (FR; Lelouch, Claude; 1971)
BFI/Monthly Film Bulletin. Apr 1971, v38, n447, p85.
Filmfacts. 1971, v14, n15, p379-81.
Films and Filming. Jun 1971, v17, n9, p74.
Hollywood Reporter. May 3, 1971, v216, n4, p3.
The New York Times. Jun 21, 1971, p38.
The New Yorker. Jun 26, 1971, v47, p85-86.
Newsweek. Jun 7, 1971, v77, p106.
The Village Voice. Jul 29, 1971, v16, n30, p51.

Cross Creek (US; Ritt, Martin; 1983)
Christian Century. Nov 9, 1983, v100, p1022-23.
Hollywood Reporter. Jun 14, 1983, p3.
Horizon. Oct 1983, v26, p44-47.
The Los Angeles Times. Sep 30, 1983, SecVI, p1.
Maclean's. Oct 10, 1983, v96, p56.
Magill's Cinema Annual, 1984. p116-20.
New York. Oct 3, 1983, v16, p88.
The New York Times. Sep 21, 1983, SecIII, p19.
The New Yorker. Oct 3, 1983, v59, p104.
Time. Sep 26, 1983, v122, p77.
Variety. May 25, 1983, p19.

Cross of Iron (GB, WGER; Peckinpah, Sam; 1977)
America. Jun 11, 1977, v136, p528.
BFI/Monthly Film Bulletin. Mar 1977, v44, p40.
Films in Review. Aug-Sep 1977, v28, p441.
Hollywood Reporter. May 3, 1977, p3.
The Los Angeles Times. May 20, 1977, SecIV, p18.
Motion Picture Herald Product Digest. May 25, 1977, p97.
The New Republic. May 28, 1977, v176, p26.
The New York Times. May 12, 1977, SecIII, p22.
The New Yorker. May 23, 1977, v53, p110-11.
Newsweek. May 23, 1977, v89, p73.
Sam Peckinpah (McKinney). p203-14.
Saturday Review. Jun 11, 1977, v4, p45.
Time. Jun 13, 1977, v109, p94.
Variety. Feb 9, 1977, p22.

Crossed Swords (Italian title: Maestro di Don Giovanni, Il) (IT, US; Krims, Milton; 1954)

BFI/Monthly Film Bulletin. Aug 1954, v21, p120.
Film Daily. Jul 28, 1954, p6.
Films in Review. Dec 1954, v5, p544.
The Films of Errol Flynn. p195-96.
Hollywood Reporter. Jul 28, 1954, p3.
Motion Picture Herald Product Digest. Jul 31, 1954, p89.
National Parent-Teacher. Nov 1954, v49, p39.
Variety. Jul 28, 1954, p6.

The Cruel Sea (GB; Balcon, Michael; 1952)
America. Aug 22, 1953, v89, p506.
BFI/Monthly Film Bulletin. May 1953, v20, p65.
Commonweal. Aug 28, 1953, v58, p520.
Farm Journal. Aug 1953, v77, p107.
Film Daily. Aug 10, 1953, p6.
Films in Review. Jun-Jul 1953, v4, p301-02.
Hollywood Reporter. Oct 14, 1953, p3.
Library Journal. Aug 1953, v78, p1321.
Life. Sep 21, 1953, v35, p73-74.
Magill's Survey of Cinema. Series II. v2, p251-54.
The Nation. Aug 29, 1953, v177, p178.
National Parent-Teacher. Oct 1953, v48, p39.
The New York Times. Aug 11, 1953, p1.
The New York Times. Aug 16, 1953, SecII, p1.
The New York Times Magazine. Apr 26, 1953, p42.
The New Yorker. Aug 15, 1953, v29, p56.
Newsweek. Aug 17, 1953, v42, p88.
Saturday Review. Aug 22, 1953, v36, p26.
Saturday Review. Jan 8, 1955, v38, p29.
Senior Scholastic. Sep 23, 1953, v63, p38.
Time. Aug 24, 1953, v62, p64.
Variety. Apr 1, 1953, p6.

Cruising (US; Friedkin, William; 1980)
Christian Century. Apr 9, 1980, v97, p420.
Films in Review. Apr 1980, v31, p242.
Hollywood Reporter. Feb 12, 1980, p3.
The Los Angeles Times. Feb 10, 1980, Calendar, p1.
Maclean's. Feb 25, 1980, v93, p53.
Motion Picture Herald Product Digest. Mar 12, 1980, p78.
The Nation. Feb 23, 1980, v230, p218.
National Catholic Reporter. Mar 28, 1980, v16, p16.
The New Republic. Mar 15, 1980, v182, p24.
New Statesman. Sep 12, 1980, v100, p24.
New West. Mar 10, 1980, v5, p66-68.
New York. Mar 3, 1980, v13, p72-73.
The New Yorker. Feb 18, 1980, v55, p126-27.
Newsday. Feb 15, 1980, SecII, p7.
Newsweek. Feb 18, 1980, v95, p92.
Philadelphia Magazine. Apr 1980, v71, p62.
Playboy. May 1980, v27, p43.
Progressive. May 1980, v44, p54.
Time. Feb 18, 1980, v115, p67.
Variety. Feb 13, 1980, p16.
The Village Voice. Feb 18, 1980, p47.

The Cry (Antonioni, 1957) *See* Grido, Il

The Cry (Czech title: Krik; Also titled: The First Cry) (CZECH; Jeres, Jaromil; 1963)
BFI/Monthly Film Bulletin. Dec 1966, v33, p179.
The Czechoslovak New Wave. p93-99.
Films and Filming. Dec 1966, v13, p6, 8.
The London Times. Oct 13, 1966, p18.
Movies Into Film. p283-85.
New Statesman. Oct 21, 1966, v72, p599.
Variety. May 13, 1964, p19.

Cry Danger (US; Parrish, Richard; 1951)
BFI/Monthly Film Bulletin. Dec 1951, v18, p375.

Christian Century. Mar 14, 1951, v68, p351.
Commonweal. Feb 9, 1951, v53, p448.
Film Daily. Feb 2, 1951, p10.
Hollywood Reporter. Jan 31, 1951, p3.
Motion Picture Herald Product Digest. Feb 10, 1951, p706.
The New York Times. Feb 22, 1951, p27.
The New Yorker. Mar 3, 1951, v27, p94.
Newsweek. Mar 5, 1951, v37, p86-87.
Time. Feb 26, 1951, v57, p103.
Variety. Feb 7, 1951, p6.

Cry, the Beloved Country (Also titled: African Fury) (GB; Korda, Zoltan; 1952)
BFI/Monthly Film Bulletin. May 1952, v19, p60.
Catholic World. Mar 1952, v174, p457.
Christian Century. Oct 15, 1952, v69, p1207.
Commonweal. Feb 8, 1952, v55, p446.
The Evolution of Character Portrayals in the Films of Sidney Poitier, 1950-1978. p35-36.
Film Criticism and Caricatures, 1943-1953. p143-44.
Film Daily. Jan 24, 1952, p 6.
Films in Review. Jan 1952, v3, p42.
The Films of Sidney Poitier. p47-50.
From Sambo to Superspade. p167-69.
Holiday. May 1952, v11, p105.
Hollywood Reporter. Sep 18, 1952, p4.
Illustrated London News. May 17, 1952, v220, p852.
Library Journal. Feb 15, 1952, v77, p311.
The London Times. Jul 12, 1950, p8.
Magill's Survey of Cinema. Series II. v2, p554-56.
Motion Picture Herald Product Digest. Jan 26, 1952, p1213.
The New Republic. Feb 11, 1952, v126, p21-22.
The New Statesman and Nation. May 3, 1952, v43, p525.
The New York Times. Jan 24, 1952, p23.
The New York Times Magazine. Jan 20, 1952, p22-23.
The New Yorker. Feb 2, 1952, v27, p53.
Newsweek. Jan 28, 1952, v39, p89.
Saturday Review. Feb 2, 1952, v35, p31.
The Spectator. Apr 25, 1952, v188, p545.
Time. Feb 18, 1952, v59, p86.
Variety. Jan 23, 1952, p6.

Cul-De-Sac (GB; Polanski, Roman; 1966)
BFI/Monthly Film Bulletin. Jul 1966, v33, p103.
Cinema. Mar 1966, v3, p13-14.
The Cinema of Roman Polanski. p83-116.
Commonweal. Nov 25, 1966, v85, p230.
Dictionary of Films. p75.
Esquire. Mar 1967, v67, p20-21.
Filmfacts. Jan 1, 1967, v9, p319-20.
Films and Filming. Jul 1966, v12, p18, 51-52.
International Film Guide. 1966, v3, p84.
International Film Guide. 1967, v4, p87.
Life. Dec 9, 1966, v61, p19.
The London Times. Jun 2, 1966, p19.
The London Times. Jun 5, 1966, p25.
Magill's Survey of Cinema. Series II. v2, p557-59.
Motion Picture Herald Product Digest. Nov 23, 1966, p632.
New Statesman. Jun 10, 1966, v71, p853.
The New York Times. Nov 8, 1966, p44.
The New York Times. Nov 20, 1966, p1.
The New Yorker. Nov 12, 1966, v42, p115.
Newsweek. Nov 21, 1966, v68, p129-30.
The Observer. Jun 5, 1966, p24.
Playboy. Feb 1967, v14, p22.
Polanski (Leaming). p66-73.

The Private Eye, the Cowboy and the Very Naked Girl. p209-10.
Private Screenings. p290-91.
Roman Polanski: A Guide to References and Resources. p21-23.
Roman Polanski (Wexman). p32-37.
Saturday Review. Dec 10, 1966, v49, p65.
Screen. Nov-Dec 1970, v11, p44-60.
Sight and Sound. Sum 1966, v35, p146-47.
The Spectator. Jun 3, 1966, v216, p695.
Take One. Jun 1967, v1, p28-30.
Time. Nov 18, 1966, v88, p122-24.
Variety. Jun 8, 1966, p6.
The Village Voice. Dec 1, 1966, v12, p27, 29.

Cure et le Bon Dieu, La *See* Jessica

Curée, La *See* The Game Is Over

The Curse of Frankenstein (GB; Fisher, Terence; 1957)
BFI/Monthly Film Bulletin. Jun 1957, v24, p70.
Film Daily. Jun 25, 1957, v111, p14.
Films and Filming. Jul 1957, v3, p24.
Hollywood Reporter. Jun 19, 1957, p3.
Motion Picture Herald Product Digest. Jun 22, 1957, p426.
The New York Times. Aug 8, 1957, p15.
One Good Film Deserves Another. p94-101.
Variety. May 15, 1957, p22.

Curtain Up (GB; Smart, Ralph; 1952)
BFI/Monthly Film Bulletin. Jun 1952, v19, p79.
Catholic World. Jan 1953, v176, p303.
Commonweal. Jan 15, 1953, v57, p378.
The Nation. Feb 14, 1953, v176, p153.
The New York Times. Feb 2, 1953, p17.
Saturday Review. Dec 20, 1952, v35 p28.
The Spectator. May 9, 1952, v188, p610.
Theatre Arts. Jan 1953, v37, p84.
Time. Feb 16, 1953, v61, p108.
Variety. May 14, 1952, p20.

Cutter's Way (Also titled: Cutter and Bone) (US; Passer, Ivan; 1981)
Film Comment. Jul-Aug 1981, v17, p18-23.
Hollywood Reporter. May 18, 1981, p3.
The Los Angeles Times. Sep 13, 1981, Calendar, p30.
Maclean's. Oct 12, 1981, v94, p68.
Magill's Cinema Annual, 1982. p119-24.
The Nation. Apr 18, 1981, v232, p476-77.
The New Republic. Aug 15, 1981, v185, p26-27.
New York. Apr 6, 1981, v14, p56.
The New York Times. Mar 20, 1981, SecIII, p6.
Newsweek. Apr 6, 1981, v97, p103.
Progressive. Sep 1981, v45, p54-55.
Time. Apr 6, 1981, v117, p68.

Cybels, ou Les Dimanches de Ville D'Avray *See* Sundays & Cybele

Cyrano de Bergerac (US; Gordon, Michael; 1950)
BFI/Monthly Film Bulletin. Oct 1951, v18, p338-39.
Christian Century. Feb 7, 1951, v68, p191.
Commonweal. Nov 24, 1950, v53, p172.
Film Daily. Nov 14, 1950, p6.
Film News. Mar-Apr 1976, v33, p27.
Films in Review. Dec 1950, v1, p39-40.
Harper's Magazine. Jan 1951, v202, p103-04.
Hollywood Reporter. Nov 14, 1950, p3.
Illustrated London News. Oct 20, 1951, v219, p640.
Journal of Popular Film. n1, 1976, v5, p68-75.
Library Journal. Dec 1, 1950, v75, p2086.
Life. Nov 20, 1950, v29, p73-75.
Magill's Survey of Cinema. Series I. v1, p400-03.
Motion Picture Herald Product Digest. Nov 18, 1950, p569.

The New Republic. Dec 4, 1950, v123, p22.
The New Statesman and Nation. Oct 6, 1951, v42, p365.
The New York Times. Nov 17, 1950, p31.
The New Yorker. Nov 18, 1950, v26, p157.
Newsweek. Nov 27, 1950, v36, p84.
Quarterly of Film, Radio and Television. Wint 1951, v6, p186-90.
Saturday Review. Nov 18, 1950, v33, p32.
Senior Scholastic. Dec 13, 1950, v57, p22.
Sight and Sound. Oct-Dec 1951, v21, p81-82.
The Spectator. Sep 28, 1951, v187, p393.
Stanley Kramer, Film Maker. p65-72.
Theatre Arts. Nov 1950, v34, p32-35.
Time. Nov 20, 1950, v56, p103.
Variety. Nov 15, 1950, p6.

Czlowiek z Marmuru *See* Man of Marble

The D.I. (US; Webb, Jack; 1957)
America. Jun 22, 1957, v97, p352.
BFI/Monthly Film Bulletin. Oct 1957, v24, p127.
Commonweal. Jun 21, 1957, v66, p303.
Film Daily. May 27, 1957, p6.
Films in Review. Aug-Sep 1957, v8, p355-56.
Motion Picture Herald Product Digest. Jun 1, 1957, p402.
The New York Times. Jun 6, 1957, p35.
The New Yorker. Jun 15, 1957, v33, p72.
Newsweek. Jun 10, 1957, v49, p114.
Saturday Review. Jun 8, 1957, v40, p30.
Time. Jun 17, 1957, v69, p96.
Variety. May 29, 1957, p6.

Daddy Long Legs (US; Negulesco, Jean; 1955)
America. May 21, 1955, v93, p223.
Catholic World. Jun 1955, v181, p223.
Commonweal. May 27, 1955, v62, p207.
Film Culture. Sum 1955, v1, p26.
Film Daily. May 4, 1955, p6.
Films and Filming. Aug 1955, v1, p17.
Films in Review. Jun-Jul 1955, v6, p289-90.
Hollywood Reporter. May 4, 1955, p3.
Library Journal. Jun 1, 1955, v80, p1321.
Life. May 23, 1955, v38, p78-82.
Magill's Survey of Cinema. Series I. v1, p404-08.
The New York Times. May 6, 1955, p17-18.
The New Yorker. May 14, 1955, v31, p145.
Newsweek. May 16, 1955, v45, p113.
Saturday Review. May 21, 1955, v38, p45.
Starring Fred Astaire. p39-46.
Time. May 9, 1955, v65, p106.
Variety. May 4, 1955, p6.

Daisies *See* Sedmikrasky

Daisy Miller (US; Bogdanovich, Peter; 1974)
Audience. Jul 1974, v7, p2-4.
BFI/Monthly Film Bulletin. Oct 1974, v41, p222.
The Classic American Novel and the Cinema. p83-94.
Commonweal. Jun 28, 1974, v100, p361-62.
Double Exposure. p145-53.
Esquire. Aug 1974, v82, p9-10.
Film. Sep 1974, n18, p19.
Film Heritage. n1, 1974, v10, p43-44.
Films and Filming. Nov 1974, v21, p33-34.
Films Illustrated. Sep 1974, v4, p6.
Films in Review. Aug-Sep 1974, v25, p437-38.
Hollywood Reporter. May 17, 1974, p3.
Independent Film Journal. May 29, 1974, v73, p9-10.
The Los Angeles Times. Jul 3, 1974, SecIV, p1.
Motion Picture Herald Product Digest. May 22, 1974, p102.
Movietone News. Jul 1974, n33, p13-16.

The Nation. Jun 15, 1974, v218, p762.
National Review. Aug 30, 1974, v26, p983-84.
The New Republic. Jun 8, 1974, v170, p20.
New Statesman. Oct 4, 1974, v88, p479-80.
New York. May 27, 1974, v7, p90-91.
The New York Times. Jun 30, 1974, SecII, p15.
The New York Times. Jun 16, 1974, SecII, p1.
The New Yorker. May 27, 1974, v50, p69-70.
Newsweek. May 27, 1974, v83, p81.
Partisan Review. Fall 1974, v41, p450-54.
Penthouse. Oct 1974, v6, p37.
PTA Magazine. Sep 1974, v69, p10.
Rolling Stone. Jun 20, 1974, p92.
Saturday Review. Jun 29, 1974, v69, p10.
Sight and Sound. Wint 1973-1974, v43, p12-15.
Sight and Sound. Fall 1974, v43, p247.
Time. Jun 3, 1974, v103, p56.
Variety. May 22, 1974, p18.
The Village Voice. Jun 27, 1974, p79-80.
The Village Voice. Jul 11-17, 1974, p71-72.

Daleka Cesta *See* Distant Journey

Dallas (US; Heisler, Stuart; 1950)
BFI/Monthly Film Bulletin. Sep 1951, v18, p329.
Christian Century. Feb 28, 1951, v68, p287.
Commonweal. Jan 26, 1951, v53, p399.
Film Daily. Nov 22, 1950, p6.
The Films of Gary Cooper. p225-26.
Hollywood Reporter. Nov 21, 1950, p3.
Motion Picture Herald Product Digest. Nov 25, 1950, p589.
The New Statesman and Nation. Oct 20, 1951, v42, p434-35.
The New York Times. Jan 13, 1951, p10.
Saturday Review. Feb 17, 1951, v34, p31.
Time. Jan 22, 1951, v57, p92.
Variety. Nov 22, 1950, p8.

Dam Busters (GB; Anderson, Michael; 1955)
America. Sep 17, 1955, v93, p603.
BFI/Monthly Film Bulletin. Jun 1955, v22, p82.
Catholic World. Aug 1955, v181, p383.
Commonweal. Sep 30, 1955, v62, p647.
Film Daily. Jun 29, 1955, p7.
Hollywood Reporter. Jun 22, 1955, p3.
The New York Times. Nov 21, 1955, SecII, p5.
Time. Aug 22, 1955, v66, p82.
Variety. Jun 1, 1955, p6.

Dames du Bois de Boulogne, Les (Also titled: The Ladies of the Bois de Boulogne) (FR; Bresson, Robert; 1946)
BFI/Monthly Film Bulletin. Mar 1966, v33, p36.
Cinema Eye, Cinema Ear. p124-28.
Confessions of a Cultist. p133-35.
Film Culture. 1959, n20, p44-52.
The Films in My Life. p188-90.
The Films of Robert Bresson. p33-41.
The London Times. Jun 17, 1965, p17.
New Statesman. Jun 25, 1965, v69, p1021.
The New York Times. Apr 4, 1964, p15.
Sequence. New Year 1951, n13, p41-43.
Sight and Sound. Spr 1962, v31, p84-88.
The Spectator. Jun 25, 1965, v214, p821.
Variety. Mar 11, 1964, p6.
The Village Voice. Apr 16, 1964, p13.

Damien-The Omen II (US; Taylor, Don; 1978)
BFI/Monthly Film Bulletin. Dec 1978, v45, p237.
Christian Century. Aug 30, 1978, v95, p803.
Films in Review. Aug-Sep 1978, v29, p438.
Hollywood Reporter. Jun 5, 1978, p3.
The Los Angeles Times. Jun 9, 1978, SecIV, p1.
Motion Picture Herald Product Digest. Jun 7, 1978, p1.

New Times. Aug 7, 1978, v11, p58.
The New York Times. Jun 9, 1978, SecIII, p6.
The New York Times. Jun 18, 1978, SecII, p17.
The New Yorker. Jun 19, 1978, v54, p85-86.
Newsweek. Jun 19, 1978, v91, p75-76.
Time. Jun 12, 1978, v111, p90.

Damn the Defiant! (Also titled: H.M.S. Defiant) (GB; Gilbert, Lewis; 1962)
America. Sep 29, 1962, v107, p823-24.
BFI/Monthly Film Bulletin. Apr 1962, v29, p46-47.
Film Daily. Aug 10, 1962, v10, p4.
Filmfacts. Sep 28, 1962, v5, p211-12.
Films and Filming. Apr 1962, v8, p33.
Films in Review. Oct 1962, v13, p488.
The Films of Dirk Bogarde. p128-30.
Hollywood Reporter. Aug 6, 1962, v6, p3.
Motion Picture Herald Product Digest. Aug 22, 1962, p641.
The New York Times. Sep 20, 1962, p29.
The New Yorker. Sep 24, 1962, v38, p141.
Newsweek. Sep 24, 1962, v60, p92.

Damn Yankees (Also titled: What Lola Wants) (US; Abbott, George; 1958)
America. Oct 25, 1958, v100, p119.
BFI/Monthly Film Bulletin. Dec 1958, v25, p152.
Catholic World. Nov 1958, v188, p154.
Commonweal. Oct 17, 1958, v69, p73.
Dance Magazine. Oct 1958, v32, p13-14.
Film Daily. Sep 11, 1958, v114, p6.
Filmfacts. Nov 5, 1958, v1, p179-80.
Films in Review. Oct 1958, v9, p456.
Hollywood Reporter. Sep 11, 1958, p3.
Library Journal. Oct 15, 1958, v83, p2825.
The Musical from Broadway to Hollywood. p70-73.
The New York Times. Sep 27, 1958, p12.
The New Yorker. Oct 4, 1958, v34, p158.
Newsweek. Sep 29, 1958, v52, p94.
Saturday Review. Sep 27, 1958, v41, p26.
Senior Scholastic. Oct 17, 1958, v73, p27.
Stanley Donen (Casper). p131-39.
Time. Sep 29, 1958, v72, p69.
Variety. Sep 17, 1958, p6.

The Damned (Also titled: Goetterdaemmerung; Caduta degli Dei, La) (WGER, IT; Visconti, Luchino; 1969)
America. Dec 27, 1969, v121, p642.
Deeper Into Movies. p108-10.
Dictionary of Films. p50.
Film 70/71. p184-87, 189-90.
Film Society Review. Feb 1970, v5, p32-35.
Films and Filming. May 1970, v16, p37-38.
Films in Review. Feb 1970, v21, p120-21.
The Films of Dirk Bogarde. p181-84.
The International Dictionary of Films and Filmmakers. v1, p75-76.
International Film Guide. 1971, v8, p181-82.
Movies Into Film. p190-96.
The New York Times. Dec 19, 1969, p67.
The New York Times. Dec 21, 1969, SecII, p3.
The New Yorker. Jan 3, 1970, v45, p61-62.
Popular Photography. Oct 1969, v45, p117.
Saturday Review. Dec 27, 1969, v52, p21.
Screen. Sum 1970, v11, p44-56.
Second Sight. p289-93.
Sight and Sound. Wint 1969-70, v39, p48-49.
Take One. 1970, v2, p29-30.
Time. Jan 5, 1970, v95, p53.
Variety. Jun 25, 1969, p6.

The Damned (Losey, 1961) *See* These Are the Damned

The Damned Don't Cry (US; Sherman, Vincent; 1950)

BFI/Monthly Film Bulletin. Sep 1950, v17, p139.
Christian Century. May 31, 1950, v67, p687.
Commonweal. May 12, 1950, v52, p127.
Film Daily. Apr 11, 1950, p6.
The Films of Joan Crawford. p173-75.
The Great Gangster Pictures. p96-97.
Hollywood Reporter. Apr 6, 1950, p3.
The London Times. Jul 31, 1950, p2.
Motion Picture Herald Product Digest. Apr 15, 1950, p263.
The New York Times. Apr 8, 1950, p9.
The New Yorker. Apr 15, 1950, v26, p100.
Newsweek. Apr 17, 1950, v35, p96.
Time. Apr 17, 1950, v55, p106.
Variety. Apr 12, 1950, p6.

Dance With a Stranger (GB; Newell, Mike; 1984)
BFI/Monthly Film Bulletin. Mar 1985, v52, p82.
Commonweal. Nov 1, 1985, v112, p608.
Hollywood Reporter. Aug 6, 1985, p3.
The Los Angeles Times. Aug 14, 1985, SecVI, p1.
Maclean's. Sep 30, 1985, v98, p88.
Magill's Cinema Annual, 1986. p125-27.
Ms. Aug 1985, v14, p72-73.
The Nation. Nov 30, 1985, v241, p595-96.
National Review. Oct 18, 1985, v37, p59.
The New Leader. Oct 21, 1985, v68, p20-21.
The New Republic. Sep 9, 1985, v193, p22.
New York. Aug 19, 1985, v18, p81-82.
The New York Times. Aug 9, 1985, SecIII, p12.
The New Yorker. Aug 26, 1985, v61, p63-65.
Newsweek. Aug 5, 1985, v106, p64.
Time. Aug 19, 1985, v126, p70-71.
Vogue. Jul 1985, v175, p30.
The Wall Street Journal. Aug 1, 1985, p17.

A Dandy in Aspic (US; Mann, Anthony; 1968)
Anthony Mann (Basinger). p31-32.
BFI/Monthly Film Bulletin. May 1968, v35, p71-72.
Christian Century. Jun 5, 1968, v85 p761-62.
Commonweal. Apr 19, 1968, v88, p146.
Film Daily. Apr 2, 1968, p6.
Film Quarterly. Fall 1968, v22, p72-73.
Filmfacts. May 15, 1968, v11, p124-26.
Films and Filming. Jul 1968, v14, p35.
Films in Review. May 1968, v19, p311-12.
Hollywood Reporter. Apr 1, 1968, p3.
Life. Mar 29, 1968, v64, p15.
The London Times. Apr 4, 1968, p11.
Motion Picture Herald Product Digest. Apr 10, 1968, p794-95.
New Statesman. Apr 12, 1968, v75, p494-95.
The New York Times. Apr 3, 1968, p40.
Senior Scholastic. Apr 11, 1968, v92, p26.
The Spectator. Apr 12, 1968, v220, p501.
Time. Apr 12, 1968, v91, pE3.
Variety. Apr 3, 1968, p22.
A Year In the Dark. p101-02.

Dangerous Mission (US; King, Louis; 1954)
America. Mar 27, 1954, v90, p694.
BFI/Monthly Film Bulletin. Jul 1954, v21, p103-04.
Film Daily. Feb 25, 1954, p10.
Hollywood Reporter. Feb 24, 1954, p3.
The London Times. Jun 14, 1954, p5.
Motion Picture Herald Product Digest. Feb 27, 1954, p2197.
National Parent-Teacher. May 1954, v48, p39.
The New York Times. Mar 6, 1954, p13.
The New Yorker. Mar 13, 1954, v30, p124.
Time. Mar 22, 1954, v63, p113.

Variety. Feb 24, 1954, p6.
Vincent Price Unmasked. p191-92.

Dangerous Moves (Also titled: Diagonale du Fou, La) (SWITZ; Dembo, Richard; 1985)
BFI/Monthly Film Bulletin. Mar 1986, v53, p77.
Films in Review. Aug 1985, v36, p424.
Hollywood Reporter. May 31, 1985, p3.
The Los Angeles Times. May 24, 1985, SecVI, p4.
Magill's Cinema Annual, 1986. p129-31.
New York. May 27, 1985, v18, p98.
The New York Times. May 24, 1985, SecIII, p10.
The New Yorker. Jun 3, 1985, v61, p119.
Variety. Apr 3, 1985, p15.

Daniel (US; Lumet, Sidney; 1983)
BFI/Monthly Film Bulletin. Sep 1983, v50, p242-43.
Films in Review. Oct 1983, v34, p500-01.
Hollywood Reporter. Aug 24, 1983, p3.
Horizon. Sep 1983, v26, p45-49.
The Los Angeles Times. Sep 23, 1983, SecVI, p1.
Maclean's. Oct 3, 1983, v96, p61.
Ms. Nov 1983, v12, p38.
The Nation. Oct 1, 1983, v237, p283-85.
National Review. Oct 14, 1983, v35, p1294.
The New Leader. Oct 3, 1983, v66, p20-21.
The New Republic. Sep 12, 1983, v189, p24-25.
New York. Sep 5, 1983, v16, p49-50.
The New York Times. Sep 4, 1983, SecII, p11.
The New Yorker. Sep 5, 1983, v59, p109-11.
Newsweek. Aug 29, 1983, v102, p65.
Progressive. Nov 1983, v47, p36.
Theatre Crafts. Nov-Dec 1983, v17, p28-31.
Time. Aug 29, 1983, v122, p61.
Variety. Aug 24, 1983, p14.
Vogue. Aug 1983, v173, p318-21.

Danton (POL, FR; Wajda, Andrzej; 1982)
American Film. Oct 1983, v9, p24.
Film Comment. Nov-Dec 1983, v19, p71-72.
Hollywood Reporter. Oct 5, 1983, p9.
The Los Angeles Times. Oct 14, 1983, SecVI, p2.
Magill's Cinema Annual, 1984. p121-25.
The Nation. Mar 12, 1983, v236, p297-99.
National Review. Nov 25, 1983, v35, p1496-98.
The New Republic. Oct 17, 1983, v189, p24-26.
New York. Oct 10, 1983, v16, p87-88.
The New York Times. Sep 28, 1983, SecIII, p19.
The New Yorker. Feb 28, 1983, v59, p104-06.
Newsweek. Oct 10, 1983, v102, p94.
Progressive. Oct 1983, v47, p36.
Sight and Sound. Aut 1983, v52, p284.
Time. Sep 26, 1983, v122, p76.
Vogue. Oct 1983, v173, p92.
Working Press Review. Mar 1983, v30, p61.

Dark at the Top of the Stairs (US; Mann, Delbert; 1960)
America. Oct 8, 1960, v104, p56.
BFI/Monthly Film Bulletin. Nov 1960, v27, p150.
Commonweal. Oct 14, 1960, v73, p73-74.
Film Daily. Sep 15, 1960, p3.
Films and Filming. Nov 1960, v7, p29.
Films in Review. Oct 1960, v11, p485-86.
Hollywood Reporter. Sep 12, 1960, p3.
Motion Picture Herald Product Digest. Sep 17, 1960, p844.
The New York Times. Sep 23, 1960, p33.
The New York Times. Sep 25, 1960, SecII, p1.
The New Yorker. Oct 1, 1960, v36, p167.
Newsweek. Sep 26, 1960, v56, p119.
Saturday Review. Sep 17, 1960, v43, p44.

Time. Sep 12, 1960, v76, p80.
Variety. Sep 14, 1960, p6.

Dark City (US; Dieterle, William; 1950)
BFI/Monthly Film Bulletin. Apr 1951, v18, p249.
Commonweal. Nov 19, 1950, v53, p122.
Dark City: The Film Noir. p101-05.
Film Daily. Aug 8, 1950, p12.
The Films of Charlton Heston. p25-27.
The Great Gangster Pictures. p99-100.
Hollywood Reporter. Aug 8, 1950, p3.
Motion Picture Herald Product Digest. Aug 12, 1950, p433.
The New York Times. Oct 19, 1950, p40.
Newsweek. Apr 10, 1950, v36, p82.
The Spectator. Apr 6, 1951, v186, p444.
Time. Nov 6, 1950, v56, p106.
Variety. Aug 9, 1950, p8.

The Dark Crystal (GB; Henson, Jim; 1982)
Hollywood Reporter. Dec 17, 1982, p3.
The Los Angeles Times. Dec 17, 1982, SecVI, p10.
Maclean's. Dec 27, 1982, v95, p46.
Magill's Cinema Annual, 1983. p130-33.
The New York Times. Dec 12, 1982, SecII, p21.
Newsweek. Dec 27, 1982, v100, p61.
Rolling Stone. Feb 23, 1983, p34.
Senior Scholastic. Dec 10, 1982, v115-22.
Time. Jan 1, 1983, v121, p82.
Variety. Dec 15, 1982, p3.

The Dark Page *See* Scandal Sheet

Darling (GB; Schlesinger, John; 1965)
America. Aug 21, 1965, v113, p190-91.
BFI/Monthly Film Bulletin. Sep 1965, v32, p132.
Catholic World. Dec 1965, v202, p190-92.
Christian Century. Jan 5, 1966, v83, p17.
Christian Science Monitor (Western edition). Sep 2, 1965, p4.
Commonweal. Aug 20, 1965, v82, p598.
Dictionary of Films. p78-79.
Esquire. Nov 1965, v64, p32, 34.
Film Quarterly. Spr 1966, v19, p40-41.
Films and Filming. Oct 1965, v12, p24.
Films and Filming. Apr 1965, v11, p52.
Films and Filming. Aug 1965, v11, p40-41.
The Films of Dirk Bogarde. p156-59.
The Films of the Sixties. p150-51.
Hollywood Reporter. Aug 4, 1965, p3.
ims in Review. Oct 1965, v16, p514-15.
John Schlesinger: A Guide to References and Resources. p45-46.
John Schlesinger (Phillips). p63-76.
Kiss Kiss Bang Bang. p193-94.
Life. Aug 27, 1965, v59, p10.
London Magazine. Nov 1965, v5, p63-65.
The London Times. Sep 16, 1965, p16.
Mademoiselle. Oct 1965, v61, p62.
Magill's Survey of Cinema. Series I. v1, p412-15.
Motion Picture Herald Product Digest. Aug 4, 1965, p337-38.
Movie. Aug 1965, n14, p45.
The Nation. Aug 30, 1965, v201, p108.
The New Republic. Sep 4, 1965, v153, p29-31.
The New Republic. Sep 25, 1965, v153, p37-38.
New Statesman. Sep 17, 1965, v70, p409.
The New York Times. Aug 4, 1965, p20.
The New Yorker. Aug 7, 1965, v41, p66.
Newsweek. Aug 16, 1965, v66, p79.
Playboy. Nov 1965, v12, p52.
Saturday Review. Aug 21, 1965, v48, p40.
Screen. 1985, v26, n1, p50-65.
Second Sight. p39-42.
Senior Scholastic. Oct 14, 1965, v87, sup18.
Sight and Sound. Aug 1965, v34, p196.
The Spectator. Sep 17, 1965, v215, p351-52.

Time. Aug 13, 1965, v86, p74.
Variety. Jul 21, 1965, p6.
The Village Voice. Aug 19, 1965, p15-16.
Vogue. Oct 1, 1965, v146, p168.
A World on Film. p206-09.

Darling, How Could You (Also titled: Rendezvous) (US; Leisen, Mitchell; 1951)
BFI/Monthly Film Bulletin. Sep 1952, v19, p130.
Catholic World. Nov 1951, v174, p145.
Film Daily. Aug 8, 1951, p6.
Hollywood Director. p288-90.
Hollywood Reporter. Aug 6, 1951, p3.
Motion Picture Herald Product Digest. Aug 11, 1951, p973.
The New York Times. Nov 9, 1951, p22.
Variety. Aug 8, 1951, p6.

Darling Lili (US; Edwards, Blake; 1970)
America. Aug 8, 1970, v123, p74-75.
BFI/Monthly Film Bulletin. Nov 1970, v30, p224-25.
Blake Edwards (Lehman and Luhr). p15-17, 214-18.
Films and Filming. Nov 1970, v17, p48.
Films in Review. Aug-Sep 1970, v21, p441.
Hollywood Reporter. Jun 23, 1970, p3.
National Review. Sep 8, 1970, v22, p959.
The New Republic. Jul 18, 1970, v163, p22.
The New York Times. Jul 24, 1970, p16.
The New York Times. Aug 9, 1970, SecII, p1.
The New Yorker. Aug 1970, v46, p70.
Newsweek. Jul 27, 1970, v76, p71.
Saturday Review. Jul 18, 1970, v53, p22.
Time. Jul 27, 1970, v96, p68.
Variety. Jun 24, 1970, p17.

A Date with a Lonely Girl See T.R. Baskin

The Daughter of Rosie O'Grady (US; Butler, David; 1950)
Film Daily. Apr 3, 1950, p6.
Hollywood Reporter. Mar 29, 1950, p3.
Motion Picture Herald Product Digest. Apr 1, 1950, p245.
The New York Times. Mar 31, 1950, p36.
The New Yorker. Apr 8, 1950, v26, p98.
Newsweek. Apr 10, 1950, v35, p83.
Variety. Mar 29, 1950, p11.

David and Bathsheba (US; King, Henry; 1951)
BFI/Monthly Film Bulletin. Oct 1951, v18, p339.
Catholic World. Oct 1951, v174, p68-69.
Christian Century. Sep 26, 1951, v68, p1111.
Commonweal. Aug 31, 1951, v54, p501.
Film Daily. Aug 15, 1951, p8.
Films in Review. Oct 1951, v2, p52-53.
The Films of Gregory Peck. p106-10.
The Films of Susan Hayward. p165-70.
Hollywood Reporter. Aug 15, 1951, p3.
Life. Aug 27, 1951, v31, p77.
Motion Picture Herald Product Digest. Aug 25, 1951, p990-91.
The New Statesman and Nation. Nov 10, 1951, v42, p530-31.
The New York Times. Aug 15 1951, p23.
The New Yorker. Aug 27, 1951, v27, p63.
Newsweek. Aug 20, 1951, v38, p90-91.
Saturday Review. Sep 8, 1951, v34, p36.
The Spectator. Nov 2, 1951, v187, p568.
Time. Aug 20, 1951, v58, p86.
Variety. Aug 15, 1951, p6.

David and Lisa (US; Perry, Frank; 1962)
America. Jan 26, 1963, v108, p154.
BFI/Monthly Film Bulletin. Feb 1964, v31, p19.
Commonweal. Jan 4, 1963, v77, p389.

Fifty Grand Movies of the 1960s and 1970s. p223-26.
Film Daily. Jan 7, 1963, p7.
Film Quarterly. Sum 1963, v16, p43-44.
Filmfacts. Jan 11, 1963, v5, p323-24.
Films and Filming. Feb 1964, v10, p27.
Films in Review. Jan 1963, v14, p47-48.
The Films of the Sixties. p80-81.
Hollywood Reporter. Dec 19, 1962, p3.
Magill's Survey of Cinema. Series II. v2, p570-73.
Motion Picture Herald Product Digest. Dec 26, 1962, p721.
Movie. Oct 1962, n3, p30.
Movie. Jul-Aug 1963, n11, p27.
The Nation. Mar 9, 1963, v196, p216.
The New Republic. Jan 5, 1963, v148, p20.
The New York Times. Dec 27, 1962, p5.
The New Yorker. Jan 12, 1963, v38, p100-01.
Newsweek. Dec 31, 1962, v60, p57.
Private Screenings. p60-61.
Saturday Review. Jan 5, 1963, v46, p30.
Sight and Sound. Wint 1963-64, v33, p41.
Time. Dec 28, 1962, v80, p60.
Variety. Sep 5, 1962, p6.

Dawn at Socorro (US; Sherman, George; 1954)
BFI/Monthly Film Bulletin. Nov 1954, v21, p160.
Catholic World. Oct 1954, v180, p65.
Film Daily. Jul 19, 1954, p6.
Hollywood Reporter. Jul 13, 1954, p3.
Motion Picture Herald Product Digest. Jul 24, 1954, p81.
National Parent-Teacher. Sep 1954, v49, p38.
The New York Times. Aug 28, 1954, p8.
Variety. Jul 14, 1954, p6.

Day for Night (French title: Nuit americaine, La) (FR; Truffaut, François; 1973)
American Scholar. 1974, v43, n3, p467-71.
Atlantic. Nov 1973, v232, p118-22.
BFI/Monthly Film Bulletin. Jan 1974, v41, p12.
Commonweal. Dec 26, 1973, v99, p87-88.
Film Heritage. 1974, v9, n3, p21-26.
Films in Review. Dec 1973, v24, p628.
François Truffaut: A Guide to References and Resources. p72-75.
François Truffaut (Insdorf). p94-101, 192-94.
The Great French Films. p225-28.
Hollywood Reporter. Sep 28, 1973, p3.
Jump Cut. May-Jun 1974, n1, p13.
The Los Angeles Times. Apr 3, 1974, SecIV, p1.
Magill's Survey of Cinema. Foreign Language Films. v2, p728-32.
Modern Photography. Feb 1974, v38, p44.
Motion Picture Herald Product Digest. Oct 3, 1974, p24.
Movie Maker. Feb 1974, v8, p82-84.
Movietone News. Apr 1974, n31, p38-39.
Movietone News. Mar 1974, n30, p32-33.
The Nation. Oct 15, 1973, v217, p382.
The New Republic. Oct 13, 1973, v169, p22.
The New York Times. Jan 9, 1974, p24.
The New Yorker. Oct 15, 1973, v49, p160.
Newsweek. Oct 29, 1973, v82, p108.
Reeling. p248-50.
Sight and Sound. Wint 1973-1974, v43, p44-45.
Time. Oct 15, 1973, v102, p72.
Variety. May 23, 1973, p34.
The Village Voice. Jan 24, 1974, p87.

Day of the Dolphin (US; Nichols, Mike; 1973)
Atlantic. Mar 1974, v233, p93-95.
Atlantic. Jan 1974, v233, p71.
BFI/Monthly Film Bulletin. Feb 1974, v41, p25-26.

Commonweal. Jan 18, 1974, v99, p389-90.
Esquire. Apr 1974, v81, p78.
Films and Filming. Feb 1974, v20, p38-39.
Films and Filming. Jan 1974, v20, p6-7.
Films in Review. Feb 1974, v25, p119-20.
The Los Angeles Times. Dec 20, 1973, SecIV, p1.
Mike Nichols (Schuth). p111-18.
Motion Picture Herald Product Digest. Jan 1, 1974, p65.
The New Republic. Jan 19, 1974, v170, p22.
New York. Jan 21, 1974, v7, p56-57.
The New York Times. Dec 20, 1973, p57.
PTA Magazine. Mar 1974, v68, p4.
Reeling. p334-35.
Rolling Stone. Feb 28, 1974, p60.
Sight and Sound. Spr 1974, v43, p117-118.
Variety. Dec 29, 1973, p12.

The Day of the Locust (US; Schlesinger, John; 1975)
America. Aug 16, 1975, v133, p71-73.
American Cinematographer. Jun 1975, v56, p722-31.
BFI/Monthly Film Bulletin. Jun 1975, v42, p132.
Commonweal. Jul 18, 1975, v102, p278.
Double Exposure. p212-18.
The Films of the Seventies. p118-20.
John Schlesinger: A Guide to References and Resources. p56-59.
John Schlesinger (Phillips). p92-108.
The Los Angeles Times. May 7, 1975, SecIV, p1.
Magill's Survey of Cinema. Series II. v2, p586-88.
The Modern American Novel and the Movies. p95-106.
Motion Picture Herald Product Digest. May 14, 1975, p93.
The Nation. May 24, 1975, v220, p636-37.
The New Republic. May 17, 1975, v172, p24.
The New Republic. Aug 16, 1975, v173, p36-38.
The New York Times. May 8, 1975, p48.
The New York Times. May 11, 1975, SecII, p11.
The New York Times. Jun 8, 1975, SecII, p11.
The New Yorker. May 12, 1975, v51, p110-14.
Newsweek. May 12, 1975, v85, p104-05.
Reeling. p624-31.
Saturday Review. May 17, 1975, v2, p48-49.
Time. May 12, 1975, v105, p58.
Variety. Apr 30, 1975, p19.
The Village Voice. May 12, 1975, p77-79.
Vogue. Oct 1975, v165, p38.

The Day the Earth Stood Still (US; Wise, Robert; 1951)
BFI/Monthly Film Bulletin. Nov 1951, v18, p355.
Christian Century. Oct 31, 1951, v68, p1263.
Cinefantastique. n4, 1976, v4, p4-23.
Cue. Sep 22, 1951, p19.
Film Daily. Sep 7, 1951, p10.
Films in Review. Oct 1951, v2, p51-52.
The Films of the Fifties. p49-52.
Future Tense: The Cinema of Science Fiction. p83-85.
Hollywood Reporter. Sep 4, 1951, p3.
Literature/Film Quarterly. n3, 1982, v10, p150-54.
Literature/Film Quarterly. Jul 1982, v10, p150-54.
Magill's Survey of Cinema. Series II. v2, p589-91.
Motion Picture Herald Product Digest. Sep 8, 1951, p1005.
The Nation. Jan 5, 1952, v174, p19.

The New Statesman and Nation. Dec 22, 1951, v42, p734.
The New York Times. Sep 19, 1951, p37.
The New Yorker. Sep 22, 1951, v27, p91.
Newsweek. Oct 1, 1951, v38, p90.
Saturday Review. Oct 6, 1951, v34, p35.
Science Fiction Gold. p39-50.
Science Fiction Studies in Film. p113-15.
Selected Film Criticism, 1951-1960. p29-30.
Senior Scholastic. Oct 31, 1951, v59, p30.
Time. Oct 1, 1951, v58, p98.
Twenty All-Time Great Science Fiction Films. p37-48.
Variety. Sep 5, 1951, p6.

Days of Heaven (US; Malick, Terrence; 1978)
BFI/Monthly Film Bulletin. Mar 1978, v46, p93.
Christian Century. Jan 3, 1979, v96, p23-24.
Commonweal. Dec 22, 1978, v105, p816-18.
Encore. Oct 16, 1978, v7, p29.
Film Comment. Sep 1978, v14, p27-28.
Films in Review. Nov 1978, v29, p568.
Hollywood Reporter. Sep 8, 1978, p3.
The International Dictionary of Films and Filmmakers. v1, p115-16.
The Los Angeles Times. Sep 17, 1978, Calendar, p11.
Maclean's. Oct 9, 1978, v91, p59-60.
Motion Picture Herald Product Digest. Sep 13, 1978, p25.
The Nation. Oct 7, 1978, v227, p356-57.
National Review. Dec 22, 1978, v30, p1607-08.
The New Republic. Sep 16, 1978, v179, p16-17.
New York. Sep 25, 1978, v11, p138-40.
The New Yorker. Sep 18, 1978, v54, p154.
Newsweek. Sep 18, 1978, v92, p97.
Rolling Stone. Nov 16, 1978, p22.
Saturday Review. Jan 6, 1979, v6, p46-47.
Time. Sep 18, 1978, v112, p93.
Variety. Sep 13, 1978, p21.

The Days of Wine & Roses (US; Edwards, Blake; 1962)
America. Feb 16, 1963, v108, p238.
BFI/Monthly Film Bulletin. Jul 1963, v30, p94.
Commonweal. Feb 1, 1963, v77, p493-94.
Film Daily. Nov 30, 1962, v30, p6.
Filmfacts. Feb 7, 1963, v6, p1-2.
Films and Filming. Jul 1963, v9, p22.
Films in Review. Feb 1963, v14, p109-10.
The Films of Jack Lemmon. p130-35.
The Films of the Sixties. p116-19.
Hollywood Reporter. Nov 29, 1962, p3.
Magill's Survey of Cinema. Series I. v1, p418-20.
Motion Picture Herald Product Digest. Dec 12, 1962, p715.
Movie. Jul-Aug 1963, n11, p14-17.
The New Republic. Feb 2, 1963, v148, p31.
The New York Times. Jan 18, 1963, p7.
The New Yorker. Jan 26, 1963, v38, p121-22.
Newsweek. Jan 28, 1963, v61, p88.
Saturday Review. Feb 2, 1963, v46, p19.
Time. Feb 1, 1963, v81, p17.
Variety. Dec 5, 1962, p11.

Dead Heat On a Merry-Go-Round (US; Gerard, Bernard; 1966)
BFI/Monthly Film Bulletin. Dec 1967, v34, p189-90.
Film Daily. Oct 11, 1966, p8.
Filmfacts. Dec 1, 1966, v9, p266-68.
Films and Filming. Jan 1968, v14, p23-24.
Films in Review. Nov 1966, v17, p584-85.
The Great Gangster Pictures. p105.
Hollywood Reporter. Oct 20, 1966, p3.
Life. Oct 14, 1966, v61, p18.
The London Times. Nov 9, 1967, p13.

Motion Picture Herald Product Digest. Oct 26, 1966, p622.
The New York Times. Oct 13, 1966, p50.
The New Yorker. Oct 22, 1966, v42, p164.
Playboy. Dec 1966, v13, p62.
The Primal Screen. p188-90.
Time. Oct 14, 1966, v88, p122.

Dead Image *See* Dead Ringer

Dead Men Don't Wear Plaid (US; Reiner, Carl; 1982)
Hollywood Reporter. Mar 22, 1982, p4.
The Los Angeles Times. May 20, 1982, SecVI, p3.
Maclean's. May 31, 1982, v95, p58.
Magill's Cinema Annual, 1983. p134-36.
The Nation. Jun 26, 1982, v234, p794.
The New Leader. Jun 14, 1982, v65, p20.
The New Republic. Jun 16, 1982, v186, p24.
The New York Times. May 21, 1982, SecIII, p8.
Newsweek. May 24, 1982, v99, p85.
Rolling Stone. Jun 10, 1982, p38.
Saturday Review. Jun 1982, v9, p64-65.
Time. May 17, 1982, v119, p84.
Variety. Mar 22, 1982, p3.

Dead Ringer (Also titled: Dead Image) (US; Henreid, Paul; 1964)
BFI/Monthly Film Bulletin. May 1964, v31, p68.
Boxoffice. Feb 3, 1964, v84, p2797.
Film Daily. Jan 31, 1964, p4.
Films in Review. Mar 1964, v15, p175.
Hollywood Reporter. Jan 23, 1964, v178, p3.
Motion Picture Herald Product Digest. Feb 5, 1964, p986.
The New York Times. Feb 20, 1964, p22.
Time. Feb 7, 1964, p101.
Variety. Jan 29, 1964, p6.

Deadlier Than the Male (GB; Thomas, Ralph; 1966)
BFI/Monthly Film Bulletin. Mar 1967, v34, p44-45.
Christian Science Monitor (Western edition). Mar 17, 1967, p10.
Film Daily. Jan 31, 1967, p7.
Filmfacts. Mar 15, 1967, v10, p39-40.
Films and Filming. Jun 1967, v13, p26-27.
The London Times. Dec 29, 1966, p6.
Motion Picture Herald Product Digest. Feb 15, 1967, p659.
The New York Times. Feb 22, 1967, p21.
Playboy. May 1967, v14, p35.
The Spectator. Dec 30, 1966, v217, p842.
Time. Mar 10, 1967, v89, p99.
Variety. Jan 25, 1967, p6.

Deadline U.S.A. (Also titled: Deadline) (US; Brooks, Richard; 1952)
BFI/Monthly Film Bulletin. Jun 1952, v19, p73.
Christian Century. Jun 11, 1952, v69, p711.
The Complete Films of Humphrey Bogart. p152-66.
Film Daily. Mar 18, 1952, p6.
Hollywood Reporter. Mar 12, 1952, p4.
Humphrey Bogart: The Man and His Films. p160-62.
Motion Picture Herald Product Digest. Mar 15, 1952, p1282.
The New York Times. Mar 15, 1952, p8.
The New Yorker. Mar 22, 1952, v28, p114.
Newsweek. Mar 31, 1952, v35, p27.
The Spectator. May 23, 1952, v188, p673.
The Tatler. Jun 4, 1952, v204, p540.
Time. Mar 31, 1952, v59, p100.
Variety. Mar 12, 1952, p6.

The Deadly Affair (GB; Lumet, Sidney; 1966)
America. Feb 4, 1967, v116, p194.

BFI/Monthly Film Bulletin. Mar 1967, v34, p40.
Christian Science Monitor (Eastern Edition). Apr 29, 1967, p6.
Commonweal. Feb 17, 1967, v85, p566.
Esquire. Mar 1967, v67, p20.
Film Daily. Jan 27, 1967, p3.
Film Quarterly. Wint 1967-68, v21, p17-18.
Filmfacts. Feb 1, 1967, v10, p1-3.
Films and Filming. Apr 1967, v13, p6-7.
Films in Review. Mar 1967, v18, p179-80.
The Great Spy Pictures. p137-38.
The London Times. Feb 2, 1967, p5.
Motion Picture Herald Product Digest. Feb 15, 1967, p658.
New Statesman. Feb 10, 1967, v73, p198.
The New York Times. Jan 27, 1967, p31.
The New Yorker. Feb 4, 1967, v42, p98.
Newsweek. Feb 6, 1967, v69, p97.
Playboy. Mar 1967, v14, p24.
Saturday Review. Jan 28, 1967, v50, p49.
Senior Scholastic. Mar 10, 1967, v90, p28.
Sidney Lumet: A Guide to References and Resources. p80-82.
Sight and Sound. Spr 1967, v36, p96.
Time. Jan 27, 1967, v89, p80.
Variety. Feb 1, 1967, p6.
The Village Voice. Feb 9, 1967, p27.

The Deadly Companions (US; Peckinpah, Sam; 1961)
BFI/Monthly Film Bulletin. Jul 1962, v29, p90-91.
Film Daily. Jun 12, 1961, v12, p6.
Filmfacts. 1961, v4, p331.
The Films of Sam Peckinpah. p7-16.
Hollywood Reporter. Jun 6, 1961, p3.
The New York Times. Apr 12, 1962, p41.
Peckinpah (Simmons). p36-40.
Sam Peckinpah (McKinney). p39-48.
Variety. Jun 7, 1961, p6.

Dear Brigitte (US; Koster, Henry; 1965)
BFI/Monthly Film Bulletin. Apr 1965, v32, p50-51.
Christian Science Monitor (Western edition). Mar 4, 1965, p2.
Film Daily. Jan 28, 1965, p4.
Filmfacts. Feb 26, 1965, v8, p13-14.
Films and Filming. Jun 1965, v11, p31.
Films and Filming. Apr 1965, v11, p39.
Films in Review. Mar 1965, v16, p178-79.
The Films of James Stewart. p233-36.
Hollywood Reporter. Jan 28, 1965, p3.
The London Times. Apr 8, 1965, p6.
Motion Picture Herald Product Digest. Feb 17, 1965, p233.
The New York Times. Jan 28, 1965, p20.
Time. Feb 5, 1965, v85, p64.
Variety. Feb 3, 1965, p6.

Dear Detective (French title: Tendre Poulet; Also titled: Dear Inspector) (FR; Broca, Philippe de; 1977)
BFI/Monthly Film Bulletin. Feb 1979, v46, p34.
Films in Review. Aug-Sep 1978, v29, p442.
Hollywood Reporter. Apr 25, 1978, p3.
The Los Angeles Times. Jun 21, 1978, SecIV, p1.
The New Leader. May 22, 1978, v61, p31.
The New York Times. Apr 24, 1978, SecIII, p16.
The New York Times. Jun 11, 1978, SecII, p21.
The New York Times. May 1, 1978, v34, p132-33.
Time. May 22, 1978, v111, p90.
Variety. Dec 21, 1977, p21.

Dear Heart (US; Mann, Delbert; 1964)
BFI/Monthly Film Bulletin. May 1965, v32, p66.

Boxoffice. Dec 14, 1964, v86, p2884.
Commonweal. Mar 5, 1965, v81, p733.
Film Daily. Dec 7, 1964, p6.
Hollywood Reporter. Dec 2, 1964, p3.
Life. Feb 5, 1965, v58, p18.
Motion Picture Herald Product Digest. Dec 9, 1964, v232, p185.
The New York Times. Mar 8, 1965, p33.
Newsweek. Mar 8, 1965, v65, p90D.
Saturday Review. Mar 13, 1965, v48, p123.
Time. Mar 12, 1965, v95, p97-98.
Variety. Dec 2, 1964, p6.
Vogue. Feb 1, 1965, v145, p99.

Dear Inspector *See* Dear Detective

Dear John (Swedish title: Kare John)
(SWED; Lindgren, Lars Magnus; 1964)
BFI/Monthly Film Bulletin. Dec 1965, v32, p179-80.
Big Screen, Little Screen. p327-28.
Christian Science Monitor (Western edition). Aug 12, 1966, p6.
Commonweal. Apr 8, 1966, v84, p81-82.
Esquire. Nov 1966, v65, p60, 62.
Film. Wint 1965-66, n44, p19-20.
Film Quarterly. Wint 1966-67, v20, p60-61.
Filmfacts. May 15, 1966, v9, p83-84.
Life. Mar 18, 1966, v60, p12.
The London Times. Nov 11, 1965, p18.
Motion Picture Herald Product Digest. Mar 30, 1966, p492.
Movie. Aut 1965, n14, p40-41.
The New Republic. Apr 9, 1966, v154, p25.
New Statesman. Nov 12, 1965, v70, p761.
The New York Times. Mar 9, 1966, p46.
Newsweek. Apr 4, 1966, v67, p99.
Playboy. May 1966, v13, p36.
The Private Eye, the Cowboy and the Very Naked Girl. p230.
Private Screenings. p243-47.
Second Sight. p62-65.
Sight and Sound. Wint 1965-66, v35, p41.
The Spectator. Nov 12, 1965, v215, p617, 619.
Time. Mar 18, 1966, v87, p109.
Variety. Dec 9, 1964, p6.
The Village Voice. Apr 7, 1966, v11, p31.

Death By Hanging (Japanese title: Koshikei) (JAPAN; Oshima, Nagisa; 1968)
BFI/Monthly Film Bulletin. Apr 1971, v38, p76.
Cinema East. p125-49.
The International Dictionary of Films and Filmmakers. v1, p245-46.
International Film Guide. 1969, v6, p113.
Magill's Survey of Cinema. Foreign Language Films. v2, p752-57.
The New York Times. Feb 15, 1974, p23.
Sight and Sound. Wint 1969-70, v39, p11.
Sight and Sound. Spr 1971, v40, p104-05.

Death in Venice (Italian title: Morte a Venezia) (IT; Visconti, Luchino; 1971)
America. Jul 10, 1971, v125, p17.
Atlantic. Sep 1971, v228, p111-13.
BFI/Monthly Film Bulletin. Apr 1971, v38, p80.
Commonweal. Sep 24, 1971, v94, p501-02.
Double Exposure. p182-88.
Double Takes. p41-42.
Film and Literature: An Introduction. p303-09.
Film Quarterly. Fall 1971, v25, p41-47.
Filming Literature. p126-30.
Films and Filming. May 1971, v17, n8, p87-88.
Films in Review. Aug-Sep 1971, v22, n7, p442-43.
The Films of Dirk Bogarde. p186-90.
The Great Romantic Films. p204-09.

Hollywood Reporter. May 25, 1971, v216, n20, p3.
Luchino Visconti: A Biography. p196-99.
Luchino Visconti (Nowell-Smith). p194-203.
Luchino Visconti (Tonetti). p141-51.
The Nation. Jun 28, 1971, v212, p829.
National Review. Aug 24, 1971, v23, p941.
The New York Times. Jun 18, 1971, p24.
The New York Times. Jun 20, 1971, SecII, p13.
The New York Times. Jun 27, 1971, SecII, p1.
The New York Times. Jul 4, 1971, SecII, p18.
The New York Times. Jul 18, 1971, SecII, p11.
The New Yorker. Apr 17, 1971, v47, p114-15.
The New Yorker. Jun 26, 1971, v47, p85.
Newsweek. Jun 28, 1971, v77, p90.
The Novel and the Cinema. p338-47.
Saturday Review. Jun 19, 1971, v54, p28.
Saturday Review. Aug 8, 1970, v53, p16-18.
Sight and Sound. Aut 1970, v39, n4, p198-200.
Take One. Jul-Aug 1970, v11, p27-28.
Time. Jul 5, 1971, v98, p66.
Variety. Apr 7, 1971, p18.
The Village Voice. Jul 8, 1971, p54.
Women and their Sexuality in the New Film. p179-90.

Death of a Gunfighter (US; Totten, Robert; 1969)
Big Screen, Little Screen. p177-79.
Film. Wint 1970, n57, p29.
Film Daily. May 7, 1969, p3.
Focus. Oct 1969, n5, p29-31.
The New York Times. May 10, 1969, p34.
Time. May 23, 1969, v93, p114.
Variety. Apr 30, 1969, p6.

Death of a Salesman (US; Benedek, Laslo; 1951)
Catholic World. Feb 1952, v174, p386.
Christian Century. Feb 20, 1952, v69, p231.
Cinema, the Magic Vehicle. v2, p86-87.
Commonweal. Dec 28, 1951, v55, p300.
Dictionary of Films. p80.
Film Daily. Dec 10, 1951, p6.
Films in Review. Jan 1952, v3, p11-14, 38-40.
The Films of Fredric March. p201-03.
Holiday. Mar 1952, v11, p14.
Hollywood Reporter. Dec 10, 1951, p3.
Library Journal. Jan 15, 1952, v77, p140.
Life. Jan 14, 1952, v32, p63-64.
Magill's Survey of Cinema. Series I. v1, p421-23.
Motion Picture Herald Product Digest. Dec 15, 1951, p1153.
The New Republic. Dec 31, 1951, v125, p22.
The New York Times. Dec 21, 1951, p21.
The New Yorker. Dec 22, 1951, v27, p62.
Newsweek. Dec 31, 1951, v38, p56-57.
Saturday Review. Dec 22, 1951, v34, p34.
Sight and Sound. Oct-Dec 1952, v22, p82-84.
Stanley Kramer, Film Maker. p73-82.
Theatre Arts. Jan 1952, v36, p36-37.
Time. Dec 31, 1951, v58, p60.
Variety. Dec 12, 1951, p6.

Death on the Nile (GB; Guillermin, John; 1978)
Bette Davis: Her Films and Career. p205-06.
BFI/Monthly Film Bulletin. Oct 1978, v45, p167.
Commonweal. Oct 13, 1978, v105, p662-63.
Films in Review. Nov 1978, v29, p565.
Hollywood Reporter. Sep 21, 1978, p3.
The Los Angeles Times. Sep 24, 1978, Calendar, p32.
Maclean's. Oct 16, 1978, v91, p70.
Motion Picture Herald Product Digest. Oct 4, 1978, p35.
New York. Oct 9, 1978, v11, p112.
The New York Times. Nov 6, 1978, np.

The New York Times. Dec 3, 1978, SecII, p13.
The New Yorker. Oct 23, 1978, v54, p152-54.
Newsweek. Oct 2, 1978, v92, p85.
Time. Oct 2, 1978, v112, p66.
Variety. Sep 27, 1978, p20.
Vogue. Oct 1978, v168, p46.

Death Wish (US; Winner, Michael; 1974)
America. Sep 21, 1974, v131, p139-40.
Before My Eyes. p31-35.
BFI/Monthly Film Bulletin. Jan 1975, v42, p7.
Cineaste. 1974, v6, n3, p37-38.
Commonweal. Aug 23, 1974, v100, p454-55.
Films in Review. Oct 1974, v25, p503-04.
The Films of Charles Bronson. p213-16.
The Films of Michael Winner. p102-09.
Hollywood Reporter. Jul 19, 1974, p3.
Independent Film Journal. Jul 24, 1974, v74, p14.
The Los Angeles Times. Jul 31, 1974, SecIV, p1.
Magill's Survey of Cinema. Series II. v2, p600-03.
Motion Picture Herald Product Digest. Jul 31, 1974, p17.
Movietone News. Sep 1974, n35, p27-28.
Movietone News. Oct 1974, n36, p14-17.
New York. Jul 29, 1974, v7, p54-55.
The New York Times. Aug 4, 1974, SecII, p1.
The New York Times. Sep 1, 1974, SecII, p1.
The New Yorker. Aug 26, 1974, v50, p48.
Newsweek. Aug 26, 1974, v84, p82.
PTA Magazine. Oct 1974, v69, p6.
Time. Aug 19, 1974, v104, p72.
Today's Filmmaker. 1974, v4, n2, p24-27.
Variety. Jul 24, 1974, p20.
The Village Voice. Aug 1, 1974, p67.

Deathtrap (US; Lumet, Sidney; 1982)
Hollywood Reporter. Mar 17, 1982, p3.
The Los Angeles Times. Mar 19, 1982, SecVI, p4.
Maclean's. Mar 29, 1982, v95, p59-60.
Magill's Cinema Annual, 1983. p137-41.
The Nation. Apr 17, 1982, v234, p473-74.
The New Republic. Apr 5, 1982, v186, p188.
The New Yorker. Apr 5, 1982, v58, p188.
Newsweek. Mar 22, 1982, v99, p84-85.
Rolling Stone. Apr 15, 1982, p72.
Saturday Review. Mar 1982, v9, p54-55.
Theater Crafts. Apr 1982, v16, p20-21.
Variety. Mar 17, 1982, p3.

The Decadent Influence *See* To Be a Crook

Decima Vittima, La *See* The Tenth Victim

Decision Before Dawn (US; Litvak, Anatole; 1951)
American Cinematographer. Feb 1952, v33, p62-63.
BFI/Monthly Film Bulletin. Sep 1951, v18, p323.
Catholic World. Nov 1951, v174, p143.
Christian Century. Jan 30, 1952, v69, p143.
Commonweal. Jan 11, 1952, v55, p350.
Film Daily. Dec 19, 1951, p6.
Films in Review. Jan 1952, v3, p40-41.
Hollywood Reporter. Dec 19, 1951, p3.
Library Journal. Jan 1, 1952, v77, p44.
Life. Dec 17, 1951, v31, p118.
The London Times. Sep 3, 1951, p8.
Motion Picture Herald Product Digest. Dec 22, 1951, p1161.
The New Republic. Jan 14, 1952, v126, p21.
The New Statesman and Nation. Sep 8, 1951, v42, p254.
The New York Times. Dec 22, 1951, p12.
The New Yorker. Jan 5, 1952, v27, p58.
Newsweek. Dec 31, 1951, v38, p56.
Saturday Review. Nov 17, 1951, v34, p6.

Saturday Review. Dec 29, 1951, v34, p20-22.
Sight and Sound. Oct-Dec 1951, v21, p79, 81.
Sight and Sound. Mar 1951, v19, p427.
The Spectator. Sep 7, 1951, v187, p295.
Time. Dec 24, 1951, v58, p59.
Variety. Dec 19, 1951, p6.

Dédée (French title: Dédée D'Anvers) (FR; Allégret, Yves; 1948)
BFI/Monthly Film Bulletin. Oct 1952, v19, p138.
Film Daily. Apr 13, 1949, p6.
The London Times. Sep 8, 1952, p8.
The New Republic. Apr 25, 1949, v120, p30.
The New York Times. Apr 9, 1949, p9.
Newsweek. May 2, 1949, v33, p83.
The Spectator. Sep 5, 1952, v188, p295.
Theatre Arts. Jun 1949, v33, p97.
Variety. Apr 13, 1949, p11.

The Deep (US; Yates, Peter; 1977)
BFI/Monthly Film Bulletin. Dec 1977, v44, p277.
Commonweal. Aug 5, 1977, v104, p499-500.
Hollywood Reporter. Jun 17, 1977, p3.
Inside The Deep. 1977.
The Los Angeles Times. Jun 17, 1977, SecIV, p1.
Motion Picture Herald Product Digest. Jun 6, 1978, p9.
New York. Jul 4, 1977, v10, p54-55.
The New York Times. May 1, 1978, SecII, p1.
The New York Times. Jun 18, 1978, p10.
The New Yorker. Jul 4, 1977, v53, p83.
Saturday Review. Jul 23, 1977, v4, p46.
Time. Jun 27, 1977, v109, p60.
Variety. Jun 22, 1977, p16.

Deep in My Heart (US; Donen, Stanley; 1954)
America. Dec 18, 1954, v92, p326.
BFI/Monthly Film Bulletin. Apr 1955, v21, p51.
Catholic World. Jan 1955, v180, p305.
Collier's. Jan 7, 1955, v135, p26-27.
Commonweal. Dec 24, 1954, v61, p334.
Dance Magazine. Jan 1955, v29, p9.
Farm Journal. Jan 1955, v79, p70.
Film Daily. Dec 1, 1954, p6.
Films in Review. Jan 1955, v6, p36-37.
The Films of Gene Kelly. p156-58.
Hollywood Reporter. Dec 1, 1954, p3.
Library Journal. Jan 15, 1955, v80, p150.
Motion Picture Herald Product Digest. Dec 4, 1954, p233.
National Parent-Teacher. Feb 1955, v49, p39.
The New York Times. Dec 10, 1954, p35.
The New Yorker. Dec 18, 1954, v30, p67.
Newsweek. Dec 20, 1954, v44, p83.
Saturday Review. Jan 8, 1955, v38, p26.
Stanley Donen (Casper). p76-83.
Time. Jan 17, 1955, v65, p74.
Variety. Dec 1, 1954, p6.

The Deer Hunter (US; Cimino, Michael; 1978)
America. Mar 3, 1979, v140, p163.
America. Nov 17, 1979, v141, p301-04.
BFI/Monthly Film Bulletin. Mar 1979, v46, p42.
Commonweal. Mar 2, 1979, v106, p115-17.
Fifty Grand Movies of the 1960s and 1970s. p165-70.
Film Comment. Mar 1979, v15, p22-24.
Films in Review. Apr 1979, v30, p241.
The Films of the Seventies. p238-44.
Harper's. Apr 1979, v258, p84-86.
Hollywood Reporter. Dec 1, 1978, p3.
Literature/Film Quarterly. Jan 1983, v11, p16-21.

The Los Angeles Times. Dec 3, 1978, Calendar, p1.
Magill's Survey of Cinema. Series I. v1, p427-31.
Martin Scorsese and Michael Cimino (Bliss). p163-93.
Motion Picture Herald Prooduct Digest. Dec 13, 1978, p55.
The Nation. Feb 24, 1979, v228, p220.
The Nation. May 12, 1979, v228, p540-41.
National Review. Feb 16, 1979, v31, p247-49.
The New Republic. May 26, 1979, v180, p22-23.
The New Republic. Dec 23, 1978, v179, p22-23.
New York. Jun 18, 1979, v12, p79-80.
New York. Dec 18, 1978, v11, p98-100.
The New York Times. Dec 15, 1978, SecIII, p5.
The New Yorker. Dec 18, 1978, v54, p66.
Newsweek. Dec 11, 1978, v92, p113.
Rolling Stone. Mar 8, 1979, p27-28.
Saturday Review. Feb 17, 1979, v6, p50-51.
Time. Dec 18, 1978, v112, p86.
Variety. Nov 29, 1978, p24.

Déesses de l'Ecran, Les *See* The Love Goddesses

The Defector (French title: Espion, L') (WGER, FR; Levy, Raoul; 1966)
America. Dec 10, 1966, v115, p785.
BFI/Monthly Film Bulletin. Nov 1967, v34, p174.
Christian Science Monitor (Eastern Edition). Feb 13, 1967, p6.
Cinema. Dec 1966, v3, p36-37.
Commonweal. Dec 2, 1966, v85, p262.
Film Daily. Nov 15, 1966, p4.
Filmfacts. Jan 1, 1967, v9, p306-08.
Films and Filming. May 1967, v13, p46-47.
Films and Filming. Mar 1969, v15, p84.
Films in Review. Dec 1966, v17, p667.
The Films of Montgomery Clift. p209-14.
The Great Spy Pictures. p141-43.
Hollywood Reporter. Dec 5, 1966, p3.
Motion Picture Herald Product Digest. Nov 23, 1966, p631-32.
The New York Times. Nov 17, 1966, p55.
The Private Eye, the Cowboy and the Very Naked Girl. p217-18.
Saturday Review. Dec 3, 1966, v49, p74.
Time. Nov 25, 1966, v88, p128.
Variety. Nov 16, 1966, p6.

The Defiant Ones (US; Kramer, Stanley; 1958)
America. Sep 27, 1958, v99, p679.
BFI/Monthly Film Bulletin. Sep 1958, v25, p124.
Catholic World. Oct 1958, v188, p65.
Commonweal. Sep 26, 1958, v68, p637-38.
The Evolution of Character Portrayals in the Films of Sidney Poitier, 1950-1978. p112-24.
Film Daily. Aug 5, 1958, p8.
Filmfacts. Oct 22, 1958, v1, p167-68.
Films in Review. Oct 1958, v9, p462-63.
The Films of Sidney Poitier. p76-79.
The Films of the Fifties. p248-74.
From Sambo to Superspade. p225-26.
Hollywood Reporter. Aug 5, 1958, p3.
Life. Aug 11, 1958, v40, p51-52.
Magill's Survey of Cinema. Series II. v2, p604-08.
The Nation. Oct 11, 1958, v187, p219.
The New Republic. Sep 1, 1958, v139, p22-23.
The New York Times. Sep 25, 1958, p29.
The New Yorker. Oct 4, 1958, v34, p159.
Newsweek. Aug 25, 1958, v52, p77.
Saturday Review. Jul 26, 1958, v41, p22-23.
Selected Film Criticism 1951-60. p30-37.
Stanley Kramer, Film Maker. p199-206.

Time. Aug 25, 1958, v72, p78.
Tony Curtis: The Man and His Movies. p72-76.
Variety. Aug 6, 1958, p6.

The Delicate Delinquent (US; McGuire, Don; 1956)
America. Jul 20, 1957, v97, p432.
BFI/Monthly Film Bulletin. Sep 1957, v24, p110-11.
Commonweal. Jul 12, 1957, v66, p376.
Film Daily. Jun 6, 1957, p6.
Films and Filming. Oct 1957, v4, p24.
The Films of the Fifties. p207-08.
Hollywood Reporter. May 28, 1957, p4.
Motion Picture Herald Product Digest. Jun 1, 1957, p401.
The New York Times. Jul 4, 1957, p16.
Newsweek. Jun 24, 1957, v69, p108.
Variety. May 29, 1957, p6.

Deliverance (US; Boorman, John; 1972)
America. Sep 2, 1972, v127, p127.
Commonweal. Sep 29, 1972, v96, p526.
Fifty Grand Movies from the 1960s and 1970s. p131-34.
Film Quarterly. Wint 1972-73, v26, n2, p39.
Filmfacts. 1972, v15, n9, p213.
Films in Review. Oct 1972, v23, n8, p506.
The Films of Burt Reynolds. p145-51.
The Films of The Seventies. p65-68.
Hollywood Reporter. Jul 12, 1972, p3.
John Boorman (Ciment). p116-33.
Life. Aug 18, 1972, v73, p8.
Magill's Survey of Cinema. English Language Films. Series I, v1 p432.
The Modern American Novel and the Movies. p293-302.
The New Republic. Aug 5, 1972, v167, p24.
The New York Times. Aug 20, 1972, SecII, p7.
The New Yorker. Aug 5, 1972, v48, p52-53.
Newsweek. Aug 7, 1972, v80, p61.
Saturday Review. Aug 5, 1972, v55, p61.
Time. Aug 7, 1972, v100, p75-76.
Variety. Jul 19, 1972, p14.

Démanty Noci *See* Diamonds of the Night

Demetrius and the Gladiators (US; Daves, Delmer; 1954)
America. Jan 26, 1954, v91, p345.
BFI/Monthly Film Bulletin. Oct 1954, v21, p143.
Catholic World. Jul 1954, v179, p301.
Commonweal. Jul 9, 1954, v60, p344.
Film Daily. Jun 4, 1954, p14.
Films and Filming. Nov 1954, v1, p19.
Films in Review. Aug-Sep 1954, v5, p365.
The Films of Susan Hayward. p192-96.
Hollywood Reporter. Jun 2, 1954, p3.
The London Times. Sep 13, 1954, p3.
Motion Picture Herald Product Digest. Jun 12, 1954, p27.
National Parent-Teacher. Sep 1954, v49, p38.
The New York Times. Jun 19, 1954, p9.
Newsweek. Jul 5, 1954, v44, p79.
One Good Film Deserves Another. p76-78.
The Tatler. Sep 22, 1954, v213, p569.
Time. Jul 5, 1954, v64, p97.
Variety. Jun 2, 1954, p6.

Demoiselles de Rochefort, Les *See* The Young Girls of Rochefort

The Demon *See* Onibaba

Demon Est Mauvais Jouer, Le *See* Return From the Ashes

Dentellièrs, Le *See* The Lacemaker

Départ, Le (Also titled: The Start; The Departure) (BELG; Skolimowski, Jerzy; 1966)

BFI/Monthly Film Bulletin. May 1968, v35, p72.
Cahiers du Cinema in English. Dec 1967, n12, p16-21.
Cinema. Wint 1967, v3, p49.
Filmfacts. Jul 15, 1968, v11, p210-11.
Films and Filming. May 1968, v14, p27.
Hollywood Reporter. Nov 16, 1966, p3.
International Film Guide. 1968, v5, p49.
The London Times. Feb 10, 1968, p19.
Motion Picture Herald Product Digest. May 1, 1968, p806.
New Statesman. Feb 9, 1968, v75, p183.
The New York Times. Sep 23, 1967, p20.
Sight and Sound. Wint 1967-68, v37, p12, 49.
The Spectator. Feb 16, 1968, v220, p208.
Time. Sep 29, 1967, v90, p100.
Unholy Fools, Wits, Comics, Disturbers of the Peace. p99-100.
Variety. May 17, 1967, p18.

Départ sans Adieu *See* Nobody Waved Goodbye

The Departure *See* Départ, Le

Deported (US; Siodmak, Robert; 1950)
Christian Century. Jan 24, 1951, v68, p127.
Commonweal. Dec 1, 1950, v53, p198.
Film Daily. Oct 19, 1950, p6.
The Great Gangster Pictures. p107-08.
Hollywood Reporter. Oct 18, 1950, p3.
Motion Picture Herald Product Digest. Oct 21, 1950, p537.
The New York Times. Nov 2, 1950, p39.
Newsweek. Nov 6, 1950, v36, p94.
The Spectator. May 26, 1950, v184, p721-22.
Variety. Oct 18, 1950, p6.

Dernier Metro, Le *See* The Last Metro

Dersu Uzala (JAPAN, USSR; Kurosawa, Akira; 1975)
Akira Kurosawa: A Guide to References and Resources. p68-70.
BFI/Monthly Film Bulletin. Jan 1978, v45, p5.
Films and Filming. Dec 1977, v24, p37.
The Films of Akira Kurosawa. p195-203.
Hollywood Reporter. Mar 30, 1975, p6.
The Los Angeles Times. Dec 20, 1977, SecIV, p14.
Magill's Survey of Cinema. Foreign Language Films. v2, p771-77.
The Nation. Jan 28, 1978, v226, p91.
Time. Oct 25, 1976, v108, p80-81.
Variety. Aug 13, 1975, p16.

Desaparecidos, Los *See* The Official Story

The Desert Fox (Also titled: Rommel, The Desert Fox) (US; Hathaway, Henry; 1951)
BFI/Monthly Film Bulletin. Oct 1951, v18, p344.
Christian Century. Nov 14, 1951, v68, p1327.
Commonweal. Nov 2, 1951, v55, p94.
Film Daily. Oct 1, 1951, p5.
Films in Review. Oct 1951, v2, p49-50.
The Films of James Mason. p98-99.
Hollywood Reporter. Sep 28, 1951, p3.
Library Journal. Oct 15, 1951, v76, p1722.
Life. Oct 8, 1951, v31, p78-79.
Motion Picture Herald Product Digest. Oct 6, 1951, p1050-51.
The New Republic. Nov 19, 1951, v125, p21.
The New Statesman and Nation. Oct 20, 1951, v42, p435.
The New York Times. Oct 18, 1951, p32.
The New York Times. Oct 28, 1951, p11.
The New Yorker. Oct 27, 1951, v27, p74-75.
Newsweek. Oct 29, 1951, v38, p92.
Saturday Review. Oct 20, 1951, v34, p28.

Senior Scholastic. Sep 26, 1951, v59, p45.
Sight and Sound. Jan-Mar 1952, v21, p134.
The Spectator. Oct 12, 1951, v187, p472.
Time. Oct 15, 1951, v58, p117-18.
Variety. Oct 3, 1951, p6.

The Desert Hawk (US; De Cordova, Frederick; 1950)
Film Daily. Aug 8, 1950, p12.
Hollywood Reporter. Aug 4, 1950, p3.
Motion Picture Herald Product Digest. Aug 12, 1950, p434.
The New York Times. Aug 26, 1950, p9.
Variety. Aug 9, 1950, p8.

Desert Hearts (US; Deitch, Donna; 1985)
BFI/Monthly Film Bulletin. Aug 1986, v53, p222.
Hollywood Reporter. Sep 10, 1985, p3.
The Los Angeles Times. Apr 25, 1986, SecVI, p1.
Ms. Nov 1985, v14, p66-67.
New York. Apr 14, 1986, v19, p90.
The New York Times. Apr 4, 1986, SecIII, p8.
Saturday Review. Jan-Feb 1986, v12, p86.
Variety. Aug 28, 1985, p13.
Vogue. Feb 1986, v176, p66.

The Desert Rats (US; Wise, Robert; 1953)
America. May 16, 1953, v89, p200.
BFI/Monthly Film Bulletin. May 1953, v20, p66.
Catholic World. May 1953, v177, p142-43.
Commonweal. May 8, 1953, v58, p122.
Films and Filming. Aug 1962, v8, p35.
Films in Review. May 1953, v4, p240.
The Films of James Mason. p114-16.
Hollywood Reporter. May 6, 1953, p3.
The New York Times. May 9, 1953, p13.
The New Yorker. May 16, 1953, v29, p131.
Newsweek. May 25, 1953, v41, p101.
Saturday Review. May 16, 1953, v36, p32.
Senior Scholastic. May 13, 1953, v62, p30.
Time. May 18, 1953, v61, p114.
Variety. May 13, 1953, p18.

Deserto Rosso, Il *See* Red Desert

Designing Woman (US; Minnelli, Vincente; 1957)
America. May 18, 1957, v97, p244.
BFI/Monthly Film Bulletin. May 1957, v24, p54.
Commonweal. May 17, 1957, v66, p183.
Film Daily. Mar 13, 1957, p6.
Films and Filming. Jun 1957, v3, p24.
Films in Review. May 1957, v8, p226.
The Films of Gregory Peck. p144-47.
Hollywood Reporter. Mar 12, 1957, p3.
Lauren Bacall: Her Films and Career. p144-48.
Magill's Survey of Cinema. English Language Films. Series II, v2, p612-615.
Motion Picture Herald Product Digest. Mar 16, 1957, v206, p297-98.
The New York Times. May 17, 1957, p20.
The New York Times Magazine. Apr 14, 1957, p24.
The New Yorker. May 25, 1957, v33, p129.
Newsweek. Apr 8, 1957, v49, p115.
Saturday Review. Mar 23, 1957, v40, p26.
Time. Apr 1, 1957, v69, p94.
Variety. Mar 13, 1957, p6.
The Village Voice. Aug 7, 1957, p6.

Desire Under the Elms (US; Mann, Delbert; 1958)
America. Mar 22, 1958, v98, p734.
BFI/Monthly Film Bulletin. May 1958, v25, p55.
Catholic World. Apr 1958, v187, p65.
Commonweal. Mar 21, 1958, v67, p639.
Cosmopolitan. Mar 1958, v144, p16.

Film Daily. Feb 12, 1958, p7.
Filmfacts. Apr 9, 1958, v1, p39-40.
Films in Review. Apr 1958, v9, p200-201.
The Films of Sophia Loren. p89-91.
Hollywood Reporter. Mar 12, 1958, p3.
Library Journal. Mar 15, 1958, p835.
Life. Feb 17, 1958, v44, p69-70.
The Nation. Apr 5, 1958, v186, p304.
The New Republic. Apr 7, 1958, v138, p22-23.
The New York Times Magazine. Dec 22, 1957, p30-31.
The New York Times Magazine. Mar 13, 1958, p24.
The New Yorker. Mar 22, 1958, v34, p95.
Newsweek. Mar 17, 1958, v51, p 106-07.
O'Neill on Film. p116-30.
Saturday Review. Mar 15, 1958, v40, p55.
Theater Arts. Apr 1958, v40, p79-81.
Time. Mar 17, 1958, v71, p106.
Variety. Feb 12, 1958, p7.

Desirée (US; Koster, Henry; 1954)
America. Nov 27, 1954, v92, p259.
BFI/Monthly Film Bulletin. Mar 1955, v22, p33-34.
Catholic World. Jan 1955, v180, p304.
Commonweal. Dec 3, 1954, v61, p255.
Film Daily. Nov 17, 1954, p10.
Films and Filming. Apr 1955, v1, p21.
Films and Filming. Jan 1955, v1, p26.
Films in Review. Dec 1954, v5, p542.
The Films of Marlon Brando. p82-89.
Hollywood Reporter. Nov 17, 1954, p3.
Library Journal. Dec 1, 1954, v79, p2315.
Life. Nov 22, 1954, v37, p197-00.
The London Times. Feb 14, 1955, p3.
Motion Picture Herald Product Digest. Nov 20, 1954, p217.
National Parent-Teacher. Jan 1955, v49, p39.
The New Statesman and Nation. Feb 19, 1955, v49, p246.
The New York Times. Nov 18, 1954, p42.
The New Yorker. Nov 27, 1954, v30, p189.
Newsweek. Nov 29, 1954, v44, p97-98.
Saturday Review. Dec 4, 1954, v37, p38-39.
The Spectator. Feb 18, 1955, v194, p190.
The Tatler. Feb 23, 1955, v215, p343.
Time. Nov 29, 1954, v64, p75.
Variety. Nov 17, 1954, p6.

Desk Set (Also titled: His Other Woman) (US; Lang, Walter; 1957)
America. Jun 1, 1957, v97, p292.
BFI/Monthly Film Bulletin. Aug 1957, v24, p97.
Commonweal. Jun 7, 1957, v66, p257.
Film Daily. May 10, 1957, p7.
Films and Filming. Aug 1957, v3, p24.
Films in Review. Jun-Jul 1957, v8, p279-80.
The Films of Katharine Hepburn. p167-71.
The Films of Spencer Tracy. p226-27.
Hollywood Reporter. May 10, 1957, p3.
Magill's Survey of Cinema. English Language Films. Series II, v2, p616-18.
Motion Picture Herald Product Digest. May 18, 1957, v207, p377.
The New York Times. May 16, 1957, p28.
The New Yorker. May 25, 1957, v33, p129.
Newsweek. May 27, 1957, v49, p118.
Saturday Review. Jun 1, 1957, v40, p23.
Time. May 27, 1957, v69, p101.
Variety. May 5, 1957, p6.

Desperate Characters (US; Gilroy, Frank D.; 1971)
America. Oct 16, 1971, v125, p293.
Commonweal. Oct 22, 1971, v95, p89.
Films in Review. Oct 1971, v22, p513-14.
Hollywood Reporter. Sep 30, 1971, p3.
The Nation. Oct 18, 1971, v213, p381.

The New Republic. Sep 25, 1971, v165, p24.
The New York Times. Sep 23, 1971, p74.
The New York Times. Dec 19, 1971, SecII, p15.
The New Yorker. Sep 25, 1971, v47, p101-04.
Newsweek. Sep 27, 1971, v78, p109.
Saturday Review. Sep 18, 1971, v54, p14.
Unholy Fools, Wits, Comics, Disturbers of the Peace. p81-86.
Variety. Jul 14, 1971, p16.
The Village Voice. Sep 23, 1971, p76.

Desperate Decision (French title: Jeune Folle, La) (FR; Allégret, Yves; 1952)
Film Daily. Nov 12, 1954, p22.
The New York Times. Nov 9, 1954, p31.
The New Yorker. Nov 20, 1954, v30, p82.
Variety. Oct 8, 1952, p12.

The Desperate Hours (US; Wyler, William; 1955)
America. Oct 8, 1955, v94, p56.
Catholic World. Nov 1955, v182, p136.
Classics of the Gangster Film. p206-08.
Commonweal. Oct 21, 1955, v63, p63-64.
The Complete Films of Humphrey Bogart. p186-87.
Film Daily. Sep 14, 1955, p6.
Films in Review. Oct 1955, v6, p411-12.
The Films of Fredric March. p213-15.
Hollywood Reporter. Sep 14, 1955, p3.
Humphrey Bogart: The Man and His Films. p175-76.
Library Journal. Oct 15, 1955, v80, p2230.
Life. Oct 10, 1955, v39, p111-12.
Magill's Survey of Cinema. Series II. v2, p619-22.
The Nation. Oct 29, 1955, v181, p369.
The New York Times. Oct 16, 1955, SecII, p5.
The New York Times. Oct 6, 1955, p25.
The New York Times. Oct 9, 1955, SecII, p1.
The New Yorker. Oct 15, 1955, v31, p182.
Newsweek. Oct 3, 1955, v46, p86-87.
Saturday Review. Oct 22, 1955, v38, p30.
Time. Oct 10, 1955, v66, p116.
Variety. Sep 14, 1955, p6.
William Wyler: A Guide to References and Resources. p134-37.
William Wyler (Anderegg). p180-84.

Desperate Search (US; Lewis, Joseph H.; 1952)
BFI/Monthly Film Bulletin. Feb 1953, v20, p23.
Film Daily. Dec 5, 1952, p4.
Hollywood Reporter. Nov 24, 1952, p3.
Library Journal. Jan 1, 1953, v78, p50.
Motion Picture Herald Product Digest. Nov 29, 1952, p1622.
Variety. Nov 26, 1952, p6.

Desperately Seeking Susan (US; Seidelman, Susan; 1985)
BFI/Monthly Film Bulletin. Sep 1985, v52, p176.
California Magazine. May 1985, v10, p52.
Commonweal. May 17, 1985, v112, p304.
Films in Review. Aug 1985, v36, p418.
Hollywood Reporter. Mar 25, 1985, p4.
The Los Angeles Times. Mar 28, 1985, SecVI, p1.
Maclean's. Apr 8, 1985, v98, p61.
Magill's Cinema Annual, 1986. p137-40.
Ms. Apr 1985, v13, p114.
The Nation. May 11, 1985, v240, p568.
National Review. Jun 14, 1985, v37, p48-49.
The New Republic. Apr 22, 1985, v192, p24.
New Statesman. Sep 6, 1985, v110, p33.
New York. Apr 22, 1985, v18, p56.
New York. Apr 1, 1985, v18, p76.
The New York Times. Mar 29, 1985, SecIII, p5.

The New Yorker. Apr 22, 1985, v61, p134.
Newsweek. Apr 8, 1985, v105, p85.
Playboy. Jul 1985, v32, p21.
Progressive. Jun 1985, v49, p39.
Rolling Stone. May 9, 1985, p27.
Texas Monthly. May 1985, v13, p180.
Time. Apr 1, 1985, v125, p76.
Variety. Mar 27, 1985, p16.
Vogue. Mar 1985, v175, p498-99.
Washingtonian. May 1985, v20, p72.
Wilson Library Bulletin. Sep 1985, v60, p67.

Destination Moon (US; Pichel, Irving; 1950)
American Cinematographer. Feb 1950, v31, p46.
BFI/Monthly Film Bulletin. Sep 1950, v17, p140.
Film Daily. Jun 26, 1950, p6.
Films in Review. Sep 1950, v1, p29-31.
The Films of George Pal. p36-46.
Focus on the Science Fiction Film. p52-65.
Future Tense: The Cinema of Science Fiction. p74-76.
Hollywood Reporter. Jun 26, 1950, p3.
Illustrated London News. Sep 2, 1950, v217, p371.
The London Times. Aug 28, 1950, p6.
Magill's Survey of Cinema. Series II. v2, p623-24.
Motion Picture Herald Product Digest. Jul 1, 1950, p366.
The New York Times. Jun 28, 1950, p32.
Science Fiction Gold. p15-26.
Science Fiction Studies in Film. p93-97.
The Spectator. Sep 8, 1950, v185, p273.
Twenty All-Time Great Science Fiction Films. p14-25.
Variety. Jun 28, 1950, p6.

Destry (US; Marshall, George; 1954)
BFI/Monthly Film Bulletin. Feb 1955, v22, p23-24.
Catholic World. Jan 1955, v180, p303.
Collier's. Oct 1, 1954, v134, p26-27.
Film Daily. Dec 7, 1954, p12.
The Great Western Pictures. p82-86.
Hollywood Reporter. Dec 2, 1954, p3.
Make It Again, Sam. p45-49.
Motion Picture Herald Product Digest. Dec 11, 1954, p241.
National Parent-Teacher. Jan 1955, v49, p39.
Variety. Dec 8, 1954, p6.

The Detective (Also titled: Father Brown) (GB; Hamer, Robert; 1954)
America. Aug 14, 1954, v91, p480.
America. Nov 13, 1954, v92, p194.
BFI/Monthly Film Bulletin. Jul 1954, v21, p98-99.
Catholic World. Oct 1954, v180, p64.
Commonweal. Nov 12, 1954, v61, p167.
Farm Journal. Dec 1954, v78, p141.
Film Daily. Oct 4, 1954, p6.
Films in Review. Nov 1954, v5, p485.
Hollywood Reporter. Sep 27, 1954, p3.
Kiss Kiss Bang Bang. p318.
Library Journal. Dec 1, 1954, v79, p2315.
Motion Picture Herald Product Digest. Oct 16, 1954, p179.
The Nation. Nov 13, 1954, v179, p429.
National Parent-Teacher. Oct 1954, v49, p39.
The New Statesman and Nation. Jun 19, 1954, v47, p787.
The New York Times. Nov 2, 1954, p25.
The New York Times Magazine. Oct 24, 1954, p40.
The New Yorker. Nov 13, 1954, v30, p210.
Newsweek. Sep 6, 1954, v44, p76.
Reporter. Dec 2, 1954, v11, p42.

Saturday Review. Sep 18, 1954, v37, p26.
Senior Scholastic. Nov 17, 1954, v65, p37.
Sight and Sound. Jul-Sep 1954, v24, p33-34.
The Spectator. Jun 11, 1954, v192, p705.
Time. Nov 15, 1954, v64, p110.
Variety. Jun 16, 1954, p6.

The Detective (US; Douglas, Gordon; 1968)
America. Jun 8, 1968, v118, p760.
BFI/Monthly Film Bulletin. Oct 1968, v35, p148-49.
Commonweal. Jun 21, 1968, v88, p410.
Film Daily. May 28, 1968, p5.
Film Quarterly. Fall 1968, v22, p73.
Filmfacts. Jul 15, 1968, v11, p185-87.
Films and Filming. Oct 1968, v15, p40.
Films in Review. Jun-Jul 1968, v19, p376-77.
The Films of Frank Sinatra. p323-34.
Five Thousand One Nights At the Movies. p144.
Hollywood Reporter. May 28, 1968, p3.
The London Times. Sep 5, 1968, p7.
Look. Mar 19, 1968, v32, p71-75.
Motion Picture Herald Product Digest. Jun 12, 1968, p822A.
Movie. Wint 1968-69, n16, p33-34.
The New York Times. May 29, 1968, p20.
Newsweek. Jun 10, 1968, v71, p86.
Saturday Review. Jun 8, 1968, v51, p57.
The Spectator. Sep 13, 1968, v221, p368.
Time. Jun 7, 1968, v91, p101.
Variety. May 29, 1968, p6.

Detective Story (US; Wyler, William; 1951)
BFI/Monthly Film Bulletin. Nov 1951, v18, p355-56.
Catholic World. Nov 1951, v174, p142.
Christian Century. Jan 16, 1952, v69, p87.
Cinema, the Magic Vehicle. v2, p100.
Commonweal. Nov 16, 1951, v55, p144.
Dark City: The Film Noir. p109-12.
Fifty From the Fifties. p91-98.
Film Daily. Sep 24, 1951, p22.
Films and Filming. Sep 1964, v10, p23.
Films in Review. Dec 1951, v2, p57.
The Films of Kirk Douglas. p80-83.
Hollywood Reporter. Sep 24, 1951, p3.
Library Journal. Nov 1, 1951, v76, p1818.
Life. Nov 19, 1951, v31, p169-70.
Magill's Survey of Cinema. Series II. v2, p628-31.
Motion Picture Herald Product Digest. Sep 29, 1951, p1041.
Movies (Farber). p42-44.
Movietone News. Sep 1974, n35, p29.
The Nation. Nov 24, 1951, v173, p457.
The New Republic. Dec 3, 1951, v125, p21.
The New Statesman and Nation. Oct 27, 1951, v42, p460-61.
The New York Times. Nov 7, 1951, p35.
The New Yorker. Nov 17, 1951, v27, p108-09.
Newsweek. Nov 5, 1951, v38, p98-99.
Quarterly of Film, Radio and Television. Wint 1952, v7, p203-09.
Saturday Review. Nov 10, 1951, v34, p27.
The Spectator. Oct 19, 1951, v187, p504.
Time. Oct 29, 1951, v58, p83.
Variety. Sep 26, 1951, p6.
William Wyler: A Guide to References and Resources. p124-27.
William Wyler (Anderegg). p173-76.

Deux Sous d'Espoir *See* Due Soldi di Speranza

Deuxieme Souffle, Le (Also titled: The Second Breath; Second Wind) (FR; Melville, Jean-Pierre; 1966)
BFI/Monthly Film Bulletin. Apr 1967, v34, p55-56.
International Film Guide. 1968, v5, p70.
The London Times. Feb 16, 1967, p8.

Magill's Survey of Cinema. Foreign Language Films. v6, p2682-87.
Melville on Melville. p111-25.
Sight and Sound. Spr 1967, v36, p85-87.
The Spectator. Feb 24, 1967, v218, p225-26.
Variety. Nov 9, 1966, p6.

The Devil at 4 O'Clock (US; LeRoy, Mervyn; 1961)
America. Oct 21, 1961, v106, p104.
BFI/Monthly Film Bulletin. Jan 1962, v29, p3-4.
Commonweal. Nov 10, 1961, v75, p175.
Film Daily. Sep 21, 1961, p6.
Filmfacts. Dec 29, 1961, v4, p313-14.
Films and Filming. Dec 1961, v8, p29.
The Films of Frank Sinatra. p171-75.
The Films of Spencer Tracy. p240-41.
The New York Times. Oct 19, 1961, p39.
Newsweek. Oct 23, 1961, v58, p101.
Saturday Review. Nov 4, 1961, v44, p37.
Time. Oct 27, 1961, v78, p55.
Variety. Sep 27, 1961, p6.

The Devil Makes Three (US; Marton, Andrew; 1952)
BFI/Monthly Film Bulletin. Jan 1953, v20, p8.
Catholic World. Oct 1952, v176, p63.
Christian Century. Dec 3, 1952, v69, p1423.
Commonweal. Sep 19, 1952, v56, p583.
Film Daily. Aug 27, 1952, p6.
Films in Review. Oct 1952, v3, p415-16.
The Films of Gene Kelly. p142-45.
Hollywood Reporter. Aug 13, 1952, p3.
Motion Picture Herald Product Digest. Aug 16, 1952, p1485.
National Parent-Teacher. Sep 1952, v47, p38.
The New York Times. Aug 30, 1952, p6.
Newsweek. Sep 15, 1952, v40, p103.
Saturday Review. Sep 20, 1952, v35, p34.
Time. Sep 8, 1952, v60, p106.
Variety. Aug 13, 1952, p6.

The Devil Never Sleeps *See* Satan Never Sleeps

The Devils (GB; Russell, Ken; 1971)
America. Sep 4, 1971, v125, p127.
BFI/Monthly Film Bulletin. Aug 1971, v38, p161.
Commonweal. Oct 1, 1971, v95, p16-17.
Film Quarterly. Spr 1972, v25, p13-25.
Filmfacts. 1971, v14, n14, p338-341.
Films and Filming. Sep 1971, v17, p49.
Films in Review. Aug-Sep 1971, v22, p437-38.
Hollywood Reporter. Jul 9, 1971, p3.
Ken Russell: A Guide to References and Resources. p27-30.
Ken Russell (Atkins). p55-65.
Ken Russell (Phillips). p103-12.
Ken Russell: The Adaptor as Creator. p137-82.
Ken Russell's Films. p118.
Life. Sep 24, 1971, v71.
National Review. Nov 5, 1971, v23, p1250.
The New Republic. Sep 11, 1971, v165, p26.
The New York Times. Jul 7, 1971, p14.
The New York Times. Aug 15, 1971, SecII, p1.
The New York Times. Sep 19, 1971, SecII, p1.
The New Yorker. Jul 24, 1971, v47, p58.
Newsweek. Jul 26, 1971, v78, p71.
Saturday Review. Jul 31, 1971, v54, p50.
Time. Jul 26, 1971, v98, p50.
Variety. Jul 14, 1971, p16.
The Village Voice. Aug 12, 1971, p47.

The Devil's Doorway (US; Mann, Anthony; 1950)
The American West in Film. p87-88.
Anthony Mann (Basinger). p89-93.
BFI/Monthly Film Bulletin. Sep 1950, v17, p140.

Commonweal. Nov 24, 1950, v53, p173.
Film Daily. May 18, 1950, p6.
The Filming of the West. p534-35.
The Films of Robert Taylor. p116-17.
The Great Western Pictures. p86-87.
Hollywood Reporter. May 15, 1950, p3.
Motion Picture Herald Product Digest. May 6, 1950, p287.
The New York Times. Nov 10, 1950, p35.
Time. Oct 9, 1950, v56, p118.
Variety. May 17, 1950, p6.

Devil's General (German title: Teufels General, Des) (WGER; Kautner, Helmut; 1957)
Commonweal. Mar 1, 1957, v65, p568.
Film. Jan-Feb 1958, n15, p24-25.
Films and Filming. Jul 1959, v5, p22.
Films in Review. Mar 1957, v8, p133.
Motion Picture Herald Product Digest. Feb 9, 1957, v206, p257.
The Nation. Jun 1, 1957, v184, p487.
The New York Times. Apr 16, 1957, p38.
Time. May 13, 1957, v69, p106.
Variety. May 6, 1955, p6.

Devil's Pitchfork *See* Ana-ta-han

Devyat'Dney Odnogo Goda *See* Nine Days of One Year

Diabolique (Also titled: Diaboliques, Les) (FR; Clouzot, Henri-Georges; 1955)
American Film. Jul-Aug 1983, v8, p66-67.
BFI/Monthly Film Bulletin. Jan 1956, v23, p2.
Cinema, the Magic Vehicle. v2, p212-14.
Commonweal. Dec 16, 1955, v63, p286.
Commonweal. Jan 12, 1962, v75, p414.
Fifty from the Fifties. p167-71.
Film Daily. Nov 22, 1955, p5.
Films and Filming. Jan 1956, v2, p23-24.
Films and Filming. Dec 1985, v31, p41-42.
Films in Review. Dec 1955, v6, p527.
The Great French Films. p256-57.
Hollywood Reporter. Mar 9, 1961, p3.
The International Dictionary of Films and Filmmakers. v1, p121-22.
The London Times. Feb 9, 1955, p11.
Magill's Survey of Cinema. Foreign Language Films. v2, p809-14.
Motion Picture Herald Product Digest. Jan 7, 1956, p730.
The Nation. Dec 10, 1955, v181, p524.
The New York Times. Nov 22, 1955, p41.
The New Yorker. Feb 12, 1955, v30, p111.
The New Yorker. Nov 26, 1955, v31, p96.
Newsweek. Nov 28, 1955, v46, p116.
Saturday Review. Dec 3, 1955, v38, p39.
Sight and Sound. Wint 1955-56, v25, p149.
Time. Dec 5, 1955, v66, p109.
Variety. Feb 23, 1955, p8.
The Village Voice. Apr 18, 1956, p6.

Diabolo Menthe *See* Peppermint Soda

Diagonale du Fou, La *See* Dangerous Moves

Dial M for Murder (US; Hitchcock, Alfred; 1954)
Alfred Hitchcock (Phillips). p127-29.
America. Jun 5, 1954, v91, p287.
The Art of Alfred Hitchcock. p229-36.
Artforum. Sum 1980, v18, p79.
BFI/Monthly Film Bulletin. Sep 1954, v21, p127-28.
Catholic World. Jun 1954, v179, p222-23.
Cinema Eye, Cinema Ear. p192-93.
Collier's. Jun 11, 1954, v133, p90-91.
Commonweal. May 28, 1954, v60, p97.
Cue. May 29, 1954, p16.
Film Daily. Apr 27, 1954, p6.

Films and Filming. Oct 1983, v29, p37.
Films in Review. Jun-Jul 1954, v5, p302-03.
The Films of Alfred Hitchcock. p163-64.
Hitchcock: The First Forty-Four Films. p119-21.
Hitchcock (Truffaut). p209-34.
Hollywood Reporter. Apr 27, 1954, p3.
Kiss Kiss Bang Bang. p321.
Library Journal. Jun 15, 1954, v79, p1168.
The London Times. Jul 19, 1954, p11.
Magill's Survey of Cinema. Series I. v1, p440-43.
Motion Picture Herald Product Digest. May 1, 1954, p2277.
New Statesman. Aug 5, 1983, v106, p29-30.
The New Statesman and Nation. Jul 24, 1954, v48, p102.
The New York Times. May 29, 1954, p13.
The New Yorker. Jun 5, 1954, v30, p62.
Newsweek. May 10, 1954, v43, p100.
Saturday Review. May 29, 1954, v37, p23.
Selected Film Criticism, 1951-1960. p31.
Sight and Sound. Oct-Dec 1954, v24, p89-90.
Sight and Sound. Sum 1976, v45, p175-79.
Sight and Sound. Wint 1982-83, v52, p32-33.
The Spectator. Jul 23, 1954, v193, p111.
The Tatler. Jul 28, 1954, v213, p164.
Time. May 24, 1954, v53, p102.
Variety. Apr 28, 1954, p6.
The Village Voice. Mar 31, 1980, v25, p43.

The Diamond Earrings *See* The Earrings of Madame De

Diamond Head (US; Green, Guy; 1963)
BFI/Monthly Film Bulletin. Jul 1963, v30, p99.
Commonweal. Mar 1, 1963, v77, p599.
Film Daily. Dec 22, 1963, p4.
Filmfacts. Feb 28, 1963, v6, p15-16.
Films and Filming. Jun 1963, v9, p22.
The Films of Charlton Heston. p133-35.
Hollywood Reporter. Dec 26, 1962, p3.
Illustrated London News. Jun 8, 1963, v242, p902.
The New York Times. Feb 21, 1963, p5.
The New Yorker. Mar 9, 1963, v39, p146-47.
Photoplay. Mar 1963, v63, p6.
Saturday Review. Jan 26, 1963, v46, p31.
Time. Feb 22, 1963, v81, p93.
Variety. Dec 26, 1962, p6.

Diamonds Are Forever (GB; Hamilton, Guy; 1971)
BFI/Monthly Film Bulletin. Feb 1971, v39, p29.
Commonweal. Jan 7, 1972, v95, p325.
Deeper into Movies. p489-90.
Esquire. Jun 1972, v77, p61-62.
Films and Filming. Mar 1972, v18, p52-53.
Films in Review. Jan 1972, v23, p54-55.
Hollywood Reporter. Dec 15, 1971, p3.
James Bond and the Cinema. p179-202.
The James Bond Films. p99-100.
James Bond's Bedside Companion. p101-03.
National Review. Feb 18, 1972, v24, p172-73.
The New York Times. Dec 18, 1971, p34.
The New York Times. Dec 26, 1971, SecII, p15.
The New Yorker. Jan 15, 1972, v47, p81-82.
Newsweek. Dec 27, 1971, v78, p61.
Saturday Review. Jan 1, 1972, v55, p22.
Time. Jan 10, 1972, v99, p50.
Variety. Dec 15, 1971, p14.
The Village Voice. Dec 16, 1971, p79.

Diamonds of the Night (Czech title: Démanty Noci) (CZECH; Nemec, Jan; 1964)
BFI/Monthly Film Bulletin. Sep 1965, v32, p132-33.
The Czechoslovak New Wave. p187-92.
Dictionary of Films. p80-81.

Film Comment. Fall 1968, v5, p72.
Filmfacts. Apr 15, 1968, v11, p92-93.
Films and Filming. Sep 1965, v11, p25.
International Film Guide. 1966, v3, p59.
The London Times. Jul 22, 1965, p15.
Movies Into Film. p285-86.
The New York Times. Mar 15, 1968, p30.
On Film. p279-80.
The Spectator. Jul 30, 1965, v215, p152.
Variety. Aug 5, 1964, p7.
A Year in the Dark. p79-80.

The Diary of a Chambermaid (French title: Journal d'une Femme de Chambre, Le) (FR, IT; Buñuel, Luis; 1964)
BFI/Monthly Film Bulletin. Sep 1965, v32, p133-34.
The Cinema of Luis Buñuel. p139-50.
Commonweal. Mar 27, 1970, v92, p63-64.
Dictionary of Films. p167-68.
Film. 1964, n41, p21.
Film Daily. Mar 9, 1965, p6.
Film Quarterly. Wint 1970-71, v24, p48-51.
Filmfacts. Apr 2, 1965, v8, p44-46.
Films and Filming. Oct 1965, v12, p31-32.
International Film Guide. 1965, v2, p71.
Life. Mar 26, 1965, v38, p15.
The London Times. Aug 5, 1965, p5.
Luis Buñuel (Aranda). p220-23.
Luis Buñuel (Durgnat). p139-50.
Luis Buñuel (Higginbotham). p118-24.
Magill's Survey of Cinema. Foreign Language Films. v2, p815-19.
Motion Picture Herald Product Digest. Mar 31, 1965, p260.
Moviegoer. Sum 1966, v3, p38-43.
The New Republic. Apr 3, 1965, v152, p23.
New Statesman. Aug 6, 1965, v70, 195-96.
The New York Times. Sep 22, 1964, p44.
The New Yorker. Mar 20, 1965, v41, p153-54.
The New Yorker. Apr 4, 1964, v40, p186.
Sight and Sound. Aut 1964, v33, p174-78.
The Spectator. Aug 6, 1965, v215, p180.
Time. Mar 19, 1965, v85, p110.
Variety. Mar 8, 1964, p7.
The World of Luis Buñuel. p257-69.

Diary of a Country Priest *See* Journal d'un Cure de Compagne, Le

The Diary of a Mad Housewife (US; Perry, Frank; 1970)
America. Sep 5, 1970, v123, p131-32.
Atlantic. Nov 1970, v226, p127-28.
BFI/Monthly Film Bulletin. Aug 1971, v38, p162.
Big Screen, Little Screen. p293-94.
Commonweal. Nov 27, 1970, v93, p222-23.
Films in Review. Oct 1970, v21, p505-06.
Hollywood Reporter. Jul 31, 1970, p3, 8.
Life. Aug 7, 1970, v69, p8.
Look. Sep 22, 1970, v34, p70.
Magill's Survey of Cinema. Second Series 1981, v2, p639.
The New Republic. Sep 5, 1970, v162, p22.
The New York Times. Aug 11, 1970, p27.
The New York Times. Aug 23, 1970, SecII, p11.
The New York Times. Nov 2, 1970, p47.
The New Yorker. Aug 15, 1970, v46, p68-69.
Newsweek. Aug 10, 1970, v76, p72.
Saturday Review. Aug 15, 1970, v53, p36.
Time. Aug 17, 1970, v96, p34.
Variety. Aug 5, 1970, p16.
Vogue. Aug 15, 1970, v156, p34.

The Diary of Anne Frank (US; Stevens, George; 1959)
America. Apr 4, 1959, v101, p52-54.
BFI/Monthly Film Bulletin. Sep 1959, v26, p82, 126.

Catholic World. Jun 1959, v189, p236.
Commonweal. Apr 10, 1959, v70, p58-59.
Film Daily. Mar 18, 1959, v115, p6.
Filmfacts. Apr 8, 1959, v2, p45-47.
Films in Review. Dec 1960, v11, p261-62.
Hollywood Reporter. Mar 18, 1959, p3.
Look. May 26, 1959, v23, p105-06.
Magill's Survey of Cinema. Series II. v2, p642-45.
McCall's. Jun 1959, v86, p6.
The New Republic. Apr 6, 1959, v140, p22.
The New York Times. Mar 19, 1959, p40.
The New Yorker. Mar 28, 1959, v35, p95.
Newsweek. Mar 30, 1959, v53, p98.
Reporter. Apr 16, 1959, v20, p36.
Saturday Review. Apr 4, 1959, v42, p29.
Senior Scholastic. Apr 10, 1959, v74, p35.
Time. Mar 30, 1959, v73, p75-76.
Variety. Mar 18, 1959, p6.

The Diary of Major Thompson *See* The French They Are a Funny Race

Die! Die! My Darling! (Also titled: Fanatic) (GB; Narizzano, Silvio; 1965)
BFI/Monthly Film Bulletin. Apr 1965, v32, p51.
Film Daily. Apr 29, 1965, p6.
Filmfacts. Jul 9, 1965, v8, p132-34.
Films and Filming. May 1965, v11, p30-31.
Films in Review. May 1965, v16, p313-14.
Hollywood Reporter. Apr 27, 1965, p3.
Life. Apr 9, 1965, v58, p10.
Motion Picture Herald Product Digest. Mar 31, 1965, p258.
The New York Times. May 20, 1965, p52.
Newsweek. Apr 5, 1965, v65, p95.
Saturday Review. Jun 12, 1965, v48, p57.
Time. Apr 2, 1965, v85, p97.
Variety. Apr 28, 1965, p6.

A Different Story (US; Aaron, Paul; 1978)
BFI/Monthly Film Bulletin. Sep 1979, v46, p194-95.
Films in Review. Aug-Sep 1978, v29, p440.
Hollywood Reporter. Apr 19, 1978, p2.
The Los Angeles Times. May 10, 1978, SecIV, p1.
Motion Picture Herald Product Digest. May 26, 1978, p89.
The New Leader. Jun 19, 1978, v61, p21-22.
New York. Jun 5, 1978, v11, p86.
The New York Times. Jun 14, 1978, SecIII, p20.
Variety. Apr 19, 1978, p26.
Vogue. May 1978, v168, p48.

The Difficult Years *See* Anni Difficili

Dim Stars of the Big Bear *See* Vaghe Stelle Dell'Orsa

Dimanche à la campagne *See* A Sunday in the Country

Dimanches de Ville D'Avray, Les *See* Sundays & Cybele

Diner (US; Levinson, Barry; 1982)
America. May 8, 1982, v146, p363.
Christian Century. Jun 9, 1982, v99, p708.
Commonweal. Aug 13, 1982, v109, p440-41.
Hollywood Reporter. Mar 3, 1982, p3.
Horizon. Dec 1982, v25, p60.
The Los Angeles Times. May 7, 1982, SecVI, p1.
Maclean's. May 3, 1982, v95, p52.
Magill's Cinema Annual, 1983. p142-46.
The Nation. Apr 24, 1982, v234, p505-06.
National Review. May 14, 1982, v34, p572.
The New Leader. May 3, 1982, v65, p19-20.
The New Republic. Apr 28, 1982, v186, p24-26.
New York. Apr 5, 1982, v15, p58.

The New York Times. Apr 2, 1982, SecIII, p3.
The New Yorker. Apr 5, 1982, v58, p180.
Newsweek. Apr 19, 1982, v99, p96.
Rolling Stone. May 13, 1982, p391.
Time. Apr 19, 1982, v119, p85.
Variety. Mar 1, 1982, p3.

Dingaka (S AFR; Uys, Jamie; 1965)
BFI/Monthly Film Bulletin. Oct 1965, v32, p150.
Film Daily. May 27, 1965, p5.
Films and Filming. Dec 1965, v12, p29-30.
Hollywood Reporter. May 27, 1965, p3.
The London Times. Oct 18, 1965, p8.
Motion Picture Herald Product Digest. Jun 9, 1965, p307.
The New York Times. Jul 1, 1965, p34.
Time. Jul 2, 1965, v86, p80.
Variety. May 19, 1965, p6.

Dinner for Adele (Also titled: Nick Carter in Prague; Adele Hasn't Had her Supper Yet) (CZECH; Lipstory, Aldrich; 1980)
Films in Review. Jun 1980, v31, p376.
Hollywood Reporter. Mar 23, 1979, p14.
The New York Times. Jun 6, 1980, SecIII, p9.
The New Yorker. Jun 2, 1980, v55, p126.

Diplomatic Courier (US; Hathaway, Henry; 1952)
BFI/Monthly Film Bulletin. Jul 1952, v19, p90.
Catholic World. Jul 1952, v175, p305.
Commonweal. Jun 27, 1952, v56, p291.
Film Daily. Jun 25, 1952, p6.
The Films of Tyrone Power. p173-75.
Hollywood Reporter. Jun 10, 1952, p3.
Library Journal. Jun 15, 1952, v77, p1071.
Motion Picture Herald Product Digest. Jun 21, 1952, p1417-18.
The New Statesman and Nation. Jun 28, 1952, v43, p771.
The New York Times. Jun 14, 1952, p12.
Newsweek. Jun 30, 1952, v39, p103.
The Spectator. Jun 20, 1952, v188, p808.
The Tatler. Jul 2, 1952, v205, p26.
Theatre Arts. Aug 1952, v36, p88.
Time. Jun 30, 1952, v59, p59.
Variety. Jun 11, 1952, p6.

The Dirty Dozen (US, GB; Aldrich, Robert; 1967)
America. Jul 1, 1967, v117, p22-23.
BFI/Monthly Film Bulletin. Nov 1967, v34, p167.
Esquire. Dec 1967, v66, p46.
Film Daily. Jun 16, 1967, p5.
Film Quarterly. Wint 1967, p36-41.
Film Quarterly. Fall 1967, p58.
Films and Filming. Oct 1967, v14, p21-22.
Films in Review. Aug-Sep 1967, v18, p445-46.
The Films of Robert Aldrich. p42-44.
The Films of the Sixties. p209-12.
Hollywood Reporter. Jun 16, 1967, p3.
Life. Jul 21, 1967, v63, p10.
Magill's Survey of Cinema. Series I. v1, p448-50.
Motion Picture Herald Product Digest. Jun 21, 1967, p695.
The New York Times. Jun 16, 1967, p36.
The New York Times. Aug 31, 1968, v44, p21-22.
The New Yorker. Jul 22, 1967, v43, p70.
Newsweek. Jul 3, 1967, v70, p78.
Saturday Review. Jun 17, 1967, v50, p47.
Sight and Sound. Aut 1967, v36, p201-02.
Take One. 1967, v1, p23-24.
Time. Jun 30, 1967, v89, p70.
Variety. Jun 21, 1967, p6.
The Village Voice. Jun 29, 1967, p23.

The Dirty Game (French title: Guerre
Secret; Also titled: Secret War) (FR,
IT, WGER, GB; Young, Terence;
Christian-Jacque; Lizzani, Carlo; 1965)
Film Daily. Apr 22, 1966, p9.
Filmfacts. Dec 1, 1966, v9, p275-76.
The Films of Henry Fonda. p190-91.
Motion Picture Herald Product Digest. May 11,
1966, p520.
Variety. Jul 21, 1965, p7.

Dirty Hands *See* Mains Sales, Les

Dirty Harry (US; Siegel, Don; 1971)
BFI/Monthly Film Bulletin. May 1972, v39,
p93.
Clint Eastwood (Guérif). p86-91.
Deeper into Movies. p85-89.
Filmfacts. 1971, v14, p525-28.
Films and Filming. Jun 1972, v18, n9, p55, 58.
The Films of Clint Eastwood. p131-41.
The Films of the Seventies. p47-51.
Hollywood Reporter. Dec 22, 1971, p3.
Magill's Survey of Cinema. Series I. v1, p451-
53.
The New York Times. Dec 23, 1971, p20.
The New York Times. May 21, 1972, SecII,
p15.
The New Yorker. Jan 15, 1972, v47, p78-81.
Newsweek. Jan 10, 1972, v79, p59.
Saturday Review. Jan 29, 1972, v55, p23.
Sight and Sound. Spr 1972, v41, p112-13.
Time. Jan 3, 1972, v99, p66.
Variety. Dec 22, 1971, p6.

Dirty Mary Crazy Larry (US; Hough, John;
1974)
BFI/Monthly Film Bulletin. Dec 1974, v41,
p272.
Films and Filming. Sep 1974, v20, p26-27.
Films Illustrated. Jun 1974, v3, p384-85.
Hollywood Reporter. May 9, 1974, p3.
Independent Film Journal. May 29, 1974, v73,
p13.
The Los Angeles Times. May 24, 1974, SecIV,
p32.
Motion Picture Herald Product Digest. Jun 5,
1974, p3.
Movietone News. Sep 1974, n35, p34.
Time. Aug 19, 1974, v104, p73.
Variety. May 15, 1974, p24.
The Village Voice. Aug 1, 1974, p71.

The Discreet Charm of the Bourgeoisie
(French title: Charme Discret de la
Bourgeoisie, Le) (SP, FR; Buñuel,
Luis; 1972)
Atlantic. Jan 1973, v231, p96-97.
Film Comment. May-Jun 1975, v14, p52-59.
Film Quarterly. Wint 1972-73, v26, p14.
Filmfacts. 1972, v15, n18, p417.
Films in Review. Jan 1973, v24, p54.
Hollywood Reporter. Oct 19, 1972, p4.
*The International Dictionary of Films and
Filmmakers.* v1, p83-85.
Life. Nov 17, 1972, v73, p30.
The Nation. Nov 13, 1972, v215, p474.
The New Republic. Dec 2, 1972, v167, p20.
The New York Times. Oct 14, 1972, p40.
The New York Times. Oct 29, 1972, SecII, p1.
The New Yorker. Nov 11, 1972, v48, p1532-55.
Newsweek. Nov 6, 1972, v80, p121.
Reeling. p70-73.
Saturday Review. Dec 2, 1972, v55, p93.
Time. Nov 6, 1972, v100, p87-88.
Variety. Sep 27, 1972, p6.

The Disorderly Orderly (US; Tashlin,
Frank; 1964)
Film Daily. Dec 16, 1964, p6.
Film Quarterly. Spr 1965, v18, p59.

Filmfacts. Jan 15, 1965, v7, p364-65.
Films and Filming. Sep 1965, v11, p29-30.
The London Times. Jul 1, 1965, p17.
The Los Angeles Times. Jan 1, 1965, p6.
Motion Picture Herald Product Digest. Jan 6,
1965, p201.
Movie. Aut 1965, n14, p45.
New Statesman. Jul 16, 1965, v70, p94.
The New York Times. Dec 24, 1964, p8.
Newsweek. Jan 4, 1965, v65, p61.
The Spectator. Jul 9, 1965, v215, p41.
Tynan Right and Left. p233-34.
Variety. Dec 16, 1964, p17.

Distant Drums (US; Walsh, Raoul; 1951)
BFI/Monthly Film Bulletin. May 1952, v19,
p64.
Christian Century. Jan 23, 1952, v69, p111.
Commonweal. Jan 18, 1952, v55, p374.
Film Daily. Nov 29, 1951, p6.
The Films of Gary Cooper. p233-34.
Holiday. Mar 1952, v11, p9.
Hollywood Reporter. Nov 29, 1951, p3.
Library Journal. Jan 15, 1952, v77, p140.
The London Times. Mar 24, 1952, p8.
Motion Picture Herald Product Digest. Dec 1,
1951, p1126.
The New Statesman and Nation. Mar 22, 1952,
v43, p346.
The New York Times. Dec 26, 1951, p19.
Newsweek. Jan 14, 1952, v39, p82.
Saturday Review. Jan 12, 1952, v35, p28.
The Spectator. Mar 28, 1952, v188, p397.
Time. Jan 21, 1952, v59, p94.
Variety. Dec 5, 1951, p6.

Distant Journey (Czechoslovakian title:
Daleka Cesta; Also titled: Ghetto
Terezin) (CZECH; Radok, Alfred;
1950)
Dictionary of Films. p77.
*Magill's Survey of Cinema. Foreign Language
Films.* v2, p832-85.
The New Republic. Sep 25, 1950, v123, p30.
The New York Times. Aug 28, 1950, p13.
Variety. Feb 27, 1952, p16.

Distant Thunder (Indian title: Ashani
Sanket) (INDIA; Ray, Satyajit; 1973)
BFI/Monthly Film Bulletin. May 1975, v42,
p99.
Commonweal. Dec 19, 1975, v102, p626-27.
Film. Feb-Mar 1974, n11/12, p27.
Film. Jan 1974, n10, p9.
Film Quarterly. Wint 1973, v27, p56-57.
Hollywood Reporter. Nov 28, 1975, p13.
*Magill's Survey of Cinema. Foreign Language
Films.* v2, p836-39.
The Nation. Nov 15, 1975, v221, p510.
The New York Times. Oct 12, 1973, p32.
The New Yorker. Nov 10, 1975, v51, p169-72.
Newsweek. Nov 17, 1975, v86, p98-99.
Time. Nov 24, 1975, v106, p85.
Variety. Aug 1, 1973, p18.
When the Lights Go Down. p68-72.

A Distant Trumpet (US; Walsh, Raoul;
1964)
BFI/Monthly Film Bulletin. May 1964, v31,
p68-69.
Boxoffice. May 18, 1964, v85, p2828.
Film Daily. May 28, 1964, p6.
Films and Filming. Jun 1964, v10, p26.
Hollywood Reporter. May 25, 1964, p3.
Motion Picture Herald Product Digest. Jun 10,
1964, p67.
The New York Times. May 28, 1964, p40.
Time. May 1, 1964, v83, pE5.
Variety. May 27, 1964, p6.

Diva (FR; Beineix, Jean-Jacques; 1980)
Christian Century. Jul 7, 1982, v99, p769.
Hollywood Reporter. Apr 7, 1982, p12.
The Los Angeles Times. Apr 1, 1982, SecVI, p1.
Maclean's. May 10, 1982, v95, p62.
Magill's Cinema Annual, 1983. p147-50.
National Review. Jun 25, 1982, v34, p777-78.
The New Republic. May 12, 1982, v186, p24-25.
New York. Apr 19, 1982, v15, p77-78.
The New York Review of Books. May 27, 1982,
v29, p44-45.
The New York Times. Apr 16, 1982, SecIII,
p17.
The New Yorker. Apr 19, 1982, v58, p165-68.
Newsweek. Apr 19, 1982, v99, p86.
Rolling Stone. Apr 29, 1982, p37.
Time. Apr 26, 1982, v119, p74.
Variety. Apr 1, 1982, p3.

The Divided Heart (GB; Crichton, Charles;
1954)
America. Aug 13, 1955, v93, p479.
BFI/Monthly Film Bulletin. Dec 1954, v21,
p171-72.
Catholic World. Sep 1955, v181, p463.
Commonweal. Aug 5, 1955, v62, p445.
Film Daily. Aug 11, 1955, p5.
Films and Filming. Jan 1955, v1, p19.
Films in Review. Oct 1955, v6, p410.
Illustrated London News. Nov 27, 1954, v225,
p962.
Life. Aug 15, 1955, v39, p79-80.
The London Times. Nov 12, 1954, p11.
*Michael Balcon Presents . . . A Lifetime of
Films.* p181.
Motion Picture Herald Product Digest. Aug 13,
1955, p554.
National Parent-Teacher. Oct 1955, v50, p39.
The New Statesman and Nation. Nov 20, 1954,
v48, p645-46.
The New York Times. Aug 4, 1955, p16.
The New Yorker. Aug 20, 1955, v31, p69.
Newsweek. Aug 22, 1955, v46, p90.
Saturday Review. Sep 17, 1955, v38, p34.
Sight and Sound. Jan-Mar 1955, v24, p145.
The Tatler. Nov 24, 1954, v214, p486.
Time. Aug 22, 1955, v66, p84.
Variety. Nov 24, 1954, p16.

The Dividing Line *See* The Lawless

Divine Madness (US; Ritchie, Michael;
1980)
BFI/Monthly Film Bulletin. Jan 1981, v49, p5.
Christian Century. Oct 29, 1980, v97, p1044.
Christian Science Monitor. Oct 16, 1980, p19.
Films in Review. Nov 1980, v31, p569.
Hollywood Reporter. Sep 15, 1980, p2.
The Los Angeles Times. Sep 21, 1980,
Calendar, p33.
Motion Picture Herald Product Digest. Oct 8,
1980, p34.
The New Republic. Oct 4, 1980, v183, p26.
The New York Times. Sep 25, 1980, SecIII, p21.
The New Yorker. Nov 10, 1980, v56, p205-06.
Variety. Sep 17, 1980, p18.

Divorce-Italian Style (Italian title: Divorzio
All' Italiana) (IT; Germi, Pietro; 1961)
America. Nov 3, 1962, v107, p1011.
BFI/Monthly Film Bulletin. Jul 1963, v30, p94-
95.
Commonweal. Oct 12, 1962, v77, p73.
Dictionary of Films. p86.
Film Daily. Sep 18, 1962, p4.
Filmfacts. Sep 28, 1962, v5, p207-09.
Hollywood Reporter. Oct 2, 1962, p3.
Motion Picture Herald Product Digest. Oct 17,
1962, p676.
The Nation. Dec 8, 1962, v195, p412.

The New Republic. Oct 8, 1962, v147, p26.
The New York Times. Sep 18, 1962, p34.
The New Yorker. Sep 29, 1962, v38, p139.
Newsweek. Oct 1, 1962, v60, p60-61.
Reruns. p160-65.
Saturday Review. Sep 22, 1962, v45, p22.
Time. Sep 28, 1962, v80, p103.
Variety. Dec 27, 1961, p6.

Do Not Disturb (US; Levy, Ralph; 1965)
BFI/Monthly Film Bulletin. Feb 1966, v33, p22.
Christian Science Monitor (Western edition). Jan 11, 1966, p6.
Film Daily. Dec 29, 1965, p4.
Films and Filming. Jan 1966, v12, p22.
Films and Filming. Feb 1966, v12, p10-12.
The Films of Doris Day. p223-28.
Hollywood Reporter. Dec 20, 1965, p3.
The London Times. Dec 23, 1965, p4.
Motion Picture Herald Product Digest. Jan 5, 1966, p435.
The New York Times. Dec 25, 1965, p17.
Newsweek. Jan 10, 1966, v67, p62.
Time. Jan 14, 1966, v87, p89.
Variety. Dec 22, 1965, p17.

Doctor at Large (GB; Thomas, Ralph; 1957)
BFI/Monthly Film Bulletin. Apr 1957, v24, p46.
Commonweal. Aug 23, 1957, v66, p523.
Film Daily. Jun 17, 1957, p6.
Films and Filming. May 1957, v3, p24.
The Films of Dirk Bogarde. p95-98.
Motion Picture Herald Product Digest. Jun 8, 1957, p411.
The New York Times. Jul 29, 1957, p15.
Variety. Apr 3, 1957, p6.

Doctor Doolittle (US; Fleischer, Richard; 1967)
BFI/Monthly Film Bulletin. Feb 1968, v35, p19.
Christian Century. May 1, 1968, v85, p594.
Commonweal. Jan 19, 1968, v87, p472.
Film Daily. Dec 20, 1967, p6.
Films and Filming. Feb 1968, v14, p22-23.
Films in Review. Jan 1968, v19, p49-50.
Hollywood Reporter. Dec 15, 1967, p3.
Life. Sep 30, 1966, v61, p122-24.
Look. Dec 12, 1967, v31, p86-90.
McCall's. Apr 1968, v95, p137.
Motion Picture Herald Product Digest. Jan 3, 1968, p755.
The New York Times. Dec 20, 1967, p55.
Newsweek. Jan 1, 1968, v71, p64.
Time. Dec 29, 1967, v90, p54.
Variety. Dec 20, 1967, p6.

Dr. Faustus (Also titled: Doctor Faustus) (GB, IT; Burton, Richard; Coghill, Neville; 1967)
America. Feb 3, 1968, v118, p166.
Christian Science Monitor (Western edition). Feb 19, 1968, p6.
Commonweal. Feb 23, 1968, v87, p625.
Film Daily. Feb 6, 1968, p6.
Film Quarterly. Spr 1968, v21, p56.
Filmfacts. Mar 1, 1968, v11, p40-42.
Filming Literature. p166-67.
Films and Filming. Jan 1967, v13, p53-55.
Films in Review. Mar 1968, v19, p176-77.
The Films of Elizabeth Taylor. p184-87.
Going Steady. p49-50.
Hollywood Reporter. Feb 6, 1968, p3.
Motion Picture Herald Product Digest. Feb 28, 1968, p777-78.
The New York Times. Feb 7, 1968, p38.
Saturday Review. Feb 17, 1968, v51, p41.

Senior Scholastic. Mar 14, 1968, v92, p28.
Time. Feb 23, 1968, v91, p95.
Variety. Oct 25, 1967, p20.
The Village Voice. Feb 22, 1968, p47.
A Year In the Dark. p34-35.

Doctor Goldfoot and the Bikini Machine (Also titled: Dr. Goldfoot and the Bikini Machine) (US; Taurog, Norman; 1965)
BFI/Monthly Film Bulletin. Aug 1966, v33, p122-23.
Film Daily. Nov 17, 1965, p6.
Filmfacts. Mar 1, 1966, v9, p23-24.
Hollywood Reporter. Nov 10, 1965, p3.
Motion Picture Herald Product Digest. Nov 24, 1965, p409.
The New York Times. Feb 17, 1966, p29.
Variety. Nov 10, 1965, p6.

Doctor in Distress (GB; Thomas, Ralph; 1963)
BFI/Monthly Film Bulletin. Sep 1963, v30, p130.
Boxoffice. Jul 6, 1964, v85, p2842.
Film Daily. Jun 18, 1964, p7.
Films and Filming. Sep 1963, v9, p31.
The Films of Dirk Bogarde. p140-42.
Motion Picture Herald Product Digest. Jul 8, 1964, p84.
The New York Times. Jul 8, 1964, p38.
Time. Jul 24, 1964, v84, p87.
Variety. Aug 7, 1963, p20.

Doctor in the House (GB; Thomas, Ralph; 1954)
America. Mar 12, 1955, v92, p630.
BFI/Monthly Film Bulletin. May 1954, v21, p73.
Catholic World. Feb 1955, v180, p383.
Commonweal. Feb 25, 1955, v61, p551.
Film Daily. Feb 24, 1955, p10.
Films and Filming. May 1957, v3, p24.
Films in Review. Mar 1955, v6, p133.
The Films of Dirk Bogarde. p70-73.
Hollywood Reporter. Mar 28, 1955, p3.
Illustrated London News. Apr 17, 1954, v224, p632.
The London Times. Mar 22, 1954, p4.
Mademoiselle. May 1955, v41, p124.
Magill's Survey of Cinema. Series II. v2, p646-49.
Motion Picture Herald Product Digest. Feb 19, 1955, p330.
The Nation. Mar 5, 1955, v180, p206.
National Parent-Teacher. Jan 1955, v49, p39.
The New Statesman and Nation. Mar 27, 1954, v47, p403.
The New York Times. Feb 19, 1955, p18.
The New Yorker. Feb 26, 1955, v31, p89.
Newsweek. Feb 28, 1955, v45, p88.
Saturday Review. Mar 12, 1955, v38, p27.
The Spectator. Mar 19, 1954, v192, p322.
The Tatler. Mar 31, 1954, v211, p604.
Time. Mar 7, 1955, v65, p106.
Variety. Apr 7, 1954, p6.

Dr. No (GB; Young, Terence; 1962)
Commonweal. Jun 21, 1963, v78, p355.
Film Daily. Mar 19, 1963, p7.
Filmfacts. Jun 13, 1963, v6, p106-8.
Hollywood Reporter. Mar 15, 1963, p3.
Illustrated London News. Oct 27, 1962, v241, p672.
James Bond and the Cinema. p21-44.
The James Bond Films. p11-22.
James Bond's Bedside Companion. p167-71.
Magill's Survey of Cinema. Series II. v2, p654-56.
The New Republic. Jun 15, 1963, v148, p36.

The New York Times. May 30, 1963, p20.
The New Yorker. Jun 1, 1963, v39, p65-66.
Newsweek. May 13, 1963, v61, p106.
Saturday Review. Jun 1, 1963, v46, p16.
Sight and Sound. Aut 1962, v31, p197.
Time. Oct 11, 1962, v80, p63.
Time. May 31, 1963, v81, p80.
Variety. Oct 17, 1962, p6.
The Village Voice. Jul 4, 1963, p9.

Dr. Strangelove or How I Learned to Stop Worrying and Love the Bomb (US; Kubrick, Stanley; 1964)
America. Mar 28, 1964, v110, p462.
American History/American Film. p219-35.
Beyond Formula. p289-91.
BFI/Monthly Film Bulletin. Feb 1964, v31, p19-20.
The Cinema of Stanley Kubrick. p111-44.
Commentary. May 1964, v37, p75-77.
Commonweal. Feb 21, 1964, v79, p632.
Confessions of a Cultist. p119-22.
Dictionary of Films. p87-88.
Directors and Directions: Cinema for the Seventies. p119-24.
Esquire. Feb 1964, v61, p26.
Fifty Grand Movies of the 1960s and 1970s. p89-92.
Film as Film: Critical Responses to Film Art. p159-69.
Film Comment. Wint 1964, v2, p40-43.
Film Comment. Sum 1965, v3, p55-57.
Film Daily. Jan 22, 1964, p14.
Film Quarterly. Spr 1964, v17, p41-42.
Film Quarterly. Fall 1964, v18, p4-11.
Films and Filming. Feb 1964, v10, p26.
Films in Review. Feb 1964, v15, p113-14.
The Films of the Sixties. p131-33.
Great Horror Movies. p131-32.
The Great Movies. p74-75.
Guts & Glory. p190-95.
Hollywood Reporter. Jan 15, 1964, p3.
The International Dictionary of Films and Filmmakers. v1, p125-26.
International Film Guide. 1965, v2, p26-29.
Kubrick: Inside a Film Artist's Maze. p79-89.
Landmark Films. p268-77.
Life. Mar 13, 1964, v56, p15.
London Magazine. May 1964, v4, p67-70.
Magill's Survey of Cinema. Series I. v1, p465-67.
Motion Picture Herald Product Digest. Feb 5, 1964, p985-86.
Movie Comedy (Byron). p179-83.
The Nation. Feb 3, 1964, v198, p127-28.
National Review. Mar 10, 1964, v16, p203-04.
The New Republic. Mar 21, 1964, v150, p28.
The New Republic. Feb 1, 1964, v150, p26-28.
New York Review of Books. Feb 6, 1964, p12-14.
The New York Times. Jan 30, 1964, p24.
The New Yorker. Feb 1, 1964, v39, p75-76.
Newsweek. Feb 3, 1964, v63, p79.
Nuclear War Films. p58-67.
On Movies. p289-93.
The Private Eye, the Cowboy and the Very Naked Girl. p58-61.
Private Screenings. p122-24.
Renaissance of the Film. p71-78.
Saturday Review. Jan 25, 1964, v47, p24.
Seventh Art. Spr 1964, v2, p2-3.
Sight and Sound. Wint 1963-64, v33, p37-38.
Stanley Kubrick: A Film Odyssey. p105-26.
Stanley Kubrick: A Guide to References and Resources. p46-49.
Stanley Kubrick Directs. p156-21.
Talking Pictures. p348-52.
Time. Jan 31, 1964, v83, p69.

Twenty All-Time Great Science Fiction Films.
p159-69.
*Unholy Fools, Wits, Comics, Disturbers of the
Peace.* p119-22.
Variety. Jan 22, 1964, p6.
The Village Voice. Feb 13, 1964, p13-14.
Vintage Films. p202-06.
A World on Film. p14-19.

Doctor Zhivago (Also titled: Dr. Zhivago)
(US; Lean, David; 1965)
America. Jan 15, 1966, v114, p94.
Atlantic Monthly. Aug 1965, v216, p58-64.
BFI/Monthly Film Bulletin. Jun 1966, v33, p86.
Christian Century. Feb 9, 1966, v83, p178.
Christian Science Monitor (Western edition).
Mar 18, 1965, p4.
Christian Science Monitor (Western edition).
Jan 4, 1966, p4.
Christian Science Monitor (Western edition).
Mar 19, 1966, p4.
Cinema. Mar 1966, v3, p46.
The Cinema of David Lean. p161-98.
Classic Movies. p138-40.
Commentary. May 1966, v41, p73-74.
Commonweal. Jan 14, 1966, v83, p441-42.
Confessions of a Cultist. p225-29.
*David Lean: A Guide to References and
Resources.* p90-92.
David Lean and His Films. p183-99.
David Lean (Anderegg). p121-32.
Esquire. Dec 1965, v64, p132.
Film Daily. Dec 23, 1965, p6.
Film Epic (Castelli). p203-27.
Film Quarterly. Fall 1966, v20, p28-34.
Films and Filming. Jul 1966, v12, p9, 12.
Films and Filming. Jul 1965, v11, p50-51.
Films in Review. Jan 1966, v17, p51-52.
The Films of the Sixties. p158-64.
Guardian. Jan 26, 1965, p11.
Hollywood Reporter. Dec 23, 1965, p3.
Illustrated London News. Dec 18, 1965, v247,
p36-37.
International Film Guide. Sum 1966, v35,
p149.
Interviews With Film Directors. p316-21.
Kiss Kiss Bang Bang. p166-68.
Life. Jan 21, 1966, v60, p48-59.
The London Times. May 29, 1965, p12.
The London Times. Aug 2, 1965, p7.
The London Times. Apr 27, 1966, p7.
Magill's Survey of Cinema. Series I. v1, p468-
70.
Marshall Delaney At the Movies. p195-97.
Motion Picture Herald Product Digest. Jan 5,
1966, p17.
Motion Picture Herald Product Digest. Jan 19,
1966, p451.
National Review. May 31, 1966, v18, p542-44.
The New Republic. Jan 15, 1966, v154, p34, 36.
New Statesman. Apr 29, 1966, v71, p624-25.
The New York Times. Dec 23, 1965, p21.
The New York Times Magazine. May 23, 1965,
p32-33.
The New Yorker. Jan 1, 1966, v41, p46-47.
Newsweek. Jan 3, 1966, v67, p54-55.
Playboy. Mar 1966, v13, p22.
*The Private Eye, the Cowboy and the Very
Naked Girl.* p168-71.
Private Screenings. p232-36.
Saturday Evening Post. Jan 15, 1966, v239,
p26-31.
Saturday Review. Jan 15, 1966, v49, p43.
Second Sight. p46-49.
Senior Scholastic. Feb 18, 1966, v88, p29.
Sight and Sound. Sum 1966, v35, p149.
The Spectator. Apr 29, 1966, v216, p527-28.
Time. Dec 31, 1965, v86, p77.
Time. Dec 24, 1965, v86, p44-45.

Variety. Dec 29, 1965, p6.
The Village Voice. Dec 30, 1965, p15.
Vogue. Feb 15, 1966, v147, p58.

Doctor's Dilemma (GB; Asquith, Anthony;
1958)
America. Jan 10, 1959, v100, p437.
BFI/Monthly Film Bulletin. May 1959, v26,
p54.
Commonweal. Jan 16, 1959, v69, p413.
Film Daily. Dec 16, 1958, p6.
Filmfacts. Jan 14, 1959, v1, p261-63.
Films in Review. Jan 1959, v10, p43.
The Films of Anthony Asquith. p173-77.
The Films of Dirk Bogarde. p110-12.
Hollywood Reporter. Dec 15, 1958, p3.
Library Journal. Jan 1, 1959, v84, p70.
The New Republic. Dec 29, 1958, v139, p22.
The New York Times. Dec 18, 1958, p2.
The New Yorker. Dec 27, 1958, v34, p60.
Saturday Review. Dec 27, 1958, v40, p21.
Time. Jan 12, 1959, v73, p72.
Variety. Dec 3, 1958, p6.

Doctor's Wives (US; Schaefer, George;
1971)
BFI/Monthly Film Bulletin. Aug 1971, v38,
p162.
Deeper into Movies. p256-63.
Filmfacts. 1971, v14, p7-10.
Films and Filming. Jul 1971, v17, p58.
Films in Review. Mar 1971, v22, p176-77.
Hollywood Reporter. Jan 26, 1971, p3.
Life. Feb 26, 1971, v70, p7.
The New York Times. Feb 4, 1971, p30.
The New Yorker. Feb 6, 1971, v47, p89.
Newsweek. Feb 15, 1971, v77, p82.
Time. Feb 13, 1971, v97, p65.
Variety. Jan 27, 1971, p17.
The Village Voice. Feb 11, 1971, p71.

Dodes'ka-Den (JAPAN; Kurosawa, Akira;
1970)
*Akira Kurosawa: A Guide to References and
Resources.* p66-68.
Cinema (Beverly Hills). Spr 1972, v7, p18-19,
20-22.
Commonweal. Jan 7, 1972, v95, p325-26.
Film Quarterly. Sum 1971, v24, p63.
Film Society Review. Nov 1971, v7, n3.
The Films of Akira Kurosawa. p184-94.
Hollywood Reporter. Jun 8, 1971, v216, n29,
p3.
The Nation. Nov 1, 1971, v213, p446.
The New York Times. Oct 30, 1970, p31.
The New York Times. Oct 6, 1971, p39.
The New York Times. Oct 18, 1974, p28.
The Samurai Films of Akira Kurosawa. p62-66.
Saturday Review. Jan 1, 1972, v55, p22.
Sight and Sound. Wint 1970-71, v40, p18.
Time. Dec 27, 1971, v98, p58-59.
Variety. Dec 9, 1970, p14.

The Does *See* Biches, Les

Dog Day Afternoon (US; Lumet, Sidney;
1975)
BFI/Monthly Film Bulletin. Nov 1975, v42,
p236.
Commonweal. Oct 24, 1975, v102, p499.
Films in Review. Nov 1975, v26, p563.
The Films of the Seventies. p129-30.
Hollywood Reporter. Sep 4, 1975, p3.
The Los Angeles Times. Oct 5, 1975, Calendar,
p1.
Magill's Survey of Cinema. Series I. v1, p474-
77.
Motion Picture Herald Product Digest. Sep 24,
1975, p29.
The Nation. Oct 11, 1975, v221, p347.
The New Republic. Oct 4, 1975, v173, p20-21.

The New York Times. Sep 22, 1975, p41.
The New York Times. Sep 28, 1975, SecII, p13.
The New Yorker. Sep 22, 1975, v51, p95.
Newsweek. Sep 29, 1975, v86, p84.
Rolling Stone. Oct 23, 1975, p29.
Saturday Review. Oct 4, 1975, v86, p84.
*Sidney Lumet: A Guide to References and
Resources.* p104-07.
Time. Oct 6, 1975, v106, p66.
Variety. Aug 27, 1975, p15.
Vogue. Oct 1975, v165, p72.

The Dogs of War (US; Irvin, John; 1981)
Film Journal. Feb 16, 1981, v84, p12-13.
Films In Review. Mar 1981, v32, p184.
Hollywood Reporter. Dec 8, 1980, p4.
The Los Angeles Times. Feb 13, 1981, SecVI,
p16.
The Nation. Mar 14, 1981, v232, p316-17.
New York. Feb 23, 1981, v14, p40.
The New York Times. Feb 2, 1981, SecII, p1.
The New York Times. Feb 13, 1981, SecIII,
p10.
The New Yorker. Mar 23, 1981, v57, p138.
Newsweek. Feb 23, 1981, v97, p61.
Rolling Stone. Mar 5, 1981, p43.

Dolce Vita, La (IT; Fellini, Federico; 1959)
America. Jun 3, 1961, v105, p410-11.
America. Oct 7, 1961, v106, p13-15.
American Cinematographer. Apr 1960, v41,
p234-35.
BFI/Monthly Film Bulletin. Sep 1972, v30,
p184.
Christian Century. Apr 19, 1961, v78, p488-90.
Cinema, the Magic Vehicle. v2, p455-59.
Classics of the Foreign Film. p244-49.
Commonweal. May 12, 1961, v74, p177.
Commonweal. May 26, 1961, v74, p221.
Esquire. Apr 1961, v58, p18.
*Federico Fellini: A Guide to References and
Resources.* p79-87.
Fellini (Budgen). p34-44.
Fellini the Artist. p112-33.
Film Daily. Apr 18, 1961, p9.
Films and Filming. Mar 1962, v7, p16-18.
Films in Review. Jun-Jul 1961, v12, p352-54.
The Films of Federico Fellini. p97-105.
The Great Films. p232-36.
The Great Movies. p154-58.
Harper's. Sep 1960, v221, p65-66A.
Hollywood Reporter. Apr 19, 1961, p3.
Hudson Review. Aut 1961, v14, p425-31.
I Lost it at the Movies. p179-96.
*The International Dictionary of Films and
Filmmakers.* v1, p130-31.
Italian Cinema (Bondanella). p323-34.
Journal of Social Issues. Jan 1964, v20, p71-96.
Kenyon Review. Spr 1962, v24, p351-56.
La Dolce Vita. 1961.
Literature and Film. p106-16.
*Magill's Survey of Cinema. Foreign Language
Films.* v2, p857-61.
Motion Picture Herald Product Digest. Apr 22,
1961, p100-01.
The Nation. Apr 29, 1961, v192, p379-80.
National Review. Jun 17, 1961, v10, p392.
The New Republic. May 1, 1961, v144, p22-23.
The New York Times. Apr 16, 1961, SecII, p7.
The New York Times. Apr 20, 1961, p30.
The New York Times. Apr 23, 1961, SecII, p1.
The New Yorker. Apr 29, 1961, v37, p126-28.
Newsweek. Apr 24, 1961, v57, p98.
On Movies. p383-85.
Renaissance of the Film. p79-90.
Saturday Review. Apr 22, 1961, v44, p33.
Saturday Review. May 20, 1961, v44, p37.
Sex Psyche Etcetera in the Film. p106-13.
Sight and Sound. Sum 1960, v29, p123-27.
Time. Apr 21, 1961, v77, p72.

Variety. Feb 17, 1960, p6.
The Village Voice. Apr 27, 1961, p13.
The Village Voice. Nov 23, 1967, p31.
A World on Film. p320-22.

A Doll's House (GB; Losey, Joseph; 1973)
America. Jul 12, 1973, v128, p564.
Commonweal. Nov 2, 1973, v99, p108-09.
Films in Review. Oct 1973, v24, p506.
Holiday. Sep 1973, v54, p8.
Joseph Losey (Hirsch). p197-207.
Magill's Survey of Cinema. English Language Films. Series II, v2, p657.
The New Republic. Jul 2, 1973, v168, p24.
The New York Times. May 23, 1973, p38.
The New York Times. Jul 3, 1973, SecII, p1.
The New York Times. Oct 2, 1973, p54.
The New Yorker. Jul 2, 1973, v49, p65.
Newsweek. Jul 11, 1973, v81, p103.
PTA Magazine. Oct 1973, v68, p8.
Time. Jul 18, 1973, v101, p58.
Variety. May 9, 1973, p6.
Variety. May 23, 1973, p18.

Domani È Troppo Tardi *See* Tomorrow Is Too Late

Domenica d'Agosto *See* Sunday in August

Domicile Conjugal *See* Bed and Board

Don Camillo *See* The Little World of Don Camillo

Dona Flor and Her Two Husbands (Portuguese title: Dona Flor e Seurs Dois Maridos) (BRAZ; Barreto, Bruno; 1977)
The Los Angeles Times. Jun 21, 1978, SecIV, p11.
Magill's Survey of Cinema. Foreign Language Films. v3, p865-67.
The New York Times. Feb 27, 1977, SecIII, p18.
Time. May 1, 1978, v111, p75.
Variety. Sep 14, 1977, p17.

Dongoko *See* The Lower Depths

Donna del Fiume, La *See* Woman of the River

Donna della Domenicia, La *See* Sunday Woman

Donne Senza Nome (Also titled: Unwanted Women; Women Without Names) (IT; Radvanyi, Geza; 1950)
BFI/Monthly Film Bulletin. May 1951, v18, p258-59.
Film Daily. Aug 8, 1951, p6.
Hollywood Reporter. Apr 21, 1952, p3.
The Nation. Sep 1, 1951, v173, p178.
The New Statesman and Nation. Apr 14, 1951, v41, p422.
The New York Times. Aug 7, 1951, p22.
Saturday Review. Aug 18, 1951, v34, p27.
Sight and Sound. May 1951, v20, p19.
The Spectator. Apr 6, 1951, v186, p444.

Donovan's Reef (US; Ford, John; 1963)
BFI/Monthly Film Bulletin. Jul 1963, v30, p95.
The Complete Films of John Wayne. p246-47.
Film Daily. Jun 24, 1963, p7.
Filmfacts. Aug 1, 1963, v6, p148-50.
Films and Filming. Aug 1963, v9, p22.
Films in Review. Jun-Jul 1963, v14, p371.
Hollywood Reporter. Jun 20, 1963, p3.
New Statesman. Jul 12, 1963, v66, p53.
The New York Times. Jul 25, 1963, SecI, p4.
The New York Times. Jul 28, 1963, SecII, p1.
The New Yorker. Aug 3, 1963, v39, p50.
The Non-Western Films of John Ford. p274-78.
Sight and Sound. Sum 1963, v32, p147.

Time. Aug 2, 1963, v82, p50.
Variety. Jun 19, 1963, p6.

Don't Bother to Knock (US; Baker, Roy; 1952)
BFI/Monthly Film Bulletin. Dec 1952, v19, p171.
Catholic World. Aug 1952, v175, p383.
Christian Century. Sep 17, 1952, v69, p1079.
Film Daily. Jul 17, 1952, p6.
The Films of Marilyn Monroe. p76-82.
Hollywood Reporter. Jul 11, 1952, p4.
Library Journal. Oct 15, 1952, v77, p1801.
Motion Picture Herald Product Digest. Jul 19, 1952, p1453-54.
The Nation. Aug 16, 1952, v175, p138.
National Parent-Teacher. Sep 1952, v47, p38.
The New York Times. Jul 19, 1952, p8.
Newsweek. Jul 28, 1952, v40, p81.
A Reference Guide to the American Film Noir. p61.
Time. Aug 11, 1952, v60, p88.
Variety. Jul 16, 1952, p6.

Don't Go Near the Water (US; Walters, Charles; 1957)
America. Nov 23, 1957, v98, p256.
BFI/Monthly Film Bulletin. Feb 1958, v25, p20.
Commonweal. Nov 29, 1957, v67, p234.
Film Daily. Nov 13, 1957, p8.
Films and Filming. Feb 1958, v4, p25.
Hollywood Reporter. Nov 12, 1957, p3.
The New York Times. Nov 15, 1957, p37.
The New York Times. Nov 24, 1957, SecII, p1.
The New Yorker. Nov 23, 1957, v33, p84.
Newsweek. Nov 18, 1957, v50, p132.
Saturday Review. Nov 30, 1957, v40, p22.
Time. Nov 25, 1957, v70, p120.
Variety. Nov 13, 1957, p6.

Don't Look Now (GB; Roeg, Nicolas; 1973)
America. Feb 23, 1974, v130, p134.
American Scholar. Sum 1974, v43, p467-68.
Atlantic. Jan 1974, v233, p94-96.
Audience. Jan 1974, v6, p8-9.
Bizarre. Aug 1974, v3, p27.
Cinefantastique. 1974, v3, n3, p30.
Commonweal. Jan 18, 1974, v99, p389-90.
Esquire. Mar 1974, v81, p70.
Fifty Grand Movies of the 1960s and 1970s. p193-96.
Film Comment. Jan-Feb 1974, v10, p2.
Film Quarterly. Spr 1974, v27, p39-43.
Films in Review. Jan 1974, v25, p49.
Interview. Jan 1974, v4, p37.
Jump Cut. Sep-Oct 1974, n3, p13-17.
The Los Angeles Times. Dec 27, 1973, SecIV, p1.
Magill's Survey of Cinema. Series II. v2, p661-65.
Millimeter. Feb 1974, v2, p40.
Motion Picture Herald Product Digest. Dec 1973, p57.
The New York Times. Dec 10, 1973, p56.
The New York Times. Dec 23, 1973, SecII, p15.
The New Yorker. Dec 24, 1973, v49, p68.
Newsweek. Dec 17, 1973, v82, p91.
Nicholas Roeg (Feineman). p83-104.
Partisan Review. 1974, v41, n2, p273-78.
Progressive. Mar 1974, v38, p54.
PTA Magazine. Mar 1974, v68, p4.
Reeling. p319-24.
Rolling Stone. Feb 28, 1974, p60-64.
Sight and Sound. Wint 1973-1974, v43, p2-8.
Time. Dec 10, 1973, v102, p104.
Variety. Oct 24, 1973, p16.

Doomed *See* Ikiru

Dorado, El (US; Hawks, Howard; 1967)
BFI/Monthly Film Bulletin. Aug 1967, v34, p120-21.
The Complete Films of John Wayne. p267-70.
Film Daily. Jun 9, 1967, p5.
Film Quarterly. Fall 1967, v21, p58-59.
The Films of Howard Hawks (Willis). p62-66.
Focus. Aut 1972, v8, p13-18.
Hollywood Reporter. Jun 12, 1967, p3.
Life. Aug 4, 1967, v63, p8.
The Making of the Great Westerns. p367-80.
Motion Picture Herald Product Digest. Jun 21, 1967, p695.
Movie. Spr 1968, v15, p36.
The New Republic. Aug 5, 1967, v157, p41.
The New York Times. Jun 29, 1967, p32.
Robert Mitchum on the Screen. p195-97.
Saturday Review. Jul 15, 1967, v50, p44.
Sight and Sound. Sum 1967, v36, p148-49.
Time. Jul 28, 1967, v90, p80.
Variety. Jun 14, 1967, p7.
The Village Voice. Jul 27, 1967, p17, 26.

Double Dynamite (US; Cummings, Irving; 1951)
BFI/Monthly Film Bulletin. Feb 1952, v19, p20.
Film Daily. Nov 13, 1951, p6.
The Films of Frank Sinatra. p67-70.
Hollywood Reporter. Nov 7, 1951, p3.
Motion Picture Herald Product Digest. Nov 10, 1951, p1101.
The New York Times. Dec 26, 1951, p19.
The Spectator. Dec 21, 1951, v187, p852-53.
Time. Nov 26, 1951, v58, p106.
Variety. Nov 7, 1951, p6.

Down Three Dark Streets (US; Laven, Arnold; 1954)
America. Mar 12, 1955, v92, p630.
BFI/Monthly Film Bulletin. Dec 1954, v21, p177-78.
Film Daily. Sep 2, 1954, p6.
Hollywood Reporter. Sep 1, 1954, p3.
Motion Picture Herald Product Digest. Sep 4, 1954, p129.
National Parent-Teacher. Oct 1954, v49, p39.
The New York Times. Sep 4, 1964, p6.
Time. Sep 27, 1954, v64, p98.
Variety. Sep 8, 1954, p6.

Downhill Racer (US; Ritchie, Michael; 1969)
America. Nov 22, 1969, v121, p508.
Deeper Into Movies. p57-59.
Directors in Action: Selections From Action. p247-51.
Film Daily. Nov 10, 1969, p22.
Film Quarterly. Spr 1970, v23, p59.
Films and Filming. Apr 1970, v16, p44.
The Films of Robert Redford. p120-27.
Life. Dec 5, 1969, v67, p18.
Magill's Survey of Cinema. Series II. v2, p670-72.
Movies Into Film. p301-03.
The New York Times. Nov 7, 1969, p36.
The New Yorker. Nov 15, 1969, v45, p179-81.
Newsweek. Nov 24, 1969, v74, p118.
Second Sight. p270.
Sight and Sound. Aut 1970, v39, p221-22.
Time. Nov 14, 1969, v94, p101.
Variety. Oct 29, 1969, p16.

Dracula (US; Badham, John; 1979)
BFI/Monthly Film Bulletin. Sep 1979, v46, p195.
Film Comment. Sep 1979, v15, p50-51.
Hollywood Reporter. Jul 6, 1979, p3.
Laurence Olivier: Theater & Cinema. p263-67.

The Los Angeles Times. Jul 13, 1979, SecIV, p1.
Motion Picture Herald Product Digest. Aug 1, 1979, p17.
New York. Jul 30, 1979, v12, p61.
The New York Times. Jun 13, 1979, SecIII, p14.
The New Yorker. Jul 30, 1979, v55, p70.
Newsweek. Jul 23, 1979, v94, p70.
Time. Jul 23, 1979, v114, p80.
Variety. Jul 4, 1979, p24.

Dracula—Prince of Darkness (GB; Fisher, Terence; 1965)
BFI/Monthly Film Bulletin. Feb 1966, v33, p22-23.
Film Daily. Feb 3, 1966, p8.
Filmfacts. Apr 1, 1966, v9, p46.
Films and Filming. Mar 1966, v12, p55-56.
Hollywood Reporter. Jan 24, 1966, p3.
The London Times. Jan 6, 1966, p8.
Motion Picture Herald Product Digest. Feb 16, 1966, p468.
The Spectator. Jan 7, 1966, v216, p13-14.
Variety. Jan 19, 1966, p6.

Dragnet (US; Webb, Jack; 1954)
America. Oct 2, 1954, v92, p26.
BFI/Monthly Film Bulletin. Dec 1954, v21, p178.
Commonweal. Sep 10, 1954, v60, p557.
Film Daily. Aug 20, 1954, p6.
Films in Review. Oct 1954, v5, p435.
Hollywood Reporter. Aug 20, 1954, p3.
Life. Aug 30, 1954, v37, p50-52.
The London Times. Jan 17, 1955, p5.
Motion Picture Herald Product Digest. Aug 21, 1954, p113.
National Parent-Teacher. Oct 1954, v49, p39.
The New York Times. Aug 21, 1954, p10.
Newsweek. Sep 13, 1954, v44, p107.
Senior Scholastic. Oct 13, 1954, v65, p25.
Time. Sep 6, 1954, v64, p87.
Variety. Aug 25, 1954, p6.

Dragonfly Squadron (US; Selander, Lesley; 1954)
BFI/Monthly Film Bulletin. Sep 1954, v21, p132.
Film Daily. Jan 29, 1954, p22.
Hollywood Reporter. Jan 28, 1954, p3.
Motion Picture Herald Product Digest. Feb 13, 1954, p2182.
Variety. Feb 3, 1954, p6.

Dragonslayer (US; Robbins, Matthew; 1981)
Hollywood Reporter. Jun 19, 1981, p2.
The Los Angeles Times. Jun 29, 1981, SecVI, p2.
Maclean's. Jul 6, 1981, v94, p54.
Magill's Cinema Annual, 1982. p125-29.
New York. Jul 20, 1981, v14, p60.
The New York Times. Jun 26, 1981, SecIII, p10.
The New Yorker. Jul 13, 1981, v57, p80-81.
Rolling Stone. Aug 6, 1981, p33-34.
Time. Jul 6, 1981, v118, p69.
Variety. Jun 24, 1981, p23.

Drango (US; Bartlett, Hall; Brieken, Jules; 1957)
BFI/Monthly Film Bulletin. May 1957, v24, p59.
Commonweal. Feb 15, 1957, v65, p512.
Film Daily. Jan 17, 1957, p6.
Films in Review. Mar 1957, v8, p131-32.
Hollywood Reporter. Jan 9, 1957, p3.
Motion Picture Herald Product Digest. Jan 12, 1957, p217-18.

Saturday Review. Feb 9, 1957, v40, p29.
Variety. Jan 16, 1957, p20.

The Draughtsman's Contract (GB; Greenaway, Peter; 1982)
Hollywood Reporter. Jul 15, 1983, p3.
The Los Angeles Times. Jul 28, 1983, SecVI, p1.
Maclean's. Aug 1, 1983, v96, p54.
Magill's Cinema Annual, 1984. p126-29.
National Review. Oct 28, 1983, v35, p1351-52.
The New Republic. May 9, 1983, v188, p26-27.
New York. Jun 27, 1983, v16, p57-58.
The New York Times. Jun 19, 1983, SecII, p23.
The New Yorker. Aug 22, 1983, v59, p76-77.
Newsweek. Jul 4, 1983, v102, p78.
Progressive. Jun 1983, v47, p41.
Time. Jul 4, 1983, v122, p73.
Variety. Jun 22, 1983, p18.
Vogue. Sep 1983, v173, p92.

A Dream of Passion (GREECE; Dassin, Jules; 1978)
America. Nov 25, 1978, v139, p384.
BFI/Monthly Film Bulletin. Mar 1979, v46, p43.
The Los Angeles Times. Oct 18, 1978, SecIV, p1.
Maclean's. Dec 18, 1978, v91, p49.
The New Republic. Nov 4, 1978, v179, p40.
New York. Nov 13, 1978, v11, p128-29.
Newsweek. Nov 13, 1978, v92, p106.
Time. Sep 11, 1978, v112, p86-87.
Variety. May 24, 1978, p34.

Dreamboat (US; Binyon, Claude; 1952)
BFI/Monthly Film Bulletin. Sep 1952, v19, p127.
Christian Century. Oct 8, 1952, v69, p1175.
Commonweal. Aug 15, 1952, v56, p462.
Film Daily. Jul 24, 1952, p4.
The Films of Ginger Rogers. p212-13.
Hollywood Reporter. Jul 21, 1952, p3.
The London Times. Aug 25, 1952, p6.
Motion Picture Herald Product Digest. Jul 26, 1952, p1461.
National Parent-Teacher. Sep 1952, v47, p37.
The New York Times. Jul 26, 1952, p9.
The New Yorker. Aug 2, 1952, v28, p56.
Newsweek. Aug 11, 1952, v40, p86.
Saturday Review. Aug 30, 1952, v35, p24.
The Spectator. Aug 22, 1952, v189, p39.
The Tatler. Sep 10, 1952, v205, p464.
Time. Aug 11, 1952, v60, p92.
Variety. Jul 23, 1952, p6.

Dreamchild (US, GB; Millar, Gavin; 1985)
BFI/Monthly Film Bulletin. Jan 1986, v53, p7.
Hollywood Reporter. Oct 22, 1985, p3.
The Los Angeles Times. Oct 18, 1985, p9.
Magill's Cinema Annual, 1986. p146-50.
The New Republic. Nov 4, 1985, v193, p25.
The New York Times. Oct 4, 1985, SecIII, p9.
The New Yorker. Oct 21, 1985, v61, p123-25.
Newsweek. Oct 28, 1985, v106, p92.
Variety. Oct 9, 1985, p22.
The Wall Street Journal. Dec 17, 1985, p24.

Dreamscape (US; Ruben, Joseph; 1984)
American Cinematographer. Jul 1984, v65, p82-85.
BFI/Monthly Film Bulletin. Oct 1984, v51, p304.
Cinefantastique. 1984, v14, n4/5, p105.
Cinefex. Nov 1984, n19, p60-71.
Film Journal. Sep 1984, v87, p27.
Films and Filming. Aug 1984, n359, p34-35.
Films in Review. Dec 1984, v35, p624-25.
Hollywood Reporter. Aug 15, 1984, p4.
The Los Angeles Times. Aug 15, 1984, SecVI, p4.

Maclean's. Sep 3, 1984, v97, p54.
Magill's Cinema Annual, 1985. p166-70.
The New York Times. Sep 2, 1984, SecII, p11-12.
The New York Times. Aug 15, 1984, SecIII, p24.
The New Yorker. Oct 1, 1984, v60, p106.
Photoplay 1984. Nov 1984, v35, p22.
Variety. May 16, 1984, p131.
The Village Voice. Aug 28, 1984, p52.

Dressed to Kill (US; De Palma, Brian; 1980)
American Film. Dec 1980, v6, p8.
BFI/Monthly Film Bulletin. Nov 1980, v48, p213.
Brian De Palma (Bliss). p88-97.
Christian Century. Sep 24, 1980, v97, p892.
Commonweal. Aug 29, 1980, v107, p466-67.
Double De Palma. p166-69.
Film Quarterly. Fall 1981, v35, p41.
Films in Review. Oct 1980, v31, p497.
Forbes. Dec 22, 1980, v126, p23.
Hollywood Reporter. Jul 24, 1980, p6.
Los Angeles. Sep 1980, v25, p222.
The Los Angeles Times. Jul 25, 1980, SecVI, p1.
Maclean's. Jan 2, 1981, v93, p48.
Maclean's. Sep 15, 1980, v93, p60.
Maclean's. Jul 29, 1980, v93, p54.
Motion Picture Herald Product Digest. Jul 23, 1980, p14.
The Nation. Aug 16, 1980, v231, p165.
National Review. Sep 19, 1980, v32, p1151-54.
National Review. Sep 5, 1980, v32, p1092.
The New Leader. Aug 11, 1980, v63, p27.
The New Republic. Aug 22, 1981, v185, p22.
The New Republic. Aug 23, 1980, v183, p24-25.
New Statesman. Sep 26, 1980, v100, p35.
New West. Aug 11, 1980, v5, p46.
New York. Jul 28, 1980, v13, p44.
The New York Times. Jul 25, 1980, SecIII, p10.
The New Yorker. Aug 4, 1980, v56, p68-72.
Newsday. Jul 25, 1980, SecII, p7.
Penthouse. Nov 1980, v12, p56-57.
Philadelphia Magazine. Oct 1980, p58.
Philadelphia Magazine. Sep 1980, v71, p66.
Playboy. Oct 1980, v27, p42.
Progressive. Oct 1980, v44, p51.
Time. Jul 28, 1980, v116, p66.
Variety. Jul 23, 1980, p18.
The Village Voice. Jul 23, 1980, p42.
The Village Voice. Sep 17, 1980, p43.

The Dresser (GB; Yates, Peter; 1983)
BFI/Monthly Film Bulletin. Apr 1984, v51, p115.
Hollywood Reporter. Nov 14, 1983, p4.
The Los Angeles Times. Dec 7, 1983, SecVI, p1.
Maclean's. Dec 12, 1983, v96, p70.
The New Republic. Dec 12, 1983, v189, p26-27.
New York. Dec 12, 1983, v16, p88-90.
The New York Times. Jun 26, 1983, SecII, p17.
The New York Times. Dec 6, 1983, p88-90.
The New York Times. Dec 4, 1983, SecII, p1.
Newsweek. Dec 5, 1983, v102, p125.
Time. Dec 12, 1983, v122, p106.
Variety. Nov 16, 1983, p16.
The Village Voice. Dec 13, 1983, p78.

Drive a Crooked Road (US; Quine, Richard; 1954)
BFI/Monthly Film Bulletin. Jul 1954, v21, p104.
Commonweal. May 14, 1954, v60, p144.
Farm Journal. May 1954, v78, p137.
Film Daily. Apr 21, 1954, p6.
Hollywood Reporter. Mar 17, 1954, p3.
Motion Picture Herald Product Digest. Mar 20, 1954, p229.

National Parent-Teacher. May 1954, v48, p39.
The New York Times. Apr 3, 1954, p19.
Newsweek. Mar 22, 1954, v43, p103.
Sight and Sound. Jan-Mar 1955, v24, p144.
Time. Apr 12, 1954, v63, p106.
Variety. Mar 17, 1954, p6.

Drole de Paroissien, Un *See* Thank Heaven for Small Favors

Drop Dead, Darling *See* Arrividerci, Baby

The Drowning Pool (US; Rosenberg, Stuart; 1975)
BFI/Monthly Film Bulletin. Sep 1975, v42, p197.
Films in Review. Oct 1975, v26, p502.
Hollywood Reporter. Jun 18, 1985, p3.
The Los Angeles Times. Jun 25, 1975, SecIV, p1.
Motion Picture Herald Product Digest. Jun 25, 1975, p25.
The New Republic. Jul 26, 1975, v173, p20.
The New York Times. Jul 26, 1975, p34.
The New York Times. Jul 6, 1975, SecII, p9.
The New Yorker. Jun 30, 1975, v51, p84.
One Good Film Deserves Another. p111-14.
Time. Jul 28, 1975, v106, p44.
Variety. Jun 18, 1975, p18.

Drum Beat (Also titled: Drumbeat) (US; Daves, Delmer; 1954)
America. Nov 27, 1954, v92, p259.
BFI/Monthly Film Bulletin. Feb 1955, v22, p19.
Commonweal. Nov 19, 1954, v61, p188.
Film Daily. Nov 10, 1954, p10.
Films and Filming. Mar 1955, v1, p22.
The Films of Alan Ladd. p201-03.
Hollywood Reporter. Nov 3, 1954, p4.
The London Times. Dec 24, 1954, p3.
Motion Picture Herald Product Digest. Nov 6, 1954, p201.
National Parent-Teacher. Jan 1955, v49, p39.
The New York Times. Nov 18, 1954, p42.
Newsweek. Dec 13, 1954, v44, p98.
Time. Nov 22, 1954, v64, p105.
Variety. Nov 3, 1954, p6.

Drums Across the River (US; Juran, Nathan; 1954)
BFI/Monthly Film Bulletin. Nov 1954, v21, p161.
Film Daily. Jun 2, 1954, p6.
Hollywood Reporter. May 10, 1952, p3.
Motion Picture Herald Product Digest. May 22, 1954, p1-2.
National Parent-Teacher. Jun 1954, v48, p39.
Variety. May 19, 1954, p6.

Du Rififi a Paname *See* Rififi in Panama

Du Rififi chez des Hommes *See* Rififi

The Duchess of Idaho (US; Leonard, Robert Z.; 1950)
Christian Century. Jul 26, 1950, v67, p903.
Film Daily. Jun 15, 1950, p8.
Hollywood Reporter. Jun 13, 1950, p3.
Motion Picture Herald Product Digest. Jun 17, 1950, p345.
The New York Times. Jul 21, 1950, p15.
Newsweek. Jul 31, 1950, v36, p78.
Time. Jul 31, 1950, v56, p62.
Variety. Jun 14, 1950, p8.

Due Nemici, I *See* The Best of Enemies

Due Soldi di Speranza (Also titled: Two Pennyworth of Hope; Two Cents Worth of Hope; Deux Sous d'Espoir) (IT; Castellani, Renato; 1951)
BFI/Monthly Film Bulletin. Jun 1953, v20, p83-84.

Catholic World. Jan 1953, v176, p304.
Commonweal. Dec 12, 1952, v57, p260-61.
Dictionary of Films. p95.
Films in Review. Dec 1952, v3, p529-30.
Motion Picture Herald Product Digest. Dec 20, 1952, p1647.
National Parent-Teacher. Jan 1953, v47, p38.
The New Statesman and Nation. May 9, 1953, v45, p547-48.
The New York Times. Dec 16, 1952, p44.
The New Yorker. Dec 20, 1952, v28, p110.
Newsweek. Dec 29, 1952, v40, p64-65.
Passion and Defiance. p141.
Saturday Review. Dec 13, 1952, v35, p26.
Theatre Arts. Aug 1952, v36, p67.
Theatre Arts. Feb 1953, v37, p81.
Variety. Jun 4, 1952, p18.

Duel At Diablo (US; Nelson, Ralph; 1966)
America. Jun 25, 1966, v114, p881.
BFI/Monthly Film Bulletin. Aug 1966, v33, p123.
Commonweal. Jul 1, 1966, v84, p419.
Film Daily. May 13, 1966, p3.
Filmfacts. Sep 1, 1966, v9, p170-71.
Films and Filming. Sep 1966, v12, p18.
The Films of Sidney Poitier. p137-41.
Hollywood Reporter. May 16, 1966, p3.
The London Times. Jun 23, 1966, p7.
Motion Picture Herald Product Digest. May 25, 1966, p527.
The New York Times. Jun 16, 1966, p53.
Playboy. Sep 1966, v13, p54, 56.
The Spectator. Jul 1, 1966, v217, p15-16.
Time. Jul 1, 1966, v88, p78.
Variety. May 18, 1966, p6.

Duel At Silver Creek (US; Siegel, Don; 1952)
BFI/Monthly Film Bulletin. Oct 1952, v19, p142-43.
Don Siegel: American Cinema (Lovell). 1977, p52-53, 63-64.
Film Daily. Jul 17, 1952, p6.
Hollywood Reporter. Jul 11, 1952, p3.
Motion Picture Herald Product Digest. Jul 12, 1952, p1442.
National Parent-Teacher. Sep 1952, v47, p37.
The New York Times. Aug 2, 1952, p7.
Newsweek. Aug 4, 1952, v40, p84.
Saturday Review. Jul 26, 1952, v35, p26.
Theatre Arts. Aug 1952, v36, p34.
Variety. Jul 16, 1952, p6.

Duel in the Jungle (US; Marshall, George; 1954)
America. Aug 28, 1954, v91, p527.
BFI/Monthly Film Bulletin. Aug 1954, v21, p120-21.
Film Daily. Aug 6, 1954, p7.
Films and Filming. Oct 1954, v1, p29-30.
Hollywood Reporter. Aug 6, 1954, p3.
The London Times. Jul 5, 1954, p11.
Motion Picture Herald Product Digest. Aug 14, 1954, p105.
National Parent-Teacher. Oct 1954, v49, p39.
Natural History. Oct 1954, v63, p380.
The New York Times. Aug 9, 1954, p13.
Time. Sep 13, 1954, v64, p110.
Variety. Jul 7, 1954, p6.

The Duellists (GB; Scott, Ridley; 1977)
BFI/Monthly Film Bulletin. Dec 1977, v44, p258.
Films in Review. Jan 1978, v29, p52.
Hollywood Reporter. Jan 20, 1978, p2.
The Los Angeles Times. Jan 27, 1978, SecIV, p1.
Motion Picture Herald Product Digest. Dec 14, 1977, p54.
The Nation. Jan 28, 1978, v226, p91-92.

New York. Jan 30, 1978, v11, p58.
The New York Times. Jan 14, 1978, p10.
The New York Times. Feb 5, 1978, SecII, p15.
The New Yorker. Jan 23, 1978, v53, p80-81.
Newsweek. Jan 30, 1978, v91, p55-56.
Saturday Review. Mar 18, 1978, v5, p59.
Time. Feb 6, 1978, v111, p66.
Variety. Jun 1, 1977, p17.
Vogue. Aug 1977, v167, p50.

Duet for Cannibals (US; Sontag, Susan; 1969)
Commonweal. Dec 5, 1969, v91, p306-07.
Deeper Into Movies. p44-45.
Figures of Light. p208-09.
Film. Wint 1970, n57, p29.
Film Comment. Sum 1970, v6, p45-47.
Films and Filming. Feb 1970, v16, p51.
Films in Review. Nov 1969, v20, p572-73.
The Nation. Nov 10, 1969, v209, p515.
The New Republic. Nov 15, 1969, v161, p32.
The New York Times. Sep 25, 1969, p51.
The New Yorker. Nov 1, 1969, v45, p141-42.
Time. Sep 26, 1969, v94, p96.
Variety. May 21, 1969, p18.
Vogue. Oct 15, 1969, v154, p64.

Dune (US; Lynch, David; 1984)
American Cinematographer. Dec 1984, v65, p62-64.
American Film. Dec 22, 1984, v10, p44.
BFI/Monthly Film Bulletin. Feb 1985, v52, p46.
Cinefantastique. 1984, v14, n4/5, p78-79.
Commonweal. Jan 11, 1985, v112, p18.
Dance Magazine. Sep 1984, v9, p108.
Film Journal. Dec 1984, v87, p6.
Film Quarterly. Spr 1985, v38, p53.
Films and Filming. Jan 1985, n358, p36.
Hollywood Reporter. Dec 3, 1984, p3.
The Los Angeles Times. Dec 14, 1984, SecVI, p8.
Maclean's. Dec 24, 1984, v97, p91.
Magill's Cinema Annual, 1985. p171-75.
The Making of Dune. 1984.
New Statesman. Dec 14, 1984, v108, p36.
New York. Jan 14, 1985, v18, p57.
The New Yorker. Dec 24, 1984, v60, p74.
Newsweek. Dec 10, 1984, v104, p93.
On Location. Dec 1984, v8, p38-39.
Playboy. Apr 1985, v32, p33.
Psychology Today. Oct 1984, v18, p70.
Rolling Stone. Dec 6, 1984, p26-28.
Texas Monthly. Jan 1985, v13, p132.
Time. Dec 17, 1984, v124, p99.
Variety. Dec 5, 1984, p16.
Washingtonian. Jan 1985, v20, p66.

E. T. The Extra-Terrestrial (US; Spielberg, Steven; 1982)
America. Jun 26, 1982, v147, p14.
Atlantic. Oct 1982, v250, p100-02.
Christian Century. Jun 23, 1982, v99, p716.
Christianity Today. Jul 16, 1982, v26, p53.
Commentary. Aug 1982, v74, p65-67.
Commonweal. Aug 13, 1982, v109, p442-45.
Hollywood Reporter. May 25, 1982, p3.
The International Dictionary of Films and Filmmakers. v1, p147-48.
The Los Angeles Times. Jun 11, 1982, SecVI, p1.
Maclean's. Jun 14, 1982, v95, p49.
Magill's Cinema Annual, 1983. p151-55.
The Nation. Jul 10, 1982, v235, p59-61.
National Review. Jul 23, 1982, v34, p909-10.
The New Republic. Jul 5, 1982, v187, p26-27.
New York. Jun 14, 1982, v15, p73-75.
The New York Times. Jun 11, 1982, SecIII, p4.
The New Yorker. Jun 14, 1982, v58, p119-22.
Newsweek. Jul 19, 1982, v100, p76.

Newsweek. May 31, 1982, v99, p62-64.
Rolling Stone. Jul 8, 1982, p25-26.
Time. May 31, 1982, v119, p54-60.
Time. Jul 19, 1982, v120, p62-64.
Variety. May 25, 1982, p3.

E Venne un Uomo *See* And There Came a
Man

The Eagle and the Hawk (US; Foster,
Lewis R.; 1950)
Film Daily. Feb 6, 1950, p11.
Hollywood Reporter. Feb 3, 1950, p3.
Motion Picture Herald Product Digest. Feb 11,
1950, p186.
The New York Times. Jul 6, 1950, p31.
Variety. Feb 8, 1950, p11.

The Earrings of Madame De (French title:
Madame De . . .; Also titled: The
Diamond Earrings; The Loves of
Madame De) (FR, IT; Ophuls, Max;
1953)
BFI/Monthly Film Bulletin. May 1954, v21,
p71.
Dictionary of Films. p203.
Film Comment. Sum 1971, v7, p67-68.
Film Daily. Jul 23, 1954, p10.
The Great French Films. p155-58.
I Lost It at the Movies. p87-90.
*The International Dictionary of Films and
Filmmakers.* v1, p272-73.
The London Times. Mar 29, 1954, p9.
Mademoiselle. Nov 1954, v40, p143.
*Magill's Survey of Cinema. Foreign Language
Films.* v2, p903-06.
Max Ophuls and the Cinema of Desire. p105-
35.
Motion Picture Herald Product Digest. Jul 31,
1954, p89-90.
The New Republic. Aug 16, 1954, v131, p21.
The New Statesman and Nation. Apr 3, 1954,
v47, p436.
The New York Times. Jul 20, 1954, p15.
Newsweek. Aug 9, 1954, v44, p80.
Saturday Review. Sep 4, 1954, v37, p26.
The Seventh Art. Sum 1964, v2, p13-14.
Sexual Stratagems. p62-71.
Sight and Sound. Apr-Jun 1954, v23, p196-97.
The Spectator. Mar 26, 1954, v192, p350.
Time. Jul 26, 1954, v64, p77.
Variety. Jul 21, 1954, p6.
Variety. Oct 21, 1953, p18.

Earthquake (US; Robson, Mark; 1974)
American Cinematographer. Nov 1974, v55,
p1325.
BFI/Monthly Film Bulletin. Jan 1975, v42, p7.
Commonweal. Apr 11, 1975, v102, p52-53.
Earthquake. 1974.
Films in Review. Jan 1975, v26, p47.
The Films of Charlton Heston. p218-20.
Hollywood Reporter. Nov 13, 1974, p3.
Independent Film Journal. Nov 27, 1974, v74,
p5.
The Los Angeles Times. Nov 15, 1974, SecIV,
p1.
Motion Picture Herald Product Digest. Nov 27,
1974, p51.
New York. Dec 2, 1974, v7, p76.
The New York Times. Nov 24, 1974, SecII, p1.
The New York Times. Nov 16, 1974, p20.
The New Yorker. Dec 2, 1974, v50, p152-54.
Newsweek. Dec 2, 1974, v84, p104.
Reeling. p511-15.
Time. Dec 9, 1974, v104, p4.
Variety. Nov 13, 1974, p18.
The Village Voice. Dec 23, 1974, p90-91.

East of Eden (US; Kazan, Elia; 1955)
America. Mar 19, 1955, v92, p659.
An American Odyssey. p194-202.
Catholic World. Apr 1955, v181, p60.
Commonweal. Mar 11, 1955, v61, p604.
*Elia Kazan: A Guide to References and
Resources.* p65-68.
Film Culture. May-Jun 1955, v1, p24.
Film Daily. Feb 16, 1955, p5.
Films and Filming. Apr 1955, v1, p24.
Films in Review. Mar 1955, v6, p129-30.
Hollywood Reporter. Feb 16, 1955, p3.
James Dean: A Biography. p61-98.
Kazan on Kazan. p120-44.
Library Journal. Mar 1, 1955, v80, p555.
Magill's Survey of Cinema. Series I. v1, p488-
93.
The Nation. Apr 2, 1955, v180, p294.
The New Republic. Apr 25, 1955, v132, p22.
The New York Times. Mar 10, 1955, p32.
The New York Times. Mar 10, 1955, p33.
The New York Times. Mar 20, 1955, SecII, p1.
The New Yorker. Mar 19, 1955, v31, p140-41.
Newsweek. Mar 7, 1955, v45, p90.
Saturday Review. Mar 19, 1955, v38, p25.
Sight and Sound. Sum 1955, v25, p32-34.
Steinbeck on Film. p137-51.
Time. Mar 21, 1955, v65, p98.
Variety. Feb 16, 1955, p6.

Easy Rider (US; Hopper, Dennis; 1969)
America. Aug 30, 1969, v121, p126.
Atlantic. Oct 1969, v224, p120-24.
Big Screen, Little Screen. p232-34.
Christian Century. Sep 10, 1969, v86, p1169.
Christian Century. Nov 19, 1969, v86, p1491.
Commonweal. Aug 8, 1969, v90, p487.
Confessions of a Cultist. p445-47.
Dictionary of Films. p97-98.
Double Takes. p95-96, 178-80.
Esquire. Sep 1969, v72, p12.
Fifty Grand Movies of the 1960s and 1970s.
p23-26.
Figures of Light. p185-88.
Film 69/70. p34-46.
Film Daily. Jul 18, 1969, p6.
Film Quarterly. Fall 1969, v23, p22-24.
Film Society Review. May 1969, v4, p35-40.
Filmfacts. 1969, v12, p265.
The Films of the Sixties. p286-88.
Focus. Oct 1969, n5, p18-19.
The Great Movies. p160-66.
Hollywood Reporter. Jun 26, 1969, p3.
*The International Dictionary of Films and
Filmmakers.* v1, p137-39.
Journal of Popular Culture. Sum 1970, v4,
p273-85.
Landmark Films. p324-35.
Magill's Survey of Cinema. Series I. v2, p494-
97.
Movies Into Film. p115-17.
The New York Times. Jul 15, 1969, p32.
The New York Times. Jul 27, 1969, SecII, p1.
Second Sight. p240-43.
Sight and Sound. Aut 1969, v38, p211.
Sight and Sound. Wint 1969-70, v39, p36-38.
Twenty-Four Times a Second. p122-33.
Variety. May 14, 1969, p6.

Eating Raoul (US; Bartel, Paul; 1982)
American Film. Oct 1982, v8, p14.
The Nation. Nov 6, 1982, v235, p474.
The New Leader. Nov 29, 1982, v65, p21.
New York. Oct 11, 1982, v15, p86.
The New York Times. Sep 25, 1982, p13.
The New Yorker. Nov 29, 1982, v58, p162-65.
Newsweek. Oct 11, 1982, v100-03.
Rolling Stone. Nov 11, 1982, p34.
Time. Oct 4, 1982, v120, p82.

Variety. Mar 24, 1982, p41.
The Village Voice. Sep 21, 1982, p38-40.

Eboli (Italian title: Cristo si è Fermato a
Eboli) (IT, ALG; Rosi, Francesco;
1980)
American Film. Mar 1980, v5, p66.
Christian Science Monitor. Apr 16, 1980, p22.
Films in Review. May 1980, v31, p313.
Hollywood Reporter. May 15, 1980, p3.
*Magill's Survey of Cinema. Foreign Language
Films.* v2, p911-14.
Motion Picture Herald Product Digest. Apr 9,
1980, p32.
The Nation. Apr 12, 1980, v230, p44.
National Review. May 30, 1980, v32, p673.
The New Republic. Apr 19, 1980, v182, p26.
New York. Mar 31, 1980, v13, p86-87.
The New York Times. Mar 23, 1980, p54.
The New Yorker. May 5, 1980, v56, p165-66.
Newsday. Mar 26, 1980, SecII, p77.
Newsweek. Mar 31, 1980, v95, p85.
Time. Apr 28, 1980, v115, p76.
Variety. Mar 21, 1979, p24.
The Village Voice. Apr 7, 1980, p37.

Echappement Libre *See* Backfire

The Eclipse (Also titled: Eclisse, L') (IT,
FR; Antonioni, Michelangelo; 1962)
America. Feb 2, 1963, v108, p181.
Antonioni (Cameron and Wood). p93-105.
Antonioni (Chatman). p99-105.
BFI/Monthly Film Bulletin. Mar 1962, v30,
p30-31.
Cinema. 1963, v1, n4, p45.
Commonweal. Dec 28, 1962, v77, p367-68.
Dictionary of Films. p98.
Filament. 1983, n3, p6-9.
Film. Spr 1963, n35, p26.
Film Criticism. 1984, v9, n1, p25-37.
Filmfacts. Jan 25, 1963, v5, p356-58.
Films and Filming. Feb 1963, v9, p33.
Films in Review. Feb1963, v14, p114.
*The International Dictionary of Films and
Filmmakers. Vol I.* p139.
Literature/Film Quarterly. 1981, v9, n3, p139-
51.
*Magill's Survey of Cinema. Foreign Language
Series.* v2, p915-18.
*Michelangelo Antonioni: A Guide to References
and Resources.* p108-14.
Motion Picture Herald Product Digest. Jan 23,
1962, p740.
Movie. Feb 1963, n8, p30.
The Nation. Jan 19, 1963, v196, p59.
The New Republic. Dec 29, 1962, v147, p26.
The New Republic. May 11, 1963, v148, p27.
The New York Times. Dec 21, 1962, p5.
The New Yorker. Dec 29, 1962, v38, p60.
Newsweek. Oct 29, 1962, v60, p87-88.
On Movies. p337-39.
Private Screenings. p57-60.
Saturday Review. Oct 27, 1962, p27.
Saturday Review. Nov 3, 1962, p41.
Sight and Sound. Spr 1963, v32, p90-91.
Time. Jan 11, 1963, v81, p89.
Variety. May 9, 1962, p7.
The Village Voice. Dec 13, 1962, p13.
World on Film. p307-13.

The Edge of Doom (US; Robson, Mark;
1950)
Christian Century. Nov 8, 1950, v67, p1343.
Commonweal. Sep 8, 1950, v52, p532-33.
Film Daily. Aug 3, 1950, p6.
Films in Review. Jul-Aug 1950, v1, p20-21.
Hollywood Reporter. Aug 3, 1950, p3.
Library Journal. Jul 1950, v75, p1201.

Motion Picture Herald Product Digest. Aug 5, 1950, p413.
The New Republic. Aug 14, 1950, v123, p23.
The New York Times. Aug 4, 1950, p13.
The New Yorker. Aug 12, 1950, v26, p46.
Newsweek. Aug 14, 1950, v36, p82.
Samuel Goldwyn Presents. p276-78.
Time. Aug 28, 1950, v56, p74.
Variety. May 9, 1950, p8.

Edge of the City (Also titled: A Man is Ten Feet Tall) (US; Ritt, Martin; 1957)
America. Feb 2, 1957, v96, p512.
American Dreaming. p23, 36.
BFI/Monthly Film Bulletin. May 1957, v24, p55.
Commonweal. Jan 25, 1957, v65, p434.
Film Culture. 1957, v3, n1, p16-18.
Film Daily. Jan 3, 1957, v111, p8.
Films and Filming. May 1957, v3, p27.
Films in Review. Feb 1957, v8, p84.
The Films of Sidney Poitier. p72-75.
From Sambo to Superspade. p224-25.
Hollywood Reporter. Dec 26, 1956, p3.
Magill's Survey of Cinema. English Language Films. Series II, v2, p692-94.
The Nation. Feb 9, 1957, v184, p125.
The New Republic. Mar 4, 1957, v136, p22.
The New York Times. Apr 15, 1956, SecII, p5.
The New York Times. Jan 30, 1957, p33.
The New York Times. Jan 31, 1957, p20.
The New York Times. Feb 3, 1957, SecII, p1.
The New York Times Magazine. Jan 20, 1957, p71.
The New Yorker. Feb 9, 1957, v32, p107.
Newsweek. Jan 7, 1957, v49, p68.
Saturday Review. Jan 12, 1957, v40, p59.
Time. Jan 14, 1957, v69, p100.
Variety. Jan 2, 1957, p6.
The Village Voice. Apr 3, 1957, p8.

Educating Rita (GB; Gilbert, Lewis; 1983)
America. Jan 28, 1984, v150, p54.
BFI/Monthly Film Bulletin. May 1983, v50, p130.
Films in Review. Nov 1983, v34, p569.
Hollywood Reporter. May 5, 1983, p3.
The Los Angeles Times. Sep 22, 1983, SecVI, p1.
Maclean's. Oct 3, 1983, v96, p63.
Magill's Cinema Annual, 1984. p136-40.
The New Republic. Nov 21, 1983, v189, p33.
The New York Times. Sep 21, 1983, SecIII, p21.
The New Yorker. Nov 14, 1983, v59, p174-75.
Saturday Review. Sep-Oct 1983, v9, p36-37.
Variety. May 4, 1983, p54.

Edvard Munch (Also titled: Edward Munch) (SWED, NOR; Watkins, Peter; 1974)
Films in Review. Nov 1976, v27, p566-67.
Independent Film Journal. Oct 29, 1976, v78, p12.
The Los Angeles Times. Dec 21, 1976, SecIV, p13.
Magill's Survey of Cinema. Foreign Language Films. v2, p924-28.
The New Republic. Oct 16, 1976, v175, p22-23.
New York. Sep 13, 1976, v9, p89-91.
The New York Times. Sep 12, 1976, SecII, p1.
The New York Times. Sep 13, 1976, p38.
The New Yorker. Sep 20, 1976, v52, p114-16.
Newsweek. Sep 27, 1976, v88, p90.
Peter Watkins (Gomez). p125-28.
The Thousand Eyes Magazine. Nov 1976, v2, p7.
Time. Oct 18, 1976, v108, p97.
Times Literary Supplement. Apr 2, 1976, p372.
Variety. Apr 14, 1976, p27.

The Effects of Gamma Rays on Man-in-the-Moon Marigolds (US; Newman, Paul; 1972)
Commonweal. Feb 9, 1973, v97, p423-24.
Filmfacts. 1972, v15, n21, p533.
Films in Review. Jan 1973, v24, n1, p56.
Hollywood Reporter. Dec 12, 1972, p3.
The New Republic. Jan 20, 1973, v168, p33-34.
The New York Times. Dec 21, 1972, p28.
The New Yorker. Dec 23, 1972, v48, p52-53.
Newsweek. Jan 1, 1973, v81, p55-56.
Reeling. p113-16.
Saturday Review. Dec 9, 1972, v55, p84.
Senior Scholastic. Feb 5, 1973, v102, p18.
Time. Jan 1, 1973, v101, p44.
Variety. Dec 13, 1972, p20.

Effi Briest (WGER; Fassbinder, Rainer Werner; 1974)
Before My Eyes. p97.
BFI/Monthly Film Bulletin. Mar 1978, v45, p45.
Fassbinder, Filmmaker. p91-91, 129.
Fassbinder (Tanam). p157-61.
Hollywood Reporter. Jun 1, 1977, p2.
The Los Angeles Times. Jun 28, 1977, SecIV, p10.
Magill's Survey of Cinema. Foreign Language Films. v2, p929-37.
Modern European Filmmakers and the Art of Adaptation. p248-62.
The New Republic. Jun 25, 1977, v176, p20-21.
The New York Times. Jun 17, 1977, SecIII, p5.
The New Yorker. Jun 27, 1977, v53, p81-82.
Variety. Jul 10, 1974, p18.

Efter Reptitionen *See* After the Rehearsal

The Egyptian (US; Curtiz, Michael; 1954)
America. Sep 4, 1954, v91, p553-54.
BFI/Monthly Film Bulletin. Dec 1954, v21, p172.
Catholic World. Oct 1954, v180, p66.
Commonweal. Sep 3, 1954, v60, p537.
Film Daily. Aug 25, 1954, p18.
Films and Filming. Nov 1954, v1, p18.
Films in Review. Oct 1954, v5, p433.
Hollywood Reporter. Aug 25, 1954, p3.
Library Journal. Oct 1, 1954, v79, p1755.
Life. Sep 6, 1954, v37, p102-03.
The London Times. Oct 18, 1954, p2.
Motion Picture Herald Product Digest. Sep 4, 1954, p130-31.
National Parent-Teacher. Oct 1954, v49, p39.
Natural History. Oct 1954, v63, p379.
The New York Times. Aug 25, 1954, p23.
The New Yorker. Sep 4, 1954, v30, p42-43.
Newsweek. Sep 6, 1954, v44, p76.
Saturday Review. Sep 4, 1954, v37, p26.
Senior Scholastic. Oct 13, 1954, v65, p25.
The Tatler. Oct 27, 1954, v214, p230.
Time. Aug 30, 1954, v64, p76.
Variety. Aug 25, 1954, p6.

Ehe der Maria Braun, Die *See* The Marriage of Maria Braun

8½ (Italian title: Otto e Mezzo) (IT; Fellini, Federico; 1963)
America. Jul 13, 1963, v109, p62.
BFI/Monthly Film Bulletin. Oct 1963, v30, p61-62.
Catholic World. Sep 1963, v197, p295-96.
Cinema. Nov-Dec 1963, v1, p44.
Classic Movies. p185-86.
Close-Up. p345-54.
Commonweal. Jul 12, 1963, v78, p425.
Dictionary of Films. p266-67.
Film and Literature: An Introduction. p259-66.
Film Comment. Sum 1963, v1, p61-62.
Film Comment. Wint 1964, v2, p48.

Film Daily. Jun 25, 1963, p10.
Film Journal. Apr 1963, n21, p116-118.
Film Language: A Semiotics of the Cinema. p140-46.
Film Quarterly. Fall 1963, v17, p43-46.
Filmfacts. Jun 11, 1963, v6, p127-28.
Filmguide to 8½. 1975.
Films and Filming. Oct 1963, v10, p21.
The Films in My Life. p271-72.
Films in Review. Aug-Sep 1963, v14, p433-35.
Great Film Directors. p290-304.
The Great Movies. p176-79.
Hollywood Reporter. Jul 11, 1963, p3.
The International Dictionary of Films and Filmmakers. v1, p350-52.
International Film Guide. 1964, v1, p66.
Italian Cinema (Bondanella). p241-45.
Italian Cinema From Neorealism to the Present. p241-45.
Landmark Films. p258-67.
Magill's Survey of Cinema. Foreign Films. v2, p939-40.
Movie. 1963, n11, p25.
The Nation. Jul 27, 1963, v197, p59-60.
The New Republic. Jul 13, 1963, v149, p28-29.
The New York Times. Jun 26, 1963, p36.
The New York Times. Jun 30, 1963, SecII, p1.
The New Yorker. Jun 29, 1963, v29, p62.
The New Yorker. Jul 6, 1963, v39, p19-20.
Newsweek. Jun 24, 1963, v61, p112.
On Movies. p15-32.
Photoplay. Sep 1963, v64, p10.
Reruns. p170-74.
Saturday Review. Jun 29, 1963, v46, p20.
Sight and Sound. Aut 1963, v32, p193.
Sight and Sound. Fall 1974, v43, p172-75.
Time. Jun 28, 1962, v81, p82.
Two Hundred Days of 8½, 1964.
Variety. May 3, 1963, p6.
The Village Voice. Jun 27, 1963, v8, p13.

Eight Iron Men (US; Dmytryk, Edward; 1952)
BFI/Monthly Film Bulletin. Feb 1953, v20, p19.
Catholic World. Nov 1952, v176, p144.
Christian Century. Nov 26, 1952, v69, p1391.
Commonweal. Jan 30, 1953, v57, p425.
Film Daily. Oct 29, 1952, p6.
Films in Review. Nov 1952, v3, p472.
Hollywood Reporter. Oct 22, 1952, p3.
Motion Picture Herald Product Digest. Oct 25, 1952, p1581.
National Parent-Teacher. Oct 1952, v47, p37.
The New York Times. Jan 2, 1953, p11.
Newsweek. Jan 5, 1953, v41, p60.
Stanley Kramer, Film Maker. p123-30.
Theatre Arts. Dec 1952, v36, p84.
Time. Dec 8, 1952, v60, p104.
Variety. Oct 22, 1952, p6.

Eight O'Clock Walk (GB; Comfort, Lance; 1954)
BFI/Monthly Film Bulletin. Mar 1954, v21, p39.
The London Times. Mar 22, 1954, p4.
Motion Picture Herald Product Digest. Jun 4, 1955, p466.
The Nation. May 21, 1955, v180, p450.
The New Statesman and Nation. Mar 27, 1954, v47, p403.
The New York Times. Apr 30, 1955, p10.
The New Yorker. May 7, 1955, v31, p131.
The Tatler. Mar 31, 1954, v211, p604.
Variety. Mar 24, 1954, p6.

Electra (Also titled: Elektra) (GREECE; Cacoyannis, Michael; 1961)
America. Jan 19, 1963, v108, p122-23.

BFI/Monthly Film Bulletin. May 1963, v30, p60.
Dictionary of Films. p100.
Esquire. Feb 1963, v59, p34.
Film Comment. 1963, v1, n4, p30.
Film Daily. Jan 2, 1963, p7.
Film Quarterly. Sum 1963, v16, p56-59.
Filmfacts. Jan 18, 1963, v5, p331-32.
Films and Filming. May 1963, v9, p24.
Films in Review. Nov 1962, v13, p561.
Hollywood Reporter. Dec 6, 1962, p3.
Motion Picture Herald Product Digest. Jan 9, 1963, p729-30.
The New Republic. Jan 19, 1963, v148, p28-29.
The New York Times. Dec 18, 1962, p5.
The New York Times Magazine. Nov 25, 1962, p92.
The New Yorker. Dec 22, 1962, v38, p78.
Newsweek. Dec 31, 1962, v60, p57.
Private Screenings. p61-62.
Saturday Review. Dec 15, 1962, v45, p29.
Time. Jan 4, 1963, v81, p58.
Variety. May 30, 1962, p6.
Variety. Sep 5, 1962, p6.

Electra Glide in Blue (US; Guerica, James William; 1973)
Commentary. Jan 1974, v58, p54-58.
Films and Filming. Mar 1974, v20, p41-42.
New Statesman. Jan 25, 1974, v87, p124.
The New York Times. Aug 20, 1973, p21.
The New York Times. Aug 26, 1973, SecII, p1.
Sight and Sound. Wint 1973-1974, v43, p54-55.
Variety. May 23, 1973, p18.

Electric Horseman (US; Pollack, Sydney; 1979)
BFI/Monthly Film Bulletin. Mar 1980, v47, p46.
The Films of Jane Fonda. p230-39.
The Films of Robert Redford. p243-50.
The Films of the Seventies. p269-71.
Hollywood Reporter. Dec 10, 1979, p3.
The Los Angeles Times. Dec 20, 1979, SecIV, p31.
Magill's Survey of Cinema. Series II. v2, p701-04.
Motion Picture Herald Product Digest. Dec 26, 1979, p58.
The New Republic. Dec 15, 1979, v181, p24-25.
The New York Times. Dec 21, 1979, SecIII, p10.
Newsweek. Dec 17, 1979, v94, p112.
Time. Dec 17, 1979, v114, p60.
Variety. Dec 5, 1979, p22.

Elektra *See* Electra

Elena et les Hommes *See* Paris Does Strange Things

Eleni (GB; Yates, Peter; 1985)
BFI/Monthly Film Bulletin. Sep 1986, v53, p269.
Commonweal. Nov 15, 1985, v112, p648-49.
Films in Review. Jan 1986, v37, p47.
Hollywood Reporter. Oct 30, 1985, p3.
Horizon. Sep 1985, v28, p19-21.
The Los Angeles Times. Nov 15, 1985, SecVI, p1.
Maclean's. Nov 18, 1985, v98, p71.
Magill's Cinema Annual, 1986. p151-55.
Ms. Dec 1985, v14, p28-29.
The Nation. Dec 28, 1985, v241, p723.
National Review. Dec 13, 1985, v37, p47-48.
The New Republic. Nov 4, 1985, v193, p24-25.
New York. Nov 11, 1985, v18, p114.
The New York Times. Nov 1, 1985, SecIII, p12.
The New Yorker. Dec 2, 1985, v61, p114-17.
Newsweek. Nov 11, 1985, v106, p81.
Theatre Crafts. Nov 1985, v19, p91-94.

Variety. Oct 30, 1985, p16.
The Wall Street Journal. Oct 31, 1985, p26.

Elephant Ca Trompe Enormement, Un *See* Pardon Mon Affaire

The Elephant Man (US; Lynch, David; 1980)
Atlantic Monthly. Nov 1980, v246, p88.
BFI/Monthly Film Bulletin. Oct 1980, v48, p192.
Christian Century. Nov 12, 1980, v97, p1108.
Christian Science Monitor. Oct 9, 1980, p18.
Cineaste. Spr 1981, v11, p28.
Encore. Nov 1980, v9, p42.
The Elephant Man: the Book of the Film. 1980.
Film Quarterly. Sum 1981, v35, p21.
Films in Review. Nov 1980, v31, p567.
Harpers. May 1981, v262, p66-68.
Hollywood Reporter. Sep 25, 1980, p3.
Horizon. Nov 1980, v23, p70.
Los Angeles. Oct 1980, v25, p246.
The Los Angeles Times. Sep 28, 1980, Calendar, p34.
Maclean's. Oct 13, 1980, v93, p66.
Magill's Survey of Cinema. Series II. v2, p705-08.
Motion Picture Herald Product Digest. Jul 24, 1980, p30.
The Nation. Oct 18, 1980, v231, p388.
National Review. Jan 23, 1981, v33, p50-51.
National Review. Jan 23, 1981, v33, p50.
The New Leader. Sep 22, 1980, v68, p18-19.
The New Republic. Oct 18, 1980, v183, p24-26.
New Statesman. Oct 10, 1980, v100, p25-26.
New West. Oct 20, 1980, v5, 1981.
New York. Nov 3, 1980, v13, p81.
The New York Times. Oct 3, 1980, SecIII, p8.
The New Yorker. Oct 27, 1980, v56, p178.
Newsday. Oct 3, 1980, SecII, p7.
Newsweek. Oct 6, 1980, v96, p71-72.
Penthouse. Jan 1981, v12, p50.
Philadelphia Magazine. Oct 1980, p53.
Playboy. Nov 1980, v27, p44.
San Francisco. Dec 1980, v22, p47.
Saturday Review. Oct 1980, v7, p92.
Sight and Sound. Wint 1980-81, v50, p64.
Time. Oct 6, 1980, v116, p92-93.
Variety. Oct 1, 1980, p20.
The Village Voice. Oct 1, 1980, p52.
Washingtonian. Jan 1981, v16, p45.
Washingtonian. Dec 1980, v16, p57.
Washingtonian. Nov 1980, v16, p63.
Washingtonian. Oct 1980, v16, p62.

Elephant Walk (US; Dieterle, William; 1954)
America. May 8, 1954, v91, p172.
BFI/Monthly Film Bulletin. Jul 1954, v21, p98.
Catholic World. Apr 1954, v179, p62-63.
Commonweal. May 7, 1954, v60, p117.
Farm Journal. May 1954, v78, p137.
Film Daily. Mar 29, 1954, p6.
Films in Review. Mar 1954, v5, p145.
The Films of Elizabeth Taylor. p106-09.
Hollywood Reporter. Mar 29, 1954, p3.
Library Journal. Apr 15, 1954, v79, p766.
The London Times. Jul 19, 1952, p11.
Look. May 4, 1954, v18, p72.
Motion Picture Herald Product Digest. Apr 3, 1954, p2245.
National Parent-Teacher. Apr 1954, v48, p39.
Natural History. Apr 1954, v63, p189.
The New York Times. Apr 22, 1954, p37.
The New Yorker. May 1, 1954, v30, p109.
Saturday Review. Apr 17, 1954, v37, p23.
Senior Scholastic. Apr 21, 1954, v64, p30.
The Tatler. Jul 28, 1954, v213, p164.
Time. Apr 19, 1954, v63, p100.
Variety. Mar 31, 1954, p6.

11 Harrowhouse (GB; Avakian, Aram; 1974)
BFI/Monthly Film Bulletin. Aug 1974, v41, p175.
Film. Sep 1974, n18, p20-21.
Films Illustrated. Sep 1974, v4, p4.
Films in Review. Oct 1974, v25, p506.
The Films of James Mason. p244-47.
Hollywood Reporter. Jun 24, 1974, p3.
Independent Film Journal. Jul 10, 1974, v74, p13-14.
Motion Picture Herald Product Digest. Jul 17, 1974, p14.
The Nation. Nov 2, 1974, v219, p443-44.
New Statesman. Aug 16, 1974, v88, p231-32.
New York. Sep 30, 1974, v7, p72-73.
The New York Times. Sep 27, 1974, p49.
The New Yorker. Oct 21, 1974, v50, p170.
Time. Oct 28, 1974, v104, p5.
Variety. Jun 26, 1974, p22.
The Village Voice. Oct 31, 1974, p110.

Elmer Gantry (US; Brooks, Richard; 1960)
America. Jul 16, 1960, v103, p463.
BFI/Monthly Film Bulletin. Feb 1961, v28, p18.
Burt Lancaster: A Pictorial Treasury of His Films. p106-08.
Burt Lancaster: The Man and His Movies. p86-122.
Commonweal. Aug 5, 1960, v72, p402.
Fifty Grand Movies of the 1960s and 1970s. p65-68.
Film Daily. Jun 24, 1960, p6.
Films and Filming. Jan 1960, v7, p30.
Films in Review. Aug-Sep 1960, v11, p431-432.
The Films of the Sixties. p32-35.
Hollywood Reporter. Jun 24, 1960, p3.
Life. Jul 18, 1960, v49, p81.
Madamoiselle. Sep 1960, v51, p57.
Magill's Survey of Cinema. Series I. SecII, p499-501.
Movie. Spr 1965, v12, p10-14.
The Nation. Aug 6, 1960, v191, p78.
The New Republic. Aug 15, 1960, v143, p20.
The New York Times. Jul 8, 1960, p16.
The New York Times. Jul 10, SecII, p1.
The New Yorker. Jul 16, 1960, v34, p57.
Newsweek. Jul 11, 1960, v56, p90-91.
Saturday Review. Jun 25, 1960, v43, p28.
Time. Jul 18, 1960, v76, p76.
Variety. Jun 29, 1960, p8.

Elopement (US; Koster, Henry; 1951)
BFI/Monthly Film Bulletin. Feb 1952, v19, p20-21.
Catholic World. Jan 1952, v174, p304.
Christian Century. Mar 5, 1952, v69, p295.
Film Daily. Nov 13, 1951, p6.
Hollywood Reporter. Nov 7, 1951, p3.
Motion Picture Herald Product Digest. Nov 17, 1951, p1110.
The New York Times. Dec 21, 1951, p21.
The New Yorker. Feb 3, 1951, v26, p74.
Newsweek. Dec 31, 1951, v38, p57.
The Spectator. Dec 28, 1951, v187, p884.
Time. Dec 31, 1951, v58, p60.
Variety. Nov 7, 1951, p6.

The Elusive Pimpernel (GB; Powell, Michael; Pressburger, Emeric; 1950)
BFI/Monthly Film Bulletin. Dec 1950, v17, p184.
The Films of David Niven. p94-96.
Sequence. New Year 1951, n13, p18.
Variety. Nov 15, 1950, p18.

Elvira Madigan (SWED; Widerberg, Bo; 1967)
BFI/Monthly Film Bulletin. May 1968, v35, p73, 94.
Cinema. Spr 1968, v4, p48.
Cinema Journal. Spr 1969, v8, p25-31.
Commonweal. Dec 22, 1967, v87, p84-85.
Film Comment. Fall 1970, v6, p64-69.
Film Heritage. Fall 1968, v4, p29-35.
Film Quarterly. Sum 1968, v21, p48-50.
Films and Filming. Oct 1968, v15, p52.
Films in Review. Dec 1967, v18, p645-46.
Harper's. Dec 1967, v236, p130-31.
Look. Apr 16, 1968, v32, p52-54.
Magill's Survey of Cinema. Foreign Language Films. v2, p961-64.
Motion Picture Herald Product Digest. Nov 1, 1967, p737.
The Nation. Nov 20, 1967, v205, p542.
The New Republic. Dec 2, 1967, v157, p20.
The New York Times. Sep 30, 1967, p26.
The New York Times. Oct 31, 1967, p37.
The New Yorker. Nov 4, 1967, v43, p164.
Newsweek. Nov 20, 1967, v70, p108.
Reruns. p205-08.
Saturday Review. Nov 18, 1967, v50, p57.
Sight and Sound. Spr 1968, v37, p101-02.
Take One. 1968, v1, p25-26.
Variety. May 10, 1967, p6.

Elvis on Tour (US; Adidge, Pierre; Abel, Robert; 1972)
Elvis: The Films and Career of Elvis Presley. p211-15.
Hollywood Reporter. Nov 2, 1972, p4.
The New York Times. Jun 17, 1973, SecII, p1.
Variety. Nov 8, 1972, p18.

The Emerald Forest (GB; Boorman, John; 1985)
BFI/Monthly Film Bulletin. Nov 1985, v52, p338.
Commonweal. Aug 9, 1985, v112, p440.
Film Comment. Nov-Dec 1985, v21, p47-48.
Hollywood Reporter. May 20, 1985, p3.
The Los Angeles Times. Jul 2, 1985, SecVI, p1.
Maclean's. Jul 15, 1985, v98, p55.
Magill's Cinema Annual, 1986. p156-60.
National Review. Aug 9, 1985, v37, p48-49.
New York. Jul 22, 1985, v18, p63-64.
The New York Times. Jul 3, 1985, SecIII, p19.
The New Yorker. Aug 12, 1985, v61, p65-67.
Newsweek. Jul 8, 1985, v106, p74-75.
Time. Jul 29, 1985, v126, p68.
Variety. May 22, 1985, p15.
The Wall Street Journal. Jul 18, 1985, p20.

The Emigrants (SWED; Troell, Jan; 1972)
America. Oct 28, 1972, v127, p347.
American Scholastic. Sum 1973, v42, p500-02.
Christian Century. Dec 13, 1972, v89, p1276-78.
Film Quarterly. Wint 1972, v26, p28-30.
Filmfacts. 1972, v15, n11, p237.
Hollywood Reporter. Mar 13, 1972, p3.
Life. Oct 13, 1972, v73, p28.
The Nation. Oct 16, 1973, v215, p349-50.
National Review. Jan 5, 1973, v25, p36.
The New Republic. Sep 20, 1972, v167, p24.
The New York Times. Sep 25, 1972, p48.
The New York Times. Oct 22, 1972, SecII, p19.
The New Yorker. Sep 20, 1972, v48, p115-18.
Newsweek. Oct 2, 1972, v80, p97.
Reeling. p25-29.
Time. Sep 25, 1972, v100, p64.

Emmanuelle (FR; Jaeckin, Just; 1974)
BFI/Monthly Film Bulletin. Oct 1974, v41, p233.
Cult Movies. p78-81.

Film. Nov 1974, n20, p19.
Films and Filming. Nov 1974, v21, p33.
Independent Film Journal. Dec 25, 1974, v75, p52.
The Los Angeles Times. Feb 2, 1975, SecIV, p15.
Motion Picture Herald Product Digest. Mar 10, 1976, p80.
New Statesman. Oct 11, 1974, v88, p516.
New York. Dec 16, 1974, v7, p92.
The New York Times. Dec 16, 1974, p47.
Time. Jan 6, 1975, v105, p60.
Variety. Jul 31, 1974, p18.

The Emperor's Baker (Czechoslovakian title: Cisaruv pekar a pekaruv cisar) (CZECH; Fric, Martin; 1952)
BFI/Monthly Film Bulletin. May 1954, v21, p69-70.
The London Times. Mar 18, 1954, p10.
The New Statesman and Nation. Mar 20, 1954, v47, p356.
The Spectator. Mar 19, 1954, v192, p322.

The Emperor's Nightingale (Czechoslovakian title: Cisaruv Slavik) (CZECH; Trnka, Jiri; 1949)
BFI/Monthly Film Bulletin. Mar 1953, v20, p31.
Films in Review. May 1951, v2, p46.
The London Times. Feb 2, 1953, p2.
Motion Picture Herald Product Digest. May 19, 1951, p854.
The New Statesman and Nation. Feb 7, 1953, v20, p31.
The New York Times. May 14, 1951, p29.
Variety. May 16, 1951, p6.

Empire des sens, Le *See* In the Realm of the Senses

The Empire Strikes Back (US; Kershner, Irvin; 1980)
America. Jun 14, 1980, v142, p504.
BFI/Monthly Film Bulletin. Jul 1980, v48, p129.
Boston Magazine. Jul 1980, v72, p47.
Chicago. Jul 1980, v29, p72.
Christian Century. Jul 30, 1980, v97, p769.
Christian Science Monitor. May 21, 1980, p19.
Christianity Today. Sep 19, 1980, v24, p28-29.
Commentary. Aug 1980, v70, p58-62.
Commonweal. Jun 6, 1980, v107, p336.
Fantasy and Science Fiction. Sep 1980, v59, p113-15.
Film Quarterly. Spr 1981, v35, p10-16.
Films in Review. Aug 1980, v31, p439.
Forbes. Dec 22, 1980, v126, p23.
Hollywood Reporter. May 12, 1980, p8.
The International Dictionary of Films and Filmmakers. v1, p449-50.
The Los Angeles Times. May 18, 1980, Calendar, p1.
Maclean's. May 26, 1980, v93, p53.
Motion Picture Herald Product Digest. Mar 28, 1980, p97.
The Nation. Jun 21, 1980, v230, p765.
National Review. Jun 13, 1980, v32, p742.
The New Leader. Jun 2, 1980, v63, p20.
New Statesman. May 23, 1980, v99, p789.
New West. Jun 16, 1980, v5, p115.
New York. May 26, 1980, v13, p67.
The New York Times. May 21, 1980, SecIII, p25.
The New Yorker. May 26, 1980, v56, p123-25.
Newsweek. May 19, 1980, v95, p105-06.
Penthouse. Sep 1980, v12, p51.
Philadelphia Magazine. Jul 1980, v71, p55-58.
Philadelphia Magazine. Aug 1980, v71, p56.
Playboy. Sep 1980, v27, p30.

Saturday Review. Jul 1980, v7, p87.
Skywalking: The Life and Films of George Lucas. p204-22.
Variety. May 14, 1980, p14.
The Village Voice. May 26, 1980, p50.
Washingtonian. Jul 1980, v15, p49-51.

The Empty Canvas (Also titled: Noia, La) (IT; Damiani, Damiano; 1964)
BFI/Monthly Film Bulletin. Jan 1968, v35, p11.
Boxoffice. Apr 27, 1964, v85, p2821.
Film Daily. Mar 19, 1964, p5.
Films in Review. Apr 1964, v15, p240.
Hollywood Reporter. Mar 10, 1964, p3.
Motion Picture Herald Product Digest. Apr 1, 1964, p19.
The New Republic. Jun 13, 1964, v150, p3.
The New York Times. May 16, 1964, p12.
The New Yorker. May 30, 1964, v40, p114.
Newsweek. May 18, 1964, v63, p102.
Time. Apr 17, 1964, v83, p128.
Variety. Mar 18, 1964, p7.

Encore (GB; French, Harold; Jackson, Pat; Pelissier, Anthony; 1951)
BFI/Monthly Film Bulletin. Dec 1951, v18, p371.
Catholic World. May 1952, v175, p142.
Christian Century. Sep 24, 1952, v69, p1111.
Commonweal. May 2, 1952, v56, p94.
Films in Review. Apr 1952, v3, p195-96.
Holiday. Jun 1952, v11, p128-30.
Hollywood Reporter. Mar 31, 1952, p3.
Library Journal. Apr 15, 1952, v77, p713.
Motion Picture Herald Product Digest. Apr 5, 1952, p1305.
The New Statesman and Nation. Nov 24, 1951, v42, p590.
The New York Times. Apr 3, 1952, p45.
The New Yorker. Apr 12, 1952, v28, p113.
Newsweek. Mar 17, 1952, v39, p96.
Saturday Review. Apr 5, 1952, v35, p28.
Sight and Sound. Jan-Mar 1952, v21, p125.
The Spectator. Nov 23, 1951, v186, p704.
Theatre Arts. May 1952, v36, p104.
Time. Apr 7, 1952, v59, p106.
Variety. Nov 21, 1951, p6.

The End (US; Reynolds, Burt; 1978)
BFI/Monthly Film Bulletin. Feb 1979, v46, p23.
Film Comment. May 1978, v14, p16-21.
Films in Review. Aug-Sep 1978, v29, p441.
The Films of Burt Reynolds. p211-15.
The Films of Myrna Loy. p252.
Hollywood Reporter. May 3, 1978, p3.
The Los Angeles Times. May 11, 1978, SecIV, p1.
Maclean's. Jun 12, 1978, v91, p70-71.
Motion Picture Herald Product Digest. May 31, 1978, p98.
New York. May 22, 1978, v11, p80.
The New York Times. May 10, 1978, SecIII, p21.
Newsweek. May 22, 1978, v91, p72.
Time. May 22, 1978, v111, p84.
Variety. May 3, 1978, p26.

End as a Man *See* The Strange One

Endless Love (US; Zeffirelli, Franco; 1981)
American Film. Jul-Aug 1981, v6, p46-48.
BFI/Monthly Film Bulletin. Sep 1981, v48, p174.
The Los Angeles Times. Jul 17, 1981, SecVI, p14.
The New Leader. Aug 10, 1981, v64, p21.
New Statesman. Oct 23, 1981, v102, p27.
New York. Jul 27, 1981, v14, p51-52.
The New York Times. Jul 17, 1981, SecIII, p6.
Newsweek. Jul 27, 1981, v98, p74.

Time. Jul 27, 1981, v118, p62.
Variety. Jul 22, 1981, p16.
The Village Voice. Jul 22, 1981, p42.

The Endless Summer (US; Brown, Bruce; 1966)
BFI/Monthly Film Bulletin. Mar 1968, v35, p45.
Christian Science Monitor (Western edition). Oct 14, 1966, p6.
Commonweal. Jul 8, 1966, v84, p441.
Film Quarterly. Fall 1967, v21, p59.
Filmfacts. Aug 15, 1966, v9, p160-61.
Films and Filming. Mar 1968, v14, p26-27.
Life. Nov 25, 1966, v61, p19.
The London Times. Feb 8, 1968, p7.
Motion Picture Herald Product Digest. Jul 13, 1966, p560A.
The New York Times. Jun 16, 1966, p53.
The New Yorker. Jul 9, 1966, v42, p78.
Newsweek. Aug 1, 1966, v68, p84.
Playboy. Nov 1966, v13, p48.
Saturday Review. Dec 10, 1966, v49, p65.
Senior Scholastic. Sep 30, 1966, v89, p33.
Time. Jul 8, 1966, v88, p84.
Variety. Jun 22, 1966, p20.

The Enemy Below (US; Powell, Dick; 1957)
America. Jan 4, 1958, v98, p404.
BFI/Monthly Film Bulletin. Feb 1958, v25, p20.
Commonweal. Jan 24, 1958, v67, p432.
Film Daily. Nov 25, 1957, p6.
Films and Filming. Mar 1958, v4, p24.
Films in Review. Jan 1958, v9, p26.
Hollywood Reporter. Nov 25, 1957, p3.
Magill's Survey of Cinema. Series II. v2, p712-14.
The Nation. Jan 11, 1958, v186, p38.
The New Republic. Mar 3, 1958, v138, p21-22.
The New York Times. Dec 26, 1957, p23.
The New Yorker. Janaury 18, 1958, v33, p95.
Newsweek. Jan 6, 1958, v51, p69.
Saturday Review. Jan 18, 1958, v41, p24.
Time. Jan 13, 1958, v71, p92.
Variety. Nov 27, 1957, p6.

Enfant Sauvage, L' *See* The Wild Child

Enfants Terribles, Les (Also titled: The Strange Ones) (FR; Melville, Jean-Pierre; 1949)
Andy Warhol's Interview. Apr 1975, v5, p43.
BFI/Monthly Film Bulletin. Dec 1952, v19, p166.
Christian Century. Dec 3, 1952, v69, p1423.
Cinema Journal. n2, 1980, v19, p25-40.
Cinema, the Magic Vehicle. v1, p514-15.
Commonweal. Aug 1, 1952, v56, p412-13.
Films and Filming. Oct 1976, v23, p41-42.
The Great French Films. p122-26.
Jean Cocteau (Gilson). p40-43.
Kiss Kiss Bang Bang. p325.
Magill's Survey of Cinema. Foreign Language Films. v2, p977-81.
Melville on Melville. p38-47.
Motion Picture Herald Product Digest. Aug 9, 1952, p1477.
The New Statesman and Nation. May 9, 1953, v45, p547.
The New Statesman and Nation. Nov 15, 1952, v44, p574-75.
The New Statesman and Nation. Aug 13, 1976, v91, p217-18.
New York. Mar 10, 1975, v8, p82-83.
The New York Times. Jul 29, 1952, p17.
The New Yorker. Aug 9, 1952, v28, p55.
Newsweek. Aug 11, 1952, v40, p87.
Saturday Review. Jul 26, 1952, v35, p27.
Saturday Review. Feb 12, 1955, v38, p43.
Sight and Sound. Oct-Dec 1952, v22, p79.

The Spectator. Nov 7, 1952, v189, p596-97.
The Tatler. Nov 19, 1952, v206, p433.
Theatre Arts. Oct 1952, v36, p72.
Time. Jul 21, 1952, v60, p96.
Variety. May 24, 1950, p20.
The Village Voice. Mar 3, 1975, p71.
The Village Voice. Mar 24, 1975, p78-79.
Vision. Spr 1962, v1, p17-19.

The Enforcer (Also titled: Murder, Inc.) (US; Windust, Bretaigne; 1951)
BFI/Monthly Film Bulletin. Sep 1951, v18, p326.
Classics of the Gangster Film. p195-98.
Commonweal. Feb 9, 1951, v53, p448.
The Complete Films of Humphrey Bogart. p157-58.
Film Daily. Jan 24, 1951, p6.
The Films of the Seventies. p157-58.
The Great Gangster Pictures. p132-33.
Halliwell's Harvest. p32-35.
Hollywood Reporter. Jan 23, 1951, p3.
Humphrey Bogart: The Man and His Films. p155.
The London Times. Aug 20, 1951, p8.
Motion Picture Herald Product Digest. Jan 27, 1951, p689.
The New Republic. Feb 12, 1951, v124, p23.
The New York Times. Jan 26, 1951, p19.
The New Yorker. Feb 3, 1951, v26, p74.
Newsweek. Feb 5, 1951, v37, p81.
The Spectator. Aug 17, 1951, v187, p212.
Time. Feb 12, 1951, v57, p90.
Variety. Jan 24, 1951, p6.
The Velvet Light Trap. Sum 1983, n20, p2-9.

Enough Rope (French title: Meurtrier, Le; Also titled: The Murderer) (FR; Autant-Lara, Claude; 1963)
Film Daily. May 5, 1966, p5.
Filmfacts. Sep 15, 1966, v9, p187-88.
Films in Review. Jun-Jul 1966, v17, p383.
Hollywood Reporter. Apr 28, 1966, p3.
Motion Picture Herald Product Digest. May 11, 1966, p519.
The New York Times. Jul 15, 1966, p34.
Saturday Review. Apr 30, 1966, v49, p53.
Time. May 6, 1966, v87, p105.
Variety. Feb 20, 1963, p6.

Enter Laughing (US; Reiner, Carl; 1967)
America. Sep 9, 1967, v117, p254-55.
BFI/Monthly Film Bulletin. Aug 1969, v36, p172.
Christian Century. Nov 1, 1967, v84, p1401.
Film Daily. Aug 1, 1967, p3.
Film Quarterly. Spr 1968, v21, p56-58.
Hollywood Reporter. Jul 31, 1967, p3.
Motion Picture Herald Product Digest. Aug 2, 1967, p710.
The New York Times. Aug 1, 1967, p24.
The New Yorker. Aug 5, 1967, v43, p64.
Newsweek. Aug 7, 1967, v70, p75-76.
Time. Aug 18, 1967, v90, p63.
Variety. Aug 2, 1967, p7.
The Village Voice. Sep 7, 1967, p29.
Vogue. Aug 1, 1967, v150, p42.

The Entertainer (GB; Richardson, Tony; 1960)
BFI/Monthly Film Bulletin. Sep 1960, v27, p124.
Commonweal. Oct 21, 1960, v73, p97.
Film Daily. Oct 5, 1960, p6.
Film Journal. Oct 1961, v18, p15-17.
Film Quarterly. Wint 1960, v14, p42.
Filmfacts. 1960, v3, p235.
Films and Filming. May 1960, v6, p21.
Films in Review. Oct 1960, v11, p486-87.
The Films of Laurence Olivier. p126-29.

The Great British Films. p184-86.
Hollywood Reporter. Dec 16, 1960, p3.
Hollywood UK. p74-79.
Laurence Olivier: Theater & Cinema. p144-48.
Magill's Survey of Cinema. Series II. v2, p720-23.
McCall's. Nov 1960, v88, p220.
Motion Picture Herald Product Digest. Oct 8, 1960, p876.
The Nation. Nov 5, 1960, v191, p355.
The New Republic. Oct 17, 1960, v143, p20-21.
The New York Times. Oct 4, 1960, p49.
The New York Times. Oct 9, SecII, p1.
The New Yorker. Oct 15, 1960, v36, p134.
Newsweek. Oct 10, 1960, v56, p104.
Sight and Sound. Aut 1960, v29, p194-95.
Time. Oct 3, 1960, v76, p73.
Variety. Aug 3, 1960, p6.
A World on Film. p183-85.

Entertaining Mr. Sloane (GB; Hickox, Douglas; 1970)
BFI/Monthly Film Bulletin. Apr 1970, v37, p72.
Films and Filming. Jun 1970, v16, p82-83.
The Great British Films. p247-50.
Magill's Survey of Cinema. Series II. v2, p724.
The New York Times. Jul 28, 1970, p22.
The New Yorker. Aug 1, 1970, v46, p69-70.
Newsweek. Aug 3, 1970, v76, p64-65.
Take One. 1970, v2, n8, p20-21.
Time. Aug 17, 1970, v96, p32.
Variety. Apr 18, 1970, p22.

Enticement *See* Sensualita

Entre Nous (Also titled: Coup de Foudre) (FR; Kurys, Diane; 1983)
Christian Century. Jul 18, 1984, v101, p722-23.
Cineaste. 1984, v13, n3, p45-47.
Commonweal. Apr 20, 1984, v111, p242-43.
Film. Dec 1983, n121, p11.
Film Comment. Mar-Apr 1984, v20, p15-17.
Films and Filming. Jan 1984, n353, p32.
Informer. Apr 1984, p3-4.
The Los Angeles Times. Feb 16, 1984, SecVI, p1.
Maclean's. Feb 20, 1984, v97, p62.
Magill's Cinema Annual, 1985. p176-80.
Ms. Dec 1983, v12, p23.
National Review. May 4, 1984, v36, p54-56.
The New Republic. Feb 27, 1984, v190, p22-24.
New York. Jan 23, 1984, v17, p57-59.
The New York Times. Jan 25, 1984, SecIII, p17.
The New York Times. Jan 29, 1984, SecII, p13.
The New Yorker. Mar 5, 1984, v60, p130.
Newsweek. Feb 6, 1984, v103, p81.
Time. Jan 30, 1984, v123, p78.
Variety. Jan 18, 1984, p26.
The Village Voice. Jan 31, 1984, p55.

Equus (US; Lumet, Sidney; 1977)
America. Nov 5, 1977, v137, p314.
BFI/Monthly Film Bulletin. Nov 1977, v44, p232.
Christian Century. Apr 5, 1978, v95, p367-68.
Films in Review. Dec 1977, v28, p629.
Hollywood Reporter. Oct 17, 1977, p3.
The Los Angeles Times. Nov 13, 1977, Calendar, p58.
Motion Picture Herald Product Digest. Oct 19, 1977, p38.
National Review. Dec 9, 1977, v29, p1444.
The New Republic. Nov 5, 1977, v117, p24-26.
The New York Times. Oct 17, 1977, p39.
The New Yorker. Nov 7, 1977, v53, p120-22.
Newsweek. Oct 24, 1977, v90, p125.
Sidney Lumet: A Guide to References and Resources. p110-14.
Time. Oct 31, 1977, v110, p91.
Variety. Oct 19, 1977, p25.

Eraserhead (US; Lynch, David; 1977)
BFI/Monthly Film Bulletin. Mar 1979, v46, p44.
Cult Movies. p86-89ee.
Film Review Annual 1981. p283-84.
The Los Angeles Times. Feb 20, 1978, SecIV, p12.
The New York Times. Oct 17, 1980, SecII, p15.
Newsweek. Sep 11, 1978, v92, p95.
Variety. Mar 23, 1977, p24.
The World of Fantastic Films. p147-50.

Erendira (WGER; Guerra, Ruy; 1983)
America. Nov 1983, v35, p56.
American Film. Sep 1984, v9, p12.
Film Journal. Jun 1984, v87, p25.
Forbes. Nov 1, 1984, v134, p13.
The Los Angeles Times. Jun 9, 1984, SecV, p8.
Magill's Cinema Annual, 1985. p181-85.
Ms. Jul 1984, v13, p48.
The New York Times. Oct 1, 1983, p16.
The New York Times. Apr 27, 1984, SecIII, p8.
The New Yorker. Jun 11, 1984, v60, p106.
Progressive. Aug 1984, v48, p40-41.
Time. Jul 23, 1984, v124, p102.
Variety. Apr 25, 1984, p22.
The Village Voice. May 8, 1984, p46.

Escapade in Japan (US; Lubin, Arthur; 1957)
America. Dec 7, 1957, v98.
BFI/Monthly Film Bulletin. Feb 1958, v25, p21.
Commonweal. Dec 13, 1957, v67, p288.
Film Daily. Sep 16, 1957, v112, p8.
Films and Filming. Feb 1958, v4, p26.
Hollywood Reporter. Sep 11, 1957, p3.
Motion Picture World. Sep 14, 1957, v208, p529-30.
The New York Times. Dec 24, 1957, p11.
The New Yorker. Jan 11, 1958, v33, p103.

Escape from Alcatraz (US; Siegel, Don; 1979)
BFI/Monthly Film Bulletin. Jan 1980, v47, p5-6.
Films in Review. Aug-Sep 1979, v30, p434.
The Films of Clint Eastwood. p209-15.
Hollywood Reporter. Jun 20, 1979, p3.
The Los Angeles Times. Jun 22, 1979, SecIV, p26.
Motion Picture Herald Product Digest. Apr 20, 1979, p20.
The New Republic. Jul 21, 1979, v181, p26.
New York. Jul 9, 1979, v12, p89-90.
The New York Times. Jun 22, 1979, v3, p5.
The New Yorker. Jul 9, 1979, v55, p75.
Time. Jul 2, 1979, v114, p72.
Variety. Jun 20, 1979, p18.

Escape from Fort Bravo (US; Sturges, John; 1953)
America. Dec 19, 1953, v90, p327.
BFI/Monthly Film Bulletin. Apr 1954, v21, p52.
Commonweal. Dec 25, 1953, v59, p307.
Film Daily. Nov 9, 1953, p6.
Films in Review. Jan 1954, v5, n1, p34.
The Films of William Holden. p146-49.
Hollywood Reporter. Nov 5, 1953, p5.
The New York Times. Jan 23, 1954, p11.
The New Yorker. Jan 30, 1954, v29, p87.
Newsweek. Dec 7, 1953, v42, p98.
Saturday Review. Dec 12, 1953, v36, p49.
Time. Dec 14, 1953, v62, p108.
Variety. Nov 11, 1953, p6.

Escape From New York (US; Carpenter, John; 1981)
Film Comment. Jul-Aug 1981, v17, p2.
Hollywood Reporter. Jun 12, 1981, p3.

Humanist. Nov-Dec 1981, v41, p49.
The Los Angeles Times. Jul 10, 1981, SecVI, p5.
Maclean's. Jul 13, 1981, v94, p48-49.
Magill's Cinema Annual, 1982. p133-37.
The New York Times. Aug 2, 1981, SecII, p15.
Newsweek. Jul 27, 1981, v98, p75.
Rolling Stone. Aug 20, 1981, p33.
Saturday Review. Aug 1981, v8, p61.
Time. Jul 13, 1981, v118, p60.

Escape From the Planet of the Apes (US; Taylor, Don; 1971)
BFI/Monthly Film Bulletin. Aug 1971, v38, p163.
Filmfacts. 1971, v14, p203-05.
Films and Filming. Oct 1971, v18, n1, p64, 66.
Films in Review. Aug-Sep 1971, v22, p438-39.
Hollywood Reporter. May 20, 1971, p3.
Journal of Popular Culture. Fall 1971, v5, p473.
The New York Times. May 29, 1971, p10.
The New Yorker. Jun 5, 1971, v47, p102-04.
One Good Film Deserves Another. p121-29.
Variety. May 26, 1971, p23.
The Village Voice. Jul 1, 1971, p54.

Escape of the Amethyst *See* Battle Hell

Escape to Nowhere (French title: Silencieux, Le) (FR, IT; Pinoteau, Charles; 1973)
Audience. Sep 1974, v7, p13-14.
BFI/Monthly Film Bulletin. May 1974, v41, p106.
Films and Filming. Jun 1974, v20, p50.
Hollywood Reporter. Aug 5, 1974, p3.
Independent Film Journal. Aug 21, 1974, v74, p9.
The Nation. Nov 2, 1974, v219, p444.
The New Republic. Aug 31, 1974, v171, p20.
New Statesman. May 10, 1974, v87, p672.
New York. Sep 2, 1974, v7, p66-67.
The New York Times. Aug 5, 1974, p30.
The New Yorker. Aug 12, 1974, v50, p78.
Time. Sep 9, 1974, v104, p3.
Variety. Mar 14, 1973, p21.

Espion, L' *See* The Defector

Et Dieu...Créa la Femme *See* And God Created Woman

Etat de Siege *See* State of Siege

Europa Fifty-One (Also titled: Europa '51; The Greatest Love) (IT; Rossellini, Roberto; 1952)
Catholic World. Apr 1954, v179, p64.
Films in Review. Feb 1954, v5, p92-93.
The Films of Ingrid Bergman. p134-36.
Hollywood Reporter. Jul 12, 1954, p3.
Magill's Survey of Cinema. Foreign Language Films. v3, p1295-99.
Motion Picture Herald Product Digest. Jan 16, 1954, p2142.
The New York Times. Jan 12, 1954, p19.
Newsweek. Jan 25, 1954, v43, p90.
Roberto Rossellini (Guarner). p50-53.
The Spectator. Feb 22, 1952, v188, p228.
Variety. Sep 24, 1952, p6.

The Europeans (GB; Ivory, James; 1979)
America. Nov 24, 1979, v141, p323.
BFI/Monthly Film Bulletin. Aug 1979, v46, p171-72.
Commonweal. Nov 23, 1979, v106, p663.
Commonweal. Dec 7, 1979, v106, p691-92.
Film Comment. Nov 1979, v15, p72.
Films in Review. Dec 1979, v30, p625.
Hollywood Reporter. Dec 11, 1979, p3.
The Los Angeles Times. Dec 16, 1979, Calendar, p54.
The Nation. Oct 27, 1979, v229, p410.

The New Republic. Oct 27, 1979, v181, p23.
New York. Dec 10, 1979, v12, p137.
The New York Times. Oct 2, 1979, SecIII, p8.
The New Yorker. Oct 15, 1979, v55, p182.
Newsweek. Oct 22, 1979, v94, p104.
Time. Oct 29, 1979, v114, p92.
Variety. May 16, 1979, p27.

Eva (Also titled: Eve) (FR, IT; Losey, Joseph; 1962)
BFI/Monthly Film Bulletin. Sep 1963, v30, p128.
Christian Science Monitor (Western edition). Dec 18, 1965, p6.
The Cinema of Joseph Losey. p106-26.
Film Daily. Jun 7, 1965, p6.
Films and Filming. Sep 1963, v9, p25.
Films and Filming. Apr 1966, v12, p32.
Illustrated London News. Aug 3, 1963, v243, p180.
Magill's Survey of Cinema. Foreign Language Films. v3, p1005-10.
Motion Picture Herald Product Digest. Jun 23, 1965, p316.
The New Republic. Apr 3, 1965, v152, p23.
New Statesman. Jul 26, 1963, v66, p121.
The New York Times. Jun 5, 1965, p21.
The New Yorker. Jun 12, 1965, v41, p102.
Newsweek. Jun 14, 1965, v65, p116.
The Private Eye, the Cowboy and the Very Naked Girl. p133-35.
Saturday Review. Feb 20, 1965, v48, p44.
The Spectator. Jul 26, 1963, v211, p110.
Time. Jun 11, 1965, v85, p108.
Variety. Oct 17, 1962, p17.

Evangile Selon Saint Matthieu, L' *See* The Gospel According to St. Matthew

Every Day Is a Holiday (Spanish title: Cabriola) (SP, US; Ferrer, Mel; 1966)
Film Daily. Jun 24, 1966, p8.
Filmfacts. Jan 15, 1967, v9, p357-58.
Films and Filming. Apr 1969, v15, p44.
Hollywood Reporter. Jun 23, 1966, p3.
Motion Picture Herald Product Digest. Jul 6, 1966, p555.
Variety. Jul 6, 1966, p6.

Every Day's a Holiday *See* Gold of Naples

Every Man for Himself (French title: Sauve Qui Peut; Vie, La) (FR; Godard, Jean-Luc; 1980)
Christian Century. Dec 3, 1980, v97, p1196.
Christian Science Monitor. Oct 9, 1980, p18.
Christian Science Monitor. Oct 30, 1980, p18.
Cineaste. Fall 1980, v10, p6.
Commonweal. Nov 21, 1980, v107, p663-64.
Film Comment. Nov-Dec 1980, v16, p67-68.
Films in Review. Jan 1981, v32, p58.
Hollywood Reporter. Oct 21, 1980, p18.
The Los Angeles Times. Jan 11, 1981, Calendar, p21.
Magill's Cinema Annual, 1982. p139-43.
The Nation. Nov 8, 1980, v231, p491-93.
The New Leader. Nov 3, 1980, v63, p19-20.
The New Republic. Nov 1, 1980, v183, p24-25.
New York. Oct 6, 1980, v13, p28.
New York. Oct 20, 1980, v13, p83-84.
The New York Times. Oct 8, 1980, SecIII, p21.
The New Yorker. Nov 24, 1980, v56, p197-98.
Newsweek. Oct 20, 1980, v96, p83-84.
Progressive. Dec 1980, v44, p52-53.
Rolling Stone. Nov 27, 1980, p32.
Time. Oct 27, 1980, v116, p94.
Variety. May 28, 1980, p15.

Everything For Sale (Polish title: Wszystko na Sprzedaz) (POL; Wajda, Andrzej; 1968)

BFI/Monthly Film Bulletin. Aug 1969, v36, p168-69.
The Cinema of Andrzej Wajda. p99-114.
Film Quarterly. Wint 1969-70, v23, p37-41.
Films and Filming. Sep 1969, v15, p58-59.
The London Times. Jun 19, 1969, p11.
Magill's Survey of Cinema. Foreign Language Films. v3, p1016-20.
New Statesman. Jun 20, 1969, v77, p883-84.
Sight and Sound. Sum 1969, v38, p139-41.
The Spectator. Jun 21, 1969, v222, p829.
Variety. Jan 1, 1969, p6.

Everything I Have Is Yours (US; Leonard, Robert Z.; 1952)
BFI/Monthly Film Bulletin. Jan 1953, v20, p8.
Catholic World. Nov 1952, v176, p144.
Christian Century. Nov 19, 1952, v69, p1367.
Commonweal. Nov 7, 1952, v57, p120.
Film Daily. Sep 29, 1952, p6.
Hollywood Reporter. Sep 24, 1952, p3.
Motion Picture Herald Product Digest. Sep 27, 1952, p1541.
National Parent-Teacher. Nov 1952, v47, p37.
The New York Times. Oct 30, 1952, p40.
Newsweek. Nov 3, 1952, v40, p106.
Time. Nov 3, 1952, v60, p104.
Variety. Sep 24, 1952, p6.

Excalibur (GB; Boorman, John; 1981)
Christian Century. May 27, 1981, v98, p619.
Christian Century. Jul 29, 1981, v98, p774-76.
Film Comment. May-Jun 1981, v17, p49-53.
Hollywood Reporter. Apr 6, 1981, p2.
John Boorman (Ciment). p178-202.
The Los Angeles Times. Jun 17, 1981, SecVI, p1.
Maclean's. Apr 27, 1981, v94, p50.
Magill's Cinema Annual, 1982. p144-47.
The Nation. May 16, 1981, v232, p612-13.
The New Leader. May 4, 1981, v64, p17.
New York. Apr 13, 1981, v14, p52.
The New York Times. Apr 10, 1981, SecIII, p11.
Newsweek. Apr 13, 1981, v97, p82.
Rolling Stone. May 14, 1981, p36-37.
Time. Apr 13, 1981, v117, p96.
Variety. Apr 8, 1981, p18.

Excuse My Dust (US; Rowland, Roy; 1951)
BFI/Monthly Film Bulletin. Jul 1951, v18, p296.
Christian Century. Jul 25, 1951, v68, p879.
Commonweal. Jul 27, 1951, v54, p380.
Film Daily. May 31, 1951, p7.
Hollywood Reporter. May 23, 1951, p3.
Library Journal. Jun 1, 1951, v76, p972.
Motion Picture Herald Product Digest. May 26, 1951, p861.
The New York Times. Jun 28, 1951, p21.
Newsweek. Jun 25, 1951, v37, p87.
Saturday Review. Jun 30, 1951, v34, p22.
Variety. May 23, 1951, p6.

Executive Action (US; Miller, Donald; 1974)
Audience. Jan 1974, v6, p13-14.
BFI/Monthly Film Bulletin. Feb 1974, v41, p26-27.
Burt Lancaster: The Man and His Movies. p124-25.
Cineaste. 1974, v6, p8-12.
Film. Feb-Mar 1974, n11/12, p15.
Films and Filming. Feb 1974, v20, p37.
Films Illustrated. Jan 1974, v3, p246.
Films in Review. Jan 1974, v25, p53.
Motion Picture Herald Product Digest. Nov 14, 1974, p49.
The New York Times. Nov 8, 1974, p60.
The New York Times. Nov 25, 1974, SecII, p1.

The New York Times. Dec 30, 1974, SecII, p1.
PTA Magazine. Feb 1974, v63, p6.
Rolling Stone. Jan 3, 1974, p70-71.
Variety. Nov 7, 1973, p19.

Executive Suite (US; Wise, Robert; 1954)
America. May 15, 1954, v92, p201.
BFI/Monthly Film Bulletin. Apr 1954, v21, p52.
Catholic World. May 1954, v179, p142.
Cinema, the Magic Vehicle. v2, p217-18.
Commonweal. Apr 30, 1954, v60, p96-97.
Film Daily. Feb 23, 1954, p6.
Films in Review. Mar 1954, v5, p138-40.
The Films of Barbara Stanwyck. p229-32.
The Films of Fredric March. p209-10.
The Films of the Fifties. p121-24.
The Films of William Holden. p150-53.
Fortune. Jan 1955, v51, p108-09.
Hollywood Reporter. Feb 23, 1954, p3.
Library Journal. Apr 15, 1954, v79, p766.
Life. Apr 19, 1954, v36, p85.
The London Times. Jun 18, 1954, p2.
Look. May 18, 1954, v18, p117-119.
Magill's Survey of Cinema. Series II. v2, p735-37.
Motion Picture Herald Product Digest. Feb 27, 1954, p2197.
National Parent-Teacher. Apr 1954, v48, p39.
The New Statesman and Nation. Jun 26, 1954, v47, p832.
The New York Times. May 7, 1954, p19.
The New Yorker. May 15, 1954, v30, p74.
Newsweek. Apr 26, 1954, v43, p102.
Newsweek. May 3, 1954, v43, p90-94.
Saturday Review. May 1, 1954, v37, p33-34.
Saturday Review. Jan 1, 1955, v38, p63.
Seeing is Believing (Biskind). p305-08.
Sight and Sound. Jul-Sep 1954, v24, p33.
The Spectator. Jun 18, 1954, v192, p734.
Starring Miss Barbara Stanwyck. p247-48.
The Tatler. Jun 30, 1954, v212, p738.
Time. May 10, 1954, v63, p108.
Variety. Feb 24, 1954, p6.

Exodus (US; Preminger, Otto; 1960)
America. Jan 7, 1961, v104, p451.
BFI/Monthly Film Bulletin. Jun 1961, v28, p74.
The Cinema of Otto Preminger. p131-35.
Commonweal. Dec 16, 1960, v73, p316.
Dictionary of Films. p106-07.
Film Daily. Dec 15, 1960, p5.
Film Quarterly. Spr 1961, v14, p56-59.
Filmfacts. 1960, v3, p301.
Films and Filming. Jun 1961, v7, p22-23.
Films in Review. Dec 1960, v11, p611-13.
The Films of Paul Newman. p91-96.
Hollywood Reporter. Dec 14, 1960, p3.
Life. Dec 12, 1960, v49, p70-77.
McCall's. Feb 1961, v88, p168.
Motion Picture Herald Product Digest. Dec 31, 1960, p973.
Movie. Sep 1962, p24-25.
The New Republic. Dec 19, 1960, v143, p21-22.
The New York Times. Dec 16, 1960, p44.
The New York Times. Jan 1, 1961, SecII, p1.
The New Yorker. Dec 17, 1960, v36, p136-37.
Newsweek. Dec 19, 1960, v56, p87-88.
Saturday Review. Dec 17, 1960, v43, p30.
Senior Scholastic (teacher's edition). Jan 25, 1961, v77, p23.
Sight and Sound. Sum 1961, v30, p146-47.
Time. Dec 19, 1960, v76, p69.
Variety. Dec 14, 1960, p6.

The Exorcist (US; Friedkin, William; 1973)
America. Feb 2, 1974, v130, p66-73.
America. Jan 19, 1974, v130, p26.
America. Feb 23, 1974, v130, p131-32.

American Cinematographer. Feb 1974, v55, p154-57.
Atlantic. Mar 1974, v233, p92-95.
Audience. Feb 1974, v6, p11-13.
BFI/Monthly Film Bulletin. Apr 1974, v41, p71.
Bizaare. Aug 1974, n3, p28.
Christian Century. Jan 30, 1974, v91, p91-92.
Christian Century. Feb 13, 1974, v91, p181-83.
Cineaste. 1974, v6, n3, p18-22.
Cinefantastique. 1974, v3, n4, p8-21.
Cinefantastique. 1974, v3, n2, p24-25.
Cinefantastique. 1974, v3, n3, p6-13.
Commentary. Mar 1974, v58, p73-75.
Commonweal. Mar 1, 1974, v99, p532-33.
Commonweal. Feb 22, 1974, v99, p499.
Critic. Mar-Apr 1974, v23, p54-56.
Esquire. Apr 1974, v83, p74.
Film. Apr 1974, n13, p22.
The Film Book Bibliography. n3998, p404.
Film Comment. May-Jun 1974, v10, p32.
Film Heritage. 1974, v9, n3, p27-29.
Film Heritage. 1974, v9, n4, p30.
Film Quarterly. Fall 1974, v27, p61-62.
Filmmakers Newsletter. Apr 1974, v7, p18-23.
Films and Filming. Apr 1974, v32, p20, p38.
Films Illustrated. Apr 1974, v32, p303-04.
Films in Review. Feb 1974, v25, p117-18.
The Films of the Seventies. p74-75.
Harper's Bazaar. Mar 1973, v106, p152.
Humanist. May-Jun 1974, v34, p42.
Independent Film Journal. Feb 4, 1974, v73, p6, 11.
Independent Film Journal. Jan 7, 1974, v73, p9.
Journal of Popular Film. 1974, v3, n2, p183-87.
Jump Cut. May-Jun 1974, n1, p3-5.
The Los Angeles Times. Dec 26, 1973, SecIV, p1.
The Los Angeles Times. Dec 30, 1973, Calendar, p1.
Magill's Survey of Cinema. English Language Films. Series I, v2, p506.
Magill's Survey of Cinema. Series I. v2, p506-09.
Media and Methods. Mar 1974, v73, p6.
Midstream. Feb 1974, v20, p68-70.
Motion Picture Herald Product Digest. Jan 16, 1974, p65.
Movietone News. Jul 1974, n33, p19-22.
Movietone News. May-Jun 1974, n32, p38.
Movietone News. Apr 1974, n31, p39-40.
The Nation. Feb 2, 1974, v218, p157-58.
National Review. Apr 12, 1974, v26, p432.
The New Republic. Feb 9, 1974, v170, p22.
New Statesman. Apr 26, 1974, v87, p581-82.
New Statesman. Mar 22, 1974, v87, p418.
New York. Jun 21, 1974, v7, p56-57.
The New York Times. Jan 28, 1974, p1.
The New York Times. Feb 3, 1974, SecII, p15.
The New York Times. Aug 4, 1974, p11.
The New York Times. Jan 27, 1974, SecII, p33.
The New York Times. May 5, 1973, SecII, p11.
The New York Times. Jan 13, 1974, SecII, p1.
The New York Times. Dec 27, 1973, p1.
The New York Times. Dec 30, 1973, SecII, p1.
The New Yorker. Jan 7, 1974, v49, p59-62.
Newsweek. Feb 11, 1974, v83, p60-64.
Newsweek. Jan 21, 1974, v83, p97.
Newsweek. Jan 7, 1974, v83, p60.
Penthouse. May 1974, v5, p35-36.
Producers Guild of America Journal. 1974, v16, n2, p16.
Reeling. p337-42.
Rolling Stone. Feb 28, 1974, p16.
Rolling Stone. Feb 14, 1974, p64-65.
Rolling Stone. Mar 28, 1974, p10-11.
Saturday Review. Feb 9, 1974, v1, p56-57.

Saturday Review. Jun 15, 1974, v1, p43-44.
Sequences. Apr 1974, n76, p40-41.
Seventeen. Sep 1973, v32, p148-49.
Sight and Sound. Spr 1974, v43, p120.
Social Policy. May-Jun 1974, v5, p71-73.
Society. May-Jun 1974, v11, p86-87.
The Story behind the Exorcist. 1974.
Take One. 1974, v4, n4, p29.
Time. Jan 14, 1974, v103, p38-39.
Time. Jan 21, 1974, v103, p44.
Times Educational Supplement. Mar 22, 1974, n3069, p70.
Variety. Dec 26, 1973, p12.
Variety. Dec 26, 1973, p12.
Variety. Dec 26, 1973, p12.
The Velvet Light Trap. Fall 1974, n13, p7-10.
The Village Voice. Apr 10, 1974, p1.
The Village Voice. May 2, 1974, p95.
William Peter Blatty on the Exorcist—From Novel to Film. 1974.

Experiment in Terror (US; Edwards, Blake; 1962)
America. Apr 28, 1962, v107, p187.
Blake Edwards (Lehman and Luhr). p33-35, 66-70.
Commonweal. Apr 20, 1962, v76, p86.
Film Daily. Mar 19, 1962, p15.
Film Quarterly. Sum 1962, v15, p63.
Filmfacts. May 11, 1962, v5, p87-88.
Films and Filming. Nov 1962, v9, p38.
Films in Review. May 1962, v13, p293-94.
Hollywood Reporter. Mar 19, 1962, p3.
Motion Picture Herald. Mar 28, 1962, p491.
Movie. Oct 1962, n3, p36.
Movie. Nov 1962, n4, p27.
The New York Times. Apr 14, 1962, p14.
The New Yorker. Apr 21, 1962, v38, p171.
Newsweek. Apr 16, 1962, v59, p110.
Variety. Mar 21, 1962, p6.

Exposed (US; Toback, James; 1983)
BFI/Monthly Film Bulletin. Nov 1983, v50, p297-98.
Dance Magazine. Feb 1983, v57, p50-51.
Hollywood Reporter. Apr 22, 1983, p3.
Maclean's. May 2, 1983, v96, p61.
The New Republic. May 23, 1983, v188, p26.
New York. May 9, 1983, v16, p84-85.
The New York Times. May 1, 1983, SecII, p17-18.
Newsweek. May 2, 1983, v101, p89.
Rolling Stone. Apr 28, 1983, p50.
Variety. Mar 16, 1983, p16.

The Exterminating Angel (Spanish title: Angel Exterminador, El; French title: Ange Exterminateur, L') (MEX; Buñuel, Luis; 1962)
BFI/Monthly Film Bulletin. Aug 1966, v33, p118.
Christian Century. Nov 15, 1967, v84, p1468.
Christian Science Monitor (Eastern Edition). Dec 1, 1967, p10.
The Cinema of Luis Buñuel. p127-36.
Cinema Texas Program Notes. Dec 5, 1979, v17, p87-92.
Commonweal. Sep 22, 1967, v86, p588.
Dictionary of Films. p11.
The Discreet Art of Luis Buñuel. p169-93.
Film. Aut 1962, n33, p20-21.
Film Culture. Sum 1966, n41, p66-67.
Film Heritage. Sum 1968, v3, p28-34.
Film Society Review. Feb 1966, p18-20.
Filmfacts. Oct 15, 1967, v10, p248-50.
Films in Review. Jun-Jul 1962, v13, p330, 332.
Hollywood Reporter. Jan 17, 1968, p3.
International Film Guide. 1964, v1, p119.
Life. Oct 6, 1967, v63, p14.
The London Times. Jun 9, 1966, p8.

Luis Buñuel (Aranda). p206-13.
Luis Buñuel (Durgnat). p125-29.
Luis Buñuel (Higginbotham). p149-58.
Magill's Survey of Cinema. Foreign Language Films. v3, p1021-24.
Motion Picture Herald Product Digest. Aug 30, 1967, p717-18.
Movie. May 1963, n9, p26-27.
New Statesman. Jul 9, 1965, v70, p59.
New Statesman. Jun 10, 1966, v71, p853.
The New York Times. Aug 22, 1967, p33.
The New Yorker. Aug 26, 1967, v43, p78-79.
Newsweek. Sep 4, 1967, v70, p72.
Playboy. Nov 1967, v14, p50.
Reflexivity in Film and Literature. p184-85.
Second Sight. p136-39.
The Spectator. Oct 26, 1962, v209, p637.
The Spectator. Jun 10, 1966, v216, p730.
Studies in the Literary Imagination. n1, 1983, v16, p7-27.
Time. Sep 8, 1967, v90, p99-100.
Variety. May 23, 1962, p6.
The Village Voice. Aug 24, 1967, p21.
The World of Luis Buñuel. p244-56.

The Exterminator (US; Glickenhaus, James; 1980)
BFI/Monthly Film Bulletin. Feb 1981, v49, p24.
The New York Times. Sep 11, 1980, SecIII, p18.
Newsday. Sep 12, 1980, SecII, p7.
Variety. Sep 17, 1980, p20.

Eye of the Needle (GB; Marquand, Richard; 1981)
Hollywood Reporter. Jul 21, 1981, p3.
The Los Angeles Times. Jul 24, 1981, SecVI, p1.
Magill's Cinema Annual, 1982. p148-50.
The Nation. Sep 19, 1981, v233, p251.
New York. Aug 10, 1981, v14, p56-57.
The New York Times. Jul 24, 1981, SecIII, p10.
Newsweek. Aug 3, 1981, v98, p50.
Rolling Stone. Aug 20, 1981, p35.
Saturday Review. Jul 1981, v8, p85.

Eye Witness (Also titled: Your Witness) (GB; Montgomery, Robert; 1950)
BFI/Monthly Film Bulletin. Feb-Mar 1950, v17, p28.
Christian Century. Nov 22, 1950, v67, p1407.
Film Daily. Jul 24, 1950, p6.
Hollywood Reporter. Jul 18, 1950, p3.
The London Times. Jan 28, 1950, p2.
Motion Picture Herald Product Digest. Jul 29, 1950, p405.
The New Republic. Sep 11, 1950, v123, p22.
The New York Times. Aug 28, 1950, p13.
Newsweek. Sep 11, 1950, v36, p89.
Time. Sep 25, 1950, v56, p98.
Variety. Feb 1, 1950, p14.

The Eyes of Laura Mars (US; Kershner, Irvin; 1978)
BFI/Monthly Film Bulletin. Nov 1978, v45, p219.
Films in Review. Oct 1978, v29, p500.
Hollywood Reporter. Aug 2, 1978, p3.
The Los Angeles Times. Aug 3, 1978, SecIV, p10.
Maclean's. Aug 21, 1978, v91, p52.
Motion Picture Herald Product Digest. Aug 23, 1978, p22.
New York. Aug 21, 1978, v11, p62.
The New York Times. Aug 4, 1978, SecIII, p10.
The New Yorker. Aug 14, 1978, v54, p53.
The New Yorker. Sep 25, 1978, v54, p137-47.
Newsweek. Aug 14, 1978, v92, p62.
Time. Aug 21, 1978, v112, p52.
Variety. Aug 2, 1978, p14.

Eyewitness (US; Yates, Peter; 1981)
American Cinematography. Apr 1981, v62, p350.
American Film. Mar 1981, v6, p49-51.
BFI/Monthly Film Bulletin. Oct 1981, v48, p202-03.
Commentary. Jun 1981, v71, p69-70.
Films In Review. Apr 1981, v32, p242-43.
Horizon. Apr 1981, v24-70-71.
The Los Angeles Times. Mar 6, 1981, SecVI, p1.
Maclean's. Mar 16, 1981, v94, p62-63.
The Nation. May 16, 1981, v232, p612-13.
The New Leader. Apr 20, 1981, v64, p20.
The New Republic. Mar 7, 1981, v184, p27.
New York. Mar 2, 1981, v14, p49-50.
The New York Times. Apr 5, 1981, SecII, p15-16.
The New York Times. Feb 27, 1981, SecIII, p12.
The New Yorker. Mar 23, 1981, v57, p141-44.
Newsweek. Mar 2, 1981, v97, p81.
Rolling Stone. Apr 16, 1981, p33-34.
Time. Mar 2, 1981, v117, p93.
Variety. Feb 18, 1981, p18.
The Village Voice. Mar 4, 1981, p41.

F.I.S.T. (US; Jewison, Norman; 1978)
America. May 20, 1978, v138, p408.
BFI/Monthly Film Bulletin. Sep 1978, v45, p174.
Films in Review. Jun-Jul 1978, v29, p375.
Hollywood Reporter. Apr 14, 1978, p3.
The Los Angeles Times. Apr 23, 1978, Calendar, p1.
Maclean's. May 15, 1978, v91, p86-87.
Motion Picture Herald Product Digest. May 10, 1978, p93.
The Nation. Jun 3, 1978, v226, p675-76.
National Review. Jun 23, 1978, v30, p792.
The New Republic. May 20, 1978, v178, p24-25.
New York. May 8, 1978, v11, p74.
The New York Times. Apr 26, 1978, SecIII, p15.
The New York Times. May 14, 1978, SecII, p17.
The New Yorker. May 8, 1978, v54, p121-23.
Newsweek. May 1, 1978, v91, p89.
Saturday Review. Jun 24, 1978, v5, p23.
Time. May 1, 1978, v111, p74.
Variety. Apr 19, 1978, p26.

Fabuleuse Adventure de Marco Polo, Le *See* Marco the Magnificent

The Fabulous Adventures of Marco Polo *See* Marco the Magnificent

The Face *See* The Magician

A Face in the Crowd (US; Kazan, Elia; 1957)
America. Jun 15, 1957, v97, p332.
An AMerican Odyssey. p219-20.
BFI/Monthly Film Bulletin. Dec 1957, v24, p147.
Cinema, the Magic Vehicle. v2, p361-62.
Commonweal. Jun 14, 1957, v66, p277-78.
Elia Kazan: A Guide to References and Resources. p71-47.
Film Culture. 1957, v3, n3, p13-14.
Film Daily. May 28, 1957, v111, p6.
Films and Filming. Sep 1957, v3, p23.
Films and Filming. Oct 1957, v4, p9.
The Films in My Life. p113-15.
Films in Review. Aug-Sep 1957, v3, p350-51.
The Films of the Fifties. p225-28.
Hollywood Reporter. May 28, 1957, p3.
Kazan on Kazan. p102-19.
Magill's Survey of Cinema. Series II. v2, p738-40.

Sight and Sound. 1984/85, v54, n1, p43-44.
Take One. Feb 1967, v1, p24-26.
Time. Nov 18, 1966, v88, p122.
Variety. Sep 14, 1966, p6.
The Village Voice. Nov 17, 1966, v12, p27-28.
The Village Voice. Nov 24, 1966, v12, p27-28.
Wilson Library Bulletin. Jan 1967, v41, p464-65.

Fail Safe (US; Lumet, Sidney; 1964)
America. Oct 17, 1964, v111, p464-65.
BFI/Monthly Film Bulletin. May 1965, v32, p67.
Commonweal. Oct 9, 1964, v81, p72.
Film Daily. Sep 11, 1964, p3.
Films in Review. Oct 1964, v15, p506-07.
The Films of Henry Fonda. p177-79.
The Fondas (Springer). p201-02.
Great Horror Movies. p132-33.
Guts & Glory. p195-201.
Hollywood Reporter. Sep 11, 1964, p3.
Life. Oct 30, 1964, v57, p12.
Motion Picture Herald Product Digest. Sep 30, 1964, p138.
National Review. Nov 17, 1964, v16, p1026-27.
The New Republic. Sep 12, 1964, v151, p26-27.
The New York Times. Sep 16, 1964, p36.
The New Yorker. Oct 10, 1964, v40, p200-01.
Newsweek. Oct 12, 1964, v64, p114.
Nuclear War Films. p68-75.
Sidney Lumet: A Guide to References and Resources. p72-74.
Sight and Sound. Spr 1965, v34, p97.
Tynan Right and Left. p227-28.
Variety. Sep 16, 1964, p6.
Vogue. Oct 15, 1964, v144, p100.

The Fair Angel *See* Foire aux Chimeres, La

The Falcon and the Snowman (US; Schlesinger, John; 1985)
BFI/Monthly Film Bulletin. Aug 1985, v52, p109.
Commonweal. Apr 5, 1985, v112, p212-13.
Films in Review. Mar 1985, v36, p180.
Hollywood Reporter. Jan 21, 1985, p3.
The Los Angeles Times. Jan 25, 1985, SecVI, p1.
Maclean's. Jan 25, 1985, v98, p49.
Magill's Cinema Annual, 1986. p165-68.
The Nation. Mar 9, 1985, v240, p280-82.
National Review. Mar 22, 1985, v37, p56-57.
The New Leader. Feb 11, 1985, v68, p19-20.
New York. Feb 4, 1985, v18, p66-67.
The New York Times. Jan 25, 1985, SecIII, p10.
The New York Times. Feb 3, 1985, SecII, p17.
The New Yorker. Feb 11, 1985, v60, p106.
Newsweek. Feb 4, 1985, v105, p75.
Saturday Review. Jan-Feb 1985, v11, p34-36.
Time. Jan 28, 1985, v125, p90.
Variety. Jan 23, 1985, p16.
Vogue. Jan 1985, v125, p90.

The Fall of the Roman Empire (US; Mann, Anthony; 1964)
America. Apr 18, 1964, v110, p553.
BFI/Monthly Film Bulletin. May 1964, v31, p69.
Boxoffice. Apr 6, 1964, v84, p2816.
Commonweal. Apr 10, 1964, v80, p91.
Film Daily. Mar 25, 1964, v124, p3-4.
Films and Filming. May 1964, v10, p22.
Films in Review. Apr 1964, v15, p245-46.
The Films of Sophia Loren. p156-61.
Hollywood Reporter. Mar 23, 1964, v179, p3.
Life. Mar 27, 1964, v56, p18.
Motion Picture Herald Product Digest. Apr 1, 1964, v231, p10, 20.
The New York Times. Mar 27, 1964, p14.
The New Yorker. Apr 4, 1964, v40, p178.
Newsweek. Apr 6, 1964, v63, p87.

The Private Eye, the Cowboy and the Very Naked Girl. p77-81.
Saturday Review. Apr 4, 1964, v47, p36.
Variety. Mar 25, 1964, p6.

Falling in Love (US; Grosbard, Ulu; 1984)
BFI/Monthly Film Bulletin. Feb 1984, v51, p31-32.
Esquire. Jul 1984, v102, p160.
Film. Feb 1984, n123, p2.
Film. Nov 1984, v130, p12.
Film Quarterly. Fall 1984, v37, p13-19.
Films and Filming. Feb 1984, n353, p36.
Films in Review. Nov 1984, v35, p569.
Hollywood Reporter. Nov 16, 1984, p3.
The Los Angeles Times. Nov 21, 1984, SecVI, p1.
Maclean's. Dec 3, 1984, v97, p69.
The New Leader. Oct 29, 1984, v67, p22.
The New Republic. Dec 10, 1984, v191, p74-75.
New York. Dec 3, 1984, v17, p141-42.
The New York Times. Aug 3, 1984, SecIII, p6.
The New Yorker. Dec 10, 1984, v60, p168.
Newsweek. Dec 3, 1984, v104, p78.
Sight and Sound. Wint 1983-84, v53, p60-61.
Time. Nov 26, 1984, v124, p105.
The Village Voice. Aug 14, 1984, p47.
Vogue. Dec 1984, v174, p350.

Falstaff *See* Chimes at Midnight

Fame (US; Parker, Alan; 1980)
BFI/Monthly Film Bulletin. Jul 1980, v47, p130.
Boston Magazine. Jul 1980, v72, p47.
Chicago. Jul 1980, v29, p72-74.
Cineaste. Fall 1980, v10, p34.
Dance Magazine. Jul 1980, v54, p42.
Films in Review. Jun 1980, v31, p373.
Hollywood Reporter. May 7, 1980, p3.
Horizon. Jul 1980, v23, p71.
Los Angeles. Jun 1980, v25, p222.
The Los Angeles Times. May 11, 1980, Calendar, p1.
Maclean's. May 19, 1980, v93, p54.
Motion Picture Herald Product Digest. May 28, 1980, p98.
National Review. Sep 5, 1980, v32, p1091.
New Orleans. Aug 1980, v14, p30-31.
The New Republic. Jun 7, 1980, v182, p22-23.
New Statesman. Jul 25, 1980, v100, p26-27.
New York. May 19, 1980, v13, p62.
The New York Times. May 16, 1980, SecIII, p14.
The New Yorker. May 26, 1980, v56, p125-26.
Newsday. May 16, 1980, SecII, p7.
Newsweek. Jun 2, 1980, v95, p87.
Philadelphia Magazine. Jul 1980, v71, p60.
Philadelphia Magazine. Aug 1980, v71, p58.
Playboy. Aug 1980, v27, p40.
Saturday Review. Jun 1980, v7, p62.
Time. Jul 21, 1980, v116, p74.
Variety. Apr 30, 1980, v298, p36.
The Village Voice. May 26, 1980, p54.
Vogue. Jun 1980, v170, p36.
Washingtonian. Aug 1980, v15, p45.
Washingtonian. Jul 1980, v15, p49.

Fame Is the Spur (GB; Boulting, Roy; 1947)
Christian Century. Jan 18, 1950, v67, p95.
Commonweal. Nov 18, 1949, v51, p180.
Film Daily. Nov 30, 1949, p6.
Hollywood Reporter. Jan 10, 1950, p3.
Motion Picture Herald Product Digest. Nov 19, 1949, p89.
The New Republic. Nov 21, 1949, v121, p22.
The New York Times. Nov 8, 1949, p34.
The New Yorker. Nov 26, 1949, v25, p86.
Newsweek. Nov 7, 1949, v34, p90.
School and Society. Dec 3, 1949, v70, p361-62.

Senior Scholastic. Dec 14, 1949, v55, p22.
Sight and Sound. Wint 1947-48, v16, p137.
Variety. Oct 8, 1947, p8.

Family Diary (Italian title: Cronaca Familiare) (IT; Zurlini, Valerio; 1963)
BFI/Monthly Film Bulletin. Jan 1964, v31, p3.
Film Daily. Nov 12, 1963, p9.
Filmfacts. Dec 11, 1963, v6, p278-79.
Films and Filming. Jan 1964, v10, p27.
Films in Review. Dec 1963, v6, p278-79.
The New York Times. Nov 12, 1963, p48.
The New Yorker. Nov 23, 1963, v39, p235.
Newsweek. Nov 18, 1963, v62, p107.
Sight and Sound. Wint 1963, v33, p41.
Variety. Sep 12, 1962, p6.

The Family Jewels (US; Lewis, Jerry; 1965)
BFI/Monthly Film Bulletin. Jan 1966, v33, p2.
Cahiers du Cinema in English. 1966, n4, p33, 39.
Film Daily. Jun 21, 1965, p6.
Films and Filming. Feb 1966, v12, p12.
Hollywood Reporter. Jun 21, 1965, p3.
The London Times. Nov 18, 1965, p8.
Motion Picture Herald Product Digest. Jul 7, 1965, p323.
New Statesman. Nov 26, 1965, v70, p853.
The New York Times. Aug 12, 1965, p30.
Variety. Jun 23, 1965, p7.

Family Plot (US; Hitchcock, Alfred; 1976)
America. Apr 3, 1976, v134, p290-91.
The Art of Alfred Hitchcock. p447-61.
BFI/Monthly Film Bulletin. Jul 1976, v43, p146-47.
Cinema Papers. Sep-Oct 1976, p172-73.
Commentary. Nov 1976, v62, p75-78.
Commonweal. May 7, 1976, v103, p306-07.
Film Bulletin. Apr 1976, v45, pC.
Film Comment. May-Jun 1976, v12, p20-22.
Film Comment. Jul-Aug 1976, v12, p2-4.
Film Heritage. 1976, v11, n4, p41-42.
Films and Filming. Aug 1976, v22, p14-15, 34.
Films in Review. May 1976, v27, p313-14.
The Films of Alfred Hitchcock. p243-45.
Hitchcock (Truffaut). p339-43.
Hollywood Reporter. Mar 19, 1976, p3.
Independent Film Journal. Apr 14, 1976, v77, p7.
The Los Angeles Times. Apr 1, 1976, SecIV, p14.
Millimeter. Jan 1976, v4, p10-13.
Motion Picture Herald Product Digest. Apr 7, 1976, p87.
The Nation. May 8, 1976, v222, p572-73.
The New Republic. Apr 24, 1976, v174, p17.
New Statesman. Aug 20, 1976, v92, p250.
New York. Apr 19, 1976, v9, p84-86.
The New York Review of Books. Jun 24, 1976, v23, p38-39.
The New York Times. Apr 11, 1976, SecII, p1.
The New Yorker. Apr 19, 1976, v52, p102-04.
Newsweek. Apr 5, 1976, v87, p85-86.
Penthouse. Aug 1976, v7, p46-47.
Saturday Review. May 1, 1976, v3, p43-44.
Sight and Sound. Fall 1976, v45, p189-90.
Take One. 1976, v5, n2, p20-22, 27.
The Thousand Eyes Magazine. May 1976, n10, p10-12.
Time. Apr 26, 1976, v107, p45.
Times Educational Supplement. Oct 22, 1976, n3203, p70.
Variety. Mar 24, 1976, p20.

The Family Secret (US; Levin, Henry; 1951)
Catholic World. Dec 1951, v174, p223.
Christian Century. Apr 2, 1952, v69, p415.
Commonweal. Feb 1, 1952, v55, p424.
Film Daily. Oct 24, 1951, p6.

Hollywood Reporter. Oct 17, 1951, p4.
Motion Picture Herald Product Digest. Oct 27, 1951, p1074.
Theatre Arts. Jan 1952, v36, p84.
Variety. Oct 24, 1951, p6.

The Family Way (GB; Boulting, Roy; 1966)
America. Jul 15, 1967, v117, p64.
BFI/Monthly Film Bulletin. Feb 1967, v34, p26-27.
Christian Science Monitor (Western edition). Jul 31, 1967, p4.
Commonweal. Jul 14, 1967, v86, p450-51.
Confessions of a Cultist. p304-06.
Film 67/68. p108-10.
Film Daily. May 8, 1967, p4.
Film Quarterly. Fall 1967, v21, p59-60.
Filmfacts. Sep 1, 1967, v10, p194-96.
Films and Filming. Apr 1967, v13, p5-6.
Hollywood Reporter. May 8, 1967, p3.
Life. May 5, 1967, v62, p12.
The London Times. Dec 22, 1966, p15.
Magill's Survey of Cinema. Series II. v2, p753-56.
Motion Picture Herald Product Digest. May 10, 1967, p682.
New Statesman. Dec 30, 1966, v72, p974.
The New York Times. Jun 29, 1967, p32.
The New Yorker. Jul 15, 1967, v43, p100-01.
Newsweek. Jul 24, 1967, v70, p75.
Playboy. Aug 1967, v14, p20.
Second Sight. p105-07.
Senior Scholastic. May 19, 1967, v90, p42.
Time. Jul 14, 1967, v90, p89.
Variety. Dec 28, 1966, p18.
The Village Voice. Aug 10, 1967, p21.

The Fan (US; Bianchi, Edward; 1981)
BFI/Monthly Film Bulletin. Jun 1981, v48, p112-13.
Commonweal. Jul 31, 1981, v108, p434-35.
Film Bulletin. Jul 1981, p37.
Film Journal. Jun 8, 1981, v84, p12-13.
The Los Angeles Times. May 18, 1981, SecVI, p1.
Maclean's. Jun 8, 1981, v94, p49-50.
The Nation. Jun 13, 1981, v232, p739-40.
The New Republic. Jun 13, 1981, v184, p24-25.
New Statesman. May 29, 1981, v101, p24-25.
New York. Jun 8, 1981, v14, p52.
The New York Times. May 22, 1981, SecIII, p8.
The New York Times. May 31, 1981, SecII, p15.
Newsweek. Jun 1, 1981, v97, p92.
Theatre Crafts. May 1981, v15, p71.
Time. Jun 22, 1981, v117, p80.
Variety. May 20, 1981, p24.
The Village Voice. May 27, 1981, p47.

Fanatic *See* Die! Die! My Darling!

Fancy Pants (US; Marshall, George; 1950)
Christian Century. Sep 20, 1950, v67, p1119.
Commonweal. Sep 29, 1950, v52, p605.
Film Daily. Jul 19, 1950, p4.
Hollywood Reporter. Jul 19, 1950, p3.
The London Times. Aug 7, 1950, p6.
Motion Picture Herald Product Digest. Jul 22, 1950, p397.
The New Republic. Sep 11, 1950, v122, p21.
The New York Times. Aug 31, 1950, p21.
The New Yorker. Sep 9, 1950, v26, p98.
Newsweek. Sep 11, 1950, v36, p87.
The Spectator. Aug 11, 1950, v185, p177.
Time. Sep 4, 1950, v56, p82.
Variety. Jul 19, 1950, p6.

Fanfan the Tulip (French title: Fanfan la Tulipe) (FR, IT; Christian-Jacque; 1951)

BFI/Monthly Film Bulletin. May 1953, v20, p66.
Cinema, the Magic Vehicle. v2, p141-42.
Commonweal. May 22, 1953, v58, p180.
Dictionary of Films. p109.
Films and Filming. Jun 1969, v15, p86.
Films in Review. Jun-Jul 1953, v4, p302.
The Great French Films. p253.
Kiss Kiss Bang Bang. p328.
The London Times. Jan 20, 1953, p3.
Motion Picture Herald Product Digest. May 23, 1953, p1847.
The New Statesman and Nation. Sep 12, 1953, v46, p286.
The New York Times. May 5, 1953, p34.
The New Yorker. May 16, 1953, v29, p130.
Newsweek. May 25, 1953, v41, p100.
Saturday Review. May 2, 1953, v36, p36.
The Tatler. Sep 16, 1953, v209, p522.
Theatre Arts. Jul 1953, v37, p88.
Time. May 11, 1953, v61, p110.
Variety. Apr 30, 1952, p18.

Fangschuss, Der *See* Coup de Grace

Fanny (US; Logan, Joshua; 1961)
America. Aug 12, 1961, v105, p616.
BFI/Monthly Film Bulletin. Aug 1961, v28, p107.
Chevalier: The Films and Career and Maurice Chevalier. p197-201.
Commonweal. Jul 14, 1961, v74, p403.
Film. Wint 1961, n30, p15.
Film Daily. Jun 1961, p6.
Film Quarterly. Fall 1961, v15, p55.
Filmfacts. Jul 28, 1961, v4, p149-51.
Films and Filming. Aug 1961, v7, p24.
Films in Review. Aug-Sep 1961, v7, p430-32.
Life. Jun 30, 1961, v50, p97-99.
Magill's Survey of Cinema. Series II. v2, p757-59.
The New Republic. Jul 24, 1961, v145, p26.
The New York Times. Jul 7, 1961, p16.
The New Yorker. Jul 8, 1961, v37, p58.
Newsweek. Jul 17, 1961, v58, p84.
Saturday Review. Jul 8, 1961, v44, p29.
Time. Jul 14, 1961, v78, p92.
Variety. Jun 21, 1961, p6.

Fanny and Alexander (Swedish title: Fanny Och Alexander) (SWED; Bergman, Ingmar; 1983)
America. Jul 23, 1983, v149, p53-54.
BFI/Monthly Film Bulletin. Apr 1983, v50, p83-84.
Christian Century. Jul 20, 1983, v100, p690.
Christianity Today. Aug 5, 1983, v27, p60.
Commentary. Sep 1983, v76, p64-67.
Film Comment. May-Jun 1983, v19, p13-16.
Films in Review. Aug-Sep 1983, v35, p439.
Hollywood Reporter. Jun 29, 1983, p3.
The Los Angeles Times. Jun 29, 1983, SecVI, p1.
Maclean's. Jul 4, 1983, v96, p53.
Magill's Cinema Annual, 1984. p146-52.
Ms. Sep 1983, v12, p39-40.
The Nation. Jul 2, 1983, v237, p27-28.
National Review. Jul 22, 1983, v35, p886-88.
The New Leader. Aug 8, 1983, v66, p20-21.
The New Republic. Jun 27, 1983, v188, p22-24.
New York. Jun 13, 1983, v16, p67.
The New York Times. Jun 17, 1983, SecIII, p8.
The New Yorker. Jun 13, 1983, v59, p117-21.
Newsweek. Jun 20, 1983, v101, p84.
Saturday Review. May-Jun 1983, v9, p41-42.
Sight and Sound. Spr 1983, v92, p141.
Time. Jun 20, 1983, v121, p75.
Variety. Sep 28, 1983, p148.
Vogue. Jun 1983, v173, p41-42.

Fantastic Voyage (US; Fleischer, Richard; 1966)
BFI/Monthly Film Bulletin. Oct 1966, v33, p151.
Christian Science Monitor (Western edition). Oct 12, 1966, p6.
Commonweal. Sep 2, 1966, v84, p557.
Esquire. May 1966, v65, p112-13.
Film Daily. Jul 25, 1966, p7.
Film Quarterly. Wint 1966-67, v20, p61.
Filmfacts. Nov 1, 1966, v9, p239-40.
Films and Filming. Nov 1966, v13, p12-13.
Films in Review. Oct 1966, v17, p522-23.
Great Horror Movies. p156-57.
The Great Spy Pictures. p170-72.
Hollywood Reporter. Jul 25, 1966, p3.
Kiss Kiss Bang Bang. p191-92.
Life. Sep 23, 1966, v61, p16.
The London Times. Sep 15, 1966, p14.
Motion Picture Herald Product Digest. Aug 3, 1966, p569A.
National Review. Nov 15, 1966, v18, p1178-79.
The New Republic. Oct 8, 1966, v155, p34-35.
New Statesman. Sep 11, 1966, v72, p407.
The New York Times. Sep 8, 1966, p43.
The New Yorker. Sep 17, 1966, v42, p225.
Newsweek. Aug 29, 1966, v68, p68.
Playboy. Dec 1966, v13, p50.
Popular Photography. Oct 1966, v59, p118-19.
Saturday Review. Sep 3, 1966, v49, p38.
Senior Scholastic. Oct 7, 1966, v89, p26.
Seventeen. Oct 1966, v25, p116-17.
Sight and Sound. Aut 1966, v35, p201.
Time. Sep 9, 1966, v88, p103.
Variety. Jul 27, 1966, p6.

Fantomas (FR, IT; Hunebelle, André; 1964)
BFI/Monthly Film Bulletin. Jun 1968, v35, p91.
Dictionary of Films. p110-11.
Filmfacts. Jun 1, 1966, v9, p87-89.
Films and Filming. Jan 1969, v15, p50.
Hollywood Reporter. May 18, 1966, p4.
The London Times. Aug 2, 1963, p15.
Motion Picture Herald Product Digest. Apr 27, 1966, p511.
The New York Times. Apr 6, 1966, p36.
Variety. Dec 2, 1964, p6.

Fantome de la Liberté, Le (FR; Buñuel, Luis; 1974)
America. Dec 7, 1974, v131, p376.
America. Feb 1, 1975, v132, p174-75.
BFI/Monthly Film Bulletin. Feb 1975, v42, p30.
Commonweal. Nov 22, 1974, v101, p190-91.
Esquire. Feb 1975, v83, p34.
Film Comment. Sep-Oct 1974, v10, p34-35.
Film Quarterly. Sum 1975, v28, p20-25.
Films in Review. Dec 1974, v25, p625-26.
Independent Film Journal. Oct 30, 1974, v74, p6.
The Los Angeles Times. Mar 19, 1975, SecIV, p9.
The Nation. Nov 16, 1974, v219, p508-09.
The New Republic. Nov 16, 1974, v171, p22.
The New York Times. Oct 20, 1974, SecII, p17.
The New Yorker. Oct 28, 1974, v50, p71.
Newsweek. Nov 4, 1974, v84, p92.
Sight and Sound. Sum 1974, v43, p170-71.
Variety. Aug 28, 1974, p20.
The Village Voice. Oct 31, 1974, p99.

Far From the Madding Crowd (GB; Schlesinger, John; 1967)
America. Nov 4, 1967, v117, p520-21.
BFI/Monthly Film Bulletin. Dec 1967, v34, p185-86.
Christian Century. Dec 20, 1967, v84, p1632-33.

Commonweal. Nov 10, 1967, v87, p169.
Film Daily. Sep 27, 1967, p3.
Film Quarterly. Wint 1967-68, v21, p61.
Films and Filming. Dec 1967, v14, p24.
Films in Review. Nov 1967, v18, p574-76.
Harper's. Jan 1968, v236, p82.
Hollywood Reporter. Sep 27, 1967, p3.
John Schlesinger: A Guide to References and Resources. p47-49.
John Schlesinger (Phillips). p92-108.
Life. Dec 8, 1967, v63, p12.
Look. Mar 21, 1967, v31, p59-65.
Magill's Survey of Cinema. Series I. v2, p157-20.
Motion Picture Herald Product Digest. Oct 4, 1967, p728.
National Review. Mar 12, 1968, v20, p252-53.
The New York Times. Oct 19, 1967, p59.
The New Yorker. Oct 28, 1967, v43, p165-66.
Newsweek. Oct 30, 1967, v70, p94.
Saturday Review. Oct 21, 1967, v50, p46.
Senior Scholastic. Nov 30, 1967, v91, p27.
Sight and Sound. Wint 1967-68, v37, p29-30.
Time. Oct 27, 1967, v90, p102.
Variety. Sep 27, 1967, p6.
The Village Voice. Nov 2, 1967, p33, 40.
Vogue. Dec 1967, v150, p174.

Farewell, My Lovely (GB; Richards, Dick; 1975)
BFI/Monthly Film Bulletin. Dec 1975, v42, p259.
Films in Review. Oct 1975, v26, p503.
The Films of the Seventies. p127-28.
Hollywood Reporter. Aug 13, 1975, p7.
The Los Angeles Times. Aug 20, 1975, SecIV, p16.
Magill's Survey of Cinema. Series I. v2, p521-23.
Motion Picture Herald Product Digest. Aug 27, 1975, p21.
The New York Times. Aug 14, 1975, p39.
The New York Times. Nov 23, 1975, SecII, p15.
Newsweek. Aug 18, 1975, v86, p73.
Raymond Chandler and Film. p171-89.
Raymond Chandler in Hollywood. p135-42.
Raymond Chandler on Screen. p172-97.
Robert Mitchum on the Screen. p225-27.
Saturday Review. Oct 4, 1975, v3, p36.
Time. Sep 1, 1975, v106, p44.
Variety. Aug 13, 19975, p16.

A Farewell to Arms (US; Vidor, Charles; 1957)
America. Jan 25, 1958, v98, p495-96.
BFI/Monthly Film Bulletin. May 1958, v25, p56.
The Classic American Novel and the Cinema. p297-304.
Commonweal. Feb 7, 1958, v67, p488.
Film Daily. Apr 1958, p21.
Film Daily. Dec 19, 1957, p11.
Films and Filming. Apr 1958, v4, p21.
Films in Review. Jan 1958, v9, p29-30.
The Films of Jennifer Jones. p149-54.
Hemingway on Film. p6-16.
Hollywood Reporter. Dec 19, 1957, p3.
Motion Picture Herald Product Digest. Dec 21, 1957, p14.
The New Republic. Feb 17, 1958, v138, p22.
The New York Times. Jan 25, 1958, p14.
The New York Times. Feb 2, 1598, SecII, p1.
The New Yorker. Feb 1, 1958, v33, p65.
Newsweek. Dec 30, 1957, v50, p61.
Saturday Review. Feb 1, 1958, v61, p27.
Time. Feb 3, 1958, v71, p80.
Variety. Dec 25, 1957, p6.

The Fascist (Italian title: Federale, Il) (IT; Salce, Luciano; 1965)
Confessions of a Cultist. p199-200.
Film Daily. Jul 1, 1965, p6.
Motion Picture Herald Product Digest. Jul 7, 1965, p324.
The New York Times. Jun 18, 1965, p28.
The New Yorker. Jul 3, 1965, v41, p58.
Private Screenings. p191-94.
Time. Jul 9, 1965, v86, p98.
Variety. Jun 23, 1965, p7.
The Village Voice. Jul 15, 1965, p11.

Fast Times at Ridgemont High (US; Heckerling, Amy; 1982)
Hollywood Reporter. Aug 11, 1982, p3.
The Los Angeles Times. Aug 13, 1982, SecVI, p16.
Magill's Cinema Annual, 1983. p156-59.
New York. Sep 27, 1982, v15, p50-51.
The New York Times. Sep 3, 1982, SecIII, p6.
The New Yorker. Nov 1, 1982, v58, p146.
Newsweek. Sept 20, 1982, v100, p92.
Time. Sep 13, 1982, v120, p86-87.
Variety. Aug 11, 1982, p3.

Fat City (US; Huston, John; 1972)
America. Sep 2, 1972, v127, p126.
American Scholar. Wint 1972, v42, p148-50.
The Cinema of John Huston. p176.
Commentary. Nov 1972, v54, p82-83.
Commonweal. Oct 6, 1972, v97, p15-16.
Filmfacts. 1972, v15, n16, p361.
Films in Review. Oct 1972, v23, p507.
Hollywood Reporter. Nov 15, 1972, p9.
John Huston (Hammen). p122-24.
Life. Aug 25, 1972, v73, p20.
Magill's Survey of Cinema. Series II. v2, p763.
The New Republic. Aug 19, 1972, v167, p25.
The New York Times. Aug 6, 1972, SecII, p1.
The New York Times. Jul 27, 1972, p20.
The New Yorker. Jul 29, 1972, v48, p53.
Newsweek. Aug 7, 1972, v80, p61.
Saturday Review. Sep 9, 1972, v55, p88.
Time. Aug 7, 1972, v100, p76.
Variety. May 24, 1972, p19.

The Fat Man (US; Castle, William; 1951)
Film Daily. Mar 30, 1951, p5.
Hollywood Reporter. Mar 30, 1951, p3.
Motion Picture Herald Product Digest. Apr 7, 1951, p794.
The New York Times. May 25, 1951, p31.
Variety. Apr 4, 1951, p6.

Father Brown *See* The Detective

Father Goose (US; Nelson, Ralph; 1964)
America. Dec 12, 1964, v111, p788.
BFI/Monthly Film Bulletin. Feb 1965, v32, p24-25.
Commonweal. Dec 4, 1964, v81, p355.
Film Daily. Nov 17, 1964, p4.
Films and Filming. Feb 1965, v11, p33.
Films in Review. Jan 1965, v16, p49-50.
The Films of Cary Grant. p262-65.
Hollywood Reporter. Nov 17, 1964, p3.
Magill's Survey of Cinema. Series II. v2, p766-69.
Motion Picture Herald Product Digest. Nov 25, 1964, p177.
The New Republic. Jan 2, 1965, v152, p21.
The New York Times. Dec 11, 1964, p55.
Saturday Review. Jan 2, 1965, v48, p31.
Variety. Nov 18, 1964, p6.

Father Is a Bachelor (US; Foster, Norman; Berlin, Abby; 1950)
Christian Century. Mar 15, 1950, v67, p351.
Film Daily. Feb 14, 1950, p6.
The Films of William Holden. p105-07.
Hollywood Reporter. Feb 10, 1950, p3.

Motion Picture Herald Product Digest. Feb 11, 1950, p186, 189.
The New York Times. Feb 23, 1950, p33.
Variety. Feb 15, 1950, p13.

Father of the Bride (US; Minnelli, Vincente; 1950)
BFI/Monthly Film Bulletin. Jul 1950, v17, p99-100.
Christian Century. Jul 12, 1950, v67, p855.
Commonweal. May 26, 1950, v52, p173.
Film Daily. May 10, 1950, p7.
The Films of Elizabeth Taylor. p81-84.
The Films of Spencer Tracy. p204-06.
The Films of the Fifties. p27-28.
Fortnight. Jun 9, 1950, v8, p31.
Hollywood Reporter. May 10, 1950, p3.
I Remember It Well. p225-29.
Library Journal. Jun 15, 1950, v75, p1058.
Magill's Survey of Cinema. Series II. v2, p770-72.
The New Republic. Jun 12, 1950, v122, p23.
The New Statesman and Nation. Jun 24, 1950, v39, p711.
The New York Times. May 19, 1950, p31.
The New Yorker. May 27, 1950, v26, p58.
Newsweek. May 29, 1950, v35, p83.
Selected Film Criticism 1941-1950. p58-59.
The Spectator. Jun 16, 1950, v184, p820.
Time. May 29, 1950, v55, p87-88.
Variety. May 10, 1950, p6.

Father Unknown *See* Né de Pere Inconnu

Father's Dilemma *See* Prima Communione

Father's Little Dividend (US; Minnelli, Vincente; 1951)
BFI/Monthly Film Bulletin. May 1951, v18, p264.
Christian Century. May 16, 1951, v68, p623.
Commonweal. Apr 27, 1951, v54, p59.
The Films of Elizabeth Taylor. p85-87.
The Films of Spencer Tracy. p207-08.
Hollywood Reporter. Feb 21, 1951, p3.
Motion Picture Herald Product Digest. Feb 24, 1951, p721.
The New Statesman and Nation. Apr 7, 1951, v41, p392.
The New York Times. Apr 13, 1951, p18.
Newsweek. Apr 30, 1951, v37, p83.
Saturday Review. Apr 14, 1951, v34, p47.
The Spectator. Mar 30, 1951, v186, p413.
Time. Apr 23, 1951, v57, p104.
Variety. Feb 21, 1951, p6.

Fatiche di Ercole, Le *See* Hercules

Fatso (US; Bancroft, Anne; 1980)
Films in Review. Apr 1980, v31, p249.
Hollywood Reporter. Feb 1, 1980, p3.
Humanist. May-Jun 1980, v40, p47.
The Los Angeles Times. Feb 1, 1980, SecV, p1.
Motion Picture Herald Product Digest. Feb 20, 1980, p74.
The New Republic. Feb 23, 1980, v182, p24-25.
The New York Times. Feb 1, 1980, SecIII, p11.
Newsday. Feb 1, 1980, SecII, p7.
Time. Feb 25, 1980, v115, p50.
Variety. Jan 30, 1980, p28.

Fatto di sangue fra due uomini per causa de un vedova *See* Blood Feud

Fear Consumes the Soul *See* Ali

Fear Strikes Out (US; Mulligan, Robert; 1957)
America. Mar 30, 1957, v96, p743.
BFI/Monthly Film Bulletin. May 1957, v24, p54.
Commonweal. Mar 29, 1957, v65, p661.
Film Daily. Feb 4, 1957, p6.

Films and Filming. Jun 1957, v3, p22-23.
Films in Review. Apr 1957, v8, p174-75.
Hollywood Reporter. Feb 4, 1957, p3.
Magill's Survey of Cinema. Series II. p773-77.
Motion Picture Herald Product Digest. Feb 9, 1957, p257.
The New York Times. Mar 21, 1957, p37.
The New York Times. Mar 24, 1957, SecII, p1.
The New Yorker. Mar 30, 1957, v33, p128.
Newsweek. Mar 25, 1957, v49, p109.
Saturday Review. Mar 23, 1957, v40, p25.
Time. Mar 18, 1957, v69, p100.
Variety. Feb 6, 1957, p6.

Fearless Fagan (US; Donen, Stanley; 1952)
BFI/Monthly Film Bulletin. Dec 1952, v19, p171.
Film Daily. Jul 7, 1952, p4.
Hollywood Reporter. Jul 7, 1952, p3.
Motion Picture Herald Product Digest. Jul 12, 1952, p1441-42.
National Parent-Teacher. Sep 1952, v47, p36.
Newsweek. Aug 25, 1952, v40, p86.
Saturday Review. Sep 6, 1952, v35, p26.
Stanley Donen (Casper). p55-57.
Time. Aug 4, 1952, v60, p78.
Variety. Jul 9, 1952, p6.

Federale, Il *See* The Fascist

Fedora (WGER; Wilder, Billy; 1979)
BFI/Monthly Film Bulletin. Aug 1979, v46, p172.
Billy Wilder (Dick). p161-67.
The Film Career of Billy Wilder. p113.
Film Comment. Jan 1979, v15, p39.
Films in Review. Jun-Jul 1979, v30, p377-78.
The Films of Henry Fonda. p245.
The Los Angeles Times. Apr 20, 1979, SecIV, p27.
The Nation. May 5, 1979, v228, p513-14.
The New Republic. May 5, 1979, v180, p122-23.
New York. May 21, 1979, v12, p63.
The New York Times. Apr 15, 1979, p35.
The New Yorker. Apr 23, 1979, v55, p122-23.
Newsweek. Apr 23, 1979, v93, p69.
Time. May 21, 1979, v113, p86.
Variety. Aug 23, 1978, p30.

The Felines *See* Joy House

Félines, Les *See* Joy House

Fellini Satyricon (Also titled: Satyricon) (IT, FR; Fellini, Federico; 1969)
America. Apr 4, 1970, v122, p376.
American Scholar. Aut 1970, v39, p679-80.
BFI/Monthly Film Bulletin. Oct 1970, v37, p200-01.
Cinema. Fall 1970, v6, p40-41.
Cinema. 1969, v5, n3, p3-13.
Classic Cinema. p317-50.
Deeper Into Movies. p160-66.
Federico Fellini: A Guide to References and Resources. p112-18.
Federico Fellini: Essays in Criticism. p161-87.
Fellini the Artist. p177-89.
Film Heritage. Sum 1971, v6, p25-29.
Film Quarterly. Sum 1970, v23, p38-42.
Films and Filming. Nov 1969, v16, p26-31.
Films and Filming. Nov 1970, v17, p47-48.
Films in Review. Apr 1970, v21, p239-41.
The Films of Federico Fellini. p132-38.
The Films of The Seventies. p21-23.
Holiday. Mar 1970, v47, p32.
Hollywood Reporter. Mar 20, 1970, p3.
Horizon. Aut 1970, v12, p42-47.
Magill's Survey of Cinema. Foreign Language Films. v3, p1059-64.
Modern European Filmmakers and the Art of Adaptation. p145-57.

Motion Picture Herald Product Digest. Feb 25, 1970, p379-80.
Movies Into Film. p211-19.
The Nation. Mar 23, 1970, v210, p347.
National Review. May 19, 1970, v22, p521.
The New Republic. Apr 4, 1970, v162, p24.
The New York Times. Mar 12, 1970, p48.
The New York Times. Mar 15, 1970, p1.
The New York Times. May 10, 1970, p11.
The New Yorker. Mar 14, 1970, v46, p134.
Newsweek. Mar 23, 1970, v75, p102.
On the Set of Fellini Satyricon. 1971.
Saturday Review. Mar 14, 1970, v53, p42.
Second Sight. p289-93.
Sight and Sound. Aut 1970, v39, p217-18.
Take One. Jul-Aug 1969, v2, p29.
Time. Mar 16, 1970, v95, p76-79.
Variety. Sep 17, 1969, p13.
The Village Voice. Jan 22, 1970, p55, 57-59.
The Village Voice. Mar 19, 1970, p51.
The Village Voice. May 14, 1970, p20.
Vogue. Apr 15, 1970, v155, p58.

Fellini's Casanova (Italian title: Casanova di Fellini, Il; Also titled: Casanova) (IT; Fellini, Federico; 1976)
America. Feb 26, 1977, v136, p170.
BFI/Monthly Film Bulletin. Aug 1977, v44, p164.
Commonweal. Apr 15, 1977, v104, p240-41.
Commonweal. Apr 29, 1977, v104, p277-78.
Film Quarterly. Sum 1977, v30, p24-31.
Films in Review. Apr 1977, v28, p245.
Hollywood Reporter. Jan 3, 1977, p4.
The Los Angeles Times. Jan 1, 1977, SecII, p10.
The Nation. Feb 26, 1977, v224, p252-53.
The New Republic. Mar 5, 1977, v176, p28-29.
The New York Times. Feb 12, 1977, p12.
The New York Times. Feb 27, 1977, SecII, p17.
The New York Times Magazine. Feb 6, 1977, p22-24.
Newsweek. Jan 24, 1977, v89, p60-61.
Saturday Review. Feb 19, 1977, v4, p40-41.
Time. Feb 21, 1977, v109, p70.
Variety. Dec 22, 1976, p20.

Femme a Sa Fenetre, Une *See* A Woman at Her Window

Femme D'A Cote, La *See* The Woman Next Door

Femme douce, Une (Also titled: A Gentle Creature) (FR; Bresson, Robert; 1969)
Cineaste. Fall 1969, v3, p6-10.
Commonweal. Aug 20, 1971, v94, p428.
Film. Wint 1970, n57, p19.
Film 71/72. p141-43.
Film Quarterly. Sum 1970, v23, p54-56.
Filmfacts. 1971, v14, n15, p366.
Films and Filming. Dec 1970, v17, p49-50.
The Films of Robert Bresson. p127-33.
The Great French Films. p217-20.
Living Images. p57-59.
Modern European Filmmakers and the Art of Adaptation. p158-72.
Movies Into Film. p388-89.
The Nation. Jun 21, 1971, v212, p796.
The New Republic. Jun 26, 1971, v164, p28.
The New York Times. Sep 18, 1969, p62.
The New York Times. Sep 28, 1969, SecII, p1.
The New Yorker. May 29, 1971, v47, p79.
Newsweek. Jun 7, 1971, v77, p106.
Robert Bresson: A Guide to References and Resources. p83-89.
Self and Cinema. p191-240.
Sight and Sound. Spr 1970, v39, p82-83.
Variety. Jun 25, 1969, p18.
The Village Voice. Oct 2, 1969, p53.

Femme est une Femme, Une *See* A Woman Is a Woman

Femme Infidele, La (Also titled: The Unfaithful Wife) (FR, IT; Chabrol, Claude; 1968)
America. Dec 13, 1969, v121, p600.
BFI/Monthly Film Bulletin. Aug 1969, v36, p161-62.
Claude Chabrol (Wood and Walker). p113-22.
Commonweal. Dec 12, 1969, v91, p337-38.
Deeper Into Movies. p66-68.
Directors and Directions: Cinema for the Seventies. p31-32.
Film 69/70. p121-23.
Film Quarterly. Sum 1970, v23, p56-58.
Films and Filming. Oct 1969, v16, p43-44.
Five Thousand One Nights At the Movies. p183.
The International Dictionary of Films and Filmmakers. v1, p155-56.
The London Times. Jun 19, 1969, p11.
Motion Picture Herald Product Digest. Nov 19, 1969, p325-26.
Movie. Wint 1969-70, n17, p16-24.
Movie. Wint 1970-71, n18, p2-9.
Movies Into Film. p266-70.
The Nation. Dec 1, 1969, v209, p612.
New Statesman. Jun 20, 1969, v77, p884.
The New York Times. Nov 10, 1969, p55.
The New Yorker. Nov 29, 1969, v45, p158.
Newsweek. Dec 1, 1969, v74, p89.
Saturday Review. Nov 22, 1969, v52, p68.
Sight and Sound. Aut 1969, v38, p209-10.
The Spectator. Jun 28, 1969, v222, p861.
Variety. Nov 27, 1968, p26.
The Village Voice. Nov 13, 1969, p55-56.

Femme Mariée, Une (Also titled: A Married Woman; The Married Woman) (FR; Godard, Jean-Luc; 1964)
BFI/Monthly Film Bulletin. May 1965, v32, p67-68.
Cahiers du Cinema in English. 1966, n3, p54-59.
Christian Science Monitor (Western edition). Nov 11, 1965, p4.
Close-Up: A Critical Perspective on Film. p212-17.
Commonweal. Sep 3, 1965, v82, p637-38.
Dictionary of Films. p393.
Film Comment. Sum 1965, v3, p31-32.
Film Daily. Aug 16, 1965, p3.
Film Quarterly. Sum 1966, v19, p42-48.
Film Society Review. Oct 1966, p19-21.
Film Society Review. Mar 1966, p11-17.
Films and Filming. Jun 1965, v11, p28-29.
Georgia Review. n3, 1976, v30, p706-24.
Jean-Luc Godard: A Guide to References and Resources. p61-64.
Jean-Luc Godard (Mussman). p191-05.
The London Times. Apr 8, 1965, p6.
Magill's Survey of Cinema. Foreign Language Films. v4, p1970-75.
Motion Picture Herald Product Digest. Sep 1, 1965, p353.
Movie. Sum 1965, n13, p2-5.
Movie Man (Thomson). p38-40.
The Nation. Oct 18, 1965, v201, p259.
The New Leader. Sep 13, 1965, v48, p31-32.
The New Republic. Sep 11, 1965, v153, p26-27.
New Statesman. Apr 9, 1965, v69, p583.
New Statesman. Sep 18, 1964, v68, p414.
The New Wave (Monaco). p145-52.
The New York Times. Dec 4, 1964, p46.
The New York Times. Aug 17, 1965, p17.
The New York Times. Aug 21, 1965, v41, p99-100.
Newsweek. Aug 30, 1965, v66, p79-80.
Playboy. Dec 1965, v12, p40.

Private Screenings. p205-07.
Saturday Review. Aug 28, 1965, v48, p28.
Sight and Sound. Sum 1965, v34, p106-11.
The Spectator. Apr 9, 1965, v214, p475.
Time. Aug 27, 1965, v86, p82.
Tynan Right and Left. p225-26.
Variety. Sep 16, 1964, p17.
The Village Voice. Sep 30, 1965, p19, 33.
Wide Angle. n3, 1976, v1, p14-16.
A World on Film. p244-46.

Ferroviere, Il *See* The Railroad Man

Ferry Cross The Mersey (GB; Summers, Jeremy; 1964)
Film Daily. Feb 1, 1965, p6.
Filmfacts. Feb 26, 1965, v8, p17-18.
Films and Filming. Feb 1965, v11, p34-35.
Hollywood Reporter. Jan 29, 1965, p3.
The London Times. Dec 3, 1964, p7.
Motion Picture Herald Product Digest. Feb 17, 1965, p234-35.
The New York Times. Feb 20, 1965, p16.
Variety. Dec 2, 1964, p6.

Fete a Henriette, La *See* Holiday For Henrietta

Fetes Galantes, Les (FR, RUM; Clair, René; 1965)
BFI/Monthly Film Bulletin. Mar 1967, v34, p41.
Cahiers du Cinema in English. 1966, n2, p80.
Films and Filming. Apr 1967, v13, p10.
The London Times. Mar 7, 1966, p9.
The London Times. Dec 15, 1966, p8.
René Clair (McGerr). p208-10.
Variety. Apr 20, 1966, p28.

Fever Heat *See* Bob le Flambeur

ffolkes (Also titled: North Sea Adventure; Assault Force) (US, GB; McLaglen, Andrew V.; 1980)
Hollywood Reporter. Apr 16, 1980, p3.
The Los Angeles Times. Apr 18, 1980, SecVI, p6.
Motion Picture Herald Product Digest. May 7, 1980, p94.
The New York Times. Apr 18, 1980, SecIII, p11.
Newsday. Feb 1, 1980, SecII, p7.
Variety. Apr 23, 1980, p18.
The Village Voice. Apr 28, 1980, p46.

Fiddler on the Roof (US; Jewison, Norman; 1971)
BFI/Monthly Film Bulletin. Jan 1972, v39, p5.
Deeper into Movies. p412-20.
Filmfacts. 1971, v14, p385-90.
Films and Filming. Feb 1972, v18, p50-51.
Films in Review. Dec 1971, v22, p639-40.
Hollywood Reporter. Nov 3, 1971, p3.
Life. Dec 3, 1971, v71, p87-90.
Life. Dec 10, 1971, v71, p16.
Magill's Survey of Cinema. Series I. v2, p527.
National Review. Feb 18, 1972, v24, p172.
The New Republic. Nov 20, 1971, v165, p28.
The New York Times. Nov 4, 1971, p52-54.
The New York Times. Nov 28, 1971, SecII, p1.
The New Yorker. Nov 13, 1971, v47, p133-39.
Newsweek. Nov 15, 1971, v78, p114.
Saturday Review. Nov 13, 1971, v54, p30.
Time. Nov 22, 1971, v98.
Variety. Nov 3, 1971, p16.
The Village Voice. Nov 18, 1971, p84.

Fidel (US; Landau, Saul; Saraf, Irving; 1968)
BFI/Monthly Film Bulletin. Feb 1971, v38, p22.
Cineaste. Wint 1970-1971, v4, p38-39.
Film Quarterly. Spr 1970, v23, p59-60.

Film Society Review. Nov 1971, v7, p43-44.
Filmfacts. 1971, v14, n17, p422.
The New York Times. Jun 26, 1971, p18.
The Village Voice. Aug 19, 1971, p53-54.

The Fiendish Plot of Dr. Fu Manchu (US; Haggard, Piers; 1980)
BFI/Monthly Film Bulletin. Oct 1980, v47, p192.
Christian Science Monitor. Aug 22, 1980, p19.
Films in Review. Oct 1980, v31, p503.
Hollywood Reporter. Aug 8, 1980, p3.
The Los Angeles Times. Aug 8, 1980, SecVI, p1.
Maclean's. Aug 25, 1980, v93, p50.
Motion Picture Herald Product Digest. Aug 20, 1980, p22.
The New York Times. Aug 8, 1980, SecIII, p3.
The New York Times. Aug 24, 1980, SecII, p17.
Newsday. Aug 8, 1980, SecII, p7.
Newsweek. Aug 18, 1980, v96, p85.
Variety. Aug 13, 1980, p23.
The Village Voice. Aug 27, 1980, p39.

Fifi La Plume (FR; Lamorisse, Albert; 1964)
BFI/Monthly Film Bulletin. Jan 1966, v33, p6.
The London Times. Dec 2, 1965, p15.
New Statesman. Jun 4, 1965, v69, p890.
New Statesman. Dec 3, 1965, v70, p900.
Variety. Jun 2, 1965, p22.

The Fifth Horseman Is Fear (Czechoslovakian title: A Paty Jezdec Je Strach; Also titled: The Fifth Rider Is Fear) (CZECH; Brynych, Zbynek; 1966)
Christian Century. Aug 14, 1968, v85, p1021.
Cinema. Fall 1968, v4, p43.
Film Comment. Fall 1968, v5, p72.
Film Daily. May 17, 1968, p8.
Filmfacts. Jul 1, 1968, v11, p168-70.
Films and Filming. Jan 1970, v16, p41-42.
Films in Review. Jun-Jul 1968, v19, p378-79.
The Los Angeles Times. Jul 21, 1968, SecIV, p1.
Magill's Survey of Cinema. Foreign Language Films. v3, p1074-78.
Motion Picture Herald Product Digest. May 22, 1968, p814.
Movies Into Film. p280-81.
The Nation. May 27, 1968, v206, p709-10.
The New York Times. May 7, 1968, p52.
The New Yorker. Jul 1, 1967, v43, p58.
Newsweek. Jun 10, 1968, v71, p87A.
Time. May 10, 1968, v91, p117.
Tynan Right and Left. p217.
Variety. Jul 27, 1966, p24.
The Village Voice. Jun 13, 1968, p47.
A Year in the Dark. p139-41.

55 Days at Peking (US; Ray, Nicholas; Marton, Andrew; 1963)
America. Jul 6, 1963, v109, p26.
BFI/Monthly Film Bulletin. Jun 1963, v30, p78-79.
Film Daily. May 1, 1963, p4.
Filmfacts. Jun 6, 1963, v6, p101-02.
Films and Filming. Jun 1963, v9, p28.
The Films of Charlton Heston. p136-41.
The Films of David Niven. p180-84.
Hollywood Reporter. May 1, 1963, p3.
Illustrated London News. May 25, 1963, v242, p822.
Movie. Jul-Aug 1963, p46.
National Review. Jul 30, 1963, v15, p72.
The New York Times. May 30, 1963, p20.
The New Yorker. Jun 1, 1963, v39, p68.
Newsweek. Jun 3, 1963, v61, p83-84.
Nicholas Ray: A Guide to References and Resources. p125-31.

Time. May 31, 1963, v81, p80.
Variety. May 1, 1963, p6.

The Fighting Seventh *See* Little Big Horn

Figures in a Landscape (GB; Losey, Joseph; 1971)
BFI/Monthly Film Bulletin. Feb 1971, v38, p23.
Filmfacts. 1971, v14, p424-26.
Films and Filming. Jan 1971, v17, n4, p49-50.
Focus. Spr 1970, n6, p47-48.
Hollywood Reporter. Jul 16, 1971, v217, n6, p3.
Joseph Losey (Hirsch). p179-80.
The New York Times. Jul 19, 1971, p31.
The New Yorker. Jul 31, 1971, v47, p55-57.
Saturday Review. Aug 14, 1971, v54, p42.
Sight and Sound. Wint 1970-71, v40, p48-49.
Time. Aug 9, 1971, v98, p63.
Variety. Jul 29, 1970, p20.

Fille en Noir, La *See* Girl in Black

Fills et des Fusile, Une *See* To Be a Crook

Film D'Amore e D'Anarchia *See* Love and Anarchy

The Final Countdown (US; Taylor, Don; 1980)
BFI/Monthly Film Bulletin. Jul 1980, v47, p131.
Christian Century. Sep 24, 1980, v97, p892.
Films in Review. Oct 1980, v31, p503.
Hollywood Reporter. Jul 18, 1980, p3.
The Los Angeles Times. Aug 1, 1980, Calendar, p1.
Motion Picture Herald Product Digest. Aug 20, 1980, p22.
The New Republic. Aug 30, 1980, v183, p25.
New York. Aug 18, 1980, v13, p70.
The New York Times. Aug 1, 1980, SecIII, p10.
Newsday. Aug 1, 1980, SecII, p10.
Newsweek. Aug 18, 1980, v96, p85.
Time. Aug 18, 1980, v116, p59.
Variety. Jul 16, 1980, p23.
The Village Voice. Jul 30, 1980, p40.

The Final Test (GB; Asquith, Anthony; 1953)
America. Mar 6, 1954, v90, p610.
BFI/Monthly Film Bulletin. May 1953, v20, p67.
The Films of Anthony Asquith. p141-49.
Kiss Kiss Bang Bang. p329.
The London Times. Apr 13, 1953, p10.
Motion Picture Herald Product Digest. Feb 13, 1954, p2183.
National Parent-Teacher. Apr 1954, v48, p38.
The New Statesman and Nation. Apr 18, 1953, v45, p456.
The New York Times. Jan 26, 1954, p21.
The New Yorker. Feb 6, 1954, v29, p100.
Newsweek. Feb 1, 1954, v43, p77.
Saturday Review. Feb 6, 1954, v37, p29.
The Spectator. Apr 10, 1953, v190, p447.
The Tatler. Apr 22, 1953, v208, p210.
Time. Feb 22, 1954, v63, p102.
Variety. Apr 15, 1953, p22.

Finders Keepers (GB; Hayers, Sidney; 1966)
BFI/Monthly Film Bulletin. Feb 1967, v34, p27.
Film Daily. Apr 6, 1967, p6.
Filmfacts. Jan 1, 1968, v10, p363.
Films and Filming. Feb 1967, v13, p37.
The London Times. Dec 8, 1966, p18.
Motion Picture Herald Product Digest. Apr 26, 1967, p679.
Variety. Dec 13, 1966, p19.

Fine and Dandy *See* The West Point Story

A Fine Madness (US; Kershner, Irvin; 1966)
America. Jun 18, 1966, v114, p861.
BFI/Monthly Film Bulletin. Sep 1966, v33, p136-37.
Cinema. Jul 1966, v3, p48.
Commonweal. May 27, 1966, v84, p284.
Film Daily. May 9, 1966, p7.
Film Quarterly. Fall 1966, v20, p59.
Filmfacts. Sep 1, 1966, v9, p176-77.
Films and Filming. Sep 1966, v12, p10.
Films in Review. Jun-Jul 1966, v17, p381-82.
Hollywood Reporter. May 9, 1966, p3.
The London Times. Jul 21, 1966, p17.
Magill's Survey of Cinema. Series II. v2, p781-83.
Motion Picture Herald Product Digest. May 18, 1966, p524A.
New Statesman. Jul 22, 1966, v72, p141.
The New York Times. Jun 30, 1966, p28.
The New Yorker. Jul 9, 1966, v42, p78.
Newsweek. Jun 27, 1966, v67, p94B.
Playboy. Aug 1966, v13, p24-25.
Saturday Review. May 21, 1966, v49, p49.
Sight and Sound. Aut 1966, v35, p201.
Time. Jul 8, 1966, v88, p84.
Variety. May 4, 1966, p6.

Finian's Rainbow (US; Coppola, Francis Ford; 1968)
America. Nov 16, 1968, v119, p501.
Astaire Dancing: The Musical Films. p400-07.
BFI/Monthly Film Bulletin. Oct 1968, v35, p149.
BFI/Monthly Film Bulletin. Jun 1985, v52, p200.
Christian Science Monitor (Western edition). Oct 11, 1968, p4.
Cinema. Fall 1968, v4, p45.
Commonweal. Nov 1, 1968, v89, p160.
Dance Magazine. Mar 1969, v43, p94-95.
Film 68/69. p157-58.
Film Daily. Oct 9, 1968, p3.
Filmfacts. Jan 1, 1968, v11, p421-23.
Films and Filming. Nov 1968, v15, p42-43.
Films in Review. Nov 1968, v19, p578-79.
Five Thousand One Nights At the Movies. p185.
Francis Ford Coppola: A Guide to References and Resources. p40-44, 85-90.
Francis Ford Coppola (Johnson). p61-69.
Going Steady. p192-93.
Harper's Magazine. Nov 1968, v237, p170.
Hollywood Reporter. Oct 9, 1968, p3.
The London Times. Oct 10, 1968, p9.
Motion Picture Herald Product Digest. Oct 23, 1968, p44.
The Musical: From Broadway to Hollywood. p119-24.
New Statesman. Oct 11, 1968, v76, p472.
The New York Times. Oct 10, 1968, p59.
The New Yorker. Oct 19, 1968, v44, p212.
Newsweek. Oct 21, 1968, v72, p101A.
Saturday Review. Oct 5, 1968, v51, p47.
Senior Scholastic. Oct 18, 1968, v93, p26.
Sight and Sound. Wint 1968-69, v38, p43-44.
Starring Fred Astaire. p449-55.
Time. Oct 25, 1968, v92, p100.
Variety. Oct 9, 1968, p6.
A Year In the Dark. p266.

Fire Down Below (US; Parrish, Robert; 1957)
America. Aug 24, 1957, v97, p532.
BFI/Monthly Film Bulletin. Jul 1957, v24, p87.
Commonweal. Aug 30, 1957, v66, p542.
Film Daily. May 29, 1957, p10.
Films and Filming. Jul 1957, v3, p24.
The Films of Jack Lemmon. p77-80.
The Films of Rita Hayworth. p198-202.

Hollywood Reporter. May 29, 1957, p3.
Motion Picture Herald Product Digest. Jun 1, 1957, p401-02.
The New York Times. Aug 9, 1957, p11.
Newsweek. Jul 15, 1957, v50, p102-03.
Time. Jul 22, 1957, v70, p78.
Variety. May 29, 1957, p6.

The Fireball (US; Garnett, Tay; 1950)
BFI/Monthly Film Bulletin. Oct 1950, v17, p154.
Film Daily. Aug 16, 1950, p7.
The Films of Marilyn Monroe. p46-47.
Hollywood Reporter. Aug 14, 1950, p3.
Motion Picture Herald Product Digest. Aug 19, 1950, p441.
The New York Times. Nov 10, 1950, p35.
Newsweek. Oct 16, 1950, v36, p93.
Robert Mitchum on the Screen. p151-53.
Variety. Aug 16, 1950, p11.

Fireball 500 (US; Asher, William; 1966)
BFI/Monthly Film Bulletin. Oct 1966, v33, p154.
Film Daily. Jun 9, 1966, p7.
Filmfacts. Jan 15, 1967, v9, p337-38.
Hollywood Reporter. Jun 8, 1966, p3.
Motion Picture Herald Product Digest. Jun 15, 1966, p543-44.
The New York Times. Nov 24, 1966, p65.
Variety. Jun 15, 1966, p6.

Firefox (US; Eastwood, Clint; 1982)
Clint Eastwood (Guérif). p151-56.
Commentary. Aug 1982, v74, p66-67.
Hollywood Reporter. Jun 14, 1982, p3.
The Los Angeles Times. Jun 18, 1982, SecVI, p1.
Maclean's. Jun 28, 1982, v95, p60.
Magill's Cinema Annual, 1983. p160-63.
New York. Jun 28, 1982, v15, p52.
The New York Times. Jun 18, 1982, SecIII, p16.
Newsweek. Jun 28, 1982, v99, p73.
Time. Jun 21, 1982, v119, p72.
Variety. Jun 14, 1982, p3.

Fireman, Save My Child (US; Goodwins, Leslie; 1954)
BFI/Monthly Film Bulletin. Feb 1955, v22, p24.
Film Daily. May 17, 1954, p6.
Hollywood Reporter. Apr 27, 1954, p3.
Motion Picture Herald Product Digest. Apr 24, 1954, p2270.
National Parent-Teacher. Jun 1954, v48, p38.
Newsweek. Apr 26, 1954, v43, p103.
Variety. Apr 28, 1954, p6.

First Blood (US; Kotcheff, Ted; 1982)
Hollywood Reporter. Oct 19, 1982, p3.
The Los Angeles Times. Oct 22, 1982, SecVI, p1.
Magill's Cinema Annual, 1983. p164-66.
New Statesman. Dec 17, 1982, v104, p53.
New York. Nov 15, 1982, v15, p108.
The New York Times. Jan 27, 1982, SecIII, p20.
Newsweek. Oct 25, 1982, v100, p119.
Time. Nov 8, 1982, v120, p85.
Variety. Oct 19, 1982, p3.
The Village Voice. Nov 23, 1982, p58.

First Communion *See* Prima Communione

The First Cry *See* The Cry

The First Deadly Sin (US; Hutton, Brian G.; 1980)
BFI/Monthly Film Bulletin. May 1981, v48, p92.
Films in Review. Jan 1981, v31, p57.
Hollywood Reporter. Oct 24, 1980, p3.

The Los Angeles Times. Oct 29, 1980, SecIV, p1.
Maclean's. Nov 17, 1980, v93, p67-68.
Motion Picture Herald Product Digest. Nov 5, 1980, p41.
The New York Times. Oct 24, 1980, SecIII, p10.
Newsday. Oct 24, 1980, SecII, p7.
Newsweek. Nov 10, 1980, v96, p108.
Time. Nov 10, 1980, v116, p64.
Variety. Oct 22, 1980, p24.
The Village Voice. Oct 28, 1980, p52.

The First Great Train Robbery *See* The Great Train Robbery

The First Legion (US; Sirk, Douglas; 1951)
BFI/Monthly Film Bulletin. Oct 1951, v18, p346.
Commonweal. May 11, 1951, v54, p117.
Douglas Sirk (Stern). p66-69.
Film Daily. Apr 20, 1951, p6.
Library Journal. Jan 1, 1951, v76, p59.
Motion Picture Herald Product Digest. Apr 14, 1951, p801.
The New Republic. May 14, 1951, v124, p23.
The New York Times. Apr 28, 1951, p9.
Newsweek. May 7, 1951, v37, p89.
Variety. Apr 11, 1951, p6.

First Monday in October (US; Neame, Ronald; 1981)
Fortune. Sep 21, 1981, v104, p58.
Hollywood Reporter. Aug 17, 1981, p2.
The Los Angeles Times. Aug 22, 1981, p3.
Maclean's. Aug 24, 1981, v94, p65.
Magill's Cinema Annual, 1982. p151-53.
The Nation. Sep 26, 1981, v233, p285.
New York. Sep 7, 1981, v14, p52-53.
The New York Times. Aug 21, 1981, SecIII, p8.
Newsweek. Aug 31, 1981, v98, p37.
Rolling Stone. Oct 1, 1981, p74.
Variety. Aug 17, 1981, p3.

First Name Carmen (French title: Prenom Carmen) (FR; Godard, Jean-Luc; 1983)
American Film. Jun 1984, v9, p33.
BFI/Monthly Film Bulletin. Feb 1984, v51, p31.
Commonweal. Sep 7, 1984, v111, p464-65.
Film. Feb 1984, n123, p2.
Film. Nov 1984, v130, p12.
Film Quarterly. Fall 1984, v37, p13-19.
Films and Filming. Feb 1984, n353, p36.
Films in Review. Nov 1984, v35, p569.
Hollywood Reporter. Aug 16, 1984, p4.
The Los Angeles Times. Aug 23, 1984, SecVI, p5.
Maclean's. Sep 17, 1984, v97, p73.
Magill's Cinema Annual, 1985. p186-91.
The New Republic. Sep 10, 1984, v191, p24-25.
New Statesman. Jan 27, 1984, v107, p27.
New York. Aug 6, 1984, v17, p58-59.
The New York Times. Aug 3, 1984, SecIII, p6.
The New Yorker. Sep 17, 1984, v60, p130-33.
Newsweek. Aug 27, 1984, v104, p68.
Progressive. Oct 1984, v48, p36-37.
Sight and Sound. Wint 1983-84, v53, p60-61.
Stills. Feb-Mar 1984, n10, p69.
The Village Voice. Aug 14, 1984, p47.

The First Nudie Musical (US; Haggard, Mark; Kimmel, Bruce; 1976)
Cult Movies 2. p59-62.
Film Bulletin. Mar 1976, v45, p36.
Filmmakers' Newsletter. Apr 1976, v9, p17-19.
Films and Filming. Jul 1976, v22, p45-47.
Independent Film Journal. Mar 17, 1976, v77, p10-11.
Independent Film Journal. Jul 8, 1977, v80, p13.

The Los Angeles Times. May 6, 1976, SecIV, p20.
Motion Picture Herald Product Digest. Mar 24, 1976, p84.
The New York Times. Sep 16, 1977, SecIII, p9.
The New York Times. Jul 25, 1977, p29.
Variety. Mar 10, 1976, p22.
The Village Voice. Aug 15, 1977, p41.

The First Time (US; Tashlin, Frank; 1952)
BFI/Monthly Film Bulletin. Apr 1952, v19, p50.
Burt Lancaster: A Pictorial Treasury of His Films. p64.
Christian Century. Jul 16, 1952, v69, p839.
Film Daily. Jan 31, 1952, p6.
Hollywood Reporter. Jan 25, 1952, p3.
Motion Picture Herald Product Digest. Jan 26, 1952, p1214.
Talking Pictures. p77-79.
Variety. Jan 30, 1952, p6.

Fist in His Pocket *See* Fists in the Pocket

A Fistful of Dollars (Italian title: Per un Pugno di Dolari; Also titled: For a Handful of Dollars; For a Fistful of Dollars) (IT, WGER, SP; Leone, Sergio; 1964)
Christian Science Monitor (Western edition). Feb 3, 1967, p4.
Clint Eastwood (Guérif). p41-45.
Film Comment. Mar-Apr 1973, v9, p8.
Film Daily. Dec 28, 1966, p4.
Film Society Review. Sep 1968, v4, p37-40.
Filmfacts. Feb 15, 1967, v10, p16-18.
Films and Filming. Sep 1967, v13, p26.
Films in Review. Mar 1967, v18, p174-75.
The Films of Clint Eastwood. p54-59.
Focus. Mar 1967, n2, p23.
Focus on Film. Spr 1972, n9, p15-16.
The Great Western Pictures. p265-67.
Hollywood Reporter. Jan 9, 1967, p3.
Italian Cinema (Bondanella). p255-57.
The London Times. Jun 8, 1967, p8.
Motion Picture Herald Product Digest. Jan 4, 1967, p646.
New Statesman. Jun 9, 1967, v73, p807.
The New York Times. Feb 2, 1967, p29.
Spaghetti Westerns. p160-91.
Take One. Feb 1967, v1, p22-24.
Variety. Nov 18, 1964, p22.
The Velvet Light Trap. 1974, n12, p31-33.
The Village Voice. Feb 9, 1967, p27.

Fists in the Pocket (Italian title: Pugni in Tasca, I; Also titled: Fist in His Pocket) (IT; Bellochio, Marco; 1965)
BFI/Monthly Film Bulletin. Jun 1966, v33, p91.
Big Screen, Little Screen. p389.
Figures of Light. p86-87.
Film 68/69. p178-79.
Filmfacts. Sep 1, 1968, v11, p226-27.
Films and Filming. Jul 1966, v12, p18.
Going Steady. p6-8.
The International Dictionary of Films and Filmmakers. v1, p378.
International Film Guide. 1967, v4, p108-09.
Italian Cinema (Bondanella). p191-93.
Life. Mar 1, 1968, v64, p8.
The London Times. Nov 18, 1965, p8.
The London Times. May 5, 1966, p20.
Magill's Survey of Cinema. Foreign Language Films. v3, p1097-03.
Motion Picture Herald Product Digest. Jan 17, 1968, p760.
The Nation. Jun 17, 1968, v206, p806.
The New Italian Cinema. p43-44.
The New Republic. Jun 15, 1968, v158, p26.
New Statesman. May 20, 1966, v71, p746.

The New York Times. May 28, 1968, p40.
The New Yorker. Jan 13, 1968, v43, p93-94.
Newsweek. Jan 22, 1968, v71, p84.
Sight and Sound. Wint 1965-66, v35, p5-6.
Sight and Sound. Wint 1967-68, v37, p14-16.
The Spectator. May 13, 1966, v216, p600.
Time. Jan 12, 1968, v91, p59.
Tynan Right and Left. p243.
Variety. Aug 25, 1965, p6.
The Village Voice. Jun 13, 1968, v13, p47.
A Year in the Dark. p159-60.

Fitzcarraldo (WGER; Herzog, Werner; 1982)
Commentary. Dec 1982, v74, p59-67.
Commonweal. Dec 3, 1982, v109, p655-56.
Film Comment. May-Jun 1982, v18, p22-23.
Film Comment. Sep-Oct 1982, v18, p56-59.
Hollywood Reporter. Oct 29, 1982, p6.
The Los Angeles Times. Oct 28, 1982, SecVI, p1.
Maclean's. Nov 8, 1982, v95, p70.
Magill's Cinema Annual, 1983. p167-72.
The New Leader. Oct 4, 1982, v65, p19-20.
The New Republic. Oct 18, 1982, v187, p24-26.
New York. Oct 25, 1982, v15, p96-97.
The New York Times. Oct 10, 1982, p89.
The New Yorker. Oct 18, 1982, v58, p173-78.
Progressive. Aug 1982, v46, p20-21.
Senior Scholastic. Dec 10, 1982, v115, p22.
Time. Oct 25, 1982, v120, p77-78.
Variety. May 28, 1982, p3.

Five (US; Oboler, Arch; 1951)
BFI/Monthly Film Bulletin. Nov 1951, v18, p356.
Christian Century. Jun 20, 1951, v68, p751.
Commonweal. May 18, 1951, v54, p143.
Film Daily. Apr 26, 1951, p11.
The New Republic. May 14, 1951, v124, p23.
The New York Times. Apr 26, 1951, p34.
The New Yorker. May 5, 1951, v27, p68.
Nuclear War Films. p11-16.
Saturday Review. May 5, 1951, v34, p26.
Science Fiction Studies in Film. p117-18.
Time. May 21, 1951, v57, p120.
Variety. Apr 25, 1951, p6.

Five Angles on Murder *See* The Woman in Question

Five Easy Pieces (US; Rafelson, Bob; 1970)
America. Oct 3, 1970, v123, p244.
BFI/Monthly Film Bulletin. Apr 1971, v38, p72.
Big Screen, Little Screen. p303-05.
Commentary. Jan 1970, v51, p92.
Esquire. Nov 1970, v74, p68.
Fifty Grand Movies of the 1960s and 1970s. p27-32.
Films in Review. Nov 1970, v21, p577.
The Films of the Sixties. p24-25.
Life. Sep 18, 1970, v69, p16.
Magill's Survey of Cinema. Series I. v2, p538.
The New Republic. Sep 26, 1970, v163, p21.
The New York Times. Sep 12, 1970, p31.
The New York Times. Sep 27, 1970, SecII, p13.
The New Yorker. Sep 19, 1970, v46, p101-03.
Newsweek. Dec 21, 1970, v76, p14.
Saturday Review. Sep 26, 1970, v53, p40-41.
Talking Pictures. p348-54.
Time. Sep 14, 1970, v96, p89.
Variety. Sep 16, 1970, p15.
Vogue. Nov 1, 1970, v156, p106.

Five Fingers (US; Mankiewicz, Joseph L.; 1952)
BFI/Monthly Film Bulletin. Apr 1952, v19, p45.
Catholic World. Apr 1952, v175, p62.
Christian Century. Apr 30, 1952, v69, p543.

Fifty from the Fifties. p99-104.
Film Daily. Feb 14, 1952, p6.
Films in Review. Apr 1952, v3, p196-97.
The Films of James Mason. p100-01.
Hollywood Reporter. Feb 13, 1952, p3.
Illustrated London News. Apr 19, 1952, v220, p676.
Joseph L. Mankiewicz (Dick). p101-07.
Library Journal. Mar 15, 1952, v77, p522.
Life. Apr 7, 1952, v32, p139-40.
Magill's Survey of Cinema. Series II. v2, p784-88.
Motion Picture Herald Product Digest. Feb 16, 1952, p1237.
The New Republic. Mar 10, 1952, v126, p22.
The New Statesman and Nation. Apr 12, 1952, v43, p434.
The New York Times. Feb 23, 1952, p7.
Newsweek. Mar 3, 1952, v39, p90-91.
Pictures Will Talk. p212-20.
Saturday Review. Mar 8, 1952, v35, p32-33.
The Spectator. Apr 4, 1952, v188, p434.
The Tatler. Apr 16, 1952, v204, p132.
Theatre Arts. Apr 1952, v36, p41.
Time. Mar 10, 1952, v59, p100.
Variety. Feb 13, 1952, p6.

The Five-Legged Sheep *See* Mouton a Cinq Pattes, Le

Five Miles to Midnight (French title: Conteau dans la Plaie, le) (FR; Litvak, Anatole; 1963)
America. Apr 20, 1963, v108, p590.
BFI/Monthly Film Bulletin. May 1963, v30, p58-59.
Commonweal. Mar 1, 1963, v77, p599.
Film Daily. Feb 21, 1963, p8.
Filmfacts. Mar 21, 1963, v6, p33-34.
Films and Filming. Jun 1963, v9, p30-31.
Films in Review. Feb 1963, v14, p113-14.
Hollywood Reporter. Feb 20, 1963, p3.
The New York Times. Mar 21, 1963, p8.
Newsweek. Mar 11, 1963, v61, p99.
Photoplay. Apr 1963, v63, p8.
Saturday Review. Mar 16, 1963, v46, p82.
Time. Apr 12, 1963, v81, pM29.
Variety. Jan 16, 1963, p20.

The 5,000 Fingers of Doctor T (US; Rowland, Roy; 1953)
America. Jun 27, 1953, v89, p345.
American Photographer. May 1953, v47, p8.
Commonweal. Jul 3, 1953, v58, p322.
Film Daily. Jul 1, 1953, p6.
Films in Review. Mar 1953, v4, p151.
Hollywood Reporter. Jun 16, 1953, p3.
Magill's Survey of Cinema. Series II. v2, p792-95.
Musical America. May 1953, v73, p9.
National Parent-Teacher. Mar 1953, v47, p26.
The New York Times. Jun 20, 1953, p8.
The New York Times. Jun 28, 1953, SecII, p1.
The New Yorker. Jun 1953, v29, p58.
Newsweek. Jun 15, 1953, v41, p100-01.
Photography. Jul 1953, v33, p98.
Saturday Review. Jun 13, 1953, v36, p30.
Stanley Kramer, Film Maker. p149-56.
Theatre Arts. May 1953, v37, p82.
Time. Jun 22, 1953, v61, p84.
Variety. Jun 17, 1953, p6.

Fixed Bayonets (US; Fuller, Sam; 1951)
Christian Century. Jan 2, 1952, v69, p31.
Commonweal. Dec 14, 1951, v55, p255.
The Director's Event. p132-34.
Film Daily. Nov 26, 1951, p6.
Holiday. Mar 1952, v11, p19.
Hollywood Reporter. Nov 21, 1951, p3.
Library Journal. Jan 1, 1952, v77, p44.

Motion Picture Herald Product Digest. Nov 24, 1951, p1117-18.
The Nation. Jan 5, 1952, v174, p18.
The New York Times. Nov 21, 1951, p20.
Newsweek. Dec 3, 1951, v38, p94.
Samuel Fuller (Hardy). p73-75.
Variety. Nov 21, 1951, p6.

The Fixer (US; Frankenheimer, John; 1968)
America. Jan 25, 1969, v120, p117.
BFI/Monthly Film Bulletin. Nov 1969, v36, p230-31.
Christian Science Monitor (Western edition). Jan 12, 1968, p4.
Commonweal. Dec 27, 1968, v89, p441-42.
Esquire. Apr 1969, v71, p38.
Film 68/69. p225-27.
Film Daily. Nov 18, 1968, p4.
Filmfacts. Jan 15, 1968, v11, p508-11.
Films in Review. Jan 1969, v20, p52-53.
Five Thousand One Nights At the Movies. p188-89.
Going Steady. p256-59.
Harper's Magazine. Jan 1969, v238, p107-08.
Hollywood Reporter. Nov 18, 1968, p3.
Life. Dec 6, 1968, v65, p14.
Motion Picture Herald Product Digest. Nov 20, 1968, p63.
Movies Into Film. p321.
The New Republic. Jan 25, 1969, v160, p22.
The New York Times. Dec 9, 1968, p59.
The New Yorker. Dec 21, 1968, v44, p86.
Newsweek. Dec 16, 1968, v72, p101-02.
Saturday Review. Nov 30, 1968, v51, p59.
Sight and Sound. Sum 1969, v38, p155-56.
Time. Dec 13, 1968, v92, p104.
Variety. Nov 20, 1968, p34.
Vogue. Dec 1968, v152, p180.

The Flame and the Arrow (US; Tourneur, Jacques; 1950)
BFI/Monthly Film Bulletin. Dec 1950, v17, p187-88.
Burt Lancaster: A Pictorial Treasury of His Films. p51-54.
Christian Century. Aug 23, 1950, v67, p1007.
Commonweal. Jul 28, 1950, v52, p392.
Film Daily. Jun 20, 1950, p8.
The Great Adventure Films. p150-55.
Hollywood Reporter. Jun 20, 1950, p3.
Life. Aug 14, 1950, v29, p51.
Motion Picture Herald Product Digest. Jun 24, 1950, p353.
The New York Times. Jul 8, 1950, p7.
The New Yorker. Jul 15, 1950, v26, p57.
Time. Jul 31, 1950, v56, p65.
Variety. Jun 21, 1950, p8.

The Flame and the Flesh (US; Brooks, Richard; 1954)
America. May 15, 1954, v91, p203.
BFI/Monthly Film Bulletin. Oct 1954, v21, p143.
Commonweal. May 21, 1954, v60, p176.
Film Daily. May 14, 1954, p12.
The Films of Lana Turner. p188-90.
Hollywood Reporter. Apr 28, 1954, p3.
Library Journal. May 15, 1954, v79, p953.
The London Times. Aug 30, 1954, p5.
Motion Picture Herald Product Digest. May 1, 1954, p2277.
The New Statesman and Nation. Aug 28, 1954, v48, p232.
The New York Times. May 3, 1954, p21.
Newsweek. May 10, 1954, v43, p102.
Saturday Review. May 29, 1954, v37, p23.
Time. May 24, 1954, v63, p106.
Variety. Apr 28, 1954, p6.

Flame of Araby (US; Lamont, Charles; 1951)
Film Daily. Nov 19, 1951, p6.
Hollywood Reporter. Nov 16, 1951, p3.
Motion Picture Herald Product Digest. Nov 24, 1951, p1118.
The New York Times. Dec 20, 1951, p41.
Variety. Nov 21, 1951, p6.

Flaming Star (US; Siegel, Don; 1960)
American Film Genres. p239-42.
BFI/Monthly Film Bulletin. Mar 1961, v28, p3.
Commonweal. Jan 13, 1961, v73, p414.
Elvis: The Films and Career of Elvis Presley. p120-23.
Film Daily. Dec 20, 1960, p6.
Filmfacts. 1960, v3, p341.
Films and Filming. Mar 1961, v7, p29.
Hollywood Reporter. Dec 19, 1960, p3.
Magill's Survey of Cinema. Series I. v2, p541-44.
Motion Picture Herald Product Digest. Dec 24, 1960, p964.
The New York Times. Dec 17, 1960, p19.
Saturday Review. Jan 7, 1961, v44, p32.
Variety. Dec 21, 1960, p6.

Flamingo Kid (US; Marshall, Garry; 1984)
BFI/Monthly Film Bulletin. Sep 1985, v52, p278.
California Magazine. Feb 1985, v10, p36.
Films in Review. Mar 1985, v36, p180.
Hollywood Reporter. Nov 27, 1984, p3.
The Los Angeles Times. Dec 21, 1984, SecVI, p8.
Maclean's. Jan 14, 1985, v98, p49.
Magill's Cinema Annual, 1985. p192-97.
The New Leader. Mar 25, 1985, v68, p21.
New Statesman. Oct 25, 1985, v100, p33.
New York. Jan 7, 1985, v18, p69.
The New York Times. Dec 21, 1984, SecIII, p25.
The New York Times. Dec 7, 1984, SecIII, p8.
The New Yorker. Jan 28, 1985, v60, p89.
Newsweek. Dec 31, 1984, v104, p65.
Playboy. Jan 1985, v32, p34.
Saturday Review. Jan-Feb 1985, v11, p82.
Time. Dec 24, 1984, v124, p66.
Variety. Nov 28, 1984, p19.
Washingtonian. Jan 1985, v20, p66.
Washingtonian. Feb 1985, v20, p33.

Flareup (US; Neilson, James; 1969)
Film Daily. Nov 25, 1969, p4.
Films and Filming. Mar 1970, v16, p42.
Hollywood Reporter. Nov 10, 1969, p3.
The New York Times. Nov 11, 1969, p42.
Variety. Nov 12, 1969, p21.

Flash Gordon (US; Hodges, Mike; 1980)
BFI/Monthly Film Bulletin. Dec 1980, v47, p235.
The Los Angeles Times. Nov 3, 1980, Calendar, p42.
Maclean's. Dec 9, 1980, v93, p60.
Motion Picture Herald Product Digest. Dec 17, 1980, p56.
The New Leader. Dec 29, 1980, v63, p18.
New York. Dec 15, 1980, v13, p56.
The New York Times. Dec 5, 1980, SecIII, p8.
The New Yorker. Jan 5, 1981, v56, p83-85.
Newsweek. Dec 8, 1980, v96, p105.
Time. Dec 22, 1980, v116, p72-73.
Variety. Dec 3, 1980, p22.

Flashdance (US; Lyne, Adrian; 1983)
BFI/Monthly Film Bulletin. Jul 1983, v50, p188.
Dance Magazine. Jul 1983, v57, p104-05.
Hollywood Reporter. Apr 18, 1983, p3.

The Los Angeles Times. Apr 19, 1983, SecVI, p1.
Magill's Cinema Annual, 1984. p158-61.
Ms. Jul 1983, v12, p34.
The New Leader. May 2, 1983, v66, p19-20.
The New York Times. Apr 15, 1983, SecIII, p13.
The New Yorker. Jun 27, 1983, v59, p94-95.
Newsweek. Apr 25, 1983, v101, p50.
Newsweek. Jul 4, 1983, v102, p55.
Rolling Stone. May 26, 1983, p64.
Time. May 9, 1983, v121, p80.
Variety. Apr 20, 1983, p12.

The Flavor of Green Tea Over Rice
(Japanese title: Ochazuke no Aji) (JAPAN; Ozu, Yasujiro; 1952)
Magill's Survey of Cinema. Foreign Language Films. v3, p1117-21.
The New Republic. Feb 10, 1973, v168, p35.
The New York Times. Jan 25, 1973, p51.
Newsweek. Feb 5, 1973, v81, p81.
Ozu (Richie). p67-68, 226-27, 237-38.
Variety. Jan 17, 1973, p20.
The Village Voice. Feb 22, 1973, v18, p73.

Flesh (US; Morrissey, Paul; 1968)
BFI/Monthly Film Bulletin. Mar 1970, v37, p45-46.
Dictionary of Films. p116.
Directors and Directions: Cinema for the Seventies. p154-56.
Filmfacts. Jan 1, 1969, v11, p409.
Films and Filming. Apr 1970, v17, p42-43.
Hollywood Reporter. Jul 18, 1969, p3.
The London Times. Jan 15, 1970, p8.
The New York Times. Sep 27, 1968, p36.
Stargazer: Andy Warhol's World and His Films. p126-27.
Variety. Oct 2, 1968, p26.
The Village Voice. Jan 9, 1969, p51.
The Village Voice. Feb 6, 1969, p51.
The Village Voice. Oct 17, 1968, p55.

Flesh And Fury (US; Pevney, Joseph; 1952)
BFI/Monthly Film Bulletin. May 1952, v19, p64.
Christian Century. May 21, 1952, v69, p631.
Commonweal. May 9, 1952, v56, p117.
Film Daily. Mar 14, 1952, p12.
Hollywood Reporter. Mar 7, 1952, p3.
Motion Picture Herald Product Digest. Mar 8, 1952, p1261.
The New York Times. Mar 28, 1952, p27.
Tony Curtis: The Man and His Movies. p36-37.
Variety. Mar 12, 1952, p16.

Fletch (US; Ritchie, Michael; 1985)
BFI/Monthly Film Bulletin. Jul 1985, v52, p214.
Films in Review. Aug 1985, v36, p420.
Hollywood Reporter. May 16, 1985, p3.
The Los Angeles Times. May 31, 1985, SecVI, p1.
Maclean's. Jun 10, 1985, v98, p64.
Magill's Cinema Annual, 1986. p169-71.
New York. Jun 3, 1985, v18, p73.
The New York Times. May 31, 1985, SecIII, p10.
Newsweek. Jun 3, 1985, v105, p65.
Time. Jun 3, 1985, v125, p71.
Variety. May 22, 1985, p14.

The Flight *See* Fuga, La

The Flight of the Eagle (Swedish title: Ingenor Andrees Luftfard) (SWED; Troell, Jan; 1982)
Film Comment. May-Jun 1983, v19, p13-17.
Hollywood Reporter. May 10, 1983, p3.
The Nation. May 4, 1983, v236, p617-18.
National Review. Jun 10, 1983, v35, p702-05.

The New Republic. May 16, 1983, v188, p24-25.
The New York Times. Apr 8, 1983, SecIII, p8.
The New Yorker. May 16, 1983, v59, p112.
Newsweek. Apr 25, 1983, v101, p50.
Saturday Review. May-Jun 1983, v9, p42.
Smithsonian. May 1983, v14, p122-24.
Variety. Apr 6, 1983, p18.

The Flight of the Phoenix (US; Aldrich, Robert; 1965)
America. Mar 5, 1966, v114, p338.
BFI/Monthly Film Bulletin. Feb 1966, v33, p14-15.
Christian Science Monitor (Western edition). Apr 13, 1966, p10.
Cinema. Mar 1966, v3, p48-49.
Commonweal. Apr 1, 1966, v84, p55-56.
Film Daily. Dec 21, 1965, p6.
Filmfacts. Feb 15, 1966, v9, p9-11.
Films and Filming. Feb 1966, v12, p9.
Films and Filming. Mar 1966, v12, p18, 51.
Films in Review. Mar 1966, v17, p182-83.
The Films of James Stewart. p240-43.
The Films of Robert Aldrich. p40-42.
Hollywood Reporter. Dec 14, 1965, p3.
Life. Feb 18, 1966, v60, p14.
The London Times. Jan 20, 1966, p17.
Magill's Cinema Annual, 1985. p549-54.
Motion Picture Herald Product Digest. Jan 5, 1966, p433-34.
Movies (Farber). p185-86.
New Statesman. Jan 21, 1966, v71, p100-01.
The New York Times. Feb 1, 1966, p26.
The New Yorker. Feb 12, 1966, v41, p140.
Newsweek. Jul 12, 1965, v66, p90.
The Private Eye, the Cowboy and the Very Naked Girl. p180-81.
Saturday Review. Jan 29, 1966, v49, p43.
Senior Scholastic. Apr 1, 1966, v88, p27.
Sight and Sound. Spr 1966, v35, p94-95.
Time. Feb 4, 1966, v87, p103.
Variety. Dec 15, 1965, p6.
The Village Voice. Apr 14, 1966, v11, p31.

Flipper (US; Clark, James B.; 1963)
BFI/Monthly Film Bulletin. Aug 1963, v30, p117.
Film Daily. May 2, 1963, p3.
Filmfacts. Jun 12, 1963, v6, p184-85.
Films and Filming. Oct 1963, v10, p25.
Films in Review. Jun-Jul 1963, v14, p368.
Hollywood Reporter. Apr 30, 1963, p3.
The New York Times. Sep 19, 1963, p23.
Variety. May 1, 1963, p6.

The Flowering Wheat *See* Blé en Herbe, Le

The Flowers of St. Francis (Italian title: Francesco, Giullare di Dio; Also titled: Francis, God's Jester; Francis, God's Fool) (IT; Rossellini, Roberto; 1950)
Catholic World. Dec 1952, v176, p224.
Cinema, the Magic Vehicle. v2, p43-46.
Commonweal. Oct 31, 1952, v57, p101-02.
Film Daily. Oct 16, 1952, p6.
Hollywood Quarterly. Sum 1951, v5, p389-400.
Italian Cinema (Leprohon). p135-36.
Motion Picture Herald Product Digest. Oct 11, 1952, p1559.
Moviegoer. Wint 1964, v1, p19-25.
The New York Times. Oct 7, 1952, p26.
The New Yorker. Oct 18, 1952, v28, p143.
Newsweek. Oct 20, 1952, v40, p122.
Passion and Defiance. p109-11.
Roberto Rossellini (Guarner). p44-49.
Time. Oct 6, 1952, v60, p102.
Variety. Sep 27, 1950, p20.

Flying Leathernecks (US; Ray, Nicholas; 1951)
BFI/Monthly Film Bulletin. Oct 1951, v18, p340.
Christian Century. Sep 26, 1951, v68, p1111.
Commonweal. Nov 2, 1951, v55, p94.
The Complete Films of John Wayne. p182.
Film Daily. Jul 18, 1951, p6.
Motion Picture Herald Product Digest. Jul 21, 1951, p937-38.
The New York Times. Sep 20, 1951, p37.
Nicholas Ray: A Guide to References and Resources. p62-65.
Time. Oct 8, 1951, v58, p114.
Variety. Jul 25, 1951, p6.

The Flying Missile (US; Levin, Henry; 1950)
BFI/Monthly Film Bulletin. May 1951, v18, p264.
Commonweal. Jan 19, 1951, v53, p376.
Film Daily. Dec 27, 1950, p6.
Hollywood Reporter. Dec 26, 1950, p3.
Motion Picture Herald Product Digest. Jan 6, 1951, p653-54.
The New York Times. Dec 25, 1950, p25.
Newsweek. Jan 15, 1951, v37, p82.
Senior Scholastic. Jan 10, 1951, v57, p30.
Time. Jan 15, 1951, v57, p80.
Variety. Dec 27, 1950, p6.

Fog *See* A Study in Terror

The Fog (US; Carpenter, John; 1980)
BFI/Monthly Film Bulletin. Nov 1980, v47, p214.
Films in Review. Mar 1980, v31, p182.
Hollywood Reporter. Jan 15, 1980, p3.
The Los Angeles Times. Feb 2, 1980, SecII, p8.
Maclean's. Feb 11, 1980, v93, p52-53.
Motion Picture Herald Product Digest. Feb 6, 1980, p70.
New York. Feb 18, 1980, v13, p78.
The New York Times. Feb 29, 1980, SecIII, p15.
The New Yorker. Feb 25, 1980, v56, p115-16.
Newsday. Feb 22, 1980, SecII, p7.
Newsweek. Mar 3, 1980, v95, p68.
Variety. Jan 16, 1980, p31.
The Village Voice. Feb 25, 1980, p40.
The World of Fantastic Films. p75-78.

Foire aux Chimeres, La (Also titled: The Fair Angel) (FR; Chenal, Pierre; 1946)
BFI/Monthly Film Bulletin. Jun 1952, v19, p80.
The Spectator. May 2, 1952, v188, p576-77.
Variety. Oct 9, 1946, p14.

Follow Me, Boys! (US; Tokar, Norman; 1966)
BFI/Monthly Film Bulletin. Feb 1967, v34, p27.
Christian Century. Feb 1, 1967, v84, p144-45.
Christian Science Monitor (Western edition). Jan 14, 1967, p6.
Commonweal. Dec 9, 1966, v85, p293-94.
Film Daily. Oct 14, 1966, p3.
Filmfacts. Jan 1, 1967, v9, p327-28.
Films in Review. Dec 1966, v17, p666-67.
Hollywood Reporter. Oct 12, 1966, p3.
The London Times. Dec 22, 1966, p15.
Motion Picture Herald Product Digest. Oct 26, 1966, p621-22.
New Statesman. Dec 30, 1966, v72, p974.
The New York Times. Dec 2, 1966, p46.
Newsweek. Dec 19, 1966, v68, p114.
Variety. Oct 12, 1966, p6.

Follow the Boys (US; Thorpe, Richard; 1963)
BFI/Monthly Film Bulletin. May 1963, v30, p65-66.

Film Daily. Feb 21, 1963, v6, p36.
Filmfacts. Mar 21, 1963, v6, p36.
Hollywood Reporter. Feb 22, 1963, v174, p3.
The New York Times. Feb 28, 1963, p8.
Photoplay. May 1963, v63, p7.
Variety. Feb 27, 1963, p6.

Follow the Sun (US; Lanfield, Sidney; 1951)
BFI/Monthly Film Bulletin. May 1951, v18, p264-65.
Christian Century. Jul 25, 1951, v68, p879.
Commonweal. May 11, 1951, v54, p117.
Film Daily. Mar 20, 1951, p6.
Hollywood Reporter. Mar 19, 1951, p3.
Library Journal. Apr 1, 1951, v76, p608.
Motion Picture Herald Product Digest. Mar 24, 1951, p765.
The New York Times. Apr 26, 1951, p34.
Newsweek. Apr 16, 1951, v37, p105.
Senior Scholastic. Apr 4, 1951, v58, p31.
The Spectator. May 11, 1951, v186, p617.
Time. Apr 30, 1951, v57, p106.
Variety. Mar 21, 1951, p6.

Folly To Be Wise (GB; Launder, Frank; 1952)
BFI/Monthly Film Bulletin. Jan 1953, v20, p4.
Hollywood Reporter. Aug 2, 1954, p3.
Kiss Kiss Bang Bang. p330.
Motion Picture Herald Product Digest. Dec 12, 1953, p2102.
The New York Times. Dec 28, 1953, p17.
The New Yorker. Jan 9, 1954, v29, p73.
Sight and Sound. Jan-Mar 1953, v22, p130.
The Spectator. Dec 5, 1952, v189, p762.
The Tatler. Dec 17, 1952, v206, p654.
Time. Jan 18, 1954, v63, p100.
Variety. Dec 10, 1952, p18.

A Fool for Love (US; Altman, Robert; 1985)
BFI/Monthly Film Bulletin. Jul 1986, v53, p195.
The Los Angeles Times. Dec 6, 1985, SecVI, p1.
Maclean's. Jan 13, 1986, v99, p46.
Magill's Cinema Annual, 1986. p172-75.
The Nation. Jan 11, 1986, v242, p25-26.
The New Republic. Dec 23, 1985, v193, p24-25.
New York. Dec 9, 1985, v18, p90-91.
The New York Times. Dec 1, 1985, SecII, p1.
The New Yorker. Jan 27, 1986, v61, p84-87.
Time. Dec 2, 1985, v126, p101.
Variety. Nov 27, 1985, p16.
The Wall Street Journal. Dec 5, 1985, p28.

The Fool Killer (Also titled: A Violent Journey) (US; Gonzalez, Servando; 1965)
Commonweal. May 7, 1965, v82, p218.
Film Daily. May 7, 1965, p3.
Filmfacts. 1969, v12, n13, p305-07.
Hollywood Reporter. Apr 28, 1965, p3.
Motion Picture Herald Product Digest. May 12, 1965, p281-82.
The New Republic. May 1, 1965, v152, p26.
The New York Times. Jun 10, 1969, p51.
Saturday Review. May 15, 1965, v48, p34.
Senior Scholastic. May 6, 1965, v86, p28.
Time. May 14, 1965, v85, p106.
Variety. Apr 28, 1965, p6.

Footloose (US; Ross, Herbert; 1984)
BFI/Monthly Film Bulletin. Apr 1984, v51, p116.
Christianity Today. Apr 20, 1984, v28, p49-50.
Dance Magazine. Mar 1984, v58, p58-60.
Esquire. Feb 1984, v101, p94.
Film Comment. May-Jun 1984, v20, p49-55.
Film Journal. Mar 1984, v87, p41.
Films and Filming. May 1984, n356, p37.

Forbidden Planet (US; Wilcox, Fred
McLeod; 1956)
America. Mar 31, 1956, v94, p724.
BFI/Monthly Film Bulletin. Jun 1956, v23,
p71-72.
Cinefantastique. 1975, v4, p4-13.
Cinefantastique. 1979, v8, p4-67.
Cult Movies. p94-98.
Film Daily. Mar 15, 1956, p6.
Films and Filming. Jul 1956, v2, p22.
Films in Review. Apr 1956, v4, p174-176.
The Films of the Fifties. p183-84.
Great Horror Movies. p146.
Hollywood Reporter. Mar 12, 1956, p3.
Magill's Survey of Cinema. Series II. v2, p805-
07.
The New York Times. May 4, 1956, p21.
The New York Times. May 6, 1956, SecII, p1.
The New Yorker. May 12, 1956, v32, p171.
Newsweek. Jun 4, 1956, v47, p98.
Photoplay. Mar 1982, v33, p48.
Saturday Review. Apr 7, 1956, v39, p23.
Science Fiction Gold. p159-70.
Time. Apr 9, 1956, v67, p112.
Twenty All Time Great Science Fiction Films.
p122-35.
Variety. Mar 14, 1956, p6.
The World of Fantastic Films. p33-34.

Force of Arms (US; Curtiz, Michael; 1951)
BFI/Monthly Film Bulletin. May 1952, v19,
p60-61.
Commonweal. Aug 31, 1951, v54, p501.
Film Daily. Aug 23, 1951, p6.
The Films of William Holden. p119-21.
Hollywood Reporter. Aug 14, 1951, p3.
Motion Picture Herald Product Digest. Aug 18,
1951, p981-82.
The Nation. Sep 15, 1951, v173, p218.
The New York Times. Aug 14, 1951, p20.
The New Yorker. Aug 25, 1951, v27, p63.
Newsweek. Sep 3, 1951, v38, p72.
Saturday Review. Sep 8, 1951, v34, p36.
Time. Sep 10, 1951, v58, p100.
Variety. Aug 15, 1951, p6.

The Forgotten Ones *See* Olvidados, Los

The Formula (US; Avildsen, John G.;
1980)
BFI/Monthly Film Bulletin. Nov 1980, v47, p6.
Christian Science Monitor. Dec 11, 1980, p19.
Films in Review. Feb 1981, v32, p121.
Hollywood Reporter. Dec 8, 1980, p3.
Maclean's. Dec 22, 1980, v93, p59.
Motion Picture Herald Product Digest. Dec 31,
1980, p57.
The New Leader. Jan 12, 1981, v64, p19-20.
New York. Dec 22, 1980, v13, p62.
The New York Times. Dec 19, 1980, SecIII,
p10.
Newsweek. Jan 19, 1981, v97, p79-80.
Science. Nov 28, 1980, v210, p990.
Time. Dec 29, 1980, v116, p59.
Variety. Dec 10, 1980, p30.

Fort Apache, the Bronx (US; Petrie, Daniel;
1981)
Christian Century. Mar 25, 1981, v98, p332.
Commentary. May 1981, v71, p73-81.
Hollywood Reporter. Feb 6, 1981, p3.
The Los Angeles Times. Feb 6, 1981, SecVI, p1.
Maclean's. Feb 16, 1981, v94, p62.
Magill's Cinema Annual, 1982. p159-62.
The Nation. Mar 7, 1981, v232, p285.
The New Leader. Feb 23, 1981, v64, p20-21.
The New Republic. Feb 21, 1981, v184, p24.
New York. Feb 9, 1981, v14, p48-49.
New York. Feb 16, 1981, v14, p60-61.
The New York Times. Feb 6, 1981, SecIII, p6.

The New Yorker. Feb 23, 1981, v57, p101-05.
Newsweek. Feb 16, 1981, v97, p81.
Rolling Stone. Mar 5, 1981, p43.
Time. Feb 16, 1981, v117, p77.
Variety. Feb 6, 1981, p3.

The Fortune (US; Nichols, Mike; 1975)
BFI/Monthly Film Bulletin. Sep 1975, v42,
p197.
Films in Review. Aug-Sep 1975, v26, p440.
The Films of Warren Beatty. p198-209.
Hollywood Reporter. May 20, 1975, p4.
The Los Angeles Times. Jun 25, 1975, SecIV,
p1.
Mike Nichols (Schuth). p129-44.
Motion Picture Herald Product Digest. Jun 11,
1975, p4.
The Nation Jun 7, 1975. v220, p702.
The New Republic. Jul 5, 1975, v173, p22.
The New York Times. May 21, 1975, p49.
The New York Times. Jun 1, 1975, SecII, p15.
The New York Times. Oct 12, 1975, SecII, p1.
Newsweek. May 26, 1975, v85, p84.
Time. May 26, 1975, v105, p76.
Variety. May 21, 1975, p19.

The Fortune Cookie (Also titled: Meet
Whiplash Willie) (US; Wilder, Billy;
1966)
America. Oct 29, 1966, v115, p527.
BFI/Monthly Film Bulletin. Jul 1967, v34,
p103-04.
Billy Wilder (Dick). p111-15.
Billy Wilder (Madsen). p142-43.
Christian Century. Nov 30, 1966, v83, p1474-
75.
Christian Science Monitor (Western edition).
Nov 18, 1966, p4.
The Film Career of Billy Wilder. p104-06.
Film Comment. Jan-Feb 1979, v15, p33-39.
Film Daily. Oct 17, 1966, p4.
Film Quarterly. Spr 1967, v20, p61.
Filmfacts. Dec 15, 1966, v9, p291-93.
Films and Filming. Aug 1967, v13, p24-25.
Films in Review. Nov 1966, v17, p587.
The Films of Jack Lemmon. p164-69.
Focus. Feb 1967, n1, p17.
Hollywood Reporter. Oct 17, 1966, p3.
Life. Nov 18, 1966, v61, p18.
The London Times. May 18, 1967, p8.
Magill's Survey of Cinema. Series II. v2, p818-
22.
Motion Picture Herald Product Digest. Oct 26,
1966, p621.
New Statesman. May 19, 1967, v73, p697-98.
The New York Times. Oct 20, 1966, p52.
The New Yorker. Oct 29, 1966, v42, p150.
Newsweek. Oct 31, 1966, v68, p111-11A.
Playboy. Dec 1966, v13, p50, 52.
Private Screenings. p290.
Saturday Review. Sep 24, 1966, v49, p30.
Second Sight. p87-90.
Senior Scholastic. Dec 2, 1966, v89, p26.
Sight and Sound. Sum 1967, v36, p147-48.
Talking Pictures. p155-56.
Time. Oct 28, 1966, v88, p111.
Variety. Oct 19, 1966, p6.
The Village Voice. Nov 3, 1966, v12, p31.

40 Pounds of Trouble (US; Jewison,
Norman; 1963)
America. Mar 2, 1963, v108, p316.
BFI/Monthly Film Bulletin. Apr 1963, v30,
p47.
Commonweal. Feb 15, 1963, v77, p541.
Film Daily. Dec 4, 1962, p5.
Filmfacts. Feb 21, 1963, v77, p541.
Films and Filming. Apr 1963, v9, p30.
The New York Times. Jan 24, 1963, p5.
The New York Times. Feb 6, 1963, p5.

The New Yorker. Feb 2, 1963, v38, p102.
Photoplay. Mar 1963, v63, p6.
Saturday Review. Feb 2, 1963, v46, p44.
Time. Feb 8, 1963, v81, p66.
Tony Curtis: The Man and His Movies. p 94-
97.
Variety. Dec 12, 1963, p6.

48 HRS. (US; Hill, Walter; 1982)
Hollywood Reporter. Nov 24, 1982, p3.
The Los Angeles Times. Dec 9, 1982, SecVI, p1.
Maclean's. Dec 13, 1982, v95, p96.
Magill's Cinema Annual, 1983. p173-77.
New York. Dec 11, 1982, v15, p95.
The New York Times. Dec 8, 1982, SecIII, p28.
Newsweek. Dec 6, 1982, v100, p51.
Time. Dec 20, 1982, v120, p82.
Variety. Nov 24, 1982, p3.

Foul Play (US; Higgins, Colin; 1978)
BFI/Monthly Film Bulletin. Dec 1978, v45,
p239.
Commonweal. Aug 18, 1978, v105, p531-32.
Films in Review. Oct 1978, v29, p501.
Hollywood Reporter. Jul 10, 1978, p2.
The Los Angeles Times. Jul 23, 1978, Calendar,
p25.
Magill's Survey of Cinema. Series II. v2, p823-
27.
Motion Picture Herald Product Digest. Jul 26,
1978, p13.
New York. Jul 31, 1978, v11, p36.
The New York Times. Jul 19, 1978, SecIII, p15.
Newsweek. Jul 24, 1978, v92, p59.
Saturday Review. Sep 16, 1978, v5, p36.
Time. Jul 31, 1978, v112, p86.
Variety. Jul 12, 1978, p18.

Four Bags Full (FR; Autant-Lara, Claude;
1957)
Film Daily. Aug 5, 1957, p6.
The New York Times. Sep 5, 1957, p32.
The New York Times. Sep 8, 1957, SecII, p1.
The New Yorker. Sep 14, 1957, v33, p94.
Newsweek. Sep 9, 1957, v50, p110.
Saturday Review. Aug 24, 1957, v40, p25.
Time. Sep 16, 1957, v70, p112.

Four Days in November (US; Stuart, Mel;
1964)
Boxoffice. Oct 19, 1964, v85, p2868.
Film Daily. Oct 8, 1964, p9.
Films in Review. Nov 1964, v15, p571-72.
Hollywood Reporter. Oct 7, 1964, p4.
Motion Picture Herald Product Digest. Oct 28,
1964, p154.
The New York Times. Oct 8, 1964, p48.
Variety. Oct 7, 1964, p6.

Four Days Leave (Also titled: Swiss Tour)
(SWITZ; Lindtberg, Leopold; 1949)
BFI/Monthly Film Bulletin. Sep 1950, v17,
p140.
Christian Century. Jun 7, 1950, v67, p719.
Film Daily. Apr 3, 1950, p6.
Hollywood Reporter. Mar 23, 1950, p3.
Motion Picture Herald Product Digest. Apr 1,
1950, p246-47.
The New York Times. Jun 9, 1950, p29.
Variety. Dec 28, 1949, p6.

4 for Texas (US; Aldrich, Robert; 1963)
BFI/Monthly Film Bulletin. Feb 1964, v31,
p25.
Film Daily. Dec 24, 1963, p4.
Filmfacts. Jan 16, 1964, v6, p316-18.
Films and Filming. Feb 1964, v10, p34.
The Films of Charles Bronson. p116-18.
The Films of Frank Sinatra. p195-97.
The Films of Robert Aldrich. p38-39.
The New York Times. Dec 26, 1963, p33.

Robert Aldrich: A Guide to References and Resources. p38-39.
Time. Jan 10, 1964, v83, p80.
Variety. Dec 25, 1963, p6.

Four Friends (US; Penn, Arthur; 1981)
America. Feb 6, 1982, v146, p96.
BFI/Monthly Film Bulletin. Jul 1982, v49, p123-24.
Film Journal. Jan 15, 1982, v85, p6.
Films in Review. Mar 1982, v33, p172-73.
Hollywood Reporter. Nov 12, 1981, p2.
The Los Angeles Times. Dec 11, 1981, SecVI, p1.
Maclean's. Dec 21, 1981, v94, p48-49.
Magill's Cinema Annual, 1982. p167-70.
The Nation. Jan 23, 1982, v234, p91.
New Statesman. Jun 25, 1982, v103, p27.
New York. Dec 21, 1981, v14, p51-52.
The New York Times. Dec 11, 1981, SecIII, p12.
The New York Times. Jan 17, 1982, SecVI, p4.
The New Yorker. Jan 4, 1982, v57, p80-81.
Newsweek. Dec 21, 1981, v98, p49.
Photoplay. Jul 1982, v33, p23.
Saturday Review. Jan 1982, v9, p53.
Sight and Sound. Spr 1982, v51, p135-36.
Time. Dec 21, 1981, v118, p82.
Variety. Nov 11, 1981, p3.

Four Guns to the Border (US; Carlson, Richard; 1954)
BFI/Monthly Film Bulletin. Jan 1955, v22, p9.
Film Daily. Sep 27, 1954, p6.
Hollywood Reporter. Sep 21, 1954, p3.
Motion Picture Herald Product Digest. Sep 25, 1954, p153.
National Parent-Teacher. Nov 1954, v49, p39.
The New York Times. Nov 6, 1954, p15.
Variety. Sep 22, 1954, p6.

The 4 Horsemen of the Apocalypse (US; Minnelli, Vincente; 1962)
America. Mar 17, 1962, v106, p801.
BFI/Monthly Film Bulletin. Apr 1962, v29, p46.
Commonweal. Mar 23, 1962, v75, p668.
Film. Sum 1962, n32, p15-16.
Film Daily. Feb 9, 1962, p11.
Film Quarterly. Sum 1962, v15, p63-64.
Filmfacts. Apr 6, 1962, v5, p53-56.
Films and Filming. May 1962, v8, p32.
Films in Review. Mar 1962, v13, p174-75.
Hollywood Reporter. Feb 8, 1962, p3.
Motion Picture Herald Product Digest. Feb 21, 1962, p452.
The New York Times. Mar 10, 1962, p10.
The New Yorker. Mar 31, 1962, v38, p127-28.
Newsweek. Mar 19, 1962, v59, p116.
Saturday Review. Mar 31, 1962, v45, p26.
Time. Mar 23, 1962, v79, p67.
Variety. Feb 14, 1962, p6.

The 400 Blows (French title: Quartre cents coups, Les) (FR; Truffaut, François; 1959)
The Adventures of Antoine Doinel: 4 Screenplays by François Truffaut. p15-58.
BFI/Monthly Film Bulletin. Apr 1960, v27, p48.
The Cinema of François Truffaut. p36-50.
Commonweal. Nov 27, 1959, v71, p265.
Film Daily. Sep 23, 1959, v116, p10.
Filmfacts. Dec 23, 1959, v2, p286-88.
François Truffaut: A Guide to References and Resources. p41-44.
Great Film Directors. p722-30.
The Great Movies. p217-18.
Hollywood Reporter. Dec 15, 1959, p3.

The International Dictionary of Films and Filmmakers. v1, p381-82.
Magill's Survey of Cinema. Foreign Language Films. v3, p1145-48.
The Nation. Nov 28, 1959, v189, p407.
The New Republic. Dec 7, 1959, v141, p21-22.
The New York Times. Nov 17, 1959, p41.
The New Yorker. Nov 28, 1959, v35, p297-98.
Newsweek. Oct 26, 1959, v54, p122.
On Movies. p375-76.
Saturday Review. Oct 3, 1959, v42, p29.
Ten Film Classics: A Re-Viewing. p121-34.
Time. Dec 14, 1959, v74, p96.
Variety. Apr 29, 1959, p20.
Vintage Films. p175-78.
The 400 Blows. 1969.

Four In a Jeep (SWITZ; Lindtberg, Leopold; 1951)
BFI/Monthly Film Bulletin. Jul 1951, v18, p291.
Christian Century. Sep 12, 1951, v68, p1063.
Commonweal. Jul 6, 1951, v54, p310.
Film Daily. Jun 12, 1951, p6.
Hollywood Reporter. Jun 1, 1951, p4.
Motion Picture Herald Product Digest. Jun 9, 1951, p878.
The New Republic. Jul 2, 1951, v125, p23.
The New Statesman and Nation. Jun 16, 1951, v41, p680.
The New York Times. Jun 12, 1951, p35.
The New Yorker. Jun 16, 1951, v27, p75.
Newsweek. Jun 18, 1951, v37, p92.
Rotha on Film. p181-83.
Saturday Review. Jun 30, 1951, v34, p22.
Sight and Sound. Aug-Sep 1951, v21, p28.
Time. Jun 18, 1951, v57, p100.
Variety. Apr 11, 1951, p22.

Four Kinds of Love *See* Bambole, Le

The Four Musketeers (Also titled: The Revenge of Milady) (GB, SP; Lester, Richard; 1975)
BFI/Monthly Film Bulletin. Apr 1975, v42, p80-81.
Films in Review. May 1975, v26, p312.
The Films of Charlton Heston. p214-15.
The Films of the Seventies. p116-17.
Hollywood Reporter. Mar 6, 1975, p3.
The Los Angeles Times. Mar 21, 1975, SecIV, p16.
Motion Picture Herald Product Digest. Apr 9, 1975, p87.
The New York Times. Mar 20, 1975, p48.
The New Yorker. Mar 31, 1975, v51, p79-81.
Newsweek. Apr 7, 1975, v85, p83.
One Good Film Deserves Another. p135-39.
Richard Lester: A Guide to References and Resources. p41.
Time. Apr 7, 1975, v105, p72-73.
Variety. Mar 12, 1975, p18.

The Four Poster (US; Reis, Irving; 1952)
BFI/Monthly Film Bulletin. Jan 1953, v20, p4-5.
Catholic World. Oct 1952, v176, p62.
Christian Century. Feb 18, 1953, v70, p207.
Commonweal. Nov 7, 1952, v57, p120.
Film Daily. Oct 8, 1952, p10.
Films in Review. Oct 1952, v3, p414-15.
Hollywood Reporter. Oct 8, 1952, p3.
Library Journal. Oct 15, 1952, v77, p1801.
Magill's Survey of Cinema. Series II. v2, p836-38.
Motion Picture Herald Product Digest. Oct 11, 1952, p1557-58.
National Parent-Teacher. Sep 1952, v47, p38.
The New York Times. Oct 16, 1952, p37.
The New York Times Magazine. Aug 24, 1952, p24-25.

The New Yorker. Oct 18, 1952, v28, p151.
Newsweek. Oct 20, 1952, v40, p122.
Saturday Review. Oct 18, 1952, v35, p31.
Stanley Kramer, Film Maker. p117-22.
Theatre Arts. Sep 1952, v36, p73.
Time. Oct 13, 1952, v60, p106.
Variety. Oct 8, 1952, p12.

The Four Seasons (US; Alda, Alan; 1981)
America. Jun 20, 1981, v114, p506-07.
Christian Century. Jul 15, 1981, v98, p746.
Commonweal. Jul 3, 1981, v108, p403-04.
Hollywood Reporter. Apr 6, 1981, p3.
The Los Angeles Times. May 22, 1981, SecVI, p1.
Maclean's. May 25, 1981, v94, p48-49.
Magill's Cinema Annual, 1982. p171-73.
Ms. Jun 1981, v9, p46-49.
The Nation. Jun 13, 1981, v232, p740-41.
National Review. v33, p913-14.
The New Republic. Jun 13, 1981, v184, p25.
New York. Jun 1981, v14, p46-47.
The New York Times. Jun 14, 1981, SecII, p17.
The New York Times. May 22, 1981, SecIII, p11.
Newsweek. May 25, 1981, v97, p74.
Rolling Stone. Jul 9, 1981, p39.
Saturday Review. Jun 1981, v8, p64-65.
Time. May 25, 1981, v117, p95.
Variety. Apr 4, 1981, p3.

Fourteen Hours (Also titled: 14 Hours) (US; Hathaway, Henry; 1951)
BFI/Monthly Film Bulletin. Apr 1951, v18, p245.
Christian Century. Sep 5, 1951, v68, p1031.
Commonweal. Mar 23, 1951, v53, p589.
Film Daily. Mar 1, 1951, p6.
Films in Review. May 1951, v2, p42-43.
Library Journal. Mar 15, 1951, v76, p535.
Life. Mar 12, 1951, v30, p114-18.
Motion Picture Herald Product Digest. Mar 3, 1951, p741.
The Nation. Mar 31, 1951, v172, p306.
The New Republic. Mar 12, 1951, v124, p22.
The New Statesman and Nation. Mar 10, 1951, v41, p272.
The New York Times. Mar 7, 1951, p43.
The New Yorker. Mar 17, 1951, v27, p107.
Newsweek. Mar 19, 1951, v37, p94-95.
Saturday Review. Mar 24, 1951, v34, p27.
Sight and Sound. Apr 1951, v19, p473-74.
The Spectator. Mar 9, 1951, v186, p309.
Time. Mar 12, 1951, v57, p96.
Variety. Feb 28, 1951, p13.

The Fourth Man (Dutch title: Vierde Man, De) (NETH; Verhoeven, Paul; 1983)
BFI/Monthly Film Bulletin. Aug 1984, v51, p252.
Commentary. Dec 1984, v78, p59.
Film Journal. Aug 1984, v87, p41.
Films and Filming. Jul 1984, n358, p18.
Films in Review. Aug-Sep 1984, v35, p430-31.
The Los Angeles Times. Jul 5, 1984, SecVI, p6.
Maclean's. Jul 9, 1984, v97, p44.
Magill's Cinema Annual, 1985. p203-07.
The New York Times. Jun 27, 1984, p21.
The New Yorker. Jul 9, 1984, v60, p84.
Newsweek. Jun 18, 1984, v103, p92.
Time. Jul 23, 1984, v124, p102.
Variety. Jul 4, 1984, p18.
The Village Voice. Jul 3, 1984, p62.

The Fox (US, CAN; Rydell, Mark; 1967)
America. Mar 2, 1968, v118, p298.
BFI/Monthly Film Bulletin. Jun 1968, v35, p91.
Christian Century. Mar 20, 1968, v85, p360-61.
Christian Science Monitor (Western edition). Feb 26, 1968, p4.
Cinema. Spr 1968, v4, p47.

Commonweal. Mar 1, 1968, v87, p656.
Esquire. Feb 1968, v69, p20.
Film 68/69. p194-99.
Film Daily. Dec 12, 1967, p6.
Film Quarterly. Spr 1968, v21, p58.
Filmfacts. Feb 1, 1968, v11, p1-3.
Films and Filming. Jul 1968, v14, p33-34.
Films in Review. Mar 1968, v19, p177-78.
Five Thousand One Nights At the Movies. p200.
Going Steady. p36-39.
Hollywood Reporter. Dec 11, 1967, p3.
Life. Feb 16, 1968, v64, p6.
Literature/Film Quarterly. 1973, v1, n1, p17-27.
Movies Into Film. p137-39.
The New Republic. Mar 9, 1968, v158, p24.
New Statesman. May 24, 1968, v75, p702.
The New York Times. Feb 8, 1968, p36.
The New York Times. Feb 25, 1968, p1.
The New Yorker. Feb 10, 1968, v43, p100.
Newsweek. Feb 19, 1968, v71, p92.
Saturday Review. Feb 10, 1968, v51, p40.
Take Twenty Two. p175-80.
Time. Feb 16, 1968, v91, p91-92.
Variety. Dec 13, 1967, p6.
The Village Voice. Mar 14, 1968, p47.
A Year In the Dark. p57-58.

Foxes (US; Lyne, Adrian; 1980)
BFI/Monthly Film Bulletin. Aug 1980, v47, p157.
Christian Science Monitor. Mar 26, 1980, p22.
Films in Review. Apr 1980, v31, p246.
Hollywood Reporter. Feb 29, 1980, p3.
The Los Angeles Times. Feb 29, 1980, SecVI, p1.
Maclean's. Apr 21, 1980, v93, p58.
Motion Picture Herald Product Digest. Mar 12, 1980, p79.
New York. Mar 10, 1980, v13, p85.
The New York Times. Feb 29, 1980, SecIII, p15.
The New Yorker. Mar 17, 1980, v56, p92.
Newsday. Feb 29, 1980, SecII, p7.
Newsweek. Mar 10, 1980, v95, p88.
Progressive. May 1980, v44, p53-54.
Variety. Mar 17, 1980, p92.
The Village Voice. Mar 10, 1980, p51.
Vogue. Mar 1980, v170, p40.

Frances (US; Clifford, Graeme; 1982)
Hollywood Reporter. Dec 1, 1982, p3.
The Los Angeles Times. Dec 3, 1982, SecVI, p1.
Magill's Cinema Annual, 1983. p178-82.
New York. Dec 13, 1982, v15, p85-86.
The New York Times. Dec 3, 1982, SecIII, p15.
Newsweek. Dec 6, 1982, v100, p152.
Time. Feb 15, 1982, v119, p62-63.
Time. Dec 13, 1982, v120, p79.
Variety. Dec 1, 1982, p3.

Francesco, Guillare di Dio *See* The Flowers of St. Francis

The Franchise Affair (GB; Huntington, Lawrence; 1951)
Motion Picture Herald Product Digest. Jun 21, 1952, p1418.
The New York Times. Jun 6, 1952, p19.
The New Yorker. Jun 14, 1952, v28, p99.
Theatre Arts. Aug 1952, v36, p88.
Time. Jul 28, 1952, v60, p72.
Variety. Feb 28, 1951, p18.

Francis (US; Lubin, Arthur; 1950)
Christian Century. May 3, 1950, v67, p575.
Commonweal. Mar 17, 1950, v51, p607.
Film Daily. Dec 13, 1949, p6.
Library Journal. Feb 15, 1950, v75, p332.
Life and Letters. Mar 1950, v64, p175.
Motion Picture Herald Product Digest. Dec 17, 1949, p121.

The New Republic. Apr 3, 1950, v122, p21.
The New Statesman and Nation. Feb 11, 1950, v39, p160.
The New York Times. May 16, 1950, p40.
The New Yorker. Mar 18, 1950, v26, p102.
Newsweek. Feb 20, 1950, v35, p87.
Time. Mar 20, 1950, v55, p95.
Variety. Dec 14, 1949, p8.

Francis, God's Fool *See* The Flowers of St. Francis

Francis, God's Jester *See* The Flowers of St. Francis

Francis Goes to the Races (US; Lubin, Arthur; 1951)
Christian Century. Aug 22, 1951, v68, p975.
Film Daily. May 18, 1951, p6.
Hollywood Reporter. May 18, 1951, p3.
The London Times. Aug 20, 1951, p8.
Motion Picture Herald Product Digest. May 26, 1951, p863.
The New York Times. Jul 25, 1951, p19.
The New Yorker. Jul 14, 1951, v27, p61.
Variety. May 23, 1951, p6.

Francis Goes to West Point (US; Lubin, Arthur; 1952)
BFI/Monthly Film Bulletin. Jan 1953, v20, p8-9.
Christian Century. Aug 27, 1952, v69, p983.
Film Daily. Jun 23, 1952, p6.
Hollywood Reporter. Jun 13, 1952, p3.
Motion Picture Herald Product Digest. Jun 14, 1952, p1397.
National Parent-Teacher. Sep 1952, v47, p36.
The New York Times. Aug 23, 1952, p10.
Newsweek. Aug 25, 1952, v40, p85.
Time. Aug 18, 1952, v60, p84.
Variety. Jun 18, 1952, p6.

Francis in the Navy (US; Lubin, Arthur; 1955)
BFI/Monthly Film Bulletin. Aug 1955, v22, n259, p123.
Clint Eastwood (Guérif). p19.
Film Daily. Jul 7, 1955, p6.
The Films of Clint Eastwood. p42-43.
Hollywood Reporter. Jun 28, 1955, v135, n14, p3.
Magill's Survey of Cinema. Series II. v2, p839-41.
National Parent-Teacher. Sep 1955, v50, p38.
The New York Times. Aug 6, 1955, p13.
Variety. Jun 29, 1955, p6.

Francis Joins the Wacs (US; Lubin, Arthur; 1954)
BFI/Monthly Film Bulletin. Nov 1954, v21, p162.
Farm Journal. Sep 1954, v78, p140.
Film Daily. Jul 7, 1954, p10.
Hollywood Reporter. Jul 1, 1954, p3.
Motion Picture Herald Product Digest. Jul 3, 1954, p49.
National Parent-Teacher. Sep 1954, v49, p37.
The New York Times. Jul 31, 1954, p6.
Variety. Jul 7, 1954, p6.

Frankie and Johnny (US; De Cordova, Frederick; 1966)
BFI/Monthly Film Bulletin. May 1966, v33, p75.
Elvis: The Films and Career of Elvis Presley. p168-70.
Film Daily. Mar 25, 1966, p6.
Filmfacts. Oct 1, 1966, v9, p201-02.
Films and Filming. Jul 1966, v12, p12-13.
Hollywood Reporter. Mar 25, 1966, p3.
The London Times. Apr 29, 1966, p17.

Motion Picture Herald Product Digest. Apr 13, 1966, p500.
The New York Times. Jul 21, 1966, p20.
Variety. Mar 30, 1966, p6.

Free Escape *See* Backfire

Freebie and the Bean (US; Rush, Richard; 1974)
BFI/Monthly Film Bulletin. Feb 1975, v42, p32.
Commonweal. Mar 14, 1975, v101, p456-57.
Films and Filming. Mar 1975, v21, p36.
Films Illustrated. Jan 1975, v4, p168.
Films in Review. Jan 1975, v26, p46.
Hollywood Reporter. Nov 14, 1974, p3.
Independent Film Journal. Nov 27, 1974, v74, p6.
The Los Angeles Times. Dec 26, 1974, SecIV, p23.
Motion Picture Herald Product Digest. Jan 15, 1974, p64.
The New York Times. Jan 20, 1974, SecII, p1.
The New York Times. Dec 26, 1974, p59.
Newsweek. Jan 13, 1975, v85, p71.
Time. Jan 20, 1975, v105, p3.
Variety. Nov 13, 1974, p6.
Women and Film. 1975, v2, n7, p90-105.

The French Connection (US; Friedkin, William; 1971)
America. Oct 23, 1971, v125, p321.
BFI/Monthly Film Bulletin. Jan 1971, v39, p6.
Commonweal. Dec 24, 1971, v95, p301.
Directors in Action: Selections From Action. p175-88.
Fifty Grand Movies of the 1960s and 1970s. p217-19.
Film Quarterly. Sum 1972, v235, p3-9.
Filmfacts. 1971, v14, p329-33.
Films and Filming. Mar 1972, v18, n6, p50.
Films in Review. Nov 1971, v22, p573-74.
The Films of the Seventies. p30-32.
Hollywood Reporter. Oct 29, 1971, p3.
Life. Nov 19, 1971, v71, p13.
Magill's Survey of Cimena. Series I, v2, p579.
The New York Times. Oct 8, 1971, p35.
The New York Times. Nov 21, 1971, SecII, p15.
The New York Times. May 21, 1972, SecII, p15.
The New Yorker. Oct 30, 1971, v47, p114.
One Good Film Deserves Another. p140-45.
Saturday Review. Nov 6, 1971, v54, p70.
Take One. Jul-Aug 1971, v3, n6, p25-28.
Time. Nov 1, 1971, v98, p109.
Variety. Oct 6, 1971, p16.
The Village Voice. Oct 21, 1971, v16, n42, p77.

The French Connection II (US; Frankenheimer, John; 1975)
Hollywood Reporter. May 14, 1975, p4.
The Los Angeles Times. May 22, 1975, SecIV, p1.
Motion Picture Herald Product Digest. May 28, 1975, p99.
The New Republic. Jun 14, 1975, v172, p20.
The New York Times. Jun 2, 1975, p24.
The New York Times. Jul 6, 1975, SecII, p19.
The New Yorker. Jun 2, 1975, v51, p92-93.
Newsweek. May 26, 1975, v105, p53.
One Good Film Deserves Another. p140-45.
Time. Jun 2, 1975, v105, p53.
Variety. May 14, 1975, p26.

The French Lieutenant's Woman (GB; Reisz, Karel; 1981)
America. Oct 17, 1981, v145, p223.
Christian Century. Oct 21, 1981, v98, p1073.
Commentary. Nov 1981, v72, p78-87.
Commonweal. Nov 6, 1981, v108, p621-22.
Double Exposure. p104-09.

Film Comment. Sep-Oct 1981, v17, p26-28.
The French Lieutenant's Woman: A Screenplay.
1981.
Hollywood Reporter. Sep 10, 1981, p4.
Horizon. Oct 1981, v24, p36-41.
The Los Angeles Times. Sep 13, 1981,
Calendar, p27.
Maclean's. Sep 21, 1981, v94, p52.
Magill's Cinema Annual, 1982. p174-78.
Making Pictures: The Pinter Screenplays. p145-
84.
Ms. Nov 1981, v10, p112.
The Nation. Oct 10, 1981, v233, p354-55.
National Review. Nov 13, 1981, v33, p1362.
The New Republic. Sep 23, 1981, v185, p22-24.
New York. Sep 28, 1981, v14, p56.
The New York Times. Sep 27, 1981, SecII, p17.
The New York Times. Sep 18, 1981, SecIII, p4.
The New York Times Magazine. Aug 30, 1981,
p24-25.
The New Yorker. Oct 12, 1981, v57, p158-62.
Newsweek. Sep 21, 1981, v98, p96.
Rolling Stone. Oct 15, 1981, p17-19.
Rolling Stone. Oct 29, 1981, p34.
Saturday Review. Oct 1981, v8, p61.
Time. Sep 7, 1981, v118, p48-50.
Variety. Sep 10, 1981, p3.

The French Line (US; Bacon, Lloyd; 1954)
BFI/Monthly Film Bulletin. Jun 1954, v21, p84.
Film Daily. Jan 5, 1954, p6.
Hollywood Reporter. Dec 30, 1953, p4.
The London Times. May 3, 1954, p4.
Look. Nov 3, 1953, v17, p106-09.
Motion Picture Herald Product Digest. Jan 9,
1954, p2134.
National Parent-Teacher. May 1954, v48, p39.
The New Statesman and Nation. May 1, 1954,
v47, p598.
The New York Times. May 15, 1954, p13.
The New Yorker. May 22, 1954, v30, p112.
Newsweek. May 31, 1954, v43, p84.
The Spectator. Apr 30, 1954, v192, p513.
The Tatler. May 12, 1954, v212, p357.
Time. May 31, 1954, v63, p72.
Variety. Jan 6, 1954, p52.

The French They Are a Funny Race
(French title: Carnets du Major
Thompson, Les; Also titled: The Diary
of Major Thompson) (FR; Sturges,
Preston; 1957)
Between Flops. p271-77.
BFI/Monthly Film Bulletin. Jan 1958, v25, p3.
Commonweal. May 24, 1957, v66, p205.
Film Daily. May 21, 1957, p8.
Films and Filming. Jan 1958, v4, p25-26.
Films in Review. Jun-Jul 1957, v8, p282.
Motion Picture Herald Product Digest. Jun 8,
1957, p411.
The New York Times. May 21, 1957, p41.
The New Yorker. Jun 1, 1957, v33, p73.
Newsweek. May 20, 1957, v49, p118.
*Preston Sturges: A Guide tor References and
Resources.* p82-84.
Saturday Review. Jun 1, 1957, v40, p23.
Time. May 27, 1957, v69, p102.
Variety. Jan 11, 1956, p22.

Frenchie (US; King, Louis; 1950)
BFI/Monthly Film Bulletin. Dec 1950, v17,
p188.
Film Daily. Dec 1, 1950, p4.
Hollywood Reporter. Nov 29, 1950, p3.
Motion Picture Herald Product Digest. Dec 2,
1950, p598.
The New York Times. Feb 12, 1951, p19.
Newsweek. Jan 22, 1951, v37, p83.
Time. Feb 19, 1951, v57, p100.
Variety. Nov 29, 1950, p14.

Frenzy (US, GB; Hitchcock, Alfred; 1972)
America. Jul 8, 1972, v127, p20.
American Scholar. Aut 1972, v41, p630-36.
The Art of Alfred Hitchcock. p435-46.
Commentary. Sep 1972, v54, p77-79.
Commonweal. Aug 11, 1972, v96, p429-30.
Film Quarterly. Fall 1972, v26, p58-60.
Filmfacts. 1972, v15, p6.
The Films in My Life. p88-92.
Films in Review. Aug-Sep 1972, v23, p429.
The Films of Alfred Hitchcock. p238-42.
Hitchcock (Truffaut). p333-39.
Hollywood Reporter. May 26, 1972, p3.
Life. Jul 2, 1972, v72, p25.
Magill's Survey of Cinema. Series II. v2, p849.
The Nation. Jul 10, 1972, v215, p27.
The New Republic. Jul 8, 1972, v167, p22.
The New York Times. Jul 30, 1972, SecII, p9.
The New York Times. Jul 22, 1972, p48.
The New Yorker. Jul 24, 1972, v48, p61-62.
Newsweek. Jul 26, 1972, v79, p83-84.
Saturday Review. Jul 24, 1972, v55, p74.
Time. Jul 19, 1972, v99, p70.
Variety. May 31, 1972, p6.

Freud (Also titled: Freud: The Secret
Passion) (US; Huston, John; 1962)
America. Jan 26, 1963, v108, p153.
BFI/Monthly Film Bulletin. Oct 1963, v30,
p140-41.
The Cinema of John Huston. p131-38.
Commonweal. Jan 4, 1963, v77, p389.
Film Comment. May-Jun 1980, v16, p25-56.
Film Daily. Dec 13, 1962, p11.
Film Quarterly. Sum 1963, v16, p50-51.
Filmfacts. Jan 4, 1962, v5, p315-17.
Films and Filming. Oct 1963, v10, p22-23.
Films in Review. Jan 1963, v14.
The Films of Montgomery Clift. p203-08.
High Fidelity and Musical America. Aug 1978,
v28, p94.
Hollywood Reporter. Dec 13, 1962, p3.
John Huston (Hammen). p99-101.
Life. Jan 4, 1963, v54, p51A-51B.
Magill's Cinema Annual, 1984. p535-541.
Motion Picture Herald Product Digest. Dec 26,
1962, p721.
The Nation. Jan 19, 1963, v196, p59.
The New Republic. Jan 5, 1963, v148, p19-20.
The New York Times. Dec 13, 1962, p37.
The New Yorker. Dec 22, 1962, v38, p77-78.
Newsweek. Dec 24, 1962, v60, p63.
Private Screenings. p55-57.
Saturday Review. Jan 5, 1963, v46, p30.
Sight and Sound. Aut 1963, v32, p196-97.
Time. Dec 28, 1962, v80, p60.
Variety. Dec 19, 1962, p6.
The Village Voice. Dec 20, 1962, p17.

Friday the 13th (US; Cunningham, Sean S.;
1980)
BFI/Monthly Film Bulletin. Jul 1980, v47,
p132.
Films in Review. Apr 1980, v31, p246.
Hollywood Reporter. May 9, 1980, p3.
The Los Angeles Times. May 15, 1980, SecIV,
p7.
The New York Times. May 10, 1980, p14.
Newsday. May 10, 1980, SecII, p22.
Variety. May 14, 1980, p14.
The Village Voice. May 19, 1980, p50.

Friendly Persuasion (US; Wyler, William;
1956)
America. Nov 17, 1956, v96, p212.
BFI/Monthly Film Bulletin. Dec 1956, v23,
p140.
Commonweal. Nov 23, 1956, v65, p206.
Fifty from the Fifties. p105-10.
Film Daily. Sep 27, 1956, p11.

Films and Filming. Dec 1956, v3, p22-23.
Films in Review. Nov 1956, v7, p459-61.
The Films of Gary Cooper. p255-58.
Hollywood Reporter. Sep 26, 1956, p3.
Magill's Survey of Cinema. Series II. v2, p852-
55.
The Nation. Nov 24, 1956, v183, p467.
The New York Times. Nov 2, 1956, p30.
The New York Times. Nov 4, 1956, SecII, p1.
The New Yorker. Nov 10, 1956, v32, p125.
Newsweek. Oct 1, 1956, v48, p88.
Saturday Review. Nov 10, 1956, v39, p28.
Time. Nov 5, 1956, v68, p110.
Variety. Sep 26, 1956, p6.
*William Wyler: A Guide to References and
Resources.* p137-41.
William Wyler (Anderegg). p187-92.

Friends (GB; Gilbert, Lewis; 1971)
America. May 8, 1971, v124, p491-92.
BFI/Monthly Film Bulletin. Oct 1971, v38,
n453, p195.
Filmfacts. 1971, v14, n11, p254-56.
Films and Filming. Nov 1971, v28, n2, p52.
Hollywood Reporter. Mar 22, 1971, p3.
The New York Times. Mar 25, 1971, p46.
Time. May 10, 1971, v97, p99.
Variety. Mar 24, 1971, p26.

The Frightened Bride *See* Tall Headlines

The Frogmen (US; Bacon, Lloyd; 1951)
BFI/Monthly Film Bulletin. Aug 1951, v18,
p306-07.
Christian Century. Aug 1, 1951, v68, p903.
Commonweal. Jul 13, 1951, v54, p335.
Film Daily. Jun 13, 1951, p6.
Films in Review. Aug-Sep 1951, v2, p41-42.
Hollywood Reporter. Jun 7, 1951, p3.
The London Times. Aug 20, 1951, p8.
Motion Picture Herald Product Digest. Jun 9,
1951, p877.
The Nation. Jul 14, 1951, v173, p37.
The New Republic. Jul 16, 1951, v125, p23.
The New Statesman and Nation. Aug 25, 1951,
v42, p204.
The New York Times. Jun 30, 1951, p8.
The New Yorker. Jul 14, 1951, v27, p72.
Newsweek. Jun 25, 1951, v37, p89.
Saturday Review. Jul 21, 1951, v34, p26.
Time. Jul 9, 1951, v58, p84.
Variety. Jun 13, 1951, p6.

Froken Julie *See* Miss Julie

From Here to Eternity (US; Zinnemann,
Fred; 1953)
America. Aug 15, 1953, v89, p486.
BFI/Monthly Film Bulletin. Dec 1953, v20,
n239, p171.
*Burt Lancaster: A Pictorial Treasury of His
Films.* p72-75.
Burt Lancaster: The Man and His Movies. p58-
62.
Catholic World. Sep 1953, v177, p461.
Collier's. Aug 1953, v132, p38-39.
Commonweal. Aug 21, 1953, v58, p488-89.
Farm Journal. Oct 1953, v77, p98.
Fifty from the Fifties. p111-18.
Film Daily. Jul 29, 1953, p6.
Films in Review. Oct 1953, v4, p428-30.
The Films of Frank Sinatra. p75-79.
The Films of Montgomery Clift. p141-50.
The Films of the Fifties. p99-102.
The Great Movies. p111-13.
Guts & Glory. p117-29.
Harper's. Oct 1953, v207, p92-93.
Holiday. Jan 1954, v15, p14.
Hollywood Reporter. Jul 29, 1953, p3.
Library Journal. Sep 1, 1953, v78, p1411.

Life. Aug 31, 1983, v35, p81-83.
Look. Aug 25, 1953, v17, p41-43.
Magill's Survey of Cinema. Series I. v2, p577.
The Nation. Aug 29, 1953, v177, p178.
National Parent-Teacher. Oct 1953, v48, p39.
The New York Times. May 10, 1953, SecVII, p8.
The New Yorker. Aug 8, 1953, v29, p51.
Newsweek. Aug 10, 1953, v42, p82.
The Platinum Years. p64-69.
Reruns. p87-92.
Saturday Review. Aug 8, 1953, v36, p25.
Sight and Sound. Jan-Mar 1954, v23, p145-46.
Time. Aug 10, 1953, v62, p94.
Variety. Jul 29, 1953, p6.

From Russia with Love (GB; Young, Terence; 1963)
America. Apr 25, 1964, v110, p580.
BFI/Monthly Film Bulletin. Nov 1963, v30, p155.
Boxoffice. Mar 2, 1964, v84, p2805.
Film Daily. Feb 27, 1964, p6.
Films and Filming. Dec 1963, v10, p27.
Films in Review. May 1964, v5, p307-09.
Hollywood Reporter. Feb 27, 1964, p3.
The James Bond Films. p23-36.
James Bond in the Cinema. p45-76.
James Bond's Bedside Companion. p172-75.
Life. Apr 3, 1964, v56, p51-52.
Magill's Survey of Cinema. Series I. v2, p582-85.
Motion Picture Herald Product Digest. Mar 4, 1964, p1.
The New Republic. Apr 25, 1964, v150, p26.
The New York Times. Apr 9, 1964, p25.
The New Yorker. Apr 18, 1964, v40, p20.
Newsweek. Apr 13, 1964, v63, p93-94.
Private Screenings. p133-34.
Reruns. p175-78.
Saturday Review. Apr 18, 1964, v47, p29.
Time. Apr 10, 1964, v83, p103.
Variety. Oct 16, 1963, p6.

From the Life of the Marionettes (Swedish title: Aus dem Leben der Marionetten) (SWED; Bergman, Ingmar; 1980)
America. Dec 20, 1980, v143, p412.
BFI/Monthly Film Bulletin. May 1981, v48, p88.
Christian Century. Dec 24, 1980, v97, p1276.
Christian Science Monitor. Dec 4, 1980, p19.
Hollywood Reporter. Nov 1, 1980, p3.
Ingmar Bergman and the Rituals of Art. p162-63.
Maclean's. Jan 19, 1981, v94, p55.
The Nation. Nov 29, 1980, v231, p586.
The New Republic. Nov 29, 1980, v183, p22-24.
New York. Nov 17, 1980, v13, p80-82.
The New York Times. Nov 7, 1980, SecIII, p6.
Newsday. Nov 7, 1980, SecII, p7.
Newsweek. Nov 17, 1980, v96, p118.
Sight and Sound. Spr 1981, v50, p133.
Time. Nov 17, 1980, v116, p109.
Variety. Jul 23, 1980, p18.
The Village Voice. Nov 12, 1980, p51.

From the Terrace (US; Robson, Mark; 1960)
America. Aug 6, 1960, v103, p522.
BFI/Monthly Film Bulletin. Sep 1960, v27, p124.
Commonweal. Aug 5, 1960, v72, p402.
Film Daily. Jun 27, 1960, p6.
Film Quarterly. Sum 1960, v13, p60.
Filmfacts. 1960, v3, p173.
Films and Filming. Sep 1960, v6, p23.
Films in Review. Aug-Sep 1960, v11, p431.
The Films of Myrna Loy. p246.
The Films of Paul Newman. p86-90.

Hollywood Reporter. Jun 27, 1960, p3.
The New York Times. Jul 16, 1960, p10.
The New Yorker. Jul 23, 1960, v36, p72-73.
Newsweek. Jul 18, 1960, v56, p88.
Saturday Review. Jul 30, 1960, v43, p24.
Time. Jul 18, 1960, v76, p76.
Variety. Jun 28, 1960, p9.

The Front (US; Ritt, Martin; 1976)
America. Oct 16, 1976, v135, p236-37.
Before My Eyes. p242.
BFI/Monthly Film Bulletin. Dec 1976, v43, p251.
Christian Century. Nov 3, 1976, v93, p963-64.
Commentary. Jan 1977, v63, p72-74.
Commonweal. Dec 3, 1976, v103, p784.
Film Bulletin. Sep-Oct 1976, v45, p36.
Films in Review. Nov 1976, v27, p566.
Hollywood Reporter. Sep 15, 1976, p2.
Independent Film Journal. Sep 17, 1976, v78, p7.
The Los Angeles Times. Sep 26, 1976, Calendar, p1.
Magill's Cinema Annual, 1986. p502-06.
Motion Picture Herald Product Digest. Oct 6, 1976, p37.
The Nation. Oct 16, 1976, v223, p378-79.
The New Republic. Oct 2, 1976, v175, p24-25.
New York. Oct 4, 1976, v9, p78-80.
The New York Times. Oct 3, 1976, SecII, p1.
The New Yorker. Oct 4, 1976, v52, p130-33.
Newsweek. Oct 4, 1976, v88, p89.
Saturday Review. Oct 2, 1976, v4, p38-39.
The Thousand Eyes Magazine. Oct 1976, v2, p8.
Time. Oct 11, 1976, v108, p88.
Variety. Sep 15, 1976, p16.
The Village Voice. Oct 4, 1976, p121.
Vogue. Nov 1976, v166, p160.
When the Lights Go Down. p170-72.
Woody Allen: His Films and Career. p158-66.

The Front Page (US; Wilder, Billy; 1974)
Audience. Jan 1975, v7, p4-5.
BFI/Monthly Film Bulletin. Feb 1975, v42, p32-33.
Billy Wilder (Dick). p115-20.
Cinema Papers. Mar-Apr 1975, v2, p62-63.
Commonweal. Jan 17, 1975, v101, p328-30.
Film. Feb 1975, n23, p21-22.
The Film Career of Billy Wilder. p110-13.
Film Heritage. 1975, v10, n3, p34-35.
Films and Filming. Mar 1975, v21, p37.
Films Illustrated. Jan 1975, v4, p166.
Films Illustrated. Feb 1975, v4, p216-18.
Films in Review. Dec 1974, v25, p626-27.
The Films of Jack Lemmon. p216-21.
Hollywood Reporter. Dec 9, 1974, p3.
Independent Film Journal. Dec 25, 1974, v75, p30.
The Los Angeles Times. Dec 15, 1974, Calendar, p1.
Motion Picture Herald Product Digest. Dec 11, 1974, p54.
Movietone News. Oct 1974, n36, p29.
The New Republic. Feb 1, 1975, v172, p20, 34.
New Statesman. Dec 27, 1974, v88, p939-40.
New York. Dec 23, 1974, v7, p70-71.
New York. Jan 20, 1975, v8, p45-46.
The New York Times. Dec 19, 1974, p59.
The New Yorker. Jan 27, 1975, v50, p94.
Newsweek. Dec 23, 1974, v84, p79.
Penthouse. Apr 1975, v6, p37-39.
Reeling. p560-65.
Sight and Sound. Fall 1974, v43, p212.
Sight and Sound. Spr 1975, v44, p124.
Time. Dec 23, 1974, v104, p4.
Variety. Dec 11, 1974, p18.
The Village Voice. Dec 23, 1974, p83-85.

Fruit Defendu, Le *See* Forbidden Fruit

Fuga, La (Also titled: The Flight) (IT; Spinola, Paolo; 1965)
Film Daily. Mar 1, 1966, p4.
Filmfacts. May 1, 1966, v9, p67-68.
Hollywood Reporter. Apr 6, 1967, p3.
Motion Picture Herald Product Digest. Mar 16, 1966, p484.
The New York Times. Mar 22, 1966, p33.
Variety. Apr 7, 1965, p30.

The Fugitive Kind (US; Lumet, Sidney; 1960)
America. Apr 30, 1960, v103, p201.
BFI/Monthly Film Bulletin. Jul 1960, v27, p90.
Commonweal. Apr 29, 1960, v72, p127.
Film Daily. Apr 13, 1960, p6.
Film Quarterly. Sum 1960, v13, p47-49.
Filmfacts. 1960, v3, p85.
Films and Filming. Aug 1960, v6, p23-24.
Films in Review. May 1960, v11, p290-92.
The Films of Marlon Brando. p122-27.
The Films of Tennessee Williams. p197-13.
Hollywood Reporter. Apr 13, 1960, p3.
McCall's. Jun 1960, v87, p179.
The New Republic. May 2, 1960, v142, p21-22.
The New York Times. Apr 15, 1960, p13.
The New York Times. Apr 24, 1960, SecII, p7.
The New Yorker. Apr 23, 1960, v36, p147.
Newsweek. Apr 25, 1960, v55, p115.
Saturday Review. Apr 23, 1960, v40, p28.
Sidney Lumet: A Guide to References and Resources. p67-69.
Sight and Sound. Sum 1960, v29, p144-45.
Tennessee Williams and Film. p60-66.
Time. Apr 18, 1960, v75, p81.
Variety. Apr 13, 1960, p6.
A World on Film. p83-85.

Full House *See* O. Henry's Full House

Full Moon in Paris (French title: Nuits de la Pleine Lune, Les) (FR; Rohmer, Eric; 1984)
BFI/Monthly Film Bulletin. Dec 1984, v51, p379.
Film Journal. Oct 1984, v87, p19.
The Los Angeles Times. Oct 4, 1984, SecVI, p5.
Magill's Cinema Annual, 1985. p208-12.
The New Republic. Oct 15, 1984, v191, p26.
New Statesman. Nov 9, 1984, v108, p34.
The New York Times. Sep 7, 1984, SecIII, p34.
Penthouse. Dec 1984, v16, p60.
Progressive. Nov 1984, v48, p39.
Sight and Sound. Wint 1984, v54, p65.
Variety. Aug 29, 1984, p16.
The Village Voice. Sep 11, 1984, p51-53.

The Fuller Brush Girl (US; Bacon, Lloyd; 1950)
Film Daily. Sep 14, 1950, p8.
Hollywood Reporter. Sep 14, 1950, p3.
Motion Picture Herald Product Digest. Sep 16, 1950, p486.
The New York Times. Oct 6, 1950, p23.
Variety. Sep 20, 1950, p6.

Fun in Acapulco (US; Thorpe, Richard; 1963)
BFI/Monthly Film Bulletin. Dec 1963, v30, p171-72.
Commonweal. Dec 13, 1963, v79, p349.
Elvis: The Films and Career of Elvis Presley. p140-45.
Film Daily. Nov 21, 1963, p6.
Films and Filming. Jan 1964, v10, p32.
The New York Times. Feb 20, 1964, p22.
Variety. Nov 20, 1963, p6.

Fun with Dick and Jane (US; Kotcheff, Ted; 1977)
BFI/Monthly Film Bulletin. May 1977, v44, p98.
Films in Review. May 1977, v28, p315.
The Films of Jane Fonda. p185-91.
Hollywood Reporter. Jan 28, 1977, p3.
The Los Angeles Times. Feb 9, 1977, SecIV, p1.
Motion Picture Herald Product Digest. Feb 2, 1977, p67.
The New Republic. Feb 26, 1977, v176, p20.
The New York Times. Feb 20, 1977, SecII, p1.
The New Yorker. Feb 28, 1977, v53, p90-91.
Newsweek. Feb 21, 1977, v89, p90-92.
Saturday Review. Feb 19, 1977, v4, p41.
Time. Feb 7, 1978, v109, p78.
Variety. Feb 2, 1977, p22.

Funeral in Berlin (GB; Hamilton, Guy; 1966)
America. Feb 4, 1967, v116, p194.
BFI/Monthly Film Bulletin. Apr 1967, v34, p56.
Christian Century. Apr 5, 1967, v84, p440-41.
Christian Science Monitor (Western edition). Jan 6, 1967, p4.
Commonweal. Feb 3, 1967, v85, p488-89.
Film Daily. Dec 13, 1966, p4.
Filmfacts. Jan 15, 1967, v9, p351-52.
Films and Filming. May 1967, v13, p26.
Films in Review. Jan 1967, v18, p55.
The Great Spy Pictures. p191-92.
Hollywood Reporter. Dec 13, 1966, p3.
The London Times. Feb 23, 1966, p10.
Marshall Delaney At the Movies. p202-05.
Motion Picture Herald Product Digest. Dec 21, 1966, p641-42.
The New Republic. Jan 14, 1967, v156, p42.
The New York Times. Dec 23, 1966, p17.
The New Yorker. Dec 24, 1966, v42, p60.
Newsweek. Jan 2, 1967, v69, p63-64.
Playboy. Mar 1967, v14, p22-23.
Saturday Review. Dec 31, 1966, v49, p36.
Senior Scholastic. Feb 10, 1967, v90, p24.
Sight and Sound. Spr 1967, v36, p96.
Take One. Apr 1967, v1, p22-23.
Time. Dec 23, 1966, v88, p75.
Variety. Feb 14, 1966, p6.

Funny Face (US; Donen, Stanley; 1957)
America. Apr 20, 1957, v97, p83.
BFI/Monthly Film Bulletin. Apr 1957, v24, p42.
Classic Movies. p52-55.
Commonweal. Apr 5, 1957, v66, p16.
Dance Magazine. May 1957, v31, p16-22.
Film Daily. Feb 13, 1957, p6.
Films and Filming. May 1957, v3, p23-24.
Films in Review. Apr 1957, v8, p171-73.
The Films of the Fifties. p217-20.
Hollywood Reporter. Feb 13, 1957, p3.
Magill's Survey of Cinema. Series II. v2, p859-61.
Motion Picture Herald Product Digest. Feb 16, 1957, v206.
The New Republic. Jun 10, 1957, v136, p22-23.
The New York Times. Jul 15, 1956, SecII, p5.
The New York Times. Mar 29, 1957, p16.
The New York Times. Apr 7, 1957, SecII, p1.
The New York Times Magazine. Mar 17, 1957, p16.
The New Yorker. Apr 6, 1957, v33, p76.
Newsweek. Apr 1, 1957, v49, p106.
Saturday Review. Apr 13, 1957, v40, p26.
Sight and Sound. Sum 1957, v27, p40.
Stanley Donen (Casper). p93-104.
Starring Fred Astaire. p407-20.
Time. Apr 1, 1957, v69, p94.
Variety. Feb 13, 1957, p6.

Funny Girl (US; Wyler, William; 1968)
Barbra: The First Decade. p156-163.
BFI/Monthly Film Bulletin. Mar 1969, v36, p48-49.
Christian Century. Nov 20, 1968, v85, p1477.
Christian Science Monitor (Western edition). Sep 25, 1968, p4.
Commonweal. Oct 11, 1968, v89, p64.
Confessions of a Cultist. p392-95.
Dance Magazine. Dec 1968, v42, p24.
Figures of Light. p114-15.
Film Daily. Sep 20, 1968, p6.
Film Quarterly. Spr 1969, v22, p59.
Filmfacts. Sep 15, 1968, v11, p239-42.
Films and Filming. May 1969, v15, p44.
Films in Review. Oct 1968, v19, p518-19.
The Films of the Sixties. p236-38.
Going Steady. p161-66.
Hollywood Reporter. Sep 20, 1968, p3.
Life. Nov 8, 1968, v65, p10.
The London Times. Jan 16, 1969, p11.
Look. Oct 15, 1968, v32, p50-53.
Magill's Survey of Cinema. Series I. v2, p589-91.
Motion Picture Herald Product Digest. Oct 2, 1968, p33.
The New Republic. Nov 9, 1968, v159, p22.
The New York Times. Sep 20, 1968, p42.
The New Yorker. Sep 28, 1968, v44, p167-70.
Newsweek. Sep 30, 1968, v72, p96.
Saturday Review. Oct 12, 1968, v51, p54.
Senior Scholastic. Dec 6, 1968, v93, p27-28.
Sight and Sound. Spr 1969, v38, p95-96.
The Spectator. Jan 24, 1969, v222, p116.
Time. Oct 4, 1968, v92, p101.
Today's Cinema. Jan 24, 1969, p12.
Variety. Sep 25, 1968, p6.
The Village Voice. Oct 10, 1968, p53-55.
Vogue. Nov 1, 1968, v152, p128.
William Wyler: A Guide to References and Resources. p158-62.
William Wyler (Anderegg). p219-25.
William Wyler (Madsen). p387-94.
A Year In the Dark. p243-44.

Funny Lady (US; Ross, Herbert; 1975)
BFI/Monthly Film Bulletin. May 1975, v42, p106.
Esquire. Jun 1975, v83, p62.
Films in Review. Apr 1975, p244.
Hollywood Reporter. Mar 3, 1975, p3.
Motion Picture Herald Product Digest. Mar 26, 1975, p83.
The New Republic. Apr 5, 1975, v172, p20.
The New York Times. Mar 12, 1975, p30.
The New York Times. Mar 16, 1975, SecII, p17.
The New Yorker. Mar 17, 1975, v51, p112-18.
Newsweek. Jul 15, 1974, v84, p83.
Newsweek. Mar 24, 1975, v85, p58-59.
One Good Film Deserves Another. p130-34.
Reeling. p605-13.
Saturday Review. Apr 19, 1975, v2, p46-47.
Time. Mar 24, 1975, v105, p9.
Variety. Mar 5, 1975, p20.

A Funny Thing Happened On the Way to the Forum (GB; Lester, Richard; 1966)
America. Oct 29, 1966, v115, p526.
BFI/Monthly Film Bulletin. Mar 1967, v34, p41.
Big Screen, Little Screen. p334.
Christian Science Monitor (Western edition). Jan 9, 1967, p6.
Commonweal. Oct 28, 1966, v85, p104, 106.
Esquire. Mar 1967, v67, p22.
Film. Wint 1966, n47, p25-26.
Film Daily. Sep 27, 1966, p3.
Film Quarterly. Sum 1966, v19, p12-16.
Film Quarterly. Wint 1966-67, v20, p61-62.

Filmfacts. Dec 1, 1966, v9, p276-79.
Films and Filming. Apr 1967, v13, p8.
Films in Review. Nov 1966, v17, p589-90.
Focus. Feb 1967, n1, p18.
Hollywood Reporter. Sep 27, 1966, p3.
Illustrated London News. Feb 4, 1967, v250, p32.
Kiss Kiss Bang Bang. p169-70.
Life. Nov 11, 1966, v61, p10, 16.
The London Times. Feb 2, 1967, p5.
Magill's Survey of Cinema. Series I. v1, p592-95.
Motion Picture Herald Product Digest. Sep 28, 1966, p603.
National Review. Feb 7, 1967, v19, p153.
The New Republic. Dec 10, 1966, v155, p36-37.
New Statesman. Feb 3, 1967, v73, p164.
The New York Times. Oct 17, 1966, p48.
The New Yorker. Oct 22, 1966, v42, p164-65.
Playboy. Dec 1966, v13, p48.
Punch. Feb 8, 1967, v252, p206-07.
Reporter. Dec 29, 1966, v35, p39.
Richard Lester: A Guide to References and Resources. p28-29.
Saturday Review. Oct 15, 1966, v49, p26.
Sight and Sound. Wint 1966-67, v36, p47.
Take One. Feb 1967, v1, p22.
Time. Oct 28, 1966, v88, p111.
Variety. Sep 28, 1966, p6.
The Village Voice. Nov 3, 1966, p31.
Vogue. Dec 1966, v148, p166.

The Furies (US; Mann, Anthony; 1950)
Anthony Mann (Basinger). p93-97.
BFI/Monthly Film Bulletin. Jul 1950, v17, p104.
Christian Century. Sep 6, 1950, v67, p1063.
Commonweal. Sep 1, 1950, v52, p510.
Film Daily. Jun 29, 1950, p7.
The Films of Barbara Stanwyck. p203-05.
The Great Western Pictures. p109-10.
Hollywood Quarterly. Wint 1950, v5, p178-81.
Hollywood Reporter. Jun 27, 1950, p3.
The London Times. Jul 24, 1950, p2.
Motion Picture Herald Product Digest. Jul 1, 1950, p365.
The New Statesman and Nation. Jul 29, 1950, v39, p123.
The New York Times. Aug 17, 1950, p23.
Newsweek. Sep 4, 1950, v36, p70.
The Spectator. Jul 21, 1950, v185, p81.
Starring Miss Barbara Stanwyck. p229.
Time. Aug 21, 1950, v56, p82.
Variety. Jun 28, 1950, p6.

The Fury (US; De Palma, Brian; 1978)
Double De Palma. p6, 11, 175.
Encore. Apr 17, 1978, v7, p31.
Films in Review. May 1978, v29, p313.
The Films of the Seventies. p216-19.
Hollywood Reporter. Mar 10, 1978, p3.
The Los Angeles Times. Mar 5, 1978, SecIV, p16.
Maclean's. Apr 3, 1978, v91, p74.
Motion Picture Herald Product Digest. Mar 22, 1978, p81.
The New Leader. Apr 24, 1978, v61, p25.
The New York Times. Apr 2, 1978, SecII, p13.
The New York Times. Mar 15, 1978, SecIII, p19.
The New Yorker. May 20, 1978, v54, p122-24.
Saturday Review. May 13, 1978, v5, p26.
Time. Mar 20, 1978, v111, p74.
Variety. Apr 19, 1978, p26.
The World of Fantastic Films. p90-91.

Fussgaenger, Der *See* The Pedestrian

Futureworld (US; Heffron, Richard T.;
1976)
BFI/Monthly Film Bulletin. Oct 1976, v43,
p213-14.
Cinefantastique. 1976, v5, n3, p25.
Films and Filming. Dec 1976, v23, p36.
Films in Review. Oct 1976, v27, p506.
Hollywood Reporter. Jul 13, 1976, p2.
Independent Film Journal. Aug 6, 1976, v78,
p8.
The Los Angeles Times. Aug 18, 1976, SecIV,
p1.
Motion Picture Herald Product Digest. Aug 18,
1976, p21.
New Statesman. Oct 22, 1976, v92, p570.
The New York Times. Aug 14, 1976, p10.
The New Yorker. Aug 30, 1976, v52, p68-70.
Science Fiction Films of the Seventies. p122-25.
Time. Sep 20, 1976, v108, p80.

GI Blues (US; Taurog, Norman; 1960)
America. Dec 3, 1960, v104, p350.
BFI/Monthly Film Bulletin. Dec 1960, v27,
p170.
Elvis: The Films and Career of Elvis Presley.
p116-19.
Film Daily. Oct 20, 1960, p6.
Filmfacts. 1960, v3, p290.
Films and Filming. Dec 1960, v7, p33.
Hollywood Reporter. Oct 19, 1960, p3.
The New York Times. Nov 5, 1960, p28.
Newsweek. Nov 14, 1960, v56, p110.
Time. Dec 5, 1960, v76, p64.
Variety. Oct 19, 1960, p16.

Gable and Lombard (US; Furie, Sidney J.;
1976)
Audience. Nov 1976, v9, p13-15.
BFI/Monthly Film Bulletin. Nov 1976, v43,
p231-32.
Commonweal. Mar 12, 1976, v103, p80.
Film Bulletin. Feb 1976, v45, p36.
Films in Review. Mar 1976, v27, p308-10.
Hollywood Reporter. Feb 10, 1976, p5.
Independent Film Journal. Feb 18, 1976, v77,
p10-11.
The Los Angeles Times. Feb 11, 1976, SecIV,
p1.
Millimeter. May 1976, v4, p28-30.
Motion Picture Herald Product Digest. Feb 18,
1976, p76.
Movietone News. Apr 1976, n49, p48.
New York. Feb 23, 1976, v9, p68.
The New York Times. Feb 22, 1976, SecII, p15.
The New York Times. Feb 12, 1976, p42.
The New Yorker. Feb 23, 1976, v52, p86.
Newsweek. Mar 15, 1976, v87, p90.
Saturday Review. Mar 20, 1976, v3, p49.
Time. Mar 1, 1976, v107, p65-66.
Variety. Feb 18, 1976, p35.
The Village Voice. Feb 23, 1976, p115-16.
When the Lights Go Down. p140-43.

Gabriela (BRAZ; Barreto, Bruno; 1983)
BFI/Monthly Film Bulletin. Oct 1984, v51,
p306.
Film Journal. Jun 1984, v87, p22.
Films and Filming. Nov 1984, n362, p36-37.
Hollywood Reporter. May 18, 1984, p11.
The Los Angeles Times. May 25, 1984, SecVI,
p2.
Magill's Cinema Annual, 1985. p213-18.
The Nation. Jun 2, 1984, v238, p683-84.
The New Republic. Jun 4, 1984, v190, p24.
New York. May 28, 1984, v17, p98.
The New York Times. May 11, 1984, SecIII,
p14.
Variety. Jan 4, 1984, p5.
The Village Voice. May 29, 1984, p60.

Gaily, Gaily (Also titled: Chicago, Chicago)
(US; Jewison, Norman; 1969)
Deeper Into Movies. p92-93.
Films and Filming. May 1970, v16, p54.
Films in Review. Feb 1970, v21, p120.
Focus on Film. Mar-Apr 1970, n2, p11-16.
Holiday. Dec 1969, v46, p28.
Hollywood Reporter. Dec 4, 1969, p3.
Life. Dec 19, 1969, v67, p10.
The New York Times. Dec 17, 1969, p62.
The New Yorker. Dec 20, 1969, v45, p70.
Newsweek. Jan 5, 1970, v75, p62.
Saturday Review. Dec 20, 1969, v52, p68.
Variety. Dec 3, 1969, p16.

Galia (Also titled: I and My Lovers) (FR,
IT; Lautner, Georges; 1965)
BFI/Monthly Film Bulletin. Jun 1966, v33, p93.
Cahiers du Cinema in English. 1966, n4, p60.
Film Daily. Dec 27, 1966, p3.
Filmfacts. Jan 15, 1967, v9, p344-45.
The London Times. Apr 21, 1966, p9.
Motion Picture Herald Product Digest. Jan 18,
1967, p650.
The Nation. Jan 16, 1967, v204, p94.
The New York Times. Dec 20, 1966, p50.
The New Yorker. Dec 24, 1966, v42, p60.
Newsweek. Dec 26, 1966, v68, p72.
Playboy. Dec 1966, v13, p49-50.
Time. Jan 27, 1967, v89, p80.
Variety. Feb 16, 1966, p18.

Gallipoli (AUSTRALIA; Weir, Peter; 1980)
Christian Century. Oct 21, 1981, v98, p1073.
Hollywood Reporter. Aug 10, 1981, p8.
Horizon. Oct 1981, v24, p70-71.
The Los Angeles Times. Aug 23, 1981,
Calendar, p32.
Maclean's. Sep 21, 1981, v94, p55-56.
Magill's Cinema Annual, 1982. p179-81.
The Nation. Sep 26, 1981, v233, p284-85.
The New Republic. Nov 4, 1981, v185, p22-23.
New York. Aug 31, 1981, v14, p52.
The New York Times. Aug 28, 1981, SecIII, p6.
Newsweek. Sep 7, 1981, v98, p82.
Progressive. Oct 1981, v45, p52-53.
Rolling Stone. Sep 17, 1981, p41.
Senior Scholastic. Nov 13, 1981, v114, p25.
Time. Sep 14, 1981, v118, p90.
Variety. Aug 6, 1981, p3.

Gambit (US; Neame, Ronald; 1966)
BFI/Monthly Film Bulletin. Jan 1967, v34, p10.
Christian Science Monitor (Western edition).
Jan 6, 1967, p4.
Commonweal. Dec 16, 1966, v85, p325.
Film Daily. Nov 17, 1966, p7.
Filmfacts. Jan 15, 1967, v9, p359-60.
Films and Filming. Feb 1967, v13, p30.
The Films of Shirley MacLaine. p141-44.
Hollywood Reporter. Nov 16, 1966, p3.
The London Times. Dec 29, 1966, p6.
Motion Picture Herald Product Digest. Nov 23,
1966, p631.
The New York Times. Dec 22, 1966, p40.
The New Yorker. Jan 7, 1967, v42, p89.
Newsweek. Jan 2, 1967, v69, p63-64.
Playboy. Mar 1967, v14, p23.
Saturday Review. Jan 7, 1967, v50, p110.
Senior Scholastic. Dec 2, 1966, v89, p26.
The Spectator. Dec 30, 1966, v217, p842.
Time. Jan 6, 1967, v89, p96.
Variety. Nov 16, 1966, p6.

The Gambler (GB; Reisz, Karel; 1974)
Audience. Dec 1974, v7, p13-14.
Before My Eyes. p87-89.
BFI/Monthly Film Bulletin. Mar 1975, v42,
p56.
Esquire. Nov 1974, v82, p44.
Film Quarterly. Spr 1975, v28, p49-50.

Films in Review. Nov 1974, v25, p567.
Hollywood Reporter. Sep 24, 1974, p3.
Independent Film Journal. Oct 2, 1974, v74,
p32.
Karel Reisz (Gaston). p105-20.
The Los Angeles Times. Oct 6, 1974, Calendar,
p30.
Motion Picture Herald Product Digest. Oct 2,
1974, p35.
The New Republic. Oct 26, 1974, v171, p20.
The New Republic. Oct 26, 1974, v171, p201.
New York. Oct 7, 1974, v7, p93-96.
The New York Times. Oct 3, 1974, p50.
The New Yorker. Oct 14, 1974, v50, p174-75.
The New Yorker. Oct 14, 1974, v50, p174-75.
Newsweek. Oct 7, 1974, v84, p95-96.
Penthouse. Dec 1974, v6, p61-62.
Reeling. p466-67.
Saturday Review. Sep 21, 1974, v2, p42-43.
Sports Illustrated. Oct 28, 1974, v41, p7.
Time. Oct 28, 1974, v104, p55.
Variety. Oct 2, 1974, p24.
The Village Voice. Oct 3, 1974, p81-82.

The Game Is Over (French title: Curée, La;
Also titled: The Kill) (FR, IT; Vadim,
Roger; 1966)
BFI/Monthly Film Bulletin. Aug 1967, v34,
p119-20.
Big Screen, Little Screen. p359-61.
Christian Science Monitor (Western edition).
Mar 6, 1967, p10.
Commonweal. Jan 27, 1967, v85, p462.
Film Daily. Jan 6, 1967, p6.
Film Quarterly. Fall 1967, v21, p60.
Filmfacts. Feb 1, 1967, v10, p8-9.
Films and Filming. Jun 1967, v13, p20.
The Films of Jane Fonda. p127-31.
Hollywood Reporter. Jan 5, 1967, p3.
Life. Feb 3, 1967, v62, p15.
The London Times. Jul 27, 1967, p6.
The London Times. Jul 31, 1967, p5.
Motion Picture Herald Product Digest. Jan 18,
1967, p649-50.
The New York Times. Jan 10, 1967, p34.
The New Yorker. Jan 14, 1967, v42, p105.
Newsweek. Jan 16, 1967, v69, p87.
Playboy. Feb 1967, v14, p20-21.
Saturday Review. Dec 31, 1966, v49, p36.
Time. Jan 13, 1967, v89, p96.
Variety. Jul 27, 1966, p6.
Vogue. Feb 15, 1967, v149, p62.

The Game of Love *See* Blé en Herbe, Le

Gamlet *See* Hamlet

Gandhi (GB, INDIA; Attenborough,
Richard; 1982)
America. Dec 18, 1982, v147, p392.
Christianity Today. Feb 4, 1983, v27, p104.
Christianity Today. Apr 22, 1983, v27, p16-22.
Christianity Today. Apr 8, 1983, v27, p12-18.
Commentary. Mar 1983, v75, p59-72.
Commonweal. Dec 17, 1982, v109, p691-92.
Commonweal. Jan 3, 1983, v110, p341-43.
Commonweal. Jan 14, 1983, v110, p20-21.
Film Comment. Jan-Feb 1983, v19, p26-29, 30-
32.
Hollywood Reporter. Nov 24, 1982, p3.
Humanist. May-Jun 1983, v43, p37-38.
The Los Angeles Times. Dec 8, 1982, SecVI, p1.
Maclean's. Dec 6, 1982, v96, p67.
Magill's Cinema Annual, 1983. p183-88.
Ms. Jan 1983, v11, p71-73.
The Nation. Jan 22, 1983, v236, p91.
National Review. Mar 4, 1983, v35, p269-70.
The New Leader. Jan 24, 1983, v66, p19-20.
The New Republic. Dec 13, 1982, v187, p26-27.
The New Republic. Mar 21, 1983, v188, p9-11.
New York. Sep 20, 1982, v15, p34-35.

New York. Dec 6, 1982, v15, p166-67.
The New York Times. Dec 8, 1982, Sec III, p21.
The New Yorker. Dec 27, 1982, v58, p72-74.
Newsweek. Dec 13, 1982, v100, p60-61.
Newsweek. Apr 25, 1983, v101, p44.
Progressive. Feb 1983, v47, p50-51.
Progressive. Mar 1983, v47, p20.
Rolling Stone. Mar 17, 1983, p35.
Smithsonian. Dec 1982, v13, p28.
Time. Dec 6, 1982, v120, p96.
Variety. Nov 23, 1982, p3.
Vogue. Apr 1983, v173, p328-29.

Garbo Talks (US; Lumet, Sidney; 1984)
Film Journal. Nov 1984, v87, p52-53.
Films in Review. Dec 1984, v35, p623-24.
Hollywood Reporter. Oct 10, 1984, p3.
The Los Angeles Times. Oct 12, 1984, SecVI, p1.
Maclean's. Oct 22, 1984, v97, p78.
The New Republic. Nov 12, 1984, v191, p33-34.
New York. Oct 22, 1984, v17, p138.
The New York Times. Oct 12, 1984, SecIII, p8.
The New York Times. Mar 25, 1984, SecII, p19.
Variety. Oct 10, 1984, p12.
The Village Voice. Oct 23, 1984, p57.

Garçon Sauvage, Le *See* Savage Triangle

Garde a vue (Also titled: Under Suspicion)
(FR; Miller, Claude; 1981)
Hollywood Reporter. Apr 15, 1982, p3.
The Los Angeles Times. Jul 15, 1982, SecVI, p6.
Magill's Cinema Annual, 1983. p189-92.
The Nation. May 15, 1982, v234, p600.
National Review. Jun 11, 1982, v34, p709.
The New Republic. May 1982, v186, p22-23.
New York. Apr 26, 1982, v15, p98-99.
The New York Times. Apr 16, 1982, SecIII, p26.
Newsweek. May 17, 1982, v99, p101.
Variety. Oct 7, 1981, p16.
The Village Voice. Apr 27, 1982, p49.

Garden of Delights (Spanish title: Jardin de
las Delicias, El) (SP; Saura, Carlos; 1971)
America. Feb 27, 1971, v124, p209.
Commonweal. Mar 12, 1971, v94, p15.
Deeper into Movies. p333-34.
Film Quarterly. Sum 1971, v24, p2-19.
Filmfacts. 1971, v14, p352-54.
Life. Mar 19, 1972, v70, p12.
The Nation. Mar 8, 1971, v212, p318.
The New Republic. Apr 3, 1971, v164, p24.
The New York Times. Sep 19, 1970, p32.
The New York Times. Feb 12, 1971, p25.
The New Yorker. Mar 13, 1971, v47, p92.
Newsweek. Mar 1, 1971, v77, p92.
Saturday Review. Feb 27, 1971, v54, p22.
Time. Sep 28, 1970, v96, p74.
Variety. Jul 16, 1970, p15.
The Village Voice. Feb 18, 1971, p55.

Garden of Evil (US; Hathaway, Henry; 1954)
America. Jul 24, 1954, v91, p426.
BFI/Monthly Film Bulletin. Oct 1954, v21, p144.
Catholic World. Jul 1954, v179, p305.
Commonweal. Jul 30, 1954, v60, p413.
Film Daily. Jul 7, 1954, p10.
Films and Filming. Dec 1954, v1, p20.
Films in Review. Aug-Sep 1954, v5, p365-66.
The Films of Gary Cooper. p245-47.
The Films of Susan Hayward. p197-99.
Hollywood Reporter. Jun 30, 1954, p3.
The London Times. Nov 22, 1954, p2.
Motion Picture Herald Product Digest. Jul 3, 1954, p49.

National Parent-Teacher. Sep 1954, v49, p38.
The New Republic. Sep 6, 1954, v131, p20.
The New Statesman and Nation. Nov 27, 1954, v48, p694.
The New York Times. Jul 10, 1954, p17.
The New Yorker. Jul 17, 1954, v30, p57.
Newsweek. Jul 26, 1954, v44, p83.
The Tatler. Dec 1, 1954, v214, p570-71.
Time. Jul 19, 1954, v64, p76.
Variety. Jun 30, 1954, p6.

The Garden of the Finzi-Continis (Italian
title: Giardino del Finzi-Contini, Il)
(IT; De Sica, Vittorio; 1971)
America. Feb 26, 1972, v126, p216.
BFI/Monthly Film Bulletin. Jul 1972, v39, p138.
Commonweal. Mar 3, 1972, v95, p428.
Filmfacts. 1971, v14, p497-500.
Films and Filming. Aug 1972, v18, p47-48.
Films in Review. Feb 1972, v23, p114.
Hollywood Reporter. Oct 12, 1971, p3.
Indelible Shadows: Film and the Holocaust. p95-98, 111-13.
Life. Feb 18, 1972, v72, p18.
Literature and Film Quarterly. Apr 1973, v1, p171-75.
National Review. Apr 28, 1972, v24, p476.
The New Republic. Feb 19, 1972, v166.
The New York Times. Dec 17, 1971, p32.
The New York Times. Jan 2, 1972, SecII, p9.
The New York Times. Aug 27, 1972, p20.
The New Yorker. Dec 18, 1971, v47, p48.
Newsweek. Dec 18, 1971, v79, p48.
Saturday Review. Jan 8, 1972, v55, p19.
Time. Jan 17, 1972, v99, p54.
Variety. Dec 23, 1970, p6.
The Village Voice. Dec 23, 1971, p71.
Vittorio De Sica: A Guide to References and Resources. p152-58.

The Garment Jungle (US; Aldrich, Robert;
Sherman, Vincent; 1957)
BFI/Monthly Film Bulletin. Aug 1957, v24, p102.
Film Daily. Apr 26, 1957, p10.
Film Noir. p112-13.
The Films and Career of Robert Aldrich. p76-79.
Hollywood Reporter. Apr 24, 1957, p3.
Motion Picture Herald Product Digest. Apr 27, 1957, p354.
New York Times. May 16, 1957, p28.
Robert Aldrich: A Guide to References and Resources. p29-30.
Saturday Review. May 18, 1957, v40, p36.
Time. Jun 3, 1957, v69, p92.
Variety. Apr 24, 1957, p6.
The Village Voice. May 15, 1957, p6.

Gas-s-s-s! (US; Corman, Roger; 1971)
Filmfacts. 1971, v14, p318.
The Films of Roger Corman. p66-69, 192-94.
Take One. May-Jun 1970, v11, n11, p32.
Variety. Aug 26, 1970, p16.
The Village Voice. May 13, 1971, v16, n19, p71-72.

Gate of Hell (Japanese title: Jigokumon)
(JAPAN; Kinugasa, Teinosuke; 1953)
America. Jan 15, 1955, v92, p407.
BFI/Monthly Film Bulletin. Jul 1954, v21, p99-100.
Catholic World. Jan 1955, v180, p302.
Classics of the Foreign Film. p210-11.
Commonweal. Dec 31, 1954, v61, p360.
Dictionary of Films. p165.
Film Culture. Mar-Apr 1955, v1, p40-41, 45-47.
Film Daily. Dec 10, 1954, p34.
Films and Filming. Jan 1955, v1, p9.

Films in Review. Aug-Sep 1954, v5, p367-68.
Hollywood Reporter. Dec 20, 1954, p3.
The International Dictionary of Films and Filmmakers. v1, p224-25.
The Japanese Film: Art and Industry. p228.
Kiss Kiss Bang Bang. p333.
Library Journal. Jan 1, 1955, v80, p63.
Life. Nov 15, 1954, v37, p90-91.
Magill's Survey of Cinema. Foreign Language Films. v3, p1193-95.
Motion Picture Herald Product Digest. Dec 4, 1954, p234.
The Nation. Dec 11, 1954, v179, p516.
National Parent-Teacher. Jan 1955, v49, p39.
The New Statesman and Nation. Jun 12, 1954, v47, p756.
The New York Times. Dec 14, 1954, p45.
The New Yorker. Jan 8, 1955, v30, p77.
Newsweek. Dec 13, 1954, v44, p98.
Reporter. Aug 11, 1955, v13, p54.
Saturday Review. Jan 1, 1955, v38, p63.
Saturday Review. Dec 11, 1954, v37, p26.
Sight and Sound. Jul-Sep 1954, v24, p32-33.
The Spectator. Jun 4, 1954, v192, p678.
The Tatler. Jun 16, 1954, v212, p638.
Time. Dec 13, 1954, v64, p100.
Variety. Nov 25, 1953, p24.
The Village Voice. Nov 23, 1955, v1, p6.

Gates of Paris (French title: Porte de Lilas)
(FR; Clair, René; 1958)
America. Feb 14, 1958, v67, p513.
Film Daily. Jan 27, 1958, v113, p6.
Films in Review. Feb 1958, v9, p92.
The Nation. Feb 1, 1958, v186, p108.
The New York Times. Jan 15, 1958, p24.
Newsweek. Feb 3, 1958, v51, p87.
René Clair (McGerr). p200-04.
Saturday Review. Jan 25, 1958, v41, p27.
Time. Feb 3, 1958, v71, p80.
Variety. Oct 23, 1957, p15.

A Gathering of Eagles (US; Mann, Delbert; 1963)
America. Aug 1963, v109, p124.
BFI/Monthly Film Bulletin. Aug 1963, v30, p117-18.
Film Daily. Jun 4, 1963, p7.
Filmfacts. Jul 18, 1963, v6, p135-37.
Films and Filming. Aug 1963, v9, p31.
Films in Review. Aug-Sep 1963, v14, p433.
Hollywood Reporter. Jun 4, 1963, v175, p3.
The New York Times. Jul 11, 1963, v21, p2.
Newsweek. Jul 22, 1963, v62, p86.
Photoplay. Aug 1963, v64, p8.
Saturday Review. Jul 6, 1963, v46, p1963.
Variety. Jun 5, 1963, p6.

Gattopardo, Il *See* The Leopard

Gauloises Bleues, Les (FR; Cournot,
Michel; 1968)
Film Daily. May 21, 1969, p6.
Filmfacts. 1969, v12, p342.
The New York Times. May 13, 1969, p42.
The New Yorker. May 24, 1969, v55, p122.
Variety. May 15, 1968, p7.

The Gauntlet (US; Eastwood, Clint; 1977)
BFI/Monthly Film Bulletin. Feb 1978, v75, p23.
Clint Eastwood (Guérif). p125-28.
Films in Review. Feb 1978, v29, p116.
The Films of Clint Eastwood. p200-03.
The Films of the Seventies. p198-99.
Hollywood Reporter. Dec 21, 1977, p3.
The Los Angeles Times. Dec 21, 1977, SecIV, p15.
Motion Picture Herald Product Digest. Jan 4, 1978, p62.

The New York Times. Dec 22, 1979, SecIII, p11.
The New Yorker. Jan 16, 1978, v53, p86.
Newsweek. Jan 2, 1978, v91, p59.
Variety. Dec 21, 1977, p20.
The Village Voice. Dec 26, 1977, p44.

Generale delle Rovere, Il (Also titled: General Delle Rovere) (IT; Rossellini, Roberto; 1959)
Commonweal. Nov 18, 1960, v73, p201.
Fifty from the Fifties. p119-22.
Filmfacts. Dec 23, 1960, v3, p293-95.
Films in Review. Oct 1959, v10, p453.
The Nation. Dec 10, 1960, v190, p463-64.
The New Republic. Dec 12, 1960, v143, p27.
The New York Times. Nov 22, 1960, p41.
The New Yorker. Nov 26, 1960, v36, p206-07.
Newsweek. Nov 14, 1960, v56, p108.
Reporter. Nov 10, 1960, v23, p42.
Reruns. p136-40.
Roberto Rossellini (Guarner). p78-82.
Saturday Review. Nov 19, 1960, v43, p39.
Time. Nov 21, 1960, v76, p89.
Variety. Sep 9, 1959, p6.

Genevieve (GB; Cornelius, Henry; 1953)
America. Feb 27, 1954, v90, 587.
BFI/Monthly Film Bulletin. Jul 1953, v20, p100-01.
Catholic World. Dec 1953, v178, p226.
Collier's. Apr 30, 1954, v133, p6.
Commonweal. Mar 12, 1954, v59, p577.
Film Daily. Feb 17, 1954, p6.
Films in Review. Dec 1953, v4, p537-38.
Halliwell's Hundred. p100-03.
Hollywood Reporter. Apr 6, 1954, p3.
Kiss Kiss Bang Bang. p335-36.
Life. Mar 8, 1954, v36, p97-98.
The London Times. Jun 1, 1953, p11.
Magill's Survey of Cinema. Series II. v2, p865-67.
Motion Picture Herald Product Digest. Feb 20, 1954, p2190.
National Parent-Teacher. Jan 1954, v48, p39.
The New Statesman and Nation. Jun 6, 1953, v45, p670.
The New York Times. Feb 16, 1954, p30.
The New York Times Magazine. Nov 8, 1953, p58.
The New Yorker. Feb 27, 1954, v30, p105.
Newsweek. Nov 30, 1953, v42, p109.
Saturday Review. Feb 13, 1954, v37, p32.
Sight and Sound. Jul-Sep 1953, v23, p30.
The Tatler. Jul 1, 1953, v209, p31.
Time. Nov 30, 1953, v62, p100.
Variety. Jul 8, 1953, p18.

Genghis Khan (US, WGER, YUGO; Levin, Henry; 1965)
BFI/Monthly Film Bulletin. Aug 1965, v32, p123-24.
Christian Science Monitor (Western edition). Aug 21, 1965, p6.
Film Daily. Apr 15, 1965, p5.
Films and Filming. Aug 1965, v11, p30.
The Films of James Mason. p168-70.
Hollywood Reporter. Apr 15, 1965, p3.
The London Times. Jun 17, 1965, p17.
Motion Picture Herald Product Digest. Apr 28, 1965, p274.
The New York Times. Jun 24, 1965, p28.
Newsweek. Jun 14, 1965, v65, p117.
Time. Jun 25, 1965, v85, p105.
Variety. Apr 21, 1965, p6.

Genou de Claire, Le *See* Claire's Knee

The Gentle Art of Seduction *See* Male Hunt

A Gentle Creature *See* Femme douce, Une

The Gentle Gunman (GB; Dearden, Basil; 1952)
BFI/Monthly Film Bulletin. Nov 1952, v19, p153.
Film Daily. Oct 16, 1953, p6.
The Films of Dirk Bogarde. p63-64.
Motion Picture Herald Product Digest. Oct 3, 1953, p2014.
National Parent-Teacher. Sep 1953, v48, p39.
The New York Times. Oct 1, 1953, p34.
The Spectator. Oct 24, 1952, v189, p533.
The Tatler. Nov 5, 1952, v206, p320.
Variety. Oct 29, 1952, p24.

Gentlemen Prefer Blondes (US; Hawks, Howard; 1953)
America. Aug 1, 1953, v89, p446.
BFI/Monthly Film Bulletin. Sep 1953, v20, p131.
Catholic World. Aug 1953, v177, p384.
Commonweal. Aug 7, 1953, v58, p442.
Film Daily. Jun 26, 1953, p6.
The Films in My Life. p71-72.
Films in Review. Aug-Sep 1953, v4, p365.
The Films of Howard Hawks. p148-49.
The Films of Marilyn Monroe. p98-104.
Hawks on Hawks. p129-30.
Hollywood Reporter. Jun 26, 1953, p3.
Howard Hawks, Storyteller. p67.
Howards Hawks (Poague). p134-38.
Library Journal. Aug 1953, v78, p1321.
Life. May 25, 1953, v34, p79-80.
Magill's Survey of Cinema. Series I. v2, p613-16.
Movie. Oct 1962, n3, p36.
The Musical: From Broadway to Hollywood. p38-42.
National Parent-Teacher. Sep 1953, v48, p39.
The New York Times. Jul 12, 1953, v2, p5.
The New Yorker. Jul 25, 1953, v29, p46.
Newsweek. Jul 27, 1953, v42, p76-77.
Saturday Review. Aug 1, 1953, v36, p27.
Time. Jul 27, 1953, v62, p88.
Variety. Jul 1, 1953, p6.

George Stevens: A Filmmaker's Journey (US; Stevens, George Jr.; 1985)
Christian Century. Jul 17, 1985, v102, p684-85.
Commonweal. May 31, 1985, v112, p343.
Film Comment. Jul-Aug 1985, v21, p66-69.
Films in Review. Aug-Sep 1985, v36, p420-21.
Hollywood Reporter. Apr 12, 1985, p3.
The Los Angeles Times. Apr 11, 1985, SecVI, p1.
The New York Times. May 3, 1985, SecIII, p8.
Time. May 6, 1985, v125, p86.
The Village Voice. Apr 30, 1985, p30.

Georgy Girl (GB; Narizzano, Silvio; 1966)
America. Nov 12, 1966, v115, p629.
BFI/Monthly Film Bulletin. Dec 1966, v33, p185-86.
Big Screen, Little Screen. p334-35.
Catholic World. Feb 1967, v204, p301-06.
Christian Century. Dec 28, 1966, v83, p1604-05.
Christian Science Monitor (Western edition). Nov 21, 1966, p12.
Commonweal. Oct 28, 1966, v85, p104.
Film Daily. Oct 7, 1966, p6.
Filmfacts. Nov 15, 1966, v9, p245-47.
Films and Filming. Nov 1966, v13, p16, 18.
Films in Review. Dec 1966, v17, p664-65.
The Films of James Mason. p175-77.
Hollywood Reporter. Oct 10, 1966, p3.
Kiss Kiss Bang Bang. p27-29.
Life. Oct 28, 1966, v61, p10.
The London Times. Oct 15, 1966, p6.
Magill's Survey of Cinema. Series II. v2, p874-76.

Motion Picture Herald Product Digest. Oct 26, 1966, p623.
Movie Comedy (Byron). p198-201.
The Nation. Nov 7, 1966, v203, p494.
The New Republic. Nov 5, 1966, v155, p42-45.
New Statesman. Oct 14, 1966, v72, p565.
The New York Times. Oct 18, 1966, p48.
The New Yorker. Oct 29, 1966, v42, p150.
Newsweek. Oct 31, 1966, v68, p108.
Playboy. Nov 1966, v13, p34.
The Primal Screen. p186-88.
Private Screenings. p289-90.
The Spectator. Oct 21, 1966, v217, p519.
Take One. 1968, v1, n9, p6-7.
Variety. Jul 13, 1966, p6.
The Village Voice. Dec 1, 1966, v12, p27, 29.
Vogue. Oct 15, 1966, v148, p79.

Gertrud (DEN; Dreyer, Carl-Theodor; 1964)
Afterimage. Spr 1974, n5, p57-64.
Cahiers du Cinema in English. 1966, n4, p7-17.
The Cinema of Carl Dreyer. p167-78.
Commonweal. Jun 24, 1966, v84, p392-93.
Confessions of a Cultist. p251-52.
Dictionary of Films. p126.
Esquire. Dec 1965, v64, p86, 88.
Film. Wint 1965-66, n44, p18.
Film Comment. Fall 1966, v4, p70-76.
Film Culture. Sum 1966, n41, p58-60.
Film Quarterly. Spr 1966, v19, p36-40.
Film Society Review. Mar 1967, p19-21.
Filmfacts. Sep 1, 1966, v9, p179-80.
Films and Filming. Jan 1969, v15, p42.
Films in Review. Oct 1965, v16, p516-17.
The Films of Carl-Theodor Dreyer. p171-90, 226-27.
Great Film Directors. p227-29.
Guardian. Mar 25, 1965, p8.
The International Dictionary of Films and Filmmakers. v1, 169-70.
The London Times. Sep 26, 1968, p15.
Magill's Survey of Cinema. Foreign Language Films. v3, p1216-19.
New York Review of Books. Nov 11, 1965, v5, p30-31.
The New York Times. Jun 3, 1966, p33.
Newsweek. Jun 13, 1966, v67, p115-16.
Sight and Sound. Spr 1965, v34, p56-58.
Sight and Sound. Wint 1985-86, v55, p40-45.
Time. Jun 24, 1966, v87, p104.
The Village Voice. Jun 2, 1966, v11, p19.

Gervaise (FR; Clément, René; 1957)
BFI/Monthly Film Bulletin. Jan 1957, v24, p2.
Commonweal. Nov 22, 1957, v67, p202-04, 210.
Film Culture. Dec 1957, v3, p14-15.
Film Daily. Nov 13, 1957, p8.
Films and Filming. Feb 1957, v3, p22.
Films in Review. Dec 1957, v8, p525.
The Great French Films. p159-62.
The Nation. Nov 23, 1957, p396.
The New York Times. Nov 12, 1957, p46.
The New York Times. Nov 17, 1957, SecII, p1.
The New York Times. Jan 19, 1958, SecII, p1.
The New Yorker. Nov 23, 1957, v33, p83.
Newsweek. Nov 11, 1957, v50, p120.
Saturday Review. Nov 16, 1957, v40, p30.
Sight and Sound. Wint 1956-57, v26, p148-50.
Variety. Sep 19, 1956, p6.

Get Carter (US; Hodges, Mike; 1971)
BFI/Monthly Film Bulletin. Apr 1971, v38, p73.
Filmfacts. 1971, v14, n1, p10-13.
Films and Filming. May 1971, v17, n8, p88-89.
Hollywood Reporter. Jan 14, 1971, p3.
The New Republic. Apr 3, 1971, v164, p24.
The New York Times. Mar 4, 1971, p40.

The New York Times. Mar 14, 1971, SecII, p11.
Saturday Review. Feb 13, 1971, v54, p42.
Sight and Sound. Spr 1971, v40, p107-08.
Time. Mar 22, 1971, v97, p77.
Variety. Jan 20, 1971, p13.
The Village Voice. Mar 18, 1971, p68.

Get Off My Back *See* Synanon

Get Out Your Handkerchiefs (French title: Preparez vos mouchers) (FR, BELG; Blier, Bertrand; 1978)
BFI/Monthly Film Bulletin. Apr 1980, v47, p74.
Films in Review. Feb 1979, v30, p122.
The Great French Films. p274-75.
The Los Angeles Times. Jan 24, 1979, SecIV, p1.
Magill's Survey of Cinema. Foreign Language Films. v3, p1225-27.
The Nation. Jan 6, 1979, v228, p27-28.
The New Republic. Jan 13, 1978, v180, p26-27.
New York. Oct 16, 1978, v11, p120.
New York. Jan 22, 1979, v12, p66-67.
The New York Times. Dec 18, 1978, SecIII, p15.
The New Yorker. Oct 16, 1978, v54, p96.
Newsweek. Jan 15, 1979, v93, p78-79.
Time. Jan 15, 1979, v113, p71.
Variety. Jan 1, 1978, p27.

The Getaway (US; Peckinpah, Sam; 1972)
Audience. Jan 1983, v5, p6.
Audience. Feb 1973, v5, p3-4.
Commentary. Mar 1973, v55, p77-78.
Commonweal. Feb 16, 1973, v97, p448.
Filmfacts. 1972, v15, n24, p627.
Filmmakers Newsletter. Mar 1973, v6, p31-33.
Films In Review. Feb 1973, v24, p120-21.
The Films of Sam Peckinpah. p65-70.
The Films of Steve McQueen. p190-99.
Hollywood Reporter. Dec 13, 1972, p3.
Life. Aug 11, 1972, v73, p47-50.
The New Republic. Feb 10, 1973, v168, p35.
The New York Times. Dec 20, 1972, p53.
The New York Times. Sep 30, 1973, SecII, p4.
The New Yorker. Dec 23, 1972, v48, p55.
Peckinpah (Simmons). p154-69.
Sam Peckinpah (McKinney). p145-56.
Sight and Sound. Spr 1973, v42, p69-74.
Time. Jan 8, 1973, v101, p53-54.
Variety. Dec 13, 1972, p15.

The Getting of Wisdom (AUSTRALIA; Beresford, Bruce; 1977)
BFI/Monthly Film Bulletin. May 1979, v46, p95.
Films in Review. Oct 1980, v31, p501.
Hollywood Reporter. Sep 28, 1978, p14.
Hollywood Reporter. Nov 29, 1978, p30.
The Los Angeles Times. Aug 24, 1980, Calendar, p34.
The Nation. Aug 30, 1980, v231-197.
The New Australian Cinema. p42-43.
The New Yorker. Sep 15, 1980, v56, p156-58.
Newsday. Aug 29, 1980, SecII, p7.
Time. Sep 8, 1980, v116, p74.
Variety. Aug 31, 1977, p19.
The Village Voice. Aug 6, 1980, p42.

Ghetto Terezin *See* Distant Journey

The Ghost and Mr. Chicken (US; Rafkin, Alan; 1966)
BFI/Monthly Film Bulletin. Jun 1966, v33, p93-94.
Film Daily. Jan 18, 1966, p7.
Filmfacts. Nov 15, 1966, v9, p259-60.
Hollywood Reporter. Jan 11, 1966, p3.
Motion Picture Herald Product Digest. Jan 26, 1966, p458.

The New York Times. Sep 22, 1966, p57.
Variety. Jan 12, 1966, p6.

Ghostbusters (US; Reitman, Ivan; 1984)
American Cinematographer. Jun 1984, v65, p62-66.
American Film. Jun 1984, v9, p78.
BFI/Monthly Film Bulletin. Dec 1984, v51, p379.
Cinefex. Jun 1984, n17, p4-53.
Film Comment. May-Jun 1984, v20, p4-5.
Film Comment. Jul-Aug 1984, v20, p52-54.
Film Journal. Jul 1984, v87, p21.
Informer. May-Jun 1984, p3.
The Los Angeles Times. Jun 8, 1984, SecVI, p1.
Maclean's. Jun 18, 1984, v97, p50.
Magill's Cinema Annual, 1985. 219-23.
Midnight Marquee. Fall 1984, n33, p29.
Millimeter. Sep 1984, v12, p142-44.
The Nation. Jul 21, 1984, v239, p59-61.
The New Republic. Aug 13, 1984, v191, p22-23.
New Statesman. Dec 7, 1984, v108, p35-36.
New York. Jun 11, 1984, v17, p66-67.
The New York Times. Jun 8, 1984, SecIII, p5.
The New York Times. Sep 29, 1984, p31.
The New Yorker. Jun 25, 1984, v60, p104-05.
Newsweek. Jun 11, 1984, v103, p80.
On Location. May 1984, v8, p42.
Photoplay. Dec 1984, v35, p47-49.
Time. Jun 11, 1984, v123, p83.
Variety. Jun 6, 1984, p20.
The Village Voice. Jun 12, 1984, p52.

Giant (US; Stevens, George; 1956)
Commonweal. Oct 26, 1956, v65, p102-03.
Film Culture. 1956, v2, p23-24.
Film Daily. Oct 10, 1956, p7.
Films and Filming. Feb 1957, v3, p21.
Films and Filming. Aug 1962, v8, p35.
Films in Review. Nov 1956, v7, p466-67.
Films in Review. May 1983, v34, p302.
The Films of Elizabeth Taylor. p120-24.
The Films of the Fifties. p193-95.
Hollywood Reporter. Oct 10, 1956, p3.
James Dean: A Biography. p125-52.
Magill's Survey of Cinema. Series I. v2, p616-19.
Movie. Nov 1962, n4, p32-33.
The Nation. Oct 20, 1956, v183, p334.
The New York Times. Oct 11, 1956, p51.
The New York Times. Oct 21, 1956, SecII, p1.
The New Yorker. Oct 20, 1956, v32, p178.
Newsweek. Oct 22, 1956, v48, p112.
Reruns. p97-101.
Saturday Review. Oct 13, 1956, v39, p28-29.
Sight and Sound. Wint 1956-57, v26, p148.
Time. Oct 22, 1956, v68, p108.
Variety. Oct 10, 1956, p6.

Giardino del Finzi-Contini, Il *See* The Garden of the Finzi-Continis

Gidget Goes to Rome (US; Wendkos, Paul; 1963)
BFI/Monthly Film Bulletin. Dec 1963, v30, p172.
Film Daily. Jul 30, 1963, p3.
Filmfacts. Aug 22, 1963, v6, p165-67.
Films and Filming. Jan 1964, v10, p31.
Hollywood Reporter. Jul 31, 1963, v176, p3.
The New York Times. Sep 12, 1963, p32.
Time. Aug 16, 1963, v82, p74.
Variety. Jul 31, 1963, p6.

Gifle, La *See* The Slap

Gigi (US; Minnelli, Vincente; 1958)
America. May 31, 1958, v99, p298-99.
The Best of MGM. p71-72.
BFI/Monthly Film Bulletin. Feb 1959, v26, p28.
Catholic World. Jun 1958, v187, p223.

Chevalier: The Films and Career of Maurice Chevalier. p175-81.
Commonweal. May 16, 1958, v118, p183.
Cosmopolitan. May 1958, v144, p76-79.
Dance Magazine. May 1958, v32, p22.
Film Daily. May 15, 1958, v113, p6.
Filmfacts. Jun 4, 1958, v1, p73-74.
Films in Review. May 1958, v9, p266-67.
Hollywood Reporter. May 15, 1958, p3.
I Remember it Well. p317-35.
Library Journal. May 1, 1958, v83, p1389.
Life. Apr 28, 1958, v44, p105-10.
Magill's Survey of Cinema. Series I. v2, p621-26.
The Nation. Jun 14, 1958, v184, p551.
The New Republic. Jun 9, 1958, v138, p22.
The New York Times. May 16, 1958, p21.
The New Yorker. May 24, 1958, v34, p73.
Newsweek. May 26, 1958, v51, p98.
Saturday Review. May 17, 1958, v40, p28.
Selected Film Criticism 1951-60. p48-49.
Time. May 19, 1958, v71, p98.
Variety. May 21, 1958, p6.
Vincente Minnelli and the Film Musical. p60-64, 142-45.
Vintage Films. p170-75.

Giornata Particolare, Una *See* A Special Day

A Girl and Guns *See* To Be a Crook

Girl Friends *See* Girlfriends

The Girl from Petrovka (US; Miller, Robert Ellis; 1974)
Films in Review. Oct 1974, v25, p504.
Hollywood Reporter. Aug 9, 1974, p3.
Independent Film Journal. Aug 21, 1974, v74, p10.
The Los Angeles Times. Aug 16, 1974, SecIV, P18.
Motion Picture Herald Product Digest. Aug 14, 1974, p24.
The New Republic. Sep 14, 1974, v171, p34.
New York. Sep 9, 1974, v7, p62-63.
The New York Times. Aug 23, 1974, p16.
Newsweek. Sep 16, 1974, v84, p79.
PTA Magazine. Nov 1974, v69, p8.
Time. Sep 16, 1974, v104, p9.
Variety. Aug 14, 1974, p16.

Girl Happy (US; Sagal, Boris; 1965)
BFI/Monthly Film Bulletin. Apr 1965, v32, p56.
Elvis: The Films and Career of Elvis Presley. p161-62.
Film Daily. Jan 22, 1965, p3.
Films and Filming. May 1965, v11, p31.
Hollywood Reporter. Jan 21, 1965, p3.
The London Times. Mar 25, 1965, p16.
Motion Picture Herald Product Digest. Feb 3, 1965, p217.
The New York Times. May 27, 1965, p28.
Saturday Review. May 29, 1965, v48, p30.

Girl in Black (Also titled: To Koritsi Me Ta Maura; Fille en Noir, La) (GREECE; Cacoyannis, Michael; 1957)
BFI/Monthly Film Bulletin. Jan 1957, v24, p3.
Commonweal. Oct 11, 1957, v67, p49.
Film. Mar-Apr 1960, n24, p16-19.
Films and Filming. Jan 1957, v3, p23-24.
Films in Review. Oct 1957, v8, p406-07.
The New York Times. Sep 17, 1957, p39.
The New York Times Magazine. Jul 21, 1957, p27.
The New Yorker. Sep 28, 1957, v33, p91.
Newsweek. Jan 28, 1957, v49, p94.
Saturday Review. Oct 5, 1957, v40, p23.
Sight and Sound. Wint 1956-57, v26, p154.

Time. Oct 7, 1957, v70, p98.
Variety. May 16, 1956, p6.

A Girl In Every Port (US; Erskine, Chester; 1952)
BFI/Monthly Film Bulletin. Dec 1952, v19, p171.
Film Daily. Jan 8, 1952, p10.
Hollywood Reporter. Dec 20, 1951, p3.
Motion Picture Herald Product Digest. Feb 16, 1952, p1237.
The New York Times. Feb 14, 1952, p23.
Time. Feb 25, 1952, v59, p71.
Variety. Dec 26, 1951, p6.

The Girl In White (Also titled: So Bright the Flame) (US; Sturges, John; 1952)
BFI/Monthly Film Bulletin. Jul 1952, v19, p96.
Catholic World. Jun 1952, v175, p223.
Christian Century. Aug 27, 1952, v69, p983.
Commonweal. Aug 8, 1952, v56, p435.
Film Daily. Mar 18, 1952, p6.
Hollywood Reporter. Mar 13, 1952, p3.
Library Journal. May 15, 1952, v77, p873.
Motion Picture Herald Product Digest. Mar 22, 1952, p1289.
The New York Times. May 31, 1952, p12.
The New Yorker. May 31, 1952, v28, p81.
Newsweek. May 19, 1952, v39, p110.
Saturday Review. May 3, 1952, v35, p31.
The Spectator. Jun 6, 1952, v188, p743.
Theatre Arts. Jun 1952, v36, p96.
Time. Jun 16, 1952, v59, p96.
Variety. May 21, 1952, p6.

A Girl Named Tamiko (US; Sturges, John; 1962)
BFI/Monthly Film Bulletin. Apr 1963, v30, p48.
Film Daily. Dec 4, 1962, p7.
Filmfacts. Mar 14, 1963, v6, p28-29.
Films and Filming. May 1963, v9, p25-26.
The New York Times. Mar 15, 1963, p8.
Newsweek. Apr 1, 1963, v61, p81.
Photoplay. Mar 1963, v63, p8.
Time. Mar 22, 1963, v81, pE10.
Variety. Dec 5, 1962, p6.

The Girl On a Motorcycle (French title: Motorcyclette, La; Also titled: Naked Under Leather) (GB, FR; Cardiff, Jack; 1968)
America. Oct 14, 1968, v119, p632.
BFI/Monthly Film Bulletin. Oct 1968, v35, p156.
Cinema. Dec 1968, v4, p35.
Commonweal. Dec 6, 1968, v89, p352.
Film Daily. Dec 4, 1968, p8.
Filmfacts. Jan 15, 1969, v11, p467-68.
Films and Filming. Oct 1968, v15, p36-37.
The London Times. Sep 12, 1968, p11.
Motion Picture Herald Product Digest. Nov 20, 1968, p64.
The New York Times. Nov 28, 1968, p66.
Variety. Jul 24, 1968, p20.

Girl with Green Eyes (GB; Davis, Desmond; 1963)
America. Sep 12, 1964, v111, p267.
BFI/Monthly Film Bulletin. Jun 1964, v31, p89.
Commonweal. Sep 4, 1964, v80, p610.
Film Daily. Jul 29, 1964, p5.
Films and Filming. Jun 1964, v10, p20.
Films in Review. Aug-Sep 1964, v15, p436.
Hollywood Reporter. Oct 8, 1964, p3.
Life. Aug 28, 1964, v57, p15.
Motion Picture Herald Product Digest. Aug 5, 1964, p97-98.
The New York Times. Aug 11, 1964, p37.
The New Yorker. Aug 22, 1964, v40, p87-88.
Newsweek. Aug 24, 1964, v64, p79.

Saturday Review. Aug 8, 1964, v47, p24.
Sight and Sound. Sum 1964, v33, p146-47.
Time. Aug 21, 1964, v84, p85.
Variety. May 20, 1964, p6.
Vogue. Dec 1964, v144, p150.

The Girlfriends *See* Biches, Les

Girlfriends (Also titled: Girl Friends) (US; Weill, Claudia; 1978)
BFI/Monthly Film Bulletin. Sep 1978, v45, p175.
Films in Review. Oct 1978, v29, p503.
Hollywood Reporter. May 11, 1978, p4.
Human Behavior. Oct 1978, v7, p77.
The Los Angeles Times. Aug 20, 1978, Calendar, p1.
Magill's Survey of Cinema. Series II. v2, p802-04.
Motion Picture Herald Product Digest. Jul 26, 1978, p5.
Ms. Aug 1978, v7, p34.
The Nation. Aug 19, 1978, v227, p156-57.
The New Republic. Aug 5, 1978, v179, p20-22.
New York. Aug 21, 1978, v11, p65-66.
The New Yorker. Aug 21, 1978, v54, p71-72.
Newsweek. Aug 28, 1978, v92, p79-80.
Saturday Review. Sep 2, 1978, v5, p28.
Time. Aug 28, 1978, v112, p57.
Variety. May 10, 1978, p23.

The Girl-Getters (Also titled: The System) (GB; Winner, Michael; 1964)
Commonweal. May 13, 1966, v84, p225.
Filmfacts. Jun 1, 1966, v9, p95-96.
Films and Filming. Oct 1964, v11, p31-32.
The Films of Michael Winner. p26-31.
Motion Picture Herald Product Digest. Jun 15, 1966, p544.
The New York Times. Apr 13, 1966, p37.
Newsweek. Apr 25, 1966, v67, p90.
Private Screenings. p253-56.
Time. Apr 29, 1966, v87, p110.
Variety. Aug 12, 1964, p6.

Girls, Les (US; Cukor, George; 1957)
America. Oct 19, 1957, v98, p92.
The Best of MGM. p118.
BFI/Monthly Film Bulletin. Dec 1957, v24, p147.
Commonweal. Oct 18, 1957, v67, p74.
Dance Magazine. Nov 1957, v31, p11.
Film Daily. Oct 2, 1957, v107, p6.
Films and Filming. Dec 1957, v4, p25.
Films in Review. Nov 1957, v8, p461.
The Films of Gene Kelly. p173-83.
George Cukor (Phillips). 155-59.
Hollywood Reporter. Oct 2, 1957, p3.
Magill's Survey of Cinema. Series II. v2, p885-88.
Motion Picture Herald Product Digest. Oct 5, 1957, v209, p553.
The New Republic. Dec 23, 1957, v137, p21.
The New York Times. Oct 4, 1957, p27.
The New York Times. Oct 14, 1957, SecII, p1.
The New Yorker. Oct 12, 1957, v33, p108.
Newsweek. Oct 14, 1957, v50, p112.
Saturday Review. Oct 19, 1957, v40, p54.
Sight and Sound. Wint 1957-58, v27, p147-48.
Time. Oct 14, 1957, v70, p112.
Variety. Oct 2, 1957, p6.

Gishiki *See* The Ceremony

Giuliette degli Spiriti *See* Juliet of the Spirits

Give Us This Day (Also titled: Christ in Concrete; Salt to the Devil) (GB; Dmytryk, Edward; 1949)
Cinema, the Magic Vehicle. v1, p511-12.

Film Criticism and Caricatures, 1943-1953. p102-04.
Film Daily. Dec 15, 1949, p6.
Hollywood Reporter. Jun 19, 1950, p3.
The Humanist. Jan-Feb 1979, v39, p60-61.
Illustrated London News. Nov 12, 1949, v215, p750.
Motion Picture Herald Product Digest. Dec 17, 1949, p122.
The New York Times. Dec 21, 1949, p41.
Shots in the Dark. p111-17.
Sight and Sound. Dec 1949, v18, p19-21.
The Spectator. Oct 28, 1949, v183, p566.
Variety. Oct 19, 1949, p8.

The Glass Bottom Boat (US; Tashlin, Frank; 1966)
BFI/Monthly Film Bulletin. Jul 1966, v33, p108-09.
Commonweal. Jul 8, 1966, v84, p441.
Film Daily. Apr 21, 1966, p5.
Film Quarterly. Fall 1966, v20, p59.
Filmfacts. Aug 15, 1966, v9, p158-60.
Films and Filming. Aug 1966, v12, p58-59.
The Films of Doris Day. p229-34.
The Great Spy Pictures. p196-97.
Hollywood Reporter. Apr 20, 1966, p3.
The London Times. Jun 23, 1966, p7.
Motion Picture Herald Product Digest. Apr 27, 1966, p509.
New Statesman. Jun 24, 1966, v71, p939-40.
The New York Times. Jun 10, 1966, p54.
Saturday Review. Jun 25, 1966, v49, p40.
Variety. Apr 20, 1966, p6.

The Glass Menagerie (US; Rapper, Irving; 1950)
Christian Century. Nov 22, 1950, v67, p1407.
Christian Science Monitor Magazine. Apr 15, 1950, p8.
Commonweal. Oct 6, 1950, v52, p631-32.
Film Daily. Sep 19, 1950, p6.
Films in Review. Oct 1950, v1, p25-26.
The Films of Kirk Douglas. p67-70.
The Films of Tennessee Williams. p33-64.
Hollywood Quarterly. Fall 1950, v5, p14-32.
Hollywood Reporter. Sep 19, 1950, p3.
Library Journal. Oct 15, 1950, v75, p1843.
Motion Picture Herald Product Digest. Sep 23, 1950, p493.
The New Republic. Oct 23, 1950, v123, p22.
The New Statesman and Nation. Nov 4, 1950, v40, p411.
The New York Times. Sep 29, 1950, p31.
The New York Times Magazine. Jun 4, 1950, p58-59.
The New Yorker. Sep 30, 1950, v26, p56.
Newsweek. Oct 9, 1950, v36, p90.
Saturday Review. Oct 14, 1950, v33, p32.
Senior Scholastic. Oct 18, 1950, v57, p28.
The Spectator. Nov 3, 1950, v185, p446.
Tennessee Williams and Film. p9-14.
Time. Oct 2, 1950, v56, p74.
Variety. Sep 20, 1950, p6.

Glass Slipper (US; Walters, Charles; 1955)
America. Apr 2, 1955, v93, p26.
BFI/Monthly Film Bulletin. Sep 1955, v22, p136.
Catholic World. Apr 1955, v181, p62.
Commonweal. Apr 15, 1955, v62, p49.
Films and Filming. Dec 1955, v2, n3, p17-18.
Films in Review. Mar 1955, v6, n3, p132-33.
Library Journal. Mar 15, 1955, v80, p642.
Motion Picture Herald Product Digest. Feb 19, 1955, p329.
The New York Times. Mar 25, 1955, p19.
The New York Times. Apr 3, 1955, SecII, p1.
The New Yorker. Apr 2, 1955, v31, p117.
Newsweek. Apr 11, 1955, v45, p113.

Saturday Review. Apr 16, 1955, v38, p27.
Time. Mar 28, 1955, v65, p98.
Variety. Feb 16, 1955, p6.

The Glenn Miller Story (US; Mann, Anthony; 1954)
America. Feb 13, 1954, v90, p518.
BFI/Monthly Film Bulletin. Feb 1954, v21, p25.
Catholic World. Feb 1954, v178, p382.
Commonweal. Feb 5, 1954, v59, p449.
Coronet. Mar 1954, v35, p6.
Film Daily. Jan 6, 1954, p6.
Films and Filming. May 1985, v30, p37.
Films in Review. Jan 1954, v5, p36.
Films in Review. Oct 1954, v5, p437-38.
The Films of James Stewart. p162-65.
Hollywood Reporter. Jan 6, 1954, p3.
Life. Mar 1, 1954, v36, p74.
The London Times. Feb 1, 1954, p10.
Look. Jan 26, 1954, v18, p84-86.
Motion Picture Herald Product Digest. Jan 9, 1954, p2133.
The Nation. May 4, 1985, v240, p520.
National Parent-Teacher. Mar 1954, v48, p38.
The New York Times. Feb 11, 1954, p33.
The New York Times. Nov 17, 1984, p11.
The New Yorker. Feb 20, 1954, v30, p103.
Newsweek. Feb 1, 1954, v43, p76.
Saturday Review. Feb 27, 1954, v37, p29.
Senior Scholastic. Mar 17, 1954, v64, p37.
The Tatler. Feb 10, 1954, v211, p226.
Time. Mar 1, 1954, v63, p90.
Variety. Mar 6, 1954, p52.

Gloria (US; Cassavetes, John; 1980)
American Dreaming. p273-81.
BFI/Monthly Film Bulletin. Mar 1981, v48, p48.
Christian Century. Dec 24, 1980, v97, p1277.
Christian Science Monitor. Sep 11, 1980, p18.
Films in Review. Nov 1980, v31, p475.
Hollywood Reporter. Sep 16, 1980, p3.
The Los Angeles Times. Oct 19, 1980, Calendar, p37.
Motion Picture Herald Product Digest. Oct 22, 1980, p28.
New York. Oct 13, 1980, v13, p62-63.
The New York Times. Oct 1, 1980, SecIII, p29.
Newsweek. Oct 6, 1980, v96, p72.
Saturday Review. Oct 6, 1980, v7, p93.
Time. Oct 6, 1980, v116, p92.
Variety. Sep 10, 1980, p30.

Glory Alley (US; Walsh, Raoul; 1952)
BFI/Monthly Film Bulletin. Dec 1952, v19, p171-72.
Commonweal. Jul 4, 1952, v56, p316.
Film Daily. May 21, 1952, p6.
Hollywood Reporter. May 16, 1952, p3.
Motion Picture Herald Product Digest. May 24, 1952, p1373.
The Nation. Aug 16, 1952, v175, p138-39.
The New York Times. Jul 30, 1952, p20.
Newsweek. Jun 16, 1952, v39, p110-11.
Time. Jun 9, 1952, v59, p106.
Variety. May 21, 1952, p6.

The Glory Guys (US; Laven, Arnold; 1965)
BFI/Monthly Film Bulletin. Feb 1966, v33, p15-16.
Film Daily. Jul 14, 1965, p7.
Film Quarterly. Fall 1965, v19, p61.
Films and Filming. Dec 1965, v12, p39.
Films and Filming. Mar 1966, v12, p53.
Hollywood Reporter. Jul 9, 1965, p3.
Motion Picture Herald Product Digest. Jul 21, 1965, p330.
Variety. Jul 14, 1965, p6.

Go For Broke! (US; Pirosh, Robert; 1951)
BFI/Monthly Film Bulletin. Jul 1951, v18, p292.
Christian Century. Jun 27, 1951, v68, p777.
Commonweal. Jun 8, 1951, v54, p214.
Film Daily. Mar 26, 1951, p6.
Hollywood Reporter. Mar 26, 1951, p3.
Magill's Survey of Cinema. Series II. v2, p889-91.
Motion Picture Herald Product Digest. Mar 31, 1951, p785.
The New Republic. Jun 4, 1951, v124, p23.
The New York Times. May 25, 1951, p31.
The New Yorker. Jun 2, 1951, v27, p83.
Newsweek. May 28, 1951, v37, p89.
Saturday Review. May 26, 1951, v34, p30.
Senior Scholastic. Apr 27, 1951, v58, p30.
Time. May 28, 1951, v57, p106.
Variety. Mar 28, 1951, p6.

Go Go Mania (Also titled: Pop Gear) (GB; Goode, Frederic; 1965)
BFI/Monthly Film Bulletin. Apr 1965, v32, p58.
Film Daily. May 27, 1965, p7.
Filmfacts. Jun 25, 1965, v8, p120-21.
Films and Filming. Oct 1965, v12, p30-31.
Motion Picture Herald Product Digest. Jun 9, 1965, p308.
The New York Times. May 20, 1965, p52.
Variety. May 26, 1965, p15.

Go, Man, Go! (US; Howe, James Wong; 1954)
America. Mar 20, 1954, v90, p666.
BFI/Monthly Film Bulletin. Jun 1954, v21, p88.
Film Daily. Jan 20, 1954, p10.
The Films of the Fifties. p112-14.
Hollywood Reporter. Jan 14, 1954, p3.
Motion Picture Herald Product Digest. Jan 23, 1954, p2157.
National Parent-Teacher. Feb 1954, v48, p38.
The New York Times. Mar 10, 1954, p29.
Newsweek. Jan 25, 1954, v43, p90.
The Spectator. May 14, 1954, v192, p578.
Time. Feb 8, 1954, v63, p96.
Variety. Jan 20, 1954, p18.

Go Tell the Spartans (US; Post, Ted; 1978)
BFI/Monthly Film Bulletin. Jul 1978, v45, p135.
Hollywood Reporter. Jun 15, 1978, p2.
The Humanist. Nov 1978, v38, p62.
The Los Angeles Times. Sep 6, 1978, SecIV, p1.
Magill's Survey of Cinema. Series II. v2, p892-95.
Motion Picture Herald Product Digest. Jun 28, 1978, p8.
The New Leader. Nov 6, 1978, v61, p19.
The New Republic. Jun 24, 1978, v178, p22-23.
Newsweek. Oct 2, 1978, v92, p85.
Saturday Review. Jul 22, 1978, v5, p38.
Time. Sep 25, 1978, v112, p92.
Variety. Jun 14, 1978, p20.

The Goalie's Anxiety at the Penalty Kick
See The Anxiety of the Goalie at the Penalty Kick

The Go-Between (GB; Losey, Joseph; 1971)
BFI/Monthly Film Bulletin. Oct 1971, v38, p195, 230.
Commonweal. Sep 17, 1971, v94, p480-81.
Fifty Classic British Films. p138-41.
Film Quarterly. Sep 1972, v25, p37-41.
Filmfacts. 1971, v14, p301-04.
Films and Filming. Oct 1971, v18, n1, p53-54.
The Great British Films. p251.
Hollywood Reporter. Jul 8, 1971, v216, n50, p3.
Joseph Losey (Hirsch). p129-41.
Life. Oct 1, 1971, v71, p10.

Magill's Survey of Cinema. Series I. v2, p633.
Making Pictures: The Pinter Screenplays. p77-102.
The Nation. Oct 4, 1971, v213, p316-17.
National Review. Dec 3, 1971, v23, p1368.
The New Republic. Sep 11, 1971, v165, p26.
The New York Times. Jul 30, 1971, p21.
The New Yorker. Jul 31, 1971, v47, p76.
Newsweek. Aug 16, 1971, v78, p76.
Saturday Review. Aug 14, 1971, v54, p42.
Sight and Sound. Aut 1970, v39, p202-03.
Sight and Sound. Sum 1971, v40, p158-59.
Time. Aug 9, 1971, v98, p36.
Variety. Jun 2, 1971, p15.
The Village Voice. Aug 12, 1971, p43, 46.

The Goddess (US; Cromwell, John; 1958)
BFI/Monthly Film Bulletin. Sep 1958, v25, p124.
Catholic World. May 1958, v187, p141.
Commonweal. May 23, 1958, v68, p206.
Film Daily. Apr 16, 1958, p8.
Filmfacts. Jul 16, 1958, v1, p97-98.
Films in Review. May 1958, v9, p271.
Hollywood Reporter. Apr 16, 1958, p3.
Magill's Survey of Cinema. Series II. p896-99.
The Nation. Jul 19, 1958, v187, p40.
The New Republic. Jun 2, 1958, v138, p19-20.
The New York Times Magazine. Sep 22, 1957, p68.
The New York Times Magazine. Jun 25, 1958, p24.
The New Yorker. Jul 5, 1958, v34, p60.
Newsweek. May 26, 1958, v51, p99.
Saturday Review. May 10, 1958, v41, p21.
Time. Jul 7, 1958, v72, p70.
Variety. Apr 23, 1958, p7.

The Godfather (US; Coppola, Francis Ford; 1972)
America. Mar 25, 1972, v126, p320-21.
America. Jul 3, 1972, v126, p596.
Christian Century. May 17, 1972, v89, p585-86.
Classics of the Gangster Film. p233-38.
Commentary. Jul 1972, v54, p88-90.
Commonweal. Apr 28, 1972, v96, p191-92.
Dreams and Dead Ends. p326-35.
Fifty Grand Movies of the 1960s and 1970s. p69-74.
Film Quarterly. Sum 1972, v25, p60-61.
Filmfacts. 1972, v15, n2,3,4,5, p69.
Films in Review. Apr 1972, v23, n4, p243.
The Films of Marlon Brando. p228-39.
The Films of the Seventies. p57-59.
Francis Ford Coppola: A Guide to References and Resources. p46-51.
The Godfather Journal. 1973.
Hollywood Reporter. Mar 8, 1972, p3.
The Hudson Review. Wint 1973, v26, p170-76.
The International Dictionary of Films and Filmmakers. v1, p174-76.
Journal of Popular Film. Spr 1973, v2, p204-8.
Life. Mar 31, 1972, v72, p16.
Life. Mar 10, 1972, v72, p40-44.
Magill's Survey of Cinema. Series I. v2, p638.
Millimeter. Nov 1974, v2, p26-29.
The Nation. Apr 3, 1972, v214, p442.
National Review. Jul 23, 1972, v24, p704-05.
The New Republic. Apr 1, 1972, v166, p26.
The New York Times. Mar 12, 1972, SecII, p1.
The New York Times. Mar 16, 1972, p56.
The New York Times. Jul 30, 1974, p59.
The New Yorker. Mar 18, 1972, v48, p132-34.
Newsweek. Mar 13, 1972, v79, p56-59.
Saturday Review. Mar 25, 1972, v55, p16.
Society. Jul 1972, v9, p34-37.
Time. Apr 3, 1972, v99, p71.
Time. Mar 13, 1972, v99, p57-58.

Variety. Mar 8, 1972, p20.
Vintage Films. p215-22.

The Godfather, Part II (US; Coppola, Francis Ford; 1974)
America. Feb 15, 1975, v132, p116.
Audience. Jan 1975, v7, p2-4.
Before My Eyes. p104-07.
BFI/Monthly Film Bulletin. Jun 1975, v42, p135.
Christian Century. Jan 22, 1975, v92, p51-52.
Cinema Papers. Jul-Aug 1975, v2, p148-49.
Classics of the Gangster Film. p248-52.
Commentary. Mar 1975, v59, p79-80.
Commonweal. May 23, 1975, v102, p146-47.
Esquire. Mar 1975, v83, p31-32.
Film. Jul 1975, n28, p22.
Film Comment. Mar-Apr 1975, v11, p2.
Films and Filming. Jul 1975, v21, p42-43.
Films Illustrated. Jun 1975, v4, p372-73.
Films in Review. Feb 1975, v26, p119-20.
The Films of the Seventies. p97-98.
Francis Ford Coppola: A Guide to References and Resources. p55-61.
Hollywood Reporter. Dec 11, 1974, p3.
Independent Film Journal. Dec 25, 1974, v75, p29.
The International Dictionary of Films and Filmmakers. v1, p175-76.
Journal of Popular Film. 1975, v4, n2, p157-63.
Jump Cut. May-Jul 1975, n7, p1.
The Los Angeles Times. Dec 17, 1974, SecIV, p1.
Magill's Survey of Cinema. Series I. v2, p644-47.
Motion Picture Herald Product Digest. Dec 25, 1974, p58.
The New Republic. Jan 18, 1975, v172, p22.
New Statesman. May 16, 1975, v88, p669.
New York. Dec 23, 1974, v7, p70-71.
The New York Times. Dec 13, 1974, p58.
The New York Times. Dec 22, 1974, SecII, p19.
The New Yorker. Dec 23, 1974, v50, p63-66.
Newsweek. Dec 23, 1974, v84, p78-79.
One Good Film Deserves Another. p146-53.
Sight and Sound. Sum 1975, v44, p187-88.
Take One. 1974, v4, n7, p30.
Time. Dec 16, 1974, v104, p70-73.
Variety. Dec 11, 1974, p16.
The Village Voice. Dec 23, 1974, p88-89.
The Village Voice. Jan 30, 1975, p71-72.
Vintage Films. p215-22.

God's Little Acre (US; Mann, Anthony; 1958)
America. Jun 13, 1958, v68.
Anthony Mann (Basinger). p185-89.
BFI/Monthly Film Bulletin. Sep 1958, v25, p124.
Cosmopolitan. Jun 1958, v144, p22.
Film Daily. May 13, 1958, p6.
Filmfacts. Aug 27, 1958, v1, p123-24.
Films in Review. May 1958, v9, p270-71.
Hollywood Reporter. May 9, 1958, p3.
Library Journal. Jul 1958, v133, p2036.
Life. May 5, 1958, v44, p93-94.
The New Republic. Jun 30, 1958, v138, p21.
The New York Times. Aug 14, 1958, p23.
Newsweek. Jun 2, 1958, v51, p90.
Time. Jun 2, 1958, v71, p84.
Variety. May 14, 1958, p6.

The Gods Must be Crazy (BOTSWANA; Uys, Jamie; 1980)
Commonweal. Oct 1984, v111, p535-36.
Los Angeles. Sep 1984, v29, p42.
The Los Angeles Times. Aug 22, 1984, SecVI, p1.
Maclean's. Aug 20, 1984, v97, p63.
Magill's Cinema Annual, 1985. p224-29.

National Review. Aug 24, 1984, v36, p59.
The New Republic. Sep 10, 1984, v191, p24.
New Statesman. Apr 23, 1982, v103, p31.
New York. Feb 4, 1985, v18, p23.
New York. Jul 30, 1984, v17, p47.
The New York Times. Jul 9, 1984, SecIII, p8.
Playboy. Oct 1984, v31, p32.
Progressive. Sep 1984, v48, p40.
Texas Monthly. Oct 1984, v12, p186.
Theatre Crafts. Oct 1985, v19, p118-19.
Time. Feb 4, 1985, v125, p83.
Variety. Jul 4, 1984, p18.

Godzilla, King of the Monsters (JAPAN; Morse, Terry; Honda, Inoshiro; 1956)
American Cinematographer. Aug 1960, v41, p488-89.
Film Daily. Apr 27, 1956, p6.
Films and Filming. Feb 1957, v3, p24.
Japanese Fantasy Film Journal. 1981, n13, p16-21.
Japanese Fantasy Film Journal. 1982, n14, p14-17.
Newsweek. May 14, 1956, v47, p126.
Sight and Sound. Wint 1956-57, v26, p24.
Variety. Apr 25, 1956, p6.
The Village Voice. Aug 3, 1982, p42.
The World of Fantastic Films. p39.

Goetterdaemmerung *See* The Damned

Gog (US; Strock, Herbert L.; 1954)
BFI/Monthly Film Bulletin. Nov 1954, v21, p162.
Film Daily. Jun 23, 1954, p10.
Films in Review. Aug-Sep 1954, v5, p368-69.
Hollywood Reporter. Jun 7, 1954, p3.
Motion Picture Herald Product Digest. Jun 12, 1954, p26.
National Parent-Teacher. Sep 1954, v49, p38.
The New Republic. Oct 25, 1954, v131, p21.
The New York Times. Aug 14, 1954, p8.
Time. Oct 19, 1953, v62, p112.
Time. Jul 19, 1954, v64, p78.
Variety. Jun 9, 1954, p6.

Goin' South (US; Nicholson, Jack; 1978)
BFI/Monthly Film Bulletin. May 1979, v46, p96.
The Los Angeles Times. Oct 1, 1978, Calendar, p1.
Maclean's. Oct 23, 1978, v91, p63.
Motion Picture Herald Product Digest. Oct 4, 1978, p34.
The Nation. Oct 21, 1978, v227, p422.
New York. Oct 30, 1978, v11, p120.
The New Yorker. Dec 11, 1978, v54, p75-76.
Newsweek. Oct 9, 1978, v92, p94.
Time. Oct 9, 1978, v112, p100.
Variety. Oct 4, 1978, p18.

Going Places (French title: Valseuses, Les) (FR; Blier, Bertrand; 1974)
Audience. Oct 1974, v7, p12-14.
Audience. Jun 1974, v6, p7-11.
BFI/Monthly Film Bulletin. Jun 1975, v42, p135.
Esquire. Sep 1974, v82, p42.
Hollywood Reporter. Jul 24, 1974, p3.
Independent Film Journal. Jun 12, 1974, v74, p12.
The Los Angeles Times. Jul 24, 1974, SecIV, p1.
Ms. Sep 1974, v3, p42-43.
The Nation. Jun 1, 1974, v218, p700-01.
The New Republic. Jul 6, 1974, v171, p20.
New York. May 20, 1974, v7, p88-89.
The New York Times. Jun 2, 1974, SecII, p11.
The New Yorker. May 20, 1974, v50, p124.
Newsweek. May 20, 1974, v83, p106-07.

Time. Jun 10, 1974, v103, p83.
Variety. Mar 27, 1974, p24.

Gold (GB; Hunt, Peter; 1974)
BFI/Monthly Film Bulletin. Aug 1974, v41, p176-77.
Films and Filming. Sep 1974, v20, p44-45.
Films Illustrated. Sep 1974, v4, p10.
Films in Review. Nov 1974, v25, p568.
Hollywood Reporter. Oct 1, 1974, p3.
Independent Film Journal. Oct 16, 1974, v74, p5-6.
Motion Picture Herald Product Digest. Oct 16, 1974, p38.
Movietone News. Nov 1974, n37, p36.
New Statesman. Sep 6, 1974, v88, p325.
New York. Oct 21, 1974, v7, p80.
The New York Times. Oct 17, 1974, p57.
The New Yorker. Oct 21, 1974, v50, p168-70.
Newsweek. Nov 18, 1974, v84, p110.
Time. Nov 4, 1974, v104, p8.
Variety. Oct 2, 1974, p22.

Gold of Naples (Italian title: Oro di Napoli, L'; Also titled: Every Day's a Holiday) (IT; De Sica, Vittorio; 1954)
BFI/Monthly Film Bulletin. Jul 1956, v23, p87.
Commonweal. Feb 22, 1957, v65, p539-40.
Film Culture. 1957, v3, n2, p13-14.
Film Daily. Mar 5, 1957, p8.
Films and Filming. Nov 1959, v6, p24-25.
Films in Review. Mar 1957, v8, p129-30.
Hollywood Reporter. May 23, 1957, p3.
Motion Picture Herald Product Digest. Mar 9, 1957, p290.
The Nation. Mar 2, 1957, v184, p194.
The New York Times. Feb 12, 1957, p30.
The New York Times. Feb 17, 1957, SecII, p1.
The New Yorker. Feb 16, 1957, v32, p123-24.
Newsweek. Feb 18, 1957, v49, p110.
Saturday Review. Feb 23, 1957, v40, p27.
Time. Feb 25, 1957, v69, p96.

The Golden Coach (French title: Carosse d'Or, Le; Italian title: Carrozza d'Oro, La) (IT, FR; Renoir, Jean; 1952)
America. Jan 30, 1954, v90, p464.
BFI/Monthly Film Bulletin. Jan 1954, v21, p3-4.
Catholic World. Dec 1953, v178, p225-26.
Commonweal. Feb 12, 1954, v59, p472-73.
Dictionary of Films. p54.
Film: A Modern Art (Sultanik). p182.
Film Comment. May-Jun 1974, v10, p38-42.
Film Daily. Jan 27, 1954, p6.
Films and Filming. Jul 1961, v7, p16.
The Films in My Life. p43-44.
Films in Review. Mar 1954, v5, p140-42.
I Lost It At the Movies. p90-93.
Jean Renoir: A Guide to References and Resources. p146-49.
Jean Renoir (Durgnat). p285-95.
Jean Renoir (Leprohon). p148-50.
Jean Renoir: The World of His Films. p93-97.
Motion Picture Herald Product Digest. Jan 23, 1954, p2158.
Movie Comedy (Byron). p223-25.
Movie Man (Thomson). p148-49.
Musical America. Jan 15, 1954, v74, p8.
My Life and My Films (Renoir). p266-68.
National Parent-Teacher. Mar 1954, v48, p39.
The New Statesman and Nation. Dec 19, 1953, v46, p796.
The New York Times. Jan 22, 1954, p30.
The New Yorker. Jan 30, 1954, v29, p86.
Newsweek. Jan 25, 1954, v43, p90.
Quarterly of Film, Radio and Television. Fall 1954, v9, p16-27.
Saturday Review. Jan 23, 1954, v37, p62-63.
Sight and Sound. Apr-Jun 1954, v23, p198-99.

Sight and Sound. Oct-Dec 1952, v22, p57.
The Social Cinema of Jean Renoir. p179-80.
Time. Feb 1, 1954, v63, p72.
Variety. Mar 11, 1953, p18.

Golden Girl (US; Bacon, Lloyd; 1951)
BFI/Monthly Film Bulletin. Feb 1952, v19, p21.
Catholic World. Dec 1951, v174, p220-21.
Film Daily. Nov 8, 1951, p6.
Hollywood Reporter. Nov 1, 1951, p4.
The London Times. Feb 4, 1952, p8.
Motion Picture Herald Product Digest. Nov 10, 1951, p1101.
The New York Times. Nov 21, 1951, p20.
Newsweek. Dec 3, 1951, v38, p95.
The Spectator. Feb 1, 1952, v188, p140.
Time. Nov 26, 1951, v58, p110.
Variety. Nov 7, 1951, p6.

The Golden Hawk (US; Salkow, Sidney; 1952)
BFI/Monthly Film Bulletin. Sep 1952, v19, p127.
Film Daily. Sep 10, 1952, p6.
Hollywood Reporter. Sep 10, 1952, p3.
Motion Picture Herald Product Digest. Sep 13, 1952, p1525.
National Parent-Teacher. Oct 1952, v47, p38.
The New York Times. Oct 18, 1952, p16.
Newsweek. Nov 3, 1952, v40, p107.
Variety. Oct 29, 1952, p24.

Golden Helmet *See* Casque D'Or

Golden Marie *See* Casque D'Or

The Golden Salamander (GB; Neame, Ronald; 1950)
Film Daily. Mar 23, 1951, p6.
Hollywood Reporter. Apr 5, 1951, p3.
Illustrated London News. Feb 18, 1950, v216, p268.
Library Journal. May 15, 1950, v75, p885.
The London Times. Feb 6, 1950, p4.
The London Times. Feb 8, 1950, p12.
Motion Picture Herald Product Digest. Mar 31, 1951, p785.
The New York Times. Mar 24, 1951, p8.
Sequence. Sum 1950, n11, p15.
Variety. Feb 8, 1950, p18.

The Golden Twenties (US; Rochemont, Richard de; 1950)
Commonweal. Mar 31, 1950, v51, p655.
Film Daily. Mar 20, 1950, p8.
Films in Review. May-Jun 1950, v1, p19-21.
Hollywood Reporter. Mar 17, 1950, p3.
Library Journal. May 15, 1956, v75, p885.
Life. Apr 17, 1950, v28, p165.
Motion Picture Herald Product Digest. Mar 18, 1950, p229.
The New Republic. May 1, 1950, v122, p22.
The New York Times. Apr 10, 1950, p15.
The New Yorker. Apr 8, 1951, v26, p98.
Rotha on Film. p161-63.
Saturday Review. May 9, 1953, v36, p39.
Time. Apr 3, 1950, v55, p92.
Variety. Mar 22, 1950, p6.

The Golden Virgin (Also titled: The Story of Esther Costello) (US; Miller, David; 1957)
BFI/Monthly Film Bulletin. Aug 1957, v24, p99.
Commonweal. Oct 11, 1957, v67, p50.
Film Daily. Sep 23, 1957, p8.
Films and Filming. Sep 1957, v3, p24.
Hollywood Reporter. Sep 17, 1957, p3.
Motion Picture Herald Product Digest. Sep 21, 1957, p538.
The New York Times. Nov 6, 1957, p43.

Saturday Review. Sep 7, 1957, v40, p25.
Time. Feb 4, 1957, v69, p90.
Variety. Aug 21, 1957, p6.

Goldfinger (GB; Hamilton, Guy; 1964)
BFI/Monthly Film Bulletin. Nov 1964, v31, p161.
Commonweal. Dec 18, 1964, v81, p422.
Fifty Grand Movies of the 1960s and 1970s. p75-78.
Film Daily. Nov 9, 1964, p6.
Films and Filming. Nov 1964, v11, p26.
Films in Review. Dec 1964, v15, p634-35.
The Films of the Sixties. p128-30.
Hollywood Reporter. Nov 9, 1964, p3.
Hollywood U.K. p194-96.
The James Bond Films. p37-50.
James Bond in the Cinema. p75.
James Bond's Bedside Companion. p176-81.
Life. Nov 6, 1964, v57, p116-19.
Magill's Survey of Cinema. Series II. v2, p904-06.
Motion Picture Herald Product Digest. Nov 25, 1964, p177.
National Review. Feb 9, 1965, v17, p116.
The New Republic. Dec 19, 1964, v151, p27.
The New York Times. Dec 22, 1964, p36.
The New Yorker. Dec 26, 1964, v40, p73.
The New Yorker. Mar 20, 1965, v41, p165-67.
Newsweek. Dec 21, 1964, v64, p72-73.
Saturday Review. Dec 12, 1964, v47, p42.
Variety. Sep 23, 1964, p6.

Gone to Earth *See* The Wild Heart

The Good Fight (US; Dore, Mary; Buckner, Noel; 1983)
The Nation. Apr 14, 1984, v238, p460-61.
The New Republic. Apr 23, 1984, v190, p24-25.
New York. Apr 2, 1984, v17, p71-73.
The New York Times. Apr 15, 1984, SecII, p21.
The New York Times. Mar 28, 1984, SecIII, p24.
Progressive. May 1984, v48, p38.
Time. Apr 9, 1984, v123, p92.
Variety. Apr 4, 1984, p21.
The Village Voice. Apr 3, 1984, p58.

Good Morning, Miss Dove (US; Koster, Henry; 1955)
America. Dec 10, 1955, v94, p314.
Catholic World. Jan 1956, v182, p305-06.
Commonweal. Dec 9, 1955, v63, p258.
Films in Review. Dec 1955, v6, p530.
The Films of Jennifer Jones. p673.
Library Journal. Dec 15, 1955, v80, p2855.
Motion Picture Herald Product Digest. Nov 19, 1955, p673.
The New York Times. Nov 24, 1955, p41.
The New Yorker. Dec 3, 1955, v31, p186.
Newsweek. Dec 5, 1955, v46, p98.
Time. Dec 5, 1955, v66, p106.
Variety. Nov 16, 1955, p6.

Good Neighbor Sam (US; Swift, David; 1964)
America. Aug 8, 1964, v111, p143.
BFI/Monthly Film Bulletin. Mar 1965, v32, p40.
Boxoffice. Jun 29, 1964, v85, p2839.
Film Daily. Jun 16, 1964, p6.
Films and Filming. Apr 1965, v2, p30-31.
The Films of Jack Lemmon. p148-52.
Hollywood Reporter. Jun 12, 1964, p3.
Motion Picture Herald Product Digest. Jun 24, 1964, p73-74.
The New York Times. Jul 23, 1964, p19.
The New Yorker. Aug 8, 1964, v40, p74.
Saturday Review. Jun 27, 1964, v47, p50.
Variety. Jun 17, 1964, p6.

The Good, the Bad, and the Ugly (Italian title: Buono, Il Brutto, Il Cattivo, Il) (IT; Leone, Sergio; 1966)
BFI/Monthly Film Bulletin. Oct 1968, v35, p154-55.
Christian Science Monitor (Eastern Edition). Jun 5, 1968, p4.
Clint Eastwood (Guérif). p50-54.
Film Comment. Mar-Apr 1973, v9, p9-10.
Film Daily. Jan 11, 1968, p8.
Filmfacts. Feb 1, 1968, v11, p7-8.
Films and Filming. Nov 1968, v15, p48-49.
The Films of Clint Eastwood. p65-69.
Going Steady. p64-65.
The Great Western Pictures. p42-44.
Hollywood Reporter. Dec 20, 1966, p3.
The International Dictionary of Films and Filmmakers. v1, p180-81.
Italian Cinema (Bondanella). p259-61.
Italian Westerns: The Opera of Violence. p66-75.
Magill's Survey of Cinema. Foreign Language Films. v3, p1252-57.
Motion Picture Herald Product Digest. Jan 17, 1968, p760.
New Statesman. Aug 30, 1968, v75, p265.
The New York Times. Jan 25, 1968, p33.
Spaghetti Westerns. p160-91.
Variety. Dec 27, 1967, p6.
The Velvet Light Trap. 1974, n12, p31-33.
A Year in the Dark. p23-24.

Good Times, Wonderful Times (US; Rogosin, Lionel; 1965)
Christian Century. Apr 19, 1967, v84, p506.
Film Daily. Jul 25, 1966, p7.
Film Society Review. May 1966, p20.
Filmfacts. Oct 1, 1966, v9, p204-05.
The London Times. Sep 3, 1965, p14.
Motion Picture Herald Product Digest. Aug 17, 1966, p582.
The Nation. Aug 8, 1966, v203, p133-34.
The New York Times. Jul 19, 1966, p34.
The New Yorker. Jul 30, 1966, v42, p64.
Newsweek. Aug 22, 1966, v68, p98.
On Film. p343-44.
Playboy. Dec 1966, v13, p54, 56.
Variety. Sep 1, 1965, p6.
The Village Voice. Aug 25, 1966, p21.
Vogue. Aug 15, 1966, v148, p50.

Goodbye, Charlie (US; Minnelli, Vincente; 1964)
America. Dec 5, 1964, v111, p757.
BFI/Monthly Film Bulletin. Apr 1965, v32, p51-52.
Boxoffice. Nov 9, 1964, v86, p2873.
Commonweal. Dec 18, 1964, v81, p421.
Film Daily. Nov 5, 1964, p10.
Films and Filming. May 1965, v11, p31-32.
Hollywood Reporter. Nov 5, 1964, p3.
Motion Picture Herald Product Digest. Nov 11, 1964, p162.
The New Republic. Feb 13, 1965, v152, p27.
The New York Times. Nov 19, 1964, p49.
Newsweek. Nov 30, 1964, v64, p100.
Time. Nov 27, 1964, v84, p109-10.
Tony Curtis: The Man and His Movies. p100-01.
Variety. Nov 11, 1964, p6.

Goodbye Columbus (US; Peerce, Larry; 1969)
America. Apr 19, 1969, v120, p484-85.
Atlantic. Jul 1969, v224, p108.
Big Screen, Little Screen. p164-67.
Christian Century. Jul 16, 1969, v86, p960.
Cineaste. Sum 1969, v3, p19-20.
Commonweal. Apr 25, 1969, v90, p172.
Confessions of a Cultist. p431-34.

Esquire. Jul 1969, v72, p130.
Figures of Light. p154-57.
Film 69/70. p79-82.
Film Daily. Mar 26, 1969, p8.
Film Quarterly. Fall 1969, v23, p34-38.
Filmfacts. 1969, v12, p121.
Films and Filming. Nov 1969, v16, p42.
Films in Review. May 1969, v20, p317.
Magill's Survey of Cinema. Series I. v2, p660-62.
Movies Into Film. p322-23.
The Nation. Apr 28, 1969, v208, p550.
The New Republic. Apr 12, 1969, v160, p24.
The New York Times. Apr 4, 1969, p43.
The New York Times. Apr 13, 1969, SecII, p1.
The New Yorker. Apr 12, 1969, v45, p171-73.
Newsweek. Apr 14, 1969, v73, p115-115A.
Saturday Review. Apr 19, 1969, v52, p50.
Time. Apr 11, 1969, v93, p104.
Unholy Fools, Wits, Comics, Disturbers of the Peace. p253-56.
Variety. Mar 19, 1969, p6.

The Goodbye Girl (US; Ross, Herbert; 1977)
America. Jan 7, 1978, v138, p20.
BFI/Monthly Film Bulletin. Mar 1978, v45, p46.
Films in Review. Dec 1977, v28, p633.
The Films of the Seventies. p200-03.
Hollywood Reporter. Nov 16, 1977, p2.
The Los Angeles Times. Dec 4, 1977, Calendar, p1.
Maclean's. Jan 23, 1978, v91, p59.
Magill's Survey of Cinema. Series II. v2, p915-17.
Motion Picture Herald Product Digest. Nov 23, 1977, p50.
The New Leader. Jan 16, 1978, v61, p25.
The New Republic. Dec 17, 1977, v177, p22.
The New York Times. Dec 1, 1977, SecIII, p17.
The New York Times. Dec 4, 1977, SecII, p13.
The New Yorker. Jan 16, 1978, v53, p83-85.
Newsweek. Dec 5, 1977, v90, p109.
Time. Nov 28, 1977, v110, p110-11.
Variety. Nov 16, 1977, p20.

Goodbye Mr. Chips (US; Ross, Herbert; 1969)
America. Nov 15, 1969, v121, p476.
Big Screen, Little Screen. p257-58.
Deeper Into Movies. p47-51.
Film 69/70. p229-35.
Film Daily. Oct 16, 1969, p5.
Films and Filming. Feb 1970, v16, p38-39.
Films in Review. May 1969, v20, p317.
Life. Nov 14, 1969, v67, p9.
Make It Again, Sam. p63-68.
Movies Into Film. p332-33.
The New York Times. Nov 6, 1969, p56.
The New Yorker. Nov 8, 1969, v45, p161-64.
Newsweek. Nov 17, 1969, v74, p122.
Saturday Review. Nov 15, 1969, v52, p64.
Time. Nov 7, 1969, v94, p100.
Variety. Oct 15, 1969, p15.

Goodbye, My Fancy (US; Sherman, Vincent; 1951)
BFI/Monthly Film Bulletin. Sep 1951, v18, p323-24.
Christian Century. Jul 11, 1951, v68, p831.
Commonweal. Jun 1, 1951, v54, p190.
Film Daily. Apr 10, 1951, p6.
The Films of Joan Crawford. p178-79.
Hollywood Reporter. Apr 10, 1951, p3.
Library Journal. Mar 15, 1951, v76, p535.
Motion Picture Herald Product Digest. Apr 14, 1951, p801.
The New York Times. May 30, 1951, p14.
The New Yorker. Jun 9, 1951, v27, p60.

Saturday Review. May 19, 1951, v34, p26.
Senior Scholastic. Apr 25, 1951, v58, p30.
Time. May 28, 1951, v57, p102.
Variety. Apr 11, 1951, p6.

The Goonies (US; Donner, Richard; 1985)
BFI/Monthly Film Bulletin. Nov 1985, v52, p341.
The Chicago Tribune. Jun 7, 1985, SecVII, p36.
Hollywood Reporter. Jun 3, 1985, p4.
The Los Angeles Times. Jun 7, 1985, SecVI, p1.
Maclean's. Jun 17, 1985, v98, p54.
Magill's Cinema Annual, 1986. p176-81.
The Nation. Jun 29, 1985, v240, p809-10.
New York. Jun 17, 1985, v18, p73.
The New York Times. Jun 7, 1985, SecIII, p19.
Newsweek. Jun 10, 1985, v105, p88.
Time. Jul 1, 1985, v125, p62.
Variety. Jun 5, 1985, p14.
The Wall Street Journal. Jun 20, 1985, p26.

Gorky Park (US; Apted, Michael; 1983)
American Cinematographer. Jan 1984, v65, p52-58.
Armchair Detective. 1984, v17, n4, p434-35.
BFI/Monthly Film Bulletin. Jan 1984, v51, p14-15.
Film Comment. Jan 1984, v20, p29-32.
Film Journal. Jan 1984, v87, p11.
Films and Filming. Feb 1984, n353, p36.
Hollywood Reporter. Dec 12, 1983, p3.
Informer. Apr 1984, p6.
The Los Angeles Times. Aug 3, 1983, SecVI, p1.
The Los Angeles Times. Dec 16, 1983, SecIV, p1.
Maclean's. Dec 19, 1983, v96, p55.
Magill's Cinema Annual, 1984. p168-73.
The Nation. Feb 4, 1984, v238, p140-41.
The New Republic. Feb 6, 1984, v190, p25-26.
New Statesman. Jan 6, 1984, v107, p26-27.
The New York Times. Jul 13, 1983, SecIII, p17.
The New York Times. Dec 16, 1983, SecIII, p6.
Newsweek. Dec 19, 1983, v102, p66.
Photoplay. Jan 1984, v35, p24-28.
Time. Dec 19, 1983, v122, p74.
Variety. Dec 14, 1983, p16.

The Gospel According to St. Matthew (Vangelo Secondo Matteo, Il; Evangile Selon Saint Matthieu, L') (IT, FR; Pasolini, Pier Paolo; 1964)
America. Feb 26, 1966, v114, p307-08.
Cahiers du Cinema in English. 1966, n3, p61-62.
Christian Century. Mar 16, 1966, v83, p335.
Christian Science Monitor (Western edition). Mar 3, 1966, p10.
Cinema. Jul 1966, v3, p47.
Commonweal. Jul 2, 1965, v82, p471-72.
Dictionary of Films. p398-99.
Film. 1964, n41, p13-14.
Film Comment. Fall 1965, v3, p22-23.
Film Daily. Feb 24, 1966, p6.
Film Quarterly. Sum 1965, v18, p43-44.
Film Society Review. Dec 1966, p20-23.
Film Society Review. Apr 1967, p36-37.
Film Society Review. Feb 1969, v4, p19-22.
Filmfacts. Mar 15, 1966, v9, p29-31.
Films and Filming. Jun 1967, v13, p23-24.
Films and Filming. Jun 1971, v17, p55-58.
Films in Review. Jan 1966, v17, p54-55.
Hollywood Reporter. Apr 8, 1966, p3.
The International Dictionary of Films and Filmmakers. v1, p502-03.
International Film Guide. 1966, v3, p99-100.
Italian Cinema (Bondanella). p182-84.
Life. Mar 11, 1966, v60, p10.
The London Times. Jun 1, 1967, p8.
Magill's Survey of Cinema. Foreign Language Films. v3, p1264-71.

Motion Picture Herald Product Digest. Mar 2, 1966, p476-77.
Movietone News. Jun 1976, n50, p34.
The New Italian Cinema. p121.
The New Republic. Mar 26, 1966, v154, p33-34.
New Statesman. Jun 9, 1967, v73, p806-07.
The New York Times. Feb 18, 1966, p23.
The New Yorker. Mar 5, 1966, v42, p157.
Newsweek. Feb 28, 1966, v67, p91.
On Movies. p437-40.
Pasolini on Pasolini. p73-98.
Pier Paolo Pasolini (Snyder). p59-70.
The Private Eye, the Cowboy and the Very Naked Girl. p234.
Reporter. Jun 30, 1966, v34, p39-40.
Saturday Review. Mar 26, 1966, v49, p46-47.
Screen. May-Jun 1969, v10, p25-28.
Second Sight. p58-61.
Senior Scholastic. Apr 1, 1966, v88, p27.
Sight and Sound. Wint 1964-65, v34, p39.
Time. Feb 18, 1966, v87, p101.
Variety. Sep 16, 1964, p17.

The Graduate (US; Nichols, Mike; 1967)
America. Jan 20, 1968, v118, p95.
BFI/Monthly Film Bulletin. Sep 1968, v35, p131.
Christian Century. Feb 21, 1968, v85, p238.
Commonweal. Jan 19, 1968, v87, p472.
Esquire. Apr 1968, v69, p40.
Fifty Grand Movies of the 1960s and 1970s. p33-36.
Film Daily. Dec 18, 1967, p8.
Film Heritage. Fall 1968, v4, p1-6.
Film Quarterly. Spr 1968, v21, p37-41.
Film Society Review. Jan 1970, v5, p36-44.
Films and Filming. Oct 1968, v15, p39-40.
Films and Filming. Nov 1968, v15, p4-8.
Films in Review. Jan 1968, v19, p55.
Films in Review. Feb 1968, p89-95.
The Films of Dustin Hoffman. p61-78.
The Films of the Sixties. p190-92.
Harper's. Mar 1968, v236, p155.
Hollywood Reporter. Dec 18, 1967, p3.
Ladies Home Journal. Apr 1968, v85, p79.
Life. Jan 19, 1968, v64, p16.
Life. Nov 24, 1967, v63, p111-12.
Look. Apr 2, 1968, v32, p71-74.
Magill's Survey of Cinema. Series I. v2, p667-71.
McCall's. Apr 1968, v95, p18.
Mike Nichols (Schuth). p45-64.
Motion Picture Herald Product Digest. Dec 20, 1967, p751.
The Nation. Jan 15, 1968, v206, p94.
National Review. May 7, 1968, v20, p459-60.
The New Republic. Dec 23, 1967, v157, p22.
The New Republic. Feb 10, 1968, v158, p20.
New York Review of Books. Mar 28, 1968, v10, p25-27.
The New York Times. Dec 22, 1967, p44.
The New Yorker. Dec 30, 1967, v43, p48.
The New Yorker. Jul 27, 1968, v44, p34-42.
Newsweek. Jan 1, 1968, v71, p63.
Reporter. Feb 8, 1968, v38, p38-39.
Reruns. p209-13.
Saturday Review. Dec 23, 1967, v50, p24.
Saturday Review. Mar 16, 1968, v51, p53.
Saturday Review. Jul 6, 1968, p14-15.
Second Sight. p160-62.
Sight and Sound. Sum 1968, v37, p160.
Sight and Sound. Wint 1968-69, v38, p49-51.
Talking Pictures. p362-65.
Time. Dec 29, 1967, v90, p55.
Trans-Action. May 1968, v5, p15-21.
Variety. Dec 20, 1967, p6.
The Village Voice. Dec 28, 1967, p33, 35.
Vogue. Feb 1, 1968, v151, p112.

Grand Patron, Un (Also titled: The
   Perfectionist) (FR; Ciampi, Yves;
   1951)
   BFI/Monthly Film Bulletin. Aug 1952, v19,
      p110.
   Commonweal. May 23, 1952, v56, p175.
   Motion Picture Herald Product Digest. May 3,
      1952, p1350.
   The New York Times. May 2, 1952, p21.
   Newsweek. May 12, 1952, v39, p102.
   Saturday Review. May 24, 1952, v35, p34.
   The Spectator. Jun 13, 1952, v188, p76.
   Variety. Jan 2, 1952, p68.
   Variety. Apr 30, 1952, p18.

Grand Prix (US; Frankenheimer, John;
   1966)
   America. Jan 28, 1967, v116, p162.
   BFI/Monthly Film Bulletin. Apr 1967, v34,
      p56-57.
   Big Screen, Little Screen. p379-80.
   Christian Science Monitor (Western edition).
      Dec 31, 1966, p6.
   Cineaste. Sum 1967, v1, p27, 29.
   The Cinema of John Frankenheimer. p149-61.
   Commonweal. Jan 20, 1967, v85, p428.
   Film Daily. Dec 22, 1966, p6.
   Film Quarterly. Sum 1967, v20, p11-22.
   Filmfacts. Jan 15, 1967, v9, p361-63.
   Films and Filming. Jun 1967, v13, p22.
   Films in Review. Jan 1967, v18, p53-54.
   Focus. Mar 1967, n2, p23.
   Guardian. Oct 20, 1966, p7.
   Hollywood Reporter. Dec 22, 1966, p3.
   Kiss Kiss Bang Bang. p11-12.
   Life. Oct 28, 1966, v61, p122-24.
   The London Times. Mar 9, 1967, p10.
   Motion Picture Herald Product Digest. Jan 4,
      1967, p645.
   The New Republic. Jan 14, 1967, v156, p41-42.
   New Statesman. Mar 17, 1967, v73, p384.
   The New York Times. Dec 22, 1966, p40.
   The New Yorker. Dec 31, 1966, v42, p60.
   Newsweek. Jan 2, 1967, v69, p63.
   Playboy. Mar 1967, v14, p24.
   Saturday Review. Jan 14, 1967, v50, p97.
   Senior Scholastic. Feb 17, 1967, v90, p18.
   Sight and Sound. Spr 1967, v36, p95-96.
   Time. Jan 13, 1967, v89, p69.
   Variety. Dec 28, 1966, p6.
   The Village Voice. Feb 16, 1967, v12, p25.

Grande Course Autour du Monde, La *See*
   The Great Race

Grandfather Frost *See* Jack Frost

The Grass Is Greener (US; Donen, Stanley;
   1960)
   America. Jan 14, 1961, v104, p480.
   BFI/Monthly Film Bulletin. Mar 1961, v28,
      p36.
   Commonweal. Jan 27, 1961, v73, p463.
   Film Daily. Nov 29, 1960, p6.
   Filmfacts. 1960, v3, p343.
   Films and Filming. Mar 1961, v7, p27.
   The Films of Cary Grant. p250-53.
   Hollywood Reporter. Nov 29, 1960, p3.
   The New Republic. Dec 26, 1960, v143, p21-22.
   The New York Times. Dec 24, 1960, p8.
   The New Yorker. Jan 7, 1961, v36, p63.
   Newsweek. Jan 2, 1961, v57, p66.
   Robert Mitchum on the Screen. p171-72.
   Stanley Donen (Casper). p159-65.
   Time. Jan 6, 1961, v77, p42.
   Variety. Nov 30, 1960, p6.

Grease (US; Kleiser, Randal; 1978)
   The Atlantic. Aug 1978, v242, p82-83.
   BFI/Monthly Film Bulletin. Sep 1978, v45,
      p175.

Commonweal. Sep 1, 1978, v105, p564-65.
Encore. Jul 10, 1978, v7, p28.
Film Comment. Jul 1978, v14, p14-16.
Films in Review. Aug-Sep 1978, v29, p437.
Hollywood Reporter. Jun 6, 1978, p4.
The Los Angeles Times. Jun 16, 1978, SecIV,
   p30.
Maclean's. Jul 10, 1978, v91, p59.
Magill's Survey of Cinema. Series II. v2, p918-
   20.
Motion Picture Herald Product Digest. Jun 28,
   1978, p5.
The Nation. Jul 1, 1978, v227, p27.
National Review. Jul 21, 1978, v30, p908.
The New Republic. Jul 1, 1978, v179, p18-19.
New York. Jun 26, 1978, v11, p58.
The New York Times. Jun 16, 1978, SecIII,
   p10.
The New Yorker. Jun 26, 1978, v54, p90-91.
Newsweek. Jun 12, 1978, v91, p92.
Time. Jun 19, 1978, v111, p78-79.
Variety. Jun 7, 1978, p28.

Greased Lightning (US; Schultz, Michael;
   1977)
   BFI/Monthly Film Bulletin. Nov 1977, v44,
      p233.
   Hollywood Reporter. Jul 13, 1977, p2.
   The Los Angeles Times. Sep 20, 1977, SecIV,
      p8.
   Motion Picture Herald Product Digest. Aug 24,
      1977, p23.
   The New York Times. Aug 4, 1977, SecIII, p14.
   The New Yorker. Aug 22, 1977, v53, p66-67.
   Newsweek. Aug 15, 1977, v90, p77.
   Sports Illustrated. Aug 15, 1977, v47, p39.
   Time. Aug 15, 1977, v110, p61.
   Variety. Jul 20, 1977, p18.

The Great Adventure (Swedish title: Stora
   Aventyret, Det) (SWED; Sucksdorff,
   Arne; 1953)
   America. Jun 4, 1955, v93, p379.
   BFI/Monthly Film Bulletin. Jan 1955, v22, p2-
      3.
   Catholic World. Jul 1955, v181, p305.
   Commonweal. Jun 3, 1955, v62, p231.
   Dictionary of Films. p357.
   Film Culture. Sum 1955, v1, p22.
   Film Daily. May 25, 1955, p6.
   Films and Filming. Nov 1954, v1, p11.
   Films and Filming. Jan 1955, v1, p21.
   Films in Review. Jun-Jul 1955, v6, p290-91.
   Kiss Kiss Bang Bang. p343-44.
   Life. Jun 13, 1955, v38, p71-72.
   The London Times. Nov 29, 1954, p10.
   *Magill's Survey of Cinema. Foreign Language
      Films.* v3, p1286-89.
   The Nation. Jun 11, 1955, v180, p510-11.
   National Parent-Teacher. Sep 1955, v50, p38.
   Natural History. Jun 1955, v64, p334.
   The New Statesman and Nation. Dec 4, 1954,
      v48, p740.
   The New York Times. May 24, 1955, p34.
   The New Yorker. Jun 11, 1955, v31, p123.
   Newsweek. May 16, 1955, v45, p112.
   On Film (Young). p249-51.
   Saturday Review. Jun 4, 1955, v38, p27.
   Senior Scholastic. Jan 12, 1956, v67, p25.
   Sight and Sound. Oct-Dec 1953, v23, p83-86,
      102.
   Sight and Sound. Jan-Mar 1955, v24, p141.
   Swedish Film Classics. p85-88.
   The Tatler. Dec 8, 1954, v214, p646.
   Time. Jun 20, 1955, v65, p91.
   Variety. May 7, 1952, p6.
   The Village Voice. Nov 2, 1955, v1, p6.

The Great Bank Robbery (US; Averback,
   Hy; 1969)
   Commonweal. Jul 25, 1969, v90, p465.
   Films and Filming. Jan 1971, v17, p50.
   Hollywood Reporter. Jun 19, 1969, p3.
   The New York Times. Sep 11, 1969, p50.
   Popular Photography. Oct 1969, v65, p117.
   Time. Jul 11, 1969, v94, p79.
   Variety. Jun 25, 1969, p6.

The Great Caruso (US; Thorpe, Richard;
   1951)
   The Best of MGM. p87-88.
   BFI/Monthly Film Bulletin. Jun 1951, v18,
      p280.
   Christian Century. Jun 6, 1951, v68, p695.
   Commonweal. May 11, 1951, v54, p117.
   Film Daily. Apr 16, 1951, p6.
   Hollywood Reporter. Apr 13, 1951, p3.
   Library Journal. May 15, 1951, v76, p883.
   Motion Picture Herald Product Digest. Apr 21,
      1951, p810.
   The New Statesman and Nation. May 19, 1951,
      v41, p560.
   The New York Times. May 11, 1951, p32.
   The New Yorker. May 19, 1951, v27, p110.
   Newsweek. May 14, 1951, v37, p98.
   Saturday Review. May 12, 1951, v34, p26.
   Sight and Sound. Apr-Jun 1952, v21, p164-65.
   Time. May 21, 1951, v57, p116.
   Variety. Apr 18, 1951, p6.

The Great Escape (US; Sturges, John;
   1963)
   America. Aug 17, 1963, v109, p178-79.
   BFI/Monthly Film Bulletin. Aug 1963, v30,
      p118.
   Combat Films. p79-115.
   Commonweal. Jul 26, 1963, v78, p458.
   Film Daily. Apr 17, 1963, p7.
   Filmfacts. Aug 15, 1963, v6, p157-59.
   Films and Filming. Jul 1963, v9, p21.
   Films in Review. Jun-Jul 1963, v14, p367-68.
   The Films of Charles Bronson. p111-15.
   The Films of Steve McQueen. p66-79.
   The Films of the Sixties. p108-09.
   The Great Adventure Films. p256-59.
   Hollywood Reporter. Apr 17, 1963, p3.
   Magill's Survey of Cinema. Series I. v2, p682-
      84.
   The New York Times. Aug 8, 1963, p19.
   The New York Times. Aug 11, 1963, SecII, p1.
   The New Yorker. Aug 24, 1963, v39, p64.
   Newsweek. Jul 15, 1963, v62, p79.
   Photoplay. Aug 1963, v64, p14.
   Saturday Review. Jul 6, 1963, v46, p16.
   Time. Jul 19, 1963, v82, p78.
   Variety. Apr 17, 1963, p6.

The Great Gatsby (US; Clayton, Jack;
   1974)
   America. Apr 20, 1974, v130, Inside Back
      Cover.
   Atlantic. Jun 1974, v233, p102.
   Audience. May 1974, v6, p5-7.
   BFI/Monthly Film Bulletin. May 1974, v41,
      p97-98.
   Christian Century. May 22, 1974, v91, p571.
   The Classic American Novel and the Movies.
      p261-67.
   Commonweal. Apr 26, 1974, v100, p188.
   Double Exposure. p98-103.
   Esquire. Jul 1974, v82, p144.
   Film. Jun 1974, n15, p8-9.
   Film Comment. Jul-Aug 1974, v10, p49-51.
   Filming The Great Gatsby. 1974.
   Films and Filming. Jun 1974, v20, p45-47.
   Films Illustrated. Apr 1974, v3, p329.
   Films Illustrated. May 1974, v3, p329.
   Films in Review. May 1974, v25, p306-07.

The Films of Robert Redford. p199-208.
Hollywood Reporter. Mar 26, 1974, p3.
Jack Clayton: A Guide to References and Resources. p37-42.
Literature/Film Quarterly. 1974, n3, v2, p207-15.
The Los Angeles Times. Mar 31, 1974, Calendar, p1.
Magill's Survey of Cinema. Series I. v2, p690-92.
Motion Picture Herald Product Digest. Mar 27, 1974, p85.
Movietone News. Apr 1974, n31, p8-12.
Ms. Jul 1974, v3, p29-30.
The Nation. Apr 6, 1974, v218, p446.
The New Republic. Apr 13, 1974, v170, p20.
New York. Apr 8, 1974, v7, p77-78.
New York. May 27, 1974, v7, p54-55.
New York Review of Books. May 2, 1974, v21, p35-37.
The New York Times. Feb 15, 1974, p52.
The New York Times. Mar 31, 1974, SecII, p1.
The New Yorker. Apr 1, 1974, v50, p93-98.
Newsweek. Apr 1, 1974, v83, p72.
Penthouse. Jul 1974, v5, p36.
Progressive. May 1974, v38, p52-53.
PTA Magazine. Jun 1974, v68, p4.
Rolling Stone. May 9, 1974, p160.
Saturday Review. May 4, 1974, v1, p57.
Sight and Sound. Spr 1974, v43, p78-79.
Sight and Sound. Sum 1974, v43, p177-78.
Time. Mar 18, 1974, v103, p82-91.
Time. Apr 1, 1974, v103, p88.
Variety. Mar 27, 1974, p14.
The Village Voice. Apr 10, 1974, p81.

The Great Manhunt *See* State Secret

The Great Missouri Raid (US; Douglas, Gordon; 1950)
BFI/Monthly Film Bulletin. Mar 1951, v18, p233.
Film Daily. Dec 1, 1950, p7.
Hollywood Reporter. Nov 29, 1950, p3.
Motion Picture Herald Product Digest. Dec 9, 1950, p605.
The New York Times. Apr 9, 1951, p31.
Saturday Review. Feb 17, 1951, v34, p30.
Time. Feb 19, 1951, v57, p102.
Variety. Dec 6, 1950, p15.

The Great Muppet Caper (US, GB; Henson, Jim; 1981)
Hollywood Reporter. Jun 24, 1981, p3.
The Los Angeles Times. Jun 27, 1981, SecII, p4.
Magill's Cinema Annual, 1982. p187-90.
The New Republic. Jul 18, 1981, v185, p26.
The New York Times. Jun 26, 1981, SecIII, p8.
Newsweek. Jul 6, 1981, v98, p75.
Rolling Stone. Aug 6, 1981, p33.
Variety. Jun 24, 1981, p3.

The Great Race (French title: Grande Course Autour du Monde, La) (US; Edwards, Blake; 1965)
America. Sep 25, 1965, v113, p349-51.
BFI/Monthly Film Bulletin. Nov 1965, v32, p163-64.
Blake Edwards (Lehman and Luhr). p168-78.
Cahiers du Cinema in English. 1966, n3, p26-27.
Commonweal. Sep 24, 1965, v82, p699-700.
Film Daily. Jun 29, 1965, p6.
Film Quarterly. Fall 1965, v19, p61.
Films and Filming. Dec 1965, v12, p29.
Films and Filming. Sep 1965, v11, p22.
Films in Review. Oct 1965, v16, p515.
The Films of Jack Lemmon. p158-63.
Hollywood Reporter. Jun 29, 1965, p3.
Life. Sep 17, 1965, v59, p8.

Life. Jul 9, 1965, v59, p84-85.
The London Times. Oct 14, 1965, p16.
Marshall Delaney At the Movies. p89-91.
Motion Picture Herald Product Digest. Jul 21, 1965, p332.
Movie. Aut 1965, n14, p41-42.
The New Republic. Nov 6, 1965, v153, p31.
New Statesman. Oct 15, 1965, v70, p574.
The New York Times. Sep 16, 1965, np.
The New Yorker. Sep 18, 1965, v41, p126.
Newsweek. Aug 2, 1965, v66, p67.
Playboy. Oct 1965, v12, p27-28.
Redbook. Nov 1965, v126, p48.
Saturday Review. Jul 17, 1965, v48, p24.
Senior Scholastic. Oct 7, 1965, v87, p22.
Sight and Sound. Wint 1965-66, v35, p43-44.
The Spectator. Oct 15, 1965, v215, p485-86.
Time. Sep 24, 1965, v86, p106.
Variety. Jun 30, 1965, p6.
The Village Voice. Dec 2, 1965, v11, p21.

The Great Santini (US; Carlino, Lewis J.; 1980)
BFI/Monthly Film Bulletin. Apr 1981, v48, p67.
Christian Century. Nov 26, 1980, v97, p1170.
Christian Science Monitor. Aug 7, 1980, p19.
Films in Review. Oct 1980, v31, p495.
Hollywood Reporter. Oct 25, 1979, p3.
The Los Angeles Times. Aug 17, 1980, Calendar, p28.
Maclean's. Sep 8, 1980, v93, p60-61.
Motion Picture Herald Product Digest. Oct 31, 1980, p41.
The Nation. Aug 2, 1980, v231-132.
The New Republic. Aug 2, 1980, v183, p26-27.
New York. Aug 4, 1980, v13, p56.
The New York Times. Jul 14, 1980, SecIII, p14.
The New Yorker. Sep 1, 1980, v56, p79-80.
Newsday. Jul 14, 1980, SecII, p30.
Time. Sep 1, 1980, v116, p59.
Variety. Oct 31, 1979, p14.

The Great Spy Chase (French title: Bardouzes, Les; Also titled: The Private Eyes) (FR; Lautner, Georges; 1964)
Film Daily. May 3, 1966, p5.
Filmfacts. Jan 1, 1967, v9, p304-05.
The Great Spy Pictures. p205.
Motion Picture Herald Product Digest. May 11, 1966, p519.
The New York Times. Oct 6, 1966, p56.

The Great Spy Mission *See* Operation Crossbow

The Great Train Robbery (Also titled: The First Great Train Robbery) (GB; Crichton, Michael; 1979)
BFI/Monthly Film Bulletin. Feb 1979, v46, p25.
Films in Review. Apr 1979, v30, p245.
Hollywood Reporter. Jan 18, 1979, p3.
The Los Angeles Times. Feb 2, 1979, SecIV, p1.
Motion Picture Herald Product Digest. Feb 21, 1979, p75.
The Nation. Feb 24, 1979, v228, p220-21.
The New Republic. Feb 24, 1979, v180, p25.
The New York Times. Feb 2, 1979, SecIII, p10.
The New Yorker. Feb 12, 1979, v54, p88-90.
Newsweek. Feb 5, 1979, v93, p79.
Saturday Review. Apr 14, 1979, v6, p40.
Time. Feb 5, 1979, v113, p144.
Variety. Jan 17, 1979, p21.

The Great Waldo Pepper (US; Hill, George Roy; 1975)
BFI/Monthly Film Bulletin. May 1975, v42, p108.
Films in Review. Apr 1975, v26, p245.

The Films of George Roy Hill. p114-26.
The Films of Robert Redford. p209-16.
Flying. Feb 1975, v96, p48.
George Roy Hill (Shores). p75-88.
Hollywood Reporter. Mar 3, 1975, p3.
The Los Angeles Times. Mar 13, 1975, SecIV, p1.
Motion Picture Herald Product Digest. Mar 12, 1975, p78.
The New Republic. Mar 22, 1975, v172, p22.
The New York Times. Mar 14, 1975, p24.
The New York Times. Mar 16, 1975, SecII, p17.
The New Yorker. Mar 24, 1975, v51, p94.
The New Yorker. Mar 17, 1975, v85, p93.
Reeling. p617-20.
Senior Scholastic. May 1, 1975, v106, p18.
Variety. Mar 5, 1975, p20.

The Great White Hope (US; Ritt, Martin; 1970)
BFI/Monthly Film Bulletin. Apr 1971, v38, p24.
Deeper into Movies. p158-61.
Film Quarterly. Spr 1971, v24, p56-57.
Hollywood Reporter. Oct 9, 1970, p3, 7.
Life. Nov 6, 1970, v69, p10.
Look. Nov 17, 1970, v34, p45.
The New Republic. Oct 31, 1970, v163, p30.
The New York Times. Oct 12, 1970, p46.
The New Yorker. Oct 17, 1970, v46, p155-57.
Newsweek. Oct 26, 1970, v76, p89.
Saturday Review. Oct 17, 1970, v53, p50.
Time. Oct 19, 1970, v96, p87.
Variety. Oct 14, 1970, p17.

The Greatest (US, GB; Gries, Tom; 1977)
BFI/Monthly Film Bulletin. Sep 1977, v44, p192.
Films in Review. Aug-Sep 1977, v28, p441.
Hollywood Reporter. May 20, 1977, p3.
The Los Angeles Times. May 19, 1977, SecIV, p14.
Motion Picture Herald Product Digest. Jun 8, 1977, p2.
The New York Times. May 21, 1977, p11.
Newsweek. May 30, 1977, v89 p63.
Sports Illustrated. May 30, 1977, v46, p45.
Time. Jun 6, 1977, v109, p76.
Variety. May 25, 1977, p21.
The Village Voice. Jun 6, 1977, p41.

The Greatest Love *See* Europa Fifty-One

The Greatest Show on Earth (US; DeMille, Cecil B.; 1952)
BFI/Monthly Film Bulletin. Mar 1952, v19, p29-33.
Catholic World. Feb 1952, v174, p384-85.
Cecil B. DeMille: A Guide to References and Resources. p107-08.
Christian Century. May 28, 1952, v69, p655.
Commonweal. Jan 25, 1952, v55, p399-400.
Cue. Jan 12, 1952, p16.
Film Daily. Jan 2, 1952, p5.
Films in Review. Feb 1952, v3, p89.
The Films of Cecil B. DeMille. p350-55.
The Films of James Stewart. p145-48.
The Films of the Fifties. p79-80.
Holiday. Mar 1952, v11, p19.
Hollywood Reporter. Jan 2, 1952, p3-4.
The London Times. Feb 14, 1952, p4.
Magill's Survey of Cinema. Series I. v2, p697-99.
Motion Picture Herald Product Digest. Jan 5, 1952, p1177.
The New Republic. Feb 11, 1952, v126, p22.
The New Statesman and Nation. Feb 23, 1952, v43, p214.
The New York Times. Jan 11, 1952, p17.
The New Yorker. Jan 19, 1952, v27, p83.
Newsweek. Jan 21, 1952, v39, p90.

Saturday Review. Jan 12, 1952, v35, p27.
Selected Film Criticism, 1951-1960. p49-50.
Senior Scholastic. Feb 6, 1952, v60, p29.
Theatre Arts. Feb 1952, v36, p33.
Time. Jan 14, 1952, v59, p90.
Variety. Jan 2, 1952, p68.

The Greatest Story Ever Told (US; Stevens, George; 1965)
America. Feb 27, 1965, v112, p296-97.
BFI/Monthly Film Bulletin. May 1965, v32, p69-70.
Catholic World. Apr 1965, v201, p76.
Christian Century. Apr 21, 1965, v82 p492-95.
Christian Science Monitor (Western edition). Mar 15, 1965, p6.
Cinema. Mar-Apr 1965, v2, p49.
Cinema. Dec-Jan 1964-65, v2, p 4-7, 26-35.
Commonweal. Mar 12, 1965, v81, p765.
The Complete Films of John Wayne. p255.
Esquire. Jul 1965, v64, p120-22.
Film Daily. Feb 15, 1965, p4.
Filmfacts. Apr 30, 1965, v8, p63-68.
Films and Filming. Jun 1965, v11, p25-26.
Films and Filming. Apr 1965, v11, p8-9.
Films in Review. Mar 1965, v16, p173-76.
The Films of Charlton Heston. p142-43.
The Films of Sidney Poitier. p129-31.
Hollywood Reporter. Feb 15, 1965, p3.
Illustrated London News. Apr 24, 1965, v246, p28.
Life. Feb 26, 1965, v58, p25.
The London Times. Apr 8, 1965, p6.
Look. Dec 29, 1964, v28, p44-45.
Motion Picture Herald Product Digest. Feb 17, 1965, p13, 24.
Motion Picture Herald Product Digest. Mar 3, 1965, p244.
The Nation. Mar 1, 1965, v200, p234.
National Review. May 18, 1965, v17, p430-32.
The New Republic. Mar 6, 1965, v152, p32.
New Statesman. Apr 16, 1965, v69, p621-22.
The New York Times. Feb 16, 1965, p40.
The New Yorker. Feb 20, 1965, v41, p137.
Newsweek. Feb 22, 1965, v65, p96B.
On Movies. p430-37.
Playboy. May 1965, v12, p34, 36.
The Private Eye, the Cowboy and the Very Naked Girl. p117-20.
Private Screenings. p172-75.
Reporter. Apr 22, 1965, v32, p36.
Saturday Review. Feb 27, 1965, v48, p41.
Senior Scholastic. Apr 8, 1965, v86, sup10.
Senior Scholastic. Mar 18, 1965, v86, p28.
The Spectator. Apr 16, 1965, v214, p506.
Surrealism and the Cinema. p30-37.
Time. Feb 26, 1965, v85, p96.
Tynan Right and Left. p226-27.
Variety. Feb 17, 1965, p7.
The Village Voice. Mar 4, 1965, v10, p15.
Vogue. Apr 15, 1965, v145, p57.
A World on Film. p28-30.

The Greek Tycoon (US; Thompson, J. Lee; 1978)
Hollywood Reporter. May 10, 1978, p3.
The Los Angeles Times. May 12, 1978, SecIV, p30.
Motion Picture Herald Product Digest. May 31, 1978, p97.
New York. May 29, 1978, v11, p67-68.
The New York Times. May 12, 1978, SecIII, p10.
The New York Times. May 21, 1978, SecII, p17.
The New Yorker. May 29, 1978, v54, p111-13.
Newsweek. May 22, 1978, v91, p78.
Saturday Review. Jun 24, 1978, v5, p52.

Time. May 22, 1978, v111, p84.
Variety. May 10, 1978, p22.

The Green Berets (US; Wayne, John; Kellogg, Ray; 1968)
BFI/Monthly Film Bulletin. Sep 1968, v35, p131-32.
Christian Science Monitor (Western edition). Jul 10, 1968, p4.
The Complete Films of John Wayne. p271-73.
Film 68/69. p103-06.
Film Daily. Jun 17, 1968, p3.
Film Quarterly. Fall 1968, v22, p73-74.
Filmfacts. Oct 1, 1968, v11, p259-60.
Films and Filming. Oct 1968, v15, p44-45.
Films in Review. Aug-Sep 1968, v19, p453-54.
The Films of the Sixties. p241-45.
Hollywood Reporter. Jun 17, 1968, p3.
Life. Jul 19, 1968, v65, p8.
The London Times. Jul 10, 1968, p19.
Motion Picture Herald Product Digest. Jun 26, 1968, p826.
The New York Times. Jun 20, 1968, p49.
The New York Times. Jun 29, 1968, v44, p24-27.
The New Yorker. Jul 6, 1968, v44, p44.
Newsweek. Jul 1, 1968, v72, p94.
Politics and Film. p145-48.
The Spectator. Aug 16, 1968, v221, p237.
Take One. 1968, v1, n11, p23-24.
Time. Jun 21, 1968, v91, p84.
Variety. Jun 19, 1968, p6.
Vietnam on Film. p33-52.
A Year In the Dark. p177-78.

Green Fire (US; Marton, Andrew; 1954)
America. Jan 1, 1955, v92, p367.
BFI/Monthly Film Bulletin. Feb 1955, v22, p20.
Commonweal. Jan 28, 1955, v61, p455.
Farm Journal. Feb 1955, v79, p149.
Film Daily. Dec 29, 1954, p4.
Films and Filming. Apr 1955, v1, p23.
Hollywood Reporter. Dec 23, 1954, p3.
The London Times. Feb 14, 1955, p3.
Motion Picture Herald Product Digest. Dec 25, 1954, p258.
National Parent-Teacher. Jan 1955, v49, p40.
The New York Times. Dec 25, 1954, p7.
Newsweek. Jan 24, 1955, v45, p94.
The Spectator. Feb 4, 1955, v194, p130.
The Tatler. Feb 16, 1955, v215, p292.
Time. Jan 10, 1955, v65, p82.
Variety. Dec 29, 1954, p6.

The Green Man (US; Day, Robert; 1957)
BFI/Monthly Film Bulletin. Oct 1956, v23, p125.
Film Daily. Jun 13, 1957, p8.
Films and Filming. Nov 1956, v3, p24.
Hollywood Reporter. Sep 27, 1957, p3.
Motion Picture Herald Product Digest. Jun 8, 1957, p410.
The New York Times. May 23, 1957, p40.
The New Yorker. Jun 1, 1957, v33, p72.
Variety. Nov 26, 1956, p15.

Greetings (US; De Palma, Brian; 1968)
BFI/Monthly Film Bulletin. Nov 1969, v36, p231-32.
Brian De Palma (Bliss). p1-7.
Cinema. 1969, v5, n2, p45.
Esquire. Apr 1969, v71, p42.
Figures of Light. p133-34.
Film Society Review. Apr 1969, v4, p37-41.
Filmfacts. Jan 15, 1969, v11, p461-62.
Films and Filming. Dec 1969, v16, p43-44.
Five Thousand One Nights At Movies. p233.
Going Steady. p261-62.
Hollywood Reporter. Jul 8, 1969, p3.
Motion Picture Herald Product Digest. Jan 1, 1969, p88.

Movies Into Film. p110-11.
The New Republic. Jan 18, 1969, v160, p23.
The New York Times. Dec 16, 1968, p61.
The New Yorker. Dec 21, 1968, v44, p91.
Time. Jan 31, 1969, v93, p75.
Variety. Dec 25, 1968, p18.

Gregory's Girl (GB; Forsyth, Bill; 1981)
Hollywood Reporter. May 14, 1982, p3.
The Los Angeles Times. Jul 20, 1982, SecVI, p1.
Magill's Cinema Annual, 1983. p193-96.
The New York Times. May 26, 1982, SecIII, p23.
Newsweek. Jun 14, 1982, v99, p89.
Time. Jun 21, 1982, v119, p72.
Variety. May 25, 1982, p3.

Gremlins (US; Dante, Joe; 1984)
America. Jun 23, 1984, v150, p493.
American Film. Jun 1984, v9, p78.
BFI/Monthly Film Bulletin. Dec 1984, v51, p382.
Cinefantastique. 1984, v14, n4/5, p109.
Film Comment. Jul-Aug 1984, v20, p50.
Film Comment. May-Jun 1984, v20, p22-27.
Film Journal. Jul 1984, v87, p22.
Films in Review. Aug 1984, v35, p411.
Hollywood Reporter. May 21, 1984, p8.
The Los Angeles Times. Jun 8, 1984, SecVI, p1.
Maclean's. Jun 4, 1984, v97, p48.
Magill's Cinema Annual, 1985. 230-35.
Midnight Marquee. Fall 1984, n33, p29.
The Nation. Jun 30, 1984, v238, p810-11.
The New Leader. Jul 9, 1984, v67, p20.
New York. Jun 18, 1984, v17, p87-88.
The New York Times. Jun 8, 1984, SecIII, p10.
Newsweek. Jun 18, 1984, v60, p99.
Time. Jun 4, 1984, v123, p64-66.
Variety. May 23, 1984, p12.

The Grey Fox (CAN; Borsos, Philip; 1983)
Christianity Today. Oct 21, 1983, v27, p47.
Film Comment. Jul-Aug 1983, v19, p78-79.
Films in Review. Dec 1983, v34, p622.
Hollywood Reporter. Jul 14, 1983, p4.
The Los Angeles Times. Aug 3, 1983, SecVI, p1.
Maclean's. Apr 11, 1983, v96, p70.
The New Republic. Aug 1, 1983, v189, p22-23.
The New York Times. Jul 13, 1983, SecIII, p17.
The New Yorker. Aug 8, 1983, v59, p87-89.
Newsweek. Aug 1, 1983, v102, p46.
Rolling Stone. Aug 18, 1983, p31.
Time. Aug 15, 1983, v122, p67.

Greystoke: the Legend of Tarzan, Lord of the Apes (GB; Hudson, Hugh; 1984)
America. May 12, 1984, v150, p363.
BFI/Monthly Film Bulletin. May 1984, v51, p150.
Cinefantastique. 1984, v14, n3, p13.
Cinema Papers. Aug 1984, n47, p268-69.
Commonweal. May 4, 1984, v111, p280.
Films and Filming. May 1984, n359, p38.
Films in Review. May 1984, v35, p302.
Hollywood Reporter. Mar 19, 1984, p4.
Humanist. Jul-Aug 1984, v44, p32-33.
The Los Angeles Times. Mar 30, 1984, SecVI, p1.
Maclean's. Apr 2, 1984, v97, p65.
Magill's Cinema Annual, 1985. p236-42.
The Nation. May 12, 1984, v238, p587-88.
National Review. Jun 1, 1984, v36, p48-49.
The New Republic. Apr 23, 1984, v190, p25.
New Statesman. Apr 13, 1984, v107, p29-30.
New York. Apr 9, 1984, v17, p66-67.
The New York Times. Apr 1, 1984, p21.
The New Yorker. Apr 2, 1984, v60, p119-21.
Newsweek. Mar 26, 1984, v103, p74-75.
Photoplay. Jun 1984, v35, p23.

Senior Scholastic Update. Apr 27, 1984, v116, p16.
Stills. Jun-Jul 1984, n12, p100.
Time. Apr 2, 1984, v123, p89.
Variety. Mar 21, 1984, p16.
Vogue. Jun 1984, v174, p52.

Grido, Il (Also titled: The Outcry; The Cry) (IT, US; Antonioni, Michelangelo; 1957)
Antonioni (Cameron and Wood). p67-71.
Dictionary of Films. p140.
Esquire. Jun 1961, v55, p57-58.
Film Criticism. 1984, v9, n1, p8-16, 38-46.
Film Daily. Oct 22, 1962, p20.
Filmfacts. Jan 4, 1962, v5, p319-20.
Films and Filming. Nov 1961, v8, p25.
Motion Picture Herald Product Digest. Jan 9, 1963, p730.
The New Republic. Dec 29, 1962, v147, p26.
The New York Times. Oct 23, 1962, p42.
Newsweek. Oct 29, 1962, v60, p87-88.
Saturday Review. Nov 3, 1962, v45, p41.
Time. Nov 16, 1962, v80, pE9.
Variety. Sep 25, 1957, p26.
A World on Film. p311.

The Grissom Gang (US; Aldrich, Robert; 1971)
America. Jun 5, 1971, v124, p595.
BFI/Monthly Film Bulletin. Dec 1971, v38, p239.
Filmfacts. 1971, v14, p166.
The Films and Career of Robert Aldrich. p166.
Films and Filming. Jan 1972, v18, n4, p52-53.
The New York Times. May 29, 1971, p10.
Robert Aldrich: A Guide to References and Resources. p53-56.
Variety. May 26, 1971, p13.
The Village Voice. Jul 15, 1971, v16,.

The Groom Wore Spurs (US; Whorf, Richard; 1951)
BFI/Monthly Film Bulletin. Jul 1951, v18, p297.
Film Daily. Feb 5, 1951, p8.
The Films of Ginger Rogers. p228-52.
Hollywood Reporter. Feb 5, 1951, p3.
Library Journal. Feb 15, 1951, v76, p343.
Motion Picture Herald Product Digest. Feb 10, 1951, p705.
Motion Picture Herald Product Digest. Feb 24, 1951, p722.
The New York Times. Mar 14, 1951, p41.
The New Yorker. Mar 24, 1951, v27, p95.
Time. Mar 12, 1951, v57, p96.
Variety. Feb 7, 1951, p6.

Grounds for Marriage (US; Leonard, Robert Z.; 1950)
BFI/Monthly Film Bulletin. Feb 1951, v18, p218-19.
Christian Century. Jan 31, 1951, v68, p159.
Film Daily. Dec 13, 1950, p14.
Hollywood Reporter. Dec 12, 1950, p3.
Motion Picture Herald Product Digest. Dec 16, 1950, p614.
The New York Times. Jan 12, 1951, p24.
Newsweek. Feb 5, 1951, v37, p81.
Time. Jun 29, 1951, v57, p104.
Variety. Dec 13, 1950, p8.

The Group (US; Lumet, Sidney; 1966)
America. Mar 26, 1966, v114, p424.
BFI/Monthly Film Bulletin. Nov 1966, v33, p163-64.
Christian Science Monitor (Western edition). Apr 27, 1966, p6.
Cinema. Jul 1966, v3, p50.
Commonweal. Mar 18, 1966, v83, p698-99.
Confessions of a Cultist. p245-48.

Esquire. Dec 1965, v64, p234-37.
Film Daily. Mar 2, 1966, p3.
Film Quarterly. Wint 1967-68, v21, p17.
Film Quarterly. Sum 1966, v19, p59-60.
Filmfacts. May 1, 1966, v9, p61-64.
Films and Filming. Sep 1966, v12, p14-15.
Films in Review. Apr 1966, v17, p250-51.
Holiday. May 1966, v39, p155-56.
Kiss Kiss Bang Bang. p83-124.
Life. Apr 8, 1966, v60, p116-17.
The London Times. Sep 13, 1966, p11.
The London Times. Sep 22, 1966, p6.
Look. Sep 7, 1965, v29, p32-36.
Mademoiselle. Sep 1965, v61, p166-68.
Motion Picture Herald Product Digest. Mar 16, 1966, p483.
National Review. May 17, 1966, v18, p480-81.
The New Republic. Apr 9, 1966, v154, p25.
New Statesman. Sep 30, 1966, v72, p488.
The New York Times. Mar 17, 1966, p35.
The New Yorker. Mar 19, 1966, v42, p173-74.
Newsweek. Mar 21, 1966, v67, p105A.
Playboy. May 1966, v13, p30.
The Private Eye, the Cowboy and the Very Naked Girl. p188-90.
Private Screenings. p247-48.
Reporter. May 19, 1966, v34, p55-56.
Saturday Review. Mar 26, 1966, v49, p46.
Sidney Lumet: A Guide to References and Resources. p78-80.
Sight and Sound. Aut 1966, v35, p200.
The Spectator. Sep 30, 1966, v217, p413.
Time. Mar 11, 1966, v87, p99.
Variety. Mar 2, 1966, p6.
The Village Voice. May 12, 1966, v11, p29.
Vogue. Apr 15, 1966, v147, p66.

Guerre du Feu, La *See* Quest for Fire

Guerre Est Finie, La (Also titled: The War Is Over) (FR, SWED; Resnais, Alain; 1966)
Alan Resnais (Kreidl). p137-53.
BFI/Monthly Film Bulletin. Nov 1966, v33, p164-65.
Big Screen, Little Screen. p373-74.
Cahiers du Cinema in English. Feb 1967, n8, p59-62.
Christian Century. Mar 15, 1967, v84, p346.
Christian Science Monitor (Western edition). Jan 22, 1968, p4.
Cineaste. Fall 1967, v1, p12-13.
Cineaste. Sum 1967, v1, p12-13.
The Cinema of Alain Resnais. p133-47.
Commonweal. Mar 3, 1967, v85, p626.
Confessions of a Cultist. p285-87.
Dictionary of Films. p141.
Esquire. May 1967, v67, p68.
Film 67/68. p126-31.
The Film Narratives of Alain Resnais. p87-100.
Film Quarterly. Sum 1967, v20, p68-69.
Film Society Review. Mar 1968, p23-27.
Filmfacts. Feb 15, 1967, v10, p11-13.
Films and Filming. Nov 1966, v13, p9, 12.
Films in Review. Mar 1967, v18, p176-77.
Harper's Magazine. Jun 1967, v234, p111-12.
Hollywood Reporter. Oct 3, 1967, p3.
International Film Guide. 1967, v4, p69.
Kiss Kiss Bang Bang. p197-202.
The London Times. Sep 1, 1966, p11.
Magill's Survey of Cinema. Foreign Language Films. v3, p1313-18.
Motion Picture Herald Product Digest. Mar 8, 1967, p655.
Movies Into Film. p67-70.
The New Republic. Mar 18, 1967, v156, p29-32.
The New York Times. Sep 23, 1966, p43.
The New York Times. Feb 2, 1967, p29.
The New Yorker. Feb 11, 1967, v42, p134.

Newsweek. Feb 20, 1967, v69, p98.
Playboy. May 1967, v14, p36, 39.
The Private Eye, the Cowboy and the Very Naked Girl. p236-38, 271.
Second Sight. p95-97.
Sight and Sound. Aut 1966, v35, p196-97.
Sight and Sound. Aut 1965, v34, p160-63.
Time. Feb 3, 1967, v89, p76.
Variety. May 18, 1966, p7.
The Village Voice. Feb 2, 1967, v12, p24.
Vogue. Mar 15, 1967, v149, p55.

Guerre Secret *See* The Dirty Game

Guess Who's Coming to Dinner (US; Kramer, Stanley; 1967)
America. Dec 16, 1967, v117, p750.
BFI/Monthly Film Bulletin. Mar 1968, v35, p35.
Commonweal. Dec 29, 1967, v87, p409.
Ebony. Jan 1968, v23, p56-58.
Esquire. Feb 1968, v69, p20.
The Evolution of Character Portrayals in the Films of Sidney Poitier, 1950-1978. p158-78.
Film Comment. Wint 1969, v5, p26-33.
Film Daily. Dec 6, 1967, p7.
Film Quarterly. Sum 1968, v21, p58.
Films and Filming. Mar 1968, v14, p4-7.
Films and Filming. Jun 1968, p29-30.
Films in Review. Jan 1968, v19, p51-52.
The Films of Katharine Hepburn. p184-88.
The Films of Sidney Poitier. p155-65.
The Films of Spencer Tracy. p248-52.
Harper's. Jan 1968, v236, p80-81.
Hollywood Reporter. Dec 6, 1967, p3.
Life. Dec 15, 1967, v63, p16.
Mademoiselle. Jan 1968, v66, p26.
Magill's Survey of Cinema. Series II. v2, p945-48.
Motion Picture Herald Product Digest. Dec 6, 1967, p747.
The Nation. Jan 1, 1968, v206, p28.
The New Republic. Dec 16, 1967, v157, p19.
The New York Times. Dec 12, 1967, p56.
The New Yorker. Dec 16, 1967, v43, p108.
Newsweek. Dec 25, 1967, v70, p70.
Reporter. Mar 21, 1968, v38, p40.
Saturday Review. Dec 16, 1967, v50, p47.
Senior Scholastic. Feb 1, 1968, v92, p20.
Stanley Kramer, Film Maker. p273-82.
Take One. 1968, v1, p23-24.
Time. Dec 15, 1967, v90, p108.
Variety. Dec 6, 1967, p6.
The Village Voice. Dec 14, 1967, p45.
Vogue. Jan 1, 1968, v151, p56.

Guichets du Louvre, Les *See* Black Thursday

A Guide for the Married Man (US; Kelly, Gene; 1967)
America. Jun 17, 1967, v116, p860.
BFI/Monthly Film Bulletin. Sep 1967, v34, p135.
Esquire. Sep 1967, v68, p28.
Film Daily. Apr 24, 1967, p3.
Films and Filming. Oct 1967, v14, p23-24.
The Films of Gene Kelly. p224-26.
Hollywood Reporter. Apr 19, 1967, p3.
Journal of Popular Culture. Spr 1970, v3, p755-66.
Motion Picture Herald Product Digest. Apr 26, 1967, p677.
The New York Times. May 27, 1967, p16.
The New Yorker. Jun 10, 1967, v43, p72.
Newsweek. Jun 5, 1967, v69, p96.
Variety. Apr 19, 1967, p6.
The Village Voice. Jul 13, 1967, p23.

The Gumball Rally (US; Ball, Chuck; 1976)
BFI/Monthly Film Bulletin. Oct 1976, v43, p214.
Films and Filming. Nov 1976, v23, p36.
Hollywood Reporter. Jul 22, 1976, p3.
Independent Film Journal. Aug 6, 1976, v78, p9.
New York. Sep 6, 1976, v9, p72-73.
The New York Times. Oct 10, 1976, SecII, p17-18.
Time. Sep 20, 1976, v108, p80.
Variety. Jul 28, 1976, p24.

Gun Glory (US; Rowland, Roy; 1957)
America. Aug 10, 1957, v97, p492.
BFI/Monthly Film Bulletin. Nov 1957, v24, p139.
Commonweal. Aug 9, 1957, v66, p472.
Film Daily. Aug 1, 1957, p6.
Hollywood Reporter. Jul 22, 1957, p3.
Motion Picture Herald Product Digest. Jul 27, 1957, p465.
The New York Times. Jul 20, 1957, p8.
Variety. Jul 24, 1957, p7.

Gun Runners (US; Siegel, Don; 1958)
BFI/Monthly Film Bulletin. Oct 1958, v25, p127.
Film Daily. Sep 15, 1958, v114, p6.
Filmfacts. Jan 7, 1959, v1, p249-50.
Films in Review. Apr 1959, v10, p217-18.
Hollywood Reporter. Sep 15, 1958, p3.
Variety. Sep 17, 1958, p7.

Gunfight at the O.K. Corral (US; Sturges, John; 1957)
America. Jun 1, 1957, v97, p292.
American Cinematographer. Jul 1957, v308, p436-37.
BFI/Monthly Film Bulletin. Jul 1957, v24, p82.
Burt Lancaster: A Pictorial History of His Films. p96-97.
Burt Lancaster: The Man and His Movies. p74-76.
Cinema, the Magic Vehicle. v2, p367-68.
Film Daily. May 10, 1957, p6.
Films and Filming. Aug 1957, v3, p26-27.
Films and Filming. Sep 1965, v10, p23.
The films of Kirk Douglas. p137-40.
The Films of the Fifties. p221-23.
Hollywood Reporter. May 10, 1957, p3.
Magill's Survey of Cinema. Series II. v2, p952-55.
Motion Picture Herald Product Digest. May 25, 1957, v207, p385.
The New York Times. May 20, 1956, SecII, p5.
The New York Times. May 30, 1957, p23.
The New York Times. Jun 9, 1957, SecII, p1.
The New Yorker. Jun 8, 1957, v33, p88.
Newsweek. Jun 3, 1957, v49, p101.
One Good Film Deserves Another. p90-93.
Saturday Review. Jun 22, 1957, v40, p25.
Time. Jun 17, 1957, v69, p96.
The Village Voice. May 15, 1957, p7.

The Gunfighter (US; King, Henry; 1950)
BFI/Monthly Film Bulletin. Aug 1950, v17, p114.
Christian Century. Jul 26, 1950, v67, p903.
Cinema, the Magic Vehicle. v2, p63-64.
Commonweal. Jul 14, 1950, v52, p346.
Film Daily. Apr 26, 1950, p5.
Film Notes (Bowser). p117-18.
Films and Filming. Jun 1964, v10, p28.
The Films of Gregory Peck. p97-102.
The Films of the Fifties. p35-38.
The Great Western Pictures. p124-25.
Hollywood Reporter. Apr 26, 1950, p3.
The London Times. Aug 14, 1950, p6.
Magill's Survey of Cinema. Series II. v2, p956-58.

The Making of the Great Westerns. p195-206.
Motion Picture Herald Product Digest. Apr 29, 1950, p277.
The New Statesman and Nation. Aug 19, 1950, v40, p200.
The New York Times. Jun 24, 1950, p7.
The New Yorker. Jun 24, 1950, v26, p65.
Newsweek. Jul 10, 1950, v36, p85.
Shots in the Dark. p213-15.
The Spectator. Aug 11, 1950, v185, p177.
Time. Jul 17, 1950, v56, p90.
Variety. Apr 26, 1950, p8.

Guns in the Afternoon *See* Ride the High Country

The Guns of Navarone (US; Thompson, J. Lee; 1961)
America. Jul 1, 1961, v105, p492-93.
BFI/Monthly Film Bulletin. Jun 1961, v28, p75-76.
Commonweal. Jun 30, 1961, v74, p353.
Film Daily. May 19, 1961, p6.
Filmfacts. Jul 14, 1961, v4, p137-39.
Films in Review. Aug-Sep 1961, v17, p430.
The Films of Anthony Quinn. p190-91.
The Films of David Niven. p166-71.
The Films of Gregory Peck. p170-73.
Life. Jun 9, 1961, v50, p120-21.
Magill's Survey of Cinema. Series I. v2, p700-03.
The New Republic. Jun 26, 1961, v144, p28.
The New York Times. Jun 23, 1961, p19.
The New Yorker. Jun 26, 1961, v67, p94.
Saturday Review. Jun 24, 1961, v44, p24.
Time. Jun 30, 1961, v77, p50.
Variety. May 3, 1961, p6.

The Guru (US; Ivory, James; 1969)
America. May 3, 1969, v120, p549.
Film 69/70. p133-34.
Film Daily. Feb 25, 1969, p8.
Filmfacts. 1969, v12, p188.
Films and Filming. Jul 1969, v15, p38.
Films in Review. Mar 1969, v20, p180.
Harper's Magazine. Apr 1969, v238, p116-17.
Life. May 16, 1969, v67, p16.
The Nation. May 5, 1969, v208, p582.
The New York Times. Apr 21, 1969, p58.
The New Yorker. May 10, 1969, v45, p135-38.
Senior Scholastic. Apr 18, 1969, v94, p20.
Sight and Sound. Sum 1969, v38, p155.
Time. May 9, 1969, v93, p105.
Variety. Feb 12, 1969, p6.

Guys & Dolls (US; Mankiewicz, Joseph L.; 1955)
America. Nov 19, 1955, v94, p224.
Catholic World. Dec 1955, v182, p217.
Commonweal. Nov 18, 1955, v63, p165.
Dance Magazine. Nov 1955, v29, p18-23.
Dance Magazine. Dec 1955, v29, p9.
Film Culture. Wint 1955, v1, n5/6, p34.
Film Daily. Nov 2, 1955, p5.
Films and Filming. Oct 1956, v3, n1, p23-24.
Films in Review. Dec 1955, v6, n10, p523-25.
The Films of Frank Sinatra. p95-100.
Joseph L. Mankiewicz (Dick). p121-26.
Library Journal. Nov 15, 1955, v80, p2594.
Motion Picture Herald Product Digest. Nov 12, 1955, p665.
The Nation. Dec 3, 1955, v181, p486.
The New Republic. Apr 23, 1956, v134, p20.
The New York Times. Mar 13, 1955, SecII, p5.
The New York Times. May 8, 1955, SecII, p5.
The New York Times. Oct 9, 1955, SecVI, p28.
The New York Times. Oct 23, 1955, SecII, p5.
The New York Times. Nov 4, 1955, p26.
The New York Times. Nov 6, 1955, SecII, p1.
The New Yorker. Nov 5, 1955, v31, p131.
Newsweek. Nov 7, 1955, v46, p117.

Samuel Goldwyn Presents. p287-91.
Saturday Review. Nov 12, 1955, v38, p25.
Time. Nov 14, 1955, v66, p116.
Time. Dec 12, 1955, v66, p34.
Variety. Nov 2, 1955, p6.

Gycklarnas afton *See* The Naked Night

Gypsy (US; LeRoy, Mervyn; 1962)
America. Nov 17, 1962, v107, p1104.
BFI/Monthly Film Bulletin. Feb 1963, v30, p16-17.
Commonweal. Nov 23, 1962, v77, p231.
Film. Spr 1963, n35, p34.
Film Daily. Sep 27, 1962, p5.
Film Quarterly. Spr 1963, v16, p58.
Filmfacts. Nov 16, 1962, v5, p259-61.
Films and Filming. Jan 1963, v9, p45.
Films in Review. Nov 1962, v13, p553-54.
Hollywood Reporter. Sep 26, 1962, p3.
Motion Picture Herald Product Digest. Oct 17, 1962, p673.
Movie. Dec 1962, n5, p40.
Movie. Jan 1963, n6, p27.
The Musical: From Broadway to Hollywood. p91-95.
The New York Times. Nov 2, 1962, p24.
The New Yorker. Nov 10, 1962, v38, p235.
Newsweek. Nov 12, 1962, v60, p96.
Saturday Review. Dec 8, 1962, v45, p50.
Time. Nov 16, 1962, v80, p97, E9.
Variety. Sep 26, 1962, p6.

Gypsy Girl *See* Sky West and Crooked

The Gypsy Moths (US; Frankenheimer, John; 1969)
America. Sep 6, 1969, v121, p144.
Burt Lancaster: A Pictorial Treasury of His Films. p112-14.
Burt Lancaster: The Man and His Movies. p140-42.
The Cinema of John Frankenheimer. p 189-99.
Film Daily. Sep 5, 1969, p5.
Filmfacts. 1969, v12, p464.
Films and Filming. Dec 1969, v16, p45-46.
Films in Review. Oct 1969, v20, p512.
Hollywood Reporter. Aug 27, 1969, p3.
Life. Sep 26, 1969, v77, p24.
The New York Times. Aug 29, 1969, p20.
The New Yorker. Aug 30, 1969, v45, p73.
Newsweek. Sep 8, 1969, v74, p82.
Sight and Sound. Wint 1969-70, v39, p51.
Variety. Aug 27, 1969, p18.

H. M. S. Defiant *See* Damn the Defiant!

Hadaka no Akima *See* The Island

Hagbard and Signe (Also titled: Roede Kappe, Den; The Red Mantle) (SWED, DEN, ICE; Axel, Gabriel; 1967)
BFI/Monthly Film Bulletin. Mar 1969, v36, p60.
Christian Science Monitor (Western edition). Jun 10, 1968, p6.
Cinema. Fall 1968, v4, p42-43.
Filmfacts. Aug 1, 1968, v11, p203-04.
Films and Filming. Apr 1969, v15, p50-51.
Films in Review. Jun-Jul 1968, v19, p377.
Hollywood Reporter. Aug 15, 1968, p3.
The New Republic. Jun 8, 1968, v158, p26.
The New York Times. May 17, 1968, p56.
The Spectator. Feb 7, 1969, v222, p180.
Time. May 10, 1968, v91, p117.
Variety. Jan 25, 1967, p21.

Hail, Mary (French title: Je Vous Salue, Marie) (FR, SWITZ; Godard, Jean-Luc; 1985)
America. Dec 14, 1985, v153, p426.
American Film. Jan 1986, v11, p38.

BFI/Monthly Film Bulletin. Aug 1985, v52, p267.
Christian Century. Jun 5, 1985, v102, p590.
Commonweal. Nov 15, 1985, v112, p648.
Film Comment. Nov-Dec 1985, v21, p61-62.
The Los Angeles Times. Nov 20, 1985, SecVI, p1.
Magill's Cinema Annual, 1986. p182-85.
New York. Oct 21, 1985, v18, p87-88.
The New York Times. Oct 7, 1985, SecIII, p16.
Saturday Review. Sep-Oct 1985, v11, p77.
Time. Oct 21, 1985, v126, p81.
Vogue. Oct 1985, v175, p92.

Hair (US; Forman, Milos; 1979)
America. Apr 7, 1979, v140, p286.
BFI/Monthly Film Bulletin. Jul 1979, v46, p146.
Commonweal. May 25, 1979, v106, p305-36.
Films in Review. May 1979, v30, p313.
The Los Angeles Times. Mar 15, 1979, SecIV, p1.
Magill's Survey of Cinema. Series II. v2, p966-68.
Motion Picture Herald Product Digest. Apr 4, 1979, p87.
The New Republic. Apr 14, 1979, v180, p40-41.
New York. Mar 19, 1979, v12, p62-63.
The New York Times. Mar 14, 1979, SecIII, p15.
The New Yorker. Apr 16, 1979, v55, p142.
Newsweek. Mar 19, 1979, v93, p102.
Time. Mar 19, 1979, v113, p88.
Variety. Mar 14, 1979, p22.

Hakuchi *See* The Idiot

Half a Sixpence (GB, US; Sidney, George; 1967)
America. Mar 9, 1968, v118, p331.
BFI/Monthly Film Bulletin. Feb 1968, v35, p20-21.
Christian Science Monitor (Western edition). Jun 10, 1968, p6.
Cinema. Sum 1967, v3, p42.
Commonweal. Mar 15, 1968, v87, p718.
Film Daily. Feb 13, 1968, p15.
Filmfacts. Mar 1, 1968, v11, p51-53.
Films and Filming. Feb 1968, v14, p24-25.
Films in Review. Mar 1968, v19, p174-75.
Motion Picture Herald Product Digest. Feb 14, 1968, p773.
The New York Times. Feb 21, 1968, p60.
The New Yorker. Mar 2, 1968, v44, p126.
Saturday Review. Feb 24, 1968, v51, p53.
Senior Scholastic. Mar 7, 1968, v92, p23-24.
Time. Mar 1, 1968, v91, p84.
Variety. Dec 27, 1967, p6.
A Year In the Dark. p51-52.

Half Angel (US; Sale, Richard; 1951)
BFI/Monthly Film Bulletin. Aug 1951, v18, p312.
Christian Century. Jul 4, 1951, v68, p807.
Commonweal. Jul 6, 1951, v54, p310.
Film Daily. Apr 10, 1951, p6.
Hollywood Reporter. Apr 9, 1951, p3.
The London Times. Jul 23, 1951, p2.
Motion Picture Herald Product Digest. Apr 14, 1951, p802.
The New Statesman and Nation. Jul 28, 1951, v42, p95.
The New York Times. Jun 16, 1951, p9.
The New Yorker. Jun 23, 1951, v27, p61.
Newsweek. May 14, 1951, v37, p100.
Time. Jun 25, 1951, v57, p90.
Variety. Apr 11, 1951, p6.

The Hallelujah Trail (US; Sturges, John; 1965)
Burt Lancaster: A Pictorial Treasury of His Films. p126-29.
Christian Science Monitor (Western edition). Oct 12, 1965, p6.
Commonweal. Jul 23, 1965, v82, p534.
Film Daily. Jun 16, 1965, p5.
Film Quarterly. Spr 1966, v19, p51.
Films and Filming. Sep 1965, v11, p27.
Films and Filming. Aug 1965, v11, p42-43.
Films in Review. Aug-Sep 1965, v16, p452.
Hollywood Reporter. Jun 16, 1965, p3.
The London Times. Jul 22, 1965, p15.
Motion Picture Herald Product Digest. Jun 23, 1965, p313.
New Statesman. Jul 23, 1965, v70, p132.
The New York Times. Jul 2, 1965, p17.
Newsweek. Jul 26, 1965, v66, p90.
Time. Jul 16, 1965, v86, p94.
Variety. Jun 16, 1965, p6.

Halloween (US; Carpenter, John; 1978)
BFI/Monthly Film Bulletin. Feb 1979, v46, p27.
Films in Review. Mar 1979, v30, p182.
Hollywood Reporter. Oct 27, 1978, p3.
The Los Angeles Times. Oct 27, 1978, SecIV, p22.
Maclean's. Feb 5, 1978, v92, p47.
Magill's Survey of Cinema. Series II. v2, p969-74.
The New Leader. Dec 18, 1978, v61, p17-18.
The New York Times. Jan 21, 1979, SecII, p13.
The New Yorker. Feb 19, 1979, v55, p128.
Newsweek. Dec 4, 1978, v92, p116.
Variety. Oct 25, 1978, p20.

Halls of Montezuma (US; Milestone, Lewis; 1950)
BFI/Monthly Film Bulletin. Apr 1951, v18, p245-46.
Christian Century. Feb 21, 1951, v68, p254.
Commonweal. Jan 19, 1951, v53, p375.
Film Daily. Dec 11, 1950, p6.
Films in Review. Mar 1951, v2, p41-42.
Illustrated London News. Apr 21, 1951, v218, p628.
Lewis Milestone (Millichap). p168-73.
Motion Picture Herald Product Digest. Dec 16, 1950, p613.
The New Republic. Jan 29, 1951, v124, p23.
The New Statesman and Nation. Apr 21, 1951, v41, p446, 448.
The New York Times. Jan 6, 1951, p9.
The New Yorker. Jan 13, 1951, v26, p53.
Newsweek. Jan 8, 1951, v37, p74.
Saturday Review. Jan 20, 1951, v34, p29-30.
Sight and Sound. May 1951, v20, p20.
The Spectator. Apr 6, 1951, v186, p444.
Time. Jan 15, 1951, v57, p78-80.
Variety. Dec 13, 1950, p8.

Hamlet (US; Colleran, Bill; 1964)
BFI/Monthly Film Bulletin. Aug 1972, v39, p163.
Esquire. Dec 1964, v62, p74.
Filmfacts. Dec 18, 1964, v7, p315-17.
Films in Review. Nov 1964, v15, p574-75.
Hollywood Reporter. Sep 24, 1964, v182, p3.
The Nation. Sep 28, 1964, v199, p175.
The New York Times. Sep 24, 1964, p46.
Variety. Sep 30, 1964, p6.

Hamlet (Also titled: Gamlet) (USSR; Kozintsev, Grigori; 1964)
Christian Science Monitor (Western edition). Oct 10, 1966, p6.
Commonweal. Feb 26, 1966, v83, p615.
Dictionary of Films. p144-45.

Esquire. Dec 1964, v62, p74.
Film. 1964, n41, p16.
Film Daily. Mar 16, 1966, p10.
Filmfacts. May 1, 1966, v9, p69-71.
Films and Filming. Feb 1965, v11, p29.
Films and Filming. Sep 1962, v8, p20.
Films in Review. Apr 1966, v17, p251-52.
Grigori Kozintsev (Leaming). p95-16.
Hollywood Reporter. Apr 28, 1966, p3.
Illustrated London News. Jan 23, 1965, v246, p32.
International Film Guide. 1965, v2, p141.
Motion Picture Herald Product Digest. Mar 30, 1966, p492-93.
The Nation. Sep 28, 1964, v199, p175.
New Statesman. Jan 8, 1965, v69, p51.
The New York Times. Mar 16, 1966, p48.
The New York Times. Sep 15, 1964, p32.
The New Yorker. Mar 26 1966, v42, p125.
Newsweek. Mar 14, 1966, v67, p99.
On Movies. p271-73.
Saturday Review. May 21, 1966, v49, p49.
Shakespeare and the Film. p146-52.
Shakespeare on Film. p218-34.
Sight and Sound. Sum 1964, v33, p144-45.
The Spectator. Jan 15, 1965, v214, p71-72.
Theater and Film. p171-81.
Tynan Right and Left. p208-09.
Variety. Jul 29, 1964, p8.

Hammett (US; Wenders, Wim; 1982)
American Cinematographer. Nov 1982, v63, p1168-76.
BFI/Monthly Film Bulletin. Nov 1982, v49, p247-48.
Films in Review. Oct 1982, v37, p488-89.
Maclean's. Sep 27, 1982, v95, p63.
New Statesman. Oct 8, 1982, v104, p28.
The New York Times. Jul 1, 1982, SecIII, p8.
Newsweek. Oct 18, 1982, v100, p96.
Rolling Stone. Oct 14, 1982, p52-53.
Variety. Jun 2, 1982, p15.

Hands Over the City (Italian title: Mani Sulla Citta, Le; Also titled: Hands Across the City) (IT; Rosi, Francesco; 1963)
BFI/Monthly Film Bulletin. Sep 1966, v33, p137-38.
Films and Filming. Oct 1966, v13, p18, 53-54.
The London Times. Jul 14, 1966, p19.
Magill's Survey of Cinema. Foreign Language Films. v3, p1330-34.
The New Italian Cinema. p162-63.
New Statesman. Jul 22, 1966, v72, p140.
The New York Times. Sep 18, 1964, p28.
The New Yorker. Aug 14, 1965, v41, p92.
Sight and Sound. Sum 1966, v35, p145-46.
The Spectator. Jul 22, 1966, v217, p123.
Variety. Sep 11, 1963, p6.

Handsome Serge *See* Beau Serge, Le

Hang 'Em High (US; Post, Ted; 1968)
BFI/Monthly Film Bulletin. Nov 1968, v35, p180.
Clint Eastwood (Guérif). p57-59.
Film Daily. Aug 2, 1968, p7.
Filmfacts. Nov 15, 1968, v11, p324-26.
Films and Filming. Nov 1968, v15, p51.
The Films of Clint Eastwood. p72-79.
Hollywood Reporter. Jul 25, 1968, p3.
The London Times. Oct 24, 1968, p17.
Motion Picture Herald Product Digest. Aug 7, 1968, p840.
The New York Times. Aug 8, 1968, p27.
Time. Aug 23, 1968, v92, p63.
Variety. Jul 17, 1968, p6.

The Hanging Tree (US; Daves, Delmer; 1959)
America. Feb 14, 1959, v100, p585.
BFI/Monthly Film Bulletin. Mar 1959, v26, p28.
Catholic World. Apr 1959, v189, p56.
Commonweal. Feb 6, 1959, v69, p497.
Film Daily. Jan 28, 1959, p8.
Filmfacts. Mar 4, 1959, v2, p19-20.
The Films of Gary Cooper. p267-68.
Hollywood Reporter. Jan 28, 1959, p3.
Library Journal. Feb 15, 1959, v84, p589.
The New Republic. Feb 16, 1959, v140, p21.
The New York Times. Feb 12, 1959, p23.
Newsweek. Feb 16, 1959, v53, p102.
Saturday Review. Feb 7, 1959, v40, p31.
Time. Feb 16, 1959, v73, p101.
Variety. Jan 28, 1959, p6.

Hanna K (FR; Costa-Gavras, Constantin; 1983)
Commonweal. Oct 21, 1983, v110, p565.
Films in Review. Nov 1983, v34, p570.
Hollywood Reporter. Sep 30, 1983, p3.
The Los Angeles Times. Oct 19, 1983, SecVI, p1.
Maclean's. Oct 10, 1983, v96, p55.
Magill's Cinema Annual, 1984. p177-81.
National Review. Nov 25, 1983, v35, p1498.
The New Republic. Oct 24, 1983, v189, p32-33.
New York. Oct 10, 1983, v16, p88-89.
Saturday Review. Nov-Dec 1983, v9, p42-43.
Time. Oct 17, 1983, v122, p89-90.

Hans Christian Anderson (US; Vidor, Charles; 1952)
BFI/Monthly Film Bulletin. Feb 1953, v20, p19-20.
Catholic World. Jan 1953, v176, p301.
Christian Century. Mar 4, 1953, v70, p271.
Commonweal. Nov 28, 1952, v57, p199-200.
Cosmopolitan. Jan 1953, v134, p24.
Cue. Nov 29, 1952, p15.
Film Daily. Nov 25, 1952, p6.
Films in Review. Jan 1953, v4, p39.
Hollywood Reporter. Nov 25, 1952, p3.
Journal of Popular Film. 1975, v4, n2 p117-23.
Library Journal. Dec 15, 1952, v77, p2170.
Life. Nov 3, 1952, v33, p84-89.
McCall's. Jan 1953, v80, p12-13.
Motion Picture Herald Product Digest. Nov 29, 1952, p1621.
Musical America. Jan 15, 1953, v73, p9.
National Parent-Teacher. Jan 1953, v47, p36.
The New Statesman and Nation. Jan 3, 1953, v45, p12.
The New York Times. Nov 26, 1952, p20.
The New York Times Magazine. Nov 2, 1952, p62-63.
The New Yorker. Dec 6, 1952, v28, p73.
Newsweek. Dec 8, 1952, v40, p92.
Samuel Goldwyn (Epstein). p126-29.
Samuel Goldwyn Presents. p283-86.
Saturday Review. Nov 29, 1952, v35, p28.
Selected Film Criticism, 1951-1960. p50-51.
Senior Scholastic. Dec 3, 1952, v61, p34.
The Spectator. Dec 19, 1952, v189, p842.
The Tatler. Dec 31, 1952, v206, p730.
Theatre Arts. Jan 1953, v37, p82.
Time. Dec 1, 1952, v60, p62.
Variety. Nov 26, 1952, p6.

Hansel and Gretel (Also titled: Hanzel and Gretel) (US; Paul, John; 1954)
BFI/Monthly Film Bulletin. Jan 1955, v22, p3.
Film Daily. Oct 7, 1954, p6.
Films and Filming. Jan 1955, v1, p20.
Films in Review. Nov 1954, v5, p485.
Hollywood Reporter. Nov 11, 1954, p3.
The London Times. Dec 15, 1954, p6.

The London Times. Dec 20, 1954, p9.
Motion Picture Herald Product Digest. Oct 16, 1954, p177.
The New York Times. Oct 11, 1954, p33.
Sight and Sound. Jan-Mar 1955, v24, p145.
The Tatler. Dec 1, 1954, v214, p571.
Variety. Oct 6, 1954, p6.

The Happiest Days of Your Life (GB; Launder, Frank; 1950)
Christian Century. Apr 4, 1951, v68, p447.
Film Daily. Sep 13, 1950, p6.
The Great British Films. p142-43.
Hollywood Reporter. May 3, 1951, p3.
Kiss Kiss Bang Bang. p346.
The London Times. Mar 13, 1950, p2.
Magill's Survey of Cinema. Series II. v3, p978-81.
Motion Picture Herald Product Digest. Sep 16, 1950, p486.
The New Republic. Oct 9, 1950, v123, p30.
The New Statesman and Nation. Mar 18, 1950, v39, p299.
The New York Times. Sep 18, 1950, p19.
The New Yorker. Sep 23, 1950, v26, p54.
Newsweek. Oct 2, 1950, v36, p85.
Senior Scholastic. Oct 25, 1950, v57, p20.
Shots in the Dark. p164-65.
The Spectator. Mar 17, 1950, v184, p338.
Time. Oct 9, 1950, v56, p112.
Variety. Mar 15, 1950, p12.

Happiness *See* Bonheur, Le

The Happy Ending (US; Brooks, Richard; 1969)
Big Screen, Little Screen. p260-65.
Double Takes. p10.
Film. Spr 1970, n58, p30.
Film Quarterly. Fall 1970, v24, p57-58.
Films and Filming. Jul 1970, v16, p42-43.
Films in Review. Feb 1970, v21, p121.
Focus. Spr 1970, n6, p43-44.
Life. Dec 19, 1969, v67, p18.
The New York Times. Dec 22, 1969, p43.
Saturday Review. Dec 27, 1969, v52, p40.
Variety. Nov 19, 1969, p14.

Happy Ever After *See* Tonight's the Night

Happy Go Lovely (GB; Humberstone, Bruce; 1951)
BFI/Monthly Film Bulletin. Apr 1951, v18, p246.
Film Daily. Jun 14, 1951, p6.
The Films of David Niven. p102-03.
Hollywood Reporter. Jun 11, 1951, p3.
Motion Picture Herald Product Digest. Jun 16, 1951, p886-87.
The New York Times. Jul 26, 1951, p17.
The Spectator. Jun 8, 1951, v186, p748-49.
Variety. Mar 7, 1951, p18.

The Happy Road (US; Kelly, Gene; 1957)
America. Jun 22, 1957, v97, p351.
BFI/Monthly Film Bulletin. Aug 1957, v24, p96.
Commonweal. Mar 15, 1957, v65, p614.
Film Daily. Jan 28, 1957, p7.
Films and Filming. Aug 1957, v3, p27.
The Films of Gene Kelly. p170-72.
Hollywood Reporter. Jan 28, 1957, p3.
Motion Picture Herald Product Digest. Feb 2, 1957, p250.
The New York Times. Jun 21, 1957, p20.
The New York Times Magazine. Apr 7, 1957, p37.
The New Yorker. Jun 29, 1957, v33, p72.
Saturday Review. Jul 6, 1957, v40, p23.
Time. Jul 1, 1957, v70, p80.
Variety. Jan 30, 1957, p6.

The Happy Time (US; Fleischer, Richard; 1952)
BFI/Monthly Film Bulletin. Sep 1952, v19, p122-23.
Catholic World. Aug 1952, v175, p381-82.
Christian Century. Jan 14, 1953, v70, p63.
Commonweal. Sep 26, 1952, v56, p607.
Film Daily. Aug 26, 1952, p6.
Films in Review. Aug-Sep 1952, v3, p356-57.
Hollywood Reporter. Aug 18, 1952, p3.
Library Journal. Aug 1952, v77, p1299.
Motion Picture Herald Product Digest. Aug 16, 1952, p1485.
The Nation. Oct 11, 1952, v175, p338.
The New York Times. Oct 31, 1952, p30.
The New Yorker. Nov 15, 1952, v28, p74.
Newsweek. Oct 13, 1952, v40, p100.
Saturday Review. Sep 6, 1952, v35, p26.
Sight and Sound. Oct-Dec 1952, v22, p79-80.
The Spectator. Oct 10, 1952, v189, p469.
Stanley Kramer, Film Maker. p109-16.
The Tatler. Oct 22, 1952, v206, p200.
Theatre Arts. Aug 1952, v36, p34.
Time. Sep 29, 1952, v60, p90.
Variety. Aug 20, 1952, p6.

The Happy Years (US; Wellman, William A.; 1950)
BFI/Monthly Film Bulletin. Jul 1951, v18, p292.
Christian Century. Nov 1, 1950, v67, p1311.
Commonweal. Aug 11, 1950, v52, p437.
Film Daily. May 25, 1950, p7.
Hollywood Reporter. May 25, 1950, p3.
Library Journal. Jun 15, 1950, v75, p1059.
Newsweek. Jul 24, 1950, v36, p68.
Variety. May 31, 1950, p6.
William A. Wellman (Thompson). p226-28.

Hard Contract (US; Pogostin, S. Lee; 1969)
Christian Century. Jun 18, 1969, v86, p842-43.
Film Daily. Apr 25, 1969, p7.
Filmfacts. 1964, v12, p196.
Films in Review. May 1969, v20, p316-17.
Movies Into Film. p354-55.
The New York Times. May 26, 1969, p53.
The New Yorker. Jun 7, 1969, v45, p114.
Saturday Review. Mar 24, 1969, v52, p37.
Time. Jul 11, 1969, v94, p79.
Variety. Apr 16, 1969, p6.

A Hard Day's Night (GB; Lester, Richard; 1964)
The Beatles in Richard Lester's A Hard Day's Night. 1964.
BFI/Monthly Film Bulletin. Aug 1964, v31, p121.
Boxoffice. Jul 27, 1964, v85, p2848.
Commonweal. Sep 18, 1964, v80, p638.
Confessions of a Cultist. p160-63.
Cult Movies. p199-202.
Dictionary of Films. p145-46.
Fifty Classic British Films, 1932-82. p118-20.
Film Daily. Jul 16, 1964, p4.
Films in Review. Oct 1964, v15, p503-05.
The Films of the Sixties. p122-23.
The Great British Films. p218-19 a Movie Comedy (Byron), p248-49.
Hollywood Reporter. Jul 21, 1964, p3.
Hollywood U.K. p234-42.
The International Dictionary of Films and Filmmakers. v1, p193-94.
Life. Aug 7, 1964, v57, p15.
Magill's Survey of Cinema. Series I. v2, p712-15.
Motion Picture Herald Product Digest. Aug 5, 1964, p97.
The New Republic. Oct 10, 1964, v151, p26.
The New York Times. Aug 12, 1964, p41.
Newsweek. Aug 24, 1964, v64, p79.

On Movies. 400-01.
Reruns. p179-82.
Richard Lester: A Guide to References and Resources. p21-23.
Saturday Review. Sep 19, 1964, v47, p30.
Seventeen. Aug 1964, v23, p236-37.
Sight and Sound. Aut 1964, v33, p196-97.
Time. Aug 14, 1964, v84, p67.
Unholy Fools, Wits, Comics, Disturbers of the Peace. p213-15.
Variety. Jul 15, 1964, p6.

Hard, Fast and Beautiful (US; Lupino, Ida; 1951)
BFI/Monthly Film Bulletin. Oct 1951, v18, p347.
Commonweal. Jul 27, 1951, v54, p380.
Film Daily. May 29, 1951, p6.
Hollywood Reporter. May 23, 1951, p4.
Motion Picture Herald Product Digest. May 26, 1951, p861.
The New York Times. Jul 2, 1951, p16.
Newsweek. Jun 8, 1951, v37, p94-95.
Saturday Review. Jun 30, 1951, v34, p23.
Time. Jun 25, 1951, v57, p93.
Variety. May 30, 1951, p6.

Hard Times (Also titled: The Street Fighter) (US; Hill, Walter; 1975)
BFI/Monthly Film Bulletin. Dec 1975, v42, p269.
Films in Review. Dec 1975, v26, p636.
The Films of Charles Bronson. p220-23.
Hollywood Reporter. Sep 30, 1975, p5.
The Los Angeles Times. Oct 8, 1975, SecIV, p14.
Motion Picture Herald Product Digest. Oct 22, 1975, p38.
The New York Times. Oct 9, 1975, p54.
The New York Times. Oct 26, 1975, SecII, p15.
The New Yorker. Oct 6, 1975, v51, p97-98.
Time. Nov 3, 1975, v106, p70.
Variety. Sep 24, 1975, p22.

The Harder They Come (JAMAICA; Henzell, Perry; 1973)
Magill's Survey of Cinema. Series II. v3, p982-84.
The Nation. Mar 5, 1973, v216, p316.
The New York Times. Feb 9, 1973, p32.
The New York Times. Jul 14, 1974, SecII, p1.
The New Yorker. Feb 24, 1973, v49, p120-22.
Reeling. p179-81.
Time. Feb 19, 1973, II v101, p64.
Variety. Sep 6, 1972, p16.

The Harder They Fall (US; Robson, Mark; 1956)
America. May 19, 1956, v95, p209.
BFI/Monthly Film Bulletin. May 1956, v23, p56.
Commonweal. Jun 1, 1956, v64, p227.
The Complete Films of Humphrey Bogart. p188-99.
Film Culture. 1956, v2, p27-28.
Film Daily. Mar 28, 1956, p10.
Films and Filming. May 1956, v2, p22-23.
Films in Review. May 1956, v7, p218.
Hollywood Reporter. Mar 23, 1956, p3.
Humphrey Bogart: The Man and His Films. p179-82.
Magill's Survey of Cinema. Series II. v3, p986-91.
The New York Times. May 10, 1956, p26.
The New York Times. May 13, 1956, SecII, p1.
The New Yorker. May 19, 1956, v32, p138.
Newsweek. May 7, 1956, v47, p99.
Saturday Review. May 12, 1956, v39, p25.
Time. May 21, 1956, v67, p114.
Variety. Mar 28, 1956, p6.

Harlow (US; Gordon, Douglas; 1965)
America. Jul 31, 1965, v113, p123-24.
BFI/Monthly Film Bulletin. Aug 1965, v32, p119-20.
Christian Science Monitor (Western edition). Jul 30, 1965, p2.
Film Daily. Jun 22, 1965, p6.
Film Quarterly. Fall 1965, v19, p62.
Films and Filming. Aug 1965, v11, p25.
Films in Review. Aug-Sep 1965, v16, p449-50.
Hollywood Reporter. Jun 22, 1965, p3.
Kiss Kiss Bang Bang. p346-47.
The London Times. Jul 1, 1965, 1965, p17.
Motion Picture Herald Product Digest. Jul 7, 1965, p322.
National Review. Aug 24, 1965, v17, p738.
New Statesman. Jul 2, 1965, v70, p23.
The New York Times. Jul 22, 1965, p24.
Newsweek. Jul 26, 1965, v66, p89-90.
Playboy. Sep 1965, v12, p56, 58.
The Private Eye, the Cowboy and the Very Naked Girl. p144-46.
Private Screenings. p198-99.
Saturday Review. Jun 5, 1965, v48, p37.
Time. Jul 23, 1965, v86, p88.
Tynan Right and Left. p234.
Variety. Jun 23, 1965, p6.

Harlow (US; Segal, Alex; 1965)
America. May 22, 1965, v112, p791-92.
Film Daily. May 12, 1965, p7.
Film Quarterly. Fall 1965, v19, p61-62.
Films in Review. Jun-Jul 1965, v16, p386-87.
The Films of Ginger Rogers. p226.
Hollywood Reporter. May 11, 1965, p3.
Motion Picture Herald Product Digest. May 26, 1965, p290-91.
The New York Times. May 15, 1965, p18.
Playboy. Sep 1965, v12, p56, 58.
Saturday Review. Jun 5, 1965, v48, p37.
Time. May 28, 1965, v85, p109.
Variety. May 19, 1965, p6.

Harold & Maude (US; Ashby, Hal; 1971)
BFI/Monthly Film Bulletin. May 1972, v39, p95.
Film Quarterly. Fall 1972, v26, p51-53.
Films and Filming. Jun 1972, v18, p51-52.
Hollywood Reporter. Dec 16, 1971, p3.
Magill's Survey of Cinema. Series I. v2, p716-19.
Movie Comedy. p204-05.
The New York Times. Dec 21, 1971, p51.
Variety. Dec 15, 1971, p18.
The Village Voice. Dec 23, 1971, p66.

The Harp of Burma *See* The Burmese Harp

Harper (Also titled: The Moving Target) (US; Smight, Jack; 1966)
America. May 21, 1966, v114, p753-54.
BFI/Monthly Film Bulletin. May 1966, v33, p72.
Big Screen, Little Screen. p348-49.
Christian Science Monitor (Western edition). Apr 4, 1966, p6.
Cinema. Dec 1966, v3, p50.
Commonweal. Apr 29, 1966, v84, p179.
Film Daily. Feb 10, 1966, p6.
Filmfacts. Jun 1, 1966, v9, p91-94.
Films and Filming. Aug 1966, v12, p57-58.
Films in Review. May 1966, v178, p312-13.
The Films of Paul Newman. p146-50.
Hollywood Reporter. Feb 10, 1966, p3.
Lauren Bacall: Her Films and Career. p168-79.
Life. Apr 1, 1966, v60, p16.
The London Times. Jun 2, 1966, p19.
The London Times Sunday Magazine. May 29, 1966, p25-27.
Motion Picture Herald Product Digest. Feb 16, 1966, p467.

New Statesman. Jun 3, 1966, v71, p819.
The New York Times. Mar 31, 1966, p43.
The New Yorker. Apr 2, 1966, v42, p162.
Newsweek. Apr 4, 1966, v67, p99.
Playboy. May 1966, v13, p26, 30.
The Private Eye, the Cowboy and the Very Naked Girl. p193-94, 230.
Saturday Review. Mar 12, 1966, v49, p46.
Second Sight. p51-53.
Sight and Sound. Sum 1966, v35, p147.
The Spectator. Jun 3, 1966, v216, p695.
Time. Apr 1, 1966, v87, p99.
Variety. Feb 16, 1966, p6.
The Village Voice. Apr 7, 1966, p31.

Harriet Craig (US; Sherman, Vincent; 1950)
BFI/Monthly Film Bulletin. Dec 1950, v17, p188.
Christian Century. Jan 3, 1951, v68, p30.
Commonweal. Nov 17, 1950, v53, p141.
Film Daily. Oct 31, 1950, p14.
The Films of Joan Crawford. p176-77.
Hollywood Reporter. Oct 27, 1950, p3.
Library Journal. Nov 15, 1950, v75, p2021.
Motion Picture Herald Product Digest. Oct 28, 1950, p545.
The New York Times. Nov 3, 1950, p31.
The New Yorker. Nov 4, 1950, v26, p139.
Saturday Review. Nov 18, 1950, v33, p32.
The Spectator. Nov 10, 1950, v185, p462, 464.
Time. Nov 6, 1950, v56, p104.
Variety. Nov 1, 1950, p6.

Harry & Son (US; Newman, Paul; 1984)
BFI/Monthly Film Bulletin. May 1984, v51, p151-52.
Film Journal. Apr 1984, v87, p37-38.
Films and Filming. May 1984, n356, p39.
Films in Review. May 1984, v35, p307-08.
Hollywood Reporter. Mar 1, 1984, p4.
The Los Angeles Times. Mar 2, 1984, SecVI, p13.
Maclean's. Mar 5, 1984, v97, p61.
The New York Times. Mar 2, 1984, SecIII, p12.
Newsweek. Mar 12, 1984, v103, p89.
Photoplay. Jun 1984, v35, p19.
Time. Mar 5, 1984, v123, p86.
Variety. Feb 29, 1984, p15.

Harry and Tonto (US; Mazursky, Paul; 1974)
America. Sep 21, 1974, v131, p139-40.
Audience. Nov 1974, v7, p11.
Before My Eyes. p49-51.
BFI/Monthly Film Bulletin. Jan 1975, v42, p9.
Christian Century. Dec 25, 1974, v91, p1229-30.
Fifty Grand Movies of the 1960s and 1970s. p227-30.
Films in Review. Oct 1974, v25, p502-03.
Hollywood Reporter. Jul 31, 1974, p3.
Independent Film Journal. Aug 7, 1974, v74, p7.
Magill's Survey of Cinema. Series II. v3, p989-91.
Motion Picture Herald Product Digest. Sep 4, 1974, p26.
Movietone News. Nov 1974, n37, p29-30.
The New Republic. Sep 14, 1974, v171, p20.
New York. Sep 2, 1974, v7, p66-67.
The New York Times. Aug 13, 1974, p24.
The New Yorker. Aug 26, 1974, v50, p46.
Newsweek. Sep 2, 1974, v84, p60-61.
Penthouse. Nov 1974, v6, p45-46.
PTA Magazine. Nov 1974, v69, p9.
Take One. 1974, v4, n5, p35.
Time. Sep 9, 1974, v104, p4.
Variety. Jul 31, 1974, p18.

Harry and Walter Go to New York (US; Rydell, Mark; 1976)
BFI/Monthly Film Bulletin. Sep 1976, v43, p191-92.
Films and Filming. Oct 1976, v23, p32-33.
Hollywood Reporter. Jun 16, 1976, p2.
Independent Film Journal. Jun 25, 1976, v78, p14-15.
The Los Angeles Times. Jul 28, 1976, SecIV, p13.
Millimeter. May 1976, v4, p12-14.
Motion Picture Herald Product Digest. Jun 30, 1976, p10.
New York. Jun 28, 1976, v9, p66-69.
The New York Times. Jun 27, 1976, SecII, p15.
Newsweek. Jun 28, 1976, v87, p77-78.
Saturday Review. Jul 24, 1976, v3, p42.
Time. Jul 12, 1976, v108, p49.
Variety. Jun 16, 1976, p18.

Harum Scarum (US; Nelson, Gene; 1965)
Elvis: The Films and Career of Elvis Presley. p165-67.
Film Daily. Nov 15, 1965, p3.
Hollywood Reporter. Oct 22, 1965, p3.
Motion Picture Herald Product Digest. Nov 10, 1965, p403.
The New York Times. Dec 16, 1965, p63.
Senior Scholastic. Jan 14, 1966, v87, p24.
Variety. Oct 27, 1965, p6.

Harvey (US; Koster, Henry; 1950)
BFI/Monthly Film Bulletin. Jan 1951, v18, p200.
Christian Century. Jan 17, 1951, v68, p95.
Commonweal. Dec 29, 1950, v53, p301-02.
Film Daily. Oct 13, 1950, p3.
Films in Review. Dec 1950, v1, p40.
The Films of James Stewart. p138-41.
Fortnight. Dec 25, 1950, v9, p32.
Halliwell's Hundred. p119-22.
Hollywood Reporter. Oct 12, 1950, p3.
Library Journal. Nov 15, 1950, v75, p2021.
Magill's Survey of Cinema. Series I. v2, p720-23.
Motion Picture Herald Product Digest. Oct 21, 1950, p538.
The New Republic. Jan 15, 1951, v124, p31.
The New York Times. Dec 22, 1950, p19.
The New Yorker. Dec 23, 1950, v26, p59.
Newsweek. Dec 25, 1950, v36, p64.
Saturday Review. Jan 6, 1951, v34, p26.
Selected Film Criticism, 1941-1950. p74-76.
Senior Scholastic. Feb 14, 1951, v58, p23.
Time. Jan 1, 1951, v57, p60-61.
Variety. Oct 18, 1950, p6.

Has Anybody Seen My Gal? (Also titled: Has Anybody Seen My Girl) (US; Sirk, Douglas; 1952)
BFI/Monthly Film Bulletin. Aug 1952, v19, p110.
Douglas Sirk (Stern). p75-78.
Film Daily. Jun 11, 1952, p7.
Hollywood Reporter. Jun 6, 1952, p3.
Library Journal. Nov 1, 1952, v77, p1893.
Motion Picture Herald Product Digest. Jun 14, 1952, p1397-98.
The New York Times. Jul 5, 1952, p7.
Newsweek. Aug 4, 1952, v40, p84.
Time. Jul 28, 1952, v60, p74.
Variety. Jun 11, 1952, p6.

Hatari (US; Hawks, Howard; 1962)
America. Jul 14, 1962, v107, p512.
BFI/Monthly Film Bulletin. Feb 1963, v30, p17.
Commonweal. Jul 29, 1962, v76, p351.
The Complete Films of John Wayne. p239-41.
Film Daily. May 24, 1962, p9.

Filmfacts. Aug 3, 1962, v5, p162-64.
Films in Review. Aug-Sep 1962, v13, p430.
Hollywood Reporter. May 16, 1962, p3.
Howard Hawks (Wood). p130-38.
Motion Picture Herald Product Digest. May 30, 1962, p572.
The New York Times. Jul 12, 1962, p19.
The New Yorker. Jul 21, 1962, v38, p39.
Newsweek. Jul 23, 1962, v60, p72.
Sight and Sound. Wint 1962-63, v32, p41.
Time. Jul 27, 1962, v80, p69.
Variety. May 23, 1962, p6.
The Village Voice. Aug 16, 1962, p6.

A Hatful of Rain (US; Zinnemann, Fred; 1957)
America. Aug 3, 1957, v97, p471.
BFI/Monthly Film Bulletin. Aug 1957, v24, p96-97.
Commonweal. Jul 26, 1957, v66, p425.
Film Culture. 1957, v3, n3, p12.
Film Daily. Jun 18, 1957, p11.
Films and Filming. Oct 1957, v4, p21-22.
Films in Review. Aug-Sep 1957, v8, p355.
Hollywood Reporter. Jun 18, 1957, p3.
Magill's Survey of Cinema. Series II. v3, p995-98.
Motion Picture Herald Product Digest. Jun 22, 1957, v207, p425.
The Nation. Aug 17, 1957, v185, p78.
The New Republic. Oct 21, 1957, v137, p22.
The New York Times. Feb 3, 1957, SecII, p5.
The New York Times. Jul 18, 1957, p18.
The New York Times. Jul 21, 1957, SecII, p1.
The New York Times Magazine. May 19, 1957, p60.
The New Yorker. Jul 27, 1957, v33, p67-68.
Newsweek. Jul 22, 1957, v50, p84.
Saturday Review. Jul 27, 1957, v40, p23-24.
Sight and Sound. Aut 1957, v27, p90-91.
Time. Aug 5, 1957, v70, p76.
Variety. Jun 19, 1957, p7.

Hatsukoi Jigokuhen *See* The Inferno of First Love

The Haunted Palace (US; Corman, Roger; 1963)
Film Daily. Aug 30, 1963, p7.
The Films of Roger Corman. p53-54, 174-75.
Hollywood Reporter. Aug 28, 1963, p3.
The New York Times. Jan 30, 1964, p24.
Newsweek. Sep 16, 1963, v62, p86.

The Haunting (US; Wise, Robert; 1963)
BFI/Monthly Film Bulletin. Jan 1964, v3, p4-5.
Commonweal. Sep 27, 1963, v79, p16.
Film Daily. Aug 22, 1963, p7.
Film Quarterly. Wint 1963-64, v17, p44-46.
Filmfacts. Jun 12, 1963, v6, p181-82.
Films and Filming. Feb 1964, v10, p27-28.
Hollywood Reporter. Aug 21, 1963, v176, p3.
Life. Aug 30, 1963, v55, p35-36.
Magill's Survey of Cinema. Series II. v3, p999-1001.
The New York Times. Sep 19, 1963, p23.
The New Yorker. Sep 28, 1963, v39, p108.
Newsweek. Sep 23, 1963, v62, p101.
Saturday Review. Sep 28, 1963, v46, p44.
Time. Oct 4, 1963, v82, p122.
Variety. Aug 21, 1963, p6.

Having a Wild Weekend (Also titled: Catch Us If You Can) (GB; Boorman, John; 1965)
BFI/Monthly Film Bulletin. Aug 1965, v32, p118-19.
Esquire. Sep 1965, v64, p44.
Films and Filming. Aug 1965, v11, p26-28.
Hollywood Reporter. Jun 21, 1965, p3.
John Boorman (Ciment). p52-57.

The London Times. Jul 8, 1965, p17.
Motion Picture Herald Product Digest. Jul 7, 1965, p323.
Movie. Aut 1965, n14, p45.
The New Republic. Sep 25, 1965, v153, p35.
New Statesman. Jul 16, 1965, v70, p94.
The New York Times. Aug 19, 1965, p35.
Newsweek. Sep 13, 1965, v66, p86.
Private Screenings. p207.
Seventeen. Jul 1965, v24, p90-91.
Sight and Sound. Wint 1969-70, v39, p20-23.
Time. Sep 3, 1965, v86, p84.
Variety. Jun 23, 1965, p7.

Hawaii (US; Hill, George Roy; 1966)
America. Nov 5, 1966, v115, p560.
BFI/Monthly Film Bulletin. Jan 1967, v34, p3-4.
Big Screen, Little Screen. p333-34.
Christian Science Monitor (Western edition). Oct 17, 1966, p4.
Commonweal. Oct 28, 1966, v85, p104.
Film Daily. Oct 5, 1966, p6.
Film Quarterly. Sum 1967, v20, p11-22.
Filmfacts. Nov 1, 1966, v9, p229-32.
Films and Filming. Mar 1967, v12, p30-31.
Films and Filming. Oct 1965, v12, p51.
Films in Review. Nov 1966, v17, p583-84.
The Films of George Roy Hill. p53-58.
George Roy Hill (Shores). p3-5.
Hollywood Reporter. Oct 5, 1966, p3.
Kiss Kiss Bang Bang. p165-66.
Life. Oct 21, 1966, v61, p10.
Life. Oct 14, 1966, v61, p69-70.
The London Times. Nov 28, 1966, p6.
The London Times. Jan 3, 1967, p6.
Look. Sep 6, 1966, v30, p48-57.
Motion Picture Herald Product Digest. Nov 23, 1966, p632.
The New Republic. Oct 22, 1966, v155, p32-33.
New Statesman. Jan 6, 1967, v73, p23.
The New York Times. Oct 11, 1966, p54.
The New Yorker. Oct 29, 1966, v42, p152.
Newsweek. Oct 24, 1966, v68, p117.
Playboy. Dec 1966, v13, p62, 66.
The Primal Screen. p177-79.
The Private Eye, the Cowboy and the Very Naked Girl. p202-03.
Saturday Review. Oct 15, 1966, v49, p26.
Senior Scholastic. Nov 11, 1966, v89, p26.
Time. Oct 21, 1966, v88, p118.
Variety. Oct 5, 1966, p6.
The Village Voice. Oct 20, 1966, v12, p27.

The Hawks and the Sparrows (Italian title: Uccellacci e Uccellini; Also titled: Bad Birds and Good Birds) (IT; Pasolini, Pier Paolo; 1966)
Christian Science Monitor (Western edition). Jan 15, 1966, p4.
Film. Wint 1966, n47, p27.
Film Culture. Fall 1966, n42, p101-05.
Film Daily. Aug 14, 1967, p12.
Film Society Review. Feb 1969, v4, p22-25.
Filmfacts. Oct 1, 1967, v10, p230-32.
The International Dictionary of Films and Filmmakers. v1, p491-92.
International Film Guide. 1968, v5, p104.
Italian Cinema (Bondanella). p184-88.
The London Times. Dec 10, 1966, p13.
Motion Picture Herald Product Digest. Aug 16, 1967, p714.
New Statesman. Dec 2, 1966, v72, p850.
The New York Times. Sep 17, 1966, p28.
The New York Times. Jul 28, 1967, p15.
Newsweek. Aug 14, 1967, v70, p84.
Pasolini on Pasolini. p99-110.
Pier Paolo Pasolini (Snyder). p73-85.
Playboy. Nov 1967, v14, p56.

Private Screenings. p283-84.
Saturday Review. Jul 29, 1967, v50, p38.
The Spectator. May 20, 1966, v216, p632.
Take One. Sep-Oct 1966, v1, p28-29.
Time. Sep 23, 1966, v88, p75.
Variety. May 26, 1966, p7.

He Ran All the Way (US; Berry, John; 1951)
BFI/Monthly Film Bulletin. Oct 1951, v18, p340-41.
Christian Century. Sep 19, 1951, v68, p1087.
Commonweal. Jul 6, 1951, v54, p310.
Film Daily. Jun 6, 1951, p6.
The Films of John Garfield. p176-84.
The Films of the Fifties. p53-54.
Hollywood Reporter. Jun 25, 1951, p3.
Library Journal. Jul 1951, v76, p1141.
Life. Jun 4, 1951, v30, p129-30.
The London Times. Sep 28, 1951, p8.
Motion Picture Herald Product Digest. Jun 9, 1951, p877-78.
The Nation. Jul 14, 1951, v173, p38.
The New Republic. Jul 16, 1951, v125, p23.
The New Statesman and Nation. Oct 6, 1951, v42, p365.
The New York Times. Jun 21, 1951, p24.
The New Yorker. Jun 30, 1951, v27, p65.
Newsweek. Jun 25, 1951, v37, p88.
Saturday Review. Jun 23, 1951, v34, p34.
Time. Jun 25, 1951, v57, p90.
Variety. Jun 6, 1951, p6.

He Who Must Die *See* Celui Qui doit Mourir

Head (US; Rafelson, Bob; 1968)
Christian Science Monitor (Eastern edition). Nov 29, 1968, p12B.
Cinema. Dec 1968, v4, p37-38.
Film Daily. Nov 12, 1968, p8.
Filmfacts. 1969, v11, p488.
Five Thousand One Nights At the Movies. p245.
Hollywood Reporter. Nov 6, 1968, p3.
Motion Picture Herald Product Digest. Nov 20, 1968, p64.
Variety. Oct 16, 1968, p28.
A Year in the Dark. p284-85.

Heart Beat (US; Byrum, John; 1980)
BFI/Monthly Film Bulletin. Sep 1980, v47, p176.
Christian Science Monitor. May 30, 1980, p19.
Commentary. Mar 1980, v69, p69.
Films in Review. Jun 1980, v31, p372.
Hollywood Reporter. Dec 4, 1979, p3.
The Los Angeles Times. Jan 19, 1980, SecII, p5.
Maclean's. Jun 28, 1980, v93, p50.
Motion Picture Herald Product Digest. May 7, 1980, p95.
The New Republic. May 24, 1980, v182, p24-25.
New York. May 12, 1980, v13, p62.
The New Yorker. May 12, 1980, v56, p130.
Newsday. Apr 25, 1980, SecII, p7.
Variety. Dec 5, 1979, p22.
The Village Voice. May 12, 1980, p50.
Vogue. Apr 1980, v170, p42.

The Heart Is a Lonely Hunter (US; Miller, Robert Ellis; 1968)
Atlantic. Oct 1968, v222, p147-49.
BFI/Monthly Film Bulletin. Jul 1969, v36, p140-41.
Christian Science Monitor (Western edition). Aug 23, 1968, p4.
Commonweal. Sep 6, 1968, v88, p598.
Esquire. Nov 1968, v70, p24.
Film 68/69. p223-25.
Film Daily. Jul 30, 1968, p4.
Filmfacts. Aug 15, 1968, v11, p207-09.
Films and Filming. Aug 1969, v15, p38, 40.

Films in Review. Oct 1968, v19, p519.
Hollywood Reporter. Jul 30, 1968, p3.
Life. Aug 30, 1968, v65, p8.
Listener. Jun 19, 1969, v81, p873.
Look. Apr 2, 1968, v32, pM14-16.
Mademoiselle. Oct 1968, v67, p72.
Magill's Survey of Cinema. Series II. v3, p1002-04.
The Modern American Novel and the Movies. p119-30.
Motion Picture Herald Product Digest. Jul 31, 1968, p835.
Movies Into Film. p41-42.
The New Republic. Sep 14, 1968, v159, p41.
The New York Times. Aug 1, 1968, p24.
The New York Times. Dec 10, 1967, p19.
The New Yorker. Aug 3, 1968, v44, p72-74.
Newsweek. Aug 12, 1968, v72, p80.
Saturday Review. Aug 10, 1968, v51, p43.
Senior Scholastic. Oct 11, 1968, v93, p24.
Sight and Sound. Sum 1969, v38, p156-57.
The Spectator. Jun 14, 1969, v222, p794.
Time. Aug 9, 1968, v92, p82.
Variety. Jul 31, 1968, p6.
Vogue. Sep 1, 1968, v152, p276.
A Year In the Dark. p198-200.

Heart Like a Wheel (US; Kaplan, Jonathan; 1983)
Film Comment. Nov-Dec 1983, v19, p63.
Hollywood Reporter. Apr 1, 1983, p3.
The Los Angeles Times. Nov 4, 1983, SecVI, p6.
Maclean's. Oct 3, 1983, v96, p62.
Magill's Cinema Annual, 1984. p182-86.
Ms. Oct 1983, v12, p36.
The New Republic. Nov 28, 1983, v189, p22.
The New York Times. Oct 6, 1983, SecIII, p30.
The New Yorker. Nov 14, 1983, v59, p170.
Newsweek. Oct 31, 1983, v102, p83.
Rolling Stone. Jun 9, 1983, p49.
Sports Illustrated. Oct 24, 1983, v59, p56.
Time. Oct 24, 1983, v122, p90.
Vogue. Jul 1983, v173, p43.

The Heart of the Matter (GB; O'Ferrall, George More; 1953)
America. Dec 4, 1954, v92, p284.
Catholic World. Jan 1955, v180, p303.
Commonweal. Dec 3, 1954, v61, p254.
Film Daily. Nov 19, 1954, p14.
Films in Review. Dec 1954, v5, p540-41.
Illustrated London News. Nov 14, 1953, v223, p784.
Literature/Film Quarterly. 1974, v2, n4, p359-63.
Motion Picture Herald Product Digest. Nov 27, 1954, p225.
The Nation. Nov 27, 1954, v179, p470.
National Parent-Teacher. Feb 1955, v49, p39.
The New Statesman and Nation. Oct 24, 1953, v46, p486-87.
The New York Times. Nov 19, 1954, p20.
The New Yorker. Nov 27, 1954, v30, p188.
Newsweek. Nov 29, 1954, v44, p92.
Reporter. Dec 30, 1954, v11, p45-46.
Saturday Review. Nov 20, 1954, v37, p31.
Sight and Sound. Jan-Mar 1954, v23, p146-47.
The Spectator. Oct 23, 1953, v191, p450.
Time. Dec 13, 1954, v64, p96.
Variety. Nov 11, 1953, p22.

Heartbeat *See* Chamade, La

The Heartbreak Kid (US; May, Elaine; 1972)
Christian Century. Mar 7, 1973, v90, p298-99.
Commonweal. Feb 23, 1973, v97, p470.
Filmfacts. 1972, v15, n21, p505.
Films in Review. Feb 1973, v24, p117.
Hollywood Reporter. Dec 13, 1972, p3.

The New Republic. Jan 6, 1973, v168, p33.
The New York Times. Dec 18, 1972, p56.
The New Yorker. Dec 16, 1972, v48, p126.
Reeling. p105-09.
Time. Jan 1, 1973, v101, p43.
Variety. Dec 13, 1972, p20.

Heartland (US; Pearce, Richard; 1979)
BFI/Monthly Film Bulletin. Jan 1981, v48, p7.
Christian Century. Dec 9, 1981, v98, p1292.
Commonweal. Oct 9, 1981, v108, p563.
Hollywood Reporter. Oct 4, 1979, p2.
The Los Angeles Times. Nov 2, 1981, SecVI, p4.
Magill's Cinema Annual, 1982. p191-94.
The New York Times. Aug 23, 1981, p65.
Progressive. Nov 1981, v45, p51.
Variety. Mar 12, 1980, p23.

Hearts of the West (Also titled: Hollywood Cowboy) (US; Zieff, Howard; 1975)
BFI/Monthly Film Bulletin. Jun 1976, v43, p126.
Films in Review. Dec 1975, v26, p633.
Hollywood Reporter. Oct 1, 1975, p4.
The Los Angeles Times. Oct 19, 1975, Calendar, p40.
Magill's Survey of Cinema. Series II. v3, p1005-07.
Motion Picture Herald Product Digest. Oct 8, 1975, p33.
The Nation. Oct 18, 1975, v221, p379-80.
The New Republic. Oct 25, 1975, v173, p20-21.
The New York Times. Oct 4, 1975, p14.
The New York Times. Oct 12, 1975, SecII, p13.
The New York Times. Nov 23, 1975, SecII, p15.
The New Yorker. Oct 13, 1975, v86, p106.
Progressive. Mar 1976, v40, p39-40.
Saturday Review. Oct 18, 1975, v3, p70.
Senior Scholastic. Dec 2, 1975, v107, p28.
Time. Oct 13, 1975, v106, p78-79.
Variety. Oct 1, 1975, p18.

Heat and Dust (GB; Ivory, James; 1983)
Films in Review. Dec 1983, v34, p624.
Hollywood Reporter. Sep 16, 1983, p3.
The Los Angeles Times. Nov 9, 1983, SecVI, p1.
Maclean's. Oct 10, 1983, v96, p56.
Magill's Cinema Annual, 1984. p187-91.
Ms. Oct 1983, v12, p37.
The New Republic. Oct 24, 1983, v189, p33.
New York. Oct 3, 1983, v16, p87-88.
The New York Times. Sep 15, 1983, SecIII, p18.
Newsweek. Sep 12, 1983, v102, p88.
Saturday Review. Sep-Oct 1983, v9, p36-37.
Sight and Sound. Wint 1982, v52, p65.

Heaven Can Wait (US; Beatty, Warren; 1978)
BFI/Monthly Film Bulletin. Oct 1978, v45, p201.
Commonweal. Aug 18, 1978, v105, p531-32.
Films in Review. Oct 1978, v29, p503.
The Films of the Seventies. p213-15.
The Films of Warren Beatty. p210-22.
Fortune. Sep 11, 1978, v98, p25-26.
Heaven Can Wait. 1978.
Hollywood Reporter. Jun 26, 1978, p3.
The Los Angeles Times. Jun 27, 1978, SecIV, p1.
Maclean's. Jul 24, 1978, v91, p58.
Magill's Survey of Cinema. Series I. v2, p727-29.
Motion Picture Herald Product Digest. Jun 26, 1978, p16.
National Review. Aug 4, 1978, v30, p970-71.
The New Republic. Jul 22, 1978, v178, p22.
New York. Jul 10, 1978, v11, p74-75.
The New York Times. Jun 28, 1978, SecIII, p17.

The New Yorker. Jul 10, 1978, v54, p83-85.
Newsweek. Jul 3, 1978, v92, p90.
Saturday Review. Sep 16, 1978, v5, p36.
Variety. Jun 28, 1978, p20.

Heaven Knows, Mr. Allison (US; Huston, John; 1957)
America. Mar 23, 1957, v96, p716.
BFI/Monthly Film Bulletin. May 1957, v24, p55.
The Cinema of John Huston. p112-13.
Commonweal. Mar 29, 1957, v65, p661.
Film Daily. Mar 15, 1957, v111, p4.
Films and Filming. Jun 1957, v3, p22.
Films in Review. Apr 1957, v8, p176-77.
Hollywood Reporter. Mar 15, 1957, p3.
John Huston (Hammen). p83-92.
Magill's Survey of Cinema. Series II. v3, p1008-11.
Motion Picture Herald Product Digest. Mar 16, 1957, v206, p297.
The New York Times. Nov 8, 1956, SecII, p8.
The New York Times. Mar 15, 1957, p22.
The New York Times. Mar 24, 1957, SecII, p1.
The New Yorker. Mar 23, 1957, v33, p103.
Newsweek. Mar 25, 1957, v49, p110.
On the Verge of Revolt. p121-36.
Robert Mitchum on the Screen. p159-60.
Saturday Review. Apr 6, 1957, v40, p27.
Time. Mar 25, 1957, v69, p106.
Variety. Mar 20, 1957, p6.

Heaven Sent *See* Thank Heaven for Small Favors

Heaven's Gate (US; Cimino, Michael; 1980)
BFI/Monthly Film Bulletin. May 1982, v49, p195-98.
Business Week. Dec 8, 1980, p29.
Commonweal. Dec 19, 1980, v107, p724-25.
Films in Review. Jun 1981, v32, p55.
Final Cut. 1985.
Hollywood Reporter. Nov 20, 1980, p3.
Magill's Cinema Annual, 1982. p195-98.
Martin Scorsese and Michael Cimino. p194-267.
Motion Picture Herald Product Digest. Dec 3, 1980, p512.
The Nation. Dec 20, 1980, v231, p684-85.
The New Republic. Dec 13, 1980, v183, p26-27.
New York. Dec 8, 1980, v13, p16, 82.
The New York Times. Dec 22, 1980, p100.
The New York Times. Nov 19, 1980, SecIII, p29.
The New York Times. Apr 24, 1981, SecIII, p10.
The New Yorker. Dec 22, 1980, v56, p100.
Newsweek. Dec 1, 1980, v96, p87-88.
Time. Dec 1, 1980, v110, p104.
Variety. Nov 26, 1980, p14.
The Village Voice. Nov 26, 1980, p50.

Heidi (SWITZ; Comencini, Luigi; 1952)
America. Jan 2, 1954, v90, p366.
BFI/Monthly Film Bulletin. Jun 1954, v21, p84-85.
Catholic World. Mar 1954, v178, p461.
Commonweal. Feb 12, 1954, v59, p473.
Farm Journal. Mar 1954, v78, p94.
Film Daily. Dec 29, 1953, p6.
Films in Review. Feb 1954, v5, p98.
Library Journal. Jan 1, 1954, v79, p56.
The London Times. Apr 19, 1954, p9.
Motion Picture Herald Product Digest. Dec 26, 1953, p2118.
National Parent-Teacher. Feb 1954, v48, p38.
The New York Times. Dec 21, 1953, p27.
The New Yorker. Dec 21, 1953, v29, p51.
Saturday Review. Jan 9, 1954, v37, p33.

Time. Jan 11, 1954, v63, p82.
Variety. Dec 31, 1952, p6.

The Helen Morgan Story (Also titled: Both Ends of the Candle) (US; Curtiz, Michael; 1957)
America. Sep 28, 1957, v97, p688.
BFI/Monthly Film Bulletin. Dec 1957, v24, p149-50.
Commonweal. Oct 4, 1957, v67, p19.
Film Daily. Sep 18, 1957, p6.
Films and Filming. Nov 1957, v4, p26.
The Films of Paul Newman. p57-60.
Hollywood Reporter. Sep 18, 1957, p3.
Motion Picture Herald Product Digest. Sep 21, 1957, p537-38.
The New York Times. Oct 3, 1957, p33.
The New York Times. Oct 6, 1957, SecII, p1.
Newsweek. Sep 30, 1957, v50, p127.
Time. Oct 14, 1957, v70, p116.
Variety. Sep 18, 1957, p6.

Hell and High Water (US; Fuller, Sam; 1954)
America. Feb 20, 1954, v90, p546.
American Magazine. Feb 1954, v157, p12.
BFI/Monthly Film Bulletin. Jun 1954, v21, p85.
Commonweal. Feb 26, 1954, v59, p524.
Film Daily. Feb 2, 1954, p6.
Films in Review. Apr 1954, v5, p195.
The Films of the Fifties. p111.
Hollywood Reporter. Feb 2, 1954, p3.
The London Times. May 10, 1954, p9.
Motion Picture Herald Product Digest. Feb 6, 1954, p2173.
National Parent-Teacher. Apr 1954, v48, p39.
The New York Times. Feb 2, 1954, p20.
The New Yorker. Feb 13, 1954, v29, p105.
Newsweek. Feb 22, 1954, v43, p106.
Samuel Fuller (Hardy). p54-59.
The Tatler. May 19, 1954, v212, p412.
Time. Feb 22, 1954, v63, p102.
Variety. Feb 3, 1954, p6.

Hell Below Zero (GB; Robson, Mark; 1954)
BFI/Monthly Film Bulletin. Mar 1954, v21, p40.
Farm Journal. Jun 1954, v78, p141.
Film Daily. May 21, 1954, p22.
The Films of Alan Ladd. p194-96.
Hollywood Reporter. Dec 15, 1953, p3.
The London Times. Jan 18, 1954, p4.
Motion Picture Herald Product Digest. May 22, 1954, p1.
National Parent-Teacher. Jun 1954, v48, p39.
Natural History. Apr 1954, v63, p188.
The New Statesman and Nation. Jan 23, 1954, v47, p98.
The New York Times. Jul 17, 1954, p7.
The Spectator. Jan 22, 1954, v192, p93.
Time. Jul 26, 1954, v64, p79.
Variety. Jan 27, 1954, p6.

Hell in the Pacific (US; Boorman, John; 1969)
America. Mar 8, 1969, v120, p288.
Commonweal. Mar 7, 1969, v89, p707-08.
Film Quarterly. Sum 1969, v22, p52-56.
Filmfacts. 1969, v12, p38.
Films and Filming. Jul 1969, v15, p54-55.
Going Steady. p336-37.
Holiday. Apr 1969, v45, p40.
John Boorman (Ciment). p80-93.
The New York Times. Feb 11, 1969, p25.
The New Yorker. Mar 1, 1969, v45, p74.
Newsweek. Feb 24, 1969, v73, p98.
Senior Scholastic. Mar 14, 1969, v94, p24.
Sight and Sound. Sum 1969, v38, p159.

Time. Feb 21, 1969, v93, p87.
Variety. Dec 11, 1969, p30.

Hell Is for Heroes (US; Siegel, Don; 1962)
American Film Genres. p197-200.
BFI/Monthly Film Bulletin. Jun 1962, v29, p81.
Cinema Texas Program Notes. Aug 8, 1976, v10, p89-93.
Combat Films. p172-91.
Commonweal. Jul 22, 1962, v76, p330.
Don Siegel (Lovell). p56.
Film Daily. May 24, 1962, p9.
Filmfacts. Jul 13, 1962, v5, p141-42.
Films and Filming. Jul 1962, v8, p35.
The Films of Steve McQueen. p141-42.
The Hollywood Professionals. v4, p129-31.
Hollywood Reporter. May 23, 1962, p3.
Motion Picture Herald Product Digest. May 30, 1962, p573.
The New York Times. Jul 12, 1962, p19.
Newsweek. Jul 16, 1962, v60, p79.
Variety. May 30, 1962, p6.

Hellcats of the Navy (US; Juran, Nathan; 1957)
BFI/Monthly Film Bulletin. Oct 1957, v24, p127-28.
Film Daily. Apr 18, 1957, p6.
The Films of Ronald Reagan. p218-21.
Hollywood Reporter. Apr 12, 1957, p3.
Motion Picture Herald Product Digest. Apr 20, 1957, p345.
Variety. May 1, 1957, p7.

Heller in Pink Tights (US; Cukor, George; 1960)
America. Mar 26, 1960, v102, p775.
BFI/Monthly Film Bulletin. May 1960, v27, p64.
Commonweal. Mar 4, 1960, v71, p629.
Film Daily. Mar 8, 1960, p8.
Film Quarterly. Spr 1960, v13, p60.
Filmfacts. 1960, v3, p57.
Films and Filming. May 1960, v6, p26.
Films in Review. Apr 1960, v11, p233-34.
The Films of Anthony Quinn. p183-85.
The Films of Sophia Loren. p106-09.
George Cukor (Phillips). p123-26.
Hollywood Reporter. Mar 7, 1960, p3.
The New York Times. Mar 17, 1960, p28.
The New York Times. Mar 20, 1960, SecII, p1.
Newsweek. Mar 14, 1960, v55, p100.
On Cukor. p236-39.
Saturday Review. Mar 5, 1960, v43, p35.
Sight and Sound. Sum 1960, v29, p147.
Time. Apr 4, 1960, v75, p81.
Variety. Mar 9, 1960, p6.

Hellfighters (US; McLaglen, Andrew V.; 1969)
Big Screen, Little Screen. p145-46.
The Complete Films of John Wayne. p274-75.
Filmfacts. 1969, v12, p29.
Films and Filming. May 1969, v15, p46.
Holiday. Apr 1969, v45, p40.
The New York Times. Feb 6, 1969, p30.
Newsweek. Feb 24, 1969, v73, p98.
Variety. Nov 27, 1968, p6.

Hello, Dolly! (US; Kelly, Gene; 1969)
Deeper Into Movies. p100-07.
Film 69/70. p240-42.
Films and Filming. Feb 1970, v16, p51-52.
Films in Review. Jan 1970, v21, p52.
The Films of Gene Kelly. p228-34.
The Hollywood Musical. p393.
Movies Into Film. p333-34.
The Musical: From Broadway to Hollywood. p131-37.
The New York Times. Dec 18, 1969, p62.
The New Yorker. Jan 3, 1970, v45, p57-58.

Saturday Review. Jan 10, 1970, v53, p30.
Time. Dec 26, 1969, v94, p52.
Variety. Dec 24, 1969, p14.

Hello, Elephant! (Italian title: Buongiorno
Elefante!; French title: Bonjour
Éléphant; Also titled: Hullo, Elephant)
(IT; Franciolini, Gianni; 1953)
BFI/Monthly Film Bulletin. Feb 1953, v20,
p22.
Film Daily. Sep 13, 1954, p6.
The London Times. Jan 12, 1953, p2.
Motion Picture Herald Product Digest. Sep 25,
1954, p154.
National Parent-Teacher. Nov 1954, v49, p38.
The New York Times. Sep 10, 1954, p18.
The Spectator. Jan 9, 1952, v190, p36.
Variety. Aug 20, 1952, p22.

Hell's Half Acre (US; Auer, John H.; 1954)
BFI/Monthly Film Bulletin. Apr 1954, v21,
p56-57.
Film Daily. Feb 19, 1954, p6.
Hollywood Reporter. Feb 5, 1954, p3.
Motion Picture Herald Product Digest. Feb 13,
1954, p2183.
National Parent-Teacher. May 1954, v48, p39.
The New York Times. Feb 27, 1954, p11.
Variety. Feb 10, 1954, p6.

The Hellstrom Chronicle (US; Green,
Walon; 1971)
BFI/Monthly Film Bulletin. Oct 1971, v38,
p197.
Cinema. Spr 1972, v7, n2, p53-54.
Commonweal. Jul 23, 1971, v94, p382-83.
Filmfacts. 1971, v14, p259-62.
Films and Filming. Mar 1972, v18, p51-52.
Films in Review. Aug-Sep 1971, v22, p439-40.
Hollywood Reporter. Jun 25, 1971, p3.
The New York Times. Jun 29, 1971, p30.
The New York Times. SecII, p9.
The New Yorker. Jul 17, 1971, v47, p54.
Newsweek. Jul 12, 1971, v78, p82.
Newsweek. Aug 2, 1971, v78, p9.
Saturday Review. Jul 24, 1971, v54, p51.
Variety. Jun 16, 1971, p22.
The Village Voice. Aug 12, 1971, p51.

Help! (GB; Lester, Richard; 1965)
Berkeley Barb. Aug 20, 1965, v1, p3.
BFI/Monthly Film Bulletin. Sep 1965, v32,
p133.
Christian Science Monitor (Western edition).
Aug 2, 1965, p4.
Confessions of a Cultist. p205-07.
Dictionary of Films. p147.
Esquire. Jun 1966, v65, p52, 54.
Film Daily. Aug 3, 1965, p6.
Film Heritage. Sum 1966, v1, p3-13.
Film Quarterly. Fall 1965, v19, p57-58.
Films and Filming. Oct 1965, v12, p27.
Films in Review. Oct 1965, v16, p513.
Help! The Beatles. 1965.
Hollywood Reporter. Aug 3, 1965, p3.
Illustrated London News. Aug 14, 1965, v247,
p38.
Kiss Kiss Bang Bang. p142-44.
The London Times. Jul 29, 1965, p14.
Magill's Survey of Cinema. Series II. v3, p1012-
15.
Motion Picture Herald Product Digest. Aug 18,
1965, p346.
Movie. Fall 1965, n14, p6-11.
Movie Comedy (Byron). p250-51.
The New Republic. Sep 25, 1965, v153, p34-35.
New Statesman. Jul 30, 1965, v70, p162-63.
The New York Times. Aug 24, 1965, p25.
The New Yorker. Aug 28, 1965, v41, p101-02.
On Movies. p403-06.

Playboy. Oct 1965, v12, p26.
Punch. Aug 4, 1965, v249, p175.
*Richard Lester: A Guide to References and
Resources.* p25-28.
Saturday Review. Aug 28, 1965, v48, p28.
Senior Scholastic. Sep 30, 1965, v87, p52.
Seventeen. Aug 1965, v24, p230-31.
Sight and Sound. Aut 1965, v34, p199-200.
The Spectator. Jul 30, 1965, v215, p151.
Time. Sep 3, 1965, v86, p84.
Tynan Right and Left. p206-07.
Variety. Aug 4, 1965, p7.
The Village Voice. Sep 9, 1965, p15.

Hemingway's Adventures of a Young Man
(Also titled: Adventures of a Young
Man) (US; Ritt, Martin; 1962)
America. Jul 28, 1962, v107, p552.
BFI/Monthly Film Bulletin. Jul 1962, v29,
p136-37.
Film Daily. Jun 19, 1962, p6.
Film Quarterly. Sum 1963, v16, p53-54.
Filmfacts. Jul 27, 1962, v5, p153-56.
Films and Filming. Oct 1962, v9, p31-32.
Films in Review. Aug-Sep 1962, v13.
Hollywood Reporter. Jun 15, 1962, p3.
I Lost It at the Movies. p200-02.
Magill's Survey of Cinema. Series II. v3, p1016-
18.
Motion Picture Herald Product Digest. Jun 20,
1962, p597.
The New Republic. Jul 16, 1962, v147, p28-29.
The New York Times. Jul 26, 1962, p17.
The New Yorker. Aug 11, 1962, v38, p46.
Newsweek. Jul 30, 1962, v60, p76.
Saturday Review. Jul 21, 1962, v45, p22.
Sight and Sound. Aut 1962, v31, p197.
Time. Jul 27, 1962, v80, p69.
Variety. Jun 20, 1962, p18.

Hennesy (GB; Sharp, Don; 1975)
BFI/Monthly Film Bulletin. Sep 1975, v42,
p198.
Hollywood Reporter. Jul 18, 1975, p5.
The Los Angeles Times. Jul 30, 1975, SecIV,
p1.
Motion Picture Herald Product Digest. Aug 13,
1975, p17.
The New York Times. Aug 1, 1975, p13.
The New York Times. Aug 3, 1975, SecII, p11.
The New Yorker. Aug 4, 1975, v51, p52.
Newsweek. Aug 11, 1975, v86, p78-79.
Senior Scholastic. Oct 21, 1975, v107, p35.
Time. Aug 18, 1975, v106, p60.
Variety. Jul 23, 1975, p20.

Henriette *See* Holiday For Henrietta

Her Twelve Men (US; Leonard, Robert Z.;
1954)
America. Aug 21, 1954, v91, p507.
BFI/Monthly Film Bulletin. Nov 1954, v21,
p162.
Catholic World. Aug 1954, v179, p383.
Commonweal. Sep 10, 1954, v60, p557.
Film Daily. Jul 7, 1954, p10.
Films and Filming. Oct 1954, v1, p29.
Hollywood Reporter. Jun 29, 1954, p3.
Library Journal. Aug 1954, v79, p1393.
The London Times. Sep 27, 1954, p10.
Motion Picture Herald Product Digest. Jul 3,
1954, p49-50.
National Parent-Teacher. Jun 1954, v48, p39.
The New York Times. Aug 12, 1954, p23.
Newsweek. Aug 16, 1954, v44, p82.
Time. Aug 30, 1954, v67, p77.
Variety. Jun 30, 1954, p6.

Herbstonate *See* Autumn Sonata

Hercules (Italian title: Fatiche di Ercole,
Le) (IT; Francisci, Pietro; 1959)
America. Jul 25, 1959, v101, p559.
The Ancient World in the Cinema. p74-75, 187-
88.
BFI/Monthly Film Bulletin. Jun 1959, v26, p71.
Film Daily. May 12, 1959, p6.
Filmfacts. Aug 5, 1959, v2, p155.
The Films of the Fifties. p271-73.
Hollywood Reporter. May 12, 1959, p3.
Library Journal. Jul 1959, v84, p2171.
The New York Times. Jul 23, 1959, p32.
Senior Scholastic. Sep 16, 1959, v75, p40.
Time. Jul 27, 1959, v74, p32.
Variety. May 13, 1959, p6.

Here Come The Nelsons (Meet the
Nelsons) (US; De Cordova, Frederick;
1952)
BFI/Monthly Film Bulletin. Apr 1952, v19,
p51.
Film Daily. Jan 21, 1952, p6.
Hollywood Reporter. Jan 16, 1952, p3.
Motion Picture Herald Product Digest. Jan 19,
1952, p1193-94.
Variety. Jul 11, 1951, p6.

Here Comes the Groom (US; Capra, Frank;
1951)
BFI/Monthly Film Bulletin. Aug 1951, v18,
p307.
Christian Century. Oct 17, 1951, v68, p1207.
Commonweal. Oct 25, 1951, v55, p64.
Film Daily. Jul 9, 1951, p10.
The Films of Bing Crosby. p193-96.
The Films of Frank Capra (Scherle and Levy).
p245-50.
The Films of Frank Capra (Willis). p156-61.
Frank Capra (Maland). p164-66.
Hollywood Reporter. Jul 6, 1951, p3.
The London Times. Jul 16, 1951, p2.
Motion Picture Herald Product Digest. Jul 7,
1951, p921.
The New Republic. Sep 24, 1951, v125, p21.
The New York Times. Sep 21, 1951, p19.
The New Yorker. Sep 29, 1951, v27, p112.
Newsweek. Oct 1, 1951, v38, p88.
Saturday Review. Aug 25, 1951, v34, p23.
The Spectator. Jul 13, 1951, v187, p62.
Theatre Arts. Sep 1951, v35, p87.
Time. Oct 15, 1951, v58, p120.
Variety. Jul 11, 1951, p6.

The Heroes of Telemark (GB; Mann,
Anthony; 1965)
Anthony Mann (Basinger). p180-82.
BFI/Monthly Film Bulletin. Dec 1965, v32,
p179.
Commonweal. Apr 1, 1966, v84, p56.
Film Daily. Nov 30, 1965, p6.
Film Quarterly. Spr 1966, v19, p52.
Filmfacts. Apr 15, 1966, v9, p55-57.
Films and Filming. Jan 1966, v12, p25-26.
Films and Filming. Dec 1965, v12, p22.
The Great Spy Pictures. p213-14.
Hollywood Reporter. Nov 30, 1965, p3.
The London Times. Nov 25, 1965, p5.
Motion Picture Herald Product Digest. Dec 8,
1965, p418.
New Statesman. Nov 26, 1965, v70, p853.
The New York Times. Mar 10, 1966, p26.
Newsweek. Feb 14, 1966, v67, p94-95.
Playboy. Feb 1966, v13, p34.
Senior Scholastic. Mar 4, 1966, v88, p20.
Time. Feb 18, 1966, v87, p101.
Tynan Right and Left. p247.
Variety. Nov 3, 1965, p6.

Hester Street (US; Silver, Joan Micklin; 1975)
BFI/Monthly Film Bulletin. Dec 1975, v42, p261.
Fifty Grand Movies of the 1960s and 1970s. p99-104.
Films in Review. Dec 1975, v26, p634.
Hollywood Reporter. Oct 31, 1975, p9.
The Los Angeles Times. Nov 23, 1975, Calendar, p36.
Magill's Survey of Cinema. Series I. v2, p741-44.
The New Republic. Oct 18, 1975, v173, p21.
The New York Times. Oct 20, 1975, p44.
The New York Times. Nov 2, 1975, SecII, p15.
The New Yorker. Nov 24, 1975, v51, p167.
Newsweek. Nov 3, 1975, v86, p87-88.
Saturday Review. Nov 15, 1975, v2, p41.
Senior Scholastic. Nov 18, 1975, v107, p36.
Time. Oct 27, 1975, v106, p73-74.
Variety. May 14, 1975, p27.
Vogue. Nov 1975, v165, p66.

The Hidden Fortress (Japanese title: Kakushi Toridi No San-Akunin; Also titled: Three Rascals in the Hidden Fortress) (JAPAN; Kurosawa, Akira; 1959)
Esquire. Aug 1961, v56, p116.
Film Quarterly. Spr 1960, v13, p59.
Filmfacts. Mar 9, 1962, v5, p31-32.
Films and Filming. May 1961, v7, p27.
The Films of Akira Kurosawa. p134-39.
Magill's Survey of Cinema. Foreign Language Series. v3, p1356-61.
The New Republic. Mar 19, 1962, v146, p28.
The New York Times. Jan 24, 1962, p24.
On Film. p115-21.
Variety. Jul 8, 1959, p6.
Variety. Nov 25, 1959, p6.
The Village Voice. Feb 1962, p11.

Hide in Plain Sight (US; Caan, James; 1980)
BFI/Monthly Film Bulletin. Jul 1980, v47, p134.
Christian Science Monitor. Apr 11, 1980, p19.
Cineaste. Sum 1980, v10, p37.
Films in Review. May 1980, v31, p309.
Hollywood Reporter. Mar 18, 1980, p3.
Motion Picture Herald Product Digest. Mar 26, 1980, p85.
The Nation. Apr 5, 1980, v230, p410-11.
The New Republic. Apr 12, 1980, v182, p25.
The New York Times. Mar 21, 1980, SecIII, p66.
Newsday. Mar 14, 1980, SecII, p8.
Newsweek. Mar 24, 1980, v95, p79.
Time. Apr 14, 1980, v115, p98.
Variety. Mar 19, 1980, p28.
The Village Voice. Mar 31, 1980, p43.

Hideg Napok (Also titled: Cold Days) (HUNG; Kovacs, Andras; 1966)
BFI/Monthly Film Bulletin. Nov 1967, v34, p168.
Magill's Survey of Cinema. Foreign Language Films. v2, p593-97.
Sight and Sound. Wint 1967-68, v37, p40-41.
Variety. Jul 27, 1966, p7.

High and Dry (Also titled: The Maggie) (GB; Mackendrick, Alexander; 1954)
America. Sep 11, 1954, v91, p574.
BFI/Monthly Film Bulletin. Apr 1954, v21, p53-54.
Commonweal. Sep 17, 1954, v60, p582.
Dictionary of Films. p204.
Farm Journal. Oct 1954, v78, p137.
Film Daily. Aug 26, 1954, p6.

Films in Review. Oct 1954, v5, p435.
Hollywood Reporter. Nov 4, 1954, p4.
The London Times. Mar 1, 1954, p9.
Motion Picture Herald Product Digest. Aug 28, 1954, p121.
National Parent-Teacher. Nov 1954, v49, p38.
The New Statesman and Nation. Mar 6, 1954, v47, p285.
The New York Times. Aug 31, 1954, p25.
The New Yorker. Sep 11, 1954, v30, p77.
Newsweek. Sep 27, 1954, v44, p98.
Reporter. Dec 2, 1954, v11, p41.
Saturday Review. Sep 18, 1954, v37, p25.
Sight and Sound. Apr-Jun 1954, v23, p199-200.
The Spectator. Feb 26, 1954, v192, p228.
The Tatler. Mar 10, 1954, v211, p428.
Time. Sep 27, 1954, v64, p6.
Time. Sep 13, 1954, v64, p106.
Variety. Mar 17, 1954, p6.

High and Low (Japanese title: Tengoku To-Jigoku) (JAPAN; Kurosawa, Akira; 1963)
Akira Kurosawa: A Guide to References and Resources. p63-64.
Filmfacts. Jan 9, 1964, v6, p309-11.
The Films of Akira Kurosawa. p163-70.
Magill's Survey of Cinema. Foreign Language Films. v3, p1363-68.
The New Republic. Nov 23, 1963, v149, p26-27.
The New York Times. Nov 27, 1963, p30.
The New Yorker. Dec 14, 1963, v39, p197.
Newsweek. Nov 25, 1963, v62, p105B.
The Samurai Films of Akira Kurosawa. p137-39.
Variety. Sep 4, 1963, p20.

The High and the Mighty (US; Wellman, William A.; 1954)
America. Jul 17, 1954, v91, p407.
Aviation Week. Jul 26, 1954, v61, p67.
BFI/Monthly Film Bulletin. Oct 1954, v21, p144.
Catholic World. Jul 1954, v179, p303.
Commonweal. Jul 16, 1954, v60, p365.
The Complete Films of John Wayne. p111.
Cue. Jul 3, 1954, p15.
Film Daily. May 28, 1954, p22.
Films in Review. Jun-Jul 1954, v5, p306-07.
Fortnight. Jun 2, 1954, v16, p40.
Hollywood Reporter. May 26, 1954, p3.
Library Journal. Jul 1954, v79, p1304.
The London Times. Sep 6, 1954, p5.
Look. Jul 27, 1954, v18, p70.
Magill's Survey of Cinema. Series II. v3, p1023-26.
Motion Picture Herald Product Digest. May 22, 1954, p9.
National Parent-Teacher. Sep 1954, v49, p38.
The New Statesman and Nation. Sep 11, 1954, v48, p294.
The New York Times. Jul 1, 1954, p21.
The New Yorker. Jul 10, 1954, v30, p59.
Saturday Review. Jul 3, 1954, v37, p33.
Selected Film Criticism, 1951-1960. p52-54.
The Tatler. Sep 15, 1954, v213, p492.
Time. Jul 12, 1954, v64, p94.
Variety. May 26, 1954, p6.
William A. Wellman (Thompson). p245-47, 309-10.

High Anxiety (US; Brooks, Mel; 1977)
America. Jan 28, 1978, v138, p63.
BFI/Monthly Film Bulletin. May 1978, v45, p91.
Films in Review. Feb 1978, v29, p118.
Hollywood Reporter. Dec 19, 1977, p3.
The Los Angeles Times. Dec 23, 1977, SecIV, p1.
Maclean's. Feb 6, 1978, v91, p60.

Mel Brooks' High Anxiety. 1977.
Motion Picture Herald Product Digest. Jan 25, 1978, p63.
National Review. Feb 7, 1978, v30, p228.
New York. Jan 16, 1978, V11, p47-48.
The New York Times. Dec 26, 1977, p26.
The New Yorker. Jan 9, 1978, v53, p70.
Newsweek. Jan 2, 1978, v91, p58.
Saturday Review. Mar 4, 1978, v5, p43.
Variety. Dec 12, 1977, p20.

High Infidelity (Italian title: Alta Infideltà; Also titled: Modern People; Sin in the Afternoon; The Scandal; Victim) (IT; Rossi, Franco; Petri, Elio; Salce, Luciano; 1964)
Christian Science Monitor (Western edition). Sep 28, 1965, p4.
Film Daily. Jul 12, 1965, p12.
Motion Picture Herald Product Digest. Jul 21, 1965, p331.
The New York Times. Jul 2, 1965, p17.
Playboy. Oct 1965, v12, p28.
Time. Jul 23, 1965, v86, p88.
Variety. Feb 26, 1964, p6.
The Village Voice. Oct 28, 1965, v11, p29.

High Lonesome (US; LeMay, Alan; 1950)
Film Daily. Aug 11, 1950, p7.
Hollywood Reporter. Aug 10, 1950, p3.
Motion Picture Herald Product Digest. Aug 12, 1950, p434.
The New York Times. Dec 8, 1950, p40.
Newsweek. Sep 25, 1950, v36, p92.
Variety. Aug 16, 1950, p11.

High Noon (US; Zinnemann, Fred; 1952)
America's Favorite Movies. p269-88.
BFI/Monthly Film Bulletin. Jun 1952, v19, p74-75.
BFI/Monthly Film Bulletin. Jun 1986, v53, p186-88.
Catholic World. May 1952, v175, p143.
Christian Century. Sep 10, 1952, v69, p1046.
Cinema, the Magic Vehicle. v2, p109-12.
Classic Film Collector. Spr 1978, n58, p20-21.
Classic Film/Video Images. May 1981, n75, p50.
Classic Movies. p23-26.
Commonweal. Jul 25, 1952, v56, p390.
Cue. Jul 26, 1952, p26.
Dictionary of Films. p149.
Fifty from the Fifties. p123-32.
Film: An Anthology. p157-58.
Film as Film: Critical Responses to Film Art. p200-07.
Film Criticism. 1976-77, v1, n3, p2-12.
Film Criticism and Caricatures, 1943-1953. p145.
Film Daily. Apr 30, 1952, p6.
Film Quarterly. Fall 1967, v21, p32-37.
The Filming of the West. p539-45.
Films and Filming. May 1986, v32, p33.
Films in Review. May 1952, v3, p243-44.
The Films of Gary Cooper. p235-37.
The Films of the Fifties. p65-68.
The Great Western Pictures. p133-35.
Hollywood Reporter. Apr 30, 1952, p4.
The International Dictionary of Films and Filmmakers. v1, p196-98.
Journal of Popular Film. 1984-85, v12, n4, p156-62.
Jump Cut. Dec 1981, n26, p9-12.
Kiss Kiss Bang Bang. p349-50.
The Last Hero. p289-95.
Library Journal. Jul 1952, v77, p1185.
Life. Aug 25, 1952, v33, p73-74.
Magic Moments From the Movies. p178.
Magill's Survey of Cinema. Series I. v2, p745-47.

The Making of the Great Westerns. p207-19.
Motion Picture Herald Product Digest. May 3, 1952, p1349.
The Nation. Apr 26, 1952, v174, p410.
National Parent-Teacher. Sep 1952, v47, p38.
New Times. Mar 18, 1977, v8, p52-58.
The New York Times. Jul 25, 1952, p14.
The New Yorker. Aug 2, 1952, v28, p55.
Newsweek. Jul 14, 1952, v40, p91.
Quarterly of Film, Radio and Television. Fall 1953, v8, p80-86.
Running Time: Films of the Cold War. p176.
Saturday Review. Jul 5, 1952, v35, p29.
Seeing Is Believing (Biskind). p44-49.
Selected Film Criticism, 1951-1960. p54-55.
Stanley Kramer, Film Maker. p99-108.
Theatre Arts. Jun 1952, v36, p45.
Time. Jul 14, 1952, v60, p92.
Variety. Apr 30, 1952, p6.
Vintage Films. p134-38.
Western Movies. p51-61.
Wide Angle. 1976, v1, n2, p4-6.

High Tension (Swedish title: Sant Hander Inte Har; Also titled: This Can't Happen Here) (SWED; Bergman, Ingmar; 1950)
BFI/Monthly Film Bulletin. Jan 1953, v20, p9.
Ingmar Bergman and the Rituals of Art. p142.
Ingmar Bergman (Cowie). p91-92.

High Time (US; Edwards, Blake; 1960)
America. Oct 1, 1960, v104, p26.
BFI/Monthly Film Bulletin. Nov 1960, v27, p156.
Blake Edwards. p58-60.
Commonweal. Oct 7, 1960, v73, p48.
Film Daily. Sep 20, 1960, p6.
Filmfacts. 1960, v3, p227.
Films and Filming. Nov 1960, v7, p32-33.
The Films of Bing Crosby. p230-32.
Hollywood Reporter. Sep 19, 1960, p3.
Life. Aug 15, 1960, v49, p37.
The New York Times. Sep 17, 1960, p15.
The New Yorker. Oct 1, 1960, v36, p168.
Time. Sep 26, 1960, v76, p94.
Variety. Sep 21, 1960, p6.

High Treason (GB; Boulting, Roy; 1951)
BFI/Monthly Film Bulletin. Nov 1951, v18, p356.
Catholic World. Jun 1952, v175, p222.
Commonweal. Jun 6, 1952, v56, p225.
Motion Picture Herald Product Digest. May 31, 1952, p1382.
The New Statesman and Nation. Nov 3, 1951, v42, p490-91.
The New Statesman and Nation. Sep 23, 1950, v40, p296.
The New York Times. May 21, 1952, p23.
The New Yorker. May 24, 1952, v28, p112.
Newsweek. May 5, 1952, v39, p100.
Saturday Review. Jun 28, 1952, v35, p27.
The Spectator. Oct 26, 1951, v187, p536-37.
Theatre Arts. Jul 1952, v36, p36.
Time. May 19, 1952, v59, p110.
Variety. Nov 21, 1951, p18.

A High Wind in Jamaica (GB; Mackendrick, Alexander; 1965)
BFI/Monthly Film Bulletin. Jul 1965, v32, p103-04.
Christian Science Monitor (Western edition). Jul 22, 1965, p2.
Commonweal. Jun 18, 1965, v82, p415.
Film Daily. Jun 2, 1965, p6.
Films and Filming. Aug 1965, v11, p29-30.
Films and Filming. Jul 1965, v11, p40.
Films in Review. Jun-Jul 1965, v16, p386.
The Films of Anthony Quinn. p206-08.

Hollywood Reporter. May 25, 1965, p3.
The London Times. May 20, 1965, p19.
Motion Picture Herald Product Digest. Jun 9, 1965, p305-06.
The New Republic. Jun 5, 1965, v152, p26.
New Statesman. May 28, 1965, v69, p857-58.
The New York Times. Jun 17, 1965, p27.
Newsweek. Jul 12, 1965, v66, p91.
Saturday Review. May 29, 1965, v48, p30.
The Spectator. May 28, 1965, v214, p689.
Time. Jul 2, 1965, v86, p80.
Variety. May 26, 1965, p6.

Highly Dangerous (GB; Baker, Roy; 1950)
BFI/Monthly Film Bulletin. Jan 1951, v18, p204.
Hollywood Reporter. Sep 10, 1951, p3.
The Spectator. Dec 15, 1950, v185, p693.
Variety. Dec 13, 1950, p25.

Highway Dragnet (US; Juran, Nathan; 1954)
BFI/Monthly Film Bulletin. Jul 1954, v21, p105.
Film Daily. Jan 28, 1954, p14.
Hollywood Reporter. Jan 20, 1954, p3.
Motion Picture Herald Product Digest. Jan 30, 1954, p2166.
The New York Times. Feb 20, 1954, p8.
Variety. Jan 27, 1954, p6.

The Hill (GB; Lumet, Sidney; 1965)
America. Oct 9, 1965, v113, p419.
BFI/Monthly Film Bulletin. Jul 1965, v32, p104.
Christian Century. Dec 15, 1965, v82, p1548.
Christian Science Monitor (Western edition). Nov 13, 1965, p6.
Cinema. Sum 1968, v4, p5-9.
Commonweal. Oct 8, 1965, v83, p25-26.
Film Daily. Oct 1, 1965, p7.
Film Quarterly. Spr 1966, v19, p52.
Films and Filming. Aug 1965, v11, p26.
Films in Review. Nov 1965, v16, p581-82.
Hollywood Reporter. Oct 1, 1965, p3.
The London Times. Jun 17, 1965, p17.
Motion Picture Herald Product Digest. Sep 29, 1965, p379.
The Nation. Oct 25, 1965, v201, p288.
The New Republic. Oct 9, 1965, v153, p29-30.
New Statesman. Jun 18, 1965, v69, p977-78.
The New York Times. Oct 4, 1965, p00.
The New Yorker. Oct 9, 1965, v41, p189-90.
Newsweek. Oct 25, 1965, v66, p113-14.
Playboy. Nov 1965, v12, p54, 56.
Private Screenings. p217.
Saturday Review. Oct 2, 1965, v48, p30.
Sight and Sound. Sum 1965, v34, p148-49.
The Spectator. Jun 18, 1965, v214, p788.
Variety. Jun 9, 1965, p6.
Vogue. Oct 15, 1965, v146, p64.

The Hindenburg (US; Wise, Robert; 1975)
BFI/Monthly Film Bulletin. Apr 1975, v43, p82.
Commonweal. Jan 2, 1975, v103, p19-20.
Films in Review. Jan 1976, v27, p53.
Hollywood Reporter. Dec 19, 1975, p8.
The Los Angeles Times. Dec 21, 1975, Calendar, p56.
Motion Picture Herald Product Digest. Dec 24, 1975, p54.
The New York Times. Dec 26, 1975, p46.
The New Yorker. Jan 19, 1976, v51, p48.
Newsweek. Dec 29, 1975, v86, p50-51.
Saturday Review. Jan 24, 1976, v3, p50.
Senior Scholastic. Feb 10, 1976, v108, p24.
Time. Dec 29, 1975, v106, p38.
Variety. Dec 24, 1975, p14.

Hired Hand (US; Fonda, Peter; 1971)
BFI/Monthly Film Bulletin. Dec 1971, v38, p240.
Commonweal. Oct 22, 1971, v95, p88.
Filmfacts. 1971, v14, p369-71.
Films and Filming. Dec 1971, v18, p50.
Hollywood Reporter. Jun 30, 1971, v216, n45, p3.
Life. Sep 17, 1971, v71, p15.
Magill's Survey of Cinema. Series II. v3, p1031-33.
The New Republic. Sep 4, 1971, v165, p26.
The New York Times. Aug 12, 1971, p29.
The New York Times. Oct 24, 1971, SecII, p11.
The New Yorker. Aug 21, 1971, v67, p62-63.
Newsweek. Aug 2, 1971, v78, p75.
Saturday Review. Aug 7, 1971, v54, p31.
Time. Aug 2, 1971, v98, p62.
Variety. Jul 7, 1971, p14.
The Village Voice. Aug 26, 1971, p51.

The Hireling (GB; Bridges, Alan; 1973)
Films in Review. Aug-Sep 1973, v24, p435.
Hollywood Reporter. Aug 10, 1973, p3.
Magill's Survey of Cinema. Series II. v3, p1034.
The Nation. Jul 2, 1973, v217, p28.
The New Republic. Jul 7, 1973, v169, p22.
The New York Times. Jul 11, 1973, p45.
The New Yorker. Jul 16, 1973, v49, p83-85.
Newsweek. Jul 2, 1973, v82, p71-71A.
Variety. May 23, 1973, p18.

Hiroshima, Mon Amour (FR, JAPAN; Resnais, Alain; 1959)
Alain Resnais (Kreidl). p53-64.
Alain Resnais, or the Theme of Time. p17-38.
Alain Resnais: The Role of Imagination. p34-52.
America. Jun 18, 1960, v103, p383.
BFI/Monthly Film Bulletin. 1960, v27, p19.
The Cinema of Alain Resnais. p66-87.
Classics of the Foreign Film. p222-25.
Commonweal. Jun 10, 1960, v72, p279.
Film Daily. May 20, 1960, p10.
The Film Narratives of Alain Resnais. p5-33.
Filmfacts. Jun 10, 1960, v3, p109-11.
Films in Review. Jun-Jul 1959, v10, p326.
The Great French Films. p171-76.
The Great Movies. p222-23.
Hiroshima, Mon Amour. 1966.
The International Dictionary of Films and Filmmakers. v1, p198-200.
The Nation. May 28, 1960, v190, p479-80.
The New Republic. Jun 13, 1960, v142, p29-30.
The New York Times. May 17, 1960, p43.
The New Yorker. Jul 11, 1959, v35, p78-80.
The New Yorker. May 28, 1960, v36, p133.
Newsweek. May 23, 1960, v55, p119.
Nuclear War Films. p17-24.
On Movies. p366-68.
Renaissance of the Film. p105-26.
Reporter. Aug 20, 1959, v21, p35-36.
Reruns. p127-31.
Saturday Review. May 21, 1960, v43, p34.
Time. May 16, 1960, v75, p88.
Variety. May 13, 1959, p7.

His Kind of Woman (US; Farrow, John; 1951)
BFI/Monthly Film Bulletin. Oct 1951, v18, p347-48.
Film Daily. Jul 13, 1951, p6.
The Great Gangster Pictures. p190-91.
Hollywood Reporter. Jul 11, 1951, p3.
The London Times. Sep 3, 1951, p8.
Motion Picture Herald Product Digest. Jul 21, 1951, p938.
The Nation. Jan 5, 1952, v174, p18.
The New York Times. Aug 30, 1951, p20.
Newsweek. Sep 10, 1951, v38, p30.

Robert Mitchum on the Screen. p116-17.
The Spectator. Aug 31, 1954, v187, p268.
Time. Sep 17, 1951, v58, p110.
Variety. Jul 18, 1951, p6.

His Majesty Mr. Jones *See* Prima Communione

His Majesty O'Keefe (GB; Haskin, Byron; 1953)
America. Feb 13, 1954, v90, p518.
BFI/Monthly Film Bulletin. Jun 1954, v21, p88.
Burt Lancaster: A Pictorial Treasury of His Films. p76-77.
Burt Lancaster: The Man and His Movies. p60-62.
Film Daily. Dec 31, 1953, p6.
Hollywood Reporter. Dec 30, 1953, p3.
Library Journal. Jan 15, 1954, v79, p139.
The London Times. May 6, 1954, p2.
Motion Picture Herald Product Digest. Jan 12, 1954, p2125.
National Parent-Teacher. Mar 1954, v48, p139.
Natural History. Mar 1954, v63, p138-39.
The New Statesman and Nation. May 1, 1954, v47, p598.
The New York Times. Feb 6, 1954, p17.
Senior Scholastic. Feb 17, 1954, v64, p30.
The Spectator. Apr 30, 1954, v192, p513.
The Tatler. May 12, 1954, v212, p356.
Time. Feb 15, 1954, v63, p96.
Variety. Dec 30, 1953, p6.

His Other Woman *See* Desk Set

Histoire d'Adéle H., L' *See* The Story of Adele H.

Histoire d'Amour, Une (FR; Lefranc, Guy; 1951)
BFI/Monthly Film Bulletin. Oct 1952, v19, p143.
The London Times. Sep 1, 1952, p8.
The New Statesman and Nation. Sep 6, 1952, v44, p264.
The Spectator. Aug 29, 1952, v189, p264.
The Tatler. Sep 10, 1952, v205, p464.
Variety. Dec 5, 1951, p22.

Histoire Immortelle, Une *See* Immortal Story

Histoire simple, Une *See* A Simple Story

The History of the World, Part I (US; Brooks, Mel; 1981)
BFI/Monthly Film Bulletin. Sep 1981, v48, p177-78.
Horizon. Jul-Aug 1981, v24, p70-71.
The Los Angeles Times. Jun 11, 1981, SecVI, p1.
The Nation. Jun 27, 1981, v232, p805.
New Statesman. Oct 9, 1981, v102, p27.
New York. Jun 22, 1981, v14, p48-49.
The New York Times. Jun 7, 1981, SecII, p13-14.
The New York Times. Jul 10, 1981, p6.
The New York Times. Jun 12, 1981, SecIII, p14.
The New Yorker. Jun 29, 1981, v57, p93-95.
Newsweek. Jun 22, 1981, v97, p87.
Playboy. Jul 1981, v28, p160-62.
Time. Jun 29, 1981, v117, p70.
Variety. Jun 10, 1981, p18.
The Village Voice. Jun 17, 1981, p43.

Hitler, a Film from Germany *See* Our Hitler

Hitler. Ein Film aus Deutschland *See* Our Hitler

Hobson's Choice (GB; Lean, David; 1954)
America. Jul 10, 1954, v91, p387.
BFI/Monthly Film Bulletin. Mar 1954, v21, p36.
Charles Laughton (Brown). p141-42.
The Cinema of David Lean. p109-18.
David Lean: A Guide to References and Resources. p82-84.
David Lean and His Films. p115-28.
David Lean (Anderegg). p81-86.
Film Daily. Jun 14, 1954, p6.
Films in Review. Aug-Sep 1954, v5, p366-67.
Hollywood Reporter. Jun 18, 1954, p3.
Illustrated London News. Mar 20, 1954, v224, p450.
Kiss Kiss Bang Bang. p351.
The London Times. Mar 1, 1954, p9.
Magill's Survey of Cinema. Series I. v2, p754-57.
Motion Picture Herald Product Digest. Jun 12, 1954, p25-26.
National Parent-Teacher. Sep 1954, v49, p38.
The New Republic. Jul 5, 1954, v131, p21.
The New Statesman and Nation. Mar 6, 1954, v47, p285.
The New York Times. Jun 15, 1954, p37.
The New Yorker. Jun 19, 1954, v30, p65.
Newsweek. Jun 21, 1954, v43, p86.
Saturday Review. Jun 19, 1954, v37, p30.
Sight and Sound. Apr-Jun 1954, v23, p198.
The Spectator. Mar 5, 1954, v192, p257-58.
The Tatler. Mar 10, 1953, v209, p428.
Time. Jan 21, 1954, v63, p102.
Variety. Mar 3, 1954, p6.

The Hole *See* Onibaba

Holiday For Henrietta (French title: Fete a Henriette, La; Henriette) (FR; Duvivier, Julien; 1952)
BFI/Monthly Film Bulletin. Jun 1954, v21, p83-84.
Cinema, the Magic Vehicle. v2, p146-47.
Farm Journal. Mar 1955, v79, p103.
Film Daily. Jan 21, 1955, p10.
Films in Review. Feb 1955, v6, p84-85.
The Great French Films. p255.
Hollywood Reporter. Jun 9, 1955, p3.
The London Times. May 5, 1954, p8.
Motion Picture Herald Product Digest. Jan 15, 1955, p290.
The Nation. Feb 19, 1955, v180, p166.
National Parent-Teacher. Apr 1955, v49, p39.
The New Statesman and Nation. Jun 5, 1954, v47, p731.
The New York Times. Jan 25, 1955, p21.
The New Yorker. Feb 5, 1955, v30, p103.
Quarterly of Film, Radio and Television. Fall 1955, v10, p11-18.
Saturday Review. Feb 12, 1955, v38, p25.
The Tatler. May 19, 1954, v212, p412.
Variety. Feb 18, 1953, p18.

Holiday For Sinners (US; Mayer, Gerald; 1952)
BFI/Monthly Film Bulletin. Dec 1952, v19, p172.
Film Daily. Jun 27, 1952, p7.
Hollywood Reporter. Jun 23, 1952, p3.
Motion Picture Herald Product Digest. Jun 28, 1952, p1426.
The New York Times. Sep 20, 1952, p13.
Newsweek. Oct 20, 1952, v40, p124.
Variety. Jun 25, 1952, p6.

The Holly and the Ivy (GB; O'Ferrall, George More; 1952)
America. Mar 6, 1954, v90, p610.
BFI/Monthly Film Bulletin. Oct 1952, v19, p138-39.

Catholic World. Mar 1954, v178, p462.
Commonweal. Feb 19, 1954, v59, p497.
Illustrated London News. Feb 7, 1953, v222, p214.
Magill's Survey of Cinema. Series II. v3, p1038-40.
Motion Picture Herald Product Digest. Feb 13, 1954, p2183.
National Parent-Teacher. May 1954, v48, p39.
The New York Times. Feb 5, 1954, p16.
Saturday Review. Feb 27, 1954, v37, p29.
The Spectator. Oct 31, 1952, v189, p565.
The Tatler. Nov 5, 1952, v206, p320.
Time. Mar 1, 1954, v63, p91.
Variety. Feb 10, 1954, p6.

Hollywood Cowboy *See* Hearts of the West

Hollywood Story (US; Castle, William; 1951)
BFI/Monthly Film Bulletin. Jun 1951, v18, p280.
Commonweal. Jun 22, 1951, v54, p261.
Film Daily. May 14, 1951, p6.
The New Republic. Jun 18, 1951, v124, p21.
The New York Times. Jun 7, 1951, p40.
The New Yorker. Jun 16, 1951, v27, p75.
Newsweek. Jun 18, 1951, v37, p94.
Time. Jun 11, 1951, v57, p110.
Variety. May 16, 1951, p6.

Hombre (US; Ritt, Martin; 1967)
America. May 20, 1967, v116, p764.
BFI/Monthly Film Bulletin. Jun 1967, v34, p88.
Commonweal. Apr 21, 1967, v86, p152.
Film Daily. Mar 10, 1967, p3.
Film Quarterly. Fall 1967, p49-58.
Films and Filming. Jun 1967, v13, p20-21.
Films in Review. Apr 1967, v18, p289.
The Films of Fredric March. p236-38.
The Films of Paul Newman. p156-60.
Hollywood Reporter. Mar 10, 1967, p3.
Magill's Cinema Annual, 1984. p547-51.
Motion Picture Herald Product Digest. Mar 15, 1967, p665-A.
The New York Times. Mar 22, 1967, p41.
Newsweek. Apr 10, 1967, v69, p99.
Saturday Review. Apr 15, 1967, v50, p45.
Senior Scholastic. Apr 7, 1967, v90, p26.
Take One. 1967, v1, p23.
Variety. Mar 15, 1967, p6.
The Village Voice. Apr 6, 1967, p31.
Vogue. Apr 1, 1967, v149, p95.

Home At Seven (Also titled: Murder On Monday) (GB; Richardson, Ralph; 1952)
America. Oct 31, 1953, v90, p139.
BFI/Monthly Film Bulletin. Mar 1952, v19, p30-31.
Commonweal. Nov 6, 1953, v59, p120.
Films in Review. Nov 1953, v4, p482-83.
Hollywood Reporter. Nov 25, 1953, p3.
Illustrated London News. Mar 8, 1952, v220, p422.
The London Times. Feb 4, 1952, p8.
Motion Picture Herald Product Digest. Oct 10, 1953, p2022.
National Parent-Teacher. Dec 1953, v48, p40.
The New Statesman and Nation. Feb 9, 1952, v43, p153-54.
The New York Times. Oct 7, 1953, p35.
The New Yorker. Oct 17, 1953, v29, p107.
Newsweek. Oct 19, 1953, v42, p104.
Saturday Review. Oct 17, 1953, v36, p38.
The Spectator. Feb 1, 1952, v188, p140.
Time. Oct 26, 1953, v62, p108.
Variety. Feb 6, 1952, p20.

Homme de Rio, L' *See* That Man From Rio

Homme d'Istanbul, L' *See* That Man in Istanbul

Homme et une Femme, Un *See* A Man and a Woman

Homme qui aimait les femmes, L' *See* The Man Who Loved Women

Homme Qui Ment, L' (Also titled: The Man Who Lies) (FR, CZECH; Robbe-Grillet, Alain; 1968)
The Film Career of Alain Robbe-Grillet. p30-33, 140.
Film Festival (Bishop). p41-44, 87-89.
Films in Review. May 1970, v21, p206-07.
The Films of Alain Robbe-Grillet. p91-115.
The London Times. Jul 2, 1968, p13.
The New York Times. Apr 14, 1970, p53.
Variety. Apr 10, 1968, p22.
The Village Voice. Apr 2, 1970, p58.

Hon Dansade en Sommar *See* One Summer of Happiness

Hondo (US; Farrow, John; 1953)
America. Dec 19, 1953, v90, p327.
BFI/Monthly Film Bulletin. Apr 1954, v21, p57.
Catholic World. Jan 1954, v178, p301.
Commonweal. Dec 25, 1953, v59, p307.
The Complete Films of John Wayne. p192-94.
Film Daily. Nov 27, 1953, p4.
Films in Review. Jan 1954, v5, p33.
Hollywood Reporter. Nov 25, 1953, p3.
Life. Dec 14, 1953, v35, p125-26.
The New Yorker. Dec 19, 1953, v29, p97.
Newsweek. Dec 14, 1953, v42, p88.
Saturday Review. Dec 5, 1953, v36, p53.
Time. Dec 14, 1953, v62, p112.
Variety. Nov 25, 1953, p6.

The Honey Pot (US; Mankiewicz, Joseph L.; 1967)
America. Jun 3, 1967, v116, p820-21.
BFI/Monthly Film Bulletin. May 1967, v34, p75.
Commonweal. Jun 2, 1967, v86, p323.
Film Daily. May 22, 1967, p5.
Film Quarterly. Fall 1967, v21, p60.
Films and Filming. Jul 1967, v13, p22.
Films in Review. Jun-Jul 1967, v18, p366-67.
The Films of Susan Hayward. p270-72.
Hollywood Reporter. May 25, 1967, p3.
Joseph L. Mankiewicz (Dick). p69-75.
Life. Jul 14, 1967, v63, p12.
Motion Picture Herald Product Digest. May 24, 1967, p687.
The New York Times. May 23, 1967, p52.
The New Yorker. Jun 3, 1967, v43, p119.
Newsweek. Jun 5, 1967, v69, p97.
Saturday Review. Jun 10, 1967, v50, p83.
Take One. Jun 1967, v1, p30-31.
Time. May 26, 1967, v89, p94.
Variety. Mar 22, 1967, p6.
The Village Voice. Jun 22, 1967, p21.

Honeysuckle Rose (US; Schatzberg, Jerry; 1980)
BFI/Monthly Film Bulletin. Oct 1980, v47, p193.
Christian Science Monitor. Aug 22, 1980, p19.
Films in Review. Oct 10, 1980, v31, p499.
Hollywood Reporter. Jul 11, 1980, p3.
The Los Angeles Times. Jul 17, 1980, SecIV, p1.
Maclean's. Jul 29, 1980, v93, p53.
Motion Picture Herald Product Digest. Jul 23, 1980, p16.
The New Republic. Aug 30, 1980, v183, p24.
New York. Aug 4, 1980, v13, p55.
The New York Times. Jul 18, 1980, SecIII, p14.

The New Yorker. Aug 18, 1980, v56, p81-86.
Newsday. Jul 18, 1980, SecII, p7.
Newsweek. Aug 4, 1980, v96, p61.
Time. Jul 28, 1980, v116, p66.
Variety. Jul 16, 1980, p23.

Hong Kong (US; Foster, Lewis R.; 1951)
American Magazine. Jan 1952, v153, p9.
BFI/Monthly Film Bulletin. Mar 1952, v19, p35.
Film Daily. Nov 20, 1951, p14.
The Films of Ronald Reagan. p186-89.
Hollywood Reporter. Nov 13, 1951, p3.
Motion Picture Herald Product Digest. Nov 17, 1951, p1110.
The New York Times. Apr 5, 1952, p20.
Newsweek. May 19, 1952, v39, p110.
Variety. Nov 14, 1951, p6.

Honky Tonk Freeway (US; Schlesinger, John; 1981)
Hollywood Reporter. Aug 20, 1981, p2.
The Los Angeles Times. Aug 21, 1981, SecVI, p1.
Maclean's. Sep 14, 1981, v94, p68.
Magill's Cinema Annual, 1982. p199-202.
New York. Mar 16, 1981, v14, p52.
Newsweek. Aug 31, 1981, v98, p36.
Senior Scholastic. Sep 4, 1981, v114, p26.
Theatre Crafts. May 1981, v15, p70-71.
Variety. Aug 21, 1981, p3.

Honky Tonk Man (US; Eastwood, Clint; 1982)
Clint Eastwood (Guérif). p155-61.
Hollywood Reporter. Dec 15, 1982, p8.
The Los Angeles Times. Dec 15, 1982, SecVI, p1.
Magill's Cinema Annual, 1983. p200-05.
The New York Times. Dec 15, 1982, SecIII, p29.
Time. Dec 20, 1982, v120, p82.
Variety. Dec 14, 1982, p3.

The Hook (US; Seaton, George; 1963)
America. Feb 23, 1963, v108, p275.
BFI/Monthly Film Bulletin. Apr 1963, v30, p42-43.
Commonweal. Mar 1, 1963, v77, p599.
Film Daily. Jan 16, 1963, p5.
Filmfacts. Feb 14, 1963, v6, p7-8.
Films and Filming. Mar 1963, v9, p37.
Hollywood Reporter. Jan 16, 1963, p3.
The New York Times. Feb 16, 1963, p5.
The New Yorker. Mar 9, 1963, v39, p145-46.
Newsweek. Mar 4, 1963, v61, p85.
Photoplay. Apr 1963, v63, p6.
Saturday Review. Feb 16,, 1963, v46, p26.
Time. Mar 1, 1963, v81, pM17.
Variety. Jan 16, 1963, p6.

Hooper (US; Needham, Hal; 1978)
BFI/Monthly Film Bulletin. Nov 1978, v45, p219.
The Films of Burt Reynolds. p216-21.
Hollywood Reporter. Jul 24, 1978, p3.
The Los Angeles Times. Aug 9, 1978, SecIV, p12.
Motion Picture Herald Product Digest. Aug 9, 1978, p17.
New Times. Aug 7, 1978, v11, p62.
New York. Aug 28, 1978, p94.
The New York Times. Aug 4, 1978, SecIII, p11.
The New Yorker. Sep 4, 1978, v54, p95-96.
Newsweek. Aug 21, 1978, v92, p67.
Senior Scholastic. Sep 21, 1978, v111, p52.
Variety. Jul 26, 1978, p20.

The Hopeless Ones *See* The Round-Up

Hopscotch (US; Neame, Ronald; 1980)
BFI/Monthly Film Bulletin. Dec 1980, v47, p236.
Films in Review. Nov 1980, v31, p567.
Hollywood Reporter. Jul 24, 1980, p3.
The Los Angeles Times. Sep 26, 1980, Calendar, p1.
Maclean's. Nov 10, 1980, v93, p72.
Motion Picture Herald Product Digest. Aug 6, 1980, p17.
The New York Times. Sep 26, 1980, SecIII, p6.
Newsday. Sep 26, 1980, SecII, p7.
Newsweek. Sep 29, 1980, v96, p78.
Saturday Review. Sep 1980, v7, p90-91.
Time. Oct 13, 1980, v116, p108.
Variety. Jul 23, 1980, p20.
The Village Voice. Oct 8, 1980, p51.

Horizons West (US; Boetticher, Budd; 1952)
BFI/Monthly Film Bulletin. Nov 1952, v19, p157.
Film Daily. Sep 24, 1952, p6.
Hollywood Reporter. Sep 19, 1952, p3.
Motion Picture Herald Product Digest. Sep 20, 1952, p1534.
The New York Times. Nov 22, 1952, p16.
Variety. Sep 24, 1952, p6.

Horror of Dracula (GB; Fisher, Terence; 1958)
America. Jun 21, 1958, v99, p358.
Film Daily. May 7, 1958, v113, p6.
Filmfacts. Jul 2, 1958, v1, p90-91.
The Films of the Fifties. p250-51.
The Great British Films. p172-74.
Hollywood Reporter. May 6, 1958, p3.
Magill's Survey of Cinema. Series I. v2, p762-65.
The New York Times. May 29, 1958, p24.
Variety. Jul 5, 1958, p22.

The Horse Soldiers (US; Ford, John; 1959)
America. Jul 4, 1959, v101, p497.
BFI/Monthly Film Bulletin. Dec 1959, v26, p154.
Catholic World. Aug 1959, v189, p394-95.
Commonweal. Jul 3, 1959, v70, p352.
The Complete Films of John Wayne. p225-26.
Cosmopolitan. Sep 1959, v147, p12.
Film Daily. Jun 12, 1959, p10.
Filmfacts. Jul 22, 1959, v2, p135-37.
Films in Review. Aug-Sep 1959, v10, p417-18.
The Films of William Holden. p1196-201.
Hollywood Reporter. Jun 12, 1959, p3.
Library Journal. Jul 1959, v84, p2172.
Life. Jun 29, 1959, v46, p55-58.
The New York Times. Jun 26, 1959, p13.
Newsweek. Jun 29, 1959, v53, p91.
Saturday Review. Jun 20, 1959, v42, p28.
Time. Jul 20, 1959, p63.
Variety. Jun 10, 1959, p6.
The Western Films of John Ford. p174-85.

The Horsemen (US; Frankenheimer, John; 1971)
BFI/Monthly Film Bulletin. Sep 1971, v38, p181.
Filmfacts. 1971, v14, p453-55.
Films and Filming. Oct 1971, v18, p58.
Hollywood Reporter. Jun 28, 1971, p3.
The New York Times. Jul 22, 1971, p27.
Time. Aug 16, 1971, v98, p55.
Variety. Jun 23, 1971, p20.
The Village Voice. Aug 5, 1971, p53.

The Horse's Mouth (Also titled: The Oracle) (GB; Richards, C. Pennington; 1953)
America. Jan 30, 1954, v90, p464.

BFI/Monthly Film Bulletin. Apr 1953, v20, p49.
Commonweal. Feb 26, 1954, v59, p525.
Motion Picture Herald Product Digest. Jan 23, 1954, p2158-59.
National-Parent Teacher. Mar 1954, v48, p38.
The New York Times. Jan 20, 1954, p33.
Saturday Review. Feb 6, 1954, v37, p29.
Variety. Jun 10, 1953, p6.

The Horse's Mouth (GB; Neame, Ronald; 1958)
America. Nov 22, 1958, v100, p254.
BFI/Monthly Film Bulletin. Mar 1959, v26, p29.
Catholic World. Jan 1959, v188, p327.
Commonweal. Dec 5, 1958, v69, p258.
Film Daily. Nov 10, 1958, p6.
Filmfacts. Dec 17, 1958, v1, p215-16.
Films in Review. Oct 1958, v9, p421-22.
Films in Review. Dec 1958, v9, p593-94.
Films in Review. Jan 1959, v10, p4.
Hollywood Reporter. Nov 10, 1958, p3.
Library Journal. Dec 1, 1958, v83, p3418.
Life. Nov 10, 1958, v40, p98-99.
Mademoiselle. Jan 1959, v40, p66.
Magill's Survey of Cinema. Series II. v3, p1054-57.
The New Republic. Dec 15, 1958, v139, p21-22.
The New York Times. Nov 12, 1598, p41.
The New York Times Magazine. Oct 26, 1958, p66-67.
The New Yorker. Nov 22, 1598, v34, p137.
Newsweek. Nov 24, 1958, v52, p113.
Saturday Review. Nov 15, 1958, v41, p26.
Sex, Psyche etcetera in the Film. p156-60.
Time. Nov 24, 1958, v72, p94.
Variety. Sep 17, 1958, p6.

The Hospital (US; Hiller, Arthur; 1971)
Atlantic. Mar 1970, v225, p139-42.
BFI/Monthly Film Bulletin. Aug 1972, v39, p164.
Deeper into Movies. p126-28.
Filmfacts. 1971, v14, p441-45.
Films and Filming. Aug 1972, v18, p50.
Films in Review. Jan 1972, v23, p53-54.
Hollywood Reporter. Dec 8, 1971, p3.
Life. Jan 28, 1972, v72, p14.
Magill's Survey of Cinema. Series I. v2, p766.
The New Republic. Jan 22, 1972, v166.
The New York Times. Dec 15, 1971, p66.
The New York Times. Apr 2, 1972, SecII, p1.
The New Yorker. Jan 31, 1970, v65, p75-76.
Newsweek. Feb 9, 1970, v75, p85-86.
Newsweek. Dec 20, 1971, v78, p88.
Time. Jan 10, 1972, v99, p50.
Variety. Dec 8, 1971, p16.

Hot Blood *See* The Wild One

Hot Millions (GB; Till, Eric; 1968)
America. Oct 12, 1968, v119, p335.
BFI/Monthly Film Bulletin. Dec 1968, v35, p193-94.
Christian Century. Dec 4, 1968, v85, p1545-46.
Film Daily. Sep 5, 1968, p3.
Filmfacts. Dec 1, 1968, v11, p355-56.
Films in Review. Oct 1968, v19, p518.
Harper's Magazine. Nov 1968, v237, p170-71.
Hollywood Reporter. Sep 3, 1968, p3.
The London Times. Oct 17, 1968, p18.
Magill's Survey of Cinema. Series II. v3, p1058-60.
Motion Picture Herald Product Digest. Sep 11, 1968, p853.
The New York Times. Sep 20, 1968, p42.
The New Yorker. Sep 21, 1968, v44, p147.
Saturday Review. Oct 19, 1968, v51, p39.
Senior Scholastic. Oct 11, 1968, v93, p23.

The Spectator. Oct 25, 1968, v221, p599.
Variety. Sep 4, 1968, p6.

The Hot One *See* Corvette Summer

Hotel (US; Quine, Richard; 1967)
America. Jan 28, 1967, v116, p162.
BFI/Monthly Film Bulletin. Apr 1967, v34, p61.
Commonweal. Feb 17, 1967, v85, p566.
Film Daily. Jan 19, 1967, p3.
Film Quarterly. Sum 1967, v20, p78-79.
Films and Filming. Apr 1967, v13, p8.
Films in Review. Feb 1967, v18, p114.
Hollywood Reporter. Jan 16, 1967, p3.
Motion Picture Herald Product Digest. Feb 1, 1967, p653.
The New York Times. Jan 20, 1967, p27.
Newsweek. Jan 30, 1967, v69, p96.
Saturday Review. Feb 4, 1967, v50, p55.
Time. Jan 27, 1967, v89, p80.
Variety. Jan 18, 1967, p6.

The Hotel New Hampshire (US; Richardson, Tony; 1984)
American Cinematographer. Mar 1984, v65, p42-43.
BFI/Monthly Film Bulletin. Nov 1984, v51, p334-35.
Film Journal. Apr 1984, v87, p35.
Films and Filming. Aug 1984, n359, p35-36.
Horizon. Mar 1984, v27, p19-20.
The Los Angeles Times. Mar 9, 1984, SecVI, p1.
Maclean's. Mar 12, 1984, v97, p66.
Magill's Cinema Annual, 1985. p243-47.
New Statesman. Nov 16, 1984, v108, p34.
New York. Mar 19, 1984, v17, p64-65.
The New York Times. Mar 9, 1984, SecIII, p8.
Newsweek. Apr 2, 1984, v103, p85-86.
Photoplay. Oct 1984, v35, p19.
Theatre Crafts. Jan 1984, v18, p22-23.
Time. Mar 19, 1984, v123, p91.
Variety. Mar 14, 1984, p20.
The Village Voice. Mar 20, 1984, p47.

Hotel Paradiso (GB; Glenville, Peter; 1966)
America. Oct 29, 1966, v115, p526.
BFI/Monthly Film Bulletin. Apr 1971, v38, p74-75.
Christian Science Monitor (Western edition). Jan 6, 1967, p4.
Film Daily. Sep 8, 1966, p3.
Filmfacts. Dec 15, 1966, v9, p287-88.
Films and Filming. Apr 1971, v17, p49.
Films in Review. Nov 1966, v17, p590-91.
Hollywood Reporter. Sep 8, 1966, p3.
Motion Picture Herald Product Digest. Sep 14, 1966, p595.
The New York Times. Oct 15, 1966, p34.
Playboy. Oct 1966, v13, p26.
Time. Oct 28, 1966, v88, p112.
Variety. Sep 7, 1966, p6.
Vogue. Dec 1966, v148, p166.

Hotel Sahara (GB; Annakin, Ken; 1951)
BFI/Monthly Film Bulletin. Aug 1951, v18, p312.
Catholic World. Nov 1951, v174, p143-44.
Film Daily. Sep 12, 1951, p6.
Films in Review. Dec 1951, v2, p56-57.
Hollywood Reporter. Nov 2, 1951, p3.
The London Times. Jul 16, 1951, p2.
Motion Picture Herald Product Digest. Sep 15, 1951, p1014.
The New Statesman and Nation. Jul 14, 1951, v42, p42.
The New York Times. Jan 1, 1952, p21.
Newsweek. Jan 14, 1952, v39, p82.
The Spectator. Jul 13, 1951, v187, p62.

Time. Sep 24, 1951, v58, p107.
Variety. Jul 18, 1951, p20.

Hothead *See* Coup de tete

Houdini (US; Marshall, George; 1953)
America. Jul 18, 1953, v89, p406.
BFI/Monthly Film Bulletin. Dec 1953, v20, n239, p177.
Catholic World. Jul 1953, v177, p304-05.
Commonweal. Jul 10, 1953, v58, p348.
Film Daily. May 21, 1953, p6.
Hollywood Reporter. May 18, 1953, p3.
The New Yorker. Jul 25, 1953, v29, p47.
Saturday Review. Jul 11, 1953, v36, p36.
Time. Jun 29, 1953, v61, p92.
Tony Curtis: The Man and His Movies. p40-42.
Variety. May 20, 1953, p6.

Hour of the Gun (US; Sturges, John; 1967)
BFI/Monthly Film Bulletin. Jan 1968, v35, p5.
Film Daily. Oct 11, 1967, p10.
Films and Filming. Jan 1968, v14, p22-23.
Hollywood Reporter. Oct 4, 1967, p4.
Magill's Survey of Cinema. Series II. v3, p1061-64.
Motion Picture Herald Product Digest. Oct 11, 1967, p729.
The New York Times. Nov 2, 1967, p58.
Variety. Oct 4, 1967, p16.

Hour of the Wolf (Swedish title: Vargtimmen) (SWED; Bergman, Ingmar; 1968)
America. May 25, 1968, v118, p716.
BFI/Monthly Film Bulletin. Aug 1968, v35, p115-16.
Christian Science Monitor (Western edition). Mar 2, 1968, p4.
Cinema. Fall 1968, v4, p40-41.
Commonweal. May 10, 1968, v88, p239.
The Cracked Lens. p160-99.
Dictionary of Films. p399.
Esquire. Jul 1968, v70, p38-39.
Figures of Light. p62-65.
Film 68/69. p130-36.
Film Comment. Spr 1970, v6, p26-31.
Film Culture. Wint-Spr 1970, v48-49, p56-60.
Film Quarterly. Wint 1976-77, v30, p23-34.
Film Quarterly. Sum 1968, v21, p33-40.
Film Quarterly. 1981, v34, n3 p26-37.
Filmfacts. May 15, 1968, v11, p122-24.
Films and Filming. Sep 1968, v14, p32-33.
Films in Review. May 1968, v19, p306-08.
Hollywood Reporter. Jul 10, 1968, p3.
Ingmar Bergman (Cowie). p241-47.
Ingmar Bergman: Essays in Criticism. p270-77.
Ingmar Bergman (Wood). p159-71.
International Film Guide. 1969, v6, p153-54.
Life. Apr 26, 1968, v64, p8.
Literature/Film Quarterly. 1980, v8, n2, p104-15.
London Magazine. Sep 1968, v8, p107-09.
The London Times. Jul 11, 1968, p11.
Magill's Survey of Cinema. Foreign Language Films. v3, p1393-97.
Motion Picture Herald Product Digest. Apr 17, 1968, p800A.
Movie. Wint 1968-69, n16, p9-12.
Movies Into Film. p230-33.
The Nation. Apr 29, 1968, v206, p582.
The New Republic. Apr 20, 1968, v158, p30.
New Statesman. Jul 12, 1968, v76, p58-59.
The New York Times. Apr 10, 1968, p50.
The New York Times. Apr 14, 1968, p1.
The New Yorker. Apr 20, 1968, v44, p163-66.
Newsweek. Apr 29, 1968, v71, p84.
Saturday Review. Apr 13, 1968, v51, p50.
Sight and Sound. Aut 1968, v37, p203-04.
The Spectator. Jul 19, 1968, v221, p97.
Time. Apr 12, 1968, v91, p105-06.

Variety. Feb 28, 1968, p22.
The Village Voice. May 30, 1968, v13, p45-46.
A Year In the Dark. p111-12, 116-17.

The Hour of Thirteen (Also titled: The
Hour of 13) (GB; French, Harold;
1952)
BFI/Monthly Film Bulletin. Dec 1952, v19,
p172.
Christian Century. Jan 7, 1953, v70, p31.
Film Daily. Oct 2, 1952, p6.
Hollywood Reporter. Sep 29, 1952, p3.
Motion Picture Herald Product Digest. Oct 4,
1952, p1549.
National Parent-Teacher. Oct 1952, v47, p38.
The New York Times. Oct 28, 1952, p37.
Newsweek. Nov 3, 1952, v40, p105.
Time. Nov 10, 1952, v60, p120.
Variety. Oct 1, 1952, p6.

The Hours of Love (Italian title: Ore
Dell'Amore, Le) (IT; Salce, Luciano;
1963)
Confessions of a Cultist. p211-12.
Film Daily. Sep 7, 1965, p14.
Motion Picture Herald Product Digest. Sep 15,
1965, p363.
The New York Times. Sep 4, 1965, p11.
The New Yorker. Sep 11, 1965, v41, p100.
Variety. Mar 27, 1963, p6.
The Village Voice. Oct 7, 1965, v10, p27.

The House By the River (US; Lang, Fritz;
1950)
BFI/Monthly Film Bulletin. Jun 1950, v17, p79.
The Cinema of Fritz Lang. p170-71.
Film Daily. Apr 4, 1950, p6.
The Films of Fritz Lang. p227-30.
*Fritz Lang: A Guide to References and
Resources.* p99-102.
Fritz Lang (Eisner). p285-94.
Hollywood Reporter. Mar 24, 1950, p3.
Library Journal. May 1, 1950, v75, p787.
Motion Picture Herald Product Digest. Apr 1,
1950, p246.
The New Republic. May 15, 1950, v122, p23.
The New York Times. May 2, 1950, p25.
Newsweek. May 15, 1950, v35, p90.
Variety. Mar 29, 1950, p11.

House Calls (US; Zieff, Howard; 1978)
BFI/Monthly Film Bulletin. Jul 1978, v45,
p159.
Films in Review. May 1978, v29, p312.
Hollywood Reporter. Mar 13, 1978, p3.
The Los Angeles Times. Mar 12, 1978,
Calendar, p1.
Motion Picture Herald Product Digest. Apr 12,
1978, p88.
The New York Times. Mar 15, 1978, SecIII,
p15.
The New Yorker. Apr 3, 1978, v54, p94-96.
Newsweek. Mar 20, 1978, v91, p95.
Time. Apr 10, 1978, v111, p72.
Variety. May 15, 1978, p21.

The House in the Square *See* I'll Never
Forget You

House of Bamboo (US; Fuller, Sam; 1955)
America. Jul 23, 1955, v93, p419.
BFI/Monthly Film Bulletin. Oct 1955, v22,
n261, p148.
Commonweal. Jul 22, 1955, v62, p399.
Film Daily. Jul 7, 1955, p6.
Films and Filming. Dec 1955, v2, n3, p19.
Hollywood Reporter. Jul 1, 1955, v135, n17, p3.
The New York Times. Jul 2, 1955, p13.
Newsweek. Jul 18, 1955, v46, p83.
Samuel Fuller (Hardy). p95-122.
Saturday Review. Jul 23, 1955, v38, p23.

Time. Aug 1, 1955, v66, p60.
Variety. Jul 6, 1955, p6.

House of Pleasure *See* Plaisir, Le

House of Wax (US; De Toth, Andre; 1953)
America. May 23, 1953, v89, p229.
BFI/Monthly Film Bulletin. Jun 1953, v20,
n233, p84.
Catholic World. Jun 1953, v177, p223-24.
Commonweal. May 1, 1953, v58, p99.
Film Daily. Apr 10, 1953, p5.
Films in Review. May 1953, v4, n5, p235-36.
The Films of Charles Bronson. p42-43.
The Films of the Fifties. p95-96.
Hollywood Reporter. Apr 10, 1953, p3.
Magill's Survey of Cinema. Series I. v2, p772.
National Parent-Teacher. Jun 1953, v47, p37.
The New York Times. Apr 11, 1953, p15.
The New Yorker. Apr 18, 1953, v29, p133.
Newsweek. Apr 27, 1953, v41, p108.
Sight and Sound. Jul-Sep 1953, v23, n1, p31.
Time. Apr 20, 1953, v61, p114.
Variety. Apr 15, 1953, p6.

The House on Telegraph Hill (US; Wise,
Robert; 1951)
BFI/Monthly Film Bulletin. Jun 1951, v18,
p280-81.
Film Daily. Mar 7, 1951, p4.
Hollywood Reporter. Mar 6, 1951, p3.
Library Journal. Jun 1, 1951, v76, p972.
Motion Picture Herald Product Digest. Mar 10,
1951, p749-50.
The New York Times. May 14, 1951, p29.
Newsweek. May 28, 1951, v37, p89.
Senior Scholastic. Mar 14, 1951, v58, p29.
Time. Jun 18, 1951, v57, p106.
Variety. Mar 7, 1951, p6.

Houseboat (US; Shavelson, Melville; 1958)
America. Dec 6, 1958, v100, p327.
BFI/Monthly Film Bulletin. Nov 1958, v25,
p140.
Catholic World. Oct 1958, v188, p64.
Commonweal. Nov 28, 1958, v69, p232.
Film Daily. Sep 5, 1958, p6.
Filmfacts. Dec 17, 1958, v1, p218-19.
The Films of Cary Grant. p238-40.
The Films of Sophia Loren. p92-94.
Hollywood Reporter. Sep 5, 1958, p3.
Life. Oct 13, 1958, v45, p56.
The New York Times. Nov 14, 1958, p24.
The New York Times Magazine. Jul 6, 1958,
p20.
The New Yorker. Nov 22, 1958, v34, p138.
Newsweek. Nov 3, 1958, v52, p106-07.
Saturday Review. Dec 6, 1958, v41, p36.
Time. Dec 1, 1958, v82, p82.
Variety. Sep 10, 1958, p6.

How Do I Love Thee (US; Gordon,
Michael; 1971)
BFI/Monthly Film Bulletin. Jun 1971, v38,
p121.
Filmfacts. 1971, v14, p106-07.
Hollywood Reporter. Sep 17, 1970, p3.
The New York Times. Feb 4, 1971, p30.
Variety. Sep 30, 1970, p15.

How the West Was Won (US; Ford, John;
Hathaway, Henry; Marshall, George;
1962)
America. Mar 30, 1963, v108, p448.
BFI/Monthly Film Bulletin. Dec 1962, v29,
p166-67.
Commonweal. Apr 5, 1963, v78, p48.
Dictionary of Films. p152.
Film Daily. Nov 7, 1962, p3.
Hollywood Reporter. Nov 7, 1962, p3.
Life. Mar 29, 1963, v54, p87-89.

Magill's Survey of Cinema. Series II. v3, p1069-
72.
Motion Picture Herald Product Digest. Nov 28,
1962, p700.
The New Republic. Apr 20, 1963, v148, p29.
The New York Times. Apr 2, 1963, p54.
The New Yorker. Apr 6, 1963, v39, p175-76.
Newsweek. Mar 4, 1963, v61, p85.
Saturday Review. Feb 23, 1963, v46, p42.
Time. Mar 22, 1963, v81, p102.
Variety. Nov 7, 1962, p6.

How to Marry a Millionaire (US;
Negulesco, Jean; 1953)
America. Nov 28, 1953, v90, p247.
Catholic World. Jan 1954, v178, p302.
Commonweal. Nov 27, 1953, v59, p198.
The Complete Films of William Powell. p250-
51.
Film Daily. Nov 5, 1953, p6.
Films in Review. Dec 1953, v4, p535-36.
The Films of Marilyn Monroe. p105-09.
Hollywood Reporter. Nov 5, 1953, p3.
Lauren Bacall: Her Films and Career. p110-19.
Library Journal. Dec 1, 1953, v78, p2098.
Life. Nov 23, 1953, v35, p137-38.
The Nation. Dec 26, 1953, v177, p574.
The New York Times. Nov 11, 1953, p37.
The New York Times. Nov 15, 1953, SecII, p1.
The New Yorker. Nov 21, 1953, v29, p133.
Newsweek. Nov 16, 1953, v42, p104.
Saturday Review. Nov 28, 1953, v36, p31.
Time. Nov 23, 1953, v62, p114.
Variety. Nov 11, 1953, p6.

How to Murder a Rich Uncle (GB; Patrick,
Nigel; 1957)
BFI/Monthly Film Bulletin. Jul 1957, v24, p87.
Film Daily. Nov 14, 1957, v112, p9.
Films and Filming. Aug 1957, v3, p25.
Hollywood Reporter. Oct 28, 1957, p3.
The New York Times. Oct 26, 1957, p19.
The New Yorker. Nov 2, 1957, v33, p167.
Variety. Oct 30, 1957, p6.

How to Murder Your Wife (US; Quine,
Richard; 1965)
America. Feb 6, 1966, v112, p202-04.
BFI/Monthly Film Bulletin. Aug 1965, v32,
p120.
Christian Science Monitor (Western edition).
Feb 17, 1965, p4.
Commonweal. Feb 12, 1965, v81, p643.
Film Daily. Jan 20, 1965, p4.
Film Quarterly. Spr 1965, v18, p60.
Filmfacts. Feb 19, 1965, v8, p9-11.
Films and Filming. Oct 1965, v12, p24-25.
Films in Review. Feb 1965, v16, p111-12.
The Films of Jack Lemmon. p153-57.
Hollywood Reporter. Jan 20, 1965, p3.
Life. Jan 29, 1965, v58, p13.
The London Times. Sep 2, 1965, p6.
Motion Picture Herald Product Digest. Feb 3,
1965, p217.
The New Republic. Feb 13, 1965, v152, p27.
New Statesman. Sep 10, 1965, v70, p368.
The New York Times. Jan 27, 1965, p26.
The New Yorker. Jan 30, 1965, v40, p114.
Newsweek. Feb 8, 1965, v65, p86.
Playboy. Apr 1965, v12, p26.
Private Screenings. p168-70.
The Spectator. Sep 10, 1965, v215, p324.
Time. Jan 29, 1965, v85, p85.

How to Steal a Million (US; Wyler,
William; 1966)
America. Aug 20, 1966, v115, p193.
BFI/Monthly Film Bulletin. Sep 1966, v33,
p137.

Christian Science Monitor (Western edition).
   Jul 22, 1966, p4.
Commonweal. Aug 19, 1966, v84, p534.
Film Daily. Jun 30, 1966, p7.
Film Quarterly. Wint 1966-67, v20, p62.
Filmfacts. Sep 1, 1966, v9, p172-73.
Films and Filming. Oct 1966, v13, p12.
Films in Review. Aug-Sept 1966, v17, p451-52.
Hollywood Reporter. Jun 30, 1966, p3.
Illustrated London News. Aug 20, 1966, v249,
   p31.
Life. Aug 5, 1966, v61, p18.
The London Times. Aug 4, 1966, p6.
Motion Picture Herald Product Digest. Jul 13,
   1966, p560A.
New Statesman. Aug 5, 1966, v72, p210.
The New York Times. Jul 15, 1966, p34.
The New Yorker. Jul 16, 1966, v42, p92.
Newsweek. Jul 25, 1966, v68, p89-90.
Playboy. Oct 1966, v13, p28, 30.
Time. Jul 22, 1966, v88, p62.
Variety. Jul 13, 1966, p6.
The Village Voice. Aug 11, 1966, v11, p21.
*William Wyler: A Guide to References and
   Resources.* p155-58.
William Wyler (Anderegg). p214-15.

How to Stuff a Wild Bikini (US; Asher,
   William; 1965)
Film Daily. Jul 16, 1965, p4.
Hollywood Reporter. Jul 23, 1965, p3.
Motion Picture Herald Product Digest. Jul 21,
   1965, p330-31.
The New York Times. Jan 12, 1967, p48.
Variety. Jul 28, 1965, p6.

**How to Succeed in Business Without Really
   Trying** (US; Swift, David; 1967)
America. Apr 1, 1967, v116, p512-13.
BFI/Monthly Film Bulletin. May 1967, v34,
   p71-72.
Christian Century. May 10, 1967, v84, p628.
Cinema. Sum 1967, v3, p49.
Commonweal. Apr 14, 1967, v86, p128.
Film Daily. Feb 15, 1967, p3.
Film Quarterly. Sum 1967, v20, p78.
Films and Filming. May 1967, v13, p28.
Films in Review. Mar 1967, v18, p180.
Hollywood Reporter. Feb 14, 1967, p3.
Life. Mar 31, 1967, v62, p10.
Motion Picture Herald Product Digest. Feb 22,
   1967, p660.
The New York Times. Mar 10, 1967, p30.
Newsweek. Mar 20, 1967, v69, p98.
Saturday Review. Mar 11, 1967, v50, p111.
Senior Scholastic. May 12, 1967, v90, p34.
Variety. Feb 15, 1967, p6.

The Howling (US; Dante, Joe; 1981)
Hollywood Reporter. Jan 30, 1981, p3.
The Los Angeles Times. Apr 15, 1981, SecVI,
   p4.
Maclean's. Jun 1, 1981, v94, p62.
Magill's Cinema Annual, 1982. p207-213.
New York. Mar 16, 1981, v14, p48.
The New York Times. Mar 13, 1981, SecIII,
   p10.
The New Yorker. May 4, 1981, v57, p164-67.
Rolling Stone. Apr 30, 1981, p61.
Time. Apr 20, 1981, v117, p85.
Variety. Jan 27, 1981, p3.

Hud (US; Ritt, Martin; 1963)
America. Jun 15, 1963, v108, p871-72.
BFI/Monthly Film Bulletin. Jun 1963, v30, p79.
Commonweal. Jun 14, 1963, v78, p328.
Esquire. Sep 1963, v60, p50.
Fifty Grand Movies of the 1960s and 1970s.
   p105-08.
Film Daily. May 7, 1963, p12.
Filmfacts. May 30, 1963, v6, p91-93.

Films and Filming. Jun 1963, v9, p26.
Films in Review. May 1963, v14, p30-34.
The Films of Paul Newman. p116-21.
The Films of the Sixties. p110-12.
Hollywood Reporter. May 7, 1963, p3.
Illustrated London News. Jun 8, 1963, v242,
   p902.
The Making of the Great Westerns. p328-41.
The New Republic. May 25, 1963, v148, p27-28.
New Statesman. Jun 7, 1963, v65, p873.
The New York Times. May 29, 1963, p36.
The New York Times. Jun 9, 1963, SecII, p1.
The New Yorker. Jun 8, 1963, v39, p166.
Newsweek. Jun 3, 1963, v61, p84.
On Movies. p299-301.
Reruns. p165-69.
Saturday Review. May 25, 1963, v46, p40.
Sight and Sound. Sum 1963, v32, p144-45.
Time. Jun 7, 1963, v81, p100.
Variety. May 8, 1963, p6.

Hue and Cry (GB; Crichton, Charles; 1947)
Dictionary of Films. p152.
Film Daily. Dec 12, 1950, p4.
Motion Picture Herald Product Digest. Dec 9,
   1950, p606.
The New York Times. Jan 9, 1951, p25.
Variety. Feb 26, 1947, p11.

Hullo, Elephant *See* Hello, Elephant!

Human Desire (US; Lang, Fritz; 1954)
BFI/Monthly Film Bulletin. Jan 1955, v22, p9.
The Cinema of Fritz Lang. p186-89.
Dictionary of Films. p152-53.
Film Daily. Aug 6, 1954, p7.
Films and Filming. Oct 1954, v1, p24.
Films and Filming. May 1955, v1, p18.
The Films of Fritz Lang. p250-52.
*Fritz Lang: A Guide to References and
   Resources.* p116-18.
Fritz Lang (Eisner). p338-43.
Fritz Lang in America. p92-97.
Hollywood Reporter. Aug 6, 1954, p3.
Motion Picture Herald Product Digest. Aug 7,
   1954, p98.
National Parent-Teacher. Oct 1954, v49, p39.
The New York Times. Aug 7, 1954, p7.
A Reference Guide to the American Film Noir.
   p86-87.
Sight and Sound. Spr 1955, v24, p198.
Variety. Aug 11, 1954, p6.

The Human Factor (US; Preminger, Otto;
   1980)
Christian Science Monitor. Feb 13, 1980, p18.
Films in Review. Mar 1980, v31, p180.
Maclean's. Feb 25, 1980, v93, p54.
Motion Picture Herald Product Digest. Aug 6,
   1980, p19.
The Nation. Feb 23, 1980, v230, p218-19.
The New Republic. Feb 16, 1980, v182, p24-25.
The New York Times. Feb 8, 1980, SecIII, p8.
The New Yorker. Feb 11, 1980, v55, p99-101.
Newsday. Feb 8, 1980, SecII, p5.
Newsweek. Mar 29, 1980, v95, p82.
Saturday Review. Mar 29, 1980, v7, p28.
Sight and Sound. Spr 1980, v50, p124.
Time. Mar 17, 1980, v115, p81.
Travels in Greeneland. p178-86.

The Human Jungle (US; Newman, Joseph
   M.; 1954)
BFI/Monthly Film Bulletin. Mar 1955, v22,
   p39.
Film Daily. Sep 22, 1954, p6.
Hollywood Reporter. Sep 14, 1954, p3.
Motion Picture Herald Product Digest. Sep 18,
   1954, p145.
National Parent-Teacher. Dec 1954, v49, p39.
The New York Times. Nov 26, 1954, p24.

Newsweek. Oct 11, 1954, v44, p112.
Saturday Review. Nov 27, 1954, v37, p29.
Senior Scholastic. Dec 8, 1954, v65, p25.
Variety. Sep 15, 1954, p6.

The Hunchback of Notre Dame (French
   title: Notre Dame de Paris) (US;
   Delannoy, Jean; 1957)
BFI/Monthly Film Bulletin. Apr 1957, v24,
   p48.
Film Daily. Nov 4, 1957, p10.
Films and Filming. Apr 1957, v3, p30.
The Films of Anthony Quinn. p166-68.
Great Horror Movies. p44-45.
Hollywood Reporter. Oct 31, 1957, p3.
Make It Again, Sam. p81-89.
The New York Times. Nov 11, 1956, SecVI,
   p22.
The New York Times. Dec 12, 1957, p35.
Time. Jan 6, 1958, v71, p77.
Variety. Nov 6, 1957, p6.

Hunger (Also titled: Sult) (DEN, NOR,
   SWED; Carlsen, Henning; 1966)
BFI/Monthly Film Bulletin. Jan 1968, v35, p6.
Figures of Light. p100-02.
Film 68/69. p127-30.
Filmfacts. Nov 15, 1968, v11, p318-20.
Films and Filming. Feb 1969, v15, p75-76.
Films in Review. Oct 1968, v19, p517.
Five Thousand One Nights At the Movies. p261.
*The International Dictionary of Films and
   Filmmakers.* v1, p458.
The New Republic. Sep 7, 1968, v159, p28.
The New York Times. Aug 13, 1968, p45.
The New York Times. Sep 14, 1966, p53.
The New Yorker. Aug 17, 1968, v44, p74.
Newsweek. Sep 2, 1968, v72, p67.
The Novel and the Cinema. p268-76.
Saturday Review. Sep 7, 1968, v51, p53.
Sight and Sound. Wint 1967-68, v37, p43.
Time. Aug 30, 1968, v92, p57.
Time. Sep 23, 1966, v88, p74-75.
Variety. May 18, 1966, p7.
A Year In the Dark. p208-09.

The Hunger (US; Scott, Tony; 1983)
Hollywood Reporter. Apr 27, 1983, p3.
Maclean's. May 16, 1983, v96, p50.
The Nation. May 21, 1983, v236, p648-49.
The New Leader. May 2, 1983, v66, p20.
Newsweek. May 9, 1983, v101, p85.

Hungry For Love *See* Love a La Carte

The Hunt (Spanish title: Caza, La) (IT;
   Saura, Carlos; 1966)
America. Jun 17, 1967, v116, p858.
BFI/Monthly Film Bulletin. Nov 1975, v42,
   p235-36.
Esquire. Aug 1967, v68, p34.
Film 67/68. p233-35.
Film Daily. May 2, 1967, p7.
Filmfacts. Jun 15, 1967, v10, p118-20.
Films in Review. Jun-Jul 1967, v18, p369.
Hollywood Reporter. Jul 28, 1967, p3.
*Journal of the University Film and Video
   Association.* 1983, v35, n3, p15-33.
Life. May 19, 1967, v62, p12.
Motion Picture Herald Product Digest. May 3,
   1967, p680A-B.
The Nation. May 15, 1967, v204, p638.
New Statesman. Oct 24, 1975, v90, p520.
The New York Times. Sep 20, 1966, p39.
The New York Times. Apr 25, 1967, p38.
The New Yorker. Apr 29, 1967, v43, p132.
Private Screenings. p282-83.
Reruns. p192-95.
Second Sight. p112-14.
The Spectator. Nov 25, 1966, v217, p680.

Time. Sep 23, 1966, v88, p74.
Variety. Jul 6, 1966, p6.

The Hunter (US; Kulik, Buzz; 1980)
BFI/Monthly Film Bulletin. Nov 1980, v47, p215.
The Films of Steve McQueen. p233-39.
Hollywood Reporter. Jul 28, 1980, p3.
The Los Angeles Times. Aug 1, 1980, SecVI, p8.
Motion Picture Herald Product Digest. Aug 6, 1980, p19.
The Nation. Aug 16, 1980, v231, p165.
The New York Times. Aug 1, 1980, SecIII, p12.
Newsday. Aug 1, 1980, SecII, p7.
Newsweek. Aug 11, 1980, v96, p69.
Rolling Stone. Aug 7, 1980, p32-35.
Variety. Jul 30, 1980, p22.
The Village Voice. Aug 6, 1980, p41.

The Hunting Party (US; Medford, Don; 1971)
BFI/Monthly Film Bulletin. Oct 1971, v38, p198.
Filmfacts. 1971, v14, p291-93.
Films and Filming. Jan 1972, v18, p58.
Focus on Film. Sum 1971, n7, p6.
Hollywood Reporter. May 27, 1971, p3.
The New York Times. Jul 17, 1971, p14.
Variety. May 26, 1971, p20.
The Village Voice. Jul 29, 1971, v16, n30, p45.

Hurry Sundown (US; Preminger, Otto; 1967)
America. Apr 29, 1967, v116, p660-62.
BFI/Monthly Film Bulletin. Oct 1967, v34, p151.
The Cinema of Otto Preminger. p153-57.
Commonweal. Apr 21, 1967, v86, p152.
Esquire. Sep 1967, v68, p20.
The Fifty Worst Films of All Time. p107-12.
Film Daily. Feb 10, 1967, p7.
Film Quarterly. Sum 1967, v20, p78-79.
Films and Filming. Nov 1967, v14, p22-23.
Films in Review. Apr 1967, v18, p238-39.
The Films of Jane Fonda. p132-36.
Hollywood Reporter. Feb 10, 1967, p3.
Life. Apr 14, 1967, v62, p21.
Motion Picture Herald Product Digest. Mar 1, 1967, p661.
The New York Times. Mar 24, 1967, p22.
Newsweek. Apr 10, 1967, v69, p96.
Saturday Evening Post. Apr 8, 1967, v240, p26-31.
Saturday Review. Mar 25, 1967, v50, p45.
Time. Mar 31, 1967, v89, p95.
Variety. Feb 25, 1967, p6.

Husbands (US; Cassavetes, John; 1970)
American Dreaming. p119-39.
BFI/Monthly Film Bulletin. May 1971, v38, p97.
Commonweal. Feb 12, 1971, v93, p469.
Films in Review. Jan 1971, v22, p46-47.
Hollywood Reporter. Dec 9, 1970, p3, 10.
Magill's Survey of Cinema. Series II. v3, p1076-79.
The Nation. Nov 30, 1970, v211, p570-71.
The New York Times. Dec 9, 1970, p63.
The New York Times. Dec 20, 1970, SecII, p3.
The New Yorker. Jan 2, 1971, v46, p48-51.
Newsweek. Dec 21, 1970, v67, p100.
Saturday Review. Dec 12, 1970, v53, p26.
Sight and Sound. Spr 1971, v40, p106.
Time. Dec 7, 1970, v96, p72.
Variety. Nov 4, 1970, p26.

Hush . . . Hush, Sweet Charlotte (US; Aldrich, Robert; 1965)
Bette Davis: Her Films and Career. p184-87.
BFI/Monthly Film Bulletin. May 1965, v32, p70.

Christian Science Monitor (Western edition). Mar 16, 1965, p4.
Commonweal. Mar 5, 1965, v81, p734.
Film Daily. Jan 14, 1965, p7.
Film Quarterly. Fall 1966, v20, p22-27.
Film Quarterly. Spr 1965, v18, p60.
Filmfacts. Apr 2, 1965, v7, p47-49.
Films and Filming. Jun 1965, v11, p33.
Films and Filming. Apr 1965, v11, p20-21.
Films in Review. Feb 1965, v16, p112-14.
The Films of Olivia De Havilland. p239-41.
The Films of Robert Aldrich. p39-40.
Hollywood Reporter. Dec 17, 1964, p3.
The London Times. Apr 29, 1965, p17.
Mother Goddam. p333-35.
Motion Picture Herald Product Digest. Jan 6, 1965, p201.
Movie. Sum 1965, n13, p44.
The New Republic. Mar 20, 1965, v152, p27.
The New York Times. Mar 4, 1965, p36.
The New Yorker. Mar 11, 1965, v41, p168-69.
Newsweek. Mar 15, 1965, v65, p98.
Playboy. Apr 1965, v12, p28.
Saturday Review. Jan 23, 1965, v48, p56.
Sight and Sound. Sum 1965, v34, p150.
Time. Mar 19, 1965, v85, p109.
Tynan Right and Left. p229.
Variety. Dec 23, 1964, p6.
The Village Voice. Jul 1, 1965, v10, p12, 14.

Hustle (US; Aldrich, Robert; 1975)
BFI/Monthly Film Bulletin. Mar 1976, v43, p53.
The Films and Career of Robert Aldrich. p187-96.
Films in Review. Nov 1975, v26, p564.
The Films of Burt Reynolds. p179-83.
Hollywood Reporter. Dec 19, 1975, p42.
Motion Picture Herald Product Digest. Dec 24, 1975, p55.
The New York Times. Dec 26, 1975, p37.
The New Yorker. Jan 26, 1976, v51, p82.
Newsweek. Jan 12, 1976, v87, p69.
Robert Aldrich: A Guide to References and Resources. p64-68.
Saturday Review. Jan 10, 1976, v3, p64.
Variety. Dec 24, 1975, p16.
Vogue. Dec 1975, v165, p54.

The Hustler (US; Rossen, Robert; 1961)
America. Oct 14, 1961, v106, p57.
BFI/Monthly Film Bulletin. Dec 1961, v28, p165-66.
Commonweal. Oct 13, 1961, v75, p71.
Fifty Grand Movies of the 1960s and 1970s. p37-40.
Film. Spr 1962, n31, p14.
Film Daily. Sep 25, 1961, p6.
Film Quarterly. Wint 1961-62, v15, p61.
Filmfacts. Oct 31, 1961, v4, p225-27.
Films and Filming. Dec 1961, v8, p30.
Films in Review. Oct 1961, v7, p488-89.
The Films of Paul Newman. p97-101.
The Films of the Sixties. p55-56.
Life. Nov 24, 1961, v51, p52.
Magill's Survey of Cinema. Series I. v2, p796-99.
The New Republic. Oct 9, 1961, v145, p28.
The New York Times. Sep 27, 1961, v35, p1.
The New Yorker. Sep 30, 1961, v37, p140-41.
Newsweek. Sep 25, 1961, v58, p111.
Saturday Review. Oct 7, 1961, v44, p37.
Sight and Sound. Wint 1961-62, v31, p40-41.
Stories Into Film. p68.
Time. Oct 6, 1961, v78, p74.
Variety. Sep 27, 1961, p6.

I Am a Camera (US; Cornelius, Henry; 1955)
BFI/Monthly Film Bulletin. Nov 1955, v22, p162.
Catholic World. Sep 1955, v181, p462.
Commonweal. Sep 9, 1955, v62, p565.
Film Culture. Sum 1955, v1, n4, p25.
Film Daily. Aug 5, 1955, p6.
Films and Filming. Nov 1955, v2, p16.
Films in Review. Oct 1955, v6, p412-13.
Hollywood Reporter. Aug 4, 1955, p3.
Life. Aug 8, 1955, v39, p57-58.
Magill's Survey of Cinema. Series I. v2, p800-02.
The Nation. Sep 3, 1955, v181, p211.
The New York Times. Jan 23, 1955, SecII, p5.
The New York Times. Aug 9, 1955, p29.
The New Yorker. Aug 20, 1955, v31, p69.
Saturday Review. Aug 6, 1955, v38, p24.
Sight and Sound. Wint 1955-56, v25, p150.
Time. Aug 15, 1955, v66, p58.
Variety. Aug 10, 1955, p6.

I Am Curious Yellow (Also titled: Jag Ar Nyfiken: Gul) (SWED; Sjoman, Vilgot; 1967)
Commonweal. May 23, 1969, v90, p293-94.
Figures of Light. p147-50.
Film 69/70. p261-67.
Film Daily. Mar 7, 1969, p4.
Film Quarterly. Sum 1969, v20, p37-42.
Filmfacts. 1969, v12, p97.
Films and Filming. Oct 1969, v16, p42-43.
Hollywood Reporter. Jun 4, 1969, p3.
I Am Curious Yellow. 1968.
Life. Mar 21, 1969, v66, p12.
Look. Apr 29, 1969, v33, p80.
Marshall Delaney At the Movies. p223-25.
Movies Into Film. p132-35, 143-45.
The Nation. Mar 24, 1969, v208, p381-82.
National Review. Jul 29, 1969, v21, p760.
The New Republic. Mar 15, 1969, v160, p22.
The New York Times. Mar 11, 1969, p42.
The New Yorker. Apr 5, 1969, v45, p97-98.
Newsweek. Mar 24, 1969, v73, p114-15.
Saturday Review. Mar 15, 1969, v52, p54.
Sex, Psyche, Etcetera in the Film. p57-63.
Time. Mar 14, 1969, v93, p98.
Variety. Nov 1, 1967, p7.
Vogue. Apr 15, 1969, v153, p34.

I and My Lovers *See* Galia

I Can Get It For You Wholesale (Also titled: This Is My Affair; Only the Best) (US; Gordon, Michael; 1951)
BFI/Monthly Film Bulletin. Apr 1951, v18, p248.
Christian Century. May 23, 1951, v68, p647.
Film Daily. Mar 15, 1951, p6.
The Films of Susan Hayward. p160-64.
Hollywood Reporter. Mar 14, 1951, p3.
Library Journal. Apr 15, 1951, v76, p720.
Motion Picture Herald Product Digest. Mar 17, 1951, p757.
The New York Times. Apr 5, 1951, p34.
The New Yorker. Apr 14, 1951, v27, p111.
Newsweek. Apr 16, 1951, v37, p106.
Saturday Review. Apr 21, 1951, v34, p28.
Time. Apr 30, 1951, v57, p104.
Variety. Mar 14, 1951, p6.

I Confess (US; Hitchcock, Alfred; 1953)
America. Mar 28, 1953, v88, p717-18.
American Photographer. Jul 1953, v47, p16.
The Art of Alfred Hitchcock. p221-28.
BFI/Monthly Film Bulletin. May 1953, v20, n232, p67.
Catholic World. Apr 1953, v177, p63.
Christian Century. Apr 5, 1953, v70, p463.

Commonweal. Mar 6, 1953, v57, p550.
Film Daily. Feb 5, 1953, p6.
Films in Review. Mar 1953, v4, p148-50.
The Films of Alfred Hitchcock. p158-61.
The Films of Montgomery Clift. p135-40.
Hitchcock: The First Forty-Four Films. p112-18.
Hitchcock (Truffaut). p200-07.
Hollywood Reporter. Feb 5, 1953, p3.
Library Journal. Mar 1, 1953, v78, p437.
Look. Apr 21, 1953, v17, p110.
Magill's Survey of Cinema. Series II. v3, p1080.
The Nation. Apr 11, 1953, v176, p314.
National Parent-Teacher. Apr 1953, v47, p40.
The New York Times. Mar 23, 1953, p28.
The New Yorker. Apr 4, 1953, v29, p82.
Newsweek. Mar 2, 1953, v41, p90.
Saturday Review. Feb 21, 1953, v36, p33-34.
Sight and Sound. Jul-Sep 1953, v23, p34.
Theatre Arts. Apr 1953, v37, p89.
Time. Mar 2, 1953, v61, p92.
Variety. Feb 11, 1953, p6.

I Could Go on Singing (GB; Neame, Ronald; 1963)
BFI/Monthly Film Bulletin. Apr 1963, v30, p43.
Commonweal. Jun 28, 1963, v78, p377.
Film Daily. Mar 12, 1963, p7.
Filmfacts. May 16, 1963, v6, p79-80.
Films and Filming. Mar 1963, v9, p34.
Films in Review. Apr 1963, v14, p238-39.
The Films of Dirk Bogarde. p137-39.
Hollywood Reporter. Mar 13, 1963, p3.
Judy: The Films and Career of Judy Garland. p180-83.
The New York Times. May 16, 1963, p42.
The New York Times. May 26, 1963, SecII, p1.
Newsweek. Apr 22, 1963, v61, p98.
Photoplay. May 1963, v63, p6.
Time. Apr 19, 1963, v81, p112.
Variety. Mar 13, 1963, p6.

I Deal in Danger (US; Grauman, Walter; 1966)
BFI/Monthly Film Bulletin. Dec 1966, v33, p186.
Film Daily. Oct 28, 1966, p7.
Filmfacts. Jan 1, 1967, v9, p321.
Films and Filming. Feb 1967, v13, p34.
Films and Filming. Mar 1969, v15, p55-56.
The Great Spy Pictures. p223-24.
Hollywood Reporter. Oct 24, 1966, p3.
Motion Picture Herald Product Digest. Nov 9, 1966, p627.
Variety. Oct 26, 1966, p6.

I Dream of Jeanie (US; Dwan, Allan; 1952)
BFI/Monthly Film Bulletin. Oct 1952, v19, p143.
Film Daily. Jun 11, 1952, p7.
Hollywood Reporter. Jun 5, 1952, p3.
Motion Picture Herald Product Digest. Jun 14, 1952, p1398.
The New York Times. Jun 26, 1952, p26.
Variety. Jun 11, 1952, p18.

I Love You, Alice B. Toklas (US; Averback, Hy; 1968)
American Film. May 1984, v9, p62-65.
BFI/Monthly Film Bulletin. Mar 1969, v36, p58-59.
Christian Science Monitor (Western edition). Oct 12, 1968, p6.
Film Daily. Sep 3, 1968, p6.
Film Quarterly. Fall 1968, v22, p75.
Filmfacts. Jan 1, 1969, v11, p410-12.
Films and Filming. Jun 1969, v15, p46-47.
The Films of the Sixties. p251-54.
Hollywood Reporter. Aug 28, 1968, p3.
The London Times. Apr 24, 1969, p15.

Motion Picture Herald Product Digest. Sep 11, 1968, p853-54.
The New Republic. Dec 7, 1968, v159, p41.
New Statesman. Apr 25, 1969, v77, p596.
The New York Times. Oct 8, 1968, p40.
The New Yorker. Oct 19, 1968, v44, p212.
Newsweek. Sep 2, 1968, v72, p67.
Saturday Review. Sep 21, 1968, v51, p47.
The Spectator. May 2, 1969, v222, p392.
Time. Nov 22, 1968, v92, p78.
Variety. Aug 28, 1968, p6.
The Village Voice. Nov 14, 1968, p45.

I Never Promised You a Rose Garden (US; Page, Anthony; 1977)
America. Aug 27, 1977, v137, p112.
Hollywood Reporter. Jul 20, 1977, p2.
The Los Angeles Times. Aug 14, 1977, Calendar, p1.
Motion Picture Herald Product Digest. Aug 3, 1977, p18.
The New York Times. Jul 15, 1977, SecIII, p10.
The New York Times. Sep 18, 1977, SecII, p15.
The New Yorker. Aug 8, 1977, v54, p45.
Newsweek. Jul 25, 1977, v90, p57.
Time. Jul 25, 1977, v110, p69.
Variety. Jul 20, 1977, p18.

I Never Sang for My Father (US; Cates, Gilbert; 1970)
America. Nov 28, 1970, v123, p473.
BFI/Monthly Film Bulletin. Jul 1971, v38, n450, p143.
Big Screen, Little Screen. p291-93.
Deeper Into Movies. p169-71.
Film 70/71. p231-32.
Film Quarterly. Spr 1971, v34, p57-58.
Films in Review. Dec 1970, v21, p645-46.
Hollywood Reporter. Oct 19, 1970, p3.
Life. Oct 30, 1970, v69, p16.
Look. Oct 6, 1970, v34, p114.
Magill's Survey of Cinema. Series II. v3, p1086-88.
National Review. Sep 8, 1970, v22, p960.
The New York Times. Oct 19, 1970, p50.
The New York Times. Nov 15, 1970, SecII, p15.
The New Yorker. Oct 31, 1970, v46, p130.
Newsweek. Nov 2, 1970, v76, p108.
Saturday Review. Nov 7, 1970, v53, p50.
Time. Oct 26, 1970, v96, p113.
Variety. Oct 21, 1970, p14.

I Saw What You Did (US; Castle, William; 1965)
BFI/Monthly Film Bulletin. Dec 1965, v32, p184.
Film Daily. May 14, 1965, p6.
Films and Filming. Jan 1966, v12, p29-30.
The Films of Joan Crawford. p216-19.
Hollywood Reporter. May 12, 1965, p3.
The London Times. Nov 18, 1965, p8.
Motion Picture Herald Product Digest. May 26, 1965, p291.
The New York Times. Jul 22, 1965, p24.
Redbook. Sep 1965, v125, p6.
Saturday Review. Sep 4, 1965, v48, p44.
Time. Jul 30, 1965, v86, p67.
Variety. May 12, 1965, p28.

I Sent a Letter to My Love (Chere Inconnue) (FR; Mizrahi, Moshe; 1981)
Hollywood Reporter. May 4, 1981, p4.
Magill's Cinema Annual, 1982. p214-17.
The Nation. May 30, 1981, v232, p676-77.
The New Republic. May 30, 1981, v184, p22-23.
New York. May 25, 1981, v14, p90.
The New York Times. May 3, 1981, p71.
Rolling Stone. Jul 9, 1981, p39.
Time. Aug 10, 1981, v118, p60-61.

Variety. May 21, 1980, p16.
Variety. Apr 19, 1981, p22.

I Shall Return *See* American Guerilla in the Philippines

I, the Jury (US; Essex, Harry; 1953)
America. Sep 12, 1953, v89, p584.
Commonweal. Sep 4, 1953, v58, p537.
Film Daily. Jul 20, 1953, p11.
Hollywood Reporter. Jul 20, 1953, p3.
Library Journal. Sep 1, 1953, v78, p1411.
The New York Times. Aug 22, 1953, p8.
The New Yorker. Aug 22, 1953, v29, p50.
Newsweek. Aug 17, 1953, v42, p90.
Saturday Review. Aug 22, 1953, v36, p27.
Time. Aug 17, 1953, v62, p90.
Variety. Jul 22, 1953, p6.

I Wanna Hold Your Hand (US; Zemeckis, Robert; 1978)
Atlantic. Aug 1978, v242, p83.
BFI/Monthly Film Bulletin. Jul 1978, v45, p160.
Films in Review. Jun-Jul 1978, v29, p376.
Hollywood Musical. p410.
Hollywood Reporter. Apr 19, 1978, p2.
The Los Angeles Times. Apr 22, 1978, SecII, p8.
Motion Picture Herald Product Digest. May 10, 1978, p94.
The New York Times. Apr 21, 1978, SecIII, p11.
The New York Times. Apr 30, 1978, SecII, p15.
Newsweek. May 1, 1978, v91, p91.
Rolling Stone. Jun 1, 1978, p8.
Time. May 9, 1978, v111, p70.
Variety. Apr 19, 1978, p26.

I Want to Live (US; Wise, Robert; 1958)
America. Nov 29, 1958, v100, p297.
BFI/Monthly Film Bulletin. Aug 1959, v26, p99.
Catholic World. Jan 1959, v188, p329.
Commonweal. Dec 12, 1958, v69, p293.
Fifty from the Fifties. p151-58.
Film Daily. Oct 28, 1958, v114, p10.
Filmfacts. Dec 10, 1598, v1, p209-10.
Films in Review. Dec 1958, v9, p591-92.
The Films of Susan Hayward. p233-34.
Hollywood Reporter. Oct 28, 1958, p3.
Library Journal. Dec 1, 1958, v83, p3418.
Magill's Survey of Cinema. Series I. v2, p813-16.
The Nation. Dec 27, 1958, v187, p504.
The New Republic. Dec 22, 1958, v139, p21.
The New York Times. Nov 19, 1958, p45.
The New Yorker. Nov 29, 1958, v34, p108.
Newsweek. Nov 17, 1958, v52, p109.
Saturday Review. Nov 29, 1958, v40, p25.
Time. Nov 24, 1958, v72, p94.
Variety. Oct 29, 1958, p6.

I Want You (US; Robson, Mark; 1951)
BFI/Monthly Film Bulletin. Jan 1952, v19, p3.
Catholic World. Feb 1952, v174, p385.
Christian Century. Feb 13, 1952, v69, p207.
Commentary. Mar 1952, v13, p275-81.
Commonweal. Dec 28, 1951, v55, p301.
Film Daily. Nov 1, 1951, p8.
Hollywood Reporter. Oct 31, 1951, p3.
Library Journal. Dec 15, 1951, v76, p2110.
Motion Picture Herald Product Digest. Nov 3, 1951, p1093.
The Nation. Jan 19, 1952, v174, p66.
The New Republic. Dec 31, 1951, v125, p22.
The New York Times. Dec 24, 1951, p9.
The New Yorker. Jan 5, 1952, v27, p58.
Newsweek. Jan 7, 1952, v39, p59.
Samuel Goldwyn Presents. p279-82.
Saturday Review. Dec 22, 1951, v34, p34.

The Spectator. Nov 30, 1951, v187, p737.
Time. Jan 28, 1952, v59, p96.
Variety. Oct 31, 1951, p6.

I Was a Communist For the FBI (US; Gordon, Douglas; 1951)
BFI/Monthly Film Bulletin. Sep 1951, v18, p324-25.
Christian Century. Jun 6, 1951, v68, p695.
Commonweal. May 18, 1951, v54, p143.
Film Daily. Apr 19, 1951, p6.
The Films of the Fifties. p61-62.
Hollywood Reporter. Apr 19, 1951, p3.
The London Times. Aug 29, 1951, p7.
Motion Picture Herald Product Digest. Apr 21, 1951, p809.
The New Statesman and Nation. Sep 1, 1951, v42, p227.
The New York Times. May 3, 1951, p34.
The New Yorker. May 12, 1951, v27, p93.
Newsweek. May 14, 1951, v37, p101.
Propaganda on Film. p117-19.
Saturday Review. May 19, 1951, v34, p26.
The Spectator. Aug 31, 1951, v187, p268.
Time. May 7, 1951, v57, p104.
Variety. Apr 25, 1951, p6.

I Was a Shoplifter (US; Lamont, Charles; 1950)
Commonweal. May 12, 1950, v52, p127.
Film Daily. Apr 12, 1950, p6.
Hollywood Reporter. Apr 7, 1950, p3.
Motion Picture Herald Product Digest. Apr 15, 1950, p262-63.
The New York Times. Apr 28, 1950, p26.
Variety. Apr 12, 1950, p22.

I Was Happy Here *See* Time Lost and Time Remembered

Ice Palace (US; Sherman, Vincent; 1960)
America. Jul 9, 1960, v103, p443.
BFI/Monthly Film Bulletin. Sep 1960, v27, p124.
Commonweal. Aug 5, 1960, v72, p403.
Film Daily. Jun 15, 1960, p8.
Filmfacts. 1960, v3, p163.
Films and Filming. Sep 1960, v6, p24.
Hollywood Reporter. Jun 15, 1960, p3.
The New York Times. Jun 30, 1960, p22.
The New Yorker. Jul 9, 1960, v36, p55-56.
Newsweek. Jul 11, 1960, v56, p91.
Saturday Review. Jul 23, 1960, v43, p31.
Time. Jul 4, 1960, v76, p51.
Variety. Jun 15, 1960, p6.

Iceman (US; Schepisi, Fred; 1984)
America. May 12, 1984, v150, p363.
Cinefantastique. 1984, v14, n4/5, p107.
Discover. Jun 1984, v5, p97.
Film Journal. May 1984, v87, p24-25.
The Los Angeles Times. Apr 12, 1984, SecVI, p1.
Maclean's. Apr 23, 1984, v97, p50.
Magill's Cinema Annual, 1985. p248-52.
Ms. Jul 1984, v13, p45-46.
The Nation. May 12, 1984, v238, p588.
The New Republic. May 14, 1984, v190, p24-25.
New York. Apr 23, 1984, v17, p100-02.
The New York Times. May 6, 1984, SecII, p17.
The New Yorker. Apr 30, 1984, v60, p99-101.
Newsweek. Apr 16, 1984, v103, p92.
Time. Apr 23, 1984, v123, p83.
Variety. Apr 11, 1984, p16.
The Village Voice. Apr 24, 1984, p54.

Ich War 19 (EGER; Konrad, Wolf; 1968)
Magill's Survey of Cinema. Foreign Language Films. v3, p1421-25.
Sight and Sound. Aut 1968, v37, p179.
Variety. Jun 19, 1968, p39.

I'd Climb the Highest Mountain (US; King, Henry; 1951)
BFI/Monthly Film Bulletin. Jun 1951, v18, p275.
Christian Century. Feb 14, 1951, v68, p222.
Film Daily. Jan 12, 1951, p6.
The Films of Susan Hayward. p152-56.
Hollywood Reporter. Jan 12, 1951, p3.
Library Journal. Feb 15, 1951, v76, p343.
Motion Picture Herald Product Digest. Jan 20, 1951, p669.
The New York Times. May 10, 1951, p38.
Newsweek. Feb 19, 1951, v37, p89.
Saturday Review. Mar 31, 1951, v34, p32.
The Spectator. Jun 22, 1951, v186, p813.
Time. Mar 5, 1951, v57, p96.
Variety. Jan 17, 1951, p11.

The Idiot (Japanese title: Hakuchi) (JAPAN; Kurosawa, Akira; 1951)
Akira Kurosawa: A Guide to References and Resources. p47-48.
BFI/Monthly Film Bulletin. Mar 1974, v41, p41.
Cinema, the Magic Vehicle. v2, p66-70.
Commonweal. May 10, 1963, v78, p198.
Dictionary of Films. p143-44.
The Films of Akira Kurosawa. p81-85.
The New Republic. May 11, 1963, v148, p27.
The New York Times. May 1, 1963, p35.
The Samuari Films of Akira Kurosawa. p60-61.
Spectator. n2, 1985, v4, p10-11.
To the Distant Observer. p299-301.
Variety. Sep 25, 1963, p6.
The Waves at Genji's Door. p50, 207.

The Idol (GB; Petrie, Daniel; 1966)
America. Sep 3, 1966, v115, p234.
BFI/Monthly Film Bulletin. Nov 1966, v33, p170-71.
Christian Science Monitor (Western edition). Jan 6, 1967, p4.
Commonweal. Sep 2, 1966, v84, p557.
Film Daily. Aug 3, 1966, p4.
Filmfacts. Oct 15, 1966, v9, p221-22.
Films and Filming. Dec 1966, v13, p12-13.
The Films of Jennifer Jones. p161-64.
Life. Sep 16, 1966, v61, p20.
The London Times. Oct 6, 1966, p18.
New Statesman. Oct 7, 1966, v72, p530.
The New York Times. Aug 11, 1966, p27.
Playboy. Oct 1966, v13, p27-28.
Time. Aug 19, 1966, v88, p78.
Variety. Aug 3, 1966, p6.

Idolmaker (US; Hackford, Taylor; 1980)
BFI/Monthly Film Bulletin. Apr 1981, v48, p68.
Films in Review. Dec 1980, v31, p631.
Hollywood Reporter. Nov 1, 1980, p3.
The Los Angeles Times. Nov 9, 1980, Calendar, p28.
Maclean's. Nov 17, 1980, v93, p66-67.
Motion Picture Herald Product Digest. Nov 19, 1980, p45.
The New Leader. Dec 1, 1980, v63, p19.
New York. Nov 24, 1980, v13, p59-60.
The New York Times. Dec 22, 1980, SecIII, p8.
The New Yorker. Dec 22, 1980, v56, p102.
Newsday. Nov 14, 1980, SecII, p7.
Time. Nov 10, 1980, v116, p64-65.
Variety. Nov 5, 1980, p22.
The Village Voice. Nov 19, 1980, p56.

Ieri, Oggi, Domani *See* Yesterday, Today and Tomorrow

If . . . (GB; Anderson, Lindsay; 1968)
America. Mar 15, 1969, v120, p713-14.
BFI/Monthly Film Bulletin. Feb 1969, v36, p25-26.

Christian Century. Jul 2, 1969, v86, p905.
Cineaste. Spr 1969, v11, p19-20.
Cinema. 1969, v5, n3, p46-47.
Cinema Journal. Fall 1971, v11, p56-57.
Commentary. Feb 1970, v49, p77-78.
Commonweal. Mar 21, 1969, v90, p21-22.
Dictionary of Films. p154.
Directors and Directions: Cinema for the Seventies. p91-95.
Fifty Classic British Films. p127-29.
Figures of Light. p134-37.
Film 69/70. p83-90.
Film Daily. Feb 20, 1969, p7.
The Film Director As Superstar. p102-09.
Film Heritage. Fall 1969, v5, p13-20.
Film Quarterly. Sum 1969, v22, p48-52.
Film Society Review. Sep 1969, v5, p30-38.
Filmfacts. 1969, v12, n4, p173-77.
Films and Filming. Mar 1969, v15, p50-51.
Films in Review. Apr 1969, v20, p255-56.
Five Thousand One Nights At the Movies. p270.
Going Steady. p346-55.
Harper's Magazine. Apr 1969, v238, p115-16.
Hollywood Reporter. May 28, 1969, p3.
Hudson Review. Aut 1969, v22, p469-76.
The International Dictionary of Films and Filmmakers. v1, p205-06.
International Film Guide. 1970, v7, p106-07.
Lindsay Anderson: A Guide to References and Resources. p53-58, 83-94.
Listener. Dec 26, 1968, v80, p872-73.
The London Times. Nov 29, 1968, p14.
The London Times. Dec 19, 1968, p14.
Magill's Survey of Cinema. Series II. v3, p1103-06.
Motion Picture Herald Product Digest. Feb 5, 1969, p109-10.
Movie. Wint 1968-69, n16, p39.
Movies Into Film. p109-10.
The Nation. Mar 17, 1969, v208, p348-49.
The New Republic. Feb 15, 1969, v160, p22.
New Society. Dec 19, 1968, p923.
New Statesman. Dec 20, 1968, v76, p882.
The New York Times. Mar 10, 1969, p54.
The New York Times. Mar 30, 1969, p1.
The New Yorker. Mar 15, 1969, v45, p152.
Newsweek. Mar 31, 1969, v73, p95.
Saturday Review. Feb 15, 1969, v52, p50.
Screen. Jan-Feb 1969, v10, p24-33.
Screen. Mar-Apr 1969, v10, p85-89.
Screen. 1975-76, v16, n4, p62-80.
Sight and Sound. Sum 1968, v37, p130-31.
Sight and Sound. Wint 1968-69, v38, p42-43.
The Spectator. Dec 20, 1968, v221, p884-85.
Take One. Nov-Dec 1968, v2, p21.
Time. Mar 21, 1969, v93, 97.
Variety. Dec 11, 1968, p30.
The Village Voice. Mar 20, 1969, v14, p43, 52.

If It's Tuesday, This Must Be Belgium (US; Stuart, Mel; 1969)
America. May 3, 1969, v120, p550.
Film Daily. Apr 14, 1969, p8.
Filmfacts. 1969, v12, p176.
Films in Review. May 1969, v20, p320.
Magill's Survey of Cinema. Series II. v3, p1113-16.
The New York Times. Apr 25, 1969, p34.
Time. May 9, 1969, v93, p105.
Travel. Jun 1969, v131, p72-75.
Variety. Apr 9, 1969, p8.

If You Feel Like Singing *See* Summer Stock

Ikiru (Also titled: Living; To Live; Doomed; Vivre; Vivre Enfin; Seul Jour, Un) (JAPAN; Kurosawa, Akira; 1952)

Akira Kurosawa: A Guide to References and Resources. p48-50.
BFI/Monthly Film Bulletin. Aug 1959, v26, p99.
Christian Science Monitor (New England Edition). Nov 10, 1960, p11.
Cinema, the Magic Vehicle. v2, p112-14.
Dictionary of Films. p155.
Film Quarterly. Sum 1960, v13, p39-41.
Filmfacts. Mar 18, 1960, v3, p37-38.
Films and Filming. Aug 1959, v5, p25.
Films in Review. Mar 1960, v11, p168.
The Films of Akira Kurosawa. p186-96.
Ikiru: A Film by Akira Kurosawa. p6-11.
The International Dictionary of Films and Filmmakers. v1, p206-07.
Japanese Cinema (Richie). p220-21.
Literature/Film Quarterly. Wint 1975, v3, p2-12.
The London Times. Jul 2, 1959, p9.
Magill's Survey of Cinema. Foreign Language Films. v3, p1440-45.
Motion Picture Herald Product Digest. Jun 11, 1960, p733.
The Nation. Mar 26, 1960, v190, p284.
The New Republic. Mar 7, 1960, v142, p28.
The New Statesman and Nation. Jul 11, 1959, v58, p48.
The New York Times. Jan 30, 1960, p13.
The New Yorker. Feb 13, 1960, v35, p125-26.
Quarterly of Film, Radio and Television. Sum 1956, v10, p354-63.
The Samurai Films of Akira Kurosawa. p138-39.
Sight and Sound. Wint 1957-58, v27, p131-33.
The Spectator. Jul 17, 1959, v203, p65.
Ten Film Classics. p48-61.
Time. Feb 15, 1960, v75, p85.
Time. Sep 21, 1962, v80, p90.
To the Distant Observer. p301-06.
Variety. May 15, 1957, p22.
The Village Voice. Feb 10, 1960, v5, p8, 10.
The Waves at Genji's Door. p229-35.
A World on Film. p374-76.

I'll Cry Tomorrow (US; Mann, Daniel; 1955)
America. Jan 28, 1956, v94, p487.
Catholic World. Nov 1955, v182, p137.
Commonweal. Jan 20, 1956, v63, p403.
Film Daily. Dec 16, 1955, p6.
Films and Filming. May 1956, v2, p24-25.
Films in Review. Feb 1956, v2, p81-83.
The Films of Susan Hayward. p219-26.
Hollywood Reporter. Dec 16, 1955, p3.
Library Journal. Feb 1, 1956, v81, p360.
Life. Jan 9, 1956, v40, p117-18.
Magill's Survey of Cinema. Series II. v3, p1117-20.
The Nation. Jan 28, 1956, v182, p78.
The New York Times. Jan 13, 1956, p18.
The New York Times. Jan 15, 1956, SecII, p1.
The New Yorker. Jan 21, 1956, v31, p110.
Newsweek. Nov 28, 1956, v46, p117.
Saturday Review. Jan 7, 1956, v39, p56.
Time. Jan 23, 1956, v67, p92.
Variety. Dec 21, 1955, p6.

I'll Get By (US; Sale, Richard; 1950)
BFI/Monthly Film Bulletin. Jan 1951, v18, p204.
Film Daily. Sep 25, 1950, p7.
Hollywood Reporter. Sep 25, 1950, p3.
Illustrated London News. Dec 16, 1950, v217, p1010.
Motion Picture Herald Product Digest. Sep 30, 1950, p501.
The New York Times. Nov 2, 1950, p39.
Newsweek. Nov 13, 1950, v36, p102.

Time. Nov 13, 1950, v56, p104.
Variety. Sep 27, 1950, p8.

I'll Never Forget What's 'Is Name (GB; Winner, Michael; 1967)
BFI/Monthly Film Bulletin. Jan 1968, v35, p5-6.
Christian Science Monitor (Western edition). May 24, 1968, p8.
Commonweal. May 17, 1968, v88, p267.
Esquire. Jul 1968, v70, p38.
Film Daily. Apr 15, 1968, p6.
Filmfacts. Jun 15, 1968, v11, p156-58.
Films and Filming. Feb 1968, v14, p26.
Films in Review. May 1968, v19, p309-10.
The Films of Michael Winner. p42-48.
Hollywood Reporter. Apr 15, 1968, p3.
Life. May 17, 1968, v64, p12.
Motion Picture Herald Product Digest. Apr 24, 1968, p801.
The New Republic. Jun 8, 1968, v158, p26, 43.
The New York Times. Apr 15, 1968, p51.
The New Yorker. Apr 27, 1968, v44, p144.
Variety. Dec 27, 1967, p6.
The Village Voice. Jun 6, 1968, p47.

I'll Never Forget You (Also titled: The House in the Square) (GB; Baker, Roy; 1951)
American Magazine. Jan 1952, v153, p9.
BFI/Monthly Film Bulletin. Nov 1951, v18, p356-57.
Film Daily. Dec 14, 1951, p6.
The Films of Tyrone Power. p170-72.
Hollywood Reporter. Dec 7, 1951, p3.
Library Journal. Jan 1, 1952, v77, p44.
Motion Picture Herald Product Digest. Dec 8, 1951, p1133.
The New Statesman and Nation. Dec 15, 1951, v42, p706.
The New York Times. Dec 8, 1951, p9.
The New Yorker. Dec 15, 1951, v27, p135-36.
The Spectator. Dec 7, 1951, v187, p772-73.
Time. Jan 14, 1952, v59, p92.

I'll See You In My Dreams (US; Curtiz, Michael; 1951)
American Magazine. Jan 1952, v153, p8.
BFI/Monthly Film Bulletin. Aug 1952, v19, p110.
Christian Century. Jan 23, 1952, v69, p111.
Commonweal. Dec 21, 1951, v55, p278.
Film Daily. Dec 12, 1951, p6.
The Films of Doris Day. p111-16.
Hollywood Reporter. Dec 6, 1951, p3.
The London Times. Jul 7, 1952, p8.
Motion Picture Herald Product Digest. Dec 8, 1951, p1133.
The New York Times. Dec 7, 1951, p35.
The New Yorker. Dec 8, 1951, v27, p69-70.
Newsweek. Dec 17, 1951, v38, p100.
The Spectator. Jul 4, 1952, v189, p15.
The Tatler. Jul 16, 1952, v205, p114.
Time. Jan 21, 1952, v59, p94.
Variety. Dec 12, 1951, p6.

I'll Take Sweden (US; De Cordova, Frederick; 1965)
Christian Science Monitor (Western edition). Jul 29, 1965, p10.
Film Daily. Jun 2, 1965, p7.
Films and Filming. Sep 1965, v11, p32.
Hollywood Reporter. Jun 1, 1965, p4.
The London Times. Jun 10, 1965, p7.
Motion Picture Herald Product Digest. Jun 23, 1965, p315.
The New York Times. Aug 12, 1965, p30.
Variety. Jun 2, 1965, p6.

Illicit Interlude (Swedish title: Sommarlek; Also titled: Summer Interlude) (SWED; Bergman, Ingmar; 1951)
BFI/Monthly Film Bulletin. Dec 1959, v26, p156.
Cinema Borealis. p72-76.
Cinema Eye, Cinema Ear. p148-52.
Dictionary of Films. p347.
Film Daily. Nov 10, 1954, p10.
Films and Filming. Dec 1959, v6, p25.
The Films of Ingmar Bergman (Donner). p79-86.
Ingmar Bergman (Cowie). p85-91.
Ingmar Bergman: Essays in Criticism. p142-43.
Ingmar Bergman (Mosley). p51-52.
Ingmar Bergman (Steene). p49-52.
Ingmar Bergman (Wood). p32-39.
Kiss Kiss Bang Bang. p444.
The London Times. Oct 19, 1959, p12.
Magill's Survey of Cinema. Foreign Language Films. v3, p1455-59.
The Nation. Nov 13, 1954, v179, p430.
The New Statesman and Nation. Jan 12, 1952, v43, p37.
The New York Times. Oct 27, 1954, p32.
The Spectator. Oct 23, 1959, v203, p556.
The Thousand Eyes Magazine. 1975, n1, p11.
Time. Nov 8, 1954, v64, p114.
Variety. Nov 28, 1951, p6.

The Illustrated Man (US; Smight, Jack; 1969)
America. May 3, 1969, v120, p550.
Big Screen, Little Screen. p162.
Commonweal. Apr 18, 1969, v90, p144.
Film Daily. Mar 11, 1969, p4.
Filmfacts. 1969, v12, p150.
Films and Filming. Aug 1969, v15, p35-36.
Hollywood Reporter. Feb 14, 1969, p3.
The New York Times. Mar 27, 1969, p52.
The New Yorker. Apr 5, 1969, v45, p50.
Senior Scholastic. Apr 25, 1969, v94, p24.
Sight and Sound. Sum 1969, v38, p159.
Time. Apr 4, 1969, v93, p92.
Variety. Feb 19, 1969, p6.
Vogue. Apr 1, 1969, v153, p148.

I'm All Right Jack (GB; Boulting, John; 1959)
Commonweal. May 27, 1960, v72, p229.
Film Daily. Feb 26, 1960, p8.
Film Quarterly. Fall 1960, v14, p51-54; 54-55.
Filmfacts. 1960, v3, p115.
Films and Filming. Sep 1959, v5, p21-22.
Films in Review. Aug-Sep, 1960, v11, p425-26.
The Great British Films. p181.
Hollywood Reporter. Jul 12, 1960, p3.
Magill's Survey of Cinema. Series II. v3, p1124-27.
McCall's. May 1960, v87, p6.
The Nation. May 14, 1960, v190, p431.
The New Republic. May 30, 1960, v142, p21.
The New York Times. Apr 26, 1960, p40.
The New York Times. May 1, 1960, SecII, p1.
The New Yorker. Nov 21, 1959, v35, p204-06.
The New Yorker. May 7, 1960, v36, p190-91.
Newsweek. May 9, 1960, v55, p112.
Saturday Review. Apr 30, 1960, v43, p24.
Time. May 2, 1960, v75, p34.
Variety. Aug 19, 1959, p6.
A World on Film. p51-53.

I'm Dancing as Fast as I Can (US; Hofsiss, Jack; 1982)
American Film. May 1982, v7, p9.
Film Journal. Mar 8, 1982, v85, p23-24.
Films in Review. May 1982, v33, p307.
The Los Angeles Times. Mar 4, 1982, SecVI, p1.
Maclean's. Mar 22, 1982, v95, p60.

The Nation. Mar 20, 1982, v234, p346-47.
The New Republic. Mar 24, 1982, v186, p25-26.
New York. Mar 15, 1982, v15, p58-59.
New York. Mar 29, 1982, v15, p82-83.
The New York Times. Mar 5, 1982, SecIII, p8.
The New York Times. Mar 7, 1982, SecII, p1.
Newsweek. Mar 8, 1982, v199, p90.
Rolling Stone. Apr 15, 1982, p71.
Saturday Review. Mar 1982, v9, p28-30.
Variety. Mar 3, 1982, p16.
The Village Voice. Mar 16, 1982, p45.

Imitation of Life (US; Stahl, John M.; 1959)
America. May 9, 1959, v101, p314.
BFI/Monthly Film Bulletin. May 1959, v26, p55.
Catholic World. May 1959, v189, p154-55.
Commonweal. Apr 17, 1959, v70, p82.
Film Daily. Feb 3, 1959, p6.
Filmfacts. May 20, 1959, v2, p81-82.
The Films of Lana Turner. p222-26.
From Sambo to Superspade. p212-13.
Hollywood Reporter. Feb 3, 1959, p3.
Library Journal. Mar 15, 1959, v84, p843.
Magill's Survey of Cinema. Series II. p1128-31.
The New York Times. Apr 18, 1959, p18.
The New Yorker. Apr 25, 1953, v35, p167-68.
Newsweek. Apr 13, 1959, v53, p118.
Saturday Review. Apr 11, 1959, v42, p28.
Time. May 11, 1959, v73, p86.
Variety. Nov 27, 1934, p15.

Immorale, L' *See* The Climax

The Immoralist *See* The Climax

Immortal Bachelor (Italian title: A Mezzanatte Va La Ronda Del Piacere) (IT; Fondato, Marcello; 1979)
Films in Review. Apr 1980, v31, p248.
Hollywood Reporter. Jan 29, 1980, p3.
The Los Angeles Times. May 10, 1980, SecII, p7.
Motion Picture Herald Product Digest. Mar 26, 1980, p84.
The Nation. Mar 15, 1980, v230, p317.
The New York Times. Feb 12, 1980, SecIII, p18.
The New Yorker. Feb 25, 1980, v56, p117-18.
Newsday. Feb 22, 1980, SecII, p7.
The Village Voice. Feb 25, 1980, p39.

Immortal Story (French title: Histoire Immortelle, Une) (FR; Welles, Orson; 1968)
BFI/Monthly Film Bulletin. May 1969, v36, p91-92.
Christian Century. Apr 2, 1969, v86, p452.
Commonweal. Feb 28, 1969, v89, p676.
Dictionary of Films. p150-51.
Figures of Light. p146-47.
Film Comment. Sum 1971, v7, p54-55.
Film Quarterly. Fall 1969, v23, p44-47.
Film Society Review. Oct 1968, v4, p23-28.
Filmfacts. 1969, v12, n2, p34-36.
Films and Filming. May 1969, v15, p38-39.
Films in Review. May 1969, v20, p181-82.
The Films of Orson Welles. p182-88.
Focus. Oct 1969, n5, p28-29.
International Film Guide. 1969, v6, p72.
The London Times. Jul 10, 1968, p8.
The London Times. Apr 3, 1969, p14.
The Magic World of Orson Welles. p286-94.
The New Republic. Mar 8, 1969, v160, p22.
New Statesman. Apr 11, 1969, v77, p524.
The New York Times. Sep 19, 1968, p62.
The New York Times. Feb 12, 1969, p33.
Newsweek. Feb 24, 1969, v73, p98.
Orson Welles: A Critical View (Bazin). p22-23.
Orson Welles (McBride). p159-65.

Sight and Sound. Wint 1968-69, v38, p31-32.
Sight and Sound. Aut 1970, v39, p194-95.
The Spectator. Apr 11, 1969, v222, p482.
Variety. Jul 17, 1968, p24.
The Village Voice. Feb 20, 1969, p46.
The Village Voice. Feb 6, 1969, p49, p53-55.
A Year In the Dark. p242.

The Importance of Being Earnest (GB; Asquith, Anthony; 1952)
BFI/Monthly Film Bulletin. Jul 1952, v19, p90.
Catholic World. Feb 1953, v176, p384-85.
Classics of the Foreign Film. p212-13.
Commonweal. Jan 2, 1953, v57, p334.
Film Daily. Dec 24, 1952, p8.
Films in Review. Feb 1953, v4, p97.
The Films of Anthony Asquith. p133-40.
Illustrated London News. Jul 5, 1952, v221, p35.
Illustrated London News. Jul 12, 1952, v221, p70.
Library Journal. Jan 1, 1953, v78, p50.
Magill's Survey of Cinema. Series I. v2, p817-21.
Motion Picture Herald Product Digest. Dec 27, 1952, p1661-62.
National Parent-Teacher. Jan 1953, v47, p38.
The New Statesman and Nation. Jul 5, 1952, v44, p12.
The New York Times. Dec 23, 1952, p17.
The New Yorker. Jan 3, 1953, v28, p35.
Newsweek. Jan 5, 1953, v41, p60.
Quarterly of Film, Radio and Television. Fall 1953, v8, p72-79.
Saturday Review. Jan 10, 1953, v36, p31.
Sight and Sound. Jul-Sep 1952, v22, p28.
The Spectator. Jun 27, 1952, v188, p852-53.
The Tatler. Jul 9, 1952, v205, p70.
Theatre Arts. Feb 1953, v37, p83.
Theatre Arts. Apr 1953, v37, p72-74.
Time. Jan 5, 1953, v61, p71.
Variety. Jun 18, 1952, p6.

In a Lonely Place (US; Ray, Nicholas; 1950)
BFI/Monthly Film Bulletin. Jun 1950, v17, p80.
Bright Lights. n3, 1978, v2, p4-7.
Cinema, the Magic Vehicle. v2, p52.
Commonweal. Jun 9, 1950, v52, p221.
Dark City: The Film Noir. p93-96.
Film Daily. May 15, 1950, p7.
The Films of Humphrey Bogart. p154-56.
The Films of the Fifties. p29-32.
Hollywood Reporter. May 17, 1950, p3.
Humphrey Bogart: The Man and His Films. p152-54.
Library Journal. Jun 1, 1950, v75, p992.
Magill's Survey of Cinema. Series II. v3, p1135-37.
Motion Picture Herald Product Digest. May 20, 1950, p301-02.
The New Statesman and Nation. May 27, 1950, v39, p606.
The New York Times. May 18, 1950, p37.
The New Yorker. May 27, 1950, v26, p58.
Newsweek. Jun 5, 1950, v35, p85.
Nicholas Ray: A Guide to References and Resources. p57-61.
Nicholas Ray (Kreidl). p32.
Quarterly Review of Film Studies. n2, 1984, v9, p101-12.
The Spectator. May 26, 1950, v184, p721.
Time. Jun 5, 1950, v55, p91.
Variety. May 17, 1950, p6.

In a Year of 13 Moons (German title: In einem Jahr mit 13 Monden) (WGER; Fassbinder, Rainer Werner; 1978)
BFI/Monthly Film Bulletin. Oct 1980, v31, p195.

Fassbinder, Filmmaker. p76-83.
Fassbinder (Tanam). p197-206.
Hollywood Reporter. Mar 27, 1979, p14.
The New York Times. Jun 12, 1980, SecIII, p18.
Newsday. Jun 27, 1980, SecII, p7.
Sight and Sound. Oct 1980, v50, p266.
Variety. Mar 7, 1979, p22.
The Village Voice. Jun 16, 1980, p41.

In Cold Blood (US; Brooks, Richard; 1967)
America. Jan 13, 1968, v118, p48.
BFI/Monthly Film Bulletin. May 1968, v35, p73-74.
Catholic World. May 1968, v207, p79-80.
Christian Century. Apr 17, 1968, v85, p488-89.
Commonweal. Jan 26, 1968, v87, p504-05.
Esquire. Mar 1968, v69, p52.
Film Daily. Dec 13, 1967, p7.
Films and Filming. May 1968, v14, p30, 35.
Films in Review. Jan 1968, v19, p47-49.
The Films of the Sixties. p206-08.
Harper's. Mar 1968, v236, p153-55.
Hollywood Reporter. Dec 13, 1967, p3.
Life. Jan 12, 1968, v64, p10.
Magill's Survey of Cinema. Series II. v3, p1138-41.
McCall's. Apr 1968, v95, p18.
Motion Picture Herald Product Digest. Dec 20, 1967, p751.
The Nation. Jan 1, 1968, v206, p28.
The New Republic. Jan 6, 1968, v158, p30.
New York Review Books. Jul 11 1968, v11, p28-30.
The New York Times. Dec 15, 1967, p60.
The New Yorker. Dec 23, 1967, v43, p47.
Newsweek. Apr 24, 1967, v69, p94.
Newsweek. Dec 25, 1967, v70, p70.
Reporter. Jan 11, 1968, v38, p38.
Saturday Review. Dec 30, 1967, v50, p33.
Senior Scholastic. May 16, 1968, v92, p36.
Sight and Sound. Sum 1968, v37, p148-59.
Sight and Sound. Aut 1968, p170-76.
Take One. 1968, v1, n9, p24-25.
Time. Dec 22, 1967, v90, p78.
Variety. Dec 13, 1967, p6.
The Village Voice. Dec 28, 1967, p33, 35.

In einem Jahr mit 13 Monden *See* In a Year of 13 Moons

In Harm's Way (US; Preminger, Otto; 1965)
America. Apr 17, 1965, v112, p588.
BFI/Monthly Film Bulletin. Jun 1965, v32, p87-88.
Christian Science Monitor (Western edition). Apr 14, 1965, p4.
Cinema. Jul-Aug 1965, v2, p50.
The Cinema of Otto Preminger (Pratley). p148-50.
Commonweal. Apr 16, 1965, v82, p117.
The Complete Films of John Wayne. p256-58.
Film Daily. Mar 31, 1965, p5.
Film Quarterly. Fall 1965, v19, p62.
Filmfacts. May 28, 1965, v8, p87-89.
Films and Filming. Oct 1965, v12, p32-33.
Films and Filming. Jun 1965, v11, p6-8.
Films in Review. Apr 1965, v16, p248-49.
Films in Review. Oct 1965, v16, p525-26.
The Films of Henry Fonda. p185-86.
The Films of Kirk Douglas. p203-206.
Hollywood Reporter. Mar 31, 1965, p3.
The London Times. May 13, 1965, p6.
Motion Picture Herald Product Digest. Apr 14, 1965, p265.
Movie. Sum 1965, n13, p14-16.
The New Republic. Apr 17, 1965, v152, p41.
New Statesman. May 21, 1965, v69, p816.
The New York Times. Apr 7, 1965, p36.

The New Yorker. Apr 17, 1965, v41, p158.
Newsweek. Apr 12, 1965, v65, p110.
Playboy. Jul 1965, v12, p28, 32.
Saturday Review. Apr 24, 1965, v48, p39.
The Spectator. May 21, 1965, v214, p665.
Time. Apr 9, 1965, v85, p101-02.
Variety. Mar 31, 1965, p6.
The Village Voice. Apr 29, 1965, v10, p12.

In Like Flint (US; Douglas, Gordon; 1967)
BFI/Monthly Film Bulletin. Jul 1967, v34, p106-07.
Film Daily. Mar 14, 1967, p15.
Films in Review. Apr 1967, v18, p241-42.
Hollywood Reporter. Mar 14, 1967, p3.
Motion Picture Herald Product Digest. Mar 29, 1967, p669.
The New York Times. Mar 16, 1967, p53.
The New Yorker. Mar 18, 1967, v43, p175.
Saturday Review. Apr 8, 1967, v50, p48.

In the Cool of the Day (US; Stevens, Robert; 1963)
BFI/Monthly Film Bulletin. Nov 1963, v30, p158.
Commonweal. Jun 28, 1963, v78, p377.
Film Daily. May 23, 1963, p7.
Filmfacts. Jun 20, 1963, v6, p112-13.
Films and Filming. Nov 1963, p23.
Films in Review. Jun-Jul 1963, v14, p370-71.
The Films of Jane Fonda. p93-97.
The Fondas (Springer). p193-95.
The New Republic. Jun 15, 1963, v148, p36.
The New York Times. May 30, 1963, p20.
Saturday Review. Jun 15, 1963, v46, p45.
Time. Jun 14, 1963, v81, p99-100.
Variety. May 15, 1963, p6.

In The Forest *See* Rashomon

In the French Style (US, FR; Parrish, Robert; 1963)
America. Oct 5, 1963, v109, p399.
BFI/Monthly Film Bulletin. Nov 1963, v30, p155.
Commonweal. Oct 4, 1963, v79, p46.
Film Daily. Sep 17, 1963, p7.
Filmfacts. Sep 26, 1963, v6, p193-94.
Films and Filming. Nov 1963, v10, p25.
Films in Review. Oct 1963, v14, p495-96.
New Statesman. Sep 27, 1963, v66, p419.
The New York Times. Sep 19, 1963, p23.
The New Yorker. Sep 28, 1963, v39, p106.
Newsweek. Sep 23, 1963, v62, p101-02.
Photoplay. Sep 1963, v64, p13.
Saturday Review. Sep 28, 1963, v46, p44.
Spectator. Oct 4, 1963, v211, p415.
Variety. Sep 18, 1963, p6.

In the Heat of the Night (US; Jewison, Norman; 1967)
America. Aug 12, 1967, v117, p160.
BFI/Monthly Film Bulletin. Oct 1967, v34, p151-52.
Christian Century. Dec 6, 1967, v84, p1560-61.
Cinema. Wint 1967, v3, p47, 48.
Commonweal. Aug 25, 1967, v86, p523-24.
Esquire. Sep 1967, v68, p20.
Film Daily. Jun 21, 1967, p3.
Film Quarterly. Wint 1967-68, v21, p61-62.
Films and Filming. Nov 1967, v14, p21-22.
The Films of Sidney Poitier. p148-54.
The Films of the Sixties. p186-89.
From Sambo to Superspade. p228-30.
Hollywood Reporter. Jun 21, 1967, p3.
Life. Jul 28, 1967, v63, p10.
Magill's Survey of Cinema. Series I. v2, p829-32.
Motion Picture Herald Product Digest. Jun 21, 1967, p696.
The New York Times. Aug 3, 1967, p26.

The New Yorker. Aug 5, 1967, v43, p64.
Newsweek. Aug 14, 1967, v70, p83.
Saturday Review. Jul 8, 1967, v50, p39.
Saturday Review. Aug 19, 1967, p45.
Senior Scholastic. Sep 28, 1967, v91, p46.
Sight and Sound. Aut 1967, v36, p206.
Take One. 1967, v1, n6, p25.
Time. Aug 11, 1967, v90, p72.
Variety. Jun 21, 1967, p6.
The Village Voice. Aug 17, 1967, p21.

In the Realm of the Senses (Japanese title: Ai No Corrida; French title: Empire des sens, L') (JAPAN, FR; Oshima, Nagisa; 1976)
Before My Eyes. p291.
Cineaste. 1977, v7, n4, p32-34, 35.
Cinema Canada. Nov 1976, n32, p10.
Cinema Papers. Sep-Oct 1976, n10, p111.
Film Comment. Sep-Oct 1976, v12, p37-38.
Film Comment. Jan-Feb 1977, v13, p32-33.
Film Comment. Jul-Aug 1977, v13, p35-36.
Film Quarterly. Wint 1976, v30, p58-61.
Independent Film Journal. Aug 19, 1977, v80, p18.
Interview. Nov 1976, v6, p35.
The Los Angeles Times. Apr 1, 1977, SecIV, p13.
Magill's Survey of Cinema. Foreign Language Films. v3, p1475-79.
The Nation. Oct 23, 1976, v223, p412.
The New Republic. Jul 2, 1977, v177, p26-27.
New Times. Aug 19, 1977, v9, p66-67.
New York. Aug 8, 1977, v10, p53-54.
The New York Times. Oct 3, 1976, p25.
The New York Times. Jul 18, 1977, p34.
The New York Times. Jul 31, 1977, SecII, p1.
Penthouse. Jan 1977, v8, p49-50.
Psychology Today. Feb 1977, v10, p18.
Take One. 1977, v5, n8, p9-10.
Take One. 1977, v5, n10, p50-51.
Times Educational Supplement. Dec 17, 1976, p18.
Variety. Feb 25, 1976, p22.
The Village Voice. Aug 8, 1977, p39-40.

In The Woods *See* Rashomon

Inadmissible Evidence (GB; Page, Anthony; 1968)
BFI/Monthly Film Bulletin. Jul 1969, v36, 141-42.
Commonweal. Aug 9, 1968, v88, p534.
Esquire. Oct 1968, v70, p92.
Figures of Light. p91-93.
Film Daily. Aug 1, 1968, p10.
Filmfacts. Sep 15, 1968, v11, p243-45.
Films and Filming. Aug 1969, v15, p34-35.
Films in Review. Aug-Sep 1968, v19, p457.
Hollywood Reporter. Jun 24, 1968, p3.
Life. Aug 16, 1968, v65, p10.
The London Times. May 22, 1969, p16.
Motion Picture Herald Product Digest. Jul 10, 1968, p830A.
The New Republic. Jul 13, 1968, v159, p22.
The New York Times. Jun 24, 1968, p44.
The New Yorker. Jun 29, 1968, v44, p62.
Newsweek. Jul 1, 1968, v72, p94-95.
The Spectator. May 23, 1969, v222, p694.
Time. Jun 28, 1968, v91, p80.
Variety. Jul 3, 1968, p6.

Inchon (KOREA, US; Young, Terence; 1982)
Christianity Today. Oct 22, 1982, v26, p63.
Film Journal. Sep 24, 1982, v85, p11-12.
The Los Angeles Times. Sep 17, 1982, SecVI, p1.
The Nation. Oct 16, 1982, v235, p380.
The New York Times. Sep 17, 1982, SecIII, p9.

Newsweek. Sep 27, 1982, v100, p76.
Variety. Sep 15, 1982, p12.

Incorrigible (French title: Incorrigible, L') (FR; Broca, Philippe de; 1975)
The Los Angeles Times. Jun 21, 1980, SecII, p11.
The New York Times. Apr 13, 1980, p47.
Variety. Oct 29, 1975, p17.
The Village Voice. Apr 28, 1980, p46.

The Incredible Journey (CAN; Markle, Fletcher; 1963)
BFI/Monthly Film Bulletin. Mar 1964, v31, p40.
Commonweal. Dec 13, 1963, v79, p349.
The Disney Films. p214-15.
Film Daily. Oct 18, 1963, p6.
Filmfacts. Dec 19, 1963, v6, p284-85.
Films and Filming. Jan 1964, v10, p31.
The New York Times. Nov 21, 1963, p43.
Newsweek. Dec 9, 1963, v62, p92.
Photoplay. Dec 1963, v64, p12.
Saturday Review. Nov 16, 1963, v46, p29.
Time. Dec 6, 1963, v82, p120.
Variety. Oct 16, 1963, p6.
Walt Disney: A Guide to References and Resources. p90-91.

The Incredible Sarah (US; Fleischer, Richard; 1976)
Audience. Jun-Jul 1976, v8, p4-6.
BFI/Monthly Film Bulletin. Nov 1976, v43, p232-33.
Film Bulletin. Sep-Oct 1976, v45, p39.
Films and Filming. Dec 1976, v23, p29-30.
Films in Review. Dec 1976, v27, p635-36.
Hollywood Reporter. Sep 1, 1976, p2.
Independent Film Journal. Nov 26, 1976, v78, p9.
The Los Angeles Times. Nov 5, 1976, SecIV, p1.
Ms. Feb 1976, v4, p52-53.
New Statesman. Nov 12, 1976, v92, p689.
New York. Nov 22, 1976, v9, p88.
The New York Times. Nov 7, 1976, SecII, p13.
The New York Times. Nov 14, 1976, SecII, p15.
The New York Times. Nov 6, 1976, p11.
The New Yorker. Nov 15, 1976, v52, p180.
Newsweek. Nov 8, 1976, v88, p107.
Saturday Review. Nov 27, 1976, v4, p41.
Variety. Sep 8, 1976, p20.
The Village Voice. Nov 29, 1976, p53.
When the Lights Go Down. p204-06.

The Incredible Shrinking Man (US; Arnold, Jack; 1957)
America. Mar 16, 1957, v96, p685.
BFI/Monthly Film Bulletin. Jul 1957, v24, p83.
Commonweal. Apr 19, 1957, v66, p65.
Film Daily. Feb 1, 1957, p6.
Films and Filming. Aug 1957, v3, p27.
Hollywood Reporter. Feb 1, 1957, p3.
Magill's Survey of Cinema. Series I. v2, p836-38.
Motion Picture Herald Product Digest. Feb 12, 1957, v206, p249-50.
The New York Times. Feb 23, 1957, p13.
Newsweek. Mar 11, 1957, v49, p106.
Variety. Feb 6, 1957, p6.

The Incredible Shrinking Woman (US; Schumacher, Joel; 1981)
BFI/Monthly Film Bulletin. Apr 1981, v48, p69.
Christian Century. Mar 25, 1981, v98, p332.
Commonweal. Feb 13, 1981, v108, p33.
Film Journal. Feb 2, 1981, v84, p39-40.
Films In Review. Apr 1981, v32, p249.
The Los Angeles Times. Jan 30, 1981, SecVI, p1.

Maclean's. Feb 9, 1981, v94, p58.
The Nation. Feb 21, 1981, v232, p221.
New Statesman. Apr 24, 1981, v101, p28-29.
New York. Feb 23, 1981, v14, p42.
The New York Times. Jan 30, 1981, SecIII, p12.
The New York Times. Feb 15, 1981, SecII, p13-14.
The New York Times. Jan 29, 1981, SecIII, p13.
The New Yorker. Mar 9, 1981, v57, p108-10.
Newsweek. Feb 9, 1981, v97, p97.
Rolling Stone. Mar 19, 1981, p45.
Time. Feb 23, 1981, v117, p110.
Variety. Jan 28, 1981, p18.
The Village Voice. Jan 28, 1981, p43.

Independence Day (US; Mandel, Robert; 1982)
BFI/Monthly Film Bulletin. Sep 1984, v51, p280.
Esquire. Jul 1982, v98, p113.
Film Journal. Jan 28, 1983, v86, p41-42.
Maclean's. Jan 24, 1983, v96, p53.
Ms. Apr 1983, v11, p70.
The New Leader. Feb 21, 1983, v66, p19-20.
New York. Feb 7, 1983, v16, p72.
The New York Times. Jan 21, 1983, SecIII, p8.
Penthouse. Mar 1983, v14, p50.
Rolling Stone. May 31, 1983, p42.
Variety. Jan 19, 1983, p21.

Indiana Jones and the Temple of Doom (US; Spielberg, Steven; 1984)
America. Jun 30, 1984, v150, p493.
American Cinematographer. Jul 1984, v60, p50-75.
BFI/Monthly Film Bulletin. Jul 1984, v51, p203.
Christianity Today. Aug 10, 1984, v28, p36.
Cinefantastique. 1984, v14, n4/5, p100.
Cinefex. Aug 1984, v18, p4-41.
Commonweal. Jun 15, 1984, v111, p374-75.
Film Comment. Jul/Aug 1984, v20, p49-51.
Film Journal. Jun 1984, v87, p21.
Films and Filming. Jul 1984, n358, p18-20.
Films in Review. Aug 1984, p35, p426.
Harper's. Aug 1984, v269, p18-19.
Hollywood Reporter. May 11, 1984, p4.
Informer. May-Jun 1984, p10-11.
Life. Jun 1984, v7, p88-94.
The Los Angeles Times. May 27, 1984, Calendar, p17.
Maclean's. Jun 4, 1984, v97, p47.
Magill's Cinema Annual, 1985. p253-58.
Midnight Marquee. Fall 1984, n33, p30.
The Nation. Jun 9, 1984, v238, p713-14.
National Review. Jul 13, 1984, v36, p51.
New Statesman. Jun 15, 1983, v107, p29-30.
New York. Jun 4, 1984, v17, p72-74.
The New York Times. May 23, 1984, SecIII, p21.
The New York Times. May 20, 1984, SecII, p1.
The New York Times. May 11, 1984, SecIII, p8.
The New Yorker. Jun 11, 1984, v60, p100.
Newsweek. Jun 4, 1984, v103, p78-79.
On Location. Jun 1984, v8, p106-10.
Penthouse. Sep 1984, v16, p54.
Photoplay. Aug 1984, v35, p19.
Photoplay. Jul 1984, v35, p29-33.
Time. May 21, 1984, v123, p82-83.
Variety. May 16, 1984, p26.
The Village Voice. Jun 5, 1984, p1.

Indiscreet (US; Donen, Stanley; 1958)
America. Jul 5, 1958, v99, p399.
BFI/Monthly Film Bulletin. Aug 1958, v25, p99.
Catholic World. Sep 1958, v187, p457.
Commonweal. Jul 18, 1958, v68, p404.
Double Takes. p14-15.
Film Daily. May 29, 1958, p6.

Filmfacts. Aug 20, 1958, v1, p117-18.
Films in Review. Aug-Sep 1958, v9, p400.
The Films of Cary Grant. p234-37.
The Films of Ingrid Bergman. p155-57.
Hollywood Reporter. May 28, 1958, p3.
Library Journal. Jul 1958, v83, p404.
Life. Jul 7, 1958, v45, p69.
The New Republic. Jul 21, 1958, v139, p21.
The New York Times. Jun 27, 1958, p18.
The New Yorker. Jul 12, 1958, v34, p99.
Newsweek. Jul 7, 1958, v52, p73.
Saturday Review. Jul 12, 1958, v41, p12.
Stanley Donen (Casper). p124-30.
Time. Jul 21, 1958, v72, p78.
Variety. May 28, 1958, p6.

Indiscretion of an American Wife (Italian title: Stazioni Termini; Also titled: Indiscretion; Terminal Station) (IT, US; De Sica, Vittorio; 1953)
America. Jul 17, 1954, v91, p407.
BFI/Monthly Film Bulletin. Sep 1954, v21, p128-29.
Catholic World. May 1954, v179, p143-44.
Commonweal. May 7, 1954, v60, p117.
Coronet. May 1954, v36, p14.
Farm Journal. Jul 1954, v78, p92.
Film Daily. Apr 30, 1954, p6.
Films and Filming. Oct 1954, v1, p20.
Films in Review. Apr 1954, v5, p191-92.
The Films of Jennifer Jones. p111-16.
The Films of Montgomery Clift. p151-56.
Hollywood Reporter. Apr 21, 1954, p3.
The London Times. Aug 5, 1954, p8.
Motion Picture Herald Product Digest. Apr 24, 1954, p2270.
National Parent-Teacher. Apr 1954, v48, p39.
The New Statesman and Nation. Aug 14, 1954, v48, p184.
The New York Times. Jun 26, 1954, p7.
Newsweek. Apr 12, 1954, v43, p104-05.
Saturday Review. Apr 24, 1954, v37, p25.
Sight and Sound. Oct-Dec 1954, v24, p87.
Time. Apr 26, 1954, v63, p110.
Variety. Apr 21, 1954, p6.

The Inferno of First Love (Japanese title: Hatsukoi Jigokuhen; Nanami) (JAPAN; Hani, Susumu; 1968)
Film Comment. Spr 1969, v5, p42-44.
Filmfacts. 1969, v12, n16, p367-69.
International Film Guide. 1969, v6, p114.
Magill's Survey of Cinema. Foreign Language Films. v3, p1480-85.
Motion Picture Herald Product Digest. Mar 12, 1969, p132.
The New York Times. Sep 5, 1969, p32.
The Village Voice. Sep 18, 1969, p49, 53.

Infidelity *See* Altri Tempi

Ingenor Andrees Luftfard *See* The Flight of the Eagle

Ingénue Libertine, L' *See* Minne

Inherit the Wind (US; Kramer, Stanley; 1960)
America. Oct 15, 1960, v104, p101.
BFI/Monthly Film Bulletin. Jul 1960, v27, p92.
Christian Century. Jan 11, 1961, v78, p48-49.
Commonweal. Nov 4, 1960, v73, p151.
Coronet. Jul 1960, v48, p12.
Film Daily. Jun 29, 1960, p10.
Film Quarterly. Fall 1960, v14, p61.
Filmfacts. 1960, v3, p249.
Films and Filming. Aug 1960, v6, p21.
Films in Review. Aug-Sep 1960, v11, p427-28.
The Films of Fredric March. p225-27.
The Films of Gene Kelly. p196-203.
The Films of Spencer Tracy. p236-39.

Hollywood Reporter. Jun 28, 1960, p3.
Life. Sep 26, 1960, v49, p77.
Look. Oct 25, 1960, v24, p126.
Magill's Survey of Cinema. Series II. v3, p1148-50.
The New Republic. Oct 31, 1960, v143, p29.
The New York Times. Oct 13, 1960, p41.
The New York Times. Oct 16, 1960, SecII, p1.
The New Yorker. Oct 22, 1960, v36, p98.
Newsweek. Oct 17, 1960, v56, p114.
Saturday Review. Oct 8, 1960, v43, p30.
Senior Scholastic (teacher's edition). Sep 14, 1960, v77, p40.
Sight and Sound. Sum 1960, v29, p147.
Time. Oct 17, 1960, v76, p95.
Variety. Jul 6, 1960, p6.

The In-Laws (US; Hiller, Arthur; 1979)
BFI/Monthly Film Bulletin. Oct 1979, v46, p209.
Hollywood Reporter. Jun 11, 1979, p3.
The Los Angeles Times. Jun 10, 1979, Calendar, p37.
Motion Picture Herald Product Digest. Jul 4, 1979, p10.
The New Republic. Jun 23, 1979, v180, p27.
The New York Times. Jun 15, 1979, SecIII, p10.
The New Yorker. Jul 2, 1979, v55, p67.
Newsweek. Jul 2, 1979, v94, p71.
Saturday Review. Oct 13, 1979, v6, p60.
Time. Jun 18, 1979, v113, p60.
Variety. Jun 13, 1979, p14.

The Inn of the Sixth Happiness (US; Robson, Mark; 1958)
America. Dec 20, 1958, v100, p380.
BFI/Monthly Film Bulletin. Jan 1959, v26, p2.
Commonweal. Dec 19, 1958, v69, p317.
Film Daily. Nov 21, 1958, p4.
Filmfacts. Dec 24, 1958, v1, p221-22, 240.
Films in Review. Jan 1959, v10, p36-37.
The Films of Ingrid Bergman. p158-67.
Good Housekeeping. Jan 1959, v148, p24.
Hollywood Reporter. Nov 18, 1958, p3.
Life. Jan 12, 1959, v46, p45.
The New York Times. Dec 14, 1958, p2.
The New Yorker. Dec 13, 1958, v34, p124-25.
The New Yorker. Dec 20, 1958, v34, p98.
Newsweek. Dec 15, 1958, v52, p114.
Saturday Review. Dec 13, 1958, v41, p26.
Senior Scholastic. Jan 30, 1959, v74, p30.
Time. Dec 22, 1958, v72, p72.
Variety. Nov 19, 1958, p6.

Innocence Unprotected (Yugoslavian title: Nevinost Bez Zastite) (YUGO; Makavejev, Dusan; 1968)
BFI/Monthly Film Bulletin. Sep 1969, v36, p190.
Directors and Directions: Cinema for the Seventies. p246-48.
Filmfacts. 1971, v14, p545.
Films and Filming. Apr 1969, v15, p54.
International Film Guide. 1969, v6, p187.
The London Times. Feb 13, 1969, p11.
The London Times. Aug 2, 1969, p19.
Magill's Survey of Cinema. Foreign Language Films. v3, p1490-95.
New Statesman. Aug 1, 1969, v78, p157.
The New York Times. Dec 12, 1969, p70.
The New York Times. Mar 26, 1971, p30.
The Spectator. Feb 21, 1969, v222, p248-49.
Variety. Jul 17, 1968, p24.
The Village Voice. Apr 1, 1971, p67.

The Innocent (Italian title: Innocente, L') (IT, FR; Visconti, Luchino; 1976)
BFI/Monthly Film Bulletin. Jan 1978, v45, p8-9.

Film Comment. Mar 1979, v15, p14-16.
Films in Review. Mar 1979, v30, p180.
The Los Angeles Times. May 3, 1979, SecIV, p4.
Luchino Visconti (Tonetti). p181-90.
Magill's Survey of Cinema. Foreign Language Films. v3, p1496-99.
Motion Picture Herald Product Digest. Feb 7, 1979, p70.
The Nation. Feb 10, 1979, v228, p157-58.
The New Republic. Feb 3, 1979, v180, p25.
New York. Jan 29, 1979, v12, p125.
The New York Times. Jan 12, 1979, SecIII, p10.
The New Yorker. Feb 12, 1979, v54, p90-92.
Time. Feb 12, 1979, v113, p74.
Variety. May 26, 1979, p20.

Innocent Young Man *See* Benjamin, or The Diary of an Innocent Young Boy

Innocente, L' *See* The Innocent

The Innocents (GB; Clayton, Jack; 1961)
America. Jan 13, 1962, v106, p480.
BFI/Monthly Film Bulletin. Jan 1962, v29, p5-6.
Cinefantastique. 1983, v13, n5, p51-55.
Commonweal. Jan 12, 1962, v75, p414.
Double Exposure. p91-97.
Fifty Classic British Films. p216-24.
Film. Spr 1962, n31, p16-17.
Film and Literature: An Introduction. p216-24.
Film Daily. Dec 13, 1961, p5.
Film News. Sep-Oct 1979, n36, p36.
Film Quarterly. Spr 1962, v15, p72.
Film Reader. 1980, n4, p201-13.
Filmfacts. Jan19, 1962, v4, p337-39.
Films and Filming. Jan 1962, v8, p32.
Films in Review. Jan 1962, v13, p43-44.
The Great British Films. p199-202.
Hollywood Reporter. Dec 13, 1961, p3.
Hollywood U.K. p162-64.
I Lost it at the Movies. p147-55.
Jack Clayton: A Guide to References and Resources. p25-29.
Life. Feb 2, 1962, v52, p45-46.
Literature/Film Quarterly. 1977, v5, n3, p198-215.
Magill's Survey of Cinema. Series II. v3, p1151-54.
Motion Picture Herald Product Digest. Dec 20, 1961, p388.
The New Republic. Jan 8, 1962, v146, p20.
The New York Times. Dec 26, 1961, p15.
The New Yorker. Jan 6, 1962, v37, p72.
Newsweek. Jan 1, 1962, v59, p52.
Saturday Review. Dec 23, 1961, v44, p38.
Sight and Sound. Sum 1961, v30, p114-15.
Sight and Sound. Wint 1961-62, v31, p39-40.
Time. Jan 5, 1962, v79, p59.
Variety. Dec 6, 1961, p6.
The Village Voice. Jan 18, 1962, p10.
A World on Film. p107-08.

Inside Daisy Clover (US; Mulligan, Robert; 1965)
America. Mar 19, 1966, v114, p397.
BFI/Monthly Film Bulletin. Jul 1966, v33, p103-04.
Christian Science Monitor (Western edition). Apr 30, 1966, p6.
Commonweal. Mar 11, 1966, v83, p667.
Film Daily. Dec 27, 1965, p10.
Film Quarterly. Spr 1966, v19, p52-53.
Film Quarterly. Fall 1966, v20, p22-27.
Filmfacts. Mar 15, 1966, v9, p36-38.
Films and Filming. Aug 1966, v12, p59-60.
Films in Review. Mar 1966, v17, p185-86.
The Films of Robert Redford. p80-85.
Hollywood Reporter. Dec 16, 1965, p3.
International Film Guide. 1967, v4, p160, 162.

Kiss Kiss Bang Bang. p352-53.
Life. Mar 25, 1966, v60, p17.
London Magazine. Aug 1966, v6, p93-97.
The London Times. May 26, 1966, p19.
Motion Picture Herald Product Digest. Jan 5, 1966, p434.
New Statesman. Jun 3, 1966, v71, p819.
The New York Times. Feb 18, 1966, p23.
The New Yorker. Feb 26, 1966, v42, p109.
Newsweek. Feb 28, 1966, v67, p91-92.
Playboy. Apr 1966, v13, p46-47.
Saturday Review. Jan 29, 1966, v49, p43.
Sight and Sound. Sum 1966, v35, p148.
Time. Feb 25, 1966, v87, p105-06.
Variety. Dec 22, 1965, p17.
The Village Voice. May 19, 1966, v11, p31, 33.
Vogue. Feb 15, 1966, v147, p58.

Inside Moves (US; Donner, Richard; 1980)
BFI/Monthly Film Bulletin. Apr 1981, v48, p69.
Christian Science Monitor. Feb 5, 1981, p19.
Films in Review. Feb 1982, v33, p119.
Hollywood Reporter. Dec 8, 1980, p8.
The Los Angeles Times. Dec 18, 1980, SecVI, p1.
The Nation. Feb 21, 1981, v232, p221.
The New York Times. Dec 19, 1980, SecIII, p18.
Newsweek. Jan 5, 1981, v96, p55.
Variety. Dec 10, 1980, p32.
The Village Voice. Dec 24, 1980, p42.

Inside North Vietnam (US; Greene, Felix; 1967)
Catholic World. Apr 1968, v207, p24-30.
Christian Century. Jan 21, 1970, v87, p87.
Christian Science Monitor (Western edition). Jan 17, 1968, p8.
Film Quarterly. Spr 1968, v21, p58-59.
Filmfacts. 1967, v10, p402.
Hollywood Reporter. Feb 29, 1968, p3.
The London Times. Feb 17, 1968, p19.
The Nation. Dec 25, 1967, v205, p701.
Newsweek. Jan 1, 1968, v71, p63.
Variety. Dec 27, 1967, p6.

Inside the Walls of Folsom Prison (US; Crane, Wilbur; 1951)
BFI/Monthly Film Bulletin. Mar 1952, v19, p35.
Film Daily. May 22, 1951, p6.
Hollywood Reporter. May 18, 1951, p3.
Motion Picture Herald Product Digest. May 19, 1951, p854.
The New York Times. May 28, 1951, p17.
Newsweek. Jun 11, 1951, v37, p102.
Saturday Review. Jun 23, 1951, v34, p34.
Variety. May 23, 1951, p6.

An Inspector Calls (GB; Hamilton, Guy; 1954)
BFI/Monthly Film Bulletin. Apr 1954, v21, p53.
Film Daily. Dec 2, 1954, p6.
Illustrated London News. Apr 3, 1954, v224, p540.
Magill's Survey of Cinema. Series II. v3, p1155-58.
Motion Picture Herald Product Digest. Dec 18, 1954, p250.
The Nation. Dec 11, 1954, v179, p517.
National Parent-Teacher. Jan 1956, v50, p39.
The New Statesman and Nation. Mar 20, 1954, v47, p356.
The New York Times. Nov 26, 1954, p24.
The New Yorker. Dec 4, 1954, v30, p228.
Newsweek. Dec 13, 1954, v44, p98.
Quarterly of Film, Radio and Television. Fall 1955, v10, p16-17.
The Spectator. Mar 12, 1954, v192, p287.

The Tatler. Mar 24, 1954, v211, p554.
Variety. Mar 23, 1954, p24.

Inspector Clouseau (US; Yorkin, Bud; 1968)
BFI/Monthly Film Bulletin. Jan 1969, v36, p11.
Christian Science Monitor (Western edition). Jun 14, 1968, p4.
Esquire. Aug 1968, v70, p22.
Film Daily. May 24, 1968, p4.
Filmfacts. Oct 15, 1968, v11, p283-84.
Films and Filming. Feb 1969, v15, p45.
Hollywood Reporter. May 22, 1968, p3.
Life. Aug 23, 1968, v65, p8.
Motion Picture Herald Product Digest. Jun 5, 1968, p819.
The New York Times. Jul 25, 1968, p26.
The New Yorker. Jul 27, 1968, v44, p80-81.
Time. Aug 9, 1968, v92, p82.
Variety. May 22, 1968, p6.
A Year In the Dark. p196-97.

Inspector Maigret (French title: Maigret Tend un Piege; Also titled: Maigret Lays a Trap) (FR; Delannoy, Jean; 1958)
Film Daily. Oct 9, 1958, v114, p6.
Filmfacts. Dec 17, 1958, v1, p217.
Library Journal. Nov 15, 1958, v83, p3237.
The New York Times. Oct 9, 1958, p47.
Newsweek. Oct 13, 1958, v52, p119.
Time. Dec 8, 1958, v72, p104.
Variety. Mar 26, 1958, p6.

Interiors (US; Allen, Woody; 1978)
America. Sep 23, 1978, v139, p180.
BFI/Monthly Film Bulletin. Dec 1978, v45, p241.
Commonweal. Sep 29, 1978, v105, p630-32.
Films in Review. Nov 1978, v29, p566.
Hollywood Reporter. Jul 28, 1978, p3.
The Los Angeles Times. Aug 27, 1978, Calendar, p1.
Maclean's. Oct 2, 1978, v91, p62.
Magill's Survey of Cinema. Series I. v2, p844-47.
Motion Picture Herald Product Digest. Aug 23, 1978, p21.
Ms. Dec 1978, v7, p30.
The Nation. Aug 19, 1978, v227, p156.
The New Republic. Sep 9, 1978, v179, p24.
New York. Aug 14, 1978, v11, p60-62.
New York Review of Books. Aug 16, 1979, v26, p18-19.
The New York Times. Aug 2, 1978, SecIII, p15.
The New Yorker. Aug 7, 1978, v54, p76-78.
The New Yorker. Sep 25, 1978, v54, p151-52.
Newsweek. Aug 7, 1978, v92, p83.
Saturday Review. Jan 6, 1979, v6, p46-47.
Time. Aug 7, 1978, v112, p57.
Variety. Aug 2, 1978, p14.
Vogue. Nov 1978, v168, p246.
Woody Allen: His Films and Career. p179-86.
Woody Allen (Palmer). p97-102.

International Velvet (GB; Forbes, Bryan; 1978)
BFI/Monthly Film Bulletin. Jul, 1978, v45, p159.
Films in Review. Oct 1978, v29, p505.
Hollywood Reporter. Jun 23, 1978, p3.
The Los Angeles Times. Jul 16, 1978, Calendar, p1.
Maclean's. Jul 24, 1978, v91, p58.
Motion Picture Herald Product Digest. Jul 26, 1978, p15.
The New York Times. Jul 19, 1978, SecIII p15.
The New York Times. Jul 30, 1978, SecII, p13.
The New Yorker. Jul 24, 1978, v54, p58.
Sports Illustrated. Jul 10, 1978, v49, p66.

Time. Jul 24, 1978, v112, p56.
Variety. Jun 28, 1978, p20.

The Internecine Project (GB; Hughes, John; 1974)
BFI/Monthly Film Bulletin. Sep 1974, v41, p200-01.
Films and Filming. Oct 1974, v21, p40.
Films Illustrated. Oct 1974, v4, p46.
Hollywood Reporter. Sep 20, 1974, p3.
The Los Angeles Times. Sep 20, 1974, SecIV, p8.
Movietone News. Sep 1974, n35, p3.
New Statesman. Sep 20, 1974, v88, p390.
Time. Nov 25, 1974, v104, p11.
Variety. Oct 2, 1974, p24.

Interrupted Melody (US; Bernhardt, Curtis; 1955)
America. May 14, 1955, v93, p193.
BFI/Monthly Film Bulletin. Aug 1955, v22, p124.
Catholic World. May 1955, v181, p143.
Commonweal. May 6, 1955, v62, p126.
Film Daily. Mar 25, 1955, p5.
Films in Review. May 1955, v6, p240-42.
Hollywood Reporter. Mar 25, 1955, p3.
Magill's Survey of Cinema. Series II. v3, p1162-65.
The New York Times. May 6, 1955, p18.
The New Yorker. May 14, 1955, v31, p145.
Newsweek. Apr 25, 1955, v45, p108.
Saturday Review. Apr 30, 1955, v38, p27.
Senior Scholastic. May 11, 1955, v66, p30.
Time. May 9, 1955, v65, p109.
Variety. Mar 30, 1955, p8.

Intimate Lighting (Czechoslovakian title: Intimní Osvetleni) (CZECH; Passer, Ivan; 1965)
The Czechoslovak New Wave. p151-57.
Figures of Light. p222-23.
Film 69/70. p119-20.
Film Library Quarterly. Fall 1971, v4, p18-21.
Film Quarterly. Spr 1967, v20, p39-41.
Films and Filming. Jun 1967, v13, p21-22.
The London Times. Nov 23, 1966, p17.
The London Times. Apr 6, 1967, p12.
New Statesman. Apr 7, 1967, v73, p482-83.
The New York Times. Sep 19, 1966, p57.
Private Screenings. p285-86.
Time. Sep 23, 1966, v88, p74.
Unholy Fools, Wits, Comics, Disturbers of the Peace. p338-39.
Variety. Aug 3, 1966, p6.
The Village Voice. Dec 4, 1969, v14, p57-58.

Intimate Relations (GB; Frank, Charles; 1953)
Films in Review. Apr 1954, v5, p195-96.
Motion Picture Herald Product Digest. Feb 20, 1954, p2190.
The New York Times. Feb 22, 1954, p15.
Saturday Review. Mar 6, 1954, v37, p28.
Time. Mar 15, 1954, v63, p102.
Variety. Mar 25, 1953, p24.

Intimní Osvetleni *See* Intimate Lighting

Into The Night (US; Landis, John; 1985)
BFI/Monthly Film Bulletin. May 1985, v52, p155.
The Los Angeles Times. Feb 22, 1985, SecVI, p1.
Maclean's. Mar 4, 1985, v98, p53.
Magill's Cinema Annual, 1986. p186-89.
The New York Times. Feb 22, 1985, SecIII, p8.
Newsweek. Mar 11, 1985, v105, p70.
Saturday Review. Mar/Apr 1985, v11, p75.
Time. Feb 25, 1985, v125, p96.
Variety. Feb 20, 1985, p23.
The Wall Street Journal. Feb 21, 1985, p28.

Invasion of the Body Snatchers (US; Siegel, Don; 1956)
BFI/Monthly Film Bulletin. Oct 1956, v23, p125.
Cinefantastique. 1973, v2, p16-19, 20-23.
Cult Movies. p154-57.
Fifty from the Fifties. p141-50.
Film Comment. Jan-Feb 1979, v15, p22-25.
Film Criticism. 1982, v7, p56-68.
Film Daily. Feb 28, 1956, p10.
Films and Filming. Feb 1969, v15, p49-50.
The Films of the Fifties. p171-74.
Focus on the Science Fiction Film. p71-77.
Halliwell's Hundred. p147-50.
Hollywood Reporter. Feb 16, 1956, p3.
The International Dictionary of Films and Filmmakers. v1, p213-14.
Journal of Popular Culture. 1979, v13, p5-16.
Jump Cut. Mar 1981, n24/25, p3-4.
Literature/Film Quarterly. 1978, v6, p285-92.
Magill's Survey of Cinema. Series I. v2, p848-51.
Motion Picture Herald Product Digest. Feb 25, 1956, p794.
Movietone. Mar 1974, n30, p1-10.
Science Fiction Gold. p171-82.
Twenty All Time Great Science Fiction Films. p136-49.
Variety. Feb 29, 1956, p6.
The World of Fantastic Films. p36-37.

Invasion of the Body Snatchers (US; Kaufman, Philip; 1978)
BFI/Monthly Film Bulletin. Mar 1979, v46, p47.
Films in Review. Feb 1979, v30, p120.
Hollywood Reporter. Dec 14, 1978, p3.
Invasion of the Body Snatchers. 1978.
The Los Angeles Times. Dec 21, 1978, SecIV, p1.
Maclean's. Dec 25, 1978, v91, p49.
Motion Picture Herald Product Digest. Jan 3, 1979, p63.
New York. Jan 8, 1979, v12, p71.
The New York Times. Dec 22, 1978, SecIII, p14.
The New Yorker. Dec 25, 1978, v54, p48.
Newsweek. Dec 18, 1978, v92, p85.
Rolling Stone. Dec 28, 1978, p22-23.
Time. Dec 25, 1978, v112, p82.
Variety. Dec 20, 1978, p27.

Invitation (US; Reinhardt, Gottfried; 1952)
BFI/Monthly Film Bulletin. Apr 1952, v19, p46.
Film Daily. Jan 25, 1952, p7.
Hollywood Reporter. Jan 22, 1952, p3.
Library Journal. Mar 1, 1952, v77, p426.
The London Times. Feb 18, 1952, p2.
Motion Picture Herald Product Digest. Jan 26, 1952, p1214.
The New York Times. Jan 30, 1952, p22.
The New Yorker. Feb 9, 1952, v27, p105.
Newsweek. Feb 11, 1952, v39, p88.
Time. Feb 4, 1952, v59, p72.
Variety. Jan 23, 1952, p6.

Invitation to a Gunfighter (US; Wilson, Richard; 1964)
BFI/Monthly Film Bulletin. Jul 1965, v32, p104-05.
Boxoffice. Oct 26, 1964, v86, p2870.
Film Daily. Oct 26, 1964, p5.
Films and Filming. Jul 1965, v11, p27.
Hollywood Reporter. Oct 21, 1964, p3.
Motion Picture Herald Product Digest. Nov 11, 1964, v232, p161-62.
The New York Times. Oct 28, 1964, p51.
Sight and Sound. Sum 1965, v34, p144-45.
Variety. Oct 21, 1964, p6.

The Ipcress File (GB; Furie, Sidney J.; 1965)
BFI/Monthly Film Bulletin. May 1965, v32, p70-71.
Christian Science Monitor (Western edition). Nov 11, 1965, p4.
Cinema. Jul-Aug 1965, v2, p49.
Commonweal. Sep 3, 1965, v82, p637.
Confessions of a Cultist. p210-11.
Film Daily. Jul 7, 1965, p4.
Film Quarterly. Sum 1966, v19, p60-64.
Films and Filming. May 1965, v11, p28.
Films and Filming. Apr 1965, v11, p40.
Films in Review. Oct 1965, v16, p513-14.
The Great Spy Pictures. p241-42.
Hollywood Reporter. Jul 6, 1965, p3.
The London Times. Mar 18, 1965, p9.
Magill's Survey of Cinema. Series II. v3, p1175-76.
The Nation. Aug 30, 1965, v201, p108.
The New Republic. Jul 24, 1965, v153, p33.
New Statesman. Mar 26 1965, v69, p504.
The New York Times. Aug 3, 1965, p35.
The New Yorker. Aug 14, 1965, v41, p92.
Newsweek. Aug 9, 1965, v66, p79.
Playboy. Sep 1965, v12, p58.
Saturday Review. Jul 31, 1965, v48, p31.
Senior Scholastic. Sep 23, 1965, v87, p32.
Sight and Sound. Sum 1965, v34, p150.
The Spectator. Mar 19, 1965, v214, p365.
Time. Aug 13, 1965, v86, p74.
Variety. Mar 24, 1965, p6.
The Village Voice. Oct 7, 1965, v10, p27.

Irma La Douce (US; Wilder, Billy; 1963)
America. Aug 3, 1963, v109, p124.
BFI/Monthly Film Bulletin. Feb 1963, v31, p20.
Billy Wilder (Dick). p104-09.
Commonweal. Jun 28, 1963, v78, p376.
The Film Career of Billy Wilder. p100-02.
Film Daily. Jun 5, 1963, p5.
Filmfacts. Jun 13, 1963, v5, p103-05.
Films and Filming. Mar 1964, v10, p25-26.
Films in Review. Aug-Sep 1963, v14, p438-39.
The Films of Jack Lemmon. p136-42.
The Films of Shirley MacLaine. p122-27.
Hollywood Reporter. Jun 5, 1963, p3.
Magill's Survey of Cinema. Series II. p1178-81.
The New Republic. Jul 13, 1963, v149, p29.
The New York Times. Jun 6, 1963, p39.
The New Yorker. Jun 15, 1963, v39, p54.
Newsweek. Jun 17, 1963, v61, p90.
Photoplay. Sep 1963, v64, p10.
Saturday Review. Jun 22, 1963, v46, p31.
Sight and Sound. Spr 1964, v33, p98.
Time. Jun 21, 1963, v81, p92.
Variety. Jun 5, 1963, p6.

The Iron Kiss *See* The Naked Kiss

The Iron Mistress (US; Gordon, Douglas; 1952)
BFI/Monthly Film Bulletin. Dec 1952, v19, p172-73.
Film Daily. Oct 20, 1952, p6.
The Films of Alan Ladd. p161-62.
Hollywood Reporter. Oct 16, 1952, p3.
Library Journal. Dec 15, 1952, v77, p2170.
The London Times. Jan 26, 1953, p2.
Motion Picture Herald Product Digest. Oct 18, 1952, p1565.
The Nation. Dec 6, 1952, v175, p536.
The New York Times. Nov 20, 1952, p39.
Newsweek. Dec 8, 1952, v40, p94.
The Spectator. Jan 23, 1953, v190, p92-93.
The Tatler. Feb 4, 1953, v207, p194.
Time. Nov 24, 1952, v60, p108.
Variety. Oct 22, 1952, p6.

Is Paris Burning? (French title: Paris Brule-t-il?) (FR, US; Clément, René; 1966)
America. Nov 26, 1966, v115, p715-16.
BFI/Monthly Film Bulletin. Jan 1967, v34, p4-5.
Christian Science Monitor (Western edition). Nov 11, 1966, p4.
Cinema. Jul 1966, v3, p4-7.
Commonweal. Dec 2, 1966, v85, p262.
Film Daily. Nov 9, 1966, p3.
Filmfacts. Dec 1, 1966, v9, p261-64.
Films in Review. Dec 1966, v17, p662-63.
The Films of Kirk Douglas. p214-16.
Hollywood Reporter. Nov 9, 1966, p3.
The London Times. Dec 1, 1966, p18.
The London Times. Dec 8, 1966, p18.
Motion Picture Herald Product Digest. Dec 22, 1965, p10, 29.
Motion Picture Herald Product Digest. Nov 16, 1966, p629.
National Review. Jan 10, 1967, v19, p47.
New Statesman. Dec 9, 1966, v72, p885-86.
The New York Times. Nov 11, 1966, p36.
The New Yorker. Nov 5, 1966, v42, p167-68.
The New Yorker. Nov 19, 1966, v42, p183.
Newsweek. Nov 21, 1966, v68, p126-26A.
Playboy. Feb 1967, v14, p20.
The Private Eye, the Cowboy and the Very Naked Girl. p212-14.
Private Screenings. p289.
Reporter. Jan 12, 1967, v36, p56.
Saturday Review. Nov 26, 1966, v49, p59.
Senior Scholastic. Jan 20, 1967, v89, p23.
Sight and Sound. Wint 1966-67, v36, p48.
The Spectator. Dec 16, 1966, v217, p788.
Time. Nov 25, 1966, v88, p122.
Variety. Oct 26, 1966, p6.

Isadora (Also titled: The Loves of Isadora) (GB; Reisz, Karel; 1968)
America. May 17, 1969, v120, p598.
BFI/Monthly Film Bulletin. Apr 1969, v36, p71-72.
Cineaste. Sum 1969, v3, p20-21.
Commonweal. May 9, 1969, v90, p234-35.
Dance Magazine. Jun 1969, v43, p29-30.
Figures of Light. p164-68.
Film 69/70. p215-28.
Film Comment. Sep-Oct 1981, v17, 29.
Film Daily. Apr 3, 1969, p4.
Film Quarterly. Sum 1969, v22, p45-48.
Filmfacts. 1969, v12, n7, p145-50.
Films and Filming. May 1969, v15, p52-53.
Films in Review. Jun-Jul 1969, v20, p375-76.
Focus. Oct 1969, n5, p27-28.
Hollywood Reporter. Dec 19, 1968, p3.
Hudson Review. Sum 1969, v22, p295-306.
Karel Reisz (Gaston). p85-102.
Listener. Mar 13, 1969, v81, p360-61.
The London Times. Mar 8, 1968, p13.
Magill's Survey of Cinema. Series II. v3, p1182-84.
Motion Picture Herald Product Digest. Apr 9, 1968, p161-62.
Movies Into Film. p356.
The Nation. May 19, 1969, v208, p644.
The New Republic. May 17, 1969, v160, p20.
New Statesman. Mar 7, 1969, v77, p338.
The New York Times. Dec 17, 1967, p19.
The New York Times. Apr 28, 1969, p33.
The New York Times. May 4, 1969, p1.
The New Yorker. Apr 26, 1969, v45, p85-86.
Newsweek. Apr 28, 1969, v73, p98.
Saturday Review. May 3, 1969, v52, p43.
Sight and Sound. Spr 1969, v38, p94.
The Spectator. Mar 14, 1969, v222, p343.
Time. Apr 18, 1969, v93, p99.
Variety. Dec 25, 1968, p6.
The Village Voice. Jul 10, 1969, p43.

The Island (Japanese title: Hadaka no Akima; Naked Island) (JAPAN; Shindo, Kaneto; 1961)
BFI/Monthly Film Bulletin. Dec 1962, v29, p166.
Commonweal. Aug 24, 1962, v76, p474.
Dictionary of Films. p143.
Film Daily. Nov 5, 1962, p8.
Filmfacts. Sep 14, 1962, v5, p195-96.
Films in Review. Oct 1962, v13, p486.
Hollywood Reporter. Nov 13, 1962, p3.
Magill's Survey of Cinema. Foreign Language Series. v4, p1534-36.
Motion Picture Herald Product Digest. Oct 3, 1962, p667-68.
The Nation. Sep 29, 1962, v195, p185-86.
The New Republic. Jul 30, 1962, v147, p29-30.
The New York Times. Sep 11, 1962, p27.
The New Yorker. Sep 22, 1962, v38, p86-87.
Newsweek. Sep 10, 1962, v60, p104.
Saturday Review. Jul 7, 1962, v45, p16.
Time. Sep 28, 1962, v80, p103.
Variety. Nov 15, 1961, p6.
A World on Film. p386-87.

The Island (US; Ritchie, Michael; 1980)
BFI/Monthly Film Bulletin. Sep 1980, v47, p50.
Films in Review. Jun-Jul 1980, v31, p374.
Hollywood Reporter. Jun 16, 1980, p4.
The Los Angeles Times. Jun 13, 1980, SecVI, p1.
Motion Picture Herald Product Digest. Jun 25, 1980, p7.
The New Leader. Jul 14, 1980, v63, p19.
The New Republic. Jun 21, 1980, v182, p25.
New York. Jun 23, 1980, v13, p57-58.
The New York Times. Jun 13, 1980, SecIII, p16.
Newsday. Oct 24, 1980, SecII, p10.
Newsweek. Jun 16, 1980, v95, p99.
Time. Jul 7, 1980, v116, p45.
Variety. Jun 4, 1980, p20.
The Village Voice. Jun 23, 1980, p44.

Island in the Sun (US; Rossen, Robert; 1957)
BFI/Monthly Film Bulletin. Aug 1957, v24, p97.
Commonweal. Jul 5, 1957, v66, p351.
Film Daily. Jun 13, 1957, p6.
Films and Filming. Sep 1957, v3, p25.
Films in Review. Aug-Sep 1957, v8, p353-54.
From Sambo to Superspade. p209-11.
Hollywood Reporter. Jun 13, 1957, p3.
Motion Picture Herald Product Digest. Jun 15, 1957, p417.
The Nation. Jun 29, 1957, v184, p574.
The New Republic. Jul 29, 1957, v137, p21.
The New Republic. Sep 16, 1957, v137, p3.
The New York Times. Jun 13, 1957, p37.
The New Yorker. Jun 22, 1957, v33, p75.
Newsweek. Oct 7, 1957, v50, p106.
Saturday Review. Jun 29, 1957, v40, p22.
Time. Jun 24, 1957, v69, p84.
Toms, Coons, Mulattoes, Mammies & Bucks. p243-45.
Variety. Jun 19, 1957, p6.

Island of Desire (Also titled: Saturday Island) (GB; Heisler, Stuart; 1952)
BFI/Monthly Film Bulletin. Apr 1952, v19, p53.
Catholic World. Jun 1952, v175, p223.
Commonweal. Aug 15, 1952, v56, p462.
Film Daily. Aug 4, 1952, p10.
Film Heritage. Sum 1970, v5, p16-20, 27-28.
Hollywood Reporter. Jul 30, 1952, p3.
The London Times. Mar 24, 1952, p8.
Motion Picture Herald Product Digest. Aug 2, 1952, p1470-71.

The New Statesman and Nation. Mar 29, 1952, v43, p373.
The Spectator. Mar 21, 1952, v188, p366.
The Tatler. Apr 2, 1952, v204, p30.
Time. Jul 28, 1952, v60, p74.
Variety. Mar 26, 1952, p6.

The Island of Dr. Moreau (US; Taylor, Don; 1977)
American Cinematographer. Aug 1977, v58, p846-56.
BFI/Monthly Film Bulletin. Oct 1977, v44, p213.
Films in Review. Oct 1977, v28, p499.
Hollywood Reporter. Jul 12, 1977, p3.
The Los Angeles Times. Jul 13, 1977, SecIV, p1.
Motion Picture Herald Product Digest. Aug 24, 1977, p23.
New York. Aug 1, 1977, v10, p65-67.
The New York Times. May 1, 1977, SecII, p1.
The New York Times. Jul 14, 1977, p12.
Newsweek. Jul 25, 1977, v90, p57.
Science Fiction Films of the Seventies. p164-67.
Senior Scholastic. May 5, 1977, v109, p25.
Time. Jul 18, 1977, v110, p87.
Variety. Jul 13, 1977, p18.

Islands in the Stream (US; Schaffner, Franklin J.; 1977)
America. Mar 19, 1977, v136, p244.
BFI/Monthly Film Bulletin. May 1977, v44, p123.
Films in Review. Apr 1977, v28, p247.
Hemingway on Film. p135-54.
Hollywood Reporter. Feb 4, 1977, p3.
The Los Angeles Times. Mar 18, 1977, SecIV, p1.
Magill's Survey of Cinema. Series II. v3, p1189-94.
The New Republic. Mar 19, 1977, v176, p20.
The New York Times. Mar 10, 1977, SecII, p17.
The New Yorker. Mar 14, 1977, v53, p125-29.
Newsweek. Mar 14, 1977, v89, p94.
Saturday Review. Mar 19, 1977, v4, p40-41.
Time. Mar 21, 1977, v109, p89.
Variety. Mar 9, 1977, p16.

Istanbul (US; Pevney, Joseph; 1957)
America. Feb 2, 1957, v96, p512.
BFI/Monthly Film Bulletin. Jan 1957, v24, p7.
Film Daily. Jan 22, 1957, p6.
Films and Filming. Jul 1969, v15, p51.
The Films of Errol Flynn. p207-08.
Hollywood Reporter. Jan 10, 1957, p3.
Motion Picture Herald Product Digest. Jan 19, 1957, p225.
The New York Times. Jan 24, 1957, p34.
Variety. Jan 16, 1957, p18.

It Grows On Trees (US; Lubin, Arthur; 1952)
BFI/Monthly Film Bulletin. Oct 1952, v19, p143.
Film Daily. Nov 10, 1952, p6.
Hollywood Reporter. Oct 31, 1952, p3.
Motion Picture Herald Product Digest. Nov 1, 1952, p1589.
National Parent-Teacher. Dec 1952, v47, p36.
The New York Times. Nov 29, 1952, p11.
Variety. Nov 5, 1952, p6.

It Happened at the World's Fair (US; Taurog, Norman; 1963)
BFI/Monthly Film Bulletin. Jul 1963, v30, p100.
Elvis: The Films and Career of Elvis Presley. p136-39.
Film Daily. Apr 3, 1963, p3.
Filmfacts. May 23,, 1963, v6, p89-90.
Films and Filming. Jul 1963, v9, p27-28.

Hollywood Reporter. Apr 2, 1963, p3.
The New York Times. May 30, 1963, p20.
Variety. Apr 3, 1963, p16.

It Happened Here (GB; Brownlow, Kevin; Mollo, Andrew; 1964)
America. Sep 10, 1966, v115, p260-61.
American Cinematographer. Mar 1966, v47, p190-93.
BFI/Monthly Film Bulletin. Jun 1966, v33, p88.
Cineaste. 1975, v6, n4, p36-37.
Film. 1964, n41, p28-29.
Film Daily. Aug 8, 1966, p15.
Filmfacts. Oct 15, 1966, v9, p224-25.
Films and Filming. Jul 1966, v12, p8.
Films in Review. Oct 1966, v17, p521-22.
Hollywood Reporter. Aug 8, 1966, p3.
How It Happened Here: the Making of a Film. 1968.
The London Times. Feb 25, 1966, p13.
The London Times. May 12, 1966, p6.
Motion Picture Herald Product Digest. Aug 17, 1966, p579.
New Statesman. May 13, 1966, v71, p702.
New Statesman. Aug 3, 1979, v98, p172-73.
The New York Times. Aug 9, 1966, p29.
The New Yorker. Aug 13, 1966, v42, p98.
Newsweek. Aug 22, 1966, v68, p98.
Private Screenings. p274-75.
Senior Scholastic. Oct 28, 1966, v89, p26.
Sight and Sound. Wint 1964-65, v34, p38-39.
Sight and Sound. Sum 1965, v34, p138-41.
The Spectator. May 13, 1966, v216, p600.
Time. Aug 26, 1966, v88, p80.
Variety. Oct 28, 1964, p7.

It's My Turn (AUSTRALIA; Weill, Claudia; 1980)
BFI/Monthly Film Bulletin. Mar 1981, v48, p50.
Christian Science Monitor. Nov 6, 1980, p16.
Film Comment. Nov-Dec 1980, v16, p34-37.
Hollywood Reporter. Oct 22, 1980, p2.
The Los Angeles Times. Oct 24, 1980, SecVI, p1.
Motion Picture Herald Product Digest. Nov 5, 1980, p44.
The Nation. Nov 15, 1980, v231, p522.
The New Republic. Oct 18, 1980, v183, p24.
New York. Nov 10, 1980, v13, p72-73.
The New York Times. Oct 24, 1980, SecIII, p12.
Newsday. Oct 24, 1980, SecII, p7.
Newsweek. Nov 3, 1980, v96, p90.
Rolling Stone. Nov 27, 1980, p54-57.
Time. Oct 27, 1980, v116, p94.
Variety. Oct 22, 1980, p24.
The Village Voice. Oct 22, 1980, p48.

It Should Happen to You (US; Cukor, George; 1954)
America. Jan 23, 1954, v90, p426.
BFI/Monthly Film Bulletin. Apr 1954, v21, p53.
Catholic World. Mar 1954, v178, p463.
Commonweal. Feb 12, 1954, v59, p473.
Cue. Jan 23, 1954, p20.
Dictionary of Films. p161.
Film Daily. Jan 20, 1954, p10.
The Films in My Life. p104-06.
Films in Review. Mar 1954, v5, p144.
The Films of Jack Lemmon. p47-51.
Fortnight. Mar 3, 1954, v16, p29.
George Cukor (Phillips). p114-15.
Hollywood Reporter. Jan 15, 1954, p3.
Life. Feb 1, 1954, v36, p37-38.
Motion Picture Herald Product Digest. Jan 16, 1954, p2141.
National Parent-Teacher. Mar 1954, v48, p39.
The New Statesman and Nation. Feb 27, 1954, v47, p252.

The New York Times. Jan 16, 1954, p10.
The New Yorker. Jan 23, 1954, v29, p81.
On Cukor. p208-12.
Saturday Review. Feb 6, 1954, v37, p28.
Selected Film Criticism, 1951-1960. p62-63.
Senior Scholastic. Apr 7, 1954, v64, p38.
Sight and Sound. Apr-Jun 1954, v23, p200.
The Spectator. Feb 19, 1954, v192, p202.
Time. Jan 25, 1954, v63, p108.
Variety. Jan 20, 1954, p6.

It Started in Naples (US; Shavelson, Melville; 1960)
BFI/Monthly Film Bulletin. Nov 1960, v27, p151.
Commonweal. Aug 19, 1960, v72, p425.
Film Daily. Jul 6, 1960, p10.
Filmfacts. 1960, v3, p205.
Films and Filming. Oct 1960, v7, p27.
The Films of Clark Gable. p248-49.
The Films of Sophia Loren. p110-13.
Hollywood Reporter. Jul 6, 1960, p3.
McCall's. Oct 1960, v88, p6.
The New Republic. Oct 3, 1960, v143, p19-20.
The New York Times. Sep 3, 1960, p7.
The New York Times. Sep 11, 1960, SecII, p1.
The New Yorker. Sep 17, 1960, v36, p169.
Newsweek. Aug 29, 1960, v56, p85.
Time. Aug 15, 1960, v76, p62.
Variety. Jul 6, 1960, p6.
A World on Film. p53-55.

It Started in Paradise (GB; Bennett, Compton; 1952)
BFI/Monthly Film Bulletin. Dec 1952, v19, p173.
Commonweal. Sep 25, 1953, v58, p610.
Motion Picture Herald Product Digest. Aug 22, 1953, p1958.
The New Statesman and Nation. Nov 8, 1952, v44, p545.
The New York Times. Jul 25, 1953, p8.
The New Yorker. Aug 1, 1953, v29, p44.
The Spectator. Oct 31, 1952, v189, p565.
The Tatler. Nov 12, 1952, v206, p376.
Variety. Nov 12, 1952, p6.

Italiano brava Gente (Also titled: The Brave Italian People; Italians, Good People) (IT, USSR; De Santis, Giuseppe; 1963)
Commonweal. Jan 28, 1966, v83, p507-08.
Film Daily. Oct 26, 1965, p6.
Filmfacts. Mar 1, 1966, v9, p21-23.
Hollywood Reporter. Oct 11, 1965, p3.
Life. Feb 11, 1966, v60, p15.
Motion Picture Herald Product Digest. Nov 10, 1965, p402.
The Nation. Feb 21, 1966, v202, p221-22.
The New York Times. Feb 4, 1966, p20.
The New Yorker. Feb 12, 1966, v41, p140-42.
Newsweek. Nov 15, 1965, v66, p125D.
Playboy. Apr 1966, v13, p44-45.
The Private Eye, the Cowboy and the Very Naked Girl. p183-84.
Saturday Review. Oct 30, 1965, v48, p75.
Variety. Oct 14, 1964, p22.
Vogue. Mar 15, 1966, v147, p59.

It's a Big Country (US; Thorpe, Richard; Sturges, John; Hartman, Don; Weis, Don; Brown, Clarence; Wellman, William A.; Vidor, Charles; 1951)
BFI/Monthly Film Bulletin. Dec 1952, v19, p166.
Catholic World. Jan 1952, v174, p305.
Christian Century. Apr 2, 1952, v69, p415.
Commonweal. Jan 25, 1952, v55, p400.
Film Daily. Nov 20, 1951, p14.
The Films of Fredric March. p204-05.
The Films of Gary Cooper. p231-32.

The Films of Gene Kelly. p131-32.
Motion Picture Herald Product Digest. Nov 24, 1951, p1117.
The New Republic. Jan 28, 1952, v126, p22.
The New York Times. Jan 9, 1952, p25.
Newsweek. Jan 21, 1952, v39, p90.
Saturday Review. Jan 5, 1952, v35, p26.
Senior Scholastic. Jan 9, 1952, v59, p26.
Theatre Arts. Feb 1952, v36, p32.
Time. Jan 28, 1952, v59, p96.
Variety. Nov 28, 1951, p6.

It's a Mad, Mad, Mad, Mad World (US; Kramer, Stanley; 1963)
America. Nov 29, 1963, v79, p284.
BFI/Monthly Film Bulletin. Jan 1964, v31, p5.
Film Daily. Nov 7, 1963, p7.
Filmfacts. Nov 21, 1963, v6, p249-52.
Films and Filming. Jan 1964, v10, p25.
The Films of Spencer Tracy. p246-47.
The New Republic. Nov 16, 1963, v149, p26-27.
New Statesman. Dec 6, 1963, v66, p851.
The New York Times. Nov 19, 1963, p47.
The New York Times. Nov 24, 1963, SecII, p1.
The New Yorker. Nov 30, 1963, v39, p127-28.
Newsweek. Nov 18, 1963, v62, p107.
Saturday Review. Nov 9, 1963, v46, p33.
Stanley Kramer, Film Maker. p251-58.
Time. Nov 22, 1963, v82, p97.
Variety. Nov 6, 1963, p6.
The Village Voice. Dec 26, 1963, p14.

It's Always Fair Weather (US; Kelly, Gene; Donen, Stanley; 1955)
America. Sep 10, 1955, v93, p575.
BFI/Monthly Film Bulletin. Nov 1955, v22, p162.
Catholic World. Oct 1955, v181, p59.
Commonweal. Sep 2, 1955, v62, p541.
Dance Magazine. Oct 1955, v29, p15.
Film Daily. Aug 22, 1955, p6.
Films and Filming. Nov 1955, v2, n2, p18-19.
Films in Review. Oct 1955, v6, p415.
The Films of Gene Kelly. p159-62.
The Films of the Fifties. p151-52.
Hollywood Reporter. Aug 22, 1955, p3.
The Nation. Oct 1, 1955, v181, p291.
The New York Times. Sep 16, 1955, p19.
The New Yorker. Sep 24, 1955, v31, p113.
Saturday Review. Sep 3, 1955, v38, p20.
Sight and Sound. Wint 1955-56, v25, p149-50.
Stanley Donen (Casper). p84-92.
Time. Sep 5, 1955, v66, p80.
Variety. Aug 24, 1955, p6.

Ivanhoe (GB, US; Thorpe, Richard; 1952)
BFI/Monthly Film Bulletin. Aug 1952, v19, p106.
Catholic World. Aug 1952, v175, p381.
Christian Century. Oct 29, 1952, v69, p1271.
Commonweal. Aug 22, 1952, v56, p485-86.
Cue. Aug 2, 1952, p25.
Film Daily. Jun 16, 1952, p4.
Films in Review. Aug-Sep 1952, v3, p355-56.
The Films of Elizabeth Taylor. p97-100.
The Films of Robert Taylor. p124-25.
The Great Adventure Films. p166-71.
Harper's Magazine. Sep 1952, v205, p92.
Hollywood Reporter. Jun 16, 1952, p3.
Library Journal. Aug 1952, v77, p1299.
Life. Aug 11, 1952, v33, p53-54.
Magill's Survey of Cinema. Series II. v3, p1202-04.
Motion Picture Herald Product Digest. Jun 21, 1952, p1417.
The Nation. Sep 27, 1952, v175, p283.
National Parent-Teacher. Sep 1952, v47, p37.
The New York Times. Aug 1, 1952, p8.
The New Yorker. Aug 9, 1952, v28, p55.
Saturday Review. Aug 2, 1952, v35, p28.

Selected Film Criticism, 1951-1960. p63-64.
Senior Scholastic. Sep 17, 1952, v61, p37.
The Spectator. Jun 20, 1952, v188, p808.
The Tatler. Jun 25, 1952, v204, p708.
Time. Aug 4, 1952, v60, p76.
Variety. Jun 11, 1952, p6.

Ivory Hunter (Also titled: Where No
   Vultures Fly) (GB; Watt, Harry; 1951)
BFI/Monthly Film Bulletin. Dec 1951, v18,
   p374.
Catholic World. Jun 1952, v175, p223.
Christian Century. Aug 13, 1952, v69, p935.
Commonweal. Jun 20, 1952, v56, p268.
Film Daily. May 21, 1952, p6.
Films in Review. Jun-Jul 1952, v3, p289-90.
Hollywood Reporter. May 16, 1952, p3.
Motion Picture Herald Product Digest. May 24,
   1952, p1373-74.
National Parent-Teacher. Sep 1952, v47, p36.
Natural History. Jun 1952, v61, p286.
Nature Magazine. Aug 1952, v45, p343.
The New York Times. Aug 19, 1952, p19.
The New Yorker. Aug 30, 1952, v28, p53.
Newsweek. Jun 16, 1952, v39, p108.
Saturday Review. Jun 7, 1952, v35, p28.
Senior Scholastic. Oct 1, 1952, v61, p20.
Theatre Arts. Jul 1952, v36, p89.
Time. Aug 25, 1952, v66, p74.
Variety. Nov 21, 1951, p18.

Jack Frost (Russian title: Morozko; Also
   titled: Grandfather Frost) (USSR;
   Row, Alexander; 1965)
BFI/Monthly Film Bulletin. Apr 1966, v33,
   p62.
Film Daily. Oct 27, 1966, p4.
Filmfacts. Jan 15, 1967, v9, p368-69.
Hollywood Reporter. Oct 14, 1966, p8.
Motion Picture Herald Product Digest. Nov 9,
   1966, p626.
Variety. Oct 19, 1966, p20.

The Jackie Robinson Story (US; Green,
   Alfred E.; 1950)
Christian Century. Jun 21, 1950, v67, p775.
Commonweal. Jun 2, 1950, v52, p198.
Film Daily. May 16, 1950, p5.
Hollywood Reporter. May 15, 1950, p4.
Motion Picture Herald Product Digest. May 20,
   1950, p301.
The New Republic. Jun 12, 1950, v122, p23.
The New York Times. May 17, 1950, p36.
Newsweek. May 29, 1950, v35, p84.
Time. Jun 5, 1950, v55, p86.
Variety. May 17, 1950, p6.

The Jackpot (US; Lang, Walter; 1950)
BFI/Monthly Film Bulletin. Nov 1950, v17,
   p173.
Christian Century. Dec 13, 1950, v67, p1503.
Commonweal. Dec 1, 1950, v53, p198.
Film Daily. Oct 2, 1950, p4.
Films in Review. Feb 1951, v2, p42.
The Films of James Stewart. p134-37.
Hollywood Reporter. Oct 2, 1950, p3.
Library Journal. Nov 1, 1950, v75, p1915.
Life. Dec 4, 1950, v29, p109-10.
Motion Picture Herald Product Digest. Oct 7,
   1950, p509.
The New Republic. Dec 11, 1950, v123, p28.
The New York Times. Nov 23, 1950, p55.
The New Yorker. Dec 2, 1950, v26, p105.
Newsweek. Nov 13, 1950, v36, p100-02.
Senior Scholastic. Nov 29, 1950, v57, p19.
The Spectator. Oct 13, 1950, v185, p385.
Time. Nov 27, 1950, v56, p100.
Variety. Oct 4, 1950, p6.

**Jacques Brel Is Alive and Well and Living
   in Paris** (US; Heroux, Denis; 1975)
Films in Review. Apr 1975, v26, p249.
Hollywood Reporter. Feb 28, 1975, p4.
The Los Angeles Times. Apr 21, 1975, SecIV,
   p21.
Motion Picture Herald Product Digest. Mar 12,
   1975, p78.
The New York Times. Feb 25, 1975, p31.
Variety. Jan 29, 1975, p17.

Jag Ar Nyfiken: Gul *See* I Am Curious
   Yellow

The Jagged Edge (US; Marquand, Richard;
   1985)
BFI/Monthly Film Bulletin. Feb 1986, v53,
   p44.
Commonweal. Nov 15, 1985, v112, p647-48.
Film Comment. Nov/Dec 1985, v21, p26-28.
Hollywood Reporter. Sep 9, 1985, p3.
Los Angeles. Oct 1985, v30, p32.
The Los Angeles Times. Oct 4, 1985, SecVI, p1.
Maclean's. Oct 14, 1985, v98, p94.
Magill's Cinema Annual, 1986. p190-92.
The Nation. Nov 23, 1985, v241, p561-62.
New York. Oct 14, 1985, v18, p84.
The New York Times. Oct 4, 1985, SecIII, p15.
The New Yorker. Nov 4, 1985, v61, p117.
Newsweek. Dec 16, 1985, v106, p82.
Time. Dec 23, 1985, v126, p79.
Variety. Sep 11, 1985, p14.
Vogue. Dec 1985, v175, p68.
The Wall Street Journal. Oct 3, 1985, p28.

Jailhouse Rock (US; Thorpe, Richard;
   1957)
BFI/Monthly Film Bulletin. Feb 1958, v25,
   p22.
Elvis: The Films and Career of Elvis Presley.
   p109-11.
Film Daily. Oct 21, 1957, p8.
The Films of the Fifties. p237-38.
Hollywood Reporter. Oct 16, 1957, p3.
Magill's Survey of Cinema. Series II. v3, p1205-
   08.
Motion Picture Herald Product Digest. Oct 19,
   1957, p570.
The New York Times. Nov 14, 1957, p41.
Time. Nov 4, 1957, v70, p111.
Variety. Oct 16, 1957, p6.

The James Dean Story (US; George, G.
   W.; Altman, Robert; 1957)
BFI/Monthly Film Bulletin. Nov 1957, v24,
   p142-43.
Film Daily. Jul 26, 1957, p6.
Films and Filming. Nov 1957, v4, p23-24.
Hollywood Reporter. Jul 24, 1957, p3.
Motion Picture Herald Product Digest. Jul 27,
   1957, p465.
The New York Times. Oct 19, 1957, p16.
Newsweek. Sep 9, 1957, v50, p111.
*Robert Altman: A Guide to References and
   Resources.* p109-11.
Saturday Review. Aug 3, 1957, v40, p20.
Sight and Sound. Aut 1957, v27, p93.
Time. Sep 9, 1957, v70, p112.

James Joyce's Women (GB; Pearce,
   Michael; 1985)
Hollywood Reporter. Oct 3, 1985, p3.
The Los Angeles Times. Sep 30, 1985, SecVI,
   p9.
Magill's Cinema Annual, 1986. p193-97.
The New Republic. Oct 14, 1985, v193, p27.
The New York Times. Sep 12, 1985, SecIII, p21.
Variety. Mar 20, 1985, p13.

Japanese War Bride (US; Vidor, King;
   1952)
BFI/Monthly Film Bulletin. Apr 1952, v19,
   p51.
Film Daily. Jan 21, 1952, p7.
Hollywood Reporter. Jan 7, 1952, p3.
Motion Picture Herald Product Digest. Jan 12,
   1952, p1185-86.
The New York Times. Jan 30, 1952, p22.
Newsweek. Feb 11, 1952, v39, p90.
Time. Feb 4, 1952, v59, p74.
Variety. Jan 9, 1952, p6.

Jardin de las Delicias, El *See* Garden of
   Delights

Jason and the Argonauts (GB; Chaffey,
   Don; 1963)
America. Aug 10, 1963, v109, p143.
BFI/Monthly Film Bulletin. Sep 1963, v30,
   p131.
Film Daily. Jun 5, 1963, p7.
Hollywood Reporter. Jun 5, 1963, p3.
The New York Times. Aug 8, 1963, p19.
The New Yorker. Aug 24, 1963, v39, p65.
Newsweek. Jul 8, 1963, v62, p78B.
Photoplay. Jul 1963, v64, p15.
Time. Jul 19, 1963, v82, p78.
Variety. Jun 5, 1963, p6.

Jaws (US; Spielberg, Steven; 1975)
American Cinematographer. Mar 1975, v56,
   p274-78.
BFI/Monthly Film Bulletin. Dec 1975, v42,
   p263.
Christian Century. Oct 1, 1975, v92, p858-60.
Commonweal. Jun 20, 1975, v102, p210-11.
Films in Review. Aug-Sep 1975, v26, p436.
The Films of the Seventies. p121-23.
Hollywood Reporter. Jun 12, 1975, p3.
Jaws. 1975.
The Jaws Log. 1975.
The Los Angeles Times. Jun 20, 1975, SecIV,
   p1.
Magill's Survey of Cinema. Series I. v2, p863-
   65.
Motion Picture Herald Product Digest. Jun 11,
   1975, p2.
The Nation. Aug 30, 1975, v221, p154.
The New Republic. Jul 26, 1975, v173, p20.
The New York Times. Jun 21, 1975, p19.
The New York Times. Jun 29, 1975, SecII, p15.
The New York Times. Aug 24, 1975, SecII, p1.
The New Yorker. Jul 7, 1975, v51, p78.
The New Yorker. Jun 23, 1975, v85, p54.
The New Yorker. Jul 28, 1975, v86, p16-17.
*On Location on Martha's Vineyard: The
   Making of the Movie Jaws.* 1975.
Saturday Review. Jul 12, 1975, v2, p50-51.
Sports Illustrated. Jun 30, 1975, v42, p6.
The Steven Spielberg Story. p40-53.
Time. Jun 23, 1975, v105, p42-44.
Time. Jul 28, 1975, v106, p47.
Variety. Jun 18, 1975, p16.

Jaws 2 (Also titled: Jaws II) (US; Szwarc,
   Jeannot; 1978)
BFI/Monthly Film Bulletin. Dec 1978, v45,
   p243.
Commonweal. Aug 4, 1978, v105, p499-500.
Encore. Jul 10, 1978, v7, p30.
Films in Review. Aug-Sep 1978, v29, p437.
The Films of the Seventies. p207-09.
Hollywood Reporter. Jun 5, 1978, p3.
The Jaws II Log. 1978.
The Los Angeles Times. Jun 16, 1978, SecIV,
   p1.
Maclean's. Jul 10, 1978, v91, p59.
Motion Picture Herald Product Digest. Jun 28,
   1978, p6.

National Review. Jul 21, 1978, v30, p908-09.
The New Republic. Jul 1, 1978, v179, p18.
New York. Jul 3, 1978, v11, p67-68.
The New York Times. Jun 16, 1978, SecIII, p10.
The New Yorker. Jun 26, 1978, v54, p90.
Newsweek. Jun 19, 1978, v91, p74.
Time. Jun 19, 1978, v111, p78-79.
Variety. Jun 7, 1978, p25.

The Jazz Singer (US; Fleischer, Richard; 1980)
BFI/Monthly Film Bulletin. Feb 1981, v48, p26.
Films in Review. Mar 1981, v32, p186.
Hollywood Reporter. Dec 8, 1980, p3.
The Los Angeles Times. Dec 18, 1980, SecVI, p4.
Motion Picture Herald Product Digest. Dec 31, 1980, p60.
The New York Times. Dec 19, 1980, SecIII, p18.
Newsweek. Jan 5, 1981, v97, p55.
Time. Jan 5, 1981, v117, p85.
Time. Jan 26, 1981, v117, p71.
Variety. Dec 10, 1980, p32.
The Village Voice. Dec 24, 1980, p1.
The Village Voice. Jan 7, 1981, p1.
Vogue. Dec 1980, v170, p42.

Je Vous Salue, Marie *See* Hail, Mary

Jeanne Eagels (US; Sidney, George; 1957)
America. Sep 28, 1957, v97, p688.
BFI/Monthly Film Bulletin. Oct 1957, v24, p122-23.
Commonweal. Oct 4, 1957, v67, p19.
Film Daily. Jul 24, 1957, p10.
Films and Filming. Oct 1957, v4, p25.
Films in Review. Oct 1957, v8, p408-12.
Hollywood Reporter. Jul 19, 1957, p3.
Motion Picture Herald Product Digest. Jul 20, 1957, p457-58.
The New York Times. Aug 31, 1957, p19.
The New Yorker. Sep 7, 1957, v33, p74.
Newsweek. Aug 12, 1957, v50, p93.
Saturday Review. Aug 17, 1957, v40, p25.
Variety. Jul 24, 1957, p6.

Jeremiah Johnson (US; Pollack, Sydney; 1972)
Commonweal. Feb 9, 1973, v97, p423.
Filmfacts. 1972, v15, n23, p561.
Films in Review. Jan 1973, v24, p53.
The Films of Robert Redford. p164-74.
Holiday. Nov 1972, v52, p22-23.
Hollywood Reporter. Dec 13, 1972, p3.
Magill's Survey of Cinema. Series II. v3, p1209-13.
The New Republic. Jan 6, 1973, v168, p24.
The New York Times. May 9, 1972, p34.
The New York Times. Dec 22, 1972, p23.
The New Yorker. Dec 30, 1972, v48, p50-51.
Newsweek. Jan 1, 1973, v81, p56.
Reeling. p143-44.
Senior Scholastic. Jan 8, 1973, v101, p24.
Sydney Pollack (Taylor). p51-55, 103-06.
Time. Jan 8, 1973, v101, p54.
Variety. May 10, 1972, p21.
Vogue. Feb 1973, v161, p66.

The Jerk (US; Reiner, Carl; 1979)
BFI/Monthly Film Bulletin. Apr 1980, v47, p68-69.
Hollywood Reporter. Dec 13, 1979, p3.
The Los Angeles Times. Dec 14, 1979, SecIV, p1.
Motion Picture Herald Product Digest. Jan 9, 1980, p62.
The New York Times. Dec 14, 1979, SecIII, p12.

The New Yorker. Dec 17, 1979, v55, p168.
Newsweek. Dec 17, 1979, v94, p112.
Variety. Dec 12, 1979, p23.

Jessica (French title: Sage-Femme, Le; Cure et le Bon Dieu, La) (FR, IT; Negulesco, Jean; 1961)
BFI/Monthly Film Bulletin. Jul 1962, v29, p92.
Chevalier: The Films and Career of Maurice Chevalier. p203-16.
Commonweal. May 4, 1962, v76, p153.
Film Daily. Mar 26, 1962, p4.
Filmfacts. Jun 1, 1962, v5, p105-06.
Films in Review. May 1962, v13, p298-99.
Hollywood Reporter. Mar 19, 1962, v169, p3.
Motion Picture Herald Product Digest. Apr 18, 1962, p524.
The New York Times. Apr 20, 1962, p20.
The New Yorker. May 19, 1962, v38, p182.
Time. Apr 20, 1962, v79, p97-98.
Variety. Mar 21, 1962, p6.

Jesus Christ Superstar (US; Jewison, Norman; 1973)
America. Sep 1, 1973, v129, p132.
The Ancient World in the Cinema. p218-20.
Christian Century. Jul 27, 1973, v90, p693-94.
Christian Century. Sep 5, 1973, v90, p859.
Christianity Today. Oct 12, 1973, v18, p47.
Commentary. Sep 1973, v56, p76-77.
Esquire. Oct 1973, v80, p44.
Films in Review. Aug-Sep 1973, v24, n7, p438.
Films In Review. Oct 1973, v24, p488-91.
Films In Review. Aug-Sep 1973, v24, p438-39.
Hollywood Reporter. Jun 25, 1973, p3.
Mademoiselle. Jul 1973, v77, p146-47.
Magill's Survey of Cinema. Series II. v3, p1216-19.
The Musical: From Broadway to Hollywood. p155-66.
National Review. Aug 17, 1973, v25, p898.
The New Republic. Jul 28, 1973, v169, p22.
The New York Times. Aug 8, 1973, v28, p1.
Newsweek. Jul 9, 1973, v82, p82.
PTA Magazine. Oct 1973, v68, p8.
Senior Scholastic. Dec 13, 1973, v103, p28-29.
Seventeen. Jul 1973, v32, p102-03.
Time. Jul 30, 1973, v102, p72.
Variety. Jun 27, 1973, p20.

Jet Pilot (US; Sternberg, Josef von, et. al.; 1957)
BFI/Monthly Film Bulletin. Dec 1957, v24, p147.
Commonweal. Oct 11, 1957, v67, p49.
The Complete Films of John Wayne. p213-15.
Film Daily. Sep 23, 1957, p9.
The Films in My Life. p74-76.
Hollywood Reporter. Sep 19, 1957, p3.
Motion Picture Herald Product Digest. Sep 21, 1957, p538.
The New York Times. Oct 5, 1957, p8.
Newsweek. Sep 23, 1957, v50, p115.
Saturday Review. Oct 12, 1957, v40, p31.
Variety. Sep 25, 1957, p6.

Jetée, La (Also titled: The Pier) (FR; Marker, Chris; 1964)
Dictionary of Films. p164.
Film Quarterly. Wint 1965-66, v19, p50-52.
Film Society Review. Jan 1967, p18-20.
Literature/Film Quarterly. Jan 1979, v7, p11-15.
Movie. Jul-Aug 1963, n11, p25.
New Statesman. Mar 18, 1966, v71, p400-01.
The New York Times. Jan 16, 1967, p27.
Sight and Sound. Aut 1984, v53, p284-88.
Sight and Sound. Aut 1966, v35, p166-68.

Jeu de Massacre (Also titled: The Killing Game; Comic Strip Hero) (FR; Jessua, Alain; 1967)
BFI/Monthly Film Bulletin. Feb 1968, v35, p21-22.
Film Comment. Mar-Apr 1973, v9, p44-45.
Film Daily. Aug 27, 1968, p6.
Hollywood Reporter. Aug 26, 1967, p3.
The London Times. May 9, 1967, p8.
The New Republic. Sep 14, 1968, v159, p22.
The New York Times. Aug 27, 1968, p36.
On Film. p336-37.
Sight and Sound. Wint 1967-68, v37, p40.
Variety. May 3, 1967, p24.

Jeune Folle, La *See* Desperate Decision

Jeux Interdits, Les *See* Forbidden Games

Jewel of the Nile (US; Teague, Lewis; 1985)
BFI/Monthly Film Bulletin. May 1986, v53, p147.
Film Comment. Nov-Dec 1985, v21, p26-28.
The Los Angeles Times. Jun 23, 1985, Calendar, p24.
The Los Angeles Times. Dec 11, 1985, SecVI, p1.
Maclean's. Dec 23, 1985, v98, p48.
The New York Times. Dec 11, 1985, SecIII, p22.
Newsweek. Dec 16, 1985, v106, p82.
Time. Dec 23, 1985, v126, p79.
Variety. Dec 11, 1985, p17.

Jigokumon *See* Gate of Hell

Jim Thorpe, All American (Also titled: Man of Bronze) (US; Curtiz, Michael; 1951)
BFI/Monthly Film Bulletin. Jul 1952, v19, p95.
Burt Lancaster: A Pictorial Treasury of His Films. p60-62.
Burt Lancaster: The Man and His Movies. p48-52.
Christian Century. Oct 24, 1951, v68, p1239.
Commonweal. Sep 14, 1951, v54, p550.
Film Daily. Jun 18, 1951, p22.
Hollywood Reporter. Jun 14, 1951, p3.
Motion Picture Herald Product Digest. Jun 16, 1951, p885.
The New Statesman and Nation. May 24, 1952, v43, p615.
The New York Times. Aug 25, 1951, p7.
Newsweek. Sep 3, 1951, v38, p73.
Senior Scholastic. Oct 3, 1951, v59, p30.
Time. Sep 24, 1951, v58, p108.
Variety. Jun 20, 1951, p6.

Jiouchi *See* Rebellion

Jio-uchi *See* Rebellion

Joe (US; Avildsen, John G.; 1970)
BFI/Monthly Film Bulletin. Apr 1971, v38, p75-76.
Films and Filming. Jun 1971, v17, p78.
Films in Review. Aug-Sep 1970, v21, p441-42.
Hollywood Reporter. Jul 16, 1970, p3.
The New Republic. Aug 22, 1970, v163, p33.
The New York Times. Jul 16, 1970, p40.
The New York Times. Aug 2, 1970, SecII, p1.
The New Yorker. Aug 15, 1970, v46, p65-66.
Newsweek. Jul 27, 1970, v76, p71.
Saturday Review. Sep 5, 1970, v53, p35.
Time. Jul 27, 1970, v96, p68.
Variety. Jul 15, 1970, p14.

Joe Butterfly (US; Hibbs, Jesse; 1957)
America. Jun 1, 1957, v97, p292.
BFI/Monthly Film Bulletin. Jul 1957, v38, p88.
Commonweal. Jun 7, 1957, v66, p257.
Film Daily. Apr 24, 1957, p6.
Hollywood Reporter. Apr 23, 1957, p3.

Motion Picture Herald Product Digest. May 4, 1957, p361.
The New York Times. May 30, 1957, p23 p56.
Variety. Apr 24, 1957, p6.

Joe Cocker/Mad Dogs & Englishmen (Also titled: Mad Dogs & Englishmen) (US; Adidge, Pierre; 1971)
BFI/Monthly Film Bulletin. Nov 1971, v38, p223.
Film Quarterly. Sum 1971, v24, p63-64.
Filmfacts. 1971, v14, p113.
Films in Review. Jun-Jul 1971, v22, p369-71.
Hollywood Reporter. Mar 19, 1971, p3.
The New York Times. Mar 30, 1971, p25.
Saturday Review. May 1, 1971, v54, p44.
Time. Apr 19, 1971, v97, p70.
Variety. Feb 3, 1971, p26.

John F. Kennedy: Years of Lightning, Day of Drums (Also titled: Years of Lightning, Day of Drums) (US; Herschensohn, Bruce; 1966)
America. Apr 23, 1966, v114, p602-03.
Big Screen, Little Screen. p346-47.
Christian Century. May 18, 1966, v83, p655-56.
Commonweal. Apr 22, 1966, v84, p154.
Film Comment. Fall-Wint 1967, v4, p22-23, 33-53.
Film Daily. Mar 22, 1966, p7.
Filmfacts. Jun 1, 1966, v9, p85-87.
Films and Filming. Nov 1966, v13, p13, 16.
Films in Review. Mar 1966, v17, p186-87.
Life. Apr 15, 1966, v60, p14.
The London Times. Jun 23, 1966, p7.
Motion Picture Herald Product Digest. Apr 13, 1966, p499.
National Review. Jul 12, 1966, v18, p694-66.
New Statesman. Jul 1, 1966, v72, p27.
The New York Times. Apr 11, 1966, p41.
The New Yorker. Apr 16, 1966, v42, p121.
Newsweek. Apr 18, 1966, v67, p109-10.
Second Sight. p66-70.
Senior Scholastic. May 6, 1966, v88, p37.
Variety. Jun 23, 1965, p26.
Vogue. Mar 15, 1966, v147, p59.

Johnny Dangerously (US; Heckerling, Amy; 1984)
BFI/Monthly Film Bulletin. Jun 1985, v52, p185.
Hollywood Reporter. Dec 19, 1984, p3.
The Los Angeles Times. Dec 21, 1984, SecVI, p4.
Maclean's. Jan 7, 1985, v98, p71.
The New York Times. Dec 21, 1985, SecIII, p25.
Newsweek. Jan 14, 1985, v105, p53.
Time. Jan 14, 1985, v125, p66.
Variety. Dec 19, 1984, p19.

Johnny Dark (US; Sherman, George; 1954)
BFI/Monthly Film Bulletin. Sep 1954, v21, p133-34.
Farm Journal. Aug 1954, v78, p101.
Film Daily. Jun 2, 1954, p6.
Hollywood Reporter. Jun 1, 1954, p4.
Motion Picture Herald Product Digest. Jun 5, 1954, p17.
The New York Times. Jun 26, 1954, p7.
Time. Jul 26, 1954, v64, p78.
Tony Curtis: The Man and His Movies. p48-49.
Variety. Jun 2, 1954, p6.

Johnny Got His Gun (US; Trumbo, Dalton; 1971)
America. Sep 4, 1971, v125, p126-27.
BFI/Monthly Film Bulletin. Nov 1972, v39, p236.
Commonweal. Oct 15, 1971, v95, p62.
Film Society Review. Oct 1971, v7, p45.

Filmfacts. 1971, v14, p582-85.
Films and Filming. Dec 1972, v19, p46-48.
Hollywood Reporter. Jul 15, 1971, p3.
The New York Times. Aug 5, 1971, p25.
The New Yorker. Aug 7, 1971, v47, p65-67.
Newsweek. Aug 9, 1971, v78, p70.
Saturday Review. Aug 28, 1971, v54, p48.
Time. Aug 30, 1971, v98, p52.
Variety. May 19, 1971, p17.

Johnny Guitar (US; Ray, Nicholas; 1954)
America. Jun 5, 1954, v91, p287.
American Film. Jul-Aug 1983, v8, p66-67.
BFI/Monthly Film Bulletin. Jul 1954, v21, p100.
Catholic World. Jun 1954, v179, p221.
Cinema, the Magic Vehicle. v2, p195-97.
Commonweal. Jun 18, 1954, v60, p270.
Cue. Jun 5, 1954, p15.
Cult Movies. p171-75.
Dictionary of Films. p166.
Film Daily. May 5, 1954, p7.
Film Reader. 1982, n5, p95-108.
The Films in My Life. p141-43.
The Films of Joan Crawford. p188-91.
The Films of the Fifties. p127-30.
Fortnight. May 19, 1954, v16, p40.
The Great Western Pictures. p165-66.
Hollywood Reporter. May 5, 1954, p3.
The International Dictionary of Films and Filmmakers. v1, p225-26.
Library Journal. Jun 1, 1954, v79, p1048.
The London Times. Jun 7, 1954, p3.
Magill's Survey of Cinema. Series I. v2, p874-76.
The Making of the Great Westerns. p237-48.
Medium. Aug 1980, v10, p33-35.
Motion Picture Herald Product Digest. May 8, 1954, p2285.
The New Statesman and Nation. Jun 12, 1954, v47, p756.
The New York Times. May 28, 1954, p19.
The New Yorker. Jun 5, 1954, v30, p63.
Newsweek. Jun 14, 1954, v43, p104.
Nicholas Ray: A Guide to References and Resources. p75-79.
Nicholas Ray (Kreidl). p43-59.
Selected Film Criticism, 1951-1960. p64-65.
The Spectator. Jun 4, 1954, v192, p678.
The Tatler. Jun 16, 1954, v212, p638.
Time. Jun 14, 1954, v63, p106.
Variety. May 5, 1954, p6.
The Velvet Light Trap. Spr 1974, n12, p19-25.
The Village Voice. Jan 13, 1982, v27, p52.

Johnny One-Eye (US; Florey, Robert; 1950)
BFI/Monthly Film Bulletin. Oct 1950, v17, p155.
Film Daily. Jun 21, 1950, p8.
Hollywood Reporter. Jun 14, 1950, p4.
Library Journal. May 1, 1950, v75, p787.
Motion Picture Herald Product Digest. Jun 24, 1950, p354.
The New York Times. Nov 17, 1950, p31.
Variety. Jun 14, 1950, p8.

A Joke of Destiny (Italian title: Scherzo del Destino Agguato Dietro L'Angelo Come Un Brigante Di Strada, Un) (IT; Wertmuller, Lina; 1983)
Film Journal. Nov 1984, v87, p20.
Film Journal. Oct 1984, v87, p18-19.
Films in Review. Nov 1984, v35, p566-67.
The Los Angeles Times. Oct 27, 1984, SecV, p1.
Magill's Cinema Annual, 1985. p259-63.
The New York Times. Sep 12, 1984, SecIII, p21.
Philadelphia Magazine. Nov 1984, v75, p83.
Variety. Sep 12, 1984, p20.
The Village Voice. Sep 25, 1984, p70.

The Joker Is Wild (US; Vidor, Charles; 1957)
America. Sep 28, 1957, v97, p688.
BFI/Monthly Film Bulletin. Dec 1957, v24, p151.
Commonweal. Oct 4, 1957, v67, p20.
Film Daily. Aug 30, 1957, p6.
The Films of Frank Sinatra. p128-35.
Hollywood Reporter. Aug 28, 1957, p3.
Motion Picture Herald Product Digest. Aug 31, 1957, p26.
The New York Times. Sep 27, 1957, p16.
The New Yorker. Oct 5, 1957, v33, p146.
Newsweek. Sep 30, 1957, v50, p126.
Time. Sep 30, 1957, v70, p98.
Variety. Aug 28, 1957, p6.

Joli Mai, Le (Also titled: The Lovely May) (FR; Marker, Chris; 1963)
BFI/Monthly Film Bulletin. Apr 1964, v31, p51-52.
Dictionary of Films. p166-67.
The Documentary Tradition. p395-97.
Film Quarterly. Sum 1964, v17, p165-66.
Film Society Review. Jan 1967, p15-18.
Filmfacts. Sep 1, 1966, v9, p173-74.
Films and Filming. May 1964, v10, p22.
The International Dictionary of Films and Filmmakers. v1, p227-28.
International Film Guide. 1964, v1, p59-60.
The London Times. Sep 11, 1963, p7.
The London Times. Mar 5, 1964, p5.
Movie. Jul-Aug 1963, n11, p25-26.
The New York Times. Jun 10, 1966, p54.
Sight and Sound. Spr 1964, v33, p93-94.
Sight and Sound. Aut 1966, v35, p165-66.
Variety. May 15, 1963, p21.

Jonah Who Will Be in the Year 2000 (French title: Jonas Qui Aura 25 Ans en l'an 2000) (SWITZ, FR; Tanner, Alain; 1976)
Cineaste. 1977, n4, v7, p24-25.
Film Quarterly. 1977, v30, n3, p36-42.
Hollywood Reporter. Oct 7, 1976, p2.
Independent Film Journal. Nov 26, 1976, v78, p11.
Jump Cut. 1977, n15, p1, 8-9.
Magill's Survey of Cinema. Foreign Language Films. v4, p1579-83.
The Nation. Oct 23, 1976, v223, p411.
New York. Nov 15, 1976, v9, p117-19.
The New York Times. Oct 2, 1976, p15.
The New York Times. Oct 24, 1976, SecII, p15.
The New Yorker. Oct 18, 1976, v52, p75-77.
A Possible Cinema: The Films of Alain Tanner. p125-50.
Take One. 1977, v5, n8, p13-14.
The Thousand Eyes Magazine. Jan 1977, v2, p21.
Time. Oct 25, 1976, v108, p81.
Variety. Aug 25, 1976, p22.
The Village Voice. Nov 1, 1976, p52-53.
When the Lights Go Down. p179-83.

Joseph Andrews (GB; Richardson, Tony; 1977)
America. May 6, 1978, v138, p366.
BFI/Monthly Film Bulletin. Apr 1977, v44, p74.
The English Novel and the Movies. p28-35.
Films and Filming. Apr 1977, v23, p29-30.
Films in Review. Nov 1977, v28, p568.
Hollywood Reporter. Mar 10, 1977, p3.
The Los Angeles Times. Nov 23, 1977, SecIV, p1.
Motion Picture Herald Product Digest. Aug 24, 1977, p21.
The New Republic. May 13, 1978, v178, p27.
The New York Times. Apr 14, 1978, SecIII, p9.

The New York Times. Jun 11, 1978, SecII, p21.
The New Yorker. Apr 24, 1978, v54, p145-46.
Theatre Crafts. Mar 1978, v12, p32-33.
Variety. Mar 16, 1978, p22.

Joshua Then, and Now (CAN; Kotcheff, Ted; 1985)
Hollywood Reporter. May 21, 1985, p3.
The Los Angeles Times. Oct 16, 1985, SecVI, p1.
Maclean's. May 20, 1985, v98, p63.
Maclean's. Sep 23, 1985, v98, p44-50.
Magill's Cinema Annual, 1986. p198-202.
The New York Times. Sep 20, 1985, SecII, p21.
Variety. May 27, 1985, p18.

Jour de Fete (Also titled: The Village Fair; The Big Day) (FR; Tati, Jacques; 1949)
BFI/Monthly Film Bulletin. Apr-May 1950, v17, p59.
Cinema, the Magic Vehicle. v2, p459-60.
Dictionary of Films. p167.
Film Criticism. n2, 1983, v7, p31-44.
Films and Filming. May 1962, v8, p19-20, 49-53.
Films and Filming. Jun 1982, v27, p39-40.
The Films of Jacques Tati. p37-39.
Illustrated London News. Apr 29, 1950, v216, p672.
Jacques Tati: A Guide to References and Resources. p62-63.
Jacues Tati (Gilliatt). p6-11.
Kiss Kiss Bang Bang. p361.
Magill's Survey of Cinema. Foreign Language Films. v4, p1584-88.
The New Statesman and Nation. Jul 2, 1982, v104, p26.
The New York Times. Feb 20, 1952, p26.
The New Yorker. Mar 1, 1952, v28, p64.
Rotha on Film. p159-60.
Saturday Review. May 19, 1956, v39, p50.
Shots in the Dark. p175-79.
Sight and Sound. Jun 1950, v19, p165-66.
Time. Mar 31, 1952, v59, p102.
Variety. May 25, 1949, p18.

Journal d'un Cure de Campagne, Le (Also titled: Diary of a Country Priest) (FR; Bresson, Robert; 1950)
America. Apr 17, 1954, v91, p80.
BFI/Monthly Film Bulletin. Jun 1953, v20, p85.
Catholic World. Jun 1954, v179, p221.
Cinema Journal. Fall 1969, v9, p13-22.
Cinema, the Magic Vehicle. v2, p39-42.
Commonweal. Apr 23, 1954, v60, p69.
Dictionary of Films. p167.
Film. Oct 1964, n1, p21-22.
Film Criticism and Caricatures, 1943-1953. p154-55.
Film Culture. 1959, n20, p44-52.
Film Daily. Apr 14, 1954, p6.
Film Forum. Feb 1952, n5, p3.
Film Heritage. n3, 1974, v9, p12-16.
Film Journal. Aug 1960, n16, p79-82.
Films and Filming. Dec 1966, v13, p28-32.
Films in Review. May 1953, v4, p239-40.
The Films of Robert Bresson. p42-66.
Great Film Directors. p97-105.
The Great French Films. p131-34.
The International Dictionary of Films and Filmmakers. v1, p230-31.
Kiss Kiss Bang Bang. p321-22.
Library Journal. May 1, 1954, v79, p852.
Literature/Film Quarterly. n1, 1976, v4, p39-45.
The London Times. Jan 1, 1952, p8.
Magill's Survey of Cinema. Foreign Language Films. v2, p820-25.
Modern European Filmmakers and the Art of Adaptation. p20-37.

National Parent-Teacher. Jun 1954, v48, p39.
The New Statesman and Nation. Apr 25, 1953, v45, p486.
The New York Times. Apr 6, 1954, p35.
The New York Times. May 2, 1954, p1.
The New Yorker. Apr 17, 1954, v30, p113.
Robert Bresson: A Guide to References and Resources. p44-50.
Saturday Review. Mar 27, 1954, v37, p25.
The Screenplay as Literature. p87-95.
Sequence. Jan 1951, n13, p6-8.
Sight and Sound. Nov-Dec 1951, v21, p76.
Sight and Sound. Jul-Sep 1953, v23, p35-39.
The Spectator. Apr 24, 1953, v190, p513.
The Tatler. Apr 29, 1953, v208, p258.
Time. May 10, 1954, v63, p108.
Transcendental Style in Film. p70-76, 78-80.
Variety. Sep 12, 1951, p18.
What Is Cinema? v1, p125-43.
Yale French Studies. 1980, n60, p233-40.

Journal d'une Femme de Chambre, Le *See* The Diary of a Chambermaid

The Journey of Natty Gann (US; Kayan, Jeremy; 1985)
BFI/Monthly Film Bulletin. Feb 1986, v53, p45.
The Chicago Tribune. Oct 15, 1985, SecV, p2.
Hollywood Reporter. Sep 10, 1985, p3.
The Los Angeles Times. Oct 11, 1985, SecVI, p1.
Magill's Cinema Annual, 1986. p203-07.
Senior Scholastic Update. Oct 4, 1985, v118, p39.
Time. Nov 25, 1985, v126, p121.
Variety. Sep 18, 1985, p18.

Joy House (French title: Félins, Les; Also titled: The Love Cage; The Felines) (FR; Clément, René; 1964)
BFI/Monthly Film Bulletin. Feb 1966, v33, p23.
Christian Science Monitor (Western edition). Nov 9, 1964, p6.
Film Daily. Nov 2, 1964, p4B.
Film Quarterly. Spr 1965, v8, p60.
Filmfacts. Apr 2, 1965, v8, p41-42.
Films and Filming. Mar 1966, v12, p10-11.
Hollywood Reporter. Nov 2, 1964, p4.
The London Times. Feb 10, 1966, p16.
Motion Picture Herald Product Digest. Nov 11, 1964, p162.
New Statesman. Feb 11, 1966, v71, p201.
The New York Times. Feb 18, 1965, p29.
The New Yorker. Feb 27, 1965, v41, p114.
Time. Feb 26, 1965, v85, p100.
Variety. Jun 24, 1964, p20.
Vogue. Oct 1, 1964, v144, p110.

Joy In the Morning (US; Segal, Alex; 1965)
Commonweal. Jun 11, 1965, v82, p385.
Film Daily. Mar 11, 1965, p10.
Films in Review. May 1965, v16, p315-16.
Hollywood Reporter. Mar 10, 1965, p3.
The London Times. Feb 24, 1965, p16.
Motion Picture Herald Product Digest. Mar 17, 1965, p249.
The New York Times. Jun 10, 1965, p38.
Saturday Review. May 8, 1965, v48, p51.
Time. Jun 11, 1965, v85, p108.
Variety. Mar 10, 1965, p6.

Jubilee Trail (US; Kane, Joseph; 1954)
BFI/Monthly Film Bulletin. Apr 1954, v21, p57.
Catholic World. Mar 1954, v178, p461.
Film Daily. Jan 20, 1954, p10.
The Great Western Pictures. p168-69.
Hollywood Reporter. Jan 15, 1954, p3.
Library Journal. Feb 15, 1954, v79, p314.

Motion Picture Herald Product Digest. Jan 23, 1954, p2158.
National Parent-Teacher. Mar 1954, v48, p39.
The New York Times. May 1, 1954, p13.
Variety. Jan 20, 1954, p6.

Judex (FR, IT; Franju, Georges; 1963)
Christian Science Monitor (Western edition). May 13, 1966, p6.
Christian Science Monitor (Western edition). Jul 25, 1964, p4.
Cinema. Dec-Jan 1964-65, v2, p50.
Confessions of a Cultist. p245.
Dictionary of Films. p169.
Film Daily. Apr 25, 1966, p3.
Film Quarterly. Spr 1967, v20, p61-62.
Film Society Review. Dec 1967, p15-16.
Filmfacts. Jul 1, 1966, v9, p114-16.
Films and Filming. Jul 1967, v13, p23-24.
Franju (Durgnat). p105-23.
The London Times. May 4, 1967, p8.
Magill's Survey of Cinema. Foreign Language Films. v4, p1603-09.
Motion Picture Herald Product Digest. Apr 27, 1966, p511.
Movie. Fall 1965, n14, p36-38.
The New York Times. Apr 26, 1966, p55.
Newsweek. May 9, 1966, v67, p98B.
Saint Cinema: Selected Writings, 1929-1970. p267-71.
Saturday Review. May 7, 1966, v49, p100.
Sight and Sound. Sum 1967, v36, p144.
Time. May 13, 1966, v87, p103.
Variety. Dec 18, 1963, p17.

Judgment at Nuremberg (US; Kramer, Stanley; 1961)
America. Jan 30, 1962, v106, p542-43.
BFI/Monthly Film Bulletin. Feb 1962, v29, p19.
Burt Lancaster: A Pictorial Treasury of His Films. p111-13.
Burt Lancaster: The Man and His Movies. p90.
Catholic World. Apr 1962, v195, p63-64.
Christian Century. Mar 14, 1962, v79, p332-33.
Commentary. Jan 1962, v33, p56-63.
Commonweal. Dec 15, 1961, v75, p318-19.
Esquire. Jan 1962, v57, p26.
Film. Spr 1962, n13, p13.
Film Daily. Oct 18, 1961, p6.
Film Quarterly. Wint 1961-62, v15, p51-53.
Filmfacts. Dec 22, 1961, v4, p299-302.
Films and Filming. Jan 1962, v8, p30.
Films in Review. Jan 1961, v8, p39-40.
The Films of Marlene Dietrich. p210-13.
The Films of Montgomery Clift. p179-202.
The Films of Spencer Tracy. p242-45.
Judy: The Films and Career of Judy Garland. p170-73.
Life. Dec 15, 1961, v51, p121-23.
Magill's Survey of Cinema. Series II. v3, p1239-42.
The Nation. Jan 6, 1962, v194, p19-20.
National Review. Apr 10, 1962, v12, p254.
The New Republic. Dec 11, 1961, v145, p26.
The New York Times. Dec 20, 1961, v36.
Newsweek. Dec 25, 1961, v58, p72.
Saturday Review. Dec 2, 1961, v44, p43-45.
Sight and Sound. Wint 1961-62, v31, p41.
Stanley Kramer, Film Maker. p225-36.
Time. Dec 15, 1961, v78, p5.
Variety. Oct 18, 1961, p6.

Judith (US, ISR; Mann, Daniel; 1965)
BFI/Monthly Film Bulletin. Apr 1966, v33, p61.
Christian Science Monitor (Western edition). Feb 18, 1966, p4.
Film Daily. Jan 13, 1966, p4.
Filmfacts. Feb 1, 1966, v9, p6-8.

Films and Filming. Mar 1966, v12, p6, 10.
Films in Review. Feb 1966, v17, p115.
The Films of Sophia Loren. p178-82.
Hollywood Reporter. Jan 12, 1966, p3.
The London Times. Feb 17, 1966, p8.
Motion Picture Herald Product Digest. Dec 23, 1964, p13-14.
Motion Picture Herald Product Digest. Jan 19, 1966, p449.
National Review. Feb 7, 1967, v19, p153.
The New York Times. Jan 21, 1966, p22.
The New Yorker. Jan 22, 1966, v41, p99.
Newsweek. May 9, 1966, v67, p98B.
Playboy. Apr 1966, v13, p42-43.
The Private Eye, the Cowboy and the Very Naked Girl. p176-78.
Saturday Review. Jan 22, 1966, v49, p49.
Saturday Review. May 7, 1966, v49, p100.
Time. May 13, 1966, v87, p103.
Variety. Jan 12, 1966, p6.

Juggernaut (US; Lester, Richard; 1974)
America. Oct 12, 1974, v131, p195.
BFI/Monthly Film Bulletin. Oct 1974, v41, p224-25.
Commonweal. Nov 1, 1974, v101, p110.
Films and Filming. Nov 1974, v21, p32.
Films Illustrated. Oct 1974, v4, p44.
Films Illustrated. May 1974, v3, p348, p51.
Films Illustrated. Jun 1974, v3, p389-91.
Films in Review. Nov 1974, v25, p568-69.
Hollywood Reporter. Sep 18, 1974, p3.
Independent Film Journal. Oct 2, 1974, v74, p31-32.
The Los Angeles Times. Sep 27, 1974, SecIV, p1.
Movietone News. Oct 1974, n36, p34-35.
New Statesman. Oct 18, 1974, v88, p549.
New York. Sep 30, 1974, v7, p72-73.
The New Yorker. Oct 1974, v50, p154.
Newsweek. Oct 7, 1974, v84, p95.
Reeling. p462-65.
Richard Lester: A Guide to References and Resources. p38-41.
Time. Oct 21, 1974, v104, p4.
Variety. Sep 18, 1974, p19.
The Village Voice. Oct 24, 1974, p97.

The Juggler (US; Dmytryk, Edward; 1953)
America. May 9, 1953, v89, p175.
BFI/Monthly Film Bulletin. Jul 1953, v20, p101.
Catholic World. Jun 1953, v177, p225.
Commentary. Jun 1953, v15, p615-17.
Commentary. Aug 1953, v16, p175.
Commonweal. May 29, 1953, v58, p201.
Film Daily. May 12, 1953, p6.
The Films of Kirk Douglas. p102-05.
Hollywood Reporter. May 1, 1953, p3.
Library Journal. May 1, 1953, v78, p806.
The New York Times. Nov 23, 1953, SecII, p5.
The New York Times. May 6, 1953, p39.
The New Yorker. May 16, 1953, v29, p131.
Newsweek. May 18, 1953, v41, p110.
Saturday Review. May 9, 1953, v36, p28-29.
Stanley Kramer, Film Maker. p140-49.
Theatre Arts. Jul 1953, v37, p88.
Time. May 4, 1953, v61, p102.
Variety. May 6, 1953, p6.

Jules & Jim (French title: Jules et Jim)
(FR; Truffaut, François; 1961)
BFI/Monthly Film Bulletin. Jul 1962, v29, p91.
Cinema. 1963, v1, n3, p32.
Cinema Journal. 1981, v21, n1, p31-58.
The Cinema of François Truffaut. p45-47.
Cinema Texas Program Notes. Apr 26, 1977, v12, p1-4.
Cinema Texas Program Notes. Apr 20, 1982, v22, p79-84.

Commonweal. May 4, 1962, v76, p153.
Confessions of a Cultist. p42-44.
Dictionary of Films. p170.
Esquire. Dec 1981, v96, p134.
Film. Aut 1962, n33, p17.
Film and Literature: An Introduction. p234-41.
Film and the Critical Eye. p458-86.
Film as Film: Critical Responses to Film Art. p210-18.
Film Culture. Sum 1962, n25, p22-23.
Film Heritage. 1974, v9, n3, p1-11.
Film Journal. Oct 1963, n22, p19-26.
Filmfacts. Jun 8, 1962, v5, p107-09.
Films and Filming. Jun 1962, v8, p31.
Finally Truffaut. p92-103.
François Truffaut (Allen). p86-97.
François Truffaut (Crisp). p58-67.
François Truffaut (Insdorf). p84-91.
The Great French Films. p187-92.
The Great Movies. p159.
Hollywood Reporter. Aug 15, 1962, p3.
I Lost It at the Movies. p195-200.
Informer. Nov 1984, p12-13.
The International Dictionary of Films and Filmmakers. Volume I. p232-33.
Journal of Aesthetic Education. Apr 1971, v5, p91-101.
Literature/Film Quarterly. 1977, v5, n3, p183-97.
Magill's Survey of Cinema. Foreign Language Series. 1985, v4, p1610-14.
The Nation. May 12, 1962, v194, p427-28.
The New Republic. May 7, 1962, v146, p28-30.
The New York Times. Apr 24, 1962, p32.
The New Yorker. May 5, 1962, v38, p184-85.
Newsweek. May 7, 1962, v59, p90.
On Movies. p377-79.
Saturday Review. May 12, 1962, v45, p50.
Sight and Sound. Aut 1962, v31, p142-43.
Sight and Sound. Spr 1963, v32, p78-82.
Time. May 4, 1962, v79, p65.
Variety. Feb 7, 1962, p6.
The Village Voice. Apr 19, 1962, p15-16.
The Village Voice. May 3, 1962, p11-12.
A World on Film. p226-30.
Yale French Studies. 1980, n60, p183-203.

Julia (US; Zinnemann, Fred; 1977)
America. Oct 22, 1977, v137, p268-69.
BFI/Monthly Film Bulletin. Dec 1977, v44, p260.
Christian Century. Dec 21, 1977, v94, p1198-99.
Commonweal. Feb 17, 1978, v105, p117-18.
Films in Review. Nov 1977, v28, p565.
The Films of Jane Fonda. p192-200.
The Films of the Seventies. p182-83.
Hollywood Reporter. Sep 19, 1977, p3.
Horizon. Oct 1977, v20, p86-90.
The Los Angeles Times. Oct 16, 1977, Calendar, p1.
Magill's Survey of Cinema. Series II. v3, p1243-46.
Motion Picture Herald Product Digest. Oct 5, 1977, p33.
The Nation. Nov 5, 1977, v225, p475-76.
National Review. Nov 25, 1977, v29, p1375-77.
The New Republic. Oct 15, 1977, v177, p32-33.
The New York Times. Oct 2, 1977, SecII, p15.
The New York Times. Oct 3, 1977, p40.
The New York Times. Dec 20, 1977, p44.
The New York Times. Mar 12, 1978, SecII, p15.
The New Yorker. Oct 10, 1977, v53, p94.
Newsweek. Oct 10, 1977, v90, p78-82.
Saturday Review. Oct 29, 1977, v5, p46.
Time. Oct 10, 1977, v110, p83.
Variety. Sep 21, 1977, p16.

Julie de Carneilhan (FR; Manuel, Jacques; 1950)
BFI/Monthly Film Bulletin. Dec 1952, v19, p173.
The Spectator. Oct 24, 1952, v189, p533.
Variety. May 24, 1950, p20.

Juliet of the Spirits (Italian title: Giulietta degli Spiriti) (IT, FR; Fellini, Federico; 1965)
America. Dec 18, 1965, v113, p784.
BFI/Monthly Film Bulletin. Mar, 1966, v33, p37-38.
Cahiers du Cinema in English. 1966, n2, p76-77.
Cahiers du Cinema in English. 1966, n5, p26-33.
Christian Century. Feb 9, 1966, v83, p178.
Christian Science Monitor (Western edition). Jan 10, 1966, p4.
Cinema. Jul 1966, v3, p46.
Commonweal. Nov 26, 1965, v83, p244-47.
Confessions of a Cultist. p215-19.
Dictionary of Films. p128-29.
Esquire. Mar 1966, v65, p18, 20.
Federico Fellini: A Guide to References and Resources. p28-32, 99-105.
Federico Fellini: Essays in Criticism. p137-51.
Fellini (Budgen). p67-84.
Fellini the Artist. p156-76.
Fellini's Road. p149-03.
Film Daily. Nov 3, 1965, p7.
Film Quarterly. Spr 1968, v21, p21-25.
Film Quarterly. Spr 1966, v19, p4-19.
Films and Filming. Mar 1965, v10, p52-53.
Films and Filming. Aug 1965, v11, p52-53.
Films and Filming. Apr 1966, v12, p52-53.
Films in Review. Dec 1965, v16, p643.
Films in Review. Jan 1966, v17, p46-47.
The Films of Federico Fellini. p118-25.
International Film Guide. 1967, v4, p107-08.
Juliet of the Spirits. p11-65.
The Landscape of Contemporary Cinema. p9-12.
Life. Nov 26, 1965, v59, p18.
London Magazine. Apr 1966, v6, p88-92.
The London Times. Oct 25, 1965, p15.
The London Times. Feb 10, 1966, p16.
The London Times. Sep 25, 1964, p16.
Magill's Survey of Cinema. Foreign Language Films. v4, p1615-17.
Motion Picture Herald Product Digest. Dec 22, 1965, p426.
The Nation. Nov 15, 1965, v201, p371-72.
The New Leader. Dec 6, 1965, v48, p32-33.
The New Republic. Nov 13, 1965, v153, p28-30.
New Statesman. Feb 11, 1966, v71, p201.
New York Review of Books. Dec 23, 1965, v5, p22-24.
The New York Times. Nov 4, 1965, p57.
The New Yorker. Nov 6, 1965, v41, p120.
Newsweek. Nov 15, 1965, v66, p124-24A.
On Movies. p350-54.
Playboy. Feb 1966, v13, p33.
The Private Eye, the Cowboy and the Very Naked Girl. p155-56.
Private Screenings. p220-25.
Quarterly Review of Film Studies. 1979, v4, n2, p193-206.
Reporter. Dec 16, 1965, v33, p45-46.
Saturday Evening Post. Jan 1, 1966, v239, p24-33.
Saturday Review. Nov 20, 1965, v48, p55.
Sight and Sound. Wint 1965-66, v35, p18-19.
The Spectator. Feb 11, 1966, v216, p167.
Studies in the Humanities. 1981, v9, n1, p22-29.
Time. Nov 12, 1965, v86, p114.
Tynan Right and Left. p255-56.

Variety. Nov 3, 1965, p6.
The Village Voice. Nov 11, 1965, v11, p23.
The Village Voice. Nov 18, 1965, v11, p23.
Vogue. Jan 1, 1966, v147, p70.
Vogue. Sep 1, 1965, v146, p274-75, 282.
A World on Film. p325-29.

Julius Caesar (US; Mankiewicz, Joseph L.; 1953)
America. Jun 13, 1953, v89, p306.
BFI/Monthly Film Bulletin. Dec 1953, v20, p172.
Catholic World. Jul 1953, v177, p303.
Commonweal. Jun 19, 1953, v58, p273-74.
Film Daily. Jun 3, 1953, p10.
Film Quarterly. Wint 1953, v8, n2, p109-38.
Films in Review. Apr 1953, v4, n4, p184-88.
Films in Review. May 1953, v4, n5, p237-39.
The Films of James Mason. p116-19.
The Films of Marlon Brando. p54-63.
Hollywood Reporter. Jun 3, 1953, p3.
Joseph L. Mankiewicz (Dick). p133-38.
Library Journal. Jun 15, 1953, v78, p1102.
Life. Apr 20, 1953, v34, p135-39.
Look. Mar 10, 1953, v17, p17-19.
Magill's Survey of Cinema. Series I. v2, p881.
National Parent-Teacher. Jan 1953, v47, p38.
The New Republic. Aug 3, 1953, v129, p20-21.
The New York Times. Nov 25, 1952, p33.
The New Yorker. Jun 13, 1953, v29, p65.
Newsweek. Jun 8, 1953, v41, p101.
Saturday Review. May 30, 1953, v36, p6.
Senior Scholastic. Sep 16, 1953, v63, p37.
Shakespeare on Film. p92-105.
Sight and Sound. Jul-Sep 1953, v23, n1, p24-27.
Sight and Sound. Oct-Dec 1953, v23, n2, p89-90.
Theatre Arts. Jun 1953, v37, p84.
Time. Jun 1, 1953, v61, p94.
Variety. Jun 3, 1953, p6.
Vintage Films. p139-42.

Julius Caesar (US; Burge, Stuart; 1970)
Filmfacts. 1971, v14, p94.
Films and Filming. Sep 1970, v16, n12, p62-63.
Hollywood Reporter. Aug 7, 1970, p3.
Look. Mar 9, 1971, v35, p31.
Variety. Jun 10, 1970, p26.
The Village Voice. Feb 25, 1971, v16, n8, p57.

Jumbo (Also titled: Billy Rose's Jumbo) (US; Walters, Charles; 1962)
BFI/Monthly Film Bulletin. Feb 1963, v30, p15.
Commonweal. Dec 21, 1962, v77, p342.
Film Daily. Dec 5, 1962, p8.
Filmfacts. Dec 21, 1962, v5, p299-301.
Films and Filming. Feb 1963, v9, p36-37.
The Films of Doris Day. p207-10.
Hollywood Reporter. Dec 5, 1962, p3.
Motion Picture Herald Product Digest. Dec 12, 1962, p713.
Movie. Jan 1963, n6, p35.
The New York Times. Dec 7, 1962, p49.
The New Yorker. Dec 15, 1962, v38, p135.
Newsweek. Dec 17, 1962, v60, p95.
Saturday Review. Dec 8, 1962, v45, p50.
Time. Dec 21, 1962, v80, p77.
Variety. Dec 5, 1962, p6.

Jumping Jacks (US; Taurog, Norman; 1952)
BFI/Monthly Film Bulletin. Oct 1952, v19, p143.
Commonweal. Jul 18, 1952, v56, p368.
Film Daily. Jun 11, 1952, p7.
Hollywood Reporter. Jun 4, 1952, p3.
The London Times. Sep 29, 1952, p10.
Motion Picture Herald Product Digest. Jun 7, 1952, p1389.
National Parent-Teacher. Sep 1952, v47, p37.

The New Statesman and Nation. Oct 4, 1952, v44, p377.
The New York Times. Jul 24, 1952, p30.
Saturday Review. Aug 9, 1952, v35, p36.
The Spectator. Sep 26, 1952, v189, p393.
Time. Aug 4, 1952, v60, p76.
Variety. Jun 4, 1952, p6.

Junge Törless, Der *See* Young Torless

Jungfrukallen *See* The Virgin Spring

The Jungle Book (US; Reitherman, Wolfgang; 1967)
BFI/Monthly Film Bulletin. Jan 1968, v35, p10.
The Disney Films (Maltin). p253-55.
Film Daily. Oct 11, 1967, p11.
Films and Filming. Mar 1968, v14, p30.
Films in Review. Dec 1967, v18, p647-48.
Hollywood Reporter. Oct 4, 1967, p3.
Motion Picture Herald Product Digest. Oct 25, 1967, p734.
The New York Times. Dec 23, 1967, p29.
Variety. Oct 4, 1967, p6.
Walt Disney: A Guide to References and Resources. p109-11.

Junior Bonner (US; Peckinpah, Sam; 1972)
Commentary. Nov 1972, v54, p83-84.
Commonweal. Sep 8, 1972, v96, p479-80.
Filmfacts. 1972, v15, n17, p410.
Films in Review. Aug-Sep 1972, v23, p435.
The Films of Sam Peckinpah. p58-64.
The Films of Steve McQueen. p183-89.
Hollywood Reporter. Jun 9, 1972, p3.
Life. Aug 11, 1972, v73, p18.
Magill's Survey of Cinema. Series II. v3, p1247-50.
The New Republic. Sep 2, 1972, v167, p26.
The New York Times. Aug 3, 1972, p24.
The New Yorker. Aug 12, 1972, v48, p53-54.
Newsweek. Jul 19, 1972, v79, p64.
Peckinpah (Simmons). p139-53.
Sam Peckinpah (McKinney). p133-42.
Saturday Review. Jul 29, 1972, v55, p70.
Senior Scholastic. Oct 2, 1972, v101, p20-21.
Time. Jul 26, 1972, v99, p68.
Variety. Jun 14, 1972, p18.

Just Across the Street (US; Pevney, Joseph; 1952)
BFI/Monthly Film Bulletin. Jul 1952, v19, p94.
Film Daily. Jun 2, 1952, p6.
Hollywood Reporter. May 23, 1952, p3.
Motion Picture Herald Product Digest. May 31, 1952, p1382.
The New York Times. Jun 28, 1952, p12.
The Spectator. Jun 6, 1952, v188, p744.
Time. Jul 7, 1952, v60, p77.
Variety. May 28, 1952, p6.

Just For You (US; Flemyng, Gordon; 1952)
BFI/Monthly Film Bulletin. Sep 1952, v19, p128.
Catholic World. Sep 1952, v175, p464.
Christian Century. Oct 29, 1952, v69, p1271.
Film Daily. Jul 31, 1952, p6.
The Films of Bing Crosby. p197-98.
Hollywood Reporter. Jul 31, 1952, p3.
Library Journal. Oct 15, 1952, v77, p1801.
The London Times. Sep 1, 1952, p8.
McCall's. Oct 1952, v80, p18-19.
Motion Picture Herald Product Digest. Aug 2, 1952, p1469.
National Parent-Teacher. Oct 1952, v47, p36.
The New York Times. Oct 9, 1952, p40.
Newsweek. Sep 22, 1952, v40, p114-15.
Saturday Review. Sep 27, 1952, v35, p27.
Senior Scholastic. Oct 22, 1952, v61, p47.
The Spectator. Aug 29, 1952, v189, p264.
Theatre Arts. Oct 1952, v36, p73.

Time. Aug 25, 1952, v60, p72.
Variety. Aug 6, 1952, p6.

Just Me *See* Ma Pomme

Just Tell Me What You Want (US; Lumet, Sidney; 1980)
Films in Review. Apr 1980, v31, p247.
The Films of Myrna Loy. p253-54.
Hollywood Reporter. Feb 6, 1980, p3.
The Los Angeles Times. Feb 8, 1980, SecVI, p1.
Motion Picture Herald Product Digest. Aug 15, 1980, p24.
The Nation. Mar 1, 1980, v230, p252.
National Review. Apr 4, 1980, v32, p425.
The New Leader. Feb 25, 1980, v63, p21-22.
The New Republic. Feb 16, 1980, v182, p25.
New York. Feb 11, 1980, v13, p66.
The New York Times. Feb 8, 1980, SecIII, p8.
The New Yorker. Feb 11, 1980, v55, p101-03.
Newsday. Feb 8, 1980, SecII, p5.
Newsweek. Feb 18, 1980, v95, p94.
Time. Feb 25, 1980, v115, p50.
Variety. Feb 6, 1980, p22.
Vogue. Mar 1980, v170, p40.

Just This Once (US; Weis, Don; 1952)
BFI/Monthly Film Bulletin. Apr 1952, v19, p51-52.
Catholic World. Feb 1952, v174, p387.
Film Daily. Jan 29, 1952, p7.
Hollywood Reporter. Jan 17, 1952, p3.
Library Journal. May 1, 1952, v77, p785.
Motion Picture Herald Product Digest. Jan 19, 1952, p1193.
The New York Times. Mar 18, 1952, p22.
Newsweek. Mar 31, 1952, v39, p87.
The Tatler. Sep 10, 1952, v205, p464.
Theatre Arts. Mar 1952, v36, p73.
Variety. Jan 23, 1952, p6.

Justice Est Faite (Also titled: Let Justice Be Done; Justice Is Done) (FR; Cayatte, André; 1950)
BFI/Monthly Film Bulletin. Nov 1951, v18, p357.
Cinema, the Magic Vehicle. v2, p48-49.
Commonweal. Feb 27, 1953, v57, p522.
Dictionary of Films. p171.
Film Daily. May 5, 1953, p6.
Films in Review. Apr 1953, v4, p199-200.
Films in Review. Oct 1950, v1, p8-10.
Motion Picture Herald Product Digest. Mar 14, 1953, p1759.
The New Statesman and Nation. Oct 27, 1951, v42, p461.
The New York Times. Mar 3, 1953, p23.
The New York Times Magazine. Feb 15, 1953, p52-53.
Saturday Review. Feb 28, 1953, v36, p39.
The Spectator. Oct 26, 1951, v187, p537.
Time. Mar 16, 1953, v61, p112.
Variety. Nov 1, 1950, p18.

Justice Is Done *See* Justice Est Faite

Kagemusha (Also titled: Shadow Warrior) (JAPAN; Kurosawa, Akira; 1980)
America. Nov 1, 1980, v143, p272.
BFI/Monthly Film Bulletin. Dec 1980, v47, p237.
Christian Century. Dec 3, 1980, v97, p1198.
Christian Science Monitor. Nov 23, 1980, p19.
Cineaste. Fall 1980, v10, p8.
Film Comment. Nov-Dec 1980, v16, p54-57, 65-66.
Film Quarterly. Wint 1980, v34, p44.
The Films of Akira Kurosawa. p204-13.
Hollywood Reporter. Oct 6, 1980, p3.
The International Dictionary of Films and Filmmakers. v1, p233-34.

The Los Angeles Times. Oct 12, 1980, Calendar, p34.
Magill's Survey of Cinema. Foreign Language Films. v4, p1622-26.
Motion Picture Herald Product Digest. Nov 19, 1980, p46.
The Nation. Nov 15, 1980, v231, p522.
The New Republic. Oct 25, 1980, v183, p32-33.
New York. Oct 27, 1980, v13, p71-72.
The New York Times. Oct 6, 1980, SecIII, p14.
Newsday. Oct 3, 1980, SecII, p7.
Newsweek. Oct 13, 1980, v96, p131-32.
Progressive. Dec 1980, v44, p52.
The Samurai Films of Akira Kurosawa. p57-133.
Saturday Review. Sep 1980, v7, p18-20.
Sight and Sound. Wint 1980-81, v50, p61.
Time. Oct 13, 1980, v116, p108.
Variety. May 21, 1980, p18.

Kaidan *See* Kwaidan

Kakushi Toridi No San-Akunin *See* The Hidden Fortress

Kaleidoscope (GB; Smight, Jack; 1966)
America. Oct 1, 1966, v115, p397.
BFI/Monthly Film Bulletin. Oct 1966, v33, p151-52.
Christian Science Monitor (Western edition). Nov 7, 1966, p4.
Film Daily. Sep 7, 1966, p3.
Film Quarterly. Wint 1966-67, v20, p62.
Filmfacts. Nov 15, 1966, v9, p247-48.
Films and Filming. Nov 1966, v13, p8-9.
The Films of Warren Beatty. p122-30.
Hollywood Reporter. Sep 7, 1966, p3.
Life. Oct 14, 1966, v61, p18.
The London Times. Sep 8, 1966, p17.
Motion Picture Herald Product Digest. Sep 14, 1966, p597-98.
National Review. Feb 7, 1967, v19, p153.
New Statesman. Sep 19, 1966, v72, p369.
The New York Times. Sep 23, 1966, p45.
The New Yorker. Oct 1, 1966, v42, p185-86.
Newsweek. Oct 10, 1966, v68, p116.
Playboy. Nov 1966, v13, p42.
Time. Sep 30, 1966, v88, p123.
Variety. Sep 7, 1966, p6.
The Village Voice. Oct 13, 1966, v11, p27.

Kanejo to Kare *See* She and He

Kangaroo (US; Milestone, Lewis; 1952)
American Cinematographer. Jul 1952, v33, p299-93.
BFI/Monthly Film Bulletin. Jul 1952, v19, p94-95.
Christian Century. Aug 6, 1952, v69, p911.
Film Daily. May 21, 1952, p6.
Films in Review. Jun-Jul 1952, v3, p292.
Good Housekeeping. Jun 1952, v134, p17.
Hollywood Reporter. May 19, 1952, p3.
Lewis Milestone (Millichap). p175-76.
Motion Picture Herald Product Digest. May 24, 1952, p1373.
The New York Times. May 17, 1952, p22.
The New Yorker. May 24, 1952, v28, p128.
Newsweek. Jun 2, 1952, v39, p87.
Saturday Review. Jun 7, 1952, v35, p28.
The Spectator. Jun 20, 1952, v188, p808.
The Tatler. Jul 2, 1952, v205, p26.
Time. Jun 2, 1952, v59, p94.
Variety. May 21, 1952, p6.

Kansas City Confidential (US; Karlson, Phil; 1952)
Film Daily. Nov 14, 1952, p7.
Hollywood Reporter. Nov 3, 1952, p3.
Motion Picture Herald Product Digest. Nov 15, 1952, p1606-07.
The Nation. Nov 8, 1952, v175, p435.

National Parent-Teacher. Feb 1953, v47, p37.
The New York Times. Nov 29, 1952, p11.
Newsweek. Dec 8, 1952, v40, p94.
Saturday Review. Nov 22, 1952, v35, p39.
Time. Nov 10, 1952, v60, p120.
Variety. Nov 5, 1952, p6.

The Karate Kid (US; Avildsen, John G.; 1984)
BFI/Monthly Film Bulletin. Sep 1984, v51, p280.
Film Journal. Jul 1984, v87, p6, 19-20.
Films and Filming. Sep 1984, n360, p39-40.
Films in Review. Aug 1984, v35, p429.
Hollywood Reporter. May 21, 1984, p16.
The Los Angeles Times. Jun 21, 1984, SecVI, p4.
Maclean's. Jun 25, 1984, v97, p50.
Magill's Cinema Annual, 1985. p264-69.
New York. Jul 23, 1984, v17, p54-55.
The New York Times. Jun 22, 1984, SecIII, p16.
The New York Times. Aug 12, 1984, SecII, p17.
Newsweek. Jun 25, 1984, v103, p69.
Photoplay. Oct 1984, v35, p20.
Sports Illustrated. Jul 9, 1984, v61, p58.
Time. Jul 2, 1984, v124, p78.
Variety. May 23, 1984, p12.
The Village Voice. Jul 10, 1984, p50.

Kare John *See* Dear John

Keep An Eye on Amelia *See* Occupe-Toi D'Amelie

The Kentuckian (US; Lancaster, Burt; 1955)
America. Sep 3, 1955, v93, p547.
BFI/Monthly Film Bulletin. Nov 1955, v22, n262, p163.
Burt Lancaster: A Pictorial Treasury of His Films. p82-83.
Burt Lancaster: The Man and His Movies. p66-67.
Catholic World. Sep 1955, v181, p464.
Film Daily. Jul 15, 1955, p5.
Films and Filming. Oct 1955, v2, p19.
Hollywood Reporter. Jul 13, 1955, p3.
The New York Times. Sep 2, 1955, p13.
The New Yorker. Sep 10, 1955, v31, p81.
Newsweek. Aug 8, 1955, v46, p76.
Sight and Sound. Aut 1955, v25, p91.
Time. Sep 26, 1955, v66, p96.
Variety. Jul 13, 1955, p6.

Kentucky Fried Movie (US; Landis, John; 1977)
Films in Review. Oct 1977, v28, p504.
Hollywood Reporter. Aug 3, 1977, p3.
The Los Angeles Times. Aug 11, 1977, SecIV, p18.
Motion Picture Herald Product Digest. Aug 24, 1977, p22.
The New York Times. Aug 11, 1977, SecIII, p14.
Time. Aug 29, 1977, v110, p76.
Variety. Aug 3, 1977, p32.

Keshoku Ichadai-onna *See* The Life of Oharu

The Key (GB; Reed, Carol; 1958)
America. Jul 26, 1958, v99, p459.
BFI/Monthly Film Bulletin. Jul 1958, v25, p84.
Catholic World. Sep 1958, v187, p458.
Commonweal. Jul 25, 1958, v68, p423.
Film Daily. Jun 12, 1958, p6.
Filmfacts. Aug 13, 1958, v1, p113-14, 300.
Films in Review. Aug-Sep 1958, v9, p400-01.
The Films of Sophia Loren. p95-98.
The Films of William Holden. p186-90.
Hollywood Reporter. Jun 11, 1958, p3.

Library Journal. Jul 1958, v83, p2036.
Life. Jul 21, 1958, v45, p73-74.
The Nation. Jul 19, 1958, v187, p40.
The New York Times. Jul 2, 1958, p23.
The New Yorker. Jul 123, 1958, v34, p99.
Newsweek. Jul 7, 1958, v52, p72.
Saturday Review. Jul 5, 1958, v41, p23.
Time. Jul 14, 1958, v72, p82.
Variety. Jun 11, 1958, p6.

Key of Keys *See* What's Up, Tiger Lily?

Key to the City (US; Sidney, George; 1950)
BFI/Monthly Film Bulletin. Jun 1950, v17, p86.
Christian Century. Mar 29, 1950, v67, p415.
Commonweal. Feb 17, 1950, v51, p511.
Film Daily. Jan 27, 1950, p6.
The Films of Clark Gable. p218-20.
Hollywood Reporter. Jan 30, 1950, p3.
Illustrated London News. Jun 10, 1950, v216, p910.
The New Republic. Feb 20, 1950, v122, p23.
The New York Times. Feb 2, 1950, p31.
Newsweek. Mar 6, 1950, v35, p84.
Time. Feb 13, 1950, v55, p88.
Variety. Feb 1, 1950, p14.

Khartoum (US, GB; Dearden, Basil; 1966)
America. Jul 16, 1966, v115, p78.
BFI/Monthly Film Bulletin. Jul 1966, v33, p104.
Cinema. Dec 1966, v3, p46.
Film Daily. Jun 15, 1966, p3.
Film Quarterly. Sum 1967, v20, p11-22.
Filmfacts. Sep 1, 1966, v9, p165-67.
Films and Filming. Aug 1966, v12, p7.
Films in Review. Aug-Sep 1966, v17, p445-46.
The Films of Laurence Olivier. p142-44.
Hollywood Reporter. Jun 15, 1966, p3.
Illustrated London News. Jun 4, 1966, v248, p16-19.
Laurence Olivier (Hirsch). p154-55.
Laurence Olivier: Theater & Cinema. p177-79.
Life. May 27, 1966, v60, p93-95.
The London Times. Apr 23, 1966, p18.
The London Times. Jun 9, 1966, p8.
Motion Picture Herald Product Digest. Jun 22, 1966, p545.
Motion Picture Herald Product Digest. Mar 2, 1966, p12-13.
New Statesman. Jun 17, 1966, v71, p902.
The New York Times. Jul 14, 1966, p28.
The New Yorker. Jul 23, 1966, v42, p75.
Newsweek. Jul 11, 1966, v68, p90.
Playboy. Sep 1966, v13, p62-63.
Saturday Review. Jul 16, 1966, v49, p43.
Second Sight. p54-57.
Senior Scholastic. Sep 30, 1966, v89, p33-34.
The Spectator. Jun 10, 1966, v216, p730.
Time. Aug 5, 1966, v88, p56.
Variety. Jun 15, 1966, p6.

Kid de Cincinnati, Le *See* The Cincinnati Kid

Kid Gallahad (US; Karlson, Phil; 1962)
BFI/Monthly Film Bulletin. Nov 1962, v29, p155.
Elvis: The Films and Career of Elvis Presley. p132-33.
Film Daily. Jul 25, 1962, p5.
Filmfacts. Jan 18, 1963, v5, p341.
Films and Filming. Dec 1962, v9, p44.
Hollywood Reporter. Jul 25, 1962, p3.
Motion Picture Herald Product Digest. Aug 8, 1962, p633.
Movie. Nov 1962, n4, p35.
The New Yorker. Mar 7, 1963, p8.
Time. Aug 3, 1962, v80, p36.
Variety. Jul 25, 1962, p6.

Kid Rodelo (SP, US; Carlson, Richard; 1966)
BFI/Monthly Film Bulletin. Aug 1966, v33, p124.
Film Daily. Jan 18, 1966, p7.
Filmfacts. Apr 15, 1966, v9, p53-54.
Hollywood Reporter. Jan 10, 1966, p3.
Motion Picture Herald Product Digest. Jan 19, 1966, p450.
The New York Times. Feb 23, 1966, p46.
Variety. Jan 19, 1966, p6.

The Kidnappers *See* The Little Kidnappers

The Kill *See* The Game Is Over

The Killer Elite (US; Peckinpah, Sam; 1975)
BFI/Monthly Film Bulletin. Mar 1976, v43, p55.
Commonweal. Jan 30, 1975, v103, p83-84.
Films in Review. Feb 1976, v27, p122.
The Films of Sam Peckinpah. p87-89.
Hollywood Reporter. Dec 18, 1975, p4.
The Los Angeles Times. Dec 18, 1975, SecIV, p32.
Motion Picture Herald Product Digest. Dec 31, 1975, p60.
The New York Times. Dec 18, 1975, p62.
The New Yorker. Jan 12, 1976, v51, p70-75.
Newsweek. Jan 12, 1976, v87, p69.
Peckinpah: A Portrait in Montage. p209-24.
Sam Peckinpah (McKinney). p193-201.
Variety. Dec 24, 1975, p14.
When the Lights Go Down. p112-19.

Killer on a Horse *See* Welcome to Hard Times

The Killers (US; Siegel, Don; 1964)
American Film Genres (Kaminsky). p52-56.
BFI/Monthly Film Bulletin. Apr 1965, v32, p52.
Boxoffice. Jun 15, 1964, v85, p2836.
Cinema Stylists. p225.
Don Siegel (Lovell). p56-57.
Film Daily. Jun 1, 1964, p15.
Films and Filming. May 1965, v11, p30.
The Films of Ronald Reagan. p222-26.
The Hollywood Professionals. v4, p131-34.
Hollywood Reporter. May 26, 1964, v180, p3.
Motion Picture Herald Product Digest. Jun 10, 1964, p66-67.
The New York Times. Jul 18, 1964, p10.
Newsweek. Aug 3, 1964, v64, p72.
Time. Jun 12, 1964, v83, p115.
Underworld USA. p160-61.
Variety. May 27, 1964, p24.

The Killing (US; Kubrick, Stanley; 1956)
American Classic Screen. Spr 1980, v4, p13-18.
BFI/Monthly Film Bulletin. Aug 1956, v23, p98.
Dark City: The Film Noir. p117-22.
Film Culture. 1956, v2, p30-31.
Film Daily. Jun 6, 1956, p6.
Films and Filming. Sep 1956, v2, p26-27.
Hollywood Reporter. May 18, 1956, p3.
Kubrick (Ciment). p58-65.
The New York Times. May 21, 1956, p20.
Newsweek. Jun 18, 1956, v47, p122.
Saturday Review. Aug 4, 1956, v39, p32.
Sight and Sound. Fall 1956, v26, p95-96.
Stanley Kubrick: A Guide to References and Resources. p36-37.
Time. Jun 4, 1956, v67, p106.
Variety. May 23, 1956, p6.

The Killing Fields (US; Joffe, Roland; 1984)
America. Mar 23, 1985, v152, p236.

BFI/Monthly Film Bulletin. Dec 1984, v51, p383.
California Magazine. Dec 1984, v9, p65.
Canadian Dimension. Sep-Oct 1985, v19, p26.
Christian Century. Jan 30, 1985, v102, p105.
Christianity Today. Jan 30, 1985, v29, p65-67.
Commonweal. Dec 14, 1984, v111, p686.
Films in Review. Jan 1985, v36, p45.
Hollywood Reporter. Oct 30, 1984, p3.
The Killing Fields, The Facts Behind the Film. 1984.
Los Angeles. Dec 1984, v29, p32.
Maclean's. Nov 26, 1984, v97, p77.
Magill's Cinema Annual, 1985. p270-76.
The Nation. Dec 1, 1984, v239, p594.
National Review. Dec 28, 1984, v36, p47-48.
The New Republic. Nov 26, 1984, v191, p24-25.
New Statesman. Nov 23, 1984, v108, p33.
New York. Nov 12, 1984, v17, p121.
The New York Times. Nov 2, 1984, SecIII, p10.
The New York Times. Dec 13, 1984, SecI, p13.
The New Yorker. Dec 10, 1984, v60, p165.
Newsweek. Nov 5, 1984, v104, p74.
Playboy. Feb 1985, v32, p17.
Saturday Review. Jan-Feb 1985, v11, p82.
Senior Scholastic Update. Jan 18, 1985, v117, p22.
Variety. Oct 31, 1984, p24.
Vogue. Jan 1985, v175, p39, 41.
Washingtonian. Feb 1985, v20, p53.

The Killing Game *See* Jeu de Massacre

The Killing of a Chinese Bookie (US; Cassavetes, John; 1976)
American Dreaming. p223-49.
Film Bulletin. Feb 1976, v45, p39.
Films in Review. Apr 1976, v27, p242.
Hollywood Reporter. Feb 18, 1976, p3.
Independent Film Journal. Mar 3, 1976, v77, p13.
The Los Angeles Times. Feb 17, 1976, SecIV, p1.
Motion Picture Herald Product Digest. Mar 10, 1976, p80.
The Nation. Feb 28, 1976, v222, p254.
The New York Times. Mar 7, 1976, SecII, p13.
Newsweek. Mar 15, 1976, v87, p89-90.
Saturday Review. Apr 3, 1976, v3, p50.
Time. Mar 8, 1976, v107, p80.
Variety. Feb 18, 1976, p35.

The Killing of Sister George (US; Aldrich, Robert; 1968)
America. Jan 18, 1969, v120, p80.
BFI/Monthly Film Bulletin. May 1969, v36, p92-93.
Christian Science Monitor (Western edition). Nov 15, 1968, p6.
Christian Science Monitor (Western edition). Feb 3, 1969, p6.
Commonweal. Jan 17, 1969, v89, p502-03.
Confessions of a Cultist. p416-17.
Esquire. Mar 1969, v71, p34.
Film 68/69. p210-11.
Film Daily. Dec 17, 1968, p7.
Film Quarterly. Spr 1969, v22, p61.
Filmfacts. Jan 15, 1969, v11, p480-82.
Films and Filming. Jun 1969, v15, p45-46.
Films in Review. Jan 1969, v20, p54.
The Films of the Sixties. p261-64.
Focus. Oct 1969, n5, p22-23.
Hollywood Reporter. Dec 18, 1968, p3.
Life. Nov 1, 1968, v65, p34-36.
The London Times. Mar 22, 1969, p3.
The London Times. Mar 27, 1969, p7.
Motion Picture Herald Product Digest. Dec 18, 1968, p84.
Movies Into Film. p43-44.
The Nation. Jan 6, 1969, v208, p30.

The New Republic. Jan 18, 1969, v160, p34.
New Statesman. Mar 28, 1969, v77, p456.
The New York Times. Dec 17, 1968, p58.
The New Yorker. Dec 21, 1968, v44, p86.
Newsweek. Dec 23, 1968, v72, p90-91.
Robert Aldrich: A Guide to References and Resources. p47-49.
Saturday Review. Jan 11, 1968, v52, p94.
The Spectator. Apr 4, 1969, v222, p449.
Time. Dec 20, 1968, v92, p83.
Variety. Dec 18, 1968, p6.
The Village Voice. Dec 26, 1968, p45.
A Year In the Dark. p319-20.

Kim (US; Saville, Victor; 1950)
BFI/Monthly Film Bulletin. Feb 1951, v18, p215.
Children's Novels and the Movies. p101-10.
Christian Century. Feb 7, 1951, v68, p191.
Commonweal. Dec 22, 1950, v53, p278.
Film Daily. Dec 6, 1950, p6.
Films in Review. Jan 1951, v2, p41-42.
The Films of Errol Flynn. p170-72.
Hollywood Reporter. Dec 5, 1950, p3.
Library Journal. Jan 1, 1951, v76, p59.
The London Times. Jan 27, 1951, p7.
The London Times. Jan 29, 1951, p8.
Motion Picture Herald Product Digest. Dec 9, 1950, p605-06.
The New York Times. Dec 8, 1950, p40.
The New Yorker. Dec 16, 1950, v26, p64.
Newsweek. Dec 18, 1950, v36, p93.
Saturday Review. Dec 16, 1950, v33, p28.
Senior Scholastic. Jan 3, 1951, v57, p24.
The Spectator. Jan 26, 1951, v186, p108.
Time. Dec 11, 1950, v56, p98.
Variety. Dec 6, 1950, p15.

Kind Lady (US; Sturges, John; 1951)
BFI/Monthly Film Bulletin. Sep 1951, v18, p325.
Christian Century. Sep 26, 1951, v68, p1111.
Commonweal. Aug 31, 1951, v54, p501.
Film Daily. Jun 20, 1951, p8.
Hollywood Reporter. Jun 18, 1951, p3.
Library Journal. Jul 1951, v76, p1141.
Motion Picture Herald Product Digest. Jun 23, 1951, p905.
The New York Times. Aug 8, 1951, p21.
The New Yorker. Aug 18, 1951, v27, p54.
Newsweek. Jul 16, 1951, v38, p84.
Time. Jul 16, 1951, v58, p93.
Variety. Jun 20, 1951, p6.

A Kind of Loving (GB; Schlesinger, John; 1961)
America. Oct 20, 1962, v107, p939.
BFI/Monthly Film Bulletin. May 1962, v29, p62.
Commonweal. Oct 5, 1962, v77, p42.
Film Daily. Oct 5, 1962, p6.
Filmfacts. Nov 16, 1962, v5, p265-66.
Films and Filming. Jun 1962, v8, p33-34.
Films in Review. Mar 1963, v14, p176-77.
The Great British Films. p203-04.
John Schlesinger: A Guide to References and Resources. p42-43.
John Schlesinger (Phillips). p41-41.
Magill's Survey of Cinema. Series I. v2, p894-96.
The New Republic. Oct 1, 1962, v147, p25-26.
The New York Times. Oct 2, 1962, v46, p1.
The New Yorker. Oct 6, 1962, v38, p158.
Saturday Review. Oct 20, 1962, v45, p34.
Sight and Sound. Sum 1962, v31, p143-44.
Time. Oct 19, 1962, v80, p92.
Variety. Apr 25, 1962, p6.

King and Country (GB; Losey, Joseph; 1964)
America. Feb 19, 1966, v114, p271.

The Los Angeles Times. Dec 17, 1978, Calendar, p1.
Maclean's. Dec 25, 1978, v91, p50-51.
Motion Picture Herald Product Digest. Dec 20, 1978, p58.
The New Leader. Jan 15, 1979, v62, p21.
New York. Jan 15, 1979, v12, p55.
The New York Times. Dec 20, 1978, SecIII, p17.
Newsweek. Dec 18, 1978, v92, p86.
Time. Jan 9, 1979, v112, p69.
Variety. Dec 13, 1978, p26.

King of the Khyber Rifles (US; King, Henry; 1953)
America. Jan 9, 1954, v90, p386.
BFI/Monthly Film Bulletin. May 1954, v21, p70.
Catholic World. Mar 1954, v178, p460.
Commonweal. Jan 29, 1954, v59, p428.
Film Daily. Dec 22, 1953, p10.
The Films of Tyrone Power. p183-85.
Hollywood Reporter. Dec 22, 1953, p3.
Library Journal. Feb 1, 1954, v79, p199.
The London Times. Apr 12, 1954, p6.
Motion Picture Herald Product Digest. Dec 26, 1953, p2117-18.
National Parent-Teacher. Feb 1954, v48, p39.
The New Statesman and Nation. Apr 17, 1954, v47, p502.
The New York Times. Dec 23, 1953, p21.
The New Yorker. Jan 2, 1954, v29, p51.
Newsweek. Jan 11, 1954, v43, p80.
Saturday Review. Jan 16, 1954, v37, p33.
Sight and Sound. Apr-Jun 1954, v23, p198.
The Spectator. Apr 9, 1954, v192, p430.
The Tatler. Apr 21, 1954, v212, p168.
Time. Jan 11, 1954, v63, p82.
Variety. Dec 23, 1953, p6.

King Rat (US; Forbes, Bryan; 1965)
America. Nov 13, 1965, v113, p608-09.
American Cinematographer. Dec 1965, v46, p777-81.
BFI/Monthly Film Bulletin. Jan 1966, v33, p2-3.
Cinema. Dec 1965, v3, p32-35.
Cinema. Mar 1966, v3, p4-8, 13-14.
Commonweal. Nov 5, 1965, v83, p148-49.
Film Daily. Oct 25, 1965, p4.
Film Quarterly. Spr 1966, v19, p53.
Films and Filming. Jan 1966, v12, p25.
Films in Review. Dec 1965, v16, p644.
Hollywood Reporter. Oct 25, 1965, p3.
Life. Nov 12, 1965, v59, p15.
The London Times. Dec 2, 1965, p15.
Magill's Survey of Cinema. Series I. v2, p911-14.
Motion Picture Herald Product Digest. Nov 10, 1965, p401.
The New Republic. Dec 4, 1965, v153, p35.
New Statesman. Dec 10, 1965, v70, p946.
The New York Times. Oct 28, 1965, p48.
The New Yorker. Oct 30, 1965, v41, p203.
Newsweek. Nov 8, 1965, v66, p113.
Playboy. Mar 1965, v12, p34.
Saturday Review. Nov 6, 1965, v48, p46.
Senior Scholastic. Nov 18, 1965, v87, p32.
Sight and Sound. Wint 1965-66, v35, p42-43.
The Spectator. Dec 3, 1965, v215, p741.
Time. Nov 5, 1965, v86, p115.
Variety. Oct 27, 1965, p6.

King Richard and the Crusaders (US; Butler, David; 1954)
America. Aug 28, 1954, v91, p527.
BFI/Monthly Film Bulletin. Nov 1954, v21, p157.
Catholic World. Sep 1954, v179, p466.
Commonweal. Sep 3, 1954, v60, p537.

Film Daily. Jul 8, 1954, p6.
Films and Filming. Oct 1954, v1, p25.
Hollywood Reporter. Jul 7, 1954, p3.
Library Journal. Sep 1, 1954, v79, p1485.
The London Times. Oct 13, 1954, p9.
The London Times. Oct 18, 1954, p2.
Motion Picture Herald Product Digest. Jul 10, 1954, p57.
National Parent-Teacher. Sep 1954, v49, p38.
The New York Times. Aug 23, 1954, p20.
The New Yorker. Aug 28, 1954, v30, p55.
Newsweek. Aug 2, 1954, v44, p78-79.
Saturday Review. Aug 14, 1954, v37, p24.
Time. Aug 23, 1954, v64, p74.
Variety. Jul 7, 1954, p6.

King Solomon's Mines (US; Bennett, Compton; Marton, Andrew; 1950)
BFI/Monthly Film Bulletin. Jan 1951, v18, p204.
Christian Century. Dec 13, 1950, v67, p1503.
Commonweal. Nov 17, 1950, v53, p141.
Film Daily. Sep 26, 1950, p6.
Films in Review. Jan 1951, v2, p42.
The Great Adventure Films. p150-55.
Hollywood Reporter. Sep 26, 1950, p3.
Illustrated London News. Dec 30, 1950, v217, p1084.
Library Journal. Oct 15, 1950, v75, p1843.
Life. Nov 13, 1950, v29, p149-50.
Magill's Survey of Cinema. Series II. v3, p1261-64.
Motion Picture Herald Product Digest. Sep 30, 1950, p501.
The New Republic. Dec 4, 1950, v123, p23.
The New Statesman and Nation. Dec 16, 1950, v40, p624.
The New York Times. Nov 10, 1950, p35.
The New Yorker. Nov 11, 1950, v26, p141.
Newsweek. Nov 20, 1950, v36, p100.
One Good Film Deserves Another. p69-72.
The Spectator. Dec 8, 1950, v185, p648.
Time. Nov 20, 1950, v56, p106.
Variety. Sep 27, 1950, p8.

Kings of the Sun (US; Thompson, J. Lee; 1963)
BFI/Monthly Film Bulletin. Apr 1964, v31, p57.
Film Daily. Dec 16, 1963, p14.
Filmfacts. Jan 9, 1964, v6, p308-09.
Films and Filming. May 1964, v10, p24-25.
The New York Times. Dec 26, 1963, p33.
Saturday Review. Jan 18, 1964, v47, p27.
Variety. Dec 18, 1963, p6.

Kiss Me Deadly (US; Aldrich, Robert; 1955)
BFI/Monthly Film Bulletin. Aug 1955, v22, p120.
Cult Movies. p188-90.
Film Daily. May 12, 1955, p7.
The Films and Career of Robert Aldrich. p36-45.
The Films in My Life. p93-94.
Hollywood Reporter. Apr 20, 1955, v134, n16, p3.
Magill's Survey of Cinema. Series II. v3, p1269-71.
National Parent Teacher. May 1955, v49, p39.
Newsweek. Apr 25, 1955, v45, p106.
Robert Aldrich: A Guide to References and Resources. p22-24.
Variety. Apr 20, 1955, p6.

Kiss Me Goodbye (US; Mulligan, Robert; 1982)
Film Journal. Dec 27, 1982, v85, p12.
Films in Review. Feb 1983, v34, p112-13.
Hollywood Reporter. Dec 22, 1982, p3.

The Los Angeles Times. Dec 22, 1982, SecVI, p1.
Magill's Cinema Annual, 1983. p209-14.
The New York Times. Dec 22, 1982, SecIII, p22.
Newsweek. Jan 3, 1983, p53.
Variety. Dec 22, 1982, p14.
The Village Voice. Dec 28, 1982, p61.

Kiss Me Kate (US; Sidney, George; 1953)
America. Nov 21, 1953, v90, p215.
BFI/Monthly Film Bulletin. Feb 1954, v21, p40.
Catholic World. Dec 1953, v178, p223.
Commonweal. Nov 20, 1953, v59, p164.
Film Daily. Oct 27, 1953, p6.
Films in Review. Dec 1953, v4, p538-40.
Hollywood Reporter. Oct 27, 1953, p3.
Library Journal. Nov 15, 1953, v78, p2009.
Life. Nov 30, 1953, v35, p121-22.
Look. Dec 1, 1953, v17, p100-01.
Magill's Survey of Cinema. Series II. v3, p1272-74.
The Musical: From Broadway to Hollywood. p43-48.
National Parent-Teacher. Dec 1953, v48, p39.
The New York Times. Nov 6, 1953, p23.
The New Yorker. Nov 14, 1953, v29, p136.
Newsweek. Nov 9, 1953, v42, p96.
Saturday Review. Nov 14, 1953, v36, p40.
Time. Nov 16, 1953, v62, p106.
Variety. Oct 28, 1953, p6.

Kiss Me, Stupid (US; Wilder, Billy; 1964)
BFI/Monthly Film Bulletin. Mar 1965, v32, p34.
Billy Wilder in Hollywood. p239-42.
Billy Wilder (Madsen). p133-39, 142.
Christian Century. Feb 3, 1965, v82, p144-45.
Christian Science Monitor (Western edition). Jan 5, 1965, p5.
Commonweal. Dec 18, 1964, v81, p421-22.
Esquire. Jun 1965, v63, p18, 20.
The Film Career of Billy Wilder. p102-04.
Film Comment. Jan-Feb 1979, v15, p33-39.
Film Daily. Dec 17, 1964, p3.
Film Quarterly. Spr 1965, v18, p60.
Filmfacts. Jan 1, 1965, v7, p339-41.
Films and Filming. Apr 1965, v11, p27-28.
Films in Review. Feb 1965, v16, p118.
Hollywood Reporter. Dec 16, 1964, p3.
The London Times. Feb 25, 1965, p16.
Motion Picture Herald Product Digest. Jan 6, 1965, p202.
The New Republic. Jan 9, 1965, v152, p26.
New Statesman. Feb 26, 1965, v69, p334.
The New York Times. Dec 23, 1964, p22.
Newsweek. Dec 28, 1964, v64, p53-54.
Playboy. Mar 1965, v12, p34.
The Private Eye, the Cowboy and the Very Naked Girl. p109-12.
Saturday Review. Jan 2, 1965, v48, p31.
See No Evil. p299-308.
Sight and Sound. Spr 1965, v34, p95.
The Spectator. Mar 5, 1965, v214, p298.
Time. Jan 1, 1965, v85, p69.
Variety. Dec 16, 1964, p6.
The Velvet Light Trap. Wint 1971-72, n3, p33-35.
The Village Voice. Jan 14, 1965, v10, p14, 16.
Vogue. Mar 1, 1965, v145, p97.

Kiss of the Spider Woman (BRAZ; Babenco, Hector; 1985)
America. Sep 28, 1985, v153, p176.
Christian Century. Aug 28, 1985, v102, p774.
Film Comment. Jul/Aug 1985, v21, p56-59.
Films in Review. Oct 1985, v36, p485.
Hollywood Reporter. May 14, 1985, p3.

The Los Angeles Times. Aug 14, 1985, SecVI, p1.
Magill's Cinema Annual, 1986. p209-13.
The Nation. Oct 26, 1985, v241, p419-21.
National Review. Sep 6, 1985, v37, p56-57.
The New Republic. Sep 2, 1985, v193, p24-25.
New York. Aug 5, 1985, v18, p60-61.
The New York Times. Jul 26, 1985, SecIII, p5.
The New Yorker. Aug 26, 1985, v61, p61-63.
Newsweek. Aug 5, 1985, v106, p64.
Time. Aug 5, 1985, v126, p71.
Variety. May 15, 1985, p14.
Vogue. Aug 1985, v175, p60.
The Wall Street Journal. Oct 15, 1985, p26.

Kiss Them for Me (US; Donen, Stanley; 1957)
America. Nov 23, 1957, v98, p256.
BFI/Monthly Film Bulletin. Feb 1958, v25, p15.
Commonweal. Nov 29, 1957, v67, p233.
Film Daily. Nov 6, 1957, p6.
Films and Filming. Jan 1958, v4, p27.
Films in Review. Dec 1957, v8, p523.
The Films of Cary Grant. p230-33.
Hollywood Reporter. Nov 6, 1957, p3.
Motion Picture Herald Product Digest. Nov 9, 1957, p593.
The New York Times. Nov 9, 1957, p31.
The New York Times. Nov 24, 1957, SecII, p1.
The New Yorker. Nov 16, 1957, v33, p109.
Newsweek. Nov 18, 1957, v50, p130.
Saturday Review. Nov 23, 1957, v40, p29.
Stanley Donen (Casper). p117-23.
Time. Nov 25, 1957, v70, p120.
Variety. Nov 6, 1957, p6.

Kiss Tomorrow Goodbye (US; Douglas, Gordon; 1950)
BFI/Monthly Film Bulletin. Dec 1950, v17, p189.
Christian Century. Oct 18, 1950, v67, p1247.
Classics of the Gangster Film. p184-87.
Dark City: The Film Noir. p97-11.
The Films of James Cagney. p194-95.
The Great Gangster Pictures. p231.
Hollywood Reporter. Aug 1, 1950, p3.
Motion Picture Herald Product Digest. Aug 5, 1950, p413.
The New York Times. Aug 5, 1950, p9.
The New Yorker. Aug 12, 1950, v26, p46.
Newsweek. Aug 14, 1950, v36, p84.
The Spectator. Nov 17, 1950, v185, p509.
Time. Sep 4, 1950, v56, p82.
Variety. Aug 2, 1950, p16.

Kizino Kizi *See* What's Up, Tiger Lily?

Klute (US; Pakula, Alan J.; 1971)
Atlantic. Nov 1971, v228, p144.
BFI/Monthly Film Bulletin. Nov 1971, v38, p222.
Commonweal. Aug 6, 1971, v94, p407-08.
Deeper into Movies. p355-57.
Film Comment. Spr 1972, v7, p32-37.
Film Quarterly. Fall 1971, v25, p55-56.
Filmfacts. 1971, v45, p109-11.
Films and Filming. Nov 1971, v18, p51.
The Films of Jane Fonda. p157-60.
The Films of The Seventies. p42-44.
Hollywood Reporter. Jun 24, 1971, p3.
Life. Jul 30, 1971, v71, p14.
Magill's Survey of Cinema. Series I. v2, p915-18.
The New York Times. Jun 24, 1971, p35.
The New Yorker. Jul 3, 1971, v47, p42-43.
Sight and Sound. Aut 1971, v40, p220-21.
Time. Jul 12, 1971, v98, p44.
Variety. Jun 30, 1971, p22.

The Village Voice. Jul 15, 1971, p55.
Women and their Sexuality in the New Cinema. p55-73.

The Knack (Also titled: The Knack, and How to Get It) (GB; Lester, Richard; 1965)
America. Jul 24, 1965, v113, p103.
BFI/Monthly Film Bulletin. Jun 1965, v32, p88.
Christian Century. Dec 15, 1965, v82, p1547-48.
Christian Science Monitor (Western edition). Aug 4, 1965, p4.
Commonweal. Jul 2, 1965, v82, p473.
Esquire. Oct 1965, v64, p36, 38.
Film Daily. Jun 30, 1965, p20.
Film Quarterly. Fall 1965, v19, p55-57.
Film Society Review. Mar 1967, p30-34.
Films and Filming. Jul 1965, v11, p14-16, 25.
Films in Review. Aug-Sep 1965, v16, p450.
Hollywood Reporter. Jun 28, 1965, p3.
Illustrated London News. Jun 19, 1965, v246, p32.
International Film Guide. 1966, v3, p85.
Kiss Kiss Bang Bang. p143-44.
The London Times. Jun 3, 1965, p17.
The London Times. May 29, 1965, p7.
Los Angeles Free Press. Jul 30, 1965, v2, p7.
Magill's Survey of Cinema. Series II. v3, p1279-81.
Motion Picture Herald Product Digest. Jul 21, 1965, p329.
Movie. Fall 1965, n14, p6-11.
Movie Comedy (Byron). p250-51.
The Nation. Aug 2, 1965, v201, p68.
National Review. Oct 5, 1965, v17, p886-88.
The New Republic. Jul 10, 1965, v153, p29-30.
New Statesman. Jun 4, 1965, v69, p890.
The New York Times. Jun 30, 1965, p42.
The New Yorker. Jun 26, 1965, v41, p82, 84.
The New Yorker. Jul 10, 1965, v41, p54.
Newsweek. Jul 5, 1965, v66, p82.
On Movies. p401-03.
Playboy. Aug 1965, v12, p24.
The Private Eye, the Cowboy and the Very Naked Girl. p140-41.
Punch. Jun 16, 1965, v248, p900.
Redbook. Nov 1965, v126, p48.
Reporter. Sep 23, 1965, v33, p64.
Richard Lester: A Guide to References and Resources. p23-25.
Saturday Review. Jul 17, 1965, v48, p24-25.
Sight and Sound. Sum 1965, v34, p148.
The Spectator. Jun 11, 1965, v214, p758.
Time. Jul 9, 1965, v86, p98.
Variety. May 19, 1965, p31.
The Village Voice. Jul 8, 1965, v10, p13.
Vogue. Aug 15, 1965, v146, p52.
A World on Film. p215-17.

Knave of Hearts (French title: Monsieur Ripois; Also titled: Lovers, Happy Lovers; Lover Boy) (GB, FR; Clément, René; 1954)
BFI/Monthly Film Bulletin. Jul 1954, v21, p100.
Catholic World. Nov 1954, v180, p140.
Cinema, the Magic Vehicle. v2, p218-19.
Dictionary of Films. p178.
Film Culture. 1957, v3, n13, p11.
Film Daily. Oct 8, 1954, p6.
Films and Filming. Dec 1966, v13, p22.
Films in Review. Dec 1954, v5, p541-42.
Kiss Kiss Bang Bang. p389-90.
The London Times. May 17, 1954, p4.
Motion Picture Herald Product Digest. Nov 13, 1954, p210.
National Parent-Teacher. Nov 1954, v49, p39.

The New Statesman and Nation. Jun 26, 1954, v47, p832.
The New York Times. Oct 1, 1954, p19.
The New York Times. Sep 9, 1965, p36.
The New Yorker. Oct 16, 1954, v30, p146.
Newsweek. Nov 8, 1954, v44, p100.
Sight and Sound. Jul-Sep 1954, v24, p31.
The Tatler. Jun 2, 1954, v212, p524.
Variety. May 5, 1954, p21.

Knife in the Head (German title: Messer Im Kopf) (WGER; Hauff, Reinhard; 1978)
BFI/Monthly Film Bulletin. Apr 1980, v47, p71.
Christian Science Monitor. May 14, 1980, p19.
Films in Review. Aug-Sep 1980, v31, p436.
Hollywood Reporter. Mar 16, 1979, p22.
The Los Angeles Times. Dec 2, 1981, Calendar, p4.
The Nation. May 17, 1980, v230, p600-02.
The New Republic. Apr 26, 1980, v182, p24-25.
New Statesman. May 2, 1980, v104, p685.
New York. Apr 28, 1980, v13, p60-61.
The New York Times. Apr 23, 1980, SecIII, p24.
The New Yorker. Apr 28, 1980, v56, p129-31.
Newsweek. May 12, 1980, v95, p93-94.
Variety. Oct 25, 1978, p20.
The Village Voice. Apr 25, 1980, p45.

Knife in the Water (Polish title: Noz W Wodzie) (POL; Polanski, Roman; 1961)
Commonweal. Nov 8, 1963, v79, p195.
Film and the Critical Eye. p495-500.
Magill's Survey of Cinema. Foreign Language Films. v4, p1663-66.
The Nation. Nov 30, 1963, v197, p373.
The New Republic. Nov 2, 1963, v149, p30.
The New York Times. Oct 29, 1963, p31.
The New York Times. Nov 3, 1963, SecII, p1.
The New Yorker. Nov 2, 1963, v39, p195.
Newsweek. Nov 4, 1963, v62, p102.
Private Screenings. p95-96.
Roman Polanski: A Guide to References and Resources. p16-18.
Roman Polanski (Wexman). p27-32.
Saturday Review. Oct 26, 1963, v46, p51.
Variety. Sep 12, 1962, p16.
Vintage Films. p198-201.

Knightriders (US; Romero, George; 1981)
American Film. May 1981, v6, p42-43.
Film Journal. Apr 20, 1981, v84, p13-14.
The Los Angeles Times. Apr 9, 1981, SecVI, p1.
The Nation. May 16, 1981, v232, p613.
The New Leader. May 4, 1981, v64, p17-18.
New York. Apr 27, 1981, v14, p64.
The New York Times. Apr 17, 1981, SecIII, p8.
The New Yorker. May 18, 1981, v57, p47-48.
Newsweek. Apr 13, 1981, v97, p82.
Rolling Stone. May 28, 1981, p52.
Time. Apr 27, 1981, v117, p54-55.
Variety. Apr 8, 1981, p20.
The Village Voice. Apr 15, 1981, p51.

Knights of the Round Table (GB; Thorpe, Richard; 1953)
BFI/Monthly Film Bulletin. Jul 1954, v21, p100-01.
Commonweal. Jan 29, 1954, v59, p425-28.
Film Daily. Dec 23, 1953, p6.
Films and Filming. Jun 1963, v5, p37.
Films in Review. Feb 1954, v5, p90-91.
The Films of Robert Taylor. p135-39.
The London Times. May 14, 1954, p8.
Motion Picture Herald Product Digest. Dec 26, 1953, p2117.

The New Statesman and Nation. May 22, 1954, v47, p661.
The New Yorker. Jan 16, 1954, v29, p85-86.
Newsweek. Jan 18, 1954, v43, p88.
Saturday Review. Jan 16, 1954, v37, p32.
The Spectator. May 21, 1954, v192, p613-14.
The Tatler. May 26, 1954, v212, p462.
Time. Jan 25, 1954, v63, p110.
Variety. Dec 23, 1953, p6.

Knock on Wood (US; Panama, Norman; 1954)
America. May 1, 1954, v91, p147.
BFI/Monthly Film Bulletin. May 1954, v21, p70.
Catholic World. May 1954, v179, p143.
Commonweal. Apr 9, 1954, v60, p15.
Film Daily. Mar 31, 1954, p10.
Films and Filming. Jan 1963, v9, p55.
Films in Review. Mar 1954, v5, p145-46.
Hollywood Reporter. Mar 31, 1954, p3.
Illustrated London News. May 15, 1954, v224, p810.
Kiss Kiss Bang Bang. p364-65.
Life. Mar 22, 1954, v36, p133-34.
The London Times. Apr 22, 1954, p9.
Look. Apr 29, 1954, v18, p75-76.
Motion Picture Herald Product Digest. Apr 3, 1954, p2245.
National Parent-Teacher. May 1954, v48, p38.
The New Statesman and Nation. May 1, 1954, v47, p363.
The New York Times. Apr 15, 1954, p34.
The New Yorker. Apr 24, 1954, v30, p80.
Newsweek. Apr 12, 1954, v43, p102.
Saturday Review. Apr 10, 1954, v37, p36.
Senior Scholastic. Apr 14, 1954, v64, p29.
The Spectator. Apr 23, 1954, v192, p485.
The Tatler. May 5, 1954, v212, p286.
Time. Apr 26, 1954, v63, p112.
Variety. Mar 31, 1954, p6.

Kokkina Fanaria, Ta *See* Red Lanterns

Kon-Tiki (Also titled: Pacific Crossing on Raft) (US; Nordemar, Olle; 1951)
BFI/Monthly Film Bulletin. Nov 1952, v19, p154.
Film Daily. Mar 23, 1951, p6.
Films in Review. May 1951, v2, p42.
Motion Picture Herald Product Digest. Mar 24, 1951, p765-66.
The New Statesman and Nation. Oct 25, 1952, v44, p478.
The New York Times. Apr 4, 1951, p35.
The New Yorker. Apr 7, 1951, v27, p68.
Time. Apr 16, 1951, v57, p106.
Time. Mar 31, 1952, v59, p100.
Variety. Mar 21, 1951, p6.

Koshikei *See* Death By Hanging

Kotch (US; Lemmon, Jack; 1971)
America. Oct 23, 1971, v125, p321.
BFI/Monthly Film Bulletin. Jun 1972, v39, p117.
Filmfacts. 1971, v14, p546-49.
Films and Filming. Jun 1972, v18, p61-62.
Films in Review. Nov 1971, v22, p572.
The Films of Jack Lemmon. p192-96.
Focus on Film. 1972, v1, n9, p5-7.
Hollywood Reporter. Sep 22, 1971, p3.
The New York Times. Oct 1, 1971, p34.
Sight and Sound. Spr 1972, v41, p111.
Time. Oct 11, 1971, v98, p81.
Variety. Sep 22, 1971, p6.
The Village Voice. Apr 20, 1972, v16.

The Koumiko Mystery (French title: Mystere Koumiko, Le) (FR; Marker, Chris; 1965)
Cinema. Sum 1968, v4, p57.

Film. Wint 1965-66, n44, p25-26.
Film 67/68. p244-45.
Filmfacts. Jun 15, 1967, v10, p113-14.
The New Yorker. Apr 15, 1967, v43, p148.
Variety. Aug 4, 1965, p28.

Koyaanisqatsi (US; Reggio, Godfrey; 1983)
American Cinematographer. Mar 1984, v65, p62-64.
BFI/Monthly Film Bulletin. Aug 1983, v50, p217.
Cinefantastique. 1983-84, v14, n2, p50.
Cineforum. Jun-Jul 1984, v24, p79-80.
Film Journal. Sep 23, 1983, v86, p10, 23.
Hollywood Reporter. Apr 15, 1983, p28.
The Hudson Review. Spr 1984, v37, p289-94.
The Los Angeles Times. Oct 6, 1983, SecVI, p5.
New Statesman. Sep 2, 1983, v106, p25-26.
The New York Times. Sep 14, 1983, SecIII, p22.
Time. Oct 17, 1983, p89-90.
Variety. Sep 14, 1983, p18.
The Village Voice. Sep 20, 1983, p60.

Kradezat na Praskovi *See* The Peach Thief

Kramer vs. Kramer (US; Benton, Robert; 1979)
America. Jan 1980, v142, p43.
BFI/Monthly Film Bulletin. Apr 1980, v47, p69-70.
Commonweal. Feb 15, 1980, v107, p87-88.
The Films of Dustin Hoffman. p203-10.
The Films of the Seventies. p265-68.
Hollywood Reporter. Nov 29, 1979, p3.
The Los Angeles Times. Dec 16, 1979, Calendar, p1.
Magill's Survey of Cinema. Series I. v2, p919-24.
Motion Picture Herald Product Digest. Dec 26, 1979, p57.
The Nation. Jan 26, 1980, v230, p90-91.
The New Republic. Dec 22, 1979, v181, p24-25.
The New York Times. Dec 19, 1979, SecIII, p23.
The New Yorker. Dec 24, 1979, v55, p81-82.
Saturday Review. Mar 1, 1980, v7, p34.
Time. Dec 3, 1979, v114, p74-81.
Time. Feb 4, 1980, v115, p77.
Variety. Nov 28, 1979, p16.

Krik *See* The Cry

Kumonosu-jo *See* Throne of Blood

Kvarteret Korpen *See* Raven's End

Kvinnors Vantan *See* Secrets of Women

Kwaidan (Also titled: Kaidan) (JAPAN; Kobayashi, Masaki; 1964)
BFI/Monthly Film Bulletin. Sep 1967, v34, p135-36.
Cinema. Mar 1966, v3, p50.
Film Daily. Nov 12, 1965, p22.
Film Society Review. Dec 1966, p25-26.
Films and Filming. Oct 1967, v14, p22.
Films in Review. Jan 1966, v17, p48-49.
The International Dictionary of Films and Filmmakers. v1, p247.
International Film Guide. 1966, v3, p103-04.
Magill's Survey of Cinema. Foreign Language Films. v4, p1672-78.
Motion Picture Herald Product Digest. Nov 24, 1965, p410.
New Statesman. Jul 28, 1967, v73, p126.
The New York Times. Nov 23, 1965, p51.
The New Yorker. Nov 27, 1965, v41, p233.
Newsweek. Nov 22, 1965, v66, p112.
Saturday Review. Nov 20, 1965, v48, p55.
Senior Scholastic. Dec 9, 1965, v87, p33.
Sight and Sound. Aut 1967, v36, p202-03.
Variety. May 26, 1965, p6.

The L-Shaped Room (GB; Forbes, Bryan; 1963)
America. Aug 31, 1963, v109, p218-19.
BFI/Monthly Film Bulletin. Jan 1963, v30, p3.
Commonweal. Jun 7, 1963, v78, p304-05.
Film Daily. May 15, 1963, p11.
Filmfacts. Jun 6, 1963, v6, p97-99.
Films in Review. Aug-Sep 1963, v14, p437.
Hollywood Reporter. May 27, 1963, p3.
Illustrated London News. Dec 22, 1962, v241, p1030.
Magill's Survey of Cinema. Series I. v2, p925-28.
National Review. Jul 30, 1963, v15, p72.
The New Republic. Jun 8, 1963, v148, p26.
New Statesman. Nov 23, 1962, v64, p752.
The New York Times. May 28, 1963, p32.
The New Yorker. Jun 1, 1963, v39, p66.
Newsweek. Jun 3, 1963, v61, p83.
Photoplay. Sep 1963, v64, p10.
Saturday Review. Jun 8, 1963, v46, p40.
Sight and Sound. Wint 1962-63, v32, p40-41.
Variety. Nov 21, 1962, p12.
The Village Voice. Jul 4, 1963, v8, p9.

The Lacemaker (French title: Dentelliers, Le) (FR, SWITZ, WGER; Goretta, Claude; 1977)
BFI/Monthly Film Bulletin. Nov 1977, v44, p230.
Hollywood Reporter. Oct 21, 1977, p16.
The International Dictionary of Films and Filmmakers. v1, p117-18.
The Los Angeles Times. Dec 18, 1977, Calendar, p60.
Magill's Survey of Cinema. Foreign Language Films. v4, p1679-83.
The Nation. Oct 22, 1977, v225, p413.
National Review. Jan 20, 1978, v30, p103-05.
The New York Times. Oct 6, 1977, SecIII, p21.
Time. Nov 7, 1977, v110, p88.
Variety. May 25, 1977, p21.

Lacombe, Lucien (FR, IT, WGER; Malle, Louis; 1974)
America. Oct 26, 1974, v131, p234.
BFI/Monthly Film Bulletin. Jul 1974, v41, p149-50.
Christian Century. May 15, 1974, v91, p543.
Christian Century. Nov 13, 1974, v91, p1074.
Commonweal. Nov 29, 1974, v101, p214-15.
Esquire. Dec 1974, v82, p23.
Film Comment. Sep-Oct 1974, v10, p36-37.
Film Comment. May-Jun 1974, v10, p2.
Films and Filming. Jul 1974, v20, p43-44.
Films Illustrated. Jun 1974, v3, p378.
Films in Review. Nov 1974, v25, p566-67.
Hollywood Reporter. Oct 2, 1974, p3.
Independent Film Journal. Oct 2, 1974, v74, p32-33.
The Los Angeles Times. May 18, 1975, Calendar, p1.
Magill's Survey of Cinema. Foreign Language Films. v4, p1684-88.
Motion Picture Herald Product Digest. Oct 2, 1974, p33.
The Nation. Oct 19, 1974, v219, p379.
The New Republic. Oct 5, 1974, v171, p18.
New Statesman. Jun 7, 1974, v87, p811-12.
The New York Times. Nov 13, 1974, SecII, p15.
The New York Times. Mar 10, 1974, p3.
The New York Times. Oct 6, 1974, SecII, p1.
The New Yorker. Sep 30, 1974, v50, p94-100.
Newsweek. Oct 14, 1974, v84, p131.
Reeling. p447-55.
Saturday Review. Oct 19, 1974, v2, p41-42.
Time. Oct 14, 1974, v104, p4.
Times Educational Supplement. Jun 14, 1974, p66.

Variety. Jan 30, 1974, p14.
The Village Voice. Oct 17, 1974, p77-78.
Vogue. Nov 1974, v164, p110.

Ladies and Gentlemen *See* The Birds, the Bees and the Italians

The Ladies of the Bois de Boulogne *See* Dames du Boulogne, Les

Ladri di Venezia *See* The Thief of Venice

Lady in a Cage (US; Grauman, Walter; 1964)
America. Jun 20, 1964, v110, p853-54.
BFI/Monthly Film Bulletin. Aug 1967, v34, p121.
Commonweal. Jun 26, 1964, v80, p423-24.
Film Daily. May 28, 1964, v124, p6.
Films and Filming. Sep 1967, v13, p22-23.
Films in Review. May 1964, v15, p305-07.
The Films of Olivia De Havilland. p237-38.
Hollywood Reporter. May 28, 1964, p3.
Motion Picture Herald Product Digest. Jun 10, 1964, p65-66.
The New Republic. Jun 20, 1964, v150, p25.
The New York Times. Jun 11, 1964, p27.
Newsweek. Jun 22, 1964, v63, p84.
Saturday Review. Jun 20, 1964, v47, p29.
Time. Jun 19, 1964, v83, p93.
Variety. Jun 3, 1964, p15.

Lady L (US, IT, FR; Ustinov, Peter; 1965)
America. Jun 18, 1966, v114, p861.
BFI/Monthly Film Bulletin. Jan 1966, v33, p3.
Christian Science Monitor (Western edition). Jun 25, 1966, p6.
Cinema. Jul 1966, v3, p49.
Commonweal. Jun 10, 1966, v84, p337-38.
Film Daily. May 11, 1966, p6.
Filmfacts. Aug 1, 1966, v9, p143-45.
Films and Filming. Jan 1966, v12, p9.
Films and Filming. Feb 1966, v12, p10.
Films in Review. Jun-Jul 1966, v17, p382.
The Films of David Niven. p194-97.
The Films of Paul Newman. p141-45.
The Films of Sophia Loren. p172-77.
Hollywood Reporter. May 11, 1966, p3.
The London Times. Nov 25, 1965, p5.
Motion Picture Herald Product Digest. May 11, 1966, p517.
New Statesman. Nov 26, 1965, v70, p852-53.
The New York Times. May 19, 1966, p51.
The New Yorker. May 21, 1966, v42, p98.
Newsweek. Jun 13, 1966, v67, p114B.
Saturday Review. May 21, 1966, v49, p48.
Sight and Sound. Wint 1965-66, v35, p44.
The Spectator. Nov 26, 1965, v215, p691.
Tynan Right and Left. p245-56.
Variety. Dec 1, 1965, p6.
Vogue. Jul 1966, v148, p30.

Lady Paname (FR; Jeanson, Henri; 1950)
BFI/Monthly Film Bulletin. Jul 1952, v19, p95.
Commonweal. Mar 16, 1951, v53, p566.
Film Daily. Mar 30, 1951, p5.
The New Republic. Apr 9, 1951, v124, p32.
The New Statesman and Nation. May 24, 1952, v43, p614-15.
The New York Times. Mar 20, 1951, p35.
The Spectator. May 16, 1952, v188, p640.
Variety. Jun 28, 1950, p18.

The Lady Pays Off (US; Sirk, Douglas; 1951)
BFI/Monthly Film Bulletin. Nov 1951, v18, p360.
Douglas Sirk (Stern). p64-65.
Film Daily. Oct 22, 1951, p6.
Hollywood Reporter. Oct 19, 1951, p3.
Motion Picture Herald Product Digest. Oct 20, 1951, p1065.

The Spectator. Oct 12, 1951, v187, p473.
Time. Nov 19, 1951, v58, p114.
Variety. Oct 24, 1951, p6.

Lady Possessed (US; Spier, William; Kellino, Roy; 1952)
BFI/Monthly Film Bulletin. Jan 1952, v19, p3.
Film Daily. Feb 28, 1952, p8.
The Films of James Mason. p102-03.
Hollywood Reporter. Feb 15, 1952, p3.
Library Journal. Mar 1, 1952, v77, p426.
Motion Picture Herald Product Digest. Feb 23, 1952, p1246.
The New York Times. Feb 15, 1952, p17.
Newsweek. Mar 3, 1952, v39, p90.
Time. Feb 25, 1952, v59, p71.
Variety. Feb 20, 1952, p6.

Lady Sings the Blues (US; Furie, Sidney J.; 1972)
Commonweal. Dec 8, 1972, v97, p228-29.
Ebony. Nov 1972, v28, p37-40.
Filmfacts. 1972, v15, n17, p389.
Life. Dec 1, 1972, v73, p28.
Life. Dec 8, 1972, v73, p42-45.
Magill's Cinema Annual, 1985. p565-69.
The New York Times. Oct 19, 1972, p56.
The New York Times. Nov 12, 1972, SecII, p1.
The New Yorker. Nov 4, 1972, v48, p152-58.
Newsweek. Nov 6, 1972, v80, p133.
Reeling. p62-69.
Saturday Review. Nov 11, 1972, v55, p81.
Time. Nov 6, 1972, v100, p86-87.
Variety. Oct 18, 1972, p18.

The Lady With the Lamp (GB; Wilcox, Herbert; 1951)
BFI/Monthly Film Bulletin. Oct 1951, v18, p341-42.
Catholic World. May 1952, v175, p144.
Illustrated London News. Sep 15, 1951, v219, p414-15.
Illustrated London News. Oct 6, 1951, v219, p526.
The New Statesman and Nation. Sep 29, 1951, v42, p338.
Saturday Review. Jan 19, 1952, v35, p33.
Senior Scholastic. May 14, 1952, v60, p24.
The Spectator. Sep 28, 1951, v187, p392-93.
Variety. Oct 3, 1951, p6.

A Lady Without Passport (US; Lewis, Joseph H.; 1950)
BFI/Monthly Film Bulletin. Dec 1950, v17, p189.
Film Daily. Jul 3, 1950, p7.
The Films of Hedy Lamarr. p211-14.
Hollywood Reporter. Jul 13, 1950, p3.
Motion Picture Herald Product Digest. Jul 15, 1950, p390.
The New York Times. Aug 4, 1950, p13.
Variety. Jul 19, 1950, p6.

The Ladykillers (GB; MacKendrick, Alexander; 1955)
America. Apr 7, 1956, v95, p43.
BFI/Monthly Film Bulletin. Jan 1956, v23, p3.
Commonweal. Feb 24, 1956, v63, p545.
Fifty Classic British Films. p88-90.
Film Culture. 1956, v2, p28-29.
Film Daily. Feb 23, 1956, p6.
Films in Review. Feb 1956, v7, p2.
The Great British Films. p165-67.
Hollywood Reporter. Feb 28, 1956, p3.
Magill's Survey of Cinema. Series I. v2, p939-41.
Motion Picture Herald Product Digest. Feb 25, 1956, p793.
The Nation. Mar 10, 1956, v182, p207.
The New York Times. Feb 21, 1956, p37.
The New York Times. Feb 26, 1956, SecII, p1.

The New Yorker. Mar 3, 1956, v32, p68.
Newsweek. Feb 20, 1956, v47, p106.
Saturday Review. Feb 4, 1956, v39, p21.
Sight and Sound. Wint 1955-56, v25, p148-49.
Time. Mar 12, 1956, v67, p112.
Variety. Dec 28, 1955, p6.

Land of the Pharoahs (US; Hawks, Howard; 1955)
America. Jul 30, 1955, v93, p439.
BFI/Monthly Film Bulletin. Nov 1955, v22, p163.
Catholic World. Aug 1, 1955, v181, p383.
Commonweal. Jul 1, 1955, v62, p330.
Film Daily. Jun 22, 1955, p6.
Films and Filming. Jun 1953, v2, p23.
The Films in My Life. p72-73.
Films in Review. Aug-Sep 1955, v6, p344.
Hollywood Reporter. Jun 21, 1955, p3.
Natural History. Sep 1955, v64, p391.
The New York Times. Sep 5, 1954, SecII, p5.
The New York Times. Jul 27, 1955, p15.
The New Yorker. Aug 6, 1955, v31, p49.
Saturday Review. Jun 25, 1955, v38, p24.
Time. Jul 4, 1955, v66, p71.
Variety. Jun 22, 1955, p6.

The Landlord (US; Ashby, Hal; 1970)
America. Jun 6, 1970, v122, p618.
BFI/Monthly Film Bulletin. Mar 1971, v38, p52.
Esquire. Oct 1970, v74, p67.
Films and Filming. Oct 1970, v17, p44-45.
Hollywood Reporter. May 21, 1970, p3, 11.
Magill's Survey of Cinema. Series II. v3, p1300-04.
The New York Times. May 21, 1970, p44.
The New York Times. Jun 14, 1970, SecII, p1.
The New York Times. Aug 2, 1970, SecII, p9.
Newsweek. Jun 1, 1970, v75, p99-100.
Saturday Review. May 30, 1970, v53, p37.
Variety. May 27, 1970, p14.

The Las Vegas Story (US; Stevenson, Robert; 1952)
BFI/Monthly Film Bulletin. May 1952, v19, p66.
Film Daily. Jan 10, 1952, p8.
Hollywood Reporter. Jan 2, 1952, p3.
Motion Picture Herald Product Digest. Jan 5, 1952, p1177.
The New York Times. Jan 31, 1952, p37.
The New Yorker. Feb 9, 1952, v27, p105.
Newsweek. Feb 11, 1952, v39, p90.
Time. Feb 11, 1952, v59, p92.
Variety. Jan 9, 1952, p6.
Vincent Price Unmasked. p187-89.

Lásky Jedne Plavovlasky *See* Loves of a Blonde

The Last Angry Man (US; Mann, Daniel; 1959)
America. Oct 31, 1959, v102, p137.
BFI/Monthly Film Bulletin. May 1960, v27, p64.
Commonweal. Nov 20, 1959, v71, p239.
Film Daily. Oct 9, 1959, p6.
Filmfacts. Nov 25, 1959, v2, p253-55.
Films in Review. Nov 1959, v10, p556-57.
Hollywood Reporter. Oct 9, 1959, p3.
McCall's. Dec 1959, v87, p6.
The New Republic. Nov 2, 1959, v141, p22.
The New York Times. Oct 23, 1959, p24.
Newsweek. Oct 26, 1959, v54, p123.
Saturday Review. Oct 17, 1959, v42, p64.
Time. Oct 26, 1959, v74, p59.
Variety. Oct 14, 1959, p6.

The Last Bridge (German title: Letzte Bruecke, Die) (AUSTRIA; Kautner, Helmut; 1957)

BFI/Monthly Film Bulletin. May 1955, v22, p70.
Commonweal. Sep 6, 1957, v66, p569.
Film Culture. Oct 1957, v3, p16-17.
Film Daily. Aug 26, 1957, p6.
Films and Filming. May 1955, v1, p20.
Films in Review. Nov 1957, v8, p462.
The New York Times. Aug 21, 1957, p22.
Newsweek. Aug 26, 1957, v50, p99.
Time. Sep 2, 1957, v70, p60.
Variety. Apr 7, 1954, p24.

The Last Detail (US; Ashby, Hal; 1973)
Audience. May 1974, v6, p8-9.
BFI/Monthly Film Bulletin. Jul 1974, v41, p150.
Christian Century. May 1, 1974, v91, p482-84.
Commentary. May 1974, v57, p61-63.
Commonweal. Apr 19, 1974, v100, p166-67.
Esquire. May 1974, v81, p32.
Film. Jun 1974, n15, p9.
Films and Filming. Jun 1974, v20, p20-21.
Films and Filming. Oct 1974, v21, p42-43.
Films Illustrated. Jun 1974, v3, p372.
The Films of the Seventies. p79-81.
Guts & Glory. p290-92.
Hollywood Reporter. Nov 28, 1973, p3.
Independent Film Journal. Feb 4, 1974, v73, p9.
Jump Cut. May-Jun 1974, n1, p11-12.
The Los Angeles Times. Dec 9, 1973, Calendar, p1.
Magill's Survey of Cinema. Series I. v2, p942-45.
Motion Picture Herald Product Digest. Feb 13, 1974, p74.
Movietone News. Mar 1974, n30, p27-29.
Ms. May 1974, v2, p29-30.
The Nation. Mar 2, 1974, v218, p283-84.
The New Republic. Feb 23, 1974, v170, p22.
New Statesman. May 31, 1974, v87, p777.
New York. Feb 11, 1974, v7, p74-75.
The New York Times. Feb 11, 1974, p50.
The New York Times. Feb 24, 1974, SecII, p1.
The New Yorker. Feb 11, 1974, v49, p95-96.
Newsweek. Feb 11, 1974, v83, p86.
Reeling. p368-72.
Rolling Stone. Mar 14, 1974, p70-71.
Sight and Sound. Sum 1974, v43, p177.
Society. Sep-Oct 1974, v11, p77-80.
Time. Feb 18, 1974, v103, p72.
Variety. Dec 5, 1973, p20.
The Village Voice. Feb 7, 1974, p61-62.

The Last Gasp *See* Breathless

Last Holiday (GB; Cass, Henry; 1950)
BFI/Monthly Film Bulletin. Jun 1950, v17, p80-81.
Films in Review. Jan 1951, v2, p42-43.
Hollywood Reporter. Oct 9, 1950, p4.
Kiss Kiss Bang Bang. p366.
Motion Picture Herald Product Digest. Nov 25, 1950, p589.
The New Republic. Dec 4, 1950, v123, p22.
The New Statesman and Nation. May 13, 1950, v39, p544.
The New York Times. Nov 14, 1950, p39.
The New Yorker. Nov 25, 1950, v26, p132.
Newsweek. Nov 27, 1950, v36, p84.
Variety. May 17, 1950, p6.

The Last Hurrah (US; Ford, John; 1958)
About John Ford. p161-62.
America. Nov 15, 1958, v100, p224-26.
BFI/Monthly Film Bulletin. Feb 1959, v26, p15.
Catholic World. Dec 1958, v188, p238-39.
Commonweal. Nov 14, 1958, v69, p176-77.
Film Daily. Oct 17, 1958, p6.
Filmfacts. Nov 26, 1958, v1, p197-98.

Films in Review. Nov 1958, v9, p512-13.
Films in Review. Jan 1959, v10, p2.
The Films of Spencer Tracy. p232-35.
Good Housekeeping. Dec 1958, v147, p24.
Hollywood Reporter. Oct 15, 1958, p3.
Library Journal. Nov 1, 1958, v83, p3098.
Magill's Survey of Cinema. Series I. v3, p945-47.
The Modern American Novel and the Movies. p215-23.
The Nation. Nov 15, 1958, v187, p367.
The New Republic. Oct 27, 1958, v139, p21.
The New York Times. Oct 24, 1958, p40.
The New Yorker. Nov 1, 1958, v34, p170.
Newsweek. Oct 27, 1958, v52, p94.
The Non-Western Films of John Ford. p76-82.
Saturday Review. Nov 1, 1958, v41, p32.
Senior Scholastic. Dec 5, 1958, v73, p33.
Time. Oct 27, 1958, v70, p42.
Variety. Oct 15, 1958, p6.

The Last Married Couple in America (US; Cates, Gilbert; 1980)
BFI/Monthly Film Bulletin. Apr 1980, v47, p70.
Commonweal. Mar 28, 1980, v107, p183.
Films in Review. Mar 1980, v31, p184.
Hollywood Reporter. Feb 6, 1980, p22.
The Los Angeles Times. Feb 8, 1980, SecVI, p7.
Maclean's. Feb 11, 1980, v93, p54.
Motion Picture Herald Product Digest. Feb 6, 1980, p72.
The Nation. Mar 1, 1980, v230, p251-52.
The New York Times. Feb 8, 1980, SecIII, p12.
Newsday. Feb 8, 1980, SecII, p6.
Variety. Feb 6, 1980, p20.
The Village Voice. Feb 18, 1980, p48.

The Last Metro (French title: Dernier Metro, Le) (FR; Truffaut, François; 1980)
BFI/Monthly Film Bulletin. Jul 1981, v48, p135.
Christian Science Monitor. Oct 30, 1980, p18.
Cineaste. Fall 1980, v10, p9.
Films in Review. Apr 1981, v32, p245.
François Truffaut: A Guide to References and Resources. p87-90.
Hollywood Reporter. Oct 24, 1980, p9.
The Los Angeles Times. Feb 22, 1981, Calendar, p23.
Magill's Survey of Cinema. Foreign Language Films. v4, p1712-17.
The Nation. Mar 7, 1981, v236, p284.
The New Republic. Feb 28, 1981, v188, p22.
New Statesman. Jun 19, 1981, v105, p26.
New York. Feb 16, 1981, v14, p58.
The New York Times. Oct 12, 1980, p71.
Newsday. Feb 11, 1981, p58.
Newsweek. Feb 23, 1981, v101, p60.
Saturday Review. Dec 1980, v7, p84.
Sight and Sound. Sum 1981, v51, p210.
Time. Feb 23, 1981, v121, p110.
Variety. Sep 17, 1980, p18.
The Village Voice. Oct 15, 1980, p49.
The Village Voice. Feb 11, 1981, p47.

The Last Movie (US; Hopper, Dennis; 1971)
Atlantic. Dec 1971, v228, p130-33.
The Fifty Worst Films of All Time. p137-42.
Filmfacts. 1971, v14, p530-33.
Hollywood Reporter. Oct 13, 1971, v218, n17, p3.
Interview. Feb 1972, v19, p35.
National Review. Dec 3, 1971, v23, p1368.
The New Republic. Oct 30, 1971, v165, p22.
The New York Times. Aug 30, 1971, p35.
The New York Times. Sep 30, 1971, p58.
The New York Times. Oct 24, 1971, SecII, p11.

The New Yorker. Oct 9, 1971, v47, p152-54.
Newsweek. Oct 18, 1971, v78, p114-15.
Saturday Review. Oct 16, 1971, v14, p63.
Take One. Jun 1972, v3, n4, p30-31.
Time. Oct 18, 1971, v98, p87.
Variety. Sep 8, 1971, p16.
The Village Voice. Oct 14, 1971, p69.

The Last of Sheila (US; Ross, Herbert; 1973)
Christian Century. Jul 4, 1973, v90, p740.
Hollywood Reporter. Jun 8, 1973, p3.
The New York Times. Jul 15, 1973, p24.
The New York Times. Jul 29, 1973, SecI, p3.
The New York Times. Jul 29, 1973, SecII, p1.
The New Yorker. Jul 23, 1973, v49, p68-69.
Newsweek. Jul 25, 1973, v81, p55.
PTA Magazine. Nov 1973, v68, p8.
Time. Jul 25, 1973, v101, p77.
Variety. May 23, 1973, p36.

The Last Picture Show (US; Bogdanovich, Peter; 1971)
BFI/Monthly Film Bulletin. Apr 1972, v39, p73.
Commonweal. Nov 5, 1971, v95, p132-33.
Commonweal. Jan 14, 1972, v95, p348-50.
Deeper into Movies. p370-75.
Fifty Grand Movies of the 1960s and 1970s. p41-44.
Film Quarterly. Spr 1972, v25, p59.
Film Society Review. Nov 1971, v7, n3, p23-24.
Filmfacts. 1971, v14, p357-63.
Films and Filming. May 1972, v18, n8, p51-52.
Films in Review. Nov 1971, v22, n9, p574.
The Films of The Seventies. p38-39.
Hollywood Reporter. Oct 8, 1971, v218, n15, p3.
Magill's Survey of Cinema. Series II. v3, p1314-17.
The Nation. Oct 25, 1971, v213, p411-12.
The New Republic. Oct 16, 1971, v165, p18.
The New York Times. Dec 14, 1970, p86.
The New York Times. Oct 4, 1971, p51.
The New York Times. Oct 17, 1971, SecII, p1.
The New York Times. Jan 23, 1972, SecII, p11.
The New York Times. Jul 23, 1972, SecII, p7.
The New York Times. Jul 30, 1973, p22.
The New Yorker. Oct 9, 1971, v47, p145-47.
Newsweek. Oct 11, 1971, v78, p57.
Saturday Review. Oct 16, 1971, v54, p63.
Sight and Sound. Spr 1972, v41, n2, p107-08.
Take One. Jan-Feb 1971, v3, n3, p22-23.
Time. Oct 11, 1971, v98, p80.
Variety. Oct 6, 1971, p16.
The Village Voice. Oct 14, 1971, v16, p69, 78-80.

The Last Remake of Beau Geste (US; Feldman, Marty; 1977)
BFI/Monthly Film Bulletin. Dec 1977, v44, p261.
Commonweal. Aug 19, 1977, v104, p532.
Films in Review. Oct 1977, v28, p500.
Hollywood Reporter. Jul 13, 1977, p3.
The Los Angeles Times. Jul 15, 1977, SecIV, p1.
Motion Picture Herald Product Digest. Aug 3, 1977, p17.
The New York Times. Jul 16, 1977, p16.
The New Yorker. Jul 25, 1977, v53, p78-79.
Surrealism and American Feature Films. p165-84.
Time. Aug 8, 1977, v110, p58.
Variety. Jul 13, 1977, p18.

Last Run (US; Fleischer, Richard; 1971)
BFI/Monthly Film Bulletin. Dec 1971, v38, p242.
Filmfacts. 1971, v14, p281-83.
Films and Filming. Apr 1972, v18, p6.

Hollywood Reporter. Jun 29, 1971, p3.
The New York Times. Jul 8, 1971, p30.
Newsweek. Jul 19, 1971, v78, p79.
Saturday Review. Jul 31, 1971, v54, p50.
Time. Jul 26, 1971, v98, p51.
Variety. Jul 7, 1971, p20.
The Village Voice. Jul 22, 1971, p60.

The Last Starfighter (US; Castle, Nick; 1984)
American Cinematographer. Nov 1984, v65, p84, 91.
BFI/Monthly Film Bulletin. Dec 1984, v51, p384.
Cinefantastique. 1984, v14, n3, p23-25.
Cinefex. Jun 1984, n17, p54-55.
Film Journal. Aug 1984, v87, p17.
Hollywood Reporter. Jul 9, 1984, p4.
The Los Angeles Times. Jul 13, 1984, SecVI, p4.
Magill's Cinema Annual, 1985. p277-81.
Midnight Marquee. Fall 1984, n33, p30.
Millimeter. Sep 1984, v12, p142-44.
Millimeter. Jun 1984, v12, p91-94.
The New York Times. Jul 13, 1984, SecIII, p5.
The New York Times. Aug 12, 1984, SecII, p17.
Newsweek. Jul 30, 1984, v104, p80.
On Location. Jun 1984, v8, p98-105.
Time. Jul 23, 1984, v124, p102.
Variety. Jul 11, 1984, p16.
The Village Voice. Jul 24, 1984, p57-58.

Last Summer (US; Perry, Frank; 1969)
America. Aug 30, 1969, v121, p126.
Big Screen, Little Screen. p228-30.
Commonweal. Aug 8, 1969, v90, p486-87.
Confessions of a Cultist. p450-51.
Figures of Light. p177-79.
Film Daily. Jun 16, 1969, p10.
Film Quarterly. Fall 1969, v23, p50-51.
Filmfacts. 1969, v12, p193.
Films and Filming. Feb 1970, v16, p37-38.
Focus. Oct 1969, n5, p34.
Holiday. Jul 1969, v46, p22.
Hollywood Reporter. Jun 30, 1969, p3.
Life. Jul 18, 1969, v67, p6.
Movies Into Film. p113-15.
The Nation. Jun 30, 1969, v108, p837.
The New Republic. Jul 12, 1969, v161, p22.
The New York Times. Jun 11, 1969, p38.
The New Yorker. Jun 28, 1969, v45, p87-88.
Newsweek. Jun 23, 1969, v73, p95.
Saturday Review. Jul 19, 1969, v52, p22.
Variety. May 21, 1969, p18.
Vogue. Aug 15, 1969, v154, p44.

The Last Sunset (US; Aldrich, Robert; 1961)
BFI/Monthly Film Bulletin. Aug 1961, v28, p114-15.
Commonweal. Jun 30, 1961, v73, p353.
Film Daily. May 24, 1961, p6.
Film Quarterly. Fall 1961, v15, p55.
Filmfacts. Aug 11, 1961, v4, p167-68.
The Films and Career of Robert Aldrich. p156.
Films and Filming. Aug 1961, v7, p27-28.
The Films of Kirk Douglas. p173-76.
The New York Times. Jun 15, 1961, p51.
Newsweek. Jul 3, 1961, v58, p72.
Robert Aldrich: A Guide to References and Resources. p32-34.
Variety. May 24, 1961, p6.

Last Tango in Paris (Italian title: Ultimo tango à Parigi, L') (IT, FR; Bertolucci, Bernardo; 1972)
America. Feb 24, 1973, v128, p171-72.
Atlantic. Apr 1973, v231, p120-23.
Christian Century. Feb 28, 1973, v90, p251-52.
Christian Century. Mar 14, 1973, v90, p321-22.

Christianity Today. Jul 6, 1973, v17, p20-22.
Commonweal. Mar 9, 1973, v98, p15-16.
Cult Movies 2. p176-77.
Esquire. May 1973, v79, p18.
Film Quarterly. Spr 1973, v26, p2-9.
Film Quarterly. Spr 1973, v26, p9-19.
Films in Review. Apr 1973, v24, n4.
The Films of Marlon Brando. p240-45.
The Films of The Seventies. p62-64.
Good Housekeeping. May 1973, v176, p102-03.
Ladies Home Journal. Apr 1973, v90, p2.
Mademoiselle. Apr 1973, v76, p246.
Mademoiselle. Jul 1973, v77, p128-29.
Magill's Survey of Cinema. Series II. v3, p1318-20.
The Nation. Feb 12, 1973, v216, p220-22.
National Review. Feb 16, 1973, v25, p226.
National Review. May 25, 1973, v25, p586.
The New Republic. Mar 3, 1973, v168, p20.
The New York Times. Oct 16, 1972, v46, p1.
The New Yorker. Oct 28, 1972, v48, p130.
Newsweek. Feb 12, 1973, v81, p54-58.
Reeling. p52-61.
Saturday Review. Aug 1973, v1, p47.
Saturday Review. Apr 1973, v1, p68-69.
Society. Apr 1973, v1, p92.
Time. Jan 22, 1973, v101, p51-55.
Variety. Oct 18, 1972, p18.
Vintage Films. p223-30.
Vogue. Apr 1973, v161, p20.
Women and their Sexuality in the New Film. p53.

The Last Time I Saw Paris (US; Brooks, Richard; 1954)
America. Dec 4, 1954, v92, p285.
BFI/Monthly Film Bulletin. Feb 1955, v22, p20.
Commonweal. Nov 26, 1954, v61, p223.
Film Daily. Nov 4, 1954, p6.
Films and Filming. Feb 1955, v1, p20.
The Films of Elizabeth Taylor. p115-19.
Hollywood Reporter. Nov 3, 1954, p3.
Library Journal. Dec 15, 1954, v79, p2438.
Motion Picture Herald Product Digest. Nov 6, 1954, p201.
National Parent-Teacher. Jan 1955, v49, p40.
The New York Times. Nov 19, 1954, p20.
The New Yorker. Dec 4, 1954, v30, p227.
Newsweek. Nov 22, 1954, v44, p106.
Reporter. Dec 30, 1954, v11, p45.
Saturday Review. Nov 20, 1954, v37, p31.
The Spectator. Apr 29, 1955, v194, p537.
The Tatler. May 11, 1955, v216, p354.
Time. Nov 22, 1954, v64, p102.
Variety. Nov 3, 1954, p6.

The Last Train from Gun Hill (US; Sturges, John; 1958)
America. Aug 15, 1959, v101, p619.
BFI/Monthly Film Bulletin. Jun 1958, v26, p72.
Catholic World. Jun 1959, v189, p238-39.
Commonweal. May 15, 1959, v70, p185.
Film Daily. Apr 16, 1959, v115, p11.
Filmfacts. Sep 2, 1959, v2, p181-82.
The Films of Anthony Quinn. p180-82.
The Films of Kirk Douglas. p155-58.
Hollywood Reporter. Apr 15, 1959, p3.
The New York Times. Jul 30, 1959, p31.
The New Yorker. Aug 8, 1959, v35, p86.
Newsweek. Aug 3, 1959, v54, p47.
Time. Aug 10, 1959, v74, p59.
Variety. Apr 15, 1959, p6.

The Last Tycoon (US; Kazan, Elia; 1976)
American Film. Mar 1976, v1, p8-14.
Atlantic Monthly. Feb 1977, v239, p92-94.
Before My Eyes. p266-68.
BFI/Monthly Film Bulletin. Apr 1977, v44, p74-75.

Commonweal. Jan 21, 1977, v104, p51-52.
Elia Kazan: A Guide to References and Resources. p89-92.
Film Bulletin. Nov-Dec 1976, v45, p7.
Films in Review. Dec 1976, v27, p633-34.
Harpers. Mar 1977, v254, p102-04.
Hollywood Reporter. Nov 18, 1976, p3.
Independent Film Journal. Nov 26, 1976, v78, p8.
The Los Angeles Times. Nov 18, 1976, SecIV, p1.
Magill's Survey of Cinema. Series II. v3, p1322-24.
Making Pictures: The Pinter Screenplays. p129-44.
Motion Picture Hearld Product Digest. Dec 8, 1976, p55.
The Nation. Dec 11, 1976, v223, p637.
The New Republic. Dec 4, 1976, v175, p20-21.
The New York Times. Mar 21, 1976, SecII, p15.
The New York Times. Nov 14, 1976, SecII, p1.
The New Yorker. Nov 29, 1976, v52, p157-60.
Newsweek. Nov 22, 1976, v88, p107-8.
Saturday Review. Dec 11, 1976, v4, p77-78.
Time. Dec 6, 1976, v108, p87-88.
Tony Curtis: The Man and His Movies. p128-29.
Variety. Nov 17, 1976, p18.
The Village Voice. Nov 15, 1976, p57.
When The Lights Go Down. p216-19.

The Last Wave (AUSTRALIA; Weir, Peter; 1977)
American Cinematographer. Apr 1978, v58, p397-99.
BFI/Monthly Film Bulletin. Apr 1978, v45, p66.
Cinema Papers. Oct 1977, n14, p151-53.
Hollywood Reporter. Apr 14, 1977, p3.
The International Dictionary of Films and Filmmakers. v1, p255-56.
Motion Picture Herald Product Digest. Dec 20, 1978, p60.
The Nation. Jan 6, 1978, v228, p28.
The New Australian Cinema. p106-12.
New York. Jan 8, 1979, v12, p71.
The New York Times. Dec 19, 1978, SecIII, p7.
The New Yorker. Jan 22, 1979, v54, p102-03.
Newsweek. Jan 15, 1979, v93, p79.
Variety. Nov 16, 1977, p21.
The World of Fantastic Films. p165-66.

Last Year at Marienbad (French title: Annee Derniere a Marienbad, L') (FR, IT; Resnais, Alain; 1961)
BFI/Monthly Film Bulletin. Mar 1962, v29, p30.
Cineaste. 1980, v10, n4, p44.
Cinema. 1963, v1, n1, p44.
Cinema Journal. Spr 1971, v10, p40-43.
The Cinema of Alain Resnais. p88-114.
Cinema Texas Program Notes. Mar 30, 1978, v14, n3, p15-19.
Commonweal. Mar 23, 1962, v75, p667-68.
Dictionary of Films. p12-13.
The Fifty Worst Films of All Times. p143-46.
Film. Spr 1962, n31, p19-21.
Film. Sum 1962, n32, p16-17.
Film as Film: Critical Responses to Film Art. p231-48.
Film Culture. Sum 1962, n25, p21-22.
Film Daily. Mar 14, 1962, p6.
Filmfacts. Mar 30, 1962, v5, p47-49.
Films and Filming. Mar 1962, v8, p32-33.
Films in Review. Apr 1962, v3, p237-38.
Hollywood Reporter. Mar 6, 1962, v169, p3.
I Lost it at the Movies. p167-71.
International Dictionary of Films and Filmmakers. Volume I. p30-32.

*Magill's Survey of Cinema. Foreign Language
Films.* v4, p1735-38.
Motion Picture Herald Product Digest. Apr 4,
1962, p501.
The Nation. Mar 24, 1962, v194, p272.
The New Republic. Mar 26, 1962, v146, p26.
The New York Times. Mar 8, 1962, p26.
The New York Times Magazine. Mar 18, 1962,
p54-55.
The New Yorker. Mar 10, 1962, v38, p89.
Newsweek. Mar 19, 1962, v59, v118.
On Movies. p369-72.
Quarterly Review of Film Studies. 1980, v5, n1,
p1-17.
Saturday Review. Mar 10, 1962, v45, p33.
Screen. 1976, v17, n1, p34-39.
Sight and Sound. Wint 1961-62, v31, p26-28.
Time. Mar 16, 1962, v79, p56.
Variety. May 10, 1967, p7.
The Village Voice. Mar 15, 1962, p13.
A World on Film. p246-51.

The Late Edwina Black *See* Obsessed

The Late Show (US; Benton, Robert; 1977)
America. Mar 19, 1977, v136, p244.
BFI/Monthly Film Bulletin. Aug 1977, v44,
p168.
Films in Review. Apr 1977, v28, p248.
Hollywood Reporter. Feb 2, 1977, p3.
Magill's Survey of Cinema. Series II. v3, p1330-
32.
Motion Picture Herald Product Digest. Aug 24,
1977, p22.
The Nation. Mar 12, 1977, v224, p315.
The New Republic. Mar 12, 1977, v176, p24.
The New York Times. Feb 11, 1977, SecIII, p4.
The New York Times. Feb 13, 1977, SecII, p1.
The New Yorker. Feb 7, 1977, v52, p109-10.
Newsweek. Feb 21, 1977, v89, p88.
Psychology Today. May 1977, v10, p24.
Saturday Review. Mar 19, 1977, v4, p41.
Time. Feb 7, 1977, v109, p78.
Variety. Feb 2, 1977, p26.

Laughing Anne (GB; Wilcox, Herbert;
1953)
BFI/Monthly Film Bulletin. Oct 1953, v20,
p144.
Film Daily. May 20, 1954, p10.
Hollywood Reporter. Apr 26, 1954, p3.
Library Journal. May 15, 1954, v79, p953.
The London Times. Sep 14, 1953, p11.
Motion Picture Herald Product Digest. May 8,
1954, p2285.
National Parent-Teacher. Jun 1954, v48, p39.
The New Statesman and Nation. Sep 19, 1953,
v46, p315.
The New York Times. May 8, 1954, p15.
The Tatler. Sep 23, 1953, v209, p584.
Variety. May 5, 1954, p21.

Laughter in Paradise (GB; Zampi, Mario;
1951)
BFI/Monthly Film Bulletin. Jun 1951, v18,
p275.
Christian Century. Jan 2, 1952, v69, p31.
Motion Picture Herald Product Digest. Dec 1,
1951, p1125.
The New Republic. Dec 3, 1951, v125, p22.
New Statesman. Jun 9, 1951, v41, p650.
The New York Times. Nov 12, 1951, p21.
Variety. Jun 17, 1951, p9.

Laughter in the Dark (GB; Richardson,
Tony; 1969)
Big Screen, Little Screen. p179-80.
Commonweal. Jun 6, 1969, v90, p344.
Confessions of a Cultist. p436-41.
Double Takes. p35-36.
Film Daily. May 14, 1969, p7.

Film Quarterly. Spr 1970, v23, p43-48.
Filmfacts. 1969, v12, p286.
Films and Filming. Nov 1969, v16, p40.
Films in Review. Jun-Jul 1969, v20, p378-79.
Movies Into Film. p47-48.
The New York Times. May 12, 1969, p53.
The New Yorker. May 24, 1969, v45, p121.
Newsweek. May 26, 1969, v73, p113.
Saturday Review. May 31, 1969, v52, p44.
Time. Jun 6, 1969, v93, p93.
*Unholy Fools, Wits, Comics, Disturbers of the
Peace.* p86-89.
Variety. May 14, 1969, p6.

The Lavender Hill Mob (GB; Crichton,
Charles; 1951)
BFI/Monthly Film Bulletin. Jul 1951, v18,
p292-93.
Catholic World. Nov 1951, v174, p143.
Christian Century. Dec 5, 1951, v68, p1423.
Cinema, the Magic Vehicle. v2, p80-81.
Commonweal. Oct 26, 1951, v55, p64.
Dictionary of Films. p187.
Film Daily. Oct 15, 1951, p6.
Films in Review. Dec 1951, v2, p56-57.
The Great British Films. p147-49.
The Great Gangster Pictures. p243.
Halliwell's Hundred. p171-73.
Hollywood Reporter. Jan 10, 1952, p3.
Kiss Kiss Bang Bang. p368.
The London Times. Jul 2, 1951, p4.
Magill's Survey of Cinema. Series I. v2, p952-
55.
Motion Picture Herald Product Digest. Oct 20,
1951, p1067.
The New Republic. Oct 22, 1951, v125, p22.
The New Statesman and Nation. Jul 7, 1951,
v42, p13-14.
The New York Times. Oct 16, 1951, p35.
The New Yorker. Oct 20, 1951, v27, p130-31.
Newsweek. Oct 22, 1951, v38, p100.
Saturday Review. Oct 13, 1951, v34, p45.
Senior Scholastic. Nov 14, 1951, v59, p26.
Sight and Sound. Aug-Sep 1951, v21, p29.
The Spectator. Jun 29, 1951, v186, p860.
Theatre Arts. Nov 1951, v35, p36-37.
Time. Oct 15, 1951, v58, p118.
Variety. Jul 4, 1951, p8.
Vintage Films. p123-25.

The Lawless (Also titled: The Dividing
Line) (US; Losey, Joseph; 1950)
Christian Century. Nov 15, 1950, v67, p1375.
The Cinema of Joseph Losey. p34-40.
Commonweal. Jul 7, 1950, v52, p318-19.
Dictionary of Films. p187.
Film Daily. Apr 12, 1950, p6.
Hollywood Reporter. Apr 7, 1950, p3.
Motion Picture Herald Product Digest. Apr 8,
1950, p253.
The New Republic. Jul 17, 1950, v123, p21.
The New York Times. Jun 23, 1950, p29.
The New Yorker. Jul 1, 1950, v26, p49.
Newsweek. Jul 24, 1951, v78, p38.
Sequence. Aut 1950, n12, p14-15.
Shots in the Dark. p180-81.
Time. Jul 3, 1950, v56, p76.
Variety. Apr 12, 1950, p6.

The Lawless Breed (US; Walsh, Raoul;
1952)
BFI/Monthly Film Bulletin. Feb 1953, v20,
p24.
Catholic World. Jan 1953, v176, p303.
Film Daily. Dec 8, 1952, p6.
Hollywood Reporter. Nov 28, 1952, p4.
Magill's Survey of Cinema. Series I. v2, p956-
58.
Motion Picture Herald Product Digest. Dec 6,
1952, p1629.

National Parent-Teacher. Jan 1953, v47, p38.
Variety. Dec 3, 1952, p6.

Lawman (US; Winner, Michael; 1971)
BFI/Monthly Film Bulletin. Apr 1971, v38,
p77.
Filmfacts. 1971, v14, n14, p354-56.
Films and Filming. Apr 1971, v17, p47.
The Films of Michael Winner. p60-65.
Hollywood Reporter. Jul 13, 1971, p3.
The New York Times. Aug 5, 1971, p25.
Variety. Mar 24, 1971, p19.

Lawrence of Arabia (GB; Lean, David;
1962)
America. Jan 5, 1963, v108, p26-28.
BFI/Monthly Film Bulletin. Feb 1963, v30,
p17-18.
Cinema. 1963, v1, n1, p43.
The Cinema of David Lean. p161-84.
Classic Film/Video Images. Mar 1980, n68,
p2X-3X.
Commonweal. Jan 18, 1963, v77, p439.
Confessions of a Cultist. p65-67.
*David Lean: A Guide to References and
Resources.* p85-89.
David Lean and His Films. p167-82.
David Lean (Anderegg). p105-20.
Film Daily. Dec 17, 1962, p5.
Film News. Jan-Feb 1977, v34, p34.
Film Quarterly. Spr 1963, v16, p56-57.
Film Quarterly. Spr 1964, v17, p51-54.
Film Society Review. May 1971, v6, p35-38.
Filmfacts. Jan 25, 1963, v5, p343-46.
Films and Filming. Feb 1963, v9, p32-33.
Films in Review. Jan 1963, v4, p42-44.
Films in Review. Mar 1985, v36, p159-62.
The Films of the Sixties. p84-87.
The Great Adventure Films. p248-55.
The Great Movies. p137-43.
Hollywood Reporter. Dec 17, 1962, p3.
Hollywood Reporter. Dec 21, 1962, p3.
International Film Guide. 1964, v1, p71-72.
*Journal of the Society of Film and Television
Arts Limited.* Wint 1962-63, n10, (entire
issue).
Life. Dec 14, 1962, v53, p118-19.
Magill's Survey of Cinema. Series I. v2, p959-
62.
Motion Picture Herald Product Digest. Jan 9,
1963, p732.
Movie Maker. Dec 8, v18, p22-23.
The Nation. Jan 19, 1963, v196, p58.
The New Republic. Jan 12, 1963, v148, p26-28.
The New York Times. Dec 17, 1962, p5.
The New Yorker. Dec 22, 1962, v38, p77.
Newsweek. Dec 24, 1962, v60, p64.
Private Screenings. p52-55.
Saturday Review. Dec 29, 1962, v45, p29-30.
Saturday Review. Jan 5, 1963, v46, p31.
Time. Jan 4, 1963, v81, p58.
Variety. Dec 19, 1962, p6.
The Village Voice. Dec 20, 1962, p16.
A World on Film. p24-27.

Lax Yeux Bandés *See* Blindfold

Laxdale Hall *See* Scotch on the Rocks

Leadbelly (US; Parks, Gordon; 1976)
BFI/Monthly Film Bulletin. Jul 1976, v43,
p149.
Film Bulletin. Mar 1976, v45, p34.
Films in Review. Jan 1976, v27, p56-57.
Hollywood Reporter. Feb 27, 1976, p6.
Independent Film Journal. Mar 17, 1976, v77,
p9-10.
The Los Angeles Times. Jul 14, 1976, SecIV,
p1.
Millimeter. Apr 1976, v4, p30-32.
New Statesman. Jun 4, 1976, v91, p752.

The New York Times. Jul 4, 1976, SecII, p11.
Newsweek. Apr 19, 1976, v87, p95-96.
Saturday Review. May 29, 1976, v3, p48.
Time. May 24, 1976, v107, p76.
Variety. Mar 3, 1976, p21.
Vogue. Jan 1976, v166, p33.

The League of Gentlemen (GB; Dearden, Basil; 1960)
America. Apr 29, 1961, v105, p227.
BFI/Monthly Film Bulletin. May 1960, v27, p65.
Filmfacts. 1961, v4, p20.
Films and Filming. May 1960, v6, p25.
Films in Review. Mar 1961, v12, p177.
Hollywood UK. p102-04.
Magill's Survey of Cinema. Series II. v3, p1340-43.
The New Republic. Jan 16, 1961, v144, p20.
The New York Times. Jan 25, 1961, p30.
The New Yorker. Jan 28, 1961, v36, p70.
Saturday Review. Jan 14, 1961, v44, p29.
Time. Feb 24, 1961, v77, p40.
Variety. Apr 13, 1960, p20.

Lease of Life (GB; Frend, Charles; 1954)
BFI/Monthly Film Bulletin. Nov 1954, v21, p157-58.
Film Daily. Dec 29, 1955, p8.
Films and Filming. Nov 1954, v1, p21.
Films in Review. Dec 1955, v6, p526-27.
The London Times. Oct 8, 1954, p10.
Motion Picture Herald Product Digest. Dec 31, 1955, p721.
The Tatler. Oct 20, 1954, v214, p166-67.
Variety. Nov 3, 1954, p6.

The Leather Boys (GB; Furie, Sidney J.; 1964)
America. Dec 11, 1965, v113, p761.
BFI/Monthly Film Bulletin. Feb 1964, v31, p20-21.
Christian Science Monitor (Western edition). Sep 12, 1966, p4.
Commonweal. Dec 3, 1965, v83, p280.
Confessions of a Cultist. p231-34.
Film Quarterly. Spr 1966, v19, p43.
Films and Filming. Jan 1964, v10, p24.
Films in Review. Feb 1966, v17, p117-18.
Life. Dec 10, 1965, v59, p20.
The London Times. Sep 23, 1963, p6.
The London Times. Jan 23, 1964, p8.
Motion Picture Herald Product Digest. Dec 8, 1965, p419.
The New Republic. Nov 20, 1965, v153, p32.
New Statesman. Jan 24, 1964, v67, p138.
The New York Times. Nov 9, 1965, p50.
The New Yorker. Nov 13, 1965, v41, p233-34.
Newsweek. Nov 22, 1965, v66, p108.
Playboy. Feb 1966, v13, p34-35.
Saturday Review. Nov 20, 1965, v48, p55.
Second Sight. p43-45.
Sight and Sound. Spr 1964, v33, p94-95.
The Spectator. Jan 31, 1964, v212, p143.
Time. Nov 19, 1965, v86 p130.
Variety. Feb 5, 1964, p6.
The Village Voice. Jan 29, 1966, v11, p23.

Lebenszeichen *See* Signs of Life

The Left Hand of God (US; Dmytryk, Edward; 1955)
America. Sep 24, 1955, v93, p631.
BFI/Monthly Film Bulletin. Nov 1955, v22, n262, p163.
Catholic World. Sep 1955, v181, p465.
Commonweal. Sep 16, 1955, v62, p589.
The Complete Films of Humphrey Bogart. p183-85.
Film Daily. Aug 25, 1955, p5.
Films and Filming. Dec 1955, v2, n3, p19.

Hollywood Reporter. Aug 24, 1955, v136, n4, p3.
Humphrey Bogart: The Man and His Films. p176-78.
The Nation. Oct 15, 1955, v181, p329.
The New York Times. Sep 22, 1955, p34.
The New Yorker. Oct 1, 1955, v31, p83.
Newsweek. Sep 26, 1955, v46, p116-17.
Time. Oct 3, 1955, v66, p96.
Variety. Aug 24, 1955, p6.

The Left-Handed Gun (US; Penn, Arthur; 1958)
Arthur Penn (Wood). p19-27.
BFI/Monthly Film Bulletin. Oct 1958, v25, p128.
Catholic World. Jul 1958, v187, p307.
Commonweal. May 23, 1958, v68, p207.
Film Daily. Apr 23, 1958, v113, p6.
Filmfacts. May 21, 1958, v1, p67.
The Films of Paul Newman. p66-70.
Hollywood Reporter. Apr 23, 1958, p3.
The New York Times. May 8, 1958, p36.
Variety. Apr 30, 1958, p6.

The Legend of Lylah Clare (US; Aldrich, Robert; 1968)
BFI/Monthly Film Bulletin. Apr 1978, v45, p67.
Cinema Texas Program Notes. Apr 29, 1975, v8, p1-4.
Film Daily. Aug 22, 1968, p9.
Film Quarterly. Wint 1968-69, v22, p57-58.
Filmfacts. Dec 1, 1968, v11, p344-46.
Films in Review. Oct 1968, v19, p515.
Five Thousand One Nights At the Movies. p323.
Hollywood Reporter. Aug 16, 1968, p3.
Life. Sep 27, 1968, v65, p8.
Motion Picture Herald Product Digest. Aug 21, 1968, p845.
The New York Times. Aug 23, 1968, p33.
The New Yorker. Sep 14, 1968, v44, p198-200.
Newsweek. Sep 9, 1968, v72, p98.
Robert Aldrich: A Guide to References and Resources. p44-47.
Saturday Review. Aug 31, 1968, v51, p31.
The Thousand Eyes Magazine. Dec 1976, v2, p15.
Time. Aug 30, 1968, v92, p57.
Variety. Jul 24, 1968, p6.
A Year In the Dark. p215-16.

Legend of the Lost (US; Hathaway, Henry; 1957)
America. Jan 18, 1958, v98, p468.
BFI/Monthly Film Bulletin. Mar 1958, v25, p36.
The Complete Films of John Wayne. p216-18.
Film Daily. Dec 17, 1957, p6.
Films and Filming. Mar 1958, v4, p27.
The Films of Sophia Loren. p85-88.
Hollywood Reporter. Dec 17, 1957, p3.
Motion Picture Herald Product Digest. Dec 21, 1957, p649.
The New York Times. Dec 23, 1957, p18.
Newsweek. Jan 6, 1958, v51, p69.
Time. Jan 20, 1958, v71, p86.
Variety. Dec 18, 1957, p6.

Lektion I Karleck, En *See* A Lesson in Love

The Lemon Drop Kid (US; Lanfield, Sidney; 1951)
BFI/Monthly Film Bulletin. May 1951, v18, p266.
Film Daily. Mar 8, 1951, p6.
Hollywood Reporter. Mar 7, 1951, p3.
The London Times. Mar 26, 1951, p8.
Motion Picture Herald Product Digest. Mar 17, 1951, p758.

The New York Times. Mar 22, 1951, p41.
The New Yorker. Mar 31, 1951, v27, p65.
Newsweek. Apr 2, 1951, v37, p86.
The Spectator. Mar 30, 1951, v186, p413.
Time. Apr 2, 1951, v57, p96.
Variety. Mar 7, 1951, p6.

Lenny (US; Fosse, Bob; 1974)
America. Dec 7, 1974, v131, Inside Back Cover.
Audience. Dec 1974, v7, p8-10.
Before My Eyes. p91-93.
BFI/Monthly Film Bulletin. May 1975, v42, p109.
Commonweal. Feb 14, 1975, v101, p397-98.
Esquire. Feb 1975, v83, p44.
The Films of Dustin Hoffman. p157-66.
Hollywood Reporter. Nov 7, 1974, p3.
Independent Film Journal. Nov 13, 1974, v74, p11.
The Los Angeles Times. Nov 17, 1974, Calendar, p1.
Magill's Survey of Cinema. Series II. v3, p1344-47.
Millimeter. Dec 1974, v2, p24-27.
Motion Picture Herald Product Digest. Nov 27, 1974, p49.
National Review. Dec 20, 1974, v26, p1468.
The New Republic. Dec 14, 1974, v171, p18.
New York. Nov 18, 1974, v7, p88.
The New York Times. Dec 1, 1974, SecII, p17.
The New Yorker. Nov 18, 1974, v50, p194-98.
Newsweek. Nov 18, 1974, v84, p103.
Reeling. p494-502.
Rolling Stone. Dec 5, 1974, n175, p42-46.
Time. Nov 25, 1974, v104, p5.
Variety. Nov 13, 1974, p3, 19.
The Village Voice. May 2, 1974, p99.

The Leopard (Italian title: Gattopardo, Il) (IT; Visconti, Luchino; 1963)
America. Sep 28, 1963, v109, p369.
BFI/Monthly Film Bulletin. Jan 1964, v31, p3-4.
Burt Lancaster: A Pictorial Treasury of His Films. p121-23.
Commonweal. Sep 20, 1963, v78, p563.
Esquire. May 1964, v61, p20.
Fifty Grand Movies of the 1960s and 1970s. p45-48.
Film Comment. Fall 1963, v1, p34-38.
Film Daily. Aug 14, 1963, p5.
Film Quarterly. Wint 1963, p35-38.
Filmfacts. Aug 29, 1963, v6, p169-71.
Films and Filming. Dec 1963, v10, p21.
Films in Review. Oct 1963, v14, p497-98.
Hollywood Reporter. Aug 14, 1963, p3.
Italian Cinema (Bondanella). p199-203.
Luchino Visconti (Tonetti). p95-107.
Magill's Survey of Cinema. Foreign Language Series. v4, p1758-62.
Movie. Jul-Aug 1963, p21-22.
The New Republic. Sep 14, 1963, v149, p26.
The New York Times. Aug 13, 1963, p25.
The New York Times. Aug 18, 1963, SecII, p1.
The New Yorker. Aug 17, 1963, v39, p54.
The New Yorker. Jul 13, 1963, v39, p70.
Newsweek. Aug 26, 1963, v62, p76-77.
On Movies. p341-42.
Reporter. Sep 12, 1963, v29, p48.
Saturday Review. Aug 24, 1963, v46, p35.
Sight and Sound. Wint 1963-64, v33, p36.
Time. Aug 23, 1963, v82, p68.
Variety. Apr 17, 1963, p7.
The Village Voice. Aug 22, 1963, v8, p13.

A Lesson in Love (Swedish title: Lektion I Karleck, En) (SWED; Bergman, Ingmar; 1954)
BFI/Monthly Film Bulletin. Jun 1959, v26, p68.
Cinema Borealis. p139-42.

Cinema Eye, Cinema Ear. p154-55.
Cinema, the Magic Vehicle. v2, p219-20.
Commonweal. Feb 12, 1960, v71, p546-47.
Film Quarterly. Sum 1960, v13, p52-53.
Filmfacts. Apr 1, 1960, v3, p53-54.
Films and Filming. Aug 1959, v5, p22-23.
Films in Review. Feb 1960, v11, p103.
The Films of Ingmar Bergman (Donner). p118-23.
Ingmar Bergman and the Rituals of Art. p130-31.
Ingmar Bergman (Cowie). p120-22.
Ingmar Bergman (Mosley). p54-56.
Ingmar Bergman (Wood). p62-66.
Magill's Survey of Cinema. Foreign Language Films. v4, p1763-68.
Motion Picture Herald Product Digest. May 21, 1960, p701.
The Nation. Mar 26, 1960, v190, p284.
The New Republic. Apr 25, 1960, v142, p20.
The New York Times. Mar 15, 1960, p46.
The New Yorker. Mar 26, 1960, v36, p148.
Newsweek. Mar 21, 1960, v55, p120.
Saturday Review. Jan 23, 1960, v43, p26.
The Thousand Eyes Magazine. 1975, n1, p19.
Time. Mar 28, 1960, v75, p104.
Variety. Nov 4, 1959, p7.
A World on Film. p275-76.

Let Justice Be Done *See* Justice Est Faite

Let's Dance (US; McLeod, Norman Z.; 1950)
Astaire Dancing: The Musical Films. p312-19.
BFI/Monthly Film Bulletin. Sep 1950, v17, p141.
Christian Century. Dec 13, 1950, v67, p1503.
Commonweal. Dec 15, 1950, v53, p254.
Film Daily. Aug 11, 1950, p7.
Hollywood Reporter. Aug 9, 1950, p3.
Motion Picture Herald Product Digest. Aug 19, 1950, p442.
The New York Times. Nov 30, 1950, p42.
The New Yorker. Dec 2, 1950, v26, p105.
Newsweek. Dec 11, 1950, v36, p92.
The Spectator. Oct 20, 1950, v185, p401.
Starring Fred Astaire. p347-53.
Time. Nov 27, 1950, v56, p98.
Variety. Sep 9, 1950, p8.

Let's Make Up *See* Lilacs in the Spring

Letzte Bruecke, Die *See* The Last Bridge

Lianna (US; Sayles, John; 1983)
Films in Review. Jun-Jul 1983, v34, p365.
Hollywood Reporter. Feb 18, 1983, p3.
The Los Angeles Times. Feb 16, 1983, SecVI, p1.
Maclean's. Feb 21, 1983, v96, p49.
Magill's Cinema Annual, 1984. p201-05.
Ms. Apr 1983, v11, p70-71.
The New Republic. Mar 14, 1983, v188, p24-25.
New York. Jan 31, 1983, v16, p55-56.
The New York Times. Feb 19, 1983, SecIII, p22.
Newsweek. Feb 7, 1983, v101, p70.
Progressive. Mar 1983, v47, p55.
Time. Mar 14, 1983, v121, p90.

Liebe in Deutschland, Eine *See* A Love in Germany

Lieutenant Robin Crusoe, U.S.N. (US; Paul, Byron; 1966)
BFI/Monthly Film Bulletin. Aug 1966, v33, p125.
Christian Science Monitor (Western edition). Jul 15, 1966, p4.
Film Daily. May 19, 1966, p5.
Filmfacts. Sep 15, 1966, v9, p183-84.
Films and Filming. Sep 1966, v12, p12, 14.

Hollywood Reporter. May 18, 1966, p3.
The London Times. Jun 30, 1966, p7.
Motion Picture Herald Product Digest. Jun 1, 1966, p533.
The New York Times. Jul 14, 1966, p28.
Saturday Review. Jul 2, 1966, v49, p37.
Variety. May 18, 1966, p6.

The Life and Times of Judge Roy Bean (US; Huston, John; 1972)
The Cinema of John Huston. p179.
Commonweal. Jan 12, 1973, v97, p327-28.
Filmfacts. 1972, v15, n24, p607.
Hollywood Reporter. Dec 7, 1972, p3.
John Huston (Hammen). p127-28.
Magill's Survey of Cinema. Series II. v3, p1363-66.
The New Republic. Jan 20, 1973, v168, p26.
The New York Times. Dec 19, 1972, v52, p1.
The New Yorker. Jan 13, 1973, v48, p86-88.
Reeling. p143-47.
Senior Scholastic. Feb 12, 1973, v102, p18.
Time. Dec 25, 1972, v100, p75.
Variety. Dec 13, 1972, p20.

Life At the Top (GB; Kotcheff, Ted; 1965)
BFI/Monthly Film Bulletin. Feb 1966, v33, p16-17.
Christian Science Monitor (Western edition). Dec 28, 1965, p4.
Cinema. Mar 1966, v3, p49.
Commonweal. Dec 24, 1965, v83, p376.
Film Daily. Dec 15, 1965, p6.
Films and Filming. Feb 1966, v12, p14-15.
Films in Review. Jan 1966, v17, p54.
Hollywood Reporter. Dec 13, 1965, p3.
Illustrated London News. Feb 13, 1965, v246, p34-35.
London Magazine. Mar 1966, v5, p57-59.
The London Times. Jan 13, 1966, p14.
Motion Picture Herald Product Digest. Dec 22, 1965, p426-27.
The New Republic. Dec 18, 1965, v153, p32-33.
New Statesman. Feb 19, 1965, v69, p289-90.
New Statesman. Jan 14, 1966, v71, p58.
The New York Times. Dec 15, 1965, p53.
The New Yorker. Dec 18, 1965, v41, p162-63.
Newsweek. Dec 27, 1965, v66, p71A-B.
Playboy. Mar 1966, v13, p23.
Saturday Review. Dec 18, 1965, v48, p42.
The Spectator. Jan 14, 1966, v216, p43.
Tynan Right and Left. p249-50.
Variety. Dec 15, 1965, p6.
The Village Voice. Feb 3, 1966, v11, p23, 27.

Life Begins Tomorrow *See* Vie Commence Demain, La

The Life of a Woman by Saikaku *See* The Life of Oharu

The Life of Brian *See* Monty Python's Life of Brian

A Life of Her Own (US; Cukor, George; 1950)
BFI/Monthly Film Bulletin. Nov 1950, v17, p173.
Christian Century. Oct 25, 1950, v67, p1279.
Film Daily. Aug 15, 1950, p6.
The Films of Lana Turner. p241-45.
George Cukor (Phillips). p116-17.
Hollywood Reporter. Aug 11, 1950, p3.
Motion Picture Herald Product Digest. Aug 12, 1950, p433-34.
The New York Times. Oct 12, 1950, p43.
The Spectator. Oct 20, 1950, v185, p401.
Time. Sep 18, 1950, v56, p107.
Variety. Aug 16, 1950, p11.

The Life of Oharu (Japanese title: Oharu; Saikaku Ichidai Onna; Keshoku Ichadai-onna; Also titled: The Life of a Woman by Saikaku) (JAPAN; Mizoguchi, Kenji; 1952)
BFI/Monthly Film Bulletin. Mar 1975, v42, p66.
Cinema, the Magic Vehicle. v2, p116-17.
Commonweal. May 8, 1964, v80, p209.
Confessions of a Cultist. p138-39.
Currents in Japanese Cinema. p181-83.
Dictionary of Films. p322-23.
Film Criticism. Spr 1980, v4, p4-15.
The International Dictionary of Films and Filmmakers. v1, p403-05.
Kenji Mizoguchi: A Guide to References and Resources. p134-37.
Magill's Survey of Cinema. Foreign Language Films. v4, p1785-90.
Mizoguchi (McDonald). p104-16.
The New York Times. Apr 21, 1964, p42.
Sexual Stratagems. p108-10.
Sight and Sound. Spr 1978, v47, p118.
The Thousand Eyes Magazine. Apr 1977, v2, p9.
Variety. Sep 17, 1952, p22.
The Village Voice. May 28, 1964, v9, p22, 25.
The Waves at Genji's Door. p259-67.

Life Upside Down (French title: Vie a l'Envers, La) (FR; Jessua, Alain; 1964)
BFI/Monthly Film Bulletin. Dec 1964, v31, p174-75.
Commonweal. Sep 17, 1965, v82, p666.
Film. 1964, n41, p14-15.
Film Comment. Mar-Apr 1973, v9, p41-45.
Films and Filming. Jan 1965, v11, p28-29.
The London Times. May 12, 1964, p15.
The London Times. Sep 8, 1964, p13.
The New Republic. Sep 11, 1965, v153, p25-26.
New Statesman. Nov 13, 1964, v68, p760.
The New York Times. Aug 18, 1965, p41.
The New Yorker. Aug 21, 1965, v41, p100.
Newsweek. Sep 6, 1965, v66, p70B.
Playboy. Nov 1965, v12, p57.
Private Screenings. p204-05.
Sight and Sound. Wint 1964-65, v34, p9-11.
Time. Sep 10, 1965, v86, p95.
Unholy Fools, Wits, Comics, Disturbers of the Peace. p113-14.
Variety. May 6, 1964, p16.
A World on Film. p267-69.

Light *See* Lumiere

Light at the Edge of the World (US; Billington, Kevin; 1971)
Filmfacts. 1971, v14, n15, p375-76.
Films and Filming. Mar 1973, v, p54.
Hollywood Reporter. Jul 7, 1971, p3.
The New York Times. Jul 17, 1971, p14.
Variety. Jul 7, 1971, p18.

The Light Touch (US; Brooks, Richard; 1951)
BFI/Monthly Film Bulletin. Dec 1951, v18, p371-72.
Christian Century. Mar 12, 1952, v69, p327.
Film Daily. Nov 13, 1951, p6.
Hollywood Reporter. Oct 29, 1951, p3.
Motion Picture Herald Product Digest. Nov 3, 1951, p1094.
The New Republic. Feb 11, 1952, v126, p22.
The New Statesman and Nation. Dec 1, 1951, v42, p623.
The New York Times. Jan 17, 1952, p23.
The New Yorker. Jan 26, 1952, v27, p89.
Newsweek. Feb 25, 1952, v39, p100.
Saturday Review. Dec 8, 1951, v34, p31.
The Spectator. Nov 30, 1951, v187, p737.

Time. Dec 10, 1951, v58, p106.
Variety. Oct 31, 1951, p6.

Lightning Strikes Twice (US; Vidor, King; 1951)
BFI/Monthly Film Bulletin. Oct 1951, v18, p342.
Christian Century. Apr 11, 1951, v68, p479.
Film Daily. Feb 27, 1951, p6.
Hollywood Reporter. Feb 20, 1951, p3.
Library Journal. Apr 1, 1951, v76, p608.
Motion Picture Herald Product Digest. Feb 24, 1951, p721.
The New Statesman and Nation. Dec 15, 1951, v42, p706.
The New York Times. Apr 13, 1951, p18.
The Spectator. Dec 7, 1951, v187, p773.
Time. Apr 2, 1951, v57, p98.
Variety. Feb 21, 1951, p6.

Lights Out *See* Bright Victory

Lilacs in the Spring (Also titled: Let's Make Up) (GB; Wilcox, Herbert; 1954)
BFI/Monthly Film Bulletin. Jan 1955, v22, p3-4.
Film Daily. Feb 7, 1956, p5.
Films and Filming. Feb 1955, v1, p19.
Films and Filming. Nov 1955, v2, p18.
The London Times. Dec 24, 1954, p3.
The New Statesman and Nation. Jan 8, 1955, v49, p43-44.
The Tatler. Jan 5, 1955, v215, p20.
Variety. Jan 5, 1955, p58.

Lili (US; Walters, Charles; 1953)
America. Apr 11, 1953, v89, p60.
BFI/Monthly Film Bulletin. Apr 1953, v20, p47.
Catholic World. Mar 1953, v176, p459.
Commonweal. Mar 13, 1953, v57, p575.
Film Daily. Mar 11, 1953, p6.
Films in Review. Apr 1953, v14, p200.
Holiday. Jan 1954, v15, p18.
Hollywood Reporter. Mar 11, 1953, p3.
Library Journal. Mar 1, 1953, v78, p437.
Life. Mar 16, 1953, v34, p77-78.
Magill's Survey of Cinema. Series II. v3, p1371-73.
National Parent-Teacher. Mar 1953, v47, p26.
The New York Times. Mar 1, 1953, SecVI, p26.
The New Yorker. Mar 21, 1953, v29, p121.
Newsweek. Mar 16, 1953, v41, p102.
Saturday Review. Mar 7, 1953, v36, p35.
Senior Scholastic. Sep 23, 1953, v63, p38.
Sight and Sound. Apr-Jun 1953, v22, n4, p199.
Time. Mar 9, 1953, v61, p100.
Variety. Mar 11, 1953, p6.

Lili Marlene (WGER; Fassbinder, Rainer Werner; 1981)
Christian Century. Sep 16, 1981, v98, p912.
Film Comment. Jul-Aug 1981, v17, p8.
Hollywood Reporter. Jul 14, 1981, p16.
The Los Angeles Times. Jul 29, 1981, SecVI, p1.
Magill's Cinema Annual, 1982. p222-25.
The Nation. Aug 22, 1981, v233, p156-57.
The New York Times. Jul 10, 1981, SecIII, p15.
The New York Times. Aug 2, 1981, SecII, p15.
Newsweek. Aug 10, 1981, v98, p69.
Progressive. Sep 1981, v45, p54.
Time. Jul 13, 1981, v118, p59.
Variety. Feb 6, 1981, p10.

Lilies of the Field (US; Nelson, Ralph; 1963)
America. Oct 12, 1963, v109, p439-40.
BFI/Monthly Film Bulletin. May 1964, v31, p75.
Ebony. Oct 1963, v18, p55-58.

The Evolution of Character Portrayals in the Films of Sidney Poitier, 1950-1978. p125-43.
Film Daily. Aug 7, 1963, p4.
Filmfacts. Oct 31, 1963, v6, p229-31.
Films and Filming. May 1964, v10, p21-22.
The Films of Sidney Poitier. p111-16.
Hollywood Reporter. Jul 23, 1963, p3.
Magill's Survey of Cinema. Series II. v3, p1374-76.
The New York Times. Oct 2, 1963, p5.
The New York Times. Oct 6, 1963, SecII, p1.
Newsweek. Oct 4, 1963, v62, p117.
Photoplay. Aug 1963, v64, p14.
Saturday Review. Sep 7, 1963, v46, p32.
Variety. Jul 3, 1963, p6.

Lilith (US; Rossen, Robert; 1964)
America. Oct 10, 1964, v111, p423.
BFI/Monthly Film Bulletin. Dec 1966, v33, p179-80.
Christian Century. Dec 2, 1964, v81, p1499-1500.
Commonweal. Oct 16, 1964, v81, p101.
Dictionary of Films. p193.
Film Comment. Fall 1970, v6, n3, p51-54.
Film Daily. Sep 21, 1964, v125, p8.
Films in Review. Oct 1964, v15, p502-03.
The Films of Warren Beatty. p88-100.
Hollywood Reporter. Sep 21, 1964, v182, p3.
Life. Oct 2, 1964, v57, p26.
Magill's Survey of Cinema. Series II. v3, p1377-81.
Motion Picture Herald Product Digest. Sep 30, 1964, v232, p137.
The New Republic. Aug 22, 1964, v151, p35-36.
The New York Times. Sep 21, 1964, p37.
The New Yorker. Oct 10, 1964, v40, p202.
Newsweek. Oct 12, 1964, v64, p115.
Sight and Sound. Sum 1966, v35, p147-48.
Time. Oct 2, 1964, v84, p130.
Variety. Sep 23, 1964, p6.
Vogue. Nov 1, 1964, v144, p64.

Limelight (US; Chaplin, Charles; 1952)
American Mercury. Nov 1952, v75, p90.
BFI/Monthly Film Bulletin. Nov 1952, v19, p154.
Catholic World. Nov 1952, v176, p142.
Chaplin: His Life and Art (Robinson). p544-72.
Chaplin: The Mirror of Opinion (Robinson). p153-55.
Chaplin's Films. p175-79.
Charles Chaplin: A Guide to References and Resources. p77-78.
Charles Chaplin (Manvell). p210-13.
Charlie Chaplin (McCabe). p21-24.
Christian Century. Feb 4, 1953, v70, p151.
Cinema, the Magic Vehicle. v2, p136-37.
Commentary. Mar 1953, v15, p295-97.
Commonweal. Oct 31, 1952, v57, p102.
Commonweal. Feb 6, 1953, v57, p451-53.
Dictionary of Films. p193-94.
Essays on Chaplin. p49-58.
Film Comment. Sep-Oct 1972, v8, p24-25.
Film Criticism and Caricatures, 1943-53. p149-50.
Film Daily. Oct 8, 1952, p10.
Films and Filming. Oct 1973, v20, p52.
Films in Review. Nov 1952, v3, p466-70.
The Films of Charlie Chaplin. p216-21.
Focus on Chaplin. p1143-48.
Harper's Magazine. Jan 1953, v206, p93.
Hollywood Reporter. Oct 10, 1952, p3.
Illustrated London News. Nov 1, 1952, v221, p738.
The International Dictionary of Films and Filmmakers. v1, p259-60.
Journal of the University Film Association. Wint 1979, v31, p33-41.

Literature/Film Quarterly. 1984, v12, n3 p202-10.
The London Times. Aug 6, 1952, p2.
The London Times. Sep 17, 1952, p2.
Magill's Survey of Cinema. Series I. v2, p978-80.
Motion Picture Herald Product Digest. Oct 11, 1952, p1557.
Movietone News. Dec 1975, n46, p9-12.
The Nation. Oct 25, 1952, v175, p393-94.
The Nation. Mar 21, 1953, v176, p247-48.
National Parent-Teacher. Dec 1952, v47, p38.
New Statesman. Jul 20, 1973, v86, p98-99.
The New Statesman and Nation. Oct 18, 1952, v44, p449-50.
The New York Times. Oct 24, 1952, p27.
The New Yorker. Oct 25, 1952, v28, p141.
Newsweek. Oct 27, 1952, v40, p112.
Reporter. Jan 6, 1953, v8, p1-2.
Saturday Review. Nov 22, 1952, v35, p23.
Saturday Review. Oct 25, 1952, v35, p29-31.
Sight and Sound. Jan-Mar 1953, v22, p123-27.
The Spectator. Oct 17, 1952, v189, p501.
The Tatler. Oct 29, 1952, v206, p268.
Theatre Arts. Nov 1952, v36, p72-77.
Time. Oct 27, 1952, v60, p88.
Variety. Oct 10, 1952, p6.
The Village Voice. Oct 1, 1964, v9, p15, 18.
What Is Cinema? v2, p124-39.

The Lion in Winter (GB, US; Harvey, Anthony; 1968)
America. Nov 9, 1968, v119, p444-45.
BFI/Monthly Film Bulletin. Mar 1969, v36, p49-50.
Christian Century. Dec 11, 1968, v85, p1578-79.
Christian Science Monitor (Western edition). Nov 1, 1968, p6.
Cinema. Fall 1968, v4, p27.
Cinema. Dec 1968, v4, p34-35.
Commonweal. Nov 22, 1968, v89, p284.
Film 68/69. p200-05.
Film Daily. Oct 18, 1968, p3.
Film Society Review. Dec 1969, v5, p36-43.
Filmfacts. Nov 15, 1968, v11, p315-18.
Films and Filming. Mar 1969, v15, p52-54.
Films in Review. Nov 1968, v19, p579-80.
The Films of Katharine Hepburn. p189-95.
Harper's Magazine. Jan 1969, v238, p109.
Hollywood Reporter. Oct 18, 1968, p3.
Life. Jul 19, 1968, v65, p48A.
The London Times. Jan 1, 1969, p13.
Look. Nov 26, 1968, v32, p100.
Magill's Survey of Cinema. Series II. v3, p1382-85.
Motion Picture Herald Product Digest. Oct 23, 1968, p43.
Movie. Wint 1968-69, n16, p39.
Movies Into Film. p347-50.
The New York Times. Oct 31, 1968, p54.
The New Yorker. Nov 9, 1968, v44, p189-92.
Newsweek. Nov 18, 1968, v72, p118.
Saturday Review. Nov 2, 1968, v51, p59-60.
Second Sight. p213-16.
Sight and Sound. Wint 1968-69, v38, p44.
The Spectator. Jan 10, 1969, v222, p51.
Take One. Jul-Aug 1968, v1, p22-24.
Time. Nov 15, 1968, v92, p107.
Variety. Oct 23, 1968, p6.
Vogue. Dec 1968, v152, p180.

Lion of the Desert (LIB, GB; Akkad, Moustapha; 1981)
The New Republic. May 16, 1981, v184, p25-26.
New York. Apr 20, 1981, v14, p52-53.

Lipstick (US; Johnson, Lamont; 1976)
Audience. Aug 1976, v9, p8-9.
BFI/Monthly Film Bulletin. Aug 1976, v43, p167-68.
Film Bulletin. Apr 1976, v45, pC.
Films and Filming. Sep 1976, v22, p38-39.
Films and Filming. Aug 1976, v22, p24-26.
Films in Review. Jun-Jul 1976, v27, p378-79.
Hollywood Reporter. Apr 2, 1976, p2.
The Los Angeles Times. Apr 2, 1976, SecIV, p21.
Millimeter. May 1976, v4, p32-36.
Movietone News. Aug 1976, n51, p11-18.
Movietone News. Apr 1976, n49, p40-41.
Ms. Jul 1976, v5, p39-40.
New York. Apr 26, 1976, v9, p72-73.
The New York Times. May 9, 1976, SecII, p13.
Newsweek. Apr 12, 1976, v87, p94.
The Thousand Eyes Magazine. May 1976, n10, p10-11.
Time. Apr 19, 1976, v107, p82.
Times Educational Supplement. Aug 20, 1976, p27.
Variety. Apr 7, 1976, p22.
The Velvet Light Trap. Fall 1976, n16, p50-51.

The Liquidator (GB; Cardiff, Jack; 1965)
BFI/Monthly Film Bulletin. Oct 1966, v33, p154-55.
Christian Science Monitor (Western edition). Nov 21, 1966, p12.
Commonweal. Nov 18, 1966, v85, p201.
Film Daily. Oct 7, 1966, p7.
Filmfacts. Dec 15, 1966, v9, p293-95.
Films and Filming. Oct 1966, v13, p18.
Hollywood Reporter. Sep 19, 1966, p3.
The London Times. Aug 25, 1966, p6.
Motion Picture Herald Product Digest. Sep 28, 1966, p604.
New Statesman. Sep 2, 1966, v72, p329-30.
The New York Times. Oct 29, 1966, p34.
Playboy. Dec 1966, v13, p52-53.
Time. Oct 21, 1966, v88, p121.
Variety. Aug 31, 1966, p6.

The List of Adrian Messinger (US; Huston, John; 1963)
America. Aug 1963, v109, p123.
BFI/Monthly Film Bulletin. Jul 1963, v30, p95.
Burt Lancaster: A Pictorial Treasury of His Films. p120-21.
The Cinema of John Huston. p139-41.
Commonweal. Jun 21, 1963, v78, p354.
Film Daily. May 29, 1963, p5.
Filmfacts. Jun 27, 1963, v6, p115-16.
Films and Filming. Jul 1963, v9, p25-26.
Films in Review. Jun-Jul 1963, v14, p364-65.
The Films of Frank Sinatra. p192-94.
The Films of Kirk Douglas. p194-97.
Hollywood Reporter. May 29, 1963, p3.
Magill's Survey of Cinema. Series II. v3, p1386-89.
The New Republic. Jun 15, 1963, v148, p33.
The New York Times. May 30, 1963, p20.
The New Yorker. Jun 8, 1963, v39, p166.
Newsweek. Jun 10, 1963, v61, p105.
Robert Mitchum on the Screen. p182-84.
Sight and Sound. Sum 1963, v32, p146-47.
Time. Jun 14, 1963, v81, p98.
Variety. May 29, 1963, p6.

Lisztomania (GB; Russell, Ken; 1975)
BFI/Monthly Film Bulletin. Oct 1975, v42, p221.
Hollywood Reporter. Oct 10, 1975, p3.
Ken Russell: A Guide to References and Resources. p39-42.
Ken Russell (Phillips). p167-76.
Ken Russell's Films. p291-325.

The Los Angeles Times. Oct 17, 1975, SecIV, p13.
Motion Picture Herald Product Digest. Oct 22, 1975, p37.
The New York Times. Oct 11, 1975, p23.
The New York Times. Oct 19, 1975, SecII, p1.
The New Yorker. Nov 24, 1975, v51, p171-72.
Newsweek. Oct 20, 1975, v86, p99.
Time. Oct 20, 1975, v66, p61.
Variety. Oct 15, 1975, p26.
When the Lights Go Down. p83-84.

Little Big Horn (Also titled: The Fighting Seventh) (US; Warren, Charles Marquis; 1951)
BFI/Monthly Film Bulletin. Oct 1951, v18, p346.
Film Daily. May 29, 1951, p6.
Hollywood Reporter. May 25, 1951, p3.
Motion Picture Herald Product Digest. Jun 2, 1951, p869.
The Nation. Jan 5, 1952, v174, p18.
The New York Times. Jul 27, 1951, p15.
Variety. May 30, 1951, p6.

Little Big Man (US; Penn, Arthur; 1970)
America. Jan 30, 1971, v74, p97.
BFI/Monthly Film Bulletin. Apr 1971, v38, p78-79.
Commonweal. Feb 5, 1971, v93, p447.
Deeper Into Movies. p212-16.
Film Quarterly. Fall 1971, v25, p30-33.
The Films of Dustin Hoffman. p105-06.
Hollywood Reporter. Dec 16, 1970, p3.
Magill's Survey of Cinema. Series I. v2, p981-84.
The Modern American Novel and the Movies. p272-81.
The New Republic. Dec 26, 1970, v163, p18.
The New York Times. Dec 15, 1970, p53.
The New Yorker. Dec 26, 1970, v46, p50-52.
Newsweek. Dec 21, 1970, v76, p98A-98B.
Saturday Review. Jan 2, 1971, v54, p60.
Sight and Sound. Spr 1971, v40, n4, p102-03.
Time. Dec 21, 1970, v96, p56-57.
Variety. Feb 16, 1970, p17.

Little Boy Lost (US; Seaton, George; 1953)
America. Sep 26, 1953, v89, p629.
BFI/Monthly Film Bulletin. Aug 1953, v20, n235, p125.
Catholic World. Oct 1953, v178, p61.
Commonweal. Oct 9, 1953, v59, p13.
Film Daily. Jul 8, 1953, p10.
Films in Review. Aug-Sep 1953, v4, n7, p367-68.
The Films of Bing Crosby. p203-06.
Hollywood Reporter. Jul 8, 1953, p3.
Library Journal. Oct 15, 1953, v78, p1840.
Life. Aug 3, 1953, v35, p65-66.
The New York Times. Sep 22, 1953, p38.
The New Yorker. Oct 3, 1953, v29, p118.
Newsweek. Sep 21, 1953, v42, p98.
Saturday Review. Oct 3, 1953, v36, p44.
Senior Scholastic. Nov 4, 1953, v63, p35.
Time. Oct 5, 1953, v62, p104.
Variety. Jul 8, 1953, p6.

Little Darlings (US; Maxwell, Ronald F.; 1980)
BFI/Monthly Film Bulletin. Jul 1980, v47, p136.
Christian Science Monitor. Apr 16, 1980, p27.
Films in Review. Apr 1980, v31, p247.
Hollywood Reporter. Mar 19, 1980, p4.
The Los Angeles Times. Mar 21, 1980, SecVI, p4.
Motion Picture Herald Product Digest. Mar 12, 1980, p79.
The New York Times. Mar 28, 1980, SecIII, p15.

Newsday. Mar 28, 1980, SecII, p7.
Variety. Mar 19, 1980, p28.
The Village Voice. Apr 7, 1980, p38.

The Little Drummer Girl (US; Hill, George Roy; 1984)
BFI/Monthly Film Bulletin. Jul 1985, v52, p219.
Film Journal. Nov 1984, v87, p50.
Hollywood Reporter. Oct 9, 1984, p3.
The Los Angeles Times. Oct 19, 1984, SecVI, p1.
Maclean's. Nov 5, 1984, v97, p62.
The New Leader. Oct 29, 1984, v67, p20-22.
The New Republic. Nov 5, 1984, v191, p26-27.
New York. Oct 29, 1984, v17, p78.
The New York Times. Oct 19, 1984, SecIII, p18.
The New York Times. Oct 14, 1984, SecII, p1.
The New York Times. Nov 25, 1984, SecII, p13.
The New Yorker. Nov 12, 1984, v60, p179-80.
Newsweek. Oct 15, 1984, v104, p118.
Time. Oct 22, 1984, v22, p10.
Variety. Oct 10, 1984, p12.
Vogue. Nov 1984, v174, p106.

Little Fauss and Big Halsy (US; Furie, Sidney J.; 1970)
BFI/Monthly Film Bulletin. Oct 1971, v38, n453, p199-200.
Commonweal. Nov 13, 1970, v93, p177.
Deeper Into Movies. p212-16.
Hollywood Reporter. Oct 12, 1970, p3.
The New York Times. Oct 22, 1970, p62.
The New Yorker. Oct 31, 1970, v40, p132.
Newsweek. Oct 26, 1970, v76, p89A.
Saturday Review. Oct 31, 1970, v53, p24.
Sight and Sound. Spr 1971, v40, n2, p108.
Time. Nov 2, 1970, v96, p95.
Variety. Oct 21, 1970, p14.

The Little Fugitive (US; Ashley, Ray; 1953)
America. Oct 24, 1953, v90, p109.
Catholic World. Nov 1953, v178, p142.
Commonweal. Oct 23, 1953, v59, p61.
Film Daily. Oct 14, 1953, p10.
Films and Filming. Dec 1954, v1, n3, p19.
Films in Review. Nov 1953, v4, n9, p481-82.
The Films of the Fifties. p97-98.
Hollywood Reporter. Sep 9, 1953, p3.
The Nation. Oct 31, 1953, v177, p358.
The New Republic. Jul 26, 1954, v131, p22.
The New York Times. Oct 7, 1953, p35.
The New York Times. Oct 18, 1953, SecII, p1.
The New Yorker. Oct 10, 1953, v29, p126.
Newsweek. Oct 19, 1953, v42, p103.
Saturday Review. Nov 7, 1953, v36, pl36.
Saturday Review. May 19, 1956, v39, p50.
Senior Scholastic. Jan 6, 1954, v63, p28.
Sight and Sound. Jan-Mar 1955, v24, n3, p145-46.
Time. Nov 2, 1953, v62, p108.
Variety. Sep 23, 1953, p24.

The Little Hut (GB; Robson, Mark; 1957)
BFI/Monthly Film Bulletin. Aug 1957, v24, p103.
Commonweal. May 17, 1957, v66, p183.
Film Daily. May 3, 1957, v111, p6.
Films and Filming. Sep 1957, v3, p25.
The Films of David Niven. p134-37.
Hollywood Reporter. May 3, 1957, p3.
Motion Picture Herald Product Digest. May 11, 1957, v207, p369.
The New York Times. May 4, 1957, p25.
The New Yorker. May 11, 1957, v33, p152.
Newsweek. May 13, 1957, v49, p116.
Saturday Review. Apr 6, 1957, v40, p27.
Time. May 27, 1957, v69, p105.
Variety. May 15, 1957, p6.

The Little Kidnappers (Also titled: The Kidnappers) (GB; Leacock, Philip; 1953)
America. Oct 2, 1954, v92, p26.
BFI/Monthly Film Bulletin. Jan 1954, v21, p4.
Catholic World. Sep 1954, v179, p467.
Commonweal. Oct 1, 1954, v60, p631.
Film Daily. Aug 24, 1954, p10.
Films in Review. Oct 1954, v5, n8, p435-36.
The New Republic. Aug 16, 1954, v131, p21.
The New York Times. Sep 1, 1954, p18.
The New York Times. Sep 5, 1954, SecII, p1.
The New Yorker. Sep 11, 1954, v30, p76.
Newsweek. Sep 20, 1954, v44, p100.
Saturday Review. Sep 18, 1954, v37, p25.
Senior Scholastic. Nov 17, 1954, v65, p37.
Time. Sep 6, 1954, v64, p86-87.
Variety. Jan 27, 1954, p26.

The Little Man *See* Anni Difficili

Little Miss Marker (US; Bernstein, Walter; 1980)
BFI/Monthly Film Bulletin. Jul 1980, v47, p136.
The Christian Science Monitor. Apr 2, 1980, p8.
Films in Review. May 1980, v31, p310.
Hollywood Reporter. Mar 19, 1980, p4.
The Los Angeles Times. Mar 21, 1980, SecVI, p8.
The New York Times. Mar 21, 1980, SecIII, p8.
Newsweek. Mar 31, 1980, v95, p85.
Time. Mar 24, 1980, v115, p81.
Variety. Mar 19, 1980, p28.
The Village Voice. Mar 31, 1980, p48.

Little Murders (US; Arkin, Alan; 1971)
America. Mar 20, 1971, v124, p292.
Atlantic. Apr 1971, v227, p98-99.
BFI/Monthly Film Bulletin. Aug 1971, v38, p166.
Commonweal. Sep 3, 1971, v94, p453-54.
Deeper into Movies. p320-25.
Filmfacts. 1971, v14, n1, p1-5.
Films in Review. Feb 1971, v22, p109.
Hollywood Reporter. Feb 1, 1971, p4.
Journal of Popular Culture. Fall 1971, v5, n2, p471-72.
Life. Feb 12, 1971, v70, p10.
National Review. Jun 15, 1971, v23, p662.
The New Republic. Feb 6, 1971, v164, p24.
The New York Times. Feb 10, 1971, p34.
The New York Times. Feb 21, 1971, SecII, p1.
The New Yorker. Mar 6, 1971, v47, p92.
Newsweek. Feb 15, 1971, v77, p82.
Saturday Review. Aug 8, 1970, v53, p19-21.
Saturday Review. Feb 6, 1971, v54, p44.
Take One. Jan-Feb 1970, v11, n9, p15-16.
Time. Feb 22, 1971, v97, p54.
Variety. Feb 3, 1971, p17.
The Village Voice. Feb 18, 1971, v16, n7.

The Little Nuns (French title: Monachine, Le) (IT; Salce, Luciano; 1963)
Film Daily. Sep 20, 1965, p5.
Filmfacts. Jul 1, 1966, v9, p110-11.
Hollywood Reporter. Sep 15, 1965, p3.
Motion Picture Herald Product Digest. Sep 29, 1965, p380.
The New York Times. Apr 28, 1966, p49.
Variety. Sep 15, 1965, p6.

The Little Prince (GB; Donen, Stanley; 1974)
America. Dec 21, 1974, v131, p411.
BFI/Monthly Film Bulletin. Aug 1975, v42, p177.
Children's Novels and the Movies. p141-50.
Films Illustrated. Jul 1974, v3, p54.
Films in Review. Dec 1974, v25, p624.

Hollywood Reporter. Nov 6, 1974, p3.
Independent Film Journal. Nov 13, 1974, v74, p12-13.
The Los Angeles Times. Dec 19, 1974, SecIV, p1.
Motion Picture Herald Product Digest. Nov 13, 1974, p45.
New York. Nov 11, 1974, v7, p106.
The New York Times. Nov 17, 1974, SecII, p17.
The New York Times. Nov 8, 1974, p44.
The New Yorker. Dec 2, 1974, v50, p154-56.
Newsweek. Nov 11, 1974, v84, p86.
Stanley Donen (Casper). p203-13.
Time. Nov 18, 1974, v104, p5.
Variety. Nov 6, 1974, p22.
The Village Voice. Dec 9, 1974, p81-82, 90.

A Little Romance (US; Hill, George Roy; 1979)
BFI/Monthly Film Bulletin. Sep 1979, v47, p197.
Films in Review. Jun-Jul 1979, v30, p377.
The Films of George Roy Hill. p138-49.
George Roy Hill (Shores). p109-21.
Hollywood Reporter. Apr 2, 1979, p4.
Laurence Olivier: Theater & Cinema. p253-61.
Motion Picture Herald Product Digest. Apr 18, 1979, p89.
The Nation. Apr 28, 1979, v228, p475-76.
The New Republic. May 5, 1979, v180, p25.
The New York Times. Apr 27, 1979, SecIII, p16.
The New Yorker. May 7, 1979, v55, p141.
Newsweek. Apr 30, 1979, v93, p81.
Saturday Review. Jul 7, 1979, v6, p41.
Time. May 7, 1979, v113, p80.
Variety. Apr 4, 1979, p20.

The Little Shop of Horrors (US; Corman, Roger; 1960)
Cult Movies. p203-05.
The Films of Roger Corman. p42-43, 142-46.
Magill's Survey of Cinema. Series II. v3, p1396-1403.

The Little World of Don Camillo (French title: Petit Monde de Don Camillo, Le; Also titled: Don Camillo) (FR, IT; Duvivier, Julien; 1952)
BFI/Monthly Film Bulletin. Mar 1953, v20, p32.
Commonweal. Jan 16, 1953, v57, p378.
Films in Review. Feb 1953, v4, p96-97.
Illustrated London News. May 2, 1953, v222, p706.
Library Journal. Jan 15, 1953, v78, p141.
The London Times. Feb 13, 1953, p9.
The London Times. Jan 20, 1953, p3.
The Nation. Feb 14, 1953, v176, p153.
The New Statesman and Nation. Feb 21, 1953, v45, p206.
The New York Times. Jan 14, 1953, p27.
The New York Times Magazine. Jan 11, 1953, p16.
The New Yorker. Jan 24, 1953, v28, p63.
Newsweek. Jan 19, 1953, v41, p96.
Passion and Defiance. p144-45.
Saturday Review. Jan 17, 1953, v36, p29.
The Spectator. Feb 20, 1953, v190, p213.
Time. Jan 19, 1953, v61, p96.
Variety. May 28, 1952, p22.

Live and Let Die (GB; Hamilton, Guy; 1973)
America. Jul 7, 1973, v129, p20.
Films in Review. Oct 1973, v24, n8, p501.
The James Bond Bedside Companion. p206-10.
The James Bond Films. p111-24.
James Bond in the Cinema. p203-20.
The New Republic. Jul 28, 1973, v169, p35.

The New York Times. Jul 28, 1973, p56.
The New York Times. Jul 15, 1973, SecII, p1.
The New York Times. Jan 6, 1974, II v1, p2.
The New Yorker. Jul 9, 1973, v49, p56-57.
Roger Moore's James Bond Diary. 1973.
Time. Jul 9, 1973, v102, p40.
Variety. Jun 27, 1973, p20.
Vogue. Sep 1973, v162, p100.

Live for Life (French title: Vivre pour Vivre) (FR; Lelouch, Claude; 1967)
America. Feb 10, 1968, v118, p202-03.
BFI/Monthly Film Bulletin. Apr 1968, v35, p56-57.
Film Daily. Dec 19, 1967, p6.
Film Quarterly. Spr 1968, v21, p59.
Films and Filming. May 1968, v14, p25-26.
Films in Review. Jan 1968, v19, p53-54.
Motion Picture Herald Product Digest. Dec 20, 1967, p753.
The New York Times. Dec 19, 1967, p59.
The New Yorker. Dec 23, 1967, v43, p47-48.
Saturday Review. Dec 23, 1967, v50, p24.
Time. Dec 29, 1967, v90, p54.
Variety. Sep 27, 1967, p26.
The Village Voice. Jan 25, 1968, p38-39.

Living *See* Ikiru

The Living Desert (US; Algar, James; 1953)
America. Nov 14, 1953, v90, p185.
Commonweal. Nov 13, 1953, v59, p142.
Dictionary of Films. p195.
The Disney Films (Maltin). p113-14.
Film Daily. Oct 2, 1953, p6.
Films and Filming. Jan 1955, v1, p8-9.
Films in Review. Nov 1953, v4, p480.
Hollywood Reporter. Oct 1, 1953, p3.
The London Times. May 17, 1954, p4.
Motion Picture Herald Product Digest. Oct 10, 1953, p2021.
The Nation. Dec 26, 1953, v177, p574.
National Parent-Teacher. Jan 1954, v48, p38.
Natural History. Oct 1953, v62, p382.
The New Statesman and Nation. May 22, 1954, v47, p661.
The New York Times. Nov 10, 1953, p38.
The New Yorker. Nov 14, 1953, v29, p135.
Newsweek. Nov 23, 1953, v42, p100.
Saturday Review. Nov 14, 1953, v36, p41.
Sight and Sound. Jul-Sep 1954, v24, p35.
The Spectator. May 14, 1954, v192, p579.
The Tatler. May 26, 1954, v212, p462.
Time. Nov 16, 1953, v62, p106.
Variety. Oct 7, 1953, p6.
Walt Disney: A Guide to References and Resources. p46.

Living it Up (US; Taurog, Norman; 1954)
BFI/Monthly Film Bulletin. Sep 1954, v21, p129.
Catholic World. Aug 1954, v179, p384.
Farm Journal. Jul 1954, v78, p92.
Film Daily. Apr 29, 1954, p6.
Hollywood Reporter. Apr 29, 1954, p3.
Motion Picture Herald Product Digest. May 1, 1954, p2277.
National Parent-Teacher. Oct 1954, v49, p39.
The New York Times. Jul 24, 1954, p6.
Saturday Review. Jul 31, 1954, v37, p35.
Time. Jul 19, 1954, v64, p76.
Variety. May 5, 1954, p6.

Lizzie (US; Haas, Hugo; 1957)
America. Apr 20, 1957, v97, p84.
BFI/Monthly Film Bulletin. Jul 1957, v24, p89.
Commonweal. Apr 19, 1957, v66, p65.
Film Daily. Mar 4, 1957, v111, p6.
Films in Review. Apr 1957, v8, p177.
Hollywood Reporter. Feb 25, 1957, p3.

America. Mar 28, 1959, v100, p754.
Catholic World. Mar 1959, v188, p501-02.
Commonweal. Feb 13, 1959, v69, p520.
Film Daily. Dec 1, 1958, v114, p6.
Filmfacts. Apr 1, 1959, v2, p39-41.
Films in Review. Feb 1959, v10, p108-09.
The Films of Montgomery Clift. p173-78.
The Films of Myrna Loy. p244-45.
Hollywood Reporter. Dec 1, 1958, p3.
The Modern American Novel and the Movies. p19-28.
The New York Times. Mar 5, 1959, p35.
The New Yorker. Mar 14, 1959, v35, p164.
Newsweek. Mar 16, 1959, v53, p95.
Reporter. Apr 2, 1959, v20, p36-37.
Time. Mar 23, 1959, v73, p95.
Variety. Dec 3, 1958, p6.

Lonesome Cowboys (US; Warhol, Andy; 1968)
Atlantic. Apr 1969, v223, p141.
BFI/Monthly Film Bulletin. Mar 1970, v37, p56.
Christian Century. Oct 29, 1969, v86, p1402.
Commonweal. Jul 25, 1969, v90, p465.
Dictionary of Films. p197.
Directors and Directions: Cinema for the Seventies. p152-53.
Filmfacts. 1969, v12, n9, p201-03.
Films and Filming. Apr 1970, v16, p43-44.
Hollywood Reporter. Nov 19, 1968, p3.
The London Times. Jan 15, 1970, p8.
Movie Comedy (Byron). p111-13.
The New York Times. May 6, 1969, p38.
Variety. Nov 13, 1968, p6.
The Village Voice. May 8, 1969, p47.

The Long Dark Hall (GB; Bushell, Anthony; Beck, Reginald; 1951)
BFI/Monthly Film Bulletin. Mar 1951, v18, p228.
Christian Century. Jul 25, 1951, v68, p879.
Commonweal. May 25, 1951, v54, p166.
Film Daily. Mar 1, 1951, p6.
Hollywood Reporter. Mar 1, 1951, p3.
Library Journal. Jun 15, 1951, v76, p1037.
The London Times. Feb 12, 1951, p6.
Motion Picture Herald Product Digest. Mar 10, 1951, p750.
The New Republic. May 21, 1951, v124, p23.
The New York Times. May 10, 1951, p38.
The New Yorker. May 19, 1951, v27, p110.
Newsweek. May 24, 1951, v37, p97.
Saturday Review. May 19, 1951, v34, p27.
The Spectator. Feb 9, 1951, v186, p177.
Time. Jun 18, 1951, v57, p104.
Variety. Feb 14, 1951, p13.

Long Day's Journey Into Night (US; Lumet, Sidney; 1962)
America. Nov 24, 1962, v107, p1158.
BFI/Monthly Film Bulletin. Aug 1964, v31, p115.
Cinema. 1963, v1, n3, p33.
Commonweal. Oct 19, 1962, v77, p94-95.
Film. Aut 1962, n33, p21.
Film Daily. Oct 10, 1962, p3.
Filmfacts. Oct 12, 1962, v5, p219-21.
Films and Filming. Jul 1964, v10, p20.
Films in Review. Oct 1962, v13, p486-88.
The Films of Katharine Hepburn. p178-83.
Hollywood Reporter. Oct 10, 1962, p3.
Life. Oct 26, 1962, v53, p70A.
Magill's Survey of Cinema. Series I. v3, p999-1003.
Motion Picture Herald Product Digest. Oct 17, 1962, p675.
Movie. Jun 1963, n10, p35.
The Nation. Oct 13, 1962, v195, p227-28.
The New Republic. Sep 24, 1962, v147, p26.

The New York Times. Oct 10, 1962, p57.
The New Yorker. Oct 20, 1962, v38, p215.
Newsweek. Oct 15, 1962, v60, p109.
Private Screenings. p51-52.
Reruns. p155-59.
Saturday Review. Oct 6, 1962, v45, p30.
Sidney Lumet: A Guide to References and Resources. p70-72.
Sight and Sound. Sum 1964, v33, p147.
Time. Oct 12, 1962, v80, p102.
Variety. May 30, 1962, p6.
A World on Film. p74-76.

The Long Good Friday (GB; Mackenzie, John; 1980)
Hollywood Reporter. Apr 20, 1982, p19.
The Los Angeles Times. May 8, 1982, SecV, p4.
Magill's Cinema Annual, 1983. p220-23.
The Nation. May 1, 1982, v234, p537.
National Review. May 14, 1982, v34, p572-74.
The New Leader. Jun 14, 1982, v65, p20.
New York. Apr 19, 1982, v15, p78.
The New York Times. Apr 2, 1982, SecIII, p12.
Rolling Stone. May 27, 1982, p39-40.
Variety. May 28, 1980, p3.

The Long Goodbye (US; Altman, Robert; 1973)
Cult Movies. p210-14.
Film Quarterly. Summer 1973, v26, n4, p46.
Film Quarterly. Sum 1973, v26, p46-48.
Films in Review. Aug-Sep 1973, v24, n7, p441.
Hollywood Reporter. Feb 28, 1973, p3.
The Nation. Nov 26, 1973, v217, p574.
The New Republic. Nov 3, 1973, v169, p20.
The New York Times. Oct 28, 1973, SecII, p1.
The New York Times. Oct 29, 1973, p42.
The New York Times. Nov 18, 1973, SecII, p1.
The New York Times. Jan 6, 1974, SecII, p1.
The New Yorker. Oct 22, 1973, v49, p133-39.
Newsweek. Oct 29, 1973, v82, p107.
PTA Magazine. Jan 1974, v68, p4.
Raymond Chandler in Hollywood. p123-34.
Reeling. p253-62.
Rolling Stone. Dec 6, 1973, p86.
Saturday Review World. Nov 6, 1973, v1, p49-50.
Sight and Sound. Wint 1973-74, v43, n1, p51.
Sight and Sound. Spr 1973, v42, p85.
Sight and Soung. Wint 1973-1974, v43, p51-52.
Time. Apr 9, 1973, v101, p83.
Variety. Mar 7, 1973, p18.
The Village Voice. Nov 1, 1973, p67-68.
The Village Voice. Nov 15, 1973, p69.

The Long Hot Summer (US; Ritt, Martin; 1958)
America. Mar 22, 1958, v98, p735.
BFI/Monthly Film Bulletin. May 1958, v25, p57.
Catholic World. May 1958, v187, p143.
Commonweal. Mar 21, 1958, v60, p639.
Cosmopolitan. Apr 1958, v144, p20.
Film Daily. Mar 5, 1958, v113, p6.
Filmfacts. May 7, 1958, v1, p55-56.
Films in Review. May 1958, v9, p201-02.
The Films of Paul Newman. p61-65.
Hollywood Reporter. Mar 5, 1958, p3.
Library Journal. Apr 1, 1958, v83, p1077.
Magill's Survey of Cinema. Series II. v3, p1421-23.
The Nation. Apr 19, 1958, v186, p352.
The New York Times. Apr 4, 1958, p16.
Newsweek. Apr 7, 1958, v51, p96.
Reporter. May 15, 1958, v18, p43-44.
Saturday Review. Apr 12, 1958, v41, p43-44.
Saturday Review. Dec 7, 1957, v40, p52-53.
Time. Mar 31, 1958, v71, p86.
Variety. Mar 5, 1958, p6.

The Long, Long Trailer (US; Minnelli, Vincente; 1954)
America. Feb 27, 1954, v90, p582.
American Magazine. Feb 1954, v157, p12.
BFI/Monthly Film Bulletin. May 1954, v21, p70-71.
Commonweal. Mar 5, 1954, v59, p554.
Film Daily. Jan 7, 1954, p10.
Films in Review. Feb 1954, v5, p96.
Hollywood Reporter. Jan 5, 1954, p3.
Library Journal. Feb 15, 1954, v79, p314.
The London Times. Apr 19, 1954, p9.
Motion Picture Herald Product Digest. Jan 9, 1954, p2133.
National Parent-Teacher. Mar 1954, v48, p38.
The New York Times. Feb 19, 1954, p24.
Newsweek. Feb 8, 1954, v43, p86-87.
Saturday Review. Feb 20, 1954, v37, p32.
The Tatler. Apr 28, 1954, v212, p216.
Time. Feb 22, 1954, v63, p102.
Variety. Jan 6, 1954, p52.

The Long Memory (GB; Hamer, Robert; 1953)
BFI/Monthly Film Bulletin. Feb 1953, v20, p20-21.
The New Statesman and Nation. Jan 31, 1953, v45, p119-20.
The New York Times. Jul 27, 1953, p15.
The Spectator. Jan 23, 1953, v190, p93.
The Tatler. Feb 4, 1953, v207, p194.
Variety. Feb 4, 1953, p20.

The Long Riders (US; Hill, Walter; 1980)
BFI/Monthly Film Bulletin. Sep 1980, v47, p178.
Film Comment. May-Jun 1980, v16, p13-19.
Films in Review. Aug-Sep 1980, v440.
Hollywood Reporter. May 7, 1980, p3.
Horizon. Jul 1980, v23, p71.
The Los Angeles Times. May 16, 1980, SecVI, p2.
Motion Picture Herald Product Digest. Mar 28, 1980, p99.
The Nation. Jun 7, 1980, v230, p699.
The New Republic. May 31, 1980, v182, p24-25.
New York. May 26, 1980, v13, p68-69.
The New York Times. May 16, 1980, SecIII, p14.
The New Yorker. May 19, 1980, v56, p143-44.
Newsday. May 16, 1980, SecII, p7.
Newsweek. Jun 2, 1980, v95, p87-88.
Sight and Sound. Aut 1980, v50, p267.
Time. Jun 16, 1980, v115, p51.
Variety. May 7, 1980, p10.

The Long Wait (US; Saville, Victor; 1954)
BFI/Monthly Film Bulletin. Aug 1954, v21, p121.
Catholic World. May 1954, v179, p145.
Commonweal. May 29, 1954, v60, p198.
Farm Journal. Jun 1954, v78, p141.
Film Daily. May 14, 1954, p12.
The Films of Anthony Quinn. p146-47.
Hollywood Reporter. Apr 28, 1954, p3.
Library Journal. May 15, 1954, v79, p953.
Motion Picture Herald Product Digest. May 1, 1954, p2278.
National Parent-Teacher. Jun 1954, v48, p39.
The New York Times. Jul 3, 1954, p9.
A Reference Guide to the American Film Noir. p204.
Time. Jun 21, 1954, v63, p104.
Variety. May 5, 1954, p6.

The Longest Day (US; Annakin, Ken; Marton, Andrew; Wicki, Bernhard; 1962)
BFI/Monthly Film Bulletin. Nov 1962, v29, p148-49.

Combat Films. p43-78.
Commonweal. Oct 26, 1962, v77, p124-25.
The Complete Films of John Wayne. p242-43.
Film Daily. Oct 3, 1962, p3.
Filmfacts. Nov 9, 1962, v5, p251-53.
Films and Filming. Dec 1962, v9, p40-41.
Films in Review. Oct 1962, v13, p481-84.
Films in Review. Nov 1962, v13, p567-68.
The Films of Henry Fonda. p168-69.
The Films of the Sixties. p82-83.
Guts & Glory. p140-63.
Hollywood Reporter. Oct 3, 1962, p3.
Journal of Popular Film. 1976, v5, n3/4, p211-32.
Magill's Survey of Cinema. Series II. v3, p1424-30.
Motion Picture Herald Product Digest. Oct 31, 1962, p683-84.
The New Republic. Nov 10, 1962, v147, p25.
The New York Times. Oct 5, 1962, p28.
The New Yorker. Oct 13, 1962, v38, p188.
Newsweek. Oct 15, 1962, v60, p105.
Robert Mitchum on the Screen. p177-79.
Saturday Review. Oct 20, 1962, v45, p34.
Time. Oct 19, 1962, v80, p91.
Variety. Oct 3, 1962, p6.

The Longest Yard (US; Aldrich, Robert; 1974)
BFI/Monthly Film Bulletin. Dec 1974, v41, p27-28.
Commonweal. Sep 27, 1974, v100, p523-24.
Film. Dec 1974, v4, p142-43.
The Films and Career of Robert Aldrich. p180-87.
Films Illustrated. Dec 1974, v4, p126.
Films in Review. Oct 1974, v25, p505-06.
The Films of Burt Reynolds. p165-70.
Hollywood Reporter. Aug 20, 1974, p4.
Independent Film Journal. Sep 4, 1974, v74, p11.
The Los Angeles Times. Sep 25, 1974, SecIV, p1.
Magill's Survey of Cinema. Series II. v3, p1341-44.
Motion Picture Herald Product Digest. Sep 4, 1974, p25.
Movietone News. Sep 1974, n35, p29-30.
New York. Sep 9, 1974, v7, p62-63.
The New York Times. Sep 15, 1974, SecII, p1.
The New Yorker. Oct 14, 1974, v50, p176.
Newsweek. Sep 16, 1974, v84, p79.
Penthouse. Nov 1974, v6, p45.
PTA Magazine. Nov 1974, v69, p9.
Reeling. p469-73.
Robert Aldrich: A Guide to References and Resources. p61-64.
Sports Illustrated. Sep 30, 1974, v41, p48-51.
Time. Sep 23, 1974, v104, p6.
Variety. Aug 28, 1974, p18.
The Village Voice. Sep 12, 1974, p76.

Look Back in Anger (GB; Richardson, Tony; 1959)
America. Sep 19, 1959, v101, p748.
BFI/Monthly Film Bulletin. Jun 1959, v26, p68.
Commonweal. Sep 4, 1959, v70, p472.
Film Daily. Sep 3, 1959, v116, p6.
Filmfacts. Oct 14, 1959, v2, p215-17.
Films in Review. Oct 1959, v10, p491-93.
Hollywood Reporter. Sep 2, 1959, p3.
Magill's Survey of Cinema. Series II. v3, p1435-38.
The Nation. Oct 3, 1959, v189, p200.
The New Republic. Sep 28, 1959, v141, p30-32.
The New York Times. Sep 16, 1959, p45.
The New Yorker. Sep 26, 1959, v35, p179-80.
Newsweek. Sep 21, 1959, v54, p124.
Reporter. Oct 15, 1959, v21, p43.

Saturday Review. Sep 12, 1959, v42, p30.
Time. Sep 28, 1959, v74, p76.
Variety. Jun 3, 1959, p6.

Looking for Mr. Goodbar (US; Brooks, Richard; 1977)
America. Nov 5, 1977, v137, p314.
BFI/Monthly Film Bulletin. Mar 1978, v45, p49.
Commonweal. Feb 3, 1978, 105, p82-83.
Films in Review. Dec 1978, v28, p629.
Hollywood Reporter. Oct 14, 1977, p3.
Human Behavior. Mar 1978, v7, p62-67.
The Los Angeles Times. Nov 20, 1978, Calendar, p1.
Motion Picture Herald Product Digest. Nov 2, 1978, p42.
Ms. Feb 1978, v6, p24.
The New York Times. Oct 20, 1977, SecIII, p19.
The New Yorker. Oct 24, 1977, v53, p147-50.
Newsweek. Oct 24, 1977, v90, p126.
Saturday Review. Dec 10, 1977, v5, p62-63.
Time. Oct 24, 1977, v110, p104.
Time. Sep 26, 1977, v110, p68-69.
Variety. Oct 19, 1977, p25.

The Looking Glass War (GB; Pierson, Frank; 1970)
BFI/Monthly Film Bulletin. Feb 1970, v37, p27.
Deeper Into Movies. p117-19.
Film Daily. Feb 9, 1970, p7.
Hollywood Reporter. Feb 4, 1970, p3.
Magill's Survey of Cinema. Series II. v3, p1439-41.
The New York Times. Feb 5, 1970, p33.
The New Yorker. Feb 21, 1970, v46, p99-100.
Saturday Review. Feb 14, 1970, v53, p16.
Variety. Feb 4, 1970, p18.

Lord Jim (GB; Brooks, Richard; 1965)
BFI/Monthly Film Bulletin. Apr 1965, v32, p52-53.
Christian Science Monitor (Western edition). Feb 19, 1965, p4.
Cinema. Mar-Apr 1965, v2, p48.
Commonweal. Mar 19, 1965, v81, p791-92.
Film Daily. Feb 24, 1965, p6.
Film Quarterly. Fall 1965, v19, p39-51.
Filmfacts. Mar 5, 1965, v8, p19-24.
Films and Filming. Feb 1965, v11, p17.
Films and Filming. Mar 1965, v11, p16-17.
Films and Filming. Apr 1965, v11, p26-27.
Films in Review. Apr 1965, v16, p249-50.
The Films of James Mason. p165-67.
Guardian. Feb 16, 1965, p9.
Hollywood Reporter. Feb 24, 1965, p3.
Illustrated London News. Feb 27, 1965, v246, p24.
Life. Mar 19, 1965, v58, p15.
Listener. Feb 25, 1965, v73, p304.
The London Times. Feb 8, 1965, p5, 16.
Motion Picture Herald Product Digest. Mar 3, 1965, p16.
Motion Picture Herald Product Digest. Mar 17, 1965, p251-52.
Movie. Sum 1965, n13, p38-39.
The Nation. Mar 22, 1965, v200, p315.
The New Republic. Mar 13, 1965, v152, p22-23.
New Statesman. Feb 19, 1965, v69, p289-90.
The New York Times. Feb 26, 1965, p18.
The New Yorker. Mar 6, 1965, v41, p94, 96.
Newsweek. Mar 8, 1965, v65, p91-92.
Playboy. May 1965, v12, p30.
Private Screenings. p175-76.
Reporter. Jun 17, 1965, v32, p46-48.
Saturday Review. Mar 6, 1965, v48, p39.
Senior Scholastic. Apr 29, 1965, v86, p33.
The Spectator. Feb 19, 1965, v214, p232.
Time. Mar 5, 1965, v85, p98.

Variety. Feb 24, 1965, p6.
The Village Voice. Apr 29, 1965, v10, p12.
Vogue. Apr 15, 1965, v145, p57.

Lord Love a Duck (US; Alexrod, George; 1966)
America. Mar 26, 1966, v114, p424-25.
BFI/Monthly Film Bulletin. Oct 1967, v34, p152-53.
Big Screen, Little Screen. p347-48.
Christian Science Monitor (Western edition). Mar 22, 1966, p12.
Commonweal. Mar 11, 1965, v83, p667.
Confessions of a Cultist. p241-43.
Film Daily. Jan 28, 1966, p6.
Film Quarterly. Sum 1966, v19, p68.
Filmfacts. Apr 1, 1966, v9, p49-50.
Films in Review. Mar 1966, v17, p181-82.
The London Times. Jun 15, 1967, p8.
Motion Picture Herald Product Digest. Feb 2, 1966, p461.
New Statesman. Jun 30, 1967, v73, p914-15.
The New York Times. Feb 22, 1966, p14.
The New Yorker. Feb 26, 1966, v42, p106.
Newsweek. Mar 7, 1966, v67, p100.
Playboy. Apr 1966, v13, p44.
Private Screenings. p252-53.
Saturday Review. Feb 12, 1966, v49, p45.
Senior Scholastic. May 13, 1966, v88, p27.
Sight and Sound. Aut 1967, v36, p204-05.
Talking Pictures. p92-95.
Variety. Jan 19, 1966, p6.
The Village Voice. Mar 17, 1966, v11, p23.

Lord of the Flies (GB; Brook, Peter; 1963)
America. Oct 5, 1963, v109, p398.
BFI/Monthly Film Bulletin. Sep 1964, v31, p131.
Esquire. Feb 1964, v61, p28.
Film Daily. Aug 22, 1963, p6.
Film Quarterly. Wint 1963-64, p31-32.
Filmfacts. Sep 5, 1963, v6, p175-77.
Films and Filming. Aug 1964, v10, p21.
Films in Review. Aug-Sep 1963, v14, p439-40.
The New Republic. Aug 17, 1963, v149, p27.
The New York Times. Aug 20, 1963, p37.
The New York Times. Aug 25, 1963, SecII, p1.
The New Yorker. Aug 31, 1963, v39, p56.
Newsweek. Aug 26, 1963, v62, p76.
Saturday Review. Aug 17, 1963, v46, p14.
Sight and Sound. Aut 1964, v33, p194-95.
Time. Aug 23, 1963, v82, p68.
Variety. May 22, 1963, p6.

The Lords of Discipline (US; Roddam, Franc; 1983)
Christian Century. Apr 13, 1983, v100, p348-49.
Hollywood Reporter. Feb 11, 1983, p3.
Horizon. May 1983, v26, p54-55.
Maclean's. Feb 21, 1983, v96, p50.
The New Leader. Feb 21, 1983, v66, p20.
New York. Feb 28, 1983, v16, p84-86.
Newsweek. Feb 21, 1983, v101, p60-61.

The Lords of Flatbush (US; Vernal, Stephen F.; Davidson, Mark; 1974)
Audience. Jun 1974, v6, p7-11.
BFI/Monthly Film Bulletin. Jun 1975, v42, p139.
Films in Review. Aug-Sep 1974, v25, p439-40.
Hollywood Reporter. May 1, 1974, p3.
Independent Film Journal. May 15, 1974, v73, p20.
The Los Angeles Times. Sep 4, 1974, SecIV, p1.
Millimeter. May 1974, v2, p44.
Motion Picture Herald Product Digest. May 22, 1974, p103.
New York. May 13, 1974, v7, p104-6.
Saturday Review. Jun 1, 1974, v1, p41.
Time. May 20, 1974, v103, p68.

Variety. Oct 2, 1974, p4.
Variety. May 1, 1974, p18.

Lost and Found (GB; Frank, Melvin; 1979)
BFI/Monthly Film Bulletin. Jul 1979, v46, p148.
Hollywood Reporter. Jun 22, 1979, p3.
Motion Picture Herald Product Digest. Aug 1, 1979, p18.
The New York Times. Jun 13, 1979, SecIII, p8.
Variety. Jun 27, 1979, p18.

The Lost Command (Also titled: The Centurions) (US; Robson, Mark; 1966)
America. Jul 16, 1966, v115, p78-79.
BFI/Monthly Film Bulletin. Aug 1966, v33, p125.
Christian Science Monitor (Western edition). Jun 10, 1966, p4.
Film Daily. May 25, 1966, p7.
Filmfacts. Oct 15, 1966, v9, p217-18.
Films and Filming. Sep 1966, v12, p8.
Films in Review. Jun-Jul 1966, v17, p379-80.
The Films of Anthony Quinn. p209-10.
Hollywood Reporter. May 25, 1966, p3.
Life. Jun 3, 1966, v60, p12.
The London Times. Jun 23, 1966, p7.
Motion Picture Herald Product Digest. May 25, 1966, p526-27.
New Statesman. Jun 24, 1966, v71, p939.
The New York Times. Sep 15, 1966, p51.
The New Yorker. Sep 24, 1966, v42, p111.
Newsweek. Sep 26, 1966, v68, p114.
Playboy. Jul 1966, v13, p26.
Saturday Review. Jun 18, 1966, v49, p50.
Time. Oct 7, 1966, v88, pLA9.
Variety. May 25, 1966, p6.

Lost Continent (US; Newfield, Sam; 1951)
BFI/Monthly Film Bulletin. Mar 1952, v19, p36.
Hollywood Reporter. Jul 20, 1951, p3.
Motion Picture Herald Product Digest. Jul 28, 1951, p946.
Variety. Jul 25, 1951, p6.

Lost Horizon (US; Jarrott, Charles; 1972)
America. Apr 7, 1973, v128, p316.
Good Housekeeping. Apr 1973, v176, p36.
Holiday. May 1973, v53, p8.
Hollywood Reporter. Mar 7, 1973, p3.
The New Yorker. Mar 17, 1973, v49, p119-21.
Newsweek. Mar 26, 1973, v81, p72.
Saturday Evening Post. Mar 1973, v245, p68-69.
Seventeen. Apr 1973, v32, p121.
Time. Apr 2, 1973, v101, p60.
Variety. Mar 7, 1973, p18.

Lost in Alaska (Also titled: Abbott and Costello Lost in Alaska) (US; Yarbrough, Jean; 1952)
BFI/Monthly Film Bulletin. Oct 1952, v19, p141.
Film Daily. Jul 30, 1952, p8.
Hollywood Reporter. Jul 25, 1952, p3.
Motion Picture Herald Product Digest. Jul 26, 1952, p1462.
National Parent-Teacher. Oct 1952, v47, p37.
Variety. Jul 30, 1952, p6.

Lost in America (US; Brooks, Albert; 1985)
BFI/Monthly Film Bulletin. Dec 1985, v52, p381.
Christian Century. Apr 24, 1985, v102, p425-26.
Commonweal. May 17, 1985, v112, p304-05.
The Los Angeles Times. Mar 15, 1985, SecVI, p1.
Maclean's. Apr 8, 1985, v98, p62.
Magill's Cinema Annual, 1986. p219-22.
The New Republic. Mar 18, 1985, v192, p26.

New York. Feb 25, 1985, v18, p58-59.
The New York Times. Feb 1985, SecIII, p5.
The New Yorker. Apr 8, 1985, v61, p120.
Newsweek. Feb 25, 1985, v105, p85.
Time. Mar 18, 1985, v125, p84.
Variety. Feb 13, 1985, p22.

The Lost One *See* Verlorene, Der

Lost Property *See* Souvenirs Perdus

Lotna (POL; Wajda, Andrzej; 1959)
The Cinema of Andrzej Wajda. p47-53.
Cinema, the Magic Vehicle. v2, p516-18.
Filmfacts. Jul 15, 1966, v9, p128.
The London Times. Nov 11, 1965, p18.
The New York Times. May 27, 1966, p33.
Politics, Art and Commitment in East European Cinema. p174-75.
Sight and Sound. Wint 1965-66, v35, p41-42.
The Spectator. Nov 12, 1965, v215, p619.
Variety. May 20, 1964, p20.

Louisa (US; Hall, Alexander; 1950)
Christian Century. Sep 6, 1950, v67, p1063.
Christian Century. Sep 20, 1950, v67, p1119.
Film Daily. May 31, 1950, p7.
The Films of Ronald Reagan. p173-75.
Hollywood Reporter. May 31, 1950, p3.
Motion Picture Herald Product Digest. Jun 3, 1950, p321.
The New York Times. Oct 25, 1950, p45.
Newsweek. Aug 21, 1950, v36, p83.
The Spectator. Jun 23, 1950, v184, p853-54.
Time. Nov 13, 1950, v56, p100.
Variety. May 31, 1950, p6.

Loulou (FR; Pialat, Maurice; 1980)
BFI/Monthly Film Bulletin. Mar 1981, v47, p51.
Christian Science Monitor. Oct 30, 1980, p18.
Film Comment. Nov-Dec 1980, v16, p67.
Films in Review. Dec 1980, v31, p631.
Hollywood Reporter. Oct 16, 1980, p34.
The Los Angeles Times. Mar 19, 1981, SecVI, p7.
Magill's Cinema Annual, 1982. p226-29.
The Nation. Nov 8, 1980, v23, p493.
New York. Oct 20, 1980, v13, p84-86.
The New York Times. Oct 8, 1980, SecIII, p20.
Newsday. Oct 10, 1980, SecII, p7.
Newsweek. Oct 20, 1980, v96, p84.
Progressive. Dec 1980, v44, p53.
Sight and Sound. Spr 1981, v50, p136.
Time. Oct 20, 1980, v116, p96.
Variety. May 28, 1980, p15.

Love a La Carte (Italian title: Adua e le Compagne; Also titled: Hungry For Love; Adua and Her Colleagues) (IT; Pietrangeli, Antonio; 1960)
BFI/Monthly Film Bulletin. Mar 1962, v29, p38.
Film Daily. Jan 5, 1965, p9.
Filmfacts. Apr 30, 1965, v8, p68-69.
Films and Filming. Mar 1962, v8, p33.
Motion Picture Herald Product Digest. Jan 20, 1965, p211.
The New Yorker. Jan 23, 1965, v40, p107.
The Spectator. Feb 2, 1962, v208, p140.
Time. Feb 12, 1965, v85, p91.
Variety. Sep 14, 1960, p20.

Love Affair, or The Case of the Missing Switchboard Operator (Yugoslavian title: Ljubavni Slucaj ou Tragedija Sluzbenice P.T.T.; Also titled: An Affair of the Heart; The Switchboard Operator; Case of the Missing Switchboard Operator; Love Dossier,

or The Tragedy of a Switchboard Operator) (YUGO; Makavejev, Dusan; 1967)
BFI/Monthly Film Bulletin. Sep 1969, v36, p189-90.
Directors and Directions: Cinema for the Seventies. p239-46.
Esquire. May 1968, v69, p84.
Figures of Light. p52-55.
Film Quarterly. Spr 1968, v21, p41-44.
Film Society Review. Sep 1968, v4, p41-43.
Filmfacts. Feb 15, 1968, v11, p23-24.
Films and Filming. Oct 1969, v16, p41-42.
The Films of the Sixties. p177-79.
International Film Guide. 1968, v5, p165-66.
Listener. Jan 11, 1968, v79, p61-62.
Motion Picture Herald Product Digest. Apr 17, 1968, p800A.
Movie Comedy (Byron). p254-55.
The Nation. Feb 26, 1968, v206, p286.
The New Republic. Feb 17, 1968, v158, p24.
The New York Times. Feb 7, 1968, p38.
Newsweek. Feb 19, 1968, v71, p92.
Variety. May 3, 1967, p6.
The Village Voice. Feb 15, 1968, p41.

Love and Anarchy (Italian title: Film D'Amore e D'Anarchia) (IT, FR; Wertmuller, Lina; 1973)
Cineaste. 1974, v6, n3, p36-37.
Commonweal. Aug 9, 1974, v100, p430-31.
Film Quarterly. Wint 1974, v61, p75-76.
Hollywood Reporter. Mar 12, 1974, p3.
Independent Film Journal. Apr 29, 1974, v73, p8.
Jump Cut. Nov-Dec 1974, n4, p8-9.
Jump Cut. Jul-Aug 1974, n2, p8-9.
The Los Angeles Times. Nov 26, 1974, SecIV, p1.
Magill's Survey of Cinema. Foreign Language Films. v4, p1839-43.
Movietone News. Sep 1974, n35, p26-27.
Ms. Jun 1974, v2, p33.
The Nation. May 4, 1974, v218, p573-74.
New York. Apr 22, 1974, v7, p90-91.
The New York Times. Jun 23, 1974, SecII, p13.
Newsweek. Apr 29, 1974, v83, p98.
Time. May 20, 1974, v103, p68.
Variety. Mar 30, 1973, p26.

Love and Death (US; Allen, Woody; 1975)
Before My Eyes. p140.
BFI/Monthly Film Bulletin. Nov 1975, v42, p241.
Commonweal. Jul 4, 1975, v102, p242.
Films in Review. Aug-Sep 1975, v26, p435.
Hollywood Reporter. Jun 10, 1975, p3.
The Los Angeles Times. Jun 11, 1975, SecIV, p1.
Magill's Survey of Cinema. Series III. v3, p1449-51.
Motion Picture Herald Product Digest. Jun 25, 1975, p6.
The Nation. Jun 28, 1975, v220, p797-98.
The New Republic. Jul 5, 1975, v173, p22.
The New York Times. Jun 11, 1975, p48.
The New York Times. Jun 22, 1975, SecII, p1.
The New York Times. Jun 29, 1975, SecII, p1.
The New Yorker. Jun 16, 1975, v51, p104.
Newsweek. Jun 23, 1975, v85, p84-85.
Time. Jun 30, 1975, v105, p76.
Variety. Jun 11, 1975, p18.
Vogue. Aug 1975, v165, p46.
Woody Allen: His Films and Career. p145-47.
Woody Allen (Palmer). p77-82.

Love and Kisses (US; Nelson, Ozzie; 1965)
BFI/Monthly Film Bulletin. Oct 1966, v33, p155.

Christian Science Monitor (Western edition).
  Nov 8, 1965, p6.
Film Daily. Aug 5, 1965, p7.
Hollywood Reporter. Aug 5, 1965, p3.
Motion Picture Herald Product Digest. Aug 18,
  1965, p346.
The New York Times. Dec 23, 1965, p21.
Variety. Aug 11, 1965, p6.

Love at First Bite (US; Dragoti, Stan; 1979)
BFI/Monthly Film Bulletin. Aug 1979, v46,
  p177.
Films in Review. Jun-Jul 1979, v30, p374.
Hollywood Reporter. Apr 6, 1979, p3.
The New York Times. Apr 13, 1979, SecIII,
  p10.
Time. May 14, 1979, v113, p76.
Variety. Apr 11, 1979, p20.

The Love Cage *See* Joy House

**Love Dossier, or The Case of the Missing
  Switchboard Operator** *See* Love Affair,
  or The Case of the Missing
  Switchboard Operator

The Love Goddesses (French title: Déesses
  de l'Ecran, Les) (US; Turell, Saul J.;
  Ferguson, Graeme; 1965)
BFI/Monthly Film Bulletin. May 1965, v32,
  p71.
Cahiers du Cinema in English. 1966, n5, p56-
  57.
Commonweal. Mar 26, 1965, v82, p22.
Film Daily. Mar 2, 1965, p3.
Filmfacts. May 28, 1965, v8, p90-92.
Films and Filming. Jul 1965, v11, p31.
Films in Review. Apr 1965, v16, p251-52.
Hollywood Reporter. Mar 2, 1965, p3.
The London Times. Apr 22, 1965, p16.
Motion Picture Herald Product Digest. Mar 17,
  1965, p249-50.
The New Republic. Mar 20, 1965, v152, p25.
The New York Times. Mar 4, 1965, p36.
The New Yorker. Mar 13, 1965, v41, p167-68.
Newsweek. Mar 8, 1965, v65, p90B.
Playboy. Jun 1965, v12, p30.
Saturday Review. Mar 20, 1965, v48, p36.
Time. Mar 19, 1965, v85, pE5.
Variety. Mar 3, 1965, p7.
The Village Voice. May 20, 1965, v10, p19-20.

Love Has Many Faces (US; Singer,
  Alexander; 1965)
Christian Science Monitor (Western edition).
  Apr 3, 1965, p4.
Commonweal. Feb 5, 1965, v81, p611.
Film Daily. Feb 10, 1965, p6.
Film Quarterly. Spr 1965, v18, p60-61.
Filmfacts. Apr 30, 1965, v8, p72-73.
Films and Filming. Dec 1965, v12, p32.
The Films of Lana Turner. p241-45.
Hollywood Reporter. Feb 5, 1965, p3.
The London Times. Oct 14, 1965, p16.
Motion Picture Herald Product Digest. Feb 17,
  1965, p234.
The New York Times. Feb 25, 1965, p24.
Newsweek. Mar 15, 1965, v65, p99.
Saturday Review. Feb 6, 1965, v48, p43.
Time. Mar 5, 1965, v85, pE7.
Variety. Feb 10, 1965, p6.

A Love In Germany (German title: Liebe in
  Deutschland, Eine) (WGER, FR;
  Wajda, Andrzej; 1983)
BFI/Monthly Film Bulletin. May 1985, v52,
  p157.
Film Journal. Dec 1984, v87, p16.
Films in Review. Feb 1985, v36, p5.
The Los Angeles Times. Nov 15, 1984, SecVI,
  p5.

Maclean's. Mar 4, 1985, v98, p53.
Magill's Cinema Annual, 1985. p283-87.
Ms. Dec 1984, v191, p75.
The New Republic. Dec 10, 1984, v191, p75.
New York. Dec 10, 1984, v17, p94-96.
The New York Times. Oct 2, 1984, SecIII, p13.
The New York Times. Oct 7, 1984, SecII, p17.
The New York Times. Nov 9, 1984, SecIII, p10.
Time. Nov 19, 1984, v124, p139.
The Village Voice. Nov 20, 1984, p55.
Vogue. May 1984, v174, p70.

Love in Las Vegas *See* Viva Las Vegas

Love in the Afternoon (US; Wilder, Billy;
  1957)
America. Sep 7, 1957, v97, p603.
American Cinematographer. Aug 1957, v308,
  p506-07.
BFI/Monthly Film Bulletin. Sep 1957, v24,
  p111.
Billy Wilder (Dick). p82-85.
The Bright Side of Billy Wilder, Primarily.
  p170, 179-80.
*Chevalier: The Films and Career of Maurice
  Chevalier.* p171-74.
Cinema, the Magic Vehicle. v2, p381.
Commonweal. Sep 13, 1957, v66, p589.
The Film Career of Billy Wilder. p89-91.
Film Culture. Oct 1957, v3, p18.
Film Daily. Jun 3, 1957, v111, p4.
Films and Filming. Sep 1957, v3, p26.
Films in Review. Aug-Sep 1957, v8, p352-53.
The Films of Gary Cooper. p259-61.
Hollywood Reporter. Jun 3, 1957, p3.
*Magill's Survey of Cinema. English Language
  Films. Series I,* v3, p1018-21.
Motion Picture Herald Product Digest. Jun 8,
  1957, v207, p409.
The New Republic. Oct 14, 1957, v137, p21.
The New York Times. Aug 24, 1957, p12.
The New York Times. Aug 25, 1957, SecII, p1.
The New Yorker. Aug 31, 1957, v33, p54.
Newsweek. Jul 1, 1957, v50, p78.
Saturday Review. Aug 10, 1957, v40, p24.
Sight and Sound. Aut 1957, v27, p94.
Time. Jul 15, 1957, v70, p100.
Variety. Jun 5, 1957, p6.

Love Is a Ball (US; Swift, David; 1963)
Commonweal. Mar 22, 1963, v77, p665-66.
Film Daily. Mar 5, 1963, p3.
Filmfacts. Apr 25, 1963, v6, p64-65.
Films in Review. Mar 1963, v14, p177-78.
Hollywood Reporter. Mar 5, 1963, p3.
The New York Times. Apr 25, 1963, p38.
Photoplay. Apr 1963, v63, p8.
Time. Apr 12, 1963, v81, pM27.
Variety. Mar 3, 1963, p6.

Love Is a Many-Splendored Thing (Also
  titled: A Many-Splendored Thing) (US;
  King, Henry; 1955)
America. Aug 27, 1955, v93, p519.
BFI/Monthly Film Bulletin. Nov 1955, v22,
  p164.
Catholic World. Oct 1955, v181, p57.
Commonweal. Sep 9, 1955, v62, p565.
Film Daily. Aug 10, 1955, p6.
Films and Filming. Nov 1955, v2, n2, p17-18.
The Films of Jennifer Jones. p123-30.
The Films of William Holden. p164-67.
Hollywood Reporter. Aug 10, 1955, v135, n44,
  p3.
Library Journal. Oct 1, 1955, v80, p2050.
Magill's Survey of Cinema. Series II. v3, p1452-
  54.
The New York Times. Apr 3, 1955, SecII, p5.
The New York Times. Aug 19, 1955, p10.
The New York Times. Aug 21, 1955, SecII, p1.
The New Yorker. Aug 27, 1955, v31, p101.

Newsweek. Aug 29, 1955, v46, p77.
Time. Sep 12, 1955, v66, p116.
Variety. Aug 10, 1955, p6.

Love Is Better Than Ever (US; Donen,
  Stanley; 1952)
Christian Century. Aug 20, 1952, v69, p959.
Film Daily. Feb 7, 1952, p10.
The Films of Elizabeth Taylor. p95-96.
Hollywood Reporter. Feb 5, 1952, p3.
Motion Picture Herald Product Digest. Feb 9,
  1952, p1230.
The New York Times. Mar 4, 1952, p23.
Newsweek. Mar 17, 1952, v39, p98.
Stanley Donen (Casper). p41-43.
Time. Mar 24, 1952, v59, p102.
Variety. Feb 6, 1952, p6.

Love Letters (Also titled: My Love Letters)
  (US; Jones, Amy; 1984)
American Cinematographer. Jan 1984, v65,
  p42-45.
American Film. Jan 1984, v9, p86.
Christian Century. Jul 25, 1984, v101, p722.
Film Journal. Feb 1984, v87, p85.
The Los Angeles Times. Apr 25, 1984, SecVI,
  p1.
Magill's Cinema Annual, 1985. p288-92.
New York. Feb 13, 1984, v17, p72-74.
The New York Times. Jan 27, 1984, SecIII, p14.
Variety. Jan 25, 1984, p24.
The Village Voice. Feb 7, 1984, p56.
Vogue. Feb 1984, v174, p52.

The Love Lottery (GB; Crichton, Charles;
  1954)
BFI/Monthly Film Bulletin. Mar 1954, v21,
  p37.
The Films of David Niven. p114-15.
The London Times. Feb 1, 1954, p10.
The Spectator. Jan 29, 1954, v192, p121.
The Tatler. Feb 10, 1954, v211, p226.
Variety. Feb 10, 1954, p6.

The Love Machine (US; Haley, Jack Jr.;
  1971)
America. Sep 4, 1971, v75, p126-27.
BFI/Monthly Film Bulletin. Apr 1972, v39,
  p74.
Filmfacts. 1971, v14, n10, p237-40.
Films and Filming. May 1972, v18, n8, p61.
Hollywood Reporter. Aug 4, 1971, p3.
The New York Times. Aug 6, 1971, p15.
Newsweek. Aug 16, 1971, v78, p76.
Time. Aug 30, 1971, v98, p52.
Variety. Aug 4, 1971, p18.
The Village Voice. Aug 19, 1971, p49.

Love Me or Leave Me (US; Vidor, Charles;
  1955)
America. Jun 4, 1956, v93, p279.
BFI/Monthly Film Bulletin. Aug 1955, v22,
  p120.
Catholic World. Jun 1955, v181, p222.
Classics of the Gangster Film. p199-202.
Commonweal. Jun 17, 1955, v62, p278-79.
Film Culture. Sum 1955, v1, n4, p26.
Film Daily. May 23, 1955, p5.
The Films in My Life. p157-58.
Films in Review. Jun-Jul 1955, v6, n6, p288-89.
The Films of Doris Day. p147-54.
The Films of James Cagney. p210-13.
Hollywood Reporter. May 23, 1955, p3.
Life. Jun 20, 1955, v38, p67-68.
Magill's Survey of Cinema. Series II. v3, p1455-
  57.
The Nation. Jul 9, 1955, v181, p30.
The New York Times. May 27, 1955, p14.
The New York Times. Jun 5, 1955, SecII, p1.
The New Yorker. Jun 4, 1955, v31, p101.
Newsweek. May 30, 1955, v45, p82.

Saturday Review. Jun 11, 1955, v38, p26.
Time. Jun 6, 1955, v65, p106.
Variety. May 25, 1955, p6.

Love Me Tender (US; Webb, Robert D.;
1956)
Commonweal. Dec 7, 1956, v65, p254.
Elvis: The Films and Career of Elvis Presley.
p102-04.
Film Daily. Nov 16, 1956, p10.
Films in Review. Dec 1956, v7, p524-25.
Hollywood Reporter. Nov 16, 1956, p3.
The New Republic. Dec 24, 1956, v135, p22.
The New York Times. Nov 16, 1956, p23.
The New York Times. Nov 18, 1956, SecII, p1.
The New Yorker. Nov 24, 1956, v32, p196.
Newsweek. Dec 3, 1956, v48, p99.
Saturday Review. Dec 8, 1956, v39, p30.
Time. Nov 26, 1956, p106.
Variety. Nov 21, 1956, p6.

The Love Root *See* Mandragola, La

Love Story (US; Hiller, Arthur; 1970)
America. Jan 30, 1971, v124, p97-98.
BFI/Monthly Film Bulletin. Apr 1971, v38,
n447, p79.
Commonweal. Feb 5, 1971, v93, p447.
Commonweal. Mar 19, 1971, v94, p40.
Deeper Into Movies. p216-20.
Film Quarterly. Spr 1971, v24, n3, p58.
Films in Review. Feb 1971, v22, n2, p106-08.
The Films of the Sixties. p19-20.
The Great Romantic Films. p196-99.
Hollywood Reporter. Dec 15, 1970, p3, 11.
The Love Story Story. 1971.
The New Republic. Jan 2, 1971, v162, p28.
The New York Times. Dec 18, 1970, p51.
The New Yorker. Dec 26, 1970, v46, p52-54.
Newsweek. Dec 28, 1970, v76, p66.
Newsweek. Feb 1, 1971, v77, p10-11.
Saturday Review. Jan 2, 1971, v54, p60.
Talking Pictures. p355-60.
Time. Dec 21, 1970, v96, p55-56.
Time. Jan 11, 1971, v97, p40-45.
Variety. Dec 16, 1970, p17.

Love That Brute (US; Hall, Alexander;
1950)
BFI/Monthly Film Bulletin. Oct 1950, v17,
p155.
Christian Century. Jun 28, 1950, v67, p800.
Film Daily. May 10, 1950, p7.
Hollywood Reporter. May 10, 1950, p3.
Motion Picture Herald Product Digest. May 13,
1950, p293.
The New York Times. May 27, 1950, p10.
Newsweek. Jun 19, 1950, v35, p89.
Time. Jun 26, 1950, v55, p95.
Variety. May 10, 1950, p6.

Love with the Proper Stranger (US;
Mulligan, Robert; 1963)
America. Feb 1, 1964, v110, p172.
BFI/Monthly Film Bulletin. Oct 1964, v31,
p145.
Commonweal. Dec 27, 1963, v79, p405.
Film Daily. Dec 20, 1963, v123, p4.
Films and Filming. Oct 1964, v11, p33-34.
Films in Review. Jan 1964, v15, p51-52.
The Films of Steve McQueen. p85-90.
Hollywood Reporter. Dec 19, 1963, v178, p3.
The Los Angeles Times. Dec 26, 1963, SecIV,
p13.
Magill's Survey of Cinema. Series I. v3, p1029-
32.
Motion Picture Herald Product Digest. Dec 25,
1964, v230, p953-54.
The New Republic. Feb 8, 1964, v150, p24.
The New York Times. Dec 26, 1963, p33.
The New Yorker. Jan 11, 1964, v39, p85.

Newsweek. Jan 6, 1964, v63, p42.
Saturday Review. Jan 4, 1964, v47, p31.
Sight and Sound. Aut 1964, v33, p196.
Time. Dec 27, 1963, v82, p57.
Variety. Dec 25, 1963, p6.
Vogue. Feb 1, 1964, v143, p64.

The Loved One (French title: Cher
Disparu, Le) (US; Richardson, Tony;
1965)
America. Oct 23, 1965, v113, p481-82.
BFI/Monthly Film Bulletin. Apr 1966, v33,
p54-55.
Cahiers du Cinema in English. 1966, n5, p56.
Christian Century. Feb 9, 1966, v83, p178.
Christian Science Monitor (Western edition).
Dec 30, 1965, p4.
Cinema. Jul-Aug 1965, v2, p9-11.
Cinema. Mar 1966, v3, p4-8, 13-14.
Esquire. Feb 1966, v65, p32.
Film Daily. Oct 13, 1965, p4.
Film Quarterly. Spr 1966, v19, p41-42.
Films and Filming. Dec 1965, v12, p14-15.
Films and Filming. Nov 1965, v12, p12-13.
Films and Filming. Jun 1966, v12, p14-15.
Films in Review. Nov 1965, v16, p580-81.
Holiday. Dec 1965, v38, p174.
Hollywood Reporter. Oct 12, 1965, p3.
Journal of The Loved One.
Kiss Kiss Bang Bang. p374-76.
Life. Oct 8, 1965, v59, p34.
Life. Oct 29, 1965, v59, p10.
Literature/Film Quarterly. Apr, 1983, v11, p83-
87.
The London Times. Feb 13, 1966, p29.
The London Times. Oct 13, 1965, p13.
The London Times. Mar 31, 1966, p17.
Motion Picture Herald Product Digest. Oct 13,
1965, p385-86.
The Nation. Nov 1, 1965, v201, p316.
National Review. Feb 8, 1966, v18, p124-26.
The New Republic. Oct 23, 1965, v153, p32-34.
New Statesman. Apr 8, 1966, v71, p512.
The New York Times. Oct 12, 1965, p57.
The New Yorker. Oct 23, 1965, v41, p198.
Newsweek. Oct 18, 1965, v66, p122.
Playboy. Dec 1965, v12, p36.
Reporter. Nov 18, 1965, v33, p40-42.
Saturday Review. Oct 23, 1965, v48, p75.
Senior Scholastic. Nov 18, 1965, v97, sup10.
Sight and Sound. Spr 1966, v35, p93-94.
The Spectator. Apr 8, 1966, v216, p434.
Time. Oct 22, 1965, v86, p121.
Tynan Right and Left. p256-57.
Variety. Oct 13, 1965, p6.
The Village Voice. Oct 21, 1965, v11, p21.
Vogue. Nov 15, 1965, v146, p69.
A World on Film. p126-27.

The Lovely May *See* Joli Mai, Le

Lovely To Look At (US; LeRoy, Mervyn;
1952)
BFI/Monthly Film Bulletin. Sep 1952, v19,
p123.
Catholic World. Jul 1952, v175, p304-05.
Christian Century. Aug 13, 1952, v69, p935.
Commonweal. Jun 20, 1952, v56, p268.
Film Daily. May 29, 1952, p6.
Hollywood Reporter. May 27, 1952, p3.
The London Times. Sep 22, 1952, p2.
Motion Picture Herald Product Digest. May 31,
1952, p1381.
National Parent-Teacher. Sep 1952, v47, p38.
The New York Times. May 30, 1952, p11.
The New Yorker. Jun 7, 1952, v28, p125.
Saturday Review. Jun 21, 1952, v35, p33.
Time. Jun 2, 1952, v59, p92.
Variety. May 28, 1952, p6.

Lover Boy *See* Knave of Hearts

Lover Come Back (US; Mann, Delbert;
1961)
America. Feb 24, 1962, v106, p699.
BFI/Monthly Film Bulletin. Feb 1962, v29,
p20.
Esquire. Nov 1962, p68.
Film. Sum 1962, n32, p20.
Film Daily. Dec 12, 1961, p3.
Filmfacts. Feb 23, 1962, v5, p17-19.
Films and Filming. Mar 1962, v8, p34.
Films in Review. Mar 1962, v13, p174.
The Films of Doris Day. p199-203.
Hollywood Reporter. Dec 12, 1961, p3.
Look. Mar 13, 1962, p54a-54c.
Motion Picture Herald Product Digest. Dec 20,
1961, p388.
The Nation. Mar 10, 1962, v194, p222.
The New York Times. Feb 9, 1962, p21.
The New Yorker. Feb 24, 1962, v38, p110.
Newsweek. Feb 19, 1962, v59, p96.
Time. Feb 16, 1962, v79, p72.
Variety. Dec 13, 1961, p6.

The Lovers *See* Amants, Les

Lovers and Other Strangers (US; Howard,
Cy; 1970)
BFI/Monthly Film Bulletin. Dec 1970, v37,
n443, p246.
Deeper Into Movies. p467.
Films and Filming. Mar 1971, v14, n6, p51, 55.
Focus on Film. Sep-Oct 1970, n4, p10-12.
Hollywood Reporter. Aug 10, 1970, p3.
Magill's Survey of Cinema. Series II. v3, p1461-
63.
The New York Times. Aug 13, 1970, p13.
The New Yorker. Aug 15, 1970, v46, p68.
Saturday Review. Aug 22, 1970, v53, p61.
Time. Aug 31, 1970, v96, p69.
Variety. Aug 12, 1970, p15.

Lovers, Happy Lovers *See* Knave of Hearts

Loves of a Blonde (Czechoslovakian title:
Lásky Jedne Plavovlasky; Also titled:
A Blonde in Love; A Blonde's Love)
(CZECH; Forman, Milos; 1965)
America. Dec 17, 1966, v115, p812-13.
BFI/Monthly Film Bulletin. Jun 1966, v33, p89.
Christian Science Monitor (Western edition).
Jan 25, 1967, p8.
Cinema. Dec 1966, v3, p49.
Commonweal. Nov 11, 1966, v85, p166.
The Czechoslovak New Wave. p131-35.
Dictionary of Films. p186.
Film. Wint 1965-66, n44, p17-18.
Film Daily. Nov 2, 1966, p7.
Film Quarterly. Fall 1967, v21, p47-48.
Filmfacts. Dec 15, 1966, v9, p285-86.
Films and Filming. Jul 1966, v12, p16, 18.
Films and Filming. Feb 1966, v12, p32-33.
Films in Review. Dec 1966, v17, p663-64.
Harper's Magazine. Dec 1966, v233, p137-38.
Hollywood Reporter. Dec 22, 1966, p4.
*The International Dictionary of Films and
Filmmakers.* v1, p251-52.
The London Times. Nov 5, 1965, p16.
The London Times. May 12, 1966, p6.
*Magill's Survey of Cinema. Foreign Language
Films.* v4, p1848-52.
The Milos Forman Stories. p59-74.
Motion Picture Herald Product Digest. Nov 9,
1966, p625-26.
Movie Comedy (Byron). p255-56.
The Nation. Nov 14, 1966, v203, p526.
New Statesman. May 20, 1966, v71, p746.
The New York Times. Sep 13, 1966, p13.
The New York Times. Oct 27, 1966, p55.
The New Yorker. Nov 5, 1966, v42, p197.
Newsweek. Sep 19, 1966, v68, p110D.

Playboy. Jan 1967, v14, p20, 22.
Politics, Art and Commitment in the East European Cinema. p215-16.
The Private Eye, the Cowboy and the Very Naked Girl. p230.
Private Screenings. p286.
Saturday Review. Oct 22, 1966, v49, p48.
Sight and Sound. Wint 1965-66, v35, p34-35.
Take One. Feb 1967, v1, p24.
Time. Sep 23, 1966, v88, p74.
Variety. Sep 1, 1965, p6.
The Village Voice. Nov 10, 1966, v12, p27.

The Loves of Isadora *See* Isadora

The Loves of Madame De *See* The Earrings of Madame De

Lovesick (US; Brickman, Marshall; 1983)
Hollywood Reporter. Feb 14, 1983, p3.
Maclean's. Feb 28, 1983, v96, p50.
The New Republic. Mar 14, 1983, v188, p25.
The New Yorker. Mar 7, 1983, v59, p128-29.
Newsweek. Feb 21, 1983, v101, p61.

Lovin' Molly (US; Lumet, Sidney; 1974)
BFI/Monthly Film Bulletin. May 1975, v42, p110.
Hollywood Reporter. Mar 13, 1974, p3.
Independent Film Journal. Mar 18, 1974, v73, p10-11.
The Los Angeles Times. May 8, 1974, SecIV, p28.
Motion Picture Herald Product Digest. Mar 27, 1974, p88.
New York. Apr 29, 1974, v7, p64-66.
New York. Apr 15, 1974, v7, p79-81.
The New York Times. Apr 15, 1974, p41.
The New Yorker. Apr 22, 1974, v50, p136.
Newsweek. Apr 15, 1974, v83, p101.
Penthouse. Mar 1974, v5, p36.
PTA Magazine. Apr 1974, v68, p6.
Sidney Lumet: A Guide to References and Resources. p100-01.
Time. Apr 22, 1974, v103, p68.
Variety. Mar 13, 1974, p18.

Loving Couples (Swedish title: Alskande Par) (SWED; Zetterling, Mai; 1965)
Big Screen, Little Screen. p328.
Cahiers du Cinema in English. Dec 1966, n6, p50-51.
Cinema. Dec 1965, v3, p48.
Commonweal. Sep 30, 1966, v84, p638.
Filmfacts. Nov 15, 1966, v9, p248-50.
Films and Filming. Sep 1965, v11, p26-27.
International Film Guide. 1966, v3, p129-30.
London Magazine. Oct 1965, v5, p80-86.
The London Times. Dec 23, 1964, p11.
The London Times. Jan 8, 1965, p14.
The London Times. Jul 15, 1965, p6.
Motion Picture Herald Product Digest. Sep 28, 1966, p604.
New Statesman. Jun 4, 1965, v69, p890.
New Statesman. Jul 23, 1965, v70, p132.
The New York Times. Sep 20, 1966, p38.
The New Yorker. Oct 1, 1966, v42, p186.
Playboy. May 1966, v13, p3, 36.
The Spectator. Jul 23, 1965, v215, p106.
Take One. Apr 1967, v1, p23.
Time. Mar 18, 1966, v87, p110.
Vogue. Apr 1, 1966, v147, p111.

Loving Couples (US; Smight, Jack; 1980)
BFI/Monthly Film Bulletin. Nov 1981, v48, p220.
Films in Review. Dec 1980, v31, p632.
Hollywood Reporter. Sep 26, 1980, p18.
The Los Angeles Times. Oct 24, 1980, SecVI, p1.
Maclean's. Nov 3, 1980, v93, p63-64.

Motion Picture Herald Product Digest. Nov 5, 1980, p43.
The New York Times. Oct 24, 1980, SecIII, p6.
Newsday. Oct 24, 1980, SecII, p10.
Newsweek. Nov 3, 1980, v96, p90.
Variety. Sep 10, 1980, p34.
The Village Voice. Nov 12, 1980, p52.

Loving You (US; Kanter, Hal; 1957)
America. Aug 3, 1957, v97, p472.
BFI/Monthly Film Bulletin. Sep 1957, v24, p111.
Elvis: The Films and Career of Elvis Presley. p105-08.
Film Daily. Jul 9, 1957, v112, p10.
Hollywood Reporter. Jul 3, 1957, p3.
Motion Picture Herald Product Digest. Jul 6, 1957, v208, p441-42.
The New York Times. Jul 18, 1957, p19.
Time. Jul 15, 1957, v70, p100.
Variety. Jul 3, 1957, p6.

The Lower Depths (Japanese title: Dongoko) (JAPAN; Kurosawa, Akira; 1957)
Cinema. 1963, v1, n2, p34.
Cinema Texas Program Notes. Aug 28, 1976, v10, n4, p67-74.
Dictionary of Films. p91.
Film Quarterly. Wint 1959, v13, p52.
Films in Review. Mar 1962, v13, p175-76.
The Films of Akira Kurosawa. p125-33.
The New Republic. Mar 19, 1962, v146, p28.
The New York Times. Feb 10, 1962, p12.
The New Yorker. Feb 17, 1962, v37, p117-19.
Time. Mar 9, 1962, v79, p91.
Variety. Mar 19, 1958, p6.
The Village Voice. Feb 8, 1962, p11.
A World on Film. p378-79.

Lowlands *See* Tiefland

Luci del Varietà *See* Variety Lights

Lucia (CUBA; Solas, Humberto; 1968)
American Anthropologist. 1977, v79, n1, p200.
BFI/Monthly Film Bulletin. Dec 1972, v39, p252-53.
Commonweal. Apr 5, 1974, v100, p109-10.
The Cuban Image. p225-36.
Film. Wint 1970, n57, p28.
Film Quarterly. Wint 1974-75, v28, p53-59.
Films in Review. May 1974, v25, p310.
Framework. Spr 1979, n10, p24-27.
The International Dictionary of Films and Filmmakers. v1, p269-70.
Jump Cut. Jul-Aug 1974, n2, p7-8.
Jump Cut. Dec 1978, n19, p21-27.
The London Times. Jun 3, 1969, p7.
Magill's Survey of Cinema. Foreign Language Films. v4, p1858-63.
Memories of Underdevelopment: The Revolutionary Films of Cuba. p111-63.
Ms. Jun 1974, v2, p29-34.
The Nation. Mar 16, 1974, v218, p349.
The New York Times. Mar 1, 1974, p16.
The New Yorker. Apr 8, 1974, v50, p108-12.
Newsweek. Apr 17, 1972, v79, p98.
Sexual Stratagems. p82-90.
Take One. Jul-Aug, 1970, v2, p20.
Variety. Jul 30, 1969, p6.
The Village Voice. Mar 7, 1974, p67.

The Luck of Ginger Coffey (CAN; Kershner, Irvin; 1964)
BFI/Monthly Film Bulletin. Jul 1965, v32, p105.
Commonweal. Sep 25, 1964, v81, p18.
Film Daily. Sep 23, 1964, v125, p6.
Films and Filming. Aug 1965, v11, p31.
Films in Review. Dec 1964, v15, p632-33.
Hollywood Reporter. Sep 21, 1964, v182, p3.

Magill's Survey of Cinema. Series II, v3, p1464-66.
Motion Picture Herald Product Digest. Oct 14, 1964, v232, p146.
The Nation. Oct 19, 1964, v199, p257-58.
The New Republic. Oct 31, 1964, v151, p28.
The New York Times. Sep 22, 1964, p44.
The New Yorker. Sep 26, 1964, v40, p193.
Newsweek. Sep 28, 1964, v64, p96D-97.
Saturday Review. Oct 3, 1964, v47, p27.
Sight and Sound. Sum 1965, v34, p149.
Time. Oct 2, 1964, v84, p124.
Variety. Sep 23, 1964, p6.
A World on Film. p128-29.

Lucky Lady (US; Donen, Stanley; 1975)
BFI/Monthly Film Bulletin. Feb 1976, v43, p31.
Films in Review. Jan 1976, v27, p57.
The Films of Burt Reynolds. p184-88.
Hollywood Reporter. Dec 16, 1975, p3.
The Los Angeles Times. Dec 28, 1975, Calendar, p1.
Motion Picture Herald Product Digest. Dec 31, 1975, p57.
The New York Times. Dec 14, 1975, SecII, p1.
The New York Times. Dec 26, 1975, p47.
The New Yorker. Dec 29, 1975, v51, p51-52.
Newsweek. Dec 29, 1975, v86, p50.
Saturday Review. Jan 24, 1976, v3, p50.
Stanley Donen (Casper). p214-19.
Time. Dec 22, 1975, v106, p22.
Variety. Dec 17, 1975, p23.
When the Lights Go Down. p106-07.

Lucky Me (US; Donohue, Jack; 1954)
America. Apr 24, 1954, v91, p119.
BFI/Monthly Film Bulletin. Jul 1954, v21, p101.
Film Daily. Apr 12, 1954, p6.
The Films of Doris Day. p137-40.
Hollywood Reporter. Apr 9, 1954, p3.
The London Times. May 31, 1954, p3.
Motion Picture Herald Product Digest. Apr 17, 1954, p2261.
National Parent-Teacher. Jun 1954, v48, p40.
The New York Times. Apr 10, 1954, p11.
The Spectator. May 28, 1954, v192, p643.
Time. May 3, 1954, v63, p102.
Variety. Apr 14, 1954, p6.

Lullaby of Broadway (US; Butler, David; 1951)
BFI/Monthly Film Bulletin. Oct 1951, v18, p348.
Christian Century. May 2, 1951, v68, p575.
Film Daily. Mar 15, 1951, p6.
The Films of Doris Day. p101-06.
Hollywood Reporter. Mar 13, 1951, p3.
Motion Picture Herald Product Digest. Mar 17, 1951, p757.
The New York Times. Mar 27, 1951, p35.
Newsweek. Apr 2, 1951, v37, p85.
The Spectator. Nov 16, 1951, v187, p640.
Time. Apr 9, 1951, v57, p108.
Variety. Mar 14, 1951, p6.

Lumiere (Also titled: Light) (FR; Moreau, Jeanne; 1976)
Commonweal. Feb 1, 1977, v104, p114.
Commonweal. Mar 4, 1977, v104, p49-50.
Film Journal. Dec 10, 1976, v78, p7-8.
Films in Review. Dec 1976, v27, p634-35.
Hollywood Reporter. Oct 19, 1976, p3.
The Los Angeles Times. Jan 12, 1977, SecIV, p1.
The Nation. Dec 11, 1976, v223, p637-38.
The New Republic. Dec 18, 1976, v175, p33.
The New York Times. Jun 30, 1976, p26.
The New Yorker. Sep 20, 1976, v52, p116.
The New Yorker. Dec 20, 1976, v52, p117-18.

The Los Angeles Times. Sep 11, 1974, SecIV, p1.
Motion Picture Herald Product Digest. Jun 5, 1974, p2.
Movietone News. Sep 1974, n35, p31.
New York. Dec 9, 1974, v7, p100-01.
The New York Times. Jan 16, 1975, p49.
Time. Oct 14, 1974, v104, p8.
Variety. Apr 24, 1974, p22.

Mad Dogs & Englishmen *See* Joe Cocker/ Mad Dogs & Englishmen

The Mad Magician (US; Brahm, John; 1954)
BFI/Monthly Film Bulletin. Aug 1954, v21, p121.
Film Daily. Apr 14, 1954, p6.
Hollywood Reporter. Mar 26, 1954, p3.
The London Times. Jul 5, 1954, p11.
Motion Picture Herald Product Digest. Mar 27, 1954, p2238.
National Parent-Teacher. May 1954, v48, p39.
The New Statesman and Nation. Jul 10, 1954, v48, p43.
The New York Times. May 20, 1954, p38.
Time. Oct 19, 1953, v62, p112.
Variety. Mar 31, 1954, p6.

Mad Max (AUSTRALIA; Miller, George; 1979)
BFI/Monthly Film Bulletin. Nov 1979, v46, p228.
The New Australian Cinema. p92-94.
The New York Times. Jun 14, 1980, p13.
Variety. May 16, 1979, p38.

Mad Max II *See* The Road Warrior

Mad Max Beyond Thunderdome
(AUSTRALIA; Miller, George; Ogilvie, George; 1985)
American Cinematographer. Sep 1985, v66, p68-80.
BFI/Monthly Film Bulletin. Oct 1985, v52, p312.
Films and Filming. Oct 1985, n373, p39.
Hollywood Reporter. Jul 8, 1985, p3.
Jet. Jul 29, 1985, v68, p28-30.
The Los Angeles Times. Jul 10, 1985, SecVI, p1.
Magill's Cinema Annual, 1986. p223-26.
The New York Times. Jul 10, 1985, SecIII, p21.
Newsweek. Jul 29, 1985, v106, p58.
Rolling Stone. Aug 29, 1985, p40-42.
Time. Jul 22, 1985, v126, p77.
Variety. Jun 26, 1985, p18.
The Wall Street Journal. Jul 18, 1985, p20.

Madame De. . . *See* The Earrings of Madame De

Madame Rosa (French title: Vie devant soi, La) (FR; Mizrahi, Moshe; 1977)
America. May 6, 1978, v138, p366.
BFI/Monthly Film Bulletin. Jun 1979, v46, p130.
Films in Review. May 1978, v29, p311.
The Great French Films. p272-73.
Hollywood Reporter. Mar 27, 1978, p2.
The Los Angeles Times. Apr 9, 1978, Calendar, p1.
Maclean's. Jun 12, 1978, v91, p70.
Magill's Survey of Cinema. Foreign Language Films. v4, p1886-94.
Motion Picture Herald Product Digest. Mar 22, 1978, p82.
The Nation. Apr 15, 1978, v226, p444.
The New Republic. Apr 29, 1978, v178, p23.
New York. Apr 24, 1978, v11, p70-71.
The New York Times. Mar 19, 1978, p54.
The New York Times. Apr 2, 1978, SecII, p13.

The New Yorker. Mar 27, 1978, v54, p122-24.
Newsweek. Apr 3, 1978, v91, p91.
Time. Apr 1978, v111, p86.
Variety. Oct 26, 1977, p20.
Vogue. May 1978, v168, p48.

Madame X (US; Rich, David Lowell; 1966)
America. May 14, 1966, v114, p706.
BFI/Monthly Film Bulletin. Nov 1966, v33, p165.
Christian Science Monitor (Western edition). Jun 3, 1966, p4.
Confessions of a Cultist. p256-59.
Film Daily. Feb 23, 1966, p8.
Filmfacts. Jun 15, 1966, v9, p102-04.
Films and Filming. Dec 1966, v13, p8-9.
The Films of Lana Turner. p246-51.
The Great Romantic Films. p184-87.
Hollywood Reporter. Feb 23, 1966, p3.
Kiss Kiss Bang Bang. p148-50.
The London Times. Oct 6, 1966, p18.
Make It Again, Sam. p108-13.
Motion Picture Herald Product Digest. Mar 2, 1966, p475-76.
The New York Times. Apr 28, 1966, p49.
Saturday Review. May 21, 1966, v49, p48.
Variety. Feb 23, 1966, p6.
The Village Voice. Jul 7, 1966, v11, p21.

Made in USA (FR; Godard, Jean-Luc; 1966)
Cahiers du Cinema in English. May 1967, n10, p16-17, 32-37.
Cineaste. Wint 1967-68, v1, p3-4.
Cineaste. Spr 1968, v1, p16-18.
Cinema. Spr 1968, v4, p50.
Film Heritage. Spr 1968, v3, p31-34.
Film Quarterly. Spr 1969, v22, p18-25.
The Films of Jean-Luc Godard. p113-21.
Jean-Luc Godard (Collet). p135-37.
The London Times. Dec 10, 1966, p13.
The New Wave (Monaco). p173-78.
The New York Times. Sep 28, 1967, p58.
Sight and Sound. Wint 1966-67, v36, p3-6.
The Spectator. Dec 16, 1966, p217, p788.
Take One. 1967, v1, p7-10.
Variety. Dec 14, 1966, p19.
The Village Voice. Oct 12, 1967, v12, p33.

Madeleine (GB; Lean, David; 1949)
BFI/Monthly Film Bulletin. Feb-Mar 1950, v17, p24.
Christian Century. Mar 28, 1951, v68, p415.
The Cinema of David Lean. p91-98.
Commonweal. Sep 15, 1950, v52, p558-59.
David Lean: A Guide to References and Resources. p79-80.
David Lean and His Films. p85-106.
David Lean (Anderegg). p69-73.
Film Daily. Aug 31, 1950, p11.
Hollywood Reporter. Aug 30, 1950, p3.
Library Journal. May 15, 1950, v75, p885.
Library Journal. Dec 1, 1952, v77, p2066.
The London Times. Feb 16, 1950, p10.
Motion Picture Herald Product Digest. Sep 2, 1950, p457-58.
The New Republic. Sep 25, 1950, v123, p30.
The New Statesman and Nation. Feb 25, 1950, v39, p216.
The New York Times. Sep 1, 1950, p17.
The New Yorker. Sep 9, 1950, v26, p98.
Sequence. Sum 1950, n11, p16.
The Spectator. Feb 24, 1950, v184, p241.
Time. Sep 18, 1950, v56, p104.
Variety. Feb 22, 1950, p6.

Mademoiselle (FR, GB; Richardson, Tony; 1966)
BFI/Monthly Film Bulletin. Feb 1967, v34, p23-24.
Film Daily. Aug 3, 1966, p22.

Filmfacts. Oct 1, 1966, v9, p199-201.
Films and Filming. Mar 1967, v13, p29-30.
Films in Review. Oct 1966, v17, p523-24.
Life. Sep 16, 1966, v61, p20.
The London Times. Jan 12, 1967, p6.
Motion Picture Herald Product Digest. Aug 17, 1966, p581-82.
The New York Times. Aug 2, 1966, p23.
The New Yorker. Aug 6, 1966, v42, p84.
Newsweek. Aug 15, 1966, v68, p84A.
Playboy. Oct 1966, v13, p24-25.
Saturday Review. Aug 27, 1966, v49, p40.
The Spectator. May 20, 1966, v216, p632.
Time. Aug 19, 1966, v88, p78.
Variety. May 18, 1966, p7.

Madigan (US; Siegel, Don; 1968)
America. Apr 13, 1968, v118, p521-22.
American Film Genres (Kaminsky). p228-32.
BFI/Monthly Film Bulletin. Apr 1968, v35, p51-52.
Christian Century. Jul 10, 1968, v85, p900.
Christian Science Monitor (Western edition). Jun 3, 1968, p4.
Cinema. Spr 1968, v4, p4-9.
Cinema Texas Program Notes. Oct 30, 1975, v9, p47-55.
Confessions of a Cultist. p352-53.
Don Siegel: American Cinema (Lovell). p72-73.
Don Siegel: Director (Kaminsky). p197-208.
Film Daily. Mar 27, 1968, p4.
Filmfacts. May 1, 1968, v11, p109-10.
Films and Filming. Apr 1968, v14, p26.
Hollywood Reporter. Mar 27, 1968, p3.
The London Times. Mar 14, 1968, p13.
Motion Picture Herald Product Digest. Apr 10, 1968, p794.
The New York Times. Mar 30, 1968, p22.
The New York Times. Jul 16, 1967, p9.
Newsweek. Apr 22, 1968, v71, p94.
Senior Scholastic. May 2, 1968, v92, p94.
Time. Apr 12, 1968, v91, p106.
Variety. Mar 27, 1968, p6.
The Village Voice. Apr 4, 1968, p47.

The Madwoman of Chaillot (US; Forbes, Bryan; 1969)
America. Oct 18, 1969, v121, p340-41.
Big Screen, Little Screen. p245-47.
Commonweal. Oct 3, 1969, v91, p21-22.
Deeper Into Movies. p31-32.
Film Daily. Jun 24, 1969, p11.
Films in Review. Oct 1969, v20, p514-15.
The Films of Katharine Hepburn. p196-99.
Good Housekeeping. Oct 1969, v169, p76.
Holiday. Nov 1969, v46, p20.
Hollywood Reporter. Jun 24, 1969, p3.
Life. Oct 31, 1969, v67, p20.
Movies Into Film. p51-52.
The New Republic. Oct 25, 1969, v161, p20.
The New York Times. Oct 13, 1969, p54.
The New Yorker. Oct 18, 1969, v45, p196.
Newsweek. Oct 27, 1969, v74, p125.
Popular Photography. Oct 1969, v65, p117.
Saturday Review. Oct 18, 1969, v52, p34.
Time. Oct 31, 1969, v94, p91.
Variety. Jun 25, 1969, p6.
Vogue. Oct 1, 1969, v154, p154.

Maestro di Don Giovanni, Il *See* Crossed Swords

The Maggie *See* High and Dry

The Magic Box (GB; Boulting, John; 1951)
BFI/Monthly Film Bulletin. Oct 1951, v18, p342-43.
Catholic World. Nov 1952, v176, p143.
Commonweal. Oct 17, 1952, v57, p38.
Fifty Classic British Films. p79-81.
Films in Review. Oct 1952, v3, p15.

Films in Review. Aug-Sep 1951, v2, p13-15.
The Films of Laurence Olivier. p108-09.
Hollywood Reporter. Oct 29, 1952, p4.
Laurence Olivier: Theater and Cinama. p118-20.
Magill's Survey of Cinema. Series II. v4, p1485-87.
Motion Picture Herald Product Digest. Sep 20, 1952, p1534.
The New Statesman and Nation. Sep 22, 1951, v42, p309-10.
The New York Times. Sep 24, 1952, p40.
The New Yorker. Sep 27, 1952, v28, p94.
Newsweek. Oct 27, 1952, v40, p112.
Saturday Review. Oct 18, 1952, v35, p30.
Sight and Sound. Jan-Mar 1952, v21, p125, 141.
The Spectator. Sep 21, 1951, v187, p360.
Time. Oct 6, 1952, v60, p100.
Variety. Sep 26, 1951, p6.

The Magic Face (US; Tuttle, Frank; 1951)
Commonweal. Nov 2, 1951, v55, p94.
Film Daily. Aug 13, 1951, p6.
Hollywood Reporter. Aug 8, 1951, p3.
Motion Picture Herald Product Digest. Aug 11, 1951, p974-75.
The New Statesman and Nation. Apr 12, 1952, v43, p434.
The New York Times. Oct 1, 1951, p19.
The New Yorker. Oct 6, 1951, v27, p70.
Newsweek. Oct 8, 1951, v38, p102-03.
Saturday Review. Oct 20, 1951, v34, p29.
Time. Oct 22, 1951, v58, p116.
Variety. Aug 8, 1951, p18.

The Magic Flute (Swedish title: Trollflojten) (SWED; Bergman, Ingmar; 1975)
America. Jan 24, 1976, v134, p55-56.
Before My Eyes. p69-72.
BFI/Monthly Film Bulletin. Feb 1976, v43, p35.
Christian Century. Oct 6, 1976, v93, p839-41.
Dissent. n2, 1976, v23, p213-15.
Film Quarterly. Fall 1976, v30, p45-49.
Films and Filming. Mar 1976, v22, p213-15.
Hi Fi. Feb 1976, v26, p16-18.
Hollywood Reporter. Nov 11, 1975, p3.
The Los Angeles Times. Dec 12, 1975, Calendar, p1.
Magill's Survey of Cinema. Foreign Language Films. v4, p1895-1900.
Medium. Nov 1976, v6, p24-25.
Movietone News. Feb 1976, n48, p33.
The Nation. Dec 6, 1975, v221, p606.
National Review. Mar 5, 1976, v28, p217-18.
The New Republic. Nov 29, 1975, v173, p22-23.
The New York Times. Nov 9, 1975, SecII, p1.
The New Yorker. Nov 17, 1975, v51, p169-71.
Opera. Nov 1975, v40, p36.
Penthouse. Jan 1976, v7, p39-40.
Saturday Review. Jan 10, 1976, v3, p65-66.
Saturday Review. Nov 29, 1975, v3, p38.
Time. Nov 24, 1975, v106, p82.
Vogue. Dec 1975, v165, p54.
When the Lights Go Down. p72-76.

The Magician (Swedish title: Ansiktet; also titled: The Face) (SWED; Bergman, Ingmar; 1958)
BFI/Monthly Film Bulletin. Nov 1959, v26, p146.
Cinema Borealis. p174-87, 303-04.
Commonweal. Sep 18, 1959, v70, p521.
Film Daily. Aug 25, 1959, v116, p6.
Filmfacts. Sep 30, 1959, v2, p203-05.
Films in Review. Oct 1959, v9, p486-89.
Ingmar Bergman and the Rituals of Art. p70-84, 100-09.

Ingmar Bergman (Cowie). p173-78.
Ingmar Bergman: Essays in Criticism. p201-14.
Magill's Survey of Cinema. Foreign Language Films. v4, p1901-04.
The Nation. Sep 26, 1959, v189, p180.
The New Republic. Oct 12, 1959, v141, p21.
The New York Times. Aug 28, 1959, p27.
The New Yorker. Sep 5, 1959, v35, p76-77.
Newsweek. Sep 7, 1959, v54, p79-80.
The Personal Vision of Ingmar Bergman. p174-84.
Saturday Review. Aug 29, 1959, p23-24.
Time. Sep 7, 1959, v74, p78.
Variety. Jan 14, 1959, p16.

The Magnet (GB; Frend, Charles; 1950)
BFI/Monthly Film Bulletin. Mar 1951, v2, p39-41.
Christian Century. Jul 11, 1951, v68, p831.
Commonweal. Mar 16, 1951, v53, p566.
Film Daily. Mar 22, 1951, p6.
Films in Review. Mar 1951, v2, p39-41.
Motion Picture Herald Product Digest. Mar 10, 1951, p750-51.
The Nation. Mar 10, 1951, v172, p238.
The New Republic. Mar 12, 1951, v124, p23.
The New York Times. Feb 27, 1951, p22.
The New Yorker. Mar 3, 1951, v27, p94.
Newsweek. Mar 12, 1951, v37, p88.
Time. Apr 2, 1951, v57, p99.
Variety. Nov 1, 1950, p6.

The Magnificent Cuckold (Italian title: Magnifico Cornuto, Il) (IT, FR; Pietrangeli, Antonio; 1964)
Filmfacts. Jul 9, 1965, v8, p130-31.
The London Times. Jun 8, 1967, p8.
Motion Picture Herald Product Digest. May 12, 1965, p283.
The New York Times. Apr 20, 1965, p42.
The New Yorker. May 1, 1965, v41, p120, 122.
Time. Apr 2, 1965, v85, p97.
Variety. Nov 25, 1964, p6.

Magnificent Obsession (US; Sirk, Douglas; 1954)
America. Aug 14, 1954, v91, p487.
BFI/Monthly Film Bulletin. Dec 1954, v21, p179.
Bright Lights. n2, 1977-78, v2, p23-26.
Catholic World. Aug 1954, v179, p383-84.
Colliers. Aug 6, 1954, v134, p6.
Commonweal. Jul 23, 1954, v60, p388.
Douglas Sirk (Stern). p93-108.
Film Daily. May 11, 1954, p6.
Hollywood Reporter. May 11, 1954, p3.
Library Journal. Aug 1954, v79, p1393.
Look. Aug 24, 1954, v18, p90.
Magill's Survey of Cinema. Series II. v4, p1491-94.
Motion Picture Herald Product Digest. May 15, 1954, p2293.
National Parent-Teacher. Sep 1954, v49, p39.
The New York Times. Aug 5, 1954, p18.
The New Yorker. Aug 14, 1954, v30, p59.
Newsweek. Aug 2, 1954, v44, p79.
Saturday Review. Jul 31, 1954, v37, p36.
Sirk on Sirk. p92-97.
Time. Aug 23, 1954, v64, p75.
Variety. May 12, 1954, p6.

The Magnificent Seven (US; Sturges, John; 1960)
America. Dec 3, 1960, v104, p351-52.
BFI/Monthly Film Bulletin. Apr 1961, v28, p44.
Commonweal. Dec 2, 1960, v73, p255.
Film Daily. Oct 6, 1960, p6.
Filmfacts. 1960, v3, p282.
Films and Filming. Apr 1961, v7, p26.

Films in Review. Nov 1960, v11, p557-58.
The Films of Charles Bronson. p89-93.
The Films of Steve McQueen. p41-48.
The Great Adventure Films. p220-23.
Hollywood Reporter. Oct 5, 1960, p3.
Horizon. May 1961, v3, p114-15.
Magill's Survey of Cinema. Series I. v3, p1039-42.
The Making of the Great Westerns. p283-98.
The New York Times. Nov 24, 1960, p48.
Newsweek. Oct 31, 1960, v56, p90.
Reporter. Mar 17, 1960, v22, p36-38.
Saturday Review. Nov 5, 1960, v43, p40.
Senior Scholastic. Jan 18, 1961, v78, p26.
Sight and Sound. Spr 1961, v30, p91-92.
Time. Dec 12, 1960, v76, p96.
Variety. Oct 5, 1960, p6.

The Magnificent Yankee (Also titled: The Man With Thirty Sons) (US; Sturges, John; 1950)
BFI/Monthly Film Bulletin. Aug 1951, v18, p308.
Christian Century. May 16, 1951, v68, p623.
Commonweal. Jan 26, 1951, v53, p399.
Film Daily. Nov 15, 1950, p3.
Films in Review. Feb 1951, v2, p33-35.
Hollywood Reporter. Nov 15, 1950, p3.
Library Journal. Feb 1, 1951, v76, p189.
Motion Picture Herald Product Digest. Nov 18, 1950, p569-70.
The Nation. Feb 3, 1951, v172, p114.
The New Republic. Jan 29, 1951, v124, p22.
The New York Times. Jan 19, 1951, p21.
The New Yorker. Jan 27, 1951, v26, p58.
Newsweek. Jan 22, 1951, v37, p83.
Saturday Review. Feb 10, 1951, v34, p29.
Senior Scholastic. Jan 10, 1951, v57, p30.
Time. Jan 8, 1951, v57, p72.

Magnifico Cornuto, Il See The Magnificent Cuckold

Magnum Force (US; Post, Ted; 1973)
America. Feb 23, 1974, v130, p134.
BFI/Monthly Film Bulletin. Feb 1974, v41, p31.
Clint Eastwood (Guérif). p100-02.
Films and Filming. Mar 1974, v20, p18-21.
Films Illustrated. Jan 1974, v3, p252.
Films In Review. Feb 1974, p118-19.
The Films of Clint Eastwood. p161-70.
The Films of The Seventies. p82-84.
Martin Scorsese and Michael Cimino. p283-87.
The New York Times. Dec 26, 1973, v60, p1.
The New Yorker. Jan 14, 1974, v49, p84.
Reeling. p342-49.
Rolling Stone. Mar 14, 1974, p71.
Variety. Dec 12, 1973, p18.
The Village Voice. Feb 7, 1974, p71.

Maigret Lays a Trap See Inspector Maigret

Maigret Tend un Piege See Inspector Maigret

The Main Chance (GB; Knight, John; 1964)
BFI/Monthly Film Bulletin. May 1965, v32, p76.
Film Daily. Jun 17, 1966, p5.
Filmfacts. Aug 1, 1966, v9, p134-35.
Films and Filming. Jul 1965, v11, p30-31.
Hollywood Reporter. Jun 14, 1966, p3.
Motion Picture Herald Product Digest. Jun 29, 1966, p552.
Variety. Jun 22, 1966, p5.

The Main Event (US; Zieff, Howard; 1979)
BFI/Monthly Film Bulletin. Aug 1979, v46, p178.
Hollywood Reporter. Jun 21, 1979, p3.

The New York Times. Jun 22, 1979, SecIII, p14.
Variety. Jun 20, 1979, p19.

Mains Sales, Les (Also titled: Dirty Hands)
(FR; Rivers, Fernand; 1951)
BFI/Monthly Film Bulletin. Oct 1952, v19, p139.
Films in Review. Aug-Sep 1954, v5, p363-64.
The London Times. Aug 25, 1952, p6.
Motion Picture Herald Product Digest. May 22, 1954, p2.
The New Statesman and Nation. Sep 6, 1952, v44, p63-64.
The New York Times. May 11, 1954, p25.
The New Yorker. May 22, 1954, v30, p113.
Newsweek. May 24, 1954, v43, p94.
Saturday Review. May 22, 1954, v37, p29.
Sight and Sound. Oct-Dec 1952, v22, p80.
Variety. Sep 12, 1951, p18.

Major Dundee (US; Peckinpah, Sam; 1965)
American Cinematographer. Feb 1965, v46, p94-95.
Christian Science Monitor (Western edition). Apr 13, 1965, p12.
Cinema. Mar-Apr 1965, v2, p48.
Cinema. Oct-Nov 1964, v2, p4-10.
Commonweal. Apr 16, 1965, v82, p118.
Film Daily. Mar 17, 1965, p2.
Film Quarterly. Spr 1965, v18, p40-42.
Filmfacts. Jun 11, 1965, v8, p105-08.
Films and Filming. Jul 1965, v11, p26-27.
Films in Review. Apr 1965, v17, p251-52.
The Films of Charlton Heston. p150-53.
The Films of Sam Peckinpah. p17-25.
The Great Western Pictures. p210-12.
Hollywood Reporter. Mar 17, 1965, p3.
International Film Guide. 1966, v3, p143.
Jump Cut. Aug 1978, n18, p17-20.
The London Times. Jun 3, 1965, p17.
Magill's Survey of Cinema. Series II. v4, p1498-1500.
Motion Picture Herald Product Digest. Mar 31, 1965, p257.
Movie. Sum 1965, n13, p45.
Movie. Aut 1965, n14, p29-32.
The New Republic. Apr 17, 1965, v152, p40.
New Statesman. Jun 11, 1965, v69, p929-30.
The New York Times. Apr 8, 1965, p45.
Newsweek. May 3, 1965, v65, p94.
Peckinpah: The Western Films. p43-76.
Playboy. Jun 1965, v12, p24, 26.
Sam Peckinpah (McKinney). p63-76.
Saturday Review. Apr 10, 1965, v48, p30.
Sight and Sound. Sum 1965, v34, p144-45.
Time. Apr 16, 1965, v85, p101.
Variety. Mar 17, 1965, p7.
The Village Voice. May 13, 1965, v10, p20.
Vogue. Apr 1, 1965, v145, p99.

A Majority of One (US; LeRoy, Mervyn; 1961)
America. Feb 10, 1962, v106, p33.
BFI/Monthly Film Bulletin. Apr 1962, v29, p47.
Commonweal. Jan 19, 1962, v75, p437.
Film Daily. Nov 19, 1961, p6.
Filmfacts. Feb 2, 1962, v5, p1-2.
Films in Review. Jan 1962, v8, p41-42.
The New York Times. Jan 12, 1962, p29.
The New Yorker. Jan 20, 1962, v37, p113.
Newsweek. Jan 29, 1962, v59, p81.
Saturday Review. Jan 27, 1962, v45, p28.
Time. Jan 19, 1962, v79, p55.
Variety. Nov 15, 1961, p6.

Make Haste To Live (US; Seiter, William A.; 1954)
BFI/Monthly Film Bulletin. May 1954, v21, p75.

Film Daily. Mar 31, 1954, p10.
Hollywood Reporter. Mar 26, 1954, p3.
Motion Picture Herald Product Digest. Apr 10, 1954, p2253-54.
National Parent-Teacher. Jun 1954, v48, p40.
The New York Times. Mar 26, 1954, p16.
The New Yorker. Apr 3, 1954, v30, p58.
The Spectator. Apr 2, 1954, v192, p386.
Variety. Mar 31, 1954, p6.

Make Me An Offer (GB; Frankel, Cyril; 1954)
BFI/Monthly Film Bulletin. Jan 1955, v22, p4.
Film Daily. Feb 28, 1956, p8.
The London Times. Dec 13, 1954, p11.
National Parent-Teacher. May 1956, v50, p39.
The New Statesman and Nation. Dec 11, 1954, v48, p786.
The New York Times. Feb 29, 1956, p35.
The Tatler. Dec 22, 1954, v214, p750.
Variety. Dec 22, 1954, p22.

Making Love (US; Hiller, Arthur; 1982)
American Film. Mar 1982, v7, p13-14.
BFI/Monthly Film Bulletin. May 1982, v49, p88.
Film Comment. May-Jun 1982, v18, p16.
Horizon. Jul-Aug 1982, v25, p62-63.
Maclean's. Apr 1, 1982, v95, p60.
Ms. Apr 1982, v10, p35.
The New Leader. Mar 22, 1982, v65, p21-22.
The New Republic. Mar 3, 1982, v186, p24-26.
The New York Times. Feb 21, 1982, SecII, p13.
Newsweek. Mar 1, 1982, v99, p70.
Progressive. May 1982, v46, p52-53.
Time. Feb 22, 1982, v119, p69.
Variety. Feb 10, 1982, p22.
The Village Voice. Feb 3, 1982, p38-40.

Mal, El *See* Rage

Male Companion (French title: Monsieur de Compagnie, Un) (FR, IT; Broca, Philippe de; 1964)
BFI/Monthly Film Bulletin. Feb 1967, v34, p28.
Christian Science Monitor (Western edition). Jun 17, 1966, p6.
Film Daily. Jan 21, 1966, p6.
Filmfacts. Mar 15, 1966, v9, p34-35.
Films in Review. Feb 1966, v17, p118.
Motion Picture Herald Product Digest. Jan 26, 1966, p457.
The New Republic. Apr 9, 1966, v154, p24-25.
The New York Times. Feb 15, 1966, p33.
The New Yorker. Feb 19, 1966, v41, p145.
Newsweek. Jan 31, 1966, v67, p85.
Playboy. May 1966, v13, p32-33.
Time. Jan 21, 1966, v87, p80.
Variety. Nov 18, 1964, p22.

Male Hunt (Also titled: Chasse a l'Homme, La; The Gentle Art of Seduction) (FR, IT; Molinaro, Edouard; 1964)
BFI/Monthly Film Bulletin. Apr 1966, v33, p58.
Commonweal. May 21, 1965, v82, p293.
Film Daily. May 10, 1965, p7.
Filmfacts. Jun 11, 1965, v8, p108-10.
Life. May 7, 1965, v58, p16.
The London Times. Feb 24, 1966, p16.
Motion Picture Herald Product Digest. Apr 28, 1965, p275.
The New York Times. Apr 20, 1965, p42.
The New Yorker. May 1, 1965, v41, p120.
Private Screenings. p185.
Time. Apr 30, 1965, v85, p109.
Variety. Oct 28, 1964, p6.

Malizia (Also titled: Malicious) (IT; Samperi, Salvatore; 1973)
Esquire. Sep 1974, v82, p44.

Films in Review. Mar 1974, v25, p186.
Hollywood Reporter. Jun 20, 1974, p3.
Independent Film Journal. Feb 4, 1974, v73, p10.
The Los Angeles Times. Jul 3, 1974, SecIV, p1.
Motion Picture Herald Product Digest. Jan 30, 1974, p72.
New York. Jun 3, 1974, v7, p76-77.
The New York Times. Jun 6, 1974, p49.
The New Yorker. Jun 17, 1974, v50, p90-91.
PTA Magazine. Apr 1974, v68, p4.
Saturday Review. Jun 1, 1974, v1, p41.
Time. Jul 1, 1974, v104, p42.
Variety. Jul 4, 1973, p18.
The Village Voice. Jun 6, 1974, p91.

Mama Turns 100 (Spanish title: Mama Cumple 100 Anos) (SP; Saura, Carlos; 1979)
The New York Times. Jan 11, 1980, SecIII, p6.
Newsday. Jan 11, 1980, SecII, p5.
Variety. Oct 3, 1979, p18.
The Village Voice. Jan 21, 1980, p54.

Mame (US; Saks, Gene; 1974)
BFI/Monthly Film Bulletin. Aug 1974, v41, p180-81.
Esquire. Jan 1974, v82, p36.
Film Heritage. 1974, v9, n4, p37-39.
Films and Filming. May 1974, v20, p51-53.
Films Illustrated. Jun 1974, v3, p372.
Films in Review. Apr 1974, v25, p243.
Focus on Film. Sum 1974, n18, p9-10.
Hollywood Reporter. Mar 11, 1974, p3.
Independent Film Journal. Mar 4, 1974, v73, p17.
The Los Angeles Times. Mar 27, 1974, SecIV, p1.
Motion Picture Herald Product Digest. Mar 13, 1974, p81.
The New Republic. Mar 23, 1974, v170, p24.
New Statesman. Jun 28, 1974, v87, p933-34.
New York. Mar 18, 1974, v7, p66, p67.
The New York Times. Mar 8, 1974, p18.
The New Yorker. Mar 11, 1974, v50, p122-24.
Newsweek. Mar 18, 1974, v83, p133.
PTA Magazine. Jun 1974, v68, p5.
Reeling. p402-04.
Saturday Evening Post. Mar 1974, v246, p36-37.
Saturday Review. Apr 6, 1974, v1, p50.
Time. Mar 25, 1974, v103, p68.
Variety. Feb 27, 1974, p16.
The Village Voice. Mar 21, 1974, p75.

A Man and a Woman (French title: Homme et Une Femme, Une) (FR; Lelouch, Claude; 1966)
America. Sep 10, 1966, v115, p260.
BFI/Monthly Film Bulletin. Mar 1967, v34, p42.
Christian Century. Mar 15, 1967, v84, p346-47.
Christian Science Monitor (Western edition). Aug 27, 1966, p6.
Christian Science Monitor (Western edition). Mar 11, 1967, p6.
Film Daily. Jul 14, 1966, p6.
Film Quarterly. Spr 1967, v20, p41-42.
Filmfacts. Sep 15, 1966, v9, p194-96.
Films and Filming. Feb 1967, v13, p28.
Films in Review. Aug-Sep 1966, v17, p452.
The Films of the Sixties. p180-81.
The Great French Films. p266.
Kiss Kiss Bang Bang. p154.
Life. Sep 9, 1966, v61, p12.
The London Times. Jan 5, 1967, p4.
The London Times. Jan 19, 1967, p6.
Magill's Survey of Cinema. Foreign Language Films. v4, p1914-17.

Motion Picture Herald Product Digest. Aug 3, 1966, p570-71.
The New Republic. Dec 24, 1966, v155, p34.
New Statesman. Jan 20, 1967, v73, p90.
The New York Times. Jul 13, 1966, p35.
The New Yorker. Jul 23, 1966, v42, p75.
Newsweek. Aug 1, 1966, v68, p84.
On Film. p306-07.
Playboy. Dec 1966, v13, p53.
The Private Eye, the Cowboy and the Very Naked Girl. p233-34.
Private Screenings. p270-74.
Saturday Review. Aug 13, 1966, v49, p38.
Second Sight. p84-86.
The Spectator. Jan 20, 1967, v218, p73.
Take One. Sep-Oct 1966, v1, p27-28.
Time. Aug 12, 1966, v88, p60.
Variety. May 18, 1966, p7.
The Village Voice. Aug 4, 1966, v11, p15.

The Man Between (GB; Reed, Carol; 1953)
America. Dec 5, 1953, v90, p279.
BFI/Monthly Film Bulletin. Nov 1953, v20, n238, p159.
Commonweal. Dec 4, 1953, v59, p225-26.
Film Daily. Nov 19, 1953, p14.
Films in Review. Jan 1954, v5, n1, p35-36.
The Films of James Mason. p110-11.
The Nation. Dec 26, 1953, v177, p574.
The New York Times. Nov 19, 1953, p14.
The New York Times. Nov 29, 1953, SecII, p1.
The New Yorker. Nov 28, 1953, v29, p131.
Newsweek. Nov 23, 1953, v42, p98.
Saturday Review. Nov 28, 1953, v36, p31.
Sight and Sound. Jan-Mar 1954, v23, n3, p144.
Time. Dec 7, 1953, v62, p104.
Variety. Sep 30, 1953, v22.

A Man Called Adam (US; Penn, Leo; 1966)
Film Daily. Jul 13, 1966, p4.
Filmfacts. Nov 1, 1966, v9, p236-37.
Hollywood Reporter. Jun 29, 1966, p3.
Motion Picture Herald Product Digest. Jul 6, 1966, p554.
The New York Times. Aug 4, 1966, p24.
Newsweek. Aug 8, 1966, v68, p80.
Playboy. Oct 1966, v13, p28.
Time. Aug 19, 1966, v88, p78.
Variety. Jun 29, 1966, p6.

A Man Called Horse (US; Silverstein, Elliot; 1970)
America. May 16, 1970, v122, p538.
BFI/Monthly Film Bulletin. Sep 1970, v37, n440, p189.
Commonweal. Jun 26, 1970, v92, p318.
Film Quarterly. Fall 1970, v24, n1, p60-61.
Films and Filming. Oct 1970, v17, n1, p45-46.
The New York Times. Apr 30, 1970, p46.
The New Yorker. May 9, 1970, v46, p118.
Newsweek. May 25, 1970, v75, p102.
Saturday Review. May 2, 1970, v53, p52.
Time. May 11, 1970, v95, p103.
Variety. Apr 29, 1970, p18.

A Man Called Peter (US; Koster, Henry; 1955)
America. Apr 9, 1955, v93, p55.
BFI/Monthly Film Bulletin. May 1955, v22, n256, p71.
Catholic World. May 1955, v181, p141-42.
Commonweal. Apr 8, 1955, v62, p14-15.
Film Culture. May-Jun 1955, v1, n3, p24-25.
Film Daily. Mar 23, 1955, p6.
Films and Filming. Jun 1955, v1, n9, p22.
Films in Review. Apr 1955, v6, n4, p187-88.
Hollywood Reporter. Mar 23, 1955, v133, n46, p3.
Library Journal. Apr 1, 1955, v80, p775.
Life. Apr 4, 1955, v38, p115-18.
The New York Times. Apr 1, 1955, p22.

The New York Times. Apr 10, 1955, SecII, p1.
The New York Times. Apr 17, 1955, SecII, p5.
The New Yorker. Apr 16, 1955, v31, p146.
Saturday Review. Apr 2, 1955, v38, p32.
Time. Apr 11, 1955, v65, p110.
Variety. Mar 23, 1955, p6.

A Man Could Get Killed (US; Neame, Ronald; Owen, Cliff; 1966)
America. May 21, 1966, v114, p754-55.
BFI/Monthly Film Bulletin. Jun 1966, v33, p94-95.
Christian Science Monitor (Western edition). May 14, 1966, p4.
Film Daily. Mar 16, 1966, p6.
Filmfacts. Jul 15, 1966, v9, p126-27.
Hollywood Reporter. Mar 15, 1966, p3.
The London Times. May 5, 1966, p20.
Motion Picture Herald Product Digest. Mar 30, 1966, p492.
The New York Times. May 12, 1966, p54.
Senior Scholastic. Apr 22, 1966, v88, p20.
Seventeen. Mar 1966, v25, p158-59.
Time. May 27, 1966, v87, p97.
Variety. Mar 16, 1966, p6.

Man Die Zijn Haar Kort Kiet Knippen, De
See The Man Who Had His Hair Cut Short

A Man Escaped *See* Condamne a Mort s'est Echappe, Un

A Man For All Seasons (GB; Zinnemann, Fred; 1966)
America. Dec 24, 1966, v115, p837-38.
BFI/Monthly Film Bulletin. May 1967, v34, p72-73.
Christian Century. Jan 25, 1967, v84, p112.
Christian Century. Jul 19, 1967, v84, p934-36.
Christian Science Monitor (Western edition). Dec 19, 1966, p4.
Christian Science Monitor (Western edition). Feb 6, 1967, p1.
Commonweal. Dec 23, 1966, v85, p349-50.
Confessions of a Cultist. p277-80.
Esquire. Mar 1967, v67, p20.
Fifty Classic British Films. p124-26.
Film Daily. Dec 12, 1966, p4.
Film Society Review. Sep 1970, v6, p41-46.
Filmfacts. Dec 15, 1966, v9, p281-84.
Films and Filming. Apr 1967, v13, p4.
Films Illustrated. Nov 1974, v4, p90.
Films in Review. Jan 1967, v18, p48-50.
The Films of the Sixties. p171-72.
The Great Adventure Films. p124-26.
Hollywood Reporter. Dec 12, 1966, p3.
Kiss Kiss Bang Bang. p189-90.
Life. Jan 6, 1967, v62, p72-74.
The London Times. Aug 18, 1966, p6.
Magill's Survey of Cinema. Series I. v3, p1053-55.
Marshall Delaney at the Movies. p100-03.
Motion Picture Herald Product Digest. Dec 14, 1966, p639.
The New Republic. Feb 25, 1967, v156, p35-36.
New Statesman. Mar 31, 1967, v73, p447.
The New York Times. Dec 13, 1966, p60.
The New Yorker. Dec 17, 1966, v42, p124.
Newsweek. Dec 19, 1966, v68, p113.
Playboy. Mar 1967, v14, p20, 22.
The Private Eye, the Cowboy and the Very Naked Girl. p218-20, 229.
Private Screenings. p295-97.
Saturday Review. Dec 17, 1966, v49, p58.
Senior Scholastic. Jan 13, 1967, v89, p18.
Sight and Sound. Spr 1967, v36, p97.
Take One. Feb 1967, v1, p30.
Take One. Apr 1967, v1, p29-30.
Time. Dec 16, 1966, v88, p119.

Variety. Dec 14, 1966, p6.
The Village Voice. Dec 22, 1966, v12, p27.
Vogue. Jan 15, 1967, v149, p44.

The Man From Button Willow (US; Detiege, David; 1965)
BFI/Monthly Film Bulletin. Apr 1966, v33, p61-62.
Film Daily. Feb 1, 1965, p6.
Hollywood Reporter. Feb 18, 1965, p3.
Motion Picture Herald Product Digest. Feb 3, 1965, p218.

Man in the Attic (US; Fregonese, Hugo; 1954)
BFI/Monthly Film Bulletin. Jun 1954, v21, p88-89.
Film Daily. Jan 11, 1954, p6.
Hollywood Reporter. Dec 18, 1953, p3.
Library Journal. Jan 15, 1954, v79, p139.
Motion Picture Herald Product Digest. Dec 26, 1953, p2119.
National Parent-Teacher. Feb 1954, v48, p39.
The New York Times. Feb 6, 1954, p17.
Newsweek. Jan 18, 1954, v43, p90-91.
Time. Jan 25, 1954, v63, p108.
Variety. Dec 23, 1953, p16.

The Man in the Glass Booth (US; Hiller, Arthur; 1975)
Hollywood Reporter. Feb 25, 1975, p3.
The Los Angeles Times. Feb 24, 1975, SecIV, p1.
The New York Times. May 20, 1975, p46.
Newsweek. Jul 21, 1975, v86, p64.
Variety. Jan 22, 1975, p34.

The Man in the White Suit (GB; Mackendrick, Alexander; 1951)
BFI/Monthly Film Bulletin. Sep 1951, v18, p326.
Catholic World. Apr 1952, v175, p64.
Christian Century. May 14, 1952, v69, p599.
Classics of the Foreign Film. p196-97.
Commonweal. May 2, 1952, v56, p94.
Fifty From the Fifties. p179-86.
Film Daily. Apr 7, 1952, p6.
Film News. Jun 1973, v30, p20.
Films in Review. Mar 1952, v3, p136-37.
Halliwell's Hundred. p191-94.
Hollywood Reporter. May 29, 1952, p4.
Illustrated London News. Aug 25, 1951, v219, p300.
The International Dictionary of Films and Filmmakers. v1, p276-77.
Kiss Kiss Bang Bang. p382-83.
The London Times. Aug 13, 1951, p6.
Magill's Survey of Cinema. Series I. v3, p1056-58.
Motion Picture Herald Product Digest. Apr 5, 1952, p1306.
The New Statesman and Nation. Aug 18, 1951, v42, p180.
The New York Times. Apr 1, 1952, p35.
The New Yorker. Apr 12, 1952, v28, p113.
Newsweek. Apr 14, 1952, v39, p96.
Saturday Review. May 10, 1952, v35, p31.
Saturday Review. Apr 5, 1952, v35, p28.
Science Fiction Studies in Film. p116-17.
Sight and Sound. Apr 1951, v19, p462-63.
Sight and Sound. Oct-Dec 1951, v21, p47-48, 78-79.
The Spectator. Aug 10, 1951, v187, p184.
Theatre Arts. Apr 1952, v36, p85.
Time. Apr 14, 1952, v59, p108.
Twenty All-Time Great Science Fiction Films. p49-58.
Variety. Aug 22, 1951, p10.

A Man Is Ten Feet Tall *See* Edge of the City

A Man Named John *See* And There Came a Man

Man of a Thousand Faces (US; Pevney, Joseph; 1957)
America. Aug 24, 1957, v97, p532.
BFI/Monthly Film Bulletin. Oct 1957, v24, p123.
Commonweal. Aug 30, 1957, v66, p542.
Film Daily. Jul 16, 1957, v112, p7.
Films and Filming. Oct 1957, v4, p22-23.
Films in Review. Aug-Sep 1957, v8, p345-47.
Hollywood Reporter. Jul 16, 1957, p3.
Magill's Survey of Cinema. Series II. v4, p1513-15.
Motion Picture Herald Product Digest. Jul 20, 1957, v208, p457.
The New York Times. Aug 18, 1957, SecII, p1.
The New York Times. Aug 14, 1957, p21.
The New Yorker. Aug 24, 1957, v33, p70.
Newsweek. Aug 19, 1957, v50, p88.
Saturday Review. Aug 17, 1957, v40, p25.
Time. Aug 26, 1957, v70, p82.
Variety. Jul 17, 1957, p6.

Man of Bronze *See* Jim Thorpe, All-American

Man of Iron *See* The Railroad Man

Man of La Mancha (US; Hiller, Arthur; 1972)
Filmfacts. 1972, v15, n4, p617.
The Films of Sophia Loren. p230-39.
Harper's Bazaar. Mar 1973, v106, p152.
Hollywood Reporter. Dec 1, 1972, p3.
The Musical from Broadway to Hollywood. p148-54.
The New York Times. Dec 1972, v60, p1.
The New Yorker. Dec 23, 1972, v48, p54.
Newsweek. Dec 18, 1972, v80, p94.
Reeling. p117-18.
Saturday Review. Dec 23, 1972, v55, p75.
Senior Scholastic. Oct 16, 1972, v101, p16.
Time. Dec 25, 1972, v100, p75-76.
Variety. Dec 6, 1972, p16.

Man of Marble (Polish title: Czlowiek z Marmuru) (POL; Wajda, Andrzej; 1977)
Horizon. Mar 1981, v24, p70-71.
The International Dictionary of Films and Filmmakers. v1, p113-14.
The Los Angeles Times. Apr 8, 1981, SecVI, p1.
The Nation. Feb 7, 1981, v232, p155-56.
The New Republic. Nov 11, 1981, v185, p37.
The New York Times. Jan 23, 1981, SecIII, p16.
Newsweek. Feb 9, 1981, v97, p95.
Progressive. Mar 1981, v45, p55.
Time. Mar 9, 1981, v117, p69.
Variety. Jun 1, 1977, p17.

Man of the West (US; Mann, Anthony; 1958)
Anthony Mann (Basinger). p144-57.
BFI/Monthly Film Bulletin. Jan 1959, v26, p3.
Commonweal. Oct 10, 1958, v69, p48.
Film Daily. Sep 17, 1958, v114, p6.
Filmfacts. Oct 22, 1958, v1, p169-70.
The Films of Gary Cooper. p265-66.
Hollywood Reporter. Sep 17, 1958, p3.
Library Journal. Oct 1958, v83, p2741.
The New York Times. Oct 2, 1958, p44.
Newsweek. Oct 6, 1958, v52, p91.
Time. Oct 6, 1958, v72, p88.
Variety. Sep 17, 1958, p6.

Man on a Swing (US; Perry, Frank; 1974)
BFI/Monthly Film Bulletin. Aug 1974, v41, p180.
Commonweal. Mar 29, 1974, v100, p85.
Films in Review. Apr 1974, v25, p247-48.

Hollywood Reporter. Mar 11, 1974, p3.
Independent Film Journal. Mar 4, 1974, v73, p17-18.
The Los Angeles Times. Feb 26, 1974, SecIV, p1.
Motion Picture Herald Product Digest. Feb 27, 1974, p77.
Movietone News. Apr 1974, n31, p34.
New York. Mar 4, 1974, v7, p58-59.
The New York Times. Feb 28, 1974, p33.
Newsweek. Mar 18, 1974, v83, p109.
PTA Magazine. Jun 1974, v68, p5.
Saturday Review. Mar 23, 1974, v1, p58.
Time. Mar 11, 1974, v103, p79.
Variety. Feb 27, 1974, p16.
The Village Voice. Mar 21, 1974, v19, p69.

Man on a Tightrope (US; Kazan, Elia; 1953)
America. Jun 6, 1953, v89, p287.
BFI/Monthly Film Bulletin. Jun 1953, v20, n233, p86.
Catholic World. May 1953, v177, p145.
Commonweal. Jun 26, 1953, v58, p298.
Film Daily. Apr 6, 1953, p11.
Films in Review. May 1953, v4, n5, p240-41.
The Films of Frederic March. p206-08.
Hollywood Reporter. Apr 1, 1953, p3.
Library Journal. May 15, 1953, v78, p897.
The New York Times. Sep 7, 1952, SecII, p5.
The New York Times. Jun 5, 1953, p9.
The New York Times. Jun 21, 1953, SecII, p1.
The New Yorker. Jun 13, 1953, v29, p66.
Newsweek. May 11, 1953, v41, p102.
Saturday Review. May 30, 1953, v36, p30.
Sight and Sound. Jul-Sep 1953, v23, n1, p32.
Time. Apr 27, 1953, v61, p108.
Variety. Apr 1, 1953, p6.

Man on Fire (US; MacDougall, Ranald; 1957)
BFI/Monthly Film Bulletin. Nov 1957, v24, p140.
Commonweal. Aug 9, 1957, v66, p472.
Film Daily. Jun 4, 1957, v111, p10.
Films and Filming. Dec 1957, v4, p25.
The Films of Bing Crosby. p225-26.
Hollywood Reporter. Jun 4, 1957, p3.
Motion Picture Herald Product Digest. Jun 8, 1957, v107, p409.
The New York Times. Aug 23, 1957, p10.
The New York Times. Aug 25, 1957, SecII, p1.
The New Yorker. Aug 31, 1957, p54.
Newsweek. Jul 8, 1957, v50, p89.
Time. Jul 8, 1957, v70, p70.
Variety. Jun 5, 1957, p6.

The Man On the Eiffel Tower (FR, US; Meredith, Burgess; 1949)
BFI/Monthly Film Bulletin. Dec 1950, v17, p189-90.
Christian Century. Feb 15, 1950, v67, p223.
Commonweal. Jan 27, 1950, v51, p438.
Film Daily. Dec 15, 1949, p8.
Library Journal. Feb 15, 1950, v75, p332.
Motion Picture Herald Product Digest. Dec 24, 1949, p130.
The New Republic. Feb 6, 1950, v122, p22.
The New Statesman and Nation. Dec 9, 1950, v40, p586.
The New York Times. Jan 30, 1950, p12.
The New Yorker. Feb 11, 1950, v25, p51.
Newsweek. Feb 6, 1950, v35, p84.
Variety. Dec 21, 1949, p8.

The Man Who Cheated Himself (US; Feist, Felix; 1950)
BFI/Monthly Film Bulletin. Feb 1951, v18, p219.
Commonweal. Feb 9, 1951, v53, p448.

Film Daily. Dec 26, 1950, p6.
Hollywood Reporter. Dec 18, 1950, p3.
The London Times. Feb 12, 1951, p6.
Motion Picture Herald Product Digest. Dec 23, 1950, p633.
The Nation. Jan 5, 1952, v174, p19.
The New Statesman and Nation. Feb 17, 1951, v41, p184.
The New York Times. Feb 9, 1951, p21.
Newsweek. Feb 19, 1951, v37, p88.
Variety. Dec 20, 1950, p6.

The Man Who Cut His Hair Short *See* The Man Who Had His Hair Cut Short

The Man Who Fell to Earth (GB; Roeg, Nicolas; 1976)
America. Jul 10, 1976, v135, p19-20.
Audience. Oct 1976, v9, p14-15.
BFI/Monthly Film Bulletin. Apr 1976, v43, p86-87.
Commonweal. Jul 16, 1976, v103, p463-64.
Cult Movies 2. p81-83.
Encounter. Jun 1976, v46, p50-52.
Film. May 1976, n37, p8.
Film Heritage. Fall, 1976, p18-25.
Film Illustrated. Apr 1976, v5, p284.
Films and Filming. May 1976, v22, p28-29.
Films and Filming. Feb 1976, v22, p26-30.
Films in Review. Aug-Sep 1976, v27, p442.
Hollywood Reporter. Jun 23, 1976, p3.
Independent Film Journal. Jun 11, 1976, v78, p9.
The Los Angeles Times. Jul 7, 1976, SecIV, p1.
Magill's Cinema Annual, 1983. p469-72.
Movietone News. Aug 1976, n51, p19-22.
The Nation. Jun 19, 1976, v222, p765.
National Review. Nov 12, 1976, v28, p1239.
New Statesman. Mar 19, 1976, v91, p380.
New York. Jun 14, 1976, v9, p63-66.
The New York Times. Jun 6, 1976, SecIII, p13.
The New York Times. Aug 22, 1976, SecII, p11.
The New York Times. Jun 7, 1976, v52, p120.
The New Yorker. Nov 8, 1976, v52, p140-42.
Newsweek. Jun 14, 1976, v87, p89.
Nicholas Roeg (Feineman). p105-30.
Penthouse. Sep 1976, v8, p46-47.
Progressive. Sep 1976, v40, p53-54.
Rolling Stone. Jul 13, 1976, p22.
Saturday Review. Jul 10, 1976, v3, p63.
Science Fiction Films of the Seventies. p119-21.
Self and Cinema. p345-461.
Sight and Sound. Fall 1976, v45, p145-47.
Take One. n4, 1976, v5, p38-39.
The Thousand Eyes Magazine. Jul-Aug 1976, n12, p6-7.
Time. Jun 14, 1976, v107, p66.
Variety. Mar 24, 1976, p20.
When the Lights Go Down. p200-01.

The Man Who Had His Hair Cut Short (Also titled: Man Die Zijn Haar Kort Kiet Knippen, De; The Man Who Cut His Hair Short) (BELG; Delvaux, André; 1966)
BFI/Monthly Film Bulletin. Feb 1967, v34, p24.
Dictionary of Films. p206-07.
Films and Filming. Jun 1967, v13, p25-26.
Films and Filming. Jan 1969, v15, p85-86.
The London Times. Nov 23, 1966, p17.
New Statesman. Apr 14, 1967, v73, p520.
Sight and Sound. Spr 1967, v36, p93-94.
The Spectator. Nov 25, 1966, v217, p680.
Variety. Sep 28, 1966, p24.

The Man Who Knew Too Much (US; Hitchcock, Alfred; 1956)
America. May 26, 1956, v95, p231.
The Art of Alfred Hitchcock. p267-82.

BFI/Monthly Film Bulletin. Jun 1956, v23, p73.
Boxoffice. Feb 1984, v120, p23-24.
Commonweal. May 25, 1956, v64, p204.
Film Comment. May-Jun 1984, v20, p9-18.
Film Daily. May 1, 1956, p6.
Films and Filming. Jul 1956, v2, p23.
Films and Filming. Oct 1962, v9, p39.
Films in Review. Jun-Jul 1956, v7, p285-86.
The Films of Alfred Hitchcock. p178-81.
The Films of Doris Day. p155-58.
The Films of James Stewart. p183-85.
Hitchcock: The First Forty-Four Films. p138-44.
Hitchcock (Truffaut). p90-94.
Hollywood Reporter. May 1, 1956, p3.
Informer. Mar 1984, p2-3.
Magill's Survey of Cinema. Series II. v4, p1519-22.
Movie. Oct 1962, n3, p4-7.
Movie. Jan 1963, n6, p8-12.
The Nation. Jun 9, 1956, v182, p498.
The New York Times. May 17, 1956, p37.
The New York Times. May 20, 1956, SecII, p1.
The New Yorker. May 26, 1956, v32, p119.
Newsweek. May 28, 1956, v47, p106.
Saturday Review. May 26, 1956, v39, p25.
Sight and Sound. Sum 1956, v26, p30-31.
Time. May 21, 1956, v67, p114.
Variety. May 2, 1956, p6.
The Village Voice. Aug 23, 1983, v28, p41.

The Man Who Lies *See* Homme Qui Ment, L'

The Man Who Loved Women (French title: Homme qui aimait les femmes, L') (FR; Truffaut, François; 1976)
Before My Eyes. p189-92.
BFI/Monthly Film Bulletin. Apr 1978, v45, p65.
Commonweal. Feb 3, 1978, v105, p82-83.
François Truffaut: A Guide to References and Resources. p81-83.
François Truffaut (Insdorf). p200-18.
Hollywood Reporter. Oct 5, 1977, p7.
The Los Angeles Times. Nov 6, 1977, Calendar, p1.
The Nation. Nov 12, 1977, v225, p510.
The New Republic. Oct 22, 1977, v177, p20.
The New York Times. Oct 1, 1977, p10.
The New Yorker. Dec 5, 1977, v53, p125-26.
Newsweek. Oct 31, 1977, v90, p96.
Saturday Review. Nov 26, 1977, v5, p46.
Time. Oct 10, 1977, v110, p84.
Variety. Apr 27, 1977, p24.
When the Lights Go Down. p354-56.

The Man Who Shot Liberty Valance (US; Ford, John; 1962)
America. Jul 16, 1962, v107, p409.
American Film. Sep 1983, v8, p72-74.
Authorship and Narrative in the Cinema. p45-84.
BFI/Monthly Film Bulletin. Jun 1962, v29, p77-78.
Cinema Texas Program Notes. Nov 4, 1976, v11, n3, p57-64.
Commonweal. May 18, 1962, v76, p211.
The Complete Films of John Wayne. p236-38.
Film Comment. Fall 1971, v7, p18-20.
Film Culture. Sum 1962, n25, p13-15.
Film Daily. Apr 11, 1962, p6.
Film Quarterly. Wint 1963-64, v17, p42-44.
Filmfacts. Jun 8, 1962, v5, p109-10.
Films and Filming. Jun 1962, v8, p33.
Films in Review. May 1962, v13, p292-93.
The Films of James Stewart. p215-18.
Hollywood Reporter. Apr 11, 1962, v169, p3.
International Dictionary of Films and Filmmakers. Volume 1. p278-80.

Magill's Survey of Cinema. Series I. v3, p1059-62.
Motion Picture Herald Product Digest. Apr 18, 1962, p524.
Movie. Wint 1977-78, n25, p1-11.
The New York Times. May 24, 1962, p29.
The New Yorker. Jul 16, 1962, v38, p102.
Quarterly Review of Film Studies. 1977, v2, n1, p75-87.
Sight and Sound. Sum 1962, v31, p146.
Sight and Sound. Wint 1978, v47, p237-41.
Sight and Sound. Spr 1982, v51, p124-29.
Time. May 7, 1962, v79, p88.
Variety. Apr 11, 1962, p6.
Wide Angle. 1978, v2, n4, p36-42.

The Man Who Would Be King (US; Huston, John; 1975)
Before My Eyes. p193.
BFI/Monthly Film Bulletin. Feb 1976, v43, p32.
The Cinema of John Huston. p187-95.
Commonweal. Jan 30, 1976, v103, p83-84.
The English Novel and the Movies. p180-86.
Films in Review. Feb 1976, v27, p122.
The Films of the Seventies. p134-35.
The Great Adventure Films. p274-79.
Hollywood Reporter. Dec 12, 1975, p3.
John Huston (Hammen). p129-33.
John Huston (Madsen). p244-48, 264-65.
John Huston, Maker of Magic. p197-202.
The Los Angeles Times. Dec 18, 1975, SecIV, p1.
Magill's Survey of Cinema. Series I. v3, p1063-66.
Motion Picture Herald Product Digest. Dec 31, 1975, p58.
The New Republic. Jan 31, 1976, v174, p24-25.
The New York Times. Dec 18, 1975, p62.
The New Yorker. Jan 5, 1976, v51, p52-55.
Newsweek. Dec 29, 1975, v86, p50-51.
An Open Book. p351-60.
Saturday Review. Jan 24, 1976, v3, p50.
Senior Scholastic. Feb 24, 1976, v108, p42.
Time. Dec 29, 1975, v106, p38.
Variety. Dec 10, 1975, p26.
When the Lights Go Down. p107-12.

The Man With a Cloak (US; Markle, Fletcher; 1951)
BFI/Monthly Film Bulletin. Dec 1951, v18, p376.
Christian Century. Jan 2, 1952, v69, p31.
Film Daily. Oct 2, 1951, p6.
The Films of Barbara Stanwyck. p208-09.
Hollywood Reporter. Oct 1, 1951, p3.
Library Journal. Nov 15, 1951, v76, p1948.
Motion Picture Herald Product Digest. Oct 6, 1951, p1050.
The New Republic. Dec 17, 1951, v125, p21.
The New York Times. Nov 28, 1951, p37.
The New Yorker. Dec 8, 1951, v27, p70.
Newsweek. Oct 29, 1951, v38, p92.
Starring Miss Barbara Stanwyck. p232-33.
Time. Oct 22, 1951, v58, p118.
Variety. Oct 3, 1951, p6.

Man With a Million (Also titled: The Million Pound Note) (GB; Neame, Ronald; 1954)
America. Jul 10, 1954, v91, p386.
BFI/Monthly Film Bulletin. Feb 1954, v21, p20-21.
Catholic World. Jun 1954, v179, p220.
Commonweal. Jul 16, 1954, v60, p365.
Film Daily. Jun 2, 1954, p6.
Films in Review. Aug-Sep 1954, v5, p362-63.
The Films of Gregory Peck. p129-31.
Hollywood Reporter. Jul 1, 1954, p3.
Kiss Kiss Bang Bang. p383-84.

Library Journal. May 1, 1954, v79, p852.
Motion Picture Herald Product Digest. May 29, 1954, p9-10.
National Parent-Teacher. May 1954, v48, p38.
The New York Times. Jun 29, 1954, p21.
Newsweek. May 31, 1954, v43, p86-86.
Saturday Review. Jul 10, 1954, v37, p25-26.
Senior Scholastic. May 12, 1954, v64, p29.
Time. May 31, 1954, v63, p72.
Variety. Jan 13, 1954, p6.

The Man With the Golden Arm (US; Preminger, Otto; 1955)
America. Jan 28, 1956, v94, p488.
Catholic World. Feb 1956, v182, p381-82.
The Cinema of Otto Preminger. p115-18.
Cinema, the Magic Vehicle. v2, p263-65.
Commonweal. Dec 30, 1955, v63, p332.
Film Daily. Dec 14, 1955, p6.
The Films of Frank Sinatra. p101-05.
Life. Dec 19, 1955, v39, p85-86.
The Nation. Jan 7, 1956, v182, p17.
The New Republic. Feb 6, 1956, v134, p22.
The New York Times. Dec 16, 1955, p38.
The New Yorker. Dec 24, 1955, v31, p52.
Newsweek. Dec 26, 1955, v46, p66-67.
Saturday Review. Dec 17, 1955, v38, p26-27.
Time. Dec 26, 1955, v66, p59.
Variety. Dec 14, 1955, p6.

The Man With the Golden Gun (GB; Hamilton, Guy; 1974)
BFI/Monthly Film Bulletin. Jan 1975, v42, p11.
Films and Filming. Dec 1974, v21, p52-53.
Hollywood Reporter. Dec 10, 1974, p3.
Independent Film Journal. Dec 11, 1974, v75, p9.
The James Bond Films. p125-34.
James Bond in the Cinema. p221-34.
James Bond's Bedside Companion. p140-42, 211-14.
The Los Angeles Times. Dec 19, 1974, SecIV, p25.
Motion Picture Herald Product Digest. Dec 25, 1974, p59.
New York. Dec 23, 1974, v7, p70-71.
The New York Times. Dec 19, 1974, p60.
Newsweek. Dec 30, 1974, v84, p56.
Time. Jan 13, 1975, v105, p5.
Variety. Dec 11, 1974, p16.

The Man With the Green Carnation *See* The Trials of Oscar Wilde

The Man With Thirty Sons *See* The Magnificent Yankee

The Man With Two Brains (US; Reiner, Carl; 1983)
Films in Review. Aug-Sep 1983, v35, p441.
Hollywood Reporter. Jun 3, 1983, p4.
The Los Angeles Times. Jun 3, 1983, SecVI, p13.
Maclean's. Jun 13, 1983, v96, p55.
Magill's Cinema Annual, 1984. p223-27.
The New York Times. Jun 3, 1983, SecIII, p8.
The New Yorker. Jun 27, 1983, v59, p90.
Newsweek. Jun 13, 1983, v101, p78.
Time. Jun 20, 1983, v121, p75.

The Manchurian Candidate (US; Frankenheimer, John; 1962)
America. Nov 24, 1962, v107, p1158.
BFI/Monthly Film Bulletin. Dec 1962, v29, p168.
The Cinema of John Frankenheimer. p81-102.
Commonweal. Nov 23, 1962, v77, p231.
Fifty Grand Movies of the 1960s and 1970s. p145-48.
Film Culture. Fall 1964, n34, p28-34.
Film Daily. Oct 16, 1962, p4.
Film Quarterly. Spr 1963, v16, p59.

Filmfacts. Nov 2, 1962, v5, p243-45.
Films and Filming. Dec 1962, v9, p37-38.
Films in Review. Nov 1962, v13, p558-59.
The Films of Frank Sinatra. p184-87.
The Films of the Sixties. p92-94.
The Great Movies. p204-05.
Hollywood Reporter. Oct 12, 1962, p3.
Life. Nov 9, 1962, v53, p93-94.
Magill's Survey of Cinema. Series II. v4, p1523-26.
Motion Picture Herald Product Digest. Oct 17, 1962, p673.
Movie. Dec 1962, n5, p35.
The New Republic. Dec 1, 1962, v147, p26.
The New York Times. Oct 25, 1962, p48.
The New Yorker. Nov 3, 1962, v38, p115.
Newsweek. Oct 29, 1962, v60, p88.
Saturday Review. Oct 27, 1962, v45, p65.
Screen. Jul-Oct 1969, v10, p160-73.
Sight and Sound. Wint 1962-63, v32, p36-37.
Time. Nov 2, 1962, v80, p101.
Variety. Oct 17, 1962, p6.

Mandabi (Also titled: The Money Order) (SENEGAL, FR; Sembene, Ousmane; 1968)
The Cinema of Ousemane Sembene, A Pioneer of African Film. p127-40.
Film Library Quarterly. 1973, v6, n3, p13-15.
Film News. Jun 1973, v30, p21.
Film Quarterly. Sum 1970, v23, p48-50.
Film Quarterly. Spr 1973, v26, p36-42.
Films and Filming. Jan 1974, v20, p45.
Magill's Survey of Cinema. Foreign Language Films. v4, p1945-49.
The New York Times. Sep 30, 1969, p41.
Newsweek. Apr 6, 1970, v75, p94.
Variety. Sep 11, 1968, p106.

Mandragola, La (Also titled: The Mandrake; The Love Root) (IT, FR; Lattuada, Alberto; 1965)
BFI/Monthly Film Bulletin. Jun 1966, v33, p95.
Commonweal. Jun 17, 1966, v84, p368.
Film Daily. Jun 3, 1966, p6.
Filmfacts. Aug 1, 1966, v9, p135-36.
The London Times. Jun 9, 1966, p8.
Motion Picture Herald Product Digest. Jun 29, 1966, p552.
The New York Times. Jun 7, 1966, p50.
The New Yorker. Jun 11, 1966, v42, p112.
Playboy. Sep 1966, v13, p54.
Time. Jun 3, 1966, v87, p93.
Variety. Mar 9, 1966, p17.

Mandy (Also titled: The Story of Mandy; The Crash of Silence) (GB; Mackendrick, Alexander; 1952)
BFI/Monthly Film Bulletin. Sep 1952, v19, p123.
Film Criticism and Caricatures, 1943-53. p146-47.
Film Daily. Apr 2, 1953, p10.
Films in Review. Mar 1953, v4, p154.
Illustrated London News. Aug 16, 1952, v221, p261.
Illustrated London News. Aug 23, 1952, v221, p304.
The London Times. Aug 4,1952, p9.
Motion Picture Herald Product Digest. Feb 21, 1953, p1733.
The New Statesman and Nation. Aug 9, 1952, v44, p160.
The New York Times. Feb 24, 1953, p21.
Newsweek. Mar 9, 1953, v41, p87.
Saturday Review. Feb 28, 1953, v36, p39.
Sight and Sound. Oct-Dec 1952, v22, p77-78.
The Tatler. Aug 13, 1952, v205, p290.
Time. Mar 9, 1953, v61, p103.
Variety. Aug 20, 1952, p22.

Maneges (Also titled: The Wanton) (FR; Allégret, Yves; 1950)
BFI/Monthly Film Bulletin. Mar 1951, v18, p228.
Cinema, the Magic Vehicle. v1, p518-19.
The New Statesman and Nation. Feb 3, 1951, v41, p138.
Sight and Sound. Mar 1951, v19, p440.
Variety. Mar 8, 1950, p6.

Manhattan (US; Allen, Woody; 1979)
America. May 12, 1979, v140, p395.
BFI/Monthly Film Bulletin. Aug 1979, v46, p179.
Commonweal. Aug 3, 1979, v106, p438-39.
Film Comment. May 1979, v15, p16-17.
Films in Review. Jun-Jul 1979, v30, p371.
The Films of the Seventies. p248-50.
Hollywood Reporter. Apr 23, 1979, p4.
The International Dictionary of Films and Filmmakers. v1, p280-81.
The Los Angeles Times. Apr 22, 1979, Calendar, p1.
Magill's Survey of Cinema. Series I. v3, p1067-69.
Motion Picture Herald Product Digest. May 16, 1979, p96.
The Nation. May 19, 1979, v228, p580-81.
The New Republic. May 19, 1979, v180, p22-23.
The New York Times. Apr 25, 1979, SecIII, p17.
The New Yorker. Apr 30, 1979, v55, p110.
Newsweek. Apr 30, 1979, v93, p78.
Saturday Review. Jul 7, 1979, p41.
Time. Apr 30, 1979, v113, p62-65, 68-69.
Variety. Apr 25, 1979, p18.
Woody Allen: His Films and Career. p187-99.
Woody Allen (Palmer). p103-17.

Mani Sulla Citta, Le *See* Hands Over the City

Manon (FR; Clouzot, Henri-Georges; 1949)
BFI/Monthly Film Bulletin. Oct 1950, v17, p149-50.
Cinema, the Magic Vehicle. v2, p473-74.
Commonweal. Feb 23, 1951, v53, p496.
Film Daily. Dec 27, 1950, p6.
Hollywood Reporter. Feb 9, 1951, p3.
The London Times. Sep 21, 1950, p6.
The Nation. Jan 13, 1951, v172, p45.
The New Statesman and Nation. Sep 30, 1950, v40, p324.
The New York Times. Dec 26, 1950, p19.
Shots in the Dark. p232-36.
The Spectator. Sep 22, 1950, v185, p312.
Variety. Apr 6, 1949, p22.

Manon des Sources (Also titled: Manon of the Springs) (FR; Pagnol, Marcel; 1952)
BFI/Monthly Film Bulletin. Apr 1954, v21, p54.
BFI/Monthly Film Bulletin. Apr 1980, v47, p81.
The French Literary Filmmakers. p45.
The London Times. Feb 22, 1954, p4.
Marcel Pagnol (Caldicott). p116-19.
The New Statesman and Nation. Feb 27, 1954, v47, p252.
The Tatler. Mar 3, 1954, v211, p362.
Variety. Feb 18, 1953, p6.

Man's Favorite Sport? (US; Hawks, Howard; 1964)
BFI/Monthly Film Bulletin. May 1964, v31, p70.
Boxoffice. Jan 27, 1964, v84, p2796.
Commonweal. Mar 6, 1964, v79, p694.
Confessions of a Cultist. p128-29.
Film Daily. Jan 21, 1964, v124, p5.

Films and Filming. Jul 1964, v10, p23.
Films in Review. Mar 1964, v15, p173-74.
The Films of Howard Hawks. p39-40.
Focus on Howard Hawks. p135-38.
Hollywood Reporter. Jan 21, 1964, v178, p3.
Howard Hawks (Wood). p138-40.
Motion Picture Herald Product Digest. Feb 5, 1964, v231, p987.
The New York Times. Feb 20, 1964, p22.
Saturday Review. Feb 29, 1964, v47, p22.
Time. Feb 28, 1964, v83, p106.
Variety. Jan 22, 1964, p6.

Mans, Le (US; Katzin, Lee H.; 1971)
BFI/Monthly Film Bulletin. Aug 1971, v38, n451, p166.
Filmfacts. 1971, v14, n13, p323-25.
Films and Filming. Sep 1971, v17, n12, p50-51.
Hollywood Reporter. Jun 15, 1971, p3.
The New York Times. Jun 24, 1971, p35.
The New York Times. Aug 7, 1971, p17.
Time. Jul 12, 1971, v98, p45.
Variety. Jun 16, 1971, p15.
The Village Voice. Jul 15, 1971, p57.

A Many-Splendored Thing *See* Love Is a Many-Splendored Thing

Mara Maru (Also titled: Maru Maru) (US; Douglas, Gordon; 1952)
BFI/Monthly Film Bulletin. Aug 1952, v19, p111.
Film Daily. Apr 21, 1952, p10.
The Films of Errol Flynn. p176-77.
Hollywood Reporter. Apr 1, 1952, p3.
Motion Picture Herald Product Digest. Apr 5, 1952, p1305.
The New York Times. Apr 24, 1952, p38.
Newsweek. May 12, 1952, v39, p103.
Variety. Apr 2, 1952, p6.

Marat/Sade (Also titled: The Persecution and Assassination of Jean-Paul Marat as Performed by the Inmates of the Asylum of Charenton Under the Direction of the Marquis De Sade) (GB; Brook, Peter; 1967)
America. Mar 4, 1967, v116, p324-25.
BFI/Monthly Film Bulletin. May 1967, v34, p73.
Cinema. Sum 1967, v3, p48-49.
Commonweal. Mar 17, 1967, v85, p682-83.
Film Daily. Feb 7, 1967, p6.
Film Quarterly. Sum 1967, v20, p54-57.
Films and Filming. May 1967, v13, p26-27.
Films in Review. Feb 1967, v18, p115-17.
Hollywood Reporter. Feb 7, 1967, p3.
Magill's Survey of Cinema. Series II. v4, p1530-32.
Motion Picture Herald Product Digest. Mar 1, 1967, p662.
The Nation. Mar 13, 1967, v204, p347.
The New York Times. Feb 23, 1967, p41.
Senior Scholastic. Mar 31, 1967, v90, p28-29.
Variety. Feb 8, 1967, p6.
The Village Voice. Mar 9, 1967, p27, 30.
Vogue. Mar 1, 1967, v149, p112.

Marathon Man (US; Schlesinger, John; 1976)
America. Nov 20, 1976, v135, p350.
BFI/Monthly Film Bulletin. Dec 1976, v43, p252-53.
Film Bulletin. Nov-Dec 1976, v45, p42.
Films in Review. Dec 1976, v27, p636.
The Films of Dustin Hoffman. p177-84.
The Films of the Seventies. p141-43.
Hollywood Reporter. Sep 29, 1976, p2.
Independent Film Journal. Oct 11, 1976, v78, p31.

Variety. Dec 23, 1964, p6.
A World on Film. p297-99.

The Marriage of Maria Braun (German title: Ehe der Maria Braun, Die) (WGER; Fassbinder, Rainer Werner; 1979)
America. Nov 24, 1979, v141, p323.
BFI/Monthly Film Bulletin. Aug 1980, v47, p155.
Films in Review. Nov 1979, v30, p567.
German Film and Literature. p276-88.
Hollywood Reporter. Nov 5, 1979, p3.
The International Dictionary of Films and Filmmakers. v1, p140-41.
The Los Angeles Times. Nov 18, 1979, Calendar, p32.
Magill's Survey of Cinema. Foreign Language Films. v4, p1966-69.
The Nation. Oct 27, 1979, v229, p411-12.
The New Republic. Sep 29, 1979, v181, p26.
The New York Times. Oct 21, 1979, SecII, p1.
The New Yorker. Oct 29, 1979, v55, p146.
Newsweek. Oct 29, 1979, v94, p105-06.
Time. Oct 22, 1979, v114, p85-86.

Marriage on the Rocks (US; Donohue, Jack; 1965)
BFI/Monthly Film Bulletin. Nov 1965, v32, p167-68.
Film Daily. Sep 20, 1965, p6.
Films and Filming. Dec 1965, v12, p32.
The Films of Frank Sinatra. p208-11.
Hollywood Reporter. Sep 20, 1965, p3.
Motion Picture Herald Product Digest. Sep 29, 1965, p377, 379.
The New York Times. Sep 16, 1965, np.
The New Yorker. Oct 2, 1965, v41, p212.
Variety. Sep 22, 1965, p6.

A Married Woman *See* Femme Marée, Une

The Married Woman *See* Femme Marée, Une

The Marrying Kind (US; Cukor, George; 1952)
American Mercury. Aug 1952, v75, p93-96.
BFI/Monthly Film Bulletin. Sep 1952, v19, p123-24.
Catholic World. Apr 1952, v175, p64.
Christian Century. Jun 11, 1952, v69, p711.
Commonweal. Mar 28, 1952, v55, p615.
Film Daily. Mar 17, 1952, p10.
Films in Review. Mar 1952, v3, p137.
George Cukor (Phillips). p112-13.
Hollywood Reporter. Mar 12, 1952, p4.
Magill's Survey of Cinema. Series II. v3, p1544-46.
Motion Picture Herald Product Digest. Mar 15, 1952, p1281.
The Nation. Apr 26, 1952, v174, p410.
The New Statesman and Nation. Nov 15, 1952, v44, p575.
The New York Times. Mar 14, 1952, p27.
The New Yorker. Mar 22, 1952, v28, p115.
Newsweek. Mar 24, 1952, v39, p109.
On Cukor. p201-04.
Saturday Review. Mar 22, 1952, v35, p30.
Sight and Sound. Oct-Dec 1952, v22, p79-80.
Sight and Sound. Spr 1955, v24, p186-91.
The Spectator. Nov 7, 1952, v189, p597.
Talking Pictures. p207-10.
The Tatler. Nov 19, 1952, v206, p432.
Theatre Arts. Apr 1952, v36, p40.
Time. Mar 17, 1952, v59, p102.
Variety. Mar 12, 1952, p6.

Marty (US; Mann, Delbert; 1955)
America. Apr 30, 1955, v93, p139.
Catholic World. Apr 1955, v181, p63.
Commentary. Sep 1955, v20, p265-69.
Commonweal. Apr 22, 1955, v62, p77.
Fifty from the Fifties. p195-220.
Film Daily. Mar 21, 1955, p6.
Films and Filming. Aug 1955, v1, n11, p17-18.
Films in Review. Apr 1955, v6, n4, p191-92.
The Films of the Fifties. p167-68.
Hollywood Reporter. Mar 21, 1955, v133, n44, p3.
Life. Apr 11, 1955, v38, p166.
Magill's Survey of Cinema. Series I. v3, p1079-82.
The Nation. Apr 30, 1955, v180, p381.
The New York Times. Sep 12, 1954, SecII, p5.
The New York Times. Mar 20, 1955, SecVI, p36.
The New York Times. Apr 10, 1955, SecII, p5.
The New York Times. Apr 12, 1955, p25.
The New York Times. Apr 17, 1955, SecII, p1.
The New York Times. Jan 8, 1956, SecII, p7.
The New Yorker. Apr 23, 1955, v31, p133-34.
Newsweek. Apr 18, 1955, v45, p100.
Saturday Review. Mar 26, 1955, v38, p25-26.
Sight and Sound. Sum 1955, v25, n1,.
Time. Apr 18, 1955, v65, p106.
Variety. Mar 23, 1955, p6.

Maru Maru *See* Mara Maru

Mary Poppins (US; Stevenson, Robert; 1964)
America. Oct 3, 1964, v111, p390.
BFI/Monthly Film Bulletin. Feb 1965, v32, p20-21.
Boxoffice. Sep 7, 1964, v85, p2858.
Commonweal. Nov 31, 1964, v81, p239.
Dance Magazine. Oct 1964, v38, p30-32.
The Disney Films. p226-31.
Film Daily. Sep 1, 1964, v125, p4.
Films in Review. Nov 1964, v15, p575-76.
The Films of the Sixties. p141-42.
Hollywood Reporter. Aug 28, 1964, v182, p3.
Life. Sep 25, 1964, v57, p28.
Magill's Survey of Cinema. Series II. v4, p1550-53.
Motion Picture Herald Product Digest. Sep 2, 1964, v232, p15.
The New York Times. Sep 25, 1964, p34.
The New Yorker. Oct 3, 1964, v40, p132.
Newsweek. Oct 5, 1964, v64, p112.
Saturday Review. Aug 22, 1964, v47, p22.
Time. Sep 18, 1964, v84, p114.
Variety. Sep 2, 1964, p6.
Walt Disney: A Guide to References and Resources. p97-98.

Mary Queen of Scots (GB; Jarrott, Charles; 1971)
America. Mar 11, 1972, v126, p264.
BFI/Monthly Film Bulletin. May 1972, v39, n460, p97.
Commonweal. Mar 17, 1972, v96, p39.
Films in Review. Jan 1972, v23, n1, p51-52.
Hollywood Reporter. Dec 20, 1971, v219, n13, p3.
The New York Times. Feb 4, 1972, p17.
Time. Jan 10, 1972, v99, p50.
Variety. Dec 22, 1971, p6.

Masculin-Féminin (Also titled: Masculine-Feminine; The Children of Marx and Coca-Cola) (FR, SWED; Godard, Jean-Luc; 1966)
BFI/Monthly Film Bulletin. Aug 1967, v34, p122.
Cahiers du Cinema in English. May 1967, n10, p19-31.

Commonweal. Oct 7, 1966, v85, p21-22.
Dictionary of Films. p212.
Film Comment. Jan-Feb 1980, v16, p9-15.
Film Culture. Fall 1966, n42, p10-11.
Film Quarterly. Sum 1967, v20, p57-60.
Film Society Review. Feb 1968, p15-17.
Filmfacts. Nov 1, 1966, v9, p237-39.
The Films of Jean-Luc Godard. p119-30.
Focus on Godard. p69-72.
Godard and Others: Essays on Film Form. p19-59.
Hollywood Reporter. Oct 13, 1966, p6.
Jean-Luc Godard: A Critical Anthology. p261-73.
Jean-Luc Godard: A Guide to References and Resources. p69-72.
Kiss Kiss Bang Bang. p155-59.
The London Times. Jun 22, 1967, p8.
The London Times. May 10, 1966, p6.
Magill's Survey of Cinema. Foreign Language Films. v4, p1976-81.
Masculine-Feminine: A Film by Jean-Luc Godard. p187-88.
Motion Picture Herald Product Digest. Oct 12, 1966, p613.
The Nation. Oct 10, 1966, v203, p366.
The New Republic. Nov 19, 1966, v155, p24-30.
New Statesman. Jun 23, 1967, v73, p885.
The New Wave (Monaco). p167-72.
The New York Times. Sep 19, 1966, p57.
Newsweek. Feb 14, 1966, v68, p94.
Playboy. Nov 1966, v13, p42.
Sight and Sound. Wint 1966, v36, p44-45.
Sight and Sound. Sum 1966, v35, p113-16.
The Spectator. Jun 30, 1967, v218, p773-74.
Take One. Sep-Oct 1966, v1, p26-27.
Time. Oct 7, 1966, v88, pLA10, 120.
Variety. May 4, 1966, p6.
The Village Voice. Oct 6, 1966, v11, p27.

Mask (US; Bogdanovich, Peter; 1985)
American Film. Mar 19, 1985, v10, p80.
California Magazine. Apr 1985, v10, p52.
Chatelaine. May 1985, v58, p6.
Christian Century. Apr 24, 1985, v102, p424.
Films in Review. Jun-Jul 1985, v36, p366.
Hollywood Reporter. Apr 25, 1985, p3.
Los Angeles. Apr 1985, v30, p38.
The Los Angeles Times. Mar 7, 1985, SecVI, p1.
Maclean's. Mar 18, 1985, v98, p55.
Magill's Cinema Annual, 1986. p231-35.
The Nation. May 11, 1985, v240, p568.
New Statesman. Jun 28, 1985, v109, p32.
New York. Mar 18, 1985, v18, p81.
The New York Times. May 5, 1985, SecII, p17.
Newsweek. Mar 4, 1985, v105, p74.
Playboy. May 1985, v32, p36.
Savvy. Apr 1985, v6, p102.
Time. Apr 22, 1985, v65, p1.
Variety. Feb 27, 1985, v318, p14.
Washingtonian. May 1985, v20, p74.
Washingtonian. Apr 1985, v20, p60.
Whole Earth Review. May 1985, p80.

The Masque of the Red Death (US; Corman, Roger; 1964)
BFI/Monthly Film Bulletin. Aug 1964, v31, p116-17.
Boxoffice. Jun 8, 1964, v85, p2834.
Film Daily. May 25, 1964, v124, p10.
Films and Filming. Aug 1964, v10, p24.
The Films of Roger Corman. p178-81.
Great Horror Movies. p87-89.
Hollywood Reporter. Jun 24, 1964, v181, p3.
Motion Picture Herald Product Digest. Jun 10, 1964, v231, p67.
The New York Times. Sep 17, 1964, p52.

Newsweek. Jun 29, 1964, v63, p87-88.
Variety. Jun 24, 1964, p7.

Masquerade (GB; Dearden, Basil; 1965)
America. May 29, 1965, v112, p809.
BFI/Monthly Film Bulletin. May 1965, v32, p76-77.
Christian Science Monitor (Western edition). Jun 8, 1965, p12.
Cinema. Aug 1965, v3, p50.
Cinema. Jul-Aug 1964, v2, p49-50.
Commonweal. May 21, 1965, v82, p292.
Film Daily. Apr 29, 1965, p6.
Film Quarterly. Sum 1965, v18, p60.
Filmfacts. Jun 25, 1965, v8, p118-20.
Films and Filming. May 1965, v11, p25.
Films in Review. May 1965, v16, p311.
Hollywood Reporter. Apr 29, 1965, p3.
Life. May 21, 1965, v58, p15.
The London Times. Apr 15, 1965, p17.
Motion Picture Herald Product Digest. Apr 28, 1965, p274-75.
The New York Times. Apr 29, 1965, p40.
The New Yorker. May 22, 1965, v41, p168.
Playboy. Jul 1965, v12, p28.
Time. May 14, 1965, v85, p106.
Variety. Apr 21, 1965, p7.

Mass Appeal (US; Jordan, Glenn; 1984)
America. Feb 2, 1985, v152, p90.
BFI/Monthly Film Bulletin. Jun 1985, v52, p185.
Commonweal. Jan 25, 1985, v112, p51.
Esquire. Jan 1985, v103, p113.
Hollywood Reporter. Dec 4, 1984, p3.
Los Angeles. Dec 1984, v29, p32.
The Los Angeles Times. Dec 13, 1984, SecVI, p9.
Maclean's. Feb 18, 1985, v98, p57.
The New Republic. Jan 28, 1985, v192, p22.
The New York Times. Dec 17, 1984, SecIII, p12.
Playboy. Jun 1985, v32, p38.
Saturday Review. Apr 1985, v11, p78.
Savvy. Feb 1985, v6, p91.
Time. Dec 24, 1984, v124, p65.
Variety. Dec 12, 1984, p1.
Washingtonian. Feb 1985, v20, p54.

Master of the World (US; Whitney, William; 1961)
America. Sep 23, 1961, v105, p811.
BFI/Monthly Film Bulletin. Oct 1961, v28, p143-44.
Film Daily. Apr 28, 1961, p6.
Filmfacts. Sep 22, 1961, v4, p208-09.
The New York Times. Sep 16, 1961, p9.
Time. Sep 22, 1961, v78, p116.
Variety. May 3, 1961, p6.

The Mating Season (US; Leisen, Mitchell; 1951)
BFI/Monthly Film Bulletin. Mar 1951, v18, p234.
Christian Century. Apr 25, 1951, v68, p543.
Commonweal. Apr 27, 1951, v54, p59.
Film Daily. Jan 12, 1951, p6.
Holiday. Jul 1951, v10, p6.
Hollywood Director. p285-88.
Hollywood Reporter. Jan 10, 1951, p3.
The London Times. Feb 12, 1951, p6.
Motion Picture Herald Product Digest. Jan 13, 1951, p661.
The New York Times. Apr 12, 1951, p41.
Newsweek. Apr 30, 1951, v37, p83.
Saturday Review. Mar 17, 1951, v34, p34.
The Spectator. Feb 9, 1951, v186, p177.
Time. Mar 26, 1951, v57, p100.
Variety. Jan 10, 1951, p13.

Matrimonio all'Italiana *See* Marriage Italian Style

A Matter of Resistance *See* Vie de Chateau, La

Max Dugan Returns (US; Ross, Herbert; 1983)
Films and Filming. Aug 1983, n347, p36.
Hollywood Reporter. Mar 21, 1983, p4.
The Los Angeles Times. Mar 29, 1983, SecVI, p1.
Magill's Cinema Annual, 1984. p228-30.
The New Republic. Apr 25, 1983, v188, p22.
New York. Apr 11, 1983, v16, p74-75.
The New York Times. Mar 29, 1983, SecIII, p8.
Newsweek. Mar 28, 1983, v101, p73.

Maytime in Mayfair (GB; Wilcox, Herbert; 1949)
Film Daily. May 8, 1952, p6.
Hollywood Reporter. May 5, 1952, p4.
Motion Picture Herald Product Digest. Apr 26, 1952, p1329.
The New York Times. Apr 23, 1952, p23.
Variety. Jun 1, 1949, p11.

McCabe & Mrs. Miller (US; Altman, Robert; 1971)
America. Sep 11, 1971, v125, p153.
Atlantic. Sep 1971, v228, p109-11.
BFI/Monthly Film Bulletin. Mar 1972, v39, n458, p53.
Commonweal. Aug 6, 1971, v94, p408.
Film Library Quarterly. Wint 1971-72, v6, n1, p14-21.
Film Quarterly. Wint 1971, v25, p49-53.
Film Society Review. Sep 1971, v7, n1, p43.
Filmfacts. 1971, v14, n9, p189-93.
Films and Filming. Apr 1972, v18, n7, p55-56.
Films in Review. Aug-Sep 1971, v22, n7, p440-41.
The Films of Robert Altman. p65-74.
The Films of Warren Beatty. p155-64.
Focus on Film. Spr 1972, n9, p8-9.
Hollywood Reporter. Jun 25, 1971, v216, n42, p3.
Life. Sep 17, 1971, v71, p15.
Look. Aug 10, 1971, v35, p44.
Magill's Survey of Cinema. Series II. v4, p1477.
National Review. Oct 22, 1971, v23, p1191.
The New Republic. Sep 4, 1971, v165, p33.
The New York Times. Jun 25, 1971, p18.
The New York Times. Jul 25, 1971, SecII, p1.
The New Yorker. Jul 3, 1971, v47, p40-42.
Newsweek. Jul 5, 1971, v78, p71-72.
Newsweek. Aug 2, 1971, v78, p9.
Robert Altman: A Guide to References and Resources. p42-44.
Robert Altman: American Innovator. p111-24.
Robert Altman (Plecki). p35-48.
Saturday Review. Jul 24, 1971, v54, p51.
Saturday Review. Aug 7, 1971, v54, p31.
Sight and Sound. Aut 1971, v40, n4, p221.
Take One. Jul-Aug 1970, v2, n12, p19-20.
Take One. Nov-Dec 1970, v3, n2, p4.
Time. Jul 26, 1971, v98, p51.
Variety. Jun 30, 1971, p22.
The Village Voice. Dec 2, 1971, v16, n48, p79.
The Village Voice. Jul 8, 1971, v16, n27, p49.

McQ (US; Sturges, John; 1974)
BFI/Monthly Film Bulletin. Apr 1974, v41, p76.
Commonweal. Mar 8, 1974, v100, p12-13.
The Complete Films of John Wayne. p301-04.
Films and Filming. Mar 1974, v20, p28.
Films in Review. Mar 1974, v25, p184-85.
Independent Film Journal. Feb 4, 1974, v73, p9-10.

The Los Angeles Times. Feb 1, 1974, SecIV, p11.
Motion Picture Herald Product Digest. Feb 13, 1974, p74.
New York. Feb 11, 1974, v7, p74-75.
The New York Times. Mar 10, 1974, SecII, p1.
The New Yorker. Feb 11, 1974, v49, p96.
PTA Magazine. Apr 1974, v68, p5.
Rolling Stone. Mar 14, 1974, p71.
Variety. Jan 23, 1974, p14.
The Village Voice. Feb 14, 1974, p68.

Me and the Colonel (US; Glenville, Peter; 1958)
America. Sep 6, 1958, v99, p609-10.
BFI/Monthly Film Bulletin. Dec 1958, v25, p151.
Catholic World. Oct 1958, v188, p64.
Commonweal. Sep 19, 1958, v68, p616.
Film Daily. Aug 6, 1958, v114, p4.
Filmfacts. Oct 8, 1958, v1, p155-56.
Films in Review. Oct 1958, v9, p458-59.
Hollywood Reporter. Aug 6, 1958, p3.
Library Journal. Oct 1, 1958, v83, p2741.
The New Republic. Oct 13, 1958, v139, p21.
The New York Times. Aug 27, 1958, p33.
The New Yorker. Sep 6, 1958, v34, p21.
Newsweek. Sep 1, 1958, v52, p57.
Saturday Review. Aug 30, 1958, v40, p23.
Time. Sep 1, 1958, v72, p60.
Variety. Aug 6, 1958, p7.

Me, Natalie (US; Coe, Fred; 1969)
Film Daily. Jul 18, 1969, p4.
Filmfacts. 1969, v12, p382.
Films and Filming. Nov 1969, v16, p42-43.
Hollywood Reporter. Jul 7, 1969, p3.
Look. Aug 26, 1969, v33, p14.
The New York Times. Jul 14, 1969, p27.
Saturday Review. Aug 2, 1969, v52, p18.
Variety. Jul 16, 1969, p28.

The Mean Season (US; Borsos, Philip; 1985)
BFI/Monthly Film Bulletin. Mar 1985, v2, p158.
Commonweal. Mar 27, 1985, v112, p180-81.
Horizon. Mar 1985, v28, p17-20.
The Los Angeles Times. Feb 14, 1985, SecVI, p1.
Maclean's. Feb 25, 1985, v98, p62.
New York. Mar 4, 1985, v18, p98.
The New York Times. Feb 15, 1985, SecIII, p10.
The New York Times. Mar 3, 1985, SecIII, p17.
The New Yorker. Mar 11, 1985, v61, p106-07.
Newsweek. Feb 25, 1985, v105, p85.
Time. Feb 25, 1985, v125, p96.
Variety. Feb 13, 1985, p19.

Mean Streets (US; Scorsese, Martin; 1973)
Atlantic. Dec 1973, v232, p132-34.
BFI/Monthly Film Bulletin. May 1974, v41, p102-3.
Magill's Survey of Cinema. Series II. v4, p1554.
Martin Scorsese and Michael Cimino. p51-63.
The Nation. Nov 5, 1973, v217, p477.
The New Republic. Oct 27, 1973, v169, p22.
New Statesman. Apr 12, 1974, v87, p524.
The New York Review of Books. Feb 7, 1974, v21, p18-22.
The New York Times. Oct 3, 1973, p38.
The New York Times. Oct 14, 1973, SecII, p1.
The New York Times. Oct 21, 1973, SecII, p1.
The New York Times. Dec 30, 1973, SecII, p11.
The New York Times. Jan 6, 1974, SecII, p1.
The New York Times. Jan 7, 1974, p38.
The New York Times. Jan 9, 1974, p24.
The New York Times. Jan 20, 1974, SecII, p1.
The New Yorker. Oct 8, 1973, v49, p157-62.
Newsweek. Oct 22, 1973, v82, p125.

Penthouse. 1974, v5, p35-36.
PTA Magazine. Dec 1973, v68, p4.
Sight and Sound. Wint 1973-1974, v43, p48-50.
Social Policy. Jan-Feb 1974, v4, p59-60.
Time. Nov 5, 1973, II v102, p100.
Variety. Oct 3, 1973, p15.
The Village Voice. May 23, 1974, p105.

Meatballs (CAN; Reitman, Ivan; 1979)
BFI/Monthly Film Bulletin. Feb 1980, v47, p24-25.
Hollywood Reporter. Jun 28, 1979, p3.
The Los Angeles Times. Jul 8, 1979, Calendar, p26.
Motion Picture Herald Product Digest. Jul 18, 1979, p16.
The New York Times. Jul 3, 1979, SecIII, p10.
Variety. Jun 27, 1979, p18.

Medicin Malgre Lui, Le *See* Three On a Couch

The Medium (IT, US; Menotti, Gian-Carlo; 1951)
BFI/Monthly Film Bulletin. May 1953, v20, p69.
Commonweal. Sep 14, 1951, v54, p550.
Film Daily. Sep 17, 1951, p12.
Films in Review. Jun-Jul 1951, v2, p40.
Hollywood Reporter. Jan 15, 1952, p3.
Kiss Kiss Bang Bang. p385.
Library Journal. Sep 1, 1951, v76, p1344.
Motion Picture Herald Product Digest. Sep 15, 1951, p1013-14.
Musical America. Apr 15, 1951, v71, p21.
The New Republic. Oct 22, 1951, v125, p21.
The New Statesman and Nation. Mar 28, 1953, v45, p368.
The New York Times. Apr 8, 1951, p60.
The New Yorker. Sep 1, 1951, v27, p43.
Newsweek. Sep 17, 1951, v38, p91.
Saturday Review. Sep 8, 1951, v34, p36.
Saturday Review. Feb 12, 1955, v38, p43.
Sight and Sound. Jul-Sep 1953, v23, p33-34.
The Spectator. Mar 27, 1953, v190, p373-74.
The Tatler. Apr 8, 1953, v209, p74.
Theatre Arts. Oct 1951, v35, p32-33.
Time. Sep 24, 1951, v58, p104.
Variety. Sep 12, 1951, p6.

Medium Cool (US; Wexler, Haskell; 1969)
America. Sep 20, 1969, v121, p203.
Atlantic. Nov 1969, v124, p203.
Big Screen, Little Screen. p241-43.
Christian Century. Nov 19, 1969, v86, p1487.
Commonweal. Sep 5, 1969, v90, p545.
Figures of Light. p192-96.
Film 69/70. p165-72.
Film Daily. Jul 25, 1969, p6.
Film Quarterly. Wint 1969-70, v23, p47-56.
Filmfacts. 1969, v12, p313.
Films and Filming. Apr 1970, v16, p45-46.
The Films of the Sixties. p281.
Focus. Oct 1969, n5, p19-20.
Holiday. Oct 1969, v46, p50.
Journal of Popular Culture. Spr 1971, v4, p933-41.
Life. Aug 15, 1969, v67, p14.
Look. Sep 23, 1969, v33, p65.
Mademoiselle. Oct 1969, v69, p54.
Magill's Survey of Cinema. Series II. v4, p1557-60.
Movies Into Film. p76-81.
The Nation. Sep 29, 1969, v109, p326.
The New Republic. Sep 20, 1969, v161, p20.
The New York Times. Aug 28, 1969, p46.
The New York Times. Aug 31, 1969, SecII, p1.
The New Yorker. Sep 13, 1969, v45, p143-44.
Newsweek. Sep 1, 1969, v74, p66.
Saturday Review. Sep 6, 1969, v52, p43-44.
Second Sight. p247-49.

Sight and Sound. Spr 1970, v39, p100-01.
Time. Aug 22, 1969, v94, p62.
Variety. Jul 30, 1969, p6.
Vogue. Oct 15, 1969, v154, p56.

Meet Danny Wilson (US; Pevney, Joseph; 1951)
Catholic World. Dec 1951, v174, p222.
Christian Century. May 28, 1952, v69, p655.
Film Daily. Jan 23, 1952, p7.
The Films of Frank Sinatra. p71-74.
Hollywood Reporter. Jan 11, 1952, p3.
The New York Times. Mar 27, 1952, p34.
Newsweek. Mar 10, 1952, v39, p102.
The Spectator. Nov 9, 1951, v187, p600-01.
Time. Feb 25, 1952, v59, p68.
Variety. Jan 16, 1952, p6.

Meet Me After the Show (US; Sale, Richard; 1951)
BFI/Monthly Film Bulletin. Oct 1951, v18, p349.
Christian Century. Dec 12, 1951, v68, p1447.
Film Daily. Aug 7, 1951, p6.
Hollywood Reporter. Aug 3, 1951, p3.
Motion Picture Herald Product Digest. Aug 4, 1951, p965.
The New York Times. Aug 16, 1951, p23.
Newsweek. Aug 20, 1951, v38, p87.
Time. Aug 27, 1951, v58, p102.
Variety. Aug 3, 1951, p6.

Meet Me At the Fair (US; Sirk, Douglas; 1952)
Catholic World. Feb 1952, v176, p385.
Commonweal. Apr 3, 1953, v57, p650.
Film Daily. Dec 12, 1952, p7.
Hollywood Reporter. Dec 5, 1952, p3.
Library Journal. Jan 15, 1953, v78, p141.
Motion Picture Herald Product Digest. Dec 13, 1952, p1637.
National Parent-Teacher. Feb 1953, v47, p36.
Sirk on Sirk. p87-88.
Time. Jan 26, 1953, v61, p98.
Variety. Dec 10, 1952, p6.

Meet Me Tonight *See* Tonight at 8:30

Meet the Nelsons *See* Here Come the Nelsons

Meet Whiplash Willie *See* The Fortune Cookie

Mélodie du Bonheur, La *See* The Sound of Music

Mélodie en Sous-Sol *See* Any Number Can Win

Melvin and Howard (US; Demme, Jonathan; 1980)
BFI/Monthly Film Bulletin. Jul 1980, v47, p136.
The Christian Science Monitor. Apr 2, 1980, p18.
Film Comment. Sep 1980, v16, p56.
Film Quarterly. Fall 1980, v34, p32.
Hollywood Reporter. Sep 8, 1980, p2.
Horizon. Dec 1980, v23, p70.
The Los Angeles Times. Mar 21, 1980, SecVI, p8.
Magill's Cinema Annual, 1982. p453-57.
Motion Picture Herald Product Digest. Dec 3, 1980, p50.
The Nation. Nov 15, 1980, v231, p524.
The New Republic. Nov 8, 1980, v183, p22.
New York. Nov 3, 1980, v13, p80.
The New York Times. Mar 21, 1980, SecIII, p8.
The New Yorker. Oct 13, 1980, v56, p174.
Newsweek. Sep 29, 1980, v96, p78.
Time. Oct 20, 1980, v116, p90.

Variety. Mar 19, 1980, p28.
The Village Voice. Mar 31, 1980, p48.

The Member of the Wedding (US; Zinnemann, Fred; 1952)
BFI/Monthly Film Bulletin. Apr 1952, v20, p47-48.
Christian Century. Mar 25, 1953, v70, p367.
Commonweal. Jan 30, 1953, v57, p424.
Cue. Jan 3, 1953, p25.
Film Daily. Dec 18, 1952, p6.
Film News. Jan-Feb 1979, v36, p28.
Films in Review. Feb 1953, v4, p95-96.
Hollywood Reporter. Dec 15, 1952, p3.
Kiss Kiss Bang Bang. p385-87.
Library Journal. Jan 15, 1953, v78, p141.
Literature/Film Quarterly. Wint 1976, v4, p28-38.
The London Times. Feb 22, 1954, p4.
Magill's Survey of Cinema. Series II. v3, p1561-64.
McCall's. Mar 1953, v80, p11.
Motion Picture Herald Product Digest. Dec 20, 1952, p1645-46.
The Nation. Jan 31, 1953, v176, p105.
National Parent-Teacher. Feb 1953, v47, p38.
The New Statesman and Nation. Feb 27, 1954, v47, p251-52.
The New York Times. Dec 31, 1952, p10.
The New Yorker. Jan 3, 1953, v28, p35.
Newsweek. Jan 12, 1953, v41, p76.
Saturday Review. Jan 10, 1953, v36, p31.
Selected Film Criticism, 1951-1960. p75-76.
Sight and Sound. Apr-Jun 1953, v22, p196-97.
Sight and Sound. Spr 1957, v26, p191-95.
The Spectator. Feb 19, 1954, v192, p201.
Stanley Kramer, Film Maker. p131-40.
The Tatler. Jul 29, 1953, v209, p211.
The Tatler. Mar 3, 1954, v211, p362.
Theatre Arts. Mar 1953, v37, p85.
Time. Dec 29, 1952, v60, p64.
Variety. Dec 17, 1952, p6.

Memoires d'un Puceau, Les *See* Benjamin, or The Diary of an Innocent Young Boy

Memories of Underdevelopment (Cuban title: Memorias de Subdesarrollo) (CUBA; Alea, Tomas Gutierrez; 1968)
BFI/Monthly Film Bulletin. Aug 1969, v36, p164.
Cineaste. 1977, v8, n1, p16-21.
Commonweal. Jul 27, 1973, v98, p405-07.
The Cuban Image. p236-48.
Film 73/74. p132-34.
Film Library Quarterly. 1973, v6, n4, p20-23.
Film Quarterly. 1972-73, v26, n2, p56-57.
Film Quarterly. 1976, v29, n2, p45-52.
Films and Filming. Apr 1969, v15, p64, 87-88.
Films and Filming. Sep 1969, v15, p64.
Hollywood Reporter. Jul 19, 1977, p3.
The International Dictionary of Films and Filmmakers. v1, p292-94.
Jump Cut. May-Jun 1974, n1, p9-11.
Jump Cut. Mar 1985, n30, p45-48.
Living Images. p198-200.
The London Times. Jun 3, 1969, p7.
The London Times. May 17, 1969, p91.
The London Times. Jul 10, 1969, p13.
Magill's Survey of Cinema. Foreign Language Films. v5, p2007-13.
Memories of Underdevelopment: The Revolutionary Films of Cuba. p41-107.
The Nation. Jun 11, 1973, v216, p764.
The Nation. Mar 30, 1985, v240, p377-78.
The New Republic. May 19, 1973, v168, p22.
New Statesman. Jul 25, 1969, v78, p125.
The New York Times. Mar 15, 1972, p52.
The New York Times. Apr 2, 1972, p1.

The New York Times. May 18, 1973, p28.
The New York Times. May 20, 1973, p13.
The New Yorker. May 26, 1973, v49, p122.
Newsweek. Apr 17, 1972, v79, p98.
Post Script. 1984, v3, n2, p65-84.
Sight and Sound. Aut 1969, v38, p212-13.
Something to Declare. p153-54.
The Spectator. Jul 19, 1969, v223, p86.
Take One. Jan-Feb 1971, v3, p14-15.
Time. Jul 23, 1973, v102, p80.
Variety. Jun 26, 1968, p6.
The Village Voice. Mar 26, 1985, v30, p45.
Wide Angle. 1980, v4, n2, p52-55.
Women and Film. 1975, v2, n7, p78-79.

The Men (Also titled: Battle Stripe) (US; Zinnemann, Fred; 1950)
BFI/Monthly Film Bulletin. Nov 1950, v17, p168.
Christian Century. Sep 13, 1950, v67, p1087.
Cinema, the Magic Vehicle. v2, p61-62.
Commonweal. Aug 4, 1950, v52, p414.
Dictionary of Films. p215-16.
Film Criticism and Caricatures, 1943-1953. p116-18.
Film Daily. May 19, 1950, p6.
Films in Review. May-Jun 1950, v1, p9-11, 21-23, 38.
The Films of Marlon Brando. p26-33.
Hollywood Reporter. May 19, 1950, p3.
Illustrated London News. Dec 2, 1950, v217, p914.
Magill's Survey of Cinema. Series II. v4, p1565-67.
Motion Picture Herald Product Digest. May 20, 1950, p301.
The Nation. Sep 2, 1950, v171, p213.
The New Republic. Jul 31, 1950, v123, p22.
The New Statesman and Nation. Nov 25, 1950, v40, p502.
The New York Times. Jul 21, 1950, p15.
The New York Times Magazine. May 28, 1950, p45.
The New Yorker. Jul 22, 1950, v26, p45.
Newsweek. Jul 17, 1950, v36, p80.
Saturday Review. Aug 26, 1950, v33, p26-28.
Shots in the Dark. p243-47.
Sight and Sound. Dec 1950, v19, p329-30.
Social Policy. Fall 1982, v13, p24-31.
The Spectator. Nov 17, 1950, v185, p509.
Stanley Kramer, Film Maker. p55-64.
Time. Jul 24, 1950, v56, p78.
Variety. May 24, 1950, p6.

Men of the Fighting Lady (US; Marton, Andrew; 1954)
America. May 22, 1954, v91, p229.
BFI/Monthly Film Bulletin. Nov 1954, v21, p162.
Catholic World. Jul 1954, v179, p304.
Film Daily. May 13, 1954, p5.
Films and Filming. Nov 1954, v1, p19.
Films in Review. Aug-Sep 1954, v5, p365.
Hollywood Reporter. May 10, 1954, p3.
Library Journal. Jun 15, 1954, v79, p1168.
The London Times. Sep 27, 1954, p10.
Motion Picture Herald Product Digest. May 15, 1954, p2293.
The New York Times. May 8, 1954, p15.
The New Yorker. May 15, 1954, v30, p74.
Newsweek. Jun 7, 1954, v43, p56.
Time. May 31, 1954, v63, p72.
Variety. May 12, 1954, p6.

Men Who Tread on the Tiger's Tail *See* Tora-no-o

Mephisto (HUNG; Szabo, Istvan; 1981)
The International Dictionary of Films and Filmmakers. v1, p294-95.

The Los Angeles Times. Mar 26, 1982, SecVI, p1.
Maclean's. Jun 7, 1982, v95, p54-55.
Magill's Cinema Annual 1982. p237-239.
The Nation. Apr 3, 1982, v234, p411-12.
National Review. Jun 25, 1982, v34, p778-79.
The New Republic. Apr 7, 1982, v186, p24-26.
New York. Apr 12, 1982, v15, p61.
The New York Times. Sep 29, 1981, SecIII, p8.
The New Yorker. May 17, 1982, v58, p128-32.
Newsweek. Apr 12, 1982, v99, p87.
Time. May 3, 1982, v119, p73.
Variety. Mar 17, 1982, p26.

The Mephisto Waltz (US; Wendkos, Paul; 1971)
BFI/Monthly Film Bulletin. Aug 1971, v38, n451, p167.
Filmfacts. 1971, v14, n4, p76-78.
Films in Review. May 1971, v22, n5, p313.
Hollywood Reporter. Feb 1, 1971, v214, n4, p3.
The New York Times. Apr 10, 1971, p10.
Time. May 3, 1971, v97, p89.
Variety. Feb 3, 1971, p17.
The Village Voice. Apr 15, 1971, v16, n15, p69.

Mépris, Le *See* Contempt

Merrill's Marauders (US; Fuller, Sam; 1962)
America. Aug 4, 1962, v107, p572.
BFI/Monthly Film Bulletin. Aug 1962, v29, p107.
Commonweal. Jul 22, 1962, v76, p330.
The Director's Event. p164-66.
Film Daily. May 15, 1962, p8.
Filmfacts. Jun 22, 1962, v5, p123-24.
Hollywood Reporter. May 8, 1962, p3.
Motion Picture Herald Product Digest. May 23, 1962, p563.
Movie. Sep 1962, n2, p32.
The New York Times. Jul 14, 1962, p23.
Samuel Fuller (Hardy). p73-85.
Time. Jul 8, 1962, v79, p66.
Variety. May 9, 1962, p6.

Merry Christmas, Mr. Lawrence (GB, JAPAN; Oshima, Nagisa; 1983)
American Film. Sep 1983, v8, p26.
Christianity Today. Oct 7, 1983, v27, p99.
Films in Review. Nov 1983, v34, p569.
Hollywood Reporter. Aug 26, 1987, p3.
The Los Angeles Times. Aug 25, 1983, SecVI, p1.
Maclean's. Oct 3, 1983, v96, p62.
Magill's Cinema Annual, 1984. p231-35.
The Nation. Oct 8, 1983, v237, p316.
The New Republic. Oct 3, 1983, v189, p22-23.
New York. Sep 12, 1983, v16, p80.
The New York Times. Aug 26, 1983, SecIII, p10.
Newsweek. Sep 12, 1983, v102, p88.
Time. Sep 12, 1983, v122, p70.

The Merry Widow (US; Bernhardt, Curtis; 1952)
BFI/Monthly Film Bulletin. Oct 1952, v19, p144.
Catholic World. Oct 1952, v176, p62.
Christian Century. Oct 1, 1952, v69, p1143.
Dictionary of Films. p216-17.
Film Daily. Jul 8, 1952, p6.
Films in Review. Aug-Sep 1952, v3, p357-58.
The Films of Lana Turner. p173-77.
Holiday. Oct 1952, v12, p24.
Hollywood Reporter. Jul 8, 1952, p3.
Motion Picture Herald Product Digest. Jul 12, 1952, p1441.
National Parent-Teacher. Oct 1952, v47, p37.
The New York Times. Sep 25, 1952, p38.
Newsweek. Oct 13, 1952, v40, p103.

Saturday Review. Sep 27, 1952, v35, p28.
The Spectator. Oct 10, 1952, v189, p469.
Time. Sep 8, 1952, v60, p106.
Variety. Jul 9, 1952, p6.

Meshi *See* Repast

Messer Im Kopf *See* Knife in the Head

Metamorphose des Cloportes, Le *See* Cloportes

The Metamorphosis of Bugs *See* Cloportes

Meteor (US; Neame, Ronald; 1979)
BFI/Monthly Film Bulletin. Jan 1980, v47, p9.
The Films of Henry Fonda. p246.
Hollywood Reporter. Oct 17, 1979, p3.
The Los Angeles Times. Oct 19, 1979, SecIV, p22.
Motion Picture Herald Product Digest. Oct 31, 1979, p44.
The New York Times. Oct 19, 1979, v3, p6.
Time. Nov 19, 1979, v114, p110.
Variety. Oct 17, 1979, p10.

Meurtier, Le *See* Enough Rope

A Mezzanatte Va la Ronda del Piacere *See* Immortal Bachelor

The Miami Story (US; Sears, Fred F.; 1954)
America. May 29, 1954, v91, p259.
BFI/Monthly Film Bulletin. Jul 1954, v21, p106.
Commonweal. May 14, 1954, v60, p144.
Farm Journal. Jun 1954, v78, p141.
Film Daily. May 11, 1954, p6.
Hollywood Reporter. Mar 31, 1954, p3.
Motion Picture Herald Product Digest. Apr 10, 1954, p2254.
National Parent-Teacher. May 1954, v48, p39.
The New York Times. May 15, 1954, p13.
Newsweek. May 24, 1954, v43, p95.
Saturday Review. May 8, 1954, v37, p26.
Time. May 17, 1954, v63, p90.
Variety. Mar 31, 1954, p6.

Mickey One (US; Penn, Arthur; 1965)
Arthur Penn: A Guide to References and Resources. p8, 36-38.
Arthur Penn (Wood). p42-51.
BFI/Monthly Film Bulletin. Jul 1966, v33, p104-05.
Cinema. Dec 1965, v3, p50.
Commonweal. Oct 22, 1965, v83, p99-100.
Esquire. Dec 1965, v64, p90, 94.
Film Daily. Sep 27, 1965, p3.
Film Quarterly. Wint 1967-68, v21, p41-48.
Films and Filming. Jul 1966, v12, p7, 13.
Films in Review. Nov 1965, v16, p582.
The Films of the Sixties. p156-57.
The Films of Warren Beatty. p101-13.
Hollywood Reporter. Sep 27, 1965, p3.
The London Times. Sep 8, 1965, p13.
The London Times. Nov 24, 1966, p7.
Magill's Survey of Cinema. Series II. v4, p1571-73.
Modernism in the Narrative Cinema. p40-55.
Motion Picture Herald Product Digest. Sep 29, 1965, p377.
The Nation. Oct 18, 1965, v201, p259.
The New Republic. Oct 9, 1965, v153, p29-30.
The New York Times. Sep 9, 1965, p36.
The New Yorker. Oct 2, 1965, v41, p211-12.
Newsweek. Oct 4, 1965, v66, p94.
Playboy. Dec 1965, v12, p38, 40.
Saturday Review. Oct 16, 1965, v48, p63.
Screen. May-Jun 1969, v10, p60-71.
Time. Oct 8, 1965, v86, pLA8.
Tynan Right and Left. p238.

Variety. Sep 8, 1965, p6.
The Village Voice. Sep 30, 1965, v10, p19, 33.

Middle Age Crazy (CAN; Trent, John; 1980)
BFI/Monthly Film Bulletin. Apr 1981, v48, p72.
Films in Review. Oct 1980, v31, p505.
Hollywood Reporter. Jul 11, 1980, p2.
The Los Angeles Times. Aug 14, 1980, SecVI, p1.
Maclean's. Sep 29, 1980, v93, p62.
Motion Picture Herald Product Digest. Sep 3, 1980, p25.
The New York Times. Oct 18, 1980, p13.
Newsday. Aug 15, 1980, SecIII, p7.
Time. Sep 15, 1980, v116, p101.
Variety. May 28, 1980, p44.
Vogue. Aug 1980, v170, p38.

Middle of the Night (US; Mann, Delbert; 1959)
America. Jul 4, 1959, v101, p497-98.
BFI/Monthly Film Bulletin. Jul 1959, v26, p83.
Catholic World. Aug 1959, v189, p393-94.
Commonweal. Jul 31, 1959, v70, p398.
Coronet. Aug 1959, v46, p18.
Film Daily. May 20, 1959, v115, p6.
Filmfacts. Jul 29, 1959, v2, p141-43.
Films in Review. Aug-Sep 1959, v10, p421-22.
The Films of Fredric March. p222.
Hollywood Reporter. May 10, 1959, p3.
Library Journal. Jun 15, 1959, p2054.
The New Republic. Jun 8, 1959, v140, p21-22.
The New York Times. Jun 27, 1959, p6.
The New Yorker. Jun 27, 1959, v35, p54.
Newsweek. Jun 22, 1959, v53, p91.
Saturday Review. May 30, 1959, v42, p27.
Time. Jun 29, 1959, v73, p62.
Variety. May 20, 1959, p6.

Midnight Cowboy (US; Schlesinger, John; 1969)
America. Jun 28, 1969, v120, p737-38.
Big Screen, Little Screen. p185-87.
Christian Century. Oct 29, 1969, v86, p1400-02.
Commonweal. Jun 20, 1969, v90, p393-94.
Esquire. Oct 1969, v72, p14.
Figures of Light. p170-74.
Film Daily. May 20, 1969, p6.
Film Quarterly. Fall 1969, v23, p20-22.
Filmfacts. 1969, v12, p169.
Films in Review. Aug-Sep 1969, v20, p447.
Journal of Popular Culture. Sum 1970, v4, p273-85.
Journal of Popular Culture. Spr 1971, v4, p933-41.
Look. Jun 24, 1969, v33, p200.
Mademoiselle. Sep 1969, v69, p74.
Magill's Survey of Cinema. Series I. v3, p1095-97.
Marshall Delaney At the Movies. p129-31.
Movies Into Film. p357-60, 401-02.
The Nation. Jun 16, 1969, v108, p774.
The New Republic. Jun 7, 1969, v160, p20.
The New York Times. May 26, 1969, p54.
The New Yorker. May 31, 1969, v65, p80.
The New Yorker. Sep 27, 1969, v65, p127.
Newsweek. Jun 2, 1969, v73, p90.
Newsweek. Jul 28, 1969, v74, p85.
Saturday Review. May 31, 1969, v52, p44.
Second Sight. p237-39.
Sight and Sound. Aut 1969, v38, p211-12.
Time. May 30, 1969, v93, p89.
Variety. May 14, 1969, p6.
Vogue. Jul 1969, v154, p52.

Midnight Express (US; Parker, Alan; 1978)
BFI/Monthly Film Bulletin. Jul 1978, v45, p139.
Films in Review. Dec 1978, v29, p635.

Hollywood Reporter. May 18, 1978, p4.
The Los Angeles Times. Oct 25, 1978, SecIV, p1.
Maclean's. Nov 6, 1978, v91, p66.
Magill's Survey of Cinema. Series II. v4, p1578-81.
Motion Picture Herald Product Digest. Oct 18, 1978, p38.
New York. Oct 16, 1978, v11, p122-23.
The New Yorker. Nov 27, 1978, v54, p182.
Newsweek. Oct 16, 1978, v92, p76.
Rolling Stone. Nov 30, 1978, p18.
Time. Oct 16, 1978, v112, p111-12.
Variety. May 24, 1978, p27.

Midnight Lace (US; Miller, David; 1960)
America. Oct 29, 1960, v104, p158.
BFI/Monthly Film Bulletin. Jan 1961, v28, p10.
Commonweal. Oct 21, 1960, v73, p96.
Film Daily. Oct 18, 1960, p6.
Filmfacts. 1960, v3, p266.
Films and Filming. Feb 1961, v7, p31-32.
The Films of Doris Day. p193-98.
The Films of Myrna Loy. p248.
Hollywood Reporter. Oct 14, 1960, p3.
Life. Oct 10, 1960, v49, p136A-136B.
Magill's Survey of Cinema. Series II. v4, p1582-86.
McCall's. Dec 1960, v88, p180.
The New York Times. Oct 14, 1960, p27.
The New Yorker. Oct 29, 1960, v36, p103.
Newsweek. Oct 24, 1960, v56, p131.
Saturday Review. Oct 22, 1960, v43, p23.
Time. Oct 24, 1960, v76, p102.
Variety. Oct 19, 1960, p6.

The Midnight Man (US; Kibbee, Roland; Lancaster, Burt; 1974)
Audience. Aug 1974, v7, p10.
BFI/Monthly Film Bulletin. Jan 1975, v42, p12.
Burt Lancaster: The Man and His Movies. p126-29.
Films in Review. May 1974, v25, p310-11.
Independent Film Journal. Apr 1, 1974, v73, p9-10.
The Los Angeles Times. May 23, 1974, SecIV, p20.
Motion Picture Herald Product Digest. Mar 27, 1974, p86.
Movietone News. Jul 1974, n33, p40.
New York. Jun 17, 1974, v103, p81.
Saturday Review. Jul 13, 1974, v1, p38.
Time. Jun 17, 1974, v103, p81.
Variety. Mar 20, 1974, p19.

A Midsummer Night's Sex Comedy (US; Allen, Woody; 1982)
BFI/Monthly Film Bulletin. Oct 1982, v49, p230-31.
Christian Century. Jun 9, 1982, v99, p708.
Commonweal. Sep 24, 1982, v109, p499-500.
Hollywood Reporter. Jul 14, 1982, p3.
The Los Angeles Times. Aug 12, 1982, SecVI, p1.
Maclean's. Jul 26, 1982, v95, p53.
Magill's Cinema Annual, 1983. p224-27.
The Nation. Sep 11, 1982, v235, p220-21.
National Review. Sep 17, 1982, v34, p1163-64.
The New Leader. Sep 6, 1982, v65, p20.
The New Republic. Aug 16, 1982, v187, p27-28.
New York. Jul 26, 1982, v15, p45-46.
The New York Times. Jul 16, 1982, SecIII, p4.
The New Yorker. Jul 26, 1982, v58, p63-64.
Newsweek. Jul 19, 1982, v100, p70.
Rolling Stone. Sep 2, 1982, p33.
Time. Aug 2, 1982, v120, p78.
Variety. Jul 13, 1982, p78.
Woody Allen: His Films and Career. p213-21.

Midway (US; Smight, Jack; 1976)
BFI/Monthly Film Bulletin. Feb 1977, v44, p19.
Films in Review. Aug-Sep 1976, v27, p439.
The Films of Henry Fonda. p235-36.
Guts & Glory. p295-300.
Hollywood Reporter. Jun 17, 1976, p2.
Independent Film Journal. Jun 25, 1976, v78, p16.
Jump Cut. Dec 30, 1976, n12/13, p13-14.
The Los Angeles Times. Jun 18, 1976, SecIV, p1.
Movietone News. Jun 1976, n50, p45.
New York. Jul 12, 1976, v9, p74.
The New York Times. Jun 19, 1976, p11.
Newsweek. Jun 28, 1976, v87, p78.
Robert Mitchum on the Screen. p228-29.
Time. Jul 12, 1976, v108, p49.
Variety. Jun 9, 1976, p7.
Variety. Jun 16, 1976, p18.
Vogue. Aug 1976, v166, p64.

Mikey and Nicky (US; May, Elaine; 1976)
Before My Eyes. p272-74.
Films in Review. Feb 1977, v28, p119.
Hollywood Reporter. Dec 21, 1976, p3.
The Los Angeles Times. Dec 25, 1976, SecIV, p1.
Magill's Cinema Annual, 1985. p576-80.
Motion Picture Herald Product Digest. Dec 29, 1976, p59.
The New York Times. Dec 17, 1976, SecIII, p10.
The New York Times. Sep 24, 1976, SecIII, p8.
Saturday Review. Jan 22, 1977, v4, p49.
Time. Jan 31, 1977, v109, p59.
Variety. Dec 22, 1976, p20.

The Milkman (US; Annakin, Ken; French, Harold; 1950)
Christian Century. Dec 27, 1950, v67, p1561.
Film Daily. Oct 17, 1950, p5.
Hollywood Reporter. Oct 10, 1950, p3.
The London Times. Sep 4, 1950, p6.
Motion Picture Herald Product Digest. Oct 14, 1950, p518.
The New York Times. Jan 1, 1951, p13.
Time. Dec 11, 1950, v56, p98.
Variety. Oct 11, 1950, p8.

The Miller's Beautiful Wife (French title: Bella Mugnaia, La; Also titled: The Miller's Wife) (IT; Camerini, Mario; 1957)
BFI/Monthly Film Bulletin. Dec 1957, v24, p149.
Commonweal. Jun 28, 1957, v66, p328-29.
Film Daily. Jun 9, 1957, v111, p6.
The New York Times. Jun 12, 1957, p40.
Time. Jun 10, 1957, v69, p98.

Million Dollar Mermaid (Also titled: The One Piece Bathing Suit) (US; LeRoy, Mervyn; 1952)
BFI/Monthly Film Bulletin. Jan 1953, v20, p10.
The Busby Berkeley Book. p168-71.
Catholic World. Dec 1952, v176, p225.
Christian Century. Jan 14, 1953, v70, p63.
Commonweal. Dec 19, 1952, v57, p284.
Film Daily. Nov 10, 1952, p6.
George Cukor (Phillips). p173.
Hollywood Reporter. Oct 31, 1952, p3.
Motion Picture Herald Product Digest. Nov 8, 1952, p1597.
National Parent-Teacher. Feb 1953, v47, p36.
The New York Times. Dec 5, 1952, p35.
The New Yorker. Dec 13, 1952, v28, p153.
Newsweek. Dec 15, 1952, v40, p101.
The Spectator. Dec 19, 1952, v189, p842.
The Tatler. Dec 31, 1952, v206, p730.

Time. Dec 15, 1952, v60, p108.
Variety. Nov 5, 1952, p6.

The Million Pound Note *See* Man With a
Million

The Miniver Story (US; Potter, H. C.;
1950)
BFI/Monthly Film Bulletin. Sep 1950, v17,
p136.
Christian Century. Dec 27, 1950, v67, p1561.
Commonweal. Oct 20, 1950, v53, p40.
Film Daily. Oct 5, 1950, p8.
Hollywood Reporter. Aug 31, 1950, p3.
Library Journal. Nov 1, 1950, v75, p1915.
The London Times. Aug 28, 1950, p6.
Motion Picture Herald Product Digest. Oct 7,
1950, p509-10.
The New York Times. Oct 27, 1950, p24.
The New Yorker. Nov 4, 1950, v26, p139.
Newsweek. Oct 30, 1950, v36, p82.
One Good Film Deserves Another. p47-49.
The Spectator. Aug 25, 1950, v185, p240.
Time. Oct 23, 1950, v56, p100.
Variety. Aug 30, 1950, p6.

Minne (Also titled: Ingénue Libertine, L')
(FR; Audry, Jacqueline; 1950)
BFI/Monthly Film Bulletin. Jul 1951, v18,
p292.
Film Daily. Apr 24, 1951, p6.
The New Republic. Apr 23, 1951, v124, p23.
The New Statesman and Nation. Jun 30, 1951,
v41, p746.
The New York Times. Apr 17, 1951, p35.
The New Yorker. Apr 28, 1951, v27, p95.
Variety. Jun 28, 1950, p18.

Minnie and Moskowitz (US; Cassavetes,
John; 1971)
American Dreaming. p140-87.
BFI/Monthly Film Bulletin. Jun 1972, v39,
n461, p118.
Filmfacts. 1971, v14, n, p690.
Hollywood Reporter. Dec 21, 1971, v219, n14,
p3.
Magill's Survey of Cinema. Series II. v4, p1594-
96.
The Nation. Jan 3, 1972, v214, p27.
The New Republic. Jan 22, 1972, v166, p24.
The New York Times. Dec 23, 1971, p16.
Newsweek. Dec 27, 1971, v78, p62.
Saturday Review. Jan 8, 1972, v55, p19.
Time. Dec 27, 1971, v98, p58.
Variety. Dec 22, 1971, p6.

Minute de Vérité, La *See* The Moment of
Truth

Miquette (FR; Clouzot, Henri-Georges;
1950)
Commonweal. Feb 23, 1951, v53, p496.
Film Daily. Feb 26, 1951, p6.
The New Republic. Feb 26, 1951, v124, p31.
Variety. May 24, 1950, p20.

The Miracle *See* The Ways of Love

Miracle in Milan *See* Miracolo a Milano

The Miracle of Our Lady of Fatima (Also
titled: The Miracle of Fatima) (US;
Brahm, John; 1952)
BFI/Monthly Film Bulletin. Apr 1953, v20,
p55.
Catholic World. Sep 1952, v175, p466.
Christian Century. Nov 12, 1952, v69, p1335.
Commonweal. Aug 29, 1952, v56, p510-11.
Film Daily. Aug 21, 1952, p6.
Hollywood Reporter. Aug 21, 1952, p3.
The London Times. Apr 6, 1953, p9.
Motion Picture Herald Product Digest. Aug 23,
1952, p1501.

National Parent-Teacher. Nov 1953, v47, p37.
The New York Times. Aug 21, 1952, p16.
Newsweek. Aug 25, 1952, v40, p86-87.
Variety. Aug 27, 1952, p6.

The Miracle Worker (US; Penn, Arthur;
1962)
America. Jun 9, 1962, v107, p389-90.
Arthur Penn (Wood). p28-40.
BFI/Monthly Film Bulletin. Aug 1962, v29,
p107-08.
Commonweal. Jun 1, 1962, v76, p258-59.
Film Daily. May 3, 1962, p7.
The Film Director As Superstar. p219-21.
Film News. Mar-Apr 1978, v35, p30-31.
Filmfacts. Jun 1, 1962, v5, p101-03.
Films and Filming. Sep 1962, v8, p29.
Films in Review. Jun-Jul 1962, v13, p356-57.
The Films of the Sixties. p77-79.
Hollywood Reporter. May 2, 1962, p3.
Life. Mar 30, 1962, v52, p89-91.
Magill's Survey of Cinema. Series II. v4, p1601-
03.
Motion Picture Herald Product Digest. May 9,
1962, p549.
Movie. Sep 1962, n2, p35.
Movie. Oct 1962, n3, p27-28.
The New Republic. Jun 4, 1962, v146, p28.
The New York Times. May 24, 1962, p29.
The New Yorker. Jun 2, 1962, v38, p79.
Newsweek. May 28, 1962, v59, p101.
Saturday Review. May 26, 1962, v45, p23.
Saturday Review. Jul 16, 1962, v45, p72.
Screen. Mar-Apr 1969, v10, p69-78.
Time. May 25, 1962, v79, p89.
Variety. May 2, 1962, p6.
The Village Voice. May 31, 1962, p11.

Miracolo a Milano (Also titled: Miracle in
Milan) (IT; De Sica, Vittorio; 1950)
BFI/Monthly Film Bulletin. Dec 1952, v19,
p166-67.
Christian Century. May 21, 1952, v69, p631.
Commonweal. Dec 21, 1951, v55, p278.
Dictionary of Films. p221.
Film Criticism. Wint 1979, v3, p24-27.
Film Criticism and Caricatures, 1943-1953.
p150-51.
Film Daily. Mar 4, 1952, p10.
Film News. May-Jun 1976, v33, p18-19.
Films and Filming. Oct 1964, v11, p15-16.
Films in Review. Apr 1951, v2, p42-43.
Films in Review. May 1951, v2, p26-30.
Hollywood Reporter. Feb 15, 1951, p3.
*The International Dictionary of Films and
Filmmakers.* v1, p300-01.
Italian Cinema (Bondanella). p93-95.
Italian Cinema (Leprohon). p125-30.
Library Journal. Feb 1, 1952, v77, p206.
*Magill's Survey of Cinema. Foreign Language
Films.* v5, p2058-63.
Movie Comedy (Byron). p261.
The Nation. Jan 19, 1952, v174, p65.
The New Republic. Dec 31, 1951, v125, p22.
The New Statesman and Nation. Nov 22, 1952,
v44, p604.
The New York Times. Dec 18, 1951, p42.
The New Yorker. Dec 22, 1951, v27, p62.
The New Yorker. Jul 6, 1957, v33, p35-53.
Newsweek. Jan 7, 1952, v39, p60.
Patterns of Realism. p163-67.
Saturday Review. Dec 15, 1951, v34, p35.
Saturday Review. May 19, 1956, v39, p51.
Sight and Sound. Apr 1951, v19, p480-81.
Sight and Sound. Jun 1951, v20, p41-42.
The Spectator. Nov 21, 1952, v189, p670.
Theatre Arts. Jan 1952, v36, p28-29.
Time. Dec 17, 1951, v58, p102.
Time. Jun 2, 1952, v59, p22.

Variety. Feb 28, 1951, p18.
*Vittorio De Sica: A Guide to References and
Resources.* p57-63.

Miracolo, Il *See* The Ways of Love

Mirage (US; Dmytryk, Edward; 1965)
America. Jun 19, 1965, v112, p887.
BFI/Monthly Film Bulletin. Oct 1965, v32,
p151.
Christian Science Monitor (Western edition).
Jul 14, 1965, p6.
Commonweal. Jun 4, 1965, v82, p357.
Film Daily. May 19, 1965, p14.
Films and Filming. Nov 1965, v12, p28.
Films in Review. Jun-Jul 1965, v16, p382.
The Films of Gregory Peck. p194-96.
Hollywood Reporter. May 19, 1965, p3.
Life. Jun 18, 1965, v58, p15.
Motion Picture Herald Product Digest. May 26,
1965, p290.
The Nation. Feb 21, 1966, v202, p222.
The New Republic. Jun 5, 1965, v152, p25.
The New York Times. May 27, 1965, p28.
The New Yorker. Jun 5, 1965, v41, p118-19.
Saturday Review. Jul 31, 1965, v48, p31.
Time. May 28, 1965, v85, p104.
Variety. May 19, 1965, p6.

The Mirror Cracked (GB; Hamilton, Guy;
1980)
BFI/Monthly Film Bulletin. Feb 1981, v47,
p28.
The Christian Science Monitor. Jan 29, 1981,
p11.
Films in Review. Feb 1981, v31, p119.
Hollywood Reporter. Dec 12, 1980, p3.
Maclean's. Dec 22, 1980, v93, p58.
Motion Picture Herald Product Digest. Dec 17,
1980, p61.
New York. Dec 29, 1980, v14, p48.
The New York Times. Jun 19, 1980, SecIII,
p14.
The New York Times. Dec 18, 1980, SecIII,
p14.
Newsweek. Jun 19, 1981, v97, p80.
Time. Dec 29, 1980, v116, p59.
Variety. Dec 17, 1980, p16.
The Village Voice. Dec 24, 1980, p41.
Vogue. Jan 1981, v171, p27.

Miserables, Les (US; Milestone, Lewis;
1952)
BFI/Monthly Film Bulletin. Oct 1952, v19,
p139-40.
Catholic World. Sep 1952, v175, p464.
Christian Century. Oct 1, 1952, v69, p1143.
Commonweal. Aug 22, 1952, v56, p486.
Film Daily. Jul 28, 1952, p6.
Hollywood Reporter. Jul 22, 1952, p3.
Lewis Milestone (Millichap). p176-77.
Library Journal. Apr 15, 1952, v77, p713.
The London Times. Sep 8, 1952, p8.
Motion Picture Herald Product Digest. Jul 26,
1952, p1462.
National Parent-Teacher. Oct 1952, v47, p36-
37.
The New York Times. Aug 15, 1952, p11.
Newsweek. Aug 18, 1952, v40, p83.
The Spectator. Sep 5, 1952, v189, p295.
Time. Aug 25, 1952, v60, p75.
Variety. Jul 23, 1952, p6.

The Misfits (US; Huston, John; 1961)
BFI/Monthly Film Bulletin. Jul 1961, v28, p92-
93.
Christian Century. Apr 5, 1961, v78, p424-25.
The Cinema of John Huston. p126-30.
Commentary. May 1961, v31, p433-36.
Commonweal. Feb 17, 1961, v73, p532.
Film Daily. Feb 1, 1961, p6.

Film Quarterly. Spr 1961, v14, p51-53.
Filmfacts. Feb 17, 1961, v4, p11-13.
Films and Filming. Jun 1961, v7, p21.
Films in Review. Feb 1961, v7, p102-03.
The Films of Clark Gable. p250-53.
The Films of Marilyn Monroe. p153-58.
The Films of Montgomery Clift. p191-96.
John Huston (Hammen). p97-102.
Magill's Survey of Cinema. Series I. v3, p1117-20.
The Making of the Great Westerns. p299-314.
Modern Photographer. v25, p24-25.
The Nation. Feb 18, 1961, v192, p154-55.
National Review. May 20, 1961, v10, p321.
The New Republic. Feb 20, 1961, v144, p26.
The New York Times. Feb 2, 1961, p24.
The New York Times. Feb 5, 1961, SecII, p1.
The New Yorker. Feb 4, 1961, v36, p86.
Newsweek. Feb 6, 1961, v57, p84.
On Movies. p285-86.
Reporter. Mar 21, 1961, v24, p46-47.
Saturday Review. Feb 1, 1961, v44, p27.
Sight and Sound. Sum 1961, v30, p142-44.
Time. Feb 3, 1961, v77, p68.
Variety. Feb 1, 1961, p6.

Mishima (Also titled: Mishima: A Life in Four Chapters) (US, JAPAN; Schrader, Paul; 1985)
American Film. Mar 1985, v10, p36.
BFI/Monthly Film Bulletin. Sep 1985, v52, p299.
Film Comment. Sep-Oct 1985, v21, p49-50.
Films in Review. Oct 1985, p36, p492.
Hollywood Reporter. May 15, 1985, p3.
The Los Angeles Times. Oct 3, 1985, SecVI, p1.
Maclean's. Sep 16, 1985, v98, p63.
Magill's Cinema Annual, 1986. p237-41.
National Review. Nov 1, 1985, v37, p68-70.
The New Republic. Oct 21, 1985, v193, p24.
New York Review of Books. Oct 10, 1985, v32, p15-17.
The New York Times. Sep 20, 1985, SecIII, p4.
Newsweek. Jun 17, 1985, v105, p89.
Newsweek. Sep 23, 1985, v106, p68.
Theatre Crafts. Oct 1985, v19, p109-12.
Variety. May 15, 1985, p14.
Vogue. Sep 1985, v175, p96.
The Wall Street Journal. Sep 24, 1985, p30.

Miss Julie (Swedish title: Froken Julie) (SWED; Sjoberg, Alf; 1951)
BFI/Monthly Film Bulletin. Jan 1952, v19, p2.
Cinema, the Magic Vehicle. v2, p49-51.
Classics of the Foreign Film. p182-85.
Commonweal. May 2, 1952, v56, p94.
Dictionary of Films. p120-21.
Film Criticism and Caricatures, 1943-1953. p133-34.
Film Daily. May 15, 1952, p6.
Films in Review. May 1952, v3, p242-43.
Hollywood Reporter. Jun 26, 1952, p3.
The International Dictionary of Films and Filmmakers. v1, p163-64.
Library Journal. May 15, 1952, v77, p873.
Magill's Survey of Cinema. Foreign Language Films. v5, p2070-74.
The New Statesman and Nation. Dec 8, 1951, v42, p664, 666.
The New Statesman and Nation. Dec 15, 1951, v42, p706.
The New York Times. Apr 8, 1952, p35.
The New Yorker. Aug 11, 1951, v27, p63.
Newsweek. Apr 28, 1952, v39, p97.
Quarterly of Film, Radio and Television. Sum 1952, v6, p414-20.
Saturday Review. Apr 26, 1952, v35, p28.
Sight and Sound. Jan-Mar 1952, v21, p122-23.
Swedish Film Classics. p77-80.

Theater and Film. p204-15.
Variety. May 16, 1951, p18.

Miss Lonely Hearts *See* Lonelyhearts

Miss Sadie Thompson (US; Bernhardt, Curtis; 1953)
America. Jan 2, 1954, v90, p366.
BFI/Monthly Film Bulletin. Jul 1954, v21, p101.
Catholic World. Feb 1954, v178, p333.
Collier's. Jul 11, 1953, v132, p14-16.
Commonweal. Jan 1, 1954, v59, p331.
Film Daily. Dec 21, 1953, p6.
Films in Review. Jan 1954, v5, p36.
The Films of Rita Hayworth. p192-97.
Hollywood Reporter. Dec 21, 1953, p3.
Library Journal. Jan 1, 1954, v79, p56.
The London Times. May 31, 1954, p3.
Motion Picture Herald Product Digest. Dec 26, 1953, p2117.
National Parent-Teacher. Feb 1954, v48, p39.
The New York Times. Dec 24, 1953, p9.
The New Yorker. Jan 9, 1954, v29, p73.
Newsweek. Dec 28, 1953, v42, p68.
The Tatler. Jun 9, 1954, v212, p586.
Time. Dec 28, 1953, 62, p57.
Variety. Dec 23, 1953, p6.

Missing (US; Costa-Gavras, Constantin; 1982)
America. Apr 3, 1982, v146, p263.
BFI/Monthly Film Bulletin. May 1982, v49, p88-89.
Christian Century. Mar 10, 1982, v99, p260-61.
Commonweal. Apr 9, 1982, v109, p211-12.
Hollywood Reporter. Jan 25, 1982, p3.
The Los Angeles Times. Feb 11, 1982, SecVI, p1.
The Los Angeles Times. Apr 8, 1982, SecVI, p1.
Maclean's. Feb 22, 1982, v95, p56.
Magill's Cinema Annual, 1983. p228-32.
The Nation. Feb 20, 1982, v234, p219-20.
The Nation. Apr 17, 1982, v234, p466-69.
National Review. Mar 5, 1982, v34, p209-10.
National Review. Mar 19, 1982, v34, p308-10.
The New Republic. Feb 17, 1982, v186, p34, p308-10.
The New Republic. Mar 10, 1982, v186, p24-25.
New York. Feb 1, 1982, v15, p44-45.
New York. Feb 22, 1982, v15, p67-68.
The New York Times. Feb 12, 1982, SecIII, p14.
The New Yorker. Mar 8, 1982, v58, p116.
Newsweek. Feb 22, 1982, v99, p69.
Rolling Stone. Apr 15, 1982, p15-18.
Saturday Review. Feb 1982, v9, p88-89.
Time. Feb 15, 1982, v119, p64.
USA Today. May, 1982, v110, p66-67.
Variety. Jan 25, 1982, p3.

The Missionary (GB; Loncraine, Richard; 1982)
Hollywood Reporter. Nov 3, 1982, p3.
The Los Angeles Times. Nov 5, 1982, SecVI, p11.
Maclean's. Nov 1, 1982, v95, p70.
Magill's Cinema Annual, 1983. p233-36.
The New Republic. Nov 29, 1982, v187, p23-24.
New York. Nov 8, 1982, v15, p62.
The New York Times. Nov 5, 1982, SecIII, p7.
Newsweek. Nov 8, 1982, v100, p90.
Variety. Nov 2, 1982, p3.

Mississippi Gambler (US; Maté, Rudolph; 1953)
BFI/Monthly Film Bulletin. Mar 1953, v20, n230, p37.
Commonweal. Mar 6, 1953, v57, p551.
Film Daily. Jan 15, 1953, p13.
The Films of Tyrone Power. p179-82.

Hollywood Reporter. Jan 9, 1953, p3.
National Parent-Teacher. Feb 1953, v47, p38.
The New York Times. Jan 30, 1953, p25.
Newsweek. Feb 9, 1953, v41, p83.
Theatre Arts. Mar 1953, v37, p88.
Time. Feb 9, 1953, v61, p99.
Variety. Jan 14, 1953, p6.

The Missouri Breaks (US; Penn, Arthur; 1976)
America. Jun 5, 1976, v134, p498-99.
Atlantic. Oct 1976, v238, p102.
Atlantic Monthly. Oct 1976, v238, p102.
Before My Eyes. p134-36.
BFI/Monthly Film Bulletin. Aug 1976, v43, p168-69.
Commentary. Jul 1976, v62, p60-61.
Commonweal. Jun 18, 1976, v103, p403-04.
Commonweal. Jul 2, 1976, v103, p436-37.
Film Bulletin. May 1976, v45, pA.
Film Comment. Jul-Aug 1976, v12, p37-40.
Films and Filming. Aug 1976, v22, p33-34.
Films in Review. Aug-Sep 1976, v27, p438-39.
Hi Fi. Oct 1976, v26, p140-41.
Hollywood Reporter. May 18, 1976, p3.
Independent Film Journal. May 28, 1976, v77, p7.
Journal of Popular Film. n2, 1976, v5, p147-55.
The Los Angeles Times. May 21, 1976, SecIV, p17.
Millimeter. Jan 1976, v4, p28-33.
The Missouri Breaks. 1976.
Movietone News. Aug 1976, n51, p38.
Movietone News. Jun 1976, n50, p43-45.
The Nation. May 29, 1976, v222, p670.
The New Republic. Jun 5, 1976, v174, p18-19.
New Statesman. Jul 9, 1976, v92, p56.
The New York Times. Jun 6, 1976, SecII, p13.
The New York Times. May 23, 1976, SecII, p17.
The New Yorker. May 31, 1976, v52, p100-01.
Newsweek. May 24, 1976, v87, p103.
Rolling Stone. Feb 12, 1976, p34-39.
Saturday Review. Jun 12, 1976, v3, p48.
Sight and Sound. Sum 1976, v45, p190-91.
The Thousand Eyes Magazine. Jun 1976, n11, p12.
Time. May 24, 1976, v107, p74.
Times Literary Supplement. Jul 23, 1976, n3190, p46.
Variety. May 19, 1976, p19.
Vogue. Jul 1976, v166, p26.

Mr. Arkadin (Also titled: Confidential File; Confidential Report) (SP; Welles, Orson; 1955)
Cinema Texas Program Notes. Oct 12, 1983, v25, p9-14.
Confessions of a Cultist. p63-65.
Dictionary of Films. p68.
Film Culture. 1956, v2, n3, p27-28.
Film Daily. Oct 22, 1962, p20.
Film Heritage. Fall 1974, v10, p31-36.
Filmfacts. Jan 25, 1963, v5, p351-53.
Films and Filming. Oct 1955, v2, p20.
The Films in My Life. p285-87.
Films in Review. Nov 1962, v13, p557.
Hollywood Reporter. Oct 8, 1962, p3.
Motion Picture Herald Product Digest. Nov 28, 1962, p699.
The New Republic. Oct 8, 1962, v147, p26.
The New York Times. Oct 12, 1962, p26.
The New Yorker. Oct 27, 1962, v38, p204.
Newsweek. Oct 15, 1962, v60, p105.
Sight and Sound. Aut 1955, v25, p86-87.
Sight and Sound. Wint 1981-82, v51, p8.
Variety. Sep 19, 1962, p6.
Variety. May 15, 1956, p6.
The Village Voice. Oct 13, 1962, p13, 17.

Mr. Belvedere Rings the Bell (US; Koster, Henry; 1951)
BFI/Monthly Film Bulletin. Sep 1951, v18, p331.
Christian Century. Dec 19, 1951, v68, p1495.
Commonweal. Aug 24, 1951, v54, p478.
Film Daily. Jul 24, 1951, p6.
Hollywood Reporter. Jul 23, 1951, p3.
The London Times. Sep 24, 1951, p8.
Motion Picture Herald Product Digest. Jul 28, 1951, p945.
The New Statesman and Nation. Sep 22, 1951, v42, p310.
The New York Times. Aug 2, 1951, p18.
The New Yorker. Aug 11, 1951, v27, p69.
Newsweek. Aug 13, 1951, v38, p80.
Saturday Review. Aug 25, 1951, v34, p24.
The Spectator. Sep 21, 1951, v187, p360.
Time. Aug 27, 1951, v58, p106.
Variety. Jul 25, 1951, p6.

Mister Buddwing (Also titled: Woman Without a Face) (US; Mann, Delbert; 1966)
America. Oct 15, 1966, v115, p468.
Film Daily. Sep 29, 1966, p4.
Filmfacts. Dec 1, 1966, v9, p274-75.
Films and Filming. Feb 1969, v15, p49.
Hollywood Reporter. Sep 14, 1966, p3.
Motion Picture Herald Product Digest. Sep 14, 1966, p596.
The New Republic. Oct 22, 1966, v155, p34.
The New York Times. Oct 12, 1966, p36.
Playboy. Nov 1966, v13, p40, 42.
Saturday Review. Oct 29, 1966, v49, p45.
Variety. Sep 14, 1966, p6.
The Village Voice. Nov 3, 1966, v12, p31.

Mister 880 (US; Goulding, Edmund; 1950)
BFI/Monthly Film Bulletin. Oct 1950, v17, p150.
Burt Lancaster: A Pictorial Treasury of His Films. p55-57.
Burt Lancaster: The Man and His Movies. p44-46.
Christian Century. Nov 29, 1950, v67, p1439.
Commonweal. Oct 20, 1950, v53, p40.
Film Daily. Aug 22, 1950, p5.
Hollywood Reporter. Aug 21, 1950, p3.
Life. Sep 11, 1950, v29, p97-98.
The London Times. Sep 11, 1950, p6.
Motion Picture Herald Product Digest. Aug 26, 1950, p449.
The New Republic. Oct 23, 1950, v123, p23.
The New York Times. Sep 30, 1950, p13.
The New Yorker. Oct 7, 1950, v26, p63.
Newsweek. Sep 25, 1950, v36, p95.
Senior Scholastic. Nov 1, 1950, v57, p27.
The Spectator. Sep 15, 1950, v185, p290.
Time. Oct 2, 1950, v56, p74.
Variety. Aug 23, 1950, p8.

Mr. Hobbs Takes a Vacation (US; Koster, Henry; 1962)
America. Jul 14, 1962, v107, p513.
BFI/Monthly Film Bulletin. Jul 1962, v29, p91.
Commonweal. Jul 6, 1962, v76, p377.
Film Daily. May 16, 1962, p8.
Filmfacts. Jul 20, 1962, v5, p147-49.
Films and Filming. Aug 1962, v8, p33.
The Films of James Stewart. p219-22.
Hollywood Reporter. May 16, 1962, p3.
Motion Picture Herald Product Digest. May 23, 1962, p563, 565.
The New York Times. Jul 16, 1962, p11.
Newsweek. Jul 25, 1962, v59, p88.
Time. Jul 6, 1962, v80, p55.
Variety. May 16, 1962, p6.

Mr. Hulot's Holiday (French title: Vacances de Monsieur Hulot, Les; Also titled: Mr. Hulot's Vacation) (FR; Tati, Jacques; 1953)
BFI/Monthly Film Bulletin. Jan 1954, v21, p6-7.
Cinema, the Magic Vehicle. v2, p121-22.
The Comic Mind. p294-97.
Commonweal. Jul 2, 1954, v60, p318.
Dictionary of Films. p396.
Film: A Modern Art (Sultanik). p183.
Film Daily. Aug 12, 1954, p5.
Films and Filming. Feb 1966, v12, p51-52.
Films in Review. Aug-Sep 1954, v5, p367.
The Films of Jacques Tati. p50-62.
The Great French Films. p147-50.
The International Dictionary of Films and Filmmakers. v1, p497-98.
Jacques Tati: A Guide to References and Resources. p64-66.
Jacques Tati (Gilliatt). p35-41, 93-94.
Kiss Kiss Bang Bang. p391.
Life. Jul 5, 1954, v37, p37-38.
Magill's Survey of Cinema. Foreign Language Films. v5, p2075-79.
Motion Picture Herald Product Digest. Jul 3, 1954, p50.
The Nation. Nov 27, 1954, v179, p470.
National Parent-Teacher. Sep 1954, v49, p39.
The New Republic. Jul 5, 1954, v131, p21.
The New Statesman and Nation. Nov 21, 1953, v46, p635.
The New York Times. Jun 17, 1954, p36.
The New Yorker. Sep 12, 1953, v29, p132.
The New Yorker. Jun 19, 1954, v30, p66.
Newsweek. Jun 21, 1954, v43, p86.
Quarterly of Film, Radio and Television. Fall 1955, v10, p19-23.
Saturday Review. Jun 19, 1954, v37, p30.
Sight and Sound. Jan-Mar 1954, v23, p148.
Time. Jul 5, 1954, v64, p77.
Variety. Apr 29, 1953, p18.
Variety. Jun 23, 1954, p6.
Wide Angle. 1977, v1, n1, p22-30.
Wide Angle. 1977, v1, n4, p54-55.
Wide Angle. 1978, v2, n1, p22-30.

Mr. Imperium (US; Hartman, Don; 1951)
Film Daily. May 14, 1951, p6.
The Films of Lana Turner. p246-53.
Hollywood Reporter. May 8, 1951, p3.
Motion Picture Herald Product Digest. May 12, 1951, p845-46.
The New York Times. Oct 15, 1951, p22.
Newsweek. Oct 22, 1951, v38, p102.
Time. Oct 22, 1951, v58, p116.
Variety. May 9, 1951, p6.

Mr. Majestyk (US; Fleischer, Richard; 1974)
BFI/Monthly Film Bulletin. Jul 1974, v41, p151-55.
Films and Filming. Jul 1974, v20, p44.
The Films of Charles Bronson. p210-12.
Hollywood Reporter. May 29, 1974, p3.
Independent Film Journal. May 29, 1974, v73, p10.
The Los Angeles Times. Jul 17, 1974, SecIV, p14.
Motion Picture Herald Product Digest. Mar 27, 1974, p86.
New Statesman. Jun 7, 1974, v87, p811-12.
New York. Jul 29, 1974, v7, p54-55.
The New York Times. Jul 18, 1974, p32.
PTA Magazine. Oct 1974, v69, p6.
Time. Sep 2, 1974, v104, p8.
Variety. May 29, 1974, p14.
The Village Voice. Aug 8, 1974, p67.

Mister Moses (Also titled: Mr. Moses) (US; Neame, Ronald; 1965)
America. May 29, 1965, v112, p809.
BFI/Monthly Film Bulletin. Jul 1965, v32, p111.
Commonweal. May 21, 1965, v82, p292.
Film Daily. Apr 13, 1965, p27.
Filmfacts. Jun 25, 1965, v8, p115-16.
Films and Filming. Aug 1965, v11, p32-33.
Films in Review. May 1965, v16, p316-17.
Hollywood Reporter. Apr 13, 1965, p3.
The London Times. Jun 10, 1965, p7.
Motion Picture Herald Product Digest. Apr 28, 1965, p274.
The New Republic. May 29, 1965, v152, p34.
New Statesman. Jun 11, 1965, v69, p930.
The New York Times. May 13, 1965, p32.
Time. May 28, 1965, v85, p106.
Variety. Apr 14, 1965, p6.

Mr. Music (US; Haydn, Richard; 1950)
BFI/Monthly Film Bulletin. Sep 1950, v17, p141.
Christian Century. Jan 10, 1951, v68, p63.
Commonweal. Dec 22, 1950, v53, p278.
Film Daily. Aug 25, 1950, p6.
The Films of Bing Crosby. p191-92.
Hollywood Reporter. Aug 25, 1950, p3.
Library Journal. Nov 1, 1950, v75, p1915.
Motion Picture Herald Product Digest. Sep 2, 1950, p458.
The New York Times. Dec 21, 1950, p34.
The New Yorker. Dec 30, 1950, v26, p51.
Newsweek. Jan 1, 1951, v37, p56.
The Spectator. Nov 10, 1950, v185, p464.
Time. Jan 1, 1951, v57, p60.
Variety. Aug 30, 1950, p6.

Mr. Potts Goes to Moscow (Also titled: Mister Potts Goes to Moscow; Top Secret) (GB; Zampi, Mario; 1952)
BFI/Monthly Film Bulletin. Dec 1952, v19, p168.
Film Daily. Apr 7, 1954, p6.
Hollywood Reporter. Mar 24, 1954, p3.
National Parent-Teacher. May 1955, v49, p39.
The New York Times. Sep 3, 1953, p15.
Newsweek. Sep 14, 1953, v42, p104.
Time. Sep 14, 1953, v62, p108.
Variety. Sep 9, 1953, p6.

Mister Roberts (US; Ford, John; LeRoy, Mervyn; 1955)
America. Jul 23, 1955, v93, p419.
BFI/Monthly Film Bulletin. Nov 1955, v72, n262, p164.
Catholic World. Jul 1955, v181, p301-02.
Commonweal. Jul 29, 1955, v62, p421-22.
The Complete Films of William Powell. p252-53.
Film Daily. May 24, 1955, p6.
Films and Filming. Nov 1955, v2, n2, p18.
Films in Review. Aug-Sep 1955, v6, n7, p340-41.
The Films of Henry Fonda. p143-46.
The Films of Jack Lemmon. p60-66.
The Films of James Cagney. p214-16.
The Films of the Fifties. p149-50.
The Fondas (Springer). p151-54.
Hollywood Reporter. May 24, 1955, v134, n40, p3.
Library Journal. Jul 1956, v80, p1576.
Life. Jun 6, 1955, v38, p82-84.
Magill's Survey of Cinema. Series I. v3, p1121-24.
The Nation. Aug 6, 1955, v181, p121.
The New York Times. May 22, 1955, SecI, p66.
The New York Times. Jul 15, 1955, p14.
The New York Times. Jul 17, 1955, SecII, p1.
The New Yorker. Jul 23, 1955, v31, p48.

Newsweek. Jul 23, 1955, v46, p83.
Saturday Review. Jul 2, 1955, v38, p30.
Sight and Sound. Wint 1955-56, v25, n3, p149.
Time. Jul 18, 1955, v66, p94.
Variety. May 25, 1955, p6.

Mrs. Pollifax-Spy (Also titled: The Unexpected Mrs. Pollifax) (US; Martinson, Leslie H.; 1971)
BFI/Monthly Film Bulletin. Mar 1971, v38, n446, p52.
Films and Filming. May 1971, v17, n8, p92-94.
Films in Review. Apr 1971, v22, n4, p235-36.
Hollywood Reporter. Mar 4, 1971, v215, n12, p6.
The New Yorker. May 17, 1971, v47.
Variety. Mar 3, 1971, p17.

Mrs. Soffel (US; Armstrong, Gillian; 1985)
BFI/Monthly Film Bulletin. Jul 1985, v52, p221.
Commonweal. Mar 8, 1985, v112, p146-47.
Hollywood Reporter. Dec 24, 1984, p3.
The Los Angeles Times. Dec 26, 1984, SecVI, p1.
The Los Angeles Times. Mar 3, 1985, Calendar, p34.
Maclean's. Feb 11, 1985, v98, p51.
New York. Jan 14, 1985, v18, p55-57.
The New York Times. Dec 26, 1984, SecIII, p5.
The New Yorker. Jan 7, 1985, v60, p66-67.
Newsweek. Jan 14, 1985, v105, p52-53.
Time. Jan 14, 1985, v125, p66.
Variety. Dec 26, 1984, p12.

Mitt Hem Ar Copacabana *See* My Home Is Copacabana

Miyamoto Musashi *See* Samurai

Moby Dick (US; Huston, John; 1956)
America. Jul 14, 1956, v95, p372.
The Cinema of John Huston. p103-11.
The Classic American Novel and the Movies. p42-51.
Commonweal. Jun 29, 1956, v64, p324.
Film Comment. May-Jun 1980, v16, p25-56.
Film Culture. 1956, v2, p3-7.
Film Daily. Jun 27, 1956, p6.
Films and Filming. Nov 1956, v3, p23.
Films in Review. Aug-Sep 1956, v7, p338-41.
The Films of Gregory Peck. p139-43.
Hollywood Reporter. Jun 27, 1956, p3.
John Huston (Hammen). p77-85, 89-91.
John Huston, Maker of Magic. p101-09.
Magill's Survey of Cinema. Series II. v4, p1623-27.
Make It Again, Sam. p120-24.
The Nation. Jul 14, 1956, v183, p46.
The New York Times. Jul 5, 1956, p18.
The New York Times. Jul 8, 1956, SecII, p1.
The New York Times. Jul 15, 1956, SecII, p1.
The New Yorker. Jul 14, 1956, v32, p83.
Newsweek. Jul 2, 1956, v48, p72.
Saturday Review. Jun 9, 1956, v39, p28.
Sight and Sound. Wint 1956-57, v26, p151-52.
Take One. May-Jun 1982, v3, p15-23.
Time. Jul 9, 1956, v68, p78.
Variety. Jun 27, 1956, p6.

The Model and the Marriage Broker (US; Cukor, George; 1951)
BFI/Monthly Film Bulletin. Feb 1952, v19, p22.
Catholic World. Feb 1952, v174, p386-87.
Commonweal. Feb 1, 1952, v55, p424.
Film Daily. Nov 19, 1951, p6.
George Cukor (Phillips). p57-58.
Hollywood Reporter. Nov 19, 1951, p3.
Motion Picture Herald Product Digest. Nov 24, 1951, p1117.
The New York Times. Jan 12, 1952, p10.

The New Yorker. Jan 19, 1952, v27, p70.
Newsweek. Jan 28, 1952, v39, p91.
The Spectator. Feb 8, 1952, v188, p173-74.
Time. Jan 14, 1952, v59, p91.
Variety. Nov 21, 1951, p6.

Modern People *See* High Infidelity

A Modern Romance (US; Brooks, Albert; 1981)
Christian Century. Jul 1, 1981, v98, p714.
Hollywood Reporter. Mar 11, 1981, p3.
The Los Angeles Times. Mar 21, 1981, SecII, p5.
Maclean's. Apr 13, 1981, v94, p55.
Magill's Cinema Annual, 1982. p241-44.
New York. Mar 30, 1981, v14, p41.
The New York Times. Mar 13, 1981, SecIII, p5.
Newsweek. Mar 30, 1981, v97, p82-83.
Rolling Stone. Apr 30, 1981, p61.
Variety. Mar 11, 1981, p3.

Modesty Blaise (GB; Losey, Joseph; 1966)
BFI/Monthly Film Bulletin. Jun 1966, v33, p89-90.
Christian Science Monitor (Western edition). Aug 31, 1966, p4.
Cinema. Dec 1965, v3, p14-17.
Cinema. Spr 1968, v4, p22-23.
The Cinema of Joseph Losey. p148-56.
Commonweal. Sep 2, 1966, v84, p557.
Encounter. Jul 1966, v27, p44-45.
Film Daily. May 9, 1966, p7.
Film Heritage. Sum 1967, v2, p3-8.
Film Quarterly. Sum 1967, v20, p63-65.
Filmfacts. Oct 15, 1966, v9, p222-24.
Films and Filming. Apr 1966, v12, p32.
Films and Filming. Jul 1966, v12, p56.
Films in Review. Jun-Jul 1966, v17, p383.
The Films of Dirk Bogarde. p160-63.
The Great Spy Pictures. p308-10.
Hollywood Reporter. May 6, 1966, p3.
Joseph Losey (Hirsch). p80-84.
The London Times. May 5, 1966, p20.
Mademoiselle. Aug 1966, v63, p92.
Motion Picture Herald Product Digest. May 25, 1966, p526.
New Society. May 5, 1966, p26.
New Statesman. May 6, 1966, v71, p662-63.
The New York Times. Aug 11, 1966, p27.
The New Yorker. Aug 13, 1966, v42, p96.
Newsweek. Aug 22, 1966, v68, p98.
Playboy. Aug 1966, v13, p23-24.
Sight and Sound. Sum 1966, v35, p142-44.
The Spectator. May 13, 1966, v216, p 600.
Time. Jul 15, 1966, v88, p81-82.
Variety. May 11, 1966, p6.
The Village Voice. Aug 18, 1966, v11, p23.

Mogambo (US; Ford, John; 1953)
America. Oct 17, 1953, v90, p82.
BFI/Monthly Film Bulletin. Dec 1953, v20, n239, p173.
Catholic World. Oct 17, 1953, v90, p82.
Commonweal. Oct 16, 1953, v59, p39.
Film Daily. Sep 15, 1953, p6.
Films in Review. Nov 1953, v4, n9, p478-80.
The Films of Clark Gable. p231-32.
Holiday. Jan 1954, v15, p17.
Hollywood Reporter. Sep 15, 1953, p3.
Library Journal. Oct 15, 1953, v78, p1840.
Life. Jan 26, 1953, v34, p80.
Magill's Survey of Cinema. Series I. v3, p1138-40.
Make It Again, Sam. p163-67.
The Nation. Nov 21, 1953, v177, p434.
National Parent-Teacher. Dec 1953, v48, p39.
Natural History. Nov 1953, v62, p429.
The New York Times. Jan 4, 1953, SecII, p5.
The New Yorker. Oct 10, 1953, v29, p127.
Newsweek. Oct 12, 1953, v42, p100-02.

The Non-Western Films of John Ford. p272-73.
Saturday Review. Oct 10, 1953, v36, p34.
Senior Scholastic. Nov 11, 1953, v63, p41.
Time. Oct 12, 1953, v62, p114.
Variety. Sep 16, 1953, p6.

Mogliamante *See* Wifemistress

Moglie del Prete, La *See* The Priest's Wife

Mohn Ist Auch Eine Blume *See* The Poppy Is Also a Flower

The Molly Maguires (US; Ritt, Martin; 1970)
America. Feb 21, 1970, v122, p200.
BFI/Monthly Film Bulletin. Jun 1970, v37, n437, p121.
Deeper Into Movies. p103-04.
Film Daily. Jan 19, 1970, p7.
Films in Review. Mar 1970, v21, n3, p182.
Hollywood Reporter. Jan 16, 1970, p3.
The New Republic. Feb 21, 1970, v162, p20.
The New York Times. Feb 9, 1970, p46.
The New Yorker. Feb 7, 1970, v65, p91.
Newsweek. Feb 16, 1970, v75, p87.
Saturday Review. Feb 14, 1970, v53, p61.
Sight and Sound. Sum 1970, v39, n3, p162-63.
Time. Feb 23, 1970, v95, p76.
Variety. Jan 21, 1970, p18.

Moment by Moment (US; Wagner, Jane; 1978)
BFI/Monthly Film Bulletin. Nov 1979, v46, p228.
Films in Review. Feb 1979, v30, p123.
Hollywood Reporter. Dec 20, 1978, p3.
The Los Angeles Times. Dec 29, 1978, SecIV, p1.
Maclean's. Dec 25, 1978, v91, p50.
Motion Picture Herald Product Digest. Dec 20, 1978, p57.
The New Republic. Jan 6, 1979, v180, p24.
New York. Dec 25, 1978, v12, p85-86.
The New York Times. Dec 22, 1978, SecIII, p18.
Newsweek. Jan 8, 1979, v93, p60.
Time. Dec 25, 1978, v112, p82-83.
Variety. Dec 20, 1978, p30.

The Moment of Truth (French title: Minute de Vérité, La) (FR; Delannoy, Jean; 1952)
BFI/Monthly Film Bulletin. Oct 1953, v20, p144-45.
Films in Review. May 1954, v5, p242.
Hollywood Reporter. Oct 22, 1954, p3.
The London Times. Sep 7, 1953, p2.
Motion Picture Herald Product Digest. May 22, 1954, p3.
The New Statesman and Nation. Sep 19, 1953, v46, p315.
The New York Times. Apr 27, 1954, p36.
Saturday Review. May 22, 1954, v37, p29.
The Spectator. Sep 4, 1953, v191, p239.
The Tatler. Sep 16, 1953, v209, p522.
Variety. Nov 12, 1952, p6.

The Moment of Truth (Also titled: Momemto della Verità, Il) (IT, SP; Cervi, Antonio; Rosi, Francesco; 1964)
America. Aug 28, 1965, v113, p226.
Christian Science Monitor (Western edition). Aug 19, 1966, p4.
Cinema. Jul 1966, v3, p49.
Film. Wint 1965-66, n44, p21.
Film Daily. Aug 9, 1965, p11.
Films and Filming. Dec 1964, v11, p5-10.
Films in Review. Oct 1965, v16, p515-16.
Hollywood Reporter. May 3, 1966, p3.
International Film Guide. 1966, v3, p100.
Kiss Kiss Bang Bang. p145-47.

Life. Sep 24, 1965, v59, p10.
The London Times. Apr 13, 1967, p6.
The London Times. Nov 10, 1965, p15.
Motion Picture Herald Product Digest. Aug 18, 1965, p346-47.
Movie. Aut 1965, n14, p39.
The New Italian Cinema. p163.
New Statesman. Apr 14, 1967, v73, p520.
The New York Times. Aug 10, 1965, p18.
The New Yorker. Aug 14, 1965, v41, p92.
Newsweek. Aug 23, 1965, v66, p81.
Saturday Review. Sep 11, 1965, v48, p51.
The Spectator. Nov 19, 1965, v215, p657.
Time. Aug 20, 1965, v86, p76.
Variety. Mar 31, 1965, p6.

Moment to Moment (US; LeRoy, Mervyn; 1966)
BFI/Monthly Film Bulletin. Jun 1966, v33, p95.
Christian Science Monitor (Western edition). May 6, 1966, p4.
Film Daily. Jan 26, 1966, p7.
Filmfacts. Apr 1, 1966, v9, p47-48.
Films and Filming. Jul 1966, v12, p56.
Films and Filming. Feb 1966, v12, p13.
Films in Review. Apr 1966, v17, p249.
Hollywood Reporter. Jan 26, 1966, p3.
The London Times. May 13, 1966, p12.
Motion Picture Herald Product Digest. Feb 2, 1966, p459, 461.
New Statesman. May 20, 1966, v71, p746.
The New York Times. Mar 3, 1966, p28.
Time. Mar 18, 1966, v87, p113.
Variety. Jan 26, 1966, p6.
Vogue. Feb 1, 1966, v147, p101.

Momento della Verità, Il *See* The Moment of Truth

Mommie Dearest (US; Perry, Frank; 1981)
Hollywood Reporter. Sep 8, 1981, p3.
Maclean's. Oct 5, 1981, v94, p56.
Magill's Cinema Annual, 1982. p245-49.
The Nation. Sep 26, 1981, v233, p284.
New York. Sep 28, 1981, v14, p58.
The New York Times. Sep 18, 1981, SecIII, p15.
The New Yorker. Oct 12, 1981, v57, p150.
Rolling Stone. Oct 29, 1981, p26-27.
Rolling Stone. Nov 12, 1981, p45.
Time. Sep 21, 1981, v118, p73.
Variety. Sep 9, 1981, p3.

Mon Oncle (Also titled: My Uncle) (FR; Tati, Jacques; 1958)
BFI/Monthly Film Bulletin. Aug 1959, v26, p102.
Commonweal. Nov 21, 1958, v69, p208.
Film Daily. Oct 23, 1958, v114, p3.
The Films in My Life. p235-37.
Films in Review. Jun-Jul 1958, v9, p292.
Films in Review. Dec 1958, p587-90.
Films in Review. Jan 1959, p4.
The Films of Jacques Tati. p43-55.
The Great French Films. p259.
Jacques Tati: A Guide to References and Resources. p66-69.
Jacques Tati (Gilliat). p22-43.
Magill's Survey of Cinema. Foreign Language Films. v5, p2085-90.
The New Republic. Dec 8, 1958, v139, p30.
The New Yorker. Nov 15, 1958, v34, p147.
Newsweek. Nov 10, 1958, v52, p98-99.
Reporter. Nov 27, 1958, v19, p36-38.
Saturday Review. Nov 15, 1958, v41, p26.
Senior Scholastic. Dec 12, 1958, p34.
Time. Dec 1, 1958, v72, p82.
Variety. May 21, 1958, p16.

Mon Oncle d'Amerique (FR; Resnais, Alain; 1980)
BFI/Monthly Film Bulletin. Dec 1980, v47, p239.
The Christian Science Monitor. Jan 15, 1981, p19.
Cineaste. Wint 1980-81, v10, p30.
Film Comment. Sep-Oct 1980, v16, p18-25.
Film Quarterly. Fall 1981, v35, p31.
The Great French Films. p233-39.
Hollywood Reporter. Dec 31, 1980, p2.
The Los Angeles Times. Dec 31, 1980, SecV, p6.
The Nation. Jan 17, 1981, v232, p60-61.
The New Republic. Jan 17, 1981, v184, p22.
New York. Jan 12, 1981, v14, p47-49.
The New York Times. Dec 17, 1980, SecIII, p25.
The New York Times. Dec 21, 1980, SecII, p19.
Newsweek. Dec 15, 1980, v96, p109.
Sight and Sound. Wint 1980-81, v50, p62.
Time. Dec 8, 1980, v116, p119.
Variety. May 21, 1980, p22.
The Village Voice. Dec 17, 1980, p65.

Monachine, Le *See* The Little Nuns

Monde Nouveau, Un *See* A Young World

Monde Sans Soleil, Le *See* World Without Sun

The Money Order *See* Mandabi

The Money Trap (Also titled: Piege Au Grisbi) (US; Kennedy, Burt; 1966)
BFI/Monthly Film Bulletin. Mar 1966, v33, p44.
Cahiers du Cinema in English. Dec 1966, n6, p55.
Christian Science Monitor (Western edition). Feb 16, 1966, p4.
Film Daily. Jan 20, 1966, p4.
Filmfacts. Jul 1, 1966, v9, p112-13.
Films and Filming. Mar 1966, v12, p57.
The Films of Rita Hayworth. p232-34.
Hollywood Reporter. Jan 18, 1966, p3.
Motion Picture Herald Product Digest. Feb 2, 1966, p461-62.
The New York Times. May 5, 1966, p59.
Newsweek. Feb 14, 1966, v67, p95.
Time. Feb 11, 1966, v87, p85.
Variety. Jan 19, 1966, p6.
The Village Voice. Mar 31, 1966, v11, p29.

Monkey Business (US; Hawks, Howard; 1952)
BFI/Monthly Film Bulletin. Oct 1952, v19, p144.
Bright Lights. 1975, v1, n3, p23-26.
Christian Century. Oct 29, 1952, v69, p1271.
Cinema Stylists (Belton). p269-76.
Cinema, the Magic Vehicle. v2, p144-45.
Commonweal. Sep 19, 1952, v56, p583.
Dictionary of Films. p226.
Film Daily. Sep 3, 1952, p6.
Film Heritage. Wint 1970-71, v6, p19-26.
The Films of Cary Grant. p213-15.
The Films of Ginger Rogers. p210-11.
The Films of Howard Hawks. p22-25.
The Films of Marilyn Monroe. p83-88.
Hollywood Reporter. Sep 2, 1952, p3.
Howard Hawks (Poague). p65-66, 80-82, 139-40.
Howard Hawks, Storyteller. p133-87.
Howard Hawks (Wood). p78-84.
Magill's Survey of Cinema. Series I. v3, p1144-46.
Motion Picture Herald Product Digest. Sep 6, 1952, p1517.
Movie. Dec 1962, n5, p21-22.
National Parent-Teacher. Nov 1952, v47, p38.

The New Statesman and Nation. Oct 4, 1952, v44, p377.
The New York Times. Sep 6, 1952, p12.
The New Yorker. Sep 13, 1952, v28, p136.
Newsweek. Sep 15, 1952, v40, p100-02.
Saturday Review. Sep 20, 1952, v35, p34.
Time. Sep 22, 1952, v60, p106.
Variety. Sep 10, 1952, p6.

Monsieur de Compagnie, Un *See* Male Companion

Monsieur Ripois *See* Knave of Hearts

Monsignor (US; Perry, Frank; 1982)
Christian Century. Oct 27, 1982, v99, p1083.
Christian Century. Dec 8, 1982, v99, p1271.
Maclean's. Nov 1, 1982, v95, p70.
The Nation. Nov 13, 1982, v235, p508.
The New Leader. Nov 29, 1982, v65, p20.
New York. Nov 8, 1982, v15, p66-67.
The New York Times. Oct 31, 1982, SecII, p15.
Newsweek. Nov 8, 1982, v100, p90.
Variety. Oct 27, 1982, p14.
The Village Voice. Nov 2, 1982, p43.

Montana (US; Enright, Ray; 1950)
Christian Century. Feb 22, 1950, v67, p255.
Commonweal. Mar 10, 1950, v51, p582.
Film Daily. Jan 5, 1950, p6.
The Films of Errol Flynn. p165-66.
Hollywood Reporter. Jan 4, 1950, p3.
The London Times. Jul 10, 1950, p2.
Motion Picture Herald Product Digest. Jan 7, 1950, p145.
The New York Times. Feb 4, 1950, p9.
The Spectator. Jul 7, 1950, v185, p13.
Variety. Jan 4, 1950, p63.

Montana Belle (US; Dwan, Allan; 1952)
BFI/Monthly Film Bulletin. Feb 1953, v20, p25.
Film Daily. Dec 3, 1952, p7.
Hollywood Reporter. Oct 29, 1952, p4.
Motion Picture Herald Product Digest. Nov 1, 1952, p1589-90.
National Parent-Teacher. Feb 1953, v47, p38.
The New York Times. Nov 8, 1952, p9.
Time. Nov 24, 1952, v60, p110.
Variety. Oct 29, 1952, p6.

Monte Carlo Baby (French title: Nous Irons a Monte Carlo) (FR; Boyer, Jean; Fuller, Lester; 1951)
BFI/Monthly Film Bulletin. Apr 1954, v21, p58.
Motion Picture Herald Product Digest. Jun 19, 1954, p33.
The New York Times. May 29, 1954, p13.
Variety. Feb 27, 1952, p16.

The Monte Carlo Story (US; Girosi, Marcello; 1957)
BFI/Monthly Film Bulletin. May 1957, v24, p56.
Film Daily. Jun 19, 1957, v111, p7.
Films and Filming. Jun 1957, v3, p23.
Films in Review. Aug-Sep 1957, v8, p356.
The Films of Marlene Dietrich. p199-202.
Hollywood Reporter. Jun 18, 1957, p3.
Motion Picture Herald Product Digest. Jun 29, 1957, v207, p433.
The New York Times. Feb 13, 1958, p23.
The New Yorker. Feb 22, 1958, v34, p76.
Newsweek. Jul 29, 1957, v50, p86.
Time. Mar 17, 1958, v71, p108.
Variety. Jun 19, 1957, p6.

Montenegro (Also titled: Pigs and Pearls) (SWED, GB; Makavejev, Dusan; 1981)
BFI/Monthly Film Bulletin. Nov 1981, v48, p221-22.
Film Journal. Nov 9, 1981, v85, p45.

Hollywood Reporter. Nov 16, 1981, p3.
The Los Angeles Times. Dec 24, 1981, SecV, p5.
Maclean's. Jan 4, 1982, v95, p51.
Magill's Cinema Annual, 1982. p250-54.
The New Republic. Nov 25, 1981, v185, p23-24.
Newsweek. Nov 16, 1981, v98, p119.
The Village Voice. Nov 4, 1981, p54.

Monterey Pop (US; Pennebaker, D. A.; 1968)
BFI/Monthly Film Bulletin. Jun 1970, v37, p134-35.
Christian Century. Jul 30,, 1969, v86, p1022.
Christian Science Monitor (Western edition). Mar 21, 1968, p15.
Film Quarterly. Fall 1969, v23, p52.
Filmfacts. 1969, v12, n4, p88-90.
High Fidelity. Feb 1986, v36, p66.
International Film Guide. 1970, v7, p227-29.
Life. Feb 7, 1969, v66, p10.
New Statesman. Jun 5, 1969, v78, p815.
The New York Times. Dec 27, 1968, p4.
The New Yorker. Mar 22, 1969, v45, p120-21.
Saturday Review. Jan 30, 1971, v54, p48.
Sight and Sound. Sum 1970, v39, p159-60.
Time. Mar 7, 1969, v93, pE9.
Variety. Sep 18, 1968, p28.
The Village Voice. Feb 6, 1969, p49, p53-55.
A Year In the Dark. p330-32.

Monty Python and the Holy Grail (GB; Gilliam, Terry; 1975)
America. May 31, 1975, v132, p428-29.
BFI/Monthly Film Bulletin. Apr 1975, v42, p84.
Commonweal. Jun 6, 1975, v102, p182.
Hollywood Reporter. Mar 13, 1975, p18.
The Los Angeles Times. Jul 23, 1974, SecIV, P1.
Magills Survey of Cinema. Series II. v4, p1633-37.
Monty Python and the Holy Grail. 1975.
Motion Picture Herald Product Digest. May 14, 1975, p94.
The New Republic. May 24, 1975, v172, p20.
The New Yorker. May 5, 1975, v51, p115-17.
Newsweek. May 19, 1975, v85, p90-91.
Time. May 26, 1975, v105, p58.
Variety. Mar 19, 1975, p32.
Vogue. Jul 1975, v165, p30.

Monty Python's Life of Brian (Also titled: The Life of Brian) (GB; Jones, Terry; 1979)
America. Sep 15, 1979, v141, p102.
BFI/Monthly Film Bulletin. Nov 1979, v46, p229.
Commonweal. Oct 26, 1979, v106, p596-97.
Hollywood Reporter. Aug 16, 1979, p3.
The Los Angeles Times. Aug 17, 1979, SecIV, p30.
Motion Picture Herald Product Digest. Aug 29, 1979, p28.
The New Republic. Sep 22, 1979, v181, p40.
The New York Times. Aug 17, 1979, SecIII, p15.
The New Yorker. Aug 27, 1979, v55, p74.
Newsweek. Sep 3, 1979, v94, p65.
Rolling Stone. Oct 18, 1979, p52.
Time. Sep 17, 1979, v114, p101.
Variety. Aug 22, 1979, p20.
The World of Fantastic Films. p99-100.

Monty Python's The Meaning of Life (GB; Jones, Terry; 1983)
Hollywood Reporter. Mar 25, 1983, p4.
Maclean's. Apr 11, 1983, v96, p69.
The New Republic. Apr 18, 1983, v188, p24-25.
New York. Apr 4, 1983, v16, p73-74.

Newsweek. Apr 4, 1983, v101, p74.
Psychology Today. Apr 1983, v17, p60-65.
Time. Mar 28, 1983, v121, p62.

The Moon in the Gutter (FR; Beineix, Jean-Jacques; 1983)
Commonweal. Oct 7, 1983, v110, p535.
Film Comment. Jul-Aug 1983, v19, p16-19.
Hollywood Reporter. Sep 6, 1983, p3.
Maclean's. Sep 19, 1983, v96, p70.
New York. Sep 12, 1983, v16, p82.
The New Yorker. Sep 19, 1983, v59, p120-25.
Newsweek. Sep 19, 1983, v102, p85.

The Moon Is Blue (US; Preminger, Otto; 1953)
Catholic World. Aug 1953, v177, p383.
The Cinema of Otto Preminger. p107-08.
Commonweal. Jul 17, 1953, v58, p396.
Film Daily. Jun 3, 1953, p10.
Films in Review. Aug-Sep 1953, v4, n7, p364-65.
The Films of David Niven. p112-13.
The Films of William Holden. p138-41.
Holiday. Jan 1954, v15, p17.
Hollywood Reporter. Jun 3, 1953, p3.
Library Journal. Jul 1953, v78, p1226.
Life. Jul 13, 1953, v35, p71-72.
Magill's Survey of Cinema. Series II. v4, p1642.
Movie. Sep 1962, n2, p17.
The Nation. Jul 4, 1953, v177, p18.
National Parent-Teacher. Sep 1953, v48,p39.
The New York Times. Feb 22, 1953, p5.
The New Yorker. Jul 18, 1953, v29, p62.
Newsweek. Jun 29, 1953, v41, p87-88.
Saturday Review. Jun 27, 1953, v36, p36.
Theatre Arts. Aug 1953, v37, p89.
Time. Jul 6, 1953, v62, p84.
Variety. Jun 3, 1953, p6.

Moonfleet (US; Lang, Fritz; 1955)
America. Jul 2, 1955, v93, p359.
Commonweal. Jun 24, 1955, v62, p305.
Films and Filming. Aug 1955, v1, n11, p17.
Fritz Lang: A Guide to References and Resources. p118-21.
Hollywood Reporter. May 9, 1955, p3.
Library Journal. Jun 1, 1955, v80, p1321.
Motion Picture Herald Product Digest. May 14, 1955, p433.
The Nation. Jul 9, 1955, v181, p31.
The New York Times. Sep 5, 1954, SecII, p5.
The New York Times. Sep 19, 1954, SecII, p5.
The New York Times. Jun 25, 1955, p9.
Newsweek. Jul 18, 1955, v46, p83.
Time. Jun 20, 1955, v65, p91.
Variety. May 11, 1955, p6.

Moonlighting (GB; Skolimowski, Jerzy; 1982)
BFI/Monthly Film Bulletin. Sep 1982, v49, p187-88.
Commonweal. Nov 5, 1982, v109, p591-93.
Hollywood Reporter. Oct 8, 1982, p14.
The Los Angeles Times. Nov 24, 1982, SecVI, p1.
Maclean's. Nov 22, 1982, v95, p71-72.
Magill's Cinema Annual, 1983. p237-40.
The New Republic. Nov 8, 1982, v187, p25.
New York. Oct 11, 1982, v15, p88-89.
The New York Times. Sep 26, 1982, p55.
Newsweek. Oct 11, 1982, v100, p103.
Progressive. Dec 1982, v46, p55.
Time. Oct 11, 1982, v120, p90.
Variety. May 26, 1982, p15.

Moonraker (GB, FR; Gilbert, Lewis; 1979)
BFI/Monthly Film Bulletin. Aug 1979, v46, p179.
Hollywood Reporter. Jun 27, 1979, p3.
James Bond and the Cinema. p259-80.

The James Bond Films. p154-60.
James Bond's Bedside Companion. p222-25.
The Los Angeles Times. Jun 29, 1979, SecIV, p1.
Motion Picture Herald Product Digest. Jul 18, 1979, p13.
The New York Times. Jun 29, 1979, SecIII, p3.
The New Yorker. Jul 9, 1979, v55, p75.
Newsweek. Jul 2, 1979, v94, p68.
Rolling Stone. Aug 23, 1979, p32-33.
Time. Jul 2, 1979, v114, p72.
Variety. Jun 27, 1979, p18.
The World of Fantastic Films. p73-74.

The Moon-Spinners (GB; Nielson, James; 1964)
BFI/Monthly Film Bulletin. Aug 1964, v31, p122-23.
Boxoffice. Jul 6, 1964, v85, p2841.
Film Daily. Jun 24, 1964, v124, p6.
Films and Filming. Aug 1964, v10, p20.
Films in Review. Dec 1964, v15, p632.
Hollywood Reporter. Jun 24, 1964, v181, p3.
Motion Picture Herald Product Digest. Jul 8, 1964, v232, p83.
The New York Times. Nov 4, 1964, p47.
Time. Nov 20, 1964, v84, p107.
Variety. Jun 24, 1964, p6.

Morgan (Also titled: Morgan, A Suitable Case For Treatment) (GB; Reisz, Karel; 1966)
America. Jun 18, 1966, v114, p861.
BFI/Monthly Film Bulletin. May 1966, v33, p71-72.
Catholic World. Feb 1967, v204, p301-06.
Christian Century. Dec 28, 1966, v83, p1604.
Christian Science Monitor (Western edition). Jun 1, 1966, p6.
Commonweal. May 13, 1966, v84, p225.
Esquire. Oct 1966, v66, p40.
Film Comment. Sep-Oct 1981, v17, p29.
Film Daily. Apr 6, 1966, p7.
Film Quarterly. Fall 1966, v20, p51-55.
Filmfacts. Jun 15, 1966, v9, p97-99.
Films and Filming. Dec 1965, v11, p6, 10.
Films and Filming. Jun 1966, v12, p6-10.
Films in Review. May 1966, v17, p311-12.
Karel Reisz (Gaston). p63-84.
Kiss Kiss Bang Bang. p25-27.
Life. May 6, 1966, v60, p16.
The London Times. Apr 14, 1966, p7.
Mademoiselle. Jun 1966, v63, p52.
Magill's Survey of Cinema. Series II. v4, p1647-49.
Marshall Delaney at the Movies. p197-99.
The Nation. Apr 25, 1966, v202, p502.
The New Republic. Apr 30, 1966, v154, p30, 32.
New Statesman. Apr 15, 1966, v71, p549.
The New York Times. Apr 5, 1966, p42.
The New Yorker. Apr 9, 1966, v42, p86.
On Movies. p406-11.
Playboy. Jun 1966, v13, p38.
The Primal Screen. p186-88.
Private Screenings. p248-52.
Reruns. p188-91.
Saturday Review. Apr 16, 1966, v49, p65.
Second Sight. p74-76.
Sight and Sound. Sum 1966, v35, p144.
The Spectator. Apr 29, 1966, v216, p528.
Time. Apr 1, 1966, v87, p99.
Time. Jun 24, 1966, v87, p80.
Tynan Right and Left. p258-59.
Variety. Apr 13, 1966, p6.
The Village Voice. Apr 21, 1966, v11, p29.

Morituri (Also titled: Saboteur; Code Name Morituri) (US; Wicki, Bernhard; 1965)
America. Sep 11, 1965, v113, p265.

BFI/Monthly Film Bulletin. Oct 1965, v32, p152.
Christian Science Monitor (Western edition). Sep 4, 1965, p6.
Commonweal. Sep 3, 1965, v82, p637.
Film Daily. Jul 22, 1965, p4.
Films and Filming. Oct 1965, v12, p25-26.
The Films of Marlon Brando. p156-63.
The Great Spy Pictures. p311-12.
Hollywood Reporter. Jul 22, 1965, p3.
Life. Sep 3, 1965, v59, p10.
The London Times. Sep 23, 1965, p8.
Motion Picture Herald Product Digest. Aug 4, 1965, p337.
New Statesman. Oct 1, 1965, v70, p493.
The New York Times. Aug 26, 1965, p40.
The New Yorker. Aug 28, 1965, v41, p102.
Newsweek. Aug 23, 1965, v66, p81.
Playboy. Oct 1965, v12, p28, 30.
Saturday Review. Aug 21, 1965, v48, p40.
Time. Sep 3, 1965, v86, p84.
Variety. Jul 28, 1965, p6.
Vogue. Sep 15, 1965, v146, p76.

Morning Departure *See* Operation Disaster

Morozko *See* Jack Frost

Morte a Venezia *See* Death in Venice

Moscow Does Not Believe in Tears
(Russian title: Moskva slyozam ne verit) (USSR; Menshov, Vladimir; 1979)
BFI/Monthly Film Bulletin. Sep 1981, v48, p180-81.
Commonweal. Jul 1981, v72, p66-67.
Film Journal. May 18, 1981, v84, p17.
Films Illustrated. Oct 6, 1981, v11, p6.
Hollywood Reporter. Apr 20, 1981, p2.
The Los Angeles Times. May 17, 1981, Calendar, p26.
Maclean's. Sep 14, 1981, v94, p70.
Magill's Survey of Cinema. Foreign Language Films. v5, p2095-100.
Ms. Aug 1981, v10, p95-97.
The New Republic. May 23, 1981, v184, p24.
New York. May 25, 1981, v14, p90.
The New York Times. May 8, 1981, SecIII, p10.
Newsweek. May 25, 1981, v97, p74.
Saturday Review. Jun 1981, v8, p64.
Time. May 11, 1981, v117, p84.
Variety. Mar 5, 1980, p26.
The Village Voice. May 6-12, 1981, p54.

Moscow on the Hudson (US; Mazursky, Paul; 1984)
BFI/Monthly Film Bulletin. Nov 1984, v51, p335-36.
Christian Century. May 9, 1984, v101, p498-99.
Cineaste. Fall 1984, v13, p60.
Commonweal. May 18, 1984, v111, p301-02.
Film Journal. May 1984, v87, p23.
Films and Filming. Oct 1984, n36, p43.
Hollywood Reporter. Mar 28, 1984, p4.
Hudson Review. Fall 1984, v37, p457-60.
The Los Angeles Times. Apr 6, 1984, SecVI, p1.
Maclean's. Apr 9, 1984, v97, p62.
National Review. Jun 1, 1984, v36, p49.
The New Republic. May 28, 1984, v190, p24-25.
New Statesman. Oct 5, 1984, v108, p34-35.
New York. Apr 16, 1984, v17, p90.
The New York Times. May 22, 1984, SecIII, p11.
The New York Times. Apr 6, 1984, SecIII, p12.
The New York Times. May 6, 1984, SecII, p17.
The New Yorker. Apr 16, 1984, v60, p138-42.
Newsweek. Apr 16, 1984, v103, p93.
Photoplay. Nov 1984, v35, p23-27.
Time. Apr 23, 1984, v123, p83.

Variety. Mar 28, 1984, p22.
The Village Voice. Apr 17, 1984, p47.

Moskva slyozam ne verit *See* Moscow Does Not Believe in Tears

Mother Didn't Tell Me (US; Binyon, Claude; 1950)
Christian Century. Apr 19, 1950, v67, p511.
Commonweal. Mar 31, 1950, v51, p655.
Film Daily. Feb 2, 1950, p9.
Hollywood Reporter. Feb 1, 1950, p3.
Library Journal. Feb 15, 1950, v75, p333.
The New York Times. Mar 4, 1950, p11.
The New Yorker. Mar 11, 1950, v26, p71.
Newsweek. Mar 13, 1950, v35, p79.
Time. Mar 20, 1950, v55, p92.
Variety. Feb 1, 1950, p14.

Motorcyclette, La *See* The Girl On a Motorcycle

Mouchette (FR; Bresson, Robert; 1966)
BFI/Monthly Film Bulletin. Apr 1968, v35, p52.
Commonweal. Nov 29, 1968, v88, p318-19.
Dictionary of Films. p228-29.
Film Heritage. n3, 1974, v9, p12-16.
Film Quarterly. Fall 1968, v22, p52-56.
Film Society Review. Oct 1968, v4, p23-28.
The Films of Robert Bresson. p115-23.
Listener. Mar 21, 1968, p10.
The London Times. Apr 5, 1967, p10.
The London Times. May 13, 1967, p7.
The London Times. Nov 25, 1967, p19.
The London Times. Mar 14, 1968, p13.
The Nation. Oct 7, 1968, v207, p348.
The New York Times. Mar 13, 1970, p29.
The New York Times. Sep 21, 1968, p26.
On Film. p334-36.
Robert Bresson: A Guide to References and Resources. p71-75.
Robert Bresson: A Guide to References and Resources. p71-75.
Sight and Sound. Sum 1968, v37, p152-53.
The Spectator. Mar 22, 1968, v220, p377.
Variety. Apr 5, 1967, p6.
The Village Voice. Mar 19, 1970, v15, p59-60.

Moulin Rouge (US; Huston, John; 1952)
American Photography. May 1953, v47, p4.
BFI/Monthly Film Bulletin. Apr 1953, v20, p48.
Catholic World. Mar 1953, v176, p459-60.
Christian Century. Apr 22, 1953, v70, p495.
The Cinema of John Huston. p94-97.
Cinema, the Magic Vehicle. v2, p130-31.
Commonweal. Feb 13, 1953, v57, p473-74.
Cue. Feb 14, 1953, p17.
Dictionary of Films. p229.
Film Daily. Dec 24, 1952, p8.
Films in Review. Mar 1953, v4, p142-48.
Holiday. Apr 1953, v13, p26-27.
Hollywood Reporter. Dec 24, 1952, p3.
Illustrated London News. Apr 4, 1953, v222, p540.
John Huston (Hammen). p68-71.
Library Journal. Feb 15, 1953, v78, p314.
Life. Jan 19, 1953, v34, p64-68.
Motion Picture Herald Product Digest. Dec 27, 1952, p1661.
The Nation. Feb 28, 1953, v176, p193-94.
National Parent-Teacher. Apr 1953, v47, p40.
The New Statesman and Nation. Mar 21, 1953, v45, p339.
The New York Times. Feb 11, 1953, p33.
The New York Times Magazine. Aug 31, 1952, p12-13.
The New Yorker. Feb 21, 1953, v29, p65.
Newsweek. Feb 23, 1953, v41, p96.
Saturday Review. Feb 14, 1953, v36, p46.

Selected Film Criticism, 1951-1960. p80-81.
Sight and Sound. Apr-Jun 1953, v22, p194-95.
The Spectator. Mar 13, 1953, v190, p307.
The Tatler. Mar 25, 1953, v207, p560.
Theatre Arts. Mar 1953, v37, p84-85.
Time. Jan 5, 1953, v61, p68.
Variety. Dec 24, 1952, p6.

Mourir a Madrid *See* To Die in Madrid

The Mouse on the Moon (GB; Lester, Richard; 1963)
BFI/Monthly Film Bulletin. Jun 1963, v30, p87.
Film Daily. May 24, 1963, p4.
Filmfacts. Aug 22, 1963, v6, p167-68.
Films and Filming. Jun 1963, v9, p29.
Hollywood Reporter. Jul 2, 1963, v176, p3.
The New York Times. Jun 18, 1963, p32.
Newsweek. Jul 1, 1963, v62, p68.
Richard Lester: A Guide to References and Resources. p19-21.
Saturday Review. Jul 20, 1963, v46, p37.
Time. Jun 21, 1963, v81, p92.
Variety. May 15, 1963, p6.

The Mouse that Roared (GB; Arnold, Jack; 1959)
America. Nov 14, 1959, v102, p212.
BFI/Monthly Film Bulletin. Aug 1959, v26, p102.
Commonweal. Oct 23, 1959, v71, p106.
Film Daily. Oct 2, 1959, v116, p6.
Filmfacts. Dec 30, 1959, v2, p291-92.
Films in Review. Dec 1959, v10, p625.
Hollywood Reporter. Oct 1, 1959, p3.
Life. Nov 9, 1959, v47, p91.
Magill's Survey of Cinema. Series I. v3, p1159-63.
The New York Times. Oct 27, 1959, p40.
The New Yorker. Nov 7, 1959, v35, p205.
Newsweek. Nov 9, 1959, v54, p120.
Reporter. Oct 1959, v21, p37-38.
Saturday Review. Sep 26, 1959, v42, p28.
Senior Scholastic. Oct 28, 1959, v75, p29.
Time. Nov 9, 1959, v74, p84.
Variety. Aug 5, 1959, p6.

Mouton a Cinq Pattes, Le (Also titled: The Sheep Has Five Legs; The Five-Legged Sheep) (FR; Verneuil, Henri; 1954)
BFI/Monthly Film Bulletin. Jan 1955, v22, p4.
Film Daily. Aug 5, 1955, p8.
Films and Filming. Jan 1955, v1, p19.
Illustrated London News. Dec 11, 1954, v225, p1074.
The London Times. Nov 29, 1954, p10.
Motion Picture Herald Product Digest. Aug 27, 1955, p570.
The Nation. Sep 3, 1955, v181, p211.
National Parent-Teacher. Oct 1955, v50, p40.
The New Statesman and Nation. Dec 25, 1954, v48, p855.
The New York Times. Aug 10, 1955, p19.
The New Yorker. Aug 20, 1955, v31, p68.
Newsweek. Aug 29, 1955, v46, p77.
The Tatler. Dec 8, 1954, v214, p646.
Time. Sep 5, 1955, v66, p80.
Variety. Aug 11, 1954, p6.
The Village Voice. Nov 23, 1955, v1, p6.

Move Over, Darling (US; Gordon, Michael; 1963)
America. Dec 21, 1963, v109, p809-10.
BFI/Monthly Film Bulletin. Apr 1964, v31, p58.
Chicago Tribune. Dec 27, 1963, v79, p405.
Film Daily. Dec 5, 1963, p6.
Filmfacts. Dec 26, 1963, v6, p289-90.
Films and Filming. Apr 1964, v10, p33-34.
Films in Review. Dec 1963, v14, p628-29.
The Films of Doris Day. p215-18.

Look. Dec 17, 1963, v27, p138.
The New York Times. Dec 26, 1963, p33.
The New Yorker. Jan 11, 1964, v39, p86.
Saturday Review. Jan 4, 1964, v47, p31.
Time. Dec 27, 1963, v82, p57.
Variety. Dec 11, 1963, p6.

Movie Movie (Also titled: Movie, Movie)
(US; Donen, Stanley; 1978)
BFI/Monthly Film Bulletin. Apr 1979, v46,
p75.
Films in Review. Mar 1979, v30, p181.
Hollywood Reporter. Nov 15, 1978, p4.
The Los Angeles Times. Dec 10, 1978,
Calendar, p57.
Motion Picture Herald Product Digest. Nov 29,
1978, p49.
The Nation. Jan 6, 1979, v228, p27.
The New York Times. Nov 22, 1978, SecIII, p9.
The New York Times. Dec 3, 1978, p13.
The New Yorker. Dec 4, 1978, v54, p192-95.
Newsweek. Nov 27, 1978, v92, p93-94.
Stanley Donen (Caspar). p220-27.
Time. Dec 11, 1978, v112, p109-10.
Variety. Nov 15, 1978, p18.

The Moving Target *See* Harper

The Mudlark (US; Negulesco, Jean; 1950)
BFI/Monthly Film Bulletin. Dec 1950, v17,
p185.
Christian Century. Feb 21, 1951, v68, p254.
Commonweal. Dec 22, 1950, v53, p278.
Film Daily. Nov 28, 1950, p10.
Films in Review. Jan 1951, v2, p39-41.
Hollywood Reporter. Oct 31, 1950, p3.
Illustrated London News. Oct 28, 1950, v217,
p702.
Illustrated London News. Nov 18, 1950, v217,
p824.
Library Journal. Jan 1, 1951, v76, p59.
Motion Picture Herald Product Digest. Dec 2,
1950, p597-98.
The New York Times. Dec 25, 1950, p25.
The New York Times Magazine. Oct 15, 1950,
p58-59.
The New Yorker. Jan 6, 1951, v26, p59.
Newsweek. Nov 13, 1950, v36, p100.
Newsweek. Dec 25, 1950, v36, p80.
Saturday Review. Dec 23, 1950, v33, p29.
Senior Scholastic. Jan 3, 1951, v57, p24.
The Spectator. Nov 10, 1950, v185, p462.
Time. Jan 1, 1951, v57, p60.
Variety. Nov 8, 1950, p6.

The Muppet Movie (GB; Frawley, James;
1979)
America. Jul 21, 1979, v141, p36.
BFI/Monthly Film Bulletin. Jul 1979, v46,
p149.
Commonweal. Aug 31, 1979, v106, p470-71.
Films in Review. Aug-Sep 1979, v30, p439.
Hollywood Reporter. May 31, 1979, p3.
The Los Angeles Times. Jun 21, 1979, SecIV,
p17.
Magill's Survey of Cinema. Series II. v4, p1668-
71.
Motion Picture Herald Product Digest. Jul 18,
1979, p14.
The New Republic. Jul 21, 1979, v181, p27.
The New York Times. Jun 22, 1979, SecIII,
p19.
The New Yorker. Jul 2, 1979, v55, p67.
Newsweek. Jul 2, 1979, v94, p67.
Time. Jul 9, 1979, v114, p72.
Variety. May 30, 1979, p16.

The Muppets Take Manhattan (US; Oz,
Frank; 1984)
BFI/Monthly Film Bulletin. Apr 1985, v52,
p117.

Film Journal. Aug 1984, v87, p16.
Hollywood Reporter. Jul 4, 1984, p4.
The Los Angeles Times. Jul 13, 1984, SecVI,
p1.
Maclean's. Jul 23, 1984, v97, p46.
The New York Times. Jul 13, 1984, SecIII, p10.
Newsweek. Jul 30, 1984, v104, p82.
Theatre Crafts. Aug-Sep 1984, v18, p14.
Time. Jul 16, 1984, v124, p71.
Variety. Jul 11, 1984, p16.

Mura di Malapaga, La *See* Au-Dela des
Grilles

Murder Ahoy! (GB; Pollock, George; 1964)
BFI/Monthly Film Bulletin. Oct 1965, v32,
p151.
Boxoffice. Sep 21, 1964, v85, p2862.
Film Daily. Sep 17, 1964, v125, p6.
Films and Filming. Dec 1965, v12, p26.
Hollywood Reporter. Sep 17, 1964, v182, p3.
Motion Picture Herald Product Digest. Sep 30,
1964, v232, p138-39.
The New York Times. Sep 23, 1964, p55.
Time. Oct 2, 1964, v84, p129.
Variety. Sep 30, 1964, p6.

Murder at the Gallop (US; Pollock, George;
1963)
BFI/Monthly Film Bulletin. Jun 1963, v30, p87.
Film Daily. Jul 8, 1963, p4.
Filmfacts. Aug 29, 1963, v6, p173-74.
Films and Filming. Jul 1963, v9, p26.
Hollywood Reporter. Jul 8, 1963, v176, p3.
The New York Times. Jun 25, 1963, p23.
Newsweek. Jul 8, 1963, v62, p78B.
Time. Jul 5, 1963, v82, p85.
Variety. May 8, 1963, p6.

Murder by Death (US; Moore, Robert;
1976)
Action. Jan-Feb 1976, v11, p12-13.
America. Sep 4, 1976, v135, p99.
BFI/Monthly Film Bulletin. Oct 1976, v43,
p216.
Commonweal. Jul 30, 1976, v103, p500.
Films and Filming. Oct 1976, v23, p35.
Films in Review. Aug-Sep 1976, v27, p443.
Hollywood Reporter. Jun 23, 1976, p2.
Independent Film Journal. Jul 9, 1976, v78,
p12-13.
The Los Angeles Times. Jun 23, 1976, SecIV,
p1.
The Nation. Jul 17, 1976, v223, p60-61.
New Statesman. Aug 27, 1976, v91, p286-87.
The New York Times. Jun 24, 1976, p26.
The New Yorker. Jun 28, 1976, v52, p62-63.
Newsweek. Jul 4, 1976, v88, p101.
Saturday Review. Jul 24, 1976, v3, p42.
Time. Jul 12, 1976, v108, p48-49.
Variety. Jun 23, 1976, p16.
Vogue. Apr 1976, v166, p184-85.

The Murder Game (GB; Salkow, Sidney;
1965)
Film Daily. Apr 22, 1966, p6.
Filmfacts. May 1, 1966, v9, p68-69.
Hollywood Reporter. Apr 13, 1966, p3.
Motion Picture Herald Product Digest. Apr 27,
1966, p511.
The New York Times. Mar 31, 1966, p43.
Variety. Apr 13, 1966, p20.

Murder in the Cathedral (GB; Hoellering,
George; 1952)
Authors on Film. p190-95.
BFI/Monthly Film Bulletin. Apr 1952, v19,
p47.
Christian Century. Apr 30, 1952, v69, p543.
Commonweal. Mar 28, 1952, v55, p616.
Film. Jan-Feb 1956, n7, p6-9.
Films in Review. Feb 1952, v3, p84-88.

Harper's Magazine. Mar 28, 1952, v55, p616.
Library Journal. Apr 1, 1952, v77, p586.
The London Times. Feb 29, 1951, p6.
Motion Picture Herald Product Digest. Apr 5,
1952, p1307.
The New Statesman and Nation. Mar 1, 1952,
v43, p244.
The New York Times. Mar 26, 1952, p35.
The New Yorker. Apr 5, 1952, v28, p117.
Newsweek. Apr 7, 1952, v39, p102.
Saturday Review. Apr 5, 1952, v35, p28.
Sight and Sound. Apr-Jun 1952, v21, p172.
The Spectator. Feb 29, 1952, v188, p261.
Theatre Arts. Feb 1952, v36, p33, 90.
Time. Sep 17, 1951, v58, p95.
Variety. Apr 2, 1952, p22.

Murder, Inc. *See* The Enforcer

Murder On Monday *See* Home At Seven

Murder on the Orient Express (US; Lumet,
Sidney; 1974)
America. Dec 21, 1974, v131, p411.
Audience. Dec 1974, v7, p10-13.
Before My Eyes. p330-32.
BFI/Monthly Film Bulletin. Dec 1974, v41,
p279-80.
Commonweal. Jan 17, 1975, v101, p329.
Esquire. Feb 1975, v83, p36.
Films and Filming. Oct 1974, v21, p44-46.
Films Illustrated. Jul 1974, v3, p430-33.
Films Illustrated. Dec 1974, v4, p128-29.
Films in Review. Dec 1974, v25, p623-24.
The Films of the Seventies. p94-96.
Focus on Film. Aut 1974, n19, p8-9.
Hollywood Reporter. Nov 20, 1976, p3.
Independent Film Journal. Nov 27, 1974, v74,
p7.
Lauren Bacall: Her Films and Career. p171-77.
The Los Angeles Times. Dec 22, 1974,
Calendar, p1.
Motion Picture Herald Product Digest. Nov 13,
1974, p47.
The Nation. Dec 14, 1974, v219, p637.
The New Republic. Dec 28, 1974, v171, p20.
New Statesman. Nov 22, 1974, v88, p750-51.
New York. Nov 25, 1974, v7, p94.
The New York Times. Nov 25, 1974, p38.
The New York Times. Dec 8, 1974, SecII, p15.
The New Yorker. Dec 9, 1974, v50, p171-72.
Newsweek. Dec 2, 1974, v84, p107.
Reeling. p518-21.
Senior Scholastic. Jan 16, 1975, v105, p20.
*Sidney Lumet: A Guide to References and
Resources*. p102-04.
Time. Dec 9, 1974, v104, p4.
Times Literary Supplement. Dec 6, 1974,
n3796, p1367-68.
Variety. Nov 20, 1974, p14.
The Village Voice. Dec 2, 1974, p81.
Vogue. Dec 1974, v164, p172-75.

Murder, She Said (GB; Pollock, George;
1961)
Film Daily. Jan 22, 1962, p4.
Filmfacts. Mar 9, 1962, v5, p32-33.
Films and Filming. Oct 1961, v8, p29.
Films in Review. Feb 1962, v13, p107.
Hollywood Reporter. Jan 12, 1962, p3.
Magill's Survey of Cinema. Series II. v4, p1672-
75.
Motion Picture Herald Product Digest. Jan 31,
1962, p427.
The Nation. Jan 20, 1962, v194, p68.
The New York Times. Jan 8, 1962, p27.
The New Yorker. Jan 20, 1962, v37, p110.
Newsweek. Jan 15, 1962, v59, p80.
Time. Jan 26, 1962, v79, p92.
Variety. Oct 18, 1961, p6.
Variety. Jan 17, 1962, p6.

My Dinner With Andre (US; Malle, Louis; 1981)
The Hollywood Reporter. Oct 13, 1981, p10.
The Los Angeles Times. Nov 1, 1981, Calendar, p28.
Magill's Cinema Annual, 1982. p255-58.
The Nation. Nov 7, 1981, v233, p483-84.
The New Republic. Nov 25, 1981, v185, p22-23.
The New Republic. Dec 23, 1981, v185, p25.
New York. Oct 19, 1981, v14, p37-40.
New York. Oct 26, 1981, v14, p96-97.
The New York Times. Oct 8, 1981, SecIII, p13.
The New Yorker. Jan 4, 1982, v57, p81-83.
Newsweek. Oct 26, 1981, v98, p78.
Time. Oct 26, 1981, v118, p94.
Variety. Sep 18, 1981, p3.

My Fair Lady (US; Cukor, George; 1964)
America. Nov 7, 1964, v111, p569-70.
BFI/Monthly Film Bulletin. Mar 1965, v32, p35.
Commonweal. Nov 13, 1964, v81, p238-39.
Confessions of a Cultist. p175-81.
Dance Magazine. Dec 1964, v38, p30-32.
Dictionary of Films. p232.
Esquire. Feb 1965, p44.
Film Daily. Oct 22, 1964, v125, p3, 6.
Films in Review. Nov 1964, v15, p570-71.
The Films of the Sixties. p137-40.
George Cukor (Philips). p161-65.
Hollywood Reporter. Oct 22, 1964, v182, p3-4.
Life. Nov 20, 1964, v57, p10.
Magill's Survey of Cinema. Series I. v3, p1170-74.
Motion Picture Herald Product Digest. Oct 28, 1964, v232, p12.
The Musical: From Broadway to Hollywood. p101-06.
National Review. Jan 12, 1965, v17, p31-32.
The New Republic. Nov 14, 1964, v151, p32.
The New York Times. Oct 22, 1964, p41.
The New Yorker. Oct 31, 1964, v40, p134-35.
Newsweek. Nov 2, 1964, v64, p96.
On Cukor. p240-45.
Saturday Review. Nov 14, 1964, v47, p40.
Sight and Sound. Spr 1965, v34, p94.
Time. Oct 30, 1964, v84, p106.
Tynan Right and Left. p209-13.
Variety. Oct 28, 1964, p6.
A World on Film. p41-42.

My Favorite Spy (US; McLeod, Norman Z.; 1951)
BFI/Monthly Film Bulletin. Dec 1951, v18, p377.
Catholic World. Dec 1951, v174, p222.
Christian Century. Jan 30, 1952, v69, p143.
Film Daily. Oct 5, 1951, p6.
The Films of Hedy Lamarr. p218-21.
Hollywood Reporter. Oct 5, 1951, p3.
Motion Picture Herald Product Digest. Oct 6, 1951, p1049.
The New Statesman and Nation. Dec 1, 1951, v42, p623.
The New York Times. Dec 26, 1951, p19.
Newsweek. Dec 24, 1951, v38, p67.
The Spectator. Nov 30, 1951, v187, p737-38.
Time. Dec 31, 1951, v58, p60.
Variety. Oct 10, 1951, p6.

My Favorite Year (US; Benjamin, Richard; 1982)
Christian Century. Oct 27, 1982, v99, p1093.
Hollywood Reporter. Sep 27, 1982, p3.
Horizon. Dec 1982, v25, p60.
The Los Angeles Times. Oct 2, 1982, SecV, p1.
Magill's Cinema Annual, 1983. p241-45.
National Review. Dec 10, 1982, v34, p1561-62.
The New Leader. Nov 29, 1982, v65, p21.
The New Republic. Nov 1, 1982, v187, p24.

New York. Oct 18, 1982, v15, p72-73.
The New York Times. Oct 1, 1982, SecIII, p10.
The New Yorker. Oct 4, 1982, v58, p132.
Newsweek. Oct 4, 1982, v100, p77.
Senior Scholastic. Nov 26, 1982, v115, p33.
Time. Sep 27, 1982, v120, p71.
Variety. Sep 24, 1982, p3.

My Forbidden Past (US; Stevenson, Robert; 1951)
BFI/Monthly Film Bulletin. Jul 1951, v18, p298.
Film Daily. Mar 23, 1951, p6.
Hollywood Reporter. Mar 21, 1951, p3.
Library Journal. Mar 1, 1951, v76, p418.
Motion Picture Herald Product Digest. Mar 31, 1951, p786-87.
The New York Times. Apr 26, 1951, p34.
Newsweek. May 7, 1951, v37, p90.
Robert Mitchum on the Screen. p114-15.
The Spectator. Jun 15, 1951, v186, p781.
Time. May 14, 1951, v57, p112.
Variety. Mar 28, 1951, p6.

My Home Is Copacabana (Swedish title: Mitt Hem Ar Copacabana) (SWED; Sucksdorff, Arne; 1965)
BFI/Monthly Film Bulletin. Mar 1966, v33, p38-39.
Christian Science Monitor (Western edition). Apr 10, 1965, p6.
Films and Filming. Mar 1965, v10, p18, 51.
Films and Filming. Apr 1966, v12, p18, 51.
International Film Guide. 1966, v3, p130.
The London Times. Jan 27, 1966, p9.
New Statesman. Feb 4, 1966, v71, p172.
On Film. p271-72.
The Spectator. Feb 4, 1966, v216, p140.
Tynan Right and Left. p252-53.
Variety. Jun 16, 1965, p16.

My Love Letters *See* Love Letters

My Man and I (US; Wellman, William A.; 1952)
BFI/Monthly Film Bulletin. Jan 1953, v19, p5.
Christian Century. Dec 3, 1952, v69, p1423.
Film Daily. Aug 25, 1952, p6.
Hollywood Reporter. Aug 15, 1952, p3.
Motion Picture Herald Product Digest. Aug 23, 1952, p1502.
The Nation. Sep 27, 1952, v175, p282.
National Parent-Teacher. Oct 1952, v47, p38.
The New York Times. Sep 6, 1952, p12.
Newsweek. Sep 22, 1952, v40, p114.
The Tatler. Dec 24, 1952, v206, p694.
Time. Sep 15, 1952, v60, p110.
Variety. Aug 20, 1952, p6.
William A. Wellman (Thompson). p239-41, 308-09.

My Man Godfrey (US; Koster, Henry; 1957)
BFI/Monthly Film Bulletin. Dec 1957, v24, p147-48.
Commonweal. Nov 1, 1957, v67, p132.
Film Daily. Sep 4, 1957, v112, p11.
Films and Filming. Nov 1957, v4, p24.
Hollywood Reporter. Sep 4, 1957, p3.
Motion Picture Herald Product Digest. Sep 7, 1957, v208, p521.
The New York Times. Oct 12, 1957, p23.
The New York Times. Oct 20, 1957, SecII, p1.
The New Yorker. Oct 19, 1957, v33, p87.
Newsweek. Nov 18, 1957, v50, p132.
Time. Oct 21, 1957, v70, p102.

My Margo *See* Margo

My Night at Maud's (French title: Ma nuit chez Maud) (FR; Rohmer, Eric; 1969)
America. Apr 11, 1970, v122, p397.

Australian Journal of Screen Theory. 1977, n2, p3-32.
BFI/Monthly Film Bulletin. Jan 1970, v377, p6-7.
Cineaste. Fall 1969, v3, p6-10.
Cineaste. Fall 1971, v7, p16-21.
Commentary. Aug 1971, v52, p84-86.
Commonweal. May 1, 1970, v92, p169-70.
Film Quarterly. Wint 1969-70, v23, p57-59.
Film Quarterly. Sum 1971, v24, p34-41.
Films and Filming. Apr 1970, v16, p54.
Films in Review. May 1970, v21, p307-08.
Magill's Survey of Cinema. Foreign Language Films. v5, p2146-51.
The Nation. Apr 27, 1970, v210, p509-10.
The New York Times. Sep 24, 1969, p50.
The New York Times. Mar 23, 1970, p49.
The New York Times. Mar 7, 1971, SecII, p1.
The New York Times. Oct 29, 1972, SecII, p1.
The New Yorker. Apr 4, 1970, v46, p115-16.
Newsweek. Feb 23, 1970, v75, p101.
Saturday Review. Feb 7, 1970, v53, p41.
Second Sight. p306-08.
Variety. May 14, 1969, p35.
The Village Voice. Sep 4, 1969, p43.
The Village Voice. Mar 26, 1970, p55-56.
The Village Voice. Apr 2, 1970, v15, p59.
The Village Voice. Jun 26, 1984, p49.

My Pal Gus (US; Parrish, Robert; 1952)
BFI/Monthly Film Bulletin. Jan 1953, v20, p5.
Commonweal. Dec 19, 1952, v57, p283.
Film Daily. Nov 14, 1952, p6.
Hollywood Reporter. Nov 7, 1952, p3.
Motion Picture Herald Product Digest. Nov 15, 1952, p1606.
Saturday Review. Dec 6, 1952, v35, p42.
Variety. Nov 12, 1952, p6.

My Sister, My Love (Swedish title: Sepkonbadd 1782; Also titled: Brother and Sister Bed) (SWED; Sjoman, Vilgot; 1966)
BFI/Monthly Film Bulletin. Feb 1967, v34, p25-26.
Christian Science Monitor (Western edition). Apr 8, 1967, p10.
Film Daily. Feb 24, 1967, p7.
Filmfacts. Apr 1, 1967, v10, p57-58.
Films and Filming. Feb 1967, v13, p35-36.
International Film Guide. 1967, v4, p145.
The New York Times. Feb 20, 1967, p45.
The New Yorker. Feb 25, 1967, v43, p132.
Playboy. Mar 1967, v14, p23-24.
Variety. Jan 18, 1967, p6.

My Six Convicts (US; Fregonese, Hugo; 1952)
BFI/Monthly Film Bulletin. Jul 1952, v19, p91-92.
Christian Century. May 7, 1952, v69, p575.
Commonweal. Apr 4, 1952, v55, p638-39.
Film Daily. Mar 12, 1952, p12.
Hollywood Reporter. Mar 10, 1952, p3.
Library Journal. Mar 15, 1952, v77, p522.
Motion Picture Herald Product Digest. Mar 15, 1952, p1281-82.
The New York Times. Mar 28, 1952, p27.
The New Yorker. Apr 5, 1952, v28, p135.
Newsweek. Mar 31, 1952, v39, p86.
Saturday Review. Mar 19, 1952, v35, p27.
The Spectator. May 23, 1952, v188, p673.
Stanley Kramer, Film Maker. p83-90.
The Tatler. Jun 4, 1952, v204, p540.
Theatre Arts. Apr 1952, v36, p85.
Time. Apr 21, 1952, v59, p108.
Variety. Mar 12, 1952, p6.

My Six Loves (US; Champion, Gower; 1963)
BFI/Monthly Film Bulletin. Jun 1963, v30, p88.
Commonweal. Apr 19, 1963, v78, p107.
Film Daily. Mar 6, 1963, p6.
Filmfacts. Mar 28, 1963, v6, p41-42.
Films and Filming. Jun 1963, v9, p34.
Hollywood Reporter. Mar 6, 1963, v174, p3.
The New York Times. Apr 4, 1963, p58.
Photoplay. May 1963, v63, p6.
Time. Apr 19, 1963, v81, p112.
Variety. Mar 6, 1963, p6.

My Son, John (US; McCarey, Leo; 1952)
American Mercury. Jun 1952, v74, p74-80.
BFI/Monthly Film Bulletin. May 1953, v20, p69-70.
Catholic World. Apr 1952, v175, p65.
Christian Century. Nov 5, 1952, v69, p1303.
Commentary. May 1952, v13, p483-85.
Commonweal. Apr 18, 1952, v56, p46.
Commonweal. Apr 25, 1952, v56, p59-60.
Film Comment. Jan-Feb 1976, v12, p16-20.
Film Daily. Mar 20, 1952, p10.
Films in Review. May 1952, v3, p239-42.
The Films of the Fifties. p63-64.
Hollywood Goes to War. p129, 132.
Hollywood Reporter. Mar 20, 1952, p3.
The Immediate Experience (Warshow). p163-71.
Journal of Popular Film. 1980, v8, n1, p44-49.
Jump Cut. Oct-Dec 1975, n9, p14-16.
Motion Picture Herald Product Digest. Mar 22, 1952, p1289.
The Nation. Mar 22, 1952, v174, p286-87.
The New York Times. Apr 9, 1952, p27.
The New Yorker. Apr 19, 1952, v28, p93.
Newsweek. Apr 14, 1952, v39, p96.
Running Time: Films of the Cold War. p94-99.
Saturday Review. Apr 19, 1952, v35, p46.
Theatre Arts. Apr 1952, v36, p42.
Time. Apr 7, 1952, v59, p104.
Variety. Mar 26, 1952, p6.

My True Story (US; Rooney, Mickey; 1951)
BFI/Monthly Film Bulletin. Jul 1951, v18, p298.
Film Daily. Mar 8, 1951, p6.
Hollywood Reporter. Mar 7, 1951, p3.
Motion Picture Herald Product Digest. Mar 10, 1951, p750.
Variety. Mar 7, 1951, p18.

My Uncle *See* Mon Oncle

My Wife's Best Friend (US; Sale, Richard; 1952)
BFI/Monthly Film Bulletin. Oct 1952, v19, p144.
Commonweal. Nov 7, 1952, v57, p120.
Film Daily. Oct 6, 1952, p6.
Hollywood Reporter. Oct 6, 1952, p3.
The London Times. Sep 29, 1952, p10.
Motion Picture Herald Product Digest. Oct 11, 1952, p1558.
The New York Times. Oct 11, 1952, p17.
The Spectator. Sep 26, 1952, v189, p393.
The Tatler. Oct 8, 1952, v206, p84.
Variety. Oct 8, 1952, p6.

Mystere Koumiko, Le *See* The Koumiko Mystery

Mystery Street (US; Sturges, John; 1950)
BFI/Monthly Film Bulletin. Aug 1950, v17, p120.
Christian Century. Sep 20, 1950, v67, p1119.
Commonweal. Sep 22, 1950, v52, p581.
Film Daily. Jun 1, 1950, p6.
Hollywood Reporter. May 17, 1950, p3.

Motion Picture Herald Product Digest. May 20, 1950, p302.
The New York Times. Jul 28, 1950, p12.
The New Yorker. Sep 16, 1950, v26, p52.
Time. Aug 7, 1950, v56, p67.
Variety. May 17, 1950, p6.

Mystery Submarine (US; Sirk, Douglas; 1950)
BFI/Monthly Film Bulletin. Jan 1951, v18, p205-06.
Commonweal. Feb 2, 1951, v53, p427.
Film Daily. Nov 24, 1950, p8.
Films and Filming. Jun 1953, v9, p31.
Hollywood Reporter. Nov 22, 1950, p3.
Motion Picture Herald Product Digest. Nov 25, 1950, p590.
The New York Times. Feb 2, 1951, p19.
Newsweek. Jan 15, 1951, v37, p82.
Variety. Nov 22, 1950, p8.

The Nada Gang (Also titled: Nada) (FR; Chabrol, Claude; 1974)
BFI/Monthly Film Bulletin. Apr 1974, v41, p77-78.
Film. Jun 1974, n15, p8.
Films and Filming. Jun 1974, v20, p48.
Films Illustrated. Jul 1974, v3, p424.
Independent Film Journal. Nov 13, 1974, v74, p13.
Motion Picture Herald Product Digest. Nov 27, 1974, p51.
The Nation. Nov 30, 1974, v219, p572.
New Statesman. May 3, 1974, v87, p634.
New York. Nov 11, 1974, v7, p106.
The New York Times. Nov 7, 1974, p56.
Newsweek. Nov 11, 1974, v84, p86.
Sight and Sound. Spr 1974, v43, p119.
Time. Dec 2, 1974, v104, p6.
Times Educational Supplement. May 10, 1974, n3076, p78.
Variety. Jun 30, 1974, p14.
The Village Voice. Nov 14, 1974, p93.

Naked Alibi (US; Hopper, Jerry; 1954)
America. Oct 9, 1954, v92, p55.
BFI/Monthly Film Bulletin. Oct 1954, v21, p148.
Catholic World. Oct 1954, v180, p64.
Farm Journal. Oct 1954, v78, p137.
Film Daily. Aug 24, 1954, p10.
Films and Filming. Oct 1954, v1, p25-26.
Hollywood Reporter. Aug 23, 1954, p3.
Motion Picture Herald Product Digest. Aug 28, 1954, p121.
National Parent-Teacher. Oct 1954, v49, p40.
The New York Times. Oct 2, 1954, p21.
Variety. Aug 25, 1954, p6.

Naked Island *See* The Island

The Naked Jungle (US; Haskin, Byron; 1954)
America. Apr 10, 1954, v91, p54.
BFI/Monthly Film Bulletin. May 1954, v21, p71-72.
Catholic World. May 1954, v179, p144.
Film Daily. Feb 15, 1954, p6.
The Films of George Pal. p79-84.
Hollywood Reporter. Feb 10, 1954, p3.
Library Journal. Mar 1, 1954, v79, p44.
The London Times. Jun 7, 1954, p3.
Motion Picture Herald Product Digest. Feb 13, 1954, p2181.
National Parent-Teacher. Apr 1954, v48, p39.
Natural History. May 1954, v63, p236-67.
The New York Times. Apr 3, 1954, p19.
Newsweek. Mar 29, 1954, v43, p86.
Saturday Review. Apr 17, 1954, v37, p23.
Senior Scholastic. Apr 21, 1954, v64, p30.
Variety. Feb 17, 1954, p6.

The Naked Kiss (Also titled: The Iron Kiss; Police Speciale) (US; Fuller, Sam; 1964)
BFI/Monthly Film Bulletin. Jun 1970, v37, p122.
Cahiers du Cinema in English. 1964, n4, p57-58.
Cinema. Sum 1967, v3, p50.
Film Quarterly. Fall 1964, v18, p62.
Filmfacts. Mar 12, 1965, v8, p31-32.
Films and Filming. Jul 1970, v16, p38-40.
The New York Times. Oct 29, 1964, p38.
Samuel Fuller (Hardy). p131-38.
Surrealism and the Cinema. p131-33.
Variety. Jan 20, 1965, p6.

The Naked Night (Swedish title: Gycklarnas afton; Also titled: Sawdust and Tinsel) (SWED; Bergman, Ingmar; 1953)
Cinema, the Magic Vehicle. v2, p149-52.
Film Daily. Jan 18, 1956, p5.
Ingmar Bergman: A Critical Biography. p112-20.
Ingmar Bergman: Essays in Criticism. p143-45.
Ingmar Bergman (Steene). p79-83.
The International Dictionary of Films and Filmmakers. v1, p190-91.
Magill's Survey of Cinema. Foreign Language Films. v5, p2166-70.
The Nation. Apr 21, 1956, v182, p349.
The New York Times. Apr 10, 1957, p27.
Newsweek. Apr 23, 1956, v47, p98.
Variety. Feb 8, 1956, p6.

The Naked Prey (US, S AFR; Wilde, Cornel; 1966)
BFI/Monthly Film Bulletin. Sep 1966, v33, p141-42.
Christian Science Monitor (Western edition). May 4, 1966, p6.
Cinema. Jul 1966, v3, p49.
Cinema. Dec 1965, v3, p44-45.
Film Daily. Mar 11, 1966, p4.
Film Quarterly. Fall 1966, v20, p59.
Filmfacts. Aug 15, 1966, v9, p161-62.
Films and Filming. Oct 1966, v13, p7, 9.
Films in Review. Apr 1966, v17, p248-49.
The Great Adventure Films. p266-69.
The London Times. Sep 22, 1966, p6.
Motion Picture Herald Product Digest. Mar 30, 1966, p491.
New Statesman. Sep 23, 1966, v72, p454.
The New York Times. Jun 15, 1966, p40.
Time. Jun 17, 1966, v87, p101.
Variety. Mar 16, 1966, p6.

The Naked Spur (US; Mann, Anthony; 1953)
America. Mar 21, 1953, v88, p689.
Anthony Mann (Basinger). p111-16.
BFI/Monthly Film Bulletin. Mar 1953, v20, p31.
Catholic World. Mar 1953, v176, p460.
Christian Century. Apr 29, 1953, v70, p527.
Commonweal. Apr 17, 1953, v58, p52.
Film Daily. Jan 21, 1953, p10.
The Films of James Stewart. p155-57.
Hollywood Reporter. Jan 9, 1953, p3.
Library Journal. Feb 15, 1953, v78, p314.
The London Times. Apr 23, 1953, p6.
Magill's Survey of Cinema. Series II. v4, p1704-09.
Motion Picture Herald Product Digest. Jun 17, 1953, p1685.
The Nation. Mar 28, 1953, v176, p274.
National Parent-Teacher. Mar 1953, v47, p27.
The New York Times. Mar 26, 1953, p37.
Newsweek. Mar 2, 1953, v41, p91.
Saturday Review. Feb 14, 1953, v36, p47.

The Spectator. Apr 10, 1953, v190, p447-48.
Time. Feb 2, 1953, v61, p78.
Variety. Jan 14, 1953, p6.

Naked Under Leather *See* The Girl On a Motorcycle

Nana (FR; Ahlberg, Mac; 1971)
BFI/Monthly Film Bulletin. May 1971, v28, n448, p102.
Filmfacts. 1971, v14, n8, p151.
Hollywood Reporter. Apr 21, 1971, p3.
The New York Times. Apr 29, 1971, p49.
Variety. May 5, 1971, p22.

Nanami *See* The Inferno of First Love

Nancy Goes to Rio (US; Leonard, Robert Z.; 1950)
Christian Century. Mar 29, 1950, v67, p415.
Film Daily. Feb 2, 1950, p9.
Hollywood Reporter. Feb 1, 1950, p3.
The New York Times. Apr 7, 1950, p22.
Time. Apr 17, 1950, v55, p108 .
Variety. Feb 1, 1950, p14.

The Nanny (GB; Holt, Seth; 1965)
America. Nov 6, 1965, v113, p542.
Bette Davis: Her Films and Career. p189-91.
BFI/Monthly Film Bulletin. Nov 1965, v32, p164.
Commonweal. Nov 19, 1965, v83, p217.
Film Daily. Oct 20, 1965, p5.
Film Quarterly. Spr 1966, v19, p53.
Films and Filming. Nov 1965, v12, p30.
Films in Review. Nov 1965, v16, p578-79.
Great Horror Movies. p89-90.
Hollywood Reporter. Oct 19, 1965, p3.
Life. Dec 3, 1965, v59, p20.
London Magazine. Dec 1965, v5, p66-69.
The London Times. Oct 7, 1965, p16.
Motion Picture Herald Product Digest. Oct 27, 1965, p393-94.
The New Republic. Dec 11, 1965, v153, p34.
New Statesman. Oct 8, 1965, v70, p534.
The New York Times. Nov 4, 1965, p57.
Playboy. Jan 1966, v13, p48.
The Spectator. Oct 15, 1965, v215, p485.
Time. Oct 29, 1965, v86, p101.
Variety. Oct 13, 1965, p6.
Vogue. Dec 1965, v146, p147.

The Narrow Margin (US; Fleischer, Richard; 1950)
BFI/Monthly Film Bulletin. Nov 1952, v19, p158.
Film Daily. Apr 2, 1952, p6.
Hollywood Reporter. Mar 26, 1952, p3.
Motion Picture Herald Product Digest. Apr 12, 1952, p1314.
The New Statesman and Nation. Dec 13, 1952, v44, p718.
The New York Times. May 5, 1952, p18.
The New Yorker. May 10, 1952, v28, p86.
Newsweek. May 19, 1952, v39, p106.
A Reference Guide to the American Film Noir. p120.
Sight and Sound. Oct-Dec 1952, v22, p80.
The Spectator. Dec 5, 1952, v189, p762.
Theatre Arts. Jul 1952, v36, p88.
Time. May 5, 1952, v59, p106.
Variety. Apr 2, 1952, p6.

Nashville (US; Altman, Robert; 1975)
America. Aug 16, 1975, v133, p71-73.
BFI/Monthly Film Bulletin. Oct 1975, v42, p221.
Commonweal. Aug 29, 1975, v102, p368-69.
Esquire. Sep 1975, v84, p34.
Film Quarterly. Wint 1975, v29, p13-25.
Films in Review. Aug-Sep 1975, v26, p7.
The Films of Robert Altman. p50-62.

The Films of the Seventies. p124-26.
Hollywood Reporter. Aug 15, 1975, p3.
International Dictionary of Films and Filmmakers. v1, p314-15.
Landmark Films. p388-97.
Magill's Survey of Cinema. Series I. v3, p1181-85.
Motion Picture Herald Product Digest. Jun 11, 1975, p1.
Nashville. 1975.
The Nation. Jul 5, 1975, v221, p28.
The New Republic. Jun 28, 1975, v172, p22.
The New York Times. Jun 12, 1975, p32.
The New York Times. Jun 15, 1975, SecII, p1.
The New York Times. Aug 10, 1975, SecII, p1.
The New Yorker. Mar 3, 1975, v51, p79-83.
The New Yorker. Jun 16, 1975, v51, p107-08.
Newsweek. Jun 30, 1975, v85, p46-50.
Reeling. p591-98.
Reruns. p238-42.
Robert Altman: American Innovator. p193-212.
Robert Altman (Plecki). p238-42.
Saturday Review. Jun 28, 1975, v2, p40-41.
Time. Jun 16, 1975, v105, p67-68.
Variety. Jun 11, 1975, p18.
Vogue. Jun 1975, v165, p102-03.

Nasty Habits (US, GB; Lindsay-Hogg, Michael; 1977)
America. Apr 9, 1977, v136, p332.
BFI/Monthly Film Bulletin. Aug 1977, v44, p171.
Commonweal. Apr 29, 1977, v104, p258.
Films in Review. May 1977, v28, p315.
Hollywood Reporter. Mar 18, 1977, p3.
The Los Angeles Times. May 6, 1977, SecIV, p1.
Motion Picture Herald Product Digest. Apr 6, 1977, p88.
The New Republic. Feb 26, 1977, v176, p20.
The New York Times. Mar 19, 1977, p11.
The New Yorker. Feb 21, 1977, v53, p115-18.
Newsweek. Mar 28, 1977, v89, p86-87.
Saturday Review. Apr 2, 1977, v4, p41.
Time. Apr 25, 1977, v109, p73.
Variety. Oct 27, 1976, p26.

National Lampoon's Animal House (Also titled: Animal House) (US; Landis, John; 1978)
BFI/Monthly Film Bulletin. Feb 1979, v46, p29.
Christian Century. Dec 6, 1978, v95, p1186.
Films in Review. Nov 1978, v29, p568.
The Films of the Seventies. p225-28.
Hollywood Reporter. Jun 23, 1978, p3.
The Los Angeles Times. Aug 4, 1978, SecIV, p1.
Maclean's. Sep 4, 1978, v91, p59.
Motion Picture Herald Product Digest. Jul 26, 1978, p16.
New York. Jul 31, 1978, v11, p65.
The New York Times. Jul 28, 1978, SecIII, p7.
The New York Times. Nov 19, 1978, SecII, p17.
The New Yorker. Aug 14, 1978, v54, p53-54.
Newsweek. Oct 2, 1978, v92, p74.
Newsweek. Oct 23, 1978, v92, p88-89.
Time. Aug 14, 1978, v112, p87.
Variety. Jun 28, 1978, p20.

National Lampoon's Vacation (US; Ramis, Harold; 1983)
Films and Filming. Oct 1983, n349, p43.
Hollywood Reporter. Jul 29, 1983, p3.
The Los Angeles Times. Jul 29, 1983, SecVI, p16.
Maclean's. Aug 15, 1983, v96, p47.
Magill's Cinema Annual, 1984. p241-46.
The New York Times. Jul 29, 1983, SecIII, p10.
Newsweek. Aug 8, 1983, v102, p55.

Native Son (ARG; Chenal, Pierre; 1951)
BFI/Monthly Film Bulletin. Jan 1952, v19, p4.
Commonweal. Jun 29, 1951, v54, p286.
Film Daily. Jun 29, 1951, p6.
Library Journal. Jul 1951, v76, p1141.
Motion Picture Herald Product Digest. Jun 23, 1951, p906.
The New Republic. Jul 2, 1951, v125, p23.
The New York Times. Jun 18, 1951, p19.
Newsweek. Jul 9, 1951, v38, p94.
Saturday Review. Jul 7, 1951, v34, p24.
Variety. Apr 25, 1951, p14.

Nattlek *See* Night Games

Nattvardsgaesterna *See* Winter Light

The Natural (US; Levinson, Barry; 1984)
America. Jun 23, 1984, v150, p493.
American Film. May 1984, v9, p16-21.
BFI/Monthly Film Bulletin. Nov 1984, v51, p337-38.
Christian Century. May 30, 1984, v101, p563-64.
Commonweal. Jun 15, 1984, v111, p373-74.
Film Journal. Apr 1984, v87, p7.
Films and Filming. Oct 1984, n36, p44.
Films and Filming. Jun 1984, n357, p42.
Films in Review. Aug-Sep 1984, v35, p427.
Hollywood Reporter. May 17, 1984, p8.
Horizon. Apr 1984, v27, p52-53.
Informer. May-Jun 1984, p4.
The Los Angeles Times. May 11, 1984, SecVI, p1.
Maclean's. May 21, 1984, v97, p65.
Millimeter. May 1984, v12, p84-86.
The Nation. Jun 2, 1984, v238, p682-83.
National Review. Jul 13, 1984, v36, p51-52.
The New Leader. Jun 11, 1984, v67, p21.
The New Republic. Jun 11, 1984, v190, p24-25.
New Statesman. Oct 19, 1984, v108, p36-37.
New York. May 21, 1984, v17, p94-95.
The New York Times. May 11, 1984, SecIII, p15.
The New York Times. May 6, 1984, SecII, p1.
The New York Times. Jun 14, 1984, SecIII, p17.
The New York Times. Apr 1, 1984, SecV, p2.
The New Yorker. May 28, 1984, v60, p100-01.
Newsweek. May 28, 1984, v103, p77.
Photoplay. Nov 1984, v35, p16-17, 20.
School Update. Sep 7, 1984, v117, p27-28.
Sport Magazine. May 1984, v75, p108.
Sports Illustrated. May 7, 1984, v60, p71.
Time. Mar 14, 1984, v123, p91.
Variety. May 9, 1984, p10.
The Village Voice. May 22, 1984, p57.
Vogue. May 1984, v174, p75.

Nazarin (MEX; Buñuel, Luis; 1959)
AFFS Newsletter. Feb 1965, p15-16.
BFI/Monthly Film Bulletin. Oct 1963, v30, p141.
Christian Century. Nov 6, 1968, v85, p1410.
Cinema Eye, Cinema Ear. p106-07.
Commonweal. Jul 26, 1968, v88, p505-06.
Dictionary of Films. p239-40.
The Discreet Art of Luis Bunuel. p113-39.
Film. Aut 1962, n33, p20-21.
Film Culture. Sum 1960, n21, p60-62.
Film Culture. Sum 1966, n41, p60-65.
Film Journal. Mar 1960, n15, p51-54.
Film Journal. Oct 1961, n18, p19.
Film Quarterly. Spr 1960, v13, p30-31.
Filmfacts. Sep 15, 1968, v11, p249-50.
Films and Filming. Oct 1963, v10, p23.
Five Thousand One Nights At the Movies. p407.
Luis Bunuel (Higginbotham). p107-10.
Motion Picture Herald Product Digest. Jul 17, 1968, p832.
The Nation. Jul 8, 1968, v207, p28-29.

The New Yorker. Jun 22, 1968, v44, p66.
Sight and Sound. Aut 1963, v32, p194-95.
Variety. May 20, 1959, p6.
A Year In the Dark. p179-80.

Né de Pere Inconnu (Also titled: Father Unknown) (FR; Cloche, Maurice; 1950)
BFI/Monthly Film Bulletin. Sep 1952, v19, p129.
The London Times. Jul 28, 1952, p8.
The Spectator. Jul 25, 1952, v189, p129.
Variety. May 16, 1951, p18.

Negatives (GB; Medak, Peter; 1968)
BFI/Monthly Film Bulletin. May 1970, v37, p109.
Film Daily. Oct 25, 1968, p6.
Filmfacts. Jan 15, 1969, v11, p431-32.
Motion Picture Herald Product Digest. Oct 23, 1968, p46.
Movies Into Film. p316-17.
The Nation. Nov 11, 1968, v207, p508.
The New Republic. Nov 23, 1968, v159, p26.
The New York Times. Oct 15, 1968, p40.
Variety. Oct 16, 1968, p6.

Network (US; Lumet, Sidney; 1976)
America. Dec 18, 1976, v135, p452.
Before My Eyes. p101.
Commonweal. Dec 3, 1976, v103, p784.
Film Bulletin. Nov-Dec 1976, v45, p39.
Films in Review. Dec 1976, v27, p635.
The Films of the Seventies. p154-56.
Hollywood Reporter. Oct 12, 1976, p1, 3.
Independent Film Journal. Oct 29, 1976, v78, p9.
The Los Angeles Times. Nov 14, 1976, Calendar, p1.
Magill's Survey of Cinema. Series I. v3, p1190-93.
Millimeter. Dec 1976, v4, p26.
The Nation. Dec 4, 1976, v223, p605-06.
The New Republic. Nov 3, 1976, v175, p22-23.
The New York Times. Nov 28, 1976, SecII, p17.
The New Yorker. Dec 6, 1976, v52, p177-80.
Newsweek. Nov 22, 1976, v88, p107.
Reruns. p243-47.
Rolling Stone. Dec 16, 1976, p41.
Saturday Review. Nov 13, 1976, v4, p44.
Sidney Lumet: A Guide to References and Resources. p107-10.
Time. Nov 29, 1976, v108, p79.
Time. Dec 13, 1976, v108, p78-79.
Variety. Oct 13, 1976, p22.
The Village Voice. Nov 29, 1976, p53.
Vogue. Nov 1976, v166, p160, 227.

Nevada Smith (US; Hathaway, Henry; 1966)
America. Jun 25, 1966, v114, p881.
BFI/Monthly Film Bulletin. Sep 1966, v33, p138.
Christian Science Monitor (Western edition). Aug 6, 1966, p6.
Commonweal. Jul 1, 1966, v84, p419.
Film Daily. Jun 1, 1966, p7.
Filmfacts. Sep 1, 1966, v9, p174-76.
Films and Filming. Oct 1966, v13, p12, 16.
The Films of Steve McQueen. p113-79.
Hollywood Reporter. May 31, 1966, p3.
The London Times. Jul 28, 1966, p7.
Motion Picture Herald Product Digest. Jun 8, 1966, p535.
New Statesman. Sep 30, 1966, v72, p177.
The New York Times. Jun 30, 1966, p28.
Newsweek. Jul 11, 1966, v68, p90.
Playboy. Jun 1966, v13, p38, 40.
Saturday Review. Jun 18, 1966, v49, p50.
The Spectator. Aug 26, 1966, v217, p261.

Time. Jul 15, 1966, v88, p81.
Variety. Jun 1, 1966, p6.

Never a Dull Moment (Also titled: Come Share My Love) (US; Marshall, George; 1950)
BFI/Monthly Film Bulletin. Jul 1951, v18, p298.
Christian Century. Jan 24, 1951, v68, p127.
Commonweal. Dec 15, 1950, v53, p254.
Film Daily. Nov 2, 1950, p6.
Hollywood Reporter. Oct 30, 1950, p3.
Library Journal. Dec 1, 1950, v75, p2086.
Motion Picture Herald Product Digest. Nov 4, 1950, p553.
The New York Times. Nov 22, 1950, p20.
The New Yorker. Dec 2, 1950, v26, p105.
Newsweek. Dec 4, 1950, v36, p82.
Time. Dec 4, 1950, v56, p96.
Variety. Nov 1, 1950, p6.

Never Cry Wolf (US; Ballard, Carroll; 1983)
Films in Review. Dec 1983, v34, p621.
Hollywood Reporter. Oct 7, 1983, p3.
The Los Angeles Times. Oct 20, 1983, SecVI, p1.
Maclean's. Oct 17, 1983, v96, p59-60.
Magill's Cinema Annual, 1984. p247-51.
The Nation. Nov 5, 1983, v237, p442.
The New Republic. Dec 5, 1983, v189, p20.
New York. Oct 24, 1983, v16, p104-05.
The New York Times. Oct 14, 1983, SecIII, p8.
The New York Times Magazine. Oct 16, 1983, p84-85.
The New Yorker. Dec 12, 1983, v59, p152-54.
Newsweek. Oct 17, 1983, v102, p98.
Rolling Stone. Nov 10, 1983, p68-70.
Time. Oct 24, 1983, v122, p92.

The Never Ending Story (German title: Unendlighe Geschichte, Die) (WGER; Peterson, Wolfgang; 1984)
American Cinematographer. Aug-Sep 1984, v65, p64-69.
American Premiere. Sum 1984, v5, p32.
BFI/Monthly Film Bulletin. Apr 1985, v52, p124.
Cinefantastique. 1983, v13, n6, p14-15.
Film Journal. Aug 1984, v87, p15-16.
Horizon. Oct 1984, v27, p60.
Informer. Aug 1984, p6.
The Los Angeles Times. Jul 20, 1984, SecVI, p1.
Maclean's. Jul 23, 1984, v97, p47.
Midnight Marquee. Fall 1984, n33, p29.
New York. Jul 30, 1984, v17, p47.
The New York Times. Jul 15, 1984, SecII, p15.
Newsweek. Jul 30, 1984, v104, p80.
Time. Jul 16, 1984, v124, p71.
Variety. Jul 4, 1984, p16.
The Village Voice. Jul 24, 1984, v29, p57-58.

Never Fear (US; Lupino, Ida; 1950)
Christian Century. Apr 5, 1950, v67, p447.
Film Daily. Jan 12, 1950, p5.
Hollywood Reporter. Jan 4, 1950, p4.
Variety. Jan 4, 1950, p63.

Never Give an Inch *See* Sometimes a Great Notion

Never on Sunday (Greek title: Potè Tin Kyriaki) (GREECE; Dassin, Jules; 1959)
Dictionary of Films. p290-91.
Films and Filming. Dec 1960, v7, p7.
Films in Review. Nov 1960, v2, p9.
Magill's Survey of Cinema. Foreign Language Films. v5, p2177-80.
The Nation. Nov 5, 1960, v191, p355.

The New Republic. Nov 14, 1960, v143, p19.
The New York Times. Oct 19, 1960, p54.
The New Yorker. Oct 29, 1960, v36, p102-03.
Newsweek. Oct 24, 1960, v56, p130.
Saturday Review. Oct 29, 1960, v43, p28.
Sight and Sound. Wint 1960-61, v30, p37-38.
Time. Oct 31, 1960, v76, p47.
The Village Voice. Sep 29, 1960, p11-12.

Never Say Never Again (US; Kershner, Irvin; 1983)
Films in Review. Dec 1983, v34, p623.
Hollywood Reporter. Oct 5, 1983, p3.
The Los Angeles Times. Oct 7, 1983, SecVI, p1.
Maclean's. Oct 24, 1983, v96, p64.
Magill's Cinema Annual, 1984. p252-57.
New York. Nov 7, 1983, v16, p100-01.
The New York Times. Oct 7, 1983, SecIII, p13.
Newsweek. Oct 10, 1983, v102, p93.
Time. Oct 17, 1983, v122, p89.

Never So Few (US; Sturges, John; 1959)
America. Jan 16, 1960, v102, p480.
BFI/Monthly Film Bulletin. Feb 1960, v27, p20.
Commonweal. Jan 22, 1960, v70, p469.
Film Daily. Dec 7, 1959, v116, p8.
Filmfacts. Feb 12, 1960, v3, p7.
The Films of Charles Bronson. p86-88.
The Films of Frank Sinatra. p154-59.
The Films of Steve McQueen. p36-40.
Hollywood Reporter. Dec 7, 1959, p8.
The New York Times. Jan 22, 1959, p15.
Newsweek. Jan 18, 1960, v55, p90.
Saturday Review. Jan 23, 1960, v43, p26.
Time. Jan 25, 1960, v75, p93.
Variety. Dec 9, 1959, p6.

Never Take No For An Answer (GB; Cloche, Maurice; Smart, Ralph; 1952)
BFI/Monthly Film Bulletin. Feb 1952, v19, p22.
Catholic World. Apr 1952, v175, p63.
Christian Century. Jul 16, 1952, v69, p839.
Commonweal. Apr 25, 1952, v56, p70.
Film Daily. Mar 19, 1952, p6.
Hollywood Reporter. Aug 4, 1952, p3.
Library Journal. May 15, 1952, v77, p873.
Life. Jun 2, 1952, v32, p58.
The New York Times. Apr 29, 1952, p32.
The New Yorker. May 10, 1952, v28, p57.
Newsweek. Apr 28, 1952, v39, p98.
The Spectator. Dec 28, 1951, v187, p884.
Theatre Arts. May 1952, v36, p104.
Variety. Dec 26, 1951, p22.

Never Too Late (US; Yorkin, Bud; 1965)
America. Dec 4, 1965, v113, p733.
BFI/Monthly Film Bulletin. Feb 1966, v33, p25.
Christian Science Monitor (Western edition). Nov 9, 1965, p4.
Film Daily. Oct 26, 1965, p3.
Films and Filming. Mar 1965, v12, p10-11.
Films and Filming. Apr 1966, v12, p10-11.
Films in Review. Dec 1965, v16, p646.
Hollywood Reporter. Oct 26, 1965, p3.
The London Times. Jan 6, 1966, p8.
Motion Picture Herald Product Digest. Nov 10, 1965, p403.
The New York Times. Nov 5, 1965, p28.
The New Yorker. Nov 13, 1965, v41, p234-35.
Newsweek. Nov 15, 1965, v66, p125A.
Variety. Oct 27, 1965, p6.

Nevinost Bez Zastite *See* Innocence Unprotected

New Faces (US; Horner, Harry; 1954)
America. Mar 13, 1954, v90, p638.
BFI/Monthly Film Bulletin. Dec 1954, v21, p173-74.

Catholic World. Apr 1954, v179, p63.
Commonweal. Mar 12, 1954, v59, p577.
Film Daily. Feb 19,1954, p6.
Films and Filming. Dec 1954, v1, p18.
Films in Review. Apr 1954, v5, p196.
Hollywood Reporter. Feb 19, 1954, p3.
Library Journal. Mar 15, 1954, v79, p541.
Motion Picture Herald Product Digest. Feb 20, 1954, p2189.
National Parent-Teacher. May 1954, v48, p39.
The New York Times. Feb 20, 1954, p8.
The New Yorker. Mar 6, 1954, v30, p62.
Newsweek. Mar 8, 1954, v43, p82.
Saturday Review. Mar 6, 1954, v37, p27.
Senior Scholastic. Mar 10, 1954, v64, p27.
The Tatler. Dec 15, 1954, v214, p705.
Time. Mar 8, 1954, v63, p96.
Variety. Feb 24, 1954, p6.

A New Kind of Love (US; Shavelson, Melville; 1963)
America. Nov 9, 1963, v109, p612.
BFI/Monthly Film Bulletin. Nov 1963, v30, p159.
Commonweal. Nov 15, 1963, v79, p226.
Film Daily. Aug 29, 1963, p6.
Filmfacts. Nov 7, 1963, v6, p238-39.
Films and Filming. Nov 1963, v10, p23.
The Films of Paul Newman. p122-25.
Hollywood Reporter. Aug 28, 1963, v176, p3.
The New Republic. Nov 9, 1963, v149, p49.
The New York Times. Oct 31, 1963, p26.
Newsweek. Oct 21, 1963, v62, p115.
Saturday Review. Sep 21, 1963, v46, p46.
Variety. Aug 28, 1963, p6.

The New Land (Swedish title: Nybyggarna) (SWED; Troell, Jan; 1973)
Audience. Dec 1973, v6, p1-2.
Christian Century. Dec 19, 1973, v90, p1259-60.
Esquire. Nov 1973, v80, p62.
Films In Review. Nov 1973, v24, p564-65.
Hollywood Reporter. Oct 12, 1973, p3.
National Review. Decmeber 7, 1973, v25, p1362.
The New Republic. Oct 6, 1973, v169, p22.
The New York Times. Oct 27, 1973, p17.
The New York Times. Nov 18, 1973, p15.
The New York Times. Aug 11, 1974, SecII, p1.
The New York Times. Jan 7, 1974, p38.
The New York Times. Nov 18, 1973, SecII, p15.
The New Yorker. Oct 15, 1973, v49, p165-66.
Newsweek. Nov 5, 1973, v82, p97-97A.
PTA Magazine. Dec 1973, v68, p5.
Reeling. p251-52.
Rolling Stone. Dec 6, 1973, p86-87.
Time. Oct 8, 1973, II v102, p97-98.
Variety. Mar 22, 1972, p36.
The Village Voice. Dec 13, 1973, p99.

A New Leaf (US; May, Elaine; 1971)
America. Apr 3, 1971, v124, p354.
BFI/Monthly Film Bulletin. Mar 1972, v39, n458, p55.
Commonweal. May 21, 1971, v94, p262.
Deeper into Movies. p340-41.
Filmfacts. 1971, v14, n3, p41-44.
Films in Review. Apr 1971, v22, n4, p332-33.
Hollywood Reporter. Mar 10, 1971, v215, n16, p3.
The New Republic. Mar 27, 1971, v164, p37.
The New York Times. Mar 12, 1971, p28.
The New York Times. Apr 25, 1971, SecII, p1.
The New Yorker. Mar 20, 1971, v47, p140.
Newsweek. Mar 22, 1971, v77, p112.
Saturday Review. Mar 27, 1971, v54, p50.
Sight and Sound. Wint 1971-72, v41, n1, p52.
Time. Mar 29, 1971, v97, p85.

Variety. Mar 10, 1971, p16.
The Village Voice. Mar 25, 1971, v16, n12, p57.

New York, New York (US; Scorsese, Martin; 1977)
America. Jul 30, 1977, v137, p56-57.
Commonweal. Jul 22, 1977, v104, p467-68.
Films and Filming. Sep 1977, v23, p16-17.
Hollywood Reporter. Jun 20, 1977, p4.
The Los Angeles Times. Jun 19, 1977, Calendar, p1.
Magill's Cinema Annual, 1984. 567-72.
Martin Scorsese and Michael Cimino. p116-23.
Motion Picture Herald Product Digest. Jul 6, 1977, p10.
The New Republic. Jul 23, 1977, v177, p18-19.
New York. Jul 11, 1977, v10, p70-73.
The New York Times. Jun 23, 1977, p21.
The New York Times. Jul 10, 1977, SecII, p11.
The New Yorker. Jul 4, 1977, v53, p82.
Newsweek. May 15, 1977, v89, p80-84.
Newsweek. Jun 27, 1977, v89, p61.
Saturday Review. Jul 23, 1977, v4, p47.
Time. Jun 27, 1977, v109, p61.
Variety. Jun 22, 1977, p16.
The Village Voice. Jun 27, 1977, p37-38.

The Next Man (US; Sarafin, Richard C.; 1976)
America. Nov 20, 1976, v135, p350.
Film Bulletin. Nov-Dec 1976, v45, p43-44.
Films in Review. Jan 1977, v28, p58-59.
Hollywood Reporter. Nov 4, 1976, p3.
Independent Film Journal. Nov 26, 1976, v78, p8-9.
The Los Angeles Times. Nov 10, 1976, SecIV, p1.
New York. Nov 22, 1976, v9, p88.
The New York Times. Nov 11, 1976, SecII, p52.
The New Yorker. Nov 15, 1976, v52, p180.
Time. Dec 20, 1976, v108, p63.
Variety. Nov 3, 1976, p26.
The Village Voice. Dec 20, 1976, p57.
When the Lights Go Down. p206.

Next Stop Greenwich Village (US; Mazursky, Paul; 1976)
Action. Mar-Apr 1976, v11, p6-10.
America. Feb 21, 1976, v134, p144.
Audience. Feb 1976, v8, p3-4.
Before My Eyes. p196.
BFI/Monthly Film Bulletin. Feb 1977, v44, p27.
Christian Century. Jul 7, 1976, v93, p638-40.
Film Bulletin. Jan 1976, v45, p25.
Filmmakers' Newsletter. Apr 1976, v9, p30-34.
Films and Filming. Nov 1976, v23, p42-43.
Films in Review. Mar 1976, v27, p184-85.
Hollywood Reporter. Jan 23, 1976, p10.
Independent Film Journal. Feb 4, 1976, v77, p7-8.
The Los Angeles Times. Feb 8, 1976, Calendar, p1.
Magill's Cinema Annual, 1985. p592-96.
Midstream. May 1976, v22, p56-58.
National Review. May 14, 1976, v28, p511-12.
The New Republic. Feb 21, 1976, v174, p20-21.
New York. Feb 9, 1976, v9, p72-73.
The New York Times. Feb 8, 1976, SecII, p19.
The New York Times. Feb 5, 1976, p24.
The New Yorker. Feb 2, 1976, v51, p79-81.
Newsweek. Feb 16, 1976, v87, p78.
Penthouse. Apr 1976, v7, p55-59.
Saturday Review. Feb 7, 1976, v3, p43.
Time. Feb 9, 1976, v107, p86.
Variety. Feb 4, 1976, p16.
The Village Voice. Feb 9, 1976, v21, p120.
When the Lights Go Down. p127-30.

The Next Voice You Hear (US; Wellman, William A.; 1950)
BFI/Monthly Film Bulletin. May 1951, v18, p259.
Case History of a Movie (Schary). 1950.
Christian Century. Jan 31, 1951, v68, p159.
Commonweal. Jun 30, 1950, v52, p295.
Film Daily. Jun 7, 1950, p3.
Films in Review. Sep 1950, v1, p31.
Films in Review. Nov 1950, v1, p1-3, 28-32.
Hollywood Quarterly. Wint 1950, v5, p105-14.
Hollywood Reporter. Jun 7, 1950, p3.
Library Journal. Jul 1950, v75, p1202.
Motion Picture Herald Product Digest. Jun 10, 1950, p329.
The New Republic. Jul 10, 1950, v123, p23.
The New York Times. Jun 30, 1950, p18.
The New Yorker. Jul 8, 1950, v26, p58.
Newsweek. Jul 10, 1950, v36, p86.
Sight and Sound. Apr 1951, v19, p466-71.
Time. Jul 10, 1950, v56, p76.
Variety. Jun 7, 1950, p8.
William A. Wellman (Thompson). p228-31.

Nicholas and Alexandra (US; Schaffner, Franklin J.; 1971)
BFI/Monthly Film Bulletin. Jan 1972, v39, n456, p12.
Deeper into Movies. p461-65.
Filmfacts. 1971, v14, n22, p553-57.
Films and Filming. Feb 1972, v18, n5, p51-52.
Films in Review. Jan 1972, v23, n1, p49-50.
The Films of Laurence Olivier. p170-73.
Hollywood Reporter. Dec 17, 1971, v219, n12, p3.
Laurence Olivier: Theater and Cinema. p202-05.
Life. Jan 14, 1972, v72, p14.
The New Republic. Jan 22, 1972, v166, p32-33.
The New York Times. Dec 14, 1971, p54.
The New York Times. Dec 19, 1971, SecII, p3.
The New Yorker. Dec 25, 1971, v47, p58.
Newsweek. Dec 20, 1971, v78, p87-88.
Saturday Review. Jan 15, 1972, v55, p17.
Sight and Sound. Wint 1971-72, v41, n1, p52-53.
Variety. Dec 8, 1971, p16.
The Village Voice. Dec 23, 1971, v16, n51, p61.

Nick Carter in Prague *See* Dinner for Adele

Nickelodeon (US; Bogdanovich, Peter; 1976)
Audience. May-Jun 1977, v9, p23.
BFI/Monthly Film Bulletin. Feb 1977, v44, p27-28.
Film. Apr 1977, n48-49.
Film Bulletin. Jan-Feb 1977, v46, p32-33.
Film Heritage. n3, 1977, v12, n3, p42-44.
Films and Filming. May 1976, v22, p45.
Films and Filming. Feb 1977, v23, p41.
Films Illustrated. Feb 1977, v6, p213-15.
Films Illustrated. Mar 1977, v6, p248.
Films in Review. Jan 1977, v28, p60.
The Films of Burt Reynolds. p197-200.
Hollywood Reporter. Dec 17, 1976, p3.
Independent Film Journal. Jan 21, 1977, v79, p20.
The Los Angeles Times. Dec 23, 1976, SecIV, p1.
Medium. Oct 1977, v7, p33.
Millimeter. Mar 1977, v5, p24.
The New Leader. Jan 17, 1977, v60, p25-26.
New Statesman. Mar 4, 1977, v93, p297.
New York. Sep 20, 1976, v9, p53.
New York. Jan 10, 1977, v10, p55-57.
The New York Times. Dec 22, 1976, p34.
The New Yorker. Jan 17, 1977, v52, p98-100.
Newsweek. Dec 27, 1976, v88, p56.

Saturday Review. Jan 22, 1977, v4, p49-50.
The Thousand Eyes Magazine. Feb 12, 1977, v2, p12.
Time. Jan 3, 1977, v109, p63.
Variety. Dec 22, 1976, p22.
The Village Voice. Jan 17, 1977, p51.

The Night (Italian title: Notte, La) (IT, FR; Antonioni, Michelangelo; 1960)
America. Apr 7, 1962, v107, p28-29.
Antonioni (Cameron and Wood). p74-92.
BFI/Monthly Film Bulletin. Mar 1962, v29, p34.
Cinema. 1963, v1, n2, p33.
Classics of the Foreign Film. p250-54.
Commonweal. Mar 9, 1962, v75, p620.
Dictionary of Films. p249-50.
Film. Spr 1962, n31, p10.
Film as Film: Critical Responses to Film Art. p266-77.
Film Culture. Spr 1962, n24, p82-83.
Film Daily. Dec 15, 1961, p8.
Film Journal. Aug 1962, n20, p84.
Filmfacts. Mar 16, 1962, v5, p35-37.
Films and Filming. Feb 1962, v8, p28.
Films in Review. Dec 1961, v12, p625.
Hollywood Reporter. Feb 20, 1962, v169, p3.
I Lost It at the Movies. p161-67.
The International Dictionary of Films and Filmmakers. v1, p327-38.
Literature/Film Quarterly. 1979, v7, n1, p36-46.
Magill's Survey of Cinema. Foreign Language Films. 1985, v5, p2239-44.
Michelangelo Antonioni: A Guide to References and Resources. p101-08.
Motion Picture Herald Product Digest. Mar 7, 1962, p469.
The Nation. Mar 10, 1962, v194, p222.
The New Republic. Feb 26, 1962, v146, p26-28.
The New York Times. Feb 20, 1962, p29.
The New Yorker. Mar 3, 1962, v38, p102-03.
Newsweek. Feb 19, 1962, v59, p96.
On Movies. p333-37.
Sight and Sound. Wint 1961-62, v31, p28-31.
Time. Feb 23, 1962, v79, p102.
Variety. Mar 29, 1961, p6.
The Village Voice. Feb 15, 1962, p11.
A World on Film. p302-07.

Night and the City (GB; Dassin, Jules; 1950)
BFI/Monthly Film Bulletin. Apr-May 1950, v17, p59-60.
Christian Century. Jul 12, 1950, v67, p855.
Commonweal. Jun 16, 1950, v52, p249.
Dictionary of Films. p244.
Film Daily. May 24, 1950, p7.
The Great Gangster Pictures. p291-92.
Hollywood Reporter. May 23, 1950, p3.
Kenyon Review. n3, 1951, v13, p535-37.
Kiss Kiss Bang Bang. p396.
Library Journal. Jun 1, 1950, v75, p992.
Motion Picture Herald Product Digest. May 27, 1950, p313.
The New York Times. Jun 10, 1950, p11.
The New Yorker. Jun 17, 1950, v26, p59.
Newsweek. Jun 19, 1950, v35, p89.
Sequence. Aut 1950, n12, p14-15.
The Spectator. Jun 16, 1950, v184, p820.
Time. Jul 3, 1950, v56, p76.
Variety. May 24, 1950, p6.

Night Beauties *See* Belles-de-Nuit, Les

The Night Does Strange Things *See* Paris Does Strange Things

Night Games (Also titled: Nattlek) (SWED; Zetterling, Mai; 1966)
BFI/Monthly Film Bulletin. Feb 1967, v34, p24-25.

Big Screen, Little Screen. p361-62.
Christian Science Monitor (Western edition). Apr 29, 1967, p6.
Commonweal. Jan 27, 1967, v85, p461.
Film Daily. Jan 3, 1967, p3.
Film Quarterly. Wint 1966-67, v20, p37-38.
Filmfacts. Jan 15, 1967, v9, p342-44.
Films and Filming. Feb 1967, v13, p29-30.
Films in Review. Jan 1967, v18, p53.
Kiss Kiss Bang Bang. p127-28.
The London Times. Dec 1, 1966, p18.
The London Times. Sep 7, 1966, p16.
Magill's Survey of Cinema. Foreign Language Films. v5, p2192-95.
Motion Picture Herald Product Digest. Jan 18, 1967, p651.
The Nation. Jan 16, 1967, v204, p94.
The New Republic. Feb 25, 1967, v156, p36.
New Statesman. Dec 9, 1966, v72, p886.
The New York Times. Dec 20, 1966, p58.
Newsweek. Jan 2, 1967, v69, p64.
Playboy. Feb 1967, v14, p20.
Variety. Sep 7, 1966, p6.
The Village Voice. Jan 5, 1967, v12, p21.

Night in Havana *See* Big Boodle

Night Moves (US; Penn, Arthur; 1975)
Before My Eyes. p131.
BFI/Monthly Film Bulletin. May 1975, v42, p112.
Films in Review. Aug-Sep 1975, v26, p440.
Hollywood Reporter. Mar 19, 1975, p22.
The Los Angeles Times. Jul 2, 1975, SecIV, p1.
Motion Picture Herald Product Digest. Jun 11, 1975, p3.
The New Republic. Jun 14, 1975, v172, p20.
The New York Times. Jun 12, 1975, p30.
The New York Times. Jul 6, 1975, SecII, p9.
The New Yorker. Jun 23, 1975, v51, p97-98.
Newsweek. Jun 16, 1975, v85, p76.
Time. Jul 21, 1975, v106, p58.
Variety. Mar 26, 1975, p18.

Night Must Fall (GB; Reisz, Karel; 1964)
BFI/Monthly Film Bulletin. Jul 1964, v31, p103.
Boxoffice. Apr 6, 1964, v84, p2815.
Commonweal. Mar 27, 1964, v80, p17.
Film Daily. Mar 19, 1964, v124, p5.
Films and Filming. Jun 1964, v10, p21-22.
Films in Review. Apr 1964, v15, p245.
Hollywood Reporter. Mar 18, 1964, v179, p3.
Motion Picture Herald Product Digest. Apr 1, 1964, v231, p17.
The New Republic. Apr 4, 1964, v150, p28.
The New York Times. Mar 19, 1964, p28.
The New Yorker. Mar 28, 1964, v40, p144.
Newsweek. Mar 30, 1964, v63, p53.
The Private Eye, the Cowboy and the Very Naked Girl. p74-77.
Sight and Sound. Sum 1964, v33, p144.
Variety. Mar 18, 1964, p6.

Night of Cabiria *See* The Nights of Cabiria

The Night of the Generals (GB, FR; Litvak, Anatole; 1967)
America. Feb 11, 1967, v116, p225.
BFI/Monthly Film Bulletin. Mar 1967, v34, p42, 113.
Cinema. Sum 1967, v3, p49.
Commonweal. Feb 24, 1967, v85, p597.
Film Daily. Feb 3, 1967, p5.
Films and Filming. Mar 1967, v13, p28.
Films in Review. Feb 1967, v18, p112-14.
Hollywood Reporter. Jan 30, 1967, p3.
Motion Picture Herald Product Digest. Feb 15, 1967, p657.
The New York Times. Feb 3, 1967, p38.
The New Yorker. Feb 4, 1967, v42, p98.

Newsweek. Feb 20, 1967, v69, p98.
Saturday Review. Feb 18, 1967, v50, p44.
Senior Scholastic. Mar 17, 1967, v90, p25.
Time. Feb 10, 1967, v89, p99.
Variety. Feb 1, 1967, p6.
The Village Voice. Feb 16, 1967, p25.

Night of the Grizzly (US; Pevney, Joseph; 1966)
BFI/Monthly Film Bulletin. Sep 1966, v33, p142.
Film Daily. Apr 15, 1966, p7.
Filmfacts. Sep 1, 1966, v9, p169-70.
Hollywood Reporter. Apr 14, 1966, p3.
Motion Picture Herald Product Digest. Apr 27, 1966, p510.
The New York Times. Jun 23, 1966, p29.
Variety. Apr 20, 1966, p6.

Night of the Hunter (US; Laughton, Charles; 1955)
America. Oct 8, 1955, v94, p56.
Catholic World. Sep 1955, v181, p465.
Charles Laughton. p142-43.
Film. Mar-Apr 1958, n16, p23-24.
Film Culture. Wint 1955, v1, n5/6, p32-33.
Film Daily. Aug 3, 1955, p4.
Films and Filming. Jan 1956, v2, n4, p22-23.
The Films in My Life. p119-20.
Films in Review. Aug-Sep 1955, v6, n7, p337-39.
The Films of the Fifties. p143-45.
Halliwell's Harvest. p181-83.
Hollywood Reporter. Jul 20, 1955, v135, p3.
Library Journal. Oct 15, 1955, v80, p2231.
Life. Aug 1, 1955, v39, p49-51.
Magill's Survey of Cinema. Series I. v3, p1200-02.
The Modern American Novel and the Movies. p204-15.
The Nation. Oct 15, 1955, v181, p328.
The New York Times. Oct 31, 1955, SecII, p5.
The New York Times. Sep 30, 1955, p23.
The New York Times. Oct 2, 1955, SecII, p1.
The New Yorker. Oct 8, 1955, v31, p159.
Newsweek. Aug 29, 1955, v46, p77.
Robert Mitchum on the Screen. p140-41.
Saturday Review. Aug 13, 1955, v38, p21.
Sight and Sound. Wint 1955-56, v25, n3, p147-48.
Surrealism and American Feature Films. p143-64.
Time. Aug 1, 1955, v66, p58.
Variety. Jul 20, 1955, p6.

Night of the Iguana (US; Huston, John; 1964)
America. Aug 15, 1964, v111, p61.
BFI/Monthly Film Bulletin. Oct 1964, v31, p146.
Boxoffice. Jul 13, 1964, v85, p2844.
The Cinema of John Huston. p142-45.
Commonweal. Aug 21, 1964, v80, p580.
Film Daily. Jul 1, 1964, v124, p3.
Films and Filming. Oct 1964, v11, p28.
Films in Review. Aug-Sep 1964, v15, p439-41.
Hollywood Reporter. Jul 1, 1964, v181, p3.
John Huston (Hammen). p106-07, 120-21.
John Huston (Madsen). p200-08.
John Huston, Maker of Magic. p155-60.
Life. Jul 10, 1964, v57, p11.
Magill's Survey of Cinema. Series II. v4, p1721-24.
Motion Picture Herald Product Digest. Jul 8, 1964, v232, p81-82.
The New York Times. Jul 1, 1964, p42.
The New Yorker. Aug 15, 1964, v40, p84-85.
Newsweek. Jul 13, 1964, v64, p85.
Saturday Review. Jul 18, 1964, v47, p22.

Sight and Sound. Aut 1964, v33, p199.
Time. Jul 17, 1964, v84, p86.
Variety. Jul 1, 1964, p6.

Night of the Living Dead (US; Romero, George; 1968)
BFI/Monthly Film Bulletin. Jan 1970, v37, p8-9.
Cinefantastique. 1973, v2, n3, p8-15.
Cinefantastique. 1975, v4, n1, p4-27.
Cinema Texas Program Notes. Sep 16, 1974, v7, p1-6.
Cinema Texas Program Notes. Nov 16, 1977, v13, p73-77.
Film Daily. Oct 21, 1968, p7.
Film Journal. 1973, v2, n2, p6-35.
Filmfacts. Jan 15, 1969, v11, p442.
Filmmaker's Newsletter. Jan 1972, v5, p19-23.
Films and Filming. Dec 1970, v17, p53, 56.
Five Thousand One Nights At the Movies. p414.
Medium. Jan 1980, v10, p46.
The New York Times. Dec 5, 1968, p59.
Newsweek. Nov 8, 1971, v78, p118.
Sight and Sound. Spr 1970, v39, p105.
Variety. Oct 16, 1968, p6.
The Village Voice. Jan 13, 1982, p52.
The Village Voice. Dec 25, 1969, p54.
Writer's Digest. Jul 1974, v54, p24-26.

The Night of the Shooting Stars (Italian title: Notte Di San Lorenzo, La) (IT; Taviani, Paolo; Taviani, Vittorio; 1983)
America. Feb 26, 1983, v148, p54.
Films in Review. Nov 1982, v33, p556.
Hollywood Reporter. Feb 15, 1983, p3.
The Los Angeles Times. Feb 16, 1983, SecVI, p1.
Maclean's. Feb 7, 1983, v96, p55.
Magill's Cinema Annual, 1984. p258-64.
The New Republic. Mar 7, 1983, v188, p24-25.
New York. Feb 7, 1983, v16, p72-73.
The New York Times. Jan 30, 1983, p34.
The New Yorker. Feb 7, 1983, v58, p117-20.
Newsweek. Feb 7, 1983, v101, p69.
Time. Feb 21, 1983, v121, p80.

Night Passage (US; Neilson, James; 1957)
America. Aug 10, 1957, v97, p492.
American Cinematographer. Mar 1957, v38, p148-49.
BFI/Monthly Film Bulletin. Sep 1957, v24, p115-16.
Commonweal. Aug 16, 1957, v66, p495.
Film Daily. May 16, 1957, v111, p9.
The Films of James Stewart. p189-92.
Hollywood Reporter. May 14, 1957, p3.
The Nation. Aug 17, 1957, v185, p79.
The New York Times. Jul 25, 1957, p28.
Variety. May 15, 1957, p22.

Night People (US; Johnson, Nunnally; 1954)
America. Mar 27, 1954, v90, p694.
BFI/Monthly Film Bulletin. Aug 1954, v21, p116.
Catholic World. May 1954, v179, p145.
Commonweal. Apr 2, 1954, v59, p650.
Film Daily. Mar 17, 1954, p6.
Films in Review. May 1954, v5, p244.
The Films of Gregory Peck. p126-28.
Hollywood Reporter. Mar 12, 1954, p3.
Library Journal. Apr 1, 1954, v79, p618.
The London Times. Jul 5, 1954, p11.
Motion Picture Herald Product Digest. Mar 20, 1954, p2229.
National Parent-Teacher. May 1954, v48, p40.
The New Statesman and Nation. Jul 17, 1954, v48, p76.
The New York Times. Mar 13, 1954, p4.

The New Yorker. Mar 27, 1954, v30, p60.
Saturday Review. Apr 3, 1954, v37, p41.
Sight and Sound. Oct-Dec 1954, v24, p67-73.
The Spectator. Jul 2, 1954, v193, p11-12.
The Tatler. Jul 14, 1954, v213, p74.
Time. Mar 22, 1954, v63, p110.
Variety. Mar 17, 1954, p6.

The Night Porter (Italian title: Portiere di Notte, Il) (IT; Cavani, Liliana; 1974)
America. Oct 26, 1974, v131, p234.
BFI/Monthly Film Bulletin. Nov 1974, v41, p255-56.
Film. Nov 1974, n20, p12.
Films and Filming. Aug 1974, v20, p56-59.
Films Illustrated. Nov 1974, v4, p84.
The Films of Dirk Bogarde. p193-94.
Hollywood Reporter. Oct 1, 1974, p4.
Independent Film Journal. Oct 17, 1974, v74, p33.
The Los Angeles Times. Oct 30, 1974, SecIV, p13.
Motion Picture Herald Product Digest. Oct 16, 1974, p38.
The New Republic. Oct 5, 1974, v171, p33.
New Statesman. Oct 25, 1974, v88, p592.
New York. Oct 7, 1974, v7, p93-96.
The New York Times. Oct 13, 1974, SecII, p1.
The New Yorker. Oct 7, 1974, v50, p151-52.
Newsweek. Oct 7, 1974, v84, p95.
Reeling. p457-60.
Take One. 1974, v4, n5, p39-40.
Time. Oct 21, 1974, v104, p12.
Variety. Apr 3, 1974, p14.
The Village Voice. Oct 17, 1974, p77-78.
Vogue. Dec 1974, v164, p86.

Night Shift (US; Howard, Ron; 1982)
BFI/Monthly Film Bulletin. Dec 1982, v49, p293-94.
Film Journal. Jul 26, 1982, v87, p19-20.
The Los Angeles Times. Jul 29, 1982, SecVI, p1.
Maclean's. Aug 9, 1982, v95, p46.
The New Republic. Sep 13, 1982, v187, p26-27.
New York. Sep 13, 1982, v15, p64.
The New York Times. Jul 30, 1982, SecIII, p8.
Newsweek. Aug 2, 1982, v100, p62-63.
Rolling Stone. Sep 2, 1982, p34.
Time. Aug 9, 1982, v120, p62.
Variety. Jul 14, 1982, p27.
The Village Voice. Aug 3, 1982, p39.

The Night They Raided Minsky's (US; Friedkin, William; 1968)
BFI/Monthly Film Bulletin. May 1969, v36, p106.
Christian Century. Jan 29, 1969, v80, p155.
Film Daily. Dec 16, 1968, p4.
Filmfacts. Jan 15, 1969, v11, p505-06.
Films and Filming. Jun 1969, v15, p52.
Five Thousand One Nights At the Movies. p414-15.
Going Steady. p293-96.
Harper's Magazine. Mar 1969, v238, p110.
Hollywood Reporter. Dec 5, 1968, p3.
International Film Guide. 1970, v7, p223-24.
The London Times. Apr 17, 1969, p14.
The London Times. Apr 19, 1969, p21.
Magill's Survey of Cinema. Series II. v4, p1725-27.
Motion Picture Herald Product Digest. Dec 18, 1968, p79-80.
The New Republic. Jan 18, 1969, v160, p23.
New Statesman. Apr 18, 1969, v77, p561.
The New York Times. Dec 23, 1968, p43.
The New York Times. Jan 18, 1969, v44, p76.
Newsweek. Dec 30, 1968, v72, p61.
Saturday Review. Dec 21, 1968, v51, p16.

Time. Jan 3, 1969, v93, p56.
Variety. Dec 4, 1968, p6.

Night Tide (US; Harrington, Curtis; 1963)
Filmfacts. Aug 22, 1963, v6, p166-67.
The New York Times. Jun 7, 1963, p37.
Saturday Review. Jan 13, 1962, v42, p50.
Time. Dec 6, 1963, v82, p119.
Variety. Sep 6, 1961, p18.

A Night to Remember (GB; Baker, Roy; 1958)
America. Jan 3, 1959, v100, p411.
Catholic World. Dec 1958, v188, p240.
Commonweal. Jan 16, 1959, v69, p413.
Film Daily. Dec 17, 1958, v114, p6.
Filmfacts. Jan 7, 1959, v1, p245-46.
Films in Review. Oct 1958, v9, p452-53.
The Great British Films. p175-77.
Hollywood Reporter. Dec 18, 1958, p3.
Library Journal. Dec 15, 1958, v83, p3507.
Magill's Survey of Cinema. Series I. v3, p1203-06.
The Nation. Jan 17, 1959, v183, p60.
The New Yorker. Dec 27, 1958, v34, p60.
Newsweek. Dec 22, 1958, v52, p81.
Saturday Review. Dec 13, 1958, v41, p26.
Senior Scholastic. Nov 21, 1958, v74, p44.
Time. Jan 5, 1959, v73, p84.
Variety. Jul 9, 1958, p16.

Night Without Sleep (US; Baker, Roy; 1952)
BFI/Monthly Film Bulletin. Dec 1952, v19, p174.
Christian Century. Dec 31, 1952, v69, p1537.
Film Daily. Oct 1, 1952, p6.
Hollywood Reporter. Sep 26, 1952, p4.
Library Journal. Nov 1, 1952, v77, p1893.
Motion Picture Herald Product Digest. Oct 4, 1952, p1550.
National Parent-Teacher. Dec 1952, v47, p38.
The New York Times. Sep 27, 1952, p13.
Variety. Oct 1, 1952, p6.

Nighthawks (US; Malmuth, Bruce; 1981)
Commentary. Jun 1981, v71, p70-71.
The Los Angeles Times. Apr 6, 1981, SecVI, p1.
Maclean's. May 4, 1981, v94, p54.
Magill's Cinema Annual, 1982. p259-61.
The New Leader. May 4, 1981, v64, p18.
The New Republic. May 2, 1981, v184, p26-27.
New York. Apr 20, 1981, v14, p53.
The New York Times. Apr 10, 1981, SecIII, p6.
Newsweek. Apr 20, 1981, v97, p93.
Time. May 11, 1981, v117, p87.
USA Today. Jul 1981, v110, p68.
Variety. Apr 6, 1981, p3.

The Nights of Cabiria (Also titled: Notti di Cabiria, Le; Cabiria; Night of Cabiria) (IT; Fellini, Federico; 1957)
BFI/Monthly Film Bulletin. May 1958, v25, p57-58.
Cinema, the Magic Vehicle. v2, p295-96.
Commonweal. Nov 22, 1957, v67, p202-04, 209.
Federico Fellini: A Guide to References and Resources. p72-79.
Film Culture. Jan 1958, v4, p18-21.
Film Quarterly. Fall 1958, v12, p43-45.
Films and Filming. Mar 1958, v4, p23.
The Films in My Life. p270-71.
Films in Review. Dec 1957, v8, p529.
The Films of Federico Fellini. p91-96.
Great Film Directors. p284-89.
Magill's Survey of Cinema. Foreign Language Films. v5, p2201-04.
The Nation. Nov 23, 1957, v185, p396.
The New York Times. Oct 29, 1957, p34.
The New York Times. Nov 3, 1957, SecII, p1.

The New Yorker. Nov 9, 1957, v33, p109.
Newsweek. Nov 4, 1957, v50, p114-15.
Saturday Review. Nov 9, 1957, v40, p28-29.
The Village Voice. Apr 10, 1969, p51, 54.

Nijinsky (US; Ross, Herbert; 1980)
BFI/Monthly Film Bulletin. Jun 1980, v47, p114.
The Christian Science Monitor. Mar 26, 1980, p22.
Dance Magazine. Apr 1980, v54, p74-78.
Dance Magazine. May 1980, v54, p38-39.
Dance Magazine. Aug 1980, v54, p51-53.
Films in Review. May 1980, v31, p307.
Hollywood Reporter. Mar 14, 1980, p3.
The Los Angeles Times. Mar 20, 1980, SecVI, p5.
The Los Angeles Times. Mar 21, 1980, SecVI, p10.
Maclean's. Mar 31, 1980, v93, p51.
Motion Picture Herald Product Digest. Mar 26, 1980, p83.
The Nation. Mar 29, 1980, v230, p380.
National Review. May 2, 1980, v32, p544.
The New Republic. Mar 29, 1980, v182, p26-27.
New York. Mar 24, 1980, v13, p45-49.
The New Yorker. Mar 24, 1980, v56, p102.
Newsday. Mar 20, 1980, SecII, p7.
Newsweek. Mar 24, 1980, v95, p78.
Saturday Review. Oct 1980, v7, p94.
Time. Mar 24, 1980, v115, p81.
Variety. Mar 12, 1980, p22.
The Village Voice. Mar 24, 1980, p47.
Vogue. Mar 1980, v170, p324-25.
Vogue. May 1980, v170, p60.

Nine Days of One Year (Also titled: Devyat'Dney Odnogo Goda) (USSR; Romm, Mikhail; 1961)
BFI/Monthly Film Bulletin. Jun 1964, v31, p87.
Commonweal. Jan 29, 1965, v81, p573.
Dictionary of Films. p84.
Esquire. May 1965, v63, p18, 20, 22.
Film Society Review. Sep 1966, p21-22.
Filmfacts. Nov 27, 1964, v7, p273-74.
Films and Filming. Nov 1965, v12, p28-29.
International Film Guide. 1965, v2, p143.
The London Times. Aug 26, 1965, p12.
The New York Times. Dec 29, 1964, p19.
The New Yorker. Jan 9, 1965, v40, p105.
On Movies. p273-76.
Sight and Sound. Sum 1964, v33, p145-46.
The Spectator. Sep 3, 1965, v215, p291-92.
Time. Jan 15, 1965, v85, p89.
Variety. Jun 27, 1962, p6.

Nine Hours to Rama (US; Robson, Mark; 1963)
America. Apr 13, 1963, v108, p504-05.
BFI/Monthly Film Bulletin. Mar 1963, v30, p32.
Commonweal. Apr 26, 1963, v78, p140-41.
Film Daily. Feb 18, 1963, p8.
Filmfacts. May 2, 1963, v6, p67-69.
Films and Filming. Mar 1963, v9, p33-34.
Films in Review. Apr 1964, v14, p236-37.
Hollywood Reporter. Feb 18, 1963, v174, p3.
The New Republic. Mar 16, 1963, v148, p27.
The New York Times. Apr 4, 1963, p58.
The New York Times. Apr 21, 1963, SecII, p1.
The New Yorker. Apr 13, 1963, v39, p157.
Newsweek. Apr 15, 1963, v61, p104-05.
Photoplay. Apr 1963, v63, p6.
Saturday Review. Apr 6, 1963, v46, p39.
Time. Apr 19, 1963, v81, p114.
Variety. Feb 20, 1963, p6.

9 to 5 (US; Higgins, Colin; 1980)
BFI/Monthly Film Bulletin. Feb 1981, v48, p30.

The Christian Science Monitor. Jan 8, 1981, p19.
Films in Review. Jan 1981, v32, p55.
The Films of Jane Fonda. p240-51.
Hollywood Reporter. Dec 15, 1980, p3.
Maclean's. Dec 15, 1980, v93, p61.
Motion Picture Herald Product Digest. Dec 17, 1980, p54.
The New Leader. Dec 29, 1980, v63, p17-18.
New York. Dec 22, 1980, v13, p61-62.
The New York Times. Dec 19, 1980, SecIII, p20.
The New York Times. Dec 9, 1980, SecIII, p20.
Newsweek. Mar 31, 1980, v95, p80.
Newsweek. Dec 22, 1980, v96, p72-73.
Rolling Stone. Dec 11, 1980, p39-41.
Time. Dec 22, 1980, v116, p73.
Variety. Dec 17, 1980, p17.
The Village Voice. Dec 24, 1980, p41.

1900 (Italian title: Novecento) (IT, FR, WGER; Bertolucci, Bernardo; 1977)
America. Dec 3, 1977, v137, p403.
BFI/Monthly Film Bulletin. Jan 1978, v45, p10.
Commonweal. Jan 6, 1978, v105, p16-18.
Commonweal. Dec 23, 1977, v104, p820.
Films in Review. Jan 1978, v29, p53.
Hollywood Reporter. Nov 4, 1977, p3.
The International Dictionary of Films and Filmmakers. v1, p328-29.
The Los Angeles Times. Dec 22, 1977, SecIV, p1.
Maclean's. Jan 9, 1978, v91, p58.
Magill's Survey of Cinema. Foreign Language Films. v5, p2211-15.
Motion Picture Herald Product Digest. Dec 14, 1977, p55.
The Nation. Oct 29, 1977, v225, p444-45.
The Nation. Nov 26, 1977, v225, p573-74.
The New Republic. Nov 26, 1977, v177, p20-21.
New York. Jun 6, 1977, v10, p73-76.
The New York Times. Oct 8, 1977, p14.
The New York Times. Oct 16, 1977, SecII, p17.
The New York Times. Nov 4, 1977, SecIII, p11.
The New Yorker. Oct 31, 1977, v53, p148-54.
Newsweek. Oct 17, 1977, v90, p101-02.
Rolling Stone. Jun 2, 1977, p33.
Time. May 2, 1977, v109, p70-71.
Time. Oct 17, 1977, v110, p99.
Variety. Jun 2, 1976, p16.
The Village Voice. Oct 24, 1977, p48.
Vogue. Sep 1976, v166, p346-48.

1918 (US; Harrison, Ken; 1985)
America. May 25, 1985, v152, p433.
Christian Century. Jun 5, 1985, v102, p589-90.
The Los Angeles Times. Jun 12, 1985, SecVI, p5.
National Review. Jun 14, 1985, v37, p49-50.
The New Republic. May 27, 1985, v192, p24-25.
The New York Times. Apr 26, 1985, SecIII, p8.
The New York Times. Apr 28, 1985, SecII, p17.
Time. May 13, 1985, v125, p68-69.
Variety. Apr 17, 1985, p10.

1941 (US; Spielberg, Steven; 1979)
BFI/Monthly Film Bulletin. Apr 1980, v47, p72.
The Films of the Seventies. p279-82.
Hollywood Reporter. Dec 13, 1979, p3.
The Los Angeles Times. Dec 14, 1979, SecIV, p1.
Motion Picture Herald Product Digest. Jan 9, 1980, p64.
The New York Times. Dec 4, 1979, SecIII, p10.
The New Yorker. Dec 24, 1979, v55, p83.
Newsweek. Dec 17, 1979, v94, p111.
Time. Apr 16, 1979, v113, p97.
Time. Dec 24, 1979, v114, p76.
Variety. Dec 19, 1979, p19.

Ninety Degrees in the Shade (Czechoslovakian title: Tricetjedna Ve Stinu; Also titled: Ninety) (GB, CZECH; Weiss, Jiri; 1965)
Filmfacts. Jan 15, 1967, v9, p363-65.
Films and Filming. Apr 1965, v11, p56.
Motion Picture Herald Product Digest. Nov 16, 1966, p630.
The New York Times. Nov 16, 1966, p52.
Newsweek. Dec 26, 1966, v68, p72.
Time. Dec 2, 1966, v88, p99.
Variety. Jul 7, 1965, p6.

No Down Payment (US; Ritt, Martin; 1957)
America. Nov 2, 1957, v98, p147-48.
BFI/Monthly Film Bulletin. Feb 1958, v25, p15.
Commonweal. Oct 25, 1957, v66, p100.
Film Daily. Sep 30, 1957, v112, p6.
Films and Filming. Dec 1957, v4, p24.
Films in Review. Nov 1957, v8, p460-61.
The Films of the Fifties. p214-16.
Hollywood Reporter. Sep 30, 1957, p3.
Motion Picture Herald Product Digest. Oct 5, 1957, v209, p553.
The New York Times. Oct 31, 1957, p41.
Newsweek. Oct 14, 1957, v50, p121-22.
Saturday Review. Oct 12, 1957, v40, p31.
Sight and Sound. Spr 1958, v27, p200-01.
Time. Oct 14, 1957, v70, p112.
Variety. Oct 2, 1957, p6.

No Highway (Also titled: No Highway In the Sky) (GB; Koster, Henry; 1951)
BFI/Monthly Film Bulletin. Aug 1951, v18, p308.
Catholic World. Oct 1951, v174, p64.
Christian Century. Nov 7, 1951, v68, p1294.
Commonweal. Nov 30, 1951, v55, p201.
Film Daily. Jul 18, 1951, p6.
The Films of James Stewart. p142-44.
The Films of Marlene Dietrich. p189-91.
The London Times. Aug 4, 1951, p6.
Magill's Survey of Cinema. Series I. v3, p1214-16.
Motion Picture Herald Product Digest. Jul 21, 1951, p937.
The New Republic. Oct 22, 1951, v125, p22.
The New York Times. Sep 22, 1951, p8.
The New Yorker. Sep 29, 1951, v27, p112.
Newsweek. Oct 8, 1951, v38, p100.
Saturday Review. Oct 6, 1951, v34, p35.
Sight and Sound. Oct-Dec 1951, v21, p60.
The Spectator. Aug 3, 1951, v187, p156.
Time. Oct 8, 1951, v58, p112.
Variety. Jul 4, 1951, p8.

No Love For Johnnie (GB; Thomas, Ralph; 1961)
BFI/Monthly Film Bulletin. Mar 1961, v28, p33.
Commonweal. Dec 29, 1961, v75, p366.
Film Daily. Dec 14, 1961, p6.
Filmfacts. Jan 12, 1962, v4, p325-27.
Films in Review. Oct 1961, v7, p484-86.
Magill's Survey of Cinema. Series II. v4, p1732-34.
The Nation. Jan 20, 1962, v194, p67-68.
The New Republic. Nov 20, 1961, v145, p22-23.
The New York Times. Dec 13, 1961, p55.
The New Yorker. Dec 16, 1961, v37, p112.
Newsweek. Dec 11, 1961, v58, p93.
Saturday Review. Nov 4, 1961, v44, p37.
Time. Dec 8, 1961, v78, p96.
Variety. Feb 22, 1961, p6.

No Man Is an Island (US; Monks, John Jr.; Goldstone, Michael; 1962)
Commonweal. Nov 2, 1962, v77, p153.

Film Daily. Aug 7, 1962, p7.
Filmfacts. Oct 19, 1962, v5, p231-32.
Films and Filming. Jan 1963, v9, p50.
Hollywood Reporter. Aug 7, 1962, p3.
Motion Picture Herald Product Digest. Aug 8, 1962, p634.
The New York Times. Oct 11, 1962, p49.
Variety. Aug 8, 1962, p6.

No Man of Her Own (US; Leisen, Mitchell; 1950)
Christian Century. Jun 7, 1950, v67, p719.
Commonweal. May 12, 1950, v52, p126.
Film Daily. Feb 21, 1950, p5.
The Films of Barbara Stanwyck. p201-02.
Hollywood Director. p282-85.
Hollywood Reporter. Feb 21, 1950, p3.
Illustrated London News. May 27, 1950, v216, p832.
Library Journal. Apr 15, 1950, v75, p708.
Motion Picture Herald Product Digest. Feb 25, 1950, p205-06.
The New York Times. May 4, 1950, p32.
The New Yorker. May 13, 1950, v26, p93.
Newsweek. May 15, 1950, v35, p89.
Starring Miss Barbara Stanwyck. p222, 227.
Time. May 15, 1950, v55, p100.
Variety. Feb 22, 1950, p6.

No Resting Place (GB; Rotha, Paul; 1951)
BFI/Monthly Film Bulletin. Aug 1951, v18, p309.
Catholic World. Sep 1952, v175, p463.
Film Criticism and Caricatures, 1943-1953. p126-27.
Film Daily. Apr 30, 1952, p6.
Films in Review. May 1952, v3, p244-45.
The London Times. Jul 16, 1951, p2.
Motion Picture Herald Product Digest. Apr 26, 1952, p1329-30.
The New Statesman and Nation. Jul 21, 1951, v42, p69.
The New York Times. May 5, 1952, p18.
The New Yorker. May 17, 1952, v28, p107.
Quarterly of Film, Radio and Television. Wint 1952, v7, p135-39.
Sight and Sound. Aug-Sep 1951, v21, p20-21.
The Spectator. Jul 20, 1951, v187, p92.
Theatre Arts. Jul 1952, v36, p37.
Variety. Aug 1, 1951, p18.

No Room For the Groom (US; Sirk, Douglas; 1952)
BFI/Monthly Film Bulletin. Sep 1952, v19, p129.
Douglas Sirk (Stern). p78-81.
Film Daily. May 8, 1952, p6.
Hollywood Reporter. May 2, 1952, p3.
Motion Picture Herald Product Digest. May 10, 1952, p1357.
The New York Times. Jun 14, 1952, p12.
Tony Curtis: The Man and His Movies. p38-39.
Variety. May 7, 1952, p6.

No Sad Songs For Me (US; Maté, Rudolph; 1950)
BFI/Monthly Film Bulletin. Jul 1950, v17, p100-01.
Christian Century. May 31, 1950, v67, p687.
Commonweal. May 5, 1950, v52, p97.
Film Daily. Apr 12, 1950, p6.
Films in Review. Jul-Aug 1950, v1, p24, 27.
Hollywood Reporter. Apr 11, 1950, p3.
Library Journal. Apr 1, 1950, v75, p570.
Life. May 15, 1950, v28, p85-86.
Motion Picture Herald Product Digest. Apr 15, 1950, p261-62.
The New Republic. May 15, 1950, v122, p22.
The New York Times. Apr 28, 1950, p26.
The New Yorker. May 6, 1950, v26, p64.
Newsweek. May 8, 1950, v35, p87.

Time. May 15, 1950, v55, p99.
Variety. Apr 12, 1950, p6.

No Sleep till Dawn *See* Bombers B-52

No Time For Flowers (US, AUSTRIA; Siegel, Don; 1952)
BFI/Monthly Film Bulletin. Jun 1954, v21, p89.
Catholic World. Feb 1953, v176, p383.
Christian Century. Apr 15, 1953, v70, p463.
Commonweal. Jan 16, 1953, v57, p378.
Film Daily. Dec 18, 1952, p6.
Films in Review. Feb 1953, v4, p98.
Hollywood Reporter. Dec 2, 1952, p3.
Motion Picture Herald Product Digest. Dec 6, 1952, p1629-30.
National Parent-Teacher. Feb 1953, v47, p38.
The New York Times. Dec 26, 1952, p20.
Newsweek. Jan 12, 1953, v41, p77.
Saturday Review. Jan 24, 1953, v36, p28.
Time. Dec 29, 1952, v60, p67.
Variety. Dec 3, 1952, p6.

No Way Out (US; Mankiewicz, Joseph L.; 1950)
BFI/Monthly Film Bulletin. Aug 1950, v17, p115.
Christian Century. Oct 11, 1950, v67, p1215.
Commentary. Oct 1950, v10, p388-91.
Commonweal. Aug 18, 1950, v52, p461.
The Evolution of Character Portrayals in the Films of Sidney Poitier, 1950-1978. p94-111.
Film Daily. Aug 2, 1950, p6.
Films in Review. Oct 1950, v1, p24-25.
From Sambo to Superspade. p161-64.
Hollywood Reporter. Aug 2, 1950, p3.
Joseph L. Mankiewicz (Dick). p81-85.
Life. Sep 4, 1950, v29, p44-46.
The London Times. Sep 25, 1950, p6.
Magill's Survey of Cinema. Series II. v4, p1735-37.
Motion Picture Herald Product Digest. Aug 5, 1950, p413.
The Nation. Oct 28, 1950, v171, p397.
Negro Digest. Dec 1950, v9, p81-83.
The New Republic. Sep 4, 1950, v123, p22.
The New Statesman and Nation. Sep 30, 1950, v40, p322, 324.
The New York Times. Aug 17, 1950, p23.
The New Yorker. Aug 26, 1950, v26, p68.
Newsweek. Aug 21, 1950, v36, p83-84.
Pictures Will Talk. p153-57.
Saturday Review. Sep 2, 1950, v33, p28-29.
Saturday Review. Oct 14, 1950, v33, p24.
Senior Scholastic. Oct 11, 1950, v57, p37.
Sequence. Aut 1950, n12, p15-16.
The Spectator. Sep 22, 1950, v185, p312.
Time. Aug 21, 1950, v56, p82.
Variety. Aug 2, 1950, p16.

No Way to Treat a Lady (US; Smight, Jack; 1968)
America. Apr 13, 1968, v118, p520-21.
BFI/Monthly Film Bulletin. Jun 1985, v35, p87.
Christian Science Monitor (Western edition). Apr 12, 1968, p4.
Commonweal. Apr 5, 1968, v88, p76.
Film 68/69. p185-88.
Film Daily. Mar 12, 1968, p5.
Filmfacts. Apr 1, 1968, v11, p63-65.
Films and Filming. Jul 1968, v14, p32-33.
Films in Review. Apr 1968, v19, p243.
Hollywood Reporter. Mar 12, 1968, p3.
The London Times. May 16, 1968, p15.
Magill's Survey of Cinema. Series II. v4, p1738-41.
Motion Picture Herald Product Digest. Mar 13, 1968, p781.
New Statesman. May 17, 1968, v75, p663.
The New York Times. Mar 21, 1968, p56.
The New Yorker. Mar 30, 1968, v44, p114-16.

Newsweek. Apr 8, 1968, v71, p120.
Saturday Review. Apr 13, 1968, v51, p50.
Senior Scholastic. Apr 11, 1968, v92, p26.
Sight and Sound. Sum 1968, v37, p155-56.
Time. Mar 29, 1968, v91, p98.
Variety. Mar 13, 1968, p6.
The Village Voice. Apr 25, 1968, p45-46.
Vogue. Apr 15, 1968, v151, p48.

Nobody Waved Goodbye (Also titled: Départ sans Adieu) (CAN; Owen, Don; 1964)
America. May 1, 1965, v112, p646-47.
BFI/Monthly Film Bulletin. Feb 1966, v33, p17-18.
Cahiers du Cinema in English. May 1967, n10, p62-63.
Catholic World. Jul 1965, v201, p279-80.
Christian Century. Jun 30, 1965, v82, p839-40.
Christian Science Monitor (Western edition). May 21, 1965, p2.
Commonweal. May 7, 1965, v82, p218.
Film. 1964, n41, p29-30.
Film Daily. May 10, 1965, p6.
Film Society Review. Sep 1966, p23-24.
Filmfacts. Jul 9, 1965, v8, p128-29.
Films and Filming. Mar 1967, v13, p28-29.
Films and Filming. Feb 1969, v15, p71-76.
Films in Review. Jun-Jul 1965, v16, p382-83.
Hollywood Reporter. Jun 3, 1965, p3.
International Film Guide. 1966, v3, p54.
Life. Jun 4, 1965, v58, p12.
The London Times. Dec 15, 1966, p8.
Motion Picture Herald Product Digest. May 12, 1965, p284.
The Nation. May 10, 1965, v200, p516.
The New Republic. May 15, 1965, v152, p32.
The New York Times. Sep 17, 1964, p52.
The New Yorker. Apr 24, 1965, v41, p163-64.
On Film. p265-66.
The Private Eye, the Cowboy and the Very Naked Girl. p124-25.
Saturday Review. May 29, 1965, v48, p31.
Senior Scholastic. Apr 8, 1965, v86, sup10.
Time. Apr 30, 1965, v85, p110.
Variety. Aug 19, 1964, p6.
The Village Voice. Sep 2, 1965, v10, p15-17.
Vogue. Jun 1965, v145, p69.

Noia, La *See* The Empty Canvas

None But the Brave (US; Sinatra, Frank; 1965)
BFI/Monthly Film Bulletin. Mar 1965, v32, p35-36.
Christian Science Monitor (Western edition). Mar 8, 1965, p4.
Commonweal. Apr 9, 1965, v82, p84.
Ebony. Oct 1964, v19, p110-12.
Film Daily. Feb 10, 1965, p7.
Film Quarterly. Spr 1965, v18, p61.
Filmfacts. Mar 5, 1965, v8, p24-26.
Films and Filming. May 1965, v11, p33.
Films in Review. Apr 1965, v16, p252-53.
The Films of Frank Sinatra. p201-04.
Hollywood Reporter. Feb 8, 1965, p3.
The London Times. Mar 11, 1965, p15.
Motion Picture Herald Product Digest. Mar 3, 1965, p243.
New Statesman. Mar 19, 1965, v69, p462.
The New York Times. Feb 25, 1965, p24.
Newsweek. Feb 15, 1965, v65, p92.
Time. Feb 26, 1965, v85, p96.
Variety. Feb 10, 1965, p6.

Norma Rae (US; Ritt, Martin; 1979)
America. Apr 7, 1979, v140, p286.
BFI/Monthly Film Bulletin. Aug 1979, v46, p180.
Films in Review. May 1979, v30, p307.
Hollywood Reporter. Feb 21, 1979, p3.

Commonweal. Oct 30, 1964, v81, p167.
Film Daily. Nov 5, 1964, p4.
Filmfacts. Jan 1, 1965, v7, p336-38.
Films and Filming. Jun 1965, v11, p28.
Films in Review. Dec 1964, v15, p637.
Ingmar Bergman (Cowie). p220-23.
Ingmar Bergman (Steene). p130-31.
Ingmar Bergman (Wood). p139-42.
Life. Oct 16, 1964, v57, p19.
The London Times. Apr 1, 1965, p5.
Movie. Sum 1965, n13, p6-9.
The New Republic. Oct 31, 1964, v151, p28.
New Statesman. Apr 2, 1965, v69, p544.
The New York Times. Oct 6, 1964, p35.
Newsweek. Oct 12, 1964, v64, p116.
Saturday Review. Nov 21, 1964, v47, p34.
Sight and Sound. Sum 1965, v34, p146-47.
Tynan Right and Left. p224-25.
Variety. Jul 1, 1964, p22.
The Village Voice. Oct 22, 1964, v10, p15.
A World on Film. p289-90.

Noz W Wodzie *See* Knife in the Water

Nuit americaine, La *See* Day For Night

Nuit de Varennes, La (FR; Scola, Ettore; 1983)
Films in Review. Apr 1983, v34, p244.
Hollywood Reporter. Mar 11, 1983, p3.
The Los Angeles Times. Mar 2, 1983, SecVI, p1.
Maclean's. Apr 4, 1983, v96, p62.
Magill's Cinema Annual 1984. p270-75.
The Nation. Mar 26, 1983, v236, p376-77.
The New Republic. Mar 21, 1983, v188, p24-25.
New York. Mar 7, 1983, v16, p95.
The New York Times. Feb 16, 1983, SecIII, p23.
The New Yorker. Mar 21, 1983, v59, p121-22.
Newsweek. Mar 7, 1983, v101, p78.
Progressive. Jun 1983, v47, p40-41.
Time. Mar 7, 1983, v121, p84.
Vogue. Jan 1983, v173, p56.

Nuits de la Pleine Lune, Les *See* Full Moon in Paris

Numero Deux (FR; Godard, Jean-Luc; 1975)
Film Journal. Aug 10, 1981, v84, p13-14.
Jump Cut. Oct-Dec 1975, n9, p12-13.
The Nation. Jul 11, 1981, v233, p60-61.
The New Republic. Aug 1, 1981, v185, p26-27.
The New York Times. Jun 19, 1981, SecIII, p12.
Take One. 1975, n12, v4, p36.
Variety. Oct 8, 1975, p20.
The Village Voice. Jun 17, 1981, p41.

The Nun *See* Religieuse, La

The Nun's Story (US; Zinnemann, Fred; 1959)
America. May 23, 1959, v101, p356.
America. Jun 27, 1959, v101, p468-71.
BFI/Monthly Film Bulletin. Sep 1959, v26, p120.
Catholic World. Jul 1959, v189, p315-16.
Commonweal. Jul 17, 1959, v70, p374.
Film Daily. May 6, 1959, v115, p6.
Filmfacts. Jul 15, 1959, v2, p129-31.
Films in Review. Jun-Jul 1959, v10, p351-54.
Good Housekeeping. Jul 1959, v149, p24.
Hollywood Reporter. May 6, 1959, p3.
Library Journal. Jun 15, 1959, v84, p2055.
Life. Jun 8, 1959, v46, p141-44.
Magill's Survey of Cinema. Series II. v4, p1759-63.
The Nation. Jul 4, 1959, v189, p20.
The New Republic. Jun 29, 1959, v140, p21.
The New York Times. Jun 19, 1959, p30.

The New Yorker. Jun 27, 1959, v35, p52.
Newsweek. Jun 29, 1959, v53, p91.
On the Verge of Revolt. p121-36.
Saturday Review. Jun 27, 1959, v42, p24.
Time. Jul 6, 1959, v74, p57.
Variety. May 6, 1959, p6.

The Nutty Professor (US; Lewis, Jerry; 1963)
BFI/Monthly Film Bulletin. Aug 1963, v30, p111.
Film Daily. May 17, 1963, p4.
Filmfacts. Jul 25, 1963, v6, p141-42.
Films and Filming. Oct 1963, v10, p31.
Hollywood Reporter. May 16, 1963, v175, p3.
The New York Times. Jul 18, 1963, p15.
The New Yorker. Aug 10, 1963, v39, p61.
Saturday Review. Jun 1, 1963, v46, p16.
Sight and Sound. Sum 1964, v33, p147.
Time. Jul 26, 1963, v82, p80.
Variety. May 22, 1963, p6.

Nybyggarna *See* The New Land

O. Henry's Full House (Also titled: Full House) (US; Negulesco, Jean; Hathaway, Henry; King, Henry; Hawks, Howard; Koster, Henry; 1952)
BFI/Monthly Film Bulletin. Oct 1952, v19, p138.
Catholic World. Oct 1952, v176, p61.
Charles Laughton (Brown). p127-31.
Christian Century. Nov 26, 1952, v69, p1391.
Film Daily. Aug 26, 1952, p6.
Films in Review. Oct 1952, v3, p416-17.
The Films of Marilyn Monroe. p89-92.
Hollywood Reporter. Aug 18, 1952, p3.
Library Journal. Nov 15, 1952, v77, p1981.
The London Times. Sep 22, 1952, p2.
Motion Picture Herald Product Digest. Aug 23, 1952, p1501.
Movie. Dec 1962, n5, p21-22.
The Nation. Nov 22, 1952, v175, p475.
National Parent-Teacher. Oct 1952, v47, p38.
The New Statesman and Nation. Oct 11, 1952, v44, p420.
The New York Times. Oct 17, 1952, p33.
Newsweek. Oct 6, 1952, v40, p113.
Saturday Review. Sep 13, 1952, v35, p34.
Senior Scholastic. Sep 13, 1952, v61, p20.
Sight and Sound. Oct-Dec 1952, v22, p77.
The Spectator. Oct 3, 1952, v189, p425-26.
The Tatler. Oct 15, 1952, v206, p144.
Theatre Arts. Dec 1952, v36, p86.
Time. Sep 22, 1952, v60, p102.
Variety. Aug 20, 1952, p6.

O Lucky Man! (GB; Anderson, Lindsay; 1973)
America. Jul 7, 1973, v129, p20.
Christian Century. Aug 15, 1973, v90, p809.
Commentary. Sep 1973, v56, p76.
Commonweal. Sep 21, 1973, v98, p502.
Filmfacts. 1973, v16, n5, p109.
Films in Review. Aug-Sep 1973, v24, n7, p434.
Hollywood Reporter. May 29, 1973, p3.
Lindsay Anderson: A Guide to References and Resources. p58-63.
Magill's Survey of Cinema. Series I. v3, p1231.
The Nation. Jul 2, 1973, v217, p27-28.
The New Republic. Jul 16, 1973, v168, p24.
The New York Times. Jul 24, 1973, SecII, p1.
The New York Times. Jul 8, 1973, SecII, p8.
The New Yorker. Jul 16, 1973, v49, p80.
PTA Magazine. Nov 1973, v68, p8.
Time. Jul 18, 1973, v101, p58.
Variety. Apr 18, 1973, p30.

O Slavnosti a Hostech *See* A Report on the Party and the Guests

Oasis (FR; Allégret, Yves; 1957)
BFI/Monthly Film Bulletin. May 1956, v23, p56-57.
Film Daily. Jan 21, 1957, v111, p6.
Films and Filming. May 1956, v2, p24.
Hollywood Reporter. Jan 9, 1957, p4.
Motion Picture Herald Product Digest. Jan 12, 1957, v206, p218.
The New York Times. Jul 7, 1960, p26.

Obchod na Korze *See* The Shop on Main Street

Obsessed (Also titled: The Late Edwina Black) (GB; Elvey, Maurice; 1951)
BFI/Monthly Film Bulletin. Mar 1951, v18, p234.
Film Daily. Sep 10, 1951, p6.
Hollywood Reporter. Aug 29, 1951, p4.
Motion Picture Herald Product Digest. Sep 1, 1951, p998.
The New York Times. Feb 6, 1952, p24.
Newsweek. Feb 18, 1952, v39, p100.
Variety. Aug 29, 1951, p20.

Obsession (US; De Palma, Brian; 1976)
America. Sep 4, 1976, v135, p99-100.
BFI/Monthly Film Bulletin. Oct 1976, v43, p217.
Commentary. Nov 1976, v62, p75-78.
Commonweal. Sep 24, 1976, v103, p628-29.
De Palma (Bliss). p40-49.
Film. Dec 1976, n44, p6.
Film Heritage. 1976, v12, n1, p33-34.
Films and Filming. Dec 1976, v23, p30.
Films in Review. Nov 1976, v27, p561-64.
Films in Review. Oct 1976, v27, p504-05.
Gore Creatures. Sep 1976, n25, p51.
Hi Fi. Nov 1976, v26, p147-48.
Hollywood Reporter. Jul 7, 1976, p2.
Independent Film Journal. Jul 23, 1976, v78, p9.
The Los Angeles Times. Sep 1, 1976, SecIV, p1.
Motion Picture Herald Product Digest. Jul 28, 1976, p17.
The New Republic. Sep 18, 1976, v175, p25.
New York. Aug 16, 1976, v9, p60-61.
The New York Times. Aug 8, 1976, SecII, p11.
The New Yorker. Aug 2, 1976, v52, p61-62.
Newsweek. Aug 9, 1976, v88, p68.
Penthouse. Nov 1976, v8, p55-57.
Saturday Review. Sep 18, 1976, v3, p41-42.
The Thousand Eyes Magazine. Sep 1976, v2, p8-9.
Time. Aug 16, 1976, v108, p58.
Variety. Jul 7, 1976, p16.
Vogue. Sep 1976, v166, p239.

Occupe-Toi D'Amelie (Also titled: Oh, Amelia!; Keep An Eye on Amelia) (FR; Autant-Lara, Claude; 1949)
Dictionary of Films. p254-55.
Film Daily. Feb 6, 1951, p6.
Halliwell's Hundred. p243-46.
The New Republic. Dec 17, 1951, v125, p20.
The New York Times. Dec 3, 1951, p22.
Newsweek. Jan 14, 1952, v39, p82.
Sight and Sound. Dec 1950, v19, p334.
Variety. Oct 19, 1949, p18.

Ocean's Eleven (US; Milestone, Lewis; 1960)
America. Aug 20, 1960, v103, p563.
BFI/Monthly Film Bulletin. Oct 1960, v27, p139.
Film Daily. Aug 5, 1960, p9.
Film Quarterly. Fall 1960, v14, p61.
Filmfacts. 1960, v3, p199.
Films and Filming. Oct 1960, v7, p27.
Films in Review. Oct 1960, v11, p493.
The Films of Frank Sinatra. p163-67.

Hollywood Reporter. Aug 5, 1960, p3.
Lewis Milestone (Millichap). p180-81.
The New Yorker. Aug 20, 1960, v36, p72.
Newsweek. Aug 22, 1960, v56, p86.
The Platinum Years. p108-11.
Saturday Review. Aug 11, 1960, p19.
Saturday Review. Aug 14, 1960, SecII, p1.
Time. Aug 22, 1960, v76, p53.
Variety. Aug 10, 1960, p6.

Ochazuke no Aji *See* The Flavor of Green Tea Over Rice

Octopussy (GB; Glen, John; 1983)
Hollywood Reporter. Jun 8, 1983, p3.
The James Bond Films. p176-78.
James Bond's Bedside Companion. p232-37.
The Los Angeles Times. Jun 10, 1983, SecVI, p1.
Maclean's. Jun 13, 1983, v96, p53.
Magill's Cinema Annual, 1984. p276-81.
New York. Jun 20, 1983, v16, p70.
The New York Times. Jun 10, 1983, SecIII, p17.
The New Yorker. Jun 27, 1983, v59, p93-94.
Newsweek. Jun 13, 1983, v101, p77-78.
Time. Jun 27, 1983, v121, p71.
Variety. Jun 8, 1983, p77.

The Odd Couple (US; Saks, Gene; 1968)
America. Jun 1, 1968, v118, p740.
BFI/Monthly Film Bulletin. Aug 1968, v35, p112.
Christian Century. Sep 11, 1968, v85, p1144.
Christian Science Monitor (Western edition). May 8, 1968, p6.
Commonweal. May 17, 1968, v88, p267.
Esquire. Aug 1968, v70, p22.
Figures of Light. p75-77.
Film Daily. Apr 30, 1968, p5.
Film Quarterly. Fall 1968, v22, p75.
Filmfacts. Jun 15, 1968, v11, p143-45.
Films and Filming. Aug 1968, v14, p24.
Films in Review. Jun-Jul 1968, v19, p379.
The Films of Jack Lemmon. p174-79.
The Films of the Sixties. p234-35.
Hollywood Reporter. Apr 30, 1968, p3.
The London Times. Jun 27, 1968, p8.
Magill's Survey of Cinema. Series I. v3, p1234-36.
Motion Picture Herald Product Digest. May 1, 1968, p805.
Movie Comedy (Byron). p174-76.
The New Republic. May 25, 1968, v158, p43.
The New York Times. May 3, 1968, p42.
Newsweek. May 13, 1968, v71, p100.
The Spectator. Jul 5, 1968, v221, p28.
Time. May 3, 1968, v91, p80-81.
Variety. May 1, 1968, p6.
The Village Voice. Jun 13, 1968, p47.
Vogue. Aug 1, 1968, v152, p60.
A Year In the Dark. p135-36.

Ode to Billy Joe (US; Baer, Max; 1976)
BFI/Monthly Film Bulletin. Aug 1976, v43, p169-70.
Film Bulletin. Apr 1976, v45, p10-19.
Films and Filming. Nov 1976, v23, p31-32.
Films and Filming. Jun 1976, v22, p25-27.
Hollywood Reporter. Jun 3, 1976, p3.
Independent Film Journal. Jun 25, 1976, v78, p14.
The Los Angeles Times. Jun 29, 1976, SecIV, p1.
Motion Picture Herald Product Digest. Jun 16, 1976, p6.
The New York Times. Aug 29, 1976, SecIII, p11.
Time. Sep 20, 1976, v108, p80.
Variety. Jun 9, 1976, p23.

The Odessa File (GB, WGER; Neame, Ronald; 1974)
BFI/Monthly Film Bulletin. Dec 1974, v41, p281.
Films and Filming. Aug 1974, v20, p37-40.
Films Illustrated. Nov 1974, v4, p86.
Films in Review. Dec 1974, v25, p624-25.
Hollywood Reporter. Oct 9, 1974, p3.
Independent Film Journal. Oct 30, 1974, v74, p5.
The Los Angeles Times. Oct 18, 1974, SecIV, p19.
Motion Picture Herald Product Digest. Oct 30, 1974, p43.
Movietone News. Nov 1974, n37, p33.
New Statesman. Oct 18, 1974, v88, p549.
New York. Nov 4, 1974, v7, p82-83.
The New York Times. Oct 19, 1974, p36.
Newsweek. Nov 11, 1974, v84, p86.
Senior Scholastic. Jan 16, 1975, v105, p20.
Time. Nov 11, 1974, v104, p8.
Variety. Oct 9, 1974, v276, p18.
Views. 1974, v6, n1, p49-50.

Odette (GB; Wilcox, Herbert; 1950)
BFI/Monthly Film Bulletin. Jul 1950, v17, p101.
Christian Century. Oct 10, 1951, v68, p1175.
Commonweal. Apr 20, 1951, v54, p38.
Film Daily. Jan 3, 1951, p6.
Hollywood Reporter. Jun 28, 1951, p3.
Motion Picture Herald Product Digest. Jan 6, 1951, p653.
The New Republic. Apr 16, 1951, v124, p30.
The New York Times. Mar 28, 1951, p33.
The New Yorker. Mar 31, 1951, v27, p65.
Newsweek. Mar 26, 1951, v37, p100.
Senior Scholastic. May 9, 1951, v58, p29.
Variety. Jun 14, 1950, p22.

Oedipus Rex (CAN; Guthrie, Tyrone; 1957)
Commonweal. Feb 8, 1957, v65, p488.
Film Daily. Jan 9, 1957, v111, p6.
Films and Filming. Aug 1956, v2, p6.
Films in Review. Oct 1956, v7, p416.
Hollywood Reporter. Mar 29, 1957, p3.
The Nation. Jan 19, 1957, v184, p66.
The New York Times. Jan 8, 1957, p26.
The New Yorker. Jan 19, 1957, v32, p96.
Newsweek. Jan 14, 1957, v49, p86.
Saturday Review. Jan 26, 1957, v40, p25.
Variety. Jan 2, 1957, p6.
The Village Voice. Feb 6, 1957, p6.

Oedipus the King (GB; Saville, Philip; 1967)
America. Oct 19, 1968, v119, p364.
BFI/Monthly Film Bulletin. Aug 1968, v35, p112-13.
Christian Science Monitor (Western edition). Jul 10, 1968, p4.
Film Daily. Sep 19, 1968, p8.
Filmfacts. Dec 15, 1968, v11, p372-74.
Films and Filming. Aug 1968, v14, p24-25.
Hollywood Reporter. Sep 18, 1968, p3.
The London Times. Feb 3, 1968, p19.
Motion Picture Herald Product Digest. Sep 25, 1968, p34.
The New York Times. Sep 19, 1968, p62.
Newsweek. Sep 30, 1968, v72, p98.
Senior Scholastic. Oct 4, 1968, v93, p26.
Time. Oct 11, 1968, v92, p104.
Variety. Jul 3, 1968, p6.

Of a Thousand Delights *See* Vaghe Stelle Dell'Orsa

Of Human Bondage (GB; Hughes, Ken; 1963)
BFI/Monthly Film Bulletin. Oct 1964, v31, p146-47.
Commonweal. Sep 25, 1964, v81, p18.
Film Daily. Sep 17, 1964, v125, p8.
Films and Filming. Nov 1964, v2, p25-26.
Films in Review. Oct 1964, v15, p499-500.
Hollywood Reporter. Jul 24, 1964, v181, p3.
The Los Angeles Times. Nov 20, 1964, SecV, p14.
Motion Picture Herald Product Digest. Sep 30, 1964, v232, p138.
National Review. Dec 29, 1964, v16, p1156.
The New York Times. Sep 24, 1964, p46.
Newsweek. Sep 28, 1964, v64, p96.
Saturday Review. Nov 21, 1964, v47, p34.
Time. Oct 2, 1964, v84, p129.
Variety. Jul 1, 1964, p6.

Of Love and Desire (US; Rush, Richard; 1963)
BFI/Monthly Film Bulletin. Mar 1964, v31, p41.
Commonweal. Oct 4, 1963, v79, p48.
Film Daily. Aug 27, 1963, p14.
Filmfacts. Oct 3, 1963, v6, p201-02.
Films and Filming. Mar 1964, v10, p29.
Hollywood Reporter. Aug 27, 1963, v176, p3.
The New York Times. Sep 12, 1963, p32.
Variety. Aug 28, 1963, p6.

An Officer and a Gentleman (US; Hackford, Taylor; 1982)
BFI/Monthly Film Bulletin. Mar 1983, v50, p74-75.
Commonweal. Oct 8, 1982, v109, p531.
Ebony. Sep 1982, v37, p112.
Films In Review. Nov 1982, v33, p539-44.
Films In Review. Oct 1982, v33, p490-91.
Hollywood Reporter. Jul 19, 1982, p3.
Horizon. Oct-Nov 1982, v25, p58-59.
The Los Angeles Times. Jul 28, 1982, SecVI, p1.
Maclean's. Aug 9, 1982, v95, p46-47.
Magill's Cinema Annual, 1983. p246-49.
National Review. Oct 15, 1982, v34, p1292-93.
The New Republic. Sep 13, 1982, v187, p26.
New Statesman. Jan 28, 1983, v105, p31.
New York. Aug 9, 1982, v15, p58-59.
The New York Times. Aug 8, 1982, SecIII, p13.
The New York Times. Aug 17, 1982, SecIII, p7.
The New Yorker. Aug 23, 1982, v58, p77-80.
Newsweek. Aug 2, 1982, v100, p62.
Progressive. Oct 1982, v46, p54-55.
Time. Aug 9, 1982, v120, p58.
Variety. Jul 19, 1982, p3.
Variety. Jul 21, 1982, p20.
The Village Voice. Aug 10, 1982, p45.

The Official Story (Also titled: Desaparecidos, Los; The Official Version) (ARG; Puenzo, Luis; 1985)
BFI/Monthly Film Bulletin. Oct 1985, v52, p308.
Commonweal. Nov 29, 1985, v112, p671-72.
Films in Review. Jan 1986, v37, p43.
Hollywood Reporter. Nov 8, 1985, p3.
The Los Angeles Times. Dec 20, 1985, SecVI, p1.
Magill's Cinema Annual, 1986. p249-54.
National Review. Jan 31, 1986, v38, p61.
New York. Nov 18, 1985, v18, p88-89.
The New York Times. Nov 3, 1985, SecII, p1.
The New York Times. Nov 8, 1985, SecIII, p6.
Newsweek. Nov 25, 1985, v106, p107.
Time. Dec 2, 1985, v126, p101.
Variety. Apr 24, 1985, p34.
Vogue. Dec 1985, v175, p72.

Oh, Amelia! *See* Occupe-Toi D'Amelie

Oh! For a Man! *See* Will Success Spoil Rock Hunter?

Oh, God! (US; Reiner, Carl; 1977)
BFI/Monthly Film Bulletin. Nov 1977, v44, p236.
Christian Century. Nov 23, 1977, v94, p1095.
Christianity Today. Dec 30, 1977, v22, p23-24.
Films and Filming. Dec 1977, v24, p32.
Hollywood Reporter. Oct 3, 1977, p3.
The Los Angeles Times. Oct 7, 1977, SecIV, p1.
Maclean's. Nov 14, 1977, v90, p88.
Motion Picture Herald Product Digest. Oct 19, 1977, p38.
New Statesman. Apr 28, 1978, v95, p577.
The New York Times. Oct 8, 1977, p13.
The New York Times. Nov 13, 1977, SecII, p15.
Newsweek. Oct 24, 1977, v90, p126.
Senior Scholastic. Nov 17, 1977, v110, p32.
Time. Oct 31, 1977, v110, p90.
Variety. Oct 5, 1977, p28.
The Village Voice. Oct 17, 1977, p53.

Oh, God! Book II (US; Cates, Gilbert; 1980)
Hollywood Reporter. Sep 30, 1980, p2.
The Los Angeles Times. Oct 3, 1980, SecVI, p1.
Motion Picture Herald Product Digest. Oct 8, 1980, p34.
The New York Times. Oct 3, 1980, SecIII, p8.
Variety. Oct 1, 1980, p20.

Oh, Heavenly Dog! (US; Camp, Joe; 1980)
Films in Review. Oct 1980, v31, p503.
Hollywood Reporter. Jul 11, 1980, p3.
The Los Angeles Times. Aug 15, 1980, SecVI, p13.
The New York Times. Nov 8, 1980, p12.
Newsday. Nov 7, 1980, SecII, p7.
Variety. Jul 16, 1980, p23.

Oh Men! Oh Women! (US; Johnson, Nunnally; 1957)
America. Mar 16, 1957, v96, p685.
BFI/Monthly Film Bulletin. May 1957, v24, p60.
Commonweal. Mar 15, 1957, v65, p615.
Film Daily. Feb 25, 1957, v111, p6.
Films and Filming. May 1957, v3, p25-26.
The Films of David Niven. p140.
The Films of Ginger Rogers. p324.
Hollywood Reporter. Feb 19, 1957, p3.
Motion Picture Herald Product Digest. Feb 23, 1957, v206, p273.
The New York Times. Feb 22, 1957, p25.
The New Yorker. Mar 2, 1957, v33, p88.
Newsweek. Mar 4, 1957, v49, p100.
Talking Pictures. p174-87.
Time. Mar 11, 1957, v69, p98.
Variety. Feb 20, 1957, p6.

Oh! What A Lovely War (GB; Attenborough, Richard; 1969)
America. Oct 25, 1969, v121, p368-70.
Big Screen, Little Screen. p248-49.
Deeper Into Movies. p17-21.
Film Daily. Sep 24, 1969, p4.
Filmfacts. 1969, v12, p385.
Films and Filming. Jun 1969, v15, p40-41.
Films in Review. Nov 1969, v20, p573-74.
The Films of Dirk Bogarde. p179-80.
The Films of Laurence Olivier. p149-51.
Focus. Oct 1969, n5, p34.
Holiday. Nov 1969, v46, p23.
Laurence Olivier: Theater & Cinema. p287-90.
Life. Oct 10, 1969, v67, p17.
Look. Nov 4, 1969, v33, p92.
Mademoiselle. Sep 1969, v69, p74.
Magill's Survey of Cinema. Series II. v4, p1767-70.

The Nation. Oct 27, 1969, v109, p452.
The New Republic. Oct 18, 1969, v161, p22.
The New York Times. Oct 3, 1969, p34.
The New York Times. Oct 19, 1969, SecII, p1.
The New Yorker. Oct 11, 1969, v45, p157-58.
Newsweek. Oct 13, 1969, v74, p116-17.
Saturday Review. Oct 4, 1969, v52, p34.
Screen. May-Jun 1969, v10, p84-90.
Second Sight. p263-65.
Sight and Sound. Spr 1969, v38, p93-94.
Variety. Apr 16, 1969, p6.
Vogue. Oct 1, 1969, v154, p150.

Oharu *See* The Life of Oharu

Oklahoma! (US; Zinnemann, Fred; 1955)
America. Oct 29, 1955, v94, p138.
Catholic World. Dec 1955, v182, p217.
Commonweal. Oct 28, 1955, v63, p90-91.
Film Culture. Wint 1955, v1, n5/6, p33-34.
Film Daily. Oct 11, 1955, p5.
Films and Filming. Oct 1956, v3, n1, p23.
Films in Review. Nov 1955, v6, n9, p462-64.
The Hollywood Musical. p345, 351.
Hollywood Reporter. Oct 11, 1955, v136, n37, p3.
Library Journal. Nov 1, 1955, v80, p2478.
Magill's Survey of Cinema. Series I. v3, p1246-48.
The Musical: From Broadway to Hollywood. p49-54.
The Nation. Oct 29, 1955, v181, p369.
The New York Times. Aug 29, 1954, SecII, p5.
The New York Times. Oct 29, 1955, SecI, p29.
The New York Times. Oct 16, 1955, SecII, p1.
The New Yorker. Oct 22, 1955, v31, p171.
Newsweek. Oct 24, 1955, v46, p106.
Saturday Review. Nov 5, 1955, v38, p27.
Time. Oct 24, 1955, v66, p104.
Variety. Oct 12, 1955, p6.

The Old Man and the Child *See* The Two of Us

The Old Man and the Sea (US; Sturges, John; 1958)
America. Oct 25, 1958, v100, p118.
BFI/Monthly Film Bulletin. Jan 1959, v26, p4.
Catholic World. Nov 1958, v188, p151.
Commonweal. Oct 3, 1958, v69, p16.
Film Daily. May 21, 1958, v113, p6.
Filmfacts. Nov 12, 1958, v1, p185-87.
Films in Review. Aug-Sep 1958, v9, p396-98.
Hemingway on Film. p135-54.
Hollywood Reporter. May 19, 1958, v10, p3.
Hollywood Reporter. Jan 1959, v10, p1.
Hollywood Reporter. Apr 1959, v10, p216.
Library Journal. Aug 1958, v83, p2150.
Life. Oct 6, 1958, v45, p124-29.
Look. Sep 2, 1958, v22, p66-67.
Magill's Survey of Cinema. Series II. v4, p1775-77.
The New Republic. Oct 6, 1958, v139, p21-22.
The New York Times. Oct 8, 1958, p41.
The New Yorker. Oct 18, 1958, v34, p154.
Newsweek. Oct 13, 1958, v51, p118-19.
Popular Photography. Oct 1958, v43, p106-08.
Saturday Review. Oct 4, 1958, v41, p26.
the Films of Spencer Tracy. p228-31.
Thee Modern American Novel and the Movies. p199-203.
Time. Oct 27, 1958, v72, p42.
Variety. May 21, 1958, p6.

Old Yeller (US; Stevenson, Robert; 1957)
America. Jan 25, 1958, v98.
BFI/Monthly Film Bulletin. May 1958, v25, p63.
Commonweal. Dec 27, 1957, v67, p336.
The Disney Films. p145-46.
Film Daily. Nov 14, 1957, v112, p12.

Films in Review. Dec 1957, v8, p528-29.
Hollywood Reporter. Nov 14, 1957, p3.
The New York Times. Dec 26, 1957, p23.
Newsweek. Dec 30, 1957, v50, p61.
Time. Jan 20, 1958, v71, p90.
Variety. Nov 20, 1957, p6.
Walt Disney: A Guide to References and Resources. p60-63.

Oliver! (GB; Reed, Carol; 1968)
BFI/Monthly Film Bulletin. Nov 1968, v35, p172-73.
Commonweal. Jan 24, 1969, v89, p528-29.
Confessions of a Cultist. p422-23.
Dance Magazine. Jun 1969, v43, p25.
Film 68/69. p159-61.
Film Daily. Dec 2, 1968, p4.
Film Quarterly. Spr 1969, v22, p62.
Filmfacts. Jan 1, 1969, v11, p387-90.
Films and Filming. Nov 1968, v15, p44-45.
Films in Review. Jan 1969, v20, p56-57.
Five Thousand One Nights At the Movies. p426.
Going Steady. p245-52.
Hollywood Reporter. Sep 30, 1968, p3.
The London Times. Sep 23, 1968, p7.
The London Times. Sep 26, 1968, p15.
The London Times. Jul 23, 1969, p11.
Look. Jan 21, 1969, v33, p66.
Magill's Survey of Cinema. Series I. v3, p1252-55.
Motion Picture Herald Product Digest. Dec 11, 1968, p75.
Movies Into Film. p329-30.
The Musical: From Broadway to Hollywood. p125-30.
The New Republic. Jan 18, 1969, v160, p23.
New Statesman. Oct 4, 1968, v76, p439.
The New York Times. Dec 12, 1968, p62.
The New York Times. Dec 29, 1968, p29.
The New Yorker. Dec 14, 1968, v44, p193-96.
Newsweek. Dec 23, 1968, v72, p89.
Saturday Review. Dec 21, 1968, v51, p16.
Time. Dec 13, 1968, v92, p104.
Variety. Oct 2, 1968, p6.

Olivia (FR; Audry, Jacqueline; 1950)
BFI/Monthly Film Bulletin. Aug 1952, v19, p106.
BFI/Monthly Film Bulletin. Oct 1983, v50, p283.
The New Statesman and Nation. Jul 5, 1952, v44, p13.
Variety. May 16, 1951, p18.

Olvidados, Los (Also titled: The Young and the Damned; The Forgotten Ones; Pity For Them) (MEX; Buñuel, Luis; 1950)
American Film. Jun 1983, v8, p14-15.
BFI/Monthly Film Bulletin. Jun 1952, v19, p76.
The Cinema of Luis Buñuel. p48-50.
Cinema, the Magic Vehicle. v2, p49.
Cinema, the Magic Vehicle. v1, p506-07.
Dictionary of Films. p258.
Film Criticism and Caricatures, 1943-1953. p144-45.
Films in Review. May 1952, v3, p245.
The International Dictionary of Films and Filmmakers. v1, p338-39.
Kiss Kiss Bang Bang. p404-05.
Luis Buñuel (Durgnat). p60-68.
Luis Buñuel (Edwards). p87-111.
Luis Buñuel (Higgenbotham). p77-82.
Luis Buñuel (Kyrou). p48-49.
Lumiere. Apr-May 1974, n33, p31.
Magill's Survey of Cinema. Foreign Language Films. v5, p2266-71.
Motion Picture Herald Product Digest. Apr 19, 1952, p1322.
Movies (Farber). p278.
Movietone News. Feb 1975, n39, p3-8.

The New Statesman and Nation. May 10, 1952, v43, p553.
The New York Times. Mar 25, 1952, p23.
The New Yorker. Dec 8, 1951, v27, p74.
The New Yorker. Mar 29, 1952, v28, p106.
Quarterly of Film, Radio and Televison. Sum 1953, v7, p392-401.
Saturday Review. Sep 15, 1951, v34, p24.
Sequence. New Year, 1952, n14, p30-32.
Seventy Years of Cinema. p174-75.
Sight and Sound. May 1951, v20, p4.
Sight and Sound. Apr-Jun 1952, v21, p167-68.
Sight and Sound. Jul-Sep 1953, v23, p21-23.
The Spectator. May 2, 1952, v188, p576.
Surrealism and the Cinema. p70-79.
Time. Mar 31, 1952, v59, p102.
Variety. May 16, 1951, p18.
The World of Luis Buñuel. p194-200.

Ombre Bianche *See* The Savage Innocents

The Omega Man (US; Sagal, Boris; 1971)
BFI/Monthly Film Bulletin. Mar 1972, v39, n458, p56.
Filmfacts. 1971, v14, n19, p493-96.
Films and Filming. May 1972, v18, n8, p54-55.
Hollywood Reporter. Jul 30, 1971, v217, n16, p3.
The New York Times. Aug 14, 1971, p13.
Time. Sep 6, 1971, v98, p61.
Variety. Aug 4, 1971, p18.
The Village Voice. Aug 26, 1971, v16, n34, p59.

The Omen (US; Donner, Richard; 1976)
BFI/Monthly Film Bulletin. Aug 1976, v43, p170-71.
Christian Century. Aug 4, 1976, v93, p689-91.
Christianity Today. Aug 6, 1976, v20, p9-10.
Cinefantastique. 1976, v5, n2, p27.
Cinefantastique. 1976, v5, n3, p40-47.
Commonweal. Sep 24, 1976, v103, p628-29.
The Fifty Worst Films of All Time. p171-76.
Filmmakers' Newsletter. Sep 1976, v9, p30-32.
Films and Filming. Nov 1976, v23, p30-31.
Films and Filming. Sep 1976, v22, p26-29.
Films Illustrated. Nov 1976, v6, p102-03.
Films in Review. Aug-Sep, 1976, v27, p440.
The Films of the Seventies. p147-49.
Gore Creatures. Sep 1976, n25, p50-51.
Hollywood Reporter. Jun 8, 1976, p2.
Independent Film Journal. Jun 25, 1976, v78, p13.
The Los Angeles Times. Jun 25, 1976, SecIV, p1.
Motion Picture Herald Product Digest. Jun 16, 1976, p5.
Movietone News. Jun 1976, n50, p32-33.
New Statesman. Sep 17, 1976, v92, p383-84.
The New York Times. Jul 25, 1976, SecII, p13.
The New Yorker. Jul 19, 1976, v52, p81.
Newsweek. Jul 12, 1976, v88, p69.
Saturday Review. Jul 24, 1976, v3, p43.
Time. Jun 28, 1976, v107, p46.
Times Educational Supplement. Dec 31, 1976, n3213, p12.
Variety. Jun 9, 1976, p23.
Vogue. Aug 1976, v166, p64.

On a Clear Day You Can See Forever (US; Minnelli, Vincente; 1970)
America. Aug 8, 1970, v123, p74.
BFI/Monthly Film Bulletin. Sep 1971, v38, n452, p184.
Big Screen, Little Screen. p288-89.
Deeper into Movies. p185.
Films in Review. Aug-Sep 1970, v21, n7, p438-39.
Hollywood Reporter. Jun 17, 1970, p3, 6.
The New Republic. Jul 18, 1970, v163, p22.
The New York Times. Jun 18, 1970, p53.
Newsweek. Jun 29, 1970, v75, p78.

Saturday Review. Jul 4, 1970, v53, p22.
Time. Jun 29, 1970, v95, p81.
Variety. Jun 17, 1970, p16.

On Any Sunday (US; Brown, Bruce; 1971)
American Cinematographer. Jan 1972, v53, n1, p44-47.
BFI/Monthly Film Bulletin. Apr 1972, v39, n459, p75.
Filmfacts. 1971, v14, n20, p503-05.
Hollywood Reporter. Jul 14, 1971, v217, n4, p3.
The New York Times. Jul 29, 1971, p42.
The New York Times. Aug 7, 1971, p17.
Newsweek. Aug 16, 1971, v78, p79.
Time. Aug 16, 1971, v98, p55.
Variety. Jul 21, 1971, p16.

On Dangerous Ground (US; Ray, Nicholas; 1951)
BFI/Monthly Film Bulletin. Jun 1952, v19, p76.
Film Comment. Mar-Apr 1975, v11, p22-23.
Film Daily. Nov 28, 1951, p6.
Hollywood Reporter. Nov 28, 1951, p3.
Library Journal. Jan 1, 1952, v77, p44.
Magill's Survey of Cinema. Series II. v4, p1784-88.
Motion Picture Herald Product Digest. Dec 1, 1951, p1125.
The Nation. Mar 22, 1952, v174, p287.
The New Republic. Jan 28, 1952, v126, p22.
The New York Times. Feb 13, 1952, p35.
Newsweek. Feb 18, 1952, v39, p103.
Nicholas Ray: A Guide to References and Resources. p66-67.
Nicholas Ray (Kreidl). p33-37.
Variety. Dec 5, 1951, p6.

On Golden Pond (US; Rydell, Mark; 1981)
American Cinematographer. May 1982, v63, p452.
BFI/Monthly Film Bulletin. Feb 1982, v49, p30.
Christian Century. Mar 31, 1982, v99, p355-56.
Christian Century. Dec 30, 1981, v98, p1371.
Commonweal. Jan 15, 1982, v109, p22-23.
Film Bulletin. Feb-Mar 1982, p50.
Films In Review. Jan 1982, v33, p47.
Films In Review. Feb 1982, v33, p102-09.
Hollywood Reporter. Nov 13, 1981, p3.
Horizon. Jul-Aug 1982, v25, p62-63.
The Los Angeles Times. Nov 29, 1981, Calendar, p37.
Maclean's. Dec 21, 1981, v94, p47-48.
Magill's Cinema Annual, 1982. p263-67.
The New Republic. Jan 20, 1982, v186, p26.
New Statesman. Mar 5, 1982, v103, p30-31.
New York. Dec 7, 1981, v14, p156.
The New York Times. Mar 29, 1982, SecIII, p11.
The New Yorker. Dec 7, 1981, v57, p198.
Newsweek. Nov 30, 1981, v98, p105.
Penthouse. Mar 1982, v13, p46-47.
Photoplay. Apr 1982, v33, p24-25, 54-55.
Saturday Review. Dec 1981, v8, p69.
Senior Scholastic. Mar 19, 1982, v114, p19.
Time. Nov 16, 1981, v118, p112-16.
Time. Apr 12, 1982, v119, p68.

On Her Majesty's Secret Service (GB; Hunt, Peter; 1969)
Deeper Into Movies. p107.
Film Daily. Dec 17, 1969, p3.
Films and Filming. Feb 1970, v16, p38.
Films in Review. Jan 1970, v21, p51-52.
Hollywood Reporter. Dec 17, 1969, p3.
The James Bond Films. p85-98.
James Bond in the Cinema. p150-78.
James Bond's Bedside Companion. p194-99.
The New York Times. Dec 19, 1969, p68.
Newsweek. Dec 29, 1969, v74, p56.

Saturday Review. Jan 10, 1970, v53, p30.
Variety. Dec 17, 1969, p16.

On Moonlight Bay (US; Del Ruth, Roy; 1951)
BFI/Monthly Film Bulletin. Mar 1952, v19, p36.
Christian Century. Oct 3, 1951, v68, p1143.
Commonweal. Aug 1951, v54, p430.
Film Daily. Jul 16, 1951, p6.
The Films of Doris Day. p107-10.
Hollywood Reporter. Jul 9, 1951, p3.
Motion Picture Herald Product Digest. Jul 14, 1951, p929.
Moving Places. p38-128.
The New York Times. Jul 27, 1951, p15.
Newsweek. Aug 6, 1951, v38, p85.
The Spectator. Apr 18, 1952, v188, p513.
Time. Aug 20, 1951, v58, p88.
Variety. Jul 11, 1951, p6.

On the Beach (US; Kramer, Stanley; 1959)
America. Dec 19, 1959, v102, p381.
BFI/Monthly Film Bulletin. Feb 1960, v27, p21.
Catholic World. May 1960, v191, p80-85.
Commentary. Jun 1960, v29, p522-24.
Commonweal. Dec 25, 1959, v71, p374.
Coronet. Dec 1959, v47, p18.
Film Daily. Dec 2, 1959, v116, p10.
Filmfacts. Jan 6, 1959, v2, p299-301.
Films in Review. Jan 1960, v11, p4-5, 36-37.
Films in Review. Feb 1960, v11, p124-25.
The Films of Gregory Peck. p165-69.
The Films of the Fifties. p285-88.
Hollywood Reporter. Dec 2, 1959, p3.
Life. Nov 30, 1959, v47, p93-95.
Magill's Survey of Cinema. Series II. v4, p1789-91.
McCall's. Nov 1959, v87, p6.
The Nation. Jan 2, 1960, v190, p20.
The New Republic. Dec 14, 1959, v141, p21-22.
The New York Times. Dec 18, 1959, p34.
The New Yorker. Jan 2, 1960, p47.
Newsweek. Dec 21, 1959, v54, p95.
Nuclear War Films. p31-38.
Saturday Review. Oct 24, 1959, v42, p32-33.
Science. Dec 18, 1959, v130, p1679.
Science Newsletter. Dec 5, 1959, v76, p390.
Stanley Kramer, Film Maker. p207-16.
Starring Fred Astaire. p435-40.
Time. Dec 28, 1959, v70, p44.
Variety. Dec 2, 1959, p6.

On the Lookout for Trains *See* Closely Watched Trains

On the Loose (US; Lederer, Charles; 1951)
Film Daily. Jul 26, 1951, p6.
Hollywood Reporter. Jul 25, 1951, p3.
Motion Picture Herald Product Digest. Jul 28, 1951, p945.
The New York Times. Jun 3, 1951, p3.
Variety. Jul 25, 1951, p6.

On the Nickel (US; Waite, Ralph; 1980)
The Christian Science Monitor. Apr 24, 1980, p19.
Films in Review. Jun-Jul 1980, v31, p375.
Hollywood Reporter. Apr 9, 1980, p2.
Horizon. Jul 1980, v23, p70.
The Los Angeles Times. Apr 6, 1980, Calendar, p1.
The Nation. May 24, 1980, v230, p636.
The New Republic. May 17, 1980, v182, p27.
The New Yorker. May 12, 1980, v56, p130-31.
Newsday. May 2, 1980, SecII, p7.
Variety. Mar 26, 1980, p21.
The Village Voice. May 19, 1980, p50.

On the Riviera (US; Lang, Walter; 1951)
BFI/Monthly Film Bulletin. Jul 1951, v18, p298-99.
Film Daily. Apr 20, 1951, p6.
Hollywood Reporter. Apr 20, 1951, p3.
Library Journal. Jul 1951, v76, p1141.
Motion Picture Herald Product Digest. Apr 28, 1951, p818.
The New Republic. Jun 4, 1951, v124, p22.
The New Statesman and Nation. Jun 16, 1951, v41, p680.
The New York Times. May 24, 1951, p47.
The New Yorker. Jun 2, 1951, v27, p83.
Newsweek. May 12, 1951, v34, p26.
Sight and Sound. Aug-Sep 1951, v21, p29.
The Spectator. Jun 8, 1951, v186, p748.
Time. May 7, 1951, v57, p100.
Variety. Apr 25, 1951, p6.

On the Waterfront (US; Kazan, Elia; 1954)
America. Aug 7, 1954, v91, p466.
American Film. May 1981, v6, p73-75.
American Quarterly. 1979, v31, n5, p666-96.
BFI/Monthly Film Bulletin. Sep 1954, v21, p129.
Business Week. Aug 7, 1954, p94-98.
Catholic World. Aug 1954, v179, p384.
Cineaste. 1982, v11, n4, p56.
Cinema, the Magic Vehicle. v2, p200-01.
Classic Movies. p154-55.
Crime Movies (Clarens). p343-45.
Cue. Jul 31, 1954, p15.
Elia Kazan: A Guide to References and Resources. p11-12.
Esquire. Jan 1982, v97, p77-78.
Film As Film: Critical Responses to Film Art. p296-304.
Film Culture. Sum 1955, v1, p4-6.
Film Culture. Jan 1955, v1, p58-60.
Film Daily. Jul 14, 1954, p8.
Film Quarterly. Fall 1975, v29, p25-38.
Films and Filming. Oct 1954, v1, p18.
Films in Review. Aug-Sep 1954, v5, p360-61.
The Films of Marlon Brando. p72-81.
The Films of the Fifties. p115-18.
Fortnight. Aug 18, 1954, v17, p32.
The Great Films. p214-17.
The Great Gangster Pictures. p298-99.
The Great Movies. p219-20.
Harper's Magazine. Aug 1954, v209, p93.
Hollywood As Historian. p159-89.
Hollywood Reporter. Jul 14, 1954, p3.
I Lost It At the Movies. p41-48.
The International Dictionary of Films and Filmmakers. v1, p341-43.
Kazan on Kazan. p102-12.
Library Journal. Jul 1954, v79, p1304.
Life. Jul 19, 1954, v37, p45-48.
Literature/Film Quarterly. 1981, v9, n4, p265-67.
The London Times. Sep 13, 1954, p3.
The London Times. Feb 22, 1955, p5.
Look. Aug 10, 1954, v18, p37-38.
Magic Moments From the Movies. p188.
Magill's Survey of Cinema. Series I. v3, p1262-64.
Motion Picture Herald Product Digest. Jul 17, 1954, p65.
Movie. Wint 1971-72, n19, p7-8.
National Parent-Teacher. Sep 1954, v49, p39.
The New Statesman and Nation. Sep 18, 1954, v48, p324.
The New York Times. Jul 29, 1954, p18.
The New York Times. Jan 6, 1980, p28-30.
The New York Times Magazine. Jul 4, 1954, p14.
The New Yorker. Jul 31, 1954, v30, p52.
Newsweek. Aug 2, 1954, v44, p78.
Reporter. Sep 23, 1954, v11, p46-47.

Running Time: Films of the Cold War. p151-66.
Saturday Review. Oct 23, 1954, v37, p8.
Saturday Review. Jan 1, 1955, v38, p63.
Saturday Review. Jul 24, 1954, v37, p25.
Seeing Is Believing (Biskind). p169-82.
Selected Film Criticism, 1951-1960. p93-96.
Senior Scholastic. Sep 15, 1954, v65, p35.
Sight and Sound. Oct-Dec 1954, v24, p85-86.
Sight and Sound. Jan-Mar 1955, v24, p127-30.
Sight and Sound. Spr 1955, v24, p214-16.
The Spectator. Sep 10, 1954, v193, p306, 308.
The Tatler. Sep 22, 1954, v213, p569.
Ten Film Classics. p86-101.
The Thousand Eyes Magazine. Jan 1976, n6, p8.
Time. Aug 9, 1954, v64, p82.
Variety. Jul 14, 1954, p6.

Once Upon a Time in America (US; Leone, Sergio; 1984)
American Film. Jun 1984, v9, p20-25.
BFI/Monthly Film Bulletin. Oct 1984, v51, p295-97.
Film Comment. Jul-Aug 1984, v20, p18-21.
Film Comment. Dec 1984, v20, p68-69.
Film Journal. Jul 1984, v87, p25.
Films and Filming. Sep 1984, n360, p41.
Films in Review. Nov 1984, v35, p568-69.
Hollywood Reporter. Jun 1, 1984, p6.
Horizon. Oct 1984, v27, p60.
The Los Angeles Times. Jun 1, 1984, SecVI, p4.
Maclean's. Jun 11, 1984, v97, p63.
The Nation. Jul 21, 1984, v239, p60.
The New Republic. Jul 2, 1984, v191, p25.
New Statesman. Oct 5, 1984, v108, p34-35.
New York. Jun 18, 1984, v17, p88.
The New York Times. Jun 1, 1984, SecIII, p8.
Newsweek. Jun 11, 1984, v103, p81.
Photoplay. Nov 1984, v35, p21.
Sight and Sound. Wint 1984, v53, p301.
Time. Jun 18, 1984, v123, p82.
The Village Voice. Jun 12, 1984, p48.
The Village Voice. Oct 23, 1984, p57.
The Village Voice. Jun 5, 1984, p59-60.

Once Upon a Time in the West (Also titled: C'era una volta il West) (IT; Leone, Sergio; 1969)
Cineaste. Sum 1969, v3, p17-18.
Commonweal. Jul 11, 1969, v90, p439.
Film Daily. Jun 4, 1969, p4.
Filmfacts. 1969, v12, p299.
Films and Filming. Oct 1969, v16, p42.
The Films of Charles Bronson. p153-58.
The Films of Henry Fonda. p211-14.
The Fondas. p259-61.
The International Dictionary of Films and Filmmakers. v1, p343-44.
The New Republic. Jun 21, 1969, v160, p22.
Newsweek. Jun 9, 1969, v73, p108.
Variety. May 28, 1969, p6.

The One and Only (US; Reiner, Carl; 1978)
BFI/Monthly Film Bulletin. Jul 1978, v45, p162.
Films in Review. Mar 1978, v29, p186.
Hollywood Reporter. Jan 24, 1978, p3.
The Los Angeles Times. Feb 3, 1978, SecIV, p1.
Motion Picture Herald Product Digest. Feb 8, 1978, p72.
New York. Feb 20, 1978, v11, p79-80.
The New York Times. Feb 3, 1978, SecIII, p10.
The New York Times. Feb 12, 1978, SecII, p15.
Newsweek. Feb 13, 1978, v91, p98-99.
Senior Scholastic. Mar 23, 1978, v110, p35-36.
Time. Feb 13, 1978, v111, p70.
Variety. Sep 25, 1978, p28.

One Day in the Life of Ivan Denisovich (GB; Wrede, Casper; 1971)
America. Jun 5, 1971, v74, p595.
BFI/Monthly Film Bulletin. Feb 1972, v39, n457, p34.
Filmfacts. 1971, v14, n16, p398-401.
Films and Filming. Apr 1972, v18, n7, p50-51.
Films in Review. Aug-Sep 1971, v22, n7, p444-45.
Hollywood Reporter. May 18, 1971, v216, n15, p3.
Life. Jun 25, 1971, v70, p12.
Marshall Delaney at the Movies. p228-31.
The Nation. Jun 7, 1971, v212, p730-31.
The New Republic. Jun 19, 1971, v164, p24.
The New York Times. May 17, 1971, p40.
The New Yorker. May 22, 1971, p47.
Newsweek. May 24, 1971, v77, p97.
Time. Mar 2, 1970, v95, p77.
Time. May 31, 1971, v97, p86.
Variety. May 19, 1971, p17.
The Village Voice. Jun 10, 1971, v16, n23, p59-60.

One Flew Over the Cuckoo's Nest (US; Forman, Milos; 1975)
Action. May-Jun 1976, v11, p6-10.
Audience. Jan 1976, v8, p9-11.
Before My Eyes. p174-78.
BFI/Monthly Film Bulletin. Feb 1976, v43, p32-33.
Christian Century. Aug 4, 1976, v93, p688-89.
Cineaste. Fall, 1976, v7, p42-43.
Cinema Papers. Mar-Apr 1976, p359.
Cinema Papers. Jun-Jul 1976, p154.
Fifty Grand Movies of the 1960s and 1970s. p235-40.
Film. Mar 1976, n35, p8.
Film Heritage. n4, 1976, v11, p43-45.
Film Illustrated. Mar 1976, v5, p244-45.
Filmmakers' Newsletter. Dec 1975, v9, p26-31.
Films and Filming. Apr 1976, v22, p30-31.
Films and Filming. Mar 1976, v22, p41-43.
Films in Review. Jan 1976, v27, p53.
The Films of the Seventies. p131-33.
Focus on Film. Wint 1976, n23, p4-5.
Hollywood Reporter. Nov 14, 1975, p3.
Independent Film Journal. Nov 26, 1975, v76, p7.
Jump Cut. Sum 1976, n10/11, p51-52.
The Los Angeles Times. Nov 21, 1975, SecIV, p1.
Magill's Survey of Cinema. Series I. v3, p1265-67.
Medium. Mar 1976, v6, p24.
The Modern American Novel and the Movies. p266-71.
Motion Picture Herald Product Digest. Nov 26, 1975, p45.
Movietone News. Feb 1976, n48, p34-36.
The Nation. Nov 29, 1975, v221, p573-74.
The New Republic. Dec 13, 1975, v173, p22-23.
New Statesman. Feb 27, 1976, v91, p269-70.
New York. Dec 1, 1975, v8, p80-83.
The New York Review of Books. Feb 5, 1976, v23, p3-4.
The New York Times. Nov 23, 1975, SecII, p1.
The New York Times. Dec 21, 1975, SecII, p17.
The New Yorker. Dec 1, 1975, v51, p131-36.
Newsweek. Nov 24, 1975, v86, p113.
Rolling Stone. Dec 4, 1975, p48-54.
Saturday Review. Jan 10, 1976, v3, p61.
Sight and Sound. Sum 1976, v45, p120.
Take One. 1976, v5, n1, p28-31.
The Thousand Eyes Magazine. Apr 1976, n9, p6.
Time. Dec 1, 1975, v106, p68.
Times Educational Supplement. Mar 5, 1976, n3170, p86.

Times Literary Supplement. Mar 19, 1976, n3862, p318.
Variety. Nov 19, 1975, p18.
The Village Voice. Jul 26, 1976, p109.
The Village Voice. Dec 1, 1975, p136.
Vogue. Feb 1976, v166, p80.
When the Lights Go Down. p84-90.

One From the Heart (US; Coppola, Francis Ford; 1982)
American Cinematographer. Jan 1982, v63, p30-31, 44-45.
Christian Century. Mar 3, 1982, v99, p250.
Film Comment. May-Jun 1981, v17, p2.
Film Comment. Mar-Apr 1982, v18, p44-45.
Films In Review. May 1982, v33, p307-08.
Francis Ford Coppola: A Guide to References and Resources. p69-74.
Hollywood Reporter. Jan 18, 1982, p4.
The Los Angeles Times. Jan 22, 1982, SecVI, p1.
The Los Angeles Times. Feb 25, 1982, SecVI, p1.
Maclean's. Feb 15, 1982, v95, p62.
Magill's Cinema Annual, 1983. p250-53.
Modern Photography. Feb 1982, v46, p55-57.
New York. Feb 1, 1982, v15, p54-55.
The New York Times. Feb 11, 1982, SecIII, p25.
The New York Times. Feb 21, 1982, SecII, p13.
The New York Times. Jan 17, 1982, SecIII, p56.
The New Yorker. Feb 1, 1982, v57, p118-20.
The New Yorker. Nov 8, 1982, v58, p48-50.
Newsweek. Jan 25, 1982, v99, p74.
Rolling Stone. Mar 19, 1982, p20-21.
Saturday Review. Mar 1982, v9, p54-55.
Sight and Sound. Sum 1982, v51, p192-93.
Time. Jan 18, 1982, v119, p76.
Time. Jan 25, 1982, v119, p71.
Variety. Jan 18, 1982, p3.
The Village Voice. Jan 27, 1982, p45.

One Is a Lonely Number (US; Stuart, Mel; 1972)
Filmfacts. 1972, v15, n11, p254.
Hollywood Reporter. Mar 20, 1972, p3.
Magill's Survey of Cinema. English Language Films. Series II, v4, p1802.
The New York Times. Jul 20, 1972, v35, p1.
Saturday Review. May 13, 1972, v55, p17.
Time. Apr 24, 1972, v99, p94.
Variety. Mar 22, 1972, p20.

One Magic Christmas (US; Borsos, Philip; 1985)
Cinema Canada. Feb 1986, p22.
Hollywood Reporter. Nov 20, 1985, p3.
The Los Angeles Times. Nov 22, 1985, SecVI, p17.
Maclean's. Dec 9, 1985, v98, p70.
New York. Dec 2, 1985, v18, p121.
The New York Times. Dec 22, 1985, SecIII, p14.
Newsweek. Dec 2, 1985, v106, p92.
Time. Nov 25, 1985, v126, p121.
Variety. Nov 20, 1985, p14.

One Man Mutiny *See* Court Martial of Billy Mitchell

The $1,000,000 Duck (US; McEveety, Vincent; 1971)
BFI/Monthly Film Bulletin. Aug 1971, v38, n451, p167.
Filmfacts. 1971, v14, n18, p445-46.
Hollywood Reporter. Jun 11, 1971, v216, n32, p3.
The New York Times. Sep 2, 1971, p41.
Variety. Jun 16, 1971, p15.

One Million Years B.C. (GB, US; Chaffey, Don; 1966)
BFI/Monthly Film Bulletin. Dec 1966, v33, p180.
Christian Science Monitor (Western edition). Apr 29, 1967, p6.
Film Daily. Feb 21, 1967, p6.
Filmfacts. Mar 15, 1967, v10, p41-42.
Films and Filming. Jan 1967, v13, p30.
Films in Review. Mar 1967, v18, p178-79.
Motion Picture Herald Product Digest. Mar 8, 1967, p664.
The New York Times. Feb 22, 1967, p21.
Newsweek. Mar 13, 1967, v69, p109.
Senior Scholastic. Feb 17, 1967, v90, p19.
The Spectator. Dec 30, 1966, v217, p842-43.
Variety. Dec 28, 1966, p18.

One Minute to Zero (US; Garnett, Tay; 1952)
BFI/Monthly Film Bulletin. Feb 1953, v20, p25.
Film Daily. Jul 21, 1952, p11.
Guts & Glory. p113-14.
Hollywood Reporter. Jul 16, 1952, p3.
Motion Picture Herald Product Digest. Jul 19, 1952, p1454.
National Parent-Teacher. Oct 1952, v47, p38.
The New York Times. Sep 20, 1952, p13.
Newsweek. Oct 6, 1952, v40, p114.
Robert Mitchum on the Screen. p122-23.
Saturday Review. Sep 20, 1952, v35, p35.
Time. Aug 25, 1952, v60, p72.
Variety. Jul 16, 1952, p6.

One on One (US; Johnson, Lamont; 1977)
BFI/Monthly Film Bulletin. Sep 1977, v44, p195.
Films and Filming. Sep 1977, v23, p40-41.
Hollywood Reporter. May 14, 1977, p2.
The Los Angeles Times. Aug 3, 1977, SecIV, p1.
Motion Picture Herald Product Digest. Jun 22, 1977, p7.
The New York Times. Aug 25, 1977, SecIII, p14.
The New York Times. Sep 4, 1977, SecII, p9.
Newsweek. Sep 5, 1977, v90, p78.
Senior Scholastic. Oct 20, 1977, v110, p47.
Sports Illustrated. Jul 11, 1977, v47, p48.
Time. Jul 25, 1977, v110, p69.
Variety. Jun 15, 1977, p21.
The Village Voice. Sep 19, 1977, p53.

The One Piece Bathing Suit *See* Million Dollar Mermaid

One Potato, Two Potato (US; Peerce, Larry; 1964)
America. Sep 19, 1964, v111, p329-31.
BFI/Monthly Film Bulletin. Feb 1967, v34, p29.
Commonweal. Sep 4, 1964, v80, p609.
Film Daily. Jul 21, 1964, v125, p6.
Films and Filming. Feb 1967, v13, p36-37.
From Sambo to Superspade. p216-19.
Hollywood Reporter. Aug 6, 1964, v181, p3.
Magill's Survey of Cinema. Second Series, v4, p1809-11.
Motion Picture Herald Product Digest. Aug 5, 1964, v232, p98.
The New York Times. Jul 30, 1964, p16.
The New Yorker. Aug 1, 1964, v40, p65.
Newsweek. Aug 3, 1964, v64, p72.
Saturday Review. Jun 6, 1964, v47, p29.
Time. May 15, 1964, v83, p69.
Time. Aug 7, 1964, v84, p89.
Variety. May 6, 1964, p6.
Vogue. Aug 15, 1964, v144, p38.

One Sings the Other Doesn't (French title: Une Chante L'Autre Pas, L') (FR, BELG, CURACAO; Varda, Agnés; 1977)
America. Oct 22, 1977, v137, p269.
Film Comment. Jul-Aug 1977, v13, p6.
Hollywood Reporter. Sep 28, 1977, p4.
Maclean's. Nov 20, 1978, v91, p67.
Motion Picture Herald Product Digest. Oct 5, 1978, p36.
Ms. Jan 1978, v6, p26.
The New Republic. Oct 8, 1977, v177, p26-27.
New York. Sep 26, 1977, v10, p58-60.
The New York Times. Sep 23, 1977, SecIII, p10.
The New Yorker. Nov 14, 1977, v53, p75-78.
Newsweek. Oct 17, 1977, v90, p102.
Saturday Review. Nov 26, 1977, v5, p46.
Time. Oct 10, 1977, v110, p84.
Variety. Feb 16, 1977, p26.

One Summer of Happiness (Swedish title: Hon Dansade en Sommar; Sommardansen; Also titled: She Only Danced One Summer) (SWED; Mattsson, Arne; 1951)
BFI/Monthly Film Bulletin. Apr 1953, v20, p47.
Cinema, the Magic Vehicle. v2, p75-76.
Dictionary of Films. p151.
Film Culture. May-Jun 1955, v1, p26.
Film Daily. Apr 7, 1955, p10.
Magill's Survey of Cinema. Foreign Language Films. v5, p2282-85.
The Nation. Apr 16, 1955, v180, p334.
The New York Times. Mar 22, 1955, p35.
Saturday Review. Sep 11, 1954, v37, p45.
Swedish Film Classics. p73-76.
Time. Mar 28, 1955, v65, p98.
Variety. Mar 5, 1952, p22.

One, Two, Three (US, WGER; Wilder, Billy; 1961)
America. Feb 3, 1962, v106, p605-06.
Billy Wilder (Dick). p70-73.
Commonweal. Jan 19, 1962, v75, p436.
Esquire. Mar 1962, v57, p204,.
The Film Career of Billy Wilder. p241-44.
The Films of James Cagney. p241-44.
The Films of the Sixties. p52-53.
I Lost it at the Movies. p150-55.
The Nation. Jan 6, 1962, v194, p20.
The New York Times. Jul 16, 1961, SecII, p5.
The New York Times. Dec 17, 1961, SecII, p9.
The New York Times. Dec 22, 1961, p17.
The New Yorker. Jan 6, 1962, v37, p70.
Newsweek. Dec 25, 1961, v58, p72-73.
Saturday Review. Jan 6, 1962, v45, p24.
Time. Dec 8, 1961, v78, p96.
Variety. Nov 29, 1961, p6.

One Way Pendulum (GB; Yates, Peter; 1964)
BFI/Monthly Film Bulletin. Mar 1965, v32, p36.
Film Comment. Jan 27, 1965, p4.
Film Daily. Jan 27, 1965, p4.
Filmfacts. Mar 12, 1965, v8, p30-31.
Films and Filming. Feb 1965, v11, p28.
Films and Filming. Nov 1964, v11, p6-9.
Films in Review. Apr 1965, v16, p253.
The London Times. Jan 28, 1965, p18.
Motion Picture Herald Product Digest. Feb 3, 1965, p219.
The New Republic. Mar 20, 1965, v152, p25.
New Statesman. Feb 5, 1965, v69, p209.
The New York Times. Mar 3, 1965, p34.
The New Yorker. Mar 11, 1965, v41, p169.
Newsweek. Mar 15, 1965, v65, p99.
The Spectator. Jan 29, 1965, v214, p138.
Time. Mar 12, 1965, v85, p97.

One Way Street (US; Fregonese, Hugo; 1950)
Christian Century. May 17, 1950, v67, p631.
Commonweal. May 12, 1950, v52, p127.
Film Daily. Apr 21, 1950, p6.
The Films of James Mason. p94-95.
Hollywood Reporter. Apr 12, 1950, p4.
Motion Picture Herald Product Digest. Apr 15, 1950, p262.
The New Republic. May 29, 1950, v122, p23.
The New York Times. May 12, 1950, p33.
Variety. Apr 12, 1950, p6.

One-Eyed Jacks (US; Brando, Marlon; 1961)
America. Apr 15, 1961, v105, p163.
BFI/Monthly Film Bulletin. Jul 1961, v28, p93.
Commonweal. Apr 14, 1961, v74, p78.
Esquire. Oct 1961, v56, p24.
Film Daily. Mar 15, 1961, p6.
Filmfacts. Apr 21, 1961, v4, p65-67.
Films in Review. Apr 1961, v7, p233-35.
The Films of Marlon Brando. p114-21.
Magill's Survey of Cinema. Series II. v4, p1795-97.
The Nation. Apr 15, 1961, v192, p330.
The New Republic. Apr 3, 1961, v144, p20-21.
The New York Times. Mar 31, 1961, p21.
The New Yorker. Apr 15, 1961, v37, p153.
Newsweek. Apr 3, 1961, v57, p90.
Saturday Review. Apr 1, 1961, v44, p26.
Time. Mar 24, 1961, v77, p72.
Variety. May 3, 1961, p6.

One-Trick Pony (US; Young, Robert; 1980)
The Christian Science Monitor. Oct 16, 1980, p19.
Films in Review. Jan 1981, v32, p57.
Hollywood Reporter. Oct 1, 1980, p2.
The Los Angeles Times. Sep 28, 1980, Calendar, p33.
Motion Picture Herald Product Digest. Oct 22, 1980, p39.
New York. Oct 20, 1980, v13, p86.
The New York Times. Oct 3, 1980, SecIII, p14.
Newsday. Oct 3, 1980, SecII, p10.
Newsweek. Oct 20, 1980, v96, p84.
Rolling Stone. Oct 30, 1980, v96, p84.
Variety. Oct 1, 1980, p20.
The Village Voice. Oct 8, 1980, p53.

Onibaba (Also titled: Oni Baba; The Hole; The Demon) (JAPAN; Shindo, Kaneto; 1964)
BFI/Monthly Film Bulletin. Dec 1966, v33, p180-81.
Dictionary of Films. p260.
Film. Wint 1966, n47, p22-23.
Film Daily. Feb 18, 1965, p6.
Film Quarterly. Fall 1965, v19, p62.
Films and Filming. Jan 1967, v13, p32, 36.
International Film Guide. 1966, v3, p105.
The London Times. Sep 27, 1966, p6.
Magill's Survey of Cinema. Foreign Language Films. v5, p2291-95.
Motion Picture Herald Product Digest. Mar 17, 1965, p250.
The Nation. Mar 1, 1965, v200, p234.
New Statesman. Nov 4, 1966, v72, p674.
The New York Times. Feb 10, 1965, p44.
The New Yorker. Feb 27, 1965, v41, p113-14.
Newsweek. Feb 8, 1965, v65, p86.
Private Screenings. p171-72.
The Spectator. Oct 28, 1966, v217, p551.
Variety. Feb 10, 1965, p7.

The Onion Field (US; Becker, Harold; 1979)
BFI/Monthly Film Bulletin. Mar 1980, v47, p51.

Films in Review. Oct 1979, v30, p498.
Hollywood Reporter. Oct 2, 1979, p3.
The Los Angeles Times. Sep 28, 1979, SecIV, p1.
Magill's Survey of Cinema. Series II. v4, p1815-17.
Motion Picture Herald Product Digest. Sep 12, 1979, p29.
The Nation. Nov 10, 1979, v229, p474.
The New Republic. Oct 13, 1979, v181, p26-27.
The New York Times. Sep 19, 1979, SecIII, p25.
The New Yorker. Oct 1, 1979, v55, p103.
Newsweek. Sep 24, 1979, v94, p107.
Time. Oct 1, 1979, v114, p85.
Variety. May 23, 1979, p23.

Only the Best *See* I Can Get It For You Wholesale

Only the Valiant (US; Douglas, Gordon; 1951)
BFI/Monthly Film Bulletin. Nov 1951, v18, p362.
Christian Century. Jun 6, 1951, v68, p695.
Film Daily. Mar 7, 1951, p4.
The Films of Gregory Peck. p103-05.
Hollywood Reporter. Mar 6, 1951, p3.
Library Journal. Feb 15, 1951, v76, p343.
The New York Times. Apr 14, 1951, p9.
Newsweek. Apr 30, 1951, v37, p82.
The Spectator. Dec 28, 1951, v187, p884.
Variety. Mar 7, 1951, p6.

Only When I Laugh (US; Jordan, Glenn; 1981)
Films in Review. Nov 1981, v32, p556-57.
Hollywood Reporter. Sep 5, 1981, p3.
The Los Angeles Times. Sep 24, 1981, SecVI, p2.
Magill's Cinema Annual, 1982. p268-71.
The Nation. Oct 31, 1981, v233, p451.
National Review. Dec 11, 1981, v33, p1498.
New York. Oct 12, 1981, v14, p83-85.
The New York Times. Sep 23, 1981, SecIII, p23.
Newsweek. Sep 28, 1981, v98, p87-88.
Saturday Review. Sep 1981, v8, p48-49.
Senior Scholastic. Nov 13, 1981, v114, p25.
Time. Oct 5, 1981, v118, p88.
Variety. Sep 16, 1981, p16.
The Village Voice. Sep 23, 1981, p51.

Operation Crossbow (Also titled: The Great Spy Mission) (GB, IT; Anderson, Michael; 1965)
America. Apr 17, 1965, v112, p587.
BFI/Monthly Film Bulletin. Jul 1965, v32, p111-12.
Christian Science Monitor (Western edition). Jul 1, 1965, pE5.
Commonweal. Apr 16, 1965, v82, p118.
Film Daily. Apr 2, 1965, p5.
Filmfacts. Jun 11, 1965, v8, p99-101.
Films and Filming. Jul 1965, v11, p30.
Films and Filming. Jun 1965, v11, p21.
Films in Review. May 1965, v16, p310-12.
The Great Spy Pictures. p348-50.
Hollywood Reporter. Apr 2, 1965, p3.
Life. Apr 16, 1965, v58, p18.
The London Times. May 20, 1965, p19.
Motion Picture Herald Product Digest. Apr 14, 1965, p265-66.
The New Republic. Apr 17, 1965, v152, p40.
The New York Times. Apr 2, 1965, p29.
The New Yorker. Apr 10, 1965, v41, p158-59.
Newsweek. Apr 5, 1965, v65, p95.
Playboy. Jul 1965, v12, p32.
Saturday Review. Apr 24, 1965, v48, p39.
Time. Apr 9, 1965, v85, p102.
Variety. Apr 7, 1965, p6.

Operation Disaster (Also titled: Morning Departure) (GB; Baker, Roy; 1951)
Commonweal. Feb 2, 1951, v53, p426.
Film Daily. Jan 10, 1951, p6.
Films in Review. Mar 1951, v2, p43-44.
Hollywood Reporter. Jan 10, 1951, p3.
Library Journal. Jan 15, 1951, v76, p124.
The London Times. Feb 24, 1950, p2.
Motion Picture Herald Product Digest. Jan 13, 1951, p661.
The Nation. Feb 3, 1951, v172, p114.
The New Republic. Jan 29, 1951, v124, p23.
The New York Times. Jan 15, 1951, p13.
The New Yorker. Jan 27, 1951, v26, p58.
Time. Feb 5, 1951, v57, p81.
Variety. Mar 1, 1950, p16.

Operation Mad Ball (US; Quine, Richard; 1957)
America. Nov 23, 1957, v98, p256.
BFI/Monthly Film Bulletin. Oct 1957, v24, p129-30.
Commonweal. Nov 15, 1957, v67, p175.
Film Daily. Sep 3, 1957, v112, p14.
Films in Review. Jan 1958, v9, p24.
The Films of Jack Lemmon. p81-85.
Hollywood Reporter. Sep 3, 1957, p3.
Motion Picture Herald Product Digest. Sep 7, 1957, v208, p521.
The New York Times. Nov 21, 1957, p38.
The New York Times. Nov 24, 1957, SecII, p1.
The New Yorker. Nov 30, 1957, v33, p145.
Saturday Review. Nov 30, 1957, v40, p22.
Time. Nov 25, 1957, v70, p122.

Operation Petticoat (US; Edwards, Blake; 1959)
America. Jan 16, 1960, v102, p481.
BFI/Monthly Film Bulletin. Feb 1960, v27, p25.
Blake Edwards (Lehman and Luhr). p53-58.
Film Daily. Sep 28, 1959, v116, p8.
Filmfacts. Dec 30, 1959, v2, p294-95.
Films in Review. v12, p598.
The Films of Cary Grant. p46-49.
Hollywood Reporter. Sep 28, 1959, p3.
Magill's Survey of Cinema. Series II. v4, p1818-21.
McCall's. Dec 1959, v87, p6.
The New York Times. Dec 6, 1959, p38.
The New Yorker. Dec 12, 1959, v35, p196.
Saturday Review. Jan 2, 1960, v43, p31.
Time. Dec 14, 1959, v70, p96.
Tony Curtis: The Man and His Movies. p80-84.
Variety. Sep 30, 1959, p6.

Operation X (Also titled: My Daughter Joy) (US; Ratoff, Gregory; 1950)
Christian Century. Mar 14, 1951, v68, p351.
The Cinema of Edward G. Robinson. p179-80.
Hollywood Reporter. Dec 12, 1950, p3.
Library Journal. Jan 15, 1951, v76, p124.
Motion Picture Herald Product Digest. Dec 23, 1950, p634.
The New York Times. Dec 11, 1950, p31.

The Oracle *See* The Horse's Mouth

Orca (Also titled: Orca. . .Killer Whale) (US; Anderson, Michael; 1977)
American Cinematographer. Oct 1977, v58, p1022-25.
BFI/Monthly Film Bulletin. Aug 1977, v44, p171.
Films and Filming. Sep 1977, v23, p31-32.
Films in Review. Oct 1977, v28, p503-04.
Hollywood Reporter. Jul 13, 1977, p3.
The Los Angeles Times. Jul 14, 1977, SecIV, p1.
Motion Picture Herald Product Digest. Aug 8, 1977, p18.

New York. Aug 1, 1977, v10, p65-67.
The New York Times. May 1, 1977, SecII, p1.
The New York Times. Jul 16, 1977, p12.
Oceans. Sep 1977, v10, p68.
Time. Aug 8, 1977, v110, p59.
Variety. Jul 13, 1977, p18.

An Orchid For the Tiger (French title: Tigre Se Parfume a la Dynamite, Le) (FR, SP, IT; Chabrol, Claude; 1965)
BFI/Monthly Film Bulletin. Oct 1966, v33, p153.
Claude Chabrol (Wood and Walker). p84-86.
The Great Spy Pictures. p481.
Variety. Dec 22, 1965, p6.

Orders to Kill (GB; Asquith, Anthony; 1958)
BFI/Monthly Film Bulletin. May 1958, v25, p58.
Commonweal. Dec 5, 1958, v69, p258.
Film Daily. Nov 28, 1958, v114, p6.
Filmfacts. Dec 24, 1958, v1, p223-24.
Films in Review. Jun-Jul 1958, v9, p292.
The Films of Anthony Asquith. p165-70.
The New York Times. Nov 18, 1958, p41.
The New Yorker. Nov 29, 1958, v34, p108.
Newsweek. Nov 24, 1958, v52, p113.
Variety. Apr 2, 1958, p6.

Ordet (Also titled: The Word) (DEN; Dreyer, Carl-Theodor; 1955)
Christian Century. Mar 12, 1958, v75, p312-13.
The Cinema of Carl Dreyer. p156-67.
Cinema, the Magic Vehicle. v2, p191-94.
Commonweal. Dec 27, 1957, v67, p336.
Dictionary of Films. p262.
Dreyer (Nash). p64-67.
Film Culture. 1956, v2, n1,, p24.
Film Culture. 1956, v2, n3, p21.
Film Culture. 1958, v4, n1, p17-18.
Film Culture Reader. p27-28.
Film Daily. Dec 5, 1957, p11.
Films in Review. Jan 1955, v6, p19-22.
The International Dictionary of Films and Filmmakers. v1, p344-45.
Kiss Kiss Bang Bang. p408.
The Nation. Dec 21, 1957, v185, p484.
National Parent-Teacher. Jan 1958, v52, p39.
The New York Times. Dec 16, 1957, p33.
Newsweek. Dec 2, 1957, v50, p96.
Quarterly of Film, Radio and Television. Spr 1956, v10, p257-61.
Quarterly of Film, Radio and Television. Wint 1956, v11, p181-82.
Sight and Sound. Wint 1955-56, v25, p126-27.
Sight and Sound. Spr 1975, v44, p108-12.
Time. Dec 16, 1957, v70, p97.
Transcendental Style in Film: Ozu, Bresson, Dreyer. p132-38.
Variety. Sep 7, 1955, p6.
The Village Voice. Dec 11, 1957, v3, p6, 12.

Ordinary People (US; Redford, Robert; 1980)
America. Oct 18, 1980, v143, p231.
BFI/Monthly Film Bulletin. Feb 1981, v48, p31.
Christian Century. Nov 26, 1980, v97, p1169-70.
The Christian Science Monitor. Sep 25, 1980, p19.
Christianity Today. Apr 24, 1981, v25, p50.
Cineaste. Spr 1981, p31.
Commonweal. Oct 24, 1980, v107, p594-95.
Film Comment. Jan-Feb 1981, v17, p49-51.
Films in Review. Nov 1980, v31, p565.
The Films of Robert Redford. p259-70.
Hollywood Reporter. Sep 15, 1980, p2.
Horizon. Nov 1980, v23, p70-71.

The Los Angeles Times. Sep 21, 1980, Calendar, p1.
Maclean's. Nov 1980, v93, p69-70.
Motion Picture Herald Product Digest. Sep 24, 1980, p29.
The Nation. Oct 11, 1980, v231, p356-57.
National Review. Apr 3, 1981, v33, p374.
The New Leader. Oct 20, 1980, v63, p20.
The New Republic. Sep 27, 1980, v183, p24.
New York. Sep 29, 1980, v13, p54.
The New York Times. Sep 19, 1980, SecIII, p6.
The New Yorker. Oct 13, 1980, v56, p184-86.
Newsday. Sep 19, 1980, SecII, p7.
Newsweek. Sep 22, 1980, v96, p76.
Progressive. Jan 1981, v45, p49.
Rolling Stone. Nov 13, 1980, v156, p136-37.
Sight and Sound. Spr 1981, v51, p138.
Time. Sep 22, 1980, v116, p78.
Variety. Sep 17, 1980, p18.
The Village Voice. Sep 17, 1980, p46.

Ore Dell'Amore, Le *See* The Hours of Love

Orfeo de Conceicao *See* Black Orpheus

Orfeu Negro *See* Black Orpheus

The Organizer (Italian title: Compagni, I) (IT; Monicelli, Mario; 1963)
America. Jun 6, 1964, v110, p804-05.
BFI/Monthly Film Bulletin. Nov 1965, v32, p162-63.
Commonweal. May 8, 1964, v80, p208-09.
Esquire. Oct 1964, v62, p62.
Film Comment. Sum 1964, v2, n3, p55-56.
Film Daily. May 15, 1964, v124, p6.
Films and Filming. Dec 1965, v12, p33-34.
Films in Review. Jun-Jul 1964, v15, p374.
Hollywood Reporter. Jun 5, 1964, v180, p3.
Life. May 15, 1964, v56, p12.
Motion Picture Herald Product Digest. May 27, 1964, v231, p59.
The Nation. May 18, 1964, v198, p516.
The New Republic. May 16, 1964, v150, p34.
The New York Times. May 7, 1964, p31.
The New Yorker. May 9, 1964, v40, p191.
Newsweek. May 11, 1964, v63, p98.
On Movies. p360-63.
The Private Eye, the Cowboy and the Very Naked Girl. p86-88.
Private Screenings. p144-46.
Saturday Review. May 9, 1964, v47, p35.
Tynan Right and Left. p243-44.
Variety. Nov 20, 1963, p14.
A World on Film. p340-42.

Orgueilleux, Les (Also titled: The Proud Ones; The Proud and the Beautiful) (FR, MEX; Allégret, Yves; 1953)
BFI/Monthly Film Bulletin. Jun 1954, v21, p85.
Catholic World. Aug 1956, v183, p382.
Film Culture. 1956, v2, n3, p26-27.
Film Daily. Jul 9, 1956, p6.
Films in Review. Aug-Sep 1956, v7, p347.
Hollywood Reporter. Aug 29, 1956, p3.
Kiss Kiss Bang Bang. p421.
The London Times. Apr 26, 1954, p2.
Motion Picture Herald Product Digest. Jun 23, 1956, p946-47.
The Nation. Jun 23, 1956, v182, p536.
National Parent-Teacher. Sep 1956, v51, p40.
The New Statesman and Nation. May 1, 1954, v47, p563.
The New York Times. May 29, 1956, p32.
The New Yorker. Jun 9, 1956, v32, p52.
Saturday Review. Feb 11, 1956, v39, p38.
Sight and Sound. Jul-Sep 1954, v24, p35.
The Spectator. Apr 23, 1954, v192, p485.
The Tatler. May 5, 1954, v212, p286.
Time. Jun 18, 1956, v67, p101.
Variety. Sep 30, 1953, p22.

Oro di Napoli, L' *See* Gold of Naples

Orphée (Also titled: Orpheus) (FR; Cocteau, Jean; 1950)
BFI/Monthly Film Bulletin. Jun 1950, v17, p81.
Cinema Journal. Spr 1972, v11, p26-33.
Classic Movies. p65-66.
Classics of the Foreign Film. p186-91.
Commonweal. Dec 15, 1950, v53, p253.
The Contemporary Cinema. p93-94.
Dictionary of Films. p263-64.
Film Daily. Nov 22, 1950, p6.
Film Journal. n2, 1956, p7.
Film Makers on Film Making. p142-54.
Films and Feelings. p239-46.
Films and Filming. Oct 1963, v10, p45-48.
Films and Filming. Feb 1978, v24, p28-33.
Films in Review. Feb 1951, v2, p38-40.
The Great French Films. p127-30.
Halliwell's Hundred. p258-61.
Illustrated London News. Jun 24, 1950, v216, p988.
The International Dictionary of Films and Filmmakers. v1, p346-47.
Jean Cocteau and His Films of Orphic Identity. p102-29.
Jean Cocteau (Gilson). p80-93.
Library Journal. Feb 1, 1951, v76, p189.
Magill's Survey of Cinema. Foreign Language Films. v5, p2316-21.
The New Republic. Dec 25, 1950, v123, p23.
The New Statesman and Nation. Jun 3, 1950, v39, p631.
The New York Times. Nov 30, 1950, p42.
The New Yorker. Dec 9, 1950, v26, p127.
Newsweek. Dec 4, 1950, v36, p83.
Quarterly Journal of Speech. Oct 1965, v51, p311-25.
Saturday Review. Apr 12, 1952, v35, p59.
Sequence. Aut 1950, n12, p20-32.
Seventy Years of Cinema. p177.
Shots in the Dark. p184-90.
Sight and Sound. Jul 1950, v19, p205-07.
The Spectator. Jun 2, 1950, v184, p756.
Time. Dec 18, 1950, v56, p92.
Variety. Jul 12, 1950, p16.

The Oscar (US; Rouse, Russell; 1966)
America. Mar 19, 1966, v114, p396-97.
BFI/Monthly Film Bulletin. Jul 1966, v33, p105.
Christian Science Monitor (Western edition). Feb 23, 1966, p4.
Cinema. Dec 1965, v3, p42.
Commonweal. Mar 11, 1966, v83, p667.
Film Daily. Feb 17, 1966, p5.
Filmfacts. Apr 15, 1966, v9, p51-53.
Films and Filming. Jul 1966, v12, p52, 56.
Films in Review. Apr 1966, v17, p246-47.
The Films of Frank Sinatra. p216-18.
Hollywood Reporter. Feb 15, 1966, p3.
Life. Mar 25, 1966, v60, p17.
The London Times. Jun 16, 1966, p7.
Motion Picture Herald Product Digest. Feb 23, 1966, p475.
New Statesman. Jun 17, 1966, v71, p904.
The New York Times. Mar 5, 1966, p16.
Newsweek. Mar 14, 1966, v67, p99.
Playboy. May 1966, v13, p30.
The Private Eye, the Cowboy and the Very Naked Girl. p185-87.
Saturday Review. Mar 12, 1966, v49, p46.
The Spectator. Jun 17, 1966, v216, p762.
Time. Mar 11, 1966, v87, p100-01.
Variety. Feb 16, 1966, p6.
Vogue. Apr 1, 1966, v147, p111.

Ostre Sledovane Vlasky *See* Closely Watched Trains

Otac Na Sluzhenom Putu *See* When Father Was Away on Business

Othello (US, IT; Welles, Orson; 1952)
The Cinema of Orson Welles. p116-27.
Film Culture. Wint 1955, v1, n5/6, p32.
Film Heritage. Fall 1969, v5, n1, p9-15.
Film Journal. 1956, n5, p1-4.
Films and Filming. Apr 1956, v2, n7, p14.
Films in Review. Aug-Sep 1955, v6, n7, p341-42.
The Magic World of Orson Welles. p212-19.
Magill's Survey of Cinema. Series II. v4, p1828.
Motion Picture Herald Product Digest. Jun 4, 1955, p465.
The Nation. Oct 1, 1955, v181, p290.
The New Republic. Oct 3, 1955, v132, p21-22.
The New York Times. Apr 1, 1951, SecII, p5.
The New York Times. Sep 13, 1955, p27.
The New York Times. Sep 18, 1955, SecII, p1.
The New Yorker. Sep 17, 1955, v31, p141.
Newsweek. May 23, 1955, v45, p120.
Orson Welles (McBride). p106-22.
Shakespeare on Film. p175-90.
Sight and Sound. Spr 1956, v25, n4, p196-97.
Time. Jun 6, 1955, v65, p106.
Variety. May 16, 1956, p6.

Othello (GB; Burge, Stuart; 1965)
Cinema. Mar 1966, v3, p47.
Commentary. Apr 1966, v41, p79-81.
Commonweal. Feb 25, 1966, v83, p614-15.
Confessions of a Cultist. p235-41.
Film Daily. Dec 21, 1965, p6.
Film Heritage. Fall 1966, v2, p18-22.
Film Quarterly. Sum 1966, v19, p48-50.
Filmfacts. Mar 1, 1966, v9, p17-20.
Films and Filming. May 1966, v12, p6, 12-13.
Films in Review. Jan 1966, v17, p52-53.
The Films of Laurence Olivier. p136-37.
Kiss Kiss Bang Bang. p211-13.
Laurence Olivier (Hirsch). p126-30.
Laurence Olivier: Theater & Cinema. p167-74.
Literature/Film Quarterly. 1973, v1, n4, p321-31.
The London Times. Dec 17, 1965, p15.
The London Times. Apr 28, 1966, p18.
Motion Picture Herald Product Digest. Jan 5, 1966, p435.
National Review. Mar 22, 1966, v18, p281-83.
New Statesman. May 6, 1966, v71, p663.
The New York Times. Feb 2, 1966, p24.
The New Yorker. Feb 19, 1966, v41, p145.
Newsweek. Jan 17, 1966, v67, p85.
The Private Eye, the Cowboy and the Very Naked Girl. p181-83.
Private Screenings. p238-42.
Saturday Review. Feb 5, 1966, v49, p60.
Senior Scholastic. Feb 11, 1966, v88, p23.
Shakespeare and the Film. p153-57.
Shakespeare on Film. p191-206.
Sight and Sound. Sum 1966, v35, p149.
The Spectator. May 6, 1966, v216, p570-71.
Time. Feb 4, 1966, v87, p103-04.
Variety. Dec 15, 1965, p6.
The Village Voice. Feb 17, 1966, v11, p21.
The Village Voice. Mar 3, 1966, v11, p23.
Vogue. Mar 1, 1966, v147, p95.

The Other Side of Midnight (US; Jarrott, Charles; 1977)
BFI/Monthly Film Bulletin. Sep 1977, v44, p196.
Films in Review. Aug-Sep 1977, v28, p437-38.
Hollywood Reporter. Jun 6, 1977, p2.
The Los Angeles Times. Jun 16, 1977, SecIV, p1.
Motion Picture Herald Product Digest. Jun 22, 1977, p6.
The New Republic. Sep 3, 1977, v177, p22-23.

New York. Jun 27, 1977, v10, p117-19.
The New York Times. Jun 9, 1977, SecIII, p16.
The New York Times. Jun 26, 1977, SecII, p1.
The New York Times. Sep 18, 1977, SecII, p17.
The New Yorker. Jul 11, 1977, v53, p84-86.
Newswseek. Jun 13, 1977, v89, p64.
Saturday Review. Jul 23, 1977, v4, p46-47.
Time. Jun 20, 1977, v109, p73.
Variety. Jun 8, 1977, p26.
The Village Voice. Jun 20, 1977, v22, p38.
The Village Voice. Jul 4, 1977, p37-38.
Vogue. May 1977, v167, p238-39.

Otokotachi *See* Tora-no-o

Otto e Mezzo *See* 8½

Our Hitler (German title: Hitler. Ein Film aus Deutschland; Also titled: Hitler, a Film from Germany) (WGER; Syberberg, Hans-Jurgen; 1977)
The Christian Science Monitor. Mar 5, 1980, p19.
Discourse. Sum 1980, n2, p60-82.
Films in Review. Mar 1980, v31, p176.
The Great German Films. p279-83.
The Los Angeles Times. Jun 22, 1980, Calendar, p29.
Magill's Survey of Cinema. Foreign Language Films. v3, p1374-81.
The New York Times. Jan 15, 1980, SecIII, p7.
Newsday. Jan 15, 1980, SecII, p32.
October. Sum 1981, n17, p99-118.
Variety. Nov 30, 1977, p20.

Our Man Flint (French title: Notre Homme Flint) (US; Mann, Daniel; 1966)
America. Feb 5, 1966, v114, p209.
BFI/Monthly Film Bulletin. Mar 1966, v33, p39.
Cahiers du Cinema in English. Dec 1966, n6, p55.
Christian Century. Apr 13, 1966, v83, p466.
Christian Science Monitor (Western edition). Feb 8, 1966, p4.
Film Daily. Jan 3, 1966, p5.
Filmfacts. Feb 15, 1966, v9, p11-13.
The Great Spy Pictures. p360-61.
Hollywood Reporter. Jan 3, 1966, p3.
The London Times. Feb 17, 1966, p8.
Motion Picture Herald Product Digest. Dec 22, 1965, p425-26.
The New York Times. Jan 26, 1966, p23.
The New Yorker. Feb 5, 1966, v41, p124-25.
Newsweek. Feb 7, 1966, v67, p84.
Playboy. May 1966, v13, p33.
The Private Eye, the Cowboy and the Very Naked Girl. p231.
Saturday Review. Feb 12, 1966, v49, p45.
Time. Feb 4, 1966, v87, p104.
Variety. Jan 12, 1966, p6.

Our Man in Havana (GB; Reed, Carol; 1960)
America. Feb 13, 1960, v102, p593-94.
BFI/Monthly Film Bulletin. Jan 1960, v27, p4.
Commonweal. Feb 12, 1960, v71, p546.
Film Daily. Jan 28, 1960, p6.
Film Quarterly. Spr 1960, v13, p60.
Filmfacts. 1960, v3, p19.
Films and Filming. Feb 1960, v6, p21.
Films in Review. Mar 1960, v11, p167-68.
Graham Greene (DeVitis). p47-50.
Hollywood Reporter. Jan 27, 1960, p3.
Life. Feb 15, 1960, v48, p61-63.
Magill's Survey of Cinema. Series II. v4, p1831-33.
McCall's. Apr 1960, v87, p6.
The Nation. Feb 13, 1960, v190, p156.
The New Republic. Feb 15, 1960, v142, p22-23.

The New York Times. Jan 28, 1960, p26.
The New York Times. Jan 31, 1960, SecII, p1.
Newsweek. Feb 8, 1960, v55, p102.
Saturday Review. Feb 6, 1960, v43, p33.
Sight and Sound. Wint 1959-60, v29, p35.
Time. Feb 8, 1960, v7, p92.
Travels in Greeneland. p145-54.
Variety. Jan 13, 1960, p7.

Our Man in Marrakesh *See* Bang, Bang, You're Dead!

Our Time (US; Hyams, Peter; 1974)
Christian Century. May 22, 1974, v91, p571.
Cineaste. 1974, v6, n3, p34-35.
Films in Review. May 1974, v25, p309.
Hollywood Reporter. Apr 4, 1974, p4.
Independent Film Journal. Apr 15, 1974, v73, p10.
The Los Angeles Times. Apr 26, 1974, SecIV, p1.
Motion Picture Herald Product Digest. Apr 10, 1974, p89.
New York. Apr 15, 1974, v7, p79-81.
The New York Times. Apr 11, 1974, p31.
Saturday Review. May 18, 1974, v1, p39.
Time. Apr 29, 1974, v103, p77.
Variety. Apr 3, 1974, vp24.
The Village Voice. May 16, 1974, v19, p107.

Our Very Own (US; Miller, David; 1950)
BFI/Monthly Film Bulletin. Mar 1951, v18, p228-29.
Christian Century. Oct 18, 1950, v67, p1247.
Commonweal. Aug 11, 1950, v52, p436.
Film Daily. Mar 20, 1950, p6.
Hollywood Reporter. Mar 20, 1950, p3.
The London Times. Feb 19, 1951, p9.
Motion Picture Herald Product Digest. Mar 25, 1950, p237.
The New Republic. Aug 14, 1950, v123, p22.
The New York Times. Jul 28, 1950, p12.
The New Yorker. Jul 29, 1950, v26, p61.
Newsweek. Aug 7, 1950, v36, p76.
Samuel Goldwyn Presents. p272-75.
Senior Scholastic. Mar 15, 1950, v56, p36.
The Spectator. Feb 16, 1951, v186, p208.
Time. Aug 7, 1950, v56, p67-68.
Variety. Mar 22, 1950, p6.

Out of Africa (US; Pollack, Sydney; 1985)
America. Feb 1, 1986, v154, p75.
Architectural Digest. Jan 1986, v43, p54.
BFI/Monthly Film Bulletin. Apr 1986, v53, p112.
Christian Century. Jan 15, 1986, v103, p35-36.
Commonweal. Jan 31, 1986, v113, p53-54.
Film Comment. Mar-Apr 1986, v22, p7-12.
Films in Review. Feb 1986, v37, p114.
Hollywood Reporter. Dec 9, 1985, p3.
Jet. Mar 17, 1986, v69, p55.
The Los Angeles Times. Dec 18, 1985, SecVI, p1.
Maclean's. Dec 23, 1985, v98, p48.
Magill's Cinema Annual, 1986. p255-60.
The Nation. Jan 25, 1986, v242, p88-89.
National Review. Feb 14, 1986, v38, p57-59.
The New Leader. Feb 10, 1986, v69, p19-20.
The New Republic. Jan 20, 1986, v194 p26-27.
New York. Jan 6, 1986, v19, p57-58.
The New York Times. Dec 18, 1985, SecIII, p17.
The New York Times Magazine. Dec 15, 1985, p54-56.
The New Yorker. Dec 30, 1985, v61, p67-68.
Newsweek. Dec 23, 1985, v106, p72-74.
Newsweek. Feb 17, 1986, v107, p61.
Time. Dec 16, 1985, v126, p82.
Variety. Dec 11, 1985, p17.
Vogue. Dec 1985, v175, p64, 246.
The Wall Street Journal. Dec 26, 1985, p6.

Outcast of the Islands (GB; Reed, Carol; 1951)
BFI/Monthly Film Bulletin. Jan 1952, v19, p4.
Catholic World. May 1952, v175, p143.
Christian Century. Jul 16, 1952, v69, p839.
Cinema, the Magic Vehicle. v2, p101.
Commonweal. May 30, 1952, v56, p197.
Film Criticism and Caricatures, 1943-1953. p136-38.
Film Culture. n1, 1956, v3, p13-14.
Film Daily. May 15, 1952, p6.
Films in Review. May 1952, v3, p238-39.
Hollywood Reporter. Jun 17, 1952, p3.
Illustrated London News. Mar 8, 1952, v220, p422.
Kiss Kiss Bang Bang. p410-11.
Library Journal. Jun 1, 1952, v77, p970.
Life. May 19, 1952, v32, p111-12.
The London Times. Jan 17, 1952, p2.
Magill's Survey of Cinema. Series II. v4, p1838-41.
Motion Picture Herald Product Digest. May 17, 1952, p1366.
The Nation. May 17, 1952, v174, p486.
The New Statesman and Nation. Jan 26, 1952, v43, p97.
The New York Times. May 16, 1952, p19.
The New York Times Magazine. Apr 20, 1952, p30-31.
The New Yorker. May 17, 1952, v28, p107.
Quarterly of Film, Radio and Televison. Wint 1952, v7, p135-39.
Saturday Review. Apr 26, 1952, v35, p28-29.
Sight and Sound. Apr-Jun 1952, v21, p166-67.
Sight and Sound. Jun 1951, v20, p48-50.
The Spectator. Jan 18, 1952, v188, p76.
The Tatler. Jan 30, 1952, v203, p186.
Theatre Arts. Jun 1952, v36, p44.
Time. Apr 28, 1952, v59, p98.
Variety. Jan 23, 1952, p6.

The Outcasts of Poker Flat (US; Newman, Joseph M.; 1952)
BFI/Monthly Film Bulletin. Jul 1952, v19, p92.
Christian Century. Jul 23, 1952, v69, p863.
Commonweal. Jun 6, 1952, v56, p224-25.
Film Daily. May 13, 1952, p12.
Hollywood Reporter. May 5, 1952, p3.
Library Journal. May 15, 1952, v77, p873.
The London Times. Jan 25, 1952, p7.
Motion Picture Herald Product Digest. May 10, 1952, p1357.
The New York Times. May 16, 1952, p19.
The New Yorker. May 24, 1952, v28, p129.
Theatre Arts. Jul 1952, v36, p88.
Time. May 26, 1952, v59, p100.
Variety. May 7, 1952, p6.

The Outcry *See* Grido, Il

Outland (US; Hyams, Peter; 1981)
Hollywood Reporter. May 15, 1981, p2.
The Los Angeles Times. May 21, 1981, SecVI, p1.
Maclean's. Jun 1, 1981, v, p94, p63.
Magill's Cinema Annual, 1982. p272-75.
The New Leader. Jun 1, 1981, v64, p21-22.
New York. Jun 1, 1981, v14, p47.
The New York Times. May 22, 1981, SecIII, p8.
The New Yorker. Jun 29, 1981, v57, p95-97.
Newsweek. Jun 1, 1981, v97, p91.
Rolling Stone. Jul 9, 1981, p38.
Technology Review. Oct 1981, v84, p76.
Time. Jun 1, 1981, v117, p75.
Variety. May 15, 1981, p3.

The Outlaw Josey Wales (US; Eastwood, Clint; 1976)
BFI/Monthly Film Bulletin. Aug 1976, v43, p171.

Clint Eastwood (Guérif). p113-19.
Commonweal. Oct 8, 1976, v103, p662-63.
Film Heritage. Fall 1976, v37, p8.
Films and Filming. Oct 1976, v23, p39-40.
Films and Filming. Aug 1976, v22, p17-19.
The Films of Clint Eastwood. p189-94.
The Films of the Seventies. p144-46.
Hollywood Reporter. Jun 29, 1976, p3.
Independent Film Journal. Aug 20, 1976, v78, p11.
The Los Angeles Times. Jun 14, 1976, SecIV, p9.
Magill's Survey of Cinema. Series II. v4, p1842-45.
Motion Picture Herald Product Digest. Aug 18, 1976, p23.
Movietone News. Oct 11, 1976, n52, p34.
New Statesman. Aug 6, 1976, v92, p189.
The New York Times. Aug 5, 1976, p26.
The New York Times. Aug 15, 1976, SecII, p13.
Newsweek. Sep 13, 1976, v88, p89.
Sight and Sound. Wint 1976, v45, p256.
The Thousand Eyes Magazine. Sep 1976, v2, p8-9.
Time. Aug 2, 1976, v108, p69.
Variety. Jun 30, 1976, p20.

Outpost in Malaya (Also titled: The Planter's Wife) (GB; Annakin, Ken; 1952)
BFI/Monthly Film Bulletin. Nov 1952, v19, p155.
Christian Century. Feb 11, 1953, v70, p175.
Commonweal. Dec 19, 1952, v57, p284.
Film Daily. Dec 4, 1952, p6.
The London Times. Sep 19, 1952, p8.
Motion Picture Herald Product Digest. Nov 15, 1952, p1606.
National Parent-Teacher. Feb 1953, v47, p38.
The New Statesman and Nation. Sep 27, 1952, v44, p349.
The New York Times. Nov 27, 1952, p49.
Newsweek. Dec 15, 1952, v40, p102.
The Spectator. Sep 19, 1952, v189, p360.
Variety. Oct 1, 1952, p6.

Outrage (US; Lupino, Ida; 1950)
BFI/Monthly Film Bulletin. Dec 1951, v18, p377.
Film Daily. Aug 24, 1950, p5.
Hollywood Reporter. Aug 23, 1950, p3.
Motion Picture Herald Product Digest. Aug 26, 1950, p450.
The New York Times. Oct 16, 1950, p30.
Newsweek. Oct 30, 1950, v36, p83.
Variety. Aug 23, 1950, p8.

The Outrage (US; Ritt, Martin; 1964)
America. Oct 31, 1964, v111, p533.
BFI/Monthly Film Bulletin. Oct 1965, v32, p147.
Commonweal. Oct 23, 1964, v81, p136.
Film Daily. Sep 30, 1964, v125, p6.
Films and Filming. Oct 1965, v12, p29-30.
Films in Review. Nov 1964, v15, p573-74.
The Films of Paul Newman. p136-40.
The Great Western Pictures. p251-53.
Hollywood Reporter. Sep 30, 1964, v182, p3.
Motion Picture Herald Product Digest. Oct 14, 1964, v232, p145-46.
The New York Times. Oct 8, 1964, p48.
Newsweek. Oct 26, 1964, v64, p118.
Variety. Sep 30, 1964, p6.

The Outsider (US; Mann, Delbert; 1961)
America. Feb 17, 1962, v106, p663.
BFI/Monthly Film Bulletin. Mar 1962, v29, p35.
Commonweal. Feb 16, 1962, v75, p542.
Film Daily. Dec 19, 1961, p6.
Film Quarterly. Sum 1962, v15, p64.

Filmfacts. 1962, v5, p50.
Filmfacts. Mar 30, 1962, v5, p50-52.
Hollywood Reporter. Dec 19, 1961, p3.
Motion Picture Herald Product Digest. Dec 27, 1961, p396.
The New York Times. Feb 8, 1962, p25.
The New Yorker. Feb 17, 1962, v37, p119.
Saturday Review. Dec 9, 1961, v44, p28.
Time. Feb 2, 1962, v79, p63.
Tony Curtis: The Man and His Movies. p90-91.
Variety. Dec 20, 1961, p6.

The Outsider (GB; Luorschi, Tony; 1979)
Films in Review. Aug-Sep 1980, v31, p441.
Hollywood Reporter. Mar 5, 1980, p30.
The Los Angeles Times. Jul 3, 1980, SecVI, p2.
The New York Times. Jun 3, 1980, SecIII, p19.
Newsday. Jun 6, 1980, SecII, p7.
Variety. Dec 5, 1979, p27.

The Outsiders (US; Coppola, Francis Ford; 1983)
Commonweal. May 6, 1983, v110, p274.
Film Quarterly. Fall 1983, v37, p29.
Films in Review. May 1983, v34, p304.
Hollywood Reporter. Mar 23, 1983, p3.
The Los Angeles Times. Mar 25, 1983, SecVI, p1.
Maclean's. Apr 4, 1983, v96, p62.
Magill's Cinema Annual, 1984. p282-88.
New York. Apr 4, 1983, v16, p73.
The New York Times. Mar 25, 1983, SecIII, p3.
Newsweek. Apr 4, 1983, v101, p74.
Rolling Stone. May 12, 1983, p55.
Senior Scholastic. Feb 4, 1983, v115, p28.
Sight and Sound. Aut 1983, v52, p287.
Time. Apr 4, 1983, v121, p78.

The Outsiders (Godard, 1964) *See* Band of Outsiders

The Owl and the Pussycat (US; Ross, Herbert; 1970)
BFI/Monthly Film Bulletin. Apr 1971, v38, n447, p81.
Deeper into Movies. p183-85.
Films in Review. Dec 1970, v21, n10, p646.
Magill's Survey of Cinema. Series II. v4, p1846.
The New Republic. Dec 5, 1970, v163, p22.
The New York Times. Nov 4, 1970, p46.
The New Yorker. Nov 14, 1970, v46, p165-66.
Newsweek. Nov 16, 1970, v76, p101.
Time. Nov 16, 1970, v96, p96.
Variety. Nov 11, 1970, p15.

PT 109 (US; Martinson, Leslie H.; 1963)
America. Jul 20, 1963, v109, p83-84.
BFI/Monthly Film Bulletin. Sep 1963, v30, p132.
Commonweal. Jul 26, 1963, v78, p458.
Film Daily. Mar 14, 1963, p5.
Filmfacts. Aug 1, 1963, v6, p145-47.
Films and Filming. Sep 1963, v9, p26, 31.
Films in Review. Aug-Sep 1963, v14, p435.
Hollywood Reporter. Mar 14, 1963, v174, p3.
The New York Times. Jun 27, 1963, p23.
The New Yorker. Jul 8, 1963, v62, p79.
Photoplay. Sep 1963, v64, p10.
Saturday Review. Jul 20, 1963, v46, p37.
Time. Jun 28, 1963, v81, p82.
Variety. Mar 20, 1963, p6.

Pacific Crossing on Raft *See* Kon-Tiki

The Pad (And How to Use It) (US; Hutton, Brian G.; 1966)
BFI/Monthly Film Bulletin. Oct 1966, v33, p155-56.
Commonweal. Sep 23, 1966, v84, p614.
Film Daily. Aug 18, 1966, p4.
Filmfacts. Oct 15, 1966, v9, p219-20.
Hollywood Reporter. Aug 17, 1966, p3.

The London Times. Sep 22, 1966, p6.
Motion Picture Herald Product Digest. Aug 31, 1966, p587-88.
The New York Times. Aug 18, 1966, p27.
The New Yorker. Aug 27, 1966, v42, p88.
Newsweek. Sep 5, 1966, v68, p88.
Playboy. Nov 1966, v13, p42, 48.
Senior Scholastic. Sep 30, 1966, v89, p34.
Time. Sep 2, 1966, v88, p66.
Variety. Aug 17, 1966, p6.
Vogue. Oct 15, 1966, v148, p79.

Padre Padrone (IT; Taviani, Vittorio; Taviani, Paolo; 1975)
Before My Eyes. p301.
BFI/Monthly Film Bulletin. Nov 1977, v44, p237.
Films in Review. Aug-Sep 1978, v29, p441.
The Los Angeles Times. Mar 3, 1978, SecIV, p1.
Magill's Survey of Cinema. Foreign Language Films. v5, p2342-47.
The Nation. Oct 15, 1975, v225, p378-79.
The Nation. Jan 7, 1978, v226, p30.
The New Republic. Jan 21, 1978, v178, p22.
The New York Times. Sep 25, 1977, p56.
The New York Times. Dec 24, 1977, p12.
The New Yorker. Oct 3, 1977, v53, p127-30.
Newsweek. Jan 16, 1978, v91, p81.
Time. Jan 16, 1978, v111, p82.
Variety. May 25, 1977, p24.

Pagan Love Song (US; Alton, Robert; 1950)
BFI/Monthly Film Bulletin. May 1951, v18, p267.
Film Daily. Dec 26, 1950, p6.
Hollywood Reporter. Dec 20, 1950, p3.
Library Journal. Jan 15, 1951, v76, p124.
Motion Picture Herald Product Digest. Dec 23, 1950, p633.
The New York Times. Dec 26, 1950, p19.
Newsweek. Jan 8, 1951, v37, p75.
Time. Jan 15, 1951, v57, p80.
Variety. Dec 20, 1950, p6.
The World of Entertainment. p289-96.

Paid in Full (US; Dieterle, William; 1949)
BFI/Monthly Film Bulletin. Nov 1949, v16, p194.
Christian Century. Apr 12, 1950, v67, p479.
Commonweal. Mar 10, 1950, v51, p580.
Film Daily. Jan 3, 1950, p6.
Hollywood Reporter. Dec 20, 1949, p3.
The London Times. Jan 9, 1950, p7.
Motion Picture Herald Product Digest. Dec 24, 1949, p130.
The New York Times. Feb 16, 1950, p28.
Newsweek. Feb 27, 1950, v35, p80.
Time. Mar 6, 1950, v55, p92.
Variety. Dec 21, 1949, p8.

Paint Your Wagon (US; Logan, Joshua; 1969)
America. Nov 15, 1969, v121, p474-75.
Big Screen, Little Screen. p69-72, 256-57.
Clint Eastwood (Guérif). p67-70.
Dance Magazine. Dec 1969, v43, p31.
Deeper into Movies. p26-30.
Film 69/70. p111-15.
Film Daily. Oct 15, 1969, p3.
Films and Filming. Mar 1970, v16, p46, 51.
Films in Review. Nov 1969, v20, p571-72.
The Films of Clint Eastwood. p94-103.
Mademoiselle. Oct 1969, v69, p190-91.
Movies Into Film. p330-32.
The Musical From Broadway to Hollywood. p138-42.
The New York Times. Oct 16, 1969, p56.
The New Yorker. Oct 25, 1969, v65, p176-79.
Newsweek. Oct 27, 1969, v74, p124.

Saturday Review. Nov 15, 1969, p64.
Time. Oct 24, 1969, v94, p100.
Variety. Oct 15, 1969, p15.

The Painted Hills (US; Kress, Harold F.; 1951)
BFI/Monthly Film Bulletin. Jul 1951, v18, p299.
Film Daily. Mar 26, 1951, p6.
Hollywood Reporter. Mar 23, 1951, p3.
Motion Picture Herald Product Digest. Mar 24, 1951, p765.
Variety. Mar 28, 1951, p6.

Painting the Clouds With Sunshine (US; Butler, David; 1951)
BFI/Monthly Film Bulletin. Feb 1952, v19, p22-23.
Film Daily. Sep 6, 1951, p8.
Hollywood Reporter. Aug 31, 1951, p3.
The London Times. Jan 28, 1952, p8.
Motion Picture Herald Product Digest. Sep 8, 1951, p1005.
The New York Times. Sep 1, 1951, p9.
The Spectator. Jan 25, 1952, v188, p109.
Variety. Sep 5, 1951, p6.

The Pajama Game (US; Donen, Stanley; Abbott, George; 1957)
BFI/Monthly Film Bulletin. Oct 1957, v24, p124.
Commonweal. Sep 13, 1957, v66, p589.
Dance Magazine. Aug 1957, v31, p36-37.
Film Daily. Aug 7, 1957, p6.
Films and Filming. Dec 1957, v4, p22-23.
Films in Review. Oct 1957, v8, p413.
The Films of Doris Day. p163-68.
Hollywood Reporter. Aug 7, 1957, p3.
Motion Picture Herald Product Digest. Aug 10, 1957, v208, p481.
The New York Times. Aug 30, 1957, p12.
The New York Times Magazine. Aug 4, 1957, v33, p40-41.
The New Yorker. Sep 7, 1957, v33, p72.
Newsweek. Sep 2, 1957, v50, p87.
Saturday Review. Aug 31, 1957, v40, p23.
Sight and Sound. Wint 1957-58, v27, p147-48.
Stanley Donen (Casper). p105-16.
Time. Sep 9, 1957, v70, p110.
Variety. Aug 7, 1957, p6.

Pal Joey (US; Sidney, George; 1957)
America. Nov 2, 1957, v98, p148.
BFI/Monthly Film Bulletin. Jan 1958, v25, p3.
Commonweal. Nov 8, 1957, v67, p150.
Film Daily. Sep 9, 1957, v112, p6.
Films and Filming. Feb 1958, v4, p23-24.
Films and Filming. Aug 1962, v8, p35.
Films in Review. Dec 1957, v8, p527.
The Films of Frank Sinatra. p136-40.
The Films of Rita Hayworth. p203-08.
Hollywood Reporter. Sep 9, 1957, p3.
Motion Picture Herald Product Digest. Sep 14, 1957, v208, p529.
The Musical: From Broadway to Hollywood. p66-69.
The New Republic. Dec 23, 1957, v137, p21.
The New York Times. Oct 28, 1957, p30.
The New York Times Magazine. Jun 9, 1957, p58.
The New Yorker. Nov 2, 1957, v33, p166.
Newsweek. Oct 28, 1957, v50, p104.
Saturday Review. Nov 2, 1957, v40, p23.
Time. Oct 28, 1957, v70, p98.
Variety. Sep 11, 1957, p6.

Pale Rider (US; Eastwood, Clint; 1985)
America. Aug 17, 1985, v153, p91.
BFI/Monthly Film Bulletin. Aug 1985, v52, p239.
Christian Century. Aug 14, 1985, v102, p740.

Commonweal. Sep 6, 1985, v112, p468-69.
Films in Review. Oct 1985, p487.
Hollywood Reporter. Mar 8, 1985, p3.
The Los Angeles Times. Jun 28, 1985, SecVI, p1.
Magill's Cinema Annual, 1986. p261-64.
New York. Jul 29, 1985, v18, p61.
The New York Times. Jun 28, 1985, SecIII, p8.
The New Yorker. Aug 12, 1985, v61, p64-65.
Newsweek. Jul 1, 1985, v106, p55.
Progressive. Sep 1985, v49, p38.
Time. Jul 1, 1985, v125, p63.
Variety. May 8, 1985, p25.
Vogue. Aug 1985, v175, p66.

Palm Springs Weekend (US; Taurog, Norman; 1963)
America. Nov 30, 1963, v109, p715.
BFI/Monthly Film Bulletin. Feb 1964, v31, p27.
Commonweal. Nov 15, 1963, v79, p225.
Film Daily. Nov 6, 1963, p6.
Filmfacts. Nov 7, 1963, v6, p237-38.
Films and Filming. Feb 1964, v10, p29-30.
The New York Times. Nov 6, 1963, p32.
Photoplay. Jan 1964, v65, p20.
Variety. Nov 6, 1963, p6.

Pandora and the Flying Dutchman (GB; Lewin, Albert; 1951)
BFI/Monthly Film Bulletin. Mar 1951, v18, p229.
BFI/Monthly Film Bulletin. b Aug 1985, v52, p261-62.
BFI/Monthly Film Bulletin. Aug 1985, v52, p261-62.
Christian Century. Mar 19, 1952, v69, p351.
Commonweal. Dec 14, 1951, v55, p254.
Film Criticism and Caricatures, 1943-1953. p120-22.
Film Daily. Oct 15, 1951, p6.
The Films of James Mason. p96-97.
Holiday. Mar 1952, v11, p11.
Hollywood Reporter. Feb 2, 1951, p3.
Library Journal. May 15, 1951, v76, p883.
The London Times. Jan 30, 1951, p12.
The London Times. Feb 3, 1951, p8.
Motion Picture Herald Product Digest. Oct 13, 1951, p1057.
The New Statesman and Nation. Feb 10, 1951, v41, p156.
The New York Times. Dec 7, 1951, p35.
The New York Times. Dec 15 1951, v27, p136.
Newsweek. Dec 17, 1951, v38, p98.
The Spectator. Feb 2, 1951, v186, p146.
Surrealism and American Feature Films. p123-40.
Time. May 28, 1951, v57, p105-06.
Variety. Oct 10, 1951, p6.

Pane, Amore, E... *See* Scandal in Sorrento

Pane, Amore e Fantasia *See* Bread, Love and Dreams

Pane e cioccolata *See* Bread and Chocolate

The Panic in Needle Park (US; Schatzberg, Jerry; 1971)
Esquire. Sep 1971, v76, p74.
Filmfacts. 1971, v14, p434-37.
Films in Review. Aug-Sep 1971, v22, n7, p443-44.
Hollywood Reporter. May 24, 1971, v216, n19, p3.
Magill's Survey of Cinema. Series II. v4, p1856-59.
The New Republic. Jun 26, 1971, v164, p28.
The New York Times. Jul 14, 1971, p19.
Newsweek. Aug 2, 1971, v78, p76.
Saturday Review. Jun 26, 1971, v54, p47.
Time. Aug 2, 1971, v98, p62.

Variety. May 26, 1971, p13.
The Village Voice. Aug 19, 1971, v16, n33, p51.

Panic in the Streets (US; Kazan, Elia; 1950)
BFI/Monthly Film Bulletin. Aug 1950, v17, p115-16.
Christian Century. Nov 8, 1950, v67, p1343.
Cinema, the Magic Vehicle. v2, p57-58.
Commonweal. Aug 18, 1950, v52, p460.
Film Culture. n2, 1956, v2, p21-22.
Film Daily. Jun 21, 1950, p7.
Films in Review. Jul-Aug 1950, v1, p17-19.
Georgia Review. n2 1985, v39, p397-10.
Hollywood Reporter. Jun 14, 1950, p3.
Life. Aug 21, 1950, v29, p87-90.
The London Times. Jul 31, 1950, p2.
Magill's Survey of Cinema. Series II. v4, p1860-62.
Motion Picture Herald Product Digest. Jun 17, 1950, p345.
Movie. Wint 1971-72, v19, p14-16.
The Nation. Sep 2, 1950, v171, p214.
The New Statesman and Nation. Aug 5, 1950, v40, p147.
The New York Times. Aug 5, 1950, p9.
Newsweek. Aug 7, 1950, v36, p75.
Saturday Review. Sep 2, 1950, v33, p28-30.
Sequence. Aut 1950, n12, p14-15.
Shots in the Dark. p208-12.
Sight and Sound. Aug 1950, v19, p241-42.
The Spectator. Jul 28, 1950, v185, p113.
Theatre Arts. Oct 1950, v34, p8.
Time. Aug 14, 1950, v56, p84.

Papa's Delicate Condition (US; Marshall, George; 1963)
America. Mar 16, 1963, v108, p382.
BFI/Monthly Film Bulletin. Sep 1963, v30, p132.
Film Daily. Feb 13, 1963, p5.
Filmfacts. Mar 7, 1963, v6, p22-23.
Films and Filming. Jul 1963, v9, p29.
Hollywood Reporter. Feb 13, 1963, v174, p3.
The New York Times. Mar 7, 1963, p8.
The New Yorker. Mar 16, 1963, v39, p143.
Time. Mar 15, 1963, v81, pM27.
Variety. Feb 6, 1963, p6.

The Paper Chase (US; Bridges, James; 1973)
Esquire. Dec 1973, v80, p88.
Magill's Survey of Cinema. English Language Films. Series I, v3, p1293.
The New York Times. Oct 17, 1973, p55.
The New York Times. Nov 4, 1973, SecII, p1.
The New York Times. Apr 3, 1974, v36, p1.
The New Yorker. Oct 29, 1973, v49, p153.
Newsweek. Nov 5, 1973, v82, p97.
PTA Magazine. Dec 1973, v68, p5.
Reeling. p263-65.
Time. Aug 20, 1973, v102, p58.
Variety. Sep 12, 1973, p36.

Paper Lion (US; March, Alex; 1968)
Christian Science Monitor (Western edition). Oct 21, 1968, p4.
Film Daily. Sep 30, 1968, p7.
Filmfacts. Jan 15, 1969, v11, p455-56.
Hollywood Reporter. Oct 7, 1968, p3.
Motion Picture Herald Product Digest. Oct 9, 1968, p36.
Movies Into Film. p317.
The New Republic. Nov 9, 1968, v159, p22.
The New York Times. Oct 24, 1968, p54.
Newsweek. Oct 28, 1968, v72, p117-18.
Senior Scholastic. Nov 8, 1968, v93, p23.
Time. Nov 22, 1968, v92, p78.
Variety. Oct 2, 1968, p28.
Vogue. Nov 15, 1968, v152, p100.

Paper Moon (US; Bogdanovich, Peter; 1973)
America. Jun 2, 1973, v128, p523.
Audience. Jul 1973, p5-6.
BFI/Monthly Film Bulletin. Jan 1974, v41, p12-13.
Chr Cent. Jul 6, 1973, v90, p659-60.
Commonweal. Jun 29, 1973, v98, p359-60.
Esquire. Feb 1973, v79, p52.
Filmfacts. 1973, v16, n3, p57.
Films and Filming. Jan 1974, v20, p41-42.
Films in Review. Jun-Jul 1973, v24, p372-73.
Holiday. Sep 1973, v54, p22.
The Nation. Jun 11, 1973, v216, p764-65.
The New Republic. Jul 9, 1973, v168, p33.
New Statesman. Nov 30, 1973, v86, p832-33.
The New York Times. May 17, 1973, p53.
The New York Times. Dec 30, 1973, SecII, p1.
The New York Times. Jan 13, 1974, SecII, p13.
The New York Times. Dec 8, 1974, SecII, p15.
The New Yorker. May 26, 1973, v49, p124-25.
Newsweek. May 28, 1973, v81, p99.
Rolling Stone. Jul 19, 1973, p28-30.
Rolling Stone. Jun 7, 1973, p66-67.
Time. May 28, 1973, v101, p88.
TV Movies. 1983-84, p583.
Variety. Apr 18, 1973, p22.
The Village Voice. Jun 21, 1973, p83-84.
Vogue. Jul 1973, v162, p12.

Papillon (US; Schaffner, Franklin J.; 1973)
Atlantic Monthly. Mar 1974, v233, p92-95.
BFI/Monthly Film Bulletin. Mar 1974, v41, p50-51.
Commonweal. Feb 1, 1974, v99, p435-36.
Esquire. Mar 1974, v82, p72.
Films and Filming. Apr 1974, v20, p38-39.
Films Illustrated. Apr 1974, v32, p300-02.
Films In Review. Jan 1974, v25, p51-52.
The Films of Dustin Hoffman. p137-46.
The Films of Steve McQueen. p200-08.
Hollywood Reporter. Dec 11, 1973, p3.
New Statesman. Mar 15, 1974, v87, p371.
The New York Times. Dec 30, 1973, SecII, p1.
The New York Times. Jan 20, 1974, v2, n1, p4.
The New Yorker. Dec 24, 1973, v49, p72-73.
Newsweek. Dec 17, 1973, v82, p92.
Reeling. p324-27.
Rolling Stone. Jan 31, 1974, p56-57.
Time. Dec 31, 1973, v102, p50.
TV Movies. 1983-84, p583.
Variety. Dec 12, 1973, p16.
The Village Voice. Jan 10, 1074, p57.

Paradise, Hawaiian Style (US; Moore, Michael; 1966)
BFI/Monthly Film Bulletin. Aug 1966, v33, p127.
Film Daily. Jun 8, 1966, p5.
Filmfacts. Sep 1, 1966, v9, p178-79.
The Films and Career of Elvis Presley. p171-73.
Films and Filming. Sep 1966, v12, p61.
Hollywood Reporter. Jun 6, 1966, p3.
The London Times. Jul 7, 1966, p17.
Motion Picture Herald Product Digest. Jun 8, 1966, p535-36.
The New York Times. Jun 16, 1966, p15.
Newsweek. Jul 11, 1966, v68, p92A.
Variety. Jun 8, 1966, p6.

Paradise Lagoon *See* Admirable Crichton

The Parallax View (US; Pakula, Alan J.; 1974)
Atlantic. Aug 1974, v234, p84-87.
BFI/Monthly Film Bulletin. Nov 1974, v41, p254-55.
Christian Century. Aug 7, 1974, v91, p778-80.
Cult Movies. p115-18.
Film. Dec 1974, n21, p18.

Filmmakers Newsletter. Sep 1974, v7, p20-24.
Films and Filming. Dec 1974, v21, p37-38.
Films and Filming. Oct 1974, v21, p48-49.
Films Illustrated. Nov 1974, v4, p90-91.
Films in Review. Aug-Sep 1974, v25, p441-42.
The Films of Warren Beatty. p174-87.
Hollywood Reporter. Jun 14, 1974, p3.
Independent Film Journal. Jun 12, 1974, v74, p9.
The Los Angeles Times. Jun 23, 1974, Calendar, p30.
Millimeter. Oct 1974, v2, p26-28.
Motion Picture Herald Product Digest. Jun 5, 1974, p1.
National Review. Nov 8, 1974, v26, p1303.
The New Republic. Jun 29, 1974, v170, p18.
New Statesman. Oct 4, 1974, v88, p479-80.
New York. Jun 24, 1974, v7, p58-59.
The New York Times. Aug 11, 1974, SecII, p11.
The New Yorker. Jun 24, 1974, v50, p82-83.
Newsweek. Jul 1, 1974, v84, p74-75.
Penthouse. Oct 1974, v6, p36-37.
Saturday Review. Jul 13, 1974, v1, p38.
Time. Jul 8, 1974, v104, p60.
Variety. Jun 19, 1974, p16.
The Village Voice. Jul 25, 1974, p71.

Parapluies de Cherbourg, Les *See* The Umbrellas of Cherbourg

The Paratrooper (Also titled: The Red Beret) (GB; Young, Terence; 1953)
America. Jun 23, 1954, v90, p427.
Catholic World. Dec 1953, v178, p225.
Commonweal. Nov 20, 1953, v59, p164.
Farm Journal. Feb 1954, v78, p108.
Film Daily. Jan 11, 1954, p6.
The Films of Alan Ladd. p192-93.
Library Journal. Dec 15, 1953, v78, p2208.
Motion Picture Herald Product Digest. Dec 26, 1953, p2118.
National Parent-Teacher. Nov 1953, v48, p35.
The New York Times. Dec 31, 1953, p9.
Newsweek. Jan 18, 1954, v43, p90.
Time. Jan 11, 1954, v63, p80.
Variety. Aug 19, 1953, p6.

Pardon Mon Affaire (French title: Elephant Ca Trompe Enormement, Un) (FR; Robert, Yves; 1976)
BFI/Monthly Film Bulletin. Mar 1978, v45, p50.
Films in Review. Jan 1978, v29, p55.
Hollywood Reporter. Jul 24, 1977, p2.
The Los Angeles Times. Sep 25, 1977, Calendar, p1.
Magill's Survey of Cinema. Foreign Language Films. v5, p2352-54.
The New York Times. Jun 22, 1977, SecIII, p22.
Saturday Review. Jun 11, 1977, v4, p44.
Time. Jul 18, 1977, v110, p88.
Variety. Oct 6, 1976, p20.

The Parent Trap (US; Swift, David; 1961)
America. Jul 15, 1961, v105, p533.
BFI/Monthly Film Bulletin. Sep 1961, v28, p131-32.
Commonweal. Jun 2, 1961, v74, p257.
Film Daily. May 9, 1961, p6.
Filmfacts. Aug 18, 1961, v4, p174-76.
Magill's Survey of Cinema. Series I. v3, p1296-98.
The New York Times. Jun 22, 1961, p23.
The New Yorker. Jun 22, 1961, p23.
Newsweek. Jun 19, 1961, v57, p96.
Saturday Review. May 27, 1961, v44, p27.
Time. Jul 7, 1961, v78, p61.
Variety. May 3, 1961, p26.

Paris Does Strange Things (French title: Elena et les Hommes; Also titled: The Night Does Strange Things) (FR; Renoir, Jean; 1957)
America. Apr 6, 1957, v97, p28.
Commonweal. Mar 22, 1957, v65, p639.
Film Daily. Feb 21, 1957, v111, p6.
Films in Review. Jun-Jul 1957, v8, p284.
Hollywood Reporter. Feb 21, 1957, p3.
Jean Renoir: A Guide to References and Resourcs. p215-18.
Jean Renoir (Durgnat). p315-26.
Motion Picture Herald Product Digest. Mar 2, 1957, v206, p282.
The New York Times. Mar 30, 1957, p13.
The New Yorker. Apr 6, 1957, v33, p78.
Variety. Mar 6, 1957, p6.

Paris Seen By... *See* Paris Vu Par...

Paris, Texas (US; Wenders, Wim; 1984)
BFI/Monthly Film Bulletin. Aug 1984, v51, p227-28.
Christian Century. Nov 21, 1984, v101, p1106.
Cinema Papers. Aug 1984, n47, p224-29.
Film Comment. Dec 1984, v20, p70.
Film Comment. May-Jun 1984, v20, p60-63.
Film Journal. Dec 1984, v87, p17-18.
Films and Filming. Jul 1984, n358, p21-22.
Hollywood Reporter. Sep 10, 1984, p3.
Maclean's. Dec 24, 1984, v97, p50.
The Nation. Oct 27, 1984, v239, p426-27.
The New Leader. Oct 29, 1984, v67, p20-21.
The New Republic. Dec 3, 1984, v191, p26-27.
New Statesman. Aug 24, 1984, v108, p27-28.
New York. Nov 19, 1984, v17, p52-53.
The New York Times. Nov 9, 1984, SecIII, p4.
The New York Times. Nov 11, 1984, SecII, p17.
The New York Times. Oct 14, 1984, p64.
Newsweek. Nov 19, 1984, v104, p132.
Paris/Texas. 1984.
Photoplay. Sep 1984, v35, p22.
Sight and Sound. Wint 1984, v53, p244-47.
Time. Dec 3, 1984, v124, p79.
Variety. May 23, 1984, p12.
The Village Voice. Nov 20, 1984, p51-52.
Vogue. Oct 1984, v174, p76.

Paris Vu Par . . . (Also titled: Paris Seen By . . .; Quartiers des Paris, Les; Six in Paris) (FR; Rouch, Jean; Chabrol, Claude; Godard, Jean-Luc; Rohmer, Eric; Pollet, Jean-Daniel; Douchet, Jean; 1965)
BFI/Monthly Film Bulletin. Apr 1966, v33, p55-56.
Filmfacts. n5, 1969, v12, p119-20.
Films and Filming. May 1966, v12, p53-54.
Movie. Aut 1965, n14, p39-40.
The New Wave. p139-41, 267-68.
The New York Times. Sep 16, 1965, p54.
Sight and Sound. Spr 1966, v35, p91-92.
The Spectator. Feb 25, 1966, v216, p228.
Variety. May 26, 1965, p7.

Park Row (US; Fuller, Sam; 1952)
BFI/Monthly Film Bulletin. Dec 1952, v19, p174.
BFI/Monthly Film Bulletin. Jan 1981, v48, p14.
Film Daily. Aug 7, 1952, p7.
Hollywood Reporter. Aug 5, 1952, p3.
Motion Picture Herald Product Digest. Aug 9, 1952, p1477.
The Nation. Nov 22, 1952, v175, p474.
National Parent-Teacher. Oct 1952, v47, p38.
The New York Times. Dec 22, 1952, p20.
Newsweek. Aug 4, 1952, v40, p84.
Samuel Fuller (Hardy). p39-44.
Theatre Arts. Jul 1952, v36, p37.

The Thousand Eyes Magazine. Feb 1977, v2, p8.
Time. Aug 4, 1952, v60, p79.
Variety. Aug 6, 1952, p6.

Partner (Also titled: Sosia, Il) (IT; Bertolucci, Bernardo; 1968)
Bernardo Bertolucci (Kolker). p23-35.
BFI/Monthly Film Bulletin. Nov 1970, v37, p220.
Films and Filming. Jan 1971, v17, p53.
Five Thousand One Nights At the Movies. p448.
International Film Guide. 1970, v7, p148.
The Los Angeles Times. Apr 18, 1974, p10.
The New Republic. Feb 9, 1974, v170, p22.
New York Magazine. Feb 11, 1974, v7, p74-75.
The New York Times. Sep 24, 1968, p52.
The New York Times. Feb 7, 1974, p46.
Rolling Stone. Mar 28, 1974, n157, p55.
Sight and Sound. Wint 1968-69, v38, p34, 51.
The Spectator. Nov 29, 1968, v221, p918-19.
The Spectator. Mar 14, 1969, v222, p343-44.
Variety. Sep 18, 1968, p6.

The Party (US; Edwards, Blake; 1968)
BFI/Monthly Film Bulletin. Apr 1969, v36, p73.
Blake Edwards (Lehman). p136-65.
Christian Science Monitor (Western edition). Apr 10, 1968, p12.
Esquire. Aug 1968, v70, p22.
Film Daily. Mar 22, 1968, p4.
Filmfacts. May 15, 1968, v11, p116-17.
Films and Filming. Jun 1969, v15, p44-45.
Five Thousand One Nights At the Movies. p448.
Hollywood Reporter. Mar 19, 1968, p3.
The London Times. Mar 6, 1969, p13.
Magill's Survey of Cinema. Series II. v4, p1866-69.
Motion Picture Herald Product Digest. Mar 27, 1968, p787.
Movie. Wint 1969-70, n17, p34-35.
The New York Times. Apr 5, 1968, p56.
The Spectator. Mar 14, 1969, v222, p343.
Variety. Mar 20, 1968, p6.
The Village Voice. Apr 11, 1968, p45.

The Party and the Guests *See* A Report on the Party and the Guests

Party Girl (US; Ray, Nicholas; 1958)
America. Nov 29, 1958, v100, p297.
BFI/Monthly Film Bulletin. Feb 1959, v26, p20.
Film Daily. Oct 22, 1958, v114, p10.
Filmfacts. Dec 10, 1958, v1, p212-13.
The Films of Robert Taylor. p163-65.
Hollywood Reporter. Oct 20, 1958, p3.
Magill's Survey of Cinema. Series II. p1870-72.
The New York Times. Oct 29, 1958, p30.
Nicholas Ray: A Guide to References and Resources. p111-15.
Nicholas Ray (Kreidl). p163-65.
Time. Nov 10, 1958, v72, p102.
Variety. Oct 22, 1958, p6.

Pasqualino Settebellezze *See* Seven Beauties

The Passenger (Italian title: Professione: Reporter) (IT, FR, SP; Antonioni, Michelangelo; 1975)
America. Jun 14, 1975, v132, p462-63.
Antonioni (Chatman). p176-212.
Atlantic. Feb 1976, v237, p106.
BFI/Monthly Film Bulletin. Jun 1975, v42, p143.
Commonweal. May 19, 1975, v102, p113-114.
Esquire. Jul 1975, v84, p16.
Film Quarterly. Sum 1975, v28, p26-30, 56-61.
Films in Review. May 1975, v26, p315.
Hollywood Reporter. Mar 26, 1975, p18.

The International Dictionary of Films and Filmmakers. v1, p374-75.
The Los Angeles Times. Apr 8, 1975, SecIV, p1.
Magill's Survey of Cinema. Foreign Language Films. v5, p2367-71.
Michelangelo Antonioni (Perry and Prieto). p133-37.
Michelangelo Antonioni's Neo-Realism. Afterword, np.
Motion Picture Herald Product Digest. Apr 23, 1975, p90.
The Nation. Apr 26, 1975, v220, p510.
The New Republic. Apr 19, 1975, v172, p22.
The New York Times. Apr 10, 1975, p46.
The New York Times. Apr 20, 1975, SecII, p1.
The New Yorker. Apr 14, 1975, v51, p112-14.
Newsweek. Apr 14, 1975, v85, p90.
The Passenger. 1975.
Saturday Review. May 3, 1975, v2, p35.
Time. Apr 14, 1975, v105, p64.
Variety. Mar 19, 1975, p29.
Vogue. Jun 1975, v165, p38.

The Passionate Sentry *See* Who Goes There!

Pat and Mike (US; Cukor, George; 1952)
BFI/Monthly Film Bulletin. Jul 1952, v19, p92.
Catholic World. Jul 1952, v175, p304.
Christian Century. Aug 6, 1952, v69, p911.
Commonweal. Jun 27, 1952, v56, p291.
Cue. Jun 21, 1952, p11.
Film Daily. May 15, 1952, p6.
The Films of Katharine Hepburn. p151-54.
The Films of Spencer Tracy. p211-12.
George Cukor (Phillips). p84-85.
Hollywood Reporter. May 13, 1952, p3.
Kiss Kiss Bang Bang. p414.
Magill's Survey of Cinema. Series II. v4, p1873-76.
Motion Picture Herald Product Digest. May 17, 1952, p1365.
The Nation. Aug 9, 1952, v175, p117.
National Parent-Teacher. Sep 1952, v47, p38.
The New Statesman and Nation. Oct 11, 1952, v44, p418, 420.
The New York Times. Jun 19, 1952, p32.
The New Yorker. Jun 28, 1952, v28, p62.
Newsweek. Jun 23, 1952, v39, p91.
On Cukor. p204-08.
Selected Film Criticism, 1951-1960. p96-97.
Sight and Sound. Jul-Sep 1952, v22, p29.
The Spectator. Oct 3, 1952, v189, p426.
Talking Pictures. p211-14.
The Tatler. Oct 15, 1952, v206, p144.
Time. Jun 16, 1952, v59, p96.
Variety. May 14, 1952, p6.

Pat Garrett & Billy the Kid (US; Peckinpah, Sam; 1973)
Christian Century. Jul 4, 1973, v90, p740.
Commonweal. Jul 13, 1973, v98, p385-86.
Film Heritage. Wint 1973-74, v19, n2, p1.
Filmfacts. 1973, v16, n3, p86.
Films in Review. Aug-Sep 1973, v24, n7, p436.
The Films of Sam Peckinpah. p71-79.
Hollywood Reporter. May 22, 1973, p3.
The New Republic. Jun 16, 1973, v168, p33.
New Statesman. Aug 31, 1973, v86, p295.
The New York Times. May 24, 1973, p53.
The New York Times. Jun 3, 1973, SecII, p1.
The New York Times. Jul 8, 1973, SecII, p8.
The New York Times. Dec 30, 1973, SecII, p1.
Newsweek. Jun 11, 1973, v81, p104.
Peckinpah (McKinney). p159-73.
Peckinpah (Simmons). p169-88.
Rolling Stone. Mar 15, 1973, p46-47.
Rolling Stone. Jul 5, 1973, p74-75.
Sight and Sound. Fall 1973, v42, p232-33.
Time. Jun 11, 1973, v101, p70.

Payment on Demand (US; Bernhardt, Curtis; 1951)
Bette Davis: Her Films and Career. p151-53.
BFI/Monthly Film Bulletin. Jun 1951, v18, p276.
Christian Century. Apr 18, 1951, v68, p511.
Commonweal. Mar 2, 1951, v53, p519.
Film Daily. Feb 20, 1951, p6.
Hollywood Reporter. Feb 15, 1951, p4.
Motion Picture Herald Product Digest. Feb 24, 1951, p722.
The New Republic. Feb 26, 1951, v124, p30.
The New York Times. Feb 16, 1951, p21.
The New Yorker. Feb 17, 1951, v27, p87.
Newsweek. Feb 26, 1951, v37, p80.
Saturday Review. Mar 17, 1951, v34, p34.
Time. Feb 26, 1951, v57, p100.
Variety. Feb 21, 1951, p6.

The Peach Thief (Also titled: Kradezat na Praskovi) (BULG; Raden, Veulo; 1964)
BFI/Monthly Film Bulletin. Dec 1965, v32, p180.
Filmfacts. n20, 1969, v12, p461-63.
Films and Filming. Jan 1966, v12, p26-27.
The London Times. Nov 4, 1965, p17.
Motion Picture Herald Product Digest. Sep 23, 1969, p264.
New Statesman. Nov 12, 1965, v70, p761.
Sight and Sound. Wint 1965-66, v35, p43.
The Spectator. Nov 5, 1965, v215, p586.
Variety. Sep 9, 1964, p24.

Peau de Banane *See* Banana Peel

Peau Douce, La *See* The Soft Skin

The Pedestrian (German title: Fussgaenger, Der) (WGER; Schell, Maximillian; 1973)
Atlantic Monthly. May 1974, v233, p132-35.
Christian Century. May 15, 1974, v91, p543-44.
Esquire. Jul 1974, v82, p144.
Films Illustrated. Jan 1974, v3, p271.
Films In Review. Apr 1974, v25, p243-45.
Independent Film Journal. Mar 18, 1974, v73, p9-10.
The Nation. Mar 16, 1974, v218, p349.
New Statesman. Dec 7, 1973, v86, p878.
New York. Mar 4, 1974, v7, p58-59.
The New York Times. Mar 1, 1974, v16, p1.
Saturday Review. Apr 6, 1974, v1, p50.
Time. Apr 8, 1974, v103, p63.
TV Movies. 1983-84, p589.
Variety. Feb 20, 1974, p5, 14.
The Village Voice. Mar 28, 1974, p81.

Peeping Tom (GB; Powell, Michael; 1960)
Cult Movies. p252-55.
The New York Times. Oct 14, 1980, p65.
Powell Pressburger and Others. p53-61.
Variety. Apr 20, 1960, p8.

Pee-Wee's Big Adventure (US; Burton, Tim; 1985)
Hollywood Reporter. Jul 26, 1985, p3.
The Los Angeles Times. Aug 9, 1985, SecVI, p1.
Magill's Cinema Annual, 1986. p265-70.
The New York Times. Aug 9, 1985, SecIII, p15.
The New Yorker. Nov 4, 1985, v61, p117.
Newsweek. Aug 26, 1985, v106, p63.
Time. Aug 26, 1985, p126, p64.
Variety. Jul 31, 1985, p14.
The Wall Street Journal. Aug 13, 1985, p22.

Peggy (US; De Cordova, Frederick; 1950)
Christian Century. Sep 20, 1950, v67, p1119.
Commonweal. Aug 11, 1950, v52, p437.
Film Daily. Jun 12, 1950, p7.
Hollywood Reporter. Jun 14, 1950, p4.

Motion Picture Herald Product Digest. Jun 17, 1950, p346.
The New York Times. Jul 21, 1950, p15.
Variety. Jun 14, 1950, p8.

Penelope (US; Hiller, Arthur; 1966)
BFI/Monthly Film Bulletin. Mar 1967, v34, p46.
Commonweal. Nov 25, 1966, v85, p230.
Film Daily. Nov 4, 1966, p7.
Filmfacts. Jan 1, 1967, v9, p305-06.
Hollywood Reporter. Nov 4, 1966, p3.
Life. Dec 9, 1966, v61, p19.
The London Times. Feb 16, 1967, p8.
Motion Picture Herald Product Digest. Nov 9, 1966, p626.
The New York Times. Nov 11, 1966, p36.
The New Yorker. Nov 19, 1966, v42, p183-84.
Newsweek. Dec 5, 1966, v68, p109.
Playboy. Feb 1967, v14, p22.
Variety. Nov 9, 1966, p6.
The Village Voice. Dec 8, 1966, v12, p27.

Pennies from Heaven (US; Ross, Herbert; 1982)
BFI/Monthly Film bulletin. Jul 1982, v15, p73-74.
Contemporary Review. May 1982, v240, p269-72.
Dance Magazine. Mar 1982, v56, p118-19.
Film Bulletin. Feb-Mar 1982, p55.
Film Comment. Mar-Apr 1982, v18, p45-46.
Films In Review. Apr 1982, v33, p241.
Hollywood Reporter. Dec 9, 1981, p3.
The Los Angeles Times. Dec 10, 1981, SecVI, p1.
Magill's Cinema Annual, 1982. p276-79.
The Nation. Jan 23, 1982, v234, p91.
National Review. Feb 5, 1982, v34, p123-24.
New York. Jan 11, 1982, v15, p73-74.
The New York Times. Feb 7, 1982, SecII, p12.
Photoplay. Jul 1982, v33, p26-27.
Photoplay. Jun 1982, v33, p36-38.
Rolling Stone. Feb 4, 1982, p31-32.
Theater Crafts. Jan 1982, v16, p24-25.

Penny Princess (GB; Guest, Val; 1952)
America. Apr 11, 1953, v89, p91.
BFI/Monthly Film Bulletin. Sep 1952, v19, p130.
Commonweal. May 22, 1953, v58, p181.
Film Daily. May 4, 1953, p6.
The Films of Dirk Bogarde. p61-62.
Hollywood Reporter. Aug 10, 1953, p3.
The London Times. Jul 21, 1952, p6.
Motion Picture Herald Product Digest. Apr 4, 1953, p1782.
National Parent-Teacher. Jun 1953, v47, p37.
The New Statesman and Nation. Jul 26, 1952, v44, p104.
The New York Times. Mar 25, 1953, p37.
Newsweek. Apr 20, 1953, v41, p104.
The Spectator. Jul 18, 1952, v188, p97.
The Tatler. Jul 30, 1952, v205, p202.
Variety. Jul 23, 1952, p18.

The People Against O'Hara (US; Sturges, John; 1951)
BFI/Monthly Film Bulletin. Nov 1951, v18, p358.
Christian Century. Oct 3, 1951, v68, p1143.
Film Daily. Aug 22, 1951, p6.
The Films of Spencer Tracy. p209-10.
Hollywood Reporter. Aug 21, 1951, p3.
Library Journal. Oct 15, 1951, v76, p1722.
Motion Picture Herald Product Digest. Aug 25, 1951, p989.
The Nation. Jan 5, 1952, v174, p19.
The New Statesman and Nation. Nov 3, 1951, v42, p491.
The New York Times. Sep 6, 1951, p39.

Newsweek. Sep 17, 1951, v38, p92.
Saturday Review. Sep 29, 1951, v34, p32.
The Spectator. Oct 19, 1951, v187, p504.
Time. Sep 17, 1951, v58, p110.
Variety. Aug 22, 1951, p10.

People Will Talk (US; Mankiewicz, Joseph L.; 1951)
BFI/Monthly Film Bulletin. Sep 1951, v18, p326-27.
Catholic World. Oct 1951, v174, p63.
Christian Century. Oct 10, 1951, v68, p1175.
Commonweal. Sep 14, 1951, v54, p550.
Film Daily. Aug 22, 1951, p6.
Films in Review. Oct 1951, v2, p47-48.
The Films of Cary Grant. p206-09.
Joseph L. Mankiewicz (Dick). p88-92.
The London Times. Aug 27, 1951, p8.
Motion Picture Herald Product Digest. Aug 18, 1951, p981.
The Nation. Sep 29, 1951, v173, p267.
The New Republic. Sep 24, 1951, v125, p21.
The New Statesman and Nation. Sep 1, 1951, v42, p227.
The New Yorker. Sep 1, 1951, v27, p43.
Newsweek. Aug 27, 1951, v38, p82.
Pictures Will Talk. p209-12.
Saturday Review. Sep 15, 1951, v34, p24.
Sight and Sound. Oct-Dec 1951, v21, p81.
The Spectator. Aug 24, 1951, v187, p239.
Time. Sep 17, 1951, v58, p106.
Variety. Aug 22, 1951, p10.

Pepe (US; Sidney, George; 1960)
America. Jan 14, 1961, v104, p480.
BFI/Monthly Film Bulletin. Apr 1961, v28, p45.
Chevalier. p195-96.
The Cinema of Edward G. Robinson. p208-12.
Commonweal. Jan 20, 1961, v73, p437.
Film Daily. Dec 21, 1960, p5.
Filmfacts. 1960, v3, p337.
Films and Filming. Apr 1961, v7, p29.
Films in Review. Feb 1961, v12, p108-09.
The Films of Frank Sinatra. p168-70.
The Films of Jack Lemmon. p113-15.
Hollywood Reporter. Dec 21, 1960, p3.
Life. Dec 19, 1960, v49, p43.
The New York Times. Dec 22, 1960, p18.
The New Yorker. Dec 31, 1960, v36, p50.
Newsweek. Jan 2, 1961, v57, p66.
Pepe. 1960.
Saturday Review. Jan 7, 1961, v44, p32.
Senior Scholastic. Feb 15, 1961, v78, p24.
Time. Jan 2, 1961, v77, p49.
Variety. Dec 21, 1960, p6.

Peppermint Soda (French title: Diabolo Menthe) (FR; Kurys, Diane; 1979)
BFI/Monthly Film Bulletin. Aug 1980, v47, p154-55.
Hollywood Reporter. Jul 19, 1979, p3.
The Los Angeles Times. Sep 11, 1979, SecV, p1.
Magill's Survey of Cinema. Foreign Language Films. v5, p2404-08.
The New Republic. Aug 4, 1979, v181, p31.
The New York Times. Jul 15, 1979, p32.
The New York Times. Jul 29, 1979, SecII, p17.
The New Yorker. Jul 30, 1979, v55, p71.
Newsweek. Jul 23, 1979, v94, p70-71.
Time. Sep 17, 1979, v114, p104.
Variety. Dec 21, 1977, p30.

Per Qualche Dollaro In Piu *See* For a Few Dollars More

Per un Pugno di Dolari *See* A Fistful of Dollars

Perfect (US; Brooks, James; 1985)
BFI/Monthly Film Bulletin. Aug 1985, v52, p249.

Film Comment. Jul-Aug 1985, v21, p2.
Hollywood Reporter. Jun 5, 1985, p3.
The Los Angeles Times. Jun 7, 1985, SecVI, p1.
Maclean's. Jun 10, 1985, v98, p62.
The New Republic. Jun 24, 1985, v192, p20-21.
New York. Jun 17, 1985, v18, p72-73.
The New York Times. Jun 7, 1985, SecIII, p18.
The New York Times. Jun 16, 1985, SecII, p19.
Newsweek. Jun 10, 1985, v105, p89.
Progressive. Aug 1985, v49, p38.
Rolling Stone. Jul 18, 1985, p39.
Time. Jun 10, 1985, v125, p83.
Variety. Jun 5, 1985, p16.

Perfect Strangers (US; Windust, Bretaigne; 1950)
Christian Century. Apr 19, 1950, v67, p511.
Commonweal. Mar 24, 1950, v51, p630.
Film Daily. Mar 1, 1950, p11.
The Films of Ginger Rogers. p226.
Hollywood Reporter. Feb 28, 1950, p3.
Library Journal. Apr 15, 1950, v75, p709.
Motion Picture Herald Product Digest. Mar 4, 1950, p214.
The New York Times. Mar 11, 1950, p8.
Newsweek. Mar 20, 1950, v35, p91.
Time. Mar 27, 1950, v55, p100.
Variety. Mar 1, 1950, p6.

The Perfectionist *See* Grand Patron, Un

Performance (GB; Roeg, Nicolas; Cammell, Donald; 1970)
America. Sep 6, 1970, v12, p132.
Art in America. Mar 1971, v59, p114-15.
BFI/Monthly Film Bulletin. Feb 1971, v38, n445, p27-28.
Deeper Into Movies. p156, 209.
Hollywood Reporter. Aug 3, 1970, p3, 11.
Magill's Survey of Cinema. Series I. v3, p1310.
The New York Times. Aug 4, 1970, p21.
The New York Times. Aug 16, 1970, SecII, p1.
The New York Times. Aug 23, 1970, SecII, p1.
Newsweek. Aug 17, 1970, v76, p85.
Nicholas Roeg (Feineman). p37-60.
Saturday Review. Aug 22, 1970, v53, p61.
Sight and Sound. Spr 1971, v40, n2, p67-69.
Time. Aug 24, 1970, v96, p61.
Variety. Aug 5, 1970, p20.

Period of Adjustment (US; Hill, George Roy; 1962)
America. Jan 19, 1963, v108, p119.
BFI/Monthly Film Bulletin. Mar 1963, v30, p33.
Commonweal. Dec 14, 1962, v77, p315.
Film Daily. Oct 29, 1962, p6.
Filmfacts. Nov 30, 1962, v5, p280-81.
Films and Filming. Mar 1963, v9, p38.
Films in Review. Dec 1962, v13, p627.
The Films of George Roy Hill. p31-35.
The Films of Jane Fonda. p88-92.
The Films of Tennessee Williams. p249-79.
George Roy Hill (Shores). p3.
Hollywood Reporter. Oct 29, 1962, p3.
Motion Picture Herald Product Digest. Oct 31, 1962, p681.
The New York Times. Nov 1, 1962, p34.
The New Yorker. Nov 10, 1962, v38, p234.
Newsweek. Nov 12, 1962, v60, p96.
Saturday Review. Nov 10, 1962, v45, p77.
Sight and Sound. Spr 1963, v32, p93.
Tennessee Williams and Film. p99-104.
Time. Nov 16, 1962, v80, p97.
Variety. Oct 31, 1962, p6.

The Persecution and Assassination of Jean-Paul Marat as Performed by the Inmates of the Asylum of Charenton Under the Direction of the Marquis De Sade *See* Marat/Sade

Persona (SWED; Bergman, Ingmar; 1966)
America. May 6, 1967, v116, p703.
BFI/Monthly Film Bulletin. Nov 1967, v34, p169-70.
Cahiers du Cinema in English. Sep 1967, n11, p30-33.
Christian Century. May 31, 1967, v84, p726.
Christian Science Monitor (Western edition). Nov 11, 1966, p4.
Cinema Borealis. p224-37, 304-05.
Cinema Journal. n1, 1979, v19, p71-85.
Classic Movies. p187.
Commentary. Dec 1967, v44, p80-82.
Commonweal. Mar 31, 1967, v86, p55-56.
Confessions of a Cultist. p289-92.
Esquire. Jun 1967, v67, p40.
Figures of Light. p13-18.
Film 67/68. p194-200.
Film Comment. Fall-Wint 1967, v4, p63-65.
Film Criticism. n2/3, 1978, v2, p72-77.
Film Culture. Wint-Spr 1970, n48-49, p56-60.
Film Daily. Mar 6, 1967, p3.
Film Heritage. Spr 1967, v2, p28-32.
Film Quarterly. Sum 1967, v20, p52-54.
Film Quarterly. n2, 1983/84, v37, p10-19.
Filmfacts. Apr 15, 1967, v10, p59-61.
Films and Filming. Dec 1967, v14, p20.
Films in Review. Apr 1967, v18, p244-46.
The Great Movies. p188-90.
Harper's Magazine. Jun 1967, v234, p111.
Hollywood Reporter. Apr 10, 1967, p3.
Horizon. n3, 1974, v16, p88-95.
Ingmar Bergman and Society. p86-91.
Ingmar Bergman and the Rituals of Art. p180-21.
Ingmar Bergman (Cowie). p227-38.
Ingmar Bergman Directs. p208-310.
Ingmar Bergman: Essays in Criticism. p253-69.
Ingmar Bergman (Mosely). p121-31.
Ingmar Bergman (Steene). p114-22.
Ingmar Bergman (Wood). p143-58.
The International Dictionary of Films and Filmmakers. v1, p361-62.
International Film Guide. 1968, v5, p137-38.
Kiss Kiss Bang Bang. p208-10.
Literature/Film Quarterly. Wint 1977, v5, p75-88.
Literature/Film Quarterly. Jan 1979, v7, p47-59.
Living Images. p340-50.
The London Times. May 4, 1967, p8.
The London Times. Sep 21, 1967, p8.
Magill's Survey of Cinema. Foreign Language Films. v5, p2418-21.
Motion Picture Herald Product Digest. Mar 15, 1967, p666.
Movie. Spr 1968, n15, p22-24.
Movies Into Film. p226-29.
The Nation. Mar 27, 1967, v204, p413-14.
The New Republic. May 6, 1967, v156, p31-34.
New Statesman. Sep 29, 1967, v73, p413-14.
The New York Times. Oct 20, 1966, p52.
The New Yorker. Mar 11, 1967, v43, p180-81.
Newsweek. Mar 20, 1967, v69, p102.
Playboy. Jun 1967, v14, p36.
The Private Eye, the Cowboy and the Very Naked Girl. p247-48.
Salmagundi. Wint 1978, n40, p131-41.
Saturday Review. Nov 18, 1967, v50, p40.
Sight and Sound. Aut 1967, v36, p186-91.
The Silence of God. p135-53.
Take One. n8, 1968, v1, p24-26.
Take One. Jul-Aug 1968, v1, p26-28.
Variety. Nov 30, 1966, p6.
The Village Voice. Mar 23, 1967, v12, p25.

Personal Affair (GB; Pelissier, Anthony; 1953)
America. Jun 19, 1954, v91, p338.

Film Daily. Feb 9, 1954, p8.
Films in Review. Apr 1954, v5, p194-95.
Holiday. Jul 1954, v16, p24.
Library Journal. Mar 15, 1954, v79, p541.
Motion Picture Herald Product Digest. Jan 9, 1954, p2133-34.
National Parent-Teacher. Jan 1954, v48, p40.
The New York Times. Oct 23, 1954, p13.
Newsweek. Feb 8, 1954, v43, p86.
Saturday Review. Feb 13, 1954, v37, p29.
Time. Mar 15, 1954, v63, p106.
Variety. Oct 28, 1953, p6.

Personal Best (US; Towne, Robert; 1982)
Commonweal. Apr 23, 1982, v109, p244-45.
Film Comment. May-Jun 1982, v18, p16-17.
Hollywood Reporter. Feb 3, 1982, p3.
The Los Angeles Times. Jan 31, 1982, Calendar, p29.
Maclean's. Mar 1, 1982, v95, p59.
Magill's Cinema Annual, 1983. p254-57.
The Nation. Feb 27, 1982, v234, p251-52.
The New Leader. Mar 22, 1982, v65, p21-22.
The New Republic. Mar 3, 1982, v186, p24-26.
New York. Mar 8, 1982, v15, p88.
New York Review of Books. Mar 18, 1982, v29, p45.
The New York Times. Feb 5, 1982, SecIII, p8.
The New Yorker. Feb 22, 1982, v58, p112.
Newsweek. Feb 8, 1982, v99, p60.
Rolling Stone. Apr 1, 1982, p34-35.
Rolling Stone. Apr 15, 1982, p24.
Sports Illustrated. Feb 1, 1982, p V56, p50-54.
Time. Feb 8, 1982, v119, p72.
Variety. Jan 27, 1982, p3.

Pete Kelly's Blues (US; Webb, Jack; 1955)
America. Sep 10, 1955, v93, p575.
BFI/Monthly Film Bulletin. Nov 1955, v22, n262, p165.
Catholic World. Oct 1955, v181, p59.
Commonweal. Sep 2, 1955, v62, p542.
Films and Filming. Nov 1955, v2, n2, p16.
Films in Review. Oct 1955, v6, n8, p410-11.
Hollywood Reporter. Jul 28, 1955, p3.
Life. Aug 29, 1955, v39, p109-10.
Motion Picture Herald Product Digest. Aug 6, 1955, p545.
The New York Times. Aug 19, 1955, p10.
The New Yorker. Aug 27, 1955, v31, p100.
Newsweek. Sep 5, 1955, v46, p66.
Saturday Review. Aug 27, 1955, v38, p23.
Time. Sep 12, 1955, v66, p114.
Variety. Aug 3, 1955, p6.

Pete 'n' Tillie (US; Ritt, Martin; 1972)
Films in Review. Feb 1973, v24, n2, p119.
Hollywood Reporter. Dec 11, 1972, p3.
The New Republic. Jan 20, 1973, v168, p26.
The New York Times. Dec 18, 1972, v56, p1.
The New Yorker. Dec 30, 1972, v48, p49-50.
Newsweek. Jan 1, 1973, v81, p56.
Reeling. p126-30.
Saturday Review. Feb 1973, v1, p71.
Time. Jan 8, 1973, v101, p54.
Variety. Dec 13, 1972, p15.

Peter Pan (US; Luske, Hamilton; Geronimi, Clyde; Jackson, Wilfred; 1953)
BFI/Monthly Film Bulletin. May 1953, v20, n232, p70.
Catholic World. Mar 1953, v176, p459.
Christian Century. Feb 25, 1953, v70, p239.
Commonweal. Feb 20, 1953, v57, p499.
The Disney Films. p107-09.
The Disney Version. p295-96.
Film Daily. Jan 14, 1953, p8.
Films in Review. Feb 1953, v4, n2, p94-95.
Hollywood Reporter. Jan 14, 1953, p8.
Library Journal. Feb 1, 1953, v78, p211.

The Nation. Dec 6, 1952, v175, p536.
The New York Times. Feb 12, 1953, p23.
The New York Times. Feb 15, 1953, SecII, p1.
The New York Times. Apr 12, 1953, SecII, p5.
Newsweek. Feb 16, 1953, v34, p62-63.
Saturday Review. Feb 7, 1953, v36, p27.
Theatre Arts. Feb 1953, v37, p84.
Time. Feb 2, 1953, v61, p78.
Variety. Jan 14, 1953, p6.
Walt Disney: A Guide to References and Resources. p43-45.

Pete's Dragon (US; Chaffey, Don; 1977)
American Cinematographer. Oct 1977, p1026-37.
Films in Review. Dec 1977, v28, p632.
Hollywood Reporter. Nov 7, 1977, p2.
The Los Angeles Times. Dec 16, 1977, SecIV, p22.
Motion Picture Herald Product Digest. Nov 16, 1977, p47.
The New York Times. Nov 4, 1977, SecIII, p6.
Time. Dec 5, 1977, v110, p105.
Variety. Nov 9, 1977, p16.
The Village Voice. Nov 14, 1977, p45.

Petit Monde de Don Camillo, Le *See* The Little World of Don Camillo

The Petty Girl (US; Levin, Henry; 1950)
Commonweal. Sep 1, 1950, v52, p509.
Film Daily. Aug 23, 1950, p6.
Hollywood Reporter. Aug 18, 1950, p3.
Motion Picture Herald Product Digest. Aug 19, 1950, p441.
The New York Times. Aug 18, 1950, p17.
Newsweek. Aug 21, 1950, v36, p83.
Time. Aug 28, 1950, v56, p72.
Variety. Aug 23, 1950, p8.

Petulia (GB; Lester, Richard; 1968)
BFI/Monthly Film Bulletin. Aug 1968, v35, p113.
Christian Century. Sep 4, 1968, v85, p1110.
Christian Science Monitor (Western edition). Jun 21, 1968, p6.
Cinema. Wint 1967, v3, p4-9, 33, 36.
Commonweal. Jun 28, 1968, v88, p443.
Confessions of a Cultist. p367-70.
Cult Movies. p259-62.
Esquire. Oct 1968, v70, p90.
Figures of Light. p87-91.
Film 68/69. p107-10.
Film Criticism. 1979, v4, n1, p65-73.
Film Daily. May 1, 1968, p10.
Film Quarterly. Fall 1968, v22, p67-70.
Filmfacts. Jul 1, 1968, v11, p159-61.
Films and Filming. Sep 1968, v14, p33-34.
Films in Review. Jun-Jul 1968, v19, p380-81.
The Films of the Sixties. p226-28.
Going Steady. p143-48.
Hollywood Reporter. Apr 26, 1968, p3.
Life. May 31, 1968, v64, p12.
The London Times. Jun 13, 1968, p15.
Magill's Survey of Cinema. Series I. v3, p1314-17.
Motion Picture Herald Product Digest. May 8, 1968, p808.
Movie. Wint 1968-69, n16, p16-27.
Movies Into Film. p346-47.
The Nation. Jul 8, 1968, v207, p209.
National Review. Sep 24, 1968, v20, p969.
The New Republic. Jun 29, 1968, v158, p22.
New Statesman. Jun 21, 1968, v75, p846-47.
The New York Times. Jun 11, 1968, p54.
The New York Times. Jun 23, 1968, p1.
The New Yorker. Jun 15, 1968, v44, p87.
Newsweek. Jun 17, 1968, v71, p90.
Ramparts Magazine. Aug 24, 1968, v7, p54.
Richard Lester: A Guide to References and Resources. p31-33, 73-80.

Second Sight. p187-90.
Sight and Sound. Sum 1968, v37, p154-55.
The Spectator. Jun 21, 1968, v220, p863.
Time. Jun 14, 1968, v91, p91.
Variety. May 1, 1968, p26.
The Village Voice. Jul 4, 1968, p33, 36.
Vogue. Jun 1968, v151, p82.
A Year In the Dark. p168-69.

Peyton Place (US; Robson, Mark; 1957)
America. Dec 21, 1957, v98, p383.
BFI/Monthly Film Bulletin. May 1958, v25, p58-59.
Commonweal. Dec 27, 1957, v67, p335.
Fifty from the Fifties. p219-28.
Film Daily. Dec 13, 1957, v112, p6.
Films and Filming. Apr 1958, v4, p22.
Films and Filming. Feb 1966, v12, p52.
Films in Review. Jan 1958, v9, p26-28.
The Films of Lana Turner. p212-15.
The Films of the Fifties. p211-13.
Hollywood Reporter. Dec 13, 1957, p3.
Magill's Survey of Cinema. English Language Films. Series I, v3, p1318-21.
Motion Picture Herald Product Digest. Dec 14, 1957, v209, p641.
The New Republic. Mar 17, 1958, v138, p21-22.
The New York Times. Jun 16, 1957, SecII, p7.
The New York Times. Aug 11, 1957, SecII, p5.
The New York Times. Aug 11, 1957, SecVI, p27.
The New York Times. Dec 13, 1957, p35.
The New York Times. Dec 15, 1957, SecII, p3.
The New Yorker. Dec 21, 1957, v33, p52.
Newsweek. Dec 23, 1957, v50, p76.
One Good Film Deserves Another. p84-89.
Saturday Review. Dec 28, 1957, v40, p23.
Time. Jan 6, 1958, p74.
Variety. Dec 18, 1957, p6.

Phaedra (US, FR, GREECE; Dassin, Jules; 1961)
Acid Test. p34-38.
BFI/Monthly Film Bulletin. Jan 1963, v30, p4-5.
Commonweal. Dec 14, 1962, v77, p316.
Film Daily. Oct 18, 1962, p7.
Filmfacts. Dec 7, 1962, v5, p288-90.
Films and Filming. Jan 1963, v9, p46-47.
Films in Review. Nov 1962, v13, p559-60.
Hollywood Reporter. Oct 18, 1962, p3.
Motion Picture Herald Product Digest. Oct 17, 1962, p674-75.
The New Republic. Nov 10, 1962, v147, p25-26.
The New York Times. Oct 19, 1962, p24.
The New Yorker. Oct 27, 1962, v38, p203.
Newsweek. Oct 29, 1962, v60, p87.
On Movies. p293-95.
Saturday Review. Nov 3, 1962, v45, p51.
Sight and Sound. Spr 1963, v32, p95.
Time. Oct 26, 1962, v80, p99.
Variety. Jun 6, 1962, p6.

The Phantom of the Paradise (US; De Palma, Brian; 1974)
BFI/Monthly Film Bulletin. May 1975, v42, p112.
Brian De Palma (Bliss). p30-39.
Cult Movies 2. p119-22.
The Films of the Seventies. p104-06.
Hollywood Reporter. Oct 29, 1974, p3.
The Los Angeles Times. Nov 1, 1974, SecIV, p1.
Make It Again, Sam. p139-44.
Millimeter. Dec 1974, v2, p20-23.
Motion Picture Herald Product Digest. Nov 13, 1974, p45.
New York. Nov 4, 1974, v7, p82-83.
The New York Times. Jan 25, 1974, p20.
The New York Times. Nov 2, 1974, p16.

The New Yorker. Nov 11, 1974, v50, p178-82.
Reeling. p488-94.
Rolling Stone. Dec 19, 1974, p11-12.
Senior Scholastic. Jan 16, 1975, v105, p20.
Time. Dec 2, 1974, v104, p4.
Variety. Oct 30, 1974, p42.

Phantom of the Rue Morgue (US; Del Ruth, Roy; 1954)
America. Mar 27, 1954, v90, p694.
BFI/Monthly Film Bulletin. Jul 1954, v21, p106.
Commonweal. Mar 26, 1954, v59, p627.
Film Daily. Feb 25, 1954, p10.
Hollywood Reporter. Feb 25, 1954, p3.
Library Journal. Apr 15, 1954, v79, p766.
The London Times. May 31, 1954, p3.
Motion Picture Herald Product Digest. Mar 6, 1954, p2206.
National Parent-Teacher. Apr 1954, v48, p39.
The New Statesman and Nation. Jun 5, 1954, v47, p731.
The New York Times. Mar 20, 1954, p10.
The Tatler. Jun 9, 1954, v212, p586.
Variety. Mar 3, 1954, p6.

Phffft (US; Robson, Mark; 1954)
BFI/Monthly Film Bulletin. Jan 1955, v22, p4-5.
Catholic World. Dec 1954, v180, p221.
Commonweal. Nov 26, 1954, v61, p224.
Farm Journal. Jan 1955, v79, p70.
Film Daily. Oct 21, 1954, p6.
Films and Filming. Jan 1955, v1, p20.
The Films of Jack Lemmon. p52-55.
Hollywood Reporter. Oct 19, 1954, p3.
The London Times. Dec 13, 1954, p11.
Motion Picture Herald Product Digest. Oct 23, 1954, p185.
National Parent-Teacher. Jan 1955, v49, p40.
The New Statesman and Nation. Dec 18, 1954, v48, p824, 826.
The New York Times. Nov 11, 1954, p43.
The New Yorker. Nov 20, 1954, v30, p80.
Newsweek. Nov 8, 1954, v44, p98.
Saturday Review. Nov 13, 1954, v37, p27.
Senior Scholastic. Dec 8, 1954, v65, p25.
The Tatler. Dec 22, 1954, v214, p750.
Time. Nov 15, 1954, v64, p110.
Variety. Oct 20, 1954, p6.

Phone Call From a Stranger (US; Negulesco, Jean; 1952)
Bette Davis: Her Films and Career. p156-57.
BFI/Monthly Film Bulletin. Mar 1952, v19, p31.
Catholic World. Mar 1952, v174, p458.
Christian Century. Apr 16, 1952, v69, p479.
Commonweal. Feb 15, 1952, v55, p471.
Film Daily. Jan 10, 1952, p8.
Hollywood Reporter. Jan 8, 1952, p3.
Library Journal. Feb 1, 1952, v77, p206.
The London Times. Jan 21, 1952, p2.
Motion Picture Herald Product Digest. Jan 12, 1952, p1185.
The New Republic. Feb 11, 1952, v126, p22.
The New Statesman and Nation. Jan 12, 1952, v43, p97.
The New York Times. Feb 2, 1952, p11.
The New Yorker. Feb 9, 1952, v27, p102.
Newsweek. Feb 4, 1952, v39, p78-79.
The Spectator. Jan 18, 1952, v188, p76.
Theatre Arts. Mar 1952, v36, p73.
Time. Feb 18, 1952, v59, p86.
Variety. Jan 9, 1952, p6.

The Pickpocket (FR; Bresson, Robert; 1959)
BFI/Monthly Film Bulletin. 1960, v27, p139.
Filmfacts. May 1969, v12, p18.
Films and Filming. Oct 1960, v7, p25.

Saturday Review. Feb 29, 1964, v47, p23.
Sight and Sound. Spr 1964, v33, p95-96.
Time. Apr 17, 1964, v83, p130.
Unholy Fools, Wits, Comics, Disturbers of the Peace. p50-52.
Variety. Jan 15, 1964, p6.

The Pirates of Penzance (US; Leach, Wilford; 1983)
Dance Magazine. Feb 1983, v57, p48-49.
Films in Review. Apr 1983, v34, p244.
Hollywood Reporter. Feb 17, 1983, p3.
The Los Angeles Times. Feb 22, 1983, SecVI, p1.
Magill's Cinema Annual. p301-06.
The New York Times. Feb 20, 1983, p80.
Newsweek. Feb 21, 1983, v101, p66.
Newsweek. Feb 14, 1983, v101, p85.
Time. Mar 7, 1983, v121, p69.
Vogue. Jan 1983, v173, p202-03.

Pirosmani (USSR; Shengelaya, Georgy; 1971)
Before My Eyes. p310-11.
BFI/Monthly Film Bulletin. Sep 1974, v41, p205.
The Most Important Art: East European Cinema After 1945. p331.
The New Republic. Jun 10, 1978, v178, p19.
The New York Times. Apr 5, 1975, p34.
The New York Times. May 26, 1978, SecIII, p8.
The New Yorker. Jun 5, 1978, v54, p94-96.
Variety. Jun 12, 1974, p24.

The Pit and the Pendulum (US; Corman, Roger; 1961)
America. Sep 2, 1961, v105, p693.
Commonweal. Sep 22, 1961, v74, p518.
The Films of Roger Corman. p32-33, 154-58.
The Films of the Sixties. p62-63.
The New York Times. Aug 24, 1961, p25.
The New Yorker. Sep 9, 1961, v37, p113.
Variety. Aug 9, 1961, p6.

Pity For Them *See* Olvidados, Los

Pixote (BRAZ; Babenco, Hector; 1981)
Film Journal. Sep 21, 1981, v85, p17.
Films in Review. v32, p559, p52.
The Hollywood Reporter. Sep 1, 1981, p2.
The Los Angeles Times. Oct 25, 1981, Calendar, p29.
Magill's Cinema Annual, 1982. p280-83.
New York. Oct 12, 1981, v14, p85.
The New York Times. May 5, 1981, SecIII, p6.
The New York Times. Sep 11, 1981, SecIII, p6.
The New Yorker. Nov 9, 1981, v57, p170.
Newsweek. Sep 28, 1981, v98, p88.
Rolling Stone. Nov 26, 1981, p49-50.
Variety. May 6, 1981, p21.

A Place in the Sun (US; Stevens, George; 1951)
BFI/Monthly Film Bulletin. Nov 1951, v18, p358-59.
Catholic World. Oct 1951, v174, p62-63.
Christian Century. Nov 14, 1951, v68, p1327.
Cinema, the Magic Vehicle. v2, p82-84.
Commonweal. Sep 7, 1951, v54, p524.
Cue. Sep 1, 1951, p18.
Fifty From the Fifties. p247-54.
Fifty from the Fifties. p55-58.
Film. Sum 1970, n59, p14.
Film Culture. n1, 1957, v3, p3, 25-26.
Film Daily. Jul 18, 1951, p6.
Film News. Nov-Dec 1977, v34, p25.
Films and Filming. Apr 1965, v11, p10-12.
Films in Review. Oct 1951, v2, p39-42.
The Films of Elizabeth Taylor. p88-92.
The Films of Montgomery Clift. p125-34.
The Films of the Fifties. p55-58.
George Stevens (Richie). p55-60.

Holiday. Aug 1951, v10, p6.
Illustrated London News. Jan 12, 1952, v220, p66.
The International Dictionary of Films and Filmmakers. v1, p366-67.
Library Journal. Jul 1951, v76, p1142.
Life. May 28, 1951, v30, p47-48.
Literature/Film Quarterly. Sum 1977, v5, p258-68.
Love in the Film. p235-39.
Magill's Survey of Cinema. Series I. v3, p1349-51.
Make It Again, Sam. p27-31.
Motion Picture Herald Product Digest. Jul 21, 1951, p937.
The Movie Makers. p90-91.
The New Republic. Sep 10, 1951, v125, p22.
The New Statesman and Nation. Dec 29,1951, v42, p757.
The New York Times. Aug 29, 1951, p20.
The New York Times Magazine. Jul 29, 1951, p35.
The New Yorker. Sep 8, 1951, v27, p107.
Newsweek. Sep 10, 1951, v38, p96.
Quarterly of Film, Radio and Television. Sum 1952, v6, p388-93.
Saturday Review. Sep 1, 1951, v34, p28-31.
Selected Film Criticism 1951-1960. p101.
Sight and Sound. Jan-Mar 1952, v21, p120-22.
The Spectator. Dec 21, 1951, v187, p852.
Theatre Arts. Aug 1951, v35, p16.
Time. Sep 10, 1951, v58, p96.
Variety. Jul 8, 1951, p6.

Places in the Heart (US; Benton, Robert; 1984)
BFI/Monthly Film Bulletin. Mar 1985, v52, p89.
Christian Century. Oct 3, 1984, v101, p9.
Christianity Today. Nov 9, 1984, v28, p78.
Commonweal. Nov 30, 1984, v111, p660-61.
Film Journal. Oct 1984, v87, p8-9, 15.
Films in Review. Oct 1984, v35, p495.
Hollywood Reporter. Sep 12, 1984, p3.
Informer. Sep-Oct 1984, p9-10.
The Los Angeles Times. Sep 21, 1984, SecVI, p1.
Maclean's. Sep 24, 1984, v97, p62.
Ms. Oct 1984, v13, p29.
The Nation. Oct 27, 1984, v239, p425-26.
National Review. Dec 14, 1984, v36, p49-50.
The New Republic. Oct 1, 1984, v191, p24.
New York. Oct 1, 1984, v17, p80.
The New York Times. Oct 7, 1984, SecII, p17.
The New York Times. Sep 21, 1984, SecIII, p8.
The New York Times. Sep 23, 1984, SecII, p19.
The New York Times. Oct 8, 1984, SecIII, p13.
The New York Times. Nov 23, 1984, SecIII, p13.
The New Yorker. Oct 15, 1984, v60, p170.
Newsweek. Sep 24, 1984, v104, p86.
Saturday Review. Nov-Dec 1984, v10, p66-67.
Time. Sep 24, 1984, v124, p70-71.
Variety. Sep 19, 1984, p20.
The Village Voice. Oct 2, 1984, p49.
Vogue. Oct 1984, v174, p72.
Vogue. Aug 1984, v174, p52-53.

Plaisir, Le (Also titled: House of Pleasure) (FR; Ophuls, Max; 1951)
BFI/Monthly Film Bulletin. Mar 1953, v20, p32-33.
Cinema, the Magic Vehicle. v2, p92-93.
Commonweal. Jun 4, 1954, v60, p223.
Dictionary of Films. p285-86.
Film Criticism. n3, 1980, v4, p17-24.
Film Criticism and Caricatures, 1943-1953. p153-54.
Film Daily. Jul 8, 1954, p6.

The Great French Films. p135-38.
Movie. Sum 1982, n29/30, p80-89.
The New York Times. May 20, 1954, p38.
The New Yorker. May 29, 1954, v30, p52-53.
Newsweek. Jul 19, 1954, v44, p86.
Saturday Review. Jun 5, 1954, v37, p27.
Sight and Sound. Apr-Jun 1953, v22, p195-96.
Sight and Sound. Jul-Sep 1952, v22, p32-34.
The Spectator. Feb 6, 1953, v190, p149.
The Tatler. Feb 18, 1953, v207, p284.
Time. Jun 14, 1954, v63, p110.
Variety. Mar 26, 1952, p16.

Planet of the Apes (US; Schaffner, Franklin J.; 1968)
America. Mar 2, 1968, v118, p301.
BFI/Monthly Film Bulletin. Apr 1968, v35, p52-53.
Christian Science Monitor (Western edition). Feb 9, 1968, p6.
Cineaste. Sum 1969, v3, p11-16, 33.
Commonweal. Feb 23, 1968, v87, p624-25.
Fifty Grand Movies of the 1960s and 1970s. p135-38.
Film 68/69. p63-64.
Film Daily. Feb 9, 1968, p3.
Film Quarterly. Fall 1968, v22, p56-58.
Film Quarterly. Sum 1968, v21, p60.
Filmfacts. Feb 15, 1968, v11, p15-17.
Films and Filming. Apr 1968, v14, p24-25.
Films in Review. Mar 1968, v19, p172-74.
The Films of Charlton Heston. p175-83.
The Films of the Sixties. p215-16.
Five Thousand One Nights At the Movies. p463.
Franklin J. Schaffner (Kim). p223-41.
Going Steady. p44-46.
Hollywood Reporter. Feb 5, 1968, p3.
Humanist. Jun 1968, v83, p178.
Life. May 10, 1968, v64, p20.
The London Times. Mar 21, 1968, p9.
Magill's Survey of Cinema. Series I. v3, p1355-57.
Media and Methods. Oct 1973, v10, p32-34.
Motion Picture Herald Product Digest. Feb 21, 1968, p776A.
The Nation. Mar 11, 1968, v206, p356.
The New York Times. Feb 9, 1968, p55.
The New York Times. Aug 19, 1973, p1.
The New Yorker. Feb 17, 1968, v43, p108.
Newsweek. Feb 26, 1968, v71, p84.
Science Fiction Studies in Film. p202-03.
Second Sight. p180-82.
Senior Scholastic. Mar 21, 1968, v92, p20.
Sight and Sound. Sum 1968, v37, p156.
The Spectator. Mar 29, 1968, v220, p415.
Time. Feb 23, 1968, v91, p95.
Variety. Feb 7, 1968, p6.
The Village Voice. Mar 15, 1973, p77-78.
The Village Voice. Mar 7, 1968, p41, 47-48.
A Year In the Dark. p37-38.

The Planter's Wife *See* Outpost in Malaya

Play It Again, Sam (US; Ross, Herbert; 1972)
Christian Century. Sep 13, 1972, v89, p906.
Commonweal. Jul 30, 1972, v96, p357.
Filmfacts. v15, n13, p299.
Films in Review. Jun-Jul 1972, v23, n6, p374.
The Films of The Seventies. p52-54.
Hollywood Reporter. Apr 19, 1972, p3.
Ladies Home Journal. Jul 1972, v89, p14.
Life. May 19, 1972, v72, p18.
Magill's Survey of Cinema. English Language Films. Series II, v4, p1909.
The New Republic. May 13, 1972, v166, p35.
The New York Times. May 5, 1972, v30, p1.
The New Yorker. May 13, 1972, v48, p104-06.
Newsweek. May 8, 1972, v79, p115.
Saturday Review. May 13, 1972, v55, p16-17.

Time. May 15, 1972, v99, p56.
Variety. Apr 19, 1972, p18.
Woody Allen: His Films and Career. p112-23.
Woody Allen (Palmer). p61-69.
Woody Allen's Play It Again, Sam. 1977.

Play It As It Lays (US; Perry, Frank; 1972)
Commonweal. Feb 2, 1973, v97, p398.
Filmfacts. 1972, v15, n20, p494.
Films in Review. Dec 1972, v23, n10, p644.
Harper's Bazaar. Nov 1972, v106, p135.
Life. Nov 3, 1972, v73, p16.
National Review. Jan 5, 1973, v25, p36.
The New Republic. Dec 9, 1972, v167, p22.
The New York Times. Nov 26, 1972, SecII, p9.
The New York Times. Oct 30, 1972, p36.
The New Yorker. Nov 11, 1972, v48, p155-58.
Reeling. p73-77.
Saturday Review. Dec 2, 1972, v55, p93.
Time. Nov 13, 1972, v100, p107.
Variety. Sep 13, 1972, p24.

Play Misty For Me (US; Eastwood, Clint; 1971)
BFI/Monthly Film Bulletin. Mar 1972, v39, p57.
Clint Eastwood (Guérif). p81-85.
Filmfacts. 1971, v14, p534-36.
Films and Filming. Apr 1972, v18, n7, p54.
The Films of Clint Eastwood. p124-30.
The Films of The Seventies. p35-37.
Hollywood Reporter. Sep 13, 1971, v217, n46, p3.
The New York Times. Nov 4, 1971, p52.
Newsweek. Nov 22, 1971, v78, p120.
Saturday Review. Nov 27, 1971, v54.
Variety. May 15, 1971, p6.
The Village Voice. Nov 11, 1971, v16, n45, p47.

The Playboy of the Western World (US; Hurst, Brian Desmond; 1963)
America. May 11, 1963, v108, p692.
Commonweal. Mar 29, 1963, v78, p22.
Filmfacts. May 9, 1963, v6, p75-76.
Films in Review. Jun-Jul 1963, v14, p368-70.
The New Republic. Mar 30, 1963, v148, p23.
The New York Times. Mar 19, 1963, p8.
The New Yorker. Mar 23, 1963, v39, p170.
Newsweek. Dec 24, 1962, v60, p63.
Time. Mar 28, 1963, v81, p92.

Playgirl (US; Pevney, Joseph; 1954)
BFI/Monthly Film Bulletin. Jun 1954, v21, p90.
Film Daily. May 17, 1954, p3.
Hollywood Reporter. Apr 19, 1954, p3.
Motion Picture Herald Product Digest. Apr 24, 1954, p2269.
National Parent-Teacher. Jun 1954, v48, p40.
The New York Times. May 15, 1954, p13.
Time. Jun 28, 1954, v63, p90.
Variety. Apr 21, 1954, p6.

Plaza Suite (US; Hiller, Arthur; 1971)
America. May 29, 1971, v124, p579.
Atlantic. Aug 1971, v228, p92-93.
BFI/Monthly Film Bulletin. Apr 1972, v39, p76.
Filmfacts. 1971, v14, p138-42.
Films and Filming. Jul 1972, v18, n10, p53.
Films in Review. Jun-Jul 1971, v22, n6, p362-63.
Hollywood Reporter. May 10, 1971, v216, n9, p3.
The New York Times. May 14, 1971, p46.
The New Yorker. May 15, 1971, v47, p129.
Newsweek. May 24, 1971, v77, p97.
Saturday Review. May 22, 1971, v54, p50.
Time. May 24, 1971, v97, p86.
Variety. May 12, 1971, p19.
The Village Voice. May 20, 1971, p61.

Please Believe Me (US; Taurog, Norman; 1950)
BFI/Monthly Film Bulletin. Jun 1950, v17, p87.
Film Daily. Mar 10, 1950, p8.
Hollywood Reporter. Mar 9, 1950, p3.
Motion Picture Herald Product Digest. Mar 11, 1950, p221.
The New York Times. Jun 12, 1950, p19.
Time. Jul 17, 1950, v56, p93.
Variety. Mar 11, 1950, p12.

Please Don't Eat the Daisies (US; Walters, Charles; 1960)
America. Apr 23, 1960, v103, p171.
BFI/Monthly Film Bulletin. May 1960, v27, p66.
Commonweal. Apr 15, 1960, v72, p65-66.
Coronet. Apr 1960, v47, p16.
Film Daily. Mar 22, 1960, p7.
Film Quarterly. Sum 1960, v13, p60.
Filmfacts. 1960, v3, p61.
Films and Filming. May 1960, v6, p25-26.
Films in Review. Apr 1960, v11, p236-37.
The Films of David Niven. p161-65.
The Films of Doris Day. p189-92.
Hollywood Reporter. Mar 22, 1960, p3.
The New York Times. Apr 1, 1960, p37.
The New York Times. Apr 3, 1960, SecII, p1.
The New Yorker. Apr 9, 1960, v36, p107.
Newsweek. Apr 11, 1960, v55, p121.
Variety. Mar 23, 1960, p6.

Please! Mr. Balzac (Also titled: En effeuillant la Marguerite) (FR; Allégret, Marc; 1956)
Film Daily. Dec 2, 1957, v112, p6.
Films in Review. Jan 1958, v9, p28.
Motion Picture Herald Product Digest. Nov 23, 1957, v209, p618.
The New York Times. Nov 18, 1957, p37.
Time. Nov 11, 1957, v70, p122.

The Pleasure Seekers (US; Negulesco, Jean; 1964)
BFI/Monthly Film Bulletin. Mar 1965, v32, p42-43.
Christian Science Monitor (Western edition). Jan 28, 1965, p2.
Film Daily. Dec 24, 1964, p4.
Films and Filming. Mar 1965, v11, p36-37.
Films in Review. Feb 1965, v16, p116-17.
The London Times. Jan 28, 1965, p18.
Motion Picture Herald Product Digest. Jan 6, 1965, p202.
The New York Times. Dec 26, 1964, p9.
Variety. Dec 30, 1964, p6.

Plein Soleil *See* Purple Noon

Plenty (US; Schepisi, Fred; 1985)
America. Oct 19, 1985, v153, p242.
BFI/Monthly Film Bulletin. Nov 1985, v52, p344.
Christian Century. Nov 6, 1985, v102, p987-88.
Commonweal. Oct 18, 1985, v112, p582.
Film Comment. Sep-Oct 1985, v21, p13-22.
Films in Review. Dec 1985, v36, p622.
Hollywood Reporter. Sep 9, 1985, p3.
The Los Angeles Times. Sep 18, 1985, SecVI, p1.
Maclean's. Sep 30, 1985, v98, p56.
Magill's Cinema Annual, 1986. p271-75.
Ms. Oct 1985, v14, p19-20.
National Review. Nov 1, 1985, v37, p70.
The New Republic. Sep 30, 1985, v193, p26-28.
New York. Sep 30, 1985, v18, p66-67.
The New York Times. Sep 19, 1985, SecIII, p22.
The New Yorker. Oct 7, 1985, v61, p128-31.
Newsweek. Sep 23, 1985, v106, p68.
Sight and Sound. Aut 1985, v54, p299.
Time. Oct 7, 1985, v126, p66.

Vogue. Oct 1985, v175, p99,110.
The Wall Street Journal. Sep 19, 1985, p28.

Plymouth Adventure (US; Brown, Clarence; 1952)
BFI/Monthly Film Bulletin. Jan 1953, v20, p5.
Catholic World. Dec 1952, v176, p223.
Christian Century. Dec 17, 1952, v69, 1487.
Commonweal. Dec 5, 1952, v57, p224.
Film Daily. Oct 20, 1952, p6.
The Films of Spencer Tracy. p213-14.
Hollywood Reporter. Oct 20, 1952, p3.
Library Journal. Dec 1, 1952, v77, p2066.
McCall's. Dec 1952, v80, p10-11.
Motion Picture Herald Product Digest. Oct 25, 1952, p1581.
National Parent-Teacher. Dec 1952, v47, p37.
The New York Times. Nov 14, 1952, p20.
The New Yorker. Nov 29, 1952, v28, p102.
Newsweek. Dec 1, 1952, v40, p83.
Publisher's Weekly. Oct 25, 1952, v162, p1808.
Saturday Review. Nov 29, 1952, v35, p29.
Senior Scholastic. Nov 19, 1952, v61, p22.
The Spectator. Feb 6, 1953, v190, p149.
The Tatler. Feb 18, 1953, v207, p284.
Theatre Arts. Dec 1952, v36, p84.
Time. Jun 9, 1952, v59, p102.
Time. Nov 24, 1952, v60, p108.
Variety. Oct 22, 1952, p6.

Pocketful of Miracles (US; Capra, Frank; 1961)
America. Dec 23, 1961, v106, p425.
Bette Davis: Her Films and Career. p170-72.
BFI/Monthly Film Bulletin. Jan 1962, v29, p8.
Commonweal. Dec 22, 1961, v75, p341.
Film Daily. Nov 2, 1961, p6.
Filmfacts. Jan 5, 1962, v14, p322.
Films in Review. Dec 1961, v7, p624.
The Films of Frank Capra (Scherle and Levy). p263-70.
The Films of Frank Capra (Willis). p136-44.
The New York Times. Dec 19, 1961, p39.
Newsweek. Dec 18, 1961, v58, p97.
Saturday Review. Nov 11, 1961, v44, p32.
Time. Dec 29, 1961, v78, p57.
Variety. Nov 1, 1961, p6.

Point Blank (US; Boorman, John; 1967)
BFI/Monthly Film Bulletin. Feb 1968, v35, p22-23.
Commonweal. Oct 6, 1967, v87, p24.
Film Daily. Sep 5, 1967, p6.
Film Heritage. Fall 1969, v5, p21-24.
Film Quarterly. Wint 1967-68, v21, p63.
Film Quarterly. Sum 1968, v21, p2-13, 40-42.
Film Quarterly. Wint 1968-69, v22, p2-14.
Films and Filming. Mar 1968, v14, p25-26.
Films in Review. Oct 1967, v18, p508.
Hollywood Reporter. Aug 31, 1967, p3.
Life. Oct 20, 1967, v63, p10.
Magill's Survey of Cinema. Series II. v4, p1913-15.
Motion Picture Herald Product Digest. Sep 6, 1967, p721.
The New York Times. Sep 19, 1967, p53.
The New Yorker. Sep 30, 1967, v43, p112.
Newsweek. Sep 25, 1967, v70, p107.
Saturday Review. Sep 30, 1967, v50, p36.
Second Sight. , p145-48.
Sight and Sound. Spr 1968, v37, p98.
Sight and Sound. Aut 1968, v37, p170-76.
Sight and Sound. Wint 1969-70, v39, p20-23, 37.
Variety. Sep 6, 1967, p6.
The Village Voice. Oct 19, 1967, p31.

Police Academy (US; Wilson, Hugh; 1984)
BFI/Monthly Film Bulletin. Jun 1984, v51, p181.
Film Journal. May 1984, v87, p25.

Films and Filming. Jul 1984, n358, p22.
Films in Review. Aug-Sep 1984, v35, p433-34.
The Los Angeles Times. Mar 22, 1984, SecVI, p1.
The New York Times. Mar 23, 1984, SecIII, p12.
Newsweek. Apr 30, 1984, v103, p61.
Photoplay. Aug 1984, v35, p21.
Time. Apr 23, 1984, v123, p83.
Variety. Mar 14, 1984, p22.
The Village Voice. Mar 27, 1984, p52.

Police Speciale *See* The Naked Kiss

The Policeman (Also titled: Aliza the Policeman) (ISR; Kishon, Ephraim; 1971)
Hollywood Reporter. Apr 6, 1972, p3.
The New York Times. Apr 7, 1972, p26.
Variety. Jun 26, 1972, p6.

Pollyanna (US; Swift, David; 1960)
America. May 28, 1960, v103, p320.
BFI/Monthly Film Bulletin. Sep 1960, v27, p130.
Commonweal. Jun 3, 1960, v72, p257.
The Disney Films. p170-71.
Film Daily. Apr 6, 1960, p10.
Filmfacts. 1960, v3, p103.
Films and Filming. Sep 1960, v6, p21.
Films in Review. May 1960, v11, p297-98.
Hollywood Reporter. Apr 6, 1960, p3.
McCall's. Jul 1960, v87, p6.
The New York Times. May 20, 1960, p26.
Newsweek. May 16, 1960, v55, p110.
Saturday Review. May 7, 1960, v43, p27.
Time. May 9, 1960, v75, p88.
Variety. Apr 13, 1960, p6.
Walt Disney: A Guide to References and Resources. p70-71.

Poltergeist (US; Hooper, Tobe; 1982)
America. Jun 26, 1982, v147, p14.
Atlantic. Oct 1982, v250, p101-02.
BFI/Monthly Film Bulletin. Sep 1982, v49, p205-06.
Christian Century. Jul 7, 1982, v99, p768.
Commonweal. Aug 13, 1982, v109, p442-45.
Films In Review. Aug-Sep 1982, v33, p430-31.
Hollywood Reporter. May 21, 1982, p3.
The Los Angeles Times. Jun 4, 1982, SecVI, p1.
Maclean's. Jun 7, 1982, v95, p54.
Magill's Cinema Annual, 1983. p263-66.
The Nation. Jul 10, 1982, v235, p59-60.
National Review. Jul 23, 1982, v34, p908-09.
New York. Jun 7, 1982, v15, p71-72.
The New York Times. Jun 4, 1982, SecIII, p16.
The New Yorker. Jun 14, 1982, v58, p122-25.
Newsweek. May 31, 1982, v99, p62-64.
Time. May 31, 1982, v119, p54-60.
Variety. May 24, 1982, p3.
The Village Voice. Jun 15, 1982, p59.

Polyester (US; Waters, John; 1981)
Film Comment. May-Jun 1981, v17, p27.
Horizon. Jul-Aug 1981, v24, p70-71.
New York. Jun 29, 1981, v14, p34-35.
The New York Times. Jun 7, 1981, SecII, p19.
Newsweek. Jun 1, 1981, v97, p91.
Time. Apr 27, 1981, v117, p54-55.
Variety. Apr 22, 1981, p22.
The Village Voice. Jun 3, 1981, p48.

Pony Soldier (US; Newman, Joseph M.; 1952)
Christian Century. Dec 17, 1952, v69, p1487.
Commonweal. Nov 21, 1952, v57, p165.
Film Daily. Dec 11, 1952, p6.
The Films of Tyrone Power. p176-78.
Hollywood Reporter. Nov 5, 1952, p3.
Library Journal. Dec 1, 1952, v77, p2066.

Motion Picture Herald Product Digest. Nov 8, 1952, p1597.
National Parent-Teacher. Jan 1953, v47, p37.
The New York Times. Dec 20, 1952, p15.
Variety. Nov 5, 1952, p6.

Pookie *See* The Sterile Cuckoo

Pool of London (GB; Dearden, Basil; 1951)
BFI/Monthly Film Bulletin. Mar 1951, v18, p229-30.
Film Daily. Aug 13, 1951, p6.
From Sambo to Superspade. p169-70.
Hollywood Reporter. Aug 7, 1951, p3.
The London Times. Feb 26, 1951, p6.
Motion Picture Herald Product Digest. Aug 11, 1951, p974.
The New Statesman and Nation. Mar 3, 1951, v41, p244.
The New York Times. Nov 28, 1951, p37.
The New Yorker. Dec 8, 1951, v27, p68.
Newsweek. Nov 19, 1951, v38, p102.
Saturday Review. Aug 25, 1951, v34, p24.
Sight and Sound. Apr 1951, v19, p474-75.
The Spectator. Feb 23, 1951, v186, p242.
Time. Oct 8, 1951, v58, p 116.
Variety. Feb 28, 1951, p18.

Poor Cow (GB; Loach, Kenneth; 1967)
America. Mar 2, 1968, v118, p300.
BFI/Monthly Film Bulletin. Feb 1968, v35, p23.
Christian Century. May 15, 1968, v85, p656.
Commonweal. Feb 16, 1968, v87, p593-94.
Esquire. May 1968, v69, p86.
Film Daily. Jan 22, 1968, p3.
Film Quarterly. Spr 1969, v22, p11-17.
Filmfacts. Feb 15, 1968, v11, p26-27.
Films and Filming. Apr 1968, v14, p26-27.
Films in Review. Mar 1968, v19, p181-82.
Five Thousand One Nights At the Movies. p464-65.
Going Steady. p30-33.
Hollywood Reporter. Jan 19, 1968, p3.
London Magazine. Feb 1968, v7, p78-80.
Motion Picture Herald Product Digest. Jan 31, 1968, p764.
Movies Into Film. p290-91.
The Nation. Feb 19, 1968, v206, p249.
The New Republic. Feb 10, 1968, v158, p20.
The New York Times. Feb 1, 1968, p28.
The New Yorker. Feb 3, 1968, v43, p92-93.
Newsweek. Feb 19, 1968, v71, p92.
Saturday Review. Mar 2, 1968, v51, p40.
Sight and Sound. Wint 1967-68, v37, p43.
Time. Feb 9, 1968, v91, p93.
Variety. Dec 13, 1967, p6.
The Village Voice. Feb 15, 1968, p41.
A Year In the Dark. p30-31.

The Poor Outlaws *See* The Round-Up

Pop Gear *See* Go Go Mania

The Pope of Greenwich Village (US; Rosenberg, Stuart; 1984)
BFI/Monthly Film Bulletin. Nov 1984, v51, p340.
Film Journal. Jul 1984, v87, p19.
Films and Filming. Oct 1984, n361, p45.
Hollywood Reporter. Jun 19, 1984, p4.
Life. Jul 1984, v7, p23-24.
The Los Angeles Times. Jun 22, 1984, SecVI, p1.
Maclean's. Jul 2, 1984, v97, p53.
The Nation. Jul 21, 1984, v239, p59-60.
The New Republic. Jul 16, 1984, v191, p24.
New York. Jun 25, 1984, v17, p62-63.
The New York Times. Jun 22, 1984, SecIII, p2.
The New Yorker. Jul 23, 1984, v60, p92-95.
Newsweek. Jun 25, 1984, v103, p68-69.
Photoplay. Dec 1984, v35, p19.

Time. Jun 25, 1984, v123, p68.
Variety. Jun 20, 1984, p17.
The Village Voice. Jun 26, 1984, p49.

Popeye (US; Altman, Robert; 1980)
BFI/Monthly Film Bulletin. Mar 1981, v48, p54.
Christian Century. Feb 18, 1981, v98, p180.
The Christian Science Monitor. Dec 18, 1980, p19.
Film Quarterly. Spr 1981, v35, p42.
Films in Review. Feb 1981, v31, p122.
Hollywood Reporter. Dec 9, 1980, p3.
Humanist. Mar-Apr 1981, p55-56.
Motion Picture Herald Product Digest. Dec 31, 1980, p60.
The New York Times. Dec 12, 1980, SecIII, p5.
Progressive. Feb 1981, v45, p51.
Robert Altman (Plecki). p117-28.
Variety. Dec 10, 1980, p30.
The Village Voice. Dec 17, 1980, p70.

Popi (US; Hiller, Arthur; 1969)
America. Jun 7, 1969, v120, p675-76.
Christian Century. Nov 5, 1969, v86, p1423-24.
Commonweal. Jun 27, 1969, v90, p416.
Film Daily. Apr 15, 1969, p6.
Film Quarterly. Fall 1969, v23, p53.
Filmfacts. 1969, v12, p258.
Films and Filming. May 1970, v16, p52.
Holiday. Jun 1969, v45, p22-23.
Life. May 30, 1969, v66, p16.
Look. Jun 10, 1969, v33, p16.
The New York Times. May 28, 1969, p34.
The New York Times. Jun 15, 1969, SecII, p1.
The New Yorker. May 31, 1969, v45, p81-82.
Newsweek. Jun 9, 1969, v73, p108.
Saturday Review. May 31, 1969, v52, p44.
Senior Scholastic. May 9, 1969, v94, p25.
Time. Jun 6, 1969, v93, p108.
Variety. Apr 16, 1969, p6.

Popiol y Diament *See* Ashes and Diamonds

The Poppy Is Also a Flower (Also titled: Mohn Ist Auch Eine Blume) (UN; Young, Terence; 1966)
Film Daily. Nov 1, 1966, p3.
Filmfacts. Jan 15, 1967, v10, p410-12.
The Films of Rita Hayworth. p235-37.
Motion Picture Herald Product Digest. Nov 9, 1966, p627.
The New York Times. Dec 14, 1967, p62.
Variety. Nov 23, 1966, p26.
Variety. May 18, 1966, p18.

Porgy and Bess (US; Preminger, Otto; 1959)
America. Jul 18, 1959, v101, p538-39.
The Cinema of Otto Preminger. p122-27.
Commentary. Sep 1959, v28, p246-48.
Commonweal. Aug 14, 1959, v70, p424-25.
Coronet. Jul 1959, v40, p74-83.
Cosmopolitan. Sep 1959, v147, p12.
Dance Magazine. Aug 1959, v33, p16-17.
Film Daily. Jun 25, 1959, v115, p25.
Filmfacts. Aug 5, 1959, v2, p149-52.
Films in Review. Aug-Sep 1959, v10, p419-20.
The Films of Sidney Poitier. p86-92.
From Sambo to Superspade. p207-09.
Hollywood Reporter. Jun 25, 1959, p3.
Library Journal. Jul 1959, v84, p2173.
Life. Jun 15, 1959, v46, p70-77.
Music America. Jul 1959, v79, p10.
The Musical from Broadway to Hollywood. p74-78.
The Nation. Jul 4, 1959, v189, p19.
The New Republic. Jul 13, 1959, v141, p22.
The New York Times. Jun 25, 1949, p20.
The New Yorker. Jul 4, 1959, v35, p65-66.
Newsweek. Jul 6, 1959, v54, p83.

Samuel Goldwyn (Epstein). p131-35.
Samuel Goldwyn Presents. p292-96.
Saturday Review. Jul 4, 1959, v42, p24-25.
Senior Scholastic. Sep 16, 1959, v75, p40.
Time. Jul 6, 1959, v74, p5.
Variety. Jul 1, 1959, p6.

Porky's (CAN; Clark, Bob; 1982)
Christian Century. Aug 18, 1982, v99, p868.
Hollywood Reporter. Nov 13, 1981, p25.
The Los Angeles Times. Mar 23, 1982, SecVI, p3.
Maclean's. Mar 29, 1982, v95, p63-64.
Magill's Cinema Annual, 1983. p267-69.
New York. Apr 26, 1982, v15, p99.
The New York Times. Apr 25, 1982, SecII, p15.
Newsweek. Apr 5, 1982, v99, p74.
Variety. Nov 13, 1981, p3.

Porte de Lilas *See* Gates of Paris

Portiere di Notte, Il *See* The Night Porter

Portrait in Black (US; Gordon, Michael; 1960)
America. Aug 13, 1960, v103, p542.
BFI/Monthly Film Bulletin. Nov 1960, v27, p152.
Commonweal. Aug 19, 1960, v72, p425.
Film Daily. Jun 6, 1960, p6.
Filmfacts. 1960, v3, p182.
Films and Filming. Nov 1960, v7, p34.
The Films of Anthony Quinn. p183-85.
The Films of Lana Turner. p227-30.
Hollywood Reporter. Jun 6, 1960, p3.
The New York Times. Jul 28, 1960, p19.
The New Yorker. Aug 6, 1960, v36, p55.
Time. Aug 15, 1960, v76, p62.
Variety. Jun 8, 1960, p6.

Portrait of Teresa (CUBA; Pastor, Vega; 1979)
BFI/Monthly Film Bulletin. Aug 1981, v48, p160.
International Dictionary of Films and Filmmakers. p391-92.
The New York Times. Apr 27, 1981, SecIII, p15.
Variety. Sep 5, 1979, p26.
Variety. Nov 7, 1979, p18.

The Poseidon Adventure (US; Neame, Ronald; 1972)
Commonweal. Apr 20, 1973, v98, p162.
Filmfacts. 1972, v15, n20, p477.
Films in Review. Jan 1973, v24, n1, p53.
The Films of The Seventies. p55-56.
Hollywood Reporter. Dec 8, 1972, p3.
Magill's Survey of Cinema. English Language Films. Series I, v3, p1361.
The New York Times. Dec 13, 1972, v61, p1.
The New Yorker. Dec 16, 1972, v48, p128.
Reeling. p109.
Saturday Evening Post. Fall 1972, v244, p68.
Saturday Review. Mar 1973, v1, p51-52.
Saturday Review. Feb 1973, v1, p71.
Senior Scholastic. Mar 5, 1973, v102, p18.
Time. Dec 18, 1972, v100, p79-80.
Variety. Dec 13, 1972, p15.

The Postman Always Rings Twice (US; Rafelson, Bob; 1981)
America. Apr 11, 1981, v144, p301.
Christian Century. May 27, 1981, v98, p619.
Commonweal. May 22, 1981, v108, p305-06.
Film Comment. Mar-Apr 1981, v17, p18-20, 25-28.
Hollywood Reporter. Mar 13, 1981, p3.
Horizon. Apr 1981, v24, p70-71.
The Los Angeles Times. Mar 20, 1981, SecVI, p1.
Maclean's. Mar 23, 1981, v94, p58-59.

Magill's Cinema Annual, 1982. p284-87.
The Nation. Apr 4, 1981, v232, p412-13.
The New Leader. Mar 23, 1981, v64, p21-22.
The New Republic. Apr 11, 1981, v184, p26-27.
New York. Mar 30, 1981, v14, p39-41.
The New York Times. Mar 20, 1981, SecIII, p12.
The New Yorker. Apr 6, 1981, v57, p160.
Newsweek. Mar 23, 1981, v97, p81.
Rolling Stone. Apr 30, 1981, p38-39.
Saturday Review. Apr 1981, v8, p84-85.
Time. Mar 23, 1981, v117, p62.
Variety. Mar 13, 1981, p3.

Posto, Il (Also titled: Sound of Trumpets) (IT; Olmi, Ermanno; 1961)
BFI/Monthly Film Bulletin. Mar 1962, v29, p36.
Commonweal. Aug 9, 1963, v78, p480.
Film and the Critical Eye. p430-57.
Film Quarterly. Sum 1964, v17, p44-45.
Films and Filming. Apr 1962, v8, p31.
Films in Review. Dec 1963, c v14, p629.
Italian Cinema (Bondanella). p173-75.
Magill's Survey of Cinema. Foreign Language Films. v6, p2842-46.
Motion Picture Herald Product Digest. Oct 30, 1963, p923.
The Nation. Nov 30, 1963, v197, p373.
The New Republic. Aug 17, 1963, v149, p27.
The New York Times. Oct 23, 1963, p36.
The New Yorker. Oct 26, 1963, v39, p205-06.
Newsweek. Oct 7, 1963, v62, p111.
Private Screenings. p82-85.
Saturday Review. Aug 17, 1963, v46, p14.
Sight and Sound. Spr 1964, v33, p78-81.
Time. Nov 1, 1963, v82, p109.
Variety. Sep 6, 1961, p6.
The Village Voice. Oct 31, 1963, p13.

Potè Tin Kyriaki *See* Never on Sunday

Practice Makes Perfect (French title: Cavaleur, La) (FR; Broca, Philippe de; 1979)
Films in Review. Oct 1980, v31, p498.
Hollywood Reporter. May 29, 1980, p3.
The Los Angeles Times. Jul 31, 1980, Calendar, p32.
The New York Times. Jul 13, 1980, p32.
Variety. Jan 24, 1979, p23.

The Premature Burial (US; Corman, Roger; 1962)
BFI/Monthly Film Bulletin. Nov 1962, v29, p156.
Film Daily. Mar 15, 1962, p7.
Filmfacts. Jun 15, 1962, v5, p117-18.
Films and Filming. Nov 1962, v9, p41.
The Films of Roger Corman. p32-34, 158-59.
Motion Picture Herald Product Digest. Mar 14, 1962, p476-77.
Movie. Nov 1962, n4, p35.
The New York Times. May 24, 1962, p29.
Newsweek. Apr 2, 1962, v59, p87.
Variety. Mar 14, 1962, p6.

Prenom Carmen *See* First Name Carmen

Preparez vos mouchers *See* Get Out Your Handkerchiefs

The President's Analyst (US; Flicker, Theodore J.; 1967)
America. Jan 20, 1968, v118, p95.
BFI/Monthly Film Bulletin. Dec 1968, v35, p195.
Commonweal. Feb 9, 1968, v87, p564.
Film Daily. Dec 21, 1967, p4.
Film Quarterly. Spr 1968, v21, p60-61.
Films and Filming. Jan 1969, v15, p49-50.
Films in Review. Feb 1968, v19, p114-15.

Hollywood Reporter. Dec 20, 1967, p3.
Life. Jan 26, 1968, v64, p8.
Magill's Survey of Cinema. Series II. v4, p1916-18.
Motion Picture Herald Product Digest. Jan 3, 1968, p755-56.
The New York Times. Dec 22, 1967, p44.
The New Yorker. Jan 6, 1968, v43, p74.
Saturday Review. Jan 6, 1968, v51, p38.
Sight and Sound. Sum 1968, v37, p155-56.
Take One. 1968, v1, n9, p22.
Time. Jan 5, 1968, v91, p74.
Variety. Dec 20, 1967, p14.

Pretty Baby (US; Malle, Louis; 1978)
America. Apr 22, 1978, v138, p328.
BFI/Monthly Film Bulletin. Nov 1979, v46, p231.
Cult Movies 2. p128-31.
Encore. May 22, 1978, v7, p34.
Film Comment. May 1978, v14, p61-66.
Films in Review. Jun-Jul 1978, v29, p372.
Hollywood Reporter. Apr 5, 1978, p8.
The Los Angeles Times. Apr 15, 1978, SecII, p11.
Maclean's. May 15, 1978, v91, p84.
Magill's Cinema Annual, 1985. p597-601.
Motion Picture Herald Product Digest. Apr 12, 1978, p85.
Ms. Apr 1978, v6, p28.
The Nation. Apr 22, 1978, v226, p484-85.
The New Republic. Apr 15, 1978, v178, p18-19.
New York. Apr 17, 1978, v11, p97-98.
The New Yorker. Apr 10, 1978, v54, p126-27.
Newsweek. Apr 10, 1978, v91, p106-07.
Rolling Stone. Apr 6, 1978, p39-41.
Saturday Review. May 27, 1978, v5, p40-41.
Time. Apr 10, 1978, v111, p70.
Variety. Apr 5, 1978, p23.

Pretty Maids All in a Row (US; Vadim, Roger; 1971)
BFI/Monthly Film Bulletin. Dec 1971, v38, p245.
Commonweal. May 14, 1971, v94, p239.
Filmfacts. 1971, v14, p38-40.
Films and Filming. Jan 1972, v18, n4, p56-57.
Hollywood Reporter. Mar 9, 1971, v215, n15, p3.
The New York Times. Apr 29, 1971, p46.
Time. May 10, 1971, v97, p100.
Variety. Aug 3, 1971, p22.
The Village Voice. May 6, 1971, v16, n18, p65.

Pretty Poison (US; Black, Noel; 1968)
BFI/Monthly Film Bulletin. Apr 1969, v36, p73-74.
Christian Science Monitor (Western edition). Oct 4, 1968, p8.
Cinema. 1969, v5, n2, p28-30.
Cult Movies. p271-73.
Film 68/69. p176-78.
Film Daily. Oct 14, 1968, p23.
Film Quarterly. Sum 1969, v22, p59-60.
Filmfacts. Jan 15, 1969, v11, p453-54.
Films and Filming. May 1969, v15, p39.
Films in Review. Feb 1969, v20, p115-16.
The Films of the Sixties. p239-40.
Five Thousand One Nights At the Movies. p470.
Going Steady. p204-07.
Hollywood Reporter. Dec 28, 1967, p3.
Jump Cut. Sum 1976, n10/11, p41-43.
The London Times. Feb 27, 1969, p7.
Motion Picture Herald Product Digest. Sep 18, 1968, p19.
The Nation. Dec 9, 1968, v207, p637-38.
New Statesman. Mar 7, 1969, v77, p338.
The New York Times. Oct 24, 1968, p55.
The New Yorker. Nov 2, 1968, v44, p180-81.
Sight and Sound. Spr 1969, v38, p99.

The Spectator. Mar 7, 1969, v222, p314.
Time. Nov 22, 1968, v92, p85.
Variety. Sep 18, 1968, p6.
The Village Voice. Dec 5, 1968, p49.

The Pride and the Passion (US; Kramer, Stanley; 1957)
America. Jul 20, 1957, v97, p432.
BFI/Monthly Film Bulletin. Nov 1957, v24, p136.
Commonweal. Jul 19, 1957, v66, p400.
Film Daily. Jun 26, 1957, v111, p7.
Films and Filming. Nov 1957, v4, p25.
Films in Review. Aug-Sep 1957, v8, p349-50.
The Films of Cary Grant. p222-26.
The Films of Frank Sinatra. p123-27.
The Films of Sophia Loren. p78-80.
Hollywood Reporter. Jun 26, 1957, p3.
Motion Picture Herald Product Digest. Jul 7, 1957, v208, p443.
The Nation. Jul 20, 1957, v185, p38.
The New York Times. Jun 29, 1957, p10.
The New York Times. Jul 7, 1957, SecII, p1.
The New Yorker. Jul 13, 1957, v33, p48-49.
Newsweek. Jul 8, 1957, v50, p88.
Saturday Review. Jul 13, 1957, v40, p25.
Time. Jul 8, 1957, v70, p70.
Variety. Jun 26, 1957, p6.

The Pride of St. Louis (US; Jones, Harmon; 1952)
BFI/Monthly Film Bulletin. Oct 1952, v19, p145.
Christian Century. May 14, 1952, v69, p599.
Film Daily. Feb 27, 1952, p6.
Hollywood Reporter. Feb 25, 1952, p3.
Motion Picture Herald Product Digest. Mar 1, 1952, p1253.
The Nation. May 13, 1952, v174, p534.
The New York Times. May 3, 1952, p17.
Newsweek. Apr 21, 1953, v39, p120.
Saturday Review. May 17, 1952, v35, p25.
Senior Scholastic. May 14, 1952, v60, p25.
Time. May 12, 1952, v59, p107.
Variety. Feb 27, 1952, p6.

Priest of Love (GB; Miles, Christopher; 1981)
The Los Angeles Times. Oct 6, 1981, SecVI, p2.
Magill's Cinema Annual, 1982. p288-91.
National Review. Dec 11, 1981, v33, p1498.
The New Republic. Oct 21, 1981, v185, p20-21.
The New York Times. Oct 11, 1981, SecIII, p1.
Saturday Review. Oct 1981, v8, p60.
Variety. Sep 30, 1981, p3.

The Priest's Wife (Also titled: Moglie del Prete, La) (IT; Risi, Dino; 1971)
America. Mar 20, 1971, v124, p292.
BFI/Monthly Film Bulletin. Apr 1971, v318, p80.
Commonweal. May 14, 1971, v94, p239.
Filmfacts. 1971, v14, p32-34.
Films in Review. Apr 1971, v22, n4, p236.
Hollywood Reporter. Feb 26, 1971, v215, n8, p3.
The New Republic. Apr 3, 1971, v164, p24.
The New York Times. Feb 27, 1971, p20.
The New York Times. Mar 7, 1971, SecII, p1.
Newsweek. Mar 15, 1971, v77, p110.
Saturday Review. Mar 20, 1971, v54, p21.
Time. Mar 15, 1971, v97, p85.
Variety. Jan 20, 1971, p22.

Prima Angelica, La *See* Cousin Angelica

Prima Communione (Also titled: First Communion; His Majesty Mr. Jones; Father's Dilemma) (IT; Blasetti, Alessandro; 1950)

BFI/Monthly Film Bulletin. Sep 1952, v19, p124.
Catholic World. Dec 1952, v176, p224.
Film Daily. Oct 23, 1952, p6.
Hollywood Quarterly. Sum 1951, v5, p389-400.
The London Times. Jul 28, 1952, p8.
Motion Picture Herald Product Digest. Oct 4, 1952, p1550.
The New Statesman and Nation. Jul 26, 1952, v44, p104.
The New York Times. Sep 23, 1952, p25.
The New Yorker. Oct 4, 1952, v28, p74.
Saturday Review. Oct 18, 1952, v35, p30.
The Spectator. Jul 25, 1952, v189, p129.
The Tatler. Aug 6, 1952, v205, p246.
Variety. Nov 1, 1950, p18.
Variety. Oct 1, 1952, p22.

Prima della Rivoluzione *See* Before the Revolution

The Prime of Miss Jean Brodie (GB; Neame, Ronald; 1969)
America. Mar 15, 1969, v120, p312-13.
Atlantic. Sep 1969, v224, p123-24.
Big Screen, Little Screen. p149-51.
Christian Century. Apr 16, 1969, v86, p521-22.
Commonweal. Mar 28, 1969, v90, p48-49.
Double Takes. p34-35.
Fifty Classic British Films. p130-32.
Figures of Light. p140-42.
Film Daily. Feb 20, 1969, p5.
Film Quarterly. Spr 1969, v22, p63.
Filmfacts. 1969, v12, p25.
Films and Filming. May 1969, v15, p54-55.
Films in Review. Apr 1969, v20, p250-52.
Focus. Oct 1969, n5, p34.
Going Steady. p355-58.
Holiday. Apr 1969, v45, p40.
Hollywood Reporter. Feb 13, 1969, p3.
Look. Apr 1, 1969, v33, p76.
Magill's Survey of Cinema. Series I. v3, p1371-72.
Movies Into Film. p46-47.
National Review. Jun 17, 1969, v21, p606.
The New Republic. Mar 1, 1969, v160, p20.
The New York Times. Mar 3, 1969, p30.
The New Yorker. Mar 15, 1969, v45, p160-61.
Newsweek. Apr 7, 1969, v73, p82.
Redbook. May 1969, v133, p38.
Saturday Review. Mar 8, 1969, v52, p36.
Senior Scholastic. May 9, 1969, v94, p25.
Time. Feb 19, 1969, p6.
Variety. Feb 19, 1969, p6.
Vogue. Apr 1, 1969, v153, p154.

The Prince and the Showgirl (GB; Olivier, Laurence; Bushell, Anthony; 1957)
America. Jul 6, 1957, v97, p392.
BFI/Monthly Film Bulletin. Jul 1957, v24, p84.
Commonweal. Jun 21, 1957, v66, p303.
Film Daily. May 15, 1957, v111, p6.
Films and Filming. Jul 1957, v3, p21-22.
Films in Review. Aug-Sep 1957, v8, p347-48.
The Films of Laurence Olivier. p120-23.
The Films of Marilyn Monroe. p135-40.
Hollywood Reporter. May 15, 1957, p3.
Laurence Olivier (Hirsch) p113-17.
Laurence Olivier: Theater and Cinema. p132-37.
Motion Picture Herald Product Digest. May 18, 1957, v207, p377.
The Nation. Jun 29, 1957, v184, p574.
The New York Times. Jun 14, 1957, p22.
The New Yorker. Jun 22, 1957, v33, p74.
Newsweek. Jun 17, 1957, v49, p111.
Saturday Review. Jun 8, 1957, v40, p30.
Sight and Sound. Sum 1957, v27, p409-41.
Time. Jun 24, 1957, v69, p84.
Variety. May 15, 1957, p6.

The Prince of Players (US; Dunne, Philip; 1955)
America. Jan 22, 1955, v92, p434-35.
BFI/Monthly Film Bulletin. Apr 1955, v22, n253, p52.
Catholic World. Feb 1955, v180, p383.
Commonweal. Jan 28, 1955, v61, p455.
Films and Filming. Mar 1955, v1, n6, p24.
Films and Filming. Sep 1955, v1, n12, p21.
Films in Review. Feb 1955, v6, n2, p79-81.
Life. Jan 24, 1955, v38, p55-56.
Motion Picture Herald Product Digest. Jan 8, 1955, p273.
The Nation. Jan 22, 1955, v180, p84.
The New York Times. Jan 12, 1955, p24.
The New York Times. Jan 16, 1955, SecII, p1.
The New Yorker. Jan 22, 1955, v30, p87.
Newsweek. Jan 24, 1955, v45, p94.
Saturday Review. Jan 22, 1955, v38, p44.
Sight and Sound. Spr 1955, v24, n4, p196-97.
Time. Feb 7, 1955, v65, p68-69.
Variety. Jan 5, 1955, p58.

Prince of the City (US; Lumet, Sidney; 1981)
America. Oct 3, 1981, v145, p184.
American Heritage. Dec 1981, v33, p70-71.
Commonweal. Oct 23, 1981, v108, p596-97.
Encore. Oct 1981, v10, p43.
Hollywood Reporter. Aug 13, 1981, p7.
Horizon. Sep 1981, v24, p30.
Horizon. Oct 1981, v24, p70-71.
The Los Angeles Times. Aug 27, 1981, SecVI, p1.
Maclean's. Aug 31, 1981, v94, p57-58.
Magill's Cinema Annual, 1982. p292-93.
The Nation. Sep 12, 1981, v233, p219.
National Review. Oct 16, 1981, v33, p1217-18.
The New Leader. Sep 21, 1981, v64, p21-22.
The New Republic. Sep 9, 1981, v185, p24.
New York. Aug 10, 1981, v14, p54-55.
New York. Aug 24, 1981, v14, p65-67.
New York. Aug 31, 1981, v14, p28-30.
New York Review of Books. Oct 22, 1981, v28, p59.
The New York Times. Aug 19, 1981, SecIII, p17.
Newsweek. Aug 24, 1981, v98, p67-68.
Progressive. Nov 1981, v45, p50.
Rolling Stone. Sep 17, 1981, p36.
Saturday Review. Aug 1981, v8, p60.
Time. Aug 17, 1981, v118, p68.
Variety. Aug 10, 1981, p3.

Prince Valiant (US; Hathaway, Henry; 1954)
America. Apr 24, 1954, v91, p117.
BFI/Monthly Film Bulletin. Jun 1954, v21, p85-86.
Catholic World. May 1954, v179, p143.
Commonweal. Apr 16, 1954, v60, p41.
Film Daily. Apr 2, 1954, p6.
Films in Review. May 1954, v5, p241-42.
Hollywood Reporter. Apr 2, 1954, p3.
Library Journal. Apr 15, 1954, v79, p766.
Life. Jan 25, 1954, v36, p108-10.
The London Times. May 3, 1954, p4.
Look. Dec 29, 1953, v17, p34-35.
Motion Picture Herald Product Digest. Apr 10, 1954, p2254-55.
National Parent-Teacher. Jun 1954, v48, p38.
The New Statesman and Nation. May 1, 1954, v47, p598.
The New York Times. Apr 7, 1954, p40.
The New Yorker. Apr 10, 1954, v30, p93.
Newsweek. Apr 19, 1954, v43, p106-07.
The Tatler. May 12, 1954, v212, p356.
Time. Apr 12, 1954, v63, p106.
Variety. Apr 7, 1954, p6.

The Prince Who Was a Thief (US; Maté, Rudolph; 1951)
BFI/Monthly Film Bulletin. Aug 1951, v18, p314.
Commonweal. Aug 3, 1951, v54, p407.
Film Daily. Jun 4, 1951, p6.
Hollywood Reporter. May 31, 1951, p3.
Library Journal. Jun 15, 1951, v76, p1037.
The London Times. Jul 23, 1951, p2.
Motion Picture Herald Product Digest. Jun 9, 1951, p879.
The New Republic. Jul 30, 1951, v125, p23.
Newsweek. Jul 19, 1951, v38, p95.
Time. Jul 23, 1951, v58, p85.
Tony Curtis: The Man and His Movies. p32-33.
Variety. Jun 6, 1951, p6.

Princess of the Nile (US; Jones, Harmon; 1954)
BFI/Monthly Film Bulletin. Oct 1954, v21, p148-49.
Film Daily. Jun 23, 1954, p10.
Hollywood Reporter. Jun 11, 1954, p3.
Motion Picture Herald Product Digest. Jun 19, 1954, p33.
National Parent-Teacher. Sep 1954, v49, p39.
The New York Times. Jun 12, 1954, p13.
Variety. Jun 16, 1954, p6.

Princess Yang Kwei Fei (Japanese title: Yokihi; Yang Kwei Fei) (JAPAN; Mizoguchi, Kenji; 1955)
Film Daily. Sep 17, 1956, p6.
The New York Times. Sep 11, 1956, p41.
Newsweek. Sep 24, 1956, v48, p114.
Saturday Review. Sep 29, 1956, v39, p22.
Time. Oct 1, 1956, v68, p90.
Variety. May 30, 1962, p6.
The Village Voice. Jun 29, 1972, p69.

Prise de Pouvoir par Louis XIV, La *See* The Rise of Louis XIV

The Prisoner of Second Avenue (US; Frank, Melvin; 1975)
BFI/Monthly Film Bulletin. Mar 1975, v42, p61.
Films in Review. Mar 1975, v26, p183.
The Films of Jack Lemmon. p222-28.
Hollywood Reporter. Dec 20, 1974, p3.
The Los Angeles Times. Mar 19, 1975, SecIV, p1.
Motion Picture Herald Product Digest. Feb 12, 1975, p70.
The New York Times. Mar 15, 1975, p18.
The New Yorker. Mar 10, 1975, v51, p68.
Newsweek. Mar 17, 1975, v85, p92.
Reeling. p600-04.
Saturday Review. Mar 8, 1975, v2, p36.
Variety. Dec 25, 1974, p16.

Prisoner of War (US; Marton, Andrew; 1954)
America. May 22, 1954, v91, p229.
BFI/Monthly Film Bulletin. Apr 1955, v22, p53.
Catholic World. May 1954, v179, p145.
Commonweal. Apr 9, 1954, v60, p15.
Film Daily. Apr 22, 1954, p7.
Films in Review. Jun-Jul 1954, v5, p305-06.
The Films of Ronald Reagan. p206-09.
Hollywood Reporter. Mar 24, 1954, p3.
Motion Picture Herald Product Digest. Apr 3, 1954, p2245.
National Parent-Teacher. May 1954, v48, p40.
The New York Times. May 10, 1954, p20.
Newsweek. May 17, 1954, v43, p101.
Saturday Review. Apr 17, 1954, v37, p24.
Variety. Mar 24, 1954, p6.

The Prisoner of Zenda (US; Thorpe, Richard; 1952)
BFI/Monthly Film Bulletin. Jan 1953, v20, p10.
Catholic World. Dec 1952, v176, p222.
Commonweal. Nov 21, 1952, v57, p165.
Film Daily. Oct 14, 1952, p6.
The Films of James Mason. p104-05.
Hollywood Reporter. Oct 14, 1952, p3.
Library Journal. Nov 15, 1952, v77, p1981.
The London Times. Jan 9, 1953, p9.
Make It Again, Sam. p151-56.
McCall's. Nov 1952, v80, p7.
Motion Picture Herald Product Digest. Oct 18, 1952, p1565.
National Parent-Teacher. Dec 1952, v47, p37.
The New York Times. Nov 5, 1952, p36.
The New York Times. Nov 15, 1952, v28, p72.
Saturday Review. Nov 8, 1952, v35, p33.
The Spectator. Jan 9, 1953, v190, p35-36.
The Tatler. Jan 21, 1953, v207, p110.
Time. Nov 3, 1952, v60, p100.
Variety. Oct 15, 1952, p6.

Prisonnière, La (Also titled: Women in Chains) (FR; Clouzot, Henri-Georges; 1968)
Commonweal. May 23, 1969, v90, p294.
Film Quarterly. Fall 1969, v23, p53-54.
Filmfacts. 1969, v12, p126.
Life. May 9, 1969, v96, p15.
Movies Into Film. p145.
The Nation. Apr 7, 1969, v208, p444.
The New York Times. Mar 27, 1969, p52.
The New Yorker. Apr 12, 1969, v45, p173.
Newsweek. Apr 14, 1969, v73, p115A.
Take One. 1970, v2, p25-26.
Time. Apr 11, 1969, v93, p104.
Variety. Nov 27, 1968, p6.
Vogue. May 1969, v153, p136.

Private Benjamin (US; Zieff, Howard; 1980)
America. Nov 29, 1980, v143, p352.
BFI/Monthly Film Bulletin. Feb 1981, v48, p32.
Cineaste. Wint 1980-81, p32.
Films in Review. Feb 1981, v32, p122.
Hollywood Reporter. Oct 7, 1980, p3.
The Los Angeles Times. Oct 10, 1980, SecVI, p1.
Motion Picture Herald Product Digest. Oct 22, 1980, p39.
New York. Nov 10, 1980, v13, p70.
The New York Times. Oct 10, 1980, SecIII, p6.
The New Yorker. Nov 10, 1980, v56, p203-05.
Newsday. Oct 10, 1980, SecII, p7.
Newsweek. Oct 20, 1980, v96, p84.
Time. Nov 24, 1980, v116, p102-03.
Variety. Oct 8, 1980, p20.
The Village Voice. Oct 22, 1980, p48.

The Private Eyes *See* The Great Spy Chase

A Private Function (GB; Mowbray, Malcolm; 1985)
BFI/Monthly Film Bulletin. Nov 1984, v51, p340.
Commonweal. Apr 19, 1985, v112, p246.
Films and Filming. Dec 1984, n363, p42.
Hollywood Reporter. Mar 15, 1985, p3.
The Los Angeles Times. Apr 24, 1985, SecVI, p1.
Maclean's. Apr 15, 1985, v98, p57.
Magill's Cinema Annual, 1986. p280-83.
The New York Times. Mar 1, 1985, SecIII, p14.
The New Yorker. Mar 25, 1985, v61, p108-09.
Newsweek. Mar 18, 1985, v105, p71.
Time. Mar 18, 1985, v125, p84.
Variety. Jan 2, 1985, p7.

The Village Voice. Mar 5, 1985, p56.
Vogue. Apr 1985, v175, p80.

Private Hell 36 (US; Siegel, Don; 1954)
America. Sep 18, 1954, v91, p601.
BFI/Monthly Film Bulletin. Dec 1954, v21, p179-80.
Film Daily. Sep 1, 1954, p6.
Hollywood Reporter. Aug 31, 1954, p3.
Motion Picture Herald Product Digest. Sep 4, 1954, p129.
National Parent-Teacher. Nov 1954, v49, p40.
The New York Times. Sep 4, 1954, p6.
A Reference Guide to the American Film Noir. p141.
Time. Sep 27, 1954, v64, p98.
Variety. Sep 1, 1954, p6.

Private Life *See* A Very Private Affair

The Private Life of Sherlock Holmes (GB; Wilder, Billy; 1970)
BFI/Monthly Film Bulletin. Jan 1971, v38, p11-12.
Billy Wilder (Dick). p106-09.
Film Quarterly. Spr 1971, v24, p45-48.
Films in Review. Nov 1970, v21, p575-76.
The Films of Sherlock Holmes. p315-22.
Magill's Survey of Cinema. Series II. v4, p1936-38.
The New York Times. Oct 30, 1970, p26.
The New Yorker. Nov 14, 1970, v46, p168.
Newsweek. Nov 2, 1970, v76, p108.
Saturday Review. Dec 5, 1970, v53, p44.
Sherlock Holmes on the Screen. p219-24.
Sight and Sound. Wint 1970-71, v40, p47-48.
Talking Pictures. p156-61.
Variety. Oct 28, 1970, p17.

The Prize (French title: Rosier de Madame Husson, Le; Also titled: The Virtuous Isidore) (FR; Boyer, Jean; 1950)
BFI/Monthly Film Bulletin. Apr 1953, v20, p49-50.
Hollywood Reporter. May 23, 1952, p4.
The New York Times. Apr 30, 1952, p33.
The New Yorker. May 10, 1952, v28, p87.
Newsweek. May 26, 1952, v39, p92.
Saturday Review. May 24, 1952, v35, p33.
Variety. Apr 30, 1952, p18.

The Prize (US; Robson, Mark; 1963)
BFI/Monthly Film Bulletin. Mar 1964, v31, p37.
Film Daily. Dec 4, 1963, p4.
Films and Filming. Mar 1964, v10, p24.
The Films of Paul Newman. p126-30.
Magill's Survey of Cinema. Series II. v4, p1941-43.
The New York Times. Jan 24, 1964, p21.
The New York Times. Feb 2, 1964, SecII, p1.
Newsweek. Jan 13, 1964, v63, p74.
Photoplay. Jan 1964, v65, p20.
Saturday Review. Jan 18, 1964, v47, p27.
Signt and Sound. Spr 1964, v33, p99.
Time. Jan 24, 1964, v83, p52.
Variety. Dec 4, 1963, p6.

Prizzi's Honor (US; Huston, John; 1985)
BFI/Monthly Film Bulletin. Oct 1985, v52, p331.
Christian Century. Jul 17, 1985, v102, p685.
Commonweal. Jul 12, 1985, v112, p407-08.
Film Comment. May-Jun 1985, v21, p53-61.
Film Comment. Sep-Oct 1985, v21, p4.
Films in Review. Aug 1985, v36, p428.
Hollywood Reporter. Jun 5, 1985, p3.
The Los Angeles Times. Jun 14, 1985, SecVI, p1.
Maclean's. Jun 17, 1985, v98, p54.
Magill's Cinema Annual, 1986. p285-89.
National Review. Jul 26, 1985, v37, p48-51.

Fifty Grand Movies of the 1960s and 1970s. p149-54.
Film and Literature: An Introduction. p206-15.
Film Daily. Jun 17, 1960, p8.
Film Quarterly. Fall 1960, v14, p47-49.
Filmfacts. 1960, v3, p153.
Filmguide to Psycho. 1973.
Films and Filming. Sep 1960, v6, p21.
Films in Review. Aug-Sep 1960, v11, p426-27.
The Films of Alfred Hitchcock. p216-20.
The Films of the Sixties. p36-38.
Great Film Directors. p496-509.
The Great Movies. p202-03.
Hitchcock (Truffaut). p189.
Hitchcock's Films. p106-14.
Hollywood Reporter. Jun 17, 1960, p3.
The International Dictionary of Films and Filmmakers. v1, p375-77.
Magill's Survey of Cinema. Series I. SecIII, p1391-94.
The Movies on Your Mind. p106-37.
The Nation. Jul 2, 1960, v191, p18.
The New Republic. Aug 29, 1960, v143, p21-22.
The New York Times. Jun 17, 1960, p37.
The New York Times. Jun 26, 1960, SecII, p1.
The New Yorker. Jun 25, 1960, v36, p70.
Newsweek. Jun 27, 1960, v55, p92.
Reruns. p116-21.
Sight and Sound. Aut 1960, v29, p195-96.
Surrealism and the Cinema. p97-101.
Time. Jun 27, 1960, v75, p51.
Twenty-Four Times A Second. p85.
Variety. Jun 22, 1960, p6.

Psycho II (US; Franklin, Richard; 1983)
Commonweal. Jul 15, 1983, v110, p399-401.
Films in Review. Aug-Sep 1983, v35, p440.
Hollywood Reporter. Jun 3, 1983, p4.
The Los Angeles Times. Jun 3, 1983, SecVI, p1.
Maclean's. Jun 13, 1983, v96, p54.
Magill's Cinema Annual, 1984. p307-12.
The New York Times. Jun 3, 1983, SecII, p14.
Newsweek. Jun 13, 1983, v101, p78.
Time. Jun 20, 1983, v121, p54.

Pugni in Tasca, I *See* Fists in the Pocket

Pulp (US; Hodges, Mike; 1973)
Commentary. Mar 1973, v55, p79.
Esquire. Jun 1973, v79, p62.
Filmfacts. 1973, v16, n3, p76.
The New York Times. Feb 9, 1973, v32, p1.
Time. Feb 26, 1973, v101, p54.
TV Movies. 1983-84, p617.
Variety. Aug 30, 1973, p18.

Pumping Iron (US; Fiore, Robert; Butler, George; 1977)
America. Feb 12, 1977, v136, p135-36.
BFI/Monthly Film Bulletin. Nov 1977, v44, p239.
Maclean's. Sep 5, 1977, v57, p90.
New Statesman. Sep 30, 1977, v94, p453.
The New York Times. Jan 19, 1977, SecIII, p20.
The New York Times. Feb 6, 1977, SecII, p1.
Newsweek. Jan 24, 1977, v89, p61.
Time. Mar 21, 1977, v109, p89.
Variety. Jul 19, 1977, p22.
The Village Voice. Jan 31, 1977, p83.

Pumping Iron II: The Women (US; Butler, George; 1985)
BFI/Monthly Film Bulletin. Nov 1985, v52, p346.
Film Comment. Jul-Aug 1985, v21, p60-64.
Hollywood Reporter. May 9, 1985, p3.
The Los Angeles Times. May 24, 1985, SecVI, p1.
Ms. Jul 1985, v14, p84-86.
New York. May 6, 1985, v18, p76.
The New York Times. May 3, 1983, SecIII, p5.

The New Yorker. May 20, 1985, v61, p34-35.
Progressive. Aug 1985, v49, p38.
Time. May 6, 1985, v125, p86.
Variety. May 1, 1985, p13.
Vogue. Jun 1985, v175, p54.
Women's Sports. Jun 1985, v6, p60.

The Pumpkin Eater (GB; Clayton, Jack; 1964)
America. Nov 28, 1964, v111, p723.
BFI/Monthly Film Bulletin. Sep 1964, v31, p131-32.
Commonweal. Nov 27, 1964, v81, p332.
Film Daily. Oct 23, 1964, v125, p6.
Films and Filming. Aug 1964, v10, p20-21.
Films in Review. Dec 1964, v15, p633.
Hollywood Reporter. Oct 23, 1964, v182, p3.
Jack Clayton: A Guide to References and Resources. p29-33.
Life. Nov 13, 1964, v57, p15.
Magill's Survey of Cinema. Series II. v4, p1947-49.
Making Pictures: The Pinter Screenplays. p27-41.
Motion Picture Herald Product Digest. Oct 28, 1964, v232, p154.
The New Republic. Dec 19, 1964, v151, p28-29.
The New York Times. Nov 10, 1964, p58.
The New Yorker. Nov 14, 1964, v40, p148-49.
Newsweek. Nov 16, 1964, v64, p102.
On Movies. p398-400.
Saturday Review. Nov 21, 1964, v47, p34.
Time. Nov 13, 1964, v84, p125.
Variety. May 20, 1964, p20.
Vogue. Jan 1, 1964, v145, p66.

Purple Noon (French title: Plein Soleil; Also titled: Blazing Sun) (FR; Clément, René; 1961)
BFI/Monthly Film Bulletin. Jul 1961, v28, p94.
Commonweal. Sep 8, 1961, v74, p497.
Esquire. Jan 1962, v57, p30.
Film Daily. Aug 16, 1961, p6.
Filmfacts. Nov 16, 1961, v4, p264-66.
Films in Review. Oct 1961, v7, p491.
The Nation. Sep 30, 1961, v193, p214.
The New York Times. Sep 1, 1961, p12.
The New Yorker. Sep 2, 1961, v37, p62.
Newsweek. Aug 21, 1961, v58, p91.
Saturday Review. Sep 23, 1961, v44, p26.
Time. Aug 18, 1961, v78, p60.
Variety. Mar 23, 1960, p6.

Purple Rain (US; Magnoli, A.; 1984)
BFI/Monthly Film Bulletin. Oct 1984, v51, p310-11.
Christian Century. Nov 21, 1984, v101, p1106-07.
Essence. Nov 1984, v15, p56.
Film Journal. Sep 1984, v87, p59-60.
Films in Review. Oct 1984, v35, p470-73, 496-97.
Hollywood Reporter. Jul 13, 1984, p4.
Informer. Aug 1984, p4.
Jet. Aug 27, 1984, v66, p46-47.
The Los Angeles Times. Jul 27, 1984, SecVI, p1.
Maclean's. Aug 13, 1984, v97, p53.
The Nation. Sep 22, 1984, v239, p251-53.
New York. Aug 13, 1984, v17, p50-51.
The New York Times. Jul 27, 1984, SecIII, p5.
The New York Times. Dec 14, 1984, SecIII, p10.
The New York Times. Aug 12, 1984, SecII, p17.
The New York Times. Jul 22, 1984, SecII, p19.
The New Yorker. Aug 20, 1984, v60, p84.
Newsweek. Jul 23, 1984, v104, p65.
On Location. Oct 1984, v8, p197.
Photoplay. Nov 1984, v35, p30-33.
Rolling Stone. Aug 16, 1984, p31.

Rolling Stone. Aug 30, 1984, p16-17.
Time. Aug 6, 1984, v124, p62.
Variety. Jul 4, 1984, p16.
The Village Voice. Jul 31, 1984, p55.

Purple Rose of Cairo (US; Allen, Woody; 1985)
America. Apr 1985, v152, p284.
Atlantic. May 1985, v255, p94-96.
BFI/Monthly Film Bulletin. Jun 1985, v52, p203.
Christian Century. Apr 24, 1985, v102, p424.
Commonweal. Apr 19, 1985, v112, p245-46.
Films in Review. Jun 1985, p36, p365.
The Los Angeles Times. Mar 1, 1985, SecVI, p1.
Maclean's. Mar 11, 1985, v98, p63.
Magill's Cinema Annual, 1986. p290-94.
National Review. May 3, 1985, v37, p56-57.
New York. Mar 11, 1985, v18, p97-98.
The New York Times. Feb 24, 1985, SecII, p1.
The New York Times. Mar 17, 1985, SecII, p19.
The New Yorker. Mar 25, 1985, v61, p104.
Newsweek. Feb 25, 1985, v105, p84.
The Progressive. May 1985, v49, p38-39.
Sight and Sound. Sum 1985, v54, p219.
Time. Mar 4, 1985, v125, p78-79.
Variety. Jun 30, 1985, p18.
Vogue. Mar 1985, v175, p92.

Pursuit of the Graf Spee (Also titled: The Battle of the River Plate) (GB; Powell, Michael; Pressburger, Emeric; 1957)
America. Nov 16, 1957, v98, p227.
BFI/Monthly Film Bulletin. Dec 1956, v23, p148.
Commonweal. Jan 24, 1958, v67, p432.
Film Daily. Oct 17, 1957, v107, p8.
Films and Filming. Dec 1956, v3, p22.
Films in Review. Dec 1957, v8, p224-25.
Motion Picture Herald Product Digest. Oct 19, 1957, v209, p569.
The Nation. Jan 11, 1958, v186, p39.
The New Republic. Mar 3, 1958, v138.
The New York Times. Dec 27, 1957, p23.
The New Yorker. Jan 11, 1958, v33, p102.
Newsweek. Jan 13, 1958, v51, p88.
Saturday Review. Sep 14, 1957, v40, p30.
Time. Jan 27, 1958, v71, p90.

Pushover (US; Quine, Richard; 1954)
BFI/Monthly Film Bulletin. Oct 1954, v21, p144.
Catholic World. Sep 1954, v179, p465.
Farm Journal. Sep 1954, v78, p140.
Film Daily. Jul 27, 1954, p6.
Films and Filming. Nov 1954, v1, p20-21.
Hollywood Reporter. Jul 23, 1954, p3.
Motion Picture Herald Product Digest. Jul 24, 1954, p81.
National Parent-Teacher. Sep 1954, v49, p39.
The New York Times. Jul 31, 1954, p6.
Newsweek. Aug 16, 1954, v44, p82.
A Reference Guide to the American Film Noir. p143-44.
Saturday Review. Aug 14, 1954, v37, p24.
Sight and Sound. Jan-Mar 1955, v24, p144.
Variety. Jul 28, 1954, p6.

Putney Swope (US; Downey, Robert; 1969)
Christian Century. Oct 22, 1969, v86, p1352.
Cineaste. Wint 1969-70, v3, p17-18.
Commonweal. Sep 5, 1969, v90, p544.
Figures of Light. p189-90.
Film 69/70. p157-64.
Film Daily. Jul 29, 1969, p20.
Filmfacts. 1969, v12, p361.
Life. Aug 22, 1969, v67, p16.
Magill's Survey of Cinema. Series II. v5, p1955-57.
Movie Comedy. p115-16.

Rabbit Run (US; Smight, Jack; 1971)
Filmfacts. 1971, v14, p491-93.
The Modern American Novel and the Movies.
p247-55.
Variety. Nov 4, 1970, p26.
Vogue. Feb 1, 1971, v157, p139.

Rachel, Rachel (US; Newman, Paul; 1968)
America. Sep 14, 1968, v119, p195.
BFI/Monthly Film Bulletin. Nov 1968, v35,
p174.
Christian Century. Oct 16, 1968, v85, p1306-07.
Christian Science Monitor (Western edition).
Sep 18, 1968, p10.
Commonweal. Sep 27, 1968, v88, p661.
Film 68/69. p116-19.
Film Daily. Aug 22, 1968, p9.
Film Quarterly. Fall 1968, v22, p77.
Filmfacts. Sep 1, 1968, v11, p223-26.
Films and Filming. Feb 1969, v15, p38-39.
Films in Review. Oct 1968, v19, p517.
The Films of Paul Newman. p170-74.
The Films of the Sixties. p249-50.
Hollywood Reporter. Aug 21, 1968, p3.
Life. Oct 4, 1968, v65, p14.
The London Times. Oct 3,1968, p8.
Magill's Survey of Cinema. Series II. v5, p1958-
61.
Motion Picture Herald Product Digest. Aug 28,
1968, p847.
Movie. Wint 1968-69, n16, p39.
Movies Into Film. p317-18.
The New Republic. Sep 7, 1968, v159, p28.
New Statesman. Oct 4, 1968, v76, p439.
The New York Times. Aug 27, 1968, p36.
The New Yorker. Sep 7, 1968, v44, p85-86.
Newsweek. Sep 16, 1968, v72, p96.
Saturday Review. Aug 24, 1968, v51, p28.
Second Sight. p198-201.
The Spectator. Oct 11, 1968, v221, p519.
Take Twenty Two. p58-59.
Time. Sep 6, 1968, v92, p78.
Variety. Aug 21, 1968, p6.
A Year In the Dark. p220-21.

Racing With the Moon (US; Benjamin,
Richard; 1984)
BFI/Monthly Film Bulletin. Aug 1984, v51,
p247-48.
Film Journal. May 1984, v87, p26.
Films and Filming. Jul 1984, n358, p22-23.
Films in Review. May 1984, v35, p305-06.
Informer. Apr 1984, p2-3.
The Los Angeles Times. Mar 23, 1984, SecVI,
p1.
Maclean's. Mar 26, 1984, v97, p53.
National Review. Jun 15, 1984, v36, p54-55.
The New Leader. Apr 16, 1984, v67, p18-19.
The New Republic. Apr 9, 1984, v190, p24.
New Statesman. Sep 14, 1984, v108, p34-35.
New York. Apr 2, 1984, v17, p71.
The New York Times. Mar 23, 1984, SecIII, p5.
The New Yorker. Apr 2, 1984, v60, p121-23.
Newsweek. Apr 2, 1984, v103, p85.
Photoplay. Sep 1984, v35, p40-41.
Time. Apr 2, 1984, v123, p89.
Variety. Feb 29, 1984, p15.
The Village Voice. May 1, 1984, v29, p47.
Vogue. Mar 1984, v174, p94.

The Racket (US; Cromwell, John; 1951)
BFI/Monthly Film Bulletin. Feb 1952, v19,
p16.
Catholic World. Dec 1951, v174, p223.
Film Daily. Oct 18, 1951, p10.
The Great Gangster Pictures. p326-27.
Hollywood Reporter. Oct 12, 1951, p3.
Library Journal. Dec 15, 1951, v76, p2110.
Motion Picture Herald Product Digest. Oct 20,
1951, p1065.

The New York Times. Dec 13, 1951, p44.
Time. Dec 10, 1951, v58, p109.
Variety. Oct 17, 1951, p6.

Rage (Spanish title: Mal, El) (US, MEX;
Gazcon, Gilberto; 1966)
BFI/Monthly Film Bulletin. Dec 1966, v33,
p187.
Christian Science Monitor (Western edition).
Dec 5, 1966, p14.
Film Daily. Nov 28, 1966, p7.
Filmfacts. Nov 1, 1967, v10, p269-70.
Hollywood Reporter. Nov 28, 1966, p3.
Motion Picture Herald Product Digest. Dec 14,
1966, p640.
Variety. Nov 30, 1966, p6.

Rage au Corps, La (Also titled: Tempest in
the Flesh) (FR; Habib, Ralph; 1954)
The New Statesman and Nation. May 7, 1955,
v49, p648.
The New York Times. Jan 19, 1957, p12.
The New Yorker. Jan 26, 1957, v32, p94.
The Tatler. May 11, 1955, v216, p354-55.
Variety. Mar 31, 1954, p6.

A Rage to Live (US; Grauman, Walter;
1965)
Cinema. Dec-Jan 1964-65, v2, p50.
Film Daily. Sep 15, 1965, p5.
Films and Filming. Mar 1965, v10, p18.
Films and Filming. Apr 1966, v12, p18.
Films in Review. Nov 1965, v16, p579-80.
Hollywood Reporter. Sep 15, 1965, p3.
The London Times. Jan 20, 1966, p17.
Motion Picture Herald Product Digest. Sep 29,
1965, p379-80.
The New York Times. Oct 21, 1965, p57.
Playboy. Apr 1965, v12, p24, 26.
Variety. Sep 15, 1965, p6.
The Village Voice. Nov 25, 1965, v11, p22.
Vogue. Nov 1, 1965, v146, p116.

Raggedy Man (US; Fisk, Jack; 1981)
Christian Century. Oct 21, 1981, v98, p107.
The Hollywood Reporter. Aug 26, 1981, p3.
The Los Angeles Times. Oct 16, 1981, SecVI,
p1.
Maclean's. Oct 19, 1981, v94, p66.
Magill's Cinema Annual, 1982. p300-03.
The New York Times. Sep 18, 1981, SecIII, p10.
Newsweek. Oct 5, 1981, v98, p78.
Rolling Stone. Nov 12, 1981, p45.
Time. Sep 28, 1981, v118, p87.
Variety. Aug 26, 1981, p3.

Raging Bull (US; Scorsese, Martin; 1980)
America. Dec 20, 1980, v143, p412.
BFI/Monthly Film Bulletin. Feb 1981, v48,
p32.
Christian Century. Mar 25, 1981, v98, p332.
The Christian Science Monitor. Dec 4, 1980,
p19.
Cineaste. Wint 1980-81, p28.
Commonweal. Jan 16, 1981, v108, p20-21.
Encore. Dec 1980, v9, p45.
Film Comment. Jan-Feb 1981, v17, p11-15.
Films in Review. Jun 1981, v32, p54.
Hollywood Reporter. Nov 10, 1980, p2.
Horizon. Jan 1981, v24, p70.
The Los Angeles Times. Nov 9, 1980, Calendar,
p1.
Maclean's. Dec 1, 1980, v93, p73.
Martin Scorsese and Michael Cimino. p124-33.
Motion Picture Herald Product Digest. Dec 3,
1980, p49.
The Nation. Dec 13, 1980, v231, p652-53.
National Review. Jan 23, 1981, v33, p52.
National Review. Mar 20, 1981, v33, p303-04.
The New Leader. Dec 1, 1980, v63, p18-19.
The New Republic. Dec 6, 1980, v183, p26-27.

New York. Dec 1, 1980, v13, p61-63.
The New York Times. Nov 14, 1980, SecIII,
p11.
The New Yorker. Dec 8, 1980, v56, p217-18.
Newsday. Nov 14, 1980, SecII, p7.
Newsweek. Nov 24, 1980, v96, p128-29.
Progressive. Feb 1981, v45, p50-51.
Sports Illustrated. Dec 1, 1980, v53, p87.
Time. Nov 24, 1980, v116, p100.
Variety. Nov 12, 1980, p26.
The Village Voice. Nov 19, 1980, p55.

Ragtime (US; Forman, Milos; 1981)
American Film. Dec 1981, v7, p38-43.
American Heritage. Apr-May 1982, v33, p42-43.
BFI/Monthly Film Bulletin. Mar 1982, v49,
p46-47.
Double Exposure. p132-37.
Essence. Jan 1982, v12, p13.
Film Comment. Jan-Feb 1982, v18, p11-15.
Hollywood Reporter. Nov 13, 1981, p3.
The Los Angeles Times. Nov 15, 1981,
Calendar, p29.
Magill's Cinema Annual, 1982. p304-07.
Ms. Feb 1982, v10, p25.
National Review. Feb 5, 1982, v34, p122-23.
The New Leader. Jan 25, 1982, v65, p21.
The New York Times. Mar 1, 1981, SecVI, p28-
31.
The New York Times. Nov 20, 1981, SecIII,
p10.
The New York Times. Dec 6, 1981, SecII, p21.
The New York Times. Nov 17, 1981, SecIII,
p11.
The New York Times. Dec 12, 1981, p21.
Penthouse. Feb 1982, v13, p50-51.
Rolling Stone. Feb 18, 1982, p28.
Sight and Sound. Wint 1980, v50, p36-37.
Theater Crafts. Jan 1982, v16, p16-21.
Variety. Nov 18, 1981, p14.
The Village Voice. Nov 18, 1981, p57.

The Raid (US; Fregonese, Hugo; 1954)
America. Sep 18, 1954, v91, p601.
BFI/Monthly Film Bulletin. Oct 1954, v21,
p145.
Commonweal. Sep 10, 1954, v60, p557.
Film Daily. Jul 23, 1954, p10.
Motion Picture Herald Product Digest. Jul 31,
1954, p89.
National Parent-Teacher. Oct 1954, v49, p38.
The New York Times. Aug 21, 1954, p10.
Newsweek. Aug 23, 1954, v44, p76.
Variety. Jun 2, 1954, p6.

Raid on Rommel (US; Hathaway, Henry;
1971)
BFI/Monthly Film Bulletin. Feb 1972, v39,
p36.
Filmfacts. 1971, v14, p182-83.
Hollywood Reporter. Feb 19, 1971, p3.
The New York Times. Apr 24, 1971, p17.
Newsweek. May 17, 1971, v77, p105.
Variety. Feb 24, 1971, p18.

Raiders of the Lost Ark (US; Spielberg,
Steven; 1981)
America. Jul 4, 1981, v145, p15.
BFI/Monthly Film Bulletin. Aug, 1981, v48,
p159-60.
Christian Century. Aug 12, 1981, v98, p810.
Christianity Today. Aug 7, 1981, v25, p48.
Commentary. Aug 1981, v72, p61-63.
Commonweal. Aug 28, 1981, v108, p470-71.
Film Comment. Jul-Aug 1981, v17, p58-59.
Hollywood Reporter. Jun 5, 1981, p3.
Humanist. Sep-Oct 1981, v41, p53-54.
*The International Dictionary of Films and
Filmmakers.* v1, p382-83.
The Los Angeles Times. Jun 7, 1981, Calendar,
p1.

Magill's Cinema Annual, 1982. p308-11.
The New Leader. Jun 29, 1981, v64, p19-20.
The New Republic. Jul 4, 1981, v185, p26-27.
New York. Jun 15, 1981, v14, p68.
The New York Times. Jun 12, 1981, SecIII, p10.
The New Yorker. Jun 15, 1981, v57, p132-35.
Newsweek. Jun 15, 1981, v97, p58-61.
Progressive. Aug 1981, v45, p54.
Raiders of the Lost Ark: An Illustrated Screenplay. 1981.
Rolling Stone. Jun 25, 1981, p20-24.
Saturday Review. Jun 1981, v8, p12-15.
Time. Jun 15, 1981, v117, p74-76.
Variety. Jun 5, 1981, p3.

The Railroad Man (Also titled: Man of Iron; Ferroviere, Il; The Railwayman) (IT; Germi, Pietro; 1956)
America. Nov 27, 1965, v113, p693-94.
BFI/Monthly Film Bulletin. Mar 1963, v30, p31.
Christian Science Monitor (Western edition). Jan 7, 1966, p4.
Commonweal. Nov 19, 1965, v83, p217.
Film Daily. Oct 11, 1965, p12.
Films and Filming. Mar 1963, v9, p35.
Italian Cinema (Leprohon). p158-60.
Motion Picture Herald Product Digest. Oct 27, 1965, p394-95.
The Nation. Nov 15, 1965, v201, p372.
The New York Times. Oct 25, 1965, p46.
Time. Oct 8, 1965, v86, pLA7.
Variety. Jun 13, 1956, p20.

The Rain People (US; Coppola, Francis Ford; 1969)
Christian Century. Dec 31, 1969, v86, p1673.
Cult Movies. p278-81.
Film Daily. Jun 23, 1969, p4.
Filmfacts. 1969, v12, p443.
Films in Review. Oct 1969, v20, p515.
Focus. Oct 1969, n5, p20-21.
Francis Ford Coppola: A Guide to References and Resources. p44-45.
Holiday. Oct 1969, v46, p52.
Hollywood Reporter. Jun 18, 1969, p3.
Magill's Survey of Cinema. Series II. v5, p1972-75.
The New York Times. Aug 28, 1969, p46.
Newsweek. Sep 8, 1969, v74, p82.
Popular Photography. Oct 1969, v65, p116.
Variety. Jun 25, 1969, p18.

The Rainbow Jacket (GB; Dearden, Basil; 1954)
BFI/Monthly Film Bulletin. Jul 1954, v21, p102.
The London Times. May 27, 1954, p4.
The New Statesman and Nation. Jun 5, 1954, v47, p731.
The Spectator. Jun 4, 1954, v192, p678.
The Tatler. Jun 9, 1954, v212, p586.
Variety. Jun 9, 1954, p6.

Rainbow 'Round My Shoulder (US; Quine, Richard; 1952)
BFI/Monthly Film Bulletin. Oct 1952, v19, p145.
Film Daily. Aug 19, 1952, p7.
Hollywood Reporter. Aug 6, 1952, p3.
The London Times. Sep 15, 1952, p10.
Motion Picture Herald Product Digest. Aug 9, 1952, p1477.
National Parent-Teacher. Sep 1952, v47, p37.
Variety. Aug 6, 1952, p6.

The Rainmaker (US; Anthony, Joseph; 1956)
America. Jan 5, 1957, v96, 399.

Burt Lancaster: A Pictorial Treasury of His Films. p90-93.
Burt Lancaster: The Man and His Movies. p72-74.
Commonweal. Jan 11, 1957, v65, p384.
Film Daily. Dec 12, 1956, p10.
Films and Filming. Mar 1957, v3, p23.
Films in Review. Jan 1957, v8, p32.
The Films of Katharine Hepburn. p159-62.
Hollywood Reporter. Dec 12, 1956, p3.
Magill's Survey of Cinema. Series I. v3, p1419-23.
The New York Times. Dec 13, 1956, p51.
The New Yorker. Dec 22, 1956, v32, p64.
Newsweek. Dec 24, 1956, v48, p69.
Saturday Review. Dec 22, 1956, v39, p33.
Time. Dec 31, 1956, v68, p46.
Variety. Dec 12, 1956, p6.

Raintree County (US; Dmytryk, Edward; 1958)
America. Dec 21, 1957, v98, p384.
BFI/Monthly Film Bulletin. Jul 1958, v25, p85-86.
Commonweal. Jan 17, 1958, v67, p409.
Film Daily. Oct 4, 1957, v112, p10.
Films in Review. Jan 1958, v9, p31-33.
The Films of Elizabeth Taylor. p125-30.
The Films of Montgomery Clift. p157-66.
Hollywood Reporter. Oct 4, 1957, p3.
Motion Picture Herald Product Digest. Oct 12, 1957, v209, p562.
The New Republic. Nov 11, 1957, v137, p22.
The New York Times. Dec 21, 1957, p22.
The New Yorker. Jan 11, 1958, v33, p102.
Newsweek. Oct 21, 1957, v50, p112.
Saturday Review. Nov 22, 1957, v40, p23.
Time. Jan 6, 1958, v71, p76.
Variety. Oct 9, 1957, p6.

Raise the Titanic (GB; Jameson, Jerry; 1980)
BFI/Monthly Film Bulletin. Dec 1980, v47, p241.
Hollywood Reporter. Aug 1, 1980, p2.
The Los Angeles Times. Aug 1, 1980, SecVI, p1.
Maclean's. Aug 11, 1980, v93, p55.
Motion Picture Herald Product Digest. Aug 6, 1980, p19.
The New Republic. Aug 30, 1980, v183, p24-25.
New York. Aug 18, 1980, v13, p71.
The New York Times. Aug 1, 1980, SecIII, p8.
Newsweek. Aug 18, 1980, v96, p85.
Variety. Aug 6, 1980, p22.

A Raisin in the Sun (US; Petrie, Daniel; 1961)
America. Apr 8, 1961, v105, p133-34.
BFI/Monthly Film Bulletin. Jul 1961, v28, p95.
Commonweal. Apr 7, 1961, v74, p46.
Ebony. Apr 1961, v16, p53-56.
Film Daily. Mar 29, 1961, p6.
Filmfacts. May 5, 1961, v4, p77-79.
Films in Review. May 1961, v7, p298.
The Films of Sidney Poitier. p97-100.
From Sambo to Superspade. p226-27.
Life. Apr 21, 1961, v50, p52D.
Magill's Survey of Cinema. Series I. v3, p1422-24.
The New Republic. Mar 20, 1961, v144, p19.
The New York Times. Mar 30, 1961, p24.
The New York Times. Jul 17, 1960, SecII, p5.
The New York Times. Apr 2, 1961, SecII, p1.
The New Yorker. Apr 8, 1961, v37, p164.
Newsweek. Apr 10, 1961, v57, p103.
Saturday Review. Mar 25, 1961, v44, p34.
Time. Mar 31, 1961, v77, p64.

Rambo: First Blood, Part II (US; Cosmatos, George P.; 1985)
BFI/Monthly Film Bulletin. Jul 1985, v52, p225.
Business Week. Aug 26, 1985, p109.
Commonweal. Jun 21, 1985, v112, p374-75.
Commonweal. Sep 20, 1985, v112, p499.
Hollywood Reporter. May 20, 1985, p3.
Life. Aug 1985, v8, p11.
The Los Angeles Times. May 22, 1985, SecVI, p1.
Maclean's. Jul 29, 1985, v98, p7.
Magill's Cinema Annual, 1986. p299-303.
Ms. Aug 1985, v14, p71-72.
The Nation. Jun 22, 1985, v240, p776-78.
The New Republic. Jul 1, 1985, v193, p16.
New York. Jun 3, 1985, v18, p72-73.
The New York Times. May 22, 1985, SecIII, p23.
The New Yorker. Jun 17, 1985, v61, p117.
Newsweek. May 27, 1985, v105, p74-75.
Newsweek. Jun 3, 1985, v105, p62-63.
Saturday Review. Jul-Aug 1985, v114, p93-94.
Sight and Sound. Aut 1985, v54, p300.
Time. May 27, 1985, v125, p91.
Time. Jun 24, 1985, v125, p72-73.
Variety. May 22, 1985, p14.

Ran (Also titled: Chaos) (JAPAN; Kurosawa, Akira; 1985)
America. Mar 29, 1985, v154, p249.
American Film. Sep 1985, v10, p20.
Film Comment. Sep-Oct 1985, v21, p48.
Film Comment. Nov 1985, v21, p60-61.
Films in Review. Jan 1986, v37, p40.
Hollywood Reporter. Jun 6, 1985, p3.
The Los Angeles Times. Dec 24, 1985, SecVI, p1.
Maclean's. Jan 6, 1986, v99, p79.
Magill's Cinema Annual, 1986. p304-08.
The New Republic. Jan 6, 1986, v194, p26-28.
New York. Sep 30, 1985, v18, p64-65.
New York. Jan 6, 1986, v19, p56-57.
The New York Times. Sep 27, 1985, SecIII, p14.
The New Yorker. Jan 13, 1986, v61, p64.
Newsweek. Jan 6, 1986, v107, p64-65.
Theatre Crafts. Feb 1986, v20, p88-93.
Time. Dec 30, 1985, v126, p83.
Variety. Jun 5, 1985, p14.
Vogue. Dec 1985, v175, p68.
The Wall Street Journal. Jan 9, 1986, p16.
World Press Review. Sep 1985, v32, p56.

Rancho Notorious (US; Lang, Fritz; 1952)
BFI/Monthly Film Bulletin. May 1952, v19, p61.
Catholic World. Apr 1952, v175, p64.
Christian Century. Apr 15, 1952, v69, p479.
The Cinema of Fritz Lang. p174-79.
The Films of Fritz Lang. p234-36.
Fritz Lang: A Guide to References and Resources. p105-08.
Fritz Lang (Eisner). p301-12.
Fritz Lang in America. p77-80.
Hollywood Reporter. Feb 6, 1952, p4.
Magill's Survey of Cinema. Series II. v5, p1976-78.
Marlene Dietrich (Dickens). p192-95.
Motion Picture Herald Product Digest. Feb 9, 1952, p1229.
Movietone News. Oct 11, 1976, n52, p16-23.
The New Statesman and Nation. Apr 19, 1952, v43, p463.
The New York Times. May 15, 1952, p39.
Newsweek. Mar 24, 1952, v39, p113.
The Tatler. Apr 23, 1952, v204, p190.
Time. Mar 10, 1952, v59, p104.
Variety. Feb 6, 1952, p6.

Rapture (IT; Allesandrini, Goffredo; 1949)
Film Daily. Apr 11, 1950, p6.
Hollywood Reporter. Apr 3, 1950, p3.
The London Times. Jul 2, 1951, p4.
Motion Picture Herald Product Digest. Apr 15, 1950, p263.
The New York Times. Dec 14, 1950, p51.
Variety. Mar 9, 1949, p20.

Rapture (FR, US; Guillermin, John; 1965)
America. Sep 18, 1965, v113, p297.
BFI/Monthly Film Bulletin. Dec 1967, v34, p191.
Christian Science Monitor (Western edition). Jan 20, 1966, p6.
Commonweal. Sep 17, 1965, v82, p666.
Film Daily. Aug 18, 1965, p6.
Films and Filming. Feb 1965, v11, p53-55.
Films in Review. Oct 1965, v16, p517.
Motion Picture Herald Product Digest. Aug 18, 1965, p345.
The New Republic. Sep 25, 1965, v153, p35.
The New York Times. Oct 25, 1965, p46.
The New Yorker. Sep 4, 1965, v41, p86.
Newsweek. Sep 13, 1965, v66, p88.
Playboy. Nov 1965, v12, p56.
Saturday Review. Sep 11, 1965, v48, p51.
Time. Aug 27, 1965, v86, p82.
Variety. Aug 25, 1965, p6.

The Rare Breed (US; McLaglen, Andrew V.; 1966)
BFI/Monthly Film Bulletin. Aug 1966, v33, p127.
Christian Science Monitor (Western edition). May 4, 1966, p6.
Film Daily. Jan 28, 1966, p3.
Filmfacts. Jun 1, 1966, v9, p94-95.
Films and Filming. Sep 1966, v12, p10-12.
The Films of James Stewart. p244-47.
Hollywood Reporter. Jan 31, 1966, p3.
The London Times. Jun 30, 1966, p7.
Motion Picture Herald Product Digest. Feb 16, 1966, p469.
The New York Times. Apr 14, 1966, p42.
Senior Scholastic. Mar 11, 1966, v88, p28.
Variety. Feb 2, 1966, p6.

Rashomon (Also titled: Rasho-Mon; In the Forest; In the Woods) (JAPAN; Kurosawa, Akira; 1950)
Akira Kurosawa: A Guide to References and Resources. p45-47.
The Ambiguous Image (Armes). p25-26.
American Film. Apr 1982, v7, p56-57.
Antioch Review. Dec 1954, v14, p492-01.
BFI/Monthly Film Bulletin. May 1952, v19, p61-62.
Catholic World. Feb 1952, v174, p385.
Christian Century. Apr 9, 1952, v69, p447.
Cinema East. p23-35.
Cinema Texas Program Notes. Mar 19, 1974, v6, p1-5.
Cinema, the Magic Vehicle. v2, p35-39.
Classic Movies. p176-77.
Classics of the Foreign Film. p192-95.
Commonweal. Jan 11, 1952, v55, p350.
The Contemporary Cinema. p143-45.
Dictionary of Films. p306.
Fifty From the Fifties. p263-68.
Film and Literature: An Introduction. p181-89.
Film and the Critical Eye. p243-71.
Film Criticism and Caricatures, 1943-1953. p140-41.
Film Culture. n10, 1956, v2, p3-5.
Film Daily. Jan 4, 1952, p8.
Film Journal. Dec 1956, n6, p6-9.
Films in Review. Jan 1952, v3, p34-37.
Films in Review. Jun-Jul 1953, v4, p277-90.
The Films of Akira Kurosawa. p70-80.

Focus on Rashomon.
The Great Films. p202-05.
Harper's Magazine. Jul 1955, v211, p54-59.
Horizon. Spr 1974, v16, p36-44.
Hudson Review. Aut 1952, v5, p420-23.
Illustrated London News. Apr 5, 1952, v220, p592.
The International Dictionary of Films and Filmmakers. v1, p383-84.
Japan Quarterly. Jan-Mar 1965, v12, p59-64.
Kiss Kiss Bang Bang. p423-24.
Landmark Films. p202-09.
Library Journal. Jan 15, 1952, v77, p140.
Life. Jan 21, 1952, v32, p53-54.
Literature/Film Quarterly. n2, 1982, v10, p120-29.
The Liveliest Art. p230-31.
Living Images. p316-24.
The London Times. Mar 14, 1952, p2.
Made Into Movies. p160-78.
Magill's Survey of Cinema. Foreign Language Films. v5, p2502-07.
Motion Picture Herald Product Digest. Jan 12, 1952, p1186.
The Nation. Jan 19, 1952, v174, p66.
The New Republic. Jan 14, 1952, v126, p22.
The New Statesman and Nation. Mar 15, 1952, v43, p302.
The New York Times. Dec 27, 1951, p18.
The New York Times. Jan 6, 1962, p1.
The New Yorker. Dec 29, 1951, v27, p60-61.
Newsweek. Jan 7, 1952, v39, p59-60.
Rashomon: A Film by Akira Kurosawa. 1969.
Renaissance of the Film. p198-10.
The Samurai Films of Akira Kurosawa. p65-71.
Saturday Review. Jan 19, 1952, v35, p33.
Sight and Sound. Oct-Dec 1951, v21, p90-91.
Sight and Sound. Jul-Sep 1952, v22, p28-29.
Sight and Sound. Oct-Dec 1954, v24, p74-78, 112.
Soundings. Wint 1973, v56, p393-11.
Soundtrack. Jun 1985, v4, p15.
Three Faces of the Film. p36-43.
Time. Jan 7, 1952, v59, p82-84.
To the Distant Observer. p296-98.
Variety. Sep 19, 1951, p24.
The Waves at Genji's Door. p46-50.

The Rat Race (US; Mulligan, Robert; 1960)
America. Jun 11, 1960, v103, p361.
BFI/Monthly Film Bulletin. Apr 1961, v28, p46.
Commonweal. Jun 10, 1960, v72, p279.
Film Daily. May 4, 1960, p6.
Filmfacts. 1960, v3, p121.
Films and Filming. Apr 1961, v7, p30.
Hollywood Reporter. May 4, 1960, p3.
McCall's. Jul 1960, v87, p6.
The Nation. Jun 11, 1960, v190, p520.
The New Republic. Jun 20, 1960, v142, p21.
The New York Times. May 26, 1960, p37.
Newsweek. Jun 6, 1960, v55, p115.
Saturday Review. May 14, 1960, v43, p29.
Time. May 30, 1960, v75, p46.
Tony Curtis: The Man and His Movies. p84.
Variety. May 4, 1960, p6.

Rattle of a Simple Man (GB; Box, Muriel; 1964)
BFI/Monthly Film Bulletin. Oct 1964, v31, p151.
Boxoffice. Feb 8, 1965, v86, p2898.
Commonweal. Jan 15, 1965, v81, p519.
Film Daily. Dec 21, 1964, v125, p3.
Films and Filming. Nov 1964, v11, p29.
The Los Angeles Times. May 22, 1965, v3, p5.
Motion Picture Herald Product Digest. Dec 23, 1964, v232, p194-95.
The Nation. Jan 18, 1965, v200, p68.

The New York Times. Dec 21, 1964, p42.
Time. Jan 8, 1965, v85, p54.
Variety. Sep 16, 1964, p19.

The Raven (US; Corman, Roger; 1963)
BFI/Monthly Film Bulletin. Oct 1963, v30, p142.
Commonweal. Feb 15, 1963, v77, p542.
Film Daily. Jan 30, 1963, p8.
Filmfacts. Feb 7, 1963, v6, p3-4.
Films and Filming. Oct 1963, v10, p25.
The Films of Roger Corman. p34-37, 53-54.
Hollywood Reporter. Jan 30, 1963, v173, p3.
The New York Times. Jan 26, 1963, p5.
Newsweek. Feb 4, 1963, v61, p78-79.
Sight and Sound. Aut 1963, v32, p198.
Time. Feb 1, 1963, v81, p81.
Variety. Feb 6, 1963, p6.

Raven's End (Swedish title: Kvarteret Korpen) (SWED; Widerberg, Bo; 1964)
BFI/Monthly Film Bulletin. Mar 1965, v32, p34-35.
Dictionary of Films. p181.
Esquire. Dec 1964, v64, p88.
Films and Filming. Apr 1965, v11, p30-31.
Films and Filming. Mar 1965, v11, p43.
International Film Guide. 1965, v2, p131.
The London Times. Feb 4, 1965, p16.
Magill's Survey of Cinema. Foreign Language Films. v5, p2502-07.
Movie. Spr 1965, n12, p45.
New Statesman. Feb 12, 1965, v69, p255.
The New York Times. Sep 10, 1965, p40.
Sight and Sound. Spr 1965, v34, p96-97.
The Spectator. Feb 12, 1965, v214, p202.
Tynan Right and Left. p213-15.
Variety. May 13, 1964, p6.
The Village Voice. May 21, 1970, v15, p55, 62.

Rawhide (US; Hathaway, Henry; 1951)
BFI/Monthly Film Bulletin. Mar 1951, v18, p235-36.
Christian Century. Jun 27, 1951, v68, p777.
Commonweal. Apr 13, 1951, v54, p14.
Film Daily. Mar 6, 1951, p4.
The Films of Susan Hayward. p157-59.
The Films of Tyrone Power. p167-69.
Hollywood Reporter. Mar 5, 1951, p3.
The London Times. Mar 5, 1951, p2.
Motion Picture Herald Product Digest. Mar 10, 1951, p749.
The New York Times. Mar 26, 1951, p19.
Newsweek. Apr 2, 1951, v37, p86.
Time. Mar 19, 1951, v57, p106.
Variety. Mar 7, 1951, p6.

The Razor's Edge (US; Byrum, John; 1984)
Film Journal. Nov 1984, v87, p52.
Film Journal. Sep 1984, v87, p8.
Films in Review. Dec 1984, v35, p625.
Hollywood Reporter. Oct 17, 1984, p3.
Humanist. Jan-Feb 1985, v45, p39-40.
The Los Angeles Times. Oct 19, 1984, SecVI, p1.
Maclean's. Nov 5, 1984, v97, p63.
The New Republic. Nov 19, 1984, v191, p27.
New York. Oct 29, 1984, v17, p81.
The New York Times. Oct 19, 1984, SecIII, p14.
Newsweek. Oct 22, 1984, v104, p99.
Time. Oct 22, 1984, v124, p89.
Variety. Oct 17, 1984, p14.
Vogue. Nov 1984, v174, p106.

Rear Window (US; Hitchcock, Alfred; 1954)
Alfred Hitchcock (Phillips). p141-42.
America. Aug 21, 1954, v91, p507.
American Cinematographer. Feb 1954, v35, p76-78.

American Film. Nov 1983, v9, p28-35.
Armchair Detective. 1985, v18, n2, p190-93.
The Art of Alfred Hitchcock. p237-50.
Artforum. May 1984, v22, p39-43.
Atlantic Monthly. Oct 1983, v252, p100.
BFI/Monthly Film Bulletin. Sep 1954, v21, p129-30.
BFI/Monthly Film Bulletin. Feb 1984, v51, p34-36.
Boxoffice. Feb 1984, v120, pR23-24.
Catholic World. Aug 1954, v179, p383.
Cineaste. 1980, v10, n3, p9-13.
Cinema Eye, Cinema Ear. p193-94.
Cinema, the Magic Vehicle. v2, p206.
Classic Images. Mar 1984, n105, p45.
Commonweal. Aug 13, 1954, v60, p463.
Commonweal. Jan 27, 1984, v111, p49-50.
Cue. Aug 7, 1954, p15.
Enclitic. 1983, v7, n1, p136-45.
Film Daily. Jul 13, 1954, p6.
Film Journal. Oct 28, 1983, v86, p24.
Films and Filming. Nov 1954, v1, p18.
Films and Filming. Dec 1959, v6, p32.
Films and Filming. Oct 1970, v17, p61.
Films and Filming. Nov 1983, v29, p38-39.
The Films in My Life. p77-80.
Films in Review. Oct 1954, v5, p427-29.
The Films of Alfred Hitchcock. p165-69.
The Films of James Stewart. p166-69.
The Great Movies. p50-52.
Hitchcock: The First Forty-Four Films. p122-28.
Hitchcock's Films (Wood). p68-76.
Hollywood Reporter. Jul 13, 1954, p3.
Illustrated London News. Oct 30, 1954, v225, p762.
Informer. Oct-Nov 1983, p2-3.
The International Dictionary of Films and Filmmakers. v1, p384-85.
Journal of the University Film and Video Association. 1985, v37, n2,, 53-65.
Life. Aug 16, 1954, v37, p88-90.
The London Times. Oct 11, 1954, p3.
Look. Sep 21, 1954, v18, p50-51.
Magill's Survey of Cinema. Series II. v5, p1983-86.
Motion Picture Herald Product Digest. Jul 17, 1954, p65.
National Parent-Teacher. Oct 1954, v49, p40.
New Orleans Review. 1985, v12, n3, p21-30.
The New Statesman and Nation. Oct 16, 1954, v48, p472.
New York Magazine. Oct 17, 1983, v16, p98.
The New York Times. Aug 5, 1954, p18.
The New York Times. Oct 9, 1983, p21.
The New Yorker. Aug 7, 1954, v30, p50.
Newsweek. Aug 9, 1954, v44, p80-81.
Post Script. Wint 1986, v5, p31-46.
Psychoanalytic Review. 1984, v71, n3, p483-500.
Saturday Review. Aug 21, 1954, v37, p31.
Selected Film Criticism, 1951-1960. p107-09.
Senior Scholastic. Sep 29, 1954, v65, p45.
Sight and Sound. Oct-Dec 1954, v24, p89-90.
The Spectator. Oct 8, 1954, v193, p433.
Take One. Nov-Dec 1968, v2, p18-20.
The Tatler. Oct 20, 1954, v214, p167.
Time. Aug 2, 1954, v64, p72.
Time. Mar 26, 1984, v123, p77-78.
Variety. Jul 14, 1954, p6.
Variety. Apr 25, 1984, p2.
The Village Voice. Aug 23, 1983, v28, p41.
The Village Voice. Oct 18, 1983, v28, p57.

Rebel Without a Cause (US; Ray, Nicholas; 1955)
America. Nov 5, 1955, v94, p168.
BFI/Monthly Film Bulletin. Jan 1956, v23, p17.
Cinema, the Magic Vehicle. v2, p262-63.
Commonweal. Nov 11, 1955, v63, p142.

Diacritics. 1980, v10, p57-66.
Esquire. Oct 1982, v98, p132-33.
Fifty from the Fifties. p269-76.
Film Culture. 1956, v2, p18-21.
Film Daily. Oct 27, 1955, p10.
Film Quarterly. 1974, v28, p32-38.
Films and Filming. Aug 1977, v23, p16-24.
Films Illustrated. Jun 1976, v5, p391-93.
Films in Review. Nov 1955, v6, p467-68.
The Films of the Fifties. p163-66.
Hollywood Reporter. Oct 21, 1955, p3.
The International Dictionary of Films and Filmmaking. v1, p385-87.
James Dean: A Biography. p99-124.
Magill's Survey of Cinema. Series II. v5, p1987-93.
Motion Picture Product Herald Digest. Oct 22, 1955, p641.
The Nation. Dec 3, 1955, v181, p486.
The New Republic. Mar 6, 1976, v174, p31-32.
The New York Times. Oct 27, 1955, p28.
The New York Times. Oct 30, 1955, SecII, p1.
The New York Times. Apr 9, 1956, p29.
The New Yorker. Nov 5, 1955, v31, p132.
Newsweek. Nov 7, 1955, v46, p117.
Nicholas Ray: A Guide to References and Resources. p83-88.
Nicholas Ray (Kreidl). p73-167.
The Platinum Years. p80-83.
Rolling Stone. Jun 20, 1974, n163, p46-48.
Rolling Stone. Oct 16, 1980, n328, p50.
Saturday Review. Nov 5, 1955, v38, p28.
Sight and Sound. Fall 1956, v26, p70-74.
Take One. 1979, v7, p15-16.
Time. Nov 28, 1955, v66, p104.
Variety. Oct 26, 1955, p6.
Vintage Films. p147-50.

Rebellion (Japanese title: Jiouchi; Jio-uchi) (JAPAN; Kobayashi, Masaki; 1967)
BFI/Monthly Film Bulletin. Mar 1968, v35, p36.
Filmfacts. Jan 15, 1969, v11, p456-58.
Films and Filming. Mar 1969, v15, p86.
The London Times. Feb 3, 1968, p19.
Motion Picture Herald Product Digest. Nov 6, 1968, p56A.
New Statesman. Feb 9, 1968, v75, p183.
The New York Times. Oct 26, 1968, p27.
The New York Times. Sep 25, 1967, p56.
Sight and Sound. Spr 1968, v37, p97-98.
The Spectator. Feb 9, 1968, v220, p176.

The Reckoning (US; Gold, Jack; 1971)
Double Takes. p36-38.
Filmfacts. 1971, v14, p118.
Films and Filming. Feb 1970, v16, p36-37.
Hollywood Reporter. Aug 20, 1969, p3.
Life. Feb 26, 1971, v70, p6-7.
The New Republic. Feb 13, 1971, v164, p24.
The New York Times. Jan 20, 1971, p20.
Newsweek. Feb 1, 1971, v77, p75.
Time. Feb 15, 1971, v97, p64.
Variety. Aug 20, 1969, p16.
The Village Voice. Jan 28, 1971, p64.

The Red Badge of Courage (US; Huston, John; 1951)
BFI/Monthly Film Bulletin. Dec 1951, v18, p373.
Catholic World. Oct 1951, v174, p65.
Christian Century. Nov 21, 1951, v68, p1359.
The Cinema of John Huston. p72-87.
Cinema, the Magic Vehicle. v2, p72-75.
The Classic American Novel and the Movies. p114-23.
Commonweal. Nov 2, 1951, v55, p93.
Dictionary of Films. p307.
Film Criticism and Caricatures, 1943-1953. p131-33.

Film Daily. Aug 24, 1951, p6.
Films in Review. Oct 1951, v2, p42-43.
Hollywood Reporter. Aug 15, 1951, p3.
John Huston (Hammen). p53-54, 99-100.
John Huston: Maker of Magic. p75-82.
Library Journal. Nov 15, 1951, v76, p1948.
Life. Sep 10, 1951, v31, p102-04.
Magill's Survey of Cinema. Series II. v5, p1994-96.
Motion Picture Herald Product Digest. Aug 18, 1951, p981.
The Nation. Nov 10, 1951, v173, p409.
The New Republic. Sep 24, 1951, v125, p20-21.
The New Statesman and Nation. Nov 24, 1951, v42, p590.
The New York Times. Oct 19, 1951, p22.
The New Yorker. Oct 27, 1951, v27, p74.
The New Yorker. May 24, 1951, v28, p32-36.
Newsweek. Oct 15, 1951, v38, p94.
An Open Book. p179-80.
Saturday Review. Sep 29, 1951, v34, p31.
Senior Scholastic. Oct 10, 1951, v59, p22.
Sight and Sound. Jan-Mar 1952, v21, p124.
Sight and Sound. May 1951, v20, p6.
Time. Oct 8, 1951, v58, p110.
Variety. Aug 15, 1951, p6.

Red Ball Express (US; Boetticher, Budd; 1952)
BFI/Monthly Film Bulletin. Aug 1952, v19, p113.
Christian Century. Jun 11, 1952, v69, p711.
Film Daily. Apr 30, 1952, p6.
Hollywood Reporter. Apr 30, 1952, p3.
Motion Picture Herald Product Digest. May 3, 1952, p1349.
The New York Times. May 30, 1952, p11.
Time. Jun 16, 1952, v59, p96.
Variety. Apr 30, 1952, p6.

The Red Balloon (French title: Ballon Rouge, Le) (FR; Lamorisse, Pascal; 1957)
America. Apr 6, 1957, v97, p28.
BFI/Monthly Film Bulletin. Dec 1957, v23, p158.
Cinema, the Magic Vehicle. p294-95.
Commonweal. Apr 5, 1957, v66, p17.
Film Culture. 1957, v3, n3, p15.
The Films in My Life. p220-22.
Films in Review. Mar 1957, v8, p132.
Hollywood Reporter. Dec 14, 1956, p4.
The Nation. Mar 30, 1957, v184, p281.
The New York Times. Mar 12, 1957, p38.
The New York Times. Mar 17, 1957, SecII, p1.
The New York Times Magazine. Feb 17, 1957, p36.
The New Yorker. Mar 23, 1957, v33, p104.
Saturday Review. Mar 16, 1957, v40, p27.
Sight and Sound. Wint 1956-57, v26, p155.
Time. Mar 18, 1957, v69, p102.
Variety. May 16, 1956, p6.

Red Beard (Japanese title: Akahige) (JAPAN; Kurosawa, Akira; 1965)
Akira Kurosawa: A Guide to References and Resources. p65-66.
Catholic Film Newsletter. Jan 30, 1969, v34, p2-3.
Cinema East. p71-87.
Dictionary of Films. p5-6.
Esquire. Dec 1965, v64, p84, 86.
Film. Wint 1965-66, n44, p16-17.
Film 69/70. p138-39.
Film Quarterly. Fall 1965, v19, p14-25.
Filmfacts. Jan 15, 1968, v11, p516-18.
Films and Filming. Feb 1969, v15, p46.
The Films of Akira Kurosawa. p171-83.
Japan: Film Image. p81-84.
The London Times. Nov 10, 1965, p15.

The London Times. Nov 14, 1968, p9.
Magill's Survey of Cinema. Foreign Language Films. v6, p2523-26.
Motion Picture Herald Product Digest. Jan 8, 1969, p96.
The New Republic. Jan 11, 1969, v160, p34.
The New York Times. Dec 20, 1968, p60.
On Film. p302-04.
The Spectator. Nov 19, 1965, v215, p657.
Time. Jan 17, 1969, v93, p67.
Tynan Right and Left. p239.
Variety. Sep 8, 1965, p6.

The Red Beret *See* The Paratrooper

Red Dawn (US; Milius, John; 1984)
American Premiere. Sum 1984, v5, p12.
BFI/Monthly Film Bulletin. Nov 1984, v51, p341-42.
Christian Century. Oct 24, 1984, v101, p996-97.
Christianity Today. Oct 19, 1984, v28, p60.
Film Journal. Sep 1984, v87, p27.
Films in Review. Oct 1984, v35, p498.
Hollywood Reporter. Aug 6, 1984, p4.
The Los Angeles Times. Aug 10, 1984, SecVI, p15.
Maclean's. Aug 20, 1984, v97, p63.
The Nation. Sep 15, 1984, v239, p219-21.
New Statesman. Nov 9, 1984, v108, p34.
New York. Aug 20, 1984, v17, p90.
The New York Times. Sep 16, 1984, SecII, p19.
The New York Times. Aug 10, 1984, SecIII, p11.
The New York Times. Aug 19, 1984, SecII, p15.
Photoplay. Dec 1984, v35, p19.
Time. Aug 27, 1984, v124, p64.
Variety. Aug 8, 1984, p14.
The Village Voice. Aug 21, 1984, p47-48, 54.

Red Desert (Also titled: Deserto Rosso, Il) (IT, FR; Antonioni, Michelangelo; 1964)
Antonioni (Cameron). p111-24.
Antonioni (Chatman). p131-33.
Antonioni's Visual Language. p93-102.
BFI/Monthly Film Bulletin. May 1965, v32, p66-67.
Christian Century. Jun 2, 1965, v82, p713.
Christian Science Monitor (Western edition). Dec 4, 1965, p6.
The Classic Cinema. p273-94.
Commonweal. Feb 26, 1965, v81, p704-05.
Confessions of a Cultist. p189-93.
Dictionary of Films. p82.
Dwight Macdonald on Film. p339-41.
Esquire. Dec 1964, v62, p68.
Film Comment. Wint 1965, v3, p71-72.
Film Culture. Sum 1966, n41, p24-30.
Film Daily. Feb 8, 1965, p4.
Film Heritage. Wint 1965-66, v1, p24-27.
Film Quarterly. Fall 1965, v19, p51-54.
Film Society Review. Apr 1967, p15-17.
Filmfacts. Mar 19, 1965, v8, p33-38.
Films and Filming. Jun 1965, v11, p27.
Films in Review. Mar 1965, v16, p180-81.
The International Dictionary of Films and Filmmakers. v1, p119-20.
International Film Guide. 1966, v3, p98-99.
Italian Cinema (Bondanella). p217-21.
Kiss Kiss Bang Bang. p30-31.
Life. Mar 5, 1965, v58, p12.
London Magazine. Jun 1965, v5, p83-87.
The London Times. Apr 1, 1965, p5.
The London Times. Sep 8, 1964, p13.
Magill's Survey of Cinema. Foreign Language Films. v6, p2527-31.
Motion Picture Herald Product Digest. Feb 17, 1965, p235.
Movie. Sum 1965, n13, p10-13.
Movie. Spr 1965, n12, p31-34.

Movie Man (Thomson). p42.
The New Republic. Feb 20, 1965, v152, p30-34.
New Statesman. Apr 2, 1965, v69, p544.
The New York Times. Feb 9, 1965, p43.
The New Yorker. Feb 13, 1965, v40, p88, 90.
Newsweek. Feb 22, 1965, v65, p96.
Playboy. May 1965, v12, p32.
Private Screenings. p177-81.
Renaissance of the Film. p211-19.
Saturday Review. Feb 20, 1965, v48, p44.
Sight and Sound. Spr 1965, v34, p76-81, 103.
Sight and Sound. Sum 1964, v33, p118-19.
The Spectator. Apr 2, 1965, v214, p439-40.
Time. Feb 19, 1965, v85, p99.
Tynan Right and Left. p223-24.
Variety. Sep 16, 1964, p6.
The Village Voice. Feb 11, 1965, v17, p14, 16.

Red Garters (US; Marshall, George; 1954)
America. Apr 3, 1954, v91, p27.
BFI/Monthly Film Bulletin. Apr 1954, v21, p59.
Catholic World. Mar 1954, v178, p461.
Commonweal. Mar 12, 1954, v59, p577.
Farm Journal. Apr 1954, v78, p165.
Film Daily. Feb 5, 1954, p6.
Films in Review. Apr 1954, v5, p193-94.
Hollywood Reporter. Feb 1, 1954, p3.
Life. Mar 15, 1954, v36, p70-71.
The London Times. Mar 22, 1954, p4.
Look. Oct 6, 1953, v17, p114-115.
Motion Picture Herald Product Digest. Feb 6, 1954, p2173.
National Parent-Teacher. Mar 1954, v48, p40.
The New York Times. Mar 27, 1954, p13.
The New Yorker. Apr 3, 1954, v30, p58.
Newsweek. Feb 15, 1954, v43, p97.
Saturday Review. Mar 20, 1954, v37, p29.
The Spectator. Mar 19, 1954, v192, p322.
Time. Feb 22, 1954, v63, p102.
Variety. Feb 3, 1954, p6.

The Red Inn (French title: Auberge Rouge, L') (FR; Autant-Lara, Claude; 1951)
BFI/Monthly Film Bulletin. Jul 1957, v24, p82.
Dictionary of Films. p18.
Film Daily. Jun 22, 1954, p6.
Films and Filming. Jul 1957, v3, p26.
The Great French Films. p252.
Hollywood Reporter. Sep 2, 1954, p3.
The New Republic. Jul 5, 1954, v131, p21.
The New York Times. Jun 8, 1954, p25.
Newsweek. Jul 26, 1954, v44, p83.
Sight and Sound. Sum 1957, v27, p42-43.
Variety. Nov 28, 1951, p6.

Red Lanterns (Greek title: Kokkina Fanaria, Ta) (GREECE; Georgiades, Vassili; 1963)
BFI/Monthly Film Bulletin. May 1965, v32, p75.
Film Daily. Mar 31, 1965, p7.
Films and Filming. May 1965, v11, p29.
Motion Picture Herald Product Digest. Mar 31, 1965, p260.
New Statesman. Mar 26, 1965, v69, p504.
The New York Times. Apr 1, 1965, p30.
The New Yorker. Apr 10, 1965, v41, p160.
Variety. May 20, 1964, p20.

Red Line 7000 (US; Hawks, Howard; 1965)
BFI/Monthly Film Bulletin. Feb 1966, v33, p18.
Film Daily. Nov 5, 1965, p6.
Film Quarterly. Spr 1966, v19, p53.
Films and Filming. Mar 1966, v12, p56-57.
Films in Review. Dec 1965, v16, p646.
The Films of Howard Hawks. p98-101.
Hollywood Reporter. Nov 4, 1965, p3.
The London Times. Dec 16, 1965, p4.

Motion Picture Herald Product Digest. Nov 24, 1965, p409.
Movie. Sum 1966, n3, p60-64.
The New York Times. Dec 9, 1965, p60.
Newsweek. Dec 27, 1965, v66, p71A.
Saturday Review. Dec 4, 1965, v48, p74.
Time. Jan 14, 1966, v87, p89.
Variety. Nov 10, 1965, p6.
The Village Voice. Dec 9, 1965, v11, p21.

The Red Mantle *See* Hagbard and Signe

Red Mountain (US; Dieterle, William; 1951)
BFI/Monthly Film Bulletin. Aug 1951, v18, p314.
Commonweal. Mar 7, 1952, v55, p544.
Film Daily. Nov 19, 1951, p6.
The Films of Alan Ladd. p156-60.
Hollywood Reporter. Nov 14, 1951, p3.
The London Times. Aug 4, 1951, p6.
Motion Picture Herald Product Digest. Nov 17, 1951, p1109.
The New York Times. Apr 26, 1952, p19.
The Spectator. Aug 3, 1951, v187, p156.
Time. Jan 21, 1952, v59, p94.
Variety. Nov 14, 1951, p6.

Red Planet Mars (US; Horner, Harry; 1952)
BFI/Monthly Film Bulletin. Oct 1952, v19, p140-41.
Film Daily. May 15, 1952, p6.
Hollywood Goes to War. p135, 137.
Hollywood Reporter. May 14, 1952, p4.
Motion Picture Herald Product Digest. May 17, 1952, p1367.
National Parent-Teacher. Sep 1952, v47, p37.
The New York Times. Jun 16, 1952, p15.
Sight and Sound. Oct-Dec 1952, v22, p81.
Variety. May 14, 1952, p20.

Red Sky at Morning (US; Goldstone, James; 1971)
America. May 29, 1971, v124, p579-80.
BFI/Monthly Film Bulletin. Jan 1972, v39, p14.
Film Quarterly. Wint 1971, v25, p57-58.
Filmfacts. 1971, v14, p54-57.
Films in Review. Jun-Jul 1971, v22, n6, p373.
Hollywood Reporter. May 3, 1971, v216, n4, p3.
The New York Times. May 13, 1971, p53.
The New York Times. May 23, 1971, SecII, p15.
Newsweek. May 31, 1971, v70, p54.
Saturday Review. May 15, 1971, v54, p18.
Variety. May 5, 1971, p16.
The Village Voice. May 20, 1971, p65.

The Redhead and the Cowboy (US; Fenton, Leslie; 1950)
BFI/Monthly Film Bulletin. May 1951, v18, p267.
Christian Century. Apr 4, 1951, v68, p447.
Film Daily. Dec 7, 1950, p6.
Hollywood Reporter. Dec 7, 1950, p3.
Motion Picture Herald Product Digest. Dec 16, 1950, p614.
The New York Times. Jun 6, 1951, p37.
Newsweek. Feb 26, 1951, v37, p80.
Saturday Review. Feb 17, 1951, v34, p30.
Variety. Dec 13, 1950, p8.

Redl Ezredes Oerst Redl *See* Colonel Redl

Reds (US; Beatty, Warren; 1982)
America. Jan 23, 1982, v146, p56.
American Heritage. Apr-May 1982, v33, p42-43.
Christianity Today. May 7, 1982, v26, p55.
Commentary. Mar 1982, v73, p56-63.
Commonweal. Feb 12, 1982, v109, p87-89.
Film Comment. Jan-Feb 1982, v18, p15-16.
Harper's. Feb 1982, v264, p74-76.

The Nation. Jan 16, 1982, v234, p58-59.
National Review. Feb 5, 1982, v34, p133.
The New Leader. Dec 28, 1981, v64, p17-18.
New York Review of Books. Mar 4, 1982, v29, p9-10.
Progressive. Feb 1982, v46, p56-57.
Rolling Stone. Jan 21, 1982, p24-25.
Saturday Review. Jan 1982, v9, p52.
Senior Scholastic. Apr 2, 1982, v114, p27.

Reflections in a Golden Eye (US; Huston, John; 1967)
BFI/Monthly Film Bulletin. Aug 1968, v35, p114.
Cinema. Spr 1968, v4, p47.
The Cinema of John Huston. p160-64.
Film Daily. Oct 10, 1967, p3.
Film Quarterly. Wint 1967-68, v21, p63.
Films and Filming. May 1968, v14, p24.
Films in Review. Nov 1967, v18, p576-77.
The Films of Elizabeth Taylor. p188-93.
The Films of Marlon Brando. p188-97.
Hollywood Reporter. Oct 9, 1967, p3.
John Huston (Hammen). p113-18, 133-37.
John Huston (Madsen). p217-21.
John Huston, Maker of Magic. p173-86.
John Huston (Pratley). p160-64.
Motion Picture Herald Product Digest. Oct 25, 1967, p733.
Movie. Spr 1968, v15, p25-26.
The New York Times. Oct 12, 1967, p59.
The New Yorker. Oct 21, 1967, v43, p137-38.
The New Yorker. Oct 28, 1967, v43, p165.
The New Yorker. Feb 10, 1968, v43, p100.
Newsweek. Oct 30, 1967, v70, p94.
Saturday Review. Oct 28, 1967, v50, p26.
Sight and Sound. Spr 1968, v37, p99-100.
Time. Oct 27, 1967, v90, p102.
Variety. Oct 11, 1967, p6.
The Village Voice. Nov 30, 1967, p39.

The Reformer and the Redhead (US; Panama, Norman; Frank, Melvin; 1950)
BFI/Monthly Film Bulletin. Oct 1950, v17, p156.
Christian Century. Jun 21, 1950, v67, p775.
Commonweal. Apr 14, 1950, v52, p17.
Film Daily. Mar 9, 1950, p6.
Hollywood Reporter. Mar 8, 1950, p3.
Library Journal. Apr 15, 1950, v75, p704, 709.
Motion Picture Herald Product Digest. Mar 11, 1950, p222.
The New York Times. Apr 10, 1950, p15.
Newsweek. Apr 24, 1950, v35, p96.
Senior Scholastic. Apr 26, 1950, v56, p25.
Time. May 1, 1950, v55, p91.
Variety. Mar 8, 1950, p6.

The Reivers (US; Rydell, Mark; 1969)
Deeper Into Movies. p93-95.
Film Daily. Dec 3, 1969, p7.
Films and Filming. Jan 1971, v17, p56, 60.
Films in Review. Feb 1970, v21, p121.
The Films of Steve McQueen. p154-63.
Hollywood Reporter. Nov 26, 1969, p3.
Life. Dec 19, 1969, v67, p10.
Magill's Survey of Cinema. Series II. v5, p2004-06.
The New York Times. Dec 26, 1969, p42.
The New Yorker. Dec 27, 1969, v45, p47.
Newsweek. Jan 5, 1970, v75, p63.
Saturday Review. Jan 3, 1970, v53, p74.
Time. Jan 5, 1970, v95, p53.
Variety. Nov 26, 1969, p14.

Religieuse, La (Also titled: The Nun; Suzanne Simonin, La Religieuse de Diderot) (FR; Rivette, Jacques; 1965)

BFI/Monthly Film Bulletin. Nov 1967, v34, p171-72.
Cahiers du Cinema in English. Jan 1967, n7, p5-7, 64.
Film Quarterly. Spr 1969, v22, p44-47.
Filmfacts. 1971, v14, n19, p486-89.
Films in Review. Aug-Sep 1971, v22, p444.
International Film Guide. 1967, v4, p71.
Modern European Filmmakers and the Art of Adaptation. p131-44.
Motion Picture Herald Product Digest. Oct 13, 1965, p387.
New Statesman. Aug 5, 1977, v94, p189.
The New Wave. p306, 315-18.
The New York Times. Sep 23, 1968, p42.
Sight and Sound. Wint 1967-68, v37, p38-39.
Sight and Sound. Sum 1966, v35, p130-33.
Variety. Mar 30, 1966, p28.
The Village Voice. Jul 22, 1971, v16, p59.
A Year in the Dark. p245-46.

The Reluctant Debutante (US; Minnelli, Vincente; 1958)
America. Aug 30, 1958, v99, p559-60.
BFI/Monthly Film Bulletin. Jan 1959, v26, p4.
Catholic World. Oct 1958, v188, p63-64.
Commonweal. Aug 29, 1958, v68, p545.
Film Daily. Aug 5, 1958, v114, p8.
Filmfacts. Oct 1, 1958, v1, p149-50.
Hollywood Reporter. Aug 4, 1958, p3.
Library Journal. Sep 1, 1958, v83, p2278.
Life. Aug 25, 1958, v45, p79.
The New Republic. Sep 8, 1958, v139, p22.
The New York Times. Aug 15, 1958, p17.
The New Yorker. Aug 23, 1958, v34, p66.
Newsweek. Aug 18, 1958, v52, p90.
Saturday Review. Aug 16, 1958, v41, p24.
Senior Scholastic. Oct 3, 1958, v72, p4.
Time. Aug 18, 1958, v72, p82.
Variety. Aug 6, 1958, p7.

Rendezvous *See* Darling, How Could You?

Rendezvous de Juillet (FR; Becker, Jacques; 1949)
Dictionary of Films. p310-11.
Films and Filming. Nov 1954, v1, p18.
The London Times. Jul 26, 1954, p5.
The New Statesman and Nation. Jul 31, 1954, v48, p132.
Sight and Sound. Oct-Dec 1954, v24, p90-91.
The Tatler. Aug 4, 1954, v213, p204.
Variety. Oct 19, 1949, p18.

Repast (Japanese title: Meshi) (JAPAN; Naruse, Mikio; 1951)
The Japanese Film: Art and Industry. p195.
Magill's Survey of Cinema. Foreign Language Films. v6, p2541-46.
New Statesman. Jun 9, 1978, v95, p795.

Repo Man (US; Cox, Alex; 1984)
BFI/Monthly Film Bulletin. Nov 1984, v51, p342-43.
Films in Review. Oct 1984, v35, p497-98.
Hollywood Reporter. May 16, 1984, p4.
The Los Angeles Times. May 3, 1984, SecIV, p1.
The New York Times. Jul 6, 1984, SecIII, p8.
The New York Times. Nov 11, 1984, SecII, p17.
The New Yorker. Apr 6, 1984, v60, p72-74.
Time. Feb 4, 1985, v125, p83.
Variety. Mar 7, 1984, p371.
The Village Voice. Jul 17, 1984, p49.

A Report on the Party and the Guests (Czechoslovakian title: O Slavnosti a Hostech; Also titled: The Party and the Guests) (CZECH; Nemec, Jan; 1968)

BFI/Monthly Film Bulletin. Apr 1969, v36, p72-73.
The Czechoslovak New Wave. p192-98.
Esquire. Jan 1969, v71, p34.
Film Society Review. Oct 1968, v4, p29-36.
Filmfacts. Jan 15, 1969, v11, p440-42.
Films and Filming. Mar 1969, v15, p45-46.
The International Dictionary of Films and Filmmakers. v1, p334-335.
International Film Guide. 1969, v6, p55-56.
The London Times. Jan 16, 1969, p11.
The New Republic. Oct 5, 1968, v159, p18.
New Statesman. Jan 31, 1969, v77, p165.
The New York Times. Sep 28, 1968, p37.
The New York Times. Sep 20, 1968, p37.
The New Yorker. Sep 21, 1968, v44, p142-43.
Variety. Aug 10, 1966, p18.
A Year In the Dark. p244-45.

Repulsion (GB; Polanski, Roman; 1965)
BFI/Monthly Film Bulletin. Jul 1965, v32, p107.
Cahiers du Cinema in English. 1966, n4, p56-57.
Christian Science Monitor (Eastern Edition). Jun 30, 1965, p4.
Cinema. Mar 1966, v3, p4-8, 13-14.
The Cinema of Roman Polanski. p51-82.
Cinema Papers. Nov-Dec 1981, n35, p438-43.
Commonweal. Oct 29, 1965, v83, p124-25.
Confessions of a Cultist. p208-10.
Dictionary of Films. p311.
Esquire. Apr 1966, v65, p60, 62.
Fifty Classic British Films. p121-23.
Film Daily. Sep 30, 1965, p4.
Film Heritage. Wint 1968-69, v4, p1-10, 25.
Film Quarterly. Spr 1966, v19, p44-45.
Film Reader. 1982, n5, p37-40.
Films and Filming. Aug 1965, v11, p28-29.
Focus on the Horror Film. p152-61.
Hollywood Reporter. Sep 30, 1965, p3.
The Horror Film (Butler). p111-22.
Horror in the Cinema. p131-43.
International Film Guide. 1966, v3, p84.
Life. Oct 8, 1965, v59, p23.
The London Times. Jun 10, 1965, p7.
Magill's Survey of Cinema. Series II. v5, p2011-13.
Motion Picture Herald Product Digest. Oct 13, 1965, p387-88.
Movie. Sum 1965, n13, p44.
Movie. Aut 1965, n14, p26-29.
The New Republic. Oct 16, 1965, v153, p31-32.
New Statesman. Jun 18, 1965, v69, p978.
The New York Times. Oct 4, 1965, p7.
The New York Times. Nov 14, 1965, p9.
The New Yorker. Oct 9, 1965, v41, p190-91.
Playboy. Oct 1965, v12, p30.
Polanski (Leaming). p59-66.
Private Screenings. p217-18.
Saturday Review. Oct 16, 1965, v48, p63.
Sight and Sound. Sum 1965, v34, p146.
The Spectator. Jun 18, 1965, v214, p788.
The Thousand Eyes Magazine. May 1976, n10, p18-19.
Time. Oct 8, 1965, v86, p115.
Tynan Right and Left. p231-33.
Variety. Jun 16, 1965, p6.
The Village Voice. Oct 7, 1965, v10, p27.
Vogue. Dec 1965, v146, p147.

Requiem for a Heavyweight (US; Nelson, Ralph; 1962)
America. Oct 27, 1962, v107, p967-68.
Film Daily. Sep 7, 1962, p7.
Film Quarterly. Spr 1963, v16, p59.
Filmfacts. Nov 2, 1962, v5, p249-50.
Films and Filming. Apr 1963, v9, p30.
Films in Review. Nov 1962, v13, p560.

The Films of Anthony Quinn. p194-95.
Hollywood Reporter. Sep 7, 1962, p3.
Magill's Survey of Cinema. Series I. v3, p1444-46.
Motion Picture Herald Product Digest. Sep 19, 1962, p657, 659.
The New Republic. Nov 24, 1962, v147, p26.
The New York Times. Oct 17, 1962, p35.
The New Yorker. Oct 20, 1962, v38, p216.
Newsweek. Oct 22, 1962, v60, p104.
Time. Oct 19, 1962, v80, p91.
Variety. Sep 12, 1962, p6.

Resurrection (US; Petrie, Daniel; 1980)
BFI/Monthly Film Bulletin. Mar 1981, v48, p56.
Films in Review. Nov 1980, v31, p565.
Hollywood Reporter. Sep 8, 1980, p2.
The Los Angeles Times. Nov 2, 1980, Calendar, p1.
Motion Picture Herald Product Digest. Nov 19, 1980, p46.
Ms. Oct 1980, v9, p21-22.
The Nation. Dec 13, 1980, v231, p653.
The New Republic. Nov 15, 1980, v183, p22-23.
New York. Nov 17, 1980, v13, p82.
The New York Times. Nov 7, 1980, SecIII, p13.
The New Yorker. Dec 22, 1980, v56, p104.
Newsday. Nov 7, 1980, SecII, p7.
Newsweek. Nov 17, 1980, v96, p117.
Saturday Review. Nov 1980, v96, p117.
Time. Nov 3, 1980, v116, p104.
Variety. Sep 10, 1980, p3.
The Village Voice. Nov 12, 1980, p52.
Vogue. Nov 1980, v170, p48.

Retour de Martin Guerre, Le *See* The Return of Martin Guerre

Retreat, Hell! (US; Lewis, Joseph H.; 1952)
BFI/Monthly Film Bulletin. Jan 1953, v20, p5-6.
Christian Century. Apr 9, 1952, v69, p447.
Film Daily. Feb 27, 1952, p6.
Guts & Glory. p114.
Motion Picture Herald Product Digest. Feb 9, 1952, p1230.
The New York Times. Feb 20, 1952, p26.
Newsweek. Mar 3, 1952, v39, p88.
Seeing is Believing (Biskind). p313-14.
The Spectator. Nov 28, 1952, v189, p731.
The Tatler. Dec 10, 1952, v206, p606.
Time. Mar 24, 1952, v59, p100.
Variety. Feb 13, 1952, p6.

Return From the Ashes (Also titled: Demon Est Mauvais Joueur, Le) (GB; Thompson, J. Lee; 1965)
BFI/Monthly Film Bulletin. Mar 1966, v33, p45-46.
Cahiers du Cinema in English. Dec 1966, n6, p55.
Christian Science Monitor (Western edition). Nov 30, 1965, p6.
Commonweal. Dec 10, 1965, v83, p315.
Film Daily. Oct 15, 1965, p7.
Films and Filming. Mar 1965, v12, p14, 18.
Films and Filming. Apr 1966, v12, p14, 18.
Films and Filming. Feb 1966, v12, p53.
Films in Review. Dec 1965, v16, p645-46.
Hollywood Reporter. Oct 15, 1965, p3.
The London Times. Feb 3, 1966, p18.
Motion Picture Herald Product Digest. Nov 10, 1965, p401-02.
New Statesman. Feb 4, 1966, v71, p172.
The New York Times. Nov 17, 1965, p53.
The New Yorker. Nov 27, 1965, v41, p234.
Newsweek. Dec 6, 1965, v66, p104.
The Spectator. Feb 4, 1966, v216, p140.
Time. Nov 26, 1965, v86, p104.

Variety. Oct 20, 1965, p6.
The Village Voice. Nov 18, 1965, v11, p23.

The Return of a Man Called Horse (US; Kershner, John; 1976)
BFI/Monthly Film Bulletin. Nov 1976, v43, p234.
Film Bulletin. Sep-Oct 1976, v45, p38.
Films and Filming. Nov 1976, v23, p29-30.
Hollywood Reporter. Jul 28, 1976, p3.
Independent Film Journal. Aug 6, 1976, v78, p8-9.
The Los Angeles Times. Aug 1, 1976, Calendar, p38.
Motion Picture Herald Product Digest. Aug 18, 1976, p21.
Movietone News. Oct 11, 1976, v52, p41.
New Statesman. Oct 29, 1976, v92, p609-10.
The New York Times. Aug 13, 1976, p13.
The New Yorker. Aug 17, 1976, v52, p82.
Saturday Review. Sep 18, 1976, v3, p41-42.
Time. Sep 13, 1976, v108, p80.
Variety. Jul 28, 1976, p18.
When the Lights Go Down. p197-98.

The Return of Martin Guerre (French title: Retour de Martin Guerre, Le) (FR; Vigne, Daniel; 1983)
Christian Century. Sep 14, 1983, v100, p816.
The Los Angeles Times. Jul 22, 1983, SecVI, p1.
Maclean's. Jun 27, 1983, v96, p53.
Magill's Cinema Annual, 1984. p318-25.
National Review. Aug 5, 1983, v39, p950-51.
New York. May 23, 1983, v16, p91-92.
The New York Times. Jun 10, 1983, SecIII, p12.
Newsweek. Jun 27, 1983, v101, p80.

Return of the Jedi (US; Marquand, Richard; 1983)
Christian Century. Jun 22, 1983, v100, p621-22.
Christianity Today. Jul 15, 1983, v27, p54-55.
Film Comment. Jul-Aug 1983, v19, p9.
Films in Review. Jun-Jul 1983, v39, p368.
Hollywood Reporter. May 16, 1983, p3.
The International Dictionary of Films and Filmmakers. v1, p447-50.
The Los Angeles Times. May 25, 1983, SecVI, p1.
Maclean's. May 30, 1983, v96, p45.
Magill's Cinema Annual, 1984. p326-31.
The Nation. Jun 18, 1983, v16, p78.
National Review. Jun 24, 1983, v236, p776-77.
The New Leader. May 30, 1983, v35, p763-64.
New York. May 30, 1983, v89, p76.
The New York Times. May 25, 1983, SecIII, p24.
The New Yorker. May 30, 1983, v59, p88-90.
Newsweek. May 30, 1983, v101, p95-96.
Time. May 23, 1983, v121, p62-65.
Time. Jun 13, 1983, v121, p70.

Return of the Living Dead (US; O'Bannion, Dan; 1985)
BFI/Monthly Film Bulletin. Dec 1985, v52, p386.
Hollywood Reporter. Jun 18, 1985, p3.
The Los Angeles Times. Aug 16, 1985, SecVI, p14.
Magill's Cinema Annual, 1986. p314-18.
The New York Times. Aug 16, 1985, SecIII, p6.
Variety. Jun 19, 1985, p25.

Return of the Pink Panther (US; Edwards, Blake; 1975)
BFI/Monthly Film Bulletin. Aug 1975, v42, p180.
Films in Review. Aug-Sep 1975, v26, p438.
The Los Angeles Times. May 20, 1975, SecIV, p1.

Motion Picture Herald Product Digest. Jun 11, 1975, p4.
The New York Times. Jun 1, 1975, SecII, p15.
The New York Times. Jun 29, 1975, SecII, p1.
The New Yorker. Jun 2, 1975, v51, p90-92.
Newsweek. Jul 21, 1975, v86, p66-67.
Time. Jul 7, 1975, v106, p46.
Variety. May 14, 1975, p26.

Return of the Secaucus 7 (Also titled: Return of the Secaucus Seven) (US; Sayles, John; 1980)
BFI/Monthly Film Bulletin. Dec 1981, v48, p254.
Christian Century. Jul 1, 1981, v98, p714.
The Christian Science Monitor. Sep 11, 1980, p18.
Cineaste. Fall 1980, p32.
Film Comment. May-Jun 1981, v17, p54-59.
Films in Review. Nov 1980, v31, p566.
Hollywood Reporter. Sep 18, 1980, p2.
The Los Angeles Times. Mar 19, 1980, SecVI, p14.
Magill's Cinema Annual, 1983. p484-89.
The Nation. Apr 4, 1981, v232, p413.
New York. Sep 15, 1980, v13, p57-58.
The New York Times. Sep 4, 1980, p68.
Newsweek. Sep 22, 1980, v96, p76.
Progressive. Jun 1981, v45, p52-53.
Rolling Stone. May 14, 1981, p36.
Time. Sep 15, 1980, v116, p101.
Variety. Mar 26, 1980, p21.
The Village Voice. Mar 4, 1980, p41.

Return of the Seven (US, SP; Kennedy, Burt; 1966)
BFI/Monthly Film Bulletin. Jan 1967, v34, p12-13.
Film Daily. Oct 13, 1966, p7.
Filmfacts. Dec 15, 1966, v9, p295-96.
Films and Filming. Feb 1967, v13, p35.
The Great Western Pictures. p207-10.
Hollywood Reporter. Oct 11, 1966, p3.
Motion Picture Herald Product Digest. Oct 12, 1966, p613-14.
The New York Times. Oct 20, 1966, p52.
Variety. Oct 12, 1966, p6.

Revenge *See* Blood Feud

The Revenge of Milady *See* The Four Musketeers

The Reward (US; Bourguignon, Serge; 1965)
BFI/Monthly Film Bulletin. Dec 1965, v32, p185.
Christian Science Monitor (Western edition). Oct 22, 1965, p4.
Cinema. Dec 1965, v3, p49.
Cinema. Mar-Apr 1965, v2, p6-7.
Film Daily. Oct 7, 1965, p7.
Films and Filming. Jan 1966, v12, p31.
Hollywood Reporter. Sep 10, 1965, p3.
The London Times. Nov 11, 1965, p18.
Motion Picture Herald Product Digest. Sep 29, 1965, p379.
The New York Times. Sep 16, 1965, p55.
Newsweek. Sep 13, 1965, v66, p87A.
Saturday Review. Jul 24, 1965, v48, p51.
The Spectator. Nov 12, 1965, v215, p617.
Time. Aug 20, 1965, v86, p76.
Variety. Feb 2, 1966, p6.

Rhapsody (US; Vidor, Charles; 1954)
America. Apr 3, 1954, v91, p27.
BFI/Monthly Film Bulletin. Apr 1954, v21, p59-60.
Catholic World. Apr 1954, v179, p62.
Commonweal. Mar 26, 1954, v59, p626.
Film Daily. Feb 17, 1954, p6.
Films in Review. Apr 1954, v5, p192-93.

The Films of Elizabeth Taylor. p103-05.
The Great Romantic Films. p264-67.
Hollywood Reporter. Feb 16, 1954, p4.
Library Journal. Mar 1, 1954, v79, p444.
Look. May 4, 1954, v18, p72.
Motion Picture Herald Product Digest. Feb 13, 1954, p2181.
National Parent-Teacher. Apr 1954, v48, p39.
The New York Times. Mar 12, 1954, p17.
The New Yorker. Mar 20, 1954, v30, p119.
Newsweek. Mar 8, 1954, v43, p82.
Saturday Review. Mar 20, 1954, v37, p28.
Time. Apr 5, 1954, v63, p106.
Variety. Feb 17, 1954, p6.

Rhinestone (US; Clark, Bob; 1984)
BFI/Monthly Film Bulletin. Jan 1985, v52, p27.
Film Journal. Aug 1984, v87, p21.
Films in Review. Aug-Sep 1984, v35, p435-36.
Hollywood Reporter. Jun 20, 1984, p4.
The Los Angeles Times. Jun 22, 1984, SecVI, p1.
Maclean's. Jul 2, 1984, v97, p53.
Millimeter. Jul 1984, v12, p52-54.
The New York Times. Jul 29, 1984, SecII, p15.
The New York Times. Jun 22, 1984, SecIII, p10.
Newsweek. Jul 2, 1984, v104, p45.
Time. Jul 2, 1984, v124, p78.
Variety. Jun 20, 1984, p17.
The Village Voice. Jul 3, 1984, p59.

Rhubarb (US; Lubin, Arthur; 1951)
BFI/Monthly Film Bulletin. Oct 1951, v18, p349.
Christian Century. Oct 24, 1951, v68, p1239.
Film Daily. Aug 6, 1951, p6.
Hollywood Reporter. Aug 2, 1951, p3.
The London Times. Sep 17, 1951, p6.
Motion Picture Herald Product Digest. Aug 4, 1951, p965.
The New Statesman and Nation. Sep 15, 1951, v42, p282.
The New York Times. Aug 31, 1951, p12.
Newsweek. Sep 3, 1951, v38, p72.
Saturday Review. Sep 22, 1951, v34, p30.
Senior Scholastic. Oct 24, 1951, v59, p21.
The Spectator. Sep 14, 1951, v187, p328.
Variety. Aug 8, 1951, p6.

Rich and Famous (US; Cukor, George; 1981)
Film Comment. Sep-Oct 1981, v17, p41-44.
Hollywood Reporter. Oct 7, 1981, p3.
The Los Angeles Times. Oct 9, 1981, v1, p1.
Maclean's. Oct 19, 1981, v94, p66.
Magill's Cinema Annual, 1982. p316-19.
The New Republic. Nov 18, 1981, v185, p26.
New York. Oct 19, 1981, v14, p87-88.
The New York Times. Oct 9, 1981, SecIII, p16.
The New Yorker. Oct 26, 1981, v57, p178.
Newsweek. Oct 12, 1981, v98, p98.
Time. Oct 12, 1981, v118, p102.
Variety. Oct 5, 1981, p3.

Rich, Young and Pretty (US; Taurog, Norman; 1951)
BFI/Monthly Film Bulletin. Sep 1951, v18, p332.
Film Daily. Jul 9, 1951, p10.
Hollywood Reporter. Jul 2, 1951, p3.
The London Times. Jul 30, 1951, p2.
Motion Picture Herald Product Digest. Jul 7, 1951, p921-22.
The New York Times. Jul 26, 1951, p17.
Newsweek. Jul 30, 1951, v38, p68.
Time. Aug 20, 1951, v58, p89.
Variety. Jul 4, 1951, p8.

Richard III (GB; Olivier, Laurence; 1955)
America. Mar 17, 1956, v94, p675-76.
Commonweal. Mar 23, 1956, v63, p643.
Film Culture. 1956, v2, p21-23.
Film Daily. Mar 8, 1956, p10.
Film News. Jan-Feb 1976, v33, p27.
Film Quarterly. Sum 1967, v20, p23-32.
Films and Filming. Dec 1955, v2, p16.
Films in Review. Mar 1956, v7, p122-26.
The Films of Laurence Olivier. p115-19.
Focus on Shakespearean Films. p131-46.
The Great British Films. p168-71.
Hollywood Reporter. Sep 25, 1956, p3.
Laurence Olivier (Hirsch). p95-109.
Laurence Olivier: Theater & Cinema. p124-31.
Literature Film Quarterly. 1976, v4, p99-107.
Magill's Survey of Cinema. Series II. v5, p2014-18.
The Nation. Mar 10, 1956, v182, p207.
The New York Times. Mar 12, 1956, p1.
The New Yorker. Dec 31, 1955, v31, p49.
The New Yorker. Mar 17, 1956, v32, p76.
Newsweek. Mar 19, 1956, v47, p105-09.
Quarterly of Film, Radio and Television. Sum 1956, v10, p399-415.
Quarterly of Film, Radio and Television. Spr 1957, v11, p280-93.
Saturday Review. Mar 10, 1956, v39, 26-27.
Shakespeare on Film. p136-47.
Sight and Sound. Wint 1955-56, v25, p144-45.
Time. Mar 12, 1956, v67, p112.
Variety. Dec 21, 1955, p6.

Richard's Things (GB; Harvey, Anthony; 1981)
Hollywood Reporter. Jun 22, 1981, p15.
The Los Angeles Times. Jul 10, 1981, SecVI, p12.
Magill's Cinema Annual, 1982. p321-23.
Ms. Oct 1981, v10, p77.
The Nation. Jul 25, 1981, v233, p91-92.
The New Republic. Jun 27, 1981, v184, p26-27.
The New York Times. Jun 28, 1981, SecII, p15.
Variety. Jan 10, 1981, p18.

Ride the High Country (Also titled: Guns in the Afternoon) (US; Peckinpah, Sam; 1962)
Cinema. 1963, v1, n3, p33.
Dictionary of Films. p312.
Film Daily. May 9, 1962, p7.
Filmfacts. Jul 6, 1962, v5, p137-38.
Films and Filming. Jun 1962, v8, p38.
Films in Review. Apr 1962, v13, p232-33.
The Films of the Sixties. p71.
The Great Adventure Films. p236-39.
Hollywood Reporter. May 7, 1962, p3.
Magill's Survey of Cinema. Series I. v3, p1447-50.
The Making of the Great Westerns. p315-28.
Motion Picture Herald Product Digest. May 16, 1962, p556.
The New York Times. Jul 21, 1962, p26.
Newsweek. Jul 16, 1962, v60, p80.
Quarterly Review of Film Studies. 1977, v2, n1, p75-87.
Quarterly Review of Film Studies. 1979, v4, n3, p379-88.
Quarterly Review of Film Studies. 1979, v4, n4, p507-08.
Saturday Review. Jul 21, 1962, v45, p22.
Sight and Sound. Sum 1962, v31, p146.
Time. Jul 13, 1962, v80, p66.
Variety. May 9, 1962, p7.

Ride the Man Down (US; Kane, Joseph; 1952)
BFI/Monthly Film Bulletin. May 1953, v20, p74.
Film Daily. Oct 29, 1952, p6.

Hollywood Reporter. Oct 27, 1952, p3.
Motion Picture Herald Product Digest. Nov 1, 1952, p1590.
National Parent-Teacher. Jan 1953, v47, p37.
Variety. Oct 29, 1952, p6.

Riders To the Stars (US; Carlson, Richard; 1954)
BFI/Monthly Film Bulletin. Jun 1954, v21, p90.
Film Daily. Feb 15, 1954, p6.
Future Tense: The Cinema of Science Fiction. p79.
Hollywood Reporter. Jan 15, 1954, p3.
The London Times. May 10, 1954, p9.
Motion Picture Herald Product Digest. Mar 27, 1954, p2237.
National Parent-Teacher. Mar 1954, v48, p40.
The New York Times. Mar 20, 1954, p10.
The Tatler. May 19, 1954, v212, p412.
Time. Mar 15, 1954, v63, p106.
Variety. Jan 20, 1954, p6.

Riding High (US; Capra, Frank; 1950)
BFI/Monthly Film Bulletin. Feb-Mar 1950, v17, p26-27.
Christian Century. May 3, 1950, v67, p575.
Commonweal. Apr 28, 1950, v52, p70.
Film Daily. Jan 12, 1950, p5.
The Films of Bing Crosby. p189-90.
The Films of Frank Capra. p151-55.
Frank Capra (Maland). p161-64.
Hollywood Reporter. Jan 9, 1950, p3.
The London Times. Mar 6, 1950, p8.
Motion Picture Herald Product Digest. Jan 14, 1950, p153.
The Nation. Jun 10, 1950, v170, p582.
The New Republic. May 1, 1950, v122, p21.
The New Statesman and Nation. Mar 18, 1950, v39, p300.
The New York Times. Apr 11, 1950, p26.
The New Yorker. Apr 22, 1950, v26, p105.
Newsweek. Apr 17, 1950, v35, p94.
The Spectator. Mar 3, 1950, v184, p274.
Time. May 1, 1950, v55, p88.
Variety. Jan 11, 1950, v137, p6.

Rififi (French title: Du Rififi chez des Hommes; Also titled: Rififi Means Trouble) (FR; Dassin, Jules; 1955)
Commonweal. Jul 6, 1956, v64, p348.
Films and Filming. Apr 1963, v9, p35.
Films in Review. Jun-Jul 1956, v7, p289-90.
The Great French Films. p257.
The Nation. Jun 23, 1956, v182, p536.
The New York Times. Jun 6, 1956, p37.
The New York Times. Jun 10, 1956, SecII, p1.
The New Yorker. Jun 23, 1956, v32, p71.
Newsweek. Jun 18, 1956, v47, p122.
Saturday Review. Jun 23, 1956, v39, p29.
Sight and Sound. Fall 1955, v25, p91.
Time. Jul 16, 1956, v68, p90.
Variety. Jun 8, 1955, p6.

Rififi in Panama (Also titled: Du Rififi a Paname; The Upper Hand) (FR, IT, WGER; De La Patelliere, Denys; 1965)
BFI/Monthly Film Bulletin. Feb 1967, v34, p26.
Film Daily. Aug 4, 1967, p7.
Filmfacts. Sep 15, 1967, v10, p224-25.
The Great Gangster Pictures. p127.
Motion Picture Herald Product Digest. Aug 16, 1967, p714-15.
Playboy. Dec 1967, v14, p46.

Rififi Means Trouble *See* Rififi

Right Cross (US; Sturges, John; 1950)
BFI/Monthly Film Bulletin. Oct 1950, v17, p157.
Commonweal. Dec 8, 1950, v53, p232.

Risky Business (US; Brickman, Paul; 1983)
Films in Review. Oct 1983, v34, p41.
Humanist. Nov-Dec 1983, v43, p41-42.
The Los Angeles Times. Aug 5, 1983, SecV, p1.
Maclean's. Aug 15, 1983, v96, p46.
Magill's Cinema Annual, 1984. p349-53.
National Review. Oct 14, 1983, v35, p1295.
The New Leader. Sep 19, 1983, v66, p19-20.
The New Republic. Sep 19, 1983, v189, p22.
New York. Aug 22, 1983, v16, p62.
The New York Times. Aug 5, 1983, SecIII, p13.
The New Yorker. Sep 5, 1983, v59, p109.
Newsweek. Aug 15, 1983, v102, p64.

The Ritz (GB; Lester, Richard; 1976)
America. Sep 4, 1976, v135, p99-100.
BFI/Monthly Film Bulletin. Dec 1976, v43, p255-56.
Film Bulletin. Sep-Oct 1976, v45, p14-17.
Film Illustrated. Apr 1976, v5, p292.
Film Illustrated. Nov 1976, v6, p108-11.
Hollywood Reporter. Aug 6, 1976, p3.
Independent Film Journal. Aug 6, 1976, v78, p7-8.
The Los Angeles Times. Oct 6, 1976, SecIV, p1.
Motion Picture Herald Product Digest. Aug 25, 1976, p26.
The New Republic. Sep 11, 1976, v175, p25.
New York. Aug 30, 1976, v9, p50-52.
The New York Times. Aug 13, 1976, SecIII, p12.
The New Yorker. Aug 23, 1976, v52, p70-71.
Newsweek. Aug 30, 1976, v88, p74.
Richard Lester: a Guide to References and Resources. p51-52.
Saturday Review. Sep 4, 1976, v3, p55.
Time. Aug 30, 1976, v108, p72.
Variety. Aug 11, 1976, p19.
The Village Voice. Jul 26, 1976, v117, 126.
Vogue. Sep 1976, v166, p239.

The River (INDIA; Renoir, Jean; 1951)
BFI/Monthly Film Bulletin. Jun 1952, v19, p77.
Christian Century. Nov 7, 1951, v68, p1294.
Commonweal. Sep 21, 1951, v54, p573.
Film Daily. Sep 7, 1951, p10.
Film News. Sep-Oct 1978, v35, p34.
Films in Review. Oct 1951, v2, p43-46.
Hollywood Reporter. Oct 17, 1951, p4.
Jean Renoir: A Guide to References and Resources. p141-45.
Jean Renoir: My Life and My Films. p248-59.
Jean Renoir: The World of His Films. p39-41, 145-47.
Library Journal. Aug 1951, v76, p1240.
Motion Picture Herald Product Digest. Sep 8, 1951, p1006.
The New Republic. Sep 10, 1951, v125, p22.
The New Statesman and Nation. May 3, 1952, v43, p525.
The New York Times. Sep 11, 1951, p33.
The New Yorker. Sep 15, 1951, v27, p107.
Newsweek. Sep 24, 1951, v38, p87.
Saturday Review. Aug 4, 1951, v34, p49-50.
Senior Scholastic. Oct 17, 1951, v59, p30.
Sight and Sound. Oct-Dec 1951, v21, p91.
Sight and Sound. Jan-Mar 1952, v21, p123-24.
The Spectator. Apr 25, 1952, v188, p545.
The Tatler. May 7, 1952, v204, p321.
Theatre Arts. Aug 1951, v35, p103.
Time. Sep 24, 1951, v58, p104.
Variety. Sep 12, 1951, p6.
The Velvet Light Trap. Wint 1974, n11, p54-56.

The River (US; Rydell, Mark; 1984)
American Cinematographer. Nov 1984, v65, p69-72.
BFI/Monthly Film Bulletin. Apr 1985, v52, p121.
Hollywood Reporter. Nov 14, 1984, p3.

Horizon. Dec 1984, v27, p18-20.
The Los Angeles Times. Dec 19, 1984, SecVI, p1.
The New York Times. Dec 16, 1984, SecII, p1.
Newsweek. Dec 31, 1984, v104, p65.
On Location. Feb 1984, v7, p38.
Variety. Nov 14, 1984, p13.
The Village Voice. Dec 25, 1984, v29, p72.

River of No Return (US; Preminger, Otto; 1954)
America. May 8, 1954, v91, p175.
BFI/Monthly Film Bulletin. Sep 1954, v21, p130-31.
The Cinema of Otto Preminger. p108-09.
Commonweal. May 21, 1954, v60, p176.
Film Daily. Apr 23, 1954, p6.
Films and Filming. Oct 1954, v1, p29.
Films in Review. Jun-Jul 1954, v5, p307.
The Films of Marilyn Monroe. p110-15.
Framework. Wint 1977, n5, p5-11.
Hollywood Reporter. Apr 23, 1954, p3.
The London Times. Aug 9, 1954, p9.
Motion Picture Herald Product Digest. Apr 24, 1954, p2269.
Movie. Sep 1962, n2, p18-19.
National Parent-Teacher. Jun 1954, v48, p40.
The New York Times. May 1, 1954, p13.
The New Yorker. May 8, 1954, v30, p70.
Newsweek. May 10, 1954, v43, p100.
The Tatler. Aug 18, 1954, v213, p288.
Time. May 17, 1954, v63, p89.
Variety. Apr 28, 1954, p6.

The Road (Fellini, 1954) *See* Strada, La

The Road (Goren, 1982) *See* Yol

The Road to Bali (US; Walker, Hal; 1952)
BFI/Monthly Film Bulletin. Jan 1953, v20, p11.
Catholic World. Jan 1953, v176, p301.
Christian Century. Jan 21, 1953, v70, p95.
Commonweal. Jan 2, 1953, v57, p334.
Film Daily. Nov 19, 1952, p6.
The Films of Bing Crosby. p199-202.
Hollywood Reporter. Nov 18, 1952, p4.
Motion Picture Herald Product Digest. Nov 22, 1952, p1613.
The New York Times. Jan 30, 1953, p25.
Newsweek. Jan 26, 1953, v41, p98.
The Spectator. Dec 5, 1952, v189, p762.
The Tatler. Dec 17, 1952, v206, p654.
Theatre Arts. Jan 1953, v37, p84.
Time. Dec 22, 1952, v60, p66.
Variety. Nov 19, 1952, p6.

The Road to Hope *See* Cammino della speranza, Il

The Road Warrior (Also titled: Mad Max II) (AUSTRALIA; Miller, George; 1981)
The Los Angeles Times. May 20, 1982, SecVI, p1.
Maclean's. May 31, 1982, v95, p58.
Magill's Cinema Annual, 1983. p277-82.
The New Republic. Oct 11, 1982, v187, p24-25.
New York. Aug 30, 1982, v15, p61.
The New York Times. Apr 28, 1982, SecIII, p24.
The New Yorker. Sep 6, 1982, v58, p96-99.
Newsweek. May 31, 1982, v99, p67.
Rolling Stone. Jun 24, 1982, p25.
Time. May 10, 1982, v119, p115.
Variety. Dec 21, 1981, p3.

Roadie (US; Rudolph, Alan; 1980)
BFI/Monthly Film Bulletin. Jun 1981, v48, p119.
Hollywood Reporter. Jul 11, 1980, p2.
Motion Picture Herald Product Digest. Jun 25, 1980, p6.

The New York Times. Jun 13, 1980, SecIII, p8.
Newsday. Jun 13, 1980, SecII, p7.
Variety. Jun 11, 1980, p20.
The Village Voice. Jun 23, 1980, p44.

Rob Roy, the Highland Rogue (Also titled: Rob Roy) (GB; French, Harold; 1953)
America. Feb 6, 1954, v90, p490.
American Magazine. Feb 1954, v157, p12.
Catholic World. Jan 1954, v178, p304.
Commonweal. Feb 19, 1954, v59, p497.
The Disney Films (Maltin). p115-16.
Farm Journal. Feb 1954, v78, p108.
Film Daily. Dec 3, 1953, p6.
Films in Review. Apr 1954, v5, p194.
Hollywood Reporter. Nov 20, 1953, p3.
Illustrated London News. Aug 8, 1953, v223, p225.
Illustrated London News. Nov 14, 1953, v223, p784.
Library Journal. Jan 15, 1954, v79, p139.
Motion Picture Herald Product Digest. Nov 23, 1953, p2086.
National Parent-Teacher. Jan 1954, v48, p38.
The New York Times. Feb 4, 1954, p21.
The New Yorker. Feb 13, 1954, v29, p105.
Newsweek. Feb 15, 1954, v43, p94.
Saturday Review. Feb 20, 1954, v37, p32.
Senior Scholastic. Feb 17, 1954, v64, p30.
The Spectator. Oct 30, 1953, v191, p478-79.
The Tatler. Nov 11, 1953, v210, p328.
Time. Feb 8, 1954, v63, p96.
Variety. Nov 4, 1953, p6.
Walt Disney: A Guide to References and Resources. p46-47.

The Robe (US; Koster, Henry; 1953)
America. Oct 3, 1953, v90, p26.
BFI/Monthly Film Bulletin. Jan 1954, v21, n240, p5.
Catholic World. Nov 1953, v178, p143.
Collier's. May 23, 1953, v131, p31-34.
Commonweal. Oct 9, 1953, v59, p12-13.
Film Daily. Sep 17, 1953, p7.
Films in Review. May 1953, v4, n5, p226-28.
The Films of the Fifties. p91-94.
Harper's. Nov 1953, v207, p92-93.
Hollywood Reporter. Sep 17, 1953, p3.
Library Journal. Oct 1, 1953, v78, p1677.
Life. Jul 27, 1953, v35, p54-59.
Look. Sep 8, 1953, v17, p70-73.
Magill's Survey of Cinema. Series II. v5, p2025.
The Nation. Oct 17, 1953, v177, p318.
The New York Times. May 17, 1953, SecII, p1.
The New Yorker. Sep 26, 1953, v28, p139.
Newsweek. Sep 28, 1953, v42, p96.
Oct 1953. v4, n8, p426-28.
Saturday Review. Oct 3, 1953, v36, p44.
Senior Scholastic. Dec 2, 1953, v63, p29.
Sight and Sound. Jan-Mar 1954, v23, n3, p143-44.
Time. Oct 12, 1953, v62, p110.
Variety. Sep 23, 1953, p6.

Robin and Marian (US, GB; Lester, Richard; 1976)
America. Mar 20, 1976, v134, p236-37.
BFI/Monthly Film Bulletin. May 1976, v43, p105.
Christian Century. Jun 23, 1976, v93, p600.
Film Bulletin. Mar 1976, v45, p34-35.
Film Heritage. 1976, v11, n4, p76-43.
Film Illustrated. Jun 1976, v5, p366.
Films and Filming. Jun 1976, v27, p28-29.
Films in Review. May 1976, v27, p308-10.
Films in Review. Apr 1976, v27, p241.
Hollywood Reporter. Mar 11, 1976, p6.
Independent Film Journal. Mar 17, 1976, v77, p9.

The Los Angeles Times. Mar 28, 1976, Calendar, p1.
Magill's Survey of Cinema. Series II. v5, p2034-41.
Millimeter. May 1976, v4, p28-30.
Motion Picture Herald Product Digest. Mar 24, 1976, p82.
Movietone News. Jun 1976, n50, p46-47.
Movietone News. Apr 1976, n49, p13-17.
The New Republic. Mar 27, 1976, v174, p22.
New Statesman. May 28, 1976, v91, p724.
New York. Mar 29, 1976, v9, p81-82.
The New York Times. Mar 14, 1976, SecII, p1.
The New Yorker. Mar 22, 1976, v52, p111-13.
Newsweek. Mar 22, 1976, v87, p83.
Richard Lester: A Guide to References and Resources. p48-49.
Robin and Marian. 1976.
Saturday Review. Apr 17, 1976, v3, p44.
Social Policy. Nov-Dec 1976, v7, p111-12.
Time. Mar 22, 1976, v107, p78.
Variety. Mar 10, 1976, p22.
The Village Voice. Mar 29, 1976, p117.
When the Lights Go Down. p157-60.

Robin and the Seven Hoods (US; Douglas, Gordon; 1964)
BFI/Monthly Film Bulletin. Jun 1964, v31, p93-94.
Commonweal. Jun 19, 1964, v80, p400.
Ebony. Jun 1964, v19, p90-92.
Film Daily. Jun 26, 1964, v124, p15.
Films and Filming. Aug 1964, v10, p21.
The Films of Bing Crosby. p235-38.
The Films of Frank Sinatra. p198-200.
Hollywood Reporter. Jun 25, 1964, v181, p3.
Life. Jul 24, 1964, v57, p11.
The Los Angeles Times. Aug 1, 1964, v3, p5.
Motion Picture Herald Product Digest. Jul 8, 1964, v232, p82.
The New York Times. Aug 6, 1964, p20.
Newsweek. Jul 6, 1964, v64, p76.
Saturday Review. May 16, 1964, v47, p29.
Time. Jul 17, 1964, v84, p88.
Unholy Fools, Wits, Comics, Disturbers of the Peace. p166-67.
Variety. Jun 24, 1964, p7.

Robinson Crusoe *See* The Adventures of Robinson Crusoe

Rocco and His Brothers (Italian title: Rocco e suoi fratelli) (IT; Visconti, Luchino; 1960)
America. Sep 23, 1961, v105, p811.
Christian Century. Nov 15, 1961, v78, p1369-70.
Commonweal. Jul 7, 1961, v74, p378.
Esquire. Apr 1961, v55, p21.
Hollywood Reporter. Sep 18, 1961, p3.
The International Dictionary of Films and Filmmakers. v1, p395-96.
Italian Cinema (Bondanella). p196-99.
Luchino Visconti (Tonetti). p79-92.
Magill's Survey of Cinema. Foreign Language Films. v6, p2566-69.
Motion Picture Herald Product Digest. Jul 8, 1961, p197.
The Nation. Sep 16, 1961, v193, p168.
The New Republic. Jul 3, 1961, v145, p32.
The New York Times. Jun 28, 1961, p40.
The New Yorker. Jul 1, 1961, v37, p41.
Saturday Review. Jul 1, 1961, v44, p24.
Time. Jul 21, 1961, v78, p56.
Variety. Sep 14, 1960, p6.

Rock and Roll High School (Also titled: Rock 'n' Roll High School) (US; Arkush, Allan; 1979)

BFI/Monthly Film Bulletin. Feb 1980, v47, p26.
Cult Movies. p298-301, 372-74.
The Films of Roger Corman. p74-76.
Hollywood Reporter. Apr 23, 1979, p3.
The New York Times. Aug 4, 1979, p10.
Rolling Stone. Jul 12, 1979, p25.
Variety. Apr 25, 1979, p19.

The Rocket Man (US; Rudolph, Oscar; 1954)
BFI/Monthly Film Bulletin. Aug 1954, v21, p122.
Film Daily. May 17, 1954, p6.
Hollywood Reporter. Apr 28, 1954, p3.
Motion Picture Herald Product Digest. May 1, 1954, p2278.
National Parent-Teacher. Jun 1954, v48, p39.
Variety. May 5, 1954, p6.

Rocketship X-M (US; Neumann, Kurt; 1950)
BFI/Monthly Film Bulletin. Aug 1950, v17, p120.
Boxoffice. Aug 2, 1976, v109, p7.
Boxoffice. Aug 7, 1978, v113, p8.
Film Daily. May 16, 1950, p5.
Future Tense: The Cinema of Science Fiction. p74-75, 78.
Hollywood Reporter. Apr 25, 1950, p3.
The London Times. Aug 7, 1950, p6.
The New Statesman and Nation. Aug 12, 1950, v40, p172, 174.
The New York Times. May 27, 1950, p10.
Newsweek. Jun 5, 1950, v35, p86.
Shots in the Dark. p216-18.
Variety. May 3, 1950, p6.

The Rocking Horse Winner (GB; Pelissier, Anthony; 1949)
BFI/Monthly Film Bulletin. Dec 1949, v16, p214-15.
Christian Century. Oct 4, 1950, v67, p1183.
Commonweal. Jun 23, 1950, v52, p272.
Film Daily. Jun 6, 1950, p7.
Film News. Jan-Feb 1977, v34, p32.
Films and Filming. Nov 1970, v17, p26-30.
From Fiction to Film: D. H. Lawrence's The Rocking Horse Winner. 1974.
The Great British Films. p137-39.
Hollywood Reporter. Jun 8, 1950, p3.
Illustrated London News. Jan 7, 1950, v216, p24.
Kiss Kiss Bang Bang. p426.
Library Journal. Apr 1, 1950, v75, p570.
Literature/Film Quarterly. Jan 1973, v1, p55-63.
Made Into Movies. p287-97.
Magill's Survey of Cinema. Series I. v3, p1462-64.
Media and Methods. Dec 1977, v14, p56-58.
Motion Picture Herald Product Digest. Jun 10, 1950, p330.
The New Republic. Jun 26, 1950, v122, p22.
The New York Times. Jun 9, 1950, p29.
The New Yorker. Jun 10, 1950, v26, p75.
Newsweek. Jun 19, 1950, v35, p90.
Saturday Review. Jun 24, 1950, v33, p34.
Time. Jun 26, 1950, v55, p96.
Wilson Library Bulletin. Oct 1978, v53, p176-77.

A Rockumentary by Martin Di Bergi *See* This Is Spinal Tap

Rocky (US; Avildsen, John G.; 1976)
Before My Eyes. p264-65.
BFI/Monthly Film Bulletin. Apr 1977, v44, p78-79.
Film Bulletin. Nov-Dec 1976, v45, p40.
Films in Review. Jan 1977, v28, p56.

The Films of the Seventies. p152-53.
Hollywood Reporter. Nov 5, 1976, p3.
Independent Film Journal. Nov 12, 1976, v78, p7-8.
The Los Angeles Times. Nov 28, 1976, Calendar, p1.
Magill's Survey of Cinema. Series II. v1, p1465-68.
Motion Picture Herald Product Digest. Nov 24, 1976, p51.
The New Republic. Nov 27, 1976, v175, p18.
New York. Oct 18, 1976, v9, p70-75.
New York. Nov 29, 1976, v9, p69-72.
The New York Times. Nov 28, 1976, p17.
The New Yorker. Nov 29, 1976, v52, p154.
Newsweek. Nov 29, 1976, v88, p113.
The Official Rocky Scrapbook. 1976.
Saturday Review. Nov 27, 1976, v4, p40-41.
Time. Nov 15, 1976, v108, p99.
Time. Dec 13, 1976, v108, p98.
Variety. Nov 10, 1976, p20.
The Village Voice. Nov 8, 1976, p12-13.
The Village Voice. Nov 22, 1976, p61.
Vogue. Jan 1977, v167, p104-05.
When the Lights Go Down. p213-16.

Rocky II (US; Stallone, Sylvester; 1979)
BFI/Monthly Film Bulletin. Oct 1979, v46, p212.
Commonweal. Sep 14, 1979, v106, p501-02.
Films in Review. Aug-Sep 1979, v30, p436.
The Films of the Seventies. p254-56.
Hollywood Reporter. Jun 13, 1979, p3.
The Los Angeles Times. Jun 17, 1979, Calendar, p1.
Magill's Survey of Cinema. Series II. v5, p2041-44.
Motion Picture Herald Product Digest. Jul 4, 1979, p9.
The New Republic. Jun 30, 1979, v180, p25.
The New York Times. Jun 5, 1979, SecIII, p14.
The New Yorker. Jul 2, 1979, v55, p66.
Newsweek. Jun 25, 1979, v93, p81-82.
Sports Illustrated. Jun 25, 1979, v50, p63.
Time. Jun 25, 1979, v113, p52.
Variety. Jun 13, 1979, p14.

Rocky III (US; Stallone, Sylvester; 1982)
Film Comment. Jul-Aug 1982, v18, p61-63.
Hollywood Reporter. May 19, 1982, p3.
The Los Angeles Times. May 28, 1982, SecVI, p1.
Maclean's. Jun 7, 1982, v95, p56.
Magill's Cinema Annual, 1983. p283-87.
The New Leader. Jun 14, 1982, v65, p19.
New York. May 31, 1982, v15, p80.
The New York Times. May 28, 1982, SecIII, p8.
The New Yorker. May 31, 1982, v58, p84-85.
The New Yorker. Aug 23, 1982, v58, p28-29.
Newsweek. May 31, 1982, v99, p70.
Rolling Stone. Jun 10, 1982, p37-38.
Saturday Review. Jun 1982, v91, p64-65.
Sports Illustrated. Jun 7, 1982, v56, p70.
Time. Jun 14, 1982, v119, p58-60.
Variety. May 19, 1982, p3.

Rocky IV (US; Stallone, Sylvester; 1985)
Commonweal. Jan 17, 1986, v113, p16-17.
Hollywood Reporter. Nov 27, 1985, p3.
The Los Angeles Times. Nov 27, 1985, SecVI, p1.
Magill's Cinema Annual, 1986. p319-23.
New York. Dec 9, 1985, v18, p90.
The New York Times. Nov 27, 1985, SecIII, p18.
Newsweek. Dec 9, 1985, v106, p92.
Newsweek. Dec 23, 1985, v106, p58-62.
Time. Dec 9, 1985, v126, p110.
Variety. Nov 27, 1985, p15.
The Wall Street Journal. Nov 27, 1985, p18.

The Rocky Horror Picture Show (GB, US;
  Sharman, Jim; 1975)
  BFI/Monthly Film Bulletin. Aug 1975, v42,
    p185.
  Hollywood Reporter. Sep 24, 1975, p15.
  *The International Dictionary of Films and
    Filmmakers.* v1, p397-98.
  The Los Angeles Times. Sep 26, 1974, SecIV,
    p15.
  Magill's Survey of Cinema. Series II. v5, p2044-
    49.
  National Review. Nov 24, 1978, v30, p1493-94.
  Newsweek. Jul 17, 1978, v92, p93.
  The Rocky Horror Picture Show Scrapbook.
    1975.
  Variety. Sep 24, 1975, p22.
  The Village Voice. Sep 19, 1977, p55.
  The World of Fantastic Films. p154-55.

Rocky Mountain (US; Keighley, William;
  1950)
  BFI/Monthly Film Bulletin. Apr 1951, v18,
    p252.
  Commonweal. Nov 17, 1950, v53, p142.
  Film Daily. Oct 4, 1950, p4.
  The Films of Errol Flynn. p167-69.
  The Great Western Pictures. p310.
  Hollywood Reporter. Oct 3, 1950, p3.
  The London Times. Feb 26, 1951, p6.
  Motion Picture Herald Product Digest. Oct 7,
    1950, p509.
  The New York Times. Nov 4, 1950, p13.
  The Spectator. Feb 23, 1951, v186, p242.
  Variety. Oct 4, 1950, p6.

Rodan (JAPAN; Honda, Inoshiro; 1957)
  BFI/Monthly Film Bulletin. Feb 1958, v25,
    p23-24.
  Commonweal. Dec 13, 1957, v67, p288.
  Film Daily. Nov 7, 1957, v112, p8.
  Films and Filming. Mar 1958, v4, p24.
  Hollywood Reporter. Nov 6, 1957, p3.

Roede Kappe, Den *See* Hagbard and Signe

Rogue Cop (US; Rowland, Roy; 1954)
  America. Sep 25, 1954, v91, p631.
  BFI/Monthly Film Bulletin. Dec 1954, v21,
    p175.
  Farm Journal. Nov 1954, v78, p73.
  Film Daily. Sep 1, 1954, p6.
  The Films of Robert Taylor. p142-44.
  Hollywood Reporter. Sep 1, 1954, p3.
  Library Journal. Oct 15, 1954, v79, p1884.
  The London Times. Nov 8, 1954, p10.
  Motion Picture Herald Product Digest. Sep 4,
    1954, p129.
  National Parent-Teacher. Nov 1954, v49, p40.
  The New Statesman and Nation. Nov 13, 1954,
    v48, p612.
  The New York Times. Sep 18, 1954, p12.
  The New Yorker. Sep 25, 1954, v30, p62.
  Newsweek. Sep 27, 1954, v44, p98.
  Senior Scholastic. Nov 17, 1954, v65, p37.
  Time. Oct 18, 1954, v64, p106.
  Variety. Sep 1, 1954, p6.

Roi de Coeur, Le *See* King of Hearts

Roi, Le *See* A Royal Affair

Rollerball (US; Jewison, Norman; 1975)
  BFI/Monthly Film Bulletin. Oct 1975, v42,
    p223.
  Commonweal. Jul 18, 1975, v102, p277.
  Films in Review. Oct 1975, v26, p503.
  The Los Angeles Times. Jun 22, 1975,
    Calendar, p1.
  Motion Picture Herald Product Digest. Jul 9,
    1975, p9.
  The New Republic. Jul 26, 1975, v173, p20.
  New Yorker. Jul 7, 1975, v51, p67-68.

Newsweek. Jul 7, 1975, v86, p56.
Saturday Review. Aug 9, 1975, v2, p54.
Sports Illustrated. Jul 7, 1975, v43, p1.
Time. Jul 7, 1975, v106, p46.
Variety. Jun 25, 1975, p23.

Rollercoaster (US; Goldstone, James; 1977)
  American Cinematographer. Jun 1977, v58,
    p592-601.
  BFI/Monthly Film Bulletin. Jan 1978, v45, p27.
  Films and Filming. Aug 1977, v23, p38-39.
  Films in Review. Oct 1977, v28, p495-98.
  The Films of Henry Fonda. p237-38.
  Hollywood Reporter. Apr 28, 1977, p2.
  The Los Angeles Times. Jun 10, 1977, SecIV,
    p1.
  Motion Picture Herald Product Digest. Jun 22,
    1977, p8.
  New York. Jul 4, 1977, v10, p54-55.
  The New York Times. Jun 11, 1977, p12.
  The New Yorker. Jun 20, 1977, v53, p90-91.
  Saturday Review. Jul 23, 1977, v4, p46-47.
  Senior Scholastic. Oct 6, 1977, v110, p31.
  Time. Jul 11, 1977, v110, p55.
  Variety. Apr 27, 1977, p20.

Roman Holiday (US; Wyler, William; 1953)
  America. Sep 5, 1953, v89, p562.
  BFI/Monthly Film Bulletin. Sep 1953, v20,
    n236, p132.
  Catholic World. Sep 1953, v177, p462.
  Commonweal. Sep 18, 1953, v58, p586.
  Film Daily. Jul 1, 1953, p6.
  Films in Review. Aug-Sep 1953, v4, n7, p363-
    64.
  The Films of Gregory Peck. p121-25.
  Hollywood Reporter. Jun 30, 1953, p3.
  Life. Aug 24, 1953, v35, p76.
  Look. Aug 11, 1953, v17, p58-59.
  Magill's Survey of Cinema. Series II. v5, p2050.
  The Nation. Sep 12, 1953, v177, p218.
  The New York Times. Jul 13, 1952, SecII, p5.
  Newsweek. Sep 7, 1953, v42, p86.
  Saturday Review. Sep 5, 1953, v36, p26.
  Sight and Sound. Oct-Dec 1953, v23, n2, p91.
  Time. Sep 7, 1953, v62, 60-62.
  Variety. Jul 1, 1953, p6.
  *William Wyler: A Guide to References and
    Resources.* p131-33.
  William Wyler (Anderegg). p176-80.
  William Wyler (Madsen). p308-12.

The Roman Spring of Mrs. Stone (GB;
  Quintero, Jose; 1961)
  America. Jan 13, 1962, v106, p481.
  BFI/Monthly Film Bulletin. Mar 1962, v29,
    p36.
  Commonweal. Dec 29, 1961, v75, p365.
  Film Daily. Nov 30, 1961, p6.
  Filmfacts. Jan 12, 1962, v4, p329-30.
  Films in Review. Jan 1962, v8, p42-43.
  The Films of Tennessee Williams. p249-79.
  The Films of Warren Beatty. p68-78.
  The Great Romantic Films. p180-83.
  The New York Times. Dec 29, 1961, p11.
  The New York Times. Jan 15, 1961, SecII, p7.
  The New Yorker. Jan 13, 1962, v37, p97.
  Newsweek. Jan 1, 1962, v59, p53.
  Saturday Review. Dec 9, 1961, v44, p28.
  Tennessee Williams and Film. p84-92.
  Time. Dec 29, 1961, v78, p57.
  Variety. Dec 6, 1961, p6.

Romancing the Stone (US; Zemeckis,
  Robert; 1984)
  BFI/Monthly Film Bulletin. Aug 1984, v51,
    p249-50.
  Christian Century. Jul 18, 1984, v101, p722.
  Commonweal. May 18, 1984, v111, p301.
  Film Journal. May 1984, v87, p24.
  Films and Filming. Jun 1984, n357, p18.

Films in Review. May 1984, v35, p303-04.
The Los Angeles Times. Mar 29, 1984, SecVI,
  p1.
Maclean's. Apr 2, 1984, v97, p66.
Millimeter. Apr 1984, v12, p166.
The New Leader. Apr 16, 1984, v67, p19.
The New Republic. May 7, 1984, v190, p26.
New Statesman. Aug 17, 1984, v108, p27-28.
The New York Times. Mar 30, 1984, SecIII,
  p19.
The New Yorker. Apr 30, 1984, v60, p101-03.
Newsweek. Apr 16, 1984, v103, p93.
Photoplay. Sep 1984, v35, p46-48.
Rolling Stone. May 24, 1984, p23-25.
Time. Apr 2, 1984, v123, p89.
Variety. Mar 28, 1984, p20.
The Village Voice. Apr 3, 1984, p49.

The Romantic Englishwoman (US; Losey,
  Joseph; 1975)
  BFI/Monthly Film Bulletin. Oct 1975, v42,
    p224.
  Commonweal. Jan 16, 1976, v103, p51-52.
  Films in Review. Jan 1976, v27, p56.
  Joseph Losey (Hirsch). p150-54.
  The Los Angeles Times. Dec 23, 1975, SecII,
    p6.
  Motion Picture Herald Product Digest. Dec 10,
    1975, p52.
  The New York Times. Nov 27, 1975, p46.
  The New York Times. Dec 14, 1975, SecII, p15.
  The New Yorker. Dec 8, 1975, v51, p165-66.
  Saturday Review. Jan 10, 1976, v3, p64.
  Variety. May 28, 1975, p19.
  When the Lights Go Down. p93-95.

Romeo and Juliet (GB, IT; Castellani,
  Renato; 1954)
  America. Dec 25, 1954, v92, p346.
  BFI/Monthly Film Bulletin. Oct 1954, v21,
    p145.
  Catholic World. Dec 1954, v180, p222.
  Cinema, the Magic Vehicle. v2, p203-04.
  Commonweal. Dec 10, 1954, v61, p289.
  Farm Journal. Nov 1954, v78, p73.
  Film Culture. Mar-Apr 1955, v1, p44-45.
  Film Daily. Dec 17, 1954, p10.
  Films and Filming. Nov 1954, v1, p15.
  Films in Review. Dec 1954, v5, p538-40.
  Hollywood Reporter. Dec 17, 1954, p3.
  Illustrated London News. Oct 2, 1954, v225,
    p559.
  Kiss Kiss Bang Bang. p426-27.
  Library Journal. Nov 15, 1954, v79, p2182.
  Life. Dec 6, 1954, v37, p133-34.
  Literature/Film Quarterly. 1973, v1, n4, p343-
    51.
  Mademoiselle. Nov 1954, v40, p143.
  Motion Picture Herald Product Digest. Dec 25,
    1954, p257.
  The Nation. Jan 8, 1955, v180, p37.
  National Parent-Teacher. Nov 1954, v49, p38.
  The New Republic. Jan 10, 1955, v132, p20.
  The New Statesman and Nation. Oct 2, 1954,
    v48, p390.
  The New York Times. Dec 22, 1954, p28.
  The New York Times Magazine. Dec 12, 1954,
    p38-39.
  The New Yorker. Jan 1, 1955, v30, p46.
  Newsweek. Dec 20, 1954, v44, p83.
  Quarterly of Film, Radio and Television. Fall
    1955, v10, p1-10.
  Saturday Review. Dec 18, 1954, v37, p26-27.
  Senior Scholastic. Jan 12, 1955, v65, p30.
  Senior Scholastic. Jan 5, 1955, v65, p6T.
  The Spectator. Sep 24, 1954, v193, p361.
  Time. Dec 20, 1954, v64, p48-49.
  Twentieth Century. Nov 1954, v156, p464-71.
  Variety. Sep 8, 1954, p6.

Romeo and Juliet (GB; Czinner, Paul; 1966)
BFI/Monthly Film Bulletin. Nov 1966, v33, p165-66.
Christian Science Monitor (Western edition). Oct 28, 1966, p4.
Dance Magazine. Oct 1966, v40, p22-24.
Film Daily. Oct 6, 1966, p4.
Filmfacts. Dec 15, 1966, v9, p299-300.
Films and Filming. Jan 1967, v13, p31-32.
Films in Review. Oct 1966, v17, p519-20.
Hollywood Reporter. Oct 3, 1966, p3.
The London Times. Oct 27, 1966, p6.
Motion Picture Herald Product Digest. Oct 12, 1966, p613.
The New York Times. Oct 6, 1966, p55.
Senior Scholastic. Nov 4, 1966, v89, p28.
Variety. Oct 5, 1966, p6.

Romeo and Juliet (GB, IT; Zeffirelli, Franco; 1968)
America. Oct 19, 1968, v119, p363-64.
BFI/Monthly Film Bulletin. Apr 1968, v35, p54.
Christian Century. Mar 26, 1969, v86, p420-21.
Christian Science Monitor (Western edition). Mar 15, 1968, p4.
Cineaste. Wint 1968-69, v2, p17, 21.
Commonweal. Oct 25, 1968, v89, p122-23.
Figures of Light. p112-14.
Film 68/69. p206-09.
Film Daily. Sep 11, 1968, p3.
Filmfacts. Oct 15, 1968, v11, p275-78.
Films and Filming. Jul 1968, v14, p34-35.
Films in Review. Oct 1968, v19, p513-14.
The Films of the Sixties. p258-60.
Five Thousand One Nights At the Movies. p500-01.
Going Steady. p185-91.
Hollywood Reporter. Jun 14, 1968, p3.
Journal of Aesthetic Education. 1977, v11, n1, p51-61.
Life. Sep 6, 1968, v65, p10.
Literature/Film Quarterly. 1973, v1, n4, p343-57.
Literature/Film Quarterly. 1977, v5, n4, p322-25.
Literature/Film Quarterly. 1980, v8, n4, p210-18.
The London Times. Mar 5, 1968, p7.
Motion Picture Herald Product Digest. Sep 4, 1968, p851-52.
Motion Picture Herald Product Digest. Sep 18, 1968, p17.
Movie. Spr 1968, n15, p40.
Movies Into Film. p107-08.
The Nation. Oct 28, 1968, v207, p444-45.
New Statesman. Mar 8, 1968, v75, p310.
The New York Times. Oct 9, 1968, p41.
The New York Times. Jan 13, 1969, p27.
The New Yorker. Apr 6, 1968, v44, p121.
The New Yorker. Oct 19, 1968, v44, p209-12.
Newsweek. Oct 14, 1968, v72, p102.
Saturday Review. Oct 5, 1968, v51, p47.
Senior Scholastic. Sep 13, 1968, v93, p33.
Shakespeare on Film. p79-91.
The Spectator. Mar 15, 1968, v220, p343.
Time. Oct 11, 1968, v92, p104.
Variety. Mar 13, 1968, p6.
Vogue. Oct 1, 1968, v152, p146.
A Year In the Dark. p264-65.

Romeo, Julie a Tina *See* Sweet Light In a Dark Room

Romeo, Juliet and Darkness *See* Sweet Light In a Dark Room

Rommel, the Desert Fox *See* The Desert Fox

Ronde, La (Also titled: Circle of Love) (FR; Ophuls, Max; 1950)
BFI/Monthly Film Bulletin. Jun 1951, v18, p276-77.
Cinema, the Magic Vehicle. v2, p58-59.
The Comic Mind. p307-10.
Commonweal. Mar 26, 1954, v59, p626.
Dictionary of Films. p319.
Film. Apr-May 1983, n115, p20.
Film and the Critical Eye. p272-89.
Film Criticism and Caricatures, 1943-1953. p124-26.
Film Daily. Oct 4, 1951, p6.
Film Quarterly. Fall 1973, v26, p35-41.
Films and Filming. May 1962, v8, p21-23, 46-48.
The Great French Films. p252.
Hollywood Reporter. Sep 21, 1951, p4.
Illustrated London News. May 5, 1951, v218, p708.
The International Dictionary of Films and Filmmakers. v1, p400-01.
Library Journal. Apr 1, 1954, v79, p618.
Life. Jan 21, 1952, v32, p56.
Magill's Survey of Cinema. Foreign Language Films. v6, p2585-88.
Max Ophuls and the Cinema of Desire. p71-85.
Modern European Filmmakers and the Art of Adaptation. p38-50.
Movie. Sum 1982, n29-30, p73-79.
Movie Comedy. p216-17.
The Nation. Apr 10, 1954, v178, p314.
The New Republic. Apr 5, 1954, v130, p21.
The New Statesman and Nation. Apr 28, 1951, v41, p476.
The New Statesman and Nation. May 7, 1982, v103, p24-25.
The New Yorker. Mar 27, 1954, v30, p56.
Newsweek. Oct 22, 1951, v38, p100.
Rotha on Film. p171-73.
Saturday Review. Nov 10, 1951, v34, p27.
Sequence. New Year 1952, n14, p33-35.
Sight and Sound. Jun 1951, v20, p47.
Sight and Sound. n2, 1982, v51, p137-38.
The Spectator. Apr 27, 1951, v186, p553-54.
Theatre Arts. Dec 1951, v35, p24-25.
Time. Oct 22, 1951, v58, p114.
Time. Jan 25, 1954, v63, p23.
Variety. Jul 12, 1950, p6.
The Village Voice. Oct 16, 1969, v14, p55-56.

Ronde, La (Vadim, 1964) *See* Circle of Love

Roogie's Bump (US; Young, Harold; 1954)
Film Daily. Sep 20, 1954, p10.
Hollywood Reporter. Sep 16, 1954, p3.
Motion Picture Herald Product Digest. Sep 25, 1954, p153.
National Parent-Teacher. Dec 1954, v49, p38.
Variety. Sep 22, 1954, p6.

Room at the Top (GB; Clayton, Jack; 1959)
BFI/Monthly Film Bulletin. Feb 1959, v26, p15.
Catholic World. Jun 1959, v189, p237-38.
Commonweal. Apr 3, 1959, v70, p22.
Commonweal. Jul 3, 1959, v70, p347-48.
Fifty Classic British Films. p94-96.
Fifty from the Fifties. p277-82.
Film Daily. Apr 10, 1959, v115, p8.
Filmfacts. May 27, 1959, v2, p87-89.
Films in Review. May 1959, v10, p303-04.
Films in Review. Jun-Jul 1959, v10, p321.
The Great British Films. p178-80.
Jack Clayton: A Guide to References and Resources. p20-25.
Landmark Films. p236-45.
Library Journal. Apr 1, 1959, v84, p1119.

Magill's Survey of Cinema. Series I. v3, p1469-71.
The Nation. Apr 25, 1959, v188, p395.
The New Republic. Apr 13, 1959, v140, p20-21.
The New York Times. Mar 31, 1959, p26.
The New Yorker. Apr 11, 1959, v35, p162.
Newsweek. Apr 6, 1959, v53, p113.
One Good Film Deserves Another. p102-05.
Reporter. May 14, 1959, v20, p38.
Saturday Review. Apr 11, 1959, v42, p28.
Time. Apr 20, 1959, v73, p78.
Variety. Jan 28, 1959, p6.

Room for One More (US; Taurog, Norman; 1952)
BFI/Monthly Film Bulletin. Aug 1952, v19, p113.
Catholic World. Jan 1952, v174, p304-05.
Christian Century. Mar 26, 1952, v69, p383.
Commonweal. Feb 1, 1952, v55, p424.
Film Daily. Jan 10, 1952, p8.
The Films of Cary Grant. p210-12.
Hollywood Reporter. Jan 10, 1952, p3.
Library Journal. Feb 1, 1952, v77, p206.
The London Times. Aug 11, 1952, p2.
Magill's Survey of Cinema. Series II. v5, p2059-62.
Motion Picture Herald Product Digest. Jan 12, 1952, p1185.
The New York Times. Jan 16, 1952, p21.
Newsweek. Jan 28, 1952, v39, p90.
Saturday Review. Jan 26, 1952, v35, p24.
The Spectator. Aug 8, 1952, v189, p184.
The Tatler. Aug 20, 1952, v205, p334.
Time. Jan 28, 1952, v59, p96.
Variety. Jan 16, 1952, p6.

Rooster Cogburn (US; Millar, Stuart; 1975)
BFI/Monthly Film Bulletin. Jan 1976, v43, p9.
The Complete Films of John Wayne. p309-14.
Films in Review. Oct 1975, v26, p506.
Hollywood Reporter. Oct 15, 1975, p3.
Motion Picture Herald Product Digest. Nov 5, 1975, p42.
The New Republic. Oct 25, 1975, v173, p20.
The New York Times. Oct 18, 1975, p22.
The New York Times. Oct 26, 1975, SecII, p15.
The New Yorker. Nov 3, 1975, v51, p140-41.
Newsweek. Oct 27, 1975, v86, p105.
Progressive. Mar 1976, v40, p39-40.
Saturday Review. Oct 18, 1975, v3, p71.
Time. Nov 10, 1975, v106, p77.
Variety. Oct 15, 1975, p26.
Vogue. Dec 1975, v165, p54.
When the Lights Go Down. p62-64.

The Roots of Heaven (US; Huston, John; 1958)
America. Nov 1, 1958, v100, p147.
BFI/Monthly Film Bulletin. Feb 1959, v26, p15.
Catholic World. Jan 1959, v188, p327-28.
The Cinema of John Huston. p119-23, 217-19.
Commonweal. Nov 7, 1958, v69, p150.
Film Daily. Oct 16, 1958, v114, p6.
Filmfacts. Nov 19, 1958, v1, p191-92.
Films in Review. Nov 1958, v9, p513-15.
The Films of Errol Flynn. p217-19.
Hollywood Reporter. Oct 16, 1958, p3.
John Huston (Hammen). p97-100.
Library Journal. Nov 1958, v83, p3098.
Life. Oct 27, 1958, v45, p105-06.
Look. Nov 25, 1958, v20, p106.
The New Republic. Nov 3, 1958, v139, p21-22.
The New York Times. Oct 16, 1958, p46.
The New Yorker. Oct 25, 1958, v34, p192.
Newsweek. Oct 27, 1958, v52, p94-95.
Saturday Review. Jul 19, 1958, v61, p36.
Saturday Review. Oct 25, 1958, v61, p25.
Senior Scholastic. Dec 5, 1958, v73, p33.

Time. Nov 3, 1958, v72, p94.
Variety. Oct 22, 1958, p6.

The Rose (US; Rydell, Mark; 1979)
BFI/Monthly Film Bulletin. Jan 1980, v47, p11-12.
Films in Review. Dec 1979, v30, p631.
Hollywood Reporter. Oct 10, 1979, p3.
The Los Angeles Times. Nov 4, 1979, Calendar, p1.
Motion Picture Herald Product Digest. Oct 31, 1979, p43.
The Nation. Dec 1, 1979, v229, p572-73.
The New York Times. Nov 7, 1979, SecIII, p23.
The New Yorker. Nov 12, 1979, v55, p97.
Newsweek. Nov 12, 1979, v94, p107.
Time. Nov 12, 1979, v114, p122.
Variety. Oct 10, 1979, p20.

The Rose Bowl Story (US; Beaudine, William; 1952)
Film Daily. Aug 27, 1952, p6.
Hollywood Reporter. Aug 22, 1952, p3.
Motion Picture Herald Product Digest. Aug 30, 1952, p1509-10.
National Parent-Teacher. Nov 1952, v47, p37.
Variety. Aug 27, 1952, p6.

Rose Marie (US; LeRoy, Mervyn; 1954)
America. Apr 10, 1954, v91, p54.
BFI/Monthly Film Bulletin. Sep 1954, v21, p135.
The Busby Berkeley Book. p180-81.
Commonweal. Apr 16, 1954, v60, p41.
Farm Journal. May 1954, v78, p137.
Film Daily. Mar 3, 1954, p10.
Films and Filming. Oct 1954, v1, p20.
Hollywood Reporter. Mar 3, 1954, p3.
Library Journal. May 15, 1954, v79, p953.
Life. Feb 22, 1954, v36, p64-65.
The London Times. Sep 6, 1954, p5.
Motion Picture Herald Product Digest. Mar 6, 1954, p2205.
National Parent-Teacher. May 1954, v48, p38.
The New York Times. Apr 2, 1954, p22.
The New Yorker. Apr 17, 1954, v30, p124.
Saturday Review. Apr 10, 1954, v37, p36.
Senior Scholastic. Apr 21,1954, v64, p30.
The Tatler. Sep 15, 1954, v213, p492.
Time. Mar 15, 1954, v63, p102.
Variety. Mar 3, 1954, p6.

The Rose Tattoo (US; Mann, Daniel; 1955)
America. Dec 24, 1955, v94, p362.
Burt Lancaster: A Pictorial Treasury of His Films. p85-87.
Burt Lancaster: The Man and His Movies. p68-70.
Catholic World. Dec 1955, v182, p218.
Commonweal. Dec 23, 1955, v63, p305.
Film Culture. Wint 1955, v1, n5/6, p36.
Films and Filming. Mar 1956, v2, n6, p16.
Films in Review. Dec 1955, v6, n10, p527-28.
The Films of Tennessee Williams. p104-20.
Hollywood Reporter. Nov 1, 1955, v130, n2, p3.
Library Journal. Nov 1, 1955, v80, p2478.
Life. Nov 28, 1955, v39, p139-40.
Magill's Survey of Cinema. Series I. v3, p1472-75.
The Nation. Jan 7, 1955, v182, p18.
The New York Times. Dec 5, 1954, SecII, p9.
The New York Times. Apr 10, 1955, SecI, p47.
The New York Times. Oct 30, 1955, SecI, p29.
The New York Times. Dec 13, 1955, p55.
The New York Times. Dec 18, 1955, SecII, p3.
The New Yorker. Dec 24, 1955, v31, p52.
Newsweek. Dec 26, 1955, v46, p65-66.
Saturday Review. Dec 10, 1955, v38, p25-26.
Sight and Sound. Spr 1956, v25, n4, p194-96.
Tennessee Williams and Film. p25-31.

Time. Dec 19, 1955, v66, p94.
Variety. Nov 2, 1955, p6.

Rosebud (US; Preminger, Otto; 1975)
BFI/Monthly Film Bulletin. Apr 1975, v42, p87.
Films in Review. May 1975, v26, p314.
Hollywood Reporter. Mar 21, 1975, p29.
The Los Angeles Times. Apr 30, 1975, SecIV, p10.
Motion Picture Herald Product Digest. Apr 9, 1975, p88.
The New York Times. Mar 25, 1975, p24.
The New York Times. May 18, 1975, SecII, p19.
The New Yorker. Apr 7, 1975, v51, p124-26.
Newsweek. Apr 7, 1975, v85, p82.
Soon to Be a Major Motion Picture. 1979.
Time. Mar 26, 1975, v105, p76.
Variety. Mar 26, 1975, p18.

Roseland (US; Ivory, James; 1977)
America. Nov 19, 1977, v137, p362.
BFI/Monthly Film Bulletin. Mar 1978, v45, p52.
Commonweal. Nov 25, 1977, v104, p757-58.
Films in Review. Dec 1977, v28, p633.
Hollywood Reporter. Oct 20, 1977, p23.
The Los Angeles Times. Nov 22, 1977, SecIV, p12.
Motion Picture Herald Product Digest. Nov 12, 1977, p52.
The Nation. Oct 22, 1977, v225, p412.
New York. Sep 26, 1977, v10, p58-60.
The New York Times. Oct 2, 1977, p66.
The New Yorker. Dec 5, 1977, v53, p126-29.
Newsweek. Oct 24, 1977, v90, p125.
Time. Oct 17, 1977, v110, p101.
Variety. Oct 5, 1977, p36.
The Village Voice. Sep 26, 1977, p58-60.
The Village Voice. Oct 31, 1977, p45-46.

Rosemary's Baby (US; Polanski, Roman; 1968)
America. Jul 20, 1968, v119, p51-52.
American Cinematographer. Sep 1982, v63, p900-03.
BFI/Monthly Film Bulletin. May 1969, v36, p95-96.
Christian Century. Sep 18, 1968, v85, p1117.
Christian Science Monitor (Western edition). Jun 22, 1968, p6.
Cineaste. Fall 1968, v2, p15.
Cinema. Fall 1968, v4, p41-42.
The Cinema of Roman Polanski. p145-73.
Cinema Papers. Nov-Dec 1981, n35, p438-43.
Commonweal. Jun 14, 1968, v88, p384-85.
Confessions of a Cultist. p373-76.
Esquire. Nov 1968, v70, p24.
Fifty Grand Movies of the 1960s and 1970s. p203-06.
Figures of Light. p83-85.
Film 68/69. p49-52.
Film Comment. Fall 1968, v5, p4-9.
Film Daily. May 29, 1968, p5.
Film Quarterly. Spr 1969, v22, p35-38.
Filmfacts. Jul 15, 1968, v11, p175-77.
Films and Filming. Mar 1969, v15, p38-39.
Films and Filming. Aug 1969, v15, p10.
Films in Review. Aug-Sep 1968, v19, p456-57.
The Films of the Sixties. p229-30.
Hollywood Reporter. May 29, 1968, p3.
The International Dictionary of Films and Filmmakers. v1, p402-03.
International Film Guide. 1969, v6, p173-74.
Journal of Popular Culture. Wint 1968, v2, p493-502.
Journal of Popular Film. 1982, v10, n3, p130-36.
The London Times. Jan 23, 1969, p7.

Look. Jun 25, 1968, v32, p91-94.
Magill's Survey of Cinema. Series I. v3, p1476-79.
Motion Picture Herald Product Digest. May 29, 1968, p817.
Movie. Wint 1968-69, n16, p39.
Movies Into Film. p181-82.
The Nation. Jul 22, 1968, v207, p60-61.
National Review. Sep 24, 1968, v20, p969.
The New Republic. Jun 15, 1968, v158, p26.
New Statesman. Jan 31, 1969, v77, p165.
The New York Times. Jun 13, 1968, p57.
The New York Times. Jul 18, 1982, p5.
The New Yorker. Jun 15, 1968, v44, p87-89.
Roman Polanski: A Guide to References and Resources. p25-27, 61-69.
Roman Polanski (Wexman). p63-69.
Saturday Review. Jun 15, 1968, v51, p49.
Screen. Mar-Apr 1969, v10, p90-96.
Sight and Sound. Wint 1968-69, v38, p17-19.
The Spectator. Jan 31, 1969, v222, p147.
Time. Jun 21, 1968, v91, p84.
Variety. May 29, 1968, p6.
The Village Voice. Jul 25, 1968, p37.
A Year In the Dark. p170-72.

Rosier de Madame Husson, Le *See* The Prize

Rotten to the Core (GB; Boulting, John; 1965)
BFI/Monthly Film Bulletin. Aug 1965, v32, p125.
Christian Science Monitor (Western edition). Aug 31, 1965, p10.
Film Daily. Jul 20, 1965, p6.
Films and Filming. Sep 1965, v11, p32-33.
The London Times. Jul 15, 1965, p6.
Motion Picture Herald Product Digest. Aug 18, 1965, p346.
The New York Times. Jul 20, 1965, p39.
Newsweek. Sep 13, 1965, v66, p87A.
Saturday Review. Jul 24, 1965, v48, p51.
The Spectator. Jul 23, 1965, v215, p106.
Time. Aug 20, 1965, v86, p76.
Variety. Jul 21, 1965, p7.

Rough Company *See* The Violent Men

Rough Cut (US; Siegel, Don; 1980)
Hollywood Reporter. Jun 16, 1980, p3.
The Los Angeles Times. Jun 19, 1980, SecVI, p1.
Maclean's. Jun 30, 1980, v93, p53.
Motion Picture Herald Product Digest. Jul 9, 1980, p9.
National Review. Jul 25, 1980, v32, p916.
The New Republic. Jul 19, 1980, v183, p22-23.
The New York Times. Jul 6, 1980, SecIII, p1.
The New York Times. Jun 19, 1980, SecIII, p19.
Newsweek. Jun 30, 1980, v95, p62.
Time. Jun 30, 1980, v115, p72.
Variety. Jun 18, 1980, p22.

The Round *See* Circle of Love

The Rounders (US; Kennedy, Burt; 1965)
BFI/Monthly Film Bulletin. Mar 1965, v32, p43.
Cinema. Dec-Jan 1964-65, v2, p49.
Film Daily. Jan 15, 1965, p3.
Film Quarterly. Sum 1965, v18, p60.
Filmfacts. Jun 11, 1965, v8, p102-03.
Films and Filming. May 1965, v11, p33.
Films in Review. Feb 1965, v16, p117.
The Films of Henry Fonda. p182-84.
Hollywood Reporter. Jan 14, 1965, p3.
The London Times. Mar 11, 1965, p15.
Motion Picture Herald Product Digest. Jan 20, 1965, p209-10.
The New Republic. Mar 20, 1965, v152, p26.

BFI/Monthly Film Bulletin. Oct 1966, v33, p152.
Christian Science Monitor (Western edition). Jun 3, 1966, p4.
Commonweal. Jun 10, 1966, v84, p337.
Film Daily. May 24, 1966, p4.
Film Quarterly. Fall 1966, v20, p28-34.
Filmfacts. Jul 15, 1966, v9, p121-23.
Films and Filming. Nov 1966, v13, p16.
Films in Review. Aug-Sep 1966, v17, p446-47.
Hollywood Reporter. May 26, 1966, p3.
Life. May 27, 1966, v60, p12.
The London Times. Aug 25, 1966, p6.
Magill's Survey of Cinema. Series II. v5, p2073-75.
Motion Picture Herald Product Digest. May 25, 1966, p525.
New Statesman. Aug 26, 1966, v72, p298.
The New York Times. May 26, 1966, p55.
The New Yorker. Jun 4, 1966, v42, p87.
Newsweek. Jun 20, 1966, v67, p102.
Playboy. Jul 1966, v13, p26.
Saturday Review. Jun 11, 1966, v49, p77.
Senior Scholastic. Sep 16, 1966, v89, p29.
The Spectator. Aug 26, 1966, v217, p261.
THe Films of the Sixties. p165-66.
Time. Jun 10, 1966, v87, p111-12.
Variety. May 25, 1966, p7.
The Village Voice. Jun 9, 1966, v11, p23.
Vogue. Jul 1966, v148, p30.

Ryan's Daughter (GB; Lean, David; 1970)
America. Dec 12, 1970, v123, p529.
BFI/Monthly Film Bulletin. Jan 1971, v38, p13.
The Cinema of David Lean. p199-205.
Commonweal. Dec 18, 1970, v93, p302-03.
David Lean: A Guide to References and Resources. p92-94.
David Lean and His Films. p148-49.
David Lean (Anderegg). p132-38.
Double Takes. p59-61.
Films in Review. Dec 1970, v21, p640-43.
The Great British Films. p240-43.
Hollywood Reporter. Nov 10, 1970, p3, 8.
Magill's Survey of Cinema. Series I. v3, p1480.
The New York Times. Nov 10, 1970, p54.
The New York Times. Nov 22, 1970, SecII, p1.
The New Yorker. Nov 21, 1970, v46, p116-18.
Newsweek. Nov 23, 1970, v76, p123.
Robert Mitchum on the Screen. p212-13.
Saturday Review. Nov 14, 1970, v53, p53.
Take One. 1970, v2, n9, p20.
Time. Nov 16, 1970, v96, p96.
Variety. Nov 11, 1970, p15.

S.O.B. (US; Edwards, Blake; 1981)
America. Aug 1, 1981, v145, p86.
Christian Century. Aug 12, 1981, v98, p810.
Hollywood Reporter. Jun 22, 1981, p5.
The Los Angeles Times. Jun 28, 1981, Calendar, p21.
Maclean's. Jul 6, 1981, v94, p52.
Magill's Survey of Cinema. p328-31.
The Nation. Aug 8, 1981, v233, p123.
National Review. Sep 18, 1981, v33, p1089-91.
The New Leader. Aug 10, 1981, v64, p21.
The New Republic. Jul 18, 1981, v185, p26-27.
New York. Jul 20, 1981, v14, p62.
The New York Times. Aug 16, 1981, SecII, p20.
The New York Times. Jul 1, 1981, SecIII, p21.
Newsweek. Jul 6, 1981, v98, p77.
Rolling Stone. Aug 6, 1981, p20-23.
Saturday Review. Jul 1981, v8, p84-85.
Time. Jul 13, 1981, v118, p58.
Variety. Jun 22, 1981, p3.

Sables du Kalahari, Les *See* Sands of the Kalahari

Saboteur *See* Morituri

Sabrina (Also titled: Sabrina Fair) (US; Wilder, Billy; 1954)
America. Sep 25, 1954, v91, p631.
BFI/Monthly Film Bulletin. Sep 1954, v21, p131.
Billy Wilder (Dick). p76-78.
Billy Wilder (Madsen). p97-100.
Catholic World. Sep 1954, v179, p465.
Cinema, the Magic Vehicle. v2, p216-17.
Commonweal. Oct 8, 1954, v61, p14.
The Complete Films of Humphrey Bogart. p176-77.
Coronet. Sep 1954, v36, p6.
Cue. Sep 25, 1954, p15.
The Film Career of Billy Wilder. p84-85.
Film Daily. Aug 2, 1954, p10.
Films and Filming. Oct 1954, v1, p20.
Films in Review. Aug-Sep 1954, v5, p361-62.
The Films of William Holden. p154-56.
Hollywood Reporter. Aug 2, 1954, p3.
Humphrey Bogart: The Man and His Films. p168-70.
Library Journal. Sep 1, 1954, v79, p1485.
Life. Oct 4, 1954, v37, p60.
The London Times. Sep 13, 1954, p3.
Magill's Survey of Cinema. Series I. v3, p1484-86.
Motion Picture Herald Product Digest. Aug 7, 1954, p97.
National Parent-Teacher. Sep 1954, v49, p39.
The New York Times. Sep 23, 1954, p43.
The New Yorker. Oct 2, 1954, v30, p130.
Newsweek. Aug 30, 1954, v44, p76.
Saturday Review. Aug 28, 1954, v37, p29-30.
Saturday Review. Oct 23, 1954, v37, p8.
Selected Film Criticism, 1951-1960. p114-15.
Senior Scholastic. Sep 15, 1954, v65, p35.
Sight and Sound. Oct-Dec 1954, v24, p91.
The Spectator. Sep 10, 1954, v193, p308.
The Tatler. Sep 22, 1954, v213, p569.
Time. Sep 13, 1954, v64, p106.
Variety. Aug 4, 1954, p6.
Woman's Home Companion. Sep 1954, v81, p10.

The Saga of Anatahan *See* Ana-ta-han

Sage-Femme, Le *See* Jessica

Saikaku Ichidai Onna *See* The Life of Oharu

Sailor Beware (US; Walker, Hal; 1951)
Christian Century. Apr 9, 1952, v69, p447.
Film Daily. Nov 29, 1951, p6.
Holiday. Feb 1952, v11, p16.
Hollywood Reporter. Nov 29, 1951, p3.
Motion Picture Herald Product Digest. Dec 1, 1951, p1125.
The New York Times. Feb 1, 1952, p17.
Newsweek. Mar 10, 1952, v39, p103.
Time. Feb 18, 1952, v59, p86.
Variety. Dec 5, 1951, p6.

The Sailor Who Fell From Grace With the Sea (GB; Carlino, Lewis J.; 1976)
BFI/Monthly Film Bulletin. Aug 1976, v43, p17.
Film Bulletin. May 1976, v45, pE.
Films and Filming. Sep 1976, v22, p32, 36-37.
Hollywood Reporter. Apr 9, 1976, p3.
Independent Film Journal. Apr 14, 1976, v77, p78.
The Los Angeles Times. May 18, 1976, SecIV, p7.
Motion Picture Herald Product Digest. Apr 14, 1976, p89.
New Statesman. Jul 30, 1976, v92, p154-55.
New York. Apr 26, 1976, v9, p72-73.
The New York Times. Apr 12, 1976, p36.
The New Yorker. Apr 26, 1976, v52, p119-21.

Newsweek. Apr 19, 1976, v87, p95.
Playboy. Jul 1976, v23, p122-27.
Saturday Review. May 15, 1976, v3, p51-52.
The Thousand Eyes Magazine. May 1976, n10, p11-12.
Time. May 10, 1976, v107, p72-74.
Variety. Apr 14, 1976, p23.

St. Elmo's Fire (US; Schumacher, Joel; 1985)
BFI/Monthly Film Bulletin. Oct 1985, v52, p316.
Commonweal. Sep 6, 1986, v112, p469-70.
Hollywood Reporter. Jun 17, 1985, p3.
The Los Angeles Times. Jun 28, 1985, SecVI, p1.
Magill's Cinema Annual, 1986. p330-33.
New York. Jul 15, 1985, v18, p66.
The New York Times. Jun 28, 1985, SecIII, p6.
Newsweek. Jul 1, 1985, v106, p55.
Time. Jul 1, 1985, v125, p63.
Variety. Jun 19, 1985, p25.
Vogue. Aug 1985, v175, p64.
The Wall Street Journal. Jun 27, 1985, p28.

St. Ives (Also titled: Saint Ives) (US; Thompson, J. Lee; 1976)
BFI/Monthly Film Bulletin. Aug 1976, v43, p175.
Films and Filming. Nov 1976, v23, p37-38.
Hollywood Reporter. Jul 21, 1976, p21.
Independent Film Journal. Sep 3, 1976, v78, p9.
The Los Angeles Times. Aug 25, 1976, SecIV, p15.
Motion Picture Herald Product Digest. Aug 25, 1976, p26.
Movietone News. Oct 11, 1976, n52, p34-35.
New York. Sep 6, 1976, v9, p72-73.
The New York Times. Sep 2, 1976, p24.
Newsweek. Sep 13, 1976, v88, p89.
Time. Oct 11, 1976, v108, p90.
Variety. Jul 21, 1976, p22.

Saint Jack (US; Bogdanovich, Peter; 1979)
America. Jun 2, 1979, v140, p454.
BFI/Monthly Film Bulletin. Sep 1979, v46, p200.
Films in Review. Aug-Sep 1979, v30, p440.
The Los Angeles Times. Aug 24, 1979, SecIV, p1.
The Nation. May 26, 1979, v228, p609-10.
The New York Times. Apr 27, 1979, v3, p4.
The New Yorker. May 7, 1979, v55, p141-42.
Newsweek. May 7, 1979, v93, p88.
Time. May 21, 1979, v113, p86.
Variety. May 2, 1979, p26.

Saint Joan (US; Preminger, Otto; 1957)
America. Jun 29, 1957, v97, p372.
American Cinematographer. Aug 1958, v38, p510-11.
BFI/Monthly Film Bulletin. Aug 1957, v24, p98.
The Cinema of Otto Preminger. p116-20.
Cinema, the Magic Vehicle. p379-80.
Commonweal. Jul 19, 1957, v66, p400-01.
Film Daily. May 8, 1957, v111, p11.
Films and Filming. Jul 1957, v3, p21.
Films in Review. Jun-Jul 1957, v8, p280-81.
Hollywood Reporter. May 8, 1957, p3.
Motion Picture Herald Product Digest. May 11, 1957, v207, p369.
The Nation. Jul 20, 1957, v185, p38.
The New Republic. Aug 12, 1957, v137, p22.
The New York Times. Jun 27, 1957, p21.
The New York Times. Jun 30, 1957, SecII, p1.
The New Yorker. Jul 6, 1957, v33, p58.
Newsweek. Jun 24, 1957, v49, p108.
Saturday Review. Jun 29, 1957, v40, p22.

Time. Jul 1, 1957, v70, p80.
Variety. May 8, 1957, p6.

Salaire de la Peur, Le *See* The Wages of Fear

Sally and Saint Anne (US; Maté, Rudolph; 1952)
BFI/Monthly Film Bulletin. May 1953, v20, p74-75.
Film Daily. Jun 23, 1952, p6.
Hollywood Reporter. Jun 20, 1952, p3.
Motion Picture Herald Product Digest. Jun 28, 1952, p1426.
National Parent-Teacher. Sep 1952, v47, p37.
Newsweek. Jul 14, 1952, v40, p90.
Variety. Jun 25, 1952, p6.

Salome (US; Dieterle, William; 1953)
America. Mar 28, 1953, v88, p718.
BFI/Monthly Film Bulletin. Jul 1953, v20, n234, p102.
Catholic World. May 1953, v177, p143.
Charles Laughton. p134-39.
Christian Century. Apr 29, 1953, v70, p527.
Commonweal. Apr 10, 1953, v58, p24.
Film Daily. Mar 13, 1953, p12.
The Films of Rita Hayworth. p187-91.
Hollywood Reporter. Mar 13, 1953, p3.
Library Journal. Apr 1, 1953, v78, p588.
The New York Times. Mar 22, 1953, SecII, p5.
The New York Times. Mar 25, 1953, p37.
The New Yorker. Apr 4, 1953, v29, p83.
Newsweek. Mar 30, 1953, v41, p92.
Saturday Review. Apr 4, 1953, v36, p43.
Theatre Arts. Apr 1953, v37, p86.
Time. Mar 30, 1953, v61, p84.
Variety. Mar 18, 1953, p6.

Salt of the Earth (US; Biberman, Herbert J.; 1954)
BFI/Monthly Film Bulletin. Nov 1954, v21, p158-59.
Cineaste. 1973, v5, n4, p53-55.
Cineaste. 1978, v9, n1, p48-49.
Cineaste. n3, 1984, v13, p30-36.
Commonweal. Apr 2, 1954, v59, p651.
Cult Movies 2. p135-38.
Dictionary of Films. p323-24.
Film Culture. Fall-Wint 1970, n50/51, p79-81.
Film Library Quarterly. Wint 1971-72, v5, p51-53.
Films and Filming. Nov 1954, v1, p20, 23.
Films in Review. Apr 1954, v5, p197.
The International Dictionary of Films and Filmmakers. v1, p405-07.
Iris. 1985, v3, n1, p91-98.
Jump Cut. Dec 30, 1976, n12/13, p19-22.
The Latin Image in American Film. p98-104.
The London Times. Sep 17, 1954, p11.
Motion Picture Herald Product Digest. Nov 24, 1965, p410.
The Nation. Apr 10, 1954, v178, p314.
The New Statesman and Nation. Sep 18, 1954, v48, p324.
The New York Times. Mar 15, 1954, p20.
The New York Times. Feb 1, 1980, p27.
The New York Times. May 3, 1982, p16.
The New York Times. Nov 1, 1965, p57.
Newsweek. Mar 29, 1954, v43, p87.
Running Time: Films of the Cold War. p173-76.
Salt of the Earth: Screenplay.
Salt of the Earth: The Story of a Film.
Sight and Sound. Oct-Dec 1954, v24, p67-73.
The Spectator. Sep 24, 1954, v193, p361.
The Tatler. Sep 29, 1954, v213, p618.
Time. Mar 16, 1953, v61, p108.
Time. Mar 29, 1954, v63, p92.
Variety. Mar 17, 1954, p6.

Variety. Apr 27, 1983, p1.
The Village Voice. May 16, 1963, v8, p13.

Salt to the Devil *See* Give Us this Day

Salto (POL; Konwicki, Tadeusz; 1965)
Christian Century. Nov 16, 1966, v83, p1416-17.
Film Society Review. Feb 1968, p18-22.
Filmfacts. Dec 15, 1966, v9, p284-85.
The Films of Steve Mcqueen. p120-30.
Motion Picture Herald Product Digest. Jul 27, 1966, p569.
The Nation. Oct 24, 1966, v203, p429.
The New York Times. Oct 4, 1966, p50.
Newsweek. Sep 5, 1966, v68, p88A.
Playboy. Jan 1967, v14, p27.
Tynan Right and Left. p238.
Variety. Sep 8, 1965, p68.

Salvador (US; Stone, Oliver; 1985)
Film Comment. Feb 1987, v23, p11.
Film Journal. Mar 1986, v89, p11-12.
The Los Angeles Times. Dec 1, 1985, Calendar, p24.
Maclean's. Jul 21, 1986, v99, p150.
Mademoiselle. Jul 1986, v92, p48.
New York. Mar 24, 1986, v19, p86.
The New Yorker. Jul 28, 1986, v62, p77-79.
Newsweek. Sep 9, 1985, v106, p89.
Newsweek. Mar 17, 1986, v107, p80.
Newsweek. Sep 9, 1985, v106, p89.
Variety. Mar 5, 1985, p14.

Sam Whiskey (US; Laven, Arnold; 1969)
Commonweal. Jul 11, 1969, v90, p439.
Film Daily. Feb 10, 1969, p10.
Filmfacts. 1969, v12, p311.
Films and Filming. Sep 1969, v15, p60-61.
The Films of Burt Reynolds. p129-33.
Hollywood Reporter. Feb 3, 1969, p3.
The New York Times. Jun 12, 1969, p52.
Variety. Feb 5, 1969, p6.

Samma no Aji *See* An Autumn Afternoon

Sammy Going South *See* A Boy Ten Feet Tall

Samurai (Also titled: Miyamoto Musashi) (JAPAN; Inagaki, Hiroshi; 1954, 1955, 1967)
Film Daily. Nov 23, 1955, p10.
Hollywood Reporter. Nov 16, 1955, p3.
Magill's Survey of Cinema. Foreign Language Films. v6, p2618-24.
Motion Picture Herald Product Digest. Nov 26, 1955, p682.
The New York Times. Jan 10, 1956, p26.
The New York Times. Oct 21, 1967, p16.
Variety. Nov 16, 1955, p6.
Variety. Nov 1, 1967, p20.
Variety. Nov 15, 1967, p20.
The Waves at Genji's Door. p115-17.

Samurai Assassin (JAPAN; Okamoto, Kihachi; 1964)
Filmfacts. Jun 11, 1965, v8, p101-02.
Motion Picture Herald Product Digest. Apr 14, 1965, p266.
The New Republic. Apr 3, 1965, v152, p23.
The New York Times. Mar 19, 1965, p27.
The New Yorker. Mar 27, 1965, v41, p168-69.
Newsweek. Mar 29, 1965, v65, p88.
Playboy. Sep 1965, v12, p54.
Sight and Sound. Mar 17, 1965, v34, p7.
Variety. Mar 17, 1965, p7.

The San Francisco Story (US; Parrish, Robert; 1952)
BFI/Monthly Film Bulletin. Jul 1952, v19, p96.
Film Daily. Apr 23, 1952, p6.
Hollywood Reporter. Apr 7, 1952, p3.

Motion Picture Herald Product Digest. Apr 12, 1952, p1314.
The New York Times. May 10, 1952, p16.
The Spectator. May 9, 1952, v188, p610.
Time. May 19, 1952, v59, p106.
Variety. Apr 9, 1952, p6.

The Sand Pebbles (US; Wise, Robert; 1966)
America. Jan 7, 1967, v116, p27.
BFI/Monthly Film Bulletin. Jun 1967, v34, p91.
Christian Century. Mar 8, 1967, v84, p313.
Christian Science Monitor (Western edition). May 15, 1967, p4.
Commonweal. Jan 20, 1967, v85, p428.
Film Daily. Dec 21, 1966, p4-5.
Film Quarterly. Sum 1967, v20, p11-22.
Filmfacts. Jan 15, 1967, v9, p329-32.
Films and Filming. Jul 1967, v13, p22-23.
Films in Review. Jan 1967, v18, p50-51.
The Films of Steve McQueen. p120-130.
Hollywood Reporter. Dec 21, 1966, p3.
Life. Jan 6, 1967, v62, p11.
The London Times. Apr 6, 1967, p12.
Motion Picture Herald Product Digest. Jan 18, 1967, p651.
Motion Picture Herald Product Digest. Jan 4, 1967, p3-4.
The New Republic. Jan 14, 1967, v156, p40-41.
New Statesman. Apr 7, 1967, v73, p483.
The New York Times. Dec 21, 1966, p48.
Newsweek. Jan 2, 1967, v69, p64.
Playboy. May 1967, v14, p34-35.
Saturday Review. Dec 24, 1966, v49, p62.
Senior Scholastic. Feb 10, 1967, v90, p24.
Time. Jan 6, 1967, v89, p96.
Variety. Dec 21, 1966, p6.

The Sandpiper (US; Minnelli, Vincente; 1965)
America. Jul 24, 1965, v113, p103.
American Cinematographer. Jul 1965, v46, p428-31.
BFI/Monthly Film Bulletin. Oct 1965, v32, p147-48.
Christian Science Monitor (Western edition). Jun 29, 1965, p2.
Cinema. Jul-Aug 1965, v2, p7-8, 14-15.
Film Daily. Jun 25, 1965, p6.
Film Quarterly. Fall 1965, v19, p62-63.
Films and Filming. Oct 1965, v12, p28-29.
Films in Review. Aug-Sep 1965, v16, p448-49.
The Films of Elizabeth Taylor. p166-70.
Hi Fidelity. Apr 1973, v23, p26.
Kiss Kiss Bang Bang. p432-33.
Life. Jul 16, 1965, v59, p22.
The London Times. Sep 9, 1965, p5.
Motion Picture Herald Product Digest. Jul 7, 1965, p321.
Movie. Aut 1965, n14, p41.
The New Republic. Jul 24, 1965, v153, p33.
New Statesman. Sep 10, 1965, v70, p368.
The New York Times. Jul 16, 1965, p14.
The New Yorker. Jul 24, 1965, v41, p87.
Newsweek. Jul 26, 1965, v66, p89.
Playboy. Oct 1965, v12, p30-31.
The Private Eye, the Cowboy and the Very Naked Girl. p141-44.
Private Screenings. p196-98.
Saturday Review. Jul 24, 1965, v48, p51.
The Spectator. Sep 10, 1965, v215, p324.
Time. Jul 16, 1965, v86, p94.
Variety. Jun 30, 1965, p6.
The Village Voice. Aug 12, 1965, v10, p15.

Sandra *See* Vaghe Stelle Dell'Orsa

Sands of the Kalahari (Also titled: Sables du Kalahari, Les) (GB; Enfield, Cy; 1965)

BFI/Monthly Film Bulletin. Jan 1966, v33, p4.
Cahiers du Cinema in English. 1966, n4, p61.
Cinema. Dec 1965, v3, p14-17.
Commonweal. Dec 10, 1965, v83, p315.
Film Daily. Oct 28, 1965, p6.
Film Quarterly. Spr 1966, v19, p53.
Films and Filming. Feb 1966, v12, p12, 16.
Films and Filming. Dec 1965, v12, p10.
Hollywood Reporter. Oct 27, 1965, p3.
The London Times. Dec 2, 1965, p15.
Motion Picture Herald Product Digest. Nov 10, 1965, p402.
New Statesman. Dec 3, 1965, v70, p899-900.
The New York Times. Nov 25, 1965, p64.
Newsweek. Dec 6, 1965, v66, p104.
The Spectator. Dec 3, 1965, v215, p741.
Time. Dec 3, 1965, v86, p103.
Variety. Oct 27, 1965, p26.

Sansho the Bailiff (Japanese title: Sansho Dayu; Also titled: The Bailiff) (JAPAN; Mizoguchi, Kenji; 1954)
BFI/Monthly Film Bulletin. Mar 1976, v43, p67-68.
Cinema, the Magic Vehicle. v2, p194-95.
Dictionary of Films. p326.
Film Comment. Mar-Apr 1973, v9, p32-40.
Film Criticism. Spr 1980, v4, p12-13.
Film Quarterly. Sum 1964, v17, p53-54.
Films Illustrated. Apr 1976, v5, p286.
The International Dictionary of Films and Filmmakers. v1, p410-11.
The Japanese Film: Art and Industry. p274.
Kenji Mizoguchi: A Guide to References and Resources. p144-46.
Magill's Survey of Cinema. Foreign Language Films. v6, p2640-45.
Mizoguchi (McDonald). p131-36.
New Statesman. Feb 20, 1976, v91, p236.
The New York Times. Dec 17, 1969, p61.
Person Views: Explorations in Film. p225-48.
Sight and Sound. Spr 1978, v47, p116-17.
The Thousand Eyes Magazine. Apr 1977, v2, p9.
Variety. Oct 6, 1954, p22.
The Village Voice. Dec 4, 1969, v14, p59.
The Waves at Genji's Door. p104-08.

Sant Hander Inte Har *See* High Tension

Santa Claus: The Movie (US; Szwarc, Jeannot; 1985)
BFI/Monthly Film Bulletin. Dec 1985, v52, p387-88.
Hollywood Reporter. Nov 25, 1985, p3.
The Los Angeles Times. Nov 27, 1985, SecVI, p1.
Magill's Cinema Annual, 1986. p334-37.
The New York Times. Nov 27, 1985, SecIII, p18.
Newsweek. Dec 2, 1985, v106, p92.
Theatre Crafts. Jan 1986, v20, p75-78.
Time. Dec 9, 1985, v126, p111.
Variety. Nov 27, 1985, p15.

The Saracen Blade (US; Castle, William; 1954)
BFI/Monthly Film Bulletin. Aug 1954, v21, p122.
Film Daily. May 20, 1954, p10.
Hollywood Reporter. May 14, 1954, p3.
Library Journal. Jun 1, 1954, v79, p1048.
Motion Picture Herald Product Digest. May 22, 1954, p2.
The New York Times. May 15, 1954, p13.
Time. Jun 14, 1954, v63, p112.
Variety. May 19, 1954, p6.

Saskatchewan (US; Walsh, Raoul; 1954)
America. Mar 20, 1954, v90, p666.
Film Daily. Feb 25, 1954, p10.

The Films of Alan Ladd. p196-97.
Hollywood Reporter. Feb 24, 1954, p3.
Motion Picture Herald Product Digest. Feb 27, 1954, p2197.
National Parent-Teacher. Apr 1954, v48, p38.
The New York Times. Mar 11, 1954, p26.
Newsweek. Mar 15, 1954, v43, p104-06.
Time. Mar 22, 1954, v63, p110.
Variety. Feb 24, 1954, p6.

Sasom I En Spegel *See* Through a Glass Darkly

The Satan Bug (US; Sturges, John; 1965)
BFI/Monthly Film Bulletin. May 1965, v32, p71.
Film Daily. Mar 8, 1965, p4.
Film Quarterly. Sum 1965, v18, p60-61.
Filmfacts. May 14, 1965, v8, p82-83.
Films and Filming. Jul 1965, v11, p27-28.
Hollywood Reporter. Mar 8, 1965, p3.
The London Times. May 6, 1965, p10.
Motion Picture Herald Product Digest. Mar 17, 1965, p249.
New Statesman. May 7, 1965, v69, p735.
The New York Times. Apr 15, 1965, p38.
Newsweek. May 3, 1965, v65, p94.
Time. Apr 30, 1965, v85, p110.
Tynan Right and Left. p231.
Variety. Mar 10, 1965, p6.

Satan Never Sleeps (Also titled: The Devil Never Sleeps) (US; McCarey, Leo; 1962)
America. Mar 10, 1962, v106, p774-75.
Commonweal. Mar 16, 1962, v75, p644.
Film Daily. Feb 23, 1962, p6.
Filmfacts. Mar 23, 1962, v5, p43-44.
Films and Filming. Apr 1962, v8, p32.
The Films of William Holden. p202-05.
Hollywood Reporter. Feb 21, 1962, v169, p3.
Motion Picture Herald Product Digest. Feb 28, 1962, p460-61.
Movie. Jun 1962, n1, p31-32.
The New York Times. Feb 22, 1962, p20.
Newsweek. Mar 12, 1962, v59, p102.
Time. Mar 9, 1962, v79, p91.
Variety. Feb 21, 1962, p6.

Saturday Island *See* Island of Desire

Saturday Night & Sunday Morning (GB; Reisz, Karel; 1960)
America. Jun 10, 1961, v105, p430.
BFI/Monthly Film Bulletin. Dec 1960, v27, p166.
Commonweal. Apr 14, 1961, v74, p79.
Esquire. Feb 61, v55, p44.
Fifty Classic British Films. p100-02.
Film Quarterly. Sum 1961, v14, p58-59.
Filmfacts. 1961, v4, p71.
Films in Review. Apr 1961, v12, p235-37.
The Great British Films. p190-92.
Hollywood UK. p80-91.
Karel Reisz (Gaston). p31-46.
Magill's Survey of Cinema. Series II. v5, p2086-88.
McCall's. May 1961, v78, p208.
The Nation. Apr 29, 1961, v192, p380.
The New Republic. Apr 17, 1961, v144, p19-20.
The New York Times. Apr 4, 1961, p44.
The New York Times. Apr 9, 1961, SecII, p8.
The New Yorker. Apr 15, 1961, v37, p154-55.
Newsweek. Apr 10, 1961, v57, p103.
On Movies. p8.
Reruns. p141-45.
Saturday Review. Apr 8, 1961, v44, p41.
Sight and Sound. Wint 1960-61, v30, p33.
Time. Mar 31, 1961, v77, p64.
Variety. Nov 9, 1960, p6.
A World on Film. p196-98.

Saturday Night Fever (US; Badham, John; 1977)
America. Jan 6, 1978, v138, p20.
BFI/Monthly Film Bulletin. Apr 1977, v45, p68.
Commonweal. Jan 20, 1978, v105, p53-54.
Dance Magazine. Mar 1978, v52, p39-41.
Encore. Jan 16, 1978, v7, p30.
The Films of The Seventies. p193-98.
Hollywood Reporter. Dec 9, 1977, p3.
The Los Angeles Times. Dec 11, 1977, Calendar, p74.
Magill's Survey of Cinema. Series II. v5, p2089-91.
Motion Picture Herald Product Digest. Dec 21, 1977, p57.
National Review. Feb 17, 1978, v30, p229.
The New Republic. Feb 11, 1978, v178, p24.
New York. Jan 9, 1978, v11, p64-65.
The New York Times. Dec 11, 1977, p15.
The New York Times. Dec 16, 1977, SecIII, p10.
The New Yorker. Dec 26, 1977, v53, p56-60.
Newsweek. Dec 19, 1977, v90, p65.
Newsweek. May 29, 1978, v91, p97.
Saturday Night Fever—Official Authorized Scrapbook. 1977.
Time. Dec 19, 1977, v110, p69-70.
Variety. Dec 14, 1977, p12.
The Village Voice. Dec 19, 1977, p49-50.
The Village Voice. Dec 26, 1977, p41.

Saturday's Hero (US; Miller, David; 1951)
Christian Century. Nov 7, 1951, v68, p1294.
Commonweal. Oct 12, 1951, v55, p14.
Film Daily. Aug 23, 1951, p6.
Hollywood Reporter. Aug 22, 1951, p3.
Motion Picture Herald Product Digest. Aug 25, 1951, p989.
The Nation. Sep 29, 1951, v173, p267-68.
The New York Times. Sep 12, 1951, p37.
Newsweek. Sep 10, 1951, v38, p98.
Senior Scholastic. Oct 24, 1951, v59, p21.
Time. Oct 15, 1951, v58, p122.
Variety. Aug 22, 1951, p10.

Satyricon *See* Fellini Satyricon

Sauve Qui Peut *See* Every Man for Himself

The Savage (US; Marshall, George; 1952)
BFI/Monthly Film Bulletin. Oct 1952, v19, p145.
Film Daily. Sep 25, 1952, p10.
Hollywood Reporter. Sep 18, 1952, p3.
Library Journal. Nov 15, 1952, v77, p1981.
Motion Picture Herald Product Digest. Sep 20, 1952, p1534.
National Parent-Teacher. Nov 1952, v47, p37.
The New York Times. Jan 2, 1953, p11.
Time. Nov 3, 1952, v60, p100.
Variety. Jan 14, 1953, p6.

The Savage Innocents (Also titled: Ombre Bianche) (US; Ray, Nicholas; 1959)
BFI/Monthly Film Bulletin. Aug 1960, v27, p108.
Commonweal. Dec 2, 1960, v73, p255.
Film Daily. Sep 22, 1960, v117, p10.
The Films of Anthony Quinn. p188-89.
Magill's Survey of Cinema. Series II. v5, p2093-95.
McCall's. Dec 1960, v88, p180.
The New Republic. Jan 2, 1961, v144, p24.
The New York Times. May 25, 1961, p31.
Nicholas Ray: A Guide to References and Resources. p116-18.
Saturday Review. Jan 28, 1961, v44, p26.
Variety. Jun 29, 1960, p9.

Savage Princess *See* Aan

Savage Sam (US; Tokar, Norman; 1963)
BFI/Monthly Film Bulletin. Sep 1963, v30, p132.
Commonweal. Jun 14, 1963, v78, p328.
Film Daily. May 23, 1963, p7.
Filmfacts. Jul 25, 1963, v6, p144.
Films and Filming. Sep 1963, v9, p24.
Hollywood Reporter. May 22, 1963, v175, p3.
The New York Times. Aug 1, 1963, p17.
Variety. May 22, 1963, p6.

Savage Triangle (French title: Garçon
Sauvage, Le; Also titled: Wild Boy)
(FR; Delannoy, Jean; 1951)
BFI/Monthly Film Bulletin. Apr 1952, v19, p45.
Film Daily. Oct 3, 1952, p6.
The London Times. Feb 22, 1952, p4.
The New York Times. Sep 30, 1952, p38.
The New Yorker. Oct 11, 1952, v28, p127.
Newsweek. Oct 13, 1952, v40, p102.
Variety. Sep 19, 1951, p6.

Save the Tiger (US; Avildsen, John G.;
1973)
America. Mar 10, 1973, v128, p226.
Audience. Apr 1973, v5, p5-6.
Christian Century. Jun 13, 1973, v90, p685.
Commentary. May 1973, v55, p81-84.
Commonweal. Mar 16, 1973, v98, p38-39.
Filmfacts. 1973, v16, n2, p29.
Filmmakers Newsletter. Apr 1973, v6, p18-19.
Films in Review. Mar 1973, v24, p181-82.
The Films of Jack Lemmon. p207-12.
Forbes. Jun 1, 1973, v111, p46.
Hollywood Reporter. Jan 30, 1973, p3.
*Magill's Survey of Cinema. English Language
Films. Series II,* v5, p2096.
The New Republic. Mar 10, 1973, v168, p28.
New Statesman. Jun 22, 1973, v86, p936-37.
The New York Times. Feb 15, 1973, p53.
The New York Times. Mar 25, 1973, SecII, p13.
The New York Times. Apr 8, 1973, p15.
The New York Times. Sep 9, 1973, SecII, p1.
The New York Times. Apr 3, 1974, p36.
The New Yorker. Feb 17, 1973, v48, p95-96.
Reeling. p167-71.
Rolling Stone. Mar 29, 1973, p64.
Saturday Review. Feb 1973, v1, p79.
Time. Feb 19, 1973, v101, p65.
Variety. Feb 7, 1973, p18.
The Village Voice. Feb 15, 1973, p79.

Sawdust and Tinsel *See* The Naked Night

Say Amen Somebody (US; Nierenberg,
George T.; 1982)
Christian Century. Jun 22, 1983, v100, p622.
Maclean's. Jul 11, 1983, v96, p46.
Ms. Sep 1983, v12, p40.
New York. Mar 21, 1983, v16, p76-77.
The New Yorker. Apr 4, 1983, v59, p124.
Rolling Stone. Mar 17, 1983, p34.
Time. May 2, 1983, v121, p76.

Sayonara (US; Logan, Joshua; 1957)
America. Dec 21, 1957, v98, p384.
America Cinematographer. Nov 1957, v38, p722-23.
BFI/Monthly Film Bulletin. Feb 1958, v25, p17.
Commonweal. Dec 13, 1957, v67, p287.
Dance Magazine. Dec 1957, v31, p14-15.
Film Culture. Feb 1958, v4, p17.
Film Daily. Nov 13, 1957, v112, p9.
Films and Filming. Jan 1958, v4, p23.
Films in Review. Dec 1957, v8, p527-28.
The Films of Marlon Brando. p102-07.
Hollywood Reporter. Nov 13, 1957, p3.
Magill's Survey of Cinema. Series II. v5, p2099-101.

The Nation. Dec 21, 1957, v185, p484.
The New York Times. Mar 10, 1957, SecII, p5.
The New York Times. Dec 1, 1957, SecII, p5.
The New York Times. Dec 6, 1957, p39.
The New York Times. Dec 8, 1957, SecII, p5.
The New Yorker. Dec 14, 1957, v33, p89.
Newsweek. Dec 9, 1957, v50, p96.
Sight and Sound. Wint 1957-58, v27, p149-50.
Time. Dec 16, 1957, v70, p94.
Variety. Nov 13, 1957, p6.

The Scalphunters (US; Pollack, Sydney;
1968)
BFI/Monthly Film Bulletin. Apr 1968, v35, p54-55.
Burt Lancaster: The Man and His Movies. p108-09.
Christian Science Monitor (Western edition). Apr 20, 1968, p12.
Film Daily. Mar 7, 1968, p3.
Film Quarterly. Sum 1968, v21, p61.
Filmfacts. May 15, 1968, v11, p118-19.
Films and Filming. Apr 1968, v14, p25.
Five Thousand One Nights At the Movies. p513.
Going Steady. p108.
Hollywood Reporter. Mar 6, 1968, p3.
The London Times. Feb 29, 1968, p15.
Motion Picture Herald Product Digest. Mar 13, 1968, p781.
New Statesman. Mar 1, 1968, v75, p280-81.
The New York Times. Apr 3, 1968, p40.
Senior Scholastic. May 9, 1968, v92, p26.
Sidney Pollack (Taylor). p41-45.
Variety. Mar 6, 1968, p6.

The Scandal *See* High Infidelity

Scandal in Sorrento (Italian title: Pane,
Amore, E...) (IT; Risi, Dino; 1957)
BFI/Monthly Film Bulletin. Apr 1957, v24, p48.
Commonweal. Jul 5, 1957, v66, p352.
Film Daily. Jun 24, 1957, v111, p8.
Films and Filming. Apr 1957, v3, p24-25.
The Films of Sophia Loren. p74-75.
The New York Times. Jun 13, 1957, p37.

Scandal Sheet (Also titled: The Dark Page)
(US; Karlson, Phil; 1952)
BFI/Monthly Film Bulletin. Apr 1952, v19, p50.
Christian Century. Mar 12, 1952, v69, p327.
Film Daily. Jan 15, 1952, p6.
Hollywood Reporter. Jan 9, 1952, p3.
Library Journal. Feb 1, 1952, v77, p206.
Motion Picture Herald Product Digest. Jan 12, 1952, p1186.
The New York Times. Jan 17, 1952, p23.
Newsweek. Jan 28, 1952, v39, p89.
The Spectator. Apr 11, 1952, v188, p481-82.
Time. Feb 4, 1952, v59, p72.
Variety. Jan 9, 1952, p6.

Scandale, Le *See* The Champagne Murders

Scanners (CAN; Cronenberg, David; 1981)
BFI/Monthly Film Bulletin. Apr 1981, v48, p78.
Film Journal. Feb 2, 1981, v84, p39.
Film Journal. Jan 15, 1981, v84, p10-11.
The Los Angeles Times. Jan 16, 1981, SecVI, p2.
Maclean's. Feb 2, 1981, v94, p51.
The New Leader. Feb 9, 1981, v64, p18.
New Statesman. Apr 17, 1981, v101, p24-25.
The New York Times. Jan 14, 1981, SecIII, p21.
Rolling Stone. Feb 19, 1981, p37.
Variety. Jan 21, 1981, p26.
The Village Voice. Jan 28, 1981, p44.

Scaramouche (US; Sidney, George; 1952)
BFI/Monthly Film Bulletin. Aug 1952, v19, p106-07.
Christian Century. Aug 6, 1952, v69, p911.
Commonweal. May 30, 1952, v56, p198.
Film Daily. May 12, 1952, p6.
The Great Adventure Films. p172-79.
Hollywood Reporter. May 12, 1952, p3.
Library Journal. Jun 1, 1952, v77, p970.
Life. May 26, 1952, v32, p72-73.
The London Times. Aug 22, 1952, p6.
Magill's Survey of Cinema. Series II. v5, p2102-05.
Motion Picture Herald Product Digest. May 17, 1952, p1365-66.
Movietone News. Nov 4, 1977, n56, p18-23.
The New York Times. May 9, 1952, p20.
Newsweek. May 19, 1952, v39, p109.
Saturday Review. Jun 14, 1952, v35, p35.
The Spectator. Aug 22, 1952, v189, p239.
The Tatler. Sep 3, 1952, v205, p418.
Time. May 26, 1952, v59, p98.
Variety. May 14, 1952, p6.

Scared Stiff (US; Marshall, George; 1953)
America. Jul 19, 1953, v89, p406.
BFI/Monthly Film Bulletin. Jul 1953, v20, n234, p110.
Catholic World. Jul 1953, v177, p304.
Film Daily. Apr 27, 1953, p15.
Hollywood Reporter. Apr 14, 1953, p3.
The New York Times. Jul 3, 1953, p10.
Newsweek. Jul 20, 1953, v42, p97.
Saturday Review. Jun 20, 1953, v36, p33.
Time. Jun 29, 1953, v61, p95.
Variety. Apr 15, 1953, p6.

The Scarf (US; Dupont, E. A.; 1951)
BFI/Monthly Film Bulletin. Jun 1951, v18, p277.
Christian Century. Jul 18, 1951, v68, p854.
Film Daily. Mar 20, 1951, p6.
Hollywood Reporter. Mar 19, 1951, p3.
Motion Picture Herald Product Digest. Mar 24, 1951, p766.
The Nation. May 26, 1951, v172, p498.
The New York Times. Apr 23, 1951, p21.
The New Yorker. Apr 28, 1951, v27, p95.
Newsweek. Apr 2, 1951, v37, p86.
The Spectator. May 11, 1951, v186, p617.
Time. Apr 2, 1951, v57, p98.
Variety. Mar 21, 1951, p6.

Scarface (US; De Palma, Brian; 1983)
American Film. Dec 1983, v9, p28-34.
BFI/Monthly Film Bulletin. Feb 1984, v51, p50-52.
Cineaste. 1984, v13, n3, p48-50.
Classics of the Gangster Films. p253-56.
Commonweal. Feb 24, 1984, v111, p17.
Film Comment. Jan-Feb 1984, v20, p66-70.
Film Journal. Jan 1984, v87, p9.
Films and Filming. Feb 1984, n353, p40.
Hollywood Reporter. Nov 30, 1983, p3.
Humanist. Mar-Apr 1984, v44, p39-40.
Informer. Dec 1983, p2.
Maclean's. Dec 12, 1983, v96, p69.
National Review. Feb 10, 1984, v36, p50-51.
The New Republic. Jan 9, 1984, v190, p24-25.
New Statesman. Jan-Feb 1984, v20, p66-70.
New York. Dec 19, 1983, v16, p70.
The New York Times. Dec 9, 1983, SecIII, p18.
The New Yorker. Dec 26, 1983, v59, p50-53.
Newsweek. Dec 5, 1983, v102, p122.
Newsweek. Dec 12, 1983, v102, p109.
Penthouse. Apr 1984, v15, p46.
Photoplay. Mar 1984, v35, p39-41.
Time. Dec 5, 1983, v122, p96.
Variety. Nov 30, 1983, p3.

Scarlet Angel (US; Salkow, Sidney; 1952)
BFI/Monthly Film Bulletin. Aug 1952, v19, p113.
Film Daily. Jun 2, 1952, p6.
Hollywood Reporter. May 28, 1952, p3.
Motion Picture Herald Product Digest. May 31, 1952, p1382.
The New York Times. Jun 21, 1952, p12.
Newsweek. Jun 23, 1952, v39, p91.
Time. Jul 7, 1952, v60, p76.
Variety. May 28, 1952, p6.

The Scarlet Spear (GB; Breakston, George; Stahl, Roy; 1953)
BFI/Monthly Film Bulletin. Mar 1954, v21, p42.
Film Daily. Mar 18, 1954, p10.
Hollywood Reporter. Mar 12, 1954, p4.
Motion Picture Herald Product Digest. Mar 27, 1954, p2238-39.
The New York Times. Apr 10, 1954, p11.
Variety. Mar 17, 1954, p6.

Scent of a Woman (Italian title: Profumo di donna) (IT; Risi, Dino; 1974)
BFI/Monthly Film Bulletin. Nov 1977, v44, p239.
Films in Review. Mar 1976, v27, p186.
Hollywood Reporter. Dec 31, 1975, p3.
Independent Film Journal. Feb 4, 1976, v77, p8-9.
The Los Angeles Times. Dec 31, 1975, SecII, p4.
Magill's Survey of Cinema. Foreign Language Films. v6, p2667-71.
Motion Picture Herald Product Digest. Feb 11, 1976, p70.
New York. Feb 9, 1976, v9, p72.
The New York Times. Jan 26, 1976, p28.
Saturday Review. Mar 6, 1976, v3, p42-43.
Variety. Jan 1, 1975, p14.
The Village Voice. Mar 1, 1976, v21, p115-16.

Scherzo del Destino Agguato Dietro L'Angelo Come Un Brigante Di Strada, Un *See* A Joke of Destiny

Sciecco Bianco, Lo *See* The White Sheik

Scorpio Rising (US; Anger, Kenneth; 1963)
Dictionary of Films. p330-31.
Film Culture. Wint 1963-64, n31, p5-9.
Film Culture. Spr 1964, n32, p9-11.
Film Culture. Spr 1966, n40, p68-71.
Film Culture Reader. p277-79.
Film Daily. Jul 13, 1966, p4.
Film Society Review. Apr 1966, p20-21.
The International Dictionary of Films and Filmmakers. v1, p416-17.
The London Times. Nov 10, 1965, p15.
The Nation. Sep 14, 1964, v199, p123-25.
The New Yorker. Apr 23, 1966, v42, p130-31.
Newsweek. Apr 25, 1966, v67, p90C.
Private Screenings. p230-32.
Variety. May 25, 1966, p6.
The Velvet Light Trap. Sum 1983, n20, p41-46.
The Village Voice. Nov 14, 1963, v9, p8.
The Village Voice. Apr 21, 1966, v11, p29.

Scotch on the Rocks (Also titled: Laxdale Hall) (GB; Eldridge, John; 1953)
Commonweal. Jul 2, 1954, v60, p318.
Film Daily. Jun 16, 1954, p6.
Films in Review. Aug-Sep 1954, v5, p368.
Motion Picture Herald Product Digest. Jun 12, 1954, p27.
National Parent-Teacher. Sep 1954, v49, p39.
The New Republic. Jul 5, 1954, v131, p21.
The New York Times. Jun 14, 1954, p18.
The New Yorker. Jun 12, 1954, v30, p70.
Variety. Jun 16, 1954, p6.

Scrooge (GB; Neame, Ronald; 1970)
BFI/Monthly Film Bulletin. Jan 1971, v38, p13-14.
Commonweal. Dec 25, 1970, v93, p327.
Dickens on Film. p336-41.
Films in Review. Dec 1970, v21, p643-44.
Hollywood Reporter. Oct 30, 1970, p3.
The New York Times. Nov 20, 1970, p29.
The New Yorker. Nov 28, 1970, v46, p175.
Newsweek. Dec 14, 1970, v76, p104A.
Saturday Review. Dec 5, 1970, v53, p44.
Scrooge. 1970.
Time. Dec 70, 1970, v96, p73.
Variety. Nov 4, 1970, p16.

Scrooge (Hurst, 1951) *See* A Christmas Carol

The Sea Chase (US; Farrow, John; 1955)
America. Jun 18, 1955, v93, p319.
BFI/Monthly Film Bulletin. Aug 1955, v22, n259, p121.
Catholic World. Jul 1955, v181, p304.
Commonweal. Jun 10, 1955, v62, p256.
The Complete Films of John Wayne. p198-99.
The Films of Lana Turner. p283-86.
Hollywood Reporter. May 12, 1955, v134, n32, p3.
Library Journal. Jun 1, 1955, v80, p1321.
Motion Picture Herald Product Digest. May 14, 1955, p433.
The New York Times. Jun 11, 1955, p8.
The New Yorker. Jun 18, 1955, v31, p65.
Newsweek. Jun 13, 1955, v45, p106.
Saturday Review. Jun 4, 1956, v38, p27.
Variety. May 18, 1955, p8.

The Sea Shall Not Have Them (GB; Gilbert, Lewis; 1954)
BFI/Monthly Film Bulletin. Dec 1954, v21, p175.
Film Daily. Jun 3, 1955, p8.
Films and Filming. Dec 1954, v1, p20.
The Films of Dirk Bogarde. p78-79.
Library Journal. Jun 15, 1955, v80, p1487.
The London Times. Dec 6, 1954, p11.
Motion Picture Herald Product Digest. Jun 4, 1955, p465.
National Parent-Teacher. Sep 1955, v50, p40.
The New Statesman and Nation. Dec 11, 1954, v48, p786-87.
The New Yorker. Jun 18, 1955, v31, p65.
Newsweek. Jun 13, 1955, v45, p106.
Saturday Review. Jun 4, 1955, v38, p27.
The Tatler. Dec 15, 1954, v214, p705.
Variety. Dec 15, 1954, p28.

Sea Wife (GB; McNaught, Bob; 1957)
BFI/Monthly Film Bulletin. May 1957, v24, p56.
Film Daily. Aug 6, 1957, v112, p8.
Films and Filming. May 1957, v3, p26.
Motion Picture Herald Product Digest. Aug 17, 1957, v208, p489.
The New York Times. Dec 5, 1957, p45.
Newsweek. Aug 26, 1957, v50, p96.
Variety. May 8, 1957, p6.

Seagulls Over Sorrento *See* Crest of the Wave

Seance on a Wet Afternoon (GB; Forbes, Bryan; 1964)
America. Dec 12, 1964, v111, p788.
BFI/Monthly Film Bulletin. Jul 1964, v31, p103-04.
Commonweal. Nov 27, 1964, v81, p331.
Film Daily. Nov 6, 1964, v125, p6.
Films and Filming. Jul 1964, v10, p21.
Films in Review. Dec 1964, v15, p635-36.
The Great British Films. p215-17.
Hollywood Reporter. Dec 4, 1964, v183, p3.

Hollywood U.K. p246-48.
Life. Dec 18, 1964, v57, p16.
Magill's Survey of Cinema. Series II. v5, p2120-23.
Motion Picture Herald Product Digest. Nov 11, 1964, v232, p163.
The Nation. Nov 30, 1964, v199, p420.
The New Republic. Dec 5, 1964, v151, p22.
The New York Times. Nov 6, 1964, p30.
The New Yorker. Nov 14, 1964, v40, p149-50.
Newsweek. Nov 16, 1964, v64, p102.
The Private Eye, the Cowboy, and the Very Naked Girl. p100-01.
Sight and Sound. Sum 1964, v33, p146.
Variety. Jun 10, 1964, p6.
Vogue. Jan 15, 1965, v145, p25.

The Searchers (US; Ford, John; 1956)
America. Jun 9, 1956, v95, p272.
American Film Genres (Kaminsky). p211-12.
The American West in Film. p56-57.
Authorship and Narrative in the Cinema. p85-136.
BFI/Monthly Film Bulletin. Aug 1956, v23, p100.
Bright Lights. 1977, v2, p4-7.
Cinema Papers. Dec 1982, n41, p510-15.
Cinema Texas Program Notes. Oct 2, 1975, v9, p27-34.
Cinema Texas Program Notes. Mar 21, 1979, v16, p43-50.
Cinema, the Magic Vehicle. v2, p.
Commonweal. Jun 15, 1956, v64, p274.
The Complete Films of John Wayne. p206-09.
Cult Movies. p310-14.
Favorite Movies. p34-43.
Film Comment. Spr 1971, v7, p56-61.
Film Daily. Mar 13, 1956, p6.
Film Heritage. 1976-77, v12, p24-30.
Film Quarterly. Wint 1980-81, v34, p9-23.
Film Reader. 1977, n2, p78-84.
Films and Filming. Sep 1956, v2, p25-26.
Films in Review. Jun-Jul 1956, v7, p284-85.
The Films of the Fifties. p180-82.
The Great Movies. p32-34.
The International Dictionary of Films and Filmmaking. v1, p417-19.
John Ford (McBride). p147-63.
Journal of Popular Film and Television. 1980, v8, p34-41.
Magill's Survey of Cinema. Series I. v4, p1502-06.
Motion Picture Herald Product Digest. Mar 31, 1956, p843.
The Nation. Jun 23, 1956, v182, p536.
New York. Mar 5, 1979, v12, p45-48.
The New York Times. May 31, 1956, p21.
The New Yorker. Jun 9, 1956, v32, p54.
Newsweek. May 21, 1956, v47, p116.
Sight and Sound. Fall 1956, v26, p94-95.
Sight and Sound. Fall 1971, v40, p210-14.
Talking Pictures. p330-35.
Time. Jun 25, 1956, p58.
University Film Association Journal. 1976, v28, p19-24.
Variety. Mar 14, 1956, p6.
Views. 1974, v5, p53-54.
The Western Films of John Ford. p160-73.
Wide Angle. 1978, v2, p36-42.
Wide Angle. 1981, v4, p65-70.

The Second Breath *See* Deuxieme Souffle, Le

Second Wind *See* Deuxieme Souffle, Le

Seconds (US; Frankenheimer, John; 1966)
America. Oct 15, 1966, v115, p467-68.
BFI/Monthly Film Bulletin. Dec 1966, v33, p181-82.

Christian Science Monitor (Western edition).
Oct 21, 1966, p4.
The Cinema of John Frankenheimer. p131-48.
Film Daily. Sep 22, 1966, p3.
Film Quarterly. Wint 1966-67, v20, p25-28.
Filmfacts. Nov 15, 1966, v9, p255-57.
Films and Filming. Jan 1967, v13, p28-29.
Films and Filming. Jan 1966, v12, p53.
Films in Review. Nov 1966, v17, p585-86.
Focus. Feb 1967, n1, p16.
Hollywood Reporter. Sep 15, 1966, p3.
International Film Guide. 1967, v4, p162-63.
The London Times. Nov 10, 1966, p16.
Magill's Survey of Cinema. Series II. v5, p2124-27.
Motion Picture Herald Product Digest. Sep 28, 1966, p603-04.
New Society. Nov 17, 1966, p768.
New Statesman. Nov 11, 1966, v72, p715.
The New York Times. Oct 6, 1966, p56.
The New Yorker. Oct 8, 1966, v42, p127.
Newsweek. Oct 17, 1966, v68, p104.
The Private Eye, the Cowboy and the Very Naked Girl. p207-08.
Saturday Review. Oct 29, 1966, v49, p45.
Senior Scholastic. Nov 4, 1966, v89, p28.
Sight and Sound. Wint 1966-67, v36, p46.
Time. Oct 14, 1966, v88, p117-18.
Variety. May 25, 1966, p24.
The Village Voice. Oct 13, 1966, v11, p27.

Secret Ceremony (GB; Losey, Joseph; 1968)
BFI/Monthly Film Bulletin. Jul 1969, v36, p142-43.
Commonweal. Dec 6, 1968, v89, p351.
Conversations With Losey. p268-69, 282-96.
Film Daily. Oct 22, 1968, p4.
Film Heritage. Sum 1970, v5, p1-6.
Film Quarterly. Spr 1969, v22, p64.
Filmfacts. Jan 15, 1969, v11, p436-37.
Films and Filming. Aug 1969, v15, p32-33.
Films in Review. Dec 1968, v19, p648-49.
The Films of Elizabeth Taylor. p203-08.
Going Steady. p207-08.
Hollywood Reporter. Oct 22, 1968, p3.
Joseph Losey (Hirsch). p167-73.
The London Times. Jun 19, 1969, p11.
Motion Picture Herald Product Digest. Oct 23, 1968, p47.
Movie. Wint 1968-69, n16, p39.
Movies Into Film. p350-51.
New Statesman. Jun 27, 1969, v77, p919-20.
The New York Times. Oct 24, 1968, p55.
The New York Times. Nov 10, 1968, p1.
Sight and Sound. Spr 1969, v38, p77-78.
The Spectator. Jun 28, 1969, v222, p861.
Time. Nov 1, 1968, v92, p101.
Variety. Oct 23, 1968, p24.

Secret de Mayerling, Le *See* The Secret of Mayerling

Secret Flight (GB; Ustinov, Peter; 1951)
Hollywood Reporter. Sep 28, 1951, p4.
Motion Picture Herald Product Digest. Jul 12, 1952, p1442.
The New York Times. Jul 3, 1952, p16.
Newsweek. Jul 14, 1952, v40, p90.
Variety. Oct 3, 1951, p24.

The Secret Fury (US; Ferrer, Mel; 1950)
Christian Century. Jun 28, 1950, v67, p800.
Commonweal. Jul 21, 1950, v52, p368.
Film Daily. Apr 26, 1950, p7.
Hollywood Reporter. Apr 26, 1950, p4.
The London Times. Jan 15, 1951, p6.
Motion Picture Herald Product Digest. Apr 29, 1950, p277.
The New York Times. Jun 22, 1950, p34.
The New Yorker. Jul 1, 1950, v26, p49.
Newsweek. Jul 3, 1950, v36, p68.

The Spectator. Jan 12, 1951, v186, p44.
Time. Jul 17, 1950, v56, p90.
Variety. Apr 26, 1950, p8.

The Secret Game *See* Forbidden Games

The Secret of Convict Lake (US; Gordon, Michael; 1951)
BFI/Monthly Film Bulletin. Sep 1951, v18, p327-28.
Film Daily. Jun 25, 1951, p6.
Hollywood Reporter. Jun 22, 1951, p3.
Motion Picture Herald Product Digest. Jun 30, 1951, p913.
The Nation. Sep 1, 1951, v173, p178.
The New Republic. Aug 27, 1951, v125, p21.
The New Statesman and Nation. Oct 27, 1951, v42, p461.
The New York Times. Aug 4, 1951, p7.
Newsweek. Aug 13, 1951, v38, p79.
Time. Aug 20, 1951, v58, p87.
Variety. Jun 27, 1951, p9.

The Secret of Mayerling (French title: Secret de Mayerling, Le) (FR; Delannoy, Jean; 1949)
Commonweal. May 25, 1951, v54, p166.
The New Republic. May 21, 1951, v124, p23.
The New Statesman and Nation. Sep 17, 1949, v38, p299.
The New York Times. May 8, 1951, p39.
Newsweek. May 21, 1951, v37, p101.
Time. Jun 4, 1951, v57, p102.
Variety. May 16, 1951, p18.

The Secret of My Success (GB; Stone, Andrew L.; 1965)
BFI/Monthly Film Bulletin. Jan 1966, v33, p7-8.
Christian Science Monitor (Western edition). Dec 6, 1965, p12.
Commonweal. Dec 10, 1965, v83, p315.
Film Daily. Sep 29, 1965, p5.
Films and Filming. Apr 1966, v12, p53.
Films and Filming. Mar 1965, v12, p53.
Hollywood Reporter. Sep 29, 1965, p3.
The London Times. Dec 19, 1965, p13.
Motion Picture Herald Product Digest. Oct 13, 1965, p387.
The New York Times. Nov 4, 1965, p57.
Time. Nov 26, 1965, v86, p103.
Variety. Sep 29, 1965, p6.

The Secret of NIMH (US; Bluth, Don; 1982)
Hollywood Reporter. Jun 16, 1982, p3.
The Los Angeles Times. Jul 2, 1982, SecVI, p1.
Maclean's. Jul 5, 1982, v95, p52.
Magill's Cinema Annual, 1983. p288-93.
The New York Times. Jul 30, 1982, SecIII, p12.
Newsweek. Jul 12, 1982, v100, p75.
Newsweek. Aug 9, 1982, v100, p70-71.
Science News. Aug 7, 1982, v122, p92-93.
Time. Jul 26, 1982, v120, p44.
Variety. Jun 16, 1982, p3.

The Secret of Santa Vittoria (US; Kramer, Stanley; 1969)
America. Dec 13, 1969, v121, p600.
Deeper Into Movies. p43-44.
Film Daily. Oct 2, 1969, p3.
Films and Filming. Nov 1968, v15, p65-68.
Films and Filming. Jul 1970, v16, p32.
Films in Review. Nov 1969, v20, p575-76.
The Films of Anthony Quinn. p227-29.
Hollywood Reporter. Oct 1, 1969, p3.
Life. Oct 24, 1969, v67, p17.
The New York Times. Oct 30, 1969, p58.
The New Yorker. Nov 1, 1969, v45, p140-41.
Newsweek. Nov 24, 1969, v74, p121A.
Saturday Review. Oct 25, 1969, v52, p32.
Stanley Kramer, Film-Maker. p283-94.

Time. Nov 7, 1969, v94, p105.
Variety. Oct 1, 1969, p17.

Secret of the Incas (US; Hopper, Jerry; 1954)
America. Jun 12, 1954, v91, p307.
BFI/Monthly Film Bulletin. Sep 1954, v21, p135-36.
Commonweal. Jun 18, 1954, v60, p270.
Film Daily. May 21, 1954, p4.
Hollywood Reporter. May 19, 1954, p3.
Motion Picture Herald Product Digest. May 22, 1954, p1.
The New York Times. May 29, 1954, p13.
Variety. May 19, 1954, p6.

Secret People (GB; Dickinson, Thorold; 1952)
BFI/Monthly Film Bulletin. Mar 1952, v19, p32-33.
A Critical History of British Cinema. p231-33.
Film Criticism and Caricatures, 1943-1953. p138-39.
Hollywood Reporter. Aug 22, 1952, p3.
The London Times. Feb 11, 1951, p2.
Motion Picture Herald Product Digest. Aug 30, 1952, p1510.
The New Statesman and Nation. Feb 16, 1952, v43, p182.
Sight and Sound. Apr-Jun 1952, v21, p168-71.
Sight and Sound. Aug-Sep 1951, v21, p25-27.
The Spectator. Feb 8, 1952, v188, p173.
Variety. Feb 12, 1952, p6.

Secret War *See* The Dirty Game

The Secret War of Harry Frigg (US; Smight, Jack; 1968)
America. Mar 16, 1968, v118, p358.
BFI/Monthly Film Bulletin. Mar 1968, v35, p43.
Christian Science Monitor (Western edition). Apr 19, 1968, p4.
Film Daily. Feb 29, 1968, p7.
Film Quarterly. Sum 1968, v21, p60-61.
Filmfacts. Apr 1, 1968, v11, p70-72.
Films and Filming. Mar 1968, v14, p27.
Films in Review. Apr 1968, v19, p243-44.
The Films of Paul Newman. p166-69.
Going Steady. p69-70.
Hollywood Reporter. Feb 28, 1968, p3.
The London Times. Feb 1, 1968, p11.
Motion Picture Herald Product Digest. Mar 13, 1968, p782.
The New York Times. Mar 5, 1968, p34.
The New Yorker. Mar 9, 1968, v44, p150.
Senior Scholastic. Apr 25, 1968, v92, p30.
Time. Mar 15, 1968, v91, p92.
Variety. Feb 28, 1968, p6.
A Year In the Dark. p61-63.

Secrets of Women (Swedish title: Kvinnors Vantan; Also titled: Waiting Women) (SWED; Bergman, Ingmar; 1952)
Cinema Borealis. p117, 119-22.
Film Quarterly. Fall 1961, v15, p45-47.
Filmfacts. Oct 6, 1961, v4, p221-22.
Films and Filming. Dec 1959, v6, p24.
The Films of Ingmar Bergman (Donner). p89-92.
Ingmar Bergman (Steene). p53-55.
Ingmar Bergman (Wood). p43-48.
The London Times. Jan 25, 1960, p3.
Magill's Survey of Cinema. Foreign Language Films. v6, p2688-93.
Motion Picture Herald Product Digest. Aug 23, 1961, p245.
National Review. Nov 4, 1961, v11, p311-13.
The New Republic. Aug 7, 1961, v145, p27-28.
The New York Times. Jul 12, 1961, p36.
The New Yorker. Jul 22, 1961, v37, p54.

Good Housekeeping. Nov 1958, v147, p24.
Hollywood Reporter. Dec 2, 1958, p3.
Library Journal. Dec 15, 1958, v83, p3507.
Magill's Survey of Cinema. Series I. v4, p1506-08.
The New Republic. Jan 5, 1959, v140, p21-22.
The New York Times. Dec 19, 1958, p2.
The New Yorker. Jan 3, 1959, v34, p59.
Newsweek. Dec 22, 1958, v52, p80.
Saturday Review. Dec 27, 1958, v41, p21.
Time. Dec 15, 1958, v72, p61.
Variety. Dec 3, 1958, p6.

Sepkonbadd 1782 *See* My Sister, My Love

Sept Fois Femme *See* Woman Times Seven

Sept Peches Capitaux, Les *See* The Seven Deadly Sins

Sept Samourais, Les *See* The Seven Samurai

September Affair (US; Dieterle, William; 1950)
BFI/Monthly Film Bulletin. Oct 1950, v17, p151.
Christian Century. Mar 21, 1951, v68, p383.
Commonweal. Feb 16, 1951, v53, p469.
Film Daily. Oct 18, 1950, p6.
Hollywood Reporter. Sep 27, 1950, p3.
Motion Picture Herald Product Digest. Oct 21, 1950, p538.
The New York Times. Feb 2, 1951, p19.
The New Yorker. Feb 10, 1951, v26, p90.
Newsweek. Feb 12, 1951, v37, p80.
Saturday Review. Feb 24, 1951, v34, p26.
The Spectator. Oct 27, 1950, v185, p422.
Time. Feb 12, 1951, v57, p88.
Variety. Sep 6, 1950, p8.

Sequestrati di Altona, I *See* The Condemned of Altona

Sgt. Pepper's Lonely Hearts Club Band (US, WGER; Schultz, Michael; 1978)
BFI/Monthly Film Bulletin. Feb 1979, v46, p32-33.
The Hollywood Musical. p410.
The Los Angeles Times. Jul 30, 1978, Calendar, p70.
Maclean's. Aug 7, 1978, v91, p58.
Motion Picture Herald Product Digest. Aug 9, 1978, p18.
New York. Aug 7, 1978, v11, p56-58.
The New York Times. Jul 21, 1978, SecIII, p16.
The New Yorker. Jul 31, 1978, v54, p64-65.
Newsweek. Jul 31, 1978, v92, p42.
The Official Sgt. Pepper's Lonely Heart's Club Band Scrapbook. 1978.
Time. Jul 31, 1978, v112, p86.

Sergeant Rutledge (US; Ford, John; 1960)
America. Jun 4, 1960, v103, p342.
BFI/Monthly Film Bulletin. Jun 1960, v27, p81.
Commonweal. Jun 17, 1960, v72, p305.
Film Quarterly. Spr 1960, v13, p60.
Filmfacts. 1960, v3, p139.
Films and Filming. Jul 1960, v6, p24-25.
Films in Review. May 1960, v11, p297.
Hollywood Reporter. Apr 8, 1960, p3.
John Ford (McBride). p164-75.
Magill's Survey of Cinema. Series II. v5, p2135-37.
The Nation. Jun 11, 1960, v190, p519.
The New York Times. May 26, 1960, p37.
The New Yorker. Jun 4, 1960, v36, p100.
Newsweek. Apr 16, 1960, v43, p32.
Sight and Sound. Sum 1960, v29, p142.
Time. Jun 13, 1960, v75, p67.
The Western Films of John Ford. p186-97.

Sergeants 3 (US; Sturges, John; 1962)
BFI/Monthly Film Bulletin. Apr 1962, v29, p54-55.
Commonweal. Mar 16, 1962, v75, p645.
Film. Sum 1962, n32, p20.
Film Daily. Jan 24, 1962, p6.
Filmfacts. Mar 16, 1962, v5, p39-40.
Films and Filming. May 1962, v8, p33-34.
Films in Review. Mar 1962, v13, p172.
The Films of Frank Sinatra. p176-80.
Hollywood Reporter. Jan 24, 1962, p3.
Motion Picture Herald Product Digest. Jan 31, 1962, p427.
The New York Times. Feb 12, 1962, p28.
Time. Feb 9, 1962, v79, p83.
Variety. Jan 24, 1962, p6.

Serial (US; Persky, Bill; 1980)
Encore. May 1980, v9, p46.
Hollywood Reporter. Mar 24, 1980, p3.
The Los Angeles Times. Mar 27, 1980, SecVI, p2.
Maclean's. Apr 7, 1980, v93, p61.
Motion Picture Herald Product Digest. Apr 9, 1980, p86.
The Nation. May 3, 1980, v230, p539-40.
The New Republic. Apr 19, 1980, v182, p26-27.
New York. Apr 14, 1980, v13, p83-84.
The New York Times. Mar 28, 1980, SecIII, p8.
The New Yorker. Apr 14, 1980, v56, p111.
Newsweek. Apr 7, 1980, v95, p68.
Time. Apr 14, 1980, v115, p99.
Variety. Mar 26, 1980, p20.

Serpico (US; Lumet, Sidney; 1973)
America. Feb 23, 1973, v130, p34.
Atlantic Monthly. Feb 1974, v233, p92-94.
BFI/Monthly Film Bulletin. Mar 1974, v41, p52-53.
Commonweal. Jan 11, 1974, v99, p366-67.
Esquire. Mar 1974, v82, p66.
Film Heritage. Sum 1974, v9, p31.
Filmmakers Newsletter. Feb 1974, v7, p30-34.
Films in Review. Feb 1974, v25, p119.
The Films of The Seventies. p71-73.
Harpers. Mar 1974, v248, p82-84.
Interview. Jan 1974, v4, p36-37.
Magill's Survey of Cinema. English Language Films. Series I, v4, p1512.
Millimeter. Feb 1974, v2, p40.
The Nation. Dec 17, 1973, v217, p668.
New Statesman. Mar 29, 1974, v87, p458.
The New York Review of Books. Feb 7, 1974, v21, p18-22.
The New York Times. Dec 6, 1973, p61.
The New York Times. Dec 16, 1973, SecII, p3.
The New York Times. Jan 6, 1974, SecII, p1.
The New Yorker. Dec 17, 1973, v49, p107-10.
Newsweek. Dec 17, 1973, v82, p91-92.
Partisan Review. Spr 1974, v41, p273-78.
Reeling. p310-18.
Rolling Stone. Jan 3, 1974, p70.
Saturday Review. Jan 12, 1974, v1, p54.
Sidney Lumet: A Guide to References and Resources. p97-100.
Time. May 7, 1973, v101, p94.
Variety. Dec 5, 1973, p20.

The Servant (GB; Losey, Joseph; 1963)
America. May 16, 1964, v110, p685-86.
BFI/Monthly Film Bulletin. Dec 1963, v30, p169.
The Cinema of Joseph Losey. p126-33.
Commonweal. Mar 20, 1964, v79, p751.
Confessions of a Cultist. p129-31.
Conversations with Losey. p224-39.
Dictionary of Films. p333-34.
Fifty Classic British Films. p115-17.
Film and the Critical Eye. p500-04.
Films and Filming. Dec 1963, v10, p24-25.

Films in Review. Apr 1964, v15, p241-42.
The Films of Dirk Bogarde. p143-46.
The Great British Films. p212-14.
Great Horror Movies. p92-94.
Hollywood Reporter. May 13, 1964, v180, p3.
Hollywood U.K. p205-18.
Joseph Losey (Hirsch). p87-111.
Life. Apr 10, 1964, v56, p12.
Magill's Survey of Cinema. Series II. v5, p2138-41.
Making Pictures: The Pinter Screenplays. p9-26.
Motion Picture Herald Product Digest. Apr 1, 1964, v231, p17-18.
The Nation. Apr 6, 1964, v198, p354-55.
The New Republic. Mar 21, 1964, v150, p27-28.
The New York Times. Mar 17, 1964, p30.
The New Yorker. Nov 30, 1963, v39, p207.
The New Yorker. Mar 21, 1964, v40, p172.
Newsweek. Mar 23, 1964, v63, p95-96.
The Private Eye, the Cowboy and the Very Naked Girl. p70-71.
Renaissance of the Film. p220-31.
Saturday Review. Mar 14, 1964, v47, p17.
Sight and Sound. Wint 1963-64, v33, p38-39.
Time. Mar 20, 1964, v83, p94a-94b.
Variety. Sep 11, 1963, p22.

Seul Jour, Un *See* Ikiru

Seven Beauties (Italian title: Pasqualino Settebellezze; Also titled: Seven Beauties, That's What They Call Him) (IT; Wertmuller, Lina; 1975)
America. Feb 7, 1976, v134, p99-100.
American Film. Jul-Aug 1976, v1, p6-7.
Audience. Apr 1976, v8, p8-10.
Before My Eyes. p23-27.
BFI/Monthly Film Bulletin. Dec 1976, v43, p254.
Cineaste. 1976, v7, n2, p2-5.
Commentary. May 1976, v61, p72-76.
Film Bulletin. Jan 1976, v45, p27.
Films in Review. Feb 1976, v27, p123.
Hollywood Reporter. Jan 22, 1976, p18.
Independent Film Journal. Jan 21, 1976, v77, p7.
Landmark Films. p398-405.
The Los Angeles Times. Mar 31, 1976, SecIV, p1.
Magill's Survey of Cinema. Foreign Language Films. v6, p2709-13.
Midstream. Jun-Jul 1976, v22, p51-52.
Motion Picture Herald Product Digest. Jan 28, 1976, p25.
Ms. May 1976, v4, p71-75.
The Nation. Feb 7, 1976, v222, p155-56.
The New Republic. Feb 14, 1976, v174, p22-23.
New York. Feb 2, 1976, v9, p24-31.
New York Review of Books. Mar 18, 1976, v23, p5.
The New York Times. Feb 17, 1976, p31.
The New York Times. Jan 25, 1976, SecII, p1.
The New York Times. Mar 7, 1976, SecII, p1.
The New Yorker. Feb 16, 1976, v51, p104.
Newsweek. Jan 25, 1976, v87, p78-79.
Progressive. May 1976, v40, p39-40.
Saturday Review. Feb 21, 1976, v3, p49-50.
The Screenplays of Lina Wertmuller. p267-334.
Self and Cinema. p87-191.
Sight and Sound. Sum 1976, v45, p134-39.
Time. Jan 26, 1976, v107, p76.
Variety. Jan 14, 1976, p20.
Vogue. Mar 1976, v166, p68.
When the Lights Go Down. p136-40.

Seven Brides for Seven Brothers (US; Donen, Stanley; 1954)
America. Jul 31, 1954, v91, p446.
The Best of MGM. p188-89.

BFI/Monthly Film Bulletin. Dec 1954, v21, p175-76.
Catholic World. Aug 1954, v179, p382.
Commonweal. Aug 13, 1954, v60, p463.
Cue. Jul 17, 1954, p15.
Dance Magazine. Aug 1954, v28, p21-23.
Farm Journal. Aug 1954, v78, p101.
Film Daily. Jun 1, 1954, p6.
Films and Filming. Oct 1954, v1, p25.
Films and Filming. Jan 1955, v1, p19.
Films and Filming. May 1969, v15, p56.
Films in Review. Aug-Sep 1954, v5, p364.
Hollywood Reporter. Jun 1, 1954, p3.
Library Journal. Aug 1954, v79, p1393.
Life. Jul 26, 1954, v37, p53-54.
Magill's Survey of Cinema. Series I. v4, p1515-18.
Motion Picture Herald Product Digest. Jun 5, 1954, p17.
National Parent-Teacher. Sep 1954, v49, p37.
The New York Times. Jul 23, 1954, p8.
The New York Times Magazine. Jul 4, 1954, p14-15.
The New Yorker. Jul 31, 1954, v30, p53.
Newsweek. Sep 20, 1954, v44, p101.
Reruns. p92-96.
Saturday Review. Jan 1, 1955, v38, p63.
Saturday Review. Aug 7, 1954, v37, p26-27.
Selected Film Criticism, 1951-1960. p118-19.
Senior Scholastic. Sep 15, 1954, v65, p35.
Sight and Sound. Jan-Mar 1955, v24, p142.
The Spectator. Dec 31, 1954, v193, p829.
Stanley Donen (Casper). p64-75.
The Tatler. Dec 22, 1954, v214, p750.
Time. Jul 12, 1954, v64, p90.
Variety. Jun 2, 1954, p6.

Seven Days in May (US; Frankenheimer, John; 1964)
America. Mar 7, 1964, v110, p323-24.
BFI/Monthly Film Bulletin. May 1964, v31, p71-72.
Burt Lancaster: A Pictorial Treasury of His Films. p124.
Burt Lancaster: The Man and His Movies. p98-101.
The Cinema of John Frankenheimer. p103-14.
Esquire. Jun 1964, p14-16.
Film Daily. Feb 4, 1964, v124, p8.
Films in Review. Mar 1964, v15, p171-72.
The Films of Kirk Douglas. p194-97.
Guts & Glory. p201-05.
Hollywood Reporter. Feb 4, 1964, v179, p3.
Look. Nov 19, 1964, v27, p90-95.
Magill's Survey of Cinema. Series II. v5, p2144-49.
Motion Picture Herald Product Digest. Feb 5, 1964, v231, p985.
The Nation. Mar 9, 1964, v198, p251-52.
The New Republic. Mar 7, 1964, v150, p35.
The New York Times. Feb 20, 1964, p22.
The New Yorker. Feb 22, 1964, v40, p112.
Newsweek. Feb 24, 1964, v63, p89.
Private Screenings. p127-29.
Saturday Review. Feb 1, 1964, v47, p25.
Time. Feb 21, 1964, v83, p94.
Variety. Feb 5, 1964, p6.

Seven Days to Noon (GB; Boulting, John; Boulting, Roy; 1950)
BFI/Monthly Film Bulletin. Sep 1950, v17, p136.
Christian Century. May 2, 1951, v68, p575.
Commonweal. Jan 12, 1951, v53, p350.
Film Criticism and Caricatures, 1943-1953. p113-14.
Film Daily. Dec 28, 1950, p6.
Films in Review. Feb 1951, v2, p36.
The Great British Films. p144-46.

Hollywood Reporter. Feb 16, 1951, p4.
Illustrated London News. Sep 30, 1950, v217, p534.
The London Times. Sep 14, 1950, p6.
Magill's Survey of Cinema. Series II. v5, p2150-52.
Motion Picture Herald Product Digest. Dec 30, 1950, p641.
The New Republic. Dec 25, 1950, v123, p22-23.
The New Statesman and Nation. Sep 23, 1950, v40, p296.
The New York Times. Dec 19, 1950, p41.
The New York Times Magazine. Dec 3, 1950, p28-29.
The New Yorker. Sep 30, 1950, v26, p64.
The New Yorker. Dec 16, 1950, v26, p144.
Newsweek. Jan 1, 1951, v37, p57.
Saturday Review. Dec 30, 1950, v33, p21-23.
Senior Scholastic. Jan 3, 1951, v57, p24.
Sight and Sound. Jan 1950, v19, p13-15.
Sight and Sound. Dec 1950, v19, p332.
The Spectator. Sep 22, 1950, v185, p312.
Time. Dec 25, 1950, v56, p56.
Variety. Aug 23, 1950, p20.

The Seven Deadly Sins (French title: Sept Peches Capitaux, Les) (FR, IT; De Filippo, Eduardo; Autant-Lara, Claude; Rossellini, Roberto; Allégret, Yves; Lacombe, Georges; Carlo-Rim; Dreville, Jean; 1951)
BFI/Monthly Film Bulletin. Jan 1953, v20, p6.
Classics of the Foreign Film. p200-01.
Commonweal. Jun 5, 1953, v58, p228.
Film Daily. Sep 9, 1953, p6.
Films in Review. Aug-Sep 1953, v4, p358-60.
Motion Picture Herald Product Digest. May 23, 1953, p1846-47.
The New Republic. Sep 4, 1953, v129, p20.
The New York Times. May 12, 1953, p31.
The New Yorker. May 23, 1953, v29, p74.
Newsweek. May 25, 1953, v41, p100.
Saturday Review. May 23, 1953, v36, p30.
Saturday Review. Jan 8, 1955, v38, p30.
The Spectator. Dec 12, 1952, v189, p809-10.
Theatre Arts. Aug 1953, v37, p87.
Time. Jun 1, 1953, v61, p96.
Variety. May 20, 1953, p16.
Variety. Jun 4, 1952, p6.

Seven Eleven Ocean Drive (Also titled: 711 Ocean Drive) (US; Newman, Joseph M.; 1950)
BFI/Monthly Film Bulletin. Jan 1951, v18, p202.
Christian Century. Aug 16, 1950, v67, p983.
Commonweal. Jul 28, 1950, v52, p391.
Film Daily. Jul 14, 1950, p5.
The Great Gangster Pictures. p351-52.
Hollywood Reporter. Jul 12, 1950, p3.
The London Times. Jan 29, 1951, p8.
Motion Picture Herald Product Digest. Jul 15, 1950, p389-90.
The New York Times. Jul 20, 1950, p21.
The New Yorker. Jul 29, 1950, v26, p61.
Newsweek. Aug 7, 1950, v36, p75.
The Spectator. Jan 26, 1951, v186, p108.
Time. Aug 7, 1950, v56, p68.
Variety. Jul 19, 1950, p6.

7 Faces of Dr. Lao (US; Pal, George; 1964)
BFI/Monthly Film Bulletin. Nov 1965, v32, p169.
Boxoffice. Mar 16, 1964, v84, p2809.
Commonweal. Apr 10, 1964, v80, p91.
Film Daily. Mar 5, 1964, v124, p6.
Films and Filming. Dec 1965, v12, p28.
The Films of George Pal. p147-58.
Great Horror Movies. p94-95.
Hollywood Reporter. Mar 2, 1964, v179, p3.

Motion Picture Herald Product Digest. Mar 18, 1964, v231, p10.
The New York Times. Jul 23, 1964, p19.
Time. Aug 7, 1964, v84, p89.
Variety. Mar 11, 1964, p6.
The World of Fantastic Films. p48-49.

Seven Men From Now (US; Boetticher, Budd; 1956)
Film Daily. Jul 11, 1956, p10.
Hollywood Reporter. Jul 11, 1956, p3.
Variety. Jul 11, 1956, p6.

The Seven Per-Cent Solution (US, GB; Ross, Herbert; 1976)
Before My Eyes. p252-54.
BFI/Monthly Film Bulletin. Feb 1977, v44, p31.
Film Bulletin. Nov-Dec 1976, v45, p7.
Films in Review. Nov 1976, v27, p567.
The Films of Sherlock Holmes. p232-42.
The Films of the Seventies. p165-66.
Hollywood Reporter. Oct 6, 1976, p2.
Independent Film Journal. Oct 11, 1976, v78, p31-32.
Laurence Olivier: Theater & Cinema. p228-31.
The Los Angeles Times. Nov 12, 1976, SecIV, p1.
Magill's Survey of Cinema. Series II. v5, p2153-55.
Millimeter. Nov 1976, v4, p32-34.
Motion Picture Herald Product Digest. Oct 6, 1976, p37.
The Nation. Nov 13, 1976, v223, p508.
The New Republic. Oct 30, 1976, v175, p30.
New York. Nov 8, 1976, v9, p76.
The New York Times. Oct 31, 1976, SecII, p17.
The New Yorker. Nov 1, 1976, v52, p145-47.
Newsweek. Nov 1, 1976, v88, p83.
Saturday Review. Oct 30, 1976, v4, p53.
The Thousand Eyes Magazine. Nov 1976, v2, p8.
Time. Nov 1, 1976, v108, p80.
Variety. Oct 6, 1976, p20.
The Village Voice. Nov 8, 1976, p53-54.
Vogue. Dec 1976, v166, p108.
When the Lights Go Down. p190-92.

The Seven Samurai (Japanese title: Shichi-nin no Samurai; French title: Sept Samourais, Les) (JAPAN; Kurosawa, Akira; 1954)
Akira Kurosawa: A Guide to References and Resources. p50-52.
BFI/Monthly Film Bulletin. Apr 1955, v22, p54.
Cineaste. 1979-80, v10, n1, p42-43.
Cinema, the Magic Vehicle. v2, p185-88.
Classic Movies. p134-35.
Commonweal. Dec 14, 1956, v65, p289.
Dictionary of Films. p339-40.
Film As Film: Critical Responses to Film Art. p251-62.
Film Culture. 1956, v2, n4, p3-7.
Film Daily. Dec 6, 1956, p6.
Film Journal. Dec 1956, n6, p6-9.
Film Quarterly. Spr 1962, v15, p55-58.
Films and Filming. Apr 1955, v1, p23.
Films in Review. Dec 1956, v7, p526.
The Films of Akira Kurosawa. p97-108.
The Great Movies. p124-28.
I Lost It At the Movies. p107-11.
The International Dictionary of Films and Filmmakers. v1, p428-30.
Japanese Cinema (Richie). p232-35.
The Japanese Film: Art and Industry. p272-73.
Japanese Film Directors. p175-79.
Life. Jan 14, 1957, v42, p92.
Literature/Film Quarterly. 1985, v13, n2, p112.
The London Times. Nov 17, 1956, p146.

Magill's Survey of Cinema. Foreign Language Films. v6, p2714-19.
Motion Picture Herald Product Digest. Nov 17, 1956, p146.
The Nation. Dec 8, 1956, v183, p507.
National Parent-Teacher. Dec 1956, v51, p39.
The New Republic. Jan 31, 1983, v188, p22-23.
The New Statesman and Nation. Feb 26, 1955, v49, p278-79.
The New York Times. Nov 20, 1956, p46.
The New York Times Magazine. Oct 28, 1956, p70-71.
The New Yorker. Dec 1, 1956, v32, p129.
Newsweek. Dec 10, 1956, v48, p119.
Private Screenings. p39-42.
Rolling Stone. Mar 1, 1983, p42.
The Samurai Films of Akira Kurosawa. p77-91, 141-44.
Saturday Review. Dec 1, 1956, v39, p54.
The Seven Samurai: A Film by Akira Kurosawa. p5-21.
Sight and Sound. Spr 1955, v24, p195-96.
Soundtrack. Jun 1985, v4, p15.
The Spectator. Feb 25, 1955, v194, p226.
The Tatler. Mar 2, 1955, v215, p391.
Time. Dec 10, 1956, v68, p102.
Variety. Sep 8, 1954, p22.
The Village Voice. Dec 28, 1982, v27, p68-69.
The Waves at Genji's Door. p91-99.
Western American Literature. 1976, v11, n3, p231-38.

Seven Thieves (US; Hathaway, Henry; 1960)
America. Feb 27, 1960, v102, p659.
BFI/Monthly Film Bulletin. Mar 1960, v27, p39.
The Cinema of Edward G. Robinson. p208.
Commonweal. Feb 26, 1960, v71, p594.
Film Daily. Jan 20, 1960, p6.
Filmfacts. 1960, v3, p45.
Films and Filming. Apr 1960, v6, p24.
Films in Review. Feb 1960, v11, p105-06.
Hollywood Reporter. Jan 19, 1960, p3.
The New Republic. Apr 4, 1960, v142, p29.
The New York Times. Mar 12, 1960, p14.
Newsweek. Mar 14, 1960, v55, p100.
Saturday Review. Feb 6, 1960, v43, p33.
Variety. Jan 20, 1960, p6.

Seven Waves Away *See* Abandon Ship

Seven Women (US; Ford, John; 1965)
America. May 14, 1966, v114, p706.
BFI/Monthly Film Bulletin. Jan 1967, v34, p6-7.
Christian Science Monitor (Western edition). May 11, 1965, p12.
Christian Science Monitor (Western edition). Feb 11, 1966, p4.
Cinema. Dec 1965, v3, p48.
Confessions of a Cultist. p248-50.
Film Comment. Fall 1971, v7, p8-17.
Film Comment. Spr 1972, v8, p56-60.
Film Daily. Dec 7, 1965, p3.
Filmfacts. Jul 1, 1966, v9, p119-20.
Films and Filming. Feb 1967, v13, p31.
Films in Review. Feb 1966, v17, p116-17.
The Films of John Ford. p279-86.
Focus. Mar 1967, n2, p19-22.
Hollywood Reporter. Dec 6, 1965, p3.
Kiss Kiss Bang Bang. p175-76.
The London Times. Nov 24, 1966, p7.
Motion Picture Herald Product Digest. Dec 22, 1965, p427.
New Statesman. Dec 2, 1966, v72, p850.
The New York Times. May 5, 1966, p59.
The Non-Western Films of John Ford. p279-85.
The Private Eye, the Cowboy and the Very Naked Girl. p227.

Sight and Sound. Wint 1966-67, v36, p43-44.
Sight and Sound. Spr 1982, v51, p124-28.
Time. May 13, 1966, v87, p104.
Variety. Dec 8, 1965, p22.
The Velvet Light Trap. Aug 1971, v2, p22-24.
The Village Voice. May 26, 1966, v11, p27.

The Seven Year Itch (US; Wilder, Billy; 1955)
America. Jun 25, 1955, v93, p339.
Billy Wilder (Dick). p78-82.
Commonweal. Jun 24, 1955, v62, p305.
The Film Career of Billy Wilder. p85-87.
Film Culture. Sum 1955, v1, n4, p22-23.
Film Daily. Jun 3, 1955, p6.
Films and Filming. Oct 1955, v2, n1, p20.
The Films in My Life. p159-61.
Films in Review. Aug-Sep 1955, v6, n7, p345.
The Films of Marilyn Monroe. p122-28.
The Films of the Fifties. p135-38.
Hollywood Reporter. Jun 3, 1955, v134, n47, p3.
Library Journal. Jul 1955, v80, p1577.
Life. May 30, 1955, v38, p87-88.
Magill's Survey of Cinema. Series I. v4, p1519-22.
The Nation. Jun 25, 1955, v180, p590.
The New Republic. Aug 8, 1955, v133, p22.
The New York Times. Sep 19, 1954, SecI, p32.
The New York Times.
The New York Times. Jun 4, 1955, p9.
The New York Times. Jun 12, 1955, SecII, p1.
The New Yorker. Jun 11, 1955, v31, p123.
Newsweek. Jun 20, 1955, v45, p94.
Time. Jun 13, 1955, v65, p100.
Variety. Jun 8, 1955, p6.

1776 (US; Hunt, Peter H.; 1972)
Filmfacts. 1972, v15, n23, p589.
Films in Review. Dec 1972, v24, n10, p642.
Hollywood Reporter. Nov 8, 1972, p3.
Life. Dec 8, 1972, v73, p30.
National Review. Dec 22, 1972, v24, p1409.
The New York Times. Nov 10, 1972, v44, p1.
The New Yorker. Nov 25, 1972, v48, p180.
Newsweek. Nov 27, 1972, v80, p100-01.
Reeling. p85-88.
Saturday Review. Dec 16, 1972, v55, p78.
Senior Scholastic. Dec 11, 1972, v101, p28.
Variety. Oct 8, 1972, p18.

The Seventh Dawn (GB; Gilbert, Lewis; 1964)
BFI/Monthly Film Bulletin. Sep 1964, v31, p136.
Boxoffice. Jul 6, 1964, v85, p2842.
Film Daily. Jun 24, 1964, v124, p6.
Films and Filming. Sep 1964, v10, p21.
Films in Review. Aug-Sep 1964, v15, p442.
The Films of William Holden. p217-20.
Hollywood Reporter. Jun 26, 1964, v181, p4.
The Los Angeles Times. Aug 21, 1964, v4, p13.
Motion Picture Herald Product Digest. Jul 8, 1964, v232, p82-83.
The New York Times. Sep 3, 1964, p24.
The New Yorker. Aug 29, 1964, v40, p79.
Time. Jul 24, 1964, v84, p87.
Variety. Jun 24, 1964, p6.

The Seventh Seal (Swedish title: Sjunde Inseglet, Det) (SWED; Bergman, Ingmar; 1958)
Bergman on Bergman. p112-19.
Change from Landmark Films. p228-29, p228-35.
Cinema Borealis. p153-60.
Cinema Eye, Cinema Ear. p158-59.
Cinema, the Magic Vehicle. v2, p288-91.
The Classic Cinema. p223-246.
Commentary. Nov 1961, v32, p391-98.

Commonweal. Nov 14, 1958, v69, p177.
Commonweal. Mar 11, 1960, v71, p647-49.
Cult Movies 2. p139-42.
Dictionary of Films. p343-44.
Encounter. Apr 1961, v16, p54-57.
Film and the Critical Eye. p290-28.
Film as Film: Critical Responses to Film Art. p351-63.
Film Culture. Apr 1959, n19, p51-61.
Film Journal. Nov 1959, v14, p9-17.
Film Quarterly. Spr 1959, v12, p42-44.
Film Quarterly. Sum 1959, v12, p3-16.
Films and Filming. Jan 1963, v9, p25-29.
Films in Review. Nov 1958, v11, p515-17.
Focus on the Seventh Seal. 1972.
Great Film Directors. p60-68.
The Great Films. p218-22.
Harper's. Dec 1958, 217, p84.
Hudson Review. Sum 1959, v12, p266-70.
Ingmar Bergman: Essays in Criticism. p148-79.
International Dictionary of Films and Filmmakers. v1, p433-35.
Journal of Aesthetics and Arts. Wint 1965, v24, p263-72.
Journal of Social Issues. Jan 1964, v20, p71-96.
Landmark Films. p228-29.
Magill's Survey of Cinema. Foreign Language Films. v6, p2720-23.
The Nation. Nov 15, 1958, v187, p367.
New Statesman. Mar 8, 1958, v55, p303.
The New York Times. Oct 14, 1958, p44.
The New York Times. Oct 19, 1958, SecII, p1.
The New Yorker. Oct 25, 1958, v34, p193.
Renaissance of the Film. p232-40.
Reporter. Feb 15, 1962, v26, p37-42.
Sight and Sound. Spr 1958, v27, p199-00.
The Spectator. Mar 14, 1958, v200, p326.
Swedish Film Classics. p93-96.
Time. Nov 10, 1958, 72, p102.
Variety. May 29, 1957, p22.
Women and their Sexuality in the new Film. p106-27.

Sex and the Single Girl (US; Quine, Richard; 1964)
BFI/Monthly Film Bulletin. Jan 1965, v32, p5.
Boxoffice. Jan 11, 1965, v86, p2889.
Commonweal. Feb 12, 1965, v81, p643.
Film Daily. Dec 23, 1964, v125, p6.
Films and Filming. Feb 1965, v11, p31.
The Films of Henry Fonda. p180-81.
The Fondas. p208.
Hollywood Reporter. Dec 23, 1964, v183, p3.
Life. Jan 8, 1965, v58, p13.
Motion Picture Herald Product Digest. Dec 23, 1964, v232, p194.
The New York Times. Dec 26, 1964, p9.
Time. Jan 1, 1965, v85, p69.
Tony Curtis: The Man and His Movies. p102-03.
Variety. Dec 23, 1964, p6.

Shadow Warrior *See* Kagemusha

Shadows of Forgotten Ancestors (Also titled: Teni Zabytykh Predkov) (USSR; Paradjanov, Sergei; 1964)
Film Comment. Fall 1968, v5, p38-48.
Film Quarterly. Sum 1966, v19, p56-59.
Filmfacts. May 1, 1967, v10, p80-81.
Films and Filming. Jun 1969, v15, p53-54.
The International Dictionary of Films and Filmmakers. v1, p464-65.
International Film Guide. 1967, v4, p167, 170.
The London Times. Nov 30, 1966, p15.
Magill's Survey of Cinema. Foreign Language Films. v6, p2730-33.
New Statesman. Apr 11, 1969, v77, p524.
The New York Times. Mar 17, 1967, p35.

Post Script. 1984, v3, n3, p16-23.
Variety. Sep 8, 1965, p68.

Shaft (US; Parks, Gordon; 1971)
America. Jul 24, 1971, v125, p48.
BFI/Monthly Film Bulletin. Jan 1972, v39, p15.
Filmfacts. 1971, v14, p346-48.
Films and Filming. Apr 1972, v18, n7, p52.
Focus on Film. Oct 1971, n8, p7.
From Sambo to Superspade. p249-50.
Hollywood Reporter. Jun 10, 1971, v216, n31, p3.
Magill's Survey of Cinema. Series II. v5, p2156-58.
The New York Times. Jul 3, 1971, p20.
The New York Times. Jul 11, 1971, SecII, p1.
The New Yorker. Aug 7, 1971, v47, p67.
Newsweek. Jul 19, 1971, v78, p80.
Time. Jul 26, 1971, v98, p51.
Variety. Jun 16, 1971, p15.
The Village Voice. Jul 8, 1971, p58.

The Shaggy Dog (US; Barton, Charles; 1959)
BFI/Monthly Film Bulletin. 1959, v26, p74.
Catholic World. May 1959, v189, p156.
Commonweal. Apr 10, 1959, v70, p59.
The Disney Films. p157-58.
Film Daily. Feb 26, 1959, v115, p6.
Filmfacts. Apr 22, 1959, v2, p61-62.
Hollywood Reporter. Feb 24, 1959, p3.
Library Journal. Apr 15, 1959, v84, p1282.
The New York Times. Mar 20, 1959, p26.
Senior Scholastic. Apr 3, 1959, v74, p57.
Time. Apr 20, 1959, v73, p78.
Variety. Feb 25, 1959, p6.
Walt Disney: A Guide to References and Resources. p60-65.

Shake Hands with the Devil (US; Anderson, Michael; 1959)
America. Jun 20, 1959, v101, p458.
BFI/Monthly Film Bulletin. May 1959, v26, p85.
Catholic World. Jun 1959, v189, p237.
Commonweal. Jun 26, 1959, v70, p327.
Cosmopolitan. Jun 1959, v146, p12-13.
Film Daily. May 8, 1959, v115, p6.
Filmfacts. Jul 8, 1959, v2, p127-28.
Films in Review. Jun-Jul 1959, v10, p359.
The Films of James Cagney. p234-36.
Hollywood Reporter. May 8, 1959, p3.
Library Journal. Jul 1959, v84, p2173.
Magill's Survey of Cinema. Series II. p2159-62.
The New York Times. Jun 25, 1959, p20.
Saturday Review. May 30, 1959, v42, p27.
Time. Jul 20, 1959, v74, p63.
Variety. May 13, 1959, p6.

Shakespeare Wallah (INDIA; Ivory, James; 1965)
America. Apr 9, 1966, v114, p526-27.
BFI/Monthly Film Bulletin. Feb 1966, v33, p19.
Christian Century. May 25, 1966, v83, p687.
Commonweal. Apr 8, 1966, v84, p81.
Esquire. Dec 1965, v64, p90.
Film. Wint 1965-66, n44, p18-19.
Film Quarterly. Wint 1966-67, v20, p33-35.
Film Society Review. Jan 1967, p24-25.
Filmfacts. Jun 1, 1966, v9, p90-91.
Films and Filming. Mar 1966, v12, p15, 18.
Films and Filming. May 1982, v27, p36-37.
Films in Review. May 1966, v17, p316-17.
Life. Apr 29, 1966, v60, p16.
The London Times. Nov 5, 1965, p16.
Motion Picture Herald Product Digest. Mar 30, 1966, p493.
New Statesman. Nov 5, 1965, v70, p708.
The New York Times. Sep 13, 1965, p42.
The New York Times. Mar 23, 1966, p40.

The New Yorker. Mar 26, 1966, v42, p126.
The Private Eye, the Cowboy and the Very Naked Girl. p231.
Saturday Review. Apr 9, 1966, v49, p55.
Second Sight. p71-73.
The Spectator. Nov 19, 1965, v215, p657.
Time. Mar 25, 1966, v87, p90.
Variety. Jul 14, 1965, p6.

Shame (Swedish title: Skammen; Also titled: The Shame) (SWED; Bergman, Ingmar; 1968)
America. Feb 15, 1969, v120, p202.
BFI/Monthly Film Bulletin. Apr 1969, v36, p76.
Christian Science Monitor (Western edition). Feb 5, 1969, p8.
Cinema Borealis. p243-54.
Commonweal. Jan 31, 1969, v89, p563.
The Cracked Lens. p200-39.
Esquire. Mar 1969, v71, p32.
Figures of Light. p125-28.
Film Heritage. Spr 1969, v4, p1-5.
Film Quarterly. Fall 1969, v23, p32-34.
Film Society Review. Jan 1969, v4, p35-39.
Filmfacts. Jan 15, 1969, v11, p427-29.
Films and Filming. Apr 1969, v15, p38.
Films in Review. Jan 1969, v20, p51-52.
Going Steady. p263-73.
Hollywood Reporter. Jan 21, 1969, p3.
Hudson Review. Sum 1969, v22, p259-60.
Ingmar Bergman (Cowie). p249-55.
Ingmar Bergman: Essays in Criticism. p278-85.
Ingmar Bergman (Wood). p171-83.
Literature/Film Quarterly. 1984, v12, n1, p34-41.
The London Times. Feb 20, 1969, p15.
Magill's Survey of Cinema. Foreign Language Films. v5, p2734-38.
Motion Picture Herald Product Digest. Dec 18, 1968, p81.
Movie. Wint 1969-70, n17, p32-34.
Movies Into Film. p233-38.
The Nation. Jan 13, 1969, v208, p61-62.
The New Republic. Jan 4, 1969, v160, p24.
New Statesman. Feb 21, 1969, v77, p268.
The New York Times. Dec 24, 1968, p14.
The New Yorker. Dec 28, 1968, v44, p56-59.
Newsweek. Dec 30, 1968, v72, p60.
Saturday Review. Jan 25, 1969, v52, p22.
Sight and Sound. Spr 1969, v38, p89-91.
The Spectator. Feb 21, 1969, v222, p248.
Take One. Sep-Oct 1968, v2, p16-18.
Time. Jan 10, 1969, v93, p68.
Variety. Oct 16, 1968, p6.
The Village Voice. Jan 2, 1969, p39.

The Shameless Old Lady (French title: Vieille Dame Indigne, La; Also titled: The Unworthy Old Woman; The Shocking Old Party) (FR; Allio, René; 1965)
America. Nov 12, 1966, v115, p631.
BFI/Monthly Film Bulletin. Sep 1972, v39, p197.
Christian Century. Dec 14, 1966, v83, p1540.
Christian Science Monitor (Western edition). Sep 30, 1966, p6.
Commonweal. Oct 7, 1966, v85, p22.
Film Quarterly. Spr 1967, v20, p63.
Filmfacts. Oct 1, 1966, v9, p197-98.
Films and Filming. Jul 1970, v16, p37-38.
Films in Review. Nov 1966, v17, p585.
Harper's Magazine. Dec 1966, v233, p139.
International Film Guide. 1966, v3, p68-69.
Kiss Kiss Bang Bang. p135-36.
The London Times. Nov 22, 1966, p14.
Motion Picture Herald Product Digest. Oct 5, 1966, p612.

The Nation. Oct 10, 1966, v203, p366.
The New Republic. Dec 10, 1966, v155, p35-36.
The New York Times. Sep 19, 1966, p57.
The New York Times. Sep 27, 1966, p52.
The New Yorker. Oct 8, 1966, v42, p127.
The New Yorker. Apr 17, 1965, v41, p185-86.
Newsweek. Oct 17, 1966, v68, p105A.
Saturday Review. Dec 10, 1966, v49, p65.
Time. Oct 7, 1966, v88, p120.
Variety. Mar 31, 1965, p6.
The Village Voice. Oct 27, 1966, v12, p25.

Shampoo (US; Ashby, Hal; 1975)
America. Aug 16, 1975, v133, p71-73.
BFI/Monthly Film Bulletin. May 1975, v42, p116.
Esquire. May 1975, v83, p42-43.
Film Quarterly. Sum 1975, v28, p61-64.
Films in Review. Apr 1975, v26, p247.
The Films of the Seventies. p113-15.
The Films of Warren Beatty. p188-97.
Hollywood Reporter. Feb 7, 1975, p3.
The Los Angeles Times. Feb 16, 1975, Calendar, p1.
Magill's Survey of Cinema. Series II. v5, p2163-66.
Motion Picture Herald Product Digest. Feb 26, 1975, p73.
The Nation. Mar 8, 1975, v220, p284.
The New Republic. Mar 8, 1975, v172, p22.
The New York Times. Feb 12, 1975, p46.
The New York Times. Feb 16, 1975, SecII, p1.
The New York Times. Apr 13, 1975, SecII, p15.
The New Yorker. Feb 17, 1975, v50, p86-90.
Newsweek. Feb 10, 1975, v85, p51.
Reeling. p557-86.
Time. Feb 24, 1975, v105, p4.
Variety. Feb 12, 1975, p28.
Vogue. Apr 1975, v165, p90, 141.

Shane (US; Stevens, George; 1953)
America. May 2, 1953, v89, p146.
BFI/Monthly Film Bulletin. Sep 1953, v20, n236, p132.
Catholic World. Jun 1953, v177, p223.
Classic Movies. p27-28.
Commonweal. May 8, 1953, v58, p121.
Fifty from the Fifties. p283-92.
Film Culture. 1957, v3, n1, p2-4, 25-32.
Film Daily. Apr 13, 1953, p6.
Films and Filming. May 1966, v12, p36-41.
Films in Review. Apr 1953, v4, n4, p195-97.
The Films of Alan Ladd. p181-89.
The Films of the Fifties. p103-06.
The Great Films. p210-13.
The Great Movies. p38-39.
Hollywood Reporter. Apr 13, 1953, p3.
Library Journal. May 1, 1953, v78, p806.
Life. Apr 27, 1953, v34, p85-86.
Magill's Survey of Cinema. Series I. v4, p1534.
The Making of the Great Westerns. p221-36.
The New York Times. Apr 24, 1953, p30.
The New Yorker. May 2, 1953, v29, p78.
Newsweek. May 4, 1953, v41, p96.
On the Verge of Revolt. p35-47.
Saturday Review. May 2, 1953, v36, p35.
Senior Scholastic. May 13, 1953, v62, p30.
Sight and Sound. Oct-Dec 1953, v23, n2, p71-76.
Time. Apr 13, 1953, v61, p104.
Variety. Apr 15, 1953, p6.

The Shanghai Story (US; Lloyd, Frank; 1954)
BFI/Monthly Film Bulletin. May 1954, v21, p76-77.
Farm Journal. Dec 1954, v78, p141.
Film Daily. Oct 4, 1954, p6.
Hollywood Reporter. Nov 26, 1954, p3.
The London Times. Apr 5, 1954, p5.

Motion Picture Herald Product Digest. Oct 2, 1954, p170.
National Parent-Teacher. Dec 1954, v49, p40.
The New York Times. Sep 25, 1954, p10.
Variety. Sep 29, 1954, p16.

Sharky's Machine (US; Reynolds, Burt; 1981)
Hollywood Reporter. Dec 16, 1981, p3.
The Los Angeles Times. Dec 18, 1981, SecVI, p6.
Magill's Cinema Annual, 1982. p324-27.
New York. Jan 11, 1982, v15, p54-55.
The New York Times. Dec 18, 1981, SecIII, p10.
Newsweek. Dec 28, 1981, v98, p65.
Time. Jan 11, 1982, v119, p88.
Variety. Dec 16, 1981, p3.

Shatranj Ke Khilari *See* The Chess Players

She (GB; Day, Robert; 1965)
BFI/Monthly Film Bulletin. May 1965, v32, p78.
Christian Science Monitor (Western edition). Aug 19, 1965, p4.
Film Daily. Apr 19, 1965, p3.
Films and Filming. Jun 1965, v11, p30.
Motion Picture Herald Product Digest. Apr 28, 1965, p275.
The New York Times. Sep 2, 1965, p36.
The New Yorker. Sep 11, 1965, v41, p100, 102.
Newsweek. Sep 20, 1965, v66, p98.
Saturday Review. May 8, 1965, v48, p51.
Time. Sep 17, 1965, v86, p127.
Variety. Apr 21, 1965, p6.

She and He (Also titled: Kanejo to Kare) (JAPAN; Hani, Susumu; 1964)
Film Daily. May 15, 1967, p7.
Filmfacts. Jun 15, 1967, v10, p109-11.
Films and Filming. Sep 1966, v12, p7-8.
The London Times. Jun 30, 1966, p7.
New Statesman. Jul 8, 1966, v72, p64.
The New York Times. Sep 26, 1964, p16.
Newsweek. May 1, 1967, v69, p87.
The Spectator. Jul 15, 1966, v215, p84.
Variety. Dec 31, 1969, p6.

She Couldn't Say No (US; Leonard, Robert Z.; 1954)
America. Mar 13, 1954, v90, p639.
Film Daily. Jan 28, 1954, p12.
Hollywood Reporter. Jan 13, 1954, p3.
Library Journal. Feb 15, 1954, v79, p314.
Motion Picture Herald Product Digest. Jan 16, 1954, p2141.
The New York Times. Feb 27, 1954, p11.
Newsweek. Mar 15, 1954, v43, p104.
Time. Mar 8, 1954, v63, p100.
Variety. Jan 13, 1954, p6.

She Only Danced One Summer *See* One Summer of Happiness

The Sheep Has Five Legs *See* Mouton a Cinq Pattes, Le

Sheila Levine Is Dead and Living in New York (US; Furie, Sidney J.; 1975)
Films in Review. Mar 1975, v26, p180.
Hollywood Reporter. Feb 3, 1975, p3.
The Los Angeles Times. Mar 27, 1975, SecIV, p12.
Motion Picture Herald Product Digest. Feb 26, 1975, p75.
The New Republic. Feb 15, 1975, v172, p34.
The New York Times. May 17, 1975, p14.
The New Yorker. Feb 2, 1975, v50, p83-86.
Reeling. p568-72.
Saturday Review. Feb 22, 1975, v2, p49.
Time. Feb 17, 1975, v105, p7.
Variety. Feb 5, 1975, p20.

Shenandoah (US; McLaglen, Andrew V.; 1965)
America. Aug 14, 1965, v113, p170.
Christian Science Monitor (Western edition). Mar 9, 1965, p4.
Commentary. Nov 1965, v40, p77-78.
Commonweal. Jun 11, 1965, v82, p384.
Film Daily. Apr 14, 1965, p3.
Films and Filming. Sep 1965, v11, p25-26.
The Films of James Stewart. p237-39.
The Great Western Pictures. p326-27.
Hollywood Reporter. Apr 14, 1965, p3.
The London Times. Jul 22, 1965, p15.
Motion Picture Herald Product Digest. Apr 28, 1965, p273.
Movie. Aut 1965, n14, p44.
The New Republic. Aug 7, 1965, v153, p36-38.
New Statesman. Jan 21, 1966, v71, p101.
The New York Times. Jul 29, 1965, p18.
The New Yorker. Jul 31, 1965, v41, p56.
Newsweek. Aug 23, 1965, v66, p81B.
Saturday Review. May 8, 1965, v48, p51.
Senior Scholastic. May 13, 1965, v86, p36.
Time. Aug 13, 1965, v86, p74.
Variety. Apr 14, 1965, p6.

Sherlock Holmes' Smarter Brother *See* The Adventures of Sherlock Holmes' Smarter Brother

She's Working Her Way Through College (US; Humberstone, Bruce; 1952)
BFI/Monthly Film Bulletin. Nov 1952, v19, p159.
Film Daily. Jun 23, 1952, p6.
The Films of Ronald Reagan. p190-92.
Hollywood Reporter. Jun 5, 1952, p3.
Motion Picture Herald Product Digest. Jun 7, 1952, p1389.
National Parent-Teacher. Sep 1952, v47, p38.
The New York Times. Jul 10, 1952, p27.
Saturday Review. Jun 14, 1952, v35, p36.
Time. Jul 21, 1952, v60, p96.
Variety. Jun 11, 1952, p6.

Shichinin no Samurai *See* The Seven Samurai

Shichi-nin no Samurai *See* The Seven Samurai

Shinbone Alley (US; Wilson, John David; 1971)
Cinema. 1969, v5, n2, p36-37.
Filmfacts. 1971, v14, p466-68.
Hollywood Reporter. Apr 8, 1971, v215, n37, p3.
The New York Times. Apr 8, 1971, p32.
The New Yorker. Apr 17, 1971, v47, p98-99.
Saturday Review. May 15, 1971, v14.
Variety. Mar 31, 1971, p6.

The Shining (US; Kubrick, Stanley; 1980)
America. Jan 14, 1980, v142, p504.
Atlantic Monthly. Aug 1980, v246, p80-83.
Christian Century. Jul 30, 1980, v97, p771.
Commonweal. Aug 1, 1980, v107, p438-40.
Encore. Aug 1980, v9, p39.
Film Comment. Jul-Aug 1980, v16, p28-32.
Humanist. Sep-Oct 1980, v40, p49-50.
Kubrick (Ciment). p135-46.
Kubrick: Inside a Film Artist's Maze. p197-237.
The Los Angeles Times. May 23, 1980, SecVI, p1.
Maclean's. Jun 16, 1980, v93, p52-53.
Magill's Survey of Cinema. Series II. v4, p2175-77.
Motion Picture Herald Product Digest. Jun 11, 1980, p3.
The Nation. Jun 14, 1980, v230, p732-33.
National Review. Jun 27, 1980, v32, p795-97.

The New Leader. Jul 14, 1980, v63, p19-20.
The New Republic. Jun 14, 1980, v182, p26-27.
New York. Jun 9, 1980, v13, p60-61.
The New York Times. May 23, 1980, SecIII, p8.
The New York Times. Jun 8, 1980, SecII, p1.
The New York Times Magazine. May 11, 1980, p42-44.
The New Yorker. Jun 9, 1980, v56, p130.
Newsweek. May 26, 1980, v95, p96-97.
Saturday Review. Jul 1980, v7, p64-65.
Stanley Kubrick: A Guide to References and Resources. p58-62.
Time. Jun 2, 1980, v115, p69.
Variety. Mar 28, 1980, p14.

Ship of Fools (US; Kramer, Stanley; 1965)
America. Aug 14, 1965, v113, p170.
American Cinematographer. Jan 1965, v46, p28-29.
BFI/Monthly Film Bulletin. Nov 1965, v32, p164-65.
Christian Century. Oct 13, 1965, v82, p1262.
Christian Science Monitor (Western edition). Oct 6, 1965, p6.
Commentary. Nov 1965, v40, p77-78.
Commonweal. Aug 6, 1965, v82, p563-64.
Film Daily. May 4, 1965, p6.
Film Quarterly. Fall 1965, v19, p39-51.
Films and Filming. Nov 1965, v12, p24.
Films in Review. Jun-Jul 1965, v16, p380-82.
Holiday. Sep 1965, v38, p120.
Hollywood Reporter. May 4, 1965, p3.
Kiss Kiss Bang Bang. p259-62.
Life. Aug 6, 1965, v59, p11.
The London Times. Oct 21, 1965, p16.
Magill's Survey of Cinema. Series II. v5, p2179-82.
Motion Picture Herald Product Digest. May 12, 1965, p281.
The New Republic. Aug 7, 1965, v153, p36-39.
New Statesman. Oct 22, 1965, v70, p616.
The New York Times. Jul 29, 1965, p18.
The New Yorker. Jul 31, 1965, v41, p56.
Newsweek. Aug 16, 1965, v66, p80.
Playboy. Aug 1965, v12, p24.
The Private Eye, the Cowboy and the Very Naked Girl. p150-53.
Private Screenings. p199-200.
Reporter. Nov 4, 1965, v33, p48-49.
Saturday Review. Jul 3, 1965, v48, p19.
Stanley Kramer, Film Maker. p265-72.
Time. Aug 6, 1965, v86, p85.
Tynan Right and Left. p244-45.
Variety. May 5, 1965, p6.
The Village Voice. Sep 30, 1965, v10, p19, 33.
Vogue. Aug 1, 1965, v146, p51.

Shoah (WGER; Lanzmann, Claude; 1985)
America. Jan 18, 1986, v154, p28-31.
Commonweal. Dec 20, 1985, v112, p702-04.
Life. Dec 1985, v8, p7.
The Los Angeles Times. Dec 27, 1985, SecVI, p1.
Magill's Cinema Annual, 1986. p339-43.
The Nation. Mar 15, 1986, v242, p313-17.
The New Republic. Dec 16, 1985, v193, p46-48.
The New Republic. Oct 28, 1985, v193, p39-40.
New York. Nov 11, 1985, v18, p29.
New York. Oct 28, 1985, v18, p130.
New York Review of Books. Dec 19, 1985, v32, p26-28.
The New York Times. Nov 3, 1985, SecIII, p1.
The New Yorker. Dec 30, 1985, v61, p70-72.
Progressive. Nov 1985, v49, p40.
Time. Nov 4, 1985, v126, p96.
Variety. May 15, 1985, p15.
Vogue. Dec 1985, v175, p74.

The Shocking Old Party *See* The Shameless Old Lady

The Shoes of the Fisherman (US;
Anderson, Michael; 1968)
America. Nov 30, 1968, v11, p576-77.
Christian Science Monitor (Western edition).
Nov 27, 1968, p16.
Commonweal. Dec 13, 1968, v89, p381-82.
Film Daily. Nov 15, 1968, p4.
Filmfacts. Jan 15, 1969, v11, p490-93.
Films in Review. Dec 1968, v19, p466-46.
The Films of Anthony Quinn. p222-24.
Focus on Film. Oct 1971, n8, p12-14.
Hollywood Reporter. Nov 15, 1968, p3.
Life. Nov 29, 1968, v65, p8.
The London Times. Jun 3, 1968, p5.
Look. Dec 10, 1968, v32, p102.
Motion Picture Herald Product Digest. Nov 27,
1968, p67.
The New York Times. Nov 15, 1968, p40.
The New Yorker. Nov 23, 1968, v44, p197-99.
Newsweek. Nov 25, 1968, v72, p108.
Saturday Review. Dec 14, 1968, v51, p48.
Time. Nov 29, 1968, v92, p106.
Variety. Nov 20, 1968, p6.

Shoot Loud, Louder . . . I Don't Understand
(Italian title: Spara Forte, Pui Forte . . .
Non Capisco) (IT; De Filippo,
Eduardo; 1966)
Christian Science Monitor (Western edition).
Jan 7, 1967, p8.
Film Daily. Jan 3, 1967, p3.
Filmfacts. Nov 1, 1967, v10, p273-74.
Hollywood Reporter. Dec 23, 1966, p3.
Motion Picture Herald Product Digest. Jan 4,
1967, p646-47.
The New York Times. Sep 21, 1967, p56.
Reporter. Oct 19, 1967, v37, p39-40.
Saturday Review. Jan 14, 1967, v50, p97.
Time. Jan 20, 1967, v89, p83.
Variety. Jan 11, 1967, p28.

Shoot Out (US; Hathaway, Henry; 1971)
BFI/Monthly Film Bulletin. Jun 1972, v39,
p122.
Filmfacts. 1971, v14, p505-06.
Hollywood Reporter. May 17, 1971, v216, n14,
p3.
The New York Times. Oct 14, 1971, p53.
Variety. May 26, 1971, p20.
The Village Voice. Nov 18, 1971, p87.

Shoot the Moon (US; Parker, Alan; 1982)
Christian Century. Feb 3, 1982, v99, p108.
Christian Century. Mar 31, 1982, v99, p355-56.
Christian Century. Apr 7, 1982, v99, p421.
Film Comment. Mar-Apr 1982, v18, p16.
Hollywood Reporter. Jan 13, 1982, p3.
Horizon. Jul-Aug 1982, v25, p62-63.
Humanist. May-Jun 1982, v42, p57.
The Los Angeles Times. Jan 22, 1982, SecVI,
p1.
Maclean's. Jan 25, 1982, v95, p57.
Magill's Cinema Annual, 1983. p295-98.
Ms. Apr 1982, v10, p35.
The Nation. Feb 27, 1982, v234, p252.
National Review. Mar 25, 1982, v34, p242-44.
The New Leader. Feb 22, 1982, v65, p21.
The New Republic. Feb 3, 1982, v186, p24-26.
New York. Jan 25, 1982, v15, p66-67.
The New York Times. Jan 22, 1982, SecIII, p13.
The New Yorker. Jan 18, 1982, v57, p104.
Newsweek. Jan 25, 1982, v99, p75.
Rolling Stone. Feb 18, 1982, p27-28.
Rolling Stone. Mar 18, 1982, p48-49.
Time. Feb 1, 1982, v119, p79.
Variety. Jan 13, 1982, p3.

Shoot the Piano Player (French title: Tirez
sur le Pianiste) (FR; Truffaut,
François; 1960)

Cinema Texas Program Notes. Mar 2, 1978,
v14, p39-44.
Confessions of a Cultist. p62-63.
Dictionary of Films. p376-77.
Film Comment. Sum 1965, v3, p24-29.
Film Culture. Wint 1962-63, n27, p14-16.
Film Daily. Jul 6, 1962, p5.
Film Quarterly. Spr 1963, v16, p3-11.
Filmfacts. Aug 10, 1962, v5, p165-66.
Films and Filming. Feb 1961, v7, p29-30.
Films and Filming. Oct 1960, v7, p22.
Focus on Shoot the Piano Player. 1972.
*Francois Truffaut: A Guide to References and
Resources.* p43-45.
Francois Truffaut (Insdorf). p26-34.
Hollywood Reporter. Jan 18, 1963, p3.
I Lost It at the Movies. p189-94.
*The International Dictionary of Films and
Filmmakers. Volume I.* p476-77.
Literature/Film Quarterly. 1977, v5, n3, p183-
97.
*Magill's Survey of Cinema. Foreign Language
Series.* 1985, v6, p2750-57.
Motion Picture Herald Product Digest. Jul 11,
1962, p616.
Movie Comedy (Byron). p231-35.
The Nation. Aug 25, 1962, v195, p80.
The New Republic. Jul 9, 1962, v147, p20-21.
The New York Times. Jul 24, 1962, p19.
The New Yorker. Aug 4, 1962, v38, p50.
Newsweek. Aug 6, 1962, v60, p76.
Saturday Review. Jul 7, 1962, v45, p16.
Time. Aug 3, 1962, v80, p36.
Variety. Aug 31, 1960, p6.
The Village Voice. Jul 26, 1962, p11.
A World on Film. p230-32.

The Shooting Party (GB; Bridges, Alan;
1985)
BFI/Monthly Film Bulletin. Feb 1985, v52,
p56.
Films in Review. Oct 1985, v36, p496.
Hollywood Reporter. Jul 5, 1985, p3.
The Los Angeles Times. Jun 27, 1985, SecVI,
p1.
Magill's Cinema Annual, 1986. p344-48.
National Review. Jul 26, 1985, v37, p50-51.
The New Republic. Jun 17, 1985, v192, p24-25.
New York. Jun 10, 1985, v18, p76.
The New York Times. May 24, 1985, SecIII, p8.
The New Yorker. Jun 17, 1985, v61, p112-14.
Newsweek. Jun 17, 1985, v105, p91.
Progressive. Jul 1985, v49, p40.
Time. Jun 10, 1985, v125, p83.
Variety. May 30, 1985, p12.

The Shootist (US; Siegel, Don; 1976)
Audience. Oct 1976, v9, p5-6.
Before My Eyes. p237.
BFI/Monthly Film Bulletin. Oct 1976, v43,
p219-20.
The Complete Films of John Wayne. p315-20.
Film. Nov 1976, v43, p2.
Filmmakers' Newsletter. Oct 1976, v9, p28-32.
Films and Filming. Oct 1976, v23, p44-45.
Films in Review. Oct 1976, v27, p504.
Hollywood Reporter. Jul 23, 1976, p2.
Independent Film Journal. Aug 6, 1976, v8, p7.
The Los Angeles Times. Aug 22, 1976,
Calendar, p1.
Magill's Survey of Cinema. Series I. v4, p1542-
44.
Motion Picture Herald Product Digest. Aug 25,
1976, p25.
The New Republic. Sep 11, 1976, v175, p24-25.
New York. Aug 30, 1976, v9, p50-52.
The New York Times. Aug 12, 1976, p38.
The New York Times. Aug 29, 1976, SecII, p11.
Newsweek. Aug 16, 1976, v88, p68.

Saturday Review. Aug 21, 1976, v3, p45.
Sight and Sound. Wint 1976, v45, p267.
The Thousand Eyes Magazine. Sep 1976, v2,
p8-9.
Time. Aug 30, 1976, v108, p72.
Variety. Jul 28, 1976, p18.
When the Lights Go Down. p197.

The Shop on Main Street (Also titled:
Obchod na Korze; The Shop on the
High Street) (CZECH; Kadar, Jan;
Klos, Elmar; 1965)
America. Feb 19, 1966, v114, p270.
BFI/Monthly Film Bulletin. Aug 1965, v32,
p120.
Christian Century. May 4, 1966, v83, p590.
Christian Science Monitor (Western edition).
Jul 8, 1965, p11.
Christian Science Monitor (Western edition).
Feb 24, 1966, p10.
Closely Watched Films. p406-10.
Commentary. Aug 1966, v42, p59.
Commonweal. Feb 4, 1966, v83, p535.
Dictionary of Films. p254.
Esquire. Dec 1965, v63, p88, 90.
Fifty Grand Movies of the 1960s and 1970s.
p241-43.
Film Comment. Fall/Wint 1967, v4, p68-72.
Film Daily. Jan 31, 1966, p4.
Film Quarterly. Sum 1965, v19, p56-59.
Film Society Review. Dec 1967, p19-20.
Filmfacts. Feb 1, 1966, v9, p1-2.
Films and Filming. Aug 1965, v11, p24-25.
Films and Filming. Jun 1965, v11, p43, 53.
Films in Review. Mar 1966, v17, p185.
Harper's Magazine. May 1966, v232, p115.
Indelible Shadows: Film and the Holocaust.
p148-49.
International Film Guide. 1966, v3, p60.
Life. Feb 4, 1966, v60, p8.
The London Times. Jun 24, 1965, p17.
*Magill's Survey of Cinema. Foreign Language
Films.* v6, p2758-62.
Motion Picture Herald Product Digest. Feb 16,
1966, p468.
The New York Times. Sep 13, 1965, p42.
The New York Times. Jan 25, 1966, p47.
The New Yorker. Jan 29, 1966, v41, p90.
Newsweek. Feb 7, 1966, v67, p83-84.
Playboy. Apr 1966, v13, p43-44.
*The Private Eye, the Cowboy and the Very
Naked Girl.* p175-76, 229.
Reruns. p183-87.
Saturday Review. Jan 22, 1966, v49, p49.
Senior Scholastic. Mar 11, 1966, v88, p28.
The Spectator. Jul 2, 1965, v215, p13, 16.
Tynan Right and Left. p218-19.
Variety. May 26, 1965, p15.
The Village Voice. Mar 10, 1966, v11, p23.
Vogue. Mar 1, 1966, v147, p100.

A Shot in the Dark (GB, US; Edwards,
Blake; 1964)
BFI/Monthly Film Bulletin. Feb 1965, v32,
p27.
Blake Edwards (Lehman & Luhr). p12-16, 28-
30.
Boxoffice. Jun 29, 1964, v85, p2840.
Commonweal. Sep 18, 1964, v80, p638.
Film Daily. Jun 22, 1964, v124, p6.
Films in Review. Aug-Sep 1964, v15, p443-44.
Hollywood Reporter. Jun 22, 1964, v181, p3.
Motion Picture Herald Product Digest. Jul 8,
1964, v232, p82.
The New York Times. Jun 24, 1964, p28.
The New Yorker. Jul 4, 1964, v40, p58.
Newsweek. Jul 6, 1964, v64, p76.
Saturday Review. Jul 11, 1964, v47, p22.

Time. Jul 10, 1964, v84, p96.
Variety. Jun 24, 1964, p6.

Shout at the Devil (GB; Hunt, Peter; 1976)
BFI/Monthly Film Bulletin. May 1976, v43, p106-07.
Film Bulletin. Nov-Dec 1976, v45, p42-43.
Films and Filming. Jun 1976, v22, p38.
Films Illustrated. May 1976, v5, p324-25.
Hollywood Reporter. Nov 4, 1976, p3.
Independent Film Journal. Nov 12, 1976, v78, p8.
The Los Angeles Times. Nov 5, 1976, SecIV, p16.
Motion Picture Herald Product Digest. Nov 10, 1976, p46.
New Statesman. Apr 16, 1976, v91, p517.
The New York Times. Nov 25, 1976, p38.
Time. Dec 20, 1976, v108, p62-63.
Variety. Apr 14, 1976, p23.

Show Boat (US; Sidney, George; 1951)
BFI/Monthly Film Bulletin. Jul 1951, v18, p294.
Bright Lights. n9, 1980, v3, p21-24.
Christian Century. Aug 1, 1951, v68, p903.
Cue. Jul 14, 1951, p18.
Film Daily. Jun 5, 1951, p5.
Hollywood Reporter. Jun 5, 1951, p3.
Library Journal. Jun 15, 1951, v76, p1037.
Life. Jul 30, 1951, v31, p48.
Magill's Survey of Cinema. Series I. v4, p1549-52.
Make It Again, Sam. p185-91.
Motion Picture Herald Product Digest. Jun 9, 1951, p877.
The New York Times. Jul 20, 1951, p14.
The New Yorker. Jul 28, 1951, v27, p73-74.
Newsweek. Jul 2, 1951, v38, p78.
Saturday Review. Jun 9, 1951, v34, p26.
Selected Film Criticism, 1951-1960. p122-23.
Show Boat: The Story of a Classical American Musical.
Time. Jul 2, 1951, v58, p94.
Variety. Jun 6, 1951, p6.
The World of Entertainment. p332-46.

Side Street (US; Mann, Anthony; 1949)
Anthony Mann (Basinger). p75-81.
BFI/Monthly Film Bulletin. Apr-May 1950, v17, p69.
Commonweal. Apr 7, 1950, v51, p678.
Film Daily. Dec 27, 1949, p6.
The Great Gangster Pictures. p357-58.
Hollywood Reporter. Dec 22, 1949, p3.
Motion Picture Herald Product Digest. Dec 24, 1949, p129-30.
The New York Times. Mar 24, 1950, p29.
Newsweek. Apr 3, 1950, v35, p79.
Time. Apr 10, 1950, v55, p94.
Variety. Dec 28, 1949, p6.

The Siege At Red River (US; Maté, Rudolph; 1954)
BFI/Monthly Film Bulletin. Jun 1954, v21, p91.
Film Daily. Apr 12, 1954, p6.
Films in Review. Apr 1954, v5, p194.
Hollywood Reporter. Mar 19, 1954, p3.
Motion Picture Herald Product Digest. Mar 27, 1954, p2237-38.
National Parent-Teacher. May 1954, v48, p40.
The New York Times. Apr 3, 1954, p19.
Time. Apr 12, 1954, v63, p108.
Variety. Mar 24, 1954, p6.

Sierra (US; Green, Alfred E.; 1950)
Film Daily. Apr 21, 1950, p6.
Hollywood Reporter. Apr 26, 1950, p3.
Library Journal. May 15, 1950, v75, p886.
Motion Picture Herald Product Digest. Apr 29, 1950, p277.

The New York Times. Sep 15, 1950, p31.
Newsweek. Sep 25, 1950, v36, p92.
Variety. Apr 26, 1950, p8.

The Sign of Leo (French title: Signe du Lion, Le) (FR; Rohmer, Eric; 1960)
Cahiers du Cinema in English. Mar 1967, n9, p62.
Cinema, the Magic Vehicle. v2, p507-08.
The London Times. Sep 29, 1966, p7.
New Statesman. Sep 30, 1966, v72, p488.
The New Wave. p288-89.
Sight and Sound. Aut 1966, v35, p199.
Sight and Sound. Spr 1960, v29, p84-85.
Variety. Jul 13, 1960, p6.

Sign of the Pagan (US; Sirk, Douglas; 1954)
America. Feb 26, 1955, v92, p575.
BFI/Monthly Film Bulletin. Jan 1955, v22, p5.
Catholic World. Jan 1955, v180, p304.
Commonweal. Dec 24, 1954, v61, p334.
Coronet. Feb 1955, v37, p6.
Farm Journal. Jan 1955, v79, p70.
Film Daily. Nov 9, 1954, p6.
Films and Filming. Jan 1955, v1, p21.
Hollywood Reporter. Nov 9, 1954, p3.
Library Journal. Dec 15, 1954, v79, p2438.
Motion Picture Herald Product Digest. Nov 13, 1954, p209.
National Parent-Teacher. Dec 1954, v49, p40.
The New York Times. Feb 14, 1954, p24.
Variety. Nov 10, 1954, p6.
Woman's Home Companion. Dec 1954, v81, p16-17.

Signe du Lion, Le *See* The Sign of Leo

Signore e Signori *See* The Birds, the Bees and the Italians

Signs of Life (German title: Lebenszeichen) (WGER; Herzog, Werner; 1968)
BFI/Monthly Film Bulletin. Jan 1974, v41, p9-10.
German Film and Literature. p217-30.
International Film Guide. 1970, v7, p130-31.
The London Times. Dec 14, 1968, p19.
Magill's Survey of Cinema. Foreign Language Films. v5, p2772-80.
Movietone News. Nov 4, 1977, n56, p8-16.
New German Cinema (Franklin). p116-17.
The New German Cinema (Sandford). p50.
The New York Times. Sep 26, 1986, p60.
Newsweek. Jun 1, 1970, v75, p99.
Variety. May 15, 1968, p28.
The Village Voice. Dec 9, 1981, p64.

The Silence (Also titled: Tystnaden) (SWED; Bergman, Ingmar; 1963)
America. Apr 4, 1964, v110, p494-95.
Bergman on Bergman. p179-95.
BFI/Monthly Film Bulletin. Jun 1964, v31, p91.
Cinema Borealis. p212-17.
Cinema Eye, Cinema Ear. p167-68.
Commonweal. Feb 28, 1964, v79, p664.
Dictionary of Films. p387.
Esquire. Aug 1964, v62, p17-18.
Film and Dreams. p139-46.
Film Comment. Sum 1964, v2, n3, p56-58.
Film Daily. Feb 6, 1964, v124, p10.
Films in Review. Mar 1964, v15, p176-78.
Hollywood Reporter. Feb 5, 1964, v179, p3.
Ingmar Bergman and Society. p78-86.
Ingmar Bergman (Colbie). p210-17.
Ingmar Bergman: Essays in Criticism. p239-52.
Ingmar Bergman (Mosley). p115-21.
Ingmar Bergman (Steene). p107-13.
The International Dictionary of Films and Filmmakers. p490-91.
Motion Picture Herald Product Digest. Feb 19, 1964, v231, p993-94.

The Nation. Feb 17, 1964, v198, p175.
National Review. May 5, 1964, v16, p368-70.
The New Republic. Feb 22, 1964, v150, p24.
The New York Times. Feb 4, 1964, p28.
The New Yorker. Feb 8, 1964, v39, p106.
Newsweek. Feb 17, 1964, v63, p92.
On Movies. p416-18.
The Personal Visions of Ingmar Bergman. p227-33.
The Private Eye, the Cowboy and the Very Naked Girl. p61-64.
Private Screenings. p124-25.
Renaissance of the Film. p255-63.
Saturday Review. Feb 8, 1964, v47, p23.
Sight and Sound. Sum 1964, v33, p142-43.
The Silence of God. p117-33.
Time. Feb 14, 1964, v83, p94.
Time. Nov 15, 1963, v82, p72.
Variety. Oct 2, 1963, p6.
A World on Film. p286-89.

The Silencers (US; Karlson, Phil; 1966)
BFI/Monthly Film Bulletin. May 1966, v33, p72-73.
Film Daily. Feb 9, 1966, p6.
Film Quarterly. Sum 1966, v19, p68-69.
Filmfacts. Mar 15, 1966, v9, p38-39.
Films and Filming. May 1966, v12, p6, 8.
Films in Review. Mar 1966, v17, p184-85.
The Great Spy Pictures. p433-35.
Hollywood Reporter. Feb 9, 1966, p3.
The London Times. Apr 7, 1966, p16.
Motion Picture Herald Product Digest. Feb 16, 1966, p467-68.
The New York Times. Mar 17, 1966, p35.
Playboy. Apr 1966, v13, p42.
Saturday Review. Apr 9, 1966, v49, p55.
The Spectator. Apr 15, 1966, v216, p469.
Time. Mar 4, 1966, v87, p105.
Variety. Feb 9, 1966, p6.

Silencieux, Le *See* Escape to Nowhere

Silent Movie (US; Brooks, Mel; 1976)
America. Sep 4, 1976, v135, p100.
Before My Eyes. p111.
BFI/Monthly Film Bulletin. Dec 1976, v43, p256.
Commonweal. Jul 30, 1976, v103, p500-01.
Films and Filming. Nov 1976, v23, p16-17.
Hollywood Reporter. Jun 30, 1976, p2.
Independent Film Journal. Jul 9, 1976, v78, p11-12.
The Los Angeles Times. Jun 27, 1976, Calendar, p1.
Motion Picture Herald Product Digest. Jul 14, 1976, p86.
The New Republic. Jul 31, 1976, v175, p20.
New York. Jul 19, 1976, v9, p84.
The New York Times. Jul 18, 1976, SecII, p1.
The New Yorker. Jul 12, 1976, v52, p84-85.
Newsweek. Jul 12, 1976, v52, p84-85.
Penthouse. Oct 1976, v8, p45-47.
Saturday Review. Aug 7, 1976, v3, p44.
Silent Movie. 1976.
Time. Jul 12, 1976, v108, p48.
Variety. Jun 23, 1976, p16.

The Silent Voice *See* Paula

Silk Stockings (US; Mamoulian, Rouben; 1957)
America. Aug 24, 1957, v97, p532.
BFI/Monthly Film Bulletin. Jul 1957, v24, p85.
Commonweal. Aug 2, 1957, v66, p450.
Film Daily. May 20, 1957, v111, p6.
Films and Filming. Aug 1957, v3, p28.
Films in Review. Aug-Sep 1957, v8, p351-52.
The Films of Peter Lorre. p217-18.
Hollywood Reporter. May 20, 1957, p3.

Magill's Survey of Cinema. English Language Films. Series I, v4, p1553-56.
Motion Picture Herald Product Digest. May 25, 1957, p207.
The New York Times. Jul 19, 1957, p11.
The New York Times. Jul 28, 1957, SecII, p1.
The New Yorker. Aug 3, 1957, v33, p48.
Newsweek. Jul 22, 1957, v50, p84.
Rouben Mamoulian (Milne). p147-60.
Saturday Review. Jul 20, 1957, v40, p27.
Starring Fred Astaire. p421-34.
Time. Jul 15, 1957, v70, p104.
Variety. May 22, 1957, p6.

Silkwood (US; Nichols, Mike; 1983)
America. Jan 28, 1984, v150, p54.
American Cinematographer. Feb 1984, v65, p50-54.
American Film. Mar 1984, v9, p50-54.
BFI/Monthly Film Bulletin. Apr 1984, v51, p121-22.
Cineaste. 1984, v13, n3, p38-40.
Commonweal. Mar 9, 1984, v111, p146-47.
Film Journal. Jan 1984, v87, p9-10.
Film Quarterly. Wint 1984, v37, p24-26.
Films and Filming. Apr 1984, n355, p41.
Films in Review. Apr 1984, v35, p231-32.
Films in Review. Mar 1984, v35, p178-79.
Hollywood Reporter. Nov 17, 1983, p3.
Informer. Dec 1983, p6.
Maclean's. Dec 26, 1983, v96, p43.
Ms. Feb 1984, v12, p30.
The Nation. Jan 14, 1984, v238, p3-4.
National Review. Mar 23, 1984, v36, p48-50.
National Review. Jan 27, 1984, v36, p20.
The New Republic. Jan 23, 1984, v190, p24-25.
New Statesman. Apr 13, 1984, v107, p29-30.
New Statesman. May 4, 1984, v107, p15.
The New York Times. Feb 12, 1984, SecII, p1.
The New York Times. Jan 1, 1984, SecII, p11.
The New York Times. Jan 7, 1984, p11.
The New Yorker. Jan 9, 1984, v59, p99-100.
Newsweek. Dec 26, 1983, v17, p96.
Newsweek. Dec 12, 1983, v102, p108.
Progressive. Feb 1984, v48, p38.
Stills. Apr-May 1984, n11, p73.
Time. Dec 19, 1983, v122, p73.
Variety. Nov 23, 1983, p14.
The Village Voice. Feb 21, 1984, p28.
Vogue. Dec 1983, v173, p354.

The Silver Chalice (US; Saville, Victor; 1954)
America. Jan 8, 1955, v92, p387.
BFI/Monthly Film Bulletin. Jun 1955, v22, n257, p85.
Catholic World. Feb 1955, v180, p382.
Commonweal. Jan 14, 1955, v61, p407.
Farm Journal. Feb 1955, v79, p149.
Film Daily. Dec 20, 1954, p6.
Films and Filming. Jun 1955, v1, p20.
The Films of Paul Newman. p39-42.
Hi Fidelity. Dec 1975, v25, p121-22.
Hollywood Reporter. Dec 17, 1954, p3.
Library Journal. Jan 15, 1955, v80, p150.
Motion Picture Herald Product Digest. Dec 25, 1954, p257-58.
National Parent-Teacher. Mar 1955, v49, p39.
The New York Times. Dec 27, 1954, p22.
The New Yorker. Jan 15, 1955, v30, p70.
Newsweek. Jan 17, 1955, v45, p87.
Saturday Review. Jan 15, 1955, v38, p32.
Time. Jan 10, 1955, v65, p82.
Variety. Dec 22, 1954, p6.

Silver Lode (US; Dwan, Allan; 1954)
BFI/Monthly Film Bulletin. Dec 1954, v21, p180.
Film Daily. May 19, 1954, p6.
The Filming of the West. p545.

Hollywood Reporter. May 12, 1954, p3.
Motion Picture Herald Product Digest. May 22, 1954, p2.
The New York Times. Jul 24, 1954, p6.

Silver Streak (US; Hiller, Arthur; 1976)
BFI/Monthly Film Bulletin. Apr 1977, v44, p80.
Film Bulletin. Nov-Dec 1976, v45, p8.
Films in Review. Jan 1977, v28, p59.
Hollywood Reporter. Nov 30, 1976, p2.
Independent Film Journal. Dec 10, 1976, v78, p7.
The Los Angeles Times. Dec 9, 1976, SecIV, p1.
Motion Picture Herald Product Digest. Dec 29, 1976, p60.
The New York Times. Dec 9, 1976, p61.
The New Yorker. Jan 17, 1977, p98-99.
Newsweek. Dec 13, 1976, v88, p107.
Saturday Review. Jan 22, 1977, v4, p49-50.
Time. Dec 13, 1976, v108, p99.
Variety. Dec 1, 1976, v18.
The Village Voice. Dec 20, 1976, p80.
When the Lights Go Down. p246-48.

Silverado (US; Kasdan, Lawrence; 1985)
America. Aug 17, 1985, v153, p91.
BFI/Monthly Film Bulletin. Jan 1986, v53, p13.
Christian Century. Jul 17, 1985, v102, p685.
Film Comment. Jul-Aug 1985, v21, p20-27.
Film Comment. Sep-Oct 1985, v21, p76-78.
Films in Review. Oct 1985, v36, p492.
Hollywood Reporter. Jul 1, 1985, p3.
The Los Angeles Times. Jul 10, 1985, SecVI, p1.
Maclean's. Jul 22, 1985, v98, p49.
Magill's Cinema Annual, 1986. p349-53.
The New Republic. Aug 5, 1985, v193, p24-25.
New York. Jul 29, 1985, v18, p60-61.
The New York Times. Jun 10, 1985, SecIII, p21.
The New Yorker. Jul 29, 1985, v61, p58-59.
Newsweek. Jul 15, 1985, v106, p54.
Progressive. Sep 1985, v49, p38.
Time. Jul 22, 1985, v126, p77.
Variety. Jul 3, 1985, p16.
Vogue. Jul 1985, v175, p35-36.

Simeon del Desierto *See* Simon of the Desert

Simon (US; Brickman, Marshall; 1980)
Hollywood Reporter. Feb 21, 1980, p3.
Maclean's. Mar 17, 1980, v93, p62-63.
Motion Picture Herald Product Digest. Mar 12, 1980, p78.
The Nation. Mar 15, 1980, v230, p316-17.
The New Republic. Mar 22, 1980, v182, p22.
New York. Mar 17, 1980, v13, p63.
The New York Times. Feb 29, 1980, SecIII, p5.
The New York Times Magazine. Feb 24, 1980, p28-30.
The New Yorker. Mar 10, 1980, v56, p130-31.
Newsweek. Mar 3, 1980, v95, p68.
Time. Mar 3, 1980, v115, p73.
USA Today. Jul 1980, v109, p67-68.
Variety. Feb 27, 1980, p20.

Simon of the Desert (Spanish title: Simeon del Desierto) (MEX; Buñuel, Luis; 1965)
Christian Century. Apr 2, 1969, v86, p452.
The Cinema of Luis Buñuel. p151-56.
Commonweal. Feb 28, 1969, v89, p676.
The Discreet Art of Luis Buñuel. p197.
Figures of Light. p144-46.
Film Culture. Sum 1966, n41, p60-65.
Film Quarterly. Wint 1965-66, v19, p47-48.
Filmfacts. n2, 1969, v12, p36-38.
Films and Filming. Jul 1969, v15, p39.
Films in Review. Mar 1969, v20, p178.

Going Steady. p315-25.
Holiday. May 1969, v45, p22.
Luis Buñuel (Aranda). p223-25.
Luis Buñuel (Durgnat). p136-38.
Luis Buñuel (Higginbotham). p124-29.
Magill's Survey of Cinema. Foreign Language Films. v6, p2790-94.
The New Republic. Mar 8, 1969, v160, p22.
New Statesman. Apr 11, 1969, v77, p524.
The New York Times. Sep 21, 1966, p42.
The New Yorker. Feb 15, 1969, v44, p109-12.
Private Screenings. p283.
Sight and Sound. Sum 1969, v38, p154-55.
The Spectator. Apr 11, 1969, v222, p482.
Take One. Sep-Oct 1966, v1, p24-26.
Tynan Right and Left. p238.
Variety. Jun 16, 1965, p16.
The Village Voice. Feb 20, 1969, v14, p46.
The World of Luis Buñuel. p273-77.

Simon the Swiss *See* The Crook

A Simple Story (French title: Histoire simple, Une) (FR; Sautet, Claude; 1978)
The Nation. Feb 16, 1980, v230, p188.
National Review. Mar 21, 1980, v32, p364-65.
New York. Feb 11, 1980, v13, p67.
The New York Times. Feb 10, 1980, p56.
The New Yorker. Feb 18, 1980, v55, p128-30.
Newsweek. Feb 18, 1980, v95, p92.
Time. Mar 10, 1980, v115, p78.
Variety. Nov 15, 1978, p19.

Sin in the Afternoon *See* High Infidelity

Singin' in the Rain (US; Kelly, Gene; Donen, Stanley; 1952)
America in the Movies. p155-58.
America's Favorite Movies. p253-68.
The Best of MGM. p193-95.
BFI/Monthly Film Bulletin. May 1952, v19, p61.
Catholic World. May 1952, v175, p142.
Christian Century. May 7, 1952, v69, p575.
Cine-Tracts. 1977, v1, n2, p27-35.
Classic Film Collector. Fall 1977, n56, p18-19.
Classic Movies. p50-51.
Commonweal. Apr 11, 1952, v56, p15.
Cue. Mar 29, 1952, p14.
Cult Movies. p321-25.
Dictionary of Films. p342-43.
Film Comment. May-Jun 1978, v14, p7-12.
Film Criticism and Caricatures, 1943-1953. p142-43.
Film Daily. Mar 14, 1952, p12.
Films and Filming. Apr 1977, v23, p20-24.
Films in Review. Apr 1952, v3, p198-99.
The Films of Gene Kelly. p133-41.
The Films of the Fifties. p69-74.
The Great Movies. p92-95.
Halliwell's Hundred. p322-25.
Hollywood Reporter. Mar 12, 1952, p3.
Iris. 1985, v3, n1, p57-70.
Landmark Films. p210-19.
Literature/Film Quarterly. 1984, v11, n2, p87-95.
Magill's Survey of Cinema. Series I. v4, p1560-63.
Motion Picture Herald Product Digest. Mar 15, 1952, p1281.
The New Statesman and Nation. Apr 26, 1952, v43, p494.
The New York Times. Mar 28, 1952, p27.
The New York Times. May 4, 1975, p15.
Newsweek. Apr 7, 1952, v39, p100.
Quarterly Review of Film Studies. 1977, v2, n3, p313-26.
Saturday Review. Apr 12, 1952, v35, p42.
Screen Education. Aut 1975, n16, p26-30.
Selected Film Criticism, 1951-1960. p123-24.

Sight and Sound. Jul-Sep 1952, v22, p29.
Singin' in the Rain: Story and Screenplay. p1-10.
The Spectator. Apr 4, 1952, v188, p434.
Stanley Donen (Casper). p44-54.
Talking Pictures. p197-200.
The Tatler. Apr 23, 1952, v204, p190.
Theatre Arts. May 1952, v36, p45.
Time. Apr 21, 1952, v59, p106.
Variety. Mar 12, 1952, p6.
Vintage Films. p131-33.
The World of Entertainment. p347-62.

The Singing Nun (US; Koster, Henry; 1966)
America. Apr 16, 1966, v114, p567.
BFI/Monthly Film Bulletin. May 1966, v33, p75-76.
Big Screen, Little Screen. p330.
Christian Science Monitor (Western edition). Apr 1, 1966, p6.
Commonweal. Apr 15, 1966, v84, p116.
Film Daily. Mar 8, 1966, p3.
Filmfacts. May 15, 1966, v9, p73-75.
Films and Filming. Dec 1965, v12, p57-58.
Films and Filming. Jun 1966, v12, p57-58.
Hollywood Reporter. Mar 8, 1966, p3.
Kiss Kiss Bang Bang. p214-17.
The London Times. Mar 24, 1966, p16.
Motion Picture Herald Product Digest. Mar 9, 1966, p482.
The New York Times. Mar 18, 1966, p33.
Newsweek. Mar 28, 1966, v67, p100.
Variety. Mar 9, 1966, p6.

Sink the Bismarck! (GB; Gilbert, Lewis; 1960)
America. Feb 20, 1960, v102, p623.
BFI/Monthly Film Bulletin. Mar 1960, v27, p33.
Film Daily. Feb 20, 1960, p6.
Filmfacts. 1960, v3, p34.
Films and Filming. Mar 1960, v6, p23.
Films and Filming. Apr 1963, v9, p35.
Films in Review. Mar 1960, v11, p174.
Hollywood Reporter. Feb 2, 1960, p3.
The New York Times. Feb 12, 1960, p22.
The New Yorker. Feb 20, 1960, v36, p162.
Newsweek. Feb 22, 1960, v55, p103.
Sight and Sound. Spr 1960, v29, p91-92.
Time. Mar 21, 1960, v75, p83.
Variety. Feb 24, 1960, p6.

Sirocco (US; Bernhardt, Curtis; 1951)
BFI/Monthly Film Bulletin. Jul 1951, v18, p299.
Commonweal. Jul 6, 1951, v54, p310.
The Complete Films of Humphrey Bogart. p159-60.
Film Daily. Jun 12, 1951, p6.
Hollywood Reporter. Jun 6, 1951, p3.
Humphrey Bogart: The Man and His Films. p156-58.
Motion Picture Herald Product Digest. Jun 9, 1951, p878.
The New Republic. Jul 2, 1951, v125, p23.
The New York Times. Jun 14, 1951, p31.
The New Yorker. Jun 23, 1951, v27, p61.
Newsweek. Jun 11, 1951, v37, p100.
Time. Jul 2, 1951, v58, p97.
Variety. Jun 6, 1951, p6.

Situation Hopeless But Not Serious (US; Reinhardt, Gottfried; 1965)
America. Oct 23, 1965, v113, p482.
Christian Science Monitor (Western edition). Nov 27, 1965, p12.
Film Daily. Nov 12, 1965, p23.
Films and Filming. Mar 1965, v11, p48-49.
Films and Filming. Oct 1969, v16, p53-54.
Films in Review. Nov 1965, v16, p582-83.

The Films of Robert Redford. p73-79.
Hollywood Reporter. Oct 6, 1965, p3.
Motion Picture Herald Product Digest. Oct 27, 1965, p394.
The New Republic. Nov 6, 1965, v153, p32.
The New York Times. Oct 14, 1965, p53.
Variety. Oct 6, 1965, p6.

Six in Paris *See* Paris Vu Par...

Sixteen Candles (US; Hughes, John; 1984)
Film Journal. Jun 1984, v87, p22-23.
Films in Review. Jun-Jul 1984, v35, p370-71.
Hollywood Reporter. May 2, 1984, p4.
The Los Angeles Times. May 4, 1984, SecVI, p9.
Maclean's. May 14, 1984, v97, p75.
New York. May 28, 1984, v17, p96.
The New York Times. May 4, 1984, SecIII, p14.
The New Yorker. May 28, 1984, v60, p101-03.
Variety. May 2, 1984, p16.
The Village Voice. May 8, 1984, p50.
Vogue. Jul 1984, v174, p49.

Sjunde Inseglet, Det *See* The Seventh Seal

Skammen *See* Shame

Skirts Ahoy (US; Lanfield, Sidney; 1952)
Christian Century. Jul 9, 1952, v69, p815.
Commonweal. Jun 13, 1952, v56, p245.
Film Daily. Apr 17, 1952, p6.
Hollywood Reporter. Apr 11, 1952, p3.
Motion Picture Herald Product Digest. Apr 12, 1952, p1313.
The New York Times. May 29, 1952, p17.
Newsweek. Jun 9, 1952, v39, p91.
Saturday Review. May 17, 1952, v35, p25.
Time. May 19, 1952, v59, p106.
Variety. Apr 16, 1952, p16.

The Sky Above, the Mud Below (French title: Ciel et la Boue, Le) (FR; Gaisseau, Pierre-Dominique; 1960)
America. Sep 1, 1962, v107, p678.
BFI/Monthly Film Bulletin. Nov 1963, v30, p163.
Cinema. 1963, v1, n3, p34.
Commonweal. Jul 29, 1962, v76, p352.
Film Daily. Jun 25, 1962, p7.
Filmfacts. Aug 10, 1962, v5, p169-70.
Films and Filming. Nov 1963, v10, p21-22.
Films in Review. Jun-Jul 1962, v13, p358-59.
Hollywood Reporter. Aug 17, 1962, p3.
The New Republic. Jul 9, 1962, v147, p21.
The New York Times. Jul 20, 1962, p40.
The New Yorker. Jul 30, 1962, v38, p68.
Newsweek. Jul 9, 1962, v60, p72.
Time. Jul 6, 1962, v80, p55.
Variety. Jun 20, 1962, p18.
Variety. May 10, 1961, p19.

Sky Full of Moon (US; Foster, Norman; 1952)
BFI/Monthly Film Bulletin. Jan 1953, v20, p11.
Film Daily. Dec 3, 1952, p6.
Hollywood Reporter. Nov 3, 1952, p3.
Motion Picture Herald Product Digest. Nov 8, 1952, p1597.
National Parent-Teacher. Feb 1953, v47, p38.
Variety. Nov 5, 1952, p6.

Sky Riders (US, GREECE; Hickox, Douglas; 1976)
BFI/Monthly Film Bulletin. May 1976, v43, p107.
Film Bulletin. Apr 1976, v45, pD-E.
Films and Filming. Jun 1976, v22, p35.
Films in Review. May 1976, v27, p315.
Hollywood Reporter. Mar 18, 1976, p3.
Independent Film Journal. Apr 14, 1976, v77, p8-9.

The Los Angeles Times. Apr 21, 1976, SecIV, p10.
Motion Picture Herald Product Digest. Apr 14, 1976, p92.
New Statesman. May 28, 1976, v91, p724.
The New York Times. Mar 18, 1976, p18.
Time. May 10, 1976, v107, p73.
Variety. Mar 24, 1976, p21.
Variety. Apr 14, 1976, p21.

Sky West and Crooked (Also titled: Gypsy Girl) (GB; Mills, John; 1965)
BFI/Monthly Film Bulletin. Mar 1966, v33, p46.
Film Daily. Jun 17, 1966, p4.
Filmfacts. Nov 15, 1967, v10, p293.
Films and Filming. Mar 1966, v12, p31-32, 58.
Life. Sep 30, 1966, v61, p17.
The London Times. Jan 20, 1966, p17.
Motion Picture Herald Product Digest. Jun 22, 1966, p546.
Newsweek. Oct 17, 1966, v68, p105A.
Variety. Feb 2, 1966, p17.

The Slap (French title: Gifle, La) (FR; Pinoteau, Charles; 1974)
Film Bulletin. Apr 1976, v45, pF.
Films in Review. Feb 1976, v27, p123.
Hollywood Reporter. Jan 22, 1976, p18.
Independent Film Journal. Feb 4, 1976, v77, p10.
The Los Angeles Times. Feb 18, 1976, SecIV, p11.
The New Republic. Feb 21, 1976, v174, p20-21.
New York. Jan 26, 1976, v9, p62.
The New York Times. Jan 19, 1976, p25.
Newsweek. Feb 16, 1976, v87, p78.
Saturday Review. Feb 21, 1976, v3, p49-50.
The Village Voice. Feb 2, 1976, p115-16.

Slap Shot (US; Hill, George Roy; 1977)
America. Mar 19, 1977, v136, p244.
BFI/Monthly Film Bulletin. Aug 1977, v44, p174.
Bijou. Apr 1977, v1, p28-31.
Films Illustrated. Jun 9, 1977, v6, p388-89.
Films in Review. Apr 1977, v28, p249.
The Films of George Roy Hill. p127-37.
George Roy Hill (Shores). p14-16, 91-97.
Hollywood Reporter. Feb 24, 1977, p3.
The Los Angeles Times. Feb 25, 1977, SecIV, p1.
The Los Angeles Times. Mar 10, 1977, SecIV, p1.
Magill's Cinema Annual, 1982. p467-70.
Motion Picture Herald Product Digest. Mar 16, 1977, p79.
Ms. Jul 1977, v6, p31.
The New Republic. Mar 19, 1977, v176, p20-21.
New York. Mar 7, 1977, v10, p76-78.
The New York Times. Feb 26, 1977, p11.
The New Yorker. Mar 7, 1977, v53, p91-93.
Newsweek. Mar 7, 1977, v89, p68-69.
Saturday Review. Apr 2, 1977, v4, p41-42.
Sports Illustrated. Mar 7, 1977, v46, p42.
Time. Mar 14, 1977, v109, p73-74.
Variety. Mar 2, 1977, p22.
The Village Voice. Mar 14, 1977, p41.

Slaughter on Tenth Avenue (US; Laven, Arnold; 1957)
America. Nov 2, 1957, v98, p148.
BFI/Monthly Film Bulletin. Dec 1957, v24, p152-53.
Commonweal. Nov 8, 1957, v67, p150.
Film Daily. Sep 17, 1957, v112, p6.
Hollywood Reporter. Sep 17, 1957, p3.
Motion Picture Herald Product Digest. Sep 21, 1957, v208, p537.
The New York Times. Nov 6, 1957, p43.
The New Yorker. Nov 16, 1957, v33, p110.

Time. Dec 2, 1957, v70, p90.
Variety. Sep 18, 1957, p6.

Slaughterhouse-Five (US; Hill, George Roy; 1972)
America. Apr 8, 1972, v126, p380.
Christian Century. Sep 20, 1972, v89, p929-30.
Commonweal. Jul 28, 1972, v94, p406.
The Films of George Roy Hill. p81-98.
George Roy Hill (Shores). p109-21.
Harper's Bazaar. May 1972, v105, p116.
Life. Apr 28, 1972, v72, p16.
National Review. Aug 1972, v24, p911-12.
The New Republic. May 13, 1972, v166, p35.
The New York Times. Jun 11, 1972, SecII, p13.
The New Yorker. Apr 1, 1972, v48, p93.
Newsweek. Apr 3, 1972, v79, p85.
Saturday Review. Apr 15, 1972, v55, p10-11.
Time. Apr 10, 1972, v99, p77.
Variety. Mar 22, 1972, p20.

Sleeper (US; Allen, Woody; 1973)
BFI/Monthly Film Bulletin. Jun 1974, v41, p135.
Commentary. May 1974, v57, p61-63.
Commonweal. Feb 22, 1974, v99, p506.
Esquire. Mar 1974, v82, p74.
Filmmakers Newsletter. Jul-Aug 1974, v7, p20-24.
Films Illustrated. May 1974, v3, p329.
Films In Review. Feb 1974, v25, p115.
Magill's Survey of Cinema. Series II. v5, p2199.
The Nation. Jan 5, 1974, v218, p27.
National Review. Feb 15, 1974, v26, p212.
New Statesman. May 3, 1974, v87, p634.
The New York Times. Dec 18, 1973, p52.
The New York Times. Dec 23, 1973, SecII, p3.
The New York Times. Jan 6, 1974, v2, n1, p2.
The New Yorker. Dec 31, 1973, v49, p47-49.
Newsweek. Dec 31, 1973, v82, p33.
Reeling. p327-32.
Rolling Stone. Jan 17, 1974, p56-47.
Sight and Sound. Sum 1974, v43, p178-79.
Time. Jan 7, 1974, v103, p60.
TV Movies. 1983-84, p705.
Variety. Dec 19, 1973, p12.
Woody Allen: His Films and Career. p134-44.
Woody Allen (Palmer). p71-76.

The Sleeping Car Murder (Also titled: The Sleeping Car Murders; Compartiment Tueurs) (FR; Costa-Gavras, Constantin; 1965)
BFI/Monthly Film Bulletin. Nov 1966, v33, p169.
Christian Science Monitor (Western edition). May 27, 1966, p6.
Commonweal. Feb 18, 1966, v83, p586.
Costa-Gavras: The Political Fiction Film. p51-61.
Film Daily. Feb 8, 1966, p14.
Film Quarterly. Spr 1968, v21, p44-46.
Filmfacts. May 1, 1966, v9, p65-66.
Films and Filming. Dec 1966, v13, p52.
Films and Filming. Apr 1965, v11, p53.
Films in Review. Apr 1966, v17, p252-53.
The London Times. Sep 15, 1966, p6.
Motion Picture Herald Product Digest. Feb 16, 1966, p469.
The Nation. Apr 4, 1966, v202, p406.
The New York Times. Mar 8, 1966, p45.
The New Yorker. Mar 12, 1966, v42, p113-14.
Playboy. Jun 1966, v13, p36.
Saturday Review. Apr 9, 1966, v49, p55.
Time. Feb 11, 1966, v87, p85.
Variety. Dec 1, 1965, p6.
Vogue. Mar 1, 1966, p147, p100.

The Sleeping City (US; Sherman, George; 1950)
Christian Century. Oct 25, 1950, v67, p1279.
Commonweal. Sep 22, 1950, v52, p581.
Film Daily. Sep 6, 1950, p6.
The Great Gangster Pictures. p363-65.
Hollywood Reporter. Sep 6, 1950, p3.
Motion Picture Herald Product Digest. Sep 9, 1950, p477.
The New Republic. Oct 9, 1950, v123, p29.
The New York Times. Sep 21, 1950, p20.
The New Yorker. Sep 30, 1950, v26, p56.
Newsweek. Oct 2, 1950, v36, p86.
Time. Sep 25, 1950, v56, p98.
Variety. Sep 6, 1950, p8.

The Sleeping Tiger (French title: Bete S'eveille, La) (GB; Losey, Joseph; 1954)
BFI/Monthly Film Bulletin. Aug 1954, v21, p117.
The Cinema of Joseph Losey. p60-66.
Conversations with Losey. p135-39.
Film Daily. Oct 28, 1954, p6.
The Films of Dirk Bogarde. p74-75.
Joseph Losey. p64-66.
The London Times. Jun 28, 1954, p3.
Motion Picture Herald Product Digest. Nov 6, 1954, p202.
National Parent-Teacher. Dec 1954, v49, p40.
The New York Times. Oct 9, 1954, p8.
The Spectator. Jun 25, 1954, v192, p778-79.
The Tatler. Jul 7, 1954, v213, p28.
Variety. Jul 7, 1954, p22.

The Slender Thread (US; Pollack, Sydney; 1965)
America. Jan 22, 1966, v114, p158.
BFI/Monthly Film Bulletin. Apr 1966, v33, p36-37.
Christian Science Monitor (Western edition). Aug 11, 1965, p12.
Commonweal. Jan 21, 1966, v83, p478.
Film Daily. Dec 14, 1965, p5.
Film Quarterly. Sum 1966, v19, p69.
Films and Filming. May 1966, v12, p51-52.
Films in Review. Jan 1966, v17, p49-50.
Hollywood Reporter. Dec 10, 1965, p3.
Kiss Kiss Bang Bang. p176-78.
The London Times. Mar 10, 1966, p14.
Motion Picture Herald Product Digest. Dec 22, 1965, p426.
New Statesman. Mar 11, 1966, v71, p351.
The New York Times. Dec 24, 1965, p24.
The New Yorker. Jan 15, 1965, v41, p71.
Newsweek. Jan 10, 1966, v67, p61-62.
Playboy. Mar 1966, v13, p23-24.
Saturday Review. Jan 8, 1966, v49, p97.
The Spectator. Mar 11, 1966, v216, p292-93.
Sydney Pollack (Taylor). p33-37.
Time. Jan 14, 1966, v87, p89.
Variety. Dec 15, 1965, p15.

Sleuth (GB; Mankiewicz, Joseph L.; 1972)
Commonweal. Apr 20, 1973, v98, p162.
Filmfacts. 1972, v15, n21, p449.
Films in Review. Feb 1973, v24, n2, p121.
The Films of Laurence Olivier. p177-81.
The Films of The Seventies. p60-61.
Harper's Bazaar. Mar 1973, v106, p152.
Hollywood Reporter. Dec 11, 1972, p3.
Joseph L. Mankiewicz (Dick). p157-63.
Magill's Survey of Cinema. English Language Films. Series I, v4, p1567.
The Nation. Jan 1, 1973, v216, p27-28.
The New Republic. Jan 20, 1973, v168, p26.
The New York Times. Dec 11, 1972, v53, p1.
The New Yorker. Dec 23, 1972, v48, p53-54.
Newsweek. Apr 3, 1972, v79, p85.
Reeling. p116.

Time. Apr 10, 1972, v99, p77.
Variety. Dec 13, 1972, p15.

The Slipper and the Rose (GB; Forbes, Bryan; 1976)
BFI/Monthly Film Bulletin. May 1976, v43, p107-08.
Films and Filming. Jun 1976, v22, p33-34.
Films and Filming. Apr 1976, v22, p36.
Films Illustrated. Apr 1976, v5, p302-03.
Films Illustrated. May 1976, v5, p325-26.
Films in Review. Dec 1976, v27, p633.
Hollywood Reporter. Nov 4, 1976, p4.
Independent Film Journal. Nov 12, 1976, v78, p8.
Independent Film Journal. Nov 26, 1976, v78, p19.
Motion Picture Herald Product Digest. Nov 24, 1976, p50.
New Statesman. Mar 26, 1976, v91, p413-14.
New York. Nov 15, 1976, v9, p117-19.
The New York Times. Nov 5, 1976, SecIII, p8.
Newsweek. Nov 29, 1976, v88, p113.
Saturday Review. Dec 11, 1976, v4, p77-78.
Variety. Apr 14, 1976, p27.

Small Change (French title: Argent de Poche) (FR; Truffaut, François; 1976)
BFI/Monthly Film Bulletin. Aug 1977, v44, p163-64.
Film Comment. Sep-Oct 1976, v12, p42-45.
Film Quarterly. Spr 1977, v30, p42-45.
François Truffaut: A Guide to References and Resources. p78-81.
François Truffaut (Insdorf). p145-51, 157-61.
Hollywood Reporter. Oct 5, 1976, p3.
Independent Film Journal. Oct 11, 1976, v78, p33.
The Los Angeles Times. Dec 22, 1976, SecIV, p1.
Magill's Survey of Cinema. Foreign Language Films. v6, p2812-15.
Motion Picture Herald Product Digest. Nov 10, 1976, p47.
The New Republic. Oct 16, 1976, v175, p22.
The New Republic. Apr 2, 1977, v176, p23-25.
New York. Oct 18, 1976, v9, p78-81.
The New York Times. Oct 10, 1976, SecII, p17.
The New York Times. Oct 1, 1976, SecIII, p11.
The New York Times. Oct 24, 1976, SecII, p15.
The New Yorker. Oct 4, 1976, v52, p129-30.
Newsweek. Sep 27, 1976, v88, p89-90.
Psychology Today. Jan 1977, v10, p19.
Saturday Review. Oct 30, 1976, v4, p53-54.
Take One. n4, 1976, v5, p38.
The Thousand Eyes Magazine. Oct 1976, v2, p7.
Time. Oct 11, 1976, v108, p88.
Times Educational Supplement. Nov 26, 1976, n3208, p70.
Variety. Mar 24, 1976, p21.
The Village Voice. Nov 1, 1976, v21, p52-53.

Small Town Girl (US; Kardes, Leslie; 1953)
BFI/Monthly Film Bulletin. May 1953, v20, n232, p75.
Catholic World. Apr 1953, v177, p64.
Film Daily. Mar 23, 1953, p14.
Hollywood Reporter. Feb 25, 1953, p3.
The New York Times. May 7, 1953, p37.
Time. Apr 13, 1953, v61, p109.
Variety. Apr 25, 1953, p6.

Smash Palace (NZ; Donaldson, Roger; 1981)
BFI/Monthly Film Bulletin. Jun 1983, v50, p166.
Film Comment. Jul-Aug 1982, v18, p2.
Films In Review. Jun-Jul 1982, v33, p362.
The Los Angeles Times. Oct 27, 1982, SecVI, p1.

Magill's Cinema Annual, 1983. p302-06.
The Nation. May 29, 1982, v234, p664-65.
The New Republic. May 26, 1982, v186, p24.
New Statesman. Jul 15, 1983, v106, p30-31.
The New York Times. Apr 16, 1982, III, p14.
The New York Times. May 9, 1982, SecII, p15-16.
The New Yorker. May 31, 1982, v58, p81-82.
Newsweek. May 31, 1982, v99, p70.
Time. May 17, 1982, v119, p84.
Variety. Sep 4, 1981, p3.
Variety. Apr 28, 1982, p18.
The Village Voice. May 4, 1982, p62.

Smile (US; Ritchie, Michael; 1975)
Before My Eyes. p187-89.
BFI/Monthly Film Bulletin. Oct 1975, v42, p226.
Commonweal. Nov 7, 1975, v102, p530.
The Los Angeles Times. Jul 9, 1975, SecIV, p16.
Magill's Survey of Cinema. Series I. v4, p1572-74.
Motion Picture Herald Product Digest. May 28, 1975, p99.
The Nation. Nov 1, 1975, v221, p443.
The New Republic. Aug 2, 1975, v173, p22.
The New York Times. Sep 28, 1975, SecII, p13.
The New York Times. Oct 9, 1975, p52.
Newsweek. Aug 4, 1975, v86, p70-71.
Saturday Review. Jun 14, 1975, v2, p49-50.
Time. Sep 8, 1975, v106, p53.
Variety. May 7, 1975, p22.

Smiles of a Summer Night (Swedish title: Sommarnattens Leende) (SWED; Bergman, Ingmar; 1957)
BFI/Monthly Film Bulletin. Nov 1956, v23, p138-39.
Cinema Borealis. p142-48.
Film Daily. Dec 31, 1957, v112, p6.
Films and Filming. Nov 1956, v3, p26.
I Lost it at the Movies. p105-07.
Ingmar Bergman: A Critical Biography. p130-34.
Ingmar Bergman and the Rituals of Art. p118-42.
Ingmar Bergman (Steene). p125-28.
The Nation. Feb 1, 1957, v186, p108.
The New York Times. Dec 24, 1957, p11.
The New Yorker. Jan 11, 1958, v33, p103.
Sight and Sound. Aut 1956, v26, p98.
Swedish Film Classics. p89-92.
Time. Jan 27, 1958, v71, p90.
Variety. May 16, 1956, p6.
Vintage Films. p151-54.

Smithereens (US; Seidelman, Susan; 1982)
The Los Angeles Times. Jan 13, 1983, SevVI, p1.
Magill's Cinema Annual, 1983. p307-10.
Ms. Feb 1983, v11, p103.
The New Republic. Dec 6, 1982, v187, p22-23.
New York. Jan 17, 1983, v16, p80-81.
The New York Times. Nov 19, 1982, SecIII, p10.
Rolling Stone. Apr 28, 1983, p52.
Time. Mar 14, 1983, v121, p90.
Variety. Jun 2, 1982, p10.

Smokey and the Bandit (US; Needham, Hal; 1977)
BFI/Monthly Film Bulletin. Aug 1977, v44, p175.
The Films of Burt Reynolds. p201-05.
Hollywood Reporter. May 18, 1977, p3.
The Los Angeles Times. Jul 29, 1977, SecIV, p9.
Motion Picture Herald Product Digest. May 25, 1977, p98.
The New York Times. May 20, 1977, SecIII, p8.

The New York Times. Dec 18, 1977, SecII, p13.
Time. Jun 20, 1977, v109, p73.
Variety. May 18, 1977, p16.

Smokey and the Bandit II (US; Needham, Hal; 1980)
Car and Driver. Nov 1980, v26, p105-11.
The Films of Burt Reynolds. p234-38.
The Los Angeles Times. Aug 21, 1980, SecVI, p3.
Maclean's. Sep 1, 1980, v93, p56.
Maclean's. Oct 6, 1980, v93, p40.
Motion Picture Herald Product Digest. Sep 3, 1980, p25.
New York. Sep 1, 1980, v13, p46-47.
The New York Times. Aug 15, 1980, SecIII, p11.
The New York Times. Aug 24, 1980, SecII, p17.
Variety. Aug 20, 1980, p20.

Smultronstallet *See* Wild Strawberries

The Sniper (US; Dmytryk, Edward; 1952)
BFI/Monthly Film Bulletin. Mar 1953, v20, p33-34.
Christian Century. Jun 18, 1952, v69, p735.
Commonweal. May 23, 1952, v56, p174.
Film Daily. Mar 19, 1952, p6.
Hollywood Reporter. Mar 14, 1952, p3.
Motion Picture Herald Product Digest. Mar 22, 1952, p1210.
The Nation. May 31, 1952, v174, p533.
The New York Times. May 10, 1952, p16.
A Reference Guide to the American Film Noir. p159-60.
Saturday Review. May 10, 1952, v35, p29.
Theatre Arts. Jun 1952, v36, p95.
Time. May 19, 1952, v59, p108.
Variety. Mar 19, 1952, p6.

The Snows of Kilimanjaro (US; King, Henry; 1952)
BFI/Monthly Film Bulletin. Nov 1952, v19, p155.
Catholic World. Nov 1952, v176, p142-43.
Christian Century. Nov 19, 1952, v69, p1367.
Commonweal. Oct 3, 1952, v56, p360.
Cue. Sep 20, 1952, p16.
Film Daily. Sep 19, 1952, p7.
Films in Review. Oct 1952, v3, p410-12.
The Films of Gregory Peck. p114-17.
The Films of Susan Hayward. p176-78.
Hemingway and Film. p106-34.
Hollywood Reporter. Sep 19, 1952, p3.
Library Journal. Oct 1, 1952, v77, p1605.
Life. Oct 6, 1952, v33, p147.
Magill's Cinema Annual, 1983. p498-503.
Motion Picture Herald Product Digest. Sep 20, 1952, p1533.
National Parent-Teacher. Nov 1952, v47, p38.
Natural History. Nov 1952, v61, p424-25.
The New Statesman and Nation. Nov 29, 1952, v44, p636.
The New York Times. Sep 19, 1952, p19.
The New Yorker. Sep 20, 1952, v28, p119.
Newsweek. Sep 29, 1952, v40, p94.
Saturday Review. Oct 11, 1952, v35, p31.
Selected Film Criticism, 1951-1960. p124-25.
The Spectator. Nov 21, 1952, v189, p670.
Theatre Arts. Nov 1952, v36, p77.
Time. Sep 22, 1952, v60, p102.
Variety. Sep 24, 1952, p6.

Snuff (US; Anonymous; 1976)
Film Bulletin. Feb 1976, v45, p14.
Film Comment. May-Jun 1976, v12, p35.
Independent Film Journal. Mar 17, 1976, v77, p16.
The Los Angeles Times. Mar 19, 1976, SecIV, p16.
New York. Mar 29, 1976, v9, p56-57.

The New York Times. May 7, 1976, SecII, p1.
The New York Times. Mar 10, 1976, p41.
Variety. Apr 7, 1976, p4.
Variety. Feb 25, 1976, p22.
The Village Voice. Apr 12, 1976, p35-36.

So Big (US; Wise, Robert; 1953)
Catholic World. Nov 1953, v178, p140.
Commonweal. Nov 6, 1953, v59, p120.
Film Daily. Oct 6, 1953, p8.
Hollywood Reporter. Sep 30, 1953, p3.
Library Journal. Nov 15, 1953, v78, p2009.
Magill's Survey of Cinema. Series II. v5, p2205.
National Parent-Teacher. Dec 1953, v48, p40.
The New York Times. Oct 22, 1953, p34.
Newsweek. Nov 9, 1953, v42, p99.
Time. Nov 9, 1953, v62, p112.
Variety. Sep 30, 1953, p6.

So Bright the Flame *See* The Girl in White

So Fine (US; Bergman, Andrew; 1981)
BFI/Monthly Film Bulletin. Jan 1982, v49, p9-10.
Film Bulletin. Oct 1981, p46.
Film Journal. Oct 5, 1981, v87, p11.
Maclean's. Nov 16, 1981, v94, p76.
New Statesman. Jan 8, 1982, v103, p22.
New York. Oct 12, 1981, v14, p84.
The New York Times. Sep 25, 1981, SecIII, p8.
The New Yorker. Oct 12, 1981, v57, p162.
Photoplay. Mar 1982, v33, p27.
Rolling Stone. Nov 12, 1981, p44-45.
Variety. Sep 23, 1981, p22.
The Village Voice. Sep 23, 1981, p54-55.

So Long At the Fair (GB; Fisher, Terence; Darnborough, Anthony; 1950)
BFI/Monthly Film Bulletin. Jun 1950, v17, p82.
Film Daily. Jan 19, 1951, p4.
Hollywood Reporter. Jan 18, 1951, p3.
Library Journal. Jun 15, 1950, v75, p1059.
Motion Picture Herald Product Digest. Jan 27, 1951, p690.
The New Republic. Feb 26, 1951, v124, p31.
The New York Times. Jan 22, 1951, p14.
Newsweek. Feb 5, 1951, v37, p80.
Senior Scholastic. Oct 25, 1950, v57, p20.
Variety. Jun 14, 1950, p34.

So This Is Paris (US; Quine, Richard; 1954)
American Magazine. Jan 1955, v159, p10.
BFI/Monthly Film Bulletin. Feb 1955, v22, p21.
Farm Journal. Jan 1955, v79, p70.
Film Daily. Nov 19, 1954, p10.
Films and Filming. Feb 1955, v1, p24.
Hollywood Reporter. Nov 15, 1954, p3.
Motion Picture Herald Product Digest. Nov 20, 1954, p217.
National Parent-Teacher. Dec 1954, v49, p39.
The New York Times. Feb 12, 1955, p11.
Senior Scholastic. Jan 12, 1955, v65, p30.
Sight and Sound. Spr 1955, v24, p200.
Tony Curtis: The Man and His Movies. p52-53.
Variety. Nov 17, 1954, p6.

So Young, So Bad (US; Vorhaus, Bernard; 1950)
BFI/Monthly Film Bulletin. Jan 1951, v18, p207.
Film Daily. Jun 1, 1950, p5.
Hollywood Reporter. Jul 21, 1950, p3.
The London Times. Jan 8, 1951, p2.
Motion Picture Herald Product Digest. Jun 3, 1950, p321.
The New Statesman and Nation. Jan 13, 1951, v41, p38.
The New York Times. Jul 24, 1950, p15.
Newsweek. May 22, 1950, v35, p90.

The Spectator. Jan 5, 1951, v186, p13.
Variety. May 31, 1950, p6.

The Soft Skin (French title: Peau Douce, La) (FR; Truffaut, François; 1964)
BFI/Monthly Film Bulletin. Dec 1964, v31, p172.
Commonweal. Nov 6, 1964, v81, p198.
Esquire. May 1965, v63, p22.
Film Daily. Oct 19, 1964, v125, p12.
Films and Filming. Jan 1965, v11, p32.
Finally Truffaut. p104-12.
François Truffaut: A Guide to References and Resources. p49-51.
François Truffaut (Insdorf). p44-50.
Life. Oct 23, 1964, v57, p15.
Motion Picture Herald Product Digest. Oct 14, 1964, v232, p146.
The Nation. Nov 30, 1964, v199, p420.
The New Republic. Nov 14, 1964, v151, p34.
The New York Times. Oct 13, 1964, p49.
The New Yorker. Oct 24, 1964, v40, p149-50.
Newsweek. Oct 26, 1964, v64, p118.
On Film. p260-62.
On Movies. p380-83.
Private Screenings. p147-49.
Saturday Review. Nov 21, 1964, v34, p34.
Sight and Sound. Aut 1964, v33, p194.
Time. Oct 16, 1964, v84, p115.
Truffaut (Allen). p98-106.
Tynan Right and Left. p200-01.
Variety. May 13, 1964, p6.

Soldier in the Rain (US; Nelson, Ralph; 1963)
Cinema. Feb 1964, v2, p48.
Commonweal. Dec 6, 1963, v79, p313.
Film Daily. Nov 19, 1963, p5.
Filmfacts. Nov 28, 1963, v6, p262-63.
Films and Filming. Sep 1965, v11, p34.
Films in Review. Jan 1964, v15, p52-53.
The Films of Steve McQueen. p80-84.
The New York Times. Nov 28, 1963, p67.
Newsweek. Dec 2, 1963, v62, p102.
Variety. Nov 20, 1963, p6.

Soldier of Orange (Dutch title: Soleaat van oranje) (NETH; Verhoeven, Paul; 1977)
Films in Review. Oct 1979, v30, p502.
Hollywood Reporter. Jun 1, 1979, p3.
The Los Angeles Times. Jun 17, 1979, Calendar, p36.
The New York Times. Aug 16, 1979, SecIII, p13.
The New Yorker. Sep 17, 1979, v55, p132.
Newsweek. Aug 6, 1979, v94, p55.
Time. Sep 17, 1979, v114, p101-02.
Variety. Jan 17, 1979, p21.

A Soldier's Story (US; Jewison, Norman; 1984)
BFI/Monthly Film Bulletin. Mar 1985, v52, p90.
Christianity Today. Oct 5, 1984, v28, p112.
Commonweal. Oct 19, 1984, v111, p558.
Ebony. Dec 1984, v40, p60.
Ebony. Nov 1984, v40, p112.
Essence. Nov 1984, v15, p82-84.
Film Comment. Dec 1984, v20, p17-19.
Film Journal. Oct 1984, v87, p18.
Film Journal. Oct 1984, v87, p6.
Films in Review. Dec 1984, v35, p621-22.
Hollywood Reporter. Aug 31, 1984, p3.
Jet. Oct 22, 1984, v67, p26-29.
The Los Angeles Times. Sep 15, 1984, SecV, p8.
Maclean's. Sep 17, 1984, v97, p75.
Millimeter. Sep 1984, v12, p165-71.
The New Republic. Oct 15, 1984, v191, p24.
New York. Oct 1, 1984, v17, p82.

The New York Times. Dec 16, 1984, SecII, p21.
The New York Times. Sep 14, 1984, SecIII, p10.
The New Yorker. Nov 26, 1984, v60, p117-19.
Newsweek. Sep 10, 1984, v104, p75.
On Location. Jul 1984, v8, p107-08.
Variety. Sep 5, 1984, p12.
The Village Voice. Sep 25, 1984, p63.

Soldiers Three (US; Garnett, Tay; 1951)
Commonweal. May 4, 1951, v54, p91
Film Daily. Mar 15, 1951, p6.
The Films of David Niven. p104-08.
Hollywood Reporter. Mar 13, 1951, p3.
Library Journal. Apr 15, 1951, v76, p720.
Motion Picture Herald Product Digest. Mar 17, 1951, p757.
The New York Times. Mar 30, 1951, p28.
The New Yorker. Apr 7, 1951, v27, p108.
Newsweek. Apr 9, 1951, v37, p85.
Variety. Mar 14, 1951, p6.

Soleaat van oranje *See* Soldier of Orange

Solomon and Sheba (US; Vidor, King; 1959)
America. Jan 23, 1960, v102, p512.
BFI/Monthly Film Bulletin. Oct 1959, v26, p148.
The Fifty Worst Films of All Time. p211-18.
Film Daily. Dec 24, 1959, v116, p8.
Filmfacts. Jan 27, 1960, v2, p336-38.
Films in Review. Feb 1960, v11, p106-07.
The Films of Tyrone Power. p209-13.
Hollywood Reporter. Dec 28, 1959, p3.
The New York Times. Dec 26, 1959, p7.
Newsweek. Jan 11, 1960, v55, p91.
Saturday Review. Jan 16, 1960, v43, p53.
Time. Jan 11, 1960, v75, p64.
Variety. Nov 4, 1959, p6.

Some Came Running (US; Minnelli, Vincente; 1958)
BFI/Monthly Film Bulletin. May 1959, v26, p56.
Commonweal. Jan 23, 1959, v49, p439.
Film Daily. Dec 18, 1598, v114, p6.
Filmfacts. Feb 4, 1959, v2, p1-3.
Films in Review. Feb 1959, v10, p111-12.
The Films of Frank Sinatra. p144-49.
The Films of Shirley MacLaine. p70-76.
The Films of the Fifties. p274-76.
Hollywood Reporter. Dec 17, 1958, p3.
Library Journal. Jan 15, 1959, v84, p184.
Magill's Survey of Cinema. Series II. v4, p2211-13.
The New Republic. Jan 12, 1959, v140, p23.
The New York Times. Jan 23, 1959, p17.
The New Yorker. Jan 31, 1959, v34, p94.
Newsweek. Dec 29, 1958, v52, p65.
Saturday Review. Jan 3, 1959, v42, p24.
Time. Jan 12, 1959, v73, p72.
Variety. Dec 24, 1958, p6.

Some Kind of Hero (US; Pressman, Michael; 1982)
BFI/Monthly Film Bulletin. Jul 1982, v49, p137.
Film Journal. Mar 22, 1982, v85, p15-16.
The Los Angeles Times. Apr 3, 1982, SecVI, p1.
The Nation. Apr 24, 1982, v234, p505-06.
The New Republic. May 5, 1982, v186, p22-23.
New Statesman. Jul 2, 1982, v104, p26.
The New York Times. Apr 2, 1982, SecIII, p14.
Newsweek. Apr 12, 1982, v99, p87.
Photoplay. Aug 1982, v33, p27.
Variety. Mar 31, 1982, p23.
The Village Voice. Apr 13, 1982, p46.

Some Like it Hot (US; Wilder, Billy; 1959)
America. Apr 25, 1959, v101, p257.
BFI/Monthly Film Bulletin. May 1959, v26, p69.

Billy Wilder (Dick). p87-91.
The Bright Side of Billy Wilder, Primarily. p152-57.
Catholic World. May 1959, v89, p156.
Classic Movies. p42-44.
Commonweal. Mar 20, 1959, v69, p652.
Coronet. May 1959, v46, p12.
Cult Movies 2. p143-46.
The Film Career of Billy Wilder. p94-96.
Film Daily. Feb 25, 1959, v115, p8.
Filmfacts. Apr 15, 1959, v2, p51-53.
Films and Filming. Jun 1959, v5, p23-24.
Films in Review. Apr 1959, v10, p240-41.
The Films of Jack Lemmon. p95-100.
The Films of Marilyn Monroe. p141-45.
The Films of the Fifties. p305-14.
Hollywood Reporter. Feb 25, 1959, p3.
The International Dictionary of Films and Filmmakers. v1, p438-39.
Journey Down Sunset Blvd. p214-29.
Library Journal. Apr 1959, v84, p1118.
Life. Apr 20, 1959, v46, p101-03.
Mademoiselle. May 1959, v49, p117.
Magill's Survey of Cinema. Series I. v4, p1578-80.
The New Republic. Mar 30, 1959, v140, p19.
The New Yorker. Apr 4, 1959, v35, p142.
Newsweek. Apr 6, 1959, v53, p113.
On the Verge of Revolt. p137-54.
Reporter. Apr 16, 1959, v20, p35-36.
Saturday Review. Mar 28, 1959, v42, p27.
Sight and Sound. Sum 1959, v28, p173.
Talking Pictures. p141-62.
Talking Pictures. p151-54.
Time. Mar 23, 1959, v73, p95.
Tony Curtis: The Man and His Movies. p78-80.
Variety. Feb 25, 1959, p6.

Somebody Loves Me (US; Brecher, Irving; 1952)
BFI/Monthly Film Bulletin. Jan 1953, v20, p11.
Catholic World. Oct 1952, v176, p64.
Christian Century. Oct 22, 1952, v69, p1239.
Film Daily. Aug 22, 1952, p6.
Hollywood Reporter. Aug 20, 1952, p3.
McCall's. Nov 1952, v80, p6.
Motion Picture Herald Product Digest. Aug 23, 1952, p1501-02.
National Parent-Teacher. Nov 1952, v47, p38.
The New York Times. Sep 25, 1952, p38.
The New Yorker. Oct 4, 1952, v28, p75.
Newsweek. Oct 6, 1952, v40, p115.
Saturday Review. Sep 27, 1952, v35, p27.
Time. Sep 29, 1952, v60, p90.
Variety. Aug 20, 1952, p6.

Somebody Up There Likes Me (US; Wise, Robert; 1956)
America. Nov 17, 1956, v96, p212.
BFI/Monthly Film Bulletin. Dec 1956, v23, p151.
Commonweal. Nov 2, 1956, v65, p129.
Film Culture. 1956, v2, p28-30.
Film Daily. Jul 3, 1956, p6.
Films and Filming. Dec 1956, v3, p24.
Films in Review. Aug-Sep 1956, v7, p344-45.
The Films of Paul Newman. p43-47.
The Films of Steve McQueen. p20-23.
Hollywood Reporter. Jul 3, 1956, p3.
Magill's Survey of Cinema. Series II. v5, p2214-17.
The Nation. Nov 24, 1956, v183, p467.
The New York Times. Jul 6, 1956, p16.
The New York Times. Jul 15, 1956, SecII, p1.
The New Yorker. Nov 3, 1956, v32, p174.
Newsweek. Oct 8, 1956, v48, p90.
Saturday Review. Aug 4, 1956, v39, p6.
Saturday Review. Sep 29, 1956, v39, p22.

Time. Nov 12, 1956, v68, p120.
Variety. Jul 4, 1956, p6.

Someone Is Killing the Great Chefs of Europe *See* Who Is Killing the Great Chefs of Europe?

Something For the Birds (US; Wise, Robert; 1952)
BFI/Monthly Film Bulletin. Jan 1953, v20, p11-12.
Film Daily. Oct 9, 1952, p6.
Hollywood Reporter. Oct 8, 1952, p4.
Motion Picture Herald Product Digest. Oct 11, 1952, p1558-59.
National Parent-Teacher. Nov 1952, v47, p38.
Natural History. Nov 1952, v61, p426.
The New York Times. Nov 15, 1952, p15.
Newsweek. Nov 17, 1952, v40, p115.
Saturday Review. Nov 1, 1952, v35, p27.
Variety. Oct 8, 1952, p12.

Something Money Can't Buy (GB; Jackson, Pat; 1952)
BFI/Monthly Film Bulletin. Sep 1952, v19, p124.
Film Daily. Oct 16, 1953, p6.
The London Times. Jul 14, 1952, p3.
Motion Picture Herald Product Digest. Oct 3, 1953, p2015.
National Parent-Teacher. Sep 1953, v48, p39.
The New Statesman and Nation. Jul 19, 1952, v44, p70.
The New York Times. Oct 1, 1953, p34.
The Spectator. Jul 11, 1952, v188, p65.
The Tatler. Jul 23, 1952, v205, p158.
Variety. Jul 16, 1952, p20.

Something of Value (US; Brooks, Richard; 1957)
America. May 25, 1957, v97, p270.
BFI/Monthly Film Bulletin. Aug 1957, v24, p98-99.
Commonweal. May 31, 1957, v66, p232.
Film Daily. Apr 30, 1957, v111, p14.
Films and Filming. Jul 1957, v3, p24-25.
Films in Review. Aug-Sep 1957, v8, p350.
The Films of Sidney Poitier. p67-71.
Hollywood Reporter. Apr 29, 1957, p3.
Motion Picture Herald Product Digest. May 4, 1957, v207, p361.
The Nation. Jun 1, 1957, v184, p486.
The New Republic. Oct 21, 1957, v137, p21.
The New York Times. May 11, 1957, p24.
The New Yorker. May 18, 1957, v33, p146.
Newsweek. May 13, 1957, v49, p115.
Saturday Review. May 18, 1957, v40, p36.
Time. May 20, 1957, v69, p124.
Variety. May 1, 1957, p6.

Something to Live For (US; Stevens, George; 1952)
BFI/Monthly Film Bulletin. Mar 1952, v19, p33.
Catholic World. Mar 1952, v174, p458.
Christian Century. Jul 30, 1952, v69, p887.
Commonweal. Mar 28, 1952, v55, p616.
Film Daily. Jan 30, 1952, p7.
Hollywood Reporter. Jan 28, 1952, p3.
The London Times. Jan 14, 1952, p8.
Motion Picture Herald Product Digest. Feb 2, 1952, p1221.
The New York Times. Mar 8, 1952, p11.
The New Yorker. Mar 15, 1952, v28, p101.
Newsweek. Mar 17, 1952, v39, p99.
Theatre Arts. Apr 1952, v36, p42.
Time. Mar 24, 1952, v59, p100.
Variety. Jan 30, 1952, p6.

Something Wicked This Way Comes (US; Clayton, Jack; 1983)
Christianity Today. May 20, 1983, v27, p48-49.
Christianity Today. May 30, 1983, v27, p71.
Hollywood Reporter. May 3, 1983, p5.
Horizon. Sep 1983, v26, p14.
Maclean's. May 9, 1983, v96, p66.

Sometimes a Great Notion (Also titled: Never Give an Inch) (US; Newman, Paul; 1971)
BFI/Monthly Film Bulletin. Jun 1972, v39, p119.
Film Quarterly. Spr 1972, v25, p59-60.
Films and Filming. Jun 1972, v18, n9, p50-51.
Films in Review. May 1972, v23, n5, p313.
The Films of Henry Fonda. p222-24.
The Films of Paul Newman. p192-97.
Hollywood Reporter. Nov 15, 1971, v218, n39, p3.
Magill's Survey of Cinema. Series II. v5, p2217-19.
The New York Times. Mar 2, 1972, p34.
Newsweek. Jan 31, 1972, v79, p84.
Time. Dec 13, 1971, v98, p60.
Variety. Nov 17, 1971, p14.

Somewhere in Time (US; Szwarc, Jeannot; 1980)
Hollywood Reporter. Sep 19, 1980, p3.
The Los Angeles Times. Oct 3, 1980, SecVI, p1.
Motion Picture Herald Product Digest. Oct 22, 1980, p38.
The New York Times. Oct 3, 1980, SecIII, p14.
Newsweek. Oct 20, 1980, v96, p86.
Senior Scholastic. Nov 28, 1980, v113, p20.
Variety. Sep 24, 1980, p18.

Sommardansen *See* One Summer of Happiness

Sommarlek *See* Illicit Interlude

Sommarnattens Leende *See* Smiles of a Summer Night

Son of Ali Baba (US; Neumann, Kurt; 1952)
BFI/Monthly Film Bulletin. Oct 1952, v19, p145.
Film Daily. Aug 19, 1952, p7.
Hollywood Reporter. Aug 13, 1952, p3.
Motion Picture Herald Product Digest. Aug 23, 1952, p1502.
National Parent-Teacher. Oct 1952, v47, p37.
The New York Times. Aug 16, 1952, p7.
Tony Curtis: The Man and His Movies. p34-35.
Variety. Aug 13, 1952, p6.

Son of Flubber (US; Stevenson, Robert; 1963)
America. Mar 2, 1963, v108, p316.
BFI/Monthly Film Bulletin. Apr 1963, v30, p50.
Commonweal. Feb 15, 1963, v77, p541.
Film Daily. Jan 10, 1963, p10.
Filmfacts. Feb 28, 1963, v6, p17-18.
Films and Filming. Mar 1963,, v9, p38-39.
Hollywood Reporter. Jan 9, 1963, v173, p3.
The New York Times. Feb 9, 1963, p5.
Newsweek. Jan 21, 1963, v61, p91.
Photoplay. Mar 1963, v63, p8.
Time. Feb 15, 1963, v81, pM21.
Variety. Jan 16, 1963, p6.

Son of Pale Face (US; Tashlin, Frank; 1952)
BFI/Monthly Film Bulletin. Sep 1952, v19, p130.
Film Daily. Jul 14, 1952, p4.
Hollywood Reporter. Jul 14, 1952, p3.
The London Times. Aug 4, 1952, p9.

Motion Picture Herald Product Digest. Jul 19, 1952, p1453.
National Parent-Teacher. Sep 1952, v47, p37.
The New York Times. Oct 2, 1952, p32.
The New Yorker. Oct 11, 1952, v28, p127.
Newsweek. Sep 15, 1952, v40, p102.
Saturday Review. Aug 9, 1952, v35, p36.
The Spectator. Aug 1, 1952, v189, p160.
Talking Pictures. p79-80.
The Tatler. Aug 13, 1952, v205, p290.
Time. Aug 18, 1952, v60, p84.
Variety. Jul 16, 1952, p6.

Sons & Lovers (GB; Cardiff, Jack; 1960)
America. Aug 13, 1960, v103, p542.
BFI/Monthly Film Bulletin. Jul 1960, v27, p94.
Commonweal. Sep 9, 1960, v72, p469.
The English Novel and the Movies. p235-47.
Film Daily. Jul 1, 1960, p6.
Film Quarterly. Fall 1960, v14, p41-42.
Filmfacts. 1960, v3, p179.
Films in Review. Aug-Sep 1960, v11, p422-24.
Hollywood Reporter. Jun 30, 1960, p3.
Life. Aug 22, 1960, v49, p43-44.
Magill's Survey of Cinema. Series II. v5, p2221-24.
The New Republic. Aug 29, 1960, v143, p21.
The New York Times. Aug 3, 1960, p35.
The New York Times. Aug 14, 1960, SecII, p1.
The New Yorker. Aug 13, 1960, v36, p56.
Newsweek. Aug 1, 1960, v56, p80.
Saturday Review. Aug 6, 1960, v43, p28.
Sight and Sound. Sum 1960, v29, p145.
Time. Aug 1, 1960, v76, p58.
Variety. May 25, 1960, p6.
A World on Film. p97-99.

The Sons of Katie Elder (US; Hathaway, Henry; 1965)
America. Sep 18, 1965, v113, p296-97.
BFI/Monthly Film Bulletin. Nov 1965, v32, p165.
Christian Science Monitor (Western edition). Aug 17, 1965, p6.
Classic Movies. p56-59.
The Complete Films of John Wayne. p259-61.
Confessions of a Cultist. p208.
Film Daily. Jul 1, 1965, p14.
Films and Filming. Dec 1965, v12, p25.
The Great Western Pictures. p332-34.
Hollywood Reporter. Jun 25, 1965, p3.
The London Times. Oct 28, 1965, p8.
Motion Picture Herald Product Digest. Jul 7, 1965, p322-23.
The New York Times. Aug 26, 1965, p40.
Newsweek. Sep 6, 1965, v66, p70B.
Saturday Review. Sep 4, 1965, v48, p44.
Time. Sep 3, 1965, v86, p84.
Variety. Jun 30, 1965, p6.
The Village Voice. Sep 9, 1965, v10, p15.

Sophie's Choice (US; Pakula, Alan J.; 1982)
America. Jan 1, 1983, v148, p15.
American Cinematographer. Apr 1983, v64, p57.
BFI/Monthly FIlm Bulletin. Apr 1983, v50, p103-4.
Contemporary Review. May 1983, v242, p269-71.
Film Journal. Dec 27, 1982, v85, p12-13.
Films In Review. Jan 1983, v34, p49-50.
Hollywood Reporter. Dec 3, 1982, p3.
The Los Angeles Times. Dec 10, 1982, SecVI, p1.
Maclean's. Dec 13, 1982, v95, p61.
Magill's Cinema Annual, 1983. p311-15.
The Nation. Jan 1, 1983, v236, p26.
The New Republic. Jan 10, 1983, v188, p40-42.
New Statesman. Apr 15, 1983, v105, p30-31.

New York. Dec 20, 1982, v15, p64.
The New York Times. Dec 10, 1982, SecIII, p12.
The New York Times. Dec 31, 1982, SecIII, p1.
The New York Times. May 9, 1982, SecII, p1.
The New Yorker. Dec 27, 1982, v58, p74-75.
Newsweek. Dec 20, 1982, v100, p87.
Psychology Today. Jan 1983, v17, p27.
Time. Dec 13, 1982, v120, p79.
Variety. Dec 7, 1982, p3.
The Village Voice. Dec 21, 1982, p71-72.

Sorcerer (Also titled: The Wages of Fear) (US; Friedkin, William; 1977)
BFI/Monthly Film Bulletin. Mar 1978, v45, p56.
Films and Filming. Aug 1977, v23, p34-35.
Films in Review. Oct 1977, v28, p500.
Hollywood Reporter. Jun 24, 1977, p3.
The Los Angeles Times. Jun 24, 1977, SecIV, p1.
Motion Picture Herald Product Digest. Jul 20, 1977, p16.
The New Republic. Jul 30, 1977, v177, p24-25.
New York. Aug 1, 1977, v10, p65-67.
The New York Times. Jun 25, 1977, p11.
The New York Times. Jul 10, 1977, SecII, p11.
The New Yorker. Jul 18, 1977, v53, p70-71.
Newsweek. Jul 4, 1977, v90, p77.
Time. Jul 11, 1977, v110, p55.
Variety. Jul 4, 1977, p26.
The Village Voice. Jul 18, 1977, p37.

The Sorrow and the Pity (French title: Chagrin et la Pitie, Le) (FR; Ophuls, Marcel; 1972)
Cineaste. Wint 1971-72, v1, p15-18.
The Film Book Bibliography. n4331, p447.
Film Quarterly. Sum 1972, v25, p56-59.
Film Society Review. Nov 1971, v7, p26-28.
Filmfacts. 1972, v15, n8, p165.
Films in Review. Apr 1972, v23, n4, p248.
Landmark Films. p338-49.
The New York Times. May 11, 1971, v46, p1.
Reruns. p228-32.
Variety. Jun 16, 1971, p22.

Sosia, Il *See* Partner

Souffle au Coeur, Le *See* Murmur of the Heart

The Sound Barrier *See* Breaking Through the Sound Barrier

The Sound of Fury (US; Enfield, Cy; 1950)
BFI/Monthly Film Bulletin. Jul 1951, v18, p294.
Commonweal. Apr 13, 1951, v54, p13.
Film Daily. Dec 6, 1950, p6.
Films in Review. Mar 1951, v2, p38.
Library Journal. Nov 15, 1950, v75, p2021.
The London Times. Jul 30, 1951, p2.
Motion Picture Herald Product Digest. Dec 9, 1950, p605.
The Nation. Feb 24, 1951, v172, p188-89.
Newsweek. Feb 12, 1951, v37, p80.
Saturday Review. Feb 3, 1951, v34, p25.
Sight and Sound. Aug-Sep 1951, v21, p23, 28.
Time. Jan 22, 1951, v57, p94.
Variety. Dec 6, 1950, p15.

The Sound of Music (Also titled: Mélodie du Bonheur, La) (US; Wise, Robert; 1965)
America. Mar 13, 1965, v112, p374-75.
American Cinematographer. Apr 1965, v46, p222-25.
BFI/Monthly Film Bulletin. May 1965, v32, p72-73.
Cahiers du Cinema in English. 1966, n4, p62.

Christian Science Monitor (Western edition). Mar 20, 1965, p4.
Christian Science Monitor (Western edition). Mar 31, 1965, pE5.
Commonweal. Mar 26, 1965, v82, p24.
Esquire. Aug 1966, v66, p20-21.
Film Daily. Mar 3, 1965, p3, 6.
Film Quarterly. Wint 1966-67, v20, p63.
Filmfacts. Apr 16, 1965, v8, p51-54.
Films and Filming. May 1965, v11, p25-26.
Films and Filming. Mar 1965, v11, p24-25.
Films and Filming. Jul 1976, v22, p40-41.
Films in Review. Mar 1965, v16, p176-77.
The Films of the Sixties. p148-49.
Hollywood Reporter. Mar 1, 1965, p3.
Kiss Kiss Bang Bang. p214-17.
Life. Mar 12, 1965, v58, p52.
The London Times. Jan 10, 1967, p10.
The London Times. Mar 25, 1965, p16.
Motion Picture Herald Product Digest. Mar 17, 1965, p14, 18.
Motion Picture Herald Product Digest. Apr 14, 1965, p268.
Movie. Wint 1976-77, n23, p39-49.
The Musical From Broadway to Hollywood. p107-12.
The New Republic. Mar 20, 1965, v152, p26.
New Statesman. Apr 16, 1965, v69, p622.
The New York Times. Mar 3, 1965, p34.
The New York Times Magazine. Nov 20, 1966, p45-47.
The New Yorker. Mar 6, 1965, v41, p96.
Newsweek. Mar 15, 1965, v65, p100.
Playboy. May 1965, v12, p30, 32.
The Private Eye, the Cowboy and the Very Naked Girl. p120-23.
Saturday Review. Mar 20, 1965, v48, p36.
Senior Scholastic. Mar 25, 1965, v86, p23.
Time. Mar 5, 1965, v85, p98.
Time. Oct 5, 1983, v122, p91.
Tynan Right and Left. p221-22.
Variety. Mar 3, 1965, p6.
Vogue. May 1965, v145, p143.

Sound of Trumpets *See* Posto, Il

Sound Off (US; Quine, Richard; 1952)
BFI/Monthly Film Bulletin. Sep 1952, v19, p130-31.
Christian Century. May 21, 1952, v69, p631.
Film Daily. Apr 11, 1952, p11.
Hollywood Reporter. Apr 3, 1952, p3.
Motion Picture Herald Product Digest. Apr 12, 1952, p1313-14.
Variety. Apr 9, 1952, p6.

Sounder (US; Ritt, Martin; 1972)
Black Films and Film-Makers. p106-08.
Children's Novels and the Movies. p214-26.
Christian Century. Apr 11, 1973, v90, p434-36.
Commonweal. Apr 20, 1973, v98, p163.
Ebony. Oct 1972, v27, p82-84.
Film Quarterly. Spr 1973, v26, p61-64.
Filmfacts. 1972, v15, n13, p285.
Films in Review. Oct 1972, v23, n8.
Holiday. Nov 1972, v52, p12.
Hollywood Reporter. Aug 15, 1972, p3.
Life. Oct 20, 1972, v73, p18.
Magill's Survey of Cinema. Series II. v5, p2228.
The Nation. Oct 16, 1972, v215, p350.
The New York Times. Sep 5, 1972, p49.
The New York Times. Nov 12, 1972, SecII, p1.
The New York Times. Oct 15, SecII, p5.
The New Yorker. Sep 30, 1972, v48, p109-11.
Newsweek. Oct 2, 1972, v80, p97.
Reeling. p21-25.
Saturday Review. Sep 16, 1973, v55, p101.
Senior Scholastic. Nov 6, 1972, v101, p22.
Time. Oct 9, 1972, v100, p57.

Variety. Aug 16, 1972, p15.
Vogue. Dec 1972, v160, p116-17.

South Pacific (US; Logan, Joshua; 1958)
America. Apr 5, 1958, v119, p27.
BFI/Monthly Film Bulletin. Jun 1958, v25, p73.
Catholic World. May 1958, v187, p144.
Commonweal. Apr 11, 1958, v68, p49-50.
Dance Magazine. May 1958, v32, p22.
Film Daily. Mar 20, 1958, v108, p8.
Filmfacts. Apr 23, 1958, v1, p47-48.
Films and Filming. Jun 1958, v4, p24-25.
Films in Review. Apr 1958, v9, p202-04.
Good Housekeeping. May 1958, v144, p22.
Hollywood Reporter. Mar 20, 1958, p3.
Library Journal. Apr 15, 1958, v83, p1180.
Life. Mar 24, 1958, v44, p82-85.
Magill's Survey of Cinema. Series I. v4, p1589-93.
The New York Times. Mar 20, 1958, p33.
The New York Times Magazine. Sep 1, 1957, p20-21.
The New Yorker. Mar 29, 1958, v34, p105.
Newsweek. Mar 31, 1958, v51, p96.
Saturday Review. Apr 5, 1958, v41, p35.
Sight and Sound. Sum 1958, v27, p250-51.
Time. Mar 31, 1958, v71, p85-86.
Variety. Mar 26, 1958, p6.

Southern Comfort (US; Hill, Walter; 1981)
Christian Century. Dec 16, 1981, v98, p1322.
Esquire. Nov 1981, v96, p116-20.
Hollywood Reporter. Sep 25, 1981, p3.
The Los Angeles Times. Sep 26, 1981, SecII, p3.
Magill's Cinema Annual, 1982. p332-35.
The New York Times. Sep 25, 1981, SecIII, p20.
The New Yorker. Nov 23, 1981, v57, p176-78.
Newsweek. Oct 5, 1981, v98, p78.
Rolling Stone. Oct 29, 1981, p33-34.
Variety. Sep 25, 1981, p3.

Southwest to Sonora *See* The Appaloosa

Souvenirs Perdus (Also titled: Lost Property) (FR; Christian-Jacque; 1950)
BFI/Monthly Film Bulletin. Jan 1953, v20, p6-7.
The New Statesman and Nation. Nov 29, 1952, v44, p635-36.
Sight and Sound. Jan-Mar 1953, v22, p130-31.
The Spectator. Nov 28, 1952, v189, p731.
The Tatler. Dec 10, 1952, v206, p606.
Variety. Jan 10, 1951, p13.

The Spanish Gardener (GB; Leacock, Philip; 1957)
America. Sep 21 1957, v97, p660.
BFI/Monthly Film Bulletin. Jan 1957, v24, p4.
Commonweal. Sep 20, 1957, v66, p614.
Film Daily. Sep 25, 1957, v112, p8.
Films and Filming. Jan 1957, v3, p26.
The Films of Dirk Bogarde. p88-90.
Hollywood Reporter. Aug 13, 1957, p3.
The New York Times. Sep 9, 1957, p21.
The New Yorker. Sep 21, 1957, v33, p77.
Saturday Review. Sep 14, 1957, v40, p30.
Sight and Sound. Wint 1956-57, v26, p155.
Variety. Jan 2, 1957, p6.

Spara Forte, Pui Forte . . . Non Capisco *See* Shoot Loud, Louder . . . I Don't Understand

Sparkle (US; O'Steen, Sam; 1976)
Film Bulletin. Mar 1976, v43, p35.
Films in Review. May 1976, v27, p315.
Independent Film Journal. Mar 31, 1976, v77, p23-24.
The Los Angeles Times. May 21, 1976, SecIV, p10.
Motion Picture Herald Product Digest. Apr 7, 1976, p88.

The New York Times. Apr 11, 1976, SecII, p15.
The New York Times. Apr 8, 1976, p43.
The New Yorker. Sep 27, 1976, v52, p125-27.
Time. May 17, 1976, v107, p72.
Variety. Apr 7, 1976, p26.
When the Lights Go Down. p165-66.

Spartacus (US; Kubrick, Stanley; 1960)
America. Nov 12, 1960, v104, p230.
BFI/Monthly Film Bulletin. Jan 1961, v28, p6.
The Cinema of Stanley Kubrick. p69-80.
Commonweal. Oct 28, 1960, v73, p124.
Esquire. Mar 1961, v55, p24.
Film Daily. Oct 7, 1960, p7.
Film Quarterly. Fall 1960, v14, p61-62.
Filmfacts. 1960, v3, p241.
Films and Filming. Jan 1961, v7, p32-33.
Films in Review. Nov 1960, v11, p553-54.
The Films of Kirk Douglas. p167-72.
The Films of Laurence Olivier. p130-32.
The Films of Stanley Kubrick. p17-26.
The Films of the Sixties. p39-41.
Hollywood Reporter. Oct 7, 1960, p3.
Kubrick (Ciment). p100-10.
Laurence Olivier: Theater & Cinema. p149-52.
Life. Oct 24, 1960, v49, p74-79.
Look. Nov 22, 1960, v24, p85-88.
Magill's Survey of Cinema. Series II. v5, p2231-34.
McCall's. Jan 1961, v88, p8.
The New Republic. Nov 14, 1960, v143, p19-20.
The New York Times. Oct 7, 1960, p28.
The New York Times. Oct 9, 1960, SecII, p1.
The New Yorker. Oct 15, 1960, v36, p133.
Newsweek. Oct 17, 1960, v56, p117.
Redbook. Jan 1961, v116, p11.
Saturday Review. Oct 1, 1960, v43, p32.
Sight and Sound. Wint 1960-61, v30, p38.
Spartacus. 1960.
Stanley Kubrick: A Film Odyssey. p63-79.
Stanley Kubrick: A Guide to References and Resources. p38-39.
Stanley Kubrick Directs. p54.
Time. Oct 24, 1960, v76, p102.
Tony Curtis: The Man and His Movies. p86.
Variety. Oct 12, 1960, p6.
A World on Film. p23-24.

A Special Day (Italian title: Giornata particolare, Una) (IT, CAN; Scola, Ettore; 1977)
BFI/Monthly Film Bulletin. Apr 1978, v45, p89.
Films in Review. Nov 1977, v28, p566.
Hollywood Reporter. Sep 28, 1977, p4.
The Los Angeles Times. Nov 2, 1977, SecIV, p1.
Maclean's. Jan 9, 1978, v91, p59.
Magill's Survey of Cinema. Foreign Language Films. v6, p2847-51.
Motion Picture Herald Product Digest. Oct 5, 1977, p36.
The New Republic. Oct 7, 1977, v177, p26-27.
New Times. Oct 14, 1977, v9, p82-83.
New York. Oct 3, 1977, v10, p71-72.
The New York Times. Sep 26, 1977, p41.
The New York Times. Oct 2, 1977, SecII, p15.
The New Yorker. Oct 17, 1977, v53, p173-74.
Time. Oct 3, 1977, v110, p96.
Variety. May 18, 1977, p20.

Special Edition: Close Encounters of a Third Kind *See* Close Encounters of a Third Kind

Special Priority Trains *See* Closely Watched Trains

Special Section (French title: Section Speciale) (FR; Costa-Gavras, Constantin; 1975)

Christian Century. Jul 9, 1975, v92, p665.
Films in Review. Jan 1976, v27, p56.
Hollywood Reporter. Dec 2, 1975, p18.
The Los Angeles Times. Dec 24, 1975, SecII, p4.
Motion Picture Herald Product Digest. Dec 10, 1975, p50.
The Nation. Dec 27, 1975, v221, p701.
The New Republic. Dec 27, 1975, v173, p24-25.
The New York Times. Dec 8, 1975, p42.
Newsweek. Dec 15, 1975, v86, p93.
Saturday Review. Nov 29, 1975, v3, p37.
Time. Dec 8, 1975, v106, p72.
Variety. May 14, 1975, p27.
Vogue. Nov 1975, v165, p66.
When the Lights Go Down. p96-98.

Speedway (US; Taurog, Norman; 1968)
BFI/Monthly Film Bulletin. Aug 1968, v35, p121.
Film Daily. May 28, 1968, p4.
Filmfacts. Oct 15, 1968, v11, p288-89.
Films and Filming. Sep 1968, v14, p40.
The Films of Elvis Presley. p192-96.
Hollywood Reporter. May 17, 1968, p3.
Motion Picture Herald Product Digest. Jul 3, 1968, p828.
The New York Times. Jun 14, 1968, p43.
A Year In the Dark. p172-73.

Spencer's Mountain (US; Daves, Delmer; 1963)
America. May 25, 1963, v108, p784-86.
BFI/Monthly Film Bulletin. Aug 1963, v30, p121.
Commonweal. Jun 14, 1963, v78, p328.
Film Daily. Feb 21, 1963, p6.
Filmfacts. May 23, 1963, v6, p888-89.
Films and Filming. Aug 1963, v9, p24-25.
Films in Review. May 1963, v16, p309-10.
The Films of Henry Fonda. p171-73.
The Fondas (Springer). p190-92.
Hollywood Reporter. Feb 19, 1963, v174, p3.
The New York Times. May 17, 1963, p26.
The New York Times. May 26, 1963, SecII, p1.
Newsweek. May 27, 1963, v61, p104.
Photoplay. Aug 1963, v64, p14.
Time. May 24, 1963, v81, p98.
Variety. Feb 27, 1963, p6.

The Spider's Stratagem (Also titled: Strategia del Rango) (IT; Bertolucci, Bernardo; 1970)
Bernardo Bertolucci (Kolker). p105-25.
Film Quarterly. Sum 1977, v25, p10-18.
Filmfacts. 1973, v16, p89.
Films in Review. Oct 1973, v24, p498.
Magill's Survey of Cinema. Foreign Language Films. v6, p2852-57.
National Review. Dec 15, 1970, v22, p1362.
The New York Times. Sep 18, 1970, p32.
The New York Times. Jan 6, 1973, p21.
Newsweek. Jan 15, 1973, v81, p66.
Time. Jan 29, 1973, v101, p88.
Variety. Sep 2, 1970, p40.
Vogue. Nov 15, 1970, v156, p74.

Spinout (Also titled: California Holiday) (US; Taurog, Norman; 1966)
BFI/Monthly Film Bulletin. Nov 1966, v33, p168.
Film Daily. Oct 20, 1966, p7.
Filmfacts. Jan 15, 1967, v9, p349-50.
The Films and Career of Elvis Presley. p174-76.
Films and Filming. Dec 1966, v13, p53.
Hollywood Reporter. Oct 14, 1966, p3.
Motion Picture Herald Product Digest. Oct 26, 1966, p623.
The New York Times. Dec 15, 1966, p60.

Time. Nov 11, 1966, v88, p108.
Variety. Oct 19, 1966, p20.

The Spiral Road (US; Mulligan, Robert; 1962)
America. Aug 11, 1962, v107, p601.
BFI/Monthly Film Bulletin. Sep 1962, v29, p129.
Film Daily. May 28, 1962, p4.
Filmfacts. Aug 31, 1962, v5, p187-88.
Films and Filming. Sep 1962, v8, p34.
Films in Review. Aug-Sep 1962, v13, p425.
Hollywood Reporter. May 28, 1962, p3.
Motion Picture Herald Product Digest. Jun 6, 1962, p580.
Movie. Sep 1962, n2, p35.
The New York Times. Aug 4, 1962, p11.
Newsweek. Aug 13, 1962, v60, p82.
Time. Aug 10, 1962, v80, p68.
Variety. May 30, 1962, p6.

The Spirit of St. Louis (US; Wilder, Billy; 1957)
America. Mar 2, 1957, v96, p630.
BFI/Monthly Film Bulletin. Jul 1957, v24, p85.
Billy Wilder (Dick). p127-30.
Commonweal. Mar 8, 1957, v65, p591.
The Film Career of Billy Wilder. p88-89.
Film Daily. Feb 20, 1957, v111, p8.
Films and Filming. Jun 1957, v3, p24.
Films in Review. Mar 1957, v8, p126-28.
The Films of James Stewart. p186-88.
Hollywood Reporter. Feb 20, 1957, p3.
Motion Picture Herald Product Digest. Mar 2, 1957, v206, p283.
The Nation. Mar 23, 1957, v184, p263.
The New York Times. Feb 22, 1957, p25.
The New York Times. Feb 24, 1957, SecII, p1.
The New York Times Magazine. Feb 10, 1957, p40.
The New Yorker. Mar 2, 1957, v33, p88.
Newsweek. Feb 25, 1957, v49, p118.
Saturday Review. Mar 9, 1957, v40, p27.
Sight and Sound. Sum 1957, v27, p38-39.
Time. Mar 4, 1957, v69, p98.
Variety. Dec 20, 1957, p6.

Splash (US; Howard, Ron; 1984)
American Cinematographer. Mar 1984, v65, p54-60.
BFI/Monthly Film Bulletin. Jun 1984, v51, p183-84.
Cinefantastique. 1984, v144, n4, p106.
Commonweal. May 4, 1984, v111, p279-80.
Esquire. Mar 1984, v101, p228-29.
Film Comment. May-Jun 1984, v20, p40-42.
Film Journal. Apr 1984, v87, p39.
Films and Filming. Jun 1984, n357, p36-37.
Films in Review. Apr 1984, v35, p240-41.
The Los Angeles Times. Mar 9, 1984, SecVI, p1.
Maclean's. Mar 19, 1984, v97, p66.
National Review. May 4, 1984, v36, p54-56.
The New Leader. Mar 5, 1984, v67, p21.
The New Republic. Apr 9, 1984, v190, p24.
New Statesman. Jun 29, 1984, v107, p28.
New York. Mar 12, 1984, v17, p90-91.
The New York Times. Mar 9, 1984, SecIII, p15.
The New Yorker. Mar 19, 1984, v60, p123-24.
Newsweek. Mar 12, 1984, v103, p89.
Photoplay. Aug 1984, v35, p22-23.
Photoplay. Aug 1984, v35, p30-31.
Time. Mar 19, 1984, v123, p91.
Variety. Feb 29, 1984, p14.
The Village Voice. Mar 13, 1984, p48-49.

Splendor in the Grass (US; Kazan, Elia; 1961)
America. Oct 14, 1961, v106, p60.
American Odyssey. p333-34.

BFI/Monthly Film Bulletin. Feb 1962, v29, p21-22.
Commonweal. Oct 27, 1961, v75, p121.
Esquire. Dec 1961, v56, p66.
Film Daily. Aug 30, 1961, p6.
Filmfacts. Oct 27, 1961, v4, p239-41.
Films in Review. Nov 1961, v7, p555-56.
The Films of the Sixties. p68-70.
The Films of Warren Beatty. p68-77.
Kazan on Kazan. p120-144.
Magill's Survey of Cinema. Series II. v5, p2238-41.
The Nation. Nov 4, 1961, v193, p363.
The New Republic. Oct 16, 1961, v145, p21.
The New York Times. Oct 11, 1961, p53.
The New York Times. May 22, 1960, SecII, p7.
The New York Times. Apr 30, 1961, SecVI, p49.
The New York Times. Oct 8, 1961, SecII, p9.
The New York Times. Oct 15, 1961, SecII, p1.
The New Yorker. Oct 14, 1961, v37, p177-78.
Newsweek. Oct 16, 1961, v58, p112.
Reporter. Nov 23, 1961, v25, p43-44.
Saturday Review. Sep 16, 1961, v44, p36.
Time. Oct 13, 1961, v78, p95.
Variety. Aug 30, 1961, p6.

Split Image (US; Kotcheff, Ted; 1982)
Hollywood Reporter. Oct 1, 1982, p3.
The Los Angeles Times. Oct 4, 1982, VI, p1.
Magill's Cinema Annual, 1983. p317-20.
National Review. Dec 10, 1982, v34, p1562.
New York. Nov 15, 1982, v15, p108.
The New York Times. Oct 4, 1982, VI, p1.
Newsweek. Oct 25, 1982, v100, p119.
Variety. Oct 1, 1982, p3.

The Sporting Club (US; Peerce, Larry; 1971)
Deeper into Movies. p259-65.
Filmfacts. 1971, v14, p407-10.
Hollywood Reporter. Mar 1, 1971, v215, n9, p3.
The New York Times. Mar 1, 1971, p22.
The New York Times. Mar 21, 1971, SecII, p16.
The New Yorker. Mar 13, 1971, v47, p89-90.
Saturday Review. Mar 13, 1971, v54, p80.
The Village Voice. Mar 25, 1971, p63.

Springfield Rifle (US; De Toth, Andre; 1952)
BFI/Monthly Film Bulletin. Mar 1953, v20, p38.
Christian Century. Nov 12, 1952, v69, p1335.
Film Daily. Sep 29, 1952, p6.
The Films of Gary Cooper. p238-40.
Hollywood Reporter. Sep 25, 1952, p3.
The London Times. Feb 16, 1953, p10.
Motion Picture Herald Product Digest. Oct 4, 1952, p1549.
National Parent-Teacher. Mar 1954, v48, p40.
The New York Times. Oct 23, 1952, p40.
The New Yorker. Nov 1, 1952, v28, p81.
Newsweek. Oct 27, 1952, v40, p114.
Senior Scholastic. Oct 22, 1952, v61, p47.
The Spectator. Feb 13, 1953, v190, p181.
Time. Nov 3, 1952, v60, p100.
Variety. Oct 1, 1952, p6.

The Spy Who Came In From the Cold (GB; Ritt, Martin; 1965)
America. Jan 15, 1966, v114, p94.
BFI/Monthly Film Bulletin. Feb 1966, v33, p19-20.
Cinema. Mar 1966, v3, p50.
Commentary. Apr 1966, v41, p81-82.
Commonweal. Feb 11, 1966, v83, p559.
Confessions of a Cultist. p221-25.
Film Daily. Dec 15, 1965, p6.
Film Quarterly. Sum 1966, v19, p60-64.
Films and Filming. Feb 1966, v12, p31.
Films and Filming. Mar 1966, v12, p10, 12.

Films in Review. Jan 1966, v17, p47-48.
The Great Spy Pictures. p450-52.
Hollywood Reporter. Dec 15, 1965, p3.
Life. Jan 7, 1966, v60, p8.
The London Times. Jan 13, 1966, p14.
Magill's Survey of Cinema. Series I. v4, p1604-07.
Motion Picture Herald Product Digest. Dec 22, 1965, p425.
The Nation. Jan 17, 1966, v202, p84.
Negative Space. p170-74.
The New Republic. Jan 1, 1966, v154, p32-33.
New Statesman. Jan 14, 1966, v71, p58.
The New York Times. Dec 24, 1965, p24.
The New Yorker. Jan 1, 1966, v41, p46.
Newsweek. Jan 3, 1966, v67, p56.
Playboy. Feb 1966, v13, p35-36.
Private Screenings. p237-38.
Saturday Review. Jan 15, 1966, v49, p44.
Senior Scholastic. Feb 4, 1966, v88, p24-25.
Sight and Sound. Spr 1966, v35, p94.
The Spectator. Jan 21, 1966, v216, p75.
Time. Dec 24, 1965, v86, p46.
Tynan Right and Left. p250-51.
Variety. Dec 15, 1965, p15.
The Village Voice. Dec 16, 1965, v11, p29.
Vogue. Feb 1, 1966, v147, p100.

The Spy Who Loved Me (GB; Gilbert, Lewis; 1977)
BFI/Monthly Film Bulletin. Aug 1977, v44, p176.
Films Illustrated. Jul 1977, v6, p412-13.
Films in Review. Oct 1977, v28, p501.
The Films of the Seventies. p188-90.
Hollywood Reporter. Jul 7, 1977, p5.
The James Bond Films. p135-53.
James Bond in the Cinema. p235-58.
James Bond's Bedside Companion. p215-21.
The Los Angeles Times. Jul 31, 1977, Calendar, p1.
Magill's Survey of Cinema. Series I. v4, p1608-11.
Motion Picture Herald Product Digest. Jul 20, 1977, p13.
New Times. Sep 2, 1977, v9, p62-63.
New York. Aug 22, 1977, v10, p58-59.
The New York Times. Jul 28, 1977, SecIII, p17.
The New York Times. Aug 21, 1977, SecII, p11.
Newsweek. Aug 8, 1977, v90, p77.
Time. Aug 8, 1977, v110, p58.
Variety. Jul 6, 1977, p17.
The Village Voice. Aug 22, 1977, p43-44.
The World of Fantastic Films. p73-74.

S*p*y*s (GB; Kershner, Larry; 1974)
BFI/Monthly Film Bulletin. Jul 1974, v41, p157.
Film. Jul 1974, n16, p21.
Films Illustrated. Jan 1974, v3, p273.
Films Illustrated. Jun 1974, v3, p378.
Hollywood Reporter. Jun 18, 1974, p3.
Independent Film Journal. Jun 26, 1974, v74, p9-10.
The Los Angeles Times. Aug 21, 1974, SecIV, p17.
Movietone News. Aug 1974, n34, p34.
New Statesman. Jul 26, 1974, v88, p129.
New York. Jul 8, 1974, v7, p74-75.
The New York Times. Aug 11, 1974, SecII, p11.
Newsweek. Jul 8, 1974, v84, p69.
Sight and Sound. Sum 1974, v43, p180-81.
Time. Jul 22, 1974, v104, p68.
Variety. Jun 19, 1974, p18.
The Village Voice. Jul 4, 1974, p59.

Stage Fright (US; Hitchcock, Alfred; 1950)
The Art of Alfred Hitchcock. p201-08.
BFI/Monthly Film Bulletin. Jun 1950, v17, p82-83.

Christian Century. May 24, 1950, v67, p663.
Commonweal. Mar 10, 1950, v51, p580.
Film Comment. Fall 1970, v6, p49-50.
Film Daily. Feb 24, 1950, p6.
Films in Review. Apr 1950, v1, p23-25.
The Films of Alfred Hitchcock. p149-52.
The Films of Marlene Dietrich. p185-88.
Hitchcock: The First Forty-Four Films. p103-05.
Hollywood Reporter. Feb 23, 1950, p3.
Illustrated London News. Jun 10, 1950, v216, p910.
Library Journal. Apr 1, 1950, v75, p570.
Magill's Survey of Cinema. Series II. v5, p2246-48.
Motion Picture Herald Product Digest. Feb 25, 1950, p205.
The New Republic. Mar 6, 1950, v122, p22.
The New Statesman and Nation. Jun 3, 1950, v39, p631.
The New York Times. Feb 24, 1950, p27.
The New Yorker. Mar 4, 1950, v26, p80.
Newsweek. Mar 13, 1950, v35, p78.
Senior Scholastic. Mar 15, 1950, v56, p36.
Sight and Sound. Jul 1950, v19, p207-08.
The Spectator. Jun 2, 1950, v184, p757.
Time. Mar 13, 1950, v55, p94.
Variety. Mar 1, 1950, p6.

Stagecoach (US; Douglas, Gordon; 1966)
America. Jun 25, 1966, v114, p880.
BFI/Monthly Film Bulletin. Jun 1966, v33, p91-100.
Christian Science Monitor (Western edition). Jun 24, 1966, p4.
Commonweal. Jul 1, 1966, v84, p419.
Dictionary of Films. p353-54.
Film Daily. May 19, 1966, p4.
Filmfacts. Aug 15, 1966, v9, p156-58.
Films and Filming. Jul 1966, v12, p12.
The Films of Bing Crosby. p239-41.
The Great Western Pictures. p342-45.
Hollywood Reporter. May 19, 1966, p3.
The London Times. Jan 14, 1965, p5.
The London Times. May 12, 1966, p6.
Make It Again, Sam. p200-04.
Motion Picture Herald Product Digest. May 25, 1966, p525-26.
New Statesman. May 20, 1966, v71, p746.
The New York Times. Jun 16, 1966, p53.
Newsweek. Jul 11, 1966, v68, p92-83.
Playboy. Jun 1966, v13, p34, 36.
Saturday Review. Jun 4, 1966, v49, p56.
Senior Scholastic. Apr 29, 1966, v88, p20.
Time. Aug 5, 1966, v88, p56.
Variety. May 25, 1966, p6.
Vogue. Jun 1966, v147, p56.

Stalag 17 (US; Wilder, Billy; 1953)
America. Jul 11, 1953, v89, p384.
BFI/Monthly Film Bulletin. Jul 1953, v20, n234, p103.
Billy Wilder (Dick). p66-70.
Catholic World. Jul 1953, v177, p306.
Commonweal. Aug 14, 1953, v58, p467.
The Film Career of Billy Wilder. p82-84.
Film Daily. May 6, 1953, p6.
Films in Review. Jun-Jul 1953, v4, n6, p302-03.
The Films of William Holden. p133-37.
Hollywood Reporter. May 6, 1953, p3.
Library Journal. Jul 1953, v78, p1226.
Life. Jul 20, 1953, v35, p59-62.
Magill's Survey of Cinema. Series II. v5, p2256.
The Nation. Jul 25, 1953, v177, p77.
The New York Times. Jul 2, 1953, p19.
The New York Times Magazine. May 17, 1953, p20.
Newsweek. Jul 13, 1953, v42, p86.
Saturday Review. Jul 4, 1953, v36, p31.
Time. May 18, 1953, v61, p114.
Variety. May 6, 1953, p6.

Stampeded *See* Big Land

The Star (US; Heisler, Stuart; 1952)
Bette Davis: Her Films and Career. p158-59.
BFI/Monthly Film Bulletin. Apr 1953, v20, p50.
Christian Century. Apr 8, 1953, v70, p431.
Film Daily. Jan 15, 1953, p13.
Hollywood Reporter. Dec 19, 1952, p3.
Magill's Survey of Cinema. Series II. v5, p2260-62.
McCall's. Mar 1953, v80, p10.
Mother Goddam. p259-61.
Motion Picture Herald Product Digest. Dec 27, 1952, p1661.
National Parent-Teacher. Mar 1953, v47, p30.
The New Statesman and Nation. Mar 7, 1953, v45, p262.
The New York Times. Jan 29, 1953, p25.
Saturday Review. Jan 31, 1953, v36, p28.
Sight and Sound. Apr-Jun 1953, v22, p193-94.
Variety. Dec 24, 1952, p6.

Star! (US; Wise, Robert; 1968)
America. Nov 16, 1968, v119, p498.
American Cinematographer. Mar 1969, v50, p294-96.
BFI/Monthly Film Bulletin. Sep 1968, v35, p134-35.
Christian Science Monitor (Western edition). Apr 9, 1968, p6.
Commonweal. Nov 1, 1968, v89, p160-61.
Dance Magazine. Mar 1969, v43, p26.
Film 68/69. p156-57.
Film Daily. Oct 23, 1968, p3.
Filmfacts. Nov 1, 1968, v11, p295-98.
Films and Filming. Sep 1968, v14, p37, 40.
Films in Review. Dec 1968, v19, p646-47.
Five Thousand One Nights At the Movies. p553.
Going Steady. p195-201.
Harper's Magazine. Nov 1968, v237, p168-70.
Hollywood Reporter. Jul 22, 1968, p3.
Life. Nov 8, 1968, v65, p10.
The London Times. Jul 19, 1968, p13.
Look. Sep 19, 1967, v31, p63-68.
Mademoiselle. Oct 1968, v67, p72.
Motion Picture Herald Product Digest. Oct 23, 1968, p43-44.
Movie. Wint 1968-69, n16, p39.
The New York Times. Oct 23, 1968, p36.
The New York Times. Oct 12, 1968, p28.
The New Yorker. Oct 26, 1968, v44, p206-09.
Newsweek. Nov 4, 1968, v72, p104.
Saturday Review. Oct 26, 1968, p51, p55.
Senior Scholastic. Oct 26, 1968, v93, p28.
The Spectator. Jul 26, 1968, v221, p135.
Variety. Jul 24, 1968, p6.
Vogue. Nov 1, 1968, v152, p120.

The Star Chamber (US; Hyams, Peter; 1983)
Maclean's. Aug 8, 1983, v96, p52.
The Nation. Aug 20, 1983, v237, p155-56.
The New Republic. Sep 19, 1983, v189, p22-23.
Newsweek. Aug 15, 1983, v102, p64.

Star 80 (US; Fosse, Bob; 1983)
America. Dec 17, 1983, v149, p395.
Films in Review. Jan 1984, v35, p56.
Hollywood Reporter. Oct 27, 1983, p3.
The Los Angeles Times. Nov 11, 1983, SecVI, p1.
Maclean's. Nov 21, 1983, v96, p54.
Magill's Cinema Annual, 1984. p374-78.
The Nation. Dec 17, 1983, v237, p643-45.
New York. Nov 21, 1983, v16, p78-79.
The New York Times. Nov 10, 1983, SecIII, p26.
The New Yorker. Nov 28, 1983, v59, p176-77.
Newsweek. Nov 14, 1983, v102, p98.

Saturday Review. Nov-Dec 1983, v9, p42.
Time. Nov 14, 1983, v122, p98.

A Star Is Born (US; Cukor, George; 1954)
America. Oct 16, 1954, v92, p83.
American Cinematographer. Feb 1984, v65, p34-40.
BFI/Monthly Film Bulletin. Jan 1955, v22, p4-5.
BFI/Monthly Film Bulletin. Jan 1984, v51, p26-27.
Bright Lights. 1974, v1, n1, p13-17.
Catholic World. Dec 1954, v180, p221-22.
Cinema, the Magic Vehicle. v2, p232-33.
Classic Images. Nov 1984, n113, p8.
Collier's. Apr 30, 1954, v133, p32-33.
Commonweal. Oct 22, 1954, v61, p60-61.
Coronet. Jul 1954, v36, p6.
Cue. Oct 23, 1954, p17.
Farm Journal. Dec 1954, v78, p141.
Fifty from the Fifties. p315-24.
Filament. 1984, n4, p48-49.
Film Daily. Sep 29, 1954, p7.
Films and Filming. Nov 1954, v1, p24.
Films and Filming. Feb 1984, v29, p41-42.
Films in Review. Nov 1954, v5, p479-82, 486-87.
The Films of the Fifties. p119-20.
George Cukor (Phillips). p150-55.
Hollywood Reporter. Sep 29, 1954, p3.
The International Dictionary of Films and Filmmakers. v1, p446-47.
Judy: The Films and Career of Judy Garland. p161-67.
Life. Sep 13, 1954, v37, p163-66.
Look. May 18, 1954, v18, p63-66.
Look. Oct 19, 1954, v18, p83-84.
Magill's Cinema Annual, 1984. p573-78.
Magill's Survey of Cinema. Series I. v4, p1619-22.
Motion Picture Herald Product Digest. Oct 16, 1954, p178-79.
National Parent-Teacher. Dec 1954, v49, p40.
New Statesman. Dec 2, 1983, v106, p30.
The New Statesman and Nation. Mar 12, 1955, v49, p356.
New York Magazine. Jul 25, 1983, v16, p67-68.
The New York Times. Oct 12, 1954, p23.
The New York Times. Apr 15, 1983, p10.
The New York Times. Jul 3, 1983, p11-12.
The New York Times Magazine. Oct 10, 1954, p25.
The New Yorker. Oct 23, 1954, v30, p161.
Newsweek. Nov 1, 1954, v44, p86.
On Cukor. p48-53.
Penthouse. Jan 1984, v15, p54.
Quarterly Review of Film Studies. 1979, v4, n3, p321-37.
Saturday Review. Oct 23, 1954, v37, p8.
Saturday Review. Oct 30, 1954, v37, p28-29.
Selected Film Criticism, 1951-1960. p130-31.
Sight and Sound. Spr 1955, v24, p194-95.
The Spectator. Jul 12, 1969, v223, p50.
Time. Oct 25, 1954, v64, p86.
Variety. Sep 29, 1954, p6.
Variety. Jun 8, 1983, p2.
The Village Voice. Jun 26, 1978, v23, p43.
The Village Voice. Jul 19, 1983, v28, p28.
Vintage Films. p143-46.

A Star Is Born (US; Pierson, Frank; 1976)
American Cinematographer. May 1977, v58, p496-98.
American Film. Jun 1977, v2, p6-7.
Audience. Jul 1977, v9, p12-13.
BFI/Monthly Film Bulletin. Mar 1977, v44, p53.
Esquire. Dec 1976, v86, p126-28.
Esquire. Sep 1976, v86, p30.
Film. Apr 1977, n48, p9.

Film Bulletin. Nov-Dec 1976, v45, p7.
Film Bulletin. Jan-Feb 1977, v46, p5-6.
Film Bulletin. Jan-Feb 1977, v46, p30.
Films Illustrated. Jan-Feb 1977, v6, p220-21.
Films Illustrated. Mar 1977, v6, p246-47.
Films Illustrated. Jun 1977, v6, p394.
Films in Review. Feb 1977, v28, p117-18.
The Films of the Seventies. p162-64.
Hollywood Reporter. Dec 20, 1976, p3.
Independent Film Journal. Jan 21, 1977, v79, p19.
The Los Angeles Times. Dec 21, 1976, SecIV, p1.
Motion Picture Herald Product Digest. Jan 12, 1977, p61.
Ms. May 1977, v5, p39-40.
The New Leader. Jan 17, 1977, v60, p25-26.
The New Republic. Jan 15, 1977, v176, p24-26.
New Statesman. Mar 25, 1977, v93, p410.
New York. Nov 15, 1976, v9, p49-60.
The New York Times. Dec 27, 1976, SecIII, p16.
The New Yorker. Jan 10, 1977, v52, p89-90.
Newsweek. Jan 10, 1977, v89, p64.
Penthouse. Apr 1977, v8, p44-45.
Rolling Stone. Feb 10, 1977, p18.
Rolling Stone. Feb 24, 1977, p66.
Saturday Review. Feb 5, 1977, v4, p41-42.
Sight and Sound. Sum 1977, v46, p177-81.
The Thousand Eyes Magazine. Jan 1977, v2, p2.
The Thousand Eyes Magazine. Feb 1977, v2, p9.
Time. Jan 3, 1977, v109, p62.
Variety. Dec 22, 1976, p20.
The Village Voice. Jan 3, 1977, v21, p35-36.
When the Lights Go Down. p240-44.

Star Trek—The Motion Picture (Also titled: Star Trek I) (US; Wise, Robert; 1979)
BFI/Monthly Film Bulletin. Feb 1980, v47, p29-30.
Chekov's Enterprise. 1980.
The Films of the Seventies. p283-88.
Hollywood Reporter. Dec 10, 1979, p21.
The Los Angeles Times. Dec 10, 1979, SecIV, p1.
The Making of Star Trek-The Motion Picture. 1980.
Motion Picture Herald Product Digest. Dec 26, 1979, p59.
The New Republic. Dec 29, 1979, v181, p20.
The New York Times. Dec 8, 1979, p14.
The New Yorker. Dec 17, 1979, v55, p167-68.
Newsweek. Dec 17, 1979, v94, p110-11.
Science Digest. Dec 1979, v86, p48-51.
Time. Dec 17, 1979, v114, p61.
Variety. Dec 12, 1979, p22.

Star Trek II—The Wrath of Kahn (US; Meyer, Nicholas; 1982)
Christian Century. Aug 18, 1982, v99, p868.
Hollywood Reporter. May 24, 1982, p3.
The Los Angeles Times. Jun 3, 1982, SecVI, p1.
Maclean's. Jun 14, 1982, v95, p51.
Magill's Cinema Annual, 1983. p321-25.
The Nation. Aug 21, 1982, v235, p156-57.
New York. Jun 21, 1982, v15, p55.
The New York Times. Jun 4, 1982, SecIII, p12.
The New Yorker. Jun 28, 1982, v58, p96-99.
Rolling Stone. Jul 22, 1982, p34.
Time. Jun 7, 1982, v119, p75.
Variety. May 24, 1982, p3.

Star Trek III (US; Nimoy, Leonard; 1984)
American Cinematographer. Aug-Sep 1984, v65, p54-63.
BFI/Monthly Film Bulletin. Jul 1984, v51, p212-13.
Cinefantastique. 1984, v14, n4/5, p8-9.

Cinefex. Aug 1984, n18, p42-67.
Film. Sep 1984, n128, p3.
Film Journal. Jul 1984, v87, p20-21.
Films and Filming. Jul 1984, n358, p24-26.
Films in Review. Aug-Sep 1984, v35, p436-37.
Hollywood Reporter. May 25, 1984, p4.
Humanist. Sep-Oct 1984, v44, p43-44.
The Los Angeles Times. Jun 1, 1984, SecIV, p1.
Maclean's. Jun 11, 1984, v97, p63.
Midnight Marquee. Fall 1984, n33, p29.
New Statesman. Jul 27, 1984, v108, p23-30.
New York. Jun 11, 1984, v17, p67.
The New York Times. Jun 1, 1984, SecIII, p14.
The New Yorker. Jul 9, 1984, v60, p85.
Newsweek. Jun 11, 1984, v103, p80-81.
On Location. Apr 1984, v7, p34.
Photoplay. Aug 1984, v35, p45.
Photoplay. Sep 1984, v35, p30-31.
Time. Jun 11, 1984, v123, p83.
Variety. May 30, 1984, p12.
The Village Voice. Jun 5, 1984, p65.

Star Wars (US; Lucas, George; 1977)
An Album of Great Science Fiction Films. p60-65.
America. Jun 25, 1977, v136, p568.
American Film. Apr 1977, v2, p8-13.
BFI/Monthly Film Bulletin. Nov 1977, v44, p243.
Christian Century. Nov 9, 1977, v94, p1044-45.
Christian Century. Jul 20, 1977, v94, p666-68.
Christianity Today. Sep 23, 1977, v21, p28-29.
Cinema Papers. Oct 1977, n14, p119.
Commonweal. Jul 8, 1977, v104, p433.
Film Comment. Jul-Aug 1977, v13, p22-23.
Film Quarterly. Spr 1981, v35, p13-20.
Films and Filming. Dec 30, 1977, v24, p29-30.
Films in Review. Aug-Sep 1977, v28, p437.
The Films of the Seventies. p173-78.
Future Tense. p260-70, 289-91.
Future Visions. p89-91.
Hollywood Reporter. May 20, 1977, p3.
The International Dictionary of Films and Filmmakers. v1, p447-48.
Journal of Popular Culture. 1977, v11, n1, p1-10.
The Life and Films of George Lucas. p131-91.
The Los Angeles Times. May 22, 1977, Calendar, p1.
Magill's Survey of Cinema. Series I. v4, p1623-26.
Motion Picture Herald Product Digest. Jun 8, 1977, p1.
The Nation. Jun 25, 1977, v224, p794.
The New Republic. Jun 18, 1977, v176, p22.
New York. Jun 20, 1977, v10, p71-73.
The New York Times. May 26, 1977, SecIII, p18.
The New York Times. Jun 5, 1977, SecII, p15.
The New York Times. Sep 4, 1977, SecII, p9.
The New Yorker. Jun 13, 1977, v53, p69-70.
The New Yorker. Sep 26, 1977, v53, p123.
Newsweek. Jun 13, 1977, v89, p81.
Newsweek. May 30, 1977, v89, p60-61.
Newsweek. Aug 29, 1977, v90, p77.
Rolling Stone. Aug 25, 1977, p40-48.
Saturday Review. Jul 9, 1977, v4, p40.
Saturday Review. Dec 10, 1977, v5, p80.
Science Fiction Films of the Seventies. p152-71.
The Star Wars Album. 1977.
Time. May 30, 1977, v109, p54-56.
Time. Jun 27, 1977, v109, p64.
Time. Jan 2, 1978, v111, p72.
Variety. May 25, 1977, p20.
The Village Voice. Jun 13, 1977, p40-41.
The Village Voice. Jul 4, 1977, p37-38.
The World of Fantastic Films. p68-70, 93-98.

Stardust Memories (US; Allen, Woody; 1980)
America. Oct 18, 1980, v143, p231.
Christian Century. Nov 12, 1980, v97.
Hollywood Reporter. Sep 25, 1980, p3.
Horizon. Dec 1980, v23, p70.
The Los Angeles Times. Sep 28, 1980, Calendar, p1.
Maclean's. Oct 6, 1980, v93, p70.
Magill's Cinema Annual, 1985. p626-31.
Motion Picture Herald Product Digest. Oct 8, 1980, p33.
The Nation. Oct 25, 1980, v231, p418-19.
National Review. Nov 28, 1980, v32, p1469-70.
The New Leader. Oct 20, 1980, v63, p19-20.
The New Republic. Oct 11, 1980, v183, p20-21.
New York. Oct 13, 1980, v13, p61-62.
The New Yorker. Oct 27, 1980, v56, p183-86.
Newsweek. Oct 6, 1980, v97, p71.
Saturday Review. Dec 1980, v7, p85.
Time. Sep 29, 1980, v116, p68.
Variety. Oct 1, 1980, p20.
Woody Allen: His Films and Career. p200-12.

Starker Als Die Nacht *See* Stronger than the Night

Starman (US; Carpenter, John; 1984)
BFI/Monthly Film Bulletin. May 1985, v52, p163.
Hollywood Reporter. Dec 3, 1984, p3.
The Los Angeles Times. Dec 13, 1984, SecVI, p1.
Maclean's. Dec 17, 1984, v97, p59.
New York. Dec 17, 1984, v17, p54-58.
The New York Times. Dec 7, 1984, SecIII, p8.
The New York Times. Dec 14, 1984, SecIII, p18.
Newsweek. Dec 17, 1984, v104, p80-82.
On Location. Nov 1984, v8, p66-68.
Time. Dec 24, 1984, v124, p65.
Variety. Dec 5, 1984, p17.
The Village Voice. Dec 25, 1984, p67-68.

Stars and Stripes Forever (Also titled: Marching Along) (US; Koster, Henry; 1952)
BFI/Monthly Film Bulletin. Feb 1953, v20, p24-25.
Catholic World. Dec 1952, v176, p224.
Christian Century. Jan 21, 1953, v70, p95.
Commonweal. Jan 2, 1953, v57, p333.
Etude. Jan 1953, v71, p10.
Film Daily. Nov 28, 1952, p4.
Hollywood Reporter. Nov 19, 1952, p3.
Library Journal. Dec 15, 1952, v77, p2170.
Motion Picture Herald Product Digest. Nov 22, 1952, p1613-14.
National Parent-Teacher. Jan 1953, v47, p37.
The New York Times. Dec 23, 1952, p17.
Newsweek. Dec 22, 1952, v40, p72.
Saturday Review. Jan 17, 1952, v36, p29.
The Spectator. Dec 26, 1952, v189, p871.
The Tatler. Jan 7, 1953, v207, p25.
Time. Dec 29, 1952, v60, p66.
Variety. Nov 19, 1952, p6.

Stars in My Crown (US; Tourneur, Jacques; 1950)
Christian Century. Aug 2, 1950, v67, p935.
Films in Review. Feb 1951, v2, p41.
Hollywood Reporter. Mar 1, 1950, p3.
Library Journal. Apr 1, 1950, v75, p571.
Motion Picture Herald Product Digest. Mar 4, 1950, p213.
The New York Times. Dec 22, 1950, p19.
Newsweek. May 15, 1950, v35, p90.
Time. Jan 8, 1951, v57, p72-73.
Variety. Mar 1, 1950, p6.

The Start *See* Départ, Le

Starting Over (US; Pakula, Alan J.; 1979)
BFI/Monthly Film Bulletin. Feb 1980, v47, p28-29.
Films in Review. Nov 1979, v30, p563.
The Films of Burt Reynolds. p222-27.
Hollywood Reporter. Sep 28, 1979, p4.
The Los Angeles Times. Sep 30, 1979, Calendar, p1.
Magill's Survey of Cinema. Series II. v5, p2267-70.
Motion Picture Herald Product Digest. Oct 17, 1979, p38.
The New Republic. Oct 20, 1979, v181, p27-28.
The New York Times. Oct 5, 1979, v3, p8.
The New Yorker. Nov 26, 1979, v55, p171-72.
Newsweek. Oct 8, 1979, v94, p69-70.
Time. Oct 8, 1979, v114, p86-87.
Variety. Oct 3, 1979, p14.

State of Seige (Italian title: Etat de Siege) (IT; Costa-Gavras, Constantin; 1973)
America. May 19, 1973, v128, p461.
Audience. May 1973, v5, p1-2.
Commentary. Sep 1973, v56, p75.
Commonweal. May 25, 1973, v98, p288-89.
The Film Book Bibliography. n4340, p448.
Film Quarterly. Fall 1973, v27, p51-54.
Filmfacts. 1973, v16, n6, p143.
Films in Review. Jun-Jul 1973, v24, n6, p373.
Hollywood Reporter. May 11, 1973, p3.
The Nation. Apr 30, 1973, v216, p572-73.
National Review. Jun 22, 1973, v25, p689.
The New Republic. May 5, 1973, v168, p24.
New Statesman. Jul 27, 1973, v86, p128.
The New York Times. Apr 14, 1973, p39.
The New York Times. Apr 22, 1973, SecII, p1.
The New York Times. Jun 24, 1973, v15, p1.
The New York Times. Apr 4, 1973, p34.
The New Yorker. Apr 14, 1973, v49, p141-44.
The New Yorker. May 12, 1973, v49, p118-21.
Newsweek. Apr 23, 1973, v81, p106.
Ramparts. Aug 1973, v12, p45-46.
Rolling Stone. Jun 21, 1973, p70-71.
Sight and Sound. Fall 1973, v42, p238.
Time. Apr 28, 1973, v101, p69.
TV Movies. 1983-84, p730.
Variety. Feb 14, 1973, p18.
The Village Voice. Apr 19, 1973, p79-82.
The Village Voice. Apr 26, 1973, p75-76.
Vogue. Jun 1973, v161, p48.

State Secret (Also titled: The Great Manhunt) (GB; Gilliat, Sidney; 1950)
BFI/Monthly Film Bulletin. Apr-May 1950, v17, p62.
Commonweal. Oct 20, 1950, v53, p40.
Film Daily. Oct 5, 1950, p8.
Films in Review. Dec 1950, v1, p41.
Hollywood Reporter. Oct 5, 1950, p3.
The London Times. Mar 17, 1950, p12.
Motion Picture Herald Product Digest. Oct 7, 1950, p510.
The New Statesman and Nation. Apr 29, 1950, v39, p484.
The New York Times. Oct 5, 1950, p38.
Newsweek. Oct 23, 1950, v36, p96.
Shots in the Dark. p172-74.
Sight and Sound. Dec 1949, v18, p10-12.
The Spectator. Apr 28, 1950, v184, p570-71.
Time. Oct 9, 1950, v56, p112.
Variety. Apr 26, 1950, p22.

Stavisky (Also titled: Stavisky. . .) (FR, IT; Resnais, Alain; 1974)
Alain Resnais (Kreidly). p165-84.
America. Feb 15, 1975, v132, p116.
BFI/Monthly Film Bulletin. Jul 1975, v42, p161.
Film Comment. Sep-Oct 1974, v10, p38.
Film Comment. Mar-Apr 1974, v10, p2.

Films in Review. Mar 1975, v26, p179.
Hollywood Reporter. Oct 2, 1974, p3.
Horizon. Sum 1976, v18, p42-47.
Independent Film Journal. Oct 16, 1974, v74, p6.
The Los Angeles Times. Feb 7, 1975, SecIV, p1.
Magill's Survey of Cinema. Foreign Language Films. v6, p2878-82.
Motion Picture Herald Product Digest. Oct 16, 1975, p40.
The Nation. Oct 19, 1974, v219, p379-80.
The New York Times. May 25, 1975, p16.
The New York Times. Sep 30, 1975, p51.
The New York Times. Nov 3, 1974, SecII, p15.
The New Yorker. Jan 20, 1975, v50, p76-78.
Newsweek. Oct 14, 1974, v84, p131.
Reeling. p552-58.
Sight and Sound. Wint 1973-1974, v43, p25.
Sight and Sound. Spr 1974, v43, p92-93.
Stavisky. 1974.
Take One. 1974, v4, n6, p24-25.
Variety. May 22, 1974, p18.
The Village Voice. May 30, 1974, p77-78.
The Village Voice. Oct 31, 1974, p112-13.

Stay Hungry (US; Rafelson, Bob; 1976)
BFI/Monthly Film Bulletin. Sep 1976, v43, p199-200.
Cineaste. n376, p7, 37-38.
Contemporary Review. Dec 1976, v229, p326-28.
Film Bulletin. May 1976, v45, pD.
Film Comment. May-Jun 1976, v12, p2-3.
Films and Filming. Nov 1976, v23, p35-36.
Films and Filming. Sep 1976, v22, p42-43.
Hollywood Reporter. Apr 23, 1976, p3.
Independent Film Journal. Apr 30, 1976, v77, p15.
The Los Angeles Times. May 12, 1976, SecIV, p1.
Motion Picture Herald Product Digest. Apr 28, 1976, p93.
Movietone News. Oct 11, 1976, n52, p39-41.
The New Republic. May 1, 1976, v174, p20-21.
New Statesman. Oct 8, 1976, v92, p490.
New York. May 3, 1976, v9, p68.
The New York Times. Apr 26, 1976, p41.
Newsweek. May 17, 1976, v67, p111.
Penthouse. Aug 1976, v7, p46-47.
Saturday Review. May 29, 1976, v3, p46.
Sight and Sound. Wint 1976, v45, p255-56.
Time. May 10, 1976, v107, p72-73.
Variety. Apr 28, 1976, p28.
Vogue. Jun 1976, v166, p63.

Staying Alive (US; Stallone, Sylvester; 1983)
Dance Magazine. Aug 1983, v57, p48-50.
Films in Review. Oct 1983, v34, p503.
Hollywood Reporter. Jul 12, 1983, p3.
The Los Angeles Times. Jul 15, 1983, SecVI, p1.
Maclean's. Jul 25, 1983, v96, p53.
Magill's Cinema Annual, 1984. p386-90.
The New Leader. Sep 19, 1983, v66, p20.
New York. Aug 1, 1983, v16, p54-55.
The New York Times. Dec 31, 1982, SecIII, p6.
The New Yorker. Aug 22, 1983, v59, p77-79.
Newsweek. Jul 25, 1983, v102, p75.
Time. Jul 18, 1983, v122, p63.

Stazioni Termini *See* Indiscretion of an American Wife

The Steel Cage (US; Doniger, Walter; 1954)
BFI/Monthly Film Bulletin. Apr 1956, v23, p50.
Film Daily. Nov 19, 1954, p14.
Hollywood Reporter. Oct 25, 1954, p3.

Motion Picture Herald Product Digest. Oct 30, 1954, p193-94.
National Parent-Teacher. Jan 1955, v49, p40.
Newsweek. Oct 13, 1954, v44, p100.
Variety. Oct 27, 1954, p7.

The Steel Helmet (US; Fuller, Sam; 1950)
BFI/Monthly Film Bulletin. Apr 1951, v18, p253.
Christian Century. Mar 14, 1951, v68, p351.
The Director's Event. p129-32.
Film Daily. Jan 15, 1951, p6.
The Films of the Fifties. p45-46.
Hollywood Reporter. Dec 28, 1950, p3.
The London Times. Mar 12, 1951, p3.
Magill's Survey of Cinema. Series II. v5, p2271-73.
Motion Picture Herald Product Digest. Jan 6, 1951, p653.
The New Republic. Feb 12, 1951, v124, p22-23.
The New York Times. Jan 25, 1950, p21.
The New Yorker. Feb 3, 1951, v26, p74.
Newsweek. Jan 29, 1951, v37, p90.
Running Time: Films of the Cold War. p151-66.
Samuel Fuller (Hardy). p100-04.
Saturday Review. Feb 3, 1951, v34, p25.
Variety. Jan 3, 1951, p67.

Steel Town (US; Sherman, George; 1952)
BFI/Monthly Film Bulletin. Apr 1952, v19, p54.
Christian Century. May 28, 1952, v69, p655.
Film Daily. Mar 6, 1952, p14.
Hollywood Reporter. Mar 5, 1952, p3.
Library Journal. Mar 15, 1952, v77, p522.
The London Times. Feb 25, 1952, p2.
Motion Picture Herald Product Digest. Mar 8, 1952, p1261.
The New York Times. May 10, 1952, p16.
Newsweek. Mar 31, 1952, v39, p87.
The Spectator. Feb 22, 1952, v188, p228.
Variety. Mar 5, 1952, p6.

The Steel Trap (US; Stone, Andrew L.; 1952)
BFI/Monthly Film Bulletin. Jan 1952, v20, p12.
Christian Century. Dec 24, 1952, v69, p1511.
Film Daily. Oct 28, 1952, p7.
Hollywood Reporter. Oct 20, 1952, p4.
Motion Picture Herald Product Digest. Oct 25, 1952, p1582.
The Nation. Dec 6, 1952, v175, p537.
National Parent-Teacher. Dec 1952, v47, p38.
The New Statesman and Nation. Dec 13, 1952, v44, p718.
The New York Times. Nov 13, 1952, p35.
The New Yorker. Nov 22, 1952, v28, p107-08.
Newsweek. Dec 1, 1952, v40, p82.
The Spectator. Dec 12, 1952, v189, p810.
Variety. Oct 22, 1952, p6.

Stella (GREECE; Cacoyannis, Michael; 1957)
BFI/Monthly Film Bulletin. Oct 1956, v23, p127.
Commonweal. May 17, 1957, v66, p183.
Film Culture. 1957, v3, n3, p17.
Film Daily. Jun 21, 1957, v111, p6.
Films and Filming. Oct 1956, v3, p26-27.
Films in Review. Apr 1957, v8, p173-74.
The New York Times. Jun 11, 1957, p40.
The New Yorker. Jun 29, 1957, v33, p73.
Saturday Review. Mar 16, 1957, v40, p27.
Sight and Sound. Aut 1956, v26, p96.
Variety. May 11, 1955, p9.
Variety. May 1, 1957, p6.

The Stepford Wives (US; Forbes, Bryan; 1975)
Esquire. Jun 1975, v83, p62.

Films in Review. Apr 1975, v26, p247.
Hollywood Reporter. Feb 12, 1975, p8.
The Los Angeles Times. Feb 13, 1975, SecIV, p15.
Motion Picture Herald Product Digest. Feb 26, 1975, p74.
The New York Times. Feb 13, 1975, p43.
The New Yorker. Feb 24, 1975, v51, p110.
Newsweek. Mar 3, 1975, v85, p70.
Reeling. p586-90.
Time. Mar 3, 1975, v105, p6.
Variety. Feb 12, 1975, p28.

The Sterile Cuckoo (Also titled: Pookie) (US; Pakula, Alan J.; 1969)
America. Nov 22, 1969, v121, p505.
Deeper Into Movies. p31, 39-43.
Film Daily. Oct 21, 1969, p4.
Film Quarterly. Spr 1970, v23, p52-54, p55-58.
Filmfacts. 1969, v12, p433.
Films and Filming. Mar 1970, v16, p39, 42.
Films in Review. Nov 1969, v20, p572.
The Films of the Sixties. p282-83.
Holiday. Nov 22, 1969, v46, p505.
Hollywood Reporter. Oct 3, 1969, v208, p3.
Life. Nov 28, 1969, v67, p18.
Magill's Survey of Cinema. Series II. v5, p2274-76.
Movies Into Film. p120-21.
The New Yorker. Nov 1, 1969, v45, p138-40.
Newsweek. Nov 3, 1969, v74, p97.
Sight and Sound. Wint 1969-70, v39, p51.
Time. Oct 31, 1969, v94, p91.
Variety. Oct 8, 1969, p15.
Vogue. Dec 1969, v154, p142.

Stevie (GB; Enders, Robert; 1978)
America. Aug 1, 1981, v145, p56.
Christian Century. Sep 16, 1981, v98, p913.
Commonweal. Sep 11, 1981, v108, p499-500.
Films In Review. Sep-Oct 1981, v32, p472-73.
Films In Review. Nov 1981, p558-59.
Ms. Nov 1981, v10, p115.
The Nation. Sep 19, 1981, v233, p251-52.
The New Republic. Jul 25, 1981, v185, p26-25.
The New York Times. Jun 19, 1981, SecIII, p8.
The New York Times. Jun 28, 1981, SecII, p15-16.
The New York Times. Nov 6, 1981, SecIII, p13.
The New York Times. Jul 19, 1981, SecII, p17-18.
Newsweek. Aug 3, 1981, v98, p51.
Progressive. Sep 1981, v45, p55.
Time. Aug 3, 1981, v118, p67.
The Village Voice. Jun 24, 1981, p49.

Still of the Night (US; Benton, Robert; 1982)
Hollywood Reporter. Nov 19, 1982, p3.
The Los Angeles Times. Nov 19, 1982, SecVI, p1.
Magill's Cinema Annual, 1983. p326-30.
The New York Times. Nov 19, 1982, SecIII, p8.
The New Yorker. Dec 13, 1982, v58, p170-73.
Newsweek. Nov 22, 1982, v100, p118.
Time. Nov 22, 1982, v120, p108.
Variety. Nov 2, 1982, p3.

The Sting (US; Hill, George Roy; 1973)
American Cinematographer. May 1974, v55, p536-37.
Audience. Feb 1974, v6, p6-8.
BFI/Monthly Film Bulletin. Jan 1974, v41, p14-15.
Christian Century. May 29, 1974, 91, p594-96.
Commonweal. Apr 12, 1974, v100, p133-34.
Esquire. Mar 1974, v82, p72.
Films and Filming. Jan 1974, v20, p41.
Films Illustrated. Jan 1974, v3, p244.
Films in Review. Jan 1974, v25, p49-50.
The Films of George Roy Hill. p99-113.

The New Yorker. Apr 20, 1957, v33, p134.
Newsweek. Apr 22, 1957, v49, p122.
Saturday Review. Apr 20, 1957, v40, p30.
Sight and Sound. Aut 1957, v27, p89-90.
Theatre Arts. May 1957, v41, p13-14.
Time. Apr 22, 1957, v69, p108.
Variety. Apr 3, 1957, p6.
The Village Voice. Jun 5, 1957, p6.

The Strange Ones *See* Enfants Terribles, Les

The Stranger (Also titled: Straniero, Lo; Stranger, Le) (IT, FR, ALG; Visconti, Luchino; 1967)
BFI/Monthly Film Bulletin. Oct 1968, v35, p151-52.
Commonweal. Feb 2, 1968, v87, p540.
Esquire. Apr 1968, v69, p42.
Film Daily. Jan 3, 1968, p6.
Film Quarterly. Sum 1968, v21, p43-45.
Films and Filming. Nov 1968, v15, p38-39.
Films in Review. Feb 1968, v19, p110-11.
Hollywood Reporter. Dec 22, 1967, p3.
Life. Feb 2, 1968, v64, p8.
Luchino Visconti (Tonetti). p116-24.
Motion Picture Herald Product Digest. Jan 17, 1968, p759.
The New Republic. Jan 13, 1968, v158, p22.
The New York Times. Dec 19, 1967, p59.
The New Yorker. Dec 30, 1967, v43, p48.
Newsweek. Jan 1, 1968, v71, p64.
Saturday Review. Jan 6, 1968, v51, p38.
Screen. Jan-Feb 1969, v10, p99-104.
Second Sight. p163-67.
Sight and Sound. Sum 1968, v37, p148-50.
Time. Dec 29, 1967, v90, p54-55.
Variety. Sep 20, 1967, p6.
The Village Voice. Jan 4, 1968, p40-41.

The Stranger Came Home *See* The Unholy Four

Stranger Than Paradise (US; Jarmusch, Jim; 1984)
American Film. Nov 1984, v10, p62.
BFI/Monthly Film Bulletin. Nov 1984, v51, p334-35.
Christian Century. Oct 24, 1984, v101, p971-72.
Film Journal. Nov 1984, v87, p54-55.
Film Journal. Dec 1984, v87, p12.
The Los Angeles Times. Nov 2, 1984, SecVI, p18.
Maclean's. Nov 26, 1984, v97, p78.
The Nation. Dec 15, 1984, v239, p658-59.
New Statesman. Oct 5, 1984, v108, p34-35.
The New York Times. Sep 29, 1984, p14.
The New York Times. Oct 21, 1984, p23.
The New Yorker. Nov 12, 1984, v60, p180.
Newsweek. Oct 8, 1984, v104, p87.
On Film. Fall 1984, n13, p65-68.
Variety. May 23, 1984, p23-24.
The Village Voice. Oct 2, 1984, p49.

Strangers On a Train (US; Hitchcock, Alfred; 1951)
American Film. Nov 1981, v7, p75-80.
The Art of Alfred Hitchcock. p209-20.
BFI/Monthly Film Bulletin. Aug 1951, v18, p309.
Bright Lights. n2, 1975, v1, p26-27.
Christian Century. Aug 8, 1951, v68, p927.
Cinema, the Magic Vehicle. v2, p71-72.
Commonweal. Jul 20, 1951, v54, p358.
Cue. Jul 7, 1951, p16.
Dictionary of Films. p358.
Film Criticism and Caricatures, 1943-1953. p127-28.
Film Culture. Sum 1966, n41, p37-38.
Film Daily. Jun 15, 1951, p6.
Film News. Wint 1980, v37, p37.

Film Quarterly. Wint 1962-63, v16, p13-14.
Films and Filming. Oct 1970, v17, p60-64.
Films in Review. Jun-Jul 1951, v2, p36-38.
The Films of Alfred Hitchcock. p153-57.
Focus on Hitchcock. p101-11.
Hitchcock: The First Forty-Four Films. p106-11.
Hitchcock (Truffaut). p193-208.
Hitchcock's Films (Wood). p55-67.
Hollywood Reporter. Jun 14, 1951, p3.
The International Dictionary of Films and Filmmakers. v1, p454-55.
Kiss Kiss Bang Bang. p442-43.
Life. Jul 9, 1951, v31, p70-72.
Literature/Film Quarterly. n1, 1985, v13, p56-65.
The London Times. Aug 4, 1951, p6.
Magill's Survey of Cinema. Series II. v5, p2298-3002.
Motion Picture Herald Product Digest. Jun 16, 1951, p885.
Movie Maker. Jan 1985, v19, p38-40.
The Nation. Jul 28, 1951, v173, p77-78.
The New Republic. Jul 16, 1951, v125, p22.
The New Statesman and Nation. Aug 11, 1951, v42, p154.
The New York Times. Jul 4, 1951, p13.
The New Yorker. Jul 14, 1951, v27, p61.
Newsweek. Jul 9, 1951, v38, p93.
Raymond Chandler in Hollywood. p103-11.
Saturday Review. Jul 14, 1951, v34, p32.
Selected Film Criticism, 1951-1960. p132.
Sight and Sound. Aug-Sep 1951, v21, p21-22.
The Spectator. Aug 3, 1951, v187, p156.
Spectator. n2, 1985, v4, p8-9.
The Thousand Eyes Magazine. Jul-Aug 1976, n12, p3-4.
Variety. Jun 20, 1951, p6.

Strangers When We Meet (US; Quine, Richard; 1960)
America. Jul 9, 1960, v103, p443.
BFI/Monthly Film Bulletin. Aug 1960, v27, p109.
Commonweal. Aug 5, 1960, v72, p403.
Film Daily. May 25, 1960, p7.
Filmfacts. 1960, v3, p151.
Films and Filming. Nov 1960, v7, p33.
The Films of Kirk Douglas. p163-66.
The Films of the Fifties. p258-59.
Hollywood Reporter. May 25, 1960, p3.
The New Republic. Jun 27, 1960, v142, p20.
The New York Times. Jun 30, 1960, p22.
The New Yorker. Sep 24, 1960, v36, p168-69.
Newsweek. Jul 4, 1960, v56, p84.
Saturday Review. Jun 11, 1960, v43, p24.
Time. Jul 4, 1960, v26, p51.
Variety. May 25, 1960, p6.

Straniero, Lo *See* The Stranger

Strategia del Rango *See* The Spider's Strategem

Straw Dogs (US; Peckinpah, Sam; 1971)
Atlantic. Apr 1972, v229, p20.
BFI/Monthly Film Bulletin. Dec 1971, v38, p249.
Commonweal. Mar 24, 1972, v96, p63-64.
Esquire. Jun 1972, v77, p61.
Film Quarterly. Fall 1972, v26, p61-64.
Films and Filming. Mar 1972, v18, n6, p54-55.
The Films of Dustin Hoffman. p127-36.
Hollywood Reporter. Dec 13, 1971, p3.
Interview. Mar 1972, v20, p35.
Life. Feb 11, 1972, v72, p14.
Magill's Survey of Cinema. Series II. v5, p2306-09.
The Nation. Feb 7, 1972, v214, p188.
The New Republic. Feb 19, 1972, v166, p24.
The New York Times. Jan 20, 1972, p50.
The New York Times. Feb 20, 1972, SecII, p11.

The New Yorker. Jan 29, 1972, v47, p80.
Newsweek. Dec 20, 1971, v78, p87.
Peckinpah (Simmons). p121-38.
Sam Peckinpah (McKinney). p115-30.
Saturday Review. Dec 18, 1971, v54, p22.
Sight and Sound. Wint 1971-72, v41, n1, p50.
Sight and Sound. Sum 1972, v41, n3, p132-33.
Time. Dec 20, 1971, v98, p84-85.
Variety. Dec 1, 1971, p16.

Streamers (US; Altman, Robert; 1983)
Film Comment. Nov-Dec 1983, v19, p74.
Hollywood Reporter. Oct 11, 1983, p3.
The Los Angeles Times. Nov 4, 1983, SecVI, p1.
Maclean's. Nov 28, 1983, v96, p70.
Magill's Cinema Annual, 1984. p391-94.
The New York Times. Oct 9, 1983, p73.
Newsweek. Nov 7, 1983, v102, p131.
Time. Oct 17, 1983, v122, p89.

The Street Fighter *See* Hard Times

A Streetcar Named Desire (US; Kazan, Elia; 1951)
American Cinematographer. Oct 1951, v32, p400.
America's Favorite Movies. p215-33.
BFI/Monthly Film Bulletin. Mar 1952, v19, p33-34.
Christian Century. Nov 28, 1951, v68, p1391.
Cinema, the Magic Vehicle. v2, p89-91.
Commonweal. Sep 28, 1951, v54, p596-97.
Cue. Sep 22, 1951, p18.
Dictionary of Films. p359.
Elia Kazan: A Guide to References and Resources. p9-10.
Fifty From the Fifties. p325-34.
Film Comment. Sum 1968, v4, p44-46.
Film Criticism and Caricatures, 1943-1953. p139-40.
Film Culture. n2 1956, v2, p22.
Film Daily. Jun 14, 1951, p7.
Filming Literature. p160-61.
Films Illustrated. Jun 1974, v3, p374.
Films in Review. Dec 1951, v2, p51-55.
The Films of Marlon Brando. p34-45.
The Films of Tennessee Williams. p65-87.
Holiday. Oct 1951, v10, p25-28.
Hollywood Reporter. Jun 14, 1951, p4.
The International Dictionary of Films and Filmmakers. v1, p455-56.
Kazan on Kazan. p66-72.
Kiss Kiss Bang Bang. p443-44.
Library Journal. Oct 15, 1951, v76, p1722.
Life. Sep 24, 1951, v31, p91-92.
Literature/Film Quarterly. n4, 1981, v9, p233-40.
The London Times. Mar 3, 1952, p8.
Magill's Survey of Cinema. Series I. v4, p1641-44.
Modern Drama. n1, 1985, v28, p139-47.
Motion Picture Herald Product Digest. Jun 16, 1951, p885-86.
Movie. Wint 1971-72, n19, p17-18.
The Nation. Oct 20, 1951, v173, p334.
The New Republic. Oct 8, 1951, v125, p21.
The New York Times. Sep 30, 1951, p27.
The New York Times Magazine. Jul 22, 1951, p34-35.
The New Yorker. Sep 29, 1951, v27, p111.
Newsweek. Oct 1, 1951, v38, p87.
Reruns. p77-81.
Saturday Review. Sep 1, 1951, v34, p28-31.
Selected Film Criticism, 1951-1960. p132-33.
Sight and Sound. Apr-Jun 1952, v21, p170-71.
The Spectator. Feb 29, 1952, v188, p260.
Tennessee Williams and Film. p15-24.
Theater and Film. p120-34.
Theatre Arts. Jul 1951, v35, p88.

Time. Sep 17, 1951, v58, p105-06.
Variety. Jun 20, 1951, p6.
The Village Voice. Jul 26, 1973, v18, p65.

Streets of Fire (US; Hill, Walter; 1984)
American Cinematographer. Feb 1984, v65, p79-82.
American Film. Jun 1984, v9, p36-42.
BFI/Monthly Film Bulletin. Sep 1984, v51, p284-85.
Dance Magazine. Jun 1984, v58, p74-75.
Esquire. Jun 1984, v101, p276-77.
Film Comment. Jul-Aug 1984, v20, p55-58.
Film Journal. Jul 1984, v87, p23-24.
Films and Filming. Oct 1984, n361, p17-19.
Films and Filming. Sep 1984, n360, p43.
Hollywood Reporter. May 31, 1984, p4.
Informer. Jul 1984, p5.
The Los Angeles Times. May 31, 1984, SecVI, p1.
Maclean's. Jun 18, 1984, v97, p50.
New Statesman. Sep 21, 1984, v108, p41-42.
New York. Jun 4, 1984, v17, p74.
The New York Times. Jun 1, 1984, SecIII, p8.
Newsweek. Jun 11, 1984, v103, p81.
Photoplay. Oct 1984, v35, p20, 24-25.
Stills. Nov-Dec 1983, n9, p41-43.
Variety. May 30, 1984, p14.
The Village Voice. Jun 5, 1984, p1.

Streetwise (US; Freeman, Joan; 1985)
BFI/Monthly Film Bulletin. Mar 1986, v53, p84.
Commonweal. May 31, 1985, v112, p343-44.
The Los Angeles Times. May 17, 1985, SecVI, p4.
Ms. Aug 1985, v14, p73.
National Review. Jun 28, 1985, v37, p45-47.
The New Republic. May 13, 1985, v192, p22-23.
The New York Times. Apr 2, 1985, SecIII, p12.
The New York Times. Nov 3, 1985, SecII, p19.
Newsweek. Apr 22, 1985, v105, p76.
Time. May 6, 1985, v125, p86.
Variety. Feb 13, 1985, p18.

Strictly Controlled Trains *See* Closely Watched Trains

Strictly Dishonorable (US; Frank, Melvin; Panama, Norman; 1951)
Christian Century. Sep 5, 1951, v68, p1031.
Commonweal. Aug 3, 1951, v54, p406.
Film Daily. Jul 3, 1951, p6.
Hollywood Reporter. Jun 29, 1951, p3.
Library Journal. Aug 1951, v76, p1240.
Motion Picture Herald Product Digest. Jul 7, 1951, p922.
The New York Times. Jul 12, 1951, p21.
The New Yorker. Jul 21, 1951, v27, p63.
Newsweek. Jul 23, 1951, v38, p84.
Saturday Review. Jul 14, 1951, v34, p32.
Theatre Arts. Sep 1951, v35, p87.
Time. Jul 23, 1951, v58, p82.
Variety. Jul 4, 1951, p8.

Stripes (US; Reitman, Ivan; 1981)
Commentary. Oct 1981, v72, p71-72.
Hollywood Reporter. Jun 15, 1981, p3.
The Los Angeles Times. Jun 26, 1981, SecVI, p1.
Magill's Cinema Annual, 1982. p336-338.
The New York Times. Jun 26, 1981, SecIII, p16.
The New York Times. Aug 9, 1981, SecII, p20.
The New Yorker. Jul 13, 1981, v57, p82-83.
Rolling Stone. Aug 6, 1981, p34-35.
Variety. Jun 15, 1981, p3.

The Stripper (US; Schaffner, Franklin J.; 1963)
Commonweal. Jun 28, 1963, v78, p377.
Film Daily. Apr 25, 1963, p4.

Filmfacts. Jun 27, 1963, v6, p118-20.
Films in Review. May 1963, v14, p310.
Hollywood Reporter. Apr 24, 1963, v175, p3.
The New York Times. Dec 20, 1963, p29.
Photoplay. Jul 1963, v64, p14.
Saturday Review. Jul 13, 1963, v46, p16.
Time. May 3, 1963, v81, p109.
Variety. May 24, 1963, p15.

Stronger Than the Night (German title: Starker Als Die Nacht) (EGER; Dudow, Slatan; 1954)
Dictionary of Films. p354.
Magill's Survey of Cinema. Foreign Language Films. v6, p2983-87.

The Student Prince (US; Thorpe, Richard; 1954)
America. Jun 12, 1954, v91, p306.
BFI/Monthly Film Bulletin. Dec 1954, v21, p180.
Catholic World. Jul 9, 1954, v179, p303-04.
Commonweal. Jul 9, 1954, v60, p344.
Film Daily. Jun 1, 1954, p6.
Films and Filming. Oct 1954, v1, p24.
Films in Review. Jun-Jul 1954, v5, p309.
Hollywood Reporter. May 25, 1954, p3.
The London Times. Oct 18, 1954, p2.
Motion Picture Herald Product Digest. May 29, 1954, p9.
The New York Times. Jun 16, 1954, p18.
The New Yorker. Jun 26, 1954, v30, p60.
Newsweek. Jun 28, 1954, v43, p72.
Time. Jun 14, 1954, v63, p106.
Variety. May 26, 1954, p6.

A Study in Terror (Also titled: Fog) (GB; Hill, James; 1965)
BFI/Monthly Film Bulletin. Dec 1965, v32, p186.
Commonweal. Apr 29, 1966, v84, p179.
Deerstalker. p222-27.
Film Daily. Apr 20, 1966, p6.
Filmfacts. Jan 1, 1966, v9, p314-15.
Films and Filming. Jan 1966, v12, p29.
Films in Review. Aug-Sep 1966, v17, p453.
The Films of Sherlock Holmes. p209-14.
Hollywood Reporter. Apr 18, 1966, p3.
Holmes of the Movies. p132-41.
The London Times. Nov 4, 1965, p17.
Motion Picture Herald Product Digest. Apr 27, 1966, p509-10.
The New York Times. Nov 3, 1966, p45.
Playboy. Jun 1966, v13, p36.
Sherlock Holmes on the Screen. p210-18.
Sight and Sound. Wint 1965-66, v35, p44.
The Spectator. Nov 5, 1965, v215, p586.
Time. Nov 25, 1966, v88, p125.
Variety. Nov 24, 1965, p6.

The Stunt Man (US; Rush, Richard; 1980)
Film Comment. Nov-Dec 1980, v16, p21-25.
Hollywood Reporter. Jun 6, 1980, p3.
The Los Angeles Times. Aug 17, 1980, Calendar, p1.
Maclean's. Oct 13, 1980, v93, p70.
Magill's Survey of Cinema. Series II. v5, p2321-36.
Motion Picture Herald Product Digest. Oct 22, 1980, p37.
The New Leader. Nov 17, 1980, v63, p18.
The New Republic. Nov 8, 1980, v183, p22-24.
New York. Oct 27, 1980, v13, p72.
The New York Times. Oct 17, 1980, SecIII, p6.
The New York Times. Dec 21, 1980, SecII, p19.
The New Yorker. Sep 29, 1980, v56, p134-36.
Newsweek. Sep 1, 1980, v96, p45.
Saturday Review. Nov 1980, v7, p82.
Time. Sep 1, 1980, v116, p58.
Variety. Jun 11, 1980, p20.

Su Donne Per L'Assassino *See* Blood and Black Lace

The Subject Was Roses (US; Grosbard, Ulu; 1968)
America. Nov 9, 1968, v119, p445.
Christian Century. Feb 5, 1969, v86, p186.
Christian Science Monitor (Western edition). Oct 21, 1968, p4.
Commonweal. Nov 29, 1968, v89, p317.
Film Daily. Sep 26, 1968, p4.
Filmfacts. Jan 1, 1969, v11, p404-06.
Films in Review. Nov 1968, v19, p579.
Going Steady. p193-94.
Hollywood Reporter. Sep 25, 1968, p3.
Motion Picture Herald Product Digest. Oct 2, 1968, p33-34.
The New York Times. Oct 14, 1968, p53.
Newsweek. Oct 28, 1968, v72, p114.
Saturday Review. Oct 19, 1968, v51, p39.
Senior Scholastic. Dec 6, 1968, v93, p28.
Variety. Sep 25, 1968, p28.
Vogue. Nov 15, 1968, v152, p96.

Submarine Command (US; Farrow, John; 1951)
BFI/Monthly Film Bulletin. Oct 1951, v18, p350.
Christian Century. Mar 26, 1952, v69, p383.
Film Daily. Aug 29, 1951, p5.
The Films of William Holden. p122-24.
Hollywood Reporter. Aug 29, 1951, p3.
Motion Picture Herald Product Digest. Sep 1, 1951, p998.
The New Statesman and Nation. Oct 13, 1951, v42, p404.
The New York Times. Jan 19, 1952, p13.
Newsweek. Nov 12, 1951, v38, p102.
The Spectator. Oct 5, 1951, v187, p426, 428.
Time. Feb 18, 1952, v59, p88.
Variety. Aug 29, 1951, p6.

The Subterraneans (US; MacDougall, Ranald; 1960)
BFI/Monthly Film Bulletin. Jul 1960, v27, p101.
Commonweal. Aug 5, 1960, v72, p403.
Film Daily. Jun 21, 1960, p8.
Film Quarterly. Fall 1960, v14, p62.
Filmfacts. 1960, v3, p190.
Films and Filming. Aug 1960, v6, p25.
Films in Review. Aug-Sep 1960, v11, p430-31.
Hollywood Reporter. Jun 21, 1960, p3.
The New York Times. Jul 7, 1960, p26.
Newsweek. Jul 18, 1960, v56, p88.
Saturday Review. Jul 9, 1960, v43, p24.
Time. Jun 20, 1960, v75, p64.
Variety. Jun 22, 1960, p6.
The World of Entertainment. p496-504.

Successo, Il (IT, FR; Morassi, Mauro; 1963)
Christian Science Monitor (Western edition). Jun 12, 1965, p6.
Commonweal. May 21, 1965, v82, p293.
Filmfacts. Jun 25, 1965, v8, p113-15.
Motion Picture Herald Product Digest. May 12, 1965, p283.
The New York Times. Apr 29, 1965, p40.
The New Yorker. May 8, 1965, v41, p168.
Newsweek. May 17, 1965, v65, p104.
Private Screenings. p185-86.
Time. May 14, 1965, v85, p105.
Variety. Oct 23, 1963, p6.

Such Good Friends (US; Preminger, Otto; 1971)
BFI/Monthly Film Bulletin. Apr 1972, v39, p79.
The Cinema of Otto Preminger. p76.
Commonweal. Mar 10, 1972, v96, p16.

Films and Filming. May 1972, v18, n81, p55-56.
Focus. Aut 1972, n8, p57-58.
Hollywood Reporter. Dec 15, 1971, p3.
Interview. Feb 1972, n19, p40.
Life. Jan 28, 1972, v72, p14.
Magill's Survey of Cinema. Series II. v5, p2329.
The New Republic. Jan 22, 1972, v166, p24.
The New York Times. Dec 22, 1971, p28.
The New Yorker. Jan 8, 1972, v47, p77-78.
Saturday Review. Jan 22, 1972, v55, p26.
Take One. Apr 1972, v3, n3, p23-24.
Time. Jan 10, 1972, v99, p50.
Variety. Dec 22, 1971, p6.

The Sucker (French title: Corniaud, Le) (FR, IT; Oury, Gérard; 1965)
America. Oct 21, 1967, v117, p451.
BFI/Monthly Film Bulletin. Jun 1966, v33, p92-93.
Christian Science Monitor (Western edition). Nov 17, 1967, p6.
Film Daily. Jun 9, 1966, p8.
Filmfacts. Dec 1, 1967, v10, p303-04.
Films and Filming. Dec 1965, v12, p10-11.
Films and Filming. Jun 1966, v12, p10-11.
Hollywood Reporter. Nov 13, 1966, p3.
The London Times. Apr 21, 1966, p9.
New Statesman. Apr 22, 1966, v71, p588-89.
The New York Times. Oct 9, 1967, p61.
Playboy. Sep 1966, v13, p58.
Saturday Review. Apr 30, 1966, v49, p53.
Variety. Apr 7, 1965, p30.

Sudden Fear (US; Miller, David; 1952)
BFI/Monthly Film Bulletin. Oct 1952, v19, p146.
Christian Century. Oct 15, 1952, v69, p1207.
Commonweal. Aug 15, 1952, v56, p462.
Film Daily. Jul 24, 1952, p4.
The Films of Joan Crawford. p182-84.
Holiday. Nov 1952, v12, p26.
Hollywood Reporter. Jul 23, 1952, p3.
Illustrated London News. Oct 4, 1952, v221, p560.
Life. Sep 1, 1952, v33, p57-58.
The London Times. Sep 22, 1952, p2.
Motion Picture Herald Product Digest. Jul 26, 1952, p1461.
The Nation. Sep 27, 1952, v175, p282.
National Parent-Teacher. Oct 1952, v47, p38.
The New Statesman and Nation. Sep 27, 1952, v44, p349.
The New York Times. Aug 8, 1952, p9.
The New Yorker. Aug 16, 1952, v28, p82.
Newsweek. Aug 18, 1952, v40, p83.
A Reference Guide to the American Film Noir. p171.
Saturday Review. Oct 18, 1952, v35, p31.
Theatre Arts. Oct 1952, v36, p73.
Time. Aug 11, 1952, v60, p90.
Variety. Jul 23, 1952, p6.

Sudden Impact (US; Eastwood, Clint; 1983)
Hollywood Reporter. Dec 7, 1983, p3.
The Los Angeles Times. Dec 9, 1983, SecVI, p19.
Maclean's. Dec 19, 1983, v96, p55.
Magill's Cinema Annual, 1984. p395-98.
New York. Jan 16, 1984, v17, p62.
The New York Times. Dec 9, 1983, SecIII, p12.
Newsweek. Dec 12, 1983, v102, p109.
Time. Dec 19, 1983, v122, p74.

Sudden Terror (Also titled: Blind Terror) (US; Hough, John; 1971)
America. Apr 24, 1971, v124, p436.
Films and Filming. Nov 1970, v17, n2, p50-51.
Hollywood Reporter. Feb 8, 1971, p3.
The New York Times. Sep 26, 1974, p24.

Suddenly (US; Allen, Lewis; 1954)
America. Oct 9, 1954, v92, p55.
BFI/Monthly Film Bulletin. Nov 1954, v21, p159.
Catholic World. Sep 1954, v179, p465-66.
Commonweal. Nov 12, 1954, v61, p168.
Farm Journal. Oct 1954, v78, p137.
Film Daily. Sep 7, 1954, p6.
Films in Review. Oct 1954, v5, p434.
The Films of Frank Sinatra. p80-83.
Hollywood Reporter. Sep 7, 1954, p3.
Life. Oct 25, 1954, v37, p134.
The London Times. Sep 20, 1954, p9.
Motion Picture Herald Product Digest. Sep 11, 1954, p137.
National Parent-Teacher. Nov 1954, v49, p40.
The New York Times. Oct 8, 1954, p27.
The New Yorker. Oct 16, 1954, v30, p147.
Newsweek. Aug 30, 1954, v44, p76-77.
A Reference Guide to the American Film Noir. p171-72.
Time. Sep 6, 1954, v64, p88.
Variety. Sep 8, 1954, p6.

Suddenly, Last Summer (US; Mankiewicz, Joseph L.; 1959)
America. Jan 9, 1960, v102, p428-29.
BFI/Monthly Film Bulletin. 1960, v27, p81.
Commonweal. Jan 1, 1960, v71, p396.
Film Daily. Dec 16, 1959, v116, p6.
Filmfacts. Jan 20, 1960, v2, p319-21.
Films in Review. Jan 1960, v11, p4, 39-41.
The Films of Elizabeth Taylor. p139-43.
The Films of Katharine Hepburn. p172-77.
The Films of Montgomery Clift. p179-84.
The Films of Tennessee Williams. p173-96.
Hollywood Reporter. Dec 16, 1959, p3.
Joseph L. Mankiewicz (Dick). p113-19.
Magill's Survey of Cinema. Series II. p2333-35.
McCall's. Feb 1960, v87, p8.
The Nation. Jan 16, 1960, v190, p59.
The New Republic. Jan 18, 1960, v142, p20.
The New York Times. Dec 23, 1959, p22.
The New Yorker. Jan 9, 1960, v35, p74-75.
Newsweek. Dec 28, 1959, v54, p64.
Reporter. Feb 4, 1960, v22, p37-38.
Saturday Review. Jan 2, 1960, v43, p31.
Tennessee Williams and Film. p49-59.
Time. Jan 11, 1960, v75, p64.
Variety. Dec 16, 1959, p6.

The Sugarland Express (US; Spielberg, Steven; 1974)
BFI/Monthly Film Bulletin. Jul 1974, v41, p158.
Dialogue. Jul 1974, v3, p22-44.
Esquire. Jun 1974, v81, p40.
Film. Jul 1974, n16, p18.
Film Quarterly. 1974, v27, n4, p2-10.
Filmmakers Newsletter. Jul-Aug 1974, v7, p30-34.
Films and Filming. Aug 1974, v20, p41.
Films and Filming. Jul 1974, v20, p29-31.
Films Illustrated. Jul 1974, v3, p422.
Films in Review. May 1974, v25, p307-08.
Hollywood Reporter. Mar 15, 1976, p3.
Independent Film Journal. Mar 18, 1974, v73, p9.
Jump Cut. Jul-Aug 1974, n2, p3.
The Los Angeles Times. Apr 5, 1974, SecIV, p1.
Magill's Survey of Cinema. Series II. v5, p2336-39.
Motion Picture Herald Product Digest. Mar 27, 1974, p86.
Movietone News. Apr 1974, n31, p26.
The New Republic. Jun 8, 1974, v170, p34.
New Statesman. Jun 14, 1974, v87, p861.
New York. Apr 1, 1974, v7, p80-81.
The New York Times. Apr 7, 1974, SecII, p11.

The New York Times. Apr 28, 1974, SecII, p1.
The New Yorker. Mar 18, 1974, v50, p130.
Newsweek. Apr 8, 1974, v83, p82.
Penthouse. Jul 1974, v5, p36.
Reeling. p404-08.
Rolling Stone. May 9, 1974, p160.
Saturday Review. May 18, 1974, v1, p39.
Time. Apr 15, 1974, v103, p92.
Variety. Mar 20, 1974, p18.
The Village Voice. May 16, 1974, v19, p97-98.

Sult *See* Hunger

Summer and Smoke (US; Glenville, Peter; 1961)
America. Nov 25, 1961, v106, p308.
BFI/Monthly Film Bulletin. Apr 1962, v29, p49.
Commonweal. Dec 1, 1961, v75, p259.
Film Daily. Nov 17, 1961, p6.
Filmfacts. Dec 1, 1961, v4, p275-77.
Films in Review. Dec 1961, v17, p621.
The Films of Tennessee Williams. p226-48.
Magill's Survey of Cinema. Series II. v5, p2339-43.
The New Republic. Nov 27, 1961, v145, p18.
The New York Times. Nov 17, 1961, p41.
The New York Times. Jan 29, 1961, SecII, p7.
The New York Times. Nov 19, 1961, SecII, p1.
The New Yorker. Nov 25, 1961, v37, p205-6.
Newsweek. Nov 20, 1961, v58, p106.
Saturday Review. Nov 11, 1961, v44, p32.
Tennessee Williams and Film. p67-83.
Time. Dec 1, 1961, v78, p76.
Variety. Sep 6, 1961, p6.

Summer Interlude *See* Illicit Interlude

Summer Madness *See* Summertime

Summer Magic (US; Neilson, James; 1963)
America. Aug 10, 1963, v109, p143.
BFI/Monthly Film Bulletin. Jul 1963, v30, p103.
The Disney Films. p212-13.
Film Daily. Jun 26, 1963, p9.
Filmfacts. Aug 15, 1963, v6, p160-61.
Films and Filming. Jul 1963, v9, p27.
Hollywood Reporter. Jun 26, 1963, v175, p3.
The New York Times. Aug 22, 1963, p19.
Variety. Jun 26, 1963, p6.
Walt Disney: A Guide to References and Resources. p89-90.

Summer of '42 (US; Mulligan, Robert; 1971)
America. May 8, 1971, v124, p492-93.
Atlantic. Jul 1971, v228, p98-99.
BFI/Monthly Film Bulletin. Aug 1971, v38, n451, p170.
Commonweal. May 21, 1971, v94, p261.
Esquire. Jul 1971, v76, p48.
Film Quarterly. Wint 1971, v25, p57-58.
Filmfacts. 1971, v14, p133-36.
Films and Filming. Sep 1971, v17, n12, p54-55.
Films in Review. May 1971, v22, n5, p310-11.
Hollywood Reporter. Apr 15, 1971, p3.
Magill's Survey of Cinema. Series I. v4, p1652-42.
The New Republic. May 29, 1971, v164, p26.
The New York Times. Apr 19, 1971, p51.
The New York Times. May 23, 1971, v2, p15.
Newsweek. Apr 26, 1971, v77, p91.
Sight and Sound. Sum 1971, v40, n3, p167.
Time. May 10, 1971, v97, p99.
Variety. Apr 21, 1971, p17.
The Village Voice. Apr 22, 1971, p69.

A Summer Place (US; Daves, Delmer; 1959)
America. Oct 31, 1959, v102, p138.

BFI/Monthly Film Bulletin. Feb 1960, v27, p22.
Commonweal. Nov 20, 1959, v71, p240.
Film Daily. Oct 9, 1959, v116, p6.
Filmfacts. Dec 2, 1959, v2, p263-65.
Films in Review. Nov 1959, v10, p562.
The Films of the Fifties. p268-70.
Hollywood Reporter. Oct 7, 1959, p3.
Magill's Survey of Cinema. Series II. v5, 2344-47.
McCall's. Dec 1959, v87, p6.
The New York Times. Oct 23, 1959, p24.
The New Yorker. Oct 31, 1959, v35, p174.
Newsweek. Oct 26, 1959, v54, p122-23.
Saturday Review. Nov 7, 1959, v42, p29.
Time. Nov 9, 1959, v74, p84.
Variety. Oct 7, 1959, p6.

Summer Stock (Also titled: If You Feel Like Singing) (US; Walters, Charles; 1950)
BFI/Monthly Film Bulletin. Dec 1950, v17, p185.
Christian Century. Oct 4, 1950, v67, p1183.
Commonweal. Sep 29, 1950, v52, p605.
Film Daily. Aug 11, 1950, p7.
Films and Filming. Sep 1964, v10, p34.
The Films of Gene Kelly. p115-19.
Hollywood Reporter. Aug 4, 1950, p3.
Judy: The Films and Career of Judy Garland. p157-60.
Motion Picture Herald Product Digest. Aug 12, 1950, p434.
The New York Times. Sep 1, 1950, p17.
The New Yorker. Sep 9, 1950, v26, p98.
Newsweek. Sep 11, 1950, v36, p87.
The Spectator. Nov 3, 1950, v185, p446.
Time. Sep 11, 1950, v56, p104.
Variety. Aug 9, 1950, p8.

Summer Wishes, Winter Dreams (US; Cates, Gilbert; 1973)
Audience. Dec 1973, v6, p4-5.
The New York Times. Oct 22, 1973, p46.
The New York Times. Jan 9, 1974, p24.
The New Yorker. Dec 10, 1973, v49, p169-72.
Newsweek. Nov 19, 1973, v82, p138-39.
PTA Magazine. Feb 1974, v68, p7.
Time. Nov 12, 1973, v102, p123-24.
TV Movies. 1983-84, p745.
Variety. Oct 24, 1973, p17.
The Village Voice. Nov 15, 1973, p81-82.

Summertime (Also titled: Summer Madness) (GB; Lean, David; 1955)
America. Jul 2, 1955, v93, p359.
Catholic World. Jul 1955, v181, p303.
The Cinema of David Lean. p119-28.
Commonweal. Jul 1, 1955, v62, p330.
David Lean: A Guide to References and Resources. p84-86.
David Lean and His Films. p133-48.
David Lean (Anderegg). p86-91.
Fifty from the Fifties. p333-40.
Film Culture. Sum 1955, v1, n4, p23-24.
Films and Filming. Nov 1955, v2, n2, p16.
Films in Review. Aug-Sep 1955, v6, n7, p342.
The Films of Katharine Hepburn. p155-58.
Halliwell's Harvest. p256-58.
Hollywood Reporter. Jun 8, 1955, v134, n50, p3.
Library Journal. Jun 15, 1955, v80, p1487.
Life. Jul 25, 1955, v39, p55-56.
Motion Picture Herald Product Digest. Jun 18, 1955, p482.
The Nation. Jul 9, 1955, v181, p30-31.
The New York Times. Aug 22, 1954, SecII, p5.
The New York Times. Sep 19, 1954, SecVI, p66-67.
The New York Times. May 31, 1955, p24.

The New York Times. Jun 22, 1955, p25.
The New York Times. Jun 26, 1955, SecII, p1.
The New Yorker. Jun 25, 1955, v31, p64.
Newsweek. Jul 4, 1955, v46, p77.
Saturday Review. Jun 18, 1955, v38, p33-34.
Sight and Sound. Aut 1955, v25, n2, p88-89.
Time. Jun 27, 19055, v65, p88.
Variety. Jun 8, 1955, p6.

The Sun Also Rises (US; King, Henry; 1957)
America. Sep 7, 1957, v97, p604.
BFI/Monthly Film Bulletin. Dec 1957, v24, p148-49.
The Classic American Novel and the Movies. p268-71.
Commonweal. Sep 13, 1957, v66, p588.
Film Culture. Oct 1957, v3, p17-18.
Film Daily. Aug 23, 1957, v112, p5.
Films and Filming. Dec 1957, v4, p23.
Films in Review. Oct 1957, v8, p405-06.
The Films of Errol Flynn. p211-13.
The Films of Tyrone Power. p199-202.
Hemingway on Film. p106-34.
Hollywood Reporter. Aug 23, 1957, p3.
Magill's Survey of Cinema. Series II. v5, p2352-54.
Motion Picture Herald Product Digest. Aug 31, 1957, v208, p514-15.
The Nation. Oct 12, 1957, v185, p251.
The New Republic. Sep 30, 1957, v137, p22.
The New York Times. May 5, 1957, SecII, p5.
The New York Times. May 26, 1957, SecVI, p66.
The New York Times. Aug 24, 1957, p12.
The New Yorker. Aug 31, 1957, v33, p54.
Newsweek. Sep 9, 1957, v50, p110.
Saturday Review. Sep 7, 1957, v40, p25.
Time. Sep 2, 1957, v70, p59.
Variety. Aug 28, 1957, p6.

The Sun Shines Bright (US; Ford, John; 1953)
BFI/Monthly Film Bulletin. Oct 1953, v20, n237, p146.
Film Daily. May 6, 1953, p6.
Films in Review. Jun-Jul 1953, v4, n6, p300-01.
Hollywood Reporter. May 1, 1953, p3.
Magill's Survey of Cinema. Series II. v5, p2355.
The New York Times. Mar 18, 1954, p25.
The Non-Western Films of John Ford. p29-45.
Sight and Sound. Oct-Dec 1953, v23, n2, p88-89.
Variety. May 6, 1953, p16.

Sunday Bloody Sunday (GB; Schlesinger, John; 1971)
America. Oct 16, 1971, v125, p292-93.
BFI/Monthly Film Bulletin. Jul 1971, v38, p146.
Commonweal. Nov 26, 1971, v95, p207.
Deeper into Movies. p289-92.
Double Takes. p233-36.
Film Comment. Sum 1972, v7, n2, p22-26.
Film Library Quarterly. Wint 1971-72, v5, n1, p14-21.
Film Quarterly. Spr 1972, v25, p56-58.
Filmfacts. 1971, v14, p273-78.
Films and Filming. May 1971, v17, n8, p83-86.
Films and Filming. Aug 1971, v17, n11, p50-51.
Films and Filming. Sep 30, 1971, v17, n39, p67.
Films in Review. Oct 1971, v22, n8, p512-13.
Hollywood Reporter. Sep 21, 1971, v218, n2, p3.
John Schlesinger. p131-34.
John Schlesinger: A Guide to References and Resources. p289-92.
Life. Oct 8, 1971, v71, p16.

Magill's Survey of Cinema. Series II. v5, p2363-66.
The Nation. Oct 18, 1971, v213, p382.
The New Republic. Oct 9, 1971, v165, p24.
The New York Times. Sep 22, 1971, p56.
The New York Times. Oct 3, 1971, SecII, p13.
The New York Times. Nov 28, 1971, SecII, p13.
The New Yorker. Oct 2, 1971, v47, p93-97.
Newsweek. Sep 27, 1971, v77, p106.
Saturday Review. Sep 25, 1971, v54, p71.
Sight and Sound. Aut 1970, v39, n4, p200-01.
Sight and Sound. Sum 1971, v40, n3, p164.
Take One. Jul-Aug 1970, v11, n12, p18-19.
Time. Sep 27, 1971, v98, p82.
Variety. Jul 7, 1971, p14.
The Village Voice. Sep 30, 1971, p67.
Women and their Sexuality in the New Film. p55-74.

Sunday in August (Italian title: Domenica d'Agosto) (IT; Emmer, Luciano; 1951)
Film Criticism and Caricatures, 1943-1953. p119-20.
Illustrated London News. Jan 27, 1951, v218, p140.
The London Times. Jan 19, 1951, p6.
The New Statesman and Nation. Jan 20, 1951, v41, p66.
Rotha on Film. p166-67.
Sequence. New Year 1951, n13, p15-16.
The Spectator. Jan 19, 1951, v186, p76.
Variety. May 3, 1950, p20.

Sunday in New York (US; Tewksbury, Peter; 1964)
BFI/Monthly Film Bulletin. Jan 1965, v32, p5.
Christian Century. Apr 8, 1964, v81, p462-63.
Commonweal. Mar 6, 1964, v79, p694.
Film Daily. Dec 20, 1963, v123, p5.
Films and Filming. Jul 1964, v10, p21-22.
Films in Review. Jan 1964, v15, p45.
The Films of Jane Fonda. p98-102.
The Fondas. p197-98.
Hollywood Reporter. Dec 18, 1963, v178, p3.
Motion Picture Herald Product Digest. Jan 8, 1964, v231, p962.
The New Republic. Feb 8, 1964, v63, p89.
The New York Times. Feb 12, 1964, p30.
Newsweek. Feb 24, 1964, v63, p89.
Saturday Review. Feb 15, 1964, v47, p33.
Sight and Sound. Wint 1964-65, v34, p41.
Talking Pictures. p70-72.
Time. Feb 14, 1964, v83, p94.
Variety. Dec 18, 1963, p6.

A Sunday in the Country (French title: Dimanche à la campagne) (FR; Tavernier, Bertrand; 1985)
American Film. Oct 1984, v10, p30-36.
BFI/Monthly Film Bulletin. Aug 1984, v51, p240.
Chicago. Dec 1984, v33, p133-34.
Christian Century. Jun 5, 1985, v102, p589.
Commonweal. Mar 8, 1985, v112, p147-48.
The Los Angeles Times. Jan 11, 1985, SecVI, p12.
Maclean's. Jan 7, 1985, v98, p69.
National Review. Feb 8, 1985, v37, p55-58.
The New Leader. Nov 26, 1984, v67, p19-20.
The New York Times. Oct 2, 1985, SecIII, p14.
Newsweek. Jan 14, 1985, v105, p52.
Playboy. Dec 1984, v31, p40.

Sunday Woman (Italian title: Donna della Domenicia, La) (IT, FR; Comencini, Luigi; 1976)
Film Bulletin. Sep-Oct 1976, v40-41.
Independent Film Journal. Oct 29, 1976, v78, p11-12.

Motion Picture Herald Product Digest. Sep 29, 1976, p35.
New York. Oct 4, 1976, v9, p78-80.
The New York Times. Sep 27, 1976, p41.
Time. Oct 11, 1976, v108, p90.
Variety. Jan 28, 1976, p15.
The Village Voice. Oct 18, 1976, p57.

Sundays & Cybele (French title: Dimanches de Ville D'Avray, Les; Cybels, ou Les Dimanches de Ville D'Avray; Sundarpat Ville d'Avray) (FR; Bourguignon, Serge; 1962)
BFI/Monthly Film Bulletin. Feb 1963, v30, p15-16.
Cineaste. Sum 1967, v1, p18-25, 28.
Cinema. 1963, v1, n4, p44.
Commonweal. Dec 7, 1962, v77, p278-79.
Film Daily. Nov 14, 1962, p4.
Film Quarterly. Spr 1963, v16, p52-53.
Film Society Review. Sep 1967, p13-15.
Filmfacts. Dec 28, 1962, v5, p307-08.
Films and Filming. Feb 1963, v9, p34-35.
Films in Review. Dec 1962, v13, p623-24.
The Great French Films. p264.
Magill's Survey of Cinema. Foreign Language Series. 1985, v6, p3002-06.
Motion Picture Herald Product Digest. Nov 28, 1962, p698.
The Nation. Dec 8, 1962, v195, p412.
The New Republic. Dec 15, 1962, v147, p26.
The New York Times. Nov 13, 1962, p43.
The New Yorker. Nov 17, 1962, v38, p209.
Newsweek. Nov 26, 1962, v60, p92.
Private Screenings. p47-51.
Saturday Review. Dec 1, 1962, v45, p75.
Time. Dec 7, 1962, v80, p51.
Variety. Sep 21, 1962, p16.
A World on Film. p258-59.

The Sundowners (US; Templeton, George; 1950)
Commonweal. May 19, 1950, v52, p152.
Film Daily. Jan 12, 1950, p6.
Filmfacts. 1960, v3, p317.
Films and Filming. Feb 1961, v7, p30.
Films in Review. Jan 1961, v12, p34-35.
Hollywood Reporter. Jan 11, 1950, p3.
Motion Picture Herald Product Digest. Jan 14, 1950, p153.
The New York Times. May 5, 1950, p17.
Newsweek. May 15, 1950, v35, p92.
Sight and Sound. Wint 1960, v30, p36-37.
Time. May 22, 1950, v55, p106.
Variety. Jan 11, 1950, p6.

The Sundowners (US; Zinnemann, Fred; 1960)
America. Dec 10, 1960, v104, p382-84.
BFI/Monthly Film Bulletin. Feb 1961, v28, p21.
Commonweal. Dec 9, 1960, v73, p279-80.
Coronet. Dec 1960, v49, p16.
Film Daily. Nov 1, 1960, p10.
Filmfacts. 1960, v3, p317.
Films and Filming. Jan 1961, v7, p34-35.
The Great Adventure Films. p230-35.
Hollywood Reporter. Oct 27, 1960, p3.
Life. Nov 7, 1960, v49, p69-70.
Magill's Survey of Cinema. Series II. v5, p2367-70.
McCall's. Nov 1960, v88, p6.
The New Republic. Jan 2, 1961, v144, p23.
The New York Times. Dec 9, 1960, p39.
The New York Times. Dec 18, 1960, SecII, p3.
The New Yorker. Dec 17, 1960, v36, p137-38.
Newsweek. Dec 19, 1960, v56, p88.
Robert Mitchum on the Screen. p166-68.
Saturday Review. Dec 31, 1960, v43, p25.
Senior Scholastic. Dec 7, 1960, v77, p31.

Sight and Sound. Wint 1960-61, v30, p36-37.
Time. Dec 19, 1960, v76, p69.
Variety. Nov 2, 1960, p6.

Sunna No Onna *See* Woman in the Dunes

Sunrise at Campobello (US; Donehue, Vincent J.; 1960)
America. Oct 8, 1960, v104, p56.
Commonweal. Oct 7, 1960, v73, p46-48.
Esquire. May 1961, v55, p44.
Film Daily. Sep 21, 1960, p7.
Film Quarterly. Wint 1960, v14, p62.
Filmfacts. 1960, v3, p229.
Films and Filming. Jul 1961, v7, p28.
Films in Review. Oct 1960, v11, p488-89.
Hollywood Reporter. Sep 20, 1960, p3.
McCall's. Dec 1960, v88, p6.
The New Republic. Oct 17, 1960, v143, p20.
The New York Times. Sep 29, 1960, p32.
The New York Times. Oct 2, 1960, SecII, p1.
The New Yorker. Oct 8, 1960, v36, p106-07.
Newsweek. Oct 10, 1960, v56, p104.
Saturday Review. Sep 24, 1960, v43, p30.
Senior Scholastic. Oct 12, 1960, v77, p31.
Sight and Sound. Spr 1961, v30.
Time. Oct 10, 1960, v76, p75.
Variety. Sep 21, 1960, p6.

Sunset Boulevard (US; Wilder, Billy; 1950)
Agee on Film. v1, p411-15.
American Cinematographer. Sep 1950, v31, p309.
BFI/Monthly Film Bulletin. Sep 1950, v17, p137.
Billy Wilder (Dick). p152-60.
Billy Wilder in Hollywood. p149-71.
Billy Wilder (Madsen). p76, 82-86.
Christian Century. Nov 15, 1950, v67, p1375.
Cinema, the Magic Vehicle. v2, p46-47.
Classic Movies. p178-79.
Commonweal. Aug 25, 1950, v52, p486.
Dictionary of Films. p362-63.
Esquire. Dec 1950, v34, p74.
Fifty From the Fifties. p341-48.
The Film Career of Billy Wilder. p78-80.
Film Daily. Apr 17, 1950, p8.
Film Reader. 1977, n2, p90-95.
Films in Review. May-Jun 1950, v1, p28-32.
The Films of Gloria Swanson. p237-43.
The Films of the Fifties. p20-24.
The Films of William Holden. p108-11.
Fortnight. Sep 1, 1950, v9, p32.
The Great Films. p198-01.
The Great Movies. p167-69.
Halliwell's Hundred. p342-45.
Hollywood Reporter. Apr 17, 1950, p3.
Illustrated London News. Sep 2, 1950, v217, p370.
The International Dictionary of Films and Filmmakers. v1, p461-62.
Kenyon Review. n3, 1951, v13, p539-42.
Kiss Kiss Bang Bang. p446-47.
Life. Jun 5, 1950, v28, p81-82.
The London Times. Aug 18, 1950, p10.
The London Times. Aug 21, 1950, p6.
Magill's Survey of Cinema. Series I. v4, p1655-59.
Motion Picture Herald Product Digest. Apr 22, 1950, p269.
The Nation. Sep 23, 1950, v171, p273-75.
New American Mercury. Dec 1950, v71, p674-78.
The New Republic. Sep 4, 1950, v123, p22.
The New Statesman and Nation. Aug 26, 1950, v40, p226, 228.
The New York Times. Aug 11, 1950, p15.
The New Yorker. Aug 19, 1950, v26, p70.
Newsweek. Jun 26, 1950, v35, p82-84.
On the Verge of Revolt. p1-12.

Quarterly Review of Film Studies. n4, 1983, v8, p19-32.
Saturday Review. Aug 19, 1950, v33, p26-27.
Saturday Review. Nov 4, 1950, v33, p26.
Selected Film Criticism, 1941-1950. p231-33.
Senior Scholastic. Jan 3, 1951, v57, p3.
Sequence. Aut 1950, n12, p16-17.
Shots in the Dark. p219-24.
Sight and Sound. Nov 1950, v19, p283-85.
Sight and Sound. Jan 1951, v19, p376.
The Spectator. Aug 18, 1950, v185, p210.
Talking Pictures. p147-50.
Time. Aug 14, 1950, v56, p82.
Time. Oct 5, 1983, v122, p43.
Variety. Apr 19, 1950, p6.
The Village Voice. Aug 18, 1960, v5, p6.

Superfly (US; Parks, Gordon; 1972)
Filmfacts. 1972, v15, n18, p445.
Hollywood Reporter. Jul 26, 1972, p3.
Magill's Survey of Cinema. Series I. v4, p1660.
The New York Times. Aug 5, 1972, p14.
The New York Times. Aug 13, 1972, SecII, p9.
The New York Times. Nov 12, 1972, SecII, p1.
Reeling. p98-104.
Time. Sep 11, 1972, v100, p78.
Time. Jul 9, 1973, v102, p40.
Variety. Aug 2, 1972, p18.

Supergirl (US; Szwarc, Jeannot; 1984)
BFI/Monthly Film Bulletin. Jul 1984, v51, p213-14.
Film Journal. Dec 1984, v87, p13-14.
Films and Filming. Jul 1984, n358, p26.
Health. May 1984, v16, p20-22.
Hollywood Reporter. Nov 20, 1984, p3.
The Los Angeles Times. Nov 21, 1984, SecVI, p4.
Maclean's. Dec 24, 1984, v97, p50.
New Statesman. Jul 20, 1984, v108, p29.
New York. Dec 3, 1984, v17, p144.
The New York Times. Nov 22, 1984, SecIII, p15.
Newsweek. Nov 26, 1984, v104, p119.
Photoplay. Aug 1984, v35, p10-12.
Time. Nov 26, 1984, v124, p105.
Variety. Jul 18, 1984, p16.
The Village Voice. Nov 27, 1984, p68.

Superman (US; Donner, Richard; 1978)
America. Jan 6, 1978, v140, p15.
BFI/Monthly Film Bulletin. Feb 1979, v46, p33.
Business Week. Dec 12, 1978, p147.
Films in Review. Feb 1979, v30, p119.
The Films of the Seventies. p232-37.
Hollywood Reporter. Dec 16, 1978, p16.
The Los Angeles Times. Dec 15, 1978, SecIV, p1.
Maclean's. Dec 25, 1978, v91, p49-50.
The Making of Superman. 1978.
Motion Picture Herald Product Digest. Jan 3, 1979, p61.
The New Leader. Jan 15, 1979, v62, p22.
The New Republic. Jan 13, 1979, v180, p27.
New York. Jan 8, 1979, v12, p70.
The New York Times. Dec 15, 1978, SecIII, p15.
The New York Times. Dec 24, 1978, SecII, p11.
The New Yorker. Jan 1, 1979, v54, p54-55.
Newsweek. Jan 1, 1979, v93, p46-51.
Newsweek. Oct 9, 1978, v92, p91.
Superman Blueprints. 1978.
Time. Nov 27, 1978, v112, p59-61.
Time. Aug 1, 1977, v110, p64-65.
Variety. Dec 13, 1978, p24.
The World of Fantastic Films. p169-70.

Superman II (US; Lester, Richard; 1981)
America. Jul 4, 1981, v145, p15.
Commonweal. Aug 28, 1981, v108, p470-71.

Hollywood Reporter. Dec 3, 1980, p2.
The Los Angeles Times. Jun 18, 1981, SecVI, p1.
Magill's Cinema Annual, 1982. p339-42.
The New Leader. Jun 29, 1981, v64, p20
New York. Jun 22, 1981, v14, p49-50.
The New York Times. Jun 19, 1981, SecIII, p8.
The New York Times. Jun 21, 1980, SecII, p17.
Newsweek. Jun 22, 1981, v97, p87.
Time. Jun 8, 1981, v117, p74-75.
Variety. Dec 3, 1980, p22.

Superman III (US; Lester, Richard; 1983)
Hollywood Reporter. Jun 9, 1983, p3.
The Los Angeles Times. Jun 17, 1983, SecVI, p1.
Maclean's. Jun 20, 1983, v96, p55.
Magill's Cinema Annual, 1984. p399-403.
The New Leader. Jun 27, 1983, v66, p22.
The New Republic. Jul 18, 1983, v189, p22-23.
The New York Times. Jun 17, 1983, SecIII, p4.
The New Yorker. Jul 11, 1983, v59, p90.
Newsweek. Jun 20, 1983, v101, p83.
Sight and Sound. Sum 1983, v53, p194.
Time. Jun 13, 1983, v121, p69.

Support Your Local Gunfighter (US; Kennedy, Burt; 1971)
BFI/Monthly Film Bulletin. Aug 1972, v39, p172.
Filmfacts. 1971, v14, p100-01.
Films and Filming. Sep 1972, v18, n12, p44.
Hollywood Reporter. May 19, 1971, v216, n16, p3.
The New York Times. May 27, 1971, p33.
Variety. May 12, 1971, p19.
The Village Voice. Jul 8, 1971, v16, n27, p59.

Support Your Local Sheriff (US; Kennedy, Burt; 1969)
America. May 3, 1969, v110, p549.
Big Screen, Little Screen. p167-68.
Film Daily. Mar 13, 1969, p7.
Filmfacts. 1969, v12, p166.
Films and Filming. Oct 1969, v16, p52.
Films in Review. May 1969, v20, p314-15.
Life. Apr 11, 1969, v66, p16.
Magill's Survey of Cinema. Series II. v5, p2380-83.
The New York Times. Apr 9, 1969, p55.
Senior Scholastic. Apr 11, 1969, v94, p21.
Sight and Sound. Sum 1969, v38, p158-59.
Variety. Feb 26, 1969, p6.

The Sure Thing (US; Reiner, Rob; 1985)
BFI/Monthly Film Bulletin. Feb 1986, v53, p50.
Films in Review. Jun 1985, v36, p368.
Hollywood Reporter. Feb 26, 1985, p3.
The Los Angeles Times. Mar 1, 1985, SecVI, p1.
Maclean's. Mar 11, 1985, v98, p62.
Magill's Cinema Annual, 1986. p369-73.
The New Leader. Mar 25, 1985, v68, p20-21.
The New Republic. Apr 8, 1985, v192, p24-25.
New York. Mar 18, 1985, v18, p80-81.
The New York Times. Mar 1, 1985, SecIII, p12.
Time. Mar 18, 1985, v125, p84.
Variety. Feb 27, 1985, p14.

Surprise Package (GB; Donen, Stanley; 1960)
America. Dec 3, 1960, v104, p352.
BFI/Monthly Film Bulletin. Nov 1960, v27, p157.
Commonweal. Sep 23, 1960, v72, p519.
Film Daily. Oct 13, 1960, p6.
Filmfacts. 1960, v3, p273.
Films and Filming. Nov 1960, v7, p31.

Hollywood Reporter. Oct 11, 1960, p3.
The New York Times. Oct 15, 1960, p26.
Stanley Donen (Casper). p155-58.
Time. Nov 14, 1960, v76, p92.
Variety. Oct 12, 1960, p6.

Surrender (US; Dwan, Allan; 1950)
BFI/Monthly Film Bulletin. Feb 1951, v18, p220.
Film Daily. Oct 10, 1950, p6.
Hollywood Reporter. Oct 9, 1950, p3.
Motion Picture Herald Product Digest. Oct 14, 1950, p518.
The New York Times. Oct 9, 1950, p21.
Variety. Oct 11, 1950, p8.

The Survivors (US; Ritchie, Michael; 1983)
Hollywood Reporter. Jun 21, 1983, p3.
Maclean's. Jun 27, 1983, v96, p53.
The New Republic. Jul 11, 1983, v189, p23-24.
The New Yorker. Jul 25, 1983, v59, p80-81.
Newsweek. Jul 4, 1983, v102, p78.
Time. Jul 4, 1983, v122, p73.

Susan Slept Here (US; Tashlin, Frank; 1954)
America. Aug 7, 1954, v91, p466.
BFI/Monthly Film Bulletin. Sep 1954, v21, p136.
Catholic World. Sep 1954, v179, p464.
Film Daily. Jun 25, 1954, p6.
Hollywood Reporter. Jun 23, 1954, p3.
The London Times. Aug 2, 1954, p9.
Motion Picture Herald Product Digest. Jun 19, 1954, p41.
National Parent-Teacher. Sep 1954, v49, p39.
The New York Times. Jul 30, 1954, p9.
The Tatler. Aug 11, 1954, v213, p244.
Variety. Jun 23, 1954, p6.

Suzanne Simonin, La Religieuse de Diderot
See Religieuse, La

Swann in Love (French title: Amour de Swann, Un) (FR, WGER; Schlöndorff, Volker; 1984)
BFI/Monthly Film Bulletin. Apr 1984, v51, p112-13.
Contemporary Review. Jun 1984, v244, p324-27.
Double Exposure. p219-29.
Film Journal. Sep 1984, v87, p16.
Film Journal. Aug 1984, v87, p15.
Films and Filming. Jun 1984, n357, p37-38.
Films in Review. Aug-Sep 1984, v35, p420.
The Los Angeles Times. Dec 20, 1984, SecVI, p1.
Maclean's. Oct 15, 1984, v97, p77.
National Review. Nov 16, 1984, v36, p55-57.
The New Republic. Jul 30, 1984, v191, p30-31.
New Statesman. Apr 6, 1984, v107, p42.
New York. Sep 24, 1984, v17, p95-96.
New York Review of Books. Aug 16, 1984, v31, p40-43.
The New York Times. Sep 14, 1984, SecIII, p4.
The New Yorker. Oct 1, 1984, v60, p112.
Newsweek. Oct 1, 1984, v104, p80.
Sight and Sound. Fall 1984, v53, p221-22.
Stills. Jun-Jul 1984, n12, p101.
Time. Oct 15, 1984, v124, p99.
Variety. Mar 21, 1984, p16.
The Village Voice. Sep 25, 1984, p59.
Vogue. Jun 1984, v174, p52.

The Swarm (US; Allen, Irwin; 1978)
BFI/Monthly Film Bulletin. Sep 1978, v45, p183.
Films in Review. Oct 1978, v29, p503.
The Films of Henry Fonda. p243-44.
The Films of Olivia De Havilland. p253-55.
Hollywood Reporter. Jul 14, 1978, p3.
The Los Angeles Times. Jul 15, 1978, SecII, p8.

Maclean's. Aug 7, 1978, v91, p58.
Motion Picture Herald Product Digest. Aug 9, 1978, p20.
The New York Times. Jul 15, 1978, p8.
The New York Times. Jul 23, 1978, SecII, p13.
The New Yorker. Jul 31, 1978, v54, p66-68.
Newsweek. Aug 14, 1978, v92, p62.
Time. Aug 21, 1978, v112, p53.
Variety. Jul 19, 1978, p20.
The World of Fantastic Films. p40, 155.

Sweet Bird of Youth (US; Brooks, Richard; 1962)
BFI/Monthly Film Bulletin. Jun 1962, v29, p78-79.
Commonweal. Mar 30, 1962, v76, p18.
Film Daily. Feb 28, 1962, p6.
Film Quarterly. Sum 1962, v15, p64.
Filmfacts. Apr 20, 1962, v5, p65-67.
Films and Filming. Jun 1962, v8, p35.
Films in Review. Apr 1962, v13, p233-34.
The Films of Paul Newman. p106-11.
The Films of Tennessee Williams. p154-72.
Hollywood Reporter. Feb 28, 1962, v169, p3.
Magill's Survey of Cinema. Series II. v5, p2387-90.
Motion Picture Herald Product Digest. Feb 28, 1962, p460.
The New Republic. Apr 16, 1962, v146, p28.
The New York Times. Mar 29, 1962, p28.
The New Yorker. Apr 7, 1962, v38, p148.
Newsweek. Apr 2, 1962, v59, p86.
Saturday Review. Mar 31, 1962, v45, p26.
Tennessee Williams and Film. p63-98.
Time. Mar 30, 1962, v79, p83.
Variety. Feb 28, 1962, p6.
A World on Film. p85-87.

Sweet Charity (US; Fosse, Bob; 1969)
America. Apr 12, 1969, v120, p455.
Big Screen, Little Screen. p168-70, 215-17.
Dance Magazine. Jul 1969, v43, p25-26.
Film Daily. Jan 29, 1969, p4.
Filmfacts. 1969, v12, p131.
Films and Filming. Apr 1969, v15, p39-40.
The Films of Shirley MacLaine. p155-59.
Holiday. Apr 1969, v45, p38.
Look. May 13, 1969, v33, p57.
The New York Times. Apr 2, 1969, p38.
The New York Times. Apr 6, 1969, SecII, p1.
Newsweek. Feb 17, 1969, v73, p100.
Saturday Review. Mar 29, 1969, v52, p39.
Senior Scholastic. May 2, 1969, v94, p28.
Sight and Sound. Spr 1969, v38, p98.
Time. Feb 21, 1969, v93, p87.
Variety. Jan 29, 1969, p6.

Sweet Dreams (US; Reisz, Karel; 1985)
BFI/Monthly Film Bulletin. Mar 1986, v53, p85.
Commonweal. Nov 15, 1985, v112, p648.
Films in Review. Dec 1985, v36, p621.
Horizon. Oct 1985, v28, p30-32.
The Los Angeles Times. Oct 2, 1985, SecVI, p1.
Maclean's. Oct 21, 1985, v98, p86.
Magill's Cinema Annual, 1986. p374-77.
Ms. Dec 1985, v14, p31.
The Nation. Nov 16, 1985, v241, p531-33.
The New York Times. Oct 2, 1985, SecIII, p17.
The New Yorker. Oct 21, 1985, v61, p122-23.
Newsweek. Oct 7, 1985, v106, p88.
Time. Oct 7, 1985, v126, p66.
Variety. Oct 2, 1985, p9.

Sweet Light In a Dark Room (Czech title: Tma; Also titled: Romeo, Juliet and Darkness; Romeo, Julie a Tina) (CZECH; Weiss, Jiri; 1960)
Film Daily. Jun 20, 1966, p6.
Film Quarterly. Wint 1960, v14, p49-50.

Filmfacts. Sep 1, 1966, v9, p167-68.
Films and Filming. Feb 1962, v8, p29.
Motion Picture Herald Product Digest. Jun 29, 1966, p552.
The New York Times. Jun 30, 1966, p28.
Private Screenings. p269-70.
Variety. Sep 14, 1960, p20.

Sweet Movie (YUGO; Makavejev, Dusan; 1974)
Film Quarterly. Wint 1974, v28, p4-10.
Hollywood Reporter. Nov 19, 1975, p15.
The Nation. Nov 1, 1975, v221, p443-44.
The New York Times. Oct 10, 1975, p32.
Self and Cinema. p87-191.
Time. Nov 3, 1975, v106, p70.
Variety. May 22, 1974, p19.

Sweet Smell of Success (US; Mackendrick, Alexander; 1957)
BFI/Monthly Film Bulletin. Aug 1957, v24, p99.
Burt Lancaster: A Pictorial Treasury of His Films. p97.
Burt Lancaster: The Man and His Movies. p76-78.
Commonweal. Jul 12, 1957, v111, p376.
Film Culture. 1957, v3, n3, p16.
Film Daily. Jun 19, 1957, v61, p7.
Film Noir. p277-78.
Films and Filming. Sep 1957, v3, p25-26.
Films in Review. Aug-Sep 1957, v8, p354.
The Films of the Fifties. p231-32.
Hollywood Reporter. Jun 19, 1957, p3.
Magill's Survey of Cinema. Series II. v5, p2391-94.
Motion Picture Herald Product Digest. Jun 22, 1957, v207, p425.
The Nation. Jul 20, 1957, v185, p39.
The New Republic. Aug 12, 1957, v137, p22.
The New York Times. Jun 28, 1957, p29.
The New York Times. Jun 30, 1957, SecII, p1.
The New Yorker. Jul 6, 1957, v33, p57.
Newsweek. Jul 1, 1957, v50, p78.
Saturday Review. Jul 6, 1957, v40, p23.
Sight and Sound. Aut 1957, v27, p89-90.
Talking Pictures. p188-95.
Time. Jun 24, 1957, v69, p84.
Tony Curtis: The Man and His Movies. p68-70.
Variety. Jun 19, 1957, p6.
The Village Voice. Aug 28, 1957, p8.

Swept Away: By an Unusual Destiny in the Blue Sea of August (Italian title: Travolti da un Isolito Destino Nell'Azuro Mare d'Agosto) (IT; Wertmuller, Lina; 1975)
Atlantic. Dec 1975, v236, p102.
Before My Eyes. p183.
BFI/Monthly Film Bulletin. Jun 1977, v44, p130.
Commonweal. Oct 10, 1975, v102, p470-71.
Film Quarterly. Spr 1976, v29, p49-53.
Films in Review. Nov 1975, v26, p568.
Hollywood Reporter. Oct 9, 1975, p7.
The Los Angeles Times. Nov 9, 1975, Calendar, p36.
Magill's Survey of Cinema. Foreign Language Films. v6, p3097-10.
Ms. Dec 1975, v4, p37-38.
The Nation. Oct 4, 1975, v221, p318.
The New Republic. Oct 18, 1975, v173, p20.
The New York Times. Sep 18, 1975, p48.
The New York Times. Sep 21, 1975, SecII, p15.
The New Yorker. Sep 22, 1975, v51, p94.
Newsweek. Oct 6, 1975, v86, p84.
The Parables of Lina Wertmuller. p30-35, 44-46.
Progressive. May 1976, v40, p39-40.
Saturday Review. Nov 1, 1975, v3, p49.

The Screenplays of Lina Wertmuller. p181-275.
Time. Oct 6, 1975, v106, p65-66.
Variety. Jan 1, 1975, p16.

The Swimmer (US; Perry, Frank; Pollack, Sydney; 1968)
America. Jun 1, 1968, v118, p739-40.
BFI/Monthly Film Bulletin. Dec 1968, v35, p196-97.
Burt Lancaster: A Pictorial Treasury of His Films. p134-35.
Burt Lancaster: The Man and His Movies. p106-07.
Christian Century. Jul 17, 1968, v85, p921-22.
Commonweal. Jun 7, 1968, v88, p361.
Film Daily. May 15, 1968, p4.
Filmfacts. Jul 1, 1968, v11, p166-68.
Films and Filming. Dec 1968, v15, p36-37.
Films in Review. Jun-Jul 1968, v19, p377-78.
Hollywood Reporter. May 15, 1968, p3.
The London Times. Oct 31, 1968, p14.
Magill's Survey of Cinema. Series II. v5, p2395-97.
Motion Picture Herald Product Digest. May 22, 1968, p813.
The New Republic. Jun 8, 1968, v158, p43.
The New York Times. May 16, 1968, p53.
The New Yorker. May 25, 1968, v44, p84.
Newsweek. May 27, 1968, v71, p94.
Saturday Review. May 25, 1968, v51, p16.
Sight and Sound. Aut 1968, v37, p206-07.
The Spectator. Nov 8, 1968, v221, p671-72.
Time. May 24, 1968, v91, p101-02.
Variety. May 15, 1968, p6.

Swing Shift (US; Demme, Jonathan; 1984)
Film Journal. Jun 1984, v87, p26.
Films in Review. Jun-Jul 1984, v35, p370.
The Los Angeles Times. Apr 13, 1984, SecVI, p1.
Maclean's. Apr 23, 1984, v97, p50.
Ms. Jul 1984, v13, p46.
National Review. Jun 15, 1984, v36, p55-56.
The New Republic. May 21, 1984, v190, p24-25.
New York. Apr 30, 1984, v17, p87-88.
The New York Times. Apr 29, 1984, SecII, p17.
The New York Times. May 4, 1984, SecIII, p8.
The New Yorker. May 14, 1984, v60, p138-40.
Newsweek. Apr 23, 1984, v103, p80.
On Location. Apr 1984, v7, p52.
Penthouse. Aug 1984, v15, p42.
Theatre Crafts. May 1984, v18, p8.
Time. Apr 23, 1984, v123, p83.
Variety. Apr 18, 1984, p10.
The Village Voice. May 1, 1984, p47.

The Swinger (US; Sidney, George; 1966)
BFI/Monthly Film Bulletin. Feb 1967, v34, p30.
Christian Science Monitor (Western edition). Nov 18, 1966, p4.
Film Daily. Nov 4, 1966, p6.
Filmfacts. Jan 15, 1967, v9, p341-42.
Films and Filming. Mar 1967, v13, p33-34.
Hollywood Reporter. Nov 1, 1966, p3.
The London Times. Dec 22, 1966, p15.
Motion Picture Herald Product Digest. Nov 9, 1966, p626.
The New York Times. Dec 15, 1966, p60.
Newsweek. Dec 26, 1966, v68, p73.
Variety. Nov 2, 1966, p6.

Swiss Family Robinson (US; Annakin, Ken; 1960)
BFI/Monthly Film Bulletin. Feb 1961, v28, p24.
Commonweal. Dec 23, 1960, v73, p341.
Coronet. Dec 1960, v49, p16.
The Disney Films. p176-78.
Film Daily. Nov 15, 1960, p10.
Filmfacts. 1960, v3, p331.

Films and Filming. Jan 1961, v7, p33.
The Great Adventure Films. p224-29.
Hollywood Reporter. Nov 9, 1960, p3.
Life. Jan 20, 1961, v50, p81-82.
Look. Dec 20, 1960, v24, p85-87.
The New York Times. Dec 24, 1960, p8.
Saturday Evening Post. Dec 10, 1960, v233, p38-39.
Saturday Review. Dec 3, 1960, v43, p36.
Time. Jan 13, 1961, v77, p47.
Variety. Nov 9, 1960, p6.
Walt Disney: A Guide to References and Resources. p73-74.

Swiss Tour *See* Four Days Leave

The Switchboard Operator *See* Love Affair, or The Case of the Missing Switchboard Operator

Sword and the Rose (US; Annakin, Ken; 1953)
America. Aug 22, 1953, v89, p507.
BFI/Monthly Film Bulletin. Jul 1953, v20, n234, p103.
Catholic World. Aug 1953, v177, p386.
Commonweal. Aug 28, 1953, v58, p520.
Film Daily. Jul 2, 1953, p8.
Hollywood Reporter. Jul 1, 1953, p3.
Library Journal. Aug 1953, v78, p1321.
The New York Times. Aug 20, 1953, p18.
The New York Times. Aug 23, 1953, SecII, p1.
The New Yorker. Aug 22, 1953, v29, p50.
Newsweek. Sep 14, 1953, v42, p105.
Saturday Review. Sep 5, 1953, v36, p26.
Time. Sep 14, 1953, v62, p111.
Variety. Jul 1, 1953, p6.

The Sword in the Stone (US; Reitherman, Wolfgang; 1963)
BFI/Monthly Film Bulletin. Feb 1964, v3, p22.
The Disney Films. p216-17.
Film Daily. Oct 3, 1963, p14.
Filmfacts. Dec 19, 1963, v6, p286-87.
Films and Filming. Jan 1964, v10, p25-26.
The New Republic. Dec 21, 1963, v149, p30.
The New York Times. Dec 26, 1963, p33.
Photoplay. Jan 1964, v65, p21.
Variety. Oct 2, 1963, p6.
Walt Disney: A Guide to References and Resources. p92-93.

Swords of Blood *See* Cartouche

Synanon (Also titled: Get Off My Back) (US; Quine, Richard; 1965)
America. May 29, 1965, v112, p810.
BFI/Monthly Film Bulletin. Mar 1966, v33, p37.
Christian Science Monitor (Western edition). May 8, 1965, p10.
Commonweal. May 28, 1965, v82, p320.
Confessions of a Cultist. p207-08.
Film Daily. May 3, 1965, p7.
Film Quarterly. Sum 1965, v18, p61.
Filmfacts. Jul 9, 1965, v8, p126-28.
Films and Filming. May 1966, v12, p11.
Films and Filming. Feb 1966, v12, p11.
Films in Review. Jun-Jul 1965, v16, p384-85.
Hollywood Reporter. May 3, 1965, p3.
Life. May 14, 1965, v58, p19.
The London Times. Jan 20, 1966, p17.
Motion Picture Herald Product Digest. May 12, 1965, p282.
The New Republic. May 29, 1965, v152, p33-34.
New Statesman. Jan 28, 1966, v71, p136.
The New York Times. May 6, 1965, p44.
The New Yorker. May 8, 1965, v41, p167-68.
Newsweek. May 17, 1965, v65, p104.
Playboy. Jun 1965, v12, p26.
Saturday Review. May 1, 1965, v48, p51.
Time. May 14, 1965, v85, p108.

Variety. May 5, 1965, p6.
The Village Voice. Sep 9, 1965, v10, p15.

The System *See* The Girl-Getters

Szegenylegenyek *See* The Round-Up

T. R. Baskin (Also titled: A Date With a
  Lonely Girl) (US; Ross, Herbert; 1971)
BFI/Monthly Film Bulletin. Apr 1972, v39,
  p69.
Filmfacts. 1971, v14, p562-64.
Films in Review. Nov 1971, v22, n9, p570-71.
Hollywood Reporter. Oct 13, 1971, v218, n17,
  p3.
The New York Times. Oct 21, 1971, p56.
The New Yorker. Oct 23, 1971, v47, p144-46.
Newsweek. Nov 1, 1971, v78, p89-90.
Saturday Review. Nov 6, 1971, v54, p70.
Variety. Oct 13, 1971, p20.
The Village Voice. Nov 25, 1971, p81.

Take Care of My Little Girl (US;
  Negulesco, Jean; 1951)
BFI/Monthly Film Bulletin. Feb 1952, v19,
  p17.
Christian Century. Aug 8, 1951, v68, p927.
Commonweal. Jul 27, 1951, v54, p380.
Film Daily. Jun 13, 1951, p7.
Motion Picture Herald Product Digest. Jun 16,
  1951, p887.
The Nation. Aug 11, 1951, v173, p118.
The New York Times. Jul 19, 1951, p20.
The New Yorker. Jul 28, 1951, v27, p74.
Newsweek. Jul 16, 1951, v38, p85.
Saturday Review. Jun 2, 1951, v34, p24.
Senior Scholastic. May 2, 1951, v58, p29-30.
Time. Jul 23, 1951, v58, p84.
Variety. Jun 13, 1951, p6.

Take Her, She's Mine (US; Koster, Henry;
  1963)
America. Nov 30, 1963, v109, p715-16.
BFI/Monthly Film Bulletin. Jan 1963, v31, p11.
Commonweal. Nov 15, 1963, v79, p225.
Film Daily. Oct 14, 1963, p4.
Filmfacts. Nov 21, 1963, v6, p254-55.
Films and Filming. Jan 1964, v10, p29-30.
Films in Review. Nov 1963, v14, p566-67.
The Films of James Stewart. p227-29.
The New York Times. Nov 14, 1963, p41.
Photoplay. Jan 1964, v65, p20.
Variety. Oct 16, 1963, p6.

Take It All *See* A Tout Prendre

The Taking of Pelham One Two Three
  (US; Sargent, John; 1974)
America. Nov 9, 1974, v131, Inside back cover.
BFI/Monthly Film Bulletin. Jan 1975, v42, p17.
Commonweal. Nov 1, 1974, v101, p110.
Films in Review. Nov 1974, v25, p568.
Hollywood Reporter. Oct 2, 1974, p3.
The Los Angeles Times. Oct 23, 1974, SecIV,
  p4.
Motion Picture Herald Product Digest. Oct 16,
  1974, p37.
The Nation. Nov 2, 1974, v219, p443.
New York. Oct 14, 1974, v7, p70-72.
The New York Times. Jan 28, 1974, p25.
The New Yorker. Oct 28, 1974, v50, p72.
Newsweek. Oct 7, 1974, v84, p95.
Variety. Oct 2, 1974, p22.
The Village Voice. Oct 31, 1974, p103.

The Taking of Power by Louis XIV *See*
  The Rise of Louis XIV

Taking Off (US; Forman, Milos; 1971)
BFI/Monthly Film Bulletin. Oct 1971, v38,
  p204.
Commonweal. May 21, 1971, v94, p262-63.
Filmfacts. 1971, v14, p61-65.

Films and Filming. Nov 1971, v18, n2, p54.
Life. Apr 2, 1971, v70, p12.
The Milos Forman Stories. p102-13, 114-24.
The Nation. Apr 19, 1971, v212, p508-09.
National Review. Jul 27, 1971, v23, p823.
The New Republic. Apr 24, 1971, v164, p22.
The New York Times. Mar 29, 1971, p40.
The New York Times. Apr 18, 1971, SecII, p1.
The New York Times. Apr 18, 1971, SecII, p13.
The New York Times. May 16, 1971, SecII,
  p11.
Newsweek. Apr 5, 1971, v77, p92.
Saturday Review. Mar 27, 1971, v54.
Sight and Sound. Aut 1971, v40, n4, p221-22.
Time. Apr 5, 1971, v97, p86.
*Unholy Fools, Wits, Comics, Disturbers of the
  Peace.* p340-44.
Variety. Mar 17, 1971, p18.
The Village Voice. Apr 1, 1971, p71, 74.

Tales After the Rain *See* Ugetsu

The Tales of Hoffman (GB; Powell,
  Michael; Pressburger, Emeric; 1951)
American Cinematographer. May 1951, v32,
  p176-77.
BFI/Monthly Film Bulletin. Jun 1951, v18,
  p277-78.
Christian Century. May 30, 1951, v68, p671.
Commonweal. Apr 20, 1951, v54, p38.
Film Daily. Apr 4, 1951, p6.
Films and Filming. Dec 1981, v27, p14-19.
Films in Review. May 1951, v2, p44-46.
Hollywood Reporter. May 31, 1951, p3.
Life. Mar 5, 1951, v30, p95-97.
Motion Picture Herald Product Digest. Apr 7,
  1951, p793.
Musical America. Apr 1951, v71, p8.
Musical America. Mar 1951, v71, p9.
The New Republic. Apr 9, 1951, v124, p22.
The New Statesman and Nation. Apr 28, 1951,
  v41, p476-77.
The New York Times. Apr 5, 1951, p34.
The New Yorker. Apr 14, 1951, v27, p111.
Newsweek. Apr 16, 1951, v37, p106-07.
Saturday Review. Apr 7, 1951, v34, p32.
Saturday Review. Apr 28, 1951, v34, p27.
Sight and Sound. May 1951, v20, p17-18.
The Spectator. Apr 27, 1951, v186, p553.
Theatre Arts. Jun 1951, v35, p40-41.
Time. Apr 23, 1951, v57, p108.
Variety. Apr 4, 1951, p6.

Tales of Ordinary Madness (IT; Ferreri,
  Marco; 1983)
The Nation. Apr 16, 1983, v236, p490.
The New Yorker. Mar 21, 1983, v59, p118-21.
Newsweek. Mar 21, 1983, v101, p71.

**Tales of the Pale and Silvery Moon After
  the Rain** *See* Ugetsu

Tall Headlines (Also titled: The Frightened
  Bride) (GB; Young, Terence; 1952)
BFI/Monthly Film Bulletin. May 1952, v19,
  p62.
Film Daily. Aug 21, 1953, p7.
The New Statesman and Nation. Apr 12 1952,
  v43, p434.
The New York Times. Aug 20, 1953, p18.
The Spectator. Apr 4, 1952, v188, p434.
Variety. Apr 23, 1952, p6.

Tall Story (US; Logan, Joshua; 1960)
America. Apr 23, 1960, v103, p170.
BFI/Monthly Film Bulletin. Jul 1960, v27, p94.
Commonweal. Apr 29, 1960, v72, p127.
Film Daily. Feb 10, 1960, p11.
Filmfacts. 1960, v3, p77.
Films and Filming. Jul 1960, v6, p26.
Films in Review. May 1960, v11, p288.
The Films of Jane Fonda. p73-77.

The Fondas. p176-77.
Hollywood Reporter. Feb 8, 1960, p3.
McCall's. May 1960, v87, p6.
The New York Times. Apr 7, 1960, p46.
Time. Apr 11, 1960, v75, p69.
Variety. Feb 10, 1960, p6.

The Tall Target (US; Mann, Anthony;
  1951)
BFI/Monthly Film Bulletin. Sep 1951, v18,
  p332.
Film Daily. Aug 7, 1951, p6.
Hollywood Reporter. Aug 1, 1951, p3.
The London Times. Jan 1, 1952, p8.
The Making of the Great Westerns. p263-72.
Motion Picture Herald Product Digest. Aug 4,
  1951, p966.
The New York Times. Sep 28, 1951, p26.
Newsweek. Sep 3, 1951, v38, p72.
Variety. Aug 1, 1951, p6.

The Tamarind Seed (GB; Edwards, Blake;
  1974)
American Cinematographer. Jul 1974, v55,
  p796-97.
BFI/Monthly Film Bulletin. Jul 1974, v41,
  p159.
Christian Century. Aug 21, 1974, v91, p805.
Hollywood Reporter. Jul 10, 1974, p3.
The Los Angeles Times. Jul 31, 1974, SecIV,
  p13.
Motion Picture Herald Product Digest. Jul 31,
  1974, p18.
New Statesman. Aug 23, 1974, v88, p263-64.
New York. Jul 15, 1974, v7, p62-63.
The New York Times. Jul 12, 1974, p41.
The New York Times. Jul 21, 1974, SecII, p1.
The New Yorker. Jul 15, 1974, v50, p58.
Newsweek. Jul 29, 1974, v84, p68-69.
Time. Aug 5, 1974, v104, p71.
Variety. Jul 10, 1974, p16.
The Village Voice. Jul 25, 1974, p75.

The Taming of the Shrew (US, IT;
  Zeffirelli, Franco; 1967)
America. Mar 25, 1967, v116, p480.
BFI/Monthly Film Bulletin. Apr 1967, v34,
  p57-58.
Christian Century. May 3, 1967, v84,.
Commonweal. Mar 24, 1967, v86, p19.
Film Daily. Mar 8, 1967, p5.
Film Quarterly. Fall 1967, v21, p61.
Films and Filming. Oct 1966, p50-52.
Films and Filming. Jun 1967, v13, p24-25.
Films in Review. Apr 1967, v18, p238.
The Films of Elizabeth Taylor. p179-83.
Hollywood Reporter. Mar 8, 1967, p3.
Look. Oct 4, 1966, v30, p58-63.
Mademoiselle. May 1967, v65, p97.
Motion Picture Herald Product Digest. Mar 29,
  1967, p669.
The New York Times. Mar 9, 1967, p43.
Newsweek. Mar 20, 1967, v69, p98.
Saturday Review. Mar 18, 1967, v50, p40.
Senior Scholastic. Apr 28, 1967, v90, p27-28.
Shakespeare on Film. p66-78.
Sight and Sound. Spr 1967, v36, p97-98.
Time. Mar 17, 1967, v89, p104.
Variety. Nov 2, 1966, p15.
Variety. Mar 1, 1967, p6.
The Village Voice. Mar 16, 1967, p25.
Vogue. Apr 15, 1967, v419, p49.

Tammy and the Bachelor (Also titled:
  Tammy) (US; Pevney, Joseph; 1957)
America. Jun 22, 1957, v97, p352.
BFI/Monthly Film Bulletin. Apr 1957, v24,
  p49.
Commonweal. Jun 7, 1957, v66, p257.
Film Daily. May 23, 1957, v111, p8.

The Films of the Fifties. p203-04.
Hollywood Reporter. May 21, 1957, p3.
Motion Picture Herald Product Digest. May 25, 1957, v207, p386.
The New York Times. Jun 15, 1957, p10.
Newsweek. Jun 10, 1957, v49, p114.
Variety. May 22, 1957, p6.

Tammy and the Doctor (US; Keller, Harry; 1963)
BFI/Monthly Film Bulletin. May 1964, v31, p79.
Film Daily. May 6, 1963, p15.
Filmfacts. Jul 18, 1963, v6, p137-38.
Films and Filming. Jul 1964, v10, p25.
The Fondas (Springer). p195-96.
Hollywood Reporter. May 6, 1963, v175, p3.
The New York Times. Jun 27, 1963, p23.
Photoplay. Jul 1963, v64, p15.
Time. Jul 12, 1963, v82, p95.
Variety. May 8, 1963, p6.

Tanganyika (US; De Toth, Andre; 1954)
BFI/Monthly Film Bulletin. Sep 1954, v21, p136-37.
Film Daily. Jun 22, 1954, p6.
Hollywood Reporter. Jun 8, 1954, p3.
Motion Picture Herald Product Digest. Jun 12, 1954, p26.
The New York Times. Jun 19, 1954, p9.
Newsweek. Jul 12, 1954, v44, p78.
Variety. Jun 9, 1954, p6.

Tanin No Kao *See* The Face of Another

Taps (US; Becker, Harold; 1981)
American Cinematographer. Apr 1982, v63, p350-53.
BFI/Monthly Film Bulletin. Mar 1982, v49, p49-50.
Christian Century. Mar 3, 1982, v99, p250-51.
Cinema Papers. Oct 1982, n40, p468-69.
Film Bulletin. Feb-Mar 1982, p54.
Film Journal. Feb 15, 1982, v85, p30.
Film Quarterly. Fall 1982, v35, p51-55.
Films In Review. Feb 1982, v33, p111-12.
Horizon. Mar 1982, v25, p70-71.
The Los Angeles Times. Dec 18, 1981, SecVI, p3.
The New Leader. Jan 25, 1982, v65, p20-21.
New Statesman. Mar 5, 1982, v103, p30-31.
New York. Dec 21, 1981, v14, p51-52.
The New York Times. Jan 17, 1982, SecII, p19.
The New York Times. Dec 20, 1981, SecIII, p28.
The New York Times. Dec 9, 1981, p18.
Photoplay. Apr 1982, v33, p25.
Senior Scholastic. Feb 19, 1982, v114, p18.
Time. Dec 14, 1981, v118, p94.
Variety. Dec 9, 1981, p18.
The Village Voice. Jan 20, 1982, p52.
The Village Voice. Dec 9, 1981, p18.

Taras Bulba (US; Thompson, J. Lee; 1962)
America. Jan 19, 1963, v108, p118-19.
BFI/Monthly Film Bulletin. May 1963, v30, p70.
Commonweal. Jan 25, 1963, v77, p461-62.
Film Daily. Dec 10, 1962, p4.
Film Quarterly. Wint 1963-64, v17, p62.
Filmfacts. Jan 11, 1963, v5, p326-28.
Films and Filming. Apr 1963, v9, p28-29.
Films in Review. Jan 1963, v14, p49.
Hollywood Reporter. Dec 10, 1962, p3.
Life. Dec 14, 1962, v53, p116-17.
Motion Picture Herald Product Digest. Dec 12, 1962, p713-14.
The New York Times. Dec 26, 1962, p5.
Newsweek. Dec 31, 1962, v60, p57.
Saturday Review. Dec 15, 1962, v45, p29.
Time. Jan 11, 1963, v81, p89.

Tony Curtis: The Man and His Movies. p92-95.
Variety. Dec 12, 1962, p6.

Target (US; Penn, Arthur; 1985)
BFI/Monthly Film Bulletin. Aug 1986, v53, p229.
Film Comment. Jul-Aug 1985, v21, p4.
Hollywood Reporter. Nov 6, 1985, p3.
The Los Angeles Times. Nov 8, 1985, SecVI, p6.
Maclean's. Nov 18, 1985, v98, p70.
The New Republic. Dec 9, 1985, v193, p24.
New York. Nov 25, 1985, v18, p89.
The New York Times. Nov 8, 1985, SecIII, p19.
The New Yorker. Dec 2, 1985, v61, p117-18.
Newsweek. Nov 18, 1985, v106, p94.
Time. Nov 18, 1985, v126, p92.
Variety. Nov 6, 1985, p26.

Targets (US; Bogdanovich, Peter; 1968)
BFI/Monthly Film Bulletin. Feb 1969, v36, p28-29.
Cinema. Spr 1968, v4, p30-33.
Confessions of a Cultist. p382-83.
Cult Movies. p339-42.
Figures of Light. p96-99.
Film 68/69. p166-68.
Film Daily. Aug 19, 1968, p4.
Film Heritage. Sum 1969, v4, p1-8.
Film Heritage. Fall 1969, v5, p1-8.
Film Quarterly. Sum 1968, v21, p61-62.
Filmfacts. Nov 1, 1968, v11, p306-08.
Films and Filming. Nov 1969, v16, p50.
Hollywood Reporter. May 6, 1968, p3.
Motion Picture Herald Product Digest. Aug 14, 1968, p841.
Movie. Spr 1968, n15, p32-33.
The New Republic. Aug 31, 1968, v159, p22.
The New York Times. Aug 14, 1968, p34.
The New York Times. Aug 25, 1968, p1.
The New Yorker. Sep 7, 1968, v44, p85.
Newsweek. Sep 9, 1968, v72, p94.
Sight and Sound. Aut 1968, v37, p188-89.
The Spectator. Sep 27, 1969, v223, p415.
Time. Sep 13, 1968, v92, p99.
Variety. May 15, 1968, p26.
The Village Voice. Aug 22, 1968, p31.

The Tarnished Angels (US; Sirk, Douglas; 1957)
America. Jan 18, 1958, v98, p468.
BFI/Monthly Film Bulletin. Jan 1958, v25, p9.
Douglas Sirk (Stern). p152-65.
Faulkner and Film. p158-68.
Film Daily. Nov 15, 1957, v112, p6.
Filmfacts. 1958, v1, p1.
Films and Filming. Feb 1958, v4, p24.
Hollywood Reporter. Nov 15, 1957, p3.
Magill's Survey of Cinema. Series II. v5, p2412-14.
Motion Picture Herald Product Digest. Nov 23, 1957, v209, p617-18.
The New York Times. Jan 7, 1958, p31.
The New Yorker. Jan 18, 1958, v33, p95.
Saturday Review. Jan 25, 1958, v41, p27.
Screen. Sum 1971, v12, p68-93.
Variety. Nov 20, 1957, p6.

Tarzan and the Lost Safari (US; Humberstone, Bruce; Stoloff, Victor; 1957)
BFI/Monthly Film Bulletin. Jan 1958, v25, p9-10.
Commonweal. May 3, 1957, v66, p127.
Film Daily. Mar 25, 1957, v111, p6.
Hollywood Reporter. Mar 25, 1957, p3.
Motion Picture Herald Product Digest. Mar 30, 1957, v206, p321.
The New York Times. Apr 13, 1957, p12.
Variety. Mar 27, 1957, p6.

A Taste of Honey (GB; Richardson, Tony; 1961)
America. Jul 2, 1962, v107, p359-60.
Commonweal. May 11, 1962, v76, p178-79.
Dictionary of Films. p367.
Film. Wint 1961, n30, p15.
Film Daily. Apr 30, 1962, p12.
Filmfacts. May 25, 1962, v5, p95-97.
Films and Filming. Nov 1961, v8, p22.
Films in Review. Jun-Jul 1962, v13, p366.
The Great British Films. p196-98.
Hollywood Reporter. Jun 28, 1962, p3.
I Lost It at the Movies. p176-80.
Magill's Survey of Cinema. Series II. v5, p2415-18.
Motion Picture Herald Product Digest. May 6, 1962, p557.
The Nation. May 19, 1962, v194, p455.
The New Republic. May 14, 1962, v146, p34.
The New York Times. May 1, 1962, p33.
The New York Times Magazine. Apr 8, 1962, p94.
The New Yorker. May 12, 1962, v38, p146-65.
Newsweek. May 7, 1962, v59, p88.
Saturday Review. Apr 14, 1962, v45, p37.
Screen. 1984, v25, n4/5, p2-21.
Sight and Sound. Aut 1961, v30, p196.
Time. May 18, 1962, v79, p93.
Variety. Sep 20, 1961, p6.
A World on Film. p185-87.

The Taste of Mackerel *See* An Autumn Afternoon

A Taste of the Fish Called Samma *See* An Autumn Afternoon

The Tattered Dress (US; Arnold, Jack; 1957)
America. Mar 23, 1957, v96, p716.
BFI/Monthly Film Bulletin. May 1957, v24, p61.
Film Daily. Feb 26, 1957, v111, p10.
Film Noir. p281.
Hollywood Reporter. Feb 26, 1957, p3.
Motion Picture Herald Product Digest. Mar 2, 1957, v206, p281.
The New York Times. Mar 15, 1957, p22.
Time. Apr 8, 1957, v69, p92.
Variety. Feb 27, 1957, p6.

Taxi Driver (US; Scorsese, Martin; 1976)
America. Mar 6, 1976, v134, p182.
Audience. Oct 1976, v9, p7-8.
Audience. Mar 1976, v8, p11-12.
Before My Eyes. p200.
BFI/Monthly Film Bulletin. Sep 1976, v43, p200-01.
Christian Century. May 12, 1976, v93, p467-69.
Cineaste. 1976, v7, n3, p34-35.
Cinema Papers. Sep-Oct 1976, n10, p170.
Commentary. May 1976, v61, p72-76.
Contemporary Review. Dec 1976, v229, p326-28.
Cult Movies 2. p150-53.
Fifty Grand Movies of the 1960s and 1970s. p117-20.
Film Bulletin. Feb 1976, v445, p35.
Film Comment. Mar-Apr 1976, v12, p4-5.
Film Comment. May-Jun 1976, v12, p26-30.
Film Comment. Jul-Aug 1976, v12, p2-4.
Film Quarterly. Sum 1976, v29, p37-41.
Films and Filming. Sep 1976, n22, p30-31.
Films and Filming. Aug 1976, v22, p42-43.
Films in Review. May 1976, v27, p308-10.
Films in Review. Mar 1976, v27, p185-86.
The Films of the Seventies. p139-40.
Independent Film Journal. Feb 4, 1976, v77, p7.

Newsweek. Aug 16, 1982, v100, p59.
Tempest. 1982.
Time. Aug 16, 1982, v120, p70.
Variety. Aug 11, 1982, p3, 20.
The Village Voice. Aug 17, 1982, p45.

Tempest in the Flesh *See* Rage au Corps, La

Tempesta, La *See* The Tempest

"10" (US; Edwards, Blake; 1979)
BFI/Monthly Film Bulletin. Jan 1980, v47, p12.
Blake Edwards (Lehman and Luhr). p214-19, 242-57.
The Films of the Seventies. p264.
Hollywood Reporter. Sep 28, 1979, p2.
Magill's Survey of Cinema. Series II. v5, p2426-29.
Motion Picture Herald Product Digest. Oct 17, 1979, p37.
The Nation. Dec 1, 1979, v229, p573-74.
The New York Times. Oct 5, 1979, SecIII, p6.
The New Yorker. Oct 29, 1979, v55, p147.
Newsweek. Oct 15, 1979, v94, p133.
Rolling Stone. Nov 29, 1979, p35-36.
Time. Oct 15, 1979, v114, p88.
Variety. Sep 26, 1979, p20.

The Ten Commandments (US; DeMille, Cecil B.; 1956)
America. Dec 1, 1956, v96, p284.
American Cinematographer. Apr 1983, v64, p46-52.
Cecil B. DeMille: A Guide to References and Resources. p108-10.
The Cinema of Edward G. Robinson. p205-09.
Commonweal. Nov 30, 1956, v65, p232-33.
Film Daily. Oct 5, 1956, p7.
Film Quarterly. Fall 1966, v20, p59-60.
Films and Filming. Oct 1956, v3, p8.
Films and Filming. Jan 1958, v4, p23-24.
Films in Review. Nov 1956, p461-63.
The Films of Cecil B. DeMille. p356-65.
The Films of Charlton Heston. p67-82.
The Films of the Fifties. p189-92.
Hollywood Reporter. Oct 5, 1956, p3.
Magill's Survey of Cinema. Series II. v5, p2430-33.
Make It Again, Sam. p205-09.
The Nation. Dec 8, 1956, v183, p506.
The New Republic. Dec 10, 1956, v135, p20.
The New York Times. Nov 9, 1956, p35.
The New York Times. Nov 11, 1956, SecII, p1.
The New York Times. Mar 25, 1984, SecII, p19.
The New Yorker. Nov 17, 1956, v32, p101.
Newsweek. Nov 5, 1956, v48, p112.
Saturday Review. Nov 10, 1956, v39, p28.
Sight and Sound. Wint 1957-58, v27, p148-49.
Surrealism and the Cinema. p30-32.
Time. Nov 12, 1956, v68, p120.
Time. Nov 19, 1956, v68, p82.
Variety. Oct 10, 1956, p6.

Ten Little Indians (GB; Pollock, George; 1965)
BFI/Monthly Film Bulletin. Mar 1966, v33, p46-47.
Christian Science Monitor (Western edition). Apr 1, 1966, p6.
Commonweal. Feb 18, 1966, v83, p586.
Film Daily. Dec 30, 1965, p4.
Filmfacts. Feb 15, 1966, v9, p13-14.
Films and Filming. Mar 1965, v12, p12.
Films and Filming. Apr 1966, v12, p12.
The London Times. Feb 3, 1966, p18.
Motion Picture Herald Product Digest. Jan 5, 1966, p436.
The New York Times. Feb 10, 1966, p33.
Time. Feb 11, 1966, v87, p85.
Variety. Dec 29, 1965, p6.

Ten Tall Men (US; Goldbeck, Willis; 1951)
BFI/Monthly Film Bulletin. Mar 1952, v19, p38.
Burt Lancaster: A Pictorial Treasury of His Films. p63.
Burt Lancaster: The Man and His Movies. p50-52.
Film Daily. Oct 26, 1951, p4.
Hollywood Reporter. Oct 24, 1951, p3.
The London Times. Mar 24, 1952, p8.
Motion Picture Herald Product Digest. Oct 27, 1951, p1073.
The New York Times. Oct 27, 1951, p10.
Newsweek. Nov 5, 1951, v38, p96.
Time. Nov 26, 1951, v58, p106.
Variety. Oct 24, 1951, p6.

Ten Thirty P.M. Summer (Also titled: 10: 30 P.M. Summer) (US, SP; Dassin, Jules; 1966)
BFI/Monthly Film Bulletin. Mar 1967, v34, p42-43.
Christian Science Monitor (Western edition). Feb 17, 1967, p4.
Commonweal. Nov 11, 1966, v85, p166.
Film Daily. Oct 20, 1966, p7.
Film Quarterly. Sum 1967, v20, p80.
Filmfacts. Dec 15, 1966, v9, p288-90.
Films and Filming. May 1967, v13, p31-32.
Films in Review. Nov 1966, v17, p587-88.
Hollywood Reporter. Oct 19, 1966, p3.
Kiss Kiss Bang Bang. p203-04.
The London Times. Feb 9, 1967, p4.
Motion Picture Herald Product Digest. Oct 26, 1966, p623.
The New Republic. Dec 10, 1966, v155, p34.
The New York Times. Oct 20, 1966, p52.
The New Yorker. Nov 5, 1966, v42, p198.
Newsweek. Nov 7, 1966, v68, p110-11.
Playboy. Dec 1966, v13, p48-49.
Private Screenings. p288-89.
Variety. Oct 19, 1966, p20.
The Village Voice. Nov 24, 1966, v12, p27-28.
Vogue. Nov 15, 1966, v148, p100.

Ten Thousand Bedrooms (US; Thorpe, Richard; 1957)
America. Apr 20, 1957, v97, p84.
BFI/Monthly Film Bulletin. May 1957, v24, p61.
Commonweal. Mar 22, 1957, v65, p639.
Film Daily. Feb 20, 1957, v111, p10.
Films and Filming. May 1957, v3, p28.
Hollywood Reporter. Feb 18, 1957, p3.
Motion Picture Herald Product Digest. Feb 23, 1957, v206, p273.
The New York Times. Apr 4, 1957, p37.
The New York Times. Apr 7, 1957, SecII, p1.
The New Yorker. Apr 13, 1957, v33, p166.
Newsweek. Apr 1, 1957, v49, p107.
Variety. Feb 20, 1957, p6.

The Tenant (French title: Locataire, Le) (FR; Polanski, Roman; 1976)
BFI/Monthly Film Bulletin. Sep 1976, v43, p193.
Commonweal. Aug 27, 1976, v103, p563-64.
Film Heritage. Fall 1976, p36-37.
Films and Filming. Oct 1976, v23, p31-32.
Films in Review. Aug-Sep 1976, v27, p441-42.
Independent Film Journal. Jun 25, 1976, v78, p15.
The Los Angeles Times. Jun 24, 1976, SecIV, p1.
Motion Picture Herald Product Digest. Jun 30, 1976, p10.
Movietone News. Oct 11, 1976, n52, p38-39.
The Nation. Jul 17, 1976, v223, p60.
The New Republic. Aug 7, 1976, v175, p27.
New Statesman. Aug 27, 1976, v91, p286-87.

New York. Jun 28, 1976, v9, p66-69.
The New York Times. Jun 27, 1976, p15.
The New Yorker. Jul 5, 1976, v52, p62-63.
Newsweek. Jun 28, 1976, v87, p78.
Roman Polanski: A Guide to References and Resources. p34-36.
Roman Polanski (Wexman). p70-76.
Saturday Review. Jul 24, 1976, v3, p42.
Sight and Sound. Sum 1976, v45, p84.
Sight and Sound. Wint 1976, v45, p253.
Time. Jul 26, 1976, v108, p68.
Variety. Jun 2, 1976, p16.
The Village Voice. Jul 26, 1976, p108.
Vogue. Aug 1976, v166, p64.

Tender Mercies (US; Beresford, Bruce; 1983)
America. Apr 23, 1983, v148, p322.
Christian Century. Aug 17, 1983, v100, p752.
Christianity Today. Jul 15, 1983, v27, p54.
Commonweal. Apr 8, 1983, v110, p210-11.
Films in Review. Apr 1983, v34, p242.
Hollywood Reporter. Mar 4, 1983, p3.
The Los Angeles Times. Mar 4, 1983, SecVI, p1.
Maclean's. May 16, 1983, v96, p52.
Magill's Cinema Annual, 1984. p409-13.
The Nation. Apr 30, 1983, v236, p553-54.
National Review. Apr 29, 1983, v35, p508-09.
The New Leader. Mar 21, 1983, v66, p21.
The New Republic. Apr 11, 1983, v188, p24-25.
New York. Mar 14, 1983, v16, p56-57.
The New York Times. Mar 4, 1983, SecIII, p8.
The New Yorker. May 16, 1983, v59, p119-21.
Newsweek. Mar 7, 1983, v101, p78.
Rolling Stone. Apr 28, 1983, p45-46.
Saturday Evening Post. Oct 1983, v255, p36-38.
Time. Mar 28, 1983, v121, p62.
Variety. Apr 1983, v173, p82.

Tender Scoundrel (French title: Tendre Voyou) (FR, IT; Becker, Jean; 1966)
Film Daily. Aug 10, 1967, p8.
Filmfacts. Jan 1, 1968, v10, p369-70.
Motion Picture Herald Product Digest. Aug 16, 1967, p715.
The New York Times. Nov 16, 1967, p58.
The New Yorker. Dec 2, 1967, v43, p154.
Variety. Oct 12, 1966, p24.

Tendre Poulet *See* Dear Detective

Tendre Voyou *See* Tender Scoundrel

Tengoku To-Jigoku *See* High and Low

Teni Zabytykh Predkov *See* Shadows of Forgotten Ancestors

Tennessee Champ (US; Wilcox, Fred McLeod; 1954)
BFI/Monthly Film Bulletin. Dec 1954, v21, p181.
Catholic World. Apr 1954, v179, p65.
Film Daily. Feb 24, 1954, p6.
Hollywood Reporter. Feb 15, 1954, p3.
Library Journal. Mar 15, 1954, v79, p541.
Motion Picture Herald Product Digest. Feb 20, 1954, p2189.
National Parent-Teacher. May 1954, v48, p40.
Newsweek. Mar 22, 1954, v43, p103.
Variety. Feb 17, 1954, p6.

The Tenth Victim (Also titled: Decima Vittima, La) (IT, FR; Petri, Elio; 1965)
BFI/Monthly Film Bulletin. Jan 1968, v35, p4.
Christian Science Monitor (Western edition). Dec 23, 1965, p4.
Cinema. Dec 1965, v3, p37-38.
Commentary. May 1966, v41, p74-75.
Commonweal. Jan 21, 1966, v83, p478.
Esquire. Jan 1966, v65, p81.
Film Daily. Dec 27, 1965, p11.

Film Quarterly. Spr 1966, v19, p53.
Films and Filming. Feb 1968, v14, p25-26.
Films and Filming. Apr 1966, v12, p57-59.
Films in Review. Jan 1966, v17, p46-47.
Great Horror Movies. p133-34, 142.
Motion Picture Herald Product Digest. Oct 27, 1965, p24.
Motion Picture Herald Product Digest. Jan 5, 1966, p435-36.
The Nation. Jan 3, 1966, v202, p27.
The New York Times. Dec 21, 1965, p46.
The New Yorker. Dec 25, 1965, v41, p56.
Newsweek. Jan 3, 1966, v67, p55.
Playboy. Mar 1966, v13, p24.
Private Screenings. p228-30.
Time. Dec 24, 1965, v86, p46.
Variety. Dec 22, 1965, p6.

Teorema (Also titled: Theorem) (IT; Pasolini, Pier Paolo; 1968)
America. May 10, 1969, v120, p569-70.
BFI/Monthly Film Bulletin. May 1969, v36, p96-97.
Big Screen, Little Screen. p173-75.
Christian Century. Dec 24, 1969, v86, p1647.
Christian Science Monitor (Western edition). May 26, 1969, p4.
Commonweal. May 16, 1969, v90, p265-66.
Commonweal. Mar 7, 1969, v89, p706-07.
Commonweal. May 23, 1969, v90, p292-93.
Directors and Directions: Cinema for the Seventies. p58-60.
Encounter. Jun 1969, v32, p41-42.
Film Comment. Jul-Aug 1983, v19, p20-23.
Film Daily. Apr 24, 1969, p20.
Film Quarterly. Fall 1969, v23, p24-29.
Film Society Review. Mar 1969, v4, p35-40.
Filmfacts. n9, 1969, v12, p204-07.
Films and Filming. Jun 1969, v15, p38-39.
Films in Review. Jun-Jul 1969, v20, p376-77.
The Great Romantic Films. p192-95.
Hollywood Reporter. May 23, 1969, p3.
International Film Guide. 1970, v7, p147-48.
Magill's Survey of Cinema. Foreign Language Films. v7, p3042-47.
Motion Picture Herald Product Digest. Apr 23, 1969, p173.
Movies Into Film. p146-49.
The Nation. May 5, 1969, v208, p582.
New Society. Apr 10, 1969, p567.
New Statesman. Apr 4, 1969, v77, p488-89.
The New York Times. Apr 22, 1969, p39.
The New Yorker. Apr 26, 1969, v45, p92-92.
Newsweek. May 5, 1969, v73, p108.
Pasolini on Pasolini. p155-62.
Pier Paolo Pasolini (Snyder). p105-19.
Saturday Review. May 10, 1969, v52, p41.
Sight and Sound. Wint 1968-69, v38, p5-6.
The Spectator. Apr 4, 1969, v222, p449.
Take One. May-Jun 1969, v2, p27-28.
Take One. Nov-Dec 1968, v2, p23.
Take One. Jan-Feb 1969, v2, p4-5.
Time. May 9, 1969, v93, p105.
Variety. Sep 18, 1968, p6.
The Village Voice. May 1, 1969, p47-48.

Teresa (US; Zinnemann, Fred; 1951)
BFI/Monthly Film Bulletin. May 1951, v18, p260.
Christian Century. Aug 15, 1951, v68, p951.
Commonweal. Mar 23, 1951, v53, p590.
Film Daily. Feb 28, 1951, p6.
Films in Review. Apr 1951, v2, p43-45.
Hollywood Reporter. Feb 28, 1951, p3.
Motion Picture Herald Product Digest. Mar 10, 1951, p750.
The Nation. Mar 10, 1951, v172, p237-38.
The New Republic. Apr 23, 1951, v124, p23.

The New Statesman and Nation. May 19, 1951, v41, p560.
The New York Times. Apr 6, 1951, p31.
Newsweek. Apr 9, 1951, v37, p86.
Saturday Review. Apr 14, 1951, v34, p47.
Senior Scholastic. Apr 18, 1951, v58, p21.
Sight and Sound. May 1951, v20, p18-19.
Sight and Sound. Mar 1951, v19, p426.
The Spectator. Apr 20, 1951, v186, p520.
Time. Apr 9, 1951, v57, p103-04.
Variety. Feb 28, 1951, p13.

Term of Trial (US; Glenville, Peter; 1963)
America. Feb 16, 1963, v108, p238.
Commonweal. Feb 8, 1963, v77, p517.
Film Daily. Jan 10, 1963, p3.
Filmfacts. Feb 14, 1963, v6, p5-6.
Films in Review. Feb 1963, v14, p111-12.
Hollywood Reporter. Jan 10, 1963, v173, p3.
The New Republic. Feb 9, 1963, v148, p30-31.
The New York Times. Jan 31, 1963, p5.
The New York Times. Feb 9, 1963, v38, p82-83.
Newsweek. Jan 28, 1963, v61, p88.
Photoplay. Mar 1963, v63, p6.
Time. Feb 15, 1963, v81, pM19.
Variety. Aug 29, 1962, p6.
The Village Voice. Feb 14, 1963, p24.

Terminal Station *See* The Indiscretion of an American Wife

The Terminator (US; Cameron, James; 1984)
BFI/Monthly Film Bulletin. Feb 1985, v52, p58.
Film Journal. Dec 1984, v87, p18.
Hollywood Reporter. Oct 26, 1984, p3.
The New York Times. Nov 9, 1984, SecIII, p10.
The New York Times. Oct 26, 1984, SecIII, p19.
Newsweek. Nov 19, 1984, v104, p132.
Time. Nov 26, 1984, v124, p105.
Variety. Oct 31, 1984, p21.
The Village Voice. Nov 13, 1984, p62.

Terms of Endearment (US; Brooks, James; 1983)
Film Comment. Nov-Dec 1983, v19, p28-32.
Films in Review. Jan 1984, v35, p54.
Hollywood Reporter. Nov 18, 1983, p3.
The Los Angeles Times. Nov 23, 1983, SecVI, p1.
Maclean's. Dec 5, 1983, v96, p69.
Magill's Cinema Annual, 1984. p414-19.
The New Republic. Dec 26, 1983, v189, p24-25.
New York. Dec 5, 1983, v16, p143-44.
The New York Times. Nov 23, 1983, SecIII, p18.
The New Yorker. Dec 12, 1983, v59, p149-52.
Newsweek. Nov 21, 1983, v102, p91-92.
Time. Nov 28, 1983, v122, p84.

Tess (GB, FR; Polanski, Roman; 1980)
America. Jan 31, 1981, v144, p83.
Christian Century. Mar 4, 1981, v98, p241.
Double Exposure. p138-44.
Hollywood Reporter. Dec 12, 1980, p3.
The Los Angeles Times. Sep 5, 1980, SecVI, p1.
Maclean's. Feb 16, 1981, v94, p61.
Magill's Cinema Annual, 1982. p471-73.
National Review. May 1, 1981, v33, p501-02.
New York. Feb 2, 1981, v14, p50-51.
The New York Times. Dec 12, 1980, SecIII, p8.
The New York Times. Apr 5, 1981, SecII, p15.
The New Yorker. Feb 2, 1981, v56, p88-89.
The New Yorker. Feb 2, 1981, v56, p88-89.
Newsweek. Dec 22, 1980, v96, p73.
Newsweek. Feb 23, 1981, v97, p60.
Newsweek. Feb 23, 1981, v97, p60.
Rolling Stone. Feb 19, 1981, p37.
Roman Polanski (Wexman). p109-26.
Senior Scholastic. Feb 6, 1981, v113, p26-27.

Time. Dec 22, 1980, v106, p73.
Variety. Nov 7, 1979, p18.

Testament (US; Littman, Lynne; 1983)
America. Nov 26, 1983, v149, p333-34.
Film Comment. Nov-Dec 1983, v19, p78-79.
Hollywood Reporter. Oct 31, 1983, p3.
The Los Angeles Times. Nov 3, 1983, SecVI, p1.
Maclean's. Nov 7, 1983, v96, p78.
Magill's Cinema Annual, 1984. p420-25.
The New Republic. Nov 28, 1983, v189, p22.
New York. Nov 14, 1983, v16, p117-18.
The New York Times. Nov 4, 1983, SecIII, p8.
Newsweek. Nov 14, 1983, v102, p98.

Teufels General, Des *See* Devil's General

Tex (US; Hunter, Tim; 1982)
Film Comment. Jul-Aug 1982, v18, p55-57.
Hollywood Reporter. Jul 26, 1982, p3.
The Los Angeles Times. Nov 19, 1982, VI, p14.
Maclean's. Aug 16, 1982, v95, p50-51.
Magill's Cinema Annual, 1983. p335-37.
National Review. Nov 26, 1982, v34, p1494-95.
New York. Oct 18, 1982, v15, p73-74.
The New York Times. Sep 28, 1982, III, p17.
The New Yorker. Oct 4, 1982, v58, p138-40.
Newsweek. Aug 2, 1982, v100, p63.
Rolling Stone. Sep 16, 1982, p32.
Time. Oct 11, 1982, v120, p89.
Variety. Jul 26, 1982, p3.

Texas Across the River (US; Gordon, Michael; 1966)
BFI/Monthly Film Bulletin. Jul 1967, v34, p110.
Christian Science Monitor (Western edition). Apr 1, 1966, p6.
Film Daily. Sep 26, 1966, p3.
Filmfacts. Jan 1, 1967, v9, p321-23.
Hollywood Reporter. Sep 13, 1966, p3.
Motion Picture Herald Product Digest. Sep 14, 1966, p595-96.
The New York Times. Nov 24, 1966, p65.
The New Yorker. Dec 4, 1966, v42, p161-62.
Newsweek. Dec 5, 1966, v68, p109-09A.
Playboy. Dec 1966, v13, p53-54.
Senior Scholastic. Nov 18, 1966, v89, p40.
Time. Dec 9, 1966, v88, p114.
Variety. Sep 14, 1966, p6.

Texas Carnival (US; Walters, Charles; 1951)
BFI/Monthly Film Bulletin. Nov 1951, v18, p363.
Commonweal. Nov 9, 1951, v55, p119.
Film Daily. Sep 17, 1951, p12.
Motion Picture Herald Product Digest. Sep 15, 1951, p1013.
The New York Times. Oct 13, 1951, p9.
Newsweek. Oct 22, 1951, v38, p103.
Time. Nov 5, 1951, v58, p120.
Variety. Sep 12, 1951, p6.

The Texas Chainsaw Massacre (US; Hooper, Tobe; 1974)
BFI/Monthly Film Bulletin. Nov 1976, v43, p258.
Cult Movies. p347-50.
Harper's. Nov 1974, v253, p108.
Hollywood Reporter. Oct 29, 1974, p3.
The Los Angeles Times. Oct 30, 1974, SecIV, p14.
Motion Picture Herald Product Digest. Nov 13, 1974, p47.
The New York Times. Sep 7, 1975, SecII, p17.
Variety. Nov 6, 1974, p20.

Thank Heaven For Small Favors (Also
titled: Drole de Paroissien, Un;
Heaven Sent) (FR; Mocky, Jean-Pierre;
1963)
BFI/Monthly Film Bulletin. Sep 1964, v31,
p134.
Film Daily. Jan 18, 1965, p5.
Filmfacts. Feb 26, 1965, v8, p16-17.
Films and Filming. Sep 1964, v10, p17.
Motion Picture Herald Product Digest. Feb 17,
1965, p235.
New Statesman. Aug 7, 1964, v68, p194.
The New York Times. Jan 14, 1965, p44.
The New Yorker. Jan 23, 1965, v40, p104, 107.

That Championship Season (US; Miller,
Jason; 1982)
Hollywood Reporter. Dec 9, 1982, p3.
The Los Angeles Times. Dec 16, 1982, SecVI,
p1.
Magill's Cinema Annual, 1983. p338-41.
New York. Dec 27, 1982, v16, p80.
The New York Times. Dec 9, 1982, SecIII, p23.
Newsweek. Aug 9, 1982, v100, p70-71.
Newsweek. Dec 20, 1982, v100, p87.
Sports Illustrated. Dec 13, 1982, v57, p71.
Variety. Dec 9, 1982, p3.

That Cold Day in the Park (US; Altman,
Robert; 1969)
Commonweal. Aug 8, 1969, v90, p487.
Film Daily. Jun 17, 1969, p4.
Film Quarterly. Fall 1969, v23, p56.
Filmfacts. 1969, v12, p277.
Films and Filming. Jun 1970, v16, p85, 88.
The New York Times. Jun 9, 1969, p59.
The New Yorker. Jun 14, 1969, v45, p84-85.
Newsweek. Jun 16, 1969, v93, p101.
Saturday Review. Jun 14, 1969, v52, p26.
Variety. May 28, 1969, p36.

That Darn Cat! (US; Stevenson, Robert;
1965)
America. Dec 11, 1965, v113, p760.
BFI/Monthly Film Bulletin. Nov 1965, v32,
p169.
Commonweal. Dec 17, 1965, v83, p349.
Film Daily. Sep 23, 1965, p3.
Films in Review. Dec 1965, v16, p642-43.
Hollywood Reporter. Sep 22, 1965, p3.
The London Times. Oct 4, 1965, p14.
Motion Picture Herald Product Digest. Oct 13,
1965, p387.
The New York Times. Dec 3, 1965, p44.
The New Yorker. Dec 11, 1965, v41, p232-33.
Senior Scholastic. Dec 2, 1965, v87, p28.
Time. Dec 10, 1965, v86, p113.
Variety. Sep 22, 1965, p6.

That Funny Feeling (US; Thorpe, Richard;
1965)
BFI/Monthly Film Bulletin. Jul 1965, v32,
p113.
Christian Science Monitor (Western edition).
Oct 14, 1965, p12.
Film Daily. Jul 30, 1965, p6.
Films and Filming. Sep 1965, v11, p28-29.
Hollywood Reporter. Jul 28, 1965, p3.
Motion Picture Herald Product Digest. Aug 18,
1965, p347.
The New York Times. Oct 21, 1965, p57.
Time. Nov 5, 1965, v86, p118.
Variety. Jun 23, 1965, p26.

That Man From Rio (French title: Homme
de Rio, L') (FR; Broca, Philippe de;
1964)
BFI/Monthly Film Bulletin. Jun 1965, v32, p87.
Commonweal. Jun 12, 1964, v80, p369.
Esquire. Sep 1964, v62, p80-81.
Film Daily. Jun 8, 1964, v124, p8.

Films and Filming. Jun 1965, v11, p24.
Hollywood Reporter. Oct 5, 1964, v182, p3.
*Magill's Survey of Cinema. Foreign Language
Films.* v7, p3034-37.
Motion Picture Herald Product Digest. Jun 24,
1964, v231, p75.
The New Republic. Sep 19, 1964, v151, p31-32.
The New York Times. Jun 9, 1964, p30.
The New Yorker. Jun 20, 1964, v40, p123.
Newsweek. Jun 22, 1964, v63, p84A.
Private Screenings. p142-43.
Saturday Review. Jul 11, 1964, v47, p22.
Sight and Sound. Sum 1965, v34, p147-48.
Time. Jun 5, 1964, v83, p99.
Variety. Mar 11, 1964, p6.
A World on Film. p236-38.

That Man in Istanbul (Also titled: Homme
d'Istanbul, L') (FR, SP; Isasi, Anthony;
1965)
BFI/Monthly Film Bulletin. Jun 1966, v33, p87.
Christian Science Monitor (Western edition).
Feb 17, 1966, p4.
Commonweal. Feb 11, 1966, v83, p559-60.
Film Daily. Jan 21, 1966, p6.
Filmfacts. Aug 1, 1966, v9, p146-47.
Hollywood Reporter. Jan 14, 1966, p3.
Life. Feb 25, 1966, v60, p10.
Motion Picture Herald Product Digest. Jan 26,
1966, p457.
The New York Times. May 19, 1966, p51.
Saturday Review. Feb 12, 1966, v49, p45.
Variety. Oct 13, 1965, p6.

That Obscure Object of Desire (French
title: Cet Obscur Object du Desir) (FR,
SP; Buñuel, Luis; 1977)
BFI/Monthly Film Bulletin. Mar 1978, v45,
p41.
Film Comment. Nov-Dec 1977, v13, p4.
Films in Review. Jan 1978, v29, p50.
Hollywood Reporter. Oct 20, 1977, p23.
Human Behavior. Feb 1978, v7, p75.
The Los Angeles Times. Dec 21, 1977, SecIV,
p1.
*Magill's Survey of Cinema. Foreign Language
Films.* v7, p3038-41.
The Nation. Oct 29, 1977, v225, p444.
The Nation. Nov 26, 1977, v225, p572-73.
New York Review of Books. Feb 23, 1978, v25,
p39-42.
The New York Times. Oct 9, 1977, p81.
The New York Times. Oct 16, 1977, SecII, p17.
The New York Times. Nov 14, 1977, p42.
The New Yorker. Dec 19, 1977, v53, p128-30.
Newsweek. Dec 5, 1977, v90, p109.
Variety. Aug 31, 1977, p18.
The Village Voice. Oct 24, 1977, p48.

That Sinking Feeling (GB; Forsyth, Bruce;
1979)
Film Journal. Mar 1984, v87, p45-46.
Maclean's. May 21, 1984, v97, p66.
The New Republic. Mar 5, 1984, v190, p24-25.
The New York Times. Feb 15, 1984, SecIII,
p21.
Variety. Feb 22, 1984, p19.
The Village Voice. Feb 28, 1984, p49.

That Splendid November (Italian title:
Bellissima Novembre, Un) (IT;
Bolognini, Mauro; 1971)
Filmfacts. 1971, v14, p326-37.
Hollywood Reporter. Apr 23, 1971, v215, n48,
p3.
The New York Times. Jun 19, 1971, p.
Variety. Jun 23, 1971, p20.

That Touch of Mink (US; Mann, Delbert;
1962)
America. Jul 7, 1962, v107, p470.

BFI/Monthly Film Bulletin. Jun 1962, v29, p84.
Commonweal. Jul 6, 1962, v76, p377.
Film Daily. May 9, 1962, p7.
Filmfacts. Jun 29, 1962, v5, p125-26.
Films and Filming. Jun 1962, v8, p37.
The Films of Cary Grant. p254-57.
The Films of Doris Day. p203-06.
Hollywood Reporter. May 9, 1962, p3.
Motion Picture Herald Product Digest. May 16,
1962, p557.
The New York Times. Jul 15, 1962, p16.
The New Yorker. Jul 23, 1962, v38, p90.
Newsweek. Jul 25, 1962, v59, p88-89.
Saturday Review. Jul 14, 1962, v45, p16.
Time. Jul 6, 1962, v80, p55.
Variety. May 9, 1962, p6.

That's Entertainment (US; Haley, Jack Jr.;
1974)
Atlantic. Jul 1974, v234, p95-97.
BFI/Monthly Film Bulletin. Oct 1974, v41,
p231-32.
Christian Century. Nov 6, 1974, v91, p1042.
Commonweal. Jun 28, 1974, v100, p361-62.
Dance Magazine. Jul 1974, v48, p30-31.
Films in Review. Aug-Sep 1974, v25, p435-37.
The Films of Elizabeth Taylor. p239-40.
Magill's Survey of Cinema. Series II. v5, p2443-
46.
Motion Picture Herald Product Digest. Apr 24,
1974, p93.
New Statesman. Oct 4, 1974, v88, p479-80.
New York. May 27, 1974, v7, p90-91.
The New York Times. Jul 7, 1974, SecII, p1.
The New Yorker. Jun 10, 1974, v50, p104-07.
Saturday Review. Jun 29, 1974, v1, p25.
Time. May 20, 1974, v103, p71.
Variety. Apr 17, 1974, p16.

That's Entertainment, Part II (US; Kelly,
Gene; 1976)
America. Jun 19, 1976, v134, p539.
Audience. Aug 1976, v8, p6-7.
BFI/Monthly Film Bulletin. Jun 1976, v43,
p130-31.
Dance Magazine. Jul 1976, v50, p70-71.
Films and Filming. Aug 1976, v22, p39-40.
Films Illustrated. Jun 1976, v5, p366.
Films in Review. Aug-Sep 1976, v27, p438.
Hollywood Reporter. May 5, 1976, p3.
Independent Film Journal. May 14, 1976, v77,
p9.
The Los Angeles Times. May 16, 1976,
Calendar, p1.
Magill's Survey of Cinema. Series II. v5, p2447-
49.
Motion Picture Herald Product Digest. May 19,
1976, p97.
Movietone News. Jun 1976, n50, p36-37.
New Statesman. May 21, 1976, v91, p691.
New York. May 24, 1976, v9, p75-76.
The New York Times. May 30, 1976, SecII,
p11.
The New Yorker. May 24, 1976, v52, p134.
Newsweek. May 31, 1976, v87, p48-51.
Penthouse. Sep 1976, v8, p46-47.
Saturday Review. May 29, 1976, v3, p46.
Time. Jun 7, 1976, v107, p74.
Variety. May 5, 1976, p18.
Variety. Jun 9, 1976, p7.
Vogue. Jun 1976, v166, p63.

That's My Boy (US; Walker, Hal; 1951)
BFI/Monthly Film Bulletin. Jun 1952, v19, p77.
Christian Century. Sep 19, 1951, v68, p1087.
Commonweal. Aug 24, 1951, v54, p478.
Film Daily. Jun 13, 1951, p7.
Hollywood Reporter. Jun 11, 1951, p3.
Motion Picture Herald Product Digest. Jun 16,
1951, p886.

The Nation. Sep 1, 1951, v173, p177.
The New York Times. Aug 2, 1951, p18.
Newsweek. Jul 23, 1951, v38, p84-85.
Saturday Review. Aug 25, 1951, v34, p23.
Time. Aug 27, 1951, v58, p104.
Variety. Jun 13, 1951, p6.

Theatre of Blood (US; Hickox, Douglas; 1973)
Commonweal. Jun 15, 1973, v98, p337.
Filmfacts. 1973, v16, n1, p1.
Films in Review. Jun-Jul 1973, v24, n6, p379.
Magill's Survey of Cinema. English Language Films. Series I, v4, p1689.
The New York Times. May 12, 1973, v19, p1.
Time. May 21, 1973, v101, p71.
TV Movies. 1983-84, p770.
Variety. Apr 25, 1973, p18.

Their First Trip to Tokyo *See* Tokyo Story

Their Secret Affair *See* Top Secret Affair

Them! (US; Douglas, Gordon; 1954)
America. Jul 3, 1954, v91, p367.
BFI/Monthly Film Bulletin. Sep 1954, v21, p131.
Catholic World. May 1954, v179, p144.
Cinefantastique. n4, 1974, v3, p22-27.
Commonweal. Jun 18, 1954, v60, p269.
Farm Journal. Jun 1954, v78, p141.
Film Daily. Apr 14, 1954, p6.
Films in Review. May 1954, v5, p244-45.
The Films of the Fifties. p107-08.
Hollywood Reporter. Apr 8, 1954, p3.
The London Times. Aug 2, 1954, p9.
Magill's Survey of Cinema. Series II. v5, p2450-53.
Motion Picture Herald Product Digest. Apr 10, 1954, p2253.
National Parent-Teacher. Jun 1954, v48, p40.
The New Statesman and Nation. Aug 7, 1954, v48, p157.
The New York Times. Jun 17, 1954, p36.
The New Yorker. Jun 26, 1954, v30, p61.
Newsweek. Jun 7, 1954, v43, p56.
Saturday Review. Jun 5, 1954, v37, p27.
Science Fiction Gold. p111-222.
Science Fiction Studies in Film. p108-12.
Seeing is Believing (Biskind). p123-26.
Senior Scholastic. May 12, 1954, v64, p29.
The Tatler. Aug 11, 1954, v213, p244.
Time. Oct 19, 1953, v62, p112.
Time. Jul 19, 1954, v64, p79.
Twentieth Century. Sep 1954, v156, p197-98.
Twenty All-Time Great Science Fiction Films. p103-11.
Variety. Apr 14, 1954, p6.

Theorem *See* Teorema

There's Always Tomorrow (US; Sirk, Douglas; 1956)
America. Feb 11, 1956, v94, p543.
Bright Lights. 1977-78, v2, p16-19.
Douglas Sirk (Stern). p135-51.
Film Daily. Jan 18, 1956, p8.
The Films of Barbara Stanwyck. p241-43.
Hollywood Reporter. Jan 12, 1956, p3.
Magill's Survey of Cinema. Series II. v5, p2457-61.
The New York Times. Jan 21, 1956, p18.
Variety. Jan 18, 1956, p6.

There's No Business Like Show Business (US; Lang, Walter; 1954)
America. Dec 18, 1954, v92, p326.
BFI/Monthly Film Bulletin. Feb 1955, v22, p22.
Commonweal. Dec 24, 1954, v61, p334.
Cue. Dec 18, 1954, p20.
Dance Magazine. Jan 1955, v29, p9.

Film Daily. Dec 8, 1954, p6.
Films and Filming. Mar 1955, v1, p21.
Films in Review. Jan 1955, v6, p33-34.
The Films of Marilyn Monroe. p116-21.
Fortnight. Feb 2, 1955, v18, p40.
Hollywood Reporter. Dec 8, 1954, p3.
The London Times. Feb 3, 1955, p5.
Look. Nov 30, 1954, v18, p74.
Motion Picture Herald Product Digest. Dec 11, 1954, p241.
National Parent-Teacher. Feb 1955, v49, p39.
The New Statesman and Nation. Feb 12, 1955, v49, p212.
The New York Times. Dec 17, 1954, p37.
The New Yorker. Dec 25, 1954, v30, p61.
Newsweek. Dec 27, 1954, v44, p60.
Saturday Review. Jan 8, 1954, v38, p26.
Selected Film Criticism, 1951-1960. p137-38.
The Spectator. Feb 4, 1955, v194, p130.
The Tatler. Feb 16, 1955, v215, p292.
Time. Jan 17, 1955, v65, p76.
Variety. Dec 8, 1954, p6.

Therese Raquin (Also titled: Thou Shalt Not) (FR; Carné, Marcel; 1953)
Films and Filming. Jul 1953, v2, n10, p23.
Sight and Sound. Sum 1956, v26, n1, p34.
Variety. Oct 7, 1953, p6.

These Are the Damned (Also titled: The Damned) (GB; Losey, Joseph; 1961)
The Cinema of Joseph Losey. p97-106.
Dictionary of Films. p78.
Film Daily. Jul 15, 1965, p6.
Film Quarterly. Fall 1965, v19, p63.
Films and Filming. May 1963, v9, p24-25.
Hollywood Reporter. Jul 16, 1965, p3.
Motion Picture Herald Product Digest. Aug 4, 1965, p38-39.
Movie. May 1963, n9, p31-34.
Movie. Jan 1963, n6, p20-21.
Movie. Jun 1962, n1, p10-11.
The New York Times. Jul 8, 1965, p35.
The Private Eye, the Cowboy and the Very Naked Girl. p148-50.
Sight and Sound. Sum 1963, v32, p143-44.
Time. Jul 30, 1965, v86, p67.
Variety. Jul 14, 1965, p6.
The Village Voice. Jul 1, 1965, v10, p12, 14.

They All Laughed (US; Bogdanovich, Peter; 1981)
Hollywood Reporter. Nov 30, 1981, p2.
The Los Angeles Times. Dec 17, 1981, SecVI, p1.
Magill's Cinema Annual, 1982. p350-55.
The New York Times. Nov 20, 1981, SecIII, p6.
Newsweek. Nov 30, 1981, v98, p105-06.
Time. Nov 23, 1981, v118, p98.
Variety. Aug 21, 1981, p3.
Variety. Aug 19, 1981, p20-21.
The Village Voice. Nov 25, 1981, p49.

They Came to Cordua (US; Rossen, Robert; 1959)
America. Oct 17, 1959, v102, p91.
BFI/Monthly Film Bulletin. Dec 1959, v26, p157.
Commonweal. Nov 13, 1959, v71, p209.
Film Daily. Sep 18, 1959, v116, p6.
Filmfacts. Nov 11, 1959, v2, p241-43.
Films in Review. Nov 1959, v10, p557-58.
The Films of Gary Cooper. p271-73.
The Films of Rita Hayworth. p214-18.
Hollywood Reporter. Sep 18, 1959, p3.
Life. Oct 26, 1959, v47, p125-28.
Look. Sep 15, 1959, v23, p52A-52C.
The New Republic. Nov 30, 1959, v141, p2.
The New York Times. Oct 22, 1959, p47.
The New Yorker. Oct 31, 1959, v35, p173.

Newsweek. Oct 5, 1959, v54, p88.
Saturday Review. Oct 31, 1959, v42, p24.
Time. Nov 2, 1959, v74, p40.
Variety. Sep 23, 1959, p6.

They Might Be Giants (US; Harvey, Anthony; 1971)
BFI/Monthly Film Bulletin. Apr 1972, v39, p80.
Filmfacts. 1971, v14, p172-75.
Films and Filming. May 1971, v17, n8, p40-41.
Films in Review. May 1971, v22, n5, p314.
The Films of Sherlock Holmes. p223-25.
Hollywood Reporter. Mar 4, 1971, v215, n12, p3.
Magill's Cinema Annual, 1972. p515-17.
The New York Times. Jun 10, 1971, p51.
Newsweek. Apr 12, 1971, v77, p113B.
Saturday Review. May 8, 1971, v14, p40.
Time. Apr 26, 1971, v97, p98.
Variety. Mar 3, 1971, p17.
The Village Voice. Jun 24, 1971, v16, n25, p60.

They Shoot Horses Don't They? (US; Pollack, Sydney; 1969)
America. Dec 27, 1969, v121, p642.
Deeper Into the Movies. p85-90.
Figures of Light. p219-22.
Film Daily. Nov 20, 1969, p3.
Film Quarterly. Sum 1970, v23, p42-47.
Film Society Review. May 1970, v5, p32-37.
Filmfacts. 1969, v12, p457.
Films and Filming. Aug 1970, v16, p40.
Films in Review. Jan 1970, v21, p48-49.
The Films of Jane Fonda. p152-56.
The Films of the Sixties. p275-76.
Focus. Spr 1970, n6, p40-42.
Focus on Film. May-Aug 1970, n3, p3-6.
Magill's Survey of Cinema. Series II. v6, p2470-73.
The Modern American Novel and the Movies. p29-39.
Movies Into Film. p81-86.
The Nation. Dec 29, 1969, v109, p742.
The New York Times. Dec 11, 1969, p63.
The New York Times. Dec 21, 1969, SecII, p20.
The New Yorker. Dec 20, 1969, v45, p62.
Newsweek. Dec 22, 1969, v74, p100-01.
The Platinum Years. p220-37.
Saturday Review. Dec 27, 1969, v52, p21.
Screening the Novel. p64-83.
Second Sight. p280-82.
Time. Dec 19, 1969, v94, p76.
Variety. Nov 26, 1969, p14.

They Were Not Divided (GB; Young, Terence; 1950)
BFI/Monthly Film Bulletin. Apr-May 1950, v17, p63.
Film Daily. May 17, 1951, p6.
The London Times. Mar 30, 1950, p8.
Motion Picture Herald Product Digest. May 19, 1951, p854-55.
Sequence. Sum 1950, n11, p10-11.
Shots in the Dark. p166-70.
The Spectator. Apr 7, 1950, v184, p461.
Variety. Apr 5, 1950, p22.

They Who Step on the Tiger's Tail *See* Tora-no-o

They Who Tread on the Tiger's Tail *See* Tora-no-o

The Thief (US; Rouse, Russell; 1952)
BFI/Monthly Film Bulletin. Dec 1952, v19, p168.
Catholic World. Nov 1952, v176, p142.
Christian Century. Dec 24, 1952, v69, p1511.
Film Daily. Oct 1, 1952, p6.
Films in Review. Nov 1952, v3, p470-71.
Hollywood Reporter. Sep 24, 1952, p3.

Life. Sep 15, 1952, v33, p103-04.
Motion Picture Herald Product Digest. Sep 27, 1952, p1541.
The Nation. Nov 8, 1952, v175, p435.
National Parent-Teacher. Dec 1952, v47, p38.
The New York Times. Oct 16, 1952, p37.
Newsweek. Oct 20, 1952, v40, p124-25.
Saturday Review. Nov 8, 1952, v35, p32.
Sight and Sound. Jan-Mar 1953, v22, p130, 138.
The Spectator. Nov 14, 1952, v189, p630.
The Tatler. Nov 26, 1952, p480.
Theatre Arts. Dec 1952, v36, p29.
Theatre Arts. Sep 1952, v36, p72.
Theatre Arts. Oct 1952, v36, p74-75.
Time. Oct 13, 1952, v60, p104.
Variety. Sep 24, 1952, p6.

Thief (US; Mann, Michael; 1981)
Christian Century. Jul 15, 1981, v98, p746.
Hollywood Reporter. Mar 20, 1981, p178.
The Los Angeles Times. Mar 22, 1981, Calendar, p1.
Maclean's. Apr 6, 1981, v94, p54.
Magill's Cinema Annual, 1982. p356-59.
The Nation. Apr 18, 1981, v232, p477.
The New Leader. Apr 20, 1981, v64, p21.
The New Republic. Apr 25, 1981, v184, p21.
The New York Times. Mar 27, 1981, SecIII, p12.
The New Yorker. May 4, 1981, v57, p158-60.
Newsweek. Mar 30, 1981, v9782.
Rolling Stone. Apr 16, 1981, p33-34.
Rolling Stone. May 14, 1981, p35.
Time. Apr 13, 1981, v117, p98.
Variety. Mar 20, 1981, p3.

The Thief of Venice (Italian title: Ladri di Venezia) (IT, US; Brahm, John; 1950)
BFI/Monthly Film Bulletin. Apr 1954, v21, p60-61.
Film Daily. Nov 14, 1952, p7.
Hollywood Reporter. Nov 12, 1952, p3.
Motion Picture Herald Product Digest. Nov 15, 1952, p1605-06.
National Parent-Teacher. Jan 1953, v47, p38.
The New York Times. Nov 28, 1952, p22.
The New Yorker. Dec 6, 1952, v28, p74.
Variety. Nov 12, 1952, p6.

Thieves Like Us (US; Altman, Robert; 1974)
American Scholar. Sum 1974, v43, p468-69.
Atlantic. Apr 1974, v233, p115-17.
BFI/Monthly Film Bulletin. Oct 1974, v41, p232-33.
Commonweal. Apr 12, 1974, v100, p133-34.
Esquire. May 1974, v81, p32.
Film Comment. May-Jun 1974, v10, p14-15.
Film Quarterly. Sum 1974, v27, p2-10.
Films in Review. Mar 20, 1974, v25, p182.
The Films of Robert Altman. p83-92.
Hollywood Reporter. Jan 23, 1974, p3.
The Los Angeles Times. Apr 4, 1974, SecIV, p1.
Magill's Survey of Cinema. Series II. v6, p2478-80.
Motion Picture Herald Product Digest. Jan 13, 1974, p73.
The Nation. Mar 2, 1974, v218, p283.
The New Republic. Mar 2, 1974, v170, p26.
New York. Feb 11, 1974, v7, p74-75.
The New York Times. Apr 7, 1974, SecII, p1.
The New Yorker. Feb 4, 1974, v49, p92.
Newsweek. Feb 18, 1974, v83, p101.
Reeling. p362-68.
Robert Altman: American Innovator. p157-76.
Robert Altman (Plecki). p65-69.
Rolling Stone. Apr 25, 1974, p68.
Saturday Review. Mar 21, 1974, v104, p30.
Sight and Sound. Fall 1974, v43, p237-39.

Time. Mar 4, 1974, v103, p63.
Variety. Feb 20, 1974, p14.
The Village Voice. Feb 21, 1974, p63.

The Thing (Also titled: The Thing From Another World) (US; Nyby, Christian; 1951)
BFI/Monthly Film Bulletin. Aug 1952, v19, p107.
Christian Century. Jul 4, 1951, v68, p807.
Cinefantastique. n2/3, 1982, v13, p59-62.
Cinefantastique. n5/6, 1982, v12, p78-85.
Cinema of the Fantastic. p53-55.
Classic Images. Jan 1983, n91, p50.
Commonweal. May 18, 1951, v54, p143.
Fifty From the Fifties. p358-64.
Film Daily. Apr 4, 1951, p6.
Films in Review. Jun-Jul 1951, v2, p38-39.
The Films of the Fifties. p43-44.
Future Tense: The Cinema of Science Fiction. p86-88.
Gore Creatures. Oct 1975, n24, p30-32.
Hollywood Reporter. Apr 4, 1951, p3.
Library Journal. May 15, 1951, v76, p883.
The London Times. Aug 4, 1952, p9.
Magill's Survey of Cinema. Series I. v4, p1712-15.
Motion Picture Herald Product Digest. Apr 7, 1951, p793.
The Nation. May 26, 1951, v172, p497.
The Nation. Jan 5, 1952, v174, p19.
The New Republic. May 21, 1951, v124, p23.
The New York Times. May 3, 1951, p34.
The New Yorker. May 12, 1951, v27, p98.
Saturday Review. Apr 21, 1951, v34, p28.
Science Fiction Gold. p27-38.
Science Fiction Studies in Film. p108-11.
Time. May 14, 1951, v57, p110.
Twenty All-Time Great Science Fiction Films. p26-30.
Variety. Apr 4, 1951, p6.

The Thing (US; Carpenter, John; 1982)
Hollywood Reporter. Jun 21, 1982, p4.
The Los Angeles Times. Jun 25, 1982, SecVI, p15.
Maclean's. Jun 28, 1982, v95, p58.
Magill's Cinema Annual, 1983. p343-48.
New York. Jun 28, 1982, v15, p53-54.
The New York Times. Jun 25, 1982, SecIII, p14.
Newsweek. Jun 28, 1982, v99, p73.
Time. Jun 28, 1982, v119, p72.
Variety. Jun 21, 1982, p3.

The Third Day (US; Smight, Jack; 1965)
BFI/Monthly Film Bulletin. Oct 1965, v32, p152.
Christian Science Monitor (Western edition). Aug 30, 1965, p4.
Film Daily. Jul 9, 1965, p4.
Films and Filming. Oct 1965, v12, p26.
Hollywood Reporter. Jul 8, 1965, p3.
Motion Picture Herald Product Digest. Jul 21, 1965, p330.
The New York Times. Aug 5, 1965, p15.
Time. Jul 30, 1965, v86, p67.
Variety. Jul 14, 1965, p6.

The Thirteenth Letter (US; Preminger, Otto; 1951)
BFI/Monthly Film Bulletin. Mar 1951, v18, p230.
Christian Century. Apr 11, 1951, v68, p479.
The Cinema of Otto Preminger. p93-94.
Commonweal. Mar 9, 1951, v53, p543.
Dictionary of Films. p70.
Film Daily. Jan 19, 1951, p4.
Films in Review. Mar 1951, v2, p44.
Hollywood Reporter. Jan 19, 1951, p3.
The London Times. Feb 19, 1951, p9.

Motion Picture Herald Product Digest. Jan 27, 1951, p689.
The New York Times. Feb 22, 1951, p27.
The New Yorker. Feb 24, 1951, v27, p94, 97.
Newsweek. Mar 5, 1951, v37, p87.
The Spectator. Feb 16, 1951, v186, p208.
Time. Feb 26, 1951, v57, p102.
Variety. Jan 24, 1951, p6.

30 Years of Fun (US; Youngson, Robert; 1963)
Commonweal. Apr 5, 1963, v78, p48.
Film Daily. Feb 14, 1963, p8.
Filmfacts. Jan 23, 1963, v6, p327-28.
Films and Filming. Aug 1963, v9, p25-26.
Films in Review. Feb 1963, v14, p110-11.
The New York Times. Dec 26, 1963, p33.
The New Yorker. Feb 16, 1963, v148, p26.
Variety. Feb 13, 1963, p6.

Thirty Six Hours (Also titled: 36 Hours) (US; Seaton, George; 1964)
America. Feb 13, 1965, v112, p230.
Christian Science Monitor (Western edition). Feb 10, 1965, p4.
Commonweal. Jan 29, 1965, v81, p572.
Film Daily. Nov 30, 1964, p12.
Film Quarterly. Spr 1965, v18, p61.
Filmfacts. Mar 12, 1965, v8, p27-28.
Films and Filming. Feb 1965, v11, p35.
The Great Spy Pictures. p472-73.
Life. Jan 29, 1965, v58, p13.
Motion Picture Herald Product Digest. Dec 9, 1964, p185.
The New York Times. Jan 29, 1965, p25.
The New Yorker. Feb 6, 1965, v40, p120.
Newsweek. Feb 8, 1965, v65, p86.
Senior Scholastic. Jan 21, 1965, v85, p22.
Sight and Sound. Wint 1964-65, v34, p41.
Time. Feb 5, 1965, v85, p64.
Variety. Dec 16, 1964, p6.

This Can't Happen Here *See* High Tension

This Could Be the Night (US; Wise, Robert; 1957)
America. May 25, 1957, v97, p272.
BFI/Monthly Film Bulletin. Aug 1957, v24, p105.
Commonweal. May 24, 1957, v66, p205.
Double Takes. p8-9.
Film Daily. Apr 9, 1957, v111, p6.
Films and Filming. Jul 1957, v3, p33.
Hollywood Reporter. Apr 9, 1957, p3.
Motion Picture Herald Product Digest. Apr 13, 1957, v207, p337.
The New York Times. May 15, 1957, p39.
The New Yorker. May 25, 1957, v33, p129.
Newsweek. May 27, 1957, v49, p118.
Saturday Review. Apr 27, 1957, v40, p25.
Time. May 20, 1957, v69, p128.
Variety. Apr 10, 1957, p6.

This Is Elvis (US; Leo, Malcolm; Solt, Andrew; 1981)
Hollywood Reporter. Apr 6, 1981, p3.
The Los Angeles Times. May 7, 1981, SecIII, p18.
Maclean's. May 25, 1981, v94, p48.
Magill's Cinema Annual, 1982. p360-63.
New York. May 18, 1981, v14, p67-68.
The New Yorker. Jun 1, 1981, v57, p132-33.
Newsweek. May 4, 1981, v97, p44.
Rolling Stone. May 28, 1981, p46-49.
Variety. Apr 6, 1981, p3.

This Is My Affair *See* I Can Get It for You Wholesale

This Is Spinal Tap (Also titled: A Rockumentary by Martin Di Bergi) (US; Reiner, Rob; 1984)

BFI/Monthly Film Bulletin. Sep 1984, v51, p285-86.
Film Journal. Apr 1984, v87, p36-37.
Films and Filming. Sep 1984, n360, p42.
Films in Review. May 1984, v35, p308-09.
Informer. Apr 1984, p4.
The Los Angeles Times. Mar 8, 1984, SecVI, p1.
The New Republic. May 21, 1984, v190, p24.
The New York Times. Mar 18, 1984, SecII, p17.
The New York Times. Apr 25, 1984, SecIII, p20.
The New York Times. Mar 2, 1984, SecIII, p6.
Newsweek. May 14, 1984, v103, p69.
Newsweek. Mar 5, 1984, v103, p81-82.
Photoplay. Oct 1984, v35, p21, 42-43.
Rolling Stone. May 24, 1984, p37-39.
Time. Mar 5, 1984, v123, p86.
Variety. Feb 29, 1984, p14.
The Village Voice. Mar 6, 1984, p52.

This Property Is Condemned (US; Pollack, Sydney; 1966)
BFI/Monthly Film Bulletin. Oct 1966, v33, p153.
Christian Science Monitor (Western edition). Sep 14, 1966, p6.
Cinema. Jul 1966, v3, p47.
Commonweal. Aug 19, 1966, v84, p533.
Film Daily. Jun 13, 1966, p6.
Film Quarterly. Wint 1966-67, v20, p61.
Filmfacts. Oct 1, 1966, v9, p206-08.
Films and Filming. Nov 1966, v13, p6, 8.
The Films of Robert Redford. p95-101.
The Films of Tennessee Williams. p120-31.
Hollywood Reporter. Jun 13, 1966, p3.
The London Times. Oct 20, 1966, p17.
Motion Picture Herald Product Digest. Jun 15, 1966, p543.
The New York Times. Aug 4, 1966, p24.
The New Yorker. Aug 27, 1966, v42, p88.
Newsweek. Aug 1, 1966, v68, p83.
Playboy. Sep 1966, v13, p56, 58.
Saturday Review. Jun 25, 1966, v49, p40.
Sydney Pollack (Taylor). p37-41.
Tennessee Williams and Film. p113-21.
Time. Jul 22, 1966, v88, p62.
Variety. Jun 15, 1966, p6.

This Sporting Life (US; Anderson, Lindsay; 1963)
America. Aug 21, 1963, v109, p219.
BFI/Monthly Film Bulletin. Mar 1963, v30, p34.
Commonweal. Aug 9, 1963, v78, p480.
Fifty Classic British Films. p109-11.
Film Daily. Jul 18, 1963, p6.
Filmfacts. Jul 25, 1963, v6, p139-41.
Films in Review. Aug-Sep 1963, v14, p437-38.
The Illustrated London News. Mar 2, 1963, v242, p318.
Lindsay Anderson: A Guide to References and Resources. p46-49.
Magill's Survey of Cinema. Series I. v4, p1726-27.
Movie. Feb 1963, p33.
The Nation. Aug 10, 1963, v197, p80.
The New Republic. Jul 20, 1963, v149, p25-26.
New Statesman. Feb 15, 1963, v65, p246.
The New York Times. Jul 17, 1963, p19.
The New York Times. Jul 21, 1963, SecII, p1.
The New York Times Mag. Apr 14, 1963, p126-27.
The New Yorker. Jul 20, 1963, v29, p72.
Photoplay. Sep 1963,, v64, p13.
Saturday Review. Jul 13, 1963, v46, p16.
Spectator. Feb 15, 1963, v210, p199.
Time. Jul 19, 1963, v82, p78.
Variety. Feb 13, 1963, p6.

This Woman Is Dangerous (US; Feist, Felix; 1952)
BFI/Monthly Film Bulletin. Jul 1952, v19, p97.
Commonweal. Mar 21, 1952, v55, p593.
Film Daily. Jan 29, 1952, p7.
The Films of Joan Crawford. p180-81.
Hollywood Reporter. Jan 24, 1952, p3.
Motion Picture Herald Product Digest. Jan 26, 1952, p1214.
The New York Times. Feb 28, 1952, p23.
The New Yorker. Mar 8, 1952, v28, p79.
Newsweek. Feb 25, 1952, v39, p100.
The Spectator. May 30, 1952, v188, p704.
The Tatler. Jun 11, 1952, v204, p606.
Time. Feb 11, 1952, v59, p94.
Variety. Jan 30, 1952, p6.

The Thomas Crown Affair (US; Jewison, Norman; 1968)
BFI/Monthly Film Bulletin. Jan 1969, v36, p7-8.
Christian Science Monitor (Western edition). Jun 24, 1968, p4.
Commonweal. Jul 12, 1968, v88, p468.
Esquire. Oct 1968, v70, p90.
Film 68/69. p110-12.
Film Daily. Jun 20, 1968, p5.
Film Quarterly. Sum 1969, v22, p60-61.
Filmfacts. Sep 1, 1968, v11, p232-34.
Films and Filming. Apr 1969, v15, p41-42.
Films in Review. Aug-Sep 1968, v19, p455.
The Films of Steve McQueen. p131-40.
Going Steady. p135-40.
Hollywood Reporter. Jun 19, 1968, p3.
The London Times. Jan 16, 1969, p11.
The London Times. May 17, 1969, p19.
Magill's Survey of Cinema. Series II. v6, p2486-89.
Motion Picture Herald Product Digest. Jun 19, 1968, p823.
Movie. Wint 1968-69, n16, p39.
The New Republic. Jul 13, 1968, v159, p33.
The New York Times. Jun 27, 1968, p48.
The New Yorker. Jul 13, 1968, v44, p82.
The Spectator. Jan 24, 1969, v222, p116.
Time. Jul 12, 1968, v92, p77.
Variety. Jun 19, 1968, p6.
The Village Voice. Aug 1, 1968, p29.
A Year In the Dark. p185-86.

Thomas l'Imposteur (Also titled: Thomas, the Imposter) (FR; Franju, Georges; 1965)
BFI/Monthly Film Bulletin. Apr 1966, v33, p57.
Christian Science Monitor (Western edition). Apr 29, 1966, p4.
Films and Filming. May 1966, v12, p18, 51.
Franju (Durgnat). p124-36.
The London Times. Feb 17, 1966, p8.
Magill's Survey of Cinema. Foreign Language Films. v7, p3071-77.
New Statesman. Feb 25, 1966, v71, p270.
The New York Times. Sep 13, 1965, p42.
Sight and Sound. Spr 1966, v35, p87-89.
The Spectator. Feb 25, 1966, v216, p228.
Variety. Apr 28, 1965, p7.

Thoroughly Modern Millie (US; Hill, George Roy; 1967)
America. Apr 1, 1967, v116, p512-13.
BFI/Monthly Film Bulletin. Nov 1967, v34, p172.
Commonweal. Apr 14, 1967, v86, p127.
Film Daily. Mar 23, 1967, p5.
Film Quarterly. Fall 1967, v21, p62.
Films in Review. Apr 1967, v18, p243.
George Ray Hill (Shores). p3-4.
Hollywood Reporter. Mar 23, 1967, p3.
Life. Apr 28, 1967, p17.

Motion Picture Herald Product Digest. Apr 12, 1967, p673.
The New York Times. Mar 23, 1967, p25.
The New Yorker. Apr 1, 1967, v43, p94.
Newsweek. Apr 10, 1967, v69, p96.
Saturday Review. Apr 15, 1967, v50, p45.
Senior Scholastic. May 12, 1967, v90, p34.
Time. Apr 7, 1967, v89, p95.
Variety. Mar 29, 1967, p6.
The Village Voice. Jun 22, 1967, p21.

Those Magnificent Men in Their Flying Machines (Also titled: Those Magnificent Men in Their Flying Machines, or How I Flew From London to Paris in Twenty-Five Hours and Eleven Minutes) (US, GB; Annakin, Ken; 1965)
BFI/Monthly Film Bulletin. Jul 1965, v32, p113.
Catholic World. Oct 1965, v202, p64.
Christian Science Monitor (Western edition). Jul 20, 1965, p4.
Christian Science Monitor (Western edition). Oct 18, 1965, p4.
Cinema. Dec 1965, v3, p48.
Commonweal. Jul 23, 1965, v82, p534.
Film Daily. Jun 1, 1965, p4.
Film Quarterly. Fall 1965, v19, p63.
Filmfacts. Jul 9, 1965, v8, p123-25.
Films and Filming. Aug 1965, v11, p31.
Films and Filming. Jul 1965, v11, p22.
Films in Review. Aug-Sep 1965, v16, p451.
Hollywood Reporter. Jun 1, 1965, p3.
Life. Jun 25, 1965, v58, p15.
The London Times. Jun 3, 1965, p17.
Look. Jan 12, 1964, v29, p44-49.
Magill's Survey of Cinema. Series II. v6, p2490-93.
Marshall Delaney At the Movies. p91.
Motion Picture Herald Product Digest. Jun 9, 1965, p305.
The New Republic. Jun 19, 1965, v152, p27.
New Statesman. Jun 11, 1965, v69, p930.
The New York Times. Jun 17, 1965, p27.
The New Yorker. Jun 19, 1965, v41, p114.
Newsweek. Jul 5, 1965, v66, p83.
Playboy. Sep 1965, v12, p53-54.
Private Screenings. p195.
Saturday Review. Jun 26, 1965, v48, p22.
Senior Scholastic. Sep 16, 1965, v87, p30-31.
The Spectator. Jun 11, 1965, v214, p758.
Time. Jun 18, 1965, v85, p100.
Variety. Jun 2, 1965, p6.
Vogue. Jul 1965, v146, p37.

Thou Shalt Not *See* Therese Raquin

A Thousand Clowns (US; Coe, Fred; 1965)
America. Feb 5, 1966, v114, p208.
BFI/Monthly Film Bulletin. Dec 1966, v33, p183.
Christian Science Monitor (Western edition). Apr 22, 1966, p6.
Commonweal. Dec 17, 1965, v83, p349.
Film. Wint 1966, n47, p26-27.
Film Daily. Nov 29, 1965, p12.
Films and Filming. Feb 1967, v13, p33.
Films in Review. Dec 1965, v16, p641-42.
Hollywood Reporter. Nov 29, 1965, p3.
Life. Jan 14, 1966, v60, p10.
The London Times. Oct 27, 1966, p10.
Mademoiselle. Feb 1966, v62, p70.
Magill's Survey of Cinema. Series I. v4, p1728-30.
Motion Picture Herald Product Digest. Dec 8, 1965, p417-18.
Movie Comedy (Byron). p202-03.
The New Republic. Dec 11, 1965, v153, p33-34.
New Statesman. Oct 28, 1966, v72, p642.

The New York Times. Dec 14, 1965, p54.
The New Yorker. Dec 18, 1965, v41, p162.
Newsweek. Jan 3, 1966, v67, p55.
Playboy. Feb 1966, v13, p34.
Saturday Review. Dec 18, 1965, v48, p42.
Sight and Sound. Wint 1966-67, v36, p46-47.
The Spectator. Oct 28, 1966, v217, p551.
Time. Dec 17, 1965, v86, p101.
Variety. Dec 1, 1965, p6.
The Village Voice. Dec 23, 1965, v11, p23.

Three Came Home (US; Negulesco, Jean; 1950)
Christian Century. May 10, 1950, v67, p599.
Claudette Colbert (Quirk). p159-61.
Commonweal. Mar 3, 1950, v51, p557.
Film Daily. Feb 10, 1950, p8.
Films in Review. Apr 1950, v1, p29-30, 48.
Hollywood Reporter. Feb 10, 1950, p3.
Library Journal. Feb 15, 1950, v75, p333.
Life. Mar 20, 1950, v28, p61-62.
The London Times. Feb 27, 1950, p8.
Motion Picture Herald Product Digest. Feb 11, 1950, p185.
The New Statesman and Nation. Mar 4, 1950, v39, p244.
The New York Times. Feb 21, 1950, p22.
The New Yorker. Mar 4, 1950, v26, p80.
The Spectator. Feb 24, 1950, v184, p241.
Variety. Feb 15, 1950, p13.

Three Coins in the Fountain (US; Negulesco, Jean; 1954)
America. May 29, 1954, v91, p259.
BFI/Monthly Film Bulletin. Aug 1954, v21, p118.
Catholic World. Jul 1954, v179, p301.
Commonweal. Jun 4, 1954, v60, p223.
Cue. May 22, 1954, p15.
Film Daily. May 12, 1954, p6.
Films and Filming. Oct 1954, v1, p29.
Films in Review. Jun-Jul 1954, v5, p303-04.
The Films of the Fifties. p131-32.
Hollywood Reporter. May 12, 1954, p3.
Library Journal. Jun 1, 1954, v79, p1048.
Life. Jun 7, 1954, v36, p151.
The London Times. Aug 23, 1954, p10.
Motion Picture Herald Product Digest. May 15, 1954, p2293.
The New Statesman and Nation. Aug 28, 1954, v48, p232.
The New York Times. May 21, 1954, p18.
The New Yorker. May 29, 1954, v30, p52.
Newsweek. May 31, 1954, v43, p85.
Saturday Review. Jun 5, 1954, v37, p27.
Selected Film Criticism, 1951-1960. p140-41.
The Spectator. Aug 20, 1954, v193, p221.
The Tatler. Sep 1, 1954, v213, p372.
Time. May 31, 1954, v63, p72.
Variety. May 12, 1954, p6.

Three Days of the Condor (US; Pollack, Sydney; 1975)
BFI/Monthly Film Bulletin. Oct 1975, v42, p226.
Commonweal. Oct 24, 1975, v102, p499.
Films in Review. Nov 1975, v26, p564.
The Films of Robert Redford. p217-24.
Hollywood Reporter. Sep 17, 1975, p4.
The Los Angeles Times. Sep 28, 1975, Calendar, p1.
Magill's Survey of Cinema. Series II. v6, p2494-97.
Motion Picture Herald Product Digest. Sep 24, 1975, p30.
The New Republic. Sep 27, 1975, v173, p52.
The New York Times. Sep 25, 1975, p60.
The New York Times. Sep 28, 1975, SecII, p1.
The New York Times. Nov 21, 1975, SecII, p13.
The New Yorker. Oct 6, 1975, v51, p98.

Newsweek. Sep 29, 1975, v86, p84-85.
Saturday Review. Sep 6, 1975, v2, p44-45.
Sidney Pollack (Taylor). p62-66, 135-36.
Time. Sep 29, 1975, v106, p77-78.
Variety. Sep 17, 1975, p18.
When the Lights Go Down. p42-43.

The Three Faces of Eve (US; Johnson, Nunnally; 1957)
America. Oct 5, 1957, v98, p28.
BFI/Monthly Film Bulletin. Nov 1957, v24, p136-37.
Commonweal. Oct 18, 1957, v67, p74.
Film Daily. Aug 21, 1957, v112, p6.
Films and Filming. Dec 1957, v4, p22.
Films in Review. Oct 1957, v8, p404-05.
Hollywood Reporter. Aug 21, 1957, p3.
Magill's Survey of Cinema. Series II. v6, p2498-501.
Motion Picture Herald Product Digest. Aug 24, 1957, v208, p505.
The New York Times. Sep 27, 1957, p16.
The New York Times. Oct 6, 1957, SecII, p1.
The New York Times Magazine. Aug 25, 1957, p54.
The New Yorker. Oct 5, 1957, v33, p145.
Newsweek. Sep 23, 1957, v50, p112.
Saturday Review. Sep 28, 1957, v40, p26.
Time. Sep 23, 1957, v70, p48.
Variety. Aug 21, 1957, p6.

Three For Bedroom C (US; Bren, Milton H.; 1952)
BFI/Monthly Film Bulletin. Dec 1952, v19, p175.
Commonweal. Jul 18, 1952, v56, p367.
Film Daily. Jun 2, 1952, p6.
The Films of Gloria Swanson. p244-46.
Hollywood Reporter. May 29, 1952, p3.
Motion Picture Herald Product Digest. May 31, 1952, p1383.
The New York Times. Jun 27, 1952, p18.
The New Yorker. Jul 5, 1952, v28, p52.
Newsweek. Jun 16, 1952, v39, p108.
Time. Jul 7, 1952, v60, p77.
Variety. Jun 4, 1952, p6.

Three Guys Named Mike (US; Walters, Charles; 1951)
BFI/Monthly Film Bulletin. Mar 1951, v18, p236.
Christian Century. Mar 28, 1951, v68, p415.
Film Daily. Feb 9, 1951, p6.
Hollywood Reporter. Feb 9, 1951, p3.
The London Times. Feb 119, 1951, p9.
Motion Picture Herald Product Digest. Feb 10, 1951, p705-06.
The New York Times. Mar 2, 1951, p21.
The New Yorker. Mar 10, 1951, v27, p94.
Senior Scholastic. Mar 7, 1951, v58, p61.
Time. Mar 19, 1951, v57, p108.
Variety. Feb 14, 1951, p13.

Three Hours to Kill (US; Werker, Alfred L.; 1954)
BFI/Monthly Film Bulletin. Jan 1955, v22, p11.
Catholic World. Oct 1954, v180, p65.
Farm Journal. Nov 1954, v78, p73.
Film Daily. Sep 13, 1954, p6.
Hollywood Reporter. Sep 8, 1954, p3.
Motion Picture Herald Product Digest. Sep 11, 1954, p137.
National Parent-Teacher. Oct 1954, v49, p40.
The New York Times. Sep 4, 1954, p6.
Newsweek. Sep 6, 1954, v44, p77.
Senior Scholastic. Nov 17, 1954, v65, p37.
Time. Oct 18, 1954, v64, p102.
Variety. Sep 8, 1954, p6.

Three Husbands (US; Reis, Irving; 1950)
BFI/Monthly Film Bulletin. Aug 1950, v17, p121.
Christian Century. Jan 31, 1951, v68, p159.
Film Daily. Nov 2, 1950, p6.
Hollywood Reporter. Nov 6, 1950, p3.
The London Times. Jul 10, 1950, p2.
Motion Picture Herald Product Digest. Nov 11, 1950, p562.
The New York Times. Mar 9, 1951, p30.
The Spectator. Jul 7, 1950, v185, p13.
Time. Dec 11, 1950, v56, p102.
Variety. Nov 8, 1950, p6.

3 into 2 Won't Go (GB; Hall, Peter; 1969)
Commonweal. Sep 26, 1969, v90, p594.
Double Takes. p101-03.
Filmfacts. 1969, v12, p356.
Films and Filming. Nov 1969, v16, p68.
Hollywood Republic. Jun 25, 1969, p3.
The New Republic. Jul 26, 1969, v161, p26.
The New York Times. Jul 3, 1969, p20.
The New Yorker. Jul 12, 1969, v45, p74.
Newsweek. Jul 21, 1969, v74, p98.
Variety. Jun 25, 1969, p18.

Three Little Words (US; Thorpe, Richard; 1950)
Astaire Dancing: The Musical Films. p300-11.
BFI/Monthly Film Bulletin. Oct 1950, v17, p158.
Christian Century. Aug 30, 1950, v67, p1031.
Film Daily. Jul 12, 1950, p6.
Hollywood Reporter. Jul 7, 1950, p3.
The London Times. Sep 18, 1950, p6.
Magill's Survey of Cinema. Series II. v6, p2502-04.
Motion Picture Herald Product Digest. Jul 8, 1950, p373.
The New York Times. Aug 10, 1950, p21.
The New Yorker. Aug 26, 1950, v26, p68-69.
Newsweek. Aug 14, 1950, v36, p82.
Starring Fred Astaire. p333-46.
Variety. Jul 12, 1950, p6.

The Three Lives of Thomasina (US; Chaffey, Don; 1963)
BFI/Monthly Film Bulletin. Jul 1964, v31, p108.
The Disney Films. p221-22.
Film Daily. Dec 16, 1963, p15.
Films and Filming. Aug 1964, v10, p25.
The New York Times. Dec 12, 1963, p46.
Variety. Dec 18, 1963, p17.
Walt Disney: A Guide to References and Resources. p95-96.

The Three Musketeers (Also titled: The Queen's Diamonds) (PANAMA; Lester, Richard; 1974)
American Scholar. Sum 1974, v43, p468-69.
Atlantic. Apr 1974, v233, p115-17.
BFI/Monthly Film Bulletin. May 1974, v41, p107.
Commonweal. Apr 12, 1974, v100, p133-34.
Esquire. May 1974, v81, p32.
Film Quarterly. Sum 1974, v27, p2-10.
The Films of Charlton Heston. p210-11.
The Films of The Seventies. p85-86.
The Los Angeles Times. Mar 28, 1974, SecIV, p1.
Motion Picture Herald Product Digest. Feb 27, 1974, p78.
The Nation. Mar 2, 1974, v218, p283.
The New Republic. Mar 2, 1974, v170, p26.
The New York Times. Apr 4, 1974, p52.
The New York Times. Apr 14, 1974, SecII, p13.
The New Yorker. Feb 4, 1974, v49, p92.
Newsweek. Feb 18, 1974, v83, p101.
Reeling. p418-19.

Christian Century. Nov 21, 1951, v68, p1359.
Film Daily. Aug 6, 1951, p6.
Hollywood Reporter. Aug 3, 1951, p3.
Motion Picture Herald Product Digest. Aug 11, 1951, p973.
The New York Times. Oct 18, 1951, p32.
Newsweek. Oct 29, 1951, v38, p94.
The Spectator. May 25, 1951, v186, p683-84.
Variety. Aug 8, 1951, p6.

Thunderball (GB; Young, Terence; 1965)
America. Jan 8, 1966, v114, p52-53.
BFI/Monthly Film Bulletin. Feb 1966, v33, p20.
Catholic World. May 1966, v203, p126-28.
Christian Science Monitor (Western edition). Dec 31, 1965, p5.
Cinema. Mar 1966, v3, p45.
Commonweal. Feb 11, 1966, v83, p559.
Esquire. Jun 1965, v63, p62.
Film Daily. Dec 20, 1965, p6.
Film Quarterly. Spr 1966, v19, p53-54.
Films and Filming. Mar 1966, v12, p56.
Films in Review. Jan 1966, v17, p46-47.
The Great Spy Pictures. p478-80.
Hollywood Reporter. Dec 21, 1965, p3.
The James Bond Films. p51-69.
James Bond in the Cinema. p73-90.
The James Bond Man: The Films of Sean Connery. p22-25, 66-67, 69-70.
Life. Jan 7, 1966, v60, p8.
The London Times. Dec 29, 1965, p10.
Look. Jul 13, 1965, v29, p45-50.
Motion Picture Herald Product Digest. Jan 5, 1966, p433.
New Statesman. Dec 31, 1965, v70, p1037.
The New York Times. Dec 22, 1965, p23.
The New Yorker. Jan 8, 1965, v41, p101-03.
Newsweek. Jan 3, 1966, v67, p56.
Playboy. Mar 1966, v13, p22.
The Primal Screen. p180-82.
Private Screenings. p226-28.
Saturday Review. Jan 15, 1966, v49, p43.
The Spectator. Dec 31, 1965, v215, p865.
Time. Dec 24, 1965, v86, p46.
Variety. Dec 22, 1965, p6.
The Village Voice. Jan 6, 1966, v11, p23.

Thunderbolt and Lightfoot (US; Cimino, Michael; 1974)
BFI/Monthly Film Bulletin. Aug 1974, v41, p185-86.
Christian Century. May 22, 1974, v91, p570.
Clint Eastwood (Guérif). p103-08.
Film. Aug 1974, n17, p20.
Films and Filming. Sep 1974, v20, p42.
The Films of Clint Eastwood. p171-75.
Jump Cut. Nov-Dec 1974, n4, p5-6.
The Los Angeles Times. May 22, 1974, SecIV, p16.
Martin Scorsese and Michael Cimino. p151-65.
Motion Picture Herald Product Digest. May 22, 1974, p101.
New Statesman. Sep 20, 1974, v88, p390.
The New York Times. May 24, 1974, p23.
Rolling Stone. Jul 4, 1974, p82.
Time. Jun 10, 1974, v103, p83.
Variety. May 29, 1974, p14.
The Village Voice. Jun 13, 1974, p97.

THX-1138 (Also titled: THX 1138-4EB) (US; Lucas, George; 1971)
Atlantic. May 29, 1971, v227, p98-99.
BFI/Monthly Film Bulletin. Jul 1971, v38, p147.
Cineaste. Sum 1968, v11, n1, p25.
Commonweal. Apr 30, 1971, v94, p191.
Film Quarterly. Spr 1974, v27, p4-9.
Filmfacts. 1971, v14, p143-45.

Hollywood Reporter. Mar 12, 1971, v215, n18, p3.
National Review. Jun 15, 1971, v23, p24.
The New Republic. Apr 10, 1971, v164, p24.
The New York Times. Mar 12, 1971, p27.
The New York Times. Mar 21, 1971, SecII, p1.
Newsweek. Mar 29, 1971, v77, p98.
Newsweek. May 31, 1971, v77, p50.
Saturday Review. Apr 3, 1971, v54, p52.
Time. Mar 29, 1971, v97, p85.
Variety. Mar 17, 1971, p18.
The Village Voice. Apr 8, 1971, p64.

Ticket to Heaven (CAN; Thomas, Ralph; 1981)
BFI/Monthly Film Bulletin. Dec 1981, v48, p255-56.
Christian Century. Feb 24, 1982, v99, p213-15.
Film Bulletin. Feb-Mar 1982, p54.
Film Journal. Dec 1, 1981, v85, p13.
Film Journal. Dec 21, 1981, v85, p13.
Films in Review. Feb 1982, v33, p110-11.
Maclean's. Sep 28, 1981, v94, p61.
The Nation. Dec 19, 1981, v233, p680-82.
New Statesman. Feb 5, 1982, v103, p26.
The New York Times. Nov 22, 1981, SecII, p17.
The New York Times. Nov 13, 1981, SecIII, p10.
The New York Times. Nov 29, 1981, SecII, p1.
The New Yorker. Nov 23, 1981, v57, p178.
Variety. May 27, 1981, p18.
The Village Voice. Nov 11, 1981, p44.

A Ticket to Tomahawk (US; Sale, Richard; 1950)
BFI/Monthly Film Bulletin. Jul 1950, v17, p102-03.
Christian Century. May 24, 1950, v67, p663.
Commonweal. May 19, 1950, v52, p152.
Film Daily. Apr 21, 1950, p6.
The Films of Marilyn Monroe. p35-37.
Hollywood Reporter. Apr 17, 1950, p4.
The London Times. Jul 17, 1950, p6.
Motion Picture Herald Product Digest. Apr 22, 1950, p269.
The New York Times. May 20, 1950, p8.
The New Yorker. May 27, 1950, v26, p62.
Newsweek. May 22, 1950, v35, p90.
Time. May 15, 1950, v55, p96.
Variety. Apr 19, 1950, p8.

Tickle Me (US; Taurog, Norman; 1965)
BFI/Monthly Film Bulletin. Aug 1965, v32, p125.
Film Daily. Jun 15, 1965, p9.
The Films and Career of Elvis Presley. p163-64.
Films and Filming. Aug 1965, v11, p33.
Hollywood Reporter. Jun 15, 1965, p3.
Motion Picture Herald Product Digest. Jun 23, 1965, p313, 315.
The New York Times. Jun 24, 1965, p28.
Variety. Jun 16, 1965, p6.

A Ticklish Affair (US; Sidney, George; 1963)
BFI/Monthly Film Bulletin. Feb 1964, v31, p28.
Film Daily. Jul 3, 1963, p7.
Filmfacts. Sep 5, 1963, v6, p178-79.
Films and Filming. Dec 1963, v10, p27-28.
Hollywood Reporter. Jul 3, 1963, v176, p3.
The New York Times. Aug 22, 1963, p19.
Time. Sep 6, 1963, v82, p84.
Variety. Jul 3, 1963, p6.

Tiefland (Also titled: Tiepland; Lowlands) (WGER; Riefenstahl, Leni; 1952)
Film in the Third Reich. p135-40.
The Films of Leni Riefenstahl. p83-06, p146-47.
Leni Riefenstahl (Berg-Pan). p163-75.

Leni Riefenstahl: The Fallen Film Goddess. p188-92.
Magill's Survey of Cinema. Foreign Language Films. v7, p3093-96.
The New York Times. Oct 7, 1981, p28.
Variety. Oct 28, 1981, p18.
The Village Voice. Oct 7, 1981, v26, p44.

Tiger Bay (GB; Thompson, J. Lee; 1959)
America. Jan 30, 1960, v102, p538.
BFI/Monthly Film Bulletin. May 1959, v26, p57.
Filmfacts. Jan 27, 1960, v2, p334-35.
Films in Review. Oct 1959, v10, p450.
Hollywood Reporter. Dec 24, 1959, p3.
Magill's Survey of Cinema. Series II. v6, p2519-21.
The New Republic. Jan 18, 1960, v142, p20.
The New York Times. Dec 15, 1959, p50.
The New Yorker. Dec 26, 1959, v35, p55.
Reporter. Jan 21, 1960, v22, p40-41.
Time. Mar 14, 1960, v75, p84.
Variety. Apr 8, 1959, p6.

Tightrope (US; Tuggle, Richard; 1984)
BFI/Monthly Film Bulletin. Nov 1984, v51, p345.
Film Comment. Sep 10, 1984, v20, p64-71.
Film Journal. Sep 1984, v87, p25.
Films in Review. Nov 1984, v35, p564-65.
Hollywood Reporter. Aug 13, 1984, p4.
Humanist. Nov-Dec 1984, v44, p43-44.
Informer. Sep-Oct 1984, p4.
The Los Angeles Times. Aug 17, 1984, SecVI, p1.
Maclean's. Sep 3, 1984, v97, p54.
Ms. Dec 1984, v13, p34.
National Review. Oct 5, 1984, v36, p55-57.
New Statesman. Nov 2, 1984, v108, p35-36.
New York. Aug 27, 1984, v17, p112.
The New York Times. Sep 23, 1984, SecII, p19.
The New York Times. Aug 17, 1984, SecIII, P6.
The New Yorker. Oct 1, 1984, v60, p112-15.
Newsweek. Aug 27, 1984, v104, p68.
Penthouse. Nov 1984, v16, p56.
Photoplay. Dec 1984, v35, p18, 24-26.
Time. Aug 27, 1984, v124, p64.
Variety. Aug 15, 1984, p14.
The Village Voice. Aug 29, 1984, p45-46.
The Village Voice. Oct 9, 1984, v29, p62.

Tigre Se Parfume a la Dynamite, Le *See* An Orchid for the Tiger

Time After Time (GB, US; Meyer, Nicholas; 1979)
BFI/Monthly Film Bulletin. Jan 1980, v47, p13.
Films in Review. Nov 1979, v30, p566.
The Films of the Seventies. p261-63.
Hollywood Reporter. Sep 7, 1979, p3.
The Los Angeles Times. Sep 23, 1979, Calendar, p1.
Magill's Cinema Annual, 1984. p579-84.
Motion Picture Herald Product Digest. Sep 26, 1979, p33.
The Nation. Nov 3, 1979, v229, p444-45.
The New Republic. Sep 29, 1979, v181, p27.
New York. Oct 8, 1979, v12, p86.
The New York Times. Sep 28, 1979, v3, p10.
The New Yorker. Oct 29, 1979, v55, p148.
Newsweek. Oct 1, 1979, v94, p77.
Rolling Stone. Nov 15, 1979, p34.
Saturday Review. Nov 10, 1979, v6, p49.
Time. Oct 8, 1979, v114, p87.
Variety. Sep 5, 1979, p16.

Time Bandits (GB; Gilliam, Terry; 1981)
Christian Century. Jan 6, 1981, v99, p33.
Film Comment. Nov-Dec 1981, v17, p49-54.
Hollywood Reporter. Nov 5, 1981, p1.

The Los Angeles Times. Nov 6, 1981, SecVI, p4.
Maclean's. Nov 16, 1981, v94, p76.
Magill's Cinema Annual 1982. p364-67.
New York. Nov 16, 1981, v14, p116.
The New York Times. Nov 6, 1981, SecIII, p8.
Newsweek. Nov 9, 1981, v98, p92.
Senior Scholastic. Dec 11, 1981, v114, p25.
Time. Nov 9, 1981, v118, p98.
Variety. Jul 20, 1981, p3.

Time Limit (US; Malden, Karl; 1957)
America. Oct 26, 1957, v98, p120.
BFI/Monthly Film Bulletin. Dec 1957, v26, p149.
Commonweal. Oct 25, 1957, v66, p98.
Film Daily. Sep 19, 1957, v112, p6.
Films and Filming. Jan 1958, v4, p24.
Films in Review. Nov 1957, v8, p463-64.
Hollywood Reporter. Sep 18, 1957, p3.
Motion Picture Herald Product Digest. Sep 21, 1957, v208, p537.
The Nation. Nov 9, 1957, v185, p332.
The New York Times. Oct 24, 1957, p37.
The New Yorker. Nov 2, 1957, v33, p165.
Newsweek. Oct 28, 1957, v50, p104.
Saturday Review. Oct 19, 1957, v40, p54.
Time. Oct 28, 1957, v70, p98.
Variety. Sep 18, 1957, p6.

Time Lost and Time Remembered (Also titled: I Was Happy Here) (GB; Davis, Desmond; 1965)
BFI/Monthly Film Bulletin. Aug 1966, v33, p120.
Commonweal. Sep 23, 1966, v84, p614.
Film Daily. Aug 12, 1966, p3.
Film Quarterly. Spr 1967, v20, p63.
Filmfacts. Nov 1, 1966, v9, p232-33.
Films and Filming. Sep 1966, v12, p59-60.
Films and Filming. Sep 1965, v11, p43-44, 46.
International Film Guide. 1967, v4, p91.
The London Times. Jul 7, 1966, p17.
Motion Picture Herald Product Digest. Aug 17, 1966, p582.
National Review. Jul 25, 1967, v19, p816.
The New York Times. Aug 30, 1966, p35.
Newsweek. Aug 29, 1966, v68, p68.
Time. Sep 2, 1966, v88, p66.
Variety. Jul 13, 1966, p6.

The Time Machine (US; Pal, George; 1960)
America. Sep 3, 1960, v103, p603.
BFI/Monthly Film Bulletin. Sep 1960, v27, p127.
The English Novel and the Movies. p187-96.
Film Daily. Jul 19, 1960, p10.
Film Quarterly. Fall 1960, v14, p62.
Filmfacts. 1960, v3, p193.
Films and Filming. Sep 1960, v6, p25.
The Films of George Pal. p113-23.
The Films of the Sixties. p45-47.
Focus on the Science Fiction Film. p118-20.
Great Horror Movies. p157-59.
H.G. Wells (Wykes). p141-50.
Hollywood Reporter. Jul 11, 1960, p3.
The New York Times. Aug 18, 1960, p19.
The New Yorker. Aug 27, 1960, v36, p54.
Saturday Review. Jul 23, 1960, v43, p31.
Senior Scholastic. Oct 5, 1960, v77, p29.
Time. Aug 22, 1960, v76, p53.
Variety. Jul 20, 1960, p6.

A Time to Live and a Time to Die (US; Sirk, Douglas; 1958)
America. Aug 16, 1958, v119, p516-17.
BFI/Monthly Film Bulletin. 1958, v25, p111.
Catholic World. Aug 1958, v187, p382.
Commonweal. Aug 1, 1958, v68, p446.
Douglas Sirk (Stern). p167-80.
Film Daily. Apr 1, 1958, v113, p4.

Filmfacts. Aug 27, 1958, v1, p124-25.
Hollywood Reporter. Apr 1, 1958, p3.
Library Journal. Jul 1958, v83, p2037.
The New Republic. Aug 18, 1958, p31.
The New York Times. Jul 10, 1958, p22.
The New Yorker. Jul 19, 1958, v34, p82.
Newsweek. Jul 28, 1958, v52, p77.
Saturday Review. Jul 12, 1958, v41, p25.
Time. Jul 28, 1958, v72, p68-69.
Variety. Apr 2, 1958, p6.

Times Gone By *See* Altri Tempi

The Times of Harvey Milk (US; Epstein, Robert; 1984)
Film Comment. Dec 1984, v20, p70-71.
Maclean's. Dec 3, 1984, v97, p69.
The Nation. Nov 24, 1984, v239, p563-64.
The New Republic. Dec 31, 1984, v191, p25.
The New York Times. Oct 26, 1984, SecIII, p16.
The New York Times. Oct 27, 1984, p15.
The New York Times. Oct 7, 1984, p86.
Newsweek. Dec 3, 1984, v104, p81.
Variety. Sep 26, 1984, p15.
The Village Voice. Oct 16, 1984, p63.

The Tin Drum (German title: Blechtrommel, Die) (WGER; Schlöndorff, Volker; 1979)
BFI/Monthly Film Bulletin. Jun 1980, v47, p107-08.
The Great German Films. p288-91.
Hollywood Reporter. Dec 28, 1979, p3.
Magill's Survey of Cinema. Foreign Language Films. v7, p3106-11.
Motion Picture Herald Product Digest. Apr 26, 1980, p89.
The New York Times. Apr 11, 1980, SecIII, p6.
Variety. May 16, 1979, p27.

The Tin Star (US; Mann, Anthony; 1957)
America. Nov 30, 1957, v98, p300.
Anthony Mann (Basinger). p136-44.
BFI/Monthly Film Bulletin. Dec 1957, v24, p153-54.
Cinema, the Magic Vehicle. v2, p365.
Commonweal. Nov 15, 1957, v67, p175-76.
Film Daily. Oct 22, 1957, v112, p6.
Films and Filming. Jan 1958, v4, p27.
The Films of Henry Fonda. p153-54.
The Fondas (Springer). p162-63.
Hollywood Reporter. Oct 15, 1957, p3.
Motion Picture Herald Product Digest. Oct 19, 1957, v209, p569.
The New York Times. Oct 24, 1957, p37.
The New York Times. Oct 27, 1957, SecII, p1.
Newsweek. Nov 11, 1957, v50, p122-23.
Time. Nov 4, 1957, v70, p107.
Variety. Oct 16, 1957, p6.

Tirez sur le Pianiste *See* Shoot the Piano Player

The Titan: The Story of Michelangelo (US; Lyford, Richard; 1949)
Christian Century. Jun 14, 1950, v67, p743.
Commonweal. Feb 10, 1950, v51, p487.
Film Daily. Jan 4, 1950, p6.
Films in Review. Mar 1950, v1, p23-25.
Hollywood Quarterly. Fall 1950, v5, p8-13.
Hollywood Reporter. Apr 25, 1950, p4.
Library Journal. Sep 15, 1949, v74, p1240.
Library Journal. May 1, 1950, v75, p787.
Magazine of Art. Feb 1950, v43, p71-72.
The New Republic. Jan 30, 1950, v122, p31.
The New York Times. Jan 23, 1950, p16.
Newsweek. Feb 6, 1950, v35, p80.
Robert Flaherty: A Guide to References and Resources. p110-11.
Saturday Review. Mar 25, 1950, v33, p26-28.
Saturday Review. Aug 23, 1952, v35, p34.
Senior Scholastic. Mar 15, 1950, v56, p36.

Still Seeing Things. p301-05.
Time. Jan 30, 1950, v55, p84.
Variety. Dec 28, 1949, p6.
Variety. Nov 19, 1980, p14.

Titanic (US; Negulesco, Jean; 1953)
America. Jun 20, 1953, v89, p326.
BFI/Monthly Film Bulletin. Jul 1953, v20, n234, p103.
Catholic World. Jun 1953, v177, p225.
Film Daily. Apr 16, 1953, p6.
Films in Review. May 1953, v4, n5, p241-42.
The Films of Barbara Stanwyck. p216-19.
Hollywood Reporter. Apr 15, 1953, p3.
Magill's Survey of Cinema. Series II. v6, p2522.
National Parent-Teacher. Jun 1953, v47, p38.
The New York Times. May 28, 1953, p27.
The New York Times. May 31, 1953, SecII, p1.
The New Yorker. Jun 6, 1953, v29, p95-96.
Newsweek. May 18, 1953, v41, p108.
Saturday Review. May 23, 1953, v36, p30.
Theatre Arts. Jun 1953, v37, p86.
Time. Apr 27, 1953, v61, p108.
Variety. Apr 15, 1953, p6.

The Titfield Thunderbolt (GB; Crichton, Charles; 1953)
America. Oct 24, 1953, v90, p109.
BFI/Monthly Film Bulletin. Apr 1953, v20, p51.
Catholic World. Oct 1953, v178, p61-62.
Commonweal. Oct 23, 1953, v59, p61.
Film Daily. Oct 20, 1953, p6.
Halliwell's Hundred. p370-73.
Hollywood Reporter. May 27, 1954, p3.
Motion Picture Herald Product Digest. Oct 3, 1953, p2014.
National Parent-Teacher. Nov 1953, v48, p35.
The New Statesman and Nation. Mar 14, 1953, v45, p295-96.
The New York Times. Oct 6, 1953, p34.
The New Yorker. Oct 17, 1953, v29, p107.
Newsweek. Oct 19, 1953, v42, p104.
Saturday Review. Oct 10, 1953, v36, p34.
Sight and Sound. Apr-Jun 1953, v22, p196.
Time. Oct 19, 1953, v62, p116.
Variety. Mar 25, 1953, p24.

Tma *See* Sweet Light In a Dark Room

To Be a Crook (Also titled: Fille et des Fusils, Une; A Girl and Guns; The Decadent Influence) (FR; Lelouch, Claude; 1965)
America. Feb 11, 1967, v116, p226.
Cineaste. Sum 1967, v1, p10.
Commonweal. Mar 10, 1967, v85, p657.
Film Daily. Feb 17, 1967, p4.
Film Quarterly. Fall 1967, v21, p60.
Filmfacts. Mar 1, 1967, v10, p32-33.
Films in Review. Feb 1967, v18, p117.
Motion Picture Herald Product Digest. Mar 15, 1967, p667.
Movies Into Film. p249.
The New York Times. Feb 7, 1967, p33.
The New Yorker. Feb 11, 1967, v42, p134.
Newsweek. Feb 6, 1967, v69, p97.
Time. Feb 3, 1967, v89, p76.
Variety. Mar 10, 1965, p6.

To Be or Not to Be (US; Johnson, Alan; 1983)
The Christian Science Monitor. Dec 19, 1983, p31.
Hollywood Reporter. Dec 12, 1983, p3.
The Los Angeles Times. Dec 16, 1983, SecVI, p22.
Maclean's. Dec 26, 1983, v96, p44.
Magill's Cinema Annual, 1984. p426-29.
The New Republic. Dec 31, 1983, v189, p24-25.
The New Yorker. Jan 9, 1984, v61, p103.

Newsweek. Dec 19, 1983, v102, p66.
Saturday Review. Jan 1984, v10, p40.

To Begin Again *See* Volver a Empezar

To Catch a Thief (US; Hitchcock, Alfred; 1955)
America. Aug 6, 1955, v93, p460.
The Art of Alfred Hitchcock. p251-57.
BFI/Monthly Film Bulletin. Dec 1955, v22, n263, p179.
Catholic World. Sep 1955, v181, p462.
Commonweal. Sep 2, 1955, v62, p541.
Film Culture. Wint 1955, v1, n5/6, p31.
Film Daily. Jul 15, 1955, p5.
Films and Filming. Dec 1955, v2, n3, p16.
The Films in My Life. p80-82.
Films in Review. Aug-Sep 1955, v6, n7, p346.
The Films of Alfred Hitchcock. p170-73.
The Films of Cary Grant. p219-21.
The Films of the Fifties. p139-40.
Hitchcock: The First Forty-Four Films. p129-32.
Hitchcock (Truffaut). p222-26.
Hollywood Reporter. Jul 14, 1955, v135, n25, p3.
Magill's Survey of Cinema. Series I. v4, p1747-51.
The Nation. Aug 20, 1955, v181, p162.
The New Republic. Nov 28, 1955, v133, p21-22.
The New York Times. Aug 5, 1955, p14.
The New York Times. Aug 21, 1955, SecII, p1.
The New Yorker. Aug 13, 1955, v31, p48.
Newsweek. Aug 1, 1955, v46, p77.
Saturday Review. Aug 27, 1955, v38, p23.
Sight and Sound. Wint 1955-56, v25, n3, p150.
Time. Aug 15, 1955, v66, p58.
Variety. Jul 20, 1955, p6.

To Die in Madrid (French title: Mourir a Madrid) (FR; Rossif, Frederic; 1963)
Christian Century. Feb 9, 1966, v83, p178.
Christian Science Monitor (Western edition). Jun 10, 1966, p4.
Commentary. May 1966, v41, p73.
Commonweal. Oct 8, 1965, v83, p25.
The Documentary Tradition. p444.
Esquire. Sep 1965, v64, p40-42.
Film Quarterly. Sum 1966, v19, p55-56.
Film Society Review. Feb 1966, p12.
Film Society Review. Feb 1971, v6, p41-46.
Films and Filming. May 1967, v13, p30-31.
Hollywood Reporter. Jan 21, 1966, p3.
Life. Sep 10, 1965, v59, p16.
The London Times. Jan 26, 1967, p6.
Motion Picture Herald Product Digest. Oct 27, 1965, p395.
The Nation. Oct 25, 1965, v201, p288.
National Review. Aug 9, 1966, v18, p793-96.
The New Republic. Jul 3, 1965, v153, p27.
New Statesman. Jan 27, 1967, v73, p125-26.
The New York Times. Sep 16, 1965, np.
The New Yorker. Sep 25, 1965, v41, p168.
Newsweek. Sep 20, 1965, v66, p96.
Playboy. Jan 1966, v13, p48.
Private Screenings. p215-17.
Saturday Review. Sep 18, 1965, v48, p32.
Sight and Sound. Spr 1967, v36, p88-92.
Time. Oct 1, 1965, v86, p117.
Variety. Mar 20, 1963, p18.

To Kill a Mockingbird (US; Mulligan, Robert; 1962)
America. Feb 23, 1963, v108, p273.
BFI/Monthly Film Bulletin. May 1963, v30, p61-62.
Commonweal. Feb 22, 1963, v77, p572.
Confessions of a Cultist. p75-77.
Film Daily. Dec 11, 1962, p4.
Film Quarterly. Spr 1963, v16, p60.
Filmfacts. 1963, v6, p13.
Films and Filming. Jun 1963, v9, p27.

Films in Review. Mar 1963, v14, p172-73.
The Films of Gregory Peck. p179-84.
Hollywood Reporter. Dec 11, 1962, p3.
Magill's Survey of Cinema. Series I. v4, p1756-59.
Motion Picture Herald Product Digest. Dec 26, 1962, p722.
Movie. Apr 1963, n9, p35.
The New Republic. Feb 21, 1963, v148, p30-31.
The New York Times. Feb 15, 1963, p10.
The New Yorker. Feb 23, 1963, v39, p125-26.
Newsweek. Feb 18, 1963, v61, p9.
Saturday Review. Jan 12, 1963, v45, p57.
Sight and Sound. Sum 1963, v32, p147.
Time. Feb 22, 1963, v81, p93.
Variety. Dec 12, 1962, p6.

To Koritsi Me Ta Maura *See* Girl in Black

To Live *See* Ikiru

To Live and Die in LA (US; Friedkin, William; 1985)
BFI/Monthly Film Bulletin. Jun 1986, v53, p182-83.
Films in Review. Jan 1986, v37, p45.
Los Angeles. Nov 1985, v30, p34.
The Los Angeles Times. Nov 1, 1985, SecVI, p4.
Magill's Cinema Annual, 1986. p379-82.
The New Republic. Nov 25, 1985, v193, p24-25.
New York. Nov 18, 1985, v18, p88.
The New York Times. Nov 17, 1985, SecII, p17.
Newsweek. Nov 11, 1985, v106, p80.
Time. Nov 18, 1985, v126, p94.
Variety. Oct 30, 1985, p16.
The Wall Street Journal. Nov 7, 1985, p30.

To Love (Swedish title: Att Alska) (SWED; Donner, Jorn; 1964)
BFI/Monthly Film Bulletin. Nov 1966, v33, p162-63.
Commonweal. Dec 11, 1964, v81, p390.
Confessions of a Cultist. p170-71.
Esquire. Feb 1965, v63, p120.
Film Daily. Nov 24, 1964, p8.
Film Quarterly. Spr 1966, v19, p34-36.
London Magazine. Dec 1965, v5, p64-66.
Motion Picture Herald Product Digest. Jan 20, 1965, p210.
The New Republic. Jan 2, 1965, v152, p21.
The New York Times. Sep 23, 1964, p54.
The New Yorker. Nov 28, 1964, v40, p204.
Sight and Sound. Aut 1966, v35, p200-01.
Time. Dec 4, 1964, v84, p111.
Variety. Sep 9, 1964, p6.
The Village Voice. Nov 26, 1964, v10, p19, 25.

To Please a Lady (US; Brown, Clarence; 1950)
Christian Century. Dec 6, 1950, v67, p1471.
Commonweal. Nov 10, 1950, v53, p122.
Film Daily. Oct 4, 1950, p4.
The Films of Barbara Stanwyck. p206-07.
The Films of Clark Gable. p221.
Hollywood Reporter. Oct 4, 1950, p3.
Motion Picture Herald Product Digest. Oct 7, 1950, p509.
The New York Times. Oct 27, 1950, p24.
Newsweek. Nov 6, 1950, v36, p94.
Saturday Review. Nov 11, 1950, v33, p28.
The Spectator. Dec 1, 1950, v185, p613.
Starring Miss Barbara Stanwyck. p229, 232.
Time. Oct 30, 1950, v56, p98.
Variety. Oct 4, 1950, p6.

To Sir, With Love (GB; Clavell, James; 1967)
America. Jun 24, 1967, v116, p880.
BFI/Monthly Film Bulletin. Oct 1967, v34, p154.
Christian Century. Sep 20, 1967, v84, p1198-99.

Ebony. Apr 1967, v22, p68-70.
Film Daily. Jun 15, 1967, p4.
Film Quarterly. Wint 1967-68, v21, p50-52.
Films and Filming. Nov 1967, v14, p25.
The Films of Sidney Poitier. p142-47.
From Sambo to Superspade. p227-28.
Hollywood Reporter. Jun 13, 1967, p3.
Magill's Survey of Cinema. Series II. v6, p2530-32.
Motion Picture Herald Product Digest. Jun 21, 1967, p696.
The New York Times. Jun 15, 1967, p56.
The New Yorker. Jun 17, 1967, v43, p92.
Newsweek. Jun 26, 1967, v69, p73.
Saturday Review. Jul 8, 1967, v50, p39.
Senior Scholastic. May 5, 1967, v90, p30.
Senior Scholastic. Apr 7, 1967, v90, p6.
Take One. 1967, v1, n6, p30.
Time. Jun 30, 1967, v89, p70.
Variety. Jun 14, 1967, p6.
The Village Voice. Dec 7, 1967, p39.

The Toast of New Orleans (US; Taurog, Norman; 1950)
BFI/Monthly Film Bulletin. Jan 1951, v18, p207.
Christian Century. Nov 29, 1950, v67, p1439.
Film Daily. Aug 24, 1950, p5.
The Films of David Niven. p99-101.
Hollywood Reporter. Aug 24, 1950, p3.
Motion Picture Herald Product Digest. Aug 26, 1950, p450.
The New York Times. Sep 30, 1950, p13.
The New Yorker. Oct 28, 1950, v26, p63.
Time. Nov 13, 1950, v56, p102.
Variety. Aug 30, 1950, p6.

Tobruk (US; Hiller, Arthur; 1967)
BFI/Monthly Film Bulletin. Apr 1967, v34, p63-64.
Film Daily. Dec 21, 1966, p7.
Films and Filming. Sep 1967, v13, p24.
Films in Review. Jan 1967, v18, p52-53.
Hollywood Reporter. Dec 20, 1966, p3.
Motion Picture Herald Product Digest. Dec 21, 1966, p641.
The New York Times. Feb 9, 1967, p33.
The New Yorker. Feb 18, 1967, v42, p143.
Variety. Dec 21, 1966, p6.

Tokyo Monogatari *See* Tokyo Story

Tokyo Olympiad (Also titled: Tokyo Orinpikku; Tokyo Olympiad 1964) (JAPAN; Ichikawa, Kon; 1965)
BFI/Monthly Film Bulletin. Nov 1965, v32, p166.
Commonweal. Jul 8, 1966, v84, p441.
Film Comment. Sum 1965, v3, p38-40.
Film Quarterly. Spr 1966, v19, p50.
Filmfacts. Jan 15, 1966, v9, p374-76.
Films and Filming. Nov 1965, v12, p25.
Hollywood Reporter. Nov 12, 1965, p3.
International Film Guide. 1966, v3, p103.
Motion Picture Herald Product Digest. Jan 26, 1966, p458.
Movie. Aut 1965, n14, p40.
New Statesman. Oct 8, 1965, v70, p533-34.
The New York Times. Nov 17, 1966, p55.
Newsweek. Oct 11, 1965, v66, p106.
Saturday Review. Dec 10, 1966, v49, p65.
Saturday Review. Dec 11, 1965, v48, p50.
Sight and Sound. Aut 1965, v34, p199.
Sight and Sound. Fall, 1977, v46, n4, p210-15.
The Spectator. Oct 8, 1965, v215, p447.
Variety. May 26, 1965, p15.

Tokyo Story (Also titled: Tokyo Monogatari; Their First Trip to Tokyo) (JAPAN; Ozu, Yasujiro; 1953)

BFI/Monthly Film Bulletin. May 1965, v32, p73.
Cinema East. p201-27.
Cinema, the Magic Vehicle. v2, p153-56.
Dictionary of Films. p378.
Favorite Movies. p202-12.
Film. Sep-Oct 1957, n13, p20-21.
Film 72/73. p59-63.
Film Criticism. Spr 1980, v4, p31-40.
Filmfacts. 1972, v15, n7, p141-44.
Films and Filming. Jul 1965, v11, p33.
Films and Filming. Nov 1983, v29, p35-36.
The International Dictionary of Films and Filmmakers. v1, p479-80.
Japan: Film Images. p53-56.
Japanese Film Directors. p84-87.
Life. May 5, 1972, v72, p22.
Living Images. p100-03.
The London Times. Mar 18, 1965, p9.
Magill's Survey of Cinema. Foreign Language Films. v7, p3119-22.
Movie. Sum 1965, n13, p32-33.
The Nation. Jun 22, 1964, v198, p638-39.
National Review. Sep 15, 1972, v24, p1023.
The New Republic. Mar 18, 1972, v166, p24.
New Statesman. Mar 19, 1965, v69, p462.
New Statesman. Oct 28, 1983, v106, p34.
The New Yorker. Apr 8, 1972, v48, p102.
Newsweek. Mar 27, 1972, v79, p103.
Quarterly of Film, Radio and Television. Sum 1956, v10, p354-63.
Sight and Sound. Wint 1957-58, v27, p131-33, 160.
Something to Declare. p79-82.
Take One. May-Jun 1971, v3, p20-21.
Transcendental Style in Film. p44-55.

Tom Brown's Schooldays (GB; Parry, Gordon; 1951)
BFI/Monthly Film Bulletin. May 1951, v18, p260-61.
Children's Novels and the Movies. p1-14.
Commonweal. Jan 25, 1952, v55, p400.
Film Daily. Oct 26, 1951, p4.
Hollywood Reporter. Oct 24, 1951, p3.
Library Journal. Nov 15, 1951, v76, p1948.
The London Times. Mar 17, 1950, p10.
The London Times. Jul 28, 1950, p7.
Motion Picture Herald Product Digest. Oct 27, 1951, p1074.
The New Republic. Jan 28, 1952, v126, p23.
The New York Times. Jan 8, 1952, p23.
The New Yorker. Jan 19, 1952, v27, p70.
Newsweek. Nov 12, 1951, v38, p99.
Senior Scholastic. Dec 12, 1951, v59, p26.
The Spectator. Apr 20, 1951, v186, p520.
Variety. May 2, 1951, p12.

Tom Horn (US; Wiard, William; 1980)
The Films of Steve McQueen. p225-32.
Hollywood Reporter. Mar 28, 1980, p3.
The Los Angeles Times. May 16, 1980, SecVI, p2.
Motion Picture Herald Product Digest. Jun 11, 1980, p3.
The New York Times. May 23, 1980, SecIII, p8.
The New Yorker. Jun 2, 1980, v56, p125-26.
Time. Jun 30, 1980, v115, p72.
Variety. Apr 2, 1980, p22.

Tom Jones (US; Richardson, Tony; 1963)
America. Nov 2, 1963, v109, p532.
BFI/Monthly Film Bulletin. Aug 1963, v30, p113.
Catholic World. Apr 1964, v199, p71-72.
Commonweal. Oct 25, 1963, v79, p141.
The English Novel and the Movies. p36-43.
Esquire. Feb 1964, v61,, p32.
Film Daily. Oct 3, 1963, p15.
Filmfacts. Oct 10, 1963, v6, p205-07.

Films and Filming. Aug 1963, v9, p22.
Films in Review. Oct 1963, v14, p496-97.
The Films of the Sixties. p100-03.
The Great Films. p237-41.
The Great Movies. p81-83.
Life. Oct 11, 1963, v55, p55.
Magill's Survey of Cinema. Series I. v4, p1760-63.
The Nation. Nov 30, 1963, v197, p374.
National Review. Feb 25, 1964, v16, p165.
The New Republic. Oct 19, 1963, v149, p27-28.
The New York Times. Oct 8, 1963, p48.
The New York Times. Oct 13, 1963, SecII, p1.
The New York Times Magazine. Sep 29, 1963, p104-05.
The New Yorker. Sep 7, 1963, v39, p98.
The New Yorker. Oct 12, 1963, v39, p169-70.
Newsweek. Oct 14, 1963, v62, p116-17.
Photoplay. Mar 1964, v65, p18.
Reporter. Nov 21, 1963, v29, p54.
Saturday Review. Oct 5, 1963, v46, p52.
Time. Oct 18, 1963, v82, p117.
Variety. Jul 31, 1963, p12.
The Village Voice. Oct 17, 1963, v8, p13.
The Village Voice. Oct 24, 1963, v8, p13.

Tom Thumb (US; Pal, George; 1958)
BFI/Monthly Film Bulletin. Jan 1959, v26, p10.
Commonweal. Dec 12, 1958, v69, p293.
Film Daily. Nov 28, 1958, v114, p6.
Filmfacts. Jan 14, 1959, v1, p255-56.
Films in Review. Jan 1959, p40.
The Films of George Pal. p101-12.
Good Housekeeping. Dec 1958, v147, p24.
Hollywood Reporter. Nov 28, 1958, p3.
Library Journal. Dec 15, 1958, v83, p3508.
Life. Dec 15, 1958, v45, p45-46.
The New York Times. Dec 24, 1958, np.
Newsweek. Dec 29, 1958, v52, p64-65.
Senior Scholastic. Nov 21, 1958, v73, p44.
Time. Jan 5, 1959, v53, p84.
Variety. Dec 3, 1958, p6.

Tommy (GB; Russell, Ken; 1975)
BFI/Monthly Film Bulletin. Apr 1975, v42, p88.
Films in Review. May 1975, v26, p311.
Hollywood Reporter. Mar 12, 1975, p14.
Ken Russell: A Guide to References and Resources. p36-39.
Ken Russell (Atkins). p82-95.
Ken Russell (Phillips). p158-67.
Ken Russell: the Adaptor as Creator. p194-03.
Ken Russell's Films. p253-91.
The Los Angeles Times. Mar 20, 1975, SecIV, p1.
Motion Picture Herald Product Digest. Apr 9, 1975, p86.
The New Republic. Apr 26, 1975, v172, p18.
The New York Times. Mar 20, 1975, p48.
The New York Times. Mar 30, 1975, SecII, p13.
The New Yorker. Apr 7, 1975, v51, p123-24.
Newsweek. Mar 24, 1975, v85, p59.
Saturday Review. May 3, 1975, v2, p35.
Senior Scholastic. May 8, 1975, v106, p23.
The Story of Tommy. 1975.
Time. Mar 31, 1975, v105, p56.
Variety. Mar 12, 1975, p18.

Tomorrow Is Another Day (US; Feist, Felix; 1951)
BFI/Monthly Film Bulletin. Mar 1952, v19, p38.
Film Daily. Aug 13, 1951, p6.
Hollywood Reporter. Aug 9, 1951, p3.
The London Times. Jan 28, 1952, p8.
Motion Picture Herald Product Digest. Aug 11, 1951, p973.
The New York Times. Aug 9, 1951, p17.

The Spectator. Jan 25, 1952, v188, p108-09.
Variety. Aug 15, 1951, p6.

Tomorrow Is Too Late (Italian title: Domani È Troppo Tardi) (IT; Moguy, Leonide; 1950)
Commonweal. Apr 25, 1952, v56, p69.
Film Daily. Apr 17, 1952, p6.
Hollywood Reporter. Nov 3, 1952, p3.
The London Times. Mar 12, 1951, p3.
Motion Picture Herald Product Digest. Apr 19, 1952, p1322.
The New Statesman and Nation. Dec 29, 1951, v42, p756.
The New York Times. Apr 14, 1952, p22.
The New Yorker. Apr 19, 1952, v28, p86.
Newsweek. May 5, 1952, v39, p101.
Saturday Review. Apr 12, 1952, v35, p41.
Theatre Arts. May 1952, v36, p104.
Time. Apr 28, 1952, v59, p96.
Variety. Nov 1, 1950, p18.

Tonight at 8:30 (Also titled: Meet Me Tonight) (GB; Pelissier, Anthony; 1952)
America. Jun 20, 1953, v89, p326.
BFI/Monthly Film Bulletin. Oct 1952, v19, p139.
Commonweal. Jun 12, 1953, v58, p249.
The London Times. Feb 13, 1952, p7.
The London Times. Sep 10, 1952, p6.
Magill's Survey of Cinema. Series II. v6, p2533-36.
Motion Picture Herald Product Digest. Jun 6, 1953, p1862.
National Parent-Teacher. Oct 1953, v48, p39.
The New Republic. Sep 21, 1953, v129, p18.
The New Statesman and Nation. Sep 20, 1952, v44, p316.
The New York Times. May 26, 1953, p33.
Newsweek. Jun 1, 1953, v41, p87.
The Spectator. Sep 12, 1952, v189, p328.
Theatre Arts. Aug 1953, v37, p87.
Time. Jun 15, 1953, v61, p106.
Variety. Sep 17, 1952, p6.

Tonight's the Night (Also titled: Happy Ever After) (GB; Zampi, Mario; 1954)
Film Daily. Nov 19, 1954, p14.
Hollywood Reporter. Nov 12, 1954, p3.
The London Times. Jul 5, 1954, p11.
Motion Picture Herald Product Digest. Nov 20, 1954, p217-18.
The Nation. Jan 8, 1955, v180, p38.
National Parent-Teacher. Mar 1955, v49, p40.
The New York Times. Dec 23, 1954, p13.
Saturday Review. Nov 27, 1954, v37, p29.
The Spectator. Jul 2, 1954, v193, p12.
The Tatler. Jul 14, 1954, v213, p74.

Too Late the Hero (US; Aldrich, Robert; 1970)
America. Jun 13, 1970, v122, p637.
BFI/Monthly Film Bulletin. Oct 1970, v37, p203.
Film Daily. May 6, 1970, p7.
The Films and Career of Robert Aldrich. p151-56.
Films and Filming. Oct 1970, v17, p44.
Hollywood Reporter. May 6, 1970, p3.
The New York Times. May 21, 1970, p46.
Robert Aldrich: A Guide to References and Resources. p52-53.
Time. Jun 8, 1970, v95, p76.
Variety. May 6, 1970, p15.
Vogue. Jul 1970, v156, p40.

Too Young to Kiss (US; Leonard, Robert Z.; 1951)
BFI/Monthly Film Bulletin. Jan 1952, v19, p8.
Catholic World. Dec 1951, v174, p222.

Christian Century. Dec 26, 1951, v68, p1521.
Film Daily. Oct 31, 1951, p10.
Hollywood Reporter. Oct 26, 1951, p3.
Motion Picture Herald Product Digest. Oct 27, 1951, p1073.
The New York Times. Nov 23, 1951, p32.
The New Yorker. Dec 1, 1951, v27, p156.
Newsweek. Dec 10, 1951, v38, p98-99.
Time. Dec 3, 1951, v58, p104.
Variety. Oct 31, 1951, p6.

Tootsie (US; Pollack, Sydney; 1982)
America. Jan 29, 1983, v148, p74.
American Cinematographer. Apr 1983, v64, p59-63.
American Film. Apr 1983, v8, p26-28.
BFI/Monthly Film Bulletin. Apr 1983, v50, p108-09.
Christian Century. Dec 22, 1982, v99, p1318.
Cinema Papers. May-Jun 1983, n43, p98-105.
Contemporary Review. Aug 1983, v243, p101-04.
Film Comment. Mar-Apr 1982, v19, p9-18.
Film Journal. Dec 27, 1982, v85, p11.
Films In Review. Feb 1983, v34, p110.
The Films of Dustin Hoffman. p211-18.
Hollywood Reporter. Dec 8, 1982, p3.
Humanist. Mar-Apr 1983, v43, p40.
The Los Angeles Times. Dec 17, 1982, SecVI, p1.
Maclean's. Dec 20, 1982, v95, p50.
Magill's Cinema Annual, 1983. p353-57.
Millimeter. Nov 1982, v10, p223.
Millimeter. Jul 1983, v11, p52-54.
Ms. Mar 1983, v11, p39-43.
The Nation. Jan 22, 1983, v236, p90-91.
National Review. Feb 4, 1983, v35, p131-33.
The New Leader. Jan 14, 1983, p66.
The New Republic. Jan 24, 1983, v188, p24-25.
New Statesman. Apr 29, 1983, v105, p34-35.
New York. Dec 27, 1982, v16, p76.
New York. Jan 3, 1983, v16, p76.
The New York Times. Dec 17, 1982, SecIII, p12.
The New York Times. Dec 19, 1982, SecII, p1.
The New York Times. Jul 13, 1982, SecIII, p7.
The New York Times. Jan 16, 1983, SecII, p1.
The New Yorker. Dec 27, 1982, v58, p68.
Newsweek. Dec 13, 1982, v100, p81.
Penthouse. Apr 1983, v14, p54.
Photoplay. Jun 1983, v34, p19.
Rolling Stone. Feb 3, 1983, p33.
Sight and Sound. Sum 1983, v52, p212-13.
Time. Dec 20, 1982, v120, p76-77.
Variety. Dec 8, 1982, p3.
The Village Voice. Dec 28, 1982, p43-45.
The Village Voice. Dec 21, 1982, p71-72.
The Village Voice. Feb 22, 1983, p36.

Top Banana (US; Green, Alfred E.; 1954)
America. Mar 13, 1954, v90, p638.
BFI/Monthly Film Bulletin. Jul 1956, v23, p93.
Commonweal. Mar 12, 1954, v59, p577.
Film Daily. Jan 27, 1954, p6.
Hollywood Reporter. Jan 27, 1954, p3.
Motion Picture Herald Product Digest. Jan 30, 1954, p2165.
National Parent-Teacher. Apr 1954, v48, p40.
The New York Times. Feb 20, 1954, p8.
The New Yorker. Mar 6, 1954, v30, p62.
Newsweek. Feb 22, 1954, v43, p107.
Saturday Review. Mar 6, 1954, v37, p27.
Time. Feb 22, 1954, v63, p102.
Variety. Jan 27, 1954, p6.

Top Secret (Zampi; 1952) *See* Mr. Potts Goes to Moscow

Top Secret (US; Abrahams, Jim; Zucker, David; 1984)
BFI/Monthly Film Bulletin. Sep 1984, v51, p286-87.

Hollywood Reporter. Jun 11, 1984, p4.
The Los Angeles Times. Jun 22, 1984, SecVI, p11.
The Nation. Jul 21, 1984, v239, p60-61.
The New York Times. Jun 24, 1984, SecII, p19.
Newsweek. Jun 25, 1984, v103, p61.
Time. Jul 2, 1984, v124, p78.
Variety. Jun 13, 1984, p18.

Top Secret Affair (Also titled: Their Secret Affair) (US; Potter, H. C.; 1957)
America. Feb 16, 1957, v96, p568.
America. Feb 16, 1957, v96, p568.
Commonweal. Feb 15, 1957, v65, p512.
Film Daily. Jan 15, 1957, v111, p6.
Films and Filming. May 1957, v3, p26.
Films in Review. Feb 1957, v8, p85.
The Films of Susan Hayward. p229-32.
Hollywood Reporter. Jan 14, 1957, p3.
Motion Picture Herald Product Digest. Jan 19, 1957, v206, p225.
The New York Times. Feb 10, 1937, SecII, p1.
The New Yorker. Feb 9, 1957, v32, p108.
Newsweek. Feb 18, 1957, v49, p110.
Saturday Review. Feb 2, 1957, v40, p25.
Time. Feb 4, 1957, v69, p92.
Variety. Jan 16, 1957, p6.

Topaz (US; Hitchcock, Alfred; 1969)
Deeper Into Movies. p99-100.
Film Daily. Dec 9, 1969, p3.
Film Heritage. Wint 1969-70, v5, p17-23.
Film Quarterly. Spr 1970, v23, p41-44.
Films and Filming. Jan 1970, v16, p39-40.
Films in Review. Feb 1970, v21, p119-20.
Focus. Spr 1970, n6, p26-27.
Hollywood Reporter. Dec 9, 1969, p3.
Movie. Wint 1970-71, n18, p10-13.
The Nation. Jan 12, 1970, v210, p29.
New York Review of Books. Feb 26, 1970, v14, p27-31.
The New York Times. Dec 20, 1969, p36.
The New Yorker. Dec 27, 1969, v45, p49-50.
Newsweek. Dec 29, 1969, v74, p55.
Saturday Review. Dec 27, 1969, v52, p41.
Sight and Sound. Wint 1969-70, v39, p49.
Time. Jan 19, 1970, v105, p67.
Variety. Nov 12, 1969, p21.

Topkapi (US; Dassin, Jules; 1964)
America. Oct 3, 1964, v111, p391.
BFI/Monthly Film Bulletin. Dec 1964, v31, p173-74.
Boxoffice. Sep 7, 1964, v85, p2858.
Commonweal. Oct 30, 1964, v81, p168.
Film Daily. Sep 9, 1964, v125, p6.
Films and Filming. Dec 1964, v11, p24.
Films in Review. Oct 1964, v15, p498-99.
Hollywood Reporter. Sep 9, 1964, v182, p3.
Life. Oct 9, 1964, v57, p55-56.
Magill's Survey of Cinema. Series II. v6, p2540-42.
Motion Picture Herald Product Digest. Sep 16, 1964, v232, p129.
The New York Times. Sep 18, 1964, p25.
The New Yorker. Sep 26, 1964, v40, p194.
Newsweek. Sep 21, 1964, v64, p107A.
Private Screenings. p150-51.
Saturday Review. Jul 20, 1964, v47, p37.
Time. Sep 18, 1964, v84, p111.
Variety. Sep 9, 1964, p6.

Tora no O o Fumu Otokotachi *See* Tora-no-o

Tora! Tora! Tora! (JAPAN, US; Fleischer, Richard; Masuda, Toshio; Fukasaka, Kinji; 1970)
BFI/Monthly Film Bulletin. Nov 1970, v37, p221-22.
Films in Review. Oct 1970, v21, p503-05.

Guts & Glory. p273-86.
Hollywood Reporter. Sep 23, 1970, p3, 15.
The New York Times. Sep 24, 1970, p62.
The New York Times. Oct 4, 1970, SecII, p1.
Newsweek. Sep 28, 1970, v76, p91-92.
Saturday Review. Oct 10, 1970, v53, p22.
Time. Oct 5, 1970, v96, p65.
Variety. Sep 23, 1970, p13.

Tora-no-o (Japanese title: Tora no O o Fumu; Otokotachi; Also titled: Men Who Tread on the Tiger's Tail; Walkers on Tigers' Tails; They Who Tread on the Tiger's Tail; They Who Step on the Tiger's Tail;) (JAPAN; Kurosawa, Akira; 1945)
Akira Kurosawa: A Guide to References and Resources. p35-36.
BFI/Monthly Film Bulletin. Aug 1952, v19, p107.
Christian Science Monitor (New England Edition). Jun 3, 1960, p11.
Filmfacts. Feb 19, 1960, v3, p16-17.
The Films of Akira Kurosawa. p30-35.
Japanese Cinema (Richie). p221-22.
The Japanese Film: Art and Industry. p226.
Motion Picture Herald Product Digest. Jul 30, 1960, p789.
The New Statesman and Nation. Jun 28, 1952, v43, p770-71.
The New York Times. Jan 11, 1960, p35.
The New Yorker. Jan 16, 1960, v35, p97-98.
The Spectator. Jun 27, 1952, v188, p853.
Variety. May 29, 1957, p22.
Variety. Jan 27, 1960, p6.
The Waves at Genji's Door. p91.

Torch Song (US; Walters, Charles; 1953)
America. Nov 7, 1953, v90, p159.
BFI/Monthly Film Bulletin. Jan 1954, v21, n240, p6.
Catholic World. Nov 1953, v178, p142.
Commonweal. Oct 30, 1953, v59, p91.
Film Daily. Oct 9, 1953, p10.
The Films of Joan Crawford. p185-88.
Hollywood Reporter. Oct 2, 1953, p3.
The New York Times. Oct 13, 1953, p34.
Newsweek. Oct 19, 1953, v42, p106.
Saturday Review. Oct 31, 1953, v36, p32.
Time. Oct 12, 1953, v62, p110.
The Village Voice. Oct 7, 1953, p6.

Torero! (SP; Velo, Carlos; 1957)
BFI/Monthly Film Bulletin. Nov 1958, v25, p147.
Commonweal. May 31, 1957, v66, p232.
Film Culture. 1957, v3, n3, p14-15.
Film Daily. May 23, 1957, v111, p8.
Films in Review. May 1957, v8, p224-25.
Hollywood Reporter. Jul 18, 1957, p3.
The Nation. Jun 1, 1957, v184, p486.
The New York Times. May 22, 1957, p29.
The New York Times Magazine. May 12, 1957, p20.
The New Yorker. Jun 1, 1957, v33, p72.
Saturday Review. May 11, 1957, v40, p27.
Time. May 6, 1957, v69, p107.

Torn Curtain (US; Hitchcock, Alfred; 1966)
America. Aug 20, 1966, v115, p192-93.
The Art of Alfred Hitchcock. p415-22.
BFI/Monthly Film Bulletin. Sep 1966, v33, p139.
Cahiers du Cinema in English. May 1967, n10, p51-60.
Christian Science Monitor (Western edition). Mar 2, 1966, p8.
Confessions of a Cultist. p268-72.
Filament. 1984, n4, p46-47.
Film. Nov 1979, n79, 25-28.

Film Daily. Jul 14, 1966, p7.
Film Quarterly. Wint 1966-67, v20, p63.
Filmfacts. Sep 15, 1966, v9, p188-90.
Films and Filming. Oct 1966, v13, p9, 12.
Films in Review. Aug-Sep 1966, v17, p451.
The Films of Alfred Hitchcock. p230-33.
The Films of Paul Newman. p151-55.
The Great Spy Pictures. p487-89.
Hitchcock's Films (Wood). p157-64.
Hollywood Reporter. Jul 14, 1966, p3.
Life. Aug 26, 1966, v61, p17.
The London Times. Aug 10, 1966, p11.
Magill's Cinema Annual, 1985. p644-48.
Motion Picture Herald Product Digest. Jul 27, 1966, p569.
New Statesman. Aug 19, 1966, v72, p267-77.
The New York Times. Jul 28, 1966, p23.
The New Yorker. Aug 6, 1966, v42, p84.
Newsweek. Aug 8, 1966, v68, p79.
Playboy. Oct 1966, v13, p28.
Politics and Film. p139-41.
Saturday Review. Aug 13, 1966, v49, p38.
Sight and Sound. Aut 1966, v35, p198.
The Spectator. Aug 12, 1966, v217, p205.
Take One. Sep-Oct 1966, v1, p16-17.
Time. Aug 5, 1966, v88, p56.
Twenty-Four Times a Second. p191-94.
Variety. Jul 20, 1966, p6.
The Village Voice. Sep 1, 1966, v11, p19.

The Touch (SWED; Bergman, Ingmar; 1971)
America. Sep 4, 1971, v125, p119-20.
BFI/Monthly Film Bulletin. Oct 1971, v38, p205.
Commonweal. Oct 8, 1971, v95, p37-38.
Film Quarterly. Wint 1971, v25, p58.
Filmfacts. 1971, v14, n20, p507.
Films and Filming. Feb 1972, v18, n5, p54-55.
Hollywood Reporter. Jul 12, 1971, v217, n2, p3.
Ingmar Bergman: A Critical Biography. p270-75.
Ingmar Bergman: Essays in Criticism. p292-96.
Life. Sep 10, 1971, v71, p35.
The New Republic. Aug 21, 1971, v165, p35.
The New York Times. Jul 15, 1971, p22.
The New York Times. Sep 12, 1971, SecII, p10.
The New Yorker. Jul 26, 1971, v98, p50-51.
Newsweek. Jul 26, 1971, v78, p70.
Saturday Review. Jul 31, 1971, v54, p50.
Sight and Sound. Aut 1971, v40, n4, p224.
Sight and Sound. Wint 1971-72, v41, n1, p42-43.
Time. Jul 26, 1971, v98, p50-51.
Variety. Jul 7, 1971, p41.
The Village Voice. Jul 29, 1971, p47.
Women and their Sexuality in the New Film. p55-74.

A Touch of Class (GB; Frank, Melvin; 1973)
Audience. Aug 1973, v6, p3.
Commonweal. May 11, 1973, v98, p238-39.
Filmfacts. 1973, v16, n6, p137.
Films in Review. Aug-Sep 1973, v24, n7, p441.
The New Republic. Jun 9, 1973, v168, p22.
The New York Times. Jun 21, 1973, p52.
The New York Times. Apr 3, 1974, p36.
The New Yorker. Apr 7, 1973, v49, p130.
Newsweek. Apr 9, 1973, v81, p110.
PTA Magazine. Oct 1973, v68, p9.
Saturday Evening Post. Nov 1973, v245, p26-27.
Time. Jul 2, 1973, v101, p62-63.
Variety. Jun 6, 1973, p18.
The Village Voice. Jul 12, 1973, p66.

Touch of Evil (US; Welles, Orson; 1958)
BFI/Monthly Film Bulletin. Jun 1958, v25, p73.
The Cinema of Orson Welles. p137-51.

Film Daily. Apr 2, 1958, v113, p6.
Filmfacts. Jul 2, 1959, v1, p89-90.
The Films in My Life. p288-91.
Films in Review. Apr 1958, v9, p206.
The Films of Charlton Heston. p89-92.
The Films of Marlene Dietrich. p208-09.
The Films of Orson Welles. p150-58.
Focus on Orson Welles. p157-63.
The Great Movies. p56-59.
Hollywood Reporter. Mar 17, 1958, p3.
The International Dictionary of Films and Filmmakers. v1, p482-84.
The Magic World of Orson Welles. p175-206.
Magill's Survey of Cinema. Series II. v6, p2543-45.
The New Republic. May 26, 1958, v138, p22-23.
The New York Times. May 22, 1958, p25.
Orson Welles (McBride). p131-40.
Reporter. Jun 26, 1958, v18, p33.
Saturday Review. Jun 7, 1958, v41, p25.
Variety. Mar 19, 1958, p16.

Tout une vie *See* And Now My Love

The Towering Inferno (US; Guillermin, John; 1974)
American Cinematographer. Feb 1975, v56, p166-69.
BFI/Monthly Film Bulletin. Feb 1975, v42, p41.
Christian Century. Jan 29, 1975, v92, p91.
Christian Century. Mar 5, 1975, v92, p231-33.
Commonweal. Apr 11, 1975, v105, p52-53.
Films in Review. Feb 1975, v26, p118-19.
The Films of Jennifer Jones. p169-71.
The Films of Steve McQueen. p209-17.
The Films of the Seventies. p99-101.
Hollywood Reporter. Dec 16, 1974, p3.
Independent Film Journal. Dec 25, 1974, v75, p29-30.
The Los Angeles Times. Dec 15, 1974, Calendar, p1.
Magill's Survey of Cinema. Series II. v6, p2250-53.
Motion Picture Herald Product Digest. Jan 15, 1974, p61.
Movie. Aut 1975, n21, p30-33.
New York. Jan 13, 1975, v8, p59.
The New York Times. Feb 4, 1975, p31.
The New Yorker. Dec 30, 1974, v50, p59.
Newsweek. Dec 30, 1974, v84, p56.
Reeling. p539-40.
Society. Nov-Dec 1975, v13, p77-79.
Time. Jan 6, 1975, v106, p6.
Variety. Dec 18, 1974, p13.

Town Without Pity (US; Reinhardt, Gottfried; 1961)
America. Oct 14, 1961, v106, p60.
BFI/Monthly Film Bulletin. Jan 1962, v29, p9.
Film Daily. Oct 13, 1961, p6.
Filmfacts. Nov 24, 1961, v4, p267-69.
Films in Review. Nov 1961, v17, p554-55.
The Films of Kirk Douglas. p177-79.
The New Republic. Nov 13, 1961, v145, p37.
The New York Times. Oct 11, 1961, p53.
The New Yorker. Oct 14, 1961, v37, p178.
Newsweek. Oct 30, 1961, v58, p77.
Saturday Review. Sep 30, 1961, v44, p28.
Variety. Oct 11, 1961, p6.

Toys in the Attic (US; Hill, George Roy; 1963)
BFI/Monthly Film Bulletin. Jan 1964, v31, p7.
Film Daily. Jun 27, 1963, p6.
Filmfacts. Aug 8, 1963, v6, p151-53.
Films in Review. Aug-Sep 1963, v14, p439.
George Roy Hill(Shores). p3-4.
Hollywood Reporter. Jun 27, 1963, v175, p3.
The New Republic. Aug 17, 1963, v149, p28.
The New York Times. Aug 1, 1963, p17.

The New York Times. Aug 11, 1963, SecII, p1.
The New Yorker. Aug 10, 1963, v39, p60.
Newsweek. Aug 12, 1963, v62, p79.
Photoplay. Sep 1963, v64, p13.
Saturday Review. Jul 20, 1963, v46, p37.
Time. Aug 9, 1963, v82, p73.
Variety. Jun 26, 1963, p6.

Track of the Cat (US; Wellman, William A.; 1954)
America. Dec 11, 1954, v92, p306.
BFI/Monthly Film Bulletin. May 1955, v22, p72.
Catholic World. Dec 1954, v180, p220.
Commonweal. Dec 10, 1954, v61, p290.
Farm Journal. Jan 1955, v79, p70.
Film Daily. Nov 15, 1954, p22.
Films in Review. Jan 1955, v6, p37-38.
Hollywood Reporter. Nov 10, 1954, p3.
Library Journal. Dec 1, 1954, v79, p2315.
Motion Picture Herald Product Digest. Nov 13, 1954, p209.
The Nation. Dec 25, 1954, v179, p558.
National Parent-Teacher. Jan 1955, v49, p40.
The New York Times. Dec 2, 1954, p38.
The New Yorker. Dec 11, 1954, v30, p177.
Newsweek. Nov 15, 1954, v44, p111.
Robert Mitchum on the Screen. p136-37.
Saturday Review. Nov 20, 1954, v37, p31.
A Short Time for Insanity. p98-99.
Time. Nov 29, 1954, v64, p75.
Variety. Nov 10, 1954, p6.
William A. Wellman (Thompson). p247-50, 310.

Trading Places (US; Landis, John; 1983)
Christian Century. Jul 20, 1983, v100, p690-91.
Hollywood Reporter. Jun 1, 1983, p3.
The Los Angeles Times. Jun 8, 1983, SecVI, p1.
Maclean's. Jun 13, 1983, v96, p53.
Magill's Cinema Annual, 1984. p430-34.
The Nation. Jul 23, 1983, v237, p92.
The New Republic. Jul 11, 1983, v189, p22-23.
New York. Jun 27, 1983, v16, p58.
The New York Times. Jun 8, 1983, SecIII, p16.
The New Yorker. Jul 11, 1983, v59, p94-95.
Newsweek. Jun 20, 1983, v101, p83-84.
Time. Jun 13, 1983, v121, p70.

Tragedy of a Ridiculous Man (Italian title: Tragedia di un uomo ridicolo) (IT; Bertolucci, Bernardo; 1981)
BFI/Monthly Film Bulletin. Jan 1982, v49, p12.
Film Journal. Feb 15, 1982, v85, p43.
Films In Review. May 1982, v33, p308.
Hollywood Reporter. Mar 9, 1982, p3.
The Los Angeles Times. Oct 15, 1982, SecVI, p10.
Magill's Cinema Annual, 1983. p361-65.
The Nation. Mar 13, 1982, v234, p315-16.
The New Republic. Mar 10, 1982, v186, p24-26.
The New York Times. Feb 12, 1982, p24.
The New Yorker. Mar 8, 1982, v58, p125-27.
Newsweek. Feb 22, 1982, v99, p68-70.
Time. Feb 15, 1982, v119, p64.
Variety. Jun 3, 1981, p15.
Variety. Feb 10, 1982, p23.
The Village Voice. Feb 23, 1982, p45, 48.

The Train (US, FR, IT; Frankenheimer, John; 1964)
America. Apr 3, 1965, v112, p466.
BFI/Monthly Film Bulletin. Dec 1964, v31, p174.
Burt Lancaster: A Pictorial Treasury of His Films. p125-26.
Christian Science Monitor (Western edition). Mar 23, 1965, p2.
Cinema. Jul-Aug 1965, v2, p48-49.
The Cinema of John Frankenheimer. p115-30.

Commonweal. Apr 2, 1965, v82, p52-53.
Film Daily. Feb 26, 1965, p4.
Film Heritage. Wint 1965-66, v1, p23-24.
Film Quarterly. Sum 1966, v19, p29-31.
Filmfacts. May 14, 1965, v8, p75-77.
Films and Filming. Dec 1964, v11, p25.
Films and Filming. Sep 1964, v10, p31.
Films in Review. Mar 1965, v16, p179-80.
Hollywood Reporter. Feb 26, 1965, p3.
The London Times. Oct 29, 1964, p5.
Magill's Survey of Cinema. Series II. v6, p2558-60.
Motion Picture Herald Product Digest. Mar 3, 1965, p241.
The Nation. Apr 6, 1965, v200, p376.
The New Republic. Mar 20, 1965, v152, p25.
The New York Times. Mar 18, 1965, p25.
The New Yorker. Mar 20, 1965, v41, p152-53.
Newsweek. Mar 22, 1965, v65, p97-97A.
Playboy. Apr 1965, v12, p26, 28.
Private Screenings. p176.
Saturday Review. Mar 13, 1965, v48, p123.
Senior Scholastic. Mar 4, 1965, v86, sup38, p26.
Sight and Sound. Wint 1964-65, v34, p40.
Time. Mar 26, 1965, v85, p98.
Variety. Sep 30, 1964, p6.
Vogue. Apr 15, 1965, v145, p57.

Trans-Europ-Express (Also titled: Trans-European Express) (FR; Robbe-Grillet, Alain; 1967)
BFI/Monthly Film Bulletin. Aug 1969, v36, p167-68.
The Film Career of Alain Robbe-Grillet. p27-30, 101-30.
Film Daily. May 13, 1968, p6.
Film Quarterly. Spr 1969, v22, p40-44.
Filmfacts. Aug 1, 1968, v11, p193-95.
Films and Filming. Jun 1969, v15, p41-42.
Films in Review. Jun-Jul 1968, v19, p377.
The Films of Alain Robbe-Grillet. p66-90.
Hollywood Reporter. Jul 8, 1968, p3.
Motion Picture Herald Product Digest. Jul 8, 1968, p3.
The Nation. Jun 3, 1968, v206, p742.
The New York Times. May 13, 1968, p52.
The New Yorker. May 18, 1968, v44, p153-54.
Newsweek. May 27, 1968, v71, p95-95A.
Sight and Sound. Spr 1968, v37, p86-90.
Time. Jun 7, 1968, v91, p101.
Variety. Jan 18, 1967, p17.
The Village Voice. May 23, 1968, p43, 45.
A Year In the Dark. p145-47.

The Trap (GB, CAN; Hayers, Sidney; 1966)
BFI/Monthly Film Bulletin. Oct 1966, v33, p156.
Filmfacts. Mar 15, 1968, v11, p56-57.
New Statesman. Sep 23, 1966, v72, p454.
Take One. Nov-Dec 1966, v1, p28-29.
Variety. Sep 21, 1966, p6.

Travolti da un Isolito Destino Nell'Azuro Mare d'Agosto *See* Swept Away: By an Unusual Destiny in the Blue Sea of August

Treasure Island (GB; Haskin, Byron; 1950)
BFI/Monthly Film Bulletin. Jul 1950, v17, p103.
Children's Novels and the Movies. p58-68.
Christian Century. Aug 23, 1950, v67, p1007.
Christian Science Monitor Magazine. Jul 29, 1950, p10-11.
Commonweal. Aug 11, 1950, v52, p437.
The Disney Films. p97-100.
Film Daily. Jun 22, 1950, p5.
Films in Review. Sep 1950, v1, p34.
Hollywood Reporter. Jun 21, 1950, p3.

Illustrated London News. Jul 8, 1950, v217, p66.
Library Journal. Jul 1950, v75, p1202.
Life. Aug 14, 1950, v29, p52-53.
Motion Picture Herald Product Digest. Jun 24, 1950, p353.
The New Republic. Sep 4, 1950, v123, p23.
The New Statesman and Nation. Jul 1, 1950, v40, p12.
The New York Times. Aug 16, 1950, p24.
The New York Times Magazine. Jun 11, 1950, p54-55.
The New Yorker. Aug 26, 1950, v26, p68.
Newsweek. Aug 28, 1950, v36, p76.
Saturday Review. Sep 9, 1950, v33, p30.
Senior Scholastic. May 17, 1950, v56, p22.
Shots in the Dark. p192-93.
The Spectator. Jun 23, 1950, v184, p853.
Time. Jul 24, 1950, v56, p78.
Variety. Jun 21, 1950, p8.
Walt Disney: A Guide to References and Resources. p40-41.

The Tree of Wooden Clogs (Also titled: Albero degli Zoccoli, L') (FR, IT; Olmi, Ermanno; 1978)
BFI/Monthly Film Bulletin. Jun 1979, v46, p115.
Films in Review. Aug-Sep 1979, v30, p433.
Hollywood Reporter. Jun 11, 1979, p2.
The International Dictionary of Films and Filmmakers. v1, p17-18.
The Los Angeles Times. Sep 14, 1979, SecIV, p1.
Magill's Survey of Cinema. Foreign Language Films. v7, p3158-61.
The Nation. Jun 16, 1979, v228, p732-33.
The New Republic. Jun 2, 1979, v180, p24-25.
The New York Times. Jul 1, 1979, SecIII, p8.
The New Yorker. Jun 18, 1979, v55, p96.
Newsweek. Jun 4, 1979, v93, p74.
Time. Jun 25, 1979, v113, p54.
Variety. May 24, 1978, p34.

Trent's Last Case (GB; Wilcox, Herbert; 1952)
BFI/Monthly Film Bulletin. Nov 1952, v19, p155-56.
Film Daily. Oct 20, 1953, p6.
Hollywood Reporter. Oct 8, 1953, p3.
The London Times. Mar 28, 1952, p8.
The Tatler. Nov 12, 1952, v206, p376.
Variety. Nov 5, 1952, p6.

The Trial (US; Welles, Orson; 1963)
America. Mar 23, 1963, v108, p420-21.
BFI/Monthly Film Bulletin. Jan 1964, v31, p6.
Christian Century. Jan 8, 1964, v81, p49-50.
The Cinema of Orson Welles. p152-77.
Commonweal. Mar 15, 1963, v77, p642.
Film and Literature: An Introduction. p250-58.
Film Daily. Feb 27, 1963, p8.
Film Quarterly. Sum 1963, v16, p40-43.
Filmfacts. Mar 14, 1963, v6, p25-27.
Films and Filming. Dec 1963, v10, p25-26.
Hollywood Reporter. Apr 25, 1963, v175, p3.
The Illustrated London News. Nov 23, 1963, v243, p810.
The Magic World of Orson Welles. p141-47.
The Nation. Mar 9, 1963, v196, p215-16.
The New Republic. Mar 2, 1963, v148, p34-35.
The New Republic. Mar 16, 1963, v148, p28.
New Statesman. Nov 15, 1963, v66, p717.
The New York Times. Feb 21, 1963, p5.
The New York Times. Feb 27, 1963, p5.
The New Yorker. Jan 12, 1963, v38, p104-06.
The New Yorker. Mar 2, 1963, v39, p132.
Newsweek. Feb 25, 1963, v61, p94.
Photoplay. May 1963, v63, p7.
Saturday Review. Mar 9, 1963, v46, p25.

Variety. Jan 2, 1963, p6.
The Village Voice. Feb 21, 1963, v8, p15.

The Trial of Billy Jack (US; Laughlin, Tom; 1974)
Hollywood Reporter. Nov 11, 1974, p3.
The Los Angeles Times. Nov 13, 1974, SecIV, p1.
Motion Picture Herald Product Digest. Nov 27, 1974, p50.
New York. Nov 25, 1974, v7, p94.
The New York Times. Dec 15, 1974, SecII, p19.
The New Yorker. Nov 25, 1974, v50, p180-83.
Newsweek. Dec 2, 1974, v84, p104.
Progressive. Mar 1975, v39, p39-40.
Time. Dec 16, 1974, v104, p6.
Variety. Nov 13, 1974, p18.
The Village Voice. Dec 2, 1974, p128.

The Trials of Oscar Wilde (Also titled: The Man With the Green Carnation) (GB; Hughes, Ken; 1960)
America. Jul 30, 1960, v103, p503-04.
BFI/Monthly Film Bulletin. Jul 1960, v27, p95.
Film Daily. Jun 29, 1960, p11.
Filmfacts. 1960, v3, p184.
Films and Filming. Jul 1960, v6, p23.
Films in Review. Aug-Sep 1960, v11, p432-33.
The Films of James Mason. p146-78.
Hollywood Reporter. Jun 23, 1960, p3.
McCall's. Sep 1960, v87, p194.
The New Republic. Jul 25, 1960, v143, p29.
The New York Times. Jun 28, 1960, p26.
The New York Times. Jul 3, 1960, SecII, p1.
The New Yorker. Jul 2, 1960, v36, p56.
Newsweek. Jul 4, 1960, v56, p84.
Newsweek. May 16, 1960, v55, p110.
Saturday Review. Jul 2, 1960, v43, p26.
Sight and Sound. Sum 1960, v29, p146.
Variety. Jun 1, 1960, p6.
A World on Film. p194-96.

Tribulations d'un Chinois en Chine, Les *See* Up To His Ears

The Tribulations of a Chinese Gentleman *See* Up To His Ears

Tribute (US; Clark, Bob; 1980)
Christian Century. Nov 26, 1980, v97, p1171.
Hollywood Reporter. Dec 1, 1980, p3.
The Los Angeles Times. Dec 17, 1980, SecVI, p1.
Maclean's. Dec 22, 1980, v93, p58.
Motion Picture Herald Product Digest. Dec 17, 1980, p54.
The New Republic. Dec 27, 1980, v183, p24.
New York. Dec 15, 1980, v13, p56-57.
The New York Times. Dec 14, 1980, p99.
The New York Times. Dec 21, 1980, SecII, p19.
Newsweek. Dec 15, 1980, v96, p109.
Time. Dec 15, 1980, v116, p68.
Variety. Dec 3, 1980, p22.

Tricetjedna Ve Stinu *See* Ninety Degrees in the Shade

Trio (GB; Annakin, Ken; French, Harold; 1950)
BFI/Monthly Film Bulletin. Aug 1950, v17, p116-17.
Christian Century. Dec 20, 1950, v67, p1535.
Commonweal. Nov 3, 1950, v53, p96.
Film Daily. Oct 17, 1950, p5.
Films in Review. Nov 1950, v1, p19-21.
Hollywood Reporter. Oct 10, 1950, p3.
Library Journal. Oct 15, 1950, v75, p1843.
Life. Oct 9, 1950, v29, p77-78.
The London Times. Jan 25, 1950, p7.
The London Times. Jul 7, 1950, p6.
Motion Picture Herald Product Digest. Oct 14, 1950, p517.

The New Republic. Nov 6, 1950, v123, p22.
The New Statesman and Nation. Aug 12, 1950, v40, p172.
The New York Times. Oct 11, 1950, p42.
The New Yorker. Oct 14, 1950, v26, p109.
Newsweek. Oct 23, 1950, v36, p96.
Saturday Review. Oct 7, 1950, v33, p50.
Shots in the Dark. p202-06.
The Spectator. Aug 4, 1950, v185, p144.
Time. Oct 30, 1950, v56, p98.
Variety. Aug 9, 1950, p9.

Trio Infernal, Le (FR, WGER, IT; Girod, François; 1974)
BFI/Monthly Film Bulletin. Jul 1975, v42, p162.
Hollywood Reporter. Nov 14, 1974, p4.
Independent Film Journal. Nov 27, 1974, v74, p7-8.
Motion Picture Herald Product Digest. Nov 27, 1974, p52.
The Nation. Nov 30, 1974, v219, p572.
New York. Nov 18, 1974, v7, p88.
The New York Times. Nov 9, 1974, p24.
Newsweek. Dec 9, 1974, v84, p114.
Time. Dec 9, 1974, v104, p104.
Variety. May 15, 1974, p28.

Tripoli (US; Price, Will; 1950)
BFI/Monthly Film Bulletin. Dec 1950, v17, p191.
Film Daily. Oct 9, 1950, p3.
Hollywood Reporter. Oct 5, 1950, p3.
Motion Picture Herald Product Digest. Oct 7, 1950, p511.
The New York Times. Nov 10, 1950, p35.
Variety. Oct 11, 1950, p8.

Trollflojten *See* The Magic Flute

TRON (US; Lisberger, Steven; 1982)
Film Comment. Jul-Aug 1982, v18, p49-54.
Hollywood Reporter. Jul 8, 1982, p3.
The Los Angeles Times. Jul 9, 1982, SecVI, p1.
Maclean's. Jul 19, 1982, v95, p40-44.
Magill's Cinema Annual, 1983. p371-76.
The New Republic. Aug 16, 1982, v187, p26-27.
New York. Jul 26, 1982, v15, p46-47.
The New York Times. Jul 9, 1982, SecIII, p8.
Newsweek. Jul 5, 1982, v100, p64-66.
Rolling Stone. Aug 19, 1982, p12-13.
Smithsonian. Jul 1982, v13, p86-95.
Time. Jul 5, 1982, v120, p62-65.
Time. Jul 19, 1982, v120, p64.
Variety. Jul 8, 1982, p3.

Trouble in the Glen (GB; Wilcox, Herbert; 1954)
BFI/Monthly Film Bulletin. Aug 1954, v21, p119.
Film Daily. Dec 3, 1954, p6.
Hollywood Reporter. Nov 26, 1954, p3.
The London Times. Jun 21, 1954, p9.
Motion Picture Herald Product Digest. Nov 27, 1954, p225.
The New York Times. Apr 11, 1955, p29.
The Spectator. Jun 18, 1954, v192, p734.
The Tatler. Jun 30, 1954, v212, p738.
Variety. Jun 30, 1954, p6.

The Trouble With Angels (US; Lupino, Ida; 1966)
America. Apr 16, 1966, v114, p568.
BFI/Monthly Film Bulletin. Jul 1966, v33, p111-12.
Christian Science Monitor (Western edition). Apr 13, 1966, p10.
Commonweal. Apr 15, 1966, v84, p118.
Film Daily. Mar 29, 1966, p5.
Filmfacts. Jun 15, 1966, v9, p99-01.
Films and Filming. Jul 1966, v12, p57.
Hollywood Reporter. Mar 28, 1966, p3.

The London Times. May 26, 1966, p19.
Motion Picture Herald Product Digest. Apr 13, 1966, p500.
The New York Times. Apr 7, 1966, p45.
Senior Scholastic. Apr 15, 1966, v88, p35.
Variety. Mar 30, 1966, p6.

The Trouble with Harry (US; Hitchcock, Alfred; 1955)
America. Nov 12, 1955, v94, p196.
The Art of Alfred Hitchcock. p259-66.
Catholic World. Dec 1955, v182, p218.
Film Culture. Wint 1955, v1, n5/6, p31.
Film Daily. Oct 17, 1955, p6.
Films and Filming. May 1956, v2, n8, p21.
Films in Review. Nov 1955, v6, n9, p465-66.
The Films of Alfred Hitchcock. p174-77.
The Films of Shirley MacLaine. p44-48.
Hitchcock: The First Forty-Four Films. p133-37.
Hitchcock (Truffaut). p226-27.
Hollywood Reporter. Oct 7, 1955, v136, n35, p3.
Library Journal. Nov 15, 1955, v80, p2595.
Magill's Survey of Cinema. Series II. v4, p1777-79.
The Nation. Nov 12, 1955, v181, p427.
The New York Times. Oct 18, 1955, p46.
The New York Times. Oct 23, 1955, SecII, p1.
Sight and Sound. Sum 1956, v26, n1, p30-31.
Time. Nov 7, 1955, v66, p114.
Variety. Oct 12, 1955, p6.

True Confessions (US; Grosbard, Ulu; 1981)
Christian Century. Dec 9, 1981, v98, p1292.
Commentary. Dec 1981, v72, p79-83.
Hollywood Reporter. Sep 2, 1981, p2.
The Los Angeles Times. Sep 25, 1981, SecVI, p1.
Maclean's. Oct 5, 1981, v94, p58-59.
Magill's Cinema Annual 1982. p368-73.
The Nation. Oct 31, 1981, v233, p451-52.
National Review. Sep 18, 1981, v33, p1091-93.
The New Leader. Oct 5, 1981, v64, p22.
The New Republic. Sep 30, 1981, v185, p24-25.
New York. Oct 5, 1981, v14, p58.
The New York Times. Sep 25, 1981, SecIII, p4.
The New Yorker. Oct 26, 1981, v57, p174-76.
Newsweek. Sep 28, 1981, v98, p87.
Rolling Stone. Oct 15, 1981, p44.
Time. Oct 5, 1981, v118, p88.
U.S. Catholic. Sep 1981, v46, p41-43.
Variety. Sep 2, 1981, p3.

True Grit (US; Hathaway, Henry; 1969)
America. Jul 19, 1969, v121, p47.
Atlantic Monthly. Sep 1969, v224, p123-24.
Commonweal. Jul 25, 1969, v90, p464-65.
The Complete Films of John Wayne. p276-80.
Confessions of a Cultist. p454-56.
Figures of Light. p183-85.
Film Daily. May 21, 1969, p4.
Filmfacts. 1969, v12, p241.
Films and Filming. Dec 1969, v16, p37-38.
Films in Review. Aug-Sep 1969, v20, p445-46.
The Films of the Sixties. p267-68.
Focus. Oct 1969, n5, p31-32.
Focus. Spr 1970, n6, p3-6.
Focus on Film. Jan-Feb 1970, n1, p3-6.
Holiday. Jul 1969, v46, p25.
Hollywood Reporter. May 19, 1969, p3.
Life. Jun 20, 1969, v66, p18.
Magill's Survey of Cinema. Series I. v4, p1780-82.
The Making of the Great Westerns. p381-94.
Movies Into Film. p177.
National Review. Sep 23, 1969, v21, p970.
The New Republic. Jul 26, 1969, v161, p26.
The New York Times. Jul 4, 1969, p9.
The New York Times. Jul 6, 1969, SecII, p1.

The New Yorker. Jul 26, 1969, v45, p67-68.
Newsweek. Jun 23, 1969, v73, p95-96.
Saturday Review. Jun 21, 1969, v52, p31.
Second Sight. p233-36.
Time. Jul 4, 1969, v94, p51.
Variety. May 21, 1969, p6.

The Truth About Spring (GB; Thorpe, Richard; 1965)
Christian Science Monitor (Western edition). Apr 24, 1965, p6.
Film Daily. Mar 23, 1965, p4.
Films and Filming. Jul 1965, v11, p35.
Films and Filming. Jun 1965, v11, p20.
Hollywood Reporter. Mar 23, 1965, p3.
The London Times. May 13, 1965, p6.
Motion Picture Herald Product Digest. Mar 31, 1965, p257.
New Statesman. May 14, 1965, v69, p774.
The New York Times. Jun 17, 1965, p27.
Variety. Mar 24, 1965, p6.

Tunes of Glory (GB; Neame, Ronald; 1960)
America. Jan 21, 1961, v104, p550.
BFI/Monthly Film Bulletin. Dec 1960, v27, p167.
Commonweal. Dec 30, 1960, v73, p365.
Esquire. Feb 1961, v55, p48.
Film Daily. Dec 28, 1960, p6.
Filmfacts. 1960, v3, p346.
Films and Filming. Dec 1960, v7, p29-30.
Films in Review. Jan 1961, v12, p37-38.
The Great British Films. p187-89.
Hollywood Reporter. Dec 20, 1960, p3.
Magill's Survey of Cinema. Series II. v6, p2573-75.
McCall's. Mar 1961, v88, p181.
The Nation. Jan 7, 1961, v192, p20.
The New Republic. Jan 16, 1961, v144, p20.
The New York Times. Dec 21, 1960, p38.
The New York Times. Jan 1, 1961, SecII, p1.
The New Yorker. Dec 24, 1960, v36, p50.
Newsweek. Jan 2, 1961, v57, p66.
Saturday Review. Jan 14, 1961, v44, p29.
Sight and Sound. Wint 1960-61, v30, p37.
Time. Dec 26, 1960, v76, p43.
Variety. Sep 14, 1960, p6.

The Turning Point (US; Dieterle, William; 1952)
BFI/Monthly Film Bulletin. Oct 1952, v19, p146.
Catholic World. Nov 1952, v176, p143.
Film Daily. Sep 18, 1952, p8.
The Films of William Holden. p129-32.
Hollywood Reporter. Sep 16, 1952, p3.
Motion Picture Herald Product Digest. Sep 20, 1952, p1533.
The Nation. Dec 6, 1952, v175, p535-36.
National Parent-Teacher. Nov 1952, v47, p38.
The New York Times. Nov 15, 1952, p15.
The Spectator. Oct 17, 1952, v189, p501.
The Tatler. Oct 29, 1952, v206, p268.
Time. Nov 3, 1952, v60, p102.
Variety. Sep 17, 1952, p6.

The Turning Point (US; Ross, Herbert; 1977)
America. Nov 19, 1977, v137, p362.
BFI/Monthly Film Bulletin. Apr 1978, v45, p73.
Dance Magazine. Oct 1977, v51, p42-50.
Dance Magazine. Dec 1977, v51, p104-06.
Film Comment. Jan 1978, v14, p60-67.
Films and Filming. Sep 1977, v23, p48-49.
Films in Review. Dec 1977, v28, p631.
The Films of Shirley MacLaine. p174-78.
The Films of the Seventies. p179-81.
Hollywood Reporter. Oct 18, 1977, p2.
The Los Angeles Times. Nov 13, 1977, Calendar, p1.

Motion Picture Herald Product Digest. Nov 21, 1977, p41.
Ms. Jan 1978, v6, p29-30.
The New Republic. Nov 19, 1977, v177, p22-23.
New York. Nov 21, 1977, v10, p89.
The New York Times. Nov 15, 1977, p54.
The New York Times. Nov 20, 1977, SecII, p15.
The New York Times. Dec 20, 1977, p44.
The New York Times. Mar 12, 1977, SecII, p15.
The New Yorker. Nov 21, 1977, v53, p183-86.
Newsweek. Nov 28, 1977, v90, p97-98.
Saturday Review. Feb 4, 1978, v5, p44.
Senior Scholastic. Feb 9, 1978, v110, p27.
Time. Nov 28, 1977, v110, p111-12.
Variety. Oct 19, 1977, p25.
The Village Voice. Nov 21, 1977, p44.
Vogue. Dec 1977, v167, p34.

Tutto a Posto e Niente In Ordine *See* All Screwed Up

Twelve Angry Men (US; Lumet, Sidney; 1957)
America. Apr 27, 1957, v97, p150.
BFI/Monthly Film Bulletin. Jun 1957, v24, p67-68.
Commonweal. Apr 19, 1957, v66, p65.
Fifty From the Fifties. p373-79.
Film Culture. 1957, v3, n2, p14-15.
Film Daily. Feb 27, 1957, v111, p6.
Films and Filming. Jun 1957, v3, p23.
The Films in My Life. p127-28.
Films in Review. May 1957, v8, p221-22.
The Films of Henry Fonda. p155-57.
The Fondas (Springer). p164-66.
Hollywood Reporter. Mar 26, 1957, p3.
Magill's Survey of Cinema. Series I. v4, p1783-85.
Motion Picture Herald Product Digest. Mar 2, 1957, v206, p281.
The Nation. Apr 27, 1957, v184, p379.
The New York Times. Apr 7, 1957, SecII, p5.
The New York Times. Apr 15, 1957, p24.
The New York Times. Apr 21, 1957, SecII, p1.
The New York Times Magazine. Mar 31, 1957, p64-65.
The New Yorker. Apr 27, 1957, v33, p66.
Newsweek. Apr 15, 1957, v49, p113.
Saturday Review. Apr 20, 1957, v40, p29.
Sidney Lumet: A Guide to References and Resources. p63-64.
Time. Apr 29, 1957, v69, p94.
Variety. Feb 27, 1957, p6.
The Village Voice. May 22, 1957, p6.

Twenty Four Hours of a Woman's Life (Also titled: Affair in Monte Carlo) (GB; Saville, Victor; 1952)
BFI/Monthly Film Bulletin. Oct 1952, v19, p146-47.
The London Times. Sep 15, 1952, p10.
The New Statesman and Nation. Sep 20, 1952, v44, p316, 318.
The Spectator. Sep 12, 1952, v189, p328.
Variety. Sep 17, 1952, p22.

20,000 Leagues Under the Sea (US; Fleischer, Richard; 1954)
America. Jan 8, 1955, v92, p387.
BFI/Monthly Film Bulletin. Jul 1955, v22, p103.
Catholic World. Feb 1955, v180, p380-81.
Cinefantastique. 1984, v14, n3, p32-36, 41.
Cinema of the Fantastic. p235-54.
Cinemamacabre. Fall 1982, n5, p36-40.
Commonweal. Dec 31, 1954, v61, p359.
The Disney Films (Maltin). p119-21.
Farm Journal. Feb 1955, v79, p149.
Film Daily. Dec 15, 1954, v6, p6.
Films and Filming. Aug 1955, v1, p17.

Films and Filming. Mar 1979, v25, p39.
Films in Review. Jan 1955, v6, p34-35.
The Films of Kirk Douglas. p114-17.
The Films of Peter Lorre. p208-10.
Future Tense: The Cinema of Science Fiction. p101-05.
The Great Adventure Films. p184-91.
Hollywood Reporter. Dec 15, 1954, p3.
Illustrated London News. Oct 9, 1954, v225, p604-05.
Library Journal. Mar 1, 1955, v80, p555.
Look. Aug 10, 1954, v18, p46-47.
Look. Dec 28, 1954, v18, p84.
Magic Moments From the Movies. p190.
Magill's Survey of Cinema. Series I. v4, p1795-97.
Motion Picture Herald Product Digest. Dec 18, 1954, p249.
National Parent-Teacher. Feb 1955, v49, p40.
Natural History. Feb 1955, v64, p112.
The New Statesman and Nation. May 28, 1955, v49, p750.
The New York Times. Dec 24, 1954, p7.
The New Yorker. Jan 1, 1955, v30, p46.
Newsweek. Dec 27, 1954, v44, p60.
Saturday Review. Jan 15, 1955, v38, p32.
Science Fiction Studies in Film. p126-28.
Senior Scholastic. Feb 2, 1955, v66, p27.
Sight and Sound. Sum 1955, v26, p36.
The Spectator. May 20, 1955, v194, p650.
The Tatler. Jun 1, 1955, v216, p524.
Variety. Dec 15, 1954, p6.
Walt Disney: A Guide to References and Resouces. p48-49.

Twice in a Lifetime (US; Yorkin, Bud; 1985)
American Film. Oct 1985, v11, p18.
Films in Review. Jan 1986, v37, p41.
Hollywood Reporter. Sep 11, 1985, p3.
The Los Angeles Times. Oct 30, 1985, SecVI, p1.
Maclean's. Nov 4, 1985, v98, p78.
Magill's Cinema Annual, 1986. p397-401.
Ms. Nov 1985, v14, p32.
The New Republic. Nov 18, 1985, v193, p28-29.
New York. Nov 4, 1985, v18, p76.
The New York Times. Oct 23, 1985, SecIII, p20.
The New Yorker. Dec 2, 1985, v61, p118.
Newsweek. Nov 25, 1985, v106, p104.
Saturday Review. Nov-Dec 1985, v11, p88.
Time. Nov 18, 1985, v126, p92.
Variety. Sep 18, 1985, p18.
The Village Voice. Oct 29, 1985, p59.
Vogue. Nov 1985, v175, p98.

Twilight of Honor (Also titled: The Charge is Murder) (US; Sagal, Boris; 1963)
BFI/Monthly Film Bulletin. Apr 1964, v31, p54-55.
Film Daily. Sep 23, 1963, p14.
Filmfacts. Nov 21, 1963, v6, p255-56.
The New York Times. Nov 14, 1963, p41.
Newsweek. Nov 25, 1963, v62, p105B.
Photoplay. Dec 1963, v64, p10.
Variety. Sep 18, 1963, p6.

Twilight Zone (US; Landis, John; Spielberg, Steven; Dante, Joe; Miller, George; 1983)
Hollywood Reporter. Jun 19, 1983, p3.
The Los Angeles Times. Jun 24, 1983, SecVI, p1.
Maclean's. Jul 4, 1983, v96, p54.
Magill's Cinema Annual, 1984. p435-40.
The New Leader. Jun 27, 1983, v66, p21-22.
The New York Times. Jun 24, 1983, SecIII, p15.
The New York Times Magazine. Dec 4, 1983, p122-26.

The New Yorker. Jul 25, 1983, v59, p81-83.
Newsweek. Jun 27, 1983, v101, p80.
Rolling Stone. Jul 7, 1983, p37.
Time. Jun 20, 1983, v121, p73.

Twilight's Last Gleaming (US; Aldrich, Robert; 1977)
BFI/Monthly Film Bulletin. Jun 1977, v44, p131.
Films in Review. Mar 1977, v28, p187.
Hollywood Reporter. Jan 28, 1977, p3.
The Los Angeles Times. Feb 10, 1977, SecIV, p1.
The New York Times. Feb 10, 1977, p48.
The New York Times. Feb 20, 1977, SecII, p1.
Robert Aldrich: A Guide to References and Resources. p68-71.
Time. Feb 21, 1977, v109, p72.
Variety. Feb 2, 1977, p22.

Twist of Fate (Also titled: Beautiful Stranger) (GB; Miller, David; 1954)
BFI/Monthly Film Bulletin. Aug 1954, v21, p120.
Film Daily. Nov 4, 1954, p7.
Hollywood Reporter. Nov 1, 1954, p3.
The London Times. Jul 19, 1954, p11.
Motion Picture Herald Product Digest. Oct 30, 1954, p194.
National Parent-Teacher. Dec 1954, v49, p40.
Newsweek. Dec 13, 1954, v44, p100.
The Tatler. Aug 4, 1954, v213, p204.
Time. Dec 6, 1954, v64, p116.

Two Cents Worth of Hope *See* Due Soldi di Speranza

The Two Enemies *See* The Best of Enemies

Two Flags West (US; Wise, Robert; 1950)
BFI/Monthly Film Bulletin. Dec 1950, v17, p186.
Christian Century. Dec 27, 1950, v67, p1561.
Commonweal. Oct 20, 1950, v53, p41.
Film Daily. Oct 10, 1950, p6.
Hollywood Reporter. Oct 9, 1950, p3.
Motion Picture Herald Product Digest. Oct 14, 1950, p518.
The New York Times. Oct 13, 1950, p23.
The New Yorker. Oct 21, 1950, v26, p101.
Sight and Sound. Dec 1950, v19, p333-34.
Time. Oct 23, 1950, v56, p100.
Variety. Oct 11, 1950, p8.

Two for the Road (GB; Donen, Stanley; 1967)
America. May 27, 1967, v166.
BFI/Monthly Film Bulletin. Sep 1967, v34, p136-37.
Christian Century. Jul 19, 1967, v83, p945.
Commonweal. May 12, 1967, v86, p236-37.
Cult Movies. p359-62.
Film Daily. Apr 28, 1967, p4.
Film Quarterly. Sum 1967, v20, p79-80.
Film Quarterly. Fall 1967, v21, p37-42.
Films and Filming. Sep 1967, v13, p20.
Films in Review. May 1967, v18, p307-08.
Hollywood Reporter. May 18, 1967, p3.
Life. May 12, 1967, v62, p16.
Magill's Survey of Cinema. Series II. v6, p2576-78.
Motion Picture Herald Product Digest. May 10, 1967, p681.
The New Republic. May 27, 1967, v156, p29-30.
The New York Times. Apr 28, 1967, p36.
Newsweek. May 15, 1967, v69, p96.
Saturday Review. May 6, 1967, v50, p45.
Second Sight. p108-11.
Sight and Sound. Aut 1967, v36, p206.
Stanley Donen (Casper). p180-85.
Variety. May 3, 1967, p6.
The Village Voice. May 11, 1967, p29.

Two for the Seesaw (US; Wise, Robert; 1962)
America. Jan 19, 1963, v108, p119.
BFI/Monthly Film Bulletin. May 1963, v30, p62.
Commonweal. Dec 14, 1962, v77, p316.
Film Daily. Oct 25, 1962, p7.
Film Quarterly. Spr 1963, v16, p60.
Filmfacts. Dec 14, 1962, v5, p291-93.
Films and Filming. May 1963, v9, p27.
Films in Review. Dec 1962, v13, p625.
The Films of Shirley MacLaine. p118-21.
Hollywood Reporter. Oct 30, 1962, p3.
Motion Picture Herald Product Digest. Oct 31, 1062, p681.
Movie. Apr 1963, n9, p35.
The New Republic. Dec 8, 1962, v147, p21-22.
The New York Times. Nov 22, 1962, p43.
The New Yorker. Nov 24, 1962, v38, p203.
Newsweek. Nov 26, 1962, v60, p91.
Robert Mitchum on the Screen. p180-81.
Saturday Review. Dec 1, 1962, v45, p27.
Sight and Sound. Spr 1963, v32, p93.
Variety. Oct 24, 1962, p6.

Two Mules for Sister Sara (US; Siegel, Don; 1970)
BFI/Monthly Film Bulletin. Sep 1970, v37, p191.
Clint Eastwood (Guérif). p71-74.
Commonweal. Jul 24, 1970, v92, p368-69.
Film Daily. Apr 22, 1970, p6.
The Films of Clint Eastwood. p112-16.
The Films of Shirley MacLaine. p160-63.
Hollywood Reporter. Apr 14, 1970, p3.
The New Republic. Aug 1, 1970, v163, p24.
The New York Times. Jun 25, 1970, p55.
The New York Times. Jul 5, 1970, SecII, p1.
The New Yorker. Jul 11, 1970, v46, p56.
Time. Jul 13, 1970, v96, p72.
Variety. Apr 15, 1970, p17.

Two of a Kind (US; Levin, Henry; 1951)
BFI/Monthly Film Bulletin. Aug 1951, v18, p315.
Film Daily. Jun 14, 1951, p6.
Hollywood Reporter. Jun 13, 1951, p3.
Motion Picture Herald Product Digest. Jun 23, 1951, p905-06.
The New York Times. Jun 30, 1951, p8.
Variety. Jun 13, 1951, p6.

The Two of Us (French title: Vieil Homme et L'Enfant, Le; Also titled: The Old Man and the Child) (FR; Berri, Claude; 1967)
America. Mar 30, 1968, v118, p423.
BFI/Monthly Film Bulletin. Apr 1968, v35, p56.
Christian Century. May 22, 1968, v85, p689-90.
Commonweal. Mar 15, 1968, v87, p717.
Film Daily. Feb 28, 1968, p8.
Filmfacts. Mar 15, 1968, v11, p47-48.
Films and Filming. Apr 1968, v14, p29.
Films in Review. Mar 1968, v19, p175-76.
Going Steady. p59-62.
The Great French Films. p267.
Indelible Shadows: Film and the Holocaust. p74-75.
Motion Picture Herald Product Digest. Feb 7, 1968, p771-72.
The New Republic. Mar 23, 1968, v158, p30.
The New York Times. Feb 20, 1968, p53.
The New Yorker. Mar 2, 1968, v44, p122.
Newsweek. Feb 26, 1968, v71, p84.
Time. Mar 8, 1968, v91, p93.
Variety. Feb 22, 1967, p6.
The Village Voice. Feb 22, 1968, p47.
A Year In the Dark. p50-51.

Two Pennyworth of Hope *See* Due Soldi di Speranza

2001: A Space Odyssey (US; Kubrick, Stanley; 1968)
America. Apr 27, 1968, v118, p586-87.
American Cinematographer. Jun 1968, v49, p412-22.
American Cinematographer. Oct 1969, v50, p997-1000.
BFI/Monthly Film Bulletin. Jun 1968, v35, p88-89.
BFI/Monthly Film Bulletin. Mar 1985, v52, p96.
Christian Century. Jun 26, 1968, v85, p844-46.
Christian Science Monitor (Western edition). Apr 12, 1968, p4.
Cineaste. Sum 1968, v2, p10-17.
Cinefantastique. 1975, v4, n1, p44-45.
Cinema. Dec 1966, v3, p4-6.
Cinema. Sum 1968, v4, p58-59.
The Cinema of Stanley Kubrick. p145-66.
Classic Movies. p67-69.
Commonweal. May 3, 1968, v88, p207-08.
Diacritics. 1984, v14, n2, p47-59.
Dictionary of Films. p386-87.
Directors and Directions: Cinema for the Seventies. p124-32.
Enclitic. 1981-82, v5-6, n1/2, p172-80.
Esquire. May 1966, v65, p114-16.
Esquire. Jul 1968, v70, p39-40.
Favorite Movies. p225-35.
Fifty Grand Movies of the 1960s and 1970s. p139-42.
Figures of Light. p70-75.
Film 68/69. p53-63.
Film and Literature. p283-92.
Film Comment. Wint 1969, v5, p6-15.
Film Culture. Wint-Spr 1970, v48-49, p53-56.
Film Daily. Apr 3, 1968, p4.
Film Heritage. Sum 1968, v3, p1-20.
Film Heritage. Wint 1968-69, v4, p31-32.
Film Journal. 1972, v2, n1, p65.
Film Quarterly. Fall 1968, v22, p58-62.
Film Quarterly. 1976, v30, n1, p12-19.
Film Society Review. Jan 1970, v5, p23-35.
Film Society Review. Feb 1970, v5, p23-27.
Filmfacts. May 1, 1968, v11, p95-99.
Filmguide to "2001: A Space Odyssey"
Films and Filming. Jul 1968, v14, p24-27.
Films in Review. May 1968, v19, p308-09.
The Films of Stanley Kubrick. p45-56.
The Films of the Sixties. p216-20.
Focus on the Science Fiction Film. p126-41.
Future Tense: The Cinema of Science Fiction. p176-81.
Going Steady. p149-51.
The Great Movies. p207-11.
Hollywood Reporter. Apr 3, 1968, p3.
Humanist. Jul 1968, v83, p214-15.
The International Dictionary of Films and Filmmakers. v1, p488-90.
International Film Guide. 1969, v6, p84-85.
Journal of Popular Culture. Sum 1968, v2, p167-71.
Journal of Popular Culture. Spr 1971, v4, p961-65.
Journal of Popular Culture. 1985, v18, n4, p53-56.
Journal of Popular Film. 1978, v6, n3, p202-15.
Kubrick (Ciment). p126-34.
Kubrick: Inside a Film Artist's Maze. p99-132.
Landmark Films. p302-13.
Life. Jun 7, 1968, v64, p20.
Life. Apr 5, 1968, v64, p24-33.
London Magazine. Jul 1968, v8, p68-72.
The London Times. Sep 7, 1968, p19.
Magill's Survey of Cinema. Series I. v4, p1798-2000.

Modern Photography. Oct 1968, v32, p16.
Motion Picture Herald Product Digest. Apr 10, 1968, p793.
Movies Into Film. p311-13.
The Nation. Jun 3, 1968, v206, p742.
National Review. Aug 13, 1968, v20, p814-15.
The New Republic. May 4, 1968, v158, p24.
New Society. May 9, 1968, p682.
New Statesman. May 3, 1968, v75, p591.
The New York Times. Apr 4, 1968, p58.
The New York Times. Apr 21, 1968, p1.
The New York Times. Jul 5, 1968, p23.
The New York Times. May 3, 1970, p1.
The New Yorker. Apr 13, 1968, v44, p150-52.
The New Yorker. Sep 21, 1968, v44, p180-84.
Newsweek. Apr 15, 1968, v71, p97.
Popular Mechanics. Apr 1967, v127, p106-09.
Popular Science. Jun 1968, v192, p62-67.
Quarterly Review of Film Studies. 1978, v3, n3, p297-316.
Reruns. p214-23.
Saturday Review. Apr 20, 1968, v51, p48.
Science Digest. May 1968, v63, p34-39.
Science Fiction Studies in Film. p163-76.
Screen. Jan-Feb 1969, v10, 104-12.
Senior Scholastic. May 9, 1968, v92, p26.
Sight and Sound. Spr 1966, v35, p57-60.
Sight and Sound. Sum 1968, v37, p153-54.
Sight and Sound. Aut 1969, v38, p204-07.
Sight and Sound. Wint 1970-71, v40, p28-33.
The Spectator. May 10, 1968, v220, p641.
Stanley Kubrick: A Film Odyssey (Phillips). p129-52.
Stanley Kubrick: A Guide to References and Resources. p49-52, 83-96.
Stanley Kubrick (DeVries). p45-46.
Stanley Kubrick Directs. p222-67.
Take One. May-Jun 1968, v1, p18-22, 29.
Time. Apr 19, 1968, v91, p91-92.
Twenty All-Time Great Science Fiction Films. p183-99.
Variety. Apr 3, 1968, p6.
Variety. Jan 15, 1969, p6.
The Village Voice. Apr 11, 1968, p45.
The Village Voice. Feb 20, 1969, p47.
Vogue. Jun 1968, v151, p76.
A Year In the Dark. p102-04.

2010 (Also titled: 2010: Odyssey Two) (US; Hyams, Peter; 1984)
Astronomy. Apr 1985, v13, p40.
BFI/Monthly Film Bulletin. Mar 1985, v52, p93.
Chatelaine. Feb 1985, v58, p4.
Christianity Today. Jan 18, 1985, v29, p66.
Commonweal. Jan 11, 1985, v112, p17.
Discover. Jan 1985, v6, p79.
Film Comment. Dec 1984, v20, p60.
Hollywood Reporter. Nov 20, 1984, p3.
Los Angeles. Dec 1984, v29, p250.
The Los Angeles Times. Dec 7, 1984, SecVI, p1.
Maclean's. Dec 10, 1984, v97, p69.
The Nation. Jan 26, 1985, v240, p88.
The New York Times. Dec 7, 1984, SecIII, p15.
Newsweek. Dec 10, 1984, v104, p94.
Omni. Dec 1984, v7, p28.
Playboy. Mar 1985, v32, p26.
Saturday Review. Jan-Feb 1985, v11, p80.
Senior Scholastic Update. Feb 1, 1985, v117, p15.
Texas Monthly. Jan 1985, v13, p130.
Time. Dec 24, 1984, v124, p66.
Variety. Nov 28, 1984, p19.
Washingtonian. Jan 1985, v20, p67.

Two Tickets to Broadway (US; Kern, James V.; 1951)
BFI/Monthly Film Bulletin. Feb 1952, v19, p23.

The Busby Berkeley Book. p167.
Film Daily. Oct 17, 1951, p6.
Hollywood Reporter. Oct 10, 1951, p3.
The London Times. Jan 7, 1952, p8.
Motion Picture Herald Product Digest. Oct 20,
  1951, p1066-67.
The New York Times. Nov 22, 1951, p47.
The New Yorker. Dec 1, 1951, v27, p144.
Newsweek. Dec 3, 1951, v38, p94.
The Spectator. Jan 4, 1952, v188, p13.
Time. Nov 19, 1951, v58, p112.
Variety. Oct 10, 1951, p6.

Two Weeks in Another Town (US;
  Minnelli, Vincente; 1962)
America. Sep 29, 1962, v107, p824.
BFI/Monthly Film Bulletin. Sep 1962, v29,
  p124.
Cinema Texas Program Notes. Mar 1977, v12,
  p39-44.
Commonweal. Sep 21, 1962, v76, p517.
Film Comment. Jan-Feb 1981, v17, p24-32.
Film Daily. Aug 10, 1962, p4.
Filmfacts. Aug 24, 1962, v5, p177-79.
Films in Review. Aug-Sep 1962, v13, p427-28.
The Films of Kirk Douglas. p185-87.
Hollywood Reporter. Aug 9, 1962, p3.
Motion Picture Herald Product Digest. Aug 22,
  1962, p642.
The New York Times. Aug 18, 1962, p10.
Newsweek. Sep 3, 1962, v60, p70.
Saturday Review. Sep 8, 1962, v45, p26.
Sight and Sound. Aut 1962, v31, p196-97.
Time. Aug 31, 1962, v80, p66.
Variety. Aug 8, 1962, p6.
The Village Voice. Feb 6, 1978, v23, p37.

Two Weeks With Love (US; Rowland, Roy;
  1950)
BFI/Monthly Film Bulletin. Dec 1950, v17,
  p191.
The Busby Berkeley Book. p162.
Christian Century. Jan 3, 1951, v68, p30.
Film Daily. Oct 11, 1950, p6.
Hollywood Reporter. Oct 11, 1950, p3.
Motion Picture Herald Product Digest. Oct 14,
  1950, p517-18.
The New York Times. Nov 24, 1950, p31.
Newsweek. Dec 11, 1950, v36, p95.
The Spectator. Nov 17, 1950, v185, p509.
Variety. Oct 11, 1950, p8.

Two Women (Italian title: Ciociara, La)
  (IT; De Sica, Vittorio; 1961)
America. Jul 1, 1961, v105, p493.
BFI/Monthly Film Bulletin. Sep 1961, v28,
  p122.
Commonweal. Apr 28, 1961, v74, p129.
Film Daily. May 12, 1961, p6.
Filmfacts. Jun 16, 1961, v4, p113-15.
Films in Review. May 1961, v17, p296-98.
The Films of Sophia Loren. p121-25.
The Films of the Sixties. p60-61.
*Magill's Survey of Cinema. Foreign Language
  Films.* v7, p3198-3201.
*Modern European Filmmakers and the Art of
  Adaptation.* p78-88.
The Nation. Jun 3, 1961, v192, p497.
The New Republic. May 22, 1961, v144, p29-30.
The New York Times. May 9, 1961, p43.
The New York Times. May 14, 1961, SecII, p1.
The New Yorker. May 20, 1961, v37, p152-53.
Reruns. p146-49.
Saturday Review. May 6, 1961, v44, p41.
Time. Apr 28, 1961, v77, p86.
Variety. May 10, 1961, p6.
*Vittorio De Sica: A Guide to References and
  Resources.* p89-95.

Two-Lane Blacktop (US; Hellman, Monte;
  1971)
Cult Movies. p363-65.
Film Quarterly. Wint 1971-72, v25, n2, p53-55.
Filmfacts. 1971, v14, p343.
Hollywood Reporter. Jun 21, 1971, v216, n38,
  p3.
Magill's Survey of Cinema. Series II. v6, p2579-
  81.
The New Yorker. Jul 10, 1971, v47, p55.
Newsweek. Jul 5, 1971, v78, p72.
Saturday Review. Jul 17, 1971, v54.
Time. Jul 12, 1971, v98, p44.
Variety. Jun 23, 1971, p46.
The Village Voice. Aug 12, 1971, p49.

Two-Minute Warning (US; Peerce, Larry;
  1976)
America. Nov 20, 1976, v135, p350.
BFI/Monthly Film Bulletin. Feb 1977, v44,
  p31.
Christian Century. Dec 15, 1976, v93, p1115-
  16.
Film Bulletin. Nov-Dec 1976, v45, p41.
Films in Review. Jan 1977, v28, p56.
Hollywood Reporter. Nov 3, 1976, p2.
Independent Film Journal. Nov 12, 1976, v78,
  p7.
The Los Angeles Times. Nov 7, 1976, Calendar,
  p34.
Motion Picture Herald Product Digest. Nov 24,
  1976, p52.
The New York Times. Jan 2, 1977, SecII, p11.
Newsweek. Nov 22, 1976, v88, p110.
Time. Dec 6, 1976, v108, p88-89.
Variety. Nov 3, 1976, p26.
The Village Voice. Nov 29, 1976, p53.

Tystnaden *See* The Silence

U.S.S. Teakettle (Also titled: You're In the
  Navy Now) (US; Hathaway, Henry;
  1951)
BFI/Monthly Film Bulletin. May 1951, v18,
  p269.
Commonweal. Mar 9, 1951, v53, p544.
Film Daily. Feb 23, 1951, p6.
The Films of Charles Bronson. p29-31.
The Films of Gary Cooper. p227-28.
Hollywood Reporter. Feb 23, 1951, p3.
Motion Picture Herald Product Digest. Mar 3,
  1951, p742-43.
The New Republic. Mar 12, 1951, v124, p23.
The New York Times. Feb 24, 1951, p11.
The New Yorker. Mar 10, 1951, v27, p93-94.
Newsweek. Mar 5, 1951, v37, p86.
Saturday Review. Apr 7, 1951, v34, p31.
Time. Mar 12, 1951, v57, p98.
Variety. Feb 28, 1951, p13.

Uccellacci e Uccellini *See* The Hawks and
  the Sparrows

Uccello dalle Piume di Cristallo, L' *See* The
  Bird With the Crystal Plumage

Ugetsu (Also titled: Ugetsu Monogatari;
  Tales of the Pale and Silvery Moon
  After the Rain; Tales After the Rain)
  (JAPAN; Mizoguchi, Kenji; 1953)
BFI/Monthly Film Bulletin. May 1962, v29,
  p64-65.
Catholic World. Sep 1954, v179, p466-67.
Cinema East. p103-22.
Cinema, the Magic Vehicle. v2, p161-63.
Classics of the Foreign Film. p208-09.
Commonweal. Sep 17, 1954, v60, p582.
Dictionary of Films. p388-89.
Favorite Movies. p61-69.
Film: A Modern Art (Sultanik). p136.
Film Comment. Mar-Apr 1973, v9, p32-40.

Film Daily. Sep 20, 1954, p10.
Films and Filming. May 1962, v8, p30.
*The International Dictionary of Films and
  Filmmakers.* v1, p492-94.
Japanese Cinema (Richie). p115.
The Japanese Film: Art and Industry. p226.
Japanese Film Directors. p47-50.
*Kenji Mizoguchi: A Guide to References and
  Resources.* p138-41.
Library Journal. Sep 1, 1954, v79, p1485.
Life. Nov 15, 1954, v37, p94.
*Magill's Survey of Cinema. Foreign Language
  Films.* v7, p3203-09.
Mizoguchi (McDonald). p116-24.
Mizoguchi (Morris). p14-20.
Motion Picture Herald Product Digest. Sep 18,
  1954, p145.
National Parent-Teacher. Dec 1954, v49, p40.
The New York Times. Sep 8, 1954, p40.
The New York Times Magazine. Aug 29, 1954,
  p52-53.
The New Yorker. Sep 18, 1954, v30, p66.
Newsweek. Sep 20, 1954, v44, p98.
Personal Views: Explorations. p225-48.
Renaissance of the Film. p306-15.
Reporter. Oct 21, 1954, v11, p41.
Saturday Review. Sep 11, 1954, v37, p44-45.
Saturday Review. Jan 1, 1955, v38, p63.
Sight and Sound. Spr 1962, v31, p97-99.
Sight and Sound. Aut 1955, v25, p80-81.
Sight and Sound. Spr 1978, v47, p116-18.
Time. Sep 20, 1954, v64, p108.
Variety. Sep 9, 1953, p6.
The Waves at Genji's Door. p103-04.

The Ugly American (US; Englund, George;
  1963)
America. Apr 27, 1963, v108, p621-23.
BFI/Monthly Film Bulletin. Jul 1963, v30, p98.
Commonweal. Apr 26, 1963, v78, p140.
Film Daily. Apr 2, 1963, p7.
Filmfacts. Apr 25, 1963, v6, p61-63.
Films and Filming. Jul 1963, v9, p21-22.
Films in Review. May 1963, v14, p305-06.
The Films of Marlon Brando. p144-49.
Hollywood Reporter. Apr 2, 1963, v174, p3.
Magill's Survey of Cinema. Series II. v6, p2584-
  86.
The New Republic. Apr 20, 1963, v148, p29.
The New York Times. Apr 12, 1963, p30.
The New York Times. Apr 21, 1963, SecII, p1.
The New Yorker. Apr 20, 1963, v29, p112-13.
Newsweek. Apr 22, 1963, v61, p98-99.
Saturday Review. Apr 20, 1963, v46, p43.
Spectator. Jun 14, 1963, v210, p779.
Time. Apr 19, 1963, v81, p111.
Variety. Apr 3, 1963, p7.
The Village Voice. Jun 6, 1963, v8, p15.

The Ugly Dachshund (US; Tokar, Norman;
  1965)
American Cinematographer. Jan 1966, v47,
  p29-32.
BFI/Monthly Film Bulletin. May 1966, v33,
  p77.
Film Daily. Jan 17, 1966, p6.
Filmfacts. Jun 1, 1966, v9, p89.
Films and Filming. Dec 1965, v12, p16.
Films and Filming. Jun 1966, v12, p16.
Films in Review. Feb 1966, v17, p115-16.
Hollywood Reporter. Dec 22, 1965, p3.
The London Times. Mar 24, 1966, p16.
Motion Picture Herald Product Digest. Jan 19,
  1966, p449.
New Statesman. Apr 1, 1966, v71, p479.
The New York Times. Apr 7, 1966, p45.
Variety. Dec 22, 1965, p17.

Ultimo tango à Parigi, L' *See* Last Tango in
  Paris

Ulysses (IT; Camerini, Mario; 1955)
Catholic World. Aug 1955, v181, p385.
Commonweal. Jul 8, 1955, v62, p354.
Films and Filming. Sep 1955, v1, n12, p20.
Films in Review. Aug-Sep 1955, v6, n7, p346.
The Films of Anthony Quinn. p140-41.
The Films of Kirk Douglas. p110-13.
Hollywood Reporter. Jun 23, 1955, v135, n11, p3.
Library Journal. Aug 1955, v80, p1674.
Magill's Survey of Cinema. Series II. v6, p2587.
Motion Picture Herald Product Digest. Jun 25, 1955, p490.
The Nation. Sep 3, 1955, v181, p211.
The New York Times. Aug 9, 1953, SecII, p3.
The New York Times. Feb 14, 1954, SecII, p5.
The New York Times. Aug 18, 1955, p17.
The New York Times. Aug 21, 1955, SecII, p1.
The New Yorker. Aug 27, 1955, v31, p99.
Saturday Review. Jul 2, 1955, v38, p30.
Time. Aug 22, 1955, v66, p82.
Variety. Dec 8, 1954, p6.

Ulysses (GB; Strick, Joseph; 1967)
America. Apr 8, 1967, v116, p539-40.
BFI/Monthly Film Bulletin. Sep 1967, v34, p137-38.
Catholic World. Mar 1967, v204, p346-51.
Commonweal. Apr 7, 1967, v86, p95.
The English Novel and the Movies. p291-300.
Esquire. Jul 1967, v68, p16.
Film Daily. Mar 15, 1967, p4.
Films and Filming. Aug 1967, v13, p21-22.
Films in Review. Apr 1967, v18, p236-38.
The Great Films. p247-50.
Harper's. Jun 1967, v234, p112.
Hollywood Reporter. May 10, 1967, p3.
Landmark Films. p278-89.
Life. Mar 31, 1967, v62, p54-56.
Magill's Survey of Cinema. Series II. v6, p2587-89.
Motion Picture Herald. Mar 29, 1967, p670.
The Nation. Mar 27, 1967, v204, p414.
The New Republic. May 6, 1967, v156, p31-34.
New York Review of Books. Jun 1967, v15, p12-13.
The New York Times. Mar 14, 1967, p55.
The New Yorker. Apr 1, 1967, v43, p93-94.
Newsweek. Mar 27, 1967, v69, p102.
Reporter. May 4, 1967, v36, p37-38.
Saturday Review. Apr 1, 1967, v50, p41.
Sight and Sound. Sum 1967, v36, p144-45.
Time. Mar 31, 1967, v89, p92.
Variety. Mar 15, 1967, p6.
The Village Voice. Apr 6, 1967, p31.
Vogue. May 1967, v149, p143.

Umberto D (IT; De Sica, Vittorio; 1952)
America. Dec 17, 1955, v94, p344.
BFI/Monthly Film Bulletin. Jan 1955, v22, p6.
Catholic World. May 1955, v181, p144.
Cinema, the Magic Vehicle. v2, p65-66.
Commonweal. Nov 25, 1955, v63, p199.
Dictionary of Films. p389-90.
Film. Mar 1955, n4, p20-21.
Film Culture. Wint 1955, v1, p30-31.
Film Daily. Nov 7, 1955, p14.
Filmfacts. Mar 1955, n4, p19-20.
Films and Filming. Nov 1964, v11, p51-54.
Films and Filming. Dec 1954, v1, p21.
Films and Filming. Jan 1956, v2, p28-29.
Films in Review. Nov 1952, v3, p472.
Hollywood Reporter. Jun 5, 1956, p3.
Hudson Review. Wint 1956, v8, p592-96.
The International Dictionary of Films and Filmmakers. v1, p495-96.
Italian Cinema (Bondanella). p62-66.
Italian Cinema (Leprohon). p130-31.
Kiss Kiss Bang Bang. p458-59.

Life. Dec 5, 1955, v39, p171-72.
Magill's Survey of Cinema. Foreign Language Films. v7, p3210-16.
The Nation. Nov 26, 1955, v181, p466.
The New Statesman and Nation. Nov 6, 1954, v48, p576.
The New York Times. Nov 8, 1955, p37.
The New York Times. Oct 30, 1955, p5.
The New York Times Magazine. Jun 5, 1955, p27.
The New Yorker. Nov 12, 1955, v31, p90.
The New Yorker. Jul 6, 1957, v33, p43-44.
Newsweek. Sep 26, 1955, v46, p114.
Patterns of Realism. p156-63.
Renaissance of the Film. p316-23.
Reporter. Dec 29, 1955, v13, p36.
Rotha on Film. p184-88.
Saturday Review. Nov 19, 1955, v38, p38.
Sight and Sound. Oct-Dec 1953, v23, p87-88.
Sight and Sound. Wint 1960-61, v30, p26-32.
Sight and Sound. Jan-Mar 1955, v24, p147-66.
Theatre Arts. Aug 1952, v36, p66.
Time. Dec 12, 1955, v66, p105.
Variety. Jun 4, 1952, p6.
Vintage Films. p126-30.
Vittorio De Sica: A Guide to References and Resources. p64-69.
What Is Cinema? v2, p79-82.

The Umbrellas of Cherbourg (French title: Parapluies de Cherbourg, Les) (FR, WGER; Demy, Jacques; 1964)
America. Jan 16, 1965, v113, p85-86.
BFI/Monthly Film Bulletin. Feb 1965, v32, p21.
Christian Science Monitor (Western edition). Feb 19, 1966, p4.
Cinema. Mar-Apr 1965, v2, p49.
Commonweal. Dec 25, 1964, v81, p454.
Dictionary of Films. p272.
Film. Wint 1964, n41, p12.
Film Comment. Spr 1965, v3, p61-63.
Film Daily. Dec 18, 1964, p4.
Film Heritage. Wint 1965-66, v1, p19-22.
Film Heritage. Spr 1967, v2, p17-24.
Film Quarterly. Spr 1966, v19, p25-29.
Filmfacts. Jan 1, 1965, v7, p330-32.
Films and Filming. Jan 1965, v11, p28.
Films in Review. Jan 1965, v16, p49.
The Great French Films. p197-200.
Hollywood Reporter. Mar 16, 1965, p3.
The International Dictionary of Films and Filmmakers. v1, p354-55.
International Film Guide. 1965, v2, p69.
Life. Dec 11, 1964, v57, p20.
Listener. Jan 21, 1965, v73, p104.
The London Times. May 12, 1964, p15.
The London Times. Oct 27, 1964, p13.
The London Times. Apr 22, 1965, p16.
Magill's Survey of Cinema. Foreign Language Films. v7, p3217-22.
Motion Picture Herald Product Digest. Jan 6, 1965, p202-03.
Movie Man (Thomson). p162-63.
The New Republic. Jan 2, 1965, v152, p21.
The New York Times. Dec 17, 1964, p50.
The New Yorker. Mar 7, 1964, v40, p141-42.
The New Yorker. Dec 19, 1964, v40, p151.
On Film. p259-60.
Playboy. Mar 1965, v12, p33-34.
The Private Eye, the Cowboy and the Very Naked Girl. p101-03.
Private Screenings. p156-59.
Saturday Review. Jan 30, 1965, v48, p40.
Sight and Sound. Wint 1964-65, v34, p37.
Sight and Sound. Sum 1964, v33, p136-39.
The Spectator. Jan 1, 1965, v214, p17.
Time. Dec 18, 1964, v84, p89.
Variety. Jun 29, 1964, p20.

The Village Voice. Feb 25, 1965, v10, p15.
Vogue. Nov 1, 1964, v144, p184-85.

Uncle Vanya (USSR; Konchalovsky, Andrei; 1972)
Filmfacts. 1972, v15, n21, p556.
Films in Review. Aug-Sep 1972, v23, n7, p431.
The Nation. Jul 19, 1972, v214, p796-97.
The New Republic. Jul 17, 1972, v166, p24.
The New York Times. May 19, 1972, v17, p1.
The New Yorker. May 27, 1972, v48, p103-06.
Variety. Jul 28, 1971, p14.

Uncommon Valor (US; Kotcheff, Ted; 1983)
BFI/Monthly Film Bulletin. Apr 1984, v51, p126.
Film Journal. Jan 1984, v87, p13.
Films and Filming. Apr 1984, n355, p42.
New York. Jan 16, 1984, v17, p62-63.
The New York Times. Feb 13, 1984, SecIII, p14.
The New Yorker. Jan 23, 1984, v59, p91-93.
Photoplay. Apr 1984, v35, p48-49.
Variety. Dec 14, 1983, p16.

Under Fire (US; Spottiswoode, Roger; 1983)
American Film. Jan 1984, v9, p38.
Esquire. Nov 1983, v100, p95.
Hollywood Reporter. Oct 17, 1983, p3.
The Los Angeles Times. Oct 21, 1983, SecVI, p1.
Maclean's. Oct 31, 1983, v96, p51.
Magill's Cinema Annual. p441-46.
Ms. Nov 1983, v12, p45.
The Nation. Nov 19, 1983, v237, p515-16.
National Review. Dec 9, 1983, v35, p1560.
The New Republic. Nov 21, 1983, v189, p32-33.
New York. Oct 24, 1983, v16, p102.
The New York Times. Oct 30, 1983, SecII, p9.
The New Yorker. Oct 31, 1983, v59, p118.
Newsweek. Oct 24, 1983, v102, p124.
Time. Nov 7, 1983, v122, p98.
Vogue. Oct 1983, v173, p92.

Under My Skin (US; Negulesco, Jean; 1950)
BFI/Monthly Film Bulletin. Apr-May 1950, v17, p63-64.
Christian Century. May 24, 1950, v67, p663.
Commonweal. Mar 24, 1950, v51, p629.
Film Daily. Mar 10, 1950, p8.
The Films of John Garfield. p167-69.
Hemingway on Film. p89-105.
Hollywood Reporter. Mar 10, 1950, p3.
Library Journal. Apr 1, 1950, v75, p571.
Motion Picture Herald Product Digest. Mar 11, 1950, p221.
The New Republic. Apr 3, 1950, v122, p22.
The New York Times. Mar 18, 1950, p9.
The New Yorker. Mar 25, 1950, v26, p100.
Newsweek. Apr 3, 1950, v35, p79.
Time. Apr 3, 1950, v55, p90.
Variety. Mar 15, 1950, p12.

Under Suspicion *See* Garde a Vue

Under the Volcano (US; Huston, John; 1984)
America. Sep 1, 1984, v151, p104.
American Cinematographer. v65, p58-63.
American Film. Jul-Aug 1984, v9, p18-26.
BFI/Monthly Film Bulletin. Jul 1984, v51, p214-15.
Commonweal. Aug 10, 1984, v111, p438-39.
Double Exposure. p205-11.
Film. Aug 1984, n127, p12.
Film Comment. Jul-Aug 1984, v20, p59-63.
Film Comment. Jan-Feb 1984, v20, p4.
Film Journal. Jul 1984, v87, p20.
Hollywood Reporter. Jun 18, 1984, p4.

Film Daily. May 18, 1966, p3.
Film Quarterly. Wint 1966-67, v20, p63.
Filmfacts. Jul 15, 1966, v9, p131-32.
Films in Review. Jun-Jul 1966, v17, p383.
Hollywood Reporter. May 17, 1966, p3.
Motion Picture Herald Product Digest. Jun 1, 1966, p533-34.
The New York Times. May 18, 1966, p37.
Playboy. Aug 1966, v13, p25-26.
Variety. Oct 27, 1965, p26.

Up To His Neck *See* Up To His Ears

The Upper Hand *See* Rififi in Panama

Uptown Saturday Night (US; Poitier, Sidney; 1974)
Black Hollywood: The Negro in Motion Pictures. p244-45.
Commonweal. Oct 18, 1974, v101, p66.
Films in Review. Aug-Sep 1974, v25, p440-41.
The Films of Sidney Poitier. p201-04.
Hollywood Reporter. Jun 12, 1974, p3.
The Los Angeles Times. Jul 21, 1974, Calendar, p28.
Motion Picture Herald Product Digest. Jun 19, 1974, p5.
Movietone News. Sep 1974, n35, p28-29.
The New York Times. Jun 17, 1974, p25.
The New York Times. Jul 28, 1874, SecII, p1.
The New Yorker. Jun 17, 1974, v50, p88-90.
Newsweek. Jun 24, 1974, v83, p80.
Time. Jul 1, 1974, v104, p42.
Variety. Jun 12, 1974, p18.
The Village Voice. Jun 27, 1974, p87.

Urban Cowboy (US; Bridges, James; 1980)
America. Jul 5, 1980, v143, p16.
Encore. Aug 1980, v9, p40.
Hollywood Reporter. Jun 2, 1980, p2.
The Los Angeles Times. Jun 11, 1980, SecVI, p1.
Maclean's. Oct 13, 1980, v93, p50-52.
Maclean's. Jun 16, 1980, v93, p53-54.
Motion Picture Herald Product Digest. Jun 11, 1980, p1.
The Nation. Jul 5, 1980, v231, p28-29.
National Review. Aug 8, 1980, v32, p975-76.
The New Leader. Jul 14, 1980, v63, p20.
The New Republic. Jun 21, 1980, v182, p24-25.
New York. Jun 16, 1980, v13, p55-56.
The New York Times. Jun 11, 1980, SecIII, p21.
The New York Times. Jun 22, 1980, SecII, p17.
The New York Times. Dec 14, 1980, SecII, p21.
The New Yorker. Jul 21, 1980, v56, p85-86.
Newsweek. Jun 9, 1980, v95, p84-85.
Rolling Stone. Jul 10, 1980, p32-37.
Time. Jun 9, 1980, v115, p74.
Variety. Jun 4, 1980, p20.

Used Cars (US; Zemeckis, Robert; 1980)
Hollywood Reporter. Jul 2, 1980, p2.
The Los Angeles Times. Jul 11, 1980, SecVI, p12.
The Nation. Sep 27, 1980, v231, p293.
The New York Times. Aug 22, 1980, SecII, p10.
The New Yorker. Nov 10, 1980, v56, p208.
Variety. Jul 2, 1980, p18.

The V.I.P.s (US; Asquith, Anthony; 1963)
America. Sep 28, 1963, v109, p369.
BFI/Monthly Film Bulletin. Oct 1963, v30, p143.
Commonweal. Oct 4, 1963, v79, p44.
Film Daily. Aug 13, 1963, p4.
Filmfacts. Sep 19, 1963, v6, p187-89.
Films and Filming. Oct 1963, v10, p21.
Films in Review. Oct 1963, v14, p492-93.
The Films of Anthony Asquith. p198-205.
The Films of Elizabeth Taylor. p162-65.
Hollywood Reporter. Aug 13, 1963, v176, p3.

The Illustrated London News. Sep 28, 1963, v243, p486.
The New Republic. Sep 28, 1963, v149, p30.
New Statesman. Sep 20, 1963, v66, p368.
The New York Times. Sep 20, 1963, p29.
The New Yorker. Sep 28, 1963, v39, p104.
Newsweek. Sep 30, 1963, v62, p84.
Photoplay. Nov 1963, v64, p10.
Saturday Review. Sep 21, 1963, v46, p46.
Time. Oct 4, 1963, v82, p122.
Variety. Aug 14, 1963, p6.

Vacances de Monsieur Hulot, Les *See* Mr. Hulot's Holiday

Vaghe Stelle Dell'Orsa (Also titled: Sandra; Of a Thousand Delights; Dim Stars of the Big Bear) (IT; Visconti, Luchino; 1965)
BFI/Monthly Film Bulletin. Dec 1965, v32, p181.
Cahiers du Cinema in English. 1966, n2, p13-21.
Christian Science Monitor (Western edition). Jan 29, 1966, p6.
Commonweal. Feb 4, 1966, v83, p535.
Dictionary of Films. p396-97.
Esquire. Feb 1966, v65, p37.
Film Daily. Jan 31, 1966, p4.
Filmfacts. Feb 1, 1966, v9, p3-5.
Films and Filming. Dec 1965, v12, p30.
Films and Filming. Sep 1965, v11, p19.
The London Times. Sep 8, 1965, p13.
Luchino Visconti (Tonetti). p109-16.
Motion Picture Herald Product Digest. Jan 26, 1966, p457-58.
New Statesman. Oct 29, 1965, v70, p667.
The New York Times. Sep 4, 1965, p11.
The New Yorker. Jan 22, 1966, v41, p96, 99.
Newsweek. Jan 31, 1966, v67, p85.
On Movies. p347-48.
Sight and Sound. Wint 1965-66, v35, p40-41.
The Spectator. Oct 29, 1965, v215, p544.
Time. Feb 11, 1966, v87, p86.
Tynan Right and Left. p241-42.
Variety. Sep 15, 1965, p6.
The Village Voice. Jan 27, 1966, v11, p23.

Valdez Is Coming (US; Sherin, Edwin; 1971)
BFI/Monthly Film Bulletin. Jul 1971, v38, p149.
Filmfacts. 1971, v14, p59-60.
Hollywood Reporter. Mar 3, 1971, v215, n11, p3.
The New York Times. Feb 10, 1970, p48.
The New York Times. Apr 10, 1971, p11.
Time. Apr 26, 1971, v97, p97.
Variety. Mar 10, 1971, p16.

Valentino (GB; Russell, Ken; 1977)
BFI/Monthly Film Bulletin. Nov 1977, v44, p244.
Dance Magazine. Dec 1977, v51, p60-61.
Film Quarterly. Wint 1977, v31, p19-24.
Films and Filming. Nov 7, 1977, p36-37.
Films in Review. Nov 1977, v28, p569.
Hollywood Reporter. Oct 19, 1977, p39.
Ken Russell: A Guide to References and Resources. p42-45.
Ken Russell (Phillips). p131-46.
The Los Angeles Times. Oct 5, 1977, SecIV, p15.
Motion Picture Herald Product Digest. Oct 19, 1977, p39.
New Times. Nov 25, 1977, v9, p83.
New York. Oct 17, 1977, v10, p96.
The New York Times. Oct 6, 1977, SecIII, p21.
The New York Times. Dec 20, 1977, p44.
The New Yorker. Nov 7, 1977, v53, p119-20.

Newsweek. Oct 17, 1977, v90, p102.
The Nureyev Valentino. 1977.
Rolling Stone. Nov 3, 1977, p78-85.
Saturday Review. Apr 30, 1977, v4, p29-32.
Time. Oct 17, 1977, v110, p98.
Variety. Sep 21, 1977, p16.
The Village Voice. Oct 31, 1977, p45-46.
Vogue. Aug 1977, v167, p149.

Valley of Eagles *See* Valley of the Eagles

Valley of the Dolls (US; Robson, Mark; 1967)
BFI/Monthly Film Bulletin. Feb 1968, v35, p28.
Film Daily. Dec 14, 1967, p4.
Films and Filming. Mar 1968, v14, p31-32.
Films in Review. Jan 1968, v19, p52-53.
The Films of Susan Hayward. p273-76.
The Films of the Sixties. p200-02.
Hollywood Reporter. Dec 14, 1967, p3.
Motion Picture Herald Product Digest. Jan 3, 1968, p756.
The New York Times. Dec 16, 1967, p51.
Ramparts Magazine. Feb 1968, v6, p66.
Time. Dec 22, 1967, v90, p78.
Variety. Dec 20, 1967, p6.
The Village Voice. Jan 25, 1968, p38-39.

Valley of the Eagles (Also titled: Valley of Eagles) (GB; Young, Terence; 1951)
BFI/Monthly Film Bulletin. Oct 1951, v18, p345.
Christian Century. Jun 25, 1952, v69, p761.
Commonweal. Apr 25, 1952, v56, p70.
Film Daily. Apr 2, 1952, p6.
Films in Review. Apr 1952, v3, p199-200.
Hollywood Reporter. Mar 14, 1952, p3.
Life. Apr 21, 1952, v32, p119-20.
Motion Picture Herald Product Digest. Mar 22, 1952, p1290.
The New York Times. Apr 11, 1952, p19.
The New Yorker. Apr 26, 1952, v28, p136.
Newsweek. Apr 7, 1952, v39, p100.
Variety. Oct 10, 1951, p18.

Valley of the Kings (US; Pirosh, Robert; 1954)
America. Jul 31, 1954, v91, p446.
BFI/Monthly Film Bulletin. Sep 1954, v21, p137.
Commonweal. Aug 6, 1954, v60, p435.
Farm Journal. Sep 1954, v78, p140.
Film Daily. Jul 8, 1954, p6.
Films and Filming. Oct 1954, v1, p30.
Films in Review. Aug-Sep 1954, v5, p368.
The Films of Robert Taylor. p140-41.
Hollywood Reporter. Jul 6, 1954, p3.
Library Journal. Aug 1954, v79, p1393.
The London Times. Aug 9, 1954, p9.
Motion Picture Herald Product Digest. Jul 10, 1954, p57.
The New York Times. Jul 22, 1954, p15.
The Tatler. Aug 18, 1954, v213, p288.
Time. Jul 26, 1954, v64, p77-78.
Variety. Jul 7, 1954, p6.

Valseuses, Les *See* Going Places

Vangelo Secondo Matteo, Il *See* The Gospel According to St. Matthew

Vanishing Point (US; Sarafin, Richard C.; 1971)
BFI/Monthly Film Bulletin. Sep 1971, v38, p185.
Cult Movies 2. p157-59.
Filmfacts. 1971, v14, p130-32.
Films and Filming. Oct 1971, v18, n1, p60.
Hollywood Reporter. Feb 1, 1971, v214, n40, p4.
The New York Times. Mar 25, 1971, p46.

Take One. Sep-Oct 1970, v3, n1, p25-26.
Variety. Feb 3, 1971, p17.

The Vanishing Prairie (US; Algar, James; 1954)
America. Aug 28, 1954, v91, p527.
Catholic World. Aug 1954, v179, p385.
Commonweal. Aug 27, 1954, v60, p513.
The Disney Films (Maltin). p117-18.
Film Daily. Aug 4, 1954, p3.
Films and Filming. Jun 1955, v1, p21.
Films in Review. Oct 1954, v5, p432-33.
Hollywood Reporter. Aug 3, 1954, p3.
Motion Picture Herald Product Digest. Aug 7, 1954, p97.
National Parent-Teacher. Sep 1954, v49, p37.
Natural History. Sep 1954, v63, p332.
The New Statesman and Nation. Apr 16, 1955, v49, p534.
The New York Times. Aug 17, 1954, p17.
The New Yorker. Aug 21, 1954, v30, p66.
Newsweek. Aug 9, 1954, v44, p80.
Reporter. Sep 23, 1954, v11, p46.
Saturday Review. Jan 1, 1955, v38, p63.
Saturday Review. Aug 21, 1954, v37, p30.
Senior Scholastic. Sep 22, 1954, v64, p37.
The Tatler. Apr 20, 1955, v216, p150.
Time. Aug 23, 1954, v64, p72.
Variety. Aug 4, 1954, p6.
Walt Disney: A Guide to References and Resources. p47-48.

Vargtimmen *See* Hour of the Wolf

Variety Lights (Italian title: Luci del Varietà) (IT; Fellini, Federico; 1950)
BFI/Monthly Film Bulletin. Nov 1960, v27, p151-52.
Cinema Eye, Cinema Ear. p15-51, 230-33.
The Cinema of Federico Fellini. p76-79.
Federico Fellini: A Guide to References and Resources. p19, 45-49.
Federico Fellini (Burke). p7-10.
Federico Fellini: Essays in Criticism. p205-28.
Film Criticism. 1979, v3, n2, p53-66.
Film Quarterly. Fall 1961, v15, p48.
The Films of Federico Fellini. p57-62.
Italian Cinema (Bondanella). p116-18.
Motion Picture Herald Product Digest. Jun 9, 1965, p307.
The New Republic. May 15, 1965, v152, p32-33.
The New York Times. May 7, 1965, p34.
The New Yorker. May 8, 1965, v41, p167.
Newsweek. May 17, 1965, v65, p104.
The Private Eye, the Cowboy and the Very Naked Girl. p132-33.
A World on Film. p325.

Vendetta (US; Ferrer, Mel; 1950)
BFI/Monthly Film Bulletin. Aug 1951, v18, p309-10.
Film Daily. Nov 24, 1950, p8.
Hollywood Reporter. Nov 22, 1950, p3.
Library Journal. Nov 1, 1950, v75, p1915.
The London Times. Jul 16, 1951, p2.
Motion Picture Herald Product Digest. Nov 25, 1950, p590.
The New York Times. Dec 26, 1950, p19.
Newsweek. Jan 8, 1951, v37, p74.
The Spectator. Jul 13, 1951, v187, p62.
Time. Jan 22, 1951, v57, p92.
Variety. Nov 22, 1950, p8.

Venetian Bird (Also titled: The Assassin) (GB; Thomas, Ralph; 1952)
America. May 9, 1953, v89, p175.
BFI/Monthly Film Bulletin. Nov 1952, v19, p159.
Illustrated London News. Oct 18, 1952, v221, p635.
Library Journal. May 15, 1953, v78, p897.

The New York Times. Apr 18, 1953, p17.
The New Yorker. Apr 25, 1953, v29, p113.
Newsweek. May 4, 1953, v41, p94.
The Tatler. Oct 22, 1952, v206, p200.
Variety. Oct 29, 1952, p24.

Vera Cruz (US; Aldrich, Robert; 1954)
America. Feb 5, 1955, v92, p490.
America in the Movies. p84-86.
BFI/Monthly Film Bulletin. Apr 1955, v22, p55.
Burt Lancaster: A Pictorial Treasury of His Films. p79-81.
Collier's. Aug 6, 1954, v134, p72-73.
Commonweal. Jan 28, 1955, v61, p455.
Film Daily. Dec 24, 1954, p4.
Films and Filming. Apr 1955, v1, p20.
The Films in My Life. p95-98.
The Films of Gary Cooper. p248-51.
The Films of Robert Aldrich. p21-22.
Hollywood Reporter. Dec 22, 1954, p3.
Library Journal. Feb 15, 1955, v80, p436.
The London Times. Feb 14, 1955, p3.
Motion Picture Herald Product Digest. Dec 25, 1954, p257.
National Parent-Teacher. Mar 1955, v49, p40.
Natural History. Feb 1955, v64, p112.
The New Statesman and Nation. Feb 19, 1955, v49, p246.
The New York Times. Dec 27, 1954, p22.
The New Yorker. Jan 15, 1955, v30, p72.
Newsweek. Jan 10, 1955, v45, p56.
Saturday Review. Jan 15, 1955, v38, p32.
The Spectator. Feb 11, 1955, v194, p158.
The Tatler. Mar 2, 1955, v215, p391.
Time. Jan 10, 1955, v65, p82.
Variety. Dec 22, 1954, p6.

The Verdict (US; Lumet, Sidney; 1982)
American Classic Screen. Mar-Apr 1983, v7, p9-11.
BFI/Monthly Film Bulletin. Feb 1982, v50, p33-34.
Christian Century. Dec 22, 1982, v99, p1318.
Christianity Today. Mar 18, 1983, v27, p48.
Film Journal. Dec 27, 1982, v85, p11-12.
Films In Review. Jan 1983, v34, p48-49.
Hollywood Reporter. Nov 24, 1982, p3.
The Los Angeles Times. Dec 16, 1982, SecVI, p1.
Maclean's. Dec 20, 1982, v95, p49.
Magill's Cinema Annual, 1983. p377-81.
Millimeter. Dec 1982, v10, p52-54.
The Nation. Dec 18, 1982, v235, p666.
National Review. Feb 4, 1983, v35, p132-33.
The New Leader. Dec 27, 1982, v65, p19-20.
The New Republic. Dec 20, 1982, v187, p24-25.
New Statesman. Feb 25, 1983, v105, p28-29.
The New Y rk Times. Jun 6, 1982, SecVII, p26-27.
New York. Dec 20, 1982, v15, p62.
The New York Times. Dec 8, 1982, SecIII, p24.
The New Yorker. Jan 10, 1983, v58, p86, 90-92.
Newsweek. Dec 6, 1982, v100, p151.
Newsweek. Feb 28, 1983, v101, p51.
Penthouse. Feb 1983, v14, p48-49.
Progressive. Mar 1983, v47, p54.
Rolling Stone. Jan 20, 1983, p14-15.
Variety. Nov 23, 1982, p3.
The Village Voice. Dec 14, 1982, p90.
The Village Voice. Jan 11, 1983, p45.
Vogue. Jan 1983, v173, p56.

Verlorene, Der (Also titled: The Lost One) (WGER; Lorre, Peter; 1951)
Cinema, the Magic Vehicle. v2, p95-96.
The Films of Peter Lorre. p201-04.
Sight and Sound. Oct-Dec 1951, v21, p91.
Sight and Sound. Wint 1966-67, v36, p45.
Variety. Sep 5, 1951, p6.

Veronika Voss (German title: Sehnsucht der Veronika Voss, Die) (WGER; Fassbinder, Rainer Werner; 1982)
America. Nov 27, 1982, v147, p334.
BFI/Monthly Film Bulletin. Jan 1983, v50, p3-4.
Films In Review. Feb 1983, v34, p111.
Hollywood Reporter. Nov 26, 1982, p15.
The Los Angeles Times. Nov 3, 1982, SecVI, p5.
Maclean's. Nov 22, 1982, v95, p74-75.
Magill's Cinema Annual, 1983. p382-86.
National Review. Oct 29, 1982, v34, p1360.
New Statesman. Mar 18, 1983, v105, p31.
New York. Nov 1, 1982, v15, p64.
The New York Times. Sep 24, 1982, SecIII, p12.
Social Policy. Wint 1983, v14, p60-62.
Time. Sep 27, 1982, v120, p58.
Variety. Feb 24, 1982, p3.

Vertigo (US; Hitchcock, Alfred; 1958)
America. Jun 7, 1958, v99, p319.
The Art of Alfred Hitchcock. p291-338.
BFI/Monthly Film Bulletin. Sep 1958, v25, p111.
Catholic World. Aug 1958, v187, p384.
Cinema, the Magic Vehicle. v2, p398-400.
The Classic Cinema. p247-72.
Commonweal. Jun 6, 1958, v68, p255-56.
Cult Movies. p375-78.
The Dark Side of Genius. p393-402.
Fifty from the Fifties. p381-88.
Film Daily. May 14, 1958, v113, p6.
Filmfacts. Jun 25, 1958, v1, p85-86.
Films in Review. Jun-Jul 1958, v9, p333-35.
The Films of Alfred Hitchcock. p185-89.
The Films of James Stewart. p193-95.
The Films of the Fifties. p381-88.
Hitchcock (Truffaut). p243-53.
Hitchcock's Films. p77-95.
Hollywood Reporter. May 12, 1958, p3.
The International Dictionary of Films and Filmmakers. v1, p506-07.
Library Journal. Jun 1, 1958, v83, p1700.
Life. Jun 23, 1958, v44, p57-58.
Magill's Survey of Cinema. Series II. v6, p2612-15.
The Nation. Jun 14, 1958, v186, p551.
The New York Times. May 29, 1958, p24.
The New Yorker. Jun 7, 1958, v34, p65.
Newsweek. Jun 2, 1958, v51, p91.
Saturday Review. Jun 7, 1958, v41, p25.
Surrealism and the Cinema. p101-08.
Time. Jun 16, 1958, v71, p97-98.
Variety. May 14, 1958, p6.

A Very Private Affair (French title: Vie Privee; Also titled: Private Life) (FR, IT; Malle, Louis; 1961)
BFI/Monthly Film Bulletin. Nov 1962, v29, p152.
Commonweal. Oct 19, 1962, v77, p95.
Film Quarterly. Spr 1963, v16, p60.
Filmfacts. Oct 19, 1962, v5, p229-30.
Films and Filming. Nov 1962, v9, p32-33.
Films in Review. Oct 1962, v13, p491.
Hollywood Reporter. Sep 28, 1962, p3.
Motion Picture Herald Product Digest. Oct 17, 1962, p675.
Movie. Oct 1962, n3, p36.
The New York Times. Sep 29, 1962, p15.
The New Yorker. Oct 13, 1962, v38, p191.
The New Yorker. Mar 3, 1962, v38, p127-28.
Newsweek. Oct 1, 1962, v60, p61.
Time. Oct 26, 1962, v80, p99.
Variety. Feb 14, 1962, p6.

A Very Special Favor (US; Gordon,
Michael; 1965)
BFI/Monthly Film Bulletin. Dec 1965, v32,
p186.
Christian Science Monitor (Western edition).
Aug 23, 1965, p4.
Film Daily. Jul 8, 1965, p7.
Films and Filming. Dec 1965, v12, p32-33.
Films in Review. Aug-Sep 1965, v16, p450-51.
Hollywood Reporter. Jul 7, 1965, p3.
The London Times. Nov 11, 1965, p18.
Motion Picture Herald Product Digest. Jul 21,
1965, p330.
New Statesman. Nov 19, 1965, v70, p798, 800.
The New York Times. Aug 26, 1965, p40.
Newsweek. Sep 13, 1965, v66, p87A.
Variety. Jul 7, 1965, p6.

Vice and Virtue (French title: Vice et la
Vertu, Le) (FR, IT; Vadim, Roger;
1963)
BFI/Monthly Film Bulletin. Sep 1963, v30,
p134.
Film Daily. Mar 22, 1965, p6.
Film Quarterly. Fall 1966, v20, p60.
Filmfacts. Apr 2, 1965, v8, p46-47.
Films and Filming. Sep 1963, v9, p26.
The London Times. Aug 1, 1963, p7.
Motion Picture Herald Product Digest. Mar 31,
1965, p259.
The New York Times. Mar 18, 1965, p25.
Newsweek. Apr 5, 1965, v65, p92.
Variety. Mar 13, 1963, p6.

Victim *See* High Infidelity

Victim (GB; Dearden, Basil; 1961)
America. Jul 2, 1962, v107, p360.
Commonweal. Feb 23 1962, v75, p569-70.
Film Daily. Feb 2, 1962, p7.
Film Forum. 1977, v1, n2, p3-22.
Filmfacts. Mar 9, 1962, v5, p29-31.
Films and Filming. Oct 1961, v8, p26.
Films in Review. Feb 1962, v13, p107-08.
The Films of Dirk Bogarde. p125-27.
Hollywood Reporter. Jan 31, 1962, p3.
I Lost It at the Movies. p181-83.
Motion Picture Herald Product Digest. Feb 7,
1962, p436-37.
The New Republic. Mar 12, 1962, v146, p35-36.
The New York Times. Feb 6, 1962, p27.
The New Yorker. Feb 10, 1962, v37, p130.
Newsweek. Feb 5, 1962, v59, p83.
Screen. Jul-Oct 1984, v25, p22-35.
Sight and Sound. Aut 1961, v30, p198-99.
Time. Feb 23, 1962, v79, p102.
Variety. Sep 6, 1961, p6.

Victoire en Chantant, La *See* Black and
White in Color

Victor/Victoria (US; Edwards, Blake; 1982)
America. May 8, 1982, v146, p363.
American Film. Sep 1982, v7, p57-64.
BFI/Monthly Film Bulletin. Apr 1982, v49,
p71.
Christian Century. May 5, 1982, v99, p547.
Commonweal. May 21, 1982, v109, p304-05.
Contemporary Review. Nov 1982, v241, p266-
69.
Film Comment. Mar-Apr 1982, v18, p46-47.
Film Comment. May-Jun 1982, v18, p18-19.
Film Journal. Mar 8, 1982, v85, p23.
Film Quarterly. Wint 1982, v36, p46-50.
Films In Review. Apr 1982, v33, p238-39.
Hollywood Reporter. Mar 15, 1982, p32.
Interview. Oct 1982, v12, p58-61.
The Los Angeles Times. Mar 14, 1982,
Calendar, p29.
Maclean's. Mar 29, 1982, v95, p59.
Magill's Cinema Annual, 1983. p387-92.

Ms. Apr 1982, v10, p37-38.
The Nation. Apr 10, 1982, v234, p441-42.
National Review. Jun 11, 1982, v34, p708.
The New Leader. May 3, 1982, v65, p20.
The New Republic. May 24, 1982, v186, p24-25.
New Statesman. Apr 2, 1982, v103, p26.
New York. Mar 22, 1982, v15, p58-59.
The New York Times. Apr 4, 1982, SecII, p15.
The New York Times. Mar 19, 1982, SecIII, p8.
The New Yorker. May 3, 1982, v58, p124.
Newsweek. Mar 22, 1982, v99, p88.
Photoplay. Apr 1982, v33, p72-74.
Photoplay. May 1982, v33, p24.
Saturday Review. Mar 1982, v9, p54-55.
Sight and Sound. Sum 1982, v51, p209.
Variety. Mar 16, 1982, p3.
Variety. Mar 17, 1982, p23.
The Village Voice. Mar 30, 1982, p38.
The Village Voice. Mar 23, 1982, p45.

The Victors (US; Foreman, Carl; 1963)
America. Feb 22, 1964, v110, p267.
BFI/Monthly Film Bulletin. Jan 1964, v31, p7.
Commonweal. Jan 17, 1964, v79, p462.
Esquire. Mar 1964, v61, p18.
Film Daily. Oct 30, 1963, p9.
Filmfacts. Dec 11, 1963, v6, p273-75.
Films and Filming. Jan 1964, v10, p26.
Films in Review. Dec 1963, v14, p624-26.
The Fondas (Springer). p196-97.
National Review. Dec 17, 1963, v15, p536-38.
The New Republic. Jan 4, 1964, v150, p22-23.
The New York Times. Dec 20, 1963, p21.
The New York Times. Dec 22, 1963, SecII, p3.
The New Yorker. Dec 28, 1963, v39, p52.
Newsweek. Dec 30, 1963, v62, p40.
Saturday Review. Dec 14, 1963, v46, p24.
Sight and Sound. Win 1963-64, v33, p40-41.
Th Films of the Sixties. p104-07.
Time. Dec 20, 1963, v82, p63.
Variety. Oct 30, 1963, p6.
Vogue. Jan 1, 1964, v143, p24.

Victory (US; Huston, John; 1981)
BFI/Monthly Film Bulletin. Jun 1981, v48,
p175.
Hollywood Reporter. Jul 20, 1981, p4.
The Los Angeles Times. Jul 31, 1981, SecVI,
p1.
Magill's Cinema Annual, 1982. p374.
The New York Times. Jul 31, 1981, SecIII, p6.
Newsweek. Aug 10, 1981, v98, p69.
Sports Illustrated. Aug 10, 1981, v55, p44.
Time. Aug 3, 1981, v118, p66.

Victory at Sea (US; Salomon, Henry; 1954)
Commonweal. Aug 6, 1954, v60, p436.
Farm Journal. Sep 1954, v78, p140.
Film Daily. May 20, 1954, p10.
Films in Review. Aug-Sep 1954, v5, p362.
The London Times. Mar 12, 1953, p4.
Motion Picture Herald Product Digest. May 22,
1954, p2.
National Parent-Teacher. Sep 1954, v49, p39.
The New York Times. Jul 14, 1954, p33.
The New Yorker. Jul 24, 1954, v30, p41.
Newsweek. Jul 19, 1954, v44, p86.
Saturday Review. Jul 10, 1954, v37, p26.
Variety. May 19, 1954, p6.

Vie a l'Envers, La *See* Life Upside Down

Vie Commence Demain, La (Also titled:
Life Begins Tomorrow) (FR; Vedres,
Nicole; 1950)
BFI/Monthly Film Bulletin. Feb 1950, v17,
p216.
Commonweal. Dec 5, 1952, v57, p224.
Films in Review. Dec 1952, v3, p530.
Illustrated London News. Jan 27, 1951, v218,
p140.

Library Journal. Jan 1, 1953, v78, p50.
The London Times. Jan 12, 1951, p8.
The New Statesman and Nation. Jan 20, 1951,
v41, p66.
The New York Times. Nov 18, 1952, p37.
Newsweek. Dec 1, 1952, v40, p82.
Rotha on Film. p164-65.
Saturday Review. Nov 22, 1952, v35, p38-39.
Sequence. New Year 1951, n13, p15.
Shots in the Dark. p262-64.
Sight and Sound. Feb 1951, v19, p414.
Sight and Sound. Nov 1950, v19, p271.
The Spectator. Jan 12, 1951, v186, p44.
Theatre Arts. Sep 1951, v35, p38-39.
Theatre Arts. Jan 1953, v37, p83.
Variety. Nov 26, 1952, p18.

Vie de Chateau, La (Also titled: A Matter
of Resistance; Chateau Life) (FR;
Rappeneau, Jean-Paul; Gérard,
Olivier; Bibowski, Nicolas; 1966)
BFI/Monthly Film Bulletin. Jun 1967, v34,
p92-93.
Cahiers du Cinema in English. 1966, n4, p60-
61.
Film Quarterly. Spr 1968, v21, p62.
Filmfacts. May 1, 1967, v10, p79-80.
Life. Jun 2, 1967, v62, p14.
The London Times. Apr 20, 1967, p8.
Motion Picture Herald Product Digest. Mar 29,
1967, p671.
The New York Times. Mar 21, 1967, p35.
The New Yorker. Mar 25, 1967, v43, p152.
Playboy. Jul 1967, v14, p26.
Variety. Feb 9, 1966, p6.

Vie devant soi, La *See* Madame Rosa

Vie, La *See* Every Man for Himself

Vie Privee *See* A Very Private Affair

Vieil Homme et L'Enfant, Le *See* The Two
of Us

Vieille Dame Indigne, La *See* The
Shameless Old Lady

Vierde Man, De *See* The Fourth Man

A View from the Bridge (French title: Vu
du Pont) (FR, US; Lumet, Sidney;
1961)
BFI/Monthly Film Bulletin. Mar 1962, v29,
p37-38.
Commonweal. Feb 9, 1962, v75, p518.
Film. Sum 1962, n32, p17-18.
Film Daily. Jan 25, 1982, p6.
Filmfacts. Feb 9, 1962, v5, p5-7.
Films and Filming. Apr 1962, v8, p29.
Films in Review. Feb 1962, v13, p102-03.
Hollywood Reporter. Jan 23, 1962, p3.
I Lost It at the Movies. p155-58.
Magill's Survey of Cinema. Series II. v6, p2616-
18.
Motion Picture Herald Product Digest. Jan 31,
1962, p427, 429.
The Nation. Feb 10, 1962, v194, p125.
The New Republic. Feb 12, 1962, v146, p26-27.
The New York Times. Jan 23, 1962, p36.
The New Yorker. Jan 27, 1962, v37, p82.
Newsweek. Jan 22, 1962, v59, p80-81.
Saturday Review. Jan 27, 1962, v45, p28.
*Sidney Lumet: A Guide to References and
Resources*. p69-70.
Sight and Sound. Spr 1962, v31, p95-96.
Time. Jan 19, 1962, v79, p55.
Variety. Oct 18, 1961, p6.
The Village Voice. Feb 22, 1962, p11.
A World on Film. p102-06.

A View to a Kill (GB; Glen, John; 1985)
BFI/Monthly Film Bulletin. Jul 1985, v52, p228.
Films in Review. Aug 1985, v36, p419.
Hollywood Reporter. May 22, 1985, p3.
Jet. Jun 24, 1985, v68, p56-58.
The Los Angeles Times. May 24, 1985, SecVI, p1.
Maclean's. Jun 10, 1985, v98, p64.
Magill's Cinema Annual, 1986. p402-05.
The New York Times. May 24, 1985, SecIII, p10.
The New Yorker. Jun 3, 1985, v61, p119-20.
Newsweek. May 27, 1985, v105, p74.
Time. Jun 10, 1985, v106, p58.
Variety. May 22, 1985, p14.

The Vikings (US; Fleischer, Richard; 1958)
America. Jun 28, 1958, v99, p77-78.
Commonweal. Jun 27, 1958, v68, p331.
Film Daily. May 20, 1958, v113, p6.
Filmfacts. Jul 23, 1958, v1, p101-02.
Films in Review. Aug-Sep 1958, v9, p402-03.
The Films of Kirk Douglas. p150-54.
Hollywood Reporter. May 20, 1958, p3.
Library Journal. Jun 15, 1958, v83, p1914.
Life. Jul 14, 1958, v45, p68-72.
The New York Times. Jun 12, 1958, p35.
The New Yorker. Jun 21, 1958, v34, p68.
Newsweek. Jun 16, 1958, v51, p102.
Saturday Review. Jun 14, 1958, v41, p28.
Time. Jun 30, 1958, v82, p82.
Tony Curtis: The Man and His Movies. p70-72.
Variety. May 21, 1958, p6.

The Village Fair *See* Jour de Fete

Village of the Damned (GB; Rilla, Wolf; 1960)
BFI/Monthly Film Bulletin. Jul 1960, v27, p101.
Commonweal. Nov 25, 1960, v73, p232.
Film Daily. Oct 28, 1960, p6.
Filmfacts. 1960, v3, p289.
Films and Filming. Aug 1960, v6, p24-25.
Films in Review. Jan 1961, v12, p39.
Hollywood Reporter. Oct 18, 1960, p3.
The New York Times. Dec 8, 1960, p43.
Time. Dec 5, 1960, v76, p63-64.
Variety. Jun 29, 1960, p8.

A Violent Journey *See* The Fool Killer

The Violent Men (Also titled: Rough Company) (US; Maté, Rudolph; 1954)
America. Feb 5, 1955, v92, p49.
American Magazine. Jan 1955, v159, p10.
Farm Journal. Feb 1955, v79, p149.
Film Daily. Jan 10, 1955, p6.
Films and Filming. Mar 1955, v1, p20.
The Films of Barbara Stanwyck. p236-38.
Hollywood Reporter. Dec 22, 1954, p3.
Motion Picture Herald Product Digest. Dec 25, 1954, p258.
National Parent-Teacher. Feb 1955, v49, p40.
The New York Times. Jan 27, 1955, p17.
Newsweek. Feb 7, 1955, v45, p74.
Starring Miss Barbara Stanwyck. p255.
Time. Jan 24, 1955, v65, p75.
Variety. Dec 22, 1954, p6.

The Virgin and the Gypsy (GB; Miles, Christopher; 1970)
BFI/Monthly Film Bulletin. Aug 1970, v37, p161-62.
The English Novel and the Movies. p257-67.
The Great British Films. p244-46.
Hollywood Reporter. Jun 9, 1970, p3,.
Magill's Survey of Cinema. Series II. v6, p2619.
The New Republic. Aug 1, 1970, v163, p24.
The New York Times. Jul 1970, p50.
The New Yorker. Jul 4, 1970, v46, p71.

Newsweek. Jul 13, 1970, v76, p92.
Saturday Review. Jul 25, 1970, v53, p37.
Sight and Sound. Aut 1970, v39, p220-21.
Time. Jul 13, 1970, v96, p72.
Variety. Jul 17, 1970, p22.

The Virgin Spring (Swedish title: Jungfrukallen) (SWED; Bergman, Ingmar; 1960)
Bergman on Bergman. p120-23.
Catholic World. Oct 1961, v194, p18-19.
Christian Century. Apr 5, 1961, v78, p424-25.
Cinema Borealis. p187-95.
Cinema Eye, Cinema Ear. p164-65.
Commonweal. Nov 25, 1960, v73, p231.
Dictionary of Films. p170-71.
Esquire. Mar 1961, v55, p30.
Film Daily. Nov 15, 1960, p10.
Film Heritage. Wint 1966-67, v2, p2-20.
Film Quarterly. Sum 1960, v13, p43-47.
Filmfacts. 1960, v3, p277.
Films and Filming. Jul 1961, v7, p26-27.
Films in Review. Nov 1960, v11, p556-57.
Ingmar Bergman: A Critical Biography. p89-95.
Ingmar Bergman: Essays in Criticism. p215-25.
McCall's. Feb 1961, v88, p167.
The Nation. Dec 10, 1960, v191, p464.
The New Republic. Dec 5, 1960, v143, p21-22.
The New York Times. Nov 15, 1960, p46.
The New York Times. Nov 20, 1960, SecII, p1.
The New Yorker. Nov 19, 1960, v36, p152.
Newsweek. Nov 21, 1960, v56, p106.
Renaissance of the Film. p324-29.
Saturday Review. Nov 12, 1960, v43, p87.
Time. Dec 5, 1960, v76, p63.
Variety. Feb 24, 1960, p6.
A World on Film. p277-79.

Viridiana (SP, MEX; Buñuel, Luis; 1961)
BFI/Monthly Film Bulletin. May 1962, v29, p65.
Christian Century. Oct 17, 1962, v79, p1259.
Cinema. 1963, n3, p33.
Commonweal. Apr 13, 1962, v76, p65.
Confessions of a Cultist. p53-60.
Dictionary of Films. p404.
The Discreet Art of Luis Bunuel. p141-68.
Film. Aut 1962, n33, p20-21.
Film as Film: Critical Responses to Film Art. p380-94.
Film Culture. Sep 1962, n24, p76-82.
Film Heritage. n2, 1961/62, v15, p55-56.
Film Quarterly. Wint 1961-62, v15, p55-56.
Filmfacts. May 11, 1962, v5, p83-84.
Films and Filming. Jun 1962, v8, p32.
Films in Review. Feb 1962, v13, p110-11.
The Great Movies. p184-87.
Hollywood Reporter. Aug 24, 1962, p3.
The International Dictionary of Films and Filmmakers. v1, p507-08.
Luis Bunuel (Aranda). p190-205.
Luis Bunuel (Higginbotham). p110-18.
Luis Bunuel (Kyrou). p77-99.
Magill's Survey of Cinema. Foreign Language Series. 1985, v7, p3295-99.
Movie. Jun 1962, n1, p14-16.
Movietone News. Feb 1975, n39, p11-13.
The Nation. Apr 14, 1962, v194, p339.
The New Republic. Apr 9, 1962, v146, p25.
The New York Times. Mar 20, 1962, p43.
The New Yorker. Mar 24, 1962, v38, p147-48.
Newsweek. Mar 26, 1962, v59, p96.
Renaissance of the Film. 330-39.
Reruns. p150-54.
Saturday Review. Feb 17, 1962, v45, p37.
Studies in the Literary Imagination. 1983, v16, n1, p7-27.
The Thousand Eyes Magazine. Feb 1976, n7, p7.

Time. Mar 30, 1962, v79, p83.
Variety. May 24, 1961, p6.
The Village Voice. Mar 22, 1962, p10.
The World of Luis Bunuel. p216-43.
A World on Film. p350-51.

The Virtuous Isidore *See* The Prize

The Visit (German title: Besuch, Der) (WGER, FR, IT, US; Wicki, Bernhard; 1964)
America. Oct 31, 1964, v111, p533.
BFI/Monthly Film Bulletin. Oct 1965, v32, p146.
Commonweal. Oct 2, 1964, v81, p43.
Film Daily. Sep 10, 1964, v125, p6.
Films and Filming. Oct 1965, v12, p30.
Films in Review. Aug-Sep 1964, v15, p445-46.
Hollywood Reporter. Sep 10, 1964, v182, p3.
Life. Oct 9, 1964, v57, p19.
Look. Jun 16, 1964, v28, p52-59.
Motion Picture Herald Product Digest. Sep 16, 1964, v232, p129.
The New York Times. Oct 22, 1964, p44.
The New Yorker. Oct 31, 1964, v40, p135-36.
Newsweek. Oct 19, 1964, v64, p109A.
Saturday Review. Nov 21, 1964, v47, p34.
Variety. May 13, 1964, p6.

Viskningar och rop *See* Cries and Whispers

Vitelloni, I (Also titled: The Wastrels; The Young and the Passionate) (IT; Fellini, Federico; 1953)
Cinema Texas Program Notes. Apr 11, 1978, v14, p67-73.
Film Culture. 1956, v2, p24-25.
Film Daily. Oct 15, 1956, p6.
Film Society Review. May 1970, v5, p42-45.
Films and Filming. Dec 1954, v1, p21.
Films in Review. Dec 1956, v7, p527-28.
The International Dictionary of Film and Filmmaking. v1, p508-10.
Literature/Film Quarterly. 1980, v8, p116-24.
The New York Times. Oct 24, 1956, p43.
The New Yorker. Nov 3, 1956, v32, p175.
Newsweek. Nov 12, 1956, v48, p130.
Saturday Review. Nov 10, 1956, v39, p28-29.
Screen. 1981, v22, p55-78.
Time. Nov 5, 1956, v68, p110.
Variety. Oct 14, 1953, p24.
Variety. Nov 14, 1956, p6.

Viva Las Vegas (Also titled: Love in Las Vegas) (US; Sidney, George; 1964)
BFI/Monthly Film Bulletin. May 1964, v31, p75.
Film Daily. May 25, 1964, v124, p10.
The Films and Career of Elvis Presley. p150-56.
Films and Filming. Apr 1964, v10, p31.
Hollywood Reporter. May 18, 1964, v180, p3.
Motion Picture Herald Product Digest. May 27, 1964, v231, p57.
The New York Times. May 21, 1964, p42.
Time. May 29, 1964, v83, p86.
Variety. May 20, 1964, p20.

Viva Maria (FR, IT; Malle, Louis; 1965)
America. Feb 5, 1966, v114, p209.
BFI/Monthly Film Bulletin. Mar 1966, v33, p39-40.
Cahiers du Cinema in English. Dec 1966, n6, p53-54.
Christian Science Monitor (Western edition). Jan 25, 1966, p4.
Cinema. Mar 1966, v3, p48.
Cinema. Mar 1966, v3, p48.
Commonweal. Jan 21, 1966, v83, p478.
Film Daily. Dec 21, 1965, p5.
Film Quarterly. Spr 1966, v19, p54.
Films and Filming. Mar 1965, v11, p6.
Films and Filming. Apr 1966, v12, p6.

Films and Filming. Jul 1965, v11, p52-53.
Films in Review. Jan 1966, v17, p46-47.
International Film Guide. 1967, v4, p70.
Life. Jan 28, 1966, v60, p8.
The London Times. Jan 15, 1966, p5.
The London Times. Apr 7, 1966, p16.
Look. May 4, 1965, v29, p64-66.
Motion Picture Herald Product Digest. Jan 5, 1966, p434-35.
The Nation. Jan 3, 1966, v202, p27-28.
New Statesman. Apr 8, 1966, v71, p512.
The New York Times. Dec 20, 1965, p48.
The New Yorker. Dec 25, 1965, v41, p56, 58.
Newsweek. Jan 3, 1966, v67, p56.
Playboy. Mar 1966, v13, p22-23.
Sight and Sound. Spr 1966, v35, p90-91.
The Spectator. Apr 15, 1966, v216, p469.
Time. Dec 31, 1965, v86 p77.
Variety. Dec 8, 1965, p6.
The Village Voice. Jan 6, 1966, v11, p23.
Vogue. Feb 1, 1966, v147, p100.

Viva Zapata! (US; Kazan, Elia; 1952)
American History/American Film. p183-201.
BFI/Monthly Film Bulletin. Apr 1952, v19, p48.
Catholic World. Mar 1952, v174, p459.
Christian Century. Apr 23, 1952, v69, p510.
Cineaste. 1976, v7, n2, p10-17.
Cinema, the Magic Vehicle. v2, p132-34.
Commonweal. Feb 29, 1952, v55, p517.
Cue. Feb 9, 1952, p16.
Dictionary of Films. p406.
Elia Kazan: A Guide to References and Resources. p10.
Film Criticism and Caricatures, 1943-1953. p141-42.
Film Daily. Feb 6, 1952, p6.
The Films of Anthony Quinn. p122-23.
The Films of Marlon Brando. p46-53.
High Fidelity. Feb 1978, v28, p102.
Holiday. May 1952, v11, p105.
Hollywood Reporter. Feb 6, 1952, p3.
Illustrated London News. Apr 19, 1952, v220, p676.
Kazan on Kazan. p88-99.
Kiss Kiss Bang Bang. p462.
The Latin Image in American Film. p94-97.
Library Journal. Feb 15, 1952, v77, p311.
Life. Feb 25, 1952, v32, p59-61.
Literature/Film Quarterly. 1975, v3, n3, p282-83.
The London Times. Mar 31, 1952, p2.
Magill's Survey of Cinema. Series I. v4, p1812-15.
Motion Picture Herald Product Digest. Feb 9, 1952, p1229.
Movie. Wint 1971-72, n19, p6.
The New Republic. Feb 25, 1952, v126, p21.
The New Statesman and Nation. Apr 5, 1952, v43, p402.
The New York Times. Feb 8, 1952, p19.
The New Yorker. Feb 16, 1952, v27, p105.
Newsweek. Feb 4, 1952, v39, p78.
Saturday Review. Feb 9, 1952, v35, p25.
Saturday Review. Feb 16, 1952, v35, p6.
Saturday Review. Mar 1, 1952, v35, p6.
Saturday Review. Apr 5, 1952, v35, p22.
Saturday Review. May 24, 1952, v35, 25.
Selected Film Criticism, 1951-1960. p145-46.
Senior Scholastic. Mar 5, 1952, v60, p26.
Sight and Sound. Apr-Jun 1952, v21, p170.
The Spectator. Mar 28, 1952, v188, p397.
Steinbeck and Film. p121-36.
The Tatler. Apr 9, 1952, v204, p82.
Time. Feb 11, 1952, v59, p92.
Variety. Feb 6, 1952, p6.

Viva Zapata: The Original Screenplay. pxi-xxxviii.
Washington Post. Feb 23, 1952, p8.

Vivement Dimanche *See* Confidentially Yours

Vivre *See* Ikiru

Vivre Enfin *See* Ikiru

Vivre pour Vivre *See* Live for Life

Voina i Mir *See* War and Peace

Volver a Empezar (Also titled: To Begin Again) (SP; Garci, Jose Luis; 1982)
Christian Century. Sep 14, 1983, v100, p816.
Hollywood Reporter. Mar 29, 1983, p3.
The Los Angeles Times. Apr 1, 1983, VI, p1.
Magill's Cinema Annual, 1983. p393-96.
The New York Times. Apr 22, 1983, p24.
The New York Times. Apr 22, 1983, SecIII, p10.
Variety. Apr 14, 1982, p18.
Variety. Apr 27, 1983, p32.
The Village Voice. May 10, 1983, p52.

Von Ryan's Express (US; Robson, Mark; 1965)
America. Jun 19, 1965, v112, p888.
BFI/Monthly Film Bulletin. Aug 1965, v32, p121.
Cinema. Jul-Aug 1965, v2, p49-50.
Film Daily. May 19, 1965, p14.
Film Quarterly. Sum 1966, v19, p29-31.
Films and Filming. Aug 1965, v11, p24.
The Films of Frank Sinatra. p205-07.
Hollywood Reporter. May 18, 1965, p3.
Life. Jul 23, 1965, v59, p16.
The London Times. Jul 1, 1965, p17.
Motion Picture Herald Product Digest. May 26, 1965, p289.
New Statesman. Jul 2, 1965, v70, p23.
The New York Times. Jun 24, 1965, p28.
The New Yorker. Jul 17, 1965, v41, p59-60.
Newsweek. Jul 12, 1965, v66, p90D-90E.
Playboy. Jul 1965, v12, p32.
Saturday Review. Jul 17, 1965, v48, p24.
Time. Jun 25, 1965, v85, p104.
Variety. May 19, 1965, p6.

Voyage of the Damned (GB, US; Rosenberg, Stuart; 1976)
Before My Eyes. p270.
BFI/Monthly Film Bulletin. Dec 1977, v44, p265.
Film Bulletin. Nov-Dec 1976, v45, p440-41.
Films and Filming. Jul 1976, v22, p16-17.
Films Illustrated. Apr 1976, v5, p304-06.
Films in Review. Jan 1977, v28, p57.
Hollywood Reporter. Nov 29, 1976, p3.
The Los Angeles Times. Dec 24, 1976, SecIV, p1.
Motion Picture Herald Product Digest. Dec 8, 1977, p55.
The New Republic. Dec 18, 1976, v175, p20.
The New York Times. Dec 23, 1976, p18.
Newsweek. Dec 27, 1976, v88, p57.
Time. Jan 10, 1977, v109, p67.
Variety. Dec 1, 1976, p18.
Vogue. Jan 1977, v167, p36.

Voyou, Le (The Hoodlum) *See* The Crook

Vsichni Dobri Rodaci *See* All My Good Countrymen

W.C. Fields and Me (US; Hiller, Arthur; 1976)
BFI/Monthly Film Bulletin. Jun 1976, v43, p132.
Film Bulletin. Apr 1976, v45, pD.
Films and Filming. Nov 1976, v23, p33-34.

Films in Review. May 1976, v27, p312-13.
Hollywood Reporter. Mar 29, 1976, p3.
Independent Film Journal. Mar 31, 1976, v77, p9-10.
The Los Angeles Times. Apr 1, 1976, SecIV, p1.
Millimeter. May 1976, v4, p28-30.
Motion Picture Herald Product Digest. Mar 24, 1976, p81.
The New Republic. Apr 3, 1976, v174, p22-23.
New York. Apr 5, 1976, v9, p80.
The New York Times. Apr 4, 1976, SecII, p19.
The New Yorker. Apr 12, 1976, v52, p114.
Newsweek. Apr 12, 1976, v87, p94.
Saturday Review. Apr 17, 1976, v3, p47.
Time. Apr 5, 1976, v107, p80.
Variety. Mar 31, 1976, p15.
Vogue. May 1976, v166, p92.

WR-Mysteries of the Organism (Also titled: WR-Misterije Organizma) (YUGO; Makavejev, Dusan; 1971)
BFI/Monthly Film Bulletin. Jan 1972, v39, p19.
Cineaste. Wint 1971-72, v5, n1, p18-21.
Film Journal. Sep 1972, v11, n1, p62-63.
Film Quarterly. Spr 1972, v25, n3, p2-13.
Film Society Review. Nov 1971, v7, n3, p20-21.
Filmfacts. 1971, v14, p608-10.
Films and Filming. May 1972, v18, n8, p56.
Interview. Feb 1972, v19, p37.
The New Republic. Nov 20, 1971, v165, p28.
The New York Times. May 24, 1971, p26.
The New York Times. Oct 14, 1971, p52.
The New York Times. Nov 7, 1971, SecII, p9.
Newsweek. Nov 1, 1971, v78, p90.
Self and Cinema. p345.
Take One. Jun 1972, v3, n4, p32-33.
Variety. Jun 9, 1971, p22.
The Village Voice. Nov 11, 1971, p47.
Women and their Sexuality in the New Film. p179-90.

The Wages of Fear (French title: Salaire de la Peur, Le) (FR, IT; Clouzot, Henri-Georges; 1953)
BFI/Monthly Film Bulletin. Apr 1954, v21, p54.
Catholic World. Mar 1955, v180, p462-63.
Cinema, the Magic Vehicle. v2, p156-57.
Commonweal. Mar 11, 1955, v61, p604.
Dictionary of Films. p323.
Film Culture. May-Jun 1955, v1, p3-7, 23.
Film Daily. Feb 24, 1955, p10.
Films and Filming. Jun 1965, v11, p34.
Films and Filming. Jan 1986, v32, p42.
Films in Review. Feb 1955, v6, p85.
The Great French Films. p151-54.
Hollywood Reporter. Oct 27, 1955, p3.
Illustrated London News. Mar 6, 1954, v224, p370.
Life. Mar 14, 1955, v38, p63-66.
The London Times. Feb 11, 1954, p3.
The London Times. Nov 30, 1956, p5.
Magic Moments From the Movies. p179-81.
Magill's Survey of Cinema. Foreign Language Films. v7, p3317-20.
Motion Picture Herald Product Digest. Mar 19, 1955, p362.
The Nation. Feb 5, 1955, v180, p126.
The Nation. Aug 6, 1955, v181, p109-10.
National Parent-Teacher. Apr 1955, v49, p40.
The New Statesman and Nation. Feb 20, 1954, v47, p222.
The New York Times. Feb 17, 1955, p23.
The New York Times Magazine. Jan 9, 1955, p49.
The New Yorker. May 16, 1953, v29, p96.
The New Yorker. Feb 26, 1955, v31, p88.
Newsweek. Feb 28, 1955, v45, p88.
Saturday Review. Feb 5, 1955, v38, p25.

Sight and Sound. Apr-Jun 1954, v23, p197-98.
The Spectator. Feb 12, 1954, v192, p173.
The Tatler. Feb 24, 1954, v211, p318.
Time. Feb 21, 1955, v65, p82.
Variety. Apr 29, 1953, p18.
Variety. Jan 16, 1985, p40.
Variety. May 26, 1954, p6.
The Village Voice. Mar 21, 1956, v1, p6, 9.
The Village Voice. May 25, 1967, v12, p31.

The Wages of Fear (Friedkin, 1977) *See* Sorcerer

Wagonmaster (US; Ford, John; 1950)
BFI/Monthly Film Bulletin. Oct 1950, v17, p151-52.
Christian Century. Jun 14, 1950, v67, p743.
Cinema, the Magic Vehicle. v2, p62-63.
Commonweal. May 19, 1950, v52, p151.
Film Daily. Apr 10, 1950, p6.
The Filming of the West. p531-33.
The Great Western Pictures. p385-86.
Hollywood Reporter. Apr 5, 1950, p3.
Magill's Survey of Cinema. Series II. v6, p2625-29.
Motion Picture Herald Product Digest. Apr 8, 1950, p254.
The New Statesman and Nation. Oct 7, 1950, v40, p347.
The New York Times. Jun 19, 1950, p17.
The New Yorker. Jul 1, 1950, v26, p49.
Sequence. New Year 1951, n13, p17.
Sight and Sound. Dec 1950, v19, p333-34.
Variety. Apr 12, 1950, p22.
The Western Films of John Ford. p128-45.

Wait Till the Sun Shines, Nellie (US; King, Henry; 1952)
BFI/Monthly Film Bulletin. Jul 1952, v19, p98.
Film Daily. May 27, 1952, p6.
Hollywood Reporter. May 26, 1952, p3.
Motion Picture Herald Product Digest. May 31, 1952, p1381.
The New York Times. Jun 28, 1952, p12.
The New Yorker. Jul 5, 1952, v28, p51.
Newsweek. Jun 23, 1952, v39, p92.
Time. Jul 21, 1952, v60, p99.
Variety. May 28, 1952, p6.

Wait Until Dark (US; Young, Terence; 1967)
America. Dec 9, 1967, v117, p723.
BFI/Monthly Film Bulletin. Aug 1968, v35, p123-24.
Film Daily. Oct 24, 1967, p5.
Film Quarterly. Spr 1968, v21, p63.
Films and Filming. Aug 1968, v14, p33.
Films in Review. Dec 1967, v18, p644-45.
Hollywood Reporter. Oct 20, 1967, p3.
Magill's Survey of Cinema. Series II. v6, p2630-32.
Motion Picture Herald Product Digest. Oct 25, 1967, p733.
The New York Times. Oct 27, 1967, p48.
Newsweek. Nov 6, 1967, v70, p93-94.
Senior Scholastic. Oct 19, 1967, v91, p21.
Variety. Oct 25, 1967, p6.
The Village Voice. Nov 2, 1967, p33, 40.

Waiting Women *See* Secrets of Women

Walk, Don't Run (US; Walters, Charles; 1966)
America. Sep 17, 1966, v115, p297.
BFI/Monthly Film Bulletin. Sep 1966, v33, p140.
Christian Science Monitor (Western edition). Aug 12, 1966, p6.
Film Daily. Jun 28, 1966, p7.
Filmfacts. Oct 15, 1966, v9, p227-28.
Films and Filming. Sep 1966, v12, p6-7.
Films in Review. Aug-Sep 1966, v17, p453.

The Films of Cary Grant. p266-69.
Hollywood Reporter. Jun 27, 1966, p3.
Life. Aug 19, 1966, v61, p11.
The London Times. Jul 21, 1966, p17.
Motion Picture Herald Product Digest. Jul 6, 1966, p553.
New Statesman. Jul 22, 1966, v72, p140-41.
The New York Times. Aug 25, 1966, p42.
The New Yorker. Sep 3, 1966, v42, p71.
Newsweek. Jul 25, 1966, v68, p89.
Playboy. Oct 1966, v13, p25-26.
Saturday Review. Sep 3, 1966, v49, p38.
Time. Jul 15, 1966, v88, p81.
Variety. Jun 29, 1966, p6.

Walk East on Beacon (US; Werker, Alfred L.; 1952)
Catholic World. May 1952, v175, p143.
Christian Century. Jul 30, 1952, v69, p887.
Commonweal. Jun 6, 1952, v56, p225.
Film Daily. Apr 29, 1952, p6.
Hollywood Reporter. Apr 30, 1952, p3.
Jump Cut. Oct-Dec 1975, n9, p14-16.
Library Journal. May 1, 1952, v77, p785.
Motion Picture Herald Product Digest. Apr 26, 1952, p1329.
The Nation. Jun 21, 1952, v174, p609-10.
The New York Times. May 29, 1952, p17.
The New Yorker. Jun 7, 1952, v28, p124.
Newsweek. Apr 21, 1952, v39, p121.
A Reference Guide to the American Film Noir. p213.
Saturday Review. Apr 19, 1952, v35, p46.
Theatre Arts. May 1952, v36, p104.
Time. May 26, 1952, v59, p103.
Variety. Apr 30, 1952, p6.

Walk Like a Dragon (US; Clavell, James; 1960)
BFI/Monthly Film Bulletin. Oct 1960, v27, p140.
Commonweal. Jun 17, 1960, v72, p305.
Film Daily. Jun 2, 1960, p7.
Filmfacts. 1960, v3, p189.
Hollywood Reporter. Jun 2, 1960, p3.
The New York Times. Sep 16, 1960, p24.
Variety. Jun 8, 1960, p6.

Walk on the Wild Side (US; Dmytryk, Edward; 1962)
America. Jul 2, 1962, v107, p360.
Cinema. 1963, v1, p33.
Commonweal. Mar 2, 1962, v75, p599.
Film. Sum 1962, n32, p20.
Film Daily. Jan 29, 1962, p4.
Filmfacts. Apr 6, 1962, v5, p57-58.
Films and Filming. Apr 1962, v8, p32.
Films in Review. Mar 1962, v13, p171-72.
The Films of Jane Fonda. p78-82.
Hollywood Reporter. Jan 29, 1962, p3.
Motion Picture Herald Product Digest. Feb 7, 1962, p436.
The New Republic. Jul 30, 1962, v147, p30.
The New York Times. Feb 22, 1962, p20.
The New Yorker. Feb 24, 1962, v38, p111.
Newsweek. Mar 5, 1962, v59, p84.
Saturday Review. Jul 28, 1962, v45, p31.
Starring Miss Barbara Stanwyck. p280.
Time. Feb 23, 1962, v79, p102.
Variety. Jan 31, 1962, p6.
The Village Voice. Feb 1, 1962, p11.

Walk Softly, Stranger (US; Stevenson, Robert; 1950)
BFI/Monthly Film Bulletin. Feb 1951, v18, p221-22.
Film Daily. Aug 29, 1950, p6.
Hollywood Reporter. Aug 23, 1950, p3.
The London Times. Jan 15, 1951, p6.

Motion Picture Herald Product Digest. Sep 2, 1950, p458.
The New York Times. Oct 16, 1950, p30.
Newsweek. Oct 23, 1950, v36, p98.
Time. Oct 30, 1950, v56, p98.
Variety. Aug 23, 1950, p8.

Walkabout (GB; Roeg, Nicolas; 1971)
America. Jul 24, 1971, v95, p48.
BFI/Monthly Film Bulletin. 1971, v38, p227.
Cinema. Fall 1971, v7, n1, p8-12.
Esquire. Aug 1971, v76, p42.
Filmfacts. 1971, v14, p250.
Films and Filming. Dec 1971, v18, n3, p53.
Hollywood Reporter. May 17, 1971, v216, n14, p3.
Life. Jun 4, 1971, v70, p16.
National Review. Oct 24, 1975, v27, p1179-80.
The New Republic. Jul 3, 1971, v, p34.
The New York Times. Jul 2, 1971, p26.
The New York Times. Jul 18, 1971, SecII, p1.
The New York Times. Sep 12, 1971, SecII, p15.
The New Yorker. Jul 10, 1971, v47, p55.
Nicholas Roeg (Feinemann). p113.
Saturday Review. Jun 5, 1971, v54, p12.
Self and Cinema. p345.
Sight and Sound. Wint 1971-72, v41, n1, p48.
Time. Jun 28, 1971, v97, p77.
Variety. May 19, 1971, p17.
The Village Voice. May 20, 1971, p66.

Walkers on Tigers' Tails *See* Tora-no-o

The Walls of Malapaga *See* Au-Dela des Grilles

Waltz of the Toreadors (GB; Guillermin, John; 1962)
BFI/Monthly Film Bulletin. May 1962, v29, p65-66.
Commonweal. Sep 7, 1962, v76, p497.
Film Daily. Aug 13, 1962, p10.
Filmfacts. Sep 7, 1962, v5, p189-91.
Films and Filming. May 1962, v8, p34.
Films in Review. Oct 1962, v13, p485-86.
Hollywood Reporter. Sep 27, 1962, p3.
Motion Picture Herald Product Digest. Sep 5, 1962, p649.
The New York Times. Aug 14, 1962, p34.
The New Yorker. Aug 25, 1962, v38, p67.
Newsweek. Aug 20, 1962, v60, p86.
Time. Aug 17, 1962, v80, p75.
Variety. May 18, 1962, p6.

Wanda Nevada (US; Fonda, Peter; 1979)
The Films of Henry Fonda. p249.
Hollywood Reporter. May 25, 1979, p3.
The Los Angeles Times. Sep 5, 1979, SecIV, p16.
Variety. May 30, 1979, p16.

The Wanton *See* Meneges

The Wanton Countess *See* Senso

War and Peace (US, IT; Vidor, King; 1956)
America. Sep 1, 1956, v95, p512.
Commonweal. Sep 14, 1956, v64, p587.
Film Comment. Sep-Oct 1973, v9, p16-15.
Film Daily. Aug 22, 1956, p7.
Films and Filming. Mar 1956, v2, p8-9.
Films and Filming. Nov 1956, v3, p13.
Films and Filming. Dec 1956, v3, p21-22.
Films in Review. Aug-Sep 1956, v7, p314-16.
Films in Review. Oct 1956, v7, p408-09.
The Films of Henry Fonda. p147-49.
The Fondas (Springer). p155-58.
The Great Adventure Films. p204-11.
Hollywood Reporter. Aug 22, 1956, p3.
Magill's Survey of Cinema. Series II. v6, p2636-39.
The New York Times. Aug 22, 1956, p26.
The New Yorker. Sep 1, 1956, v32, p55.

Newsweek. Jul 30, 1956, v48, p53-56.
Newsweek. Sep 3, 1956, v48, p88.
Saturday Review. Sep 8, 1956, v39, p32-33.
Sight and Sound. Wint 1956-57, v26, p152.
Time. Sep 10, 1956, v68, p116.
Variety. Aug 22, 1956, p6.
A Year In the Dark. p131-33.

War and Peace (Russian title: Voina i Mir)
(USSR; Bondarchuk, Sergei; 1963-67)
America. May 18, 1968, v118, p679-81.
BFI/Monthly Film Bulletin. Mar 1969, v36,
p54-55.
Christian Century. Oct 2, 1968, v36, p54-55.
Christian Science Monitor (Western edition).
Apr 29, 1968, p4.
Classic Movies. p141-44.
Commonweal. May 24, 1968, v88, p300.
Dictionary of Films. p407.
Film 68/69. p216-22.
Film Daily. Apr 29, 1968, p4.
Film Heritage. Spr 1969, v4, p11-16, p25-26.
Filmfacts. Jun 1, 1968, v11, p127-31.
Films and Filming. May 1969, v15, p60-63.
Films and Filming. Jun 1969, v15, p47, 50.
Films in Review. Jun-Jul 1968, v19, p373-75.
Harper's Magazine. Jul 1968, v237, p110.
Hollywood Reporter. Apr 29, 1968, p3, 15.
*The International Dictionary of Films and
Filmmakers.* v1, p511-12.
International Film Guide. 1967, v4, p166-67.
International Film Guide. 1968, v5, p159.
Life. Jun 14, 1968, v64, p20.
London Magazine. Mar 1969, v8, p57-64.
The London Times. Jan 23, 1969, p7.
Look. Jul 9, 1968, v32, pT4.
*Magill's Survey of Cinema. Foreign Language
Films.* v7, p3325-28.
Motion Picture Herald Product Digest. May 8,
1968, p807.
Movies Into Film. p38-41.
The Nation. May 13, 1968, v206, p645-46.
The New Republic. May 18, 1968, v158, p24.
New Society. Jan 23, 1969, p136.
The New York Times. Oct 24, 1967, p27.
The New York Times. Apr 29, 1968, p50.
The New Yorker. May 4, 1968, v44, p163-64.
Newsweek. May 6, 1968, v71, p120.
Observer. Feb 9, 1969, p35.
Redbook. Jul 1968, v131, p34.
Saturday Review. May 11, 1968, v51, p56-57.
Second Sight. p191-93.
Senior Scholastic. Nov 15, 1968, v93, p26-27.
Sight and Sound. Spr 1969, v38, p97-98.
The Spectator. Jan 31, 1969, v222, p147.
Take One. Jun 1968, v1, p28-29.
Time. May 3, 1968, v91, p80.
Variety. Jul 28, 1965, p6.
Variety. May 10, 1967, p6.
Variety. Feb 14, 1968, p16.
Variety. May 1, 1968, p6.
Vogue. Jul 1968, v152, p20.
A Year in the Dark. p131-32.

The War Game (GB; Watkins, Peter; 1962)
Afterimage. Apr 1984, v11, p5-10.
America. May 6, 1967, v116, p703.
American Film. Oct 1982, v8, p64.
BFI/Monthly Film Bulletin. Mar 1964, v31,
p46.
Dictionary of Films. p412.
Esquire. Jul 1967, v68, p14.
Esquire. Nov 1967, v68, p52.
Film 67/68. p122-25.
Film Comment. Fall 1965, v3, p2-19.
Film Quarterly. Fall 1967, v21, p45-47.
Film Society Review. Jan 1968, p10-12.
Filmfacts. May 15, 1967, v10, p90-91.
Films and Filming. Jun 1966, v12, p62-63.

Independent. Oct 1984, v7, p22-24.
Journal of Popular Film. 1973, v2, n2, p201-03.
Journal of Popular Film. 1983, v11, n1, p25-41.
Life. Apr 7, 1967, v62, p20.
The London Times. Sep 23, 1964, p6.
The Nation. Sep 26, 1966, v203, p269.
The New Documentary in Action. p151-63.
The New Republic. May 13, 1967, v156, p32-34.
New Statesman. Apr 28, 1967, v73, p592.
New Statesman. Aug 9, 1985, v110, p13-14.
New Statesman. Aug 16, 1985, v110, p32.
The New York Times. Mar 20, 1967, p26.
The New Yorker. Apr 1, 1967, v43, p94.
Newsweek. Apr 3, 1967, v69, p89A.
Nuclear War Films. 109-15.
On Film. p340-42.
Playboy. Jul 1967, v14, p30.
Private Screenings. p280-81.
Quarterly Review of Film Studies. 1980, v5, n4,
p501-18.
Second Sight. p102-04.
Senior Scholastic. Oct 28, 1966, v89, p26.
Sight and Sound. Spr 1966, v35, p92-93.
Take One. Jun 1967, v1, p31-32.
Tynan Right and Left. p254-55.
Variety. Sep 7, 1966, p18.
Variety. Aug 7, 1985, p58.
The Village Voice. May 5, 1966, v11, p13.
The Village Voice. Mar 23, 1967, v12, p25.
Vision. 1979, v4, n1, p5-7.

War Hunt (US; Sanders, Denis; 1962)
BFI/Monthly Film Bulletin. Oct 1963, v30,
p144.
Commonweal. Jun 22, 1962, v76, p330.
Film Daily. Apr 2, 1962, p7.
Film Quarterly. Sum 1962, v15, p53-55.
Filmfacts. Oct 26, 1962, v5, p237-38.
Films and Filming. Nov 1963, v10, p25.
The Films of Robert Redford. p67-72.
Hollywood Reporter. Mar 7, 1962, v169, p3.
Motion Picture Herald Product Digest. Apr 4,
1962, p500.
The Nation. Aug 25, 1962, v195, p80.
The New York Times. Aug 8, 1962, p35.
The New Yorker. Aug 18, 1962, v38, p68.
Newsweek. Aug 20, 1962, v60, p86.
Time. Aug 3, 1962, v80, p36a-36b.
Variety. Mar 14, 1962, p6.

The War Lord (Also titled: Seigneur de la
Guerre, Le) (US; Schaffner, Franklin
J.; 1965)
BFI/Monthly Film Bulletin. Jan 1966, v33, p5.
Cahiers du Cinema in English. 1966, n4, p62.
Cinema. Dec 1965, v3, p49.
Commonweal. Dec 10, 1965, v83, p315.
Film Daily. Oct 5, 1965, p4.
Film Quarterly. Spr 1966, v19, p54.
Films and Filming. Feb 1966, v12, p6.
Films and Filming. Jan 1966, v12, p10.
Films in Review. Nov 1965, v16, p583.
The Films of Charlton Heston. p150-53.
Hollywood Reporter. Oct 4, 1965, p3.
The London Times. Dec 16, 1965, p4.
Motion Picture Herald Product Digest. Oct 13,
1965, p386.
New Statesman. Jan 7, 1966, v71, p24.
The New York Times. Nov 18, 1965, p55.
The New Yorker. Dec 4, 1965, v41, p112.
Newsweek. Dec 6, 1965, v66, p106.
Sight and Sound. Spr 1966, v35, p73-75.
The Spectator. Dec 24, 1965, v215, p842.
Time. Nov 26, 1965, v86, p103.
Variety. Oct 6, 1965, p6.
The Village Voice. Dec 23, 1965, v11, p23.

The War Lover (GB; Leacock, Philip; 1962)
BFI/Monthly Film Bulletin. Jul 1963, v30,
p104.

Film Daily. Oct 25, 1962, p6.
Filmfacts. Mar 7, 1963, v6, p20-21.
The Films of Steve McQueen. p61-65.
Hollywood Reporter. Oct 24, 1962, p3.
Motion Picture Herald Product Digest. Oct 31,
1962, p681-82.
Variety. Oct 24, 1962, p6.

War of the Worlds (US; Haskin, Byron;
1953)
America. Aug 29, 1953, v89, p526.
BFI/Monthly Film Bulletin. May 1953, v20,
n232, p70.
Collier's. Oct 4, 1953, v130, p50-51.
Film Daily. Mar 9, 1953, p7.
Films in Review. May 1953, v4, n5, p241.
Hollywood Reporter. Mar 2, 1953, p3.
Library Journal. Jun 1, 1953, v78, p985.
Look. May 19, 1953, v17, p118-19.
Magill's Survey of Cinema. Series II. v6, p2639.
National Parent-Teacher. May 1953, v47, p38.
The New York Times. Aug 14, 1953, p10.
The New York Times. Aug 1953, SecII, p1.
Saturday Review. Sep 12, 1953, v36, p47.
Science Fiction Gold. p87-88.
Twenty All Time Great Science Fiction Films.
p90-102.
Variety. Mar 4, 1953, p18.

Wargames (US; Badham, John; 1983)
Christian Century. Jul 20, 1923, v100, p691.
Commonweal. Aug 12, 1983, v110, p433-34.
Commonweal. Sep 9, 1983, v110, p469-70.
Esquire. Jul 83, 1983, v100, p110-11.
Film Comment. Jul-Aug 1983, v19, p11.
Films in Review. Aug-Sep 1983, v35, p442.
Hollywood Reporter. May 9, 1983, p3.
Horizon. Sep 1983, v26, p14.
Humanist. Sep-Oct 1983, v43, p39-40.
Journal of Popular Film and Television. Spr
1983, v11, p25.
The Los Angeles Times. Jun 3, 1983, SecVI, p1.
Magill's Cinema Annual, 1983. p458-61.
The Nation. Jul 23, 1983, v237, p91-92.
The New Leader. Jun 27, 1983, v66, p22.
The New Republic. Jul 4, 1983, v189, p24.
New York. Jun 6, 1983, v16, p84-85.
The New York Times. Jun 3, 1983, SecIII, p17.
The New Yorker. Jun 13, 1983, v59, p121-22.
Newsweek. May 30, 1983, v101, p96.
Rolling Stone. Jun 23, 1983, p43.
Saturday Review. Jul-Aug 1983, v9, p38-39.
Time. May 30, 1983, v121, p74.

Warrendale (CAN; King, Allan; 1966)
Cinema. 1969, v5, n1, p45.
Figures of Light. p102-05.
Film 68/69. p190-93.
Film Comment. Fall 1969, v5, p60-61.
Film Quarterly. Wint 1967-68, v21, p52-54.
Filmfacts. Dec 15, 1968, v11, p375-77.
Films and Filming. Nov 1968, v15, p52, 54.
International Film Guide. 1968, v5, p53.
Life. Oct 18, 1968, v65, p16.
The London Times. Jan 13, 1968, p19.
The Nation. Sep 30, 1968, v207, p318.
The New Republic. Sep 21, 1968, v159, p24.
The New York Times. Sep 17, 1968, p50.
The New Yorker. Sep 21, 1968, v44, p148.
Newsweek. Sep 23, 1968, v72, p110.
Saturday Review. Sep 28, 1968, v51, p54.
Second Sight. p202-04.
Sight and Sound. Wint 1967-68, v37, p44-46.
Take One. n7, 1967, v1, p23.
Time. Sep 29, 1967, v90, p101.
Variety. May 3, 1967, p24.
The Village Voice. Sep 21, 1967, p29.

Washington Story (US; Pirosh, Robert;
1952)
Christian Century. Aug 27, 1952, v69, p983.

Commonweal. Jul 18, 1952, v56, p368.
Film Daily. Jul 7, 1952, p4.
Hollywood Reporter. Jun 27, 1952, p3.
Motion Picture Herald Product Digest. Jun 28, 1952, p1425.
National Parent-Teacher. Sep 1952, v47, p37.
The New York Times. Jul 2, 1952, p22.
The New Yorker. Jul 12, 1952, v28, p76.
Newsweek. Jul 14, 1952, v40, p90.
Saturday Review. Jul 19, 1952, v35, p29.
Saturday Review. Nov 1, 1952, v35, p27.
Theatre Arts. Aug 1952, v36, p35.
Time. Jul 14, 1952, v60, p94.
Variety. Jul 2, 1952, p6.

The Wastrels *See* Vitelloni, I

Waterloo (USSR; Bondarchuk, Sergei; 1971)
America. Apr 10, 1971, v124, p390-92.
Commonweal. May 14, 1971, v94, p238.
Filmfacts. 1971, v14, p70-73.
Films and Filming. Jan 1971, v17, n4, p48-49.
Films in Review. May 1971, v22, n5, p311-12.
Hollywood Reporter. Apr 1, 1971, v215, n32, p3.
National Review. May 4, 1971, v23, p489-90.
The New Republic. Jun 19, 1971, v164, p24.
The New York Times. Apr 1, 1971, p50.
The New Yorker. Apr 10, 1971, v47, p130.
Newsweek. Apr 19, 1971, v77, p126.
Saturday Review. Apr 17, 1971, v54, p53.
Time. Apr 19, 1971, v97, p70.
Variety. Nov 4, 1970, p16.

Watermelon Man (US; Van Peebles, Melvin; 1970)
America. Jun 6, 1970, v122, p618.
BFI/Monthly Film Bulletin. Sep 1970, v37, p191-92.
Esquire. Oct 1970, v74, p68.
Films and Filming. Sep 1970, v16, p63, 68.
From Sambo to Superspade. p245-46.
Hollywood Reporter. May 25, 1970, p3.
The New York Times. May 28, 1970, p33.
The New Yorker. Jun 6, 1970, v46, p85.
Newsweek. May 25, 1970, v75, p102.
Saturday Review. Jun 13, 1970, v53, p26.
Variety. Jun 3, 1970, p17.

The Way It Goes *See* A Tout Prendre

Way of a Gaucho (US; Tourneur, Jacques; 1952)
BFI/Monthly Film Bulletin. Jul 1953, v20, p111-12.
Film Daily. Oct 6, 1952, p6.
Hollywood Reporter. Oct 2, 1952, p3.
Library Journal. Nov 15, 1952, v77, p1981.
The London Times. Jul 27, 1953, p3.
Motion Picture Herald Product Digest. Oct 4, 1952, p1549.
National Parent-Teacher. Nov 1952, v47, p38.
The New Statesman and Nation. Jul 25, 1953, v46, p102.
The New York Times. Nov 5, 1952, p36.
Newsweek. Nov 3, 1952, v40, p104.
The Tatler. Aug 5, 1953, v209, p252.
Variety. Oct 8, 1952, p6.

Way . . . Way Out (US; Douglas, Gordon; 1966)
BFI/Monthly Film Bulletin. Jun 1967, v34, p97.
Christian Science Monitor (Western edition). May 27, 1966, p6.
Film Daily. Oct 18, 1966, p21.
Filmfacts. Dec 15, 1966, v9, p296-97.
Films and Filming. Jul 1967, v13, p26.
Hollywood Reporter. Oct 18, 1966, p3.
The London Times. Apr 27, 1967, p8.
Motion Picture Herald Product Digest. Oct 26, 1966, p622.

The New York Times. Oct 27, 1966, p55.
Variety. Oct 19, 1966, p6.

The Ways of Love (Italian title: Miracolo, Il; Also titled: The Miracle) (IT, FR; Rossellini, Roberto; Renoir, Jean; Pagnol, Marcel; 1950)
American Film. Jul-Aug 1977, v2, p26-32.
American Film. Jun 1977, v2, p26-32.
Commonweal. Jan 12, 1951, v53, p351.
Film Comment. Sum 1968, v4, p41-44.
Film Criticism and Caricatures, 1943-1953. p108-09.
Film Daily. Jan 4, 1951, p6.
Films in Review. May 1951, v2, p1-6.
Hollywood Reporter. Mar 1, 1951, p4.
Illustrated London News. Feb 18, 1950, v216, p268.
Italian Cinema (Bondanella). p103-04.
Italian Cinema (Leprohon). p117-18.
Library Journal. Mar 1, 1951, v76, p418.
Life. Jan 15, 1951, v30, p59-60.
Life and Letters. Mar 1950, v64, p173-74.
The London Times. Jan 27, 1950, p7.
The Nation. Jan 13, 1951, v172, p45.
The Nation. Feb 3, 1951, v172, p104-05.
The New Republic. Jan 1, 1951, v124, p23.
The New Statesman and Nation. Feb 4, 1950, v39, p129.
The New York Times. Dec 13, 1950, p50.
The New Yorker. Dec 16, 1950, v26, p64.
Newsweek. Dec 18, 1950, v36, p93.
Saturday Review. Jan 27, 1951, v34, p28.
Sequence. Sum 1950, n11, p12.
Shots in the Dark. p134-38.
The Spectator. Feb 3, 1950, v184, p145.
Time. Dec 18, 1950, v56, p94.
Time. Feb 19, 1951, v57, p61.
Time. Feb 19, 1951, v57, p60-61.
Variety. Dec 20, 1950, p18.

The Wayward Bus (US; Moffat, Ivan; 1957)
BFI/Monthly Film Bulletin. Aug 1957, v24, p106.
Commonweal. Jun 21, 1957, v66, p303.
Commonweal. Jul 19, 1957, v66, p401-02.
Film Daily. May 27, 1957, v111, p6.
Films and Filming. Sep 1957, v3, p24.
Hollywood Reporter. May 27, 1957, p3.
Motion Picture Herald Product Digest. Jun 1, 1957, v207, p402.
The New York Times. Jun 6, 1957, p35.
The New Yorker. Jun 15, 1957, v33, p72.
Newsweek. May 27, 1957, v49, p119.
Time. Jun 17, 1957, v69, p99.

We Are All Murderers (French title: Nous Sommes Tous des Assassins; Also titled: Are We All Murderers?) (FR; Cayatte, André; 1952)
Cinema, the Magic Vehicle. v2, p102-07.
Dictionary of Films. p251.
Film Culture. n1, 1957, v3, p15-16.
Film Daily. Jan 10, 1957, p6.
Films in Review. Feb 1957, v8, p83-84.
The Great French Films. p254.
Library Journal. Jan 15, 1957, v82, p183.
The London Times. Feb 2, 1957, p251.
Motion Picture Herald Product Digest. Feb 2, 1957, p251.
The Nation. Jan 26, 1957, v184, p86.
National Parent-Teacher. Feb 1957, v51, p39.
The New Statesman and Nation. Oct 3, 1953, v46, p373.
The New York Times. Jan 9, 1957, p27.
The New Yorker. Jan 19, 1957, v32, p95.
Newsweek. Jan 21, 1957, v49, p84.
Saturday Review. Jan 26, 1957, v40, p25.
Sight and Sound. Jan-Mar 1954, v23, p144-45.

Variety. May 28, 1952, p24.
The Village Voice. Feb 27, 1957, v2, p6.

The Weak and the Wicked (GB; Thompson, J. Lee; 1954)
BFI/Monthly Film Bulletin. Feb 1954, v21, p21-22.
Film Daily. Jul 29, 1954, p6.
Hollywood Reporter. Jul 20, 1954, p3.
The London Times. Feb 8, 1954, p4.
Motion Picture Herald Product Digest. Jul 24, 1954, p82.
The New Statesman and Nation. Feb 13, 1954, v47, p190.
The New York Times. Aug 21, 1954, p10.
The Spectator. Feb 5, 1954, v192, p145.
The Tatler. Mar 17, 1954, v211, p500.
Variety. Feb 17, 1954, p6.

Wedding Bells *See* Royal Wedding

Wee Geordie (GB; Launder, Frank; 1955)
America. Dec 22, 1956, v96, p360.
Commonweal. Oct 19, 1956, v65, p73.
Film Daily. Oct 5, 1956, p6.
Films and Filming. Oct 1955, v2, p18.
Films in Review. Dec 1956, v7, p525-26.
The New York Times. Oct 8, 1956, p31.
The New Yorker. Oct 20, 1956, v32, p179.
Newsweek. Oct 15, 1956, v48, p132.
Saturday Review. Oct 20, 1956, v39, p59.
Time. Oct 29, 1956, v68, p74.

Weekend (French title: Week-End, Le) (FR, IT; Godard, Jean-Luc; 1967)
BFI/Monthly Film Bulletin. Aug 1968, v35, p116-17.
Christian Science Monitor (Western edition). Jul 29, 1968, p6.
Classic Movies. p116-17.
Confessions of a Cultist. p400-06.
Figures of Light. p109-12.
Film 68/69. p32-42.
Film and Revolution. p45-60.
Film Quarterly. Wint 1970-71, v24, p2-14.
Film Quarterly. Wint 1968-69, v22, p35-43.
Film Society Review. Oct 1968, v4, p38-44.
Filmfacts. Oct 1, 1968, v11, p255-56.
Films and Filming. Feb 1969, v15, p34.
Films and Filming. Jun 1970, v16, p96-05.
The Films of Jean-Luc Godard. p162-71.
Five Thousand One Nights At the Movies. p643.
Focus on Godard. p74-78.
Going Steady. p167-74.
The Great French Films. p267-68.
The Great Movies. p206.
The International Dictionary of Films and Filmmakers. v1, p517-18.
Jean-Luc Godard: A Guide to References and Resources. p87-89.
Jean-Luc Godard (Collet). p148-55.
Jean-Luc Godard (Kreidl). p167-70.
The London Times. Jul 4, 1968, p13.
Magill's Survey of Cinema. Foreign Language Films. v7, p3339-43.
Movie. Wint 1968-69, n16, p29-33.
Movie Comedy (Byron). p186-89.
The New Wave. p198-203.
New York Free Press. Oct 17, 1968, v1, p8.
The New York Times. Sep 28, 1968, p36.
The New Yorker. Feb 3, 1968, v43, p80-81.
The New Yorker. Oct 5, 1968, v44, p141-45.
Self and Cinema. p87-190 80, v49, p22-24 -80 e v49, p22-24.
Sight and Sound. Sum 1968, v37, p151-52.
Sight and Sound. Wint 1979/80, v49, p22-24.
The Spectator. Jul 12, 1968, v221, p62.
Take One. 1968, v1, n11, p23.
Time. Nov 1, 1968, v92, p100-01.
Variety. Jan 10, 1968, p6.
The Village Voice. Nov 21, 1968, p51-52.

Vogue. Sep 15, 1968, v152, p74.
Weekend and Wind From the East: Two Films by Jean-Luc Godard. p5-15.
A Year In the Dark. p251-53.

Weekend At Dunkirk (Also titled: Week-End a Zuydcoote) (FR, IT; Verneuil, Henri; 1964)
Film Daily. May 20, 1966, p4.
Filmfacts. Aug 1, 1966, v9, p140-41.
Films and Filming. Aug 1966, v9, p140-41.
Motion Picture Herald Product Digest. May 25, 1966, p528.
The New York Times. May 19, 1966, p51.
Variety. Dec 30, 1964, p6.

Weekend With Father (US; Sirk, Douglas; 1951)
American Magazine. Jan 1952, v153, p8.
BFI/Monthly Film Bulletin. Jan 1952, v19, p8.
Christian Century. Jan 30, 1952, v69, p143.
Commonweal. Feb 1, 1952, v55, p424.
Douglas Sirk (Stern). p72-75.
Film Daily. Nov 26, 1951, p6.
Hollywood Reporter. Nov 23, 1951, p3.
Motion Picture Herald Product Digest. Dec 1, 1951, p1126.
The Spectator. Dec 7, 1951, v187, p773.
Time. Jan 7, 1952, v59, p85.
Variety. Nov 28, 1951, p6.

Welcome, Mr. Marshall (Spanish title: Bienvenido, Mr. Marshall) (SP; Berlanga, Luis G.; 1952)
BFI/Monthly Film Bulletin. Mar 1955, v22, p31-31.
Dictionary of Films. p32-33.
Film Daily. Nov 13, 1956, p10.
Films and Filming. May 1955, v1, p20.
Magill's Survey of Cinema. Foreign Language Films. v7, p3344-48.
Motion Picture Herald Product Digest. Jun 30, 1956, p954.
The New Statesman and Nation. Jan 29, 1955, v49, p139.

Welcome to Hard Times (Also titled: Killer on a Horse) (US; Kennedy, Burt; 1967)
America. May 20, 1967, v116, p764.
BFI/Monthly Film Bulletin. May 1970, v37, p99-100.
Cinema. Sum 1967, v3, p50.
Esquire. Aug 1967, v68, p30.
Film Daily. Mar 27, 1967, p4.
Film Quarterly. Fall 1967, v21, p49-58.
Films in Review. May 1967, v18, p310.
The Films of Henry Fonda. p195-97.
Hollywood Reporter. Mar 24, 1967, p10.
Life. May 26, 1967, v62, p14.
Motion Picture Herald Product Digest. Mar 29, 1967, p670-71.
The New York Times. May 2, 1967, p56.
The New Yorker. May 13, 1967, v43, p181.
Newsweek. May 8, 1967, v69, p104.
Second Sight. p115-18.
Time. May 12, 1967, v89, p102.
Variety. Mar 29, 1967, p26.
The Village Voice. Apr 6, 1967, p31.

Welcome to L.A. (US; Rudolph, Alan; 1976)
America. May 7, 1977, v136, p431-32.
Audience. Oct 1977, v9, p21-22.
Before My Eyes. p286.
BFI/Monthly Film Bulletin. Oct 1977, v44, p216-17.
Commonweal. Apr 1, 1977, v104, p214-15.
Film Bulletin. Mar 1977, v46, p32.
Film Comment. Jan-Feb 1977, v13, p10-13.
Film Heritage. Fall 1976, v12, p1-7.

Films and Filming. Oct 1977, v24, p10-11.
Films Illustrated. Nov 1977, v7, p88.
Films in Review. May 1977, v28, p311.
Independent Film Journal. Feb 4, 1977, v79, p9.
Movietone News. Sep 16, 1977, n55, p14-18.
The Nation. Mar 26, 1977, v224, p380-81.
The New Leader. Feb 14, 1977, v60, p23-24.
The New Republic. Apr 2, 1977, v176, p22-23.
New Statesman. Nov 11, 1977, v94, p665-66.
New Times. Apr 15, 1977, v8, p67-70.
New York. Mar 12, 1977, v10, p63-65.
The New York Times. Mar 11, 1977, SecIII, p18.
The New York Times. Sep 18, 1977, SecII, p17.
The New Yorker. Mar 21, 1977, v53, p112-15.
Newsweek. Feb 21, 1977, v89, p88.
Saturday Review. Mar 19, 1977, v4, p40-42.
Take One. 1977, v5, n10, p10-11.
Time. Nov 22, 1976, v108, p95.
Variety. Dec 1, 1976, p18.
The Village Voice. Mar 21, 1977, p22.
When the Lights Go Down. p283-85.

The Well (US; Popkin, Leo C.; Rouse, Russell; 1951)
Catholic World. Oct 1951, v174, p65.
Christian Century. Feb 6, 1952, v69, p175.
Film Daily. Sep 7, 1951, p10.
Hollywood Reporter. Sep 5, 1951, p3.
The London Times. Feb 18, 1952, p2.
Motion Picture Herald Product Digest. Sep 8, 1951, p1005.
The Nation. Aug 11, 1951, v173, p118.
The New Republic. Nov 5, 1951, v125, p22.
The New Statesman and Nation. Feb 23, 1952, v43, p214-15.
The New York Times. Sep 27, 1951, p37.
The New Yorker. Oct 6, 1951, v27, p69-70.
Newsweek. Sep 24, 1951, v38, p88.
Saturday Review. Sep 22, 1951, v34, p30.
Sight and Sound. Apr-Jun 1952, v21, p171-72.
Time. Oct 8, 1951, v58, p108.
Variety. Sep 5, 1951, p6.

We're Not Married (US; Goulding, Edmund; 1952)
BFI/Monthly Film Bulletin. Aug 1952, v19, p108.
Catholic World. Aug 1952, v175, p382.
Christian Century. Aug 13, 1952, v69, p935.
Commonweal. Jan 18, 1952, v55, p374.
Film Daily. Jul 1, 1952, p6.
The Films of Ginger Rogers. p209.
The Films of Marilyn Monroe. p72-75.
Hollywood Reporter. Jun 23, 1952, p3.
The London Times. Jul 28, 1952, p8.
Motion Picture Herald Product Digest. Jun 28, 1952, p1425.
National Parent-Teacher. Sep 1952, v47, p40.
The New York Times. Jul 12, 1952, p16.
The New Yorker. Jan 12, 1952, v27, p51.
Newsweek. Jan 14, 1952, v39, p82.
Saturday Review. Jan 12, 1952, v35, p27.
The Spectator. Aug 1, 1952, v189, p160.
The Tatler. Aug 6, 1952, v205, p246.
Theatre Arts. Jan 1952, v36, p84.
Time. Jan 7, 1952, v59, p82.
Variety. Jun 25, 1952, p6.

West of Zanzibar (GB; Watt, Harry; 1954)
BFI/Monthly Film Bulletin. May 1954, v21, p72.
Catholic World. Jan 1955, v180, p304.
Film Daily. Dec 7, 1954, p12.
Hollywood Reporter. Dec 7, 1954, p3.
The London Times. Mar 29, 1954, p9.
Motion Picture Herald Product Digest. Dec 11, 1954, p241.
National Parent-Teacher. Jan 1955, v49, p38.

Natural History. Dec 1954, v63, p472.
The New Statesman and Nation. Apr 3, 1954, v47, p436.
The New York Times. Jan 18, 1955, p31.
Newsweek. Jan 31, 1955, v45, p80.
Variety. Apr 7, 1954, p6.

The West Point Story (Also titled: Fine and Dandy) (US; Del Ruth, Roy; 1950)
BFI/Monthly Film Bulletin. Apr 1951, v18, p250.
Christian Century. Dec 20, 1950, v67, p1535.
Commonweal. Jan 19, 1951, v53, p376.
Film Daily. Nov 16, 1950, p6.
The Films of Doris Day. p91-94.
The Films of James Cagney. p191-93.
Hollywood Reporter. Nov 14, 1950, p5.
The London Times. Jul 16, 1951, p2.
Motion Picture Herald Product Digest. Nov 18, 1950, p569.
The New York Times. Dec 23, 1950, p11.
Newsweek. Dec 25, 1950, v36, p64-65.
The Spectator. Jul 20, 1951, v187, p92.
Time. Dec 4, 1950, v56, p96.
Variety. Jan 15, 1950, p6.

West Side Story (US; Wise, Robert; Robbins, Jerome; 1961)
America. Oct 28, 1961, v106, p134-36.
BFI/Monthly Film Bulletin. Apr 1962, v29, p49-50.
Commonweal. Oct 20, 1961, v75, p93.
Dance Magazine. Oct 1961, v35, p14-15.
Esquire. Feb 1962, v57, p28-29.
Film Daily. Sep 27, 1961, p6.
Filmfacts. Nov 3, 1961, v4, p245-48.
Films in Review. Nov 1961, v7, p549-52.
The Films of the Sixties. p65-67.
I Lost it at the Movies. p141-47.
Life. Oct 20, 1961, v51, p80-87.
Magill's Survey of Cinema. Series I. v4, p1826-29.
National Review. Jul 31, 1962, v13, p73-74.
The New Republic. Oct 23, 1961, v145, p28-29.
The New York Times. Jul 3, 1960, SecII, p5.
The New York Times. Oct 15, 1961, SecII, p7.
The New York Times. Oct 19, 1961, p39.
The New York Times. Oct 22, 1961, SecII, p1.
The New Yorker. Oct 21, 1961, v37, p196.
Newsweek. Oct 23, 1961, v58, p101-02.
On Movies. p286-87.
Reruns. p122-26.
Saturday Review. Oct 14, 1961, v44, p40.
Theatre Arts. Nov 1960, 44, p12-13.
Time. Oct 20, 1961, v78, p94.
Variety. Sep 27, 1961, p6.

Westward the Women (US; Wellman, William A.; 1951)
American Cinematographer. Jan 1952, v33, p14-15.
BFI/Monthly Film Bulletin. Feb 1952, v19, p19.
Catholic World. Jan 1952, v174, p305-06.
Christian Century. Feb 27, 1952, v69, p263.
Commonweal. Jan 18, 1952, v55, p374.
Film Daily. Nov 20, 1951, p6.
The Films of Robert Taylor. p122-23.
Hollywood Reporter. Nov 15, 1951, p3.
Motion Picture Herald Product Digest. Nov 24, 1951, p1118.
The New York Times. Jan 1, 1952, p21.
The New Yorker. Jan 12, 1952, v27, p51.
Newsweek. Jan 14, 1952, v39, p82.
Saturday Review. Jan 12, 1952, v35, p27.
The Spectator. Dec 14, 1951, v187, p815-16.
Theatre Arts. Jan 1952, v36, p84.
Time. Jan 7, 1952, v59, p82.
Variety. Nov 21, 1951, p6.
William A. Wellman (Thompson). p235-38.

Wetherby (GB; Hare, David; 1985)
America. Sep 28, 1985, v153, p176.
BFI/Monthly Film Bulletin. Feb 1985, v52, p70.
Christian Century. Aug 28, 1985, v102, p774.
Commonweal. Nov 1, 1985, v112, p608.
Film Comment. Sep-Oct 1985, v21, p18-22.
Films in Review. Oct 1985, v36, p490.
The Los Angeles Times. Sep 6, 1985, SecVI, p1.
Maclean's. Sep 2, 1985, v98, p49.
Magill's Cinema Annual, 1986. p406-10.
Ms. Oct 1985, v14, p19-20.
The New Leader. Jul 1, 1985, v68, p22.
The New Republic. Aug 12, 1985, v193, p24-26.
New York. Jul 29, 1985, v18, p61.
The New York Times. Jul 19, 1985, SecIII, p12.
The New Yorker. Oct 7, 1985, v61, p131-32.
Newsweek. Aug 5, 1985, v106, p64.
Time. Aug 19, 1985, v126, p70-71.
Variety. Feb 20, 1985, p22.

What a Way to Go! (US; Thompson, J. Lee; 1964)
BFI/Monthly Film Bulletin. Jul 1964, v31, p104.
Boxoffice. Apr 13, 1964, v84, p2817.
Commonweal. May 1, 1964, v80, p177-78.
Film Daily. Mar 31, 1964, v124, p13.
Films and Filming. Aug 1964, v10, p22-23.
Films in Review. Jun-Jul 1964, v15, p372-73.
The Films of Paul Newman. p131-35.
The Films of Shirley MacLaine. p128-33.
Hollywood Reporter. Mar 31, 1964, v179, p3.
Life. May 8, 1964, v56, p14.
Motion Picture Herald Product Digest. Apr 15, 1964, v231, p25.
The New Republic. May 30, 1964, v150, p26.
The New York Times. May 15, 1964, p44.
The New Yorker. May 16, 1964, v40, p191.
Newsweek. May 18, 1964, v63, p100.
Private Screenings. p134-35.
Robert Mitchum on the Screen. p189-90.
Time. May 22, 1964, v83, p104.

What Did You Do in the War, Daddy? (US; Edwards, Blake; 1966)
America. Aug 27, 1966, v115, p214.
BFI/Monthly Film Bulletin. Dec 1966, v33, p183-84.
Blake Edwards (Lehman). p184-88, 192.
Christian Science Monitor (Western edition). Jul 15, 1966, p4.
Commonweal. Sep 23, 1966, v84, p615.
Film Daily. Jun 29, 1966, p5.
Filmfacts. Nov 15, 1966, v9, p251-52.
Films and Filming. Nov 1966, v13, p54-55.
Hollywood Reporter. Jun 29, 1966, p3.
The London Times. Oct 20, 1966, p17.
Motion Picture Herald Product Digest. Jul 6, 1966, p554.
The New York Times. Sep 1, 1966, p28.
The New Yorker. Sep 10, 1966, v42, p103.
Newsweek. Jul 25, 1966, v68, p89.
The Primal Screen. p188-90.
Time. Sep 16, 1966, v88, p117.
Variety. Jun 29, 1966, p6.

What Ever Happened to Baby Jane? (US; Aldrich, Robert; 1962)
America. Nov 17, 1962, v107, p1104.
Bette Davis: Her Films and Career. p173-75.
BFI/Monthly Film Bulletin. Jun 1963, v30, p81-82.
Cinema. 1963, v1, n3, p32.
Cinema Texas Program Notes. Mar 29, 1976, v10, p31-37.
Commonweal. Nov 23, 1962, v77, p231.
Confessions of a Cultist. p77-82.
Film Daily. Oct 26, 1962, p7.
Film Quarterly. Spr 1963, v16, p60-61.

Filmfacts. Nov 9, 1962, v5, p256-58.
Films and Filming. Apr 1963, v9, p28.
Films in Review. Dec 1962, v13, p622-23.
The Films of Joan Crawford. p208-11.
The Films of the Sixties. p75-76.
Hollywood Reporter. Oct 26, 1962, p3.
Magill's Survey of Cinema. Series II, v6, p2649-53.
Motion Picture Herald Product Digest. Nov 14, 1962, p689-90.
Movie. Mar-Apr 1963, n8, p6-7.
The New York Times. Nov 7, 1962, p48.
The New Yorker. Nov 17, 1962, v38, p209.
Newsweek. Nov 12, 1962, v60, p96.
Robert Aldrich: A Guide to References and Resources. p34-36.
Saturday Review. Nov 10, 1962, v45, p27.
Time. Nov 23, 1962, v80, p70.
Variety. Oct 31, 1962, p6.
The Village Voice. Nov 22, 1962, p13.

What Lola Wants *See* Damn Yankees

What Price Glory? (US; Ford, John; 1952)
BFI/Monthly Film Bulletin. Jan 1953, v20, p7.
Christian Century. Sep 24, 1952, v69, p1111.
Commonweal. Sep 5, 1952, v56, p535.
Film Daily. Jul 30, 1952, p8.
The Films of James Cagney. p201-03.
Hollywood Reporter. Jul 28, 1952, p3.
Motion Picture Herald Product Digest. Aug 2, 1952, p1469.
The Nation. Oct 11, 1952, v175, p338.
National Parent-Teacher. Oct 1952, v47, p38.
The New York Times. Aug 23, 1952, p10.
The New Yorker. Aug 16, 1952, v28, p81.
Newsweek. Sep 1, 1952, v40, p64.
The Non-Western Films of John Ford. p94-96.
Sight and Sound. Jan-Mar 1953, v22, p131.
Theatre Arts. Sep 1952, v36, p73.
Time. Aug 18, 1952, v60, p86.
Variety. Jul 30, 1952, p6.

What's New Pussycat? (US, FR; Donner, Clive; 1965)
America. Jul 3, 1965, v113, p27.
BFI/Monthly Film Bulletin. Oct 1965, v32, p148.
Cahiers du Cinema in English. 1966, n2, p75-76.
Commonweal. Jul 2, 1965, v82, p473.
Esquire. Nov 1965, v64, p34, 36, 38.
Film Daily. Jun 23, 1965, p5.
Film Quarterly. Spr 1966, v19, p25-29.
Films and Filming. Oct 1965, v12, p27-28.
Films in Review. Aug-Sep 1965, v16, p446-47.
The Films of the Sixties. p152-53.
Hollywood Reporter. Jun 23, 1965, p3.
Life. Jul 9, 1965, v59, p12.
The London Times. Aug 26, 1965, p12.
Motion Picture Herald Product Digest. Jul 7, 1965, p321-22.
Movie. Fall 1965, n14, p12-16.
Movie Comedy (Byron). p145-46.
The Nation. Aug 2, 1965, v201, p68.
The New Republic. Jul 10, 1965, v153, p30-31.
New Statesman. Sep 3, 1965, v70, p331.
The New York Times. Jun 23, 1965, p49.
The New Yorker. Jun 26, 1965, v41, p78.
Newsweek. Jul 12, 1965, v66, p90E.
Playboy. Sep 1965, v12, p55.
The Private Eye, the Cowboy and the Very Naked Girl. p139-40.
Private Screenings. p194-95.
Saturday Review. Jul 17, 1965, v48, p25.
Sight and Sound. Aut 1965, v34, p201.
The Spectator. Sep 3, 1965, v215, p291.
Time. Jul 2, 1965, v86, p80.
Variety. Jun 23, 1965, p6.

The Village Voice. Jul 8, 1965, v10, p13.
The Village Voice. Aug 5, 1965, v10, p14.

What's the Matter With Helen? (US; Harrington, Curtis; 1971)
BFI/Monthly Film Bulletin. Dec 1971, v38, n455, p252.
Films and Fiming. Jan 1972, v18, n4, p53.
Hollywood Reporter. Jun 9, 1971, v216, n30, p3.
The New York Times. Jul 1, 1971, p62.
Sight and Sound. Wint 1971-72, v41, n1, p53.
Variety. Jun 9, 1971, p17.
The Village Voice. Jul 1971, v16, n29, p65.

What's Up, Doc? (US; Bogdanovich, Peter; 1972)
Commentary. Jul 1972, v54, p90-91.
Commonweal. May 19, 1972, v96, p263-64.
Deeper into Movies. p426-34.
Filmfacts. 1972, v15, n3, p45.
Hollywood Reporter. Mar 8, 1972, p3.
Life. Apr 7, 1972, v72, p14.
National Review. Jul 23, 1972, v24, p705.
The New Republic. Apr 1, 1972, v166, p26.
The New York Times. Mar 10, 1972, p42.
The New York Times. Mar 19, 1972, SecII, p1.
The New York Times. Apr 16, 1972, SecII, p11.
The New Yorker. Mar 25, 1972, v48, p121.
Newsweek. Mar 20, 1972, v79, p113.
Saturday Review. Apr 8, 1972, v55, p56.
Senior Scholastic. May 8, 1972, v100, p22.
Variety. Mar 8, 1972, p20.
Vogue. Jul 1972, v159, p28.

What's Up, Tiger Lily? (Also titled: Kizino Kizi; Key of Keys) (US, JAPAN; Allen, Woody; 1966)
America. Dec 10, 1966, v115, p785.
BFI/Monthly Film Bulletin. Mar 1976, v43, p65.
Christian Science Monitor (Western edition). Mar 13, 1967, p6.
Film Daily. Oct 6, 1966, p4.
Filmfacts. Jan 15, 1967, v9, p354-55.
The Great Spy Pictures. p508-09.
Hollywood Reporter. Oct 4, 1966, p3.
Motion Picture Herald Product Digest. Oct 12, 1966, p614.
The New York Times. Nov 18, 1966, p33.
Newsweek. Oct 10, 1966, v68, p114.
Playboy. Feb 1967, v14, p21.
The Private Eye, the Cowboy and the Very Naked Girl. p217.
Saturday Review. Nov 5, 1966, v49, p45.
Time. Oct 14, 1966, v88, p117.
Variety. Oct 5, 1966, p6.
The Village Voice. Dec 8, 1966, v12, p27.
Woody Allen: His Films and Career. p53-66.

The Wheeler Dealers (Also titled: Separate Beds) (US; Hiller, Arthur; 1963)
BFI/Monthly Film Bulletin. Aug 1964, v31, p123.
Commonweal. Nov 29, 1963, v79, p285.
Film Daily. Sep 27, 1963, p14.
Filmfacts. Nov 28, 1963, v6, p259-60.
Films in Review. Nov 1963, v14, p563-64.
The New Republic. Nov 23, 1963, v149, p29.
The New York Times. Nov 15, 1963, p25.
Newsweek. Dec 2, 1963, v62, p102.
Photoplay. Dec 1963,, v64, p10.
Time. Nov 29, 1963, v82, p103.
Variety. Sep 25, 1963, p6.

When Father Was Away on Business (Yugoslavian title: Otac Na Sluzhenom Putu) (YUGO; Kasturia, Emir; 1985)
BFI/Monthly Film Bulletin. Dec 1985, v52, p383.
Commonweal. Nov 29, 1985, v112, p672.

Films in Review. Jan 1986, v37, p43.
The Los Angeles Times. May 21, 1985, SecVI, p3.
Magill's Cinema Annual, 1986. p411-15.
National Review. Nov 29, 1985, v37, p57-59.
New York. Oct 21, 1985, v18, p88.
The New York Times. Sep 28, 1985, p14.
Newsweek. Oct 28, 1985, v106, p92.
Time. Oct 21, 1985, v126, p83.
The Wall Street Journal. Oct 17, 1985, p26.

When in Rome (US; Brown, Clarence; 1952)
BFI/Monthly Film Bulletin. Jun 1952, v19, p82.
Film Daily. Mar 6, 1952, p12.
Hollywood Reporter. Feb 28, 1952, p3.
Motion Picture Herald Product Digest. Mar 1, 1952, p1253.
The New York Times. May 12, 1952, p21.
Newsweek. Apr 28, 1952, v39, p98.
The Spectator. May 30, 1952, v188, p704.
The Tatler. Jun 11, 1952, v204, p606.
Time. May 5, 1952, v59, p108.
Variety. Mar 5, 1952, p6.

When Willie Comes Marching Home (US; Ford, John; 1950)
BFI/Monthly Film Bulletin. Mar-Apr 1950, v17, p45-46.
Christian Century. Mar 29, 1950, v67, p415.
Commonweal. Mar 17, 1950, v51, p607.
Film Daily. Jan 4, 1950, p6.
Hollywood Reporter. Jan 4, 1950, p3.
The London Times. Mar 13, 1950, p2.
Motion Picture Herald Product Digest. Jan 7, 1950, p145.
The New Republic. Mar 6, 1950, v122, p22.
The New Statesman and Nation. Mar 18, 1950, v39, p299.
The New York Times. Feb 18, 1950, p9.
The New Yorker. Feb 25, 1950, v26, p105.
Newsweek. Feb 20, 1950, v35, p87-88.
The Non-Western Films of John Ford. p89-93.
The Spectator. Mar 17, 1950, v184, p338.
Time. Mar 6, 1950, v55, p92.

When Worlds Collide (US; Maté, Rudolph; 1951)
BFI/Monthly Film Bulletin. Sep 1951, v18, p333.
Catholic World. Nov 1951, v174, p144.
Christian Century. Dec 12, 1951, v68, p1447.
Cinema of the Fantastic. p152-53.
Film Daily. Aug 28, 1951, p7.
Films in Review. Oct 1951, v2, p51.
The Films of George Pal. p56-71.
Future Tense: The Cinema of Science Fiction. p85-86.
Hollywood Reporter. Aug 28, 1951, p3.
The London Times. Sep 17, 1951, p6.
Motion Picture Herald Product Digest. Sep 1, 1951, p998.
The New Statesman and Nation. Sep 22, 1951, v42, p310.
The New York Times. Feb 7, 1952, p30.
Newsweek. Mar 3, 1952, v39, p88.
Saturday Review. Nov 10, 1951, v34, p28.
Science Fiction Gold. p51-62.
Science Fiction Studies in Film. p98-99.
Senior Scholastic. Nov 28, 1951, v59, p22.
Soundtrack. Sep 1985, v4, p18.
The Spectator. Sep 14, 1951, v187, p328.
Time. Nov 12, 1951, v58, p114.
Variety. Aug 29, 1951, p6.

When You Comin' Back, Red Ryder? (US; Katselas, Milton; 1979)
Commonweal. Apr 13, 1979, v106, p215-16.
Films in Review. May 1979, v30, p310.
Hollywood Reporter. Feb 9, 1979, p10.

The Los Angeles Times. Feb 16, 1979, SecIV, p23.
Motion Picture Herald Product Digest. Feb 21, 1979, p75.
The New York Times. Feb 9, 1979, SecIII, p14.
Newsweek. Feb 26, 1979, v93, p81.
Time. Mar 12, 1979, v113, p76.
Variety. Feb 7, 1979, p29.

Where Danger Lives (US; Farrow, John; 1950)
BFI/Monthly Film Bulletin. Jan 1951, v18, p208.
Film Daily. Jun 21, 1950, p8.
Hollywood Reporter. Jun 16, 1950, p3.
The London Times. Jan 8, 1951, p2.
Motion Picture Herald Product Digest. Jun 24, 1950, p353-54.
The New York Times. Jan 1, 1951, p13.
Newsweek. Jan 8, 1951, v37, p74.
Robert Mitchum on the Screen. p112-13.
Time. Dec 18, 1950, v56, p92.
Variety. Jun 21, 1950, p8.

Where Eagles Dare (US; Hutton, Brian G.; 1969)
America. Apr 5, 1969, v120, p428.
Clint Eastwood (Guérif). p63-66.
Film Daily. Jan 3, 1969, p3.
Filmfacts. 1969, v2, p107.
Films and Filming. Apr 1969, v15, p40.
The Films of Clint Eastwood. p86-93.
Life. Mar 28, 1969, v66, p12.
The New York Times. Mar 13, 1969, p50.
Time. Mar 28, 1969, v93, p89.
Variety. Dec 11, 1968, p6.

Where No Vultures Fly *See* Ivory Hunter

Where the Bullets Fly (GB; Gilling, John; 1966)
BFI/Monthly Film Bulletin. Dec 1966, v33, p188.
Film Daily. Nov 23, 1966, p6.
Filmfacts. Nov 1, 1967, v10, p262-63.
The Great Spy Pictures. p511-12.
Hollywood Reporter. Nov 22, 1966, p3.
The London Times. Nov 3, 1966, p7.
Motion Picture Herald Product Digest. Dec 7, 1966, p635.
The New York Times. Sep 7, 1967, p50.
Variety. Nov 9, 1966, p6.

Where the Lillies Bloom (US; Graham, William A.; 1974)
Christian Century. Jan 30, 1974, v91, p108-9.
Films in Review. May 1974, v25, p308.
Hollywood Reporter. Mar 4, 1974, p3.
Independent Film Journal. Feb 18, 1974, v73, p10.
The Los Angeles Times. Apr 21, 1974, Calendar, p1.
Motion Picture Herald Product Digest. Jan 13, 1974, p36.
Movietone News. Apr 1974, n31, p35.
New York. Jun 10, 1974, v7, p74.
The New York Times. Jun 8, 1974, p18.
PTA Magazine. Feb 1974, v68, p7.
Time. Feb 11, 1974, v103, p65.
Variety. Feb 6, 1974, p18.

Where the River Bends *See* Bend of the River

Where the Sidewalk Ends (US; Preminger, Otto; 1950)
BFI/Monthly Film Bulletin. Sep 1950, v17, p137-38.
Christian Century. Aug 30, 1950, v67, p1031.
The Cinema of Otto Preminger. p92-93.
Commonweal. Jul 21, 1950, v52, p368.
Film Daily. Jun 26, 1950, p6.

The Great Gangster Pictures. p412-13.
Hollywood Reporter. Jun 26, 1950, p3.
Motion Picture Herald Product Digest. Jul 1, 1950, p365.
The New Republic. Jul 24, 1950, v123, 23.
The New York Times. Jul 8, 1950, p7.
The New Yorker. Jul 15, 1950, v26, p57.
Newsweek. Jul 24, 1950, v36, p68-69.
Time. Jul 31, 1950, v56, p64.
Variety. Jun 28, 1950, p6.

Where the Spies Are (GB; Guest, Val; 1965)
BFI/Monthly Film Bulletin. Apr 1966, v33, p64-65.
Christian Science Monitor (Western edition). Feb 15, 1966, p12.
Film Daily. Dec 7, 1965, p3.
Filmfacts. Feb 15, 1966, v9, p14-16.
The Films of David Niven. p198-201.
The Great Spy Pictures. p512-13.
Hollywood Reporter. Dec 3, 1965, p3.
The London Times. Mar 3, 1966, p18.
Motion Picture Herald Product Digest. Dec 8, 1965, p418.
New Statesman. Mar 4, 1966, v71, p308.
The New York Times. Jan 27, 1966, p29.
The New Yorker. Feb 12, 1966, v41, p142.
Playboy. Apr 1966, v13, p45-46.
Time. Jan 28, 1966, v87, p88.
Variety. Dec 8, 1965, p22.

Where's Charley? (GB; Butler, David; 1952)
BFI/Monthly Film Bulletin. Aug 1952, v19, p114.
Film Daily. Jul 2, 1952, p6.
Hollywood Reporter. Jun 26, 1952, p3.
Kiss Kiss Bang Bang. p463.
The London Times. Jul 29, 1952, p7.
The London Times. Aug 4, 1952, p9.
Motion Picture Herald Product Digest. Jun 28, 1952, p1425-26.
National Parent-Teacher. Oct 1952, v47, p37.
The New York Times. Jun 27, 1952, p18.
The Spectator. Aug 1, 1952, v189, p160.
Variety. Jul 2, 1952, p6.

Where's Poppa? (US; Reiner, Carl; 1970)
Cult Movies. p383-85.
Deeper into Movies. p183-87.
Film Quarterly. Sum 1971, v24, p60-63.
Hollywood Reporter. Nov 10, 1970, p6.
The New Republic. Dec 5, 1970, v163, p22.
The New York Times. Nov 11, 1970, p35.
The New York Times. Dec 6, 1970, SecII, p5.
The New Yorker. Nov 14, 1970, v46, p166-68.
Newsweek. Nov 23, 1970, v76, p123-123A.
Saturday Review. Nov 28, 1970, v53, p56.
Time. Dec 14, 1970, v96, p102.
Variety. Nov 11, 1970, p15.

The Whipped (US; Enfield, Cy; 1950)
Film Daily. Apr 3, 1950, p6.
Hollywood Reporter. Feb 13, 1950, p3.
Motion Picture Herald Product Digest. Apr 1, 1950, p245.
Variety. Feb 15, 1950, p13.

The Whisperers (GB; Forbes, Bryan; 1967)
BFI/Monthly Film Bulletin. Oct 1967, v34, p154-55.
Commonweal. Aug 11, 1967, v86, p495-97.
Esquire. Oct 1967, v68, p28.
Film Daily. Jul 12, 1967, p4.
Films and Filming. Nov 1967, v14, p27.
Films in Review. Aug-Sep 1967, v18, p441.
The Great British Films. p230-32.
Hollywood Reporter. Jul 12, 1967, p3.
Life. Sep 8, 1967, v63, p8.

Magill's Survey of Cinema. Series II. v6, p2654-57.
Motion Picture Herald Product Digest. Jul 12, 1967, p704.
The New York Times. Aug 1, 1967, p24.
The New Yorker. Aug 12, 1967, v43, p72.
Newsweek. Aug 7, 1967, v70, p75.
Saturday Review. Aug 19, 1967, v50, p45.
Second Sight. p129-31.
Senior Scholastic. Sep 21, 1967, v91, p34.
Sight and Sound. Aut 1967, v36, p205-06.
Take One. 1967, v1, n7, p25-26.
Time. Aug 4, 1967, v90, p73.
Variety. Jul 12, 1967, p6.
The Village Voice. Aug 10, 1967, p21.

The Whistle At Eaton Falls (US; Siodmak, Robert; 1951)
Business Week. Aug 11, 1951, p46-48.
Christian Century. Mar 12, 1952, v69, 327.
Film Daily. Aug 2, 1951, p6.
Hollywood Reporter. Aug 1, 1951, p3.
Motion Picture Herald Product Digest. Aug 4, 1951, p966.
The New Republic. Nov 5, 1951, v125, p22.
The New York Times. Oct 11, 1951, p49.
The New Yorker. Oct 20, 1951, v27, p131.
Newsweek. Aug 20, 1951, v38, p88.
Saturday Review. Aug 18, 1951, v34, p26.
Senior Scholastic. Sep 19, 1951, v59, p34.
Sight and Sound. Apr-Jun 1952, v21, p171-72.
Time. Aug 13, 1951, v58, p100.
Variety. Aug 1, 1951, p6.

Whistle Down the Wind (GB; Forbes, Bryan; 1961)
America. May 19, 1962, v107, p278.
Commonweal. Apr 20, 1962, v76, p86.
Film Daily. Mar 5, 1962, p7.
Filmfacts. Jun 1, 1962, v5, p103-05.
Films and Filming. Sep 1961, v7, p27-28.
Films in Review. May 1962, v13, p295.
The Great British Films. p193-95.
Hollywood Reporter. Feb 27, 1962, v169, p5.
Magill's Survey of Cinema. Series II. v6, p2658-61.
Motion Picture Herald Product Digest. Mar 7, 1962, p468.
The Nation. May 12, 1962, v194, p428.
The New Republic. May 28, 1962, v146, p28.
The New York Times. Apr 23, 1962, p34.
The New Yorker. Apr 28, 1962, v38, p142.
Newsweek. Apr 30, 1962, v59, p98.
Screen International. Aut 1961, v30, p199.
Time. Apr 6, 1962, v79, p96.
Variety. Aug 2, 1961, p7.

White Christmas (US; Curtiz, Michael; 1954)
America. Nov 6, 1954, v92, p165.
BFI/Monthly Film Bulletin. Nov 1954, v21, p159.
Catholic World. Nov 1954, v180, p139.
Collier's. Oct 15, 1954, v134, p74.
Commonweal. Oct 29, 1954, v61, p94.
Farm Journal. Oct 1954, v78, p137.
Film Daily. Aug 27, 1954, p8.
Films and Filming. Dec 1954, v1, p18.
Films in Review. Dec 1954, v5, p543.
The Films of Bing Crosby. p207-10.
Hollywood Reporter. Aug 27, 1954, p3.
Life. Oct 11, 1954, v37, p158-59.
The London Times. Nov 3, 1954, p6.
Motion Picture Herald Product Digest. Sep 4, 1954, p130.
National Parent-Teacher. Dec 1954, v49, p39.
The New Statesman and Nation. Nov 13, 1954, v48, p612.
The New York Times. Oct 15, 1954, p16.
The New Yorker. Oct 23, 1954, v30, p162.

Newsweek. Oct 11, 1954, v44, p110.
Saturday Review. Oct 30, 1954, v37, p29.
Senior Scholastic. Oct 27, 1954, v65, p29.
Time. Oct 25, 1954, v64, p87.
Variety. Sep 1, 1954, p6.
Woman's Home Companion. Nov 1954, v81, p16-17.

White Corridors (GB; Jackson, Pat; 1951)
BFI/Monthly Film Bulletin. Jul 1951, v18, p294-95.
Catholic World. Jul 1952, v175, p305.
Commonweal. Aug 8, 1952, v56, p435.
Film Daily. Jul 9, 1952, p6.
Films in Review. Aug-Sep 1952, v3, p359.
Motion Picture Herald Product Digest. Jun 21, 1952, p1418.
The New Statesman and Nation. Jun 23, 1951, v41, p707-08.
The New York Times. Jul 16, 1952, p21.
The New Yorker. Jul 26, 1952, v28, p59.
Newsweek. Jun 23, 1952, v39, p94.
Saturday Review. Jun 28, 1952, v35, p27.
Sight and Sound. Aug-Sep 1951, v21, p20-21.
Theatre Arts. Aug 1952, v36, p88.
Time. Jul 14, 1952, v60, p96.
Variety. Jun 27, 1951, p9.

White Nights (US; Hackford, Taylor; 1985)
American Film. Dec 1984, v10, p25.
BFI/Monthly Film Bulletin. Apr 1986, v53, p121.
Dance Magazine. Nov 1985, v59, p50-55.
Films in Review. Jan 1986, v37, p40.
Hollywood Reporter. Nov 5, 1985, p3.
The Los Angeles Times. Nov 22, 1985, SecVI, p1.
Magill's Cinema Annual, 1986. p416-19.
The New York Times. Nov 22, 1985, SecIII, p10.
The New Yorker. Nov 18, 1985, v61, p153-55.
Variety. Nov 6, 1985, p26.
The Wall Street Journal. Nov 14, 1985, p28.
White Nights, Portrait of a Film. 1985.

The White Sheik (Italian title: Sceicco Bianco, Lo) (IT; Fellini, Federico; 1952)
Cinema Eye, Cinema Ear. p21-23.
Cinema Texas Program Notes. Nov 5, 1974, v7, p1-4.
Dictionary of Films. p329.
Federico Fellini: A Guide to References and Resources. p50-54.
Federico Fellini: Essays in Criticism. p220-39.
Federico Fellini: Variety Lights to La Dolce Vita. p13-18.
Fellini (Budgen). p30-32.
Fellini the Artist. p37-47.
Film Criticism. 1979, v3, n2, p53-66.
Film Daily. Apr 27, 1956, p6.
The Films of Federico Fellini. p63-68.
Italian Cinema (Bondanella). p118-25.
Kiss Kiss Bang Bang. p463-64.
Magill's Survey of Cinema. Foreign Language Films. v7, p3372-76.
Mastering the Film and Other Essays. p91-96.
Motion Picture Herald Product Digest. May 19, 1956, p899.
The New York Times. Apr 26, 1956, p37.
Private Screenings. p32-34.
Variety. Oct 1, 1952, p22.

The White Tower (US; Tetzlaff, Ted; 1950)
BFI/Monthly Film Bulletin. Sep 1950, v17, p138.
Christian Century. Jul 26, 1950, v67, p903.
Commonweal. Jul 14, 1950, v52, p345.
Film Daily. Jun 15, 1950, p8.
Hollywood Reporter. Jun 14, 1950, p3.

Illustrated London News. Sep 2, 1950, v217, p370.
Library Journal. Jul 1950, v75, p1202.
The London Times. Aug 21, 1950, p6.
Motion Picture Herald Product Digest. Jun 17, 1950, p346.
The New Republic. Jul 10, 1950, v123, p23.
The New York Times. Jul 3, 1950, p9.
The New Yorker. Jul 8, 1950, v26, p58.
Newsweek. Jul 3, 1950, v36, p69.
Time. Jul 17, 1950, v56, p90.
Variety. Jun 14, 1950, p8.

White Voices (Also titled: Voci Bianche, Le) (IT, FR; Campanile, Pasquale Festa; Franciosa, Massimo; 1964)
Commonweal. Apr 23, 1965, v82, p158.
Film Daily. Apr 9, 1965, p4.
Filmfacts. Jun 25, 1965, v8, p121-22.
Motion Picture Herald Product Digest. Apr 14, 1965, p266.
The New Republic. Mar 27, 1965, v152, p29-30.
The New York Times. Apr 13, 1965, p32.
The New Yorker. Apr 24, 1965, v41, p165.
Saturday Review. Feb 6, 1965, v48, p43.
Time. Apr 16, 1965, v85, p102.
Variety. Oct 21, 1964, p6.

Who Goes There! (Also titled: The Passionate Sentry) (GB; Kimmins, Anthony; 1952)
BFI/Monthly Film Bulletin. Jul 1952, v19, p98.
The London Times. Feb 25, 1952, p2.
The New Statesman and Nation. Jun 21, 1952, v43, p729.
The Spectator. Jun 13, 1952, v188, p76.
The Tatler. Jun 25, 1952, v204, p708.
Variety. Jun 25, 1952, p20.

Who Is Harry Kellerman & Why Is He Saying Those Terrible Things About Me? (US; Grosbard, Ulu; 1971)
BFI/Monthly Film Bulletin. May 1972, v39, n460, p102.
Filmfacts. 1971, v14, n11, p256-59.
Films and Filming. Jun 1972, v18, n9, p53.
Hollywood Reporter. Jun 16, 1971, v216, n35, p3.
Look. Jul 27, 1971, v35, p39.
The New Republic. Sep 18, 1971, v165, p22.
The New York Times. Jul 14, 1970, p30.
The New York Times. Jun 16, 1971, p40.
The New York Times. Jun 20, 1971, SecII, p13.
The New York Times. Sep 2, 1971, p39.
The New Yorker. Jul 10, 1971, v47, p56-57.
Newsweek. Jun 28, 1971, v77, p90.
Saturday Review. Jul 3, 1971, v54, p18.
Variety. Jun 16, 1971, p15.
The Village Voice. Jun 24, 1971, v16, n25, p60.

Who Is Killing the Great Chefs of Europe? (Also titled: Someone Is Killing the Great Chefs of Europe) (US; Kotcheff, Ted; 1978)
BFI/Monthly Film Bulletin. Feb 1979, v46, p34.
Encore. Nov 6, 1978, v7, p32.
Films in Review. Nov 1978, v29, p565.
Hollywood Reporter. Sep 18, 1978, p3.
The Los Angeles Times. Oct 5, 1978, SecIV, p19.
Motion Picture Herald Product Digest. Oct 18, 1978, p37.
The New Republic. Oct 14, 1978, v179, p25.
New York. Oct 16, 1978, v11, p121.
New York. Jan 30, 1978, v11, p46.
The New York Times. Oct 6, 1978, p6.
The New Yorker. Nov 13, 1978, v54, p223-25.
Newsweek. Oct 9, 1978, v92, p92.

Saturday Review. Nov 25, 1978, v5, p52.
Variety. Sep 20, 1978, p24.

Who Was That Lady? (US; Sidney, George; 1960)
America. Apr 23, 1960, v103, p172.
BFI/Monthly Film Bulletin. Jun 1960, v27, p86.
Commonweal. Jan 22, 1960, v71, p470.
Film Daily. Jan 4, 1960, p6.
Filmfacts. 1960, v3, p82.
Films and Filming. Jun 1960, v6, p22.
Hollywood Reporter. Jan 6, 1960, p3.
McCall's. Mar 1960, v87, p6.
The New York Times. Apr 16, 1960, p10.
Time. Mar 14, 1960, v75, p84.
Tony Curtis: The Man and His Movies. p82-84.
Variety. Jan 16, 1960, p6.

Who's Afraid of Virginia Woolf (Also titled: Who's Afraid of Virginia Woolf?) (US; Nichols, Mike; 1966)
America. Jul 30, 1966, v115, p121.
America. Aug 6, 1966, v115, p141-43.
BFI/Monthly Film Bulletin. Aug 1966, v3, p121.
Christian Century. Jul 27, 1966, v83, p937-38.
Christian Century. Oct 5, 1966, v83, p1215.
Christian Science Monitor (Western edition). Jul 2, 1966, p12.
Cinema Journal. 1980, v19, n2, p41-55.
Commonweal. Jul 22, 1966, v84, p474.
Confessions of a Cultist. p259-62.
Dictionary of Films. p417.
Figures of Light. p1-4.
Film Quarterly. Fall 1966, v20, p45-48.
Filmfacts. Aug 15, 1966, v9, p149-52.
Filming Literature. p161-63.
Films and Filming. Sep 1966, v12, p6.
Films in Review. Aug-Sep 1966, v17, p448-50.
The Films of Elizabeth Taylor. p171-78.
The Films of the Sixties. p177-79.
Life. Jun 10, 1966, v60, p87-91.
The London Times. Jul 7, 1966, p17.
Look. Feb 8, 1966, v30, p42-48.
Mademoiselle. Sep 1966, v63, p100.
Magill's Survey of Cinema. Series I. v4, p1842-44.
Marshall Delaney at the Movies. p96-98.
Mike Nichols (Schuth). p27-44.
Motion Picture Herald Product Digest. Jul 6, 1966, p553.
Moving Image. Mar-Apr 1982, n5, p55-59.
National Review. Sep 20, 1966, v18, p943-46.
New Statesman. Jul 15, 1966, v72, p103.
The New York Times. Jun 30, 1966, p28.
The New York Times. Jul 10, 1966, p1.
The New Yorker. Jul 2, 1966, v42, p64-65.
Newsweek. Jul 4, 1966, v68, p84.
Playboy. Sep 1966, v13, p54.
The Private Eye, the Cowboy and the Very Naked Girl. p234-35.
Private Screenings. p265-69.
Renaissance of the Film. p228-37.
Saturday Review. Jul 9, 1966, v49, p40.
See No Evil. p318-28.
Sight and Sound. Aut 1966, v35, p198-99.
The Spectator. Jul 15, 1966, v217, p84.
Theater and Film. p228-37.
Time. Jul 1, 1966, v88, p78.
Variety. Jun 22, 1966, p6.
The Village Voice. Jul 28, 1966, v11, p19.
Vogue. Aug 1, 1966, v148, p59.

Who's Been Sleeping in My Bed? (US; Mann, Daniel; 1963)
America. Dec 21, 1963, v109, p810.
BFI/Monthly Film Bulletin. Feb 1964, v31, p29.
Commonweal. Dec 27, 1963, v79, p406.
Film Daily. Dec 5, 1963, p6.

Filmfacts. Jan 2, 1964, v6, p300-02.
Films and Filming. Mar 1964, v10, p28-29.
The New York Times. Dec 26, 1963, p33.
Photoplay. Jan 1964, v65, p210.
Time. Jan 10, 1964, v83, pE3.
Variety. Dec 4, 1963, p6.

Who's Minding the Store? (US; Tashlin, Frank; 1963)
America. Jan 11, 1964, v110, p55.
BFI/Monthly Film Bulletin. Feb 1964, v31, p23.
Commonweal. Dec 13, 1963, v79, p349.
Film Daily. Nov 27, 1963, p7.
Filmfacts. Dec 26, 1963, v6, p293-94.
Films and Filming. Feb 1964, v10, p31.
The New York Times. Nov 28, 1963, p67.
Variety. Nov 20, 1963, p6.

Whose Life Is it Anyway? (US; Badham, John; 1981)
BFI/Monthly Film Bulletin. Feb 1982, v49, p32-33.
Hollywood Reporter. Nov 24, 1981, p2.
The Los Angeles Times. Dec 4, 1981, SecVI, p1.
Maclean's. Dec 21, 1981, v94, p47.
Magill's Cinema Annual, 1982. p378-81.
The New Republic. Dec 30, 1981, v185, p24-25.
New York. Dec 21, 1981, v14, p51.
The New York Times. Dec 2, 1981, SecIII, p23.
Newsweek. Dec 14, 1981, v98, p124-25.
Saturday Review. Nov 1981, v8, p56.
Time. Dec 14, 1981, v118, p92.

The Widower *See* An Autumn Afternoon

Wifemistress (Italian title: Mogliamante) (IT; Vicario, Marco; 1977)
BFI/Monthly Film Bulletin. May 1979, v46, p100.
Commonweal. Mar 16, 1979, v106, p146.
Films in Review. Mar 1979, v30, p180.
Hollywood Reporter. Jan 17, 1979, p4.
The Los Angeles Times. Mar 9, 1979, SecIV, p1.
The Nation. Feb 10, 1979, v228, p157-58.
The New York Times. Jan 7, 1979, p43.
The New York Times. Dec 16, 1979, SecII, p19.
Newsweek. Feb 12, 1979, v113, p74.
Variety. Nov 16, 1977, p21.

The Wild Angels (US; Corman, Roger; 1966)
Christian Science Monitor (Eastern Edition). Aug 26, 1966, p4.
Confessions of a Cultist. p272-74.
Filament. 1982, n2, p4-5.
Film Daily. Jul 5, 1966, p4.
Film Quarterly. Wint 1966-67, v20, p63.
Filmfacts. Jan 15, 1967, v9, p372-73.
Films and Filming. Jul 1969, v15, p53.
The Films of the Sixties. p181-84.
Hollywood Reporter. Jul 6, 1966, p3.
Journal of Popular Film. 1976, v5, n3/4, p263-72.
The London Times. Sep 3, 1966, p6.
Marshall Delaney at the Movies. p98-100.
Motion Picture Herald Product Digest. Jul 6, 1966, p554-55.
The New York Times. Dec 22, 1966, p40.
Saturday Review. Aug 27, 1966, v49, p40.
Saturday Review. Sep 10, 1966, v49, p53.
Sight and Sound. Wint 1968-69, v38, p47-48.
The Spectator. Sep 16, 1966, v217, p351.
Take One. Nov-Dec 1966, v1, p27-28.
Variety. Jul 20, 1966, p6.
The Village Voice. Sep 15, 1966, v11, p27.

The Wild Blue Yonder (US; Dwan, Allan; 1951)
Christian Century. Feb 13, 1952, v69, p207.

Film Daily. Dec 5, 1951, p6.
Hollywood Reporter. Nov 30, 1951, p3.
Motion Picture Herald Product Digest. Dec 8, 1951, p1133-34.
The New York Times. Jan 2, 1952, p20.
Newsweek. Jan 14, 1952, v39, p82.
Variety. Dec 5, 1951, p6.

Wild Boy *See* Savage Triangle

The Wild Bunch (US; Peckinpah, Sam; 1969)
America. Jul 5, 1969, v121, p20.
America. Jul 19, 1969, v121, p47-48.
The American West in Film. p122-27.
Big Screen, Little Screen. p339-41.
Christian Century. Aug 20, 1969, v86, p1095.
Cineaste. Wint 1969-70, v3, p18-20.
Classic Movies. p30-32.
Commonweal. Jul 25, 1969, v90, p465.
Confessions of a Cultist. p447-49.
Cult Movies. p386-89.
Dictionary of Films. p418-19.
Figures of Light. p179-83.
Film Comment. Fall 1970, v6, p55-57.
Film Daily. Jun 26, 1969, p6.
Film Heritage. Wint 1969-70, v5, p1-10.
Film Society Review. Nov 1969, v5, p31-37.
Filmfacts. 1969, v12, p217.
Films in Review. Aug-Sep 1969, v20, p446-47.
The Films of the Sixties. p269-71.
The Films of William Holden. p234-38.
Focus. Oct 1969, n5, p5-8.
The Great Movies. p40-47.
Hollywood Reporter. Jun 16, 1969, p3.
The International Dictionary of Films and Filmmakers. v1, p521-25.
Life. Jul 25, 1969, v67, p8.
Magill's Survey of Cinema. Series I. v4, p1845-47.
The Making of the Great Westerns. p395-408.
Movies Into Film. p173-76.
The Nation. Jul 14, 1969, v209, p61.
The New Republic. Jul 19, 1969, v161, p24.
The New York Times. Jun 26, 1969, p45.
The New Yorker. Jul 5, 1969, v45, p74-75.
Newsweek. Jul 14, 1969, v74, p85.
Reruns. p224-27.
Sam Peckinpah (McKinney). p81-98.
Saturday Review. Jul 5, 1969, v52, p21.
Saturday Review. Sep 27, 1969, v52, p39.
Second Sight. p244-46.
Sight and Sound. Aut 1969, v38, p208-09.
Time. Jun 20, 1969, v93, p85.
Variety. Jun 18, 1969, p6.

The Wild Child (French title: Enfant Sauvage, L') (FR; Truffaut, François; 1970)
America. Oct 3, 1970, v123, p244.
BFI/Monthly Film Bulletin. Feb 1971, v38, p21-22.
The Cinema of François Truffaut. p226-27.
Commonweal. Oct 2, 1970, v93, p20-21.
Film Quarterly. Spr 1971, v24, p42-45.
Films in Review. Nov 1970, v21, p570-71.
François Truffaut: A Guide to References and Resources. p62-65.
François Truffaut (Insdorf). p162-27.
Hollywood Reporter. Sep 11, 1970, p3.
Magill's Survey of Cinema. Foreign Language Films. v8, p3392-96.
The Nation. Sep 28, 1970, v211, p285-86.
The New Republic. Oct 3, 1970, v163, p20.
The New York Times. Sep 11, 1970, p32.
The New York Times. Sep 13, 1970, SecII, p1.
The New Yorker. Sep 12, 1970, v46, p67-69.
The New Yorker. Mar 21, 1970, v46, p144.
Newsweek. Dec 21, 1970, v76, p14.
Second Sight. p328-30.

Sight and Sound. Wint 1970-71, v40, n1, p46.
Time. Sep 21, 1970, v96, p100.
Variety. Feb 18, 1970, p21.

The Wild Country (US; Totten, Robert; 1971)
BFI/Monthly Film Bulletin. May 1971, v38, n448, p105.
Filmfacts. 1971, v14, p149.
Films in Review. Feb 1971, v22, n2, p108-09.
Hollywood Reporter. Jan 13, 1971, p3.
Variety. Jan 13, 1971, p24.

The Wild Heart (Also titled: Gone to Earth) (GB; Powell, Michael; Pressburger, Emeric; 1950)
Commonweal. Jun 20, 1952, v56, p268.
Film Daily. May 29, 1952, p6.
The Films of Jennifer Jones. p97-102.
Hollywood Reporter. May 28, 1952, p4.
Library Journal. Jun 15 1952, v77, p1071.
Motion Picture Herald Product Digest. May 31, 1952, p1382.
National Parent-Teacher. Sep 1952, v47, p40.
The New York Times. May 29, 1952, p17.
Newsweek. Jun 9, 1952, v39, p90.
Saturday Review. Jun 28, 1952, v35, p27.
Sequence. New Year 1951, n13, p18.
Time. Jun 9, 1952, v59, p102.
Variety. Sep 27, 1950, p8.
Variety. Jun 4, 1952, p6.

Wild in the Streets (US; Shear, Barry; 1968)
BFI/Monthly Film Bulletin. Dec 1968, v35, p197-98.
Christian Century. Dec 25, 1968, v85, p1626.
Christian Science Monitor (Western edition). Jun 14, 1968, p4.
Commonweal. Jun 21, 1968, v88, p410.
Commonweal. Jul 12, 1968, v88, p469-71.
Esquire. Oct 1968, v70, p92.
Film 68/69. p173-75.
Film Daily. May 7, 1968, p6.
Film Society Review. May 1968, p22-25.
Filmfacts. Aug 1, 1968, v11, p191-93.
The Films of the Sixties. p224-25.
Five Thousand One Nights At the Movies. p654.
Going Steady. p108-10.
Hollywood Reporter. May 8, 1968, p3.
Life. Jul 26, 1968, v65, p10.
The London Times. Sep 9, 1968, p4.
The London Times. Nov 8, 1968, p13.
Motion Picture Herald Product Digest. May 15, 1968, p812.
The Nation. Jun 17, 1968, v206, p805-06.
The New York Times. May 30, 1968, p21.
Newsweek. Jun 3, 1968, v71, p104.
Second Sight. p194-97.
Senior Scholastic. Sep 27, 1968, v93, p33.
The Spectator. Nov 8, 1968, v221, p671.
Time. May 24, 1968, v91 p104.
Variety. May 8, 1968, p6.
A Year In the Dark. p162-63, 173-75.

Wild Is the Wind (US; Cukor, George; 1957)
America. Jan 18, 1958, v98, p468.
American Cinematographer. Jan 1958, v39, p24-25.
BFI/Monthly Film Bulletin. Apr 1958, v25, p43.
Commonweal. Jan 10, 1958, v67, p383.
Film Daily. Dec 11, 1957, v112, p6.
Films and Filming. Mar 1958, v4, p28.
The Films of Anthony Quinn. p169-70.
George Cukor (Phillips). p121-23.
Hollywood Reporter. Dec 11, 1957, p3.
Motion Picture Herald Product Digest. Dec 14, 1957, v209, p641.

The New Republic. Jan 20, 1958, v138, p21.
The New York Times. Dec 12, 1957, p35.
The New Yorker. Dec 21, 1957, v33, p52.
Saturday Review. Dec 28, 1957, v40, p23.
Sight and Sound. Spr 1958, v27, p202.
Time. Dec 16, 1957, v70, p94.
Variety. Dec 11, 1957, p6.

The Wild North (Also titled: The Big North) (US; Marton, Andrew; 1952)
BFI/Monthly Film Bulletin. Mar 1952, v19, p39.
Film Daily. Jan 24, 1952, p6.
Hollywood Reporter. Jan 15, 1952, p3.
The London Times. Jan 28, 1952, p8.
Motion Picture Herald Product Digest. Jan 19, 1952, p1193.
The New York Times. May 12, 1952, p21.
Newsweek. Mar 17, 1952, v39, p96.
The Spectator. Jan 25 1952, v188, p108.
Theatre Arts. Feb 1952, v36, p33.
Time. Jun 2, 1952, v59, p96.
Variety. Jan 16, 1952, p6.

The Wild One (Also titled: Hot Blood) (US; Benedek, Laslo; 1954)
America. Jan 16, 1954, v90, p407.
Catholic World. Jan 1954, v178, p304.
Cinema, the Magic Vehicle. v2, p168-69.
Commonweal. Feb 5, 1954, v59, p449.
Cue. Jan 2, 1954, p14, 16.
Dictionary of Films. p419.
Farm Journal. Feb 1954, v78, p108.
Fifty From the Fifties. p389-95.
Film Daily. Jan 20, 1954, p10.
Films and Filming. Mar 1955, v1, p24.
Films and Filming. Jun 1955, v1, p22.
Films and Filming. Apr 1968, v14, p24.
Films in Review. Dec 1953, v4, p533-35.
The Films of Marlon Brando. p64-71.
The Films of the Fifties. p86-87.
Fortnight. Jan 6, 1954, v16, p32.
Hollywood Reporter. Dec 23, 1953, p4.
Library Journal. Jan 1, 1954, v79, p56.
Life. Jan 18, 1954, v36, p95-96.
Magill's Survey of Cinema. Series II. v6, p2668-71.
Metro. Spr 1981, n57, p64-65.
Motion Picture Herald Product Digest. Dec 26, 1953, p2118.
National Parent-Teacher. Jan 1954, v48, p40.
New Statesman. Feb 23, 1968, v75, p247.
The New Statesman and Nation. Apr 9, 1955, v49, p504.
The New York Times. Dec 31, 1953, p9.
The New York Times Magazine. Nov 29, 1953, p34.
Newsweek. Dec 14, 1953, v42, p88.
Saturday Review. Jan 2, 1954, v37, p58.
Selected Film Criticism, 1951-1960. p147.
Sight and Sound. Sum 1955, v25, p30-31.
Stanley Kramer, Film Maker. p157-66.
Stories into Film. p110-31.
Time. Jan 18, 1954, v63, p100.
Variety. Dec 23, 1953, p6.

The Wild Party (US; Ivory, James; 1975)
BFI/Monthly Film Bulletin. Sep 1975, v42, p206.
Films in Review. Oct 1975, v26, p506.
Motion Picture Herald Product Digest. Jun 25, 1975, p8.
Time. Aug 18, 1975, v106, p61.
Variety. Jun 18, 1975, p16.
Vogue. Jul 1975, v165, p30.

Wild River (US; Kazan, Elia; 1960)
America. Jun 11, 1960, v103, p361.
An American Odyssey. p229-33.
BFI/Monthly Film Bulletin. Aug 1960, v27, p110.

Commonweal. Jun 17, 1960, v72, p306.
Elia Kazan: A Guide to References and Resources. p74-77.
Film Daily. May 26, 1960, p6.
Film Quarterly. Sum 1960, v13, p50-51.
Filmfacts. 1960, v3, p127.
Films and Filming. Aug 1960, v6, p32.
Films in Review. Jun-Jul 1960, v11, p356-57.
The Films of Montgomery Clift. p185-91.
Hollywood Reporter. May 24, 1960, p3.
Kazan on Kazan. p130-38.
Magill's Survey of Cinema. Series II. v6, p2672-74.
The Nation. Jun 11, 1960, v190, p520.
The New York Times. May 27, 1960, p22.
The New Yorker. Jun 4, 1960, v36, p99.
Saturday Review. Jun 4, 1960, v43, p26.
Time. Jun 6, 1960, v75, p47.
Variety. May 25, 1960, p6.

Wild Rovers (US; Edwards, Blake; 1971)
America. Jul 10, 1971, v125, p17.
BFI/Monthly Film Bulletin. Nov 1971, v38, n454, p228.
Blake Edwards (Lehman and Luhr). p39-40.
Filmfacts. 1971, v14, n9, p198-201.
Films and Filming. May 1971, v17, n8, p26-27.
Films and Filming. Dec 1971, v18, n3, p49.
Hollywood Reporter. Jun 18, 1971, v216, n37, p3.
The New York Times. Jun 24, 1971, p35.
Saturday Review. Jul 10, 1971, v54, p12.
Time. Jul 26, 1971, v98, p51.
Variety. Jun 23, 1971, p20.
The Village Voice. Jul 22, 1971, v16, n29, p61.

Wild Strawberries (Swedish title: Smultronstallet) (SWED; Bergman, Ingmar; 1957)
America. Aug 1, 1959, v101, p576.
Bergman on Bergman. p131-49.
Cinema Borealis. p160-70.
Cinema Eye, Cinema Ear. p159-63.
Cinema. Fall 1971, v11, p52-57.
Cinema, the Magic Vehicle. v2, p346-48.
Classics of the Foreign Film. p232-35.
Commonweal. Jul 31, 1959, v70, p398.
Dictionary of Films. p344-45.
Fifty From the Fifties. p397-406.
Film and Literature: An Introduction. p189-96.
Film and the Critical Eye. p329-61.
Film Comment. Spr 1965, v3, p68-78.
Film Quarterly. Fall 1959, v13, p44-47.
Films and Filming. Dec 1958, v5, p24.
Films in Review. Apr 1959, v10, p231-32.
Ingmar Bergman: A Critical Biography (Cowie). p156-66.
Ingmar Bergman: Essays in Criticism. p179-201.
Ingmar Bergman (Steene). p70-76.
The International Dictionary of Films and Filmmakers. v1, p435-36.
Landmark Films. p232, 260.
Magill's Survey of Cinema. Foreign Language Films. v8, p3397-3400.
The Movies on Your Mind. p169-94.
The Nation. Jul 4, 1959, v189, p19.
New Orleans Review. 1983, v10, n4, p5-15.
The New Republic. Apr 27, 1959, v140, p20.
The New York Times. Jun 23, 1959, p37.
The New Yorker. Jul 25, 1959, v35, p44.
Newsweek. Jul 6, 1959, v54, p83.
Reporter. Jul 19, 1959, v21, p37-38.
Reruns. p102-05.
Sight and Sound. Wint 1958/59, v28, p35.
Sight and Sound. Wint 1960/61, v30, p44-46.
Swedish Film Classics. p97-100.
Ten Film Classics. p102-20.
Time. Jul 13, 1959, v74, p68.

Variety. Sep 24, 1958, p6.
The Village Voice. Jul 1, 1959, p6, 11.
A World on Film. p270-73.

Will Penny (US; Gries, Tom; 1968)
BFI/Monthly Film Bulletin. Mar 1968, v35, p38.
Christian Science Monitor (Western edition). Mar 11, 1968, p4.
Commonweal. Mar 22, 1968, v88, p23-24.
Film 68/69. p172-73.
Film Daily. Feb 27, 1968, p8.
Filmfacts. Jun 1, 1968, v11, p136-38.
Films and Filming. Mar 1968, v14, p28.
Films in Review. Apr 1968, v19, p240-41.
The Films of Charlton Heston. p170-74.
Five Thousand One Nights At the Movies. p655.
The Great Western Pictures. p401-02.
Hollywood Reporter. Feb 26, 1968, p3.
Magill's Survey of Cinema. Series II. v6, p2675-77.
Motion Picture Herald Product Digest. Feb 28, 1968, p777.
The New York Times. Apr 11, 1968, p51.
Saturday Review. Mar 9, 1968, v51, p93.
Senior Scholastic. Apr 4, 1968, v92, p26.
Time. May 10, 1968, v91, p118.
Variety. Feb 28, 1968, p6.
A Year In the Dark. p113.

Will Success Spoil Rock Hunter? (Also titled: Oh! For a Man!) (US; Tashlin, Frank; 1957)
America. Sep 7, 1957, v97, p604.
Commonweal. Aug 30, 1957, v66, p542.
Film Daily. Jul 29, 1957, v112, p6.
Films and Filming. Oct 1957, v4, p25.
The Films of the Fifties. p241-43.
Hollywood Reporter. Jul 29, 1957, p3.
Magill's Survey of Cinema. Series II. v6, p2678-81.
Motion Picture Herald Product Digest. Aug 3, 1957, v208, p473.
The New Republic. Oct 14, 1957, v137, p21.
The New York Times. Sep 12, 1957, p3.
The New Yorker. Sep 21, 1957, v33, p75.
Newsweek. Aug 12, 1957, v50, p94.
Saturday Review. Aug 31, 1957, v40, p23.
Talking Pictures. p73-89.
Time. Aug 19, 1957, v70, p78.
Variety. Jul 31, 1957, p6.

Willard (US; Mann, Daniel; 1971)
BFI/Monthly Film Bulletin. Nov 1971, v38, n454, p228.
Filmfacts. 1971, v14, n9, p208-11.
Films and Filming. Nov 1971, v18, n2, p52.
Hollywood Reporter. Jun 11, 1971, v216, n32, p3.
Journal of Popular Culture. Fall 1971, v5, n2, p573.
Life. Aug 27, 1971, v71, p65.
The New York Times. Jun 19, 1971, p16.
The New Yorker. Aug 7, 1971, v47, p65.
Time. Jul 26, 1971, v98, p51.
Time. Aug 23, 1971, v98, p47.
Variety. Jun 16, 1971, p22.
The Village Voice. Jul 1, 1971, v16, n26, p53.

Willie and Joe Back at the Front *See* Back at the Front

Willie and Phil (US; Mazursky, Paul; 1980)
Atlantic Monthly. Sep 1980, v246, p103-05.
Christian Century. Sep 24, 1980, v97, p892.
Hollywood Reporter. Aug 15, 1980, p4.
The Los Angeles Times. Aug 15, 1980, SecVI, p12.
Maclean's. Aug 25, 1980, v93, p50.
Motion Picture Herald Product Digest. Aug 20, 1980, p21.

Ms. Oct 1980, v9, p18.
The Nation. Sep 20, 1980, v231, p261.
New York. Aug 25, 1980, v13, p58.
The New York Times. Aug 15, 1980, SecIII, p6.
The New York Times. Aug 17, 1980, SecII, p13.
The New York Times. Sep 7, 1980, SecII, p19.
The New Yorker. Sep 1, 1980, v56, p74-76.
Newsweek. Aug 25, 1980, v96, p74.
Saturday Review. Aug 1980, v7, p70-71.
Time. Aug 18, 1980, v116, p59.
Variety. Aug 13, 1980, p23.
Vogue. Aug 1980, v170, p38.

Willy Wonka and the Chocolate Factory (US, GB; Stuart, Mel; 1971)
BFI/Monthly Film Bulletin. Dec 1971, v38, n455, p252.
Children's Novels and the Movies. p191-96.
Filmfacts. 1971, v14, n12, p286-88.
Films and Filming. Jan 1972, v18, n4, p50.
Focus on Film. Oct 1971, n8, p9-10.
Hollywood Reporter. May 24, 1971, v216, n19, p3.
Look. Aug 24, 1971, v35, p35.
The New York Times. Jul 1, 1971, p61.
The New York Times. Sep 12, 1971, SecII, p10.
Variety. May 26, 1971, p13.

Winchester '73 (US; Mann, Anthony; 1950)
The American West in Film. p88-90.
Anthony Mann (Basinger). p97-102.
BFI/Monthly Film Bulletin. Aug 1950, v17, p117-18.
Christian Century. Aug 9, 1950, v67, p959.
Commonweal. Jun 16, 1950, v52, p248.
Film Daily. Jun 8, 1950, p7.
The Films of James Stewart. p128-30.
The Great Western Pictures. p402-04.
Hollywood Reporter. Jun 7, 1950, p4.
The London Times. Jul 10, 1950, p2.
Magill's Survey of Cinema. Series I. v4, p1848-52.
Motion Picture Herald Product Digest. Jun 10, 1950, p329.
The New York Times. Jun 8, 1950, p38.
Newsweek. Jul 3, 1950, v36, p69.
Sequence. Aut 1950, n12, p18-19.
The Spectator. Jul 7, 1950, v185, p13.
Time. Jun 19, 1950, v55, p93.
Variety. Jun 7, 1950, p8.

Wind Across the Everglades (US; Ray, Nicholas; 1958)
America. Sep 20, 1958, v99.
BFI/Monthly Film Bulletin. Nov 1958, v25, p141.
Catholic World. Nov 1958, v188, p153.
Commonweal. Sep 12, 1958, v68, p593.
Film Daily. Aug 20, 1958, v114, p6.
Filmfacts. Oct 15, 1958, v1, p165-66.
Hollywood Reporter. Aug 20, 1958, p3.
Magill's Survey of Cinema. Series II. v6, p2687-93.
The New York Times. Sep 12, 1958, p21.
The New Yorker. Sep 20, 1958, v34, p593.
Newsweek. Sep 8, 1958, v52, p94.
Nicholas Ray: A Guide to References and Resources. p107-11.
Saturday Review. Sep 6, 1958, v41, p28.
Time. Sep 22, 1958, v72, p73.
Variety. Aug 20, 1958, p6.

The Wind and the Lion (US; Milius, John; 1975)
BFI/Monthly Film Bulletin. Aug 1975, v42, p185.
Films in Review. Oct 1975, v26, p502.
The Los Angeles Times. May 22, 1975, SecIV, p1.
Motion Picture Herald Product Digest. May 28, 1975, p97.

A Neglected Art. p162-63, 888.
The New York Times. May 23, 1975, p22.
The New York Times. Jul 15, 1975, SecII, p15.
Newsweek. Jul 21, 1975, v86, p66.
Time. Jun 9, 1975, v105, p60.
Variety. May 21, 1975, p19.

The Wings of Eagles (US; Ford, John; 1957)
America. Feb 16, 1957, v96, p567.
BFI/Monthly Film Bulletin. Apr 1957, v24, p44.
Commonweal. Feb 22, 1957, v65, p538-39.
The Complete Films of John Wayne. p210-12.
Film Daily. Jan 30, 1957, v111, p6.
Films and Filming. May 1957, v3, p23.
Films in Review. Mar 1957, v8, p132-33.
Hollywood Reporter. Jan 29, 1957, p3.
Magill's Survey of Cinema. Series I. v4, p1853-58.
Motion Picture Herald Product Digest. Feb 2, 1957, v206, p249.
The New York Times. Feb 1, 1957, p28.
The New York Times. Feb 10, 1957, SecII, p1.
The New York Times. Feb 24, 1957, SecII, p1.
The New Yorker. Feb 9, 1957, v32, p108.
Newsweek. Feb 11, 1957, v49, p89.
The Non-Western Films of John Ford. p136-44.
Saturday Review. Feb 9, 1957, v40, p29.
Time. Mar 11, 1957, v69, p100.
Variety. Jul 30, 1957, p6.
The Velvet Light Trap. Aug 1971, v2, p13-15.

Winning (US; Goldstone, James; 1969)
America. Jun 7, 1969, v120, p675.
Big Screen, Little Screen. p230-31.
Commonweal. Jun 13, 1969, v90, p368.
Figures of Light. p174-77.
Film Daily. May 14, 1969, p6.
Film Quarterly. Fall 1969, v23, p57-58.
Filmfacts. 1969, v12, p230.
Films and Filming. Dec 1969, v16, p46, 52.
The Films of Paul Newman. p175-78.
Holiday. Jul 1969, v46, p24-25.
Life. Jun 6, 1969, v66, p16.
The New Republic. Jun 14, 1969, v160, p32.
The New York Times. May 23, 1969, p35.
The New Yorker. May 31, 1969, v45, p80-81.
Newsweek. Jun 2, 1969, v73, p90C.
Saturday Review. May 24, 1969, v52, p37.
Time. May 16, 1969, v93, p113.
Variety. May 7, 1969, p6.

The Winning Team (US; Seiler, Lewis; 1952)
BFI/Monthly Film Bulletin. Nov 1952, v19, p159.
Catholic World. Jul 1952, v175, p306.
Film Daily. May 28, 1952, p7.
The Films of Ronald Reagan. p193-97.
Hollywood Reporter. May 22, 1952, p3.
Motion Picture Herald Product Digest. May 24, 1952, p1373.
The New York Times. Jun 21, 1952, p12.
Newsweek. Jul 7, 1952, v40, p78.
Time. Jul 14, 1952, v60, p98.
Variety. May 28, 1952, p6.

The Winslow Boy (GB; Asquith, Anthony; 1948)
BFI/Monthly Film Bulletin. Sep 1948, v15, p126.
Christian Century. Jul 5, 1950, v67, p831.
Cinema, the Magic Vehicle. v1, p484.
Commonweal. Jun 23, 1950, v52, p271.
Film Daily. Mar 8, 1950, p10.
Films in Review. Apr 1950, v1, p25-27.
Films in Review. Nov 1950, v1, p25-27.
Halliwell's Harvest. p280-83.
Hollywood Reporter. Mar 3, 1950, p3.
Library Journal. Apr 1, 1950, v75, p571.

Motion Picture Herald Product Digest. Mar 11, 1950, p222.
The New Republic. Jun 26, 1950, v122, p22.
The New York Times. Jun 7, 1950, p34.
The New Yorker. Jun 3, 1950, v26, p52.
Newsweek. May 15, 1950, v35, p93.
Senior Scholastic. Apr 5, 1950, v56, p29.
Sight and Sound. Wint 1948-49, v17 p182.
Time. Apr 10, 1950, v55, p90.
Variety. Sep 29, 1948, p18.

Winter Light (Swedish title: Nattvardsgaesterna) (US; Bergman, Ingmar; 1962)
America. May 18, 1963, v108, p722-23.
BFI/Monthly Film Bulletin. Jun 1963, v30, p79.
Catholic World. Aug 1963, v197, p335-36.
Christian Century. Nov 20, 1963, v80, p1436-37.
Christian Century. Sep 16, 1964, v81, p1144-45.
Cinema Borealis. p208-12.
Commonweal. May 17, 1963, v78, p225-26.
Filmfacts. May 23, 1963, v6, p85-87.
Films and Filming. Jun 1963, v9, p27-28.
Films in Review. May 1963, v14, p299-301.
Hollywood Reporter. Apr 8, 1963, v174, p3.
Ingmar Bergman: Essays in Criticism. p226-38.
Magill's Survey of Cinema. Foreign Language Films. v7, p3405-08.
The Nation. Jun 15, 1963, v196, p515.
The New Republic. May 11, 1963, v148, p26-27.
The New York Times. May 14, 1963, p32.
The New York Times. May 19, 1963, SecII, p1.
The New Yorker. May 18, 1963, v39, p173.
Newsweek. May 27, 1963, v61, p103-04.
Saturday Review. May 18, 1963, v46, p37.
Sight and Sound. Sum 1963, v32, p146.
Time. May 24, 1963, v81, p98.
Variety. Feb 20, 1963, p6.
The Village Voice. Nov 7, 1963, v8, p15.

Wir Kinden Vom Bahnof 200 *See* Christiane F.

Wise Blood (US, WGER; Huston, John; 1979)
BFI/Monthly Film Bulletin. Jan 1980, v47, p13.
Double Exposure. p175-81.
Hollywood Reporter. Oct 12, 1979, p2.
The Los Angeles Times. Dec 12, 1979, SecIV, p1.
The New York Times. Sep 29, 1979, p12.
The New York Times. Oct 7, 1979, SecII, p1.
The New York Times. Feb 17, 1980, p68.
Variety. Jun 6, 1979, p22.

With a Song in My Heart (US; Lang, Walter; 1952)
BFI/Monthly Film Bulletin. Apr 1952, v19, p55.
Catholic World. Apr 1952, v175, p62-63.
Christian Century. Jun 4, 1952, v69, p687.
Commonweal. May 9, 1952, v56, p116.
Cue. Apr 5, 1952, p16, 29.
Film Daily. Feb 20, 1952, p6.
The Films of Susan Hayward. p171-75.
Hollywood Reporter. Feb 20, 1952, p3.
Magill's Survey of Cinema. Series II. v6, p2694-97.
Motion Picture Herald Product Digest. Feb 23, 1952, p1245.
The New York Times. Apr 5, 1952, p20.
Newsweek. Apr 21, 1952, v39, p120.
Saturday Review. May 3, 1952, v35, p31.
Selected Film Criticism, 1951-1960. p148.
Senior Scholastic. Apr 23, 1952, v60, p23.
The Spectator. Apr 18, 1952, v188, p512.
Theatre Arts. May 1952, v36, p45.
Time. Apr 7, 1952, v59, p106.
Variety. Feb 20, 1952, p6.

Without a Trace (US; Jaffe, Stanley R.; 1983)
Christian Century. Apr 13, 1983, v100, p347-48.
Commonweal. Feb 25, 1983, v110, p112-14.
Hollywood Reporter. Feb 1, 1983, p3.
Ms. Apr 1983, v11, p69-70.
The New Leader. Feb 21, 1983, v66, p19.
The New Republic. Mar 7, 1983, v188, p25.
Newsweek. Feb 7, 1983, v101, p69-70.
Time. Feb 14, 1983, v121, p80.

Witness (US; Weir, Peter; 1985)
BFI/Monthly Film Bulletin. May 1985, v52, p166.
Christian Century. Apr 10, 1985, v102, p341-42.
Christianity Today. Mar 15, 1985, v29, p52.
Commonweal. Mar 22, 1985, v112, p179-80.
Dance Magazine. Feb 1985, v59, p66-67.
Film Comment. May-Jun 1985, v21, p5-6.
Films in Review. Apr 1985, v36, p245.
Hollywood Reporter. Jan 25, 1985, p3.
The Los Angeles Times. Feb 8, 1985, SecVI, p1.
Maclean's. Feb 18, 1985, v98, p57.
Magill's Cinema Annual, 1986. p421-25.
National Review. Apr 5, 1985, v37, p56-58.
The New Republic. Feb 18, 1985, v192, p24.
New York. Feb 11, 1985, v18, p72.
The New York Times. Feb 8, 1985, SecIII, p18.
The New York Times. Feb 25, 1985, v61, p78-81.
Newsweek. Mar 11, 1985, v105, p69-70.
Newsweek. Feb 11, 1985, v105, p73.
Sight and Sound. Sum 1985, v54, p221.
Time. Feb 18, 1985, v125, p90-91.
Variety. Jan 30, 1985, p18.

Witness for the Prosecution (US; Wilder, Billy; 1957)
America. Feb 15, 1958, v98, p577.
BFI/Monthly Film Bulletin. Feb 1958, v25, p18.
Billy Wilder (Dick). p134-39.
Charles Laughton (Brown). p143-45.
Cinema, the Magic Vehicle. v2, p362.
Commonweal. Feb 14, 1958, v67, p513.
The Film Career of Billy Wilder. p91-93.
Film Daily. Nov 27, 1957, v112, p6.
Films and Filming. Mar 1958, v4, p25-26.
Films and Filming. Mar 1963, v9, p42.
Films in Review. Mar 1958, v9, p144-45.
The Films of Marlene Dietrich. p203-07.
Hollywood Reporter. Nov 27, 1957, p3.
Magill's Survey of Cinema. Series I. v4, p1862-66.
The Nation. Mar 8, 1958, v186, p216.
The New York Times. Aug 11, 1957, SecVI, p26.
The New York Times. Feb 7, 1958, p16.
The New York Times. Feb 23, 1958, SecII, p1.
The New Yorker. Feb 15, 1958, v33, p80.
Newsweek. Jan 20, 1958, v51, p90.
Saturday Review. Feb 15, 1958, v41, p30.
Time. Jan 27, 1958, v71, p90.
Variety. Dec 4, 1957, p6.

Witness to Murder (US; Rowland, Roy; 1954)
BFI/Monthly Film Bulletin. Jun 1954, p91.
Commonweal. May 14, 1954, v60, p145.
Farm Journal. Jun 1954, v78, p141.
Film Daily. Apr 26, 1954, p6.
The Films of Barbara Stanwyck. p226-28.
Hollywood Reporter. Apr 14, 1954, p3.
Motion Picture Herald Product Digest. Apr 17, 1954, p2261.
National Parent-Teacher. Jun 1954, v49, p40.
The New York Times. Apr 16, 1954, p16.
Newsweek. Apr 19, 1954, v43, p106.

A Reference Guide to the American Film Noir. p214-15.
Saturday Review. May 8, 1954, v37, p27.
Starring Miss Barbara Stanwyck. p248.
Time. May 10, 1954, v63, p112.
Variety. Apr 21, 1954, p6.

Wolfen (US; Wadleigh, Michael; 1981)
Encore. Sep 1981, v10, p42.
Hollywood Reporter. Oct 20, 1981, p2.
The Los Angeles Times. Nov 12, 1981, SecVI, p1.
Maclean's. Aug 10, 1981, v94, p46.
Magill's Cinema Annual, 1982. p382-87.
The New Republic. Sep 9, 1981, v185, p24-25.
New York. Aug 10, 1981, v14, p57.
The New York Times. Oct 9, 1981, p92.
Newsweek. Aug 3, 1981, v98, p51.
Time. Aug 3, 1981, v118, p67.

A Woman at Her Window (French title: Femme a Sa Fenetre, Une) (FR; Granier-Deferre, Pierre; 1976)
Hollywood Reporter. Jun 19, 1978, p2.
The Nation. Jul 8, 1978, v227, p62.
The New York Times. Jun 8, 1978, SecIII, p14.
The New Yorker. Jun 12, 1978, v54, p114-15.
Time. Sep 11, 1978, v112, p88.
Variety. Oct 27, 1978, p28.

The Woman in Question (Also titled: Five Angles on Murder) (GB; Asquith, Anthony; 1950)
BFI/Monthly Film Bulletin. Nov 1950, v17, p169-7.
Film Daily. Feb 28, 1952, p10.
The Films of Anthony Asquith. p129-30.
The Films of Dirk Bogarde. p55-56.
Motion Picture Herald Product Digest. Feb 23, 1952, p1246.
The New York Times. Feb 19, 1952, p24.
The New Yorker. Mar 8, 1952, v28, p102.
Newsweek. Mar 3, 1952, v39, p88.
The Spectator. Oct 13, 1950, v185, p385.
Time. Mar 17, 1952, v59, p106.
Variety. Oct 18, 1950, p6.

The Woman in Red (US; Wilder, Gene; 1984)
BFI/Monthly Film Bulletin. Oct 1984, v51, p311-12.
Film Journal. Sep 1984, v87, p27.
Films and Filming. Oct 1984, p49-50.
Hollywood Reporter. Aug 15, 1984, p4.
The Los Angeles Times. Aug 17, 1984, SecVI, p4.
Maclean's. Aug 27, 1984, v97, p55.
New Statesman. Oct 12, 1984, v108, p35-36.
New York. Sep 3, 1984, v17, p57.
The New York Times. Aug 15, 1984, SecIII, p24.
Photoplay. Nov 1984, v35, p22.
Time. Aug 27, 1984, v124, p64.
Variety. Aug 15, 1984, p14.
The Village Voice. Aug 28, 1984, p52.

Woman in the Dunes (Japanese title: Suna No Onna; Also titled: The Woman of the Dunes) (JAPAN; Teshigahara, Hiroshi; 1964)
BFI/Monthly Film Bulletin. Jun 1965, v32, p88-89.
Cinema East. p36-50.
Close-Up. p284-90.
Dictionary of Films. p361.
Film Comment. Wint 1965, v3, n1, p56-60, 64-65.
Films and Filming. Jun 1965, v11, p32-33.
Films in Review. Dec 1964, v15, p631-32.
The International Dictionary of Films and Filmmakers. v2, p458-59.

BFI/Monthly Film Bulletin. Aug 1976, v43, p177.
Film Bulletin. May 1976, v45, pB.
Films and Filming. Sep 1976, v22, p34-35.
The Films of Michael Winner. p110-15.
Hollywood Reporter. Apr 29, 1976, p2.
Independent Film Journal. Jun 11, 1976, v78, p11.
The Los Angeles Times. May 26, 1976, SecIV, p1.
Motion Picture Herald Product Digest. Jun 16, 19766, p8.
Movietone News. Jun 1976, n50, p38.
New Statesman. Jul 16, 1976, v92, p89-90.
New York. Jun 4, 1976, v9, p63-66.
The New York Times. May 27, 1976, p30.
Newsweek. Jun 14, 1976, v87, p90.
Variety. May 5, 1976, p18.

The Wooden Horse (GB; Lee, Jack; 1950)
BFI/Monthly Film Bulletin. Sep 1950, v17, p138.
Christian Century. Dec 12, 1951, v68, p1447.
Hollywood Reporter. Nov 1, 1951, p4.
The London Times. Jul 13, 1950, p8.
Motion Picture Herald Product Digest. Sep 8, 1951, p1006.
The New York Times. Aug 29, 1951, p20.
Newsweek. Oct 8, 1951, v38, p100.
Sight and Sound. Nov 1950, v19, p286-88.
Variety. Aug 2, 1950, p16.

Woodstock (US; Wadleigh, Michael; 1970)
BFI/Monthly Film Bulletin. Aug 1970, v37, p173.
Film Daily. Mar 27, 1970, p3.
Film Quarterly. Sum 1970, v23, p61.
Films in Review. May 1970, v21, p304-05.
Hollywood Reporter. Mar 27, 1970, p3.
The New York Times. Mar 27, 1970, p22.
The New York Times. Apr 5, 1970, SecII, p1.
The New York Times. Apr 19, 1970, SecII, p11.
Second Sight. p297-99.
Sight and Sound. Sum 1970, v39, n3, p159-60.
Variety. Apr 1, 1970, p14.

The Word *See* Ordet

The World According to Garp (US; Hill, George Roy; 1982)
Christianity Today. Sep 17, 1982, v26, p57.
Commentary. Sep 1982, v74, p61-64.
Commonweal. Sep 10, 1982, v109, p468-69.
Hollywood Reporter. Jul 2, 1982, p3.
Horizon. Oct-Nov 1982, v25, p58-59.
The Los Angeles Times. Jul 23, 1982, SecVI, p1.
Maclean's. Aug 2, 1982, v95, p50.
Magill's Cinema Annual, 1983. p397-402.
Ms. Sep 1982, v11, p14-16.
The Nation. Sep 4, 1982, v175, p187-89.
National Review. Sep 3, 1982, v34, p1096-97.
The New Leader. Sep 6, 1982, v65, p19-20.
The New Republic. Aug 30, 1982, v187, p26-27.
New York. Aug 2, 1982, v15, p46-47.
The New York Times. Jul 23, 1982, SecIII, p13.
The New Yorker. Aug 23, 1982, v58, p74-77.
Newsweek. Jul 26, 1982, v100, p77.
Progressive. Sep 1982, v46, p52-53.
Rolling Stone. Aug 19, 1982, p33.
Time. Aug 2, 1982, v120, p78.
Variety. Jul 2, 1982, p3.

World For Ransom (US; Aldrich, Robert; 1954)
Film Daily. Jan 29, 1954, p22.
Hollywood Reporter. Jan 27, 1954, p3.
Motion Picture Herald Product Digest. Feb 13, 1954, p2182-83.
The New York Times. Jun 5, 1954, p11.

Robert Aldrich: A Guide to References and Resources. p18-19.
Variety. Feb 3, 1954, p6.

The World in His Arms (US; Walsh, Raoul; 1952)
BFI/Monthly Film Bulletin. Aug 1952, v19, p108.
Christian Century. Sep 17, 1952, v69, p1079.
Commonweal. Sep 19, 1952, v56, p583.
Film Daily. Jun 17, 1952, p6.
The Films of Anthony Quinn. p126-27.
The Films of Gregory Peck. p118-20.
Hollywood Reporter. Jun 17, 1952, p3.
Library Journal. Aug 1952, v77, p1299.
Life. Sep 8, 1952, v33, p60.
The London Times. Aug 18, 1952, p8.
Motion Picture Herald Product Digest. Jun 21, 1952, p1417.
The Nation. Sep 27, 1952, v175, p283.
National Parent-Teacher. Sep 1952, v47, p40.
The New Statesman and Nation. Aug 23, 1952, v44, p210.
The New York Times. Oct 10, 1952, p21.
The New Yorker. Oct 18, 1952, v28, p151.
Saturday Review. Aug 2, 1952, v35, p28.
The Spectator. Aug 15, 1952, v189, p215.
The Tatler. Aug 27, 1952, v205, p376.
Theatre Arts. Sep 1952, v36, p73.
Time. Aug 28, 1952, v60, p72.
Variety. Jun 18, 1952, p6.

The World of Apu (Also titled: Apur Sanshar) (INDIA; Ray, Satyajit; 1959)
America. Oct 15, 1959, v104, p101.
The Apu Trilogy. 1971.
Classic Movies. p180-81.
Classics of the Foreign Film. p226-31.
Commonweal. Sep 16, 1960, v72, p497.
Filmfacts. Oct 14, 1960, v3, p223-25.
Films in Review. Mar 1960, v11, p166-67.
The Great Films. p227-31.
Hollywood Reporter. Nov 28, 1960, p3.
The International Dictionary of Films and Filmmakers. v1, p36-38.
McCall's. Jan 1961, v88, p8.
The Nation. Nov 5, 1960, v191, p355.
The New Republic. Jun 6, 1960, v142, p22.
The New York Times. Oct 5, 1960, p45.
The New Yorker. Oct 8, 1960, v36, p107.
Newsweek. Sep 26, 1960, v46, p118.
Reporter. Nov 10, 1960, v23, p44.
Saturday Review. Sep 10, 1960, v43, p32.
Time. Sep 26, 1960, v76, p94.
Variety. Sep 23, 1959, p18.

The World of Henry Orient (US; Hill, George Roy; 1964)
America. Apr 18, 1964, v110, p554.
BFI/Monthly Film Bulletin. Jul 1964, v31, p104.
Commonweal. Apr 3, 1964, v80, p43.
Film Daily. Mar 16, 1964, v124, p4.
Films and Filming. Jul 1964, v10, p20-21.
Films in Review. Apr 1964, v15, p242-43.
George Roy Hill. p103-07.
Hollywood Reporter. Mar 16, 1964, v179, p3.
Motion Picture Herald Product Digest. Mar 18, 1964, v231, p9.
The New Republic. Apr 18, 1964, v150, p26.
The New York Times. Mar 20, 1964, p27.
The New Yorker. Mar 28, 1964, v40, p144.
Newsweek. Mar 30, 1964, v63, p52-53.
Private Screenings. p132-33.
Saturday Review. Apr 4, 1964, v47, p36.
Time. May 15, 1964, v83, p69.

The World of Suzie Wong (US; Quine, Richard; 1960)
BFI/Monthly Film Bulletin. Feb 1961, v28, p26.
Commonweal. Nov 11, 1960, v73, p179-80.
Film Daily. Nov 14, 1960, p10.
Filmfacts. 1960, v3, p285.
Films and Filming. Feb 1961, v7, p30-31.
Films in Review. Dec 1960, v11, p615.
The Films of William Holden. p196-201.
Hollywood Reporter. Nov 10, 1960, p3.
The New York Times. Nov 11, 1960, p36.
The New York Times. Nov 27, 1960, SecII, p1.
The New Yorker. Dec 10, 1960, v36, p153.
Newsweek. Nov 21, 1960, v56, p107.
Saturday Review. Nov 26, 1960, v43, p29.
Time. Nov 28, 1960, v76, p56.
Variety. Nov 16, 1960, p6.

World Without Sun (French title: Monde Sans Soleil, Le) (FR, IT; Cousteau, Jacques-Yves; 1964)
Christian Science Monitor (Western edition). Jan 7, 1965, p6.
Commonweal. Dec 25, 1964, v81, p453.
Film Daily. Dec 22, 1964, p6.
Filmfacts. Jan 8, 1965, v7, p342-44.
Films in Review. Jan 1965, v16, p44-45.
Hollywood Reporter. Dec 18, 1965, p3.
Motion Picture Herald Product Digest. Jan 20, 1965, p209.
The New Republic. Jan 23, 1965, v152, p37.
The New York Times. Dec 23, 1964, p22.
The New Yorker. Jan 2, 1965, v40, p64.
Playboy. Feb 1965, v12, p24.
Senior Scholastic. Jan 7, 1965, v85, p14T, 25.
Seventeen. Feb 1965, v24, p56.
Time. Dec 25, 1964, v84, p65.
Variety. Nov 4, 1964, p18.
Vogue. Mar 1, 1965, v145, p97.

The World's Greatest Lover (US; Wilder, Gene; 1977)
America. Jan 28, 1978, v138, p63.
BFI/Monthly Film Bulletin. Apr 1978, v45, p74.
BFI/Monthly Film Bulletin. Jun 1978, v45, p126.
Films in Review. Feb 1978, v29, p117.
Hollywood Reporter. Nov 18, 1977, p3.
Maclean's. Jan 9, 1978, v91, p59-60.
Motion Picture Herald Product Digest. Dec 14, 1977, p56.
The New York Times. Dec 19, 1977, p44.
Newsweek. Jan 2, 1978, v91, p58.
Time. Dec 26, 1977, v110, p72.
Variety. Nov 16, 1977, p20.
The Village Voice. Dec 19, 1977, p78.

Wozzeck (WGER; Klaren, Georg; 1947)
BFI/Monthly Film Bulletin. Mar 1953, v20, p34.
Filmfacts. Sep 14, 1962, v5, p200.
German Film and Literature. p132-45.
The New York Times. Mar 3, 1962, p13.
The New Yorker. Mar 10, 1962, v38, p90.
Sequence. New Year 1951, n13, p37-38.

Written on the Wind (US; Sirk, Douglas; 1956)
America. Jan 26, 1957, v96, p492.
BFI/Monthly Film Bulletin. Nov 1956, v23, p139.
Commonweal. Dec 28, 1956, v65, p334.
Douglas Sirk (Stern). p135-51.
Film Comment. Nov-Dec 1975, v11, p18-24.
Film Comment. Mar-Apr 1976, v12, p20-25.
Film Daily. Sep 20, 1956, p47.
The Films in My Life. p148-50.
Hollywood Reporter. Sep 20, 1956, p3.

The International Dictionary of Film and Filmmakers. v1, p528-29.
Lauren Bacall: Her Films and Career. p138-43.
Literature/Film Quarterly. 1982, v10, p155-61.
Magill's Survey of Cinema. Series I. v4, p1876-79.
The Modern American Novel and the Movies. p40-52.
The New York Times. Jan 12, 1957, p12.
The New Yorker. Jan 26, 1957, v32, p95.
Newsweek. Feb 4, 1957, v49, p90.
Time. Feb 4, 1957, v69, p90.
Variety. Sep 26, 1956, p6.
Wide Angle. 1980, v4, p28-35.

The Wrong Box (GB; Forbes, Bryan; 1966)
America. Sep 10, 1966, v115, p261.
BFI/Monthly Film Bulletin. Jul 1966, v33, p105-06.
Christian Century. Oct 12, 1966, v83, p1243-44.
Christian Science Monitor (Western edition). Jul 30, 1966, p4.
Film Daily. Jul 21, 1966, p6.
Film Quarterly. Wint 1966-67, v20, p63.
Filmfacts. Sep 15, 1966, v9, p190-92.
Films and Filming. Jul 1966, v12, p6.
Films in Review. Aug-Sep 1966, v17, p450.
Illustrated London News. May 28, 1966, v248, p32-33.
The London Times. May 26, 1966, p19.
Magill's Survey of Cinema. Series II. v6, p2718-20.
Motion Picture Herald Product Digest. Aug 3, 1966, p570.
The Nation. Aug 8, 1966, v203, p134.
New Statesman. May 27, 1966, v71, p788.
The New York Times. Jul 20, 1966, p46.
The New Yorker. Jul 30, 1966, v42, p64.
Newsweek. Aug 1, 1966, v68, p83.
Playboy. Oct 1966, v13, p24.
The Private Eye, the Cowboy and the Very Naked Girl. p230.
Saturday Review. Aug 13, 1966, v49, p38.
Senior Scholastic. Sep 23, 1966, v89, p25.
Sight and Sound. Sum 1966, v35, p149.
Time. Aug 12, 1966, v88, p59.
Variety. Jul 1, 1966, p6.
The Village Voice. Aug 11, 1966, v11, p21.
Vogue. Sep 1, 1966, v148, p207.

Wrong Is Right (US; Brooks, Richard; 1982)
Hollywood Reporter. Apr 1, 1982, p3.
The Los Angeles Times. Apr 16, 1982, SecVI, p1.
Maclean's. May 17, 1982, v96, p62.
Magill's Cinema Annual, 1983. p403-06.
The New York Times. Apr 16, 1982, SecIII, p8.
Newsweek. Apr 26, 1982, v99, p75.
Saturday Review. May 1982, v9, p56.
Variety. Apr 1, 1982, p3.

The Wrong Man (US; Hitchcock, Alfred; 1957)
America. Jan 5, 1957, v96, p399.
American Cinematographer. Feb 1957, v38, p84-85.
The Art of Alfred Hitchcock. p283-90.
Commonweal. Jan 25, 1957, v65, p434.
Film Daily. Jan 3, 1957, v111, p8.
Films and Filming. Apr 1957, v3, p26.
The Films in My Life. p83-86.
Films in Review. Jan 1957, v8, p33-34.
The Films of Alfred Hitchcock. p182-84.
The Films of Henry Fonda. p150-52.
The Fondas (Springer). p159-61.
Hitchcock: The First Forty-Four Films. p145-52.
Hitchcock (Truffaut). p239-42.
Hollywood Reporter. Dec 21, 1956, p3.

Magill's Survey of Cinema. Series I. v4, p1880-83.
The Nation. Jan 5, 1957, v184, p27.
The New York Times. Apr 9, 1956, p21.
The New York Times. Apr 29, 1956, SecII, p7.
The New York Times. Dec 24, 1956, p8.
The New Yorker. Jan 5, 1957, v32, p61.
Newsweek. Jan 7, 1957, v49, p68.
Saturday Review. Jan 19, 1957, v40, p49.
Sight and Sound. Spr 1957, v26, p211.
Time. Jan 14, 1957, v69, p100.
Variety. Jan 2, 1957, p6.

Wszystko na Sprzedaz *See* Everything For Sale

Wuthering Heights (GB; Fuest, Robert; 1971)
America. Mar 6, 1971, v124, p244.
BFI/Monthly Film Bulletin. Jun 1971, v38, n449, p127.
The English Novel and the Movies. p76-77.
Filmfacts. 1971, v14, n5, p85-87.
Films and Filming. Jul 1971, v17, n10, p50-51.
Films in Review. Feb 1971, v22, n2, p105-06.
Make It Again, Sam. p210-14.
The New York Times. Feb 19, 1971, p23.
Newsweek. Mar 15, 1971, v77, p110.
Saturday Review. Jan 16, 1971, v54, p40.
Time. Mar 1, 1979, v97, p79.
Variety. Dec 16, 1970, p17.
The Village Voice. Apr 1, 1971, v16, n13, p73.

Xanadu (US; Greenwald, Robert; 1980)
BFI/Monthly Film Bulletin. Oct 1980, v47, p199.
Dance Magazine. Aug 1980, v54, p42-45.
Hollywood Reporter. Aug 14, 1980, p3.
The Los Angeles Times. Aug 11, 1980, SecVI, p1.
New York. Sep 1, 1980, v13, p46.
The New York Times. Aug 9, 1980, p10.
Newsday. Aug 9, 1980, SecII, p24.
Newsweek. Aug 18, 1980, v96, p85.
Variety. Aug 13, 1980, p23.

Xica (Also titled: Xica da silva) (BRAZ; Diegues, Carlos; 1976)
The Los Angeles Times. Oct 4, 1982, VI, p4.
Magill's Cinema Annual, 1983. p407-10.
Ms. Dec 1982, v11, p29-30.
The Nation. Oct 1982, v235, p348.
The New York Times. Sep 10, 1982, III, p6.
Newsweek. Sep 20, 1982, v100, p97.
Variety. Dec 1, 1976, p38.

Yang Kwei Fei *See* Princess Yang Kwei Fei

Yangtse Incident *See* Battle Hell

Yankee Buccaneer (US; De Cordova, Frederick; 1952)
BFI/Monthly Film Bulletin. Jan 1953, v20, p13.
Film Daily. Sep 18, 1952, p8.
Hollywood Reporter. Sep 12, 1952, p3.
Motion Picture Herald Product Digest. Sep 13, 1952, p1525.
Time. Oct 20, 1952, v60, p116.
Variety. Sep 17, 1952, p6.

Yankee Pasha (US; Pevney, Joseph; 1954)
BFI/Monthly Film Bulletin. May 1954, v21, p77-78.
Film Daily. Apr 7, 1954, p6.
Hollywood Reporter. Mar 12, 1954, p4.
Library Journal. Apr 1, 1954, v79, p618.
Motion Picture Herald Product Digest. Mar 13, 1954, p2213.
National Parent-Teacher. Apr 1954, v48, p40.
The New York Times. Apr 19, 1954, p19.
Newsweek. Apr 12, 1954, v43, p104.
Time. Apr 12, 1954, v63, p110.
Variety. Mar 17, 1954, p6.

Yanks (GB, US; Schlesinger, John; 1979)
America. Nov 3, 1979, v141, p263.
BFI/Monthly Film Bulletin. Oct 1979, v46, p214.
Films in Review. Nov 1979, v30, p562.
Hollywood Reporter. Sep 14, 1979, p3.
John Schlesinger (Phillips). p161-72.
The Los Angeles Times. Sep 16, 1979, Calendar, p1.
Motion Picture Herald Product Digest. Sep 12, 1979, p30.
The Nation. Nov 3, 1979, v229, p445.
The New Republic. Oct 6, 1979, v181, p24.
New York. Oct 1, 1979, v12, p120-22.
The New York Times. Sep 19, 1979, SecIII, p17.
The New Yorker. Oct 1, 1979, v55, p104-05.
Newsweek. Sep 24, 1979, v94, p102.
Time. Oct 1, 1979, v114, p84.
Variety. Sep 19, 1979, p18.

The Year of Living Dangerously (AUSTRALIA; Weir, Peter; 1983)
American Film. Jan 1984, v9, p38.
Christian Century. Apr 13, 1983, v100, p347.
Films in Review. Feb 1983, v34, p13.
Hollywood Reporter. Jan 26, 1983, p3.
The Los Angeles Times. Feb 17, 1983, SecVI, p1.
Maclean's. Feb 21, 1983, v96, p49.
Magill's Cinema Annual, 1983. p462-67.
Ms. Apr 1983, v11, p73.
The Nation. Feb 19, 1983, v236, p218-19.
National Review. Mar 18, 1983, v35, p335-37.
The New Leader. Mar 21, 1983, v66, p20-21.
The New Republic. Feb 7, 1983, v188, p24.
New York. Jan 24, 1983, v16, p62-63.
The New York Times. Jan 21, 1983, SecIII, p4.
The New Yorker. Feb 21, 1983, v59, p120.
Newsweek. Jan 24, 1983, v101, p66.
Rolling Stone. Feb 17, 1983, p38.
Time. Jan 17, 1983, v121, p63.

The Year of the Dragon (US; Cimino, Michael; 1985)
BFI/Monthly Film Bulletin. Jan 1986, v53, p15.
Films in Review. Oct 1985, v36, p496.
Hollywood Reporter. Aug 12, 1985, p3.
The Los Angeles Times. Aug 16, 1985, SecVI, p1.
Maclean's. Aug 26, 1985, v98, p53.
Magill's Cinema Annual, 1986. p426-30.
National Review. Sep 20, 1985, v37, p46-49.
The New Republic. Sep 16, 1985, v193, p30-32.
New York. Aug 26, 1985, v18, p101-02.
The New York Times. Aug 16, 1985, SecIII, p10.
The New Yorker. Sep 9, 1985, v61, p72-74.
Newsweek. Aug 19, 1985, v106, p69.
Time. Aug 19, 1985, v126, p71.
Variety. Aug 14, 1985, p16.
The Wall Street Journal. Aug 15, 1985, p24.

Years of Lightning, Day of Drums *See* John F. Kennedy: Years of Lightning, Day of Drums

The Yellow Cab Man (US; Donohue, Jack; 1950)
Christian Century. Apr 26, 1950, v67, p543.
Commonweal. Apr 14, 1950, v52, p17.
Film Daily. Feb 21, 1950, p5.
Hollywood Reporter. Feb 16, 1950, p3.
Motion Picture Herald Product Digest. Feb 18, 1950, p21.
Motion Picture Herald Product Digest. Feb 25, 1950, p206-07.
The New York Times. Mar 27, 1950, p19.
Variety. Feb 22, 1950, p6.

The Yellow Canary (US; Kulik, Buzz; 1963)
BFI/Monthly Film Bulletin. Jun 1963, v30, p90.
Commonweal. Jun 21, 1963, v78, p355.
Film Daily. Apr 16, 1963, p4.
Filmfacts. Jun 6, 1963, v6, p99-100.
Films and Filming. Jun 1963, v9, p29.
Hollywood Reporter. Apr 16, 1963, v174, p3.
The New York Times. May 16, 1963, p42.
Newsweek. May 27, 1963, v61, p104.
Photoplay. Jul 1963, v64, p14.
Variety. Apr 17, 1963, p6.

The Yellow Rolls-Royce (GB; Asquith, Anthony; 1964)
America. May 29, 1965, v112, p809.
BFI/Monthly Film Bulletin. Feb 1965, v32, p23.
Christian Science Monitor (Western edition). Jun 11, 1965, p4.
Commonweal. May 28, 1965, v82, p319.
Film Daily. Feb 5, 1965, p4.
Film Quarterly. Spr 1965, v18, p62.
Films and Filming. Feb 1965, v11, p7-8, 30.
Films in Review. Jun-Jul 1965, v16, p385-86.
The Films of Anthony Asquith. p206-14.
The Films of Ingrid Bergman. p169-73.
The Films of Shirley MacLaine. p138-40.
Hollywood Reporter. Jan 11, 1965, p3.
Motion Picture Herald Product Digest. Feb 17, 1965, p233.
The New Republic. Apr 24, 1965, v152, p24.
The New York Times. May 14, 1965, p42.
The New Yorker. May 22, 1965, v41, p167-68.
Playboy. May 1965, v12, p32, 34.
Private Screenings. p170-71.
Saturday Review. May 29, 1965, v48, p30-31.
The Spectator. Jan 8, 1965, v214, p45.
Tynan Right and Left. p215-16.
The Village Voice. May 20, 1965, v10, p19-20.

Yellow Submarine (GB; Dunning, George; 1968)
Atlantic. Jan 1969, v223, p116.
BFI/Monthly Film Bulletin. Sep 1968, v35, p136-37.
Christian Century. Mar 19, 1969, v86, p386-88.
Christian Science Monitor (Western edition). Aug 5, 1968, p6.
Cinema Texas Program Notes. Jan 16, 1978, v13, p33-37.
Dictionary of Films. p424.
Esquire. Dec 1968, v70, p86.
Figures of Light. p117-18.
Film 68/69. p152-54.
Film Daily. Oct 30, 1968, p3.
Filmfacts. Dec 1, 1968, v11, p335-36.
Films and Filming. Sep 1968, v14, p46-47.
Films in Review. Dec 1968, v19, p650-51.
Going Steady. p228-35.
Hollywood Reporter. Jul 23, 1968, p3.
Journal of Popular Culture. Wint 1974, v8, p619-33.
Magill's Survey of Cinema. Series II. v6, p2728-30.
Movies Into Film. p198-209.
The Nation. Dec 9, 1968, v207, p638.
The New Republic. Nov 16, 1968, v159, p18.
The New York Times. Nov 14, 1968, p56.
The New York Times. Nov 17, 1968, p1.
The New Yorker. Nov 30, 1968, v44, p153-54.
Newsweek. Nov 25, 1968, v72, p108.
Saturday Review. Nov 16, 1968, v51, p77.
Sight and Sound. Aut 1968, v37, p204-05.
The Spectator. Jul 26, 1968, v221, p134-35.
Take One. May-Jun 1968, v1, p26.
Time. Nov 22, 1968, v92, p78.
Time. Dec 27, 1968, v92, p42-47.
Variety. Jul 24, 1968, p6.
The Village Voice. Nov 14, 1968, p45, 49.

The Village Voice. Jun 19, 1969, p43.
The Village Voice. Jun 26, 1969, p43, 47.
A Year In the Dark. p289-91.

Yentl (US; Streisand, Barbra; 1983)
Film Comment. Jan-Feb 1984, v20, p48.
Films in Review. Jan 1984, v35, p57.
Hollywood Reporter. Nov 4, 1983, p3.
The Los Angeles Times. Nov 18, 1983, SecVI, p1.
Maclean's. Nov 28, 1983, v96, p69.
Magill's Cinema Annual, 1983. p468-72.
The New Republic. Dec 19, 1983, v189, p22.
New York. Nov 28, 1983, v16, p111-12.
The New York Times. Nov 18, 1983, SecIII, p10.
The New Yorker. Nov 28, 1983, v59, p170.
Newsweek. Nov 28, 1983, v102, p109-10.
Time. Nov 21, 1983, v122, p93.
Vogue. Dec 1983, v173, p355.

Yesterday Girl (German title: Abschied von Gestern) (WGER; Kluge, Alexander; 1966)
BFI/Monthly Film Bulletin. Apr 1967, v37, p55.
Films and Filming. May 1967, v13, p27-28.
German Film and Literature. p193-16.
International Film Guide. 1968, v5, p78.
The London Times. Dec 10, 1966, p13.
The London Times. Feb 23, 1967, p10.
Magill's Survey of Cinema. Foreign Language Films. v7, p3454-58.
New Statesman. Feb 24, 1967, v73, p271.
The New York Times. Sep 22, 1967, p57.
On Film. p307-08.
Sight and Sound. Spr 1967, v36, p95.
Variety. Sep 14, 1966, p24.

Yesterday, Today and Tomorrow (Italian title: Ieri, Oggi, Domani) (IT; De Sica, Vittorio; 1963)
America. May 23, 1964, v110, p748-49.
BFI/Monthly Film Bulletin. Oct 1964, v31, p145.
Boxoffice. Apr 6, 1964, v84, p10.
Film Comment. Wint 1964, v2, n1, p43-44.
Film Daily. Mar 17, 1964, v124, p6.
Films and Filming. Oct 1964, v11, p29-30.
Films in Review. Mar 1964, v15, p174-75.
The Films of Sophia Loren. p150-55.
Life. Apr 10, 1964, v56, p49-50.
Motion Picture Herald Product Digest. Apr 1, 1964, v231, p18.
The New Republic. Mar 14, 1964, v150, p27-28.
The New York Times. Mar 18, 1964, p46.
The New Yorker. Mar 21, 1964, v40, p173-74.
Newsweek. Mar 30, 1964, v63, p52.
Saturday Review. Mar 21, 1964, v47, p24.
Time. Mar 13, 1964, v83, p101.
Variety. Apr 1, 1964, p23.
A World on Film. p296-97.

Yojimbo (JAPAN; Kurosawa, Akira; 1961)
BFI/Monthly Film Bulletin. Jul 1970, v37, p143.
Commonweal. Oct 12, 1962, v77, p72-73.
Film Daily. Oct 17, 1962, p10.
Filmfacts. Nov 30, 1962, v5, p275-76.
Films and Filming. Aug 1970, v16, p46.
Films in Review. Nov 1962, v13, p561.
The Films of Akira Kurosawa. p147-55.
I Lost It at the Movies. p215-20.
Literature/Film Quarterly. 1980, v8, n3, p188-96.
Magill's Survey of Cinema. Foreign Language Series. 1985, v7, p3462-66.
Massachusetts Review. 1975, v16, p158-68.
Motion Picture Herald Product Digest. Oct 17, 1962, p675-76.

The New Republic. Sep 17, 1962, v147, p27-28.
The New York Times. Oct 16, 1962, p34.
Newsweek. Oct 22, 1962, v60, p104.
Saturday Review. Sep 15, 1962, v45, p26.
Variety. Aug 30, 1961, p6.
The Village Voice. Oct 25, 1962, p13.
A World on Film. p379-81.

Yokihi *See* Princess Yang Kwei Fei

Yol (Also titled: The Road) (TURK, SWITZ; Goren, Serif; 1982)
Hollywood Reporter. Nov 18, 1982, p3.
The Los Angeles Times. Nov 12, 1982, SecVI, p13.
Magill's Cinema Annual, 1983. p411-15.
New York. Nov 15, 1982, v15, p109.
The New York Times. Oct 6, 1982, SecIII, p28.
Newsweek. Oct 25, 1982, v100, p120.
Time. Oct 18, 1982, v120, p96-97.
Variety. May 18, 1982, p3.

You For Me (US; Weis, Don; 1952)
BFI/Monthly Film Bulletin. Nov 1952, v19, p159-60.
Film Daily. Jul 23, 1952, p6.
Motion Picture Herald Product Digest. Jul 26, 1952, p1462.
National Parent-Teacher. Oct 1952, v47, p38.
The New York Times. Sep 25, 1952, p38.
Saturday Review. Aug 30, 1952, v35, p24.
Variety. Jul 23, 1952, p6.

You Light Up My Life (US; Brooks, James; 1977)
BFI/Monthly Film Bulletin. Apr 1978, v45, p75.
Films in Review. Jan 1978, v29, p54.
Hollywood Reporter. Aug 4, 1977, p7.
The Los Angeles Times. Sep 21, 1977, SecIV, p11.
Motion Picture Herald Product Digest. Oct 21, 1977, p30.
The New York Times. Sep 1, 1977, SecII, p11.
Time. Dec 26, 1977, v110, p98.
Variety. Aug 10, 1977, p16.

You Only Live Twice (GB; Gilbert, Lewis; 1967)
America. Jun 24, 1967, v116, p880-81.
BFI/Monthly Film Bulletin. Aug 1967, v34, p122-23.
Esquire. Mar 1967, v67, p73-85.
Film Daily. Jun 14, 196 7, p3.
Film Quarterly. Fall 1967, v21, p62.
Films in Review. Aug-Sep 1967, v18, p441-42.
Hollywood Reporter. Jun 15, 1967, p3.
The James Bond Films. p70-83.
James Bond in the Cinema. p125-49.
James Bond's Bedside Companion. p187-94.
Motion Picture Herald Product Digest. Jun 28, 1967, p698.
The New Republic. Jul 15, 1967, v157, p27.
The New York Times. Jun 14, 1967, p40.
The New Yorker. Jun 24, 1967, v43, p74.
Newsweek. Jun 26, 1967, v69, p73.
Time. Jun 30, 1967, v89, p73.
Variety. Jun 14, 1967, p6.

The Young and the Damned *See* Olvidados, Los

The Young and the Passionate *See* Vitelloni, I

Young At Heart (US; Douglas, Gordon; 1954)
America. Feb 5, 1955, v92, p490.
American Magazine. Jan 1955, v159, p11.
BFI/Monthly Film Bulletin. Mar 1955, v22, p37.
Catholic World. Feb 1955, v180, p381.
Classic Images. Nov 1985, n125, p10-11.

Christian Century. Jun 4, 1952, v69, p687.
Hollywood Director. p291-93.
Hollywood Reporter. Feb 27, 1952, p3.
Motion Picture Herald Product Digest. Mar 1, 1952, p1254.
The Nation. Sep 27, 1952, v175, p282.
The New York Times. Jun 7, 1952, p22.
The New Yorker. Jun 14, 1952, v28, p100.
Time. Jun 23, 1952, v59, p98.
Variety. Feb 27, 1952, p6 .po 52o.

The Young One *See* The Strange One

The Young Philadephians (Also titled: The City Jungle) (US; Sherman, Vincent; 1959)
America. May 30, 1959, v101, p397.
BFI/Monthly Film Bulletin. Jun 1959, v26, p67.
Catholic World. Jul 1959, v189, p317.
Commonweal. May 22, 1959, v70, p205.
Film Daily. Apr 29, 1959, v115, p6.
Filmfacts. Jun 10, 1959, v2, p101-02.
Films in Review. Jun-Jul 1959, v10, p355-57.
The Films of Paul Newman. p81-85.
Hollywood Reporter. Apr 29, 1959, p3.
Library Journal. May 15, 1959, v84, p1593.
The New York Times. May 22, 1959, p32.
Newsweek. Jun 1, 1959, v53, p92.
Time. Jun 1, 1959, v73, p60.
Variety. Apr 29, 1959, p6.

Young Sherlock Holmes (US; Levinson, Barry; 1985)
BFI/Monthly Film Bulletin. Apr 1986, v53, p122.
Commonweal. Jan 17, 1986, v113, p16.
Hollywood Reporter. Nov 22, 1985, p3.
Humanist. Mar-Apr 1986, v46, p43-44.
The New Republic. Dec 30, 1985, v193, p25.
New York. Dec 16, 1985, v18, p78-79.
The New York Times. Dec 4, 1985, SecIII, p21.
The New Yorker. Jan 27, 1986, 61, p87-89.
Time. Dec 9, 1985, v126, p110.
Variety. Nov 27, 1985, p16.

The Young Stranger (US; Frankenheimer, John; 1957)
America. Mar 30, 1957, v96, p744.
BFI/Monthly Film Bulletin. Jun 1957, p68.
The Cinema of John Frankenheimer. p35-43.
Commonweal. Apr 26, 1957, v66, p98.
Film Culture. Dec 1957, v3, p15.
Film Daily. Feb 18, 1957, v111, p6.
Films and Filming. Apr 1957, v3, p24.
Films in Review. May 1957, v8, p225.
Hollywood Reporter. Dec 27, 1956, p3.
Motion Picture Herald Product Digest. Feb 16, 1957, v26, p265.
The Nation. Apr 27, 1957, v184, p380.
The New York Times. Apr 9, 1957, p40.
The New York Times. Apr 14, 1957, SecII, p1.
The New York Times Magazine. Mar 10, 1957, p42.
The New Yorker. Apr 20, 1957, v33, p135.
Saturday Review. Feb 16, 1957, v40, p28.
Sight and Sound. Spr 1957, v26, p212.
Variety. Mar 20, 1957, p6.

Young Torless (German title: Junge Törless, Der) (WGER, FR; Schlöndorff, Volker; 1966)
BFI/Monthly Film Bulletin. Jul 1968, v35, p99.
Esquire. Nov 1968, v70, p28.
Film 68/69. p179-81.
Film Daily. Aug 5, 1968, p6.
Film Quarterly. Wint 1966-67, v20, p42-44.
Filmfacts. Oct 15, 1968, v11, p289-90.
Films and Filming. Jul 1968, v14, p27-28.
German Film and Literature. p176-92.
Harper's Magazine. Dec 1967, v235, p132.
International Film Guide. 1967, v4, p78.

Literature/Film Quarterly. Oct 1985, v13, p215-21.
The London Times. May 9, 1968, p8.
Magill's Survey of Cinema. Foreign Language Films. v8, p3476-81.
Motion Picture Herald Product Digest. Aug 14, 1968, p842.
The New York Times. Sep 25, 1967, p56.
The New York Times. Jul 23, 1968, p27.
The New Yorker. Jul 27, 1968, v44, p80.
On Film. p300-02.
Time. Sep 29, 1967, v90, p100.
Variety. Apr 27, 1966, p19.

Young Winston (GB; Attenborough, Richard; 1972)
America. Dec 28, 1972, v127, p347.
The Film Book Bibliography. n4438, p461.
Filmfacts. 1972, v15, n14, p309.
Films in Review. Dec 1972, v23, n10, p643.
Life. Nov 10, 1972, v73, p22.
The New Republic. Nov 4, 1972, v167, p22.
The New York Times. Oct 11, 1972, v54, p1.
The New Yorker. Oct 14, 1972, v48, p147-48.
Newsweek. Oct 16, 1972, v80, p106.
Reeling. p36-40.
Saturday Review. Nov 25, 1972, v55, p79.
Senior Scholastic. Jan 8, 1973, v101, p25.
Time. Oct 30, 1972, v100, p109.
Variety. Jul 26, 1972, p14.

Young Wives' Tale (GB; Cass, Henry; 1951)
Film Daily. Jun 25, 1954, p6.
Hollywood Reporter. Jun 21, 1954, p3.
Motion Picture Herald Product Digest. Nov 29, 1952, p1623.
The New York Times. Nov 4, 1952, p33.

A Young World (French title: Monde Nouveau, Un) (FR, IT; De Sica, Vittorio; 1966)
Commonweal. Jun 3, 1966, v84, p314-15.
Film Daily. May 25, 1966, p9.
Filmfacts. Jul 15, 1966, v9, p124-26.
Films in Review. Jun-Jul 1966, v17, p380-81.
Life. Jun 10, 1966, v60, p12.
The New York Times. May 17, 1966, p52.
The New Yorker. Jun 4, 1966, v42, p87.
Newsweek. Jun 13, 1966, v67, p114A.
Private Screenings. p262-65.
Saturday Review. May 28, 1966, v49, p45.
Variety. Apr 6, 1966, p24.

Your Witness *See* Eye Witness

You're in the Navy Now *See* U.S.S. Teakettle

Yours, Mine and Ours (US; Shavelson, Melville; 1968)
America. May 11, 1968, v118, p649.
BFI/Monthly Film Bulletin. Apr 1968, v35, p62.
Christian Science Monitor (Western edition). May 13, 1968, p4.
Film Daily. Apr 26, 1968, p4.
Filmfacts. Jun 1, 1968, v11, p141-42.
Films and Filming. Apr 1968, v14, p27-28.
Films and Filming. May 1968, v14, p27-28.
Films in Review. May 1968, v19, p312.
The Films of Henry Fonda. p201-05.
Hollywood Reporter. Apr 23, 1968, p3.
Life. May 3, 1968, v64, p12.
The London Times. May 30, 1968, p13.
Motion Picture Herald Product Digest. Apr 24, 1968, p801.
The New York Times. Apr 25, 1968, p53.
The New Yorker. Jun 22, 1968, v44, p68.
Time. Apr 24, 1968, p6.
Variety. Apr 24, 1968, p6.
A Year In the Dark. p124-25.

Z (FR, ALG; Costa-Gavras, Constantin; 1969)
America. Dec 20, 1969, v121, p619.
Costa-Gavras: The Political Fiction Film. p76-105, 220-64.
Deeper Into Movies. p78-84.
Film 69/70. p27-33.
Film Daily. Nov 21, 1969, p3.
Film Quarterly. Wint 1969-70, v23, p64.
Film Society Review. Dec 1969, v5, p28-35.
Films and Filming. Dec 1969, v16, p38-39.
Films in Review. Jan 1970, v21, p50.
Focus. Spr 1970, n6, p45-46.
The Great French Films. p213-16 Films, p76-105.
Hollywood Review. Dec 29, 1969, p3.
The International Dictionary of Films and Filmmakers. v1, p533-34.
International Film Guide. 1970, v7, p16.
Landmark Films. p314-23.
Life. Dec 19, 1969, v67, p10.
The Nation. Dec 22, 1969, v209, p710.
The New Republic. Dec 13, 1969, v161, p22.
The New York Times. Dec 9, 1969, p69.
The New Yorker. Dec 13, 1969, v45, p168.
Newsweek. Dec 15, 1969, v74, p105.
Saturday Review. Dec 13, 1969, v52, p28.
Sight and Sound. Wint 1969-70, v39, p47-48.
Take One. 1969, v2, p20-21.
Time. Dec 5, 1969, v94, p113.
Variety. Feb 26, 1969, p30.
Vogue. Nov 15, 1969, v154, p56.

Zabriskie Point (US; Antonioni, Michelangelo; 1970)
America. Feb 21, 1970, v122, p199-200.
Antonioni (Chatman). p159-75.
BFI/Monthly Film Bulletin. May 1970, v37, p102.
Commonweal. Mar 6, 1970, v91, p620-21.
The Fifty Worst Films of All Time. p277-82.
Film Daily. Feb 9, 1970, p3.
Film Quarterly. Spr 1970, v23, p35-38.
Films in Review. Mar 1970, v21, p177-79.
Hollywood Reporter. Feb 10, 1970, p3.
Michelangelo Antonioni: A Guide to References and Resources. p125-29.
The Nation. Feb 23, 1970, v210, p220-21.
The New Republic. Mar 14, 1970, v162, p20.
The New York Times. Feb 10, 1970, p52.
The New York Times. Feb 15, 1970, SecII, p1.
The New York Times. Feb 22, 1970, SecII, p15.
The New Yorker. Feb 21, 1970, v75, p87.
Saturday Review. Feb 21, 1970, v53, p34.
Sight and Sound. Sum 1970, v39, p124-26.
Time. Feb 23, 1970, v95, p76.
Variety. Feb 11, 1970, p16.

Zarak (US; Young, Terence; Canutt, Yakima; Gilling, John; 1957)
America. Jan 5, 1957, v96, p399.
BFI/Monthly Film Bulletin. Jan 1957, v24, p10.
Film Daily. Jan 4, 1957, v111, p8.
Films and Filming. Feb 1957, v3, p23.
Hollywood Reporter. Dec 21, 1956, p3.
The New York Times. Dec 27, 1956, p22.
Newsweek. Jan 14, 1957, v49, p86.
Variety. Dec 26, 1956, p6.

Zardoz (US; Boorman, John; 1974)
BFI/Monthly Film Bulletin. Apr 1974, v41, p83-84.
Commonweal. Feb 22, 1974, v99, p506.
Cult Movies. p174-77.
Cult Movies 2. p174-76.
Esquire. Apr 1974, v83, p74.
Film Quarterly. 1974, v27, n4, p49-57.
Hollywood Reporter. Jan 17, 1974, p3.
Independent Film Journal. Feb 18, 1974, v73, p10.

Jump Cut. Sep-Oct 1974, n3, p5-8.
The Los Angeles Times. Feb 3, 1974, Calendar, p1.
Motion Picture Herald Product Digest. Feb 13, 1974, p76.
New Statesman. Mar 22, 1974, v87, p418.
New York. Feb 11, 1974, v7, p74-75.
The New York Times. Feb 7, 1974, p46.
The New York Times. Mar 17, 1974, SecII, p1.
Reeling. p374-78.
Rolling Stone. Mar 28, 1974, p55.
Time. Feb 18, 1974, v103, p71-72.
Variety. Jan 30, 1974, p13.
The Village Voice. Feb 28, 1974, p63-64.

Zazie dans le Métro (Also titled: Zazie) (FR; Malle, Louis; 1960)
Commonweal. Dec 8, 1961, v75, p285.
Esquire. Feb 1962, v57, p24.
Magill's Survey of Cinema. Foreign Language Films. v8, p3498-3500.
Modern European Filmmakers and the Art of Adaptation. p63-77.
The New Republic. Dec 18, 1961, v145, p28-29.
The New York Times. Nov 21, 1961, p45.
The New Yorker. Nov 25, 1961, v37, p204-05.
Newsweek. Nov 27, 1961, v58, p88.
Time. Nov 21, 1960, v76, p61.
Variety. Nov 23, 1960, p20.

Zelig (US; Allen, Woody; 1983)
America. Aug 6, 1983, v149, p73.
Christian Century. Aug 17, 1983, v100, p752.
Christianity Today. Sep 2, 1983, v27, p81.
Commentary. Nov 1983, v76, p61-65.
Commonweal. Sep 9, 1983, v110, p468-69.
Films and Filming. Oct 1983, n349, p42.
Hollywood Reporter. Jul 28, 1983, p4.
The Los Angeles Times. Jul 29, 1983, SecVI, p1.
Maclean's. Aug 1, 1983, v96, p50.
Magill's Cinema Annual, 1984. p473-78.
The Nation. Sep 17, 1983, v237, p220.
National Review. Aug 5, 1983, v35, p950.

The New Leader. Sep 19, 1983, v66, p19.
The New Republic. Aug 15, 1983, v189, p24-25.
New York. Jul 18, 1983, v16, p51-52.
The New York Times. Jul 15, 1983, SecIII, p8.
The New Yorker. Aug 8, 1983, v59, p84.
Newsweek. Jul 18, 1983, v102, p72.
School Update. Nov 11, 1983, v116, p11.
Sight and Sound. Aut 1983, v52, p283.
Time. Jul 11, 1983, v122, p67.

Zero Hour! (US; Bartlett, Hall; 1957)
America. Nov 30, 1957, v98, p300.
BFI/Monthly Film Bulletin. Jan 1958, v25, p11.
Commonweal. Dec 6, 1957, v67, p255.
Film Daily. Nov 4, 1957, v112, p10.
Films in Review. Dec 1957, v8, p524.
Hollywood Reporter. Oct 23, 1957, p3.
Motion Picture Herald Product Digest. Oct 26, 1957, v209, p577.
The New York Times. Nov 14, 1957, p41.
Time. Dec 9, 1957, v70, p112.
Variety. Oct 23, 1957, p6.

Zorba the Greek (GREECE, US; Cacoyannis, Michael; 1964)
America. Jan 30, 1965, v112, p176.
BFI/Monthly Film Bulletin. Apr 1965, v32, p53-54.
Boxoffice. Jan 4, 1965, v86, p2888.
Commonweal. Jan 15, 1965, v81, p519-20.
Dictionary of Films. p431.
Film Daily. Dec 16, 1964, v125, p6.
Films and Filming. May 1965, v11, p26-27.
Films in Review. Jan 1965, v16, p46-47.
The Films of Anthony Quinn. p204-05.
The Films of the Sixties. p145-47.
Hollywood Reporter. Dec 16, 1964, v183, p5.
Kiss Kiss Bang Bang. p195-96.
Life. Jan 15, 1965, v58, p8.
Magill's Survey of Cinema. Series I. v4, p1904-06.
Motion Picture Herald Product Digest. Dec 23, 1964, v232, p193.
The New Republic. Jan 16, 1965, v152, p26.

The New York Times. Dec 18, 1964, p25.
The New Yorker. Dec 19, 1964, v40, p151.
Newsweek. Jan 4, 1965, v65, p60.
Saturday Review. Jan 16, 1965, v48, p35.
Time. Dec 25, 1964, v84, p65.
Variety. Dec 16, 1964, p6.

Zorro, the Gay Blade (US; Medak, Peter; 1981)
BFI/Monthly Film Bulletin. Jan 1982, v49, p12-13.
New York. Aug 10, 1981, v14, p56.
The New York Times. Jul 24, 1981, SecIII, p16.
The New Yorker. Jul 24, 1981, v57, p74-79.
Newsweek. Aug 3, 1981, v98, p50.
Time. Aug 10, 1981, v11, p60-61.
Variety. Jul 22, 1981, p16.
The Village Voice. Jul 22, 1981, p41.

Zulu (GB; Enfield, Cy; 1963)
America. Jul 25, 1964, v111, p94-95.
BFI/Monthly Film Bulletin. Feb 1964, v31, p23-24.
Boxoffice. Jun 22, 1964, v85, p2838.
Film Daily. Jun 11, 1964, v124, p4.
Films and Filming. Feb 1964, v10, p30.
Films in Review. Jun-Jul 1964, v15, p373.
The Great Adventure Films. p260-65.
Hollywood Reporter. Feb 3, 1964, v179, p3.
Life. Jul 3, 1964, v57, p20.
Magill's Survey of Cinema. Series II. v6, p2749-52.
Motion Picture Herald Product Digest. Jun 24, 1964, v231, p74.
The New Republic. Jun 20, 1964, v150, p26.
The New York Times. Jul 8, 1964, v150, p26, 38.
The New Yorker. Jul 18, 1964, v40, p93.
Newsweek. Jul 13, 1964, v64, p85.
Time. Jul 10, 1964, v84, p96.
Variety. Jan 29, 1964, p6.

Director Index

Aaron, Paul
A Different Story

Abbott, George
The Cheat *
Damn Yankees
Manslaughter *
The Pajama Game
The Sea God *

Abel, Robert
Elvis on Tour

Abrahams, Jim
Airplane
Top Secret

Adidge, Pierre
Elvis on Tour
Joe Cocker/Mad Dogs &
Englishmen

Adlon, Percy
Celeste

Adolfi, John
Alexander Hamilton *
The King's Vacation *
The Man Who Played
God *
The Millionaire *
The Show of Shows *
Sinners' Holiday *
A Successful Calamity *
Voltaire *

Ahlberg, Mac
Nana

Akkad, Moustapha
Lion of the Desert

Alberini, Filoteo
Presa di Roma *

Alda, Alan
The Four Seasons

Aldrich, Robert
Apache
Attack!
The Big Knife
The Choirboys
The Dirty Dozen
The Flight of the Phoenix
4 for Texas

The Garment Jungle
The Grissom Gang
Hush . . . Hush, Sweet
Charlotte
Hustle
The Killing of Sister George
Kiss Me Deadly
The Last Sunset
The Legend of Lylah Clare
The Longest Yard
Too Late the Hero
Twilight's Last Gleaming
Vera Cruz
What Ever Happened to
Baby Jane?
World For Ransom

Alea, Tomas Gutierrez
Memories of
Underdevelopment

Alexandre, Robert
Monastery *

Alexandrov, Grigori
A Russian Jazz Comedy *

Alexrod, George
Lord Love a Duck

Algar, James
The Living Desert
The Vanishing Prairie

Allégret, Marc
Blackmailed
Fanny *
Gribouille *
Orage *
Please! Mr. Balzac
Razumov *

Allégret, Yves
Dédée
Desperate Decision
Maneges
Oasis
Orgueilleux, Les
The Seven Deadly Sins

Allen, Irwin
The Story of Mankind
The Swarm

Allen, Lewis
Suddenly
The Uninvited *

Allen, Woody
Annie Hall
Bananas
Broadway Danny Rose
Interiors
Love and Death
Manhattan
A Midsummer Night's Sex
Comedy
Purple Rose of Cairo
Sleeper
Stardust Memories
What's Up, Tiger Lily?
Zelig

Allesandrini, Goffredo
Rapture

Allio, René
The Shameless Old Lady

Altman, Robert
Buffalo Bill and the Indians
or Sitting Bull's History
Lesson
California Split
Come Back to the Five &
Dime Jimmy Dean,
Jimmy Dean
Countdown
A Fool for Love
The James Dean Story
The Long Goodbye
M*A*S*H
McCabe & Mrs. Miller
Nashville
Popeye
Quintet
Streamers
That Cold Day in the Park
Thieves Like Us
Three Women

Alton, Robert
Pagan Love Song

Ames, Winthrop
Snow White *

Amkino
Spain in Flames *

Amy, George
Kid Nightingale *
She Had to Say Yes *

Anderson, John Murray
The King of Jazz *

Anderson, Lindsay
Britannia Hospital
If . . .
O Lucky Man!
This Sporting Life

Anderson, Michael
All the Fine Young
Cannibals
Around the World in Eighty
Days
Battle Hell
Conduct Unbecoming
Dam Busters
Logan's Run
Operation Crossbow
Orca
The Quiller Memorandum
Shake Hands with the Devil
The Shoes of the Fisherman

Anger, Kenneth
Scorpio Rising

Annakin, Ken
Across the Bridge
Battle of the Bulge
Hotel Sahara
The Longest Day
The Milkman
Outpost in Malaya
Swiss Family Robinson
Sword and the Rose
Those Magnificent Men in
Their Flying Machines
Trio

Annaud, Jean-Jacques
Black and White in Color
Coup de tete
Quest for Fire

Anonymous
Snuff

Anthony, Joseph
The Rainmaker

Antonioni, Michelangelo
Avventura, L'
Blow-Up
The Eclipse
Grido, Il
The Night
The Passenger

Red Desert
Story of a Love Affair
Zabriskie Point

Apfel, Oscar C.
Brewster's Millions *
The Ghost Breaker *
The Heart Bandit *
The Man from Home *
Ready Money *
The Squaw Man *
The Unafraid *

Apted, Michael
Agatha
Coal Miner's Daughter
Continental Divide
Gorky Park

Archainbaud, George
The Big Brain *
Her Jungle Love *
The Lost Squadron *
The Silver Horde *
Some Like It Hot *
State's Attorney *
Thanks for the Memory *

Argento, Dario
The Bird With the Crystal
Plumage

Arkin, Alan
Little Murders

Arkush, Allan
Rock and Roll High School

Arliss, Leslie
The Man in Grey *
Saints and Sinners *
The Wicked Lady *

Armand, Denis
Dark Rapture *

Armstrong, Gillian
Mrs. Soffel
My Brilliant Career

Arnold, Jack
Creature From the Black
Lagoon
The Incredible Shrinking
Man
The Mouse that Roared
The Tattered Dress

Arnshtam, L.
Three Women *

Arzner, Dorothy
The Bride Wore Red *
Christopher Strong *
Craig's Wife *
Merrily We Go to Hell *
Nana *
Paramount on Parade *
Sarah and Son *
The Wild Party *

Ashby, Hal
Being There
Bound for Glory
Coming Home
Harold & Maude
The Landlord
The Last Detail
Shampoo

Asher, William
Beach Blanket Bingo
Beach Party
Fireball 500
How to Stuff a Wild Bikini

Ashley, Ray
The Little Fugitive

Asquith, Anthony
The Browning Version
A Cottage on Dartmoor *
Court-Martial
Doctor's Dilemma
The Final Test
French Without Tears *
The Importance of Being
    Earnest
The Lucky Number *
Moscow Nights *
Orders to Kill
Pygmalion *
Shooting Stars *
Tell England *
Underground *
The V.I.P.s
The Winslow Boy
The Woman in Question
The Yellow Rolls-Royce
The Young Lovers

Attenborough, Richard
A Bridge Too Far
A Chorus Line
Gandhi
Oh! What A Lovely War
Young Winston

Audry, Jacqueline
Minne
Olivia

Auer, John H.
The Crime of Dr. Crespi *
Hell's Half Acre
S.O.S.—Tidal Wave *

Autant-Lara, Claude
Blé en Herbe, Le
Enough Rope
Four Bags Full
Occupe-Toi D'Amelie

The Red Inn
The Seven Deadly Sins

Avakian, Aram
Cops and Robbers
11 Harrowhouse

Averback, Hy
The Great Bank Robbery
I Love You, Alice B. Toklas

Avery, Charles
A Submarine Pirate *

Avildsen, John G.
The Formula
Joe
The Karate Kid
Rocky
Save the Tiger

Axel, Gabriel
Hagbard and Signe

Babenco, Hector
Kiss of the Spider Woman
Pixote

Bacon, Lloyd
Action in the North
    Atlantic *
Boy Meets Girl *
Broadway Gondolier *
Brother Orchid *
Cain and Mabel *
Call Me Mister
Captain Eddie *
Cowboy from Brooklyn *
Devil Dogs of the Air *
Espionage Agent *
Ever Since Eve *
The Famous Ferguson
    Case *
Fifty Million Frenchmen *
Fireman, Save My Child *
Footlight Parade *
Forty-Second Street *
The French Line
The Frisco Kid *
The Frogmen
The Fuller Brush Girl
Gold Diggers of 1937 *
Golden Girl
Home Sweet Homicide *
I Wonder Who's Kissing
    Her Now? *
In Caliente *
Indianapolis Speedway *
Invisible Stripes *
The Irish in Us *
It Happens Every Spring *
Knute Rockne, All
    American *
Larceny, Inc. *
Manhattan Parade *
Marked Woman *
Mary Stevens, M.D. *
Moby Dick *
Mother Is a Freshman *
The Office Wife *
The Oklahoma Kid *
The Picture Snatcher *
Racket Busters *
San Quentin *
The Singing Fool *

A Slight Case of Murder *
Submarine D-1 *
The Sullivans *
Wings of the Navy *

Badger, Clarence
Doubling for Romeo *
Hands Up! *
It *
No, No, Nanette *
A Poor Relation *
She's a Sheik *
Shooting of Dan McGrew *

Badham, John
American Flyers
Bingo Long Traveling All
    Stars & Motor Kings
Blue Thunder
Dracula
Saturday Night Fever
Wargames
Whose Life Is it Anyway?

Baer, Max
Ode to Billy Joe

Baggot, King
Human Hearts *
The Notorious Lady *
Tumbleweeds *

Baker, George D.
Revelation *

Baker, Roy
Don't Bother to Knock
Highly Dangerous
I'll Never Forget You
A Night to Remember
Night Without Sleep
Operation Disaster

Bakshi, Ralph
American Pop

Balcon, Michael
The Cruel Sea
The Ware Case *

Ball, Chuck
The Gumball Rally

Ballard, Carroll
The Black Stallion
Never Cry Wolf

Ballin, Hugo
Baby Mine *

Balshofer, Fred J.
The Masked Rider *

Bancroft, Anne
Fatso

Banks, Monty
Smiling Along *
We're Going to Be Rich *

Barkas, Geoffrey
Tell England *

Barker, Reginald
The Bargain *
Civilization *
The Coward *
The Girl from Outside *
The Great Divide *
The Italian *
The Typhoon *
The Wrath of the Gods *

Barnes, A. W.
White Cargo *

Barreto, Bruno
Dona Flor and Her Two
    Husbands
Gabriela

Barrymore, Lionel
Madame X *
The Rogue Song *
Ten Cents a Dance *

Bartel, Paul
Eating Raoul

Barthelet, Arthur
Sherlock Holmes *

Bartlett, Hall
All the Young Men
The Caretakers
Drango
Zero Hour!

Barton, Charles
Car 99 *
The Last Outpost *
Ma and Pa Kettle At the
    Fair
The Shaggy Dog

Baum, L. Frank
The Magic Cloak of Oz *
The Patchwork Girl of Oz *

Bava, Mario
Blood and Black Lace

Baxter, John
Love on the Dole *

Beal, Frank
The Inside of the White
    Slave Traffic *

Beatty, Warren
Heaven Can Wait
Reds

Beaudine, William
Her Bodyguard *
Little Annie Rooney *
Make Me a Star *
Penrod and Sam *
The Rose Bowl Story
Sparrows *
Three Wise Girls *

Beaumont, Harry
Beau Brummel *
The Broadway Melody *
Dance, Fools, Dance *

Enchanted April *
Faithless *
The Floradora Girl *
The Great Lover *
Our Blushing Brides *
Our Dancing Daughters *
Should Ladies Behave? *
When Ladies Meet *

Beck, Reginald
The Long Dark Hall

Becker, Harold
The Black Marble
The Onion Field
Taps

Becker, Jacques
Antoine et Antoinette *
Casque D'Or
Goupi Mains Rouge *
Rendezvous de Juillet

Becker, Jean
Backfire
Tender Scoundrel

Beebe, Ford
Flash Gordon's Trip to
    Mars *

Behrendt, Hans
Danton *

Beineix, Jean-Jacques
Diva
The Moon in the Gutter

Bell, Monta
The King on Main Street *
Man, Woman, and Sin *
The Snob *
The Torrent *
Young Man of Manhattan *

Bellochio, Marco
China Is Near
Fists in the Pocket

Benedek, Laslo
Bengal Brigade
Death of a Salesman
The Wild One

Benjamin, Richard
City Heat
My Favorite Year
Racing With the Moon

Bennett, Chester
The Painted Lady *

Bennett, Compton
It Started in Paradise
King Solomon's Mines
The Seventh Veil *
That Forsyte Woman *

Benoit-Levy, Jean
Ballerina *
Maternelle, La *
Mort du Cygne, La *
Youth in Revolt *

Brenon, Herbert
Beau Geste *
The Case of Sergeant
   Grischa *
Dancing Mothers *
A Daughter of the Gods *
The Fall of the Romanoffs *
Ivanhoe *
A Kiss for Cinderella *
Laugh, Clown, Laugh *
Living Dangerously *
Lummox *
Neptune's Daughter *
The Passing of the Third
   Floor Back *
Peter Pan *
The Spanish Dancer *
12:10 *
War Brides *
Yellow Sands *

Bresson, Robert
Argent, L'
Au Hasard, Balthazar
Condamne a Mort s'est
   Echappe, Un
Dames du Bois de Boulogne,
   Les
Femme douce, Une
Journal d'un Cure de
   Campagne, Le
Mouchette
The Pickpocket

Brest, Martin
Beverly Hills Cop

Bretherton, Howard
Ladies They Talk About *

Brickman, Marshall
Lovesick
Simon

Brickman, Paul
Risky Business

Bridges, Alan
The Hireling
The Shooting Party

Bridges, James
The China Syndrome
The Paper Chase
Urban Cowboy

Brieken, Jules
Drango

Broca, Philippe de
Cartouche
Dear Detective
Incorrigible
King of Hearts
Male Companion
Practice Makes Perfect
That Man From Rio
Up To His Ears

Bromly, Alan
The Angel Who Pawned Her
   Harp

Brook, Clive
On Approval *

Brook, Peter
Lord of the Flies
Marat/Sade

Brooks, Albert
Lost in America
A Modern Romance

Brooks, James
Perfect
Terms of Endearment
You Light Up My Life

Brooks, Mel
Blazing Saddles
High Anxiety
The History of the World,
   Part I
The Producers
Silent Movie
Young Frankenstein

Brooks, Richard
Blackboard Jungle
The Brothers Karamazov
Cat on a Hot Tin Roof
Crisis
Deadline U.S.A.
Elmer Gantry
The Flame and the Flesh
The Happy Ending
In Cold Blood
The Last Time I Saw Paris
The Light Touch
Looking for Mr. Goodbar
Lord Jim
The Professionals
Something of Value
Sweet Bird of Youth
Wrong Is Right

Brower, Otto
Paramount on Parade *

Brown, Bruce
The Endless Summer
On Any Sunday

Brown, Clarence
Ah, Wilderness! *
Angels in the Outfield
Anna Christie *
Anna Karenina *
Chained *
Conquest *
The Eagle *
Edison, the Man *
Emma *
Flesh and the Devil *
A Free Soul *
The Goose Woman *
The Gorgeous Hussy *
The Human Comedy *
Idiot's Delight *
Inspiration *
Intruder in the Dust *
It's a Big Country
Letty Lynton *
National Velvet *
Night Flight *
Of Human Hearts *
Plymouth Adventure

Possessed *
The Rains Came *
Romance *
Smouldering Fires *
The Son-Daughter *
Song of Love *
They Met in Bombay *
To Please a Lady
When in Rome
The White Cliffs of Dover *
Wife Versus Secretary *
A Woman of Affairs *
The Yearling *

Brown, Harry Joe
I Love That Man *
Sitting Pretty *

Brown, Karl
Stark Love *

Brown, Melville
Behind Office Doors *
Check and Double Check *

Brown, Rowland
Blood Money *
Hell's Highway *
Quick Millions *

Browning, Tod
The Dangerous Flirt *
The Devil Doll *
Dracula *
Freaks *
Iron Man *
London After Midnight *
Mark of the Vampire *
Miracles for Sale *
Under Two Flags *
The Unknown *
West of Zanzibar *
The Wicked Darling *

Brownlow, Kevin
It Happened Here

Bruckman, Clyde
The General *
The Man on the Flying
   Trapeze *
Movie Crazy *

Brunn, F.
The Marriage of Corbal *

Brusati, Franco
Bread and Chocolate

Bryant, Charles
Salome *

Brynych, Zbynek
The Fifth Horseman Is Fear

Buckland, Wilfred
Rose of the Rancho *

Buckner, Noel
The Good Fight

Bucquet, Harold S.
Adventures of Tartu *
Dr. Kildare's Strange Case *
On Borrowed Time *
The Secret of Dr. Kildare *
Young Dr. Kildare *

Bulgakov, Leo
Marusia *

Buñuel, Luis
The Adventures of Robinson
   Crusoe
Age d'Or, L' *
Belle de Jour
Chien Andalou, Un *
The Diary of a
   Chambermaid
The Discreet Charm of the
   Bourgeoisie
The Exterminating Angel
Fantome de la Liberté, Le
Nazarin
Olvidados, Los
Simon of the Desert
That Obscure Object of
   Desire
Viridiana

Burge, Stuart
Julius Caesar
Othello

Burton, David
Confessions of a Co-Ed *
Dancers in the Dark *
Lady by Choice *
Let's Fall in Love *

Burton, Richard
Dr. Faustus

Burton, Tim
Pee-Wee's Big Adventure

Bushell, Anthony
The Long Dark Hall
The Prince and the Showgirl

Bushman, Francis X.
In the Diplomatic Service *

Butler, David
Ali Baba Goes to Town *
April in Paris
Bright Eyes *
Calamity Jane
Captain January *
Caught in the Draft *
The Command
A Connecticut Yankee *
The Daughter of Rosie
   O'Grady
Delicious *
Doubting Thomas *
East Side of Heaven *
Handle With Care *
High Society Blues *
Just Imagine *
Kentucky *
King Richard and the
   Crusaders
The Little Colonel *
The Littlest Rebel *
Look for the Silver Lining *

Lullaby of Broadway
Painting the Clouds With
   Sunshine
Pigskin Parade *
Road to Morocco *
San Antonio *
Straight, Place and Show *
Sunny Side Up *
Tea For Two
Thank Your Lucky Stars *
That's Right, You're
   Wrong *
The Time, the Place and the
   Girl *
Where's Charley?
You're a Sweetheart *

Butler, George
Pumping Iron
Pumping Iron II: The
   Women

Butler, Robert
The Barefoot Executive

Buzzell, Edward
At the Circus *
Easy to Wed *
Fast Company *
Honolulu *
Neptune's Daughter *
Paradise for Three *
A Woman of Distinction

Byrum, John
Heart Beat
The Razor's Edge

Caan, James
Hide in Plain Sight

Cabanne, Christy
Annapolis Salute *
Diana of the Follies *
Enoch Arden *
Flirting with Fate *
Jane Eyre *
The Lamb *
The Martyrs of the Alamo *
The Outcasts of Poker
   Flats *
Restless Youth *
Smashing the Spy Ring *
Storm Over the Andes *
We Who Are About to Die *
The World Gone Mad *

Cacoyannis, Michael
Electra
Girl in Black
Stella
Zorba the Greek

Cahn, Edward L.
Law and Order *
Merry-Go-Round *

Cain, Christopher
The Stone Boy

Camerini, Mario
The Miller's Beautiful Wife
Ulysses

Cameron, James
The Terminator

Cammell, Donald
Performance

Camp, Joe
Oh, Heavenly Dog!

Campanile, Pasquale Festa
White Voices

Campbell, Colin
The Crisis *
The Garden of Allah *
In the Days of the
    Thundering Herd *
Little Orphan Annie *
The Rosary *
The Spoilers *

Camus, Marcel
Black Orpheus

Canutt, Yakima
Zarak

Capellani, Albert
The Feast of Life *
Out of the Fog *
The Red Lantern *

Capra, Frank
American Madness *
Arsenic and Old Lace *
The Bitter Tea of General
    Yen *
Broadway Bill *
Dirigible *
Forbidden *
Here Comes the Groom
It Happened One Night *
It's a Wonderful Life *
Ladies of Leisure *
Lady for a Day *
Long Pants *
Lost Horizon *
Meet John Doe *
The Miracle Woman *
Mr. Deeds Goes to Town *
Mr. Smith Goes to
    Washington *
Platinum Blonde *
Pocketful of Miracles *
Rain or Shine *
Riding High
State of the Union *
The Strong Man *
You Can't Take It With
    You *
The Younger Generation *

Cardiff, Jack
The Girl On a Motorcycle
The Liquidator
Sons & Lovers
Young Cassidy

Carewe, Edwin
Resurrection *
Resurrection *
The Spoilers *

Carey, Harry
Love's Lariat *
The Master Cracksman *

Carlino, Lewis J.
The Great Santini
The Sailor Who Fell From
    Grace With the Sea

Carlo-Rim
The Seven Deadly Sins

Carlsen, Henning
Hunger

Carlson, Richard
Four Guns to the Border
Kid Rodelo
Riders To the Stars

Carné, Marcel
Bizarre, Bizarre *
Children of Paradise *
Drole de Drame *
Hotel du Nord *
Le Jour se Lève *
Marie du Port
Quai des Brumes *
Therese Raquin
Visiteurs du Soir, Les *

Carpenter, John
Escape From New York
The Fog
Halloween
Starman
The Thing

Cartier, Henri
Return to Life *

Carver, H.P.
The Silent Enemy *

Caserini, Mario
The Last Days of Pompeii *

Cass, Henry
Castle in the Air
Last Holiday
Young Wives' Tale

Cassavetes, John
A Child Is Waiting
Faces
Gloria
Husbands
The Killing of a Chinese
    Bookie
Minnie and Moskowitz
Woman Under the Influence

Castellani, Renato
Due Soldi di Speranza
Romeo and Juliet

Castle, Nick
The Last Starfighter

Castle, William
The Americano
The Fat Man
Hollywood Story

I Saw What You Did
The Saracen Blade

Cates, Gilbert
I Never Sang for My Father
The Last Married Couple in
    America
Oh, God! Book II
Summer Wishes, Winter
    Dreams

Cavalcanti, Alberto
Dead of Night *
Nicholas Nickelby *

Cavalier, Alain
Chamade, La

Cavani, Liliana
The Night Porter

Cayatte, André
Justice Est Faite
We Are All Murderers

Cervi, Antonio
The Moment of Truth

Chabrol, Claude
Beau Serge, Le
Biches, Les
Bonnes Femmes, Les
The Butcher
The Champagne Murders
Cousins, Les
Femme Infidele, La
The Nada Gang
An Orchid For the Tiger
Paris Vu Par . . .

Chaffey, Don
Jason and the Argonauts
One Million Years B.C.
Pete's Dragon
The Three Lives of
    Thomasina

Champion, Gower
Bank Shot
My Six Loves

Chaplin, Charles
The Bank *
Charlie Chaplin's Burlesque
    on Carmen *
The Circus *
City Lights *
A Dog's Life *
Easy Street *
The Gold Rush *
The Great Dictator *
The Immigrant *
The Kid *
A King in New York
Limelight
Modern Times *
Monsieur Verdoux *
One A.M. *
The Pilgrim *
The Rink *
Shoulder Arms *
The Tramp *
A Woman of Paris *

Chaplin, Sydney
A Submarine Pirate *

Chapman, Michael
All the Right Moves

Charell, Eric
Caravan *
Casbah *
The Congress Dances *

Chenal, Pierre
Alibi, L' *
Crime et Châtiment *
Foire aux Chimeres, La
Native Son

Cherviakov, Evgeny
Prisoners *

Christensen, Benjamin
Witchcraft Through the
    Ages *

Christian-Jacque
The Dirty Game
Disparus de Saint-Agil, Les *
Fanfan the Tulip
Pearls of the Crown *
Souvenirs Perdus

Christy, Howard
Sing, Sinner, Sing *

Chukhari, Grigoi
Ballad of a Soldier

Chytilova, Vera
Sedmikrasky

Ciampi, Yves
Grand Patron, Un

Cimino, Michael
The Deer Hunter
Heaven's Gate
Thunderbolt and Lightfoot
The Year of the Dragon

Clair, René
And Then There Were
    None *
Beaute du Diable, La
Belles-de-Nuit, Les
Break the News *
The Crazy Ray *
Dernier Milliardaire, Le *
Entr'acte *
Fetes Galantes, Les
The Flame of New Orleans *
Forever and a Day *
Gates of Paris
The Ghost Goes West *
I Married a Witch *
It Happened Tomorrow *
An Italian Straw Hat *
Million, Le *
Nous la Liberté, À *
Quatorze Juillet *
Sous les Toits de Paris *

Clark, Bob
A Christmas Story
Porky's
Rhinestone
Tribute

Clark, James B.
And Now Miguel
Flipper

Clarke, Shirley
The Cool World

Clavell, James
To Sir, With Love
Walk Like a Dragon

Clayton, Jack
The Great Gatsby
The Innocents
The Pumpkin Eater
Room at the Top
Something Wicked This
    Way Comes

Clemens, William
Man Hunt *
Nancy Drew, Reporter *

Clément, René
Au-Dela des Grilles
Forbidden Games
Gervaise
Is Paris Burning?
Joy House
Knave of Hearts
Purple Noon

Clifford, Graeme
Frances

Clifton, Elmer
Boots *
Down to the Sea in Ships *
Peppy Polly *

Cline, Edward
The Bank Dick *
Breaking the Ice *
Go Chase Yourself *
In the Next Room *
Million Dollar Legs *
My Little Chickadee *
Never Give a Sucker an
    Even Break *
One Week *
So This Is Africa *

Cloche, Maurice
Né de Pere Inconnu
Never Take No For An
    Answer

Clouzot, Henri-Georges
Diabolique
Manon
Miquette
Prisonniére, La
The Wages of Fear

Cocteau, Jean
Beauty and the Beast *
The Blood of a Poet *
Orphée

Coe, Fred
Me, Natalie
A Thousand Clowns

Coen, Joel
Blood Simple

Coffman, Joe W.
Pagliacci *

Coghill, Neville
Dr. Faustus

Coleman, C. C., Jr.
The Legion of Terror *

Colleran, Bill
Hamlet

Collins, James W. Horne
Alimony *

Collins, John H.
Blue Jeans *

Colombier, Pierre
Roi S'Amuse, Le *

Comencini, Luigi
Bambole, Le
Bread, Love and Dreams
Heidi
Sunday Woman

Comfort, Lance
Bedelia *
Eight O'Clock Walk
Old Mother Riley,
   Detective *

Compton, Richard
Macon County Line

Connelly, Marc
The Green Pastures *

Conrad, William
Brainstorm

Conway, Jack
Alias Jimmy Valentine *
Arsene Lupin *
Boom Town *
Dragon Seed *
Hell Below *
Honky Tonk *
The Hucksters *
Lady of the Tropics *
Let Freedom Ring *
Libeled Lady *
Lombardi, Ltd. *
Love Crazy *
Never Give a Sucker a
   Break *
The New Moon *
Red Headed Woman *
Saratoga *

A Tale of Two Cities *
Too Hot to Handle *
The Unholy Three *
The Unholy Three *
Untamed *
Viva Villa! *
A Yank at Oxford *

Cook, Fielder
A Big Hand For the Little
   Lady
Patterns
Prudence and the Pill

Cooper, Merian C.
Chang *
The Four Feathers *
Grass *
King Kong *

Coppola, Francis Ford
Apocalypse Now
The Conversation
The Cotton Club
Finian's Rainbow
The Godfather
The Godfather, Part II
One From the Heart
The Outsiders
The Rain People
Rumble Fish

Corman, Roger
Big Bad Mama
Bloody Mama
Gas-s-s-s!
The Haunted Palace
The Little Shop of Horrors
The Masque of the Red
   Death
The Pit and the Pendulum
The Premature Burial
The Raven
The Wild Angels

Cornelius, Henry
Genevieve
I Am a Camera
Passport to Pimlico *

Corrigan, Lloyd
The Beloved Bachelor *
Follow Thru *
Murder on a Honeymoon *
Night Key *
No One Man *

Cosmatos, George P.
Rambo: First Blood, Part II

Costa-Gavras, Constantin
Clair de Femme
The Confession
Hanna K
Missing
The Sleeping Car Murder
Special Section
State of Seige
Z

Costello, Maurice
Mr. Barnes of New York *

Couffer, Jack
Ring of Bright Water

Cournot, Michel
Gauloises Bleues, Les

Courville, Albert de
Seven Sinners *

Cousteau, Jacques-Yves
World Without Sun

Coward, Noel
In Which We Serve *

Cowen, William
Oliver Twist *

Cox, Alex
Repo Man

Crabtree, Harold
Caravan *

Crane, Frank
Thaïs *

Crane, Wilbur
Inside the Walls of Folsom
   Prison

Crichton, Charles
Battle of the Sexes
Dead of Night *
The Divided Heart
Hue and Cry
The Lavender Hill Mob
The Love Lottery
The Titfield Thunderbolt

Crichton, Michael
Coma
The Great Train Robbery

Crisp, Donald
Don Q., Son of Zorro *
The Navigator *

Cromwell, John
Abe Lincoln in Illinois *
Algiers *
Ann Vickers *
Anna and the King of
   Siam *
Banjo on My Knee *
Caged
The Company She Keeps
Dead Reckoning *
Double Harness *
The Enchanted Cottage *
For the Defense *
The Goddess
I Dream Too Much *
In Name Only *
Jalna *
Little Lord Fauntleroy *
Made for Each Other *
The Mighty *
Of Human Bondage *
Of Human Bondage *
The Prisoner of Zenda *
The Racket
Rich Man's Folly *

The Silver Cord *
Since You Went Away *
So Ends Our Night *
Son of Fury *
Spitfire *
Street of Chance *
Sweepings *
The Texan *
To Mary—With Love *
Tom Sawyer *
Unfaithful *
The Vice Squad *
The World and the Flesh *

Cronenberg, David
Scanners

Crosland, Alan
The Beloved Rogue *
Big Boy *
Don Juan *
General Crack *
The Jazz Singer *
On with the Show *
Song of the Flame *
Three Weeks *
Viennese Nights *
Youthful Folly *

Cruze, James
Beggar on Horseback *
The City That Never
   Sleeps *
The Covered Wagon *
Gangs of New York *
The Great Gabbo *
Hollywood *
I Cover the Waterfront *
Mr. Skitch *
Old Ironsides *
Once a Gentleman *
The Pony Express *
Prison Nurse *
Sailor Be Good *
Sutter's Gold *
Washington Merry-Go-
   Round *

Cukor, George
The Actress
Adam's Rib *
Bhowani Junction
A Bill of Divorcement *
The Blue Bird
Born Yesterday
Camille *
The Chapman Report
David Copperfield *
Dinner at Eight *
A Double Life *
Gaslight *
Girls About Town *
Girls, Les
Heller in Pink Tights
Holiday *
It Should Happen to You
Keeper of the Flame *
A Life of Her Own
Little Women *
The Marrying Kind
The Model and the Marriage
   Broker
My Fair Lady
Our Betters *
Pat and Mike
The Philadelphia Story *
Rich and Famous

Rockabye *
Romeo and Juliet *
The Royal Family of
   Broadway *
A Star Is Born
Susan and God *
Sylvia Scarlett *
Tarnished Lady *
Two-Faced Woman *
What Price Hollywood? *
Wild Is the Wind
The Women *
Zaza *

Cummings, Irving
Belle Starr *
Cameo Kirby *
The Cisco Kid *
Curly Top *
The Dolly Sisters *
Double Dynamite *
Down Argentine Way *
Everything Happens at
   Night *
Flesh and Blood *
Girls' Dormitory *
Hollywood Cavalcade *
In Old Arizona *
Just Around the Corner *
Lillian Russell *
Little Miss Broadway *
Louisiana Purchase *
The Mad Game *
Merry-Go-Round of 1938 *
My Gal Sal *
The Poor Little Rich Girl *
The Story of Alexander
   Graham Bell *
Vogues of 1938 *
The White Parade *

Cunningham, Sean S.
Friday the 13th

Curtiz, Michael
The Adventures of Robin
   Hood *
Alias the Doctor *
Angels With Dirty Faces *
Black Fury *
The Boy From Oklahoma
The Breaking Point
Bright Leaf
Bright Lights *
British Agent *
Cabin in the Cotton *
Captain Blood *
Captains of the Clouds *
Casablanca *
The Case of the Curious
   Bride *
The Charge of the Light
   Brigade *
Daughters Courageous *
Dive Bomber *
Doctor X *
Dodge City *
The Egyptian
Female *
Flamingo Road *
Force of Arms
Four Daughters *
Four Wives *
Four's a Crowd *
Front Page Woman *
The Gamblers *

Gold Is Where You Find
It *
Good Time Charlie *
Goodbye Again *
The Helen Morgan Story
I'll See You In My Dreams
Jim Thorpe, All American
The Kennel Murder Case *
The Keyhole *
Kid Galahad *
Life With Father *
The Mad Genius *
Mammy *
Mildred Pierce *
Mission to Moscow *
Mystery of the Wax
Museum *
Night and Day *
Noah's Ark *
Passage to Marseilles *
The Perfect Specimen *
Private Detective 62 *
The Private Lives of
Elizabeth and Essex *
The Proud Rebel
Romance on the High Seas *
Roughly Speaking *
Santa Fe Trail *
The Sea Hawk *
The Sea Wolf *
Stolen Holiday *
The Story of Will Rogers
The Third Degree *
This Is the Army *
Twenty Thousand Years in
Sing Sing *
Under a Texas Moon *
The Unsuspected *
The Walking Dead *
White Christmas
The Woman from Monte
Carlo *
Yankee Doodle Dandy *
Young Man With a Horn

Cutts, Graham
The Rat *
The Sign of the Four *

Czinner, Paul
As You Like It *
Dreaming Lips *
Escape Me Never *
Romeo and Juliet
A Stolen Life *
Traumende Mund, Der *

D'Abbabie D'Arrast, Harry
A Gentleman of Paris *
Laughter *
Raffles *
Service for Ladies *
Topaze *

Da Costa, Morton
Auntie Mame
The Music Man

Dali, Salvador
Chien Andalou, Un *

Dalrymple, Ian
Storm in a Teacup *

Dalsheim, Friedrich
The Wedding of Palo *

Daly, William Robert
Uncle Tom's Cabin *

Damiani, Damiano
The Empty Canvas

Dante, Joe
Gremlins
The Howling
Twilight Zone

Darnborough, Anthony
The Astonished Heart
So Long At the Fair

Daroy, Jacques
Generals Without Buttons *

Dassin, Jules
Brute Force *
The Canterville Ghost *
Celui Qui doit Mourir *
A Dream of Passion
The Naked City *
Never on Sunday
Night and the City
Phaedra
Promise at Dawn
Reunion in France *
Rififi
Ten Thirty P.M. Summer
Thieves' Highway *
Topkapi
Two Smart People *

Davenport, Harry
The Island of Regeneration *

Daves, Delmer
The Battle of the Villa
Fiorita
Bird of Paradise
Broken Arrow
Cowboy
Dark Passage *
Demetrius and the
Gladiators
Destination Tokyo *
Drum Beat
The Hanging Tree
Pride of the Marines *
Spencer's Mountain
A Summer Place
3:10 to Yuma

Davidson, Mark
The Lords of Flatbush

Davis, Desmond
Girl with Green Eyes
Time Lost and Time
Remembered

Davis, Ossie
Cotton Comes to Harlem

Davis, Owen
The Great Gatsby *

Dawley, J. Searle
An American Citizen *
The Battle of Trafalgar *
Caprice *
Frankenstein *
In the Bishop's Carriage *
Leah Kleschna *
Snow White *
Tess of the D'Urbervilles *
Uncle Tom's Cabin *

Dawn, Norman
For the Term of His Natural
Life *

Day, Robert
The Green Man
She

Dean, Basil
The Constant Nymph *
Escape *
Sing As We Go *

De Antonio, Emile
Rush to Judgment

Dearden, Basil
The Blue Lamp
Cage of Gold
Dead of Night *
Frieda *
The Gentle Gunman
Khartoum
The League of Gentlemen
Masquerade
Pool of London
The Rainbow Jacket
Victim
Woman of Straw

Decoin, Henri
Abus de Confiance *
Strangers in the House *

De Cordova, Frederick
Bedtime For Bonzo
Bonzo Goes to College
The Desert Hawk
Frankie and Johnny
Here Come The Nelsons
I'll Take Sweden
Peggy
Yankee Buccaneer

De Courville, Albert
An Englishman's Home *
There Goes the Bride *

De Filippo, Eduardo
The Seven Deadly Sins
Shoot Loud, Louder . . . I
Don't Understand

De Grasse, Joseph
The Girl I Loved *
The Mark of Cain *
The Old Swimmin' Hole *

Deitch, Donna
Desert Hearts

Delannoy, Jean
The Hunchback of Notre
Dame
Inspector Maigret
The Moment of Truth
Savage Triangle
The Secret of Mayerling

De La Patelliere, Denys
Marco the Magnificent
Rififi in Panama
Taxi for Tobruk

De Limur, Jean
Jealousy *
The Letter *
The Slipper Episode *

Del Ruth, Roy
About Face
Always Leave Them
Laughing *
The Babe Ruth Story *
Blessed Event *
Born to Dance *
Broadway Melody of 1936 *
Broadway Melody of 1938 *
Bulldog Drummond Strikes
Back *
Bureau of Missing Persons *
Captured *
The Chocolate Soldier *
The Desert Song *
Du Barry Was a Lady *
Folies Bergere *
Here I Am a Stranger *
Hold Everything *
It Had to Happen *
It Happened on 5th
Avenue *
Kid Millions *
Lady Killer *
The Little Giant *
The Maltese Falcon *
The Mind Reader *
My Lucky Star *
On Moonlight Bay
On the Avenue *
Phantom of the Rue Morgue
Private Number *
The Star Maker *
Stop, You're Killing Me
Tail Spin *
Taxi! *
Thanks a Million *
Three Faces East *
The West Point Story
Winner Take All *

Delvaux, André
The Man Who Had His
Hair Cut Short

Dembo, Richard
Dangerous Moves

DeMille, Cecil B.
The Affairs of Anatol *
Brewster's Millions *
The Buccaneer *
The Captive *
Carmen *
The Cheat *
Chimmie Fadden *
Cleopatra *
The Crusades *

The Devil Stone *
The Dream Girl *
Dynamite *
The Ghost Breaker *
The Golden Chance *
The Greatest Show on Earth
Joan the Woman *
The King of Kings *
Land of Liberty *
The Little American *
Madam Satan *
Male and Female *
The Man from Home *
Manslaughter *
Maria Rosa *
Northwest Mounted Police *
Old Wives for New *
The Plainsman *
Reap the Wild Wind *
The Road to Yesterday *
Rose of the Rancho *
Samson and Delilah *
Saturday Night *
The Sign of the Cross *
The Squaw Man *
The Squaw Man *
The Story of Dr. Wassell *
The Ten Commandments
The Ten Commandments *
This Day and Age *
The Unafraid *
Unconquered *
Union Pacific *
The Warrens of Virginia *
The Whispering Chorus *
Why Change Your Wife? *
The Woman God Forgot *

Demme, Jonathan
Melvin and Howard
Stop Making Sense
Swing Shift

Demy, Jacques
Bay of Angels
Lola
The Umbrellas of Cherbourg
The Young Girls of
Rochefort

De Palma, Brian
Blow Out
Body Double
Carrie
Dressed to Kill
The Fury
Greetings
Obsession
The Phantom of the
Paradise
Scarface

De Santis, Giuseppe
Bitter Rice *
Italiano brava Gente

De Seta, Vittorio
Almost a Man

Desfontaines, Henri
Queen Elizabeth *

De Sica, Vittorio
After the Fox
Bicycle Thief *

Froelich, Carl
Luise, Konigin von
    Preussen *

Fuest, Robert
Wuthering Heights

Fukasaka, Kinji
Tora! Tora! Tora!

Fuller, Lester
Monte Carlo Baby

Fuller, Sam
The Baron of Arizona
The Big Red One
Fixed Bayonets
Hell and High Water
House of Bamboo
Merrill's Marauders
The Naked Kiss
Park Row
Pickup on South Street
The Steel Helmet

Furie, Sidney J.
The Appaloosa
The Boys in Company C
Gable and Lombard
The Ipcress File
Lady Sings the Blues
The Leather Boys
Little Fauss and Big Halsy
Sheila Levine Is Dead and
    Living in New York

Gable, Martin
The Lost Moment *

Gabor, Pal
Angi Vera

Gaillord, Robert
Mr. Barnes of New York *

Gaisseau, Pierre-Dominique
The Sky Above, the Mud
    Below

Gallone, Carmine
My Heart Is Calling You *
Scipio Africanus *

Gance, Abel
Grande Amour de
    Beethoven, Une *
J'Accuse *
Louise *
Lucrezia Borgia *
Napoleon *
Roue, La *
That They May Live *

Gandera, Felix
Double Crime sur la Ligne
    Maginot *

Garci, Jose Luis
Volver a Empezar

Gardner, Cyril
Perfect Understanding *
The Royal Family of
    Broadway *

Garfein, Jack
The Strange One

Garmes, Lee
Angels Over Broadway *

Garnett, Tay
Bad Company *
Bataan *
The Black Knight
Cause For Alarm
Cheers for Miss Bishop *
China Seas *
A Connecticut Yankee in
    King Arthur's Court *
The Cross of Lorraine *
Destination Unknown *
Eternally Yours *
The Fireball
The Joy of Living *
Love Is News *
Okay America *
One Minute to Zero
One Way Passage *
The Postman Always Rings
    Twice *
Prestige *
Professional Soldier *
Slave Ship *
Soldiers Three
S.O.S Iceberg *
Stand-In *
Trade Winds *

Gaskill, Charles
The Breath of Araby *

Gasnier, Louis
Gambling Ship *
Kismet *
Slightly Scarlet *

Gavronsky, M.
Beethoven Concerto *

Gazcon, Gilberto
Rage

Genina, Augusto
Squadrone Bianco, Lo *

George, G. W.
The James Dean Story

Georgiades, Vassili
Red Lanterns

Gerard, Bernard
Dead Heat On a Merry-Go-
    Round

Gérard, Olivier
Vie de Chateau, La

Gering, Marion
The Devil and the Deep *
Jennie Gerhardt *
Ladies of the Big House *

Madame Butterfly *
Pick Up *
Rose of the Rancho *
Rumba *
Thunder in the City *

Germi, Pietro
Alfredo Alfredo
The Birds, the Bees and the
    Italians
Cammino della speranza, Il
The Climax
Divorce-Italian Style
The Railroad Man
Seduced and Abandoned

Geronimi, Clyde
Alice in Wonderland
Cinderella
Peter Pan

Gibbons, Cedric
Tarzan and His Mate *

Gilbert, Lewis
Admirable Crichton
Alfie
Cast a Dark Shadow
Damn the Defiant!
Educating Rita
Friends
Moonraker
The Sea Shall Not Have
    Them
The Seventh Dawn
Sink the Bismarck!
The Spy Who Loved Me
You Only Live Twice

Giler, David
The Black Bird

Gilliam, Terry
Brazil
Monty Python and the Holy
    Grail
Time Bandits

Gilliat, Sidney
Dulcimer Street *
The Notorious Gentleman *
State Secret

Gilling, John
Where the Bullets Fly
Zarak

Gilmore, Stuart
The Virginian *

Gilroy, Frank D.
Desperate Characters

Gimbel, Peter
Blue Water, White Death

Girod, François
Trio Infernal, Le

Girosi, Marcello
The Monte Carlo Story

Gish, Lillian
Remodeling Her Husband *

Gist, Robert
An American Dream

Glen, John
For Your Eyes Only
Octopussy
A View to a Kill

Glenville, Peter
Beckett
The Comedians
Hotel Paradiso
Me and the Colonel
Summer and Smoke
Term of Trial

Glickenhaus, James
The Exterminator

Godard, Jean-Luc
Alphaville
Band of Outsiders
Breathless
Contempt
Every Man for Himself
Femme Mariée, Une
First Name Carmen
Hail, Mary
Made in USA
Masculin-Féminin
Numero Deux
Paris Vu Par . . .
Pierrot Le Fou
Weekend
A Woman Is a Woman

Goddard, Charles L.
The Exploits of Elaine *

Godfrey, Peter
The Girl from Jones Beach *
That Hagen Girl *
The Two Mrs. Carrolls *
The Woman in White *

Golan, Menachem
Margo

Gold, Jack
The Reckoning

Goldbeck, Willis
Ten Tall Men

Goldblatt, M.
Gypsies *

Goldstone, James
Red Sky at Morning
Rollercoaster
Winning

Goldstone, Michael
No Man Is an Island

Gonzalez, Servando
The Fool Killer

Goode, Frederic
Go Go Mania

Goodman, Daniel Carson
Week End Husbands *

Goodman, Edward
Women Love Once *

Goodwins, Leslie
Fireman, Save My Child
Mexican Spitfire *
Tarnished Angel *

Gordon, Bert I.
Picture Mommy Dead

Gordon, Douglas
Harlow
I Was a Communist For the
    FBI
The Iron Mistress

Gordon, Michael
Another Part of the Forest *
Cyrano de Bergerac
For Love or Money
How Do I Love Thee
I Can Get It For You
    Wholesale
Move Over, Darling
Pillow Talk
Portrait in Black
The Secret of Convict Lake
Texas Across the River
A Very Special Favor

Gordon, Steve
Arthur

Goren, Serif
Yol

Goretta, Claude
The Lacemaker

Goulding, Edmund
Blondie of the Follies *
Claudia *
The Constant Nymph *
Dawn Patrol *
The Devil's Holiday *
The Flame Within *
Forever and a Day *
Grand Hotel *
The Great Lie *
Mister 880
Nightmare Alley *
The Old Maid *
Paramount on Parade *
The Razor's Edge *
Reaching for the Moon *
Riptide *
That Certain Woman *
The Trespasser *
We Are Not Alone *
We're Not Married *
White Banners *

Gout, Albert
Adam and Eve

Graham, William A.
Where the Lillies Bloom

Grandon, F. J.
The Adventures of
Kathlyn *

Granet, Bert
The Locket *

Granier-Deferre, Pierre
Cloportes
A Woman at Her Window

Grant, James Edward
The Angel and the
Badman *

Grant, Lee
Tell Me a Riddle

Grauman, Walter
I Deal in Danger
Lady in a Cage
A Rage to Live

Green, Alfred E.
Baby Face *
Colleen *
Dangerous *
Dark Hazard *
The Dark Horse *
Disraeli *
The Duke of West Point *
Ella Cinders *
Four Faces West *
The Ghost Breaker *
The Girl From 10th
Avenue *
The Golden Arrow *
The Goose and the
Gander *
The Gracie Allen Murder
Case *
The Green Goddess *
Irene *
It's Tough to Be Famous *
The Jackie Robinson Story
The Jolson Story *
King of the Turf *
Let's Get Married *
Little Lord Fauntleroy *
The Man from Blankley's *
More Than a Secretary *
The Narrow Corner *
Old English *
Parachute Jumper *
The Rich Are Always With
Us *
Ride a Crooked Mile *
Sierra
Silver Dollar *
Smart Money *
Sweet Music *
Thoroughbreds Don't Cry *
Top Banana
Two in a Crowd *
Union Depot *

Green, Guy
The Angry Silence
Diamond Head
The Mark
A Patch of Blue

Green, Walon
The Hellstrom Chronicle

Greenaway, Peter
The Draughtsman's Contract

Greene, Felix
Inside North Vietnam

Greenwald, Robert
Xanadu

Grémillon, Jean
Gueule d'Amour *

Gribble, Harry Wagstaff
Madame Racketeer *

Gries, Tom
Breakheart Pass
The Greatest
Will Penny

Griffith, D. W.
Abraham Lincoln *
The Adventures of Dolly *
After Many Years *
America *
Antony and Cleopatra *
As You Like It *
The Avenging Conscience *
Balked at the Altar *
The Battle *
The Battle at Elderbush
Gulch *
The Battle of the Sexes *
The Battle of the Sexes *
The Birth of a Nation *
Broken Blossoms *
A Corner in Wheat *
A Country Cupid *
The Curtain Pole *
Dream Street *
Drums of Love *
A Drunkard's Reformation *
Enoch Arden, Part 1 *
Enoch Arden, Part 2 *
The Escape *
Fighting Blood *
A Fool's Revenge *
For Love of Gold *
The Girl Who Stayed at
Home *
Gold Is Not All *
The Great Love *
The Greatest Question *
The Greatest Thing in Life *
Hearts of the World *
His Trust *
His Trust Fulfilled *
Home, Sweet Home *
The House with Closed
Shutters *
The Idol Dancer *
In Old Kentucky *
Intolerance *
Isn't Life Wonderful? *
Judith of Bethulia *
Julius Caesar *
Lady of the Pavements *
Leatherstocking *
Lines of White on a Sullen
Sea *
The Lonedale Operator *
The Lonely Villa *

The Love Flower *
The Massacre *
The Mothering Heart *
The Muskateers of Pig
Alley *
One Exciting Night *
Orphans of the Storm *
Pippa Passes *
Ramona *
The Redman's View *
The Romance of Happy
Valley *
Sally of the Sawdust *
Scarlet Days *
1776 *
Simple Charity *
The Song of the Wildwood
Flute *
The Sorrows of Satan *
The Struggle *
A Summer Idyl *
That Chink at Golden
Gulch *
That Royle Girl *
The Thread of Destiny *
True Heart Susie *
The Twisted Trail *
An Unseen Enemy *
The Violin Maker of
Cremona *
Voice of the Violin *
Way Down East *
The Way of Man *
The White Rose *

Griffith, Edward H.
The Animal Kingdom *
Another Language *
Biography of a Bachelor
Girl *
Café Metropole *
Holiday *
Honeymoon in Bali *
I'll Take Romance *
Ladies in Love *
Lady With a Past *
Next Time We Love *
No More Ladies *
Rebound *
Young and Willing *

Grinde, Nick
Love Is on the Air *
Million Dollar Legs *
Shopworn *
This Modern Age *

Grosbard, Ulu
Falling in Love
The Subject Was Roses
True Confessions
Who Is Harry Kellerman &
Why Is He Saying Those
Terrible Things About
Me?

Grune, Karl
The Marriage of Corbal *
Pagliacci *

Guazzoni, Enrico
Quo Vadis? *
Re Burlone, Il *

Guerica, James William
Electra Glide in Blue

Guerra, Ruy
Erendira

Guest, Val
Penny Princess
Where the Spies Are

Guichard, Charles
The Kreutzer Sonata *

Guillermin, John
The Blue Max
Death on the Nile
King Kong
Rapture
The Towering Inferno
Waltz of the Toreadors

Guitry, Sacha
Bonne Chance *
Champs Élysees *
Pearls of the Crown *
Roman d'un Tricheur, Le *

Guthrie, Tyrone
Oedipus Rex

Haas, Hugo
Lizzie
Strange Fascination

Habib, Ralph
Companions of the Night
Rage au Corps, La

Hackford, Taylor
Against All Odds
Idolmaker
An Officer and a Gentleman
White Nights

Haggard, Mark
The First Nudie Musical

Haggard, Piers
The Fiendish Plot of Dr. Fu
Manchu

Hale, Sonnie
Gangway *
Head Over Heels in Love *
Sailing Along *

Haley, Jack Jr.
The Love Machine
That's Entertainment

Hall, Alexander
Because You're Mine
Down to Earth *
Exclusive *
Goin' to Town *
Good Girls Go to Paris *
Here Comes Mr. Jordan *
I Am the Law *
Little Miss Marker *
Louisa
Love That Brute *
Madame Racketeer *
My Sister Eileen *
Sinners in the Sun *
There's Always a Woman *

There's That Woman
Again *
This Thing Called Love *
The Torch Singer *
Up Front
Yours for the Asking *

Hall, Peter
3 into 2 Won't Go

Halperin, Victor
Supernatural *
White Zombie *

Hamer, Robert
Dead of Night *
The Detective
Kind Hearts and Coronets *
The Long Memory

Hamilton, Guy
The Battle of Britain
The Best of Enemies
Diamonds are Forever
Funeral in Berlin
Goldfinger
An Inspector Calls
Live and Let Die
The Man With the Golden
Gun
The Mirror Cracked

Hamilton, William
Seven Keys to Baldpate *

Hancock, John
Baby Blue Marine
Bang the Drum Slowly

Hand, David
Bambi *
Snow White and the Seven
Dwarfs *

Hani, Susumu
The Inferno of First Love
She and He

Hardwicke, Sir Cedric
Forever and a Day *

Hare, David
Wetherby

Harrington, Curtis
Night Tide
What's the Matter With
Helen?

Harris, James B.
The Bedford Incident

Harrison, Ken
1918

Hart, Harvey
Bus Riley's Back in Town

Hart, William S.
Blue Blazes Rawden *
Hell's Hinges *
The Poppy Girl's Husband *

The Primal Lure *
Wolf Lowry *

Hartman, Don
Holiday Affair *
It's a Big Country
Mr. Imperium

Harvey, Anthony
The Abdication
The Lion in Winter
Richard's Things
They Might Be Giants

Harvey, Laurence
The Ceremony

Haskin, Byron
His Majesty O'Keefe
The Naked Jungle
Treasure Island
War of the Worlds

Hathaway, Henry
The Black Rose
Brigham Young—
    Frontiersman *
Call Northside 777 *
The Desert Fox
Diplomatic Courier
Down to the Sea in Ships *
Fourteen Hours
Garden of Evil
Go West, Young Man *
Home in Indiana *
The House on 92nd Street *
How the West Was Won
Johnny Apollo *
Kiss of Death *
Legend of the Lost
Lives of a Bengal Lancer *
Nevada Smith
North to Alaska
O. Henry's Full House
Peter Ibbetson *
Prince Valiant
Raid on Rommel
Rawhide
The Real Glory *
Seven Thieves
Shoot Out
The Sons of Katie Elder
Souls at Sea *
Spawn of the North *
Ten Gentlemen from West
    Point *
13 Rue Madeleine *
Trail of the Lonesome
    Pine *
True Grit
U.S.S. Teakettle
Wing and a Prayer *

Hauff, Reinhard
Knife in the Head

Hawks, Howard
Air Force *
Ball of Fire *
Barbary Coast *
The Big Sky
The Big Sleep *
Bringing Up Baby *
Ceiling Zero *
Come and Get It *

The Criminal Code *
The Crowd Roars *
The Dawn Patrol *
Dorado, El
Fazil *
Gentlemen Prefer Blondes
A Girl in Every Port *
Hatari
His Girl Friday *
I Was a Male War Bride *
Land of the Pharoahs
Man's Favorite Sport?
Monkey Business
O. Henry's Full House
Only Angels Have Wings *
The Outlaw *
Red Line 7000
Red River *
Rio Bravo
Rio Lobo
The Road to Glory *
Scarface: Shame of a
    Nation *
Sergeant York *
A Song is Born *
Tiger Shark *
To Have and Have Not *
Today We Live *
Trent's Last Case *
Twentieth Century *

Hawks, Kenneth
Such Men Are Dangerous *

Haydn, Richard
Mr. Music

Hayers, Sidney
Finders Keepers
The Trap

Hecht, Ben
Actors and Sin
Angels Over Broadway *
Crime Without Passion *
The Scoundrel *
Soak the Rich *
Specter of the Rose *

Heckerling, Amy
Fast Times at Ridgemont
    High
Johnny Dangerously

Heerman, Victor
Animal Crackers *
Paramount on Parade *

Heffron, Richard T.
Futureworld

Heffron, Thomas N.
Are You a Mason? *

Heifetz, Joseph
Baltic Deputy *

Heisler, Stuart
Along Came Jones *
Beachhead
The Biscuit Eater *
Blue Skies *
Chain Lightning
Dallas

Island of Desire
The Remarkable Andrew *
Smash Up—The Story of a
    Woman *
The Star
Storm Warning
Tulsa *

Hellman, Monte
Two-Lane Blacktop

Henabery, Joseph
His Majesty, the American *
The Man from Painted
    Post *
A Sainted Devil *

Henley, Hobart
The Big Pond *
Laughing Bill Hyde *
Roadhouse Nights *

Henreid, Paul
Dead Ringer
For Men Only

Henson, Jim
The Dark Crystal
The Great Muppet Caper

Henzell, Perry
The Harder They Come

Hepworth, Cecil M.
Rescued by Rover *

Herbert, Hugh
He Knew Women *

Herbier, Marcel L'
Argent, L' *
Bonheur, Le *
Citadelle du Silence *
Eldorado *
Entente Cordiale *
Mystere de la Chambre
    Jaune, Le *
Rasputin *
Veille d'Armes *

Heroux, Denis
Jacques Brel Is Alive and
    Well and Living in Paris

Herschensohn, Bruce
John F. Kennedy: Years of
    Lightning, Day of Drums

Herzog, Werner
Aguirre, the Wrath of God
Fitzcarraldo
Nosferatu, The Vampyre
Signs of Life

Heyes, Douglas
Beau Geste

Hibbs, Jesse
Joe Butterfly

Hickox, Douglas
Entertaining Mr. Sloane
Sky Riders
Theatre of Blood

Higgin, Howard
Hell's House *
Perfect Sap *

Higgins, Colin
The Best Little Whorehouse
    in Texas
Foul Play
9 to 5

Hill, George
The Big House *
Hell Divers *
Min and Bill *
The Secret Six *
Tell It to the Marines *
Through the Dark *

Hill, George Roy
Butch Cassidy and the
    Sundance Kid
The Great Waldo Pepper
Hawaii
The Little Drummer Girl
A Little Romance
Period of Adjustment
Slap Shot
Slaughterhouse-Five
The Sting
Thoroughly Modern Millie
Toys in the Attic
The World According to
    Garp
The World of Henry Orient

Hill, James
Born Free
A Study in Terror

Hill, Robert
Flash Gordon's Trip to
    Mars *

Hill, Walter
Brewster's Millions
48 HRS.
Hard Times
The Long Riders
Southern Comfort
Streets of Fire

Hiller, Arthur
The Americanization of
    Emily
Author! Author!
The Hospital
The In-Laws
The Lonely Guy
Love Story
Making Love
The Man in the Glass Booth
Man of La Mancha
Penelope
Plaza Suite
Popi
Promise Her Anything
Silver Streak
Teachers
Tobruk

W.C. Fields and Me
The Wheeler Dealers

Hillyer, Lambert
Barbara Frietchie *
Dracula's Daughter *
The Invisible Ray *
The Narrow Trail *
The Poppy Girl's Husband *
The Toll Gate *
Wagon Tracks *

Hiscott, Leslie
The Triumph of Sherlock
    Holmes *

Hitchcock, Alfred
The Birds
Blackmail *
Dial M for Murder
Elstree Calling *
Family Plot
Foreign Correspondent *
Frenzy
I Confess
Jamaica Inn *
Juno and the Paycock *
The Lady Vanishes *
Lifeboat *
The Lodger *
The Man Who Knew Too
    Much
The Man Who Knew Too
    Much *
The Manxman *
Marnie
Mr. and Mrs. Smith *
Murder! *
North by Northwest
Notorious *
Number Seventeen *
The Paradine Case *
Psycho
Rear Window
Rebecca *
Rich and Strange *
The Ring *
Rope *
Sabotage *
Saboteur *
The Secret Agent *
Shadow of a Doubt *
The Skin Game *
Spellbound *
Stage Fright
Strangers On a Train
Suspicion *
The Thirty-Nine Steps *
To Catch a Thief
Topaz
Torn Curtain
The Trouble with Harry
Under Capricorn *
Vertigo
Waltzes From Vienna *
The Wrong Man
Young and Innocent *

Hoagland, Herbert C.
Pershing's Crusaders *

Hochbaum, Werner
The Eternal Mask *

Hodges, Mike
Flash Gordon
Get Carter
Pulp

Hoefler, Paul L.
Africa Speaks *

Hoellering, George
Hortobagy *
Murder in the Cathedral

Hofsiss, Jack
I'm Dancing as Fast as I Can

Hogan, James
Bulldog Drummond Escapes *
Ebb Tide *
Last Train from Madrid *
Scandal Street *
The Texans *

Holden, Lansing C.
She *

Holmes, Ben
We're on the Jury *

Holt, Seth
The Nanny

Holubar, Allen
The Heart of Humanity *

Honda, Inoshiro
Godzilla, King of the Monsters
Rodan

Hooper, Tobe
Poltergeist
The Texas Chainsaw Massacre

Hopkins, Arthur
His Double Life *

Hopper, Dennis
Easy Rider
The Last Movie

Hopper, E. Mason
Getting Gertie's Garter *
Janice Meredith *

Hopper, Jerry
The Atomic City
Naked Alibi
Secret of the Incas

Horan, Charles
Polly of the Circus *

Horne, James
The Bohemian Girl *
College *
Way Out West *

Horner, Harry
Beware, My Lovely
New Faces
Red Planet Mars

Hough, John
Dirty Mary Crazy Larry
Sudden Terror

Howard, Cy
Lovers and Other Strangers

Howard, Leslie
Mister V *
Pygmalion *
Spitfire *

Howard, Noel
Marco the Magnificent

Howard, Ron
Cocoon
Night Shift
Splash

Howard, William K.
Back Door to Heaven *
Evelyn Prentice *
Fire Over England *
Mary Burns, Fugitive *
The Power and the Glory *
The Princess Comes Across *
Rendezvous *
Sherlock Holmes *
Transatlantic *
Vanessa: Her Love Story *

Howe, James Wong
Go, Man, Go!

Hubbard, Lucien
Mysterious Island *

Hudson, Hugh
Chariots of Fire
Greystoke: the Legend of Tarzan, Lord of the Apes

Hughes, Howard
Hell's Angels *
The Outlaw *

Hughes, John
The Breakfast Club
The Internecine Project
Sixteen Candles

Hughes, Ken
Arrivederci, Baby
Chitty Chitty Bang Bang
Of Human Bondage
The Trials of Oscar Wilde

Hughes, Rupert
Patria *
Souls for Sale *

Humberstone, Bruce
Charlie Chan at the Olympics *
Happy Go Lovely
Hello, Frisco, Hello *

I Wake Up Screaming *
King of the Jungle *
She's Working Her Way Through College
Sun Valley Serenade *
Tarzan and the Lost Safari
Three Little Girls in Blue *
To the Shores of Tripoli *
Westward Passage *
While New York Sleeps *

Hunebelle, André
Fantomas

Hunt, Peter
Gold
On Her Majesty's Secret Service
Shout at the Devil

Hunt, Peter H.
1776

Hunter, Tim
Tex

Huntington, Lawrence
The Franchise Affair

Hurst, Brian Desmond
A Christmas Carol
The Fugitive
The Playboy of the Western World
Prison Without Bars *

Huston, John
Across the Pacific *
The African Queen
Annie
The Asphalt Jungle
The Barbarian and the Geisha
Beat the Devil
The Bible . . . In the Beginning
Fat City
Freud
Heaven Knows, Mr. Allison
In This Our Life *
The Life and Times of Judge Roy Bean
The List of Adrian Messinger
The Maltese Falcon *
The Man Who Would Be King
The Misfits
Moby Dick
Moulin Rouge
Night of the Iguana
Prizzi's Honor
The Red Badge of Courage
Reflections in a Golden Eye
The Roots of Heaven
The Treasure of the Sierra Madre *
Under the Volcano
The Unforgiven
Victory
We Were Strangers *
Wise Blood

Huston, John, et. al.
Casino Royale

Hutton, Brian G.
The First Deadly Sin
The Pad (And How to Use It)
Where Eagles Dare

Hyams, Peter
Busting
Capricorn One
Our Time
Outland
The Star Chamber
2010

Ichikawa, Kon
The Burmese Harp
Tokyo Olympiad

Inagaki, Hiroshi
Samurai

Ince, John
The Battle of Shiloh *

Ince, Ralph
Dynamite Smith *
The Juggernaut *
Lucky Devils *
Our Mrs. McChesney *

Ince, Thomas H.
The Alien *
The Battle of Gettysburg *
The Coward *
The Cup of Life *
Peggy *
War on the Plains *

Ingraham, Lloyd
Hoodoo Ann *

Ingram, Rex
The Arab *
Black Orchids *
The Conquering Power *
The Four Horsemen of the Apocalypse *
The Garden of Allah *
Mare Nostrum *
The Prisoner of Zenda *
The Reward of the Faithless *
Scaramouche *
Shore Acres *
Trifling Women *
Turn to the Right *
Where the Pavement Ends *

Irvin, John
The Dogs of War

Irving, George Henry
The Jungle *

Isasi, Anthony
That Man in Istanbul

Ivanovsky, A. V.
Dubrovsky *

Ivens, Joris
Borinage *
The Four Hundred Million *

The New Earth *
Song of the Heroes *
The Spanish Earth *

Ivory, James
The Bostonians
The Europeans
The Guru
Heat and Dust
Quartet
Roseland
Shakespeare Wallah
The Wild Party

Iwerks, Ub
Steamboat Willie *

Jaccard, Jacques
A Knight of the Range *

Jackson, Pat
Encore
Something Money Can't Buy
White Corridors

Jackson, Wilfred
Cinderella
Peter Pan

Jacoby, Georg
Tales from the Vienna Woods *

Jacopetti, Gualtiero
Africa, Addio

Jaeckin, Just
Emmanuelle

Jaffe, Stanley R.
Without a Trace

Jaglom, Henry
Always

Jameson, Jerry
Raise the Titanic

Jancso, Miklos
The Round-Up

Jarmusch, Jim
Stranger Than Paradise

Jarrott, Charles
Lost Horizon
Mary Queen of Scots
The Other Side of Midnight

Jason, Leigh
The Bride Walks Out *
Career
The Flying Irishman *
The Mad Miss Manton *
That Girl from Paris *

Jaxon, Wilfrid
Alice in Wonderland

Jeanson, Henri
Lady Paname

Second Honeymoon *
Sentimental Journey *
Sitting Pretty *
There's No Business Like
  Show Business
Tin Pan Alley *
When My Baby Smiles at
  Me *
Wife, Doctor and Nurse *
With a Song in My Heart

Langley, Noel
The Pickwick Papers

Lanzmann, Claude
Shoah

Lattuada, Alberto
Anna
Mandragola, La
Tempest

Laughlin, Michael
Strange Invaders

Laughlin, Tom
The Trial of Billy Jack

Laughton, Charles
Night of the Hunter

Launder, Frank
The Belles of St. Trinians'
The Blue Lagoon *
Folly To Be Wise
The Happiest Days of Your
  Life
I See a Dark Stranger *
The Notorious Gentleman *
Wee Geordie

Lautner, Georges
Galia
The Great Spy Chase

Laven, Arnold
Anna Lucasta *
Down Three Dark Streets
The Glory Guys
Sam Whiskey
Slaughter on Tenth Avenue

Lawson, John Howard
Blockade *

Leach, Wilford
The Pirates of Penzance

Leacock, Philip
The Little Kidnappers
The Spanish Gardener
The War Lover

Lean, David
Blithe Spirit *
Breaking Through the Sound
  Barrier
The Bridge on the River
  Kwai
Brief Encounter *
Doctor Zhivago
Great Expectations *
Hobson's Choice

Lawrence of Arabia
Madeleine
Oliver Twist *
Ryan's Daughter
Summertime

Lear, Norman
Cold Turkey

Le Bargy, Charles
The Assassination of the
  Duke de Guise *

Lederer, Charles
On the Loose

Lee, Jack
The Wooden Horse

Lee, Rowland V.
The Bridge of San Luis
  Rey *
Captain Kidd *
Cardinal Richelieu *
The Count of Monte
  Cristo *
Desire *
Love from a Stranger *
Mother Carey's Chickens *
The Mysterious Dr. Fu
  Manchu *
The New Adventures of Dr.
  Fu Manchu *
One Rainy Afternoon *
Paramount on Parade *
Service DeLuxe *
Son of Frankenstein *
The Sun Never Sets *
The Three Musketeers *
The Toast of New York *
Tower of London *
Zoo in Budapest *

Leeds, Herbert I.
Five of a Kind *

Lefranc, Guy
Histoire d'Amour, Une

Legoshin, Vladimir
The Lone White Sail *

Lehmann, Maurice
The Courier of Lyons *

Leisen, Mitchell
Arise My Love *
Artists and Models Abroad *
Behold My Wife *
The Big Broadcast of 1937 *
The Big Broadcast of 1938 *
Captain Carey, U.S.A.
Cradle Song *
Darling, How Could You
Death Takes a Holiday *
Dream Girl *
Easy Living *
Four Hours to Kill *
Frenchman's Creek *
Golden Earrings *
Hands Across the Table *
Hold Back the Dawn *
I Wanted Wings *
Kitty *

Lady in the Dark *
The Mating Season
Midnight *
No Man of Her Own
Remember the Night *
Swing High, Swing Low *
Take a Letter Darling *
Thirteen Hours by Air *
To Each His Own *
Young Man With Ideas

Lelouch, Claude
And Now My Love
The Crook
Live for Life
A Man and a Woman
To Be a Crook

LeMay, Alan
High Lonesome

Lemmon, Jack
Kotch

Leni, Paul
Backstairs *
The Cat and the Canary *
The Man Who Laughs *
Waxworks *

Leo, Malcolm
This Is Elvis

Leonard, Arthur
Pocomania *

Leonard, Robert Z.
After Office Hours *
B. F.'s Daughter *
The Bachelor Father *
Circe, the Enchantress *
Dancing Lady *
The Divorcee *
The Duchess of Idaho
Escapade *
Everything I Have Is Yours
The Firefly *
Girl of the Golden West *
The Great Ziegfeld *
Grounds for Marriage
Her Twelve Men
In the Good Old
  Summertime *
Let Us Be Gay *
Lovers Courageous *
Maytime *
A Mormon Maid *
Nancy Goes to Rio
Piccadilly Jim *
Pride and Prejudice *
Princess Virtue *
The Restless Sex *
She Couldn't Say No
Strange Interlude *
Susan Lenox: Her Fall and
  Rise *
Too Young to Kiss
Ziegfeld Girl *

Leone, Sergio
A Fistful of Dollars
For a Few Dollars More
The Good, the Bad, and the
  Ugly

Once Upon a Time in
  America
Once Upon a Time in the
  West

Lerner, Carl
Black Like Me

LeRoy, Mervyn
Anthony Adverse *
Any Number Can Play *
The Bad Seed
Big City Blues *
Blossoms in the Dust *
The Devil at 4 O'Clock
Elmer the Great *
Escape *
Five Star Final *
Fools for Scandal *
A Gentleman's Fate *
Gold Diggers of 1933 *
Gypsy
Hard to Handle *
High Pressure *
I Am a Fugitive from a
  Chain Gang *
I Found Stella Parish *
Johnny Eager *
The King and the Chorus
  Girl *
Little Caesar *
Little Women *
Lovely To Look At
Madame Curie *
A Majority of One
Million Dollar Mermaid
Mister Roberts
Moment to Moment
Oil for the Lamps of
  China *
Page Miss Glory *
Quo Vadis
Rose Marie
Stand Up and Fight *
Sweet Adeline *
They Won't Forget *
Thirty Seconds Over
  Tokyo *
Three Men on a Horse *
Three on a Match *
Tonight or Never *
Tugboat Annie *
Two Seconds *
Waterloo Bridge *
Without Reservations *
The World Changes *

Le Saint, E. J.
The Soul of Kura-San *

Lester, Mark L.
Commando

Lester, Richard
The Bed Sitting Room
The Four Musketeers
A Funny Thing Happened
  On the Way to the Forum
A Hard Day's Night
Help!
Juggernaut
The Knack
The Mouse on the Moon
Petulia
The Ritz
Robin and Marian

Royal Flash
Superman II
Superman III
The Three Musketeers

Levin, Henry
And Baby Makes Three *
April Love
Belles on Their Toes
Bernardine
Come Fly With Me
The Family Secret
The Flying Missile
Genghis Khan
Jolson Sings Again *
Murderers Row
The Petty Girl
Two of a Kind

Levin, Moissei
Poet and Tsar *

Levinson, Barry
Diner
The Natural
Young Sherlock Holmes

Levy, Ralph
Bedtime Story
Do Not Disturb

Levy, Raoul
The Defector

Lewin, Albert
The Moon and Sixpence *
Pandora and the Flying
  Dutchman
The Picture of Dorian
  Gray *

Lewis, Cecil
How He Lied to Her
  Husband *

Lewis, Herschell G.
Blood Feast

Lewis, Jerry
The Family Jewels
The Nutty Professor
The Patsy
Three On a Couch

Lewis, Joseph H.
Desperate Search
Gun Crazy *
A Lady Without Passport
Retreat, Hell!
The Return of October *
The Three Musketeers *

Liberatore, Ugo
Bora Bora

Linder, Max
Seven Years Bad Luck *
The Three Must-Get-
  Theirs *

Lindgren, Lars Magnus
Dear John

Lindsay-Hogg, Michael
Nasty Habits

Lindtberg, Leopold
Four Days Leave
Four In a Jeep

Lipscomb, James
Blue Water, White Death

Lipstory, Aldrich
Dinner for Adele

Lisberger, Steven
TRON

Littman, Lynne
Testament

Litvak, Anatole
All This and Heaven Too *
The Amazing Dr.
   Clitterhouse *
Anastasia
Be Mine Tonight *
Blues in the Night *
Decision Before Dawn
Equipage, L' *
Five Miles to Midnight
Mayerling *
The Night of the Generals *
Out of the Fog *
The Sisters *
The Snake Pit *
Sorry, Wrong Number *
This Above All *
Tovarich *
The Woman I Love *

Lizzani, Carlo
Crazy Joe
The Dirty Game

Lloyd, Frank
Berkeley Square *
Black Oxen *
Cavalcade *
East Lynne *
Forever and a Day *
Hoopla *
The Howards of Virginia *
If I Were King *
Madame X *
Maid of Salem *
Misérables, Les *
Mutiny on the Bounty *
Oliver Twist *
A Passport to Hell *
Rulers of the Sea *
The Shanghai Story
The Sin Flood *
Son of the Gods *
A Tale of Two Cities *
Under Two Flags *
Wells Fargo *

Lloyd, Harold
Feet First *

Lloyd, Rollo
Her Private Affair *

Loach, Kenneth
Poor Cow

Loader, Jayne
The Atomic Cafe

Logan, Joshua
Bus Stop
Camelot
Fanny
I Met My Love Again *
Paint Your Wagon
Picnic
Sayonara
South Pacific
Tall Story

Logan, Stanley
First Lady *
Women Are Like That *

Lombardo, Lou
Russian Roulette

Loncraine, Richard
Brimstone and Treacle
The Missionary

Lord, Del
Trapped by Television *

Lorentz, Pare
The Plow That Broke the
   Plains *
The River *

Lorre, Peter
Verlorene, Der

Losey, Joseph
Accident
The Big Night
Blind Date
Boom
The Boy with Green Hair *
Concrete Jungle
A Doll's House
Eva
Figures in a Landscape
The Go-Between
King and Country
The Lawless
M
Modesty Blaise
The Prowler
The Romantic
   Englishwoman
Secret Ceremony
The Servant
The Sleeping Tiger
These Are the Damned

Lubin, Arthur
The Beloved Brat *
Buck Privates *
California Straight Ahead *
Eagle Squadron *
Escapade in Japan
Francis
Francis Goes to the Races
Francis Goes to West Point
Francis in the Navy
Francis Joins the Wacs
Hold That Ghost *
I Cover the War *
It Grows On Trees
The Phantom of the Opera *
Rhubarb

Lubitsch, Ernst
Angel *
Anne Boleyn *
Bluebeard's Eighth Wife *
Cluny Brown *
Design for Living *
Eternal Love *
Flamme, Die *
Forbidden Paradise *
Heaven Can Wait *
If I Had a Million *
Kiss Me Again *
Lady Windermere's Fan *
The Love Parade *
Madame Dubarry *
The Man I Killed *
The Marriage Circle *
The Merry Widow *
Monte Carlo *
Ninotchka *
One Hour With You *
Paramount on Parade *
The Patriot *
Rosita *
The Shop Around the
   Corner *
The Smiling Lieutenant *
So This Is Paris *
The Student Prince *
That Lady in Ermine *
That Uncertain Feeling *
Three Women *
To Be or Not to Be *
Trouble in Paradise *

Lucas, George
American Graffiti
Star Wars
THX-1138

Ludwig, Edward
Adventure in Manhattan *
Big Jim McLain
Caribbean
The Fighting Seabees *
The Last Gangster *
The Man Who Reclaimed
   His Head *
Swiss Family Robinson *
That Certain Age *

Lumet, Sidney
The Anderson Tapes
Bye Bye Braverman
Daniel
The Deadly Affair
Deathtrap
Dog Day Afternoon
Equus
Fail Safe
The Fugitive Kind
Garbo Talks
The Group
The Hill
Just Tell Me What You
   Want
Long Day's Journey Into
   Night
Lovin' Molly
Murder on the Orient
   Express
Network
The Pawnbroker
Prince of the City
Serpico
Twelve Angry Men

The Verdict
A View from the Bridge

Lumiere, Louis
Arroseur Arrose, L' *
Lumiere First Program *
Sortie des Ouvriers de
   l'Usine Lumiere *

Lund, O. A. C.
The Dollar Mark *

Luorschi, Tony
The Outsider

Lupino, Ida
Hard, Fast and Beautiful
Never Fear
Outrage
The Trouble With Angels

Luske, Hamilton
Alice in Wonderland
Cinderella
Peter Pan
Pinocchio *

Lyford, Richard
The Titan: The Story of
   Michelangelo

Lynch, David
Dune
The Elephant Man
Eraserhead

Lyne, Adrian
Flashdance
Foxes

Lynwood, Burt
Shadows of the Orient *

MacArthur, Charles
Crime Without Passion *
The Scoundrel *
Soak the Rich *

MacDonald, David
The Brothers *
Christopher Columbus *
This Man in Paris *
This Man Is News *

MacDonald, J. Farrell
The Patchwork Girl of Oz *

MacDougall, Ranald
Man on Fire
The Subterraneans

MacFadden, Hamilton
Charlie Chan Carries On *

Machaty, Gustav
Ecstasy *

Mackendrick, Alexander
A Boy Ten Feet Tall
High and Dry
A High Wind in Jamaica
The Ladykillers

The Man in the White Suit
Mandy
Sweet Smell of Success
Tight Little Island *

MacKenna, Kenneth
Always Good-Bye *
The Spider *

Mackenzie, John
The Long Good Friday

Maggi, Luigi
The Last Days of Pompeii *

Magnoli, A.
Purple Rain

Makavejev, Dusan
Innocence Unprotected
Love Affair, or The Case of
   the Missing Switchboard
   Operator
Montenegro
Sweet Movie
WR-Mysteries of the
   Organism

Malaparte, Curzio
Strange Deception

Malden, Karl
Time Limit

Malick, Terrence
Days of Heaven

Malle, Louis
Alamo Bay
Amants, Les
Atlantic City
Black Moon
Crackers
Lacombe, Lucien
A Murmur of the Heart
My Dinner With Andre
Pretty Baby
A Very Private Affair
Viva Maria
Zazie dans le Métro

Malmuth, Bruce
Nighthawks

Mamoulian, Rouben
Applause *
Becky Sharp *
Blood and Sand *
City Streets *
Dr. Jekyll and Mr. Hyde *
The Gay Desperado *
Golden Boy *
High, Wide and
   Handsome *
Love Me Tonight *
The Mark of Zorro *
Queen Christina *
Silk Stockings *
The Song of Songs *
We Live Again *

Mandel, Robert
Independence Day

Melford, George
East of Borneo *
Hidden Pearls *
Pettigrew's Girl *
The Sea Wolf *
The Sheik *

Melies, Georges
Cinderella *
The Impossible Voyage *
The Magic Lantern *
Voyage dans la Lune, Le *

Melville, Jean-Pierre
Bob le Flambeur
Deuxieme Souffle, Le
Enfants Terribles, Les

Mendes, Lothar
Flight for Freedom *
The Four Feathers *
The Man Who Could Work
    Miracles *
Moonlight Sonata *
Paramount on Parade *
Payment Deferred *
Power *
Strangers in Love *

Menotti, Gian-Carlo
The Medium

Menshov, Vladimir
Moscow Does Not Believe
    in Tears

Menzel, Jiri
Capricious Summer
Closely Watched Trains

Menzies, William Cameron
Always Good-Bye *
I Loved You Wednesday *
Ladies of the Jury *
The Spider *
Things to Come *

Mercanton, Louis
Queen Elizabeth *

Meredith, Burgess
The Man On the Eiffel
    Tower

Messter, Oskar
Excursion *

Meyer, Nicholas
Star Trek II—The Wrath of
    Kahn
Time After Time

Meyers, Zion
Sidewalks of New York *

Middleton, Edwin
The Pool Sharks *

Miles, Bernard
Chance of a Lifetime

Miles, Christopher
Priest of Love
The Virgin and the Gypsy

Milestone, Lewis
All Quiet on the Western
    Front *
Anything Goes *
Arch of Triumph *
Betrayal *
The Captain Hates the Sea *
The Front Page *
The Garden of Eden *
The General Died at
    Dawn *
Hallelujah, I'm a Bum *
Halls of Montezuma
Kangaroo
Miserables, Les
Mutiny on the Bounty
New York Nights *
The Night of Nights *
The North Star *
Ocean's Eleven
Of Mice and Men *
Paris in Spring *
Rain *
The Red Pony *
The Strange Love of Martha
    Ivers *
A Walk in the Sun *

Milius, John
Conan the Barbarian
Red Dawn
The Wind and the Lion

Millar, Gavin
Dreamchild

Millar, Stuart
Rooster Cogburn

Millarde, Harry
Over the Hill to the
    Poorhouse *

Mille, William C. de
Conrad in Quest of His
    Youth *
Miss Lulu Bett *
The Passion Flower *
Two Kinds of Women *

Miller, Claude
Garde a vue

Miller, David
Billy the Kid *
Captain Newman, M.D.
The Golden Virgin *
Lonely are the Brave
Midnight Lace
Our Very Own
Saturday's Hero
Sudden Fear
Twist of Fate

Miller, Donald
Executive Action

Miller, George
Mad Max
Mad Max Beyond
    Thunderdome
The Road Warrior
Twilight Zone

Miller, Jason
That Championship Season

Miller, Robert Ellis
Any Wednesday
The Girl from Petrovka
The Heart Is a Lonely
    Hunter

Mills, John
Sky West and Crooked

Milton, Robert
Outward Bound *

Miner, Worthington
Hat, Coat, and Glove *

Minkin, Adolph
Professor Mamlock *

Minnelli, Vincente
An American in Paris
The Bad and the Beautiful
The Bandwagon
Bells Are Ringing
Brigadoon
Cabin in the Sky *
The Clock *
The Courtship of Eddie's
    Father
Designing Woman
Father of the Bride
Father's Little Dividend
The 4 Horsemen of the
    Apocalypse
Gigi
Goodbye, Charlie
The Long, Long Trailer
Lust for Life
Madame Bovary *
Meet Me in St. Louis *
On a Clear Day You Can
    See Forever
The Pirate *
The Reluctant Debutante
The Sandpiper
Some Came Running
Tea and Sympathy
Two Weeks in Another
    Town
Undercurrent *
Yolanda and the Thief *
Ziegfeld Follies *

Mizoguchi, Kenji
The Life of Oharu
Princess Yang Kwei Fei
Sansho the Bailiff
Ugetsu

Mizrahi, Moshe
Black Thursday
I Sent a Letter to My Love
Madame Rosa

Mocky, Jean-Pierre
Thank Heaven For Small
    Favors

Moeller, Philip
The Age of Innocence *
Break of Hearts *

Moffat, Ivan
The Wayward Bus

Moguy, Leonide
Mioche, Le *
Tomorrow Is Too Late

Molander, Gustaf
Intermezzo *
A Woman's Face *

Molinaro, Edouard
Cage Aux Folles, La
Cage Aux Folles II, La
Male Hunt

Mollo, Andrew
It Happened Here

Monicelli, Mario
Casanova '70
The Organizer

Monks, John Jr.
No Man Is an Island

Montgomery, Robert
Eye Witness
Lady in the Lake *
Ride the Pink Horse *

Moore, Michael
Paradise, Hawaiian Style

Moore, Robert
Chapter Two
The Cheap Detective
Murder by Death

Morassi, Mauro
Successo, Il

Moreau, Jeanne
Adolescente, L'
Lumiere

Morin, Edgar
Chronicle of a Summer

Morrissey, Paul
Flesh

Morse, Terry
Godzilla, King of the
    Monsters
Young Dillinger

Mouizy, Andre
Sans Famille *

Mowbray, Malcolm
A Private Function

Mulligan, Robert
Baby, the Rain Must Fall
Bloodbrothers
Come September
Fear Strikes Out
Inside Daisy Clover
Kiss Me Goodbye
Love with the Proper
    Stranger
The Rat Race
The Spiral Road
Summer of '42
To Kill a Mockingbird
Up the Down Staircase

Murata, Minoru
Souls on the Road *

Muriel, Emilio Gomez
The Wave *

Murnau, F. W.
Faust *
Four Devils *
The Last Laugh *
Nosferatu *
Sunrise *
Tabu *

Murphy, Dudley
Confessions of a Co-Ed *
The Emperor Jones *
"...one-third of a nation" *

Murphy, Ralph
Our Neighbors, the Carters *
The Song of the Eagle *
Top of the Town *

Musso, Jeff
Puritan, Le *

Mutrux, Floyd
American Hot Wax

Muybridge, Eadweard
Animals in Motion *

Myton, Fred
Princess Virtue *

Nagy, Endre
A Chess Maniac *

Narizzano, Silvio
Die! Die! My Darling!
Georgy Girl

Naroditsky, Arcady
Young Pushkin *

Naruse, Mikio
Kimiko *
Repast

Neame, Ronald
The Chalk Garden
First Monday in October
Gambit
The Golden Salamander
Hopscotch
The Horse's Mouth
I Could Go on Singing

Reitherman, Wolfgang
The Jungle Book
The Sword in the Stone

Reitman, Ivan
Ghostbusters
Meatballs
Stripes

Renoir, Jean
Bête Humaine, La *
Boudu Savé Des Eaux *
Chienne, La *
Chotard et Compagnie *
Crime de Monsieur Lange,
　Le *
Diary of a Chambermaid *
The Golden Coach
Grande Illusion, La *
The Lower Depths *
Madame Bovary *
Marseillaise, La *
Nana *
Nuit du Carrefour, La *
Paris Does Strange Things
Partie de Campagne, Une *
Regle du Jeu, Le *
The River
The Southerner *
Swamp Water *
This Land Is Mine *
Toni *
Vie Est a Nous, La *
The Ways of Love
Woman on the Beach *

Resnais, Alain
Guerre Est Finie, La
Hiroshima, Mon Amour
Last Year at Marienbad
Mon Oncle d'Amerique
Providence
Stavisky

Reynaud, Emile
Autour D'Une Cabine *

Reynolds, Burt
The End
Sharky's Machine

Rich, David Lowell
Madame X

Rich, John
Boeing Boeing

Rich, Richard
The Black Cauldron

Richards, C. Pennington
The Horse's Mouth

Richards, Dick
Farewell, My Lovely

Richardson, Ralph
Home At Seven

Richardson, Tony
The Border
The Charge of the Light
　Brigade

The Entertainer
The Hotel New Hampshire
Joseph Andrews
Laughter in the Dark
The Loneliness of the Long
　Distance Runner
Look Back in Anger
The Loved One
Mademoiselle
A Taste of Honey
Tom Jones

Richter, W.D.
The Adventures of Buckaroo
　Banzai Across the Eighth
　Dimension

Riefenstahl, Leni
The Blue Light *
Olympiad *
Tiefland
Triumph des Willens *

Riesner, Charles F.
Caught Short *
Flying High *
It's in the Air *
Murder Goes to College *

Rilla, Wolf
Village of the Damned

Ripley, Arthur
I Met My Love Again *

Ripploh, Frank
Taxi Zum Klo

Risi, Dino
Bambole, Le
The Priest's Wife
Scandal in Sorrento
Scent of a Woman

Riskin, Robert
When You're in Love *

Ritchie, Michael
The Bad News Bears
The Candidate
Divine Madness
Downhill Racer
Fletch
The Island
Semi-Tough
Smile
The Survivors

Ritt, Martin
Back Roads
Conrack
Cross Creek
The Front
Edge of the City
The Great White Hope
Hemingway's Adventures of
　a Young Man
Hombre
Hud
The Long Hot Summer
The Molly Maguires
No Down Payment
Norma Rae
The Outrage
Pete 'n' Tillie

Sounder
The Spy Who Came In
　From the Cold

Rivers, Fernand
Mains Sales, Les

Rivette, Jacques
Celine and Julie Go Boating
Religieuse, La

Roach, Hal
The Devil's Brother *
His Royal Slyness *
The Housekeeper's
　Daughter *
Lonesome Luke's Wild
　Women *
One Million B.C. *
Safety Last *

Roach, Hal Jr.
One Million B.C. *

Robbe-Grillet, Alain
Homme Qui Ment, L'
Trans-Europ-Express

Robbins, Jerome
West Side Story

Robbins, Matthew
Dragonslayer

Robert, Yves
Pardon Mon Affaire

Roberts, Stephen
The Ex-Mrs. Bradford *
The Lady Consents *
The Man Who Broke the
　Bank at Monte Carlo *
One Sunday Afternoon *
Romance in Manhattan *
Star of Midnight *
The Story of Temple
　Drake *

Robertson, John S.
Annie Laurie *
Baby Mine *
Beyond Victory *
Bright Shawl *
Captain of the Guard *
Dr. Jekyll and Mr. Hyde *
The Enchanted Cottage *
Little Orphan Annie *
Our Little Girl *
Sentimental Tommy *
The Single Standard *
Tess of the Storm Country *
The Test of Honor *
39 East *

Robins, Matthew
Corvette Summer

Robison, Arthur
The Student of Prague *
Warning Shadows *

Robson, Mark
Bedlam *
The Bridges at Toko-Ri
Bright Victory
Champion *
Earthquake
The Edge of Doom
From the Terrace
The Harder They Fall
Hell Below Zero
Home of the Brave *
I Want You
The Inn of the Sixth
　Happiness
The Little Hut
The Lost Command
My Foolish Heart *
Nine Hours to Rama
Peyton Place
Phffft
The Prize
Valley of the Dolls
Von Ryan's Express

Rochemont, Louis de
The March of Time *

Rochemont, Richard de
The Golden Twenties

Roddam, Franc
The Lords of Discipline

Roeg, Nicolas
Bad Timing: A Sensual
　Obsession
Don't Look Now
The Man Who Fell to Earth
Performance
Walkabout

Roemer, Michael
Nothing But a Man

Rogell, Albert S.
City Streets *
Mamba *
Start Cheering *
You May Be Next *

Rogers, Charles
Babes in Toyland *

Rogosin, Lionel
Good Times, Wonderful
　Times

Rohmer, Eric
Beau Mariage, Le
Chloe in the Afternoon
Claire's Knee
Collectionneuse, La
Full Moon in Paris
The Marquise of O . . .
My Night at Maud's
Paris Vu Par . . .
Pauline at the Beach
The Sign of Leo

Roland, George
The Wandering Jew *

Romero, George
Creepshow
Knightriders
Night of the Living Dead

Romm, Mikhail
Lenin in 1918 *
Lenin in October *
Nine Days of One Year
The Thirteen *

Room, Abram
Death Bay *

Rooney, Mickey
My True Story

Rosen, Phil
Abraham Lincoln *
The Calling of Dan
　Matthews *
The President's Mystery *
West of the Pecos *

Rosenberg, Stuart
The Amityville Horror
The April Fools
Brubaker
Cool Hand Luke
The Drowning Pool
The Pope of Greenwich
　Village
Voyage of the Damned

Rosenthal, Rick
Bad Boys

Roshal, Gregori
Paris Commune *

Rosi, Francesco
Bambole, Le
Bizet's Carmen
Eboli
Hands Over the City
The Moment of Truth

Rosmer, Milton
The Dreyfus Case *
Everything Is Thunder *
The Great Barrier *

Ross, Herbert
California Suite
Footloose
Funny Lady
The Goodbye Girl
Goodbye Mr. Chips
The Last of Sheila
Max Dugan Returns
Nijinsky
The Owl and the Pussycat
Pennies from Heaven
Play It Again, Sam
The Seven Per-Cent Solution
T. R. Baskin
The Turning Point

Rossellini, Roberto
Europa Fifty-One
The Flowers of St. Francis
Generale delle Rovere, Il
Germany, Year Zero *
Open City *

The Last Days of Pompeii *
Mighty Joe Young *
The Most Dangerous
    Game *

Schrader, Paul
American Gigolo
Blue Collar
Cat People
Mishima

Schultz, Carl
Careful He Might Hear You

Schultz, Michael
Car Wash
Cooley High
Greased Lightning
Sgt. Pepper's Lonely Hearts
    Club Band

Schumacher, Joel
The Incredible Shrinking
    Woman
St. Elmo's Fire

Schunzel, Reinhold
Amphitryon *
Balalaika *
The Ice Follies of 1939 *
Rich Man, Poor Girl *
Viktor und Viktoria *

Schuster, Harold
Dinner at the Ritz *
So Dear to My Heart *
Wings of the Morning *

Schwab, Laurence
Follow Thru *

Scola, Ettore
Bal, Le
Nuit de Varennes, La
A Special Day

Scorsese, Martin
After Hours
Alice Doesn't Live Here
    Anymore
King of Comedy
Mean Streets
New York, New York
Raging Bull
Taxi Driver

Scott, Oz
Bustin' Loose

Scott, Ridley
Alien
Blade Runner
The Duellists

Scott, Sherman
Beasts of Berlin *

Scott, Sidney
Charlie's Aunt *

Scott, Tony
The Hunger

Sears, Fred F.
The Miami Story

Seaton, George
Airport
Anything Can Happen
Apartment for Peggy *
The Big Lift
Chicken Every Sunday *
The Counterfeit Traitor
The Country Girl
For Heaven's Sake
The Hook
Little Boy Lost
Miracle on 34th Street *
The Shocking Miss Pilgrim *
Teacher's Pet
Thirty Six Hours

Sedgwick, Edward
The Cameraman *
Dough Boys *
Free and Easy *
Hook and Ladder *
Parlor, Bedroom and Bath *
The Passionate Plumber *
Pick a Star *
Saturday's Millions *
A Southern Yankee *
Speak Easily *
Spite Marriage *
What! No Beer? *

Segal, Alex
All the Way Home
Harlow
Joy In the Morning

Seidelman, Susan
Desperately Seeking Susan
Smithereens

Seiler, Lewis
Career Woman *
Charlie Chan in Paris *
Crime School *
Dust Be My Destiny *
Frontier Marshall *
The Great K and A Train
    Robbery *
Guadalcanal Diary *
King of the Underworld *
Star for a Night *
The Winning Team
You Can't Get Away With
    Murder *

Seiter, William A.
Allegheny Uprising *
Borderline
The Case Against Mrs.
    Ames *
A Chance at Heaven *
Dimples *
Diplomaniacs *
Girl Crazy *
Going Wild *
Hot Saturday *
If You Could Only Cook *
In Person *
Life Begins in College *
Make Haste To Live
The Moon's Our Home *
One Touch of Venus *
Orchids to You *
Professional Sweetheart *

The Richest Girl in the
    World *
Roberta *
Room Service *
Sally, Irene and Mary *
Sons of the Desert *
Stowaway *
Sunny *
Susannah of the Mounties *
Thanks for Everything *
This Is My Affair *
Three Blind Mice *
You Were Never Lovelier *

Seitz, George B.
Between Two Women *
The Docks of San
    Francisco *
Exclusive Story *
A Family Affair *
The Hardys Ride High *
Judge Hardy and Son *
The Last of the Mohicans *
Life Begins for Andy
    Hardy *
Love Finds Andy Hardy *
Out West With the Hardys *
Six Thousand Enemies *
The Thirteenth Chair *
The Three Wise Guys *
Thunder Afloat *
The Vanishing American *
Yellow Jack *

Selander, Lesley
Battle Zone
Dragonfly Squadron

Selwyn, Edgar
The Mystery of Mr. X *
The Sin of Madelon
    Claudet *
Skyscraper Souls *

Selznick, Arna
The Care Bears Movie

Sembene, Ousmane
Mandabi

Sennett, Mack
Hypnotized *
I Surrender Dear *
Mabel at the Wheel *
Tillie's Punctured
    Romance *

Seton, Marie
Time in the Sun *

Shane, Maxwell
City Across the River *

Sharman, Jim
The Rocky Horror Picture
    Show

Sharp, Don
Bang, Bang, You're Dead!
Hennesy

Sharpsteen, Ben
Dumbo *
Pinocchio *

Shavelson, Melville
Beau James
Cast a Giant Shadow
Houseboat
It Started in Naples
A New Kind of Love
Yours, Mine and Ours

Shaw, Harold
The Fool's Awakening *

Shear, Barry
Wild in the Streets

Sheldon, Sidney
The Buster Keaton Story

Shengelaya, Georgy
Pirosmani

Sherin, Edwin
Valdez Is Coming

Sherman, George
Against All Flags
Back at the Front
The Bandit of Sherwood
    Forest
Calamity Jane and Sam
    Bass *
Dawn at Socorro
Johnny Dark
The Sleeping City
Steel Town

Sherman, Lowell
Bachelor Apartment *
Broadway Thru a Keyhole *
False Faces *
The Greeks Had a Word for
    Them *
High Stakes *
Morning Glory *
Night Life of the Gods *
The Royal Bed *
She Done Him Wrong *

Sherman, Vincent
Across the Pacific *
The Adventures of Don
    Juan *
Affair in Trinidad
Backfire
The Damned Don't Cry
The Garment Jungle
Goodbye, My Fancy
The Hard Way *
Harriet Craig
The Hasty Heart *
Ice Palace
Lone Star
Mr. Skeffington *
Nora Prentiss *
Old Acquaintance *
The Return of Doctor X *
Saturday's Children *
The Young Philadelphians

Shindo, Kaneto
The Island
Onibaba

Shumlin, Herman
Confidential Agent *
Watch on the Rhine *

Sidney, George
Anchors Aweigh *
Annie Get Your Gun
Bathing Beauty *
Bye Bye Birdie
Cass Timberlaine *
Half a Sixpence
The Harvey Girls *
Jeanne Eagels
Key to the City
Kiss Me Kate
Pal Joey
Pepe
The Red Danube *
Scaramouche
Show Boat
The Swinger
A Ticklish Affair
Viva Las Vegas
Who Was That Lady?
Young Bess

Sidney, Scott
Tarzan of the Apes *

Siegel, Don
Baby Face Nelson
The Beguiled
The Big Steal *
The Black Windmill
Coogan's Bluff
Dirty Harry
Duel At Silver Creek
Escape from Alcatraz
Flaming Star
Gun Runners
Hell Is for Heroes
Invasion of the Body
    Snatchers
The Killers
Madigan
No Time For Flowers
Private Hell 36
Riot in Cell Block 11
Rough Cut
The Shootist
Two Mules for Sister Sara
The Verdict *

Siegmann, George
Spirit of '76 *

Silver, Joan Micklin
Hester Street

Silverstein, Elliot
Cat Ballou
A Man Called Horse

Simon, S. Sylvan
Four Girls in White *
The Road to Reno *
Spring Madness *
These Glamour Girls *

Sinatra, Frank
None But the Brave

Stroheim, Erich von
Blind Husbands *
The Devil's Pass-Key *
Foolish Wives *
Greed *
The Merry Widow *
Merry-Go-Round *
Queen Kelly *
The Wedding March *

Stroyeva, Vera
Revolutionists *

Stuart, Mel
Four Days in November
If It's Tuesday, This Must
   Be Belgium
One Is a Lonely Number
Willy Wonka and the
   Chocolate Factory

Sturges, John
Bad Day at Black Rock
The Capture
Escape from Fort Bravo
The Girl In White
A Girl Named Tamiko
The Great Escape
Gunfight at the O.K. Corral
The Hallelujah Trail
Hour of the Gun
It's a Big Country
Kind Lady
The Last Train from Gun
   Hill
The Magnificent Seven
The Magnificent Yankee
Marooned
McQ
Mystery Street
Never So Few
The Old Man and the Sea
The People Against O'Hara
Right Cross
The Satan Bug
Sergeants 3

Sturges, Preston
The Beautiful Blonde From
   Bashful Bend *
Christmas in July *
The French They Are a
   Funny Race
The Great McGinty *
The Great Moment *
Hail the Conquering Hero *
The Lady Eve *
The Miracle of Morgan's
   Creek *
The Palm Beach Story *
The Sin of Harold
   Diddlebock *
Sullivan's Travels *
Unfaithfully Yours *

Sucksdorff, Arne
The Great Adventure
My Home Is Copacabana

Summers, Jeremy
Ferry Cross The Mersey

Sutherland, Edward
Champagne Waltz *
Diamond Jim *

Dixie *
Every Day's a Holiday *
Fireman Save My Child *
The Flying Deuces *
Follow the Boys *
The Gang Buster *
International House *
June Moon *
Mississippi *
Mr. Robinson Crusoe *
Murders in the Zoo *
Palmy Days *
Paramount on Parade *
Poppy *
Sky Devils *
The Social Lion *
Too Much Harmony *

Swickard, Charles
Hell's Hinges *

Swift, David
Good Neighbor Sam
How to Succeed in Business
   Without Really Trying
Love Is a Ball
The Parent Trap
Pollyanna
Under the Yum Yum Tree

Syberberg, Hans-Jurgen
Our Hitler

Szabo, Istvan
Budapest Tales
Colonel Redl
Mephisto

Szwarc, Jeannot
Jaws 2
Santa Claus: The Movie
Somewhere in Time
Supergirl

Taggart, Errol
Women Men Marry *

Talankin, Igor
Tchaikovsky

Talcamoto, Iwao
Charlotte's Web

Tallas, Gregg
The Barefoot Battalion

Tanner, Alain
Jonah who will be 25 in the
   Year 2000

Tarich, Yuri
Wings of a Serf *

Tarkovsky, Andrei
Andrei Rublev

Tashlin, Frank
The Alphabet Murders
Artists and Models
Caprice
The Disorderly Orderly
The First Time
The Glass Bottom Boat

Son of Pale Face
Susan Slept Here
Who's Minding the Store?
Will Success Spoil Rock
   Hunter?

Tati, Jacques
Jour de Fete
Mr. Hulot's Holiday
Mon Oncle

Taurog, Norman
The Adventures of Tom
   Sawyer *
A Bedtime Story *
The Big Broadcast of 1936 *
Big City *
Boys Town *
The Bride Goes Wild *
Broadway Melody of 1940 *
The Caddy
College Rhythm *
Doctor Goldfoot and the
   Bikini Machine
Fifty Roads to Town *
Finn and Hattie *
GI Blues
Girl Crazy *
Huckleberry Finn *
It Happened at the World's
   Fair
Jumping Jacks
Living it Up
Lucky Night *
Mad About Music *
Mrs. Wiggs of the Cabbage
   Patch *
Palm Springs Weekend
The Phantom President *
Please Believe Me
Presenting Lily Mars *
Reunion *
Rhythm on the Range *
Rich, Young and Pretty
Room for One More
Skippy *
Speedway
Spinout
The Stooge
Strike Me Pink *
Tickle Me
The Toast of New Orleans
The Way to Love *
Words and Music *
You Can't Have
   Everything *
Young Tom Edison *

Tavernier, Bertrand
The Clockmaker
Coup de Torchon
A Sunday in the Country

Taviani, Paolo
The Night of the Shooting
   Stars
Padre Padrone

Taviani, Vittorio
The Night of the Shooting
   Stars
Padre Padrone

Taylor, Don
Damien-The Omen II
Escape From the Planet of
   the Apes
The Final Countdown
The Island of Dr. Moreau

Taylor, Sam
Coquette *
Devil's Lottery *
Exit Smiling *
For Heaven's Sake *
The Freshman *
Girl Shy *
Hot Water *
Kiki *
My Best Girl *
The Taming of the Shrew *
Tempest *
Why Worry? *

Taylor, William Desmond
Anne of Green Gables *
The Diamond From the
   Sky *
He Fell in Love with His
   Wife *
His Majesty, Bunker Bean *
Huckleberry Finn *
Johanna Enlists *
Tom Sawyer *

Teague, Lewis
Jewel of the Nile

Templeton, George
The Sundowners

Tennyson, Pen
Convoy *

Teshigahara, Hiroshi
The Face of Another
Woman in the Dunes

Tetzlaff, Ted
Fighting Father Dunne *
The White Tower *
Window *

Tewksbury, Peter
Sunday in New York

Thiele, William
Drei von der Tankstelle,
   Die *
The Jungle Princess *
London by Night *
Waltz Time *

Thomas, Augustus
The Jungle *

Thomas, Gerald
Carry on Nurse

Thomas, Ralph
The Clouded Yellow
Deadlier Than the Male
Doctor at Large
Doctor in Distress
Doctor in the House
No Love For Johnnie

Ticket to Heaven
Venetian Bird

Thompson, J. Lee
Cape Fear
For Better, For Worse
The Greek Tycoon
The Guns of Navarone
Kings of the Sun
MacKenna's Gold
Return From the Ashes
St. Ives
Taras Bulba
Tiger Bay
The Weak and the Wicked
What a Way to Go!

Thomson, Frederick
The Christian *
The Goose Girl *
Nearly a King *

Thornby, Robert
The Trap *

Thorpe, Richard
Above Suspicion *
All the Brothers Were
   Valiant
Athena
The Black Hand
Carbine Williams
The Crowd Roars *
A Date With Judy *
Double Wedding *
The Earl of Chicago *
The First Hundred Years *
Follow the Boys
Fun in Acapulco
The Great Caruso
Huckleberry Finn *
It's a Big Country
Ivanhoe
Jailhouse Rock
Knights of the Round Table
Man-Proof *
Night Must Fall *
On an Island With You *
The Prisoner of Zenda
The Student Prince
Tarzan Finds a Son *
Ten Thousand Bedrooms
That Funny Feeling
This Time for Keeps *
Three Little Words
Three Loves Has Nancy *
The Toy Wife *
The Truth About Spring
The Voice of Bugle Ann *

Till, Eric
Hot Millions

Tinling, James
Pepper *
Sharpshooters *
Under the Pampas Moon *

Toback, James
Exposed

Tokar, Norman
The Boatniks
Follow Me, Boys!

Savage Sam
The Ugly Dachshund

Totten, Robert
Death of a Gunfighter
The Wild Country

Tourjansky, Victor
Dark Eyes *
The Lie of Nina Petrovna *
Liebesmelodie *

Tourneur, Jacques
Anne of the Indies
Berlin Express *
Canyon Passage *
Cat People *
Circle of Danger
The Flame and the Arrow
I Walked With a Zombie *
Nick Carter, Master
   Detective *
Out of the Past *
Stars in My Crown
Way of a Gaucho

Tourneur, Maurice
Alias Jimmy Valentine *
Aloma of the South Seas *
Avec le Sourire *
Barbary Sheep *
The Blue Bird *
Carnival of Sinners *
The Closed Road *
A Girl's Folly *
Jealous Husbands *
Katia *
Koenigsmark *
The Last of the Mohicans *
The Last of the Mohicans *
The Life Line *
Lorna Doone *
The Man of the Hour *
The Mother *
Never the Twain Shall
   Meet *
The Pit *
A Poor Little Rich Girl *
The Pride of the Clan *
Prunella *
Treasure Island *
Trilby *
The Velvet Paw *
Victory *
Volpone *
The White Circle *
The White Heather *

Towne, Robert
Personal Best

Trauberg, Ilya
China Express *
The Son of Mongolia *

Trauberg, Leonid
The Return of Maxim *
The Youth of Maxim *

Trenker, Luis
The Doomed Battalion *
Rebell, Der *

Trent, John
Middle Age Crazy

Trimble, Laurence
Everybody's Sweetheart *

Trivas, Victor
Song of the Streets *

Trnka, Jiri
The Emperor's Nightingale

Troell, Jan
The Emigrants
The Flight of the Eagle
The New Land

Truffaut, François
Bed and Board
The Bride Wore Black
Confidentially Yours
Day for Night
Fahrenheit 451
The 400 Blows
Jules & Jim
The Last Metro
The Man Who Loved
   Women
Shoot the Piano Player
Small Change
The Soft Skin
Stolen Kisses
The Story of Adele H.
The Wild Child
The Woman Next Door

Trumbo, Dalton
Johnny Got His Gun

Trumbull, Douglas
Brainstorm

Tryon, Glenn
Beauty for the Asking *

Tucker, George Loane
The Middleman *
The Miracle Man *
The Prisoner of Zenda *
Traffic in Souls *

Tuggle, Richard
Tightrope

Turell, Saul J.
The Love Goddesses

Tuttle, Frank
The Big Broadcast *
College Holiday *
Dangerous Money *
Dangerously Yours *
Doctor Rhythm *
The Glass Key *
Her Wedding Night *
Here Is My Heart *
I Stole a Million *
Kid Boots *
Love Among the
   Millionaires *
Lucky Jordan *
The Magic Face *
No Limit *
Paramount on Parade *
Paris Honeymoon *
Roman Scandals *
Symphony of Six Million *

This Gun for Hire *
This Is the Night *
This Reckless Age *
Waikiki Wedding *

Ucicky, Gustav
The Immortal Vagabond *
Morgenrot *
Savoy Hotel 217 *

Ulmer, Edgar G.
The Black Cat *

Ustinov, Peter
Billy Budd
Lady L
Secret Flight

Uys, Jamie
Dingaka
The Gods Must be Crazy

Vadim, Roger
And God Created Woman
Barbarella
Circle of Love
The Game Is Over
Pretty Maids All in a Row
Vice and Virtue

Valentin, Albert
Amphitryon *

Van Dyke, W. S.
After the Thin Man *
Andy Hardy Gets Spring
   Fever *
Another Thin Man *
The Cuban Love Song *
The Devil Is A Sissy *
Eskimo *
Forsaking All Others *
Guilty Hands *
His Brother's Wife *
I Live My Life *
I Take This Woman *
It's a Wonderful World *
Journey for Margaret *
Love on the Run *
Manhattan Melodrama *
Marie Antoinette *
Naughty Marietta *
Never the Twain Shall
   Meet *
Penthouse *
Personal Property *
The Prize Fighter and the
   Lady *
Rage in Heaven *
Rosalie *
Rose Marie *
San Francisco *
Sweethearts *
Tarzan, the Ape Man *
They Gave Him a Gun *
The Thin Man *
Trader Horn *
White Shadows in the South
   Seas *

Van Horn, Buddy
Any Which Way You Can

Van Peebles, Melvin
Watermelon Man

Varda, Agnés
Bonheur, Le
Cleo from 5 to 7
One Sings the Other Doesn't

Varnel, Marcel
Chandu, the Magician *
Let George Do It *
The Silent Witness *

Vasiliev, D. I.
Alexander Nevsky *

Vasiliev, Georgi
Chapayev *
The Defense of
   Volochayevsk *

Vasiliev, Sergei
Chapayev *
The Defense of
   Volochayevsk *

Vedres, Nicole
Vie Commence Demain, La

Velo, Carlos
Torero!

Venturini, Edward
The Headless Horseman *

Verhoeven, Paul
The Fourth Man
Soldier of Orange

Vernal, Stephen F.
The Lords of Flatbush

Vernay, Robert
Face To the Wind

Verneuil, Henri
Any Number Can Win
Boulanger de Valorgue, Le
Forbidden Fruit
Mouton a Cinq Pattes, Le
Weekend At Dunkirk

Vertov, Dziga
Kino Eye *
Three Songs of Lenin *

Vicario, Marco
Wifemistress

Vidor, Charles
Cover Girl *
A Farewell to Arms
Gilda *
The Great Gambini *
Hans Christian Anderson
It's a Big Country
The Joker Is Wild
Ladies in Retirement *
Love Me or Leave Me
My Son, My Son *
Rhapsody
A Song to Remember *
Thunder in the East

Vidor, King
Bardeleys the Magnificent *
Beyond the Forest *
The Big Parade *
Billy the Kid *
Bird of Paradise *
Boheme, La *
The Champ *
The Citadel *
Comrade X *
The Crowd *
Cynara *
Duel in the Sun *
The Fountainhead *
Hallelujah! *
H. M. Pulham, Esq. *
Japanese War Bride *
Lightning Strikes Twice
Northwest Passage *
Not So Dumb *
Our Daily Bread *
Peg O' My Heart *
Ruby Gentry
Show People *
So Red the Rose *
Solomon and Sheba
Stella Dallas *
The Strangers Return *
Street Scene *
The Texas Rangers *
The Turn in the Road *
War and Peace
The Wedding Night *
Wild Oranges *

Viertel, Berthold
The Magnificent Lie *
The Passing of the Third
   Floor Back *
Rhodes *
The Wiser Sex *

Vigne, Daniel
The Return of Martin
   Guerre

Vignola, Robert G.
The Scarlet Letter *
When Knighthood Was in
   Flower *

Vigo, Jean
A Propos de Nice *
Atalante, L' *
Zero for Conduct *

Vincent, James
Gold and the Woman *

Visconti, Luchino
Bellissima
Boccaccio 70
The Damned
Death in Venice
The Innocent
The Leopard
Ossessione *
Rocco and his Brothers
Senso
The Stranger
Vaghe Stelle Dell'Orsa

Vojteck, Jasny
All My Good Countrymen

Year Produced Index

1882
Animals in Motion *

1894
Autour D'Une Cabine *
Sioux Indian Dance *

1895
Arroseur Arrose, L' *
Sortie des Ouvriers de
l'Usine Lumiere *

1896
American Biograph First
Program *
Edison First Program *
The Kiss *
Lumiere First Program *
The Vanishing Lady *

1898
Battlefield Scenes *
A Chess Maniac *
Elopement on Horseback *
Excursion *

1899
Astor Battery on Parade *
Cinderella *
Jeffries-Sharkey Fight *
Love and War *
The Windsor Hotel Fire *

1900
The Adventures of Happy
Hooligan *
Dressing Room Scenes-Adolf
Zinc *
Grandma's Reading Glass *
Vaudeville *

1901
Attack on a China Mission *
Mary Jane's Mishap *

1902
The Life of an American
Fireman *
The Magic Lantern *
Voyage dans la Lune, Le *

1903
Chicago-Michigan Football
Game *
The Gay Shoe Clerk *
The Great Train Robbery *
Uncle Tom's Cabin *

1904
The Impossible Voyage *
The Land Beyond the
Sunset *
The Mermaid *
Personal *
The Story of the Kelly
Gang *

1905
How Jones Lost His Roll *
Life of an American
Policeman *
Presa di Roma *
President Roosevelt's
Inauguration *
Rescued by Rover *
Revolution in Russia *
Scenes and Incidents, Russo-
Japanese Peace
Conference *
The Seven Ages *

1906
The Dream of a Rarebit
Fiend *
The Ex-Convict *
Humorous Phases of Funny
Faces *
The Kleptomaniac *

1907
Rescued from an Eagle's
Nest *

1908
The Adventures of Dolly *
After Many Years *
Antony and Cleopatra *
As You Like It *
The Assassination of the
Duke de Guise *
Balked at the Altar *
The Bank Robbery *
A Drunkard's Reformation *
For Love of Gold *
Julius Caesar *
The Last Days of Pompeii *
The Merry Widow *
The Redman and the
Child *
Richard III *
Romeo and Juliet *
Samson and Delilah *
Sherlock Holmes *
Song of the Shirt *
The Taming of the Shrew *

1909
The Battle in the Clouds *
Camille *
A Corner in Wheat *
The Curtain Pole *
A Fool's Revenge *
The Heart of a Race Tout *
Hiawatha *
In Old Kentucky *
Incidents in the Life of
Napoleon and Josephine *
Launcelot and Elaine *
Leatherstocking *
The Life of Moses *
Lines of White on a Sullen
Sea *
The Lonely Villa *
The Merry Wives of
Windsor *
A Midsummer Night's
Dream *
Nero *
Pippa Passes *
The Prince and the Pauper *
Princess Nicotine *
The Redman's View *
Resurrection *
Tosca, La *
The Violin Maker of
Cremona *
Voice of the Violin *
The Way of Man *

1910
All on Account of the Milk *
The Burlesque Queen *
Doctor Jekyll and Mr.
Hyde *
The Fall of Babylon *
Francesca da Rimini *
Frankenstein *
The Fugitive *
Gold Is Not All *
The House with Closed
Shutters *
The Lad from Old Ireland *
The Life of Moses *
Othello *
Ramona *
1776 *
Simple Charity *
The Song of the Wildwood
Flute *
A Summer Idyl *
That Chink at Golden
Gulch *
The Thread of Destiny *
The Twisted Trail *
Uncle Tom's Cabin *
The Vampire *
The Wizard of Oz *

1911
The Battle *
The Battle of Trafalgar *
Cinderella *
The Colleen Bawn *
A Country Cupid *
David Copperfield *
The Deluge *
A Doll's House *
Enoch Arden, Part 1 *
Enoch Arden, Part 2 *
The Fall of Troy *
Fighting Blood *
Gunga Din *
Hamlet *
Help Wanted *
His Trust *
His Trust Fulfilled *
The Lonedale Operator *
Mr. Jones at the Ball *
The Poisoned Flume *
Romeo and Juliet *
Rory O'More *
The Scarlet Letter *
She *
Sherlock Holmes Jr. *
A Tale of Two Cities, Part
I *
A Tale of Two Cities, Part
II *
A Tale of Two Cities, Part
III *
Thais *
The Two Orphans *
Vanity Fair *
The Violin Maker of
Nuremberg *

1912
Conquete du Pole, A La *
A Dash Through the
Clouds *
The Delhi Dunbar *
Dr. Jekyll and Mr. Hyde *
From the Manger to the
Cross *
The Kerry Gow *
The Last Stand of the
Dalton Boys *
The Massacre *
The Muskateers of Pig
Alley *
The New York Hat *
Oliver Twist *
The Painted Lady *
Queen Elizabeth *
Richard III *
An Unseen Enemy *
War on the Plains *

1913
The Adventures of
Kathlyn *
Anthony and Cleopatra *
The Battle at Elderbush
Gulch *
The Battle of Gettysburg *
The Battle of Shiloh *
Cabiria *
Caprice *
The Count of Monte
Cristo *
In the Bishop's Carriage *
The Inside of the White
Slave Traffic *
Ivanhoe *
The Last Days of Pompeii *
Leah Kleschna *
Misérables, Les *
The Mothering Heart *
The Prisoner of Zenda *
Quo Vadis? *
The Sea Wolf *
The Student of Prague *
Tess of the D'Urbervilles *
Traffic in Souls *

1914
An American Citizen *
The Avenging Conscience *
The Bargain *
The Battle of the Sexes *
Beating Back *
Brewster's Millions *
The Christian *
The Dollar Mark *
The Escape *
The Exploits of Elaine *
A Florida Enchantment *
The Ghost Breaker *
A Good Little Devil *
Home, Sweet Home *
The Hoosier Schoolmaster *
Hypocrites *
In the Days of the
Thundering Herd *
John Barleycorn *
Judith of Bethulia *
The Jungle *
Mabel at the Wheel *
The Magic Cloak of Oz *
The Man from Home *
The Man of the Hour *
The Master Cracksman *
The Militant Suffragette *
Mr. Barnes of New York *
The Mother *
My Official Wife *
Neptune's Daughter *
The Patchwork Girl of Oz *
The Perils of Pauline *

Films followed by an asterisk (*) are listed in Film Review Index Volume 1: 1882–1949.

The Earl of Chicago *
East Side of Heaven *
An Englishman's Home *
Entente Cordiale *
Espionage Agent *
Eternally Yours *
Everything Happens at
    Night *
Fast and Furious *
Fast and Loose *
Fifth Avenue Girl *
The Fighting Sixty-Ninth *
Fin du Jour, La *
First Love *
Five Came Back *
The Flying Deuces *
The Flying Irishman *
Four Feathers *
Four Girls in White *
The Four Hundred Million *
Four Wives *
French Without Tears *
Frontier Marshall *
Full Confession *
A Girl Must Live *
Golden Boy *
Gone With the Wind *
Good Girls Go to Paris *
Goodbye, Mr. Chips *
The Gorilla *
The Gracie Allen Murder
    Case *
A Great Citizen *
The Great Man Votes *
The Great Victor Herbert *
Gulliver's Travels *
Gunga Din *
The Hardys Ride High *
Harvest *
Here I Am a Stranger *
Hollywood Cavalcade *
Honeymoon in Bali *
Honolulu *
Hotel for Women *
Hotel Imperial *
The Hound of the
    Baskervilles *
The Housekeeper's
    Daughter *
Huckleberry Finn *
The Hunchback of Notre
    Dame *
I Met a Murderer *
I Stole a Million *
The Ice Follies of 1939 *
Idiot's Delight *
In Name Only *
Indianapolis Speedway *
Inspector Hornleigh *
Intermezzo, a Love Story *
Invisible Stripes *
Invitation to Happiness *
Island of Lost Men *
It's a Wonderful World *
Jamaica Inn *
Jesse James *
Joe and Ethel Turp Call on
    the President *
Juarez *
Judge Hardy and Son *
Kid Nightingale *
King of the Turf *
King of the Underworld *
Lady of the Tropics *
Land of Liberty *
Lenin in 1918 *
Let Freedom Ring *
Let Us Live *

The Light That Failed *
The Lion Has Wings *
The Little Princess *
Louise *
Love Affair *
Lucky Night *
Made for Each Other *
The Magnificent Fraud *
Maisie *
Man About Town *
The Man in the Iron Mask *
Man of Conquest *
Meet Dr. Christian *
Mexican Spitfire *
Midnight *
The Mikado *
Million Dollar Legs *
Miracles for Sale *
Mr. Moto Takes a
    Vacation *
Mr. Smith Goes to
    Washington *
Nancy Drew, Reporter *
Never Say Die *
News Is Made at Night *
Nick Carter, Master
    Detective *
The Night of Nights *
Ninotchka *
Nurse Edith Cavell *
Of Mice and Men *
Off the Record *
The Oklahoma Kid *
The Old Maid *
On Borrowed Time *
On Your Toes *
"...one-third of a nation" *
Only Angels Have Wings *
Otages, Les *
Our Neighbors, the Carters *
Persons in Hiding *
Pocomania *
The Private Lives of
    Elizabeth and Essex *
Quick Millions *
Raffles *
The Rains Came *
Rasputin *
The Real Glory *
Reform School *
Regle du Jeu, Le *
Remember? *
Reno *
The Return of Doctor X *
Rio *
The Roaring Twenties *
Rose of Washington
    Square *
Rulers of the Sea *
Sable Cicada *
Saint Louis Blues *
School for Husbands *
Scipio Africanus *
Second Fiddle *
The Secret of Dr. Kildare *
Secret Service of the Air *
Sergeant Madden *
Shchors *
Six Thousand Enemies *
Smashing the Spy Ring *
Some Like It Hot *
Son of Frankenstein *
Song of the Streets *
Sorority House *
S.O.S.—Tidal Wave *
The Spirit of Culver *
Stagecoach *
Stand Up and Fight *

Stanley and Livingstone *
The Star Maker *
The Stars Look Down *
A Stolen Life *
The Story of Alexander
    Graham Bell *
The Story of Vernon and
    Irene Castle *
The Streets of New York *
The Sun Never Sets *
Susannah of the Mounties *
Swanee River *
Tail Spin *
Tarzan Finds a Son *
Television Spy *
Tell No Tales *
That's Right, You're
    Wrong *
These Glamour Girls *
They Made Me a Criminal *
They Shall Have Music *
This Man in Paris *
The Three Musketeers *
Three Smart Girls Grow
    Up *
Thunder Afloat *
Time in the Sun *
Topper Takes a Trip *
Tower of London *
Trois Valses *
Twelve Crowded Hours *
U-Boat 29 *
The Under-Pup *
Union Pacific *
We Are Not Alone *
When Tomorrow Comes *
Wife, Husband and Friend *
Wings of the Navy *
The Wizard of Oz *
A Woman's Face *
The Women *
Women in the Wind *
Wuthering Heights *
Yes, My Darling Daughter *
You Can't Cheat an Honest
    Man *
You Can't Get Away With
    Murder *
Young Mr. Lincoln *
Youth in Revolt *
Zenobia *

1940
Abe Lincoln in Illinois *
All This and Heaven Too *
Aloma of the South Seas *
Angels Over Broadway *
Arise My Love *
The Bank Dick *
The Biscuit Eater *
Blondie on a Budget *
Boom Town *
Brigham Young—
    Frontiersman *
Broadway Melody of 1940 *
Brother Orchid *
Chad Hanna *
Charlie Chan in Panama *
Christmas in July *
Comrade X *
Convoy *
Dark Command *
Dr. Cyclops *
Dr. Ehrlich's Magic Bullet *
Dr. Kildare's Strange Case *
Down Argentine Way *
Edison, the Man *
Escape *

Fantasia *
Foreign Correspondent *
Four Sons *
The Fugitive *
The Grapes of Wrath *
The Great Dictator *
The Great McGinty *
His Girl Friday *
The Howards of Virginia *
I Take This Woman *
Irene *
Johnny Apollo *
Kitty Foyle *
Knute Rockne, All
    American *
Let George Do It *
The Letter *
Life Begins for Andy
    Hardy *
Lillian Russell *
The Long Voyage Home *
The Man I Married *
The Mark of Zorro *
The Mortal Storm *
My Favorite Wife *
My Little Chickadee *
My Son, My Son *
Night Train *
Northwest Mounted Police *
Northwest Passage *
One Million B.C. *
Our Town *
The Philadelphia Story *
Pinocchio *
Pride and Prejudice *
The Primrose Path *
Rebecca *
Remember the Night *
The Return of Frank
    James *
The Road to Singapore *
Road to Zanzibar *
Santa Fe Trail *
Saturday's Children *
The Sea Hawk *
The Shop Around the
    Corner *
Strike Up the Band *
Susan and God *
Swiss Family Robinson *
They Drive by Night *
They Knew What They
    Wanted *
The Thief of Bagdad *
This Thing Called Love *
Tin Pan Alley *
Tom Brown's School Days *
Waterloo Bridge *
The Westerner *
When the Daltons Rode *
Young Tom Edison *

1941
Adam Had Four Sons *
Back Street *
Ball of Fire *
Belle Starr *
Billy the Kid *
The Birth of the Blues *
Blood and Sand *
Blossoms in the Dust *
Blues in the Night *
The Bride Came C.O.D. *
Buck Privates *
Caught in the Draft *
Charley's Aunt *
Cheers for Miss Bishop *
The Chocolate Soldier *

Citizen Kane *
The Corsican Brothers *
The Devil and Daniel
    Webster *
The Devil and Miss Jones *
Dive Bomber *
Dr. Jekyll and Mr. Hyde *
Dumbo *
Eagle Squadron *
The Flame of New Orleans *
49th Parallel *
The Great Lie *
Hellzapoppin' *
Here Comes Mr. Jordan *
High Sierra *
H. M. Pulham, Esq. *
Hold Back the Dawn *
Hold That Ghost *
Honky Tonk *
How Green Was My
    Valley *
Hudson's Bay *
I Wake Up Screaming *
I Wanted Wings *
In This Our Life *
Johnny Eager *
King's Row *
Ladies in Retirement *
Lady Be Good *
The Lady Eve *
The Little Foxes *
Louisiana Purchase *
Love Crazy *
Love on the Dole *
Major Barbara *
The Maltese Falcon *
Man Hunt *
The Man Who Came to
    Dinner *
Meet John Doe *
Mr. and Mrs. Smith *
Mister V *
My Favorite Blonde *
My Gal Sal *
Never Give a Sucker an
    Even Break *
One Foot in Heaven *
Out of the Fog *
Penny Serenade *
Rage in Heaven *
The Sea Wolf *
Sergeant York *
The Shanghai Gesture *
Smilin' Through *
So Ends Our Night *
Somewhere I'll Find You *
The Strawberry Blonde *
Sullivan's Travels *
Sun Valley Serenade *
Suspicion *
Swamp Water *
That Hamilton Woman *
That Uncertain Feeling *
They Died with Their Boots
    On *
They Met in Bombay *
This Above All *
Tobacco Road *
Tom, Dick, and Harry *
Two-Faced Woman *
The Wagons Roll at Night *
The Well-Digger's
    Daughter *
Western Union *
Wild Geese Calling *
The Wolf Man *
A Yank in the R.A.F. *
Ziegfeld Girl *

Claudine
The Clockmaker
Conrack
The Conversation
Cousin Angelica
Craze
Crazy Joe
Daisy Miller
Death Wish
Dirty Mary Crazy Larry
Earthquake
Edvard Munch
Effi Briest
11 Harrowhouse
Emmanuelle
Executive Action
Fantome de la Liberté, Le
For Pete's Sake
Freebie and the Bean
The Front Page
The Gambler
The Girl from Petrovka
The Godfather, Part II
Going Places
Gold
The Great Gatsby
Harry and Tonto
The Internecine Project
Juggernaut
Lacombe, Lucien
Lenny
The Little Prince
The Longest Yard
The Lords of Flatbush
Lovin' Molly
Macon County Line
Mame
Man on a Swing
The Man With the Golden
 Gun
McQ
The Midnight Man
Mr. Majestyk
Murder on the Orient
 Express
The Nada Gang
The Night Porter
The Odessa File
Our Time
The Parallax View
The Phantom of the
 Paradise
Scent of a Woman
The Slap
S*p*y*s
Stavisky
The Sugarland Express
Sweet Movie
The Taking of Pelham One
 Two Three
The Tamarind Seed
The Texas Chainsaw
 Massacre
That's Entertainment
Thieves Like Us
The Three Musketeers
Thunderbolt and Lightfoot
The Towering Inferno
The Trial of Billy Jack
Trio Infernal, Le
Uptown Saturday Night
Where the Lillies Bloom
Woman Under the Influence
Young Frankenstein
Zardoz

1975

The Adventures of Sherlock
 Holmes' Smarter Brother
At Long Last Love
Barry Lyndon
The Black Bird
Black Moon
Conduct Unbecoming
Cooley High
The Day of the Locust
Dersu Uzala
Dog Day Afternoon
The Drowning Pool
Face to Face
Farewell, My Lovely
The Fortune
The Four Musketeers
The French Connection II
Funny Lady
The Great Waldo Pepper
Hard Times
Hearts of the West
Hennesy
Hester Street
The Hindenburg
Hustle
Incorrigible
Jacques Brel Is Alive and
 Well and Living in Paris
Jaws
The Killer Elite
Lisztomania
Love and Death
Lucky Lady
The Magic Flute
The Man in the Glass Booth
The Man Who Would Be
 King
Monty Python and the Holy
 Grail
Nashville
Night Moves
Numero Deux
One Flew Over the Cuckoo's
 Nest
Padre Padrone
The Passenger
Picnic at Hanging Rock
The Prisoner of Second
 Avenue
Return of the Pink Panther
The Rocky Horror Picture
 Show
Rollerball
The Romantic
 Englishwoman
Rooster Cogburn
Rosebud
Royal Flash
Russian Roulette
Seven Beauties
Shampoo
Sheila Levine Is Dead and
 Living in New York
Smile
Special Section
The Stepford Wives
The Story of Adele H.
Swept Away: By an Unusual
 Destiny in the Blue Sea of
 August
Three Days of the Condor
Tommy
The Wild Party
The Wind and the Lion

1976

Alex and the Gypsy
All the President's Men
America at the Movies
Baby Blue Marine
The Bad News Bears
Bingo Long Traveling All
 Stars & Motor Kings
The Blue Bird
Bound for Glory
Breakheart Pass
Budapest Tales
Buffalo Bill and the Indians
 or Sitting Bull's History
 Lesson
Bugsy Malone
Car Wash
Carrie
Family Plot
Fellini's Casanova
The First Nudie Musical
The Front
Futureworld
Gable and Lombard
The Gumball Rally
Harry and Walter Go to
 New York
In the Realm of the Senses
The Incredible Sarah
The Innocent
Jonah who will be 25 in the
 Year 2000
The Killing of a Chinese
 Bookie
King Kong
The Last Tycoon
Leadbelly
Lipstick
Logan's Run
Lumiere
The Man Who Fell to Earth
The Man Who Loved
 Women
Marathon Man
The Marquise of O . . .
Midway
Mikey and Nicky
The Missouri Breaks
Murder by Death
Network
The Next Man
Next Stop Greenwich Village
Nickelodeon
Norman . . . Is That You?
Obsession
Ode to Billy Joe
The Omen
The Outlaw Josey Wales
Pardon Mon Affaire
The Return of a Man Called
 Horse
The Ritz
Robin and Marian
Rocky
The Sailor Who Fell From
 Grace With the Sea
St. Ives
The Seven Per-Cent Solution
The Shootist
Shout at the Devil
Silent Movie
Silver Streak
Sky Riders
The Slipper and the Rose
Small Change
Snuff
Sparkle
A Star Is Born

Stay Hungry
Sunday Woman
Taxi Driver
The Tenant
That's Entertainment, Part
 II
Two-Minute Warning
Voyage of the Damned
W.C. Fields and Me
Welcome to L.A.
A Woman at Her Window
Won Ton Ton, the Dog
 Who Saved Hollywood
Xica

1977

The American Friend
Annie Hall
Black and White in Color
Black Sunday
Bobby Deerfield
A Bridge Too Far
The Chess Players
The Choirboys
Close Encounters of a Third
 Kind
Cross of Iron
Dear Detective
The Deep
Dona Flor and Her Two
 Husbands
The Duellists
Equus
Eraserhead
Fun with Dick and Jane
The Gauntlet
The Getting of Wisdom
The Goodbye Girl
Greased Lightning
The Greatest
High Anxiety
I Never Promised You a
 Rose Garden
The Island of Dr. Moreau
Islands in the Stream
Joseph Andrews
Julia
Kentucky Fried Movie
The Lacemaker
The Last Remake of Beau
 Geste
The Last Wave
The Late Show
Looking for Mr. Goodbar
MacArthur
Madame Rosa
Man of Marble
Nasty Habits
New York, New York
1900
Oh, God!
One on One
One Sings the Other Doesn't
Orca
The Other Side of Midnight
Our Hitler
Pete's Dragon
Providence
Pumping Iron
Rollercoaster
Roseland
Saturday Night Fever
Semi-Tough
The Sentinel
Slap Shot
Smokey and the Bandit
Soldier of Orange
Sorcerer

A Special Day
The Spy Who Loved Me
Star Wars
That Obscure Object of
 Desire
Three Women
The Turning Point
Twilight's Last Gleaming
Valentino
Wifemistress
The World's Greatest Lover
You Light Up My Life

1978

American Hot Wax
Autumn Sonata
The Betsy
The Big Fix
The Big Sleep
Bloodbrothers
Blue Collar
The Boys from Brazil
The Boys in Company C
The Buddy Holly Story
Cage Aux Folles, La
California Suite
Capricorn One
The Chant of Jimmy
 Blacksmith
The Cheap Detective
Coma
Comes a Horseman
Coming Home
Convoy
Corvette Summer
Damien-The Omen II
Days of Heaven
Death on the Nile
The Deer Hunter
A Different Story
A Dream of Passion
The End
The Eyes of Laura Mars
F.I.S.T.
Foul Play
The Fury
Get Out Your
 Handkerchiefs
Girlfriends
Go Tell the Spartans
Goin' South
Grease
The Greek Tycoon
Halloween
Heaven Can Wait
Hooper
House Calls
I Wanna Hold Your Hand
In a Year of 13 Moons
Interiors
International Velvet
Invasion of the Body
 Snatchers
Jaws 2
King of the Gypsies
Knife in the Head
Midnight Express
Moment by Moment
Movie Movie
National Lampoon's Animal
 House
The One and Only
Pretty Baby
Sgt. Pepper's Lonely Hearts
 Club Band
A Simple Story
Stevie
Straight Time

Country Produced Index

Algeria
Bal, Le
The Battle of Algiers
Eboli
The Stranger
Z

Argentina
The Marijuana Story
Native Son
The Official Story

Australia
Breaker Morant
Careful He Might Hear You
The Chant of Jimmy
  Blacksmith
Gallipoli
The Getting of Wisdom
It's My Turn
The Last Wave
Mad Max
Mad Max Beyond
  Thunderdome
My Brilliant Career
Picnic at Hanging Rock
The Road Warrior
The Year of Living
  Dangerously

Austria
Colonel Redl
The Last Bridge
Liebesmelodie *
No Time For Flowers
Tales from the Vienna
  Woods *

Belgium
Départ, Le
Get Out Your
  Handkerchiefs
The Man Who Had His
  Hair Cut Short
One Sings the Other Doesn't

Botswana
The Gods Must be Crazy

Brazil
Bye Bye Brazil
Dona Flor and Her Two
  Husbands
Gabriela
Kiss of the Spider Woman
Pixote
Xica

Bulgaria
The Peach Thief

Canada
A Tout Prendre
The Apprenticeship of
  Duddy Kravitz
Atlantic City
The Changeling
The Fox
The Grey Fox
The Incredible Journey
Joshua Then, and Now
The Luck of Ginger Coffey
Meatballs
Middle Age Crazy
Nobody Waved Goodbye
Oedipus Rex
Porky's
Quest for Fire
Running Brave
Scanners
A Special Day
Ticket to Heaven
The Trap
Warrendale

China
Light of Asia *
Sable Cicada *

Cuba
Lucia
Memories of
  Underdevelopment
Portrait of Teresa

Curacao
One Sings the Other Doesn't

Czechoslovakia
All My Good Countrymen
Black Peter
Capricious Summer
Closely Watched Trains
The Cry
Diamonds of the Night
Dinner for Adele
Distant Journey
Ecstasy *
The Emperor's Baker
The Emperor's Nightingale
The Fifth Horseman Is Fear
Homme Qui Ment, L'
Intimate Lighting
Janosik *
Loves of a Blonde
Ninety Degrees in the Shade

A Report on the Party and
  the Guests
Sedmikrasky
The Shop on Main Street
Sweet Light In a Dark
  Room

Denmark
Day of Wrath *
Gertrud
Hagbard and Signe
Hunger
Ordet
The Wedding of Palo *

East Germany
Ich War 19
Stronger Than the Night

France
A Nos Amours
A Propos de Nice *
Abus de Confiance *
Adolescente, L'
Age d'Or, L' *
Alibi, L' *
Alphaville
Amants, Les
Amarcord
The Amazing Monsieur
  Fabre
The American Friend
And God Created Woman
And Now My Love
And There Came a Man
Antoine et Antoinette *
Any Number Can Win
Argent, L' *
Arroseur Arrose, L' *
The Assassination of the
  Duke de Guise *
Atalante, L' *
Atlantic City
Atlantide, L' *
Au Hasard, Balthazar
Auberge Rouge, L' *
Au-Dela des Grilles
Autour D'Une Cabine *
Avec le Sourire *
Avocate d'Amour *
Backfire
Bal, Le
Ballerina *
Bambole, Le
Banana Peel
Band of Outsiders
Barbarella
Bay of Angels
Beau Mariage, Le
Beau Pere

Beau Serge, Le
Beaute du Diable, La
Beauty and the Beast *
Bed and Board
Belle de Jour
Belle Équipe, La *
Belle Nivernaise, La *
Belles-de-Nuit, Les
Benjamin, or The Diary of
  an Innocent Young Boy
Bête Humaine, La *
Betrayal *
Biches, Les
The Birds, the Bees and the
  Italians
Bitter Victory
Bizarre, Bizarre *
Bizet's Carmen
Black and White in Color
Black Orpheus
Black Thursday
Blé en Herbe, Le
Blood and Black Lace
The Blood of a Poet *
Bob le Flambeur
Boccaccio 70
Bonheur, Le
Bonheur, Le *
Bonne Chance *
Bonnes Femmes, Les
Boudu Savé Des Eaux *
Boulanger de Valorgue, Le
The Brain
Breathless
The Bride Wore Black
Burn!
The Butcher
Cage Aux Folles, La
Cage Aux Folles II, La
Camille *
Captain Black Jack
Carnet de Bal, Un *
Carnival in Flanders *
Carnival of Sinners *
Caroline Cherie
Cartouche
Casanova '70
Casque D'Or
Celine and Julie Go Boating
Celui Qui doit Mourir
César *
Chamade, La
The Champagne Murders
Champs Élysees *
Chien Andalou, Un *
Chienne, La *
Children of Paradise *
Chloe in the Afternoon
Chotard et Compagnie *
Chronicle of a Summer
Cinderella *

Circle of Deceit
Circle of Love
Citadelle du Silence *
Clair de Femme
Claire's Knee
Cleo from 5 to 7
The Climax
The Clockmaker
Cloportes
Club des Femmes *
Coeur Fidele *
Collectionneuse, La
Companions of the Night
Condamne a Mort s'est
  Echappe, Un
The Confession
Confidentially Yours
Congolaise
Conquete du Pole, A La *
Contempt
The Cop
Coup de Grace
Coup de tete
Coup de Torchon
The Courier of Lyons *
Courrier-Sud *
Cousins, Les
Crainquebille *
The Crazy Ray *
Crime de Monsieur Lange,
  Le *
Crime et Châtiment *
The Crook
Dames du Bois de Boulogne,
  Les
Danton
Dark Eyes *
David Golder *
Day for Night
Dear Detective
Dédée
The Defector
Dernier Milliardaire, Le *
Desperate Decision
Deuxieme Souffle, Le
Diabolique
The Diary of a
  Chambermaid
The Dirty Game
The Discreet Charm of the
  Bourgeoisie
Disparus de Saint-Agil, Les *
Diva
Don Quixote *
Double Crime sur la Ligne
  Maginot *
Drame de Shanghai, Le *
Drole de Drame *
The Earrings of Madame De
The Eclipse
Eldorado *

Films followed by an asterisk (*) are listed in Film Review Index Volume 1: 1882–1949.

Emmanuelle
Enfants Terribles, Les
Enough Rope
Entente Cordiale *
Entr'acte *
Entre Nous
Equipage, L' *
Escape from Yesterday *
Escape to Nowhere
Eva
Every Man for Himself
Face To the Wind
Fall of the House of Usher *
Fanfan the Tulip
Fanny *
Fantomas
Fantome de la Liberté, Le
Farrebique *
Fellini Satyricon
Femme douce, Une
Femme du Boulanger, La *
Femme Infidele, La
Femme Mariée, Une
Fetes Galantes, Les
Fifi La Plume
Fin du Jour, La *
First Name Carmen
Five Miles to Midnight
Foire aux Chimeres, La
Forbidden Fruit
Forbidden Games
Four Bags Full
The 400 Blows
The French They Are a
   Funny Race
Full Moon in Paris
Galia
The Game Is Over
Garde a vue
Gates of Paris
Gauloises Bleues, Les
Generals Without Buttons *
Gens du Voyage, Les *
Gervaise
Get Out Your
   Handkerchiefs
The Girl On a Motorcycle
Going Places
The Golden Coach
Golgotha *
The Gospel According to St.
   Matthew
Goupi Mains Rouge *
Grand Jeu, Le *
Grand Patron, Un
Grande Amour de
   Beethoven, Une *
Grande Illusion, La *
The Great Spy Chase
Gribouille *
Guerre Est Finie, La
Gueule d'Amour *
Hail, Mary
Hanna K
Harvest *
Heartbeat *
Hiroshima, Mon Amour
Histoire d'Amour, Une
Holiday For Henrietta
Homme du Jour, L' *
Homme Qui Ment, L'
Hotel du Nord *
I Sent a Letter to My Love
Immortal Story
The Impossible Voyage *
In the French Style
In the Realm of the Senses
Incorrigible

The Innocent
Inspector Maigret
Is Paris Burning?
An Italian Straw Hat *
J'Accuse *
Jessica
Jetée, La
Jeu de Massacre
Joli Mai, Le
Jonah who will be 25 in the
   Year 2000
Jour de Fete
Journal d'un Cure de
   Campagne, Le
Joy House
Judex
Jules & Jim
Julie de Carneilhan
Juliet of the Spirits
Justice Est Faite
Katia
King of Hearts
Knave of Hearts
Koenigsmark *
The Koumiko Mystery
The Kreutzer Sonata *
The Lacemaker
Lacombe, Lucien
Lady L
Lady Paname
The Last Metro
Last Tango in Paris
Last Year at Marienbad
Le Jour se Lève *
The Lie of Nina Petrovna *
Life Upside Down
Liliom *
The Little World of Don
   Camillo
Live for Life
Lola
Louise *
Loulou
Love and Anarchy
A Love In Germany
The Lower Depths *
Lucrezia Borgia *
Lumiere
Lumiere First Program *
Ma Pomme
Madame Bovary *
Madame Rosa
Made in USA
Mademoiselle
Mademoiselle Docteur *
The Magic Lantern *
The Magnificent Cuckold
Mains Sales, Les
Male Companion
Male Hunt
A Man and a Woman
The Man On the Eiffel
   Tower
The Man Who Loved
   Women
Mandabi
Mandragola, La
Maneges
Manon
Manon des Sources
Marco the Magnificent
Marie du Port
Marius *
The Marquise of O . . .
Marriage Italian Style
Marseillaise, La *
Masculin-Féminin
Maternelle, La *

Mayerling *
Merlusse *
The Mermaid *
Million, Le *
Minne
Mioche, Le *
Miquette
Miracle of the Wolves *
Misérables, Les *
Misérables, Les *
Mr. Flow *
Mr. Hulot's Holiday
The Moment of Truth
Mon Oncle
Mon Oncle d'Amerique
Monastery *
Monte Carlo Baby
The Moon in the Gutter
Moonraker
Mort du Cygne, La *
Mouchette
Mouton a Cinq Pattes, Le
A Murmur of the Heart
My Night at Maud's
Mystere de la Chambre
   Jaune, Le *
The Nada Gang
Nana
Nana *
Napoleon *
Né de Pere Inconnu
The Night
The Night of the Generals
1900
Nous la Liberté, À *
Nuit de Varennes, La
Nuit du Carrefour, La *
Numero Deux
Oasis
Occupe-Toi D'Amelie
Olivia
One Sings the Other Doesn't
Orage *
An Orchid For the Tiger
Orgueilleux, Les
Orphée
Otages, Les *
Pardon Mon Affaire
Paris Does Strange Things
Paris Vu Par . . .
Paris-Mediterranée *
Partie de Campagne, Une *
The Passenger
The Passion of Joan of Arc *
Pauline at the Beach
Pearls of the Crown *
Pension Mimosas *
Pépé le Moko *
Peppermint Soda
Phaedra
The Pickpocket
Pierrot Le Fou
Plaisir, Le
Please! Mr. Balzac
Poil de Carotte *
Practice Makes Perfect
Prisonniére, La
The Prize
Promise at Dawn
Providence
Puritan, Le *
Purple Noon
Quai des Brumes *
Quartet
Quatorze Juillet *
Queen Elizabeth *
Querelle
Quest for Fire

Rage au Corps, La
Rapture
Rasputin *
Razumov *
The Red Balloon
Red Desert
The Red Inn
Regle du Jeu, Le *
Religieuse, La
Rendezvous de Juillet
The Return of Martin
   Guerre
Revolution in Russia *
Rififi
Rififi in Panama
The Rise of Louis XIV
Roi S'Amuse, Le *
Roman d'un Tricheur, Le *
Ronde, La
Roue, La *
A Royal Affair
Samson and Delilah *
Sans Famille *
Savage Triangle
Second Bureau *
The Secret of Mayerling
Seduced and Abandoned
The Seven Deadly Sins
The Shameless Old Lady
Shoot the Piano Player
The Sign of Leo
A Simple Story
The Sky Above, the Mud
   Below
The Slap
The Sleeping Car Murder
The Slipper Episode *
Small Change
The Soft Skin
Song of the Streets *
The Sorrow and the Pity
Sortie des Ouvriers de
   l'Usine Lumiere *
Sous la Lune du Maroc *
Sous les Toits de Paris *
Souvenirs Perdus
Special Section
Stavisky
Stolen Kisses
The Story of Adele H.
The Stranger
Strangers in the House *
Successo, Il
The Sucker
A Sunday in the Country
Sunday Woman
Sundays & Cybele
Swann in Love
Taxi for Tobruk
The Tenant
Tender Scoundrel
Tendre Ennemie, Le *
The Tenth Victim
Tess
Thais *
Thank Heaven For Small
   Favors
That Man From Rio
That Man in Istanbul
That Obscure Object of
   Desire
That They May Live *
Therese Raquin
Thomas l'Imposteur
To Be a Crook
To Die in Madrid
Toni *
Tosca, La *

The Train
Trans-Europ-Express
The Tree of Wooden Clogs
Trio Infernal, Le
Trois Valses *
The Two of Us
The Umbrellas of Cherbourg
Up To His Ears
The Vanishing Lady *
Veille d'Armes *
A Very Private Affair
Vice and Virtue
Vie Commence Demain, La
Vie de Chateau, La
Vie Est a Nous, La *
A View from the Bridge
Visages D'Enfants *
The Visit
Visiteurs du Soir, Les *
Viva Maria
Volpone *
Voyage dans la Lune, Le *
The Wages of Fear
The Ways of Love
We Are All Murderers
Weekend
Weekend At Dunkirk
The Well-Digger's
   Daughter *
What's New Pussycat?
White Voices
The Wild Child
A Woman at Her Window
A Woman Is a Woman
The Woman Next Door
Woman Times Seven
World Without Sun
Yoshiwara *
The Young Girls of
   Rochefort
Young Torless
A Young World
Youth in Revolt *
Z
Zazie dans le Métro
Zero for Conduct *

Great Britain
Abandon Ship
Accident
Accused *
Across the Bridge
Action for Slander *
Admirable Crichton
The Adventures of Chico *
The African Queen
After the Fox
Alfie
Alfred the Great
The Alphabet Murders
The Amateur Gentleman *
The Amorous Adventures of
   Moll Flanders
The Angel Who Pawned Her
   Harp
Angels One Five
The Angry Silence
Another Country
Another Man's Poison
Arabesque
Aren't We All? *
Arrivderci, Baby
The Astonished Heart
Attack on a China Mission *
Bad Timing: A Sensual
   Obsession
Bang, Bang, You're Dead!
Bank Holiday *

Marat/Sade
The Mark
The Marriage of Corbal *
Mary Jane's Mishap *
Mary Queen of Scots
Masquerade
Maytime in Mayfair
Men Are Not Gods *
Merry Christmas, Mr.
    Lawrence
Michael and Mary *
The Middleman *
The Mikado *
The Mill on the Floss *
Mimi *
The Mirror Cracked
The Missionary
Mr. Potts Goes to Moscow
Mister V *
Modesty Blaise
Montenegro
Monty Python and the Holy
    Grail
Monty Python's Life of
    Brian
Monty Python's The
    Meaning of Life
Moonlight Sonata *
Moonlighting
Moonraker
The Moon-Spinners
Morgan
Moscow Nights *
The Mouse on the Moon
The Mouse that Roared
The Muppet Movie
Murder! *
Murder Ahoy!
The Murder Game
Murder in the Cathedral
Murder, She Said
The Music Lovers
My Heart Is Calling You *
The Nanny
Nasty Habits
Negatives
Nell Gwyn *
Never Take No For An
    Answer
Next of Kin *
Nicholas Nickelby *
Night and the City
Night Mail *
Night Must Fall
The Night of the Generals
A Night to Remember
Night Train *
Nine Days a Queen *
Ninety Degrees in the Shade
No Highway
No Love For Johnnie
No Resting Place
The Notorious Gentleman *
Number Seventeen *
O Lucky Man!
Obsessed
Octopussy
Odd Man Out *
The Odessa File
Odette
Oedipus the King
Of Human Bondage
Oh! What A Lovely War
O.H.M.S. *
Oliver!
Oliver Twist *
On Approval *

On Her Majesty's Secret
    Service
One Day in the Life of Ivan
    Denisovich
One Million Years B.C.
One of Our Aircraft Is
    Missing *
One Way Pendulum
Operation Crossbow
Operation Disaster
Orders to Kill
Othello
Our Man in Havana
Outcast of the Islands
Outpost in Malaya
The Outsider
The Outsider *
Pagliacci *
Pandora and the Flying
    Dutchman
The Paratrooper
The Passing of the Third
    Floor Back *
The Passing of the Third
    Floor Back *
Passport to Pimlico *
Peeping Tom
Penny Princess
Performance
Personal Affair
Petulia
Piccadilly Incident *
The Pickwick Papers
Pool of London
Poor Cow
Power *
Priest of Love
The Prime of Miss Jean
    Brodie
The Prince and the Showgirl
Prison Without Bars *
The Prisoner of Zenda *
A Private Function
The Private Life of Don
    Juan *
The Private Life of Henry
    VIII *
The Private Life of Sherlock
    Holmes
Promise Her Anything
The Promoter
Prudence and the Pill
The Pumpkin Eater
Pursuit of the Graf Spee
Pygmalion *
Quartet
The Queen of Spades
The Quiller Memorandum
The Rainbow Jacket
Raise the Titanic
The Rat *
Rattle of a Simple Man
The Red Shoes *
Rembrandt *
Repulsion
Rescued by Rover *
Reserved for Ladies *
Return From the Ashes
Rhodes *
Rich and Strange *
Richard III
Richard's Things
The Ring *
Ring of Bright Water
The Ritz
Rob Roy, the Highland
    Rogue
The Robber Symphony *

Robin and Marian
The Rocking Horse Winner
The Rocky Horror Picture
    Show
The Roman Spring of Mrs.
    Stone
Rome Express *
Romeo and Juliet
Romeo and Juliet
Romeo and Juliet
Room at the Top
Rotten to the Core
A Royal Divorce *
Royal Flash
The Ruling Class
A Run For Your Money
Ryan's Daughter
Sabotage *
Sailing Along *
The Sailor Who Fell From
    Grace With the Sea
Saints and Sinners *
Sally in Our Alley *
Sanders of the River *
Sands of the Kalahari
Saturday Night & Sunday
    Morning
The Scarlet Pimpernel *
The Scarlet Spear
School for Husbands *
Scotch on the Rocks
Scrooge
The Sea Shall Not Have
    Them
Sea Wife
Seance on a Wet Afternoon
The Secret Agent *
Secret Ceremony
Secret Flight
The Secret of My Success
Secret People
The Servant
Seven Days to Noon
The Seven Per-Cent Solution
Seven Sinners *
The Seventh Dawn
The Seventh Veil *
She
The Shooting Party
A Shot in the Dark
Shout at the Devil
Sidewalks of London *
The Sign of the Four *
The Silent Witness *
Sing As We Go *
Sink the Bismarck!
Sixty Glorious Years *
The Skin Game *
Sky West and Crooked
The Sleeping Tiger
Sleuth
The Slipper and the Rose
Smiling Along *
So Long At the Fair
Something Money Can't Buy
Song of Ceylon *
The Song of Freedom *
Sons & Lovers
South Riding *
The Spanish Gardener
Spitfire *
The Spy Who Came In
    From the Cold
The Spy Who Loved Me
S*p*y*s
Stairway to Heaven *
The Stars Look Down *
State Secret

Stevie
A Stolen Face
A Stolen Life *
Stop the World, I Want to
    Get Off
Storm in a Teacup *
A Study in Terror
Summertime
Sunday Bloody Sunday
Surprise Package
The Tales of Hoffman
Talk of the Devil *
Tall Headlines
The Tamarind Seed
A Taste of Honey
Tell England *
Ten Little Indians
Tess
That Sinking Feeling
There Goes the Bride *
These Are the Damned
They Were Not Divided
The Thief of Bagdad *
Things to Come *
The Third Man *
The Thirty-Nine Steps *
This Man in Paris *
This Man Is News *
Those Magnificent Men in
    Their Flying Machines
3 into 2 Won't Go
The Three Maxims *
Thunder in the City *
Thunderball
Tiger Bay
Tight Little Island *
Time After Time
Time Bandits
Time Lost and Time
    Remembered
The Titfield Thunderbolt
To Sir, With Love
To the Victor *
Tom Brown's Schooldays
Tommy
Tonight at 8:30
Tonight's the Night
A Touch of Class
Transatlantic Tunnel *
The Trap
Treasure Island
Trent's Last Case *
The Trials of Oscar Wilde
Trio
The Triumph of Sherlock
    Holmes *
Troopship *
Trouble in the Glen
The Truth About Spring
Tunes of Glory
12:10 *
Twenty Four Hours of a
    Woman's Life
Twist of Fate
Two for the Road
U-Boat 29 *
Ulysses
Under the Red Robe *
Underground *
The Unholy Four
Vacation from Marriage *
Valentino
Valley of the Eagles
Venetian Bird
Victim
Victoria the Great *
A View to a Kill
Village of the Damned

The Virgin and the Gypsy
Voyage of the Damned
Walkabout
Waltz of the Toreadors
Waltz Time *
Waltzes From Vienna *
The Wandering Jew *
The War Game
The War Lover
The Ware Case *
The Weak and the Wicked
Wee Geordie
We're Going to Be Rich *
West of Zanzibar
Wetherby
Where the Bullets Fly
Where the Spies Are
Where's Charley?
The Whisperers
Whistle Down the Wind
White Corridors
Who Goes There!
The Wicked Lady *
The Wild Heart
Willy Wonka and the
    Chocolate Factory
Wings of the Morning *
The Winslow Boy
The Woman in Question
The Woman of Dolwyn *
Woman of Straw
Women in Love
The Wooden Horse
The Wrong Box
Wuthering Heights
Yank in London *
Yanks
The Yellow Rolls-Royce
Yellow Sands *
Yellow Submarine
You Only Live Twice
Young and Innocent *
Young Cassidy
The Young Lovers
Young Winston
Young Wives' Tale
Zulu

Greece
The Barefoot Battalion
A Dream of Passion
Electra
Girl in Black
Never on Sunday
Phaedra
Red Lanterns
Sky Riders
Stella
Zorba the Greek

Hungary
Angi Vera
Budapest Tales
A Chess Maniac *
Colonel Redl
Hideg Napok
Hortobagy *
Mephisto
The Round-Up

Iceland
Hagbard and Signe

India
Aan
Charulata
The Chess Players

Spain
Adam and Eve
Blood Wedding
Brief Vacation
The Chimes at Midnight
Cousin Angelica
The Discreet Charm of the
  Bourgeoisie
Every Day Is a Holiday
A Fistful of Dollars
For a Few Dollars More
The Four Musketeers
Garden of Delights
Kid Rodelo
Mama Turns 100
Mr. Arkadin
The Moment of Truth
An Orchid For the Tiger
The Passenger
Return of the Seven
Taxi for Tobruk
Ten Thirty P.M. Summer
That Man in Istanbul
That Obscure Object of
  Desire
Torero!
Viridiana
Volver a Empezar
Welcome, Mr. Marshall

Sweden
After the Rehearsal
The Atonement of Gösta
  Berling *
Au Hasard, Balthazar
Autumn Sonata
Cries and Whispers
Dear John
Edvard Munch
Elvira Madigan
The Emigrants
Face to Face
Fanny and Alexander
The Flight of the Eagle
From the Life of the
  Marionettes
The Girl from the Marsh
  Croft *
The Great Adventure
Guerre Est Finie, La
Hagbard and Signe
High Tension
Hour of the Wolf
Hunger
I Am Curious Yellow
Illicit Interlude
Intermezzo *
A Lesson in Love
Loving Couples
The Magic Flute
The Magician
A Man There Was *
Masculin-Féminin
The Militant Suffragette *
Miss Julie
Montenegro
My Home Is Copacabana
My Sister, My Love
The Naked Night
The New Land
Night Games
Now About These Women
One Summer of Happiness
Persona
Raven's End
Secrets of Women
The Seventh Seal
Shame

The Silence
Sir Arne's Treasure *
Sir Arne's Treasure *
Smiles of a Summer Night
Through a Glass Darkly
To Love
The Touch
The Virgin Spring
Wild Strawberries
Witchcraft Through the
  Ages *
A Woman's Face *

Switzerland
Boheme, La
The Chimes at Midnight
Dangerous Moves
The Eternal Mask *
Four Days Leave
Four In a Jeep
Hail, Mary
Heidi
Jonah who will be 25 in the
  Year 2000
The Lacemaker
Providence
Wings Over Ethiopia *
Yol

Turkey
Yol

United Nations
The Poppy Is Also a Flower

United States
Aaron Slick From Punkin
  Crick
The Abdication
Abe Lincoln in Illinois *
Abie's Irish Rose *
Abilene Town *
About Face
About Mrs. Leslie
Above and Beyond
Above Suspicion *
Abraham Lincoln *
Abraham Lincoln *
Absence of Malice
The Absent Minded
  Professor
Accent on Youth *
The Accused *
Ace in the Hole
Across the Pacific *
Across the Wide Missouri
Act of Violence *
Act One
Action in the North
  Atlantic *
Actors and Sin
The Actress
The Actress *
Adam Had Four Sons *
Adam's Rib *
Adorable *
Adventure *
Adventure in Baltimore *
Adventure in Manhattan *
The Adventures of Buckaroo
  Banzai Across the Eighth
  Dimension
The Adventures of Captain
  Fabian
The Adventures of Dolly *
The Adventures of Don
  Juan *

The Adventures of Hajji
  Baba
The Adventures of Happy
  Hooligan *
The Adventures of
  Kathlyn *
The Adventures of Marco
  Polo *
The Adventures of Mark
  Twain *
The Adventures of Robin
  Hood *
The Adventures of Robinson
  Crusoe
The Adventures of Sherlock
  Holmes *
The Adventures of Sherlock
  Holmes' Smarter Brother
Adventures of Tartu *
The Adventures of Tom
  Sawyer *
Advise and Consent
Affair in Trinidad
An Affair to Remember
The Affairs of Anatol *
The Affairs of Annabel *
The Affairs of Annabelle *
Africa Speaks *
The African Queen
After Hours
After Many Years *
After Office Hours *
After the Fox
After the Thin Man *
Against All Flags
Against All Odds
Agatha
The Age of Consent *
The Age of Innocence *
Agnes of God
The Agony and the Ecstasy
Ah, Wilderness! *
Air Force *
Air Mail *
Airplane
Airport
Airport 1975
The Alamo
Alamo Bay
Alcatraz Island *
Alex and the Gypsy
Alexander Hamilton *
Alexander the Great
Alexander's Ragtime Band *
Algiers *
Ali Baba Goes to Town *
Alias Jimmy Valentine *
Alias Jimmy Valentine *
Alias Nick Beal *
Alias the Deacon *
Alias the Doctor *
Alibi *
Alice Adams *
Alice Doesn't Live Here
  Anymore
Alice in Wonderland
Alice in Wonderland *
Alice's Restaurant
Alien
The Alien *
Alimony *
All About Eve
All Fall Down
All My Sons *
All Night Long
All of Me
All on Account of the Milk *

All Quiet on the Western
  Front *
All That Heaven Allows
All That Jazz
All the Brothers Were
  Valiant
All the Fine Young
  Cannibals
All the King's Men *
All the President's Men
All the Right Moves
All the Way Home
All the Young Men
All This and Heaven Too *
Allegheny Uprising *
Aloma of the South Seas *
Aloma of the South Seas *
Along Came Jones *
Along the Great Divide
Altered States
Alvarez Kelly
Always
Always Goodbye *
Always Good-Bye *
Always Leave Them
  Laughing *
Amadeus
Amarilly of Clothes-Line
  Alley *
The Amazing Dr.
  Clitterhouse *
America *
America, America
America at the Movies
American Biograph First
  Program *
An American Citizen *
An American Dream
American Flyers
The American Friend
American Gigolo
American Graffiti
American Guerilla in the
  Philippines
American Hot Wax
An American in Paris
American Madness *
American Pop
An American Tragedy *
An American Werewolf in
  London
The Americanization of
  Emily
The Americano
America's Answer *
The Amityville Horror
Anastasia
Anatomy of a Murder
Anchors Aweigh *
And Baby Makes Three *
. . . And Justice for All
And Now Miguel
And So They Were
  Married *
And Then There Were
  None *
The Anderson Tapes
Androcles and the Lion
The Andromeda Strain
Andy Hardy Gets Spring
  Fever *
Andy Warhol's Dracula
Andy Warhol's Frankenstein
Angel *
The Angel and the
  Badman *
Angel Face
Angel on My Shoulder *

Angelo My Love
Angels in the Outfield
Angels Over Broadway *
Angels Wash Their Faces *
Angels With Dirty Faces *
Animal Crackers *
The Animal Kingdom *
Animals in Motion *
Ann Vickers *
Anna and the King of
  Siam *
Anna Christie *
Anna Christie *
Anna Karenina *
Anna Lucasta *
Annapolis Salute *
Anne of Green Gables *
Anne of the Indies
Annie
Annie Get Your Gun
Annie Hall
Annie Laurie *
Annie Oakley *
Another Dawn *
Another Language *
Another Part of the Forest *
Another Thin Man *
Anthony Adverse *
Antony and Cleopatra *
Any Number Can Play *
Any Wednesday
Any Which Way You Can
Anything Can Happen
Anything Goes *
Apache
The Apartment
Apartment for Peggy *
Apocalypse Now
The Appaloosa
Applause *
The April Fools
April in Paris
April Love
The Arab *
Arabian Nights *
Arch of Triumph *
Are Parents People? *
Are You a Mason? *
Argent, L'
Arise My Love *
Arizona *
The Arizona Kid *
Around the World in Eighty
  Days
Around the World Under
  the Sea
The Arrangement
Arrowsmith *
Arsene Lupin *
Arsene Lupin Returns *
Arsenic and Old Lace *
The Art of Love
Arthur
Artists and Models
Artists and Models *
Artists and Models Abroad *
As You Desire Me *
As You Like It *
As You Like It *
As Young As You Feel
Ask Any Girl
The Asphalt Jungle
Assault on a Queen
Assignment—Paris
Astor Battery on Parade *
At Long Last Love
At the Circus *
At War With the Army

Elusive Isabel *
Elvis on Tour
Emma *
The Emperor Jones *
The Emperor Waltz *
The Emperor's
    Candlesticks *
The Empire Strikes Back
Enchanted April *
The Enchanted Cottage *
The Enchanted Cottage *
Enchantment *
The End
The End of St. Petersburg *
Endless Love
The Endless Summer
The Enemy Below
The Enforcer
Enoch Arden *
Enoch Arden, Part 1 *
Enoch Arden, Part 2 *
Enter Laughing
Equus
Eraserhead
Escapade *
Escapade in Japan
Escape *
Escape *
The Escape *
Escape from Alcatraz
Escape from Fort Bravo
Escape From New York
Escape From the Planet of
    the Apes
Eskimo *
Espionage *
Espionage Agent *
The Eternal City *
The Eternal Grind *
Eternal Love *
Eternally Yours *
Evangeline *
The Eve of St. Mark *
Evelyn Prentice *
Ever in My Heart *
Ever Since Eve *
Every Day Is a Holiday
Every Day's a Holiday *
Every Night at Eight *
Everybody Sing *
Everybody's Old Man *
Everybody's Sweetheart *
Everything Happens at
    Night *
Everything I Have Is Yours
Exclusive *
Exclusive Story *
The Ex-Convict *
Excuse My Dust
Excuse My Dust *
Executive Action
Executive Suite
The Exile *
Exit Smiling *
Ex-Lady *
The Ex-Mrs. Bradford *
Exodus
The Exorcist
Experiment in Terror
The Exploits of Elaine *
Exposed
The Exterminator
Extra Girl *
The Eyes of Laura Mars
Eyes of Youth *
Eyewitness
F.I.S.T.
A Face in the Crowd

Face to Face
Faces
The Facts of Life
Fade to Black
Fail Safe
Faithless *
The Falcon and the
    Snowman
The Fall of Babylon *
The Fall of the Roman
    Empire
The Fall of the Romanoffs *
Falling in Love
False Faces *
Fame
A Family Affair *
Family Honeymoon *
The Family Jewels
Family Plot
The Family Secret
The Famous Ferguson
    Case *
The Fan *
The Fan
Fancy Pants
Fanny
Fantasia *
Fantastic Voyage
A Farewell to Arms
A Farewell to Arms *
The Farmer Takes a Wife *
The Farmer's Daughter *
Fashions of 1934 *
Fast and Furious *
Fast and Loose *
Fast and Loose *
Fast Company *
Fast Life *
Fast Times at Ridgemont
    High
Fat City
The Fat Man
Father Goose
Father Is a Bachelor
Father of the Bride
Father Was a Fullback *
Father's Little Dividend
Fatso
Fazil *
Fear Strikes Out
Fearless Fagan
The Feast of Life *
A Feather in Her Hat *
Feet First *
Female *
ffolkes
Fiddler on the Roof
Fidel
The Fiendish Plot of Dr. Fu
    Manchu
Fifth Avenue Girl *
55 Days at Peking
Fifty Million Frenchmen *
Fifty Roads to Town *
Fifty-Second Street *
Fighter Squadron *
Fighting Blood *
Fighting Father Dunne *
The Fighting O'Flynn *
The Fighting Seabees *
The Fighting Sixty-Ninth *
The Final Countdown
A Fine Madness
The Finger Points *
Finian's Rainbow
Finn and Hattie *
Fire Down Below
The Fireball

Fireball 500
The Firefly *
Firefox
Fireman, Save My Child
Fireman, Save My Child *
Fireman Save My Child *
Fires of Faith *
First Blood
The First Deadly Sin
The First Hundred Years *
First Lady *
The First Legion
First Love *
First Monday in October
The First Nudie Musical
The First Time
Five
Five Came Back *
Five Easy Pieces
Five Fingers
Five Graves to Cairo *
Five of a Kind *
Five Star Final *
The 5,000 Fingers of Doctor
    T
Fixed Bayonets
The Fixer
The Flame and the Arrow
The Flame and the Flesh
Flame of Araby
The Flame of New Orleans *
The Flame Within *
Flaming Star
Flamingo Kid
Flamingo Road *
Flareup
Flash Gordon *
Flash Gordon
Flash Gordon's Trip to
    Mars *
Flashdance
Flesh
Flesh *
Flesh and Blood *
Flesh And Fury
Flesh and the Devil *
Fletch
Flight for Freedom *
The Flight of the Phoenix
Flipper
The Flirt *
Flirtation Walk *
Flirting with Fate *
The Floradora Girl *
A Florida Enchantment *
The Florentine Dagger *
A Florida Enchantment *
The Flying Deuces *
Flying Down to Rio *
Flying High *
The Flying Irishman *
Flying Leathernecks
The Flying Missile
The Fog
Folies Bergere *
The Follies Girl *
Follow Me, Boys!
Follow the Boys
Follow the Boys *
Follow the Fleet *
Follow the Sun
Follow Thru *
A Fool for Love
The Fool Killer
A Fool There Was *
Foolish Wives *
The Fool's Awakening *
Fools for Scandal *
A Fool's Revenge *

Footlight Parade *
Footloose
For Heaven's Sake *
For Heaven's Sake *
For Love of Gold *
For Love of Ivy
For Love or Money
For Men Only
For Pete's Sake
For the Defense *
For Whom the Bell Tolls *
Forbidden *
The Forbidden City *
Forbidden Paradise *
Forbidden Planet
Force of Arms
Force of Evil *
A Foreign Affair *
Foreign Correspondent *
Forever *
Forever Amber *
Forever and a Day * /
The Formula
Forsaking All Others *
Fort Apache *
Fort Apache, the Bronx
The Fortune
The Fortune Cookie
40 Pounds of Trouble
48 HRS.
Forty-Second Street *
Foul Play
The Fountainhead *
Four Daughters *
Four Days in November
Four Devils *
Four Faces West *
The Four Feathers *
4 for Texas
Four Friends
Four Girls in White *
Four Guns to the Border
The 4 Horsemen of the
    Apocalypse
The Four Horsemen of the
    Apocalypse *
Four Hours to Kill *
The Four Hundred Million *
Four Men and a Prayer *
The Four Poster
The Four Seasons
Four Sons *
Four Sons *
Four Wives *
Four's a Crowd *
Fourteen Hours
The Fox
Foxes
The Foxes of Harrow *
Frances
Francesca da Rimini *
Francis
Francis Goes to the Races
Francis Goes to West Point
Francis in the Navy
Francis Joins the Wacs
Frankenstein *
Frankenstein *
Frankenstein Meets the
    Wolfman *
Frankie and Johnny
Frankie and Johnny *
Freaks *
Free and Easy *
A Free Soul *
Freebie and the Bean
The French Connection
The French Connection II

The French Line
Frenchie
Frenchman's Creek *
Frenzy
The Freshman *
Freshman Year *
Freud
Friday the 13th
Friendly Persuasion
Friends and Lovers *
Frisco Jenny *
The Frisco Kid *
The Frogmen
From Here to Eternity
From the Manger to the
    Cross *
From the Terrace
From This Day Forward *
The Front
The Front Page
The Front Page *
Front Page Woman *
Frontier Marshall *
Frontier Marshall *
The Fugitive *
The Fugitive *
The Fugitive *
The Fugitive Kind
Full Confession *
The Fuller Brush Girl
Fun in Acapulco
Fun with Dick and Jane
Funny Face
Funny Girl
Funny Lady
The Furies
The Fury
Fury *
Futureworld
GI Blues
G Men *
Gable and Lombard
Gabriel Over the White
    House *
Gaily, Gaily
Gallant Lady *
Gambit
The Gamblers *
Gambling Ship *
The Gang Buster *
The Gang's All Here *
Gangs of New York *
Gangster's Boy *
Garbo Talks
The Garden of Allah *
The Garden of Allah *
The Garden of Allah *
The Garden of Eden *
Garden of Evil
Garden of the Moon *
The Garment Jungle
Gaslight *
Gas-s-s-s!
A Gathering of Eagles
The Gaucho *
The Gauntlet
The Gay Deception *
The Gay Desperado *
The Gay Divorcee *
The Gay Shoe Clerk *
The General *
General Crack *
The General Died at
    Dawn *
Genghis Khan
Gentle Julia *
Gentleman Jim *
A Gentleman of Paris *

Books Consulted

About John Ford. Lindsay Anderson. New York: McGraw-Hill Co., 1983.

Acid Test. John Simon. New York: Stein & Day, 1963.

The Adventures of Antoine Doinel: Four Autobiographical Screenplays by François Truffaut. New York: Simon and Schuster, 1971.

The Age of the American Novel. Claude-Edmonde Magny. New York: Frederick Ungar, 1972.

Agee on Film. James Agee. New York: Grosset & Dunlap, 1967.

Akira Kurosawa: A Guide to References and Resources. Patricia Erens. Boston: G. K. Hall & Co., 1979.

Alain Resnais. John Francis Kreidl. Boston: Twayne Publishers, 1977.

Alain Resnais; or, the Theme of Time. John Ward. Garden City, NY: Doubleday, 1968.

Alain Resnais: The Role of the Imagination. James Monaco. New York: Oxford University Press, 1978.

An Album of Great Science Fiction Films. Frank Manchel. New York: Franklin Watts, 1976.

Alfred Hitchcock. Gene D. Phillips. Boston: Twayne, 1984.

Alfred Hitchcock's Psycho. Edited by Richard Anobile. New York: Avon, 1975.

Alice's Restaurant. Venable Herndon and Arthur Penn. New York: Doubleday, 1970.

Alien. Alan D. Foster. Secaucus, N.J.: Warner Publications, 1979.

Alphaville: A Film by Jean-Luc Godard. New York: Simon & Schuster, 1966.

The Ambiguous Image. Ray Armes. Bloomington: Indiana University Press, 1976.

America, America. Elia Kazan. New York: Stein and Day, 1962.

America at the Movies or "Santa Maria, It Had Slipped My Mind." Michael Wood. New York: Basic Books, 1975.

America in the Dark: Hollywood and the Gift of Reality. David Thomson. New York: William Morrow, 1977.

American Dreaming: The Films of John Cassavetes and the American Experience. Raymond Carney. Berkeley: University of California Press, 1985.

American Film Genres. Stuart M. Kaminsky. Dayton, OH: Pflaum Publishing Co., 1974.

American History-American Film. John E. O'Connor and Martin A. Jackson. New York: Frederick Ungar Publishing Co., 1979.

An American Odyssey: Elia Kazan and American Culture. Thomas H. Pauly. Philadelphia: Temple University Press, 1983.

American Skeptic: Robert Altman's Genre-Commentary Films. Ann Arbor: Pierian Press, 1982.

The American West on Film: Myth and Reality. Richard A. Maynard. Rochelle Park, N.J.: Hayden, 1974.

America's Favorite Movies. Rudy Behlmer. New York: Frederick Ungar Publishing Co., 1982.

Anatomy of a Motion Picture. Richard Griffith. New York: St. Martin's Press, 1959.

The Ancient World in the Cinema. Jon Solomon. South Brunswick, N.J.: A. S. Barnes and Company, 1978.

Andrzej Wajda: Polish Cinema. Edited by Colin MacArthur. London: British Film Institute, 1970.

Anthony Mann. Jeanine Basinger. Boston: Twayne Publishers, 1979.

Antonioni. Ian Cameron and Robin Wood. New York: Praeger, 1969.

Antonioni: Or, The Surface of the World. Seymour Chatman. Berkeley and Los Angeles: University of California Press, 1985.

Antonioni's Visual Language. Ned Rifkin. Ann Arbor, MI: UMI Research Press, 1982.

The Apu Trilogy. Robin Wood. New York: Praeger, 1971.

The Art of Alfred Hitchcock: Fifty Years of His Motion Pictures. Donald Spoto. Garden City, N.Y.: Doubleday & Co., 1979.

The Art of Walt Disney. Christopher Finch. New York: Harry N. Abrams, Inc., 1973.

Arthur Penn. Robin Wood. New York: Praeger, 1970.

Arthur Penn: A Guide to References and Resources. Boston: G. K. Hall & Co., 1980.

Astaire Dancing: The Musical Films. John Mueller. New York: Alfred A. Knopf, 1985.

Authors on Film. Edited by Harry M. Geduld. Bloomington: University of Indiana Press, 1972.

Authorship and Narrative in the Cinema. William Luhr and Peter Lehman. New York: G. P. Putnam's Sons, Capricorn Books, 1977.

Autumn Sonata. Ingmar Bergman. New York: Pantheon, 1978.

Awake in the Dark. Edited by David Denby. New York: Vintage, 1977.

Barbra—The First Decade: The Films and Career of Barbra Streisand. James Spada. Secaucus, N.J.: Citadel Press, 1974.

Basil Rathbone: His Life and His Films. Michael B. Druxman. South Brunswick and New York: A. S. Barnes and Company, 1972.

The Battle of Britain: The Making of a Film. Leonard Mosley. New York: Stein and Day, 1969.

The Beatles in Richard Lester's A Hard Day's Night. Edited by J. Philip Defranco. New York: Penguin, 1977.

Beauty and the Beast. Edited and Annotated by Robert M. Hammond. New York: New York University Press, 1970.

Before My Eyes: Film Criticism and Comment. Stanley Kauffmann. New York: Harper, 1980.

Behind the Scenes of Otto Preminger. Willi Frischauer. New York: William Morrow, 1974.

Ben Hecht: Hollywood Screenwriter. Jeffrey B. Martin. Edited by Diane Kirkpatrick. Ann Arbor, MI: UMI Research Press, 1984.

Bernardo Bertolucci. Robert Phillip Kolker. New York: Oxford University Press, 1985.

The Best of MGM: The Golden Years (1928-59). James Robert Parish and Gregory W. Mank. Westport, CT: Arlington House, 1981.

Bette Davis: Her Films and Career. Gene Ringgold. Secaucus, N.J.: The Citadel Press, 1985.

Between Flops: A Biography of Preston Sturges. James Curtis. New York: Harcourt, Brace, Jovanovich, 1982.

Beyond Formula: American Film Genres. Stanley J. Solomon. New York: Harcourt, Brace, Jovanovich, 1982.

The Big Book of B Movies: Or, How Low Was My Budget. Robin Cross. New York: St. Martin's Press, 1981.

Big Screen, Little Screen. Rex Reed. New York: The Macmillan Company, 1971.

Billy Wilder. Bernard F. Dick. Boston: Twayne Publishers, 1980.

Billy Wilder. Axel Madsen. London: Secker & Warburg in Association with the British Film Institute, 1968.

Billy Wilder in Hollywood. Maurice Zolotow. New York: G. P. Putnam's Sons, 1977.

Black Film as Genre. Thomas Cripps. Bloomington: University of Indiana Press, 1978.

Black Films and Film-Makers: A Comprehensive Anthology from Stereotype to Superhero. Compiled by Lindsay Patterson. New York: Dodd, Mead & Co., 1975.

Blake Edwards. Peter Lehman and William Luhr. Athens: Ohio University Press, 1981.

Blow-Up: A Film. Michelangelo Antonioni and Tonino Guerra. New York: Simon and Schuster, 1971.

The Bonnie and Clyde Book. Compiled and Edited by Sandra Wake and Nicola Hayden. New York: Simon & Schuster, 1972.

Brian De Palma. Michael Bliss. Metuchen, N.J.: The Scarecrow Press, 1983.

The Bright Side of Billy Wilder, Primarily. Tom Wood. Garden City, N.Y.: Doubleday, 1970.

Burt Lancaster: A Pictorial Treasury of His Films. Jerry Vermilye. New York: Falcon Enterprises, Inc., 1971.

Burt Lancaster: The Man and His Movies. Allan Hunter. New York: St. Martin's Press, 1984.

The Busby Berkeley Book. Tony Thomas and Jim Terry with Busby Berkeley. Greenwich, CT: New York Graphic Society, 1973.

Butch Cassidy and the Sundance Kid. William Goldman. New York: Bantam, 1969.

The Carry-On Book. Kenneth Eastaugh. North Pomfret, VT: David and Charles, 1978.

Case History of a Movie. Dore Schary and Charles Palmer. New York: Random House, 1950.

A Casebook on Film. Charles Thomas Samuels. New York: Van Nostrand Reinhold Company, 1970.

A Cast of Lions: The Story of the Filming of Born Free. Carl Foreman. London: William Collins, 1966.

Cecil B. DeMille: A Guide to References and Resources. Sumiko Higashi. Boston: G. K. Hall & Co., 1985.

Chaplin: His Life and Art. David Robinson. New York: McGraw-Hill, 1985.

Chaplin: The Mirror of Opinion. David Robinson. London: Secker & Warburg, 1983.

Chaplin's Films. Uno Asplund. Newton Abbot, Devon, England: David and Charles, 1973.

Charles Chaplin. Roger Manvell. Boston: Little, Brown, 1974.

Charles Chaplin: A Guide to References and Resources. Timothy Lyons. Boston: G. K. Hall & Co., 1979.

Charles Laughton: Hollywood's Magic People. William Brown. New York: Falcon Enterprises, Inc., 1970.

Charlie Chaplin. John McCabe. New York: Doubleday, 1978.

Chekov's Enterprise. Walter Koenig. New York: Pocket Books, 1980.

Chevalier: The Films and Career of Maurice Chevalier. Gene Ringgold and DeWitt Bodeen. Secaucus, N.J.: The Citadel Press, 1973.

Children's Novels and the Movies. Edited by Douglas Street. New York: Frederick Ungar Publishing Co., 1983.

China Is Near. Marco Bellochio. New York: The Orion Press, 1969.

Cinema: The Novel into Film. Edited by Frank N. Magill. Pasadena, CA: Salem Press, 1980.

Cinema Borealis: Ingmar Bergman and the Swedish Ethos. Vernon Young. N.Y.: David Lewis, 1971.

Cinema East: A Critical Study of Major Japanese Films. Keiko I. McDonald. Rutherford, N.J.: Fairleigh Dickinson University Press, 1983.

Cinema Examined: Selections from Cinema Journal. Edited by Richard Dyer MacCann and Jack C. Ellis. New York: E. P. Dutton, Inc., 1982.

Cinema Eye, Cinema Ear: Some Key Film-Makers of the Sixties. John Russell Taylor. New York: Hill and Wang, 1964.

The Cinema of Alain Resnais. Roy Armes. New York: A. S. Barnes, 1968.

The Cinema of Alfred Hitchcock. Peter Bogdanovich. New York: The Museum of Modern Art Film Library, 1963.

The Cinema of Andrzej Wajda. Bolestaw Michatek. New York: A. S. Barnes, 1973.

The Cinema of Carl Dreyer. Tom Milne. New York: A. S. Barnes & Co., 1971.

The Cinema of David Lean. Gerald Pratley. South Brunswick, N.J.: A. S. Barnes, 1974.

The Cinema of Edward G. Robinson. James Robert Parish & Alvin H. Marill. New York: A. S. Barnes, 1972.

The Cinema of François Truffaut. Graham Petrie. New York: A. S. Barnes & Co., 1970.

The Cinema of Frank Capra. Leland A. Poague. South Brunswick, N.J.: A. S. Barnes and Company, 1975.

The Cinema of Fritz Lang. Paul M. Jensen. New York: A. S. Barnes, 1969.

The Cinema of Howard Hawks. Peter Bogdanovich. New York: The Library of the Museum of Modern Art, 1962.

The Cinema of John Ford. John Baxter. New York: A. S. Barnes, 1971

The Cinema of John Frankenheimer. Gerald Pratley. New York: A. S. Barnes and Company, 1969.

The Cinema of John Huston. Gerald Pratley. South Brunswick and New York: A. S. Barnes and Co., 1977.

The Cinema of Joseph Losey. James Leahy. New York: A. S. Barnes, 1967.

The Cinema of Luis Buñuel. Freddy Buache. Translated by Freddy Graham. London: Tantivy Press, 1973.

The Cinema of Orson Welles. Peter Bogdanovich. New York: The Library of the Museum of Modern Art, 1961.

The Cinema of Orson Welles. Peter Cowie. South Brunswick and New York: A. S. Barnes and Company, 1973.

The Cinema of Otto Preminger. Gerald Pratley. New York: A. S. Barnes and Company, 1971.

The Cinema of Ousmane Simbene, A Pioneer of African Film. Francoise Pfaff. Westport, CT: Greenwood Press, 1984.

The Cinema of Roman Polanski. Ivan Bulter. Boston: Twayne, 1985.

The Cinema of Satyajit Ray. Chidinanda Da Gupta. Bangalore, India: 1978.

Cinema of the Fantastic. Chris Steinbrunner and Burt Goldblatt. New York: Saturday Review Press, 1972.

Cinema Stylists. John Belton. Metuchen, N.J.: The Scarecrow Press, 1983.

Cinema, the Magic Vehicle: A Guide to Its Achievement. Journey Two: The Fifties. Adam Garbicz and Jacek Klinowski. New York: Schocken Books, 1983.

Cinema Verité. M. Ali Issari. East Lansing: Michigan State University, 1971.

The Cinematic Muse: Critical Studies in the History of French Cinema. Columbia: University of Missouri Press, 1979.

The Classic American Novel and the Movies. Edited by Gerald Peary and Roger Shatzkin. New York: Frederick Ungar Publishing Co., 1977.

The Classic Cinema: Essays in Criticism. Edited by Stanley J. Solomon. New York: Harcourt Brace Jovanovich, Inc., 1973.

Classic Movies. Neil Sinyard. Salem, N.H.: Salem House, 1985.

Classsics of the Foreign Film: A Pictorial Treasury. Parker Tyler. New York: The Citadel Press, 1962.

Classics of the Gangster Film. Robert Bookbinder. Secaucus, N.J.: The Citadel Press, 1985.

Classics of the Horror Film. William K. Everson. Secaucus, N.J.: The Citadel Press, 1974.

Claude Chabrol. Robin Wood and Michael Walker. New York: Praeger, 1970.

Claude Lelouch: Film Director. Peter Lev. Rutherford, N.J.: Fairleigh Dickinson University Press, 1983.

Claudette Colbert. Lawrence J. Quirk. New York: Crown Publishing, Inc., 1985.

The Cleopatra Papers. Jack Brodsky and Nathan Weiss. New York: Simon & Schuster, 1963.

Clint Eastwood. Francois Guérif. Translated from the French by Lisa Nesselson. New York: St. Martin's Press, 1986.

Close Encounters of a Third Kind: A Document of the Film. Edited by Thomas Durwood. New York: Ballantine Books, 1978.

Close Encounters of a Third Kind: Diary. Bob Balaban. New York: Paradise Press, 1978.

Closely Watched Films: The Czechoslovak Experience. Antonin J. Liehm. White Plains, N.Y.: International Arts & Sciences Press, 1974.

Closely Watched Trains. Bohumil Hrabal and Jiri Menzel. New York: Simon & Schuster, 1971.

Close-up: A Critical Perspective on Film. Marsha Kinder and Beverle Huston. New York: Harcourt, 1972.

Combat Films: American Realism, 1945–1970. Steven Jay Rubin. Jefferson, N.C.: McFarland, 1981.

The Comic Mind: Comedy and the Movies. Gerald Mast. Chicago: University of Chicago Press, 1979. Second Edition.

The Complete Films of Humphrey Bogart. Clifford McCarty. Secaucus, N.J.: The Citadel Press, 1965.

The Complete Films of John Wayne. Steve Zmijewsky, Boris Zmijewsky, and Mark Ricci. Secaucus, N.J.: The Citadel Press, 1983.

The Complete Films of William Powell. Lawrence J. Quirk. Secaucus, N.J.: The Citadel Press, 1986,

Confessions of a Cultist: On the Cinema, 1955-1959. Andrew Sarris. New York: Simon and Schuster, 1970.

The Contemporary Cinema. Penelope Huston. Baltimore, MD: Penguin Books, 1963.

The Contemporary World as Seen on Film. Robert Fulford. Toronto: P. Martin Associates, 1974.

Conversations with Losey. Michel Ciment. New York: Methuen, 1985.

Copperfield '70. George Curry. New York: Ballantine, 1970.

Costa-Gavras: The Political Fiction Film. John J. Michalczyk. Cranbury, N.J.: Associated University Press, 1984.

The Cracked Lens: The Crisis of the Artist in Bergman's Films of the Sixties. Salwa Eva Fulciham Tighrarian. Ann Arbor, MI: University Microfilm International, 1984.

The Creation of Dino De Laurentiis' King Kong. Bruce Bahrenburg. New York: Pocket Books, 1976.

Crime Movies: An Illustrated History. Carlos Clarens. New York: W. W. Norton & Company, 1980.

Critical Approaches to Fellini's 8½. Albert Edward Benderson. New York: Arno Press, 1974.

A Critical History of the British Cinema. Roy Armes. New York: Oxford University Press, 1978.

The Cuban Image: Cinema and Cultural Politics in Cuba. Michael Chanan. Bloomington: Indiana University Press, 1986.

Cult Movies: The Classics, the Sleepers, the Weird, and the Wonderful. Danny Peary. New York: Dell Publishing Co., Inc., 1981.

Cult Movies 2. Danny Peary. New York: Dell Publishing Co., 1985.

Currents in Japanese Cinema. Tadao Sato. Tokyo: Kodansha International, 1982.

The Czechoslovak New Wave. Peter Hames. Berkeley: University of California Press, 1985.

Dark City: The Film Noir. Spencer Selby. Jefferson, N.C.: McFarland, 1984.

The Dark Side of Genius: The Life of Alfred Hitchcock. Donald Spoto. Boston: Little, Brown and Company, 1983.

David Lean. Michael A. Anderegg. Boston: Twayne Publishers, 1984.

David Lean: A Guide to References and Resources. Louis Castelli and Caryn L. Cleeland. Boston: G. K. Hall & Co., 1985.

David Lean and His Films. Alain Silver and James Ursini. London: Leslie Frewin, 1974.

David O. Selznick's Hollywood. Written and Produced by Ron Haver. Designs by Thomas Ingalls. New York: Alfred A. Knopf, 1980.

Deeper Into Movies. Pauline Kael. Boston: Little, Brown and Company, 1973.

Deerstalker: Holmes and Watson on Screen. Ron Haydock. Metuchen, N.J.: Secaucus, 1978.

The Detective in Film. William K. Everson. Secaucus, N.J.: The Citadel Press, 1972.

Dickens and Film. A. L. Zambrano. New York: Gordon Press, 1977.

Dictionary of Films. George Sadoul. Translated, Edited, and Updated by Peter Morris. Berkeley: University of California Press, 1972.

Directors and Direction: Cinema for the Seventies. John Russell Taylor. New York: Farrar, Straus & Giroux, 1975.

The Director's Event: Interviews with Five American Film-Makers. Eve Sherman and Martin Rubin. New York: Atheneum, 1970.

Directors in Action: Selections from Action. Edited by Bob Thomas. Indianapolis, IN: The Bobbs-Merrill Company, 1973.

The Discreet Art of Luis Buñuel. Gwynne Edwards. London: Marion Boyars, 1982.

The Disney Films. Leonard Maltin. New York: Crown Publishers, Inc., 1973

The Disney Version. Richard Schickel. New York: Simon & Schuster, 1968.

Documentary: A History of the Non-Fiction Film. Erik Barnouw. New York: Oxford University Press, 1974.

The Documentary Tradition: From Anook to Woodstock. Lewis Jacobs. New York: Hopkinson and Blake, 1971.

Don Siegel: American Cinema. Alan Lovell. London: The British Film Institute, 1975.

Don Siegel: Director. Stuart M. Kaminsky. N.Y.: Curtis Books, 1974.

Double De Palma: A Film Study with Brian De Palma. Susan Dworkin. New York: Newmarket, 1984.

Double Exposure: Fiction into Film. Joy Gould Boyum. New York: New American Library, 1981.

Double Takes: Notes and Afterthoughts on the Movies, 1956–76. Alexander Walker. London: Elm Tree Books, 1977.

Douglas Sirk. Michael Stern. Boston: Twayne Publishers, 1979.

Dreams and Dead Ends. Jack Shadoian. Cambridge, MA: MIT Press, 1977.

Dwight Macdonald On Movies. See *On Movies*.

Each Man in His Own Time. Raoul Walsh. New York: Farrar, Strauss & Giroux, 1974.

Earthquake: The Story of a Movie. George Fox. New York: Signet Books, 1974.

Easy Rider. Peter Fonda, Dennis Hopper and Terry Southern. New York: New American Library, 1969.

Elia Kazan: A Guide to References and Resources. Lloyd Michaels. Boston: G. K. Hall & Co., 1985.

Elvis: The Films and Career of Elvis Presley. Steven Zmijewsky and Boris Zmijewsky. Secaucus, N.J.: Citadel Press, 1983.

The English Novel and the Movies. Edited by Michael Klein and Gillian Parker. New York: Frederick Ungar, 1981.

Essays on Chaplin. André Bazin. New Haven, CT: University of New Haven Press, 1985.

The Evolution of Character Portrayals in the Films of Sidney Poitier: 1950–1978. Samuel L. Kelley. New York: Garland, 1982.

Faces. John Cassavetes. New York: New American Library, 1970.

Fassbinder. Translated by Ruth McCormick. New York: Tanam Press, 1981.

Fassbinder, Filmmaker. Ronald Hayman. New York: Simon & Schuster, 1984.

Faulkner and Film. Bruce Kawin. New York: Frederick Ungar Publishing, 1977.

Favorite Movies: Critics' Choices. Philip Nobile. New York: Macmillan Publishing Co., 1973.

Federico Fellini: A Guide to References and Resources. John C. Stubbs. Boston: G. K. Hall & Co., 1978.

Federico Fellini: Essays in Criticism. Edited by Peter E. Bondanello. New York: Oxford University Press, 1978.

Federico Fellini: The Search for a New Mythology. Charles B. Ketcham. New York: Paulist Press, 1976.

Federico Fellini: Variety Lights to La Dolce Vita. Frank Burke. Boston: Twayne, 1984.

Fellini. Suzanne Budgen. London: The British Film Institute, 1966.

Fellini. Angelo Solmi. New York: Humanities Press, 1968.

Fellini on Fellini. Federico Fellini. New York: Delacorte-Seymour Lawrence, 1976.

Fellini Satyricon. Edited by Dario Zonelli and Translated by Eugene Walter and John Matthews. New York: Ballantine, 1970.

Fellini the Artist. Edward Murray. New York: Frederick Ungar Publishing Co., 1976.

Fellini's Road. Donald P. Costello. Notre Dame, IN: Notre Dame University Press, 1983.

Fifty Classic British Films. 1932-1982: A Pictorial Record. Anthony Slide. New York: Dover Publications, Inc., 1985.

Fifty from the Fifties: Vintage Films from America's Mid-Century. David Zinman. New York: Arlington House Publishers, 1979.

Fifty Grand Movies of the 1960s and 1970s. David Zinman. New York: Crown Publishers, 1986.

The Fifty Worst Films of All Time (and how they got that way). Harry Medved and Randy Dreyfuss. New York: Popular Library, 1978.

Figures of Light: Film Criticism and Comment. Stanley Kauffmann. New York: Harper and Row, 1971.

Film: A Modern Art. Aaron Sultanik. New York: Cornwall Books, 1986.

Film: An Anthology. Edited by Daniel Talbot. New York: Simon & Schuster, 1959.

Film and Dreams: An Approach to Bergman. Vladimir Petric. South Salem, NY: Redgrave Publishing Co., 1981.

Film and Literature: An Introduction. Morris Beja. New York: Longman, 1971.

Film and Literature: Contrasts in Media. Fred H. Marcus. Scranton, PA: Chandler Publishing Co., 1971.

Film and Revolution. James Roy MacBean. Bloomington: Indiana University Press, 1975.

Film and the Critical Eye. Dennis De Nitto and William Herman. New York: Macmillan, 1975.

Film and the Liberal Arts. T. J. Ross. New York: Holt, Rinehart and Winston, 1970.

The Film and the Public. Roger Manvell. Baltimore, MD: Penguin Books, 1955.

Film Art: An Introduction. David Bordwell and Kristin Thompson. Reading, MA: Addison-Wesley, 1979.

Film as Film: Critical Responses to Film Art. Joy Gould Boyum and Adrienne Scott. Boston: Allyn and Bacon, 1971.

The Film Career of Alain Robbe-Grillet. William F. Van West. Boston: G. K. Hall & Co., 1977.

The Film Career of Billy Wilder. Steve Seidman. Boston: G. K. Hall & Co., 1977.

Film Criticism and Caricature—1943-1953. Richard Wilmington. London: Paul Elek, 1975.

Film Culture Reader. Edited by P. Adams Sitney. New York: Praeger, 1970.

The Film Director as Superstar. Joseph Gelmis. Garden City, NY: Doubleday, 1970.

Film Epic. Louis Phillip Castelli. Ann Arbor, MI: UMI Research Publications, 1977.

Film Festival. Tom and Helen Bishop. New York: Grove Press, 1969.

Film in the Third Reich: A Study of the German Cinema, 1933-1945. David Stewart Hull. Berkeley: University of California Press, 1969.

Film Language: A Semiotics of the Cinema. Christian Metz. New York: Oxford University Press, 1974.

The Film Narratives of Alain Resnais. Freddy Sweet. Ann Arbor, MI: UMI Research Press, 1981.

Film Noir. An Encyclopedic Reference to the American Style. Alain Silver and Elizabeth Ward. Woodstock, NY: The Overlook Press, 1979.

Film Notes. Edited by Eileen Bowser. New York: Museum of Modern Art, 1969.

Film Semiotics Put to Empirical Test: Leone's Western Trilogy. Lane Roth. Ann Arbor, MI: UMI, 1977.

Film 67/68. Edited by Richard Schichel and John Simon. New York: Simon & Schuster, 1968.

Film 68/69. Edited by Richard Schichel and John Simon. New York: Simon & Schuster, 1969.

Film 69/70. Edited by Joseph Morgenstern and Stefan Kanfer. New York: Simon & Schuster, 1970.

Film 70/71. Edited by David Denby. New York: Simon & Schuster, 1971.

Film 71/72. Edited by David Denby. New York: Simon & Schuster, 1972

Film 73/74. Edited by Jay Cocks and David Denby. New York: Simon & Schuster, 1974.

Filmguide to 8½. Ted Perry. Bloomington: Indiana University Press, 1975.

Filmguide to Psycho. James Naremore. Bloomington: Indiana University Press, 1973.

Filmguide to The Battle of Algiers. Joan Mellon. Bloomington: Indiana University Press, 1973.

Filmguide to "2001: A Space Odyssey." Carolyn Geduld. Bloomington: Indiana University Press, 1973.

Filming Literature: The Art of Screen Adaptation. Neil Sinyard. New York: St. Martin's Press, 1986.

The Filming of the West. Jon Tuska. Garden City, N.Y.: Doubleday, 1976.

Filmmakers on Filmmaking. Harry M. Geduld. Bloomington: Indiana University Press, 1967.

The Films and Career of Robert Aldrich. Edwin T. Arnold and Eugene L. Miller. Knoxville, TN: University of Tennessee Press, 1986.

The Films in My Life. François Truffaut. Translated by Leonard Mayhew. New York: Simon and Schuster, 1978.

The Films of Akira Kurosawa. Donald Richie. Berkeley: University of California Press, Revised Edition, 1984.

The Films of Alain Robbe-Grillet. Roy Armes. Philadelphia: John Benjamin North America, Inc., 1981.

The Films of Alan Ladd. Marilyn Henry and Ron De Sourdis. Secaucus, N.J.: The Citadel Press, 1981.

The Films of Alfred Hitchcock. Robert A. Harris and Michael S. Lasky. Secaucus, N.J.: The Citadel Press, 1976.

The Films of Anthony Asquith. R. J. Minney. South Brunswick and New York: A. S. Barnes & Co., 1976.

The Films of Anthony Quinn. Alvin H. Marill. Secaucus, N.J.: The Citadel Press, 1975.

The Films of Barbara Stanwyck. Homer Dickens. Secaucus, N.J.: The Citadel Press, 1984.

The Films of Bette Davis. See *Bette Davis: Her Films and Career.*

The Films of Bing Crosby. Robert Bookbinder. Secaucus, N.J.: The Citadel Press, 1977.

The Films of Boris Karloff. Richard Bojarski and Kenneth Beale. Secaucus, N.J.: The Citadel Press, 1974.

The Films of Burt Reynolds. Nancy Streebeck. Secaucus, N.J.: Citadel Press, 1982.

The Films of Carl-Theodor Dreyer. David Bordwell. Berkeley: University of California Press, 1981.

The Films of Cary Grant. Donald Deschner. Secaucus, N.J.: The Citadel Press, 1973.

The Films of Cecil B. DeMille. Gene Ringgold and DeWitt Bodeen. Secaucus, N.J.: The Citadel Press, 1974.

The Films of Charles Bronson. Jerry Vermilye. Secaucus, N.J.: The Citadel Press, 1980.

The Films of Charlie Chaplin. Gerald D. McDonald, Michael Conway, and Mark Ricci. New York: Bonanza Books, 1977

The Films of Charlton Heston. Jeff Rovin. Secaucus, N.J.: The Citadel Press, 1977.

The Films of Clark Gable. Gabe Essoe. New York: The Citadel Press, 1970.

The Films of Clint Eastwood. Boris Zmijewsky and Lee Pfeiffer. Secaucus, N.J.: Citadel Press, 1982.

The Films of David Niven. Gerard Garrett. Secaucus, N.J.: The Citadel Press, 1976.

The Films of Dirk Bogarde. Margaret Hinxman and Susan d'Arcy. London: Literary Services and Production, 1974.

The Films of Doris Day. Christopher Young. Secaucus, N.J.: Citadel Press, 1977.

The Films of Dustin Hoffman. Douglas Brode. Secaucus, N.J.: Citadel Press, 1983.

The Films of Elizabeth Taylor. Jerry Vermilye and Mark Ricci. Secaucus, N.J.: The Citadel Press, 1976.

The Films of Errol Flynn. Tony Thomas, Rudy Behlmer, and Clifford McCarty. New York: The Citadel Press, 1969.

The Films of Federico Fellini. Claudio G. Fava and Aido Vigano. Secaucus, N.J.: The Citadel Press, 1985.

The Films of Frank Capra. Victor Scherle and William Turner Levy. Secaucus, N.J.: The Citadel Press, 1977.

The Films of Frank Capra. Donald C. Willis. Metuchen, N.J.: The Scarecrow Press, 1974.

The Films of Frank Sinatra. Gene Ringgold and Clifford McCarty. Secaucus, N.J.: The Citadel Press, 1980.

The Films of Fredric March. Lawrence J. Quirk. New York: The Citadel Press, 1971.

The Films of Fritz Lang. Frederick W. Ott. Secaucus, N.J.: The Citadel Press, 1979.

The Films of Gary Cooper. Homer Dickens. New York: The Citadel Press, 1970.

The Films of Gene Kelly: Song and Dance Man. Tony Thomas. Secaucus, N.J.: The Citadel Press, 1974.

The Films of George Pal. Gail Morgan Hickman. South Brunswick and New York: A. S. Barnes and Company, 1977.

The Films of George Roy Hill. Andrew Horton. New York: Columbia University Press, 1984.

The Films of Ginger Rogers. Homer Dickens. Secaucus, N.J.: The Citadel Press, 1975.

The Films of Gloria Swanson. Lawrence J. Quirk. Secaucus, N.J.: The Citadel Press, 1984.

The Films of Gregory Peck. John Griggs. Secaucus, N.J.: The Citadel Press, 1984.

The Films of Hedy Lamarr. Christopher Young. Secaucus, N.J.: The Citadel Press, 1978.

The Films of Henry Fonda. Tony Thomas. Secaucus, N.J.: The Citadel Press, 1983.

The Films of Howard Hawks. Donald C. Willis. Metuchen, N.J.: The Scarecrow Press, 1975.

The Films of Ingmar Bergman. Joan Donner. New York: Dover, 1972.

The Films of Ingrid Bergman. Lawrence J. Quirk. New York: The Citadel Press, 1970.

The Films of Jack Lemmon. Joe Baltake. Secaucus, N.J.: The Citadel Press, 1977.

The Films of Jacques Tati. Brent Maddock. Metuchen, N.J.: The Scarecrow Press, 1977.

The Films of James Cagney. Homer Dickens. Secaucus, N.J.: The Citadel Press, 1972.

The Films of James Mason. Clive Hirschhorn. London: LSP Books, 1975.

The Films of James Stewart. Ken D. Jones, Arthur F. McClure, and Alfred E. Twomey. South Brunswick and New York: A. S. Barnes and Company, 1970.

The Films of Jane Fonda. George Haddad-Garcia. Secaucus, N.J.: The Citadel Press, 1981.

The Films of Jean-Luc Godard. Edited by Ian Cameron. New York: Praeger, 1970.

The Films of Jeanette MacDonald and Nelson Eddy. Eleanor Knowles. South Brunswick and New York: A. S. Barnes and Company, 1975.

The Films of Jennifer Jones. W. Franklyn Moshier. San Francisco: Published by the Author, 1978.

The Films of Joan Crawford. Lawrence J. Quirk. New York: The Citadel Press, 1968.

The Films of John Garfield. Howard Gelman. Secaucus, N.J.: The Citadel Press, 1982.

The Films of John Wayne. See *The Complete Films of John Wayne.*

The Films of Josef von Sternberg. Andrew Sarris. New York: Museum of Modern Art, 1966.

The Films of Katharine Hepburn. Homer Dickens. New York: The Citadel Press, 1971.

The Films of Kirk Douglas. Tony Thomas. Secaucus, N.J.: The Citadel Press, 1972.

The Films of Lana Turner. Lou Valentino. Secaucus, N.J.: The Citadel Press, 1976.

The Films of Laurence Olivier. Margaret Morley. Secaucus, N.J.: 1978.

The Films of Leni Riefenstahl. David B. Hinton. Metuchen, N.J.: Scarecrow, 1978.

The Films of Marilyn Monroe. Michael Conway and Mark Ricci. Secaucus, N.J.: The Citadel Press, 1964.

The Films of Marlene Dietrich. Homer Dickens. New York: The Citadel Press, 1968.

The Films of Marlon Brando. Tony Thomas. Secaucus, N.J.: The Citadel Press, 1973.

The Films of Michael Winner. Bill Harding. London: Frederick Muller Limited, 1978.

The Films of Montgomery Clift. Judith M. Kass. Secaucus, N.J.: The Citadel Press, 1979.

The Films of Myrna Loy. Lawrence J. Quirk. Secaucus, N.J.: The Citadel Press, 1980.

The Films of Olivia de Havilland. Tony Thomas. Secaucus, N.J.: The Citadel Press, 1983.

The Films of Orson Welles. Charles Higham. Berkeley: University of California Press, 1970.

The Films of Paul Newman. Lawrence J. Quirk. New York: The Citadel Press, 1971.

The Films of Peter Lorre. Stephen D. Youngkin, James Bigwood, and Raymond G. Cabana, Jr. Secaucus, N.J.: The Citadel Press, 1982.

The Films of Rita Hayworth: The Legend and Career of a Love Goddess. Gene Ringgold. Secaucus, N.J.: The Citadel Press, 1974.

The Films of Robert Altman. Alan Karp. Metuchen, N.J.: The Scarecrow Press, 1981.

The Films of Robert Bresson. Anonymous. New York: Praeger, 1969.

The Films of Robert Redford. James Spada. Secaucus, N.J.: The Citadel Press, 1984.

The Films of Robert Taylor. Lawrence J. Quirk. Secaucus, N.J.: The Citadel Press, 1975.

The Films of Roger Corman: Brilliance on a Budget. New York: Arco Publishing, Inc., 1982.

The Films of Ronald Colman. Lawrence J. Quirk. Secaucus, N.J.: The Citadel Press, 1977.

The Films of Ronald Reagan. Tony Thomas. Secaucus, N.J.: The Citadel Press, 1980.

The Films of Sam Peckinpah. William Parrill. Hammond, LA: Bay-Wulf Books, 1980.

The Films of Sherlock Holmes. Chris Steinbrunner and Norman Michaels. Secaucus, N.J.: The Citadel Press, 1978.

The Films of Shirley MacLaine. Christopher Paul Denis. Secaucus, N.J.: The Citadel Press, 1980.

The Films of Shirley Temple. Robert Windeler. Secaucus, N.J.: The Citadel Press, 1978.

The Films of Sidney Poitier. Alvin H. Marill. Secaucus, N.J.: The Citadel Press, 1978.

The Films of Sophia Loren. Tony Crawley. Secaucus, N.J.: Citadel Press, 1976.

The Films of Spencer Tracy. Donald Deschner. New York: The Citadel Press, 1979.

The Films of Stanley Kubrick. Daniel DeVries. Grand Rapids, MI: William B. Eerdmans Publishing Company, 1973.

The Films of Steve McQueen. Casey St. Charnez. Secaucus, N.J.: Citadel Press, 1984.

The Films of Susan Hayward. Eduardo Moreno. Secaucus, N.J.: The Citadel Press, 1979.

The Films of Tennessee Williams. Gene D. Phillips. Cranbury, N.J.: Art Alliance, 1980.

The Films of the Fifties. Douglas Brode. Secaucus, N.J.: The Citadel Press, 1976.

The Films of the Seventies. Robert Bookbinder. Secaucus, N.J.: Citadel Press, 1982.

The Films of the Sixties. Douglas Brode. Secaucus, N.J.: The Citadel Press, 1980.

The Films of Tyrone Power. Dennis Belafonte with Alvin H. Marill. Secaucus, N.J.: The Citadel Press, 1979.

The Films of Warren Beatty. Lawrence J. Quirk. Secaucus, N.J.: The Citadel Press, 1979.

The Films of William Holden. Lawrence J. Quirk. Secaucus, N.J.: The Citadel Press, 1973.

Final Cut: Dreams and Disaster in the Making of Heaven's Gate. Steven Bach. New York: William Morrow & Co., Inc., 1985.

Finally Truffaut. Don Allen. New York: Beaufort Books, 1985.

The Five Lives of Ben Hecht. Doug Fethering. New York: Zoetrope, 1980.

Five Thousand One Nights at the Movies. Pauline Kael. New York: Holt, Rinehart and Winston, 1982.

Focus on Blow-Up. Edited by Roy Huss. Englewood Cliffs, N.J.: Prentice-Hall, 1971.

Focus on Chaplin. Donald W. McCaffrey. Englewood Cliffs, N.J.: Prentice-Hall, 1971.

Focus on Godard. Edited by Royal S. Brown. Englewood Cliffs, N.J.: Prentice-Hall, 1972.

Focus on Hitchcock. Edited by Albert J. LaValley. Englewood Cliffs, N.J.: Prentice-Hall, 1972.

Focus on Howard Hawks. Joseph McBride. Englewood Cliffs, N.J.: Prentice-Hall, 1972.

Focus on Orson Welles. Edited by Ronald Gottesman. Englewood Cliffs, N.J.: Prentice-Hall, 1976.

Focus on Rashomon. Edited by Donald Richie. Englewood Cliffs, N.J.: Prentice-Hall, 1972.

Focus on Shakespearean Films. Edited by Charles W. Eckert. Englewood Cliffs, N.J.: Prentice-Hall, 1972.

Focus on Shoot the Piano Player. Edited by Leo Braudy. Englewood, N.J.: Prentice-Hall, Inc., 1972.

Focus on the Horror Film. Roy Huss and T. J. Ross. Englewood Cliffs, N.J.: Prentice-Hall, 1972.

Focus on the Science Fiction Film. Edited by William Johnson. Englewood Cliffs, N.J.: Prentice-Hall, Inc., 1972.

Focus on the Seventh Seal. Edited by Birgitta Steene. Englewood Cliffs, N.J.: Prentice-Hall, 1972.

The Fondas: The Films and Careers of Henry, Jane and Peter Fonda. John Springer. New York: The Citadel Press, 1970.

The 400 Blows. François Truffaut and Marcell Moussy. New York: Grove Press, 1969.

Francis Ford Coppola. Robert K. Johnson. Boston: Twayne, 1977.

Francis Ford Coppola: A Guide to References and Resources. Joel S. Zuker. Boston: G. K. Hall & Co., 1984

François Truffaut. C. G. Crisp. New York: Praeger, 1972.

François Truffaut. Annette Insdorf. Boston: Twayne, 1978.

François Truffaut: A Guide to References and Resources. Eugene P. Walz. Boston: G. K. Hall & Co., 1982.

Franju. Raymond Durgnat. Berkeley: University of California Press, 1968.

Frank Capra. Charles J. Maland. Boston: Twayne Publishers, 1980.

Franklin J. Schaffner. Kim Erwin. Metuchen, N.J.: Scarecrow Press, 1985.

The French Lieutenant's Woman: A Screenplay. Harold Pinter. Boston: Little, Brown and Company, 1981.

The French Literary Filmmakers. John J. Michalczyk. East Brunswick, N.J.: Art Alliance Press, 1980.

Fritz Lang. Robert A. Armour. Boston: Twayne Publishers, 1977.

Fritz Lang. Lotte H. Eisner. New York: Oxford University Press, 1977.

Fritz Lang: A Guide to References and Resources. E. Ann Kaplan. Boston: G. K. Hall & Co., 1981.

Fritz Lang in America. Peter Bogdanovich. New York: Praeger, 1967.

From Fiction to Film: D. H. Lawrence's The Rocking Horse Winner. Gerald R. Barrett and Thomas L. Erskine. Encino, CA: Dickinson Publishing Co., 1974.

From Sambo to Superspade: The Black Experience in Motion Pictures. Daniel J. Leab. Boston: Houghton Mifflin Company, 1975.

Future Tense: The Cinema of Science Fiction. John Brosnan. New York: St. Martin's Press, 1978.

George Cukor. Gene D. Phillips. Boston: Twayne Publishers, 1982.

George Roy Hill. Edward Shores. Boston: Twayne Publishers, 1983.

George Stevens, An American Romantic. Donald Richie. New York: Museum of Modern Art, 1970.

The German Cinema. Roger Manvell and Heinrich Fraenkel. New York: Praeger, 1971.

German Film & Literature: Adaptations and Transformations. Edited by Eric Rentschler. London: Methuen, 1986.

German Literature and Film: Adaptions and Transformations. Edited by Eric Rentschler. New York: Methuen, 1986.

Gillo Pontecorvo's The Battle of Algiers. Franco Solinas and Gillo Pontecorvo. New York: Scribner's, 1973.

Godard and Others: Essays on Film Form. Louis P. Giannetti. Cranbury, N.J.: Associated University Press, 1975.

The Godfather Journal. Ira Zuckerman. New York: Manor Books, 1972.

Going Steady. Pauline Kael. Boston: Little, Brown & Co., 1970.

The Golden Age of "B" Movies. Doug McClelland. Nashville, TN: Charter House, 1978.

Graham Greene. A. A. DeVitis. Boston: Twayne Publishers, 1986.

Graham Greene: The Films of His Fiction. Gene B. Phillips. New York: Columbia University Teachers College, 1974.

The Great Adventure Films. Tony Thomas. Secaucus, N.J.: The Citadel Press, 1976.

The Great British Films. Jerry Vermilye. Secaucus, N.J.: The Citadel Press, 1978.

Great Film Directors: A Critical Anthology. Les Braudy and Morris Dickstein, Editors. New York: Oxford University Press, 1978.

The Great Films: Fifty Golden Years of Motion Pictures. Bosley Crowther. New York: G. P. Putnam's Sons, 1967.

The Great French Films. James Reid Paris. Secaucus, N.J.: The Citadel Press, 1983.

The Great Gangster Pictures. James Robert Parrish and Michael R. Pitts. Metuchen, N.J.: The Scarecrow Press, Inc., 1976.

The Great German Films. Frederick W. Ott. Secaucus, N.J.: Citadel Press, 1986.

Great Horror Movies. Favius Friedman. New York: Scholastic Book Services, 1974.

The Great Movies. William Bayer. New York: Grosset and Dunlap, 1973.

The Great Romantic Films. Lawrence J. Quirk. Secaucus, N.J.: The Citadel Press, 1974.

The Great Spy Films. Leonard Rubenstein. Secaucus, N.J.: The Citadel Press, 1979.

The Great Spy Pictures. James Robert Parrish. New York: The Scarecrow Press, 1974.

The Great Western Pictures. James Robert Parrish and Michael R. Pitts. Metuchen, N.J.: The Scarecrow Press, 1976.

Grigori Kozintsev. Barbara Leaming. Boston: Twayne, 1980.

Guts & Glory: Great American War Movies. Lawrence H. Suid. Reading, MA.: Addison Wesley Publishing Company, 1978.

H. G. Wells in the Cinema. Alan Wykes. London: Jupiter Books, 1977.

Jean-Luc Godard: A Guide to References and Resources. Julia Lesage. Boston: G.K. Hall & Co., 1979.

Jean-Marie Straub. Richard Roud. London: Secker and Warburg, 1971.

Jiri Menzel and the History of "The Closely Watched Trains." Joseph Skrorecky. New York: Columbia University Press, 1982.

John Boorman. Michael Ciment. Translated by Gilbert Adair. London: Faber and Faber, 1986.

John Ford. Peter Bogdanovich. Berkeley: University of California Press, 1968.

John Ford. Joseph McBride and Michael Wilmington. New York: Da Capo Press, 1975.

John Huston. Scott Hammen. Boston: Twayne, 1985.

John Huston. Axel Madsen. Garden City, N.Y.: Doubleday, 1978.

John Huston: Maker of Magic. Stuart Kaminsky. Boston: Houghton Mifflin, 1978.

John Schlesinger. Gene D. Phillips. Boston: Twayne Publishers, 1981.

John Schlesinger: A Guide to References and Resources. Nancy J. Brooker. Boston: G. K. Hall & Co., 1978.

John Wayne and the Movies. Allen Eyles. South Brunswick, N.J.: A. S. Barnes & Co., 1976.

Joseph L. Mankiewicz. Bernard F. Dick. Boston: Twayne Publications, 1983.

Joseph Losey. Foster Hirsch. Boston: Twayne Publishers, 1980.

Journal of The Loved One. Terry Southern. New York: Random House, 1965.

Journey Down Sunset Boulevard: The Films of Billy Wilder. Neil Sinyard and Adrian Turner. Ryde, Isle of Wight: BCW Publishing, 1979.

Judy: The Films and Career of Judy Garland. Joe Morella and Edward Z. Epstein. New York: The Citadel Press, 1969.

Juliet of the Spirits. Federico Fellini and Tullio Pinelli. New York: Ballantine Books, 1966.

Karel Reisz. Georg Gaston. Boston: Twayne Publishers, 1980.

Kazan on Kazan. Michael Ciment. New York: Viking, 1974.

Ken Russell. Edited by Thomas R. Atkins. New York: Monarch Press, 1976.

Ken Russell. Gene D. Phillips. Boston: Twayne Publishers, 1979.

Ken Russell: A Guide to References and Resources. Diane Rosenfeldt. Boston: G. K. Hall & Co., 1978.

Ken Russell: The Adaptor as Creator. Joseph A. Gomez. London: Frederick Muller Limited, 1976.

Ken Russell's Films. Ken Hanke. Metuchen, N.J.: The Scarecrow Press, Inc., 1984.

Kenji Mizoguchi: A Guide to References and Resources. James Dudley Andrew. Boston: G. K. Hall & Co., 1981.

The Killing Fields: The Facts Behind the Movie. Christopher Hudson. New York: Dell, 1984.

King Vidor. John Baxter. New York: Monarch Press, 1976.

King Vidor on Film Making. King Vidor. New York: David McKay Co., Inc., 1972.

Kino. Jay Leyda. Princeton, N.J.: Princeton University Press, 1983. Revised Edition.

Kiss Kiss Bang Bang. Pauline Kael. New York: Bantam Books, 1969.

Kubrick. Michael Ciment. Translated from the French by Gilbert Adair. New York: Holt, Rinehart and Winston, 1980.

Kubrick: Inside a Film Artist's Maze. Thomas Allen Nelson. Bloomington: Indiana University Press, 1982.

La Dolce Vita. Federico Fellini, Tullio Penilli, Ennio Flaiano, and Brunello Rondi. New York: Ballantine Books, 1961.

Ladd: The Life, the Legend, the Legacy of Alan Ladd. Beverly Linet. New York: Arbor House, 1979.

Landmark Films: The Cinema of Our Century. William Wolf with Lillian Kramer Wolf. New York: Paddington Press, Ltd., 1979.

The Landscape of Contemporary Cinema. Leon Lewis and William David Sherman. Buffalo, N.Y.: Buffalo Spectrum Books, 1967.

The Last Hero: A Biography of Gary Cooper. Larry Swindell. New York: Doubleday, 1980.

The Latin Image in American Film. Allen L. Woll. Los Angeles: UCLA Latin American Center Publications, 1977.

Lauren Bacall: Her Films and Career. Lawrence J. Quirk. Secaucus, N.J.: The Citadel Press, 1986.

Laurence Olivier. Foster Hirsch. Boston: Twayne Publishers, 1979.

Laurence Olivier: Theater & Cinema. Robert L. Daniels. New York: A. S. Barnes and Company, Inc., 1980.

Leni Riefenstahl. Renata Berg-Pan. Boston: Twayne, 1980.

Leni Riefenstahl: The Fallen Film Goddess. Glenn B. Infield. New York: Thomas Y. Crowell, 1976.

Lewis Milestone. Joseph A. Millichap. Boston: Twayne, 1981.

Lindsay Anderson: A Guide to References and Resources. Boston: G. K. Hall & Co., 1979.

The Liveliest Art. Arthur Knight. New York: New American Library, 1959.

Living Images: Film Comment and Criticism. Stanley Kauffman. New York: Harper & Row, 1975.

Love in the Film. William K. Everson. Secaucus, N.J.: The Citadel Press, 1970.

The Love Story Story. Marvin Saunders. New York: National Publishers, Inc., 1970.

Luchino Visconti. Geoffrey Nowell-Smith. New York: The Viking Press, 1973.

Luchino Visconti. Claretta Tonetti. Boston: Twayne Publishers, 1983.

Luchino Visconti: A Biography. Gaia Servadio. New York: F. Watts, 1983.

Luis Buñuel. Raymond Durgnat. Berkeley: University of California Press, 1968.

Luis Buñuel. Virginia Higginbotham. Boston: Twayne Publishers, 1979.

Luis Buñuel: A Critical Biography. Francisco Aranda. Translated and Edited by David Robinson. New York: Da Capo Press, Inc., 1976.

Luis Buñuel: An Introduction. Ado Kyrou. Translated by Adrienne Foulke. New York: Simon and Schuster, 1963.

Made Into Movies: From Literature to Film. Stuart Y. McDougal. New York: Holt, Rinehart and Winston, 1985.

The Magic Factory: How MGM Made an American in Paris. Donald Knox. New York: Praeger, 1973.

Magic Moments from the Movies. Elwy Yost. Garden City, N.J.: Doubleday, 1978.

The Magic World of Orson Welles. James Naremore. New York: Oxford University Press, 1978.

Magill's Cinema Annual, 1982-1986. Edited by Frank N. Magill. Englewood Cliffs, N.J.: Salem Press, 1982-1986.

Magill's Survey of Cinema. English Language Films. Series I and II. Edited by Frank N. Magill. Englewood Cliffs, N.J.: Salem Press, 1980-1981.

Magill's Survey of Cinema. Foreign Language Films. Edited by Frank N. Magill. Englewood Cliffs, N.J.: Salem Press, 1985.

Make It Again, Sam: A Survey of Movie Remakes. Michael B. Durxman. South Brunswick, N.J.: A. S. Barnes, 1975.

The Making of Dune. Ed Naha. New York: Berkley Books, 1984.

The Making of Star Trek: The Motion Picture. Susan Sackett and Gene Roddenberry. New York: Pocket Books, 1977.

The Making of Superman. David Michael Petrou. New York: Warner Publications, 1978.

The Making of the Great Westerns. William R. Meyer. New Rochelle, N.Y.: Arlington House, 1979.

Making Pictures: The Pinter Screenplays. Joanne Klein. Columbus: Ohio State University Press, 1985.

Mank: The Wit, World, and Life of Herman Mankiewicz. Richard Meryman. New York: Morrow, 1978.

Marcel Pagnol. C.E.J. Coldicott. Boston: Twayne, 1977.

Marshall Delaney at the Movies. Robert Fulford. Toronto: Peter Martin, 1974.

Martin Scorsese and Michael Cimino. Michael Bliss. Metuchen, N.J.: The Scarecrow Press, 1985.

Masculine-Feminine: A Film by Jean-Luc Godard. Jean-Luc Godard. New York: Grove Press, 1969.

Mastering the Film and Other Essays. Charles Thomas Samuels. Knoxville: University of Tennessee Press, 1977.

Max Ophuls and the Cinema of Desire. Alan Larson Williams. New York: Arno Press, 1980.

Mel Brooks' High Anxiety. Mel Brooks, Ron Clark, Rudy DeLuca, and Barry Levinson. New York: Grosset and Dunlap, 1977.

The MGM Years. Laurence B. Thomas. New York: Columbia House, 1972.

Melville on Melville. Edited by Rui Noguevia. New York: Viking Press, 1971.

Memories of Underdevelopment. Edited by Michael Myerson. New York: Grossman, 1973.

Michael Balcon Presents. . .A Lifetime of Films. Michael Balcon. London: Hutchinson, 1969.

Michelangelo Antonioni: A Guide to References and Resources. Ted Perry and Rene Prieto. Boston: G. K. Hall & Co., 1986.

Michelangelo Antonioni's Neo Realism. Robert J. Lyons. New York: Arno, 1976.

Mickey Mouse: 50 Happy Years. Edited by David Bain and Bruce Harris. New York: Harmony Books, 1977.

Midnight Movies. Stuart Samuels. New York: Collier Books, 1983.

Mike Nichols. H. Wayne Schuth. Boston: Twayne, 1978.

The Milos Forman Stories. Antonin J. Liehm. White Plains, N.Y.: International Arts & Sciences Press, 1975.

A Mirror for England: British Movies from Austerity to Affluence. Raymond Durgnat. New York: Praeger Publishers, 1971.

The Missouri Breaks. Thomas McGuane. New York: Ballantine Books, 1976.

Mizoguchi. Keiko I. McDonald. Boston: Twayne, 1984.

Mizoguchi. Peter Morris. Ottawa: Canadian Film Institute, 1967.

The Modern American Novel and the Movies. Edited by Gerald Perry and Roger Shatzhin. New York: Frederick Ungar, 1978.

Modern European Filmmakers and the Art of Adaptation. Edited by Andrew S. Horton and Joan Magretta. New York: Ungar, 1981.

Modernism in the Narrative Cinema: The Art of Film as a Genre. William Charles Siska. New York: Arno, 1980.

Monty Python and the Holy Grail. Terry Gilliam. New York: Methuen, 1977.

More About All About Eve. Joseph L. Mankiewicz and Gary Carey. New York: Random House, 1972.

The Most Important Art: East European Cinema After 1945. Mira and Antonin J. Liehm. Berkeley: University of California Press, 1977.

Mother Goddam: The Story of the Career of Bette Davis. Whitney Stine. New York: Hawthorne Books, 1974.

Movie Comedy. Edited by Stuart Byron and Elisabeth Weis. New York: Grossman, 1977.

Movie Journal: The Rise of the American Cinema, 1959-1971. Jonas Mekas. New York: Macmillan, 1972.

Movie Man. David Thomson. New York: Stein and Day, 1967.

The Moviemakers. Alice Fleming. New York: St. Martin's Press, 1973.

Movies. Manny Farber. New York: The Stonehill Publishing Company, 1971.

Movies and Methods: An Anthology. Edited by Bill Nichols. Berkeley: University of California Press, 1976.

Movies Into Film. John Simon. New York: Dial Press, 1971.

The Movies on Your Mind. Harvey R. Greenberg. New York: Saturday Review Press-Dutton, 1975.

Movies Plus One. William S. Pechter. New York: Horizon Press, 1982.

Moving Places: A Life at the Movies. Jonathan Rosenbaum. New York: Harper, 1980.

The Musical From Broadway to Hollywood. Michael Druxman. New York: A. S. Barnes, 1980.

My Life with Cleopatra. Walter Wanger and Joe Hyams. New York: Bantam Books, 1963.

The Name Above the Title: An Autobiography. Frank Capra. New York: The Macmillan Company, 1971.

Narration in Light: Studies in Cinematic Point of View. George M. Wilson. Baltimore: The Johns Hopkins University Press, 1986.

Nashville. Joan Tewkesbury. New York: Bantam Books, 1976.

Negative Space. See *Movies.*

A Neglected Art. Roy M. Prendergast. New York: New York University Press, 1977.

The New American Cinema: A Critical Anthology. Gregory Battcock. New York: E. P. Dutton, 1967.

The New Australian Cinema. Edited by Scott Murray. Associate Editor Peter Bellby. London: Elm Tree Books, 1980.

The New Documentary in Action: A Casebook in Film-Making. Alan Rosenthal. Berkeley: University of California Press, 1971.

New German Cinema. John Sandford. New York: Barnes & Noble, 1980.

The New Italian Cinema: Studies in Dance and Despair. Rick Trader Witcombe. New York: Oxford University Press, 1982.

The New Wave. James Monaco. New York: Oxford University Press, 1976.

Nicholas Ray. John Francis Kreidl. Boston: Twayne Publishers, 1977.

Nicholas Ray: A Guide to References and Resources. Blaine Allen. Boston: G. K. Hall & Co., 1984.

Nicholas Roeg. Neil Feineman. Boston: Twayne, 1978.

The Non-Western Films of John Ford. J. A. Place. Secaucus, N.J.: The Citadel Press, 1979.

The Novel and the Cinema. Geoffrey Wagner. Rutherford, N.J.: Fairleigh Dickinson University Press, 1975.

Novels Into Film. George Bluestone. Berkeley: University of California Press, 1957.

Nuclear War Films. Edited by Jack B. Shaheen. Carbondale, IL: Southern Illinois University Press, 1978.

The Nureyev Valentino. Alexander Bland. New York: Dell, 1977.

The Official Rocky Scrapbook. Sylvester Stallone. New York: Grosset and Dunlap, 1977.

The Official Sgt. Pepper's Lonely Hearts Club Band Scrapbook. Robert Stigwood and Anthony Dee. New York: Wallaby, 1980.

On Cukor. Gavin Lambert. New York: G. P. Putnam's Sons, 1972.

On Film: Unpopular Essays on a Popular Art. Vernon Young. Chicago: Quadrangle Press, 1972.

On Location...On Martha's Vineyard. Edith Blake. Orleans, MA: Lower Cape Publishing, 1975.

On Movies. Dwight Macdonald. Introduction by John Simon. New York: A Da Capo Paperback, 1981.

On the Set of Fellini Satyricon: A Behind-the-Scenes Diary. Eileen Lanouette Hughes. New York: Morrow, 1971.

On the Verge of Revolt. Brandon French. New York: Ungar, 1978.

One Good Film Deserves Another. Michael Druxman. South Brunswick, N.J.: A. S. Barnes, 1977.

O'Neill on Film. John Orlando. Rutherford, N.J.: Fairleigh Dickinson University Press, 1982.

An Open Book. John Huston. New York: Alfred A. Knopf, 1980.

Orson Welles. Maurice Bessy. New York: Crown, 1971.

Orson Welles. Joseph McBride. New York: Viking Press, 1972.

Orson Welles: A Critical View. André Bazin, Translated by Jonathan Rosenbaum. New York: Harper & Row, 1978.

Orson Welles, Actor and Director: An Illustrated History of the Movies. Joseph McBride. New York: Jove Publications, Harcourt, Brace, Jovanovich, 1977.

Ozu. Donald Richie. Berkeley: University of California Press, 1974.

The Parables of Lina Wertmuller. Ernest Ferlita and John R. May. New York: Paulist Press, 1977.

Paris Texas. Sam Shepard. Berlin: Nordlingen, 1984.

Pasolini on Pasolini. Interview with Oswald Stock. Bloomington: Indiana University Press, 1969.

The Passenger. Mark Peploe, Peter Wollen and Michelangelo Antonioni. New York: Grove Press, 1975.

Passion and Defiance: Film in Italy from 1942 to the Present. Maria Liehm. Berkeley: University of California Press, 1984.

Patterns of Realism. Roy Armes. South Brunswick, N.J.: A. S. Barnes and Company, 1971.

Paul Muni: His Life and His Films. Michael B. Druxman. South Brunswick: A. S. Barnes and Company, 1974.

Peckinpah: A Portrait in Montage. Garner Simmons. Austin: University of Texas Press, 1976.

Personal Views: Explorations in Films. Robin Wood. London: Gordon Fraser, 1976.

The Personal Vision of Ingmar Bergman. See *The Films of Ingmar Bergman.*

Peter Watkins. Joseph Gomez. Boston: Twayne, 1979.

A Pictorial History of the Western Film. William K. Everson. Secaucus, N.J.: The Citadel Press, 1969.

Pictures Will Talk: The Life and Films of Joseph L. Mankiewicz. Kenneth L. Geist. New York: Scribner's, 1978.

Pier Paolo Pasolini. Stephen Snyder. Boston: Twayne Publishers, 1980.

The Platinum Years. Bob Willoughby. Text by Richard Schickel. New York: A Ridgeway Press Book/Random House, 1974.

Polanski: A Biography. Barbara Leaming. Simon & Schuster, 1981.

Politics and Film. Leif Furhammer and Folke Isaksson. New York: Praeger, 1971.

Politics, Art and Commitment in the East European Cinema. David W. Paul. New York: St. Martin's Press, 1983.

Portrait of a Director. Marie Seton. Bloomington: Indiana University Press, 1970.

A Portrait of All the President's Men. Jack Hirshberg, New York: Warner Books, 1976.

Possible Cinema: The Films of Alain Tanner. Jim Leach. Metuchen, N.J.: Scarecrow, 1984.

Powell Pressburger and Others. Edited by Ian Christie. London: The British Film Institute, 1978.

Preminger: An Autobiography. Otto Preminger. Garden City, NY: Doubleday, 1977.

Preston Sturges: A Guide to References and Resources. Ray Cywinski. Boston: G. K. Hall & Co., 1984.

The Primal Screen: Essays on Film and Related Subjects. Andrew Sarris. New York: Simon & Schuster, 1973.

The Private Eye, the Cowboy, and the Very Naked Girl. Judith Crist. New York: Holt, Rinehart & Winston, 1968.

Private Screenings. John Simon. New York: Macmillan, 1967.

Propaganda on Film: A Nation at War. Richard A. Maynard. Rochelle Park, N.J.: Hayden, 1975.

Pursuits of Happiness: The Hollywood Comedy of Remarriage. Stanley Cavell. Cambridge, MA: Harvard University Press, 1981.

Raiders of the Lost Ark: The Illustrated Screenplay. Lawrence Kasdan. New York: Ballantine Books, 1981.

Rashomon. Akira Kurosawa and Shinobu Hashimoto. New York: Grove Press, 1969.

Raymond Chandler and Film. William Luhr. New York: Frederick Ungar Publishing Co., 1982.

Raymond Chandler in Hollywood. Al Clark. New York: Proteus, 1982.

Raymond Chandler on Screen: His Novels into Film. Stephen Pendo. Metuchen, N. J.: The Scarecrow Press, 1976.

Realism and the Cinema: A Reader. Edited by Christopher Williams. London: Routledge & Kegan Paul, in Association with the British Film Institute, 1980.

Reeling. Pauline Kael. New York: Warner Books, 1976.

A Reference Guide to the American Film Noir: 1940-1958. Robert Ottoson. Metuchen, N.J.: Scarecrow Press, 1981.

Reflexivity in Film and Literature From Don Quixote to Jean-Luc Godard. Robert Stam. Ann Arbor, MI: UMI Research Press, 1985.

Renaissance of the Film. Edited by Julius Bellone. New York: Collier Books, 1970.

René Clair. Celia McGerr. Boston: Twayne Publishers, 1980.

René Clair: A Guide to References and Resources. Naomi Greene. Boston: G.K. Hall & Co., 1984.

Reruns: Fifty Memorable Films. Bosley Crowther. New York: G. P. Putnam's Sons, 1978.

A Ribbon of Dreams: The Cinema of Orson Welles. See *The Cinema of Orson Welles.*

Richard Lester: A Guide to References and Resources. Diane Rosenfeldt. Boston: G. K. Hall & Co., 1978.

Robert Aldrich: A Guide to References and Resources. Alain Silver and Elizabeth Ward. Boston: G. K. Hall & Co., 1979.

Robert Altman. Gerard Plecki. Boston: Twayne, 1985.

Robert Altman: A Guide to References and Resources. Virginia Wright Wexman and Gretchen Bisplinghoff. Boston: G. K. Hall & Co., 1984.

Robert Altman: American Innovator. Judith M. Kass. New York: Popular Library, 1978,

Robert Bresson: A Guide to References and Resources. Jane Sloane. Boston: G. K. Hall & Co., 1984.

Robert Flaherty: A Guide to References and Resources. William T. Murphy. Boston: G. K. Hall, 1978.

Robert Mitchum on the Screen. Alvin H. Marill. South Brunswick and New York: A. S. Barnes, 1978.

Roberto Rossellini. Jose Luis Guarner. New York: Praeger, 1970.

Robin and Marian. James Goldman. New York: Bantam Books, 1976.

The Rocky Horror Picture Show Book. Bill Henkin. New York: Hawthorne, 1979.

Roger Moore's James Bond Diary. Roger Moore. Greenwich, CT: Fawcett, 1973.

Roman Polanski. Virginia Wright Wexman. Boston: Twayne Publishers, 1985.

Roman Polanski: A Guide to References and Resources. Gretchen Bisplinghoff and Virginia Wright Wexman. Boston: G. K. Hall & Co., 1979.

Rotha on Film: A Selection of Writings on the Cinema. Paul Rotha. Fair Lawn, N.J.: Essential Books, 1958.

Rouben Mamoulian. Tom Milne. Bloomington: Indiana University Press, 1969.

Run Through, A Memoir. John Houseman. New York: Simon & Schuster, 1972.

Running Away from Myself. Barbara Deming. New York: Grosset Publishing, 1969.

Running Time: Films of the Cold War. Nora Sayre. New York: The Dial Press, 1982.

Saint Cinema, Selected Writings, 1929-1970. Herman G. Weinberg. New York: DBS Publications, 1970.

Salt of the Earth: Screenplay. Michael Wilson and Deborah S. Rosenfelt. Old Westbury, N.Y.: Feminist Press, 1978.

Salt of the Earth: The Story of a Film. Herbert Biberman and Michael Wilson. Boston: Beacon Press, 1965.

Sam Peckinpah. Doug McKinney. Boston: Twayne Publishers, 1979.

Samuel Fuller. Phil Hardy. New York: Praeger, 1970.

Samuel Goldwyn. Lawrence J. Epstein. Boston: Twayne Publishers, 1981.

Samuel Goldwyn Presents. Alvin H. Marill. South Brunswick and New York: A. S. Barnes and Company, 1976.

The Samurai Films of Akira Kurosawa. David Dresser. Ann Arbor, MI: UMI Research Press, 1983.

Saturday Night Fever—Official Authorized Scrapbook. New York: Paradise Press, 1978.

Science Fiction Films of the Seventies. Craig W. Anderson. Jefferson, N.C.: McFarland, 1985.

Science Fiction Gold. Dennis Saleh. New York: McGraw-Hill, 1979.

Science Fiction Studies in Film. Frederick Pohl. New York: Ace Books, 1981.

The Screen Plays of Lina Wertmuller. Lina Wertmuller. New York: Quadrangle, 1977.

Screening the Novel: Rediscovered American Fiction in Film. Gabriel Miller. New York: Frederick Ungar Publishing Co., 1980.

The Screenplay as Literature. Douglas Garrett Winston. Cranbury, N.J.: Fairleigh Dickinson University Press, 1973.

Scrooge. Elaine Donaldson. Nashville: Aurora Publishers, 1970.

Sean Connery. Michael Feeney Callan. New York: Stein & Day, 1983.

Second Sight: Notes on Some Movies, 1965-1970. Richard Schickel. New York: Simon and Schuster, 1972.

See No Evil. Jack Vizzard. New York: Simon & Schuster, 1970.

Seeing Is Believing: How Hollywood Taught Us to Stop Worrying and Love the Fifties. Peter Biskind. New York: Pantheon Books, 1983.

Seen Any Good Dirty Movies Lately? James Arnold. Cincinnati, OH: St. Anthony Messenger Press, 1972.

Selected Film Criticism, 1941-1950. Edited by Anthony Slide. Metuchen, N.J.: The Scarecrow Press, Inc., 1984.

Selected Film Criticism, 1951-1960. Anthony Slide. Metuchen, N.J.: The Scarecrow Press, 1984.

Self and Cinema: A Transformalist Perspective. Beverle Houston and Marsha Kinder. Pleasantville, NY: Redgrave, 1980.

The Seven Samurai: A Film by Akira Kurosawa. Shinolou Hashimoto and Hideo Oguni. New York: Simon & Schuster, 1970.

Seventy Years of Cinema. Peter Cowie. New York: A. S. Barnes & Co., 1969.

Sex, Psyche, Etcetera in the Film. Parker Tyler. New York: Horizon Press, 1969.

Sexual Strategems: The World of Women in Film. Edited by Patricia Erens. New York: Horizon Press, 1979.

Shakespeare and the Film. Roger Manvell. South Brunswick, N.J.: A. S. Barnes & Co., 1979.

Shakespeare on Film. Jack J. Jorgens. Bloomington: University of of Indiana Press, 1977.

Sherlock Holmes on the Screen: The Motion Picture Adventures of the World's Most Popular Detective. Robert W. Pohle, Jr. and Douglas C. Hart. South Brunswick and New York: A. S. Barnes and Company, 1977.

A Short Time for Insanity: An Autobiography. William A. Wellman. New York: Hawthorn Books, 1974.

Shots in the Dark. Edited by Roger Manvell. London: Allen Wingate, 1951.

Show Boat: The Story of a Classical American Musical. Miles Kreuger. New York: Oxford University Press, 1977.

Sidney Lumet: A Guide to References and Resources. Stephen E. Bowles. Boston: G. K. Hall & Co., 1979.

The Silence of God: Creative Response to the Films of Ingmar Bergman. New York: Harper & Row, 1969.

Silent Movie. Mel Brooks, Ron Clark, Rudy DeLuca and Barry Levinson. New York: Ballantine Books, 1976.

Singin' in the Rain: Story and Screenplay. Betty Comden and Adolph Green. New York: Viking, 1972.

Sirk on Sirk. Douglas Sirk and Jon Halliday. New York: Viking, 1972.

Skywalking. The Life and Films of George Lucas. Dale Pollock. New York: Ballantine, 1984.

The Social Cinema of Jean Renoir. Christopher Faulkner. Princeton, N.J.: Princeton University Press, 1986.

Something to Declare: Twelve Years of Films Abroad. John Ivan Simon. New York: C. N. Potter, 1983.

Soon to Be a Major Motion Picture. Theodore Gershuny. New York: Holt, Rinehart & Winston, 1980.

Spaghetti Westerns: Cowboys and Europeans from Karl Marx to Sergio Leone. Christopher Frayling. London: Routledge and Kegan Paul, 1981.